Congress and the Nation

Congress and the Nation

VOLUME XIII • 2009–2012

POLITICS AND POLICY IN THE 111TH AND 112TH CONGRESSES

Los Angeles | London | New Delhi
Singapore | Washington DC

Los Angeles | London | New Delhi
Singapore | Washington DC

FOR INFORMATION:

CQ Press
An Imprint of SAGE Publications, Inc.
2455 Teller Road
Thousand Oaks, California 91320
E-mail: order@sagepub.com

SAGE Publications Ltd.
1 Oliver's Yard
55 City Road
London, EC1Y 1SP
United Kingdom

SAGE Publications India Pvt. Ltd.
B 1/I 1 Mohan Cooperative Industrial Area
Mathura Road, New Delhi 110 044
India

SAGE Publications Asia-Pacific Pte. Ltd.
3 Church Street
#10-04 Samsung Hub
Singapore 049483

Printed in the United States of America.

Cataloging-in-publication data is available from the Library of Congress.

ISBN 978-1-4522-7034-0

This book is printed on acid-free paper.

Volume Editor: David R. Tarr
Acquisitions Editor: Jim Brace-Thompson
Assistant Editor: Laura Notton
Developmental Editors: Diana Axelsen and Carole Maurer
Reference Systems Manager: Leticia Gutierrez
Production Editor: Olivia Weber-Stenis
Copy Editor: Jon Preimesberger
Typesetter: C&M Digitals (P) Ltd.
Proofreader: Lawrence W. Baker
Indexer: Sheila Bodell
Cover Designer: Candice Harman
Marketing Manager: Carmel Schrire

14 15 16 17 18 10 9 8 7 6 5 4 3 2 1

Summary Table of Contents

Tables, Figures, and Boxes xv

Introduction xvii

Chapter 1 Politics and National Issues 3

Chapter 2 Economic Policy 47

Chapter 3 Homeland Security 205

Chapter 4 Foreign Policy 223

Chapter 5 Defense Policy 263

Chapter 6 Transportation, Commerce, and Communications 319

Chapter 7 Energy and Environment 363

Chapter 8 Agricultural Policy 407

Chapter 9 Health and Human Services 419

Chapter 10 Education Policy 473

Chapter 11 Housing and Urban Aid 497

Chapter 12 Labor and Pensions 515

Chapter 13 Law and Justice 547

Chapter 14 General Government 597

Chapter 15 Inside Congress 639

Chapter 16 The Obama Presidency 689

Appendix 715

Indexes 1005

Contents

Tables, Figures, and Boxes xv
Introduction xvii

Chapter 1 Politics and National Issues

Introduction 3
- 2009 Chronology 13
  - The Legislative Year 13
  - The Political Year 17
- 2010 Chronology 19
  - The Legislative Year 19
  - The Political Year 22
- 2011 Chronology 27
  - The Legislative Year 27
  - The Political Year 30
- 2012 Chronology 31
  - The Legislative Year 31
  - The Political Year 35

Chapter 2 Economic Policy

Introduction 47
- Downs and (Somewhat) Ups of the Economy 51
- Federal Reserve Actions 60
- Troubled Asset Relief Program (TARP) 60
- Obama's Stimulus 61
- 2010 Tax Cuts 66
- "Fiscal Cliff" and Budget Cuts 66
- Regulatory Reforms 68
- Bank "Stress Tests" 69
- Basel III 70
- More Financial Scandals 70

Chronology of Action on Economic and Regulatory Policy 73
- 2009–2010 75
  - TARP Funds Released 75
  - Economic Stimulus 78
  - Credit Card Restrictions 84
  - 2010 Jobs Creation Bill 85
  - Financial Regulation Overhaul 88
  - Small Business Assistance 102
- 2011–2012 104
  - Attempts to Weaken Financial Regulation 104
  - Cordray Nomination to Lead CFPC 105
  - Job Creation Legislation 106
  - Employee Payroll Tax Cut 108
  - Small Business Regulation Eased 110

Chronology of Action on Budget and Tax Policy 111
- 2009–2010 119
  - Fiscal 2009 Omnibus Appropriations 119
  - Second Fiscal 2009 Supplemental 122
  - Fiscal 2010 Budget Resolution 123
  - 2009 Budget Enforcement Rules 126
  - Fiscal 2010 Appropriations 127
  - 2009 Debt Ceiling Increase 134
  - Fiscal 2011 Budget Resolution 134
  - Fiscal 2011 Spending Bills 137
  - Fiscal 2010 War Supplemental 138
  - Border Security Supplemental Spending 139
  - Teachers, Medicaid Supplemental 140
  - 2010 Debt Ceiling Increase 141
  - Budget Enforcement Rules—PAYGO 142
  - Presidential Debt Panel Fails 142
  - Bush Administration Tax Cuts Extended 144

Estate Taxes 146
Tax Breaks Extension 147
2011–2012 149
Fiscal 2011 Omnibus Appropriations 150
Fiscal 2012 Budget Resolution 156
Debt Limit, Budget Control Act 160
Balanced-Budget Amendment 167
Congressional Deficit Committee 168
Fiscal 2012 Continuing Resolutions 168
Fiscal 2012 "Minibus" Appropriations 170
Fiscal 2012 Omnibus Appropriations 172
Disaster Assistance 176
Fiscal 2013 Budget Resolution 177
House Reconciliation Bill 180
Fiscal 2013 Continuing Resolution 180
Fiscal 2013 Appropriations Roundup 181
Fiscal Cliff 185
Hurricane Sandy Supplemental Funds 189
Chronology of Action on Trade Policy 191
Introduction 191
2009–2010 193
South Korea, Colombia, Panama Trade Pacts 193
Trade with China 193
2011–2012 195
South Korea, Colombia, Panama Trade Pacts 195
Trade Adjustment Assistance Extended 199
Export-Import Bank Reauthorization 200
Trade Measures Package 200
Russian Trade Normalization 201

Chapter 3 Homeland Security

Introduction 205
Chronology of Action on Homeland Security 208
2009–2010 208
USA PATRIOT Act 208
Fiscal 2010 Homeland Security Appropriations 209
Chemical Plant Security 212
Border Security Funding 212
2011–2012 214
USA PATRIOT Act 214
FISA Extension 215
Cybersecurity 217
Coast Guard Reauthorization 218
Border Entry Points 219

Chapter 4 Foreign Policy

Introduction 223
Afghanistan Policy: Eleven Years and an Uncertain Outcome 229
Chronology of Action on Foreign Policy 232
2009–2010 232
Fiscal 2009 State–Foreign Operations Funding 232
Fiscal 2009 Supplemental Appropriations 233
Pakistan Aid Authorization 236
Iran Sanctions 238
State Department Authorization Bill 241
Fiscal 2010 State–Foreign Operations Funding 243
Fiscal 2010 Intelligence Authorization 245
Fiscal 2011 State–Foreign Operations Funding 248
2011–2012 249
Fiscal 2011 State–Foreign Operations Funding 249
Use of Force in Libya 250
Fiscal 2011 and 2012 Intelligence Authorization 250
Fiscal 2012 State–Foreign Operations Funding 252
Fiscal 2013 Intelligence Authorization 254
Iran Sanctions 255
Fiscal 2013 State–Foreign Operations Funding 258
International Treaty on Disability Rights 258

Chapter 5 Defense Policy

Introduction 263
Chronology of Action on Defense Policy 267

2009–2010 267

Defense Acquisitions Rules 267
Fiscal 2009 War Supplemental 269
Fiscal 2010 Defense Authorization 273
Veterans' Health Programs 280
Fiscal 2010 Defense Appropriations 280
Fiscal 2010 Military Construction Appropriations 284
Fiscal 2010 War Supplemental 286
"Don't Ask, Don't Tell" Repeal 288
New START Treaty Approval 289
Fiscal 2011 Defense Authorization 291
Fiscal 2011 Defense Appropriations 295

2011–2012 296

Fiscal 2011 Defense Appropriations 296
Fiscal 2011 Military Construction-VA Appropriations 297
Fiscal 2012 Defense Authorization 299
Fiscal 2012 Defense Appropriations 304
Fiscal 2013 Defense Authorization 307
Fiscal 2013 Defense Appropriations 312

Guantanamo Transfers Restricted 314

Chapter 6 Transportation, Commerce, and Communications

Introduction 319

Chronology of Action on Transportation, Commerce, and Communications 321

2009–2010 321

Cash for Clunkers 321
Surface Transportation Authorization 324
FAA Reauthorization 327
Airline Safety and Pilot Training 332
FCC Reform and Internet Access 332
Satellite and Cable Programming 335
Internet Gambling 338
Notarization Legislation 339

2011–2012 340

Surface Transportation 340
FAA Reauthorization 349
FCC and Internet Access 354
Internet Gambling 358
Internet Piracy 358

Chapter 7 Energy and Environment

Introduction 363

Chronology of Action on Energy and Environment 366

2009–2010 366

Climate Change 367
Environmental Protection Agency Regulation 372
National Climate Service 373
Public Lands 374
Offshore Drilling 374
Other Oil Production Legislation 376
Yucca Mountain Nuclear Waste 377
Lead Pipes 378
Air Pollution Grants 378
Algal Blooms 378
Recycling Electronic Products 379
Low-level Nuclear Waste 379
Formaldehyde Emissions 379
Solar Energy Technology 380
Clean Water Act 380
Green Schools 380
Wastewater Treatment 381
Wind Energy 381
Energy Department Research Programs 381
Energy-efficient Home Improvements 381
Electric Grid Protection 382
Interior and Environment Funds 382

2011–2012 386

Environmental Protection Agency Regulations 386
Keystone Pipeline 390
Oil and Gas Production 392
Yucca Mountain Nuclear Waste 394
Energy Projects Loans 395
Incandescent Light Bulbs 395
Copper Mining 395
Airlines and Carbon Emissions 396
Nuisance Dust 396
California Water 397
Hydropower 397
Clean Air Act 397
Federal Lands 398
Mining on Public Lands 399
Chemical Safety Standards 399

Coal Regulations 399
Hunting and Fishing 400
Pipeline Safety 401
Utilities and Environmental Regulations 401
Interior and Environmental Funds 401

Chapter 8 Agricultural Policy

Introduction 407

Chronology of Action on Agricultural Policy 409

2009–2010 409

Food Safety 409
Fiscal 2010 Agriculture Appropriations 412
Black Farmers 413

2011–2012 414

Omnibus Farm Legislation 414

Chapter 9 Health and Human Services

Introduction 419

Chronology of Action on Health 421

2009–2010 421

Health Care Overhaul 421
Non-Health Revenue Provisions 444
Children's Health Insurance Program (CHIP) 445
Tobacco Regulation 448
Medicare Physician Payments 450
Ryan White AIDS Act Reauthorization 452
Medicaid and Education Spending 453

2011–2012 455

Health Overhaul Repeal 455
Food and Drug Administration User Fees 460
Medicare Physician Payments 463

Chronology of Action on Human Services 465

2009–2010 465

Child Nutrition 465

2011–2012 468

Nutrition Programs 468

Chapter 10 Education Policy

Introduction 473

Chronology of Action on Education Policy 476

2009–2010 476

Federal Student Loans 476
Education Jobs Fund 479
Race to the Top 480
D.C. School Vouchers 481
College Savings Accounts 481
Student Punishment 481
College Campus Fire Safety 482

2011–2012 483

Elementary and Secondary Education Act 483
Federal Student Loans 485
Pell Grants 486
Student Aid Rules 487
Immigrant Student Visas 489
Student Visa Mills 489
D.C. School Vouchers 490
Charter Schools 491
Rural Schools 491
Antibullying and Gang Prevention 491
Adult Literacy 492
Race to the Top 492

Chapter 11 Housing and Urban Aid

Introduction 497

Chronology of Action on Housing and Urban Aid 500

2009–2010 500

Mortgage Relief Assistance 500
Mortgage Lender Regulation 502
Mortgage Insurance Premiums 503
Homebuyer Tax Credit 503
Section 8 Voucher Program 505
Home Improvement Rebates 506
Covered Bonds 507
Drywall Safety 508

2011–2012 509

Foreclosure Aid 509
Affordable Housing 510
Fannie and Freddie Executive Pay 510
Drywall Safety 511

Government-Sponsored Enterprises 511
Homeless Children and Youth 512

Chapter 12 Labor and Pensions

Introduction 515
Chronology of Action on Labor and Pensions 517
2009–2010 517
Unemployment Compensation 517
COBRA Subsidy 525
Job Creation and Protection 527
Education Jobs Fund 528
Gender-Based Wage Discrimination 528
Wage Parity 529
Minimum Wage for U.S. Territory Workers 529
Minimum Wage for Guam Construction Workers 530
Executive Pay 530
Executive Bonuses 531
Shareholder Oversight of Executive Pay 532
Union Card Check 533
Public Safety Workers 534
2010–2011 535
Unemployment Compensation 535
Labor Union Regulations 537
Union Organizing Rules 539
Rail and Aviation Union Elections 539
Minimum Wage 540
Federal Worker Pension Contributions 541
Welfare Law Changes 544

Chapter 13 Law and Justice

Law and Law Enforcement: Introduction 547
Chronology of Action on Law Enforcement 553
2009–2010 553
Hate Crimes 553
Legal Settlements 555
Immigration 556
Undocumented Children 556
Impeachment of Federal Judges 557
Journalism Sources 559
Firearms 559
Guantánamo Detainees 560
Smuggling of Illegal Immigrants 561
Patent Law Overhaul 561
COPS Authorization 561
Penalties for Crack Cocaine 562
Animal Crush Videos 562
Internet Schemes 563
Caller ID Spoofing 563
Law Enforcement on Tribal Lands 563
Railroad Mergers 564
Pricing Floors 564
Missing Persons 564
Haitian Children 565
Social Security Lawsuits 565
Witness Protection Plans 565
Bankruptcy Judgeships 565
TV Coverage of Court Proceedings 565
Administrative Changes to Federal Courts 566
Internet Gambling 566
Sex Tourism 566
Cyberstalking 567
Apology for Slavery and Segregation 567
2011–2012 568
Patent Law Overhaul 568
Violence Against Women Act 571
Holder Held in Contempt of Congress 573
Fiscal 2012 Appropriations 574
Concealed Handguns 575
Appellate Judgeships 576
Detention of Illegal Immigrants 577
Treatment of Suspected Terrorists 578
Prison Deaths 578
Abortion 578
Property Rights 579
Attorneys' Fees 579
Trade Secrets 580
Holocaust Survivors 580
Drug Traffickers 580
Same-sex Couples 581
Child Pornography 581
Highly Skilled Legal Immigrants 582
Low-Immigration Regions 582
Elderly and Disabled Refugees 583
The Supreme Court, 2008–2012 584

Chapter 14 General Government

Introduction 597

Chronology of Action on General Government 600

2009–2010 600

Merit-Based Pay Plan 600
Federal Worker Pay 600
Postal Service Retiree Benefit 601
Federal Teleworking 601
Whistleblower Protection 601
Parental Leave for Federal Workers 602
Federal Worker Software Sharing 603
Domestic Partner Benefits 603
Community Service Programs 604
NASA Reauthorization 605
America COMPETES Act Reauthorization 607
Federal Science Programs 609
National Flood Insurance 610
Earthquake Hazard 611
FEMA Independence 611
Government Agencies Efficiency 612
Improper Payments Elimination 612
Information Overclassification 613
Plain Writing 613
Deceptive Use of "Census" 614
Immigration Status on Census 614
E-Mail Records Protection 614
Cybersecurity Research 615
Filing Federal Regulations 615
FDR Memorabilia 615
Presidential Records 616
National Women's History Museum 616
American-Made U.S. Flags 616
Apology to Native Americans 617
Indian Health Service 617
Indian Tribes Recognition 617
Indian Casino Land 618
Native Hawaiian Government 618
Puerto Rico Political Status 619

2011–2012 621

Federal Workforce Pensions 621
Federal Worker Pay 621
Federal Employee Intelligence Leaks 622
Hatch Act Modernization 622
Whistleblower Protection 623
Federal Employee Domestic Partnerships 623
Tax Delinquents and Federal Work 624
Peace Corps Volunteer Protection 624
National Flood Insurance 624
Superstorm Sandy Disaster Relief 625
FEMA Shelters 626
Constellation Space Program 626
Postal Service Overhaul 627
Mark Twain Commemorative Coin 629
Contractors Withholding Rule 630
Small Business Federal Contracting 630
Regulatory Oversight 631
Restrictions on Regulations 632
Federal Reserve Audit 633
Government Spending Accountability 633
OMB Performance Standards 633
Improper Payments Elimination 634
GAO Authority 634
Excess Public Properties 634
American Community Survey 635
FTC and the National Gallery 635

Chapter 15 Inside Congress

Introduction 639

Chronology of Action on Congress: Members and Procedures 642

2009–2010 642

Organization: 111th Congress 642
Burris Appointment 647
D.C. Representation 648
Senate Appointments 650
Pocket Veto 650
Online Disclosure of Expenditures 650
Architect of the Capitol 651
U.S.-Made Goods in the Capitol 651
Ethics Probes 651

2011–2012 661

Organization: 112th Congress 661
STOCK Act 665
Senate Confirmation 668
House Office of General Counsel 669
Going Green at the Capitol 670
Printing Bills and Resolutions 670
Pocket Edition Constitution 670
Ethics Probes 670

Chronology of Action on Congress:
Election Issues 677

2009–2010 677

Campaign Finance 678
Shareholder Approval of Campaign Spending 679
Defunding ACORN 680

2011–2012 681

Campaign Finance 681
Presidential Election Campaign Fund 682
Election Assistance Commission 682

Chronology of Action on Congress:
Pay and Benefits 683

2009–2010 683

Congressional Pay 683
Ineligibility Clause 684

2011–2012 685

Congressional Pay 685
Members' Pay and Sequestration 685
Online Advertising 685
Disclaimers in Mailings 685

Chapter 16 The Obama Presidency

The Presidency of Barack Obama, 2009–2012 689

Domestic Policy 692

Foreign Policy 698

Reelection Campaign 702

Appointments 704

Appendix

Glossary of Congressional Terms 715
The Legislative Process in Brief 745

Key Votes 749

2009 Key Votes 751
2010 Key Votes 767
2011 Key Votes 785
2012 Key Votes 803

Congress and Its Members 823

Senate Membership in the 111th Congress 825
House Membership in the 111th Congress 826
Membership Changes, 111th and 112th Congresses 829
Senate Membership in the 112th Congress 831
House Membership in the 112th Congress 832
Members of Congress, 2009–2013 835
Congressional Leadership and Committees, 111th and 112th Congresses 843
Postelection Sessions 857
Senate Cloture Votes, 1917–2012 860
Attempted and Successful Cloture Votes, 1919–2012 871
House Discharge Petitions since 1931 872
Congressional Reapportionment, 1789–2010 873
The Presidency 875
President Obama's First Inaugural Address 877
President Obama on the State of Economy 879
President Obama's Address at Cairo University in Egypt 883
President Obama's Address on Accepting the Nobel Peace Prize 888
President Obama's Address on Climate Change 892
President Obama's 2010 State of the Union Address 893
President Obama's 2011 State of the Union Address 899
President Obama's Statement on Death of Osama bin Laden 905
President Obama's 2012 State of the Union Address 906
President Obama's Statement on Winning Reelection in 2012 912
Presidential Vetoes, 2009–2012 915
President Obama's Continuing Defense Appropriations for Fiscal 2010 915
President Obama's Veto of Notarization Legislation 915

Political Charts

Summary of Presidential Elections, 1789–2012 919
Victorious Party in Presidential Races, 1860–2012 922
2008 Presidential Election 924

2008 Electoral Votes and Map 925
2012 Presidential Election 926
2012 Electoral Votes and Map 927
Distribution of House Seats and Electoral Votes 928
Party Affiliations in Congress and the Presidency, 1789–2015 929
111th Congress Special Elections, 2009 Gubernatorial Elections 931
2010 Election Returns for Governor, Senate, and House 932
112th Congress Special Elections, 2011 Gubernatorial Elections 941
2012 Election Returns for Governor, Senate, and House 942
Results of House Elections, 1928–2012 950
Governors, 2009–2013 956

Public Laws
111th Congress 2009–2011 961
112th Congress 2011–2012 985

Index to Legislation by Public Law Number 1005

Index 1009

Tables, Figures, and Boxes

Tables

Partisanship in Congress 7

Age Structure of Congress, 1949–2011 9

Presidential Vote by Region 11

Incumbents Reelected, Defeated, or Retired, 1946–2012 12

Number of Public Laws Enacted, 1975–2012 15

Recorded Vote Totals 21

Blacks in Congress, 1947–2011 32

Women in Congress, 1947–2011 33

Hispanics in Congress, 1947–2011 34

House of Representatives Vote by Region 43

Federal Budget, Fiscal 1993–Fiscal 2012 117

Deficit History, 1929–2012 117

Public Debt 124

Taxes and Other Revenues as Percentage of Gross Domestic Product, 1935–2013 149

Annual Caps on Spending 166

Trade Balances 192

Figures

A Look at the Economy, 1996–2012 50

Federal Budget Receipts 118

Outlays for International Affairs 225

Outlays for National Defense 264

Outlays for Veterans 280

Outlays for Transportation 320

Outlays for Natural Resources and Environment 364

Outlays for Energy 365

Outlays for Agriculture 408

Outlays for Medicare and Medicaid 420

Outlays for Health 422

Outlays for Income Security 466

Outlays for Education 474

Outlays for Community and Regional Development 498

Outlays for Social Security 516

Outlays for Law Enforcement 548

Outlays for Science, Space, and General Government 598

Boxes

Congressional Leadership, 2009–2013 5

Passages 10

Congress in 2009 13

Congress in 2010 19

Congress in 2011 28

Speaker Boehner and the Hastert Rule 29

Congress in 2012 31

Money in Elections 36

Republicans Control House Redistricting 42

Economic Leadership 48

A Look at the Economy 1996–2012 50

Federal Reserve Actions during the Financial Crisis and Recession 56

Troubled Asset Relief Program: What Did TARP Do? 62

Major Actions on Economic and Financial Regulation Policy 76

Other Actions to Restore Economic Activity 79
Bernanke Given New Term as Federal Reserve Chair 86
Major Actions on Budget and Tax Policy 114
A Budget Glossary 120
Growing Public Debt 124
Backdoor Spending Caps in the Senate 137
Key Players in 2011 Debt Limit Negotiations 164
Two Minor Tax Bills Enacted 169
Extensions of Trade Adjustment Assistance, Trade Preferences, GSP 194
U.S. Trade Representative 195
Homeland Security Leadership 207
Foreign Policy Leadership 226
Iraq Policy Left a Radically Different Nation 234
U.S. War Casualties 2001–2012 236
Defense Leadership 274
Cybersecurity and Coast Guard Reauthorization 298
Transportation, Commerce, and Communications Leadership 323
Economic Stimulus Included Transportation, Broadband Funding 325
Energy, Environment Leadership 367
Economic Stimulus Bill Boosted Energy Strategy 368
Transportation Bill Eases Environmental Requirements 387
Agriculture Leadership 410
Health and Human Services Leadership 422
Health Care Overhaul: House vs. Senate 423
Obama Speaks on Health Care to Joint Session of Congress 430
Abortion Becomes an Eleventh-Hour Issue 432
Supreme Court Upholds Health Overhaul 455
Health Law Changes 456
Abortion Continues to Roil Health Law 458
Education Leadership 477
E-Reader Accessibility 479
529 Plans for College Savings 487
New Rules for For-Profit Career Colleges 488
Physical Education Report, Legislation 490
RESPECT Project, STEM Masters 493
Housing Leadership 499
PACE Loans: Property-Assisted Clean Energy Borrowing 501
Public Housing Market 505
Fannie, Freddie, and the Bailout 511
Labor Leadership 518
Permanent and Temporary Unemployment Benefit Programs 520
Cost of Living Changes Proposed for Social Security 542
Justice Leadership 549
Other Major Legal Legislation Considered by Congress 2009–2013 550
Supreme Court Confirmations 585
Supreme Court Upholds Health Care Legislation 586
NASA and Climate Change 607
Plutonium 238 608
Alaska Bypass 629
Giffords Assassination Attempt 643
Capitol Hill Dress Code 644
Sign-on Letters 645
Harry Reid's Remarks about Obama 646
Rangel: Counts and Convictions 657
House Transition Team 661
Sexual Misadventures Led to Resignations 671
Citizens United Ruling 677
Campaign Ads on Public TV 681
President Barack Obama's Cabinet 705

Introduction

The four years from 2009 to 2013, the period of the 111th and 112th U.S. Congresses and the first presidential term of Barack Obama, were dominated by one overriding event: the most devastating economic recession since the Great Depression of the 1930s. The reaction of both Congress as an institution and the presidency to this crisis foreshadowed much of the interplay between the two institutions—and the political parties—that was to dominate the full term of the newly elected president.

The Democratic Party, which controlled all of the 111th Congress, moved aggressively on legislation—principally spending, financial regulation, and health care—that the Republican Party largely voted against. The GOP's reluctance to provide many votes in favor of the Democratic initiatives in the first two years hardened into unyielding opposition to Obama in the 112th Congress after Republicans took control of the House in 2010 elections. Democrats still controlled the Senate but with their party in a decided House minority—plus GOP use of the Senate filibuster to block most legislation and many presidential appointments it opposed—Congress fell into gridlock and came close to closing down the federal government and causing the nation to default on its debt.

The president did win Senate approval of two new Supreme Court justices even though Republican support was lukewarm. The 110th Congress (2009–2011) with Democratic majorities, passed the far-reaching Affordable Care Act seeking to bring health insurance to thousands of Americans, and financial regulation seeking to prevent future economic crises of the type that caused the devastating recession. Legislation beyond the major items on economic and health issues also passed during the four years, but many other issues proved too controversial to move ahead in a deeply divided Congress, perhaps most notably immigration reform and serious debate on climate change. *(See box, major legislation, p. xx)*

Nevertheless, the four years were defined by the economic woes from the recession and, institutionally, the deepening animosity between the political parties and the barely concealed hostility of much of the GOP toward the president.

THE BUBBLE BURSTS

The economic crisis started, although unobtrusively, in mid-2006 as real estate price increases slowed from a torrid pace earlier in the decade and then collapsed as the housing market bubble—clearly visible in hindsight—burst. From there, things got worse.

Housing prices sank in much of the nation by mid-2007 and spread globally into 2008 and 2009. Thousands of homeowners found their mortgages were larger than the house's value and fell into default. Foreclosures spread and banks, whose complicated and shady lending practices were now exposed, were threatened with failure.

A pivotal moment in the global economic crisis occurred in September 2008, when the venerable Wall Street investment bank Lehman Brothers collapsed under the weight of toxic financial constructs in the housing market, particularly in so-called subprime mortgages taken out by thousands of borrowers whose earnings and creditworthiness barred them from conventional lending. When hard times came, this swath of lending became the lynchpin of the economic downturn.

First Lehman Brothers collapsed, and then other even larger banks nearly did also, which froze the global lending system. With lending largely unavailable to businesses and individuals, economic activity plunged and jobs disappeared by the thousands, with unemployment eventually spiking at over 10 percent. Moreover, household net worth—the difference between asset values (such as stocks or a house's value) and liabilities—declined by 20 percent, the Federal Reserve Board (Fed) calculated.

This was the crisis in which the United States and most of the developed world found itself as America was making a transition from the Republican administration of George W. Bush to the Democratic victor in 2008, Obama.

THE NEW TEAM IN WASHINGTON

The inauguration of Obama as the nation's forty-fourth president, on an exceptionally frigid day in Washington, D.C., initially seemed to presage a new national start from a decade of unexpected terrorism attacks on American soil and in other nations, wild economic swings, and the waging of wars in Afghanistan and Iraq. The former was a war brought on by the September 11, 2001, terrorist attacks in New York City and near Washington, D.C. The latter was a war of choice by the United States that was based on arguments made to the public and to Congress about weapons of mass destruction that turned out to be false. At first, both had popular support, but together as they dragged on through the decade, war weariness grew in America. A main campaign theme of Obama in 2008 was that he would bring these wars to an end.

Still, the immediate matter before the new administration was what to do about the economic collapse.

Obama and his financial team did not come into office in January 2009 in an economic vacuum. The Democratically controlled Congress and the Republican George W. Bush administration in 2008, seeing the damage of the housing collapse, responded in a variety of ways, starting as early as February that year with a stimulus bill estimated to cost $134 billion over six years. Even more importantly Congress in late 2008 passed a $700 billion bill—known as the Troubled Asset Relief Program (TARP)—that initially was intended to buy up toxic assets in the banking system. In fact, as new information emerged about the shakiness of the entire system, substantial amounts of the funds went instead to bail out most of the nation's largest financial institutions, including both commercial and Wall Street investment banks, with loans and direct infusion of cash. In addition, a chunk went to prop up two of the nation's largest auto companies (Chrysler and General Motors), which were near bankruptcy as car sales disappeared. *(Congress and the Nation Vol. XII, p. 163)*

Even with this running start, few doubted that the economy needed more help, although some economists and many Republicans argued that numerous earlier recessions quickly proved self-correcting and so relatively little government action was appropriate. Even some Obama advisors, to their later regret, were reluctant to push for a large-scale government stimulus of the economy.

One other component of the national government, the Fed—the nation's central bank—saw the danger starkly. As it happened, the Fed chair, Ben Bernanke, who was a scholar of the Great Depression, understood better than most where the current situation might lead. To that end he led the central bank into previously unexplored ways of propping up the economy—most notably a policy called quantitative easing that essentially involved pumping billions of dollars into the economy through the Fed's unique power to create new money.

But in the White House and Congress, the key actors, facing dangers of unknown parameters, had to decide how much and what kind of economic stimulus was needed. The answer was legislation that provided $787.2 billion in spending on a variety of activities including $575.3 billion in new funding over eleven years for projects intended to save or create jobs such as road construction and energy initiatives; programs to assist the jobless, such as extended emergency unemployment benefits and food stamps; education programs; and initiatives to expand health information technology and the extension of broadband service to rural areas. Included in that $787.2 billion total was $211.8 billion in tax cuts over eleven years for individuals and businesses.

HOW TO USE THIS BOOK

Readers can access information in several ways. The sixteen chapters are listed in the Summary Table of Contents *(page v)*. An outline of each chapter, including boxes, tables, graphs, and other related material, is provided in the detailed Table of Contents *(page vii)*.

For specific topics turn to the complete index at the end of the volume *(page 1009)*. Throughout the book page references to related subjects in other chapters are provided. These page "flags" are designed to speed research across an array of subjects.

The Introduction provides an overview of political and legislative activity and a thumbnail description of each chapter's content.

The legislation, which was thereafter known as the stimulus bill, passed with the support of three congressional Republicans out of a total 212 GOP senators and representatives who cast ballots on the key votes on the measure. This voting pattern was to be replicated time and again over the four years as the two parties increasingly talked past one another rather than debating, and reconciling, their differences.

HEALTH CARE AND FINANCIAL REGULATION

Although economic matters were foremost in Washington in early 2009, the Obama administration and its Democratic allies in Congress decided the time was ripe to move legislatively on two other fronts: one an immediate child of the economic crisis and the other a Democratic goal for more than half a century.

The first was new financial regulation to proscribe the excesses of banks and other new investment institutions that underpinned the collapse of the housing market and near collapse of the global financial system. It took a year and a half to enact the legislation and was opposed at every turn by the financial industry and Republicans in Congress. Indeed, the GOP spent much of the rest of Obama's first term trying to undo key provisions of the reform.

The second was a far-reaching overhaul of the American health care system to provide nearly universal health care coverage for the nation. The goal was to add up to 30 million individuals to the insurance rolls, to slow the rising cost of health care, to help lower-income citizens get health insurance, to set minimal insurance coverage standards, and to end an array of insurance company practices, such as coverage denial for preexisting conditions, that affected even those who had coverage. Some Obama advisers counseled against going after so big a target while the economy was still a wreck, but the president decided otherwise.

Debate on the legislation, known formally as the Affordable Care Act and derisively by opponents as "Obamacare," lasted more than a year before enactment in March 2010 and involved multiple high-wire acts in both chambers—ranging from the always controversial issue of abortion coverage to stapling together a sixty-vote margin in the Senate to end the GOP's filibuster. As with financial regulation, Republicans spent much of the rest of the 111th Congress and all of the 112th Congress trying to defund or even repeal the law. With Obama holding the veto pen, and no chance of a congressional override, these efforts were seen mostly as Republican efforts looking ahead to the next elections, and in 2010 they struck gold but in 2012 struck out.

A TALE OF TWO ELECTIONS

Democrats in 2008 had won almost everything they could hope for: the White House—historically electing an African American that few thought possible only a few decades after the civil rights changes from the 1960s—and solid control of Congress, with a commanding House majority and an almost filibuster-proof Senate majority, although implementing the latter proved far more challenging than the numbers suggested.

The next round, the 2010 midterm elections, was another matter entirely. Republicans were energized by a variety of issues that an out-of-power opposition party often welcomes as a road map back into power. Most powerfully, the economic doldrums, snail-pace advances in job creation and economic recovery (even though the actual recession had ended months earlier), the continuing aftermath of housing collapse with many losing their homes to foreclosure, and—perhaps most powerful of all—the sweeping changes contained in the health care reform legislation. Into this volatile mix of national angst marched a new force that came to be known as the Tea Party. It was initially a more or less genuine spontaneous coming together of groups around the nation that saw in actions taken in Washington, and especially at the White House, a vast overreaching by the federal government. Later the Tea Party phenomena evolved into a more conventional political role as professional politicians sought to harness its energies to specific election campaigns. But for the Republican Party in 2010 the Tea Party overall could not have come at a better time.

With much of the electorate harboring deep doubts about the nation's course and the Democratically controlled government's response, the GOP—using Tea Party energy where possible—rode to a stunning sweep in House elections in 2010, picking up sixty-three seats to regain control of the House for the first time since 2006 and significantly narrowing the Democratic majority in the Senate. Even President Obama said the Democratic Party took a "shellacking."

It was this "shellacking" on election day that gave birth to the gridlock Congress that prevailed for the following two years in the 112th Congress. Although legislation was passed during the period, including some bills of significance, much of the time was spent posturing for political gain with eyes set firmly on the 2012 national elections when the president was up for reelection.

But unlike 2010, the Republican Party whiffed in 2012. President Obama won a convincing—if slightly smaller—margin in the popular vote and a commanding majority in the electoral votes by winning nearly all the large and vigorously contested battleground states. Republicans retained House control while losing some seats; to the party's embarrassment, the GOP also lost the total national vote for House seats. That did not matter to House control because redistricting after the 2010 census allowed drawing congressional district lines in favor of GOP candidates, the long-standing tradition of gerrymandering that was done by both parties when opportunity allowed.

But that loss of the total national House vote, along with the clear national rejection of the Republican's presidential candidate, left many political observers, even staunch Republicans, wondering if the Grand Old Party had lost touch with substantial numbers of American voters—especially younger persons, women, and minorities.

LEGISLATION AND POLITICS: 2009–2013

This book continues a series begun in 1965 with the publication of *Congress and the Nation Vol. I,* which covered national government and politics from 1945 to 1964. Subsequent volumes, published every four years, covered the same subjects over the two congresses of each succeeding administration. As with the preceding volumes, this edition is divided into a series of chapters focusing on various substantive subjects such as economic and regulatory policy, commerce, law and justice, and health and welfare. This volume, as with recent ones, contains sixteen chapters, an extensive appendix, and a comprehensive index. Following are brief summaries of the chapters and the highlights of events described in them.

Chapter 1 Politics and National Issues

This chapter is an overview of the four-year period 2009 through 2012, the four years of Obama's first presidential term, and the 111th Congress and 112th Congress. The major legislative and the political events noted here are covered in more detail in subsequent chapters.

Chapter 2 Economic Policy

President Obama took office in 2009 during the most severe economic downturn since the 1930s, the repercussions of which were to dominate his entire first term even though the recession technically ended in mid-2009.

The crisis reached into nearly every important part of American life: soaring unemployment that reached above 10 percent and still was above 7 percent after four years; decimated state government budgets that forced deep spending cuts; a near total collapse of the domestic auto industry; and a financial crisis that brought down many banks and left many others—even some of the largest—on life support from the federal government.

MAJOR LEGISLATION BEFORE CONGRESS DURING OBAMA'S FIRST TERM

The two congresses of President Obama's first term in office were widely seen as diametrically opposed, with the first, the 111th from 2009 to 2011, highly productive and the second, the 112th from 2011 to 2013, largely an exercise in political gridlock. While correct in many respects, this picture distorts to an extent the legislative work done in the 112th Congress and tends to hide a useful national debate about the appropriate role of government in society and especially the national government that was prompted by the actions of the 111th Congress, which was completely controlled by Democrats. In the 112th Congress Republicans controlled the House, giving them a platform to challenge the wisdom of much that was done by Democrats two years earlier. Although little of the Democrats' handiwork was undone, GOP attempts to do so highlighted a strikingly different view of national government.

Following are brief descriptions of major issues considered over the four-year period in most subject areas examined in this volume, except for general government and Congress. Legislative action in those two areas can be found in Chapters 14 and 15.

Economic Recovery

TARP money. The Senate in 2009 approves release of $350 billion in funds provided in 2008 under the Troubled Asset Relief Program (TARP), intended to help stabilize the financial sector.

Economic stimulus. Congress in 2009 passes legislation providing an estimated $787.2 billion in new spending and tax cuts to help economic recovery.

Payroll tax cut. Legislators in 2010 clear a bill reducing by two percentage points the employee payroll tax for Social Security, which with other provisions was expected to give the economy a $180 billion boost in 2011. The action also continues tax cuts approved in 2001 and 2003 through the end of 2012.

In the 112th Congress the payroll tax cut is extended through 2012. All tax reductions from 2001 and 2003 are permanently extended except those for the wealthy whose rates return to higher levels, and automatic across-the-board cuts in federal discretionary funding are put in place.

Jobs and Unemployment

Unemployment compensation. Legislation extends emergency unemployment benefits for an additional fourteen weeks, the first of several contentious extensions throughout Obama's first term. The 112th Congress extends the benefits through 2013.

Jobs creation. Congress provides payroll tax relief and other incentives to employers who hire unemployed workers.

Help for states. A $26.1 billion bill passes in 2010 to help state and local governments avoid laying off teachers and maintain Medicaid health coverage for the poor.

Help for business. Congress in 2010 clears legislation providing tax incentives and expanded credit access to small businesses to encourage hiring or retaining workers.

Financial Regulation

Financial regulation. A comprehensive overhaul of the financial regulatory system is enacted in 2010 over objections of almost all Republicans to prevent future financial excesses such as those that collapsed the U.S. housing market and nearly collapsed the international financial system.

Credit cards. Congress in 2009 clears a bill to set new restrictions on when credit card companies could increase interest rates and fees.

Funding Government and Paying the Bills

Funding government. The appropriations process moves relatively smoothly in the 111th Congress with Democrats in control but starts to unravel in 2010, requiring short stop-gap fixes to keep the government open, a practice that becomes common. The appropriations process comes fully off the rails in the 112th Congress as Republicans, now in the House majority, and Senate Democrats and the White House see the world entirely differently. House GOP members, buoyed by a big majority and the energy of new Tea Party members, demand deep cuts in federal spending.

Talks between the president and the House Republican Speaker over a "grand bargain" on taxes and spending collapse, followed by much finger-pointing on blame. Continued maneuverings on spending and taxes dominate the rest of the 112th Congress, with mainly short-term agreements reached to prevent government closings.

Debt limit. The 111th Congress raises the national debt limit in two steps, at the end of 2009 and in early 2010.

In the 112th Congress House conservatives demand deep spending cuts before supporting another debt ceiling hike, waving off warnings of global financial chaos if the United States defaults on its debt obligations. The Senate minority leader and the vice president strike a deal to increase the limit requiring automatic across-the-board federal spending cuts if further spending and tax agreements are not reached—an arrangement known as a sequester. Few expect the sequester to kick in, but it does in 2013.

Homeland Security

Legislation is relatively light during Obama's first term, but Congress over the four years extends key provisions of the Patriot Act involving controversial issues of obtaining business records, using wiretaps, and obtaining legal permission to follow individuals deemed possible terrorist threats but not affiliated with a formal organization.

The 112th Congress updates the 1978 Foreign Intelligence Surveillance Act involving provisions about to expire that authorized the intelligence community to wiretap certain foreigners who were in touch with people in the United States, without getting individual warrants.

Foreign, Defense Policy

No serious challenges to Obama's foreign policies occur during his first two years in office, and legislators support two top presidential commitments: withdrawing U.S. troops from Iraq while boosting troop levels in Afghanistan.

START treaty. The Senate ratifies a new nuclear arms control treaty with Russia that called for reducing the arsenals in both countries.

Iran sanctions. Both Congresses impose sanctions against Iran in an attempt to thwart that country's presumed ambitions to build nuclear weapons. Existing sanctions are expanded in mid-2010 against multinational companies that helped Iran develop its domestic petroleum refining capacity. A key provision tightens limits on payments to Iran through foreign banks.

Weapons systems. The Obama administration succeeds in killing two multibillion weapons system that had strong congressional support because of jobs they provided in many states: the Air Force's F-22 fighter and a second, "alternative" engine for the F-35 fighter, being developed as the next generation warplane for the Air Force, Marine Corps, and Navy.

Intelligence authorization. Congress clears a compromise fiscal 2010 intelligence authorization bill, primarily to allow legislators to reassert oversight role of the intelligence community and permit them to make policy changes affecting the sixteen U.S. intelligence agencies and intelligence-related activities of the U.S. government.

Afghanistan, Iraq, and Pakistan. Despite increasing partisanship, legislators back, or at least make no serious attempt to overturn, Obama's policies in Iraq and Afghanistan. Congress also approves vast increases in aid to the governments of Afghanistan and neighboring Pakistan—despite concern that the Pakistani military was aiding rebels fighting the Afghanistan government that the United States was trying to keep in power.

Transportation, Commerce, and Communications

Surface transportation, FAA. Legislators in 2012 complete action on a long-stalled reauthorization of the Highway Trust Fund, although long-term financing issues remain unresolved. They also reauthorize the Federal Aviation Administration. But administration proposals on guaranteeing everyone equal access to the Internet—known as net neutrality—go nowhere.

Energy and Environment

The biggest issues in this area—what to do about climate change, or even to accept that it exists—is just too big for legislators to get their arms around. Democrats in the 111th Congress get into the stimulus bill tens of billions of dollars in initiatives designed to increase energy efficiency and boost renewable energy industries. Republicans charge the efforts would interfere with the free market. Congress considers dozens of other issues but end 2012 with little to show for the effort.

Health and Human Services

Health care reform. Along with economic legislation, a bitter and drawn-out battle between the parties in the 111th Congress results in the most far-reaching overhaul of the American health system since Medicare was created in the mid-1960s.

CHIP, tobacco, AIDS. Legislators also deal with a raft of other health matters: they expand the Children's Health Insurance Program (CHIP); give the Food and Drug Administration the power to regulate tobacco products; and reauthorize the Ryan White HIV/AIDS program without much controversy.

Education

Legislators fail to reauthorize the No Child Left Behind law, which many states criticized for its stringent requirements. Congress does, however, remove the federal government from the business of guaranteeing student loans offered by private lenders. Lawmakers also provide funding to state and local governments to avert teacher layoffs.

Housing Policy

The housing market collapse and the wave of foreclosures that came in its wake focus legislators' minds. Legislators allow easier access to mortgage modifications but fall far short of sweeping proposal from advocates of stressed homeowners. Legislators do provide a tax credit for first-time homebuyers.

Law and Justice

Supreme Court. The Senate confirms two new appointments by President Obama to fill vacancies created by retirements, but the new justices do not change the ideological balance on the Court.

Patent law. Congress overhauls provisions of the nation's patent laws, in a bipartisan effort that had eluded legislators for years.

Job discrimination, hate crimes. Democrats in the 111th Congress push through a bill to make it easier for workers to file wage discrimination lawsuits against their employers. They also expand federal hate crimes law to include crimes against people because of their sexual orientation, gender, or disability.

Immigration, Guantánamo Bay detainees. Reform of immigration laws proves too controversial for resolution. And the Obama administration's effort to close the U.S. detainee facility at Guantánamo Bay, Cuba, never gets traction in the face of strong opposition from Republicans and some Democrats.

The nation had survived many recessions since the 1930s but this one was unusual because, in addition to its severity, it was sparked by an intense financial crisis that started in the United States and spread worldwide.

Timely and sustained action by Washington—notably an unprecedented bailout of Wall Street banks and other companies, a series of interest rate cuts and financial guarantees by the Federal Reserve Bank, and a one-time injection of "stimulus" spending and tax cuts—helped prevent the recession from deepening into a 1930s-style Great Depression. Massive infusions of taxpayer cash kept hundreds of banks afloat (even as more than 300 others failed) and ensured that the nation's credit system would not collapse.

Even with the government's remarkable success in helping contain the economic damage, many taxpayers were deeply angered by the use of tax dollars to bail out giant Wall Street banks—the very banks whose risky bets had sparked the financial crisis. Perhaps more than any other single action, this propping up of wealthy banks significantly poisoned the nation's political atmosphere. The bailout program, called the Troubled Asset Relief Program (TARP), had to be forced through Congress in the fall of 2008, when Obama's predecessor, George W. Bush, was still in office. It was never popular to begin with, and quickly became a public symbol of everything that was wrong on Wall Street and in Washington. This was despite the fact that the bailout clearly rescued the financial system at a critical moment and wound up with a net cost to taxpayers, after repayments and profits, of only about $24 billion of its initial price tag of more than $700 billion.

These developments are examined in the overview section that begins this chapter, and are explored in greater detail in the following sections on economic and regulatory policy, taxes and budget, and trade policy.

Economic and regulatory policy. Within three weeks of Obama's swearing-in ceremony, Congress had approved $787.2 billion in new spending and tax cuts to spur economic growth, preserve jobs, and help those most affected by the recession. It was the largest economic stimulus bill in the nation's history—and, apart from a temporary payroll tax cut enacted a year later, the only significant measure enacted in the president's first term dedicated solely to economic recovery.

Eighteen months later, Congress in July 2010 passed far-reaching reforms to the nation's financial regulatory system intended to prevent any future financial crisis similar to the one that plunged the country into recession, a significant victory for the president and advocates of reigning in Wall Street excesses. But opponents spent the next two years trying to undo parts of the law, and they succeeded in delaying implementation of many of its most important provisions.

The widely differing views between Democrats and Republicans on how to repair the stumbling economy and faltering financial system fed into the partisanship that characterized Obama's first term and that was most intensely displayed in the legislative disputes over taxing and spending that nearly drove the government into financial default.

Attempts to inject new or additional stimulus into the economy got caught up in the legislative battles over the budget when Republicans insisted on offsetting the costs with other spending cuts. Whether larger or longer stimulus would have helped the economy recover faster remained a controversy that economists—and politicians of every stripe—continued to debate. What seemed clear is that after four years the two parties seemed no closer—and perhaps even farther apart—on resolving their differences over the role of government in the nation's economy.

Taxes and budget policy. Even though the 111th Congress in the first two years of Obama's presidency passed historic legislation, including overhauls of the nation's health care and financial regulation systems and the largest economic stimulus program ever enacted, by the end of Obama's first term legislators were more likely to be remembered for the deep partisan disputes over federal spending and tax policy that at times threatened to shut down the government and even throw it into default. Although last-minute compromises averted these disasters, they failed to resolve the underlying issues.

The gridlock on federal spending and tax policy flowed from both economic and political factors. The immediate causes grew out of the 2008 financial crisis and subsequent economic recession. The resulting decline in tax receipts and jump in federal spending on safety net programs and other emergency measures led to a near tripling of the federal budget deficit in fiscal 2009 to $1.4 trillion.

But political issues, and fundamental differences between Democrats and Republicans about government action, greatly complicated resolution of the economic problems, including a soaring public deficit. Over three decades the two parties had grown more and more polarized over their differing views on taxes, spending, and the role of government. Broadly speaking, Democrats favored government intervention in the marketplace in an effort to ensure fair treatment for producers, workers, and consumers and to provide safety nets to the less privileged. Republicans in contrast supported smaller government, preferring less regulation, taxation, and spending.

On a deeper level, Democrats and Republicans were engaged in a long-standing debate about the proper distribution of the federal tax burden across income levels, and—by extension—over income and wealth inequality in American society. Democrats consistently tried to provide tax cuts for lower- and middle-income taxpayers and raise taxes on the wealthiest 1 percent to 2 percent of the population. Republicans, in turn, accused Democrats of "class warfare" and pointed to studies suggesting that roughly 50 percent of Americans did not have to pay income tax (although most workers paid Social Security taxes, plus state and local taxes including sales and property taxes for home owners and, indirectly, renters as well).

Trade policy. Trade policy was not a top priority issue during Obama's first term but Congress did take important actions. Legislators in 2011 endorsed three trade pacts—one with South Korea, a major U.S. trading partner; the others, both smaller in scope, with Colombia and Panama. All three agreements were initially negotiated during George W. Bush's presidency and then renegotiated by the Obama administration to include stronger protections for labor and the environment. The agreements passed handily, but only after Congress resolved a difficult and related dispute over extending expanded trade adjustment assistance for displaced workers.

Congress at the end of 2012 approved legislation establishing permanent normal trade relations with Russia. The removal of decades-old trade restrictions—originally intended to protest human rights violations by the Soviet Union but kept in place for two decades after the collapse of Soviet communism—was expected to lead to expanded commerce between the two countries.

Over Republican objections, Congress also reauthorized the Export-Import Bank, which provided direct loans, financing, and loan guarantees to support the export of American goods and services. Obama had made the legislation a high priority because it supported U.S. jobs.

Chapter 3 Homeland Security

Even though candidate Obama repeatedly criticized the policies of the incumbent Bush, faulting the outgoing president on both domestic and international security issues, once in office Obama's actions on homeland security were not significantly different overall, as he continued many Bush administration policies opposed by civil libertarians and privacy advocates. The new president pursued different courses from Bush in various areas, but many of the homeland security–related arguments that began on Capitol Hill during the Bush years were refought again with Obama in the White House.

The Obama administration faced a myriad of issues, ranging from border security to cybersecurity to an extension of the controversial Patriot Act. During Obama's first term, the country also had to deal with natural and human-caused disasters including a massive oil spill off the Gulf Coast in 2010 and Hurricane Sandy on the East Coast in 2012.

In Congress lawmakers confronted a variety of issues on national security. Legislators eventually extended three controversial provisions in the Patriot Act. Congress increased funding for security along the U.S. border with Mexico, in part because of increased violence in Mexico from drug wars. Lawmakers extended warrantless wiretapping provisions that prompted heated debate. In addition, they considered but did not in every case resolve issues ranging from Coast Guard funding to cybersecurity to security at chemical plants.

Chapter 4 Foreign Policy

Obama came onto the world stage as a celebrity president, a man with almost rock-star drawing power that got him a respectful, often adoring, hearing in his early international travels. But as the new president, with little international experience, began dealing with tough global challenges, much of that warm-and-fuzzy aura wore away. By the end of his first term, Obama was struggling to keep up with a bewildering number of foreign crises or near-crises. Back home, he often faced harsh criticism, though little direct action in terms of legislation, from hostile Republicans in Congress who insisted he had diminished American influence in the world.

Obama appeared to have two new priorities on his agenda: softening the world's image of the United States, which had been tarnished by the often-brusque behavior of the preceding Bush administration, especially with the invasion and occupation of Iraq that began in 2003; and a "pivot" toward a greater focus on U.S. interests in Asia, largely as a means of restraining China's influence as it became a global economic, and eventually strategic, superpower.

If there was one big global surprise during Obama's first term, it came from a totally unexpected place: the Arab world. Popular protests against corrupt, autocratic governments began in Tunisia in December 2010 and quickly spread across North Africa and into the Arabian peninsula and the eastern Mediterranean. The protests became known as the "Arab Spring" or the "Arab Awakening."

Chapter 5 Defense Policy

President Obama's first term appeared to mark a transition period for the U.S. defense establishment after the long wars and massive buildup of his predecessor, President Bush. The winding down of U.S. military involvement in Iraq, a temporary "surge" of U.S. forces in Afghanistan before a planned withdrawal in 2014, and the early stages of defense spending cuts mandated by Congress all suggested that the military and its missions might look substantially different—and certainly leaner—in the years to come.

Perhaps the gravest warning sign for the Pentagon was the congressional inability, or unwillingness, to shield it (and related national security agencies, such as the Central Intelligence Agency) from across-the-board budget cuts that newly empowered conservative Republicans demanded throughout the government.

A government-wide budget deal negotiated in 2011 called for reducing previously projected defense spending by $487 billion over the following decade (a cut of about 9 percent, according to some estimates). More immediately, 2011 budget legislation included the Pentagon in potential across-the-board spending cuts, known as the "sequester." Few expected when the deal was negotiated that the sequester cuts actually would go into effect, but it did when an expected broader agreement on spending did not emerge.

Congress delayed the mandatory sequester cuts until March 2013 but failed to prevent them from going into effect, thus subjecting most Pentagon spending for the remainder of fiscal 2013 to an across-the-board cut of 7.8 percent. The Pentagon made thousands of cutbacks in response, including furloughing all of its 800,000 civilian employees for twenty-two days.

Despite the cuts, the Congressional Budget Office estimated early in 2013 that defense spending would continue to grow through the remainder of the decade, but at a much lower rate than in previous years and likely below the level of inflation.

Chapter 6 Transportation, Commerce, and Communications

Transportation and communication issues were recurring themes during President Obama's first term, but legislative efforts had mixed results as the White House and Congress focused primarily on combating the economic recession.

Obama promoted infrastructure and highway projects as an avenue for job creation, and they became one of the cornerstones of a $787.2 billion economic stimulus package early in the 111th Congress. Lawmakers and the administration also offered the struggling automobile industry additional relief through a short-term auto trade-in program dubbed "cash for clunkers." But lawmakers were not so quick to embrace other initiatives, and negotiations continued for months or, in several cases, years.

Lawmakers attempting to complete long-term reauthorizations of laws governing surface transportation programs and the Federal Aviation Administration (FAA) frequently were frustrated as Obama placed a higher priority on overhauling laws governing financial services and health care and—for a time—on legislation to control climate change. That left little time, energy, or political capital to move other broad measures.

Although it took some time, Congress eventually passed a twenty-seven-month highway reauthorization bill and a four-year FAA reauthorization as a sign of bipartisan cooperation. But those laws ultimately were criticized for not resolving several major issues and providing patchwork solutions to problems. The final highway measure, for example, avoided resolving long-term funding for the highway fund. Obama also had to relinquish hope for two of his major initiatives in the second session of Congress: high-speed rail and a national infrastructure bank.

The Obama administration also came into office in January 2009 with several priorities in telecommunications, including implementation of a rule on "network neutrality"—a concept to essentially ensure equal access to the Internet for all consumers and content providers—that regulators issued over congressional Republican objections. It sought to subsidize broadband access in rural areas and to limit how much telecommunication companies could charge for access to high-speed lines. These issues remained unresolved.

Chapter 7 Energy and Environment

National elections in 2008 were initially seen as foreshadowing a dramatic shift from the environmental and energy policies of the administration of President Bush. Whereas Bush had ties to the oil and gas industry, Obama spoke often of the need for more "green-collar" jobs and a greater reliance on emerging renewable and solar energy policies. He promised to begin combating climate change, which he characterized as one of the major challenges facing society, and put a greater stress on ensuring clean air and water.

Democratic lawmakers and the new president won a major, and early, victory in 2009. A sweeping economic stimulus package contained tens of billions of dollars in initiatives designed to increase energy efficiency and boost renewable energy industries. These included provisions to make the electric grid more reliable, provide loan guarantees and grants for renewable energy generation and transmission, help Americans make their homes more energy-efficient, and develop technologies to reduce dependence on foreign oil.

Republicans warned that the provisions would interfere with the free market and plunge the government deeper into debt. But supporters said the proposals would not only put the United States on a more sustainable path but were also critical to helping the nation recover from the deep economic recession and compete globally.

The stimulus, however, was the Democrats' high-water mark on energy and environmental issues, partly because legislative activity focused on immediate economic recovery and health care reform. But an equally important reason throughout Obama's first term was that the most prominent issue on the environmental agenda was climate change. The notion of regulating greenhouse gases proved deeply unpopular with many in Congress, especially conservatives and members from states and districts with a strong reliance on the coal industry. Once Republicans won control of the House in 2010 elections, Obama's environmental agenda was essentially dead because most members in the GOP caucus were fundamentally hostile to its key parts.

Energy legislation fared no better. In June 2009, a Senate committee approved a bipartisan measure, seen as a component of the climate bill, that would have sharply increased electricity generated from renewable sources, opened vast new areas of the Gulf of Mexico to oil and gas drilling, and made it easier to site power transmission lines. But it died along with climate legislation.

Chapter 8 Agricultural Policy

The four years of President Obama's first term were unproductive on agricultural legislation. Congress unsuccessfully attempted to pass a major five-year farm bill in 2012. Although the Senate approved the legislation in June 2012, it fell victim to political battles in the House and did not make it to the floor for a vote. Many farm-related programs were extended through October 1, 2013, as part of a last-minute deal, approved in January 2013. (The complete farm law was finally extended in early 2014.)

The five-year bill was designed to replace the previous multiyear farm bill, which was set to expire on September 30, 2012.

A major controversy in the 2012 farm bill involved the food stamp program, officially known as the Supplemental

Nutrition Assistance Program (SNAP). At a time of escalating controversy over spending and budget deficits some members, notably conservative Republicans, sought steep funding cuts in the program. Food stamp supporters argued that especially during tough economic times the program's funding should not be slashed.

A new food safety law, signed by President Obama on January 4, 2011, was perhaps the most significant agriculture-related legislation enacted during this period. The law gave new authority to the Food and Drug Administration (FDA) to regulate food products. Among the FDA's new powers were the ability to call for mandatory food recalls, to install a more effective system to track food and trace sources of food-borne illnesses, to inspect food facilities on the basis of risk, and to increase oversight of imported food.

Chapter 9 Health and Human Services

Health issues—and legislation—along with economic recovery measures characterized President Obama's first term in the White House.

Although he had more than a few difficulties with Congress in his four years he will be remembered as a president who succeeded in passing a major health overhaul, placing him alongside Lyndon B. Johnson, who saw enactment of Medicare in the 1960s.

It was not pretty. In fact, it was downright ugly at times. But as Obama himself pointed out, the bill he signed March 23, 2010, came "after almost a century of trying."

Republicans, however, rode doubts about even the health law to electoral victory, reclaiming the House in the 2010 elections. But Democrats retained control of the Senate, and thus managed to fend off repeated GOP efforts through the 112th Congress to repeal or otherwise undermine the nascent health law.

But while the health overhaul was center stage during all four years of Obama's first term, when it came to other health issues Congress did manage to pass important legislation. For example, early in 2009, Congress for the first time approved legislation to give the Food and Drug Administration the power to regulate tobacco products. Like the health overhaul, it was the culmination of a battle that had raged for decades and had pitted health advocates against powerful moneyed interests: growers, manufacturers, and sellers of tobacco products.

The fully Democratic-controlled 111th Congress, with a Democratic president, also managed in 2009 to do what its predecessor tried and failed to do: expand the Children's Health Insurance Program (CHIP).

For the first time, Congress managed to reauthorize the Ryan White HIV/AIDS program in 2009 without the usual regional and urban-rural clashes that had slowed earlier renewal efforts. The program, first passed at the height of the nation's AIDS epidemic in 1990, provided funding to states and cities for services and medications for those with AIDS and HIV and to prevent the further spread of the virus.

One major health policy item Congress did not solve during the four years, however, was to fix a continuing problem with the way doctors were paid under the Medicare program. A glitch created by a 1997 budget bill required Congress to repeatedly do a so-called "doc fix" to prevent doctors from getting a 21 percent pay cut that lawmakers feared and doctors threatened could have jeopardized seniors' ability to find physicians to care for them.

Chapter 10 Education Policy

On one of the most controversial and important education issues—reauthorization of the No Child Left Behind law, a signature piece of legislation for former President Bush—Congress struck out during the four years of Obama's first term. Complaints about the new law, which for the first time tied federal education aid to improvements in students' test scores, emerged early after its enactment in 2002, spread across the political spectrum, and never went away. But a clear path to fixing the measure proved elusive.

In March 2011, President Obama challenged Congress to rewrite the law by the start of the fall school year. Key Senate and House members promised swift action but reauthorization of the law, which had expired in 2007, did not occur. Little expectation existed that the job would be completed in 2012, during a presidential election year, and no meaningful progress was made. A hyperpartisan atmosphere, philosophical differences, and powerful stakeholder lobbying, for example, from teachers unions, stymied congressional efforts.

The most noteworthy education policy-related action taken by the 111th Congress was removing the federal government from the business of guaranteeing student loans offered by private lenders. Lawmakers also provided funding to state and local governments to avert teacher layoffs. A new competitive grant program called Race to the Top sought to improve and reform the educational system.

The 112th Congress, while unable to reauthorize the No Child Left Behind Act, did roll back a scheduled student loan interest rate increase, authorized funding for a federal school voucher program in the District of Columbia, and kept the budget ax from falling heavily on the Pell grant program for college expenses.

Chapter 11 Housing and Urban Aid

Housing policy remained a high priority in President Obama's first term as the ravages of the deep recession that started two years earlier continued to threaten a huge swath of American homeowners and devastated the nation's home-building industry.

In the aftermath of the housing market collapse from the recession, the 111th Congress helped alleviate some borrowers' worries by allowing easier access to mortgage modifications and by increasing federal deposit insurance coverage. Lawmakers also twice extended a tax credit for first-time homebuyers and created a credit for existing homeowners who bought a new home. The 112th Congress, with bitter partisanship growing after Republicans took control of the House, was less active in housing policy. The House passed bills to terminate some federal mortgage aid programs and to establish minimum annual premiums for mortgage insurance offered by the Federal Housing Administration, but none was taken up for consideration by the Senate. Congress did clear legislation to curtail the sale of unsafe drywall for use in building construction.

Chapter 12 Labor and Pensions

Organized labor fared much less well than they had hoped during President Obama's first term in the White House, disappointing leaders who had put union muscle behind Democratic campaigns.

Initially, labor's priorities meshed well with those of the new administration, primarily in the economic stimulus law that Obama and Democratic leaders pushed through Congress early in 2009. The stimulus law, signed on the heels of passage of a long-sought measure aimed at helping workers sue employers for wage discrimination, provided hope to labor unions that the party then controlling both the executive and legislative branches could move forward on a range of other priorities.

But Democrats' success on subsequent initiatives was more limited than labor had hoped because Congress faced continuing pressure to rein in federal spending and Republicans, who took control of the House in the 112th Congress beginning in 2011, pushed back against costly proposals and sought to unravel what they viewed as cumbersome regulations throughout government, including labor rules.

However, Obama and Democrats did achieve several extensions of unemployment benefits for workers still unable to find jobs. They repeatedly beat back GOP attempts to offset the cost and eventually extended benefits up to ninety-nine weeks.

Democrats also helped the long-term unemployed by including in the economic stimulus law a subsidy to help individuals and families cover premiums for health care under a federal law called COBRA, although that subsidy eventually was eliminated in budget negotiations. The stimulus law and other legislation also continued aid to workers who either lost their jobs or faced reduced hours and wages as a result of trade agreements.

Chapter 13 Law and Justice

Congressional action on law and justice issues during Obama's first term largely fell into two categories. Several significant pieces of legislation that had previously resisted legislative solution were cleared by Congress and signed by the president, either because they enjoyed bipartisan support or because Democrats, using their majorities in the 111th Congress during 2009–2010, were able to force them through. But other issues, particularly immigration, proved far too divisive to advance.

In 2009, Democrats pushed through two priorities. The first was a labor priority to make it easier for workers to file wage discrimination lawsuits against their employers. The second was an expansion of federal hate crimes law to include crimes against people because of their sexual orientation, gender, or disability.

Despite diminished numbers, conservatives also scored some victories. Republicans, joined by a number of Democrats, repeatedly blocked the administration's efforts to close the U.S. detainee facility at Guantánamo Bay, Cuba. Lawmakers attached provisions to several of the annual spending bills that placed restrictions on moving the prisoners and on shuttering the detention center. Republicans and pro-gun rights Democrats also came together successfully in 2009 to attach a provision to credit card legislation that would allow loaded firearms into national parks.

Although the chambers were controlled by different parties in the 112th Congress, legislators in some ways became more productive on law and justice issues.

Lawmakers achieved a longstanding goal by clearing a bipartisan overhaul of federal patent law—an issue that had eluded resolution for years. They then managed a four-year extension of three provisions of the antiterrorism law known as the Patriot Act, despite the concerns of a number of lawmakers on the left and right. In the closing days of the 112th Congress, the House and Senate worked to give an important victory to Obama and Senate Intelligence Chair Dianne Feinstein, D-Calif., by clearing a five-year renewal of a post–September 11 foreign intelligence law.

In addition, the Senate confirmed President Obama's two nominations to fill Supreme Court vacancies, both with relatively little rancor because the two new justices were widely seen as fully qualified and because their addition to the court did not alter its generally conservative judicial philosophy.

Chapter 14 General Government

Congress considered an array of legislation on issues as widely varying as disaster relief and federal employees.

The natural disaster that became known as Superstorm Sandy, which hit the East Coast in October 2012, raised once again the federal government's approach to budgeting for such events. Typically, Congress funded federal emergency efforts at a low level but then had to provide huge amounts when disaster struck, which it did with Sandy's devastating effects on coastal states—especially New Jersey and New York.

But many other lower-profile issues went before Congress. Legislators in 2009 terminated the National Security Personnel System (NSPS), a merit-based pay plan for the Department of Defense civilian workforce established in 2003 on grounds that it was an exceptionally poorly constructed effort to motivate federal works. In 2010 Congress imposed a freeze on pay for most federal civilian employees for two years, from January 1, 2011, to December 31, 2012, later extended to the end of 2013.

Legislation also was approved authorizing $58.4 billion for the National Aeronautics and Space Administration

(NASA) for fiscal 2011 through 2013. It directed NASA to retain its shuttle-related workforce through fiscal 2011, but it also authorized the agency to foster the development of commercial capabilities in keeping with the Obama administration's push to shift the U.S. human spaceflight program toward commercial carriers.

Congress in 2010 cleared legislation aimed at reducing the overclassification of information and promoting the sharing of unclassified information.

Chapter 15 Inside Congress

Entrenched partisanship was reflected in members' inability to find common ground on issues and to fashion legislative solutions to the nation's problems. It also served to change the way Congress as an institution has functioned. The changes, which had evolved over time, included vastly reduced use of conference committees to resolve Senate-House differences, the extension of the Senate filibuster to require—in effect—a supermajority of sixty votes to pass anything, and the expansion of secret holds by unnamed senators to block consideration of legislation.

Although both chambers initiated or continued a raft of ethics violations, most led nowhere, with members facing questions about their conduct being cleared. One investigation, however, was different. The House, for the first time since 1983, imposed the punishment of censure on one of its own—the amiable chair of the powerful House Ways and Means Committee, Charles B. Rangel, D-N.Y. While the litany of wrongdoing was long, Rangel maintained that the evidence against him showed no corruption and no acts for personal gain.

Congress also experienced a rare event in an attempted assassination of a sitting member. Rep. Gabrielle Giffords, a three-term Arizona Democrat, was speaking to constituents outside a supermarket in Tucson on January 8, 2011, when a gunman open fire on the crowd. Severely wounded in the head, Giffords survived the assassination attempt that killed six and injured thirteen others. The shooting was the first serious physical assault on a sitting member of Congress since the November 1978 killing of Rep. Leo J. Ryan, D-Calif., on an airstrip in Guyana just before the Jonestown massacre.

Congress reacted swiftly to a 2010 U.S. Supreme Court ruling in *Citizens United v. Federal Election Commission* (558 U.S. 310) that struck down provisions of the 2002 Bipartisan Campaign Reform Act (commonly known as McCain-Feingold, after its congressional sponsors) prohibiting corporations and unions from making independent political expenditures. However, with deep divides between the parties, no legislation to soften or reverse the decision cleared.

Chapter 16 The Obama Presidency

This chapter examines the election of Sen. Barack Obama, of Illinois, as the forty-fourth president of the United States and the major events of the four years of his first term in office, leading to his reelection in 2012.

Appendix

The appendix contains a variety of supplementary material, including Senate and House key votes (highlighted in boldface in the legislative chapters) during the four-year period, with charts showing how each member voted; a glossary of congressional terms; an explanation of how a bill becomes law; lists of committee and subcommittee chairs; biographical data on members of Congress between 2009 and 2013; presidential vetoes; and major presidential speeches and messages to Congress and elsewhere. In addition, the appendix includes extensive political charts, including presidential, House, Senate, and gubernatorial election returns for the period. Other tables record members who died or switched parties and special elections that were held. Finally, the appendix includes a complete list of public laws enacted during the four years.

Contributors

This volume has been prepared under the direction of editors at CQ Press, an imprint of SAGE Publications Inc. The chapters and the appendices were prepared and edited by a group of veteran reporters, many of whom covered Congress for Congressional Quarterly Inc. and other Washington, D.C., news organizations. The principal contributors were John Felton, Martha Gottron, David Hosansky, Kenneth Jost, Deborah Kalb, Christina Lyons, Colleen McGuiness, Julie Rovner, and David R. Tarr, who also served as volume editor for this edition. Judy Schneider and Michael Koempel at the Congressional Research Service in the Library of Congress reviewed, corrected, and expanded the glossary of legislative terms that appears in the appendix.

At SAGE Publications developmental editors Diana Axelsen and Carole Maurer made numerous useful suggestions to improve the manuscript. Editing and production at Sage was under the direction of Eric Garner and was ably shepherded through by Olivia Weber-Stenis. The manuscript was expertly edited by Jon Preimesberger. The index to the volume was prepared by Sheila Bodell. Doug Goldenberg-Hart at CQ Press and Jim Brace-Thompson at SAGE were the sponsoring editors.

CQ Press editors also wish to express their thanks to those dedicated reporters and editors on the *CQ Weekly* magazine and the *CQ Almanac* for their assistance in preparation of this edition.

CHAPTER 1

Politics and National Issues

Introduction 3

2009 Chronology 13

2010 Chronology 19

2011 Chronology 27

2012 Chronology 31

Politics and National Issues

Democrat Barack Obama was elected president in 2008 on a platform of hope and change but in the midst of the worst economic recession since the 1930s. He arrived in Washington with an ambitious agenda topped by a promise to jumpstart the economy and accelerate job creation. He also promised to change the way business was done in Washington—to reach out to Republicans to fashion bipartisan solutions to the nation's problems.

Four years later, as Obama prepared to begin his second term in office following a comfortable reelection victory, he could claim success on several important aspects of his agenda. The economy was growing again, if slowly, and the unemployment rate, though still high, had declined from its peaks. Congress had passed two landmark measures: the Affordable Care Act, extending health insurance coverage to nearly every American, and financial regulatory reform, designed to prevent the excesses that had led to the collapse of the financial industry and subsequent recession. The president had ended one lengthy and draining war and was winding down another. And in its last major act of his first term, Congress fulfilled an Obama campaign pledge to begin to pay down the national debt by raising taxes on the wealthy while holding tax rates for everyone else steady.

Yet the president failed to deliver on the one promise where success might have made action on other parts of his agenda possible. Far from compromising on solutions to problems, the two parties intensified the partisanship that had been steadily deepening in Washington for several decades. Most of the significant legislation adopted during Obama's first term was acted on in the first two years when Democrats controlled both the House and the Senate and had the numbers and discipline needed to overcome solid opposition from Republican legislators. That changed after the 2010 elections when voter concern over increased federal spending in the face of a still ailing economy gave Republicans, many of them affiliated with the conservative Tea Party movement, control of the House and narrowed the Democratic edge in the Senate. For the next two years, Congress was in almost complete gridlock as the two parties repeatedly clashed over spending and tax policy, to the exclusion of almost all other matters.

The policy arguments themselves had not changed much over the decades. Democrats had always had a more expansive view of government, seeing government's role as one of ensuring that all citizens had access to basic rights and services and were protected from the excesses of the marketplace. Republicans, in contrast, saw a much narrower role for the federal government, one that kept taxes and spending low, promoted economic growth through a largely unfettered free market system, and left social regulation mainly to the states.

What was different was an unwillingness of either side to seek workable compromises to their differences. Where once the House and Senate might agree to split the differences over spending on various government programs, each now insisted that the other side concede. As a result, legislators again and again found themselves playing a game of chicken as they approached fiscal deadlines such as the limit on the federal government's borrowing authority or the expiration of a spending or tax bill. The crises were always averted at the last minute, typically by delaying a decision on the underlying problem for a few more months or another year.

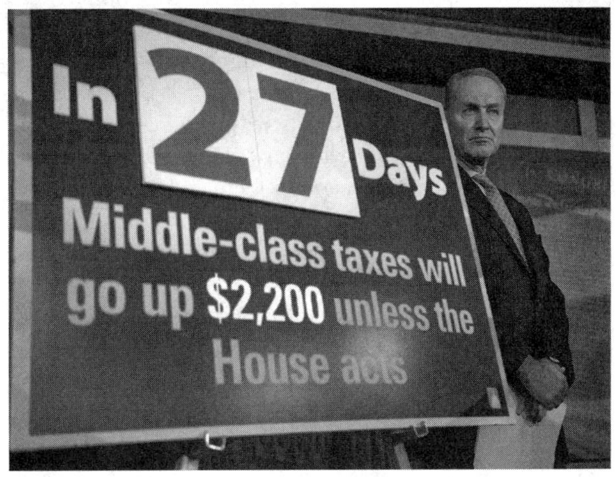

Sen. Chuck Schumer, D-N.Y., attends a news conference in the Capitol on December 5, 2012, calling on the House to act on a Senate-passed tax cut bill that would help the middle class.
Source: Photo By Tom Williams/CQ Roll Call

The comity that once prevailed, or at least papered over, differences between parties, chambers, and individual legislators also ebbed over the four years as deference to the institutions of government gave way to personal attacks. Much of the disrespect was aimed at Obama. Perhaps the most egregious incident came from Joe Wilson, a Republican representative from South Carolina, who yelled "You lie" at the president as he delivered a speech on health care to a joint session of Congress in September 2009. Wilson later apologized. But members of both parties and Obama himself were guilty of using disparaging terms to characterize one another.

All these factors merged to affect both the tone and the substance in Washington. As one scholar put it, Congress became less "communitarian" and more individualistic, less deliberative, and more responsive to media and other outside forces. Others were less charitable, describing Congress as "dysfunctional" and the atmosphere as "poisonous." By the end of 2012, close observers and ordinary citizens were beginning to question whether Congress as an institution was on the verge of collapse or, more plausibly that, simply incapable of resolving differences in order to govern.

RISE OF MODERN PARTISANSHIP

Congressional partisanship was nothing new. Historians often cite periods in the late 1800s and early 1900s when congressional factions were figuratively, if not literally, at each other's throats. In the modern era, partisanship began growing in the late 1960s and early 1970s, when the Vietnam War divided the Democratic Party and social issues such as abortion became rallying points for conservatives in both parties. Still, a broad ideological range could be found in both parties. Conservative Democrats and liberal Republicans had voting records that were so similar to their ideological counterparts in the opposing party that people said "there wasn't a dime's worth of difference" between the two parties.

Those crosscurrents began to disappear in the 1980s as previous tendencies pulling House candidates toward the political center weakened. Increasingly, districts were drawn to all but guarantee a win by one party or the other, a perpetual campaign cycle took hold requiring constant fund raising and continual candidate positioning, and agendas were designed in part to avoid fractures within each party. *(Redistricting box, p. 42)*

An important additional development was the emergence of an array of new communication channels at the end of the twentieth century and early in the twenty-first that included talk-radio stations with acerbic political commentary, cable TV channels that also multiplied and expanded the voices of argument and dissent, an increasingly robust Internet that allowed anyone to opine to the world, and social media such as Facebook and Twitter that broadened the political debate. Users of these tools, in some although not all situations, often tended not so much to debate as to demonize persons (and political parties) that held differing views of appropriate public policy.

By the turn of the new century, the two parties were no longer working to persuade the other of the merits of their agenda but battling for numerical supremacy. Whichever party dominated in the numbers then tried to impose its ideological platform, working within its own ranks to assemble the necessary votes and reaching out to the other side only when necessary—and only as far as needed—to advance its goals. The minority party worked just as hard to block the other party in hopes that it would regain the majority in the next election so that it could impose its own goals.

The eight years of George W. Bush's presidency from 2001 to 2009 saw an intensification of partisanship, particularly in the final two years, when Democrats were in control of both chambers of Congress but did not have either the presidency or the numbers in the Senate to overcome filibusters, let alone a presidential veto. Those frustrations looked as if they might disappear after the 2008 elections, when Democrats won the presidency and both houses of Congress for the first time since 1992.

A FAST START

Obama and congressional Democrats moved quickly to leverage what they saw as significant political capital coming from the historic election to put an ambitious policy agenda in place. With the nation reeling from a deep recession, sparked by a near collapse of the nation's financial sector, about two-thirds of the public said they had faith in the new leader, who had campaigned on the themes of change and hope.

Early in the first session, Democrats won enactment of a $787 billion economic stimulus measure aimed at putting the nation on the road to recovery. They also embarked on what would be a tortuous but ultimately successful effort to enact a historical overhaul of the health care system, fulfilling Obama's campaign promise to provide medical coverage to the uninsured. House Democrats also pushed through a controversial plan to overhaul regulation of the financial services industry, an equally controversial "cap-and-trade" plan to limit industrial greenhouse gas emissions, and a measure aimed at helping state governments and private businesses create or retain jobs.

Most of this legislation was passed over solid Republican opposition. In the House, Speaker Nancy Pelosi, D-Calif., presided over a caucus that was large enough to pass legislation on its own and even allow a few politically vulnerable members to defect when it served their purposes, so long as most Democrats went along. When Democrats were divided among themselves, Pelosi would try to reshape the offending provisions just enough to secure the needed votes. On the House version of the health care legislation, for example, Democratic leaders allowed antiabortion Democrats to offer an amendment restricting coverage for the practice. The amendment was

CONGRESSIONAL LEADERSHIP, 2009–2013

111th Congress

Senate

President Pro Tempore: Robert C. Byrd, D-W.Va./Daniel K. Inouye, D-Hawaii[1]
Majority Leader: Harry Reid, D.-Nev.
Majority Whip: Richard J. Durbin, D-Ill.
Democratic Caucus Vice Chair: Charles E. Schumer, D-N.Y.
Democratic Policy Committee Chair: Byron L. Dorgan, D-N.D.
Minority Leader: Mitch McConnell, R-Ky.
Minority Whip: John Kyl, R-Ariz.
Republican Conference Chair: Lamar Alexander, R-Tenn.

House

Speaker of the House: Nancy Pelosi, D-Calif.
Majority Leader: Steny Hoyer, D-Md.
Majority Whip: James E. Clyburn, D-S.C.
Democratic Caucus Chair: John B. Larson, D-Conn.
Minority Leader: John A. Boehner, R-Ohio
Minority Whip: Eric Cantor, R-Va.
Republican Conference Chair: Mike Pence, R-Ind.

112th Congress

Senate

President Pro Tempore: Daniel K. Inouye, D-Hawaii/Patrick J. Leahy, D. Vt.[2]
Majority Leader: Harry Reid, D-Nev.
Majority Whip: Richard J. Durbin, D-Ill.
Democratic Conference Vice Chair: Charles E. Schumer, D-N.Y.
Democratic Policy Committee Chair: Charles E. Schumer, D-N.Y.
Minority Leader: Mitch McConnell, R-Ky.
Minority Whip: John Kyl, R-Ariz.
Republican Conference Chair: Lamar Alexander, R-Tenn.

House

Speaker of the House: John A. Boehner, R-Ohio
Majority Leader: Eric Cantor, R-Va.
Majority Whip: Kevin McCarthy, R-Calif.
Republican Conference Chair: Jeb Hensarling, R-Texas
Minority Leader: Nancy Pelosi, D-Calif.
Minority Whip: Steny Hoyer, D-Md.
Assistant Democratic Leader: James E. Clyburn, D-S.C.

NOTES:

1. Byrd died on June 28, 2010; Inouye was sworn in the same day.
2. Inouye died December 17, 2012; Leahy was sworn in the following day.

adopted, angering abortion rights supporters but gaining passage of the bill.

In a few cases, a handful of Republicans defected to provide the winning margin to a Democratic initiative. Perhaps the most significant was on a measure to cap greenhouse gas emissions at specified levels. The bill was high on the president's priority list, but many moderate Democrats feared it would hurt economic conditions in their districts. When months of negotiations and White House lobbying efforts failed to win over enough Democrats, Pelosi and her leadership found eight Republicans who provided the margin of victory. (The effort came to naught because the Senate never took up the legislation.)

Where House Democrats were so divided that no workable consensus could be found, the Democratic leadership adopted a tactic common in the Senate of simply not bringing the legislation to the floor. That happened on a Senate-passed bill to give the District of Columbia voting representation in Congress, a move that most House Democrats endorsed. But the Senate bill also carried an amendment repealing the city's strict gun registration laws and barring it from prohibiting the possession of firearms. After months of trying unsuccessfully to round up enough votes to pass the Senate measure, the House Democratic leadership gave up and let the Senate bill die.

The basic dynamics of moving legislation were essentially the same in both chambers, but the Senate's customs and procedures gave the minority many more options for blocking or delaying legislation. The opposition, for example, can refuse unanimous consent to take up legislation or a nomination. Amendments that are not germane to the issue at hand may be offered on the floor. Individual members can impose secret "holds" on bills or nominations, preventing their consideration for as long as the member maintains the hold. A hold may be placed because a member objects to a nominee or because a member is seeking to gain something else in return for giving up the hold. In February 2010, for example, Republican Richard Shelby of Alabama placed a "blanket hold" on at least seventy nominations for a few days in an attempt to win funding for two defense-related projects that would bring thousands of jobs to his state.

In recent years, the most visible obstructing tactic was the threat of a filibuster. Filibusters could be brought to an end only after a motion to invoke cloture was introduced and passed by a supermajority of sixty votes—a high hurdle in recent decades when the majority in the Senate rarely had more than simple majority. A successful vote to invoke cloture limited the remaining debate on the issue to thirty hours, which meant debate could stretch over several days, or even weeks depending on the Senate's schedule.

Filibuster threats had become so routine in recent years that Senate Majority Leader Harry Reid, D-Nev., began to file cloture motions on controversial measures even before a filibuster threat was made. To avoid the time lost in going through the formal cloture procedure, Senate leaders frequently simply agreed to set sixty-vote thresholds for passage of amendments and bills that would otherwise require simple majorities. (Reid would eventually institute filibuster reform in 2013 that required only a simple majority vote for certain presidential nominations.)

The increased use of cloture motions to move legislation, and the need to round up sixty votes to pass them, could discourage the majority party from taking up a nomination or legislation altogether. Failure to win a cloture vote often killed legislation outright—a House-passed immigration bill died in the final days of the 2010 session when a cloture vote in the Senate failed by five votes. Inaction could be just as lethal. Several of Obama's judicial and executive branch nominees ultimately withdrew in the face of inaction in the Senate. In other instances, Democratic leaders were forced to alter legislation in search of the necessary votes. In late 2009, Reid abandoned a public health care option in the Senate version of the health care legislation to help secure the votes of a bloc of centrist Democrats. *(Cloture vote table, p. 860)*

A REVERSAL OF FORTUNE

By the end of 2009, as the federal budget deficit reached unprecedented levels. Republican charges that the Democrats agenda was misdirected began to resonate with the public. The debate over the health care act had divided the public as well as the parties in Congress. Even its common name, "Obamacare," was polarizing; initially a derisory term, it was eventually embraced by the president and his administration. Combined with measures passed at the end of President George W. Bush's term to bail out troubled financial institutions on Wall Street and collapsing automakers in Detroit, the action coming out of Washington was too much too fast for many voters. As the year ended, public opinion polls showed steadily decreasing support for the president, the Democratic Congress, and their agenda.

Then, in January 2010, the momentum changed abruptly with the victory of Republican Scott P. Brown in a special election in heavily Democratic Massachusetts to take the seat of the late Sen. Edward M. Kennedy, who had died the previous year. Brown was given almost no chance at the outset of the special election campaign, but he was able to capitalize on escalating discontent about the pending health care legislation and his Democratic opponent's poorly run campaign.

By late summer, opinion polls were showing pronounced momentum for Republican candidates across the country. The surge was most notable among independent voters, whose nearly two-to-one support had swept in Democrats in 2006 and 2008 but who had dramatically shifted to the Republican side by a similar margin by mid-2010. In November, the GOP won a net of sixty-three seats in the House and significantly narrowed the Democrat's Senate majority.

Partisan and nonpartisan observers alike agreed that the nation's economic troubles were the starting point for any discussion of the Democrats' election year losses. "This is all because the economy is genuinely bad, and Democrats have over promised and under delivered in the view of most voters," said Larry J. Sabato, director of the University of Virginia's Center for Politics, shortly before the election.

Another factor in the elections was the growth of the Tea Party movement, a loosely knit group of strongly (some said extremely) conservative activists willing to take on anyone who did not agree with their viewpoints. From the beginning of his presidency, these conservatives billed Obama as a "socialist," and they were dismayed as well by many of the Republican positions taken during the Bush administration.

On their own, in prosperous times, such ideologically driven individuals and groups probably would have had a far less decisive impact than they did in 2009 and 2010 and later. Their rhetoric was extreme, their candidates often inexperienced. In less tumultuous times, many of their candidates would have been dismissed as unelectable, which some turned out to be.

But in 2009 and 2010, two phenomena worked together to give these conservatives a voice in Republican politics it might otherwise never have attained.

The first was Sarah Palin, the former Alaska governor who had emerged as a political force as the 2008 Republican vice presidential candidate. After the 2008 election, Palin established herself as the leader of a wave of charged-up conservative women proudly wearing the "Mama Grizzly" label she bestowed on them. Often using the online platforms of Facebook and Twitter, Palin figuratively roamed the nation, dropping endorsements in Republican primaries, sometimes transforming also-rans into contenders.

At the same time, a segment of conservative voters—who would have opposed what they considered Obama's activist agenda no matter what it called for—fashioned themselves in the same light as the yeoman patriots who fought British tyranny during the Revolutionary era, fueling the rapid rise of a populist Tea Party movement and candidates who came to be called Tea Party favorites. Some of the more extreme activists in the Tea Party movement may have overshadowed what was a genuine bubbling discontent among parts of American society about the direction that the nation was headed as increasing numbers of citizens did not look or think like many typical Tea Party devotees, who tended to be older, largely white, relatively well off economically, and have somewhat higher levels of educational attainment. (One newspaper reporter who covered the Tea Party wrote a book about the phenomena titled *Boiling Mad: Inside the Tea Party America.*) In spite of the angry public face of Tea Party adherents, scholars and reporters soon discovered that they were not utterly opposed to all government activity; they typically were warm and outspoken supporters of federal programs that benefited themselves, especially Social Security and Medicare.

In any event, by 2010, there were at least two elements to the Tea Party: the intentionally loosely knit grassroots movements in each state, and organized national groups such as the Tea Party Express. The former opened an enthusiasm gap between the Democratic and Republican parties in virtually every state, even in those where Democrats held a widespread registration advantage, such as Pennsylvania and Illinois. The latter group operated much like a political party, funneling financial resources, paid media, and get-out-the-vote operations to like-minded candidates. The formalized Tea Party groups had spokespersons and media-savvy leaders who ultimately became the faces of the anti-establishment movement.

GOP congressional contenders who rode the support of Tea Party activists to primary victories over Republican establishment candidates included some of the most prominent of the year's Senate candidates, although their record on Election Day was spotty. Perhaps of more importance, many Republican candidates in both the House and Senate aimed their campaigns at more conservative voters, which would have the effect of shifting GOP legislators to the right even if they did not hold the extreme views of the Tea Party activists. When all the votes were counted, the ranks of House Democratic moderates were thinned dramatically, with most of their seats won by more conservative Republicans. The same held true in the Senate, where several moderates in both parties either retired or were defeated and in most cases replaced by more conservative legislators. These shifts, not only in party numbers but in ideology, would have significant repercussions in the 112th Congress, which was the most partisan on record, as well as on the 2012 presidential and congressional elections.

A LAST GASP OF PRODUCTIVITY

Obama conceded that his party had suffered a "shellacking" at the polls in 2010. In a lame duck session, he also conceded on one of his key promises—to raise the income tax rates for the highest-income earners while leaving them unchanged for middle- and low-income taxpayers. Because the across-the-board tax cuts put in place by the GOP in the first years of the Bush administration were set by law to expire at the end of the year, action was needed in the lame duck session to prevent a big tax increase on all Americans from taking place on January 1, 2011.

Partisanship in Congress, 2009–2012

The table shows the percentage of times that the majority of one party voted against the majority of the other. The data show that divisions between the parties were at or near record levels throughout President Barack Obama's first term. In the 111th Congress, roughly three out of four votes split the two parties in the Senate; the same was true for the House in the 112th Congress. These were the highest percentages of party unity votes since Congressional Quarterly began this study in 1953.

	2009	*2010*	*2011*	*2012*
Party unity (% of votes in which majority of party voted together)				
House Democrats	91	89	87	87
House Republicans	87	88	91	90
Senate Democrats	91	91	92	92
Senate Republicans	85	89	86	80
Partisan votes (% of total)				
House	50.9	40.0	76.8	72.8
Senate	72.0	78.6	57.1	59.8

Republicans vehemently opposed a tax increase for the wealthy, and the outcome of the midterm elections left Obama with little leverage to force his preferences through in the short time remaining in the session. In a last-minute deal, Obama and the Democrats agreed to extend the Bush-era tax rates for all taxpayers for two more years in return for an extension of expanded unemployment benefits and a year-long reduction in the employee payroll tax of two percentage points that, with other items, was expected to pump as much as $180 billion into the economy.

The deal, considered a political masterstroke by many even as it infuriated the liberal base of the president's party, signaled a change in Obama's approach to leading. After two years of achieving his priorities by negotiating primarily with Democrats, he found himself forced to bargain with Republicans. For the next two years, the president would have to adjust his governing style to deal with a Republican Party determined to make him a one-term president and Democrats wary about where he might lead them.

Despite the fallout from the elections, the 2010 lame duck session proved remarkably—and unexpectedly—productive. In addition to extending the income tax cuts and reducing the employee payroll tax, Congress also repealed the 1993 "don't ask, don't tell" doctrine that prohibited openly gay people from serving in the military, passed a food safety bill that had been pending for some months, and ratified the New Strategic Arms Reduction Treaty (START) with Russia. In addition, the House passed the so-called DREAM (Development, Relief, and Education for Alien Minors) Act, which would have provided a path to citizenship for hundreds of thousands of adult children of illegal immigrants. Over the next two years, as Congress found itself caught in gridlock over spending, taxing, and debt reduction, the few weeks between the 2010 midterm elections and the end of the year stood out as a high point of congressional activity.

DESCENT INTO GRIDLOCK

Politics trumped governing during the 112th Congress, making it one of the least productive in modern times and one of the most polarized. Repeatedly, the two parties shunned compromise in favor of taking positions that would appeal to their political base in the 2012 elections. Although both the GOP leader in the House, Speaker John A. Boehner of Ohio, and the Democratic Senate majority leader, Harry Reid of Nevada, operated under an informal rule in which they brought to the floor only legislation that had the support of a majority of their caucus, each ultimately had to rely on votes from the opposing party to push through the few significant measures that actually reached the president's desk. For the most part, however, the majority party in each chamber resorted to calling up bills that they knew would be unacceptable to the majority in the other chamber to illustrate the differences between the two parties.

House GOP leaders, encouraged by a large crop of freshman conservatives with ties to the Tea Party, began the 2011 session promising to move the chamber in a new direction. In the first weeks of the new Congress, House Republicans voted to defund the health care law, relax environmental regulations, ban the use of federal money to support Planned Parenthood and other abortion providers, and amend the Constitution to require a balanced budget, all measures that were nonstarters with Senate Democrats.

Boehner learned early on that the conservative members of his caucus would not hesitate to threaten a government shutdown or a default on the federal debt as leverage to achieve their policy goals. That became apparent when conservatives refused to endorse the spending cap proposed by GOP leaders on an omnibus appropriations bill funding the entire government for the rest of the fiscal 2011 and forced them to take a lower one. The move resulted in a two-month stalemate with Senate Democrats that ultimately involved leadership talks with Vice President Joseph R. Biden Jr., before both chambers agreed on a cap similar to that originally proposed by the House leaders.

The final agreement was reached only moments before the government would have had to shut down most federal operations for lack of funding. Boehner had to rely on eighty-one Democrats who voted for passage, after fifty-nine Republicans—nearly a quarter of his caucus—voted no on the measure. Most Democrats opposed the bill because they said the cuts were too deep.

An even bigger potential disaster loomed over Washington for most of the summer as House conservatives threatened to let the government's borrowing authority lapse as the GOP and Democrats struggled to come to agreement on a debt ceiling measure. Failure to raise the statutory debt limit would have thrown the government into default. Seeking some degree of accommodation with Republicans, Obama tried more than once to reach a "grand bargain" with Boehner to both raise taxes and cut entitlement spending in an effort to set Washington on a more sustainable fiscal path. The efforts failed when House conservatives refused to contemplate a tax increase.

In the end, and again at the eleventh hour, a compromise was reached to raise the debt ceiling and put in place a mechanism for making across-the-board spending cuts in the future if Congress could not reach agreement on individual spending bills. And once again Boehner had to rely on Democratic support to pass the measure because sixty-six Republicans voted no.

In the Senate, the situation was reversed, with Majority Leader Reid having to rely on Republican votes to pass any legislation. With his caucus down to fifty-three members (including two independent senators who caucused with the Democrats) after the 2010 elections, Reid not only needed to keep his caucus together but also find compromises that would attract at least seven GOP senators to avoid filibusters. And any compromise that was acceptable to seven Republicans was likely to be acceptable to several more. The debt ceiling increase in 2011, for example, was passed 74–26, with a large majority of both caucuses voting for it.

On some occasions, Reid resorted to a messaging strategy similar to that followed in the House. He called up bills that he knew would not pass so that he could illustrate where the parties disagreed. In October 2011, for example, he brought a version of Obama's proposed $447 billion jobs plan to the floor, where two Democrats joined all Republicans to reject a cloture motion on the measure.

Obama's leadership during this period was often held up for discussion, with some political observers saying he allowed events to get out of his control and others contending that he did the best he could under challenging circumstances. Whatever the case, Obama found little common ground with House Republicans and was held at least partly responsible for a government that appeared dysfunctional. In the weeks following the debt limit crisis, public approval ratings for both the president and Congress took a nose dive.

The president at times also found himself to the right of many in the Democratic caucus. House Democrats split their vote on the debt ceiling compromise down the middle, with ninety-five siding with Obama and voting for it and ninety-five voting against it. More than three-fourths of the House Democrats and more than half of the Senate Democrats voted against a free trade agreement with Colombia. That pact and two others passed only with strong Republican support and a compromise between the two parties on a job training program for displaced workers.

Obama and the Democrats held together at the end of 2011 and the beginning of 2012 when Republicans reluctantly agreed first to a two-month extension of the employee

Age Structure of Congress, 1949–2011

Year	*House*	*Senate*	*Congress*
1949	51.0	58.5	52.2
1951	52.0	56.6	52.9
1953	52.0	56.6	52.9
1955	51.4	57.2	52.5
1957	52.9	57.9	53.8
1959	51.7	57.1	52.7
1961	52.2	57.0	53.1
1963	51.7	56.8	52.7
1965	50.5	57.7	51.8
1967	50.8	57.7	52.1
1969	52.2	56.6	53.0
1971	51.9	56.4	51.9
1973	51.1	55.3	52.0
1975	49.8	55.5	50.9
1977	49.3	54.7	50.3
1979	48.8	52.7	49.5
1981	48.4	52.5	49.1
1983	45.5	53.4	47.0
1985	49.7	54.2	50.5
1987	50.7	54.4	51.4
1989	52.1	55.6	52.8
1991	52.8	57.2	53.6
1993	51.7	58.0	52.9
1995	50.9	58.4	52.3
1997	51.6	57.5	52.7
1999	52.6	58.3	53.7
2001	55.4	59.8	56.2
2003	54.0	59.7	55.1
2005	55.0	60.4	56.0
2007	55.9	61.7	57.1
2009	57.2	63.1	58.2
2011	56.7	62.2	57.7

NOTE: Table shows average age of members at the beginning of each Congress.

payroll tax reduction, before okaying a full-year one. Conservatives said the reduction was too expensive and insisted that the cost be offset by spending cuts elsewhere. When Democrats rejected the offsets, Republicans decided the political costs of opposing a tax reduction as the nation entered an election year were too great.

LOOKING TO THE ELECTIONS

Messaging, rather than legislating, took central stage in 2012. In the House, the GOP continued to pass measures that had no chance of acceptance in the Senate, including numerous votes to repeal, change, or deny funding for all or part of the president's signature health care act. By the end of the 112th Congress at the beginning of 2013, the House had taken nearly forty votes on the issue, including several after the Supreme Court ruled in June 2012 that the main parts of the law were constitutional.

The House vote early in 2012 to embrace a budget blueprint that significantly reduced federal spending and called for a radical reordering of entitlement programs such as Social Security and Medicare also put Mitt Romney, the likely Republican presidential nominee, on notice. The vote in favor of the plan made it hard for Romney to distance himself from it, and he ended up choosing the plan's author, Paul D. Ryan of Wisconsin, as his running mate.

Several of the skirmishes in the Senate involved Obama's nominations to administrative or judicial posts. Although most of the nominees were eventually confirmed, months could pass before the Republicans would let a vote go forward or the Democrats had rounded up enough Republican support to reach the sixty-vote threshold for cutting off debate. An extreme example was Obama's nomination of Richard Cordray to head the new Consumer Financial Protection Board created under the financial regulatory overhaul measure in 2010 over strong Republican objections. In an attempt to win changes to the law and delay its implementation, Senate Republicans rejected a cloture motion on Cordray's nomination in December 2011 and then tried to prevent the president from making a recess appointment by convening a pro forma session every three days—a tactic devised by Senate Majority Leader Harry Reid in 2007 to block recess appointments by President Bush.

Obama gave Cordray a recess appointment anyway. The Supreme Court said it would review the constitutionality of the appointment in its 2013–2014 term. In the meantime, Obama reached an agreement with Senate Republicans that allowed Cordray's nomination to go forward. He was confirmed in July 2013, nearly two years after he was first nominated.

In September 2012, the two parties agreed to suspend action on the fiscal 2012 appropriations process to avoid any chance of a government shutdown before the elections—although reaching that agreement nearly shut down the government. The two parties also put off any discussion of the income tax cuts that were set to expire at the end of the year at the same time that across-the-board spending cuts were scheduled to take effect. The potential combination of higher taxes and less government spending, termed the fiscal cliff, threatened political mayhem if not a return to economic recession. Each side hoped that a victory at the polls would allow their viewpoint to prevail.

The issue was largely settled when voters in November 2012 returned Obama to the White House and strengthened the Democratic numbers in both the House and the Senate. Observing that elections had consequences, Obama took a hard-line stance during the lame duck session, insisting that tax rates on wealthy Americans be allowed to return to the higher rates that prevailed before the Bush-era reductions, while the reduced rates for middle- and lower-income were made permanent.

House Republicans once again demanded deep spending cuts, the extension of all the Bush-era tax cuts regardless of income level, and no tax increases. Once again Boehner and Obama came close to working out a deal, but it fell apart at the last minute apparently when the conservative members of his caucus balked. That left it to Biden and Senate Minority Leader Mitch McConnell to work out a compromise that raised tax rates for those earning more than $400,000, put off the automatic spending cuts until March 1, 2013, and extended benefits for the long-term unemployed, among other things.

Only eight senators, five Republicans and three Democrats, voted against the compromise. Despite the overwhelming Senate vote for the deal and concerns that Republicans would be blamed if the compromise were not passed and rates on all taxpayers rose, two-thirds of the House Republican caucus still voted against the legislation. Boehner had to turn to the Democrats for the votes necessary to clear the bill.

That vote, which was taken on January 1, 2013, was the last the House took in the 112th Congress. In a controversial move, Boehner put off action on a Senate-passed bill providing disaster aid for areas devastated by Hurricane Sandy, primarily in the heavily Democratic areas of Connecticut, New Jersey, and New York. Disaster aid had been a sore point between the two parties all year, with Democrats vehemently objecting to Republican insistence that any aid be offset by savings elsewhere in the budget. Boehner's decision so angered northeastern lawmakers of both parties that the Speaker announced a vote would be taken on a first installment of the aid on the first legislative day in 2013.

The polarization in Congress delayed or left undone many authorization bills as well as spending bills. Congress needed more than four years and twenty-three short-term bills before it managed to clear a comprehensive reauthorization of the

PASSAGES

Several notable passages occurred during the four years, with the retirement of two Supreme Court justices and the deaths of two long-time senators.

In 2009, Sonia Sotomayor, who sat on the U.S. Court of Appeals for the Second District, became the first Hispanic to serve on the court. She replaced Justice David H. Souter, who had announced his retirement earlier in the year. In 2010, Elena Kagan, the first woman dean of Harvard Law School and the U.S. solicitor general since early 2009, was confirmed for the seat left vacant by the retirement of Justice John Paul Stevens. Kagan was the first court nominee in thirty-nine years with no experience as a judge.

Neither nomination was ever in real doubt of confirmation, in part because neither woman was expected to alter the court's ideological balance. Nonetheless, both justices won only tepid support from Republicans. Sotomayor was confirmed by a vote of 68–31; Kagan by a vote of 63–37. The two women joined Ruth Bader Ginsburg to bring the number of women serving on the court to three for the first time in history. The only other woman to serve, Justice Sandra Day O'Connor, had retired in 2005. *(Sotomayor, Kagan confirmations, pp. 585, 711)*

Edward M. Kennedy, Democrat of Massachusetts, the last surviving son of the Kennedy dynasty, died on August 25, 2009, at the age of seventy-seven, having spent nearly forty-seven years in the Senate. Known across the nation as an emphatic and tireless advocate of progressive causes, he was likely to be remembered among his Senate colleagues of both parties as perhaps the most pragmatic dealmaker in modern times, someone who was as eager as he was skilled at working with almost anyone to get things done.

Robert C. Byrd, Democrat of West Virginia, the longest-serving senator in history, died on June 28, 2010, at age ninety-two, having spent fifty-one years, five months, and twenty-five days in an institution that he loved passionately and whose traditions he fiercely defended. He was not a legendary force for the remaking of social or foreign policy. But as much as anyone he embodied the power of oratory to shape the making of public policy, the influence a single senator could exercise over questions both profound and mundane, and the ability to leverage seniority into largess for his constituents. He also was known as a fierce defender of congressional prerogatives, especially those of the Senate, and of fidelity to the Constitution as he understood it.

A passage of another sort was the unwinding of the wars in Iraq and Afghanistan that had begun under President George W. Bush. The last U.S. combat troops left Iraq at the end of 2011, bringing to an uneasy close a war that began in March 2003 when troops from the United States and several other countries invaded Iraq in search of weapons of mass destruction. The weapons, it was later learned, never existed, but the invasion toppled the country's despotic leader, Saddam Hussein, a primary goal of the Bush administration.

The Afghan war had begun in October 2001, when the United States and its allies invaded the country to hunt down al Qaeda terrorist leader Osama bin Laden and overthrow the militant Islamist Taliban government that ruled the government. Although the Taliban was driven out of power within two months, bin Laden was not found until May 2, 2011, when a Navy Seal team shot and killed him during a raid on bin Laden's secret compound in Pakistan. Obama had promised that most U.S. troops would leave Afghanistan at the end of 2014, but as of mid-2013 a security agreement that would allow about 10,000 trainers and other personnel to remain in the country was still pending.

Although Obama fulfilled his campaign promise to end the wars, he was unable make good on a related one—closing the detainee camp at the U.S. Naval Station in Guantánamo Bay, Cuba. Republicans routinely won enough support from Democrats to place restrictions on the release of the detainees and to bar funding for closing the facility.

Federal Aviation Administration in February 2012. Although Congress reauthorized surface transportation programs in 2012, it was unable to agree on a funding source for many of them. Congress failed repeatedly to conclude a reform of federal farm and nutrition programs, largely because Democrats refused to accept Republican demands for deep cuts in food stamps.

Other highly controversial issues rarely came up for consideration, either because of a lack of consensus in the public or strong lobbying pressures. Opposition from the energy lobby combined with skepticism over the dangers of climate change to quash any meaningful discussion of legislation about global warming, for example. Deeply conflicting views among the public on illegal immigration kept comprehensive reform legislation from advancing.

Strong opposition from gun-rights advocates, including the powerful National Rifle Association, kept legislators from engaging in full debate over gun control even in the wake of an assassination attempt on one of their own. Democratic Rep. Gabrielle Giffords was critically shot in the head during a "meet and greet" in her Arizona district in January 2011. Giffords, who resigned from Congress in early 2012 to concentrate on her recovery, and her husband, former astronaut Mark Kelly, began a campaign to find solutions to the gun problem after a mass shooting in a Newtown, Connecticut, elementary school on December 14, 2012, killed twenty-six people, including twenty six- and seven-year-old children.

Presidential Vote by Region

Democrat Barack Obama in 2008 received more votes any other presidential candidate in history, winning 69.5 million votes to Senator John McCain's 59.9 million, for a margin of victory of nearly 9.5 million votes, or 7.2 percentage points. Four years later, in 2012, Obama won reelection by a less impressive but still comfortable margin, taking 65.9 million votes to former governor Mitt Romney's 60.9 million for a margin of just under 5 million votes, or 3.9 percentage points.

The regional vote in both races was similar, with Republican Romney dominating the southern states and Democrat Obama in full command of the eastern and western regions and splitting the twelve midwestern region but winning the vote-heavy states of Michigan, Ohio, Illinois, Minnesota, and Wisconsin. *(National vote breakdown by state, pp. 924, 926)*

	Popular Votes		*Electoral Votes*	
		2008		
Region	*Obama*	*McCain*	*Obama*	*McCain*
East	59%	37%	117	5
Midwest	54	45	97	27
South	46	53	55	113
West	55	42	96	28
National	53	46	365	173
		2012		
Region	*Obama*	*Romney*	*Obama*	*Romney*
East	59%	21%	112	5
Midwest	51	38	80	38
South	44	54	42	133
West	54	43	98	30
National	51	47	332	206

THE 2012 ELECTIONS

Although a broad swath of the public expressed disgust and even anger over the inability of their elected officials to work together on issues affecting the country, those frustrations were not reflected in their voting patterns. Despite their efforts to make him a one-term president, Obama handily won reelection to a second term. Key to Obama's victory was his campaign's success in turning out the same groups of voters who had propelled him into office in 2008—women, the young, blacks, Hispanics, and independents.

Obama also benefited from the rightward shift of the Republican nominating process that had his opponent, Mitt Romney, tacking to the right to win the nomination, only to have to move back toward the political center without losing the Republican base. That was a difficult transit that left many voters unclear about exactly where the former Massachusetts governor stood on the political spectrum. In many ways, Romney may have been his own worst enemy. He appeared uncomfortable on the campaign trail, and he made a series of ill-timed or poorly worded gaffes that made many voters feel that the wealthy businessman was out of touch with ordinary Americans. That impression became almost impossible to erase after comments he made at a private fund-raiser were made public. In those remarks, Romney described 47 percent of the electorate as "takers" who did not pay taxes and who relied on the government for handouts.

Republicans, who once had high hopes that the 2012 elections would give them control of both the White House and Congress, were also disappointed at their net loss of two seats in the Senate. Still, Senate Democrats would need support from at least some Republicans to pass legislation in the 113th Congress. The GOP remained in firm control of the House, losing a net of eight seats.

Few political observers expected anything more than continuing polarization and deadlock in Congress coming out of the 2012 voting. The House elections, under newly drawn district lines in most states, reflected the one-party dominance of most districts and marked the departure from the House, through retirement or defeat, of another cluster of the steadily dwindling group of moderate Democrats and Republicans. Almost half of the three dozen House members whose voting patterns showed them to be the most likely to cross party lines—ten Democrats and seven Republicans—would not be returning in the 113th Congress. *(Effects of redistricting, box, p. 42)*

The Senate too lost more moderates, several of them to retirement. Most were replaced by more conservative Republicans or more liberal Democrats. One of the retirees, Republican Olympia Snowe of Maine, was blunt in her reason for leaving: she was frustrated by "an atmosphere of polarization and 'my way or the highway' ideologies" that she said had "become pervasive in campaigns and in our

Incumbents Reelected, Defeated, or Retired, 1946–2012

Year	*Retired*	*Total seeking reelection*	*Defeated in primaries*	*Defeated in general election*	*Total reelected*	*Percentage of those seeking reelection*
House						
1946	32	398	18	52	328	82.4
1948	29	400	15	68	317	79.3
1950	29	400	6	32	362	90.5
1952	42	389	9	26	354	91.0
1954	24	407	6	22	379	93.1
1956	21	411	6	16	389	94.6
1958	33	396	3	37	356	89.9
1960	27	405	5	25	375	92.6
1962	24	402	12	22	368	91.5
1964	33	397	8	45	344	86.6
1966	23	411	8	41	362	88.1
1968	24	408	4	9	395	96.8
1970	30	401	10	12	379	94.5
1972	40	392	14	13	366	93.4
1974	43	391	8	40	343	87.7
1976	47	384	3	13	368	95.8
1978	49	382	5	19	358	93.7
1980	34	398	6	31	361	90.7
1982	31	387	4	29	354	91.5
1984	22	409	3	16	390	95.4
1986	38	393	2	6	385	98.0
1988	23	408	1	6	401	98.3
1990	27	407	1	15	391	96.1
1992	65	368	19	24	325	88.3
1994	48	387	4	34	349	90.2
1996	49	384	2	21	361	94.0
1998	33	402	1	6	395	98.3
2000	32	405	3	6	396	97.8
2002	35	398	8	8	382	96.0
2004	29	404	2	7	395	97.8
2006	27	404	2	22	380	94.1
2008	32	403	4	19	380	94.3
2010	36	397	4	54	339	85.4
2012	39	391	13	27	351	89.8

Year	*Retired*	*Total seeking reelection*	*Defeated in primaries*	*Defeated in general election*	*Total reelected*	*Percentage of those reelection seeking*
Senate						
1946	9	30	6	7	17	56.7
1948	8	25	2	8	15	60.0
1950	4	32	5	5	22	68.8
1952	4	31	2	9	20	64.5
1954	6	32	2	6	24	75.0
1956	6	29	0	4	25	86.2
1958	6	28	0	10	18	64.3
1960	4	29	0	1	28	96.6
1962	4	35	1	5	29	82.9
1964	2	33	1	4	28	84.8
1966	3	32	3	1	28	87.5
1968	6	28	4	4	20	71.4
1970	4	31	1	6	24	77.4
1972	6	27	2	5	20	74.1
1974	7	27	2	2	23	85.2
1976	8	25	0	9	16	64.0
1978	10	25	3	7	15	60.0
1980	5	29	4	9	16	55.2
1982	3	30	0	2	28	93.3
1984	4	29	0	3	26	89.7
1986	6	28	0	7	21	75.0
1988	6	27	0	4	23	85.2
1990	3	32	0	1	31	96.9
1992	7	28	1	4	23	82.1
1994	9	26	0	2	24	92.3
1996	13	21	1	1	19	90.5
1998	4	30	0	3	27	90.0
2000	5	29	0	6	23	79.3
2002	5	28	1	3	24	85.7
2004	8	26	0	1	25	96.2
2006	4	29	1	6	23	79.3
2008	5	30	0	5	25	83.3
2010	12	25	3	2	21	84.0
2012	10	23	1	1	21	91.3

SOURCE: Norman J. Ornstein, Thomas E. Mann, and Michael J. Malbin, *Vital Statistics on Congress, 2001–2002* (Washington, D.C.: American Enterprise Institute, 2002); *CQ Weekly*, selected issues; Richard Scammon, Alice McGillivray, and Rhodes Cook, *America Votes* (Washington, D.C.: CQ Press, 2001) various editions; Harold W. Stanley and Richard G. Niemi, *Vital Statistics on American Politics 2013–2014* (Washington, D.C., CQ Press/Sage 2013).

NOTE: The column titled Retired does not include persons who died or resigned before the election except, in the case of deaths, for candidates whose name remained on the ballot. Some numbers in the table involved incumbents defeated in primaries but who won as independents in the general election. For details on these and other special cases, consult footnotes in Stanley/Niemi *Vital Statistics on American Politics 2013–2014.*

governing institutions," a situation that she thought was unlikely to change in the near future.

Given the even greater polarization in Congress as a result of the 2012 elections and the difficult deadlines the 113th Congress would face as soon as it reconvened in January 2013, Snowe's prediction of continuing gridlock seemed right on the mark. What effect the continuing partisan battles would have on the political system, Congress as an institution, or the nation's well-being remained a matter of conjecture.

2009

The Legislative Year

The most significant moment in the 2009 session came on the last day, when Senate Democrats succeeded in passing a historic overhaul of the nation's health care system. The December 24 vote was the culmination of a year-long drive by congressional Democrats to prevail on their new president's top priority. It also epitomized the dynamic that dominated the first session of the 111th Congress: Democrats eager to deliver on President Barack Obama's ambitious first-year agenda and Republicans determined to stop them.

A handful of bills won near-unanimous support, and a few individuals struggled to find common ground on major issues such as health care and financial regulation. But neither party showed much willingness to compromise, which meant that the Democratic majority had to maintain an exceptional level of party unity. Just a few highly controversial issues—gun rights, bank bailouts, and war policy—unraveled the otherwise tight Democratic majorities. Democrats' ability to enact an economic stimulus package, move health care legislation through both chambers, and push a climate change bill through the House depended almost entirely on resolving debates within the party and sometimes negotiating with a handful of Republicans—not on building a broad consensus on any of those issues.

MAKING HISTORY

For one day, however, partisanship was out of sight. On January 20, the nation and many around the world watched the historic inauguration of Barack Obama as the forty-fourth president of the United States and the first African American ever to lead the country. A record crowd, estimated at 1.8 million, filled the Mall in Washington, D.C., between the U.S. Capitol and the Lincoln Memorial and lined the nearby streets to watch the new president take the oath of office as his wife, Michelle, held the same gilt-edged Bible used for Abraham Lincoln's first inauguration.

Even as he took office, Obama was already reordering his priorities to grapple with the immediate challenge of the most severe economic crisis since the Great Depression in the 1930s. His economic team had worked closely for weeks with the outgoing administration on the crisis, but it would be up to the new administration to push legislation through Congress to ease swiftly rising unemployment, cope with increasing numbers of home foreclosures, and set the economy on a path to recovery. He also inherited the wars in Iraq and Afghanistan, growing public anger over the massive use of federal funds in late 2008 to rescue collapsing Wall Street financial firms, and a swelling federal deficit.

The high public expectations for the president were based in part on the assumption that the return of government in which both the White House and Congress were controlled by the same political party would allow the Democrats to accomplish their goals, just as the Republicans had been expected to do when they controlled Congress during much of the first six years of George W. Bush's presidency from 2001 to 2009. Liberals, in particular, saw Obama's election as a repudiation of the GOP policies and a mandate for their own—and were often unprepared for the compromises that the Democratic congressional leadership and the White House would make to get things done.

Nor were the Democrats prepared for the Republican's fierce opposition to nearly every proposal the Democrats put forth. Despite two devastating losses—of Congress in 2006 and the White House in 2008—Republicans clearly had no intention of retreating. They launched early rhetorical salvos at the Democrats and voted en masse against bills such as the economic stimulus package. By late spring, they were taking the offensive, using parliamentary guerrilla tactics to frustrate Democratic initiatives and raise their profile on tax and spending issues, the deficit, and Obama's top campaign priority, health care.

The polarization was more evident in the Senate, where Republicans routinely threatened to filibuster legislation, forcing Democrats to round up the sixty votes needed to invoke cloture and limit floor debate. Majority Leader Harry Reid, D-Nev., began the year with fifty-eight senators in his caucus, including two independents. In July, the Democratic

CONGRESS IN 2009

The first session of the 111th Congress began at 12 p.m. on January 6, 2009. The House was in session on 159 days, for a total of 1,247 hours, and adjourned *sine die* at 10:31 a.m. on December 25, 2009. The Senate was in session on 191 days, for a total of 1,421 hours, and adjourned *sine die* at 10:19 a.m. on December 24, 2009.

Members introduced 9,071 bills and resolutions during the year, more than double the 4,815 introduced in 2008, but fewer than the 9,227 introduced in 2007. Congress cleared 125 bills that became public law. President Barack Obama vetoed one bill. *(Public laws table, p. 15; presidential vetoes, p. 915)*

The House took 987 roll-call votes (excluding quorum calls) in 2009, 299 fewer than in 2008. The Senate took 397 recorded votes during the year, 182 fewer than in 2008. *(Recorded votes table, p. 21)*

caucus grew to sixty members with the party switch of former Republican Arlen Specter of Pennsylvania and the arrival of Minnesota Democrat Al Franken following an extended election dispute from 2008. Reaching the magic number of sixty did not make Reid's job any easier, however. As the legislative stakes rose over the summer and fall, he had to work harder than ever to keep his party united.

The simultaneous rise in partisan conflict and party unity was reflected in Congressional Quarterly's annual vote studies, which showed that a record 72 percent of Senate roll-call votes pitted a majority of Democrats against a majority of Republicans. On average, Senate Democrats stayed with their party on 91 percent of those votes. Republicans averaged 85 percent, largely because two or three moderates sometimes voted with the Democrats, pulling down the score. *(Partisanship table, p. 7)*

On the other side of the Capitol, the party divide was not as stark. A majority of House Democrats voted against a majority of House Republicans 57 percent of the time.

House Speaker Nancy Pelosi, D-Calif., was one of the most powerful Speakers in congressional history and led the largest majority either party had had in sixteen years, 256 members at the start of the year. She was unapologetic about her determination to prevail, which meant mustering 218 votes if every member voted. But Pelosi often needed to call on all of her persuasive and dealmaking skills to build consensus within her party. Members of the Democratic caucus included the Blue Dog Coalition of fiscal conservatives whose top priority was reducing the deficit, as well as members of the Congressional Progressive Caucus, who advocated increased spending for social programs and the Black Caucus, concerned with aiding minority and low-income communities.

The difficulty could be seen in the leadership's narrow victories on high-priority legislation. Pelosi mustered 219 votes for a global warming bill, 220 votes for passage of the House health care overhaul, and 223 votes for legislation creating a new regulatory regime for the financial services industry. On average, Democrats voted with their leadership on 91 percent of the year's 502 party unity votes. Republicans held together 87 percent of the time.

JOB NUMBER ONE: THE ECONOMY

The repercussions from the collapse of the financial services sector in 2008 were still playing out as the Obama administration took office. Economic growth fell 8.3 percent in the fourth quarter of 2008, just before Obama took office, and the unemployment rate was climbing. Public anger was mounting over government recovery efforts that seemed to favor Wall Street over Main Street and the potential need for hundreds of billions more in taxpayer dollars to stem the crisis. Although the financial meltdown and legislation to bail out faltering financial firms had occurred under President Bush, Obama and the Democrats, by virtue of winning the elections, were now responsible for restoring the economy.

The Senate gave Obama an important victory on January 15, five days before he was inaugurated, when it rejected a GOP joint resolution that would have prevented him from using the second half of the $700 billion authorized in 2008 under the Troubled Assets Relief Program (TARP) passed late in President Bush's term. Although the House passed a companion measure, its vote was symbolic, because both chambers had to endorse the disapproval resolution for it to take effect. *(TARP background, pp. 60, 62)*

Beyond preserving access to TARP funds, the first legislative priority for congressional Democrats and the White House was enactment of a $787 billion economic stimulus bill that had been in the works since soon after the 2008 election. The final measure provided $575.3 billion in new spending over eleven years, primarily for programs intended to save or create jobs, assist unemployed workers, and support education. It also provided $211.8 billion in individual and business tax cuts. *(Stimulus legislation, pp. 61, 78)*

The House passed its version of the measure with relative ease on January 8, but the Senate was able to pass its bill only after a group of moderates negotiated a version that dropped some Democratic items, thereby winning the support of three additional Republicans and allowing Reid to clear the sixty vote hurdle for bringing the bill to the floor. The bill cleared on February 13, but already it had become the centerpiece of Republican claims that spending under the Democrats was out of control and that the majority was denying Republicans any input in legislation—charges that the GOP would repeat again and again throughout the 111th Congress.

Over Republican objections, House Democrats also passed a $154 billion "Jobs for Main Street Act" that would have invested in infrastructure and public service jobs, as well as providing help for families and small businesses struggling during the recession. It was the last House vote of the session and came as the unemployment rate hovered around 10 percent. *(Jobs legislation, pp. 85, 106)*

The Senate did not act on that measure in 2009, but in November it combined two popular proposals—more generous federal unemployment benefits and more help for homebuyers—into a single bill that won near-unanimous support in both chambers. *(Details, pp. 500, 517)*

CLEARING THE TO-DO LIST

Earlier in the year, in another rare instance of bipartisanship, members of both parties came together on legislation to curb what many saw as abusive practices by credit card companies. The measure imposed new disclosure requirements on the companies and new restrictions on when the companies could increase interest rates and fees.

Even before Obama delivered his first address to Congress, Democrats cleared legislation that had been on their agenda for years but that had been blocked under Bush. One measure made it easier for employees to challenge wage discrimination. Another expanded the Children's Health Insurance Program, which served children in low-income

Number of Public Laws Enacted, 1975–2012

Year	*Public Laws*	*Year*	*Public Laws*
1975	205	1994	255
1976	383	1995	88
1977	223	1996	245
1978	410	1997	153
1979	187	1998	241
1980	426	1999	170
1981	145	2000	410
1982	328	2001	136
1983	215	2002	241
1984	408	2003	198
1985	240	2004	300
1986	424	2005	169
1987	242	2006	248
1988	471	2007	161
1989	240	2008	321
1990	410	2009	125
1991	243	2010	258
1992	347	2011	90
1993	210	2012	193

families that were not poor enough to qualify for Medicaid but could not afford private insurance. In June, the Democrats achieved another long-sought goal when Obama signed into law legislation that gave the Food and Drug Administration the power to regulate tobacco products. *(Details, pp. 445, 448, 528)*

HEALTH CARE

On February 24, in an address to Congress, the new president laid out his legislative priorities. At the center was an overhaul of the nation's health care system. Obama also asked Congress to create a market-based cap-and-trade system to reduce carbon emissions that contributed to greenhouse gases, for wide-ranging reforms in education, and for a new regulatory system for the financial industry that would prevent a repeat of the events that precipitated the financial crisis in 2007–2008. Although progress was made on each of these priorities, Congress completed action only on health care and financial regulation reform and then not until 2010.

The president and Democratic congressional leaders had hoped to finish the health care reform bill by the end of 2009, but they had underestimated the difficulty of putting together a measure that could attract enough votes to pass in both chambers. The goal was to come as close as possible to achieving universal health care coverage, while slowing the growth of health care costs, making health insurance affordable to lower-income Americans, and setting minimal coverage standards for the health insurance industry. *(Health care legislation, p. 421)*

Republicans were adamant in their opposition to the bill, claiming that the government was trying to socialize health care and deprive individuals of their right to make private decisions about health care including matters of life and death. In a nationwide campaign against the measure, they charged that the Democrats' plan would recklessly drive up health care costs, raise middle-class taxes, slash Medicare services, and force employers to cut jobs in the middle of the recession.

In the House, Speaker Pelosi worked for weeks, negotiating, cajoling, and fine-tuning as she rounded up votes for the bill in her own caucus. To nail down the last votes, she agreed to antiabortion language that she and most House Democrats opposed. The House then passed the bill November 7, with just two votes to spare.

In the Senate, Majority Leader Reid could not count on any Republican votes. With Minority Leader Mitch McConnell of Kentucky using every available parliamentary means to delay action on the bill, Reid kept the Senate in session seven days a week for twenty-five days before he was able to round up all fifty-eight Democrats and two Independents needed to invoke cloture and vote on the bill. In doing so, he dropped a proposed public health insurance option that was a core element of the House bill and a key element of the bill for liberals in both chambers. He also agreed to pay for part of the costs of the bill with an excise tax on high-cost insurance plans that many Democrats said would affect middle-class families as well as the wealthy.

Still, Republicans balked. After Reid won a first cloture vote on the bill December 21, McConnell forced two more cloture votes and insisted on using most of the thirty hours of debate permitted after each successful votes to end a filibuster. Not until December 24, was the Senate able to pass its version of the health care legislation, again with no Republican support.

The two leaders' assessments of the legislation were as opposite as their positions on the measure. "We are reshaping the nation. . . . With this vote, we're rejecting a system in which one class of people can afford to stay healthy while another cannot," Reid declared before the first cloture vote. "For the first time in American history, good health will not depend on wealth."

McConnell's response: "Mark my words, this legislation will reshape the nation, and Americans have already issued their verdict—they don't want it."

OTHER UNFINISHED BUSINESS

Congress also made headway on another of Obama's top priorities—legislation to overhaul the U.S. financial regulatory structure to prevent future banking crises such as the one in 2008 that precipitated the economic recession. The House in December passed a sweeping measure that included a process for managing and, if necessary, dissolving financial institutions whose operations were threatening the stability of the entire financial sector. The measure also proposed a new consumer protection agency to police consumer financial products such as credit cards and home mortgages, new restrictions on executive compensation, and federal regulation of the multibillion-dollar over-the-counter market in financial derivatives. A Senate committee began work on a companion measure. *(Financial regulation, p. 88; consumer protection, pp. 96, 105)*

The House also narrowly passed a carbon cap-and-trade system, but only after a major White House lobbying effort and numerous concessions made to members from coal-producing, manufacturing, and farm states who feared business constituents would be hurt by the bill. Similar legislation stalled in the Senate behind the debate on health care reform, but sharp differences also made it unlikely that the Senate would produce a bill in the second session. *(Climate change legislation, p. 367)*

Several other House-passed bills also stalled in the Senate, as that chamber worked on health care reform. Among them was a measure to make the federal government the sole originator of federal student loans, cutting out the role of private companies as middlemen, and reauthorizations of surface transportation and aviation programs. Legislators were sharply divided over the length of the multiyear authorizations, the amount of money to approve, and how to pay for the costs of the programs. *(Student loans, pp. 476, 485)*

SPENDING BILLS AND THE DEBT LIMIT

President Obama followed up his speech laying out his legislative priorities with a detailed version of the fiscal 2010 budget, released in early May. In keeping with a campaign pledge, Obama asked that the temporary income tax cuts enacted during the Bush administration be made permanent for low- and middle-income taxpayers but that they be raised for affluent Americans. He also called for the elimination of a variety of special tax provisions for businesses and counted on raising $646 billion by selling pollution credits as part of the carbon cap-and-trade system.

Congressional Democrats endorsed much of Obama's ambitious agenda in a $3.6 trillion budget resolution that set the stage for the year's spending and tax debates. Before turning to the fiscal 2010 spending bills, however, Congress needed to finish work on nine of the twelve annual funding bills for fiscal 2009 that Democratic leaders had deliberately left undone at the end of 2008 in hopes that they would have control of the White House and bigger majorities in Congress after the 2008 elections. The gamble paid off, when Obama signed into law on March 11 a $1.1 trillion omnibus spending bill that included $19 billion more for domestic spending than Bush had said was acceptable and that allowed many increases in domestic spending that Democrats had been unable to win in the previous Congress.

In June Congress passed and Obama signed a supplemental $105.9 billion spending bill for fiscal 2009, primarily for operations in Iran and Afghanistan and related costs. The bill was a tough sell to Democrats who were disappointed that Obama, who had promised to withdraw combat troops from Iraq by August 31, 2010, was now planning to leave 50,000 soldiers there until the end of 2011 for training and other purposes.

Partisanship broke out in earnest in the House as the fiscal 2010 spending bills began to come to the floor in June. Republicans proposed more than 100 amendments to the commerce-justice-science appropriations bill, the first spending measure to reach the floor. Democrats responded with a rule that allowed no more than thirty-three amendments, and Republicans retaliated with a series of parliamentary delaying tactics that brought action to a crawl. On June 18, the House took fifty-three votes on the bill, a modern record for a single day.

From then on, House Democrats broke with tradition by using restrictive rules for every spending bill. Republicans still succeeded in slowing action, but the House managed to pass all twelve bills before the end of July.

The process bogged down in the Senate, where individual senators have wide latitude for delaying action. The chamber passed just four spending bills before the August recess and just one more in the early fall. Appropriators finally packaged six bills into a single package that cleared December 13. The last appropriations bill, for defense, was held back as a vehicle for other unfinished legislation. It cleared December 19, after Democrats, who insisting on continued production of the F-22 fighter plane against the Pentagon's wishes, backed down in the face of a direct veto threat from Obama.

In what was to become the first of several battles on the issue over the next four years, Congress cleared a $290 billion increase in the federal debt ceiling that was expected to tide the Treasury over until early 2010. Democratic leaders had hoped to raise the debt ceiling by as much as $1.8 trillion to avoid having to raise it again before the 2010 midterm elections. But the idea ran into opposition from Republicans and resistance from centrist Democrats in both chambers, forcing the leaders to settle for the short-term bill. The last increase had come earlier in 2009, when Congress boosted the ceiling by $789 billion to cover the cost of the economic stimulus law. *(Debt ceiling actions, pp. 134, 141, 142, 160, 168)*

SOTOMAYOR CONFIRMATION

The Senate on August 6 confirmed Sonia Sotomayor as the first Hispanic and third woman to sit on the Supreme Court. She was sworn in on August 8, replacing David H. Souter, who had announced his plans to retire three months earlier. Sotomayor had been serving on the U.S. Court of Appeals for the Second Circuit.

Sotomayor's confirmation was never in serious doubt, particularly after her cautious and virtually mistake-free performance during four days of confirmation hearings. Nonetheless, a majority of the Republican opposed her as being too liberal, and perhaps racist, for the high Court. They focused on her association with a legal advocacy group for Puerto Ricans (Sotomayor's parents immigrated to New York from Puerto Rico), and on a phrase she had used in several past speeches to the effect that "a wise Latina" judge would often reach a better conclusion than a white male.

GOP leaders, however, decided not to attempt a filibuster against the nomination, judging that such a move was highly unlikely to succeed. On the confirmation vote, nine Republicans joined fifth-seven Democrats and two independents to vote for Sotomayor; thirty-one Republicans voted against confirmation.

The Political Year

A dozen congressional seats changed hands in 2009, reflecting the largest between-elections turnover since 1974. Four senators, including the president-elect himself, and five House members resigned their seats to become part of the new Obama administration. The other three shifts, all in the Senate, were precipitated by the resolution of a disputed election, a death, and a resignation. In addition, one senator and one House member changed their party affiliation in 2009.

Six of the senators whose service began during the year, five Democrats and one Republican, were all appointees, and all were of the same party as their predecessors. The arrival of the seventh—Democrat Al Franken, the winner of a contested election that had kept one of Minnesota's Senate seats empty for the first six months of the year—created the first sixty-vote majority in the Senate for either party since 1980. With the switch of Pennsylvania's Arlen Specter from Republican to Democrat in April, the party now had a "filibuster-proof" majority that allowed it to advance several legislative priorities, the most important of which was the health insurance law.

All five seats that were filled by special election were won by Democrats. One of the winners, in upstate New York, took away a House seat that had been in Republican hands since the late nineteenth century. *(Membership changes, table, p. 829)*

ADMINISTRATION-RELATED VACANCIES

The most prominent lawmaker to depart to join the new administration was, of course, Barack Obama. The first sitting member of Congress to be elected president since Democratic Sen. John F. Kennedy of Massachusetts in 1960, Obama resigned his Senate seat on November 16, 2008. But the circumstances surrounding the appointment of his successor, Democrat Roland W. Burris, a former treasurer and attorney general of Illinois, were so controversial that Burris was not sworn in until January 15, 2009, eleven days after the 111th Congress convened.

Senate Majority Leader Harry Reid, and Majority Whip Richard J. Durbin, D-Ill., initially opposed the seating of Burris because he had been appointed by Democratic Gov. Rod R. Blagojevich after Blagojevich was indicted on an array of public corruption charges, including trying to sell the Senate appointment to the highest bidder. (Blagojevich was subsequently impeached and removed from office, and in 2011 was found guilty of several public corruption charges and sentenced to fourteen years in prison.) Reid and Durbin relented after Burris promised them he had done nothing untoward to get the job. But in November, the Senate Ethics Committee admonished him for being less than candid about the matter. Burris did not seek election to the seat in 2010.

The other person elected to national office in November 2008, Joseph R. Biden, was elected both vice president and senator from Delaware, becoming only the sixth person in history to win a seventh full Senate term. He resigned the Senate seat January 15 and was succeeded by Ted Kaufman, a former chief of staff to Biden. Kaufman made clear from the outset that he would not run in the 2010 special election to complete Biden's term.

Obama chose two senators to fill cabinet posts—Hillary Rodham Clinton of New York to be secretary of state, and Ken Salazar of Colorado to be secretary of the Interior. Clinton was succeeded by Democrat Kirsten Gillibrand, who had just started her second term in the House. In 2010 Gillibrand won a special election to complete the last two years of Clinton's term. Salazar was succeeded by Michael Bennett, superintendent of the Denver public school system. In 2010, Bennett ran successfully for a full term.

The four House members appointed to the Obama administration were Democrat Rahm Emanuel of Illinois, who resigned January 2 to become Obama's chief of staff; Democrat Hilda L. Solis, of California, who resigned February 24 after her confirmation as secretary of labor; Democrat Ellen O. Tauscher, who resigned July 26 after her confirmation as undersecretary of state for arms control and international security; and Republican John M. McHugh of New York, who resigned after his September 16 confirmation as secretary of the Army. McHugh's seat was the only one in which the opposing party won the special election.

OTHER SENATE VACANCIES

Franken was sworn in as the junior senator from Minnesota on July 7, 245 days after Election Day 2008 and 182 days after the 111th Congress convened. Franken's seating closed the sixth-longest Senate vacancy since direct election of senators began in 1912 and the longest since a seven-month vacancy in 1975 that resulted from a disputed election for an open seat in New Hampshire.

Franken was making his first bid for elective office after a career as a writer and actor on NBC's *Saturday Night Live* and a satirist of Republicans as a best-selling author and radio talk show host. He defeated incumbent Norm Coleman, who was seeking a second term. The initial tally put Coleman ahead by 215 votes and triggered an automatic hand recount under Minnesota law. That recount, finished on January 5, 2009, put Franken ahead by 255 votes. Coleman contested the outcome in state court, where a three-judge panel heard several weeks of testimony and ruled for Franken on April 13. Coleman then appealed to the Minnesota Supreme Court, which ruled for Franken, 5–0, on June 30. Coleman then conceded rather than pursue his case in federal court. In the end, the official margin of victory for Franken was 312 votes out of 2.9 million cast.

Sen. Edward M. Kennedy, the surviving icon of one of the nation's most prominent Democratic political dynasties, died August 25, opening the seat that he had held for forty-seven years. A few days before he died, Kennedy asked the Massachusetts Legislature to change the state law that barred the governor from filling Senate vacancies by appointment. On September 24, the state senate cleared legislation giving Massachusetts governor Deval Patrick the authority to name an interim successor who could serve until a special election set for January 19, 2010. The next day Patrick appointed Paul G. Kirk Jr., a former member of Kennedy's staff and a former chair of the Democratic National Committee. Kirk said that he would not be a candidate in the special election. That race was won by a Republican, Scott P. Brown.

In Florida, Mel Martinez, who had been elected to the Senate in 2004, abruptly announced August 7 that he would resign as soon as Gov. Charlie Crist, a fellow Republican, decided on a successor. Martinez's resignation took effect September 9, a day before the appointed successor, George LeMieux, was sworn in. LeMieux, who had served Crist in a variety of jobs, said he would not seek to hold the seat in 2010. Martinez, who had served as Secretary of Housing and Urban Development during the first three years of George W. Bush's presidency and as chair of the Republican party in 2006 and 2007, gave no reason for his departure. Two weeks after leaving office, he was named a partner in the government affairs practice of DLA Piper, a prominent lobbying and law firm in Washington, D.C.

PARTY SWITCHES

Specter's switch from Republican to Democrat, announced April 28, enlarged the party's caucus to fifty-nine members, counting the two independents who caucused with the Democrats, Joseph I. Lieberman of Connecticut and Bernard Sanders of Vermont. The last Senate party switch had been in 2001, when James M. Jeffords of Vermont left the GOP to become a Democrat, giving majority control to his new party halfway through the session. Before Jeffords's switch, the Senate had been split 50–50, giving Republican Vice President Dick Cheney the tie-breaking vote. *(Congress and the Nation Vol. XI, p. 708)*

Specter's switch also reduced the number of reliable GOP Senate moderates. Early in 2009, for example, he was one of only three Republican senators who voted in favor of President Obama's economic stimulus package. In announcing his switch, Specter noted that the Republican Party had moved far to the right on the political spectrum since his first election in 1980 and that he now found his "political philosophy more in line" with that of the Democratic Party. It was also true that Specter was likely to face a strong challenge to his renomination to the Republican ticket in 2010 from Patrick J. Toomey, a former House member and president of the Conservative Club for Growth. Specter had barely beaten Toomey in the 2004 primary and was considered the underdog in what was expected to be a rematch in 2010. In the event, Specter lost his Democratic primary race to Joe Sestak, who then lost the general election to Toomey.

A party switch also occurred in the House where Parker Griffith of Alabama left the Democrats to become a Republican on December 22, after the first session had ended. Griffith was the first House member to switch from the majority to the minority caucus since 1999, when Michael P. Forbes of New York switched to Democrat from Republican. The most recent House member to switch parties had been Rodney Alexander of Louisiana, who joined the GOP in 2004 when Republicans held the majority.

In his first year, Griffith broke with the Democrats on 30 percent of the party unity votes, more often than all but eight others in the caucus. He had been expected to have a difficult time winning reelection as a Democrat, and changing parties apparently did not improve his chances—he lost the Republican nomination in 2010 to Mo Brooks, picking up only 33 percent of the vote.

GUBERNATORIAL ELECTIONS

In a harbinger of electoral events that were to follow in 2010, voters in New Jersey and Virginia replaced their Democratic governors with Republicans. In New Jersey, former U.S. attorney Chris Christie narrowly bested incumbent Jon Corzine in a three-way race, while in Virginia, the state attorney general, Bob McDonnell, handily defeated the Democratic nominee, Creigh Deeds, a state senator. In the 2010 elections, Republicans wrested six governorships from the Democrats *(2010 elections, p. 30)*

Corzine, who was seeking a second term in office, started the race behind Christie in the polls, in part because of the severe economic downturn, voter dissatisfaction with various steps Corzine had taken to bring the state's budget under control, and a corruption scandal that caught up several Democratic policymakers in the state. Polls showed Corzine narrowing the gap with Christie, but he fell short on Election Day. Christie, who had taken a tough anticorruption stance during the campaign, won 48.5 percent of the vote to Corzine's 44.9 percent. An independent candidate, environmental expert Christopher Daggett, won 5.8 percent.

In Virginia, McDonnell and Deeds were running to succeed Democrat Tim Kaine, who was barred by state law from seeking a second term. Deeds, a rural state senator, overcame primary opposition from Brian Moran, a state delegate and brother of U.S. Rep. Jim Moran, R-Va., and Terry McAuliffe, former chair of the Democratic National Committee and chair of Hillary Clinton's 2008 presidential campaign. But he trailed behind McConnell, who ran as a "compassionate conservative," throughout the fall and lost the general election by eighteen percentage points. McDonnell's 58.6 percent was the highest percentage vote any candidate for governor in the state had received since 1961.

2010

The Legislative Year

In a year in which Democrats lost their sixty-vote Senate majority and partisanship ruled the day in the run-up to the 2010 midterm elections, the second session of the 111th Congress was remarkably productive. In the first half of the year, Democrats muscled through two legacy-making victories for President Barack Obama—the broadest expansion of health care coverage since the creation of Medicare in 1965 and a sweeping rewrite of the way the nation's financial industry is regulated. Then, in a lame duck session after the elections, Congress passed a handful of important measures, including an extension of expiring tax cuts, repeal of the "don't ask, don't tell" policies that barred openly gay people from serving in the military, and ratification of a nuclear arms treaty with Russia. *(Health care, p. 421; financial regulation, p. 88; gays in military, p. 288; arms treaty, p. 289)*

But the increasingly tense partisanship took its toll during the regular legislative session, particularly on spending and deficit issues. In January, the Senate defeated a bipartisan attempt to set up a mechanism to help control the deficit even as it voted to raise the debt limit ceiling by $1.9 billion, enough to last into early 2011. In an early sign that the annual appropriations process was in trouble, Democrats made minimal effort to pass a fiscal 2011 budget resolution to guide spending and tax decisions. Growing voter concern over the deficit and Republicans' determination to paint the Democrats as deaf to those worries left Democrats with little appetite for engaging in spending fights that Republicans could use against them during the election campaign. As a result, Congress passed none of the twelve regular spending bills, instead funding the government through a series of continuing resolutions.

Partisanship also doomed a Democratic plan to pass a massive jobs creation bill and a House-passed bill that aimed at limiting the effect of a January Supreme Court ruling that lifted campaign financing restrictions on corporations, nonprofits, and unions. A House-passed bill that would have allowed legal status for some undocumented children of illegal immigrants died when the Senate was unable to invoke cloture to end a filibuster. *(Court decision, p. 584)*

A SEAT SHIFT IN THE SENATE

Three weeks after the session began, Republican Scott P. Brown won a special election to fill the seat left vacant by Democrat Edward M. Kennedy, who had died in August 2009. The election reduced the Democratic caucus to fifty-nine, including the Senate's two Independents, instead of the sixty members Democratic leaders needed to overcome Republican delaying tactics. Brown's election also reinforced the confidence of the Republicans that there was no harm—and possibly considerable gain—in opposing every element of the ambitious legislative agenda championed by President Obama and the Democrats.

Brown's victory was widely recognized as one of the biggest political upsets of recent history. A previously little-known state senator, Brown defeated the state's attorney general, Martha Coakley, who had been considered a shoo-in in the heavily Democratic state but by all accounts ran a lackluster campaign. In addition to displaying a vote-winning folksy demeanor, Brown ran against Obama's health care reform, which had become unpopular in the state that had enacted a similar health care system earlier in the decade.

HEALTH CARE REFORM

Brown's election diminished the possibility that Democrats could prevail on another vote if any changes were made to the version of health care reform the Senate had passed at the end of 2009. But many House Democrats were unhappy with various aspects of the Senate bill and agreed to support it only after Democratic leaders, with Obama's support, developed a companion reconciliation bill that made numerous changes to the underlying Senate-passed health bill. Among the changes were increased subsidies to help uninsured people buy health coverage beginning in 2014 and increases in certain taxes and fees to help pay for the expanded coverage. The reconciliation bill also removed many provisions, criticized as "sweetheart deals," that had

CONGRESS IN 2010

The second session of the 111th Congress began at noon on January 5, 2010. The House adjourned *sine die* at 6 p.m. on December 22, 2010. The Senate adjourned *sine die* at 8:03 p.m. on December 22, 2010. The House was in session on 127 days for a total of 879 hours. The Senate was in session on 158 days, for a total of 1,075 hours.

A total of 4,604 bills and resolutions were introduced in the two chambers in 2010, nearly half as many as the 9,079 introduced in 2009 and only slightly fewer than the 4,815 in 2008. Congress cleared 259 bills, 258 of which were signed into public law. President Barack Obama vetoed one bill, the second veto of his presidency. *(Public laws table, p. 15; presidential vetoes, p. 915)*

The House took 660 roll-call votes (excluding quorum calls) in 2010, 327 fewer than in 2009. The Senate took 299 recorded votes, 98 fewer than in 2009. *(Recorded votes table, p. 21)*

been inserted in the original Senate bill to secure its passage. In a significant but unrelated move, the reconciliation bill also made the government the sole originator of federal student loans and increased the maximum Pell grant for low-income students. *(Health care bill details, p. 421)*

House Democrats, nervous about clearing the Senate version of the health bill before the Senate had agreed to the reconciliation, had hoped that Congress could complete action on the reconciliation bill before the House took up the underlying Senate-passed health bill. Had the Senate not approved the reconciliation bill, the House might have voted against clearing the Senate health bill. House leaders had to scrap that plan, however, when the Senate parliamentarian said a reconciliation could only change existing law. The House cleared the Senate-passed health reform bill March 21 by a seven-vote margin. It then passed the reconciliation bill on another close vote.

In the Senate, Republicans did everything they could to disrupt debate on the reconciliation bill, forcing Democrats to vote on a lengthy series of amendments designed to make them take politically tough votes and to help the GOP win the public opinion war. Democrats defeated amendment after amendment, before passing the bill March 25. Three Democrats joined forty Republicans to oppose the measure, which required only a simple majority to pass. A GOP challenge to two minor provisions dealing with higher education was upheld by the parliamentarian, forcing the measure back to the House, which cleared it later the same day, 220–207. Republicans in both the Senate and House vowed to campaign on a promise to repeal the law in the next Congress.

The health care overhaul bill, as modified by the reconciliation bill, required most Americans to have health insurance coverage by 2014. Uninsured individuals and small businesses could shop for health plans in state-run marketplaces, and low-income families could get subsidized premiums. Among other things, the law barred health insurers from denying coverage for preexisting conditions and allowed parents to keep their children on their insurance policies until age twenty-six. The cost of the law, estimated at nearly $1 trillion over ten years, was offset by cuts in Medicare payments to hospitals, increased Medicare taxes on the wealthy, and higher fees for top-of-the-line health insurance policies and certain medical-device makers.

FINANCIAL SERVICES REGULATORY REFORM

Three months after passing health care reform, Congress gave President Obama another of his top priorities when it cleared a bill making the most substantial changes in financial regulation since the Great Depression in the 1930s. The legislation, which grew out of the events that precipitated the financial crisis of 2007–2008, gave financial industry regulators broad new authority and created agencies to oversee consumer lending and to determine whether changing financial practices posed a threat to the overall economy. The legislation gave the Federal Deposit Insurance Corporation (FDIC) broad powers to take over and wind down huge financial corporations on the verge of collapse. Trading in derivatives, a largely unregulated market involving complex securities, also came under closer federal scrutiny.

The House had passed its version of the legislation in late 2009 with no Republican support. In the Senate, House Banking Committee Chair Christopher J. Dodd, D-Conn., continued negotiating into early 2010 before introducing a bill that could win his panel's approval. Dodd guided the bill through Senate floor debate virtually unscathed in May, with help from Scott P. Brown, who voted with the Democrats to invoke cloture and then, with support from three additional Republicans, on final passage.

Lawmakers then convened a genuine conference committee to resolve differences in the House and Senate versions. The conference committee had been used less and less during the decade; instead, the majority tended to trade amended bills back and forth between the chambers until they could agree or one chamber receded.

The conferences committee reached a compromise in late June, which the House passed relatively easily on June 30. In the Senate, Majority Leader Harry Reid, D-Nev., had to hold up action following the death of Robert C. Byrd, the venerable Democrat from West Virginia who had served a half-century in the Senate. Byrd's death, plus the continued opposition of Wisconsin Democrat Russ Feingold, left Reid short of the sixty votes he needed to invoke cloture. Three Republicans—Olympia Snowe and Susan Collins, both of Maine, and Scott Brown—eventually agreed to vote with the Democrats first to invoke cloture and then to support adoption of the conference report, which passed on July 15.

Although the legislation provided direction and set requirements, the regulatory agencies were given the responsibility of turning it into reality, which was expected to be a lengthy process. The financial industry, which strongly opposed the measure, took every opportunity to delay implementation, challenging various elements of the bill at every step of the regulatory process. For the remainder of Obama's first term, Republicans also sought to delay or repeal various aspects of the measure, delay confirmation of key presidential appointees, and deny funding, particularly for the new consumer protection agency.

KAGAN CONFIRMED

In August, the Senate confirmed Obama's second nomination to the Supreme Court. Elena Kagan took the seat of Justice John Paul Stevens, who had retired at the end of the 2009–2010 session after thirty-five years on the bench. Kagan, the first female dean of Harvard Law School and the solicitor general since 2009, was the first nominee in thirty-nine years not to have any experience as a judge. Democrats argued she would bring a real-world perspective to the court, while Republicans argued that she lacked the necessary background for the high court. *(Kagan confirmation, p. 585)*

Recorded Vote Totals

Following are the recorded vote totals between 1953 and 2012. The figures do not include quorum calls or two House roll calls in 2011 and 2012 that were vitiated. The numbers, while high during President Barack Obama's first term, did not set records. The highest total for the Senate was 688 recorded votes in 1976. The highest number in the House was 1,177 in 2007.

Also in 2007 Congress set a new record for the highest number of recorded votes ever taken in a single year: 1,619. But the 95th Congress (1977–1979) still held the record for the most votes taken in a single Congress: 2,696.

Year	*House*	*Senate*	*Total*
1953	71	89	160
1954	76	171	247
1955	76	87	163
1956	73	130	203
1957	100	107	207
1958	93	200	293
1959	87	215	302
1960	93	207	300
1961	116	204	320
1962	124	224	348
1963	119	229	348
1964	113	305	418
1965	201	258	459
1966	193	235	428
1967	245	315	560
1968	233	281	514
1969	177	245	422
1970	266	422	688
1971	320	423	743
1972	329	532	861
1973	541	594	1,135
1974	537	544	1,081
1975	612	602	1,214
1976	661	688	1,349
1977	706	635	1,341
1978	834	516	1,350
1979	672	497	1,169
1980	604	531	1,135
1981	353	483	836
1982	459	465	924
1983	498	371	869
1984	408	275	683
1985	439	381	820
1986	451	354	805
1987	488	420	908
1988	451	379	830
1989	368	312	680
1990	510	326	836
1991	428	280	708
1992	473	270	743
1993	597	395	992
1994	497	329	826
1995	867	613	1,480
1996	454	306	760
1997	633	298	931
1998	533	314	847
1999	609	374	983
2000	600	298	898
2001	507	380	887
2002	483	253	736
2003	675	459	1,134
2004	543	216	759
2005	669	366	1,035
2006	540	279	819
2007	1,177	442	1,619
2008	688	215	903
2009	987	397	1,384
2010	660	299	959
2011	945	235	1,180
2012	656	251	907

The Democratic majority, the announcement by five Republicans that they would support the nomination, and Kagan's own competent performance during her confirmation hearing all but ensured her confirmation. Nonetheless, she received five fewer votes than Sonia Sotomayor did in 2009, demonstrating an increasing reluctance among senators to back nominees selected by presidents of the opposing party. With Kagan joining Sotomayor and Ruth Bader Ginsberg, the Supreme Court had three women members on the bench for the first time in its history.

PREELECTION GRIDLOCK

Democratic leaders returned from the summer recess in mid-September with a high-profile to-do list that included the annual defense authorization bill, immigration legislation, a food safety bill, an extension of some or all of the Bush-era tax cuts, and some of the fiscal 2011 appropriations bills. Their plans were quickly scuttled by bitter partisanship combined with political nervousness and legislative lethargy brought on by campaign pressures.

Congress managed to clear three bills—the first intelligence authorization measure to be enacted in six years; a reauthorization of the National Aeronautics and Space Administration (NASA); and a bill aiding small businesses, which were widely viewed as major drivers of job creation. Before they returned home in early October to campaign, legislators also cleared a short-term continuing resolution to carry the government past the elections.

The November 2 elections reversed the tide that had swept Obama into office and increased Democratic congressional majorities in 2008. Energized by the highly conservative Tea Party movement, Republicans gained control of the House and increased their numbers in the Senate, leaving the president facing the prospect of a far more conservative Congress for the remainder of his first term.

ORGANIZING THE NEXT CONGRESS

Congress convened for one week on November 15, primarily to organize for the next Congress. The House also dealt with an ethics case involving New York Democrat Charles B. Rangel, who had served in Congress for twenty terms.

As expected and without opposition, the Republican Caucus chose Minority Leader John A. Boehner, R-Ohio, to be the new Speaker of the House in the 112th Congress. His leadership team included Eric Cantor of Virginia as majority leader and Kevin McCarthy of California as majority whip. *(Leadership table, p. 5)*

On the Democratic side, Nancy Pelosi of California, the powerful Speaker in the 110th and 111th Congresses, returned to the minority leader position she held in 2007 before Democrats took control of the House. But first she had to overcome an open challenge from Blue Dog Coalition leader Heath Shuler of North Carolina. Although Pelosi won the caucus nomination handily, 150–43, the fact that the vote even took place indicated the depth of the frustrations among Democrats following the elections. Pelosi's second in command, Majority Leader Steny Hoyer of Maryland, was tapped to become minority whip; John B. Larson of Connecticut continued as caucus chair. A new position, assistant minority leader, was added to keep Majority Whip James E. Clyburn of South Carolina on the leadership team.

In the Senate Harry Reid, D-Nev., and Mitch McConnell, R-Ky., retained their positions as Senate majority leader and minority leader, respectively. Majority Whip Richard J. Durbin, D-Ill., and Minority Whip Jon Kyl, R-Ariz., also kept their positions.

On November 18, the House Committee on Standards of Official Conduct found Rangel guilty of eleven counts of misconduct in a case that dated to 2008 and included failing to pay taxes, inaccurately reporting his income, and improperly soliciting donations for an education center bearing his name. On December 2, the House censured Rangel, who had been reelected in November, forcing him to stand in the well of the House as Pelosi read an oral rebuke. It was the first time in twenty-seven years that the House had censured a member. *(Ethics investigations, p. 651)*

LAME DUCK SURPRISE

When Congress reconvened for its lame duck session after a Thanksgiving break, events moved quickly—and unexpectedly. Few were expecting the session to accomplish much more than intensifying political partisanship. However, Obama's December decision to break a long-standing stalemate on taxes changed the dynamic.

The White House compromise on taxes, negotiated principally by Vice President Joseph R. Biden Jr. with McConnell and other GOP leaders, extended the 2001 and 2003 income tax cuts, including those for the wealthiest taxpayers, for two years, as well as extending the expiring estate tax with more generous terms. The bill also contained a thirteen-month extension of federal emergency unemployment benefits and an unprecedented one-year reduction in employees' payroll taxes, both provisions aimed at stimulating the economy.

Liberal Democrats were furious with the White House concession on taxes. In the House, they initially prevailed on Pelosi to keep the Obama plan off the floor and instead pass a version that would have let the tax breaks for the well-off expire, among other things. But two overwhelming favorable votes for the measure in the Senate forced the House Democrats to retreat. On a key vote in the Senate on December 13, where sixty votes were needed to pass almost any piece of legislation or approve a nomination, eighty-three senators voted to cut off debate on the Obama compromise. Two days later, the Senate passed the measure handily, leaving House Democrats little room to maneuver. The House cleared the legislation, averting a substantial hike in income tax rates that would have taken place on January 1, 2011, if Congress had not acted.

The following day, after months of maneuvering, the Senate cleared a House-passed bill repealing the ban, adopted in 1993, preventing openly gay people from serving in the military. The repeal, a key victory for the president, gained momentum after it received backing from Robert M. Gates, the widely respected secretary of defense who as a Republican had also held that post under President Bush, as well as from the chair and vice chair of the Joint Chiefs of Staff. *(Details, p. 288)*

In the frenzied weeks before adjourning, Congress also cleared a long-stalled food safety bill, a continuing resolution providing funding for the government through March 11, 2011, and a defense authorization bill that had been stripped of most controversial items, including the already cleared repeal of the "don't ask, don't tell" policy and a directive to continue funding the development of a second, competing engine for the F-35 Joint Strike Fighter. The Pentagon had opposed the funding. *(Details, p. 266)*

In the last substantive vote of the session, the Senate approved ratification of the New START treaty with Russia, an action that had seemed out of reach only a week or two earlier, given the busy lame duck agenda. Ratification, which required support of two-thirds of those voting, was largely the result of a determined effort by Reid and an intense White House lobbying campaign led by Biden. Both Reid and the administration had assessed the treaty would have less chance of ratification in the next Congress. *(Details, p. 289)*

The Political Year

After disastrous performances in the previous two congressional elections, Republicans surged back in 2010, picking up sixty-three seats to regain control of the House for the first time since 2006 and significantly narrowing the Democratic majority in the Senate. In President Obama's words, the Democratic Party took a "shellacking."

It was the largest net gain of House seats for either party in the midterm elections since 1938, when the GOP won eighty-one seats in what had been an increasingly lopsided Democratic chamber during the first six years of Franklin D. Roosevelt's presidency. The rapid swing in 2010 was the result of a potent coalescence of forces: a stagnant economy, the sudden emergence of a movement of ideologically driven conservative activists, a broad sense that the federal government was overreaching under the Democrats, and a shift in the demographics of those who came out to vote.

The 2010 Republican tidal wave cut a wide swath in the House, upending long-term incumbents such as moderate Democrat James L. Oberstar, a thirty-four-year veteran from Minnesota, as well as dozens from marginal districts who owed their seats in part to the Democratic tides in the previous two election cycles. In the Senate, Republicans gained a net of six seats, knocking out incumbent Democrats

Russ Feingold of Wisconsin and Blanche Lincoln of Arkansas, while picking up open seats in Illinois, Indiana, North Dakota, and Pennsylvania.

The 2010 elections were likely to have repercussions for years to come. The Republican Party wrested six governorships from the Democrats, for a total of twenty-nine. The party also picked up twenty-one state chambers, and then flipped another, the Louisiana Senate, in a special election in February. That gave the GOP control of, or a tie in, sixty-one of ninety-nine state chambers, including Nebraska's nominally nonpartisan unicameral legislature, which was mostly Republican. Those gains were expected to boost the GOP's clout in the redistricting that would occur as a result of the 2010 Census.

FACTORS IN THE GOP SURGE

Several factors helped explain the rise of the GOP in the 2010 elections. Although the recession had technically ended in mid-2009, its effects were still taking their toll. The economy was growing again—but slowly, and there were nowhere near enough jobs for all those who wanted them. Unemployment reached 10.6 percent in January 2010, roughly double the usual rate, and hovered just under 10 percent for the rest of the year. Although the recession began under President George W. Bush, many voters held Obama and the Democratic Congress responsible for not fixing the economy faster.

"This is all because the economy is genuinely bad, and Democrats have over-promised and under-delivered in the view of most voters," said Larry J. Sabato, director of the University of Virginia's Center for Politics, shortly before the election. "People know what they see, and they use midterm elections to send their public officials a message. This is a classic message-sending, checks and balances election generated by a deeply dissatisfied public."

Many political analysts also cited the unpopularity of the legislative record of the Democratic Congress and growing public concern over rapidly rising federal deficits. To many voters, the $787 billion economic stimulus passed in Obama's first month in office and the health care overhaul and financial regulatory reform measures passed in 2010, together with the bailout of the financial and auto industries at the end of the Bush administration, appeared to be government overreach. "What I hear all across my state are three words: 'Enough is enough,'" Sen. Kent Conrad, D-N.D., said after the elections.

These frustrations contributed to the growth of the Tea Party movement, a loosely knit and vocal group of conservative activists who were not shy about pushing their viewpoints on cutting federal spending and the role of federal government. GOP congressional contenders who rode the support of Tea Party activists to primary victories over Republican establishment candidates included some of the most prominent of the year's Senate candidates, although their record on Election Day was spotty. Tea Party candidates were not able to oust Reid in Nevada or Michael Bennett in Colorado, and they lost a colorful race in Delaware. But Republican Rand Paul easily bested his Democratic opponent in Kentucky.

Yet, for all the talk of disaffected Democrats and angry taxpayers, self-described independent voters still played the role of power brokers. They remained the unpredictable—and often decisive—factor in determining who would control the White House and Congress, an important lesson that was not lost on the strategists looking toward future elections.

Constituting more than one-fourth of all voters, this constituency included millions of Americans who seemed perpetually angry about the perceived failures of the government in Washington and were deeply distrustful of both parties. The tendency of independent voters to rage against the mainstream political machine, no matter which party was in control, could clearly be seen in exit polls as published by CNN.

In 2008, independent voters favored Democratic House candidates by 51 percent to 43 percent, making common cause with liberal activists to punish Republicans for what they regarded as failures of the Bush administration. But in 2010, independents swung over to join with conservative activists who lashed back against Obama's policy agenda. Independents favored GOP House candidates over Democrats 56 percent to 38 percent. The prominence of this frustrated but relatively nonideological amalgamation of voters in tipping national elections meant both parties faced the prospect of navigating a minefield of difficult strategic and tactical decisions over the following two years.

Turnout in 2010, at 41.5 percent, was typical for midterm elections. But shifts in that turnout contributed significantly to the results. The shift in the age of those who voted was one critical factor. Young voters ages eighteen to twenty-four reverted to their nonvoting habits in 2010, after turning out in greater-than-usual numbers in 2008 to support Obama. The 2008 exit polls showed that 10 percent of the total electorate was made up of these young voters, who split 62 percent to 35 percent in favor of Obama. That group was nearly as Democratic-leaning in 2010 (58 percent to 39 percent), but was only half as large as a percentage of all voters.

That change gave more clout to the oldest voters, ages sixty-five and older, who made up 15 percent of the voters in 2008 but 23 percent in 2010. That made their big swing—from a slight Democratic edge of 49 percent to 48 percent in 2008 to a daunting 59–38 edge in favor of Republicans in 2010—a major factor in the GOP gains.

HOUSE ELECTIONS

The Republican gain of sixty-three House seats far exceeded not only the thirty-nine they needed to wrest control from the Democrats but also their gain of fifty-two seats in 1994, when they won control of the House for the first time in forty years. Their majority of 242 members in the 112th Congress was the largest they had had since the 80th Congress in 1947–1948. House Minority Leader John A. Boehner of Ohio, the Speaker-in-waiting for the new Congress, repeatedly fought back tears while delivering his victory speech on election night. "For far too long," he said, "Washington has been doing what's best for Washington and not what's best for the American people. And tonight that begins to change."

Few targeted Democrats were safe from the GOP wave, and Republicans also pulled off several long-shot surprises. Three House committee chairs fell: Oberstar, who headed the Transportation and Infrastructure Committee; John M. Spratt Jr., of South Carolina, head of the Budget Committee; and Ike Skelton of Missouri, who headed the Armed Services panel.

Democratic losses were particularly large in several big states, including Florida, New York, Ohio, and Pennsylvania, where a total of eighteen incumbents lost. Prominent among the casualties were first- and second-term Democrats who represented suburban swing districts. In New York and Pennsylvania, the GOP more than tripled what had been nominal representation. The damage was not confined to big states, however; Republicans captured the at-large seats in both Dakotas as well as both seats in New Hampshire.

Democrats captured just three seats—an open seat in Delaware and two held by GOP incumbents: Charles K. Djou of Hawaii, who had won his seat in a special election earlier in the year, and Anh "Joseph" Cao, who had been elected in 2008 and who was the only Republican to vote for passage of the House health care bill in 2009.

Democrats suffered heavy House losses in the South and the coal-rich Ohio River Valley—two areas where, to be competitive, down-ballot Democrats on the ticket in 2012 would have to run well ahead of Obama, who performed weakly there in 2008. At least a quarter of the seats the Republicans picked up were in staunchly conservative districts where Democrats were unlikely to make competitive races again anytime soon.

Bernie Pinsonat, an independent pollster with Southern Media & Opinion Research, said one reason Democrats were likely to have a particularly hard time winning back many of their losses was that the national party had lost touch with a large part of America. "Most of the things that Democrats are pushing nationally are truly disliked by Southern voters," he said. "We don't like big government. We don't like taxes. Unions don't have a foothold of any consequence. . . . The national Democratic Party is winning on the coast with those messages, but in the heartland, and especially in the South, their constituencies and the people that they kowtow to are not popular."

SENATE ELECTIONS

The 2010 Senate elections were marked by the rise and impact of the Tea Party movement, a set of colorful candidates, dramatic shifts of fortune and opportunities lost—and a flood of outside spending that made it, by any measure, the most expensive midterm elections yet. The conservative uprising that had energized the Republican Party for eighteen months led to a gain of six seats for the GOP. But it also saddled the party with a few Senate candidates who could not win, leaving the Democrats in control of the Senate by a single seat. With the support of the Senate's two independents, who typically voted with the Democrats, the party could count on a fifty-three seat majority to the GOP's forty-seven.

Despite their losses, the overwhelming feeling among Democratic senators was one of relief, especially after their leader, Harry Reid of Nevada, managed to pull out a victory in his own reelection race, overcoming abysmal poll ratings and a concerted effort by conservative activists to unseat him. Republicans also took satisfaction in the results, despite coming up short of a majority. Their greater numbers would make it that much harder for the Democrats to push through an agenda the GOP opposed.

The marquee races generally involved conservative Republicans taking on establishment Democrats or, in some cases, incumbents in their own party in primaries. Their record was mixed.

- Nevada's Sharron Angle, a former GOP state representative, ran a well-financed challenge to Reid, losing in the end by five percentage points.
- Alaska's Joe Miller, a Republican lawyer, scored a stunning upset over incumbent Lisa Murkowski in the GOP primary. Murkowski then mounted an improbable write-in campaign that returned her to the Senate for the 112th Congress.
- Colorado's Ken Buck, a rural county Republican district attorney, defeated former lieutenant governor Jane Norton for the right to challenge Democrat Michael Bennett but lost by about two points. Bennett had been appointed to the seat in 2009 to replace Democrat Ken Salazar, who had resigned to become Obama's interior secretary.
- Kentucky's Rand Paul, an eye doctor and son of libertarian Rep. Ron Paul of Texas, easily bested Democratic state attorney general Jack Conway after trouncing Kentucky Secretary of State Trey Grayson in the GOP primary.
- Delaware's Christine O'Donnell slipped past heavy primary favorite Michael N. Castle, a GOP moderate, who had held Delaware's only House seat for eighteen years. O'Donnell then lost by almost twenty points to Democrat Chris Coons, a county commissioner who had been given virtually no chance of defeating Castle.

None of these Republican standard-bearers ran anything approaching a flawless campaign. Angle made several highly publicized gaffes, including one when she told a group of Hispanic students that some of them looked "a little more Asian to me." Paul caused a stir when he questioned whether the Civil Rights Act should apply to businesses and when he proposed that Medicare beneficiaries be subject to a $2,000 deductible as a way of trimming the budget. O'Donnell ran into problems after video clips in which she discussed religion, sex, the occult, and other aspects of her personal life were widely circulated. One campaign ad featured her assuring voters, "I am not a witch." Yet, it was symbolic of how toxic the political atmosphere had turned for Democrats that, among all these once-long-shot candidates, only O'Donnell was a clear underdog on Election Day.

The contest for the Senate majority involved many more races than those targeted by the Tea Party, however. Ultimately, it came down to a handful of key states where Democrats worked hard to protect prominent Democrats who suddenly looked vulnerable, including Barbara Boxer of California and Joe Manchin III of West Virginia, along with Reid and Bennett.

Republicans ended up defeating two incumbents and flipping four open seats held by Democrats, while not losing a single Republican seat. In Wisconsin, three-term Democrat Russ Feingold fell to Republican businessman John Thompson by about five percentage points, while Blanche Lincoln of Arkansas lost by nearly twenty-one points to GOP representative John Boozer. Republicans claimed open Democratic seats in Indiana, Illinois, North Dakota, and Pennsylvania. Democrats retained open Democratic seats in Connecticut, Delaware, and West Virginia.

Although it was not the historic upset that changed the face of the House, the Republican Senate performance was an important shift that reflected public unhappiness with the Democrats. In an ordinary year, the views expressed by many of the GOP candidates on fiscal issues, and in many cases on hot-button social issues, might have helped Democrats to brand their opponents as extremists.

Even in the highly charged political environment of 2010, national Republican strategists had serious doubts about the electability of some of the Tea Party favorites. Those who associated themselves with the Tea Party demanded absolute fealty to the conservative principles the movement espoused. That ultimately posed a potential conflict with a large segment of independent voters who, while leaning Republican in November, also by and large wanted the parties to stop bickering and work out effective solutions to the nation's problems.

STATE ELECTIONS

The Republican surge of 2010 put the GOP in control of redrawing congressional districts for nearly half of the 435 seats in the U.S. House of Representatives. Of the thirty-seven contests for governor's seats in 2010, eighteen switched party control, and Republicans won twelve of these, for a net gain of six. Equally important for redistricting, Republicans won control of both legislative chambers in twenty-five states, up from fifteen before the election. In twenty of these seats, the governor was also Republican. Republicans had majorities in ten of the eighteen states that were slated to gain or lose seats in reapportionment.

Governorships. The GOP was practically handed four of the governorships, when Democratic governors, because of term limits, could not run again for office in the heavily Republican states of Kansas, Oklahoma, Tennessee, and Wyoming. Republicans also added to their number in a Rust Belt rout, winning open Democratic seats in Michigan, Pennsylvania, and Wisconsin and defeating incumbent Democrats Ted Strickland of Ohio and Chet Culver of Iowa. Republicans also held on to GOP seats in Florida and Texas.

When the vote counting was done, Republicans held twenty-nine governorships, Democrats twenty, and an independent one.

Democrats scored a big takeover in California, where Democrat Jerry Brown won to succeed term-limited Republican Arnold Schwarzenegger. Brown had been governor of the state previously from 1975 to 1983. The Democrats also held on to the governorship of New York, electing Andrew Cuomo to the seat once held by his father, Mario Cuomo. Democrats also were able to offset some of their losses in the Midwest by taking back traditionally Democratic strongholds such as Hawaii, where longtime Democratic Rep. Neil Abercrombie won the governorship.

GOP hopes of winning several governorships in the Northeast failed to materialize. Democrat Dan Malloy won to succeed retired Republican Jodi M. Rell in Connecticut. Republicans were also unable to defeat Massachusetts governor Deval Patrick despite his mediocre job approval numbers, and they lost open seats in Vermont and Rhode Island. Former Sen. Lincoln Chafee, previously a liberal-leaning Republican, won in Rhode Island as an independent. Republicans picked up the governorship in Maine when two more-liberal candidates divided the Democratic and independent vote. Third-party candidates were also significant factors in Massachusetts, Minnesota, Colorado, and Illinois, although none of them won.

Statehouses. After the 2010 elections, Republicans held about 54 percent of all state legislative seats, the most at any time since after the 1928 elections. It was the largest gain by either party since 1966, surpassing the Democratic gains in the post-Watergate election of 1974, and the largest number of legislative seats Republicans had held since the 1928 election.

Republicans were in control of twenty-five state legislatures, Democrats controlled sixteen, and eight were split between the two parties. (Nebraska has a nonpartisan, unicameral legislature.) The GOP was particularly excited about its gains in Michigan, Ohio, Pennsylvania, and Wisconsin, all of which would have GOP majorities in both chambers and the governorship.

SPECIAL ELECTIONS

Eleven special elections were held in 2010, yielding six victories for the Republicans and five for the Democrats. The GOP did not win any special elections in 2009.

Senate. In addition to the upset victory of Republican Scott P. Brown in Massachusetts, there were four other special elections for Senate seats, all held on November 2 to coincide with the general elections. In Delaware, the contest between Coons, the victor, and O'Donnell was to serve the remainder of the full term of Joseph R. Biden Jr., who left after the 2008 elections to become vice president. The term was scheduled to end in January 2015. Ted Kaufman had been appointed to fill the seat until the general election.

In Illinois, Republican Rep. Mark Steven Kirk, won election to take the seat being vacated for the rest of the 111th Congress by Democrat Roland W. Burris. Kirk also won a new six-year term. Burris had been appointed to hold Barack Obama's seat until the general election. In New York, Kirsten Gillibrand easily won election as the state's junior senator after being temporarily appointed to the job to replace Hillary Rodham Clinton, who had resigned to become secretary of state.

Democratic governor Joe Manchin III became the first newly elected senator from West Virginia in a quarter century after being elected to finish the term of Democrat Robert C, Byrd, who died June 28. Byrd's term ended in January 2012. Manchin replaced Carte P. Goodwin, whom he had appointed to fill the seat until the special election. Goodwin's appointment on July 16 had been eagerly awaited by Senate leaders because it restored the Democratic caucus in the Senate to fifty-nine seats against the Republicans' forty-one.

House. Republicans won four of the six special elections for House seats in 2010, but one of the victories was short-lived. Charles J. Djou, a Honolulu city council member, won a May 22 race for a seat that had been held by Democrat Abercrombie, who had resigned in February to run for governor in a race that he won. In November, Djuo was defeated for a full term by Democrat Colleen Hanabusa, who had served as Hawaii Senate president.

In the other Republican victories, Tom Graves, a Georgia state representative won a special election on June 8 to replace Republican Nathan Deal, who gave up his House seat to run, successfully, for governor. Graves was unopposed in November for a full term. In Indiana, state senator Marlin Stutzman won a special election on November 2 to replace Republican Mark Souder, who had resigned May 21 after admitting to an affair with an aide. In New York, Republican Tom Reed, the former mayor of Corning, won a special election to fill out the term of Democrat Eric Massa, who had resigned in March after being accused of sexually harassing male staff members. Both Stutzman and Reed simultaneously won full two-year terms starting in January 2011.

On the Democratic side, Florida state senator Ted Deutch won a special election on April 13 to replace Democrat Robert Wexler, who had resigned to head the nonprofit Center for Middle East Peace and Economic Cooperation. In Pennsylvania, Mark Critz, won a May 18 special election to replace John Murtha, who had died February 8. Both Deutch and Critz won election to a full term in November in rematches with their special election opponent—Critz by a narrow margin.

2011

The Legislative Year

The 112th Congress's first session was widely characterized as paralyzed and dysfunctional. Public confidence in the divided Congress reached a new low. A year-end Gallup survey, conducted December 15–18, showed that 11 percent of Americans approved of the job lawmakers were doing, the lowest congressional approval rating in Gallup history. Congressional scholar Norman J. Ornstein brought the issue to the fore in an article in *Foreign Policy* magazine that the editors titled "Worst. Congress. Ever."

A fleeting show of unity occurred early in the session in the wake of a January 8 mass shooting and assassination attempt that left Rep. Gabrielle Giffords, D-Ariz., severely wounded. In a symbolic act, Democrats and Republicans sat in pairs at the State of the Union address. But even before President Barack Obama's January 25 address, House Republicans—back in control after four years as the minority—began the session with an attempt to repeal his signature health care overhaul. They subsequently took repeated runs at the health care law; environmental regulation, especially efforts to mitigate climate change; the 2010 financial services regulation law; the administration's energy policies; and government spending in general.

The standoffs frequently began within the splintered House GOP caucus, where all but a few dozen members also belonged to the conservative Republican Study Committee. More than a third of the House Republicans, eighty-seven, were freshmen, many of whom owed their elections in large part to the conservative budget and tax-cutting Tea Party movement. Several of the freshmen did not regard those goals as negotiable.

The new dynamic in the House put Speaker John A. Boehner, R-Ohio, in the delicate position of playing two roles: the partisan leader of a caucus that included more determined social and fiscal conservatives than at any time in recent memory, and a practical dealmaker trying to reach agreements to avert government shutdowns and other crises largely of Congress's own making. To achieve his goal of not relying on Democrats' votes, Boehner had to appeal to the hard-line conservatives without losing his more moderate members; in many cases, Boehner found he had little room to maneuver.

On the other side of the Capitol, the Democrats' narrow Senate majority of fifty-one members (plus the generally reliable votes of two independents) and a de facto requirement for sixty votes to move legislation forward often kept the chamber from doing little more than blocking House-passed bills, which Democratic senators did with regularity. Democratic alternatives met a similar fate, denied a supermajority by the Republicans. Still, when crises loomed, it was often Majority Leader Harry Reid, D-Nev., and Minority Leader Mitch McConnell, R-Ky., who found a way to broker a deal that the House was forced to accept.

Not surprisingly, the votes in both chambers frequently broke along party lines. In the House, 75.8 percent of the roll-call votes pitted the majority of one party against the majority of the other—the highest percentage of any session in the fifty-eight years that Congressional Quarterly had measured party unity votes. In the Senate, where Reid had to hold his caucus together and pick up a handful of moderate Republicans to pass any legislation that was the least bit controversial, 57.1 percent of the roll-call votes divided the two parties. *(Table, p. 7)*

So profound was the partisan enmity and distrust that it could not be bridged even by the most powerful single players from each party. Obama and Boehner were unable to finalize a "grand bargain" on the deficit that they spent much of the summer negotiating in almost total secrecy. The year was so dominated by fiscal issues—spending, taxes, and the size of the federal debt—that Congress cleared only a few pieces of significant legislation, including a patent law overhaul, a defense authorization bill, and three trade agreements that had been held up for years.

ROUND ONE ON SPENDING

The sharp differences were on display early in the year, when House Republicans set out to cut fiscal 2011 spending. Democrats had handed them the opportunity by leaving all twelve of the fiscal 2011 appropriations bills unfinished when they controlled Congress the previous year. House leaders sought to cap spending at $1.05 trillion, but GOP conservatives rebelled and forced Boehner to accept a lower cap in a bill to cover spending for the rest of the fiscal year.

A commitment by Boehner to an open process led to dozens of amendments, including conservative proposals to defund the health care law, roll back Environmental Protection Agency (EPA) regulations of climate change emissions, and take a variety of other actions that were anathema to Democrats. The resulting bill won a majority in the House in February and allowed conservatives to begin laying out their agenda, but it had no chance of passing in the Senate, which rejected it in March.

The stalemate dragged on for two months before both chambers agreed on an omnibus bill that contained $1.05 trillion in fiscal 2011 discretionary spending, about $39 billion below the previous year's level. The cuts included $12 billion in reductions that Republicans had won as the price of three stopgap continuing resolutions, or CRs, to keep the government running while they continued to negotiate.

The final deal was reached with only minutes to spare before most federal operations would have been stopped for lack of funding. It was the first of three times that the government almost closed down in 2011. Several Tea Party Republicans said the cuts were not deep enough, but they looked ahead to tackling the deficit more aggressively as part of the fiscal 2012 budget resolution and the impending battle over raising the debt limit.

CUTTING THE BUDGET

The day after the fiscal 2011 spending bill cleared, the House easily adopted a fiscal 2012 budget resolution—a congressional framework for the year's spending and tax decisions—that proposed a $1.02 trillion cap on discretionary spending, excluding war costs. The House resolution, adopted April 15, also included nonbinding plans for major changes in entitlements. It contained controversial proposals to switch Medicare from a fee-for-service program to a federal subsidy and to change Medicaid from a formula-based program into a block grant that states could allocate as they chose. Although the ideas were popular among Republicans, they drew public criticism from the elderly, some of whom were shown on TV carrying signs reading "Hands Off My Medicare." Other nonbinding provisions called for overhauling the tax code, including setting a top rate of 25 percent, down from 35 percent, and extending 2003 tax cuts enacted in 2001 and 2003.

Written to appeal to the House majority, the measure got no Democratic votes; it was rejected by the Senate, as was a Democratic alternative. A budget resolution was later made unnecessary by enactment of fiscal statutory spending caps for fiscal 2012 under the debt limit law.

DEBT LIMIT INCREASE

The battle over fiscal 2011 funding was only a prelude to what all sides recognized would be the fight of the year over whether, and by how much, to increase the legal limit on the federal debt. The Treasury Department notified Congress that it needed an increase by August 2. After that, Treasury Secretary Timothy F. Geithner said, the federal government would be unable to borrow money to finance the deficit and the government would be in default.

House GOP conservatives saw the need to increase the debt limit increase as giving them leverage to achieve drastic spending cuts. Some Tea Party advocates maintained that letting Treasury hit the limit would not be the disaster it was made out to be.

Talks continued from early May until the end of July, with high-profile White House negotiations in June and early July led first by Vice President Joseph R. Biden Jr. and then, as the deadline neared, by Obama. Republicans rejected tax increases and insisted that spending cuts exceed the amount of the increase in the debt ceiling. Democrats were adamant that the two sides reach a "balanced" agreement that involved both spending cuts and revenue increases. Obama upset many Democrats late in the game when he put at least some entitlement cuts on the table as well.

After a handful of private meetings, the president and the Speaker were on the cusp of a deal toward the end of July to cut the deficit by almost $4 billion over ten years—a "grand bargain" involving both revenue increases and reductions to entitlements. But it soon became clear to both sides that it would be difficult to sell such a compromise to their congressional rank and file. Republican legislators were already crying foul over the talk of additional taxes, while Democrats were uncomfortable with the likely ratio of at least $3 in spending cuts for every dollar in new revenue. Complicating matters was a proposal from three senators in each party, known as the "Gang of Six," that appeared to go further than what Obama and Boehner had been discussing and that received Obama's support.

On a gloomy final weekend in July, with the Speaker having broken off a second round of talks initiated by Obama—and with the two chambers at loggerheads and the debt limit deadline only hours away—McConnell brokered a deal with Reid and Biden.

The resulting law—cleared August 2 and known as the Budget Control Act of 2011—effectively allowed Obama to increase the debt ceiling by $900 billion immediately. Central to the deal was the creation of a bipartisan Joint Select Committee on Deficit Reduction to recommend by the end of the year at least $1.2 trillion in budget cuts over ten years. If the target was not met, automatic cuts, known as a sequester, would go into effect. The measure also set discretionary spending limits for eleven years, with a $1.04 trillion cap for fiscal 2012.

Each side blamed the other for the failure to achieve a broader agreement. Democrats said the two sides were

CONGRESS IN 2011

The first session of the 112th Congress began at noon, January 5, 2011. The House adjourned *sine die* at 11:56 a.m. on January 3, 2012. The Senate adjourned at 11:01 a.m. on December 30, 2011. The Senate was in session for a total of 1,102 hours over 170 days. The House was in session 993 hours over 175 days.

Members introduced 6,903 bills and resolutions in 2011, compared with 4,604 in 2010 and 9,079 in 2009. Congress cleared ninety bills that were enacted into law, the lowest total since 1995 when eighty-eight bills became law. President Barack Obama issued no vetoes. *(Public laws table, p. 15; presidential vetoes, p. 915)*

The House took 945 roll-call votes (excluding quorum calls and one vote that was vitiated) in 2011, 285 more votes than it took in 2010. The Senate took 235 recorded votes, sixty-four fewer than in 2010. *(Recorded votes table, p. 21)*

SPEAKER BOEHNER AND THE HASTERT RULE

For much of his first two years as Speaker of the House, Ohio Republican John A. Boehner followed a governing strategy under which legislation is brought to the floor only if a majority of the majority party supports it. But on a few key votes, Boehner was forced to deviate from the principal, known as the Hastert Rule after J. Dennis Hastert, an Illinois Republican who was Speaker of the House from 1999 until 2007.

Perhaps the most conspicuous breach of the strategy came on January 1, 2013, when almost two-thirds of the 236-member House Republican caucus voted against the compromise legislation that kept the nation from going over the fiscal cliff. That measure, which raised tax rates on high-income earners while holding them steady for other earners, passed with 172 Democratic votes and just eighty-five Republican votes.

Several other times in the 112th Congress, bills passed the House with a majority of Democrats voting yes against a majority of Republicans voting no:

- A bill reducing the number of positions requiring Senate confirmation cleared July 31 with the support of 116 Democrats and 95 Republicans, while 115 Republicans voted against it. *(Details, p. 668)*
- Legislation to extend trade adjustment assistance to U.S. workers displaced by foreign trade cleared in October 2011, with all 189 Democrats supporting it along with just 118 of 240 Republicans. The measure came to the floor as part of a deal with the Obama administration that allowed trade agreements with Colombia, Panama, and South Korea to pass the same day. *(Details, p. 199)*
- A bill to make veterinary workers eligible for programs designed for public health employees passed in March 2011, as 185 Democrats voted yes along with ninety-five Republicans, while 138 GOP lawmakers were opposed.

Hastert was not always able to follow his own rule, either. On several occasions during his tenure, Democrats passed significant legislation over strong Republican opposition. Nonetheless, in a radio interview after the vote on the fiscal cliff, Hastert warned that deviations from the rule had better be rare. "Maybe you can do it once, maybe you can do it twice, but when you start making deals when you have to get Democrats to pass the legislation, you are not in power anymore," he said.

close to a deal but that Boehner could not deliver his caucus. Boehner said the president had "moved the goal posts" by seeking more tax revenue after he and Boehner had shaken hands on an accord. While Congress was tied up in the debilitating process, other legislation largely languished.

GETTING TO FISCAL 2012

The real fight over fiscal 2012 appropriations occurred not on the bills themselves but on a stopgap funding measure that was required to keep the government operating while lawmakers finished the twelve regular bills. The controversy was over whether to offset extra emergency disaster assistance for fiscal 2011 included in the continuing resolution.

A standoff between the majority parties in the House and Senate led to another impending furlough of government workers. House GOP conservatives were adamant that fiscal 2011 disaster funding be paid for by cutting spending elsewhere in the budget. Democrats dug in their heels, saying that recovery efforts at home traditionally did not require offsets. The dispute was resolved only when the Federal Emergency Management Agency (FEMA) juggled its accounts to avoid a need for the fiscal 2011 funds. The final agreement was negotiated by Reid and McConnell, and the bill cleared October 4.

Congress had to pass three more short-term bills, none of which inspired conflict, before finishing, but lawmakers cleared the twelve bills in two packages in November and December with relative ease. The main disputes were over policy riders, primarily in the House versions of the legislation, most of which were dropped.

GIVING UP, TRIGGERING A SEQUESTER

High hopes for the deficit committee were dashed in November, when the bipartisan panel gave up, acknowledging that it could not resolve the disputes that had sunk the grand bargain in July. Under the debt limit law, the group's failure triggered $1.2 trillion in automatic spending cuts spread over a decade, beginning in January 2013. The cuts were to fall equally on defense and nondefense accounts, including both discretionary and some mandatory spending. *(Deficit committee, sequester, pp. 168, 185, 189)*

Top Pentagon officials and members of the Armed Services committees quickly warned that the defense budget could not withstand such deep cuts, and thoughts turned to undoing or replacing the sequester in 2012. Obama said he would not sign a bill overturning the automatic cuts. The inability of the committee to come up with recommendations also left in place the discretionary caps for fiscal 2012 that were set in the debt limit law.

TURNING TO JOBS

After the August recess and with the battle over the debt limit ended at least in the short term, the debate shifted to jobs. The unemployment rate had hovered around 9 percent since the first of the year, and poll after poll showed it was the top issue on people's minds. Obama seized the initiative in September, releasing a broad jobs proposal before a joint session of Congress and crisscrossing the country calling for lawmakers to "pass this bill."

Republicans joined in the call for job creation, but they rejected Obama's proposals for aid to help states prevent layoffs of first-responders and teachers and for funding for infrastructure and transportation projects. Part of the reason: Senate Democrats wanted to pay for the stimulus funding with higher taxes on the wealthy, a nonstarter for Republicans.

With the prospects for a jobs stimulus package dead, Democrats focused in December on a central piece of Obama's jobs package, a proposal to expand and extend a one-year reduction in the Social Security payroll tax paid by employees. The debate developed into a standoff that dragged into the waning days of the year.

Democrats maintained that the tax break, along with an extension of federal supplemental unemployment benefits that was packaged with it, would put more money in people's pockets and the resulting spending would boost the economy. Republicans said the proposals were too expensive and would not produce jobs. However, the potential political costs of opposing a tax reduction, a key GOP campaign issue, led House Republicans to pass a two-year extension. They proposed to offset the costs in part by cutting funding for the 2010 health care overhaul and increasing Medicare premiums for better-off beneficiaries, ideas that Senate Democrats rejected.

In the end, the Senate passed a two-month extension (PL 112-78) of the existing program, which reduced the payroll tax paid by employees to 4.2 percent of their income, down from 6.4 percent. Boehner refused to consider the bill, reflecting the wishes of his caucus, but with the December 31 expiration of the program days away, he was forced into an embarrassing reversal, clearing the extension. *(Payroll tax action, p. 108)*

The Political Year

It was a relatively quiet year at the ballot box. Four special elections were held in 2011 to fill empty seats in the House of Representatives. Three of the seats were vacated in the wake of alleged sexual or financial misconduct. Four races for governor also took place in 2011; none of them resulted in a change of party control.

HOUSE SPECIAL ELECTIONS

In New York, two seats changed party in upset victories. On May 24, Democrat Kathy Hochul won an upstate New York district that had been in the GOP hands for more than four decades. The Erie County clerk defeated Republican Jane Corwin, 47 percent to 43 percent, with Tea Party nominee Jack Davis winning 9 percent. The seat had been abruptly vacated in February by Christopher Lee, a Republican, after disclosure of his involvement in an online dating incident. Hochul narrowly lost her bid for reelection in 2012 after her district was altered by redistricting. *(Lee scandal, p. 671; membership changes, table, p. 829)*

In a heavily Democratic district in New York City, Republican Bob Turner, a former television network executive, defeated Democratic state assembly member David I. Weprin in a special election on September 13. The seat had been held by Democrat Anthony Wiener, who resigned in June in a scandal over his online sexual improprieties. In 2012, after seeing his district made even more Democratic and losing the Republican nomination for the U.S. Senate seat held by Kirsten Gillibrand, Turner opted not to stand election for a full term. *(Wiener scandal, p. 671)*

Democratic Los Angeles city council member Janice Hahn won a July 12 special election to replace longtime Democratic representative Jane Harmon, who had resigned in February to become head of a Washington think tank. The election was California's first test in a congressional race of its so-called "jungle" primary, in which the top two vote winners advance to a runoff regardless of their party. In Nevada, former Republican state senator Mark Amodei won a landslide victory over Democratic state treasurer Kate Marshall in a September 13 special election. Amodei replaced Republican Dean Heller, who had resigned May 9 after being appointed to replace John Ensign in the Senate. Ensign had resigned amid allegations of financial and sexual misconduct. *(Ensign scandal, pp. 651, 671)*

GOVERNORSHIPS

In Louisiana, Republican Bobby Jindal won 60 percent of the vote against nine opponents, escaping the need for a runoff election and securing a second term in office. In Mississippi, Lieutenant Governor Paul Bryant, a Republican, defeated Hattiesburg mayor Johnny DuPree, a Democrat, with 61 percent of the vote. Bryant replaced Haley Barbour, who was barred from running by term limits. In Kentucky, Democratic incumbent Steve Beshear easily won reelection against David L. Williams, the president of the state Senate, and an independent candidate, Gatewood Galbraith.

A court ruling forced a special election in West Virginia to replace Democrat Joe Manchin III, who had won election in November 2010 to complete the term of the late Robert C. Byrd. Earl Ray Tomblin, a Democrat and president of the state Senate, succeeded Manchin as governor while continuing to hold his senate seat and office. Multiple lawsuits were filed objecting to this arrangement, and in January 2011, the state supreme court ordered a special election to be held in May. Tomblin narrowly won the election against Republican businessman Bill Maloney and three other candidates.

2012

The Legislative Year

The 2012 legislative session was one of the least productive in recent memory. Mired in partisan gridlock over federal spending and tax policy, legislators of both parties spent much time in futile battles devoted to disparaging opponents and positioning themselves for the November election.

Some of the more significant legislation was cleared during the lame duck session following Obama's comfortable November 6 reelection victory. The most significant moment came on the last day of the session, when lawmakers narrowly avoided taking the country over what was known as the fiscal cliff, a combination of huge tax increases and automatic, across-the-board spending cuts that were scheduled to take effect at the start of 2013.

The public noticed; twice during the year, in February and August, the Gallup poll approval rating for Congress fell to 10 percent. The average for the year was 15 percent, the lowest since the pollster had begun asking Americans their opinions of lawmaker performance nearly four decades earlier. With the Republican House and Democratic Senate unable to agree on policy matters, Congress sent relatively few pieces of legislation to President Barack Obama's desk. A total of 193 bills became public law—by far the lowest election-year total in decades. *(Laws enacted, table, p. 15)*

Much of the dysfunction took place in the House, where Speaker John A. Boehner of Ohio struggled to keep both the Tea Party advocates on his right flank and the more moderate wing of the Republican Party unified. A follower of the "Hastert rule"—a practice of bringing to the floor only bills that he could pass with a majority of his party—Boehner gave up on a House bill on more than one occasion because he could not solidify the support of his caucus. He could rarely count on Democrats, even if he had wanted to. An exception was the fiscal-cliff legislation, which he ended up forcing through the House by relying on Democrats to make up for Republican defectors. *(Hastert rule, box, p. 29)*

On the other hand, the GOP majority was able to unite on most bills, many of them meant to showcase Republican positions that had little if any support from Democrats and no hope in the Senate.

The partisanship was reflected in the relatively large number of votes on which members of each party stuck with their own caucus. An annual study by CQ/Roll Call (formerly Congressional Quarterly) found that in 72.8 percent of the 657 roll-call votes taken in the House, a majority of one party voted against a majority of the other, the highest rate in a presidential election year since CQ began doing the study. The overall percentage of so-called party unity in the House for the two sessions of the 112th Congress was the highest since 1953. *(Partisanship, box, p. 7)*

In the Democratic Senate, Majority Leader Harry Reid of Nevada also largely followed the Hastert rule. Party unity was reflected in 60 percent of the roll-call votes cast. Reid also sought to cast Republicans as the party of "no" by bringing up bills he knew they would reject by denying him the sixty-vote supermajority needed to prevent a filibuster.

A steady stream of retirements throughout the year signaled members' dissatisfaction, with a number of departing lawmakers citing the paralyzing partisanship in Congress.

BUDGETS AND SPENDING

Obama kicked off the fiscal 2013 congressional budget season February 13 with a budget proposal that called for increased tax rates for high-income earners while retaining current lower rates for other taxpayers. His spending plan complied with a $1.047 trillion cap for fiscal 2013 discretionary budget authority set under the hard-fought

---

CONGRESS IN 2012

The second session of the 112th Congress began at noon January 3, 2012, and kept going until a few minutes before noon, January 3, 2013. (The Senate never adjourned *sine die* for that session.) Both chambers conducted significant legislative business after December 31 for the first time since 1970. The Senate met on 153 days for a total of 930 hours. The House met for 152 days for a total of 725 hours.

A total of 5,395 bills and resolutions were introduced in 2012, compared with 6,903 in 2011 and 4,604 in 2010. Congress cleared 193 bills that were signed into public law. For the second year in a row, President Barack Obama issued no vetoes. *(Public laws table, p. 15; presidential vetoes, p. 915)*

The House took 656 roll-call votes (excluding quorum calls and a vote that was vitiated) in 2012, 289 fewer than in 2011 and the lowest number of roll calls in the House since 2006. The Senate took 251 recorded votes in 2012, sixteen more than in 2011. *(Recorded votes table, p. 21)*

Blacks in Congress, 1947–2011

Congress	*Senate*	*House*
80th (1947–1949)	0	2
81st (1949–1951)	0	2
82nd (1951–1953)	0	2
83rd (1953–1955)	0	2
84th (1955–1957)	0	3
85th (1957–1959)	0	4
86th (1959–1961)	0	4
87th (1961–1963)	0	4
88th (1963–1965)	0	5
89th (1965–1967)	0	6
90th (1967–1969)	1	5
91st (1969–1971)	1	9
92nd (1971–1973)	1	12
93rd (1973–1975)	1	15
94th (1975–1977)	1	16
95th (1977–1979)	1	16
96th (1979–1981)	0	16
97th (1981–1983)	0	17
98th (1983–1985)	0	20
99th (1985–1987)	0	20
100th (1987–1989)	0	22
101st (1989–1991)	0	24
102nd (1991–1993)	0	26
103rd (1993–1995)	1	39
104th (1995–1997)	1	38
105th (1997–1999)	1	37
106th (1999–2001)	0	37
107th (2001–2003)	0	36
108th (2003–2005)	0	39
109th (2005–2007)	1	40
110th (2007–2009)	1	40
111th (2009–2011)	1	41
112th (2011–2013)	0	42

NOTE: House totals reflect the number of members at the start of each Congress and exclude nonvoting delegates. Senate figure for 111th Congress was as of January 15, 2009. President-elect Barack Obama of Illinois resigned his Senate seat in November 2008. African American Roland W. Burris assumed the seat on January 15, 2009.

negotiations that produced the 2011 Budget Control Act (PL 112-25), but shifted funding around to boost spending on infrastructure, education, and job creation programs, among other things. The White House said if Obama's budget were accepted in full, it would serve as an alternative to the pending automatic spending cuts that were on the minds of many in Congress.

In late March, the House adopted a fiscal 2013 budget resolution that would have limited discretionary appropriations to $1.028 trillion—$19 billion below the cap set in 2011. All of the new cuts would have come from domestic spending. The GOP plan was written by Budget Chair Paul D. Ryan, R-Wis., who later in the year became the party's vice presidential nominee. The measure, which also included several GOP policy initiatives including radical reforms of entitlement programs, was uniformly rejected by Democrats and did not get beyond a procedural challenge in the Senate. Although the budget resolution does not become law, it would have set common House-Senate tax and spending guidelines for the year.

Although they were far apart on budget issues, Democrats and Republicans joined forces in September to suspend the fiscal 2013 appropriations process and clear legislation that continued existing spending through March 27, 2013. The agreement was negotiated by the White House and a bipartisan congressional leadership team. Both parties wanted to avoid any chance of a government shutdown before the election and remove partisan fights over appropriations from the expected year-end clash over the fiscal cliff. The continuing resolution (PL 112-175) increased spending by 0.6 percent for most federal programs and agencies.

MAKING IT INTO LAW

Despite the partisan combat, several notable bills did become law. One of the first orders of business at the start of the year was completing legislation that renewed federal emergency unemployment benefits and extended a reduction in employees' Social Security payroll tax rates to 4.2 percent from 6.2 percent. The bill also blocked a sharp scheduled drop in reimbursement rates for doctors who served Medicare patients. By most accounts, the debate over the payroll tax cut bruised Republics who had insisted on offsetting spending cuts and resisted Democratic efforts to pay for the extension with a "millionaire's surtax." *(Unemployment compensation, p. 535; payroll taxes, p. 108; doctor reimbursements, p. 463)*

After a battle of almost three years and a series of ups and downs during the session, lawmakers reached agreement on a two-year bill that reauthorized federal highway, transit, and other surface transportation programs through fiscal 2014 at existing levels, with some inflationary increases, and allowed the collection of revenue and the expenditure of money from the Highway Trust Fund. The agreement gave the White House a jobs bill, which it had sought, while enabling Republicans to scale back federal regulation of transportation projects, in part by speeding up environmental reviews. *(Highway legislation, p. 340)*

Boehner had championed a five-year version that would have significantly modified federal highway and transit programs, including the elimination of dedicated funding for mass transit projects. It would have covered part of the growing shortfall in Highway Trust Fund financing by dedicating new revenues from a proposed increase in domestic oil and gas production. But, with many Tea Party conservatives skeptical that infrastructure was worth spending more than was in the Highway Trust Fund, Boehner could not find enough support in his fractured caucus to bring the bill to the floor. The final legislation, negotiated between the two chambers, contained enough sweeteners for conservatives that it got through the House and became law.

Students and their families got a one-year reprieve from a scheduled increase in student loan interest rates in legislation that was attached to the transportation bill. The popular measure extended the existing 3.4 percent rate

Women in Congress, 1947–2011

Congress	*Senate*	*House*
80th (1947–1949)	1	7
81st (1949–1951)	1	9
82nd (1951–1953)	1	10
83rd (1953–1955)	1	12
84th (1955–1957)	1	17
85th (1957–1959)	1	15
86th (1959–1961)	1	17
87th (1961–1963)	2	18
88th (1963–1965)	2	12
89th (1965–1967)	2	11
90th (1967–1969)	1	10
91st (1969–1971)	1	10
92nd (1971–1973)	1	13
93rd (1973–1975)	1	16
94th (1975–1977)	0	17
95th (1977–1979)	2	18
96th (1979–1981)	1	16
97th (1981–1983)	2	19
98th (1983–1985)	2	22
99th (1985–1987)	2	22
100th (1987–1989)	2	23
101st (1989–1991)	2	28
102nd (1991–1993)	3	29
103rd (1993–1995)	7	48
104th (1995–1997)	8	48
105th (1997–1999)	9	51
106th (1999–2001)	9	56
107th (2001–2003)	13	59
108th (2003–2005)	14	59
109th (2005–2007)	14	64
110th (2007–2009)	16	71
111th (2009–2011)	17	74
112th (2011–2013)	17	72

NOTE: House totals reflect the number of members at the start of each Congress and exclude nonvoting delegates.

through June 2013. Without the bill, the rate would have reverted to 6.8 percent on July 1, 2012, affecting an estimated 7.4 million undergraduate students who had federally subsidized Stafford loans. *(Student loans, p. 485)*

Obama called on Congress to extend the student loan interest rate and publicly campaigned for it on college campuses. Republicans initially rejected the idea, calling it a campaign ploy, but came on board after GOP presidential candidate Mitt Romney agreed that Congress should keep the interest rate low. A compromise reached in the Senate paid the cost by making changes in pension law and shortening the time frame for the interest subsidies.

In other action, Congress allowed the Food and Drug Administration to continue collecting the fees that supported the approval process for prescription drugs and medical devices, pushed through two rounds of legislation toughening economic sanctions against Iran in hope of forcing that country's government to end its alleged nuclear weapons program, and cleared a Federal Aviation Administration (FAA) reauthorization bill in February (PL 112-95) that left in place a National Mediation Board ruling, strongly opposed by Republicans, that made it easier for airline and railroad workers to unionize. Failure to reach agreement on the reauthorization had shut down nonessential FAA operations for two weeks in summer 2011. *(FDA legislation, p. 460; Iran, p. 255; FAA, p. 349)*

Congress also demonstrated that it could move quickly when it wanted to. Less than five months after *60 Minutes* aired a potentially politically damaging story suggesting that legislators might have used knowledge gained in the course of their duties to profit in the stock market, Congress cleared legislation making clear that insider trading prohibitions applied to all members and employees of Congress, as well as to all officials and staff of the executive and legislative branches. *(Insider trading, p. 665)*

UNFINISHED LEGISLATION

Several major pieces of legislation died at the end of the session after the two parties failed to find agreement on key provisions. One of the biggest was a huge, multiyear bill to reauthorize and modify federal farm and nutrition programs. The Senate passed a five-year bill in June; but a separate version never made it to the House floor, GOP leaders said they did not have the votes, largely because conservative members wanted even deeper cuts to food stamps, officially known as the Supplemental Nutrition Assistance Program, than were proposed in the bill. *(Farm legislation, p. 414)*

Leaders of the House and Senate Agriculture committees pushed until the bitter end to clear a reauthorization bill, but in the end, negotiators on the fiscal-cliff package included a simple extension of existing law, which sent the agriculture committees back to the drawing boards for the 113th Congress.

Despite agreement on both sides of the aisle that action was needed to save the cash-strapped Postal Service from financial losses that threatened its operations, differences between the two chambers prevented lawmakers from completing legislation. Nor was bipartisan alarm over the threat of cyberattacks enough for Democrats and Republicans to narrow their differences over the proper scope and nature of federal involvement in strengthening the defenses of vital, privately owned computer networks. Although both chambers passed bills to reauthorize the Violence Against Women Act. they could not agree on a Senate provision that would have extended the law's protections to tribal lands. *(Postal service, p. 627; cybersecurity, p. 217; Violence Against Women, p.571)*

A low point might have been reached on the last day of the session, however, when Boehner put off further action on a measure to provide disaster relief to victims of Superstorm Sandy until early 2013. The delay infuriated members from New York and New Jersey, whose states suffered devastating damage from the October 29 storm, and brought unusually harsh criticism of Boehner from members of his own caucus. Facing a bipartisan backlash from Northeastern lawmakers, Boehner quickly announced that a vote on an initial aid installment would

Hispanics in Congress, 1947–2011

Congress	*Senate*	*House*
80th (1947–1949)	1	1
81st (1949–1951)	1	1
82nd (1951–1953)	1	1
83rd (1953–1955)	1	1
84th (1955–1957)	1	1
85th (1957–1959)	2	0
86th (1959–1961)	2	0
87th (1961–1963)	2	1
88th (1963–1965)	1	3
89th (1965–1967)	1	4
90th (1967–1969)	1	4
91st (1969–1971)	1	5
92nd (1971–1973)	1	6
93rd (1973–1975)	1	6
94th (1975–1977)	1	6
95th (1977–1979)	0	5
96th (1979–1981)	0	6
97th (1981–1983)	0	7
98th (1983–1985)	0	10
99th (1985–1987)	0	11
100th (1987–1989)	0	11
101st (1989–1991)	0	11
102nd (1991–1993)	0	11
103rd (1993–1995)	0	17
104th (1995–1997)	0	17
105th (1997–1999)	0	18
106th (1999–2001)	0	18
107th (2001–2003)	0	19
108th (1993–2005)	0	24
109th (2005–2007)	2	23
110th (2007–2009)	3	23
111th (2009–2011)[1]	3	25
112th (2011–2013)	2	24

NOTE: Totals reflect the number of members at the start of each Congress and exclude nonvoting delegates. For the 112th Congress, House members include three of Portuguese ancestry and belong to the Congressional Hispanic Caucus or the Congressional Hispanic Conference.

[1]One senator, Ken Salazar (D-Colo.), who was a member of the Senate when the 111th Congress convened, resigned on January 21, 2009, to become secretary of the Interior in the cabinet of President Barack Obama. His replacement, appointed by the Colorado governor, was not Hispanic. A House member, Hilda Solis, resigned in February 2009 to become secretary of labor.

be held on the first legislative day of the 113th Congress, with a subsequent package considered by January 15.

GOP PRIORITIES FRUSTRATED

Several GOP-sponsored bills and amendments that prevailed in the House were rejected or never taken up by the Democratic Senate but gave House Republicans a chance to take a stand on GOP policy priorities in an election year.

In addition to trying to cut appropriations below the Budget Control Act caps, House Republicans passed numerous measures to alter the budget process, including bills to require the Congressional Budget Office to take into account how legislation might affect economic growth in calculating the resulting revenue or cost—a method known as dynamic scoring—and a measure to give the president line-item veto authority over discretionary spending.

Other GOP legislation would have repealed, defunded, or ratcheted back Obama's signature 2010 health care overhaul, including abolishing an independent panel charged with curbing Medicare spending growth. The attempts came both before and after a historic Supreme Court ruling in June that the overhaul could go forward largely as written, although states could opt out of a provision that expanded the state-federal Medicaid program for the poor without losing all of their federal Medicaid funds.

Republicans took their opposition to "Obamacare" on the road as a central issue in their fall campaign, but Obama's reelection largely took the wind out of their sails. *(Court decision, pp. 584, 586)*

The House GOP energy agenda included efforts to ease regulations and expand the availability of new federal lands for drilling, including areas off the coastal United States, in the Gulf of Mexico, and in Alaska's Arctic National Wildlife Refuge. The House also passed a package of measures that would have rolled back fuel economy standards, barred regulation of greenhouse gas emissions, and ceded authority over coal waste to the states. Republican said the bills would combat what they called Obama's "war on coal." The 2010 Dodd-Frank regulatory overhaul of the financial services industry was another Republican target, with bills to delay, modify, or repeal parts of the law. Although some of those bills had support from House Democrats, they, too, were ignored in the Senate.

THE FISCAL CLIFF

Several important bills that had stalled before the election came back to life in the lame duck session that followed Obama's comfortable victory over his Republican challenger, former governor Mitt Romney of Massachusetts. Among the last acts to clear during the year were three dealing with the nation's security: a defense authorization measure that approved more money and more weapons than the Defense Department sought; a five-year renewal of a foreign-intelligence law in the final days of the session; and an intelligence authorization bill covering sixteen U.S. intelligence agencies. *(Defense authorization, p. 307; foreign intelligence renewal, p. 215; intelligence authorization, p. 250)*

The most important measure, however, was a bill to avert the fiscal cliff of higher taxes and spending reductions that threatened to tumble the economy back into recession. Legislators had stalled all year on addressing the matter, and did not agree until New Year's Day 2013 to a compromise with Obama on a measure (PL 112-240) to raise taxes on the wealthiest Americans and put off automatic, across-the-board spending cuts until March 1, 2013. *(Fiscal cliff, p. 185)*

The more than $500 billion in pending tax increases was a result of the January 1 expiration of individual income tax cuts and other reductions enacted under President George W. Bush in 2001 and 2003. The $109 billion in automatic spending cuts had been ordered under the 2011 Budget Control Act—itself the product of cliffhanger negotiations—after a committee created by the act failed to agree on an alternative plan to reduce the deficit by $1.2 trillion over ten years. The sequester was due to take effect January 2.

Throughout the year, House Republicans, led by Boehner, demanded deep spending cuts, the extension of all the Bush-era tax cuts regardless of income, and no tax increases. Democrats, led by Obama, proposed extending the tax cuts for everyone but the wealthiest Americans, no changes in entitlement program benefits and smaller spending cuts.

Negotiations began in earnest after Thanksgiving, with Obama and Boehner eager to reach agreement but reluctant to give much ground. At one point, with the talks stalled, Boehner tried to have the House pass what he called a Plan B—a tax cut extension for all but those earning $1 million or more a year. House Republicans balked, and Boehner left it to Senate Minority Leader Mitch McConnell of Kentucky to work out a deal with the White House, led by Vice President Joseph R. Biden Jr.

An agreement was reached on New Year's Eve, which the Senate easily passed the next day. House Republicans were a tougher sell. After considering a plan to amend the bill and send it back to the Senate, Boehner found enough GOP votes to clear the measure with the support of House Democrats. Nearly two-thirds of House Republicans voted against the bill, which passed with the support of all but sixteen Democrats. *(Legislative action, p. 147)*

Democrats ended the year wondering whether they could have gotten more of what they wanted by driving a harder bargain. Republicans emerged from the fight angry, rebellious, and eager to cut spending in future budget battles. They would have their opportunity early in the 113th Congress, when the sequester deal and the fiscal 2013 government funding were scheduled to expire at about the same time Congress would need to act on raising the debt limit.

The Political Year

The November 6 election, which had loomed over both sessions of the 112th Congress, ended with President Barack Obama winning a second term, dashing Republican hopes that former Massachusetts governor Mitt Romney would be the next occupant of the White House. Republicans also were unable to win control of the Senate, which had seemed within their grasp early in the campaign season. Instead, they lost two seats. The party easily retained control of the House, losing just a handful of seats to the Democrats.

The presidential campaign featured two quite different visions of how to push the sluggish economic recovery forward and particularly how to create jobs. Romney called for slashing government spending to cut the deficit while rolling back regulation, which he said hobbled businesses. He spoke out for tax cuts for all Americans, including the wealthy, whom Republicans called the "job creators."

Obama called for increasing taxes on the wealthy and portrayed Romney as being out of touch with the needs of ordinary Americans and seeking to protect the rich. He said that investments in such things as education and infrastructure were crucial to America's future and should be balanced with deficit reduction.

The outcome of the presidential race opened a lengthy period of soul-searching for Republicans, with some members of the GOP saying that the party had been captured by conservatives who did not appreciate or understand the coalition of young people, women, blacks, and Hispanics that put Obama over the top. But the party remained deeply divided over the proper remedy.

Republicans' net loss of just eight seats in the House left them with a healthy majority of 234 seats to 201 for the Democrats. Conservatives, particularly those affiliated with the Tea Party movement, quickly threw down a gauntlet, saying that while Obama had won the presidency, they had won their districts and would reflect the views of their constituents.

In the Senate, no Democratic incumbent was defeated, and the party lost only the seat of departing Sen. Ben Nelson of Nebraska. Democrats won two Republican-held seats as well as the seat in Connecticut held by independent Joseph I. Lieberman. The party added another vote when Maine independent Angus King chose to caucus with the Democrats; King replaced Republican Olympia Snowe, who had not run for reelection. That gave the Democrats fifty-three seats as well as the votes of the Senate's two independents; Republicans had forty-five members. The overall outcome left the government divided and provided little hope that the partisan gridlock would give way anytime soon.

PRESIDENTIAL ELECTION

President Barack Obama won a clear reelection battle over Republican Mitt Romney in the November 6 presidential balloting. In securing 332 electoral college votes to Romney's 206, Obama became the third president in a row to win a second term, something that had not happened since the early nineteenth century with Thomas Jefferson, James Madison, and James Monroe.

Although handicapped by an anemic economy and mixed success in foreign policy, the fifty-one-year-old president—the first African American to hold the office—retained the support of the coalition of youth, women, and especially people of color that had provided his margin of victory four years earlier.

Nevertheless, the victory was less resounding than in 2008. Sixty-five-year-old Romney, a former one-term governor of Massachusetts and successful business executive, managed to trim Obama's margin from seven percentage

MONEY IN ELECTIONS

The 2011–2012 election cycle was the most expensive on record. According to an April 2013 report by the Federal Election Commission (FEC), more than $7 billion was spent on the presidential and congressional elections—about $3.2 billion by the candidates, $2 billion by political parties, and $2.1 billion by outside political action committees (PACs) and other interest groups.

Presidential Race

President Barack Obama's campaign raised about $738 million, according to the report, substantially more than the approximately $483 million of the campaign of his opponent, Mitt Romney. But Republican Party and political action committees pushed the totals raised for both candidates well above $1 billion each. Obama's total was down from the $760 million he raised in 2008, but Romney took in almost twice as much as John McCain, Obama's rival that year. McCain, a senator from Arizona, raised $239.7 million according to the FEC.

For the first time since 1976, when it began, neither presidential candidate accepted public financing for either the primary cycle or the general election. Obama and Romney each could have received $91.2 million for the general election but in return could not have accepted any private contributions, although party, PAC, and independent expenditures on their half could still have been made. Obama had also declined the public financing in 2008, the first time a presidential nominee had done so.

A new factor in campaign financing was the ability of political organizations and individuals to spend unlimited amounts of money to influence an election so long as they did not coordinate their advertising or other activities with the political campaign they were supporting. A Supreme Court decision ruling in 2010 *(Citizens United v. Federal Election Commission,* 558 U.S. 310) struck down laws limiting such spending as a violation of free speech under the First Amendment. *(Citizens United decision, pp. 586, 677)*

Democrats warned that the ruling would allow wealthy individuals and organizations to buy elections by pouring money into ad campaigns and drowning out the voices of less well-funded groups. In one respect they were correct. According to the FEC, these groups reported spending about $607 million in 2012, nearly ten times as much as in the 2008 presidential election before the court ruling. Of the $465.3 million independent organization and individuals spent opposing a specific presidential candidate, $330.5 million was aimed at Obama; less than half that amount, $134.9 million, was directed against Romney.

The new rules allowed individuals to give to independent organizations without disclosing their donations. Thus, total giving by individuals could not be determined, but at least three of the largest givers were also high on the list of the world's wealthiest. Charles and David Koch, whose fortunes came from the oil, gas, and chemical industries and who were long supporters of libertarian causes, said that they would donate $60 million of their own money to conservative campaigns; that did not count donations that Koch Industries and other Koch affiliated organizations made in the 2012 election cycle. Sheldon Adelson, a casino and hotel magnate, and his wife reportedly donated between $100 million and $150 million during the 2012 election cycle, much of it on behalf of former House Speaker Newt Gingrich of Georgia, who sought the GOP presidential nomination.

The two largest "super PACs" were organized by longtime Republican operatives and spent most of their funding on television ads attacking Obama. Restore Our Future, created by former Romney campaign managers, reported spending $142.1 million. American Crossroads, founded by Karl Rove and Ed Gillespie, together with sister organization Crossroads Grassroots Policy Strategies, reported spending $174.5 million.

Congressional Races

Spending by Senate candidates totaled nearly $748 million, according to the FEC report—$316 million by Democratic candidates; $418 million by Republican candidates; and the remainder by third-party contestants. The most expensive Senate race was in Massachusetts, where Democrat Elizabeth Warren defeated incumbent Scott P. Brown. Warren's receipts totaled $42.2 million, about $7 million more than Brown raised. Of the five Senate candidates who spent $30 million or more, only Warren won a seat.

The most money raised on behalf of a single Senate candidate was $50.1 million for Republican Linda McMahon of Connecticut, who lost to challenger Christopher Murphy, who had only a fifth as much money to spend. Much of McMahon's campaign money came from McMahon herself, who had lost a similarly expensive race for governor two years earlier.

Spending by House candidates totaled $1.1 billion, according to the FEC—$479 million by Democrats and $604 million by Republicans. The most expensive race was that between two Democratic incumbents thrown into the same California district by redistricting. The winner, Brad Sherman, spent $6.4 million, according to the FEC. The loser, Howard L. Berman, reported spending $5.8 million. In another California race, independent Bill Bloomfield spent $9.8 million, much of it his own money, in a losing challenge to Democrat Henry Waxman.

Other high-spending challengers included Democrats Alan Grayson, who spent $5.4 million, and Tammy Duckworth of Illinois, who spent $5.3 million. Grayson, known for his incendiary comments, was first elected to Congress in 2008 but lost a bid for reelection in 2010. He easily won election to a redrawn district in 2012. Duckworth, a helicopter pilot and Iraq war veteran, lost her first bid for Congress in 2006. She won her 2012 with 55 percent of the vote.

points in 2008 to four percentage points in 2012, which meant Obama had a victory margin of just under 5 million votes compared to 9.5 million in 2008. Obama's winning margin dropped from 53 percent in 2008 to 51 percent four years later. In addition his electoral college margin dropped from 365 in 2008 to 332 in 2012.

That result was not the outcome that many Republicans, including Romney, had anticipated. In 2010 Republicans scored a smashing victory in the midterm congressional elections amid broad discontent over the president's and his party's legislative record—a victory that many in the party thought indicative of a resurgence of GOP strength at the presidential level.

Republicans took back the House that year by winning a net sixty-three seats, a modern-day record, and they had inched closer to a Senate majority. Over the next two years, GOP optimism grew, as the nation's unemployment rate continued above 8 percent and polls showed sustained and widespread disapproval of Obama's health care overhaul legislation and numerous environmental and financial regulatory measures.

What Republicans did not recognize was that they were appealing to a minority of voters, especially to those who were white and male, while Obama and the Democrats were busy resurrecting a grand coalition made up of liberals, nonwhite ethnic groups, and the young that had pushed the president over the top in 2008 but that had also largely sat out the midterm elections two years later. With a bankroll that eventually approached $1 billion, the Obama campaign team set out early to identify and keep in close touch with its voting base.

Narrowing the GOP Field

Convinced that 2012 was the GOP's year, a large number of candidates began presidential primary campaigns. Running on the far right of the political spectrum were former senator Rick Santorum of Pennsylvania and Rep. Michele Bachmann of Minnesota. Others seeking the nomination included Romney, Texas governor Rick Perry, former House Speaker Newt Gingrich of Georgia, libertarian representative Ron Paul of Texas, business executive Herman Cain—the former chief executive officer (CEO) of Godfather's Pizza and once a Federal Reserve Bank governor—and Jon Huntsman Jr., who had been Obama's ambassador to China from 2009 to 2011 and served as governor of Utah from 2005 to 2009.

With little backing from voters or donors, and embarrassing gaffes in televised debates, Bachmann, Perry, and Cain faded quickly before many votes were cast. Huntsman never gained traction.

The results of the initial contests in winter 2012—the Iowa caucuses and New Hampshire and South Carolina primaries—were mixed. Romney, who was viewed at the outset as the probable consensus candidate, easily won New Hampshire, while Santorum eked out a straw vote win in Iowa, and Gingrich won South Carolina to establish a beachhead in the South.

Ten days later, Romney decisively won Florida and used that victory as a springboard to mount a sustained campaign in which he positioned himself as a solutions-oriented business executive whose lack of experience in the nation's capital was a plus. He pressed on as an anti-Washington breath of fresh air, and it paid off. Neither Santorum nor Gingrich could match the juggernaut that Romney was crafting. With worries that a long primary season might leave whoever won the nomination bruised and tattered, most of the Republican establishment closed ranks behind Romney.

By late spring, he had largely sewn up the nomination, winning most of the big industrial Midwestern states. Most of his party rivals gave up over the course of a few weeks, although Paul, an iconoclast who often ruffled as many Republican as Democratic feathers, kept up his campaign until the party convention.

Romney's Slow Start

Having taken many conservative positions during the primary season, even referring to himself as a "severe conservative," Romney had several months before the convention to establish his credentials with more moderate voters. His basic message was that the president had failed to fix the economy and that he, Romney, had the skills and experience that were needed to do the job. He frequently mentioned his stint as a partner at Bain Capital, a private equity firm that bought failing businesses in hopes of turning them around, and as the CEO of the Salt Lake City Winter Olympics in 2002.

But the Obama campaign was able to muddy that message with a series of hard-hitting television ads aired starting in May that characterized Bain Capital as a job destroyer and Romney as a wealthy executive who was out of touch with middle America. The Romney campaign did little to directly counter the ads; some of his campaign aides later said they regretted not taking the opportunity to show Romney's more personal side, but they also admitted they had only limited funds to spend on the campaign until after the formal nomination.

A high-profile summer trip to Britain, Poland, and Israel meant to showcase Romney as a leader on the international scene also backfired, when he made a number of comments that were widely seen as undiplomatic. The British prime minister took offense when Romney appeared to question London's ability to provide adequate security at the Summer Olympics. During a stop in Israel, he offended Palestinians and others when he suggested that cultural differences explained why Israelis were more successful economically that Palestinians.

With no significant challenger from within his party, Obama and his reelection team used the time that ordinarily would have been spent on a nomination campaign to set up an expansive voter outreach effort. The Obama campaign, working from its headquarters in the president's home town of Chicago, set up a field office operation in swing states and a database that allowed them to determine on a house-to-house basis which voters were likely to go to the polls and who they were likely to vote for. That effort would prove decisive on Election Day.

Romney had one major decision to make before the GOP convention: choosing a running mate. Among the most prominent possibilities were Sens. Marco Rubio of Florida and Rob Portman of Ohio, both of whom represented competitive states whose large number of electoral votes had the potential to push the GOP ticket over the top in a close election. In addition, Rubio, whose parents fled from Cuba before the Castro revolution, could attempt an appeal to Latino voters, a segment that had trended Democratic in recent elections.

Portman was seen as a solid and popular conservative from a state critical to Republican victories. No GOP presidential nominee had ever won the nationwide contest without taking Ohio. Other possible choices included governors Chris Christie of New Jersey and Bob McDonnell of Virginia.

But Romney opted for youth and ideas, choosing Rep. Paul D. Ryan of Wisconsin, chair of the House Budget Committee. The seven-term conservative representative had immersed himself in federal budget details and favored a dramatic shift in fiscal policy, including a gradual change in Medicare, the federal government's health insurance plan for seniors, from traditional payments to a privatized, voucher-based program. Ryan also had pushed for an overhaul of the tax system that would lower income tax rates while reducing eligibility for a variety of deductions. In fourteen years in the House, Ryan had gained a reputation as a reliable conservative who was willing to advocate significant departures in government policy.

His conservative approach was a stark contrast to the liberal image of incumbent Vice President Joseph R. Biden Jr. Also, at forty-two, Ryan represented a youthful alternative to the vice president, who would turn seventy shortly after the election and had been an elected official in Washington since Ryan was two years old.

For their quadrennial conventions just before the fall campaign, both parties chose their sites with electoral-vote strategy in mind. Republicans met August 27–30 in Tampa, Fla., the heart of the Sunshine State with its twenty-nine electoral votes. Obama had carried the state in 2008 by three points against GOP nominee John McCain. The following week, the Democrats renominated Obama and Biden in Charlotte, N.C. Four years earlier, the Tar Heel State had given the Democratic ticket its slimmest margin of victory, about half a percentage point, in any of the twenty-eight states Obama won that year.

With the nominees a foregone conclusion and no significant platform controversies to be resolved, neither convention held much drama. The threat of Tropical Storm Isaac disrupted the start of the GOP convention, forcing the party to cancel the first day's activities. Another disruption of sorts occurred on the last evening, when actor Clint Eastwood delivered a meandering speech to an empty chair that he said represented an invisible Obama. The unscripted speech, which immediately was repeatedly seen on the Internet and through social media, was applauded in the convention hall but nearly overshadowed Romney's acceptance speech in the subsequent press coverage.

The Fall Campaign

After the conventions, with the nation's unemployment rate still stuck at or near 8 percent, the Romney-Ryan team kept up the attacks on the administration, saying not enough was being done to pull the country out of its economic tailspin. The Democrats acknowledged that economic recovery was slow but said that, compared with the low point reached around the time Obama came into office, life had gotten better for many Americans.

In particular, Republicans attacked the administration for its treatment of small businesses, which the GOP said were being suffocated by higher taxes and more regulation. Even before the conventions, the Romney campaign seized on a comment the president made at a July rally in Roanoke, Va., when he said, "If you've got a business, you didn't build that." Obama added, "If you were successful, somebody along the line gave you some help." The president's campaign said Obama was trying to explain that commercial enterprises needed government infrastructure and other benefits. The Romney camp saw it differently, saying the administration undervalued free enterprise at the expense of government intervention. Republicans plastered their convention hall with signs proclaiming "We Built It."

Just two weeks into the fall campaign, however, Romney's efforts on the economy were tripped up by the September 17 release of a videotaped speech he had made four months earlier at an intimate, private fund-raising event. "All right, there are 47 percent who are with [Obama], who are dependent upon government, who believe that they are victims, who believe the government has a responsibility to care for them, who believe that they are entitled to health care, to food, to housing, to you name it," Romney said. "That's an entitlement. The government should give it to them. And they will vote for this president no matter what."

The nominee backpedaled from the statement, but the tape's release had done its damage, reinforcing a key Democratic message that Romney and Republicans were out of touch with typical Americans. For much of the campaign, Romney had touted his business acumen and management skills. But suddenly those traits did not sit well with a populace nearly half of which the candidate had essentially claimed were "takers" rather than "makers" in the American economy.

Romney also sought to call into question the president's foreign policy. In an initial salvo, Romney said the State Department and Pentagon were failing to retain the global respect that the George W. Bush administration had developed in its eight years. During his acceptance speech at the Republican National Convention, Romney said Obama had squandered his first foray into foreign policy by embarking on an "apology tour" in the Middle East, wrongly framing bold Bush administration initiatives like the war in Iraq as excesses that Obama would rein in. Obama countered that he had made no apologies but had talked about better ties and more cooperation in his visit to the region.

In the most dramatic overseas incident during the campaign, on September 11, a group that U.S. officials initially described as protesters set the U.S. diplomatic compound in Benghazi, Libya, ablaze, killing the American ambassador, J. Christopher Stevens, and three other U.S. diplomats. Romney jumped on the administration for a statement it had issued earlier in response to demonstrations against the release of an anti-Muslim film by an independent California producer. "It's disgraceful that the administration's first response was not to condemn attacks on our diplomatic missions," Romney said, "but to sympathize with those who waged the attacks."

Romney met with immediate criticism for questioning the president in the midst of a foreign crisis. But he pursued the issue in a subsequent nationally televised debate, accusing the administration of attempting to cover up a failure to protect the embassy against terrorists by trying to blame "protesters." Obama made Romney look uninformed by citing a Rose Garden appearance immediately after the attacks where the president called the disaster an "act of terror." The moderator quickly confirmed that the record showed Obama was correct, although Republicans continued to press the issue.

Misplaced Optimism

As the final month of campaigning got under way, Romney caught a break at the first of the three nationally televised debates. From the outset of the ninety-minute prime-time October 3 broadcast in Denver, Obama appeared at turns aloof and distracted, while Romney hammered away at the administration's performance on the economy, regulation, and health care. By a hefty margin, postdebate polls gave the victory that night to the challenger.

Obama took the hint. In two subsequent forums with Romney later in October, the president appeared to recover his edge, engaging his opponent much more forcefully as the two sparred over foreign policy and domestic issues.

Most polls showed Obama and Biden slightly ahead through October, but Romney and Ryan closed their campaign with a vigorous effort to knock off the Democrats in a few big states, focusing on Ohio, Pennsylvania, and Florida.

Both campaigns were momentarily halted in the wake of Hurricane Sandy, which battered the coastlines of New Jersey, New York, and Connecticut on October 29, displacing tens of thousands of people and destroying millions of dollars of homes, businesses, and infrastructure. Although some Republicans complained that Obama may have won some votes with his visit to New Jersey two days later, where he was warmly praised by Republican governor Chris Christie for the government's emergency response to the disaster, subsequent polls did not show any decisive shifts in voters' affections.

Convinced that they would prevail, Romney and his campaign staff were unprepared for his loss. According to several subsequent reports, Romney's concession speech was delayed in part because he had only prepared a victory speech.

When all the votes were counted, Obama had won 65.9 million votes, or 51.1 percent of the votes, to Romney's 60.9 million votes, or 47.2 percent (third-party candidates accounted for the remaining percentage). Obama won all but two of the states that he had taken four years earlier—he was on the short end of yet another close contest in North Carolina but lost Indiana by a large margin. *(2012 vote returns, table, p. 926)*

Of the ten largest states, only North Carolina and Texas eluded his grasp. With the exception of Florida, which he won by a little less than one percentage point, his victories in the competitive states were by three points or more. In winning the overall national popular vote by 3.9 percentage points, Obama racked up double-digit margins in states with heavy urban concentrations, including the Northeast, the West Coast, and his home state of Illinois. By far Romney's strongest performance geographically was in the South, where Obama won only Virginia and Florida. Obama carried every other region of the country by at least several points.

Political analyst Rhodes Cook noted that Romney, typical of GOP presidential candidates, won most of the nation's 3,100 plus counties and jurisdictions such as independent cities. But Obama, typical of Democratic candidates, won in voter-rich jurisdictions. Of thirty-nine counties with more than one million in population, Obama won thirty-five, providing a margin of almost eight million votes compared to Romney's three million margin elsewhere in the nation.

Observers credited Obama's margin of victory to a sophisticated ground game, which targeted his support down to the precinct and neighborhood level, and focused on key Democratic constituencies, including women, youth, Latinos, and African Americans. Polls showed that those voters were much more receptive to the Democratic message, while the Republicans seemed to be focusing on conservative white men.

As he had in 2008, Obama carried well more than 90 percent of the black vote, although it was a slightly smaller proportion than four years before. He increased his popularity among Latinos, who gave him two-thirds of their vote, providing him substantial victories in battleground states like Colorado and Virginia. Those under age thirty also gave him a healthy portion of their votes.

But Cook also noted that the 2012 election continued an emerging pattern of declining competiveness in most states. After 2000 the number of competitive states—under the widely used rule of thumb of a margin of less than 5 percent—was eleven in 2004, six in 2008, and four in 2012. In 1960, by comparison, competitive states numbered twenty, steadily dropping to a dozen in 2000.

The official count of the electoral votes, which had been cast on December 17, 2012, took place at the Capitol on January 4, 2013. For the second election in a row, there were no "faithless electors" who cast their vote for someone other than expected.

Republican Soul-Searching

In the aftermath of the presidential election, many senior Republicans began a period of soul-searching. Just hours after Romney's defeat, Speaker John A. Boehner, R-Ohio, spoke words similar to those of others in the GOP worried about its failure to achieve broad support, especially among minorities: "What Republicans need to learn is: How do we speak to all Americans? You know, not just the people who look like us and act like us, but how do we appeal to all Americans?"

In trying to reach such constituencies, some leading party officials said, conservatives should not abandon their basic principles but should frame them in a way that would not appear to be uncaring or cold-hearted.

Others, including the vanquished nominee himself, defended the direction of the campaign and said Obama had managed to win support mainly with promises of government largess to his varied electoral constituencies. In what he thought was a private conference call with financial backers the week after his loss, Romney said Obama's initiatives, especially with minorities and youth, "were very generous in what they gave to those groups," whereas he said he had focused on "big issues" such as defense policy and building a stronger economy.

The health care overhaul, Romney said, played to many of those constituencies by expanding mandatory coverage (attractive to the poor), increasing the availability to contraceptives (popular with women), and requiring that children be given the option of insurance coverage under their parents' plans until age twenty-six (drawing the youth).

Whatever the reasons, the GOP faced an uphill battle against the national trend in demographics, reinforced in large states with huge metropolitan areas that were strongly Democratic. In 2012, with what they believed was one of their best chances ever to win a solid presidential mandate, Republicans instead prolonged what had become an overall twenty-year losing cycle.

Democrats had won the popular vote in five out of six presidential elections, and their only popular vote loss, in 2004, was by two points. It was a significant reversal from the 1968–1988 era, when Republicans won five of six presidential elections, four of which each netted their candidate more than 400 electoral votes.

SENATE ELECTIONS

After the 2010 midterm elections, Democratic prospects in the Senate appeared dismal. The party had lost six seats and together with two independents who caucused with the Democrats, held fifty-three seats, seven short of the number needed to invoke cloture and cut off filibusters. Moreover, Democrats were defending twenty-one of thirty-three seats going into the 2012 elections. But in a twist of fate that only the most optimistic of the party faithful could have predicted, Democrats emerged from the November 6 elections with an expanded majority.

Each of the thirty-three Senate races was called within twenty-four hours of the closing of the polls. It was emblematic of the party's convincing Senate victories and of the kind of night that Democrats enjoyed overall. Democratic Senate candidates won in battleground states that ran nearly the length of the broad red-to-blue spectrum.

Not one Democratic incumbent was defeated, and the party lost only the seat of departing Sen. Ben Nelson of Nebraska. Democrats won two Republican-held seats and added another vote when former Maine Gov. Angus King, an independent, chose to caucus with the party. Overall, Democratic candidates for the Senate won about eleven million more votes than did Republican opponents.

Once in danger of losing his hold on the majority, Sen. Harry Reid, D-Nev., could look forward to a fortified caucus, two seats larger than that of the 112th Congress. This success could be attributed, at least in part, to his choice of Patty Murray of Washington to lead the Democratic Senatorial Campaign Committee, which recruited candidates whom even Republicans viewed as strong and which helped direct campaigns that were clearly superior to their GOP opponents' efforts.

Several pivotal events of the 2012 Senate campaigns brought about changes with lasting effects on the control of the chamber's business. The erosion of the conventional wisdom—that Republicans would capture the chamber—began early in the campaign cycle, and two New England women from different political parties were central to that chipping away.

The most obvious pickup opportunity for Democrats was in Massachusetts, where Republican incumbent Scott P. Brown was seeking a full term in a state that Barack Obama ended up winning by twenty-three points. The search for a challenger in the solidly Democratic state had been surprisingly fruitless; only a few brave souls stepped forward to take on Brown, a prodigious fundraiser with a personable style attractive to blue-collar Democrats and conservative Republicans alike. Brown had surprised the political world with a special-election upset in 2010, when he won the seat of the late Edward M. Kennedy. But Democrats were convinced that in a presidential election, where the electorate was bigger and more Democratic, the right candidate could defeat Brown.

They found that person in Elizabeth Warren, a Harvard law professor and prominent consumer advocate, who officially entered the race in mid-September 2011. She raised $3.2 million in her first six weeks, a stunning sum that set the pace for a fund-raising race with Brown. For the next year, polls showed a tight race, but Warren won by more than seven percentage points.

Republicans had appeared to be on track to take over the Senate until the end of February, when Maine Republican Olympia J. Snowe made a surprise retirement announcement. With merely two weeks until the candidate filing deadline, she gave Senate Republican leaders just a few hours' notice for the party to find a replacement.

The news provided a shot in the arm for Democrats and essentially changed the narrative of the 2012 cycle. It also set up an odd three-candidate dynamic in which national Democrats shunned their own nominee, Cynthia Dill, in favor of King, once he had formally entered the race. Democrats ran ads critical of the GOP candidate without saying whom to vote for. Meanwhile, national Republicans publicly propped up Dill to help take away votes from King and slammed King in television ads—to no avail. King won handily, and, as widely expected, aligned with the Democrats on Capitol Hill for committee assignments and on procedural issues.

Democrats also gained after two Republican candidates in Republican-leaning states, Rep. Todd Akin in Missouri and Indiana state Treasurer Richard E. Mourdock, made off-the-cuff statements on rape and pregnancy that alienated women and moderates. Both men "made huge, self-inflicted mistakes and hurt the Republican brand nationwide, and they both lost in states that should have been strong Republican opportunities," Republican media strategist Erik Potholm said.

In Missouri, Democratic incumbent Claire McCaskill was as close to "dead in the water" as any incumbent could be. But Democrats' hopes for McCaskill's survival perked up when the GOP in August nominated Akin, the candidate perceived as the weakest general-election contender because of his conservative ideology. McCaskill even ran an ad in July that looked negative but was actually intended to help Akin's chances in the GOP primary.

Even so, McCaskill's chance at a second term seemed long until a fateful Sunday in August, when a local television interview with Akin aired. Akin lit a firestorm when he referred to "legitimate rape" and concluded that the female body was biologically able to forestall pregnancies that might be caused by rape.

That comment set up a narrative from which Akin never recovered and that claimed a second victim, when Mourdock in Indiana said, at a candidate debate in October against Democratic representative Joe Donnelly, that "even when life begins in that horrible situation of rape, it is something that God intended to happen." Still, the Indiana Senate race probably would not have been among the competitive ones had longtime Republican senator Richard G. Lugar not run a poor primary campaign. For example, Lugar did not even own or rent a home in the state, and Mourdock and conservative activist groups pounced on that.

In addition to Missouri, the three Democrat-held seats most likely to flip to Republicans were Montana, Nebraska, and North Dakota. Akin sunk in Missouri, while Republicans were successful in Nebraska.

But the last two races to be called were the ones that stung the most for the GOP and were perhaps the greatest success stories for Democrats. Sen. Jon Tester of Montana and former North Dakota Attorney General Heidi Heitkamp won in states that Republican presidential nominee Mitt Romney carried by more than thirteen points.

These races underscored the importance of likability and genuineness in a candidate, with both Tester and Heitkamp considered to have a big edge in those categories. Tester's pitch, as a Montana farmer, in TV ads that ran constantly over the summer buffered him from the attacks that came from Rep. Denny Rehberg and the National Republican Senatorial Committee. The same went for Heitkamp, who withstood a twenty-point Romney victory in the state. She beat Rep. Rick Berg by a single percentage point.

Obama defeated Romney in all five presidential battleground states with Senate contests: Florida, Nevada, Ohio, Virginia, and Wisconsin. Democrats were defending all but Nevada. If a Republican was to win in any of these, he would have had to outperform Romney. Only Sen. Dean Heller of Nevada accomplished that task, and he did so by just a fraction of a point. Many analysts put the onus on his opponent, Democratic Rep. Shelley Berkley and her vast underperformance compared with the president's support. Heller defeated her by slightly more than one percentage point.

In 2010, both Florida and Ohio elected Republican governors and senators. As a result, Democratic senators Bill Nelson and Sherrod Brown were high on the list of endangered incumbents. But whether because of a different environment or weak GOP candidates, neither race materialized and both incumbents won with relative ease.

Republicans were also counting on victories from two former governors—George Allen of Virginia, also a former senator, and Tommy G. Thompson of Wisconsin. The GOP, having defeated Democrat Russ Feingold in 2010, saw Wisconsin as a prime pickup. Hopes were further raised when it became clear that Rep. Tammy Baldwin, a Madison liberal, would be the Democratic nominee and after Republican governor Scott Walker held off a recall challenge. But after a bloody, expensive, and late GOP primary, Thompson emerged cash-strapped and unable to perform up to expectations.

In Virginia, Obama carried the state, and former Democratic governor Tim Kaine outran the president by appealing to Romney voters with his message of ending the gridlock in Washington. Republican outside groups spent about $30 million against Kaine, their largest sum for any congressional race.

HOUSE ELECTIONS

House members in both parties found reason to celebrate after the November 6 election: For each of them, the results could have been much worse. Republicans, who executed a carefully fashioned strategy of using [to shore up their incumbents, while making strong plays against Democrats, kept their majority by a wide margin. They suffered a net loss of eight seats. That was a short casualty list, given that President Barack Obama easily won reelection and Democrats were picking up seats in the Senate in Republican regions. Democrats, meanwhile, could revel in gaining, rather than losing, House seats.

Redistricting played a significant role in the House elections. "We benefited from places where redistricting benefited us and we got hurt by places where redistricting hurt us," said Jef Pollock, an influential Democratic pollster. "In many ways, it was that simple." In Illinois, for example, Democrats in the legislature carved an intricate map that let them pick up four seats in the state. Republicans gained three seats in North Carolina, where GOP state legislators had added Republican voters to four districts held by Democrats, inducing two of the Democrats to retire. Republicans picked up seats in Indiana and Pennsylvania, both states where the party controlled redistricting.

Because Republicans controlled more levers of power in more states and, thus, the redrawing of more districts, they had a considerable edge going into the year. For example, Republicans won a majority of the House delegations in the key Midwest battlegrounds states of Michigan, Ohio, Pennsylvania, and Wisconsin even though Obama carried all four states. Despite this skewed result in House races, produced by party-controlled redistricting, Democrats won a kind of moral victory when their House candidates nationally polled about 1.4 million more votes for all districts together than their GOP opponents. Although it did not help Democrats gain back House control, it did suggest that, nationally, public sentiment leaned more to Democrats than a count of seats controlled suggested. *(Republicans and House redistricting, box, this page)*

With redistricting diluting competitiveness, and no large Democratic wave, it made sense that the House results skewed toward the natural partisan lean of many districts. Incumbents such as Democrat Larry Kissell of North Carolina and Republicans Joe Walsh of Illinois and Ann Marie Buerkle of New York were voted out of seats where their party identification did not match that of the majority of their constituents. That was part of the reason New England did not elect a single Republican House member to the new Congress. New Hampshire GOP Reps.

REPUBLICANS CONTROL HOUSE REDISTRICTING

The Republican Party in 2012 retained a commanding majority in the U.S. House, 234 to 201, even while losing to Democrats the aggregate national tally for representatives by nearly 1.4 million votes. The discrepancy was even larger, 2.4 million votes in favor of Democrats, in districts where there was a competitive election in which both parties had a candidate. There were 310 of those in 2012 House races; Republicans won 209, Democrats 181.

The reason was simple enough: Republicans controlled most of the decennial process of redrawing House district lines that follows each national census. And that resulted from the GOP's overwhelming victories nationally in the 2010 elections in which the party captured the lion's share of state legislatures and governor's offices, where nearly all the redistricting work goes on.

Almost half the districts in the nation, 202 of 435, were located in states where Republicans had the majorities to draw the lines to fit the needs of their candidates, according to political analyst Rhodes Cook.

The process, commonly derided as gerrymandering after the nineteenth-century governor Elbridge Gerry of Massachusetts, who drew one district's lines (for a state office) that produced a shape resembling a salamander, is not a specialty of Republicans. Democrats, when they enjoy a state legislative majority, have produced district lines favoring their candidates. Both parties in many cases reach a truce by creating district configurations that mainly serve to protect incumbents.

But in the redistricting done after the 2010 census, Republicans fully controlled the process in eighteen states that resulted in 144 GOP seats to fifty-eight Democratic ones. In the seven states controlled by Democrats, their party won thirty-four seats to the GOP's thirteen. Seven states have taken the process out of the hands of politicians and turned it over to independent commissions. In those states fifty-nine seats were won by Democrats to thirty-three by Republicans. Of those seven states, one—California—has become so heavily Democratic that it resulted in a Democratic House majority of thirty-eight seats to the GOP's fifteen, which skewed the total results. Four of the other six produced largely balanced congressional delegations; the other two—Hawaii and Idaho—gave, respectively, total control to Democrats or Republicans.

The 2012 election results resulted in another notable trend: a decreasing number of competitive House races. The number of races decided with under 52 percent of the vote fell to thirty-three in 2012, from fifty-five in 2010.

Frank Guinta and Charles Bass were both defeated. Strong Republican challengers also failed to dislodge Democrats John F. Tierney of Massachusetts and David Cicilline of Rhode Island.

If Democrats maintained their hold in New England, the GOP grip on House delegations appeared to be stronger than ever in the South, the nation's largest region. Republicans held 108 seats in the thirteen Southern states, compared with just forty-seven for the Democrats. *(House vote by region, table, below)*

Meanwhile, survivors of past presidential waves fell. Pennsylvania Democrat Mark Critz, who survived three multimillion-dollar races in two years, lost reelection in a district that voted decisively for Mitt Romney. Similarly, freshman Republican Robert Dold lost in an Illinois district Republicans had held for nearly thirty years because of the president's strong, double-digit performance there. Only a handful of House members won reelection in districts that their party's presidential candidates did not carry, for example Democrats Jim Matheson of Utah and Nick J. Rahall II of West Virginia, as well as Republican Chris Gibson of New York.

Altogether, forty House members were defeated in the 2012 election cycle thirteen in primaries, and twenty-seven in the general election. *(Incumbents reelection table, p. 12)*

Many of the defeats involved districts where two incumbents were forced to run against each other as a result of redistricting. In California, two longtime Democratic incumbents, Brad Sherman and Howard Berman, were not only thrown into the same district but ran against each other twice—first, in the primary, where they came in first and second in the state's new nonpartisan primary system, and then in the general election, which Sherman won.

Redistricting also gave the GOP an edge in future cycles because the GOP-drawn congressional maps were set to remain in place, almost without exception, for a decade, until the next census in 2020. Only twelve Republicans won election by a margin of 5 percentage points or less; Democrats had eighteen members in that category.

SPECIAL HOUSE ELECTIONS

Two special House elections were held during the year to fill vacancies. In Oregon, Democrat Suzanne Bonamici was elected January 31 to fill a vacancy for the Portland-area First District House seat left vacant since August 2011, when fellow Democrat David Wu resigned after several disclosures of bizarre personal behavior and an allegation of sexual misconduct. Bonamici, a lawyer and state senator, won 54 percent of the vote against Republican Rob Cornilles and easily won election to a full term in November.

In Arizona, Democrat Ron Barber defeated Republican Jesse Kelly, 52 percent to 45 percent, in the June 12 election to succeed Rep. Gabrielle Giffords. Giffords stepped down in January to continue her rehabilitation after an assassination attempt a year before that left her seriously wounded. Barber, an aide to Giffords, also sustained injuries at the Tucson event where Giffords was attacked and six people died. Barber narrowly won election to a full term in November. *(Giffords attack, p. 640)*

House of Representatives Vote by Region

The Republican Party retained control of the House through all but four years following the election of Republican George W. Bush as president in 2000 and his successor Democrat Barack Obama in 2008. The exception was the four years between 2006 and 2010 election when Democrats won a solid House majority as national weariness with the Bush administration and the Iraq war gave Democrats an opportunity to regain control. But in 2010 Democrats were again relegated to the minority as the economic downturn that began in 2008 dragged on and as the GOP aggressively attacked Obama initiatives, especially the controversial overhaul of health insurance. The GOP dominance after 2000 reflected the party's control throughout all but four years of the previous decade. Republican strength was anchored in southern states and supported by solid, if less overwhelming, majorities in the midwestern region. Democrats had commanding leads in western and eastern states.

	South			*West*		*Midwest*		*East*			*Total House*		
	R	*D*	*I*	*R*	*D*	*R*	*D*	*R*	*D*	*I*	*R*	*D*	*I*
2000	81	55	1	43	50	57	48	40	59	1	221	212	2
2002	85	57	0	46	52	61	39	37	57	1	229	205	1
2004	91	51	0	45	53	60	40	36	58	1	232	202	1
2006	85	57	0	41	57	51	49	25	70	0	202	233	0
2008	80	62	0	35	63	45	55	18	77	0	178	257	0
2010	102	40	0	43	55	65	35	32	63	0	242	193	0
2012	108	41	0	39	63	59	35	28	62	0	234	201	0

SOURCE: Compiled from Rhodes Cook, *America Votes 30: 2011–2012, Election Returns by State* (Washington, D.C.: CQ Press, 2013).

NOTE: R: Republican. D: Democrat. I: Independent. The following groups of states make up the four regions. South: Alabama, Arkansas, Florida, Georgia, Kentucky, Louisiana, Mississippi, North Carolina, Oklahoma, South Carolina, Tennessee, Texas, and Virginia. West: Alaska, Arizona, California, Colorado, Hawaii, Idaho, Montana, Nevada, New Mexico, Oregon, Utah, Washington, and Wyoming. Midwest: Illinois, Indiana, Iowa, Kansas, Michigan, Minnesota, Missouri, Nebraska, North Dakota, Ohio, South Dakota, and Wisconsin. East: Connecticut, Delaware, Maine, Maryland, Massachusetts, New Hampshire, New Jersey, New York, Pennsylvania, Rhode Island, Vermont, and West Virginia.

Four special elections were held on November 6. In Kentucky's Fourth District, Republican Thomas Massie won a special election to complete the term of Republican Geoff Davis, who had resigned in July. In New Jersey's Tenth district, Democrat Donald M. Payne Jr. won a special election to complete the term of his father, Donald M. Payne, who had died March 2012. In Washington's First District, Democrat Suzan DelBene won election to complete the term of Democrat Jay Inslee, who had resigned in March to run for governor. Massie, Payne, and DelBene also won election to a full term in office starting in 2013.

In the fourth special election, Democrat David Curson, a former union representative won election to complete the term of Republican Thaddeus McCotter, who resigned his seat in Michigan's Eleventh District in July 2012 as a result of a political scandal. Curson's term was one of the shortest on record; he did not run for a full term. The Democratic nominee for the full term, Syed Taj, lost to Republican Kerry Bentivolio who had lost to Curson in the special election.

GUBERNATORIAL RACES

Republicans added one governorship to their side of the roster in the 2012 elections, bringing the national balance to thirty Republicans, nineteen Democrats, and one independent. Eleven governorships were at stake, with six incumbents running for reelection, all of whom won.

In the five open races, the only state to change hands was North Carolina, where Democrat Beverly Perdue decided not to seek reelection after serving one term in office. The first woman governor of the state, Perdue narrowly won election in 2008 over Republican Pat McCrory, the former mayor of Charlotte. The certainty of a rematch combined with a difficult state economy and her falling popularity in the polls were reportedly factors in her decision to retire. McCrory won the 2012 contest handily with 54.6 percent of the total vote, defeating the state's lieutenant government, Walter Dalton.

Democrats held on to three of the other open seats, while Republican Rep. Mike Pence of Indiana replaced fellow Republican Mitch Daniels, a former head of the federal Office of Management and Budget under George W. Bush. Daniels was barred by term limits from seeking a third term. The only close race was in Montana, where Democrat Steve Bullock, the state's attorney general, defeated former Rep. Rick Hill to succeed Brian Schweitzer, who was ineligible to run for a third term. Bullock won 48.9 percent of the vote to Hill's 47.3 percent.

Earlier in the year, Republican Scott Walker of Wisconsin won a recall election against Tom Barrett, defeating Barrett by a slightly higher margin than he had in the 2010 regular governor's elections. Democrats, angry at Walker for limiting collective bargaining rights for state employees early in his term, won a petition campaign to force the recall election. Walker was only the third governor in U.S. history to face a recall and the first to win. The two recalled governors were Lynn Frazier of North Dakota in 1921 and Gray Davis of California in 2003. *(Davis recall, Congress and the Nation Vol. XI, p. 20)*

STATEHOUSE RACES, BALLOT INITIATIVES

Republicans held onto control of twenty-six state legislatures, the same number they had going into the elections. Democrats initially appeared to be in control of nineteen statehouses, while the number of states in which party control was split between the two chambers fell from eight to four. In December, however, a handful of Democrats in the New York State Senate broke away to caucus with Republicans, giving that party control; Democrats retained control of the New York State Assembly. The other states with split control were Iowa, Kentucky, New Hampshire, and Virginia.

In a victory with historical importance, Republicans in Arkansas won control of the Senate and held onto their narrow House majority, giving the GOP control of the eleven states of the Confederacy. It was the first time since Reconstruction that Republicans had controlled the Arkansas statehouse. In what could only be described as a rout, Democrats won 118 GOP seats in the New Hampshire House for a total of 221 out of 400.

In a departure from recent years, voters in three states (Maine, Maryland, and Washington) passed ballot initiatives allowing same-sex marriage, while voters in Minnesota voted down a constitutional amendment defining marriage as a union between a man and a woman. Arizona was the only other state to reject a ban on same-sex marriages, and voters in that state reversed themselves two years later. Before 2012, thirty-two states had voted to bar same-sex marriages.

Colorado and Washington became the first states in the nation to legalize and control recreational use of marijuana; Oregon rejected a similar proposal. Massachusetts joined the small but growing number of states legalizing the drug for medical purposes; Arkansas vetoed a similar measure. Alabama, Missouri, Montana, and Wyoming approved legislative measures that would block implementation of the Affordable Care Act, joining four states—Arizona, Missouri, Ohio, and Oklahoma—that earlier had approved similar measures. Florida voters disapproved a similar measure.

According to the National Conference of State Legislatures, 174 ballot initiatives were put before voters in thirty-eight states, the most since 2006, when voters were presented with 204 initiatives.

CHAPTER 2

Economic Policy

Introduction	47
Chronology of Action on Economic and Regulatory Policy	73
2009–2010	75
2011–2012	104
Chronology of Action on Budget and Tax Policy	111
2009–2010	119
2011–2012	149
Chronology of Action on Trade Policy	191
2009–2010	193
2011–2012	195

Economic Policy

At the end of the George W. Bush administration (2001–2009) and during the first months of President Barack Obama's first term in office beginning in 2009, the United States endured its longest and deepest recession since the 1930s. In addition to its severity, the recession was unusual because it was sparked by an intense financial crisis that started in the United States and spread worldwide. The combination of the two events helped explain why much of the world, particularly the United States and other industrialized countries, were still digging out from the recession a half-decade after it began.

Timely and sustained action by Washington—notably an unprecedented bailout of Wall Street banks and other companies, a series of interest rate cuts and financial guarantees by the Federal Reserve Bank, and a one-time injection of "stimulus" spending and tax cuts—helped prevent the recession from deepening into a 1930s-style Great Depression. Massive infusions of taxpayer cash kept hundreds of banks afloat (even as more than 300 others failed) and ensured that the nation's credit system would not collapse. In the early months of 2009, according to a Congressional Oversight Panel, the federal government guaranteed or insured $4.4 trillion in face value of financial assets.

Despite the government's remarkable success in helping contain the economic damage, public disgust with the use of tax dollars to bail out giant Wall Street banks—the very banks whose risky bets had sparked the financial crisis—helped poison the nation's political atmosphere. The bailout program, called the Troubled Asset Relief Program (TARP), had to be forced through Congress in the fall of 2008, was never popular to begin with, and quickly became a public symbol of everything that was wrong on Wall Street and in Washington. This was despite the fact that the bailout clearly rescued the financial system at a critical moment and wound up with a net cost to taxpayers, after repayments and profits, of only about $24 billion of its initial price tag of more than $700 billion.

President Obama succeeded in getting the Democratic-controlled Congress early in 2009 to pass a $787.2 billion package of spending measures and tax cuts to stimulate the economy. Most economists said that measure did, in fact, help boost the economy temporarily. Whatever success the stimulus had, however, quickly faded from memory, and Republicans were able to gain political leverage in 2010 by linking it to the unpopular bailout and assailing it as a costly government program that had boosted the federal deficit.

By early 2013, the U.S. economy finally seemed on the way to a genuine recovery, although at a pace that was agonizingly slow. Economic growth had been sustained for every quarter since the middle of 2009, but often just barely in the positive zone. The snail's pace was especially frustrating for millions of people who still could not find jobs or, at best, could find only part-time or low-wage employment. The nominal unemployment rate remained stuck at 7.6 percent in mid-2013, well above what economists considered a "normal" range of 5 to 6 percent.

Potential evidence of faster economic improvement appeared in the spring of 2013, when the housing market seemed to be recovering, the stock markets were still in a bullish mood for the most part, and consumers expressed renewed confidence in the future. The positive signs of 2013 were all the more remarkable because the country had fallen off a supposed "fiscal cliff" at the beginning of

REFERENCES

Discussion of economic policy for the years 1945–1964 may be found in *Congress and the Nation Vol. I*, pp. 337–458; for the years 1965–1968, *Congress and the Nation Vol. II*, pp. 119–182, 253–305; for the years 1969–1972, *Congress and the Nation Vol. III*, pp. 53–145; for the years 1973–1976, *Congress and the Nation Vol. IV*, pp. 49–149; for the years 1977–1980, *Congress and the Nation Vol. V*, pp. 205–287; for the years 1981–1984, *Congress and the Nation Vol. VI*, pp. 27–120; for the years 1985–1988, *Congress and the Nation Vol. VII*, pp. 27–136; for the years 1989–1992, *Congress and the Nation Vol. VIII*, pp. 31–161; for the years 1993–1996, *Congress and the Nation Vol. IX*, pp. 31–148; for the years 1997–2001, *Congress and the Nation Vol. X*, pp. 33–170; for the years 2001–2004, *Congress and the Nation Vol. XI*, pp. 35–167; for the years 2005–2008, *Congress and the Nation Vol. XII*, pp. 51–59.

ECONOMIC LEADERSHIP

President Barack Obama took office at the low point of the worst recession in the United States since the Great Depression of the 1930s. Leading the president's economic team were two men who had been instrumental late in the administration of President George W. Bush for working to stabilize the financial sector after its near collapse and to unfreeze credit markets, Treasury Secretary Timothy F. Geithner and Federal Reserve Chair Ben S. Bernanke. Both men remained in their positions for the duration of Obama's first term. Turnover was higher in other key economic policy positions.

Treasury Secretary

Geithner, as president of the Federal Reserve Bank of New York, had worked closely in 2008 with Bernanke and President Bush's Treasury secretary, Henry M. Paulson, to design the bailout legislation and other federal interventions that were widely credited with staving off an even worse financial and economic crisis. Geithner, nominated to succeed Paulson, was confirmed in January 2009 by the relatively narrow vote of 60–34, in large part because of the unpopularity of the bailouts with both conservative Republicans, who thought they were too costly, and liberal Democrats, who thought Geithner had not been tough enough on Wall Street banks. Although Geithner had strong supporters, these were criticisms the secretary was never able to overcome. He was also criticized for failing to come up with a workable plan to deal with the millions of mortgage foreclosures that resulted from the burst housing bubble.

Geithner got off to a rocky start at Treasury, when the Dow Jones Industrial Average fell nearly 200 points during a speech he gave in February 2009 outlining a new plan to stabilize the financial system. A month later, Republicans began calling for his resignation in response to public outrage over bonuses paid to executives at American International Group (AIG), the insurance giant that had received one of the largest government bailouts. Later in the year, Geithner implemented new reforms of the bailout fund, known as TARP, or the Troubled Asset Relief Program; by the time he left office in early 2013, the government had sold, or had announced plans to sell, its remaining holdings in AIG, General Motors, and banks. TARP had ended, with all but about $25 billion of the $700 billion authorized (later reduced to $475 billion) returned to the government. *(TARP, pp. 61, 62)*

Geithner was also heavily involved in the administration's push for reform of the financial regulatory system, which was enacted in 2010. After passage of the Dodd-Frank act, Geithner worked to defend the law from attacks by various elements of the financial community as well as from legislators who sought to slow or prevent its implementation. *(Financial reform, pp. 68, 88)*

With the Republican takeover of the House in 2011, Geithner's role shifted to helping defend the president's position in the deficit and debt battles with the GOP that threatened on occasion to close the government and send it into default. Geithner also played a role in international financial policy, trying to persuade China of the need for a more balanced economy and to encourage European leaders to deal with the euro crisis before it precipitated another global downturn.

Federal Reserve

Appointed by President Bush, Bernanke began his first term as chair of the Federal Reserve (Fed) on February 1, 2006. Like others, Bernanke was slow to react to the growing housing crisis. But when the financial and economic crises hit, the Fed lent hundreds of billions of dollars to banks and businesses, supported the federal takeover of mortgage giants Fannie Mae (Federal National Mortgage Association) and Freddie Mac (Federal Home Loan Mortgage Corporation), and backed the creation of TARP. Nominating Bernanke to a second four-year term in April 2009, Obama credited Bernanke with preventing a second Great Depression. The Senate confirmed him in 2010; his term ran through January 2014. *(Confirmation, p. 86)*

Although the Fed's mandate is to keep inflation in check while striving for maximum employment, Bernanke argued that with interest rates low, the Fed could concentrate on actions that would encourage investment and ultimately job creation. To that end, the Federal Reserve engaged in a strategy of buying Treasury bonds and mortgage securities, and exchanging bonds with shorter maturities for ones with longer maturities, all in an effort to drive down long-term interest rates. In addition to what came to be called "quantitative easing," the Fed also began to describe publicly its long-term strategy so that investors might better be able to anticipate rises in interest rates and other policy changes.

While these actions kept interest rates extraordinarily low, unemployment rates remained persistently high, hovering in the 7.5 percent range at the end of 2012. While liberals criticized Bernanke for not doing more to bring down the jobless rate, conservatives worried that the Federal Reserve had created the conditions for interest rates to soar once the economy recovered. For his part, Bernanke lamented that the uncertainty created by the continual congressional wrangling over spending and tax levels was undermining investor confidence and slowing the recovery.

Office of Management and Budget

Obama had two directors of the Office of Management and Budget (OMB) in his first term, each succeeded for a period of time by the same acting director. The first director was Peter S. Orszag, an economist who served from January 2007 to November 2008 as director of the nonpartisan Congressional Budget Office, where he called attention to the long-term problems of steadily rising health care spending. His first job in the Obama administration was to promote economic stimulus while keeping the budget deficit under control. But he soon focused on health care reform, where he was credited by many for developing the analytical foundation on which the president's Affordable Care Act rested. *(Health care legislation, p. 421)*

Orszag left the administration in June 2010 and eventually settled at Citicorp, where he was vice chair of global banking. Obama named Jeffrey Zients, chief performance officer and deputy director of the OMB, as the agency's acting director. A management consultant, Zients had worked for Bain Capital and for the business consulting firms Advisory Board and Corporate Executive Board.

In November 2010, Obama named Jacob (Jack) Lew as OMB director, the same job Lew held during the Clinton administration, where he won praise for his role in bringing about the Balanced Budget Act of 1997 (PL 105-33), a bipartisan effort that resulted in a short series of federal surpluses. A lawyer by training, Lew brought extensive experience with Congress and inside the White House to the job. Widely respected on Capitol Hill, he worked as domestic policy adviser to House Speaker Thomas P. "Tip" O'Neill from 1979 through 1986. Following years in the Bill Clinton administration, as an academic, and on Wall Street, he was recruited by Secretary of State Hillary Rodham Clinton in 2009 to help rebuild her department's budget and influence after years of decline. It was, by all accounts, a successful effort.

Lew served little more than a year before Obama named him White House chief of staff in January 2012 to replace the departing William Daley. Once again, Zients was called on to fill in as acting director at OMB. At the beginning of his second term, Obama nominated Lew as Treasury Secretary; in September 2013, Zients was named head of the National Economic Council. Sylvia Mathews Burwell, former president of the Walmart Foundation, was named OMB director in April 2013.

National Economic Council

Established by President Clinton, the National Economic Council (NEC) was intended to coordinate the administration's economic policies. Obama's first NEC director was Lawrence Summers, a Treasury secretary in the Clinton administration and former president of Harvard, who had served on Obama's economic advisory term during the presidential campaign. By all accounts, Summers was an exceptionally intelligent, sometimes brilliant, economist and an adviser that Obama came to rely on, especially during the depths of the economic crisis at the end of 2008 and the beginning of 2009. But Summers was also widely criticized for not supporting stronger stimulus measures or steps to help struggling homeowners reduce their mortgage balances. By several accounts, Summers also had difficult relations with some of Obama's other top economic advisers, including former Fed chair Paul Volcker.

Summers left his job at the midway point in Obama's first term and was replaced by Gene B. Sperling, who also had served as NEC director during President Clinton's first term. In Obama's White House, Sperling represented the White House in budget negotiations with Congress and helped design several of the president's economic initiatives including the American Jobs Act, the extension of Transition Adjustment Assistance, the universal dislocated workers program, and the small business tax credit. Sperling remained as NEC director well into Obama's second term.

Council of Economic Advisers

The Council of Economic Advisers was created in 1946 to advise the president on national economic policy and is the body responsible for producing the president's annual economic report. Obama had three council chairs during his first term. Christina D. Romer, an economics professor at the University of California, Berkeley, and a strong advocate of massive stimulus to restart the economy and put people back to work, was the first.

In late 2010, she was succeeded by Austan Goolsbee, an economics professor at the University of Chicago and a longtime adviser to Obama. When Goolsbee left in August 2011 to return to Chicago, he was succeeded by Alan B. Krueger, a Princeton economics professor interested, among other things, in the effect of education and minimum wages on earnings and employment. He left the CEA in August 2013 to return to Princeton and was succeeded in 2013 by Jason Furman, who had been serving as Obama's deputy director of the National Economic Council.

A Look at the Economy 1996–2012

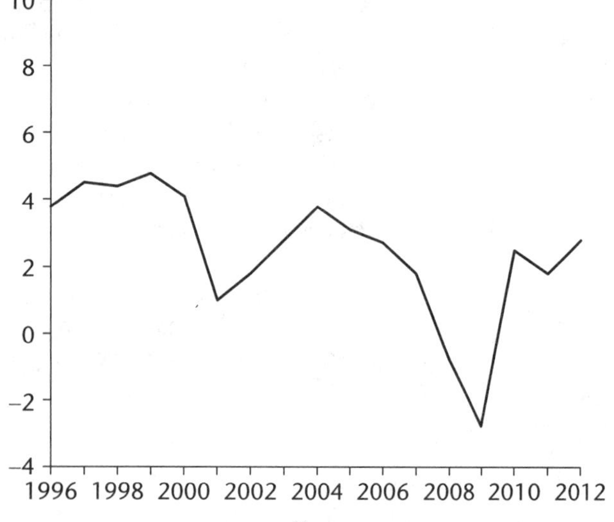

. . . declined during the early 1990s but a prolonged recovery followed that lasted to 2000. President George W. Bush's first term (2001–2005) was marked by a mild recession, followed by a mild recovery. Economic growth in his second term (2005–2009) slowed gradually until December 2007, when the country entered deep recession. The economy contracted 8.3 percent in the fourth quarter of 2008 and 5.4 percent in the first quarter of 2009. By 2010 the economy was growing again, albeit slowly, for the remainder of President Barack Obama's first term.

Growth: Annual changes in real GDP, measured in chained 2009 dollars

SOURCE: Commerce Department, Bureau of Economic Analysis.

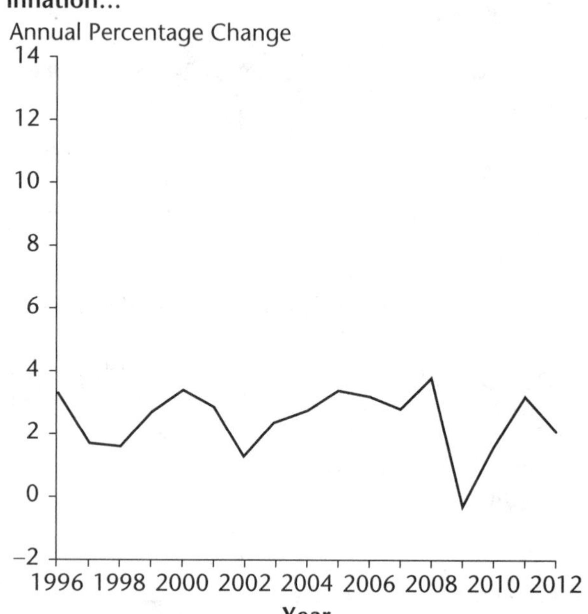

. . . stayed relatively consistent and tame for most of the 1990s and the first years of the 2000s. It rose somewhat before the 2008 recession but never approached the historically high levels it did leading up to the recession of the early 1980s. During President Obama's first term, deflation was at times a larger concern than inflation.

Inflation: Annual change in the consumer price index for all urban consumers, expressed as an annual average rate.

SOURCE: Labor Department, Bureau of Labor Statistics.

Unemployment...

Annual Percentage Average

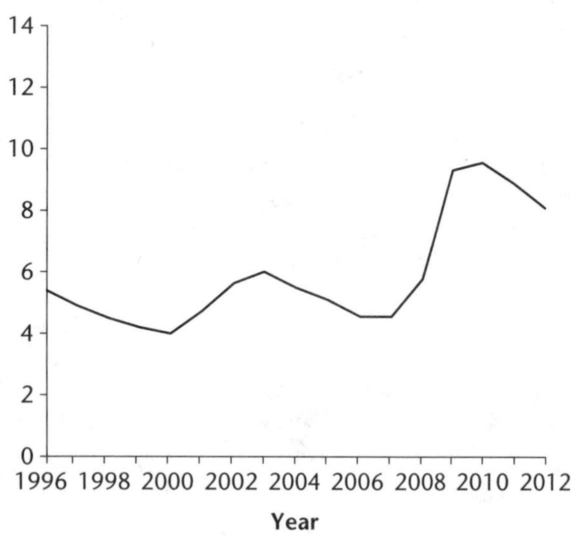

. . . surged after the 1990–1991 recession but then steadily declined until the early 2000s, when it experienced a slight uptick before settling at about 5 percent. As recession took hold in 2008, unemployment began to rise, reaching a high point of 10.6 percent in January 2010 before falling back to around 7.5 percent in the last quarter of 2012.

Unemployment: Annual rate of unemployment for all civilian workers (does not include the military).

SOURCE: Labor Department, Bureau of Labor Statistics.

Interest Rates . . .

Annual Percentage Average

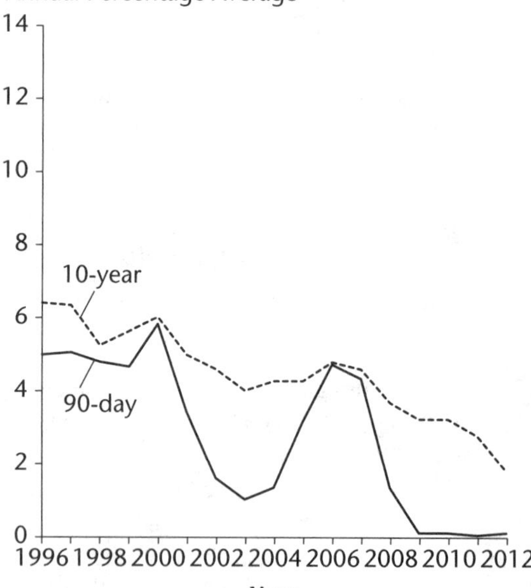

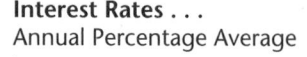

. . . on short- and long-term Treasury securities fell in 2003 to their lowest levels in almost thirty years, then rose slightly as the Fed tried to engineer a "soft landing" for the booming housing market. In late 2008, interest rates fell again and remained low as the Fed intervened in an effort to stimulate the slumping economy.

Interest rates: Annual average for ninety-day Treasury bills and ten-year Treasury notes, adjusted for constant maturities.

SOURCE: Federal Reserve.

the year: some taxes had risen, and Congress and the president had failed to get themselves out of a self-imposed straitjacket of spending cuts.

The U.S. economy was rocketing ahead when compared to those in most other industrialized countries, notably western Europe and Japan. Many countries in the seventeen-member eurozone seemed to be falling into a second bout of recession by late 2012 and early 2013. Europe was dragged down in large part by continuing discord over how to resolve a sovereign debt crisis that had forced five countries (Greece, Ireland, Italy, Portugal, and Spain) to be bailed out by their partner nations. Deflation and general economic stagnation continued to linger in Japan, which in 2013 began a high-risk experiment that attempted to reflate the economy with a mammoth expansion of the money supply.

Growth in most developing countries had slowed during the global financial crisis but in some cases appeared to be resuming at a somewhat quicker pace from 2012 onward. China remained the great global engine of growth, its insatiable appetite for everything from copper to wood helping boost commodity-exporting countries in Africa, Latin America, and elsewhere in Asia. But even China was not immune to the lingering impact of the economic uncertainty elsewhere, its growth having cooled from the double-digit rates of much of the 2000s to the high single digits since 2008.

Downs and (Somewhat) Ups of the Economy

The U.S. economy fell into a recession, defined as negative growth of the gross domestic product (GDP), during the fourth quarter of 2007. Except for modest growth in the second quarter of 2008, the economy stayed in recession through the second quarter of 2009. By nearly every measure, this eighteen-month period represented the longest and deepest recession the United States had experienced since the Great Depression of the 1930s, which was much longer and more severe.

During the recession, the economy shrunk by about 5 percent, or by about $680 billion. On an annual basis, the economy declined by 0.3 percent in 2008 and by 3.1 percent in 2009. The worst period was the last quarter of 2008 when the economy shrank by an astonishing 8.9 percent on an annualized basis—the worst single quarter since the recession of 1957–1958.

A measure used by economists showed the damage done by the recession in even starker terms: the "output gap," or the difference between what the economy could have produced and what it actually did produce during the recession, was 8.1 percent, according to data from the Federal Reserve Bank of St. Louis. A new worry arose in 2009 when the economy briefly experienced deflation (as measured by the consumer price increase) for the first time since the 1950s recession. Economists and policymakers fretted for months about the possibility of long-term deflation, an affliction that had troubled Japan for nearly two decades but eventually did not occur in the United States. Deflation, in economic terms, occurs when prices continue to fall (in contrast to inflation, the much better understood phenomena experienced by shoppers on every trip to the grocery store). Although falling prices seem a good thing on the face of it, in fact they create a vicious downward cycle in part because consumers, expecting lower prices in the future, delay purchases, which in turn constricts business activity, forces businesses to cut prices yet again, and leads to job layoffs.

Another measure showed just how much money the recession cost American households: the net worth of households (called "household wealth" by economists) fell more than $16 trillion during 2008 and 2009—a decline of 24 percent from the 2007 peak of $67 trillion. Another study by the Federal Reserve Bank of St. Louis, published in late May 2013, said that, on average, families had made back only 45 percent of their lost net worth, after accounting for inflation and population growth. "A conclusion that the financial damage of the crisis and recession largely has been repaired is not justified," the report said.

THE RECOVERY

As measured by statistics, the economy began recovering in mid-2009, and it grew, sometimes rapidly and sometimes slowly, for every quarter into the first half of 2013. It grew by 2.4 percent in 2010, by 1.8 percent in 2011, by 2.2 percent in 2012, and by 1.8 percent during the first quarter of 2013. Most midyear projections had GDP growth for all of 2013 in the range of 1.5 to 2 percent.

The growth was so minimal that, until well into 2012, many Americans talked and acted as if the recession was still under way. It was not until May 2013 that the Conference Board's "Consumer Confidence Index" showed that overall attitudes about the economy had improved to prerecession levels. Even so, substantially more people (26 percent) still said business conditions were "bad" than said business conditions were "good" (19 percent).

As the Federal Reserve study showed, in nominal terms some of the losses in household wealth had been recovered by the end of 2012. However, the bulk of the regained wealth came from the rising stock markets, which benefited primarily high-income households. Lower-income households, particularly those hit by unemployment, recovered little if any of the wealth they had lost, often because their homes had lost value and even been confiscated by lenders through foreclosure proceedings. An April 2013 study of census data by the Pew Research Center said that from 2009 to 2011, the wealthiest 7 percent of households had grown an average of 28 percent wealthier (to nearly $3.2 million), while household wealth in the other 93 percent had dropped by 4 percent (to an average of $134,000).

UNEMPLOYMENT

For many people, the question of whether the economy technically was growing mattered less than whether they had jobs and could pay their monthly bills. For millions of people, the distressing answer to that question, for an uncomfortably long time, was "no."

The unemployment rate, which stood at about 4.6 percent in 2007, zoomed to nearly 9 percent in April 2009 and peaked at 10.1 percent in October 2009, months after the recession officially ended, as measured by economic statistics. This double digit figure was only the second time since the Great Depression; the unemployment rate hit 10.8 percent in 1981.

Unemployment then fell slowly, but regularly, finally dropping below 8 percent in late 2012. As of June 2013, the rate stood at 7.6 percent—still high by historical standards, four years after the end of a recession. Moreover, much of the improvement in the rate actually represented bad news: workers who could not find jobs simply gave up and left the labor force, or they took part-time jobs and thus were no longer classified as unemployed.

The unemployment figures represented national averages, which disguised much worse employment pictures for some sectors of society. As of early 2013, the unemployment rate stood at 13.8 percent for African Americans, at 12 percent for those without a high school diploma, at 23.4 percent for young people aged sixteen to nineteen and not in school, and at 38 percent among African American youth. Moreover, three million people said they had been looking for work for more than a year. These figures began improving later in 2013 but still were high by historical standards.

For pessimists, the unemployment news was even worse than those so-called headline unemployment rates indicated. In February 2013, a broader measure of national unemployment—including some 800,000 people who had given up looking for work and some 8 million people who said they were working part-time but wanted a full-time job—was 14.4 percent.

Federal Reserve Chair Ben S. Bernanke, in August 2012, said the decline of unemployment was "painfully slow" and was "likely to remain far above levels consistent with maximum employment for some time." He added: "The stagnation of the labor market in particular is a grave concern not only because of the enormous suffering and waste of human talent it entails, but also because persistently high levels of unemployment will wreak structural damage on our economy that could last for many years."

Among other things, Bernanke was alluding to the fact that the recession accelerated what economists considered as the natural process in which businesses were shedding low-skill jobs (and workers) and replacing them with smaller numbers of higher-skill jobs (and workers). Some jobs in high-technology fields went unfilled because businesses could not find workers with the required skills. In contrast, millions of blue-collar jobs—especially in manufacturing—continued to disappear, permanently. The workers who had held those jobs found themselves unemployed or, at best, juggling two or more low-wage, part-time jobs, often in the service sector.

The flip side of the dismal unemployment figures was that millions of people did find jobs. From mid-2009 through February 2013, the economy showed a net increase of some four million nonfarm jobs. The job growth was not consistent, with some months showing increases of more than 200,000 jobs, while some other months showed well under 100,000 jobs. However, job growth did appear to strengthen as the economic recovery took hold, averaging more than 200,000 per month from November 2012 through April 2013.

Nearly all the job growth was in the private sector. The net job-creation figures would have been much higher had governments at all levels not eliminated more than 800,000 workers, as of May 2013, because of budget cuts since 2009.

DELEVERAGING

The root cause of the 2007–2008 financial crisis was that too many people and businesses got themselves too deeply in debt, mainly as a result of the unsustainable housing boom. Banks packaged billions of dollars of debt into opaque financial instruments that few people understood or bothered to examine. Those debts came crashing down, first on the United States, then on the rest of the world. In both theoretical and practical terms, the recession thus was a process of what economists call "deleveraging": everyone from individuals to giant multinational banks and corporations cutting expenses in a desperate rush to reduce their indebtedness.

The Federal Reserve reported in February 2013 that a measure called the "household debt service ratio" (basically, how much households owed compared to personal disposable income) had fallen to a level last seen in 1983. Americans still loved their credit cards, but they became more cautious in using them: "Revolving credit," mostly credit card debt, fell from more than $1 trillion in 2008 to about $850 billion from 2010 onward. Similarly, the debt levels for nonfinancial corporations had fallen to the lowest level since 2000.

The process of shedding debt, although a short-term necessity, had long-term consequences, some of them negative, according to economists. The most obvious was that consumers were reluctant to spend; this was a problem because consumer spending drove more than two-thirds of the entire economy. Another downside was that many individual investors sought only safe havens (even those with negligible returns, such as U.S. Treasury bills) and shunned even investments that would have been attractive in a better environment and might have stimulated business growth.

Although flush with cash (some of it from the government bailout), banks also were reluctant to make loans except to their very best and safest customers. This meant that some businesses, especially small ones, struggled to find the money to expand production or develop new products or services. Moreover, an unusually high proportion of the corporate bonds issued during 2012 appeared to be earmarked for refinancing existing debt, rather than expanding or opening new lines of business, according to the Federal Reserve. Research and development, long one of the key strengths of the U.S. economy, lagged because of business caution. The resulting lack of innovation could have potential long-term negative implications for the productivity and vitality of business and industry at all levels.

The Federal Reserve pumped more than $2 trillion into the economy from late 2008 through early 2013, a stimulus that helped keep the economy afloat but did not push banks to open their credit windows or consumers to open their wallets. The *Financial Times* observed in October 2012: "Central banks can create money, but they cannot force people to spend it."

FINANCIAL MARKETS

After falling to a low in March 2009, equity markets began a reasonably steady march upward that was still underway as of mid-2013. The Dow Jones Industrial Average, which had sunk to 6,547 in March 2009, recovered all of its capitalization by early 2013 and hit 15,000 for the first time in May 2013. The broader Standard & Poor's 500 index, which had fallen to a low of 676 in March 2009, rose by 13 percent during 2012 and stood above 1,600 for the first time in late May 2013. Bloomberg news service said in May 2013 that four years of a bull market had added about $11.5 trillion in market value.

Another important measure was in the bond market, often a better gauge of where the economy is headed than the stock markets. Spreads on investment-grade corporate bonds, which had reached 600 basis points in December 2008, fell to just above 25 basis points early in 2013 (a basis point is one hundredth of one percentage point). This demonstrated a marked improvement in lenders' attitudes about the creditworthiness of corporate borrowers.

HOUSING MARKET

If overborrowing was the root cause, a collapse of the overheated housing market, starting in 2006, was the main driving force behind both the financial crisis and the recession. By 2013 the housing market was on the mend, but it was clear that at least several more years would be needed before the market could recover fully, if indeed that was possible.

Housing starts, which had run at an annual pace of more than two million during the housing boom, tumbled to just above 400,000 in 2009, then began a slow recovery. At the end of 2012, the figure topped 900,000, still less than one-half the precrisis record but a positive sign nonetheless.

New home sales increased about 15 percent in 2012, but that followed the record-low year of 2011, when only 302,000 new homes were sold nationwide. Sales of existing homes rose more than 9 percent in 2012, the biggest increase in five years, according to the National Association of Realtors. By May 2013, a prime indicator of housing prices—the Case-Shiller index of twenty cities—found that prices had risen on average 10.9 percent above the previous year, the biggest jump since April 2006, just before the housing market began to swoon. These percentage increases were so high in large part because the market had fallen so much, meaning that any increase would be striking. The sales price index, for example, was still 28 percent below its previous peak of mid-2006.

Another positive sign for the housing market, according to the Commerce Department, was that houses were again beginning to sell relatively quickly. In September 2006, just as the market was beginning to cool, the medium sales time nationally was 3.4 months. That reached a high of 14.4 months in March 2010, but then declined to just 4.6 month in January 2013.

The other side of this positive news was that millions of homeowners were still suffering. At the end of 2012, according to Treasury figures, 10.4 million homeowners were still "under water" (with mortgage balances greater than their home values). Also, more than 3.3 million homeowners were "seriously delinquent" in their mortgage payments. The monthly number of foreclosure completions, which had exceeded 80,000 for much of 2008 through 2010, declined to about 40,000 during 2012, but that still was high by historical standards, Treasury Department officials said.

The government and the mortgage industry did make extensive efforts to help homeowners in trouble, but the programs reached only a minority of those in need. The Treasury Department reported in March 2013 that its Making Home Affordable program, funded by the Wall Street bailout program, had helped 1.5 million homeowners avoid foreclosure. That figure included aid to 350,000 homeowners in 2012 alone, Treasury said. In addition, the government set new standards for the mortgage servicing industry in hopes of preventing abuses that contributed to the problems in the housing market. A private industry program had reduced mortgage payments for some 3.5 million homeowners.

One explanation for the government's slowness in helping homeowners, according to some critics, was that one arm of the government—the regulator that controlled the mortgage-guarantee agencies Fannie Mae and Freddie Mac—resisted the rest of the government's policy of giving breaks on mortgages. The Federal Housing Finance Agency reportedly worried that reducing payments and principals on underwater mortgages would cut into the agencies' profits, thereby imperiling their ability to climb out from a mountain of their own debt.

The fact that it took so long for the housing market to begin recovering was all the more remarkable because houses remained relatively affordable, certainly compared to the super-hot market of the mid-2000s. Home sale prices, which fell every quarter from mid-2007 to mid-2011, were still about 12 percent below their April 2007 peak, as of early 2013, according to the Federal Housing Finance Agency. Just as important, mortgage rates were at record lows, thanks in large part to the low-interest policies of the Federal Reserve Bank. The national average rate for a thirty-year fixed mortgage was just over 6 percent in late 2008; by late 2012 it had fallen to about 3.5 percent, the lowest since banks began offering long-term mortgages in the 1950s.

One explanation was that banks—having gone overboard in the early 2000s by passing out mortgages to just about anyone—were now imposing very strict credit conditions and turning away all but the most creditworthy applicants. Another explanation was the basic one of money: millions of people were still unemployed, or underemployed, and therefore could not hope to buy a house or were having trouble paying mortgages on the houses they occupied.

Yet another problem that emerged in the aftermath of the financial crisis was that some banks, especially the giant ones that operated nationally, were engaging in dubious practices that unnecessarily damaged millions of homeowners. Examples included wrongful evictions, extremely high fees, and a process called "robo-signing" in which banks automatically processed thousands of foreclosures without carefully examining to see if the action was necessary or even justified.

State attorneys general in March 2012 settled wrongful-foreclosure allegations against five banks—Ally Financial, Bank of America, Chase, Citibank, and Wells Fargo—by ordering them to provide $17 billion in aid "to borrowers who have the intent and ability to stay in their homes." Of that amount, $10.2 billion was designated to reduce the loan principals for about 1 million "under water" homeowners. Critics said this agreement gave the banks far too much leeway to claim credit for actions they were already taking, such as donating or even demolishing homes they had repossessed but could not sell.

Federal regulators also, belatedly, got involved in the issue of unscrupulous and unnecessary foreclosures. Responding to a public outcry about wrongful evictions, federal regulators in November 2011 ordered ten banks and mortgage servicing companies to review nearly four million foreclosures; that work was done by consulting firms at an estimated cost of $1 billion. The reviews took so long, and were so fraught with allegations that the consultants were colluding with the banks, that the Comptroller of the Currency and the Federal Reserve Bank called a halt to it in January 2013 and instead ordered the banks to pay a total of $8.5 billion to the affected homeowners. That amount included $3.3 billion in cash payments and $5.2 billion in assistance such as loan modifications. The affected companies were Aurora, Bank of America, Citibank, JP Morgan Chase, MetLife Bank, PNC, Sovereign, SunTrust, U.S. Bank, and Wells Fargo.

BEHIND THE SLOW RECOVERY

Economists and other experts offered a multitude of explanations for why the recovery, once it took hold in the second half of 2009, was so tentative and its results were so uneven across society. The foremost and most widely accepted explanation, of course, was that the recession had been deeper and longer than any of the ten previous downturns since World War II—so a recovery would take longer, and be more halting, than usual. Robert J. Samuelson, economics columnist for the *Washington Post,* articulated this view in his typically straightforward fashion in November 2012: "The financial crisis and Great Recession scared the wits out of most Americans—not just consumers but also corporate managers, bankers, and small-business owners. They are reacting accordingly. They're cautious, risk-averse and defensive. They're spending less and saving more."

A similar explanation, offered for example by Janet Yellen, vice chair of the Federal Reserve Bank in February 2013, was that the economy had been exceptionally crippled by twin events: the bursting of an "unprecedented housing bubble" followed by a severe financial crisis. "These developments robbed homeowners of wealth built over a generation, impaired their access to credit, decimated retirement savings, and shattered the confidence of consumers," she said. "Businesses slashed capital spending and payrolls, and real GDP contracted by 4.7 percent, more than twice the average for the ten other recessions since World War II." (Later in the year, Yellen was nominated by President Obama to replace Ben S. Bernanke as head of the Federal Reserve when his term expired in early 2014.)

If excessive, and excessively risky, borrowing caused the financial crisis, the recession lingered in large part because borrowing suddenly became so difficult for individuals and businesses. Homeowners—including those "under water" because their mortgage balances now exceeded the value of their homes, and those whose homes had lost equity—could no longer use their homes as sources of ready cash, or giant ATM machines, as had been the popular practice in the 2000s.

Although banks had money to lend, thanks in part to low interest rates resulting from Federal Reserve policies, they were slow to relax the tighter terms and conditions for loans they had imposed once the financial crisis hit. This was especially true for consumer loans, including mortgages, which were much harder for average borrowers to obtain than during the free-spending and borrowing days before the recession.

For businesses, continued uncertainty about the economy led to pronounced caution about making capital investments or hiring workers. Corporate profits rose in most sectors, but until the last half of 2012 the profits, for most companies in most sectors, resulted more from increased efficiencies than from increased production.

Many businesses also used their profits to build cash reserves or buy back shares from the public rather than expanding their businesses.

Signs of rising production finally began appearing toward the end of 2012, for example in the Commerce Department's monthly report on new orders for manufactured durable goods (those with life spans of three or more years). These orders increased for the last four months of 2012 and two of the three first months of 2013.

Other factors not directly related to the financial crisis conspired to prolong the recession. One was that energy prices rose dramatically, by an average of about 30 percent, from late 2011 through early 2012, putting another brake on consumer spending during a period important for economic growth. Energy prices declined thereafter and well into 2013, giving consumers more encouragement to spend. Government cutbacks at all levels also were a drag on the recovery, according to most economists. The Commerce Department estimated that retrenchment by state and local governments had reduced GDP growth by 0.2 percentage points in 2010, by 0.4 points in 2011, and by 0.2 points in 2012. Tax increases—notably the expiration of a temporary payroll tax cut at the end of 2012—and spending cuts at the federal level were projected to pare economic growth in 2013 by 1.5 percentage points below what it otherwise would have been, according to the Congressional Budget Office.

The steady improvement in stock markets showed that some sectors of society prospered despite the lingering economic uncertainty. Wall Street banks, hedge funds, and other investors who profited by moving vast quantities of money from one place to another were doing very well indeed. Banks, including ones the federal government had bailed out in late 2008, reported record increases in profits during the first quarter of 2013. The Federal Deposit Insurance Corp. (FDIC) said the nation's banks earned more than $40 billion early in the year, and that 90 percent of reporting banks had been profitable. One reason for the high profits was that banks were able to reduce the reserves they set aside to cover losses to the lowest level since early 2007. This step caused some nervousness among regulators, who warned that they would watch closely to make sure the banks were not taking undue risks, as they had done in the run-up to the financial crisis. It also was unclear how long banks could continue making the cuts in spending and capital reserves that had boosted their profits.

GLOBAL IMPACT

By 2011, it was clear that the U.S. economy was in relatively better shape than most other industrialized countries, particularly in the eurozone and Japan. In contrast to the continuing contraction, or at best stagnation, in most of those other countries, at least the U.S. economy was growing, if slowly.

The most intense and long-lasting consequences of the financial crisis and economic recession were evident in Europe. Some countries whose banks had engaged in particularly risky behavior during the mid-2000s boom—notably Finland, Iceland, and Ireland—had struggled to emerge from under an avalanche of debt resulting from the collapse of their banking systems.

Other countries, some of which had little or nothing to do with the misbehavior of banks, suddenly found themselves on the short end of bets placed by investors who believed they could no longer service their sovereign debts. This created a rolling crisis across Europe, hitting Spain, Portugal, Italy, and eventually worst of all, Greece. *Financial Times* economist columnist Martin Wolf observed that during the 2000s the governments in most of the troubled countries (Greece being the exception) actually had been more frugal, with relatively lower public deficits, than supposedly "virtuous" countries such as Germany. What got those countries into trouble, Wolf said, was a balance-of-payments problem, resulting from imports and the borrowing necessary to pay for them. Whatever the cause, the so-called "peripheral" members of the eurozone were in deep crisis and had to be rescued. Starting in 2009, European leaders cobbled together a succession of stop-gap measures, including bailouts of the affected countries underwritten by a temporary "stability" fund that was made permanent in 2013.

One of the most important steps came on July 26, 2012, when the new president of the European Central Bank, Mario Draghi, said: "Within our mandate, the ECB is ready to do whatever it takes to preserve the euro." This unequivocal statement reassured markets and governments that the eurozone would, somehow, be kept intact. Draghi's intervention also created the possibility, but did not guarantee, that governments in some of the most troubled economies would have the resources to get their fiscal houses in order.

Even so, Europe was beset by intense disagreements over how deeply and how far to push austerity measures, first in the countries in deepest trouble but also in other countries where indebtedness had become a way of life. Germany, with the largest economy acting as the eurozone's paymaster, also had become its taskmaster—demanding at every step that bailed-out countries adopt spending cuts and free-market measures that Berlin believed were necessary to set them on a more virtuous path. The austerity measures that Germany demanded resulted in job losses and intense short-term misery, especially in Greece, giving rise to angry protests that the cure was worse than the disease, at least for the short term.

Europe's troubles did not stay there, just as the American origins of the financial crisis were not confined to the United States. Federal Reserve Chair Bernanke acknowledged in May 2013 that the "severe fiscal and financial strains in Europe, by weighing on U.S. exports and financial markets, have also restrained U.S. economic growth over the past couple of years. However, since last summer, financial conditions in the euro area have improved

FEDERAL RESERVE ACTIONS DURING THE FINANCIAL CRISIS AND RECESSION

Starting in August 2007 the Federal Reserve Bank (Fed) responded aggressively to signs of an international financial crisis, first by using its standard monetary tools (cutting interest rates), then by pumping more than $2 trillion into the economy. Following is a summary of the Fed's major crisis-related actions from late 2007 through early 2013 under the leadership of Fed Chair Ben S. Bernanke.

Interest Rate Actions

Beginning in August 2007, the Fed moved quickly to push down interest rates, first with a 0.5 percent cut in the discount rate (the rate depository banks pay the Fed for short-term loans), from 6.25 percent to 5.75 percent. The Fed lowered the rate again in September to 5.25 percent, then in October to 5 percent; by the end of 2008 the rate was 0.5 percent.

The Fed acted in parallel to cut the federal funds rate (the national average of the rate at which banks make short-term loans to one another), starting from a high of 5.25 percent as of August 2007 to 4.75 in September 2007, then over the next six months to 2 percent. On October 29, 2008, the Fed lowered it again to 1 percent. The Fed said at the time that the rate cut "should help over time to improve credit conditions and promote a return to moderate economic growth." About six weeks later, on December 16, 2008, the Fed cut the federal funds rate to a range of 0 to 0.25 percent (effectively, as low as it could go) and projected that an "exceptionally low" federal funds rate would be maintained "for some time."

As part of its follow-up "communications" strategy to bolster economic growth, the Fed gradually extended its projection for how it would keep interest rates at what economists call the "zero bound." Following are the Fed's key interest rate announcements:

- On March 18, 2009, the Fed said it anticipated that the "exceptionally low" federal funds rate would likely be maintained "for an extended period." This was intended to keep long-term interest rates from rising.
- On August 9, 2011, the Fed set a target date (mid-2013) as the end of the period during which the Fed anticipated it would keep the federal funds rate at "exceptionally low levels." The Fed subsequently moved back the end target date incrementally to mid-2015.
- On January 25, 2012, the Fed set a "longer-run goal" of 2 percent inflation.
- On December 12, 2012, the Fed changed the threshold for ending "exceptionally low levels" of the federal funds rate from "at least through mid-2015" to "at least as long as the unemployment rate remains above 6-1/2 percent," contingent on low inflation (that is, no more than 2.5 percent). This marked the first time the Fed had ever cited a specific economic, noninflation-related objective, such as employment, as the target for its interest rate actions.
- On May 22, 2013, Bernanke reaffirmed to Congress that the Fed would continue its "highly accommodative monetary policy as long as needed to support continued progress toward maximum employment and price stability."

Crisis Programs

Shortly after the initial outbreak of the financial crisis in August 2007, the Fed worked with other central banks to pump hundreds of billions of dollars into financial markets. The Fed also created a series of "crisis" programs from December 2007 through November 2009, all of which were intended, according to Bernanke, to provide "liquidity directly to borrowers and investors in key credit markets." The bigger goal was to inject liquidity into the financial system, thereby increasing confidence among lenders in the hope they would boost loans to businesses that would help jump-start the economy.

Lending under these programs peaked at $1.5 trillion in December 2008, according to the Fed. Most emergency lending facilities were allowed to expire in February 2010, by which point the total had fallen to about $200 million.

Following are summaries of the Fed's major crisis-related programs:

- Term Auction Facility, created on December 12, 2007, made short-term loans to banks at a rate set by an auction. Loans had to be collateralized by each bank turning over securities to the Fed until the loan was repaid. At its peak, the program loaned $150 million per auction. The Fed began winding down the program in September 2008 and held the final auction in March 2010. All loans were repaid in full, with interest.
- Term Securities Lending Facility, created on March 11, 2008, loaned Treasury securities to primary dealers (banks that buy and sell Treasury securities directly with the New York Fed) for one-month terms; all loans were collateralized. The Fed closed this program in February 2010.
- Primary Dealer Credit Facility, created on March 16, 2008 (in conjunction with the collapse of investment firm Bear Stearns and its purchase by JP Morgan Chase), allowed primary dealers to borrow money in exchange for collateral. The Fed closed this program in February 2010.

- Asset-Backed Commercial Paper Money Market Mutual Fund Liquidity Facility, created on September 19, 2008, provided a market for commercial paper sold by money market funds and thus enabled them to stay in business. The Fed created the program after a major money market, the Reserve Fund, was unable to pay back depositors $1 for each $1 they had in the fund (it "broke the buck" in common parlance). The Fed closed this program in February 2010.
- Money Market Investor Funding Facility, created on October 21, 2008, also provided liquidity to money market mutual funds (and later certain other funds that were similar to money market funds). The Fed closed the program in October 2009.
- Commercial Paper Funding Facility, created on October 7, 2008, enabled the Fed to provide liquidity to nonfinancial firms by accepting their commercial paper as collateral for short-term loans. The Fed closed the program in February 2010.
- Term Asset-Backed Securities Loan Facility (TALF). Created on November 25, 2008, and began operating on March 1, 2009, as a joint program of the Fed and the Treasury (using money from the TARP "bailout" program) to encourage credit availability to households and businesses. Before its lending was closed on June 30, 2010, TALF supported the origination of nearly three million auto loans, more than one million student loans, nearly 900,000 loans to small businesses, 150,000 other business loans, and millions of credit card loans, according to the Fed.

Large-Scale Asset Purchases

A third, longer-term leg of the Fed's actions to support the economy entailed an unprecedented series of what the Fed called "asset purchases": buying giant blocks of Treasury bills, mortgage-backed securities, and other financial instruments. These steps had two purposes: They pumped large amounts of money into the economy (basically the equivalent of printing money), and they helped push down interest rates, especially for mortgages and other long-term loans. These purchases also had a dramatic impact on the Fed's balance sheet, ballooning it from about $900 billion in late 2006 to more than $3 trillion early in 2013. In effect, the Fed pumped more than $2 trillion into the economy.

Almost as important as the purchases themselves was the Fed's evolving characterization of how long it would continue its unconventional policies. Over time, as it increased its purchases, the Fed broadened the time horizon for its actions while always citing the slowness of the economic recovery as a justification.

By the spring of 2013, Fed officials openly began talking about the eventual need to wind down the asset purchases, but only after the economy had improved even more. Despite the cautious nature of its comments, the very idea that the Fed someday would reduce, and eventually stop, its large-scale asset purchases rattled markets. Investors knew that day would come, but apparently had forgotten about it.

The Fed began its asset purchases on November 25, 2008, when it announced plans to purchase up to $100 billion of debt owed by government-related agencies ("agency debt") and $500 billion of mortgage-backed securities. The Fed's asset purchases became known as "Quantitative Easing (QE)," a term popular among economists to describe Fed actions that had the same impact as printing money. As time went on, three phases of quantitative easing became apparent, along with a related program called "Operation Twist."

Following is a summary of all four phases:

- **QE1.** On March 18, 2009, the Fed announced a purchase commitment that, when combined with the November 2008 announcement, totaled $300 billion in Treasury securities, $200 billion of federal agency debt, and $1.3 trillion of securities backed by mortgages guaranteed by Fannie Mae (Federal National Mortgage Association), Freddie Mac (Federal Home Loan Mortgage Corporation), and other government-related agencies.

In September 2009 the Fed said it would complete those purchases in the first quarter of 2010, which was done. The Fed then announced in November 2009 that it would purchase only $175 billion of federal agency debt because of the limited availability of those securities.

On August 10, 2010, following the completion of its purchases, the Fed said that maturing assets would be replaced with U.S. Treasury securities to prevent its balance sheet from shrinking.

- **QE2.** With economic expansion still slow, the Fed on November 3, 2010, announced it would purchase an additional $600 billion in Treasury bills at a pace of $75 billion per month; this was completed by the end of June 2011. During and after this QE2 process the Fed continued the practice of replacing maturing

(Continued)

FEDERAL RESERVE ACTIONS DURING THE FINANCIAL CRISIS AND RECESSION (Continued)

securities with Treasury security purchases; most of these had maturity lengths between thirty months and ten years.

- **Operation twist.** The Fed took no further policy actions for about six weeks after QE2 finished, then on September 21, 2011, announced the Maturity Extension Program, called "Operation Twist" after a similar program in 1961 (and which referred to a 1960s dance craze known as "the twist"). Under it, the Fed purchased $400 billion in long-term Treasury securities and sold an equal amount of short-term Treasury securities from its portfolio—thus extending the lifespan of the securities it held.

This program was designed to end by June 2012, but near that date the Fed extended the program to the end of 2012, resulting in the purchase/sale of an additional $267 billion in Treasury securities. This program had no impact on the size of the Fed balance sheet, bank reserves, or the monetary base. In their statements, Bernanke and other Fed officials suggested Operation Twist would provide additional stimulus but less than an equal amount of QE. Operation Twist lasted until December 12, 2012.

- **QE3.** Noting continuing slow economic growth, the Fed on September 13, 2012, said it would resume large-scale purchases of $40 billion of mortgage-backed securities each month. The Fed gave no end date but said its purchases would continue until labor markets improved substantially, in a "context of price stability"; in other words, the Fed was looking for reduced unemployment as well as low inflation.

As the end of Operation Twist neared, the Fed on December 12, 2012, said it would continuing buying $45 billion of long-term Treasury securities per month, the same rate as under Operation Twist. These purchases would be done by expanding the balance sheet, thus making them quantitative easing. Combined with the $40 billion in mortgage-backed securities, this made a total of $85 billion per month, with no announced end date or limit on total purchases. The Fed also said it would continue its monthly purchases at that level until job market conditions improved.

Bernanke told Congress in May 2013 that the Fed's Open Market Committee would reconsider its QE3 policy sometime in the "next few meetings." That statement led some investors to fear the policy would end sooner rather than later and caused rapid swings in the stock market.

Impact of the Fed's Actions

The Federal Reserve insisted that the unprecedented nature and scale of its actions had helped stabilize the economy and had prevented a serious recession from deteriorating into another 1930s-style Great Depression. Most economists and other experts appeared to agree with that claim, although there was less agreement about the direct impact of individual Fed programs. Some critics, however, said the Fed had endangered the economy over the long term by effectively printing money—and thus heightening the risk of rampant inflation. One or two members of the Fed's rate-setting panel, the Federal Open Market Committee, began voicing similar concerns in 2012, saying the Fed needed to begin winding down its actions slowly to avoid another bubble economy and inflation.

In one of his most detailed comments on the actions of the Fed under his watch, Bernanke in August 2012 pointed to the obvious, that the Fed's actions "have significantly lowered long-term Treasury yields." The cumulative effect of the asset purchases was to reduce rates on ten-year Treasury securities by 80 to 120 basis points (0.8 to 1.2 percent), a result Bernanke called "economically meaningful." These actions also reduced yields on corporate bonds and mortgage-backed securities, contributing to the rebound in the stock markets. He said one model, developed by Fed economists, suggested that as of 2012 the Fed's purchases may have raised output by nearly 3 percent and increased private payroll employment by more than 2 million jobs, compared to what might have happened otherwise. In effect, the Fed's actions "have provided meaningful support to the economic recovery while mitigating deflationary risks," Bernanke said.

In the three-plus years after the Fed began its quantitative easing, mortgage rates and yields on Treasury bills rapidly dropped to their lowest levels in decades. However, it took much longer for private borrowing to respond to the lower rates, generally because businesses and individuals for the most part were still in the process of "deleveraging": paying down debts they had incurred before the financial crisis began.

somewhat, which should help mitigate the economic slowdown there while also reducing the headwinds faced by the U.S. economy."

Nearly all of the developing world was growing at a much faster pace than either Europe or the United States. China led the pack, with annual growth rates of around 9

In addition, banks were still cautious about their lending and had imposed much stricter criteria on potential borrowers than at any time in the recent past. Instead of loaning out all the money they received through various Fed programs, banks parked much of it at the Fed and earned interest on what was nearly "free" money. The low rates helped some banks earn record profits in 2012, just four years after the economy nearly imploded because of their risky lending practices. A handful of critics worried that the Fed's loose-money policies might weaken the dollar unacceptably. The dollar did decline for much of 2009 and 2010 but then stabilized.

One undeniable result of the Fed's many actions was that they kept a lid on the government's borrowing costs. The Fed's net income in 2012 was a record $91 billion, $88.9 billion of which was paid to the Treasury. Because the money came from the government, in effect the Fed was allowing the government to borrow interest-free. Fears that the Fed's unconventional policies would lead to losses were proven unfounded.

Criticisms of the Fed's Actions

Some critics argued that the historically low interest rates hurt savers, including older people on fixed incomes, who depended on interest earnings, which had plummeted as a result of the Fed's actions. Conversely, these critics said the only direct beneficiaries of Fed policies were the wealthy, who were using money borrowed at low interests to engage in tactics similar to those that caused the 2007–2008 financial crisis.

In a similar line of argument, author William D. Cohan argued that exceptionally low rates encouraged what economists called "reaching for yield": looking for investments, however risky, that promised higher returns. Cohan wrote in the *Washington Post* on December 28, 2012, that "Bernanke's quantitative easing helps Wall Street's banks and traders, a dynamic that could be setting us up for another financial crisis as investors again seek out higher-yielding, lower-quality investments that Wall Street is only too happy to provide."

As time passed, an increasing number of economists and other observers worried about the Fed's exit strategy: how and when it would stop buying massive quantities of Treasury bills and mortgage-backed securities and begin selling off its gigantic portfolio of those assets. If interest rates somehow rose faster than expected, the argument was that the Fed might find itself with billions of dollars worth of securities that were rapidly losing their value. If the Fed unloaded its portfolio too quickly, the already-battered bond market could collapse. Hedge fund manager Mitch Feierstein wrote in a November 2012 Huffington Post blog that the Fed's holdings amounted to a "monetary neutron bomb" that inevitably would explode.

Even some of Bernanke's colleagues on the Open Market Committee dissented, arguing that the Fed's stimulus risked overheating the economy and driving up inflation. Jeffrey Lacker, president of the Federal Reserve Bank of Richmond, voted against Bernanke's policy all through 2012. In a September 2012 speech, he warned that "a commitment to provide stimulus beyond the point at which the recovery strengthens and growth increases implies too great a willingness to tolerate higher inflation."

Kansas City Fed President Esther George took over the dissenting role as a member of the Open Market Committee in 2013. Market turbulence in the spring of 2013 also suggested that many investors, particularly bond buyers, were becoming increasingly concerned about the Fed's exit strategy.

Although Bernanke acknowledged all these criticisms—especially the argument that low rates hurt savers—he insisted that the Fed's policies would not necessarily risk inflation or another bubble economy. Most important, he argued that the Fed's policies had helped stabilized the economy.

Bernanke insisted, in an August 2012 speech, that the alternative, of doing nothing, posed the danger that the recession "would have been deeper and the current recovery would have been slower than has actually occurred." Bernanke expanded that defense in testimony to the Senate Banking Committee in February 2013: "We do not see the potential costs of the increased risk-taking in some financial markets as outweighing the benefits of promoting a stronger economic recovery and more-rapid job creation." The Fed also was monitoring the nation's investment climate to head off the danger that investors would take undue risks in the search for higher yields, he said.

percent all during the postcrisis period—but this record still fell short of the double-digit growth China had experienced for much of the 2000s. China's expansion slowed further in 2012 and showed signs of continued relative sluggishness in 2013. Most other developing countries in Asia, Africa, and Latin America experienced growth rates of 5 percent or better throughout the period, although some of the biggest "emerging markets"—notably Argentina and Brazil—were struggling to stay in positive territory as of early 2013. The one major exception to the growth trend was the nonoil-producing Arab Middle East, caught in continuing stagnation that was worsened by the turmoil resulting from the so-called Arab Spring.

The one common thread, especially in the industrialized countries, was that governments remained uncertain about how to prevent another financial crisis, or, at best, they took tentative actions hedged with compromises. As the Brookings Institution–*Financial Times* Global Economic Recovery tracking index described it in an April 2013 report: "Politicians around the world continue to avoid tough structural reforms, instead relying on central banks to continue propping up growth. Policy and political uncertainty remain sources of drag that could prevent the world economy from attaining liftoff, raising the risk of a crash."

Federal Reserve Actions

The most consistent—and possibly the most effective—action by the federal government to stimulate the economy came from neither the White House nor Capitol Hill, but from inside an austere-looking marble building on Constitution Avenue in Washington, D.C. There, the Federal Reserve Bank (Fed) issued a stream of orders from late 2007 well into 2013 that had the effect of driving down interest rates and making available hundreds of billions of dollars for banks to lend and businesses to spend.

Fed Chair Ben S. Bernanke said that there was "limited historical experience" of this type of economic and financial crisis to guide the Fed. As a result, Bernanke said he and his colleagues "have been in the process of learning by doing." The doing had three major elements:

- Driving down interest rates (long the Fed's main tool to heat up, or cool off, the economy) to historically low levels, as a way encouraging lending and renewed consumer spending, especially in the near-dormant housing market;
- Several programs, all with nearly indecipherable names, that loaned money under various conditions to banks and other financial firms to keep them afloat and to encourage them to lend to businesses and individuals;
- Buying a large chunk of the government's debt, along with bundles of securities backed by federally insured mortgages, which also kept interest rates low and was intended to stimulate spending on business investment, housing, and consumer durables such as automobiles. By February 2013, the Fed's purchases had more than tripled the size of its balance sheet to $3.1 trillion.

Some of the Fed's most important steps were taken in coordination with other central banks. One of the most important was a dramatic cut, from 2 percent to 1 percent, in the key interest rate controlled by the Fed, on October 8, 2008; five other central banks took comparable action on the same day.

Bernanke said in August 2012 that the combined effect of the bank's actions had "provided meaningful support to the economic recovery while mitigating deflationary risks." Most economists shared that assessment, although an increasingly vocal minority insisted that the Fed had heightened the potential risk of inflation while providing only marginal stimulus to the economy. By mid-2013, everyone was wondering how long the Fed would continue its extraordinary monetary policies; nervous investors repeatedly roiled the stock markets when they thought they saw hints the Fed might be preparing to withdraw the punch bowl from the party. *(Details of the Fed's actions, box, pp. 56–59)*

Troubled Asset Relief Program (TARP)

An emergency effort by the Bush administration in the fall of 2008 to blunt the impact of the financial crisis continued to have aftereffects throughout President Barack Obama's first term in office—many of them positive but some with serious political consequences. That effort was the Emergency Economic Stabilization Act of 2008 (PL 110-343), which created a program officially known as the Troubled Asset Relief Program (TARP) but more widely known as the "bailout" of Wall Street.

The bill approved a maximum of $700 billion in federal funding to keep U.S. banks and other financial entities from failing, although that total amount was never spent. Even though TARP unquestionably succeeded in its goal of stabilizing the financial system at a perilous moment, it never succeeded in shaking the stigma of having bailed out Wall Street banks that had helped cause a recession. *(Details, p. 62)*

When it proposed TARP to Congress in September 2008, days after the collapse of the big investment firm Lehman Brothers, the Bush administration said the money would be used to buy so-called "toxic assets" (mostly mortgage-backed securities that had plummeted in value) from banks so they could clean up their balance sheets and resume their normal financial activities. But after Congress approved TARP, the administration decided a more practical solution was to invest directly in troubled banks—in essence injecting capital to make them more stable. The Bush, and later Obama, administrations eventually used TARP funds to bolster more than 700 banks around the country, although most of the money went to the big Wall Street banks at the heart of the financial crisis.

In addition, President Bush used TARP money to rescue the giant insurance company American Insurance Group (AIG), which faced collapse because it had guaranteed trillions of dollars worth of "credit default swaps" that were in danger of being called. Weeks before leaving office, Bush also extended short-term loans to General Motors and Chrysler, and their financing arms, when they faced the real possibility of shutting down. President Obama expanded those loans to a total of $80 billion, effectively rescuing the companies and enabling them to stay in business and, eventually, repay the government in full.

The Bush and Obama administrations also used TARP money for programs to help homeowners facing default on the mortgages and for several programs to revive the credit markets for auto loans, credit card debt, and small business loans. The government got back its $19 billion investments, with profits, from the credit market programs but, as expected, received no direct payback from the mortgage subsidies and other housing programs, which provided much less relief than originally anticipated.

TARP quickly became one of the most unpopular government programs of all time—based almost entirely on incorrect public perceptions that nearly all of the money had gone to bail out Wall Street banks and would never be recovered. Public anger at the program helped fuel anti-government sentiment at the heart of the "Tea Party" movement that brought Republicans to power in the House of Representatives in 2010. Within a couple years, however, public opinion polls showed strengthening support for some aspects of TARP, especially its rescue of the auto industry.

Obama's Stimulus

Congress in February 2009 passed an economic stimulus bill (PL 111-5), urged by President Obama, with an estimated total price tag of $787.2 billion. Of that amount, $575.3 billion was for new spending over eleven years and $211.8 billion was for tax cuts for individuals and businesses, over the same time period. President Barack Obama signed the legislation (American Recovery and Reinvestment Act of 2009) into law on February 17, 2009. *(Stimulus legislative action, p. 78)*

The stimulus was the result of political compromises that inevitably reduced its potential impact on the economy. Some of the president's economic advisors originally had advocated a much larger stimulus, in the neighborhood of $1.2 trillion, but the amount was sharply reduced because of Republican opposition in the Senate. In a generally unsuccessful attempt to lure Republican votes, Democrats and the administration also loaded the bill with tax cuts, some of which likely would have passed Congress separately anyway, notably a one-year provision to spare middle-income taxpayers from the alternative minimum tax, at a cost of nearly $70 billion.

News media accounts generally characterized the stimulus as a massive spending program intended to pump money into what the administration called "shovel-ready" projects such as highways, roads, and bridges. In fact, only $45.2 billion of the total was earmarked for transportation projects; most of the rest of the direct spending was for a grab-bag of priorities, such as $20 billion for the Supplemental Nutrition Assistance Program (SNAP, also known as food stamps), $10 billion for biomedical research, $15.6 billion to increase the amount of Pell grants to college students, and $29.2 billion for various other education programs. One of the few items directly related to the economy was a $39.2 billion earmark to extend, through the end of 2009, the additional thirty-three weeks of extra unemployment benefits for jobless workers who had exhausted their initial twenty-six weeks of payments.

In lobbying for the stimulus, the Obama administration claimed it would create or save some 3.5 million jobs—a figure based on standard economic modeling derived from the amounts of money in the law, but one that Republicans criticized as overly optimistic.

In an August 2011 report, the Congressional Budget Office (CBO) cited a range of estimates of the employment impact of the stimulus; during the peak year of 2010, the report estimated that 1.8 million to 5.2 million jobs could be attributed to the stimulus, the range depending on various assumptions. These estimates were based in part on reports from agencies and companies that received money from the stimulus.

The CBO also estimated that in the second quarter of 2011, the stimulus lowered the unemployment rate by a range of 0.5 to 1.6 percentage points below what it would have been otherwise. Reporting to Congress in February 2013, the president's Council of Economic Advisors used a slightly different calculation, saying the stimulus had enabled the economy to create or save six million "employment years"—the equivalent of six million people having a job for one year.

The president's 2013 economic report to Congress also said the stimulus had played "a significant role in the turnaround of the economy" in the previous two years. The report estimated that the stimulus was responsible for increasing the gross domestic product (GDP) by an average of more than 2 percent in each quarter through early 2011, with the impact tailing off thereafter because the stimulus was intended to be temporary. The earlier CBO report estimated that the stimulus had boosted the GDP by 0.8 to 2.5 percent in the second quarter of 2011. In terms of increasing economic output, the CBO said, the most successful parts of the stimulus were the spending components; tax cuts, especially those for high-income earners, had less impact.

Congressional Republicans who had opposed the stimulus argued that it was a failure and had succeeded only in increasing the government's budget deficit. They based their argument on the fact that the economy did not turn around nearly as quickly as Obama's advisors had predicted would happen once the stimulus was in place. In particular, Republicans cited the fact that unemployment did not decline to 7 percent in 2010, as the White House had projected would happen.

TROUBLED ASSET RELIEF PROGRAM: WHAT DID TARP DO?

The federal government's most visible, and controversial, response to the financial crisis was a program pushed through a reluctant Congress in September and October 2008 by President George W. Bush. Officially it was called the Troubled Asset Relief Program (TARP) but was almost universally known, and widely scorned, as "the bailout" of Wall Street banks and other firms. *(TARP legislation, Congress and the Nation Vol. XII, p. 154)*

The TARP legislation (the Emergency Economic Stabilization Act of 2008, PL 110-343) authorized up to $700 billion, a figure that stuck in the public's memory but that was never spent in full. The $700 billion total later was reduced to $475 by the Dodd-Frank banking reform act (PL 111-203). *(Dodd-Frank legislation, p. 88)*

The Bush administration initially sold TARP to Congress as a way of buying failed mortgage bonds and other so-called "toxic assets" from troubled banks, which could then clean up their balance sheets and resume normal lending activities. Over time, however, the administrations of both Bush and his successor, Barack Obama, used the TARP funds to take huge financial stakes in (and in some cases even gain control of) banks, insurance companies, and eventually automobile manufacturers—all with the goal of keeping those businesses afloat and preventing further damage to the economy.

By late 2012 and early 2013, the government had sold back the vast majority of shares it had bought with TARP funds, in most cases at substantial profits. According to a March 2013 report by the Treasury Department, the government spent a total of $418 billion of TARP funds and gained back all but $55.5 billion.

Moreover, the Congressional Budget Office estimated in October 2012 that the actual net cost to the government of all TARP programs was only $24 billion—far below the $700 billion "bailout" figure widely reported by the news media. Most of that $24 billion was used to help homeowners avoid foreclosure on failed mortgages and was never intended to be returned, a Treasury report added.

The Treasury Department, which administered TARP, insisted that "by any reasonable standard, TARP worked: it helped stop widespread financial panic, it helped prevent what could have been a devastating collapse of our financial system, and it helped many struggling homeowners keep their homes."

The TARP legislation also created the bipartisan Congressional Oversight Panel to monitor the Treasury Department's administration of the program. Although it was critical of some Treasury actions, this panel nevertheless said in its final report in March 2011 that, while TARP did not deserve full credit for averting another Great Depression, it "restored a measure of calm and stability" at a "moment of profound uncertainty." TARP did this, the panel said, "in part by providing capital to banks but, more significantly, by demonstrating that the United States would take any action necessary to prevent the collapse of its financial system."

That was not the popular perception of TARP, however. Politicians and other critics on the right decried TARP as a "taxpayer bailout" that got the government too deeply involved in the workings of private enterprise. Critics on the left worried that the government failed to use the leverage of TARP's money to hold Wall Street banks accountable for their risky dealings that endangered the economy. Critics across the ideological spectrum worried about the "moral hazard" of bailing out irresponsible businesses, such as banks or auto companies, which could then reasonably expect to be bailed out the next time.

Public views about specific aspects of TARP varied over time and depended on whose bailout was at issue. Throughout 2009 and 2010, most opinion polls showed strong negative views toward all of TARP's bailouts, even of the auto industry, the one bailout that undeniably saved many jobs. In a survey conducted for Bloomberg news service in October 2010, 60 percent of respondents said most of the TARP money invested in banks would never be recovered, even though government reports at the time indicated the investments would be profitable. Another survey in 2010 showed that only about one-third of Americans remembered that President Bush had pushed the bailout bill through Congress, rather than President Obama.

By early 2012, public opinion had shifted somewhat, according to a survey by the Pew Research Center for the People & the Press. A survey in February 2012 showed that a solid majority (56 percent) believed bailing out the auto industry was "mostly good for the economy"—an exact reversal of findings in October 2009. By contrast, a slight majority (52 percent) continued to believe in 2012 that the government's investments in banks and financial institutions in 2008 were "the wrong thing" even though those investments actually made money in addition to stabilizing the financial system.

Bank Bailouts

The original intended purpose of TARP was to save the nation's banking system, and by all accounts it succeeded in doing that, even though hundreds of financial institutions—some large ones but most of them smaller community institutions—were allowed to fail. The government spent $245 billion in five different programs to rescue banks, generally by injecting capital that allowed them to absorb losses and continue in business.

The largest of the bank-saving efforts was the Capital Purchase Program, which ultimately invested $205 billion in 707 banks, most of them small community banks. Of that amount, $125 billion went to the nation's eight largest banks, which held more than one-half of the nation's bank assets in 2008, and the rest to smaller banks. In return for the money, the government received preferred stock or debt securities.

Treasury said the largest single investments were $25 billion (in Citigroup and Bank of America, each) and the smallest was $301,000. As of the end of 2012, the government still had about $7 billion invested in 212 banks and had received $220 billion in income under the program, including repayments, interest, and fees, thus yielding a net profit of more than $20 billion. About $3 billion had been written off as losses.

Two other rescue programs were aimed at the big banks considered "too big to fail" because their collapse would have caused widespread damage to the country's and the world's financial system. In the end, only two major banking companies, Citigroup and Bank of America, received funds.

Under the Targeted Investment Program, Treasury purchased $20 billion in preferred stock from Bank of America and $20 billion from Citigroup (in each case these amounts were in addition to $25 billion under the Capital Purchase Program). The two banks bought the stock back in December 2009, at a combined profit for the government of $4.5 billion.

Under the related Asset Guarantee program, the Treasury, the Federal Reserve, and Federal Deposit Insurance Corporation (FDIC) agreed to share potential losses on a $301 billion pool of Citigroup's assets. As a premium, Treasury and the FDIC received $7.1 billion in preferred stock. The arrangement was terminated in December 2009, without the government having to make guarantee payments or spend any funds. The government kept $5.3 billion of the $7.1 billion in preferred stock, which had been converted into trust preferred securities. The program was closed with a $3 billion profit for the government. Overall, the government made a profit of about $12 billion on its various support programs for Citigroup.

Bank of America originally was also intended for support under the Asset Guarantee Program but withdrew before the government invested funds. Even so, the government earned a $425 million fee because the bank's value increased after the aid was announced.

Yet another related TARP program, the Community Development Capital Initiative, focused on helping financial institutions that served low-income communities and small businesses. This program spent a total of $570 million, with a projected loss of about $110 million as of late 2012.

AIG Insurance

Acting together, the Treasury and the Federal Reserve bought a total of $182.3 billion worth of shares (representing more than 90 percent of the company's stock) in the troubled insurance giant AIG; the Federal Reserve share was $112.5 billion and Treasury's was $69.8 billion. AIG, which had been the world's largest insurance company, faced collapse in late 2008 because it had guaranteed trillions of dollars worth of mortgage-based credit default swaps, which basically were insurance policies against securities going bad. When the housing market collapsed, AIG's customers demanded billions of dollars in payments on those guarantees, money that AIG did not have. Government officials feared that allowing the collapse of AIG would have further endangered credit markets already reeling from the earlier failure of Lehman Brothers, a Wall Street firm.

Once it was rescued, AIG sold off nearly one-half of its business and emerged as a much smaller company selling insurance, rather than the riskier financial products that had gotten it into trouble. By December 2012 the Treasury and the Federal Reserve had recouped in full the $182.3 billion investment and realized a cumulative profit of $22.7 billion (most of it from the Fed's larger investment, which went to the Treasury). AIG in March 2013 bought back the last $25 million worth of warrants (options to buy shares) held by the government, thus clearing the government of any direct financial interest in the company.

The Congressional Oversight Panel that monitored TARP, in its final report in March 2011, cast doubt on the Bush administration's assertion in late 2008 that it had no choice but to rescue AIG with cash bailouts after two banks (JP Morgan Chase and Goldman Sachs) refused to step in. Even considering that a crisis was afoot, the government could have sought out other potential rescuers, the panel said, or at least forced AIG's creditors and to accept payments of less than 100 cents on the dollar.

"The AIG rescue illustrated the tangled nature of relationships on Wall Street," the panel said. "Everyone involved in AIG's rescue had the mindset of either a banker or a banking regulator. The discussions did not include other voices that might have brought different ideas and a broader view of the national interest. It is unsurprising, then, that the American public remains convinced that the rescue was designed by Wall Street to help fellow Wall Streeters, with less emphasis given to protecting the public trust."

Auto Industry

Along with the bank bailouts, probably the best-known use of TARP funds was to prevent General Motors and Chrysler, two of the country's three biggest auto manufacturers, from going out of business. Both GM and Chrysler faced serious long-term problems, stemming in large part from bad business decisions as well as "legacy" costs such as unfunded pension obligations. By late 2008 both were running large losses and struggling to obtain credit just to keep operating.

GM and Chrysler went into bankruptcy in 2009, but some $80 billion in government investments through TARP helped them restructure their businesses and emerge again as viable companies. The Obama administration said the government aid had helped save about one million jobs in the auto industry and made it possible for GM, Chrysler, and their suppliers to add another 290,000 new jobs. Ford, the other big U.S. automaker, was in much better shape and did not need or request direct government assistance.

The first government aid came under President Bush, who in December 2008 used TARP funds to extend $13.4 billion in short-term loans to GM and $4 billion to Chrysler but hesitated to extend deeper, long-term involvement since he was about to leave office. The Bush administration also loaned $5 billion to General Motors Acceptance Corp., GM's lending agency, and $1.5 billion to Chrysler's loan arm, Chrysler Financial.

President Obama in March 2009 offered additional help on the condition that the companies develop plans for long-term success. The government invested a total of $50 billion, from TARP funds, in GM through early 2009, gaining control of more than 60 percent of the company's stock. GM went through a one-month "managed" bankruptcy in mid-2009, emerging as a much smaller company. Unions gave up jobs, original shareholders lost much of their investments, and dozens of dealerships were closed.

(Continued)

TROUBLED ASSET RELIEF PROGRAM: WHAT DID TARP DO? (Continued)

By the end of 2012 Treasury had sold about two-thirds of its shares in GM, and it announced plans to sell all remaining GM shares, subject to market conditions, within the following twelve to fifteen months. Two days later, GM repurchased 200 million shares of common stock for $5.5 billion.

The government invested $12.4 billion in Chrysler, which also underwent a bankruptcy process in mid-2009. The government in 2011 sold its 9.9 percent stake in the company to the Italian automaker Fiat for $11.1 billion, incurring a $1.3 billion loss; this was one of the few losses in the "bailout" portions of TARP.

In a program not directly related to the GM bailout, the government also invested $17.2 billion to buy about 75 percent of the shares in Ally Financial, the successor to the former General Motors Acceptance Corp. Ally then became a main source of financing for Chrysler dealers. The Treasury had recovered $5.8 billion of its investment in Ally as of late 2012 and planned to recoup the balance after Ally's mortgage arm went through bankruptcy and its international auto finance operations had been sold.

In total, government support under TARP for the three firms was $79.6 billion, of which $48 billion had been recovered as of early 2013.

The government provided another $413 million in loans to auto suppliers who had been caught short by the financial difficulties of GM and Chrysler. Congress and the Obama administration in 2009 also established a program (known as "Cash for Clunkers") that gave rebates to people who traded in their old cars for newer, more efficient models. This program boosted car sales for a few months, at a cost of $2.9 billion. *(Cash for clunkers, p. 321)*

Housing Programs

Shortly after taking office, President Obama launched several programs, using TARP funds, to help homeowners who were facing foreclosure because their homes had lost value during the financial crisis. Millions of homeowners had suddenly found that their homes were worth less than the balances on their mortgages; these homeowners were said to be "under water," and banks foreclosed on many of them. By the end of 2012, banks and other mortgage-holders had filed foreclosures against nearly thirteen million homeowners, according to RealtyTrac; at least one-fourth of the foreclosures took place before Obama's mortgage-rescue efforts got under way.

The government allocated $45.6 billion in TARP funds for these housing programs, but as of mid-2013 had spent less than one-fourth of that total. Unlike the bailouts of banks, AIG, and the auto industry, the government did not expect to get any of this money back.

The most important of the government's programs was the Home Affordable Modification Program, which paid mortgage services to modify first-lien mortgages so homeowners would have lower monthly payments. The Treasury in April 2013 said that more than 1.1 million homeowners had received permanent mortgage modifications under the program, typically saving them more than $500 per month. During almost four years, the program had saved homeowners an estimated $19 billion in mortgage payments, Treasury said. More than 100,000 of these homeowners also got modifications of second liens under a related program.

Another program, called Principal Reduction Alternative, gave incentives for companies servicing nongovernment guaranteed loans to reduce the principal on mortgages valued at 115 percent or more of current home values. This program benefited more than 100,000 homeowners through 2012.

The Obama administration in 2010 introduced a related program, the Hardest Hit Fund, that provided up to $7.6 billion to eighteen states, plus the District of Columbia, that were most affected by the collapse of the housing market. The money went to each state's housing agency and was targeted to helping unemployed homeowners pay their mortgages while they looked for work. Less than one-fourth of the money allocated to this program had been spent as of early 2013.

Although these programs helped a combined total of some 1.5 million homeowners avoid foreclosure, according to Treasury figures, that total was only a fraction of the number of homeowners nationwide who were in serious trouble, and well below the three to four million homeowners Treasury initially had hoped to help. A separate program run by the Federal Housing Authority, not funded by TARP, had modified 1.7 million mortgages through early 2013.

The government's programs also reached fewer homeowners than did a voluntary program of the mortgage industry called Hope Now. That program resulted in nearly 5 million mortgage modifications from 2007 through 2012, according to a statement by the program. However, Hope Now provided few details about the conditions for these modifications or how much homeowners saved. *(2009–2012 housing legislation, p. 497)*

Credit Market Programs

One of the least publicized aspects of TARP was a series of programs intended to restart credit markets that finance auto loans, credit card debt, mortgages, and small business loans. The Treasury pumped $19 billion into these markets in late 2008. Nearly all of the investments had been concluded as of early 2013 and earned the government small profits. The programs were the following:

- **Public-Private Investment Program.** This program was intended to support the private mortgage market—the parts not guaranteed by government-related agencies. The government used $18.6 billion in TARP money to invest in nine funds, managed by private companies, that bought securities consisting of residential and commercial mortgages from banks, insurance companies, and other institutions. This was the one TARP program that came close to fulfilling the original intended purpose of TARP: to buy "toxic assets" from banks so they could start lending again. By early 2013 the government had received back all of its investment, plus $331 million in profits.
- **Small Business Administration 7(a) Securities Purchase Program.** This program, an Obama administration initiative in 2010, used $368 million in TARP funds to buy the guaranteed portion of more than 1,000 Small Business Administration (SBA) loans to small businesses. The purpose was to inject liquidity into a market that had stagnated during the recession, and thus make it easier for

small businesses to get new loans. The program ended in January 2012, having earned a profit of $8 million.

- **Term Asset-Backed Securities Loan Facility (TALF).** Jointly administered by the Federal Reserve and the Treasury, this program lent money to investors willing to buy pools of securities backed by a variety of nonmortgage loans. Nearly all the money came from the Fed, with Treasury using TARP funds only to help cover losses. The Treasury said the program enabled "nearly 3 million auto loans, more than 1 million student loans, nearly 900,000 small business loans, 150,000 other types of business loans, and millions of credit card loans." The Treasury originally committed $20 billion to protect against potential losses, but that amount was reduced in stages to $1.4 billion. Lending under the program was closed in 2010. As of early 2013, TALF had earned the government about $700 million.

Executive Compensation

After Congress passed the TARP law in 2008, news reports revealed that several banks receiving federal bailouts were continuing to pay large bonuses to top executives—the same executives whose excessive risk-taking had gotten the banks into trouble. Angry members of Congress, mostly Democrats, demanded action, and got it as part of President Obama's economic stimulus legislation in February 2009. The stimulus imposed what were intended to be restrictions on executive compensation at all banks and other firms receiving TARP bailouts, including: a ban on so-called "golden parachutes" for departing executives, a limit on bonuses to one-third of total compensation, adoption of "clawback" provisions to force bankers to give back bonuses based on "materially inaccurate performance criteria," and creation of compensation committees composed entirely of independent, nonexecutive directors. To avoid these restrictions, some banks paid back their bailout funds early.

Follow-up regulations gave the government extra supervision over pay practices at seven companies bailed out by TARP: AIG, Bank of America, Chrysler, Chrysler Financial, Citigroup, General Motors, and GMAC/Ally Financial. Executive salaries at these firms was regulated by an Office of Special Master at the Treasury Department. The office was headed during 2009 and 2010 by lawyer Richard Feinberg, famed as the administrator of several compensation funds, such as those compensating victims of the September 2001 terrorist attacks and of the 2010 BP oil spill in the Gulf of Mexico. Feinberg and his successor Pat Geoghegan established several guidelines cutting compensation and executive perks at the seven companies and generally limiting pay to the levels at similar companies.

Testifying to a House subcommittee in February 2013, Geoghegan said she and Feinberg had cut total pay for the top twenty-five executives at the seven firms by more than 50 percent and restructured pay packages for those executives so that most of the pay was in the form of stocks "so that executives are not just focused on short-term results and are not encouraged to take excessive risks."

The Congressional Oversight Panel praised the standards that Feinberg had put in place but criticized his office's "lack of transparency." The panel also complained that Feinberg had failed to force executives to give back $1.7 billion in compensation that he had found to be "inappropriate" but not "contrary to the public interest."

Criticism

Very few critics, of whatever ideological persuasion, argued that the government should have done nothing in late 2008 and early 2009 when the financial system seemed to teeter on the verge of collapse. However, there appeared to be little consensus about whether TARP, as originally conceived and eventually administered, was the right approach.

Critics took numerous lines of attack against the various TARP programs, generally depending on each critic's ideological inclinations. Some conservatives argued that the government had no business intervening in private markets—even if the goal was to save the economy—and in any event should not have used tax dollars to take controlling shares of the companies being rescued. This line of criticism was reflected in numerous bills filed by Republicans seeking to scale back TARP's programs or dispense with TARP altogether. The new Republican majority in the House following the 2010 elections passed two bills (HR 830 and HR 839) early in 2011 to end two of TARP's main mortgage-relief programs. Neither bill was acted on by the Senate.

Some liberals insisted that the goals of TARP might have been sound but that both the Bush and Obama administrations failed to impose enough conditions on the rescued companies. Critics said, for example, that the government should have demanded that banks resume lending and accept stricter government oversight; some also insisted the government should have forced banks and other companies to oust top executives responsible for risky decisions that got their businesses into trouble. In effect, critics such as economist Joseph Stiglitz said the government created "moral hazard" by rewarding, rather than punishing, bankers and others who had acted in ways that caused severe damage to the economy.

This line of criticism came not just from politicians and academics but from one of the men who knew most about how TARP operated: Neil Barofsky, the special inspector general who monitored TARP during its first two years of operation. Barofksy, a former prosecuting attorney, was highly critical of how both the Bush and Obama administrations managed TARP.

After resigning early in 2011, he wrote a book, the subtitle of which pretty much summed up his views: *Bailout: An Inside Account of How Washington Abandoned Main Street While Rescuing Wall Street.* In a July 2012 interview on the *Rachel Maddow Show* on the cable channel MSNBC, Barofsky said that both the Bush and Obama administrations "consistently chose the interests of Wall Street banks over that of homeowners, over that of the broader economy." Barofsky said TARP money would have been better spent on a program of breaking up the "too large to fail" big banks, returning the financial system to the days when banks took in deposits and made loans and did not engage in risky, complex financial transactions. He also said banks and other recipients of TARP funds were never forced to explain how they used taxpayer money.

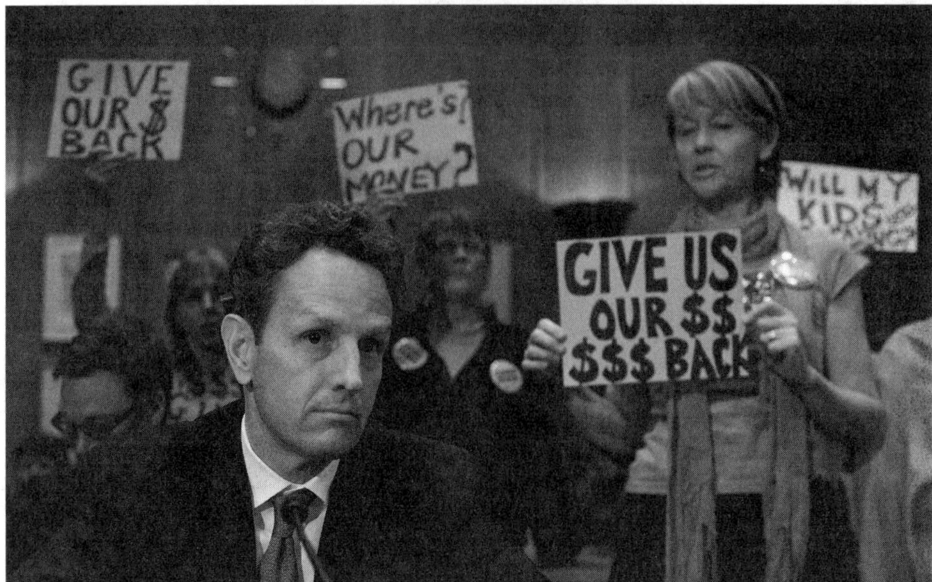

Demonstrators from the group Code Pink hold signs as Treasury Secretary Timothy Geithner testifies at a hearing of the Congressional Oversight Panel for the Troubled Asset Relief Program (TARP), in Washington, D.C., on April 21, 2009.
Source: Photo by Joshua Roberts/ Bloomberg via Getty Images

Administration officials later acknowledged that some of their projections about the impact of the stimulus had been overly optimistic, largely because the economy was in even worse shape in late 2008 and early 2009 than was understood at the time.

Although most economists argued in 2010 and 2011 that another dose of fiscal stimulus was warranted, the heated political debate over the first stimulus contributed to the poisoned atmosphere in Washington and ensured that Congress would not pass a second measure labeled as "stimulus." Given that reality, Obama did not push for a similar follow-up program, even though the economy continued to lag into 2012. In the years after 2009, the heavy lifting on the stimulus front was carried by the Federal Reserve, which pumped more than $2 trillion into the economy and kept interest rates artificially low.

2010 Tax Cuts

With the political environment precluding additional stimulus programs based on spending, tax cuts became the one option for politicians who wanted to be seen as doing something for the economy. After the midterm elections brought antitax Republicans to power in the House, a lame duck Congress in December 2010 passed and President Obama signed a grab-bag of programs under the title of the "Tax Relief, Unemployment Insurance Reauthorization, and Job Creation Act of 2010" (PL 111-312). *(Legislative action, p. 144)*

The law extended for two years the series of tax cuts from the Bush administration (all of which had been scheduled to expire at the end of 2010); extended unemployment benefits for an additional thirteen months; and allowed for a more rapid tax deduction (called "expensing") of business expenses during 2011.

"Fiscal Cliff" and Budget Cuts

By late 2012, many analysts insisted that the impact of budget cuts (at all levels of government, from localities through states and the federal government) was hampering the economic recovery and at least partially offsetting the Federal Reserve quantitative easing and other stimulus programs. Data from the White House indicated that governments had laid off some 800,000 workers in the previous three years—about one-fourth as many jobs as the private sector had created.

Concerns about the economic impact of government spending cuts grew dramatically as the nation neared what Federal Reserve Chair Ben S. Bernanke had dubbed the "fiscal cliff": the January 1, 2013, convergence of broad tax increases and across-the-board spending cuts. Some $500 billion in increased income and other taxes were scheduled to take effect with the expiration of the so-called Bush tax cuts approved in 2001 and 2003 during the presidency of George W. Bush. In addition, Congress and President Obama in 2011 had agreed to impose $109 billion in automatic, across-the-board spending cuts, known as a sequester, at the beginning of 2013 unless they had reached some other agreement to cut the budget deficit. The point of these two deadlines was to force a political compromise, because in recent years politicians in Washington seemed able to accomplish something only when they faced a deadline. Bernanke and other economists warned, however, that failure to avert a combination of big tax increases and government spending cuts could strangle the fragile economic recovery and might even force the nation back into a sustained recession.

Having just won reelection, President Obama seemed to have the upper hand as the lame duck Congress began grappling with its responsibilities. Obama agreed to allow a continuation of the Bush tax cuts for middle-income taxpayers but insisted that the "wealthy" should pay more, to help bring down the deficit and protect safety net programs for the poor. Republicans demanded continuation of all the tax cuts, plus major budget cuts.

After weeks of wrangling, Obama essentially came out ahead on a deal reached at the very last minute, on New Year's Day 2013. An agreement approved first by the Senate and then rammed through a reluctant Republican-controlled House extended the Bush tax cuts for individuals with incomes below $400,000 and for households below $450,000. Rates would rise to the pre-2001 level for incomes above those amounts. The agreement also postponed the sequester cuts for two months (and reduced the total amount of cuts by $24 billion), giving the new Congress time to look for an alternative. The deal also allowed a temporary, 2 percentage point cut in Social Security taxes to expire. President Obama signed the American Taxpayer Relief Act (PL 112-240) into law on January 2, just avoiding the fiscal cliff. *(Legislative action p. 144)*

Smarting from their perceived defeat on the tax hikes for the wealthy, Republicans vowed not to do another deal with Obama unless he accepted budget cuts larger than what would take place when the sequester went into effect. Thus deadlocked, the two sides never really tried to reach agreement during the first two months of 2013, and the sequester cuts took effect on March 1, 2013. Under the cuts, $85 billion in budget cuts for the remaining seven months of fiscal 2013 were to be shared equally between the Defense Department and all other branches of government (except for debt service, Social Security payments, and a list of other government obligations). Unless Congress acted to avert or modify cuts for fiscal 2014 and later years, a similar level of sequester cuts would take place for fiscal 2014 and subsequent years.

The stated justification for the sequester cuts was to reduce the size of the budget deficit, but other events, including improvements in the economy—however sluggish—appeared to be accomplishing that task at a much faster rate. The Congressional Budget Office (CBO) in May 2013 projected that the 2103 fiscal year deficit would be $642 billion, still a huge amount but the smallest deficit since fiscal 2008 and $200 billion less than the CBO had projected just three months earlier. Just over half the difference came from increased revenues from individual and corporate taxes (some of it because of economic improvements). Another $97 million came from increased payments to the Treasury from the government-sponsored mortgage guarantee agencies: the Federal National Mortgage Association (Fannie Mae) and the Federal Home Loan Mortgage Corporation (Freddie Mac).

FANNIE MAE AND FREDDIE MAC

Many Republicans in Congress, backed by some economic experts and journalistic commentators, said that two of the institutions most responsible for the financial crisis were Fannie Mae and Freddie Mac, the quasi-federal agencies that provided most of the financing for the housing market. Both had engaged in some of the riskiest mortgage-bundling activities that helped undermine the entire financial system; however, the extent of their responsibility for imperiling the global financial system was subject to dispute.

The two agencies bought vast quantities of mortgages from banks and other lenders, then bundled them into securities, which in turn were bought by investors—with a promise that Fannie Mae and Freddie Mac would guarantee the securities if the underlying mortgages failed. Fannie Mae and Freddie Mac tried to cover their potential losses by charging fees to the original lenders.

Fannie Mae and Freddie Mac had started their lives as government entities but were later were turned into semipublic, semiprivate agencies called "government-sponsored enterprises." Although they long had made large profits by selling mortgage securities to investors, both agencies started regularly losing large sums of money in the last half of 2007, as the housing market plummeted. By the height of the financial crisis in late 2008, they were in deep trouble, uncertain whether they could meet their obligations on $1.2 trillion worth of bonds and $3.7 trillion worth of mortgage-backed securities they had guaranteed.

The Bush administration essentially returned Fannie Mae and Freddie Mac to government control on September 7, 2008—one week before the fateful collapse of Lehman Brothers set off the worst stage of the financial crisis. The government acted under the terms of the Housing and Economic Recovery Act (PL 110-289), passed weeks earlier. That law created a new regulator, the Federal Housing Finance Agency (FHFA), for Fannie Mae and Freddie Mac (both of which previously had reported to the Office of Federal Housing Enterprise Oversight), and for the Federal Home Loan Banks, which had been regulated by the Federal Housing Finance Board. The law gave the new FHFA oversight powers that were similar to those exercised by the agencies regulating commercial banks. *(Details, Congress and the Nation Vol. XII, p. 629)*

The FHFA put both Fannie Mae and Freddie Mac under conservatorship but allowed them to continue operating; they remained in that state as of the end of 2013. The Bush administration initially set a $100 billion limit on how much money the government would use to bail out the agencies. That amount turned out to be insufficient, and by March 2009 the government had pumped $187.5 billion into Fannie Mae and Freddie Mac, nearly two-thirds of it into the larger Fannie Mae. This money came from funds authorized by the Housing and Economic Recovery Act and was separate from the bank bailouts under TARP.

By 2012, according to a December 2012 report by the online investigative news service ProPublica, the government had "almost completely taken over" the country's home mortgage market. While banks and other institutions continued to issue mortgages, the vast majority of those loans needed to be guaranteed by someone, and that someone increasingly was the government. ProPublica reported that Fannie Mae and Freddie Mac guaranteed 69 percent of all new mortgages issued in the first nine months of 2012. Two other agencies, the Government National Mortgage Association (or Ginnie Mae, part of the Department of Housing and Urban Development) and the Department of Veterans Affairs guaranteed another 21 percent, meaning that government-sponsored agencies backed 90 percent of all new mortgages—more than triple the percentage when the housing boom began to fade in 2006.

The ProPublica report also noted that Congress had treated Fannie Mae and Freddie Mac "as a private kitty, raiding them for cash." In 2010, Congress used fees from the two agencies to fund part of a temporary cut in the Social Security payroll tax.

Regulatory Reforms

One apparent lesson from the financial crisis was that the government's regulation of the banking industry had been lax—or, at the very least, ineffective. Some critics said the failure of government oversight had been a main, possibly even the most important, reason that banks had engaged in risky lending. Others insisted that faulty government regulation was only partly to blame and that banks simply took advantage of lending (and profit) opportunities that later went bad.

Even as that debate raged, by the time President Obama took office there was a wide consensus that U.S. banking regulations needed revision; the question was how to do it. Many Democrats and some economists wanted tough new regulations, and better regulatory authorities, while most Republicans sided with the banking industry in arguing that too-tough regulations would drive business overseas and harm the economy.

DODD-FRANK LEGISLATION

Months after taking office, President Obama came down on the side of new regulations to make it more difficult for banks to get themselves, and the entire country, into another financial crisis. In June 2009 he proposed a major overhaul of federal legislation on regulation of the financial industry. That set off a furious legislating and lobbying campaign, which ended a little over a year later in the adoption of a bill with the weighty name of Wall Street Reform and Consumer Protection Act (PL 111-203). The law was almost universally known as Dodd-Frank, after its chief sponsors: Senate Banking Committee Chair Christopher J. Dodd, D-Conn., and House Financial Services Committee Chair Barney Frank, D-Mass. *(Legislative action, p. 88)*

The bill was the product of numerous compromises, many of them demanded by the banking industry, which insisted that tighter regulations would damage their businesses and the overall economy. It also emerged from Congress primarily with support from Democrats. Although most said they wanted banking reforms, and had successfully pushed to weaken several key provisions opposed by bankers, all but a handful of Republicans voted against the final legislation.

Opponents sought unsuccessfully throughout 2011 and 2012 to undo key Dodd-Frank provisions. For example, in July 2012 the Republican majority in the House passed a provision in a larger antiregulatory bill (HR 4078) to prohibit the Commodity Futures Trading Commission (CFTC) and the Securities and Exchange Commission (SEC) from proposing new Dodd-Frank rules until conducting a cost-benefit analysis justifying them. The Senate did not act on the measure. The Republican presidential candidate in 2012, Mitt Romney—the former governor of Massachusetts and former private equity executive running with substantial support from Wall Street—called outright for repealing and replacing the law, though he declined to be specific about any replacement. Romney and other critics complained that the law effectively guaranteed that the government would again bail out any big banks that got into serious trouble, thereby enshrining the concept that some banks were "too big to fail." Dodd-Frank supporters insisted this was not the case; for example, Federal Deposit Insurance Commission (FDIC) Chair Sheila Bair said in an April 2011 speech that Dodd-Frank provisions ensured that "there will be no more bailouts."

Behind the scenes, banking industry lobbyists were successful in delaying or watering down many of the 398 regulations that Congress mandated for enforcement of the law. By the spring of 2013, just more than one-half of the rules that were supposed to be in place at that time had been finished. Regulations directly concerning banks—as opposed to other sectors of the financial services industry—were the furthest behind: fewer than one-third were in place, according to the Davis Polk & Wardwell law firm. Several of the most contested regulations also faced lawsuits once they were in place.

The bill was incredibly complex, but its central purpose was to curb the sorts of risky financial betting practices and unscrupulous lending that had led to the financial crisis. Dodd-Frank was based on the belated recognition that the financial services industry had grown so much more complex than when existing banking laws and regulations were written, many of them decades earlier, and that U.S. banks and their cousins had become intimately linked to the global banking system.

If Dodd-Frank had one basic principle, it was adoption of the concept that the failure of banks, especially large ones, could pose a fundamental risk to the overall financial system, and thus the entire economy. The law therefore added avoiding systemic risk to the list of characteristics at the heart of government banking regulations, some of them dating from the 1860s: adequate capital to cover losses, government-guaranteed deposit insurance, and overall safety and soundness of banks to minimize the chance of default.

To monitor systemic risk, Dodd-Frank created the Financial Stability Oversight Council, consisting of representatives from several government agencies and chaired by the Treasury secretary. This council's charter was to detect risks to the overall financial system before they could do damage. A major provision gave the government authority to mandate the orderly liquidation of "systemically important" financial institutions that were failing. The Bush administration said it lacked such authority in September 2008, which was the reason it allowed Lehman Brothers to fail, the step that set off the worst periods of the financial crisis. Dodd-Frank required the largest bank holding companies to give the government plans (commonly referred to as "living wills") for their own orderly liquidation in times of crisis; regulators were reviewing those plans in late 2012 and early 2013.

The law also reduced, from five to four, the number of agencies involved in regulating banks: the Federal Reserve, the FDIC, the Comptroller of the Currency, and the National Credit Union Administration. One widely criticized bureau, the Office of Thrift Supervision, was combined with the other agencies, notably the Office of the Comptroller of the Currency, which took over responsibility for all federally chartered thrift institutions. Other agencies regulated financial services carried out by nonbanks; for example, the SEC continued to regulate securities exchanges and dealers and public corporations, and the CFTC regulated futures trading (including derivatives) and was given new responsibility to regulate risk-trading deals known as swaps, which previously had been largely unregulated. Dodd-Frank also made the Federal Reserve the primary regulator of all financial firms (whether banks or not) that the Financial Stability Oversight Council designated as "systemically significant" because of their size or complexity.

Perhaps the single most controversial element of Dodd-Frank was the creation of a Bureau of Consumer Financial Protection, with oversight of all regulations concerning financial transactions by consumers. Dodd-Frank established the bureau as an independent office within the Federal Reserve; its jurisdiction covered nearly the entire range of consumer financial dealings, including banking accounts, mortgages, debt collection, credit cards, and the processing of financial data. However, business lobbying of Congress resulted in the exemption of consumer transactions by several types of businesses, including merchants (when they extend credit directly to customers), automobile dealers, real estate agents, insurance companies, and banks with $10 billion or less in assets.

The banking lobby fiercely opposed creation of this agency, and opposition by Republicans forced President Obama to back down from his plan to appoint Harvard professor Elizabeth Warren as its first director; Warren had been one of the agency's chief advocates. Obama then named former Ohio attorney general Richard Cordray as head of the bureau through a "recess appointment." Warren went on to win election to the Senate in 2012 as a Democrat in Massachusetts. Cordray faced an uphill battle in 2013 to win Senate confirmation of a permanent appointment to the post but was finally confirmed in July by a substantial margin, 66–34.

Another highly disputed provision of Dodd-Frank was the so-called Volcker rule, named after its chief proponent, former Federal Reserve Chair Paul A. Volcker. The rule, which Congress watered down before adopting it, limited the ability of depository banks (those whose deposits are insured by the government) from engaging in "propriety trading," in other words speculative trading on their own behalf, for example by sponsoring a hedge fund. Banking lobbyists continued to demand the rule be weakened, arguing that it would make U.S. firms uncompetitive. As of the end of 2013, regulations to put it into place had not yet been finished.

Bank "Stress Tests"

Starting in the spring of 2009, the Treasury and the Federal Reserve conducted so-called "stress tests" to determine if the nation's nineteen largest banks and bank holding companies had strong enough capital reserves to survive another financial crisis or severe economic recession. The 2010 Dodd-Frank banking reform legislation made the tests an annual requirement.

Even before conducting the 2009 tests, the government said that any bank found to be potentially insolvent would be given more capital under TARP if it could not raise the necessary capital privately. That announcement helped calm the markets. However, some critics said it amounted to an implicit guarantee that the government would do whatever was necessary to prevent more bank collapses—and thus ratified the notion that some banks were, indeed, "too big to fail."

Results of the 2009 tests, released on May 7, showed that ten of the nineteen bank holding companies needed to increase their capital reserves to levels advocated by regulators. These included some of the large banks that had been bailed out by TARP, notably Bank of America and Citigroup. By far the weakest was the financing arm of General Motors, which was in the process of transforming into a broader bank called Ally Financial.

Tests in subsequent years showed that most major U.S. banks could weather a major economic downturn, although with difficulty in some cases. The 2012 tests were the most rigorous, based on what the Federal Reserve called a "deep recession" in which unemployment reached 13 percent and stock prices fell by one-half. Even under those extreme conditions, all but four of the nineteen tested banks (those with assets of $10 billion or more) were able to meet the minimum standards for capital ratios. The four were Ally Financial, Citigroup, MetLife, and SunTrust; Ally financial was the weakest of the four, by far. MetLife later sold off its banking operations to focus on its core insurance business.

In an April 2012 speech, Daniel K. Tarullo, a member of the Federal Reserve Board of Governors, said the tests showed that most banks "have made considerable progress" in planning for their survival in the event of an economic crisis. "However, there appears to be room for improvement at virtually every firm, and at some firms the amount of work needed is still significant," he said.

Banks in Europe faced stress tests in 2011, which showed dismal results for eight large institutions. Even so, the European tests were widely criticized because they failed to catch problems that showed up later in several banks during the eurozone crisis. The European Banking Authority announced in May 2013 that the next tests would not be conducted until 2014, allowing time for the European Central Bank to examine the quality of assets claimed by some of the banks.

Basel III

Internationally, the most important regulatory response to the financial crisis—at least in terms of potential impact—was the adoption in September 2010 of tighter bank capital requirements under the Basel Accords supervised by the Bank for International Settlements, headquartered in Basel, Switzerland. These 2010 requirements stiffened ones adopted in 1988 (called "Basel I") and a second set adopted in 2004 ("Basel II"), so the latest requirements were called "Basel III." In essence, Basel III doubled (and in some cases nearly tripled) the amount of capital banks must hold as a percentage of their overall assets. Basel III added even tougher requirements for banks considered to be "globally systemic" because their failure could damage the entire global financial system.

The Basel III requirements were complex, and were stoutly resisted by the international banking community, which argued they would hinder growth by reducing their ability to make loans. The rules were supposed to take effect on January 1, 2015, but banks successfully lobbied for a four-year delay, meaning that the requirements would not take effect, at the earliest, until 2019—nearly nine years after they were proposed.

U.S. regulators also struggled to adopt domestic rules in compliance with Basel III, finally issuing a proposal amending bank capital rules in June 2012. In its February 2013 Monetary Report to Congress, the Federal Reserve said the reforms "will raise the quantity of capital that must be held by U. S. banking firms, improve the quality of regulatory capital of those firms, and strengthen the risk-weight framework of U.S. bank capital rules."

In Europe, where many banks were closely connected to those in the United States, similar, and related, debates over tightening banking regulations dragged on for years after the financial crisis. European leaders in June 2012 announced plans for what they called an "effective single supervisory mechanism" for all banks in the seventeen eurozone countries; the most likely regulator would be the European Central Bank. Although the leaders ratified those plans the following November, subsequent disagreements over the details held up further steps well into 2013. The delays and continued posturing in key capitals raised questions about when—and even if—Europe would have continent-wide rules and procedures governing the banking industry.

More Financial Scandals

The reputation of major banks and investment firms—heavily damaged by the events of the financial crisis—suffered yet more bruising in subsequent years with revelations of market manipulations and other types of fraudulent schemes.

MF GLOBAL HOLDINGS LTD.

The New York–based brokerage firm MF Global collapsed in October 2011 and filed for bankruptcy after a bad bet on European debt failed, prompting investors, clients, and partners to flee the firm. It was the eighth-largest bankruptcy in U.S. history and the largest since the collapse of Lehman Brothers in September 2008.

The firm's failure would have been big news in any event, but the impact was magnified by the fact that it was headed by John Corzine, a former CEO of Goldman Sachs who later served as U.S. senator from New Jersey and that state's Democratic governor before returning to Wall Street to head MF Global in 2010. News reports said Corzine's ambition had been to develop MF Global, a 225-year-old firm that had specialized in brokering commodities, into a giant investment banking firm rivaling his former company, Goldman Sachs.

Corzine reportedly sought to achieve this ambition by driving his employers to make increasingly risky trades, the very kinds of trades that years earlier had made him one of the most successful investors on Wall Street. The riskiest was a $6.3 billion trade in 2011, on the company's own behalf, on bonds of heavily indebted countries in Europe. The *Wall Street Journal* reported that Corzine, under pressure from credit rating agencies, had made the trade in a desperate gamble to shore up the company's profits. That trade turned sour during one of the worst periods of the European banking crisis in the fall of 2011. MF Global's customers demanded their money back, forcing the company into court-protected bankruptcy on October 31, 2011.

The failure of MF Global exploded into a major political issue—largely because of Corzine's political background—when bankruptcy investigators discovered that the company had inappropriately spent about $1.6 billion in customers' trading accounts, which were supposed to be off-limits to use by the company on its own behalf. Corzine denied wrongdoing, but customers filed civil suits accusing him and his managers of failing to fulfill their fiduciary duties. Former FBI Director Louis J. Freeh, appointed as bankruptcy trustee representing MF Global's creditors, alleged in April 2013 that Corzine "knew, or should have known" about his firm's failure to institute adequate risk controls. The Commodity Futures Trading Commission in June 2013 filed civil charges against Corzine, alleging that he violated his obligation to protect customers' money. Corzine denied any wrongdoing.

Much of the $1.6 billion allegedly misappropriated by the company belonged to farmers, ranchers, and other businesses who used MF Global to reduce their risks from the fluctuating prices of commodities. James Giddens, the government-appointed trustee on behalf of the company's clients, received 27,000 claims and was able to resolve nearly all of them by mid-2012, eventually returning full payouts. JP Morgan Chase, which held some $1.2 billion on behalf of MF Global and handled the company's trades, agreed to return about half of the funds in June 2012 and the remainder in March 2013.

Freeh negotiated a separate agreement under which secured creditors would get back most of their money (some of them receiving 100 percent) while unsecured creditors received one-third or even less of their claims. That agreement went into effect in June 2013, when Freeh stepped down and was succeeded by a three-member panel of trustees.

In addition to raising the profile of the MF Global case, Corzine's connections to the Democratic Party gave Republicans an issue with which to attack Democrats in general and the Obama administration in particular. In a November 2012 report, Republicans on the House Financial Services Subcommittee on Oversight and Investigations targeted Corzine personally in a sweeping denunciation, saying that "the responsibility for failing to maintain the systems and controls necessary to protect customer funds rested with Corzine." The panel also accused the Securities and Exchange Commission (SEC) and the Commodities Futures Trading Commission (CFTC) of failing to share information about MF Global, leaving each of the regulators "with an incomplete understanding of the company's financial health."

LOSSES BY JP MORGAN CHASE

One of the few major U.S. banks to emerge relatively unscathed from the 2008–2009 financial crisis was the biggest one, JP Morgan Chase, headed by aggressive, well-publicized Chief Executive Officer Jamie Dimon. But even that company got its comeuppance in 2012 when it acknowledged that its London-based chief investment office had placed hedging bets years earlier that turned into big losses. The bank initially estimated the losses at about $2 billion, but by year's end the total had ballooned to more than $6 billion. Even that huge sum posed no inherent risk to such a big bank (with more than $2 trillion in assets), but the losses were deeply embarrassing for Dimon and his company and, more important, raised troubling new questions about the adequacy of international financial regulations.

The first hints of JP Morgan's problems emerged in March 2012 with newspaper reports about huge day-to-day swings in the bank's gains and losses. By April, some reports in the financial press suggested the bank could lose $1 billion or more on bad investments that were described as hedges against the U.S. economy again turning sour. Dimon at the time referred to the reports as "a complete tempest in a teapot." Then on May 10, a somewhat chastened Dimon held a conference call with investors acknowledging that the failed investment had resulted in a loss of "slightly more than $2 billion." Dimon described the trading strategy that led to the loss as "flawed, complex, poorly reviewed, poorly executed and poorly monitored."

The day after Dimon's statement, the bank's stock dropped by 9 percent, or about $14 billion. Several investors then filed class action shareholder suits, alleging they had been misled. The trades by the London office quickly became widely known as "whale trades" because they were so large.

Within weeks Dimon had forced out several top managers, including Ina R. Drew, who headed the investment unit that managed the trades. An internal bank review, published in July, cited Drew's unit for "ineffective" risk management and for exercising "poor" judgment in some of its trades. Dimon himself was called to testify before congressional committees. He acknowledged his bank had made mistakes but insisted he had been unaware of the bad trades, even though Drew reported directly to him.

The bad trades had cost the bank at least $6.2 billion as of the end of 2012. Dimon saw his pay cut by the bank's board—from $23 million in 2011 to $11.5 million in 2012.

The scandal also seemed to reveal yet more weaknesses in the U.S. banking regulatory system, despite the still-incomplete changes mandated by the Dodd-Frank law. Numerous critics noted that JP Morgan's chief regulator, the office of the Comptroller of the Currency, had failed to ask tough and timely questions about the problematic trades. "Regulators already have the authority to prevent excessively risky activities," wrote James Barth, senior finance fellow at the Milken Institute and the Lowder Eminent Scholar in Finance at Auburn University. "They simply must use that authority. If regulators won't use the powers they possess, what good does it do to give them even tougher powers?"

A sternly worded report by the Senate's Permanent Subcommittee on Investigations, issued on May 15, 2013, said the JP Morgan case presented "another warning signal about the ongoing need to tighten oversight of banks' derivative trading activities, including through better valuation techniques, more effective hedging documentation, stronger enforcement of risk limits, more accurate risk models, and improved regulatory oversight." The panel said its investigation also raised questions about "broader, systemic problems related to the valuation, risk analysis, disclosure, and oversight of synthetic credit derivatives held by U.S. financial institutions."

Other critics suggested that the JP Morgan case was the latest demonstration that some of the biggest banks had simply grown too big and should be split into smaller pieces, either voluntarily or by the government if necessary. One such advocate was Sheila Bair, the former chair of the Federal Deposit Insurance Corporation (FDIC). Appearing on CNN shortly after Dimon acknowledged the losses, she said the situation showed that "even with very good management these institutions are just too big to manage, and especially when dealing with very complex derivatives instruments trying to hedge risk in large securities trading books, even the best of managers can stumble." She suggested a better alternative would be "smaller, simpler institutions, ones that have more focused management on particular business lines."

Dimon and other bank executives rejected Bair's line of reasoning, insisting that their large institutions were more efficient, and had greater depth of expertise, than smaller ones. Large banks, they said, were inherently no riskier than any other large enterprise.

THE LIBOR SCANDAL

Just when it seemed that the reputation of multinational banks could not fall any further, another major scandal erupted in mid-2012 with revelations that more than a dozen large banks for years had manipulated a key index used to determine global interest rates. The index was the London Interbank Offered Rate (LIBOR), created in 1986 and controlled by the British Bankers Association. An average of interest rates submitted by London banks, it was used worldwide to establish rates for some $10 trillion in loans (including mortgages, student loans, and other consumer loans) and more than $300 trillion worth of derivatives contracts.

Questions about the credibility of the LIBOR-rate setting process had circulated within the international financial community for years and had even been reported by the business press. In April 2008 the *Wall Street Journal* raised questions about the rate's validity; banks and even the International Monetary Fund rejected the newspaper's claims at the time. However, in June of that year, Timothy F. Geithner, then president of the Federal Reserve Bank of New York and later the Treasury secretary, wrote the Bank of England drawing attention to problems with LIBOR and making recommendations "for enhancing the credibility" of the rate-setting mechanism.

The questions about LIBOR emerged into a large-scale scandal in June 2012 when U.S. and British regulators, who had been investigating LIBOR for more than a year, settled fraud charges against Barclays, the giant London bank, extracting a $453 million settlement. One of the regulators, the CFTC, said Barclays from 2005 to 2009 had "repeatedly attempted to manipulate and made false, misleading or knowingly inaccurate submissions" concerning LIBOR and a similar European-wide rate called EURIBOR. The commission received $200 million of the total settlement; it was the largest civil fine the commission had ever imposed. The LIBOR scandal also cost the jobs of Barclays' high-profile, hard-charging chief executive officer, Bob Diamond, an American banker, and his boss, Barclays' Chair Marcus Agius.

Regulators suggested that Barclays and other banks had manipulated LIBOR for two reasons: to make it appear that the banks were in better financial condition than they actually were, and to profit from the marginal differences between the rates they reported and the rates they actually charged.

In December 2012, regulators in Switzerland, the United Kingdom, and the United States settled charges, similar to those against Barclays, with the Swiss bank UBS and its international affiliates. The bank agreed to pay $1.5 billion in fines. Regulators said UBS had reported false rates from 2005 to 2010. Explaining the case against UBS, U.S. Assistant Attorney General Lanny A. Breuer said on December 19 that "the bank's conduct was simply astonishing." The bank manipulated LIBOR, he said, "so UBS traders could maximize profit on their trading positions, and so the bank wouldn't appear vulnerable to the public during the financial crisis." The Justice Department also accused two former UBS traders, Thomas Hayes and Roger Darin, of conspiring to manipulate LIBOR.

U.S. and British authorities reached a similar agreement in February 2013 with the Royal Bank of Scotland and its Japanese subsidiary. The bank paid fines totaling $612 million to settle wire fraud charges related to LIBOR rate-setting.

Dozens of investors, companies, and borrowers (led by the city of Baltimore) filed lawsuits in the United States alleging they had been defrauded by the British banks. Those suits were consolidated into one case in the U.S. federal court for the southern district of New York. In March 2013, the judge in that case, Naomi Reice Buchwald, dismissed, on technicalities, many of the most important claims, including the central allegation that banks had conspired to manipulate the LIBOR rates.

An insider account of LIBOR rate-rigging appeared on July 27, 2012, when the *Financial Times* published an article in which a former trader for Morgan Stanley, Douglas Keenan, said banks had "misreported" their rates to the LIBOR mechanism since at least 1991.

Attempting to protect London's status as a world financial capital, in the face of the LIBOR scandal, the British government in September 2012 established new regulations covering LIBOR, which took effect in April 2013. The government also demanded a new rate-setting mechanism and in July 2013 chose NYSE Euronext (which owned the New York Stock Exchange) to run a revised LIBOR.

Chronology of Action on Economic and Regulatory Policy

Barack Obama was sworn in as the nation's forty-fourth president in January 2009 during the deepest recession since the Great Depression of the 1930s. Within three weeks of his inauguration, Congress had approved $787.2 billion in new spending and tax cuts to spur economic growth, preserve jobs, and help those most affected by the recession. It was the largest economic stimulus bill in the nation's history—and the only significant measure enacted in the president's first term dedicated solely to economic recovery.

Little more than a year later, Congress in July 2010 passed legislation making the most sweeping reforms to the nation's financial regulatory system since the Great Depression. The legislation, intended to prevent any future financial crisis similar to the one that had plunged the country into severe recession, was a significant victory for the president. But opponents spent the next two years trying to undo parts of it and delay its implementation.

The widely differing views between Democrats and Republicans on how to repair the stumbling economy and faltering financial system contributed to the partisanship that characterized Obama's first term and that was most intensely displayed in the legislative disputes over taxing and spending that nearly drove the government into financial default. Indeed, many Democratic attempts to inject a new or additional stimulus into the economy got caught up in the legislative battles over the budget when Republicans insisted on offsetting the costs with other spending cuts. Whether a larger or longer stimulus would have helped the economy recover faster remained a controversy that economists—and politicians of every stripe—continued to debate. What seemed clear is that after four years the two parties seemed no closer—and perhaps even farther apart—to resolving their differences over the role of government in the nation's economy.

REFERENCES

Discussion of economic policy for the years 1945–1964 may be found in *Congress and the Nation Vol. I,* pp. 337–458; for the years 1965–1968, *Congress and the Nation Vol. II,* pp. 119–182, 253–305; for the years 1969–1972, *Congress and the Nation Vol. III,* pp. 53–145; for the years 1973–1976, *Congress and the Nation Vol. IV,* pp. 49–149; for the years 1977–1980, *Congress and the Nation Vol. V,* pp. 205–287; for the years 1981–1984, *Congress and the Nation Vol. VI,* pp. 27–120; for the years 1985–1988, *Congress and the Nation Vol. VII,* pp. 27–136; for the years 1989–1992, *Congress and the Nation Vol. VIII,* pp. 31–161; for the years 1993–1996, *Congress and the Nation Vol. IX,* pp. 31–148; for the years 1997–2001, *Congress and the Nation Vol. X,* pp. 33–170; for the years 2001–2004, *Congress and the Nation Vol. XI,* pp. 35–167; for the years 2005–2008, *Congress and the Nation Vol. XII,* pp. 51–59.

Discussion of financial regulation activity for the years 1945–1964 may be found in *Congress and the Nation Vol. I,* pp. 337–386; for the years 1965–1968, *Congress and the Nation Vol. II,* pp. 253–279; for the years 1969–1972, *Congress and the Nation Vol. III,* pp. 135–145; for the years 1973–1976, *Congress and the Nation Vol. IV,* pp. 107–117; for the years 1977–1980, *Congress and the Nation Vol. V,* pp. 253–265; for the years 1981–1984, *Congress and the Nation Vol. VI,* pp. 83–93; for the years 1985–1988 *Congress and the Nation Vol. VII,* pp. 109–136; for the years 1989–1992, *Congress and the Nation Vol. VIII,* pp. 113–161; for the years 1993–1996, *Congress and the Nation Vol. IX,* pp. 109–148; for the years 1997–2000, *Congress and the Nation Vol. X,* pp. 120–144; for the years 2001–2004, *Congress and the Nation Vol. XI,* pp. 123–144; for the years 2005–2008, *Congress and the Nation Vol. XII,* pp. 136–162.

ECONOMIC STIMULUS

To be sure, Congress approved additional stimulus measures during the four years to boost the economy, including a temporary suspension of part of the employee payroll tax and extensions of emergency unemployment benefits. Even before Obama was sworn in, Congress acted to allow the release of the second $350 billion in the Troubled Asset Relief Program (TARP) used to bail out failing financial institutions (the total amount was subsequently reduced to $475 billion). At the end of 2010, Congress also agreed to continue income tax cuts enacted in 2001 and 2003 for two more years. A return to the higher rates of the early 2000s would likely have created a serious drag on an economy that was still struggling to get back on its feet.

But public concerns over the dramatic increase in the federal budget deficit combined with Republican opposition to the president's legislative priorities served to quell any push for new stimulus measures. After the 2010 congressional elections returned control of the House to the Republicans and significantly narrowed the Democratic advantage in the Senate, the congressional and political conversation focused almost single-mindedly on spending cuts and deficit reduction. Proposals for direct measures to spur the economy or protect jobs were watered down, combined with other legislation to get passed, or dropped altogether.

The odds against passing a second large stimulus package became clear at the end of 2009, when the House only narrowly approved a job creation package; thirty-eight Democrats broke ranks to join all Republicans in opposition. Squabbling among Senate Democrats in the face of united Republican opposition prevented the full package from moving forward in that chamber although measures to extend unemployment benefits, prevent widespread layoffs of public school teachers, and encourage small businesses to hire or retain workers all won approval. At the end of 2010, Congress also agreed to reduce for one year the employee payroll tax by two percentage points, a move that was expected to inject tens of billions into the economy. The reduction was later extended for a second year; employee payroll taxes then returned to their regular levels.

A second jobs package fared no better than the first. Obama introduced his job creation plan to a joint session of Congress in September 2011, when the unemployment rate was still hovering around 9 percent, and poll after poll had shown that jobs were the top issue on voters' minds. He then crisscrossed the country calling on lawmakers to "pass this bill."

Republicans joined in the call for job creation but quickly rejected Obama's proposals for funds to help states prevent layoffs of teachers and first responders and to support infrastructure and transportation projects. GOP legislators particularly objected to Obama's proposal to pay for the programs by raising income taxes on the wealthy.

In a separate but closely related area of economic help through government action, Democrats narrowly won an extension of another of their priorities when Republicans agreed to an extension of an expanded Trade Adjustment Assistance for workers displaced by foreign trade. The GOP willingness to accept the legislation was a condition for Democratic support for three free-trade agreements originally negotiated during the administration of George W. Bush. Obama submitted the pacts with South Korea, Colombia, and Panama to Congress for approval in 2011 after renegotiating parts of the pact to strengthen worker and environmental protections. *(Trade pacts, trade adjustment assistance, pp. 193, 195, 199)*

The two parties also repeatedly wrangled over extensions of unemployment benefits, which were considered one of the more effective ways to help the economy because recipients were likely to spend the money rather than investing it or saving it. Democrats managed to fend off Republican efforts to offset the costs of the supplemental benefits but in 2012, as the economy showed some modest signs of improving, legislators agreed to provisions reducing eligibility and shortening the payment period for some jobless workers. *(Unemployment benefits, pp. 517, 535)*

FINANCIAL REGULATION

Voter disgust with Wall Street and its excesses drove passage of the financial regulation reforms over objections from the industry and its supporters in Congress. The wide-ranging measure touched on virtually all areas of financial regulation, from reducing systemic risk and liquidating large failing institutions, to regulating the over-the-counter derivatives market for the first time, to monitoring hedge funds, to setting up a new independent agency to monitor consumer financial products and mortgage lending practices. The bill's chief sponsors made several compromises to secure necessary support for the bill, but it still won only a handful of Republican votes.

For the next two years, Republican legislators, backed by elements of the financial industry, tried, largely unsuccessfully, to change various aspects of the landmark legislation. But, unlike the Affordable Care Act, Obama's signature health reform legislation, the bill's opponents never tried to repeal the measure altogether, in part because of its popularity with voters. *(Affordable Health Care Act, p. 421)*

2009–2010

Economic policy in President Barack Obama's first two years in office was devoted almost exclusively to getting the country out of recession and preventing the circumstances that caused it from happening again. Democrats, who controlled both the House and Senate, handed him two early and important victories, both with virtually no Republican support in the House and small but crucial GOP support in the Senate. In July 2010, they gave him a third victory when they passed sweeping financial regulatory reform legislation.

The first victory came even before Obama was sworn in to serve as the nation's forty-fourth president, when the Senate on January 15, 2009, took action that released $350 billion from the Troubled Asset Relief Program (TARP) to shore up the floundering financial industry. A month later, on February 17, the new president signed into law a $787.2 billion plan to pump up the badly faltering economy with a combination of new spending meant to create or retain jobs and tax cuts.

By the end of 2009, however, with the public growing increasingly concerned about mounting federal deficits, Congress lost its appetite for large direct stimulus measures. Although House Democrats managed to narrowly win passage of a $154 billion job creation bill, the Senate was unwilling to go along; the final bill, passed in March 2010, was about a tenth that amount. Although it offered some stimulus to the housing market through a homebuyer's tax credit and mortgage assistance, Congress never directly confronted the home foreclosure crisis that continued to dampen the housing market throughout Obama's first term. *(Housing issues, p. 500)*

Congress took several actions, however, to ease the economic burden for specific sectors particularly hard hit by the recession, including extending supplemental unemployment benefits and aiding small businesses to encourage them to hire new workers. At the end of 2010, as part of legislation to extend the income tax cuts first enacted in 2001 and 2003, Congress reduced employee payroll taxes to stimulate consumer spending. *(Details, p. 144)*

Legislators found more common ground, at least initially, on regulatory reform of financial institutions. Congress in April 2009 easily passed legislation to curb what were widely seen as abusive practices by credit card companies. Partisanship was firmly back in place during consideration of the financial regulatory reform measure, however, with Republicans by and large opposing the Democratic bill, as did much of the financial industry. The measure, which passed only with the support of a handful of Senate Republicans, created an orderly process for shutting down faltering financial institutions before they created a wider crisis, brought derivatives trading under federal regulation for the first time, and established an independent consumer protection bureau within the Federal Reserve to look out for the financial interests of consumers.

TARP Funds Released

In an important win for the incoming Obama administration, the Senate on January 15, 2009, rejected an attempt to block the release of $350 billion authorized to stabilize the reeling financial industry. The House subsequently voted to withhold the funds, but it was a purely symbolic action since the Senate had already decided the issue.

In reality, the release of the funds was not in question: President Obama had made clear he would veto the measure to disapprove of the release if lawmakers cleared it. But Democrats did not want that to be the way their new president entered office. The money was the second half of the $700 billion authorized by the 2008 law (PL 110-343) that created the Troubled Asset Relief Program (TARP). Under the law, the release of the $350 billion was contingent on a written request from the president. Congress could pass a resolution of disapproval, but it had to act within fifteen days of receiving the request. *(Congress and the Nation Vol. XII, p. 154; What Did TARP Do?, box, p. 62)*

At Obama's urging, President George W. Bush requested the funds on January 12. "I have talked to the president-elect about this subject," Bush said at a news conference. "And I told him that if he felt that he needed the $350 billion, I would be willing to ask for it."

Sen. David Vitter, R-La., introduced a disapproval resolution the next day, amid intense lobbying by Obama's team, led by his top economic adviser, Lawrence H. Summers, for the release of the funds. "With the first half of the rescue package now committed, President-elect Obama believes the need is imminent and urgent," Summers said in a letter to congressional leaders. "We cannot afford to wait."

Release of the funds did little to stem criticism of the program. Later in the year, the House passed two bills that showed the continuing concern about the use of the TARP funds. The first (HR 1242) proposed stricter oversight; the second (HR 2847) sought to redirect some TARP funds to a variety of programs to create jobs. The Senate did not take up either bill.

On December 9, 2009, Treasury Secretary Timothy F. Geithner notified congressional leaders that, as permitted by the law, he was extending the program until October 3, 2010. He said future spending would be confined to three areas: limiting foreclosures, helping small banks, and increasing support for consumer, small business, and mortgage loans.

BACKGROUND

The Obama administration's request for the additional TARP funds came as the program faced withering criticism in Congress, particularly from Republicans, and a sharp populist backlash in the country. Bush's Treasury

MAJOR ACTIONS ON ECONOMIC AND FINANCIAL REGULATION POLICY

Following are brief descriptions, in chronological order, of the major actions on economic and financial regulation policy in the 111th and 112th Congresses.

2009

January 15. Senate rejects motion to block the release of $350 billion from the Troubled Asset Relief Fund (TARP). The action has the effect of releasing the funds, which would be withheld only if both chambers voted to block the release. The House subsequently votes to block the funding.

February 13. Senate clears HR 1 (PL 111-5) to pump an estimated $787.2 billion in new spending and tax cuts into the economy over eleven years. Roughly three-fourths of the new funding will be spent in the first two years. No Republicans vote for the measure in the House; three Republicans vote for it in the Senate.

June 18. Senate clears an auto trade-in rebate program (HR 2346—PL 111-32), known as "cash for clunkers," to help the struggling car industry. The popular program goes through the $1 billion allocated to it almost immediately, and a second $2 billion authorized in early August goes nearly as quickly. The Obama administration ends the program when the additional funding is nearly exhausted, declaring it a success. *(Auto rebates, p. 321)*

November 5. House clears a bill (HR 3548—PL 111-92) extending emergency unemployment benefits under the stimulus bill for an additional fourteen weeks. It is the first of a series of contentious extensions that keep the emergency benefits in place throughout Obama's first term. *(Unemployment benefits, p. 517)*

2010

March 18. Senate clears a $17.6 billion measure (HR 2847—PL 111-147) to provide payroll tax relief and other incentives to employers who hired unemployed workers. The original version of the jobs bill, passed by the House in 2009, would have provided $154 billion for infrastructure projects, aid to help state and local governments preserve public-sector jobs, and additional assistance to families affected by the recession.

July 15. Senate clears a comprehensive overhaul of the financial regulatory system (HR 4173—PL 111-203) over the objections of almost all Republican legislators and many financial institutions. Sought by the Obama administration, the Dodd-Frank bill is designed to prevent in the future the types of excesses that led to the collapse of the housing market and the near collapse of the international financial system. During the 112th Congress, opponents of the measure try to repeal or change parts of the measure and to delay implementation.

August 10. House clears a $26.1 billion measure (HR1586—PL 111-226) to help state and local governments avoid laying off teachers and maintain Medicaid health coverage for the poor. More generous versions of both provisions had been included in the House jobs bill passed in 2009.

September 23. House clears legislation (HR 5297—PL 111-240) providing tax incentives and expanded access to credit to small businesses; the measure is aimed at encouraging small businesses to hire or retain workers.

December 17. House clears legislation (HR 4853—PL 111-312) reducing by two percentage points the employee payroll tax. Together with an extension of emergency unemployment benefits through the end of 2011 and some other smaller measures, the bill is expected to give the economy

Department had told Congress that it needed the funding to purchase "toxic assets" from financial institutions whose failure could rock the entire economy. But Treasury officials quickly concluded that the funds would be most effective if they were used to provide loans to major financial institutions and regional banks, and many members felt they had been misled. Legislators and the public were also angered by Bush's decision to use some TARP funds to bail out AIG, the giant insurance company that was facing collapse because it had guaranteed trillions of dollars worth of "credit default swaps" that were in danger of being called.

Many Republicans were also upset by Bush's decision to use some bailout funds to assist domestic automakers and worried that the Obama administration might use funds for other industries as well. Obama expanded the short-term loans to General Motors and Chrysler but did not aid any other industry. Liberal Democrats, meanwhile, were angry that most of the money was going to Wall Street rather than having some of it used to help stem the home foreclosures brought on, in part, by firms that had pushed subprime mortgages. Some of that anger dissipated in May when Congress passed a mortgage assistance bill (S 896—PL 111-22) that used some TARP funding to offset the costs of easing the mortgage crisis. *(Mortgage assistance, p. 500)*

Lawmakers, including a congressional TARP oversight panel, questioned Treasury's handling of the program, including an apparent lack of accountability. The TARP oversight panel issued a report in December 2008 that raised a host of questions, saying for example that it was "unclear whether there have been any efforts to assess the business plans, the management, or the accounting and general transparency of firms receiving aid." The report also said Treasury had administered the program "without seeking to monitor the use of funds provided to specific a $180 billion boost in 2011. The payroll tax reduction is part of a broader package continuing the 2001 and 2003 tax cuts through the end of 2012. Had the tax cuts been allowed to expire, income tax rates for all taxpayers would have returned to their higher levels of 2001, exerting a short-term drag on the economy. PL 111-312 also continues through fiscal 2011 several popular business tax breaks that had been allowed to expire at the end of 2009.

2011

September 8. In a speech to a joint session of Congress, Obama proposes a $447 billion package of programs to stimulate the economy and create jobs and then embarks on a countrywide campaign to build support for the plan. In the face of Republican opposition, Congress passes only a small part of the program—tax credits for companies that hire unemployed veterans. A $35 billion package of state aid aimed at preventing layoffs of first responders and educators and a $60 billion measure to fund infrastructure and transportation projects dies in the Senate. Other job creation measures are set aside as the two parties in the Senate wrangled over extension of the employee payroll tax reduction and unemployment benefits.

October 12. House clears legislation (HR 2832—PL 112-40) restoring many of the expanded benefits under the Trade Adjustment Assistance (TAA) program initiated in the 2009 economic stimulus bill although not always at the same levels. The legislation is part of a compromise involving approval of three free-trade pacts favored by Republicans; Democrats oppose approval of those pacts without the TAA expansion.

December 8. Senate rejects a motion to impose cloture and end debate on the nomination of Richard Cordray as director of the new Consumer Financial Protection Bureau. All fifty-two members of the Democratic caucus and just one Republican vote for cloture; sixty votes are needed for approval of the motion. Obama subsequently seats Cordray in a controversial recess appointment.

December 23. Senate clears a bill (HR 3765—PL 112-78) extending the employee payroll tax cut and supplemental jobless benefits for the long-term unemployed for two months, through February 29, 2012. The bill also blocks a drastic reduction in payments to physicians who serve Medicare patients. The measure is passed at the last moment after rancorous fights in which neither chamber can agree on a plan to finance a longer-term extension of the programs.

2012

February 17. Senate clears legislation (HR 3630—PL 112-96) extending the payroll tax cut and long-term supplemental unemployment benefits and postponing the scheduled drop in Medicare reimbursement rates for physicians through the end of the year.

2013

January 1. Congress clears the fiscal cliff legislation (HR 8—PL 112-240) permanently extending all Bush-era income tax cuts except those for the wealthy and making automatic across-the-board cuts in federal discretionary funding. The measure also extends through 2013 supplemental jobless benefits for the long-term unemployed as well as the block on reducing Medicare physicians' payments. The payroll tax reduction is not extended.

financial institutions," focusing instead on the larger impact the injection of funds would have on the economy.

Lawmakers grilled Treasury official Neel Kashkari at a December 10, 2008, House Financial Services Committee hearing. Spencer Bachus of Alabama, the committee's ranking Republican, said he wondered whether Bush's Treasury Secretary, Henry M. Paulson Jr., or Kashkari, "back when they were still working for Goldman Sachs, ever agreed to a deal in which billions of dollars changed hands based on a two-page application without asking what the money was going to be used for and whether it was going to be paid back."

Kashkari cited the speed with which Treasury had to act to stem a financial disaster. "A program as large and complex as the TARP would normally take many months and years to establish," Kashkari said in prepared testimony. "But we don't have the luxury of first building the operation, then designing our programs and then executing them."

Committee Chair Barney Frank, D-Mass, saved his sharpest criticism for what he said was Treasury's unwillingness to use TARP money to help forestall foreclosures. Frank said that violated the intent of the law and would make it harder for Treasury to secure congressional approval of the second $350 billion.

Obama and his team assured lawmakers that they would make the program transparent and impose strict conditions on the use of the remaining funds. In telephone calls, meetings, and letters, they also pledged to focus on helping struggling homeowners avoid foreclosure.

LEGISLATIVE ACTION

The Senate rejected Vitter's disapproval resolution (S J Res 5) on January 15 by a **key vote of 42–52 (R 33–6; D 8–45; I 1–1)**. "This was a test of leadership at a time when leadership was desperately needed in our country," said Senate Majority Leader Harry Reid, D-Nev. *(2009 key votes, p. 751)*

The Obama team had been lobbying Congress intensely for a week before the vote, but the outcome remained in doubt until the afternoon of the vote, when Summers sent a letter, requested by the Republican caucus, to leaders of both parties providing additional details about the conditions the president-elect proposed attaching to the $350 billion in TARP funding. The administration pledged that any substantial new investment of TARP funds would have to be reviewed and approved by the president, and Congress would be notified before any action was taken.

Obama also promised that the TARP program would remain focused on "preventing systemic consequences in the financial and housing markets." He said Treasury would commit $50 billion to $100 billion to "a sweeping effort to address the foreclosure crisis." To reassure Republicans, the administration added that it did not intend to use TARP funds "to implement an industrial policy."

In addition, companies receiving government aid would have to meet certain conditions, including a requirement that executive compensation above a certain level be paid in restricted stock or other forms that could not be cashed out until the government had been repaid.

CONTINUING EFFORTS TO CURB TARP

Even though Senate rejection of the disapproval resolution allowed the funding to be released, the House cast two TARP votes—one to bar the release of the funds, and the other to restrict their use; the latter was intended to demonstrate members' unhappiness with the bailout fund. On January 21, the House voted 260–166 on a bill (HR 384) to impose significant restrictions on the use of the $350 billion. The following day, members passed the House version of the disapproval resolution (H J Res 3) by a vote of 270–155.

Frank, who sponsored HR 384, acknowledged that the Senate was unlikely to consider the bill. But he said it would set a marker for the administration when it allocated the TARP funds, and he counted as a victory Obama's commitment to devote substantial sums to mitigate foreclosures. The House-passed bill called for using $40 billion to $100 billion for the purpose.

Republicans, who voted overwhelmingly against the original bailout, largely opposed Frank's bill, with only eighteen voting for it. "The legislation still puts us on the road of picking winners and losers in our economy," said Jeb Hensarling, R-Texas.

Near the end of the session, on December 2, 2009, the House passed a bipartisan bill (HR 1242) aimed at bolstering oversight of the increasingly unpopular TARP. The legislation, sponsored by Carolyn B. Maloney, D-N.Y., passed 421–0, but the Senate did not consider it.

Congress put an end to new action under the TARP program with passage of financial regulation overhaul legislation in July 2010 (HR 4173—PL 111-203). That law reduced from $700 billion to $475 billion the amount authorized to be spent under the TARP program and barred any new TARP programs after June 25, 2010. Any unspent TARP funds and any repayments were to be used to help reduce the deficit. The TARP program had been scheduled to end on October 3, 2010. Two years later, in October 2012, the Congressional Budget Office estimated that the actual net cost to the government of all TARP programs was only $24 billion—far below the $700 billion "bailout" figure widely reported by the news media.

Economic Stimulus

Less than a month after his inauguration, President Barack Obama was handed a significant legislative victory, when Congress agreed to pump an estimated $787.2 billion into the economy to keep it from sinking further into recession. The speedy action on the stimulus bill, along with the release of $350 billion from the Troubled Asset Relief Program (TARP), approved by Congress in January even before the president was sworn into office, attested to the gravity of the country's economic situation. But passage of the stimulus bill with almost no support from Republicans was a harbinger of the bitter partisan rift on tax and spending measures that would consume Congress for the next four years and beyond.

The bill (HR 1—PL 111-5), which Obama signed into law on February 17, 2009, provided $575.3 billion in new funding over eleven years for a wide range of programs. These included projects intended to save or create jobs such as road construction and energy initiatives; programs to assist the jobless, such as extended emergency unemployment benefits and food stamps; education programs; and initiatives to expand health information technology and the extension of broadband service to rural areas. In addition, the legislation provided $211.8 billion in tax cuts over eleven years for individuals and businesses.

The final bill was not as expansive as Obama and many Democrats had envisioned because Democrats had to pare the provisions to attract enough GOP votes in the Senate. The final version more closely resembled the bill that had passed in the Senate—a compromise worked out among moderates that helped garner the votes of three Republicans in that chamber. That they were the only members of the GOP in either chamber to vote for the bill was a disappointment for Obama, who had insisted for weeks that the effort have bipartisan support.

Congressional Democrats and leaders of Obama's economic team had been working since the 2008 election to draft elements of a package they hoped would help jumpstart the economy. Although he was still president-elect, Obama came to Capitol Hill shortly after the new Congress convened, meeting with leaders from both parties to push a package he said would create or save three million jobs and put an extra $500 into the pockets of individual taxpayers.

House Democratic leaders unveiled details of a stimulus plan January 15 that called for $550 billion in spending and

OTHER ACTIONS TO RESTORE ECONOMIC ACTIVITY

In addition to release of the last TARP funds, passage of the initial economic stimulus, and other job-creating legislation discussed in this chapter, Congress passed additional legislation in President Barack Obama's first term to aid Americans hard hit by recession and to help get the faltering economy growing again. These measures, covered in more detail elsewhere in this volume, are summarized below.

Supplemental Unemployment Benefits

Although extended despite Republican objections, Congress maintained supplemental unemployment benefits for jobless workers throughout President Obama's first term. The benefits were first extended as part of the economic stimulus bill. Four short-term extensions were required in 2010. In all four cases, prolonged legislative battles led to the expiration of the benefits and required that the new short-term extension be retroactive. The final bill extended the benefits through 2011.

After another highly contentious legislative battle, Congress at the end of 2011 continued the long-term unemployment benefits for another two months, through February 2012. In 2012, Congress agreed to two more short-term extensions, both times as part of legislative packages to deal with an array of fiscal deadlines. The last extension, part of the fiscal cliff legislation signed into law on January 2, 2013, continued the benefits, with some changes, through December 2013. *(Details, pp. 517, 535)*

Mortgage Assistance

Congress cleared legislation (S 896—PL 111-22) in May 2009, aimed at helping homebuyers stave off foreclosures. The bill made it easier for borrowers to seek mortgage modifications under the $300 billion Hope for Homeowners program enacted in 2008 (PL 110-289). That program was initially expected to help 400,000 home owners, but only a handful actually sought to have their mortgages refinanced. Critics blamed high fees and minimal participation by lenders. Although S 896 eased some of the requirements of the 2008 law, it did not include a controversial House-passed provision that would have allowed bankruptcy judges to modify the terms of mortgages on primary residences that were undergoing foreclosure. *(Background on housing crisis, p. 497; details of S 896, p. 500)*

Homebuyer Tax Credit

A homebuyer tax credit, first enacted in July 2008, was extended and expanded twice in 2009 as lawmakers looked for ways to respond to the weak housing market that was a drag on the economy. Congress extended the popular program through November 2009 as part of the economic stimulus package enacted in February (HR 1—PL 111-5). Weeks before the credit was set to expire, Congress cleared a new extension that pushed the credit into the spring of 2010. Concerned that additional extensions would drain the program of its stimulus affect, supporters promised that the November 2009 extension would be the last. *(Homebuyer tax credit, p. 503)*

Employee Payroll Tax Reduction, Income Tax Cut Extension

To pump more money into the still-wobbly economy, Congress in 2010 reduced by 2 percentage points the Social Security payroll tax employees would pay in 2011. The provision was part of a larger tax bill extending tax cuts enacted during the presidency of George W. Bush on individual income taxes, dividends, and capital gains for two years through 2012. The payroll tax reduction was later extended through 2012 but then allowed to lapse. *(Payroll tax reduction, pp. 108, 144, 146; tax cut extension, p. 185)*

Cash for Clunkers

In a bid to help the struggling domestic auto industry, Congress in 2009 created a temporary auto trade-in program (PL 111-32) and quickly poured additional money into it when the program proved wildly popular (PL 111-47). The program, known as "cash for clunkers," offered rebates of up to $4,500 to consumers who traded in old gas-guzzlers and purchased or leased new, fuel-efficient vehicles. The size of the rebate depended on the improvement in fuel efficiency between the old vehicle and the new. After the additional funding was nearly exhausted, the administration proclaimed the program a success and ended it. *(Details, p. 321)*

$275 billion in tax breaks. They acknowledged that the legislation would balloon the federal budget deficit but called it vital to preventing further erosion in the economy. Preliminary figures showed that the economy had shrunk by 8.9 percent in the last quarter of 2008 and that the unemployment rate had jumped from about 4.7 percent in 2007 to nearly 9 percent in April 2009 and peaked at 10.1 percent in October 2009. *(Unemployment figures, p. 50)*

Republicans rejected the plan, as they would throughout the debate, saying it focused too much on spending and not enough on tax cuts and that it was designed to promote Democratic policy goals rather than boost the economy.

On January 28, the House passed a slightly less expensive version of the package with relative ease. But the Senate needed another two weeks while moderates of both parties negotiated a compromise that could win the sixty votes required to overcome points of order and avert a filibuster. Top House Democrats were unhappy about cuts the Senate made to spending on some of their priority programs, particularly education, but they had to accept many of the reductions to get the final bill through the Senate. The "split the difference" approach often used by House and Senate conferees did not work for this legislation.

As Congress considered the legislation, Obama traveled to several hard-hit areas of the country and had the first news conference of his presidency in an effort to convince the nation that the bill was necessary to stimulate the sagging economy. "It is only government that can break the vicious cycle where lost jobs lead to people spending less money, which leads to even more layoffs," he said in a prime time news conference February 9. "And breaking that cycle is exactly what the plan that's moving through Congress is designed to do."

The Congressional Budget Office (CBO) estimated that the combined effects of the spending and revenue provisions would increase the deficit by $184.9 billion in fiscal 2009, $399.4 billion in 2010, and $787.2 billion over ten years. To accommodate some of this increase, the bill raised the debt limit to $12.1 trillion from $11.3 trillion. CBO said 74 percent of the bill's appropriations would be spent by the end of fiscal 2010, essentially meeting the Obama administration's goal of having 75 percent out the door by that time. *(Major provisions, p. 82)*

HOUSE ACTION

In the week following the January 15 release of the House leadership's draft, the Appropriations, Ways and Means, and Energy and Commerce committees each amended and approved their portions of the legislation.

The Appropriations Committee voted 24–13, along straight party lines, on January 21 to approve a collection of spending provisions (HR 679—H Rept 111-4) that was expected to cost $361 billion over eleven years. The legislation included $90 billion for infrastructure programs, which supporters said would quickly create jobs. Many of the other provisions reflected top Democratic priorities, including $41 billion for education programs, $43 billion for increased unemployment benefits and job training, $39 billion for health care assistance to those who lost their jobs, and $20 billion to increase food stamp benefits. It proposed $87 billion for a temporary increase in the Medicaid matching rate and $20 billion to encourage the use of health information technology.

The Ways and Means Committee approved a $275.1 billion package of tax cuts for individuals and businesses, as well as an expansion of health insurance programs and electronic medical records. The panel approved the legislation (HR 598—H Rept 111-8, Parts 1 and 2) by a party-line vote of 24–13 on January 22, after rejecting eighteen Republican amendments.

The single costliest provision of the Ways and Means bill was Obama's signature "Making Work Pay" tax credit, a $500 income tax credit for workers in 2009 and 2010 to offset payroll taxes. The credit was refundable, meaning that workers who did not earn enough to pay income taxes would receive the money as a check. Other large tax breaks included an increase in the earned-income tax credit (EITC) for families with three or more children, expanded eligibility for the refundable portion of the child tax credit in 2009 and 2010, and a new $2,500 partially refundable tax credit for college tuition and other expenses, an Obama initiative known as the American Opportunity Tax Credit.

The Energy and Commerce Committee approved its portion of the recovery plan by voice vote January 22 (HR 629—H Rept 111-7). The measure included provisions to direct $54 billion to energy projects, extend insurance coverage for people who lost their jobs, and provide $20 billion to accelerate the use of electronic medical records, which was expected to increase efficiency, lower health care costs, and reduce medical errors. It also included nearly $3 billion in funding to extend broadband Internet infrastructure to poorly served areas.

House leaders combined the provisions into a single, $819.5 billion bill (HR 1), which passed by a vote of 244–188 on January 28. Despite Obama's attempts to woo Republicans, including a trip to Capitol Hill, none voted for the bill.

Republicans wanted the bill tilted much more toward tax cuts, an idea they pushed in meetings with Obama. The tax title did contain several items Republicans liked, such as a $15 billion expansion of the carryback provisions for net operating losses. But Democratic leaders indicated they were not inclined to adopt GOP proposals just to make the final tally look more bipartisan.

"The opposition to this bill can speak out against this recovery plan all they want," said Majority Leader Steny H. Hoyer of Maryland. "But their policies have not worked. . . . Americans voted for change. They voted for a new direction. That's what we're going to get."

During the floor debate, the House handily rejected Republican amendments to strike the appropriations title of the bill, to remove $800 million for Amtrak, and to recommit the bill with instructions that it be reported back with an additional $36 billion for highway infrastructure and an additional $24 billion for the Army Corps of Engineers, while dropping more than $100 billion in funding for new or unauthorized programs.

A GOP substitute that included a reduction in income tax rates in the bottom two brackets was also rejected by a wide margin. Republicans said their plan would create more jobs at a lower cost.

SENATE ACTION

The Finance and Appropriations committees approved separate pieces of the Senate's stimulus package. The measure included a $69.8 billion adjustment to the alternative minimum tax (AMT). Without the adjustment, the AMT, which was aimed at the wealthy, was expected to hit millions of additional middle-income taxpayers in 2009. House Democrats had left the AMT fix out of their bill on the grounds that it could pass easily on its own and would take up funding in the stimulus that could be used for other purposes.

The Appropriations Committee approved a $365.6 billion spending package (S 336) on January 27, with four Republicans joining all seventeen Democrats in voting for the measure. S 336 included funding for a broad array of initiatives, including highway and transit projects and renewable-energy and energy efficiency incentives. It included billions for school modernization, public housing, veterans' health facilities, and national parks. Other funds were targeted to border security, environmental cleanup, and construction and renovation of Pentagon facilities.

The Finance Committee approved what it calculated to be a $522 billion package of tax and health provisions (S 350) on January 27. Moderate Olympia J. Snowe of Maine was the only Republican to back the measure. In addition to the AMT patch amendment, the committee approved a manager's amendment calling for a $9 billion tax credit for investment to extend broadband technology to rural and underserved areas; the credit was later reduced to $7 billion before Senate passage.

Other provisions of the Finance Committee bill were similar to those in the House bill, including the Making Work Pay and American Opportunity tax credits, expansion of the child tax credits, and carryback of net operating losses experienced in 2008 and 2009. The bill also proposed $130 billion for health care, with a large package of funding to help states with Medicaid costs.

The Senate passed a somewhat slimmed-down version of the bill by a vote of 61–37 on February 10, following eight days of debate and a seemingly endless string of amendments. As with their House counterparts, Senate Democratic leaders said they had hoped Republicans would support the bill, but they were not prepared to agree to major changes to win that support. Senate Republicans echoed many of the complaints of their House colleagues, contending that the Senate's stimulus package would spend too much without doing enough to generate new jobs and get the economy back on track. They said they had been effectively shut out of the legislative process.

The crucial tally occurred February 9, when the Senate agreed, by a **key vote 61–36 (R 3–36; D 56–0; I 2–0),** to limit debate on a substitute amendment that it then adopted by unanimous consent. The amendment reflected the work of a bipartisan group of moderates, led by Susan Collins, R-Maine, and Ben Nelson, D-Neb. The group included as many as twenty centrists from both parties who wanted to back Obama's call for a stimulus bill to help pull the economy out of recession but worried the package was too big to win a bipartisan majority on the Senate floor. They began meeting early in the week of the vote. But even as the group worked behind the scenes to trim the bill, senators on the floor were seeking to expand it. The substitute brought the cost of the bill to $780 billion, down from the $940 billion version that initially came to the floor. But amendments adopted on the floor boosted the final cost of the Senate-passed bill to $838.1 billion. *(2009 key votes, p. 751)*

The debate took on added urgency February 6, when the Labor Department released figures showing the economy had lost an additional 598,000 jobs in January 2009 and unemployment had risen to 7.6 percent. "These numbers demand action," said Obama, who had generally favored a package of about $800 billion. "There may be provisions in the bill that need to be left out and some that need to be added. But broadly speaking, it is the right size."

Republicans, including Sen. John McCain of Arizona and Senate Minority Leader Mitch McConnell of Kentucky, protested that the final Senate version bill was still too costly. "Americans realize that a bill which was meant to be timely, targeted and temporary has instead become a Trojan horse for pet projects and expanded government," McConnell said.

FINAL ACTION

The conference report (H Rept 111-16) was filed February 12, and the House adopted it on February 13 on a **key vote of 246–183 (R 0–176; D 246–7).** Hours later, the Senate cleared the bill, 60–38. *(2009 key votes, p. 751)*

Democratic leaders in the Senate began the roll-call vote early enough that Friday to allow Joseph I. Lieberman, I-Conn., an Orthodox Jew, to cast his vote before sundown. And they kept the roll call going late into the evening so that Sherrod Brown, D-Ohio, could fly back from a memorial service for his mother.

The final deal was driven largely by the three centrist Republicans who supported the Senate bill. The votes of Arlen Specter of Pennsylvania (who switched parties later in the year), Collins, and Snowe were essential to overcoming procedural hurdles in the Senate. The three negotiated directly with Senate leaders and the White House. *(Specter party switch, p. 17, 18)*

Conferees restored some of the funding the Senate cut from its bill but kept the measure below $800 billion, which was the upper limit acceptable to the three Republicans. Of the total, $311.2 billion was discretionary budget authority, about $50 billion less than in the House-passed bill but about $21 billion more than in the Senate version.

The administration and Democratic leaders said the final bill would create or save 3.5 million jobs over the following two years, half a million less than what they said the House-passed version would have produced.

Negotiators made significant changes to a variety of provisions throughout the bill. Among many compromises, they trimmed the Making Work Pay tax credit, honoring Obama's pledge of providing tax cuts for 95 percent of taxpayers but at a reduced cost from what he had proposed. Conferees also reduced the scope and cost of the net operating loss carryback provision. Like the House and Senate bills, it allowed companies to use losses to offset profits going back five years, but it applied only to losses suffered in 2008 and was confined to small businesses making $15 million or less.

The final version dropped the Senate's proposal for a new $15,000 credit for all homebuyers. Instead, the bill extended the existing first-time homebuyer credit to homes purchased before December 1, 2009, and increased the credit. Conferees also dropped House provisions to set aside a combined $20 billion to repair and modernize schools and institutions of higher education. Instead, the final bill specified that part of a $53.6 billion state fiscal stabilization fund for education could be used to modernize, although not repair, such facilities. *(Homebuyer credit, p. 503)*

Conferees retained the $69.8 billion one-year adjustment to the AMT added in the Senate and split the difference between the two chambers on a formula for allocating an $86.8 billion Medicaid funding increase to states. *(Medicaid funding, p. 453)*

The final version included the Senate version of a "Buy American" provision aimed at ensuring that only U.S.-manufactured iron and steel was used in public construction projects funded under the bill. The final bill stated that the provision should be applied in a manner consistent with international trade agreements—a nod to concerns of the business community and the Obama administration that the provision could set off trade battles with Canada, the European Union, and other trade partners.

Republicans objected strongly to the way the conference was conducted. "They've been working in secret," said House Minority Leader John A. Boehner of Ohio, who called for Democrats to obey a nonbinding motion that the House had adopted, 403–0, on February 10. The motion instructed House conferees to insist that lawmakers have at least forty-eight hours to read the conference report before a vote.

Democrats defended the process, saying they had considered GOP ideas, held committee markups, allowed floor amendments, and acted as openly as they could given the time constraints. However, they did not allow any amendments in conference, did not describe the bill, and held no discussion beyond opening statements.

MAJOR PROVISIONS

Following are major provisions of the economic stimulus bill President Obama signed into law February 17 (HR 1—PL 111-5). Figures for tax cuts are in revenue reductions as calculated by the Joint Committee on Taxation. Figures for mandatory spending are in estimated outlays. Those for appropriations are in new budget authority. Eleven-year cost estimates for tax cuts and mandatory spending (in parentheses) are for fiscal years 2009 through 2019.

Appropriations

Education and training. The new law provided $53.6 billion for a new State Fiscal Stabilization Fund to prevent cutbacks and layoffs in local school districts and to modernize schools. Other spending on education and training included $15.6 billion to increase the maximum Pell grant to college students by $500, $13.0 billion for Title I basic local school grants for disadvantaged students, $12.2 billion for special-education programs, and $4.0 billion for job training, including state formula grants for adult, dislocated-worker, and youth programs.

Transportation. The law included $45.2 billion for highway construction projects, rail transportation, and mass transit.

Low-income assistance. HR 1 allocated $20.0 billion for additional Supplemental Nutrition Assistance Program (SNAP, formerly food stamps), to increase the monthly benefit by 13.6 percent, $2.0 billion to provide child care services for an additional 300,000 children in low-income families, and $2.1 billion to allow an additional 124,000 children to participate in Head Start and Early Head Start programs. Another $8 billion was allocated to public housing programs.

Health. $10.0 billion was appropriated for biomedical research in such areas as cancer, Alzheimer's disease, heart disease, and stem cells, and for improvements in the facilities of the National Institutes of Health.

Environment and science. A total of $13.2 billion was allocated for environmental cleanup of former weapons production and energy research sites, improvements in local clean- and drinking-water infrastructure; and EPA cleanup activities, including the superfund hazardous-waste program. The National Science Foundation received $3.0 billion for facilities modernization and education programs, whereas NASA received $1 billion for climate science, aviation safety, and exploration.

Energy. HR 1 appropriated $11.0 billion to modernize the nation's electric utility grid, including activities related to the "smart" grid, $5.0 billion for the Weather Assistance Program, and a total of $22.2 billion for a variety of energy efficiency, renewable energy, and other "green" programs.

Other. The law also appropriated $7.2 billion to expand broadband Internet access and usage in underserved areas; $4.0 billion to support law enforcement efforts; $2.8 billion for various Department of Homeland Security projects; $3.1 billion for repair, restoration; and improvement of public facilities on public and tribal lands, and $6.5 billion to improve and modernize Defense Department family housing, hospitals and child care, and to improve energy efficiency in other facilities.

Individual Tax Cuts

"Making Work Pay" credit. A new refundable tax credit of up to $400 for working individuals ($800 for joint filers) was put in place for 2009 and 2010. Refundable credits could be received in the form of a check to families that paid little or no taxes. The credit was calculated at a rate of 6.2 percent of earned income and was phased out for taxpayers with adjusted gross incomes in excess of $75,000 for individuals and $150,000 for married couples filing jointly. ($116.2 billion)

Alternative minimum tax relief. The amount of income exempt from the AMT was increased for one year to $46,700 for individuals and $70,950 for joint filers. The new law also allowed individuals to use nonrefundable personal credits to offset their regular tax liability and AMT liability in 2009. ($69.8 billion)

Retiree assistance. Retirees and disabled individuals receiving Social Security benefits were slated to receive a one-time payment of $250. The payment was also available to those receiving Supplementary Security Income benefits or Railroad Retirement benefits and disabled veterans getting benefits from the Department of Veterans Affairs. ($14.2 billion)

Earned-income tax credit. The EITC was increased in 2009 and 2010 for families with three or more children. Under the provision, the credit rose to 45 percent of the first $12,570 of earned income. ($4.7 billion)

Child credit. Eligibility for the refundable portion of the child tax credit was expanded. In 2009 and 2010, the child tax credit was refundable up to 15 percent of the taxpayer's earned income in excess of $3,000; the floor had previously been $8,500. ($14.8 billion)

Tuition credit. A modification in 2009 and 2010 of the HOPE scholarship credit included giving it a new name: the American Opportunity Tax Credit. The maximum amount of the revised credit, which applied to the cost of tuition and related expenses, increased to $2,500, up from $1,800 under previous law. The new law increased the adjusted gross income level at which the credit began to phase out to $80,000 for individuals and $160,000 for married couples filing jointly, up from $50,000 for individuals and $120,000 for joint filers. The credit was available for four years, and 40 percent of it was refundable. Previously, the credit had been available for only two years and none of it could be refunded. ($13.9 billion)

Homebuyer credit. The refundable tax credit—equal to 10 percent of the purchase price of a house—for first-time homebuyers was extended to homes purchased before December 1, 2009. The maximum for the credit was increased from $7,500 to $8,000, and the law waived a requirement that the funds be repaid in fifteen years. ($6.6 billion)

Business Tax Cuts

Bonus depreciation. The new law extended through 2009 a provision that allowed businesses to write off 50 percent of the cost of capital investment expenditures in the first year. ($5.1 billion)

Net operating losses. Also expanded was a provision that allowed businesses to use current net operating losses to offset profits in prior years. The new law allowed businesses with gross receipts of $15 million or less to carry back losses in 2008 for five years, up from two years under previous law. ($947 million)

Energy production credit. A credit for wind electricity generation producers was extended by three years, making it available for facilities placed in service through December 31, 2012. The law also extended the placed-in-service date for three years (through December 31, 2013) for other renewable-energy facilities, including those using biomass, geothermal energy, and hydropower. ($13.1 billion)

Health information technology. The new law also provided incentive payments to physicians and other medical providers who made meaningful use of electronic health records by 2012. ($20.8 billion)

Tax-Exempt Bonds

The law created two new categories of tax credit bonds. Tax credit bonds provide investors with a federal tax credit in lieu of an exemption for interest payments. The first, known as the Build America bond program, could be issued by state and local governments for the construction, rehabilitation, or repair of public school facilities or for the acquisition of land on which a public school facility would be constructed. The law authorized $22 billion in bonds, $11 billion in each of 2009 and 2010. ($9.9 billion)

The second category of tax credit bonds was for investment in economic recovery zones. The law authorized $10 billion in recovery zone economic development bonds and $15 billion in recovery zone facility bonds. (Estimated eleven-year cost: $5.4 billion)

Mandatory Programs

Unemployment compensation. The law continued until December 31, 2009, the existing thirty-three weeks of extra unemployment benefits granted workers who exhausted their initial twenty-six weeks of assistance. The law also boosted average jobless benefits by $25 a week and gave states additional assistance. ($39.2 billion) *(Unemployment compensation extensions, pp. 517, 535)*

COBRA. The law provided a 65 percent subsidy for health insurance premiums under the program created by the Consolidated Omnibus Budget Reconciliation Act (COBRA), which allowed people who lost their jobs to temporarily retain their employer-sponsored health insurance. The subsidy was good for up to nine months for workers who lost their jobs and health coverage before January 1, 2010. Under the previous law, the jobless person had to assume the full cost of the premiums, including the former employer's share. ($25.1 billion) *(Details, p. 525)*

Displaced workers. Trade Adjustment Assistance programs were expanded, including extending TAA to trade-affected service workers and to workers affected by outsourcing to all countries. The new law also reauthorized all TAA programs, which expired at the end of 2007, through December 31, 2010. ($1.6 billion) *(Details, p. 199)*

Medicaid. Federal Medicaid reimbursements to states were increased by 6.2 percent for the period beginning

October 1, 2008, and ending December 31, 2010. States with high unemployment rates were to receive additional assistance. ($86.6 billion)

TARP Restrictions

Restrictions on executive compensation at all banks and other firms receiving TARP bailouts, including a ban on so-called "golden parachutes" for departing executives, a limit on bonuses to one-third of total compensation, "claw-back" provisions to force bankers to give back bonuses based on "materially inaccurate performance criteria," and creation of compensation committees composed entirely of independent, nonexecutive directors. *(Executive compensation, p. 65)*

Debt Limit Increase

An increase in the statutory ceiling on federal government borrowing to $12.104 trillion from $11.315 trillion.

Credit Card Restrictions

Propelled by popular anger over what many considered arbitrary or even predatory practices by lenders in the midst of a deep recession, Congress cleared a bill to set new restrictions on when credit card companies could increase interest rates and fees. The bill was a priority for President Barack Obama, and lawmakers met his deadline of finishing it by the Memorial Day recess. Obama signed the measure on May 22, 2009 (HR 627—PL 111-24).

The House had passed similar legislation in 2008, but the Senate did not take it up, and it died at the end of the session. This time, although many Republicans criticized federal restrictions on private lenders, the outcry against practices such as retroactive rate increases led to overwhelming votes for the legislation in both chambers. *(Congress and the Nation Vol. XII, p. 149)*

LEGISLATIVE ACTION

The House passed HR 627 (H Rept 111-88) on April 30, on a bipartisan vote of 357–70. Before passage, and over opposition from the credit card industry, the House adopted several changes requested by the Obama administration to tighten some of the restrictions. In a statement issued after the vote, Obama continued his push for strong legislation. "While Americans have a responsibility to live within their means and pay what they owe," he said, "credit card companies have a responsibility to set rules that are fair and transparent."

The Senate Banking, Housing and Urban Affairs Committee narrowly approved a version (S 414—S Rept 111-16) on March 31 with sharper limitations on the ability of credit card companies to raise interest rates.

In a rare instance of bipartisanship in a bitterly divided Congress, the Senate passed a compromise version of the bill on May 19 on a **key vote of 90–5 (R 35–4; D 53–1; I 2–0).** *(2009 key votes, p. 751)*

To win that bipartisan support, Christopher J. Dodd, D-Conn., and Richard C. Shelby, R-Ala., respectively the chair and the ranking minority member of the Banking committee, negotiated for several weeks, finally agreeing on a compromise that scaled back some of the committee-approved restrictions. Still, the Senate version was stricter than the House-passed measure.

The Senate bill also carried an amendment pushed by gun rights advocates that allowed visitors to national parks and wildlife refuges to carry loaded firearms. The House cleared the Senate bill, first adopting the credit card provisions, 361–64, and then agreeing to the gun provisions, 279–147. The divided vote allowed Democrats who opposed the gun provisions to vote no on that portion of the bill without jeopardizing passage of the credit card provisions. *(Firearms in parks, p. 559)*

Slapped with a major defeat, the banking industry continued to oppose the bill, saying it would force firms to raise interest rates and reduce credit lines for all customers, including those who were current on their payments. Concerned that some financial institutions were taking advantage of consumers in the interim before the measure took effect, the House passed a bill (HR 3639) in November 2009 to speed enforcement by putting the new regulations into effect immediately, but the Senate did not act on the measure.

MAJOR PROVISIONS

Rates and fees. The new law allowed credit card companies to increase the annual percentage rate, fees, or finance charges on existing balances before the specified termination date only if the rate was pegged to a variable index or was the result of the expiration of a promotional rate, or if a minimum payment was not received within sixty days of the due date. The bill also required forty-five days' notice to the cardholder of such an increase, stating that it would last no longer than six months. The notice had to fully describe the change in annual percentage rate and how the increase would affect the cardholder's current balance.

The law prohibited "double-cycle billing"—the practice of computing interest charges based on the current and previous billing cycle—if the consumer had repaid the previous balance within the grace period. Statements had to be sent out at least twenty-five days before the due date.

The law also required that promotional rates remain valid for at least six months and that initial interest rates be locked in for at least one year after initial activation. The practice of "universal default," in which card issuers raised interest rates because the consumer was delinquent in paying other creditors, was prohibited.

Credit card companies were required to apply monthly payments above the required minimum to the balance with the highest interest rate, or to all balances equally. Companies could not apply the payments to the debt with the lowest interest rate first, thus boosting their interest charges. Companies were also prohibited from charging for payment processing, such as on-time payments by phone, and from charging a fee when a credit card balance went above a specified limit, unless the consumer expressly chose to permit the company to complete transactions that pushed the account over the limit.

Disclosure requirements. The new law required credit card companies to provide consumers with statements, in a conspicuous place, that included the type of any transaction that bore a separate interest rate, such as balance transfers or cash advances, and a warning that making only minimum payments would increase consumer costs. The report had to include the number of months needed to pay off the consumer's balance based on minimum payments and the total cost, including interest and principal payments. The statement also had to include the date on which a late payment fee would be charged and the amount of the fee, as well as any rate increase that would apply.

Protections for young consumers. Credit card companies were barred from issuing a card to an individual under twenty-one who failed to show a reasonable ability to pay or did not have a cosigner and from offering promotional items to students on campus or at school events. Colleges were required to publicly disclose any credit card marketing agreements made with a credit card company.

Gun possession. The law barred any regulation that would prohibit an individual from possessing a firearm in any national park or national wildlife refuge, if the individual was legally allowed to possess a gun. The gun possessor also had to comply with the law of the state in which the park or refuge was located.

Effective date. Companies were required to implement the forty-five-day notice requirement within ninety days of the bill's enactment. All other provisions took effect nine months after enactment.

2010 Jobs Creation Bill

The top item on the Democrats' economic agenda for 2010 was tackling the nation's double-digit unemployment. Enactment of a $17.6 billion jobs bill in March 2010 was seen as the first victory in that drive. President Barack Obama signed the bill into law March 18 (HR 2847—PL 111-147).

Yet, the final bill was far smaller than the $154 billion version the House initially adopted in December 2009 and contained few of its provisions to create or retain jobs. Moreover, Democrats' hopes that the legislation would provide momentum for other items on their jobs agenda were quickly dashed. The importance assigned to deficit control, along with partisan bickering in the Senate, stymied a number of initiatives. By the end of the year, only two other significant pieces of jobs legislation had been enacted: one aimed at preventing widespread teacher reductions and the other to help small business. *(Teacher spending supplemental, p. 479; small business, p. 102)*

The centerpiece of the March jobs bill was $13 billion over ten years in payroll tax relief for employers who hired unemployed workers. The bill also extended expensing rules for small businesses, authorization for highway programs, and the Build America bond program, which was aimed at making it easier for state and local governments to invest in infrastructure and clean-energy projects.

2009 LEGISLATIVE ACTION

With unemployment hovering at 10 percent, House Speaker Nancy Pelosi, D-Calif., saw to it that her party went on record favoring a jobs bill before leaving Washington at the end of 2009. In its last vote of the session, the House passed a $154 billion bill aimed largely at creating and retaining jobs. At the same time, the close 217–212 vote, and the effort required to win it, signaled future difficulties for the party in addressing the recession in a time of soaring deficits.

The House bill, dubbed the Jobs for Main Street Act, was broken into three broad categories: $48.3 billion for infrastructure projects, $26.7 billion in assistance to state and local governments to preserve public service jobs, and additional assistance to families affected by the recession. It also would have extended unemployment insurance and health insurance subsidies for jobless workers through June 2010 at a cost of $53.3 billion and extended the authorizations for surface transportation and for certain small-business loan programs through the end of fiscal 2010. *(Unemployment benefits, pp. 517, 535; COBRA subsidies, p. 525; surface transportation, p. 324)*

Programs in the first two categories were to be paid for by shifting funds from the Troubled Asset Relief Program (TARP), the unpopular $700 billion program created in 2008 (PL 110-343) to stabilize the battered financial industry. Funding for the third piece of the package, which covered programs such as extended unemployment benefits, was to be treated as emergency spending, which was not subject to Congress's self-imposed budget limits.

House Democrats had talked for weeks about passing a substantial package to kick-start job creation. But public concern about federal spending and record-high deficits made the plan a hard sell to some within the Democratic Caucus. Adding to Democratic resistance, the bill came up just after the House passed a $636 billion defense appropriations bill (PL 111-118) and a $290 billion increase in the federal debt ceiling (PL 111-123). The bill also followed a $787.2 billion economic stimulus bill (PL 111-5) that Democrats had pushed to enactment early in the year. *(Defense appropriations, p. 280; debt limit, p. 134; stimulus, p. 78)*

Republicans argued that the jobs bill demonstrated the failure of earlier Democratic economic plans, including the stimulus law. The infrastructure component of the bill included money for highways, public transportation, Amtrak capital improvements, state and local clean water programs, and public housing. The public service provisions were aimed at helping states to retain or create public

BERNANKE GIVEN NEW TERM AS FEDERAL RESERVE CHAIR

Ben S. Bernanke won a second term as head of the Federal Reserve in January 2010, when the Senate confirmed him by a wide margin after weeks of wrangling over the nomination. Still, he received a record number of "no" votes for the Fed chair.

Bernanke, who had parried attacks on the central bank's hands-off approach leading up to the financial crisis as well as its aggressive intervention afterward, was confirmed January 28 on a **key vote of 70–30 (R 22–18; D 47–11; I 1–1)**. The vote was preceded by another critical vote, when the Senate voted 77–23 to limit debate on the nomination. *(2010 key votes, p. 767)*

The vote foreshadowed the difficulty the Fed would encounter later in the year as Congress debated reining in the central bank's powers as part of an overhaul of financial services regulations. Yet, just as with Bernanke's confirmation, lawmakers ultimately opted to leave the Fed's authority intact. *(Financial regulatory reform, p. 88)*

Given the Fed's role in the financial crisis, Bernanke's path to a second term as chair of the central bank's Board of Governors was rocky from the start. He led the central bank in pumping trillions of dollars into the financial system to keep it afloat and was deeply involved in the unpopular $700 billion bank bailout enacted in 2008 (PL 110-343). But Bernanke was also hailed as the man who saved America from a second Great Depression. He was *Time* magazine's Person of the Year for 2009.

Similarly, senators opposed to the nomination tended to view Bernanke from two different perspectives. Opponents within the Democratic Caucus said Bernanke and the Fed had been blind to the needs of average Americans, opting instead to rescue the biggest firms on Wall Street at the expense of workers. Republicans objected to the scope of the Fed's intervention in markets and financial institutions.

Several days before the vote, when it appeared that the nomination could be in trouble, the White House began lobbying strongly for his confirmation. The administration portrayed the vote as a test of financial stability, and Democratic leaders promised members other opportunities to vent their anger with the banking system. Bernanke met with Senate Majority Whip Richard J. Durbin, D-Ill., to discuss a range of concerns of Democratic senators, including transparency and accountability at the Fed and its role in consumer protection.

The thirty votes against Bernanke set a record, almost double the sixteen votes cast against Fed Chair Paul A. Volcker in 1983, when he was up for a second term as head of the central bank. Volcker faced criticism for his extremely tight monetary policy to combat inflation.

Bernanke was confirmed by voice vote in 2006 for his first four-year term as chair, with just one senator, Jim Bunning, R-Ky., raising objections to his nomination. Bernanke was also confirmed that year for a fourteen-year term as a member of the Federal Reserve's Board of Governors. That term runs until 2020. *(Bernanke's 2006 confirmation, Congress and the Nation Vol. XII, box, p. 143)*

sector jobs at a time when they were facing severe budget cuts. The money was intended to support jobs in education, law enforcement, and firefighting; provide grants for job training in high-growth and emerging job sectors; and fund college work-study programs and summer jobs.

Knowing the jobs bill was likely to stall, Democrats included shorter extensions of many of the same programs in the fiscal 2010 defense appropriations bill.

During floor debate, Democrats stressed their desire to redirect funds from Wall Street to Main Street. Appropriations Chair David R. Obey of Wisconsin said the TARP money would be used "to preserve the jobs of teachers, firemen, policemen, prison guards, you name it, and at the same time provide another boost to construction of infrastructure projects around the country."

Republicans took to the floor to condemn the jobs measure as the latest example of Democratic spending run amok. Calling the bill "son of stimulus," they argued that it demonstrated the failure of earlier Democratic economic plans. Republicans also opposed the use of TARP funds, arguing that any money not spent for the original purpose should be returned to the Treasury to reduce the deficit.

In keeping with commitments made earlier in the year to the Blue Dog Coalition of fiscally conservative House Democrats, the leadership used the rule for floor debate (H Res 976) to automatically add the provisions of a House-passed "pay-as-you-go" bill (HR 2920) that required most new tax cuts and increases in entitlement spending to be offset so they did not add to the deficit. *(Details, p. 142)*

2010 LEGISLATIVE ACTION

The Senate voted, 70–28, on February 24, 2010, to amend the 2009 House-passed bill substituting a smaller $15 billion jobs measure. Majority Leader Harry Reid, D-Nev., pulled the four main provisions from a broader, $85 billion bipartisan draft bill negotiated by Finance Committee Chair Max Baucus, D-Mont., and the committee's top Republican, Charles E. Grassley of Iowa.

Reid's amendment offered tax relief for businesses that hired or retained workers and proposed to extend surface transportation programs, the Build America bond program, and expensing rules for small businesses. In assembling the amendment, Reid dropped more than $31 billion in tax-cut extensions from the Baucus-Grassley plan, drawing fire from Republicans, who initially withheld their support. The tax provisions that Reid left out would have extended through 2010 a raft of tax breaks that expired at the end of 2009, including the research and development tax credit, tax incentives for the production of biodiesel, and a state sales tax deduction for individuals. *(Tax breaks extension, p. 144)*

The Baucus-Grassley compromise also would have extended through the end of May federal unemployment insurance and health insurance subsidies for laid-off workers, temporarily put off a cut in Medicare physicians' payment rates, and extended provisions of the counterterrorism law known as the Patriot Act. *(Medicare pay, p. 450; Patriot Act, p. 208)*

A spokesperson said Reid pared down the bill after his caucus members raised concerns about the makeup of the Baucus-Grassley draft and Reid sensed Republican unwillingness to accept the whole Baucus-Grassley plan. Liberals also objected, in particular, that the business tax breaks were scheduled to last to the end of the year, whereas benefits for jobless workers' families would last only through May.

Before passage, leaders won a 62–34 vote to waive the chamber's pay-as-you-go budget rules. Judd Gregg, R-N.H., objected particularly to provisions to transfer $19.5 billion from the general fund to the Highway Trust fund. "This isn't so much a jobs bill as it is a debt bill," Gregg said later.

The House passed the amended Senate bill March 4, after making changes negotiated by the Democratic leadership to convince party members who were dissatisfied with the Senate version. The March 4 vote was 217–201.

The changes were aimed at mollifying three groups within the Democratic caucus. At the insistence of fiscally conservative "Blue Dog" Democrats, the cost of the tax cuts was fully offset, mainly through accounting gimmicks.

In a nod to members of the Congressional Black Caucus, the revised House bill added language requiring that 10 percent of the funds for certain programs authorized under the bill go to small businesses "controlled by socially and economically disadvantaged individuals." The caucus complained that the bill concentrated on business and should do more to help low-income and minority communities that were hit especially hard by the recession.

James L. Oberstar, D-Minn., the chair of the Transportation and Infrastructure Committee, had held up the bill over objections that the surface transportation extension would fund certain programs based on earmarks in the last long-term surface transportation law. He said that would give 58 percent of the programs' funding to California, Illinois, Louisiana, and Washington and provide no funding to twenty-two states. But Oberstar backed off, saying the revised bill would allow certain discretionary funds to be allocated among all states. Hours after the bill cleared, Oberstar won voice vote passage of legislation (HR 4853) to alter the distribution method, but the Senate did not act on the measure.

The Senate cleared the jobs bill by a vote of 68–29 on March 17 after Democrats held off another GOP budgetary challenge. Republicans insisted that even the considerably slimmed-down bill was not deficit neutral.

MAIN PROVISIONS

Employer payroll tax forgiveness. Employers were exempted from paying Social Security payroll taxes in 2010 on the wages of unemployed workers hired after February 3 and before January 1, 2011. The newly hired workers could not have been employed for more than forty hours during the sixty-day period before their hiring.

Business retention credit. An existing general business tax credit was increased for employers who retained newly hired workers in 2010. The increase was the lesser of $1,000 or 6.2 percent of the wages paid to each worker who was hired at some point during the year and retained for fifty-two consecutive weeks.

Expensing. Businesses could deduct from taxable income the amount of an investment in the year the investment was made. The measure increased for one year—from $125,000 to $250,000—the amount that businesses could write off in 2010 for certain investments made in that tax year. Previous law had provided the higher amount for 2008 and 2009 but reverted to $125,000 for 2010. The increase was phased out for property costing more than $800,000—an increase from the previous threshold of $500,000.

Build America bonds. The bill expanded and made permanent a qualified tax-credit bond initiative, known as the Build America bond program, created under the 2009 stimulus law (PL 111-5). The program gave state and local governments the option of offering tax-credit bonds—which provided federal tax credits to investors instead of interest payments—in lieu of tax-exempt bonds. The purpose was to encourage investment by alleviating the need for the state or local government to make interest payments. The extension applied to clean renewable-energy bonds, qualified school construction bonds, and qualified energy conservation bonds, among others.

Surface transportation reauthorization. Highway, mass transit, and road safety programs were extended through December 31, 2010. The bill authorized appropriations to be distributed in the same amounts as in fiscal 2009, provided contract authority, and extended the authority to spend money from the Highway Trust Fund. The last long-term authorization (PL 109-59) had expired in 2009, and highway, transit, and safety programs had been kept alive through a series of short-term extensions.

The bill also transferred $19.5 billion from the general fund to the Highway Trust Fund and restored $8.7 billion in contract authority that had been rescinded on September 30, 2009. *(Surface transportation legislation, p. 324)*

Financial Regulation Overhaul

In a major victory for President Barack Obama, Congress in July 2010 cleared a sweeping overhaul of the nation's financial regulatory system, known as Dodd-Frank after its chief sponsors, Sen. Christopher J. Dodd, D-Conn., and Rep. Barney Frank, D-Mass. The historic legislation promised to alter banking and securities law going back as far as 1933. Obama signed the bill (HR 4173—PL 111-203) into law on July 21.

The legislation was a response to the financial crisis that had begun in 2007 and led to the deepest recession since the Great Depression in the 1930s. Work on the bill came in the midst of a weak recovery at a time when voters were fed up with multibillion-dollar bailouts, double-digit unemployment rates, and the evaporation of their retirement savings. The law touched nearly every major piece of twentieth century financial regulatory law, from New Deal–era banking and securities acts to the legislation that grew out of the savings and loan crisis of the late 1980s and early 1990s.

For the first time, a process was put in place to assess and mitigate the risks of huge financial institutions whose activities or condition could pose a danger to the financial system. The legislation created an orderly process for tightening restraints on faltering institutions and, in extreme cases, shutting down a business that continued to pose a risk despite previous intervention. Lawmakers intended the process to prevent future bailouts and eliminate the assumption that the government would step in to salvage huge companies because they were considered "too big to fail." The law established a new level of transparency in financial markets, especially in derivatives trading, where complex securities such as currency swaps came under federal regulation for the first time.

A new consumer protection agency was created to watch over the interests of consumers and include them as part of the equation when regulators examined the state of the economy as a whole. Although the Federal Reserve (Fed) was put under new oversight, early attempts to greatly curtail its role were set aside, and the central bank gained major new responsibilities. In addition to retaining its regulation of federally chartered banks, it housed the new consumer agency and was given a central role in bringing risky financial institutions under federal restrictions.

From the beginning, the White House endorsed reform, saying that the status quo was unacceptable and that financial institutions needed to change the way they did business. The financial services industry, business groups, and many Republicans pushed back, calling the overhaul package as untoward government intrusion in the markets and warning that it could end up quashing any nascent economic recovery.

As a result, passage of the bill through the legislative process was lengthy and intense as supporters worked to concede only what was absolutely necessary to get the measure through Congress. The House passed its version of the bill on December 11, 2009. The Senate followed suit, passing its version May 20, 2010. Conferees thought they had reached a compromise agreement after two weeks of negotiation, only to be forced to come back and make changes that were considered crucial to securing the sixty votes needed to overcome a threatened Republican filibuster in the Senate. It still took Senate leaders until July 15 to assemble the votes to clear the bill.

Passage of the overhaul did little to diminish opposition to the legislation. As they did with the health care overhaul, congressional opponents continued their efforts to repeal or modify provisions they did not like and to slow implementation of the new regulations. *(2011–2012 action, p. 104)*

The Congressional Budget Office (CBO) estimated the total cost of the legislation at $26.9 billion over ten years and said all of it would be offset under the bill.

The last major revision of federal financial regulation laws came in 1999, when Congress repealed the Glass-Steagall Act of 1933. Among other things, that law barred commercial banks from engaging in investment banking. Various developments eroded that separation over the years, including the rise of international banking. Nonetheless, many observers said allowing banks to engage in both commercial and investment activities had contributed to the depth of the financial crisis. *(Glass-Steagall repeal, Congress and the Nation Vol. X, p. 130)*

HIGHLIGHTS

Dealing with Systemic Risks. For the first time, a government apparatus was created to identify and monitor companies that had become so large or interconnected that their failure could threaten the entire financial system. The law created a new Financial Stability Oversight Council made up of existing financial regulators, with the Treasury secretary at the helm, to monitor potential systemwide risks and make recommendations to the Fed. With a two-thirds majority vote, the council could subject a nonbank company to the Fed's regulatory powers. Also by a two-thirds vote, the council could approve a decision by the Fed to break up a large company that posed a grave threat to the financial system, but only as a last resort. New rules also limited banks' proprietary trading and their ability to invest in hedge funds and private equity funds.

An orderly process was created for the Federal Deposit Insurance Corporation (FDIC) to liquidate large failing companies whose collapse would pose a risk to the financial system. The liquidation required the assent of the Treasury secretary, the president, and two regulators and could be used only as a last resort after remediation efforts had failed. Costs of liquidating companies would be covered by the sale of their assets and by assessments on large financial institutions levied by the FDIC.

Protecting Consumers. An independent Consumer Financial Protection Bureau (CFPB) was created within the Federal Reserve system to look out for consumers' interests, with a director appointed by the president and confirmed by the Senate. The bureau was responsible for enforcing consumer protection laws, as well as consumer regulations for banks and credit unions with assets of more than $10 billion, mortgage-related businesses, payday lenders, and others. The bureau's regulations would generally not preempt state laws that provided greater protection for consumers.

Federal Reserve Powers. The Fed was a central part of the new regime, albeit with some new restrictions on its powers. It was given responsibility for identifying risks and setting heightened standards for financial institutions that were so large or interconnected that they would pose risks to the financial system as a whole if they were to collapse. The Fed could impose increasingly stringent regulations on faltering financial institutions in an effort to help them avoid collapse. The Fed also retained its oversight of federally chartered bank holding companies.

The Fed could no longer provide emergency loans for individual institutions, and the Treasury had to approve all Fed emergency lending aimed at the financial system as a whole. The emergency lending authority had played a prominent role in enabling the Fed to make emergency loans to rescue American International Group (AIG) and other troubled companies in 2008.

The Government Accountability Office (GAO) was charged with conducting a one-time audit of all Fed emergency loan programs created during the financial crisis. It also was given the authority to audit future emergency lending and other Fed transactions, with a two-year delay on releasing the results. Conferees declined to open the Fed's most sensitive monetary policy discussions to examination.

Regulating Derivatives. The law brought the over-the-counter financial derivatives market under significant government regulation. Many derivatives had to be traded on exchanges and routed through clearinghouses, with regulators examining trades before they were cleared. Regulators could impose margin requirements for those derivatives that were not required to go through a clearinghouse. Banks were required to spin off their riskiest derivatives-trading operations to affiliates.

Offsets. A major source of offsets was a provision to immediately end the Troubled Asset Relief Program (TARP), which was created in 2008 (PL 110-343) to salvage huge failing financial institutions.

Another source was higher premium fees for the FDIC's Deposit Insurance Fund for banks with more than $10 billion in assets. CBO estimated that the TARP change would result in $11 billion in savings, whereas the increased FDIC fees would generate a net $5.7 billion in revenue.

HOUSE ACTION

Still in the throes of multibillion-dollar efforts to rescue the financial industry and pull the economy out of recession, President Obama and congressional Democrats began his presidency vowing to put in place a new regulatory structure that could prevent a repeat of the meltdown of 2008. With so many of the largest financial institutions relying on the federal government for life support, and others failing entirely, the Obama administration made regulatory overhaul a core component of its agenda. Many of the administration's legislative proposals were similar to major provisions in the House bill, including the creation of a new systemic-risk regulator and a consumer financial protection agency, and efforts to bring the derivatives market under federal regulation for the first time.

In the House, the Financial Services Committee spent more than fifty hours debating the nine separate bills that made up the package that came to the floor. Throughout the process, Frank, the committee chair, had to struggle to balance the White House's wishes and Democratic leadership priorities against heavy lobbying from the still-influential financial industry. Although the president's main priorities remained largely intact, Frank made several changes to accommodate concerns within his own party. For example, he agreed to limit the reach of the consumer protection agency to allay fears that it would unduly burden smaller community banks with another layer of regulation.

Three of the nine bills were especially controversial. One bill (HR 3795) brought the financial derivatives market under government regulation. Regulation was virtually nonexistent in the relatively opaque $580 trillion over-the-counter derivatives market, where many trades and contracts were executed privately between individual parties. The measure was prompted in part by the 2008 implosion and subsequent bailout of insurance giant AIG, which had taken major risks by purchasing mortgage-related derivatives. The company rang up huge losses when the real estate market soured, prompting a massive government bailout.

The committee adopted an amendment by Frank to increase transparency in the derivatives market by requiring that transactions between two financial institutions that were processed through a clearinghouse be executed on a public exchange, where specifics of the deal would become public. The change drew fire from Republicans and the financial services industry, but it brought the bill more in line with the position of the Obama administration.

Another bill (HR 3126) created a Consumer Financial Protection Agency charged with overseeing consumer financial products. House Republicans universally opposed the legislation, and the U.S. Chamber of Commerce poured $2 million into an effort to kill it. They said the legislation would subject businesses to unnecessarily onerous restrictions and would limit credit for consumers. "It's not about protecting consumers," said Spencer Bachus of Alabama, the committee's top Republican. "It's about a new government bureaucracy making decisions for us."

Consumer groups argued that the agency was essential to protect individuals who were exploited by complicated products that had failed spectacularly in the previous two years.

Topping the list was the collapse in 2007 of the subprime mortgage market, which brought widespread foreclosures that homeowners and banks were still grappling with five years later. Banks sought but failed to win a major concession: strong preemption of state consumer regulations. Under Frank's bill, states were allowed to issue tougher consumer regulations than those adopted by the federal government.

The third House bill (HR 3996) became the centerpiece of the package. It established a Financial Oversight Council and created a process to manage, and potentially even dismantle, financial institutions whose condition posed a risk to the economy as a whole. "Our goal is to: A, make it less likely that [failures] will happen, and B, to be able to deal with it better when it does," Frank said.

Other critical features of the bill required the Securities and Exchange Commission (SEC) to monitor hedge funds for systemic risk, including authorizing the agency to require investment advisers to disclose the identity, investments, and affairs of their clients. The SEC was also required to strengthen regulation of credit rating firms, which were under fire for their role in the freeze-up of the financial markets. To help the agency with these new responsibilities, the House bill expanded the SEC, authorized an additional $9.9 billion for its activities over six years, and established new standards for investment advisers and broker-dealers. The SEC had faced stinging criticism for its failure to uncover a multibillion-dollar Ponzi scheme by broker Bernard Madoff that was revealed in 2008. *(Madoff, Congress and the Nation Vol. XII, p. 140)*

Once the House committee had acted on the individual bills, Frank combined them into a composite bill (HR 4173), which the House passed, 223–202, on December 11. No Republican voted for the bill; twenty-seven Democrats, many of them members of the fiscally conservative Blue Dog Coalition, also voted against it. Republicans blasted the overall bill as a job killer that could restrict credit and would put taxpayers on the hook to bail out failing financial firms.

The rule for floor debate added a provision authorizing the use of $22.1 billion from the TARP to offset part of the bill's cost.

Through three days of debate and votes on dozens of amendments, Frank and other Democratic leaders fended off efforts to kill critical elements of the bill, including the proposed consumer protection agency and provisions to police large financial institutions, while accommodating several changes to satisfy concerns from moderate and business-friendly members of their own caucus. Still, Frank was forced to accept some changes to get the bill passed. For example, he was unable to eliminate the provision to allow the GAO to audit the Federal Reserve.

SENATE ACTION

The Senate Banking, Housing, and Urban Affairs Committee began in November to consider an overhaul package drafted by Dodd, the committee's chair. The package proposed a single federal banking regulator and a powerful new agency to monitor broad risks to the financial system, while stripping a substantial amount of regulatory power from the Federal Reserve.

The proposal met with strong GOP resistance. After the committee broke into bipartisan groups to work on various parts of the bill, Dodd and ranking Republican Richard C. Shelby of Alabama ended the year on an optimistic note, saying in a joint statement that they had made "meaningful progress" and expected action early in 2010.

The two senators overestimated the progress that had been made. After months of bipartisan closed-door negotiations failed to produce a bill, Dodd introduced legislation on March 15, 2010. The chair had held at least two rounds of talks with GOP committee members and negotiated alternately with Shelby and with Bob Corker, R-Tenn. Dodd then focused on panel Democrats to gain their support. The Banking Committee approved the bill (S 3217—S Rept 111-176) a week later on a party-line vote.

Senate floor debate on the bill began April 26 and proceeded in fits and starts until May 20, when the Senate passed HR 4173 after inserting the text of S 3217, 59–39.

Four Republicans broke with their party to support the bill. They were Olympia J. Snowe and Susan Collins of Maine, Charles E. Grassley of Iowa, and Scott P. Brown of Massachusetts. Two Democrats—Russ Feingold of Wisconsin and Maria Cantwell of Washington—voted no.

The definitive vote leading to Senate action occurred hours earlier, when the Senate agreed 60–40, to invoke cloture on the final version of the bill, bringing the prolonged debate to close. Just a day earlier, the Senate had rejected an attempt to limit the debate, 57–42. The critical votes came from Brown, who switched to support cloture, and Arlen Specter, D-Pa., who was absent for the first of the two cloture votes. (Majority Leader Harry Reid, D-Nev., shifted to the "no" side in the first of the two votes to preserve his parliamentary right to move to reconsider at a later point.)

Republicans began their delaying tactics the day Reid first tried to bring the bill up on the floor, sticking together to defeat three cloture motions in as many days. But a key compromise and the Democrats' strategy of using the repeated votes to portray Republicans as opposing a crackdown on Wall Street excesses eventually worked. Republicans called off their filibuster April 28, allowing the Senate to proceed to the bill, but they promised many amendments.

To end the filibuster, Democrats agreed to drop a $50 billion resolution fund, financed by fees on big banks, that would have been used to cover the cost of liquidating failed companies. Republicans argued that the fund's existence would ensure future bailouts and force healthy banks to pay for the errors of risky institutions and regarded its elimination as a victory. Shelby, who had been negotiating for weeks with Dodd on the amendment, said the change would make it clear "that backdoor bailouts are impossible."

Instead, the FDIC would be able to tap a credit line at the Treasury Department to liquidate large companies. The Treasury would be repaid from assets of the failed institution. Creditors of the failing company would have to pay back any funds received in excess of what they would have been awarded in a traditional bankruptcy proceeding in liquidation. If that was insufficient, the FDIC would levy assessments on financial institutions with total consolidated assets of $50 billion or more.

During the weeks of floor debate on the bill, the Senate took roll-call votes on twenty-eight amendments. Despite intense lobbying by the American Bankers Association and others in the financial services industry, Dodd managed to keep the core provisions of the bill mostly intact.

Among the most controversial amendments was an amendment by Shelby that would have drastically scaled back the scope and powers of the consumer protection agency. It was rejected 38–62. Republicans argued that the bill would give the agency unchecked power. They particularly wanted to ensure that financial regulators could intervene if the new agency issued rules that would compromise the safety and soundness of the banks. Dodd responded that he was not willing to weaken consumer protections, "given the enormous abuses we have seen."

Also rejected, 39–59, was an amendment by Saxby Chambliss, R-Ga., to strike the provisions on derivatives and replace them with language that would require more disclosure of swaps and allow the SEC and Commodity Futures Trading Commission (CFTC) to apply new requirements to swap transactions. Republicans, in particular, wanted to ensure that companies that used derivatives to hedge risk associated with market fluctuations—rather than for trading—would not be subject to the bill's requirements that they clear their trades or place them on a public exchange. The existing legislation had a relatively narrow exemption for such end users.

Republicans and a few Democrats also opposed provisions that would force depository institutions to spin off their lucrative business in derivatives, which were partially blamed for the market meltdown that prompted the legislation. The language was championed by Blanche Lincoln, D-Ark., who was locked in a tough primary race. Democratic leaders did not want to drop the language out of concern that it would hurt Lincoln's chances, and the calculus continued when she survived a May 18 primary election but was forced into a June runoff. Having failed to minimize the provisions in the Senate, the industry turned their hopes to the conference.

The Senate adopted, 96–0, an amendment by Bernard Sanders, I-Vt., to require the GAO to complete an audit of the Fed within one year and require the central bank to disclose the names of the financial institutions that had gotten emergency financial assistance since December 2007, the amounts, the dates the assistance was provided, the terms of repayment, and the "specific rationale" for creating the emergency lending programs. The details would amount to the clearest picture yet of the central bank's lending activities during the 2008–2009 financial meltdown.

The amendment was weaker than the House language, which would have allowed monetary policy reviews. Nonetheless, Fed Chair Ben S. Bernanke wrote a strongly worded letter to Dodd expressing "deep concern" about Sanders's original language, saying the requirements could interfere with the independence of the Fed's monetary policy and damage its credibility in financial markets.

The Senate also adopted, 63–36, a Dodd amendment to require the Treasury Department to conduct a study on ending the federal conservatorship of mortgage-lending giants Fannie Mae and Freddie Mac that began in September 2008. The amendment required the Treasury to report to Congress by January 31, 2011. *(2008 action, Congress and the Nation Vol. XII, p. 153)*

Amendments to end the conservatorship of Fannie and Freddie Mac within thirty months of the bill's enactment and dismantle the two companies if they were not financially viable at that point and to cap government funding of the two mortgage lenders at $200 billion and place their balance sheets on the federal budget until the end of any federal conservatorship or receivership were both rejected.

FINAL ACTION

After two weeks of negotiations punctuated by an all-night marathon session the final day, House and Senate Democratic conferees reached agreement on the bill in the early morning on June 25. The legislation was renamed the Dodd-Frank Act in honor of the bill managers. Afterward, with tears running down his cheeks, Frank hugged Dodd, who was retiring at year's end. But four days later, Frank was forced to reconvene the conference to scrap plans to cover the cost of the overhaul through fees levied on large financial institutions and hedge funds.

Under the original conference agreement, the FDIC would have been authorized to raise up to $19 billion over five years through assessments on financial institutions with assets of $50 billion or more and on hedge funds that managed more than $10 billion in assets. The proceeds could not have been used for any other purpose, and after twenty-five years, any unused money would have gone to pay down the national debt.

Democrats dropped the Senate plan after it became clear that several moderate Senate Republicans, including Brown, Snowe, and Collins, would not support the conference report if it included the assessment. With the June 28 death of a Senate icon, Democrat Robert C. Byrd of West Virginia, Reid was down to a fifty-eight-member caucus. At least two Democrats were talking of opposing the bill, so he could not afford to lose the three GOP votes. *(Byrd death, p. 10)*

Democrats agreed to replace the bank fees with funds freed up by immediately ending TARP and to authorize the FDIC to increase premium fees for large banks. Democrats rejected an alternative that would have used money from the 2009 economic stimulus legislation (PL 111-5) instead.

The chief hurdle to completing the original conference report was Lincoln's proposed ban on derivatives trading by depository institutions. Under the final compromise, banks were required to divert their riskiest derivatives—those related to commodities, energy, metals, agriculture, equities, and below-investment-grade credit default swaps—into a separately capitalized entity walled off from federally insured deposits.

However, they were allowed to keep their business in derivatives tied to interest rate swaps, which represented a huge swath of the market. They also could continue to trade in derivatives related to foreign exchange swaps, credit, gold and silver, investment-grade credit default swaps, and any transaction to hedge risk. House Democrats had warned repeatedly that their chamber would not be able to pass the overall legislation if Lincoln's tougher provision were retained.

Conferees also struck an eleventh-hour deal on the so-called Volcker rule, which proposed to curb proprietary trading by banks. It was named after Paul A. Volcker, a former chair of the Federal Reserve Board of Governors. The final version was not as restrictive as the original Senate provision, which would have completely banned banks from using their own money to buy or sell securities in financial markets to turn a profit. The provision that negotiators accepted gave the regulators less discretion in implementing the Volcker rule, but it loosened the requirements on banks, allowing them to have up to 3 percent of their tangible common equity in a hedge fund or private equity firm.

Frank filed the conference report (H Rept 111-517) on June 29, and the House adopted it the next day by a **key vote of 237–192 (R 3–173; D 234–19)**. Fourteen more legislators—eleven Democrats and three Republicans—voted for the final version than had supported the original house version passed in December 2009. 2010 *(2010 key votes, p. 767)*

The House voted 198–229, along party lines, to reject a motion to recommit the bill with instructions to add language by Ron Paul, R-Texas, that would have given the GAO significantly expanded audit authority over the Fed, including the ability to monitor some of the central bank's most sensitive monetary policy deliberations. It also would have expanded exemptions from margin requirements for commercial businesses that used financial derivatives to hedge their business risks.

A final vote in the Senate was delayed while Reid searched for the sixty votes he needed to prevent a Republican filibuster. The American Bankers Association and others in the financial services industry redoubled their efforts to defeat the bill. "Congress consistently underestimates the complexity and size of the regulations resulting from new laws," the association's chief executive, Edward L. Yingling, said. Dodd worked to keep the pressure on his colleagues. "If we scrap it, we're right back without any of these protections," Dodd said. "It'll be a generation before the Congress comes back to deal with these issues again."

Reid finally obtained commitments from Republicans Collins, Snowe, and Brown, and the Senate cleared the bill July 15, on a **key vote of 60–39 (R: 3–38; D 55–1; I 2–0)**. Feingold remained the lone Democrat holdout opposing the bill. *(2010 key votes, p. 767)*

Obama issued a statement the same day saying the bill would provide "the strongest consumer financial protections in history." He also pledged, "There will be no more taxpayer-funded bailouts. Period. If a large financial institution should ever fail, this reform gives us the ability to wind it down without endangering the broader economy. And there will be new rules to make clear that no firm is somehow protected because it is 'too big to fail,' so that we don't have another AIG."

MAJOR PROVISIONS

Following are the major provisions of the Dodd-Frank Wall Street Reform and Consumer Protection Act (PL 111-203) that President Obama signed into law into law on July 21, 2010.

Financial Stability Oversight Council

The law established a Financial Stability Oversight Council, responsible for monitoring and addressing systemwide risks to U.S. financial stability. The council, which was required to meet at least quarterly, was to be funded through the Office of Financial Research created under the law.

The council's membership consisted of federal regulators. The voting members were the Treasury secretary, who was also the chair; the chair of the Federal Reserve Board; the comptroller of the Office of the Currency; the director of the Consumer Financial Protection Bureau; the director of the Federal Housing Finance Agency; the chair of the Securities and Exchange Commission; the chair of the Federal Deposit Insurance Corporation; the chair of the Commodity Futures Trading Commission; the chair of the National Credit Union Administration Board; and an independent insurance adviser appointed by the president. Several nonvoting members could serve in advisory roles.

The council was charged with monitoring the financial services market to identify potential threats to the financial stability of the United States. It also was directed to monitor domestic and international regulatory developments and proposals, facilitate information sharing among its member agencies, and identify potential regulatory gaps.

If the council determined that a nonbank financial company posed a systemic risk to the country's financial stability, it could vote to require the Fed to supervise and regulate the company and require the company to register with the Fed. Such a decision required a two-thirds majority vote of the council, including an affirmative vote from the chair. It could also recommend more stringent standards that the Federal Reserve could apply to such financial institutions, including higher risk-based capital, resolution plans, leverage, and concentration limits.

Office of Financial Research

The law created an Office of Financial Research within the Treasury Department, headed by a director appointed by the president and confirmed by the Senate to a six-year term. The office was charged with supporting the council by collecting data and conducting research on potential risks to the U.S. financial system.

The office was funded through assessments made by the Fed on nonbank financial companies and bank holding companies that had total consolidated assets of at least $50 billion. The provision was to take effect two years after enactment of the bill. In the interim, the Fed would provide funding for the office.

"Winding Down" Failing Institutions

"Orderly liquidation." The law created an "orderly liquidation" process run by the FDIC for the purpose of "winding down" or dismantling large, failing financial institutions in a manner that minimized the risk to the overall financial system. This authority could be used only if the Treasury secretary determined—in consultation with the president and based on written recommendations from two other federal regulators—that the financial company was in default or at risk of default, that its failure would seriously damage U.S. financial stability, and that there was no viable private-sector alternative. The process was intended for rare circumstances, with the bankruptcy code continuing to serve as the primary path for winding down a failing institution. The FDIC could not take an equity interest in or become a shareholder of the financial institution or any subsidiary.

The liquidation process was part of an effort to end the expectation among market participants that certain companies were "too big to fail" and that the government would step in to bail them out.

The Treasury was the source of the initial funds to cover the up-front costs of winding down a failed institution. The government would then establish a repayment plan and recoup losses first from shareholders and unsecured creditors and, if necessary, from risk-based assessments on financial companies with assets of more than $50 billion. Taxpayers were explicitly protected from losses associated with the use of this authority.

Process. If it was determined that a financial company had to be liquidated, the Treasury secretary would notify the FDIC and the company. If the company's board of directors agreed to the appointment of the FDIC as receiver, the Treasury secretary would make the appointment. If the board did not agree, the secretary would petition the U.S. District Court for the District of Columbia for an order authorizing the appointment of the FDIC as receiver.

Alternatively, if they deemed a financial company to be in default or in serious danger of default, the Fed and FDIC could request that the Treasury secretary appoint the FDIC as receiver. The judicial review process still applied. Under this scenario, the Fed and FDIC would provide the Treasury secretary with a written recommendation that evaluated whether the financial company was in default or in danger of default; described the effect such a failure would have on U.S. financial stability; recommended steps that should be taken; showed why there were no likely private sector alternatives; showed why bankruptcy was not appropriate; evaluated the effect on creditors, shareholders, and counterparties; and described the effect the default would have on low-income, minority, or underserved communities.

The secretary also had to consider the cost to the Treasury Department and the possibility that government intervention could increase excessive risk-taking by creditors, shareholders, or counterparties because of a belief that the government would limit the downside risk associated with investing in or doing business with a failing institution.

Liability and bankruptcy. The company's board of directors could not be held liable to shareholders or creditors for consenting to the appointment of a receiver. However, the FDIC could hold directors and officers liable for monetary damages in the case of gross negligence. The law expedited federal court consideration of cases brought by the FDIC against directors, officers, employees, and agents of a financial company that was in the process of being liquidated. If an orderly liquidation was triggered, existing bankruptcy proceedings would be dismissed and new bankruptcy proceedings could not be filed.

If an orderly liquidation was triggered and the FDIC was made receiver, the law assumed that creditors and shareholders would take losses and that the management team would be removed. In addition, management, board members, and other individuals responsible for the failure would bear financial losses through restitution or other actions. All those that had a right to the claims would be treated in similar fashion, unless the FDIC determined that not doing so would enhance the value of firm assets for sale. Unsecured claims of the United States would have, at a minimum, a higher priority than liabilities of the financial company that counted as regulatory capital.

Expanded Federal Reserve Powers

The law for the first time gave the Fed formal responsibility for identifying, measuring, monitoring, and mitigating risks to U.S. financial stability. A company with at least $50 billion in consolidated assets that had recently been classified as a bank holding company and that received financial assistance under the TARP (PL 110-343) was automatically subject to Fed supervision and regulation. However, the Fed could not authorize any federal financial assistance.

Under the law, the Fed had the authority—on its own or on the recommendation of the Financial Stability Oversight Council—to establish prudential standards for nonbank financial companies that it supervised and for large bank holding companies, those with total consolidated assets of $50 billion or more. The standards had to be more stringent than those for other financial institutions and could be increasingly restrictive depending on the risk posed by the companies.

To limit the chances that an institution in the early stages of trouble would end up failing, the Fed, together with the FDIC and the council, was directed to prescribe restrictions such as limits on capital distributions, acquisitions, and asset growth. For a company in the later stages of financial distress, Fed action could include requiring them to write plans to restore or raise capital, setting limits on transactions with affiliates, requiring management changes, and requiring asset sales.

Each nonbank financial company supervised by the Fed and each large bank holding company had to report periodically to the Fed, the Financial Stability Oversight Council, and the FDIC on its resolution plan, a blueprint for the company's rapid and orderly resolution in the event that it faced material financial distress or failure.

If the Fed and the FDIC jointly determined that a company's resolution plan was not credible and would not facilitate an orderly liquidation under the bankruptcy code, the company would be required to submit a new plan. If the company did not resubmit a satisfactory plan, the Fed, in consultation with the Financial Stability Oversight Council and the FDIC, could impose more stringent regulatory requirements or require the company to divest itself of certain assets or operations.

The Fed, in conjunction with other regulators, was charged with conducting semiannual stress tests on large bank holding companies and nonbank financial companies under its supervision to evaluate whether the individual institutions had the capital, on a total consolidated basis, to absorb losses that could result from adverse economic conditions.

The law directed the Fed to require large bank holding companies and nonbank financial companies that it supervised to maintain a debt-to-equity ratio of no more than 15-to-1, if the council determined that the company posed a grave threat to U.S. financial stability and that the requirement was necessary to mitigate the risk.

The computation of capital for purposes of meeting capital requirements had to consider the company's off-balance-sheet activities.

Unless they provided prior notice to the Fed, large holding companies and nonbank financial companies supervised by the Fed were barred from acquiring or controlling any company that did not engage in banking activities and had $10 billion or more in total consolidated assets. The Fed was directed to take the criteria outlined in the Bank Holding Act (PL 84-511) for acquisitions and mergers into consideration when reviewing the proposed transaction, as well as the level of risk that the acquisition posed to the U.S. financial system.

The Fed was authorized to set capital reserve levels for savings and loan holding companies and limit asset purchases or sale transactions with company insiders. The central bank was also directed to examine the activities of nondepository subsidiaries of depository holding companies to determine the safety and soundness of the subsidiary's activities.

Limits on Fed Authority

The law placed new limits on the Fed's emergency powers. Under previous law, the Fed was authorized to lend to an individual company under "unusual and exigent circumstances," provided that the borrower was unable to secure adequate credit accommodations from other banking institutions. The Fed rarely used this clause until the 2008 crisis in the financial services industry, when it played a central role and loaned money to several institutions, including American International Group (AIG).

The new law prohibited the Fed from providing emergency loans to an individual company. Any lending program had to be approved by the Treasury and be designed to provide liquidity to the system and not to aid a single, failing financial company. Collateral or other security for loans had to be sufficient to protect taxpayers from losses, and the Fed was required to report to Congress within seven days any time it provided lending. The report had to include information that justified issuing the loan; the identity of the loan recipients; and the date, amount, form, and material terms of the assistance.

The GAO was directed to conduct a one-time audit of the Fed's emergency lending between December 2007 and the enactment of this law. The audit had to start within thirty days of enactment and be completed within one year, after which the GAO was required to submit a report to Congress.

In a significant departure from previous law, the GAO was authorized to audit future Fed functions, including open-market transactions and discount window advances. But the GAO had to delay its report to Congress and the public to ensure that the information would not have adverse effects on the financial markets.

Financial Institution Regulatory Changes

The law abolished the Office of Thrift Supervision (OTS) and transferred its functions to the Office of the Comptroller of the Currency (OCC), which was given responsibility for supervising federal thrifts; the FDIC, which was responsible for supervising state-chartered thrifts; and the Federal Reserve, which was responsible for supervising thrift holding companies. The OTS, a bank regulator that was housed within the Treasury, oversaw savings associations and holding companies that primarily took deposits and loaned them out for residential mortgages.

The law placed a three-year moratorium on the FDIC's ability to approve new applications for deposit insurance for an industrial loan company, credit card bank, or trust bank that was owned or controlled by a commercial company. Commercial companies included all affiliates that derived at least 15 percent of their revenue from nonfinancial activities.

The law temporarily suspended exceptions permitted under the Bank Holding Company Act that allowed commercial companies to own banks. The law required a study of the implications of removing the exceptions before further action was taken.

Bank holding companies were required to provide the Fed with information on all company activities, including subsidiary activities, for the purpose of identifying and addressing risks throughout the entire organization. The law removed the so-called Fed-lite provisions under the Gramm-Leach-Bliley Act of 1999 (PL 106-102), which limited the Fed's ability to obtain information on the activities of bank holding subsidiaries.

The Federal Reserve Act was amended by expanding the list of interaffiliate-covered transactions to include credit exposure from a securities borrowing, lending, or derivatives transaction. This provision was an effort to address risks that affiliates could pose to banks when they engaged in risky derivatives transactions and incurred significant losses.

The law tightened national bank lending limits—the percentage of bank capital that could be loaned to a single borrower—by treating credit exposure on derivatives, repurchase agreements, and reverse repurchase agreements as extensions of credit. Lending limits, which prevent overexposure to any single borrower and the risk that the borrower would not repay the loan, are considered a key component of bank safety and soundness.

The Fed and other federal regulators were directed to try to make capital requirements for bank holding companies, savings and loan holding companies, and insured depository institutions "countercyclical." The amount of capital that a company was required to maintain would increase in times of economic expansion and decrease in times of economic contraction, consistent with the safety and soundness of the company.

Proprietary trading. The law placed new limits on propriety trading by the largest financial institutions, with exceptions and discretion for regulators. The provision was referred to as the Volcker rule after former Fed Chair Paul A. Volcker, who advocated such restrictions. The final version was not as restrictive as the original Senate bill, which would have completely banned banks from using their own funds to buy or sell securities in financial markets to gain a profit.

With major exceptions, the final bill prohibited insured depository institutions and bank holding companies supervised by the Fed from engaging in proprietary trading or acquiring any ownership interest in a hedge fund or private equity fund. Nonbank financial companies that were supervised by the Fed and engaged in such activities were subject to additional capital requirements and quantitative limits.

Exceptions to the restrictions on proprietary trading included brokerage activities that involved buying securities with the anticipation that they would be quickly sold to a client, the traditional practice of buying and selling derivatives to hedge risks, and advisory services to a separately capitalized hedge fund.

Big banks were required to reduce their holdings in a hedge fund or private equity fund to no more than 3 percent of the fund's capital, and the holdings had to be "immaterial" to the banking institution. The bank's aggregate holdings in all private equity and hedge funds could not exceed more than 3 percent of the bank's Tier 1 capital.

Concentration limits. Financial companies were prohibited from merging or consolidating with another company if it would result in the new company having consolidated liabilities that exceeded 10 percent of the total amount of consolidated liabilities for all financial companies. The Financial Stability Oversight Council's recommendation would also be considered in such cases.

Regulators could not approve an application for an interstate merger if the resulting insured depository institution, bank holding company, or savings and loan company would control more than 10 percent of the total deposits of insured depository institutions in the United States.

Payment, Clearing, Settlement

Generally, financial market utilities were designated as "systemically important" based on the aggregate monetary value of the transactions they processed and the effect their failure would have on clearing, settlement, and payment systems, as well as on counterparties and the U.S. financial system. The designation required a two-thirds vote by the Financial Stability Oversight Council, including an affirmative vote by the chair.

In general, the Federal Reserve was authorized to set risk management standards for systemically important financial utilities and the payment, clearing, and settlement activities of financial institutions. The CFTC and the SEC also could set standards for the institutions they regulated, but if the council and the Fed determined that the requirements were insufficient, they could impose the standards they determined were needed.

The standards had to address risk management policies and procedures; margin and collateral requirements; participant or counterparty default policies and procedures; the ability of the institution to complete timely clearing and settlement of financial transactions; and capital and financial resource requirements for designated financial market utilities.

FDIC Changes

The law directed the FDIC to change the way it calculated the assessment base used to determine the size of an institution's deposit insurance premiums. The new base was equal to the institution's total assets minus the sum of its tangible equity and long-term unsecured debt. The change would be made unless the FDIC could show that the new calculation would reduce the effectiveness of the risk-based assessment system or increase the risk of loss to the Deposit Insurance Fund.

The FDIC was required to take the steps needed to ensure that the reserve ratio of depository institutions reached 1.35 percent of insured deposits, or the comparable percentage of the assessment base, by September 30, 2020. In setting the assessments, the FDIC was directed to offset the effects on insured depository institutions that had total consolidated assets of less than $10 billion.

The law made permanent an increase in the maximum amount covered by deposit insurance to $250,000 per account. The previous maximum of $100,000 had been temporarily increased to $250,000 through December 31, 2013. The new increase was retroactive to January 1, 2008.

The FDIC was authorized to guarantee the debt of solvent insured depository institutions and their holding companies during times of severe economic distress and under specific conditions. The Fed and the FDIC first had to agree, by a two-thirds vote in each agency, that there was a "liquidity event"—a threat to the liquidity of the financial markets. They also had to find that failure to take action would have serious adverse effects on financial stability and that the guarantees were necessary to avoid or mitigate those effects.

The terms and conditions of the short-term FDIC guarantee had to be approved by the Treasury secretary, who, in consultation with the president, would determine the maximum amount of guarantees. Fees for the guarantees had to be set to cover all expected costs. Any losses that occurred would be recouped from the companies that received the guarantees. The program also had to be approved by Congress.

The law prohibited the FDIC from using this systemic-risk authority to establish a widely available debt guarantee program and required the FDIC to become receiver of any insured depository institution that defaulted on its debt guarantee.

The GAO was directed to audit any FDIC debt guarantee program that resulted from a liquidity event.

Consumer Financial Protection Bureau

The law created a Consumer Financial Protection Bureau (CFPB) with the authority to ensure that existing consumer protection laws were comprehensive, fair, and vigorously enforced. The CFPB was established as an independent body within the Fed, headed by a director appointed by the president and confirmed by the Senate to a five-year term. The bureau was charged with overseeing a broad range of retail financial products, including checking accounts, private student loans, credit cards, and mortgages.

The CFPB was responsible for implementing and enforcing federal laws to ensure that markets for consumer financial products and services were fair, transparent, and competitive, and that consumers were protected from unfair, deceptive, and abusive acts and practices, and from discrimination. Previous law prohibited unfair or deceptive acts or practices, but the addition of abusive acts was designed to ensure that the bureau was empowered to cover instances when providers took unreasonable advantage of consumers.

The consumer bureau was given the authority and accountability to issue rules applicable to all financial institutions, including depository institutions that offered financial products and services to consumers. It also had examination and enforcement authority over compliance with consumer protection laws by large banks and nonbank financial institutions, as well as by all insured depository institutions and credit unions with more than $10 billion in assets. The banking regulators retained this authority for insured depository institutions and credit unions with assets of $10 billion or less.

In monitoring for risks, the consumer bureau was directed to consider a variety of factors, including the extent to which the risks that a consumer financial product or service might disproportionately affect traditionally underserved consumers.

The law made clear that the bureau was meant to operate without interference from the Fed, including in writing rules, issuing orders, appointing or removing employees, and carrying out examinations and enforcement actions.

Funding for the CFPB also was independent of the congressional appropriations process, with the goal of increasing the bureau's independence. The Fed was directed to transfer the amount determined by the bureau's director as reasonably necessary for the bureau's annual budget but not in excess of a specified percentage of the Fed's total operating expenses as reported in its 2009 annual report. Funding was capped at 10 percent of the Fed's operating expenses for fiscal 2010, 11 percent for fiscal 2011 and 12 percent for fiscal 2013 and each year thereafter, adjusted for inflation.

Generally, the bureau's regulations could not preempt state laws that provided greater protection for consumers. However, state law could be preempted in limited circumstances for national banks, federal savings associations, and nondepository institutions.

State attorneys general had the power to enforce CFPB regulations, but they, along with state regulators, had to consult with or notify the bureau and federal financial regulators before initiating such actions. The law generally did not permit a state attorney general to bring a civil action in the name of the state against a national bank or federal savings institution unless it was to enforce a regulation prescribed by the CFPB under a provision of this law or in other limited circumstances.

Certain individuals employed at nondepository institutions were also subject to supervision by the consumer bureau, including those that originated or serviced mortgage loans or other consumer financial products. Personal tax advisers, lawyers, insurance professionals under state supervision, and others could be exempt under specified circumstances. Others outside the bureau's purview included auto dealers, accountants, and real estate brokers.

The Financial Stability Oversight Council could set aside a final regulation promulgated by the bureau if, in the view of two-thirds of the council, the regulation would put the safety and soundness of the banking system or the stability of the U.S. financial system at risk. Also, the law exempted nonfinancial companies from the CFPB's oversight. For example, dentists, doctors, small retailers, and others who simply allowed their customers to pay bills over time were excluded from the bureau's authority.

Derivatives Regulations

The law brought the over-the-counter financial derivatives market under significant government regulation for the first time. Derivatives contracts based on the underlying value of an asset, such as stocks, interest rates, currencies, or commodities, were often used by companies to hedge risk. But they could also be used for speculation, which generally involved betting on the price movements of an underlying asset, often without owning that asset and without trying to hedge risk. One type of derivative known as swaps involved two counterparties that exchanged the benefits of one's security for the benefits of the other's.

Regulatory authority. The law established a framework for regulating a broad range of participants and products in the over-the-counter derivatives market, requiring that many routine derivatives be routed through clearinghouses and then traded on exchanges. Custom swaps could still be traded over the counter, but they had to be reported to central repositories.

The CFTC and the SEC were authorized to write and enforce rules for the swaps and security-based swaps markets, respectively, and to achieve as much consistency as possible. Swaps are generally based on commodity-oriented assets, whereas security-based swaps are based on a variety of assets including company securities, interest rates, and currencies. Banking regulators retained exclusive authority to enforce provisions for capital and margin for banks and branches or agencies of foreign banks.

The law imposed new capital, margin, reporting, recordkeeping, and business conduct rules for companies that dealt in derivatives, requiring banks to "spin off" their riskiest derivatives trading operations into affiliates. Banks were allowed to retain operations for interest rate swaps, foreign exchange swaps, and gold and silver swaps, among others, but they were required to move trading in agriculture, uncleared commodities, most metals, and energy swaps to affiliates. Depository institutions could be forced to move derivatives trading desks into nonbank affiliates or divest from these activities.

The law prohibited the federal government from providing financial assistance to any swap-based institution. There were several exceptions, however, including for an insured depository institution that had a swap entity affiliate, as long as the depository institution was part of a bank holding company or savings and loan holding company supervised by the Fed. An insured depository institution was also exempt if it limited its swap activities to hedging and similar risk reduction directly related to its depository operations.

Market regulation. All over-the-counter derivatives transactions between dealers and large-market participants had to go through a registered clearinghouse, provided that a clearinghouse accepted the derivative for clearing. The role of the clearinghouse was to examine the particulars of a derivatives contract and, if it accepted the contract for clearing, to guarantee that both sides of the deal would abide by the terms. Clearinghouses were required to submit each swap product or category of swap products to the CFTC or SEC, which would determine whether the transaction needed to be cleared, based on criteria in this law.

A swap that was cleared had to be traded through an exchange, a registered swap execution facility, or a foreign swap execution facility. This provision applied to transactions that had been accepted for trading on an exchange and that involved either dealers (companies that buy and sell derivatives for their own accounts) or major market participants (nondealers who maintain substantial net positions outside of hedging purposes). It did not apply to transactions that were completed before enactment. Clearing and being traded on an exchange would make many of the details of a derivatives contract, such as pricing, widely available.

The clearing requirements did not apply to a swap product if one of the counterparties was not a financial entity, was using swap products to hedge or mitigate commercial risk, and notified the SEC or CFTC how it generally met the financial obligations associated with entering into noncleared swap transactions. An affiliate of a company that qualified for an exception could also qualify for the exception, but only if it used the swap products to hedge commercial risk. The exception did not apply if the affiliate was a swap dealer.

The law established regulations for the foreign exchange swap product market, which was valued at roughly $60 trillion and was the second-largest component of the swap market. The Treasury secretary could allow exemptions under certain conditions.

A derivatives-clearing organization could be exempt from registering to clear swap products if the organization was subject to comparable, comprehensive supervision and regulation by the CFTC or SEC, or by the appropriate government authorities in the home country in the case of a foreign derivative.

Swap products that were not accepted for clearing by any derivatives clearing organization had to be reported to a swap product data repository or, if no repository would accept the swap product, to the CFTC or SEC. Individuals or businesses engaged in a swap transaction that was not accepted for clearing were required to provide the CFTC or SEC with reports on the swap products they held. They were required to maintain proper books and records and were subject to review by the respective regulator.

Regulators had the authority to impose margin requirements on dealers and major participants for uncleared swaps to ensure that they had adequate financial resources to meet obligations. In setting margin requirements, regulators could permit the use of noncash collateral as long as doing so was consistent with preserving the financial integrity of the swaps markets and with preserving the stability of the U.S. financial system.

The CFTC and the SEC were to establish limits on the number of positions, other than true hedge positions, that an individual or business could hold with respect to swap products. A list of exempt commodities had to be established within 180 days of the date of enactment, and a list of exempt agricultural commodities had to be established within 270 days of enactment.

The SEC and CFTC were also charged with seeking, to the maximum extent practicable, to diminish, eliminate, or prevent excessive speculation; deter and prevent market manipulation, squeezes, and corners; ensure sufficient market liquidity for hedgers; and ensure that the price discovery function of the underlying market was not disrupted.

Executive Compensation

The law required that shareholders in a public company have a chance at least once every three years to cast a nonbinding advisory vote on executive compensation, a provision known as "say on pay." Brokers who were not beneficial owners of a security were prohibited from voting through company proxies unless the beneficial owner had instructed the broker to vote on his behalf.

The law also provided for shareholder votes on any generous severance package, or "golden parachute," for an outgoing executive in the event of a merger or acquisition. The vote would not overrule a decision by the board of directors, create or imply any change to the board's fiduciary duties, or restrict the ability of shareholders to make proposals for inclusion in proxy materials related to executive compensation.

Federal financial regulators were required to monitor incentive-based payment arrangements larger than $1 billion by financial institutions and prohibit such arrangements if the regulators determined jointly that they could threaten the financial institutions' safety and soundness or could have serious adverse effects on economic conditions or financial stability.

The law required a series of steps to prevent potential conflicts of interest by a company's board members. It also expanded disclosure requirements and provided for the potential recovery of compensation in specified circumstances. Board committees that set compensation policy had to consist only of directors who were independent. Any compensation consultants that were hired also had to be independent.

Companies were required to tell shareholders about the relationship between executive compensation and the company's financial performance, and to have a policy to recover money erroneously paid to executives based on finances that later had to be restated because of an accounting error. They also had to disclose in the annual proxy statement whether employees or members of the board could hedge or offset any decrease in the market value of the equity securities granted.

Hedge Fund Registration

The law eliminated existing exemptions from SEC registration requirements for hedge fund managers and private equity firms—lightly regulated pools of capital with a limited number of investors that often used aggressive trading or investment strategies. The intent was to eliminate a perceived regulatory gap and strengthen recordkeeping, examination, and disclosure requirements for hedge funds and private equity firms. The law also increased the SEC's ability to take and enforce actions against these firms if necessary.

Under previous law, investment advisers with fewer than fifteen clients were exempt from having to register, and a hedge fund counted as a single client even if it had multiple investors. The new law eliminated this "private adviser" exemption.

Venture capital firms were exempted from the SEC registration requirement, but they had to maintain records and provide the SEC with reports that were necessary to protect the public interest. Investment advisers of private funds with less than $150 million in assets under management were also exempted.

Hedge fund advisers were required to submit reports to the SEC describing the assets they had under management, the amount of leverage used, counterparty risk exposure, trading and investment positions, valuation policies, types of assets held, and other information the SEC deemed to be important.

To reduce the possibility of future Ponzi schemes, advisers were required to ensure the safeguarding of client assets over which the adviser had custody. As part of this requirement, the adviser was required to seek verification of assets under custody by an independent public accountant.

Federal Insurance Office

The law created a Federal Insurance Office within the Treasury Department, with a director who was appointed by the Treasury secretary and who also served as an adviser on the new Financial Stability Oversight Council. The new office was not a federal regulator or supervisor. Rather, its tasks were to monitor all aspects of the insurance industry, make recommendations to the council that certain insurers be designated as nonbank financial institutions subject to Federal Reserve supervision, assist department administration of the Terrorism Risk Insurance Program, coordinate federal efforts and establish federal policy on prudential aspects of international insurance matters, and consult with states on insurance issues of national importance.

The office was charged with handling all lines of insurance except crop, health, and long-term-care insurance. The new Federal Insurance Office was authorized to identify and narrowly preempt state insurance laws that were inconsistent with international insurance agreements. However, national insurance regulators could not issue regulations for insurance rates, premium limits, sales and underwriting practices, state antitrust laws, or capital or solvency requirements.

Insurance regulators in an insurer's home state had sole regulatory authority over nonadmitted insurance, including the collection and allocation of premium tax obligations. Nonadmitted insurance provided coverage for unusual risks and was typically unavailable in the traditional insurance marketplace. The majority of these policies were purchased by sophisticated commercial entities to cover commercial risk, although some individuals also purchased such coverage.

The law regulated the reinsurance market, where insurance companies bought insurance to reduce their own risk. If the insurer's home state was accredited by the National Association of Insurance Commissioners or had solvency requirements substantially similar to the association's guidelines, the home state had sole responsibility for regulating the financial solvency of the reinsurer.

Access

The law included initiatives to encourage the provision of financial products and services that were appropriate and accessible for many individuals who were not fully incorporated into the financial mainstream, including so-called "underbanked" consumers, who relied on nontraditional forms of credit and often were unable to save securely for future needs such as buying a home or paying education expenses.

The law also created a pool of capital to enable community development financial institutions to establish and maintain small-dollar loan programs, creating an alternative to payday or car title loans in local communities.

The Treasury Department was authorized to establish a multiyear program of grants, cooperative agreements, financial agency agreements, and similar contracts to promote initiatives to expand access for low- and moderate-income individuals to mainstream financial institutions.

Offsets

TARP repayment. The $700 billion authorized for the TARP was reduced to $475 billion under the law, and no unspent TARP funds could be redirected to new spending. Repayment of TARP funds had to be returned to the Treasury and used to reduce the deficit. The Treasury could not initiate any new programs under TARP after June 25, 2010. The effect was to end the TARP operation ten weeks ahead of the scheduled date of October 3, 2010.

Unused stimulus money. The law required that unused funds provided under the 2009 economic stimulus law (PL 111-5) be returned to the Treasury by December 31, 2012, and used to help reduce the federal deficit. The president could waive these requirements if he determined that it was not in the best interest of the nation to rescind a specific unobligated amount.

Debit Card Fees

The law instructed the Federal Reserve to set limits on the amount banks and payment networks could charge merchants for using debit cards and the debit card transaction network. Debit cards were understood to include any card approved for use through a payment card network to debit an account, as well as general-use prepaid cards, but not paper checks. Regulations for the amount of any interchange transaction fee that an issuer could receive or charge for an electronic debit transaction had to be reasonable and proportional to the cost incurred by the issuer with respect to the transaction.

Issuers with less than $10 billion in assets were exempt from the debit card provision. The law also exempted debit cards or general-use prepaid cards provided under a federal, state, or local government-administered payment program if the card could be used only to transfer debit funds, monetary value, or other assets that had been provided under the government program.

Credit Rating Agencies

Credit rating agencies evaluated the relative risk of default of various securities and debt instruments. Their critical gatekeeper role in the debt market was functionally similar to that of securities analysts, who evaluated the quality of securities in the equity market, and auditors, who reviewed the financial statements of companies.

The law broadened the SEC's powers to regulate credit rating agencies, also known as Nationally Recognized Statistical Rating Organizations. A new Office of Credit Ratings was established in the SEC to examine rating agencies at least once a year and make key findings public.

The SEC was authorized to issue new rules requiring the agencies to set up internal controls over the ratings process, establish an independent board of directors, make greater disclosures to the public and investors, and develop universal ratings across asset classes and types of issuers. The SEC was also authorized to deregister a credit rating agency that consistently provided inaccurate ratings over time.

Each credit rating agency was required to disclose information about the assumptions underlying its procedures and methodologies; the data it relied on to determine the credit rating; if applicable, how the agency used servicer or remittance reports to conduct surveillance of the credit rating; and information that could be used by investors and other users of credit ratings to better understand ratings in each class issued by the agency.

To address conflicts of interest inherent in the ratings business, the law required rating agencies to prohibit compliance officers from working on ratings, methodologies, or sales and to prevent other employees from selling ratings services and rating the securities. A credit agency had to conduct a one-year look-back review when an employee went to work for a company that offered or underwrote a security or money market instrument subject to a rating by the agency. The look back was to determine whether the employee was giving the company a better rating than it deserved in exchange for future employment. The rating agency also had to report the employee's new job to the SEC.

To reduce the reliance on ratings, the law required that references to credit ratings be removed from certain regulations, policies, and procedures used by federal agencies and that the agencies use a new standard to judge creditworthiness.

The law provided investors with a private right of action to bring suit against a credit rating agency for a knowing or reckless failure to conduct a reasonable investigation of the facts or to obtain analysis from an independent source.

The SEC was directed to establish a system that prohibited issuers of structured financial products from selecting the rating agency that provided the initial credit rating. This practice was common in the rating of various mortgage-related, asset-backed securities and collateralized debt obligations that played a central role in the 2008 crisis. Many of those structured products turned out to have a much poorer credit quality than that designated by a rating agency.

Mortgage Rules, Predatory Lending

The law established minimum national standards for mortgage brokers and institutions, including banks that provided home mortgages. The standards were to be issued as regulations by the CFPB.

The standards had to require that a lender or originator of a home loan ensure that a borrower had a reasonable ability to repay the loan at the time the loan was made. The determination had to be based on verified and documented information, including the borrower's credit history, income, and other factors.

Certain low-risk loans, or "qualified mortgages," were exempt from the law's loan standards. A qualified mortgage was a mortgage with a term of thirty years or less, and the lender could not allow the delay of the payment of principal or an increase in the principal balance, among other requirements.

The law prohibited prepayment penalties—fees assessed on borrowers for repaying the principal ahead of schedule—for any mortgage that did not meet the standards for a qualified mortgage. When a loan was first made, originators had to offer a version of the loan that did not include a prepayment penalty. For mortgages that met the law's underwriting standards, the law limited prepayment penalties to 3 percent of the outstanding balance in the first year of the loan, 2 percent in the second year, and 1 percent in the third year. After the three-year period, no prepayment penalties could be assessed.

Lenders were barred from providing any financial incentives, including payments known as "yield spread premiums," to mortgage brokers for steering consumers to loans with higher interest rates. Mortgage originators could not receive payments that varied based on the terms of the loan, other than the amount of the principal.

Mortgage originators that violated their obligations under the act could be sued, with maximum liability per violation of up to three times the total amount of lender fees, plus the consumer's costs including reasonable attorney fees.

The Home Ownership and Equity Protection Act of 1994 (PL 103-325) addressed certain deceptive and unfair practices in home equity lending by establishing requirements for certain loans with high interest rates, high fees, or both. The law affected refinancing and home equity installment loans that also met the definition of a high-rate or high-fee loan. The law did not cover loans to buy or build homes, reverse mortgages, or home equity lines of credit. The new law revised the benchmarks for determining loans subject to the heightened standards under the Home Ownership and Equity Protection Act.

It defined "high-cost home loans" as a primary residence mortgage with an annual interest rate higher than 6.5 percent, or 8.5 percent if the dwelling was personal property and the loan was smaller than $50,000. For a second mortgage or other subordinate loan on the property, a mortgage with an annual percentage rate higher than 8.5 percent qualified as a high-cost mortgage.

The law barred balloon payments for high-cost mortgages, which included scheduled mortgage payments that were more than twice as large as the average of earlier scheduled payments. It prohibited defaulting on an existing loan that was being refinanced by a high-cost loan. It limited late fees to no more than 4 percent of the amount of payment past due, along with other restrictions.

No high-cost loan could accelerate the indebtedness of a loan. No lender could directly or indirectly finance, in connection with any high-cost mortgage, any prepayment fee or penalty payable by the borrower if the lender held the note for the underlying loan. The provision did not apply if the payment schedule was adjusted to the seasonal or irregular income of the consumer.

Lenders could not conclude a high-risk mortgage loan without first getting a written appraisal of the property. Parties to a real estate transaction were prohibited from influencing the independent judgment of an appraiser through collusion, coercion, or bribery, among other activities.

An Office of Housing Counseling was established in the Department of Housing and Urban Development (HUD) to carry out and coordinate homeownership and rental housing counseling programs. A national public service campaign was established to promote housing counseling with a website and toll-free hotline. The law also authorized funds for counseling grants to HUD-approved groups or agencies.

The law appropriated funds to make available $1 billion in assistance through an Emergency Homeowners Relief Fund, established by HUD to provide emergency loans to help jobless homeowners make mortgage payments while they were out of work.

The law also provided $1 billion for a third round of funding for the Neighborhood Stabilization Program, through which HUD assisted state and local government efforts to finance the purchase and redevelopment of foreclosed homes and residential properties. In addition, it authorized a HUD-administered grant program to help agencies that provided legal assistance related to homeownership to low- and moderate-income people.

Investor Protections

The law set new standards for investment advisers and broker-dealers, increased authorized funding for the SEC over the following five years, and expanded the commission's authority to set more stringent rules to protect investors. It gave the SEC additional authority to conduct investigations, assess penalties for violations, and impose enforcement actions.

A new Office of Investor Advocate and an ombudsman at the SEC were established to assist investors in their dealings with the commission. The law also authorized the SEC to impose a fiduciary duty on broker-dealers and investment advisers to protect retail customers.

An investor protection fund was to be established in the Treasury to pay awards to whistleblowers and fund the activities of the SEC inspector general. The law provided incentives and protections for whistleblowers who provided information relating to a violation of the securities laws that led to successful SEC enforcement actions.

The law updated statutes related to the Securities Investor Protection Corporation (SIPC) by increasing the minimum assessments on members, raising penalties for fraud, and establishing civil and criminal penalties against any person who misrepresented membership in the SIPC. It also increased the limit on the SIPC's borrowing from the Treasury Department from $1 billion to $2.5 billion.

The SEC received new authority to increase public reporting of aggregate information on short selling, prohibit manipulative short sales, and require that customers be notified that they could choose not to allow their securities to be used in connection with short sales.

Securitization

Securitization involves the process of turning a nonmarketable asset into a marketable asset. Different loan-oriented assets—usually corporate loans, mortgages, and corporate bonds—are packaged together and then cut up into groups, or "tranches." Bonds are issued from those tranches and are secured by the cash flows generated from the underlying assets. The riskiest tranches pay the highest interest on bonds, which also carry a greater risk of default. The process was heavily used in the packaging of subprime mortgage loans and had also been used for a variety of purposes on Wall Street and in the corporate world.

The law required securitizers to retain an economic interest in a material portion of the credit risk for any asset that the securitizer sold or transferred to a third party. In general, firms using securitization were required to retain at least 5 percent of the credit risk. Regulators had discretion to set lower minimums for securitized assets with lower risks. The expectation was that the requirement would force securitizers to focus more on the quality of the underlying assets, thereby reducing excessive risk-taking.

The law provided exemptions for the Farm Credit System and any residential, multifamily or health care facility mortgage loan asset or securitization that was insured or guaranteed by the federal government. Regulators were required to provide total or partial exemptions for municipal securities and for securitizations of assets issued or guaranteed by a federal agency, as long as the exemption was in the public interest and for the protection of investors.

Other Provisions

Funds to foreign governments. The law amended the Bretton Woods Agreement Act (PL 79-171) to require the Treasury secretary to instruct the U.S. executive director of the International Monetary Fund (IMF) to review any IMF proposals that would issue a loan to a country whose public debt was higher than its recent annual gross domestic product or to a country that was not eligible for assistance from the International Development Association. If the review indicated that the loan was not likely to be paid in full, the director would be directed to oppose it.

Conflict minerals from the Congo. All companies that were required to report to the SEC were required to disclose to the agency if minerals extracted during the course of their business operations originated in the Democratic Republic of Congo or adjoining countries. The disclosure report had to describe the measures taken to exercise due diligence on the source and chain of custody of the minerals. Essential in the manufacture of consumer electronics and other devices, these minerals, rich sources of which are located in the eastern Congo, are mined in conditions of armed conflict and human rights abuses. The U.S. government was required to develop a strategy to address the illicit minerals trade in the region and a map to address links between conflict minerals and armed groups.

Mine safety. The law required mining companies to disclose mine safety violations that were material to investors.

Payments for resource extraction. The law required public disclosure to the SEC of any payment related to the commercial development of oil, natural gas, and minerals made to the United States or to a foreign government.

Small Business Assistance

Congress cleared a bill in September 2010 aimed at bolstering small businesses by expanding their access to credit and providing some tax incentives. The aim was to enable small businesses to grow and to hire or retain workers. The White House strongly supported the legislation, calling small business the "backbone of the American economy." Obama had called for many of the legislation's initiatives in his State of the Union address in January.

In the aftermath of the financial crisis, small businesses, along with their many supporters in Congress, said that it had become virtually impossible to persuade risk-weary banks to lend to them. As a result, small businesses were not creating new jobs at the pace they had been before the crisis. According to some estimates, companies with fewer than 500 employees had created about two-thirds of all new jobs between 1990 and 2005, and those with fewer than fifty workers created more than a third of them.

The centerpiece of the bill was a $30 billion Small Business Lending Fund designed to help community banks make loans to small businesses, which was combined with tax incentives that were expected to cost $12 billion over ten years. The tax breaks included an extension of a provision that allowed small businesses to carry back tax credits over five years and excluded proceeds from some small-business stock from capital gains taxes. The bill also clamped down on businesses that cheated on their taxes. Companies that failed to file returns, for instance, could be fined up to $1.5 million, up from $250,000.

The lending fund emerged as the biggest point of contention, especially in the Senate. Many Republicans called it a smaller version of the Troubled Asset Relief Program (TARP) created in 2008 (PL 110-343) to bail out the financial industry.

Democratic leaders ultimately agreed to drop $1.5 billion in agricultural disaster assistance and a revenue-raising offset that had already been used in a state aid measure to win a few GOP votes.

LEGISLATIVE ACTION

The House passed its version of the bill by a vote of 241–182 on June 17, 2010. The Financial Services Committee had approved the measure (HR 5297—H Rept 111-499) in a 42–23 vote on May 19. In addition to establishing a $30 billion lending fund, the legislation would have created a $2 billion state small-business credit initiative and a $1 billion Small Business Administration program for investments in "early stage" businesses.

The measure included $3.6 billion in tax breaks over eleven years, provided in a separate bill (HR 5486) that the House passed, 247–170, on June 15. The tax measure was automatically incorporated into the lending bill under a rule for floor debate that covered both pieces of legislation. The main tax benefit was a one-year, 100 percent exclusion from capital gains taxes for profits on certain small-business stock. The provision would have cost $2 billion more than the final version, because it would have applied to stock purchased after March 15, rather than after the date of enactment, as in the final bill. The House tax bill included $7.1 billion in offsets over eleven years from changes to the inheritance tax and the tax credit for producers of cellulosic biofuel that began on January 1, 2009, under the Food, Conservation, and Energy Act of 2008.

The measure faced stronger opposition in the Senate, where it moved forward only with the help of two departing Republican lawmakers, George LeMieux of Florida and George V. Voinovich of Ohio. They voted with the Democrats first on September 14 to invoke cloture on a substitute amendment by Finance Chair Max Baucus, D-Mont., that contained the substance of the final bill; the vote was 61–37. They voted with the majority on September 16 to invoke cloture, ending a GOP filibuster than had delayed the legislation for weeks. (Three-fifths of the total Senate—that is, sixty senators—are required to invoke cloture.) Finally the two Republicans joined the Democrats to vote for passage of the amended version of the bill on September 16. The tally on those two votes was 61–38. In all, the Senate took six cloture votes before managing to pass the measure.

The partisan maneuvering had been going on since July. Democrats had wanted to pass the bill by the August recess, but Republicans complained that they were not given a fair chance to get votes on their amendments. Minority Leader Mitch McConnell, R-Ky., sought an agreement, which was not forthcoming, that would have allowed eight amendments, including votes on the estate tax, nuclear energy loan guarantees, and border security.

During the debate on the bill, the Senate also rejected two motions to invoke cloture on amendments to change a requirement in the health care overhaul (PL 111-148, PL 111-152) that, beginning in 2012, businesses file informational reports to the Internal Revenue Service (IRS) for each vendor to whom they paid more than $600 in a tax year. One amendment would have repealed the requirement altogether; the other would have raised the thresholds for reporting. The provision was repealed in 2011 *(1099 repeal, p. 455)*

In final action, the House chose to accept the Senate version, clearing the bill, 237–187, on September 23. Although House leaders expressed some disappointment with the Senate package, it was clear that sending an altered version back to the Senate would have doomed the legislation. Instead, they emphasized the need for the legislation and said it would be critical in any effort to spur job creation.

President Barack Obama signed the measure into law September 27 (HR 5297—PL 111-240).

MAJOR PROVISIONS

The new $30 billion fund was created within the Treasury Department to enable the department to invest in community banks and other small financial institutions with less than $10 billion in risk-based assets, in an effort to expand the availability of credit to small businesses.

The measure authorized the appropriation of whatever sums were necessary to pay the cost of the $30 billion in investment. As an incentive, interest that the bank owed to the Treasury was tied to how much the bank expanded its small-business lending in the first two years and could go as low as 1 percent. Institutions that did not increase their small-business lending in the first two years could be charged rates of up to 7 percent. Participating banks were required to repay the capital investment within ten years. The Treasury had to use any proceeds to pay down the public debt. Institutions on the Federal Deposit Insurance Corporation's "problem bank" list were ineligible for the program.

The bill provided $1.5 billion for the creation of a small-business credit initiative to assist states with efforts to increase the amount of capital made available to small businesses by private lenders.

Tax Breaks

The new law authorizing $12 billion in tax incentives included:

- A 100 percent exclusion from taxation of capital gains on certain small-business stock held for five years. The 2009 economic stimulus law (PL 111-5) included a 75 percent exclusion rate for stock acquired between February 17, 2009, and January 1, 2011.
- A provision that allowed certain small businesses to carry back unused general business tax credits to offset taxes paid over the previous five years. Ordinarily, the carryback period was one year.
- A provision that allowed small businesses to use the general business credit to offset liability under the alternative minimum tax in 2010.
- A one-year extension of a "bonus depreciation" provision from the economic stimulus law. The extension allowed small businesses to immediately write off 50 percent of the cost of new equipment placed in service in 2010.
- A temporary increase in the amount businesses could deduct for certain capital expenditures in the year the expenditures were made. The maximum deduction in 2010 and 2011 was $500,000, up from $250,000, and was phased out once the expenditures exceeded $2 million, up from $800,000. The definition of property eligible for the deduction was also expanded.
- A deduction in 2010 for health insurance costs in computing self-employment taxes.

Revenue Raisers

The Joint Tax Committee estimated that revenue-raising tax changes would bring in $14.5 billion over ten years, more than paying for the tax breaks. Among the tax changes was one that made it easier for the IRS to seize property from certain federal contractors to pay the contractors' tax liability. The bill also allowed distributions from certain retirement accounts to be rolled over to Roth IRAs; the distributions would be treated as gross income. Taxes on Roth accounts were paid up front, rather than being deferred. A third change required taxpayers who received rental income to file informational returns to the IRS on payments made to service providers such as plumbers.

2011–2012

With Washington's attention focused almost exclusively on federal debt, deficits, spending, and taxes in anticipation of the 2012 elections, legislators took little action on other facets of economic policy during the 112th Congress. An effort by President Barack Obama and Democratic leaders to shift congressional attention to jobs—the issue that many polls showed was uppermost on voters' minds—met with little success. By the end of the 2011, the two parties were at loggerheads over an extension of the payroll tax cut first enacted in 2010. That issue was resolved at the beginning of 2012.

But with the exception of legislation to help small business attract capital, Congress took no other major direct actions on economic stimulus policy, although a surface transportation authorization bill passed in 2012 was expected to help create jobs, and trade adjustment assistance to some unemployed workers was extended in connection with ratification of three free trade agreements in 2011. *(Surface transportation details, p. 340; trade adjustment assistance, p. 199)*

For their part, House Republicans spent considerable time trying to delay or revise portions of the Dodd-Frank financial regulatory reform bill that they vehemently opposed. Only one minor bill embodying a change that both parties agreed to was passed. Senate Republicans also blocked confirmation of President Obama's nominee, Richard Cordray, to head the controversial Consumer Financial Protection Bureau. Obama gave Cordray a recess appointment in January 2012, contributing to another fight with Republicans over other presidential nominees that was not resolved until well into 2013.

Attempts to Weaken Financial Regulation

Almost every Republican lawmaker opposed the 2010 regulatory overhaul of the financial industry known as Dodd-Frank (PL 111-203), and during the 112th Congress many called for its full repeal. However, GOP leaders in both chambers declined to push legislation to do away with the law in its entirety, as they did for the 2010 health care overhaul law (PL 111-148, PL 111-152). Unlike the health care law, the financial rules rewrite remained broadly popular with the public. *(Dodd-Frank passage, p. 88; health care overhaul law repeal, p. 455)*

Instead, Republicans sought to delay or restructure specific elements of the law and tried to block President Barack Obama's nominee to lead the Consumer Financial Protection Bureau (CFPB), the agency at the center of the battle. Obama installed his pick, Richard Cordray, in a controversial recess appointment January 4, 2012. *(Cordray nomination, p. 105)*

CONSUMER BUREAU

The CFPB, which was the first federal financial regulatory agency established to serve as a watchdog solely for consumers, officially opened its doors in July 2011. A top priority for Democrats, the agency had broad authority to protect borrowers seeking mortgages, credit cards, and other financial products. GOP lawmakers strongly opposed its creation and argued that far too much power was concentrated in the director's position. They also complained that Congress lacked authority to oversee the bureau because it was housed in the independent Federal Reserve and its funding was not subject to the regular appropriations process.

In May 2011, forty-four Republican senators signed a letter pledging to prevent confirmation of a director for the agency unless its structure was substantially changed. They called for creation of a board to replace the single director and for making the agency's funding subject to appropriations. They also said other financial regulators should be able to more easily overrule any CFPB actions deemed a danger to individual banks or the financial system as a whole. Congressional Democrats and the Obama administration rejected each of those demands, which they said would gut the agency's authority.

Over the objections of Democrats, the GOP-controlled House passed legislation (HR 1315) in July 2011 with some of those changes; the bill did not advance in the Democratic Senate.

DERIVATIVES

House Republicans also continued to push a series of bills to scale back parts of the law, with a particular focus on the regulation of derivatives. Companies and financial institutions had long purchased financial derivatives contracts to hedge against risks associated with ordinary business operations, ranging from fluctuations in interest rates to the price of jet fuel. But derivatives trading that was related to defaults on mortgage-backed securities had helped to sink the insurance giant American International Group and fueled the 2008 financial crisis that eventually prompted government bailouts.

As part of Dodd-Frank, Congress empowered the Commodity Futures Trading Commission (CFTC) and the Securities and Exchange Commission (SEC) to place new restrictions on derivatives trading. In May 2011, the House Agriculture and Financial Services committees approved legislation (HR 1573—H Rept 112-109, Parts 1 and 2) to delay new derivatives regulations for up to eighteen months, until September 30, 2012. In addition to extending the deadline, the bill required that the CFTC and SEC finish drafting a number of definitions first, including those for swap dealers and security-based swap agreements. It also required that the agencies solicit public comment on the time and resources required to develop systems and infrastructure necessary to comply with any regulations.

Democrats charged that Republicans were using stalling tactics to try to push back implementation of the law in hopes that a future GOP administration would be able to weaken the rules or repeal them. Republicans said they wanted to ensure that the regulators got the rules right so that lawmakers did not have to revisit the derivatives issue in a few years.

The heads of the regulatory agencies did not want the deadlines extended. They had already delayed completing several crucial rules governing the new system amid uncertainty over how best to proceed. The bill, which never came to the House floor had support from a number of business and interest groups, including the U.S. Chamber of Commerce, the Business Roundtable, and the American Petroleum Institute.

END USERS

Lawmakers on both sides of the aisle were in greater accord on the need to maintain exemptions in the law for nonfinancial companies, known as end users, which relied on derivatives to hedge financial and other market-based risks. In November, the House Financial Services Committee approved a bill (HR 2682—H Rept 112-343, Part 1) to shield end users from some new rules. The full House passed the bill, 370–24, on March 26, 2012.

In June 2012, GOP senators sought to attach the end users bill as an amendment to a farm bill on the Senate floor, but they were rebuffed. That language was a top priority of business groups that said regulators had ignored the law's intent to shield end users from the burden of margin requirements. Senate Democrats, particularly those from agricultural states, remained concerned about the possible hit to end users but resisted new legislation to address the issue. Instead, they called on regulators to act.

OTHER ACTION

Other efforts to loosen new financial rules were derailed in the wake of JP Morgan Chase & Co.'s multibillion-dollar trading loss in May 2012 that came from a London office of the company; especially in an election year, lawmakers did not want to be seen as watering down financial regulations against the backdrop of JP Morgan's news. For example, a House Agriculture Committee markup of legislation to exempt certain derivatives from the overhaul's clearing and margin requirements was abruptly postponed and never rescheduled.

Democrats and Republicans did come together in one instance that touched on Dodd-Frank, although even that episode showed how difficult it was for lawmakers to find common ground on the law. The banking industry strongly supported a bill (HR 4014) clarifying that privileged information sent by financial institutions to the Consumer Financial Protection Bureau was protected as confidential and not subject to third-party subpoenas.

The House passed the bill by voice vote March 26, 2012, but action bogged down in the Senate, where several Republicans objected to passage by unanimous consent. The GOP senators wanted a chance to make more sweeping changes to Dodd-Frank and declined to let the bill advance. Democrats refused to budge, and the bill sat in legislative limbo for months. Ultimately, the GOP senators dropped their holds, and the Senate cleared the bill by unanimous consent December 11. Obama signed the bill into law on December 20 (PL 112-215).

Cordray Nomination to Lead CFPC

A key delaying tactic Senate Republicans used to obstruct implementation of the Dodd-Frank financial services regulation law (PL 111-203) was their refusal to confirm President Barack Obama's nomination of Richard Cordray as director of the Consumer Financial Protection Bureau (CFPB). In a move to keep the CFPB from getting off the ground, Senate Republicans on December 8, 2011, rejected, 53–45, a cloture motion on the nomination of Cordray, who was serving as chief of enforcement at the bureau. Sixty votes were required to invoke cloture; only one Republican, Scott P. Brown of Massachusetts, supported the cloture motion. Under the overhaul law, the agency could not exercise all of its authority without a director in place.

Obama had nominated Cordray, a former Ohio attorney general, for director of the CFPB on July 18, 2011. Cordray was seen as a more conciliatory pick than Harvard law professor Elizabeth Warren, a chief proponent of creating the new bureau who was favored by many consumer advocates but had become a lightning rod for criticism from Republicans and the financial industry.

Seeking to prevent Obama from making a recess appointment, Republicans prevented both chambers from adopting a formal adjournment resolution when Congress left town in December. The Senate was thus required to convene a pro forma session every three days.

Under the Constitution, the president can make recess appointments when vacancies arise during a Senate recess, but the Constitution does not specify a recess of any particular duration. A 1993 Justice Department memorandum interpreted the constitutional language to mean more than three days, and recent presidents had not made appointments when the Senate was out of session for three days or less. Senate Majority Leader Harry Reid, D-Nev., originated the process of holding pro forma sessions in November 2007 to block recess appointments by President George W. Bush.

On January 4, 2012, Obama gave recess appointments to Cordray and two nominees to the National Labor Relations Board (NLRB). Because the appointments were made when the Senate was in pro forma session, Republicans strongly objected. Three federal courts subsequently ruled that the NLRB nominations were unconstitutional, and the Supreme Court in June 2013 said it would consider the question in its 2013–2014 term.

In the interim, Obama renominated Cordray to the directorship on January 24, 2013. With Senate Republicans continuing to obstruct action on several presidential nominations, Majority Leader Harry Reid, D-Nev., threatened to invoke the "nuclear option" to end the practice of filibustering executive branch nominations. A last-minute compromise that involved the president pulling the two controversial NLRB nominations cleared the way for a vote on Cordray's nomination.

On July 16, 2013, the Senate voted 71–29 to invoke cloture on the nomination and then voted 66–34 to confirm him. Cordray, who had been serving as acting director of the CFPB, was sworn into office July 17, 2013, nearly two years to the day after he was first nominated.

Job Creation Legislation

After a crippling, months-long battle over the deficit that left both Congress and the White House exhausted and the public expressing dismay, President Barack Obama tried to seize the initiative in September 2011 by changing the subject to the top priority issue for Americans: jobs. But the rhetoric that had paralyzed Congress quickly returned, and while lawmakers considered several jobs bills, only one relatively small measure was enacted by the end of the year.

Obama began on September 8 by calling on a joint session of Congress to approve a $447 billion package of programs to stimulate the economy and create jobs. Four days later, he sent a bill to Capitol Hill that contained the details of his plan. In the weeks that followed, Obama stumped the country, calling day after day for Congress to pass his bill. His rhetoric was clearly partisan, a contrast with his approach during the summer debate on the debt limit, when he had tried in vain to win Republican support for a compromise. In a sample of his more combative approach, Obama took his call for spending on infrastructure to the site of a bridge connecting the home states of House Speaker John A. Boehner, R-Ohio, and Senate Minority Leader Mitch McConnell, R-Ky. *(Debt limit, p. 160)*

Faced with a halting economic recovery and stubbornly high unemployment, lawmakers, too, were looking to put jobs at the top of the legislative agenda. Despite questions from members of both parties about the effectiveness of the Obama proposals, Senate Democrats initially sought to pass the president's plan as a whole. They ran into a GOP filibuster, prompted chiefly by their proposal to finance the cost with a surtax on household income above $1 million.

On a deeper level, Democrats and Republicans were engaged in a long-standing debate about the proper distribution of the federal tax burden across income levels. Democrats consistently tried to provide tax cuts for lower and middle-income taxpayers and raise taxes on the wealthiest 1 percent to 2 percent of the population. Republicans, in turn, accused Democrats of "class warfare" and pointed to studies suggesting that roughly 50 percent of Americans did not have to pay income tax (although most workers paid Social Security taxes, plus state and local taxes including sales and property taxes for home owners).

As Obama continued to crisscross the country promoting his plan, Senate Majority Leader Harry Reid, D-Nev., sought to advance individual pieces of the package as stand-alone bills. Two such measures—a $35 billion package of state aid aimed at preventing layoffs of first responders and educators and a $60 billion measure to fund infrastructure and transportation projects—met the same fate: Republicans blocked both measures because they also would have been financed by a surtax on incomes higher than $1 million.

The House and Senate managed to agree on a small piece of the president's plan—tax credits for companies that hired unemployed veterans and encouraged job training for outgoing military service members—after linking it to a House GOP proposal to repeal a federal tax withholding requirement for payments to contractors (HR 674—PL 112-56). *(Tax withholding repeal, p. 169)*

That momentum did not translate into progress on extending the payroll tax cut and unemployment benefits, however. The Joint Select Committee on Deficit Reduction, created in August under the debt limit law, had been expected to deal with those two issues as part of its work. But when that panel disbanded in late November without producing a legislative proposal, matters grew more complicated. *(Deficit committee, p. 168)*

Specific talk of job creation dissipated, and the focus turned to the cost to American workers and the unemployed if payroll tax cuts and jobless aid were not renewed for 2012. That debate developed into a standoff that was ultimately resolved with, first, a two-month extension at the end of 2011 and then a full-year extension in February 2012. *(Payroll tax cut, pp. 79, 108, 144, 146)*

THE PRESIDENT'S PLAN

Obama's $447 billion bill, unveiled at a September 12 Rose Garden event, combined tax breaks with spending on infrastructure and public sector jobs, help for the unemployed, and extension of the payroll tax break. "This is the bill that Congress needs to pass," the president said. "No games, no politics, no delays."

Some of the proposals were aimed at creating jobs and spurring hiring; others were intended to put cash in people's pockets in an effort to increase demand and encourage more economic activity.

Major elements of the plan included $240 billion in tax breaks from extending and expanding a reduction in payroll taxes. Congress had agreed to a one-year reduction in the employee portion of the Social Security payroll tax, to

4.2 percent from 6.2 percent, as part of a tax agreement (PL 111-312) in late 2010 that also included an extension of George W. Bush–era tax cuts. Obama proposed further lowering the tax to 3.1 percent for employees, allowing the same break for employers on the first $5 million in wages, and dropping the rate even more for businesses that increased their payrolls through new hires. *(2010 tax law, p. 144)*

Other spending in the plan included $50 billion to upgrade highway, transit, rail, and aviation facilities; $35 billion for states to hire or retain teachers and first-responders; and $54.6 billion to extend emergency unemployment benefits and provide state reemployment services. The plan called for $450 billion in offsets, chiefly from limiting itemized deductions for couples with $250,000 or more in adjusted gross income ($200,000 or more for individuals).

Conservatives argued that the infrastructure spending, state aid, and jobless benefits provided under the 2009 economic stimulus law (PL 111-5) had done little to spur job growth. And although many economists contended that the 2007–2009 recession would have been harsher without congressional action, in politics it was always hard to take credit for not allowing things to get worse. *(Stimulus, p. 48)*

LEGISLATIVE ACTION

Overall Package

The Senate demonstrated conclusively on October 11 that the Obama package as a whole had no future, although GOP leaders said they could work with parts of it. The Senate rejected a cloture motion that would have limited debate and allowed senators to proceed to the bill (S 1660). The vote was 50–49, well short of the sixty votes needed.

Before bringing Obama's bill to the floor, Senate Democratic leaders turned to what they saw as a more populist tax message. Instead of curtailing itemized deductions—which Democrats worried might look like a tax increase on the middle class—they proposed a 5.6 percent surtax on joint income exceeding $1 million ($500,000 for individuals).

Senate Republicans countered with their own proposal, which they claimed could create five million new jobs. It called for a constitutional amendment requiring a balanced federal budget and a presidential line-item veto. It would have reduced the corporate tax rate to no more than 25 percent, allowed repatriation of overseas earnings at a lower tax rate, and repealed a 3 percent withholding from payments to government contractors.

The GOP package contained fifteen regulatory overhaul proposals that the sponsors said would promote growth. It also called for expanding offshore energy production, shortening the approval process for energy projects, and prohibiting the Environmental Protection Agency from using the Clean Air Act (PL 101-549) to regulate greenhouse gases.

At a news conference to release their legislation, Republicans attacked the president's policies and tactics. "If we really want to get our economy growing again, the first step we should take is to totally repeal his agenda, repeal Obamacare, repeal Dodd-Frank, repeal all these harmful regulations," said Sen. Ron Johnson, R-Wis., referring to the 2010 health care (PL 111-148, PL 111-152) and financial regulatory (PL 111-203) overhauls. *(Health care, p. 421; financial regulation, pp. 88, 104)*

After the defeat of the Obama package, Senate Democratic leaders moved to a strategy of forcing individual votes on popular portions of the bill to put Republicans in a difficult spot.

Teachers, First Responders

Reid first carved out a portion of the package (S 1723) that would have allocated $30 billion in grants to state and local governments to hire or retain teachers and $5 billion in grants to governments and other groups to pay for law enforcement officers and emergency personnel. The cost would have been offset through a 0.5 percent surtax on household income above $1 million.

McConnell sharply criticized the measure as a "bailout" for state governments that were struggling to deal with tepid economic growth and a resulting shortfall in tax receipts. Republicans also objected strongly to what they said was a permanent tax increase to pay for short-term programs.

On October 20, the Senate rejected, 50–50, a motion to invoke cloture and move to the measure.

Transportation, Infrastructure

Next up was a Democratic bill (S 1769) aimed at creating jobs through a short-term infusion of $50 billion for road, bridge, rail, transit, and airport projects, offset by a 0.7 percent surcharge on income exceeding $1 million. Democrats titled it the Rebuild America Jobs Act.

For the longer term, the bill would have established a national infrastructure bank with $10 billion in seed money for future transportation projects with public and private financing. The bank was seen as funding larger projects with regional and national impact, and lawmakers from both parties had publicly backed the idea. In May, the U.S. Chamber of Commerce and the AFL-CIO joined together in supporting it.

On November 3 the Senate rejected, 51–49, a motion to invoke cloture and move to the measure. Later the same day, the Senate voted, 47–53, against proceeding to a Republican counterproposal (S 1786) that would have reauthorized federal surface transportation programs for two years and enacted a variety of GOP-favored regulatory overhaul proposals. The costs would have been offset by a $40 billion rescission of unspecified federal funds.

Although the Rebuild America Jobs Act never got off the ground, Congress in 2012 reached agreement, after lengthy controversies, on legislation reauthorizing federal highway, transit, and other surface transportation programs through fiscal 2014. Democrats hailed the measure as a means of creating jobs as well as improving the nation's infrastructure. *(Details, p. 340)*

Veterans' Jobs, Contractor Withholding

Congress did clear one sliver of Obama's jobs plan—to create programs that would reduce unemployment among veterans—combining it with a repeal of a withholding requirement for payments to government contractors.

The bill (HR 674) began in the House as a measure devoted to the tax-withholding repeal. The Senate took up the House-passed bill and passed it November 10, after adding the provisions to boost veterans' employment. Senators voted, 94–1, to add the veterans language and passed the bill 95–0. The House cleared it, 422–0, on November 16. President Obama signed the measure into law November 21 (PL 112-56). *(Details, p. 169)*

Employee Payroll Tax Cut

After a months-long standoff, Congress passed legislation (HR 3765—PL 112-78) at the end of December 2011 to extend for just two months an expiring cut in employees' Social Security payroll taxes that had been enacted in December 2010. Lawmakers also agreed to convene a joint House-Senate conference committee early in 2012 to work out a year-long extension of the payroll tax cut. That bill was enacted February 22 (HR 3630—PL 112-96) as part of a bill to continue supplemental federal unemployment benefits and block a drop in reimbursements to Medicare physicians.

The main stumbling block to reaching agreement on a full-year extension was the issue of whether or how to offset the cost. The issue became the subject of a bitter debate between the parties and a year-end split among House Republicans over how to proceed. The prospect of a failure to renew the popular tax cut heightened the drama and forced the House to give in to Senate demands for a short-term extension to allow more time for negotiations, and then for Republicans to give into the Democrats and forgo their demand for offsets.

Private forecasters estimated that ending the payroll tax cut would have reduced growth of the gross domestic product by at least half a percentage point in 2012, with most of the damage being felt at the start of the year. The White House said that without an extension, the average middle-class family would see a tax increase of $1,000 in 2012.

Extending the tax cut was the centerpiece of a jobs package that Obama unveiled in September 2011 and stumped for in appearances across the country. Congress had agreed to a one-year reduction in the employee portion of the Social Security payroll tax, to 4.2 percent from 6.2 percent, as part of a broader tax agreement (PL 111-312) in late 2010.

The 2010 law did not affect the 6.2 percent share paid by employers. In his jobs plan, Obama proposed further lowering the tax to 3.1 percent for employees, allowing the same break for employers on the first $5 million in wages and dropping the rate even more for businesses that increased their payrolls.

SENATE ACTION

Senate Democrats tried repeatedly and unsuccessfully to pass legislation incorporating all or parts of Obama's jobs package but were never able to get close to the sixty votes needed to cut off debate. As the end of the year approached, Democrats began to focus on the impending expiration of two programs that benefited middle-class workers: the reduction in the payroll tax and benefits for the long-term unemployed.

Republicans were reluctant to support the payroll tax extension, mainly because Democrats wanted to pay for it by imposing a surtax on household income of more than $1 million. Some also argued that the cut would have a negative impact on the social Security Trust Fund. For weeks Democrats and Obama hammered the Republicans over refusing to cut taxes for the middle class while protecting millionaires.

On December 1, the Senate turned down motions to proceed to Democratic and Republican versions (sixty votes were needed to invoke cloture). The vote on the Democrats' bill was 51–49; the motion on the GOP plan was rejected 20–78.

The Democrats' bill (S 1917) would have paid for a one-year extension of the payroll tax break with a 3.25 percent surtax on adjusted gross income above $1 million. Like Obama's plan, the Democrats' measure would have cut the employer share to 3.1 percent from 6.2 percent for the first $5 million of a company's wage costs. The GOP bill (S 1931) was a one-year continuation of the 2010 tax cut, offset in part by extending an existing pay freeze for federal workers for three years beyond 2012. Their bill would have required taxpayers with annual income above $1 million to pay higher premiums for Medicare and barred them from receiving unemployment or food stamp benefits. It also would have created an option on tax forms for millionaires to pay more tax than they owed if they so chose.

In a near-repeat of the previous week, the Senate on December 8 again rejected motions to proceed to a modified Democratic bill and a reprise of the previously rejected GOP measure. The Democratic plan (S 1944), rejected on a vote of 50–48, would have cut the employee share of the tax to 3.1 percent for 2012 but left the employers paying 6.2 percent. To pay for the smaller bill, Democrats proposed a 1.9 percent surtax on income greater than $1 million, beginning in 2013 and expiring after ten years. An additional $38.1 billion was to come from increasing fees that mortgage lenders paid to Fannie Mae and Freddie Mac, the government-run mortgage-financing companies. The legislation also adopted the GOP proposal to prohibit millionaires from claiming unemployment benefits and food stamps but not the requirement that those in that income group pay higher Medicare premiums.

Republicans said they were not consulted on the revised offering and first learned about the details in media reports. They offered the same plan they put forth the previous week (S 1931), with similar results: A motion to proceed was rejected in a 22–76 vote.

HOUSE-SENATE STALEMATE

By mid-December, with public support for a continuation of the payroll tax reduction running high, House GOP leaders were ready to back the payroll extension but not the offset. On December 13, House Republicans passed a bill (HR 3630) that combined a one-year extension of the existing payroll tax cut with provisions to extend modified emergency unemployment benefits for a year and block the decrease in Medicare physicians' pay for two years. The near-party-line vote was 234–193.

To offset the costs, the bill proposed spending cuts and other savings provisions, including increasing Medicare premiums on higher-income beneficiaries, cutting funds for elements of the 2010 health care law (PL 111-148, PL 111-152), increasing loan guarantee fees charged by Fannie Mae and Freddie Mac, extending the pay freeze for federal employees, and requiring federal workers to contribute more toward their retirement. The bill also contained environmental provisions rejected by Democrats, particularly one to speed up a decision on whether to build the Keystone XL oil pipeline from Canada to the Gulf of Mexico. *(Keystone pipeline, p. 390)*

Recognizing the potential fallout for Republicans if Democrats succeeded in blaming them for not extending the lower payroll tax rate, especially during the holiday season, Senate Minority Leader Mitch McConnell, R-Ky., worked out a deal with Majority Leader Harry Reid, D-Nev., on a two-month bill. The measure covered the tax cut, unemployment benefits, and the Medicare "doc fix." As a sweetener for Republicans, it also included the Keystone XL pipeline provision. The cost of the measure was offset by a noncontroversial increase in the fees charged by Fannie Mae and Freddie Mac for guaranteeing loans.

The Senate backed the bipartisan extension as an amendment to the House-passed bill. In a rare Saturday session December 17, senators adopted the amendment on a **key vote of 89–10 (R 39–7; D 49–2; I 1–1)**. They then passed the bill by unanimous consent, setting up what was expected to be a December 19 vote in the House to clear the measure. With that done, senators went home for the year. *(2011 key votes, p. 785)*

All year long, House Speaker John A. Boehner, R-Ohio, had struggled, largely unsuccessfully, to persuade Republican members aligned with the Tea Party to accept compromises on economic policies they did not like. Boehner reportedly had hopes that a two-month extension would be acceptable to conservatives, especially because of the pipeline provision, which they strongly backed. Instead, he faced a revolt. In a conference call with the House GOP caucus shortly after the Senate vote, conservatives made it clear to Boehner that they would not go along with the Senate. Many Republicans questioned the purpose of a two-month extension, arguing that it would raise uncertainty, especially for small businesses. After the call, Boehner adamantly rejected the Senate bill, saying it was unacceptable to his chamber and insisting on a House-Senate conference on the full-year House measure.

House leaders avoided a formal vote on the Senate bill, thereby protecting their members from having to vote against a tax cut. Instead, on December 20, the House disagreed on a motion to accept the Senate amendment on a **key vote of 229–193 (R 229–7; D 0–186)**, and appointed conferees on the full-year bill. Reid said that the Senate's measure was bipartisan and that he had no intention of bringing his chamber back. *(2011 key votes, p. 785)*

With the tax cut about to expire and Obama maintaining that the Senate's two-month extension was the only viable compromise, the House Republicans were increasingly isolated. Not only had public sentiment turned against them, but Senate Republicans overwhelmingly supported the two-month measure. Some Senate Republicans, including McConnell, suggested publicly that House leaders change course and clear the Senate bill. In a December 22, 2011, editorial, headlined "The GOP Payroll Fiasco," the *Wall Street Journal* lambasted House Republicans, suggesting that they were pursuing a strategy that "might end up re-electing the president before the 2012 campaign even begins in earnest."

Finally, after refusing for several days to go against his caucus, Boehner bowed to the intense pressure, announcing December 22 that the House would vote on the Senate's two-month extension. He held another conference call with his caucus, but this time he was not soliciting input. He told members the House would pass the bill by unanimous consent, a procedure that did not require more than a few members to be present.

On December 23, the House gave unanimous consent to a bill (HR 3765) that was nearly identical to the Senate's measure. The Senate quickly cleared the modified bill, also by unanimous consent. As part of the deal, Reid agreed to appoint conferees on HR 3630, which he did on January 3, 2012.

CONFERENCE ACTION

With the two-month extension expiring on February 29, the House-Senate conference on HR 3630 convened amid expectations that the payroll debate would again go down to the wire as Democrats and Republicans wrangled over offsets for the tax reduction. But apparently fearing continued wrath from the public, Republican conferees gave up the battle and conferees completed their work with unusual speed. A majority of the conferees from both parties signed off on the deal early February 16. The House agreed to the conference report, 293–132, on February 17, and the Senate cleared it, 60–36, just minutes later. President Obama signed the bill on February 22.

Obama, who since September 2011 had pounded away on the campaign circuit on the need for an extension, praised the legislation, calling it "the right thing for our families and for our economy." Reflecting the rare bipartisan warmth, Rep. Dave Camp, R-Mich., chair of the Ways and Means Committee and an influential member of the conference committee, expressed satisfaction with the compromise: "The American people expect and deserve that their elected officials will work together. These days, that does not happen as often as it should," he said.

In addition to the reduction from 6.2 percent to 4.2 percent in the personal Social Security tax for the remainder of 2012, HR 3630 (PL 112-96) also extended federal unemployment benefits and Medicare reimbursement rates for physicians (known as the "doc fix") through the end of the year. The basic federal welfare program, Temporary Assistance to Needy Families (TANF), was extended through September 30, 2012. No revenue was included to cover the estimated $93.3 bill cost of the payroll tax reduction, but Congress added offsets and made other changes to reduce the costs of the other programs. The final measure was silent on the Keystone pipeline. *(TANF, p. 556)*

Small Business Regulation Eased

Congress cleared legislation in March 2012 to loosen securities regulations on smaller businesses in an effort to help them attract capital and foster job growth. The vote was the culmination of a months-long bipartisan push to ease financial regulations for some companies in the hope of spurring job creation. President Barack Obama signed the legislation into law (HR 3603—PL 112-106) on April 5, 2012.

Business leaders had long maintained that certain Securities and Exchange Commission (SEC) rules should be relaxed to better reflect changing investment practices and to reduce regulatory costs for smaller companies. In September 2011, President Obama joined that chorus when he urged Congress to "cut away the red tape that prevents too many rapidly growing startup companies from raising capital and going public."

The House passed several measures in November 2011 intended to do just that. One bill exempted companies that plan to sell $50 million in shares as part of a public offering from having to register with the SEC; the existing threshold was $5 million. Another bill eliminated an SEC rule that prohibited small, privately held companies from advertising to solicit investors. A third bill allowed companies to employ "crowd-funding," or the use of social media and the Internet, to raise capital from the public without having to register with the SEC.

Although some senators introduced companion measures, the broader deregulation effort largely fell off the radar until House Majority Leader Eric Cantor of Virginia bundled these bills together, as well as a few others, into a single piece of legislation. The bill, named the Jumpstart Our Business Startups Act, or JOBS Act, included new provisions to raise the threshold for the number of shareholders a company or bank could have before triggering an SEC registration. It also included provisions to allow certain companies to sell shares to the public without complying with some audit requirements in the 2002 Sarbanes-Oxley law (PL 107-204). *(Sarbanes-Oxley, Congress and the Nation Vol. X, p. 130)*

On March 8, 2012, with Obama's endorsement, the House passed the measure 390–23. On March 22, the Senate passed a slightly amended version of the bill on a **key vote of 73–26 (R 46–0; D 26–25; I 1–1)**. The lopsided vote, which had the support of all Senate Republicans and half the Democrats, belied the misgivings of a number of lawmakers who tried unsuccessfully to add consumer protections to the bill.

The Senate initially balked at the bill, after securities experts and regulators worried that the House version, by raising the threshold for federal regulation of companies and lifting other regulations for small companies, would leave investors vulnerable to fraud. A few days later, however, Senate Democrats reversed course and decided not to advance their own bill, largely because of the overwhelming vote for passage in the House and the president's support for the measure. Still, some Senate Democrats sought to delay the fast-moving measure in hopes of making changes.

The House cleared the amended version of HR 3606 on March 27, on a **key vote of 380–41 (R 235–0; D 145–41).** *(2012 key votes, p. 803)*

Chronology of Action on Budget and Tax Policy

During President Barack Obama's first term, lawmakers passed several historic pieces of legislation, including overhauls of the nation's health care and financial regulation systems and the largest economic stimulus program ever enacted. Yet by the end of 2012, Congress was more likely to be remembered for the deep partisan disputes over federal spending and tax policy that at times threatened to shut down the government and even throw it into default. Although last-minute compromises averted these disasters, they did little to resolve the underlying issues, making it a near-certainty that similar gridlock would continue to threaten congressional productivity in Obama's second term.

The gridlock on federal spending and tax policy was a consequence of both economic and political factors. The immediate causes grew out of the 2008 financial crisis and subsequent economic recession. The resulting decline in tax receipts and jump in federal spending on safety net programs and other emergency measures led to a near tripling of the federal budget deficit in fiscal 2009 to $1.4 trillion, a steep increase in the federal debt—and to widespread concern among voters.

The thornier factors were political. During the previous three decades the two parties had grown more and more polarized over their differing views on taxes, spending, and the role of government. Broadly speaking, Democrats favored government intervention in the marketplace in an effort to ensure fair treatment for producers, workers, and consumers and to provide safety nets to the less privileged, especially during economic downturns. Republicans in contrast supported smaller government, preferring less regulation, taxation, and spending. By the time the 111th Congress convened in 2009 with Democrats in control of both chambers and the White House, the gridlock reflected differences not only between the parties but within the parties themselves and between the House and the Senate.

REFERENCES

Discussion of tax policy for the years 1945–1964 may be found in *Congress and the Nation Vol. I,* pp. 397–442; for the years 1965–1968, *Congress and the Nation Vol. II,* pp. 141–182; for the years 1969–1972, *Congress and the Nation Vol. III,* pp. 77–96; for the years 1973–1976, *Congress and the Nation Vol. IV,* pp. 83–106; for the years 1977–1980, *Congress and the Nation Vol. V,* pp. 231–251; for the years 1981–1984, *Congress and the Nation Vol. VI,* pp. 63–82; for the years 1985–1988, *Congress and the Nation Vol. VII,* pp. 75–107; for the years 1989–1992, *Congress and the Nation Vol. VIII,* pp. 87–112; for the years 1993–1996, *Congress and the Nation Vol. IX,* pp. 83–107; for the years 1997–2000, *Congress and the Nation Vol. X,* pp. 87–119; for the years 2001–2004, *Congress and the Nation Vol. XI,* pp. 86–122; for the years 2005–2008, *Congress and the Nation Vol. XII,* pp. 60–135.

Discussion of federal budget policy for the years 1945–1964 may be found in *Congress and the Nation Vol. I,* pp. 387–395; for the years 1965–1968, *Congress and the Nation Vol. II,* pp. 127–140; for the years 1969–1972, *Congress and the Nation Vol. III,* pp. 63–75; for the years 1973–1976, *Congress and the Nation Vol. IV,* pp. 57–81; for the years 1977–1980, *Congress and the Nation Vol. V,* pp. 211–230; for the years 1981–1984, *Congress and the Nation Vol. VI,* pp. 33–61; for the years 1985–1988, *Congress and the Nation Vol. VII,* pp. 33–74; for the years 1989–1992, *Congress and the Nation Vol. VIII,* pp. 37–86; for the years 1993–1996, *Congress and the Nation Vol. IX,* pp. 37–82; for the years 1997–2000, *Congress and the Nation Vol. X,* pp. 40–86; for the years 2001–2004, *Congress and the Nation Vol. XI,* pp. 44–85; for the years 2005–2008, *Congress and the Nation Vol. XII,* pp. 60–135.

Over the next four years, these struggles intensified, seeming to harden a bit more each time an attempt to reconcile the differences fell apart. Another factor was the rising influence of the conservative Tea Party movement on the Republican Party's extreme right wing; legislators affiliated with this movement showed little willingness to compromise on budget and tax matters. As a result, by the end of the 112th Congress, the two parties appeared farther apart than ever on resolving their political and philosophical differences over the size and shape of the federal budget. Meanwhile, the federal debt continued to grow. For fiscal 2012, it stood at $16 trillion, or 103 percent of gross domestic product (GDP).

A GROWING FOCUS ON THE DEFICIT

During Obama's first year in office, legislators were focused primarily on economic stimulus, health care reform, and financial regulatory reform. The Democratic majority in both chambers was able to push through the annual budget resolution and the regular spending bills. Republicans, particularly in the House, objected angrily to the tactical procedures the Democrats used to keep bills moving, and they retaliated with delaying measures of their own. On a single day in June, for example, GOP House members forced a record fifty-three roll-call votes.

By the beginning of 2010, however, widening public concern over the deficit and the pending November midterm elections were making legislators in both parties nervous. Neither chamber was able to pass either the annual budget resolution (although the House did so indirectly) or any of the regular annual spending bills. Instead, the government was funded after October 1, 2010, through a series of continuing resolutions, or CRs—a procedure that would become almost standard practice over the next four years.

The increasing federal debt and the pending expiration of income tax cuts, enacted in 2001 and 2003, also became focal points of contention. Although the annual appropriations process tended to focus on discretionary funding, two-thirds of the federal budget involved mandatory spending, including entitlement programs such as Social Security, Medicare, and Medicaid, which were consuming an increasing portion of the federal budget as the population aged and health care costs rose. Without reforms, spending on these programs was projected to reach unsustainable levels in the relatively near future. In 2013, the Medicare trust fund, for example, was projected to begin running out of funds by 2026, requiring either changes in the program or an infusion of funding from general revenues.

In February 2010, Congress agreed to raise the debt ceiling by $1.9 trillion only after moderates in the Senate insisted that the president appoint a bipartisan commission to recommend ways to reduce the federal budget deficit as well as to curb the growth of entitlement spending and slow the increase in the debt over the long term. In early December the commission announced that eleven of its eighteen members had supported a set of proposals that addressed spending, tax reform, and entitlement reform—three members short of the number needed to send the plan to a promised vote in Congress. The commission's exercise was the first of several failed attempts to find a "grand bargain" to put the nation's fiscal house in better balance.

Income tax cuts, a signal victory of George W. Bush's presidency, were scheduled to expire at the end of 2010. Republicans insisted that they be made permanent. Democrats wanted to continue the reduced tax rates only for those individuals earning less than $200,000 a year ($250,000 for a couple). Although neither party was in favor of letting the tax cuts expire, Democratic leaders in both chambers had refused to bring up the matter before the midterm elections. Any momentum Democrats might have hoped to gain from the elections was quickly dashed when midterm voters gave control of the House to Republicans and increased their numbers in the Senate.

With economists warning that an increase in tax rates could throw the economy back into full recession, the Democrats, including the president, had little room to maneuver in the lame duck session. In a move that angered many in his party, Obama worked out a deal with Republican leaders to extend the tax cuts unchanged for two years, through December 31, 2012, in return for an extension of emergency jobless benefits and a reduction of two percentage points in the employee payroll tax.

A LINE IN THE SAND

As the new Congress convened in 2011, with Republicans now in control of the House following the 2010 elections, the federal government was nearing the limits of its borrowing authority, which was expected to expire sometime in the summer (in May the deadline was pushed to August 2). House Republicans made it clear from the beginning that they viewed their new majority as a mandate from the voters to hold the line on spending. In the first few weeks, they insisted on spending reductions as the price of their support for keeping the government operating through the end of the fiscal year.

In anticipation of the battle to come on raising the debt ceiling, President Obama offered a budget plan that called for $4 trillion in deficit reduction over several years through a combination of spending cuts and tax increases, the so-called grand bargain. He also created a bipartisan congressional panel to flesh out the plan and present it to Congress for approval before the August 2 deadline.

The House immediately countered with a budget resolution that called for greatly reduced domestic spending, no new taxes, and spending offsets to any increase in the debt ceiling. The Democrats' response to the president's plan was lukewarm, with some saying it went too far and others not far enough. But they were uniformly opposed to the Republican plan. To demonstrate their opposition, Senate Democrats voted unanimously against the resolution. The House returned the compliment, taking a symbolic vote rejecting a GOP-sponsored bill to raise the debt ceiling with no accompanying budget cuts.

Led by Vice President Joseph R. Biden Jr., the congressional panel met for several weeks in May and June, reportedly making some headway on possible spending reductions. When those talks broke down in late June over taxes, Obama entered the negotiations, which appeared to be making progress, albeit in fits and starts.

Then, on July 22, House Speaker John A. Boehner, R-Ohio, announced he was pulling out of the talks. Although Boehner blamed the impasse on the Democrats for "moving the goalposts" on revenue at the last minute, it seemed clear that he could not muster a majority of his party's caucus to support a revenue increase of any size. During a news conference, a visibly angry president lashed out at Republicans for walking away from what he described as a generous package of spending and entitlement cuts, along with increases in revenue by eliminating loopholes and deductions and overhauling the tax code rather than raising tax rates.

Concern began to mount about the real possibility of a government default as day after day passed with no breakthrough. Finally, Senate Republican Minority Leader Mitch McConnell, Ky., concerned that a default would be blamed on the GOP and guarantee Obama reelection in 2012, reached out to Biden to restart negotiations. On July 31, Senate leaders announced a compromise had been found, which both chambers approved on August 1.

The compromise paired a two-step increase in the debt ceiling, with each step tied to across-the-board cuts (known as "sequester") in discretionary spending, both for domestic programs and the Pentagon. The sequester cuts, which were to take effect at the beginning of calendar year 2013, were intended to be so painful, for both parties, that the prospect would force them to reach some kind of compromise instead.

Although the compromise averted a government default, it did little to resolve the underlying spending and taxing questions. Liberal Democrats were furious with Obama for not winning higher tax rates for high-income earners and for supporting legislation that could lead to cuts in entitlement programs. Conservative Republicans, especially those aligned with the Tea Party movement, complained that the spending reductions were too small.

Less than two months later, another crisis erupted over passage of a continuing resolution. Angered that the CR set the spending cap at the amount agreed to in the August debt ceiling bill, rather than the lower amount approved in the House budget resolution, Tea Party caucus members in the House voted with Democrats against a CR. It was the first clear defeat of the GOP House leadership since Republicans had taken control in January.

Boehner managed to get a revised CR through the House, but the measure was rejected by Senate Democrats opposed to offsets for disaster aid. Yet another last-minute compromise was required before the CR was passed and a shutdown of the government avoided.

In 2012, the budget debate took place on the campaign trail rather than in the halls of Congress. In a rare bipartisan move, legislators agreed to operate the government under a CR for the first six months of fiscal 2013, postponing another fight over spending levels until after the November elections, when Congress would have to deal once again with the expiring Bush-era tax cuts as well as the automatic across-the-board spending cuts that were scheduled to take place at the beginning of the year. Inaction would lead to tax increases for all taxpayers at the same time that government spending was reduced, a concurrence of events that could send the country over what Federal Reserve Board Chair Ben Bernanke dubbed a "fiscal cliff," jeopardizing the growth of the still struggling economy.

TEETERING ON THE FISCAL CLIFF

In November 2012 Obama decisively won election to a second term, campaigning on a platform to raise taxes on the rich while preventing a tax hike for the middle class. Despite that victory, Republicans held firm to their position that the Bush-era tax rates should be made permanent for all taxpayers, although many worried they would be blamed if no agreement could be reached and the tax cuts expired.

At the same time, some GOP legislators were eager to forestall the automatic across-the-board spending cuts that were scheduled to take effect at the beginning of 2013 because they applied equally to defense and domestic spending and did little to reduce entitlement spending.

Obama turned to both the public and businesses to put pressure on Republicans to yield on taxes. In private talks, the president and Boehner reportedly came near a compromise in which Boehner agreed to increased revenue in return for concessions from Obama. Then, in a surprise move, Boehner announced that the House would vote on "Plan B," a bill that would allow tax rates to rise on annual incomes above $1 million but keep all other tax rates in place. A few hours later, he was forced to pull the measure from the floor when it became clear that his caucus would not support it. Once again, the government was teetering on the edge of the fiscal cliff.

The debate then shifted to the Senate, where the two party leaders, Democrat Harry Reid of Nevada and the GOP's McConnell, tried but failed to reach a compromise. In a replay of the debt ceiling crisis, McConnell once again phoned Biden at the eleventh hour and the two men worked out a compromise on New Year's Eve, just hours before the midnight reversion to higher tax rates.

The final compromise, which was cleared on January 1, allowed the two top tax rates to return to their pre-2001 levels and postponed the sequester cuts for two months. It

MAJOR ACTIONS ON BUDGET AND TAX POLICY

Following, in chronological order, are the major actions on budget and tax policy taken during the 111th and 112th Congresses.

2009

February 13. Senate clears economic stimulus bill (HR 1—PL 111-5), which provides $787.2 billion for a series of stimulus programs and raises the federal ceiling to $12.104 trillion from $11.315 trillion.

February 25. Senate clears HR 1105 (PL 111-8), an omnibus appropriations package that completes action on the nine spending bills left unfinished at the end of the 110th Congress.

April 29. House and Senate adopt a budget resolution (S Con Res 13) setting spending and taxing parameters for fiscal 2010. The resolution, passed with no Republican votes, sets discretionary spending for the year at $1.09 trillion and gives authorizing committees until October 15 to report health care and student loan reconciliation bills, which are not subject to a filibuster in the Senate. This becomes the only budget resolution to pass both chambers during Obama's first term. *(Health care, p. 421; student loans, p. 476)*

September 25. Senate clears legislation (HR 2918—PL 111-68) appropriating fiscal 2010 funds for the legislative branch and continuing appropriations for the rest of the government through October 31. The legislative branch bill is the only spending measure to clear Congress before the start of the 2010 fiscal year.

October 29. Senate clears the fiscal 2010 spending bill for the Interior Department and environmental programs (HR 2996—PL 111-88), which also continues funding through December 18 for those federal departments and agencies whose spending bills have not yet cleared. An omnibus bill covering six of the regular spending bills clears December 13, and the final spending bill, for defense, clears December 19.

December 24. Senate clears HR 4314 (PL 111-123) raising the federal debt ceiling $290 billion to $12.394 trillion. The increase is expected to extend the government's borrowing authority into early 2010.

2010

February 4. House clears a resolution (H J Res 45—PL 111-139) raising the federal debt ceiling $1.9 billion to $14.294 trillion. The government's budget authority is expected to last into early 2011. The Senate passes the resolution after moderates insist that the president create a bipartisan commission to address the nation's fiscal problems. At the insistence of House Republicans, the measure also reinstitutes pay-as-you-go budget rules. In exchange, the House adopts a self-executing rule that concurs in the Senate-passed debt ceiling increase before clearing H J. Res 45.

Spring. Neither chamber enacts a fiscal 2011 budget resolution. The Senate Budget Committee approves a resolution in April setting discretionary spending for the year at $1.122 trillion. In July the House indirectly adopts a $1.121 trillion limit as part of the rule for debate on an unrelated spending bill.

September 30. Unable to clear any of the regular appropriations bills for fiscal 2011, Congress clears the first of four short-term continuing resolutions that keeps the government operating at fiscal 2010 levels through March 4, 2011.

November 2. Voters in the midterm elections return control of the House to Republicans and substantially narrow the Democrats' majority in the Senate. Several legislators affiliated with or sympathetic to the conservative Tea Party movement are also elected. These two factors, combined with a presidential reelection battle in November 2012, complicate the process for reaching a bipartisan agreement on spending and taxing issues for the remainder of Obama's first term.

December 3. A commission created by President Obama earlier in the year announces that, although a majority of the committee supports a set of recommendations to address the nation's long-term fiscal problems, the panel is three votes short of the number needed to send the recommendations to Congress.

December 17. The House clears a bill (HR 4853—PL 111-312) extending all of the Bush-era tax cuts for two years. Without this action, income taxes would have returned to their higher levels in 2001. To prevent that, Obama strikes a last-minute deal with Republicans that continues tax cuts for the wealthy and revives the estate tax—two provisions that the president and Democrats had long sought to overturn. In return, Obama wins an extension of expanded unemployment benefits and a year-long reduction in the employee payroll tax of two percentage points that, with other items, is expected to pump as much as $180 billion into the economy. Democrats, particularly in the House, are highly critical of the deal, charging Obama with caving to the GOP.

2011

April 13. In a major speech, Obama offers a broad outline of a proposal to reduce the deficit by $4 trillion over four years through a combination of spending cuts and tax hikes and calls for creation of a bipartisan congressional panel led by the vice president to flesh out the proposal and present it to Congress for action before August 2, when the government is expected to reach statutory limits on its borrowing authority.

April 14. Senate clears legislation (HR 1473—PL 112-10) making appropriations for the entire government for the remainder of fiscal 2011. The spending bill provides $1.05 trillion in discretionary budget authority, a reduction of nearly $40 billion from existing law; many of the controversial policy riders attached by GOP conservatives in the House are omitted. The original House version made even deeper reductions, but Democrats balked at both the spending cuts and the policy riders. Three short-term continuing resolutions (CRs) and the threat of a government shutdown are required before a compromise is reached. Even then, the new Republican leadership requires Democratic votes to pass the bill.

April 15. House passes a budget resolution (H Con Res 34) for fiscal 2012 setting discretionary spending at $1.019 trillion and proposing radical changes in Medicare, Medicaid, and other entitlement programs. The plan is almost diametrically opposed to Obama's plan.

May 25. Senate rejects the House budget plan, the Obama budget proposal, and two other Republican plans. In a symbolic action on May 31, the House rejects a bill raising the debt ceiling without spending cuts. The two actions demonstrate the difficulty of reaching a compromise on a deficit reduction/debt limit bill.

Late June. Talks led by Vice President Joseph R. Biden Jr. fall apart over the issue of increasing taxes. Obama begins talks with House and Senate congressional leaders. The Tea Party caucus demand for deep cuts and no tax increases grows louder, while Senate Democrats worry that Obama will make major concessions on entitlement reforms they oppose.

July 9. House Speaker John A. Boehner, R-Ohio, announces he is giving up the search for a "grand bargain," blaming the impasse on the White House demands for revenue increases. He calls for a short-term solution primarily involving spending cuts.

July 11. Obama rejects a short-term bill, saying he had accepted entitlement reforms and the GOP needed to accept revenue increases.

July 19. House passes legislation (HR 2560) making an increase in the debt limit contingent on passage of a constitutional amendment requiring a balance budget, setting fiscal 2012 discretionary spending at $1.019 trillion, and tying future spending to the growth of the nation's gross domestic product (GDP).

July 22. Boehner pulls out of the talks with the president, saying Obama "moved the goalposts" on revenue.

July 29. House passes a short-term bill requiring $917 billion in deficit reduction to offset a $900 billion increase in the debt ceiling. The debt limit increase is also conditional on a balanced-budget constitutional amendment. The Senate rejects the House bill the same day but Senate Democrats cannot muster a sixty-vote majority to close off debate and pass a bill of their own.

July 31. Senate Minority Leader Mitch McConnell, R-Ky., and Biden announce they have reached a compromise. The Budget Control Act of 2011 allows for an immediate increase of $900 billion in the debt ceiling and makes further increases conditional on passing a debt reduction deal; failing that, an across-the-board spending cut, known as a sequester, will occur.

July 31. By the end of July, House Republicans pass six regular fiscal 2012 appropriations bill, all hewing to the spending limits set in the House budget resolution. The Senate passes only one and puts off action on the others.

August 2. Senate clears the compromise on the debt limit (S 365—PL 112-25), averting a government default on its debts. The House passes the bill August 1, with Democratic support.

August 5. Standard and Poor's cuts its rating on U.S. Treasury debt from AAA for the first time, saying the deficit deal falls short of what is needed. A CNN poll released August 8 shows Congress's approval rating at 14 percent.

September 21. House rejects a continuing resolution (HR 2608), supported by the leadership, which continues fiscal 2012 funding for government operations through November 18. Forty-eight Republicans, many of them associated with the conservative Tea Party caucus, join almost all House Democrats to vote against the bill, which adheres to $1.043 trillion limit set in the August debt limit bill. The GOP conservatives insist on the lower spending cap set in the House budget resolution as well as offsets for disaster funding in the bill.

September 23. House passes a slightly revised version of HR 2608, which the Senate tables later in the day. With the start of fiscal 2012 fast approaching, yet another threat of government shutdown looms.

October 4. House clears HR 2608 (PL 112-36) extending fiscal 2012 funding for government operations through November 18, 2011. A compromise involving the disaster aid offsets clears the way for final action, but not before a four-day continuing resolution is adopted on September 29.

November 17. Senate clears omnibus legislation (HR 2112—PL 112-55) covering three regular fiscal 2012 appropriations bills. The bill also continues funding for the rest of the government through December 16.

November 18. House fails to approve a constitutional amendment requiring a balanced budget, falling twenty-three

(Continued)

MAJOR ACTIONS ON BUDGET AND TAX POLICY (Continued)

votes short of the two-thirds majority needed for passage. The House vote effectively kills the amendment.

November 21 . The Joint Select Committee on Deficit Reduction created by the Budget Control Act in August announces that it is unable to reach an agreement on a plan to reduce the deficit by $1.2 trillion over ten years. Under the law, the committee's failure means that automatic across-the-board spending cuts will begin in January 2013 unless Congress takes action to achieve the desired savings.

December 17. Senate clears omnibus legislation (HR 2055—PL 112-74) covering fiscal 2012 spending for the remaining nine regular appropriations bills, after a compromise involving legislation extending an employee payroll tax deduction is resolved. Two more continuing resolutions are needed to keep the government operating before Obama signs the bill December 23.

2012

May 16. Senate rejects motion to consider a budget resolution (H Con Res 112) passed by the House on March 29. The House resolution set the cap for fiscal 2013 discretionary spending at $1.028 trillion, $19 billion less than agreed to in the 2011 Budget Act, and included several policy initiatives that Democrats oppose.

July 25. In the opening skirmish of what turned out to be a months-long battle over tax and spending policy, the Senate passes a bill (S 3412) allowing the 2001 and 2003 reductions in upper-income tax rates to expire at the end of the year, as scheduled.

August 1. House passes its tax legislation (HR 8), continuing all income tax rates at the reduced levels enacted in 2001 and 2003. No further action is taken on the issue until after the November elections.

September 22. Senate clears a continuing resolution for fiscal 2013 (H J Res—PL 112-175) that funds the federal government through March 31, 2013. The discretionary spending cap is set at $1.047 trillion, slightly above the fiscal 2012 cap and the amount agreed to in the 2011 Budget Control Act. None of the regular fiscal 2013 bills have cleared Congress as of September 22, and action is needed to avoid a government shutdown on October 1, 2012, the start of the new fiscal year. The result of a compromise between the White House and the Senate and House leadership of both parties, the legislation pushes any disagreements over spending levels past the 2012 elections and removes the issue from the expected end-of-year clash over expiring income tax cuts and a pending across-the-board spending cut, collectively known as the fiscal cliff.

November 6. President Obama handily wins a second term in the general elections. Republicans lose eight seats in the House but retain a solid majority; the number of new members identifying with the Tea Party movement increases markedly. Democrats increase their majority in the Senate by two seats but still fall five votes short of the sixty needed to cut off debate with no help from the GOP.

November 16. Obama and Boehner begin talks on tax policy, with Obama insisting on raising the tax rate for wealthy earners and the Speaker just as adamantly refusing to go along. The two men meet periodically until early December, narrowing their differences on both tax increases and deficit reduction.

December 20. Realizing that any grand compromise he might make with the president is unlikely to be accepted by his caucus, Boehner abruptly breaks off talks with the White House and announces the House will vote on "Plan B," which would allow tax rates on the wealthy to rise on January 1, 2013, but keep all other income tax cuts in place. The bill is abruptly pulled from the floor when it becomes clear that it will not win enough Republican votes to pass.

December 31. In a last-ditch attempt at a compromise, McConnell and Biden began new talks that result in an agreement in which income tax rates for the two top brackets are returned to their pre-2001 levels and the automatic sequester is postponed for two months, through February 28, 2013. The measure also extends emergency unemployment benefits but does not renew the employee payroll tax reduction, which expired at the end of the year.

2013

January 1. The House clears HR 8 (PL 112-240) as amended to incorporate the agreement reached by McConnell and Biden. The Senate passes it earlier in the day. Obama signs HR 8 into law January 2. The measure keeps the country from going over the fiscal cliff but leaves the 113th Congress facing almost immediate decisions. The government is expected to reach its legal debt limit in early 2013. The automatic sequester will take effect on March 1 if Congress does not act to replace it before then, and the continuing resolution on fiscal 2013 funding for the government is scheduled to expire March 27.

also extended emergency unemployment benefits but did not renew the employee payroll tax reduction, which expired at the end of 2012.

Although the compromise kept the country from going over the fiscal cliff, it did nothing to solve the underlying disagreements over taxing and spending.

When the 113th Congress convened, it would be facing not only the automatic sequestration, but the expiration of the continuing resolution funding the government as well as the need for another increase in the debt ceiling.

FALLING DEFICIT, RISING DEBT

By one measure, the congressional focus on driving down the budget deficit seemed somewhat misplaced. In fiscal 2008, even as the country fell into recession, the annual budget deficit stood at $459 billion, or 3.2 percent of the nation's GDP. By most economic standards, that was an acceptable level of debt. Over the next year, however, as recession deepened, revenues fell off and federal safety net programs such as unemployment insurance and food stamps began to grow. At the end of fiscal 2009, the federal deficit ballooned to $1.4 trillion, or 10.1 percent of GDP.

As the economy began to grow again and troubled banks paid back most of what they had "borrowed" from the government, tax receipts began to grow, and the draw on safety net programs began to slow. In addition, many of the emergency spending measures adopted as part of the stimulus ended at the end of fiscal 2010. The budget deficit began to fall that year and stood at $1.1 trillion at the end of fiscal 2012, or 7 percent of GDP. In fiscal 2013, the deficit fell dramatically to an estimated $642 million, according to the Congressional Budget Office (CBO) projections.

The federal debt was another matter, however. The public debt doubled in Obama's first term, rising from $5.8 trillion, or 54.0 percent of GDP, in 2008 to $11.3 trillion, or 72.6 percent of GDP, in 2012. That was roughly twice as high as the average for the previous four decades. Given the pressures of an aging population, rising health care costs, an expansion of federal subsidies for health insurance, and growing interest payments on the federal debt, the CBO warned that the debt was on an upward—and unsustainable—path.

Federal Budget, Fiscal 1993–Fiscal 2012 *(Billions of dollars)*

Year	*Revenues*	*Outlays*	*On-budget Surplus or Deficit*	*Social Security*	*Total Surplus or Deficit*	*Public Debt*
1993	$1,154.3	$1,409.4	$–300.4	$45.3	$–255.1	$3,248.4
1994	1,258.6	1,461.8	–258.8	55.7	–203.2	3,433.1
1995	1,351.8	1,515.7	–226.4	62.4	–164.0	3,604.4
1996	1,453.1	1,560.5	–174.0	66.6	–107.4	3,734.1
1997	1,579.3	1,601.1	–103.2	81.4	–21.9	3,772.3
1998	1,721.7	1,652.5	–29.9	99.2	69.3	3,721.1
1999	1,827.5	1,701.8	1.9	123.7	125.6	3,632.4
2000	2,025.2	1,789.0	86.4	149.8	236.2	3,409.8
2001	1,991.4	1,862.8	–32.4	160.7	128.2	3,319.6
2002	1,853.1	2,010.9	–317.4	159.7	–157.8	3,540.4
2003	1,782.3	2,159.9	–538.4	160.8	–377.6	3,913.4
2004	1,880.1	2,292.8	–568.0	155.2	–412.7	4,295.5
2005	2,153.6	2,472.0	–493.6	175.3	–318.3	4,592.2
2006	2,406.9	2,655.1	–434.5	186.3	–248.2	4,829.0
2007	2,568.0	2,728.9	–342.2	186.3	–160.7	5,035.1
2008	2,524.0	2,982.5	–641.8	181.5	–454.6	5,803.1
2009	2,105.0	3,517.7	–1,549.7	137.0	–1,412.7	7,544.7
2010	2,162.7	3,457.1	–1,371.4	77.0	–1,294.4	9,018.9
2011	2,303.5	3,603.1	–1,366.8	67.2	–1,299.6	10,128.2
2012	2,450.2	3,537.1	–1,148.9	61.9	–1,087.0	11,281.1

SOURCE: Executive Office of the President, Office of Management and Budget, *Budget of the United States Government, Fiscal Year 2014, Historical Tables* (Washington, D.C.: Government Printing Office, 2013), Table 1.1.

Deficit History, 1929–2012 *(Fiscal years in billions of dollars)*

Fiscal Year	*Receipts*	*Outlays*	*Surplus or Deficit (–)*	*Surplus/ deficit as % of GDP*
1929	$3.9	$3.1	$0.7	—
1933	2.0	4.6	–2.6	–4.5%
1939	6.3	9.1	–2.8	–3.2
1940	6.5	9.5	–2.9	–3.0
1945	45.2	92.7	–47.6	.5
1950	39.4	42.6	–3.1	–1.1
1955	65.5	68.4	–3.0	–0.8
1960	92.5	92.2	0.3	–0.1
1965	116.8	118.2	–1.4	–0.2
1969	186.9	183.6	3.2	–0.3
1970	192.8	195.6	–2.8	–0.3
1975	279.1	332.3	–53.2	–3.4
1980	517.1	590.9	–73.8	–2.7
1981	599.3	678.2	–79.0	–2.6
1982	617.8	745.7	–128.0	–4.0
1983	600.6	808.4	–207.8	–6.0
1984	666.5	851.9	–185.4	–4.8
1985	734.1	946.4	–212.3	–5.1
1986	769.2	990.4	–221.2	–5.0
1987	854.4	1,004.1	–149.7	–3.2
1988	909.3	1,064.5	–155.2	–3.1
1989	991.2	1,143.8	–152.6	–2.8
1990	1,032.1	1,253.0	–221.0	–3.9
1991	1,055.1	1,324.2	–269.2	–4.5
1992	1,091.3	1,381.6	–290.3	–4.7
1993	1,155.0	1,409.4	–255.1	–3.9
1994	1,258.7	1,461.8	–203.2	–2.9
1995	1,351.8	1,515.7	–164.0	–2.2
1996	1,453.1	1,560.5	–107.4	–1.4
1997	1,579.3	1,601.1	–21.9	–0.3
1998	1,721.7	1,652.5	69.3	0.8
1999	1,827.5	1,701.8	125.6	1.4
2000	2,025.2	1,789.0	236.2	2.4
2001	1,991.1	1,862.8	128.2	1.3
2002	1,853.1	2,010.9	–157.8	–1.5
2003	1,782.3	2,159.9	–377.6	–3.4
2004	1,880.1	2,292.8	–412.7	–3.5
2005	2,153.6	2,472.0	–318.3	–2.6
2006	2,406.9	2,655.1	–248.2	–1.9
2007	2,568.0	2,728.9	–160.7	–1.2
2008	2,524.0	2,982.5	–458.6	–3.2
2009	2,105.0	3,517.7	–1,412.7	–10.1
2010	2,162.7	3,457.1	–1,294.4	–9.0
2011	2,303.5	3,603.1	–1,299.6	–8.7
2012	2,450.2	3,537.1	–1,087.0	–7.0

SOURCE: Executive Office of the President, Office of Management and Budget, *Budget of the United States Government, Fiscal Year 2014, Historical Tables* (Washington, D.C.: Government Printing Office, 2013), Tables 1.1, 1.2.

NOTE: GDP: Gross domestic product.

Federal Budget Receipts

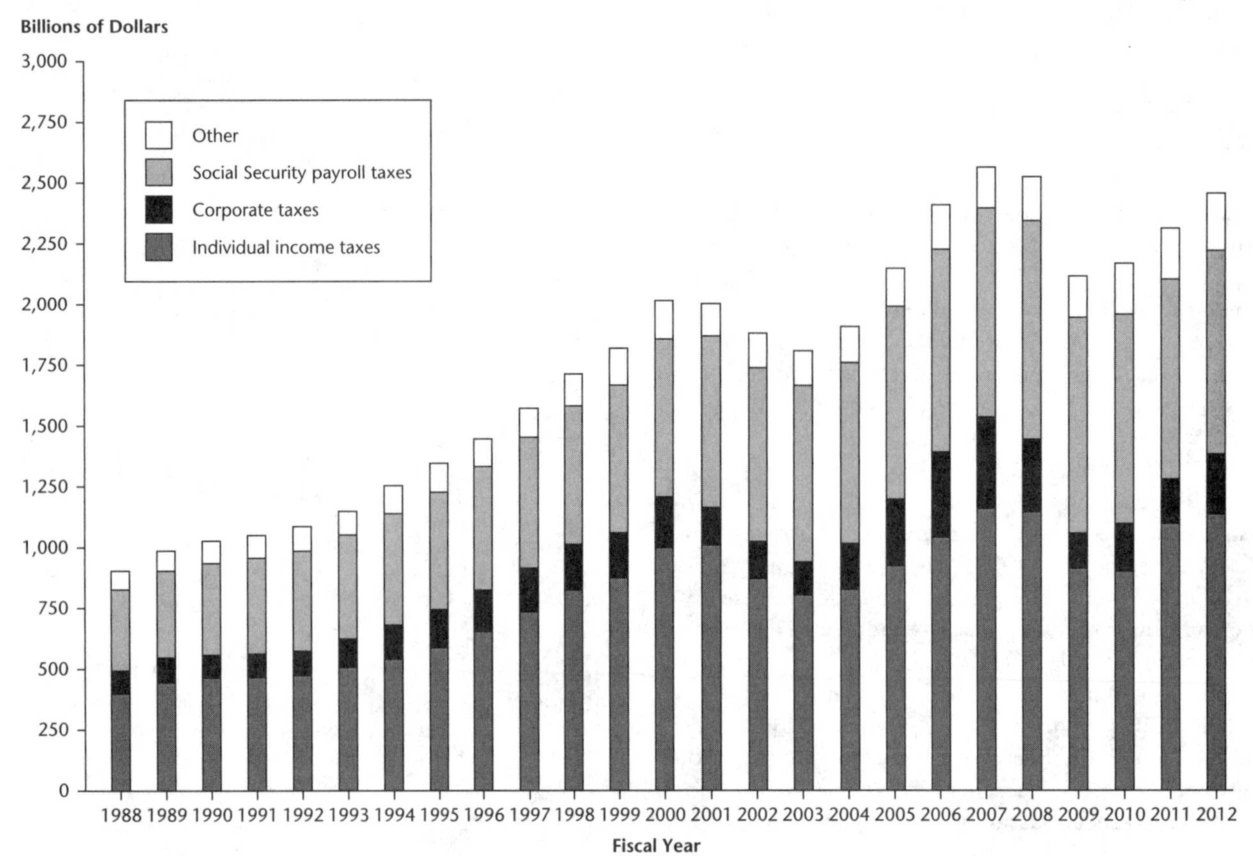

SOURCE: Office of Management and Budget, *Historical Tables, Budget of the United States Government: Fiscal Year 2014* (Washington, D.C.: U. S. Government Printing Office, 2013), Table 2.1.

2009–2010

Democrats began 2009 optimistic that Congress could write a budget and complete all of its work on the twelve annual appropriations bills without having to resort to a multibill omnibus spending package. But the appropriators' plate was too full and the pace in the Senate was too slow to bring that plan to fruition. Before the appropriations committees could begin in earnest on the annual spending bills for fiscal 2010, they had to approve the discretionary funding that was part of an economic stimulus package, close the books on fiscal 2009, and win passage of a supplemental fiscal 2009 bill to support operations in Iraq and Afghanistan.

All of this resulted in a late start for the year's regular appropriations season. Legislators completed action on a fiscal 2010 budget resolution in April; it was to be the first and last budget resolution both chambers approved during President Barack Obama's first term. The House passed all twelve of its fiscal 2010 bills before the August recess, as well as budget enforcement rules. But the process bogged down in the Senate as a result of partisan bickering and the amount of time consumed by work on health care overhaul legislation. In the end, six of the bills cleared separately; the other six were packaged into a year-end omnibus.

The appropriations process all but fell apart in 2010. Congress managed to pass three fiscal 2011 supplemental spending bills, including one to finance the winding down of the wars in Iraq and Afghanistan. But neither chamber was able to pass a budget resolution for fiscal 2011, and Democrats ultimately abandoned any effort to pass individual spending bills. Instead, legislators kept the government functioning through a series of short-term continuing resolutions, three of them in the lame duck session that followed the 2010 election in which Republicans took control of the House in 2011 and that narrowed the Democratic majority in the Senate.

Legislators did succeed in one area that would become more troublesome in the next Congress: increasing the debt ceiling limit twice—a short-term increase at the end of 2009 and then another increase at the beginning of 2010 that was large enough to see the government through the 2010 elections. The second debt limit increase included requirements that Congress offset any increases in mandatory spending or reductions in revenues by other mandatory spending cuts or tax increases.

By the end of 2010, relations between the two parties and the two chambers were rapidly deteriorating. That the two parties had come no closer to resolving their different philosophies on the appropriate levels of taxation, spending, and debt was made abundantly clear at the end of the year when a bipartisan panel of current and former legislators and outside experts appointed by the president to recommend solutions to the country's fiscal problems failed to reach a consensus.

At the same time, Obama broke a long stalemate over taxes, agreeing to a deal with Republican leaders that infuriated liberal Democrats, particularly in the House. At issue was the expiration of the income tax cuts enacted in 2001 and 2003 under President George W. Bush that were set to expire at the end of the year. Both parties wanted to extend the tax cuts to avoid steep tax hikes, but the Republicans wanted to extend the cuts for all taxpayers, while the Democrats wanted to end them for those in the highest tax brackets.

With the country only slowly working itself out of recession, unemployment lines still long, and an increasingly partisan Congress facing a series of votes on several important issues in addition to taxes, the president agreed to a compromise. Tax cuts for all taxpayers were extended for two years, as was the estate tax, which Democrats had long sought to eliminate. In exchange, Obama won a thirteen-month extension of federal emergency jobless benefits and a one-year reduction in employees' payroll taxes. The two provisions were expected to quickly inject tens of billions of dollars into the economy.

The compromise on the tax bill did little to bridge the philosophical differences between the two parties on fiscal issues—differences that were to drive the domestic legislative agenda throughout the 112th Congress.

Fiscal 2009 Omnibus Appropriations

In 2008 Democratic leaders pushed final action on all but three of the regular fiscal 2009 spending bills—those related to national security—into the 111th Congress instead of engaging in a fight with President George W. Bush, who had threatened to veto domestic spending bills that exceeded his request. They gambled, correctly, that they would come out of the November 2008 elections with larger majorities in both chambers and a Democrat in the White House who would support their spending priorities. A continuing resolution that kept the programs operating through March 6, 2009, gave them a new deadline. *(Congress and the Nation Vol. XII, p. 124)*

The Democratic election victory and Barack Obama's inauguration ensured that the Democrats would be able to write appropriations measures more to their liking. Staff and members of the House and Senate Appropriations subcommittees began working on the package in mid-November 2008, and Democratic aides said in late December that the legislation was mostly complete.

The omnibus provided about $31 billion, or 8 percent, more in discretionary funding than was included in the fiscal 2008 versions of the nine bills. The new amount was about $19 billion more than Bush sought; Bush had threatened to veto spending bills that exceeded his request.

A BUDGET GLOSSARY

Appropriations. A bill that gives legal authority to spend or obligate money from the U.S. Treasury. The Constitution prohibits money to be drawn from the Treasury "but in Consequence of Appropriations made by Law."

By congressional custom, an appropriations bill originates in the House. It is not supposed to be considered by the full House or Senate until a related measure authorizing the funding is enacted. An appropriations bill grants the actual budget authority approved by the authorization bill, though not necessarily the full amount permissible under the authorization.

Budget authority. The authority for federal agencies to spend or otherwise obligate money, accomplished through the enactment of appropriations bills.

Budget outlays. Money that is actually spent in a given fiscal year, as opposed to money that is appropriated for that year. One year's budget authority can result in outlays over several years, and the outlays in any given year result from a mix of budget authorities from that and other years.

Budget resolution. A concurrent resolution that is adopted by both chambers of Congress but does not require the president's signature. The measure sets a strict ceiling on discretionary budget authority, along with nonbinding recommendations about how the spending should be allocated. The budget resolution may also contain "reconciliation instructions" requiring authorizing and tax-writing committees to propose changes in existing law to meet deficit-reduction goals.

Continuing resolution. A joint resolution, cleared by Congress and signed by the president, to provide new budget authority for federal agencies and programs whose regular appropriations bills have not been enacted. These resolutions, also known as CRs or continuing appropriations, are used to keep agencies operating when, as often happens, Congress does not complete action on the regular appropriations process by the beginning of the fiscal year; if uncovered by either a regular appropriation or a CR, a federal agency must shut down.

Discretionary spending. Programs that Congress can finance as it chooses through appropriations (usually within the parameters set by authorization bills). About a third of the federal budget is financed by discretionary funding (the rest is financed by mandatory spending). Examples of discretionary spending include all federal agencies, Congress, the White House, the federal courts, the military, and activities from space exploration to child nutrition.

Emergency spending. Spending that the president and Congress have designated as an emergency requirement. Emergency spending is not subject to limits on discretionary spending set in the annual budget resolutions or to pay-as-you-go rules. The designation is intended for unanticipated spending, such as funding needed to respond to disasters. However, most of the appropriations for the Iraq war were designated as emergency spending, and Congress from time to time will designate spending as "emergency" to escape the discretionary spending limits.

Fiscal year. The budget year, which runs from October 1 of one calendar year through September 30 of the next year.

Mandatory spending. Spending on programs, made up mostly of entitlements, whose eligibility requirements are written into law. Anyone who meets those requirements is entitled to the money until Congress changes the law. Examples include Social Security, Medicare, Medicaid, unemployment benefits, food stamps, and federal pensions.

Another major category of mandatory spending is the interest paid to holders of federal government bonds. Social Security and interest payments are permanently appropriated. Although budget authority for some entitlements is provided through the appropriations process, appropriators have little or no control over the money. Mandatory spending accounts for about two-thirds of federal spending.

Outlays. Amounts of actual government spending. Outlays consist of payments to liquidate obligations incurred in previous fiscal years as well as the current fiscal year, including net lending of funds under budget authority. In federal budget accounting, net outlays are calculated by subtracting the amount of refunds and various kinds of reimbursements from actual spending.

Reconciliation. The process by which tax laws and spending programs are changed, or reconciled, to reach outlay and revenue targets set in the congressional budget resolution. Special rules in the Senate limit debate on reconciliation bills and prohibit extraneous or nongermane amendments. Established by the 1974 Congressional Budget Act, reconciliation was first used in 1980.

Revenues. Taxes, customs duties, some user fees, and most other receipts paid to the federal government. Some receipts and user fees show up as "negative outlays," however, and do not count as revenue.

Sequestration. A procedure for canceling budgetary resources—that is, money available for obligation or spending—to enforce budget limitations established in law. Sequestered funds are no longer available for obligation or expenditure.

Democrats expected to have a relatively easy time completing the omnibus by the time the continuing resolution was set to expire. The House passed the omnibus with relative ease February 25, but action sputtered briefly in the Senate when Republicans and a few Democrats insisted on continuing the debate to allow colleagues to offer numerous amendments. To allow for extended debate, Congress cleared a short-term continuing resolution (PL 111-6) that kept the programs running through March 11.

After seven days of debate, the Senate passed the bill unchanged, clearing it for the president. Republicans berated Democrats over both the cost of the bill and the inclusion of thousands of special projects, or earmarks, requested by individual lawmakers. They pointed to campaign promises by Obama to overhaul the earmark process, which had come under fire because of its perceived excesses and related felony convictions of lawmakers and aides. *(Ethics probes, Congress and the Nation Vol. XII, pp. 822, 838; earmarks, p. 74)*

According to an analysis by the watchdog group Taxpayers for Common Sense, the omnibus contained $7.7 billion in earmarks disclosed by members. When added to earmarks in the three bills enacted in 2008, the total came to $14.3 billion, which the group said was $500 million less than the fiscal 2008 total. Obama called the bill "imperfect," but he defended most of the spending. "I also find it ironic," he said, "that some of those who railed the loudest against this bill because of earmarks actually inserted earmarks of their own—and will tout them in their own states and districts."

HOUSE ACTION

The House passed the omnibus package by a vote of 245–178 on February 25, the day before Obama issued his budget for fiscal 2010. The spending bill included increases for a variety of programs—from education to infrastructure to scientific research—that Democrats said were neglected while the Bush administration focused on security spending. The bill ramped up funding for state and local law enforcement and crime prevention programs by $495 million, to $3.2 billion. It increased funding for the Energy Department's Office of Science to $4.8 billion. Funding for Section 8 affordable-housing vouchers administered by Department of Housing and Urban Development grew to $7.5 billion.

The legislation also included cuts in several Bush administration priorities, for example by requiring that the District of Columbia school voucher program be reauthorized by Congress and approved by the D.C. government to receive federal funding after the 2009–2010 academic year. The Democratic majority was not expected to reauthorize the school voucher program. A number of programs that received more than they had in fiscal 2008 also got funds as part of the $787.2 billion stimulus package (PL 111-5) enacted February 17—a fact Republicans repeatedly cited as evidence that the omnibus was too costly. For instance, the measure included $6.5 billion for the National Science Foundation, $363 million more than it received in fiscal 2008. In addition, the agency received $3 billion in the stimulus law. *(Stimulus, p. 78)*

The rule for floor consideration of the bill included an amendment to eliminate a cost-of-living increase for members of Congress that was scheduled to take effect automatically in January 2010.

Republicans and Democrats traded barbs on the House floor. GOP leaders urged that the bill be scrapped and that the government be funded at or near fiscal 2008 levels for the rest of the year. "Like many of my colleagues, I'm embarrassed by this omnibus spending bill and the process that created it," said Jerry Lewis of California, the top Republican on the Appropriations Committee. "Even as the president talks about the need to put our economic house in order, this House continues to spend and spend and spend and spend."

Appropriations Chair David R. Obey, D-Wis., reminded Republicans that Bush had requested most of the funding in the bill. Although GOP members chastised Democrats about the amount of earmarked money in the bill, Democrats noted that Republicans had requested 40 percent of the earmarked funding.

SENATE ACTION

The Senate cleared the bill by voice vote March 10, nearly two weeks after the House had acted. The floor debate began on March 3, and Majority Leader Harry Reid, D-Nev., vowed to clear the measure before the March 6 expiration of the long-term continuing resolution. But Republicans insisted on their right to offer myriad amendments. Reid was unable to get the sixty votes needed to invoke cloture and limit debate until he agreed to move a brief continuing resolution that would allow time for Republicans to offer their amendments and get roll-call votes.

Democrats defeated every amendment, ensuring that the already delayed measure would not have to be returned to the House for another vote. Speaker Nancy Pelosi, D-Calif., had threatened to reject any changes and keep the government operating on a continuing resolution for the rest of the fiscal year. Minority Leader Mitch McConnell, R-Ky., decried what he called a missed opportunity to "impose some kind of restraint" after the Senate rejected the GOP amendments, several of which would have cut the cost of the bill.

The amendment Democrats viewed as the biggest threat was a proposal to repeal the statutory provision that gave lawmakers an automatic cost-of-living pay raise each year unless they voted to reject it. The Senate agreed, 52–45, to table (or kill) the amendment.

After six days of debate, the Senate agreed, 62–35, to invoke cloture, clearing the way for the final vote. President Obama signed the bill (the Omnibus Appropriations Act of 2009) on March 11 (HR 1105—PL 111-8).

Second Fiscal 2009 Supplemental

Congress next took up the second fiscal 2009 supplemental (HR 2346—PL 111-32), which provided $105.9 billion in emergency fiscal 2009 funds, most of it related to operations in Iraq and Afghanistan. Other items in the bill included $7.7 billion for pandemic flu preparation and $5 billion to leverage additional lending by the International Monetary Fund (IMF).

The total in the bill was $13.7 billion, or 15 percent, more than Obama had requested, $9.3 billion more than the House had put in its initial bill, and $14.6 billion more than in the Senate-passed version. About $77.2 billion went to the Defense Department, including funds for military construction. Congress denied the president's request for money to close the detention facility at the U.S. naval station at Guantánamo Bay, Cuba, and placed restrictions on the movement of detainees. *(Guantánamo detainees, p. 314)*

It was the second supplemental appropriations bill to provide war funding for fiscal 2009. A bill enacted in June 2008 (PL 110-252) included $65.9 billion in "bridge funding" for the first half of the fiscal year, which began October 1, 2008. *(Congress and the Nation Vol. XII, p. 129)*

Democratic leaders expected the new bill to be less controversial than those cleared in the previous few years when Democrats tried to use the must-pass measures to carry spending and policy provisions opposed by Republican President George W. Bush. With Obama in the White House, those confrontations were absent. Both chambers passed their respective versions by overwhelming margins.

But several Senate provisions complicated negotiations on a final bill. They included $5 billion requested by the president to leverage additional lending by the IMF, which Republicans said would take money away from the troops and should be considered in a separate bill.

A provision that would have barred the release of photos showing abuse of detainees in U.S. custody pitted many Senate Democrats against more liberal members of their caucus. It was not until the Senate conferees received assurances from Obama that he would use his executive authority to block release of the photos that they were willing to agree to a conference report that did not include that provision.

The bill also included a new program, dubbed "cash for clunkers," that offered $1 billion in rebates to people who traded in their old cars for newer, more fuel efficient models. *(Cash for clunkers, p. 321)*

HOUSE ACTION

The House passed a $96.7 billion supplemental spending bill (HR 2346—H Rept 111-105), 368–60, on May 14, 2009. The rule for floor debate (H Res 434) automatically added language to explicitly prohibit the use of funds in the bill to release any Guantánamo detainees into the United States. It also required the president to provide detailed reports to Congress before bringing any detainee to the United States for prosecution or releasing a detainee to a foreign country. The rule, which was adopted, 247–178, allowed no other amendments.

Top Republicans lambasted the rule as preventing them from making the Guantánamo restrictions tougher. Jerry Lewis of California, the ranking Republican on the Appropriations Committee, accused Democratic leaders of being "more sensitive to the rights of known terrorists than the rights of . . . elected members of this body."

Harold Rogers, R-Ky., tried unsuccessfully to send the bill back to committee to add $3 billion in defense spending, shift funds from foreign aid to antidrug activities on the U.S.-Mexico border, and maintain Pentagon control of Pakistan counterinsurgency funds. The motion was defeated, 191–237.

SENATE ACTION

The Senate passed HR 2346 by a vote of 86–3 on May 21, 2009, after inserting its $91.3 billion version of the bill (S 1054—S Rept 111-20). Unlike disputes over previous supplemental defense bills for military operations in Iraq and Afghanistan, which focused on war policy, the floor controversy this time was over the Guantánamo Bay, Cuba, detention center and the fate of the military detainees. During the debate, the Senate adopted, 90–6, a Democratic amendment that removed the $80 million approved by the committee for closing the facility and barred the use of funding in the bill to transfer, release, or incarcerate any Guantánamo detainees to or within the United States.

Before passing the measure, the Senate adopted by voice vote an amendment by Lindsey Graham, R-S.C., and Joseph I. Lieberman, I-Conn., to bar the release of photos showing alleged prisoner abuse by U.S. soldiers taken from September 11, 2001, to January 22, 2009, if the defense secretary certified that release of the pictures would endanger U.S. citizens or troops or contractors serving abroad. It also rejected, 30–64, an amendment by Jim DeMint, R-S.C., to delete the $5 billion for the IMF.

FINAL ACTION

On June 12, 2009, House and Senate negotiators filed a conference report (H Rept 111-151) on the bill. But it took several more days of scrambling before House leaders were confident they had the votes from their own caucus to adopt the report. With Republicans lining up against the measure, Pennsylvania Democrat John P. Murtha, chair of the House Defense Appropriations Subcommittee, and others worked to contain defections among House liberals.

The chief sticking point was the Senate provision to bar the release of detainee photos. Top House leaders said the language had to be dropped to get the conference report through their chamber, where many liberal Democrats sharply opposed the Senate amendment. But Senate Democratic leaders argued they needed to retain the provision to avoid a filibuster and because it enjoyed widespread support there.

The conference stalled June 11 while Senate Democrats debated whether to accept a decision by the leaders of both chambers to drop the language. But after a phone call from the president and a letter sent to senior appropriators, the Senate Democrats agreed to support the deal, accepting Obama's pledge to use his executive authority to block release of the photos anytime soon. In his letter, Obama wrote that he would "continue to take every legal and administrative remedy available to me to ensure the [Defense Department] detainee photographs are not released."

Meanwhile, the U.S. Circuit Court of Appeals for the Second Circuit on June 11 granted a motion, put forth by the administration, to stay the court's previous order directing release of the photos.

The House adopted the conference report, 226–202, on June 16, 2009, with only five Republicans in support and thirty-two Democrats voting "nay," down from the fifty-one Democrats who voted against the House version in May. Some liberal Democrats switched to "yea" because they supported the IMF funding or because they were persuaded by leaders to toe the line. The Senate cleared the bill, 91–5, on June 18, and Obama signed it into law on June 24, 2009.

Fiscal 2010 Budget Resolution

Congressional Democrats set the stage for debates in 2009 on appropriations, health care, and tax levels with a $3.6 trillion budget resolution (S Con Res 13) that was adopted in both chambers with no Republican votes. "This budget was hugely important for the president," said Senate Budget Chair Kent Conrad, D-N.D. "This is the starting point for everything he wants to do."

Although Democrats endorsed much of President Barack Obama's ambitious agenda, they felt somewhat constrained by public concern and reservations within their own caucus about the rapidly growing deficit. The resolution, a congressional document that set the parameters for the year's tax and spending legislation, contained two key elements: a total for discretionary spending and instructions for reconciliation bills.

The budget resolution gave the House and Senate Appropriations committees a discretionary spending cap of $1.1 trillion for the annual appropriations bills, about $10 billion less than Obama had requested. (Most of the budget was for existing mandatory programs that were already written into law and were largely outside the appropriators' control.) The resolution recommended that the appropriators allocate $556.1 billion in discretionary funds for defense activities, matching the president's request, but leaving less than he requested for domestic programs.

The reconciliation instructions, which were available only through the budget resolution, gave Democrats the option of pushing Obama's health care overhaul through Congress with little or no Republican support. Reconciliation bills were protected from delaying tactics in the Senate, which meant Democrats would need only a simple majority to pass the measure rather than the sixty votes needed to invoke cloture and quash a filibuster. The budget resolution also allowed use of the reconciliation process for legislation sought by the president to sharply curtail the role of private lenders in the federal student loan program.

Republicans, joined by some Democrats, objected to the idea of using reconciliation for something as sweeping as an overhaul of health care policy. Democratic leaders said they would use it for health care only if bipartisan negotiations failed. They were also quick to point out that Republicans used the process in the past to move their priorities, including the 2001 and 2003 tax cuts (PL 107-16, PL 108-27), which added to the deficit. *(Health care debate, p. 421)*

Both parties portrayed the budget resolution as a turning point for the country that would either lead the nation to a brighter future or over a cliff, depending on who was speaking. Democrats heralded it as promoting key investments in health care, education, and renewable-energy programs, while also starting the process of putting the soaring deficit on a downward trajectory. "Today, for the first time in many, many years, we have a president's budget on the floor that is reflective of our national values," declared House Speaker Nancy Pelosi, D-Calif. "It is a foundation for how we go forward into the future."

Republicans, who had little to no role in writing the measure, denounced it as a blueprint for a huge expansion of the role of government that would push the federal debt to dangerous levels. House Minority Leader John A. Boehner, R-Ohio, said it was "nothing short of an audacious move to a big socialist government in Washington, D.C."

Budget watchdog groups also expressed concern over the amount of debt that would result from the plan. "While we welcome congressional efforts to improve the deficit picture, we worry that this budget resolution falls short of putting us on a fiscally sustainable path," the Committee for a Responsible Federal Budget said in a release. "We are also concerned that it relies on some unlikely assumptions and does not contain sufficiently strong budget rules."

HIGHLIGHTS

Discretionary Spending

The measure set a $1.1 trillion cap on the fiscal 2010 discretionary spending, which appropriators could allocate among the twelve annual spending bills. The cap did not include emergency spending or costs of overseas deployments. It did include about $3 billion for "program integrity initiatives" aimed at reducing costs and making programs more efficient. The resolution recommended that $556.1 billion of the total be used for defense, including Defense

GROWING PUBLIC DEBT

The public debt is the amount owed to the public, American or foreign, through individual or institutional purchase of government securities such as bonds. The remainder of the federal debt is the amount the government has borrowed from government trust funds such as Social Security. The latter is an intragovernmental transaction but is still an obligation that must be paid someday and carries interest the same as debt owed to the general public.

Public Debt *(Millions of dollars)*

Fiscal Year	Total Public Debt	As a % of GDP	Total Federal Debt	As a % of GDP
1990	$ 2,411.6	42.0%	$3,206.3	55.9%
1991	2,689.0	45.3	3,598.2	60.7
1992	2,999.7	48.1	4,001.8	64.1
1993	3,248.4	49.4	4,351.0	66.1
1994	3,433.1	49.3	4,643.3	66.6
1995	3,604.4	49.2	4,920.6	67.0
1996	3,734.1	48.5	5,181.5	67.1
1997	3,772.3	46.1	5,369.2	65.4
1998	3,721.1	43.1	5,478.2	63.2
1999	3,632.4	39.8	5,605.5	60.9
2000	3,409.8	35.1	5,628.7	57.3
2001	3,319.6	33.0	5,769.9	56.4
2002	3,540.4	34.1	6,198.4	58.8
2003	3,913.4	36.2	6,760.0	61.6
2004	4,295.5	37.3	7,354.7	63.0
2005	4,592.2	37.5	7,905.3	63.6
2006	4,829.0	37.1	8,451.4	64.0
2007	5,035.1	36.9	8,950.7	64.6
2008	5,803.1	40.5	9,986.1	69.7
2009	7,544.7	54.0	11,875.9	85.1
2010	9,018.9	62.9	13,528.8	94.3
2011	10,128.2	67.8	14,764.2	98.9
2012	11,281.1	72.6	16,051.0	103.2
2013*	12,403.6	76.6	17,249.2	106.5

SOURCE: Executive Office of the President, Office of Management and Budget, *Budget of the United States Government, Fiscal Year 2014, Historical Tables* (Washington, D.C.: Government Printing Office, 2013), Table 7.1.

NOTE: GDP: Gross domestic product. * Estimate

Department military activities and Energy Department nuclear weapons programs. The Congressional Budget Office (CBO), which issued an annual recalculation of the president's budget, put the defense request at $557.1 billion. Both numbers excluded funds for military operations in Iraq and Afghanistan.

Tax Cuts

The resolution assumed that the government would receive $764 billion less in revenue over five years than the amount that the CBO estimated would be collected during the same period under existing law. The reduction was meant to allow for an extension of President George W. Bush's 2001 and 2003 tax cuts, such as the 10 percent tax bracket, the $1,000 per child tax credit, and marriage penalty relief, for households earning less than $250,000; a three-year adjustment to prevent the alternative minimum tax (AMT), intended for high-income taxpayers, from affecting millions of additional middle-class households; and a permanent extension of 2009 estate tax levels (45 percent with a $7 million exemption for couples filing jointly and $3.5 million for individuals, both indexed to inflation).

Congress could provide other tax breaks, such as expanding the refundable child tax credit, but the revenue loss had to be offset.

The budget did not make room for Obama's proposal to extend the Making Work Pay program, which provided a payroll tax credit to most workers, beyond its expiration at the end of 2010. Obama had hoped to pay for the program, estimated at $536.7 billion over ten years, with revenues from the carbon cap-and-trade system. *(Cap-and-trade details, p. 367)*

Deficit and Debt

The measure allowed a $1.23 trillion deficit in fiscal 2010, $146 billion less than under Obama's budget. Under the budget resolution, the deficit was projected to drop to

$523.4 billion in fiscal 2014, with a cumulative five-year total of $3.87 trillion. The cumulative debt was projected to grow from $7.7 trillion in fiscal 2009 to $11.5 trillion in fiscal 2014. Measured as a percentage of the economy, the method preferred by economists, this meant going from 55 percent of gross domestic product (GDP) to 66.7 percent of GDP.

Reconciliation Instructions

The resolution included instructions that gave authorizing committees until October 15 to report health care and student loan reconciliation bills, which were not subject to a filibuster in the Senate. That would spare supporters from having to secure the sixty votes required in that chamber to limit debate. The resolution also carried provisions to create "reserve funds"—essentially permission to exceed the discretionary cap—to accommodate a possible health care overhaul, revision of student loan programs, and a number of other legislative proposals, provided they did not add to the deficit. There was no placeholder figure for future spending to aid the financial sector. A deficit-neutral reserve fund for clean energy or climate change legislation was the leadership's alternative to allowing the use of reconciliation for cap-and-trade legislation.

Two-year VA budget

The measure included a provision, long sought by veterans' groups, to allow Congress to provide advance fiscal 2011 appropriations for Department of Veterans Affairs (VA) medical accounts. *(Two-year funding, p. 280)*

OBAMA BUDGET REQUEST

President Obama sent Congress details of his $3.6 trillion fiscal 2010 budget request May 7, 2009. The budget fleshed out a summary released February 26 that highlighted the new president's main priorities for the year, including overhauling health care, addressing climate change, and making college more affordable.

According to the White House Office of Management and Budget (OMB), which had prepared the request, the budget would provide a total of $1.3 trillion in discretionary budget authority for fiscal 2010—25 percent more than President George W. Bush had requested for fiscal 2009. The CBO in its June report put the total request at $3.7 trillion, but essentially agreed on the discretionary portion, calculating it at $1.3 trillion. Congress used the CBO numbers, which also are used throughout this account.

In his first address to a joint session of Congress on February 24, Obama telegraphed the sweep of his plans to alter the tax and spending priorities of the previous decade. The "day of reckoning has arrived, and the time to take charge of our future is here," he said. It was time, he continued, to "invest in areas like energy, health care, and education that will grow our economy, even as we make hard choices to bring our deficit down. That is what my economic agenda is designed to do."

To help pay for his priorities, Obama proposed tax increases on affluent Americans who had enjoyed years of reductions under President George W. Bush, while retaining the Bush-era tax cuts for low- and middle-income taxpayers. Obama also proposed eliminating a variety of special tax provisions for businesses, including provisions directed at hedge fund managers and others the administration said had been allowed to avoid paying their share. The president called for selling carbon emission credits to polluters as part of a cap-and-trade system to combat climate change. He also asked Congress to squeeze savings from a variety of government accounts.

The budget request included a $250 billion placeholder to cover losses from further efforts to address the financial crisis, even as the administration began to use the second half of the $700 billion bailout of the Troubled Asset Relief Program (TARP) enacted in late 2008 (PL 110-343). The placeholder anticipated as much as $750 billion in additional borrowing to cover bank capital infusions and asset purchases, according to the administration. *(TARP, pp. 60, 75; Congress and the Nation Vol. XII, p. 154)*

Obama called for a "reserve fund" of $634 billion over ten years to cover an expansion of health care, although the budget gave no details about what an overhaul would look like. It did say, however, that $316 billion of the cost would be covered by savings from Medicare and Medicaid programs, such as reducing Medicare overpayments, prescription drug prices, and hospital readmissions. The remainder would come from higher taxes on the wealthy, particularly a cap on income tax deductions.

Republicans were quick to criticize the proposal as a tax increase that would exacerbate the recession at a time when capital was needed for investment. The administration said the proposed tax increases would not occur until after the economy was expected to rebound.

Of the $646 billion expected from enactment of a cap-and-trade system for carbon emissions, Obama proposed to dedicate $120 billion to renewable-energy programs. The rest would be used to help extend indefinitely the Making Work Pay tax credit in the economic stimulus law (PL 111-5), at a cost of $537 billion. The idea was that extending this tax cut for most working families would help offset higher energy costs resulting from the cap-and-trade program. *(Economic stimulus, p. 78)*

The assumptions undergirding the administration's budget were more optimistic than comparable projections issued early in the year by industry economists and the CBO. By the time details of the budget were released in May, those predictions had grown more pessimistic.

One reason for the differences was that the administration's projections assumed enactment of the president's budget, including various savings and benefits from his health care plans. The administration's assumptions also anticipated that the economic stimulus law and continuing efforts to shore up the financial industry would blunt the recession, resulting in a bounce-back in the economy in

2010 and a decline in the jobless rate. For example, the administration expected the economy, as measured by GDP, to contract by 1.2 percent in calendar year 2009 after the cost of inflation was taken into account.

The CBO, on the other hand, projected in January that GDP would shrink by 2.2 percent in 2009. The agency adjusted its estimates in March to project a steeper, 3.0 percent decline in 2009. And the Blue Chip Consensus, an average of about fifty top private forecasters, in February anticipated a reduction in GDP of 1.9 percent in 2009. A more pessimistic Blue Chip report in April projected a decline in GDP of 2.6 percent in 2009.

For 2010, the budget projected GDP growth of 3.2 percent. That was well above the CBO's January expectation for a 1.5 percent expansion (increased to 2.9 percent in March) and the Blue Chip February forecast of 2.1 percent growth (reduced to 1.8 percent in April). The Obama administration expected an unemployment rate of 7.9 percent in 2010—higher than average but well below the 9 percent projected by the CBO in both reports and the 8.7 percent (increased to 9.5 percent in April) by the Blue Chip forecasters.

LEGISLATIVE ACTION

The House adopted its budget resolution (H Con Res 85—H Rept 111-60) by a vote of 233–196 on April 2, 2009, after defeating substitutes put forward by groups from both parties. All Republicans and twenty Democrats voted "nay." Among the defeated alternatives was one that would have cut both discretionary and mandatory spending with the aim of balancing the budget in ten years; one that would have frozen nondefense, nonveterans' discretionary spending for five years and made the 2001 and 2003 tax cuts permanent, among other changes; one that would have cut defense spending, created a universal health plan and increased domestic spending; and one, by the Congressional Black Caucus, that would have repealed the 2001 and 2003 tax cuts for the highest earners and put the extra revenue into health care, education, job training, and other programs.

The Senate adopted its plan (S Con Res 13—S Print 111-16) by a vote of 55–43 on April 2, the same day the House acted. The measure had no GOP support and was opposed by two Democrats.

During the two days of debate leading up to the vote, senators considered dozens of amendments, rejecting most of them, including one by Republican Jeff Sessions of Alabama to freeze nondefense discretionary spending for two years. Sessions and other Republicans argued that the recently enacted $787 billion economic stimulus bill (PL 111-5) had provided domestic programs with ample funding and that the budget resolution should take deficit concerns into account. Democrats dismissed the GOP premise, arguing that the increases were needed for the many agencies that had not received adequate funding during the presidency of George W. Bush. The Senate rejected the amendment on April 1 on a **key vote of 40–58 (R 39–2; D 1–54; I 0–2)**. *(2009 key votes, p. 751)*

The Senate also went on record opposing use of the filibuster-proof reconciliation process to move cap-and-trade climate change or clean energy bills. The amendment was adopted by a vote of 67–31. Cap-and-trade supporters attempted to blunt the amendment by permitting it to be waived if the Senate determined climate change was a threat to the economy, public health, or national security. The waiver amendment failed, 42–56, on a procedural vote.

House and Senate Democrats agreed on a compromise resolution on April 29, Obama's 100th day in office. The House adopted the conference report (H Rept 111-89) by a vote of 233–193. The Senate followed suit, 53–43.

The most difficult issues in conference were the reconciliation instructions and demands from fifty-one fiscally conservative House Democrats in the Blue Dog Coalition that the leadership address the huge deficits envisioned in the budget. A pledge from House leaders that they would support stricter deficit control measures going forward appeased most of the Blue Dogs. Pelosi and Majority Leader Steny H. Hoyer, D-Md., promised that the House would consider key tax bills only if they were subject to statutory pay-as-you go rules. Such rules required all new tax cuts and new entitlement program spending to be offset by equivalent tax increases or spending cuts elsewhere. *(Budget rules, this page and p. 142)*

Senate Budget Chair Kent Conrad, D-N.D., said he had opposed inclusion of the reconciliation instructions "at every step of the way, publicly and privately" during the conference but was overruled by top party leaders. He said he still believed the process would not be used for a health care overhaul.

2009 Budget Enforcement Rules

Against a backdrop of growing public anger over Washington's seeming inability to gain control of the deficit, Democrats in both chambers were eager to put budget enforcement rules into law. But Republicans were not interested in helping them out and Democrats could not settle differences within their own caucus, leaving the issue unresolved at the end of the session.

The White House and House Democratic leaders supported the enactment of pay-as-you-go (PAYGO) budget rules that would prevent new entitlement or tax laws from adding to the deficit. The Blue Dog Coalition, a group of more than fifty fiscally conservative House Democrats, made a commitment to PAYGO legislation as one of its central demands of the year.

Under a deal struck in April, the Blue Dogs essentially agreed to support the fiscal 2010 budget resolution (S Con Res 13) in exchange for a written pledge from Speaker Nancy Pelosi, D-Calif., and House Majority Leader Steny H. Hoyer, D-Md., that four pieces of priority legislation would be fully offset or would carry long-term PAYGO provisions. The pledge covered potential bills to extend expiring middle-class tax cuts, prevent the alternative minimum tax from hitting more taxpayers, adjust the estate tax law, and eliminate scheduled cuts in pay rates for Medicare physicians.

Democratic leaders followed up July 22, winning passage of a stand-alone PAYGO bill (HR 2920). The vote was 265–166, with twenty-four Republicans supporting the measure. Before passing the bill, the House rejected, 169–259, a GOP substitute offered by Paul D. Ryan of Wisconsin that would have dropped the PAYGO provisions and set caps on discretionary spending in fiscal years 2011 through 2013. It would have limited deficits to a specified percentage of the gross domestic product in fiscal years 2010 through 2019.

In line with the April agreement, House Democratic leaders also used the rules for floor debate to attach the provisions of HR 2920 to bills aimed at revising the formula for Medicare payments to doctors (HR 3961) and adjusting the estate tax (HR 4154), as well as to a broad bill aimed at creating jobs (HR 2847). The House passed those measures, but the bills went no further. Democrats put off considering an alternative minimum tax bill and the expiring middle-class tax cuts until 2010. *(Medicare pay rates, p. 450; estate tax, p. 146; jobs bill, pp. 85, 527)*

Senate Democrats did not support the PAYGO provisions. Instead moderates wanted to establish a bipartisan commission to recommend ways to reduce both the deficit and long-term debt. They wanted the provisions written into statutes to guarantee that Congress would have to vote on the recommendations.

Both House and Senate moderates tried to use the urgency of a year-end increase to the debt limit as leverage to get their budget enforcement proposals enacted. House leaders were not averse to the Senate commission proposal as long as they also got the PAYGO provisions that were critical to the Blue Dogs. But Senate Budget Chair Kent Conrad, D-N.D., was critical of the House approach, arguing that exempting the four bills would be too costly and that a statutory PAYGO requirement should be part of a broader deficit and debt reduction effort.

A bipartisan group of senators insisted that any long-term debt limit increase also include provisions from a debt commission bill (S 2853) that Conrad and Budget ranking Republican Judd Gregg of New Hampshire had written with bipartisan support. With time running out for increasing the debt ceiling—and with the Senate absorbed in a lengthy debate over a historic health care overhaul—the leadership agreed to a short-term debt limit increase, putting the issue of budget enforcement off until 2010. *(2009 debt limit legislation, p. 134)*

Fiscal 2010 Appropriations

Despite good intentions, the only fiscal 2010 bill to clear by October 1, 2009, the start of the new fiscal year, was for the legislative branch. A continuing resolution attached to that bill kept the rest of the government operating until October 31. Congress subsequently cleared separate bills for Agriculture, Energy-Water, Interior-Environment, and Homeland Security. Departments funded by the remaining bills received stopgap appropriations through December 18 under the Interior-Environment appropriations bill. That left seven bills, six of which were enacted in the Transportation–Housing and Urban Development conference report (PL 111-117). The Defense bill was the last spending bill of the year and became a vehicle for short-term extensions of federal unemployment insurance, surface transportation programs, and a number of other expiring programs.

House appropriations subcommittees had begun marking up the fiscal 2010 bills in June, the full Appropriations Committee was finished by July 22, and the House passed the last of the bills July 30. To act that swiftly, however, Democrats adopted floor rules that strictly limited amendments and infuriated Republicans, who charged that the majority was curtailing the open debate process that was traditional for the appropriations bills. Democrats countered that they were responding to what they regarded as GOP efforts to disrupt the appropriations process.

After Republicans initially tried to offer 103 amendments to the Commerce-Justice-Science bill, the first fiscal 2010 measure to come to the floor, Democrats imposed a rule that allowed just thirty-three amendments. The rule was adopted June 17 by a **key vote of 221–201 (R 0–174; D 221–27)**. Angry Republicans responded by finding other procedural tools. In one day, the House took a total of fifty-three roll-call votes on the bill—a modern record. The struggle continued through July, with House Democrats using closed rules and Republicans offering amendments and motions to reduce spending, alter Democratic priorities, and slow the process with procedural challenges. *(2009 key votes, p. 751)*

Senate appropriators marked up all but the defense bill by the end of July, but partisan wrangling on the floor, the Senate's generally slower pace, and a full agenda led the chamber to pass only four of the measures before the August recess. The Senate passed five more spending bills in the fall, but too little time was left to hold conferences and produce final versions of all the separate bills. By late November, the Senate was deeply engaged in the health care debate.

The six-bill omnibus was assembled from the Commerce-Justice-Science, financial services, Labor-HHS-Education, Military Construction-VA, State-Foreign Operations, and Transportation-HUD bills, and it cleared December 1, 2009.

The Senate interrupted what had become an around-the-clock debate on health care to clear the last of the spending bills, for the Defense Department, on December 19.

Following are brief descriptions of each of the fiscal 2010 appropriations bills.

LEGISLATIVE BRANCH, CONTINUING RESOLUTION

Breaking with recent practice, Congress made the legislative branch appropriations bill the first fiscal 2010 spending measure to reach the president's desk and the only one to be enacted by the start of the new fiscal year.

Lawmakers typically are unwilling to be seen as putting Congress's operations ahead of the rest of the government. But the fiscal 2010 bill was the only one of the twelve annual spending measures ready to clear by September 30, and Democratic leaders chose to use the noncontroversial measure as a vehicle for a continuing resolution. The continuing resolution (CR) was must-pass legislation required to keep government agencies operating while lawmakers tried to finish the eleven remaining appropriations bills. President Obama signed the legislative branch bill into law October 1 (HR 2918—PL 111-68).

The $4.7 billion measure funded the operations of the House and Senate. It also paid for the offices and legislative agencies that supported congressional operations, including the Capitol police, architect of the Capitol, Congressional Budget Office (CBO), Library of Congress, Government Accountability Office (GAO), and Government Printing Office.

The total was $254 million, or about 6 percent, above the previous year's spending, not counting $99 million in emergency fiscal 2009 funds, and $386 million, or about 8 percent, less than the amounts requested by the agencies and reflected in Obama's budget. The House received $1.4 billion under the measure; the Senate received $926 million. The bill also allocated about $5 million to replace the House's aging electronic voting system.

The House passed a $3.7 billion legislative branch bill (HR 2918—H Rept 111-160) by a vote of 232–178 on June 19. The Senate passed a $4.6 billion version of the bill by a vote of 67–25 on July 6, after substituting the text of its own version, S 1294 (S Rept 111-29), and adding the House funding. The House adopted the conference report (H Rept 111-265) by a vote of 217–190 on September 25, and the Senate cleared the bill, 62–38, on September 30.

The conference report included the CR, a fact that drew strong objections from Republicans in both chambers, who argued that Democrats had inserted the CR into the conference report, which could not be amended, to deny lawmakers a chance to consider and amend the CR. Several Republican senators objected in particular to a provision of the CR that allowed the Postal Service to postpone a payment intended to prefund its retiree health benefits. The conference report won just five GOP votes in each chamber.

AGRICULTURE APPROPRIATIONS

Congress cleared the fiscal 2010 Agriculture spending bill (HR 2997—PL 111-80) in mid-October, with extra funding for struggling dairy farmers. The grand total of $121.2 billion was $2.7 billion less than requested, $2.6 billion less than in the House bill and $3.4 billion below the Senate total. Most of the reduction resulted from a $3 billion drop in the amount provided for food stamps in the final bill, compared with the request and the House and Senate versions. Conferees also provided about $300 million less for the Women, Infants, and Children (WIC) food and nutrition program than in either bill and $525 million less than Obama requested.

About 80 percent of the bill was mandatory funding for programs such as crop supports and food stamps, much of it required under the 2008 farm bill (PL 110-246). The remainder—$23.4 billion—was for discretionary programs, including WIC, some conservation accounts, rural development, foreign food aid, and some farm programs. The inclusion of $350 million in subsidies to ease the effects of declining milk prices was a victory for Sen. Bernie Sanders, I-Vt., and other well-positioned dairy-state Democrats. The bill also funded the Food and Drug Administration (FDA). Total discretionary spending was about $2.7 billion more than was available for the same programs in fiscal 2009, not counting emergency fiscal 2009 funding appropriated for these programs as part of the economic stimulus measure (PL 111-5) passed in February. *(Stimulus, p. 78)*

The House passed (HR 2997—H Rept 111-181) by a vote of 266–160 on July 9. The Senate passed HR 2997 by a vote of 80–17 on August 4, after substituting its own version (S 1406—S Rept 111-39). The House adopted the conference report on the bill (H Rept 111-279) by a vote of 263–162 on October 7, and the Senate cleared the bill, 76–22, the next day.

ENERGY, WATER APPROPRIATIONS

At the end of October, Congress easily cleared a $34 billion bill to fund the Energy Department, Army Corps of Engineers, and water projects carried out by the Interior Department. The annual bill was popular in Congress because it was the source of federal funding for more than a thousand water projects across the country. A few members complained each year about the number of special projects inserted by individual members, but lawmakers were rarely willing to cut any of these earmarks because they all benefited.

All but about $500 million in the fiscal 2010 bill was discretionary funding that appropriators could allocate among programs as they saw fit. The discretionary total of $33.5 billion was an increase of less than 1 percent over the amount in the regular fiscal 2009 law (PL 111-8) but about 3 percent, or $929 million, less than Obama requested. However, programs funded by the Energy-Water bill had received an additional $57.8 billion in emergency fiscal 2009 appropriations, mainly under the economic stimulus law (PL 111-5).

Negotiations on the final fiscal 2010 bill were uneventful. The House and Senate versions were only $452 million apart on discretionary spending, and minor differences over research funding for hydrogen technology, fuel cell, and other alternative energy sources were quickly resolved. Lawmakers warned, however, that a fight could be brewing for fiscal 2011. The White House envisioned funding in the economic stimulus law as a down payment on a decade of robust new spending on energy research. That meant energy appropriators could have to confront the difficult question of whether and how to sustain the spending levels.

The House passed HR 3183 (H Rept 111-203) by a 320–97 vote on July 17, 2009. The measure won bipartisan support even though Republicans complained that the rule for debate allowed consideration of only twenty-one of 103 amendments filed. The Senate passed the $34.3 billion bill (HR 3183) July 29 by a vote of 85–9, after inserting the text of S 1436 (S Rept 111-45). It rejected efforts to kill earmarked projects and subject all contracts and grants to competitive bidding.

Negotiators from the two Appropriations committees filed a conference report on the bill (H Rept 111-278) on September 30, and the House adopted it, 308–114, the next day. Action was held up in the Senate, however, where Tom Coburn, R-Okla., was angry that the final legislation did not require public disclosure of reports called for under appropriations bills. That language had been in the Senate-passed version of the legislation.

Democratic leaders were forced to hold a cloture vote to limit debate on October 14, which was adopted 79–17. Still the Senate did not clear the measure for nearly another twenty-six hours, when it finally voted, 80–17, on October 15 to adopt the conference report. President Obama signed the measure into law October 28 (HR 3183—PL 111-85).

HOMELAND SECURITY APPROPRIATIONS

In October 2009, Congress cleared a $44.1 billion fiscal 2010 spending bill for the Department of Homeland Security (HR 2892—PL 111-83), after rejecting Republican efforts to bar the Obama administration from bringing detainees held at Guantánamo Bay, Cuba, to the United States for trial.

The total, virtually equal to Obama's request, provided an increase of $2.5 billion, or 7 percent, over the previous year (not counting emergency funding for fiscal 2009). Discretionary funding made up $42.6 billion of the total; the bill also contained $242 million for overseas deployment. The measure covered spending for customs and border inspection, immigration and customs enforcement, the Transportation Security Administration, the Coast Guard, and the Federal Emergency Management Agency, among other agencies and programs.

The legislation won bipartisan support with remarkably little debate on both floors. In drafting the final bill, House and Senate conferees essentially split the difference between the smaller House bill, passed in June, and the larger version passed by the Senate in July. The final measure included 176 member earmarks, compared with 157 when the House voted on the bill. It also included eight presidentially directed spending items.

Republicans tried at every stage of the process to add language that would prevent Guantánamo detainees from entering the United States, but Democratic leaders argued that such provisions could interfere with efforts to prosecute the individuals. The final bill prohibited the release of detainees into the United States but allowed them to be transferred for trial under specific conditions. *(Detainees, p. 314)*

The final bill also omitted several provisions that Republicans had succeeded in adding to the Senate version, including a requirement that the Southwest border fence be double-layered along its entire 700 miles to further reduce pedestrian crossings and permanent authorization for the E-Verify system, a voluntary program that allowed employers to verify the immigration status of newly hired workers electronically. The bill extended the program for three years, as requested.

The House passed HR 2892 (H Rept 111-157) by a vote of 389–37 on June 24, after lengthy GOP protests over limits set by Democrats on amendments. Republicans expressed outrage that the rule governing the debate allowed only fourteen floor amendments with a ten-minute time limit for each. The Senate passed HR 2892, 84–6, on July 9 after three days of debate. Before taking up the bill, the Senate substituted the text of its own measure (S 1298—S Rept 111-31).

The House adopted the conference report (H Rept 111-298) on the final bill by a vote of 307–114 on October 15, after Democratic leaders fended off one last GOP attempt to attach language banning the transfer of detainees from Guantánamo to the United States. The Senate cleared the bill by a vote of 79–19 on October 20, and President Obama signed it into law on October 28.

INTERIOR, ENVIRONMENT, CONTINUING RESOLUTION

The fiscal 2010 spending bill for the Interior Department and environmental programs cleared easily on October 29, 2009, and was signed by President Obama the next day, helped along by the addition of must-pass provisions to fund much of the federal government until December 18 (HR 2996—PL 111-88). (Details, p. 382)

The $32.3 billion bill consisted almost entirely of discretionary spending. The two chambers were only about $200 million apart on discretionary accounts, and conferees roughly split the difference. The annual bill funded the Interior Department, the Environmental Protection Agency (EPA), and programs such as the Smithsonian Institution and the endowments for the arts and humanities. It also covered the Agriculture Department's Forest Service and the Department of Health and Human Services' Indian Health Service.

The $32.2 billion in the bill for discretionary programs was just $85 million less than Obama requested. It was $4.7 billion, or about 17 percent, more than the same programs received in the fiscal 2009 law. However, the economic stimulus law enacted in February (PL 111-5) steered an additional $11 billion in fiscal 2009 funds to programs covered by the bill. Counting that money and a small amount for mandatory programs, the fiscal 2010 bill was a drop of $6.5 billion, or about 17 percent, below total fiscal 2009 funding.

The main controversies arising from the bill were over policy issues rather than spending. In a debate that anticipated future EPA action, the Senate turned back an effort to limit EPA's authority to regulate carbon dioxide. Over the objections of environmental groups, conferees exempted thirteen steam-powered ships on the Great Lakes from EPA emissions regulation. Conferees also agreed to bar the use of funds in the bill to require permits for greenhouse gas emissions from livestock producers or to require greenhouse gas emissions reporting from manure management systems. The House had agreed, 267–147, on October 27 to a nonbinding resolution instructing conferees to insist on the House reporting exemption. *(EPA regulation, pp. 367, 386)*

The final bill also contained restrictions on transferring detainees held at Guantánamo Bay, Cuba, that mirrored most of the detainee provisions in the Homeland Security appropriations bill enacted October 28 (PL 111-83). *(Guantánamo detainees, p. 314)*

With seven of the fiscal 2010 appropriations bills unfinished and the first temporary funding law (PL 111-68) about to expire, Democrats added a new continuing resolution to the conference report. The measure extended funding through December 18, mostly at 2009 levels, for departments and programs whose funding bills had not cleared. Republicans in both chambers criticized inclusion of the continuing resolution in the bill and chastised Democrats for not getting the regular fiscal 2010 spending bills finished on time. But there was little they could do: without a temporary extension, agencies funded by the seven unfinished spending bills could not operate.

The House passed HR 2996 (H Rept 111-180) by a vote of 254–173 on June 26. Members rejected, 169–259, an amendment by Jim Jordan, R-Ohio, to reduce spending in the bill by $5.8 billion to match levels in fiscal 2008. The Senate passed the $32.2 billion bill by a vote of 77–21 on September 24, after blocking a GOP effort to prevent the EPA from regulating greenhouse gas emissions.

Final action came on October 29, when the House adopted the conference report (H Rept 111-316) by a vote of 247–178, and the Senate cleared the bill, 72–28, later the same day.

FISCAL 2010 OMNIBUS

Six regular appropriations bills were folded into a single bill in late November when it became clear that Congress would not be able to complete action on each of them individually. The House had passed all six measures, but the Senate, which was consumed with the health care bill toward the end of the year, was unable to complete action in time for differences between the House and Senate versions to be resolved in conference. Five bills (Commerce-Justice-Science, Financial Services, Labor–Health and Human Services–Education, Military Construction–Veterans Affairs, and State–Foreign Operations) were rolled into an omnibus measure that came to the floor as a conference report on the Transportation–Housing and Urban Development spending measure (HR 3288). The House adopted the conference report (H Rept 111-366) by a vote of 221–202 on December 10, 2009. The Senate interrupted its marathon health care debate on December 13 to clear the bill, 57–35. President Obama signed the omnibus into law December 16 (HR 3288—PL 111-117).

Commerce-Justice-Science

Conferees provided a total of $68.2 billion for the departments of Commerce and Justice and for major science programs such as National Aeronautics and Space Administration (NASA). More than 90 percent of the Commerce-Justice-Science funding, or $64.4 billion, was for discretionary programs—an increase of $6.8 billion, or 12 percent, over the level enacted for fiscal 2009 (PL 111-8) and virtually the same as the president's request. The Census Bureau accounted for more than half the increase, which was provided to help fund the 2010 decennial count. In addition, the separate economic stimulus bill enacted in February (PL 111-5) provided another $16.2 billion in emergency fiscal 2009 funds for programs covered by the bill.

With Democrats in charge of both chambers and the White House, debate on the Commerce-Justice-Science bill was largely free of the policy fights that had bedeviled it in previous years. Instead, the legislation became ensnared in partisan procedural maneuvering in both chambers. In the House, which passed HR 2847 (H Rept 111-149), 259–157, on June 18, Republicans forced a long series of procedural votes after Democrats blocked them from debating amendments. Although the Senate debate was tamer, a partisan impasse over a single amendment delayed the vote by more than three weeks, pushing it into November.

Democrats fended off repeated attempts by Republicans to add language that would have prevented the administration from putting detainees from the U.S. facility in Guantánamo Bay, Cuba, on trial in the United States. Like several of the other spending bills, the measure barred detainees from coming to the United States for any other reason and established a number of reporting requirements before the administration could move the prisoners or close the facility. Obama had set a January 2010 deadline for shuttering the prison. *(Detainees, p. 314)*

The Senate passed its version of HR 2847 (S Rept 111-34), 71–28, on November 5, after voting 60–39 to invoke cloture and shut out several nongermane amendments that had been tying up consideration of the measure.

Financial Services

The fiscal 2010 financial services spending bill provided $46.3 billion, with $24.2 billion devoted to discretionary programs. The discretionary amount was virtually the same as Obama's request and about $1.6 billion, or 7 percent, more than fiscal 2009 spending, excluding $6.9 billion in emergency fiscal 2009 appropriations provided in the economic stimulus law enacted in February (PL 111-5).

The annual bill funded the Treasury Department and agencies such as the Securities and Exchange Commission (SEC), the Small Business Administration (SBA), and the General Services Administration (GSA), as well as the federal judiciary and the District of Columbia. However, most of the funding went to two accounts: the Internal Revenue Service (IRS) and the Office of Personnel Management (OPM). For fiscal 2010, the IRS received $12.1 billion. OPM, the government's human resources department, received $20.4 billion, almost all of it mandatory funds for civil service pension plans and retiree health benefits.

The House passed HR 3170 (H Rept 111-202), 219–208, on July 16. House debate on the bill was marked by discontent from Republicans and some moderate Democrats over a leadership decision to limit the number of amendments to seventeen and exclude any that dealt with abortion services or private school vouchers in the District of Columbia. The rule setting the limits (H Res 544) was narrowly adopted, 216–213, with thirty-nine Democrats opposed.

The Senate Appropriations Committee approved its version of the bill on July 9 (S 1432—S Rept 111-43), 29–1. But the stand-alone financial services bill never reached the Senate floor.

To the chagrin of many Republicans, Democrats lifted a number of social policy restrictions on the District of Columbia that had been part of the Financial Services bill in previous years. The final bill allowed the District to implement a decade-old medical marijuana ballot initiative, use local funds for abortion, spend federal dollars on needle exchange programs, and provide benefits for domestic partners. The bill continued funding for the D.C. voucher program for private schools, a favorite of Republicans, but only for students already enrolled in the program and with new testing and evaluation requirements. Many Democrats believed that vouchers diverted funding from public education.

The final bill also allowed hundreds of auto dealerships that lost franchise agreements as part of General Motors Corp. and Chrysler LLC's 2009 bankruptcy proceedings to argue their cases before an independent arbitration panel. The two automakers had taken billions of dollars in government help as they restructured, and their actions had sparked a storm of opposition from angry lawmakers with terminated dealerships in their districts. The provision represented a compromise from the original House-approved language that would have required reinstatement of the dealerships. The White House had opposed that provision, saying it would jeopardize the survival of the two auto companies.

Labor–Health and Human Services–Education

Democrats won major increases for health and education programs under the fiscal 2010 spending bill for the departments of Labor, Health and Human Services (HHS), and Education. The largest of the fiscal 2010 spending bills, the measure provided a total of $730.6 billion. Less than a quarter of that—$163.6 billion—went to discretionary accounts. The rest was mandatory spending to pay for huge entitlement programs, mainly Medicare and Medicaid; the two health care programs received a total of $518.8 billion. The discretionary funding was $11.3 billion, or 7 percent, more than the same programs received in fiscal 2009 and $2 billion more than Obama requested. It was also more than appropriators in either chamber initially sought.

The Education Department received $68.2 billion, $46.3 billion for fiscal 2010 and $21.9 billion in advance fiscal 2011 funding. Many education programs needed advance funding because of the difference between the school year and the fiscal year. The total was $854 million, or 1 percent, more than regular fiscal 2009 appropriations. However, if emergency appropriations for fiscal 2009 were factored in, it was a 58 percent drop.

The Labor Department received $16.2 billion—$846 million, or 5 percent, less than the regular fiscal 2009 appropriations and roughly the same as requested. However, the department also received $4.4 billion in emergency fiscal 2009 funds under the stimulus law. The bulk of the fiscal 2010 total—$10.9 billion—was for the Employment and Training Administration and included $3 billion for grants to states and $1.4 billion for assistance for dislocated workers.

The House passed a stand-alone Labor–Health and Human Services–Education bill HR 3293 (H Rept 111-220), 264–153, on July 24, with $163.4 billion for discretionary programs. The Senate Appropriations Committee approved a slightly smaller, $163.1 billion version (HR 3293—S Rept 111-66) later the same month. The measure never reached the Senate floor and was instead folded into the six-bill omnibus spending package.

Debate over the Labor-HHS-Education bill in both chambers was fairly muted, focused less on the specific expenditures and more on the overall state of health care, as lawmakers ramped up for their fight over plans to overhaul the nation's health care system.

Republicans complained that the bill was far too costly, particularly given that the programs it covered had gotten a total of $136.6 billion in February under the economic stimulus law (PL 111-5). Democrats argued that health and education programs had been severely underfunded for years under President George W. Bush and a GOP-controlled Congress.

On one of the most controversial issues, conferees followed the House bill in eliminating a long-standing ban on federal funding for needle exchange programs, which were designed to reduce transmission of HIV/AIDS and other diseases among users of intravenous drugs. The final bill allowed such funding, with exceptions in the case of locations deemed inappropriate by local health officials.

Like the House and Senate bills, the final version dropped funding for abstinence-only sex education, which had been expanded under Bush, in favor of a new teenage pregnancy prevention program. The bill included $110 million for the program to provide "medically accurate and age-appropriate" approaches, including abstinence, to reduce teen pregnancy. Republicans said the change would encourage more teenage sex, but Democrats argued that teaching only abstinence resulted in more pregnancies.

Conferees retained provisions of previous law that prohibited the use of federal funds for research that created or destroyed human embryos. They also continued the ban on using funds to pay for abortion, except in cases of rape, incest, or danger to the woman's life.

Military Construction–Veterans Affairs

The Military Construction–Veterans (VA) portion of the fiscal 2010 omnibus spending bill provided $134.6 billion for the VA and for Defense Department military construction projects in fiscal 2010. More than 80 percent of the funding was for veterans affairs, including health services and veterans' benefits. In addition, the bill included $48.2 billion in advance appropriations for three veterans' medical accounts in fiscal 2011. For years, veterans' groups had pushed for the change to a two-year budget in an effort to ensure that veterans' services were not disrupted by the frequent delays in the annual appropriations bill. Legislation enacted earlier in the year (PL 111-81) authorized the two-year budget cycle.

Total funding for fiscal 2010 was about $7.8 billion more than the programs received in fiscal 2009. Putting aside $4.5 billion in emergency fiscal 2009 funds under the economic stimulus bill, the fiscal 2010 bill provided $12.2 billion more than the same programs got in fiscal 2009.

There was virtually no controversy over the bill, and amounts in the House- and Senate-passed versions were only about $200 million apart. Both included the fiscal 2011 advance funding. The House passed HR 3082 (H Rept 111-188) by a vote of 415–3 on July 10. The Senate passed it, 100–0, on November 17, after amending it with the text of S 1407 (S Rept 111-40). No further action occurred on the stand-alone bill; Democratic appropriators agreed on a compromise version and included it in the year-end omnibus package.

State–Foreign Operations

The omnibus appropriated $48.9 billion to pay for State Department operations and foreign assistance programs. The top line was $1.8 billion, or 4 percent, less than the total amount appropriated for fiscal 2009. But when $4.3 billion in emergency appropriations provided in other bills and $9.7 billion in extra funds in a separate war spending bill were taken out of the equation, the amount appropriated for fiscal 2010 became an increase of $12.1 billion, or 33 percent, over the previous year.

Virtually all of the funding, $48.8 billion, was for discretionary accounts and was generally in line with earlier versions of the bill passed by the House (HR 3081—H Rept 111-187) and approved by the Senate Appropriations Committee (S 1434—S Rept 111-44) in July.

But the figure was $3.3 billion below Obama's request, making the measure the only nondefense spending bill to provide significantly less than the president wanted. The biggest differences were a $1.3 billion cut from Obama's request for State Department operations and $1.1 billion less than requested to finance foreign sales of U.S. weapons. However, the fiscal 2009 war supplemental, which was enacted six months earlier (PL 111-32), had provided $4 billion in extra funding for those accounts.

The fiscal 2010 funding included $2.6 billion in economic aid to Afghanistan, the largest amount for any country, and $1.5 billion in economic and military assistance to Pakistan.

Left out of the final bill was a Senate provision that would have put into statute an action taken by Obama in January to rescind the so-called Mexico City restrictions on international family-planning aid. The Mexico City policy, first announced by President Ronald Reagan in 1984, went beyond the prohibition in existing law against using federal funds for abortion. The policy barred U.S. funding from going to nongovernmental organizations that performed or actively promoted abortion as a method of family planning, even if the group used its own money. Exceptions were allowed in cases of rape or incest, or when the life of the woman was in danger.

The omnibus also largely retained language approved by the House that overruled a move by Obama to reject congressional conditions on funding for the World Bank, the International Monetary Fund (IMF), and other international financial institutions, banks. The final bill also set specific requirements for continued U.S. participation after five years in a new IMF lending facility.

Transportation–Housing and Urban Development

In addition to appropriating $122.1 billion for the departments of Transportation (DOT) and Housing and Urban Development (HUD), the omnibus measure provided a significant boost for the creation of a national high-speed rail network, a priority for President Obama. The bill cleared near the end of the session, after the conference report became the vehicle for a year-end omnibus that contained five other unfinished spending bills.

Discretionary spending for the two departments and related programs accounted for $67.9 billion of the total—about $970 million, or 1 percent, less than Obama requested. Most of the remainder was mandatory spending appropriated from the Highway Trust Fund. DOT and HUD had also received a combined total of $63.8 billion in extra fiscal 2009 appropriations under the economic stimulus law (PL 111-5) that cleared in February. *(Stimulus, p. 78)*

Conferees agreed to provide $2.5 billion for high-speed rail, more than double the White House request. The House had called for $4 billion, with $2 billion of that available for a new national infrastructure bank that Obama was backing. The final bill did not provide for the bank, which was never authorized.

Appropriators said the absence of new laws to reauthorize surface and aviation programs precluded them from providing bigger transportation funding increases. They also said their hands were tied by an expected multibillion-dollar shortfall in the federal Highway Trust Fund, which had its own dedicated revenue stream that came mainly from an excise tax on motor fuels and was outside the appropriators' control.

With the House and Senate Transportation committees unable to agree on a long-term reauthorization of surface transportation programs, Congress had passed a series of short-term extensions of existing law, which did not address the shortfall. Before leaving for the August recess, Congress cleared a bill that provided a $7 billion injection of Treasury funds to keep the trust fund solvent. *(Highway Trust Fund, p. 324)*

The final version of the Transportation-HUD portion of the omnibus also carried a controversial provision, added in the Senate, to allow Amtrak passengers to carry guns in their checked bags.

DEFENSE APPROPRIATIONS

Democratic leaders put the must-pass defense appropriations bill at the end of the line of fiscal 2010 spending measures, holding it until they determined what last-minute legislation it should take with it. Congress cleared the measure, with several small add-ons, on December 19, and President Obama signed it the same day (HR 3326—PL 111-118).

The bill provided $636.4 billion in discretionary spending for the Defense Department—$508.1 billion for regular Pentagon activities and $128.2 billion to support ongoing operations in Iraq and Afghanistan and related activities. It was the first time since 2001 that war funding had been included in the regular defense budget.

Appropriators said the Pentagon would probably need additional fiscal 2010 funding the following spring to support Obama's planned surge of troops in Afghanistan. The bill also included $290 million in mandatory funds for retirement and disability benefits for employees of the Central Intelligence Agency (CIA), along with $10.7 billion in permanently appropriated funds for retiree health benefits.

The discretionary total was $3.8 billion, or just .06 percent, less than Obama requested, and $11.4 billion, or 2 percent, more than enacted for fiscal 2009. However, the comparison with fiscal 2009 included $70 billion in emergency appropriations provided for that year under a supplemental bill enacted in June (PL 111-32). Without that funding, the fiscal 2010 bill total was about 13 percent over the previous year.

The measure largely followed the administration's outlines, including no funding for additional F-22 Raptor fighter jets. Congress gave up on the plane after plans to fund it drew a direct veto threat from the president. Conferees retained funding for two programs that had drawn less direct veto warnings: the troubled VH-71 presidential helicopter and an alternate engine for the F-35 Joint Strike Fighter. But the final bill modified the spending, and the veto threat ebbed considerably given the importance of defense funding, especially in wartime. *(Fighter controversies, p. 263)*

The measure provided additional funds for equipment depleted by the wars in Iraq and Afghanistan, including new combat vehicles, new battle gear for the Army National Guard and reserves, military pay raises, and quality-of-life improvements for the troops and their families. It reduced spending below fiscal 2009 levels for missile defense, new nuclear weapons, and other futuristic programs such as the Future Combat Systems.

As was typically the case, the annual spending bill largely mirrored the companion defense authorization measure (PL 111-84). *(Defense authorization, p. 273; appropriations details, p. 280)*

The final bill also carried a series of provisions that extended authorizations through February 28, 2010, for several expiring programs, including several provisions of the antiterrorism law known as the Patriot Act; a delay in a scheduled cut in Medicare physician payments; highway, transit, highway safety, and motor carrier safety programs; federal unemployment benefits for workers who had exhausted their regular state benefits; and a 65 percent subsidy for health insurance coverage under the COBRA law for workers who had lost their job. *(Patriot Act, p. 208; pay, p. 450; surface transportation, p. 324; unemployment, p. 324; COBRA, p. 525)*

The House passed HR 3326 (H Rept 111-230), 400–30, on July 30. The Senate passed an amended version of the bill (HR 3326—S Rept 111-74), 93–7, on October 6. Negotiations over Defense appropriations were relatively smooth; major funding levels were generally similar in the House- and Senate-passed versions of the bill, and policy differences were minimal. Instead of holding a formal conference to reconcile the differences, appropriators reached agreement on a final measure through informal negotiations. The House adopted the compromise as a substitute amendment by a vote of 395–34 on December 16, shortly before leaving for the year. The Senate took a break from its ongoing debate on the health care overhaul to clear the bill, 88–10, on December 19.

2009 Debt Ceiling Increase

With the Treasury Department warning that it would run up against the statutory limit on the federal debt by the end of the year, Congress cleared a short-term $290 billion increase in December 2009 that was expected to tide the Treasury over until early 2010 (HR 4314—PL 111-123).

Treasury Secretary Timothy F. Geithner notified lawmakers in August that Congress would need to raise the debt limit by mid-October. The deadline was subsequently extended until the end of December as a result of higher-than-anticipated corporate tax revenue and steps taken by Treasury officials to buy time.

Using some procedural sleight-of-hand, the House approved an increase in the debt ceiling in April without having to actually vote directly on the increase. Under what was known as the Gephardt rule (after former representative and House majority leader Richard Gephardt, D-Mo.), the House was deemed to have passed a joint resolution (H J Res 45) raising the limit to $13.0 trillion once both chambers adopted the conference report on the fiscal 2010 budget resolution (S Con Res 13). *(Budget resolution, p. 134)*

(Republicans, when they regained control of the House in 2011 following the 2010 midterm elections, repealed the Gephardt rule.)

But the Senate had no comparable procedure, and the leadership put off acting on the measure. For one thing, Democrats wanted a higher ceiling to avoid an election-year vote. And by November, they were embroiled in a marathon health care debate that left no room for negotiations on a debt bill.

House leaders were still hoping in December to pass a $1.8 trillion debt increase. They considered including it in the defense appropriations bill, which would have made it difficult for Republicans to oppose. But they had to give up in the face of objections from moderates within their own party.

In the House, fiscally conservative Blue Dog Democrats said they would not vote for a major debt limit increase unless it included statutory pay-as-you-go restrictions that would require offsets for most new mandatory spending or tax cuts. The House passed such a bill (HR 2920) in July, but the Senate never acted on it. *(Budget enforcement, p. 126)*

Across the Capitol, a bipartisan group of senators tied their support for a large debt increase to the inclusion of legislation (S 2853) by Budget Committee Chair Kent Conrad, D-N.D., and the panel's ranking Republican, Judd Gregg of New Hampshire, that would create a bipartisan task force or commission to review government debt and fiscal policies. Congress would be required to vote on the commission's recommendations.

With no time to work out a compromise, House and Senate Democrats agreed to the temporary increase, which put off the pain for only a few months. The House passed the short-term bill by a vote of 218–214 on December 16. In its last vote of the session, the Senate cleared the measure, 60–39, on December 24.

Congress had raised the debt limit by more than $2.5 trillion since 2008 to well as efforts to rescue the faltering financial sector and respond to the struggling economy. The last increase had come earlier in 2009, when Congress boosted the ceiling by $789 billion, to $12.1 trillion, to cover the cost of the economic stimulus law (PL 111-5). *(Stimulus, p. 78)*

Fiscal 2011 Budget Resolution

Congress's annual budget process derailed early in 2010 in the face of widespread public concern about the deficit and lawmakers' focus on the upcoming November election. As a result, there was no bicameral fiscal 2011 budget resolution.

The Senate Budget Committee approved a five-year budget resolution in April (S Con Res 60) that would have set an upper limit of $1.1 trillion on discretionary spending for fiscal 2011, but the Senate never took it up.

Unable to overcome competing objectives among members of the Democratic caucus, the House Budget Committee did not act on a budget plan. Instead, House Democratic leaders indirectly won adoption of a scaled-back, one-year $1.1 trillion discretionary spending limit as part of the rule for debate on an unrelated spending bill.

The annual budget resolution outlines Congress's tax-and-spending policies. It also requires the majority party to show how its policies would affect the deficit over five years—a requirement that made many Democrats uneasy as they looked to the fall election. Although a budget resolution does not become law, it sets a cap on discretionary spending for the annual appropriations bills that is enforced through House and Senate rules.

The lack of a budget resolution was part of a larger collapse of the budget and appropriations process in 2010 that ended with none of the regular appropriations bills enacted and government spending largely continued at fiscal 2010 levels through March 4, 2011. *(Fiscal 2011 appropriations, p. 137)*

Congress was unable to reach final agreement on the budget in 1998, 2002, 2004, and 2006, but this was the first time since the modern budget process took effect in 1976 that the House failed to hold a floor vote on its own version of the resolution.

Democrats had been highly critical on the three occasions when GOP-controlled Congresses failed to produce a final House-Senate budget. Republicans repaid the favor in 2010 by lambasting Democrats for not putting forward a five-year fiscal 2011 outline, arguing it was evidence the majority did not have a plan to curtail the deficit.

House Democrats said their one-year approach would restrain spending for fiscal 2011, while a deficit commission established by President Obama developed recommendations for taming the deficit over time.

OBAMA'S FISCAL 2011 BUDGET

President Barack Obama released a $3.8 trillion fiscal 2011 budget on February 1, 2010, that proposed to put the brakes on domestic discretionary spending, but the president left the daunting problem of the nation's rapidly growing debt to a bipartisan commission that he pledged to create. *(Debt commission, p. 142)*

Obama proposed that spending on domestic discretionary programs not exceed $447 billion a year in each of the following three fiscal years and that for the next seven years the total be allowed to grow no faster than the rate of inflation. The White House estimated this plan would save $250 billion over ten years. The plan was not an across-the-board cut but rather a flexible freeze—individual departments and agencies could receive more or less funding.

The budget reflected multiple and sometimes conflicting goals. Obama called for reducing the long-term deficit while pumping money into the economy in the short run to promote recovery. He proposed tax cuts for the middle class, as he had promised during his election campaign, while allowing previous tax cuts for the well-to-do to expire at the end of the year, resulting in a sharp increase for those taxpayers. "When I look at this budget, I strongly agree with the president's budget in the short term," said Kent Conrad, D-N.D., chair of the Senate Budget Committee. "It is absolutely imperative that we not allow the economy to slip back into recession." But, he said, "I have strong disagreement with the long term."

Republicans said they supported the idea of a freeze in discretionary spending but were quick to point out that the budget would not contain the growth in mandatory spending and said that the discretionary savings would be "puny" in comparison with the deficits being racked up.

On jobs, both sides attacked the president's plan to devote $100 billion to employment-bolstering initiatives. Liberal Democrats said it was not enough, especially considering the country's infrastructure needs, which were potentially a major source of employment. Republicans warned about the public's aversion to more spending. Republicans also argued that a proposal to allow higher taxes on the wealthy would put a damper on job growth and said that Democrats would try another version of the 2009 economic stimulus bill (PL 111-5) under a different name. *(Stimulus bill, p. 78)*

The White House's Office of Management and Budget (OMB), which prepared the president's budget, put the total request for discretionary spending in fiscal 2011 at $1.4 trillion in outlays ($1.3 trillion in budget authority). The Congressional Budget Office (CBO) issued its annual recalculation of the budget in March based on slightly different economic and technical assumptions. The CBO estimated the discretionary request at $1.4 trillion in outlays ($1.3 trillion in budget authority). Congress generally used the CBO's estimates, which are used in the following account.

Of the total, $733.1 billion in budget authority was requested for defense, including Defense Department war-related activities and nuclear weapons programs at the Department of Energy. Of the total, about $159 billion was designated for operations in Iraq and Afghanistan. The CBO said the total was an increase of $16 billion, or 2 percent, above total fiscal 2010 funding.

For nondefense discretionary programs, the request included $536.8 billion, a drop of $19.4 billion, or 3.5 percent, from total fiscal 2010 spending. However, the overall figure included international affairs, which stood to receive a 2.5 percent increase, to $58.8 billion, under Obama's budget. Appropriations classified as "security-related" accounted for another $14 billion increase over previous funding. A major factor in Obama's plan to reduce the domestic discretionary budget was a proposal, rejected by Congress in 2009, to shift $18 billion for the Pell college grant program from discretionary to mandatory spending.

Among the domestic accounts that stood to get increases above fiscal 2010 spending were those for health programs, slated for a $1.7 billion increase, and energy programs, up by $1.1 billion. Obama proposed cuts for other agencies, including the departments of Agriculture and Housing and Urban Development.

The budget included a total of $47 billion in supplemental spending requests for fiscal 2010. Of that, $31 billion was intended for military activities and $4 billion for diplomatic operations and foreign aid. Obama also requested $5 billion for disaster relief and almost $5 billion to settle claims against the government by Black farmers and American Indians. *(Lawsuits, p. 555)*

The CBO calculated that the changes to mandatory programs proposed in Obama's budget would increase net mandatory outlays above existing law by $99 billion in fiscal 2011 and $1.9 trillion from 2011 through 2020. Total mandatory spending under the budget would be $2.2 trillion in fiscal 2011 and $25.8 trillion over a decade. The CBO said the biggest anticipated increase came from Obama's health insurance overhaul (PL 111-148, PL 111-152), which the administration at the time estimated would increase mandatory outlays by $6 billion in 2010 and $593 billion over ten years. *(Health care overhaul, p. 421)*

While shifting funds for Pell grants from discretionary to mandatory accounts cut discretionary spending under the budget, it boosted mandatory spending by $374 billion over ten years. Proposals to extend or expand various refundable tax credits amounted to a projected ten-year increase in outlays of $401 billion.

The Joint Committee on Taxation (JCT), whose estimates were used by the CBO, projected that tax changes proposed in the budget would reduce revenue by $213 billion in fiscal 2011 and $1.4 trillion over ten years, compared with existing law. Obama proposed an extension for middle-class taxpayers of cuts enacted under President George W. Bush in 2001 and 2003 (PL 107-16, PL 108-27). Those lower taxes were set to expire at the end of 2010, and without new legislation, rates would rise to levels set in previous law. The extension was projected to reduce revenues by $95 billion in fiscal 2011 and $2.2 trillion over ten years. *(Bush-era tax cuts, Congress and the Nation Vol. XI, pp. 89, 105)*

Obama wanted to permanently extend the tax rates on income, capital gains, and dividends at 2010 levels for married taxpayers' income below $250,000 and single taxpayers' income of less than $200,000. But rates for income above those amounts would rise to the much higher rates set under previous law. Capital gains and dividends would be taxed at 20 percent instead of the 15 percent rate in effect in 2010. The child tax credit, which was doubled to $1,000 in 2001, would also be extended under the budget.

The president also proposed to revive the estate tax retroactively at 2009 levels with a $3.5 million per-person exemption and a 45 percent top rate. The tax expired at the end of 2009.

To prevent the alternative minimum tax (AMT) from reaching millions of additional taxpayers each year, Congress regularly passed a one-year expansion of exemptions under the tax. Obama proposed to make the 2009 exemptions permanent and index them to inflation, at an estimated cost of $66 billion in fiscal 2011 and $577 billion over ten years.

A series of proposed changes to the U.S. system of taxing the international income of multinational corporations was projected to raise revenues by $6 billion in fiscal 2011 and $127 billion over ten years. Obama also proposed a "financial crisis responsibility fee" on the largest banks to recover costs of the financial bailout that was projected to raise $8 billion in fiscal 2011 and $90 billion over ten years.

The CBO estimated that under Obama's budget, the fiscal 2011 deficit would decline to $1.3 trillion, or 9 percent of the gross domestic product (GDP), from $1.5 trillion, or 10 percent of GDP, in fiscal 2010. Still, the fiscal 2011 deficit would be $346 billion higher than it would with no changes in the law. Over ten years, deficits under Obama's policies would total $9.8 trillion, or 5.2 percent of GDP. *(Deficit table, p. 117)*

The broad economic outlook that provided the underpinning for the budget demonstrated that the administration was counting on an economic rebound, which was essential to its two main election year priorities: reducing the deficit and creating jobs.

The administration's near-term projection for the jobless rate—9.2 percent in 2011, down from an estimated 10 percent in 2010—was in line with the most recent estimate from the Blue Chip consensus of private forecasters released in January. Over the longer term, the White House expected unemployment to stay above 6 percent through 2014 before gradually decreasing to 5.2 percent by 2020.

The White House forecast that the economy would expand by an inflation-adjusted 3.8 percent in 2011—faster than the 3.1 percent Blue Chip estimate and the 1.9 percent CBO forecast. After 2011, the White House projected that the GDP would grow by 4.3 percent in 2012 and that growth would be 4 percent or greater through 2014 before gradually declining to 2.5 percent in 2019.

The average post–World War II expansion rate was roughly 3.3 percent; sustained growth higher than 4 percent had not occurred since the Internet boom of the late 1990s. Then, economic growth and government budget-balancing deals drove the federal budget from deficit into surplus.

Despite the seeming optimism in the economic forecast, however, administration budget documents conveyed uncertainty about whether the recovery would be as vigorous as the recession was deep and about whether the financial crisis was really over for good. In the "Analytical Perspectives" that accompanied the budget submission, OMB said its economic growth estimates were slightly lower than the historical average for a post-recession rebound, in part because of the inherent uncertainty of the economic and financial climate. Officials acknowledged that they had been overly optimistic the previous year when they predicted a decline in unemployment that did not materialize.

SENATE ACTION

The Senate Budget Committee approved a five-year fiscal 2011 budget resolution (S Con Res 60) on April 22 that would have provided up to $1.1 trillion in fiscal 2011 discretionary budget authority, compared with $1.3 trillion in Obama's request. The panel rejected Obama's proposal to reclassify a portion of Pell grant funding as mandatory spending. The committee approved the measure 12–10, with Russ Feingold, D-Wis., joining all the Republicans in opposition.

According to Conrad, the plan would reduce the deficit from $1.5 trillion, or 9.8 percent of gross domestic product, in fiscal 2010 to $545 billion, or 3 percent of GDP, in fiscal 2015. The resolution called for freezing nonsecurity discretionary spending for three years and assumed that taxes would be cut by $780 billion.

Republicans won a key battle in restricting the use of reconciliation instructions that would have made specific legislation exempt from Senate filibuster rules. Reflecting the growing unease over the reconciliation process, most recently used to push "corrections" to the health care overhaul to enactment (PL 111-152), seven Democrats joined Republicans to require sixty votes in the Senate to overcome a point of order against reconciliation bills that proposed new spending in excess of 20 percent of what the relevant authorizing committee was instructed to save. The amendment, offered by ranking Republican Judd Gregg of New Hampshire, was adopted, 16–6, with Conrad's support.

The full Senate took no action on the committee measure.

HOUSE ACTION

Deliberations in the House were complicated by the efforts of some members of the Democratic rank and file and the fiscally conservative Blue Dog Coalition to make what Budget Chair John M. Spratt Jr., D-S.C., described as cuts to the president's budget that they "could take home and talk about." As a result, the House Budget Committee did not act on a budget resolution.

Instead, House Democratic leaders won adoption of their one-year budget plan (H Res 1493), which they called a "budget enforcement resolution," without requiring a direct vote. They inserted a provision that automatically adopted the resolution as part of the rule for floor debate on an unrelated fiscal 2010 war supplemental bill (HR 4899). The House adopted the rule (H Res 1500), 215–120, on July 1. *(Supplemental, p. 269)*

"We're saying this package is a functional equivalent of a budget resolution," Spratt said. Progressives, including House Appropriations Chair David R. Obey, D-Wis., resisted the proposal, which cut from Obama's budget request, but the fiscal hawks prevailed.

The resolution, which affected only the House, set an overall discretionary limit of $1.1 trillion in budget authority for the twelve House fiscal 2011 appropriations bills. The limit was well below the comparable request made by Obama and $1 billion below the amount in the Senate committee's budget resolution. The resolution also allowed an additional appropriation of $538 million, which would count against fiscal 2010 limits even if it was spent in fiscal 2011, for "program integrity" initiatives by various agencies to combat waste, fraud, and abuse. The resolution also stipulated that any savings that resulted from enactment of recommendations made by the presidential debt commission be used only for deficit reduction.

Fiscal 2011 Spending Bills

The regular appropriations process ground to a halt in 2010. Congress did not complete action on any of the regular fiscal 2011 spending bills and instead kept the government operating under a series of bills known as continuing resolutions, or CRs.

The meltdown began early in the year, when the Democratic majority declined to produce a bicameral budget resolution that would have set spending levels for fiscal 2011 and given the appropriators a common framework for writing the spending bills. The Senate Budget Committee approved a budget resolution in April that would have set a $1.122 trillion cap on discretionary spending—about $4 billion less than President Barack Obama requested—but the measure went no further. In the absence of action by the House Budget Committee, the House in July indirectly adopted a one-year, $1.121 trillion discretionary spending limit. *(Fiscal 2011 budget resolution, p. 134)*

REGULAR BILLS STALL

As the session progressed, the spending process grew more acrimonious. With growing voter anxiety over deficit spending and midterm elections approaching, Republicans stepped up their attacks on Democrats as big spenders. Democratic leaders made only halting progress on the twelve annual appropriations bills over the summer.

Facing GOP calls to cut spending, Senate Appropriations Chair Daniel K. Inouye, D-Hawaii, volunteered to set a discretionary cap of $1.114 trillion. But Senate Republicans argued for a $1.108 trillion limit, and Majority Leader Harry Reid, D-Nev., and Inouye appeared to accept that demand. *(Discretionary caps, box, above)*

BACKDOOR SPENDING CAPS IN THE SENATE

In a months-long effort, two senators failed to persuade their colleagues to set explicit caps on discretionary spending. But while they may have lost the battle, they won the war when Senate Democratic appropriators finally agreed to write spending bills that did not exceed the caps the two senators were seeking.

Republican Jeff Sessions of Alabama and Democrat Claire McCaskill of Missouri began their campaign in late January when Sessions offered an amendment to debt limit legislation (H J Res 45) that would have held discretionary spending in fiscal 2011 and the four subsequent years to fiscal 2010 levels. The amendment was voted down, 56–44 (by unanimous consent, the Senate agreed that sixty votes were necessary for passage).

Over the next few months, the two senators offered variants of their amendment three more times, only to see it defeated on procedural motions. The closest they came to their goal was a 59–41 vote on March 4, 2010, on a motion to waive the Budget Act and allow consideration of the amendment. Another attempt, on March 18, failed on a vote of 56–40.

The pair tried one final time, with an amendment that would have capped discretionary spending at $1.108 trillion through fiscal 2014. It fell on June 9, when the Senate again rejected a waiver motion on a **key vote of 57–41 (R 40–0; D 16–40; I 1–1).** *(2010 key votes, p. 767)*

Despite the rejection, Minority Leader Mitch McConnell, R-Ky., and other Republicans announced at a Senate Appropriations Committee meeting in July that they would not vote for any bill that exceeded the discretionary spending caps in the Sessions-McCaskill amendment. Senate Appropriations Chair Daniel K. Inouye, D-Hawaii, pushed for a $1.114 trillion cap, but he eventually relented and began writing spending bills that come in under the $1.108 trillion level.

The Senate Budget Committee had recommended a cap of $1.122 trillion for fiscal 2011, but the committee's budget resolution was never acted on by the full Senate. *(Fiscal 2011 budget resolution, p. 134)*

In the end, the House passed just two of the regular appropriations bills—one for the Department of Veterans Affairs and military construction, and the other for the departments of Transportation and Housing and Urban Development. None of the other House bills went beyond subcommittee markups. The Senate Appropriations Committee approved all but the Interior measure, but none of the bills reached the floor.

FIRST CONTINUING RESOLUTION

Returning from their August recess, Democrats had an extensive legislative agenda (including passage of some regular appropriations bills) they hoped to clear before leaving Washington at the end of September to campaign at home for the midterm elections. But partisan sparring blocked action on all but a short-term funding bill. The Senate passed a continuing resolution, on September 29, 69–30, to continue funding through December 3, 2010. Just after midnight September 30, the House cleared the bill, 228–194. Later that day, the president signed it (HR 3081—PL 111-242).

Although most funding for fiscal 2011 was held to fiscal 2010 levels, the CR shifted some funding from one program to another and added a few policy prescriptions. In one significant shift, the CR added an extra $624 million to help the National Nuclear Security Administration (NNSA) implement certain critical nuclear programs, including those connected to an agreement with Russia, known as New Strategic Arms Reduction Treaty (START; Treaty Doc 111-5). A vote on approval of the treaty's ratification was awaiting Senate action. *(Treaty, p. 289)*

The CR also authorized mortgage giants Fannie Mae and Freddie Mac, along with the Federal Housing Administration, to continue buying and guaranteeing mortgages up to $729,750 in expensive housing markets through September 30, 2011. The limit was set to drop to $625,000 after December 31, 2010.

THREE LAME DUCK CONTINUING RESOLUTIONS

The November elections gave Republicans control of the House in the next Congress and forty-seven seats in the Senate. It also changed the political calculus in the 2010 lame duck session.

Republicans began calling for a short-term funding measure that would last only into the beginning of 2011, giving them an early opportunity to cut spending. Democrats tried to find a way to fund the government through the end of fiscal 2011 to allow them to enact their priorities. As deliberations continued with no agreement in sight, another short-term CR became necessary. The House passed a two-week resolution continuing funding through December 18 (H J Res 101) on a largely party-line vote of 239–178 on December 1. The Senate cleared the measure by voice vote December 2 (H J Res 101—PL 111-290).

In a last-ditch effort to protect their domestic-spending priorities, House Democrats passed a bill (HR 3082) on December 8 that would have kept funding at the fiscal 2010 level of $1.09 trillion through the end of the fiscal year. It would have shifted money around, however, providing billions in additional spending for the Defense Department and for favored domestic programs. The bill passed 212–206 with no GOP support.

The bill also included $159 billion for war operations in Afghanistan and Iraq, as Obama requested. In addition, it carried the text of a food safety bill (S 510) that the Senate passed November 30. The language was appended in an attempt to get around a constitutional problem: the Senate-passed bill included revenue provisions, which had to originate in the House.

The CR stalled in the Senate, however, and a Democratic attempt to pass a full omnibus package that included all of the fiscal 2011 spending bills was blocked by Republicans. The omnibus package included $8 billion in earmarks and would have exceeded fiscal 2010 discretionary spending by $18 billion. Inouye had expected to get enough GOP votes to block a filibuster, but Republicans abruptly withdrew their support, dooming the effort.

With time running out, Senate Democrats conceded. On December 21, the Senate voted, 79–16, to pass HR 3082 after amending it to freeze fiscal 2011 spending for most programs at fiscal 2010 spending levels through March 4, 2011. The House cleared the bill, 193–165, later the same day, and the president signed it into law December 22 (PL 111-322).

The final measure included provisions that froze federal nonmilitary pay for two years; increased the rate of funding for student Pell grants to maintain the existing maximum grant; and allowed the Low Income Home Energy Assistance Program to spend more money to account for the higher obligations that usually occur during the winter. As in the earlier CRs, it allowed Fannie Mae and Freddie Mac to continue to back high-cost-area home mortgages.

The bill also increased the rate of spending for the Veterans Benefits Administration and continued higher funding for nuclear weapons labs, a step that was crucial to winning enough support in the Senate to ratify the New START agreement. It also authorized a Navy plan to buy twenty Littoral Combat Ships from two different contractors, and it extended the authorization for highway and other surface transportation programs through March 4, 2011. The authorization had been set to expire on December 31, 2010. *(Surface transportation authorization, p. 324)*

Fiscal 2010 War Supplemental

With Republicans tipping the balance, the House in July 2010 cleared a $58.8 billion fiscal 2010 supplemental spending bill devoted primarily to paying for operations in Iraq and Afghanistan. President Barack Obama signed the legislation on July 29, 2010 (HR 4899—PL 111-212).

Republicans in both chambers generally supported the bill, while House Democrats were sharply divided. Among those voting against the final version was House Appropriations Committee Chair David R. Obey, D-Wis. In floor remarks, Obey told his colleagues he had "the highest respect and appreciation" for U.S. troops but said they are "being let down by the inability of the governments of Afghanistan and in some instances Pakistan to do their parts."

When Obama sent his fiscal 2011 budget to Congress in February, he requested $33 billion in supplemental fiscal 2010 funds, including $30 billion for deployments to Afghanistan and $1 billion to train Iraqi security forces. Subsequent requests for funds for disaster aid, veterans health programs, and other purposes brought the total to $64.4 billion.

From the outset, Obey and many other House Democrats wanted to add billions of dollars for domestic needs, particularly to avoid the layoffs of tens of thousands of teachers nationwide at a time when state budgets were stretched thin and funds for the purpose in the 2009 economic stimulus law (PL 111-5) were running out. Democratic leaders spent several months trying to come up with a package that could win enough votes in the Senate to surmount a filibuster.

A steady stream of negative news about the situation in Afghanistan, including reports of pervasive corruption in the Afghan government as well as criticism of the administration's approach to the war, complicated congressional deliberations.

With disagreement among Democrats slowing action in the House, Democratic leaders took the somewhat unorthodox approach of letting Senate appropriators go first. The Senate passed the bill, 67–28, on May 27. The key procedural vote took place just hours before passage when the Senate invoked cloture, 69–29, limiting the debate. An effort led by Tom Harkin, D-Iowa, to include the money to prevent teacher layoffs failed to win enough support to block a filibuster.

The House on July 1 adopted an amendment to the $58.8 billion Senate-passed measure that added $22.8 billion for schools and other Democratic domestic priorities.

Under a complicated rule for floor debate, the House amendment was divided into several parts, which gave antiwar Democrats a chance to vote to wind down the U.S. military presence in Afghanistan. At the same time, it allowed fiscal conservatives in the Democratic Blue Dog Coalition to oppose the additional domestic spending without having to vote against the $58.8 billion in the Senate version. The rule, which also automatically approved Democrats' plan for a one-year budget, was adopted, 215–210. The rule had no GOP support and thirty-eight Democratic defectors.

The House adopted Obey's domestic spending amendment, 239–182, with fifteen Democrats and all but three Republicans voting "no." Three antiwar amendments were handily defeated, including a proposal by Barbara Lee, D-Calif., to limit the use of the military funding for Afghanistan to activities related to withdrawing troops and protecting civilian and military personnel. That amendment was rejected July 1 on a **key vote of 100–321 (R 7–164; D 93–157)**. *(2010 key votes, p. 767)*

The Senate on July 22 refused to accept the $22.8 billion domestic spending amendment added in the House. By a vote of 46–51, senators rejected a motion to limit debate on the amended House version of the bill. Instead, the Senate agreed by unanimous consent to send its original version back to the House.

With members about to leave for the August recess, the House had little choice but to clear the narrower bill. On July 27, it did so on a key vote of **308–114 (R 160–12; D 148–102)**. *(2010 key votes, p. 767)*

To allow antiwar Democrats another chance to express their concerns, House leaders gave floor time to a resolution (H Con Res 301), sponsored by Dennis J. Kucinich, D-Ohio, that would have directed the president to remove troops from Pakistan within thirty days. The resolution, rejected by a vote of 38–372, invoked the 1973 War Powers Resolution (PL 93-148), which provided that Congress could force the withdrawal of troops fighting abroad if there had not been a declaration of war or explicit statutory authorization. The White House had always refused to recognize the act, regardless of who was president, arguing that it was unconstitutional.

The $58.8 billion total for the bill—which was about equal to Obama's amended request—consisted of $45.4 billion in discretionary spending and $13.4 billion in mandatory funds.

The main discretionary items included $33.4 billion for the Pentagon, which appropriators said included funding for the addition of 30,000 troops in Afghanistan as part of the administration's surge program; $5.1 billion for the Federal Emergency Management Agency (FEMA) to help pay for the costs of previous disasters, including hurricanes Katrina and Rita, the Midwest floods of 2008, and California wildfires; $2.9 billion for aid in response to the January 12, 2010, earthquake in Haiti; and $162 million related to the Gulf of Mexico oil spill.

The mandatory funding was for the Veterans Affairs (VA) Department to cover claims by Vietnam War veterans exposed to the defoliant Agent Orange. The VA had extended coverage in 2009 to veterans who were exposed to Agent Orange and then developed B-cell leukemia, Parkinson's disease, or ischemic heart disease, a condition marked by reduced blood supply to the heart.

Border Security Supplemental Spending

Congress agreed in August 2010 to provide $600 million requested by President Barack Obama to increase patrol activities along the Southwest border. The president signed the supplemental spending bill into law on August 13 (HR 6080—PL 111-230).

"Violence on the Mexican side of the border has intensified because of turf battles among murderous transnational criminal organizations competing for drug-, alien- and weapon-trafficking business," said David E. Price, D-N.C., chair of the House Homeland Security Appropriations Subcommittee. "This funding is urgently needed to counter the pressures our law enforcement agencies in our border communities currently face."

After an unsuccessful attempt to add border security funds to the fiscal 2010 war supplemental spending bill (PL 111-212), the House passed a separate $701 million border security supplemental spending bill (HR 5875) on July 28.

The cost of the measure, which passed by voice vote, was partially offset with $100 million in rescissions, but the bill included no revenue provisions. Unlike the bill that later became law, it would have required the Defense Department to pay the full costs associated with deploying National Guard troops along the border in fiscal 2010 and 2011.

The Senate passed an amended version of the bill by unanimous consent on August 5, shortly before adjourning for a five-week recess. The Senate amendment reduced the bill's total to $600 million and allocated some of the money differently. Most significantly, the costs were fully offset by the addition of a provision to temporarily increase fees paid by companies applying for H-1B and L visas. (An H-1B visa allows U.S. employers to temporarily employ foreign workers in specialty occupations; L visas allow foreign employees of an international company to relocate to an international corporation's U.S. office.)

The House bristled at the Senate's addition of revenue provisions, which under the Constitution must originate in the House. So, during a one-day session on August 10, the House agreed by voice vote to pass its own identical bill (HR 6080). The Senate cleared the legislation by unanimous consent in a one-day session August 12.

Major provisions in the bill included $254 million for Customs and Border Protection, including funds that appropriators said would send 1,500 new patrol agents and two additional unmanned aerial drones to the border to help stem the flow of illegal immigrants and drugs; $196 million for the Justice Department for increased border-related law enforcement activities; and $80 million for Immigration and Customs Enforcement, including funds for communications equipment.

In addition to rescinding $100 million in previously enacted spending, the measure increased to $2,000 and $2,500, respectively, the fees that companies paid when they submitted applications for H-1B and L employee visas.

Teachers, Medicaid Supplemental

Members of the House interrupted their August 2010 recess to return to Washington and clear a $26.1 billion bill that provided funds to help state and local governments prevent layoffs of teachers and maintain Medicaid health coverage of the poor. President Barack Obama signed the bill into law on August 10, the day it cleared (HR 1586—PL 111-226).

The supplemental funding demonstrated the clear divide between those who believed in more government spending to foster economic recovery and those who believed government was already spending enough. Democrats said the measure would boost the economy and protect vulnerable state and local government jobs. Most Republicans criticized it as an election-year sop by Democrats to teachers' unions, among their biggest campaign supporters.

The teacher aid was popular among House Democrats, 236 of whom had voted to add it to a war supplemental spending bill in July. The Senate, however, had killed the idea when it considered that bill. *(2010 war supplemental, p. 286)*

Following that vote, Majority Leader Harry Reid, D-Nev., and Patty Murray, D-Wash., both of whom were facing tough election challenges, pushed for a vote on a stand-alone version of the Medicaid-education supplemental. The bill Reid used as a vehicle for the domestic supplemental funding was a long-term authorization bill for the Federal Aviation Administration (FAA). Both chambers had passed differing versions of the bill and final action was pending, when Reid moved to replace the language in that bill with the supplemental funding package. *(FAA, p. 327)*

The Senate passed the bill on August 5 by a **key vote of 61–39 (R 2–39; D 57–0; I 2–0)**, with Republicans Susan Collins and Olympia J. Snowe of Maine joining all members of the Democratic caucus. *(2010 key votes, p. 767)*

Passage was virtually assured after the Senate August 4 agreed, 61–38, to invoke cloture, limiting the length of the debate. Still, many Democrats were unhappy that part of the bill was offset through an $11.9 billion reduction in funds for food stamp benefits and a $1.5 billion reduction in funds for renewable-energy programs.

The successful cloture vote in the Senate and calls from state officials for quick action prompted Speaker Nancy Pelosi, D-Calif., to call the House back into session. New York governor David A. Paterson, a Democrat, warned that about thirty states had budgeted on the assumption that the federal funds would arrive. The chamber cleared the measure August 10 by a **key vote of 247–161 (R 2–158; D 245–3)**. *(2010 key votes, p. 767)*

The vote represented a small victory for Democratic leaders who for months had been unable to deliver on their promises of more ambitious help. Enactment was a victory, in particular, for liberal Democrat David R. Obey of Wisconsin, chair of the House Appropriations Committee, who was retiring at the end of the Congress and had made preventing planned teacher layoffs his top priority.

The final bill appropriated $10 billion for a new Education Jobs Fund. It directed the Education Department to use the funds to provide aid to local school districts to prevent layoffs in elementary and secondary schools. Under a "maintenance of effort" requirement, states that received aid could not reduce their education funding in fiscal 2011. *(Additional details and provisions, p. 479)*

The measure appropriated $16.1 billion over two years to extend for six months, through June 30, 2011, an enhanced federal matching rate for state Medicaid programs. The 2009 economic stimulus law (PL 111-5) authorized the extra funding under the Federal Medical Assistance Percentage, but that provision was set to expire on December 31, 2010.

The cost of the bill was covered primarily through eliminating a 13.6 percent increase in food stamp benefits that was enacted in the stimulus law, as of March 31, 2014, reducing mandatory spending by $11.9 billion over ten years. The measure also rescinded previously appropriated but unspent funds from the economic stimulus law and from the Defense Department, reducing spending by $2.8 billion over ten years. It raised $9.8 billion over ten years by closing a number of tax loopholes related to the foreign income of U.S.-based multinational corporations.

2010 Debt Ceiling Increase

Amid an increasingly acrimonious debate over the government's worsening fiscal condition, congressional Democrats succeeded in clearing a record increase in the statutory ceiling on federal borrowing. The increase was large enough to spare the majority party from having to take another vote on the politically painful issue before the November 2010 election.

The joint resolution raised the Treasury Department's borrowing limit to $14.294 trillion, a $1.9 trillion increase above the last ceiling, which was enacted in December 2009. President Barack Obama signed the bill into law February 12, 2010 (H J Res 45—PL 111-139). *(Debt ceiling table, p. 124)*

Budget-conscious moderates in the House won the inclusion of pay-as-you-go (PAYGO) budget rules that required Congress to offset new entitlement spending and tax cuts to avoid increasing the deficit. However, the provisions exempted several major pieces of legislation that were expected during the year. *(Budget enforcement, p. 142)*

Senate Democrats won a public pledge from Obama to create a bipartisan commission that would make recommendations on debt reduction. The president made the commitment after the Senate rejected a proposal to create a debt commission by statute. *(Debt commission, p. 142)*

The majority party had no choice but to clear some increase in the debt limit. The alternative was a government default, with potentially disastrous consequences for both the United States and global economies. But the vote was politically uncomfortable, especially in the midst of a yawning deficit and an increasingly angry electorate. In line with traditional practice, the minority voted against the increase in both chambers.

Democrats tried to clear a long-term increase in the debt ceiling at the end of 2009, but conflict over the debt commission, favored in the Senate, versus the PAYGO rules, insisted on by the House, sank the effort. Instead, Congress cleared a short-term bill (PL 111-123), creating the need for a new bill in early 2010. *(2009 debt limit action, p. 134)*

The Senate passed the debt limit increase (H J Res 45) by a vote of 60–39 along straight party lines January 28. By agreement, sixty votes were required. With no Republican support, Senate Majority Leader Harry Reid, D-Nev., had to secure the votes of Democratic moderates who were unwilling to support a large debt increase without a credible plan to reduce the deficit.

Kent Conrad, D-N.D., chair of the Budget Committee, and Judd Gregg of New Hampshire, the panel's ranking Republican, attempted to create a bipartisan debt commission, or "fiscal task force," by law. The Senate and House would have been bound to vote on the panel's recommendations—a key point for supporters.

But many senators from both parties were uneasy about a provision that would require Congress to hold straight up-and-down votes—without any amendments—on any recommendation supported by a supermajority on the proposed panel. The Conrad-Gregg amendment became a key test of whether lawmakers would commit to such a vote. In the end, they showed an unwillingness to force themselves to go on record for or against a yet-to-be-determined deficit reduction plan. The amendment fell on January 26, seven votes shy of the sixty-vote requirement. The **key vote was 53–46 (R 16–23; D 36–22; I 1–1)**. *(2010 key votes, p. 767)*

The following night, Obama pledged in his State of the Union address to create a similar commission by executive order. He issued the order February 18. *(Text of address, p. 893)*

Because the commission had not been created in statute, there was no legal requirement that Congress vote on the panel's recommendations. Conrad and his group waited to accept the plan until they had written assurances from Reid and House Speaker Nancy Pelosi, D-Calif., backed by Vice President Joseph R. Biden Jr., that the recommendations would receive floor votes. Pelosi pledged to hold a vote on the recommendations if the Senate passed them first.

In other action during the floor debate, the Senate adopted, 60–40, along party lines, an amendment to write the PAYGO budget rules into law. House leaders had made it clear that support for the commission in their chamber hinged on the pay-as-you-go amendment.

The House on February 4 adopted a self-executing rule (H Res 1065) that concurred in the Senate-passed debt ceiling. The vote was 217–212. The House then concurred in the Senate's PAYGO amendment, 233–187, clearing the resolution.

Budget Enforcement Rules—PAYGO

For the first time in more than a decade, Congress enacted statutory pay-as-you-go (PAYGO) budget rules as part of a joint resolution increasing the ceiling on the federal debt. The budget provisions were attached to the debt measure at the insistence of the House in exchange for an agreement by the Senate to a presidentially appointed commission on the federal debt. The White House "strongly" supported the PAYGO provisions, as well as the rest of the debt limit legislation. President Barack Obama signed the measure into law February 12 (H J Res 45—PL 111-139). *(Debt limit, p. 141; debt commission, below)*

The statutory rules required that new legislation that changed existing mandatory spending or revenue laws be "budget neutral," meaning that it would not increase the deficit. A report by the Office of Management and Budget (OMB) at the end of each session had to show whether the combination of all such legislation would increase the deficit; if so, the increase had to be offset through sequestration, or automatic across-the-board cuts, in many, but not all, mandatory programs. The rules did not apply to discretionary spending, which is enacted separately under the annual appropriations bills.

PAYGO rules were originally enacted in 1990 under the Budget Enforcement Act, part of a huge budget reconciliation bill (PL 101-508). The provisions were extended in 1997 (PL 105-33), but they expired at the end of 2002. Subsequent efforts to restore PAYGO rules were unsuccessful, mainly because of partisan disagreements over whether to cover both entitlements and taxes or, as Republicans wanted, to apply the rules to taxes only. *(Congress and the Nation Vol. VII, p. 55; Vol. X, p. 50; Vol. XI, p. 60)*

Both chambers adopted internal PAYGO rules, but as rules, they had no enforcement mechanism and were regularly waived to pass legislation that had the net effect of increasing the budget deficit. The House passed a PAYGO bill in 2009 (HR 2920), but the Senate did not act on it.

However, when Republicans regained control of the House following the 2010 elections, they put into the chamber's rules a new "cut-as-you-go" requirement that made it out of order to consider a bill or joint resolution that would have the net effect of increasing mandatory spending. The rule replaced the "pay-as-you-go" rule, which applied to both mandatory spending increases and tax cuts and allowed increases or mandatory spending reductions to be used to offset each other.

MAJOR PROVISIONS

Under the new statutory rules, legislation with PAYGO implications had to include an estimate by the Congressional Budget Office (CBO) of the budgetary effect, if one was available. OMB was required to maintain continuously updated scorecards showing the five- and ten-year effects of PAYGO-related legislation brought to the floor during the session. Within fourteen days of the end of a session, OMB had to issue a public report on the net effects on the deficit of the year's legislation subject to PAYGO rules.

A key feature of the rules was provisions on sequestration. If OMB determined that the net effect was an increase in the deficit over five or ten years, the agency would develop a sequestration order that would reduce entitlement and mandatory programs by enough to offset the shortfall. The president would then issue the sequestration order. A number of programs were exempt from the across-the-board cuts, including Social Security, certain veterans' programs, net interest on the debt, some refundable tax credits, and certain low-income and economic recovery programs.

Items designated as emergency spending were excluded from OMB's PAYGO calculations. However, in the Senate, a three-fifths majority was required to waive a point of order against emergency spending in a bill. If the point of order was sustained, the emergency items would be dropped automatically.

The law also effectively made four categories of legislation exempt from the PAYGO requirements through December 31, 2011: a permanent extension of middle-class tax cuts enacted during the presidency of George W. Bush (PL 107-16, PL 108-27); a five-year extension of the so-called Medicare "doc fix" to prevent cuts in Medicare payments to physicians; a two-year extension of the 2009 estate tax exemptions and rates; and a similar two-year reprieve for legislation to keep the alternative minimum tax from hitting millions more households. *(Estate tax, p. 146)*

LEGISLATIVE ACTION

On January 28, the Senate voted, 60–40, to add the statutory PAYGO provisions to the debt limit legislation. Republicans unanimously opposed the amendment, calling it "full of holes." The Senate passed the debt limit bill, 60–39, later the same day. By agreement, at least sixty votes were required on both votes.

Inclusion of the PAYGO language was essential to getting House support for the debt limit. The House in turn accepted a presidentially created bipartisan deficit control commission, a compromise with Senate moderates who opposed the PAYGO provision, especially because it excluded the four pieces of legislation.

On February 4, the House adopted a self-executing rule (H Res 1065) that concurred in the debt ceiling portion of the Senate-passed bill. Members then concurred in the Senate's PAYGO provisions, 233–187, clearing the joint resolution.

Presidential Debt Panel Fails

President Barack Obama's eighteen-member debt commission fell short of the votes needed to send its plan to address the nation's fiscal problems to Capitol Hill. Leaders from both parties nonetheless said the panel's proposals, released on December 3, 2010, would be part of the continuing debate.

The bipartisan commission—formally, the National Commission on Fiscal Responsibility and Reform—was charged with making recommendations to reduce the deficit to about 3 percent of gross domestic product (GDP) by fiscal 2015, as well as to address the growth of entitlement spending and the need to slow the increase in the debt over the long term.

The commission had little authority on its own to force action. Its power lay in how much the president and party leaders stood behind its proposals. Senate Majority Leader Harry Reid, D-Nev., pledged in writing to bring the recommendations to the floor for a vote if a supermajority of the panel supported them, and Speaker Nancy Pelosi, D-Calif., promised to hold a vote if the Senate passed them. Only eleven of the eighteen members supported the panel's recommendations, three short of the fourteen needed to force a vote in Congress.

Obama established the commission by executive order on February 18, 2010. He had pledged to do so in his January 27 State of the Union address, the day after the Senate rejected an attempt to create a similar panel by statute. Senate moderates made the founding of such a commission a condition of their support for a critical increase in the ceiling on the federal debt. *(Debt limit, p. 141; State of Union address, p. 893)*

The commission was led by presidential appointees Erskine Bowles, former chief of staff to President Bill Clinton, and former Republican senator Alan K. Simpson of Wyoming. Obama also appointed four more members, and the rest were named by the House and Senate majority and minority leaders. Obama named Dave Cote, chief executive of the technology firm Honeywell; Ann Fudge, a former chief executive of Young & Rubicam Brands; Alice Rivlin, a former Federal Reserve official and former director of the Congressional Budget Office and Office of Management and Budget; and Andy Stern, president of the Service Employees International Union.

Pelosi appointed Democratic representatives John M. Spratt Jr. of South Carolina, chair of the Budget Committee; Xavier Becerra of California, vice chair of the Democratic caucus; and Jan Schakowsky of Illinois. House Minority Leader John A. Boehner, R-Ohio, appointed Republican representatives Paul D. Ryan of Wisconsin, Ways and Means ranking member Dave Camp of Michigan, and Jeb Hensarling of Texas.

Reid appointed Democratic senators Kent Conrad of North Dakota, chair of the Budget Committee; Finance Committee Chair Max Baucus of Montana; and Majority Whip Richard J. Durbin of Illinois. Senate Minority Leader Mitch McConnell, R-Ky., appointed Republican senators Judd Gregg of New Hampshire, ranking member of the Budget Committee; Michael D. Crapo of Idaho; and Tom Coburn of Oklahoma.

Throughout the spring and summer, the panel held a series of public and private meetings. On November 10, with little fanfare and on short notice, the two leaders of the commission released a draft proposal that suggested, among scores of other proposals, an eventual increase in the Social Security retirement age to sixty-nine; an end to many tax breaks, including the popular home mortgage deduction; trimming federal Medicare payments; charging admission to Smithsonian facilities; and raising the federal gas tax.

Some fellow commissioners praised the boldness of Bowles and Simpson, but reaction to the suggested solutions was, at best, less than enthusiastic among the sixteen other members of the panel, especially lawmakers. Republicans Ryan, Camp, and Hensarling, for example, stressed the positive but came nowhere near endorsing the draft. "This is a provocative proposal, and while we have concerns with some of their specifics, we commend the co-chairs for advancing the debate," the three said in a joint statement. "We will continue to work toward solutions that help spur economic growth and restrain the explosive growth of government spending."

On the left, the response was generally blunter. Democrat Schakowsky ripped into the Social Security and Medicare proposals. "We can all agree that the fiscal path we are on is unsustainable, and something must be done," she said, "but it certainly cannot be done on the backs of America's elderly and disabled." Pelosi expressed similar sentiments, calling the plan "unacceptable."

Traditional Democratic allies used sharper daggers. An example: "The chairmen of the deficit commission just told working Americans to 'drop dead,'" said AFL-CIO President Richard Trumka.

Bowles and Simpson were unable to bridge these differences, even though they delayed the vote until December 3 in an unsuccessful effort to round up the necessary backing. The eleven members who voted for the report were Bowles, Coburn, Conrad, Cote, Crapo, Durbin, Fudge, Gregg, Rivlin, Simpson, and Spratt.

KEY RECOMMENDATIONS

The following are highlights of the commission proposals:

Discretionary Spending

- Cap discretionary spending through 2020, generating savings of $200 billion in 2015 alone.
- Adopt immediate discretionary cuts, totaling about $50 billion in 2015, including a reduction of the federal workforce, a three-year freeze on lawmakers' pay, a 15 percent cut in White House and congressional budgets and elimination of all earmarks.
- Require equal-share cuts in security and nonsecurity spending.
- Require the president to propose annual limits for war spending.
- Establish a disaster fund to budget ahead for catastrophes.
- Increase the federal gas tax by 15 cents a gallon and dedicate the revenue to the Highway Trust Fund.

Comprehensive Tax Overhaul

- Reduce the size and number of tax breaks and other tax expenditures, which totaled about $1.1 trillion a year.
- Permanently repeal the alternative minimum tax.
- Reduce the top individual tax rate to between 23 percent and 29 percent.
- Establish a single corporate tax rate between 23 percent and 29 percent.

Health Care Cost Containment and Savings

- Develop an improved formula for paying Medicare physicians and fully offset the cost of any annual increase in doctors' reimbursement rates.
- Give the Centers for Medicare and Medicaid Services more authority to combat Medicare fraud and waste, resulting in savings of $1 billion in 2015.
- Increase cost sharing for Medicare enrollees, saving $10 billion in 2015.
- Require health care plans to offer rebates for brand-name drugs in Medicare Part D, reducing anticipated costs by billions in 2015.
- Reduce payments to hospitals for medical education, saving $6 billion through 2020.
- Require states to take on more responsibility for Medicaid administrative costs, saving $260 million in 2015.
- Implement aggressive medical-malpractice changes.
- Establish a long-term budget for total health care spending.

Mandatory Savings

- Bring civil service and military pensions more in line with standard practices in the private sector, resulting in savings of up to $70 billion through 2020.
- Reduce spending on agriculture subsidies, saving $10 billion through 2020.
- Authorize the Pension Benefit Guaranty Corporation to increase premiums to cover budget shortfalls, saving $16 billion through 2020.
- Extend the Federal Communications Commission's authority to auction radio spectrum licenses.

Social Security Changes

- Gradually transition to a more progressive benefit formula.
- Gradually increase the early- and full-retirement ages.
- Enhance benefits for the very old and the long-term disabled.
- Allow beneficiaries to collect half their benefits at age sixty-two.
- Create a hardship exemption for those who cannot work past sixty-two but who do not qualify for disability benefits.
- Gradually increase the portion of wages subject to Social Security tax until it covers 90 percent of wages by 2050.

Bush Administration Tax Cuts Extended

Less than a week before Congress adjourned the 111th Congress on December 22, 2010, lawmakers cleared an $857.8 billion tax and unemployment benefits package that extended George W. Bush–era tax cuts for all Americans for two years. Had Congress not acted, the tax cuts would have expired on December 31, returning income tax rates to the higher levels that prevailed in 2000. President Barack Obama signed the bill into law December 17 (HR 4853—PL 111-312).

The legislation reflected a deal that Obama had reached with Republican leaders in early December. Most Democrats, particularly those in the House, were sharply critical of the agreement, saying Obama had capitulated to Republicans. They were especially angry that the deal extended tax breaks for the wealthy and revived the estate tax on the GOP's more generous terms. But Obama also won some concessions: most significantly a thirteen-month extension of federal emergency unemployment benefits, a year-long reduction in employees' Social Security payroll taxes, and other items that, together, were expected to give the economy a $180 billion boost over the following year. At a signing ceremony for the bill, he praised leaders from both parties and called the legislation "a substantial victory for middle-class families across the country." *(Estate tax, p. 146; payroll tax deduction, pp. 108, 146; unemployment benefits, p. 535)*

The bill did not include spending cuts or tax increases to pay for any of the provisions.

LEGISLATIVE ACTION

Democrats, including Obama, had long called for extending the tax cuts on income, capital gains, and dividends only for individuals making less than $200,000 a year and families making less than $250,000—and letting tax rates for wealthier Americans return to their previous higher rates. But Republicans insisted the tax cuts should be made permanent for all income levels. They also had blocked efforts to extend unemployment benefits past November 30 without corresponding cuts in other spending. *(2001, 2003 tax cuts, Congress and the Nation Vol. XI, pp. 89, 105)*

Democrats had been divided all year over what to do about the expiring tax cuts. Their leaders in both chambers had refused to vote—or undertake any serious debate—on an extension of the cuts before the midterm elections, leaving Obama with little leverage in November when Republicans won the House and made significant gains in the Senate for the next Congress.

After the election, the White House and a small bipartisan group of lawmakers began negotiations aimed at striking a deal. But with Republicans refusing to settle for anything less than a full extension of all the tax cuts, House Democrats took matters into their own hands. The House voted, 234–188, largely along partisan lines December 2 in favor of a measure (HR 4853) to permanently extend the 2001 and 2003 Bush tax cuts for incomes up to $200,000 for individuals and $250,000 for couples filing jointly. Incomes above those levels would have been taxed at higher, 2001 rates beginning January 1, 2011.

Even Democratic leaders in the House acknowledged that the proposal could not get enough votes in the Senate. Majority Leader Steny H. Hoyer, D-Md., acknowledged that the House-passed bill would not be the final product but would serve as the vehicle for a compromise being negotiated in the Senate. Twenty House Democrats voted against the measure, while three Republicans supported it.

Although the White House welcomed the House vote and reaffirmed Obama's position that extending the middle-class breaks "is the most important thing we can do for our economy right now," the administration acknowledged that the GOP would block any proposal that did not also include a multiyear extension of high-income tax cuts.

That reality was confirmed in a Saturday session on December 4, when the Senate demonstrated that excluding the wealthy from the income tax extension was a nonstarter. Senators rejected, 53–36, a motion to limit debate on a proposal offered by Finance Chair Max Baucus, D-Mont., that would have made the income tax cuts permanent for individuals earning less than $200,000 and couples making less than $250,000. It would have reinstated the estate tax at 2009 levels and extended unemployment insurance benefits, as well as extending a slew of expiring tax provisions. The Senate also rejected cloture, 53–37, on an amendment by Charles E. Schumer, D-N.Y., that would have permanently extended the tax cuts on income under $1 million.

Two days later, on December 6, Obama announced the agreement with GOP leaders. Liberals' anger—over both the deal and the fact they had been excluded from the negotiations—bubbled over on December 9, when a united bloc of House Democrats won approval of a nonbinding resolution calling on Speaker Nancy Pelosi, D-Calif., to keep the Obama-brokered package off the floor.

Obama criticized Democratic opposition to his plan. "I know there's some people in my own party and in the other party who would rather prolong this battle, even if we can't reach a compromise. But I'm not willing to let working families across this country become collateral damage for political warfare here in Washington. And I'm not willing to let our economy slip backwards just as we're pulling ourselves out of this devastating recession."

The day after reaching the compromise with Republicans, Obama sent Vice President Joseph R. Biden Jr., back to his old stomping ground in the Senate to lobby former colleagues. On December 10, Obama also brought former president Bill Clinton to the White House press room to pitch the legislation at a news conference, where he spoke at length.

Democratic opposition to the deal had been more restrained in the Senate than in the House, and the chamber had been expected to pass the bill. But the overwhelming 81–19 vote on December 15 came as something of a surprise and added strong momentum for the House to clear the measure unchanged. The key vote came December 13, when the Senate agreed to invoke cloture and thereby limit debate on the bill on a **key vote of 83–15 (R 37–5; D 45–9; I 1–1)**, far more than the sixty votes required. *(2010 key votes, p. 767)*

The bill was only slightly changed from the original agreement. In an effort to end the standoff between House Democrats and the White House, leaders had included several renewable-energy incentives, including an extension of a popular renewable-energy grant program and an extension of ethanol subsidies.

Final action came just before midnight on December 17, when the House cleared the bill on a **key vote of 277–148 (R 138–36; D 139–112)**. The vote followed a last-gasp attempt by liberals to derail the package. Their policy and procedural objections created a chaotic atmosphere that forced the party's leaders to shift the voting well into the night. *(2010 key votes, p. 767)*

Having surrendered on trying to pare the income tax cuts to apply only to the lower and middle classes, upset liberals turned their attention instead to the estate tax. Ultimately, the House leadership allowed only one amendment, a proposal to set a 45 percent tax rate on estates worth more than $3.5 million for individuals and $7 million for couples. The amendment was defeated, 194–233.

Had the amendment been adopted, the altered bill would have returned to the Senate, where it was certain to have been rejected in light of the delicate negotiations on the issue that had brought Republicans and a smattering of conservative Democrats on board.

Before the vote on the amendment, Pelosi took the floor to denounce the GOP estate tax rate for the wealthy. "Members will have to make up their minds as to how we go forward on the bill," she said, "but I hope that all of them in their consideration of it will vote for the . . . amendment, which addresses the most egregious—with stiff competition, mind you, in this bill—the most egregious provision when it comes to fairness, reducing the deficit, and not creating jobs."

All of the yes votes on the amendment came from Democrats. The few dozen party members who voted no seemed to have come to the same conclusion as their colleagues in the Senate—that the bill included plenty of provisions that they supported, such as the thirteen-month extension of expanded jobless benefits and the AMT "patch," and that the clock was not on their side.

MAJOR PROVISIONS

Following are highlights of the tax and unemployment bill. Estimated costs over ten years are given in parentheses; in some cases, part of the cost is counted as outlays rather than lost revenue.

Individual Tax Cuts

The bill extended provisions of the 2001 and 2003 tax laws for all income levels for 2011 and 2012 at a cost of $407.6 billion over ten years—more than 45 percent of the bill's total price tag. The extensions included:

- Lower marginal income tax rates, including continuation of the 10 percent bracket created under the 2001 law, as well as the retention of the reduced 25 percent, 28 percent, 33 percent, and 35 percent brackets ($186.8 billion).
- The maximum child tax credit of $1,000, as well as provisions that expanded eligibility for the refundable portion ($71.7 billion).
- Relief from the so-called marriage penalty through an increase in the standard deduction for married couples filing jointly ($17.9 billion).
- Simplified rules and expanded eligibility for the earned-income tax credit and provisions that increased the income range at which the credit phased out for married couples ($8.9 billion).

Dividends and Capital Gains

The two-year extension of individual tax cuts included the maximum rate of 15 percent on capital gains and dividends. The tax rate for capital gains for taxpayers in the two lowest brackets may be zero ($53.2 billion).

Alternative Minimum Tax

A two-year "patch" increased the amount of income that was exempt from the alternative minimum tax (AMT) and allowed various nonrefundable personal credits to be claimed against the tax. The exemption was set at $47,450 for individuals and $72,450 for couples filing jointly in 2010, increasing to $48,450 and $74,540, respectively, in 2011. The purpose was to prevent an estimated 25 million additional taxpayers from falling under the AMT, which was created to prevent wealthy taxpayers from escaping taxes ($136.7 billion).

Estate Tax

The estate tax, which lapsed at the end of 2009, was reinstated for two years at a 35 percent top rate for estates worth more than $5 million. The top rate in 2009 was 45 percent with a $3.5 million exemption. Without congressional action, the tax would have reverted to the pre-2001 level, with a 55 percent top rate and $1 million exemption. (Estimated cost: $68.1 billion over ten years.) *(Details, this page)*

"Tax Extenders"

The bill extended a number of expired tax provisions through fiscal 2011 at a total ten-year cost of $55.3 billion. They included the research and experimentation credit, a deduction for state and local sales taxes in lieu of state income taxes, an above-the-line deduction for qualified education expenses, temporary expensing rules for small businesses, and tax incentives for biodiesel and renewable diesel fuel. *(Details, p. 147)*

Unemployment Insurance

The bill extended, through the end of 2011, emergency federal unemployment insurance benefits for jobless workers who had exhausted their state benefits. The extension was retroactive to November 30, 2010, the last time the benefits, which could provide as much as ninety-nine weeks of assistance in some states, had expired ($56.5 billion) *(Details, p. 535)*

Payroll Tax Reduction

Employees' half of the payroll tax was reduced to 4.2 percent from 6.2 percent in 2011. The employer's half was unchanged. Self-employed individuals were subject to a rate of 10.4 percent instead of 12.4 percent ($111.7 billion).

Estate Taxes

Congress revived the estate tax for two years as part of a year-end package that centered on an extension of expiring income tax cuts and unemployment benefits (HR 4853—PL 111-312). The bill restored the tax for 2011 and 2012 at a top rate of 35 percent of the value of estates in excess of $5 million per spouse. It also set a 35 percent tax rate on gifts of $1 million or more given before death in 2010 and unified the gift tax with the estate tax in 2011.

The estate tax had long been a sore point between the two parties. Most Republicans wanted to do away altogether with what many of them called the "death tax." Most Democrats wanted to retain the tax, arguing that repealing it not only would be an expensive giveaway to the wealthy but would also increase the federal budget deficit. In 2001, a compromise of sorts was reached, when Congress agreed to phase out the estate tax gradually until it vanished for one year in 2010. The phaseout was part of the 2001 tax cut law (PL 107-16), which was set to expire December 31, 2010. After that, the tax was set to reappear at the 55 percent top rate that had been in effect before 2001, with a per-person exemption of $1 million. *(2001 law, Congress and the Nation Vol. XI, p. 89; Vol. XII, p. 96)*

Most Democrats and virtually all Republicans opposed the zigzag scenario. But they disagreed on the remedy: Republicans hoped to keep the tax at zero or at least make it as low as possible, while liberal Democrats wanted a less generous exemption and rate than that set for 2009.

Supporters of maintaining some levy on the richest estates also worried that restoring the tax once it was eliminated would be very difficult.

2009 LEGISLATIVE ACTION

Both the House and Senate took action on extending the estate tax in 2009, but no final compromise was reached. In April, ten Senate Democrats joined all Republicans in favor of an amendment to the fiscal 2010 budget resolution (S Con Res 13) that allowed for a 35 percent top rate and an exemption of $5 million per person, indexed for inflation. The amendment was dropped in conference, but the 51–48 floor vote demonstrated how difficult it would be for Democrats wanting a lower exemption to prevail in that chamber.

The House voted, 225–200, on December 3, to pass a bill (HR 4154) to make the 2009 exemption of $3.5 million and tax rate of 45 percent permanent, with no inflation adjustment for the exemption in future years. All Republicans and twenty-six Democrats opposed the bill, with most arguing that it would not go far enough in scaling back the politically unpopular tax. The Joint Committee on Taxation calculated that the extension would cost the Treasury $65.7 billion over six years and $233.6 billion over eleven years, compared with returning to the pre-2001 tax rate and exemption levels.

Many of the bill's opponents said they would have backed an alternative (HR 3905) that would have gradually brought the top tax rate down to 35 percent and pushed the exemption up to $5 million. Democratic leaders did not allow that bill to come to the floor.

The House voted, 234–186, to table (or kill) a motion to recommit the bill and replace the text with a permanent repeal. Members also rejected, 187–233, a similar motion to recommit the bill with instructions to substitute a repeal lasting through 2011.

As the end of the session neared, House and Senate leaders tried to negotiate an extension of anywhere from two months to two years, which would have been attached to the defense appropriations package (HR 3326). But they could not reach agreement. Senate Finance Committee Chair Max Baucus, D-Mont., tried to bring up a two-month extension by unanimous consent December 16, but Republicans blocked him.

2010 LEGISLATIVE ACTION

Through most of 2010, the estate tax legislation languished in the Senate because of a standoff within the Democratic caucus. Most in the party preferred to pass something similar to the House bill. But others, including Blanche Lincoln of Arkansas, wanted lower rates and a larger exemption. She and Republican Jon Kyl of Arizona worked out a compromise that would have set the top rate at 35 percent and applied it to the value of estates in excess of $5 million a person.

The plan stalled when Senate leaders decided to hold off on addressing all the expiring Bush-era tax cuts, including lower income tax rates, until after the November election. Senators remained deadlocked after the election, and with the clock ticking and lower income tax rates about to expire, Obama negotiated an $857.8 billion tax and unemployment benefits package with Republican leaders.

Liberal House Democrats were furious—first, that the plan included the Lincoln-Kyl compromise on the estate tax when Obama and most Democrats had long advocated letting the rate rise and the threshold decline; second, that the deal, announced on December 6, extended lower income tax rates for the wealthy; and third, that the Democrats had been shut out of the negotiations. On December 9, a solid bloc of House Democrats approved a nonbinding resolution calling on Speaker Nancy Pelosi, D-Calif., not to bring the package to the floor.

But after a surprisingly lopsided 81–19 Senate vote for the bill—and a warning from the GOP that a change in the estate tax provision would kill the deal—House Democrats had little choice. The leadership allowed only one floor amendment, which would have set a 45 percent rate on individuals' estates worth more than $3.5 million and couples' estates worth more than $7 million. The amendment, which Pelosi urged her caucus to back, was defeated 194–233; all of the support came from Democrats.

The House then cleared the bill, 277–148, after midnight December 17, with 112 Democrats voting nay.

Tax Breaks Extension

After trying in vain for most of the 111th Congress, lawmakers during the 2010 lame duck session cleared legislation that extended several dozen popular tax breaks that had expired at the end of 2009. The provisions became law as part of a large tax package that President Barack Obama negotiated with Republican leaders in December. The centerpiece of the bill was the continuation of 2001 and 2003 tax cuts enacted under President George W. Bush, but the measure also included several other items, among them a long list of so-called tax extenders—tax breaks that Congress usually renewed a year or two at a time. Obama signed the measure December 17 (HR 4853—PL 111-312). *(Tax package, p. 144)*

Lawmakers had considered a variety of proposals to renew the extenders, but disagreements over what else to include in the legislation and how to pay for it doomed the efforts until the end of the session. The final bill had no offsets.

LEGISLATIVE ACTION

The House passed legislation (HR 4213) in December 2009 that would have extended more than forty expiring tax provisions at an estimated cost of $31 billion over ten years. The bill would have been fully offset, mainly through a proposed change in the treatment of "carried interest" earned by venture capitalists and private equity managers who used their investors' money to purchase struggling companies, reshape them, and sell them at a profit. The managers got a flat fee, which was taxed at ordinary income tax rates of up to 35 percent. They also received a stake in the profits, or carried interest, which was taxed at capital gains rates, which in 2009 topped out at 15 percent. Under the House bill, the carried interest would be taxed as regular income and was expected to raise roughly $24.6 billion over ten years.

On March 10, 2010, after eight days of debate, the Senate passed, 62–36, a greatly expanded version of the 2009 House bill. The measure had a price tag in excess of $100 billion. Before passage, Majority Leader Harry Reid, D-Nev., twice mustered more than the sixty votes needed to halt a GOP filibuster. Two motions to invoke cloture—first on the substance of the Senate amendment and then on the bill itself—were adopted 66–34 and 66–33.

Like the original House bill, the measure would have provided about $31 billion in tax break extensions, including the research and development credit, the deduction for teachers' out-of-pocket expenses, and incentives for producing biofuels. It also would have extended tax breaks for people affected by natural disasters, allowed favorable tax treatment for farm equipment, and provided tax incentives for investment in economically distressed areas.

In addition to the tax breaks, the bill would have extended federal unemployment benefits and health insurance subsidies for jobless workers, as well as flood insurance and small-business programs. Other provisions would have extended an adjustment for Medicare doctors' payment, given states a temporary increase in federal Medicaid payments and reauthorized satellite TV law. Most of the extended tax breaks were offset with revenue-raisers, but the other provisions were not. *(Small-business assistance, p. 102; physician payment rates, p. 450; flood insurance, p. 610)*

By the time the measure reached the House floor in late May 2010, the package had swollen to $200 billion, the result of an agreement between Democratic chairs of the Senate Finance and House Ways and Means committees. But with the electorate in an antideficit mood, which was shared by many within their own party's caucus, House Democratic leaders were forced to sharply scale back their ambitions for the package, sending a $113 billion version of the bill back to the Senate on May 28.

The House passed the bill by adopting two amendments. Members agreed to tax-cut and social-spending extensions by a vote of 215–204, and adopted the change to Medicare doctor payments, 245–171. The cuts in the $200 billion package came from the social safety-net extensions. The tax proposals were offset, but the extensions of Medicare payment rates and unemployment benefits were not.

The bill included several new revenue-raisers, the most controversial of which was a proposed change in the tax treatment of "carried interest" earned by real estate investors, venture capitalists, and private equity fund managers. Under the bill, 50 percent of carried-interest earnings, which were taxed as capital gains under existing law, would have been taxed at the higher rate applicable to ordinary income until 2013, when 75 percent would be taxed at the higher rate. Republicans argued that the provision would discourage long-term investment, particularly in startup companies.

Despite an appeal from the president and the House vote, Senate Democrats were unable to break a deadlock over the bill. Reid pulled the measure from the floor June 24 after failing to garner sixty votes for a motion to invoke cloture, which would have ended a GOP filibuster. The vote was 57–41. Several attempts to pare back the bill failed, and Democrats eventually jettisoned the extenders and other provisions and passed the bill, 59–39 on July 20 with only the unemployment extension intact. The House cleared it, 272–152, two days later, and the president signed hours after that (HR 4213—PL 111-157). *(Unemployment, p. 517)*

Although the Senate action appeared to end hopes of passing the extensions, most of the provisions were revived and became law at the end of the year, thanks to the impending expiration of the Bush-era income tax breaks. The inclusion of the tax extenders in the package was relatively noncontroversial.

The Senate passed the package, 81–19, on December 15. The House cleared the measure, 277–148, on December 17, and President Obama signed it into law the same day (HR 4853—PL 111-312).

MAJOR PROVISIONS

The business, energy, and individual extenders renewed for 2010 and 2011 were expected to cost $55.3 billion over ten years. Temporary investment incentives added $21.8 billion. Estimated ten-year costs are given in parentheses.

Business extensions included the research and development tax credit, which generally covered 20 percent of a business' qualified research costs above a certain level ($13.3 billion); a provision that allowed restaurants and retail businesses to recover the costs of improvements over an accelerated, fifteen-year period ($3.6 billion); and a provision that allowed financial service companies to defer U.S. taxes on income earned overseas from active financing operations until the income was transferred to the United States ($9.2 billion).

Energy extensions included a production tax credit for biodiesel and biomass diesel, as well as a ten-cents-per-gallon credit for small agri-biodiesel producers ($2 billion); and tax credits for alcohol fuels and fuel mixtures ($4.9 billion).

Individual extensions included deduction of individual state and local sales taxes in lieu of itemized deductions for state and local income taxes ($5.5 billion); deduction of qualified tuition and other education expenses ($1.2 billion); and an above-the-line deduction for teachers' out-of-pocket classroom expenses ($390 million).

Investment incentives included a full deduction for small businesses in 2011 for the cost of investments in plants and equipment in the year the items were placed in service, rather than depreciating the cost over time. For 2012, they could write off up to 50 percent in the first year ($20.9 billion).

2011–2012

Congress lurched from one fiscal crisis to the next throughout the 112th Congress, always staving off fiscal disaster at the last minute but never fully resolving the issues that drove members to crisis in the first place. Pushed by a large group of legislators who identified with the conservative Tea Party movement, House Republicans insisted on lowering the federal deficit with deep cuts in federal spending, including reductions in entitlement programs such as Medicare and Medicaid and no increases in taxes. Democrats adamantly rejected that position, arguing that the deficit should be addressed by a combination of spending cuts, revenue increases, and a restructuring of entitlement programs.

The crisis in 2011 came over raising the federal debt ceiling. For months conservative House Republicans refused to budge on their demands for slashed federal spending in return for their vote in support of raising the debt level. A series of negotiations, including talks between President Barack Obama and House Speaker John A. Boehner, R-Ohio, came to naught. Not until July 30, just three days before the deadline to avoid default, were Vice President Joseph R. Biden Jr. and Senate Minority Leader Mitch McConnell, R-Ky., able to put together a deal that could pass both chambers. The bill finally cleared on August 2, meeting the deadline with just a few hours to spare. Even then, Standard and Poor's cut its rating on U.S. Treasury debt from AAA for the first time.

The unprecedented battle over the debt limit was the culmination of months of discord over budget policy, which began early in the year when deadlocks over proposed cuts in fiscal 2011 appropriations led to a series of continuing resolutions (CRs) and to the brink of a government shutdown.

Legislators next turned to the fiscal 2012 budget. House Republicans quickly passed a budget resolution that proposed radical changes in entitlement programs along with substantial spending cuts in discretionary spending. The Democratic Senate firmly rejected the House resolution but did not pass its own resolution.

Although the debt ceiling legislation set discretionary budget caps for fiscal 2012 appropriations, GOP conservatives in the House made it clear they would block any appropriations bills that did not reduce discretionary spending even more. That meant Boehner would have needed Democratic votes to pass bills with a higher spending level. A government shutdown was narrowly averted when Congress managed to clear a continuing resolution as the new fiscal year was beginning. Although they needed three more CRs, legislators finally managed to clear all twelve fiscal 2012 appropriations bills before the end of 2011.

The year 2012 opened with Congress and the president facing not only November elections but what came to be known as the "fiscal cliff"—a combination of huge tax increases that would take effect at the start of 2013 when tax cuts enacted during the administration of George W. Bush expired and automatic across-the-board spending cuts were required if Congress did not meet the deficit targets set in the debt ceiling legislation.

For the first few months of the year, relatively little of note happened, with both parties spending much of their

Taxes and Other Revenues as Percentage of Gross Domestic Product, 1935–2013

Fiscal Year	*Individual Income*	*Corporate Income*	*Social Insurance*	*Excise*	*Other*	*Total*
1935	0.8%	0.8%	—	2.1%	1.6%	5.2%
1940	0.9	1.2	1.8%	2.0	0.7	6.8
1945	8.3	7.2	1.6	2.8	0.5	20.4
1950	5.8	3.8	1.6	2.8	0.5	14.4
1955	7.3	4.5	2.0	2.3	0.5	16.6
1960	7.9	4.2	2.8	2.3	0.8	17.9
1965	7.1	3.7	3.2	2.1	0.8	17.0
1970	8.9	3.2	4.4	1.6	0.9	19.0
1975	7.8	2.6	5.4	1.1	1.0	17.9
1980	9.0	2.4	5.8	0.9	1.0	19.0
1985	8.1	1.5	6.4	0.9	0.9	17.7
1986	7.9	1.4	6.4	0.7	0.9	17.4
1987	8.4	1.8	6.5	0.7	0.9	18.4
1988	8.0	1.9	6.7	0.7	0.9	18.2
1989	8.3	1.9	6.7	0.6	0.9	18.4
1990	8.1	1.6	6.6	0.6	1.0	18.0
1991	7.9	1.7	6.7	0.7	0.9	17.8
1992	7.6	1.6	6.6	0.7	0.9	17.5
1993	7.8	1.8	6.5	0.7	0.8	17.6
1994	7.8	2.0	6.6	0.8	0.8	18.1
1995	8.1	2.1	6.6	0.8	0.9	18.5
1996	8.5	2.2	6.6	0.7	0.8	18.8
1997	9.0	2.2	6.6	0.7	0.8	19.2
1998	9.6	2.2	6.6	0.7	0.9	19.9
1999	9.6	2.0	6.6	0.8	0.9	19.8
2000	10.2	2.1	6.6	0.7	0.9	20.6
2001	9.7	1.5	6.8	0.6	0.8	19.5
2002	8.1	1.4	6.6	0.6	0.7	17.6
2003	7.2	1.2	6.5	0.6	0.7	16.2
2004	6.9	1.6	6.3	0.6	0.7	16.1
2005	7.5	2.2	6.4	0.6	0.7	17.3
2006	7.9	2.7	6.3	0.6	0.7	18.2
2007	8.4	2.7	6.3	0.5	0.7	18.5
2008	8.0	2.1	6.3	0.5	0.7	17.3
2009	6.6	1.0	6.4	0.4	0.7	15.1
2010	6.3	1.3	6.0	0.5	1.0	15.1
2011	7.3	1.2	5.5	0.5	0.9	15.4
2012	7.3	1.6	5.4	0.5	1.0	15.8
2013*	7.6	1.8	5.9	0.5	0.9	16.7

SOURCE: Office of Management and Budget, *Historical Tables, Budget of the United States Government: Fiscal Year 2014* (Washington, D.C.: U.S. Government Printing Office, 2013). Table 2.3.

NOTE: The Social Insurance category includes Social Security, Medicare, railroad, and other retirement programs, and unemployment insurance. The Other category principally includes estate and gift taxes and customs duties. * Estimate time disparaging each other and positioning themselves for the November election. In a deal brokered by the White House and a bipartisan congressional leadership team, legislators agreed in September to suspend the fiscal 2013 appropriations process and clear legislation that continued spending through March 27, 2013. The move averted a government shutdown right before the election; it also removed disputes over appropriations from the coming fight over the fiscal cliff.

Although the two chambers had passed competing tax bills in July, negotiations to avoid the fiscal cliff did not get serious until after the November elections. Even then, there were several weeks of twists and turns before Congress and the president were able to agree on a compromise that preserved the income tax cuts for all but the highest-income earners and pushed off the sequestration for three months. The legislation was not cleared until January 1, 2013.

Although the compromise averted the immediate fiscal cliff, it left several major issues, including a hike in the debt ceiling and how to make required spending cuts, for the 113th Congress, which appeared likely to be even more divided than the 112th.

Fiscal 2011 Omnibus Appropriations

Deep differences over federal spending priorities and deficit reduction kept the two parties from completing the 2011 appropriations process until April 2011, when the fiscal year was more than half over. Congress cleared a package of fiscal 2011 bills (HR 1473—PL 112-10) April 14 that provided $1.1 trillion in discretionary budget authority, a $39.9 billion reduction from existing law, including $12 billion in cuts that had been made in three earlier stopgap measures. President Barack Obama signed the measure into law the following day.

Democrats, who controlled both chambers in the 111th Congress, had left all twelve of the fiscal 2011 spending bills on the table when they adjourned in December 2010. Before leaving, they cleared a measure that gave the next Congress until March 4, 2011, to find a solution. That measure (PL 111—322) kept most programs at the previous year's levels but allowed a long list of exceptions, which resulted in an annualized cost of $1.2 billion above the total enacted for fiscal 2010. *(2010 action, p. 137)*

The March 4 deadline came and went, with the GOP-controlled House and the Democratic-run Senate at loggerheads over spending cuts. Lawmakers kept the government limping along with a series of three short-term spending bills known as continuing resolutions (CRs). Federal agencies became increasingly critical of the stopgap approach to funding; the Pentagon warned that the funding uncertainty was affecting the already-challenging transition from military to civilian leadership in Iraq as well as U.S. efforts in Afghanistan.

The conservative House Republican Study Committee, buttressed by a sizable class of freshmen swept into office in January 2011 on promises to slash spending, demanded deep cuts. That set up a conflict with the Senate and the White House, both of which initially balked at any trimming. In trying to cobble together a majority in the House, Speaker John A. Boehner of Ohio was forced to walk a fine line in negotiating a deal that would minimize defections among Republicans committed to bigger cuts while getting enough moderate Democrats on board to make up the difference.

The following chronicles the fiscal disputes and stopgap spending bills that preoccupied Congress in the winter and early spring of 2011 and that helped to set the stage for the dramatic confrontations over taxing and spending that dominated the 112th Congress.

EARLY LIMITS

House Republicans began setting the stage for significant spending cuts during the opening days of the session. The rules of the House (H Res 5), which were adopted January 5 on a 238–191 party-line vote, gave Budget Committee Chair Paul D. Ryan, R-Wis., the authority to set the discretionary spending caps for the remainder of fiscal 2011. Under the regular budget process, the annual caps were established as part of a budget resolution that was adopted by both chambers, but Congress had not passed a budget resolution for fiscal 2011. *(Details, p. 156)*

The House majority followed up on the rule January 25 by adopting a resolution (H Res 38) instructing Ryan to set a ceiling on nonsecurity discretionary spending that was at or below levels enacted for fiscal 2008—before Congress had plowed hundreds of billions of dollars into bailing out the financial services sector and stimulating an economy that was in recession. The resolution, which was adopted 265–165, translated into a $58 billion reduction from Obama's fiscal 2011 request of $478 billion for nonsecurity discretionary programs. *(Obama request, p. 157)*

OPENING GOP GAMBIT

Compelled by conservative Republicans, the House passed a bill (HR 1) on February 19 to fund the government for the remainder of fiscal 2011. It would have provided $1.0 trillion in discretionary budget authority, $100 billion below Obama's fiscal 2011 request—a GOP goal set in the 2010 campaign—and $61.5 billion below the existing spending rate based on the December CR. The reductions were to come almost entirely from nondefense discretionary spending. The bill passed, 235–189, with no Democratic support.

Boehner and other House GOP leaders had planned to pass a more modest version of the bill, which would have reduced overall discretionary spending by $74 billion below Obama's request and by about $32 billion compared with existing spending. The leadership proposal unveiled February 9 would have cut almost $41 billion from nonsecurity spending and provided a net $8 billion increase for security-related programs. Appropriations Chair Harold Rogers, R-Ky., quickly released allocations, known as 302(b)s, dividing the total among the twelve appropriations bills. But GOP conservatives led by freshman members of the Tea Party movement rebelled, forcing the leaders to go back to the drawing board and produce a revised version of HR 1, which went to the floor.

That measure contained a full defense appropriations bill with $516 billion in base funding and $157.8 billion for the wars in Afghanistan and Iraq, 3 percent less than requested but 2 percent more than provided under the fiscal 2010 law. Boehner promised members they could offer as many amendments as they wanted—a sharp contrast with years of tight Democratic control of the floor. The free-wheeling debate took ninety hours and 107 roll-call votes. The House rejected, 147–281, an attempt by the Republican Study Committee to cut an additional $22 billion by reducing most accounts by 5.5 percent. Continuing appropriations for the departments of Homeland Security, Veterans Affairs, and State would have been exempt, along with aid to Israel.

The drive for spending cuts led to approval of a Republican amendment that struck $450 million in funds opposed by the Pentagon for an alternative engine for the F-35 Joint Strike Fighter. The House had rejected the administration proposal in the past, but this time the amendment was adopted 233–198.

A large number of adopted amendments reflected Republican policy priorities. They included language to bar the use of funds made available by the bill to pay salaries to implement any portion of the 2010 health care overhaul (PL 111-148, PL 111-152). The amendment—one of several aimed at killing all or part of the overhaul—was adopted, 241–187. No Republican voted against the amendment; three Democrats supported it.

Other GOP amendments adopted by the House would have prohibited the Environmental Protection Agency (EPA) from regulating greenhouse gas emissions from stationary sources, barred the EPA from regulating surface coal mining operations, stopped any federal funding for Planned Parenthood Federation of America, Inc., or any of its affiliates, and reduced funding for the National Endowment for the Arts.

On March 9, the Senate rejected both the House-passed measure and a rival Democratic spending plan that called for much more modest cuts. The House-passed bill was defeated, 44–56, with all Democrats voting against it. Three of the chamber's most conservative Republicans (Jim DeMint of South Carolina, Mike Lee of Utah, and Rand Paul of Kentucky) also voted no, signaling that hard-line budget hawks would press for even deeper cuts.

The Democratic alternative would have made $4.7 billion in cuts compared with existing law, taking the funds from both defense and nondefense discretionary programs. It was rejected 42–58, with ten Democrats and Vermont independent Bernard Sanders voting against the measure; some said they wanted deeper cuts and others favored smaller reductions.

STALEMATE AND TEMPORARY MEASURES

Before the Senate acted, Congress had cleared a two-week CR (H J Res 44—PL 112-4), good through March 18. The measure was cleared on March 2, just two days before the existing CR expired. At the insistence of House GOP leaders, the legislation cut $4 billion from existing law as embodied in the December CR, but it did not contain the controversial policy riders favored by GOP conservatives.

The bill passed by overwhelming bipartisan margins in both chambers, allowing both parties to say they were reining in appropriations while buying time for what was expected to be a tougher spending showdown later in the month.

The cuts were relatively noncontroversial: $1.2 billion from terminating eight programs that Obama had labeled as wasteful in his recently released fiscal 2012 budget request, and $2.7 billion from eliminating earmarks contained in fiscal 2010 spending laws and presumably carried over in the December CR.

With the immediate threat of a government shutdown averted, negotiations on a more permanent bill got under way at the Capitol on March 3, with Vice President Joseph R. Biden Jr. leading the administration's team. The meeting included the four top congressional leaders: Boehner; Senate Majority Leader Harry Reid, D-Nev.; Senate Minority Leader Mitch McConnell, R-Ky.; and House Minority Leader Nancy Pelosi, D-Calif.

Despite sporadic negotiations, the standoff over a longer-term bill continued, and Congress avoided a shutdown with another CR (lasting only three weeks) through April 8. The House passed the measure, 271–158, on March 15, the Senate cleared it, 87–13, on March 17, and the president signed it the next day. (H J Res 48—PL 112-6).

The measure cut another $6 billion from existing funding, meeting GOP demands for $2 billion in spending cuts per week. House Republican leaders, who drafted the bill, once again found relatively noncontroversial places to cut, mainly programs targeted by Obama for elimination and 2010 earmarks that had not yet been canceled.

Although Boehner prevailed, the vote indicated potential trouble for the Speaker. Fifty-four members of his caucus defected, most of them unhappy over the exclusion of policy riders, forcing him to rely on Democratic votes to pass the measure. Leaders in both parties and chambers said this CR should be the final short-term extension, acknowledging that stopgap funding was no way to run a government.

A planned one-week recess left lawmakers with only two weeks to break the impasse. With a government shutdown looking more likely by the day, negotiators alternated between closed-door bargaining and public posturing. Finally, with a midnight deadline little more than an hour away and federal workers prepared for furloughs, a deal was announced April 8. It took another week to write the bill and clear it.

One last short-term measure (HR 1363), which was good through April 15 and cut an additional $2 billion, kept the government operating in the interim. The Senate passed the temporary bill (HR 1363—PL 112-8) by voice vote April 8, and the House cleared it, 348–70, after midnight.

CLOSING THE BOOKS ON FISCAL 2011

Just five-and-a-half months were left in the fiscal year when the House passed the final bill, 260–167, on April 14. The Senate cleared the measure, 81–19, later the same day. In the end, Boehner lost fifty-nine Republicans—less than a quarter of the GOP caucus—who joined 108 Democrats in opposing the measure. Among GOP members in the Tea Party caucus, thirty-five voted for the bill and twenty-one against it. Although he won a large majority of Republicans, Boehner had to secure support from at least three dozen Democrats. In the end, eighty-one House Democrats voted for the package, including Minority Whip Steny H. Hoyer, D-Md.; Pelosi voted against it.

The minority leader said that because her caucus was not part of the negotiations, she felt "no ownership" for the agreement. She said Democrats who opposed the bill were expressing dissatisfaction not with the president, but rather "about the particulars" of the legislation. Hoyer said he voted for the package to keep the government open and to allow the House to "move on and address other pressing issues, like job creation and the budget for next year."

The Congressional Budget Office (CBO) issued an estimate the day of the vote saying the $1.1 trillion bill would reduce actual spending by just $352 million in fiscal 2011. The appropriators based their estimates on budget authority, the authority given in the spending bills, while the CBO was looking at outlays, the money that would actually be spent during the fiscal year. The CBO pegged the overall reduction in outlays at $20 billion to $25 billion compared with fiscal 2010 spending. The budget office said the vast majority of the reductions would fall in the five-year period from fiscal 2012 through 2016.

The $39.9 billion in budget authority cuts was a compromise between Boehner's last offer of $40 billion, down from an earlier plan to offer $61.5 billion, and Reid and Obama's figure of $38 billion, up from an earlier plan for $33 billion.

Democrats prevailed in blocking most of the major GOP policy provisions, although they agreed to allow separate votes to enable members to go on the record on abortion and on "defunding" the health care overhaul. Both proposals—offered as enrolling resolutions—were adopted in the House but killed in the Senate.

The House adopted, 241–185, a resolution (H Con Res 36) that would have blocked federal funding of Planned Parenthood, but the Senate rejected it, 42–58. Antiabortion lawmakers had tried for years to cut funding for the organization because its services included providing abortions. The House also adopted, 240–185, a resolution (H Con Res 35) that would have barred the use of funds to implement the health care overhaul, but the Senate rejected it, 47–53.

Although the bill reduced funding for the EPA, it did not bar the agency from regulating greenhouse gas emissions.

Some conservative activists took umbrage at what they regarded as paltry savings under the bill. "If House Republicans vote for the bipartisan compromise," RedState.org blogger Erick Erickson wrote shortly before the vote, "they should be driven into the street by the Tea Party movement and horsewhipped—metaphorically speaking. In reality, they should be primaried."

Still, Boehner emerged relatively unscathed within his caucus. GOP dissenters consistently blamed Democrats, rather than the Speaker, for what they considered a failed bill. "This is the first time we've all been in this environment—the first time we've had a Republican majority dealing with this president, first time we've had a Republican majority dealing with the Senate," Boehner said at one point. "Understand that this process that we're in is likely to be repeated a number of times."

MAJOR PROVISIONS

The fiscal 2011 appropriations package (HR 1473—PL 112-10) contained all twelve of the annual appropriations bills. Following is a brief summary of each bill.

Agriculture

Funding for Agriculture Department food safety, international food aid, and nutrition programs were largely protected from bigger cuts sought by the Republican-controlled House—but the programs did not escape unscathed. The Senate Appropriations Committee called the measure "very austere."

The bill provided $125.4 billion, most of it in mandatory funding for programs such as farm supports and food stamps. Discretionary funding was set at $20 billion, roughly $3 billion below the fiscal 2010 level and $3 billion less than President Obama requested. Discretionary programs would have received $1.9 billion less under the earlier GOP version passed by the House (HR 1).

The Women, Infants, and Children (WIC) nutrition program received $6.7 billion, a reduction from fiscal 2010 levels but less than the cut proposed by the House. Appropriators said in a statement that the final bill would "fully fund participation in the program" and that the decrease from fiscal 2010 was because of lower-than-anticipated participation.

The Food and Drug Administration received an increase, but funding for the Food Safety and Inspection Service (the nation's primary foreign food assistance program), and rural housing and community programs, was reduced, though not to the levels in HR 1. Total savings from limitations on spending under the 2008 farm bill were $1.5 billion, some of which came from cuts for administering mandatory programs. The result was an 11 percent reduction from fiscal 2010 spending but an increase of 33 percent over the amount in HR 1.

Commerce-Justice-Science

Programs funded under the annual Commerce-Justice-Science appropriations bill were among the hardest-hit. Total discretionary funding was set at $53.4 billion—about $10.9 billion, or 17 percent, less than the amount appropriated in fiscal 2010, and 14 percent less than Obama requested. The House-passed GOP bill (HR 1) would have provided $775 million less.

More than half the shortfall, $6.2 billion, represented a cut for the Census Bureau, whose budget had previously been raised to cover its needs for carrying out the 2010 census. The Census Bureau cut accounted for nearly all of the reduction for the Commerce Department, which received $7.6 billion under the spending package, $6.5 billion less than in fiscal 2010.

The Justice Department received $27.4 billion, about $700 million less than in fiscal 2010 and $2.3 billion less than the president sought. The largest Justice Department cuts came from state and local law enforcement assistance grants, including the Community Oriented Policing Services (COPS) program. The Legal Services Corporation, the country's largest provider of civil legal aid for the poor, received $405 million, $15 million below fiscal 2010 funding. HR 1 would have cut the service, another GOP target, by $55 million.

The bill provided $18.5 billion for the National Aeronautics and Space Administration (NASA), a cut of about $200 million from fiscal 2010 and $515 million less than requested. The bill effectively nullified a provision in the fiscal 2010 appropriations law (PL 111-117) that barred the use of appropriated funds to terminate the Constellation space exploration program or to create new space exploration programs unless such activities were provided for in later appropriations laws. Policy language in the bill barred NASA or the Office of Science and Technology Policy from using funds in the bill to develop or carry out any program with China or any Chinese-owned company unless specifically authorized by law. That provision also prohibited using appropriated funds to host Chinese officials at NASA facilities.

Defense

Defense was the only department to receive a funding increase under the omnibus spending package. The bill provided $513 billion in base defense spending, $5 billion more than enacted in fiscal 2010, but roughly $18.1 billion less than the president requested for fiscal 2011. In addition, the bill included $157.7 billion for overseas contingency operations, mainly military activities in Afghanistan and Iraq. The amount equaled the president's request.

The defense title fully funded a 1.4 percent pay raise for military personnel. The deal added about $670 million more than requested to cover shortfalls in military personnel accounts that resulted from delays in reaching agreement on fiscal 2011 spending levels.

The bill did not include funds for the controversial F-35 Joint Strike Fighter alternative-engine program, which the president and Defense Secretary Robert M. Gates had ordered terminated.

Increased funding in the bill included an additional $850 million for the National Guard and reserves to address shortfalls in equipment. The bill also provided money to replace helicopters and fixed-wing aircraft lost in battle, and it included $2.5 billion for intelligence, surveillance, and reconnaissance programs identified by Gates as a high priority for troops overseas.

A total of $3.4 billion went to fully fund Mine Resistant Ambush Protected vehicles. Funds also were added to test and procure "double-V" hull modification for the Stryker vehicle, for added protection from improvised explosive devices.

The overseas contingency operations funding also included $11.6 billion for the Afghanistan Security Forces Fund, $1.5 billion for the Iraq Security Forces Fund, $500 million for the Commander's Emergency Response Program, $400 million for the new Afghanistan Infrastructure fund, and $800 million for the Pakistan Counterinsurgency fund.

Energy-Water

The Energy Department, Army Corps of Engineers, and Interior Department water projects received a total of $31.8 billion under the spending package. That was a decrease of $1.7 billion, or 5 percent, from fiscal 2010 spending for the same programs, but $1.9 billion more than in the original House-passed GOP bill (HR 1).

The bill provided $25.6 billion for the Department of Energy, $10.5 billion below the fiscal 2010 level. Nearly half the department's total, $10.7 billion, was devoted to the National Nuclear Security Administration (NNSA), an agency charged with ensuring the safety, security, and reliability of the country's nuclear weapons stockpile. Obama had pledged to increase funding for modernization of the aging nuclear weapons stockpile and facilities as part of getting Senate support for the New Strategic Arms Reduction Treaty with Russia in 2010. *(New START Treaty, p. 289)*

The department's energy efficiency and renewable energy programs received $1.8 billion, down 18 percent, but the Science Office, which funded work on basic energy research, nuclear physics, biological and environmental sciences, and other related endeavors, received $4.9 billion, about the same as in fiscal 2010.

The new Advanced Research Projects Agency-Energy (ARPA-E) office, which provided short-term funding for research into promising but high-risk energy technologies, received $180 million. The House bill would have cut the amount to $50 million.

The Army Corps of Engineers, charged with carrying out civil flood control, navigation, and ecosystem restoration projects throughout the country, received $4.9 billion,

9 percent below the fiscal 2010 level. The bill provided $1.1 billion for Interior water projects in the western United States, $578 million less than in fiscal 2010.

Financial Services

Agencies funded through the Financial Services appropriations title received a total of $22 billion in the spending package (PL 112-10), about 10 percent less than comparable fiscal 2010 discretionary funding and 14 percent less than requested. However, the total was $1.5 billion higher than the level that would have been provided under the earlier House-passed bill (HR 1).

The funding covered the Treasury Department; the White House and Executive Office of the President; the federal judiciary; the District of Columbia; and numerous independent agencies. The spending package cut most Treasury and Executive Office of the President accounts and reduced funding for construction of new federal buildings by more than $800 million.

The bill provided $12.1 billion, equal to the fiscal 2010 level and $600 million more than in HR 1, for the IRS, which accounted for the bulk of the Treasury Department budget. The bill provided a $13 million increase for the inspector general of the Troubled Asset Relief Program (TARP; PL 110-343), enacted in 2008 to bail out the financial services industry; the purpose was to provide oversight of the remaining TARP assets. (*TARP oversight, pp. 75, 76*)

Republican lawmakers won yearly audits, by both private-sector firms and the Government Accountability Office, of the new Consumer Financial Protection Bureau created by the 2010 financial regulatory overhaul (PL 111-203). But Democrats were successful in blocking GOP attempts to restrict the bureau's funding stream to $80 million rather than the roughly $400 million it was expected to receive from the Federal Reserve, where it was to be housed starting in July 2011. Democrats also staved off GOP efforts to cut funding for the Securities and Exchange Commission (SEC) and Commodity Futures Trading Commission (CFTC), which were given broad new responsibilities under the financial regulation law. *(Overhaul, p. 88)*

Policy provisions from the earlier House bill that were dropped included language that would have restricted funding for the implementation of "net neutrality" policies, which bar Internet providers from discriminating between different kinds of content and applications. Restrictions on the Presidential Election Campaign Fund and the use of District of Columbia funding for needle exchange programs to combat the HIV/AIDS epidemic were also omitted.

Homeland Security

The Department of Homeland Security received $41.8 billion in discretionary funds—$800 million, or 2 percent, below the fiscal 2010 level and $1.9 billion below the president's request. The total was $250 million more than would have been provided in the earlier House-passed Republican bill. It was the first time since the department was created in late 2002 that its appropriations had been reduced compared with the previous fiscal year.

Homeland security grants to state and local police, firefighters, and other first-responders were cut to $2.2 billion, down $815 million from the fiscal 2010 level but still $80 million more than in the earlier House bill.

The Federal Emergency Management Agency (FEMA) Disaster Relief Fund received $2.7 billion, a $1.1 billion hike from fiscal 2010 to help cover a shortfall going all the way back to 2005 and Hurricane Katrina. Congress typically provided much of the disaster relief funding on an emergency basis because of the difficulty in calculating the ultimate cost of hurricanes and other catastrophes. The spending package made the funding discretionary, which appropriators said required other discretionary reductions across the board for the department.

The bill also provided $9.9 billion for Customs and Border Protection, including funds sufficient to maintain the existing 21,370 Border Patrol agents; $8.9 billion for the Coast Guard; $5.5 billion for Immigration and Customs Enforcement; and $7.7 billion for the Transportation Security Administration (TSA). It capped the full-time TSA airport screening staff at 46,000. The total included funding for 500 advanced-imaging-technology machines for airports.

Interior-Environment

The Environmental Protection Agency (EPA) bore the brunt of the cuts made in the $29.6 billion interior-environment title of the bill, but the agency emerged from the appropriations showdown with most of its regulatory powers intact. Overall, programs funded through the interior-environment title were reduced by $2.6 billion, or 8 percent, from fiscal 2010. The total was $1.8 billion more than would have been provided under a House-passed Republican bill (HR 1).

Under the final spending package, the EPA received $8.8 billion for fiscal 2011, a reduction of roughly $1.5 billion, or 17 percent, from fiscal 2010 levels and 58 percent of the total cuts in the title. Still, the spending agreement offered the agency a reprieve from far deeper cuts included in the original House-passed bill, which would have reduced funding by $3.3 billion from fiscal 2010. It also omitted House riders targeting EPA policies, including greenhouse gas restrictions and other air and water regulations. However, House Republican appropriators said funding for climate change programs was cut $49 million, or 13 percent, across the spending bill.

Two popular programs that helped finance state and local clean water and drinking water infrastructure improvements were cut by about $1 billion, to $2.5 billion. The EPA was a longtime target for congressional Republicans, who accused the agency of pursuing an overly aggressive regulatory agenda.

Many Interior Department programs also experienced at least some funding reductions.

Labor–Health and Human Services–Education

The departments of Labor, Health and Human Services (HHS), and Education received a total of $157.7 billion in discretionary funding under the spending package, a reduction of $5.5 billion, or about 3 percent, from fiscal 2010. Democrats, however, preserved funding for several programs that House Republicans wanted to zero out, including family planning, Race to the Top grants for well-performing public schools, and the Corporation for Public Broadcasting (CPB). Democrats also fended off most, but not all, of the GOP policy riders.

Many programs that were spared the eradication House Republicans sought in their initial fiscal 2011 spending plan (HR 1) experienced modest to severe cuts under the final measure. Republicans made their mark in a few policy areas, including a provision ensuring that no taxpayer funds, either local or federal, could be used to pay for abortions in the District of Columbia.

Yet many Democratic priorities were protected. The bill provided $14.5 billion for Title I grants to school districts, the same amount enacted for fiscal 2010, and it included $23 billion for Pell grants, maintaining the existing maximum award of $5,550.

The Corporation for Public Broadcasting (CPB), which received appropriations two years in advance and funded National Public Radio and the Public Broadcasting Service, underwent a significant cut but was spared the threat of elimination. For the rest of fiscal 2011, the CPB received $6 million. Republicans noted that the figure represented an $80 million cut from enacted fiscal 2010 funding levels.

One of the final issues to be ironed out in negotiating the overall spending package concerned Planned Parenthood. Although existing law barred the use of federal funding to cover abortions, Republicans said that public funding enabled Planned Parenthood to use its private donations for abortions. The bill reduced the program's funding from $317 million in fiscal 2010 to $300 million, a 5 percent cut. The House GOP bill would have eliminated the funding.

The Centers for Disease Control and Prevention received $5.7 billion, 11 percent less than in fiscal 2010. The bill did not specify spending levels for international HIV/AIDS programs, which received $119 million in fiscal 2010. Community health centers, which provided primary care to millions of low-income people, were cut by $600 million, or 27 percent, from the enacted fiscal 2010 level of $2.2 billion.

Legislative Branch

Congress cut its own operating expenses by about 2 percent compared with fiscal 2010 but made exceptions for the Capitol Police and the CBO. The increases reflected bipartisan consensus that both agencies carried a heavy burden. In an era of increased security concerns there were heightened calls for protecting lawmakers, while the CBO had to keep up with scoring a perennial onslaught of legislation.

The bill reduced House and Senate office operating budgets by 5 percent. In January, the House had adopted a resolution (H Res 22) that made a 5 percent reduction in the fiscal 2011 and 2012 budgets for the offices of House leaders, members, and most committees—except the Appropriations Committee, which had its budget cut by 9 percent under the resolution. The Senate had voted twice to shave its budget by 5 percent.

The spending deal included $1.3 billion for all House staff salaries and office expenses—$55 million less than in fiscal 2010. Senate staff salaries and office expenses fell by $10 million, to about $916 million. Lawmakers did not have to furlough staff, however, as had been proposed by the earlier House-passed spending bill.

Military Construction–Veterans Affairs

The final fiscal 2011 spending bill provided a substantial increase for veterans' programs while cutting back funds for Pentagon military construction projects. Military construction projects received $16.6 billion of the total, a reduction of $6.6 billion, or about 28 percent, but discretionary funding for the Department of Veterans Affairs (VA) rose to $58.8 billion, a gain of about 8 percent above fiscal 2010.

The VA total included $51.1 billion, or 14 percent above fiscal 2010 funding, for VA medical accounts. That was made up of $580 million in new funds for fiscal 2011 and $50.6 billion in advance funds for fiscal 2012. The health administration also could count on $48.2 billion in advance budget authority that had been appropriated the previous year. The system of advance funding guaranteed that the money would be there each year, even if the spending bill was delayed.

The Veterans Benefits Administration received $64.5 billion, including a $448 million boost over fiscal 2010 to process a backlog of disability claims. The measure provided $4.3 billion for treatment and housing programs to aid homeless veterans, as requested, including $799 million in direct programs to combat homelessness.

The cuts in military construction were relatively painless and came mostly from the conclusion of spending on the 2005 round of base closures and realignments. Some other military construction initiatives were being slowed down for various reasons.

State–Foreign Operations

The spending package provided $48.3 billion for State Department and foreign operations. At $8.4 billion, discretionary spending for U.S. diplomatic and development programs remained at approximately the same level as in fiscal 2010.

International organizations and financial institutions took some of the biggest cuts. U.S. contributions to the United Nations and other international organizations dropped by 20 percent, from $1.7 billion to $1.3 billion, compared with fiscal 2010. The Millennium Challenge Corporation, a quasi-independent U.S. development agency, received $205 million less than in fiscal 2010 and $380 million less than requested. Funding for international economic and development assistance was reduced to $8.4 billion, down $379 million from fiscal 2010 levels (not including supplemental spending). That was $1.9 billion less than the president's fiscal 2011 request. Salaries for foreign service officers were frozen.

Some programs escaped far more severe reductions proposed in HR 1. Global health and child survival programs, a top priority for the Obama administration and a main target of the earlier House-passed bill, received $7.8 billion in funding—$850 million more than the original House bill had proposed. Democrats succeeded in eliminating House language that would have barred funding for international aid groups that offered or discussed abortion as a method of family planning. Direct funding for abortions remained illegal.

Transportation—Housing and Urban Development

The bill provided no funding for high-speed rail programs in fiscal 2011, a setback for what Obama considered a legacy transportation project akin to the Interstate Highway System. The rail account was part of the Transportation—Housing and Urban Development (HUD) spending bill, the section of the spending package that took the deepest cuts. Overall, the departments and related agencies received $55.5 billion in discretionary funds, about $12.3 billion, or 18 percent, less than enacted in fiscal 2010 and about 20 percent less than Obama requested. The House-passed GOP version of the bill (HR 1) would have cut $3.1 billion more.

The decision on high-speed rail essentially cut the remaining $1 billion that had not already been slashed by earlier bills. It also rescinded $400 million in high-speed rail money from fiscal 2010 appropriations. When combined with reductions made by earlier short-term continuing resolutions, the total cuts to high-speed rail funding for fiscal 2011 came to $2.9 billion.

The bill also included $41.1 billion for the federal-aid highway program, the same level provided in fiscal 2010 and in HR 1. However, it did not include $650 million for road and bridge improvements.

Among the biggest cuts in the bill was a $2.5 billion rescission of highway contract authority. The authority allowed states to assign federally reimbursable contracts across broad program categories, such as bridge and highway maintenance. The Senate Appropriations Committee said states were not able to use all of their existing contract authority, "so this rescission is not expected to affect states' ability to invest in roads and bridges."

One Obama administration initiative that survived was the so-called TIGER program, which provided competitive grants for significant transportation projects in metropolitan and rural areas. Although the program was cut by about 12 percent, to $528 million, the earlier House-passed bill would have provided no fiscal 2011 funding and rescinded unobligated balances from fiscal 2010.

In the housing area, Congress increased funding for HUD Section 8 low-income housing vouchers to $18.4 billion, about $233 million more than enacted in fiscal 2010. Homeless assistance grants were boosted by about $40 million over fiscal 2010 levels, to $1.9 billion. But funds were reduced for the Community Development Block Grant program, the Public Housing Capital Fund, and the Public Housing Operating Fund.

Fiscal 2012 Budget Resolution

For the second year in a row, Congress failed in 2011 to adopt a joint budget resolution setting annual spending, tax, and deficit targets for the coming year. The new Republican majority in the House pushed through a resolution that proposed deep spending cuts for fiscal 2012 together with radical changes in major entitlement programs such as Medicare and Medicaid. The Democratic Senate rejected that plan, as well as President Barack Obama's budget request, but did not adopt a budget of its own.

The stalemate that resulted was overtaken by an August agreement on a much-contested debt limit law (PL 112-25) that included caps on discretionary appropriations for fiscal years 2012 and 2013. The fiscal 2012 cap of $1.0 trillion was less than 1 percent above fiscal 2011 spending. *(Debt limit bill, p. 160)*

The fiscal 2012 budget request from President Obama and the House budget resolution starkly outlined the major differences between the two parties on federal tax and spending policy as well as their underlying philosophies on the role of government. As the year progressed and the 2012 elections drew nearer, those differences became more and more difficult to bridge.

The debate began in early February—in the midst of a tense partisan battle over the deficit and the twelve unfinished spending bills from the previous year—when House Budget Committee Chair Paul Ryan, R-Wis, released the GOP resolution, followed several days later by the release of the White House's budget request. The president called for a five-year freeze on domestic discretionary spending; a return to higher tax rates for wealthy Americans; and investments in infrastructure, innovation, and education to boost the economy.

In sharp contrast, the Ryan budget proposal, dubbed "The Path to Prosperity," would slash domestic spending to levels prevailing before fiscal 2008, when the recession began and freeze it there for five years. The plan also called for radical changes in the financing of and eligibility for Medicare and Medicaid.

Although Democrats were less than thrilled with Obama's budget proposals—some thought that it was too stringent, while others thought even deeper cuts were needed—virtually all Democrats in both the House and Senate rejected the Ryan proposal nearly out of hand. It took another two months, however, for the drama to reach what seemed like a foregone conclusion—rejection in the Senate of both the House GOP plan and the president's proposal.

OBAMA BUDGET REQUEST

President Obama, releasing his fiscal 2012 budget on February 14, requested $3.7 trillion in outlays for fiscal 2012 and proposed a freeze in domestic discretionary spending over the following five years. The White House's Office of Management and Budget (OMB) said the proposal would reduce the annual deficit by more than $1.1 trillion over a decade.

Obama proposed to preserve tax cuts for the middle class after 2012, when they were set to expire, while allowing taxes on upper-income taxpayers to rise and increasing taxes on multinational corporations.

The White House said the budget would responsibly reduce spending and trim the deficit, while investing in education, innovation, and infrastructure to make Americans more competitive in a global economy. "It puts us on a path towards having a sustainable federal budget where the deficit comes down to a level where we're not adding to the debt by the middle of the decade," said OMB Director Jacob (Jack) Lew. "In short, it's a program where we will live within our means and still invest in the future."

Democrats greeted the plan with varying levels of support, with some moderates preferring somewhat deeper cuts and liberals fearing proposed cuts went too far. Not surprisingly, many interest groups quickly urged Congress to reject reductions to programs they favored—in particular a high-profile proposal to cut almost in half a program to help low-income Americans pay their heating bills.

The budget drew blistering criticism from Republicans who were calling for much more sweeping reductions in spending for both fiscal 2011 and 2012. Fiscal hawks complained that at a time of record deficits and with a national debt approaching the size of the economy's annual output, the president's budget offered no suggestions for curbing entitlement spending or actually reducing the debt.

A bipartisan fiscal commission that Obama had appointed in 2010 to study those issues had produced a plan in December 2010 to trim borrowing by $4 trillion over a decade through spending cuts, an overhaul of the tax system, and deep changes to entitlement programs. But many of the proposals, particularly such fundamental changes as raising the retirement age for Social Security, were deemed too controversial and were left to be addressed through bipartisan negotiations in the future. *(Debt commission, p. 142)*

"If you look at the history of how these deals get done, typically it's not because there's an Obama plan out there," the president said. "It's because Democrats and Republicans are both committed to tackling this issue in a serious way."

The nonpartisan Congressional Budget Office (CBO) released its annual analysis of the president's budget in April, saying the plan would add $9.5 trillion to the debt over ten years—$2.3 trillion more than the White House had estimated—and would fail to stabilize government debt levels, as the administration said it would. The CBO said the difference resulted largely from its use of less optimistic economic assumptions and its decision not to count what it said were unspecified offsets that the administration was counting on to pay for two expensive initiatives: increased spending for transportation infrastructure and a permanent prevention of scheduled cuts in Medicare physician reimbursement rates. The administration took issue with that conclusion.

The CBO's estimates for the president's budget were used by Congress and are also used in the following summary of the main provisions in the president's requests.

Spending

The CBO said Obama's budget would result in $3.7 trillion in outlays—the money agencies would actually spend during the year—an increase of $69 billion, or 2 percent, over a baseline showing what the CBO calculated would be spent without any changes in law.

The budget called for $1.3 trillion in fiscal 2012 discretionary budget authority, the spending authority provided to the agencies in the annual appropriations bills. The total, including the costs of military operations in Iraq and Afghanistan, was $17 billion below the CBO's baseline. Discretionary funding accounted for less than one-third of the budget.

Obama called on Congress to slice billions from grant and loan programs, including community block grants, programs that helped state and local governments finance water infrastructure improvements, and low-income energy assistance. The administration also proposed reducing health care spending by $62 billion to offset the cost of a two-year delay in slashing payments to physicians who treated Medicare patients. The budget also proposed some increases, including $53 billion over six years to jump-start the development of a high-speed rail system.

The budget included $578 billion in base discretionary funding for the Pentagon, plus $118 billion for the wars in Afghanistan and Iraq and related costs. The amount for the base budget was up by $5 billion above fiscal 2011 spending, but the war funding was a decrease from the previous year's $159 billion. (The administration also requested $9 billion in nondefense funds for activities related to the wars in fiscal 2012, effectively bringing the war total to $127 billion.)

Obama requested $553 billion for nondefense programs (including the $9 billion for war-related expenses). The total was a drop of $8 billion from fiscal 2011 spending. Nearly half the difference, however, was the result of a certain-to-be-rejected proposal to shift funding in transportation spending from discretionary to mandatory accounts.

The budget was projected to result in $2.1 trillion in fiscal 2012 mandatory outlays—spending that occurred automatically under various laws such as those governing Medicare, Medicaid, and some farm programs. The CBO said that was an increase of about $49 billion above the baseline amount. Virtually all of the increase was attributed to Obama's proposals to increase and reclassify funding for transportation programs as mandatory and to prevent reductions in Medicare's payment rates for physicians for ten years. The budget was silent on the spiraling costs under existing law of Medicare, Medicaid, Social Security, and other programs that experts said would eventually overwhelm the government's finances.

The CBO estimated that if Obama's budget proposals were enacted, the fiscal 2012 deficit would be $1.2 trillion, or 7.4 percent of the gross domestic product (GDP). It would exceed the baseline deficit by $83 billion. The agency said that deficits would decline in succeeding years, although they would "still add significantly to federal debt." The deficit would shrink to 4.1 percent of GDP by 2015 but grow in later years, reaching 4.9 percent of GDP in 2021.

Overall, the agency said, deficits would total $9.5 trillion between 2012 and 2021—$2.7 trillion more than the CBO's baseline and $2.3 trillion more than the administration estimated. Federal debt held by the public would double, growing from $10.4 trillion (69 percent of GDP) at the end of 2011 to $20.8 trillion (87 percent of GDP) at the end of 2021.

Tax Package

The president's tax proposals skirted the big question on the minds of most congressional tax experts—whether the White House would throw its support behind the first comprehensive rewrite of the tax code in twenty-five years. Obama had begun talking about a tax overhaul after he accepted a compromise with Republicans in December 2010 that extended tax cuts from 2001 and 2003 for all income brackets for two years. Since then, however, the president and his advisers had sent conflicting signals about their commitment to tax reform.

The CBO said the main budgetary impact of the president's initiatives would come from his tax proposals. The agency said proposed tax changes would reduce revenue compared with the CBO's baseline in every year of the next decade, for a total reduction of about 6 percent over the period from 2012 through 2021. Revenue would, nevertheless, rise as a share of GDP from 16 percent in 2012 to 19 percent in 2021.

The following are major elements of Obama's tax policy proposals, with ten-year cost and revenue estimates (in parentheses) from Congress's Joint Committee on Taxation. In some cases, the revenue provisions also had outlay costs, which are not reflected here.

Individual tax cuts. Most of the individual tax breaks from 2001 and 2003 (PL 107-16, PL 108-27) had already been extended through December 31, 2012, under the December 2010 tax compromise (PL 111-312). (*Extension, p. 144*)

Obama-proposed extensions beyond that date included:

- Making permanent the lower individual income tax brackets created in 2001 and 2003 for all but high-earning taxpayers—individuals making more than $200,000 annually and joint filers making more than $250,000 ($1.2 trillion).
- Indexing the amount exempt from the alternative minimum tax to inflation, using fiscal 2011 levels as the base ($683 billion).
- Making permanent so-called marriage relief, designed to prevent married people from paying more taxes together than they would if they were single ($315.7 billion).
- Extending low rates on capital gains and dividends, capped at 15 percent for individuals making less than $200,000 annually and joint filers making less than $250,000 ($120.7 billion).
- Extending the top rate of 20 percent on dividends and capital gains, instead of the higher rates applied to ordinary income, for high earners after 2012 ($95.8 billion).
- Maintaining the estate tax at 2009 levels, with a $3.5 million per person exemption and a 45 percent top rate ($238.8 billion).
- Retaining the $1,000 per-child tax credit ($237.7 billion).
- Reducing the earnings threshold for the refundable portion of the child tax credit ($79.8 billion).
- Extending a $2,500-per-year tax credit for college tuition and other expenses ($90.3 billion).

The president proposed tax breaks for business included making permanent the tax credit for spending on research and extending provisions that allowed small businesses to take a larger deduction for the cost of investments in the year they were made, in lieu of depreciating the cost over time.

The proposal included several provisions to generate revenue, including limiting to a maximum of 28 percent the tax rate at which high-income taxpayers could take itemized deductions; limiting the ability of corporations to defer taxes on profit earned overseas or to shift income to foreign subsidiaries and making other changes in the U.S. international tax system; and eliminating various tax incentives for the production of oil, natural gas, and coal.

Economic Assumptions

Central to Obama's budget request was an assumption that the economy would regain much of the vigor it had lost during the recession that ran from December 2007 through June 2009. In particular, administration forecasters anticipated that GDP growth would return to close to historical norms fairly quickly and that the economy's underlying strength was not harmed by severe job losses during the economic contraction.

In the short term, the White House was less optimistic than many private economists. Over the longer term, however, the administration saw a faster and more expansive recovery than did other forecasters, with the economy making up more of the ground lost during the recession. OMB assumed that the economy would grow by 3.6 percent in 2012, after taking inflation into account, while the consensus of fifty private forecasters surveyed by Blue Chip Economic Indicators projected 3.3 percent growth.

The administration forecast a pickup to a 4.4 percent growth rate in 2013, followed by 4.3 percent in 2014, 3.8 percent in 2015, and 3.3 percent in 2016. Over the longer term, the White House anticipated that GDP would expand at a rate slightly below 3 percent a year, which was consistent with many other economic projections that anticipated an increase in retirements by baby boomers acting as a brake on future growth.

The administration projected a slow decline in unemployment—down to 7.5 percent in 2013—within a percentage point or so of the rates projected by the CBO and private forecasters. The administration, the CBO, and private forecasters were in general agreement that inflation would edge up to 2 percent above the following few years and remain there for the rest of the decade.

HOUSE ACTION

The House Budget Committee approved Ryan's controversial budget plan (H Con Res 34—H Rept 112-58) by a vote of 22–16 on April 6. The measure constituted the most sweeping statement of governing philosophy that House Republicans had made since taking control of the chamber at the start of the 112th Congress. It raised fundamental questions about the fate of Medicare and Medicaid, the size and reach of the federal government, tax policy, and the nation's debt burden.

"These programs are growing themselves into bankruptcy," Ryan said, referring to the two federal health care programs, which had become increasingly expensive as the nation's population aged. "We're at a tipping point." Democrats denounced the plan, charging that it would dismantle Medicare and Medicaid while shielding the rich through tax cuts.

Measured against estimates of what would be spent under existing law, Ryan's plan would have cut spending by $5.8 trillion over ten years and reduced projected deficits by $1.6 trillion. Although the budget resolution called for broad changes to entitlement programs, actually modifying the programs would have required Congress to clear separate legislation, and the budget did not provide an easy way to do that.

Significantly, it did not include reconciliation instructions, which would have allowed such legislation to pass with a simple majority in the Senate, rather than requiring supporters to assemble the sixty votes needed to overcome a filibuster—a high hurdle for Senate Republicans who numbered just forty-seven.

The resolution would have held fiscal 2012 discretionary spending, excluding war costs, to $1.0 trillion, paring about $102 billion from Obama's budget request. Ryan recommended allocating $360 billion of that to nonsecurity spending, which included all discretionary spending outside of defense, homeland security, and Veterans Affairs. The total was equal to nonsecurity spending in fiscal 2006, according to the committee staff. That left $659 billion for security-related programs, a $3 billion increase over Obama's request.

The most controversial proposal, which brought an instant clamor from senior citizens and others, called for restructuring the government's two landmark health care programs, Medicare and Medicaid. The budget proposed to provide the next generation of Medicare recipients with fixed subsidies to buy coverage through government-certified private health care plans of their choice. Under existing law, the program was a fee-for-service system, with the amount of federal funding tied to beneficiaries' use of the program for qualified services.

The Ryan plan also would replace the existing formula-based Medicaid program, which provided health care to the poor and disabled, with a block grant system under which states would receive a set amount of funding from the federal government. The individual states would have greater latitude to design their own programs and determine who would be eligible for the benefits.

The proposal would repeal most of the provisions in the 2010 health care overhaul (PL 111-148, PL 111-152) but preserve almost $500 billion in savings from the law's cuts to Medicare. Ryan said his plan would reinvest those savings in the program.

The resolution called for "fundamental tax reform," including proposals to reduce the top individual and corporate tax rates from 35 percent to 25 percent. The plan did not say what the lower brackets would be or who would fall into them. The plan also called for offsets by altering or eliminating unspecified individual and corporate tax credits and deductions, to keep overall revenue between 18 and 19 percent of GDP. Ryan said the goal was not to raise more revenue but to foster economic growth by promoting a simpler and more efficient tax system.

The Ryan plan also would extend all the Bush-era tax cuts, including those for high-income earners, and continue the estate tax at the existing rate of 35 percent, with $5 million exempt from the tax. The revenue loss was measured in trillions of dollars compared with existing law.

The budget resolution also made several other proposals that would cut spending. Among them were a binding cap on total spending as a percentage of GDP, a requirement that any increase in the statutory debt level be accompanied by spending reductions, privatization of the mortgage giants Fannie Mae and Freddie Mac, and a reduction in the federal workforce and a freeze on federal pay.

The House adopted the budget resolution on April 15, almost exactly twenty-four hours after finishing action on fiscal 2011 appropriations in a package that cut a total of $39.9 billion from fiscal 2010 levels. The **key vote was 235–193 (R 235–4; D 0–189).** *(2011 key votes, p. 785)*

In a pro forma exercise, the House considered and rejected several substitutes offered by the Democrats and by various caucuses. But it was also clear that the GOP budget, facing solid opposition in the Senate, had no chance of becoming the instrument for setting fiscal policy on Capitol Hill for fiscal 2012.

SENATE ACTION

In a series of votes on May 25, the Senate rejected the House-adopted budget plan, Obama's February budget request, and two proposals offered by Republicans.

Senate Majority Leader Harry Reid, D-Nev., scheduled the vote on the House resolution to force Senate Republicans to embrace or abandon the controversial plan. A motion to proceed to the bill was rejected on a **key vote of 40–57 (R 40–5; D 0–50; I 0–2).** Although the outcome was not a surprise, it underscored the inability of conservative Republicans to advance their program in a sharply divided Congress. *(2011 key votes, p. 785)*

The Senate defeated the motion to consider Obama's budget by a vote of 0–97. Separate proposals by Republicans Patrick J. Toomey of Pennsylvania and Rand Paul of Kentucky were rejected by votes of 42–55 and 7–90, respectively.

Debt Limit, Budget Control Act

A long and bitterly partisan standoff over raising the federal debt ceiling and slashing government spending ended August 2, hours before the Treasury Department was set to lose its borrowing authority. Treasury Secretary Timothy F. Geithner and President Barack Obama had warned with increasing urgency that failure to meet the deadline could result in a U.S. default, with potentially catastrophic consequences for the U.S. and world economies. Obama signed the legislation into law August 2, shortly after it was cleared (S 365—PL 112-25).

The bill, known as the Budget Control Act of 2011, created a two-step process for increasing the $14.3 trillion debt ceiling, with each step tied to cuts in the deficit. The first step provided for an initial $900 billion increase in the debt ceiling, paired with $917 billion in spending cuts over ten years. To achieve the spending cuts, the law set discretionary spending caps for fiscal 2012 through 2021. The limit for fiscal 2012 was $1.0 trillion, a reduction of less than 1 percent from fiscal 2011.

The law required the formation of a twelve-member bipartisan, bicameral joint committee tasked with recommending an additional $1.5 trillion in deficit reduction. If Congress enacted $1.2 trillion to $1.5 trillion in cuts, the debt ceiling could be raised by an equal amount. If less than $1.2 trillion was enacted, automatic across-the-board reductions—a process known as sequestration—would be triggered in January 2013 to reach the $1.2 trillion level, allowing the borrowing limit to be increased by that amount. *(Debt committee, p. 168; 2012 action on sequestration, p. 185)*

The bill solved the immediate default crisis, but it left major spending and taxing decisions unresolved, and those issues would come back to haunt legislators for the remainder of the 112th Congress. The prolonged debate that preceded passage sorely challenged the leadership in Congress and the White House, and it created widespread public disgust with Washington, especially Congress. An August 8 CNN poll showed Congress's approval rating at 14 percent.

Three days earlier, on August 5, Standard and Poor's cut its rating on U.S. Treasury debt from AAA for the first time, saying the deficit deal fell short of what was needed and that the "political brinkmanship" that characterized the debate indicated that further progress would remain a "contentious and fitful process."

The statutory ceiling on federal borrowing had been raised seventy-eight times since 1960. Although the process was often difficult, the specter of a default on U.S. government obligations had always brought the parties to some compromise. What was new this time was that a sizable group of House Republicans, many of them freshmen, appeared willing to allow a default rather than to compromise on their demands for spending cuts. Some sixty to eighty identified themselves with the conservative Tea Party movement and had promised during the 2010 campaign to fight to slash the deficit and the federal debt. They argued that the problem was the debt, not the debt limit.

The Tea Party Republicans succeeded in pulling their party's leadership to the right and torpedoing what became known as a "grand bargain," a prospective deal that would have achieved several trillion dollars in deficit reduction through a combination of spending cuts, revenue increases, and restructuring of entitlement programs such as Medicare. Although Republicans could rightly claim to have changed the terms of debate in Washington by putting the focus on significant debt reduction, most conservatives expressed disappointment. They said the final deal was too small and failed to require congressional passage of a balanced-budget amendment before the debt limit was raised. In the end, 45 percent of the Tea Party caucus voted against the bill.

On the other end of the spectrum, liberal Democrats were furious that the measure required no new taxes on top earners and could lead to cuts in entitlement programs in the second phase of deficit reduction. Most were critical of Obama for surrendering on those issues. Only 20 percent of the Progressive Caucus and 40 percent of the Congressional Black Caucus voted for the bill; others supported the measure only reluctantly.

PRECURSORS

The stage for the unprecedented battle over the debt limit was set early in the year, when Republicans held out for significant spending cuts as part of completing the appropriations process for fiscal 2011. The result was a series of continuing resolutions (CRs), most lasting for a matter of weeks. At one point, deadlock over proposed cuts nearly led to a government shutdown. Together, the CRs reduced spending by $39.9 billion over ten years, compared with existing law. The final continuing resolution for fiscal 2011 was cleared on April 14 (PL 112-10). *(Fiscal 2011 omnibus, p. 150)*

Almost exactly twenty-four hours after signing off on the last CR, the House passed a fiscal 2012 budget resolution (H Con Res 34) that telegraphed the next battle over spending cuts. The GOP plan, drafted by Budget Committee Chair Paul D. Ryan, R-Wis., called for fundamental changes to entitlement programs, especially Medicare; a goal of reducing nonsecurity spending below fiscal 2008 levels for five years; and a requirement that any increase in the debt be accompanied by spending reductions. It proposed a cap of $1.0 trillion on fiscal 2012 discretionary spending. *(Budget resolution, p. 156)*

Democrats pilloried the proposed cuts, especially a plan to change the fee-for-service Medicare program into subsidies for private health care and replace the existing formula-based Medicaid program with a block grant system. When the Senate defeated a motion to proceed to the House resolution, the measure was effectively dead, but it continued to provide a reference point for the House majority.

STAKING OUT POSITIONS

On April 13 in a major speech on the deficit, Obama provided a broad outline of a plan to reduce the deficit by $4 trillion over twelve years through $2 trillion in spending cuts, including reductions from defense and entitlement programs; $1 trillion by limiting tax breaks and closing tax loopholes; and $1 trillion from the resulting reduction in interest payments on the debt.

Obama called on House and Senate leaders from both parties to appoint members to a panel to be led by Vice President Joseph R. Biden Jr. He said the meetings would begin in May, with a goal of reaching a final agreement to reduce the deficit by the end of June, giving Congress a month to clear the legislation by the August 2 deadline.

Biden Group

The Biden group began slowly in early May. The participants were House Majority Leader Eric Cantor, R-Va.; Senate GOP Whip Jon Kyl of Arizona; Senate Appropriations Chair Daniel Inouye, D-Hawaii; Senate Finance Chair Max Baucus, D-Mont.; and top House Democrats James E. Clyburn of South Carolina and Chris Van Hollen of Maryland. The administration team was led by White House budget director Jacob J. Lew and subsequently by Geithner.

Almost immediately, Speaker John A. Boehner, R-Ohio, laid down a marker that he would stick by throughout the process: the one thing that was off the table was tax increases. In a speech to the Economic Club of New York on May 9, he also said flatly, "Without significant spending cuts and reforms to reduce our debt, there will be no debt limit increase. And the cuts should be greater than the accompanying increase in debt authority the president is given. We should be talking about cuts of trillions, not just billions."

Democrats strongly opposed any entitlement cuts and called for the package to include higher tax rates for top earners. They also insisted that an increase in the debt limit be large enough to last through the end of 2012, after the next election. That was expected to mean the ceiling would have to be raised by at least $2.4 trillion.

Federal Reserve Chair Ben S. Bernanke on May 12 urged lawmakers to depoliticize the debate and not engage in brinkmanship. "Using the debt limit as a bargaining chip is quite risky. We don't know exactly what would happen if the debt limit was not approved," he warned.

Some of the biggest names in the business and financial world officially jumped into the debate with a May 11 letter to congressional leaders warning that "failure to increase the statutory debt limit in a timely fashion could have a significant and long-lasting negative impact on the U.S. economy." The letter, which had been expected for some time, was signed by several dozen groups, including the U.S. Chamber of Commerce, National Association of Manufacturers, Financial Services Roundtable, and Securities Industry and Financial Markets Association.

The Biden talks took on added importance after high hopes for an agreement from a bipartisan group of senators known as the "Gang of Six" collapsed. The group consisted of Budget Chair Kent Conrad, D-N.D.; Majority Whip Richard J. Durbin, D-Ill.; Mark Warner, D-Va.; Saxby Chambliss, R-Ga.; Tom Coburn, R-Okla.; and Michael D. Crapo, R-Idaho. Their talks began as an effort to implement the December 2010 recommendations of a bipartisan fiscal commission created by Obama. Coburn announced May 17 that he was dropping out of the Gang of Six after expressing pessimism about the prospects for reaching an agreement. The group's most prominent fiscal conservative, Coburn had wanted entitlement cuts that included immediate reductions for Medicare beneficiaries. Democrats objected and refused to budge on the issue. *(Fiscal commission, p. 142)*

As the Biden talks continued, the vice president and Cantor said they were closing in on around $2 trillion in potential spending cuts. But it was never clear how the two sides could bridge the wide gap over taxes and further spending cuts.

Signs of an Impasse

On May 25, the Senate provided another look at just how hard it was going to be to get a compromise through that chamber. In a series of votes, the Senate rejected the Ryan budget plan, Obama's fiscal 2012 budget request issued in February, and two proposals offered by Senate Republicans. *(Budget resolution, Obama budget request, pp. 156, 157)*

In a purely symbolic action, the House on May 31 rejected, 97–318, a GOP-introduced bill (HR 1954) to raise the debt limit by $2.4 trillion without spending cuts.

The impasse was beginning to stir the financial markets, leading both sides to express urgency over getting a deal. On June 2, one of the premier credit-rating agencies, Moody's Investors Service, made headlines by announcing it would downgrade its rating of U.S. debt if the nation defaulted. Even if the limit were raised for the near term, the company said, without a credible long-term deficit reduction plan, it might downgrade the overall outlook for the nation's credit rating.

Obama-Boehner Talks

Just when the Biden talks were seen as entering a critical week, they fell apart, and the onus for a deal abruptly shifted to Obama and Boehner. Cantor announced June 23 that he was pulling out because of the Democrats' continued insistence on increasing taxes. "Regardless of the progress that has been made, the tax issue must be resolved before discussions can continue," he said.

Obama conducted bipartisan talks at the White House with the top House and Senate leaders through much of July; Boehner was the key congressional negotiator because he had to get whatever was decided through the House.

The Speaker was in the toughest spot, negotiating under intense pressure from the Tea Party caucus, which was becoming increasingly vociferous in its demand for deep cuts and no tax increases. A few members, including presidential hopeful Michele Bachmann, R-Minn., opposed increasing the debt limit under any circumstances. Members also began signing a pledge to oppose a boost in the debt limit unless Congress sent a balanced-budget constitutional amendment to the states for ratification.

In the Senate, GOP leaders began drawing a subtle distinction between themselves and House Republicans, sounding more flexible on modest revenue increases through closing tax loopholes and possibly raising user fees, steps they said would not be the same as increasing taxes. In what became their mantra, Democrats argued that the issue was not just about taxes per se but also about taking a "balanced" approach that would require the wealthy—specifically oil companies, hedge fund managers, and taxpayers making more than $500,000 a year—to do their part by accepting tax increases.

They also were growing increasingly wary over rumors that Obama would entertain changes in Medicare and Social Security as part of the mix. "We are not going to reduce the deficit or subsidize tax cuts for the rich on the backs of America's seniors and working families," House Minority Leader Nancy Pelosi, D-Calif., said of her caucus after a July 8 meeting with the president. "No benefit cuts in Medicare and Social Security."

In another symbolic vote, the Senate agreed, 74–22, to a motion by Majority Leader Harry Reid, D-Nev., to limit debate on proceeding to a nonbinding measure (S 1323) that called for Americans with incomes above $1 million to contribute more to deficit reduction.

GATHERING CRISIS

With the deadline growing closer, a sense of crisis pervaded the Capitol. Both chambers canceled one-week recesses in early July to remain in town while the White House talks went on. The tax issue remained the stumbling block to an agreement.

Then on Saturday, July 9, at the start of what was to be a pivotal weekend of staff talks, Boehner announced that he was giving up the search for a grand bargain. He said White House demands for revenue increases sank such a deal and that he would aim instead for a smaller package that was closer to the more than $2 trillion in spending cuts that Biden and congressional negotiators had discussed in June. His position was a departure from his earlier opposition to a short-term deal, which could force him to muster majorities for yet another extension.

Two days later Obama rejected a short-term bill. During a news conference, he said he had accepted entitlement changes that were unpopular within his party and called on Republicans to do the same on revenue. "I will not sign a thirty-day or a sixty-day or a ninety-day extension. That is just not an acceptable approach," he said. He also warned that finding a solution was not going to get easier as the country approached the November 2012 elections. "So we might as well do it now," he said.

Contingency Plan

Senate Minority Leader Mitch McConnell, R-Ky., who was concerned that the GOP might take the heat if the stalemate was not broken, unveiled what he called a "last choice" option on July 12. "What we're not going to be a party to in the Senate is a default," McConnell said. His plan was to shift the political burden to Obama, allowing him to raise the ceiling in three increments over the following year and a half. Along with each request, the president would have to submit a set of budget cuts. Lawmakers would have chances to block each increase with a resolution of disapproval, but Obama would almost certainly veto it, and an override would be unlikely.

The proposal initially received only lukewarm support, but as the crisis continued, it began to look like the plan might offer the only way to avoid a default. Over the next few days, Reid and McConnell worked behind the scenes to put together a modified version that could pass the Senate, but they were unable to clinch a deal.

On July 14, Obama publicly called on negotiators to give him a plan by the weekend. "It's decision time," he said. Although continuing to call for a grand bargain, he expressed some openness to a McConnell-style approach.

But House GOP leaders found themselves facing a potential uprising among Tea Party backers, who saw McConnell as backing down from their vow to require major spending cuts and budget control mechanisms in exchange for a debt ceiling increase.

On July 19, the House passed what supporters called a "cut, cap, and balance" bill (HR 2560) that would have made an increase in the debt limit contingent upon the passage of a balanced-budget constitutional amendment. It also would have capped fiscal 2012 discretionary spending at $1.0 trillion, the level set in the House-passed budget resolution, and limited annual federal spending to 19.9 percent of gross domestic product by fiscal 2021, down from an estimated 22.5 percent for fiscal 2012.

The House passed the bill by a vote of 234–190 on July 19, with nine Republicans voting in opposition and five Democrats supporting it. Three days later, in a strict party-line vote, the Senate tabled a motion to proceed to consideration of the legislation, 51–46.

As the public standoff continued, the bipartisan Gang of Six unexpectedly reemerged, with a proposal for $3.7 trillion in deficit reduction in the next ten years, including new revenue through a tax code overhaul. Conrad said the plan's total savings were based on a mix of 74 percent spending cuts and 26 percent tax increases.

Although the proposal did not address the immediate debt limit crisis, it was the first bipartisan plan that paired spending cuts with revenue increases. It drew optimistic comments from many corners, giving moderates a plan to rally around. Obama held a news conference supporting the plan, which essentially put him on record as favoring a revenue increase of roughly $1 trillion.

Speaker's Withdrawal

The negotiations reached a new crisis point on July 22, when Boehner announced he was withdrawing from the leadership talks with the president.

At an early-evening news conference a half-hour after Boehner issued his statement, a visibly angry Obama said he had offered a generous deal that would cut deeply into programs popular with his political supporters, including more than $1 trillion in cuts to discretionary spending and $650 billion in cuts to entitlement programs, mainly Medicare, Medicaid, and Social Security. The plan, he said, also would yield $1.2 trillion in additional revenue without increasing tax rates, by eliminating loopholes and deductions and overhauling the tax code. "It is hard to understand why Speaker Boehner would walk away from this kind of deal," Obama said. He also said that the Speaker had not returned the president's phone calls before making his announcement.

Boehner responded that the White House had "moved the goalposts on revenue" at the last minute, adding $400 billion to the $800 billion in new revenue he thought the two had agreed to; the $800 billon would have come largely from a bookkeeping change. "The only way to get that [new] revenue," said Boehner, "was to raise taxes." He reiterated his original demand for spending cuts greater than the increase in the debt limit, along with no new taxes.

The Speaker said he would now work directly with Senate leaders to try to negotiate a deal.

FINAL NEGOTIATIONS

With the White House negotiations dead and August 2 just nine days away, Boehner and Reid went their separate ways.

After an embarrassing few days that showed deep splits within the GOP caucus, Boehner narrowly won House passage of a short-term bill (S 627) that required $917 billion in deficit reduction in exchange for a $900 billion debt ceiling increase. The July 29 vote was 218–210.

Boehner had to postpone the vote by a day until he could corral Tea Party Republicans. He was able to do so only by adding language to make a debt limit increase conditional on passage by both chambers of a balanced-budget constitutional amendment. Under the bill, $400 billion of the initial debt ceiling increase would occur when the president certified that it was needed, and the other $500 billion would be subject to a congressional resolution of disapproval.

The president could get a subsequent $1.6 trillion increase only if $1.8 trillion in deficit reductions were enacted and both chambers passed a balanced-budget constitutional amendment. The addition of the balanced-budget provision was enough to win a majority in the House, but it made the bill all the more unacceptable in the Senate.

Reid tried unsuccessfully to engage McConnell in negotiations during the day. That evening, the Senate tabled, or killed, the short-term House GOP bill, 59–41. Reid and McConnell had a series of angry exchanges on the Senate floor, during which it became clear that Reid did not have the sixty votes necessary to get cloture and advance his own plan.

Although Reid's plan shared some features with Boehner's, it effectively would have guaranteed a debt limit increase lasting through 2012, as Obama demanded. It proposed $2.2 trillion in deficit reduction over ten years and allowed for a $2.4 trillion rise in the debt ceiling through a two-step process. An initial $416 billion increase could occur immediately, with a second, $784 billion hike available subject to a congressional resolution of disapproval. After that, the president could seek another $1.2 trillion, again subject to a congressional resolution of disapproval.

Like the House bill, it required the creation of a joint bipartisan twelve-member committee to recommend deficit reduction legislation that the House and Senate would be required to vote on by December 23. But the debt limit increase would not be dependent on enactment of the committee's recommendations.

KEY PLAYERS IN 2011 DEBT LIMIT NEGOTIATIONS

Central players in the battle over the debt limit and deficit reduction bill included:

Joe Biden. Vice President Joseph R. Biden Jr. was the lead negotiator for the White House. He held a series of bipartisan negotiations in May and June with six members of the congressional leadership that at one point was seen as the most likely venue for reaching an agreement. The talks collapsed in late June when House Majority Leader Eric Cantor, R-Va., withdrew. At the end, however, it was negotiations between Biden and Senate Minority Leader Mitch McConnell, R-Ky., that produced a deal that both chambers could pass.

Barack Obama. The president held out for a "grand bargain" until almost the end, but he left much of the early negotiating to Biden. After those talks collapsed in late June, Obama took center stage, negotiating with Speaker John A. Boehner, R-Ohio, and other key players. He gave a prime-time speech to the nation in an effort to apply pressure, especially on GOP negotiators. Although he sought to meet Republicans halfway by putting entitlements on the table, to the dismay of most Democrats, he never offered a detailed proposal of his own.

The one demand he would not give up—that the debt limit increase be enough to last through 2012 and the presidential election—was embodied in the final agreement.

Tea Party Caucus. The group that stood out for having its act together was the collection of Tea Party activists and sympathizers, a minority in the GOP caucus whose influence far outstripped its size. Many Republican members were more afraid of the Tea Party—which had a record in 2010 of defeating GOP establishment candidates in primary contests—than of their own leadership. Perhaps most important in explaining their influence was the fact that Congress was hopelessly polarized, which meant that other forces were not able to band together as they would have in the past to defeat a group of outliers.

Tea Party backers never let up the pressure on their leaders to block any tax increase and to guarantee cuts through adoption of a balanced-budget amendment to the Constitution. On a more fundamental level, they were decisive in ensuring that the debt limit would not be raised without equal or larger spending cuts.

John Boehner. Speaker John A. Boehner, R-Ohio, became the central congressional player during much of the negotiations because the House was the tougher place to sell a deal. He had to navigate the tricky divide between the ardent Tea Party faction, with its support from free-enterprise groups such as the Club for Growth, and more moderate Republicans, many of whom were allied with the business community. He held firm to his no-taxes vow, although at some points he seemed to consider closing loopholes as a possible source of revenue. He engaged twice in talks with Obama about a grand bargain but walked away both times in the face of unbending pressure from Tea Party supporters. The episodes left both men frustrated and angry—Obama asked Republicans what they would "say yes to," and Boehner said negotiating with the White House was like "dealing with Jell-O."

Harry Reid. Senate Majority Leader Harry Reid, D-Nev., consistently pressed for tax increases on top earners while

Tumultuous Weekend

The following day, Saturday, July 30, a mood of gloom settled over the Capitol as both chambers were gaveled into session. McConnell said forty-three Republican senators had signed a letter promising to oppose Reid's proposal, thereby ensuring it would not get the sixty votes needed to thwart a filibuster.

On the other side of the Capitol, the House demonstrated what everyone already knew, rejecting a GOP-introduced replica of Reid's plan (HR 2693) by a vote of 173–246. All options seemed to have been exhausted.

But by afternoon, the tone began to shift as news that McConnell was negotiating with Biden spread through the Capitol. "Our country is not going to default for the first time in history. That is not going to happen," the minority leader said on the floor. "We now have, I think, a level of seriousness with the right people at the table."

It took another day, but at 8:30 p.m. on Sunday, July 31, Reid and McConnell appeared together on the Senate floor to announce that an agreement had been reached. "I am relieved to say leaders from both parties have come together for the sake of our economy to reach a historic, bipartisan compromise that ends this dangerous standoff," Reid said. McConnell told senators, "We can assure the American people tonight that the United States of America will not for the first time in our history default on its obligations."

Obama made his own announcement on national television soon after, keeping up the pressure on all parties to ensure that the compromise deal was cleared by August 2. "We're not done yet," he said.

Final Push

On August 1, all the suspense was in the House, where each party had to contribute a significant number of votes to pass the bill.

Boehner told his troops that while the legislation was not "the greatest deal in the world," it guaranteed that taxes would not be raised and that spending cuts would exceed the size of the debt ceiling increase. The threat to defense protecting entitlement programs. He did a balancing act, providing the votes Obama needed while protecting the political needs of senators in his own caucus, twenty-one of whom were up for reelection in 2012. He held back, seeing what Boehner could get through the House before asking the Senate to vote.

The contours of the final deal—the creation of a joint deficit reduction committee in particular—bore Reid's fingerprints. He successfully defended Medicare, Medicaid, and Social Security, warning Obama that significant changes in entitlement programs simply would not fly in the Senate unless revenue was also on the table.

Mitch McConnell. With more moderates in positions of influence within the Senate GOP caucus, Mitch McConnell, R-Ky., was in a position to be more flexible than Boehner. McConnell was hailed by many as the indispensable man of the debt ceiling debate, receiving much of the credit for a final deal that avoided a default while also delivering Republicans a victory they had not foreseen just weeks earlier.

McConnell was adamant throughout that the GOP hold the line against tax increases, but he was also vocal about his concerns that a default could cripple the party and virtually ensure Obama's reelection. Convinced that the White House would not concede to significant spending cuts without revenue increases—and worried that Republicans would take the blame—McConnell released his contingency plan with discretionary cuts only, key elements of which became part of the final bill.

At the last moment, when all hope of a settlement seemed to have vanished, it was McConnell who reached out to Biden to seal the final deal.

Nancy Pelosi. For House Minority Leader Nancy Pelosi, D-Calif., who led the least powerful faction in Congress, the debt ceiling negotiations were all about playing defense: limiting the spending cuts in domestic programs and protecting key entitlements. "This is the most important assignment given to the Democratic leadership going to the table: make sure there are no cuts in benefits in Medicare, Medicaid, and Social Security. That was achieved," she said at the end. She also helped make sure that the automatic budget cuts, which were later triggered when the joint committee failed to reach agreement, hit defense-related and domestic programs equally. Pelosi's clout increased when the parameters of a final deal began to take shape and it became clear that many House Republicans would not support it, making Democratic votes critical.

"Gang of Six." A bipartisan group of senators known as the "Gang of Six" worked to produce a plan that would reduce the deficit by $4 trillion over a decade. The talks began as an effort to implement the December 2010 recommendations of a bipartisan fiscal commission created by Obama. For a time, the group was regarded as the most promising venue for a deal. However, neither Reid nor McConnell was supportive of a group that was considering tax increases and entitlement revisions as part of a broad plan. The Gang of Six was displaced by the Biden negotiations, although it came back briefly near the end, when prospects for a deal looked grim, to offer a detailed proposal.

spending from the automatic-cut mechanism sparked some last minute push-back from Republicans on the House Armed Services Committee, but Boehner was able to calm them by warning that the Pentagon might do worse if negotiations continued.

The House then passed the bill on a **key vote of 269–161 (R 174–66; D 95–95)**. One of the Democrats who cast a yes vote was Gabrielle Giffords of Arizona. Her surprise appearance seven months after she had been severely wounded in a shooting spree in her hometown brought several standing ovations from colleagues on both sides of the aisle, adding a bit more drama to an already-dramatic day. *(2011 key votes, p. 785; Giffords shooting, p. 640)*

Although the deal left many Democrats angry and many Republicans unsatisfied, there was never any real doubt that the Senate would approve the plan, because few senators wanted to be seen as favoring a default. The Senate sent the bill to the president August 2 by agreeing to a motion to concur in the House amendment on a **key vote of 74–26 (R 28–19; D 45–6; I 1–1)**. *(2011 key votes, p. 785)*

MAJOR PROVISIONS

Following are the major provisions of the Budget Control Act of 2011 (PL 112-25), which President Obama signed into law on August 2:

Debt Limit Increase

The new law created a two-step process for increasing the statutory limit on the federal debt by at least $2.1 trillion and not more than $2.4 trillion in fiscal 2012 through 2021.

In the first step, the president could seek a $900 billion increase immediately. Of the total, $400 billion was available as soon as Obama notified Congress that the debt was within $100 billion of the limit. The other $500 billion occurred automatically, unless it was blocked by the adoption of a resolution of disapproval. The resolution was subject to presidential veto, and a two-thirds majority vote was required to enact a bill through a veto override.

The debt limit increase was paired with discretionary spending cuts made elsewhere in the law.

In the second step, the president could seek a subsequent increase of as much as $1.5 trillion. The size of the second increase would be determined by actions Congress took to curtail growth in the debt. If, by January 15, 2012, a new joint committee had recommended and Congress had enacted $1.5 trillion in additional savings for fiscal 2012–2021, the second increase in the debt limit would be $1.5 trillion. Alternatively, the debt limit was to increase by $1.5 trillion if a constitutional amendment requiring a balanced budget was sent to the states for ratification.

If savings of less than $1.5 trillion and more than $1.2 trillion were enacted, the increase in the debt limit would be equal to the amount of the deficit reduction. If less than $1.2 trillion in savings were enacted, the debt limit would be increased by $1.2 trillion. The second debt limit increase would also be subject to a congressional resolution of disapproval, which could be vetoed.

The law established procedures to expedite consideration of debt limit increase resolutions of disapproval in the House and Senate. A resolution that applied to the first-round debt limit increase had to be enacted within fifty calendar days of the president requesting the increase. The resolution that applied to the second-round debt limit increase had to be enacted within fifteen calendar days of the president's request.

Discretionary Spending Caps

The law set statutory caps on appropriations for fiscal 2012 through 2021. The savings were expected to amount to $917 billion over ten years, according to the Congressional Budget Office (CBO), when compared with the CBO's March estimate and after taking into account savings enacted as part of the omnibus fiscal 2011 appropriations bill (PL 112-10). The expected ten-year savings included $741 billion in reduced outlays from discretionary spending accounts, $20 billion in reduced outlays from mandatory spending accounts, and $156 billion in reduced interest payments on the federal debt. The caps effectively served as the 302(a) limits on total discretionary spending allowed for the year, which usually were provided by the annual budget resolution.

The law allowed spending above the caps for "emergencies" and for the global war on terrorism. It defined emergencies as those situations that required new budget authority and outlays for the prevention or mitigation of, or response to, loss of life or property, or an unanticipated threat to national security. Emergency appropriations for disasters could not exceed the average annual amount provided for disasters over the previous ten years, excluding the highest and lowest years.

The discretionary caps could also be adjusted to finance activities aimed at reducing waste, fraud, and abuse in Medicare, Medicaid, and the Children's Health Insurance Program, and to conduct continuing disability reviews of beneficiaries in the Disability Insurance and Supplemental Security Income programs.

Annual Caps on Spending

Fiscal Year	*Cap in Trillions of Dollars*	*Year-to-Year Change*
2011	$1.050	
2012	1.043	−0.7%
2013	1.047	0.4
2014	1.066	1.8
2015	1.086	1.9
2016	1.107	1.9
2017	1.131	2.2
2018	1.156	2.2
2019	1.182	2.2
2020	1.208	2.2
2021	1.234	2.2

NOTE: The table shows the annual caps for each fiscal year and the percentage change from the previous year. The caps essentially amounted to an actual freeze for fiscal 2012 and fiscal 2013 and a "real," or inflation-adjusted, freeze for the remaining eight years.

Enforcement of the discretionary spending caps was to be accomplished in several ways. It would not be in order in the House or the Senate to consider any legislation that would cause discretionary spending to exceed the caps. The requirement could be waived in the Senate by a vote of three-fifths of the membership, or sixty votes.

If Congress was found to have exceeded the spending caps, automatic, across-the-board spending cuts would occur within capped discretionary accounts fifteen days after Congress adjourned at the end of a session. The automatic mechanism was similar to the system of spending "sequesters" enacted as part of the 1985 Gramm-Rudman antideficit law (PL 99-177). *(Congress and the Nation Vol. VII, p. 44)*

Any sequestration would be carried out by the Office of Management and Budget. The OMB and the CBO were required to coordinate in estimating levels of enacted discretionary spending. The president could exempt any military personnel accounts from sequestration, provided that the required savings were achieved through across-the-board reductions in the remainder of the Defense Department budget.

For fiscal 2012 and fiscal 2013, the law created a "firewall" between security and nonsecurity spending. Security spending was defined as discretionary spending for the Defense, Homeland Security, and Veterans Affairs departments; the National Nuclear Security Administration; the intelligence community management account; and all budget accounts in international affairs.

For fiscal 2012 and 2013, the law also established other budgetary limits, as if a budget resolution had been adopted for each year. If a budget resolution for either fiscal 2012 or fiscal 2013 were adopted, it would supersede those additional budgetary controls.

Joint Deficit Reduction Committee

The bill ordered that a Joint Select Committee on Deficit Reduction be created to recommend an additional $1.5 trillion in deficit reduction over ten years, on which

Congress would have to vote by December 23. The law did not take any aspects of the federal budget off the table to reduce future deficits, including additional discretionary spending reductions, entitlement cuts, or revenue increases.

The joint committee was to be composed of twelve members, with three each appointed by the majority and minority leaders of the Senate and the Speaker and minority leader of the House. The Speaker and the Senate majority leader each were to name one committee member to serve as co-chair.

The members and co-chairs had to be appointed within fourteen calendar days of enactment. Members would serve for the life of the joint committee. Seven members of the committee would constitute a quorum for purposes of voting, meeting, and holding hearings.

The joint committee had to consider any recommendations from standing House and Senate committees with respect to changes in law necessary to meet the deficit reduction goal, with those committees reporting their recommendations to the joint committee by October 14, 2011. The joint committee was required to complete its work by November 23 and issue a report by December 2 including its findings, conclusions, and recommendations, as well as the CBO estimates.

If a majority of the joint committee agreed on the recommendations and accompanying legislative language, the House and Senate would be required to vote on the recommendations by December 23, with no amendments allowed. Enactment had to occur by January 15, 2012, to avoid automatic spending cuts. The president would be allowed to request a debt limit increase equal to the amount of deficit reduction, not to exceed $1.5 trillion.

If the joint committee's efforts—and subsequent congressional action—did not achieve at least $1.2 trillion in deficit reduction, automatic spending cuts, or sequesters, would be triggered to achieve the desired savings. The amount of any sequester would be equal to the portion of the $1.2 trillion savings target that was not achieved and would be spread equally across nine fiscal years. The first automatic cuts would take effect January 2, 2013, and fall equally on defense and nondefense accounts, including both discretionary spending and some mandatory, or entitlement, spending. The second sequester would occur a month later, when the president submitted his budget for fiscal 2014, and would be accomplished by changing the caps on that year's discretionary spending levels and imposing across-the-board cuts in eligible mandatory programs. Subsequent sequesters would occur each year with the submission of the president's budget request.

As under Gramm-Rudman, Medicaid, Social Security, veterans' programs, and many programs targeted to low-income Americans would be largely exempt from automatic cuts. Medicare cuts could amount to no more than 2 percent of the program's outlays, and they would affect only payments to providers, not to beneficiaries.

Pell Grants and Student Loans

The law provided $17 billion over two years in mandatory spending to help fill a gap in the federal Pell grant program—$10 billion in fiscal 2012 and $7 billion in fiscal 2013.

Beginning July 1, 2012, the measure eliminated the ability of graduate and professional students to take out subsidized Stafford loans while they were in school, unless a student was enrolled in a program leading to a degree or certificate or a program necessary for a teaching credential. The existing annual and cumulative loan limits for unsubsidized loans would be adjusted to permit students to borrow additional money in the unsubsidized loan program.

The law eliminated the Education Department's authority to provide incentive payments for on-time repayment of student loans disbursed on or after July 1, 2012. It also explicitly prohibited the department from creating any incentives for on-time repayment of student loans.

Balanced-Budget Amendment

The law required both the House and Senate to vote sometime between October 1 and December 31 on a balanced-budget amendment to the Constitution. Numerous procedural protections sought to ensure that a balanced-budget amendment would be considered on the floor of each chamber, including measures passed by the other body. The law did not specify what version of a balanced-budget amendment each chamber had to consider, and it did not make an increase in the debt limit contingent on passing such an amendment or sending it to the states for ratification.

Balanced-Budget Amendment

Toward the end of 2011, both the House and the Senate rejected proposed constitutional amendments requiring a balanced budget. The votes were required by the end of the year under the terms of the debt limit law passed in August (PL 112-25).

The House vote came in mid-November as a special bipartisan panel pursued ultimately fruitless discussions on ways to reduce the budget deficit. The rejection came on a **key vote of 261–165 (R 236–4; D 25–161)** in favor of the bill (H J Res 2) on November 18, twenty-three votes short of the two-thirds majority needed under the Constitution to send such a measure to the states for ratification. *(2011 key votes, p. 785)*

It was the first House floor action on a balanced-budget amendment since 1995, the year when Republicans last took over the chamber. That measure passed easily but was blocked in the Senate by two votes. *(Congress and the Nation Vol. IX, p. 80)*

The rejected amendment would have required that total outlays in any given year not exceed the total amount of revenue taken in unless a three-fifths majority of Congress voted to make an exception. It also would allow

Congress to waive the balanced-budget requirement with a simple majority vote in years when a declaration of war was in effect.

Supporters cast the proposal as a necessary step to rein in budget deficits and force fiscal responsibility. Democratic opponents warned that a balanced-budget requirement could threaten Social Security and leave the country unable to deal with natural disasters and recessions. Others warned of a straitjacket effect in dealing with economic downturns, especially when government counter-cyclical programs—such as unemployment compensation, normally offset some of the effects of recessions.

In the days before the vote, the Democratic leadership pressed party members to oppose the measure, but the amendment won the votes of more than two dozen Democrats, most of them moderates. The GOP leadership had its own difficulties keeping its caucus in line. Four Republicans ultimately voted against it, including Rules Committee Chair David Dreier, R-Calif., who had supported a similar amendment in 1995.

Although the House rejection effectively killed the amendment, the Senate put itself on record opposing a balanced-budget amendment on December 14, when it defeated two competing proposals. The Republican version (S J Res 10), rejected, 47–53, on strict party lines, would have set up a two-thirds threshold in both chambers for approving revenue increases and established a cap for federal spending at 18 percent of the economy's annual output.

The Democratic version (S J Res 24), which was rejected, 21–79, did not include either a spending cap or a threshold for revenue increases. It would have taken Social Security receipts and outlays off the books and prohibited Congress from passing any tax cut for millionaires if the government was running a deficit.

Congressional Deficit Committee

A special congressional committee on deficit reduction, created under the August debt limit law, was unable to achieve its mandate and effectively disbanded November 21.

The Budget Control Act (PL 112-25) raised the federal debt limit in the wake of a half-year's worth of abortive negotiations between congressional leaders and President Barack Obama over how to slow the growth of the government's debt. As part of the deal, the law established the Joint Select Committee on Deficit Reduction and charged it with reaching agreement on a plan to reduce the deficit by at least $1.2 trillion over a decade. The deadline was November 23. If the panel had achieved its goal, Congress would have had until December 23 to vote on the plan in the form of legislation that would have been immune from amendment and procedural roadblocks. *(Debt limit law, p. 160)*

Under the law, the committee's failure to meet the statutory goal led to automatic across-the-board spending cuts beginning in January 2013. (Budget Control Act, p. 160)

The members of the committee—three Democrats and three Republicans from each of the two chambers—were appointed in August by the top four congressional leaders. The committee was led by Republican Rep. Jeb Hensarling of Texas and Democratic Sen. Patty Murray of Washington. The Republican members from the House were Dave Camp and Fred Upton of Michigan and from the Senate Jon Kyl of Arizona, Rob Portman of Ohio, and Patrick J. Toomey of Pennsylvania. The House Democrats were Xavier Becerra of California, James E. Clyburn of South Carolina, and Chris Van Hollen of Maryland, and Senate Democrats Max Baucus of Montana and John Kerry of Massachusetts.

The panel, dubbed the "supercommittee" because of its extraordinary scope and power, started work September 8, when it held its first full meeting. It was the committee's only meeting open to the public, outside of four hearings used to question experts on approaches to controlling the debt. Although the panel drew criticism for a lack of transparency, its membership in whole or in part met dozens of times in private, striving to meet its goal.

Over several weeks of intense discussion, the details of proposals offered by both sides began to leak out. Democrats proposed plans that included a mix of tax increases and spending cuts in the $2 trillion to $3 trillion range. Republicans offered plans that would save more than $2 trillion primarily through spending cuts. Both sides moved out of their comfort zones—Republicans offered up to $300 billion in new tax revenue, while Democrats put forth proposals to trim hundreds of billions of dollars from federal health care programs—before the talks briefly collapsed.

Ultimately, the Republican revenue offers were not of a magnitude sufficient to satisfy Democrats. And Republicans complained that Democratic proposals to trim entitlement programs fell short of adequately stemming their rapid growth.

After a last-minute flurry of activity on November 21 to see whether a deal might be reached, the committee gave up and its members went home. The end came two days before the panel's deadline, in the face of a requirement that the plan be available for forty-eight hours after the Congressional Budget Office had assessed its fiscal impact before a vote could be held.

Under the terms of the debt limit law, the panel did not officially terminate until January 31, 2012. Nonetheless, its work was finished after it lost its privilege to submit legislation that would have been handled under expedited rules.

Fiscal 2012 Continuing Resolutions

Congress had enacted none of the regulation fiscal 2012 appropriations bills before passing the Budget Control Act of 2011 on August 2 and leaving for its summer

TWO MINOR TAX BILLS ENACTED

Congress enacted two minor tax bills in 2011 with a minimum of controversy. One repealed a tax reporting requirement that was included in the 2010 health care overhaul but had provoked dissent from many quarters, including the White House. The second combined a repeal of tax withholding on government payments to federal contractors with incentives for employers to hire disabled veterans.

Tax Reporting Requirement

President Barack Obama called for the repeal of the tax reporting requirement in his January State of the Union address, and the White House said it was "pleased Congress has acted to correct a flaw" in the law. Although House Republicans cast the bill as a first step in overturning the health care overhaul (PL 111-148, PL 111-152), it was the only significant change they were able to make during the session. *(Health care repeal, p. 455; State of the Union text, p. 899)*

The repeal stripped a requirement that businesses and real estate owners report on an IRS Form 1099 any individual vendor to whom they paid $600 or more in a year, beginning in 2012. The provision had been expected to raise about $19 billion by reducing unreported income and was included to help pay for the health care overhaul.

But small businesses said it would be a paperwork nightmare. And business groups, including the Chamber of Commerce and the National Federation of Independent Business, lobbied hard for the repeal.

In a voice vote February 2, the Senate agreed to an amendment to an unrelated bill (S 223) that would have repealed the 1099 provisions and offset the revenue loss by rescinding $44 billion in unobligated discretionary funds.

The House did not take up that amendment, but instead approved a bill (HR 4) that fully offset the repeal by allowing the government to recapture a larger share of overpayments to people receiving subsidies for the new health insurance exchanges.

Although Democrats warned that the offset would amount to a hefty tax hike on low- and middle-income families, the bill passed, 314–112, March 3. The Senate cleared the bill on April 5 by a vote of 87–12. President Obama signed the bill April 14 (HR 4—PL 112-9)

Contractor Tax Withholding Repeal

President Obama on November 21, 2011, signed legislation (HR 674—PL 112-56) that repealed a provision of a law enacted in 2006 (PL 109-222) requiring federal, state, and local governments to withhold 3 percent of payments to outside vendors for goods and services. Employers and government agencies complained that complying with the mandate would divert money from job creation and result in more paperwork.

The tax-withholding requirement had never been implemented because Congress and the executive branch had delayed doing so until January 1, 2013. In September, Obama proposed another delay as part of a larger plan to boost employment. On October 27, the House handily passed the legislation (HR 674—H Rept 112-253) to repeal the requirement altogether. To cover the estimated $11.2 billion cost, the House then repealed a provision in the 2010 health care overhaul (PL 111-148, PL 111-152) that allowed people to exclude Social Security benefits from their income when applying for health benefits, such as Medicaid, and subsidies to purchase private insurance in new state-run exchanges.

The Senate passed the bill, 95–0, on November 10, after adding a tax incentive for businesses to hire unemployed veterans—part of Obama's jobs agenda. The House cleared the measure, 422–0, on November 16.

The legislation provided tax credits to companies that hired veterans with service-connected disabilities who had been unemployed for at least six months out of the previous year. It provided smaller tax credits to those that hired vets who were not disabled or had been unemployed for shorter periods. It also extended existing credits for hiring veterans through 2012 and required the Department of Veterans Affairs (VA) to establish a retraining program by July 1, 2012. To pay for the veterans' provisions, the bill postponed a scheduled reduction in fees charged to veterans who obtained VA-guaranteed mortgages until fiscal 2017.

recess. When legislators returned in September, members of both parties were determined to finish work on the bills by the end of the session. But they were nearly derailed by disputes over passing a continuing resolution (CR) by October 1, the start of the fiscal year, that would keep the government running while congressional leaders considered how to bring the appropriations process to a close.

It was the third time in 2011 that congressional inability to arrive at an agreement nearly led to a crisis in government operations. In April, Congress narrowly averted a government shutdown when it cleared legislation to fund the government for the rest of fiscal 2011. In August, lawmakers nearly ran out of time in a dispute over raising the government's debt ceiling; a failure to meet that deadline would have caused the United States to default.

LEGISLATIVE ACTION

The September battle in the House over the fiscal 2012 continuing resolution divided not only the two parties but the GOP caucus itself, a split that would continue to make life difficult for Speaker John A. Boehner, R-Ohio, in the fiscal battles to come.

The chief disputes concerned how much to provide in emergency disaster relief and how much to offset it, and whether to reduce the rate of fiscal 2012 spending below what had been agreed to in the August debt limit law (PL 112-25). By late summer, a series of natural disasters, including floods, fires, and Hurricane Irene, had nearly depleted the funding available to respond to such calamities. Republicans in general were pushing for the offsets, and conservatives in particular for lower spending levels, with Democrats firmly opposed to both. *(Emergency disaster aid, p. 176)*

In an embarrassing upset, forty-eight Republicans, many associated with the conservative Tea Party caucus, joined 182 Democrats on September 21 to scuttle a bill (HR 2608) put forward by the Republican leadership. The vote was 195–230. It was the first clear roll-call defeat for the GOP leaders since they took control of the chamber in January.

The conservatives were angry that HR 2608, which ran through November 18, set fiscal 2012 funding at an annualized rate of $1.043 trillion, the spending cap set in the hard-fought debt limit law. They argued for going back to a $1.019 trillion cap, which the House had adopted as part of a GOP budget resolution (H Con Res 34) the House had passed in the spring. *(Budget resolution, pp. 156, 159)*

Democrats were generally unwilling to vote for the CR; they wanted more disaster funding and, more importantly, they rejected the proposed offset. The GOP bill included $1 billion in immediate, fiscal 2011 funding for the Federal Emergency Management Agency (FEMA) Disaster Relief Fund and the Army Corps of Engineers' flood control program. The GOP bill more than offset the $1 billion by cutting $1.5 billion from a program, backed by Democrats, that provided loan guarantees to automakers to produce fuel-efficient vehicles. It also made an additional $2.7 billion in disaster relief available in fiscal 2012.

Two days later, Boehner returned with a slightly revised bill that kept funding at the $1.043 trillion level but added a $100 million cut to a loan guarantee program that had helped Solyndra, a solar-energy company supported by President Barack Obama. Solyndra had later gone bankrupt, causing embarrassment for the administration. The House passed the bill 219–203 on September 23, with only two dozen Republicans voting against it.

Boehner succeeded mainly by arguing to conservatives that their continued opposition would bolster the leverage of Democrats who were seeking more disaster aid.

On September 15, several days before the House rejected the version of HR 2608, Majority Leader Harry Reid, D-Nev., set up a vote on an amendment to an unrelated bill (H J Res 66) to demonstrate that Senate Democrats had the support of a small group of GOP senators who were willing to provide $6.9 billion for the FEMA disaster fund, with no offsets. The amendment to H J Res 66 was adopted on a **key vote of 62–37 (R 10–37; D 50–0; I 2–0)**. *(2011 key votes, p. 785)*

On September 23, shortly after the House passed the revised version of its CR, the Senate voted 59–36 to table, or kill, it. Several Democrats were adamant that Congress not set a precedent of requiring offsets for disaster aid.

Amid renewed speculation about a government shutdown and with Congress scheduled to be out of town until October 3, Reid and Senate Minority Leader Mitch McConnell, R-Ky., came up with a compromise. They were aided by news from FEMA that it had figured out how to free up enough money to last through the end of the fiscal year. That meant Reid and McConnell could drop the $1 billion in fiscal 2011 money, thus eliminating the issue of offsets, and accept the House's $2.7 billion disaster spending total for fiscal 2012.

The Senate adopted the compromise on HR 2608, 79–12, on September 26. The House cleared it, 352–66, when it returned October 4. Obama signed HR 2608 into law October 5 (PL 112-36).

To give the House time to act, the Senate on September 26 passed a four-day continuing resolution (HR 2017—PL 112-33) by voice vote, and the House cleared it by unanimous consent September 29 in a pro forma session.

It took three more stopgap measures to keep the government operating until an omnibus spending bill was signed December 23. The first of these was included in a three-bill spending package (PL 112-55) and lasted through December 16. Two more were needed—a one-day measure (PL 112-67) good through December 17 and a final extension (PL 112-68) through December 23.

Fiscal 2012 "Minibus" Appropriations

Congress on November 17, 2011, sent President Barack Obama the first installment of the twelve overdue fiscal 2012 appropriations bills in the form of a three-bill "minibus," which he signed into law November 18 (HR 2112—PL 112-55). The package, which contained the Agriculture, Commerce-Justice-Science, and Transportation-Housing and Urban Development appropriations bills, won bipartisan support in both chambers. The House adopted the conference report (H Rept 112-284) by a vote of 298–121, with the support of 165 Democrats and 133 Republicans. The Senate easily cleared the bill, 70–30, later the same day.

AGRICULTURE

The fiscal 2012 agriculture spending bill provided significantly more than House Republicans wanted for food and nutrition programs, blocked some school lunch nutrition standards, and liberalized a new means test for farm subsidies.

The measure provided $137 billion for the Agriculture Department and Food and Drug Administration (FDA), including $19.8 billion in discretionary funding and $367 million in emergency spending for disaster relief. The discretionary amount was about $387 million, or 2 percent, below fiscal 2011 spending and $2.5 billion, or 11 percent, less than Obama requested. It was slightly less than the Senate proposed but $2.5 billion more than in the House-passed version.

Most of the funding in the bill—$116.8 billion—was for mandatory programs. Nearly $99 billion of it went to food and nutrition—including the Supplemental Nutrition Assistance Program (SNAP), known as food stamps, and child nutrition programs—an increase of $16 billion over fiscal 2011 and $6.6 billion more than the request. The House bill would have provided $8.6 billion less in mandatory food and nutrition funding.

Conferees included controversial policy language blocking the Agriculture Department from implementing proposed new standards that would have limited white potatoes and starchy vegetables in school meals. The deal began to roll back some of the authority the Agriculture Department gained under a 2010 law (PL 111-296) to set new standards for healthier school meals. Companies and trade associations trying to protect their shares of the $9.5 billion school food industry had been fighting the preliminary nutrition regulations since the Agriculture Department released them in January.

Nutrition advocates fared better in fending off cuts to the Women, Infants and Children (WIC) nutrition program, which was paid for with discretionary funds. Democrats complained that cuts included in the version of the spending bill passed by the GOP-led House would have turned away 700,000 clients. Conferees agreed to fund the program at $6.6 billion—slightly less than the fiscal 2011 level of $6.7 billion but $570 million more than under the House bill.

Some of the additional money came from a $928 million reduction in mandatory funding for conservation programs that helped farmers and ranchers reduce runoff, prevent soil erosion, and provide habitats for wildlife.

Conferees protected funding for the FDA to carry out the 2010 food safety law (PL 111-353). They largely accepted the Senate's overall funding level of $2.5 billion for the FDA, excluding user fees, virtually the same as the amount provided in fiscal 2011. *(Food safety, p. 409)*

On June 16, the House passed HR 2112 (H Rept 112-101) 217–203 after two days of debate and votes on scores of amendments. Nineteen Republicans joined all Democrats in voting against it—the Democrats decrying what they said were draconian spending cuts, and the Republicans arguing the cuts were not deep enough. The Senate version (S Rept 112-73) approved by the Senate Appropriations Committee became the vehicle for the three-bill omnibus.

COMMERCE-JUSTICE-SCIENCE

The "minibus" legislation provided $60 billion for the Commerce and Justice departments and several science agencies. Of the total, $52.7 billion was discretionary budget authority, with another $200 million in disaster aid. The discretionary funding was $583 million below the fiscal 2011 level and $4.9 billion less than Obama requested. But it was slightly more than the Senate Appropriations Committee had approved and $2.5 billion more than House GOP appropriators had agreed to.

Two prominent programs that House Republicans had hoped to zero out, one for neighborhood policing and another for a National Aeronautics and Space Administration (NASA) space telescope, won a reprieve. The House version would have eliminated funding for the Community Oriented Policing Services (COPS) program, which provided grants for local police departments to hire officers. It also proposed no funding for NASA's James Webb Space Telescope, the successor to the Hubble Space Telescope and a main component of NASA's plans for the next decade.

Under the minibus bill, the COPS program got $199 million, which was still a 60 percent cut compared with fiscal 2011. The Senate panel had approved $256 million for the program. The bill provided $530 million for the telescope, the same as the figure proposed by the Senate. The reduction from fiscal 2011 for the COPS program was part of a general cut in funds for state and local law enforcement grants, although, again, they were not as deep as House GOP appropriators proposed. The $2.2 billion in the bill for the grants was a 20 percent cut from fiscal 2011 funding. Several other federal law enforcement programs, including the Federal Bureau of Investigation (FBI) and the federal prison system, received more than they had in fiscal 2011.

Policy language in the bill included House provisions that made permanent three firearms-related provisos, including one that required the destruction of identification information for approved firearms purchasers within twenty-four hours of notification that an individual passed a background check.

It also modified language backed by the Senate that barred funds for operations similar to a botched Justice Department gun-tracking program known as Operation Fast and Furious, a sting operation on the Southwest border that resulted in a large number of guns remaining on the streets. The measure forbade the use of funds—except for national background checks—for federal law enforcement to facilitate the transfer of operable guns to suspected drug cartel agents unless they were being continuously monitored.

On another issue, the conference report barred NASA and the Office of Science and Technology Policy from formally collaborating with China or Chinese-owned companies unless explicitly authorized by law.

The House Appropriations Committee approved the commerce-justice-science spending measure (HR 2596—H Rept 112-169) in July, and the Senate Appropriations Committee approved its version (S 1572—S Rept 112-78). Neither chamber took floor action on the legislation before it was folded into the minibus.

TRANSPORTATION–HOUSING AND URBAN DEVELOPMENT

Overall, the bill provided $109.4 billion in spending for the departments of Transportation and Housing and Urban Development. Of the total, $55.6 billion was discretionary appropriations, including $1.8 billion in disaster funds. The rest was mainly in the form of obligations permitted from the Federal Highway Trust Fund. The discretionary total was essentially equal to fiscal 2011 funding (PL 112—10), but it was $19.4 billion less than President Obama requested, mainly because Congress eliminated funding for two of his signature initiatives: high-speed rail and a national infrastructure bank.

Obama sought $53 billion over six years for high-speed rail. The Senate Appropriations Committee would have set aside $100 million in fiscal 2012; House appropriators left out any funding. House and Senate aides said the conference committee's actions were not expected to affect the phases of individual projects that were already paid for.

The White House also sought $5 billion for a national infrastructure bank that would support private investment in new roads, bridges, mass transit, and other public works. Although the bill provided no funds for the initiative, it included $500 million for national infrastructure investments commonly referred to as the TIGER program, and language prioritizing rail, highway, and transit projects that improved or expanded existing systems. It also included a modified Senate provision appropriating $600 million for capital investments in surface transportation infrastructure.

The stand-alone transportation-HUD bill did not advance beyond subcommittee approval in the House and full committee approval in the Senate (S 1596—S Rept 112—83) before being added to the minibus.

Fiscal 2012 Omnibus Appropriations

As the end of the session drew near, Senate leaders hoped to package the remaining appropriations bills in a series of "minibuses" made up of two or three spending bills. That plan collapsed after senators threatened to offer a long list of amendments that could have tied up the Senate for days. Instead, leaders decided to wrap the remaining nine measures into one bulky omnibus package.

House Republican leaders also favored the omnibus approach because it spared them from scheduling difficult spending votes that would divide their majority. As was the case with the first minibus, each vote would have required the GOP to count on backing for passage from Democrats, because many conservative GOP members were likely to oppose the measures.

House and Senate conferees began work on the omnibus in early December 2011, using the unfinished military construction–veterans affairs spending bill (HR 2055) as the vehicle to cover the nine overdue fiscal 2012 spending measures.

Negotiations went relatively smoothly, and the conference report was largely finished by December 12, when the measure became ensnared in partisan wrangling over separate legislation to extend an expiring Social Security payroll tax reduction. *(Employee payroll tax, pp. 79, 108, 146)*

Senate Democratic leaders, concerned that House Republicans might leave town without cutting a deal on the payroll tax cut, delayed signing the conference report on the spending bill. "They are twinned up at this point, these two issues," Senate Majority Whip Richard J. Durbin, D-Ill., said on December 13. A White House official, speaking on background, said President Barack Obama would not sign the appropriations package until a bipartisan agreement was in hand to continue the payroll tax reduction.

Republicans blasted Senate Democrats for allowing the quarrel over the tax cut bill to get in the way of finishing the appropriations process. At that point, Speaker John A. Boehner, R-Ohio, maneuvered around Senate Majority Leader Harry Reid, D-Nev.; House Republicans filed a stand-alone bill (HR 3671) that contained the text of the conference report on the omnibus, which was essentially finished, and they threatened to go ahead with a vote, forcing the Senate to act.

Conferees quickly agreed to settle some small remaining differences, including removing several provisions that the House had included in its bill, such as language that would have changed restrictions on travel and remittances to Cuba. Conferees filed their report December 15, and the House adopted it the following day, 296–121. The Senate cleared the package, 67–32, on December 17 in a rare Saturday session. Obama signed the measure into law December 23 (HR 2055—PL 112-74).

The $915 billion measure was consistent with the $1.0 trillion cap on fiscal 2012 discretionary spending set by the debt limit law. It included the text of the underlying military construction–veterans bill and eight other spending measures: Defense, Energy-Water, Financial Services, Homeland Security, Interior-Environment, Labor–Housing and Urban Development–Education, Legislative Branch, and State–Foreign Operations. Following are brief summaries of each of the nine bills.

DEFENSE

The Defense spending title of the omnibus bill provided $518.1 billion for the base Pentagon budget—which excluded war funding—an increase of $5 billion from fiscal 2011 but $20.8 billion less than Obama requested. The bill also provided $115 billion for overseas contingency operations—principally activities in Afghanistan—$2.8 billion less than requested and $42.7 billion less than was appropriated for fiscal 2011.

In all, the bill provided $633.2 billion in discretionary budget authority for the Defense Department and generally reflected decisions made in the companion defense authorization law (PL 112-81). The base Pentagon spending level was driven largely by the August debt limit law (PL 112-25), which put a $684 billion cap on security spending for fiscal 2012, excluding war-related funding. *(Defense authorization, p. 299)*

The security spending had to be spread among the departments of Defense, Homeland Security, and State, plus foreign aid, intelligence and nuclear security programs. The final total for Pentagon spending, the product of tough negotiations that required compromises from both chambers, was $5 billion higher than anticipated under the $684 billon cap. To provide those funds, negotiators cut back on the amount allocated for other security accounts. Even then, they had to shift some spending to the overseas contingency account, which was not limited by the caps.

The House passed a stand-alone defense bill (HR 2219—H Rept 112-110) in July, before the caps had been set, which would provide $648.7 billion in discretionary spending. That was about 2 percent more than the $630.6 billion agreed to by Senate appropriators in September (S Rept 112-77), after the security spending ceiling had become law. The final bill was closer to the Senate committee version.

Appropriators included about $1 million to pay for an independent study of U.S. efforts in Afghanistan and Pakistan. Although the amount was small, the move reflected unease over U.S. operations in both nations. The bill also included several prohibitions related to transferring terrorism detainees from the Guantánamo Bay, Cuba, detention facility. The language was similar to that in the fiscal 2011 defense spending law (PL 112-10).

The legislation required a report from the Pentagon on about $100 billion in planned efficiency savings between fiscal 2012 and 2016 identified by the military services and ordered by the defense secretary at the time, Robert M. Gates. The Pentagon was permitted to use the savings to bolster other, high-priority funding needs.

House and Senate negotiators minimized cuts to the deeply troubled F-35 Joint Strike Fighter program, reducing the president's proposal for thirty-two fighters by just one aircraft but trimming the request for advance procurement dollars for future jets. They included no funding for the controversial F-35 alternative engine, and made many other cuts in various programs. *(Defense spending details, p. 304)*

ENERGY-WATER

For the energy and water programs of the Department of Energy, the Army Corps of Engineers, and the Interior Department's Bureau of Reclamation, the omnibus bill provided $32.1 billion, less than 1 percent above fiscal 2011 spending and not enough to keep up with inflation. The total was $4.5 billion less than Obama requested.

On one of the most contentious issues, the final bill left out funding that the House had sought to review the license application for the nuclear waste disposal site at Yucca Mountain, Nev., and a provision to block the Obama administration's plans to shut down the facility. The Nuclear Regulatory Commission had begun to close down its review of the license application and had received $10 million in fiscal 2011 for the "orderly closure" of the facility. The bill provided $10 million for the agency to assess the safety of storing spent fuel. *(Yucca Mountain controversy, pp. 377, 394)*

Conferees on the bill also dropped a House provision that would have prohibited the use of funds to implement revised guidance by the Energy Department and the Army Corps of Engineers. The revised guidance expanded the definition of areas covered by the Clean Water Act.

In a win for conservatives, the final bill included a House-backed amendment that barred the Energy Department from implementing new energy efficiency standards for light bulbs. The standards were created without controversy and with bipartisan support in a 2007 energy law (PL 110-140) and were scheduled to take effect in 2012, but critics cast the standards as a ban on the incandescent light bulb and an attack on personal liberty.

Lawmakers squeezed in small funding increases for some programs, including those for energy efficiency and renewable energy, science, and nuclear nonproliferation. The bill included increases of 6 percent for nuclear energy and 5 percent for nuclear weapons activities.

The House passed a stand-alone version of the bill by a vote of 219–196 on July 15 after more than a week of debate and more than forty roll-call votes. Republicans managed to hold the bill intact, fending off Democratic attempts to reduce restrictions and increase funding for clean-water rules and renewable-energy programs. Democrats were particularly critical of using high-speed rail funds as an offset for $1 billion in disaster funding.

The version reported by Senate Appropriations Committee (S. Rept 112-75) on September 7 was $2 billion higher than House version. It included $1 billion for disaster aid with no offsets. *(Disaster aid, p. 176)*

FINANCIAL SERVICES

The Financial Services spending bill, with funding for the Treasury Department and other general government agencies, provided $44.2 billion, including $21.5 billion in discretionary spending authority. The discretionary total was $4.2 billion, or 16 percent, less than Obama requested and $222 million below the fiscal 2011 level (PL 112-10), roughly a 1 percent decrease.

Few of the most controversial policy riders sought by Republicans were retained in the omnibus. The biggest disagreements concerned how much to give the agencies charged with implementing the 2010 Dodd-Frank financial regulatory law (PL 111-203) and the 2010 health care overhaul (PL 111-148, PL 111-152). *(Dodd-Frank, p. 88; health care overhaul, p. 421)*

House Republicans opposed increasing the budget for the Securities and Exchange Commission (SEC), in part as an attack on the Dodd-Frank legislation and also reflecting a historical GOP dislike of the agency. They said the SEC should be overhauled and made more efficient. Senate Democrats countered that the agency needed more resources to handle its new responsibilities under Dodd-Frank. In the end, lawmakers compromised and provided $1.3 billion for the SEC, a $136 million increase above fiscal 2011.

Democrats also staved off GOP efforts to constrain the Consumer Financial Protection Bureau (CFPB), newly established by Dodd-Frank to protect borrowers seeking mortgages, credit cards, and other financial products. The bureau was housed within the Federal Reserve, received its money from the Fed, and was not subject to congressional appropriations. GOP lawmakers objected to this arrangement, saying it did not allow for congressional oversight, and House appropriators included a provision in their bill to bring the new credit bureau under their purview. Senate appropriators held firm in their opposition, and the provision did not make it into the omnibus.

Republicans also took aim at the 2010 health care law by proposing to limit Internal Revenue Service (IRS) spending on it and to prohibit the agency from implementing mandates for employers to provide employees with health insurance. They also sought to prevent individuals from being required to enroll in health care plans, a provision that was scheduled to go into effect in 2014. The omnibus did not include those policy prohibitions, but it also did not include the funding increase requested by the president to cover the new responsibilities.

The Financial Services appropriations measure was the venue for other policy battles that prolonged the debate over the omnibus as a whole. Republicans were successful in attaching policy riders to continue an existing prohibition on special presidential assistants, often referred to as "czars," related to health care, climate change, the auto industry, and urban affairs. In another GOP win, the bill maintained a ban on the use of federal and local tax money for abortions in the District of Columbia and barred the use of federal money for needle exchange programs.

Much of the final behind-the-scenes wrangling centered on U.S. policy toward Cuba. Ultimately, at the behest of the White House, the conference report on the bill left out provisions sought by Cuba hawks to reimpose restrictions on Cuba travel from the George W. Bush administration.

Both appropriations committees reported versions of the Financial Services spending measure (HR 2434—H Rept 112-136; S 1573—S Rept 112-79), but neither chamber took any floor action before the bill was folded into the omnibus.

HOMELAND SECURITY

The Department of Homeland Security received $41.3 billion, including $39.6 billion for discretionary programs. The discretionary amount was $2 billion below fiscal 2011 funding (PL 112-10) and about $4 billion less than the president requested, not including $4.6 billion in disaster funding that he requested in September. First-responder grants and other state and local programs took a particularly big hit. Most of the department's other major agencies received small increases for 2012.

The House passed a stand-alone Homeland Security bill (HR 2017—H Rept 112-91), and the Senate Appropriations Committee approved an amended version (S Rept 112-74), but that was as far as the stand-alone measure advanced. Much of the controversy over the stand-alone bill focused on emergency disaster aid. Under the 2011 debt limit law (PL 112-25), which set caps on fiscal 2012 discretionary spending, Congress was allowed to appropriate up to $11.3 billion in disaster aid without cutting other spending to pay for it. Republicans insisted, however, that the debt crisis necessitated offsets. Many Democrats argued that disaster aid traditionally was not offset and that it should be treated in the same way as the billions of dollars in war funding that had not been paid for.

Lawmakers ultimately resolved the issue by breaking out the disaster aid into a separate, $8.1 billion bill (PL 112-77), which included $6.4 billion for the Federal Emergency Management Agency. The funding was not offset. *(Disaster aid, p. 176)*

In a move to force Senate Democrats to put their opposition to offsetting the costs on the record, the House adopted a related measure (H Con Res 94) that directed the House enrolling clerk to add provisions to the disaster aid bill making across-the-board rescissions of 1.8 percent to discretionary accounts in most fiscal 2012 spending bills before HR 3672 was sent to the president's desk. The Senate rejected the resolution.

Although the shortfall in disaster funding was more than made up by the separate disaster relief bill, state and local grants, primarily directed to first-responder programs, were cut by about $840 million, or 39 percent, from fiscal 2011, getting $1.3 billion. The bill provided $2.4 billion for firefighters and emergency management performance grants, a cut of about $1 billion, or 30 percent.

INTERIOR-ENVIRONMENT

The interior-environment title in the omnibus provided $29.2 billion, all but $55 million of which was discretionary spending. The discretionary total was 1 percent, less than provided in fiscal 2011 (PL 112-10) and 7 percent, less than Obama requested.

Efforts by the House Republican majority to make deep cuts in spending for the Environmental Protection Agency (EPA) and to roll back a large number of environmental regulations fell short. The EPA received $8.5 billion, compared with $7.1 billion in the House bill.

Most of the myriad policy riders the House had included to limit the EPA's regulatory authority were dropped in the final spending agreement. Among them was a one-year delay of EPA regulations on greenhouse gas emissions from stationary industrial sources. *(EPA regulations, p. 386)*

The final bill cut $14 million from clean air and climate research programs, $14 million from air regulatory programs, and $12 million from the EPA's regulatory development office. It also directed the president to report to Congress on how much the federal government spent on climate change programs in fiscal 2011.

The House began floor debate on its bill (HR 2584—H Rept 112-151) in late July but never returned to it after the August recess. Senate appropriators did not mark up a bill.

LABOR–HEALTH AND HUMAN SERVICES–EDUCATION

The departments of Labor, Health and Human Services (HHS), and Education experienced cutbacks in fiscal 2012, but House Republicans were unable to use the spending bill to make the kind of sweeping cuts and program changes they had sought. In particular, the bill left largely intact funding for implementing the 2010 health care overhaul, although a few programs were cut back.

About three-quarters of the $723.9 billion appropriated in the Labor–Health and Human Services–Education bill was mandatory funding, primarily for the Medicare and Medicaid programs. The discretionary total was $156.3 billion—$1.1 billion less than in the fiscal 2011 law (PL 112-10) and $24.5 billion below Obama's request.

The measure did include some provisions sought by House Republicans, including limits on the authority of the National Labor Relations Board in permitting electronic unionization elections and a delay in implementing mine safety rules on exposure to coal dust. *(Union election rules, p. 534)*

Social conservatives won provisions prohibiting federal funding for needle exchange programs in the District of Columbia, providing $5 million for abstinence-only sex education, and barring HHS from using any funds for activities supporting gun control.

Although the bill did not strike at the heart of the health care overhaul (PL 111-148, PL 111-152), it did rescind $10 million of the $15 million appropriated in fiscal 2011 for a board charged with finding ways to reduce Medicare spending and making recommendations to Congress beginning in 2014. The bill also rescinded $400 million for the law's loan program to help health insurance cooperatives operate in state markets.

The funding bill also did not meet conservatives' goals of eliminating other health programs, including one that paid for medical services such as contraception and cancer screenings, primarily for low-income women. The president's Race to the Top competitive education grant program continued to receive funding, but it was cut by more than 20 percent from the fiscal 2011 level, to $550 million. The House proposal would have zeroed out the program, while Senate appropriators would have matched fiscal 2011 levels. *(Race to the Top, pp. 480, 492)*

Funding for the two largest education formula grants was increased. Title I grants for school districts with a high percentage of low-income students were funded at $14.5 billion, $60 million above the fiscal 2011 level. Programs to aid states in providing services for students with disabilities received $11.6 billion, an increase of $100 million above fiscal 2011. As expected, the bill maintained the maximum Pell grant award of $5,550 but tightened some eligibility requirements in order to help pay for it.

Funding for the three departments was folded into the omnibus after Congress made little progress on a stand-alone version of the bill. Senate appropriators approved legislation (S 1599—S Rept 112-84) in September, but the measure never made it to the floor. House GOP leaders released a bill (HR 3070) without committee action.

LEGISLATIVE BRANCH

Careful not to put Congress's funding ahead of money for other agencies, appropriators left spending for legislative operations until the end of the year, when it was included in the omnibus package. The House had passed a stand-alone legislative branch bill (HR 2551—H Rept 112-148) in July, and the Senate Appropriations Committee approved its version (S Rept 112-80) in September.

The bill funded the operations of the House and Senate. It also paid for the offices and legislative agencies that supported congressional operations, including the Capitol Police, the Architect of the Capitol, the Government Accountability Office (GAO), the Congressional Budget Office, the Library of Congress, and the Government Printing Office.

The bill was the smallest and least controversial of the annual spending bills. It also was the only one based on a budget request from Congress rather than the president. The bill allocated $1.2 billion for the House of Representatives, a reduction of $86 million, or nearly 7 percent, compared with fiscal 2011. The Senate allocation was $869 million, $46 million, or 5 percent, less than in fiscal 2011. The bill did not contain funds for representatives' or senators' salaries, which were paid from a permanent appropriation.

MILITARY CONSTRUCTION

The spending bill for military construction and the Department of Veterans Affairs (VA) provided $137.4 billion, including about $73.7 billion in discretionary spending. The remainder of the funding was for mandatory programs, virtually all of it for the Veterans Benefits Administration.

The discretionary amount was about $2 billion below Obama's request and $3.2 billion below the fiscal 2011 level (PL 112-10). The reductions, which came out of military construction funds, were more than twice what was initially expected, because appropriators had to make room for an increase in defense funding under an overall cap for security spending set by the 2011 debt limit law (PL 112-25).

The Defense Department was prohibited from using funds from the bill to build or modify facilities in the United States to house anyone who had been held at the U.S. detention center at Guantánamo Bay, Cuba. It could, however, make improvements at that facility.

The bill provided $52.5 billion in advance fiscal 2013 funding for the VA's three primary programs: medical services, medical facilities, and medical administration accounts. The bill included only $509 million in new funding for fiscal 2012, but the VA also had access to $50.6 billion in advance funds appropriated the previous year. The Veterans' Health Administration estimated it would treat more than 6.1 million patients in 2012.The bill also allocated $63.9 billion for disability compensation, pensions, GI bill benefits, and other programs.

The military construction spending bill served as the vehicle for the omnibus bill. The House passed HR 2055 (H Rept 112-94) 411–5, June 14. During floor debate, the House agreed, 204–203, to strip language from the bill that would have blocked funding for construction projects that involved "project labor agreements" requiring that the work go to unionized laborers. Twenty-six Republicans, many representing heavily unionized districts, joined 177 Democrats in voting for the amendment.

The Senate passed its version of the spending bill (S Rept 112-29), on July 20 in a 97–2 vote.

STATE–FOREIGN OPERATIONS

The omnibus bill provided $53.5 billion for the State Department and foreign operations—the combined total of the base budget and money for overseas contingency operations, which funded operations mainly in Afghanistan and Iraq. The total was $5.2 billion, or nearly 11 percent, more than was provided in fiscal 2011 (PL 112-10), although it was $6.2 billion less than Obama requested.

Much of the increase above fiscal 2011 came in the contingency operations account, which was bumped up to $11.2 billion from the $8.7 billion proposed in the Senate bill. The base budget was $42.3 billion, between what the Senate and House panels had sought. (Another $510 million was paid for by rescissions from previous funding.)

Under the debt limit deal enacted in August (PL 112-25), the State–Foreign Operations section of the omnibus was lumped in with the Defense and Homeland Security departments, and the Military Construction–VA department in a competition for dollars. By shifting money to the contingency account, which was not limited under the security spending cap, appropriators were able to preserve more funding for the State Department and for foreign assistance. The governments that faced the most scrutiny under the bill included Pakistan and Egypt. The bill also tightened the reins on aid to the Palestinian Authority.

The bill omitted some provisions advocated by House Republicans regarding the United Nations, including proposals to restructure how the United States paid its dues and to block all funding to the U.N. Population Fund (UNFPA). The legislation appropriated $35 million for the UNFPA on the condition that none of the money go to funding abortion. It also prohibited other aid money from going to abortion services but did not include more controversial language sought by House Republicans to reimpose the so-called Mexico City policy, which barred funding to any international aid group that funded or promoted abortion as a method of family planning. On the flip side, the bill left out language added by Senate Democrats that would have permanently blocked the Mexico City policy. *(Fiscal 2012 funding, p. 252; Mexico City policy background, pp. 244, 245)*

Conferees also dropped Republican-backed language to rescind a line of credit of more than $100 million to the International Monetary Fund. Congress had approved the credit line in 2009. GOP members objected to providing U.S. funds to help bail out some of Europe's debt-ridden economies.

Versions of a stand-alone bill advanced only as far as the Senate Appropriations Committee (S 1601—S Rept 112-85) and the House State–Foreign Operations Subcommittee.

Disaster Assistance

Controversy over how to pay for disaster relief continued until nearly the end of the 2011 session, when House Republicans passed a separate package of assistance legislation and forced Senate Democrats to go on the record against offsetting the $8.1 billion cost with cuts elsewhere.

The relief package, which provided continuing aid and recovery assistance for natural disasters that had occurred over the preceding year, was passed by the House, 351–67, on December 16. The Senate cleared the bill the next day, 72–27, and President Barack Obama signed it December 23 (HR 3672—PL 112-77).

The bill contained $6.4 billion for Federal Emergency Management Agency's Disaster Relief Fund and $1.7 billion for the Army Corps of Engineers. The House also adopted, 255–165, a related offsetting measure (H Con Res 94) directing the clerk of the House to add language making across-the-board rescissions of 1.8 percent to discretionary accounts in most fiscal 2012 spending bills before HR 3672 was sent to the president's desk.

The proposed offset was designed to keep total nonwar discretionary spending for fiscal 2012 at the $1.0 trillion limit, even though the debt limit law allowed for as much as $11.3 billion in additional disaster aid that did not count under the cap. The Senate rejected the offsets, 43–56, on December 17, with all Democrats except Ben Nelson of Nebraska voting no. The Senate action blocked the rescissions.

Fiscal 2013 Budget Resolution

In a near replay of the action in 2011, the Republican-controlled House passed a budget resolution for fiscal 2013 that was anathema to Democrats, and the Senate refused to take it up. It was the third year in a row that Congress failed to reach agreement on setting parameters on congressional spending and taxing decisions for the year. The standoff once again signaled the deep differences between the two parties on fiscal policies as well as the difficulties Congress would face throughout 2012 as it struggled to deal with decisions on spending, taxes, and deficit control.

In one sense, the budget was less important than it might have been because the fiscal 2013 discretionary spending limits that normally would be proposed in a budget had already been set at $1.0 trillion in the 2011 debt limit law known as the Budget Control Act (PL 112-25). *(Budget act, p. 160)*

Yet, failure to reach agreement left hanging the issue of automatic spending cuts of $1.2 trillion that were set to begin in January 2013, known as a sequester, which many members of Congress wanted to prevent. In early February, President Barack Obama released a fiscal 2013 budget proposal that the White House said would serve as a replacement for the so-called sequester if it were accepted in full. The spending cuts were required under the Budget Control Act once a special joint congressional committee was unable to agree on deficit reduction legislation in November 2011. *(Deficit committee, p. 168)*

There was little likelihood, particularly in an election year, that many of the main features in Obama's proposals would be accepted. The president again proposed to continue tax cuts for middle-income families enacted in 2001 and 2003 (PL 107—16, PL 108-27), while allowing them to expire for higher-income taxpayers. He again proposed to boost spending on job creation, transportation, infrastructure projects, education, and research, while making relatively small cuts to Medicare, Medicaid, and other mandatory programs.

In stark contrast, the House budget resolution called for spending cuts that exceeded those agreed to in 2011 as part of a contentious deal that produced the Budget Control Act. All of the new cuts were to come from domestic spending. The resolution (H Con Res 112) would have limited discretionary appropriations in fiscal 2013 to $1.028 trillion—$19 billion below the $1.047 trillion set by the 2011 budget act (PL 112-25) and the amount President Obama proposed. The GOP wanted to cancel the discretionary portion of the sequester—which amounted to $98 billion, including $55 billion in cuts to the military—to prevent those Pentagon reductions and allow for even higher defense spending. It would have replaced the $98 billion with a combination of $19 billion saved by lowering the 2013 discretionary cap and a separate "reconciliation" bill (HR 5652) that would pare more than $261 billion from mandatory spending over ten years. *(Reconciliation bill, p. 180; Budget Act, p. 160)*

Reconciliation bills, which could only be used as part of a budget resolution, benefited from expedited rules in the Senate, requiring only fifty-one votes to pass, rather than the sixty votes needed to overcome a filibuster. The House subsequently passed a reconciliation bill, but it would have received the special protection only if both chambers had adopted the budget resolution.

The House resolution was drawn up by Budget Committee Chair Paul D. Ryan, R-Wis, who later in the year was selected by GOP presidential candidate Mitt Romney as his vice presidential running mate. The GOP resolution contained several policy provisions that were unacceptable to most Democrats, such as repealing the 2010 health care law (PL 111-148, PL 111-152), revising Medicare, and making what the committee report on the resolution called "fundamental reform" in Medicaid. The resolution also called for an overhaul of the income tax system. *(Health care law, p. 421)*

House appropriators stuck with the $1.028 trillion discretionary cap when they wrote their annual spending bills, leading the White House to issue veto threats against all of them. Senate appropriators ignored the House resolution and used the higher figure for their spending bills. In the end, over conservatives' objections, Democratic and Republican leaders set the House caps aside, instead winning enactment in September of a law that continued appropriations for six months at the $1.047 trillion level. *(Fiscal 2013 appropriations, p. 181)*

PRESIDENT'S BUDGET REQUEST

Obama sent Congress a $3.8 trillion fiscal 2013 budget on February 13, slightly above the $3.7 trillion in outlays enacted for fiscal 2012. The administration said the budget would reduce accumulated deficits by more than $3 trillion over a decade.

That document reflected priorities the White House had emphasized the previous year—and that the president would continue to emphasize throughout his campaign for reelection. Combining short-term job creation proposals with longer-term deficit control measures, it called for trimming the deficit in a way that the president said would "balance" tax increases with spending cuts and do little harm to the fragile economic recovery.

During congressional hearings after the release of the budget, administration officials stressed that the plan would bring deficits down to about 3 percent of the gross domestic product (GDP), a level that they said would stabilize the debt as a share of the economy, at least in the near term.

Democrats generally applauded Obama's budget while Republicans assailed it, charging that its claim of budgetary savings relied on unwise tax increases and gimmicks such as counting the declining costs of the wars in Afghanistan and Iraq as spending cuts that would save $848 billion.

The nonpartisan Congressional Budget Office (CBO) released its annual analysis of the president's budget in March, saying Obama's plan would add $6.4 trillion to the accumulated debt over ten years—$294 billion less than the administration estimated but $3.5 trillion more than if the budget proposals were not enacted. The CBO was measuring Obama's proposal against a baseline that reflected the level of taxes and spending if existing law continued unchanged. The CBO's estimates for the president's budget were used by Congress and are used in the following account as well.

Highlights of Budget Proposal

The CBO said the budget would result in $3.7 trillion in outlays—the money that actually would be spent during the year—$137 billion more than without any changes in law. Obama's budget complied with the $1.047 trillion cap for fiscal 2013 discretionary budget authority set under the Budget Control Act. The administration adjusted the request downward to $1.043 trillion because it was seeking to transfer about $4 billion in fiscal 2013 surface transportation funding to the mandatory part of the ledger—a plan with little support in Congress. In addition, the budget included $104 billion that was not covered by the caps, mainly for war costs in Afghanistan and Iraq and for disaster aid.

The discretionary total included $552 billion for the base Defense Department budget and $88 billion for the wars in Afghanistan and Iraq and related costs. The CBO said the base budget was down $2 billion compared with fiscal 2012 spending; the war funding was a decrease of $27 billion from the previous year. (The administration also requested more than $8 billion in nondefense funds for activities related to the wars, effectively bringing the war total to $97 billion.)

Obama proposed more than $2 billion in fiscal 2013 cuts in Pentagon weapons programs, including a plan to stop buying C-27J cargo aircraft, which was projected to save $480 million. He also called for new fees and co-payment increases for Tricare, the military health care program.

The budget included $507 billion for nondefense programs, including the $8 billion for war-related expenses. The total was a drop of about $22 billion from fiscal 2012 spending. Winners under the budget included high-speed rail, for which Obama requested $2.7 billion, and state and local homeland security programs, which would get a $518 million increase, to $2.9 billion. Obama also requested $5 billion for a new competitive grant program for state and local school districts.

According to the CBO calculations, outlays for mandatory programs would be $1.2 trillion higher than under the CBO baseline. The biggest single cause of the increase was the president's proposal to reclassify most surface transportation funding as mandatory, which the CBO said would cause a $486 billion boost in mandatory spending over ten years. Another $366 billion of the increase came from various proposals to increase refundable tax credits such as the earned income tax credit; the cost counted as outlays. Another major factor was a $271 billion increase from a proposal to freeze Medicare physician pay rates at 2012 levels, rather than letting them decline by 27 percent in January 2013 as scheduled under existing law.

Cuts in outlays for mandatory spending under Obama's budget included savings in the Medicare and Medicaid programs and eliminating direct payments to farmers.

Tax Proposals

Obama offered a mix of new and familiar tax proposals designed to strengthen manufacturing, boost hiring across the economy, and collect more revenue from people with higher incomes. Taken together, the CBO said, the president's proposals would reduce revenue by $61 billion in 2012 and $228 billion in 2013.

To aid manufacturers, Obama again proposed a permanent extension and expansion of the research and development tax credit. One of the most significant new proposals was a call to double the value of the biggest tax break for manufacturers—the domestic manufacturing deduction—in cases where manufacturing was considered to be "advanced," while eliminating the deduction for oil companies. Companies that scaled back overseas operations could claim a 20 percent tax credit against the cost of new domestic factories. Another tax credit was designed to help companies moving to communities that had recently suffered significant job losses.

To encourage job growth, the budget included a temporary 10 percent tax credit for companies that increased their payrolls up to $500,000. The budget also called for extending "100 percent expensing" for another year, to encourage investment by allowing companies to deduct the full cost of equipment immediately rather than over several years.

A key feature, promoted in previous Obama budgets, dealt with the tax cuts enacted in 2001 and 2003 that were set to expire at the end of 2012. Obama proposed to extend the tax rates on individual income up to $200,000 and household income up to $250,000, while allowing rates for the top two tax brackets to rise as scheduled from 33 percent and 35 percent to the pre-2001 rates of 36 percent and 39.6 percent.

The budget also called for returning the estate tax to its 2009 level by setting the top rate at 45 percent, with an exemption of $3.5 million per person. Absent congressional action by January 2013, the estate tax rate was set to jump from 35 percent to 55 percent, with the exemption falling to $1 million per person from its inflation-indexed level of $5.1 million in 2012.

According to the CBO, the 2013 deficit would decline from $1.171 trillion in 2012 to $977 billion under Obama's budget. The new shortfall would be 6.1 percent of the gross domestic product and $365 billion more than the $612 billion in red ink projected in the CBO's baseline.

Between 2013 and 2022, deficits would total $6.4 trillion, or 3.2 percent of projected GDP, $3.5 trillion more than under the CBO baseline.

A major contributor to the CBO's calculation of the deficit under Obama's budget was the fact that, under the agency's mandate to measure the effects compared with existing law, it had to assume that all the 2001 and 2003 tax breaks would expire on schedule.

Economic Assumptions

The administration was relatively cautious in the economic assumptions that underpinned the budget, forecasting slow growth compared with that of past recoveries. The White House noted that "financial markets here and in Europe have been troubled by concerns about weak economic growth and the sustainability of fiscal policy in some European countries. The drag from a European slowdown could hold back the U.S. economy."

Still, the administration projected that GDP would grow by 2.7 percent in 2012, after accounting for inflation, and by 3 percent in 2013. The administration's growth forecasts were more optimistic than the Blue Chip consensus of private economists, which projected GDP growth of 2.2 percent in 2012 and 2.6 percent in 2013. They were also much more optimistic than the CBO's projections of 2 percent in 2012 and 1.1 percent in 2013.

As it always did, the White House forecast assumed that Congress would agree to all of the administration's budget recommendations. The administration also assumed a yearlong extension of the 2010 payroll tax cut and federal support for expanded unemployment benefits, both of which it credited with stimulating the economy. The CBO assumed that both policies would expire, removing what the administration said was a significant stimulus for growth.

The White House locked down its unemployment projections in November 2011, before a surge in payroll growth and a drop in the jobless rate to 8.3 percent, the lowest since early 2009, in January. As a result, the administration projected unemployment of 8.9 percent in 2012 and 8.6 percent in 2013. That was higher than the Blue Chip forecast of 8.3 percent in 2012 and 7.9 percent in 2013. The CBO was more pessimistic on unemployment figures, projecting 8.9 percent in 2012 and 9.2 percent in 2013.

HOUSE ACTION

The House Budget Committee adopted Ryan's plan (H Con Res 112—H Rept 112-421) by the barest of margins, 19–18, on March 21, with two GOP freshmen joining all Democrats in voting no.

In a renewed bid to advance his plan to restructure federal health care programs, Ryan adjusted the controversial Medicare premium support plan he had offered in 2011. That proposal would have provided new Medicare beneficiaries with fixed subsidies that could be used to buy coverage through government-certified plans. His fiscal 2013 proposal would have given seniors a government subsidy to help them buy health insurance but allowed them to use it for the traditional fee-for-service Medicare program if they wished. *(2012 budget resolution, p. 156)*

Democrats blasted the plan, calling the subsidies vouchers that would not keep up with inflation and warning that the program would end the government's promise to ensure health care benefits for seniors.

The White House was blunt, too. In a posting to the Office of Management and Budget website, Acting Director Jeff Zients said that, in addition to the "roughly $1 trillion in cuts in the Budget Control Act, it would be difficult to overstate the radicalism of the domestic cuts proposed. . . . In 2013, it would cut annual nondefense funding by 5 percent. By 2014, the resolution would cut this funding by 19 percent in purely nominal terms. Over a decade, the resolution would cut more than $1 trillion in nondefense spending on top of the reductions the president has already signed into law. The cuts in nondefense discretionary funding are nearly three times as deep as the cuts under the so-called sequester—cuts that we and most objective analysts have always regarded as unwise and unacceptable."

Overcoming objections from conservatives in their caucus who wanted deeper spending cuts, House GOP leaders won adoption of their fiscal 2013 budget resolution March 29 by a **key vote of 228–191 (R 228–10; D 0–181)**. *(2012 key votes, p. 803)*

As was traditional, the House considered several alternative budgets but rejected all of them by wide margins. Among the alternatives was a proposal based on the debt reduction framework put forth by the co-chairs of the presidential debt commission in 2010. That plan would have trimmed the deficit by more than $4 billion over ten years, with two-thirds of the savings coming from spending cuts and one-third from revenue increases. *(Presidential debt panel, p. 142)*

As passed by the House, H Con Res 112 replaced the Budget Control Act's fiscal 2013 discretionary spending cap of $1.047 trillion with a lower $1.028 trillion limit. The measure provided $554 billion for defense—$8 billion more than the cap set by the law and $63 billion more than if the scheduled sequester were to occur. Nondefense programs, which included domestic appropriations as well as international affairs funding, were essentially capped at $474 billion ($27 billion below the level set by the budget law and $16 billion more than under the sequester).

Over the following nine years, discretionary spending for defense would be above the annual limits set in the Budget Control Act, while nondefense discretionary spending would be well below the law's caps.

In other spending changes, the resolution reduces the federal workforce by 10 percent over three years, and froze federal pay through 2015, eliminated federal subsidies for high-speed rail, limited the growth of federal financial aid for college students and focused it on low-income students, and consolidated job-training programs.

Most of the alternative savings replacing the sequester were to be achieved through the separate budget reconciliation bill. The budget resolution instructed six House committees to find mandatory savings equal to $261.5 billion over ten years. The major change would come from giving Medicare beneficiaries a government subsidy, starting in 2023, to buy health insurance from either a qualified private plan or the traditional fee-for-service Medicare. Costs would be contained by the competition between the plans for seniors' business and by a limit on per capita program growth.

Other savings would come from converting both the federal share of Medicaid spending and the food stamp program into block grants, implementing time limits and work requirements for low-income assistance programs and capping the amount of federal payments, capping noneconomic damages in medical liability lawsuits, repealing exchange subsidies for health insurance and making other changes to the 2010 health care overhaul, and reducing fixed payments to farmers and revising support for crop insurance.

On taxes, the resolution would consolidate the six existing individual income tax brackets into two brackets set at 10 percent and 25 percent, reduce the corporate tax rate to 25 percent, and repeal the alternative minimum tax. It would also broaden the tax base to maintain overall revenue between 18 percent and 19 percent of gross domestic product.

SENATE ACTION

In a news conference March 20, the day Ryan released his House plan, Senate Budget Chair Kent Conrad, D-N.D., made it clear that he did not intend to revisit what he said was a settled budget. Conrad ultimately presented the Senate Budget Committee with a draft plan modeled on the presidential debt panel recommendations.

The Conrad plan would have consolidated the six tax brackets into three, setting them at 12 percent, 22 percent, and 28 percent. It would have set the corporate tax rate at 28 percent and repealed the alternative minimum tax. The proposal assumed an overhaul of Medicare and Social Security, cuts in certain agricultural subsidies, and changes to the military and civil retirement systems.

But Conrad and Majority Leader Harry Reid, D-Nev., said they would not try to bring a budget resolution to the floor. Conrad said the overwhelming vote against the Simpson-Bowles framework in the House had helped convince him the "timing is not yet right" for a vote on his plan in the Senate. Rather, he said he hoped his proposal would spur negotiations on a long-term spending plan aimed at reducing the deficit before Congress faced a series of major tax and spending decisions after the election.

Senate Republicans sought to put Democrats on the defensive May 16, lambasting the majority party for not bringing a budget resolution to the floor in three years. The Republicans tried, without success, to bring up several GOP proposals, as well as the House-passed resolution and what they said was a version of the president's fiscal 2013 budget. A motion to proceed to consideration of H Con Res 112 was rejected May 16 on a **key vote of 41–58 (R 41–5; D 0–51; I 0–2)**. *(2012 key votes, p. 803)*

Conrad said the Budget Control Act allowed him to provide authorizers and appropriators with budget allocations to move forward on fiscal 2013 bills, chiding Republicans for suggesting those levels did not exist. "Maybe my colleagues missed it when they were voting on it," he said.

House Reconciliation Bill

In an effort to force Senate Democrats to act on a budget resolution, or at least embarrass them because they opted not to, House Republicans followed up their fiscal 2013 budget resolution in May with legislation to replace across-the-board spending cuts scheduled for 2013 with reductions to mandatory social programs. Democrats responded that the GOP proposals unfairly targeted the poor and others in need of government help.

The House GOP bill (HR 5652—H Rept 112-470) would cancel $98 billion in automatic cuts to discretionary funding set to take effect in January 2013, including $55 billion in cuts to the military. The primary aim was to prevent those Pentagon reductions and allow for even higher defense spending. The bill would replace those automatic cuts, known as a sequester, with a $19 billion cut in the discretionary cap for fiscal 2013 and with "reconciliation" savings recommended by six House committees that over a decade would pare more than $310 billion from mandatory spending.

The House passed the reconciliation bill, 218–199, on May 10, mostly along party lines. The vote was taken after Democrats and Republicans spent much of the week engaged in an emotional debate about their different approaches to reducing the deficit. No Democrats voted in favor of the measure, and sixteen Republicans—many of them moderates from the East and Midwest—voted against it.

Democrats agreed that they did not want the automatic cuts required under the 2011 Budget Control Act (PL 112-25) to occur. But they wanted the substitute reductions to come from cutting tax exemptions that "benefit special interests" and from raising the income tax rate for high-income earners.

The White House threatened to veto the House bill, and in the Senate, Majority Leader Harry Reid, D-Nev., stuck to his decision not to allow floor time for a budget resolution, a precondition for considering a reconciliation bill under expedited procedures.

Fiscal 2013 Continuing Resolution

In a rare instance of bipartisan unity, congressional Democrats and Republicans agreed to push the fiscal 2013 appropriations process past the November 2012 elections and into the following year. President Barack Obama signed the resulting continuing resolution (CR) into law (H J Res 117—PL 112-175) on September 28, just two days before the start of the fiscal year. The measure continued appropriations at slightly above the fiscal 2012 level through March 27, 2013.

With none of the twelve fiscal 2013 spending bills even close to clearing, the White House and a bipartisan congressional leadership team had negotiated the agreement in August. Neither party wanted the threat of a government shutdown hanging over the November elections, a likely problem if they had tried to reach a year-long agreement. Both also preferred to remove the issue from the expected year-end clash over expiring tax law and a pending across-the-board spending cut, collectively known as the fiscal cliff.

The measure increased spending by 0.6 percent for most federal programs and agencies and left agencies operating in a kind of limbo for the following six months, running on appropriations laws enacted in 2011 and without the ability to make major changes in their budgets or operations.

Democrats signed off on the six-month CR only after it was agreed that it would reflect the $1.047 trillion fiscal 2013 discretionary spending cap set in the 2011 Budget Control Act (PL 112-25). House GOP conservatives wanted the CR instead to reflect the $1.028 trillion limit that had been part of the House-adopted fiscal 2013 budget resolution (H Con Res 112). They were reluctant to come aboard but ultimately agreed that the chance for deeper cuts in 2013 if they succeeded in taking the White House and the Senate made it worth supporting the stopgap bill. *(2011 Budget Control Act, p. 160; 2013 budget resolution, p. 177)*

In exchange, they demanded the measure not be used as a vehicle for a slew of unrelated measures, a common practice with CRs. About three dozen exceptions were included to address some pressing needs, such as advancing weather satellites and fighting wildfires. But appropriators said this limited number of special measures did not scratch the surface of the changes that were needed.

Even the Pentagon, which enjoyed great favor with conservative Republicans, faced limits on its operations under the bill. "The CR is stringent on defense," said Norm Dicks of Washington, the ranking Democrat on both the House Appropriations Committee and its defense subcommittee. "DoD requested limited authority for new starts and changes in production and procurement rates. Those requests were denied."

Some House conservatives objected to the CR's extensions of domestic programs they had been working to curtail or end. For example, the CR extended the 1996 welfare overhaul law, known as Temporary Assistance for Needy Families (TANF; PL 104-193). Authorization for the program was scheduled to run out on September 30. Republicans opposed an administration plan to allow states to apply for waivers from TANF's work participation requirements. However, the CR simply reauthorized the welfare program without mentioning the waivers. *(Welfare law, Congress and the Nation Vol. IX, p. 578)*

LEGISLATIVE ACTION

The House passed the continuing resolution by a vote of 329–91 on September 13, after House conservatives dropped threats to try to squeeze out more savings. A majority from each party voted for passage, with seventy generally conservative Republicans and twenty-one Democrats—a mix of left- and right-leaning members—in opposition.

Despite the lopsided vote, the stopgap funding bill prompted little enthusiasm among House members. Spending bills often carry suggestions and sometimes very specific directions from lawmakers for agencies to improve their operations, but the CR provided only broad guidance on spending. "The CR, some say, at least lets us keep the government open," said David E. Price of North Carolina, the ranking Democrat on the House Homeland Security Appropriations Subcommittee. "But merely averting a shutdown is hardly an achievement."

The Senate cleared the measure, 62–30, in a rare Friday-to-Saturday session that extended until just before dawn September 22, marking the end of a week of delays that threatened the chamber's plans to adjourn for the election campaign. Just one Democrat, Joe Manchin III of West Virginia, voted no, while a dozen Republicans voted with the majority.

One reason for the delays was a threat by Rand Paul, R-Ky., to stall all Senate business until he received a vote on a bill (S 3576) to cut off aid to certain countries including Pakistan, Egypt, and Libya. The bill was rejected, 10–81, with all the yes votes coming from conservative Republicans.

Besides the vote on the Paul bill, the Senate took up two other bills as part of the deal to break the CR logjam: a sense of Congress resolution (S J Res 41) from Lindsey Graham, R-S.C., urging "diplomatic and economic pressure" to deter Iran from developing nuclear weapons capability, and a bill (S 3525) sponsored by Jon Tester, D-Mont., who faced a tight reelection race, to ease restrictions on hunters and sportsmen. The Graham resolution won agreement, 90–1. The Tester bill was rejected, 50–44, on November 26 in a procedure that required sixty votes.

Fiscal 2013 Appropriations Roundup

None of the fiscal 2013 appropriations bills cleared during the second session of the 112th Congress, in 2012. Instead, lawmakers sent President Barack Obama a continuing resolution (CR) that provided spending through March 27, 2013, at an annualized rate of 0.6 percent above fiscal 2012 levels for most federal programs. Obama signed the bill into law September 28 (H J Res 117—PL 112—175). *(Continuing resolution, p. 180)*

Before passing the CR, the House had passed eleven of the twelve regular bills, and the Senate had passed five. None of them had gone to conference. The White House threatened to veto all the House-passed bills because they did not conform to limits set in the 2011 debt limit law, known as the Budget Control Act (PL 112—25). That law set a fiscal 2013 discretionary spending cap of up to $1.047 trillion. The nondefense bills would have limited discretionary funding to a lower, $1.028 trillion level called for in the House-adopted fiscal 2013 budget resolution. The House defense bill, by contrast, exceeded the cap under the debt limit law. The Senate did not act on the resolution. *(2013 budget resolution, p. 177; budget act, p. 160)*

The following account summarizes major actions that were taken on each of the individual spending bills before the six-month CR was enacted.

AGRICULTURE

The Appropriations committees in both chambers approved versions of the fiscal 2013 spending bill for the Agriculture Department's food and nutrition programs, the Food and Drug Administration, and other related agencies and programs.

Senate appropriators went first, approving a $142.2 billion measure (S 2375—S Rept 112—163) on April 26. The House Appropriations Committee version (HR 5973—H Rept 112—542), approved June 19, would have provided $140.8 billion.

The Senate bill included higher amounts for rural development and international food aid. Senate appropriators would have provided about $375 million more than their House counterparts for agriculture programs and $120 million more for the Women, Infants and Children program.

The House bill included $180 million for the Commodity Futures Trading Commission (CFTC), 12 percent below fiscal 2012 levels and 41 percent less than the president requested. Democrats expressed concern that cuts to the CFTC would come at a time when the agency was working to implement the 2010 Dodd-Frank financial regulatory overhaul (PL 111—203), a law that many Republicans strongly opposed. *(Dodd-Frank, p. 88)*

COMMERCE-JUSTICE-SCIENCE

The House passed a fiscal 2013 bill (HR 5326—H Rept 112-463) to fund the departments of Commerce and Justice, along with science programs such as the National Aeronautics and Space Administration (NASA). Senate appropriators approved a committee version of the measure (S 2323—S Rept 112-158), but the legislation went no further.

Overall funding levels in the two versions were relatively similar. One main difference concerned NASA, which would have received $1.8 billion more under the Senate version.

The House-passed bill included a number of GOP policy riders that seemed certain to set up a fight with the Senate. For example, one amendment adopted on the floor would have barred the use of funds to pursue lawsuits aimed at overturning or invalidating specific immigration laws in eight states. Amendment supporters said there were more than ten million "unauthorized aliens" in the country and that states needed to be able to enforce laws if the federal government refused to do so.

The House also adopted an amendment that would have barred the use of funds to pay for the 2010 health care overhaul (PL 111-148, PL 111-152). A third would not have allowed funding to contravene the Defense of Marriage Act (PL 104-199), which defined marriage as the union of one man and one woman. *(Health care overhaul, p. 421; Defense of Marriage Act, Congress and the Nation Vol. IX, p. 746)*

DEFENSE

The House passed a fiscal 2013 Republican-sponsored Defense Department spending bill (HR 5856—H Rept 112-493) that would have boosted Pentagon funds beyond limits set in the 2011 Budget Control Act (PL 112-25). Senate Democratic appropriators approved a version (S Rept 112-196) that stayed within the spending caps but did so partly by shifting money from the base Pentagon budget to the Overseas Contingency Operations account, which funded operations in Afghanistan and Iraq and did not count under the statutory caps.

The House bill, passed on July 19, included $518 billion for the nonwar, or base, Pentagon budget—virtually the same as the amount enacted for fiscal 2012—and $87.7 billion for contingency account. Although the total was cut by more than $1 billion during floor consideration, the base budget was still almost $7 billion higher than the cap for defense set by the budget law. Members rejected an amendment that would have reduced the bill's funding by $7.6 billion, dropping it to about the amount authorized under the budget act.

More than a dozen antiwar lawmakers from both parties called during the debate for an end to U.S. fighting in Afghanistan. However, the House rejected an amendment that would have cut spending for overseas contingency operations by $20.8 billion and limited the use of funds for Afghanistan operations to the safe and orderly withdrawal of U.S. troops.

The House also adopted an amendment to prohibit the use of funds in the bill to reduce U.S. nuclear forces and to implement or modify key Pentagon documents on military strategy and capabilities. Another amendment would have barred funding to reduce the number of delivery vehicles for nuclear weapons.

The Senate Appropriations Committee version of HR 5856 included $511.2 billion for the base budget but boosted contingency funding to $93 billion.

In what was seen as a significant blow to the Air Force's bid to lower its budget, both panels added funds for weapons that the Air Force wanted to retire including aircraft, Global Hawk surveillance drones, and Aegis cruisers.

Appropriators also rejected plans to reduce funding for submarines and destroyers. Appropriators in both chambers rejected a request from the president for $4.4 billion in advance funding for high-frequency communications satellites, as well as his request to increase fees for the military's Tricare health care system.

ENERGY-WATER

Conflict over the nuclear waste depository in Yucca Mountain, Nev., was one of the main factors separating a House-passed fiscal 2013 Energy-Water spending bill and a version approved by the Senate Appropriations Committee.

The House passed a $32.2 billion bill (HR 5325—H Rept 112-462) for the Energy Department, the Army Corps of Engineers, and Interior Department water projects on June 6. The amount was $1.6 billion below the fiscal 2012 appropriation and $1.5 billion less than requested. The measure would have prohibited the Obama administration from closing Yucca Mountain—which it was in the process of doing—and appropriated $25 million to keep the site operational.

It included $7.6 billion to maintain and refurbish nuclear weapons, an increase of about $300 million above the fiscal 2012 level. It would have reduced funding for the Energy Department's energy efficiency and renewable energy programs and research projects by $430 million from 2012, about $890 million less than Obama requested.

The Senate Appropriations Committee version (S 2465—S Rept 112-164), approved on April 26, would have provided about $1.3 billion more than the House version and authorized the Energy Department to establish a pilot project for consolidating spent nuclear fuel at one or more interim storage sites. The bill included $535 million more than the House version for energy efficiency and renewable energy and about the same amount as in the House bill for nuclear-weapons programs.

FINANCIAL SERVICES

The House and Senate Appropriations committees approved versions of the fiscal 2013 spending bill for the Treasury Department and a number of regulatory agencies, including the Securities and Exchange Commission (SEC), as well as for the federal judiciary and the District of Columbia. Although the funding levels were not that far apart, the panels appeared on a collision course over House GOP efforts to target the 2010 laws overhauling health care (PL 111-148, PL 111-152) and creating new regulations for the financial services industry (PL 111-203). However, the legislation went no further in either chamber.

The Senate panel sought to boost funding substantially for the financial regulators charged with implementing the Dodd-Frank regulatory overhaul, increasing funding for the Commodity Futures Trading Commission (CFTC) by 50 percent, to $308 million, compared with the fiscal 2012 level and boosting funding for the SEC by 19 percent to $1.6 billion. House appropriators funded the agency under the Agriculture bill, which proposed to cut the CFTC's account to $180 million. The Senate panel voted along party lines to reject an amendment that would have barred the Internal Revenue Service (IRS) from using its funds to implement the individual mandate of the 2010 health care law.

The bill approved by the House Appropriations Committee contained provisions to prohibit the transfer of funds between the IRS and the Department of Health and Human Services to implement the health care overhaul law. The panel rejected a Democratic effort to increase funding for the SEC, IRS, the Office of Management and Budget, and the judiciary.

HOMELAND SECURITY

Conflicts over immigration enforcement and airline passenger fees were among the differences that separated the House and Senate versions of the bill for the Homeland Security Department. The measures were only about $650 million apart on total funding.

The legislation passed the House and won approval from the Senate Appropriations Committee but went no further.

After a lengthy debate, much of it focused on a proposed increase in aviation security fees, Senate appropriators backed a $46.7 billion bill (S 3216—S Rept 112-169) on May 22. The total was $1 billion below the fiscal 2012 level and would have marked the third consecutive year of cuts for homeland security. Responding to an administration request, the bill increased the security fees from as little as $2.50 to a flat $5 for a one-way trip.

The House passed a $46 billion version of the bill (HR 5855—H Rept 112-492) on June 7. Immigration issues took center stage during the floor debate. Among several GOP amendments adopted was one to block funds for the White House's use of what GOP critics dubbed "administrative amnesty" by prioritizing the removal of dangerous illegal immigrants while easing enforcement actions against those attending college or serving in the military. *(Immigration issues, pp. 556, 577)*

INTERIOR-ENVIRONMENT

The House Appropriations Committee approved a controversial bill (HR 6901—H Rept 112-589) to provide $28.1 billion to fund the Interior Department, the Environmental Protection Agency (EPA), the Forest Service, and related agencies. The total was $1.2 billion below the fiscal 2012 level and $1.7 billion below Obama's request. The bill never came to the House floor, however, nor did Senate appropriators act on the measure.

During a two-day markup, House appropriators focused much of their attention on policy riders and the GOP's plan to reduce spending for the EPA by 17 percent. The committee proposed to slash spending for the Land and Water Conservation Fund—which paid for public lands acquisitions—by 80 percent from fiscal 2012, bringing the program to its lowest funding level since it was created in

1965. Financial assistance for water treatment through the Clean Water State Revolving Fund was cut in half, and climate change programs were cut by more than a quarter.

Other policy riders in the bill included language to allow the extension of grazing permits on federal land without the required National Environmental Policy Act (PL 91-190) review and to double the length of grazing permits from ten to twenty years. The bill also would have barred the EPA from changing or issuing guidance or rules clarifying the federal jurisdiction of the Clean Water Act (PL 92-500).

LABOR–HEALTH AND HUMAN SERVICES–EDUCATION

The Senate Appropriations Committee approved a bill to fund the departments of Labor, Health and Human Services (HHS), and Education, and the House Labor–HHS–Education Subcommittee approved a draft measure. Sharp differences over discretionary spending limits and policy riders were expected to generate fights between the two chambers, but the legislation went no further in either chamber.

Senate appropriators approved their bill (S 3295—S Rept 112-176) on June 14, agreeing to $158.8 billion in discretionary spending, after the Democratic majority rebuffed Republican attempts to add language restricting the authority of the National Labor Relations Board and curbing funds for a provision of the 2010 health care overhaul law.

The House subcommittee approved a draft July 18 that the panel said would provide $150 billion in discretionary funding. Over vehement objections from Democrats, the bill proposed to rescind $1.6 billion for the Center for Medicare and Medicaid Innovation and $15 million for the Independent Payment Advisory Board, which was charged with recommending steps to lower Medicare spending growth. It proposed to block any new discretionary funding for the health care overhaul in fiscal 2013.

The draft also would have blocked funding for Race to the Top, Obama's signature competitive education grant program, and prohibited support for National Public Radio. It would have eliminated funding for Title X, which paid for such medical services as contraception and cancer screenings, primarily for low-income women. Planned Parenthood would have gotten no funding unless it agreed not to perform abortions or provide referrals to places that did.

LEGISLATIVE BRANCH

The House on June 8 passed a $3.3 billion fiscal 2013 legislative branch spending bill (HR 5882—H Rept 112-511), mainly for members' office expenses and the cost of congressional agencies, such as the Capitol Police, the Architect of the Capitol, and the Library of Congress. By tradition, the House bill excluded Senate expenses, which were added by the other chamber.

The Senate Appropriations Committee approved a $4.3 billion version of the bill (S Rept 112-197) on August 2. The legislation went no further, however.

The House bill would have trimmed or maintained the budgets of most Capitol Hill agencies compared with fiscal 2012 spending, while boosting funding by 6 percent for the Capitol Police, 2 percent for the Government Accountability Office, and 1 percent for the Congressional Budget Office.

The amended version of the bill approved by Senate appropriators provided $61 million for a costly project to restore the Capital Dome. Similar to the House-passed bill, the original Senate proposal would have zeroed out that funding.

MILITARY CONSTRUCTION–VETERANS AFFAIRS

With spending levels closely aligned, the House-passed and Senate committee–approved versions of the bill for military construction and the Department of Veterans Affairs (VA) were relatively noncontroversial and were expected to pose few problems for lawmakers negotiating a final bill. But the legislation never got that far.

The House passed its $148.3 billion Military Construction–VA bill (HR 5854—H Rept 112-491) on May 31. The measure included $71.1 billion for discretionary programs, matching the fiscal 2012 level but $694 million less than Obama requested. Before passing the bill, the House voted 218–198 to strip a labor provision that would have barred agencies from requiring companies bidding for construction contracts to accept collective bargaining agreements known as project labor agreements. Although GOP leaders backed the provision, moderate Republicans and others from big union districts voted to take it out.

The Senate Appropriations Committee approved a $148.5 billion version of the measure (S 3215—S Rept 112-168) on May 22. The panel said the bill would provide $71.9 billion in discretionary funds, including $54.5 billion in advance fiscal 2014 appropriations for veterans' medical care.

STATE–FOREIGN OPERATIONS

House and Senate appropriators had distinctly different views on how much to spend on State Department operations and U.S. foreign affairs, with the Senate committee proposing about 8 percent more than its House counterpart. But the fiscal 2013 bill did not get beyond committee markups.

The House Appropriations Committee approved a bill (HR 5857—H Rept 112-494) May 17 that would have provided $48.5 billion, $5 billion below the fiscal 2012 level and $6.3 billion below Obama's request. The total met the president's request for $8.2 billion for overseas contingency operations, related mainly to the wars in Afghanistan and Iraq.

In a familiar fight, the panel defeated, largely along party lines, proposals from three Democrats to allow U.S. funding for the U.N. Population Fund. The underlying bill blocked money for the fund, which oversaw reproductive health programs in the developing world. The panel also retained language to reinstate the "Mexico City" policy, which prohibited funding for international aid groups that promoted abortion as a method of family planning.

On May 24, Senate appropriators approved $52.3 billion (S 3241—S Rept 112-172), well above the House amount but still $1.2 billion below the fiscal 2012 level. In a unanimous vote, the committee agreed to withhold $33 million of the $250 million in the bill for military aid to Pakistan to protest the country's treason conviction of a doctor who helped the United States find al Qaeda leader Osama bin Laden.

Senate appropriators broke ranks with the House panel by including $44.5 million for the U.N. Population Fund. The panel not only rejected the reinstatement of the Mexico City policy, it also adopted a proposal to allow U.S. funding for international aid groups that provided information on abortion.

In another difference with the House, Senate appropriators included $1 billion for a new account to help respond to political transitions taking place across North Africa and the Middle East as a result of the Arab spring. The administration asked for $770 million for the fund. The House committee denied the administration's request.

TRANSPORTATION–HOUSING AND URBAN DEVELOPMENT

Appropriators in the two chambers were $1.8 billion apart on discretionary spending in their versions of the fiscal 2013 spending bill for the departments of Transportation and Housing and Urban Development. The bill did not advance beyond the committee stage in either chamber, however.

The Senate Appropriations Committee approved a bill (S 2322—S Rept 112-157) April 19 that would have provided $53.4 billion in discretionary spending, virtually equal to the amount requested. Including limits on money that could be spent from the Highway Trust Fund, the total came to $105.5 billion.

After a debate that stretched over three days, the House on June 29 passed a spending bill (HR 5972—H Rept 112-541) that proposed to cut overall funding for transportation programs by $1.9 billion and housing programs by $3.9 billion, compared with fiscal 2012 levels. Overall, the bill included $51.6 billion in discretionary funding, $2.2 billion less than the fiscal 2012 level, not counting disaster spending in that year. When trust fund limits were included, the bill's total rose to $103.6 billion.

Both the House and Senate bills would have allowed $39.9 billion to be obligated from the Highway Trust Fund for the federal-aid highway program and transit formula and bus grants—the same amount as enacted in fiscal 2012, not counting disaster spending. But the two measures differed on several remaining provisions. The House measure would have zeroed out a grant program for infrastructure projects with national or regional significance, known as TIGER grants, which received $500 million in fiscal 2012, a funding level Senate appropriators sought to continue.

The House bill would have increased funding for the Community Development Block Grant program over the Senate bill's level, but cut grants for commuter and light rail capital projects, which the Senate bill proposed increasing. The Senate panel proposed to fund Choice Neighborhoods, a program to revitalize distressed housing and encourage economic development, at the existing $120 million level; the House bill would have provided no funding.

Fiscal Cliff

Lawmakers came close to tipping the country over what had come to be known as the fiscal cliff in 2012 but pulled back at the last minute. On New Year's Day 2013, they agreed to a plan that averted a combination of drastic tax increases and automatic, across-the-board spending cuts scheduled to take effect at the start of the new year. President Barack Obama signed the measure into law January 2 (HR 8—PL 112-240).

The crisis had loomed all year, and the House and Senate passed dueling tax bills in July, but negotiations turned serious only after the November election. Hopes for some kind of grand bargain quickly faded, however, as Democrats and Republicans dug in. Although it resolved the immediate fiscal cliff crisis, the 112th Congress left several larger issues, including a new debt limit and a critical plan for spending cuts, for the next Congress.

The more than $500 billion in scheduled tax increases set to take place was a result of the January 1 expiration of individual income tax cuts and other reductions enacted under President George W. Bush in 2001 and 2003 (PL 107-16, PL 208-27). The $109 billion in automatic spending cuts, known as a sequester, had been ordered under the 2011 Budget Control Act (PL 112-25) and was set to take effect January 2. *(2001, 2003 tax cuts, Congress and the Nation Vol. XI, pp. 89, 105; 2011 Budget Control Act, p. 160)*

Economists almost universally had warned that the combination of suddenly higher taxes and lower federal spending could jeopardize the still fragile recovery from the financial crisis and recession that gripped the country beginning in late 2007. The Congressional Budget Office estimated that the more than $600 billion hit to the economy from going over the fiscal cliff could lower real gross domestic product by half a percent in 2013.

Obama held a strong hand as the end-of-year negotiations began. His decisive reelection in November followed a campaign in which he focused on increasing taxes on the rich and preventing a tax hike for the middle class. Separate polls showed a majority of the public agreed with his position. Congressional Democrats backed the president and also insisted that there should be minimal, if any, cuts in spending for social and infrastructure programs.

Republicans, however, held firm to their position that the Bush-era tax rates should be made permanent for all taxpayers regardless of income and that any deal should consist primarily of spending cuts. House Speaker John A. Boehner, R-Ohio, whose ability to win support from his fractious GOP caucus was regarded as crucial to any deal, said immediately after the election that the issue of tax rate hikes was not negotiable, but he indicated that Republicans would consider "revenue" increases if they were part of an overhaul of the tax code that curbed deductions and credits.

Democrats said an overhaul simply would not raise enough money to meet the required deficit reduction target and would require unacceptable cuts to programs that benefited the middle class. House Minority Whip Steny H. Hoyer, D-Md., challenged Republicans to come up with specific cuts, which they declined to do.

Some Republicans maintained that going over the cliff might not be such a bad thing, although many in the GOP realized the public would likely blame them for the massive tax hike. Republicans also were anxious to prevent the sequester because half the reduction would come from national security spending; they preferred to shift a larger share of the cuts to domestic programs. On the other hand, some Democrats said that allowing the sequester might be preferable because it would cut defense spending more than might otherwise be the case, but Democratic defense hawks and the administration rebuffed that idea.

Virtually no one wanted the existing tax cuts to expire for middle-class families (although some members of both parties thought they might have more leverage over taxes when the new Congress convened). The core of the last-minute deal permanently extended the lower 2001 and 2003 tax cuts for individual income below $400,000 and household income below $450,000, while letting the rate go back to the pre-2001 figure of 39.6 percent for income above those thresholds.

The agreement also put off the sequester for two months, while offsetting the two-month cancellation of the spending cuts with $24 billion in combined alternative spending cuts and higher revenue from changing Roth retirement account rules. It also extended federal unemployment benefits but did not extend a two-percentage-point reduction in the employee's share of the Social Security payroll tax to 4.2 percent, which had been enacted as a stimulus measure in 2010 (PL 111-312). *(Payroll tax deduction, pp. 79, 108, 144, 146)*

Although Congress escaped the immediate crisis, huge problems were left on the table, including the need to increase the debt limit in early 2013. Treasury Secretary Timothy F. Geithner warned that the government would reach the legal limit on total borrowing on December 31, 2012, but could take extraordinary measures to give lawmakers two months of breathing room. Other potential crises involved deciding what to do about the sequester after March 1, and completing the fiscal 2013 appropriations process before a temporary bill expired March 27. The prospect of renewed crises was expected to reduce Obama's chances to push a robust legislative agenda through Congress. *(Fiscal 2013 continuing resolution, p. 180)*

BACKGROUND

Congress had nearly allowed the Bush-era tax cuts to expire at the end of 2010, the date set in the original law. In December, in another battle of brinksmanship, Obama and Republican leaders reached a deal that continued all the cuts, including those for the wealthy, for two years, in exchange for an extension of federal unemployment compensation benefits and a one-year reduction of two percentage points in the employees' share of Social Security payroll. In two separate actions at the end of 2011 and the beginning of 2012, Congress extended the payroll tax reduction for another year, through the end of 2012. *(Tax cut extension, p. 147; payroll tax , pp. 79, 108, 144, 146)*

The sequester—itself the product of cliffhanger negotiations—was put in place as part of the 2011 Budget Control Act after a committee created by the act failed to agree on an alternative plan that would reduce the deficit by $1.2 trillion over ten years. Under the 2011 law, a total of $109 billion in automatic across-the-board reductions in federal spending for fiscal 2013 were scheduled to begin on January 2. The automatic cuts were split evenly between defense and nondefense programs and applied primarily to discretionary spending. Most spending under entitlement programs, such as Social Security, was not affected by the sequester.

The automatic cuts under the sequester had been required as part of a deal to raise the debt ceiling, but both parties wanted to find ways to forestall them. In May, the House narrowly passed a reconciliation bill (HR 5652) that would have replaced the sequester for 2013 with reductions in several mandatory spending programs. The Senate did not take up the measure. *(House reconciliation bill, p. 180)*

EARLY SKIRMISHING

The House and Senate passed separate tax bills in July, as each party sought to hone its position on the expiring income tax cuts in advance of the November elections.

The Senate passed the Democrats' bill (S 3412), 51–48, on July 25 after rejecting a GOP substitute (S 3413), 45–54, earlier in the day. The most striking difference between the competing measures was their treatment of the top two tax brackets. The Democrats wanted to allow upper-income tax rates enacted in 2001 and 2003 to expire as scheduled at the end of the year. The GOP version would have continued them for all taxpayers.

Signaling a line of attack for the fall, Senate Minority Leader Mitch McConnell of Kentucky and other Republicans repeatedly referred to the Democratic bill as a large tax increase on family farms because it would not prevent a scheduled increase in the estate tax at the end of the year.

The House passed its bill (HR 8) on August 1 mostly along party lines, 256–171. The measure was nearly identical to the Senate GOP bill. The following day, members passed, 232–189, a second bill (HR 6169) that would have set in motion the process for an overhaul of the tax code in 2013.

The Senate Democratic leadership vowed that the GOP legislation would be dead on arrival, and the White House issued a veto threat. But no further action took place as legislators and the president all hit the campaign trail.

POSTELECTION POSITIONING

Immediately after Obama's decisive reelection, there were several days of cautious optimism that an agreement might be reached. Boehner announced that Republicans would consider "new revenue" under the "right conditions," a break with the GOP position before the elections. Obama indicated he would consider other sources for some of the revenue he wanted from wealthy taxpayers. *(Obama reelection, p. 35)*

But both sides soon retreated to their previous stances, particularly on tax rates for the well-to-do, and the maneuvering began. Obama flatly rejected allowing the top income rate to remain at 35 percent, even if other new revenue was part of the picture. He said the presidential election had been about different visions of the economy and taxes and that he had won that fight. House Republicans countered that he may have been reelected as president, but they had won in their districts and would not contemplate raising the top rate. Boehner put the onus on Obama, saying, "This is his moment to work on a solution that can pass both chambers."

Obama responded November 14 with a call to Congress to reassure the middle class immediately by eliminating the impending tax increase on the 98 percent of taxpayers who made less than $250,000. Then, he said, lawmakers should adopt a "framework" for additional savings in 2013 by rewriting the tax code and restructuring federal health programs. "I want a big deal. . . . I want a comprehensive deal," he said.

On November 16, Obama and Boehner opened talks. Boehner had the support of House Majority Leader Eric Cantor, R-Va., and Budget Chair and GOP vice presidential candidate Paul D. Ryan, R-Wis., important allies from the fiscally conservative wing of the party. But the speaker still led a caucus that was far more hard-line in its stance than were Senate Republicans, with some arguing that higher revenue should come, not from any increase in taxes, but only from the economic growth that they believed would be spurred by spending cuts.

Obama turned to the public to build pressure on the Republicans, launching a campaign-style appeal outside the Beltway to sell his position on taxes. The impending sequester seemed to come up rarely.

At the end of November, Treasury Secretary Geithner, the cabinet official taking the lead in the White House negotiations, delivered a new proposal from Obama. It called for $1.6 trillion in revenue over ten years from taxes on high-income earners, postponement of the sequester, renewal of unemployment benefits, a patch for the alternative minimum tax (AMT), $400 billion in trims from federal health programs, and a mechanism that would allow the president to increase the debt ceiling on his own, unless two-thirds of Congress disapproved.

Republicans dismissed the package as largely a rehash of the fiscal 2013 budget proposal that Obama had presented in February. They were particularly outraged at the proposal that they give up control over the debt limit, which they hoped to use as leverage for bigger spending cuts. McConnell told the *Wall Street Journal* that he laughed aloud when the proposal was presented to him. At the same time, Obama's willingness to put entitlement cuts in the mix incensed liberal Democrats.

PRIVATE TALKS BETWEEN OBAMA, BOEHNER

By early December, Obama and Boehner seemed to be moving closer to a deal. A *Washington Post*—Pew Research Center poll released December 5 reinforced GOP leaders' concern over the damage Republicans were doing to their own image. It showed that 53 percent of those surveyed would blame the Republicans for a failure to avoid the fiscal cliff, while 27 percent would blame the president.

Meanwhile, in part at Obama's behest, businesses stepped up their pressure for some kind of a deal, warning of the damage failure would do to the fragile economic recovery. The Business Roundtable, an association of chief executive officers of major U.S. companies, launched a campaign called "It's Time to Act" with ads calling for the two sides to reach an agreement. A newly formed bipartisan business group initiated a "Fix the Debt" campaign, placing ads and lobbying lawmakers for action.

In private talks with Obama, Boehner made major concessions, proposing to let taxes rise on incomes above $1 million and to put off a fight over the debt limit if Obama agreed to significant changes to Medicare and Social Security. Obama reportedly put new offers on the table as well, lowering his demand for new revenue from the highest earners from $1.6 trillion to $1.2 trillion and increasing the threshold to family income exceeding $400,000, up from $250,000.

He also reportedly offered to consider a GOP demand to change the measure of inflation to the so-called chained Consumer Price Index (CPI). Many economists said the alternative measure of inflation, which assumed that consumers would substitute cheaper products rather than purchasing the same basket of goods each month, better reflected the real inflation rate. Most Democrats opposed it, however, because it would lead to smaller cost-of-living increases for Social Security recipients. *(Consumer price index changes, box, p. 542)*

Obama dropped his insistence that a renewal of the payroll tax holiday be part of a deal, although he insisted on an extension of federal unemployment benefits. He also was reported to want new stimulus spending and agreement on a debt limit increase that would cover two years.

Boehner revisited proposals that he and Obama had discussed during the 2011 debate that led to the Budget Control Act, including $1.4 trillion in savings from the domestic-spending side of the ledger over ten years, with an $800 billion target for additional taxes. In a sign that he was trying to fend off turmoil on his own right flank, Boehner on December 3 stripped plum committee assignments from four rebellious Republicans.

Then, in a surprise move that ended up diminishing the Speaker's role as a negotiator, Boehner suddenly broke off the negotiations with Obama. Realizing that his latest offer could not win support from his conference, he announced that the House would pass "Plan B," which would protect income under $1 million from tax increases without addressing spending cuts or the sequester.

Despite Boehner's public statements that his tax bill would pass, conservatives remained unconvinced, objecting in particular to the lack of spending cuts in the bill. To woo conservatives, House leaders at the last minute proposed a separate spending reduction bill (HR 6684) that would have replaced the sequester set to begin in January 2013 with a $19 billion reduction in spending caps and a $300 billion cut in entitlement spending over ten years. The House had passed a similar plan in May as part of a budget reconciliation bill on a vote of 218–199.

But Boehner had badly misread his members. On December 20, the sequester replacement measure passed even more narrowly than it had in May; the **key vote was 215–209 (R 215–21; D 0–188)**. *(2012 key votes, p. 803)*

Moreover, the sequester replacement did little to persuade conservatives to support the Plan B tax measure. After hours of trying to whip up conservative votes for the tax measure, Boehner pulled the bill from the floor in a stunning reversal that demonstrated the difficulty of getting any deal through the House.

"Now it is up to the president to work with Senator Reid on legislation to avert the fiscal cliff," the Speaker said. "The House has already passed legislation to stop all of the January 1 tax rate increases and replace the sequester with responsible spending cuts that will begin to address our nation's crippling debt. The Senate must now act."

MCCONNELL-BIDEN COMPROMISE

At Obama's urging, Senate Majority Leader Harry Reid, D-Nev., and Minority Leader Mitch McConnell, R-Ky., undertook what seemed a last-ditch effort to save the negotiations. Should the talks fail, Obama warned, he would ask Reid to hold a Senate vote on a stripped-down proposal to block the tax hike on income of less than $250,000 and extend federal emergency unemployment insurance. Reid said he would schedule a vote for December 31.

With much of the actual negotiations conducted by staff, Reid indicated a willingness to limit the tax increase to family income above $450,000 a year. McConnell wanted $550,000. Republicans also briefly reintroduced the use of chained CPI, a demand Democrats flatly rejected, especially in the absence of a broader deal. (A chained CPI was a different calculation of consumer prices than currently used to determine annual Social Security cost-of-living benefit increases. Many economists argued that it would more accurately reflect cost of living expenses for senior citizens, but adopting it also was expected, over a long period, to reduce Social Security benefits.) *(Details, box, p. 542)*

Democrats wanted to delay the sequester until 2015 without other cuts and to extend unemployment benefits, the "doc fix" for Medicare, and farm subsidies. They also wanted rates on dividends and capital gains to rise to 20 percent from the existing 15 percent for those above the threshold. On December 29, Reid threw in the towel. "At this stage, we are not able to make a counteroffer. The Republican leader has told me that—he just said here that he is working with the vice president. I wish them well."

Unable to reach an agreement with Reid, McConnell had, indeed, turned to Vice President Joseph R. Biden Jr., reportedly asking him on the phone: "Does anyone down there know how to make a deal?"

The compromise came together on New Year's Eve, barely three hours before the midnight deadline for a reversion to the higher tax rates. The final hurdles were reportedly ironing out provisions on the sequester and the estate tax.

Biden hurried to the Capitol to brief Senate Democrats, while McConnell urged GOP senators to accept the plan. Republicans gave up their pledge for no new taxes, accepting tax increases on income higher than $450,000 for a couple, without corresponding spending cuts. Democrats had already yielded on their goal of increasing taxes on income of more than $250,000, which enraged some in their party.

Democrats won on higher rates for capital gains and dividends for those with income higher than the thresholds. The final estate tax rate of 40 percent was midway between the GOP's preference for 35 percent and Democrats' insistence on 45 percent. The $5 million exemption was higher than the 3.5 percent Democrats wanted and closer to the 5.2 percent Republicans sought. Democrats gave in to a GOP demand that the exemption be adjusted for inflation.

Republicans agreed to a two-month delay in the sequester, paid for with spending cuts, split relatively evenly between domestic and defense, and taxes from the expansion of Roth IRAs. Defense Secretary Leon E. Panetta reportedly campaigned hard to ensure that the sequester would be addressed, but he had urged a yearlong replacement that would ease the pressure on defense spending.

On January 1, the Senate passed the resulting bill (HR 8) by a **key vote of 89–8 (R 40–5; D 47–3; I 2–0).** After a brief flurry of talk about potential amendments, Boehner brought the bill to the House floor knowing that only a minority of his caucus would support it. The bill passed on a **key vote of 257–167 (R 85–151; D 172–16)** later the same day, clearing the legislation for the president. *(2012 key votes, p. 803)*

MAJOR PROVISIONS

Tax Provisions

The Congressional Budget Office (CBO) estimated that the tax changes in the fiscal cliff legislation would cost about $279.8 billion in fiscal 2013. Most of that—about $206.5 billion—came from extending tax cuts passed during the George W. Bush administration in 2001 and 2003 (PL 107-16, PL 108-27) and by indexing the income threshold for the alternative minimum tax, or AMT, for inflation.

The legislation permanently extended the Bush-era tax rates on ordinary income of up to $400,000 for individuals and $450,000 for married couples. The rates were 10 percent, 25 percent, 28 percent, and 33 percent, compared with 15 percent, 28 percent, and 31 percent if the 2001 and 2003 tax cuts had been allowed to expire. For income above the thresholds, however, the rate was allowed to increase from 35 percent to 39.6 percent, which the White House said would bring in $620 billion in revenue that would have been lost had the laws been allowed to expire.

The nominal tax rate on long-term capital gains and dividends was increased from 15 percent to 20 percent for individuals with annual incomes above $400,000 and married couples above $450,000. The bill also retained a 2010 health care law (PL 111-148, PL 111-152) provision that set a new 3.8 percent surtax on investment income for individuals earning more than $200,000 and joint filers with earnings above $250,000.

The personal exemption phaseout and the phaseout of itemized deductions, called the Pease provision, were reinstated for single tax filers with annual incomes above $250,000 and for joint filers with incomes above $300,000. Itemized deductions could not be reduced by more than 80 percent.

The legislation maintained the estate tax exemption at $5 million, indexed for inflation, and raised the tax rate for estates above that value from 35 percent to 40 percent. The exemption could be transferred to a spouse at death, resulting in a maximum exemption of $10 million. The exemption was indexed for inflation.

The income threshold for the alternative minimum tax was raised to $50,600 for single filers and $78,750 for joint filers. The threshold was permanently indexed to inflation, ending an era when Congress repeatedly passed temporary "patches" to prevent the alternative tax system from capturing more middle-income families.

The legislation extended for five years the tax credits included in the 2009 stimulus law (PL 111-5), including a $2,500 college tuition credit and expansions of the child tax credit and earned income tax credit. The "bonus depreciation" was extended for one year, allowing businesses to write off half of the cost of new property in 2013 instead of depreciating it over a longer period. This extension was designed to give businesses an incentive to invest in equipment.

A package of tax "extenders" that expired at the end of 2011 was renewed retroactively through the end of 2013, including business tax extenders worth about $63 billion, according to the CBO. The tax breaks included broad measures such as a credit for business research and development expenses as well as a state and local sales tax deduction and industry-specific provisions. Financial services companies and manufacturers with financing arms were allowed to defer taxes on income earned overseas from active financing operations.

Sequester

The second key part of the legislation put off cuts under the sequester until the following March 1 and reduced the amount of the 2013 sequester by $24 billion, to $85 billion, for the remainder of the year. The delay in the sequester was offset by $24 billion over ten years, split evenly between cutting spending and accelerating transfers to Roth individual retirement accounts (IRAs), which were subject to taxes. To achieve the spending cuts, discretionary spending caps were lowered by $4 billion for fiscal 2013, from $1,047 trillion to $1,043 trillion, and by $8 billion for 2014, from $1,066 trillion to $1,058 trillion.

Other Provisions

The final bill extended through 2013 federal emergency unemployment benefits for workers who had exhausted their twenty-six weeks of federal-state benefits; the cost was not offset.

A scheduled 26.5 percent cut in reimbursement rates for physicians serving Medicare patients was postponed through 2013. The $25.2 billion, ten-year cost was offset, mainly by recouping certain Medicare overpayments to hospitals. *("Doc" fix, p. 463)*

The fiscal cliff legislation extended most of the provisions of the 2008 farm law (PL 110-246) through the end of fiscal 2013, averting a sharp rise in milk prices at the beginning of 2013. Congress had been unable to reach an agreement on a five-year extension before the end of the 112th Congress. *(Farm bill, p. 414)*

Several tax incentives were also extended for renewable energy, particularly wind power. *(Details, p. 185)*

Hurricane Sandy Supplemental Funds

A Senate-passed bill to provide money for recovery efforts from Superstorm Sandy died at the end of the 112th Congress when House Republican Speaker John A. Boehner,

R-Ohio, decided to put off a vote until the new Congress convened. Outrage from the affected public and from East Coast politicians of both parties helped make the disaster aid an early priority when the 113th Congress was seated in early January 2013, with the House quickly clearing disaster aid for Sandy victims in two separate bills.

The hurricane struck the East Coast on October 29, 2012, killing at least 146 people and causing tens of billions of dollars in damage, primarily along the New Jersey, New York, and Connecticut coastlines. The Obama administration responded to the destruction with a $60.4 billion administration request, and the Senate passed a bill (HR 1) on December 28, by a **key vote of 62–32 (R 12–32; D 48–0; I 2–0)** that would have provided that amount, most of it designated as emergency spending. *(2012 key votes, p. 803)*

House leaders proposed consideration of the Senate measure, and members of the New York and New Jersey delegations said they expected a vote on the measure. But after passage of the fiscal cliff deal just before midnight on New Year's Day, Boehner closed off any additional votes for the 112th Congress. The disaster aid legislation officially died at noon January 3; legislation from one Congress does not carry over into the next.

Republican Rep. Peter T. King of New York and Republican governor Chris Christie of New Jersey led the attacks on the Speaker for his decision to keep the measure from the floor. On *Fox News* on January 2, King called Boehner's decision a "disgrace" and "immoral."

Many conservative Republicans opposed the legislation, however, because it did not contain cost offsets. Others said the bill contained funding for construction projects that could not be called true emergencies. House Oversight and Government Reform Chair Darrell Issa, R-Calif., for example, said the Senate-passed bill had directed too much money and resources to congressional districts outside the area affected by the storm.

The first House vote came January 4, 2013, on a $9.7 billion bill (HR 41—PL 113-1) to boost the borrowing authority for the National Flood Insurance Program, which the Senate cleared the same day. The Federal Emergency Management Agency had warned that without additional borrowing authority, the flood insurance program would soon run out of money for processing claims for storm damages.

Eleven days later, on January, 15, 2013, the House passed the larger disaster aid legislation (HR 152—PL 113-2) by a narrower margin of 241–180. The chamber backed the bill after adding $33.5 billion in short- and long-term recovery and mitigation spending to an underlying $17 billion measure that would have addressed only the immediate needs of communities hit by the October storm. Fiscal conservatives were unsuccessful in their earlier push to offset the $17 billion in spending with across-the-board cuts to domestic and defense spending.

The combination of the proposed additional spending with a previously enacted $9.7 billion flood insurance bill fell just short of the estimated $60.4 billion requested by the White House and passed by the Senate in December. The Senate cleared the supplemental spending bill on January 28, 62–36, and the president signed it into law the following day.

Chronology of Action on Trade Policy

Not surprisingly, given the global economic turndown and the high unemployment rate at home, trade policy sat on a back burner for much of President Barack Obama's first term. Congress in 2011 endorsed three trade pacts—one with South Korea, a major U.S. trading partner; the others, both smaller in scope, with Colombia and Panama. All three agreements were initially negotiated during George W. Bush's presidency and then renegotiated by the Obama administration to include stronger protections for labor and the environment. The agreements passed handily, but only after Congress had resolved a difficult and related dispute over extending expanded trade adjustment assistance for displaced workers.

Congress at the end of 2012 approved legislation establishing permanent normal trade relations with Russia. The removal of decades-old trade restrictions—originally intended to protest human rights violations by the Soviet Union but kept in place for two decades after the collapse of Soviet communism—was expected to lead to expanded commerce between the two countries. Over Republican objections, Congress also reauthorized the Export-Import Bank, which provided direct loans, financing, and loan guarantees to support the export of American goods and services. Obama had made the legislation a high priority because it supported U.S. jobs.

As had happened for some years, members of both parties periodically railed against China's trade practices, which were widely perceived as unfair. In particular, legislators complained about China's apparent suppression of the value of its main unit of currency, the yuan, vis-à-vis the dollar, as a way to keep Chinese exports cheap and imports expensive. The House passed legislation in 2010 to pressure China into revaluing its currency, but no further action was taken. China had been allowing the yuan to appreciate slowly against the dollar since 2005. It suspended the revaluation in 2008 in the face of the global credit crunch, and then resumed the appreciation midway through Obama's first term. By the end of 2012, the value of the yuan had risen about 35 percent against the dollar since 2005—not nearly enough to quiet complaints from U.S. businesses and politicians.

TRADE BALANCES

The global economic downturn in 2009 improved the U.S. trade deficit, at least momentarily. Exports of U.S. goods and services slowed in 2009, but U.S. imports slowed even more, bringing the current account—the net balance of exports, imports, and income and other transfers—to its lowest point since 2001. By the end of 2012, both U.S. exports and imports had begun to climb again, although the 2012 account deficit, at $440 billion, was still two-thirds lower than it had been in 2008. Trade in goods was by far the largest component of the current account, and goods imported into the United States continued to outstrip the export of goods. In contrast, U.S. trade in services showed a steadily growing surplus, partially offsetting the goods deficit.

REFERENCES

Discussion of trade action for the years 1945–1964 may be found in *Congress and the Nation Vol. I,* pp. 172–207; for the years 1965–1968, *Congress and the Nation Vol. II,* pp. 49–116; for the years 1969–1972, *Congress and the Nation Vol. III,* pp. 119–134; for the years 1973–1976, *Congress and the Nation Vol. IV,* pp. 125–137; for the years 1977–1980, *Congress and the Nation, Vol. V,* pp. 267–276; for the years 1981–1984, *Congress and the Nation Vol. VI,* pp. 95–112; for the years 1985–1988, *Congress and the Nation Vol. VII,* pp. 139–166; for the years 1989–1992, *Congress and the Nation Vol. VIII,* pp. 165–200; for the years 1993–1996, *Congress and the Nation Vol. IX,* pp. 151–184; for the years 1997–2000, *Congress and the Nation Vol. X,* pp. 147–170; for the years 2001–2004, *Congress and the Nation Vol. XI,* pp. 145–167; for the years 2005–2008, *Congress and the Nation Vol. XII,* pp. 197–213.

China remained the United States' second-largest trading partner, after Canada, but the balance of trade between the United States and China was skewed, with the value of U.S. imports from China roughly four times greater than the value of U.S. exports to China. China was also the United States's largest creditor, holding $1.2 trillion in U.S. Treasury notes at the end of 2012. Japan was a close second with $1.1 trillion in holdings.

Trade Balances *(Millions of dollars)*

Year	*Current Account*	*Goods*	*Services*	*Other*
2000	–$416,317	–$446,942	$69,605	–$38,981
2001	–396,697	–422,512	60,173	–34,358
2002	–457,800	–475,842	57,678	–39,635
2003	–518,657	–542,273	51,728	–28,113
2004	–629,327	–666,364	61,466	–24,430
2005	–739,796	–784,133	76,219	–31,882
2006	–798,478	–838,788	86,389	–46,079
2007	–713,389	–822,743	123,677	–14,323
2008	–681,343	–833,957	131,655	20,959
2009	–381,636	–510,550	126,893	2,021
2010	–449,471	–650,156	150,777	49,908
2011	–457,725	–744,139	187,301	99,113
2012	–440,416	–741,475	206,819	94,240

SOURCE: Bureau of Economic Analysis, Department of Commerce, "U.S. International Transactions."

NOTE: The current account balance includes the balances on trade in goods, services, income, and net unilateral transfers such as private remittances. Income and transfers makes up the "other" column.

OBAMA TRADE POLICY

As a senator from Illinois starting in 2005 and then as a presidential candidate in 2008, Obama was not a vocal advocate of free trade. As with many Democrats, he was wary that free-trade agreements favored countries with cheaper labor and lower labor standards over American-produced goods, costing some U.S. workers their jobs. As a president faced with a stubbornly high jobless rate, Obama came to see expanded trade as a means of creating jobs at home. The free-trade pact with South Korea, for example, was expected to lead to the creation of as many as 280,000 American jobs.

In addition to calling for ratification of the three pending trade agreements in 2011, Obama's administration took several other steps aimed at increasing jobs through trade. In 2010 the president set a goal of doubling U.S. exports, to create as many as two million new jobs by 2014. That target seemed possible until 2012, when export growth slowed markedly. The administration also stepped up the number of challenges the United States lodged with the World Trade Organization (WTO) to what it claimed were other countries' unfair trade practices, and it took several administrative steps to make it easier for American companies, especially small businesses, to sell their goods and services abroad.

The Obama administration also continued to pursue a regional trade agreement with several Pacific Rim countries that had been initiated by the Bush administration. Hosting the annual Asia-Pacific Economic Cooperation summit in Honolulu in November 2011, Obama announced that the "broad outlines" of a Trans-Pacific Partnership (TPP) agreement had been reached. Japan subsequently joined the negotiations, bringing to twelve the number of countries participating in the talks, and in 2013 Obama said he hoped an agreement would be signed by the end of the year.

Many observers suggested that U.S. participation in the Trans-Pacific Partnership talks, which excluded China, was motivated as much by a desire to counter China's economic influence in the region as to liberalize trade. "TPP is an attempt to regain the initiative by opening up Asia-Pacific markets more fully to U.S. business," David Pilling of the *Financial Times* wrote in 2011. Detractors, including many Democrats, sharply criticized the administration for not making details of the unfolding agreement public, and they appeared to be lining up opposition to whatever agreement might emerge.

As Obama's second term began in 2013, the administration announced that it would soon begin talks with the European Union (EU) aimed at forging a Trans-Atlantic Trade and Investment Partnership (TIPP). An agreement between the two would be the world's biggest trade pact, covering about 50 percent of global economic output. Such a pact had long been suggested, but the proposals never gained much traction because neither side wanted to undermine the long-running Doha Round of world trade negotiations, which were launched at the WTO Ministerial Conference in November 2001, in Doha, Qatar. That calculus changed after the Doha talks appeared to be all but dead and with China's rise to become the world's second-largest economy

Whether either the TPP or TIPP talks could be successful might depend on the administration's ability to renew its "fast-track," or trade promotion, authority, a procedure under which Congress could approve or reject a trade pact but not amend it. Both U.S. and foreign trade negotiators considered fast-track authority critical in ensuring the carefully negotiated agreements could not be undone by a congressional majority unhappy with specific elements of the pact. But Congress had allowed the president's fast-track authority to expire as of July 1, 2007 (the three trade pacts approved in 2011 had all been negotiated before then and were thus covered by fast-track rules). *(Background, Congress and the Nation Vol. XII, p. 197)*

In 2012, the Obama administration indicated that renewal of fast-track authority would be required before the TPP talks could be concluded. Obama's biggest opponents in any renewal fight were likely to come from his party; in general, most Republicans favored the authority. In 2011, Republicans in the Senate sought to force the issue, offering an amendment to revive fast-track authority through 2013. "Without trade authority, there will be no other trade agreements," said the amendment's author, Minority Leader Mitch McConnell, R-Ky. "We all know that. And that's why I've been a strong advocate for granting this president the same trade promotion authority that every other president has enjoyed since 1974." The amendment failed, 45–55; only one Democrat voted for the amendment.

2009–2010

Pending trade agreements with Panama, Colombia, and South Korea put together during the presidency of George W. Bush remained on hold in the 111th Congress as the Obama administration reviewed U.S. trade policy. The only trade action Congress took in 2009 was to clear a one-year extension of two sets of existing trade preferences for developing countries.

In 2010, the House passed a measure to address the trade imbalances between China and the United States, but the Senate took no action. Lawmakers on Capitol Hill, especially those from states with high volumes of manufacturing exports, had long complained that China artificially suppressed the value of its currency to make its own exporters more competitive on price.

South Korea, Colombia, and Panama Trade Pacts

President Barack Obama, an advocate for stronger labor and environmental protections in trade deals, declined to ask for congressional approval of the trade pacts with South Korea, Colombia, and Panama negotiated by the Bush administration. The president said the Office of the U.S. Trade Representative was reviewing all three to ensure that they met its labor and environmental standards and preserved market access for U.S. goods.

Skepticism about the pending trade agreements abounded in both chambers, reflecting historically high U.S. unemployment rates and declining public support for trade liberalization.

The Bush administration sent the Colombia agreement to Congress in 2008, but Speaker Nancy Pelosi, D-Calif., delayed action indefinitely through a change in House rules that previously had guaranteed expedited consideration. *(Congress and the Nation Vol. XII, p. 211)*

The Panama and Colombia pacts had strong support from the business community, as well as from generally protrade Democrats, such as Senate Finance Chair Max Baucus of Montana and House Ways and Means Chair Charles B. Rangel of New York. But critics voiced concerns about Panama's banking secrecy laws, while top House Democrats raised doubts about violence against labor unions in Colombia. Meanwhile, the Obama administration raised the prospect of reopening negotiations on a South Korea trade pact in response to complaints from the struggling U.S. auto industry.

Trade with China

Legislation to give the Commerce Department new tools to pressure China's government into revising its currency practices passed with strong bipartisan support in the House but was not taken up in the Senate. The bill, HR 2378, the Currency Reform for Fair Trade Act, which passed on a **key vote of 348–79 (R 99–74; D 249–5)** on September 29, 2010, demonstrated a deep level of public and congressional unease with China's trade practices and, to some degree, with what was seen as the inability of the White House to remedy the situation. *(2010 key votes, p. 767)*

Most experts agreed that the Chinese government maintained its currency, the renminbi, at an artificially low value to keep Chinese exports cheap and imports expensive. Congressional criticism had been muted because of China's role as the U.S. government's most important creditor. But slow economic recovery and continued high unemployment made China a target for congressional ire and demands for economic retaliation through tariffs or other measures.

The vote came just before Congress left town for the fall election campaign. With the election approaching, rank-and-file Democrats made it clear that they wanted an opportunity to vote on the legislation, and the House Ways and Means Committee quickly revised an earlier version of the bill, addressing concerns that it would violate World Trade Organization (WTO) rules. The committee approved the bill by voice vote on September 24 (HR 2378—H Rept 111-646).

The bill would have overturned a long-standing rule that effectively made it difficult to consider an undervalued currency as an illegal export subsidy that could lead to economic sanctions. The measure's stated purpose was "to clarify that countervailing duties may be imposed to address subsidies relating to a fundamentally undervalued currency of any foreign country." Countervailing duties are levied by governments on certain imports to offset the price advantage that the import's producer gained from government subsidies.

In essence, the measure would have changed the law so that Commerce could not dismiss a claim just because nonexporters in a foreign country also received the same subsidy. The department was to retain the power to make the final decision on whether to impose countervailing duties.

The bill had strong backing from labor unions. The Economic Policy Institute estimated that the growth in the U.S. trade deficit with China had caused the loss or displacement of 2.4 million U.S. jobs, mostly from the manufacturing sector, from 2001 to 2008.

The U.S. business community was split. Small and mid-size U.S.-based manufacturers, which faced intense competition from Chinese imports, were the primary members of the business community pushing for the currency legislation. In contrast, the National Retail Federation, whose members brought in huge quantities of goods from China, opposed the legislation. Many corporations and business groups also worried that the bill would invite Chinese retaliation.

Despite strong bipartisan support for the legislation in the Senate, the issue cooled after the election. A packed lame duck calendar thwarted efforts to schedule a vote on the issue, and the House measure died at the end of the session.

EXTENSIONS OF TRADE ADJUSTMENT ASSISTANCE, TRADE PREFERENCES, GSP

Although they did it in fits and starts, legislators continued two sets of trade preferences throughout President Barack Obama's first term. Both the Andean Trade Preference Act and the Generalized System of Preferences (GSP) were scheduled to expire on July 31, 2013, as a result of several extensions during the four-year period.

The Andean trade preference measure waived duties on imports from Colombia, Ecuador, and Peru. The GSP provided duty-free entry for a broad array of imports from more than 100 developing countries. In late 2009, Congress sent the president legislation (HR 4284—PL 111-124) that extended both sets of waivers for one year through December 31, 2010.

At the end of 2010, Congress extended the Andean Trade Preference Act for just six weeks, through February 12, 2011, as part of a broader bill (HR 6517—PL 111-344) that also extended the Trade Adjustment Assistance Act (TAA). The February 12 expiration date came and went with no congressional action. Not until October 2011, when Congress passed legislation (HR 3078—PL 112-42) that approved the free-trade agreement between the United States and Colombia, were the Andean preferences extended, this time through July 31, 2013.

By the time of the October 2011 extension, membership in the Andean preference group had dwindled to just one South American country. Bolivia had been excluded in 2008 because of its lack of cooperation in antidrug efforts. Peru left the group at the beginning of 2011 when its individual trade agreement with the United States came into effect. Colombia and Panama left it in October 2011 when broader trade pacts with the United States were approved. That left only Ecuador, which withdrew in June 2013 in protest over Edward Snowden, the former U.S. government employment who had intentionally made public classified information.

The extension of the GSP followed an even more tortuous path. It technically expired at the end of 2010. In September 2011, the Senate used House-passed legislation (HR 2832), extending it to carry an extension of an amended version of the TAA, which assisted workers who had lost their jobs as a result of foreign trade. Never particularly popular with Republicans, the TAA had grown even more controversial after it was expanded to cover trade-affected service workers as part of the economic stimulus bill passed in February 2009 (HR 1—PL 111-5). Republicans, however, favored approval of three free trade pacts—with South Korea, Colombia, and Panama—and the Obama administration and congressional Democrats conditioned their approval of the trade agreements on passage of the TAA legislation. HR 2832 (PL 112-40) continued the GSP through July 31, 2013. The amended TAA was extended through December 31, 2013. *(Details, p. 199)*

2011–2012

In the first major trade action of President Barack Obama's first term, Congress in 2011 approved three free-trade pacts that had been negotiated doing the administration of President George W. Bush and then renegotiated by the Obama administration. Congress easily cleared the agreements, after resolving a related dispute over trade adjustment assistance for displaced workers.

Late in 2012, just before the session adjourned, Congress also passed legislation establishing permanent normal trade relations with Russia. The law, which removed decades-old restrictions, was expected to lead to expanded trade between the two countries. At the same time, however, the legislation touched off new tensions by imposing new sanctions on individual Russians who greatly violated human rights, such as involvement with extrajudicial killings or torture.

In other actions, Congress reauthorized the Export-Import Bank over Republican objections, and it approved a package extending several trade measures.

South Korea, Colombia, Panama Trade Pacts

In a display of bipartisanship that was rare in the 112th Congress, lawmakers in October 2011 easily cleared three long-stalled free-trade agreements. Legislation approving the agreements and making the necessary changes in U.S. law were signed on October 21.

Final action on the trade pacts with South Korea, Colombia, and Panama provided a victory for President Obama, who had embraced the agreements as part of his jobs campaign. The president won another, related victory when the House cleared an extension of trade adjustment assistance for workers displaced by foreign trade. *(Details, p. 199)*

The South Korea free-trade pact was seen as the most economically important pact since the 1994 North American Free Trade Agreement (NAFTA). As congressional debate focused mainly on the benefits to automakers and cattle ranchers, the loudest cheerleaders for the pact were U.S. financial services companies, including big banks such as Citigroup and Goldman Sachs, and insurers eager for access to the South Korean market. The agreement allowed U.S. banks to take full ownership of Korean institutions, provided a gateway to business in other Asian countries, and broke down barriers to investment and cross-border transactions.

The Colombia agreement was the most controversial of the three, drawing opposition from a number of Democrats and from most of organized labor over Colombia's long record of violence against union activists. Obama sought to address those concerns when he signed an "action plan" in April 2011 with Colombian President Juan Manuel Santos, requiring Colombia to pass laws to protect labor organizers and prosecute individuals charged with violence against labor leaders.

U.S. TRADE REPRESENTATIVE

The Senate confirmed Barack Obama's choice of Ron Kirk as his chief trade representative by a vote of 92–5 on March 18, 2009. Kirk's nomination moved forward after Finance Committee Chair Max Baucus, D-Mont., dismissed the nominee's underpayment of $10,000 in taxes as an "honest mistake."

The fifty-four-year-old former mayor of Dallas promised senators during his March 9 confirmation hearing that his priority would be enforcing existing U.S. trade laws, not negotiating new trade agreements—a popular approach in a Congress wary of new trade liberalization measures during a time of mounting U.S. job losses.

The underlying theme of the hearing was the public's largely skeptical attitude toward trade, which had helped eviscerate congressional support for trade agreements. Kirk said he would call for a comprehensive review of pending trade agreements with Panama, Colombia, and South Korea, which had been negotiated by the Bush administration but had not been submitted to Congress for approval. Kirk oversaw the revisions of those pacts, which Congress ratified in 2011. He also helped guide the administration's tougher stance on trade laws, bringing several successful charges of unfair trade practices against China and other countries during his tenure.

Kirk remained in his post until March 2013. His successor, Michael Frooman, previously served as Obama's deputy national security adviser for international economic affairs and was instrumental in revising the three trade pacts and in developing other aspects of the administration's trade policy.

Kirk had served as Texas secretary of state in 1994 before becoming the mayor of Dallas. Upon leaving the administration, he joined the Dallas offices of Gibson, Dun, and Crutcher, an international law firm, where he was expected to play a leading role in corporate mergers, acquisitions, and other dealings around the world.

The U.S.-Panama pact, by contrast, was relatively noncontroversial. U.S. trade with Panama was minimal compared with U.S.-South Korea trade, and there were no concerns over violence against trade unionists.

The three agreements were negotiated under the Bush administration but stalled in 2007, when Democrats, who argued that the deals would cost U.S. jobs, took control of Congress. When Republicans regained the House majority in 2011, the measures were seen as among the few potential opportunities for bipartisan cooperation.

Obama began to look more favorably on the agreements as he sought to woo the business community, which viewed them as a priority. In 2009, he struck a new deal with the South Korean government on auto tariffs. The deal won the endorsement of Ford Motor Co. and the United Auto Workers, although not that of other major labor organizations.

Before submitting the deals to Congress, however, Obama insisted that lawmakers renew expanded benefits under the Trade Adjustment Assistance (TAA) program. The benefits, originally part of the 2009 economic stimulus law (PL 111-5), expired on February 12, 2011. Republican conservatives balked at an extension because they considered the program, which provided assistance to workers displaced by foreign trade, ineffective and too expensive. Republican House leaders pulled legislation to extend the TAA from the floor in February when it became clear the measure would not receive the two-thirds vote required to pass under suspension of the rules.

The administration persisted, working with Ways and Means Chair Dave Camp, R-Mich., and Senate Finance Chair Max Baucus, D-Mont., to assemble a scaled-back TAA package that would renew some of the stimulus provisions. In September, the Senate passed a bill (HR 2832) that included the compromise TAA package. After receiving assurances from GOP leaders that the House would clear the TAA bill, Obama formally submitted the trade agreements October 3. *(TAA, p. 199)*

The House prepared the way for passage on October 11 when it adopted the rule on the three bills on a **key vote of 281–128 (R 232–1; D 49–127)**. Because the trade deals and the implementing legislation were subject to so-called fast-track procedures, the bills had to receive an up-or-down vote in both chambers, without amendment, within ninety days of its submission. No trade agreement submitted to Congress under those procedures had ever been rejected. *(2011 key votes, p. 785)*

The most recent version of fast-track rules, known formally as trade promotion authority, had been enacted in 2002 (PL 107-210). The procedure was generally viewed as crucial in assuring U.S. negotiating partners that once they reached agreement on a trade deal, they would not see it revised by Congress. Although the law lapsed in June 2007, the three agreements qualified for the expedited consideration because they were negotiated before that date. An attempt by the Senate majority leader to revive fast-track rules was rejected, 45–55, on an almost straight party-line vote, during debate on the related trade adjustment assistance legislation *(Congress and the Nation Vol. XII, p. 209)*

SOUTH KOREA

The United States and South Korea signed their free-trade agreement June 30, 2007. The Bush administration, however, did not submit the legislation because of differences with the Democratic Congress over South Korea's treatment of U.S. autos and beef. Most observers said South Korea maintained one of the most protected markets for auto imports in the industrialized world and one of the most closed agricultural markets in the Organisation for Economic Co-operation and Development.

In particular, South Korea periodically banned most imports of U.S. beef products because of fears relating to mad cow disease. U.S. exporters also complained about the lack of transparency in South Korea's trading and regulatory systems, together with nontariff barriers in almost every major product sector.

Before the agreement, U.S. industrial goods faced an average tariff of 6.2 percent in South Korea; Seoul's exports entered the United States at an average tariff of 2.8 percent. The United States was South Korea's third-largest trading partner—the largest was China—while South Korea was the seventh-largest U.S. trading partner. Principal U.S. imports from South Korea included cell phones, semiconductor circuits, autos and auto parts, and steel. Major U.S. exports to South Korea included semiconductors, machinery, aircraft, and agricultural products. The International Trade Commission (ITC) estimated that annual U.S. exports to Korea would increase by $9.7 billion to $10.9 billion as a result of tariff reductions alone.

On December 3, 2010, Obama and President Lee Myung-bak of South Korea announced that they had reached an agreement to include trade changes in phase-out periods for tariffs on autos and to allow a larger number of U.S. cars into South Korea under U.S. safety standards. The beef issue was not entirely resolved.

The House passed the South Korea agreement on a 278–151 vote October 12. The Senate cleared the bill a few hours later on a vote of 83–15. President Obama signed the legislation October 21 (HR 3080—PL 112-41).

As outlined by the Ways and Means Committee, the United States–Korea Free Trade Agreement Implementation Act included the following:

Manufacturing. Granted immediate duty-free status to 80 percent of U.S. industrial and consumer exports to South Korea, with duties on the remaining products to be phased out within 10 years.

Motor vehicles and parts. Required South Korea to cut immediately its tariffs on U.S. autos by half and fully eliminate them after five years. The 2010 modification also addressed safety and environmental standards and other nontariff barriers to U.S. auto exports. South Korea committed to strengthen transparency and to help prevent the emergence of new nontariff barriers and discriminatory taxes.

The ITC estimated that U.S. exports of passenger vehicles to South Korea would increase by 54 percent as a result of tariff cuts alone and that exports of motor vehicles and parts would increase an additional 41 to 56 percent as a result of the removal of nontariff barriers.

Agriculture. Granted immediate duty-free access to more than half of existing U.S. exports of farm products to South Korea. In 2010, the country was the fifth-largest market for U.S. agriculture, with sales totaling $5.3 billion. The average tariff on U.S. agriculture exports to South Korea was 54 percent, while South Korean agricultural exports to the United States faced average tariffs of 9 percent.

South Korea agreed to eliminate its 40 percent tariff on U.S. beef over a fifteen-year period, while retaining the right to impose temporary safeguard tariffs in response to any potential surge in imports. It did not, however, change rules limiting the importation of U.S. beef to that of cattle that were less than thirty months old.

South Korea was allowed to maintain extensive quotas and tariffs on the importation of rice and oranges. Under the agreement, South Korea agreed to formalize its recognition of the equivalence of the U.S. meat, poultry, and processed-foods inspection systems.

Services. Required Korea to increase market access, national treatment, and regulatory transparency for U.S. service companies beyond the levels afforded by the World Trade Organization's General Agreement on Services. The agreement eliminated numerous barriers to South Korea's financial, insurance, telecommunications, audiovisual, express delivery, and professional services markets, including ending many restrictions that allowed only South Korean nationals to provide professional services.

South Korea was the eighth-largest importer of services, with a market worth $580 billion a year, which the House Ways and Means Committee said made "improved market access for U.S. services critical."

Investment protection. Required Korea to provide a more secure legal framework for U.S. investors operating there. The deal covered all forms of investment, including enterprises, debt, and intellectual property.

Intellectual property. Required South Korea to adopt higher standards for the protection of intellectual property rights, such as copyrights, patents, trademarks, and trade secrets. Each partner was required to grant national treatment to nationals of the other, and all laws, regulations, and procedures were to be made public. The agreement also lengthened terms for copyright protection, covered electronic and digital media, and increased enforcement. Both countries were obliged to provide appropriate civil and criminal remedies for willful violators of intellectual property rights.

Labor. Required each nation to adopt and enforce five core International Labor Organization (ILO) standards: freedom of association, recognition of the right to collective bargaining, elimination of all forms of forced or compulsory labor, effective abolition of child labor, and elimination of discrimination with respect to employment and occupation.

The two countries stipulated that it was inappropriate to weaken or reduce domestic labor protections to encourage trade or investment, and each was required to enforce its domestic labor laws with respect to minimum wages, hours of work, and occupational safety and health.

Environment. Required both countries to enforce their domestic environmental laws and establish a dispute settlement process to enforce such obligations. Each government agreed not to weaken or reduce environmental laws to attract trade or investment.

COLOMBIA

The Colombia free-trade agreement was signed November 22, 2006, and modified in 2007 to reflect a deal between congressional leaders and the Bush administration on topics that included labor, environment, intellectual property, investment, and government procurement. Bush submitted implementing legislation to Congress in early 2008.

Most Democrats still opposed the accord, however, arguing that violence against Colombian labor leaders was unacceptable. Led by Speaker Nancy Pelosi, D-Calif., the House Democratic majority was able to postpone consideration of the agreement indefinitely, despite fast-track rules that theoretically required a vote. Over vehement GOP objections, the chamber in April 2008 adopted an amendment to House rules making fast-track provisions inapplicable to the Colombia agreement. *(Congress and the Nation Vol. XII, p. 211)*

In April 2011, the Obama administration negotiated an "action plan" with new Colombian President Juan Manuel Santos, under which Colombia agreed to pass laws to protect labor organizers and prosecute individuals charged with violence against labor leaders. During the summer the U.S. trade representative stated that Colombia had met the requirements outlined in the action plan, but a number of Democrats expressed skepticism and voted against the pact. In the House, which passed the pact 262–167, only nine Democrats voted for it. Thirty Democrats voted against it in the Senate, which cleared it October 12, 2011, on a **key vote of 66–33 (R 44–2; D 21–30; I 1–1)**. President Obama signed the legislation on October 12. (HR 3078—PL 112-42). *(2011 key votes, p. 785)*

Colombia already enjoyed duty-free access on 90 percent of its exports to the United States under the 1991 Andean Trade Preference Act (PL 102-182). The average U.S. tariff on the remaining Colombian goods was 3 percent, while Colombia imposed an average rate of 12.5 percent on U.S. goods entering that country. Colombia was the third-largest U.S. export market in Latin America, after Mexico and Brazil.

The ITC estimated that annual U.S. exports to Colombia would increase by $1.1 billion under the agreement.

As outlined by the Ways and Means Committee, the United States–Colombia Trade Promotion Agreement Implementation Act, included the following:

Manufacturing. Granted immediate duty-free access to 80 percent of U.S. exports of consumer and industrial goods to Colombia, with an additional 7 percent receiving duty-free access within five years. Tariffs on the remaining products were to be phased out within ten years. The ITC estimated that exports of U.S. motor vehicles and parts would grow by 43.8 percent.

Agriculture. Granted immediate duty-free access to 77.5 percent of U.S. agricultural product lines; tariffs on almost 93 percent of agricultural product lines were to be phased out within 10 years.

Textiles and apparel. Granted immediate duty-free and quota-free treatment to all U.S. textiles and apparel products that met the agreement's rules of origin. The pact allowed temporary tariff relief if imports proved damaging to domestic producers.

Services. Required market access, national treatment, and regulatory transparency in most service sectors, including financial services, engineering, architecture, real estate, telecommunications, and computers. The agreement gave U.S. financial companies the right to establish subsidiaries or branches for banks and insurance companies. Overall, the pact was expected to reduce barriers in the banking sector by more than half. The service sector accounted for more than half of Colombia's gross domestic product, making improved market access for U.S. services a major priority.

Investment protection. Required that a secure legal framework be provided for U.S. investors operating in Colombia. U.S. investors would have similar protections to those that foreign investors had in the United States, including due process and the right to receive fair market value for property in the event of an expropriation.

Intellectual property. Required Colombia to set higher standards for the protection of intellectual property rights, such as copyrights, patents, trademarks, and trade secrets. Each partner was required to grant national treatment to nationals of the other, and all laws, regulations, and procedures were to be made public. The agreement also lengthened terms for copyright protection, covered electronic and digital media, and increased enforcement. Both countries were obliged to provide appropriate civil and criminal remedies for willful violations of intellectual property rights.

Labor. Required each nation to adopt and enforce the five core ILO standards. Each country was required to enforce its existing laws on work conditions, minimum wages, hours of work, and occupational safety and health. Each country agreed not to weaken or waive its labor laws to affect trade or investment with the other. Under the action plan, Colombia committed itself to taking specific steps to address issues related to violence against union members, worker rights, and worker cooperatives.

Environment. Required both countries to enforce their domestic environmental laws and to establish a dispute settlement process to enforce such obligations. Each government agreed not to weaken or reduce environmental laws to attract trade or investment and to implement voluntary, market-based mechanisms to protect the environment.

PANAMA

On October 12, the Panama agreement was passed by the House on a vote of 300–129. Later that day it was approved by the Senate, 77–22, and signed by President Obama (HR 3079—PL 112-43). The agreement had been signed on June 28, 2007, but was held up by an unrelated dispute over the killing of a U.S. service member in Panama. Panama already received duty-free treatment on almost all of its exports to the United States under the Andean Trade Preference Act. The average tariff on U.S. industrial exports was 7 percent, with some tariffs as high as 81 percent.

As outlined by the House Ways and Means Committee, the United States–Panama Trade Promotion Agreement Implementation Act included the following:

Consumer and industrial goods. Gave immediate duty-free treatment to 87 percent of U.S. industrial and consumer exports to Panama, with duties on the remaining products phased out within ten years.

Agriculture. Gave immediate duty-free access to half of all U.S. agricultural exports, with tariffs on the remaining products phased out at varying stages. U.S. agriculture exports to Panama faced an average tariff of 15 percent, whereas more than 99 percent of Panamanian agricultural exports entered the United States duty-free.

Apparel and textiles. Gave immediate duty-free and quota-free treatment to many U.S. textiles and apparel products that met the agreement's rules of origin. Because Panama was a huge intermediate destination point for international trade and had its own duty-free zone, U.S. apparel producers raised the issue of illegal trans-shipment of goods that did not meet rules of origin. The agreement contained consultation provisions to encourage Panamanian monitoring and compliance with trans-shipment rules.

Services. Provided market access, national treatment, and regulatory transparency in most service sectors, including retail trade, financial services, and professional services. The service sector accounted for 78 percent of Panama's gross domestic product.

Labor. Required each nation to adopt and enforce the five core ILO standards. The two nations agreed not to weaken or waive their labor laws to promote trade or investment.

Environment. Required both countries to enforce their domestic environmental laws and to establish a dispute settlement process to enforce such obligations. Each government entered a binding agreement not to weaken or reduce environmental laws to attract trade or investment.

Intellectual property. Required Panama to adopt higher standards for the protection of intellectual property rights, such as copyrights, patents, trademarks, and trade secrets. Each partner was required to grant national treatment to nationals of the other, and all laws, regulations, and procedures were to be made public. The agreement also lengthened terms for copyright protection, covered electronic and digital media, and increased enforcement. Both countries were obligated to provide appropriate civil and criminal remedies for willful violations of intellectual property rights. Also, Panama was required to adopt new pharmaceutical standards that reflected a bipartisan understanding as developed by congressional leadership and the U.S. trade representative in a May 2007 agreement.

Trade Adjustment Assistance Extended

In 2011 Congress extended a program of enhanced assistance to U.S. workers displaced by foreign trade as part of a deal that also won approval for three free-trade agreements. President Barack Obama signed the worker aid bill into law on October 21, 2011 (HR 2832—PL 112-40).

The basic Trade Adjustment Assistance (TAA) program, which was set to expire on February 12, 2012, was extended through December 31, 2013, as the linchpin in a deal to get final action on trade agreements with South Korea, Colombia, and Panama. The legislation also extended some, but not all, of the new features of the TAA program that had been added as part of Obama's 2009 economic stimulus law (PL 111-5) and extended once at the end of 2010 (PL 111-344) to February 12, 2011. *(Stimulus, p. 78)*

Democratic supporters saw help for workers whose jobs were lost or cut back because of increased imports or outsourcing as essential to their votes for the three trade bills, and Obama refused to send Congress the legislation to implement the pacts until a deal had been worked out on TAA.

The program, first enacted in 1962, offered a variety of benefits and reemployment services to help unemployed workers prepare for and obtain new jobs. The TAA program for workers was run by the Labor Department. A comparable program for companies was administered by the Department of Commerce, which also oversaw a third component created under the economic stimulus law to serve communities hurt by foreign trade.

The stimulus expansion also extended TAA to cover service sector workers, expanded access for manufacturing and secondary workers, and significantly increased funding for training. It also increased a health care tax credit for unemployed workers, made permanent a reemployment wage insurance program, and increased overall funding.

For months, GOP lawmakers rejected Democratic demands to renew the expanded version of TAA, with many conservatives questioning the cost and effectiveness of the program and arguing that the stimulus expanded it to unacceptable levels. They also argued that many of the program's components were duplicated in other job training and assistance programs. In February 2011, conservative opposition forced House leaders to pull a TAA extension from the floor. It had been set to be considered under suspension of the rules, a procedure that required a two-thirds majority vote for passage.

Despite Republican opposition, the Obama administration, along with many congressional Democrats, continued to insist that the program be renewed as part of a deal on the trade pacts. A breakthrough came in June, when House Ways and Means Chair Dave Camp, R-Mich., Senate Finance Chair Max Baucus, D-Mont., and Obama administration officials put together a scaled-back TAA package that renewed some, but not all, of the stimulus provisions.

They still had to work out how to tie the compromise to the trade bills, however. House Republicans rejected an attempt by the Senate Finance Committee to tuck the TAA provisions into a bill approving the South Korea pact. In August, Senate leaders announced that they had agreed on a plan to consider TAA and the trade bills separately but in tandem.

In September, the Senate passed the TAA provisions after attaching them to a bill (HR 2832) that also renewed the General System of Preferences (GSP), a program that allowed duty-free imports from developing countries. *(Box, p. 194)*

On October 3, Obama announced that he was sending the three trade bills to Capitol Hill, where they were considered under expedited procedures. In a single day, October 12, the House passed and the Senate cleared the trade bills, and the House immediately cleared the TAA extension.

MAJOR PROVISIONS

The TAA extension restored many of the expanded benefits that had been available temporarily under the stimulus act, although the 2011 version was not always as generous. According to the Congressional Research Service, the extension included the following major provisions:

Eligibility. The stimulus law expanded eligibility for TAA to include workers and companies in the service industry and broadened the criteria for participation in both programs to include jobs negatively affected by imports or by shifts in production to any foreign country. Previously, the program was limited to producers of articles, and the outsourcing had to be to a country that was a partner in one of several U.S. trade agreements. The 2011 extension reflected the stimulus act.

Income support. Previous law provided up to 104 weeks of cash payments for workers enrolled in full-time training, rising to 130 weeks if the worker also was getting remedial training. The stimulus law increased those totals to 130 weeks, rising to a maximum of 156 weeks. The 2011 TAA law provided up to 117 weeks of income support, rising to 130 weeks for some workers who met new criteria. The income support program was generally available to qualified workers who were getting training and whose unemployment benefits had expired.

Training. The 2011 deal capped annual training funds at $575 million, the same limit that was set in the stimulus and $355 million more than under previous law.

Health benefit. The law renewed a health care tax credit for workers in the program but scaled it back to cover 72.5 percent of premiums, down from 80 percent under the stimulus law. Previously, the level had been set at 65 percent. The credit had been one of the primary targets of conservative ire.

Community program. The TAA program for communities, created under the stimulus law, was repealed.

GSP. The bill extended the GSP until July 31, 2013, and made it retroactive to the previous expiration date of December 31, 2010.

Export-Import Bank Reauthorization

Lawmakers voted overwhelmingly in May 2012 to reauthorize the Export-Import Bank (Ex-Im), bringing an end to a weeks-long standoff in which conservatives from both chambers attempted to derail the legislation. The bill, the Export-Import Bank Reauthorization Act of 2012, which President Barack Obama signed on May 30, 2012 (HR 2072—PL 112-122), extended the credit financing agency's charter through September 30, 2014, and incrementally increased its lending cap. For fiscal 2014, the bank was authorized to lend up to $140 billion, up from $100 billion under existing law.

Renewing the bank charter was a priority for Obama. The agency provided direct loans, financing, and loan guarantees to support the purchase of American products overseas for the official purpose of creating U.S. jobs. Its charter was set to expire on May 31, 2012, and the bank also was close to reaching its lending cap. Most of the nation's foreign competitors maintained similar export banks.

Final action came after a number of attempts in both the House and the Senate to block the bill. The proposed renewal divided Republicans who were caught between their allies in the business community, who sought passage, and free-market advocacy groups that opposed government-backed export financing as a form of corporate welfare.

Established business groups argued that the bank played an important role in keeping the United States competitive with other countries that financed their own exports and in creating and sustaining jobs. The U.S. Chamber of Commerce and the National Association of Manufacturers favored the reauthorization, and both warned that they would include votes on the legislation on their annual congressional scorecards.

Conservative advocacy groups such as the Club for Growth and Heritage Action strongly opposed the bill, arguing that it would interfere with free-market principles.

Senate Democrats first tried to reauthorize the bank in March but were blocked by Republicans. Maria Cantwell, D-Wash.—whose state was home to Boeing Co., the bank's biggest beneficiary—offered an amendment to a jobs bill (HR 3606) that would have extended Ex-Im's authorization into 2015 and gradually raised its lending cap to $140 billion. Many expected the amendment to be adopted with broad bipartisan support, but Republicans backed off in deference to objections from House conservatives who did not want the Ex-Im language added. With a nearly unanimous GOP caucus in opposition, supporters fell five votes short of the sixty needed to shut off debate when the Senate voted 55–44 on March 20 against cloture.

The House Financial Services Committee had approved a version of HR 2072 in 2011 that would have extended the authorization through fiscal 2015, with a $160 billion cap. But House Majority Leader Eric Cantor, R-Va., was pushing an alternative proposal to reauthorize the bank for only one year and raise the lending cap to $113 billion. Cantor also wanted to add reporting and analysis requirements to the bank's charter, including a provision requiring additional scrutiny of aircraft-related loans. That was a nod to concerns raised by Delta Air Lines Inc., which complained that the bank undermined its global competitive position by helping international carriers purchase Boeing planes.

After weeks of negotiations, Cantor reached agreement with House Minority Whip Steny H. Hoyer, D-Md., on a compromise bill. The measure included some changes in bank operations aimed at increasing transparency in a bid to appeal to conservative critics, but it was closer to what Senate Democrats had first proposed.

Despite vociferous dissent from dozens of conservative Republicans, the House passed the compromise, 330–93, on May 9. No Democrat voted against the bill, while dozens of GOP conservatives bucked their leadership to support it.

The Senate easily cleared the bill on a 78–20 vote on May 15 after turning back several Republican amendments that would have curbed the bank's activities. Majority Leader Harry Reid, D-Nev., sought to clear the bill by unanimous consent after House passage. But faced with a possible GOP filibuster unless he allowed attempts to modify the bill, he agreed to permit five GOP amendments. The deal required a sixty-vote majority for adoption of each amendment as well as for passage. None of the amendments received more than thirty-seven votes.

Trade Measures Package

In 2012, Congress cleared legislation to extend a package of several trade measures. The House passed the bill (HR 5986—PL 112-163) by voice vote, and the Senate cleared it by unanimous consent on August 2, 2012.

The legislation authorized a three-year extension of preferential treatment for Africa-produced garments made from third-country fabrics under the African Growth and

Opportunity Act (PL 106-200) and added the new country of South Sudan to that program. It also made some technical changes to language in the free-trade agreement with the Dominican Republic and Central America and renewed import restrictions on Myanmar (PL 108-61), formerly known as Burma, for three years.

If Congress had not cleared the legislation before leaving town for its August recess, the import sanctions on Myanmar would have expired. Although the Obama administration had moved to ease a number of existing sanctions on the Southeast Asian nation after a series of economic and government changes, officials said they wanted to keep existing laws on the books as leverage should Myanmar's leaders reverse course.

Russian Trade Normalization

On December 14, 2012, President Barack Obama signed legislation, which went under the unwieldy title of the "Russia and Moldova Jackson-Vanik Repeal and Sergei Magnitsky Rule of Law Accountability Act of 2012" (HR 6156—PL 112-208) establishing permanent normal trade relations with Russia. The law lifted decades-old restrictions, paving the way for expanded U.S.-Russia trade. The legislation also targeted Russian human rights violators.

Enactment marked the culmination of a months-long effort to lift trade restrictions left over from the cold war era that bill supporters said had put U.S. companies at a disadvantage after Russia joined the World Trade Organization (WTO) in August. Proponents said the measure would boost the U.S. economy by easing access to the Russian market and leveling the playing field with other nations that already had normalized their trade with Moscow.

The bill repealed the Jackson-Vanik amendment, language included in the 1974 trade act (PL 93-618) targeting communist countries that restricted Jewish emigration. *(Jackson-Vanik, Congress and the Nation Vol. IV, p. 131)*

Business groups, including the U.S. Chamber of Commerce, lobbied heavily for the legislation. The United States exported roughly $11 billion in goods to Russia in 2011, and business groups said that could double or triple with Russian membership in the WTO.

According to the President's Export Council, U.S. firms accounted for only 4.5 percent of Russia's imports, while Europe held a 40 percent share and China an additional 16 percent. Without congressional action, business advocates warned, the United States would fall further behind. Supporters also argued that with the cold war long over, Jackson-Vanik had served its purpose and was no longer necessary.

The AFL-CIO, however, opposed the measure. "Given Russia's widespread corruption . . . and pervasive bribery, there is little reason to believe that Russia will comply with World Trade Organization rules or that U.S. workers will reap substantial benefits from Russia's accession," the AFL-CIO said in a letter to lawmakers.

The push to normalize trade relations with Russia began in December 2011. The Obama administration and its congressional allies spent months building support within a wary Congress. Human rights advocates in both chambers, however, opposed repealing the law without new methods to counteract human rights violations.

To win support from these and other lawmakers, the administration agreed to include human rights provisions directed at Russians responsible for gross human rights violations, such as extrajudicial killings or torture, and explicitly targeted those tied to the case of Russian lawyer and anticorruption activist Sergei Magnitsky. Magnitsky died in a Moscow prison after being wrongfully detained, beaten, and denied medical care. These moves won the support of top lawmakers in both parties and cleared the way for the legislation to move forward. The Senate Finance Committee and House Ways and Means Committee approved Jackson-Vanik repeal bills with virtually no opposition in July.

Proponents had hoped to clear the legislation before, or shortly after, Russia joined the WTO. But congressional leaders were initially wary of bringing the measure to the floor. Democratic leaders were concerned that organized labor's opposition to the bill might siphon votes from their caucus. Meanwhile, House GOP leaders did not want to force incumbents to take a vote shortly before the 2012 elections that might make them appear soft on the heavy-handed government of Russia's President Vladimir V. Putin.

After Congress returned from the elections, the obstacles to the bill appeared to melt away, and lawmakers sent the House version, with somewhat narrower human rights language, to the president during the lame duck session.

Although Russians were eager to gain preferential trade status with the United States, they were irate about the Magnitsky language. In December the Russian parliament retaliated by approving legislation banning Americans from adopting Russian children, outlawing some U.S.-funded nongovernmental organizations, and banning visas and freezing assets of Americans accused of violating Russians' human rights.

LEGISLATIVE ACTION

With Russia on the verge of joining the WTO, the Senate Finance Committee unanimously approved a measure to repeal Jackson-Vanik (S 3406—S Rept 112-226) on July 18. Included was the text of legislation (S 1039—S Rept 112-191), approved by the Foreign Relations Committee on June 26, requiring that the State Department compile a list of people involved in Magnitsky's death or who were responsible for "gross violations" of the rights of individuals seeking to expose illegal activities by Russian government officials. Individuals on the list would not be able to get U.S. visas, and the Treasury Department would be required to freeze their U.S. assets. The language was broader than that in the final bill, potentially affecting human rights violators anywhere in the world.

The House Ways and Means Committee gave voice vote approval to a companion bill (HR 6156—H Rept 112-632) on July 26. Because the House panel did not have jurisdiction over human rights legislation, the bill was silent on the issue. However, committee leaders from both parties supported adding such language before it moved to the House floor.

The House on November 16 passed the bill on a **key vote of 365–43 (R 227–6; D 138–37),** after adopting a rule for floor debate that added the language from legislation (HR 4405) that the Foreign Affairs Committee had approved by voice vote June 7. That bill sanctioned Russians involved in the Magnitsky affair as well as human rights violators by denying them entry into the United States and freezing their U.S.-linked assets. The White House voiced strong support for the legislation.

Despite some lingering concerns among some Democratic senators, the Senate made no effort to amend the House bill, clearing it December 6 on a **key vote of 92–4 (R 46–0; D 45–3; I 1–1).** *(2012 key votes, p. 803)*

CHAPTER 3

Homeland Security

Introduction 205

Chronology of Action on Homeland Security

2009–2010 208

2011–2012 214

Homeland Security

During his 2008 presidential campaign, Barack Obama had repeatedly criticized the policies of the then incumbent, George W. Bush, faulting the president for actions in both the domestic and international arenas. But once Obama took office, while the new president hewed to a different course from Bush in many areas, Obama's actions on homeland security were not significantly different overall from those of his predecessor, as he continued many Bush administration policies opposed by civil libertarians and privacy advocates in Congress and elsewhere. Indeed, many of the same disputes regarding homeland security that had begun on Capitol Hill during the Bush years were fought again with Obama in the White House.

Obama's inauguration in January 2009 was less than a decade removed from the September 11, 2001, terrorist attacks in New York City and just outside Washington, D.C., that had led to the creation of the new Department of Homeland Security (DHS). The Obama administration, particularly Janet Napolitano, his secretary of homeland security, faced a myriad of issues, ranging from border security to cybersecurity to an extension of the controversial USA PATRIOT Act. The acronym refers to the formal title of the legislation, the USA Uniting and Strengthening America by Providing Appropriate Tools Required to Intercept and Obstruct Terrorism Act (PL 107-56, but it is commonly known simply as the Patriot Act). During Obama's first term, the country also had to deal with natural and human-caused disasters such as a massive oil spill off the Gulf Coast in 2010 and Hurricane Sandy in the Northeast in 2012. Different parts of Napolitano's department had to respond depending on the type of disaster, including the Coast Guard and the Federal Emergency Management Agency (FEMA). FEMA's flawed response to Hurricane Katrina in 2005 was widely condemned as a disaster in itself, and the Obama administration sought to improve the agency's performance.

In Congress, lawmakers confronted a variety of issues on national security. They passed short-term measures to extend three controversial provisions in the Patriot Act before granting a longer-term extension. They increased funding for security along the U.S. border with Mexico, in part because of increased violence in Mexico from drug wars. They extended warrantless wiretapping provisions that prompted heated debate. In addition, lawmakers dealt with issues ranging from Coast Guard funding to cybersecurity to security at chemical plants.

PATRIOT ACT

In the wake of the September 11, 2001, terrorist attacks, Congress passed the Patriot Act, a measure strongly backed by President Bush and by most members of Congress. Although it strengthened the federal government's ability to combat terrorism, in subsequent years increasing numbers of lawmakers questioned some parts of the law, particularly those seen as infringing on civil liberties.

Nevertheless, in 2009–2010, Congress renewed three controversial provisions of the law for two months and then for an additional year. The first provision, dealing with "business records," gave the Federal Bureau of Investigation (FBI) broad powers to seek a special federal court order for "any tangible thing" relating to possible terrorist activity. The second provision, involving "roving wiretaps," empowered investigators, after getting court orders, to track terrorist suspects who changed their mode of communication. The third was the "lone wolf" provision, under which investigators could seek warrants from the secret Foreign Intelligence Surveillance Court to follow terrorists not affiliated with a foreign power or recognized organization. The court had been established under the Foreign Intelligence Surveillance Act (FISA) of 1978.

The Obama administration sought to retain the provisions with as few changes as possible. Senate Judiciary Committee Chair Patrick Leahy, D-Vt., and House Judiciary Committee Chair John Conyers Jr., D-Mich., each sponsored bills that would have extended the law's business

REFERENCES

Discussion of homeland security policy for the years 2001–2004 may be found in *Congress and the Nation Vol. XI*, pp. 175–225; for the years 2005–2008, *Congress and the Nation Vol. XII*, pp. 217–261.

records and wiretap provisions through 2013, with modifications. Leahy's bill would also have reauthorized the lone-wolf provision; Conyers's would not.

However, neither bill made it to the floor. Instead, with time running short in the session, congressional leaders included a short-term, two-month extension of the three provisions as part of the fiscal 2010 defense appropriations bill. Congress later passed a one-year extension of the provisions, leaving a longer extension to the 112th Congress, which approved a four-year measure.

GOVERNMENT MONITORING

The controversial issue of warrantless wiretapping was an important subject before Congress in 2012. At issue were provisions of a 2008 law that were about to expire that authorized the intelligence community to wiretap the communications of certain foreigners who were in touch with people in the United States, without getting individual warrants. In a major victory for President Obama, Congress extended the provisions through 2017.

The 2008 law, part of President Bush's antiterrorism efforts, updated FISA. Under FISA, the government needed to get a warrant from the special FISA court before engaging in foreign surveillance in situations where one person was a U.S. citizen. Bush had authorized a secret program after the September 11 attacks that tracked U.S. citizens and others in the United States in an effort to look for terrorist links.

Although Obama supported extending the provisions, civil libertarians were opposed. Most House Democrats voted against the bill. In the Senate, Ron Wyden, D-Ore., put a hold on the measure that slowed down the bill's progress, although he eventually lifted his hold.

FUNDING FOR BORDER SECURITY AND THE COAST GUARD

In reaction to increasing violence in Mexico, Congress voted in August 2010 to give $600 million toward additional equipment and personnel for U.S. patrol activities along the U.S.-Mexican border. Lawmakers voiced concerns about the ongoing problem of illegal immigration and the growing problem of serious crime in Mexico related to drug wars.

Under the bill, the DHS's Customs and Border Protection agency received an extra $254 million, which included funding for 1,500 new patrol agents, two additional unmanned aerial drones, and millions of dollars worth of communications equipment. The Justice Department received $196 million to increase border-related law enforcement activities. The Immigration and Customs Enforcement arm of the DHS received $80 million, including money for communications equipment.

In the House, Democratic sponsors said the bill was necessary in light of recent criminal activity, but Republicans complained that the spending was no panacea.

"Violence on the Mexican side of the border has intensified because of turf battles among murderous transnational criminal organizations competing for drug-, alien-, and weapon-trafficking business," said Rep. David E. Price, D-N.C., Chair of the Homeland Security Appropriations Subcommittee. "This funding is urgently needed to counter the pressures our law enforcement agencies in our border communities currently face."

But many Republicans questioned what they called a short-term fix. "Why are we taking up this piecemeal approach" instead of "real solutions?" asked Rep. Harold

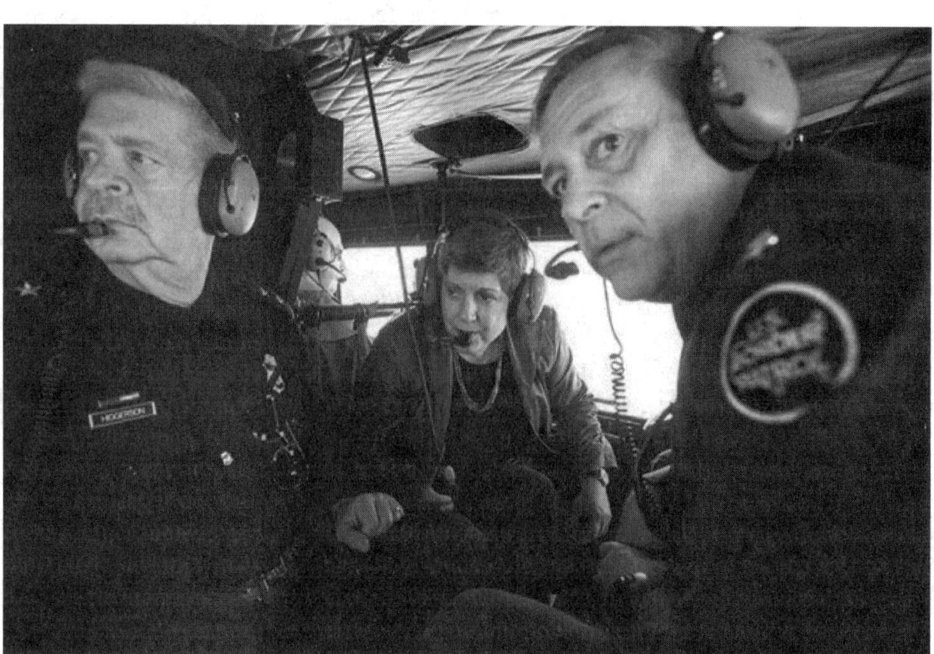

Homeland Security Secretary Janet Napolitano, center, flies over the U.S.-Mexico border by helicopter with U.S. Customs and Border Protection officials David P. Higgerson, left, and Michael Pryzbyl, right, on February 5, 2013, near Clint, Texas.
Source: Official White House Photo by Lawrence Jackson

HOMELAND SECURITY LEADERSHIP

On December 1, 2008, President Barack Obama announced that Janet Napolitano, then in her second term as Arizona's Democratic governor, would be his secretary of homeland security. "She understands as well as anyone the danger of an unsecure border," Obama said of Napolitano. As the chief executive of a border state, Napolitano had extensive experience with the controversial issue of illegal immigration. She signed a law that set tough sanctions on employers who intentionally hired illegal immigrants, and she was the first governor to seek a National Guard presence along the U.S.-Mexican border. But she was not a supporter of President Bush's plan to construct a border fence. In 2003, Arizona under Napolitano became the first state to establish its own homeland security strategy. As governor, she criticized Congress for failing to pass legislation on immigration reform.

Napolitano narrowly won her first gubernatorial term in November 2002, but easily won reelection four years later. Arizona, a traditionally Republican state, was becoming politically competitive, in important part because of an increasing Hispanic population. She endorsed Obama for president in January 2008.

Her nomination met little resistance in Congress. The Senate confirmed her by voice vote on January 20, 2009. She became the third secretary of the department.

As secretary of DHS, a still-new department with sprawling responsibilities, Napolitano faced a constant set of crises, including a continuing terrorist threat, illegal immigration, a drug war along the U.S.-Mexican border, and continuing scrutiny of FEMA.

On the terrorism front, Napolitano ran into controversy in the wake of an attempted terrorist bombing of a Northwest Airlines flight heading to Detroit from Amsterdam on Christmas day 2009. When a passenger, Umar Farouk Abdulmutallab, was caught after trying to detonate a bomb, Napolitano stated that "the system worked," a comment that provoked considerable criticism, particularly from her political opponents.

In addition to terrorism issues, her department was charged with handling natural or human-made disasters, including the aftermath of Hurricane Sandy in 2012 and a massive oil spill in the Gulf in 2010. *(Offshore oil drilling, p. 374)*

Meanwhile, as the debate over immigration continued with little progress on legislation, Napolitano was a vigorous advocate of a path to citizenship for persons illegally in the United States. During her tenure at DHS, however, the rate of deportations of illegal immigrants increased.

Napolitano remained in her position into the start of Obama's second term, but resigned at the end of August 2013 to head the University of California system.

Rogers, R-Ky. "Further securing our borders is an urgent priority that shouldn't wait."

In December 2012, Congress passed a two-year Coast Guard reauthorization bill. The Coast Guard's mission in the post–September 11 era had moved away from its longtime focus on search-and-rescue efforts. As part of the DHS, the Coast Guard increasingly focused on port security and tracking down drug smugglers and illegal immigrants at sea.

CYBERSECURITY AND CHEMICAL PLANT SECURITY

Although cybersecurity was high on the congressional agenda in 2012, and lawmakers on both sides of the aisle agreed that something needed to be done quickly to protect the computer systems connected to the country's defense and financial infrastructure, Congress did not produce legislation.

The House did pass a cybersecurity bill that sought to promote the voluntary sharing of information concerning cyber threats between the federal government and the private sector. The Senate rejected efforts by Senate Majority Leader Harry Reid, D-Nev., to bring another cybersecurity measure to a vote.

With respect to chemical plant security, Congress opted to extend the Department of Homeland Security's authority to create performance standards for chemical plants seen as potential terrorist targets. Rather than make the authority permanent, lawmakers opted for a series of short-term extensions.

Chronology of Action on Homeland Security

2009–2010

The first two years of President Barack Obama's term featured Democratic control of the White House and both houses of Congress. But even with this advantage, Democrats had difficulty passing their program, including legislation on homeland security. Unlike arguments on some other issues, especially health care reform, arguments over homeland security issues did not necessarily take place along partisan lines; lawmakers from both parties took issue with the president's views.

When it came to the renewal of three provisions in the Patriot Act, a sweeping antiterrorism measure enacted after the September 11, 2001, attacks in New York and outside Washington, D.C., Congress opted for short-term extensions rather than a multiyear continuation of the law. The provisions, which provided the federal government with new and often expansive tools to fight terrorism, were controversial. Many civil libertarians, including some in Congress, were staunchly opposed to the new powers, believing they threatened people's privacy. Although the Obama administration and many lawmakers supported legislation that included a longer-term extension, the measures never made it to either the House or the Senate floor, and, with time running out, shorter-term extensions were approved.

On another issue, chemical plant security, Congress also opted for the short-term approach, approving extensions to a law that authorized the Department of Homeland Security (DHS) to create performance standards for chemical plants that could be possible terrorist targets, rather than making the authority permanent.

Congress also succeeded in approving $600 million for additional personnel and equipment to be used to patrol the border with Mexico. Lawmakers had been concerned about both illegal immigration and increased drug-related violence.

Although homeland security for the Obama administration was a lower-profile issue than during the eight years of George W. Bush's presidency (2001 to 2009), there were times when it gained prominence. For example, on Christmas Day 2009, a man was caught on a Northwest Airlines flight bound from Amsterdam to Detroit attempting to detonate a bomb. When Homeland Security Secretary Janet Napolitano said that "the system worked," she came in for criticism, particularly from Republicans. On May 1, 2010, a bomber attempted to set off a device in a parked vehicle in Times Square in New York City; the bomb was discovered before it did any damage. Other issues brought homeland security to Americans' attention. In April 2010, a massive oil spill in the Gulf of Mexico focused attention on how the federal government responded to a disaster. Mindful of the lingering negative associations plaguing the Bush administration after Hurricane Katrina, the Obama administration attempted to react more nimbly.

USA PATRIOT Act

The 111th Congress, faced with the task of renewing three controversial provisions of the antiterrorism law called the USA PATRIOT Act, opted to act on a short-term extension, first renewing the measures for two months at the end of 2009 and then for an additional year in early 2010. *(2011 action, p. 214)* The law had been passed in 2001 (PL 107-56). *(Congress and the Nation Vol. XI, p. 187; Congress and the Nation Vol. XII, p. 222)*

The first provision, dealing with "business records," gave wide powers to the Federal Bureau of Investigation (FBI) to seek a special federal court order for "any tangible thing"—something that could include DNA information, blood samples, or a list of books a person was reading—that officials believed was necessary as part of an investigation into terrorist activity. The government needed to provide a statement of facts that demonstrated reasonable grounds to believe the information officials wanted was related to the investigation; the courts were told to presume that the material was relevant if the government could connect it to a foreign power or its agent.

The second provision involved "roving wiretaps." It gave investigators the power to get court orders enabling them to track terrorist suspects who changed their mode of communication; the investigators could tap various phones, cell phones, or Internet connections.

The third was known as the "lone wolf" provision. Under this section, investigators could ask for warrants from the Foreign Intelligence Surveillance Court to follow suspected terrorists who were not affiliated with a foreign power or recognized organization. *(Background on foreign intelligence surveillance, Congress and the Nation Vol. V, p. 720; Congress and the Nation Vol. XII, pp. 249, 251)*

The first two provisions were part of the original 2001 Patriot Act (PL 107-56), the sweeping antiterrorist measure that Congress passed after the terrorist attacks of September 11, 2001. The third provision was added in 2004 (PL 108-458). The three were reauthorized in 2006 (PL 109-177). But while most of the Patriot Act was made permanent, the three controversial provisions were placed under a sunset date—an automatic expiration date—of December 31, 2009, in order to give Congress more oversight over them.

The Patriot Act, which provided the federal government with a broad range of powers designed to combat terrorism, had long been controversial among civil liberties groups and their supporters in Congress, who charged that it interfered with the Fourth Amendment's protections against unreasonable searches and seizures. Although some civil libertarians had hoped that President Obama would be more inclined to their point of view than was the administration of his predecessor, George W. Bush, they were disappointed on a variety of fronts.

The Obama administration wanted to retain the three provisions, changing them as little as possible. In September 2009, the Justice Department wrote Sen. Patrick Leahy, D-Vt., the chair of the Senate Judiciary Committee, seeking the renewal of all three. The department did say that it would consider additional protections relating to privacy, if those protections did not affect the provisions' usefulness.

COMMITTEE ACTION

Leahy and House Judiciary Committee Chair John Conyers Jr. (D-Mich.) each sponsored bills that would have extended the business records and wiretap provisions through 2013, with some modifications. Leahy's bill also would have reauthorized the lone-wolf provision; Conyers's did not. In addition, both bills called for a new end date to another government investigative power known as "national security letters" used in counterterrorism investigations, and new parameters for issuing and challenging those letters. In addition, both bills called for a reduction to seven days from thirty days in the amount of time that law enforcement agents had before they notified a target of a delayed-notice "sneak and peek" search warrant under the Patriot Act.

The Justice Department supported the Leahy bill; civil libertarians preferred the Conyers bill.

The Senate Judiciary Committee approved Leahy's bill on October 8, 2009, on an 11–8 vote, calling for a reauthorization of the three provisions with some minor modifications, as well as a four-year sunset for national security letters. Most of the committee's Democrats backed the bill, along with Republicans Jon Kyl of Arizona and John Cornyn of Texas. Democrats voting against the bill were Russ Feingold of Wisconsin, Arlen Specter of Pennsylvania, and Majority Whip Richard Durbin of Illinois.

Initially, Leahy's bill (S 1692) would have set up a three-part framework that the government would need to meet to employ the business records authority. It would have needed to prove that it had reasonable grounds to think the materials in question involved a foreign power or its agent and that the materials were related to actions of a foreign-agent suspect under investigation or someone in contact with or known to that suspect. Leahy later eliminated the three-part test in a deal with Sen. Dianne Feinstein, D-Calif., who did not want the government's counterterrorism powers lessened. Feinstein was chair of the Senate's Select Committee on Intelligence and a staunch defender of the law. One exception was made for library records.

On the House site, the House Judiciary Committee approved the Conyers bill (HR 3845) with minor modifications on a 16–10 vote on November 5.

SHORT-TERM EXTENSIONS

However, neither bill made it to the floor of either the House or the Senate. With time running out, congressional leaders opted to include a short-term, two-month extension of the three provisions as part of the fiscal 2010 defense appropriations bill (PL 111-118), HR 3326. The House approved legislation on December 16, on a vote of 395–34; the Senate cleared the defense measure on December 19, on a vote of 88–10; and President Obama signed it on December 19. *(Defense appropriations, p. 280)*

A longer-term extension remained a possibility, perhaps including the modifications proposed in the House and Senate bills. With the extension set to expire February 28, 2010, however, rather than dealing with the intricacies of a longer-term answer, Congress again chose a short-term extension. This time it was a one-year extension, HR 3961, of the existing three provisions, lasting until February 28, 2011. The Senate approved the extension by voice vote on February 24, 2010, and the House cleared the measure on a vote of 315–97 on February 25. President Obama signed it (PL 111-141) into law on February 27.

Fiscal 2010 Homeland Security Appropriations

In 2009, Congress approved a fiscal 2010 spending bill (HR 2892—PL 111-83) for the Department of Homeland Security that totaled $44.1 billion, about the same amount that President Obama had requested. It was $231 million less than the amount for fiscal 2009. Of the total, $42.6 billion was for discretionary spending, and $242 million was for overseas deployment. President Obama signed the bill into law on October 28, 2009.

One significant controversy surrounding the legislation involved the issue of whether detainees from the U.S. prison at Guantánamo Bay, Cuba, could be brought into the United States for trial. The Obama administration wanted to be able to do that, but many congressional Republicans were opposed and tried to insert language into the bill blocking the detainees from entering the United States for trial. In the end, the Republicans failed to win backing for a complete ban, but they did succeed in putting restrictions on the transfer of the prisoners. *(Guantánamo restrictions, box, p. 314)*

HOUSE ACTION

The House Appropriations Committee approved its version of the fiscal 2010 homeland security bill by voice vote on June 12, 2009. The Homeland Security Appropriations Subcommittee had approved a draft of the bill on June 8, also by voice vote. The $44 billion House bill contained $42.4 billion in discretionary spending.

Under the bill, the Customs and Border Protection agency would receive $10 billion, $82 million less than Obama had requested and $147 million more than the fiscal 2009 total. The Federal Emergency Management Agency (FEMA) would get $7.4 billion, $118 million more than the White House request and $390 million more than the fiscal 2009 total. The Transportation Security Administration (TSA) would receive $7.7 billion, $85 million less than what Obama had wanted and $712 million more than in fiscal 2009.

Much of the debate at the markup centered on issues that did not involve funding, but rather were authorization and policy issues, including Guantánamo. Rep. Harold Rogers, R-Ky., the subcommittee ranking member, offered an amendment to restrict the administration's ability to move detainees from Guantánamo to the United States. The department would need to engage in thorough threat assessments of any detainees that were supposed to be transferred to the United States, put detainees on TSA's "no-fly" list, and refuse them immigration benefits such as visas, U.S. admissions, and refugee classifications. One justification Republicans offered for those restrictions was concern about radicalization of inmates at U.S. prisons.

On the Democratic side, subcommittee Chair David Price of North Carolina and committee Chair David Obey of Wisconsin argued that the administration's efforts to prosecute detainees could be hampered by these restrictions. Both lawmakers agreed to vote for the amendment once it was changed to say that it would not affect prosecutions. That change came in an amendment offered by full committee ranking member Jerry Lewis, R-Calif.

Another issue involved the E-Verify program, a government electronic system under which employers could check whether their workers were legally in the country. The Obama administration had sought to extend the program for three years. The House bill called for a two-year extension. An amendment by Rep. Ken Calvert, R-Calif., to extend the program permanently was rejected on a 21–36 vote.

Controversy also arose over the rule under which the bill would be considered in the House. The procedures approved by the Rules Committee allowed just fourteen floor amendments and limited the time for debate on each. Various GOP amendments, including the effort to extend E-Verify permanently, were not included in the procedures. In protest, Republicans called for six motions to adjourn the House and asked for roll-call votes each time their motion was rejected.

However, the bill itself passed easily, on a 389–37 vote, on June 24. Among the amendments approved during floor debate was one offered by Price that called for an additional $10 million for firefighting grants, and extra money for programs such as the Western Hemisphere Travel Initiative. It carried on a vote of 345–85. Also adopted, on a 282–148 vote, was an amendment by Rep. Peter King, R-N.Y., to add $50 million to the Domestic Nuclear Detection Office; $40 million of that money would be for the Securing the Cities initiative.

SENATE ACTION

The Senate Appropriations Committee approved its version of the bill (S 1298) on June 18 on a 30–0 vote. The Senate bill provided $44.3 billion for homeland security programs. The Senate bill included $42.7 billion in discretionary funding. This was $337 million more than the amount in the House bill but represented $104 million less than what the Obama administration had requested.

The Senate bill called for a three-year extension of E-Verify. It asked for $10.2 billion for Customs and Border Protection, $5.4 billion for Immigration and Customs Enforcement, not counting fees, $10.2 billion for the Coast Guard, $7.7 billion for the TSA, and $4.2 billion for grants and training.

The bill included $18 million to allow the Coast Guard's Loran-C program, a land-based navigation system, to continue for six months. The Obama administration and its immediate predecessors had sought to cut funding for the program, and the Obama administration had argued that eliminating it would save $36 million in fiscal 2010 and $190 million over a five-year period. Sen. Susan Collins, R-Maine, argued that the program was a crucial backup to GPS systems. The House bill included $36 million for Loran-C.

The Senate approved the bill 84–6 on July 9. There were some differences with the House bill. For example, Sen. Jeff Sessions, R-Alabama, was able to get a provision into the Senate version calling for a permanent E-Verify system; House Republicans had failed in their efforts to have a similar amendment included. The amendment, which also called for requiring all federal contractors to check their workers under E-Verify, was approved by voice vote. The

Senate accepted an amendment by Sen. Charles Grassley, R-Iowa, to allow private-sector employers to check all their workers under E-Verify; the system as it stood allowed only new employees to be checked. It was approved by voice vote. The Senate also accepted 54–44 an amendment by Sen. Jim DeMint, R-S.C., stating that all 700 miles of border fence mandated by Congress must be constructed in a way designed to halt pedestrian traffic.

CONFERENCE AND FINAL ACTION

House and Senate conferees faced few differences in the funding in the two bills, but a number on policy issues.

Perhaps the most contentious was about Guantánamo detainees. Republicans sought to include language to prohibit the detainees from being transferred to the United States. The House on October 1 approved a motion by Harold Rogers, R-K.y, to instruct its conferees on the issue, on a vote of 258–163. Several House provisions limited the transfer of detainees. Democratic conferees agreed to incorporate some of the provisions. One prohibited detainees from being released into the United States and required the president to send reports to Congress before a detainee's being brought to the United States for prosecution, before a detainee was released to another country, and before the Guantánamo facility would be closed. In addition, it stated that all of the Guantánamo detainees must be put on airlines' "no-fly" list.

Conferees did not approve another amendment backed by Rogers to ban the government from moving detainees to U.S. ground for prosecution. That amendment failed on a 6–10 vote. An amendment proposed by Jerry Lewis to stop the administration from going ahead with a January executive order to look over details of the Guantánamo prison in advance of its closure was rejected on a vote of 6–9.

On the issue of fencing the Southwest border with a barrier that would block pedestrians, Republicans complained that the conferees had not included Senate provisions requiring such a fence.

When it came to E-Verify, the conferees agreed with the Obama administration proposal to extend it for three years, turning aside the Republican amendment to make it permanent. In addition, the Senate proposal to allow employers to check on all employees and not just new hires was not included, nor was another Senate amendment to require all federal contractors to use E-Verify. A new federal regulation already had accomplished that goal, according to the conference report.

On the Coast Guard's Loran-C program, conferees decided to include language in the bill requiring a shutdown of the program if top officials agreed that it was no longer needed.

Republicans mounted one last effort to include language barring the Guantánamo detainees from arriving on U.S. soil. Before the House voted on the conference report, Rogers tried to send the bill back to conference with instructions to eliminate language stating that detainees could be sent to the United States for prosecution or incarceration. But his effort failed on a 193–224 vote.

The House voted 307–114 on October 15 to adopt the conference report. On October 20, the Senate cleared the bill, on a 79–19 vote, and the president signed it on October 28.

MAJOR PROVISIONS

Customs and Border Protection. Appropriated $10.1 billion, which was less than 1 percent more than the president had requested, and 3 percent more than the amount in fiscal 2009, without counting fees and emergency funds. Anticipated fees totaled about $1.4 billion. Included in the overall total was $3.8 billion to support 20,163 border patrol agents, up 6,000 since 2006, and $800 million for border fencing and technology related to the fencing.

Immigration and Customs Enforcement. Appropriated $5.4 billion, an increase of 9 percent from the previous year, not including emergency funds. This amount was almost the same as the president had requested. In addition, anticipated fees of $305 million took the overall total for fiscal 2010 to $5.7 billion. Approximately $1.5 billion went to identifying and removing criminal aliens facing deportation. The bureau was required to maintain 33,400 beds for detainees.

Transportation Security Administration. Appropriated $7.7 billion for the TSA, a 10 percent increase from the previous year, not counting emergency spending. It was about 2 percent less than the Obama administration had requested. Aviation security accounted for the majority of TSA money, getting $5.3 billion and an extra $860 million for federal air marshals. Included in the aviation security money was $1 billion to obtain and install systems to detect explosives at airports.

Coast Guard. Appropriated $10.1 billion for the Coast Guard, 4 percent more than the previous year and about 2 percent more than requested. That amount included $1.2 billion for a program to replace old aircraft and ships. The final bill, however, withheld $50 million pending the receipt of reports on costs and plans that were overdue. Also included was $242 million to be used against pirates off the Somali coast and for overseas contingency operations in the Persian Gulf.

Federal Emergency Management Agency. Appropriated $7.1 billion for FEMA, an increase of about 2 percent from fiscal 2009, not counting emergency funds, and about 2 percent less than Obama had asked for. The majority, $4.2 billion, went to training and grants, mostly for first-responders at the state and local level. This amount was a decrease of about 1 percent from the previous year, not including $540 million in emergency funding, but was an increase of almost 8 percent above what Obama had asked for. The money included $950 million for state grants; $887 million for grants to high-risk urban areas; $600 million for rail, transit, and port security grants; $340 million for performance grants; and $810 million for firefighter assistance grants. In addition, the bill included $1.5 billion for FEMA's disaster relief fund, which was about 16 percent more than in fiscal 2009 and only about three-fourths of the amount the Obama administration had asked for.

Earmarks. The bill included 176 member earmarks and eight presidentially directed spending items.

Chemical Plant Security

The 111th Congress extended DHS authority to create performance standards for chemical plants seen as potential terrorist targets. The authority was continued by short-term extensions through the remainder of President Obama's first term in office.

Legislation passed in 2006 (PL 109-295), fiscal 2007 Homeland Security appropriations, gave the department the authority to set regulations for these high-risk plants and close them if they failed to comply. Those changes were to expire three years later. In separate legislation, Congress, in 2007, gave the DHS permanent regulatory power over the chemical industry. *(Congress and the Nation Vol. XII, pp. 229, 260)*

The House in 2009 sought unsuccessfully to make the temporary authority permanent. On June 23, the House Homeland Security Committee, on a party-line vote of 18–11, approved a measure (HR 2868) that included provisions opposed by Republicans and industry groups. One provision gave the DHS power to force a chemical plant to use so-called "inherently safer technologies" designed to minimize the consequences of a possible terrorist attack. Republicans also objected to provisions that would permit broad civil lawsuits.

On October 21, the House Energy and Commerce Committee voted 29–18, again on a party line vote, to approve an amended version of HR 2868. In addition, the committee approved a second bill, HR 3258, that focused on the security of drinking-water and wastewater systems. This bill also included the provision giving the DHS authority to require companies to minimize the consequences of an attack—for example, by changing their storage facilities or their processes, or substituting different chemicals.

The bill allowed civilians to sue the department for failure to enforce security standards properly. Rep. Edward J. Markey, D-Mass., earlier introduced an amendment that the committee's Energy and Environment subcommittee approved during its markup that removed a provision allowing citizen lawsuits against companies, substituting instead language allowing citizens to petition DHS to enforce security standards more effectively.

The full committee retained the Markey amendment as part of the bill approved by the House on November 6, when it passed HR 2868 on a vote of 230–193. This version of the bill included water provisions taken from HR 3258. The bill called for giving the Environmental Protection Agency (EPA) the authority to regulate water security at community water systems that served more than 3,300 people and other water systems that the EPA considered possible security risks. The measure called for $900 million over three years for chemical plant security and $1.3 billion over five years for water and wastewater plant security.

The Senate did not act on the measure in 2009. Congress decided instead to extend the chemical security regulations through October 31 in a continuing resolution (PL 111-68) and then to clear a one-year reauthorization of the existing law in the fiscal 2010 Homeland Security appropriations bill (PL 111-83). Additional extensions followed that continued the DHS powers through the 112th Congress.

Border Security Funding

Congress voted in August 2010 to provide $600 million toward additional equipment and personnel for U.S. patrol activities along the border with Mexico. Lawmakers expressed concern about the ongoing problem of illegal immigration across the border as well as the growing problem of serious crime in Mexico related to drug wars.

The House on July 28, by voice vote, passed a $701 million border security supplemental spending bill (HR 5875), after having attempted unsuccessfully to attach border security money to the fiscal 2010 war supplemental spending bill (PL 111-212). Under the bill, the Defense Department would pay for costs connected to the deployment of National Guard troops along the border in fiscal years 2010 and 2011. The measure's cost was partially offset with rescissions totaling $100 million; the bill did not include revenue provisions.

In a surprise move, the Senate, which had not been expected to act on the bill at that point, approved an amended version by unanimous consent on August 5. The House version was amended with a substitute bill (S 3721) sponsored by Sen. Charles Schumer, D-N.Y. The Schumer bill totaled $600 million. It sought 1,500 new agents, two unmanned aerial drones, and communications equipment. The Senate version offset the bill's costs by setting a temporary increase in companies' payments for H-1B and L visas. Schumer had introduced his bill only hours before, and it had only a handful of Democratic cosponsors. After Schumer spoke on the floor that evening asking for passage of his bill and Sen. John McCain, R-Ariz., withdrew several amendments he had tried to offer, the measure picked up support, including from McCain, and easily passed before the Senate headed out of town for its summer recess.

But the House members criticized the inclusion of revenue provisions in a Senate-originated bill, a procedure that under the Constitution was a prerogative of the House.

Meeting for a one-day session on August 10, the House approved by voice vote a bill (HR 6080) identical to the

Senate bill. The Senate then returned briefly from its vacation to hold a one-day session on August 12, and it cleared the bill by unanimous consent that day. President Obama signed it into law (PL 111-230) on August 13.

MAJOR PROVISIONS

As signed into law, PL 111-230 contained the following major provisions:

- Provided the Customs and Border Protection agency with $254 million, including money to send 1,500 new patrol agents and two additional unmanned aerial drones to protect the border against drugs and illegal immigrants.
- Provided the Justice Department with $196 million to step up law enforcement activities related to the border.
- Provided the Immigration and Customs Enforcement agency with $80 million, which included money for communications equipment.
- Provided companies that applied for H-1B and L employee visas an increase of $2,000 and $2,500, respectively, on the fees they paid.
- Rescinded $100 million in previously enacted spending.

2011–2012

The 2010 midterm elections were a setback for President Barack Obama and the Democrats and a victory for Republicans, who took back control of the House from the Democrats after four years in the minority. Conservative Republicans backed by the Tea Party clashed with Democrats and even with more traditional members of the GOP, and much of the 112th Congress, especially as the 2012 election grew closer, was caught in gridlock, with most major issues receiving little serious attention.

Nevertheless, Congress was able to pass some major legislation dealing with homeland security issues, a subject that often did not break down neatly along traditional party lines. In 2011, lawmakers approved a four-year extension of three controversial provisions of the antiterrorism bill known as the Patriot Act. The 111th Congress had passed two short-term extensions, handing the issue on to its successor.

The 112th Congress first approved a three-month extension before passing the longer extension and sending it to Obama for his signature. The three provisions in question gave wide-ranging powers to the federal government to investigate possible terrorist activity. Civil libertarians condemned the measures as interfering with people's privacy. In an indication of the importance of this issue, congressional leaders of both parties forged a compromise plan that allowed the multiyear extension to go forward.

In a victory for President Obama, Congress also approved a multiyear extension, through 2017, to warrantless wiretapping provisions, also highly controversial and opposed by civil libertarians as well as some liberal Democrats in Congress. The legislation extended powers given to the intelligence community to wiretap without getting individual warrants particular foreigners who were contacting people in the United States. President George W. Bush had backed the initial legislation, and Obama was equally supportive.

Another success came when Congress approved a two-year Coast Guard reauthorization bill. The Coast Guard had gone through many changes since its inclusion in the new Department of Homeland Security as its mission moved from traditional search-and-rescue efforts to a focus on port security and tracking illegal immigrants and drug smugglers at sea. The legislation took more than a year to get through Congress.

One area in which Congress failed to act upon was cybersecurity, although it had been high on lawmakers' to-do lists as the 112th Congress began. Although lawmakers agreed that protecting the computer systems connected to the country's defense and financial infrastructure was crucial, they were not able to produce completed legislation. The House passed a cybersecurity bill, but Senate leaders were not able to bring a Senate version to a vote.

USA PATRIOT Act

The 112th Congress on May 26, 2011, cleared a four-year extension to 2015 of Patriot Act provisions (S 990—PL 112-14) that were about to expire. President Barack Obama signed the legislation the same day. The previous Congress had passed short-term extensions to three controversial provisions.

The first provision, known as the "business records" provision, gave the FBI wide powers to seek a special federal court order for "any tangible thing," which could include, for example, DNA information, blood sample, or a list of books a person was reading. Government officials, however, were required to show reasonable grounds to believe the information sought was connected to an investigation, and courts were to presume the material was relevant if the government could link it to a foreign power or its agent.

The second provision, known as "roving wiretaps," empowered investigators, after obtaining court orders, to follow terrorist suspects who changed their mode of communication. Investigators were allowed to tap various phones, cell phones, or Internet connections.

The third provision, called the "lone wolf" provision, permitted investigators to ask for warrants from the Foreign Intelligence Surveillance Court to conduct surveillance on suspected terrorists who were not affiliated with a foreign power or recognized organization.

Provisions one and two had been included in the original 2001 Patriot Act (PL 107-56), a massive antiterrorist measure approved by Congress in the wake of the terrorist attacks of September 11, 2001. The third provision was added in 2004 (PL 108-458). The three had been reauthorized in 2006 (PL 109-177, PL 109-178). But whereas most of the Patriot Act was made permanent, the three controversial provisions were given an expiration date (known as a sunset provision) of December 31, 2009, to enable Congress to review them periodically. Congress had agreed in December 2009 to extend the provisions for two months and then voted in February 2010 to extend them for another year, through February 2011. *(2009–2010 action, p. 208)*

Under the Patriot Act, the federal government was given a wide range of powers aimed at fighting terrorism. The law was controversial among civil liberties groups and their backers in Congress, who believed that it interfered with the Fourth Amendment's protections against unreasonable searches and seizure.

Although many Republicans wanted the three provisions made permanent, civil libertarians maintained that the provisions—in particular the idea of obtaining library, bookstore, and other business records—was too intrusive.

NEW SHORT-TERM EXTENSION

The three provisions were set to expire on February 28, 2011, but Congress voted once again for a temporary extension. But the road to that extension was rocky, pitting civil libertarians against supporters of the provisions. Initially, the House had considered an extension that would run through December 8, 2011. The bill (HR 514) failed 277–148 when it was brought up under suspension of the rules that require a two-thirds majority for passage. Then the bill was brought up again, this time under a procedural rule that barred amendments and needed only a simple majority to pass, which it received in a 275–144 vote on February 14.

In the Senate, Majority Leader Harry Reid, D-Nev., and Minority Leader Mitch McConnell, R-Ky., agreed to reduce the extension to three months, to May 27. The Senate approved that extension February 15, 86–12, and the House cleared it February 17, 279–143. The president signed the bill (PL 112-3) into law on February 25.

FOUR-YEAR EXTENSION

The issue of a longer-term bill remained a high-priority item. The Senate Judiciary Committee on March 10, 2011, approved a bill (S 193) in a 10–7 vote to extend the provisions through 2013. Committee Chair Patrick Leahy, D-Vt., said that the measure took a middle ground between the concerns of law enforcement and the intelligence community on the one hand, and civil liberties and privacy concerns on the other. Under the bill, law enforcement officials would face tougher standards when accessing library and bookseller records, and the government would have to prove that the records and information it wanted were relevant to an authorized investigation. The bill also set restrictions on government use of "national security letters," which were secret demands for records and other information, in counterterrorism investigations. The committee's ranking Republican, Charles Grassley of Iowa, wanted a simple extension of the three provisions. Republican Mike Lee of Utah joined the committee's Democrats in voting for the measure.

The House Judiciary Committee, meanwhile, took a different approach. Along mostly party lines, the committee voted to approve a bill (HR 1800) to extend the first two Patriot Act provisions, the "business records" and "roving wiretap" sections, through 2017. The bill, sponsored by committee Chair H. James Sensenbrenner Jr. of Wisconsin, made the "lone wolf" provision permanent. House Republicans did not include the restrictions found in the Senate bill. Democratic efforts to limit or block government access to library and bookseller records were rejected.

A potential standoff was averted just before the May 27 expiration date when top congressional leaders, in a move that indicated how important this measure had become, agreed on a compromise plan. House Speaker John Boehner, R-Ohio, Senate Majority Leader Harry Reid, D-Nevada, and Senate Minority Leader Mitch McConnell, R-Ky., agreed on a measure to extend the three provisions for four years, through June 1, 2015, claiming a middle ground between the House and Senate expiration dates. The plan eliminated the Senate's proposed new restrictions on access to records and national security letters.

In floor action, Sen. Rand Paul, R-Ky., concerned about civil liberties issues, attempted to delay passage of the bill, thus allowing the three provisions to expire. Ultimately, Paul was allowed to offer two amendments, both of which were defeated. One prevented government investigators from using the "business record" provision to get the background forms filled out by gun purchasers who buy guns from licensed dealers; it was tabled, or killed, 85–10. The second limited authority to request suspicious-activity reports to law enforcement agencies; it was tabled 91–4.

On May 26, 2011, the Senate passed the compromise bill from committee on a **key vote of 72–23 (R 41–4; D 30–18; I 1–1).** The House cleared that version the same day on a **key vote of 250–153 (R 196–31; D 54–122).** *(2011 key votes, p. 785)*

President Obama, who was on an official European trip, signed the bill that day. The congressional action came one day after James Clapper Jr., the director of national intelligence, warned Reid and McConnell in writing that continued delay on extending the provisions was risky. But opponents of the extension argued that Osama bin Laden's death May 1 during a U.S. raid on his compound had changed the situation and that Congress should not be hasty in reauthorizing the provisions.

FISA Extension

In 2012, Congress, shortly before adjournment, extended through 2017 the provisions of a controversial 2008 law (PL 110-261) that authorized the intelligence community to wiretap without getting individual warrants particular foreigners who were in touch with people in the United States. The extension was widely viewed as a major victory for the Obama administration and Senate Intelligence Chair Dianne Feinstein, D-Calif., one of the bill's most ardent backers.

The law involved was the 1978 Foreign Intelligence Surveillance Act (FISA) (PL 95-511) and later updates following the September 11, 2001, terrorist attack on the United States. The legislation making the extension was HR 5949 (PL 112-238).

BACKGROUND

Warrantless wiretapping, a topic that sparked fierce arguments from supporters and opponents, was a high priority on Congress's 2012 agenda. At issue were provisions of a 2008 law (PL 110-261) that were set to expire at the end of 2012. *(FISA, Congress and the Nation Vol. V, p. 720; 2008 action, Congress and the Nation Vol. XII, pp. 249, 251)*

The 2008 law, part of President George W. Bush's antiterrorism efforts following the September 11, 2001, attacks, was exceptionally controversial. It updated the 1978 FISA act, which had been a congressional response to concerns over widespread wiretapping during the administration of President Richard Nixon and revelations by a select congressional committee known as the Church Committee, chaired by Sen. Frank Church, D-Idaho, that warrantless electronic surveillance dated back to the administration of President Franklin D. Roosevelt.

Under FISA, the government needed to get a warrant from a special FISA court before engaging in foreign surveillance in situations where one person was a U.S. citizen. FISA court cases were sealed. If there was an emergency, the president could authorize electronic surveillance to obtain foreign intelligence without court approval for up to three days. In the event of a congressional declaration of war, the time frame would expand to fifteen days. If the surveillance only involved foreigners and was unlikely to affect U.S. citizens or residents, the time frame could expand to up to a year.

After the September 11 attacks, President Bush authorized a secret program that tracked U.S. citizens, permanent residents, tourists, and foreigners in the United States in an effort to look for terrorist links. In January 2007, the administration stated that this program, which had been reported by the *New York Times* in December 2005, had been reviewed by the FISA court and that several orders had been granted. On May 1, 2007, National Intelligence Director Michael McDonald asked Congress to update FISA, citing technological advances and arguing that the new law should permit warrantless surveillance of foreigners suspected of terrorism whether or not they were communicating with people in the United States. Bush, on July 28, asked Congress to pass legislation updating FISA. Congress cleared a six-month temporary bill on August 4, 2007, that made it easier for the government to conduct electronic surveillance.

The subsequent 2008 bill offered additional authority for executive branch spying and dismissal of lawsuits against phone companies that had helped with a warrantless wiretapping plan undertaken by the National Security Agency under presidential authority. Under the law, the attorney general and the director of national intelligence could jointly approve investigations lasting up to one year that involved surveillance of those who were not "U.S. persons" and were "reasonably believed to be located outside the United States." In addition, the law authorized authorities to obtain electronic communications and other information within the country relating to U.S. individuals who were out of the country. Under the law, warrantless surveillance was permitted if it did not intentionally target U.S. people or those located in the United States; foreign agents were excluded. Among the restrictions included in the bill was a prohibition on intentional targeting of a U.S. person, directly or indirectly, and a requirement that the collecting of intelligence be done under the Fourth Amendment.

Similar to his predecessor, Obama was eager to see this approach continue. James R. Clapper Jr., the director of national intelligence, argued that retaining the FISA law was essential to antiterrorism efforts. But civil liberties groups and various liberal Democrats in Congress were vociferously opposed to reauthorizing the law. They were concerned about how the communications of U.S. citizens would be affected under the program.

HOUSE ACTION

House action on the legislation took place relatively quickly. On June 19, 2012, the House Judiciary Committee approved a bill (HR 5949—H Rept 112-645, Part 2) that extended the provisions for five years, through the end of 2017. The vote was 23–11, mostly along party lines; three Democrats voted for the bill.

During debate, the committee rejected an amendment offered by Rep. John Conyers of Michigan, the committee's ranking Democrat, to set June 1, 2015, as the expiration date. Conyers cited privacy concerns for efforts to shorten the time frame. The amendment was rejected on a 12–12 vote. Committee Chair Lamar Smith, R-Texas, argued that the bill, which he had sponsored, took a balanced stance between the protection of the national interest and the civil liberties of U.S. citizens.

Also rejected, 11–20, was a proposal by Rep. Sheila Jackson Lee, D-Texas, to require the Justice Department and the intelligence community to provide Congress with an estimate of how many Americans' communications had been monitored.

The panel also rejected, 14–17, an attempt by Rep. Jerrold Nadler, D-N.Y., to require the attorney general to release unclassified summaries of findings by the FISA court including interpretations of the warrantless surveillance authority.

The bill won unanimous support, 17–0, from the House Permanent Select Intelligence Committee. Both Chair Mike Rogers, R-Mich., and ranking member C. A. Dutch Ruppersberger, D-Md., praised the bill.

On the House floor, most House Democrats voted against the bill even though President Obama supported it. The bill passed September 12 on a 301–118 vote. On the roll call, 111 of 185 Democrats opposed the measure, along with seven Republicans. A group of opponents including the American Civil Liberties Union sent letters on September 11 asking House members to vote against a straight renewal of the provisions; the opposing groups sought additional restrictions on and stronger oversight of the program, and more information released on Americans affected by the surveillance.

SENATE AND FINAL ACTION

The Senate passed the House bill, 72–23, without amendments, on December 28, 2012, clearing the measure for the president. He signed it December 30 (PL 112-238).

The Senate Intelligence Committee approved a measure (S 3276—S Rept 112-174) to reauthorize the warrantless wiretapping provisions through June 2017. Democrats Ron Wyden of Oregon and Mark Udall of Colorado voted against it; the bill was approved May 22 on a vote of 13–2. Committee Chair Feinstein and ranking Republican Saxby Chambliss of Georgia put out a bipartisan statement expressing their desire for quick floor action. In the statement, they noted that while the measure would continue to allow intelligence to be collected on noncitizens outside the country, the government would still need a specific court order to go after the communications of a U.S. citizen or permanent legal resident.

The Senate Judiciary Committee voted July 19 along party lines, 10–8, to extend the provisions for two and a half years. Committee Chair Patrick Leahy, D-Vt., said a five-year bill would represent too lengthy a time frame without the completion of implementation and compliance reviews. Under the bill, the intelligence community inspector general was required to review the 2008 law. On a 3–15 vote, the committee turned down a proposal by Sen. Mike Lee, R-Utah, to explicitly prohibit acquisition of a particular American's communications or a search through collected communications to look for e-mails or phone calls of an American. Exemptions would be offered if the person had agreed to the search, was under threat, or was subject to a surveillance order. Also voting for Lee's amendment were Democrats Richard Durbin of Illinois and Chris Coons of Delaware. Durbin voted against the bill at first, but opted to vote for it to break a 9–9 tie.

Progress in the Senate stalled when Wyden put a hold on the bill, blocking it from reaching the floor. He expressed concerns that loopholes in the bill could lead to abuse of information pertaining to American citizens, and that there were not enough data to indicate whether the bill's safeguards were strong enough. Later, Wyden lifted his hold in exchange for being able to offer an amendment on the floor requiring the director of national intelligence to report to Congress on collection of any domestic phone or e-mail communications under the 2008 law. Wyden's amendment was rejected on a vote of 43–52.

Also rejected were two other amendments. The first, a substitute amendment by Leahy, set a June 2015 expiration date. It also required the intelligence community inspector general review the implementation of surveillance authorities and report to Congress by the end of 2014. That amendment was defeated, 38–52. The second, by Jeff Merkley, D-Ore., required the government to disclose FISA court decisions, orders, or opinions on surveillance requests if such disclosure did not conflict with national security interests. It was rejected, 37–54.

Cybersecurity

Congress began 2012 with agreement across party lines that swift legislative action was needed to protect the computer systems connected to the country's infrastructure in such critical areas as defense and finance. But despite the unusual bipartisan sentiment, no final legislation resulted.

Security experts warned repeatedly about serious and continuing threats to the U.S. computer networks that endangered national security. According to these experts, countries such as China, Iran, and Russia were working to obtain data, intellectual property, and corporate and government secrets that could lead to greater destabilization and disruption through larger attacks in the future. Some experts disagreed, saying the threat of a major attack was exaggerated.

Because an estimated 85 to 90 percent of the nation's crucial computer networks were under the control of the private sector rather than the government, cybersecurity legislation had to persuade or require businesses to participate in any effort to strengthen security standards.

HOUSE ACTION

The House, on April 26, 2012, passed a cybersecurity bill (HR 3523—H Rept 112-445) on a 248–168 vote. This measure sought to promote voluntary sharing between federal agencies and private organizations of information relating to cyber threats.

The House bill, sponsored by Rep. Mike Rogers, R-Mich., the chair of the Select Intelligence Committee, had been approved by the intelligence committee on December 1, 2011, on a vote of 17–1. Among its provisions were incentives to participating businesses, including one to bar lawsuits from actions they had taken in good faith. Under the bill, private organization could decide how much information to share with other private firms or with the government. In addition, the bill called for the director of national intelligence to set parameters for permanent or temporary security clearances that would enable the government to share information with relevant businesses or individuals.

Many civil liberties advocates opposed the legislation. But Rogers and Rep. C. A. Dutch Ruppersberger of Maryland, the intelligence panel's top Democrat, defended the bill, arguing that the information sharing would be voluntary and that amendments to the bill had boosted its privacy and civil liberties provisions.

In addition to H.R. 3523, the House also passed three other cybersecurity bills that were less controversial.

Under one of these bills, passed by voice vote on April 26 (HR 4257—H Rept 112-455), federal agencies would be required to continually monitor security controls on their information systems, as well as conduct assessments to protect the systems from cyber-intrusions. The Oversight and Government Reform Committee had approved the bill by voice vote April 1.

Another bill (HR 2096—H Rept 112-264), approved on April 27 on a 395–10 vote, sought to reauthorize and expand federal cybersecurity programs. The legislation required that federal agencies develop a plan for the overall direction of federal cybersecurity. The bill reauthorized the National Science Foundation's cybersecurity programs. It also directed the National Institute of Standards and Technology to set federal government cybersecurity standards. This bill had been approved by the Science, Space and Technology Committee on a voice vote on July 21, 2011.

A third bill (HR 3834—H Rept 112-420), also approved on April 27 by voice vote, sought to establish a strategic plan for the government's Networking and Information Technology Research and Development. The Science, Space and Technology Committee had approved the measure February 7 by voice vote.

SENATE ACTION

The Senate twice turned back efforts by Majority Leader Harry Reid, D-Nev., to bring another cybersecurity bill (S 3414) to a vote. Cloture votes to end debate failed in August and November.

The Senate bill, which was brought directly to the floor without committee action, was intended to promote information-sharing, as with the House legislation, but gave the Department of Homeland Security the key role of coordinating the process and the power to set voluntary security standards for especially important private digital infrastructure. These provisions were opposed by the U.S. Chamber of Commerce and Republican congressional leaders, who were concerned that the voluntary standards could become mandatory.

The legislation was sponsored by Sen. Joseph Lieberman, I-Conn. Under earlier versions of the measure, the Department of Homeland Security was given power to set mandatory standards, an approach opposed by many Republican lawmakers and business groups, including the Chamber of Commerce. After sponsors agreed to weaken those provisions, the measure gained enough support to win a cloture vote July 26 to begin floor debate. The vote was 84–11.

Still, many opponents of the bill, both in the GOP and among industry groups, remained unsatisfied. They sought tougher protections against lawsuits that could result from industry's sharing information with the government, opposed widening DHS's cybersecurity responsibilities, and feared that voluntary standards could become mandatory.

Negotiations continued on alternatives, but the process became unwieldy as senators tried to include unrelated amendments, and time was running out before adjournment. Reid attempted twice to end debate and bring the bill to a vote, but failed first on August 2 by a **key vote of 52–46 (R 5–40; D 45–6; I 2–0)** and again on November 14 by a 51–47. Sixty votes were required to invoke cloture to end debate. *(2012 key votes, p. 803)*

Coast Guard Reauthorization

The effort took more than a year, but Congress in December 2012 succeeded in passing a two-year Coast Guard reauthorization bill (HR 2838—PL 112-213).

Following terrorist attacks on the United States in 2001, the Coast Guard's mission shifted from its longtime focus on search-and-rescue efforts. Under the Homeland Security Act of 2002, the Coast Guard was transferred from the Department of Transportation to the new Department of Homeland Security. As part of the DHS, the Coast Guard focused increasingly on port security and intercepting drug smugglers and illegal immigrants at sea. *(2006 reauthorization, Congress and the Nation Vol. XII, p. 228)*

The House initially passed the Coast Guard reauthorization bill (HR 2838—H Rept 112-229) on November 15, 2011, by voice vote. One major issue dividing lawmakers involved the rules under which ships could dump wastewater. Under the House bill, existing law—under which the EPA, the fifty states, and the Coast Guard all were involved in setting standards—would be replaced by one overall standard that would follow International Maritime Organization rules. This proposal, backed by House Republicans, faced opposition from Democrats, who argued that states should have the ability to set stricter standards when dealing with pollution or invasive species.

Another controversial issue was the fate of the Coast Guard's two aging heavy-duty icebreaker ships, the *Polar Star* and the *Polar Sea*. The House bill called for the *Polar Star* to be decommissioned within three years and the *Polar Sea* to be decommissioned within six months; however, the White House said it would oppose the bill because of that provision. The Obama administration, arguing that the bill would create "a significant gap in the nation's ice-breaking capacity," wanted the *Polar Star* reactivated by December 2012, with its lifespan extended another seven to ten years. The Coast Guard wanted the other ship, the *Polar Sea*, decommissioned because of serious problems related to its age. But the bill approved by the House on November 15 included the icebreaker ship provisions opposed by the White House.

The bill called for $25.8 billion for the Coast Guard for fiscal 2012 through fiscal 2014. It also called for maintaining the active-duty personnel of the Coast Guard at 47,000.

Ten months later, on September 22, 2012, the Senate by unanimous consent approved its version of HR 2838 (no committee report.) Under the Senate version, the Coast Guard would get an average of about $7 billion annually. The bill also sought to increase the Coast Guard's active-duty ranks to 49,350 in fiscal 2014.

The Senate bill differed from the House on the two icebreakers, which were almost forty years old. Under the Senate bill, the Coast Guard was forbidden to transfer, dismantle, recycle, or give away either ship. The bill stated that the ships' home port would continue to be in Seattle. This approach gained increasing support from both parties as senators pointed out that the Coast Guard was already in the middle of a project to retrofit the *Polar Star*.

In addition, the Senate bill did not include the new national wastewater standard proposed in the House bill.

The House on December 5 made additional changes before approving it by voice vote. The House did not include the national wastewater standards, and instead called for a one-year continuation of a moratorium blocking the EPA or states from requiring certain permits—for the discharge of laundry or wash waste, or engine fluids—from vessels that are less than seventy-nine-feet long.

On the icebreaker issue, the House banned the DHS from decommissioning the *Polar Sea* or *Polar Star* unless a department analysis found that reactivating the *Polar Sea* would not be cost-effective. The bill also required an analysis submitted to Congress, in the event of a planned reactivation of the *Polar Sea*.

The amended bill called for authorizing about $17.4 billion for the Coast Guard in fiscal 2013–2014, and authorized an active-duty force of 47,000.

The Senate on December 12 accepted the House changes, clearing the bill by voice vote. President Barack Obama signed the bill into law on December 20 (PL 112-213).

MAJOR PROVISIONS

As signed into law, PL 112-213 contained the following major provisions:

- Specified the Coast Guard would have 47,000 active-duty employees in fiscal 2013 and 2014.
- Authorized $8.6 billion for fiscal 2013 and slightly more for fiscal 2014.
- Prohibited the Coast Guard from disposing of its two aging heavy-duty icebreakers without convincing Congress of the need to do so. Directed the Coast Guard to demonstrate a strategy for keeping icebreaking vessels working until additional ones could be built.
- Prohibited the Coast Guard from using a sixth National Security cutter until the Coast Guard was able to show the performance of similar ships already in use.
- Required the DHS to provide Congress with a report on the Coast Guard's ability to deal with a rise in commercial activity in the waters near Alaska's North Slope.

Border Entry Points

The House in 2012 gave voice vote approval to a bill (HR 1299) to require the Obama administration to come up with a comprehensive plan for securing U.S. border entry ports within five years. The bill, passed on May 30, required the DHS to submit to Congress a plan that details how the department would achieve "operational control" of the borders, or between the ports of entry.

The Customs and Border Protection agency used "operational control" when referring to areas where their agents are deployed. Some House Republicans criticized the Obama administration's border security strategy after the Government Accountability Office reported that only 44 percent of the nearly 2,000-mile southwest border was under "operational control" at the end of fiscal 2010.

"We want to be careful about spending money in an ad hoc fashion, and developing a comprehensive and coherent plan to achieve 'operational control' of both borders is certainly our goal," said bill sponsor Candice S. Miller, R-Mich.

The Senate did not take up the measure.

CHAPTER 4

Foreign Policy

Introduction 223

Afghanistan Policy: Eleven Years and an Uncertain Outcome 229

Chronology of Action of Foreign Policy 232

2009–2010 232

2011–2012 249

Foreign Policy

Barack Obama came onto the world stage as a celebrity president, a man with almost rock-star drawing power that got him a respectful, often adoring, hearing in his early international travels. But as the new president, with little previous international experience, began dealing with tough global challenges, much of that warm-and-fuzzy aura quickly wore away. By the end of his first term, Obama was struggling to keep up with a bewildering number of foreign crises or near-crises. Back home, he often faced harsh criticism, though little direct action in terms of legislation, from hostile Republicans in Congress who insisted he had diminished American influence in the world.

All new presidents come to office with seemingly fresh agendas of foreign affairs priorities but then find themselves besieged by intractable age-old problems as well as unexpected events beyond their control. Obama appeared to have two new priorities on his agenda: first, refurbishing the world's image of the United States, which had been tarnished by the often brusque behavior of the administration of his predecessor, George W. Bush, especially with the invasion and occupation of Iraq that began in 2003; and, second, a "pivot" toward a greater focus on U.S. interests in Asia, largely as a means of restraining China's influence as it became a global economic, and eventually strategic, superpower.

Even while emphasizing these priorities, Obama needed to deal with unavoidable existing ones. He had promised in his election campaign to wind down the U.S. military role in Iraq while at the same time securing some kind of victory in Afghanistan. The president also decided to tackle one of the most intractable of all international problems: the decades-long conflict between the Israelis and the Palestinians. And although the pivot to Asia was in part intended to reduce America's focus on the Middle East, Obama needed to deal with another problem in that region: Iran, which insisted on pursuing a nuclear program that the rest of the world suspected was intended to produce nuclear weapons.

ARAB AWAKENING

If there was one big global surprise during Obama's first term, it came from a totally unexpected place: the Arab world. Popular protests against corrupt, autocratic governments began in Tunisia in December 2010 and quickly spread across North Africa and into the Arabian peninsula and the eastern Mediterranean. The protests became known as the "Arab Spring" or the "Arab Awakening."

During 2011, much of the Arab world was dramatically transformed, at least in terms of governance. Gone were some of the region's longest-serving and most authoritarian rulers: President Ben Ali of Tunisia, who fled after the first protests in his country; President Hosni Mubarak of Egypt, ousted by the military after public protests and eventually replaced, after elections, by the long-suppressed Muslim Brotherhood (which in turn was forced out of office by the military in mid-2013); Libyan dictator Muammar Gaddafi, forced from power during a civil war and killed; and President Ali Abdullah Saleh of Yemen, who was injured in a failed assassination attempt and later resigned.

Antigovernment protests erupted at least to some degree in nearly every other Arab country, in most cases to die down after leaders made concessions or used heavy-handed suppression. The most violent and long-lasting conflict of all came in Syria, where a disparate coalition of

REFERENCES

Discussion of foreign policy for the years 1945–1964 may be found in *Congress and the Nation Vol. I*, pp. 91–232; for the years 1965–1968, *Congress and the Nation Vol. II*, pp. 49–116; for the years 1969–1972, *Congress and the Nation Vol. III*, pp. 853–948; for the years 1973–1976, *Congress and the Nation Vol. IV*, pp. 847–912; for the years 1977–1980, *Congress and the Nation Vol. V*, pp. 31–95; for the years 1981–1984, *Congress and the Nation Vol. VI*, pp. 123–197; for the years 1985–1988, *Congress and the Nation Vol. VII*, pp. 169–251; for the years 1989–1992, *Congress and the Nation Vol. VIII*, pp. 203–297; for the years 1993–1996, *Congress and the Nation Vol. IX*, pp. 187–250; for the years 1997–2000, *Congress and the Nation Vol. X*, pp. 173–231; for the years 2001–2004, *Congress and the Nation Vol. XI*, pp. 229–300; for the years 2005–2008, *Congress and the Nation Vol. XII, pp.* 270–327.

Syrian protesters chant slogans and hold posters during a demonstration demanding that Syria's President Bashar Assad step down, in front of the Arab League headquarters building in Cairo, Egypt, on Sunday, May 15, 2011. Hundreds of Syrians fled to neighboring Lebanon to escape a violent crackdown against an antigovernment uprising that claimed the lives of more than 800 civilians. The poster in Arabic reads "People want Assad to step down."
Source: AP Photo/Amr Nabil

rebels challenged the dictatorial regime of President Bashar al-Assad, who used the full weight of his military to fight back.

Obviously caught off guard by the intensity of these protests, the Obama administration seemed to have no overall strategy—if, indeed, any unified strategy was possible in response to situations that varied so dramatically—and instead used case-by-case tactics. The administration quickly sided with protesters in Egypt, withdrawing longtime U.S. support for Mubarak just as he seemed to be teetering in February 2011. One month later, the United States and its North Atlantic Treaty Organization (NATO) allies lent air and naval support to a variety of rebel groups fighting to overthrow Gaddafi in Libya; that effort succeeded in August 2011 when the rebels captured Tripoli and then, in October, captured and killed Gaddafi.

Obama's intervention in Libya generated a significant amount of grumbling in Congress, particularly among those opposed to yet another U.S. military commitment in the Middle East. Congressional leaders also insisted the president had not consulted adequately with them ahead of time. The only significant congressional action, however, was adoption of a resolution by the House on June 3, 2011, demanding that the president explain "national security interests" for acting in Libya.

The outcome of the Libya rebellion turned tragic for the United States a year later, in September 2012, when armed men attacked the U.S. consulate and another building in Benghazi, killing Ambassador Christopher Stevens and three other U.S. personnel. Outraged Republicans in Congress immediately accused Obama, Secretary of State Hillary Clinton, and other administration officials of not doing enough to protect the diplomats and of covering up that failure. Some Republicans also responded by demanding a halt to U.S. aid to Libya, which Washington had begun providing after the fall of Gaddafi. Despite the high level of political rhetoric, Congress did not block the aid. One political casualty, however, was Susan E. Rice, the U.S. ambassador to the United Nations, whom Obama reportedly had wanted to name as secretary of state in his second term. After Republicans loudly accused Rice of making misleading statements about the Benghazi attack, she withdrew as a candidate. Obama instead named Senate Foreign Relations Committee Chair John Kerry to the post to succeed Clinton.

SYRIA AND IRAN

In contrast to its initially assertive stance toward Libya, the Obama administration was cautious—Republicans and even some Democrats in Congress said timid—in responding to the more complex and violent civil war in Syria. Early in 2012, Sen. John McCain, R-Ariz., and others began demanding that the administration provide weapons to some of the Syrian rebels and establish "no-fly" zones in Syria to protect the rebels and civilians from President Assad's air force.

Although giving diplomatic and eventually "nonlethal" support to the rebels, the administration rejected outright intervention in Syria. According to government officials, the country already had too many weapons, creating no-fly zones was risky, and it was unclear that the United States could have positive influence on the course of events. Saudi Arabia, Qatar, and several other Arab nations supplied weapons to their favored rebel groups, but efforts by the rebels to form a truly unified opposition to Assad foundered. By mid-2013 nearly 100,000 people had died, and Assad appeared to be gaining the upper hand against the feuding rebels.

Outlays for International Affairs

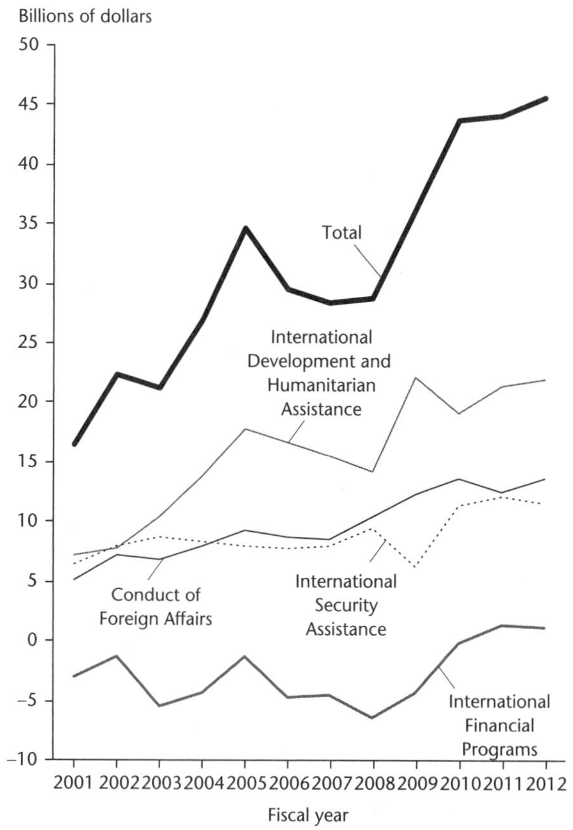

SOURCE: Office of Management and Budget, *Historical Tables, Budget of the United States Government: Fiscal Year 2013* (Washington, D.C.: U.S. Government Printing Office, 2012), Table 3.2.

NOTE: Total line includes some expenditures not shown separately.

Spurred in part by lobbying from pro-Israel groups, Congress was even more assertive in insisting that the Obama administration take a tough stance toward Iran and its suspected program to develop nuclear weapons. Throughout his first term, Obama tightened long-standing U.S. economic sanctions against Iran and imposed new ones, all with the intention of forcing the rulers in Tehran to negotiate a deal ending its weapons-oriented work in exchange for international aid for its strictly civilian nuclear energy programs.

Even so, Congress, in the election years of 2010 and 2012, passed legislation imposing even more sanctions against Iran and attempting to force the president to adopt a more aggressive posture in negotiations over the nuclear issue. Obama in 2012 also faced direct pressure over Iran from Israel's prime minister, Benjamin Netanyahu, who repeatedly called on the United States to enforce, by military means if necessary, a "red line" prohibiting Iran from developing the capability to build nuclear weapons—as opposed to stated U.S. policy of stopping Iran from having the weapons themselves. Netanyahu stopped just short of endorsing Obama's Republican opponent in the presidential elections, Mitt Romney, who also was critical of the president's Iran policy.

IRAQ AND AFGHANISTAN

Amid the challenges of the Arab Spring and Iran, Obama also had to deal with the priorities he inherited from President Bush in Iraq and Afghanistan. In some ways, Iraq was the easier of the two challenges. By the time Obama took office, Iraq was relatively calm, certainly compared with the sectarian violence that had raged just three years earlier. President Bush's "surge" of U.S. troops—combined with a decision by key Sunni leaders to cooperate, albeit grudgingly, with the United States and the Shiite-led government in Baghdad—had helped reduce the violence and enabled Iraq to begin rebuilding after decades of war and international sanctions. *(Iraq and Afghan policy, pp. 229, 234)*

Obama had promised in his campaign to "end" the U.S. military campaign in Iraq within sixteen months. He fell short of that goal but did succeed in pulling out the last U.S. troops in mid-December 2011, in compliance with a mutual agreement President Bush had negotiated with Iraq. Although some Republicans criticized Obama for "abandoning" Iraq, Congress made no substantial effort to interfere with his policies there.

Afghanistan was a more difficult situation for Obama to address for two reasons. First, the Bush administration had shifted its attention to Iraq from Afghanistan, in the years after invading Afghanistan in 2001 to oust the Taliban regime, which had harbored the al Qaeda terrorist network responsible for the terrorist attacks on the United States. The U.S.-backed government in Kabul was corrupt and weak, and Taliban insurgents had gained effective control over much of the countryside, especially in the south and east. A second challenge for Obama was one he set for himself. Candidate Obama in 2008 had said the war in Afghanistan was one the United States had to "win" because it essentially was a war against terrorism. Obama did not identify what he meant by winning, however, and by 2009 it was unclear what kind of victory was possible in any event.

Attempting to keep his campaign promise, Obama increased the U.S. military presence in Afghanistan in two stages during 2009: first, adding 21,000 troops (including 4,000 to boost the training of Afghan security forces), then with 33,000 more troops as part of a temporary "surge." Congress supported both of these steps. The surge, combined with other actions, seemed to be effective in reducing, if not stopping, the level of the Taliban insurgency. Obama said in June 2011 that the surge had accomplished most of its goals, and so the 33,000 additional troops would be withdrawn by September 2012, just before the U.S. elections.

The surge troops did come home, leaving behind an Afghanistan somewhat more at peace than before. The situation was far from stable, however, and relations between the Obama administration and President Hamid Karzai had become increasingly toxic, raising serious questions about how enduring the successes in Afghanistan would be.

FOREIGN POLICY LEADERSHIP

President Barack Obama brought in a team of Washington veterans to handle foreign policy, most of whom had substantially more experience on the international stage than did the relatively young president. By far the most recognizable face, in the entire cabinet, was Hillary Rodham Clinton, the former first lady and senator from New York—and defeated rival of Obama for the Democratic presidential nomination—whom the new president chose as his secretary of state.

Clinton's deputy was James Steinberg, who was deputy national security advisor when her husband, Bill Clinton, was president. Steinberg was succeeded in July 2011 by veteran ambassador William J. Burns, who had served most recently as undersecretary for political affairs. Burns was only the second serving career diplomat to become deputy secretary; the first was Lawrence Eagleburger, during the administration of George H. W. Bush (1989–1993).

As national security advisor, Obama chose the widely respected retired Marine Corps General James L. Jones Jr., who had served as commandant of the marines and had commanded NATO forces in Europe. Jones stepped down in October 2010, reportedly after losing a number of intramural battles within the administration. He was succeeded by his deputy, Tom Donilon, another Washington veteran who, among other things, had been chief of staff to Secretary of State Warren Christopher during Bill Clinton's first term (1993–1997).

State Department

Clinton won confirmation as secretary of state from her colleagues in an overwhelming 94–2 vote on January 21, 2009. The only "no" votes came from Republicans Jim DeMint of South Carolina and David Vitter of Louisiana.

Another Republican, John Cornyn of Texas, briefly held up Clinton's nomination, forcing a roll-call vote rather than permitting her to be confirmed by voice vote in time for inauguration day, a courtesy afforded seven other members of President Obama's cabinet. Cornyn eventually yielded and then voted to approve Clinton, saying he had concluded after conversations with her that she was well qualified for the job. But he said he remained concerned about potential conflicts of interest regarding the Clinton Foundation run by her husband, former president Clinton. The previous December, when Obama had announced his choice of Senator Clinton to head the State Department, the transition team revealed an agreement with the foundation that required annual disclosure and some limits on soliciting foreign contributions. Cornyn and some fellow senators urged still greater transparency.

During her confirmation hearing before the Foreign Relations Committee, Clinton touched on virtually every international challenge confronting the new administration. Distinguishing the Obama administration's approach from that of its predecessor, Clinton stressed the need for "more equilibrium" between diplomatic and military approaches to international issues. The committee voted 16–1 on January 15 to send Clinton's name to the floor as soon as Obama was sworn in.

Clinton, who was first elected to the Senate in 2000 as her husband was wrapping up his second term and was reelected in 2006, resigned her seat shortly after the Senate confirmed her.

During her tenure as secretary of state, Clinton was an indefatigable world traveler, setting a new record for her position by visiting 112 countries in four years. Clinton told one interviewer in 2010 that her main task was to "restore American leadership" in the world. Most independent assessments of her tenure, and of Obama's overall foreign track record during the first term, concluded that American "leadership" had not been, and probably could not have been, restored to the dominant level of the immediate post–cold war era. However, Obama and Clinton together generally succeeded in reducing the hostility toward the United States that had been widespread around the world during much of the preceding George W. Bush administration. If Clinton could claim no landmark achievements, such as a major peace treaty, she could legitimately claim to have been an effective ambassador for U.S. interests in an increasingly multipolar world.

By late 2012 Clinton made it clear that she did not wish to continue as secretary of state in Obama's second term. Washington insider speculation immediately focused on two possible successors: U.N. ambassador Susan E. Rice and Senate Foreign Relations Committee Chair John Kerry. Rice came under strong Republican attack because of comments she made—based on information from the Central Intelligence Agency (CIA) that later proved inaccurate—about the attack on the U.S. consulate in Benghazi, Libya, that killed the U.S. ambassador. Rice withdrew her name from consideration, and Obama ultimately chose Kerry.

United Nations

The Senate confirmed Susan E. Rice, a former senior diplomatic official in the Clinton administration, to be the second-youngest U.S. ambassador to the United Nations and the first African American woman to hold the post. Her confirmation came on a voice vote on January 22.

The forty-four-year-old Rice had served as a National Security Council official and later as assistant secretary of state for African affairs during the Clinton years. She also was one of Obama's top foreign policy advisors during the 2008 presidential campaign.

"My most immediate objective, should I be confirmed," she told the Foreign Relations Committee at her January 15 hearing, "will be to refresh and renew America's leadership in the United Nations and bring to bear the full weight of our influence, voice, resources, values, and diplomacy."

Rice addressed a broad range of challenge awaiting her as U.N. envoy, including climate change, global diseases, weapons proliferation, and refugee crises.

Rice said she and other top nominees "feel passionately that we must do more to end the genocide in Darfur," the region of Sudan where hundreds of thousands had died and been displaced in a conflict with the central government. However, she backed off comments made in 2007 that seemed to lay out a path to U.N.-authorized military action in Darfur, saying the authorization of a U.N.-African Union peacekeeping force had changed the situation.

Obama had signaled a desire to develop a closer U.S. relationship with the United Nations, including elevation of the ambassador job to cabinet-level status after it was downgraded by President George W. Bush.

Director of National Intelligence

The Senate on January 28, 2009, confirmed retired U.S. Navy Admiral Dennis Blair as the third person to hold the title of director of national intelligence (DNI). Congress in 2004 had created the post to coordinate all the nation's sixteen intelligence agencies, in the wake of perceived intelligence failures before the September 11, 2011, terrorist attacks against New York and Washington. Blair succeeded Michael McConnell, who had served in the post for two years and had followed the first DNI, former diplomat John Negroponte. *(U.S. intelligence community, box, Congress and the Nation Vol. XII, p. 291)*

Blair was confirmed by voice vote, with little controversy. He had held numerous high-level posts, including as commander-in-chief of the U.S. Pacific Command from 1999 to 2002, as an associate director of the CIA, and as a staff member of the National Security Council.

Despite his experience, Blair during 2009 engaged in numerous turf battles with the person who, technically, reported to him: CIA Director Leon Panetta. Most important, according to press reports, Blair insisted on having the right to choose the chief intelligence officers in foreign countries—a post traditionally held by the CIA station chief. Panetta reportedly argued that he, as CIA director, had the prerogative. After months of bickering, the White House ultimately sided with Panetta in November 2009. Six months later, on May 20, 2010, following several other controversies over alleged intelligence failures, Blair resigned under pressure from the White House. Obama nominated James R. Clapper Jr., a retired lieutenant general in the U.S. Air Force, to succeed Blair.

Central Intelligence Agency

On February 12, 2009, the Senate unanimously confirmed Leon Panetta as director of the CIA, adding to the Californian's already-long resume of public service. Panetta succeeded Air Force Lt. General Michael V. Hayden, who had held the post since May 2006.

Panetta had been a member of the House of Representatives from 1977 to 1993, serving for four years as chair of the Budget Committee. President Bill Clinton named him to head the Office of Management and Budget in January 1993 and then, a little more than one year later, promoted Panetta to be White House chief of staff—a post Panetta held until the beginning of Clinton's second term in January 1997. Panetta then moved back to his home in California and served on numerous boards and commissions.

When Panetta moved to the Pentagon in 2011, replacing Robert Gates, President Obama nominated Army General David H. Petraeus to replace Panetta at the CIA. The Senate confirmed the highly respected military officer, 94–0, on June 30, 2011.

Intelligence Committee Chair Dianne Feinstein, D-Calif., and top panel Republican Saxby Chambliss of Georgia praised Petraeus for his continued service.

The shifts by Panetta and Petraeus again highlighted the modern era of cooperation between the Defense Department and the civilian spy program. "The nomination of David Petraeus comes at a pivotal moment in our history as we face threats from across the globe," Chambliss said. "As a war fighter, he brings a unique perspective, having seen firsthand the tactical value of accurate and timely intelligence."

The confirmation vote came one year after a similarly swift confirmation of Petraeus to be commander of U.S. forces in Afghanistan. The general was one of the most recognizable military officers of his generation. He became the face of the "surge" of troops into Iraq in 2007, was credited with turning around an unpopular war, and was the author of the U.S. policy on counterinsurgency operations. However, Petraeus resigned on November 9, 2012, following revelation that he had had an extramarital affair with a coauthor of his autobiography, Paula Broadwell.

ISRAEL AND THE PALESTINIANS

One of the president's foreign policy successes proved to be short-lived. Upon taking office Obama quickly dispatched former Senate majority leader George Mitchell to the Middle East in hopes of restarting peace talks between Israel and the Palestinians. Mitchell, who in 1998 had successfully mediated an end to the sectarian "troubles" in northern Ireland, worked diligently to bring Israeli Prime Minister Netanyahu and Palestinian President Mahmoud Abbas to the negotiating table.

At Mitchell's insistence, Israel agreed to a limited ten-month "freeze" of settlement-building on the West Bank, and the two sides entered into peace talks in September 2010. But the talks lasted only three weeks and accomplished little other than to harden positions on both sides. Mitchell resigned from his peace-making, and the Obama administration made only token efforts to revive the talks during the remaining two years of the president's first term.

Aside from annually providing $3 billion in no-strings-attached aid to Israel, Congress was remarkably quiet about Israel-Palestinian matters during Obama's term. In one of its few legislative actions on the issue, Congress in late 2011 barred economic aid to Abbas's Palestinian Authority if it, in the future, became a full member of the United Nations or any of its agencies. The Palestinians had unsuccessfully sought U.N. membership but had been able to join the U.N. Educational, Scientific, and Cultural Organization before the congressional restriction took effect. The Palestinians did succeed in getting Palestine's U.N. membership upgraded to Non-Member Observer State status in 2012, but that step did not result in a complete cutoff of U.S. aid.

PIVOT TOWARD ASIA

Even while continuing to focus on areas of traditional U.S. interests, especially in the Middle East, the Obama administration from its earliest days signaled an intention to devote more attention to Asia. The rise of China and India as economic powers, and in China's case as a strategic power as well, coupled with traditional U.S. alliances with Japan, South Korea, and the countries of Southeast Asia, suggested that Asia would be as much of a concern to Washington during the twenty-first century as Europe and the Middle East had been in the twentieth century.

The administration signaled a heightened interest in Asia during its first two-plus years in office, but then, in November 2011, launched what Secretary of State Clinton called a "pivot" and other officials called a "rebalancing" toward the region. Obama, in a speech to the Australian parliament, said broadly that he wanted to ensure that "the United States will play a larger and long-term role in shaping this region and its future."

Administration officials did not make crystal clear what the pivot entailed, but they did describe a series of goals that, in sum, suggested an intention to protect the rest of Asia from the prospect of an overly aggressive China. National Security Advisor Tom Donilon referred specifically to this in an op-ed column in the *Financial Times*, saying U.S. goals included ensuring "that emerging powers build trust with their neighbors and that disagreements are resolved peacefully without threats or coercion." This last comment seemed to refer to, among other things, an increasingly testy disagreement between China and Japan over ownership of a chain of islets in the South China Sea.

The administration accompanied this rhetoric with several modest actions, including beefing up U.S. troop deployments in Australia and naval deployments in Singapore, returning naval ships to the Subic Bay base in the Philippines for the first time in two decades, and joining the East Asia Summit, a multilateral diplomatic organization. The administration also pledged that any future reductions in Pentagon spending would not come at the expense of U.S. interests in the Asia-Pacific or Middle East regions, apparently signaling that deployments elsewhere might be the first to be cut.

Despite the apparent China focus of the pivot, Obama completed his first term without facing a major crisis in relations with Beijing. One potential crisis came in the spring of 2012 when blind Chinese activist Chen Guangcheng escaped from house arrest at his home in Shendong province and, with help, made his way to the U.S. Embassy in Beijing, where he sought refuge. After tense negotiations, Chen was allowed to leave China, with his family, for study in the United States.

CHANGES IN MYANMAR

The administration's Asia focus converged with domestic developments in Myanmar (also known as Burma) to produce one of the few significant changes in U.S. policy during Obama's first term. After decades of repression by its military government, Myanmar experienced something close to a political revolution in 2011, including the release from house arrest of internationally celebrated opposition leader Aung San Suu Kyi, the release of political prisoners, and democratic elections in April 2012 that were won overwhelmingly by Suu Kyi's National League for Democracy.

In response, the United States in July eased its long-term sanctions against Myanmar, and in November, President Obama became the first sitting U.S. president ever to visit the country. The United States also restored diplomatic relations with Myanmar for the first time in twenty-two years. In September, Aung San Suu Kyi traveled to the United States, where she received the Congressional Gold Medal, awarded in 2008, honoring her battle for democracy.

Afghanistan Policy: Eleven Years and an Uncertain Outcome

President Barack Obama made one final military push in Afghanistan before deciding to end America's decade-long attempt to transform that society. The president in 2009 ordered a "surge" of U.S. forces in Afghanistan, a temporary boost of 33,000 troops that helped dampen insurgent attacks but that left uncertain the fate of Afghanistan's weak, embattled government after the United States and its allies withdrew nearly all their military forces in 2014.

By early 2013, the eleven-year U.S. involvement in Afghanistan had cost at least $600 billion, and by some estimates well above $1 trillion. More than 2,100 Americans had been killed, and some 18,000 had been wounded. *(Iraq and Afghanistan casualties, box, p. 236)*

Most U.S.-based assessments early in 2013 fell into either a glass half-full or glass half-empty category. Optimists, in the minority, tended to emphasize vast improvements in the Afghan security forces and an overall decline in violence provoked by insurgents. Pessimists noted that the Afghan army remained heavily dependent on Western forces and the Kabul government was mired in corruption and incompetence.

The United States, with strong international support, had invaded Afghanistan in October 2001 to oust an Islamist regime, known as the Taliban, that had provided sanctuary to the al Qaeda terrorist network responsible for the September 11 attacks in New York and Washington, D.C.

The invasion easily pushed the Taliban from power in Kabul but did not destroy them as a fighting force. Backed by neighboring Pakistan, and with some popular support, particularly in the southern and eastern parts of Afghanistan, the Taliban and related militias waged a guerrilla war that even the mighty U.S. military struggled to contain.

After eleven years of war and a massive infusion of U.S. aid, most of Afghanistan was safer than before, but large parts of the country remained insecure. Just as worrisome, from Washington's perspective, the Kabul government led by Hamid Karzai was increasingly at odds with U.S. policy makers. Karzai had been hand-picked for the job in late 2001 by Afghan leaders with the strong backing of the United States and other western governments. Karzai had twice (in 2004 and 2009) won election as president; in both cases, the Western-financed elections were troubled by delays and serious irregularities.

Afghan forces had increasingly assumed responsibility for security, starting in the relatively quiet Bamiyan province in 2011. During the next two years, Afghan units assumed partial or even full responsibility for hundreds of missions in other provinces, including some that had been the most violent. Even so, Afghan forces continued to rely heavily on the United States for crucial support, notably air support and logistics. For example, Afghanistan did not have its own air force—a big shortcoming for military operations in a mountainous country with few roads that was almost as large as Texas.

Obama in January 2013 announced an accelerated schedule for shifting overall security responsibility to the Afghans as part of a plan to withdraw all, or nearly all, 66,000 U.S. combat troops by the end of 2014. On June 18, 2013, Afghanistan officially assumed lead responsibility for security throughout the country. By that time, the Afghan security forces, which had not even existed a dozen years earlier, numbered some 350,000, most of whom had received training, uniforms, and equipment from the United States and its North Atlantic Treaty Organization (NATO) allies.

However, as of mid-2013, the Obama administration was still debating how many troops to leave in Afghanistan after 2014. One of the alternatives reportedly under consideration was a so-called zero option of no U.S. troops, not even trainers, if Karzai and his successor did not improve cooperation with Washington. The two countries were attempting to negotiate a bilateral security agreement that would take the place of the existing Status of Forces agreement providing for the U.S. military presence.

OBAMA'S "SURGE"

President Obama, who had said during his 2008 election campaign that "we have to win" in Afghanistan, inherited a fragile situation in that country. His predecessor, George W. Bush, had ordered an invasion to oust the Taliban but then quickly shifted his attention—and many more U.S. military resources—to Iraq, which he ordered invaded in March 2003. In subsequent years, Washington pumped billions of dollars of aid into Afghanistan, but never as much as most experts said was needed to rebuild the country after a quarter-century of war (the Soviet Union had invaded and occupied the country in the 1980s while civil war raged during the 1990s). The U.S. military and several European allies battled the Taliban and tried to build a new Afghan army, but these security efforts also fell demonstrably short of what was needed to bring peace.

By the time Obama took office, the United States had slightly more than 32,000 troops in Afghanistan; this was about one-fourth as many as were then in Iraq, a country of comparable population and, by that time, fewer security challenges. Two months later, on March 27, 2009, the president announced the deployment of 21,000 additional U.S. forces, 4,000 of whom would be assigned to training Afghan security forces.

Obama called the situation in Afghanistan "increasingly perilous" and argued that "America must no longer deny resources to Afghanistan because of the war in Iraq." He laid out two primary goals for U.S. involvement in Afghanistan: defeating al Qaeda and its allies (meaning the

Taliban) and eliminating safe havens for terrorists in Afghanistan and Pakistan. The Pentagon also shifted commanders in Afghanistan, sending in General Stanley McChrystal (who had headed Special Operations) to replace General David McKiernan.

Acting on a recommendation by McChrystal, Obama on December 1, 2009, announced that he would send an additional 30,000 troops to Afghanistan to "reverse the Taliban's momentum" and bolster the Afghan government and security forces. The president said this "surge" would be temporary and that the withdrawal of additional U.S. forces from Afghanistan would begin in July 2011, a date that was widely interpreted as a "deadline" signaling the eventual U.S. withdrawal of all troops.

In response to such talk, Obama insisted the extent and pace of any drawdown would be determined by conditions on the ground. He also said that the Afghan government would take over lead responsibility for security during 2012. Obama requested $11.6 billion in fiscal 2011 and $12.8 billion for fiscal 2012 to train and equip Afghan security forces; Congress approved both requests.

Obama's surge proved popular with Republicans in Congress, but it divided Democrats, many of whom opposed any escalation of U.S. involvement in Afghanistan. In the early summer of 2010, a group of liberal Democrats in the House mounted an effort to speed up the withdrawal of U.S. forces there, rather than adding to them.

The House on July 1 rejected a troop withdrawal amendment proposed by Barbara Lee, D-Calif., to the fiscal 2010 supplemental spending bill (HR 4899) for war operations. Ninety-three Democrats and seven Republicans supported Lee's amendment, which was rejected on a **key vote of 100–321 (R 7–164; D 93–157).** *(2010 key votes, p. 767)*

AFGHANISTAN EXIT

A NATO summit Lisbon in November 2010 resulted in an agreement that the transition to Afghan security leadership (a process called *inteqal*) would begin in early 2011 and be completed by the end of 2014. Even so, officials said at the time that some U.S. forces likely would remain after 2014. Most other U.S. partners announced plans to withdraw their forces during 2012 or 2013.

On June 22, 2011, Obama announced that the surge had accomplished most of U.S. goals and that a drawdown of the 33,000 U.S. surge troops would take place by September 2012. During a visit to Afghanistan the following May, Obama said U.S. withdrawals "will continue at a steady pace, with more and more of our troops coming home." By the end of 2014, he said, "the Afghans will be fully responsible for the security of their country."

About 10,000 of the surge forces were withdrawn during 2011, and the last of the surge forces left Afghanistan on schedule on September 20, 2012. That step cut the U.S. total in country to about 68,000, roughly the presurge level.

News media reports suggested that much of the success of the surge was based on the work of dozens or even hundreds of local militias, some financed by the United States and the Afghan government but others independent of any outside influence. This was the opposite approach from Washington's early, post-2001 effort, which emphasized disarming militias in hopes of strengthening the role of the Afghan national security forces. Some observers thought the local warlords might become the chief sources of power once the Western allies withdraw.

INSIDER ATTACKS

Another chronic problem facing the United States and its NATO allies was the prevalence of so-called insider attacks: bombings and other attacks against Western military targets by disgruntled members of the Afghan security forces. The International Crisis Group, a nonprofit, nongovernmental think tank, reported that insider attacks accounted for 13 percent of deaths suffered in 2012 by the U.S.-led military alliance.

One of the most spectacular of these incidents was a December 2009 attack on a CIA base in Khost that killed seven CIA officers. Responsibility was claimed by the Haqqani network, which operated in the North Waziristan area of Pakistan and was called a "veritable arm" of Pakistan's intelligence services by Joint Chiefs of Staff Chair Mike Mullen in September 2011.

In regular reports to Congress, the Pentagon cited numerous "metrics" to bolster claims that the security situation had improved in Afghanistan during the troop surge. In its December 2012 report, "Progress toward Security and Stability in Afghanistan," the Pentagon cited sharp declines in Taliban attacks and the improved capabilities of the Afghan security forces. In particular, the Pentagon said Afghan forces took the lead in the vast majority of military operations, even though the army continued to rely heavily on international support.

"The areas of the country influenced by the insurgents and the ability of the insurgency to attack the population have been significantly diminished," the report said. "Although challenges remain and progress in Afghanistan has been uneven in many areas, the security gains resulting from the surge are clear."

The report then went on to list some of the remaining "challenges," which seemed to be the same ones that had been present for all of the past decade: "The insurgency's safe havens in Pakistan, the limited institutional capacity of the Afghan government, and endemic corruption remain the greatest risks to long-term stability and sustainable security in Afghanistan."

An even blunter assessment came from James E. Jeffrey, a former U.S. ambassador to Iraq, quoted in a December 2012 *Washington Post* report summarizing the situation in Afghanistan. "The problem with Afghanistan is, it's not going to look like success," Jeffrey said. "It's still going to be backward and totally corrupt, with not enough government infrastructure and a huge burning insurgency. This is terribly complicated and hard stuff under the best of circumstances, and these are the worst."

CONGRESSIONAL ACTION

Despite growing concern on Capitol Hill that the long war in Afghanistan had become a losing proposition—or, at the very least, not a winning one—Congress repeatedly voted to give President Obama the money and authority he requested to continue the war. Before, and especially after, the president's troop surge was under way, both houses of Congress from 2009 through 2011 repeatedly defeated proposals to speed up U.S. troop withdrawals.

Even so, members of Congress in both parties questioned whether the United States had clear objectives in Afghanistan or could meet its objectives given the weakness of the Afghan government and what some members described as "double-dealing" by Pakistan. One of the most persistent critics in 2009 and 2010 was House Appropriations Committee Chair David R. Obey, D-Wis. Obey repeatedly pushed the Obama administration to provide more justification for continued aid to both Afghanistan and Pakistan, saying for example in a floor debate in July 2009 that U.S. soldiers in the field were "being let down by the inability of the governments of Afghanistan and in some instances Pakistan to do their parts."

The most intense battle over Afghanistan came on May 25–26, 2011, when the House defeated two amendments to the fiscal 2012 defense authorization bill (HR 1540) intended to push for a faster withdrawal. The closer of the two votes was a 204–215 rejection on May 26 of an amendment requiring the administration to develop a plan to accelerate the transition to Afghan-led security. *(Defense legislation, p. 273)*

Even while turning down attempts to reverse administration policy, Congress did occasionally dock some of the administration's specific requests for Afghanistan. For example, Congress in 2009 cut $900 million from the $7.5 billion requested for training and equipping the Afghan security forces. As part of the fiscal 2010 defense appropriations bill (HR 3326—PL 111-118), Congress shifted the bulk of that money, $825 million, to the purchase of heavy-duty troop carriers known as Mine-Resistant Ambush Protected vehicles. *(Fiscal 2010 defense appropriations, p. 280)*

Congress also supported Obama's requests for substantial aid to Pakistan. This support came despite a widespread belief that Pakistan was playing both sides of the street: continuing to support the Taliban (which Pakistan had sponsored during the five years when the Taliban ruled Afghanistan) while at the same time getting money and weapons from the United States to combat elements of al Qaeda and other extremists based in the rugged mountain regions of northwestern Pakistan.

An important test came in 2009 when Congress approved two "counterinsurgency" funds for Pakistan: a $400 million fund administered by the Pentagon to aid Pakistan's security forces, and a $700 million "counterinsurgency capability" fund, administered by the State Department, for aid over three fiscal years to Pakistan's civilian institutions. These funds were included in a fiscal 2009 supplemental appropriations bill (HR 2346—PL 111-32), primarily for operations in Iraq and Afghanistan. Even in doing so, Congress demanded a report from Obama outlining the extent to which both Afghanistan and Pakistan deserved continued U.S. aid. *(Fiscal 2009 supplemental, p. 269)*

Another, more modest, test came in 2012 when the Senate Appropriations Committee called for withholding aid to Pakistan's military until the defense secretary certified that Pakistan was keeping U.S. supply lines open to Afghanistan and was not supporting militant extremists or imprisoning the man credited with tipping U.S. forces off to the whereabouts of al Qaeda leader Osama bin Laden. The committee added this provision to its version (S 3254—S Rept 112-173) of the fiscal 2013 Defense authorization bill.

Members were angered by the conviction, in a Pakistani court, of Dr. Shakil Afridi for helping the United States find bin Laden in his compound in Abbottabad, Pakistan. On May 1, 2011, a U.S. Navy SEAL special operations team infiltrated into Pakistan and attacked the compound where bin Laden and members of his family had been in hiding. Bin Laden was killed. On May 23, 2012, Afridi was found guilty of treason and sentenced to thirty-three years in prison. The final bill (HR 4310—PL 112-239) included the provision but with a waiver authority allowing the president to provide the aid if he found it was in the national interest.

In considering that same bill in December 2012, the Senate voiced its displeasure with the president's decision to enter into a "strategic partnership" agreement with Afghanistan without consulting Congress beforehand. Obama and Karzai on May 1 had signed a Strategic Partnership Agreement providing the basis for continued U.S. military presence, as advisors and trainers, after 2014.

By voice vote, the Senate adopted an amendment by Jeff Sessions, R-Ala., to seize 50 percent of unobligated funds for the Executive Office of the President if the president did not submit to Congress details of a bilateral security agreement with Afghanistan thirty days before entering into the agreement. In May, the United States entered into an enduring strategic partnership with Afghanistan. Congress was not consulted on the framework or substance of the agreement.

The final bill required periodic consultations with Congress on the status of such an agreement and required that the text be provided to Congress before an agreement was finalized. *(Fiscal 2013 defense authorization bill, p. 307)*

Chronology of Action on Foreign Policy

2009–2010

The Democratic-led Congress offered no serious challenges to President Barack Obama's foreign policies during his first two years in office. Indeed, Congress generally supported two of the new president's most important initiatives: withdrawing U.S. troops from Iraq while boosting troop levels in Afghanistan. The Senate also ratified a new nuclear arms control treaty with Russia that called for reducing the arsenals in both countries.

Given the greater emphasis on the economy and Obama's health care initiative, foreign policy, for the most part, was a secondary concern on Capitol Hill during 2009 and 2010. Some Republicans expressed anxiety about the pullback from Iraq, even though the preceding administration of George W. Bush had signed an agreement under which U.S. troops would leave by the end of 2011. Many Democrats were concerned about escalating the American role in Afghanistan, which Bush had invaded in 2001 following the September 11 terrorist attacks. But for the most part, the overall mood about the rest of the world seemed somewhat subdued on Capitol Hill, certainly when compared with many fierce battles of the past, most recently the agony about Iraq during the middle years of Bush's presidency.

One of the few notable legislative accomplishments in foreign affairs was the Senate's ratification on December 22, 2010, of the new nuclear arms Strategic Arms Reduction Treaty (START) with Russia. The Bush administration had begun negotiations on a treaty to update several previous agreements, but the Obama team brought the treaty to a conclusion in April 2010. In general, the agreement called for each country to cut its nuclear arsenal by about 30 percent below the levels of the most recent treaty, dating from 2002.

The new treaty had broad support from the nation's foreign policy establishment, including both Republicans and Democrats, but a handful of conservative Republican senators raised objections, insisting the agreement would cut the U.S. arsenal so deeply that it would harm U.S. national security and that Moscow could not be trusted to keep its side of the bargain. After Republicans scored well in the November 2010 midterm elections, recapturing control of the House and slightly increasing their numbers in the Senate, opponents sought to postpone action until 2011, when Republicans would have a stronger shot at preventing the two-thirds majority needed for treaty approval. But key Senate leaders maneuvered to push ahead during the lame duck session. A cloture vote on December 21 killed a potential filibuster, and the Senate approved ratification of the treaty the following day by a 71–26 vote.

Congress did take the initiative, or at least it claimed to be doing so, on one foreign policy matter: imposing sanctions against Iran in an attempt to thwart that country's presumed ambitions to build nuclear weapons. In June 2010, with midterm elections on the horizon, Congress passed legislation expanding existing sanctions against multinational companies that helped Iran develop its domestic petroleum refining capacity. Signed into law by President Obama, the bill (HR 2194—PL 111-195) was the most recent of numerous U.S. attempts to damage Iran's economy and thus pressure the Tehran government into canceling its nuclear program.

Congress had less success, however, in coming to agreement on routine funding legislation for the State Department and foreign aid programs. Congress failed, for fiscal years 2009, 2010, and 2011, to pass stand-alone appropriations bills for those programs and instead folded them into numerous continuing resolutions and omnibus spending bills covering most other government functions.

Fiscal 2009 State–Foreign Operations Funding

Congress failed to approve a stand-alone fiscal 2009 appropriations bill for the State Department and foreign operations. Instead, funding at fiscal 2008 levels was included in two continuing resolutions (one in September 2008, the other in March 2009). Eventually, in March 2009, Congress adopted a final omnibus measure covering nine separate appropriations bills, including State and foreign operations.

The House State–Foreign Operations Appropriations Subcommittee approved an unnumbered bill for fiscal 2009 on July 16, 2008, but no further action was taken on it, either by the full House Appropriations Committee or by the House.

The Senate Appropriations Committee reported its comparable bill (S 3288—S Rept 110-425) on July 18, but the full Senate did not act.

With Congress failing to act, funding for these programs was included in a continuing resolution (HR 2638—PL 110-329) passed by Congress in September 2008; this measure ran through March 6, 2009. Another continuing resolution (PL 111-6) included funding for the second week of March 2009, as final action was under way on omnibus legislation. The House on February 25, 2009, approved what was to become the omnibus spending bill (HR 1105). The Senate cleared the measure by voice vote on March 10, and President Barack Obama signed it into law (PL 111-8) on March 11.

The omnibus bill included a total of $40.5 billion for State Department and foreign operations spending in fiscal 2009. This was $1.5 billion less than President George W. Bush had requested in February 2008 (President Obama did not submit a new request once he took office) and $50 million below the fiscal 2008 level.

An unnumbered joint committee print explaining the bill said a priority was increasing the "capacity and capabilities" of State Department personnel. The department's decision to move positions to Iraq and Afghanistan early in the Bush administration had "depleted" capabilities elsewhere, the report said, leading to vacancies at "many posts overseas" and inhibiting language training.

Within the foreign aid programs, the bill mandated a significant increase for development assistance: $1.8 billion for fiscal 2009, which was $176.4 million above fiscal 2008 and $160.9 million above the request. The bill also made major adjustments in the Economic Support Fund program, providing $3 billion, which was $574.6 million above the fiscal 2008 level but $146.6 million below the request. Major changes in the requested specific country-level amounts included a $25 million increase, to $732 million, for Afghanistan; a $28.2 million cut, to $425 million, for Pakistan; a $47.6 million increase, to $200 million for Colombia; and a $37 million increase, to $121.2 million, for Haiti.

As in the past, Israel was by far the largest recipient of military aid: $2.4 billion, combined with $170 million provided by the fiscal 2008 supplement (PL 110-252) for a total of $2.6 billion. Congress earmarked another $1.3 billion for military aid to Egypt.

In addition to the amounts included in the omnibus spending bill, President Obama's economic "stimulus" bill (the American Recovery and Reinvestment Act, HR 1—PL 111-5), included $602 million for programs generally covered by the State–Foreign Operations bill. That total included $290 million for the State Department's Capital Investment Fund (computer upgrades and similar work), $220 million for water quality programs and other work by the U.S.-Mexico International Boundary Water Commission, $90 million for "urgent domestic facilities requirements" for the State Department's passport and training operations, and $2 million for the State Department's inspector general. *(Stimulus legislation, p. 78)*

Fiscal 2009 Supplemental Appropriations

A fiscal 2009 supplemental appropriations bill (HR 2346—PL 111-32), cleared by Congress on June 24, 2010, was devoted primarily to military operations in Afghanistan and Iraq but also included money for State Department and foreign operations. Those funds included:

- $3.6 billion, provided under the Defense Department, for fiscal years 2009 and 2010, to expand and improve the security forces in Afghanistan.
- Two new funds to bolster the Pakistani security forces. One, totaling $700 million to be available through fiscal 2011, was a newly created Pakistan Counterinsurgency Capability Fund to improve the counterinsurgency operations of the Pakistani security forces. This fund was to be administered by the State Department "with the concurrence of" the Pentagon. The bill also created a $400 million Pakistan Counterinsurgency Fund, available through fiscal 2010, administered by the Pentagon "with the concurrence of" the State Department, The latter fund was intended to provide equipment, supplies, training and facilities for the Pakistani security forces in its counterinsurgency work.
- $1.4 billion, as requested by President Obama, for economic and diplomatic assistance to Pakistan and $2.4 billion for economic aid to Afghanistan, which was $800 million more than the president's request.
- Additional funds for oversight, U.S. embassy costs, and other purposes.
- $5 billion requested by the president to leverage $108 billion in additional lending by the International Monetary Fund (IMF); this amount was included in the Defense section of the bill.
- The bill authorized, subject to subsequent appropriations, $3.7 billion for the U.S. contribution to the fifteenth replenishment of resources for the World Bank's International Development Association, which made interest-free loans to the world's poorest countries.

IRAQ POLICY LEFT A RADICALLY DIFFERENT NATION

A central plank of Barack Obama's 2008 presidential campaign was his promise to withdraw U.S. troops from Iraq within sixteen months after taking office. As president, Obama adjusted the specifics of that promise but stuck to its core, pulling the last remaining U.S. soldiers from Iraq on December 18, 2011, in accordance with a U.S.-Iraq agreement he inherited from the administration of President George W. Bush.

The Americans left behind an Iraq radically different from the one that U.S. and allied forces had invaded in March 2003 to oust long-time dictator Saddam Hussein. Saddam was long gone by late 2011, replaced by an elected, albeit increasingly authoritarian and sectarian-minded, government controlled by the majority Shiites, who long had suffered under Saddam's dictatorship.

Economically, parts of Iraq had recovered and were doing better than in many previous years, especially the all-but-independent Kurdish region in the north and Shiite areas of the south that benefited from spending by the central government. But many areas of Iraq continued to be economically depressed, and Iraq as a whole remained behind most of its neighbors in the United Nation's measurements of education, health, and other aspects of human well-being.

Also diminished, if not entirely gone by 2011, was the U.S. ability to dictate or even just guide events both large and small in Iraq. In the four or five years immediately after Saddam was overthrown, U.S. civilian and military officials exercised significant control over most major government decisions in Iraq—largely determining, through aid allocations, military presence, and pure pressure, nearly everything from the overall shape of the government to where new power plants would be built.

As the number of U.S. troops dwindled, along with Washington's obsession with Iraq's future, so, too, did the U.S. ability to shape the course of events in Iraq. Prime Minister Nouri al-Maliki and his close colleagues in the Baghdad government insisted on their right to govern their country. The Bush administration, then the Obama team, gradually ceded to Baghdad a responsibility that had become both onerous and unpopular back home.

In 2011, fearing renewed instability and sectarian conflict in Iraq, the Obama administration attempted to extend the previously agreed end-of-year deadline for the last U.S. troops to leave. Pentagon officials reportedly wanted to keep 16,000 or so troops in the country to finish training Iraqi security forces and to retain a source of leverage over the Maliki government. But by midyear, Maliki had rejected Washington's last request for the continued presence of a much smaller force of about 5,000 troops, leading to the mutual decision to withdraw all of them.

In the year-and-a-half after the final American withdrawal, the political and security stability that Washington had worked so hard to enforce in Iraq seemed increasingly fragile. Prime Minister Maliki forced from office key Sunni leaders (including one of the three vice presidents), leading to complaints that he was seeking complete control of the government by his faction of Shiites. Sunni insurgents, some linked to an Iraqi wing of al Qaeda, renewed their bombings and other attacks against Shiite targets and government security forces. Their apparent intent was to spark a renewal of the intense intercommunal conflict that had nearly torn Iraq apart in 2006 before being contained by a massive short-term "surge" of 26,000 additional U.S. forces.

U.S. Troop Presence

In February 2009, shortly after taking office, President Obama outlined his plan for ending all U.S. combat operations in Iraq by the end of August 2010—roughly the sixteen months he had pledged during his campaign for the "end" of the Iraq war. At the time of this announcement, slightly more than 140,000 U.S. troops remained in Iraq.

On August 31, 2010, Obama said his plan had been fulfilled and that U.S. combat operations in Iraq had formally ended. At that point, 47,000 U.S. troops remained in the country. With the president's announcement, the U.S. military ended what it had called "Operation Iraqi Freedom," which had begun with the March 2003 invasion of Iraq, and initiated what it called "Operation New Dawn." The number of troops in Iraq dropped steadily over the following fifteen-plus months as the military withdrew both its personnel and tons of weapons and equipment.

On December 18, 2011, the last 500-some troops headed south into Kuwait, the principal staging ground for U.S. operations in Iraq. That ended a U.S. military presence that at one point numbered more than 170,000 combat and support personnel at some 500 bases around Iraq. This last trip south went without incident, in sharp contrast to the initial postinvasion years when nearly every movement of U.S. troops in Iraq was subject to conflict of some sort.

Even after the troops left, some 16,000 U.S. personnel remained in Iraq, nearly one-half of whom were security contractors training Iraqi personnel in the use of U.S. -supplied aircraft and other equipment and protecting the U.S. Embassy in Baghdad and other diplomatic facilities. That total was reduced to under 13,000 at the end of 2012. Many of the contractors were former U.S. military personnel. Moreover, as of March 2013 some 200 U.S. military personnel were still in Iraq as part of the training mission.

The Costs of Iraq

By February 2013, 4,475 U.S. service personnel had died in Iraq-related operations, according to Pentagon figures. In addition, more than 32,000 had been injured, many of them severely. More than 100,000 U.S. service personnel deployed to Iraq and/or Afghanistan also were diagnosed with post-traumatic stress disorder (PTSD) from 2003 through 2012, according to a compilation by the Congressional Research Service. The military's treatment of PTSD cases—and often its reluctance or even outright refusal to acknowledge PTSD claims—became a significant public issue during the Iraq war years. *(War casualties in Iraq, Afghanistan, box, p. 236)*

Other countries that participated in the U.S.-led invasion and occupation of Iraq also suffered casualties, although to a far lesser extent. The United Kingdom lost 179 service personnel, and other countries assisting the United States lost 139, according to a count through 2011 by the independent website icasualties.org (formally the Iraq Coalition Casualty Count).

The number of Iraqi civilians and security personnel killed and wounded in the years following the 2003 invasion likely will never be known. A group that sought to track Iraqi casualties, Iraq Body Count, estimated that at least 111,000 Iraqis were killed in the ten years starting with the 2003 invasion. The vast majority were civilians killed in sectarian battles between Shiites and Sunnis. Icasualties.org counted the deaths of 8,825 Iraqi security personnel from 2005 through mid-2011.

The direct and indirect financial costs to the United States for its role in Iraq were immense. Depending on what was counted, and who was doing the counting, the Iraq adventure eventually would cost the United States anywhere from $1 trillion to $4 trillion, or possibly even more. The lower end of that range counted only the extra costs to the military of fighting and maintaining troops in Iraq, U.S. postwar aid to Iraq, and similar costs that were directly attributable to the U.S. presence in Iraq through 2011.

The higher war cost estimates, provided by economists at Brown and Harvard universities, also included longer-term costs, such as disability payments and medical care for Iraq war veterans, interest payments on money the government borrowed to pay for Iraq, and even, in some estimates, the "opportunity cost" of forgoing other government priorities because of the Iraq war.

One of the smallest components of the total was U.S. economic and military aid to Iraq, which totaled $56.8 billion from fiscal years 2003 through 2012, according to January 2013 analysis by the Congressional Research Service. The biggest components of that total were $20.8 billion for relief and reconstruction, primarily during fiscal 2004, and $20.4 billion in Pentagon aid to the Iraqi security forces, two-thirds of it in fiscal years 2005 through 2007.

Congressional Action

Although many Republicans had sharply criticized Obama's campaign promise to "end" the Iraq war, saying that withdrawing U.S. forces would endanger hard-won gains, Congress generally went along with his budget requests and other Iraq policies once he became president.

For the first time since the United States invaded Afghanistan in 2011, Congress in late 2009 included funding for war operations in a regular appropriations bill, rather than paying war costs out of supplemental spending bills. The action came in the fiscal 2010 defense appropriations bill (HR 3326—PL 111-118) cleared in December 2009. Congress made only relatively minor changes in Obama's requests for Iraq spending. *(Defense appropriations, p. 280)*

One notable congressional action related to Iraq came in 2009, during consideration of a fiscal 2009 supplemental (HR 2346—PL 111-32) devoted primarily to spending on the Iraq and Afghanistan wars. The bill included a provision that would have barred the release of photos showing abuse of detainees in U.S. custody. Publication in April 2004 of photographs showing U.S. soldiers abusing Iraqi prisoners at the Abu Ghraib prison near Baghdad had caused a worldwide scandal that sent America's reputation plummeting, especially in the Arab world. In subsequent years some journalists, human rights activists, and others pushed for release of official photos from Abu Ghraib, but military leaders and many members of Congress staunchly opposed any such publication. It was not until the Senate conferees received assurances from Obama that he would use his executive authority to block release of the photos that they were willing to agree to a conference report that did not include the provision barring the release. *(Supplemental appropriations, p. 269)*

By 2010, many members of Congress were becoming annoyed at the Iraqi government's increasingly assertive stance toward the United States. One apparent manifestation of this came in action on the fiscal 2011 defense authorization bill (HR 6523—PL 111-383), which cut $500 million from the president's $2 billion request for equipment and supplies for the Iraqi security forces. The bill required the Baghdad government to pay at least 20 percent of the cost of procuring items or services from the United States, other than major military equipment. In deliberations over the follow-up defense appropriations bill, the House approved the full $2 billion request, but the Senate bill cut it in half, to $1 billion. The final fiscal 2011 defense spending measure, included in an omnibus appropriations bill (HR1473—PL 112-10), split the difference between the two chambers at $1.5 billion, but did not include the authorization bill's 20 percent matching requirement for the Iraqi government. *(Fiscal 2011 defense authorization, p. 291; defense appropriation, p. 295)*

U.S. WAR CASUALTIES 2001–2012

War in Iraq

Year	Killed in Action	Noncombat Deaths	Wounded in Action
2001	0	0	0
2002	0	0	0
2003	315	171	2,420
2004	713	133	8,002
2005	673	171	5,944
2006	704	116	6,411
2007	764	139	6,112
2008	221	92	2,045
2009	74	74	678
2010	19	41	328
2011	34	20	219
2012	1	0	0
Total	**3,518**	**957**	**32,159**

NOTE: Figures include Operation Iraqi Freedom (2003–2010) and Operation New Dawn (2010–2012)

War in Afghanistan

Year	Killed in Action	Noncombat Deaths	Wounded in Action
2001	3	8	33
2002	18	31	74
2003	17	28	99
2004	25	27	217
2005	66	32	268
2006	65	33	403
2007	83	34	748
2008	132	23	795
2009	271	40	2,145
2010	438	62	5,249
2011	360	54	5,216
2012	237	76	2,963
Total	**1,715**	**448**	**18,210**

SOURCE: Defense Casualty Analysis System, U.S. Department of Defense (https://www.dmdc.osd.mil/dcas/pages/casualties.xhtml).

Pakistan Aid Authorization

Congress in 2009 opened the way for Pakistan to receive as much as $7.5 billion in nonmilitary U.S. aid over five years. The authorization was part of President Barack Obama's broad strategy on Afghanistan. It was intended to encourage Pakistan's cooperation in U.S.-supported initiatives to root out terrorist safe havens along the border between the two countries. Obama signed the bill into law October 15, 2009 (S 1707—PL 111-73).

The bill authorized $1.5 billion a year, triple what Pakistan had been getting, to strengthen the country's democratic institutions, improve national and regional health care initiatives, and support public education. The actual funding, however, still had to be provided through the appropriations process.

Although the authorization covered a five-year period, the bill expressed the sense of Congress that the economic aid should be extended through fiscal 2019. Lawmakers and the White House stressed that the bill demonstrated a more enduring U.S. commitment to the fragile ally—one not based on support for the Pakistani military or the party in power there.

The House and Senate had passed competing aid bills in June. The final measure was the result of negotiations among Senate Foreign Relations Committee Chair John Kerry, D-Mass.; the panel's ranking Republican, Richard G. Lugar of Indiana; and House Foreign Affairs Chair Howard L. Berman, D-Calif., along with input from the Obama administration.

HOUSE COMMITTEE ACTION

The House Foreign Affairs Committee approved its Pakistan aid bill (HR 1886—H Rept 111-129) by voice vote May 20 after adopting a manager's amendment, also by voice vote.

The bill proposed authorizing $1.5 billion a year from fiscal 2010 through 2013 to assist social and economic development in Pakistan, $700 million in fiscal 2010 to help Pakistan fight insurgency and terrorism in that country, and $400 million a year through fiscal 2013 for other Pakistani security assistance. It prohibited specified military assistance to Pakistan after 2010 unless the president determined that the country was cooperating with U.S. nuclear nonproliferation efforts and making progress in combating terrorist groups.

Changes made by Berman's manager's amendment included:

- Reducing proposed annual military aid to $400 million from $600 million in the original bill. For Pakistan to receive the aid, the president would have to determine that the country was cooperating in dismantling nuclear supply networks and fighting terrorist groups.
- Making it slightly easier for the president to waive the conditions on military aid by modifying the wording to allow a waiver if the president determined it was "important" to U.S. national security interests, rather than "vital," as under the original bill.
- Dropping mention of Pakistan's nemesis, India, and referring instead only to "neighboring countries." The provision required that Pakistan make progress on ensuring that its military and its intelligence agency did not support groups that mounted terrorist attacks on other nations. The language was retained in the final bill.

Although the administration pushed back against conditions on the aid, members of the committee were eager to require some accountability from Pakistan. Michael McCaul,

R-Texas, introduced an amendment to condition military aid on access to Abdul Qadeer Khan, the so-called "father" of Pakistan's nuclear weapons program, who reportedly helped other countries obtain nuclear weapons technology. Berman argued that a requirement in the bill for access to Pakistanis involved in nuclear proliferation would have the same effect. Naming Khan, a hero to many in Pakistan, in the bill would only undermine U.S. efforts, Berman argued.

Berman agreed to modify the condition to require "direct access" and to name Khan in the committee's report rather than the bill, and McCaul withdrew his amendment.

The bill authorized $700 million in fiscal 2010 and undetermined funds in fiscal 2011–2012 for a Pakistan Counterinsurgency Capabilities Fund. The fund was to be administered by the State Department, rather than by the Pentagon, which administered counterinsurgency aid in fiscal 2009. Appropriators and authorizers argued that the program belonged under the State Department, which traditionally administered such programs.

The committee defeated, by voice vote, a GOP substitute amendment that would have authorized $1.5 billion for nonmilitary aid and $700 million for the counterinsurgency fund and required the president to submit to Congress a comprehensive strategy for Pakistan. The amendment, offered by Ileana Ros-Lehtinen of Florida, the panel's top Republican, dropped other elements of the bill, including conditions on the aid.

HOUSE FLOOR ACTION

The House passed the bill, 234–185, on June 11. Under the rule that governed the floor debate, once the Pakistan bill had passed, it was automatically added to a separate State Department authorization bill (HR 2410), a move aimed at enhancing the prospects for both measures.

The House bill included a proposal first introduced as stand-alone legislation (HR 1318) by Chris Van Hollen, D-Md., to remove tariffs on some products imported from Afghanistan and parts of Pakistan. Retail and textile groups lobbied against the provision.

Republicans allied themselves with Obama in opposing restrictions on military aid, saying they would excessively restrict the administration's flexibility to implement its strategy in Afghanistan.

"If the president is unable to make these determinations, then we should be asking ourselves much deeper questions about what we really hope to achieve in Pakistan," Berman responded.

The House rejected, 173–246, another attempt by Ros-Lehtinen to limit the bill to authorizing $1.5 billion in aid from fiscal 2010 through 2013 and requiring the administration to submit a strategy to Congress.

SENATE ACTION

The Senate Foreign Relations Committee voted 16–0 on June 16 to approve a bill (S 962—S Rept 111-33) sponsored by Kerry and Lugar. Without fanfare or debate, the Senate passed the measure by voice vote on June 24.

The measure called for $1.5 billion a year for humanitarian and economic development aid in fiscal 2010 through 2014. The House authorization was for four years instead of five. The bill included restrictions on military aid similar to those in the House measure. And like the House-passed version, it allowed the conditions to be waived if the administration determined it would be "important" to U.S. national security interests.

Included in the bill were two proposals by Robert Menendez, D-N.J. One required that the administration provide Congress with "criteria and benchmarks" before distributing the assistance. A second proposed authorizing an additional $10 million for the inspectors general of the State Department and U.S. Agency for International Development, bringing the authorized funding level to $30 million a year.

FINAL ACTION

Negotiations among Berman, Kerry, Lugar, and the White House produced a compromise, which was introduced as a new bill (S 1707) in both chambers on September 24. The Senate passed the measure by voice vote the same day, and the House cleared it, also by voice vote, September 30.

The final bill dropped Van Hollen's proposal to provide trade preferences for some Pakistani and Afghan products. The plan was the most significant difference between the two original bills. Sen. Charles E. Grassley, R-Iowa, said that he did not object to establishing trade preferences but that the proposal's labor regulations were overly intrusive and could discourage future investors.

MAJOR PROVISIONS

Following are the bill's major provisions:

Economic assistance. The bill authorized $1.5 billion a year in nonmilitary assistance in fiscal 2010 through 2014, an approach that was designed to put U.S. aid on a long-term, nonmilitary footing. The bill required that all assistance, and all payment-related information, flow through duly elected civilian authorities; withheld $750 million each year until the President's Special Representative to Afghanistan and Pakistan certified to Congress that Pakistan "has made or is making reasonable progress" toward achieving standards for political reform, reduction of corruption, civil liberties and other governance goals; authorized $30 million per year to audit use of the funds.

Security assistance. The bill authorized funding for arms and training in fiscal 2010 through 2014, but left the amount open. The funds could not be released until the secretary of State certified that, in the previous year, the Pakistani government had demonstrated a sustained commitment to combating terrorist groups, and that Pakistani security forces were not subverting the country's political or judicial process.

Counterinsurgency funds. The bill authorized the transfer of fiscal 2010 funds to the Pakistan Counterinsurgency Capabilities Fund, created under the 2009 supplemental spending bill (PL 111-32). The fund was to be administered by the State Department in consultation with the Pentagon.

Nuclear proliferation. None of the security assistance funding could be released until the secretary of state certified that Pakistan's government was continuing to cooperate in efforts to dismantle nuclear weapon supplier networks, including providing direct access to Pakistani nationals associated with such networks. Unlike the report that accompanied the original House-passed bill, it did not specifically refer to rogue nuclear scientist Abdul Qadeer Khan and his role in establishing a nuclear proliferation network.

Presidential waiver. The president could waive the conditions placed on U.S. economic and security assistance if doing so was "important" to U.S. national security interests.

Regional strategy. The president was required to produce a comprehensive regional security strategy to eliminate terrorist threats and close safe havens in Pakistan.

Iran Sanctions

Legislation aimed at pressuring Iran to suspend its nuclear weapons program cleared in June 2010. President Barack Obama signed the measure into law July 1 (HR 2194—PL 111-195).

The bill tightened existing sanctions against multinational companies that assisted Iran in developing its domestic refining capacity and expanded the restrictions to apply to companies that sold refined petroleum products to that nation. The measure also increased the number of sanctions available to the president beyond those provided under the 1996 Iran Sanctions Act (PL 104-172).

Rep. Brad Sherman, D-Calif., said the best part of the bill was the language on procurement, which required prospective federal contractors to certify that they were not engaging in any sanctionable activity as defined in the bill and levied penalties for a false certification. Sherman was a longtime proponent of tough sanctions against the Iranian regime for its alleged nuclear weapons program. Advocates said the real impact would depend on the willingness of the Obama administration to enforce the provisions.

House Foreign Affairs Chair Howard L. Berman, D-Calif., and Senate Banking Chair Christopher J. Dodd, D-Conn., resisted pressure from the White House to broaden the president's waiver authority, including a blanket exemption for companies based in countries that were participating in other forms of sanctions. Although the final bill did not include the blanket exemptions, it permitted the president to waive sanctions for such companies when a waiver would be in the national interest.

Obama used the 1996 law in the fall of 2009 to impose sanctions on Naftiran Intertrade Company, an Iranian oil company based in Switzerland. It was the first time any administration had used the law's sanctions.

The legislation followed revelations that Iran had assembled many of the main elements for a nuclear weapon. Iranian President Mahmoud Ahmadinejad insisted the nuclear program was for peaceful purposes only, but Iran had no working civil nuclear power reactors and only one that was close to being finished. The government also rebuffed calls from the Obama administration and other Western leaders to ship its uranium supply overseas. In November 2009, the Iranian cabinet approved a plan to construct ten new enrichment facilities. The government also ignored a year-end deadline set by Obama for Iran to engage in negotiations on its nuclear program.

BACKGROUND

U.S. sanctions targeting Iran's petroleum sector had been in place for more than a decade. The 1996 Iran-Libya Sanctions Act (PL 104-172) established penalties for foreign companies that invested $20 million or more in Iran's energy industry. Under a 2006 law (PL 109-293) the sanctions were expanded and reauthorized through 2011. (Libya was dropped because of the country's cooperation on antiterrorist efforts.) *(PL 104-172, Congress and the Nation Vol. IX, p. 239; PL 109-293, Congress and the Nation Vol. XII, p. 299)*

However, no company had ever been penalized for such investments, largely because of strong opposition from the European Union (EU). In 1998, President Bill Clinton waived, on national security grounds, sanctions against a foreign investment consortium that had won a $2 billion contract to develop Iran's South Pars offshore gas field. In return for the waiver, the EU and Russia promised greater cooperation on counterterrorism and on limiting the transfer of technology to Iran.

Since the 1990s, a number of foreign firms (including French, Italian, British, Dutch, and Canadian energy companies) had decided to enter the Iranian energy sector. More recently, Japanese and Chinese firms had also decided to enter the Iranian energy market on a larger scale.

Existing law applied to investment in Iran's oil sector but not to the sale of gasoline or equipment to develop its refineries. Financial institutions were not subject to sanctions for facilitating investments in Iran's oil industry. The president also was not required to begin or conclude an investigation, or make a determination regarding sanctionable activities.

Oil experts also said that Iran had plenty of time to take countermeasures to blunt potential sanctions, including expanding its refining capacity, retrofitting cars to run on natural gas, and removing subsidies on imported fuel. Another challenge facing both the multilateral and bilateral sanction regimes was that Iran continued to set up new front companies, allowing it to keep one step ahead of whatever new sanctions were imposed.

Both bills were designed to pressure Iran to suspend its nuclear weapons program by imposing sanctions on multinational companies that supported the nation's efforts to buy or produce gasoline and other refined petroleum products or to construct or expand its oil refineries.

Although Iran is rich in oil, its refineries could not keep up with demand, and it imported 40 percent of its gasoline supply. Among the largest multinational companies providing the imports were BP (United Kingdom), Vitol (Switzerland), Total (France), and Shell (the Netherlands).

Iran's leaders boasted that they were invulnerable to any U.S.-led squeeze on its gasoline supply as a result of new supply agreements with other countries and planned to increase the output of the country's petrochemical plants.

House Foreign Affairs Committee Chair Berman said he would expect such claims. "My own evaluation," he said, "is that this gets right to the heart of their economic future."

Others were less sanguine. "It would be wonderful if that was the case," said Patrick Clawson, deputy director for research at the Washington Institute for Near East Policy. "But Venezuela has more than sufficient refining capacity to meet Iran's refined-products needs, and [Venezuelan President Hugo] Chávez has visited with Iran more than any other leader. . . . He would be delighted for the opportunity to show he is standing up to the United States."

Berman and other supporters said the bill was not an alternative to President Obama's policy of seeking a dialogue with Iran but rather a way to strengthen the president's hand.

HOUSE FLOOR ACTION

The House passed its Iran sanctions bill, 412–12, on December 15, 2009. The measure focused on penalties for supplying gasoline or providing equipment that Iran could use to expand or construct domestic refineries.

The Foreign Affairs Committee had approved the bill (HR 2194—H Rept 111-342, Part 1) by voice vote October 28.

The bill called for expanding the 2006 law and reauthorizing it through 2016, with changes that included:

- Expanding the sanctions to include financial institutions, insurers, underwriters, foreign subsidiaries, and nongovernmental organizations, among others.
- Adding liquefied natural gas (LNG), oil, and LNG tankers to the items that could not be supplied to Iran.
- Requiring the president to investigate a company immediately after receiving credible information that it was violating the law's prohibitions and make a determination within 180 days.
- Prohibiting federal contracts with U.S. or foreign firms that met the criteria for sanctions.
- Barring civil nuclear cooperation with any country that allowed its citizens or companies to provide equipment, technology, or materials that aided Iran's nuclear weapons program.

House Republicans pushed for tough sanctions and wanted them in place as quickly as possible. "Diplomacy and sanctions are not mutually exclusive," Mike Pence of Indiana, chair of the House Republican Conference, said during the Foreign Affairs markup.

Despite Berman's assurances, a handful of committee members from both parties still expressed concern that the bill would undermine the administration's negotiations.

A separate bill (HR 1327) passed by the House on October 14 outlined procedures for states, local governments, and educational institutions to divest from or prevent investment in companies that had at least $20 million invested in Iran's energy sector. The measure, which passed by a vote of 414–6, also included a prohibition on legal action against asset managers who divested from such investments or elected not to make them. That bill went no further.

SENATE COMMITTEE ACTION

The Senate Banking, Housing and Urban Affairs Committee approved its bill (S 2799—S Rept 111-99) by a vote of 23–0 on October 29, 2009.

Chair Christopher J. Dodd, D-Conn., said Democrats had faith in Obama's engagement strategy with Iran and he hoped the president would not have to use the sanctions, but he added that he wanted the committee to report the bill in case negotiations failed. Richard C. Shelby of Alabama, the panel's ranking Republican, was not as keen on prospects for talks with Iran but said action on sanctions legislation would send a strong message.

The committee gave voice vote approval to an amendment by Bob Corker, R-Tenn., urging the president to continue pursuing multilateral sanctions against Iran. Corker warned that the bill's unilateral sanctions would have no effect, particularly without the support of China and Russia.

In addition to the sanctions related to supplying refined petroleum or equipment to help Iranian refineries, the bill included the following provisions:

- Established a Treasury Department freeze on the assets of Iranian officials.
- Prohibited the U.S. government from contracting with companies that supplied Iran with communications-monitoring or -jamming technology.
- Codified a ban on U.S. trade with Iran, with an exception for the export of food, medicine, humanitarian aid, and the exchange of information materials.

- Required the United States to work with Iran's trading partners to prevent the reexport of sensitive dual-use technology to Iran through third countries and to subject those countries to restrictions on exports if they refused U.S. assistance.
- Authorized states, local governments, and mutual funds to divest from firms investing in Iran's energy sector and shield private asset managers from lawsuits over fiduciary duties. The provisions were similar to those in the separate House-passed bill.

SENATE FLOOR ACTION

The Senate passed its more expansive bill, without amendments, by unanimous consent on January 28, 2010. It later inserted the text into HR 2194 and passed that bill by unanimous consent on March 11. The bill included provisions that directed the president to freeze assets of Iranian officials and prohibit the U.S. government from providing contracts to companies that supplied Iran with communications-monitoring technology.

The bill also included provisions to authorize states, local governments, and mutual funds to divest from firms investing in Iran's energy sector, and to shield private-asset managers from lawsuits over fiduciary duties. It proposed to require the United States to work with Iran's trading partners to prevent the reexport of sensitive dual-use technology to Iran through third countries, and subject those countries to restrictions on exports if they refused U.S. assistance. In addition, it sought to codify the Treasury Department's ban on trade with Iran, with an exception for the export of food, medicine, and humanitarian aid and the exchange of information materials.

CONFERENCE AND FINAL ACTION

House and Senate negotiators filed a conference report on the bill (H Rept 111-512) on June 23, 2010. The Senate adopted the report by a vote of 99–0 the following day, and the House cleared the bill, 408–8, hours later. The final measure followed the contours of the Senate bill.

MAJOR PROVISIONS

Following are the bill's major provisions:

Oil and Gas

The bill amended the Iran Sanctions Act to require the president to impose three or more sanctions if a company knowingly made an investment of $20 million or more in any twelve-month period that contributed to Iran's ability to develop its petroleum resources. The sanctions applied to companies that

- Provided goods, services, technology, information, or support that would allow Iran to maintain or expand its domestic production of refined petroleum products, including any assistance in the construction, modernization, or repair of refineries.
- Provided Iran with refined petroleum products or contributed to the country's ability to import refined petroleum resources, including providing ships, vehicles, or other means of transportation to deliver the products. The bill expanded the list of petroleum resources to include items such as LNG, oil, and LNG tankers.

New Sanctions

The bill established three new sanctions that could be imposed on companies that did not comply with the law's requirements. The president could bar access to foreign exchanges in the United States, prohibit access to the U.S. banking system, and bar property transactions in the United States.

The six existing sanctions were denial of U.S. Export-Import Bank loans, denial of licenses for the export of military technology, denial of U.S. bank loans exceeding $10 million in one year, a prohibition on being a primary U.S. government bond dealer, a prohibition on government procurement, and a prohibition on allowing a company to import certain items.

Increased Penalties

The measure increased criminal penalties on U.S. companies for violating the law, increasing fines from $10,000 to $1 million and jail time from ten to twenty years.

Federal Procurement

U.S. and foreign firms that violated the law could not enter into procurement contracts with the federal government. This included companies that exported sensitive communications technology to Iran for use in "monitoring, jamming, or other disruption of communications by the people of Iran."

Human Rights

The president was required to impose sanctions on human rights violators in Iran.

Financial Activities

U.S. banks were forbidden to open or maintain accounts for foreign financial institutions that facilitated transactions by the Islamic Revolutionary Guard Corps or with Iranian entities that were designated under the International Emergency Economic Powers Act (IEEPA) for support of acquisition of weapons of mass destruction or support of terrorism.

Banks were accountable for actions by their foreign subsidiaries. The president was required to freeze the assets of individuals who had engaged in activities such as terrorism or weapons proliferation under IEEPA sanction.

Nuclear Cooperation

The bill prohibited new civil nuclear cooperation agreements with countries that did not take action against individuals or companies that had contributed materially to Iran's nuclear weapons program or Iran's program to produce a nuclear-capable missile.

Investigations

The bill required the president to investigate reports of sanctionable activities and report to Congress, instead of stating that the president "should" conduct such investigations, as under previous law.

RELATED LEGISLATION AND EXECUTIVE ACTIONS

President Obama and the 111th Congress took other actions to stiffen sanctions against Iran and companies or countries doing businesses with Iran. These steps included the following legislation:

- The fiscal 2010 Energy and Water appropriations bill (PL 111-85), signed on October 28, 2009, prohibited the use of U.S. funds to fill the Strategic Petroleum Reserve with products from firms that sell more than $1 million worth of gasoline to Iran.
- The omnibus fiscal 2010 appropriations bill (PL 111-117) denied U.S. Export-Import (Ex-Im) Bank credits to any firm that sold gasoline and related equipment and services to Iran. This provision was aimed at India-based Reliance Industries, Ltd., which had sold gasoline to Iran until late 2008 and had received Ex-Im financing guarantees.
- The fiscal 2012 Pentagon authorization bill (PL 112-81), signed on December 31, 2011, targeted Iran's Central Bank and the financial institutions that did business with it—effectively denying such institutions access to U.S. financial markets. In its key provision, the bill required the president to prevent any foreign bank from opening any account in the United States (and to impose strict limits on any existing accounts) if the bank processed nonoil related payments through the Iranian Central Bank. The president could apply these sanctions to banks processing oil-related payments if the global oil market was adequately supplied. The president could also exempt a bank from the sanctions if the bank's home country had significantly reduced its oil purchases from Iran. President Obama in 2012 and 2013 made use of this provision to exempt banks in nineteen countries, most of them in Europe.

State Department Authorization Bill

Following a pattern that had become common, Congress left legislation to reauthorize State Department programs unfinished in 2010, denying the authorizers a chance to set new policy prescriptions for the department's activities. Funding for existing programs continued flowing at fiscal 2010 levels under a short-term continuing resolution (HR 3082—PL 111-322) that was good through March 4, 2011.

The House passed a two-year version of the reauthorization bill in 2009 (HR 2410—H Rept 111-136), sponsored by Foreign Affairs Chair Howard L. Berman, D-Calif. It would have authorized $20.5 billion in fiscal 2010 and $20.4 billion in fiscal 2011 for State Department programs, the Peace Corps, U.N. peacekeeping dues, and other international programs. According to the Congressional Budget Office (CBO), the bulk of the authorization in both years—$18.7 billion and $19.3 billion, respectively—was devoted to State Department operations and activities and related agencies.

The bill did not include foreign economic or military aid. The measure would have authorized the hiring of 1,500 new Foreign Service officers and 700 additional staff members at the U.S. Agency for International Development. The number of Peace Corps volunteers would have increased significantly from the existing figure of about 8,000.

Berman said House passage was an important step in his efforts to get Congress "back into exercising its legislative responsibilities" on the foreign policy front.

The Senate Foreign Relations Committee approved its reauthorization bill (S 2971—S Rept 111-301) by voice vote on April 27, 2010, marking the first time since 2005 that the panel had considered such an expansive measure. The one-year measure, introduced by Chair John Kerry, D-Mass., and ranking member Richard G. Lugar, R-Ind., covered only fiscal 2011. By that point, fiscal 2010 appropriations had already been determined. Rather than specifying hard dollar amounts, it authorized "such sums as necessary." CBO estimated the total authorization for fiscal 2011 would come to $20.9 billion, of which $19.2 billion would go to the State Department.

But as a result of gridlock in the Senate, the foreshortened election year schedule, and the low priority the leadership gave to the bill, the measure never reached the Senate floor and died at the end of the 111th Congress.

HOUSE COMMITTEE ACTION

The House Foreign Affairs Committee gave voice vote approval May 20, 2009, to a bill (HR 2410—H Rept 111-136) sponsored by Berman. Democrats turned back a number of GOP amendments on social issues during the daylong markup. The panel also considered a variety of amendments on narrow issues such as religious freedom in Vietnam and Venezuela, military funding for Israel, and peace in the Darfur region of Sudan.

Almost all of the authorization levels matched President Obama's fiscal 2010 request. The bill included $1.8 billion in fiscal 2010 for membership dues to international organizations, $2.3 billion for contributions to ongoing U.N. peacekeeping activities, and whatever was necessary to pay unpaid past dues—long a sore spot for some members of Congress.

Sponsors said the funding would allow hiring of 1,500 new State Department Foreign Service officers and 700 additional staff at the U.S. Agency for International Development (USAID). It also would allow for the number of Peace Corps volunteers to increase significantly from the existing level of about 8,000. It included authorization for a pay increase for junior Foreign Service officers assigned overseas, bringing their pay in line with the higher salaries of those stationed in Washington.

Republicans criticized the bill as being too expensive, preempting administration policy reviews that were under way, and giving the United Nations a blank check.

Berman tried to avoid the perennial controversy over funding for overseas family-planning groups by inserting language clarifying that the measure would not alter existing law prohibiting the use of U.S. aid to pay directly for abortions overseas. But the provision did not satisfy antiabortion Republicans.

Among the amendments considered, the committee:

- Rejected on a 17–22 party-line vote the most contentious amendment, offered by Christopher H. Smith, R-N.J. The proposal would have added antiabortion policy to language authorizing an Office for Global Women's Issues at the State Department. "It is absolutely imperative that women never be regarded or reduced to the status of objects or second-class citizens," he said. "The same is true, I would respectfully submit to my colleagues, of unborn children." Democrats said abortion provisions should not be added, noting that existing law already barred funding for abortion overseas.
- Adopted by voice vote a manager's amendment that removed potentially controversial language that would have extended to same-sex partners overseas the same benefits given to spouses and dependents, such as access to U.S. health care and moving expenses. Berman said Secretary of State Hillary Rodham Clinton had told him she would implement these benefits without legislation.
- Rejected by voice vote an amendment by Mike Pence, R-Ind., to strike language to track international discrimination based on sexual orientation and promote decriminalization of homosexuality. He proposed to replace it with a broad statement of support for universal human rights that did not mention sexual orientation. "It's not about a gay-rights agenda," said Bill Delahunt, D-Mass. "It's about violence against gays."
- Rejected by voice vote a GOP substitute that would have authorized about $2.8 billion less than Berman's bill. It would have dropped language in the bill to authorize payment of arrears to the United Nations and increase the cap on contributions to U.N. peacekeeping operations. Republicans said that would save $100 million a year.

HOUSE FLOOR ACTION

The House passed the bill by a vote of 235–187 on June 10. Under the rule for floor debate, a Pakistan aid bill that passed the following day was automatically added to the State Department measure, a move aimed at enhancing the chances for both bills.

It was the first time in four years the chamber had passed a State Department authorization bill. Most efforts in previous years to send the president a separate State Department bill bogged down, often because of disputes over policy language on abortion and other contentious issues. The last time such an authorization was enacted was 2002 (PL 107-228), in a law that covered fiscal 2002–2003. Since then, policy changes had been left to appropriators, who funded the programs through annual spending bills. *(Congress and the Nation Vol. XI, p. 250)*

Ileana Ros-Lehtinen of Florida, the ranking Republican on the Foreign Affairs Committee, urged her colleagues to reject the measure, arguing that it was far too costly: "This bill calls for exorbitant spending in the absence of true reform and does not take the difficult but necessary step of setting priorities."

Democrats used the rule governing floor debate to quash plans by Smith to repeat his effort to add antiabortion policy to language authorizing an Office for Global Women's Issues.

In action on some of the more than two dozen floor amendments, the House:

- Agreed by voice vote to a proposal by Michael N. Castle, R-Del., to authorize the State Department to suspend issuing diplomatic visas for countries that refused to repatriate citizens who had committed crimes or immigration violations in the United States.
- Rejected, 205–224, an amendment by Ros-Lehtinen to withhold $4.5 million from U.S. contributions to the International Atomic Energy Agency, an amount equal to the monetary value of nuclear technical cooperation the agency provided to Iran, Syria, Sudan, and Cuba in 2007.
- Rejected, 174–250, a motion by Dan Burton, R-Ind., to return the bill to committee with instructions that it be reported back immediately after replacing the text with a requirement for sanctions on companies that directly contributed to Iran's ability to develop or import refined-petroleum products.

SENATE COMMITTEE ACTION

The Senate Foreign Relations Committee approved Kerry's authorization bill (S 1524—S Rept 111-122) by a vote of 15–3 on November 17. Kerry acknowledged that the legislation, which focused on reshaping federal foreign aid programs, was limited in scope. But he called it an "important first step" to modernizing and rebuilding foreign assistance. He said the momentum for a foreign aid overhaul is "reaching a crescendo."

The bill called for $255 million over six years to establish a council within the executive branch to research and evaluate foreign assistance. It also proposed to establish, within USAID, an assistant administrator for policy and strategic planning and a bureau that would develop policy and long-term strategy, evaluate program effectiveness, and establish resource and workforce allocation criteria.

Democrat Jim Webb of Virginia joined two panel Republicans—James M. Inhofe of Oklahoma and Johnny Isakson of Georgia—in voting against the bill. He said he agreed with the goals but voiced concern over the cost and timing, pointing to a State Department letter urging the committee to delay approving the measure until a new USAID administrator was confirmed. The Senate did not confirm economic development specialist and physician Rajiv Shah to the post until December 8.

The bill directed the administrator to put together a strategy to promote development with the goal of reducing global poverty. It proposed career guidelines for Foreign Service and civil service officers that included rotation among agencies, governments, or international organizations. It also included a requirement that all federal departments and agencies make publicly available on their websites comprehensive and accessible information about U.S. foreign assistance by program and by country.

Fiscal 2010 State–Foreign Operations Funding

Congress cleared a $48.9 billion bill to pay for State Department operations and foreign assistance programs during fiscal 2010 as part of a year-end omnibus appropriations package. President Barack Obama signed the omnibus into law December 16 , 2009 (HR 3288—PL 111-117).

The top line was $1.8 billion, or 4 percent, less than the total amount appropriated for fiscal 2009. But when $4.3 billion in emergency appropriations provided in other bills and $9.7 billion in extra funds in a separate war spending bill were taken out of the equation, the picture changed dramatically. The amount appropriated for fiscal 2010 became an increase of $12.1 billion, or 33 percent, above the previous year.

Virtually all of the funding, $48.8 billion, was for discretionary accounts and was generally in line with earlier versions of the bill passed by the House and approved by the Senate Appropriations Committee in July. But the figure was $3.3 billion below Obama's request, making this the only nondefense spending bill to provide significantly less than the president wanted. The biggest differences were a $1.3 billion cut from Obama's request for State Department operations and $1.1 billion less than requested to finance foreign sales of U.S. weapons. However, the war supplemental, which was enacted six months earlier (PL 111-32), had provided $4 billion in extra funding for those accounts.

The fiscal 2010 funding included $2.6 billion in economic aid to Afghanistan, the largest amount for any country, and $1.5 billion in economic and military assistance to Pakistan.

HOUSE COMMITTEE ACTION

The House Appropriations Committee approved a $49 billion version of the bill (HR 3081—H Rept 111-187) by voice vote June 23. Of the total, $48.8 billion was discretionary spending, about $80 million more than in the final bill.

Some Republicans criticized the bill's cost, but Kay Granger of Texas, the ranking Republican on the State–Foreign Operations Subcommittee, said she did not object as long as Democrats stuck to a plan to avoid supplemental spending bills in the future. The subcommittee drafted the bill and approved it by voice vote June 17.

Family Planning

Subcommittee Chair Nita M. Lowey, D-N.Y., won her panel's approval to expand family-planning funding to $648 million by emphasizing that the bill would not undo any existing abortion restrictions. "I want to make this very clear," she reiterated in the full committee. "The bill does not change any provisions of law that restrict funding for abortion or otherwise condition family-planning assistance." The amount was $55 million above the president's request.

Iran Sanctions

The full committee agreed to add language to bar the U.S. Export-Import Bank from providing or guaranteeing credit to companies that provided Iran with significant amounts of refined petroleum or aided its domestic petroleum industry. Although Iran was a major oil exporter, it lacked refining capacity and had to import up to 40 percent of its gasoline. Mark Steven Kirk, R-Ill., who drafted the Iran language with Lowey, said it targeted Reliance Industries Limited, a large Indian company that had sold refined petroleum to Iran in the past and had also received $900 million in loan guarantees from the Export-Import Bank.

James P. Moran, D-Va., opposed the language, citing the public protests going on in Iran over election fraud. "The smartest thing we can do right now is to stay out of the Iranian revolution so it is the Iranians' revolution, not ours," he said.

The Iran sanctions were added as part of a manager's amendment that was adopted by voice vote.

Detainees

The committee adopted by voice vote an amendment by Jerry Lewis of California, the panel's ranking Republican, to block aid to any country that agreed to accept detainees from the U.S. facility in Guantánamo Bay, Cuba, unless the administration notified Congress in advance. Conferees changed this to a statement in the conference report requiring a report to Congress in advance of any such transfer.

International Monetary Fund

An amendment by Granger, adopted by voice vote, added language to sunset U.S. participation in the new International Monetary Fund (IMF) lending facility after five years. The language was modified in the final bill to set specific requirements for continued participation after five years. The amendment also proposed that U.S. support be limited to 20 percent of the total.

HOUSE FLOOR ACTION

The House passed the bill, 318–106, on July 9, after voting overwhelmingly to overrule a move by Obama to reject congressional conditions on funding for international banks. The bill was otherwise virtually unchanged from the committee version. As they had on previous spending bills, Democratic leaders imposed a so-called structured rule for the floor debate that allowed consideration of a limited number of specific amendments.

During the debate, the House adopted, 429–2, an amendment by Kirk to roll back a signing statement that Obama released June 26 on the war supplemental. Obama signed the bill, but he asserted constitutional authority to overlook requirements set in the bill for U.S. actions in the World Bank, the IMF, and other international financial institutions. The language of the amendment was largely retained in the final bill. "Let me give my constitutional friends over there another constitutional lesson," Financial Services Chair Barney Frank, D-Mass., said. "The notion that the administration can take the money and pick and choose what it wants to do with the conditions is unacceptable."

The House rejected, 174–256, an amendment by John Culberson, R-Texas, to cut $506 million from multilateral programs.

SENATE COMMITTEE ACTION

Setting up a potential conflict with the House, the Senate Appropriations Committee voted to add language to the bill that would effectively repeal the Mexico City policy. The policy, first announced by President Ronald Reagan in 1984, went beyond the prohibition in existing law against using federal funds for abortion. The policy barred U.S. funding for nongovernmental organizations that performed or actively promoted abortion as a method of family planning, even if the group used its own money. Exceptions were allowed in cases of rape or incest, or when the life of the woman was in danger. *(Congress and the Nation Vol. XII, pp. 283, 284, 287, 303, 314–315, 317; additional Mexico City background, Congress and the Nation Vol. XI, pp. 247, 294)*

The panel approved its $48.8 billion version of the bill (S 1434—S Rept 111-44) by a vote of 29–1 on July 9, the same day the House passed its bill. The slightly smaller Senate bill differed from the House version by only about $160 million.

Judd Gregg of New Hampshire, the ranking Republican on the State–Foreign Operations Appropriations Subcommittee, said the $2.7 billion in the bill for Afghanistan raised a "red flag." "We are putting a massive amount into Afghanistan," he said, adding: "We put . . . a lot of money into Iraq and a lot of it was not well used. We don't want to do that in Afghanistan."

Mexico City Policy

The committee adopted, 17–10, an amendment by Frank R. Lautenberg, D-N.J., stating that organizations would not be denied U.S. aid solely on the basis of health care services that they provided using non-U.S. funds, as long as the services were legal in the country where they were provided as well as in the United States. Sam Brownback, R-Kan., cast the lone vote against the bill, saying he could not support it with the Lautenberg language. The proposal "is a bad foreign policy," he said, arguing the money could be better spent elsewhere.

Travel Documents

The panel adopted by voice vote an amendment by George V. Voinovich, R-Ohio, to create a pilot project to study the use of passport cards as proof of identity and citizenship for U.S. nationals traveling between the United States and Canada. The final bill included a study that also included travel to and from Mexico.

CONFERENCE AND FINAL ACTION

The Senate never took up the State–Foreign Operations bill. Senate floor action was slowed by weeks of partisan bickering, and the Senate was later consumed by the debate on the health care overhaul. Democratic appropriators instead agreed on a compromise version of the bill and included it in the year-end omnibus package, which they inserted into the conference report on the Transportation, Housing and Urban Development spending measure (HR 3288).

The House adopted the conference report (H Rept 111-366) by a vote of 221–202 on December 10. The Senate interrupted the health care debate to clear the omnibus bill, 57–35, on December 13. *(Omnibus package, p. 127)*

MAJOR PROVISIONS

Following are the major components of the State–Foreign Operations section of the omnibus spending bill. Increases of less than 2 percent were below the rate of inflation.

Diplomatic programs. Authorized $8.2 billion for diplomatic and consular programs, with $1.6 billion of that devoted to security upgrades at U.S. embassies. The total accounted for about half of the $16.1 billion provided for State Department operations.

USAID. Authorized $1.7 billion for operational expenses of the U.S. Agency for International Development (USAID), the federal agency responsible for administering U.S. foreign assistance programs. The amount was close to the request and about $735 million more than nonemergency fiscal 2009 funding.

Global health. Authorized $7.8 billion for global health and child survival programs, $665 million more than in the regular fiscal 2009 law. The total included the following:

- $5.8 billion for programs to fight global HIV/AIDS and the related diseases of tuberculosis and malaria. The amount was $200 million more than fiscal 2009 funding and $100 million more than requested. In addition, the Labor–Health and Human Services–Education section of the omnibus legislation provided almost $1 billion in international AIDS funding, bringing the total U.S. contribution to more than $7 billion.
- $2.4 billion for child survival and health programs—including $32 million for polio treatments and $33 million for micronutrient programs.

Development assistance. Authorized $2.5 billion, about $215 million less than requested but $720 million more than regular fiscal 2009 funding, for long-term development programs, including $1.2 billion for agriculture and food security and $925 million for basic education programs.

Climate change. Authorized $1.3 billion for bilateral and multilateral assistance to promote clean-energy, environment, biodiversity, and climate change programs worldwide—$437 million less than requested but $603 million more than the fiscal 2009 level.

Millennium Challenge Corporation. Authorized $1.1 billion, which was $320 million less than requested but $230 million above fiscal 2009 funding. The program, a signature initiative of President George W. Bush, was aimed at providing aid to countries that adopted democratic and free-market policies.

International peacekeeping. Authorized $2.1 billion, which was $264 million below the previous level and $135 million less than requested. The measure also changed the authorized level of U.S. assessments for U.N. peacekeeping activities from 27.1 percent to 27.3 percent.

International financial institutions. Authorized $2 billion, about $550 million more than the fiscal 2009 level but $298 million less than the request. The total included $1.3 billion for the World Bank and set a 20 percent limit on the U.S. participation in a new IMF global lending program. It also placed restrictions on continued U.S. participation after five years.

Bilateral economic and military assistance. Authorized amounts for key countries included the following:

- $2.6 billion for humanitarian, reconstruction, and related assistance for Afghanistan, including $2 billion in economic support funds. The total was equal to fiscal 2009 funding, but about $15 million less than requested. Congress withheld a portion of the economic support funds pending certification by the State Department that the national and local authorities in Afghanistan were fully cooperating with U.S.-funded narcotics eradication and interdiction efforts.
- $1.5 billion in assistance for Pakistan, $124 million less than the president's request but $18 million more than the previous level. The total included $1 billion for general economic assistance and $238 million in foreign military financing.
- $467 million in economic, antidrug, and humanitarian assistance to Iraq, $142 million below the fiscal 2009 level including supplemental appropriations and $33 million less than requested.
- $2.2 billion in military assistance for Israel to be provided in the form of cash grants within thirty days of enactment. Israel was the only country given this favored treatment. Funding under the war supplemental brought Israel's aid total for fiscal 2010 to $2.8 billion, the amount requested.
- $1.3 billion in aid for Egypt—$1.0 billion for military grants and $250 million in economic assistance. The military grants were equal to the previous level; the economic aid exceeded it by $50 million. When combined with funding under the supplemental, the total equaled Obama's $2.8 billion request.

International family planning. Authorized $525 million in assistance for voluntary international population-planning programs, roughly equal to the fiscal 2009 level and the president's request. The measure also provided $55 million for the U.N. Population Fund. Obama promised money for the fund, a move President Bush had often blocked.

Left out of the final bill was a Senate provision that would have put into statute an action taken by Obama in January to rescind the so-called Mexico City restrictions on international family-planning aid.

Fiscal 2010 Intelligence Authorization

After months of negotiations—and to the surprise of many observers—Congress cleared a compromise fiscal 2010 intelligence authorization bill before adjourning for the campaign season. It was the first reauthorization of the nation's intelligence agencies in six years. President Barack Obama signed the measure into law October 7, 2010 (HR 2701—PL 111-259).

Negotiations on the bill had pushed enactment beyond the end of the fiscal year, but members of the House and Senate Intelligence committees persisted, in part to enable Congress to reassert its oversight role of the intelligence community.

Because fiscal 2010 had ended before the bill was enacted, the measure did not authorize specific funding. Instead, it allowed lawmakers to make policy changes affecting the sixteen U.S. intelligence agencies and intelligence-related activities of the U.S. government, including the National Security Agency (NSA), the Central Intelligence Agency (CIA), and the Federal Bureau of Investigation (FBI).

The most recent intelligence bill, which was a major overhaul, had been enacted in 2004 (PL 108-487). Subsequent authorization bills were stymied largely by disagreements between Congress and President George W. Bush over attempts to restrict the use by the CIA and other intelligence agencies of certain interrogation procedures, including waterboarding, or simulated drowning. *(2004 legislation, Congress and the Nation Vol. XI, p. 263)*

The main controversy in the 111th Congress concerned the extent to which lawmakers should be briefed on such procedures. The White House had threatened to veto earlier House and Senate versions of the bill over proposed new notification requirements for sensitive spy activities. The Obama administration argued that the provisions would intrude on the executive branch's traditional authority over national security.

The president was required under the National Security Act of 1947 to keep the House and Senate Intelligence committees "fully and currently informed" of intelligence activities. The law enumerated specific procedures for briefings on covert actions, including allowing the president to limit notification to the so-called Gang of Eight—the Democratic and Republican leaders in both chambers, and the chair and the ranking members of the House and Senate Intelligence panels—if the executive branch determined that such limitations were warranted by extraordinary circumstances affecting vital U.S. interests.

Many lawmakers said the executive branch had overused its ability to limit briefings to the Gang of Eight under Bush, and many argued that Congress could have provided greater oversight of initiatives such as the government's warrantless surveillance program if the entire committee had been notified of them sooner.

The notification controversy was exacerbated by two events in 2009. The first was a partisan fight over exactly when Speaker Nancy Pelosi, D-Calif., had been informed about the use of harsh interrogation techniques such as waterboarding.

The second occurred when CIA Director Leon E. Panetta told the House Intelligence Committee in June that the panel had not been notified about a secret program that began in 2001, reportedly designed to capture or kill leaders of the al Qaeda terrorist network abroad.

The House Intelligence Committee approved a bill (HR 2701) in June 2009 that would have given the Intelligence committees the authority to set the guidelines on when the executive branch could limit briefings to the Gang of Eight. Faced with a White House veto threat over this and other provisions, Democratic leaders pulled the measure from the floor schedule.

In September 2009, the Senate passed a version of the legislation (S 1494) that would have allowed the executive branch to continue deciding what briefings to limit to the Gang of Eight. But it would have required that all panel members receive a description of the main features of the intelligence activity or covert action, as well as the reasons for not briefing the full committee.

Both chambers passed revised bills in 2010, but they could not agree on the disclosure requirements, among other things. Most observers believed the bill was dead, but further negotiations produced an agreement, which the Senate passed and the House cleared.

HOUSE FLOOR ACTION

The House on February 26 passed a revised version of its 2009 bill (HR 2701—H Rept 111-186) that dropped several controversial provisions approved by the Intelligence Committee. The vote was 235–168.

The changes, adopted 246–166 in a manager's amendment, replaced language that would have allowed the intelligence committees to write guidelines on when the administration could restrict sensitive briefings to the Gang of Eight. Under the amendment, by Intelligence Chair Silvestre Reyes, D-Texas, the administration could limit the full committees' access, but only if the president certified that the action was required by extraordinary circumstances affecting vital U.S. interests.

After 180 days, the director of national intelligence (DNI) would have to report to all members of the Intelligence committees on the subject involved or reissue the certification. All notifications would have to be in writing.

House Democrats spent months negotiating the revised notification language, but the White House renewed its veto threat against both the House and Senate bills. Other provisions that attracted veto warnings included language in both bills that would have authorized the Government Accountability Office (GAO) to conduct intelligence and counterintelligence oversight at the direction of Congress.

Reyes's amendment left intact provisions requiring the president to provide the "legal authority" under which an activity was conducted but removed a requirement to include dissenting legal views.

The manager's amendment originally included a fifteen-year prison sentence for intelligence personnel found to be using cruel, inhuman, or degrading interrogation techniques and jail time of up to five years for medical professionals who enabled those interrogations. Reyes supported the provisions but removed them when it became clear they would derail the bill.

The bill included language to prohibit the CIA from hiring contractors to conduct interrogations of detainees and required that the DNI provide a comprehensive report to Congress on the use of contractors.

The House rejected, 186–217, a motion to recommit by Peter Hoekstra of Michigan, the ranking Republican on the Intelligence Committee, which would have, among other things, required the CIA director to make public an unclassified version of briefings to members of Congress on the use of enhanced interrogation techniques.

SENATE FLOOR ACTION

In a bid to jump-start the legislation, which had never gone to a formal conference, the Senate passed a new, compromise bill (S 3611—S Rept 111-223) by unanimous consent on August 5, shortly before leaving for the August recess. Its authors urged the House, which had already adjourned, to clear the measure when it returned briefly for a special session called to clear a state education and Medicaid funding package (HR 1586). *(HR 1586 action, p. 453)*

The intelligence bill embodied an agreement reached by White House officials and top leaders of the intelligence committees from both parties. But it lacked changes sought by Pelosi in the congressional notification procedures. Pelosi had backed the notification of all Intelligence Committee members of sensitive spy operations.

Instead, the bill proposed several modifications to existing procedures, such as clarifying when the executive branch should notify Congress of a program, including factors such as whether a program risked significant loss of life or expenditure of funds.

The Senate Intelligence Committee had approved the bill, 15–0, in a closed session July 13. The bill required several reports on the use of contractors, as well as new procedures designed to track cost overruns on major purchases. It did not include proposed language to prevent the reading of *Miranda* warnings against self-incrimination to those detained outside the United States.

FINAL ACTION

Despite general expectations that the bill was dead at that point, leaders of the intelligence committees continued to pursue a compromise, and on September 27, the Senate adopted an amendment to the House-passed bill (HR 2701) that reflected an agreement reached by Pelosi, the White House, and the leaders of the House and Senate intelligence committees. The Senate adopted the amendment by unanimous consent. The House on September 29 agreed by a **key vote of 244–181 (R 1–172; D 243–9),** clearing the bill for the president. Opposition by House Republicans reflected dissatisfaction that the bill excluded several of their proposals that had been in earlier versions of the legislation, such as the provision to forbid officials from reading *Miranda* rights to terrorism suspects. *(2010 key votes, p. 767)*

The final dispute in the negotiations was over the notification provisions. Pelosi declared satisfaction with the final language.

Lawmakers also had to resolve the dispute over how much authority the GAO should have to audit spy agencies at the direction of Congress. The new language required the director of national intelligence (DNI) to come up with a directive on GAO access to the intelligence community.

MAJOR PROVISIONS

Following are major unclassified elements of the bill:

Expanded oversight. The bill repealed the Gang of Eight provision and established in statute that the president was required to brief all members of the intelligence committees within 180 days of certain intelligence actions. However, it allowed the president to limit the briefings if the president certified that not disclosing the information was justified by extraordinary circumstances affecting vital U.S. interests.

In such cases, the president had to notify all committee members that a restricted finding had been provided and give them a "general description" of the subject. Within 180 days, all members of the intelligence committees had to be given access to the finding or notification, unless the president renewed the certification. The president also had to keep a record of members who received the briefing.

The bill required the president to consider a list of criteria in determining whether Congress had to be notified of a covert activity. The criteria included whether the activity involved significant risk of loss of life or disclosing intelligence sources or methods, was particularly costly, or might damage U.S. diplomatic relations if it was disclosed.

The information on a covert activity had to be submitted in writing and include the legal basis under which it was being conducted.

GAO review. The bill required the DNI to issue a directive by May 1, 2011, on access for GAO personnel to audit certain intelligence agencies. The directive had to be submitted to Congress before it could go into effect.

The House-passed bill would have given the GAO the authority to audit intelligence agencies at the direction of Congress. The White House threatened to veto any measure that included such language.

DNI powers. The bill provided some expansion of the DNI's powers, including authorization to conduct a review of any "failure or deficiency" by an intelligence agency and recommend corrective or punitive action. The head of any agency that ignored the DNI's recommendation had to notify the intelligence committees and give the reasons for not complying.

Inspector general. The bill established an office of inspector general for the intelligence community under the DNI. The inspector general was to be appointed by the president and confirmed by the Senate and could be removed only by the president.

Contractors. The DNI was instructed to provide a comprehensive report to the Intelligence and Armed Services committees by February 1, 2011, on the use of contractors, including the guidance given by the individual intelligence agencies on hiring and assignment, and an assessment of the costs of hiring contract personnel compared with that of using government employees.

For major projects such as spy satellites, the DNI was empowered to assess the costs and risks associated with the acquisition and, in the case of significant cost overruns, go so far as to terminate the acquisition.

Interrogation techniques. The bill required the DNI, in coordination with the attorney general and defense secretary, to submit a report to the intelligence committees on policies and procedures issued to comply with an executive order released by Obama on January 22, 2009, requiring the intelligence agencies to comply with rules banning cruel, inhuman, or degrading treatment of prisoners.

Disclosure of covert agents. The maximum sentence for individuals with authorized access to classified information who intentionally disclosed any information identifying a covert agent was increased from ten to fifteen years.

Cybersecurity. The bill required the intelligence agencies responsible for cybersecurity programs authorized by presidential findings to report to Congress on the legality of their operations. The DNI was directed to report to Congress within a year with guidelines to improve the capabilities of the intelligence community and law enforcement agencies to protect U.S. cybersecurity.

Guantánamo Bay detainees. The DNI, in consultation with the directors of the CIA and Defense Intelligence Agency, was required to make public an unclassified summary of intelligence relating to recidivism of detainees who were, or had been, held at Guantánamo Bay, Cuba, and an assessment of the likelihood that those detainees would engage in terrorism or communicate with persons in terrorist organizations.

Congressional commissions. A Foreign Intelligence and Information Commission was established in Congress to evaluate efforts by the DNI to achieve strategic integration of the often competing elements of the intelligence community.

Fiscal 2011 State–Foreign Operations Funding

The bill that provided spending for the State Department and U.S. foreign aid in fiscal 2011 stalled during 2010 after winning approval in a House subcommittee and in the full Senate Appropriations Committee. Programs under the bill were funded mostly at fiscal 2010 levels through March 4, 2011, under the continuing resolution signed into law on December 22 (PL 111-322). Fiscal 2011 appropriations eventually were incorporated into an omnibus spending bill (HR 1473—PL 112-10), which cleared April 14, 2011. *(Omnibus legislation, p. 150; foreign operations section, p. 155)*

The House State–Foreign Operations Subcommittee approved a draft bill by voice vote June 30, 2010, that would have provided $52.8 billion, $4 billion less than requested but $3.9 billion more than in fiscal 2010. The Senate full committee approved a $54.2 billion bill (S 3676) by a vote of 18–12 on July 29. Virtually all of the funding was discretionary.

The House and Senate measures called for $16.6 billion and $17.5 billion, respectively, for the State Department and related agencies; $23.2 billion and $23.4 billion, respectively, for bilateral aid; and $5.4 billion each for foreign military financing. Both bills included about $8.2 billion for Global Health and Child Survival programs, about $460 million above fiscal 2010 spending.

Several significant policy issues separated the two bills. In drafting the House bill, subcommittee Chair Nita M. Lowey, D-N.Y., cut off aid for nonhumanitarian aid for Afghanistan until the country's government sorted out allegations that vast sums of money had been lost to corruption. The bill included the amount requested for the assistance, but none of the $3.9 billion was designated for Afghanistan. The Senate bill included $2.6 billion for the Afghanistan aid. House Republicans warned that withholding significant sums could hurt the U.S.-led war effort and the strategy on the ground at a pivotal moment in the conflict.

The subcommittee adopted a handful of GOP amendments, including one by Ander Crenshaw of Florida to prohibit the use of funds to transfer detainees from the U.S. facility in Guantánamo Bay, Cuba, to any other country unless the secretary of state certified that the receiving nation met certain requirements.

The Senate bill included a controversial amendment by Frank R. Lautenberg, D-N.J., that would have codified an Obama administration order repealing the "Mexico City" policy, which barred aid to international organizations that performed or promoted abortions, whether or not they used their own money. It was adopted, 19–11.

"It's time to put aside the politics on women's lives," Lautenberg argued. "Let them make their decisions. Let them make their choices." Sam Brownback, R-Kan., said he was "very saddened" by the amendment. "It's us funding abortions overseas," he said. "There are a lot of people in the country that find this deeply offensive."

The language had been approved by the committee the previous year but was stripped out before the fiscal 2010 bill (PL 111-117) reached the floor.

2011–2012

One of the truisms in foreign policy circles holds that if the Middle East is quiet today, there is no guarantee it will remain so tomorrow. Despite President Barack Obama's failed effort early in his term to push through new peace talks between Israel and the Palestinians, and partly because of the U.S. military drawdown from Iraq, the Middle East had been relatively quiet in 2009 and up until the end of 2010. But that situation changed dramatically starting in December 2010 when antigovernment protests exploded in an astonishing number of Arab countries. By the end of 2011, long-time dictatorial regimes had been swept aside in Tunisia, Egypt, Libya, and Yemen—and autocrats in many other countries were forced to make unprecedented concessions just to stay in power.

The outburst of popular protests known as the "Arab Spring" caught the Obama administration by surprise and seemed to befuddle most members of Congress as well. When vast crowds of protesters gathered in central Cairo, the United States withdrew its long-standing support for Egyptian President Hosni Mubarak, thus contributing to (but not causing) his fall from power—and prompting Republican complaints that Washington had undermined an important ally in the region.

A much more serious, and partisan, point of contention involved a country that had only rarely been high on Washington's radar screen in recent years: Libya. When antigovernment rebels launched attacks against the regime of Muammar Gaddafi, some congressional hawks demanded U.S. intervention to support the rebels. In March 2011, the administration did join its North Atlantic Treaty Organization (NATO) allies in providing air and naval support to the rebels, a step that proved crucial in driving Gaddafi from power in August.

A year later, however, armed men attacked the U.S. consulate in Benghazi, Libya, killing the U.S. ambassador and three other American personnel. Coming less than three months before the U.S. elections, this incident gave congressional Republicans ammunition to attack the administration for failing to protect the diplomats. Republicans also focused their ire on Susan E. Rice, the U.S. ambassador to the United Nations, who had given what turned out to be a misleading press briefing on the incident. The partisan attacks succeeded in derailing Rice's ambitions to be secretary of state in Obama's second term and took some luster off the reputation of her boss, Secretary of State Hillary Clinton.

In terms of legislation, Congress enacted new rounds of sanctions against Iran in 2012, all intended to punish the country economically for its alleged program to build nuclear weapons. Congress also managed, for four straight fiscal years, to adopt legislation authorizing the nation's intelligence programs. This type of legislation had languished frequently in the past, particularly during the presidency of George W. Bush. However, the presence of widely respected former House member Leon E. Panetta as Obama's CIA director appeared to be one of several factors enabling Congress to resume what was supposed to be standard practice. That success did not apply to State Department and foreign aid programs, however, which Congress continued to handle in omnibus spending bills because of its inability to pass freestanding legislation for those and many other agencies.

Despite the increased level of partisanship on Capitol Hill following the Republican takeover of the House, Congress did back, or at least did not attempt to overturn, Obama's policies in Iraq and Afghanistan. Some Republicans worried that the U.S. military withdrawal from Iraq at the end of 2011 would endanger hard-won stability in the country, but such anxieties seemed to be swept aside by the electorate's weariness with years of conflict there and the fact that Iraq seemed relatively calm. Similarly, Congress rejected a handful of attempts by liberal Democrats to prevent or end the president's "surge" of more than 30,000 additional troops to Afghanistan, which started in late 2009 and concluded just before the 2012 elections. Congress also approved vast increases in aid to the governments of Afghanistan and neighboring Pakistan—in the latter case despite widespread concern that the Pakistani military was not so secretly aiding rebels fighting the very government in Afghanistan that the United States was trying to keep in power.

Congress praised the U.S. covert operation that, in May 2011, killed al Qaeda leader Osama bin Laden in his compound in Abbottabad, Pakistan. But even that major success took on partisan tones when Democrats gave Obama credit for approving the mission and Republicans sought to diminish the president's role.

Fiscal 2011 State-Foreign Operations Funding

Congress in 2010 and early 2011 passed three continuing resolutions to fund government programs, including the State Department and related foreign operations, for fiscal 2011. Ultimately, all twelve appropriations bills were folded into omnibus legislation (HR 1473—PL 112-10) that cleared on April 14, 2011, more than halfway into the fiscal year. President Barack Obama signed the bill into law the next day. *(Omnibus legislation, p. 150)*

The spending package provided $48.3 billion for State Department and foreign operations, keeping discretionary spending for U.S. diplomatic and development programs at approximately the same level as in fiscal 2010.

The sum was $8.4 billion, or 15 percent, less than Obama's request for fiscal 2011—a smaller cut than the $11.7 billion proposed in an earlier version of the spending bill (HR 1) passed by House Republicans. It was about $500 million less than fiscal 2010 funding.

International organizations and financial institutions took some of the biggest cuts. U.S. contributions to the United Nations and other international organizations dropped by 20 percent, from $1.7 billion to $1.3 billion, compared with fiscal 2010.

The Millennium Challenge Corporation, a quasi-independent U.S. development agency, got $205 million less than in fiscal 2010 and $380 million less than requested.

The funding for international economic and development assistance was reduced to $8.4 billion, down $379 million from fiscal 2010 levels (not including supplemental spending). That was $1.9 billion less than the president's fiscal 2011 request. Pay for Foreign Service officers was frozen.

Some programs escaped far more severe reductions proposed in HR 1. Global health and child survival programs, a top priority for the Obama administration and a main target of the earlier House-passed bill, received $7.8 billion in funding—$66 million more than in fiscal 2010 and $850 million more than what the House proposed.

Democrats succeeded in eliminating House language that would have barred funding for international aid groups that offered or discussed abortion as a method of family planning. Direct funding for abortions remained illegal.

Use of Force in Libya

The outbreak of the so-called Arab Spring protests across North Africa and the Middle East in late 2010 and early 2011 produced a confused response in the United States. Some politicians, experts, and commentators argued for forceful U.S. action to support what they perceived as democratic forces, while many others worried about the United States getting bogged down in yet more Middle East conflicts.

President Obama's administration took different, but substantive, approaches to two of the rebellions during 2011, one in Egypt and the other in Libya. In the case of Egypt, the United States withdrew its backing for the authoritarian president, Hosni Mubarak, at a crucial moment when tens of thousands of protesters had all but paralyzed Cairo and other major cities. Mubarak resigned on February 11, succeeded by a military council that later held elections, which were won by the long-suppressed Muslim Brotherhood.

A rebellion in neighboring Libya against longtime dictator Muammar Gaddafi eventually brought a more direct U.S. intervention. Various rebel groups, which in previous years had never been able to sustain a campaign against Gaddafi, took advantage of the regional upheaval to renew their fight and quickly gained substantial support, both within Libya and internationally. By late February European leaders demanded that Gaddafi resign, and British Prime Minister David Cameron proposed a no-fly zone to prevent Gaddafi from using his air force against the rebels.

The U.S. Senate took up the idea of a no-fly zone in a resolution (S Res 85) adopted by unanimous consent on March 1. That measure called on the U.N. Security Council to authorize an internationally enforced no-fly zone. After some Arab leaders endorsed the idea, the Obama administration announced its support, and the Security Council authorized a no-fly zone in Libya on March 17. U.S. forces joined those from France and other North Atlantic Treaty Organization (NATO) countries in patrolling the skies of Libya on March 19; two days later, Obama wrote to congressional leaders formally notifying them of the action, under the terms of the 1974 War Powers Resolution. *(Congress and the Nation Vol. IV, p. 849)*

Obama's decision to intervene in Libya, however cautiously, brought competing responses from members of Congress. Some in both parties said the president was too timid and too late to have much of an impact on the situation and that a more aggressive backing of the anti-Gaddafi rebels was necessary. A surprising number of Democrats (and some libertarian Republicans), particularly in the House, condemned the intervention as risking another U.S. war in the Middle East, even as the United States was withdrawing from Iraq and struggling with its commitments in Afghanistan. Congressional leaders also were annoyed that the president acted without formally consulting with them.

Rep. Dennis J. Kucinich, the liberal Ohio Democrat who had been a vociferous critic of the Iraq war, led the outright opposition to intervention in Libya and in late May gained significant support, from both Democrats and Republicans, for a proposal requiring the president to withdraw all U.S. forces from in or near Libya by mid-June 2011. Seeking to head off the Kucinich measure, House Speaker John A. Boehner, R-Ohio, put together a rival resolution (H Res 292) criticizing the president for failing to "provide Congress with a compelling rationale based upon United States national security interests for current U.S. military activities regarding Libya" and demanding a formal report including such a justification. The resolution also voiced opposition to the deployment of ground troops in Libya—a step the president had not planned. The House adopted that resolution on June 3 on a **key vote of 268–145 (R 223–10; D 45–135)**. *(2011 key votes, p. 785)*

Fiscal 2011 and 2012 Intelligence Authorization

Congress during 2011 cleared a fiscal 2011 authorization bill for the nation's intelligence community and began work on a fiscal 2012 version. The bills provided authorization for sixteen intelligence agencies and intelligence-related activities of the U.S. government, including the

Office of the Director of National Intelligence (DNI), the Central Intelligence Agency (CIA), and the National Security Agency (NSA), as well as foreign intelligence activities of the departments of Defense, State, and Homeland Security.

The legislation also authorized covert action programs, research and development, and projects related to information dissemination. The overall cost and most of the provisions were classified.

President Obama signed the fiscal 2011 bill into law June 8 (HR 754—PL 112-18).

Enactment—even though it was eight months into the fiscal year—marked a victory for the authorizers, who had struggled to pass an annual bill. The fiscal 2010 law (PL 111-259) had marked the first time in six years that a bill authorizing the intelligence agencies had been enacted, but that measure was finished so close to the end of the fiscal year that it did not contain a classified annex with the dollar amounts and personnel ceilings for each intelligence program. *(2010 legislation, p. 245)*

The fiscal 2011 bill included a classified annex, and, according to House Democrats, tracked closely with fiscal 2011 funding that had already been appropriated. It was estimated to cost a little more than $80 billion, based on statements made by House Intelligence Chair Mike Rogers, R-Mich., and on the $80.1 billion price tag for the fiscal 2010 version.

FISCAL 2011 INTELLIGENCE AUTHORIZATION

The House Select Intelligence Committee approved the fiscal 2011 bill (HR 754—H Rept 112-72) by a 7–6 party-line vote in a closed session March 10.

The bill included a provision aimed at making it more difficult for government employees to leak information to the public, other governments, or rogue agents. The language was included in response to recent incidents of government information that had appeared on the website Wiki Leaks. The proposal required that the DNI establish an "insider threat detection program"—an automated system using networks, computer servers, routers, databases, websites, and other methods of communications to detect prohibited transfers of information.

The House passed the bill on May 13 by an overwhelming bipartisan vote of 392–15, in contrast to the party split in committee in March. Democrats had opposed the original bill's termination of certain CIA positions, including those of counterintelligence analysts, but the final bill did not end those jobs.

The Senate Select Intelligence Committee voted 12–3 in a closed markup March 15 to approve a version of the bill (S 719—S Rept 112-12) that reportedly was very similar to the House committee measure. In one significant difference, however, it would have required Senate confirmation of the NSA director, a provision the White House had opposed the previous year.

It also included language aimed at reducing leaks of classified information, and it required that intelligence networks have "capabilities" to monitor threats of internal leaks.

The Senate committee's bill reached a standstill because of a hold placed by Ron Wyden, D-Ore., who objected to a provision aimed at punishing former intelligence community officials who violated their nondisclosure agreements. Wyden argued that the language would threaten the rights of whistleblowers.

The Senate instead cleared the House bill by voice vote May 26.

FISCAL 2012 INTELLIGENCE AUTHORIZATION

The House passed the fiscal 2012 bill (HR 1892) by a vote of 384–14 on September 9.

Before passage, members gave voice vote approval to a manager's amendment by Rogers that struck two provisions that had contributed to a White House veto threat against the bill: one requiring that the national intelligence director provide Congress with certain documents relating to the transfer of detainees held at Guantánamo Bay, Cuba, and one requiring Senate confirmation of the NSA director.

The House Select Intelligence Committee had included those provisions in the version (H Rept 112-197) that it approved by voice vote May 26.

The bill required the administration to provide Congress with a report on how al Qaeda leader Osama bin Laden was located and killed. Bin Laden had been killed by U.S. forces in Pakistan and buried at sea May 2. The committee adopted the language, by Mike Thompson, D-Calif., by voice vote. "It's a huge issue, and because it was such a covert operation, I was afraid that some of the facts might be lost or distorted," he said.

The House, also by voice vote, adopted an amendment by Frank R. Wolf, R-Va., to create a counterterrorism competitive analysis council of outside experts to advise the national intelligence director and Congress on how the intelligence community should respond to the evolving threat of terrorism and domestic radicalization.

The Senate Select Intelligence Committee approved a version of the bill (S 1458—S Rept 112-43) on July 28 that drew opposition from several members because it included a three-year extension of a 2008 law (PL 110-261) that overhauled electronic-surveillance guidelines set by the Foreign Intelligence Surveillance Act (FISA) of 1978. The House version did not include an extension. *(Congress and the Nation Vol. XII, p. 251)*

Because of the extension, Wyden said he would oppose any attempt to pass the measure on the floor by unanimous consent. Wyden said the Senate should not pass another FISA extension until the Intelligence Committee addressed concerns about the number of Americans being monitored under the FISA law. Wyden's objection thus killed the Senate bill.

Fiscal 2012 State–Foreign Operations Funding

Fiscal 2012 appropriations for the State Department and foreign operations accounts were included in omnibus legislation (HR 2055—PL 112-74), cleared December 17, 2011, and were signed into law on December 23, 2011. Versions of a stand-alone bill had advanced only as far as the full Senate Appropriations Committee and the House State–Foreign Operations Subcommittee. *(Omnibus legislation, p. 172)*

House-Senate conferees on the bill avoided deep cuts in funding for the State Department and U.S. foreign aid, but the bill required a number of conflict-ridden countries to meet strict conditions before they received assistance.

The bill provided $53.5 billion, a combined total of the base budget and money for overseas contingency operations (OCO), which funded operations mainly in Afghanistan and Iraq. The total was more than would have been provided under either the House or Senate versions. It was $5.2 billion, or nearly 11 percent, more than was provided in fiscal 2011 (PL 112-10), although it was $6.2 billion less than Obama had requested.

Much of the increase above fiscal 2011 came in the contingency operations account, which was bumped up to $11.2 billion from the $8.7 billion proposed in the Senate bill. The base budget was $42.3 billion, between amounts the Senate and House panels had sought. (Another $510 million was paid for by rescissions from previous funding.)

Under the debt limit deal enacted in August (PL 112-25), the State–Foreign Operations account was lumped in with Defense, Homeland Security, Military Construction, and Veterans Affairs in a competition for dollars. By shifting money to the contingency account, which was not limited under the security spending cap, appropriators were able to preserve more funding for the State Department and for foreign assistance.

The governments that faced the most scrutiny under the bill included Pakistan and Egypt. The bill also tightened the reins on aid to the Palestinian Authority. The bill omitted some provisions advocated by House Republicans regarding the United Nations, including proposals to restructure how the United States paid its dues and to block all funding to the U.N. Population Fund (UNFPA).

The legislation appropriated $35 million for the UNFPA on the condition that none of the money go to funding abortion. It also prohibited other aid money from going to abortion services but did not include more controversial language sought by House Republicans to reimpose the so-called Mexico City policy, which barred funding to any international aid group that funded or promoted abortion as a method of family planning.

On the flip side, the bill left out language added by Senate Democrats that would have permanently blocked the Mexico City policy.

The measure did withhold 15 percent of the funds for U.N. agencies until audits were made fully available to the United States and were published on a website. In total, U.S. contributions to the United Nations and other international organizations were $2.6 billion down from the $3.3 billion the president requested for fiscal 2012.

The bill tracked closely with the Senate version in authorizing and partially funding capital increases for the World Bank and four associated regional development banks. Conferees also dropped Republican-backed language to rescind a line of credit of more than $100 million to the International Monetary Fund (IMF). Congress approved the credit line in 2009. GOP members objected to providing U.S. funds to help bail out some of Europe's debt-ridden economies.

HOUSE SUBCOMMITTEE ACTION

The State–Foreign Operations Appropriations Subcommittee gave voice vote approval July 27 to a draft bill that would have slashed discretionary funding to $47.2 billion, including $39.6 billion in regular funding and $7.6 billion for overseas contingencies.

The bill included tough conditions on assistance to countries (other than Israel) in the Middle East and South Asia and curbs on funds going to a number of multilateral institutions and would have codified the Mexico City policy in law.

According to a committee aide, the bill would have cut nearly $700 million in aid from the president's $1.1 billion request for Pakistan. To get the remaining assistance, Islamabad would have been required to make demonstrable progress in combating extremist groups, investigate how Osama bin Laden was able to hide in Pakistan, and allow U.S. military trainers to return to the country.

The draft sought to condition military and economic assistance to Egypt on the secretary of state's certification that the government was adhering to its peace treaty with Israel, which received full funding with no strings attached. To receive its funding, Egypt also could not be controlled by foreign terrorists, which under certain interpretations could include the popular Muslim Brotherhood.

The legislation took aim at one of Republicans' favorite targets, the United Nations, providing $3 billion for U.N. dues and peacekeeping operations, $500 million less than requested. It would have prohibited funding for the U.N. Human Rights Council, a body that included many countries notorious for human rights abuses, as well as the U.N. Population Fund and a U.N. panel on climate change.

The draft also would have rescinded a $108 billion tranche of funding the United States committed to in 2009 to help expand the borrowing capacity of the IMF. The IMF was a key player in responding to the international banking collapse and the European Union sovereign debt crisis, but it had alienated some Republicans with its bailouts of countries such as Greece, which they considered to be irresponsible.

SENATE COMMITTEE ACTION

The Senate Appropriations Committee approved its bill (S 1601—S Rept 112-85) by a vote of 28–2 on September 21, after adding language on the Palestinians and proposing to permanently lift the Mexico City policy. The $50.1 billion bill included $44.6 billion in discretionary funds and provided $8.7 billion for overseas contingency operations (OCO).

During the markup, the committee:

- Adopted by voice vote an amendment by Lindsey Graham, R-S.C., aimed at forcing the administration to react to a push by the Palestinian Authority for U.N. recognition, absent an agreement negotiated with Israel. The proposal directed the secretary of state to make recommendations to congressional appropriators, particularly with respect to closing the Washington, D.C., office of the Palestine Liberation Organization.
- Adopted, 18–12, an amendment by Frank R. Lautenberg, D-N.J., to codify in statute Obama's lifting of the Mexico City ban at the start of his administration. "It's time to stop playing politics with women's lives," Lautenberg said, while Lindsey Graham, R-S.C., warned that the language had no chance in the GOP-led House.

The committee bill included:

- $14 billion for the State Department, plus more than $4 billion in the OCO account.
- $1.4 billion for the U.S. Agency for International Development (USAID), plus $106 million for OCO.
- $19.6 billion in bilateral economic assistance, plus $1.5 billion in OCO funds. The total included $7.9 billion for global health programs, $2.6 billion for development assistance, and $4.4 billion for the Economic Support Fund, including $1.2 billion from OCO.
- $5.3 billion for foreign military financing, plus $990 million from the OCO account.
- $2.9 billion for international financial institutions.

The Senate bill contained restrictions on assistance to certain countries, including requirements for Egypt related to free and fair elections. All funds to Pakistan depended on the government's cooperation with the United States in the war against terrorism, including against the Haqqani network and al Qaeda. It would have provided $1 billion for the Pakistan Counterinsurgency Capability Fund.

CONFERENCE AND FINAL ACTION

House and Senate appropriators negotiated a final version of the State–Foreign Operations bill as part of the nine-bill end-of-year omnibus package. The conferees filed their report on the omnibus (H Rept 112-331) on December 15. The House adopted the report, 296–121, on December 16, and the Senate cleared the bill, 67–32, the following day.

MAJOR PROVISIONS

Following are the bill's main components of the legislation:

State Department. $13.4 billion for department operations. The amount was a cut of $2.6 billion from fiscal 2011, but the OCO account provided an additional $4.5 billion for a total of $17.8 billion. About two-thirds of the combined funds, $11 billion, was devoted to diplomatic and consular programs, including security protection.

USAID. $1.3 billion for the operating expenses of the USAID plus $255 million from the OCO account, equal to fiscal 2011 funding.

Global health. $8.2 billion for global health and child survival, about $340 million more than in fiscal 2011. The total included $5.9 billion to combat HIV/AIDS, with $1.1 billion of it going to the Global Fund to Fight AIDS, Tuberculosis, and Malaria. The conference report specified that none of the funds could be used for needle-exchange programs.

International financial institutions. $2.6 billion, an increase of about $675 million over fiscal 2011 funding. The total included $1.9 billion for the World Bank.

Bilateral economic and military assistance. $3 billion for the Economic Support Fund plus $2.8 billion from the OCO account, about $180 million less than in fiscal 2011; and $2.5 billion for development assistance, equal to the fiscal 2011 level. The bill also provided $5.2 billion in foreign military financing plus $1.1 billion from OCO funding, about $940 million more than in the previous year. The bill included $1.6 billion for migration and refugee assistance plus about $230 million from OCO, $1.1 billion more than in fiscal 2011.

Assistance for key countries included:

- $850 million in counterinsurgency funds within the OCO account for Pakistan, with restrictions. Lawmakers already had frozen nearly $700 million in counterinsurgency assistance to Pakistan as part of the fiscal 2012 defense authorization bill (PL 112-81) until the secretaries of defense and state reported on Pakistan's efforts to counter the smuggling of homemade bomb material into Afghanistan, as well as to fight extremist groups within its borders. The appropriations bill added to those restrictions, blocking all but development aid to Pakistan until the secretary of state certified that a range of conditions had been met, including cooperating with the United States in counterterrorism efforts and issuing visas for U.S. military trainers and aid workers in a timely manner. The secretary could waive the requirements on national security grounds. An enterprise fund for Pakistan, which was included in the Senate draft, did not make the bill's final cut.

- $3.1 billion in military assistance to Israel.
- $1.6 billion in aid for Egypt, including $1.3 billion for military grants and $250 million in economic assistance. But given the uncertainty surrounding the future leadership in Cairo, lawmakers defied the White House by setting a range of conditions on aid to Egypt, which was second only to Israel as a foreign aid recipient. Funds for Egypt could not be released until the secretary of state certified that the government was living up to its obligations under the 1979 peace treaty with Israel. Before providing any military aid, the secretary also had to certify that the Egyptian government was supporting the transition to civilian rule. As with Pakistan, these restrictions included a national security waiver.
- The bill authorized debt relief for Egypt, a high priority for Cairo, as well as the creation of new "enterprise funds" to encourage private investment in Egypt, Tunisia, and Jordan.
- Most of the $700 million requested for the Palestinian Authority. However, the governing body for the West Bank territory could not receive any economic support funding, which had been a key factor in the territory's growing economy, if it became a full member state in the United Nations or any associated agency after the date of the bill's enactment. That meant the Palestinian Authority got a pass for joining the U.N. Educational, Scientific and Cultural Organization in October, before the bill went into effect.
- $11.2 billion was authorized for the OCO account, $2.5 billion more than requested. This reflected the decision to shift funding for a number of programs, including those noted above, to this specific account. There was no separate OCO account in the fiscal 2011 appropriations.

Fiscal 2013 Intelligence Authorization

Congress cleared a fiscal 2013 intelligence authorization bill at the end of the session. It was the fourth straight fiscal year that lawmakers had sent the president an authorization bill, following six calendar years during which Congress was unable to agree on a policy measure for the intelligence community. President Obama signed the bill into law January 14, 2013 (S 3454—PL 112-277).

Leaders of the House and Senate Intelligence committees worked to make the legislation relatively noncontroversial, reasoning that it was the only opportunity for lawmakers to put their stamp on spy agency budgets and policies.

The process began smoothly, but near year's end, the bill became caught up in a dispute among senators over efforts to crack down on leaks of classified information after a spate of high-profile spy operation disclosures during the summer of 2012. In the end, lawmakers agreed to delete the most controversial provisions, opening the way for the bill to clear.

The measure authorized funding for sixteen U.S. intelligence agencies, including the Office of the Director of National Intelligence (DNI), the Central Intelligence Agency (CIA), and the National Security Agency (NSA), as well as for foreign intelligence activities of the Federal Bureau of Investigation (FBI); the departments of Defense, State and Homeland Security; and other agencies.

Although the figures were classified, the final version of the legislation authorized funds below the fiscal 2012 budget but above Obama's request, according to the leaders of the House and Senate Intelligence panels. Obama called for a total of $71.8 billion for the spy agencies for fiscal 2013, about $6.8 billion less than the level for fiscal 2011, the most recent declassified budget total.

HOUSE COMMITTEE ACTION

After meeting behind closed doors May 17, the House Select Committee on Intelligence announced that it had voted 19–0 to approve a fiscal 2013 intelligence bill (HR 5743—H Rept 112-490). The committee said that while the bill would cut total funding, it would boost resources for counterintelligence against foreign spies and protect commercial satellite contracts from some proposed cuts.

Most of the details were classified. The committee said the new bill was "significantly below last year's enacted budget but up modestly from the president's budget request."

According to the panel, the measure proposed to freeze total personnel at the fiscal 2012 level while authorizing a funding increase for counterintelligence against foreign spies and bolstering counterterrorism efforts. It also sought to boost oversight of spending by domestic intelligence agencies and to authorize a new Defense Clandestine Service under the Pentagon. The new agency was intended to reorganize the department's human intelligence collection, according to C. A. Dutch Ruppersberger of Maryland, the panel's ranking Democrat. Not all the money for the agency was authorized, pending additional information from the administration.

Ruppersberger also noted a restoration of some of the proposed cuts to commercial imagery, referring to the administration's reported request to reduce funding from $540 million to $250 million for commercial satellite contracts. The intelligence community and the military used those contracts to supplement their own satellites.

HOUSE FLOOR ACTION

The House passed the bill by a vote of 386–28 on May 31. During the debate, the House:

- Adopted by voice vote an amendment by Michigan Democrat John Conyers Jr. to require the DNI to provide Congress with an assessment of the consequences of a military strike against Iran within sixty days of the legislation's enactment. A cadre of Republicans from both chambers had been calling for stiffer provisions that would require Obama to become more confrontational with Iran over its nuclear program.

- Adopted by voice vote an amendment from Henry Cuellar, D-Texas, to authorize the director of national intelligence to share border security information with Canada and Mexico.
- Adopted by voice vote an amendment by Republican Sue Myrick of North Carolina to require a report from the director of national intelligence that would identify and assess various risks in information technology supply chains.
- Rejected, 180–235, a motion to recommit the bill to the committee and report it back immediately with an amendment that would require the heads of the intelligence community to prevent intelligence and information about U.S. military capability from being stolen by or improperly transferred to a foreign state or state sponsor of terrorism.

SENATE COMMITTEE ACTION

The Senate Select Intelligence Committee voted 14–1 to approve its version of the bill (S 3454—S Rept 112-192) in a closed-door markup July 24. Chair Dianne Feinstein, D-Calif., said in a written statement that the bill "authorizes intelligence funding to counter terrorist threats, prevent proliferation of weapons of mass destruction, enhance counterintelligence, conduct covert actions, and collect and analyze intelligence around the globe."

The markup came amid a growing concern over leaks prompted by recent coverage in the *New York Times* that cited anonymous administration officials. The coverage focused on the administration's use of unmanned aerial vehicles in Yemen and Pakistan to kill those suspected of terrorism and the administration's involvement in the computer worm known as Stuxnet, a cybertool used to disrupt Iran's nuclear-enrichment facilities.

Leaders of both the House and Senate panels decided they needed to act to halt the flow of classified information into news outlets. They collaborated on language that was added to the Senate bill and approved by the Intelligence Committee.

The most controversial provisions would have placed restrictions on the intelligence community's ability to provide background briefings to reporters unless certain conditions were met, required the DNI to establish a procedure for taking away the pensions of former intelligence agency employees who violated their nondisclosure agreements, and prohibited former government officials with security clearances from taking on a commentary role with the media for one year after departing the intelligence community.

SENATE FLOOR AND FINAL ACTION

The Senate passed the bill by voice vote December 28 after a prolonged delay over objections by critics of the leak provisions, and the House cleared the measure, 373–29, on December 31.

Sen. Ron Wyden, D-Ore., had placed a hold on the bill over those provisions, saying that he shared his colleagues' concerns about leaks but that the provisions would do more harm than good. Other senators joined him in publicly criticizing the leaks language.

Feinstein said she would have been willing to remove some of the provisions drawing the most heated objections to advance the legislation, but Republicans objected to that idea. Eventually, she and her panel's vice chair, Saxby Chambliss, R-Ga., agreed to take out the most controversial provisions.

Iran Sanctions

Congress in 2012 pushed through two rounds of legislation toughening economic sanctions against Iran in hopes of forcing that country's government to end its alleged nuclear weapons program. Congress cleared the first measure, the Iran Threat Reduction and Syria Human Rights Act (HR 1905—PL 112-158) just before the August recess. Shortly before that bill cleared, President Barack Obama imposed new sanctions of his own through an executive order.

Leading sanctions hawks in the Senate, who said the August bill did not go far enough, succeeded in attaching additional sanctions to the 2013 Defense Department authorization bill (HR 4310—PL 112-239), which cleared in December and which Obama signed on January 2, 2013. The Iran provisions were known as the Iran Freedom and Counter-Proliferation Act. *(Defense authorization, p. 307)*

The August stand-alone measure expanded the list of activities that could trigger sanctions against third parties to include providing insurance for vessels shipping Iranian oil, purchasing Iranian debt, and supporting port facility construction and management. Under the bill, any commercial activity with Iran's oil and natural gas sectors—including financial services, insurance, technology, transportation and infrastructure—was deemed a sanctionable offense. The measure also increased sanctions against entities dealing with the Iranian Revolutionary Guard Corps, Tehran's paramilitary wing.

In a key provision, the bill tightened limits on payments to Iran through foreign banks. It required that any money owed to Iran for legal transactions (such as for oil sales), be placed in an account in the country with primary jurisdiction over the foreign bank making the transaction. The purpose was to prevent Iran from obtaining hard currency for its oil sales; instead, Iran would have to use the money earned from oil sales to buy products in the countries that bought Iranian oil.

Ileana Ros-Lehtinen, R-Fla., chair of the House Foreign Affairs Committee and the bill's sponsor, said the legislation represented the strongest sanctions ever enacted against Iran. However, some hawks in both parties wanted even stronger language, for example listing the entire Iranian energy sector as a "zone of primary proliferation concern," as proposed in a separate bill (HR 4317) introduced in the House in March. Instead, that language was included in a nonbinding section of the enacted measure, stating it was the "Sense of Congress" that the energy sector qualified as such a zone.

SENATE FLOOR ACTION

The Senate on May 21 passed by voice vote its version of the House-approved measure (HR 1905) to expand the 1996 Iran Sanctions Act by adding an assortment of penalties for those doing business with Iran, including new sanctions against those anywhere in the world who knowingly entered into ventures with Iran that would help the country to receive nuclear-weapons knowledge or technology. *(1996 sanctions legislation, Congress and the Nation Vol. IX, p. 239)*

Before the vote, supporters inserted the text of a bill (S 2101) reported by the Senate Banking, Housing, and Urban Affairs Committee on February 13. The House version included stronger sanctions, such as denying visas to Iranian government officials with ties to terrorism and blocking U.S. government contact with such officials absent a presidential waiver.

Republicans, including Sen. Lindsey Graham of South Carolina, successfully added language echoing President Obama in saying that all options, including military intervention, remained on the table to prevent Iran from obtaining a nuclear weapon.

But Graham's new language on possible military options prompted another language addition by Rand Paul, R-Ky., that specified that nothing in the bill should be deemed to authorize the use of military force against Iran or Syria. Paul said that he did not object to the addition of language to satisfy Graham. "I'm not saying that military is never an option. I'm just saying you have to have a vote on it," Paul said.

FINAL ACTION

Negotiations between Ros-Lehtinen and Senate Banking Chair Tim Johnson, D-S.D., produced the compromise bill, which the House passed, 421–6, on August 1. The Senate cleared the measure by voice vote later the same evening.

Just hours after Capitol Hill leaders released the compromise bill, the White House followed up with an executive order that focused on many of the same sectors of the Iranian economy. The Obama administration created new tools similar to those in the legislation to crack down on the National Iranian Oil Company. And as the bill did, the administration sought to close loopholes in existing energy sector sanctions to block ways third parties could pay for or ship Iranian oil. The White House also broadened existing sanctions on Iran's petrochemical industry.

In a separate move, the Treasury Department announced it would impose sanctions against two violators of existing laws: the Bank of Kunlun in China and Elaf Islamic Bank in Iraq. Administration officials said July 31 that the two banks had processed significant financial transactions for blacklisted Iranian banks, facilitating the movement of millions of dollars that might have been used for proliferation activities.

MAJOR PROVISIONS

Following are major provisions of the 2012 stand-alone law (PL 112-158):

Petroleum-Related Sanctions

The bill expanded the number of activities that could trigger sanctions to include making certain petroleum resource agreements with Iran, purchasing Iranian debt, and supporting port facility construction and management. It also lowered the dollar threshold that could trigger certain sanctions. It targeted any entity that

- Worked in Iran's petroleum, petrochemical, or natural gas sectors.
- Provided goods, services, infrastructure, or technology to Iran's oil and natural gas sectors, including financial services, consulting, and maintenance and repair.
- Conducted oil-for-gold or other swap transactions with Iran.
- Insured or reinsured investments in Iran's oil sector.
- Engaged in joint ventures with the National Iranian Oil Company.
- Engaged in uranium mining with Iran anywhere in the world.

Insurance and Shipping

The bill required sanctions against countries or companies that

- Knowingly sold, leased, or provided a vessel, or provided insurance, reinsurance or any other service for the transport—to or from Iran—of goods that could contribute materially to the Iranian government's nuclear-weapons activities or could support acts of international terrorism. Sanctions could include the confiscation of the entity's property in the United States.
- Provided insurance or reinsurance to the National Iranian Oil Company, the state-run conglomerate at the center of Tehran's energy industry, or to the National Iranian Tanker Company.

- Helped Iran evade oil sanctions through reflagging ships or concealing the origin of Iranian crude. Sanctioned vessels could be prevented from landing at a port in the United States for up to two years.

Central Bank of Iran

The bill codified and strengthened existing sanctions against Iran's central bank:

- Limited the repatriation of currency to the Iranian government for countries that had exemptions from sanctions against the Iranian Central Bank for the purposes of crude-oil purchases, and eliminated pass-through trade via third-party countries.
- Required sanctions against any entity that knowingly purchased, subscribed to, or facilitated the issuance of Iranian sovereign debt, including government bonds, or the debt, including bonds, of any entity owned or controlled by the government of Iran.

Human Rights

- Required sanctions against Iranian government officials or those acting on the government's behalf—including members of paramilitary organizations—that the president determined are responsible for violations of human rights after the June 12, 2009, elections in that country. The measure focused in particular on the use of information technology to suppress citizens.
- Required sanctions against those who provided information technology, goods or services, or weapons or ammunition that contributed to the suppression of human rights in Iran. Sanctions under the bill could also apply to entities engaged in censorship.

Revolutionary Guards

- Provided for sanctions against U.S. and foreign commercial enterprises that knowingly conducted business with any entity owned or controlled by Iran's Islamic Revolutionary Guard Corps as well as any instrumentality, subsidiary, affiliate, or agent of Iran's Revolutionary Guards.
- Authorized sanctions against individual members of the Revolutionary Guards, including restricting property and financial transactions and denying U.S. visas.

Syria Sanctions

The measure codified and authorized a number of sanctions targeting human rights abusers in Syria, including:

- Those responsible for the commission of serious human rights abuses against Syrian citizens or their family members. Penalties included restrictions on financial and property transactions.
- Companies or entities that provided the Syrian government with goods or technologies likely to be used to commit human rights abuses, including firearms or ammunition, rubber bullets, police batons, pepper or chemical sprays, stun grenades, electro-shock weapons, tear gas, water cannons, and surveillance technology.

Other Provisions

- Denied visas to Iranian government officials with ties to Iran's nuclear development program, terrorism, or the commission of serious human rights abuses against citizens of Iran or their family members.
- Tightened civil penalties against parent companies of foreign subsidiaries of U.S. institutions found to have violated sanctions.
- Required filings with the Securities and Exchange Commission to disclose business ties with Iran.
- Barred visas for any Iranian citizen seeking to attend school in the United States to further a career in the energy sector of Iran or in nuclear science or nuclear engineering.
- Stated that nothing in the bill should be construed as a declaration of war or an authorization of the use of force against Iran or Syria.

AMENDMENT TO DEFENSE BILL

Building on their success at the end of 2011—when they persuaded the Senate to attach tough sanctions against Iran's Central Bank to the fiscal 2012 Pentagon authorization bill—Democrat Robert Menendez of New Jersey and Republican Mark S. Kirk of Illinois in November introduced an amendment to the Senate version of the fiscal 2013 defense authorization bill (S 3254) that blacklisted Iran's energy, shipping, and shipbuilding sectors as well as its ports.

Although the White House succeeded in watering down Congress's latest Iran sanctions initiative, lawmakers demonstrated their determination to press for a tougher policy toward Iran by forcing a reluctant administration to accept another round of sanctions. A Senate amendment containing the new sanctions was adopted without a dissenting vote. The latest measure, attached to the annual defense authorization bill, was intended to put additional economic pressure on Tehran as it considered a new round of diplomatic negotiations on its nuclear program. *(Fiscal 2012 defense bill, p. 299; fiscal 2013 defense bill, p. 307)*

Menendez and Kirk had initially considered restrictions that would have effectively imposed an international trade embargo by requiring all countries to reduce nonpetroleum sales to Iran significantly. The senators also wanted to force other countries to freeze Iranian foreign currency reserves.

The administration warned that such moves could cause a diplomatic backlash. With the help of several influential senators—Armed Services Chair Carl Levin, D-Mich., the manager of the defense bill; Foreign Relations Chair John Kerry, D-Mass.; and Banking Chair Tim Johnson, D-S.D.—the White House persuaded Kirk and Menendez to delete or dilute some of their toughest language. The measure barred all transactions with Tehran's energy, shipping, and shipbuilding sectors and its ports, as well as sales to Iran of metals including graphite, aluminum, steel, and metallurgical coal that are used in those sectors and in other manufacturing.

The legislation continued to allow countries to buy oil from Iran if they demonstrated every 180 days that they had significantly reduced their purchases or for 120 days if a nation "faced exceptional circumstances that prevented it from significantly reducing purchases."

It also banned the sale to Iran of certain metals, including graphite, aluminum, steel, and metallurgical coal used in the energy and shipbuilding sectors, as well as other industrial processes. It designated Iran's state broadcaster and its president as human rights abusers for their broadcasting of forced confessions and show trials, blocking their assets and preventing other entities from doing business with them and banning any travel to the United States.

Much of the new sanctions language came from proposals left out of legislation that President Obama reluctantly signed into law in August. That law expanded sanctions targeting financial institutions, including Iran's Central Bank, that Tehran used to facilitate its oil trade and maintain its economy.

The Senate adopted the Menendez amendment to S 3254 on November 30 on a **key vote of 94–0 (R 43–0; D 49–0; I 2–0).** *(2012 key votes, p. 803)*

The Senate provisions survived almost entirely intact in the final version of the defense authorization bill. President Obama signed PL 112-239 into law on January 2, 2013.

Fiscal 2013 State–Foreign Operations Funding

For the seventh year in a row (ever since fiscal 2007), appropriations for the State Department and other foreign operations were included in an omnibus spending bill for fiscal 2013 rather than in freestanding legislation. Moreover, because the fiscal 2103 spending bill for state and foreign operations did not get beyond committee markups, money for those programs was folded into a continuing resolution (H J Res 117—PL 112-175) signed by the president just three days before the October 1 start of the fiscal year. *(Continuing resolution, p. 180)*

LEGISLATIVE ACTION

House and Senate appropriators had distinctly different views on how much to spend on State Department operations and U.S. foreign affairs, with the Senate committee proposing about 8 percent more than its House counterpart.

The House Appropriations Committee agreed by voice vote May 17 to approve a bill (HR5857—H Rept 112-494) that would have provided $48.5 billion, $5 billion below the fiscal 2012 level and $6.3 billion below President Barack Obama's request. The total met the president's request for $8.2 billion for overseas contingency operations, related mainly to the wars in Afghanistan and Iraq.

In a familiar fight, the panel defeated—largely along party lines—proposals from three Democrats to allow U.S. funding for the United Nations Population Fund. The underlying bill blocked money for the fund, which oversaw reproductive health programs in the developing world.

An amendment from New York's Nita M. Lowey, the top Democrat on the State-Foreign Operations Subcommittee, would have provided $39 million for the U.N. fund if certain conditions were met. Her proposal, rejected 23–27, included a ban on U.S. contributions going to China, whose family-planning policies were widely criticized. Lowey's amendment also would have struck language in the bill to reinstate the "Mexico City policy," which prohibited funding for international aid groups that provided abortions, promoted their legalization, provided counseling on the termination of pregnancies, or promoted abortion as a method of family planning.

Senate appropriators voted 29–1 on May 24 to approve a $52.3 billion bill (S 3241—S Rept 172), well above the House amount but still $1.2 billion below the fiscal 2012 level.

In a unanimous 30–0 vote, the Senate committee agreed to withhold $33 million from the $250 million in the bill for military aid to Pakistan to protest the country's treason conviction of a doctor who helped the United States find al Qaeda leader Osama bin Laden.

Senate appropriators broke ranks with the House panel by including $44.5 million for the U.N. Population Fund. The panel not only omitted the reinstatement of the Mexico City policy, it adopted, 18–12, a proposal from New Jersey Democrat Frank R. Lautenberg to allow U.S. funding for international aid groups that provided information on abortion.

In another difference with the House, Senate appropriators included $1 billion for a new account to help respond to political transitions taking place across North Africa and the Middle East as a result of the Arab Spring. The administration asked for $770 million for the fund. The House committee denied the administration's request.

International Treaty on Disability Rights

For decades, treaties negotiated at the United Nations have fared poorly once they reached the U.S. Senate for ratification. Some treaties, such as the Law of the Sea treaty, negotiated in 1982, never even reached the full Senate for a vote.

Disability rights and human rights advocates had hoped that a new treaty, the U.N. Convention on the Rights of Persons with Disabilities, might fare better because it was modeled after the U.S. Americans with Disabilities Act and therefore would have little, if any, direct impact in the United States. The treaty was intended to bring other countries up to U.S. standards on the treatment of persons with disabilities. It was widely supported by disability rights groups and veterans' organizations, as well as former officials from both Republican and Democratic administrations. Republican Sens. John McCain of Arizona and John Barrasso of Wyoming were prominent backers, as was former Senate Republican leader (and 1996 presidential candidate) Robert Dole of Kansas, who had been the prime sponsor of the U.S. disabilities law.

But the treaty ran into vociferous opposition from conservative groups, which launched a nationwide campaign portraying it as an infringement on U.S. sovereignty. Opponents also warned that the treaty would enable international tribunals to intrude in domestic policy on issues such as child care and abortion.

Among the leading opponents was Heritage Action, the lobbying arm of the conservative think tank Heritage Foundation. The group warned senators that it would keep score of those who backed the treaty. Many Republicans, in fact, had signed a letter to Majority Leader Harry Reid, D-Nev., that they would oppose any treaty taken up during the lame duck-session of Congress that followed the November election.

As the Senate prepared for debate after Thanksgiving, one Republican critic, Mike Lee of Utah, said opponents had the votes to block the treaty. Even the presence on the floor of Dole, now eighty-nine years old, did not change the outcome when the Senate voted on December 4. Thirty-eight Republicans voted against the treaty, enough to deny it the two-thirds majority necessary for ratification. Just one of the thirty-six GOP senators who had signed the letter to Reid, Scott P. Brown of Massachusetts (who had just lost a reelection bid), voted for the disability treaty.

Senate Foreign Relations Chair John Kerry of Massachusetts, who had shepherded the bill through his committee by a 13–6 vote, declared it "one of the saddest days I've seen in almost twenty-eight years in the Senate."

The Senate December 4, 2013, rejected the treaty (Treaty Doc 112-7) by a **key vote of 61–38 (R 8–38; D 51–0; I 2–0).** *(2012 key votes, p. 803)*

CHAPTER 5

Defense Policy

Introduction	263
Chronology of Action on Defense Policy	267
2009–2010	267
2011–2012	296

Defense Policy

President Barack Obama's first term appeared to mark a transition period for the U.S. defense establishment after the long wars and massive buildup of his predecessor, President George W. Bush (2001–2009). The winding down of U.S. military involvement in Iraq, a temporary "surge" of U.S. forces in Afghanistan before a planned withdrawal in 2014, and the early stages of defense spending cuts mandated by Congress all suggested that the military and its missions might look substantially different—and certainly leaner—in the years to come.

Perhaps the gravest warning sign for the Pentagon was the congressional inability, or unwillingness, to shield it (and related national security agencies, such as the Central Intelligence Agency) from across-the-board budget cuts that newly empowered conservative Republicans demanded throughout the government, especially after their significant gains in the 2010 midterm elections. These cuts were in addition to major reductions advocated by defense secretaries Robert M. Gates and Leon Panetta as part of their plans to reform the military budget.

A government-wide budget deal negotiated in 2011 called for reducing previously projected defense spending by $487 billion over the following decade (a cut of about 9 percent, according to some estimates). More immediately, the 2011 Budget Control Act (PL 112-25) included the Pentagon in potential across-the-board spending cuts, known as the "sequester," as part of the so-called "fiscal cliff" at the end of 2012. *(Budget Control Act, p. 160; fiscal cliff, p. 185)*

Few expected at the time the 2011 deal was negotiated that the sequester cuts actually would go into effect. President Obama and many others portrayed the budget deal as a forcing mechanism to achieve a broader agreement on spending and taxes. The broader deal never emerged, however, in large part because many House Republicans elected in 2010 were more interested in cutting federal spending—even defense spending—than in negotiating agreements they insisted would allow the government to continue growing.

Congress delayed the mandatory sequester cuts until March 2013 but failed to prevent them from going into effect, thus subjecting most Pentagon spending for the remainder of fiscal 2013 to an across-the-board cut of 7.8 percent. The Pentagon made thousands of cutbacks in response, including furloughing all of its 800,000 civilian employees for twenty-two days.

Despite the cuts, the Congressional Budget Office estimated early in 2013 that defense spending would continue to grow through the remainder of the decade, but at a much lower rate than in previous years and likely below the level of inflation. Hagel, like his predecessors, warned that persistent budget-cutting would force the country to choose between reducing the size of its military forces (particularly the army) and modernizing its planes, ships, and other armaments.

WINDING DOWN WARS

The political maneuvering over the budget took place in the midst of—and in part reflected—new uncertainties about the U.S. military's mission in the era following expensive U.S. adventures in Afghanistan and Iraq. The military remained sized and equipped to fight major land and sea battles, as well as to suppress terrorism and insurgencies such as those the United States attempted to defeat in the years after the September 2001 terrorist attacks in New York City and just outside Washington, D.C.

REFERENCES

Discussion of defense policy for the years 1945–1964 may be found in *Congress and the Nation Vol. I*, pp. 237–334; for the years 1965–1968, *Congress and the Nation Vol. II*, pp. 827–890; for the years 1969–1972, *Congress and the Nation Vol. III*, pp. 191–252; for the years 1973–1976, *Congress and the Nation Vol. IV*, pp. 153–197; for the years 1977–1980, *Congress and the Nation Vol. V*, pp. 125–176; for the years 1981–1984, *Congress and the Nation Vol. VI*, pp. 201–257; for the years 1985–1988, *Congress and the Nation Vol. VII*, pp. 273–340; for the years 1989–1992, *Congress and the Nation Vol. VIII*, pp. 335–412; for the years 1993–1996, *Congress and the Nation Vol. IX*, pp. 253–323; for the years 1997–2000, *Congress and the Nation Vol. X*, pp. 235–311; for the years 2001–2004, *Congress and the Nation Vol. XI*, pp. 303–366; for the years 2005–2008, *Congress and the Nation Vol. XII*, pp. 331–401.

Outlays for National Defense

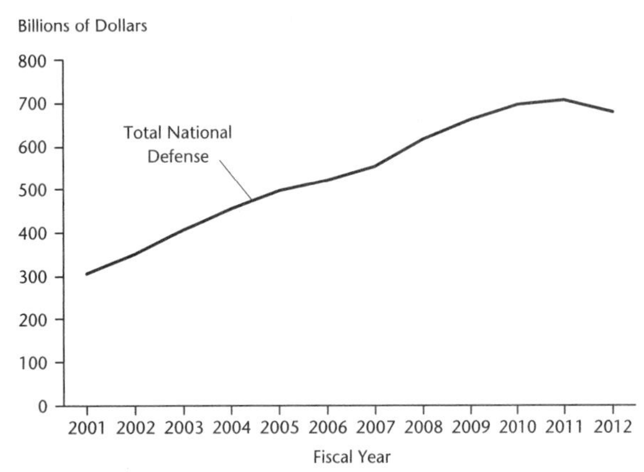

SOURCE: Office of Management and Budget, *Historical Tables, Budget of the United States Government: Fiscal Year 2013* (Washington, D.C.: U.S. Government Printing Office) 2012 Table 3.2.

NOTE: Most of the expenditures, approximately 95 percent, were for military activities of the Department of Defense. Atomic energy defense activities accounted for most of the remainder.

In addition to imposing spending cuts, Congress appeared to end, at least for the time being, the Pentagon's status as the one government agency that could always be assured of having its budget adopted in a timely manner. In the past, the Defense Department's authorization and appropriations bills were always among the very few "must-pass" items capable of surmounting the partisan bickering and legislative gridlock on other issues. But, from 2010 onward, Congress struggled with defense spending, just as it did with every other agency of government. Congress failed to pass independent defense appropriations bills for fiscal years 2011, 2012, and 2013. In each case, Congress did incorporate the equivalent of full spending bills into omnibus bills, but only after the October 1 start of each fiscal year.

By the time Obama entered office, however, the costs and duration of the Iraq and Afghanistan wars clearly had sapped public support for similar military campaigns overseas. Polls repeatedly showed that Americans were tired of foreign wars and were increasingly eager to focus instead on problems at home. In addition to the human impact—thousands of lives lost or ruined by severe injuries—the government had borrowed heavily to finance the wars. Iraq and Afghanistan had directly cost about $1.4 trillion through fiscal 2012, according to the Congressional Budget Office, with indirect costs (such as interest payments and long-term care for veterans) likely doubling that amount.

The new president's priorities reflected deep public anxieties about Iraq, by far the more deadly and costly of the two wars. Indeed, among the chief promises of his 2008 campaign were to "end" the war in Iraq while achieving a rapid, if unspecified, victory in Afghanistan. Obama did succeed in securing a U.S. military withdrawal from Iraq, but nearly two years later than he had originally hoped. The last U.S. troops crossed from Iraq into Kuwait in December 2011, on schedule with an agreement negotiated with Iraq by the Bush administration. *(Iraq withdrawal, p. 234)*

Even as he was planning the exit from the Iraq conflict he had long opposed, Obama found himself deepening the U.S. military role in the war in Afghanistan. This was the war he told Americans they needed to "win," although he was careful not to define what such a victory would entail. The president shuffled military commanders in Afghanistan and in 2009 ordered a temporary "surge" that boosted the U.S. troop level to a peak of just above 100,000 in March 2011. The surge succeeded in tamping down resistance by the Taliban and other antigovernment forces, and it enabled Afghan security forces to begin taking the lead in many military operations. Obama declared the surge a success and ordered the extra troops home by September 2012, months before the presidential election. Afghanistan remained an unstable place, however, with a weak, corrupt government facing insurgent factions that appeared to be waiting for the last U.S. troops to leave, possibly as early as 2014. *(Afghanistan, p. 229)*

DEFENSE LEADERSHIP CHANGES

President Obama's postelection decision to retain Robert M. Gates as secretary of defense was widely praised at the time. Gates had served as President Bush's defense secretary since December 2006. More important, the retention of Gates brought a measure of stability to the armed forces during the political transition in Washington and the winding down of the war in Iraq. As a Republican serving in a Democratic administration, Gates had credibility both within the military community and across party lines on Capitol Hill. *(Leadership, box, p. 274)*

Gates was a plain-spoken individual who was not afraid to challenge conventional wisdom—a characteristic that unsettled some in Washington but also added political heft to his decisions and his recommendations to the White House. Although a staunch advocate for the military, Gates understood that the nation's fiscal realities would require restraint in defense spending, and he challenged entrenched interests, including those on Capitol Hill, that promoted outdated weapons systems and unnecessary programs.

As defense secretary under President Bush, Gates supervised the U.S "surge" in Iraq—an influx of troops that was at least partly responsible for the dramatic decrease in sectarian violence there starting in 2007. During his tenure in the Obama administration, Gates oversaw the main stages of the U.S. military withdrawal from Iraq (completed six months after he left office) and he orchestrated the troop surge into Afghanistan.

Gates took a leadership role in the 2010 repeal of the "don't ask, don't tell" law that had barred openly gay people

U.S. Defense Secretary Leon Panetta (back row, second from left) attends a symbolic flag-lowering ceremony marking the end of U.S. forces' mission in Iraq at a U.S. army base west of Baghdad, on December 15, 2011.
Source: AFP Photo/Ali Al-Saadi

from serving in the military. Gates accepted the argument that gays should be allowed to serve, but he also wanted the change to be handled carefully, to minimize disruptions and dissension within the ranks. Gates's strong support, along with somewhat less enthusiastic assent from the military chiefs, helped get the repeal legislation through Congress in late 2010, after the midterm elections. The job of implementing the repeal fell to Gates's successor, however. *(Don't ask repeal, p. 288)*

Gates retired after serving for the first two-and-a-half years of Obama's first term. As his replacement, Obama chose Leon Panetta, another widely respected Washington veteran who had served eight terms in the House of Representatives, had been White House chief of staff for President Bill Clinton, and was currently serving as director of the Central Intelligence Agency. Panetta also was a budget expert, having chaired the House Budget Committee and been Clinton's first head of the Office of Management and Budget. Panetta reportedly was reluctant to take the Pentagon job because he wanted to retire to his family walnut farm in California, but ultimately he gave in to presidential persuasion.

Panetta was widely expected to focus much of his attention on controlling Pentagon spending in a new era of budget restraint. Indeed, one of his successes was winning reluctant agreement from military chiefs to the $487 billion in ten-year budget cuts mandated by the 2011 Budget Control Act. "It was no mean feat to lead the Joint Chiefs through the process where you take almost $500 billion out of what they thought they were going to get and keep them all on the reservation and to have them genuinely feel as if they'd played a role in defining how that would happen," Maren Leed, of the Center for Strategic and International Studies, told Reuters news service.

Late in his nineteen-month tenure, however, Panetta issued grave warnings about the impact of the across-the-board reductions that went into effect early in 2013 because the president and Congress could not agree on an alternative. Panetta said the cuts resulted from a "goofy meat-ax approach" that endangered national security.

In February 2013, just before leaving office, Panetta warned that "partisan dysfunction" in Washington was threatening the U.S. economy as well as national security. "My fear is that there is a dangerous and callous attitude that is developing among some Republicans and some Democrats, that these dangerous cuts can be allowed to take place in order to blame the other party for the consequences," Panetta told an audience at Georgetown University. "This is a kind of 'so what?' attitude that says, 'Let's see how bad it can get in order to have the other party blink.'"

As with Gates, Panetta ended up spending a significant portion of his tenure dealing with a sensitive personnel issue, in Panetta's case that of allowing women to serve in combat units. Women increasingly had taken on, or been assigned, roles that put them in or near combat zones, but long-standing practice—and a formal policy dating to 1994—forbade them from serving with units formally engaged in combat. In January 2013, just before leaving office, Panetta ended the policy. "They're fighting and they're dying together. And the time has come for our policies to recognize that reality," he said.

F-22 CANCELLATION

An age-old truism in Washington was that major weapons systems, once begun, were extremely difficult and sometimes almost impossible to bring to an end. Contractors tended to spread work on planes, ships, armored vehicles, and other major programs among dozens or even hundreds of facilities in many states, thus ensuring broad political support for those systems on Capitol Hill, even after Pentagon chiefs wanted to move on to new weapons.

One weapon that for several years seemed to be immune to cancellation turned out to be more vulnerable than some people had thought: the Air Force's F-22 fighter.

After years of planning, the administration of President Bill Clinton (1993–2001) began building F-22 fighters during fiscal 1999. The F-22, known as the Raptor, was designed to be the world's most advanced air-to-air combat aircraft, replacing the Air Force's F-15, which was first introduced in the mid-1970s. (The Air Force also was to receive its version of the F-35 Joint Strike Fighter to replace its F-16s from the same era).

The Bush administration, starting with its fiscal 2006 budget, proposed ending production of the F-22 at 187 planes—far short of the 750 planes the Air Force had originally wanted. Bush's aides insisted 187 planes would be enough to meet the Air Force's needs. In addition, some Pentagon officials cited concerns about the exceptionally high maintenance needs of the F-22, which often had to be grounded for repairs after as little as an hour or two of flying time. The question of how many planes to buy reportedly led to internal disputes within the Pentagon, resulting in the forced resignations in 2008 of the secretary and chief of staff of the Air Force, both of whom wanted more than 187 planes.

Shortly after coming into office, the Obama administration repeated the Bush administration's proposal to end procurement of the F-22 and, instead, simply requested money to shut down production, plus funds to upgrade electronics on existing planes. The Obama White House also threatened to veto any bill that included funding for F-22s in addition to the 187 already procured.

Under that pressure, Congress in 2009 essentially ended funding for additional copies of the plane. While acting on the fiscal 2010 defense authorization bill, the House and Senate Armed Services committees both supported additional funding, but the White House used a veto threat in July to get the money stripped from the final bill (HR 2647—PL 111-84). Congressional supporters of the plane—particularly from Georgia, Texas, and other states where production had been concentrated—made numerous efforts to revive the funding, but none got anywhere.

F-35 ALTERNATIVE ENGINE

For as long as anyone on Capitol Hill could remember, the annual defense authorization and appropriations bills had been favorite targets of legislators for special interest provisions affecting their districts and states. Usually these came in the form of "earmarks" mandating that certain amounts be spent for certain projects that just happened to benefit certain districts. An exceptionally large, and long-running, version of an earmark came to an end during 2011 when Congress stopped including funding for a second, "alternative" engine for the F-35 fighter, being developed as the next generation warplane for the Air Force, Marine Corps, and Navy.

The F-35's main engine was built by defense contractor Pratt and Whitney at its plants in Connecticut. But starting in 1995 Congress pushed the Pentagon to fund an alternative engine as a backup and potential competitor to the Pratt and Whitney model. Work on the second engine was handled by a consortium of GE Transportation and Rolls-Royce, which had plants in Cincinnati and Indianapolis (as well as in England). The Pentagon supported the second engine until 2006, when the Bush administration asked Congress to drop the project. When it came into office, the Obama administration also wanted to kill the second engine. Congress refused and continued funding the engine through 2010. As of 2009, according to the Congressional Research Service, Congress had provided about $2.5 billion for the second engine.

The second engine debate finally wound down in April 2011 when the Pentagon, taking advantage of the lack of congressional action on a fiscal 2011 defense appropriations bill, announced an end to the program. Congress then included no funding for the second engine in its fiscal 2012 defense appropriations bill, which was folded into an omnibus spending measure for the year. GE and Rolls Royce initially decided to continue the program at their own expense but dropped that effort in December 2011.

Despite the debate over the second engine and repeated cost overruns, Congress consistently supported the main F-35 project, which was the Pentagon's largest single procurement program with a planned total of 2,456 planes: the F-35A for the Air Force, the F-35B for the Marine Corps, and the F-35C for the Navy. For example, the fiscal 2013 defense authorization bill (PL 112-329) included $5.4 billion for procurement ($1 billion below the president's request) and $2.7 billion for research and development on the plane.

Chronology of Action on Defense Policy

2009–2010

Despite its overall focus on the economy and health care, Congress managed to accomplish several important national security–related tasks during the first two years of President Barack Obama's first term.

Major accomplishments included Senate ratification of a nuclear arms control treaty—called New START—with Russia, repeal of the "don't ask, don't tell" rule that had prevented gays from serving openly in the military, and approval of an overhaul of the Pentagon's procedures for acquiring expensive new weapons systems.

Congress also ended funding for the Air Force's F-22 warplane—which the Bush and Obama administrations both wanted to cancel. Much less to the administration's liking, Congress prevented Obama from keeping his 2008 campaign promise to close the detention center at Guantánamo Bay, Cuba, which had held hundreds of suspected terrorists. Congress also made it virtually impossible for the administration to bring the terrorism suspects to the United States for trial in federal courts.

The presence of Democratic majorities in both chambers—majorities that generally supported the first Democratic president in eight years—was one factor contributing to the list of accomplishments. Another was the continued presence of Robert M. Gates at the Pentagon through the first half of 2011. Obama asked Gates, a highly regarded Republican appointed by President George W. Bush, to continue as defense secretary, and Gates's influence with members of both parties on Capitol Hill served Obama well. Yet another factor was the determination by administration officials and Democratic leaders to take advantage of the lame duck session following the 2010 midterm elections that brought Republicans to power in the House. The New START treaty and the "don't ask" legislation—along with the defense authorization bill for fiscal 2011—all came in that lame duck session. Congress managed to pass the regular defense authorization and appropriations during 2009 and 2010, in contrast to the legislative gridlock that became a regular feature once conservative Republicans took control of the House in 2011.

More broadly, the 111th Congress also took place in the context of new phases in the two major conflicts stemming from the September 2001 terrorist attacks against New York and Washington, D.C. Keeping his 2008 campaign promise, Obama withdrew the last U.S. troops from Iraq in December 2011, leaving behind an increasingly authoritarian and sectarian-minded government in Baghdad over which Washington now exerted little control. Even as U.S. troops were leaving Iraq, more were headed to Afghanistan under a temporary "surge" the president ordered in late 2009 in hopes of reversing a deteriorating security situation there. The more than 30,000 extra troops came home in stages, with the last ones leaving Afghanistan two months before the 2012 U.S. presidential elections. Even so, more than 60,000 U.S. troops remained in Afghanistan, fighting what had become America's longest-ever war.

Congress regularly approved funding for the two wars, with only modest levels of controversy. House Democrats attempted to use a fiscal 2010 war supplemental to highlight the fact that spending on the wars was coming at the expense of domestic priorities; that effort may have gained some sympathy in certain congressional districts, but it had no chance of becoming law. Through 2010, money for the wars was included in supplemental spending bills rather than through the regular appropriations process. This had the effect of making the defense budget appear smaller than it really was.

Defense Acquisitions Rules

Congress raced early in 2009 to get a bill overhauling the Pentagon's acquisition process to the White House by Memorial Day, the target President Barack Obama had set for the legislation. The bill cleared without a "nay" vote in either chamber, and Obama signed it May 22 (S 454—PL 111-23).

The legislation was aimed at getting a handle on the cost overruns and project delays that plagued many Defense Department programs. The Government Accountability

Office (GAO) issued a report in March stating that the ninety-six major defense initiatives studied would cost $1.6 trillion, $296 billion more than initially estimated. The average delay in providing initial capabilities for a program was twenty-one months. The GAO said that such programs were started with inadequate technical knowledge, resulting in unrealistically low estimates of the time and money needed to accomplish goals.

The bill targeted the largest programs, which made up about 20 percent of the Defense Department's total procurement. It created new oversight procedures for the procurement process, which supporters said they hoped would limit cost growth, deliver weapons and other equipment to war fighters on time, and prevent conflicts of interest within major acquisitions programs.

SENATE ACTION

The Senate Armed Services Committee voted 26–0 on April 2 to approve an acquisition overhaul bill (S 454) written by Democratic Chair Carl Levin of Michigan and the panel's ranking Republican, John McCain of Arizona. The committee gave voice vote approval to a substitute amendment that modified several parts of the original measure that had drawn criticism from the Pentagon and the defense industry. Levin said the substitute did not incorporate all the changes, and he acknowledged the bill would make some people uncomfortable. "But the acquisition system needs tough medicine," he said.

The bill proposed a number of steps to attack soaring weapons costs and delayed deliveries. It required the Pentagon to take advantage of competition as much as possible in the acquisition of its top-dollar weapons and to ensure that two or more teams of companies produced prototypes of any major new weapon. In response to industry concerns, the substitute amendment allowed a waiver for that provision if the costs outweighed the benefits.

The substitute, as with the original bill, proposed barring arrangements that involved organizational conflicts of interest. But in response to an industry recommendation, the modified version allowed for companies to set up separate affiliates, segregated from the parent firm, to perform systems engineering functions.

The substitute also required that programs with critical cost problems be terminated unless the Pentagon could certify that the initiative was indispensable.

The Senate passed the bill, 93–0, on May 7, 2009. The Congressional Budget Office (CBO) estimated that the measure would cost about $90 million in fiscal 2010 through 2014. CBO was unable to quantify how much any gains in acquisitions efficiency and effectiveness might save the government.

HOUSE ACTION

The House Armed Services Committee approved its version of the legislation (HR 2101—H Rept 111-101), 59–0, on May 7, the same day the Senate passed its bill. The House measure, sponsored by Chair Ike Skelton, D-Mo., and ranking Republican John M. McHugh of New York, had three significant features not found in the Senate bill.

The first was a requirement that the defense secretary designate a subordinate official within the office of the secretary of defense to serve as the principal adviser throughout the life of all major contracts, with responsibility for overseeing cost estimates, systems engineering, and performance assessment. The Senate bill required this official to be appointed by the president and subject to Senate confirmation.

The second was a requirement that distressed programs enter an "intensive care" program, which would mandate annual reviews and flag them for congressional oversight. Finally, the House bill proposed a system to track cost growth for major programs before a final decision was made to go ahead with the project. "It's before Milestone B when 75 percent of a program's costs are actually determined," Skelton said. "No such process exists today."

In a complicated procedure, the House voted, 428–0, on May 13 to adopt a rule that, in one stroke, passed HR 2101, inserted the text into S 454, and passed S 454 as amended. CBO estimated that the House bill would cost $55 million over five years.

CONFERENCE AND FINAL ACTION

House and Senate negotiators filed a conference report on the bill (H Rept 111-124) on May 20. The Senate adopted the report, 95–0, the same day, and the House cleared the bill, 411–0, on May 21, allowing Obama to sign it the Friday before Memorial Day.

The key compromise struck in conference involved the creation of the new director of cost assessment and program evaluation. Like the Senate measure, the bill required the president to appoint a director of cost assessment and program evaluation, subject to Senate confirmation. Like the House version, it put the position within the office of the secretary of defense.

The Cost Assessment Improvement Group, an existing independent auditor for procurement projects, was transferred to the director's office and placed under the deputy director for cost assessment, as the Senate wanted.

McHugh called the bill a "critical measure" that "portends the opportunity to save literally hundreds and hundreds of millions of taxpayer dollars . . . [and] ensures that every tax dollar we do spend goes appropriately to providing the best weapons systems we can to keep those brave men and women in uniform safe."

MAJOR PROVISIONS

As enacted PL 111-23 contained the following major provisions:

- Created a new director of cost assessment and program evaluation to serve as the principal adviser to the secretary of defense and other senior Pentagon officials throughout the life of major contracts, with responsibility for overseeing cost estimates, systems engineering, and performance assessment.

- Required the defense secretary to select new directors, one for developmental test and evaluation and one for systems engineering.
- Required program managers to notify the Pentagon's Milestone Decision Authority if the total cost of a program grew beyond 25 percent before a final decision was made to go ahead, a point known as Milestone B. Required the Milestone Decision Authority to review the program and submit a report to the congressional defense committees identifying the root causes of the cost increases or schedule delays. Required the authority to recommend terminating the program or granting it a waiver. If the program were not terminated, the most recent milestone would be rescinded, and in most cases the program would have to regain approval before proceeding.
- Required the Pentagon's Milestone Decision Authority to review a troubled program that received a waiver at least annually until it met specified criteria and to flag the program every time the Pentagon sent budget documents to Congress.
- Required each major weapons acquisition program to include provisions to ensure competition at both the prime contract and subcontract level throughout the program's life cycle.
- Required the department to provide uniform guidance and tighten existing requirements for so-called organizational conflicts of interest by contractors in major defense acquisition programs. At issue were situations in which a single company was hired to provide systems engineering and technical assistance for a major weapons program and, at the same time, was involved in the development or production of that weapon. The bill listed issues that should be addressed and suggested remedies such as dual sourcing and seeking competitive prototypes, but it did not set specific requirements, as the Senate version had. The department was allowed to "unbundle" some contracts to make it easier for small businesses to bid on them.

Fiscal 2009 War Supplemental

Congress cleared a $105.9 billion fiscal 2009 supplemental spending bill in June 2009 that was devoted mainly to military operations in Iraq and Afghanistan in the final months of fiscal 2009. President Barack Obama signed the measure into law June 24, 2009 (HR 2346—PL 111-32).

The total for the bill was $13.7 billion, or 15 percent more than Obama's request, $9.3 billion more than the House put in its initial bill, and $14.6 billion more than in the Senate-passed version. About $77.2 billion went to the Defense Department, including funds for military construction.

It was the second supplemental appropriations bill to provide war funding for fiscal 2009. A bill enacted in June 2008 (PL 110-252) included $65.9 billion in "bridge funding" for the first half of the fiscal year, which began October 1, 2008. *(Congress and the Nation Vol. XII, p. 387)*

Democratic leaders expected the new bill to be less controversial than those cleared in the previous few years when Democrats tried to use the must-pass measures to carry spending and policy provisions opposed by Republican president George W. Bush. With Obama in the White House, those confrontations were absent. Both chambers passed their respective versions by overwhelming margins.

But a number of Senate provisions complicated negotiations on a final bill. They included $5 billion requested by the president to leverage additional lending by the International Monetary Fund, which Republicans said would take money away from the troops and should be considered in a separate bill.

A provision that would have barred the release of photos showing abuse of detainees in U.S. custody pitted many Senate Democrats against more liberal members of their caucus. It was not until the Senate conferees received assurances from Obama that he would use his executive authority to block release of the photos that they were willing to agree to a conference report that did not include that provision.

The main components of the bill included:

Personnel. $18.7 billion for military personnel, including $2.8 billion in unrequested funds to cover unbudgeted personnel costs resulting from higher-than-projected recruiting and retention levels. The bill also appropriated $534 million for additional pay for more than 185,000 service members whose enlistments had been involuntarily extended under "stop-loss" orders since September 11, 2001.

Operation and maintenance. $32.5 billion for costs related to war operations, which was $1.8 billion, or 5 percent, less than the president requested.

Procurement. $25.8 billion to refurbish or replace equipment worn out or damaged in Iraq and Afghanistan, which was about $4 billion, or 18 percent, more than requested. The total included $2.7 billion for C-17 and C-130 transport aircraft, most of which was not requested, and $4.5 billion, $1.9 billion more than requested, for lightweight Mine Resistant Ambush Protected (MRAP) vehicles mainly for use in Afghanistan. The bill provided $1.1 billion, $350 million less than Obama sought, to procure and develop countermeasures to roadside bombs and mines, which accounted for more than half of U.S. casualties in Iraq.

Military construction. $2.7 billion, which was $431 million more than requested. The total included funding for hospital construction and transition facilities for injured service members. It also included money for U.S. military facilities at home, in Afghanistan, and elsewhere.

Aid to Pakistan and Afghanistan. The bill included:

- $3.6 billion to expand and improve Afghan security forces and $400 million for a Pakistan Counterinsurgency Fund created under the bill. Both amounts reflected the president's request and were part of the total for operation and maintenance.
- $400 million for a new Pakistan Counterinsurgency Fund and $700 million for a Pakistan Counterinsurgency Capability Fund.
- $1.4 billion, as requested, for economic and diplomatic assistance to Pakistan and $2.4 billion for economic aid to Afghanistan, which was $800 million more than the president's request.
- Additional funds for oversight, U.S. embassy costs, and other purposes.

Health care. $1.1 billion for military health care costs, slightly more than requested.

International Monetary Fund. $5 billion requested by the president to leverage $108 billion in additional lending by the IMF.

Pandemic flu. $7.7 billion for efforts to address a potential flu pandemic. Obama initially requested $1.5 billion but asked for another $5 billion in June, citing the spread of the H1N1 "swine" flu virus.

Guantánamo Bay detainees. No funds for the costs of closing the detention facility at the U.S. naval station at Guantánamo Bay, Cuba. Obama requested $80 million.

HOUSE COMMITTEE ACTION

The House Appropriations Committee approved a $96.7 billion supplemental spending bill (HR 2346—H Rept 111-105) by voice vote May 7, after a contentious debate over the fate of the Guantánamo detention center.

Obama had urged Congress to approve the measure quickly and to refrain from loading it with earmarks or unnecessary projects.

The bill included $81.3 billion to pay for the Pentagon's ongoing war operations in Afghanistan and Iraq—$7.8 billion more than requested. Among the biggest differences were $4.8 billion for MRAP vehicles mainly for use in Afghanistan, $2.2 billion more than requested; $3.1 billion in unrequested funds for C-17 and C-130 transport aircraft; $17.9 billion for military personnel, $1.8 billion more than requested; and $734 million in unrequested funds for additional pay for more than 170,000 service members whose enlistments had been involuntarily extended since September 11, 2001.

The bill also included $10 billion for various foreign aid and international stabilization programs and $1.9 billion for pandemic flu preparedness. The committee included no money for closing the Guantánamo Bay detention facility.

It required the president to send Congress a report in early February 2010 on the extent to which the governments of Afghanistan and Pakistan were demonstrating the necessary commitment to warrant the continuation of aid. Appropriations Chair David R. Obey, D-Wis., backed off from previous statements that the report should be a "fish or cut bait" assessment, saying that it was not a precursor to withholding funding. Jerry Lewis of California, the committee's ranking Republican, objected to various "add-ons" that he said should be handled in regular appropriations bills.

During the markup, the committee:

- Rejected, 21–36, an amendment by Todd Tiahrt, R-Kan., to bar the use of funds in the bill to transfer or release Guantánamo Bay detainees to the United States.
- Rejected, 20–32, an amendment by Frank R. Wolf, R-Va., to place a moratorium on the transfer or release of detainees until October 1, 2009, and to require the president to submit a plan for each detainee before transferring or releasing them into the United States.
- Adopted, by voice vote, an alternative Democratic amendment by Obey to require the president to report to Congress on the administration's plans for Guantánamo by October 1, 2009.
- Adopted, by voice vote, an Obey amendment to provide $400 million in fiscal 2010 funds for Pakistan counterinsurgency under the authority of the Pentagon. Secretary Robert M. Gates and Secretary of State Hillary Rodham Clinton had testified that only the Pentagon had the ability to distribute the funds. But Obey included report language stating that it was the committee's intent that the State Department regain authority over counterinsurgency money after fiscal 2010. In addition, $400 million was provided for Pakistan counterinsurgency under the control of the State Department.
- Adopted by voice vote an amendment by C. W. Bill Young of Florida, ranking Republican on the Appropriations Subcommittee, to restore $2.5 billion in unspent fiscal 2009 funding, which was to be rescinded in the initial draft of the bill, to address military personnel shortfalls. That move brought the total price of the bill to $96.7 billion.

HOUSE FLOOR ACTION

The House passed the $96.7 billion bill, 368–60, on May 14. The rule for floor debate (H Res 434) automatically added language to explicitly prohibit the use of funds in the bill to release any Guantánamo detainees into the United States. It added provisions to require the president to provide detailed reports to Congress before bringing any detainee to the United States for prosecution or releasing a detainee to a foreign country. The rule, which was adopted, 247–178, allowed no other amendments.

Top Republicans lambasted the rule as preventing them from making the Guantánamo restrictions tougher. Lewis accused Democratic leaders of being "more sensitive to the rights of known terrorists than the rights of . . . elected members of this body." However, Young urged passage of the bill despite the detainee issue.

Key Democrats, meanwhile, signaled that they had grave doubts about continuing the U.S. commitment to a war effort that had dragged on since 2001 with no end in sight. "If we're going to go down that road," Obey said, "I want the president to get everything that he asked for and then some to maximize his chances for success, and that is what this bill does. I frankly have very little faith that it will work."

Harold Rogers, R-Ky., tried unsuccessfully to send the bill back to committee to add $3 billion in defense spending, shift funds from foreign aid to anti-drug activities on the U.S.-Mexico border, and maintain Pentagon control of Pakistan counterinsurgency funds. The motion was defeated, 191–237.

SENATE COMMITTEE ACTION

The Senate Appropriations Committee agreed, 30–0, on May 14 to approve a $91.3 billion version of the bill (S 1054—S Rept 111-20). The total was about $5.4 billion below that of the bill the House passed about an hour later.

Committee Chair Daniel K. Inouye, D-Hawaii, and ranking Republican Thad Cochran of Mississippi urged members to save amendments for the Senate floor. Republicans said they would offer amendments on Guantánamo at that time.

Following are some of the major differences between the House-passed and Senate committee bills:

- The Senate appropriators included $80 million, as requested, to close the Guantánamo Bay prison and transfer the detainees off the base. But they made the funding conditional on the release of an administration plan for detainee relocation and permitted prisoners to be moved only to other countries. Senate Majority Whip Richard J. Durbin, D-Ill., said he was not sure whether the final bill would contain the money for closing the prison, but he highlighted the legislation's demand for more details from the administration before funds could be disbursed. "I think the president was right" about the need to close the prison, Durbin said. "But he needs to come up with a plan about how that's going to be accomplished, how these detainees are going to be moved to other locations."
- The Senate measure included $5 billion to support International Monetary Fund (IMF) lending. The House bill had no IMF funding.
- The bill included $21.9 billion for procurement, about $6 billion less than in the House bill. Among other things, it did not contain the $3.1 billion added by the House for new C-17 and C-130 aircraft.
- The total for the State Department and foreign affairs was $6.9 billion, roughly matching the administration request but about $2.6 billion less than in the House bill.
- The appropriators matched what at the time was the administration's $1.5 billion request for flu preparedness, compared with $1.9 billion in the House bill.
- Although both the Senate and House bills included $400 million in the Pentagon budget for counterinsurgency programs in Pakistan, the Senate committee did not include a second counterinsurgency fund under State Department authority.

SENATE FLOOR ACTION

The Senate passed HR 2346 by a vote of 86–3 on May 21, after inserting its $91.3 billion version of the bill.

Unlike disputes over previous war supplementals, which focused on war policy, the floor controversy this time was over the Guantánamo Bay detention center and the fate of the military detainees. During the debate, the Senate adopted, 90–6, a Democratic amendment that removed the $80 million for closing the facility and barred the use of funding in the bill to transfer, release, or incarcerate any Guantánamo detainees to or within the United States. The change, offered by Inouye, was an attempt by Democratic leaders to defuse GOP attacks over the prospect of detainees entering the United States. But Inouye also said the amendment was "not a referendum on closing Guantánamo," adding, "Let me be very clear: We need to close the Guantánamo prison."

Republicans saw the issue as giving them political traction. "President Obama intends to bring a Gitmo detainee to New York to be tried in our criminal courts," said Saxby Chambliss, R-Ga., referring to the administration's plans to try a detainee on charges related to the 1998 bombings of U.S. embassies in Kenya and Tanzania. "I fear this is the start of a long process of transferring detainees to the United States, where, I believe, legal technicalities will ultimately allow some of them to be freed."

On other amendments, the committee:

- Adopted by voice vote an amendment by Lindsey Graham, R-S.C., and Joseph I. Lieberman, I-Conn., to bar the release of photos showing alleged prisoner abuse by U.S. soldiers taken from September 11, 2001, to January 22, 2009, if the defense secretary certified that release of the pictures would endanger U.S. citizens or troops or contractors serving abroad. The certification would last for three years, and the Pentagon could renew it. The provisions would take precedence over the Freedom of Information Act (FOIA), which a federal court had said required release of the photos.
- Adopted, 92–3, an amendment by Minority Leader Mitch McConnell, R-Ky., to require the president to submit a report to Congress every ninety days on the Guantánamo prisoner population. The president also would have to report to Congress before transferring any detainee to a foreign country.
- Rejected, 30–64, an amendment by Jim DeMint, R-S.C., to delete the $5 billion for the IMF.

CONFERENCE AND FINAL ACTION

House and Senate negotiators filed a conference report on the bill June 12. But it took several more days of scrambling before House leaders were confident they had the votes from their caucus to adopt the report. With Republicans lining up against the measure, Pennsylvania Democrat John P. Murtha, chair of the House Appropriations Subcommittee, and others worked to contain defections among House liberals.

The House adopted the conference report (H Rept 111-151), 226–202, on June 16, with only five Republicans in support and thirty-two Democrats voting "nay," down from the fifty-one Democrats who voted against the House version in May. Some liberal Democrats switched to "yea" because they supported the IMF funding or because they were persuaded by leaders to toe the line. The Senate cleared the bill, 91–5, on June 18.

The chief sticking point was the Senate provision to bar the release of detainee photos, but conferees also wrestled with other issues, some of which popped up late in the process.

Detainee Photos

The dispute over barring release of the photos under the FOIA reflected conflicting needs of House and Senate leaders and tied up the conference for days. Top House leaders said the language had to be dropped to get the conference report through their chamber, where many liberal Democrats sharply opposed the Senate amendment. But Senate Democratic leaders argued they needed to retain the provision to avoid a filibuster and because it enjoyed widespread support there.

The conference stalled June 11 while Senate Democrats debated whether to accept a decision by the leaders of both chambers to drop the language. But after a phone call from Obama and a letter sent to senior appropriators, the Senate Democrats agreed to support the deal, accepting the president's pledge to use his executive authority to block release of the photos anytime soon. In his letter, Obama wrote that he would "continue to take every legal and administrative remedy available to me to ensure the [Defense Department] detainee photographs are not released."

Several Democratic conferees who had strongly opposed release of the prisoner photos, including Sen. Dianne Feinstein, D-Calif., said Obama's eleventh-hour intervention allowed them to support the conference report.

Meanwhile, the U.S. Court of Appeals for the Second Circuit on June 11 granted a motion, put forth by the administration, to stay the court's previous order directing release of the photos. "To the best of my knowledge, it was a complete coincidence," Feinstein said.

Guantánamo Bay Detainees

The final bill established a list of restrictions on handling Guantánamo detainees that was repeated in several later appropriations bills:

- It barred the release of detainees into the United States.
- Detainees could not be brought into the country except to be prosecuted. In that case, the president had to submit a detailed plan to Congress, including the costs, possible risks, and steps being taken to mitigate those risks. The president also was required to notify the state to which a prisoner was being transferred.
- The bill required the president to provide detailed reports to Congress before releasing or transferring detainees to another country or closing the Guantánamo facility.

Pandemic Flu

Citing growing concern over the potential spread of the H1N1 flu virus, Obama on June 2 requested $5 billion for flu preparedness, in addition to $1.5 billion requested in April. As part of the request, the president also asked for authority to transfer funds from already-appropriated accounts, in case of a "dire emergency" related to the flu. Conferees agreed to provide a total of $7.7 billion—$1.9 billion in fiscal 2009 appropriations and $5.8 billion that would be available in such an emergency.

Cash for Clunkers

Conferees inserted a provision that established a voluntary program dubbed "cash for clunkers" and provided $1 billion for rebates to people who traded in older cars and bought newer, more fuel-efficient vehicles. The House had passed a bill (HR 2751) authorizing $4 billion for the program on June 9, but the Senate had not acted on it. *(Cash for clunkers legislation, p. 321)*

Sen. Judd Gregg, R-N.H., tried in conference to remove the money, calling it a thinly veiled bailout for the auto industry, but he was defeated, 13–17. Before clearing the bill, the Senate agreed, 60–36, to a procedural motion that blocked another attempt by Gregg to eliminate the vehicle trade-in provision.

International Monetary Fund

Like the Senate version, the agreement provided an increase in the U.S. quota in the IMF that was expected to cost the U.S. Treasury about $5 billion. "The big problem for us is the IMF money, because it basically comes out of the hide of the defense part of the supplemental," Young said. "The supplemental is supposedly all about paying for Afghanistan and Iraq."

Pakistan Aid

The agreement followed both bills in providing $400 million for a new Pakistan Counterinsurgency Fund and gave the Pentagon control over the funds. It also established a second fund, the Pakistan Counterinsurgency Capability Fund, under the State Department as proposed by the House but gave it $700 million through 2011, instead of $400 million for 2010 as in the House bill. The conferees expressed concern about allowing the aid to be controlled by the Pentagon, noting that assistance programs were traditionally handled by the State Department.

Other Funding Decisions

Negotiators scaled back several of the unrequested items that House appropriators had added. The bill included $2.7 billion for five C-130 transport planes and eight C-17 cargo planes that were neither requested by the administration nor in the Senate's bill. The House bill proposed $3.1 billion for 11 C-130s and the eight C-17s.

- The $18.7 billion provided for personnel shortfalls was more than in either chamber's bill. The measure included $534 million for stop-loss payments to service members whose duty had been extended; the Senate bill had no stop-loss funds.
- Conferees included the House requirement that Obama send Congress a report with his fiscal 2011 budget that outlined the extent to which the governments of Afghanistan and Pakistan demonstrate a level of commitment that justified continued aid.

Fiscal 2010 Defense Authorization

President Barack Obama in 2009 signed legislation authorizing $680.2 billion in discretionary fiscal 2010 defense spending despite his objections to authorizing $560 million for a backup engine for F-35 fighter jets. Obama won a bigger fight, however, using a veto threat to persuade Congress to give up on funding procurement of additional F-22 Raptor fighter jets, which the Defense Department said were not needed. Obama signed the bill October 28 (HR 2647—PL 111-84).

The annual bill authorized national security programs in the Defense and Energy departments and included $130 billion in contingency funds to pay for the wars in Iraq and Afghanistan. It authorized a pay raise for troops; additional funds for equipment depleted by the wars, including new combat vehicles and new battle gear for the Army National Guard and reserves; and restrictions on bringing detainees held at Guantánamo Bay, Cuba, to the United States for trial.

The conference report received fewer votes in both chambers than in most years, largely because of the inclusion of an unrelated, Senate-passed provision that broadened federal hate crimes law to cover crimes committed because of the victim's gender, sexual orientation, or disability.

The bill authorized $680.2 billion in discretionary funds: $550.2 billion for the base defense budget plus the $130 billion for overseas contingency operations. The discretionary amount was roughly equal to the president's request but 4 percent more than authorized in the fiscal 2009 law (PL 110-417).

Including mandatory programs such as retiree benefits, discretionary programs that did not need new authorization and some programs outside the jurisdiction of the Armed Services committees, the bill's grand total came to $692.8 billion.

The measure authorized billions of dollars for development and procurement of ships, planes, vehicles, satellites, and other weapons systems, while ratifying many of Secretary Robert M. Gates's proposals to scale back major weapons programs that were popular in the districts of individual members. Conferees went along with the administration's proposed termination of not only the F-22, but also the C-17 transport plane. They also agreed to reduce spending on missile defenses. But they defied the administration on the second F-35 engine, betting correctly that they had modified the plan enough to avoid a veto.

Senate Armed Services Chair Carl Levin, D-Mich., said the final bill "reflects almost all of the decisions of the secretary of defense and the president to terminate troubled programs, delay programs for which requirements are not yet defined, re-orient programs and systems to deal with today's threats, and apply the lessons gained from more than seven years of war."

HOUSE COMMITTEE ACTION

The House Armed Services Committee approved its fiscal 2010 defense authorization bill (HR 2647—H Rept 111-166, Parts 1 and 2) by a vote of 61–0 in a marathon markup that ended in the early morning of June 17, 2009. As approved by the committee, the bill proposed $680.5 billion in discretionary spending: $550.5 billion for the base budget and $130 billion for the wars in Iraq and Afghanistan. Six of the panel's subcommittees marked up portions of the bill under their jurisdictions the previous week, making only a handful of changes.

One of the biggest disputes came over Democrats' support for Obama's plan to restructure missile defense programs and reduce spending by $1.2 billion, to $9.3 billion.

"No shortcoming is more apparent in this mark than in the area of national missile defense," said Howard P. "Buck" McKeon of California, the committee's ranking Republican. Although he supported much of the bill, he said that "in a year where Iran and North Korea have demonstrated the capability and intent to pursue intercontinental ballistic missiles and nuclear weapon programs—the elements of a genuine national security threat—it would be irresponsible not to fund programs that provide long-range missile defense that protects the homeland."

DEFENSE LEADERSHIP

One of President Barack Obama's first decisions following his election in 2008 arguably was one of his most important—and certainly was one of his most widely applauded: to retain Robert M. Gates as secretary of defense. President George W. Bush had appointed Gates, a former director of the Central Intelligence Agency (CIA), to head the Pentagon in 2006 following midterm elections that proved disastrous for Republicans in large part because of public unease with the Iraq war. A no-nonsense but low-key administrator, Gates restored a measure of calm and stability to a military establishment rattled by years of controversy during the tenure of outgoing Defense Secretary Donald H. Rumsfeld. Gates managed to do this even while paring back the defense budget and curtailing weapons systems and other programs he regarded as wasteful and unnecessary.

A Republican, Gates continued serving longer in the Obama administration than many observers had expected—all though 2009 and 2010 and during the first half of 2011. He officially retired on July 2, 2011. As a farewell ceremony, President Obama gave Gates the Presidential Medal of Freedom and called him "one of the nation's finest public servants."

To succeed the popular Gates, Obama turned to another figure with numerous Washington credentials who also was widely respected by Republicans and Democrats alike: CIA Director Leon Panetta. During his lengthy public service career, the California Democrat had served in the House from 1977 to 1993 and was chair of the House Budget Committee before becoming President Bill Clinton's director of the Office of Management and Budget (OMB) and then chief of staff.

The Armed Services Committee approved Panetta's nomination for the post by voice vote June 14. The Senate confirmed him one week later by a vote of 100–0.

Panetta's nomination came at a time when the Pentagon faced the prospect of significant budget cuts; Obama had already proposed to reduce security spending by $400 billion over twelve years. Panetta's background in budgeting was seen as one of his many assets. Praise for Panetta came from both political parties.

Armed Services Chair Carl Levin, D-Mich., highlighted his work with Gates to foster strong cooperation between the civilian and military intelligence apparatus, leading to the killing of al Qaeda chieftain Osama bin Laden in May. "The raid on the bin Laden compound epitomizes the way in which the CIA and the Defense Department are finally working together to support each other in counterterrorism operations, and Director Panetta deserves credit for this close coordination," Levin said.

"Leon Panetta heading up the Defense Department is just a home-run choice. I've known Leon for quite a while, and I just want to let the country know that I think the president made a very wise decision," Lindsey Graham, R-S.C., said.

Afghanistan Command

David H. Petraeus, who became the most famous and lauded American military leader of his generation during the Bush administration, continued his remarkable service during the Obama administration—only to fall from grace in late 2012 because of an extramarital affair.

A larger-than-life figure who seemed to personify the best features of the American military, Petraeus quickly rose to the top ranks of the army during the war in Iraq, leading President Bush's 2006–2007 "surge" there and heading the U.S. Central Command. President Obama in 2010 put Petraeus in charge of a similar, if smaller-scale, U.S. "surge" in Afghanistan.

Obama announced his nomination of Petraeus on June 23, 2010, immediately after relieving Army Gen. Stanley A. McChrystal of his command. McChrystal had been forced to step down after *Rolling Stone* magazine quoted disparaging remarks he had made about the Obama administration.

"War is bigger than any one man or woman, whether a private, a general or a president," Obama remarked. "The conduct represented in the recently published article does not meet the standard that should be set by a commanding general," he said. "It undermines the civilian control of the military that is at the core of our democratic system."

Democrats rebuffed a proposal by Michael R. Turner of Ohio, ranking Republican on the Strategic Forces Subcommittee, to spend $120 million to deploy forty-four interceptors in Alaska, as planned under the Bush administration, offset by a reduction for nonproliferation programs. The bill supported Gates's plan to limit the number to thirty interceptors, which the Pentagon said was adequate.

The committee agreed, 35–27, to replace Turner's language with an amendment expressing the sense of Congress that the number of interceptors should be driven by military commanders' assessments of threats and requirements.

"For too many years we have not taken a balanced approach to missile defense," said Armed Services Chair Ike Skelton, D-Mo. "We have spent far too much money on programs that do not protect us from the threats that truly exist. Democrats support a missile defense system that actually works and will keep Americans safe. Today's legislation accomplishes that goal."

Petraeus, who was serving as the head of Central Command, also had written the new U.S. counterinsurgency operations policy, which he put to use during the surge in Iraq. Senate endorsement was never in doubt because Petraeus was widely respected on Capitol Hill. The Senate confirmed his nomination, 99–0, on June 30, one day after the Armed Services Committee agreed by voice vote to send it to the floor.

In a statement after the Senate vote, President Obama said he was "extremely grateful" for the quick action. "Petraeus's unrivaled experience will ensure we do not miss a beat in our strategy to break the Taliban's momentum and build Afghan capacity," he said.

John McCain of Arizona, ranking Republican on the Armed Services Committee, praised McChrystal's career without discussing his departure. But McCain also praised Petraeus and said Obama's decision to nominate him to succeed McChrystal demonstrated the president's continued commitment to the U.S. mission in Afghanistan. "He has proved that we can win wars," McCain said of Petraeus, "and we need to give him every opportunity."

At the same time, McCain reiterated his opposition to the July 2011 target date Obama had set to begin a withdrawal of U.S. troops from Afghanistan. Republicans raised the issue repeatedly in Petraeus's June 29 confirmation hearing, saying the deadline sent a mixed message to U.S. allies and enemies alike. They said the president should clearly state that the withdrawal would be based solely on conditions on the ground.

Petraeus, however, left no doubt about his support for the president's plan. He said the withdrawal date helped convey to Afghans the need to take over their own security quickly and build a sustainable government. "As the president has also indicated," the general told the Senate committee, "July 2011 is not a date when we will be rapidly withdrawing our forces and 'switching off the lights and closing the door behind us.'" But he also acknowledged that continued military operations were likely to remain difficult.

Petraeus had served in Afghanistan for just one year when Obama named him as CIA director, succeeding Panetta. *(Petraeus to CIA, p. 227)*

Petraeus had served at the CIA for only fourteen months, however, when the Federal Bureau of Investigation uncovered his extramarital affair with a woman who had been his biographer. Petraeus resigned three days after the November 2012 elections, creating an embarrassing scandal for just-reelected President Obama. The scandal also ensnared General John Allen, one of Petraeus's successors as the top commander in Afghanistan.

Joint Chiefs of Staff

Admiral Michael Mullen, appointed chair of the Joint Chiefs of Staff by President Bush in 2007, continued to serve during the early years of Obama's first term, retiring in September 2011.

Obama had been expected to name Marine Corps Gen. James Cartwright, who was serving as Joint Chiefs vice chair, to succeed Mullen. But Cartwright reportedly ran afoul of other senior Pentagon brass because of assumptions that he had given private advice to the White House on military issues, including troop levels in Afghanistan. The president told Cartwright in late May that he would not get the top job, and Cartwright retired from the military.

Obama then chose as the next chair of the Joint Chiefs Army Gen. Martin Dempsey, who had been army chief of staff for little over one month. He had held a number of senior posts, including as commander of the 1st Armored Division during the 2003 invasion of Iraq and later as commanding general of the U.S. Army Training and Doctrine Command at Fort Eustis, Va.

Obama named Dempsey as his choice on May 29, 2011, along with his nomination of Navy Adm. James A. Winnefeld Jr. as vice chair. The president also named Army Gen. Ray Odierno to succeed Dempsey as army chief of staff.

The Senate confirmed Dempsey, Winnefeld, and Odierno on August 2—all by unanimous consent.

The committee also adopted, 36–26, an amendment by Rick Larsen, D-Wash., to allow the Defense Department to use $343 million either for the proposed missile defense system in Poland and the Czech Republic or for another long-range missile system in Europe, as long as it was endorsed by the secretary of defense. The language was substituted for a Turner amendment that would have designated the money only for a long-range missile defense system in Europe, offset by reductions in nuclear nonproliferation accounts.

During the markup, the committee adopted, 31–30, an amendment by Rob Bishop, R-Utah, to shift $369 million from defense environmental cleanup to buying parts for twelve F-22 Raptors that would need to be fully funded in fiscal 2011. Bishop said buying the parts would keep the F-22 production line open.

The bill authorized $6 billion for twenty-eight F-35s, one less aircraft each for the Air Force and Navy than requested, and $3.9 billion for research and development.

The cuts made room for $603 million for research, development, and procurement of a second engine. The primary engine was being made by Pratt & Whitney, largely in Connecticut, while the alternative was being developed by General Electric Co. and Rolls-Royce in Ohio, Indiana, and elsewhere. The Pentagon opposed continued production of the second engine as unnecessary and wasteful; proponents said the competition would result in a better engine at a lower cost. At stake was perhaps $60 billion worth of multiyear business. The White House had left itself some room to maneuver, warning that the president's advisers would recommend a veto if the authorization of a second engine would "seriously disrupt" the overall F-35 program.

The panel adopted, 35–25, a substitute Guantánamo amendment by Skelton to block the use of funds authorized in the bill to release or transfer any Guantánamo detainees to U.S. jails until 120 days after the president submitted a detailed plan to Congress. Skelton's substitute replaced language in an amendment by J. Randy Forbes, R-Va., that would have prevented the president from releasing or transferring the detainees unless a list of requirements was satisfied sixty days in advance.

HOUSE FLOOR ACTION

The House passed the bill, 389–22, on June 25, one day after the White House warned that authorizing funds to procure additional F-22 fighters or a second F-35 engine was likely to result in a veto. The statement said it was the collective judgment of administration officials that the 187 F-22 fighter planes were "sufficient to meet operational requirements."

The rule for floor debate automatically incorporated the provisions of a House-passed measure (HR 2990) expanding the ability of disabled veterans to receive simultaneous military retirement and veteran's disability payments, a policy known as concurrent receipt.

Members adopted sixty-five amendments before passing the bill. During the debate, the House:

- Adopted, 224–193, an amendment by Rush D. Holt, D-N.J., to require the videotaping of all military interrogations, with some exceptions, with appropriate security classifications.
- Adopted by voice vote as part of an en bloc amendment a proposal by Alcee L. Hastings, D-Fla., to allow the International Committee of the Red Cross to have access to detainees at Bagram Air Base in Afghanistan.
- Rejected, 171–244, an amendment by Trent Franks, R-Ariz., to increase funding for missile defense by $1.2 billion with offsetting reductions coming from defense environmental cleanup. It also would have stated that it was U.S. policy to continue missile defense testing.
- Rejected, 138–278, an amendment by Jim McGovern, D-Mass., that would have required the secretary to report to Congress by December 31, 2009, on an exit strategy for U.S. military forces in Afghanistan.

SENATE COMMITTEE ACTION

The Senate Armed Services Committee approved its version of the bill (S 1390—S Rept 111-35) by a vote of 26–0 on June 25. The bill authorized $679.8 billion for Energy Department programs and included $129.3 billion for operations in Iraq and Afghanistan.

The committee voted to close its markup proceedings to the public and reporters, prompting strong objections from Claire McCaskill, D-Mo. She argued that the committee was doing the public's work and that there was no valid reason for holding the meetings in secret.

Levin, the committee chair, countered that the closed markup was necessary to be able to discuss classified information freely and for reasons of expediency. "The need to go in and out of classified information very quickly . . . would make it a much clumsier kind of a markup" if it were open, Levin said.

Although the committee broke with the administration on F-22 procurement and the second F-35 engine, it supported Gates's plan to terminate many troubled defense programs, including large portions of the Army's Future Combat Systems, the VH-71 presidential helicopter, and several components of ballistic missile defense. "I don't think anybody's looking for a battle here with the White House at all," Levin said. But, he added, "obviously, we're not in lockstep."

Despite the opposition of Democratic Chair Levin and ranking committee Republican John McCain of Arizona, the panel agreed, 13–11, to authorize $1.8 billion to procure seven additional F-22 fighter planes beyond the 187 already procured, extending the production line into 2009. "We will fight that more on the floor," McCain said.

The committee voted, 12–10, to add $439 million for the alternative engine program and also added money for eighteen F-18 planes for the Navy, rejecting the administration's plan to procure only nine.

The bill included language to prohibit contractors from interrogating detainees held by the military. It also specified certain rules of evidence for the forthcoming trials of detainees held at Guantánamo, including the inadmissibility of statements obtained through torture or through cruel, inhuman, or degrading treatment.

SENATE FLOOR ACTION

The Senate passed its bill, 87–7, on July 23, then inserted the text into HR 2647 in preparation for conference and approved the amended bill by voice vote. Senators spent nearly two weeks debating amendments, many involving high-profile issues.

The Senate on July 21, in a **key vote of 58–40 (R 15–25; D 42–14; I 1–1),** adopted an amendment by Levin and McCain reversing the provision that would have authorized $1.8 billion for additional F-22 aircraft. The vote ended the hopes of those who backed continued production by demonstrating that the provision could not get through the Senate. Obama used a brief Rose Garden appearance to thank the Senate. "Our budget is a zero-sum game, and if more money goes to F-22s, it is our troops and citizens who lose," he said. *(2009 key votes, p. 751)*

John P. Murtha, D-Pa., chair of the House Appropriations Subcommittee, subsequently prevailed on a House vote to eliminate the F-22 funds from the defense appropriations bill (HR 3326), saying that the Senate vote had made the effort futile.

In another victory for Obama, the Senate adopted by voice vote an amendment by independent Joseph I. Lieberman of Connecticut to bar continued spending on a second engine for the F-35 until the defense secretary certified that such a program would reduce the fighter program's costs, improve the planes' readiness, and not disrupt the program's development or result in fewer fighters procured. Lieberman argued that the alternative engine would take money that should be used to buy more of the warplanes, citing a July 22 letter from Gates.

The Senate rejected, 38–59, a competing amendment by Evan Bayh, D-Ind., that would have withheld 10 percent of the funding for the F-35 unless sufficient money was made available to continue development of a second engine. Bayh's amendment would have paid for the engine by cutting $439 million from the authorization for C-130 transport planes for special operations forces in Iraq and Afghanistan. Bayh said the planes were already funded by the supplemental spending law.

The Senate adopted by voice vote an amendment by Minority Whip Jon Kyl, R-Ariz., to require a report from the administration on its plan to accomplish three goals: to modernize U.S. nuclear weapons; to enhance their safety, security, and reliability; and to maintain the missiles, submarines, and aircraft that delivered them. The report would be due to Congress within thirty days of enactment or at the time a follow-on strategic arms reduction treaty with Russia was delivered to the Senate for approval, whichever happened sooner. The amendment also urged that such a treaty not limit missile defenses, military capabilities in space, or advanced conventional arms.

The Senate also adopted by voice vote an amendment by Lieberman and others that would require the Pentagon to spend $353 million in fiscal 2009 and 2010 funds only for a European missile defense system that met certain criteria—mainly, that it be able to defend not only Europe but also the United States from Iranian missiles. Lieberman said he did not want the administration to dispense with the land-based missile defense system that Bush had wanted to deploy in Poland and the Czech Republic in favor of sea-based or other options if those alternatives were not as capable.

Judiciary Chair Patrick J. Leahy, D-Vt., won voice-vote adoption of an amendment to broaden the scope of hate crimes laws, after the Senate agreed, 63–28, to invoke cloture, thereby limiting debate on the proposal. *(Hate crimes, p. 553)*

The Senate avoided a huge fight with the House when it rejected, 58–39, an amendment by John Thune, R-S.D., to allow individuals to carry concealed firearms across state lines if they had valid permits or were legally entitled by their state of residence to do so. Under an agreement announced July 20, amendment supporters needed sixty votes to win its adoption. Thune said he decided to offer the amendment on the defense bill after Democrats pushed their hate crimes amendment.

CONFERENCE AND FINAL ACTION

An informal House-Senate conference began in late July, with conferees hoping to complete the final bill in September. They nearly met their target. The House adopted the conference report (H Rept 111-288) by a vote of 281–146 on October 8. The Senate cleared the bill, 68–29, on October 22 after earlier voting 64–35 to limit debate.

House members, mainly Republicans, who were outraged that conferees retained the Senate-passed hate crimes language, either held their noses and voted for the conference report or, as in the case of Minority Leader John A. Boehner of Ohio, voted against it. "Frankly, I'm offended by it," said Boehner.

MAJOR PROVISIONS

Following are major provisions of the fiscal 2010 defense authorization:

Base Defense Department Budget

The base defense budget of $550.2 billion was composed of $533.7 billion for the Defense Department of and $16.4 billion for Energy Department nuclear weapons programs.

The Defense Department authorization included $156.2 billion for operations and maintenance; $136 billion for military personnel; $105 billion for procurement; and $79.3 billion for research, development, test, and evaluation.

F-35 Engine

Conferees authorized $560 million to continue development of the alternative engine for F-35 Joint Strike Fighters. But instead of taking the funding out of the money authorized for the plane itself, as the House had done, negotiators agreed to authorize the full $6 billion requested for thirty F-35s, plus another $560 million for the competitive engine program. Levin expressed optimism that the change would satisfy the White House. But Lieberman said he was "deeply disappointed" that the bill would authorize the second engine. "I will continue to fight this wasteful earmark at every step—and expect the president to veto any appropriations bill that includes the alternate engine."

The bill included $6 billion for procurement of the thirty F-35s requested by Obama—ten for the Air Force and twenty for the Navy—plus $2 billion for research and development, $215 million more than requested.

F-22 Procurement

The veto warning on the F-22, however, was unambiguous. On July 13, Obama wrote to the majority and minority leaders of the Senate Armed Services Committee saying he would veto the final bill if it authorized funding to procure additional F-22 fighters. The program had been plagued by cost overruns, technical problems, and questions about its utility given the kind of low-level conflicts that were becoming the norm. The Air Force, which had fought previous attempts to end the program, in April endorsed a proposal by Gates to stop procurement after fiscal 2009, limiting the fleet to 187 planes.

As recently as June, Congress had directed, in the supplemental war-spending law (PL 111-32), that no funds could be used to shut down the F-22 production line. But faced with the veto threat and the Senate unwilling to go beyond the 187-plane limit sought by the administration, conferees had no choice but to drop the authorization for additional aircraft. The bill did authorize $569 million for research and development and $288 million for modifications to existing aircraft and called for a report on the potential for foreign military sales of the fighter jet. *(Supplemental war appropriations, p. 269)*

Navy Warplanes

The bill authorized $1.5 billion for 18 F/A-18 E/Fs (Super Hornets), about $500 million and nine more aircraft than requested. It also authorized a multiyear contract for additional F/A-18 aircraft. In addition, the bill authorized $1.6 billion, as requested, for twenty-two new EA-18G Growler electronic warfare planes.

Guantánamo Bay Detainees

The agreement blocked the use of funding in the bill to release detainees held at Guantánamo into the United States. Detainees could not be transferred to U.S. jails unless several conditions were met, including a requirement that the president submit a plan to Congress for incarcerating the detainees while minimizing the risk to national security.

Shipbuilding

The conference agreement authorized the following for major Navy vessels:

- $1.1 billion, as requested, for advance procurement for the Navy's next-generation surface combat ship, the DDG-1000, and $2.3 billion for its predecessor, the DDG-51.
- $1.1 billion, slightly more than requested, for procurement of the LPD-17 San Antonio–class amphibious ship.
- $1.7 billion, as requested, for the Littoral Combat Ship, a small surface combat ship for use in coastal waters.
- $3.9 billion, as requested, for the Virginia-class attack submarine, including full funding for one and advance procurement for two additional subs to be built in fiscal 2011 and beyond.
- $85 million, as requested, to terminate a program to procure a fleet of new VH-71 presidential helicopters. The program was six years behind schedule, and the cost had doubled to $13 billion. Navy officials had canceled the program in May.

Future Combat Systems

Conferees approved $2.5 billion, the amount requested, for two elements of the terminated Future Combat Systems program that were expected to continue as separate programs. The bill also authorized $216 million, a reduction of $211 million from Obama's request, to terminate the Manned Ground Vehicle program, a central feature of what was once envisioned as a system of integrated battlefield weapons and reconnaissance instruments linked by computer software. The program had become so complex and expensive that even supporters questioned its viability. In April, Gates announced plans to restructure the program. The Pentagon said Gates concluded that the planned suite of eight ground vehicles "did not adequately reflect the lessons of counterinsurgency and close-quarters combat in Iraq and Afghanistan."

Missile Defense

The bill authorized $9.3 billion for missile defense programs, as requested by Obama, a $1.2 billion reduction from the amount the George W. Bush administration had proposed for fiscal 2010. The bill increased authorized funding for proven missile defense systems such as the Aegis, BMD, and THAAD systems, but zeroed out futuristic programs such as the kinetic energy interceptor and multiple-kill vehicle.

The bill maintained funding for the initial deployment of a national missile defense system based in Alaska and California and limited the number of interceptors to thirty, as requested, instead of the forty-four planned under Bush. It also supported Obama's decision, announced in September, to shelve Bush's controversial plans for missile defense sites in Poland and the Czech Republic and shift to a ship- and land-based approach using smaller and far less costly missiles. The bill allowed the administration to reallocate fiscal 2009 money that had been slated for the missile sites. It also permanently extended a prohibition on deploying long-range missile defense interceptors in Europe until the department certified that the interceptors would be operationally effective and had the ability to accomplish the mission.

Energy Department Nuclear Programs

The conference agreement authorized $16.5 billion for defense-related activities at the Energy Department, $88 million more than Obama's request. The total included:

- $10 billion for the nuclear weapons laboratories and for programs under the National Nuclear Security Administration. Within that amount, the bill authorized $6.4 billion to maintain a reliable and secure weapons stockpile and $2.2 billion for nuclear nonproliferation programs.
- $6.4 billion for environmental cleanup at contaminated defense sites and for nuclear waste disposal.

Afghanistan and Iraq

The agreement authorized the president's request of $130 billion in contingency funds for the wars in Iraq and Afghanistan and the general war on terrorism. Funding authorized elsewhere in the bill could also be used to support those operations.

The overseas contingency section authorized $88.3 billion for operations and maintenance accounts, $23.9 billion for procurement, and $14.1 billion for personnel. It included $6.1 billion for Mine Resistant Ambush Protected (MRAP) vehicles in addition to $600 million authorized in the base defense budget; the total was $1.2 billion more than Obama requested. Another $2.1 billion, the amount requested, was authorized for countermeasures to prevent improvised explosive device (IED) attacks. The bill also authorized the $7.5 billion requested by Obama for training and equipping the Afghan security forces.

Military Detainees

Detainee provisions in the final bill included:

- A ban on using funds in the bill to release any Guantánamo detainee into the United States, its territories, or possessions. It also prohibited transferring any of the detainees to jails in the United States for prosecution or incarceration until forty-five days after the president sent Congress a report on the risks and other implications.
- A Senate proposal to prohibit contractors from handling interrogation of detainees.
- A Senate ban on military and intelligence officials reading *Miranda* rights to "enemy belligerents." As a result of a 1966 Supreme Court ruling in *Miranda v. Arizona* (384 U.S. 436), police were required to inform criminal suspects of their right to remain silent and to have an attorney. Some in Congress expressed concerns that detainees might be less likely to divulge intelligence of use to the military if they were told up front that they need not answer any questions.
- A version of the House requirement that, with certain exceptions, U.S. officials inform the International Committee of the Red Cross "as soon as practicable" of the detention of an individual at the Bagram facility in Afghanistan and give the Red Cross access to the prisoner if the organization requested it. The conferees said they took no position on whether the protections for prisoners of war contained in the Geneva Conventions applied to detainees at Bagram.
- A version of the House revision of the rules for the military commissions that considered detainees' cases. The bill prohibited the use of coerced testimony, limited the use of hearsay evidence, and altered procedures for handling classified information. Levin said defendants would have fairer and fuller access to resources, representation, witnesses, and documentary evidence.
- The Senate's ban on the use of contractors as interrogators but with modifications intended to reduce White House opposition. Conferees included a limited time waiver in exceptional circumstances and allowed private contractors to provide support services such as training interrogators.
- A modified version of the House requirement that interrogations be videotaped. The bill required the electronic recording of each "strategic intelligence interrogation" conducted at a Defense Department facility that was physically removed from the battlefield. It did not apply to military personnel involved in "direct combat operations." The secretary of defense could waive the requirement for thirty-day periods if he believed that national security demanded it and Congress had been notified.

Concurrent Receipt

The conferees did not include a one-year provision, requested by the president and approved by the House, that would have expanded the ability of some disabled veterans to receive both military retirement pay and veteran disability compensation, a benefit known as "concurrent receipt." The conference report said the administration did not present offsets.

Other Major Provisions

In other major provisions, the bill authorized:

- $28 billion for the department's health program for service members and military retirees, their survivors, and their dependents, roughly equal to the president's request. An additional $1.3 billion was authorized in the war funding section of the bill.
- An average 3.4 percent pay increase for military personnel in fiscal 2010, one-half a percentage point more than the president's request. The bill also extended certain special pay and bonuses for active-duty and reserve personnel.
- $2.2 billion, the amount Obama requested, for construction and renovation of new and existing family housing, including new barracks and dormitories.
- $6.9 billion for new equipment for National Guard and reserve units, $600 million, or 10 percent, more than the administration's request. The conferees

noted that severe equipment shortfalls persisted across nondeployed National Guard and reserve units and could affect their ability to respond to domestic emergencies.

- A ceiling of 1,425,000 active-duty military personnel in fiscal 2010, equal to the president's request and 55,227 above the existing level. The total included 562,400 for the army; 328,800 for the Navy; 331,700 for the Air Force; and 202,100 for the Marine Corps. The bill also set a combined ceiling of 854,500 National Guard, reserve units, and Coast Guard forces, equal to the administration's request and 6,444 more than in fiscal 2009. It limited to 78,851 the number of reserve personnel that could be placed on active duty in fiscal 2010.
- $8 billion to continue the 1990 and 2005 rounds of base realignment and closure.

Veterans' Health Programs

Congress put key veterans' health programs on a two-year budget cycle in an effort to make the funding more predictable and avoid disruptions. President Barack Obama signed the bill on October 22, 2009 (HR 1016—PL 111-81).

For years, the Department of Veterans Affairs (VA) health care system had been plagued by consistently late and, at times, inadequate budgets. In nineteen of the previous twenty-two years, the regular appropriations bills that funded the VA were not enacted until after the start of the fiscal year—often months afterward—a trend that continued in 2009. With growing numbers of veterans returning from the wars in Iraq and Afghanistan, the VA also had to ask for more money for health care programs than it received under the regular appropriations bill, leading Congress to insert extra funding into supplemental spending bills.

Veterans' service organizations said advance funding was critical to alleviating the long waits for treatment, personnel shortages, and construction delays that could result when appropriations bills were late.

The legislation required that the president's budget include discretionary amounts for the coming fiscal year and the one that followed for three VA health programs—medical services, medical support and compliance, and medical facilities. Similarly, the regular appropriations bill for the VA had to include advance discretionary budget authority for the following fiscal year for the three accounts. The VA was required to provide an annual report to Congress by July 31 of each year detailing cost estimates.

The House passed HR 1016 (H Rept 111-171) by a vote of 409–1 on June 23. The Senate passed the bill by voice vote August 6, after inserting its own, slightly different version (S 423). The two chambers sent the bill back and forth, agreeing on a final version that the Senate cleared by voice vote October 13.

Outlays for Veterans

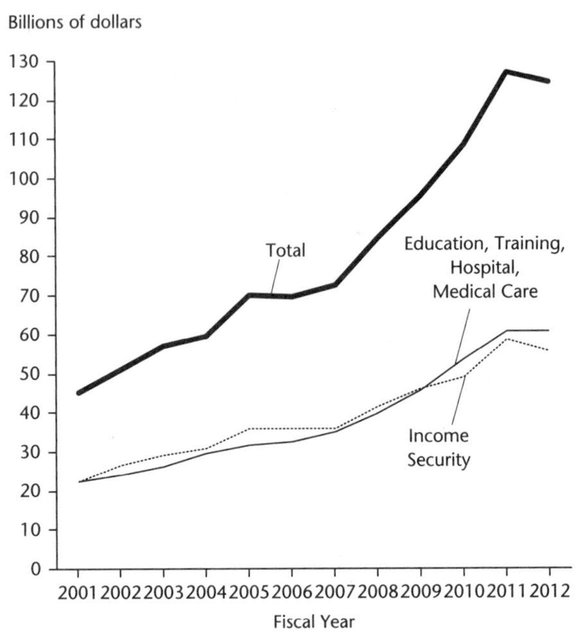

SOURCE: Office of Management and Budget, *Historical Tables, Budget of the United States Government: Fiscal Year 2013* (Washington, D.C.: U.S. Government Printing Office, 2012), Table 3.2.

NOTE: Total line includes expenditures not shown separately.

The fiscal 2010 Military Construction–VA spending bill included $48.2 billion in advance appropriations for the medical accounts in fiscal 2011. The bill was enacted in December as part of an omnibus spending package (PL 111-117). *(Omnibus appropriations, p. 127)*

Fiscal 2010 Defense Appropriations

Democratic leaders put the must-pass appropriations bill at the end of the line of fiscal 2010 spending measures, holding it until they had determined what last-minute legislation it should take with it. Congress cleared the measure, with several small add-ons, on December 19, 2009, and President Barack Obama signed it the same day (HR 3326—PL 111-118).

The bill provided $636.4 billion in discretionary spending for the Defense Department—$508.1 billion for regular Pentagon activities and $128.2 billion to support ongoing operations in Iraq and Afghanistan and related activities. It was the first time since 2001 that war funding had been included in the regular defense budget.

Appropriators said the Pentagon would probably need additional fiscal 2010 funding the following spring to support Obama's planned surge of troops in Afghanistan.

The bill also included $290 million in mandatory funds for Central Intelligence Agency (CIA) retirement and disability benefits, along with $10.7 billion in permanently appropriated funds for retiree health benefits.

The discretionary total was $3.8 billion, or just .06 percent, less than Obama requested and $11.4 billion, or 2 percent, more than enacted for fiscal 2009. However, the comparison with fiscal 2009 included $70 billion in emergency appropriations provided for that year under a supplemental bill enacted in June (PL 111-132). Without that funding, the fiscal 2010 bill total was about 13 percent above the previous year.

The measure largely followed the administration's outlines, including no funding for additional F-22 Raptor fighter jets. Congress gave up on the plane after plans to fund it drew a direct veto threat from the president. Conferees retained funding for two programs that had drawn less direct veto warnings: the troubled VH-71 presidential helicopter and an alternate engine for the F-35 Joint Strike Fighter. But the final bill modified the spending, and the threat ebbed considerably given the importance of defense funding, especially in wartime.

The measure provided additional funds for equipment depleted by the wars in Iraq and Afghanistan, including new combat vehicles, new battle gear for the Army National Guard and reserves, military pay raises, and quality-of-life improvements for the troops and their families. It reduced spending below fiscal 2009 levels for missile defense, new nuclear weapons, and other futuristic programs such as the Future Combat Systems.

As was typically the case, the annual spending bill largely mirrored the companion defense authorization measure (PL 111-84). Negotiations over defense appropriations were relatively smooth: Major funding levels were generally similar in the House- and Senate-passed versions of the bill, and policy differences were minimal.

HOUSE SUBCOMMITTEE ACTION

The House Defense Appropriations Subcommittee gave voice vote approval July 16 to a draft $636.3 billion bill that was about $3.8 billion less than Obama requested. The total consisted of $508 billion for regular accounts and $128.2 billion for operations in Iraq and Afghanistan. Subcommittee Chair John P. Murtha, D-Pa., said the savings came from some program cuts, a reduction in contractors, and moving some operations money into the war funding section of the bill. Jerry Lewis of California, the ranking Republican on the full committee, said the bill would be a 4.5 percent funding increase over fiscal 2009, while the increase allocated for other appropriations bills averaged 12 percent. He said it was "the wrong way to prioritize spending."

The draft, which the panel considered in a closed-door markup, funded several troubled programs that Obama and Gates wanted to cap or terminate, including:

- $369 million in unrequested funds for advanced procurement of twelve additional F-22 fighters.
- $5.6 billion for twenty-eight F-35s, about $400 million and two planes less than requested, and $4 billion for development costs, $430 million more than requested. Procurement savings and extra development money helped provide $560 million for the alternative engine.
- $485 million to complete five VH-71 presidential helicopters, $400 million more than requested. The troubled helicopter program had cost billions of dollars before Obama sought to end it. Murtha said after so much investment, it was necessary to get something out of the program.
- $674 million to purchase three C-17s. Like the Bush administration, Obama wanted to end the transport plane program.
- None of the funds requested to close the Guantánamo Bay, Cuba, detention facility. Murtha said the Pentagon could ask for the money again once a plan for shuttering the prison was complete.

HOUSE COMMITTEE ACTION

The full House Appropriations Committee approved the bill (HR 3326—H Rept 111-230) by voice vote July 22, making few changes to the subcommittee draft.

However, Subcommittee Chair Murtha said he would end his quest to continue funding for the purchase of new F-22 fighter jets and pledged to work to reapportion the funds before the House passed the bill. He said that a 58–40 vote by the Senate the previous day to strip its fiscal 2010 defense authorization bill of budget authority for additional F-22s rendered the House's funding effort futile. "That ended the debate," he said, also citing Obama's veto threat.

The committee gave voice vote approval to a manager's amendment by Murtha that included language to bar the use of funds to release prisoners from Guantánamo into the United States. Prisoners could not be brought to the United States for trial until two months after the president submitted a report to Congress on a list of issues.

HOUSE FLOOR ACTION

The House agreed to strip the money for procuring additional F-22 fighter jets before passing the bill, 400–30, on July 30. But the measure still retained the F-35 engine and helicopter funds.

The White House warned in a statement July 28 that the president's senior advisers would recommend he veto the bill if it would "seriously disrupt" the F-35 fighter program or interfere with plans to start a new competition for the VH-71 program.

The House adopted, 269–165, a manager's amendment that reallocated the $369 million for advance procurement of F-22s to other programs. The funds were shifted, in part, to purchase spare engines for the fleet of 187 F-22s and to close down the production line.

Republicans argued that the need to maintain air superiority and the threat of advanced fighters being built by competitors such as Russia required adding more planes to the force. But Murtha said it would take sixty-six votes in the Senate to override a veto "and there's no chance of getting that kind of vote."

Murtha predicted that other White House objections would be resolved in conference, averting a veto. "Every year we have conflict [with the administration]," he said. "But we're a different branch of government, and we try to do what we think is right, and in the end we compromise."

The House soundly rejected nine amendments offered by Jeff Flake, R-Ariz., aimed at stripping out some $2.7 billion in member projects, or earmarks, in the bill.

SENATE COMMITTEE ACTION

The Senate Appropriations Committee approved an amended version of the bill on September 10 that called for $636.3 billion—$508 billion for regular accounts and $128.2 billion for operations in Afghanistan and Iraq—virtually the same as in the House bill. The vote on the measure (HR 3326—S Rept 111-74) was 30–0. The primary differences between the House and Senate bills lay in how they handled particular weapons systems and procurement decisions.

"There has been much discussion this year about proposals by the administration to cut funding for unneeded weapons programs," said Daniel K. Inouye, D-Hawaii, chair of the committee and its subcommittee. "The vice chair and I have reviewed each of the proposals by the administration [and] while we are not in complete agreement with the judgment of administration officials, we have . . . supported the requests of our leaders."

The committee-approved bill:

- Did not include funds for additional F-22s or the alternative engine for the F-35, and included only the funding needed to eliminate the VH-71 production line and to open up competition for a new presidential helicopter.
- Diverged with the president on the C-17, approving $2.6 billion to procure ten new cargo planes. That exceeded the more modest House proposal by $1.8 billion and seven planes. During the August recess, eighteen senators had written to Inouye and ranking Republican Thad Cochran of Mississippi, urging continued production of the C-17. Ending the program, they wrote, would "not only undermine our national security, but severely degrade our ability to maintain a viable and competitive aerospace industry."
- Included a prohibition on releasing, transferring, or jailing Guantánamo Bay detainees in the United States, without an exception.
- Differed with the House on the Arleigh Burke–class DDG-51 destroyer, calling for $3.7 billion to pay for the construction of two ships in fiscal 2010 and $329 million for advance procurement for two more ships in fiscal 2011. The House bill included $1.9 billion for one DDG-51 and $329 million for advance procurement. Inouye said funding for an additional destroyer was meant to keep the production line open and cut costs for the program.
- Included $6.7 billion for Mine Resistant Ambush Protected (MRAP) vehicles, about $1.2 billion more than Obama's request. The House bill had included $3.6 billion.

SENATE FLOOR ACTION

The Senate passed the bill, 93–7, on October 6. During debate, the Senate:

- Adopted, 91–7, a bipartisan amendment to delay the retirement of about 250 aging tactical aircraft. Christopher S. Bond, R-Mo., and Patrick J. Leahy, D-Vt., co-chairs of the Senate's National Guard Caucus, sponsored the amendment.
- Adopted, 77–21, an amendment by Inouye to require that congressional earmarks for for-profit companies be subject to the same acquisition rules as items requested by the administration. The amendment, which was retained in the final bill, was an alternative to a proposal by John McCain, R-Ariz., rejected by voice vote, that would have required all Pentagon earmarks to for-profit companies to be competitively bid.
- Adopted by voice vote an amendment by Joseph I. Lieberman, I-Conn., and Jeff Sessions, R-Ala., to prevent reprogramming of between $50 million and $151 million provided for ground-based interceptor missile development. Sessions said the amendment was in response to the president's reversal of Bush's plan to establish a missile defense system in Poland and the Czech Republic. It was not in the final bill.
- Rejected, 30–68, an amendment by McCain that would have removed the funding for ten Boeing C-17 cargo planes. McCain urged his colleagues to support the administration's position that the additional aircraft were not needed, but appropriators insisted the planes were necessary to upgrade an aging fleet.
- Rejected several GOP amendments to strike earmarks. An amendment by Tom Coburn of Oklahoma to bar the funding of earmarks in Pentagon operations and maintenance accounts fell, 25–73, while one by McCain to strike a $9.5 million earmark for a hypersonic wind tunnel research program in Montana was rejected, 43–55.
- Rejected, 38–60, an amendment by John Barrasso, R-Wyo., that would have denied funds for the CIA's Center on Climate Change. Barrasso questioned whether the center would shift CIA resources away from addressing the much greater threat of a terrorist attack.

FINAL ACTION

Instead of holding a formal conference to reconcile differences between the House and Senate versions of the bill, appropriators reached agreement on a final measure through informal negotiations.

The House adopted the compromise as a substitute amendment by a vote of 395–34 on December 16, shortly before leaving for the year. The Senate took a break from its ongoing debate on the health care overhaul to clear the bill, 88–10, on December 19.

MAJOR PROVISIONS

Following are major components of PL 111-118 (the Department of Defense Appropriations Act of 2010):

Aircraft

The measure provided $13.3 billion for Air Force aircraft procurement and $18.6 billion for Navy aircraft, including:

- $6.8 billion, matching the request, for thirty F-35 Joint Strike Fighter aircraft, a multirole fighter with versions for the Air Force, Navy, and Marine Corps.
- $4 billion for research and development, including $465 million in unrequested funds to continue development and initial procurement of an alternative engine. Two teams were working separately on the engine: United Technologies' Pratt and Whitney on the one hand, and U.K.-based Rolls-Royce, partnered with General Electric, on the other. The Pentagon had been trying to eliminate the Rolls-Royce team, saying the competition was unnecessary and too costly, but lawmakers insisted it would lead to a better engine. To mollify the administration, conferees included extra money for the engine, rather than dipping into the procurement funding as the House had proposed.
- No funding for additional F-22 fighters. The bill provided $569 million for research and development and $177 million for modifications to existing F-22s. The program had been plagued by cost overruns, technical problems, and questions over the need for the plane, which was geared toward defending against the Soviet Union rather than for the low-intensity fighting that had become typical. In its statement of administration policy on the bill, the White House said "the collective judgment of the service chiefs and secretaries of the military departments" was that 187 F-22s, the last of which was to be completed in fiscal 2009, were "sufficient to meeting operational requirements."
- $2.6 billion for ten unrequested C-17 cargo planes, as the Senate wanted. The House had included $763 million for three planes. The administration strongly opposed the funding, saying in a statement, "The 205 C-17s in the force and on order, together with the existing fleet of C-5 aircraft, are sufficient to meet the department's future airlift needs, even under the most stressing situations."
- $1.6 billion for eighteen next-generation F-18 Super Hornet fighters—$495 million and nine aircraft more than requested and included in the Senate bill, and equal to the House plan. The bill also appropriated $1.6 billion, as requested and included in both bills, for twenty-two new EA-18G Growler electronic warfare planes, a variant of the F/A-18F.
- $129 million for the VH-71 presidential helicopter, which Secretary of Defense Robert M. Gates had targeted for termination as a wasteful and troubled program. The Navy officially canceled the program in May, and the White House warned that including funds could prompt a veto. The president instead requested $85 million to terminate the program. Conferees said the amount they provided would keep the program viable as a competitor in a follow-on helicopter program. The House had included $485 million to make the five helicopters in the works operational. The Senate called for $30 million to begin development of a follow-on helicopter, but did not include funding for continued work on the existing aircraft.

Shipbuilding

The bill provided $15 billion for Navy shipbuilding programs, including:

- $1.4 billion for the DDG-1000 land attack destroyer, about $300 million more than requested and included in the House bill, and close to the Senate amount. The bill also provided multiyear procurement authority and $1.9 billion for the DDG-51 Arleigh Burke–class destroyer, predecessor to the DDG-1000. The amount was similar to the House level and Obama's request; the Senate bill called for $3.7 billion. The final bill provided an additional $579 million in advanced funding to restart production of the DDG-51.
- $3.9 billion, as requested and included in both bills, for construction and long-lead components for the next ships in the Virginia class of new attack submarines, planned to replace retiring Los Angeles class and constitute the bulk of the attack submarine force in the future. The bill also provided $2 billion in advanced procurement funding for two additional submarines to be built in fiscal 2011 and beyond.
- $1.1 billion for procurement of two San Antonio–class LPD-17 amphibious ships, equal to the request and the amount in both bills.
- $1.1 billion, as passed by the Senate, for two Littoral Combat Ship vessels, $300 million and one ship less than requested, and $1.1 billion and two ships less than in the House bill. The measure also provided $425 million for research and development.

Missile Defense

The bill included $9.3 billion for missile defense programs, equal to the amount in the president's request and the House and Senate bills, but 7 percent below fiscal 2009 funding. The bill increased funding over existing levels for proven missile defense systems such as the Aegis ballistic missile defense and THAAD, and continued funding for the kinetic energy interceptor that the president wanted to terminate.

The bill included the president's request of $51 million for continued research and development of a sea-based missile defense system that would focus on protecting Europe from short- and medium-range Iranian missiles. The administration announced in September that it would pursue the new program in place of a controversial Bush administration plan to build a missile interceptor site in Poland and the Czech Republic.

Future Combat Systems

The bill included the Senate-approved amount of $2.2 billion for continued development of a restructured version of the Future Combat Systems. The amount was $330 million, or 12 percent, less than the president's request and about $150 million less than the House amount. Development of the army system, planned as a computer-linked array of reconnaissance and battlefield weapons, had become so expensive and unwieldy that the Pentagon called a temporary halt to the manned ground vehicle component and began restructuring the program.

Health

The bill included $30.5 billion for the department's health program, which included $1.3 billion provided as part of the war funding. The total was $1.3 billion more than Obama requested, about $625 million more than in the Senate bill, and $550 million less than the House wanted.

Military Pay

The bill provided for a 3.4 percent average pay increase for the military, 0.5 percentage points above the request.

Overseas Contingency Operations

The bill appropriated $128.2 billion to support ongoing operations in Iraq, Afghanistan, and elsewhere—although other money in the bill could be used as well. The amount was virtually the same as requested, although conferees allocated some of the funds differently. For example, the bill provided:

- $6.6 billion to train and equip Afghan security forces, about $900 million less than the $7.5 billion requested.
- $6.3 billion for Mine Resistant Ambush Protected (MRAP) vehicles for Afghanistan, $825 million more than requested, with funds shifted from the account for Afghan security forces.
- $5 billion for an Overseas Contingency Operations Transfer Fund created under the bill to allow the Pentagon to transfer funds among accounts as U.S. forces shifted focus from Iraq to Afghanistan.
- $1.2 billion for the Commanders' Emergency Response Program, $300 million less than requested. The fund provided a pool of money that U.S. military commanders could use for small reconstruction projects; it also had been used to put insurgents on the U.S. payroll. Commanders deemed the fund vital, but auditors said it was poorly managed. Conferees withheld $500 million pending a report from the Pentagon.
- $1.9 billion for a program to counter improvised explosive devices (IEDs), the main cause of U.S. casualties in Iraq. About $100 million of the total was included in the regular budget. The total was $216 million less than requested.
- None of the $100 million requested for shutting down the U.S. detention facility at Guantánamo Bay, Cuba. The bill also barred the use of any funds to release detainees from the prison into the United States. Detainees could be transferred to the United States for trial, but only after the president submitted a report to Congress detailing the risks and costs involved and steps that would be taken to mitigate any danger.

The final bill also carried a series of provisions that extended authorizations through February 28, 2010, for a number of expiring programs, including:

- Several provisions of the antiterrorism law known as the Patriot Act. *(Patriot Act, p. 208)*
- A delay in a scheduled cut in Medicare physician payments, commonly referred to as "the doc-fix." *(Medicare payments, p. 450)*
- Authorization for highway, transit, highway safety, and motor carrier safety programs. *(Surface transportation, p. 324)*
- Extended federal unemployment benefits for workers who had exhausted their regular state benefits. *(Unemployment, p. 517)*
- A 65 percent subsidy for health insurance coverage under the COBRA law for workers who had lost their jobs. *(Unemployment, p. 525)*

Fiscal 2010 Military Construction Appropriations

Congress in late 2009 included funding for military construction programs and the Veterans Affairs (VA) Department during fiscal year 2010 as part of a year-end omnibus appropriations package. President Barack Obama signed the omnibus into law on December 16 (HR 3288—PL 111-117). *(Omnibus funding legislation, p. 127)*

The bill appropriated $109.6 billion for the VA and $24.7 billion for department construction projects, including overseas contingency projects. The military construction total was about $6 billion less than total fiscal 2009 appropriations, which included $2.9 billion in emergency funding. Leaving out the emergency money, the bill provided $3.1 billion less than the programs got in fiscal 2009.

HOUSE COMMITTEE ACTION

The House Appropriations Committee gave voice vote approval June 23 to a bill (HR 3082—H Rept 111-188) that called for $133.7 billion in fiscal 2010 funding for the VA and military construction, about $230 million more than the White House requested. It also included $48.2 billion veterans' health care programs for fiscal 2011. The Military Construction–Veterans Affairs Subcommittee, which drafted the bill, approved it by voice vote June 16.

The bill included $24.6 billion for Pentagon military construction projects, family housing, and base realignment and closure, about $230 million more than Obama requested. The total included $1.4 billion for army and Air Force overseas construction projects.

HOUSE FLOOR ACTION

The House passed the bill by a vote of 415–3 on July 10 with only minor changes. Republicans complained about the Democrats' use of a "structured rule," which limited amendments to specific proposals approved by the majority-controlled Rules Committee. GOP lawmakers argued that Democrats were breaking with a precedent of considering spending bills under open rules that set no limits on amendments or time. Democratic leaders replied that structured rules were necessary because Republicans had been unwilling to agree to any limits, starting with the Commerce-Justice-Science bill, the first of the fiscal 2010 spending measures to reach the House floor. The rule (H Res 622) was adopted, 241–179, with no Republican support.

SENATE COMMITTEE ACTION

The Senate Appropriations Committee approved a $133.9 billion version of the bill (S 1407—S Rept 111-40), 30–0, on July 7. The Military Construction–Veterans Affairs Subcommittee had approved a draft by voice vote the previous day. The total was about $200 million more than in the House-passed version and $430 million more than the White House requested. As with the House bill, it included $48.2 billion for VA health accounts in fiscal 2011.

The bill called for $24.6 billion for military construction, virtually the same as House appropriators provided for comparable programs. The total included the $1.4 billion for overseas contingency operations.

SENATE FLOOR ACTION

The Senate passed HR 3082, 100–0, on November 17, after amending it with the text of S 1407.

During the debate, senators agreed, 57–43, to table (or kill) an amendment by James M. Inhofe, R-Okla., that would have prohibited the use of funds in the bill to build or modify a facility in the United States to hold detainees from the U.S. facility at Guantánamo Bay, Cuba, permanently or temporarily.

Republicans tried repeatedly to attach language to various bills that would prevent the Obama administration from bringing detainees to the United States for trial. Inhofe argued that terrorism suspects should be tried in tribunals, not in U.S. federal courts and not in the United States. "If you want terrorists here, then vote against this amendment," he said.

Democrats said the administration was already bringing detainees to the United States for trial and that Inhofe's amendment would only make the facilities that held them less secure. Attorney General Eric H. Holder Jr. had announced November 13 that five suspected terrorists being held at Guantánamo Bay would be tried in federal courts in New York City.

FINAL ACTION

The Military Construction–Veterans Affairs bill was the ninth and last of the twelve fiscal 2010 spending bills to reach the Senate floor. Shortly afterward, the Senate plunged into a marathon debate over a health care overhaul that left no time to consider individual spending bills or conference reports. Instead, Democratic appropriators agreed on a compromise version of the bill and included it in the year-end omnibus package, which they inserted into the conference report on the Transportation and Housing and Urban Development, and Related Agencies spending measure (HR 3288). *(Omnibus package, p. 127)*

The House adopted the conference report (H Rept 111-366) by a vote of 221–202 on December 10. The Senate broke briefly from the health care debate to clear the omnibus bill, 57–35, on December 13.

The $24.7 billion included in the bill for military construction included:

- $11.8 billion for operational facilities, barracks, child care centers, and other facilities for active-duty units.
- $1.6 billion for readiness centers and operational facilities for the Army National Guard, Air Guard, and army, Navy, Marine Corps, and Air Force reserve forces.
- $2.3 billion to construct, operate, and maintain housing for military personnel and families.
- $8 billion for base realignment and closure costs, mainly to support activities related to the 2005 round of base closings.
- $1.4 billion, the amount Obama requested, for overseas contingency operations—the construction of army and Air Force facilities to support operations and previously scheduled troop deployments to Afghanistan.

Fiscal 2010 War Supplemental

With Republicans tipping the balance, the House in July 2010 cleared a $58.8 billion fiscal 2010 supplemental spending bill devoted primarily to paying for operations in Iraq and Afghanistan. President Barack Obama signed the legislation on July 29, 2010 (HR 4899—PL 111-212).

Republicans in both chambers generally supported the bill, while House Democrats were sharply divided. Among those voting against the final version was Appropriations Chair David R. Obey, D-Wis. In floor remarks, Obey told his colleagues he had "the highest respect and appreciation" for U.S. troops but said they are "being let down by the inability of the governments of Afghanistan and in some instances Pakistan to do their parts."

When Obama sent his fiscal 2011 budget to Congress in February, he requested $33 billion in supplemental fiscal 2010 funds, including $30 billion for deployments to Afghanistan and $1 billion to train Iraqi security forces. Subsequent requests for funds for disaster aid, veterans' health programs, and other purposes brought the total to $64.4 billion.

From the outset, Obey and many other House Democrats wanted to add billions of dollars for domestic projects, particularly to avoid the layoffs of tens of thousands of teachers nationwide at a time when state budgets were stretched thin and funds for the purpose in the 2009 economic stimulus law (PL 111-5) were running out. Democratic leaders spent several months trying to come up with a package that could win enough votes in the Senate to surmount a filibuster.

A steady stream of negative news about the situation in Afghanistan, including reports of pervasive corruption in the Afghan government as well as criticism of the administration's approach to the war, complicated congressional deliberations.

The Senate passed a bill in May that focused on war spending. After lengthy negotiations among Democrats, the House accepted the Senate's bill but added $22.8 billion, mainly for domestic programs. The Senate decisively rejected the add-ons and sent its original version back to the House. The latest word from the Defense Department was that it would need the funds in mid-August. With members about to leave for the August recess, the House had little choice but to clear the narrower bill, but it did so only with the support of 160 Republicans.

SENATE COMMITTEE ACTION

With disagreement among Democrats slowing action in the House, Democratic leaders took the somewhat unorthodox approach of letting Senate appropriators go first. The Senate Appropriations Committee approved the $58.8 billion bill by a vote of 30–0 on May 13 (HR 4899—S Rept 111-188).

Appropriations Chair Daniel K. Inouye, D-Hawaii, deliberately kept the measure spare, rejecting bids for school aid and focusing the bill on the wars, veterans, and disaster relief. Inouye took a $5.1 billion disaster aid bill that the House had passed in March, stripped out $600 million for summer jobs that also had been in the bill, and inserted the funding for the wars and related expenses and for Agent Orange claims.

SENATE FLOOR ACTION

The Senate passed the bill, 67–28, on May 27. The key procedural vote took place just hours before passage when the Senate invoked cloture, 69–29, limiting the debate.

Senate Democratic leaders were somewhat defensive about the more modest amount of spending in their bill, compared with what Obey and others in the House were trying to do. "President Obama has drastically scaled down the size of the supplemental and encouraged the defense budgeting process to better incorporate wartime spending, but there is still a dire need for this supplemental," Jack Reed, D-R.I., said at a May 26 news conference seeking to rally support for the measure.

Inouye was able to fend off pressure from his left flank. Sen. Tom Harkin, D-Iowa, had been pressing to include the money to prevent teacher layoffs, but he was unable to assemble the necessary sixty votes.

Republicans offered several amendments, including proposals to add funds for border security and the prosecution of illegal immigrants, as well as to provide offsets for the bill's cost, but all of them were rejected.

HOUSE COMMITTEE ACTION

In a sign of the growing worries about the government's reliance on borrowed money, efforts in the House Appropriations Committee to mark up a more sweeping $84 billion measure ran aground. Obey postponed a scheduled May 27 session, and the markup was never held.

"At some point, they have to be hearing from their constituents that enough is enough," said Jeb Hensarling, R-Texas, a conservative who was serving on a fiscal commission created by Obama to make budget and deficit reduction recommendations. Hensarling's view was echoed by fiscally conservative Democrats. *(Deficit reduction commission, p. 142)*

The draft bore the strong stamp of Obey, a progressive set to retire at the end of the 111th Congress, who signaled his intent to spend his final months in the House battling to get more money for schools and other programs he had long supported. Obey's draft included $23 billion for schools.

Before the House markup was postponed, intense negotiations involving both chambers and parties had only seemed to widen the differences among Democrats.

HOUSE FLOOR ACTION

The House on July 1 adopted an amendment to the $58.8 billion Senate-passed measure that added $22.8 billion for schools and other Democratic domestic priorities.

The decision to add the domestic funding meant postponing further action until mid-July, because the Senate had already adjourned for the July Fourth recess. Republicans complained that Democrats could easily have gotten the supplemental funds to the Pentagon by July 4 by simply accepting the Senate version.

Under a complicated rule for floor debate, the House amendment was divided into several parts, which gave antiwar Democrats a chance to vote to wind down the U.S. military presence in Afghanistan. At the same time, it allowed fiscal conservatives in the Democratic Blue Dog Coalition to oppose the additional domestic spending without having to vote against the $58.8 billion in the Senate version. The rule, which also automatically approved Democrats' plan for a one-year budget, was adopted, 215–210. The rule had no GOP support and thirty-eight Democratic defectors.

The House adopted Obey's domestic spending amendment, 239–182, with fifteen Democrats and all but three Republicans voting "no." The amendment included:

- $10 billion to enable school districts to avoid laying off teachers for the coming school year. Obey said the funding was fully offset and would help keep 140,000 school employees on the job.
- $5 billion to cover a shortfall in Pell grants for low-income college students.
- $1 billion for a summer jobs program, a high priority for the Congressional Black Caucus.
- $701 million to increase security activities along the U.S.-Mexico border, including the hiring of 1,200 additional Border Patrol agents. To help offset the added spending, Obey proposed rescinding $800 million in previously appropriated funds for education overhaul programs, including President Obama's signature "Race to the Top" initiative that provided competitive education grants to states.

The White House issued a statement expressing support for the extra funding for teachers and for Pell grants but warned of a potential veto if the proposed rescissions remained in the final bill. The White House made a similar threat regarding amendments intended to curb military operations in Afghanistan. A group of thirteen senators, led by Evan Bayh, D-Ind., sent a letter to Inouye opposing the proposed rescissions.

Three antiwar amendments were handily defeated, but not before an impassioned debate over the direction of the war and an unusual vote by Speaker Nancy Pelosi, D-Calif., for one of the proposals resisted by the White House.

"The echoes of Vietnam are in this chamber," said Steve Cohen, D-Tenn. "That was a war we couldn't win, and some people wouldn't accept it." Cohen said the money should be spent at home instead.

Jack Kingston, R-Ga., countered: "War is complicated. War does not always go your way. . . . I think it's very important for us to let the military make these decisions."

During the debate, the House:

- Rejected, 25–376, an amendment to strike military funding for Afghanistan from the bill.
- Rejected, on a **key vote of 100–321 (R 7–164; D 93–157)** a proposal by Barbara Lee, D-Calif., to limit the use of the military funding for Afghanistan to activities related to withdrawing troops and protecting civilian and military personnel. *(2010 key votes, p. 767)*
- Rejected, 162–260, an amendment by Jim McGovern, D-Mass., to require that Obama send Congress a new intelligence estimate on Afghanistan by January 31, 2011, and a plan by April 4, 2011, for redeploying U.S. troops. Funds for Afghanistan could not be spent after July 2011 for any purpose other than beginning a troop drawdown, unless Congress voted otherwise. Pelosi voted for the proposal.

FINAL ACTION

The Senate on July 22 refused to accept the $22.8 billion domestic-spending amendment, paving the way for final action on the bill. By a vote of 46–51, senators rejected a motion to limit debate on the amended House version of the bill. Instead, the Senate agreed by unanimous consent to send its original version back to the House.

"While I would have preferred that the Senate take up and pass HR 4899 as further amended by the House, an amendment that addressed several additional critical needs, I understand that we were not going to get sixty votes for that to happen," Inouye said.

As expected, the House accepted the Senate version, clearing it by a **key vote of 308–114 (R 160–12; D 148–102)** on July 27. By then, the Pentagon had indicated that it could hold out until early August. *(2010 key votes, p. 767)*

To allow antiwar Democrats another chance to express their concerns, House leaders gave floor time to a resolution (H Con Res 301), sponsored by Dennis J. Kucinich, D-Ohio, that would have directed the president to remove troops from Pakistan within thirty days. The resolution, rejected by a vote of 38–372, invoked the 1973 War Powers Resolution (PL 93-148), which provided that Congress could force the withdrawal of troops fighting abroad if there had been a declaration of war or explicit statutory authorization. All presidents since the 1973 legislation passed had refused to recognize the act, arguing that it was unconstitutional.

MAJOR HIGHLIGHTS

The $58.8 billion total for the bill—which was about equal to Obama's amended request—consisted of $45.4 billion in discretionary spending and $13.4 billion in mandatory funds. The main components of the bill included:

Defense Department. $33.4 billion for the Pentagon, which appropriators said included funding for the addition of 30,000 troops in Afghanistan as part of the administration's surge program. Major elements included:

- $24.6 billion for operations and maintenance.
- $1.8 billion for military personnel.
- $4.9 billion for procurement.
- $2.6 billion for the Afghan Security forces and $1 billion for the Iraqi Security forces.
- $656 million for military construction.

Disaster aid. $5.1 billion for the Federal Emergency Management Agency (FEMA) to help pay for the costs of previous disasters, including hurricanes Katrina and Rita, the Midwest floods of 2008, and California wildfires.

Haiti. $2.9 billion for aid in response to the January 12 earthquake in Haiti.

Oil spill. $162 million related to the 2010 Gulf of Mexico oil spill at the British Petroleum rig Deepwater Horizon.

Veterans Affairs. $13.4 billion in mandatory funding for the Veterans Affairs (VA) Department to cover claims by Vietnam War veterans exposed to the defoliant Agent Orange. The VA had extended coverage in 2009 to veterans who were exposed to Agent Orange and then developed B-cell leukemia, Parkinson's disease, or ischemic heart disease, a condition marked by reduced blood supply to the heart.

"Don't Ask, Don't Tell" Repeal

After years of battling and months of legislative maneuvering, gay rights advocates won a landmark victory as Congress cleared legislation repealing the "don't ask, don't tell" law that banned openly gay people from serving in the military. President Obama signed the legislation into law December 22, 2010 (HR 2965—PL 111-321).

"We are not a nation that says, 'Don't ask, don't tell,' " Obama said at a signing ceremony. "We are a nation that says, 'Out of many, we are one.' " In a statement after the bill cleared, Obama said, "By ending 'Don't Ask, Don't Tell,' no longer will our nation be denied the service of thousands of patriotic Americans forced to leave the military, despite years of exemplary performance, because they happen to be gay. And no longer will many thousands more be asked to live a lie in order to serve the country they love."

Although the Defense Department was given latitude on how and when to carry out the provisions, the legislation essentially overturned a 1993 law (PL 103-160) that had been the subject of heated political controversy for nearly a generation. Obama had promised to end the seventeen-year-old law during his presidential campaign, and in his 2010 State of the Union address, he vowed to work with Congress to make that a reality. *(Text, 893; 1993 law, Congress and the Nation Vol. IX, pp. 284, 257)*

The repeal had strong backing from Defense Secretary Robert M. Gates as well as Joint Chiefs Chair Adm. Mike Mullen and Vice Chair Gen. James E. Cartwright. They cited a Pentagon survey, made public November 30, that found that 70 percent of U.S. military personnel surveyed believed a change in the law would have positive, mixed, or no effects.

Gates said he would not allow the change until he was satisfied that all necessary training and education was completed across the military. The secretary, in particular, had warned he did not want the law overturned by the courts, which could require an immediate change and allow little time for the military to prepare. Concern that the courts would act before Congress did was heightened by judicial rulings that the existing policy was unconstitutional. Those rulings were under appeal.

The chiefs of the army, Marine Corps, and Air Force were more hesitant. In testimony before the Senate Armed Services Committee on December 3, they expressed varying degrees of concern about the potential effect of the repeal on military morale and readiness, and they agreed that the change should not happen soon.

After the vote clearing the bill, Aubrey Sarvis, the executive director of the Servicemembers Legal Network, an advocacy group, cautioned gay and lesbian service members to continue to abide by the "don't ask, don't tell" limitations until the repeal was implemented. "Even with this historic vote," Sarvis wrote, "service members must continue to serve in silence until repeal is final."

The question of allowing gays and lesbians to serve openly in the U.S. military had been a topic of national debate for almost two decades. The 1993 law became the basis for the military's "don't ask, don't tell" policy. The law itself banned service by military personnel who engaged in homosexual conduct, including declaring their homosexuality or marrying someone of the same sex. It did not address the issue of sexual "orientation" or prohibit commanders from asking about an individual's orientation, although that became part of the Pentagon policy.

LEGISLATIVE ACTION

Before passing its version of the 2011 defense authorization bill (HR 5136) on May 28, the House adopted an amendment to repeal the 1993 law, conditional on the Pentagon finishing its review of the implications of a repeal and top administration officials certifying that it would not hurt readiness. The amendment, by Patrick J. Murphy, D-Pa., reflected an agreement backed by the Pentagon and the White House. It was adopted May 27, 2010, on a **key vote 234–194 (R 5–168; D 229–26).** *(2010 key votes, p. 767)*

In the Senate, the Armed Services Committee approved a defense bill (S 3454) on May 27 that contained identical repeal language. The language by Joseph I. Lieberman, I-Conn., was adopted 16–12. All but one Democrat, Jim Webb of Virginia, voted for it, while all but one Republican, Susan Collins of Maine, voted "nay."

The bill never reached the Senate floor because of a GOP filibuster sparked by the "don't ask, don't tell" language and other controversial provisions, as well as Republican complaints about a limit on the number of amendments that could be offered. When the second cloture motion on the bill was rejected December 9, it was clear that the repeal language, among other provisions, had to be dropped if the defense authorization was to have a chance of becoming law.

At that point, Lieberman and Collins introduced a stand-alone version of the repeal language; Murphy and Majority Leader Steny H. Hoyer, D-Md., did the same in the House. With the clock running out on the session, Democratic leaders took a crucial step to shorten the time the Senate would spend on the bill. They inserted the repeal into an unrelated bill (HR 2965) that both chambers had passed in different forms, passed it 250–175 on December 15, and sent the amended measure back to the Senate. Under Senate rules, that prevented a filibuster on a motion to take up the bill.

With all Democrats present and eight Republicans voting yes, the Senate on December 18, 2010, cleared the bill by a **key vote of 65–31 (R 8–31; D 55–0; I 2–0).** *(2010 key votes p. 767)*

The vote came hours after senators voted, 63–33, to limit floor debate. The eight Republicans backing the repeal were Collins and Olympia J. Snowe of Maine, Lisa Murkowski of Alaska, George V. Voinovich of Ohio, Mark Steven Kirk of Illinois, Scott P. Brown of Massachusetts, John Ensign of Nevada, and Richard M. Burr of North Carolina.

Pivotal backing for the bill in the Senate came from Webb, who said he had received a letter from Gates dated December 17 confirming that his earlier concerns about the repeal's potential effect on unit cohesion could be addressed.

Most of the votes against final passage came from conservative Republicans, some of whom suggested that the time devoted to the vote on "don't ask, don't tell" hurt the chances that they would support approval of ratification of an arms control treaty with Russia (Treaty Doc 111-5), another item on the Senate's end-of-session agenda.

Obama's 2008 opponent in the presidential race, Senate Armed Services ranking Republican John McCain of Arizona, called the procedural vote to limit floor debate on the repeal measure "a very sad day."

"So here we are about six weeks after an election that repudiated the agenda of the other side," McCain said of the midterm election results. "We are jamming or trying to jam major issues through the Senate of the United States because they know they can't get it done beginning next January 5," when the new Congress was set to convene with a GOP-controlled House and a larger force of Republicans in the Senate.

GOP strategist John Ullyot, a former spokesperson for the Senate Armed Services panel, suggested that the Republicans who sided with McCain were battling a strong social trend against their viewpoint.

"Republican opposition had a 'going-through-the motions' feel to it, and the tone seemed cranky and outdated," Ullyot said. "We will probably all look back in five years and wonder what the fuss was about and see this as a missed opportunity to move the party to the center on what is likely to be viewed by future generations as a major vote on social policy."

MAJOR PROVISIONS

In overturning the 1993 law, the bill specified that the repeal would take effect only after the president transmitted to the Armed Services committees in both houses written certification signed by the president, secretary, and Chair of the Joint Chiefs of Staff, stating that ending the ban would not harm the military. The certification had to indicate that the officials had considered the report on the department's review of the existing policy; that the Defense Department had prepared the necessary policy and regulations; and that their implementation would be consistent with standards of military readiness, military effectiveness, unit cohesion, and recruiting and retention of the armed forces. If all conditions were met, then the relevant provision of law would be repealed, effective sixty days after the certification. Until then, existing law remained in effect.

The measure also stipulated that it could not be construed to require the provision of benefits in violation of the Defense of Marriage Act (PL 104-199), which defined "marriage" as a legal union between one man and one woman as husband and wife, and defined "spouse" as referring only to a person of the opposite sex who was a husband or a wife. *(Defense of Marriage Act, Congress and the Nation Vol. IX, p. 746)*

New START Treaty Approval

Democrats scored their biggest victory of the 2010 lame duck session on the final day of the 111th Congress, when the Senate approved a nuclear arms treaty with Russia that continued the long tradition of bilateral arms accords ratified by the world's two preeminent nuclear powers.

Action on the new strategic arms reduction treaty, known as New START (Treaty Doc 111-5), sealed a hard-fought victory for President Barack Obama and proved a stinging rebuke to Republican leaders who sought to block a vote. *(Background on arms control agreements, box, Congress and the Nation Vol. XI, p. 364)*

Vice President Joseph R. Biden Jr., who led the Obama administration's lobbying effort on the treaty, presided over the Senate for the final ballot.

"This treaty will enhance our leadership to stop the spread of nuclear weapons and seek the peace of a world without them," Obama said at a news conference afterward. "The strong bipartisan vote in the Senate sends a powerful signal to the world that Republicans and Democrats stand together on behalf of our security."

The vote on the "resolution of advice and consent to ratification" followed a tireless White House lobbying effort reinforced by strong Pentagon backing and the support of a veritable who's who of the nation's foreign policy establishment, not to mention the senator long seen as Republicans' unchallenged expert on the subject: Richard G. Lugar of Indiana, the ranking member on the Senate Foreign Relations Committee. The many high-profile supporters included five former secretaries of state: Colin L. Powell, James A. Baker III, Lawrence S. Eagleburger, George P. Shultz, and Henry A. Kissinger.

The intense administration effort and the determination of Senate Majority Leader Harry Reid, D-Nev., to finish the bill before adjournment helped overcome staunch opposition to a vote before 2011 from Senate Minority Leader Mitch McConnell, R-Ky., and Jon Kyl, R-Ariz., the minority whip and GOP point man on the treaty.

Obama and Russian President Dmitry Medvedev signed the treaty in April 2010 after almost a year of talks. Obama said he deemed it "an important first step forward" in global nonproliferation efforts. But, he added, "it is just one step on a longer journey."

The administration and members of the arms control community regarded the treaty as the sort of modest, straightforward agreement that the White House could get done relatively swiftly before mounting more-ambitious negotiations. There was also broad support for resuming inspection of Russia's nuclear weapons program.

Some arms control advocates even worried that the negotiated cuts to deployed nuclear warheads, which amounted to a 30 percent reduction from the levels of the 2002 Moscow Treaty (approved by the Senate, 95–0, in 2003) were too slight. *(2003 action, Congress and the Nation Vol. XI, p. 363)*

Some Republicans, however, maintained that the treaty could have a negative impact on the nation's missile defenses and national security. They also warned that Russia's record on past treaties demonstrated that it should not be trusted.

Kyl had far less experience on nuclear issues than Lugar, but he was passionate and determined, and, for most of the debate, the GOP caucus followed his lead. The White House spent months negotiating with him, acceding to his demands for guarantees on funding for modernization of the nation's aging nuclear stockpile and a firm commitment to missile defense.

But when Kyl continued his opposition, maintaining that there was not enough time for sufficient debate, administration officials turned their focus to securing the nine necessary Republican votes, one by one. That strategy was seen initially as a last resort—and possibly futile—but the gamble paid off.

The treaty officially entered into force on February 5, 2011, with the exchange of Instruments of Ratification between Secretary of State Hillary Rodham Clinton and Russian Foreign Minister Sergey Lavrov in Munich.

SENATE COMMITTEE ACTION

The Senate Foreign Relations Committee voted 14–4 on September 16, 2010, to send the resolution of ratification to the floor. Three Republicans—Lugar, Bob Corker of Tennessee, and Johnny Isakson of Georgia—joined all the committee Democrats in support.

Before the vote, the panel gave voice vote approval to a Lugar substitute that added new conditions on how the treaty would be implemented. The language stated that the resolution would not "impose any limitations on the deployment of missile defenses"—a key concern raised by Republicans on the panel. The amendment also required the president to submit to Congress a plan for dealing with any future resource shortfalls associated with paying for his ten-year, $180 billion plan to modernize the U.S. nuclear weapons stockpile.

By amending the resolution of ratification, the panel was able to include its input on the treaty without reopening negotiations.

Lugar's changes were sufficient to persuade Corker and Isakson to back the treaty, and both Lugar and John Kerry of Massachusetts, chair of the Foreign Relations Committee, expressed optimism that the accord would win the necessary support from the full Senate.

SENATE FLOOR ACTION

Thirteen Republicans joined all fifty-eight members of the Democratic caucus to approve the resolution of ratification on a **key vote of 71–26 (R 13–26; D 56–0; I 2–0)** on December 22, 2010. *(2010 key votes, p. 767)*

In a pivotal test, the Senate voted, 67–28, on December 21 to bring debate on the treaty to a close; Democrats had the help of eleven Republicans. The success of the cloture vote started the clock on a potential thirty hours of debate, but with the outcome clear, opponents allowed a final vote the following afternoon.

Democrats, led by Kerry, fended off attempts to alter the treaty, which would certainly have killed it. Before the final vote, the Senate adopted by voice vote two Republican amendments to the resolution.

The first, sponsored by Arizona Republican John McCain, Connecticut independent Joseph I. Lieberman, and several others, required the president to certify that the United States did not recognize Russia's argument that the treaty would be viable only when the United States was not building up its missile defenses. The amendment also added language making clear that Congress did not see the treaty's preamble as legally binding.

The other amendment, offered by Kyl, required the president to certify a way forward to fund the facilities that were part of the U.S. nuclear weapons complex.

The president sent a letter to senators December 18 affirming the administration's commitment to the U.S. missile defense program, and another the following week saying he would request the necessary money to fund modernization of the nation's nuclear stockpile. Lamar Alexander, R-Tenn., cited Obama's letter as a determining factor in his support for New START.

Treaty supporters lost a few senators thought to have been on the fence. Orrin G. Hatch, R-Utah, and Lindsey Graham, R-S.C., lined up with Kyl. McCain and Mark Steven Kirk, R-Ill., also voted against the resolution. "I don't understand why we can't wait five more weeks to ratify," Graham said.

For the Obama administration, the answer was clear: ratifying the treaty would have been even more difficult, if not impossible, in the next Congress, when Republicans would control forty-seven seats and the Democratic Caucus would be reduced to fifty-three senators, down from fifty-eight senators in the 111th Congress.

MAJOR PROVISIONS

Following are the major provisions of the New START agreement:

- No more than 1,550 deployed warheads per side.
- No more than 700 deployed launchers and bombers per side.
- No more than 800 nuclear-capable missile launchers and heavy bombers per side.
- Each side allowed to make up to eighteen short-notice on-site inspections per year. Regular inspections were part of the START accord that had expired in December 2009.
- Parties required to exchange data by keeping an extensive database with numbers, types, and locations of items limited by the treaty.
- Interference with the other side's satellite observations prohibited. The treaty provided for exchange of test data (telemetry) on up to five missile flight tests annually.
- Conversion of nuclear missile launchers into ballistic missile defense launchers was prohibited.
- No limit on the number or capabilities of ballistic missile defenses.
- More flexible rules for what had to be done to eliminate a launcher or heavy bomber from the counted supply.
- Mobile ICBMs subject to ICBM launcher limits.

Fiscal 2011 Defense Authorization

The House cleared a stripped-down fiscal 2011 defense authorization bill on the last day of the 111th Congress, two days before Christmas 2010 and three months into the fiscal year. President Barack Obama signed the measure into law on January 7, 2011 (HR 6523—PL 111-383). The bill nearly became the first defense authorization in forty-nine years not to reach the president's desk.

The fiscal 2011 bill authorized $724.6 billion for national security programs, at the departments of Defense and Energy, roughly equal to the president's request for $725.9 billion and about 7 percent more than was authorized under the fiscal 2010 law (PL 111-84).

Although most of the funding could be provided through the appropriations process without an authorization, the bill included some must-pass provisions, such as a 1.4 percent pay raise for military personnel, and it allowed both the House and Senate Armed Services committees to weigh in with policy prescriptions for numerous defense programs. For example, it barred the release into the United States, or the transfer to the United States, of detainees from the U.S. facility at Guantánamo Bay, Cuba, in fiscal 2011.

Of the total authorization, $565.9 billion was considered the base defense budget and $158.7 billion was dedicated to the wars in Afghanistan and Iraq and the general war on terrorism.

There was little disagreement over general funding levels, despite worries about the deficit. The chief stumbling block was language that would have repealed the 1993 law (PL 103-160) known as "don't ask, don't tell," which barred openly gay personnel from serving in the military.

The final version, negotiated by leaders of the House and Senate Armed Services committees, omitted the language on gay service members as well as controversial language on abortions and authorization for an alternative engine for the F-35 Joint Strike Fighter. The bill did not set specific funding levels for particular programs in most cases.

The House passed an initial version of the bill (HR 5136) in May that would have authorized $725.9 billion for defense programs in fiscal 2011, including $159.3 billion specifically for operations in Iraq and Afghanistan. Lawmakers added "don't ask, don't tell" repeal language on the floor. The bill also authorized unrequested funds for the alternative engine for the F-35, a provision that elicited a veto threat from the White House.

The Senate Armed Services Committee approved a companion measure (S 3454), also in May. The bill would have authorized $725.7 billion for defense programs and included a provision to repeal "don't ask, don't tell." That language, and to a lesser degree a provision to allow privately funded abortions in overseas military hospitals, effectively prevented the bill from reaching the Senate floor.

After the Senate rejected two attempts to cut off a filibuster, it became clear that the measure could not pass without significant revision. At that point, proponents of a "don't ask, don't tell" repeal, including Sen. Joseph I. Lieberman, I-Conn., introduced stand-alone legislation in both chambers. That bill cleared December 18 (PL 111-321). *(Repeal action, p. 288)*

In the meantime, the chairs of the House and Senate Armed Services committees announced that they had reached agreement on a scaled-back fiscal 2011 defense authorization that did not include "don't ask, don't tell" or any other controversial provisions. The measure sailed through Congress, clearing just as the session was about to end.

HOUSE COMMITTEE ACTION

The House Armed Services Committee approved a $725.9 billion authorization bill (HR 5136—H Rept 111-491, Parts 1 and 2) by a vote of 59–0 on May 19. The panel's six subcommittees had each drafted sections of the measure, which included $159.3 billion to support operations in Afghanistan and Iraq and reflected some differences with the Obama administration over priorities.

As approved by the committee, the bill would have:

- Made no changes to the "don't ask, don't tell" policy.
- Prohibited the transfer of detainees from Guantánamo to the United States unless the president submitted a comprehensive disposition plan and risk assessment report to Congress. The language by Chair Ike Skelton, D-Mo., adopted 31–28, replaced a proposal by J. Randy Forbes, R-Va., that would have barred the transfer or release of any detainees into the United States.
- Authorized $485 million in fiscal 2011 for an alternative engine for the F-35.
- Authorized $11 billion for the F-35 fighter but withheld 25 percent of the funding until the Pentagon certified that all funds for development and procurement of the fighter's propulsion system had been spent. It also limited the funding to thirty jets, rather than the forty-two requested by Obama, until certain conditions were met.
- Authorized $500 million to fund eight additional F/A-18 Super Hornet aircraft beyond the twenty-two that the president requested. The language by Todd Akin, R-Mo., was adopted by voice vote.
- Prohibited the Air Force or the Air National Guard from retiring fighter aircraft in fiscal 2011 until the Government Accountability Office (GAO) completed a review of the fighter jet inventory, language added by Frank A. LoBiondo, R-N.J., and Gabrielle Giffords, D-Ariz.
- Approved a 1.9 percent pay raise for military personnel—half a percentage point more than requested. The Congressional Budget Office (CBO) estimated the increase would cost an additional $2.4 billion over five years.
- Preserved the Pentagon's ability to convert more jobs held by contractors to full-time civilian employee positions. The language, by Jim Langevin, D-R.I., was adopted by voice vote.

HOUSE FLOOR ACTION

The House passed the bill, 229–186, on May 28, after agreeing the previous day to add a repeal of "don't ask, don't tell." The repeal amendment, by Patrick J. Murphy, D-Pa., was adopted 234–194. Reflecting an agreement announced by the Pentagon and the White House, it allowed for implementation only after the Pentagon finished a review of the implications of a repeal and top administration officials certified that it would not hurt readiness.

During the floor action, the House also:

- Adopted, 282–131, a procedural motion by Forbes that had the effect of toughening the Guantánamo language to bar the transfer or release of any detainees into the United States.
- Rejected, on a **key vote of 193–231 (R 57–116; D 136–115),** an amendment by Chellie Pingree, D-Maine, to strike the $485 million for the second F-35 engine, which she called "a complete waste of money." *(2010 key votes, p. 767)*
- Adopted, 218–210, an amendment by Anna G. Eshoo, D-Calif., to allow the GAO to investigate intelligence agencies at the request of congressional committees. The proposal was opposed by the administration.

Hours before the House passed the bill, the White House Office of Management and Budget released a statement saying that Obama's advisers would recommend he veto the bill if it authorized funding for the second F-35 engine. The White House also strongly objected to the limits on procurement of the F-35 jets and warned of a veto if the bill would "seriously disrupt" the program.

SENATE COMMITTEE ACTION

The Senate Armed Services Committee approved its version of the bill (S 3454—S Rept 111-201) by a mostly party-line vote of 18–10 in a closed-door session May 27. The bill totaled $725.7 billion, about $200 million less than in the president's request or the House bill, and included $159.3 billion for operations in Afghanistan and Iraq.

The contentiousness of the measure was underscored May 28 when the panel's ranking Republican, John McCain of Arizona, departed from tradition by not joining Chair Carl Levin, D-Mich., at a news conference after the markup.

As approved by the committee, the bill would have:

- Repealed the "don't ask, don't tell" law. The amendment, by Lieberman—which was identical to the language approved in the House—was adopted 16–12. The amendment prompted warnings from Republicans that they would filibuster the bill on the floor.
- Allowed abortions to be performed at military hospitals, if paid for with private money.
- Directed the president to send 6,000 National Guard troops to the U.S.-Mexico border. The provision, by McCain, was adopted 15–13 and was strongly opposed by the White House.

- Authorized a 1.4 percent across-the-board pay raise for military personnel—the amount requested by the president, but less than the 1.9 percent in the House bill.
- Omitted authorization for a second F-35 engine. Levin said he hoped it would be added in conference.
- Met Obama's request of $11.5 billion to purchase forty-two F-35 jets.
- Authorized six additional F/A-18s.

SENATE FLOOR ACTION

Chances for clearing the bill—and with it repeal of the "don't ask, don't tell" law—seemed all but lost December 9, when Republicans blocked an attempt to take up the measure. The Senate voted, 57–40, to reject a motion to invoke cloture and end a GOP filibuster. Democrats attracted only one Republican supporter, Susan Collins of Maine, and fell three votes short of the sixty needed.

It was the second time Republicans had prevented the Senate from proceeding to the bill. The first cloture motion was defeated, 56–43, on September 21 amid partisan wrangling in advance of the midterm elections; Reid voted "no" on procedural grounds to preserve his right to seek another vote later.

Prospects for further action were clouded by the limited time remaining on the Senate calendar and a Republican caucus that had stayed nearly united on its vow to hold up all legislation until major tax and spending bills were completed.

COMPROMISE BILL

Considered problematic just two weeks earlier, the defense authorization cleared easily in the final day of the session after leaders agreed on a stripped-down version (HR 6523) that dropped a number of disputed provisions, most notably the "don't ask, don't tell" repeal. The House passed the new version, 341–48, on December 17. The Senate passed it by unanimous consent December 22, after removing a small provision that would have authorized funds for the victims of atrocities committed by the Japanese forces that occupied Guam during World War II. The House cleared the measure by voice vote December 22.

In modifying the bill, the leaders also dropped the provisions requiring that National Guard troops be deployed to the Southwest border and allowing privately funded abortions in military hospitals. Authorization to continue developing a second F-35 engine was also deleted.

However, the bill still contained significant policy provisions. The managers included language similar to that in the House bill to bar the use of authorized fiscal 2011 Pentagon funds to release or transfer to the United States any of the Guantánamo detainees who were not U.S. citizens. Sen. Mark Steven Kirk, R-Ill., had threatened to block the revised bill without the ban. In signing the bill, the president issued a statement opposing the provision as a "dangerous and unprecedented challenge to critical executive branch authority."

The bill also prohibited the use of funding authorized by the bill to construct or modify facilities in the United States to detain or imprison any of the detainees.

Aides said the requirement that the Iraqi government pay 20 percent of the cost of certain types of equipment could save the U.S. government about $300 million.

The final bill included provisions aimed at strengthening oversight of not only weapons contracts but the acquisition of services such as systems engineering and logistics. The authorizers took aim at particular initiatives that had experienced trouble. The Pentagon was required to set up a management process to more closely monitor results in the F-35 Joint Strike Fighter program, which had been hit by technical setbacks that created years of delay and billions of dollars in additional costs. In their managers' statement, the authorizers also said "Congress expects" continued production of F-18 fighter jets in the meantime "to prevent our naval air power from losing significance in our nation's arsenal."

MAJOR PROVISIONS

The authorization for the Pentagon's base budget included $168.2 billion for operations and maintenance, $138.5 billion for military personnel costs, and $110.4 billion for procurement.

Following are some of the bill's main components:

Missile Defense

More than $10 billion was authorized for missile defense programs, $1 billion above the fiscal 2010 level. The bill supported funding for the initial deployment of a national missile defense system based in Alaska and California, as well as the Obama administration's new plan for missile defense in Europe—a largely sea-based system focused on protecting Europe from short- and medium-range Iranian missiles. Obama's strategy replaced President George W. Bush's controversial plan to locate antimissile interceptors and radar facilities in Poland and the Czech Republic.

The committee said it fully supported the president's new approach to missile defense, but it limited the funds for deployment until host countries signed and ratified the necessary agreements. The bill also limited deployment until the secretary certified that the technology was effective, based on successful, realistic flight testing.

The measure also authorized $205 million for Israel's "Iron Dome" antimissile defense system.

It repealed an existing ban on contracting with a foreign government or foreign business for research, development, testing, or evaluation related to missile defense.

Aircraft

The base Pentagon authorization for aircraft procurement included $14.7 billion for the Air Force, $18.9 billion for the Navy, and $5.9 billion for the army.

The military's tactical aircraft included three major programs—the F/A-18 Super Hornet, the primary strike aircraft of both the Navy and the Marine Corps; the Air Force's F-22A Raptor, which had ended production; and the joint service F-35 Joint Strike Fighter, which had just entered initial production.

The GAO estimated that the total cost of the three aircraft programs could be more than $400 billion, with annual production costs of $14 billion to $18 billion, before inflation. Continued cost overruns and extended development times had reduced the department's buying power, with the result that the Pentagon planned to replace existing aircraft with about one-third fewer new planes than originally planned.

The bill neither endorsed nor prevented additional spending on an alternative engine for the F-35. Congress had continued the second engine, built by Rolls-Royce and General Electric, over the objections of the Pentagon, which argued that the engine being built by Pratt & Whitney was reliable and that the funding was sorely needed elsewhere in the defense budget. Proponents argued that the competition would produce a more cost-effective and reliable engine.

Ground Combat Vehicle

The Ground Combat Vehicle was the army's proposed replacement for armored fighting vehicles that were part of the Future Combat Systems, a complex, technically challenged, and costly system that was canceled in 2009. The bill authorized the administration's request of $461 million for the vehicle, but it withheld some of the funds until the authorizers received requested program documentation.

Navy Shipbuilding

The bill authorized $15.7 billion for Navy ship construction and refurbishment.

National Guard and Reserve Equipment

The authorizers said severe equipment shortfalls continued across nondeployed National Guard and reserve units, particularly among items that were critical for dual-use roles of combat operations and domestic emergencies. The bill, therefore, authorized $7.2 billion, $700 million or 10 percent more than requested, for the guard and reserves. The total included funding for aircraft missiles, wheeled and tracked combat vehicles, ammunition, small arms, and tactical radios.

Personnel

The bill set a ceiling of 1.4 million on the number of total active-duty military personnel in fiscal 2011, equal to the president's request and 7,400 above the authorized fiscal 2010 level. The total included 569,400 for the army, 328,700 for the Navy, 332,200 for the Air Force, and 202,100 for the Marine Corps. The limit for the National Guard and reserve units was 856,200. The number of reserve personnel that could be placed on active duty was limited to 78,846, roughly the same as in fiscal 2010.

Military Pay Raise

Military personnel received a 1.4 percent across-the-board pay raise, equal to the president's request.

Health Program

The bill authorized $31 billion for the Pentagon's defense health care programs, plus an additional $1.4 billion as part of the Iraq-Afghanistan section of the bill.

Nuclear Weapons Programs

About $17.7 billion was authorized for defense-related activities at the Energy Department. The total included the president's request of $11.2 billion for operating nuclear weapons laboratories and for programs operated by the National Nuclear Security Administration, and $6.5 billion for environmental restoration, waste management, and other defense activities, also equal to the request. The National Nuclear Security Administration funding was $1.2 billion more than the fiscal 2010 level, with $624 million of the extra funding to maintain the existing nuclear stockpile and $551 million for nonproliferation efforts. The stockpile funding was tied to congressional approval of the New Strategic Arms Reduction Treaty, which was ratified the day the defense bill cleared. *(Treaty approval, p. 289)*

Military Construction

The bill authorized $18.2 billion for military construction and family housing projects, including $2.7 billion for base realignment and closure and $1.8 billion for family housing. Additional funds were included in the war funding section of the bill.

Overseas Contingency Operations

The bill authorized the president's request of $158.7 billion specifically for the wars in Afghanistan and Iraq and the general war on terrorism, although funding authorized elsewhere in the bill could be used to support those operations as well.

The measure also authorized $33.1 billion that had been provided in the fiscal 2010 supplemental appropriations act (PL 111-212) for the surge of additional forces in Afghanistan and in support of relief operations in Haiti in the aftermath of a major earthquake.

The fiscal 2011 total included $114 billion for operations and maintenance, $24.7 billion for procurement, and $15.3 billion for personnel.

Among the individual accounts, the bill authorized:

- $3.4 billion for Mine Resistant Ambush Protected (MRAP) vehicles.
- $3.5 billion to procure and develop countermeasures to prevent improvised explosive device attacks.
- $11.6 billion, as requested, for training and equipping Afghanistan's security forces.

- $1.5 billion for the Iraqi security forces, $500 million less than requested. The Iraqi government was required to pay at least 20 percent of the cost of procuring items or services, other than major military equipment.
- $4 billion in special transfer authority within the overseas contingency account in fiscal 2011.
- $506 million for the Commanders' Emergency Response Program, which provided U.S. military commanders in Iraq and Afghanistan with funds for use in small humanitarian and reconstruction projects.

Fiscal 2011 Defense Appropriations

The annual defense spending bill for fiscal 2011, typically considered a must-pass measure, was left unfinished along with all the other fiscal 2011 appropriations measures during 2010. The bill funding the Defense Department and U.S. intelligence agencies did not get beyond markups in the House Defense Appropriations Subcommittee and in the full Senate Appropriations Committee.

Programs under the bill were funded, mostly at fiscal 2010 levels, through March 4, 2011, under a continuing resolution signed into law on December 22 (PL 111-322). This was the first of four continuing resolutions, which extended funding through March 2011. The final fiscal 2011 continuing resolution (HR 1473—PL 112-10) became law on April 15, 2011. *(Continuing resolution, p. 138)*

The House Subcommittee approved its draft of annual spending bill by voice vote July 27, proposing to appropriate $671 billion in fiscal 2011; this was $12.2 billion more than enacted for fiscal 2010 but $7.3 billion less than President Obama requested. The Senate committee's version (S 3800—S Rept 111-295), approved 18–12 on September 16, called for only slightly less—$669.9 billion.

Both the House and Senate totals included $157.7 billion for military operations in Iraq and Afghanistan, leaving $513.3 billion and $512.2 billion, respectively, for basic Pentagon accounts. Obama had requested $157.9 billion for the overseas operations. The fiscal 2011 law that authorized the appropriations (PL 111-383) allowed for $158.7 billion.

Major issues in the fiscal 2011 defense spending bill included:

F-35 Engine

House appropriators ignored a White House veto threat in approving $450 million for the F-35 Joint Strike Fighter alternative engine, made by General Electric and Rolls-Royce. Supporters wanted the Pentagon to equip some F-35s with that engine, while powering others with a Pratt & Whitney version. They said competition would mean better engines at lower cost, plus a diminished risk that technical problems would ground all F-35s. Obama and Defense Secretary Robert M. Gates countered that any such benefits were outweighed by the increased cost, and the White House had threatened to veto a measure that included funds for the second engine.

The Senate bill did not include the funds, and the issue became further complicated by the continuing resolution. Because the stopgap bill continued spending at fiscal 2010 levels, it included more than $430 million appropriated that year for research and development for the second engine. However, the expenditure was not authorized in the fiscal 2011 defense authorization law.

Other Major Issues

Both the House and Senate spending bills included funding for the 1.4 percent military pay raise that Obama recommended. The House version followed the administration's wishes in omitting funds for additional C-17 transport planes.

The House subcommittee also approved the full $2 billion that the White House requested for additional training and equipment for Iraqi security forces—a controversial allocation in the view of those in Congress who thought Iraq should be paying more for its own defense. The Senate bill would have cut the request in half, providing $1 billion. (The defense authorization law approved $1.5 billion and required that the Iraqi government pay at least 20 percent of the cost of procuring items or services, other than major military equipment.)

Both bills would have provided $31.5 billion for the Defense Department's health program, about $2.2 billion above the fiscal 2010 level; Obama requested $300.9 billion.

2011–2012

The January 2011 arrival on Capitol Hill of dozens of new conservative Republicans determined to impose their brand of fiscal austerity had broad legislative consequences, even for the defense budget. The 112th Congress struggled to pass any spending bills, including those for the Defense Department—long a priority for earlier generations of Republicans. Instead, Congress folded defense spending into omnibus appropriations bills for fiscal years 2011, 2012, and 2013, possibly marking an end to the status of defense bills as "must-pass" legislation.

In adopting the Budget Control Act of 2011 (PL 112-25), Congress also set the stage for long-term cutbacks in defense spending—or, at least reductions in the growth of the defense budget. The law required $487 billion in cuts from the planned defense budget over the next decade. It also included the Pentagon, along with domestic programs, in a series of mandatory cutbacks (called a "sequester") that would take effect at the beginning of 2013 if Congress and the president failed to agree on an alternative approach to cutting the deficit. The sequester cuts did begin to bite, although not until March 2013. Pentagon officials warned that continuing a similar level of cuts in future years could endanger national security. *(Budget Control Act, p. 160)*

The 112th Congress also brought to an end one of the most contentious defense spending issues in recent years—a battle over a second, or alternative, engine for the new F-35 warplane being built for the Air Force, Marine Corps, and Navy. The Pentagon had approved an official engine for the one-engine plane, but members representing districts where an alternative engine might be built had pushed funding for it since the 1990s, arguing that competition would lead to a better product. The George W. Bush administration dropped its support for the second engine in 2006, but Congress continued funding it until 2011, when combined opposition from the Obama administration and antispending Republicans doomed the project. *(F-35 action, 111th Congress, pp. 266, 295)*

Another kind of turnover occurred in 2011, when Robert M. Gates retired as defense secretary, after spending four-and-a-half years in the post. President Bush had turned to Gates in late 2006 to rescue support for the Iraq war, following the disastrous results for Republicans in that year's midterm elections. Gates urged a temporary "surge" of troops into Iraq—an increase in the number of troops that, combined with other domestic factors in Iraq, succeeded in tamping down violence from insurgent forces there. Starting in 2009, Gates oversaw a similar U.S. troop surge into Afghanistan, where antigovernment forces had made headway in part years earlier after the Bush administration turned its attention to the Iraq war. *(Defense leadership, pp. 264, 274)*

Gates also initiated restructuring and cost-cutting efforts that trimmed some of the Pentagon's bureaucracy. His successor, in mid-2011, was former House member and Washington insider Leon Panetta, a budget expert who made further defense spending cuts and began the process of dealing with across-the-board cuts mandated by the 2011 Budget Control Act.

Following the lead of its predecessor, the 112th Congress continued restrictions on the president's ability to close down, or even transfer terrorism suspects from, the detention center at Guantánamo Bay, Cuba. Congress barred the administration from spending money to close the center, and it imposed restrictions that made it all but impossible for suspects to be tried in federal courts in the United States.

Fiscal 2011 Defense Appropriations

Congress failed to finish work on any of its fiscal 2011 appropriations bills during the election year of 2010 and instead passed a series of four continuing resolutions that ran through March 2011. Congress finally finished the fiscal 2011 appropriations process early in 2011, passing an omnibus continuing resolution (HR 1473—PL 112-10), which President Barack Obama signed on April 15, 2011. *(Appropriations actions, p. 150)*

In the interim, the House—now under Republican leadership—on February 19, 2011, passed HR 1 to fund all federal agencies through the remaining months of the fiscal year. Adopted by a partisan vote of 235–189, the bill would have provided $505.2 billion for the base defense budget.

During consideration of the Republican omnibus bill, on February 16, the House adopted an amendment by Tom Rooney, R-Fla., stripping $450 million in research and development funds for a controversial second engine for the F-35 Joint Strike Fighter plane for the military services. The Bush and Obama administrations had opposed the alternative engine project, which had support from lawmakers in districts where General Electric Co. was doing the work. House adoption of the Rooney amendment killing the funds was on a **key vote of 233–198 (R 110–130; D 123–68).** *(2011 key votes, p. 785)*

The Senate debated HR 1 in early March but did not finish because of a Republican filibuster. During its debate, the Senate considered, but rejected on a 42–58 vote, an alternative proposed by Appropriations Committee Chair Daniel Inouye, D-Hawaii. The Inouye amendment would have provided $503.1 billion for base defense programs.

The final omnibus bill signed into law largely incorporated provisions from the Inouye amendment. The bill provided $513 billion in base defense spending,

$5 billion more than enacted in fiscal 2010, although it was roughly $18.1 billion less than the president requested for fiscal 2011.

In addition, the bill included $157.7 billion for overseas contingency operations, mainly military activities in Afghanistan and Iraq. The amount equaled the president's request.

Funding for military construction, covered in a separate title, was reduced from fiscal 2010 levels. *(Military construction, this page)*

The defense title fully funded a 1.4 percent pay raise for military personnel. The deal added about $670 million more than requested to cover shortfalls in military personnel accounts that resulted from delays in reaching agreement on fiscal 2011 spending levels.

The base defense funding included:

- $126.7 billion for military personnel, including funding for an active-duty end strength of 1,432,000, plus another 846,200 in the National Guard and reserve units.
- $165.6 billion for operations and maintenance.
- $102.1 billion for procurement.
- $75 billion for research and development.
- $32.8 billion for defense health programs—the fastest-growing part of the department, partly because of a general rise in medical costs and partly because of congressionally imposed increases in benefits.

The bill did not include funds for the controversial F-35 Joint Strike Fighter alternative-engine program, which the president and Defense Secretary Robert M. Gates had ordered terminated.

Some of the biggest cuts from the president's request included:

- $9 billion across all operations and maintenance accounts "due to programmatic adjustments, historic under-execution and unsupported requests for civilian personnel increases."
- $2.2 billion from the government-wide civilian pay freeze, which Obama had sought, and changes in economic assumptions.
- $2.2 billion from the F-35 Joint Strike Fighter program because of production and testing delays.
- $2 billion from about fifty programs because of underperformance, terminations, and schedule delays.
- $735 million from civilian pay.

Increased funding in the bill included an additional $850 million for National Guard and reserve units to address shortfalls in equipment. The bill also provided money to replace helicopters and fixed-wing aircraft lost in battle, and it included $2.5 billion for intelligence, surveillance, and reconnaissance programs identified by Gates as a high priority for troops overseas.

A total of $3.4 billion went to fully fund Mine-Resistant Ambush-Protection All-Terrain Vehicles. Funds also were added to test and procure "double-V" hull modification for the Stryker vehicle, for added protection from improvised explosive devices.

The overseas contingency operations funding also included:

- $11.6 billion for the Afghanistan Security Forces Fund.
- $1.5 billion for the Iraq Security Forces Fund.
- $500 million for the Commander's Emergency Response Program.
- $400 million for the new Afghanistan Infrastructure fund.
- $800 million for the Pakistan Counterinsurgency fund.

Fiscal 2011 Military Construction –VA Appropriations

The final fiscal 2011 omnibus spending bill (HR 1473—PL 112-10) provided a substantial increase for veterans' programs while cutting back funds for Pentagon military construction projects.

The bill appropriated a total of $141.3 billion, including $73.3 billion in discretionary budget authority, which was $3.3 billion below the fiscal 2010 level. Military construction projects received $16.6 billion of the total, a reduction of $6.6 billion, or about 28 percent, but discretionary funding for the Department of Veterans Affairs (VA) rose to $58.8 billion, a gain of about 8 percent over fiscal 2010.

The VA total included $51.1 billion, or 14 percent above fiscal 2010 funding for Veterans Health Administration medical accounts. That was made up of $580 million in new funds for fiscal 2011 and $50.6 billion in advance funds for fiscal 2012. The health administration also could count on $48.2 billion in advance budget authority that had been appropriated the previous year. The system of advance funding guaranteed that the money would be there each year, even if the spending bill was delayed.

The Veterans Benefits Administration got $64.5 billion, including a $448 million boost over fiscal 2010 to process a backlog of disability claims. The measure provided $4.3 billion for treatment and housing programs to aid homeless veterans, as requested, including $799 million in direct programs to combat homelessness.

"The subcommittee's main priority was to ensure that the VA had sufficient resources so as not to adversely impact services provided to veterans," Senate appropriators said in a statement.

The cuts in military construction were relatively painless and were mostly attributable to the conclusion of spending on the 2005 round of base closures and realignments. Some other military construction initiatives were

CYBERSECURITY AND COAST GUARD REAUTHORIZATION

Congress during the four years of President Barack Obama's first term confronted two issues of importance to national security policy: cybersecurity and reauthorization for the Coast Guard. Legislators late in the days of the 112th Congress completed a Coast Guard bill, but failed on the more controversial issue of cybersecurity.

Cybersecurity Issues

At the start of 2012 there was broad, bipartisan agreement that the threat to the computer systems of the nation's defense, financial, and other critical infrastructure sectors was so severe that Congress needed to act quickly. But sharp differences over the proper role of government and concern over privacy stalled cybersecurity bills in both chambers, and the year ended without any legislation signed into law. *(House and Senate action, p. 217)*

The House passed a cybersecurity bill (HR 3523) in April that focused on fostering information sharing on cyberthreats between the federal government and the private sector. A Senate proposal (S 3414) contained information-sharing provisions, but it also would have placed the Department of Homeland Security in a coordinating role and given it the power to create voluntary security standards for the most vital private digital infrastructure. Republican leaders and the U.S. Chamber of Commerce strongly opposed that language, saying that in practice, the voluntary standards could harden into mandatory regulations. The Senate twice rejected efforts by Majority Leader Harry Reid, D-Nev., to bring the bill to a vote.

Looming over the cybersecurity negotiations was the possibility that the White House would issue an executive order implementing some key provisions from the Senate bill. Administration officials, along with both opponents and supporters of the Senate measure, agreed that such action would be less than a perfect solution, as it would lack some of the liability protections for companies that shared threat information that only legislation could provide.

Cybersecurity was a particularly complex issue for Congress because the private sector owned an estimated 85 percent to 90 percent of the nation's most crucial computer networks. That meant any catastrophic attack would almost surely target industry in some way. Therefore, any legislation had to wrestle with such topics as whether or how to require that businesses comply with security regulations, as well as what kind of incentives could nudge businesses to protect their networks on their own.

Many security experts believed the threat to the nation's computer networks represented the nation's most dangerous national security challenge. They warned that a number of countries were actively targeting U.S. corporate and military cybersystems—countries including Iran, Russia, and, most of all, China. Besides looking to steal data, intellectual property, and other corporate and government secrets, such cyberattacks attempted to establish footholds through which more extensive attacks could be launched at later dates—attacks that could disable or disrupt financial, commercial, and physical infrastructure, those experts said. Some experts, however, thought that the threat of major cyberattacks was vastly overstated.

Coast Guard Reauthorization

The Senate in mid-December 2012 cleared legislation reauthorizing the Coast Guard after a thirteen-month legislative effort. President Barack Obama signed the measure into law December 20 (HR 2838—PL 112-213). *(Legislative action, p. 218)*

Because the Coast Guard's job description had changed so dramatically over the previous decade, lawmakers were eager to spell out how they wanted that expanded mission executed. Major partisan disagreements over the bill would likely have doomed legislation authorizing another agency, but legislators made substantial concessions in December to find a compromise that would ensure that their guidance for the Coast Guard became law.

A major dispute in the legislation was over rules for the wastewater that ships could dump. Under existing law, regulations were being set by a combination of the Environmental Protection Agency (EPA), states, and the Coast Guard. The House passed a reauthorization bill in November 2011 that would have overridden the differing ballast water regulations with a relatively lenient, blanket standard. Democrats in both chambers, however, said the provision would trample on the rights of states that needed to set stricter standards to prevent pollution or combat invasive species.

Ultimately, House Republicans agreed to forfeit the ballast water section before passing the final version of the bill. The concession signaled swift sign-off in the Senate a week later.

Congress had last cleared a Coast Guard authorization in 2010 (PL 111-281) and, before that, in 2006 (PL 109-241). In 2002, the agency became a part of the new Department of Homeland Security, where its responsibilities expanded beyond traditional maritime search-and-rescue tasks to focus largely on port security and missions to track down drug smugglers and illegal immigrants on the high seas.

being slowed for various reasons. For instance, two projects in Bahrain were being deferred because of unrest in that country, and spending was curtailed for the construction of facilities to support a planned Marine Corps buildup in Guam because of bid savings, delays in execution, and unresolved land use issues there.

Military-family housing programs received the requested amount of $1.8 billion.

Fiscal 2012 Defense Authorization

After a quick conference, Congress cleared a $662.4 billion fiscal 2012 defense authorization bill in the waning days of the session. President Barack Obama signed the measure into law on December 31, 2011 (HR 1540—PL 112-81).

A clash between Senate Armed Services Committee leaders and the White House over detainee policies nearly jeopardized the sprawling annual Pentagon policy bill, which had become law every year for the previous half-century. But an eleventh-hour compromise appeased the Obama administration, which ultimately lifted a veto threat.

The bill authorized funding for Pentagon programs and for nuclear weapons activities at the Department of Energy. The total included $530 billion in discretionary funding for the base defense budget, consisting of regular Pentagon operations; $115.5 billion for military operations in Afghanistan, Iraq, and the general war on terrorism; and $16.9 billion for national security programs at the Energy Department.

The overall total was $26.6 billion less than Obama's $689 billion request and $62.3 billion below fiscal 2011 funding, bringing it in line with caps placed on security spending in the August 2011 debt limit law, the Budget Control Act (PL 112-25). The $662.4 billion represented almost 60 percent of total discretionary spending in fiscal 2012. *(Debt limit, p. 160; fiscal 2011 authorization, p. 291)*

Although the money was provided in the annual appropriations bill, the measure was needed to authorize several military programs, as well as a 1.6 percent across-the-board pay raise for the armed forces, but it also allowed Congress to prescribe wide-ranging policies for defense programs. *(Defense appropriations, p. 304)*

An analysis by the Congressional Research Service listed major reductions in the bill compared with the president's request, including:

- $4 billion to take account of Obama's plan to reduce the number of troops in Afghanistan.
- $1.6 billion from the $12.8 billion requested for the Afghan army and police.
- $1.5 billion from army operations and maintenance accounts.
- $595 million from the $3.2 billion requested for Mine Resistant Ambush Protected (MRAP) vehicles.
- $435 million from the $884 million requested for the army to develop a new armored combat vehicle.

HOUSE COMMITTEE ACTION

After more than twelve hours of debate starting May 11 and spilling into the early hours of May 12, the House Armed Services Committee approved its bill (HR 1540—H Rept 112-78, Parts 1 and 2) by a vote of 60–1. The $690.1 billion bill included $553 billion for the Defense Department, $18.1 billion for national security programs at the Energy Department, and $118.9 billion for the wars in Iraq and Afghanistan. The total was $1.1 billion more than proposed by the administration and $35 billion less than was authorized for fiscal 2011.

Six subcommittees drafted portions of the bill the week of May 2, long before the new caps on security spending were imposed in the August debt limit law.

Full committee Chair Howard P. "Buck" McKeon, R-Calif., included a series of restrictions aimed at requiring that any cuts from Pentagon spending be justified by a thorough look at the effect on military missions. The provisions were a response to an Obama administration proposal that the defense budget be cut by $400 billion over the following twelve years. The bill also required competition for components throughout the life of a weapons program.

A provision in the bill, adopted in the Subcommittee on Tactical Air and Land Forces, threatened to reignite the debate over funding an alternative engine for the F-35. The plan allowed for building another engine if the existing Pratt & Whitney engine failed to meet certain goals and required additional funding. The House earlier in the year rejected funding for a second engine being developed by General Electric Corp (GE). The Obama administration opposed spending money on an alternative engine, and the Pentagon formally determined that it was unneeded and too costly.

A provision added by the Seapower and Projection Forces Subcommittee limited money for a program to replace the Marine Corps' Expeditionary Fighting Vehicle until the Navy secretary provided Congress with a cost analysis for the replacement program. The Pentagon had terminated the vehicle because of costs. A 2010 Government Accountability Office report found that the unit price for the program since 2000 had increased by 176.5 percent, to $24.3 million. Todd Akin, R-Mo., raised concerns that the proposed replacements would not perform as well.

During the markup, the committee voted to confront the administration on a number of issues but deferred at least one big vote—on the future of the war in Afghanistan—for the floor. The committee:

- Rejected, 22–38, an amendment by ranking Democrat Adam Smith of Washington that would have removed a provision in the bill barring the Defense Department from spending any money to transfer or release detainees from the facility in Guantánamo Bay, Cuba, into the United States.
- Adopted, 33–27, an amendment to prohibit the Pentagon from implementing a repeal of "don't ask, don't tell" until the chiefs of the army, Air Force, Navy, and Marine Corps certified that the change would not "degrade the readiness, effectiveness, cohesion, and morale of combat arms units." The amendment was offered by Duncan Hunter, R-Calif. Under the 2010 repeal, only the chair of the Joint Chiefs of Staff, the defense secretary, and the president had to certify

that the ban would not harm military readiness. In recent testimony, the chiefs had sounded increasingly unconcerned about the effects of the repeal on personnel in combat.

- Adopted, 55–5, an amendment by Robert E. Andrews, D-N.J., to allow GE to work on the alternative F-35 engine as long as it used its own funds, while allowing the Defense Department to own the alternative-engine technology. GE had announced it planned to work on the engine on its own through fiscal 2012, but the company and its partner, Rolls-Royce, announced December 2 that they were reversing that decision. Mike Coffman, R-Colo., withdrew an amendment that would have prohibited funding for the second engine, saying he would wait until the bill moved to the House floor.
- Adopted, 35–26, an amendment by Doug Lamborn, R-Colo., to block the president from unilaterally reducing the U.S. nuclear weapons stockpile below levels agreed to in the New START agreement. It also sought to block the retirement of weapons covered under New START until the president moved forward on his promises to modernize U.S. nuclear facilities.
- Adopted, 39–22, an amendment by Vicky Hartzler, R-Mo., to clarify that marriage in the armed forces would be interpreted as a legal union between a man and a woman.
- Adopted, 38–23, an amendment by Akin to limit marriage ceremonies at military installations to couples consisting of a man and a woman.

HOUSE FLOOR ACTION

The House passed the bill by an overwhelming vote of 322–96 on May 26. The White House issued a lengthy set of objections, threatening to veto the measure over provisions related to terrorism and detainees, nuclear weapons, and the alternative F-35 engine.

Floor debate on the bill lasted three days and included scores of amendments, many of which were consolidated as the House rushed toward adjournment for the Memorial Day weekend. In the end, the House took roll-call votes on thirty-one amendments.

Among its actions, the House:

- Rejected, 165–253, an amendment by Smith to reverse language that would bar the transfer of alleged terrorists detained overseas and at Guantánamo to the United States. The Obama administration hoped to try some detainees in U.S. courts.
- Adopted, 246–174, an amendment by Vern Buchanan, R-Fla., to require all foreign terrorism suspects to be tried by military commissions.
- Rejected, 204–215, an amendment by Jim McGovern, D-Mass., and Walter B. Jones, R-N.C., to require the administration to produce a plan with a specific time frame for the accelerated transition of military operations to the Afghan government. Obama had said that he would begin a troop drawdown in Afghanistan in July but had not given details. The close vote signaled that since the May 2 killing of al Qaeda leader Osama bin Laden and increased calls for cuts in federal spending, Congress was raising more questions about the U.S. role in Afghanistan. Twenty-six Republicans backed the amendment, while only eight Democrats opposed it.
- Adopted, 416–5, an amendment by John Conyers Jr., D-Mich., to bar the use of funds authorized in the bill to put U.S. armed forces or private security contractors on the ground in Libya unless the purpose was to rescue a service member from imminent danger. The United States, under North Atlantic Treaty Organization (NATO) leadership, was engaged in air strikes officially aimed at protecting civilians in what turned into a civil war between rebels and forces loyal to Libyan dictator Muammar Gaddafi. The administration had stressed from the outset that it would not send in ground forces.
- Rejected, 187–234, an amendment offered by Justin Amash, R-Mich., liberal Democrats Barbara Lee of California and Conyers, and Republicans Ron Paul of Texas and Walter B. Jones of North Carolina. The amendment would have struck a provision in the bill that sought to revise the 2001 use-of-force law, which had authorized the invasion of Afghanistan.
- Adopted, 269–151, an amendment by Jeff Flake, R-Ariz., to strip $348 million for a Pentagon fund to buy unspecified weapons proposed by individual lawmakers.

SENATE COMMITTEE ACTION

The Senate Armed Services Committee approved a $682.5 billion defense authorization bill (S 1253—S Rept 112-26) on a 26–0 vote in a closed-door markup June 16. The panel's six subcommittees met June 14 and 15 to approve their separate portions of the bill.

The overall authorization—which was $6.4 billion below Obama's request—included $547.1 billion for the base Pentagon budget, $117.3 billion for the wars, and $18.1 billion for Energy Department programs. The bill required the administration to report to Congress on a semiannual basis on progress in Afghanistan. The committee also pared $5 billion from the president's request for war operations, based on his plan to begin withdrawing U.S. troops from Afghanistan. In addition, the panel cut $1.6 billion out of the $12.8 billion request for equipment and training for the Afghan army and national police.

After passage of the deficit-control law, the Senate committee on November 14 approved a second version of the defense bill (S 1867) that reduced the spending total by $27.3 billion.

Authorizers took the unusual step of requiring that the next batch of F-35 fighters be under a fixed-price contract, shifting 100 percent of the burden of cost growth linked to program delays and design problems to Lockheed Martin. The provision reflected the panel's growing impatience with the enormous growth in cost of the F-35 program. The average cost to develop and acquire each plane had nearly doubled since 2001, with total acquisition costs reaching $385 billion.

The measure also required that the defense undersecretary for acquisition, technology, and logistics produce a report on plans for implementing provisions of the Weapon Systems Acquisition Reform Act of 2009 (PL 111-23) for the F-35 program. It also barred funding for the second engine.

A bipartisan provision required military detention for the core group of al Qaeda detainees suspected of plotting or carrying out attacks against the United States, although it allowed for a national security waiver of that requirement. It also proposed permanent limitations on the transfer of detainees at Guantánamo to foreign countries, aiming to make sure enough steps were taken to prevent recidivism. It also barred the use of Pentagon funding to build facilities in the United States to house Guantánamo detainees.

SENATE FLOOR ACTION

After resolving a dispute over military detainees that dominated most of two weeks of debate, the Senate passed the second version of the defense bill (S 1867), totaling a $661.6 billion, by a vote of 93–7 on December 1. The total was $28.4 billion less than passed by the House. The chamber then inserted the language into the House bill (HR 1540) in preparation for conference.

The Armed Services Committee had taken the unusual step on October 14 of revising the bill to cut the authorization by $21 billion, a reduction that was needed to bring it within the spending cap for national security set in the debt limit law.

The revised bill included $527.3 billion for the base Defense Department budget, plus $116.8 billion for overseas contingency operations and $17.5 billion for programs in the Energy Department. The total authorization was $27.3 billion less than Obama's budget request.

Three days after the new bill came out, the White House renewed its veto threat, singling out detainee provisions that it said would "micromanage the work of our experienced counterterrorism professionals, including our military commanders, intelligence professionals, seasoned counterterrorism prosecutors, or other operatives in the field." Administration officials were particularly opposed to language requiring that members of al Qaeda and its affiliates, including those captured in the United States, be held in military rather than civilian custody, although the bill allowed for a waiver on national security grounds. The statement warned of a veto against any bill that "challenges or constrains the president's critical authorities to collect intelligence, incapacitate dangerous terrorists, and protect the nation."

The divisions over detainee policy set a contentious tone in the early days of the floor debate, as Armed Services Committee leaders shrugged off the veto threat and opposed Democratic efforts to strike or revise the terrorism-related language. Armed Services Chair Carl Levin, D-Mich., who backed the detainee language, found himself in the unusual position of publicly battling political allies, such as Democrats Patrick J. Leahy of Vermont, the Chair of the Judiciary Committee, and Dianne Feinstein of California, the Chair of the Select Intelligence Committee.

During the floor debate, the Senate:

- Rejected, 45–55, an attempt by Feinstein to limit mandatory military custody to suspected terrorists captured outside the United States.
- Adopted, on a **key vote of 99–1 (R 46–1; D 51–0; I 2–0)**, a last-minute compromise between Feinstein and Armed Services Committee leaders stating that detainee language in the bill would not affect existing law related to the detention of U.S. citizens and lawful residents, effectively leaving the contested issue to the Supreme Court. Feinstein and others had warned that the bill would expose U.S. citizens accused of terrorist activities to the military's control with no limit on the time they could be held and interrogated. She also said other committees should have a chance to consider the language. *(2011 key votes, p. 785)*
- Adopted, 100–0, an amendment by New Jersey Democrat Robert Menendez and Illinois Republican Mark Steven Kirk to prevent any foreign company doing business with the Central Bank of Iran from having access to the U.S. financial system. Hours before the unanimous Senate vote, Treasury and State Department officials came to Capitol Hill to plead with senators to hold off on a push to collapse Iran's central bank, warning among other things that such sanctions would cut into Iran's oil sales and lead to a rise in global oil prices.
- Adopted by unanimous consent an amendment by Roger Wicker, R-Miss., to clarify that military chaplains would not be required to perform a marriage if they had a moral objection to doing so.
- Adopted by unanimous consent an amendment by Kelly Ayotte, R-N.H., to require the Pentagon to complete a full-scale audit of the department's finances by September 30, 2014, three years ahead of schedule. The Pentagon was one of only two cabinet-level departments that were unable to audit their books. Even defense hawks had grown impatient, saying it was impossible to determine how much money the department needed when defense officials could not track their own spending.

CONFERENCE ACTION

Conferees signed off on the final version of the bill and filed a report December 12 that included enough changes on detainees, Iran sanctions, and other issues to avert a veto.

The House adopted the conference report (H Rept 112-329) by a vote of 283–136 on December 14, and the Senate cleared the bill, 86–13, the next day.

The detainee provisions in the final bill closely resembled language in the Senate version, including a controversial new policy requiring al Qaeda members and affiliates who were not U.S. citizens to be held in military, rather than civilian, custody. The Senate bill contained a national security waiver, but that did not satisfy the administration.

Seeking to mollify the White House and other critics who were concerned that requiring military custody could interfere with civilian law enforcement, conferees added new language. It stated that the section would not affect "existing criminal enforcement and national security authorities of the Federal Bureau of Investigation or any other domestic law enforcement agency," whether or not a detainee was in military custody. The final bill also gave the waiver authority to the president rather than the secretary of defense.

White House Press Secretary Jay Carney said in a written statement that the president would ask for changes if the law hurt the work of civilian counterterrorism officials or undercut "our commitment to the rule of law."

Conferees rejected several controversial terrorism-related provisions from the original House version, including language that would have updated the 2001 law that authorized the war on terrorism (PL 107-40), a move that opponents argued would have given the commander in chief nearly boundless authority to conduct military operations.

Also omitted was House GOP language that would have required the United States to classify all foreign terrorists as enemy combatants and prosecute them in military tribunals.

To address other administration objections, House and Senate negotiators agreed to tweak a provision unanimously approved by the Senate to create new sanctions targeting the Central Bank of Iran, a move intended to force the country to abandon its alleged nuclear weapons program. Senior administration officials argued that they needed more flexibility to avoid sanctioning companies from nations deemed to be cooperating with U.S. efforts to pressure Tehran. Conferees provided some new flexibility, including changing the conditions for a waiver from "vital national security interest" to simply "national security interest."

The bill also set new policy for the troubled F-35 Joint Strike Fighter, the most expensive program on the Pentagon's books. The plane's history had been marked by soaring prices and technical difficulties. The final bill required the plane's maker, Lockheed Martin Corp., to pay out of pocket for all cost overruns on the sixth batch of aircraft. The Defense Department and Lockheed Martin had a tentative agreement in place to share the cost burden for overruns on the fifth batch.

Senate negotiators quietly dropped a provision that would have required the Pentagon to complete a full financial audit by 2014, three years ahead of schedule. The move came after pressure from the Pentagon and amid opposition from House members. The bill required the Defense Department to send Congress a plan by May 2012 on how it would complete an audit by September 30, 2014.

On another controversial issue, the conference report left out several House amendments aimed at limiting the 2010 repeal (PL 111-321) of the "don't ask, don't tell" policy that had barred openly gay people from serving in the military. The bill did allow military chaplains to decline to officiate at any marriage if doing so would violate their conscience or moral principles.

The final bill also contained less stringent provisions on reducing the U.S. nuclear arsenal than the House had passed, basically requiring notification and reports if the administration wanted to reduce the number of nuclear weapons.

Over public objections from the military's most senior leaders, the bill made the National Guard Bureau chief a member of the Joint Chiefs of Staff. The expansion of the elite Joint Chiefs marked a historic victory for Guard boosters on Capitol Hill, who had fought for years to make the Guard's top officer the equivalent in stature to the chiefs of the individual services.

MAJOR PROVISIONS

Following are the main provisions of the fiscal 2012 defense authorization:

Missile Defense

$10.5 billion for missile defense programs, slightly more than the fiscal 2011 level and the president's request. The total included funding for the initial deployment of a national missile defense system based in Alaska and California and the Obama administration's plan for missile defense in Europe. The Obama plan called for a largely sea-based missile defense system focused on protecting Europe from short- and medium-range Iranian missiles.

The measure also authorized $216 million for cooperative missile defense programs with Israel, $110 million more than requested.

Aircraft

The military's tactical aircraft included three major programs—the F-18 Super Hornet, the primary strike aircraft of both the Navy and the Marine Corps; the Air Force's F-22A Raptor, which had ended production; and the joint service F-35 Joint Strike Fighter, which had just entered initial production. The authorization included:

- $6.2 billion to procure thirty-one F-35s, one aircraft fewer than requested. The measure authorized no funds for an alternative engine, which was opposed by the administration. The Joint Strike Fighter was planned as a fighter aircraft with different versions that would serve the Air Force, Navy, and Marine Corps. Massive cost overruns had plagued the program. The House and the Senate would have met the president's request for $6.6 billion.

- $2.3 billion toward procurement of twenty-eight F/A-18 E/Fs and $1 billion for twelve EA-18G Growler electronic-warfare planes. The House would have authorized $2.4 billion, as requested, for the F-18s; the Senate would have authorized $1.8 billion.

Navy Shipbuilding

The bill authorized $14.9 billion for construction of twelve Navy vessels, including:

- $4.7 billion for two Virginia-class attack submarines, which were being built to replace retiring Los Angeles–class submarines and constitute the bulk of the future attack submarine force. The amount was only slightly less than requested and recommended by both chambers.
- $2.1 billion for one DDG-51 Arleigh Burke–class destroyer, as requested and passed by both chambers.
- $1.8 billion for four Littoral Combat Ship—fast, maneuverable, relatively inexpensive vessels built to operate in shallow coastal waters. The amount was just slightly less than requested and recommended by both chambers.

Ground Combat Vehicle

The bill included $449 million to develop the army's proposed replacement for a manned ground vehicle component that was part of the Future Combat Systems, a program that had been canceled two years earlier. The conferees said in their report that before the army started another major development program that could cost from $30 billion to $40 billion, lawmakers had to be convinced that the Ground Combat Vehicle would be significantly more capable than an upgraded version of existing vehicles. The amount was a little more than half what was requested and approved by both chambers.

Marine Corps Expeditionary Fighting Vehicle

The bill prohibited obligating funds for this vehicle pending a report to Congress. The Pentagon had recently terminated the amphibious-vehicle program, which had been plagued by technological problems, delays, and cost overruns.

Personnel

The bill set a ceiling on the number of total active-duty military personnel at 1,422,600 in fiscal 2012, equal to the president's request but 9,800 less than the existing level. The total included 562,000 for the army, 7,400 less than the existing level; 325,700 for the Navy; 332,800 for the Air Force; and 202,100 for the Marine Corps. The Defense Department had proposed reducing the size of the active-duty army by 27,000 soldiers and the active-duty Marine Corps by 15,300 marines beginning in fiscal 2015.

The measure also set a ceiling of 857,100 on selected reserve personnel, equal to the administration's request and 900 more than the fiscal 2011 level. Selected reserves included the National Guard and the reserve forces of the services and the Coast Guard. Approximately 40 percent of army troops who served in Iraq and Afghanistan were from the reserves. The agreement limited the number of reserve personnel that could be placed on active duty to 78,414 in fiscal 2012.

Military Pay

A 1.6 per cent pay increase for military personnel, equal to the president's request. The bill also extended certain special pay and bonuses for active-duty and reserve personnel.

Defense Health Program

$33.1 billion for defense health care programs. The total—which included $1.2 billion authorized in the section on Iraq and Afghanistan—was $350 million less than requested or recommended by the Senate and about $117 million less than in the House bill. The military health care system was the fastest-growing part of the defense budget, rising from about 6 percent of the base budget to 10 percent over the previous decade. The increase was partly because of a general rise in medical costs and partly because of congressionally required increases in benefits.

The measure allowed the first increase in out-of-pocket fees for participants in the military's Tricare health care program since the mid-1990s. Annual fee increases could not exceed the general rate of inflation.

Nuclear Weapons Programs

$16.9 billion for national security programs at the Energy Department, $1.1 billion less than requested. The total included $11.1 billion for operating nuclear weapons laboratories and for programs operated by the National Nuclear Security Administration (NNSA) and $5.8 billion for environmental restoration, waste management, and other defense activities. The NNSA total was $713 million below the president's request, while environmental spending was $420 million less than requested.

The conference agreement did not include a House-passed provision to limit the use of funds for any of fiscal years 2011 through 2017 to retire, dismantle, eliminate, or remove from deployed status any covered U.S. nuclear system as required by the New START agreement with Russia. Instead, the final bill required the president to notify Congress before any nuclear reductions were made and codified an existing requirement that the

Armed Services committees be briefed before changes to U.S. nuclear war plans were instituted.

Military Construction

$13.1 billion for military construction, base realignment and closure, and family housing, $1.7 billion less than requested.

Overseas Contingency Operations

The $115.5 billion for the wars in Afghanistan and Iraq and other antiterrorism activities was $2.4 billion less than requested. It was $3.4 billion less than the House recommended and $1.4 billion less than was in the Senate bill. However, funding authorized elsewhere in the bill also could be used to support those operations. The overseas contingency operations section authorized $86.2 billion for operations and maintenance, $15.1 billion for procurement, and $11.2 billion for personnel.

The total included:

- $2.6 billion for MRAP vehicles.
- $2.5 billion to develop and procure measures to counter IED attacks.
- $255 million in unrequested funds to procure additional M-1 Abrams tanks.
- $11.2 billion to train and equip Afghanistan's security forces, $1.6 billion less than requested. The total included $6.5 billion for the Afghan army and $4.6 billion for its national police.
- $400 million, $75 million less than requested, for the Afghanistan Infrastructure Fund to undertake high-priority, large-scale infrastructure projects in support of the civil-military campaign.
- $1.1 billion, as requested, for the Pentagon's Pakistan Counterinsurgency Fund.
- $400 million, $25 million less than requested, for the Commanders' Emergency Response Program (CERP), which provided U.S. commanders with funds for small humanitarian and reconstruction projects. The bill did not authorize the use of the CERP in Iraq, where remaining U.S. forces were operating in a strictly training and advisory capacity.

Fiscal 2012 Defense Appropriations

For the second fiscal year in a row, Congress failed to pass a separate defense spending bill for fiscal 2012—a piece of legislation historically considered "must pass." In fact, the full Senate never acted on the stand-alone defense bill reported by its Appropriations Committee. Congress instead folded defense into an omnibus appropriations bill (HR 2055—H Rept 112-74) in mid-December, more than two months after the fiscal year had begun.

The bill included a total of $633.2 billion for defense spending, a net of $23.6 billion below the president's request, plus $13.1 billion for military construction, which was $1.7 billion below the request. The grand total for defense thus was $646.3 billion, a net of $25.3 billion below the request and $42.4 billion below the fiscal 2011 appropriations, according to an analysis by the Congressional Research Service.

HOUSE COMMITTEE ACTION

The Defense Appropriations Subcommittee approved a draft of a defense spending bill by voice vote June 1. Senior GOP appropriators at the closed-door markup reportedly expressed serious reservations about the mission in Afghanistan, but further discussion was put off for the full-committee markup.

The full House Appropriations Committee reported its defense bill (HR 2219—H Rept 112-110) on June 16. The bill would have provided $648.7 in discretionary budget authority. It included $530.5 billion for the base Pentagon budget, $8.9 billion below the administration's request, and $118.6 billion for overseas contingency operations, $842 million more than the president sought.

The bill included language requiring the Pentagon to withhold 75 percent of the $1.1 billion allocated for the Pakistan Counterinsurgency Fund until the defense secretary provided lawmakers with a report on such issues as the country's security capabilities, U.S. objectives in Pakistan, and how Pakistan was combating terrorist groups.

While Obama administration officials stressed that a strong relationship with Pakistan was vital in the battle against terrorist groups, lawmakers were raising concerns about reported links between Pakistan's military and intelligence units to terrorist and extremist organizations. War fatigue was mounting after nearly ten years of U.S. involvement in Iraq and Afghanistan, and congressional questions about the war in Afghanistan had grown louder since the May 1 killing of al Qaeda leader Osama bin Laden.

During the markup, the full committee adopted by voice vote an amendment by Jeff Flake, R-Ariz., to give Congress thirty days to review the report on Pakistan before aid could be released. The committee also adopted by voice vote an amendment by Frank R. Wolf, R-Va., to allocate $1 million for an independent, private commission to study and make recommendations on the war in Afghanistan, the situation in Pakistan, and the region in general.

Major elements of the bill included:

- $9.4 billion for procurement and research on the F-35. No money was provided for the alternative engine.
- $2.4 billion for the Navy F-18 and $1 billion for the EA-18G variant.
- No funds for the F-22.
- $4.8 billion toward procurement of two Virginia-class submarines.
- $1.8 billion for four Littoral Combat Ships.
- $1.8 billion for one LPD amphibious transport ship.
- $768 million for research on the army Ground Combat Vehicle.

- $12.8 billion for the Afghanistan security forces and $475 million for infrastructure in Afghanistan.
- $1.1 billion for Pakistan counterinsurgency capabilities.
- $32.3 billion in the base budget, plus $1.2 billion in the contingency operations section, for defense health programs.
- A 1.6 percent military pay raise.

HOUSE FLOOR ACTION

The full House passed HR 2219 on July 8, 2011, by a vote of 335–87, after three days of debate and recorded votes on nearly three dozen amendments, many of them aimed at curbing U.S. military involvement in Afghanistan as well as support operations in Libya.

The bill would have appropriated $638.3 billion, which was a net cut of $8.1 billion from the president's request. The bill actually cut $8.9 billion from various accounts but also added $842 million for war-related expenses, most of it for National Guard and reserve units.

During debate, members defeated amendments that would have reduced funding for the ongoing U.S. military operations, especially in Afghanistan. Proposed reductions in spending for reconstruction in those countries attracted more support. Numerous amendments proposed cutting the bill's $475 million for construction of water, power, and transportation projects in Afghanistan. Steve Cohen, D-Tenn., offered an amendment that would have moved $200 million from the fund to deficit reduction. The House narrowly rejected it, 210–217. But the substantial support, despite opposition from both the Obama administration and bipartisan leaders of the Appropriations Committee, signaled the degree of disaffection with the assistance.

Efforts to cut military aid to Afghanistan and Pakistan drew less support, but the number of such efforts revealed disquiet among a coalition of liberals and conservatives.

In action on some of the other amendments, the House:

- Rejected, 119–306, a Cohen amendment that would have cut $4 billion out of the funds for training and equipping Afghan army and police units and used the money to reduce the deficit.
- Rejected, 140–285, an amendment by Ted Poe, R-Texas, that would have reduced aid to Pakistan's military. Poe called Pakistan "more and more an unfaithful ally."
- Rejected, 133–295, an amendment by John Garamendi, D-Calif., to reduce funding for the war in Afghanistan by $20.9 billion and use the funds for deficit reduction.
- Rejected, 176–249, an amendment by Scott Rigell, R-Va., to bar the use of funds in the bill for U.S. and NATO operations in Libya.
- Adopted, 225–201, an amendment by Tom Cole, R-Okla., to bar expenditures to arm, train, or advise the rebels in Libya. The administration had already stressed that it would not take such action.
- Adopted, 212–208, a proposal from Justin Amash, R-Mich., to strike a section of the bill that would block the Defense Department from contracting out functions unless it would result in savings.
- Adopted, 236–184, an amendment by Tim Huelskamp, R-Kan., to bar spending to implement a training curriculum for military chaplains related to the repeal of the "don't ask, don't tell" policy, which prevented openly gay men and women from serving in the military. The policy had been conditionally repealed in December 2010.

After the House acted, Congress in August adopted the Budget Control Act (PL 112-25), the debt limit law that required reductions in all discretionary spending accounts, including for the Pentagon but exempting war-related costs.

SENATE COMMITTEE ACTION

Pentagon nonwar funding would have been frozen at the fiscal 2011 level under the version of the bill written by Senate appropriators (HR 2219—S Rept 112-77). The measure, which the Appropriations Committee approved 30–0 on September 15, called for $630.6 billion in discretionary funds. It would have provided $513 billion for base Pentagon programs, $25.9 billion less than Obama requested and $18 billion less than in the House-passed version. War funding was set at $117.5 billion, about $260 million less than requested and $1.1 billion less than in the House bill.

"This was a difficult allocation to meet, and I will caution my colleagues that any further reductions to the Department of Defense budget could be detrimental to our military forces," said committee Chair Daniel K. Inouye, D-Hawaii, who had set the defense allocation to meet the terms of the debt limit law.

The panel's Defense Subcommittee, which Inouye also headed, approved the measure by voice vote September 13.

The bill provided $705 million less than the House version for the F-35, and $1.6 billion less for training Afghan security forces. Other major elements of the bill included:

- $8.6 billion for procurement and research on the F-35. No money was included for the alternative engine.
- $2.3 billion for the Navy F-18 and $1.1 billion for the EA-18G variant.
- No funds for the F-22.
- $4.8 billion for two Virginia-class submarines.
- $1.8 billion for four Littoral Combat Ships.
- $1.8 billion for one LPD amphibious transport ship.
- $240 million for research on the army Ground Combat Vehicle.
- $11.2 billion for the Afghanistan Security Forces and $400 million for infrastructure in Afghanistan.
- A 1.6 percent military pay raise.
- The full Senate did not act on the committee's bill.

FINAL ACTION

A House-Senate compromise, which largely tracked the Senate committee bill, was included in fiscal 2012 omnibus appropriations, HR 2055, reported by conferees (H Rept 112-331) on December 15. The House agreed to the compromise on December 16 by a vote of 296–121; the Senate acted on December 17 by a vote of 67–32. President Obama signed the bill on December 23, 2011 (PL 112-74). *(Omnibus legislation, p. 172)*

MAJOR PROVISIONS

Following are major components of PL 112-74 (the Department of Defense Appropriations Act of 2012):

Spending by Category

Divided into the main spending categories, the bill appropriated:

- $163.1 billion in the base budget, $7.7 billion less than Obama requested, to operate and maintain U.S. forces and to maintain materials and facilities worldwide. Another $89 billion in the overseas contingency operations section brought the total for operations and maintenance to $252.1 billion—more than one-third of total military expenditures. The account included training, supplies, and equipment maintenance as well as administrative functions, environmental restoration, cooperative threat reduction efforts, humanitarian assistance, and many other programs.
- $131.1 billion within the base budget, $1 billion less than requested, for military personnel, including costs of pay, allowances, bonuses, survivor benefits, and permanent change-of-station moves. An additional $11.6 billion provided in the overseas contingency operations section brought the total to $142.7 billion.
- $104.6 billion in the base budget for procurement, $9.8 billion less than requested, plus $13.6 billion in the overseas contingency account, for a total of $118.2 billion.

Missile Defense

$10 billion for missile defense programs, roughly equal to the request. The total included $990 million for the Aegis ballistic-missile defense system, $30 million more than requested. The sea-based system was meant to be the centerpiece of a new missile defense system proposed for Europe. Other expenditures included $662 million for the Patriot PAC-3 antimissile interceptor and $1 billion for ballistic-missile defense testing.

Tactical Aircraft

$17.7 billion for aircraft for the Navy, $13 billion for Air Force planes, and $5.4 billion for army aircraft, including:

- $9 billion for the procurement and continued research on the F-35 Joint Strike Fighter, versions of which were intended for the Air Force, Navy, and Marine Corps. The bill included no funding for the alternative engine for the aircraft. The Defense Department formally terminated the alternative-engine program on April 25. General Electric and its partner, Rolls-Royce, announced December 2 that they were reversing an earlier decision to use their own money to fund development of the alternative engine through the end of fiscal 2012.
- $2.3 billion for 28 F/A-18 E/Fs Super Hornet aircraft for the Navy and $1 billion for 12 new EA-18G Airborne Electronic Attack aircraft, a variant of the F/A-18F fighter.
- No funds for the F-22A Raptor fighter, the Air Force's next-generation premier fighter, designed to have both air-to-air and air-to-ground fighter capabilities. The program was originally slated to cost $96 billion for 750 planes. Only 188 aircraft had been built for more than $63 billion, making it the most costly jet fighter ever, six times as expensive as the F-15 it was meant to replace. Although numerous attempts had been made to keep the F-22 program alive, no new aircraft had been funded in the previous two years. The plane had yet to be used in combat operations in Iraq, Afghanistan, or Libya. The Pentagon had said that the existing fleet of F-22s was sufficient for meeting defense requirements.

Shipbuilding

$14.9 billion for Navy ship construction and refurbishment, roughly equal to the request, including:

- $4.7 billion, as requested, for construction and long-lead components for the next two boats in the Virginia class of new attack submarines, which were slated to replace retiring Los Angeles–class subs and constitute the bulk of the attack submarine force in the future. The Virginia class was designed with improved capabilities in stealth, surveillance, special warfare, and flexibility to be adapted to new missions.
- $2.1 billion, as requested, for the next DDG-51 vessel. The DDG-51 Arleigh Burke–class of Navy destroyers provided improved radar, fleet defense, missile defense, and land attack capabilities to the Navy's surface fleet. The DDG-1000 was supposed to have replaced the DDG-51 but had run into numerous problems.
- $1.8 billion, as requested, for four Littoral Combat Ship vessels, a small, specialized variant of the DD(X) family of future surface combat ships. The fast, maneuverable, relatively inexpensive vessel was built to operate in shallow coastal waters.
- $1.8 billion, as requested, for procurement of one San Antonio–class LPD-17. The amphibious warfare ship was developed to transport and land elements of a landing force for expeditionary-warfare missions.

The ship could incorporate both a flight deck and a well deck and could support landing craft or amphibious vehicles.

Ground Combat Vehicle

$449 million, about half what Obama requested, for the vehicle that the army proposed as a replacement for armored fighting vehicles in Heavy and Stryker brigade combat teams. The Ground Combat Vehicle was intended to replace the manned ground vehicle component of the Future Combat Systems, which had been canceled two years earlier. The first variant of the army vehicle was scheduled to be prototyped in 2015 and fielded by 2017.

Defense Health Program

The base budget included $32.5 billion for defense health care programs, roughly equal to the president's request. The overseas contingency section appropriated another $1.2 billion. The military health care system was the fastest-growing part of the defense budget, rising from about 6 percent of the base budget to 10 percent over the previous decade. Active-duty troops received free health care, and their families received care at little or no cost, depending on the coverage they chose. Wounded, disabled, and indigent veterans received care through the Veterans Affairs Department.

Military Pay

The bill paid for a 1.6 percent across-the-board pay raise for military personnel, as requested by Obama.

Detainees

The measure barred the use of funds to transfer or release Khalid Sheikh Mohammed or other detainees held on or after June 24, 2009, at the U.S. Naval Station at Guantánamo Bay, Cuba, into the United States. It prohibited the transfer of a detainee to a foreign country until the defense secretary certified that certain conditions had been met, including the receiving country taking steps to ensure that the individual could not engage in any terrorist activity.

The measure also prohibited the use of any funds to construct or modify any facility in the United States to detain or imprison individuals being held at the Guantánamo facility. The administration had proposed purchasing the Thomson Correction Center in Illinois to house some Guantánamo detainees.

Overseas Contingency Operations

Although the agreement appropriated $115 billion specifically for the wars in Afghanistan and Iraq and the general war on terrorism, funding elsewhere in the bill could be used to support those operations. The measure included:

- $2.6 billion for Mine Resistant Ambush Protected (MRAP) vehicles and $2.4 billion to procure and develop countermeasures to prevent improvised explosive device (IED) attacks.
- $1 billion in unrequested funding to address shortfalls in equipment for the National Guard and reserve units.
- Ability for the Defense Department to transfer $4 billion among accounts within the overseas contingency section.
- $11.2 billion for training and equipping Afghanistan's security forces, $1.6 billion less than requested. The total included $6.5 billion for the Afghan army and $4.6 billion for its national police. The bill also provided $400 million for the Afghanistan Infrastructure Fund, established to undertake high-priority, large-scale infrastructure projects in support of the civil-military campaign in Afghanistan. (Another $850 million in counterinsurgency assistance to the security forces of Pakistan—including military forces, police forces, and the Frontier Corps—was provided in the State–Foreign Operations section of the omnibus bill.)
- $400 million, $25 million less than requested, for the Commanders' Emergency Response Program in Afghanistan. The fund gave U.S. commanders money to use for small humanitarian and reconstruction projects.

Fiscal 2013 Defense Authorization

In one of its final acts of 2012, Congress cleared a measure authorizing $633.3 billion in discretionary spending for national defense programs, approving more money and more weapons than the Defense Department sought. President Barack Obama signed the bill into law January 2, 2013 (HR 4310—PL 112-329).

The bulk of the authorization, $527.5 billion, was for the base Pentagon budget. The amount was $2.1 billion more than Obama requested. The rest of the bill consisted of $88.5 billion for the war in Afghanistan and other overseas contingencies—virtually the same as requested—although other funds in the bill could also be used. The agreement also authorized $17.4 billion for nuclear defense activities carried out by the Energy Department, about $400 million less than requested.

Overall, the $633.3 billion total was $1.7 billion above the president's request.

Lawmakers worked diligently to limit the number of controversial issues in the bill and managed to complete a final House-Senate conference in a little more than three days. But despite the relative comity in the effort, there were difficult moments relating to detainees, alternative fuels, same-sex marriages, abortions, and Iran sanctions.

Detainees. Lawmakers clashed over detention policies up until the end of the conference, finally dropping a provision in the Senate version that was billed as a guarantee against indefinite incarceration of U.S. citizens captured in the United States in the war on terrorism.

The final law included some tough detainee language, largely from the House bill. The one provision in the House bill that the administration had said might trigger a veto—permanently blocking the transfer of detainees from the detention facility at Guantánamo Bay, Cuba—was rolled back to a one-year restriction, matching provisions in the past two defense policy laws signed by Obama. *(Fiscal 2012 law, p. 314; Guantánamo detainee issues, p. 299)*

The bill prohibited the use of funds to construct or modify facilities in the United States to house detainees transferred from Guantánamo.

The House prevailed in including a host of reporting requirements on recidivism among released detainees and the use of naval vessels as detention facilities. House conferees also managed to include a provision requiring prior notice before the transfer of third-country nationals detained in Afghanistan. This provision reflected concerns about the decision by Iraq to release a Hezbollah operative captured in Iraq by U.S. forces and turned over to Iraqis with the expectation that he would be tried in Iraqi courts. The fear was that, as the war in Afghanistan wound down, similar events could occur there.

Lawmakers also included a House provision ensuring that the writ of habeas corpus applied to Americans detained as terrorists, ensuring their access to U.S. courts.

Biofuels. Conferees reached several other tough compromises, including language allowing the Pentagon to proceed with its plans to fund a biofuels refinery, but they fenced off the $70 billion in funding until the departments of Energy and Agriculture contributed an equal amount.

Abortion. The bill retained a Senate provision allowing the use of Pentagon funds to pay for abortions for service members in the case of rape or incest.

Gay marriage. The bill retained a House provision making it clear that military chaplains could decide whether to preside over same-sex marriage ceremonies. But the compromise measure did not include House language that would have barred gay marriages from taking place on military property.

Iran. The law included Senate language on Iran sanctions but increased the time to implement the sanctions, to 180 days from ninety days in most cases, as the White House requested. *(Iran sanctions, pp. 238, 255)*

Missile defense. The bill did not mandate the construction of an East Coast missile site, as the House wanted, but authorized the study of three potential sites, two on the East Coast.

HOUSE COMMITTEE ACTION

In a bipartisan vote held after more than sixteen hours of debate, the House Armed Services Committee approved its fiscal 2013 defense policy bill (HR 4310—H Rept 112-479, Parts 1 and 2) on May 9 by a vote of 56–5. Six subcommittees had approved sections of the bill April 26 and April 27, 2012.

The bill proposed to authorize $528.6 billion for the base Defense Department budget, $88.5 billion for overseas contingency operations, and $18.1 billion for the Energy Department's atomic energy activities. The total was $3.6 billion more than the president requested and $8 billion more than prescribed under the 2011 Budget Control Act (PL 112-25). *(2011 budget act, p. 160)*

Committee member John Garamendi, D-Calif., said that by ignoring the spending caps, Republicans were placing the full burden of future spending cuts on domestic discretionary funding and holding defense harmless moving forward.

Members opted to defer discussion of some controversial issues, such as military detainee policy at Guantánamo Bay, until the bill reached the House floor. The bill contained language prohibiting the defense secretary from using fiscal 2013 funds to transfer or release Guantánamo detainees to a foreign country or entity.

During the markup, the committee:

- Adopted, 37–24, a proposal by Steven M. Palazzo, R-Miss., to prohibit the use of military installations for same-sex marriage ceremonies.
- Adopted, 44–18, a Rob Wittman, R-Va., amendment to bar the use of funds in the bill to propose, plan for, or execute an additional Base Realignment and Closure (BRAC) round. *(2005 base closings, Congress and the Nation Vol. XII, p. 370)*
- Adopted by voice vote an amendment by ranking committee Democrat Adam Smith of Washington to require the Pentagon to declare when each of its troubled F-35 fighter variants would reach "initial operational capability."
- Rejected, 29–33, an amendment by Garamendi to strike a provision in the bill requiring that the Pentagon build a new missile defense site on the East Coast before 2016. "Let's deal with the deficit and not spend our money foolishly," Garamendi said. "Does Iran have an intercontinental ballistic missile? No, they don't." Republicans criticized Garamendi's proposal, saying the threat from Iran or a nonstate actor was coming. "It's always astonishing to me that we kind of cavalierly suggest that we don't need missile defense against some of the most dangerous weapons of mankind," Arizona Republican Trent Franks said.
- Rejected a raft of amendments by Loretta Sanchez of California, the ranking Democrat on the Strategic Forces Subcommittee. One, rejected by voice vote, would have blocked funding for new antiballistic missile interceptors until there was a successful intercept missile in testing. Another proposal, rejected 26–37, would have cut spending by $358 million for the Ground-based Midcourse Defense system, which was aimed at intercepting nuclear warheads in space.

HOUSE FLOOR ACTION

Despite multiple White House veto threats, the House easily passed the bill on a 299–120 vote on May 18, 2012.

Defense Secretary Leon E. Panetta criticized House lawmakers for exceeding the funding limits laid out in the budget control law. That prompted Armed Services Chair Howard "Buck" McKeon, R-Calif., to write a letter to Panetta saying that "those caps take the Defense Department right to the razor's edge. They cut through any fat that may have existed and right into the muscle." McKeon repeated the metaphor as the House wrapped up debate on the bill.

"I wish we were wrong, and I would hope that we could continue to cut defense, cut it to the bone, cut it to the marrow, and we could just live one big happy life," he said, "but history shows that isn't the way things work."

Among the many amendments considered, the House:

- Adopted, 249–171, an amendment by Florida Republican Tom Rooney directing the Defense Department to hold detainee trials at Guantánamo Bay and not in the United States.
- Rejected, on a **key vote of 182–238 (R 19–219; D 163–19)**, language to authorize the transfer of individuals captured within the United States to military authorities. The amendment also would have guaranteed that no terrorist suspect could be held indefinitely without charge or trial in the United States and barred the use of military commissions for those detained on U.S. soil, regardless of their country of origin. Tribunals for U.S. citizens were already barred by law. The amendment was co-sponsored by Smith and Justin Amash, a Republican freshman from Michigan. *(2012 key votes, p. 803)*

Support for the Adams-Amash amendment came from an unlikely coalition of Democrats and Tea Party Republicans. The alliance was bound together by a fervor for protecting civil liberties, but defenders of the bill said that the proposed changes were unnecessary. The outside organizations that backed Smith and Amash also made strange bedfellows: liberals at the American Civil Liberties Union and Win Without War joined forces with conservatives at places such as Young Americans for Liberty, Take Back Washington, and the Tenth Amendment Center.

The fiscal 2012 defense authorization law (PL 112-81) affirmed that existing law pertaining to Americans detained at home was unchanged and stated that the government could detain terrorism suspects regardless of nationality under the 2001 law authorizing the Afghanistan war (PL 107-40). *(Congress and the Nation Vol. XI, p. 234)*

By not expressly prohibiting the detention of Americans on U.S. soil, the law was seen as sanctioning it by many on both the left and the right. Obama, in signing the defense bill, issued a statement saying that detaining Americans without trial was unnecessary and he would not do it, but did not say he lacked the authority to do it.

- Adopted, 243–173, a detainee amendment offered by Louie Gohmert, R-Texas, to clarify that the bill and the 2001 Afghanistan authorization law did not deny the right to trial in federal civilian courts or any other constitutional right for persons detained in the United States who were entitled to such rights. Smith said the Gohmert proposal would do nothing to change existing law.
- Adopted, 241–179, an amendment by Tom Price, R-Ga., to prohibit the president from unilaterally entering into any agreement that would decrease the size of the U.S. nuclear arsenal to a level below that in the New START agreement with Russia, approved in 2010. *(New START Treaty, p. 289)*

Michael R. Turner, R-Ohio, chair of the Armed Services Subcommittee on Strategic Forces, had already succeeded in committee in attaching language to bar funding for nuclear weapons reductions required under the New START pact unless certain conditions were met. House Republicans had included similar language in their fiscal 2012 defense authorization bill, but it was ultimately dropped in conference.

One of the main conditions that Turner's language set was that the White House would have to live up to funding pledges for the modernization of the nation's aging nuclear stockpile, delivery systems, and nuclear laboratories. As part of its efforts to secure support for New START among Republican senators, the administration had pledged to increase spending to upgrade these facilities and systems, but GOP members in both chambers accused the White House of reneging on its promises.

- Adopted, 220–201, an amendment by Scott Rigell, R-Va., to replace pending automatic budget cuts, known as a sequester, with an equal amount of cuts in discretionary spending. The amendment would allow lawmakers to cut less from Pentagon spending and more from domestic programs than would be the case under the sequester, which required that half the reductions be from defense.
- Adopted, 211–209, a controversial amendment by Roscoe G. Bartlett, R-Md., to prevent federal agencies from requiring contractors to sign collective-bargaining agreements, known as project labor agreements, as a condition of winning a federal construction contract.
- Rejected, 170–252, an amendment by Barbara Lee, D-Calif., to reduce the overall authorization by $8 billion, bringing it in line with the caps set in the 2011 budget act.
- Rejected, 209–211, a Mike Coffman, R-Colo., amendment to allow contractors to perform functions that

were restricted to Pentagon civilian employees and repeal a prohibition against public-private competition for certain Defense Department functions.

Afghanistan/Pakistan

The House voted to cut reimbursements to Pakistan in half, from the $1.3 billion request to $650 million. The Appropriations Committee bill had barred any of the aid unless the administration certified that Pakistan was cooperating with U.S. operations against al Qaeda and similar groups based in the country.

The House also adopted two amendments cutting nearly $600 million from the budget for Afghanistan: $412 million from incentive pay for Afghan security forces (transferring $149 million instead to incentive pay for U.S. forces) and $175 million from the Afghan Infrastructure Fund.

The House rejected, 113–303, an amendment from Barbara Lee that would have limited the use of funding for Afghanistan operations to the purpose of facilitating the withdrawal of troops.

The Rules Committee had barred an amendment by Massachusetts Democrat Jim McGovern that was likely to have garnered more votes. His proposal would have required Obama to accelerate the U.S. withdrawal from Afghanistan, mandating the full transfer of combat operations to the Afghan government by the end of 2013 and military and security operations by the end of 2014.

Veto Threat

In its veto threat, the White House said that the House legislation threatened to "impede the ability of the administration to execute the new defense strategy and to properly direct scarce resources." The new strategy was focused on a leaner, more flexible military.

The bill, for instance, included a provision requiring that the Air Force keep eighteen surveillance drones—the so-called Global Hawk Block 30s—in the fleet until at least the end of 2014. The Global Hawk program was nearly shut down two years earlier under a law that terminated programs that went over budget by more than 25 percent. The Defense Department said that retiring the drone and using the cold war–era U-2 manned spy planes could save $2.5 billion over five years.

The White House objected to the total funding level because it exceeded the budget caps. The Congressional Budget Office estimated that proposals in the bill, including the East Coast missile defense site and others, would add $57 billion to the Pentagon's budget from 2014 through 2017.

Detainee provisions in the bill also drew a veto threat, as did nuclear arsenal provisions, with the White House singling out Turner's provisions for complying with New START, which the White House said "would set onerous conditions on the administration's ability to implement the treaty."

SENATE COMMITTEE ACTION

The Senate Armed Services Committee approved its version of the defense bill (S 3254—S Rept 112-173) by a vote of 26–0 on May 24, 2012, following a two-day closed markup.

Like the House panel, the committee left discussion of some of the controversial provisions, such as the treatment of terrorism-related detainees, for the floor. The measure called for $631.4 billion in discretionary funds: $525.8 billion for the base Defense Department budget, $88.2 billion for the war in Afghanistan, and $17.4 billion for Department of Energy nuclear weapons and safety programs. The total was just under Obama's request and about $4.1 billion more than the amount called for under the 2011 budget law.

The committee proposed to withhold aid to Pakistan's military until the defense secretary certified that the country was keeping U.S. supply lines to Afghanistan open and was not supporting militant extremists or imprisoning the man credited with tipping U.S. forces off to the whereabouts of al Qaeda leader Osama bin Laden. Lawmakers were angered by the recent conviction of Dr. Shakil Afridi for helping the United States find bin Laden in his compound in Abbottabad, Pakistan. The doctor was found guilty of treason and sentenced to thirty-three years in prison. The final bill included the provisions with waiver authority if the president found it was in the national interest.

Like the House bill, the measure authorized a 1.7 percent pay raise for service members and rejected the Obama administration's proposal to raise Tricare health care insurance fees as a way to reduce personnel costs.

The Senate measure ignored an Air Force request to reduce the authorization for the Air National Guard. The branch's proposal would have eliminated A-10 fighter aircraft at Selfridge Air National Guard Base, near Detroit, and C-27J cargo aircraft planned for Battle Creek Air National Guard Base, also in Michigan. "We rejected the Air Force plan and fully funded the equipment and personnel for the Air Guard," said Armed Forces Chair Carl Levin, D-Mich.

The committee did consent to Air Force requests to mothball the Global Hawk Block 30 aircraft and retire the C-5 transport plane.

Levin noted that he and other members were concerned over the Air Force's proposed cuts. As a result, the bill would create a national advisory commission to make recommendations to Congress on the structure of the Air Force.

In a departure from their House colleagues, Senate authorizers did not embrace the effort to make the Pentagon build an antimissile battery on the East Coast.

During the markup, the panel:

- Adopted, 16–10, an amendment by Jeanne Shaheen, D-N.H., to bring the Defense Department in line with federal policies by allowing military health insurance to cover abortion services for women in uniform who were the victims of rape or incest.

- Adopted, 13–12, an amendment by John McCain, R-Ariz., to curb the Defense Department's use of biofuels. Specifically, it barred the use of funds for the production or purchase of an alternative fuel if the cost exceeded that of traditional fossil fuels used for the same purpose, except in continued testing.

"We voted, I'm happy to say, to restrict the Department of the Navy to a reasonable approach rather than spending $244 a gallon," McCain said. "We believe—at least a slim majority believes—that's the job of the Department of Energy, not the Department of Defense."

The Pentagon argued that it was a national security priority and an operational necessity to diversify the types of fuel it used in its aircraft, ships, tanks, and trucks.

SENATE FLOOR ACTION

The Senate passed its bill by a vote of 98–0 on December 4, 2012, after six months of legislative wrangling to get the measure to the floor and five days of expedited debate. Eight days later, the Senate agreed by unanimous consent to insert a slightly modified version of the language from S 3254 into HR 4310 in preparation for going to conference with the House.

The most controversial provisions included an amendment to prohibit the transfer of those in custody at Guantánamo Bay to the United States. The Senate adopted the language as an amendment sponsored by Kelly Ayotte, R-N.H., on a 54–41 vote. "They're not mere criminals who have committed a burglary in your neighborhood," Ayotte said. "They have committed acts of terror against our country, and they are very, very dangerous individuals."

California Democrat Dianne Feinstein countered that the United States already had 180 terrorists in maximum security in federal prisons within the country. But Lindsey Graham, R-S.C., said U.S. citizens did not want to close Guantánamo and "bring these crazy bastards that want to kill us all to the United States."

The Senate adopted, 67–29, a Feinstein amendment to bar the detention of a U.S. citizen or permanent resident apprehended in the United States without charge or trial.

Among actions on a raft of other amendments, the Senate:

- Adopted, 94–0, a Robert Menendez, D-N.J., amendment to bar all transactions with Iran's energy, shipping, and shipbuilding sectors and its ports. The amendment also proposed to ban the sale to Iran of certain materials, including graphite, aluminum, steel, and metallurgical coal used in those sectors as well as other industrial processes. The House bill stated simply that it was U.S. policy "to prevent Iran from threatening the United States, its allies or Iran's neighbors with a nuclear weapon."
- Adopted by voice vote an amendment by Jeff Sessions, R-Ala., to seize 50 percent of unobligated funds for the Executive Office of the President if the president did not submit to Congress details of a bilateral security agreement with Afghanistan thirty days before entering into the agreement. In May, the United States entered into an enduring strategic partnership with Afghanistan. Congress was not consulted on the framework or substance of the agreement. The final bill required periodic consultations with Congress on the status of such an agreement and required that the text be provided to Congress before an agreement was finalized.
- Adopted by unanimous consent a package of amendments, including one by John Hoeven, R-N.D., expressing the sense of the Senate that the United States should maintain a triad of strategic nuclear delivery systems and that the nation was committed to modernizing the component weapons and delivery systems of that triad.
- Adopted, 62–37, an amendment by Mark Udall, D-Colo., striking the restrictions on the Defense Department's ability to use alternative fuels.
- Adopted, 54–41, an amendment by Kay Hagan, D-N.C., to explicitly allow the Defense Department to use biofuels even if the cost exceeded the price of traditional fossil fuels.
- Adopted by voice vote a McCain amendment authorizing additional Marine personnel at U.S. embassies in light of the September attack in Benghazi, Libya. The language was retained in the final bill.
- Adopted, 92–6, a McCain amendment requiring a classified Pentagon report on the possibility of limited U.S. military action against Syria's air force, including an assessment of possible air strikes, the deployment of air defense systems in neighboring countries and the imposition of no-fly zones over population centers. The provision was not included in the final bill.

FINAL ACTION

House and Senate negotiators reached agreement on a final version of the bill and filed their conference report (H Rept 112-705) on December 18. The House adopted the report, 315–107, on December 20, 2012, and the Senate cleared the bill, 81–14, the following day.

MAJOR PROVISIONS

As enacted, the bill included the following major spending provisions:

Missile defense. The agreement authorized a total of $9.8 billion for missile defense programs, including funding for the initial deployment of a national missile defense system based in Alaska and California, and the Obama administration's plan for missile defense in Europe. The measure also increased the amount authorized for cooperative antimissile programs with Israel, including $680 million for Israel's "Iron Dome" system, which proved successful in shooting down missiles launched from the Gaza Strip in November.

Drones. The Air Force was required to keep the eighteen Global Hawk Block 30 unmanned aerial vehicles in the fleet until at least the end of 2014; officials had hoped to save $2.5 billion over the following five years by mothballing the vehicles. The bill authorized an additional $260 million in unrequested funds to maintain the aircraft.

Reserve aircraft. The law permitted the Air Force to retire some, but not all, of several other kinds of aircraft it had sought to stand down as part of a controversial cost-savings plan for the Air National Guard and reserve units. In the end, the bill restored 106 Air National Guard and Air Reserve aircraft and about 5,400 personnel slots that had initially been targeted for cuts. Among them were relatively short-range cargo planes, the C-130 and C-27. The bill required the Air Force to maintain thirty-two more of those planes than the service's most recent proposal recommended but let Air Force officials determine which aircraft they wanted to maintain in the fleet.

Benefits. Conferees blocked most of the administration's proposed increase in out-of-pocket fees for participants in the military's Tricare health care program.

Aircraft. The measure authorized the following for major aircraft:

- $5.4 billion for procurement and $2.7 billion for research and development of the F-35 Joint Strike Fighter. The plane was planned as a multirole fighter aircraft based on a common airframe and components for use by the Air Force, Navy, and Marine Corps. Massive cost overruns had plagued the program.
- $2 billion for F/A-18 E/F Super Hornets and $1 billion for EA-18G Growler electronic warfare planes.
- $1.3 billion for V-22 tilt-rotor Osprey aircraft for the Marines.

Shipbuilding. The agreement authorized $14.3 billion for major Navy vessels, $726 million more than requested, including:

- $4.9 billion for two Virginia-class attack submarines, which were planned to replace retiring Los Angeles-class submarines and constitute the bulk of the future attack submarine force.
- $3.5 billion for the DDG-51 Arleigh Burke–class destroyer program.
- $1.8 billion for Littoral Combat Ships—small, specialized vessels that were a variant of the DDG for use in coastal waters.
- Abandon the planned retirement of three naval cruisers.

Military construction. $10.4 billion for construction at military facilities, previous Base Realignment and Closure (BRAC) costs and construction of housing for military families. The measure barred the use of funds "to propose, plan for or execute" a new BRAC round.

Military pay raise. An average 1.7 percent pay increase for military personnel in fiscal 2013, equal to the president's request.

Defense Health Program. $32.6 billion for the Pentagon health program for service members and military retirees, their survivors, and their dependents.

Afghanistan. A prohibition on U.S. commanders hiring locals as security guards at U.S. bases in Afghanistan. This was in response to so-called "insider attacks" on U.S. personnel by local Afghan guards.

Heavy-armor production lines. $276 million in unrequested funds to keep open production lines for the Abrams tank and Bradley Fighting Vehicle.

Fiscal 2013 Defense Appropriations

For the third fiscal year in a row, Congress failed to agree on an independent defense appropriations bill before the October 1 beginning of the fiscal year. Instead, the defense programs were funded for fiscal 2013 through March 27, 2013, under the continuing resolution enacted September 28, 2012 (H J Res 117—PL 112-175). *(Continuing resolution action, p. 180)*

The House in July passed a fiscal 2013 Republican-sponsored defense spending bill that would have boosted Pentagon funds beyond limits set in the 2011 Budget Control Act (PL 112-25). Senate Democratic appropriators stuck with the spending caps, but did so partly by shifting money from the base Pentagon budget to the Overseas Contingency Operations (OCO) account, which funded operations in Afghanistan and Iraq and did not count under the statutory caps.

Appropriators in both chambers rejected a request from the president for $4.4 billion in advance funding for high-frequency communications satellites.

HOUSE ACTION

The House voted 326–90 on July 19, 2012, to pass its version of the defense spending bill (HR 5856), which included $518 billion for the nonwar, or base, Pentagon budget—virtually the same as the amount enacted for fiscal 2012—and $87.7 billion for OCO. As originally reported by the House Appropriations Committee (H Rept 112-493) on May 25, the bill would have provided $519.2 billion for the base budget and $88.2 billion, as requested, for OCO accounts. Although the total was reduced by more than $1 billion during floor consideration, the base budget was still almost $7 billion more than the cap for defense set by the budget law.

The House agreed to the $1 billion reduction on an amendment by Mick Mulvaney, R-S.C., that was adopted, 247–167. The amendment excluded from the reduction military personnel, the Defense health programs, and overseas contingency operations. Members rejected, 171–243, a Barbara Lee, D-Calif., amendment that would have reduced the bill's funding by $7.6 billion, dropping it to about the amount authorized under the budget act.

More than a dozen antiwar lawmakers from both parties called during the debate for an end to U.S. fighting in Afghanistan. However, the House rejected, 107–312, a Lee amendment that would have cut spending for overseas contingency operations by $20.8 billion and limited the use of funds for Afghanistan operations to the safe and orderly withdrawal of U.S. troops.

The chamber did adopt, 228–191, an amendment by Steve Cohen, D-Tenn., to reduce the Afghanistan Infrastructure Fund by $175 million. Cohen said the program was giving Afghan rulers a chance to "put money in their pockets" rather than helping the people. C. W. Bill Young, R-Fla., opposed the amendment, arguing that "those responsible for fighting the fight" said they needed the funds as part of getting U.S. troops out of Afghanistan.

An amendment by Walter B. Jones, R-N.C., adopted by voice vote, cut $412 million in Afghan Security Forces funding and transferred the funds to an OCO account to provide incentive pay for U.S. service members in Afghanistan.

The House agreed by voice vote to an amendment by Ted Poe, R-Texas, that eliminated $650 million, half the amount in the bill, for aid to Pakistan under the coalition support fund programs. The funds were reimbursement for the cost of counterinsurgency operations. But lawmakers were highly critical of Pakistan's efforts to curtail Taliban attacks and the fact that U.S. and Afghan forces had to increase security because of defense gaps along the border.

However, the House rejected, 149–270, an attempt by David Cicilline, D-R.I., to simply eliminate the account. Members adopted, 235–178, a Michael R. Turner, R-Ohio, amendment to prohibit the use of funds in the bill to reduce U.S. nuclear forces, implement the Nuclear Posture Review Implementation Study, modify the Secretary of Defense Guidance for Employment of Force, or change the Joint Strategic Capabilities Plan, Pentagon documents on military strategy and capabilities. An amendment by Rick Berg, R-N.D., adopted 232–183, barred funding to reduce the number of delivery vehicles for nuclear weapons.

The House adopted, 247–166, an amendment by Steve King, R-Iowa, to prohibit funds from being used in contravention of the Defense of Marriage Act (PL 104-199), which defined marriage as the union of one man and one woman.

SENATE COMMITTEE ACTION

The Senate Appropriations Committee approved an amended version of HR 5856 by a vote of 30–0 on August 2, 2012. The reported bill (S Rept 112-196) included $511.2 billion for the base budget but boosted OCO funds to $93 billion.

In maneuvering to create more room under the budget act's defense spending limit, the committee moved $4.1 billion from the Pentagon's request for operations and maintenance in the base budget to the war accounts to fund such items as depot maintenance for vehicles and other equipment used in combat. It transferred $1.6 billion in procurement and research funding to the OCO account to buy and develop new weapons, such as unmanned aerial vehicles.

Both the House and Senate bills included unrequested funds that were seen as a significant blow to the Air Force's bid to cut costs by divesting itself of personnel and aircraft, including new high-flying surveillance drones used in Iraq and Afghanistan, and cargo aircraft used by the National Guard. The panels added funds for weapons that the Air Force wanted to retire, including aircraft, Global Hawk surveillance drones, and Aegis cruisers. They rejected plans to reduce funding for submarines and destroyers.

As in previous years, both chambers rejected a request from Obama to increase fees for the military's Tricare health care system.

Guantánamo Transfers Restricted

In one of his first acts as president, and following through on a campaign promise, Barack Obama signed Executive Order 13492 ordering the U.S. military detention facility at Guantánamo Bay, Cuba, to be closed within a year. The January 22, 2009, executive order sharply differentiated Obama's approach from that of President George W. Bush, who established the controversial facility, to hold suspected terrorists, shortly after the September 11, 2001, terrorist attacks against New York and Washington, D.C.

Nearly 800 suspected terrorists were held at Guantánamo in the subsequent eleven-plus years; more than 600 were transferred to Afghanistan, Saudi Arabia, Pakistan, and other countries, but 166 remained there as of July 2013, according to the *New York Times*. Nine detainees died while awaiting resolution of their cases. Only one detainee was transferred to the United States for trial: Ahmed Ghailani, who was convicted on charges related to the 1998 bombings of the U.S. embassies on Kenya and Tanzania.

Obama's action set off a debate in Congress over the fate of the prison and the detainees—a debate that continued, in various forms, throughout Obama's first term. Leading Republicans argued vociferously against closing the Guantánamo facility and repeatedly sought to block any attempt to bring detainees from the prison to the United States for any reason.

Democrats supported a number of restrictions on the president's authority to close Guantánamo, but most opposed provisions that would have interfered with the administration's ability to prosecute detainees in the United States. Even so, Congress did impose restrictions that prevented Obama from following through on his commitment to close Guantánamo, which, in fact, remained open all through his first term. Congress also effectively forced the administration to retreat from a plan to try at least some Guantánamo detainees in U.S. civilian courts, thus forcing all cases to be heard by military commissions.

Congress adopted restrictions during 2009 as part of the fiscal 2009 supplemental for Iraq and Afghanistan (PL 111-32) and the fiscal 2010 appropriations bills for the departments of Defense (PL 111-118), Homeland Security (PL 111-83), and Interior (PL 111-88), and in the year-end omnibus spending bill (PL 111-117). The annual defense authorization bill (PL 111-84) also included some of the restrictions. *(Defense, p. 280; Homeland, p. 129; Interior, p. 129; omnibus, p. 130; defense authorization, p. 273; supplemental, p. 122)*

In 2010, Congress continued most of those same restrictions, or added new ones, as part of the fiscal 2010 supplemental appropriations bill (PL 111-212), the fiscal 2011 defense authorization bill (PL 111-383), and the fiscal 2011 intelligence authorization (PL 111-259). The House May 28, 2010, in action on the fiscal 2011 defense authorization bill (HR 5136), on a **key vote** of **282–131 (R 168–1; D 114–130)**, again signaled its opposition to closing Guantánamo. The key vote came on a motion adding to the bill an amendment barring the transfer or release of any detainees held there. *(Supplemental, p. 138; defense authorization, p. 291; intelligence authorization, p. 250; 2010 key votes, p. 767)*

Congress included similar restrictions in various pieces of legislation in 2011 and 2012, the net result of which was to keep Guantánamo functioning. Among these were restrictions in the defense portion of an omnibus fiscal 2012 appropriations bill (PL 112-74); the fiscal 2012 defense authorization bill (PL 112-81); and the fiscal 2013 defense authorization bill (PL 112-329). Notably, Congress in 2011 used the fiscal 2012 defense authorization bill to address a broad change of issues related to Guantánamo and the detention of terrorism suspects, including those who held U.S. citizenship. President Obama rejected several of the provisions as unnecessarily intruding on his executive power, but he signed the bill into law despite his objections. *(Fiscal 2012 omnibus, p. 172; fiscal 2012 defense authorization, p. 299; fiscal 2013 defense authorization, p. 307)*

The political power of the Guantánamo issue was illustrated even following the 2012 elections, when Obama was reelected and Democrats retained control of the Senate. On November 29, less than a month after the national vote, during consideration of the fiscal 2013 defense authorization bill (S 3254), the Senate in a **key vote of 54–41 (R 44–0; D 9–40; I 1–1)** approved an amendment to block the transfer of detainees from Guantánamo to the United States. The fact that nine Democrats supported this amendment, despite a veto threat by the White House, showed how much success Republicans had in using the Guantánamo issue to portray Democrats as soft on national security. Even so, the veto threat persuaded conferees to leave the provision out of the final bill. *(2012 key votes, p. 803)*

One result of these congressional restrictions was that most prisoners remained in a kind of limbo status at Guantánamo. The government could not or would not prosecute them (in many cases because of lack of evidence) and other countries refused to accept them. In 2013 several dozen prisoners went on a mass hunger strike to protest their seemingly permanent detention; all were force-fed until the hunger strikers dropped their protest.

Congress imposed restrictions that generally prohibited the release of any detainees within the United States or any U.S. territories. Congress also set conditions for bringing prisoners into the country for detention or trial. There also were preconditions for transferring detainees to a third country and on closing the Guantánamo prison. Congress flatly rejected Obama's request for $80 million to close the facility; the fiscal 2009 war supplemental, for example, prohibited any spending for that purpose.

Republicans tried repeatedly to include a flat ban on any detainees coming to the United States. Democrats initially were concerned enough over GOP political attacks that forty-eight Senate Democrats joined Republicans on May 20, 2009, in voting 90–6 to add the prohibition to the fiscal 2009 supplemental. The restriction was softened in conference, and Democrats fought off GOP attempts to insert the language into fiscal 2010 bills.

The sharpest debate was over trying Guantánamo detainees in U.S. federal courts and housing them in U.S. prisons.

In a decision that had already been forecast, Attorney General Eric H. Holder Jr. announced November 13, 2009, that five of the detainees, including the self-proclaimed mastermind of the September 11 attacks, Khalid Sheikh Mohammed, would be transferred to lower Manhattan for a civilian trial. He said five others would go before military commissions.

During a November 5, 2009, debate on the fiscal 2010 Commerce-Justice-Science spending bill, the Senate voted 54–45 to table (or kill) an amendment by Lindsey Graham, R-S.C., to preempt the administration by barring the use of Justice Department funds to prosecute anyone linked to the September 11 terrorist attacks in a U.S. federal court. The amendment attracted a bipartisan group of cosponsors, including Virginia Democrat Jim Webb, Connecticut independent Joseph I. Lieberman, and Arizona Republican John McCain.

"Our civilian courts are not designed to deal with war criminals; the military system is," Graham said. Mohammed "didn't rob a liquor store, he didn't commit a crime under domestic criminal law. He took this nation to war, and he killed 3,000 of our citizens, and he needs to have justice rendered in the system that recognizes that we're at war."

Senate Minority Leader Mitch McConnell, R-Ky., was equally adamant. "The right forum for bringing war criminals to justice is in military commissions at the secure facility we already have at Guantánamo. Not—I repeat, not—in civilian courts in U.S. communities," he said.

On November 17, 2009, four days after Holder's announcement, fifty-six Senate Democrats voted to kill a GOP amendment that would have barred the administration from using funds in the fiscal 2010 Military Construction–VA spending bill to "construct or modify a facility in the United States or its territories to permanently or temporarily hold any individual held at Guantánamo Bay, Cuba." The amendment, by James M. Inhofe of Oklahoma, was tabled, 57–43.

"We are not afraid of these guys," said Patrick J. Leahy, D-Vt., chair of the Senate Judiciary Committee. "They're murderers. They're criminals. Let's just prosecute them." He continued, "Why would the Senate pass an amendment that suggests that our country and the brave men and women who staff these prisons cannot handle these prisoners or that they are not up to the task?"

Sen. John D. Rockefeller IV, D-W.Va., said he would be happy to lock up the detainees in his home state. "These are supermax prisons," he said. "I would imagine we could guard these guys pretty well, don't you?"

Senate Majority Whip Richard J. Durbin, D-Ill., said a November 17, 2009, letter from Holder and the Defense and Homeland Security secretaries strengthened Democrats' resolve. The officials said that closing Guantánamo was in the national interest, that al Qaeda terrorists had used its existence as a recruiting tool, and that Inhofe's amendment would hurt efforts to close down the facility.

HIGHLIGHTS

Details of the Guantánamo-related provisions varied from bill to bill, including the duration of the restrictions. Most provisions applied only to funds appropriated or authorized by the specific bill, although a few were permanent. Following are the main provisions adopted during 2009, most of which were repeated, sometimes in modified form, in the following three years:

Release

No one detained at Guantánamo as of June 24, 2009, could be released into the United States or any U.S. territories.

Prosecution

No one detained at Guantánamo as of June 24, 2009, could be brought to the United States for trial until forty-five days after the president submitted a classified report to Congress that included:

- A risk assessment on whether the individual might instigate an act of terrorism within the United States or might attempt to radicalize other inmates if transferred to a U.S. prison.
- The costs associated with transferring the individual.
- The legal rationale and associated court demands for transfer.
- A copy of a notification to the governor of the state to which the individual would be transferred, together with a certification from the attorney general that the individual posed little or no security risk to the United States.
- An assessment of any risk to U.S. national security or to its citizens, including members of the armed services, posed by the transfer.
- A plan to mitigate any of the risks reported.

Detainee Transfer

No one detained at Guantánamo as of June 24, 2009, could be released to a foreign country until fifteen days after the president sent Congress a classified report that included:

- The individual's name and destination.
- An assessment of any risk posed to the national security of the United States or its citizens, including members of the armed services, and a plan to mitigate any risk.

- The terms of any agreement with the destination country, including any financial assistance related to the transfer.

Guantánamo Bay Closure

Before closing the Guantánamo detention facility, the president was required to send Congress a classified report describing the disposition or legal status of each individual who was detained at the facility on the date the bill was enacted. The fiscal 2011 defense authorization (PL 111-383) also prohibited the use of funding authorized by the bill to construct or modify facilities in the United States to imprison any of the Guantánamo detainees.

No-Fly List

The homeland security appropriations law directed the department to put any detainee ever held at Guantánamo on the Transportation Security Administration's no-fly list, unless the president certified that the person posed no threat to the United States, its citizens, or its allies. This provision was permanent.

Immigrants

No individual detained at Guantánamo as of June 24, 2009, could receive immigration benefits, including a visa, admission into the United States, parole into the United States, or classification as a refugee or applicant for asylum. The provision was included in the homeland security appropriations law and was permanent.

Recidivism

The fiscal 2011 intelligence authorization (PL 111-259) required the director of national intelligence to make public an unclassified summary of intelligence relating to recidivism of detainees who had been released from Guantánamo. The report also was to assess the likelihood that released detainees would engage in terrorism or communicate with persons in terrorist organizations.

MILITARY COMMISSIONS ACT

In addition to attempting to close the Guantánamo Bay detention center, Obama tried, early in his presidency, to stop the use of military commissions to try non-U.S. citizens held at Guantánamo on terrorism charges. President George W. Bush had established the commissions in 2001 as a means of trying the terrorism defendants under special military rules that gave the defendants fewer rights than they would have enjoyed in either the civilian courts or the standard courts-martial system. The Supreme Court, in the *Hamdan v. Rumsfeld* (548 U.S. 557) ruling of 2006, invalidated Bush's rules for the commissions. After Congress wrote new rules later in 2006 to satisfy the court's objections, the commissions resumed their work and convicted three defendants during the Bush years, 2001–2009.

President Obama halted proceedings before the military commissions in January 2009 and ordered a review of them. The Obama administration said in May 2009 that it was considering restarting the commissions under new rules. A presidential task force released a preliminary report on July 2009 saying that the commissions were appropriate for some of the terrorism cases but most cases should be shifted to the federal courts. On November 13, 2009, Attorney General Holder ordered the cases of the five so-called "September 11 conspirators" (including alleged mastermind Khalid Sheikh Mohammed) transferred to the Southern District courts in New York. Five other terrorism suspects were to face trials before military commissions.

Congress, in the meantime, adopted new rules for the military commissions as part of the fiscal 2010 Defense Authorization Act (PL 111-84), which cleared in October 2009. That law contained only some of the changes the Obama administration had proposed. Among the changes adopted by Congress were:

- The new law tightened prohibitions on the use of statements elicited through torture, as well as cruel, inhumane, or degrading treatment. Such statements could not be admitted into evidence, regardless of when the statements were made.
- The 2009 law established new procedures for the use of classified or "sensitive" information. These procedures included the closing of evidentiary hearings when classified information was to be presented, the sealing of records including that information, and limits on questioning witnesses who might disclose classified material.

The new law imposed new restrictions on the use of hearsay evidence. Previously, such evidence was admissible in trial unless the defendant could prove that it was unreliable. Under the new law, the prosecution had to demonstrate that hearsay evidence was reliable before it could be used.

Republicans and some Democrats consistently demanded that the Obama administration rely on the commissions as the principle venue for prosecuting alleged terrorists. For example, in considering the fiscal 2012 Defense authorization bill (HR 1540), the House on May 26, 2011, on a **key vote of 246–173 (R 228–7; D 18–166)** adopted an amendment requiring any foreign terrorism suspects accused of attacking the United States or U.S. personnel be tried only by a military commission. *(2011 key votes, p. 785)*

CHAPTER 6

Transportation, Commerce, and Communications

Introduction	319
Chronology of Action on Transportation, Commerce, and Communications	321
2009–2010	321
2011–2012	340

Transportation, Commerce, and Communications

Transportation and communication issues were recurring themes in national debates during President Barack Obama's first term, but legislative efforts had inconsistent results as the White House and Congress primarily searched for ways to help Americans cope with a deepening recession and tussled over how to rein in the federal budget and tamp down a growing deficit.

Obama saw infrastructure and highway projects as an avenue for job creation, and they became one of the cornerstones of a $787 billion economic stimulus package (HR 1—PL 111-5) that Democratic leaders rushed through Congress in the opening of the 111th session. Lawmakers and administration officials also offered the struggling automobile industry—to which President George W. Bush had granted financial assistance just before departing office—additional relief through a short-term auto trade-in program dubbed "cash for clunkers." But Congress was not so quick to embrace other initiatives, and negotiations continued for months or, in several cases, years.

Lawmakers attempting to complete long-term reauthorizations of laws governing surface transportation programs and the Federal Aviation Administration (FAA) frequently were frustrated as Obama placed a higher priority on overhauling laws governing financial services and health care and, for a time, on legislation to control climate change. That left little time, energy, or political capital to move other broad measures.

Legislators interested in passing long-term legislation addressing transportation issues also had to contend with concerns about the potential cost of such bills amid the economic recession, particularly following Obama's high-priced stimulus measure. Such fiscal concerns made it especially difficult to persuade lawmakers to devise a long-awaited solution to rebuild a rapidly dwindling Highway Trust Fund long dependent on gas taxes that had become a less reliable source of consistent revenue. Instead, Congress repeatedly issued short-term extensions of previous authorizations until it approached the 2012 elections, when Obama's decision to run against a "Do Nothing Congress" helped create impetus for passage of longer-term legislation.

The president and congressional leaders hailed passage of a twenty-seven-month highway reauthorization bill and a four-year FAA reauthorization as a sign of bipartisan cooperation and commended both as important for job creation. But those laws ultimately were criticized for not resolving several major issues and providing patchwork solutions to problems. The final highway measure, for example, avoided resolving long-term funding for the highway fund by pulling money from the general fund and other Treasury sources to fill out the authorized term of the law. Obama also had to relinquish hope for two of his major initiatives in the second session of Congress—high-speed rail and a national infrastructure bank. Meanwhile, partisan squabbling over the FAA reauthorization measure ultimately led to a two-week shutdown of certain FAA operations, frustrating workers and passengers.

The Obama administration also came into office in January 2009 with several priorities in telecommunications,

REFERENCES

Discussion of transportation, commerce, and communications policy for the years 1945–1964 may be found in *Congress and the Nation Vol. I*, pp. 517–562, 1159–1185; for the years 1965–1968, *Congress and the Nation Vol. II*, pp. 227–251, 281–305, 779–823; for the years 1969–1972, and *Congress and the Nation Vol. III*, pp. 147–187, 659–700; for the years 1973–1976, *Congress and the Nation Vol. IV*, pp. 146–147, 433–451, 505–555; for the years 1977–1980, *Congress and the Nation Vol. V*, pp. 291–362; for the years 1981–1984, *Congress and the Nation Vol. VI*, pp. 261–286, 289–329; for the years 1985–1988, *Congress and the Nation Vol. VII*, pp. 357–413; for the years 1989–1992, *Congress and the Nation Vol. VIII*, pp. 415–464; for the years 1993–1996, *Congress and the Nation Vol. IX*, pp. 327–398; for the years 1997–2000, *Congress and the Nation Vol. X*, pp. 318–338; for the years 2001–2004, *Congress and the Nation Vol. XI*, pp. 371–405; for the years 2005–2008, *Congress and the Nation Vol. XII*, pp. 405–440.

Outlays for Transportation

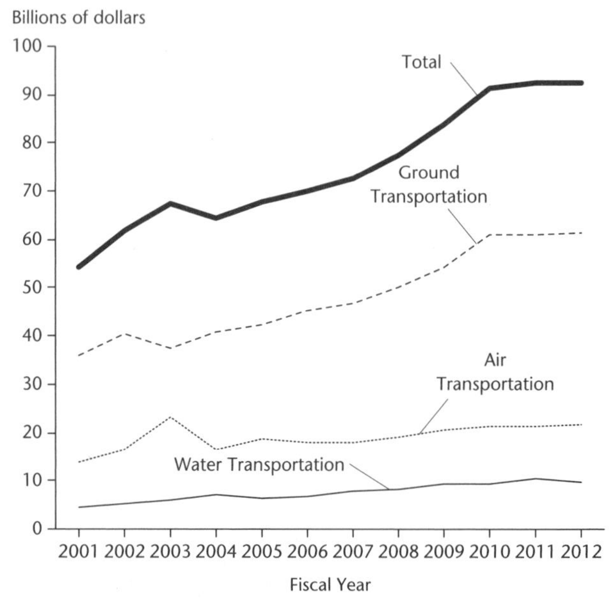

SOURCE: Office of Management and Budget, *Historical Tables, Budget of the United States Government: Fiscal Year 2013* (Washington, D.C.: U.S. Government Printing Office, 2012), Table 3.2.

NOTE: Total line includes some expenditures not shown separately.

including implementation of a rule on "network neutrality"—essentially a concept to ensure equal access to the Internet for all consumers and content providers—that regulators issued over congressional Republican objections. It sought to subsidize broadband access in rural areas and to limit how much telecommunication companies could charge for access to high-speed lines. Meanwhile, conservative Republicans frequently charged the Federal Communications Commission (FCC) with overreach, and made some brief, unsuccessful attempts to overhaul its authority.

Further technological innovation leading, for example, to the expansion of wireless broadband and related wireless devices such as the iPhone—coupled with an increased demand among consumers and businesses to download and transfer movies, music, and images in a more rapid format—further pressured Washington to analyze telecommunications laws. Moreover, lawmakers had to consider measures that would continue to enable the satellite industry to more easily compete with cable providers, even while recognizing that the growing competition in that sector would no longer necessitate the same federal assistance in the near future.

Debate on Capitol Hill continued without resolution on many of these issues, as well as several other communication initiatives that had lingered from previous sessions of Congress, including regulation of online gambling and taxation of Internet sales. An attempt in the House and Senate to crack down on digital piracy prompted widespread debate and controversy in 2012. Bill managers ultimately pulled the legislation amid pressure from lobbyists, but members of Congress vowed to find a resolution to the issue in the subsequent years.

On Capitol Hill, August 3, 2011, Rep. Steven LaTourette, R-Ohio, speaks to furloughed Federal Aviation Administration (FAA) civil engineers Mike MacDonald, left, and their lobbyist, Erin Barry, concerning extending the FAA's funding authority, which expired at midnight July 22, 2011, and idled approximately 70,000 construction-related workers and furloughed 4,000 FAA employees across the country.
Source: Photo by Melina Mara/The Washington Post via Getty Images

Chronology of Action on Transportation, Commerce, and Communications

2009–2010

Democrats retained control of both the House and Senate during the 111th Congress (2009–2010), and with Democrat Barack Obama in the White House, expectations were high for progress on a stack of lingering issues. But many transportation and communications issues were not high on the priority list of the White House or Senate leaders, particularly as several continuing partisan disagreements became even more difficult to resolve in the face of budgetary constraints.

House and Senate lawmakers representing states long dependent on the automobile industry quickly gained bipartisan support for legislation creating a vehicle trade-in program to boost sales of new cars and trucks, but agreement remained out of reach on two broad measures critical to the transportation industry and to states seeking to move on infrastructure programs: reauthorization of a 2005 surface transportation law and a 2003 law governing Federal Aviation Administration (FAA) programs, both of which had expired.

While various proposals were set forward in both chambers, Congress ultimately granted short-term extensions of the previous authorizations for highway and FAA programs. But a February 2009 crash of a regional jet in Buffalo, N.Y., provided an impetus for lawmakers to pass legislation instituting some new airline safety and pilot training standards.

Lawmakers also failed to resolve several lingering issues related to the communications industry, particularly those related to rapid growth in the Internet and wireless industry from growing consumer demand. The issue of net neutrality, a concept intended to ensure that networks that provide access to the Internet did not control how consumers use the Internet and did not discriminate against any content provider, became the center of fierce debate that pitted congressional Republicans against the Federal Communications Commission (FCC) and various sectors of the industry. Lawmakers also resumed discussions from previous years about how to extend broadband access and how to reform the Universal Service Fund (USF), created in 1997 to expand telecommunications services nationwide. Congress did clear a measure to the White House to reauthorize a law governing how satellite carriers of television programming distribute local broadcast stations to their customers.

Cash for Clunkers

In 2009, Congress approved a total of $3 billion for a program dubbed "cash for clunkers" that offered consumers who traded in their old vehicles rebates to be used toward the purchase or lease of newer, more fuel-efficient vehicles. The program was immediately popular, although some conservatives criticized it as another auto industry bailout. The legislation was one of the first pieces of legislation enacted by the 111th Congress (HR 2346—PL 111-32).

The aim of the program, initially outlined in legislation by Rep. Betty Sutton, D-Ohio, was to provide further assistance to the domestic automobile industry, which was suffering amid the global financial crisis as sales dropped and the credit crisis squeezed automaker's finances. Before President George W. Bush left office in early 2009, he had transferred $24.9 billion from the Troubled Assets Relief Program (TARP)—a fund to stabilize the financial services industry authorized in 2008 under the Emergency Economic Stabilization and Recovery Act (PL 110-343)—to provide some relief to two major automakers: General Motors Corp. and Chrysler LLC. *(TARP developments, pp. 62, 75; background on TARP enactment and auto industry assistance, Congress and the Nation Vol. XII, pp. 154, 159)*

After taking over the White House following his victory in 2008, President Obama moved swiftly to prevent an auto industry collapse. The Obama administration put the two automakers into government-led bankruptcies even while many local dealerships were being closed. Lawmakers sought ways to stimulate demand for new cars and trucks and remove old, fuel-inefficient vehicles from the roads and help avert closure of thousands more dealerships.

Language from Sutton's bill, later negotiated with Sen. Debbie Stabenow, D-Mich. (both legislators from states heavily dependent on the auto industry), offered rebates of up to $4,500 to consumers who traded in old vehicles to buy or lease new, fuel-efficient cars. The administration supported the program, and Ford Motor Co.—the only U.S. automaker that was not receiving federal funding—strongly pushed it.

Although many environmental advocates contended there were better ways to promote sales of fuel-efficient vehicles, the idea enjoyed broad support in Congress. Lawmakers cleared the program on June 16 as part of the supplementary war spending bill, HR 2346. *(Supplemental bill, pp. 122, 269)*

Initial funding was quickly exhausted, prompting Congress to add more dollars to the program through separate legislation. *(For details, see the following section)*

HOUSE ACTION

On May 20, the House Energy and Commerce Committee adopted by voice vote an amendment to climate change legislation (HR 2454) to create under the National Highway Traffic Safety Administration a "Cash for Clunkers Temporary Vehicle Trade-In Program." The amendment, sponsored by Democrat Tammy Baldwin of Wisconsin, was a modified version of a bill (HR 1550) introduced by Sutton. While the committee then approved the climate change bill, 33–25 (H Rept 111-137), Sutton that same day introduced Baldwin's version of her vehicle trade-in proposal as a stand-alone measure (HR 2640). Stabenow offered a companion bill (S 1135) in the Senate.

Sutton's bill, like the provision in the climate change legislation, included authorization for vouchers ranging from $3,500 to $4,500 for consumers who traded in older vehicles, with the vouchers to be used to offset the cost of newer fuel-efficient vehicles. Under the measure, the program would be retroactive to March 30, 2009, and continue until March 31, 2010. Consumers who purchased or leased a fuel-efficient vehicle after March 30 but before the measure was enacted, and could verify they owned an eligible trade-in vehicle that they disposed of properly, would be eligible for a cash rebate.

After weeks of negotiations with Stabenow, Sutton revised the measure, introducing a new version (HR 2751) on June 8, which the House passed the following day by a vote of 298–119 under suspension of the rules, a fast-track procedure that prevents amendments and requires a two-thirds majority for approval. The bill included a $4 billion authorization for the program and called for it to begin upon enactment of the legislation, rather than be retroactive to March 30. The measure also made ineligible for the rebate any vehicles made before model year 1984, and reduced the proposed fine for violation of any provision of the bill from $25,000 to $15,000.

The Senate, however, did not act on HR 2751.

FINAL ACTION

House Democrats immediately added a provision to the conference report on the 2009 war supplemental measure (HR 2346—H Rept 111-151) to set up the program and provide an initial $1 billion for rebates. Sen. Judd Gregg, R-N.H., tried to remove the provision from the spending bill in conference, calling it a bailout for the auto industry and contending it would further increase the deficit. His move was defeated, 13–17.

The House adopted the conference report on the war supplemental by a vote of 226–202 on June 16. The Senate cleared the bill, 91–5, on June 18. Before doing so it voted, 60–36, for a procedural motion blocking another move by Gregg to cut the trade-in provision. *(War supplemental, pp. 122, 269)*

MAJOR PROVISIONS

As signed into law by President Barack Obama on June 24, 2009, the supplemental appropriations bill for fiscal 2009 (HR 2346—PL 111-32) contained the following major provisions under Title XIII Consumer Assistance to Recycle and Save:

- Authorized rebates of $3,500 to $4,500 to consumers seeking to trade in their older vehicles for more fuel-efficient ones, with the amount of the rebate dependent on the improvement in fuel efficiency between the old vehicle and the new one.
- Required the National Highway Traffic Safety Administration (NHTSA) to draft, within one month, regulations to implement the program.
- Made eligible for trade-in vehicles that were drivable, continuously insured by the same owner for at least one year, and manufactured before 1984 (or before 2001 for certain medium-duty trucks), and had a combined estimated federal fuel economy standard of no more than eighteen miles per gallon.
- Made eligible for trade-in four classes of vehicles: cars; sport utility vehicles and small vans and pickup trucks; larger light-duty pickup trucks and vans; and medium-duty pickup trucks and cargo trucks and vans.
- Made eligible for purchase for the rebate vehicles with a manufacturer's suggested price below $45,000 and in compliance with specific emissions standards.
- Required NHTSA to issue rebates directly to auto dealers when they sell eligible vehicles between July 1, 2009, and November 1, 2009.

TRANSPORTATION, COMMERCE, AND COMMUNICATIONS LEADERSHIP

Retiring House member Ray LaHood of Illinois was among the Republicans to whom President Barack Obama turned for his cabinet picks, selecting him to head the Transportation Department. LaHood would become a relatively well-known cabinet member as he tackled with his trademark civility several high-profile issues, and Obama would rely on him throughout his first term.

LaHood had served on the House Appropriations Committee in Congress and had a reputation as a low-key moderate who got along well with members on both sides of the aisle. He was one of only three Republicans in the class of 1994 who refused to sign the "Contract with America," the GOP's policy manifesto that year. He had strong political skills after three decades on Capitol Hill, as both an aide and a member, and had built a relationship with Obama when they served together in Congress. The president would rely on him to help push forward his plans for infrastructure spending. He won easy confirmation by the Senate in a voice vote in January 2009.

He had the task of managing $27.5 billion authorized in the 2009 economic stimulus law for transportation infrastructure and took on such high-profile issues as air traffic controllers sleeping on the job, distracted driving (or texting while driving), and long tarmac delays for airline passengers. Although the process was long, he helped work out deals on long-term reauthorizations of the surface transportation and Federal Aviation Administration laws. But his history of dealmaking on the Hill did not help him convince the GOP to support Obama's plans for spending billions on high-speed rail lines or creating a national infrastructure bank to complement existing federal programs to fund infrastructure.

In February 2009, Obama selected former Washington governor Gary F. Locke, a Democrat, to be commerce secretary; Locke became the first Chinese American to serve in that capacity, just as he had been the first Chinese American in the country to hold the title of governor. He had extensive experience in trade and was confirmed by the Senate, by unanimous consent, in March after assuring senators that his department would retain management, in a professional manner, of the 2010 census.

Locke was not a visible figure during Obama's first two years in office, in part because the administration's focus was primarily on health care and financial services reform. But Locke earned the admiration of many executives of companies both big and small as he worked to help improve exports as part of his role for the National Export Initiative that aimed to double U.S. exports in five years. He also helped to get several trade deals signed, including one with South Korea.

In May 2011, Obama nominated Locke as U.S. ambassador to China. His next commerce secretary nominee, business executive John E. Bryson, also a Democrat, survived a difficult confirmation process in 2011. Bryson had been chair from 1990 to 2008 of Edison International, the company that owns California's largest utility, and was a director on the boards of Boeing Co. and Walt Disney Co. Obama lauded Bryson's role as an industry executive supporting clean energy initiatives, but several Republicans opposed his stance on some environmental issues, especially climate change. Bryson also had to assure senators from coal industry states that he would look out for traditional energy industries. He also was founder of Natural Resources Defense council. The Senate confirmed his nomination by a vote of 74–26 in October.

Under Bryson, Commerce investigated Chinese government subsidies that U.S. firms said were artificially driving down the prices of Chinese products sold in the United States. The department also imposed antidumping tariffs of more than 31 percent on Chinese solar panels, which caused an outcry from Beijing. He also was tasked with continuing the export initiative.

Bryson resigned the following June because of health issues and was succeeded by deputy secretary Rebecca Blank.

President Obama chose Julius Genachowski to serve as chair of the Federal Communications Commission (FCC), and the Senate easily confirmed his nomination on June 29, 2009. A son of immigrants, Genachowski had spent more than a decade working in the media and technology industries, including as chief of business operations and general counsel at IAC/InterActiveCorp, special advisor at the private equity firm General Atlantic, and cofounder of the technology incubator LaunchBox Digital.

He had worked in the FCC in the 1990s as chief counsel to Chair Reed Hundt and as special counsel to General Counsel William Kennard (who later served as chair). He also served as a law clerk at the U.S. Supreme Court and as an aide for the House select committee investigating the Iran-contra affair during the presidency of Ronald Reagan in the 1980s and for then-representative Charles E. Schumer, D-N.Y.

During Genachowski's tenure from June 2009 to May 2013, the FCC worked to implement a National Broadband Plan, Obama's initiative to expand the availability of high-speed Internet. He also oversaw an overhaul of the Universal Service Fund to move it from supporting telephone service to broadband and planned for the auction of 500 megahertz of broadband spectrum.

While Genachowski's commission was lauded for moving forward on broadband access 'it faced strong criticism from congressional Republicans for possibly overreaching its authority, such as when it released regulations on Internet service providers and network owners to ensure net neutrality. Yet a few citizen groups charged that he did not go far enough to protect consumers.

- Required NHTSA to base rebates on the type of new vehicle purchased, type of trade-in vehicle, and fuel economy of both. To qualify for a $3,500 rebate, for example, a new car had to get at least four miles per gallon more than the trade-in, with a twenty-two miles per gallon minimum; for a $4,500 rebate, a new car must get at least ten miles per gallon more than the trade-in, with a twenty-two miles per gallon minimum.
- Limited program to one rebate per person.
- Required auto dealers to certify that the engine of the trade-in vehicle would be disabled and the vehicle would be crushed or shredded.

ADDITIONAL PROGRAM FUNDING

The initial $1 billion in funding for the program was depleted by late July, less than a week after it was fully implemented. The House, in separate action on July 31, passed by a **key vote of 316–109 (R 77–95; D 239–14)** a bill (HR 3435) drafted by Democrat David Obey of Wisconsin, chair of the Appropriations Committee, to add another $2 billion to the program, with funds offset by pulling money from the economic stimulus law enacted in February. The money was to be shifted from the Energy Department's renewable energy loan-guarantees program, which appropriators would replenish later. *(2009 key votes, 75)*

The Senate cleared the bill on August 6 by a 60–37 roll-call vote, after Democrats defeated several amendments offered by Republicans who criticized the legislation as another bailout. President Obama signed the legislation on August 7 (PL 111-47).

Nearly all the additional funding was distributed a few weeks later; the administration called the program a major success and ended it.

Surface Transportation Authorization

Congress in 2009 and 2010 cleared six short-term extensions of the previous authorization of surface transportation programs, which was enacted in 2005 and expired on September 30, 2009. Extension of the $286.5 billion law, called the Safe, Accountable, Flexible, and Efficient Transportation Equity Act: A Legacy for Users, or SAFETEA-LU (PL 109-59), had eluded lawmakers for years, and the next reauthorization proved to be just as difficult as Congress revisited many issues that had been left unresolved. *(Congress and the Nation Vol. XII, p. 407; 2011–2012 action, p. 340)*

Lawmakers ultimately cleared a separate measure (PL 111-46), enacted on August 7, 2009, to move $7 billion from the Treasury to prevent the Highway Trust Fund from running out of money. President Barack Obama signed the bill (HR 3357) on August 7.

A major debate continued from previous Congresses focused on how to maintain the dwindling Highway Trust Fund that had provided funding for most surface transportation programs and projects since its inception in 1956. The fund was primarily financed by gas taxes, but that revenue had been dwindling as people were driving less since the start of the recession in 2007 and more drivers were buying hybrid cars. Moreover, future fuel economy standards were expected to further decrease motor fuel consumption. Politically, few lawmakers wanted to impose on their constituents a higher gas tax, which had not been increased since the 18.4-cents-per-gallon rate set in 1993. Diesel taxes that same year had been set at 24.4 cents per gallon.

Meanwhile, House and Senate committees had different views on how to approach a rewrite of the highway bill. Early in the 111th Congress, James L. Oberstar, D-Minn., chair of the House Transportation and Infrastructure Committee, sought a six-year, $500 billion reauthorization bill to overhaul all highway, transit, and other federal transportation programs and to consolidate several of those programs. Oberstar, who was known for his deep understanding of policy issues and became committee chair in 2007, touted the bill as one of the most important steps in surface transportation policy since the Interstate Highway System was created during the administration of President Dwight D. Eisenhower in the 1950s. House Speaker Nancy Pelosi, D-Calif., lauded his proposal as a way to create jobs.

But the Obama White House and other key Democrats, particularly in the Senate, did not believe the time was right for such an expansive piece of legislation. The administration was focusing on its top priorities of health care and financial regulatory overhaul, and it was coping with increased criticism of government spending in the wake of the financial services industry and auto industry bailouts and passage of a $787.2 billion economic stimulus measure (HR 1—PL 111-5) that Obama signed into law in February. Obama and Secretary of Transportation Ray LaHood requested that Congress simply maintain the 2005 law through the spring of 2011 and put off consideration of a long-term bill until after the 2010 midterm elections. *(Health care, p. 421; financial regulation, p. 88; stimulus, p. 78; financial crisis overview, p. 47)*

Meanwhile, Rep. Charles B. Rangel, D-N.Y., in 2009 was chair of the House Ways and Means Committee, the panel responsible for finding revenue for the highway bill. Rangel was trying to help tackle the government's broader financial challenges and address calls for tax reforms. (Further complicating matters, Rangel had been under investigation by the ethics committee regarding his personal finances and political dealings. He announced in March 2010 he would take a leave of absence as chair while the investigation continued, and the House ultimately voted to censure him.) *(Congressional ethics probes, pp. 651, 670)*

A House Transportation panel approved a draft of Oberstar's bill, but that measure stalled when the White House indicated it would not support a hike in the gas tax. Three Senate committees approved bills to simply extend the existing authorization through March 2011. The Senate

ECONOMIC STIMULUS INCLUDED TRANSPORTATION, BROADBAND FUNDING

President Barack Obama's first major legislative victory was congressional passage of a $787.2 billion economic stimulus package (HR 1—PL 111-5) that included billions of funding for some of his priorities, including transportation infrastructure and expansion of broadband service to rural areas. The White House and Democrats contended funding for these initiatives and others would create jobs and revive the nation's struggling economy, particularly as projects approved for funding under the bill would have to meet a "Buy American" provision when purchasing certain materials. *(Stimulus legislation, p. 78)*

Democrats sought to craft a bill that would enable immediate funding for infrastructure projects that were ready to go, with special attention to highways, bridges, public transit, Amtrak, and airports. Democratic governor Edward G. Rendell of Pennsylvania, chair of the National Governors Association, said there were $136 billion in infrastructure projects ready and awaiting funding.

The final measure included $27.5 billion for highway infrastructure projects under the Federal Highway Administration (FHWA), including $550 for transportation improvements on Indian reservations and federal lands, $20 million for highway surface transportation and technology training; and $20 million for disadvantaged business enterprises bonding assistance. The law required that states receiving funds give priority to projects that could award contracts within 120 days of the law's enactment, were included in an approved state or local transportation improvement program, were located in economically distressed areas, and were planned to be completed within three years. State funding was based on a formula in the fiscal 2008 omnibus spending law (PL 110-161).

The measure also included:

- $1.1 billion for the Federal Aviation Administration's Airport Improvement Grant program.
- $1.5 billion for the National Surface Transportation System for grants for a surface transportation project expected to significantly affect a metropolitan area, region, or the nation.
- $8 billion for the Federal Railroad Administration for capital grants for intercity passenger rail service projects. Required that preference be given to projects that can be awarded within 180 days of the law's enactment and that support the development of intercity high speed rail.
- $1.3 billion to Amtrak for capital and debt service grants, including $450 million for grants for security improvements. Required that no more than 60 percent of remaining funds be spent on the northeast corridor, and barred funds to subsidize Amtrak's operating losses.
- $6.9 billion to the Federal Transit Administration for transit capital assistance grants.
- $750 million for capital expenditures for fixed guideway infrastructure projects such as modernizing existing transit systems through upgrades and repairs.
- $750 million for capital investment grants for New Starts and Small Starts projects (created under the 2005 surface transportation law) that had started, or were about to start, construction.
- $100 million for grants to small shipyards.

The final measure included a provision in the Senate bill requiring that any public construction projects funded under the law use only U.S.-manufactured iron and steel. The law stated that the provision should be applied in a manner consistent with international trade agreements because business groups and the administration feared it otherwise could set off trade disputes with Canada, the European Union, and other trading partners.

The measure also included $7.2 billion to expand broadband Internet infrastructure to poorly served areas. Representatives of business, state and local governments, and other organizations moved quickly for some of those funds. The Commerce Department's National Telecommunications and Information Administration (NTIA) received $4.7 billion for broadband grants, and the Agriculture Department's Rural Utilities Service (RUS) received $2.5 billion to expand broadband access in rural areas.

The funding was intended to help improve connections to rural communities that had insufficient broadband access; expand computer and broadband access at hospitals, schools, libraries, and other public places; and fund projects aimed at spurring broadband demand. The money was to be distributed in two rounds, and projects had to be substantially completed with two years and fully completed within three years.

The agencies immediately began disbursing grants amid reports of a critical need to expand broadband access. A Knight Foundation commission in late 2009 warned in a 140-page paper that the United States was at risk of creating "second-class citizens" in the digital age if it did not ensure universal access.

But as lawmakers in the 112th Congress debated initiatives to expand broadband access, Republicans concerned about duplicating subsidies pushed through the House a proposal (HR 1343) for the federal government to halt awarding grants under the Broadband Technologies Opportunities program created under the stimulus law and recoup any unused funds. A companion bill (S 1659) was introduced in the Senate but did not advance further.

during the 111th Congress never considered a long-term reauthorization measure.

HOUSE SUBCOMMITTEE ACTION

The House Transportation and Infrastructure Subcommittee on Highways and Transit approved a draft of Oberstar's six-year, $500 billion bill by voice vote on June 24, 2009. That draft proposed to nearly double federal authorizations for surface transportation, including $337.4 billion for federal highway programs, $99.8 billion for public transit, $12.6 billion for highway and motor carrier safety, and $50 billion to develop eleven high-speed rail corridors to link major metropolitan areas. It also proposed changes to the approval process for surface transportation projects.

The measure raised several controversial issues that would plague lawmakers and slow debate for the next several years:

Financing the Highway Trust Fund. Subcommittee Chair Peter A. DeFazio, D-Ore., suggested a tax on energy speculation to raise about $190 billion for the Highway Trust Fund over six years, but Rangel rejected it, contending voters would not support the bill's $500 billion price tag in any event. Oberstar suggested Congress use general taxpayer money to pay for a multiyear bill for two years and thereby give the depleted trust fund time to recover. This, he said, would buy lawmakers time to consider financing options as part of a long-term reauthorization.

Distribution of highway funds. For decades, states had been locked in a dispute about how highway trust funds were distributed, with states such as Florida and Ohio complaining they gave more than they got back. The issue had slowed debate of SAFETEA-LU, but that law ultimately included a funding formula that was to guarantee that by fiscal 2008, every state would get back at least 92 cents in federal highway funds for each dollar it paid into the fund. Oberstar left this section of his bill blank but made clear he favored a solution for more equitable distribution.

Davis-Bacon wage rules. The Depression-era law (PL 71-798), enacted in 1931, required contractors on federal projects to pay locally prevailing wages. Florida Republican Connie Mack during subcommittee debate offered an amendment to remove the wage requirements from the law, but he was opposed by many Democrats. Oberstar promised to hold debate on the issue later. *(Davis-Bacon legislation, Congress and the Nation Vol. 1, p. 633)*

SENATE COMMITTEE ACTION

In 2009, three Senate committees—Environment and Public Works; Banking, Housing, and Urban Affairs; and Commerce, Science, and Transportation—approved bills that were to be incorporated into an eighteen-month extension of the existing surface transportation law. However, Sen. Max Baucus, D-Mont., chair of the Senate Finance Committee responsible for the revenue title of the bill, was focused on health care legislation and did not take up highway funding legislation.

Because the Environment and Public Works Committee also was distracted at the time with a climate change measure, it postponed a long-term rewrite. On July 15 it voted 18–1 to approve a bill to extend the authorization for the Highway Trust Fund at existing levels for eighteen months at a cost of about $41 billion in fiscal 2010 and $20.5 billion in 2011 (S1498—S Rept 111-59). Before approving the measure, the panel rejected, 5–14, a proposal by Christopher S. Bond, R-Mo., to bar a scheduled rescission of $8.7 billion in budget authority when the 2005 reauthorization law expired at the end of September. Sen. Barbara Boxer, D-Calif., chair of the Environment and Public Works Committee, wanted to send a clean extension to the floor without policy changes.

The Commerce, Science and Transportation Committee on July 21 approved by voice vote a bill to reauthorize the safety titles of the 2005 law for eighteen months (S 1496—no written report). The committee had jurisdiction over the National Highway Traffic Safety Administration, the Federal Motor Carrier Safety Administration, and the Transportation Department's enforcement of hazardous-materials regulations.

Two days later, the Banking, Housing, and Urban Affairs Committee quickly approved, without debate, an eighteen-month extension of the transit section of the 2005 law (S 1533—S Rept 111-61). The measure included provisions to reauthorize programs under the Federal Transit Administration and continue funding for grant programs, including urbanized-area formula grants, rail modernization grants, and buses and bus facility grants.

SHORT-TERM EXTENSIONS

Congress extended the highway authorization law three times in 2009 and three times in 2010. The first one-month extension, to October 31, 2009, was included in a stopgap spending bill attached to the fiscal 2010 appropriations bill for the legislative branch (HR 2918—PL 111-68).

A three-month extension that included a repeal of the scheduled $8.7 billion rescission stalled in the Senate because Republicans opposed a Democratic proposal to offset costs with money from the Troubled Asset Relief Program. Then a six-month extension stalled when the GOP balked at a vote without debate. Ultimately, lawmakers attached an extension through December 18 to another stopgap spending bill, itself attached to the fiscal 2010 Interior-Environment spending legislation (HR 2996—PL 111-88).

A subsequent extension to continue programs and authorizations to February 28, 2010, was attached to the defense appropriations legislation (HR 3326—PL 111-118). Oberstar repeatedly had refused to agree to a six-month extension, insisting a long-term reauthorization could be completed. But he ultimately persuaded colleagues to include in a jobs bill (HR 2847), which the House passed December 16, 2009, $27.5 billion in road and transit funding and an extension of the 2005 highway law through September 30, 2010. The jobs legislation also included a provision to repeal a restriction blocking the Highway Trust Fund from earning interest and to restore $20 billion to the fund.

When the jobs legislation stalled in the Senate, Democrats then attached a sixty-day extension to the conference report for the defense spending bill (HR 3326) that cleared Congress December 19, 2009 (PL 111-118).

On February 24, 2010, the Senate voted, 70–28, to amend the 2009 House-passed jobs bill (HR 2847) with a smaller $15 billion measure. Before passage, leaders won a 62–34 vote to waive the chamber's pay-as-you-go budget rules. Judd Gregg, R-N.H., objecting to provisions to move $19.5 billion from the general treasury to the Highway Trust fund, stated: "This isn't so much a jobs bill as it is a debt bill."

The House passed the bill March 4, 2010, by a vote of 217–201, after making changes negotiated by Democratic leaders to appease some in the rank and file. That included an agreement by Oberstar to address a distribution formula for highway funds at a later date. Oberstar did not like the way trust funding would be distributed under the measure because it was based on formulas in the 2005 surface transportation law that, he argued, effectively would send 58 percent of the money to just four states—California, Illinois, Louisiana, and Washington—while providing no funds to twenty-two states.

The Senate cleared the jobs bill, 68–29, on March 17 and the president signed it the next day (HR 2847—PL 111-147). The measure included an extension of mass transit and highway programs through December 31, 2010, authorized appropriations to be distributed in the same amounts as in fiscal 2009, and extended authority to make expenditures from Highway Trust Fund. *(Jobs legislation, p. 85)*

The measure also transferred $19.5 billion from the general fund to the Highway Trust Fund and restored $8.7 billion in contract authority that had been rescinded on September 30, 2009, when the 2005 law expired. That rescission had rolled back authorized contract authority that had exceeded the funding ceiling set by appropriators. Each of the three earlier extensions had been attached to spending bills based on the fiscal 2009 funding levels, which included the rescission. The American Association of State Highway and Transportation Officials had lobbied Congress to restore the funding to pre-rescission levels.

On December 21, 2010, the House passed a continuing resolution (HR 3082) negotiated with the Senate to keep government agencies operating. That continuing resolution, signed into law December 22, included provisions to extend highway, transit, and road safety programs through March 4, 2011, as well as provisions addressing the highway funding formula (PL 111-322).

HIGHWAY FUNDING FORMULA

After the Senate cleared the $17.6 billion jobs bill (PL 111-147), the House on March 17, 2010, passed by voice vote a measure (HR 4853) to change how some of the highway trust funding in the jobs bill would be distributed. (That same bill also initially included an extension of Federal Aviation Administration ([FAA] authorization.) Under the jobs legislation, funding for two highway programs was distributed to twenty-nine states that had received earmarks in the 2005 law. The new bill shifted funding to all fifty states based on their share of fiscal 2009 highway funds. It also sought to redistribute "bonus" highway funds to thirteen state highway programs rather than six programs identified in the jobs bill.

The House passed another bill (HR 4915) on March 24, 2010, that included the funding formula change Oberstar sought as well as a three-month extension of authorization for FAA programs. But the Senate was reluctant to take up either, in part because the bills were opposed by senators from the four states—including Majority Whip Richard J. Durbin of Illinois plus senators in California, Louisiana, and Washington—that would gain under the formula that was authorized by the 2005 law and had been left unchanged in the jobs bill. House Democrats also sought to include the formula change in legislation extending a number of tax breaks in existing law.

On March 26, as both chambers headed into a two-week spring recess, the Senate cleared a simple FAA extension (HR 4957—PL 111-153) by voice vote, about thirteen hours after House passage, without the highway funding formula language. President Obama signed the legislation on March 31.

The continuing resolution (HR 3082), which Congress cleared in December 2010 to fund the government through the end of fiscal 2011, addressed the highway funding formula, but its language focused on distribution across programs, not on states.

FAA Reauthorization

Debate on a long-term reauthorization of the Federal Aviation Administration (FAA) had started in the 110th Congress (2007–2008) without resolution, and a final measure continued to elude lawmakers through the 111th Congress. As it had during the previous three years, Congress in 2009 and 2010 kept aviation programs operating under several short-term extensions.

The last full FAA reauthorization was enacted in 2003 (PL 108-176) and had expired on September 30, 2007. The House passed a four-year reauthorization in 2007, but the measure died in the Senate. As a result, Congress in 2007 and 2008 granted short-term extensions of the agency's authority to collect various excise taxes and fees and to spend the money through the Airport and Airway Trust Fund for its responsibilities, which included air traffic control, weather services, navigation, training and emergency services, and administration of grants to local airports. The last extension passed in the 110th Congress was set to expire in March 2009. *(2003 reauthorization, Congress and the Nation Vol. XI, p. 382; FAA extensions, Congress and the Nation Vol. XII, p. 437)*

As soon as the 111th Congress set to work, disputes resumed on several issues that had stalled the earlier reauthorization efforts, including disagreements over whether existing airline fuel and passenger ticket taxes should be replaced with user fees—an issue that had loomed during President George W. Bush's second term (2005–2009). President Obama's fiscal 2010 budget proposed dropping fuel and ticket taxes in favor of user fees, which the administration said would create a more direct relationship between funding and costs. But many lawmakers opposed stepping into a dispute that had pitted major passenger airlines, which legislators contended carried more of the cost of air traffic control under the current system, against the general aviation industry, which feared it would pay more under the user fee system.

Other issues that further delayed action on a final reauthorization included disputes on pilot safety standards, standards for inspections of facilities overseas, continuation of antitrust immunity for certain airlines, rules for resolving labor disputes, and a proposal that would make it easier for Federal Express employees to unionize.

At the opening of the 111th Congress, Senate leaders sought a way to extend FAA authority through the end of the year. House Transportation Chair James L. Oberstar, D-Minn., who was working on a four-year reauthorization, said he would support a short-term extension, but the committee's ranking Republican, John Mica of Florida, balked. On March 18, the House passed by voice vote a short-term extension that the Senate cleared later that day and sent to the president (PL 111-112). That measure extended authorization of an aviation and revenue collections program through the end of fiscal 2009, and extended authority to collect aviation taxes and fees at existing rates.

A few months later, in May 2009, the House passed a three-year FAA reauthorization (HR 915) and the Senate Commerce, Science, and Transportation Committee followed with approval of a two-year version (S 1451) in July.

In March 2010, the full Senate passed a two-year reauthorization (HR 1586, originally a tax bill) after including provisions from the 2009 Commerce Committee bill. The House reacted by passing the same vehicle, but only after replacing the Senate language with that of its three-year bill (HR 915) as well as language from a pilot training bill that it had passed in 2009.

The House and Senate bills shared some similar provisions. Both, for example, aimed to expedite development of a modernized air traffic control system called Next Generation Air Transportation System (or NextGen) and increased the general aviation jet fuel tax to 36 cents from 21.8 cents per gallon. But the House bill granted a three-year authorization of $53.5 billion, while the Senate bill granted a two-year authorization of $34.1 billion.

A number of other disputes continued to divide House and Senate transportation committee members, including whether to increase the number of long-distance flights to and from Ronald Reagan Washington National Airport; whether to increase the maximum landing fees airports could charge on passenger tickets; how to address a labor provision that pitted Federal Express against United Parcel Service concerning unionization by employees; and how to resolve an antitrust immunity issue. (Senate Majority Leader Harry Reid of Nevada ultimately used the unfinished bill as a vehicle to enact unrelated provisions increasing Medicaid funding to states and to appropriate supplemental funds to avoid teacher layoffs—PL 111-226). *(Medicaid, p. 479; teacher layoffs, p. 453)*

HOUSE COMMITTEE ACTION

On March 5, 2009, the House Transportation and Infrastructure Committee gave voice vote approval to a $70 billion, three-year FAA reauthorization measure (HR 915—H Rep 111-119) that Oberstar had introduced the month before and was similar to a bill the House had passed during the 110th Congress *(Congress and the Nation Vol. XII, pp. 437–439)*.

The committee's bill included several controversial provisions, including one that the European Union (EU) strongly opposed because it required the FAA to inspect foreign air repair stations twice a year and to conduct drug and alcohol tests on workers at those stations. The EU threatened to withhold its agreement to a pending deal between the FAA and the EU's aviation safety counterpart, contending that the two bodies had comparable safety requirements and should accept each other's inspection and certification findings, with some exceptions. Critics of the provision pushed lawmakers to drop it, contending it could lead the EU to retaliate by, for example, requiring inspections of U.S. repair stations for compliance with its own standards. The Aerospace Industries Association also said the provisions could put tens of thousands of jobs at risk at the 1,237 U.S.-based repair stations that work on foreign aircraft.

But Oberstar would not budge on the provision and said the EU's objections were "drummed up." He claimed the EU's counterpart to FAA had not existed long enough and did not have enough inspectors to enforce its standards. "They're not doing the same kind of work, the same level of inspections, that we are," he said in early March.

Before the committee approved the bill, it adopted a manager's amendment by voice vote that included language requiring the Government Accountability Office (GAO) to study a practice in which airlines are granted antitrust immunity for certain routes. The practice, called "code sharing," occurs when an airline books flights for passengers on another airline's plane. Airlines have been granted antitrust immunity for these arrangements, which are common for international routes and permit airlines to coordinate prices and schedules along certain routes. Oberstar said he feared the arrangements could lead to more foreign ownership of U.S. airlines.

The manager's amendment also included provisions to require airlines to print the phone number of the Transportation Department's new consumer protection division on tickets, require the FAA to find a way to limit access to flight decks on all-cargo aircraft, and order the GAO to recommend minimum compensation standards for lost baggage.

Although Mica raised concerns about the antitrust and code-sharing provisions, he said he supported the bill.

The three-year authorization (for fiscal 2009 to fiscal 2012) included:

- $39.3 billion for FAA operations. Of that amount, $6 million each year would be appropriated from the Airport and Airway Trust Fund to the transportation secretary to finance airline data collection and analysis by the Bureau of Transportation Statistics.
- $1 billion for FAA research, engineering, and development.
- $16.2 billion for the AIP for airport planning and development and noise compatibility planning and programs.
- $13.4 billion for FAA air navigation facilities and equipment.
- $200 million for the Essential Air Service (EAS) Program, which provided subsidies to air carriers to continue flights into small communities that otherwise would be unprofitable.
- $105 million for the Small Community Air Service Development Program.

The bill also included provisions to:

- Increase the maximum passenger facility charge (PFC), which is the airport landing fees added in the price of a ticket—to $7 from $4.50.
- Increase to thirty-four from twenty-four the number of flights at Ronald Reagan Washington National Airport that could exceed a 1,250-mile limit. The number of flights had been at the center of a recurring dispute in which westerners typically pushed for more access while local communities, particular by in Virginia where the Reagan airport is located, sought minimize excessive aircraft noise.
- Require a new, retroactive labor dispute process.
- Require passenger airlines to submit to the Transportation Department a proposed plan to care for passengers on planes delayed on tarmacs for an extended time. This issue had been debated during the previous Congress when members were inundated with complaints from airline passengers who had been stranded for hours in parked planes because of bad weather.

HOUSE FLOOR ACTION

On May 21, 2009, the House passed the FAA reauthorization bill (HR 915) by a 277–136 vote, after reducing the overall authorization from $70 billion to $53.5 billion to fund aviation programs from fiscal 2010 through fiscal 2012. Republicans strongly objected to the bill, particularly to a provision regarding a binding arbitration process between the FAA and the air traffic controllers union. This was the same provision included in the 2007 House-passed FAA reauthorization bill that drew a veto threat from President George W. Bush. Under the provision, parties in a stalled labor dispute would be sent back to the bargaining table for forty-five days while the old contract remained in effect. Under a 1996 law, the FAA could impose its last contract offer if talks reached an impasse and Congress did not intervene.

Another provision in the bill was designed to remove Federal Express's status as an "express carrier" under the 1926 Railway Labor Act (because it was founded as an air freight company) and place it under the 1935 National Labor Relations Act, the law under which United Parcel Service was organized. The change would allow most Federal Express workers to organize locally rather than just nationally, which is more difficult. United Parcel Service (UPS), the International Brotherhood of Teamsters, and the Transportation Trades Department of the American Federation of Labor–Congress of Industrial Organizations (AFL-CIO) said Federal Express's trucking operations should fall under the National Labor Relations Act, which currently governed UPS trucking.

Mica also objected to the provision requiring FAA inspections of certain overseas aircraft repair stations twice a year, and to a requirement that workers at the facilities pass drug and alcohol tests. The measure also included the provision to end, in three years, antitrust immunity that had been granted to certain airline partnerships that allowed them to collaborate on setting prices and schedules.

The rule for floor debate on the bill, approved by the Rules Committee on the previous day, automatically added to the measure provisions to increase the excise taxes on fuel for noncommercial aviation. The provisions, endorsed by the Ways and Means Committee, would increase the tax on jet fuel from 21.8 to 35.9 cents per gallon and the tax on gasoline to 24.1 from 19.3 cents per gallon. The general aviation lobby indicated it preferred these increases to any option involving new user fees.

The bill also increased authorized spending for facilities and equipment to support development of NextGen and for airport infrastructure improvement grants.

The House bill also included language requiring the FAA to launch a rulemaking process to revise and update safety standards for airport firefighters, and required the rule to be finalized within two years of the bill's enactment. Airports complained the changes were unnecessary and would be too expensive, particularly for small, rural airports.

The bill raised the maximum passenger facility charge to $7 from $4.50. It also aimed to give the Transportation Department further leeway to reduce airline over scheduling, set health and safety standards for flight attendants, and provide protections for passengers held for extended periods in planes on the tarmac.

Pilot safety was another major issue following a fatal February regional jet crash in Buffalo, New York. An investigation had determined the plane's pilots were not trained in flying techniques to prevent such a crash. The House in its FAA bill adopted an amendment mandating a GAO study of all commercial pilot training and certification programs. Later, on October 14, the House passed a separate bill to increase pilot training and standards and require the FAA to build a comprehensive database of pilot records (HR 3371—H Rept 111-284).

Before final passage, the House rejected, 154–263, a motion by John Campbell, R-Calif., to essentially block funding under the Essential Air Service program for the airport in the hometown of Pennsylvania Republican John P. Murtha, chair of the Defense Appropriations subcommittee. Campbell argued the airport had received more than $150 million in federal funds since 1990 through the program and spending earmarks. He likened it to the famed "Bridge to Nowhere" project in Alaska. "And this surely is the airport for no one," Campbell stated. His motion was one of a series of GOP attacks against the earmarking practices of Murtha. (*Congress and the Nation Vol. XII, p. 414)*

SENATE COMMITTEE ACTION

On July 21, 2009, the Senate Commerce, Science, and Transportation Committee approved by voice vote a $35 billion, two-year FAA reauthorization bill (S 1451—S Rept 111-82). The bill included funding authorizations of $9.3 billion for fiscal 2010 and $9.6 billion for fiscal 2011 for operations; $3.5 billion for fiscal 2010 and $3.6 billion for fiscal 2011 for air navigation facilities and equipment; and $4 billion for fiscal 2010 and $4.1 billion for fiscal 2011 for airport planning and development and noise compatibility planning and programs.

The measure, introduced earlier in the month by John D. Rockefeller IV, D-W.Va., chair of the Commerce, Science, and Transportation Committee, paralleled the House bill in that it did not call for aviation system user fees. It also focused on accelerating the deployment of NextGen air traffic technologies and included language requiring that NextGen plans account for the incorporation of currently unknown technologies. It mandated development of an Air Traffic Control Modernization Oversight board to review the FAA's modernization programs, budget, and strategic plans and recommend which FAA facilities should be consolidated or eliminated.

Lawmakers again wrangled over the permitted number of daily flights at Ronald Reagan Washington National Airport. The panel turned back an amendment by Maria Cantwell, D-Wash., similar to the House bill, that would have permitted another ten long-distance, "beyond the perimeter" flights at the airport per day. Byron L. Dorgan, D-N.D., chair of the Aviation Operations subcommittee, said the original bill did not address a change to the number of flights because there was so much disagreement.

Members did include an amendment by Dorgan to require the FAA to maintain a database of all pilot performance records. The bill also encompassed a "passenger bill of rights" requiring air carriers and airports to devise plans to care for passengers during long tarmac delays and to devise plans to allow passengers to deplane after three hours of delay. Airlines also would have to publish online a list of chronically delayed flights and the performances of such flights.

Other bill provisions increased safety requirements for helicopter and fixed-wing emergency medical service operators and patients. It also focused on the safety of unmanned aircraft, commuter airlines, and FAA oversight of airlines and aircraft repair stations.

The bill proposed an increase in funding for emergency service operators subsidies and small community air service grants, and aimed to streamline the passenger facility charge approval process, but did not increase maximum PFC levels.

But action by the Senate Finance Committee, which was responsible for the revenue portion of the bill, languished as Democratic leaders had to grapple with the contentious issues of taxes and user fees. They opted instead for a short-term, three-month extension to buy more time, and the House followed suit, also preparing a three-month extension. The House on September 23, 2009, passed its three-month extension (HR 3607) by voice vote. The Senate cleared the House measure the following day by voice vote, and the president signed it on October 1 (PL 111-69).

SENATE FLOOR ACTION

On March 22, 2010, the Senate passed a two-year FAA reauthorization bill by a vote of 93–0, after inserting into a House-passed bill provisions similar to the Commerce, Science, and Transportation Committee–approved bill (S 1451) and including an aviation trust fund revenue title. The legislative vehicle the Senate used was an unrelated tax bill from the House, HR 1586. The Senate bill authorized $34.5 billion for FAA operations for fiscal years 2010 and 2011.

The bill included a provision to create a pilot program allowing up to six airports to collect passenger ticket fees with no statutory limit. It also required a special account be created within the Airport and Airway Trust Fund that would provide $400 million annually to fund NextGen implementation. Funds in the account, which was to be created by October 2010, would be generated from the excise tax on noncommercial jet fuel, which the bill would increase to 35.9 cents from 21.8 cents per gallon.

The bill also included provisions to:

- Require pilots hired by airlines to have 800 hours of flight experience, up from 250 for first officers.
- Require the FAA to create a database of pilots' performance histories.
- Streamline the approval process for passenger facility change but did not increase maximum PFC levels.

- Increase disclosure requirements on the part of airlines and contingencies for substantially delayed flights.
- Increase funding for Essential Air Service (EAS) subsidies and small community air service grants.
- Propose a research grant program for undergraduate students and students at technical colleges to examine training requirements for aircraft maintenance and the impact of new technology on training requirements for pilots and air traffic controllers.

FINAL HOUSE ACTION

The House approved the Senate-revised HR 1586 on March 25, 2010, after substituting by a 276–145 roll call its committee-approved bill (HR 915) to authorize $53.5 billion for FAA programs for three years. Under a rule governing floor debate, the bill also incorporated language from another measure (HR 3371) that targeted stricter safety standards for pilots. The FAA provisions never survived as the Senate later used HR 1586 for other purposes. *(See Short-term extensions, below)*

The bill proposed changes to the organization of NextGen, including strengthening the director's role. The bill increased authorized spending—at an average of 3.5 percent to 4 percent per year—to support development of NextGen air traffic modernization initiatives and for airport infrastructure improvement grants under the Airport Improvement Program, which provided grants for airport planning and development and other projects. The Senate version granted slightly higher amounts for NextGen with hopes of further accelerating its development.

In another controversial move, lawmakers retained a provision in the bill to repeal antitrust immunity granted to certain airline alliances enabling U.S. and international airlines to collaborate on prices and schedules for certain routes. The bill aimed to end the antitrust immunity status within three years, after which time an airline would have to reapply for the status. Airlines called the plan unwarranted government intrusion, while the provision's supporters said the antitrust protection hurt competition and could enable a monopoly on some routes. The Senate version of the bill did not address the issue.

The bill as approved would allow another twelve slots at Ronald Reagan Washington National Airport, ten of them for flights beyond a 1,250 mile perimeter. The ten would replace existing short-distance slots. Existing law limited to twenty-four the number of flights daily that could go beyond the perimeter.

Like the Senate bill, a revenue portion of the title included a proposed increase in the general aviation gasoline tax to 24.1 from 19.3 cents per gallon and in the general aviation jet fuel tax to 35.9 from 21.8 cents per gallon, a recommendation made by the transportation committee and supported by the Ways and Means Committee that drafted the full revenue title. The title was included in the House-passed version as an amendment on the floor.

Other provisions of the bill:

- Increased from $4.50 to $7 the maximum passenger fee airports could tack onto the price of a ticket. It maintained an existing rule that no more than two passenger fees could be charged per each one-way flight, meaning a round trip maximum would be $28 with the new maximum fees.
- Required a study of the impact on airports of accommodating passengers with connecting flights and whether various levels of passenger fees should be scheduled for connecting passengers versus those at originating and destination airports. The Senate version did not include an increase in passenger fee cap.
- Required every pilot in an airline cockpit to have an Airline Transport Pilot certificate that, among other things, required 1,500 hours of flight time.
- Created a centralized database of pilot records, but with more extensive information than called for under the Senate bill.
- Barred Congress from considering legislation that would use less than 90 percent of revenue from the aviation trust fund annually. Senate bill continued a 100 percent requirement.

SHORT-TERM EXTENSIONS

The 111th Congress in 2009 and 2010 repeatedly found a long-term reauthorization bill out of reach as disputes lingered regarding excise taxes on tickets, long-distance flights in and out of Ronald Reagan Washington National Airport, antitrust immunity for airline alliances, and treatment unionization rules applicable to Federal Express employees under labor laws. Repeated short-term extensions of the FAA authorization were necessary to continue the Airport Improvement Program (AIP), which provided grants for airport planning and development and other projects, and revenue collection into the aviation trust fund. Ultimately, Senate Majority Leader Harry Reid, D-Nev., used HR 1586 as a vehicle for education jobs funding and other issues, replacing the FAA authorization language.

On October 1, 2009, President Barack Obama signed the fiscal year 2010 Federal Aviation Administration Extension Act (HR 3607—PL 111-69) that continued authority to the end of the calendar year. On December 16, 2009, he signed the fiscal year 2010 Federal Aviation Administration Extension Act, Part II (HR 4217—PL 111-116), extending authority through March 31, 2010.

The next extension—the Federal Aviation Administration Extension Act of 2010—was enacted, providing an extension to April 30, 2010, at which time the Airport and Airway Extension Act of 2010 (HR 5147—PL 111-161) was signed and provided yet another extension through July 3, 2010. The day before that extension expired, the president signed a measure (HR 5611—PL 111-197) that continued authority to August 1.

On August 1, 2010, the Airline Safety and Federal Aviation Administration Extension Act of 2010 (HR 5900—PL 111-216) was enacted. The act included several airline safety provisions adopted from the House and Senate versions of HR 1586. Another extension (HR 6190—PL 111-249) continued FAA authorization and trust fund revenue collections through the end of that calendar year. That made for a total of sixteen short-term extensions since the full authorization expired at the end of fiscal 2007 (eight in the 110th Congress and eight in the 111th Congress).

The final extension cleared that year (HR 6473—PL 111-329) lasted through March 31, 2011.

Airline Safety and Pilot Training

Airline safety and pilot training became a major issue following the crash of a Continental Connection regional jet in Buffalo, N.Y., in February 2009 that killed all fifty passengers and crew members onboard. Lawmakers began studying issues related to pilot fatigue and pilot training standards and questioned potential differences in training and operational standards between regional and network carriers.

The House Transportation and Infrastructure Committee in October 2009 approved the Airline Safety and Pilot Training Improvement Act of 2009 (HR 3371—H Rept 111-284) and the House passed the legislation on October 14.

Provisions of that bill were included in the House-passed Federal Aviation Administration (FAA) reauthorization bill (HR 1586) in March 2010, and later included in the Airline Safety and Federal Aviation Administration Extension Act of 2010 (HR 5900) that the House passed on July 29, 2010, and the Senate cleared on July 30, 2010. It was signed by President Barack Obama on August 1, 2010 (PL 111-216).

Sen. Jim DeMint, R-S.C., had sought unanimous consent on the Senate floor in June to pass the stand-alone House-passed aviation safety measure. But Sen. Byron L. Dorgan, D-N.D., chair of the Commerce, Science, and Transportation Committee's panel on aviation, objected and insisted that airline safety language be included in a long-term FAA reauthorization.

The bipartisan airline safety measure, with language written by Sen. Kirsten Gillibrand, D-N.Y., and others, increased minimum flight hours required to hold a commercial pilot's license from 250 to 1,500.

The measure included language calling on the FAA to ensure that pilots are properly trained on how to recover from stalls, as well as language requiring airlines to create mentoring and leadership training programs. The measure also required the FAA to create a database, accessible to all airlines, that included every pilot's comprehensive record (rather than just the previous five years, as currently required). The Senate FAA reauthorization bill (S1451), as approved by the Commerce Committee, also included language requiring the FAA to maintain such a database, but the House reauthorization bill did not address the issue. The House bill did include language requiring the FAA to track scientific research on pilot fatigue and required airlines to create FAA-approved fatigue risk management systems.

The airline safety language of the new law included a "truth in advertising" provision to require online ticket agents to disclose the actual operators of each segment of a flight. Many major airlines had regional partners operating short flights on a contract basis. The flight labeled as Continental Connection that crashed in New York was operated by Colgan Air. Other provisions required pilots hired by the airlines to have 800 hours of flight experience; required the FAA to perform random on-site inspections of regional air carriers annually; provided a range of passenger rights, including limited waiting time on the tarmac; and created an Aviation Safety Whistleblower Investigation Office with the FAA.

FCC Reform and Internet Access

The 111th Congress focused on a scattering of telecommunications reform issues, primarily related to Internet access, but no final legislation was enacted.

Among the issues that faced increasing scrutiny was whether the federal government should impose regulations on Internet service providers and network owners to ensure equal access to the Internet, a topic dubbed "net neutrality." The administration, lawmakers, and industry companies also debated how to expand wireless broadband service to rural areas, with the Obama administration pushing for reform of the Universal Service Fund (USF) that had been created under the Telecommunications Act of 1996 (PL 104-104) to expand telecommunications services nationwide. *(Congress and the Nation Vol. IX, pp. 352, 387)*

Congress in 2006 started to consider overhauling the 1996 telecommunications law that focused primarily on deregulation of the telephone industry and promoting competition. Debate on rewriting the law to reflect changes in the modern telecommunications market repeatedly stalled amid disagreements among major companies and between the political parties on a range of issues. In 2009, the Federal Communications Commission (FCC) and Congress tried to draft more narrowly focused measures rather than a full rewrite of the 1996 law, still to no avail. But it set the stage for debate in following Congresses.

NET NEUTRALITY

The FCC in 2005 started to outline principles to ensure consumers access to any legal Internet content and services they desired and to benefit from competition among network, service, and content providers. The FCC also began to take actions to oversee Internet access, particularly as it responded to President Barack Obama's goal of expanding broadband services throughout the nation, including hard-to-reach rural areas. But Republicans and others balked, contending the FCC was stepping outside its authorization. A debate over whether and how to regulate providers followed in the 111th Congress, but without resolution. *(Congress and the Nation Vol. XII, p. 427)*

Background

The underlying principle of net neutrality is to ensure that networks that provide access to the Internet do not control how consumers use the Internet and do not discriminate against any content providers. Some lawmakers and observers contended more policies were needed to manage and oversee network providers' prioritization of Internet traffic. They said network providers might otherwise create a multitiered Internet where content providers pay for varying service levels, thereby potentially discriminating in the allocation of access to content providers on the basis of fees paid.

Others contended that existing laws and policies—including a 2005 FCC Internet Policy Statement outlining principles to preserve an open Internet—and a competitive marketplace were sufficient to prevent or deter networks from discriminatory practices. Large phone and cable companies, which opposed further regulation, insisted they needed flexibility to manage Internet traffic.

The FCC Internet Policy Statement outlined four principles to preserve an open Internet. It stated that consumers were entitled to access legal Internet content of their choice, to run applications and services of their choice, to connect to legal devices of their choice provided they did not harm the network, and to benefit from competition among network, service, and content providers. After the FCC approved the policy, members of Congress debated whether the FCC had authority to implement those standards on its own or needed legislative authorization.

The FCC first tried to enforce its open Internet principles in 2008 when it ordered Comcast, the nation's largest cable company, to stop blocking peer-to-peer service connections, which essentially allow file sharing between computers without the need of an intermediate server. Such connections can require substantial bandwidth and often are associated with online piracy. A federal appeals court in 2010 said the new open Internet principles were outside FCC's purview, but Comcast by then had changed its practices and pledged to comply with the principles. Meanwhile, Democratic congressional leaders vowed to overhaul or at least revise federal communications law.

Administrative and Congressional Action

The 2009 economic stimulus law touched on the issue with provisions requiring the National Telecommunications and Information Administration, in consultation with the FCC, to establish "nondiscrimination and network interconnection obligations" for grant participants in the Broadband Technology Opportunities Program—a new program intended to extend broadband service to rural areas. Later that year, Energy and Commerce Chair Henry A. Waxman, D-Calif., announced his support for net neutrality. *(Stimulus legislation, p. 78)*

In May 2010, FCC Chair Julius Genachowski announced he would move to regulate broadband access providers under Title II of the Communications Act, which governed telephone services. But he would seek to focus rules primarily on the administration's priority of enforcing net neutrality and expanding broadband access. While broadband access providers were upset, Senate Commerce Chair John Jay Rockefeller, D-W.Va., and House Energy and Commerce Chair Waxman backed the plan, as did consumer groups. Republicans, led by Minority Leader John A. Boehner, R-Ohio, opposed it. Boehner said it "amounts to a government takeover of the Internet, and yet another government takeover of a large portion of the private sector by the Obama administration."

The following month, the FCC voted 3–2 along party lines to begin its formal process for shifting jurisdiction—to classify broadband Internet access services under Title II of the Communications Act—of broadband Internet access, and Democrats supported Genachowski. "In the short term this is the right course and the right thing to do," Rockefeller said of FCC's regulatory move. "In the long term, however, I believe we need to develop consensus to update the law, further safeguard consumers and spur universal broadband deployment."

Rep. Edward J. Markey, D-Mass., called Genachowski's approach "the right response for carefully cutting the Gordian knot that has tied up our nation's broadband networks in regulatory uncertainty since the Comcast decision." But he also sought a legislative approach, introducing a bill (HR 3458) to create a policy of open nondiscriminatory Internet access. The bill, which Waxman supported, also required network providers to offer unbundled, or standalone, Internet access service and to disclose the speed, nature, and limitations of different service types, and to disclose network management practices.

Republicans moved to block the FCC action, but their efforts did not gain traction in the Democratic-controlled Congress. Sen. John McCain, R-Ariz., and Rep. Marsha Blackburn, R-Tenn., in October 2009 introduced matching bills (S 1836, HR 3924) to prevent the agency from imposing further regulations regarding Internet services, except those related to national security, public safety, federal or state law enforcement, or the Universal Service Fund. Rep. Gene Green, D-Texas, sponsored a resolution in July 2010 (H Con Res 311) to make clear that Congress determines FCC's regulatory authority as related to Internet services. Another bill (HR 5257), offered by Rep. Cliff Stearns, R-Fla., called on the FCC to prove a "market failure" before its institutes new Internet access regulations.

Waxman and Rick Boucher, D,-W.Va., chair of the subcommittee on Communications, Technology and the Internet, pledged to work with industry, public interest groups, and Republicans on a solution to satisfy all parties. Rep. Joe L. Barton, R-Texas, the ranking Republican on the Energy and Commerce Committee, was among those who refused to support the proposal, issuing a statement saying that "there is a widespread view that there is not sufficient time to ensure that Chair Waxman's proposal will keep the Internet open without chilling innovation and job creation." He suggested Congress "consider the issue deliberately." In September 2010, Waxman announced that it was clear that bipartisan support could not be obtained. "I do not close the door on moving legislation this Congress," Waxman said. "Cooler heads may prevail after the elections." Senate Minority Leader Mitch McConnell, R-Ky., also pledged to continue to fight the regulations in the next Congress.

On December 21, 2010, the FCC adopted, again by a party-line, 3–2 vote, its Open Internet Order, with plans for implementation the following year. The order, vigorously opposed by Republicans, entailed three rules governing transparency, no blocking, and no unreasonable discrimination. It also created an Open Internet Advisory Committee to evaluate effects of the rules and make further recommendations to the FCC. It was implemented on November 20, 2011, but several appeals of the rules had already been filed immediately after they were published in the *Federal Register* sixty days earlier. Those appeals were consolidated for review in the D.C. Circuit of the U.S. Court of Appeals. Although the court eventually in January 2014 struck down the Open Internet Order as going too far, it affirmed the FCC's role in regulating the Telecommunications Act and net neutrality. Supporters and opponents of net neutrality in Congress vowed to take up new legislation on the issue.

BROADBAND ACCESS AND THE UNIVERSAL SERVICE FUND

Lawmakers had taken up concerns about the role of broadband and the future of the Universal Service Fund (USF) in the 110th Congress, and debate continued and expanded in the 111th Congress as the Obama administration continued Bush's priority on expanded access. Once again, divisions among major telecommunications companies as well as between the political parties about the role of government regulation forestalled agreement on how or whether to further manage the industry to ensure expansion. *(Congress and the Nation Vol. XII, p. 427)*

Background

Universal access to the telecommunications network had been a basic tenet of federal communications policy since passage of the 1934 Communications Act and had been preserved by Congress with the Telecommunications Act of 1996. But technological innovation, such as the development of wireless smart phones such as iPhone and much faster networks, led to increasing demands by consumers, business, and government for access to high-speed services to transfer music, movies, and photos. The result was a demand for more sophisticated networks that did not clearly fall under purview of existing law.

Regulators and lawmakers became particularly concerned about the need to extend the reach of wireless broadband to rural areas, where communications companies saw little economic incentive to expand to serve relatively few customers, and about the viability and future of the USF in response to the changes in technology and the marketplace. The USF, authorized by the 1996 telecommunications law, was created in 1997 to bring affordable phone service to areas with little or no service. Large telecommunications and wireless carriers supported the fund by contributing some of their interstate and long-distance revenue, usually passing those costs on to consumers. As more consumers switched to wireless and Internet phone services, the contribution base dwindled.

Congressional and Administrative Action

The 2009 economic stimulus law called on the FCC to develop a National Broadband Plan to ensure every American has "access to broadband capability," with a detailed strategy to make the service affordable and widely available. FCC released its plan in March 2010, with provisions to overhaul the fund and auction off spectrum to expand wireless broadband networks.

At a hearing that month before the House Energy and Commerce Communications Subcommittee, Waxman said he wanted to revise and expand the fund to incorporate broadband, but he raised concerns about issuing redundant subsidies. Republicans also suggested that modifying the $7.1 billion fund to expand residential broadband would duplicate the $7.2 billion provided in the economic stimulus package for that purpose.

In November of that year, Boucher, who was chair of the Energy and Commerce subcommittee overseeing telecommunications issues, and Lee Terry, R-Neb., circulated a draft bill to reform the USF and authorize the FCC to use the funds to expand broadband service to rural areas. Under the legislation the FCC was to devise a system allowing wireless companies to bid for USF support. The existing system allowed all carriers in a market served by USF to receive the same subsidy that the land-line carrier in that market was paid. In some markets, the USF funded several vendors, who then selectively chose certain service areas most beneficial to their business interests. Boucher's proposal aimed to expand the funding base to include providers of Voice over Internet Protocol (VoIP) telephone services and broadband (allowing delivery of voice and multimedia communications over IP networks), but also capped the growth of the fund. It also directed the FCC to study how to increase contributions to the USF in ways other than the existing system of assessing fees based on a percentage of a carrier's long-distance and international phone revenue.

The legislation (HR 5828), introduced July 22, 2010, was similar to legislation lawmakers had introduced in the past but failed to receive consideration in part because the panel's former chair, Markey of Massachusetts, had not supported such legislation. Boucher also forged some agreement among companies who previously had staked out opposing positions on reform. Major telecom companies such as Verizon and AT&T, as well as some midsize carriers and rural businesses that received USF funds, indicated support for the plan. The cable industry wanted to confine USF support for broadband services to areas without access. Boucher's panel held a hearing on September 16, 2010, but continued divisions on the issue remained clear.

Meanwhile, Doris Matsui, D-Calif., pushed legislation (HR 3646) to expand an FCC program known as Lifeline to cover broadband. Lifeline provided subsidized telephone service to low-income Americans. Her efforts were backed by panel Democrats Markey, Mike Doyle of Pennsylvania, and Anna G. Eshoo of California, as well as Waxman. Boucher's initial discussion draft of his own bill did not include Matsui's proposal, but he said he was willing to consider including it. But his measure did not move forward.

On the Senate side, Senator Rockefeller on December 11, 2009, introduced a bill (S 2879) to call on the FCC to create a two-year pilot program of an expansion of the Lifeline program that included broadband services. The Senate Commerce Committee held hearings on USF reform, but took no action before the end of the session.

Satellite and Cable Programming

Congress in 2010 cleared a measure (S 3333—PL 111-175) reauthorizing through 2014 a 2004 law (PL 108-447) governing how satellite TV carriers distribute local broadcast stations to their customers. The Satellite Television Extension and Localism Act (STELA) of 2010 aimed to satisfy cable and satellite industries, broadcasting industry, and content providers who had long sought a compromise on issues dealing with copyright law and its application to local broadcasts distributed through cable or satellites. *(Congress and the Nation Vol. XI, p. 397)*

It extended existing law permitting satellite providers to compete with cable operators by transmitting local broadcast signals in the same market and by reducing copyright rates for certain network signals.

A major concern prompting lawmakers to act was that without an extension of an existing compulsory license, satellite providers would have to negotiate with individual broadcasters. The original intent of the license provision when approved by Congress was to enable the satellite TV industry, just starting out, to better compete with the cable industry. Lawmakers from both parties predicted it would be the last time the compulsory license was renewed.

The final measure incorporated provisions approved by two House and two Senate committees and sought to resolve several major issues, including whether DISH network, a satellite company, should be forced to carry a high-definition signal of public broadcasts and be required to expand broadcasting into rural areas. The bill included provisions to modernize and simplify license processes. Some lawmakers saw it as a way to ensure access to satellite programming in rural markets.

While lawmakers negotiated on the final reauthorization, Congress approved short-term extensions of the law. The first was attached to a defense appropriations bill (HR 3326—PL 111-118) and provided an extension until February 28, 2010. The second extension (HR 4851—PL 111-157) provided authorization until May 31 and was combined with an extension of unemployment benefits and an extension of Medicare physician payments.

BACKGROUND

Before 2010, Congress had approved several measures governing the retransmission of broadcast television signals by satellite television operators to improve competition among satellite providers and cable television operators and to increase programming choices for consumers. Among the measures enacted into law were the 1988 Satellite Home Viewer Act, the Satellite Home Viewer Act of 1994, the 1999 Satellite Home Viewer Improvement Act, and the 2004 Satellite Home Viewer Extension and Reauthorization Act. The measures made the regulatory framework for satellite and cable more similar, although differences remained. *(Congress and the Nation Vol. VII, p. 407; Vol. IX, p. 358; Vol. X, p. 338)*

Several provisions of the 2004 law were set to expire in 2009, including those that

- Provided satellite operators that retransmit certain nonlocal or "distant" TV signals to their subscribers with an efficient and low-cost way to license the copyrighted works within those signals. It provided for a per-subscriber, per-signal, per-month royalty fee.
- Provided satellite operators that retransmit to their subscribers signals of "significantly viewed" stations that are outside the local market a royalty-free license for the copyrighted works in those signals.
- Barred a television broadcast station that provides retransmission consent from engaging in exclusive contracts with companies to carry content or failing to negotiate in good faith.

HOUSE COMMITTEE ACTION

On September 16, 2009, the House Judiciary Committee approved, 34–0, a reauthorization bill (HR 3570) that was praised for incorporating several difficult industry compromises. But it did not solve a dispute over compulsory copyright licenses for certain local broadcasts retransmitted over cable or satellite.

Howard L. Berman, D-Calif., warned the cable and satellite industry not to expect renewal of the compulsory license, which Congress mandated in the 1980s to encourage the growth of the emerging paid TV. That license allowed cable and satellite providers to carry local and distant broadcast signals without producers' permission, which meant that producers could not negotiate for license fees or terms of use of their intellectual property. The bill maintained the status quo.

The measure included language essentially requiring DISH Network to provide local TV service to all 210 markets, including twenty-eight rural markets that had not been served. In exchange, it would waive a court injunction barring DISH from selling "distant signals"—or out-of-market broadcast stations—to subscribers, which broadcasters said violated their copyright. The measure also reflected a compromise between content providers and cable providers that required the cable industry to pay about $85 million in back copyright obligations over the subsequent five years.

The measure included provisions calling on satellite TV providers that carried "multicast" affiliates, where multiple signals could be broadcast on one channel, to continue carrying them. Within three years, they would have to carry any multicast affiliate that existed.

On June 25 the House Energy and Commerce Subcommittee on Communications, Technology, and the Internet approved a reauthorization measure (HR 2994) introduced by Chair Rick Boucher, D-Va. On October 14, the full committee gave voice-vote approval to the measure, which made relatively minor changes to existing law and was not as comprehensive as the Judiciary Committee's bill.

The measure included a provision requiring the FCC to devise a more specific definition of an "unserved" household to enable satellite providers to better transmit distant network broadcasts to such households.

The committee adopted, 31–20, an amendment by Anna G. Eshoo, D-Calif., to require satellite providers to provide high-definition signals of public broadcasts such as the Public Broadcasting System (PBS) by 2011. In 2008, the FCC had passed regulations to bar satellite TV providers from choosing selectively among high-definition signals and to require that they all carry high-definition signals in a market by 2013. Eshoo said all satellite providers except the DISH Network had agreed to begin airing PBS in high definition before 2013.

Boucher opposed the amendment, fearing it would disrupt compromises already made in the underlying bill to grant DISH relief from a court injunction barring it from selling out-of-market "distant signals" to certain subscribers, provided DISH offered local service to all 210 TV markets, including rural markets.

The committee also adopted a substitute amendment to permit the satellite provider EchoStar to import distant signals into "short markets" or areas where viewers do not have access to the major network broadcast affiliates. But satellite providers could not air programming from different time zones at an earlier time than it would normally appear in that time zone. It also included language requiring the FCC to conduct a study on the height and structural requirements for over-the-air antennas, and to study access for households in rural areas.

SENATE COMMITTEE ACTION

The Senate Judiciary Committee on September 24 approved, by voice vote, its reauthorization bill (S 1670) updating rebroadcasting rules for satellite TV providers. It aimed to make it easier for DIRECTV and DISH Network to provide "distant signals" in local markets. But the measure did not include language like that in the House measure requiring DISH to provide local TV service to all 210 markets, including rural markets, in exchange for granting it access to these subscribers.

Other provisions in the measure aimed to allow satellite providers to carry any low-power station in a local market. Under existing law, they could only carry a low-power station to subscribers within twenty to thirty-five miles of the station's transmitter. The bill also set new royalty rates for 2009 and encouraged satellite providers and copyright holders to negotiate their own rate deals. The panel adopted an amendment by Chair Patrick J. Leahy, D-Vt., directing the Copyright Office to study phasing out the compulsory statutory license.

Meanwhile, Senate Commerce Committee Chair John D. Rockefeller IV, D-W.Va., introduced a separate five-year reauthorization measure (S 2764) that included language similar to an amendment included in the House Energy bill to force DISH Network to carry local public broadcasting channels in high definition in markets where it already provided local signals in high definition. Part of the intent was to pressure completion of negotiations between the Association of Public Television Stations and DISH, which indicated it intended to launch another satellite in part to carry local PBS affiliates in high definition by 2013. But the House bill set a deadline of 2011. If a deal were reached between the carrier and the public stations by the time the bill was enacted, it would nullify that requirement.

The committee approved the bill by voice vote November 19. The bill included provisions barring satellite carriers from offering distant network signals in markets in which the carrier offers local service and barring providers from showing programming from different time zones earlier than would appear in that time zone. The committee also approved an amendment by voice vote by Claire McCaskill, D-Mo., calling on carriers to submit reports to the FCC defining local markets.

HOUSE AND SENATE FLOOR ACTION

On December 3 the House passed, 394–111, a full reauthorization measure (HR 3570) that incorporated provisions from the bills approved by the Energy and Commerce and Judiciary committees—just weeks before the current law (PL 108-447) was set to expire. Ultimately, pending Senate action on its reauthorization measures, House leaders attached an extension until February 28,

2010, of the satellite television distribution law to the fiscal 2010 defense appropriations bill (HR 3326), which the Senate ultimately cleared and President Obama signed December 19, 2009 (PL 111-118).

The Senate was faced with some major differences between its two committee bills, including language requiring Dish Network to carry local high-definition public TV broadcasts. Senators also needed to address language in the House-passed bill requiring DISH to provide local TV service to all 210 markets, including rural markets, in exchange for permission to sell certain kinds of programming to those subscribers. As negotiations languished, existing law was extended again, through the end of May (PL 111-157).

On May 7, 2010, the Senate passed by voice vote its reauthorization legislation (S 3333) that included language similar to that in a broad package of federal program extensions (HR 4213). The measure required language similar to that in the House bill that required DISH Network to expand local broadcasting to unserved rural markets in exchange for a waiver of the injunction. Language also called for a court-appointed "special master" to audit DISH to determine its compliance with existing laws.

FINAL ACTION

The House cleared the Senate-passed bill (S 3333) by voice vote on May 12. President Obama signed it on May 27 (PL 111-175), extending compulsory license programs, thereby allowing satellite providers to compete with cable operators by transmitting local broadcast signals in the same market and by reducing copyright rates for certain network signals. Lamar Smith called it "the single most important copyright bill to be considered by this Congress to date." Boucher said it would ensure rural homes would continue to have access to satellite network delivery. Many lawmakers warned they expected it to be the last extension of what had been intended to be a temporary license for satellite providers.

PL 111-175 extended through December 31, 2014, laws governing satellite television providers and updated the law to account for digital TV transition, which was considered complete, and eliminated the term *analog* in the law.

Under existing law, satellite providers could import distant signals from any market, but could not offer such signals to households that can receive the signal of an out-of-market network affiliate over the air. The measure permitted satellite carriers to use their distant signal license to provide an affiliate of that network into the market area.

The law included provisions waiving the injunction against DISH Network and requiring DISH to expand local broadcasting to rural markets not currently served. A court-appointed special entity, in cooperation with the Government Accountability Office, would have to audit DISH to determine its compliance with the agreement to expand local broadcasting.

The measure permitted satellite providers to carry public television stations from within a certain state if the station is part of a statewide network. Other provisions:

- Required satellite operations to pay a fee to retransmit local over-the-air signals, calculated on the basis of the number of households that receive the signals. The fees established would have to "most clearly represent the fair market value of secondary transmissions."
- Altered the way royalties are charged to cable operators, making them based on content received by local areas that receive service, rather than by content distributed across multiple areas regardless if it is seen by viewers.
- Required copyright royalty judges, rather than the Library of Congress, to be responsible for setting the compulsory royalty fees.
- Expanded the license for low-power stations that serve small communities to cover an entire market. Under existing law, satellite providers were permitted to carry low-power station within twenty to thirty-five miles of the station's transmitter.
- Modernized and simplified license processes.

CABLE PROGRAMMING

Lawmakers in 2010 ventured to step into a dispute between Fox and Cablevision Systems Corp. over rules under the 1992 Cable Act (PL 102-385) governing programming, but a deal reached between the companies forestalled any action.

In January 2010, the FCC voted 4–1 to remove a loophole in the 1992 Cable Act (PL 102–385) that allowed cable companies to withhold programming, including regional sports networks and premium content, from rivals. Program access provisions in the law had pertained to content specifically delivered via satellite.

Cable industry executives that fall appealed to Congress and the FCC to revamp rules under the law regarding retransmission. At issue was an unresolved dispute between Fox and Cablevision over fees the cable provider would pay the content producer. A stalemate in negotiations resulted in Cablevision customers being blacked out during the 2010 World Series.

FCC said it had limited authority to step into the dispute and turned to Congress, even though cable companies and some public policy advocates said the FCC did have such authority. Sen. John Kerry, D-Mass., member of the Senate Commerce Committee, drafted legislation to force broadcasters and cable companies into binding arbitration if FCC finds neither side is negotiating in good faith. Sen. Frank Lautenberg, D-N.J., also wanted to move on legislation.

By November, the issue was set aside temporarily when News Corp. reached agreement with Cablevisions Systems Corp. and DISH Network that restored News Corp.'s Fox program to Cablevision and DISH subscribers and ended the blackout.

Kerry and Lautenberg hoped to return to the issue in the next Congress, but expressed doubt that legislation would move if Republicans gained control of the House, as the GOP did in the mid-term voting in 2010.

Internet Gambling

The long-simmering issue of Internet gambling continued to be debated in the 111th Congress, with opponents of a 2006 law seeking to turn back regulations that banks deemed burdensome and unfair. But lingering disputes between supporters of that law and those who wanted to legalize Internet gambling forestalled progress on any new legislation.

A 1961 law barred interstate betting on sporting events, but foreign websites for many years had taken bets from U.S. consumers. In 2006, Congress tried to crack down on that practice by passing a law barring banks from processing check and credit card payments to gambling sites—a measure strongly backed by Republicans and included in a port security law (PL 109-347). But banks opposed the law, saying it would place an unfair and unfunded burden on them to police online gambling. *(Congress and the Nation Vol. XII, p. 423; Anticrime legislation 1950–1964, Congress and the Nation Vol. I, p. 1671)*

Sen. John Kyl, R-Ariz., who was a principal backer of the 2006 law, initially held up Treasury Department nominations until Secretary Timothy F. Geithner agreed to go ahead with the regulations that June.

The Treasury Department implemented new rules on June 1, 2010, to comply with the law as it pertained to credit cards. The law had aimed to stop the flow of Internet gambling money in five payment systems: card systems, money transmissions systems, wire transfers, check, and the Automated Clearing House System. But Treasury deemed the latter three forms of money flow to be too difficult to track and exempted them from the regulations' requirement. But Treasury did require anyone operating those three systems and who did business with illegal Internet gambling operators to adopt policies to enable them to identify their customers' business, employ customer agreements barring such transactions, and detail ways to deal with "tainted transactions" when they are identified.

Before the rules were fully implemented, a federal appeals court, ruling in a case brought by the Interactive Media Entertainment and Gaming Association, concluded that the gaming law was not unconstitutionally vague. The court said the law "itself does not make any gambling activity illegal"; rather, the definition of "unlawful Internet gambling" references federal and state laws related to gambling. Therefore, the court said, "to the extent that [there is] a vagueness problem, it is not with the Act, but rather with the underlying state law."

Critics, who had previously gained a six-month delay in the rules, let them go forward, with many hoping the resulting chaos they predicted would lead to the antigambling law's unraveling by Congress. Some lawmakers said the new rules could not stop Internet gambling, were an infringement on individual liberty, or were a lost opportunity to collect tax revenue. Meanwhile, committees held several hearings on legislative ways to loosen restrictions.

HOUSE ACTION

Rep. Barney Frank, D-Mass., chair of the House Financial Services Committee, sponsored legislation (HR 2267) to repeal the 2006 law. On July 28, 2010, his panel approved the measure by a 41–22 vote. His bill, supported by banks, would allow financial institutions to process bets made online but would require licensed Internet gambling operators to bar access by minors and residents of states where such gambling was not allowed. The bill also included language requiring operators of such websites to enforce bet limits.

Frank wanted the bill to be moved with a companion tax bill (HR 4976) sponsored by Jim McDermott, D-Wash., that included language imposing a 2 percent federal tax on online gambling operators and a 0.25 percent tax on online wagers. The bill directed that revenue be used to foster care and arts programs, but others—including Democrats—eyed such revenue as a method to help partially refill states' coffers (states at that time faced an estimated $121 billion revenue shortfall, according to the Center on Budget and Policy Priorities). Frank's bill aimed to allow Treasury to collect fees from license holders to cover costs of reviewing and examining them to ensure compliance.

Opponents of the bill included social conservatives who objected to gambling, sports leagues, and those concerned about exposure of gambling to children.

SENATE ACTION

Sen. Ron Wyden, D-Ore., and Sen. Judd Gregg, R-N.H., in 2010 drafted a plan to remodel the tax code and included a proposal to legalize some types of Internet gambling, such as poker, and then tax them.

While that proposal languished, Sen. Robert Menendez, D-N.J., introduced a bill (S 1597) to create a federal licensing program similar to that in the House bill, but it would permit only those Internet gambling operations that offered online games "in which success is predominantly determined by the skill of the players, including poker, chess, bridge, mahjong, and backgammon." He also introduced a proposal to impose a 5 percent fee on online gaming operators.

At the end of the year, three senior House Republicans pressed Senate Majority Leader Harry Reid of Nevada—whose state is home of the headquarters of such major gaming companies as Caesars Entertainment Corp.—not to move legislation legalizing online gambling. The three House members—Spencer Bachus of Alabama, the ranking Republican on Financial Services; Dave Camp of Michigan, the ranking Republican on Ways and Means; and Lamar Smith of Texas, the ranking Republican on Judiciary—feared

Reid might fold provisions licensing Internet poker into some other bill before the end of the session.

But lobbying on the issue remained heavy on Capitol Hill, with the American Gaming Association—the trade group for big Las Vegas casinos—as well as two big casino companies, MGM and Caesars, joining the push for legalization.

Notarization Legislation

In 2010, Congress quickly and with little controversy cleared legislation (HR 3808) that included provisions requiring state and federal courts to recognize notarizations affecting interstate commerce that were done by a notary in another state. But the measure, titled the Interstate Recognition of Notarizations Act of 2010, quickly became embroiled in election-year political debate regarding bank foreclosures. Questions about the potential effects of the bill led to a rare veto by President Barack Obama during his first term in office. *(Veto message, p. 915)*

The House cleared the bill, introduced by Robert B. Aderholt, R-Ala., under suspension of the rules on April 27, 2010. The Senate Judiciary Committee quickly discharged the bill by unanimous consent on September 27, 2010, sending it to the floor where it was passed the same day by unanimous consent.

But that month, concerns were raised after reports that Bank of America Corp., JP Morgan Chase & Co., and Ally Financial, Inc., had basically rubber-stamped foreclosures without reviewing documents to determine whether the property seizures were warranted. Some feared the bill could make it easier for banks to bypass property oversight in foreclosure proceedings by facilitating automated "robo-signing foreclosures" without a sufficient vetting. Conservative commentator Michelle Malkin called it a "bipartisan TARP-style banking bailout bill," likening it to the financial services overhaul measure.

President Obama pocket vetoed HR 3808 (by withholding his approval) on October 8, 2010, saying he felt further discussions were necessary. "The authors of this bill no doubt had the best intentions in mind when trying to remove impediments to interstate commerce," Obama said in his veto message.

The House on November 17 voted, 185–235, against overriding the veto. A two-thirds majority in both chambers is required to override a presidential veto. Robert B. Aderholt, R-Ala., the bill sponsor, said there was a misunderstanding and insisted there was no connection to recent foreclosure documentation problems. Obama said he would work with Aderholt and others to resolve the issue.

2011–2012

The 112th Congress posed new partisan obstacles for legislative action as Republicans took over the House and the Democrats' majority in the Senate narrowed as a result of the 2010 midterm elections. Increasingly, the political focus—pushed vigorously by Republicans and their Tea Party allies—was on fiscal belt-tightening by cutting federal spending. In spite of the controversial and often bitter disagreements over the national budget, lawmakers managed to come to terms on long-awaited reauthorizations of two major transportation laws governing surface transportation and aviation programs and projects.

With national elections less than two years away, lawmakers cleared a reauthorization of the surface transportation law, ending three years of debate that had required a total of sixteen short-term extensions of highway programs.

Many critics charged that the long-awaited legislation failed to resolve such problems as securing stable funding for highway and transit projects, while other groups, including the U.S. Chamber of Commerce and the American Automobile Association, applauded the federal investment that would enable states to move forward with construction projects. The White House touted it as a jobs bill, while the Republicans proudly proclaimed success at expediting environmental reviews of transportation projects, thereby easing some of the regulatory hurdles for states. But the unusually short two-year authorization reflected the harsh reality that lawmakers found ways to cover funding for the Highway Trust Fund in the short term but did not resolve how to make up for a continued decrease in revenue to the fund over the long term.

Congress also cleared a measure reauthorizing Federal Aviation Administration (FAA) programs for slightly more than two years, closing negotiations among lawmakers that had languished for several years and required multiple short-term extensions to continue programs and projects and to collect various excise taxes. The final measure addressed several long-term debates by, for example, providing an increase in slots for certain flights at Ronald Reagan National Airport close to Washington, D.C., directed resolutions for union disputes, and set restrictions on subsidies from the Essential Air Service program that assisted rural airports.

But lawmakers did not go along with President Barack Obama's request for funding for two of his signature initiatives: high-speed rail and a national infrastructure bank. Obama had sought $53 billion over six years for high-speed rail development, and Senate appropriators were willing to set aside $100 million for fiscal 2012, but House appropriators were not, and it was left out by the conference committee that negotiated the Transportation, Housing, and Urban Development spending bill for fiscal 2012, which Congress cleared and the president signed into law November 18 (HR 2112—Pl 112-55). Obama also had sought $5 billion for a national infrastructure bank to help finance new roads, bridges, mass transit, and other public works. The bill did not specifically provide funds for the initiative, but did include $500 million for national infrastructure investments (known as the TIGER [Transportation Investment Generating Economic Recovery] program), as well as provisions based on Senate language to appropriate $600 million for capital investments in surface transportation infrastructure.

Congress also continued discussions regarding various competing views of the FCC's role in regulating the Internet to ensure fair competition and to address Obama's goal of expanding broadband to rural areas, but with little resolved. Lawmakers did clear authorization for the FCC to begin auctions of spectrum for wireless broadband use as a component of its National Broadband Plan, which both parties agreed could bring needed revenue into the federal treasury, but they had to resolve differences on how FCC could conduct the auctions. Lawmakers also continued discussions on regulating Internet gambling and how the to block foreign websites' piracy of music, movies, and other copyrighted digital content. But heavy lobbying on both issues ground negotiations to a halt.

Surface Transportation

In 2011 and 2012 Congress passed nine short-term extensions of existing surface transportation law before it cleared legislation (HR 4348—PL 112-141) reauthorizing federal highway, transit, and other surface transportation programs through fiscal 2014 at existing levels with some inflationary increases—about $105 billion each for fiscal 2013 and 2014—and extending fiscal 2012 authorizations to the end of the fiscal year. Authorizations totaled an estimated $118 billion. The extensions of the exceptionally popular programs were among the rare achievements of the 112th Congress as Democrats and Republicans, deeply divided on most issues, headed into the 2012 national elections in which the four-year term of President Barack Obama was the central issue between the parties. *(2009 action, p. 324)*

Obama touted the Moving Ahead for Progress in the 21st Century Act or MAP-21 (PL 112-141) as a jobs bill and hailed its passage as an example of bipartisan cooperation he hoped would influence lawmakers debating other major initiatives. But the final measure was more limited than some had hoped and had been long delayed by partisan and intraparty wrangling. Many observers criticized it as a patchwork of short-term fixes and berated lawmakers for still not resolving the problems of maintaining the

Highway Trust Fund, instead choosing to temporarily replenish the fund through changes to pension rules, a transfer from a fund meant to clean up leaking underground storage tanks, and some general fund transfers.

"Well, we've known for a long time that people are driving less and driving more fuel-efficient cars," Transportation Secretary Ray LaHood said after a January 31, 2012, speech to the Aero Club of Washington. "And we know that the Highway Trust Fund is deficient and that it wasn't what it once was." Obama had proposed in his State of the Union Address earlier that month using half the savings from drawing down U.S. troops in Iraq and Afghanistan to pay for infrastructure investments. The nonpartisan Congressional Budget Office at the time showed the trust fund's balance in fiscal 2011 was $22 billion and estimated that balance would be spent down to $12 billion in 2012, $3 billion in 2013, and zeroed out the remaining years when the general fund revenues Congress had injected into it were exhausted.

Reaching a final deal on this and other issues in the 112th session became further complicated not only by partisan battles but also by disputes within the House GOP caucus. When Republicans took control of the House in 2011, John L. Mica, R-Fla., who became the chair of the House Transportation and Infrastructure Committee, followed the example of former chair James L. Oberstar, D-Minn., in seeking a long-term reauthorization measure. But Mica pushed a five-year measure that looked much different from that written by his predecessor. For one, the new chair hoped to cover costs in part by encouraging public-private partnerships, and he wanted to push it through quickly. But, like Oberstar (who had lost reelection the previous fall), he did not have support in the White House or within the congressional leadership.

House Speaker John A. Boehner of Ohio had his own plans. He first outlined his vision for infrastructure spending in September 2011 in the hopes of securing conservative support, making clear he wanted to move the bill in tandem with expanded energy production.

House leaders introduced a five-year, $260 billion proposal (HR 7) on January 31, 2012, that proposed significant modifications to federal highway and transit programs. The bill proposed to meet a gap between authorized funds and expected revenues from the Highway Trust fund by tapping royalties from an expansion of oil and gas drilling on public lands and in federal waters—a major conservative priority but one that Democrats had strongly opposed. The bill also proposed cutting Amtrak funding by 25 percent, increasing the allowable truck weights on interstate highways, and reducing funds for such transportation projects as bicycle lanes and pedestrian walkways. It did not create a national infrastructure bank that President Obama advocated, but it proposed $1 billion for the Transportation Infrastructure Finance and Innovation Act program that encourages private-public partnerships.

The bill also proposed streamlining the process for approving surface transportation projects to get federal money flowing quicker and to revise the formulas used for distributing funds to the states. Further, the bill included language requiring states with large numbers of structurally deficient bridges to spend a portion of their federal funds on fixing those bridges. States also would have more ability to institute tolls on interstates to finance major highway projects, and commercial roadside rest stops would be permitted on federally funded highways.

Boehner sought to sell the package to his fractious Republican caucus that was wary of anything resembling the 2009 stimulus law, which most Republicans vigorously opposed. The proposal had rankled some conservatives—including Budget Chair Paul Ryan, R-Wis., who wanted to keep down discretionary spending. Boehner—one of the eight House Republicans who had opposed the 2005 law transferring $8 billion from the Treasury's general fund to the highway trust fund—attempted to appeal to Tea Party followers and deficit hawks by insisting the legislation was not a "jobs" bill (contrary to his earlier efforts to link it to jobs) and highlighting provisions to streamline environmental approvals, eliminate duplicative and wasteful programs, and expand oil and gas drilling. He also noted the bill, which the GOP called the American Energy and Infrastructure Financing Act, did not include earmarks or any new taxes. Nevertheless, conservative groups called the measure "bloated" and contended it would create further budgetary problems. *(2005 legislation, Congress and the Nation Vol. XII, p. 439)*

Democrats primarily objected to the bill's provisions to expand oil and gas drilling, and they complained that the GOP did not consult them during the bill's drafting.

Further complicating the debate, the new GOP-controlled House approved a rules package removing a restriction that barred appropriators from meddling with multiyear transportation spending. That in effect abolished a point of order that had prohibited the chamber from considering a spending bill that reduced authorized highway and transit spending levels—a restriction created to ensure the trust funds were only used for transportation projects. Those who supported the rule change said they wanted to ensure lawmakers did not spend more on transportation projects than could be financed by the trust fund.

Another potential hurdle to easy passage of the bill was a rule regarding earmarks. Traditionally, passage of a highway bill was considered a relatively easy task, as appropriators and transportation committee members inserted provisions to authorize spending for special projects in their districts—so-called earmarks. Both the House and the Senate pledged a two-year ban on earmarks for the 112th Congress, following on the heels of moratoriums instituted in the previous session, and the ban seemed to slow the urgency to pass a long-term reauthorization measure among lawmakers. But the Congressional Research Service

(CRS) reported that the ban would not prevent members from directing transportation funds in certain directions because funding formulas could still be configured to favor certain districts, states, or projects. "Soft" earmarks that simply identified a project—without specifying a funding amount—as a congressional priority in a spending bill report was still permissible. Members also could continue to call or write the Transportation Department to urge support for certain projects, and they could influence state and local planning procedures.

Ultimately the GOP was unable to come to agreement on certain terms in the House bill, while Democrats opposed provisions to expand oil drilling, expedite the Keystone XL pipeline that was to bring oil from Canadian tar sands to the United States, and curtail pensions for federal workers. Boehner had to pull the measure from the floor. He ultimately maneuvered a complicated rule on the floor that allowed members to cast separate votes on transportation, energy, and pension provisions. The energy proposals of HR 3409 were the only ones to pass, 237–187, on February 16.

The House passed a three-month extension of highway programs and offered that as a basis for negotiations with the Senate, which in March 2012 had passed a two-year $109 billion bill. A compromise was reached in time to get a final bill to President Obama before congressional leaders' self-imposed deadline of June 30. The final bill was included in a package that contained provisions to freeze interest rates on government-backed student loans and extend federal flood insurance. *(For details, see pp. 476, 610)*

SENATE COMMITTEE ACTION

Highway Authorization

The Environment and Public Works Committee on November 9, 2011, approved by an 18–0 vote a bipartisan measure (S 1813) to authorize $85.3 billion for highway programs for fiscal years 2012 and 2013. It essentially maintained existing levels of spending, but it did not address Highway Trust Fund revenues, leaving a $12 billion gap between the authorization level and expected revenue level. That task was left to the Finance Committee.

The bill included provisions to consolidate ninety transportation programs into about thirty, and to guarantee each state the same percentage of highway funding it had received under the last transportation law, but with no state receiving less in aid than 95 percent of what it paid into the trust fund. Federal-aid highway programs would be structured around five core programs, and a new program would aim to improve the movement of freight on highways and among different modes of transportation. States would no longer have to spend federal funds on "enhancements" projects such as bicycle paths and sidewalks, and environmental reviews of highway projects would be expedited.

Bus and Truck Safety

On December 14, 2011, the Commerce, Science, and Transportation Committee approved on a party-line vote of 13–11 a measure (S 1950) that contained the bus and truck safety provisions of the highway reauthorization. That bill included a requirement that commercial trucks be equipped to provide electronic records to ensure compliance with hours-of-service rules. It also required that buses be equipped with seat belts and advanced window glazing to prevent passengers from being ejected.

Highway Safety and Research

The Commerce, Science, and Transportation Committee on December 14, 2011, also approved by voice vote a highway safety bill (S 1449—Rept 112-261) that called on the Transportation Department to consider motor vehicle safety rules to mitigate pedal obstruction and to set minimum performance standards for electronic systems. The panel also approved two highway safety measures sponsored by Sen. Frank R. Lautenberg, D-N.J. One bill, S 1952, addressed hazardous materials transportation safety and another, S 1953, aimed to improve transportation research.

Revenues

On February 7, 2012, the Finance Committee approved its draft measure by a vote of 17–6. The measure extended through 2015 the excise taxes that finance the Highway Trust Fund and extended authority to spend money from the fund through fiscal 2013. It included provisions to transfer $4 billion from the Leaking Underground Storage Tank Trust Fund to the highway fund, and to direct certain import tariffs into the highway fund and deny or revoke passports from those with federal tax debts of more than $50,000. The committee adopted by voice vote an amendment by Jeff Bingaman, D-N.M., to change tax requirements for long-term highway leases.

Republicans contended the measure diverted funding from the general fund to the highway fund, increased revenues for two years to pay for a two-year authorization bill, and included offsets unconnected or only loosely related to highways and transportation.

HOUSE COMMITTEE ACTION

The House version of the bill included proposals adopted by four committees, with the Transportation Committee taking the lead on authorization for the highway program, the Natural Resources Committee addressing bills to expand oil and gas drilling, the Energy and Commerce Committee approving a proposal to ensure approval of the Keystone XL pipeline, and the Ways and Means Committee addressing revenue for transportation and infrastructure programs. All bills were to be folded into the main surface transportation reauthorization bill (HR 7).

Oil and Gas Royalties

The Committee on Natural Resources on February 1, 2012, approved three proposals to expand onshore and offshore drilling that were intended to be folded into HR 7 to offset the cost of highway projects and programs. One bill (3407), approved 29–13, would open a portion of Alaska's Arctic National Wildlife and Refuge to oil and gas exploration and drilling. The second bill (HR 3410), approved 25–19, would permit lease sales for drilling off the coast of southern California and in the eastern Gulf of Mexico. The third bill (HR 3408—H Rept 112-392), approved 27–16, aimed to promote oil shale development—a proposal opposed by Democrats who wanted further studies on the impact of oil shale activities on water resources. Democrats contended all three proposals, which were not included in the Senate legislation (S 1813), would not fill the estimated $12 billion funding gap for transportation and infrastructure programs for two years. Some conservative groups said the GOP proposals were not in line with the user-fee principle of funding transportation infrastructure.

Highway Programs

Partisan rancor weighed down the Transportation and Infrastructure Committee markup before members approved a bill (HR 7—H Rept 112-397) by a 29–24 vote on February 2, 2012. The bill reauthorized highway and transit programs through fiscal 2016 at a cost of about $260 billion, consolidated or eliminated about seventy programs, and aimed to streamline environmental reviews for transportation projects.

Debate largely centered on issues related to Amtrak, local hiring, the "Buy America" program, and set-aside funding for "transportation enhancement" projects in the surface transportation program. The panel adopted a proposal by Peter A. DeFazio, D-Ore., to remove language that would have allowed the president to issue an expedited permit for any transportation infrastructure project within two years of the bill's enactment if the president determined it would benefit the country economically.

Tax Provisions

The Ways and Means Committee on February 3 approved, 20–17, a measure (HR 3864—H Rept 112-396) to extend motor fuels taxes and nonfuel excise taxes on heavy highway vehicles and tires at existing rates through fiscal 2018. The measure aimed to fund infrastructure projects from projected revenues from leases for oil and gas drilling on public lands and in federal waters. The measure also included language to end the transfer of all motor fuel taxes to the Highway Trust Fund mass transit account, instead funding the account with a one-time $40 billion transfer from an unnamed source and renaming it the "Alternative Transportation Account."

Keystone XL Oil Pipeline

The Energy and Commerce Committee on February 7 approved, 33–20, a bill (HR 3548) that aimed to shift permitting authority for the Keystone XL pipeline to the Federal Energy Regulation Commission (FERC) and give the commission thirty days to approve a permit for a 1,700-mile pipeline from western Canada to Texas refineries. The GOP had objected to Obama's earlier rejection of the pipeline proposal. The panel adopted a substitute amendment by voice vote to specify that no presidential permits were required for the construction, operation, and maintenance of the pipeline, and that FERC could not impose further conditions for the project. *(Keystone details, p. 390)*

Pension Contributions

The Rules Committee on February 14 approved a resolution guiding debate on the bill (HR 7) and included the text of legislation (HR 3813) sponsored by Dennis A. Ross, R-Fla., and approved 22–16, by the Oversight and Government Reform Committee (H Rept 112-394), to increase employee contributions to the Civil Service Retirement System and the Federal Employee Retirement System by 1.5 percent over three years. Those revenues would help pay for the $260 billion highway bill. But shortly later lawmakers decided to use that revenue to help pay for a payroll tax cut bill, requiring the GOP to find other revenue for the highway bill even while they were struggling to rally the caucus around the energy provisions in the measure.

SENATE FLOOR ACTION

The Senate easily passed its version of a two-year, $109 billion surface transportation reauthorization, called the Moving Ahead for Progress in the 21st Century Act (MAP-21, S 1813), by a vote of 74–22 on March 14, 2012. Bills approved at committee level were combined in the final measure.

The bill maintained funding for highways and transit programs at existing levels, adjusted for inflation. It also included provisions to reduce the number of highway programs from about ninety to thirty, and to structure the Federal Aid Highway Program around five "core" programs rather than seven. It proposed to end the Equity Bonus Program created by the 2005 law to ensure states received at least 92 percent of money they had contributed to the Highway Trust Fund by 2008, but would set each state's share equal to funding received under the previous law, reduced to exclude privatized highways, and assurance that each state receives at least 95 percent of the funds it contributes through gas taxes.

The measure also included provisions to expedite the environmental review process and accelerate project completion. It proposed $10.5 billion for each of the two fiscal years for transit programs.

During floor debate, John Hoeven, R-N.D., offered an amendment to provide for approval of the Keystone XL pipeline between Canada and the United States. It also would have required that the route for the pipeline in Nebraska be submitted by the state of Nebraska, and would provide for certain environmental protections. The Senate March 8 rejected Hoeven's amendment by a **key vote of 56–42 (R 45–0; D 11–40; I 0–2)** *(2012 key votes, p. 803)*.

The Senate also:

- Adopted, 76–22, an amendment by Bill Nelson, D-Fla., to redirect 80 percent of Clean Water Act penalties related to the Deepwater Horizon oil spill and explosion to a trust fund for Gulf Coast restoration. It also authorized $1.4 billion for the Land and Water Conservation Fund over two years, with the cost offset by a one-year delay of a rule granting multinational corporations flexibility in accounting for interest costs.
- Adopted, 50–47, an amendment by Jeff Bingaman, D-N.M., to bar privatized highways from receiving federal-aid funds.

SHORT-TERM EXTENSION

House GOP leaders retreated from Mica's bill just before President's Day when it became clear they would not have the votes. With the previous extension of highway programs and expenditures (PL 112-30) set to expire on March 31, 2012, there was a move to put the Senate's two-year bill on the floor. But Mica wanted another short-term extension to buy time to resolve differences on his long-term bill. The House on March 29 passed, 266–158, a three-month extension (HR 4281), with ten Republicans voting against it and thirty-seven Democrats supporting it. The Senate cleared that measure by voice vote later the same day, and the president signed it March 30 (PL 112-02).

The House followed up with passage of a bill (HR 4348) on April 18 to extend authorizations to the end of the fiscal year. The extension measure, passed by a vote of 293–127 (with sixty-nine Democrats and 224 Republicans voting for it), also included a provision to expedite approval of the Keystone XL Pipeline to bring oil from Canadian tar sands to the United States, a move that prompted a veto threat from the White House. The measure also included language from a bill (S 1400) to create a Gulf Coast Restoration Trust Fund and the text from a section of the House five-year reauthorization bill (HR 7) that would expedite environmental reviews for highway and transit projects. Language also was incorporated from a bill (HR 2273) that would shift, from the Environmental Protection Agency (EPA) to the states, responsibility for regulating fly ash, a residue of coal combustion. Concerns about the use of recycled ash in concrete and paving materials had become a growing concern since a storage ditch in Tennessee burst in December 2008, covering more than 300 acres with toxic ash and contaminating two nearby rivers.

The Senate then agreed by unanimous consent to substitute the language of its two-year highway bill (S 1813) and pass the amended bill (HR 4348) on April 24, sending it to conference. After rejecting a Democratic move to instruct conferees to accept the Senate-passed bill, the House voted unanimously on April 25 to go to conference to negotiate differences between the widely different bills.

Senate Majority Leader Harry Reid named fourteen conferees to the committee to negotiate differences between the chambers, while the House named thirty-three conferees. Under pressure to complete the bill before the previous short-term extension expired on June 30, the House adopted the conference report on the bill (HR 4348—H Rept 112-557) by a vote of 373–52 on June 29. The Senate cleared the bill by a vote of 74–19 shortly afterward.

Before final passage of the reauthorization, Congress had approved since fiscal 2008 three transfers from the general fund, totaling $29.7 billion, to replenish the Highway Trust Fund, according to the CRS.

The following are some of the key decisions made by negotiators:

State spending flexibility. As part of a deal to get House Republicans to drop demands for quick approval of the Keystone XL oil pipeline and limits on coal ash regulation, the Senate agreed to grant states more flexibility in spending funds provided through the Surface Transportation Program that had been intended for "enhancements" projects such as highway beautification or bicycle or pedestrian paths. Under the agreement, half of those funds would be directed to local Metropolitan Planning Organizations for such enhancement projects, but states could choose how to spend the other half—whether on the same type of projects or other transportation needs.

Equity Bonus. The bill ended the Equity Bonus Program created by the 2005 highway law. Instead it guaranteed a state share based on the 2005 law and a 95-cent return (in fiscal 2014) on each dollar that a state's highway users paid to the highway fund.

Tax provisions. The conference report kept most current Highway Trust Fund taxes, including the 18.4 cents-per-gallon levy on gasoline and the 24.4 cents-per-gallon surcharge on diesel purchases, in place through fiscal 2016, two years beyond the bill's policy authorizations.

The report funded surface transportation programs at existing levels through September 2014. But because Highway Trust Fund receipts would fall short of the spending requirements, revenue from fuel taxes and other excise taxes were to be supplemented with $21.2 billion in transfers from the Treasury general funds and other money, including $2.4 billion from the Leaking Underground Storage Tank Trust Fund for fiscal 2012. The costs of those transfers would be offset by revenue from two pension-related changes proposed by Reid, as well as a Republican proposal to reduce the amount of time that students are eligible for an in-school interest subsidy. The offsets also would pay for the student loan measure.

Keystone Pipeline. Boehner dropped the provision mandating quick approval of the Keystone pipeline, as well as the provision limiting EPA regulation of coal ash, when the Senate dropped $1.4 billion in funding for the Land and Water Conservation Fund. House Republicans drew criticism from some usual allies for yielding on demands to drop the provisions, while conservation advocates lamented that the Senate gave up on revenue for the conservation fund.

Regional Restoration Fund. The conference agreement created a regional restoration fund to be supported with fines in connection with the 2010 BP Deepwater Horizon oil spill and explosion and paid to states in the Gulf region, which could spend the money on environmental restoration. The so-called RESTORE Act, included as an amendment to the Senate-passed highway bill (S 1813), funneled 80 percent of Clean Water Act (PL 92-500) penalties assessed against parties responsible for the oil spill to the new trust fund. The House had included placeholder language for the trust fund in February as part of an energy package (HR 3408) that was set to be rolled into that chamber's highway reauthorization effort (HR 7). The money had been scheduled to be directed to the general Treasury. But in agreeing to the deal, conferees essentially cut $651 million in Medicaid funds to Democratic Sen. Mary Landrieu's state of Louisiana to help offset the cost of the measure.

Lawmakers at the time also faced deadlines to prevent an increase in student loan interest rates and to reauthorize federal flood insurance, so attached to the conference report measures extending for an additional year the 3.4 percent interest rate for new federally subsidized student loans, and to overhaul the federal flood insurance program to help make it actuarially sound.

MAJOR PROVISIONS

As signed into law on July 6, the Moving Ahead for Progress in the 21st Century Act—MAP-21 (PL 112-141) included the following major provisions:

Budget and Contract Authority

Authorization. Authorized about $105 billion for fiscal 2013 and fiscal 2014 combined—roughly the same as existing levels with some adjustment for inflation—and extended fiscal 2012 authorization to end of fiscal year, for a total of about $118 billion.

Unobligated balances. Directed the Transportation Department to redistribute unused obligation authority each fiscal year to states that were able to use the funds.

Budget Control Act of 2011. When the Budget Control "Super Committee" failed to reach an agreement in November 2011 on spending reductions across the federal budget, the Budget Control Act of 2011, which came to be known as the sequester, called for certain funding cuts to take place—an automatic move lawmakers were able to avert at the end of the year with a procedure that delayed the cuts another three months, giving them more time for negotiations (which ultimately failed). Several surface transportation programs and activities were expected to be exempted from the sequestration under the Balanced Budget and Emergency Deficit Control Act of 1985, according to the CRS: federal-aid highways; highway traffic safety grants; National Highway Traffic Safety Administration operations and research and National Driver Register; motor carrier safety operations, programs, and grants; and transit formula and bus grants. But the $739 million of annual contract authority and the Federal Transit Administration New Starts program, which was supported with general fund revenues, were not expected to be exempt. (*Sequester action, p. 185*)

Highway Programs

MAP-21 authorized $82.0 billion in guaranteed spending for federal-aid highway programs over two years—$41.0 billion for fiscal 2013 and $41.0 billion for fiscal 2014—and extended existing authorization levels through fiscal 2012.

To meet the funding levels, it provided for general fund transfers of $6.2 billion in fiscal 2013 and $12.6 billion in fiscal 2014, and transferred $2.4 billion of the balance of the Leaking Underground Storage Tank Trust Fund to the Highway Trust Fund for fiscal 2012. The Congressional Budget Office estimated the highway account of trust fund would retain a balance of $4.1 billion at the end of the MAP-21 authorization period, with the mass transit account expected to have a balance of $0.5 billion, according to CRS.

The measure eliminated the Equity Bonus Program and instead guaranteed a state share based on the 2005 law and a 95 percent return (in fiscal 2014) on each dollar it paid into the highway account.

Core Highway Programs

MAP-21 consolidated and reduced by about two-thirds many of the existing highway programs. Most federal-aid highway funds were for five activities, known as core programs, that were apportioned to the states based on a new funding formula that was in part based on existing allocations. While previous laws used individual program formulas to determine each state's apportionments under each program, the 2012 law had an annual authorization for each major program and a single funding formula.

The 2012 law authorized for the five core programs plus metropolitan transportation planning a total of $37.5 billion for fiscal 2013 and $37.8 billion for fiscal 2014. By core program it authorized:

National highway maintenance. $43.7 billion for the National Highway Performance Program that supports maintenance of the National Highway System, which combined the former Interstate Maintenance Program, the

National Highway System Program, and the Highway Bridge Program's on-system component.

Surface transportation program. $20.1 billion to provide states with flexible funding to be used on any federal-aid highway, bridge, public road, or transit capital projects, or bicycle or pedestrian paths. Permitted these funds to be used for Appalachian Development Highway System Projects with no state match, or for "enhancement projects" also funded under the Transportation alternatives program.

Highway safety. $4.8 billion for the Highway Safety Improvement Program created under the 2005 law to improve safety on roads by correcting hazardous conditions, such as dangerous intersections. $220 million to continue a program to install protective devices at railway-highway crossings.

Air quality. $4.4 billion for state and local governments to spend on transportation projects to help meet Clean Air Act goals. Expanded program eligibility to include such projects as telecommuting, ridesharing, and road pricing, as well as the addition of turn lanes. Permitted states to obligate these program funds for a project in a "nonattainment area"—an area that does not meet the federal air quality standards—regardless of the pollutant the project intends to reduce, and for projects that entail electric and natural gas vehicle infrastructure. Required the Transportation Department to build a database with details on all air quality-related projects and to work with EPA to determine their cost-effectiveness. Permitted states to spend funds for operating costs of transit projects previously eligible for program funding, but not on a project involving the construction of new roads or lanes available to single-occupant vehicles at all times.

Transportation alternatives. $1.6 billion for a revised program that targeted certain transportation alternatives. Changed the former Transportation Enhancements Program and other nonmotorized transportation programs, and combined them with the former recreational trails and safe-route-to-schools program under a new program entitled Transportation Alternatives. Set each state's fund to be a 2 percent set aside of its total highway funding and equal to the amount each state set aside for transportation enhancements in fiscal 2009.

Other Highway Grant Programs

MAP-21 authorized amounts for several nonapportioned programs:

Emergency Relief Program. Clarified eligibility criteria regarding roads and bridges damaged by natural disasters or catastrophic failures from an external cause. Mandated that total cost of an emergency relief project not exceed the cost of repair reconstruction of a comparable facility. Allowed the 180-day emergency period during which the federal government would pay 100 percent of repair costs to be adjusted to account for the time that damaged facilities cannot be accessed.

Territorial and Puerto Rico highways. $40 million and $150 million annually, respectively, for fiscal years 2013 and 2014.

Appalachian highways. Incorporated eligibility for the Appalachian Development Highway System Program into the national highways program and the Surface Transportation Program. Provided 100 percent federal funding to complete projects. Required each Appalachian state, within one year of bill's enactment, to create a plan for completing designated corridors.

National and regional projects. Authorized $500 million for fiscal 2013 for a new program to help finance critical high-cost surface transportation infrastructure projects that would generate national and regional economic benefits, such as boosting economic competitiveness, reduce congestion, improve national energy security, improve transport of freight and people, and improve highway safety.

Ferries and terminals. $67 million for each of fiscal years 2013 and 2014 for construction of ferry boats and facilities. Did not include set-asides for specific states but provided a new apportionment formula per project.

Federal and Native American lands. Created three components under a Federal Lands and Tribal Transportation Program with specific authorizations:

- $450 million annually for the Tribal Transportation Program, previously the Indian Reservation Roads Program.
- $300 million annually for the Federal Lands Transportation Program, which combined the former park roads and parkways program and refuge roads program.
- $250 million annually for the Federal Lands Access Program, which replaced the public lands highway program.

Highway Trust Fund and Taxes

- Extended authority through fiscal 2014 to expend funds from the Highway Trust Fund, the Sport Fish Restoration and Boating Trust Fund, and the Leaking Underground Storage Tank (LUST) Trust Fund.
- Extended the excise taxes that finance the Highway Trust Fund through fiscal 2016, including motor fuel taxes, such as the 18.3 cents-per-gallon tax on gasoline, the 24.3 cents-per-gallon tax on diesel fuels, and other excise taxes imposed on heavy highway vehicles or tires. Another 0.1 cent tax also is collected on those fuels and placed in the LUST trust fund.
- To cover expected shortfalls in the Highway Trust Fund through fiscal 2014, transferred $18.8 billion from the general Treasury fund, and $2.4 billion from the LUST trust fund.
- Offset the cost of transfers from the general treasury and the LUST trust fund by changing the method by

which businesses determine investment in employee defined-benefit pension plans, bringing in an estimated $9.4 billion over ten years; increased employer-paid insurance premiums paid to the Pension Benefit Guaranty Corporation, raising about $11.5 billion over ten years.

Highway Tax Payment to States

Eliminated the Equity Bonus Program that under previous law had set the rate of return for each state on the money it contributed to the highway account of the Highway Trust Fund through gas taxes. Instead, it set each share for fiscal 2013 and fiscal 2014 based on the apportionment it received in fiscal 2013, adjusted in fiscal 2014 to ensure each state receives at least 95 percent of its highway tax contribution.

Tolls and Innovative Financing

Interstate toll roads. Permitted construction of new interstate highways as toll roads, and allowed toll lanes to be added to existing interstate highways provided the number of free lanes are not reduced. Eliminated a previous rule that a toll agreement first had to be executed with the Federal Highway Administration.

TIFIA program. Authorized $750 million in fiscal 2013 and $1 billion in fiscal 2014, up from an annual authorization of $122 million, for programs under the 1998 Transportation Infrastructure Finance and Innovation Act (TIFIA) that provided federal credit or loan assistance for major investment in transportation. Modified rules for credit assistance to permit approval for a program of related projects, rather than limiting approval to single projects. Maintained the minimum cost for an eligible project to $50 million, or $15 million for an eligible intelligent transportation system project. Added a minimum threshold of $25 million for rural infrastructure projects, set aside 10 percent of funds for such projects, and required that loans for rural projects be offered at half the Treasury rate. Defined rural projects as any within an area other than city with 250,000 or more inhabitants. Increased maximum share of costs TIFIA may provide from 33 percent to 49 percent.

Highway Safety Programs

Authorized $670 million in fiscal 2013 and $680 million in fiscal 2014 for highway safety programs operated by NHTSA, including:

- $235 million each fiscal year for grants to state governments for highway safety programs.
- $22.5 million in fiscal 2013 and $23.1 million in fiscal 2014 for a new grant program to help states implement laws making distracted driving or texting while driving a primary offense.
- $13.3 million in fiscal 2013 and $13.6 million in fiscal 2014 for a new grant program to help states implement graduated driver licensing laws that limit the use of cell phones, driving at night, and carrying passengers not related to the driver.
- $38.4 million in fiscal 2013 and $39.4 million in fiscal 2014 for grants to help states make traffic safety information system improvements;
- $42.4 million in fiscal 2013 and $43.5 million in fiscal 2014 for occupant protection grants;
- $139.1 million in fiscal 2013 and $142.8 million in fiscal 2014 for grants to state government to implement impaired driving countermeasures.
- $4 million in fiscal 2013 and $4.1 million in fiscal 2014 for a motorcycle safety incentive grant program for states.
- $5 million in each fiscal year for a national driver register program and $29 million in each year for a high visibility enforcement program.

Barred states from using any federal highway safety grant funds to buy, operate, or maintain automated speed or red light cameras. Ended a state safety belt incentive grant program.

Federal Motor Carrier Safety Administration

Authorized $342 million in fiscal 2013 and $345 million in fiscal 2014 for the Federal Motor Carrier Safety Administration to manage safety issues regarding commercial interstate freight trucking and interstate bus passenger travel. Added new provisions that:

- Required, by 2015, every commercial vehicle involved in interstate commerce to be equipped with an electronic onboard recorder to ensure compliance with regulations regarding driving hours.
- Increased penalties for carriers operating without registration.
- Required the Transportation Department to create minimum entry-level training requirements for commercial drivers.
- Required Transportation to create a national clearinghouse with data of substance and alcohol test results of commercial drivers.
- Required Federal Transportation Administration to develop a national public transportation safety plan addressing all modes of public transportation. Gave FTA authority to set minimum safety standards for transit rail systems and oversee state safety oversight programs. Authorized $22 million annually for formula grants to help states finance participation in the new safety program. There had been high-profile incidents on heavy-rail transit systems in D.C. and Chicago that led to pressure for federal regulation.
- Required inventory of state laws requiring freight truck size and weight.

Public Transportation

Authorized $10.6 billion in fiscal 2013 and $10.7 billion in fiscal 2014 for the programs under the Federal Public Transportation Act—slight increases from the nearly $10.5 billion authorized in fiscal 2012. About 80 percent of that amount was to come from the mass transit account of the Highway Trust Fund; the remaining 20 percent was authorized to come from the general fund.

Capital Investment Grants

Maintenance program. Authorized $2.1 billion in fiscal 2013 and nearly $2.2 billion in fiscal 2014 for a new State of Good Repair (SGR) Grant Program, formerly the Fixed Guideway SGR Program. Two components of the program would finance projects to maintain fixed guideway transit systems and public transportation projects on a high-occupancy vehicle facility.

Bus and bus facilities. Authorized $422 million in fiscal 2013 and $428 million in fiscal 2014, down from $984 million in fiscal 2012. State distribution of funds, formerly based on earmarks, was required to be distributed based on a formula with each state and territory receiving a minimum allocation and remaining funds distributed according to population and service levels.

New starts. Authorized $1.9 billion for each of fiscal years 2013 and 2014, a slight decrease from the fiscal 2012 level of $2.0 billion, for major capital investment grants—known as New Starts grants for new or existing fixed-guideway transit systems or extensions to existing transit systems (previously funds could only be used for new projects, but MAP-21 permitted funds to be used for existing systems provided the project increased the corridor's capacity by at least 10 percent). Simplified project approval process for all projects.

Small starts. Further simplified approval process for projects requesting $75 million or less and with a project cost of $250 million or less, called "small starts" projects. Allowed projects to include corridor-based bus rapid transit. Required funds to come from same account as New Starts projects. Created pilot program for three projects to expedite New Starts project delivery.

Transportation Planning

- Required the Department of Transportation to develop performance measures to address seven national goals ranging from safety to environmental sustainability and reduced project delivery delays. Shortened the average review time for new transportation projects from fifteen years to seven, in part by requiring various environmental reviews to proceed concurrently and by exempting emergency road, highway, and bridge reconstruction from review under the National Environmental Policy Act (PL 91-190).
- Required the Transportation Department to compile best practices on how the public and private sector could work together to develop, finance, construct, and operate transportation infrastructure.
- Maintained a requirement that states and metropolitan planning organizations (MPOs), representing areas of at least 50,000 people, develop long-range transportation improvement plans. Instituted new requirement that states incorporate a performance-based approach that meets national standards.
- Required MPOs in areas with more than one million people that are in nonattainment or maintenance for air quality to draft performance plans linking projects with targets for emissions and congestion reduction.
- Permitted state transportation departments to accelerate a project by employing a general contractor or construction manager during the design phase, with the potential to be employed for construction. Such projects would receive 5 percent more federal funds.
- Required the Department of Transportation to create a demonstration project to streamline the process of relocating homes and businesses displaced by transportation projects by offering lump-sum payments for acquisition and relocation.

Environmental Review

- Created a process for the Department of Transportation (DOT) to ensure issues are resolved and deadlines are met for projects that require an environmental impact statement under the National Environmental Policy Act (NEPA). Established financial penalties for DOT to impose on agencies that fail to issue or deny permit, license, or other approval in a certain time frame. Permitted DOT to provide technical assistance—such as staff, training, and expertise—for certain projects to help expedite them.
- Eased requirements on states, enabling them to assume federal authority to determine whether projects would significantly impact the environment. Required DOT to propose a rule to enable certain highway, bridge, and highway safety projects to require limited documentation if they deemed to not significantly affect the environment.
- Required the Government Accountability Office (GAO) to examine state laws regulating environmental reviews of surface transportation projects and identify states with laws equivalent to federal laws. Required the GAO to determine the cost of carrying out federal environmental reviews that duplicate state reviews.

Hazardous Materials

- Authorized $42 million in fiscal 2014 and $43 million in fiscal 2014 for hazardous materials transportation programs.
- Required DOT to study transportation of hazardous material in external piping—called wetlines—of cargo tanks, then issue regulations.

- Required DOT to determine whether state hazardous materials permits meet federal standards.
- Removed minimum penalties for violations of hazardous materials transportation laws and increased maximum penalty level to $175,000.

Miscellaneous Provisions

- Required DOT to designate three broad groups of projects as categorical exclusions from NEPA review and to draft regulations for each designation: emergencies, projects within a right-of-way, and projects that receive limited federal assistance.
- Required DOT to launch a program to review and develop consistent procedures for environmental permitting and procurement requirements.
- Required DOT to compare the completion times for projects under the new law with those completed under the 2005 law.
- Directed the administration to each year spend all revenues in the harbor maintenance trust fund to operate and maintain the nation's federally maintained ports.
- Set standards for the National Park Service to restore natural quiet at the Grand Canyon.
- Authorized to the end of fiscal 2012 the Secure Rural Schools and Community Self-Determination program that helped counties finance public schools, road improvements, and forest restoration projects around national forests. (The program sought to compensate for declining timber revenues from logging on federal lands.)
- Extended through fiscal 2013 funding for Payments in Lieu of Taxes program that provided federal funds to local governments to offset losses in property taxes because of nontaxable federal lands within their boundaries.
- Capped at $15 million per year the abandoned mine land reclamation payments made to states that had finished high-priority reclamation projects.
- Created a Gulf Coast Restoration Trust Fund, and required that 80 percent of penalties paid for those responsible for 2010 Deepwater Horizon oil spill be directed to Gulf states for environmental restoration projects.
- Prohibited use of convict labor for federal-aid highway projects unless convicts are on parole, supervised releases, or probation.

FAA Reauthorization

Lawmakers resumed work on a long-term reauthorization of Federal Aviation Administration (FAA) programs in 2011, which in 2012 became one of the few measures Congress passed as partisan politics intensified heading into the presidential elections. Congress cleared the $63.4 billion bill—formally known as the FAA Modernization and Reform Act—in early February 2012, and President Barack Obama signed it February 14, 2012 (HR 658—PL 112-95). *(111th Congress action, p. 327)*

The bill authorized $13.4 billion for the Airport Improvement Program (AIP), which provided grants for airport planning and development and other projects; $10.9 billion for FAA facilities and equipment; $384 billion for FAA operations; and $672 million for research, engineering, and development. The final agreement included $461 million over four years for the Essential Air Service (EAS) program that provides subsidies for airlines to fly to rural communities, included changes to the EAS program that aimed to save the federal government more than $15 million. It also set deadlines and performance standards for the Next Generation Air Transportation System project (called NextGen), requiring implementation of an updated air traffic control system in the largest airports by 2015.

Up to that point, Congress had cleared twenty-three short-term extensions of the FAA authorization over five years. At the opening of the 112th Congress, Senate Majority Leader Harry Reid, D-Nev., had declared that a full reauthorization of federal aviation programs coincided with his top priority of creating jobs. Yet negotiations repeatedly stalled in 2011, just as they had during previous sessions. Partisan rancor had intensified since Republicans won control of the House in the 2010 elections, particularly as the parties grappled with how to address the continued recession and repeated calls for spending reductions.

Debate continued over how to continue to finance maintenance of the air traffic control system as well as the NextGen project. The airline industry favored user fees over the existing fuel taxes, but Transportation Secretary Ray LaHood had hinted that President Obama had no desire to switch to user fees. The issue had seemed to be resolved three years earlier when both sides, and a bipartisan majority of lawmakers in Congress, agreed to drop the idea of a user fee and instead increase the tax rate on some aviation fuel. But that deal was never codified in law because a full FAA reauthorization had not been enacted since 2007.

The House and Senate produced bills with major differences that centered on the length and cost of authorization, allocation of long-distance terminal slots at Ronald Reagan Washington National Airport, and subsidies to underserved rural airports—issues that had not been resolved during the previous Congresses. The House bill also included language to rescind a National Mediation Board ruling that made it easier for airline and railroad workers to unionize, which Senate Democrats strongly opposed.

Ultimately, continued delay of a final measure caused a lapse in authority beginning on July 23, 2011, forcing the shutdown of nonessential FAA operations for two weeks, a furlough of 3,500 employees, a halt of hundreds of airport construction projects, and a loss of $25 million to $30 million a day in federal excise taxes.

At the end of the year, conferees were instructed by congressional leaders to resolve disagreements on issues other than the union ruling dispute, which was left to leadership to resolve. The final version ultimately left in place the union rule, which made it easier for airline and railway employees to unionize, but, over union protests, raised to 50 percent from 35 percent the number of workers who needed to show interest before holding a vote on a new union election.

SENATE ACTION

On February 8, 2011, the Senate Finance Committee approved by voice vote a revenue title for the bill. That language, drafted by Finance Chair Max Baucus, D-Mont., increased the tax on jet fuel from 21.8 to 36 cents per gallon, raising an estimated $400 million annually to go into the Air Traffic Control System Modernization Account in the Airport and Airway Trust Fund to finance the NextGen program. The measure also included a surcharge of 14.1 cents per gallon on fuel used by aircraft with multiple owners, known as fractional aircraft.

In early 2011, Democratic leaders brought directly to the floor—bypassing a committee markup—a reauthorization bill (S 223) nearly identical to a bill that had died in the chamber the previous Congress.

Early in debate Republicans tried to attach an amendment to repeal Obama's 2010 health care overhaul law. *(Health care legislation, p. 421)*

But on February 17, after more than two weeks of debate, senators agreed, 96–2, to invoke cloture and end debate. Hours later, they passed the reauthorization bill by a vote of 87–8 after incorporating the Finance Committee's tax title.

Overall, the Senate's bill included an authorization of $17 billion for fiscal 2010 and $17.5 billion for fiscal 2011; the latter amount including $9.6 billion for operations and maintenance and $4.1 billion for the AIP, which provided grants for airport planning and development and other projects.

The bill included "passenger bill of rights" provisions that would, among other things, require airlines to develop an emergency contingency plan to enable passengers to leave a plane parked on a tarmac for more than three hours.

Sen. John McCain, R-Ariz., attempted unsuccessfully to end the EAS program, arguing it was unnecessary because most Americans had access to larger airports. Senators did approve language by Tom Coburn, R-Okla., requiring airports receiving EAS funds to have an average of at least ten passengers daily, except in Alaska, and that those airports be located at least ninety miles from a medium- or large-sized airport, up from seventy miles under existing law.

While the bill was on the floor, the Obama administration announced on February 4 it would award collective bargaining rights to Transportation Security Administration screeners, as allowed under existing law. Former president George W. Bush had not done so, and the issue divided pro- and anti-union senators. The White House announcement came one week after it announced it would halt expansion of the Screening Partnership Program, which allowed some airports to use private contractors instead of government employees for screening duties. That move also angered Republicans.

HOUSE COMMITTEE ACTION

The House Transportation and Infrastructure Committee on February 16, 2011, approved, 34–25, a $59.7 billion, four-year FAA reauthorization bill (HR 658—H Rept 112-29, Parts 1 and 2) that included a controversial provision to nullify a rule governing rail and aviation union elections, an issue not addressed in the Senate bill. The provision aimed to overturn a National Mediation Board rule that changed the way ballots are counted, allowing the outcomes of union-representation elections in airline and rail industries governed by the Railway Labor Act to be determined by a majority of votes cast.

The bill authorized $15.4 billion for the FAA in fiscal 2011 and $14.9 billion in each of the following three years. That fiscal 2011 authorization included $9.4 billion for FAA operations and maintenance and $3.2 billion for the AIP, which provided grants for airport planning and development and other projects.

The bill added ten long-distance slots at Reagan National to accommodate five round-trip flights, and proposed to phase out the EAS program by October 1, 2013, except in Alaska and Hawaii. The EAS was created to protect rural areas dependent on air service when the airline industry was deregulated in the 1970s. Although often criticized as wasteful government spending, the program was popular with lawmakers from rural states.

On March 16, the committee approved by voice vote a bill (HR 1079) to extend aviation programs and taxes and expenditure authority for the Airport and Airway Trust Fund through May 31, 2011. The previous extension (PL 111-329) was set to expire March 31. The House and Senate passed the extension March 29 and the president signed it on March 31 (PL 112-7). The measure also authorized about $2.5 billion in contract authority for the AIP from October 1, 2010, through the end of May 2011.

Ways and Means Committee. The House Ways and Means Committee, responsible for revenue, approved a bill (HR 1034—H Rept 112-44) on March 16 to extend existing aviation excise taxes and authorize expenditure authority for the Airport and Airway Trust Fund. The panel did not follow the Senate's path of increasing jet fuel taxes.

Science Committee. On March 17, the House Science, Space, and Technology Committee voted along party lines, 17–13, to approve a bill (HR 970) to reduce to fiscal 2008 levels the authorizations for aviation research and development funding for fiscal 2011 through fiscal 2014. It included authorizations of $165 million for fiscal 2011 and $147 million annually for fiscal 2012 through fiscal 2014. The levels were lower than those authorized by the Senate-passed bill.

HOUSE FLOOR ACTION

On April 1, 2011, the House passed its FAA reauthorization bill (HR 658), which combined the three committee bills, by a vote of 223–196, with Republicans contending the measure would lead to efficiencies and prioritize safety while saving money. The bill included language authorizing funding for the FAA at 2008 levels, or $4 billion less than the existing levels, according to Tom Petri, R-Wis., chair of the Aviation Subcommittee. Democrats said such reductions would hurt jobs and reduce safety.

For fiscal 2011 through fiscal 2014, the House bill included authorizations of $12.2 billion for airport planning and development and noise compatibility programs, $10.5 billion for air navigation facilities and equipment, and $36.9 billion for operations. The bill also ended the EAS program.

During debate, the House turned back, by a vote of 206–220, an attempt by Jerry F. Costello, D-Ill., and Steve LaTourette, R-Ohio, to remove a provision to repeal the National Mediation Board's ruling on counting unionization ballots that made it easier for airline and railway employees to organize. The White House threatened to veto any bill that included a repeal provision.

The bill included language permitting ten additional long-distance flights at Reagan National Airport, and a possible eight more for incumbent air carriers, for flights beyond the existing 1,250-mile perimeter limit.

The House also adopted, 215–209, an amendment by Bill Shuster, R-Pa., to require the FAA to tailor regulations for different parts of the industry and to do a cost-benefit analysis before issuing regulations. Families and friends of victims of the 2009 regional jet crash in New York criticized the provision, saying it could reduce aviation safety, and Shuster said he would not seek its inclusion in a final bill.

FINAL ACTION

The Senate amended the House bill (HR 658) on April 7, 2011, by replacing the text with that of its own two-year FAA reauthorization (S 223), which had been passed in February. It then passed the measure by unanimous consent, setting the stage for House-Senate negotiations over differences.

SHORT-TERM EXTENSIONS

Meanwhile, FAA functions continued under short-term extensions of authority.

The House, on May 23, and the Senate, on May 24, approved a one-month extension, through June, of federal aviation programs (HR 1893—PL 112-16).Then the House, on June 24, and the Senate, on June 27, passed another extension (HR 2279—PL 112-21) through July 22.

One partisan dispute carried over into the next stop-gap extension (HR 2553) that the House passed July 20, 2011, on a **key vote of 243–177 (R 230–6; D 13–171),** causing a cessation of FAA operations and construction projects. *(2011 key votes, p. 785)*

In the extension, the House GOP included a provision—dubbed a policy rider—by John L. Mica, R-Fla., to deny EAS support for certain small airports. EAS paid airlines a subsidy to keep regular service to small airports that would otherwise be unprofitable. The vote was a show of force by the new House Republican majority because the rider eliminated subsidies for a handful of airports that included those in states represented by key Senate Democratic negotiators on the long-term FAA bill: Commerce, Science, and Transportation Chair John D. Rockefeller IV of West Virginia, Finance Chair Max Baucus of Montana, and Majority Leader Harry Reid of Nevada. Senate Democrats, angered over the obvious provocation, rejected the provision and a two-week stalemate ensued, causing a lapse in authorization.

Lawmakers eventually agreed to clear the House bill with the promise that LaHood would waive the subsidy cuts. The Senate cleared the extension bill by unanimous consent August 5, and Obama signed it the same day (PL 112-27). Immediately, Rep. Frank A. LoBiondo, R-N.J., introduced legislation, cosponsored by Mica, to provide back pay to FAA employees for the two weeks they had been furloughed.

The House on January 24, 2012, and the Senate on January 26 passed another extension (HR 3800—PL 112-91) by voice vote. While the chambers worked on resolving differences between the bills in 2012, the Transportation Department extended penalties for long tarmac delays to foreign carriers operating in the United States. A rule issued in April extended a 2009 regulation requiring domestic airlines to allow passengers to leave if the airplane had idled for more than three hours.

FINAL NEGOTIATIONS

In late 2011, activity on most legislation, including the FAA authorization, was set aside while lawmakers focused on federal debt ceiling issues and languishing fiscal 2012 spending bills. On September 13, the House passed, by voice vote, a bill (HR 2887) to extend FAA programs through January 31, 2012. (That same bill extended surface transportation programs through March 31, 2012). Yet Mica remained optimistic that negotiators could complete work on a full reauthorization. He along with Sen. Rockefeller, Rep. Nick J. Rahall II, D-W.Va., and Sen. Kay Bailey Hutchison, R-Texas, (ranking committee members) directed committee aides to resolve differences on all issues other than the union provision—leaving that to leadership.

At the start of 2012, House Speaker John A. Boehner, R-Ohio, and Senate Majority Leader Reid agreed to leave in place the National Mediation Board (NMB) rule but create an initial hurdle to calling a certification vote by raising to 50 percent from 35 percent the number of eligible members of a bargaining unit who must petition the board to call a new election. The two major pilot unions supported the agreement, but unions representing other airline workers did not. The agreement also set other requirements, such as public hearings for all substantive NMB rulemakings and Governmental Accountability Office audits of the NMB at least every two years.

By the end of the month, Rockefeller declared that all disputes related to the long-term reauthorization had been resolved.

On January 31, 2012, conferees met to finalize remaining differences and approve the legislation authorizing $15.9 billion annually for federal aviation programs through fiscal 2015. The House adopted the conference report on the bill (HR 658—H Rept 112-381) on February 3, 2012, by a 248–169 roll call, and the Senate cleared it on February 6 by a 75–20 vote.

The measure authorized $63.4 billion over four years for capital programs, including $3.4 billion annually for the AIP, about $2.7 billion annually for the FAA's facilities and equipment and between $9.5 billion and $9.7 billion annually for FAA operations. It also extended existing taxes on fuel, cargo, flights, and tickets, and called on the FAA to accelerate the air traffic control modernization program and made changes to the AIP.

Some of the controversial issues the conferees addressed:

Long-distance flights from Reagan National. The conference agreement permitted another sixteen slots for nonstop flights beyond the 1,250-mile perimeter limit at Ronald Reagan Washington National Airport, for a total of twenty round-trip flights per day. The Senate had authorized twenty-four additional flights; the House had okayed ten.

Essential Air Service program. The measure included an authorization of $190 million annually for the EAS program to subsidize airlines serving rural communities. The Senate had increased the existing authorization while the House ended it by October 1, 2014. But the conference deal also changed the program to save an estimated more than $15 million. Airports not in the program could not join, and those renewing contracts faced new restrictions: subsidies were capped at $1,000 per passenger, and eligible airports were defined as those with fewer than ten passengers per day and at least 175 miles from the nearest hub airport.

The new subsidies cap essentially affected two airports: one in Ely, Nev., Reid's home state, and the other in Alamogordo, N.M.

Under the distance criteria, subsidized service to nine airports could be eliminated. However, the measure spared service to the airport in the state of Commerce Committee Chair Rockefeller, which was beyond the 175-mile limit but below the ten passenger limit. The new rules gave the transportation secretary authority to waive the distance requirement for airports with fewer than ten passengers. Moreover, state and local officials could apply to the secretary for exceptions by presenting a plan to carry at least ten passengers per day at a subsidy below the cap.

Union provision. The NMB ruling, which changed the way union election ballots were counted, remained under the agreement. But the agreement increased the proportion of eligible members—to 50 percent from 35 percent—needed to petition for new elections. The House bill repealed the May 2010 rule that allowed union certification when only a majority of the employees who actually vote in the election vote for certification. The Senate measure did not address the provision, and the administration opposed repealing the 2010 rule, which had changed the previous law that required certification by a vote of a majority of all airline workers, not just those who vote.

Repair station inspections. The final measure required the FAA to create a system to inspect certified foreign repair stations annually, consistent with international agreements. It also required drug and alcohol testing for repair station employees, and called on the FAA to report annually to Congress on the oversight of repair stations.

MAJOR PROVISIONS

As signed into law by President Barack Obama on February 14, 2012, HR 658 (PL 112-95)—the FAA Modernization and Reform Act of 2012—included the following major provisions:

FAA Operations. Authorized $38.4 billion for the main FAA operations account, including $9.7 billion for fiscal 2012, $9.5 billion for fiscal 2013, $9.6 billion for fiscal 2014, and $9.7 billion for fiscal 2015.

Airport Improvement Program. The legislation authorized the following for the AIP:

- Provided $13.4 billion in contract authority from the Aviation Trust Fund for the AIP, which provides grants to airports for projects. Authorized almost $3.4 billion for each of fiscal years 2012 through 2015. Capped at $20 million the amount of discretionary AIP funds that could support terminal development projects at nonhub or small-hub primary airports; previous law did not have a cap, and some lawmakers raised concerns that some airports might overbuild their terminals.
- Expanded project eligibility for airport development funds to include the purchase of firefighting and rescue equipment that service aircraft seating more than nine and fewer than thirty-one passengers; previous law limited the size of aircraft to those with more than twenty seats and fewer than thirty-one. Increased flexibility for states with short construction seasons to ensure they do not lose grant eligibility under the AIP and to allow funds to cover costs of relocating airport facilities under certain criteria.
- Expanded eligibility to 95 percent from 90 percent of the federal government's share for an AIP project for certain airports in economically distressed communities that participate in the Essential Air

Service program and meet unemployment or other economic criteria.

- Expanded the Contract Tower Program, under which FAA fully covers the operating costs of air traffic control towers, to include certain low-activity air traffic control towers.
- Amended project approval requirements for AIP to include only airports that have a master plan for solid-waste generation and recycling.
- Expanded the airport privatization pilot program, created in 1996, to ten airports from five.

Facilities and equipment. Provided $10.9 billion from the aviation trust fund for the facilities and equipment account, or about $2.7 billion for each fiscal year through fiscal 2015.

Research. Authorized $672 million over four years—about $168 million annually—for research, engineering, and development account. Required FAA to develop technologies and ways to prevent defects and malfunctions in all classes of unmanned aircraft that could cause a catastrophic failure.

Airport and Airway Trust Fund. Extended through fiscal 2015 the authority to expend money from the fund. Limited resources available from the fund to 90 percent of the revenue and interest credited to the fund. Previous law permitted all receipts to be used for aviation programs.

Next Generation Air Transport System. Required the capital projects that are part of the NextGen program to modernize FAA's air traffic control to be included in the Airway Capital Investment Plan. Called on FAA to create a plan to put in place NextGen navigation procedures at the thirty-five busiest U.S. airports by 2015.

Directed FAA to develop a plan within 180 days to accelerate certification of NextGen technologies by updating project deadlines, identifying specific activities needed for certification, setting staffing requirements, assessing use of third parties, and establishing performance metrics to measure FAA progress.

Essential Air Service. Authorized $461 million over four years for the EAS program: $143 million in fiscal 2012, $118 million in fiscal 2013, $107 million in fiscal 2014, and $93 million in fiscal 2015 (in addition to the $50 million already authorized from certain FAA fees). Limited the program to communities already participating. Limited subsidies to those routes costing less than $1,000 per passenger. Permitted the subsidy to airports in the contiguous forty-eight states with an average of ten or more passengers per day and within 175 miles from the nearest large- or medium-hub airport to qualify. Exceptions were made for airports in Alaska and Hawaii. The Transportation Department could waive requirements to protect certain other airports.

Passenger facility charges. Made permanent a pilot program for passenger facility charges (fees assessed by airports and collected by airlines) that allowed up to five airports to use the charges to fund intermodal ground access projects under flexible standards.

Taxes. Extended through fiscal 2015 excise taxes that funded the Airport and Airway Trust Fund. Maintained the tax rate on aviation gas used for noncommercial aviation at 19.3 cents per gallon and the tax on aviation-grade kerosene used for noncommercial purposes at 21.8 cents per gallon. The tax on commercial aviation fuel was maintained at 4.3 cents per gallon. Other taxes extended included the 7.5 percent ticket tax; the tax on each flight segment, adjusted annually for inflation; the tax on international flights, adjusted annually for inflation; and the 6.25 percent tax on air cargo.

TSA's Screening Partnership Program. Made changes to the Transportation Security Administration (TSA) Screening Partnership Program, which allows airports to opt out of using TSA workers. Gave the TSA 120 days to consider applications and required the agency to report to Congress and the airports all reasons for denying applications.

FAA personnel. Raised the threshold of members petitioning to hold an election from 35 percent to 50 percent. Required a runoff election if no option received a majority vote and created a new dispute-resolution process. Authorized the NMB to carry out the Railway Labor Act that governs union elections of airline employees.

Created a new dispute resolution process for employees if the FAA and a bargaining units did not reach agreement under which the Federal Mediation and Conciliation Service would be brought in unless the parties agreed to an alternative procedure.

FAA safety. Required the FAA to establish, within one year, a system to annually inspect certified foreign-aircraft repair stations, consistent with international agreements. Required drug and alcohol testing for repair station employees in accordance with such agreements.

- Eliminated the requirement that air carriers conduct an additional annual "line-check" evaluation for airline pilots older than sixty.
- Required flight attendants to be able to read, speak, and write English, and required flight attendants and gate agents to be trained to recognize and handle intoxicated and disruptive passengers.
- Required FAA, within six months, to begin drafting a rule to require commercial pilots who accept additional flight assignments to count that additional flying time toward the commercial flight time limitations.
- Directed the FAA to begin rules, by June 1, to improve safety of flight crew, medical personnel, and passengers on helicopters providing air ambulance services under federal regulations, and to address additional helicopter emergency medical services training.
- Required the Transportation Department to devise a plan to integrate unmanned aerial systems into the

national airspace system, by September 30, 2015, and to determine, within six months, whether unmanned aircraft could operate safely within the system.

- Created an independent Aviation Safety Whistleblower Investigation Office within the FAA to investigate complains about safety submitted by employees of FAA or certified entities.

Consumer Protections and Service Improvements

- Excessive delays. Required air carriers and airports using aircraft with more than thirty seats and participating in commercial air transport to detail how they would allow passengers to deplane following "excessive" tarmac delays. Also required the Transportation Department to report monthly on diverted and cancelled flights, and to maintain a hotline for consumer complaints.
- Cell phones. Required the FAA to study the impact of the use of cell phones by passengers during flights.
- Military personnel. Expressed the sense of Congress that all U.S. air carriers should provide reduced air fares for all active duty military personnel, allow them to modify or cancel tickets without penalties, and waive baggage fees for a minimum of three bags.
- Flight restrictions at Reagan National. Permitted sixteen additional slots for flights exceeding a 1,250-mile perimeter distance from the Ronald Reagan Washington National Airport. (Law at that time limited the number of flights to twenty-four slots per day.)

Miscellaneous Provisions

- Environmental provisions. Barred operation after December 31, 2015, of civil subsonic jets weighing up to 75,000 pounds unless they comply with certain noise levels level restrictions.
- Park air tours. Permitted exemptions from the Air Tour Management Program (which governed air tour operations in and around national parks) for parks with fifty or fewer commercial air tour flights annually unless a management plan is deemed necessary to protect resources. Provided National Park Service flexibility in managing Crater Lake National tours.
- Aviation insurance. Extended FAA aviation insurance program for domestic airlines through 2021.
- Criminal information databases. Authorized FAA to access criminal information databases operated by the Justice Department and by the states.
- Flight area. Required FAA to report to Congress, within 180 days, on proposed changes to the D.C. Metropolitan Area Special Flight Rules Area to improve general aviation access to airports in the region.
- Airport names. Barred the Transportation Department from using funds authorized under the measure to name or rename any project or programs under the bill after an individual currently serving in Congress.
- Commercial spaceflight. Barred FAA from proposing regulations on the commercial spaceflight program until October 1, 2015.

FCC and Internet Access

Republicans in the 112th Congress, now in control of the House, increased their criticism of the Federal Communications Commission (FCC), contending the agency was repeatedly overreaching its authority. They moved to overhaul the agency's authorization and set limits and preconditions for rulemaking. While none of those efforts became law in the face of Democratic opposition in the Senate and the White House, the issue promised to resurface in future years.

As Congress prepared to adjourn in 2011, the FCC was awaiting confirmation of two nominees to fill the open Democratic and Republican seats on the commission. But Charles E. Grassley, R-Iowa, was blocking full Senate confirmation of the nominees (one of whom, Jessica Rosenworcel, was an aide to Sen. Jay Rockefeller, D-W.Va.), to protest FCC Chair Julius Genachowski's rejection of his request for records related to the FCC's review of plans of a company known as LightSquared for a new national wholesale broadband network. The FCC initially granted the company conditional approval, then moved to revoke it after a government study suggested that broadband use of the spectrum could interfere with global positioning systems.

Genachowski said Grassley did not chair a committee with jurisdiction over the FCC, but Grassley maintained that made no difference. "It not only sets a dangerous precedent for a federal agency to unilaterally set the rules on how it engages with Congress—it also prevents any meaningful ability for the vast majority of Congress to inform themselves of how an agency works," Grassley said. Meanwhile, Rockefeller, who chaired the Senate Commerce Committee with jurisdiction over broadcast spectrum, moved to block Grassley's investigation into Lightsquared's proposal. Grassley did not lift his hold until the following April, after the House Energy and Commerce Committee requested documents on Grassley's behalf.

Meanwhile, lawmakers could not reach agreement on how and whether to implement net neutrality rules governing the Internet. But compromise was reached to authorize the FCC's planned auctions of donated telecommunications broadcast spectrum, thereby freeing up more bandwidth allocation for public safety as well as for wireless networks and allowing the FCC to move forward with its plan for national broadband access.

FCC OVERHAUL

Republicans charged the FCC with exceeding its authority in antitrust oversight. In a case involving Comcast, the nation's largest cable company, for example, lawmakers criticized the FCC for pressuring the company to make commitments such as offering channels aimed at racial minorities before the agency would approve Comcast's purchase of NBC Universal in 2011. Republicans and industry critics said those requirements were unrelated to the antitrust concerns under the FCC's purview.

Rep. Greg Walden, R-Ore., chair of the Communications and Technology Subcommittee of the House Energy and Commerce Committee, in late 2011 introduced a bill (HR 3309) to overhaul how the FCC operates, requiring it to demonstrate the necessity of any new regulations, restricting the types of conditions the agency could impose on corporate mergers, and mandating the agency set binding timelines for its proceedings. The FCC would have to clearly identify the existence of market failure, consumer harm, or regulatory barriers before it adopted new rules with an estimated economic impact of at least $100 million. The agency also would have to show that the benefits of any new regulations outweighed the costs, and it would have to include in its notices of proposed rules the text of the regulation. The FCC also would have to issue a rule setting deadlines for decisions or other matters that require action by the commission.

Supporters of the bill said it would increase transparency and accountability. "One of the biggest sectors of our economy is controlled by three people," said Walden, referring to the majority rule of the five-member board. But Democrats and the White House contended the measure would create unnecessary obstacles to the agency's efforts to protect consumers. Rep. John Dingell, D-Mich., a longtime member of the Energy and Commerce Committee and a critic of the FCC, said Congress should take a stronger role overseeing the agency rather than seek legislation.

In March 2012, the Energy and Commerce Committee approved Walden's bill by a largely party-line, 31–16, vote, and the full House passed it later that month, 247–174. The House approved several amendments, including one by Florida Republican Mario Diaz-Balart requiring the FCC to publicly release its decisions regarding Freedom of Information Act requests. Another Texas Democrat, Al Green, sought to clarify that the bill would not impede the agency from ensuring effective communication systems to alert the public of emergency weather conditions.

In the Senate, a similar FCC reform measure (S 1784) introduced by Dean Heller, R-Nev., did not advance before the close of the session.

NET NEUTRALITY

Lawmakers in the 112th Congress again failed to reach consensus on net neutrality, a concept intended to ensure that networks that provide access to the Internet did not control how consumers use the Internet and did not discriminate against any content provider.

Many members involved in the issue were awaiting a pending court decision on the FCC's 2010 Open Internet Order that entailed three rules governing transparency, no blocking, and no unreasonable discrimination. It also created an Open Internet Advisory Committee to evaluate effects of the rules and make further recommendations to the FCC. While some members stood behind the FCC rules, others, particularly Republicans, maintained the FCC had overstepped its authority and that Internet regulation could be harmful.

House Energy and Commerce Chair Fred Upton, R-Mich., along with Republicans Greg Walden of Oregon and Lee Terry of Nebraska—the chair and vice chair of the Communications and Technology Subcommittee—said FCC Chair Genachowski in a March 7, 2011, letter did not provide enough evidence the commission had performed a market analysis to determine a need for net neutrality rules. Genachowski's letter, a response to a March 3 Republican request for analysis, pointed to several parts of the commission's December order on the subject, including what the FCC chair said was a market analysis that found limited competition in fixed broadband markets. But the Republicans contended that the Internet already was open and that rules would only stifle investment in broadband systems.

Walden in February 2011 introduced a measure (H J Res 37) to nullify the FCC rules. The House Energy and Commerce Committee approved the resolution on March 15, 30–23. The full House on April 8 passed the resolution, 240–179, voting under the 1996 Congressional Review Act (PL 104-121), that allows Congress to nullify an agency's regulations with a majority vote of both chambers.

Walden stated: "The FCC power grab would allow it to regulate an interstate communication service on barely more than a whim and without any additional input from Congress." The Internet, he said, "is open and innovative thanks to the government's hands-off approach." But Rep. Jared Polis, D-Colo., said rules were needed to prevent "a major shift in power on the Internet to the broadband providers from the content providers." He said nonprofit and religious groups, for example, feared they would be consigned to a lower tier because they could not afford a high-priced premium service. "So your Web page from Nike might load faster than your Web page from the Catholic Church because, if there was tiered access, who would be more likely to pay for the speed of the access?"

In the Senate Rockefeller, chair of the Commerce Committee, said he was "disappointed that House leadership wants to undo the integrity of the FCC's process and unravel their good work." The Senate did not take up the House resolution.

Other similar measures that did not see action included a proposal by Rep. Marsha Blackburn, R-Tenn., to bar the FCC from issuing regulations regarding Internet services unless it was to protect national security or public safety and a proposal (HR 166) by Rep. Cliff Stearns, R-Fla., to require the FCC to prove that there is "market failure" before it issued Internet access regulations. In the Senate, Maria Cantwell, D-Wash., in January 2011 offered a bill

(S 74) to strengthen open access protections, essentially codifying into law the FCC's 2005 and 2010 principles. Other measures sought to prevent or delay implementation of the Open Internet Order.

In December 2011, the House also included in its jobs bills (HR 3630) provisions to bar the FCC from imposing network access or management rules on licensees, but those provisions were dropped before the bill was cleared for the president. Language was attached to the House fiscal 2011 spending measure (HR 1) to bar the FCC from using funds to implement the order, but lawmakers again dropped it before clearing the bill. A similar provision was included in the original fiscal 2012 financial services and general government appropriations bill (HR 2434), but not in a final consolidated spending law.

BROADBAND ACCESS

On February 10, 2011, President Obama announced "The Wireless Innovation and Infrastructure Initiative" to expand wireless broadband access to 98 percent of Americans, which the administration said would reduce the deficit by almost $10 billion. His plan, initially announced in his State of the Union address, aimed to help businesses obtain high-speed wireless services (the new "4G" technology) and create a national wireless network for public safety. *(Broadband 2008 legislation, background, Congress and the Nation Vol. XII, p. 435)*

Under his proposal, up to 500 megahertz (MHz) of spectrum would be freed up, primarily from voluntary auctions and more efficient use of government spectrum, although legislation would be required for the auctions. The initiative called for $5 billion and reform of the Universal Service Fund to ensure extension of wireless into rural areas. It also called for $3 billion of the spectrum auction proceeds to be dedicated to research and development of new wireless technologies. Another $10.7 billion would be requested to develop and deploy a national wireless network for public safety.

Republicans, however, raised concerns about more tax dollars being dedicated potentially before the last round of funding had been spent. "Let's ensure our resources are being used wisely," Energy and Commerce Committee Chair Fred Upton, R-Mich., said in February. Greg Walden, R-Ore., chair of the Communications and Technology Subcommittee, held a hearing on oversight of the $7.2 billion for broadband grants included in the economic stimulus law. The panel on April 5 approved, by voice vote, legislation (HR 1343) sponsored by Rep. Charles Bass, R-N.H., to terminate awards made under the Broadband Initiatives Program or the Broadband Technology Opportunities Program established by the 2009 economic stimulus law (PL 111-5), and to require the federal treasury to recoup broadband funds that had not been used. It was passed by the House by voice vote on October 5, but did not move further.

In June 2011, Rep. Doris Matsui, D-Calif., introduced legislation (HR 2163) calling on the FCC to create a program to subsidize Internet services, similar to the Lifeline program for telephone services. In October, the FCC took the initiative and voted to spend billions of dollars to subsidize broadband service in rural areas through a "Connect America Fund"—taking funds that were to be directed to landline operations at rural phone companies. The agency released rules for redirecting the estimated $4.5 billion in spending to broadband. The fund was part of the agency's $8 billion universal service system. The FCC said the funding would provide broadband access to seven million Americans who had not been able to get a high-speed connection because companies had no incentive to extend lines to rural areas with few customers. The FCC also lauded it as a way to create hundreds of thousands of jobs.

Obama's fiscal 2013 budget proposal also retained the president's priority of expanding coverage, proposing increased funding for FCC and the Commerce Department's National Telecommunications and Information Administration—two agencies leading an effort to increase availability of spectrum in order to expand wireless broadband. Some of the new spectrum would come from giving the FCC new authority to auction off spectrum from commercial broadcasters.

The FCC in April 2012 voted to gather information on a plan calling on businesses to invest in telephone and broadband expansion, basically revamping the Universal Service Fund. Then it announced in August that it had decided, in a party-line 3–2 vote, to suspend deregulation of the "special access" market, high-capacity broadband lines providing phone and Internet service to businesses, that were lines typically owned by major telecommunications companies. Those companies were required to lease them to smaller companies, but Democrats became concerned about reports that those companies were charging unfair rates to lease special access lines.

Meanwhile, with the presidential campaign in full swing, the Republican Party in its platform that fall criticized the execution of the administration's goal of universal connectivity, and criticized efforts to reform the Universal Service Fund. The platform asserted that the Obama administration "inherited from the previous Republican Administration 95 percent coverage of the nation with broadband. It will leave office with no progress toward the goal of universal coverage—after spending $7.2 billion more."

SPECTRUM AUCTION

The FCC outlined in its National Broadband Plan a timeline for getting 300 megahertz (MHz) of spectrum in the pipeline by 2015 through auction, with an additional 200 MHz opened up for auction by 2020. That would almost double the amount of spectrum that was available for wireless data at the time. But its auction proposal required congressional authorization, which it hoped to obtain in 2011 in time to begin the process in 2012 or 2013 that would ensure spectrum was clear for use in 2015. But it was not until 2012 that it obtained authorization to begin designing the auction and identifying the spectrum to be sold at auction.

Both parties generally agreed on the use of incentive auctions, but they disagreed on how the FCC should be permitted to conduct the auctions. Republicans drafted legislation to limit the commission's ability to set conditions on the auctions, but Senate Democrats opposed that restriction. Meanwhile, the lack of additional spectrum threatened to further slow down wireless networks, and many in the wireless industry predicted a "spectrum crisis."

House Committee Action

The House Energy and Commerce Subcommittee on Communications and Technology on December 1, 2011, approved, 17–6, a draft bill by Chair Greg Walden, R-Ore., that authorized the FCC to conduct spectrum auctions, to provide 10 MHz of electromagnetic spectrum known as the "D block" for use by first responders, and enabled the FCC to auction spectrum released voluntarily by broadcasters who would receive a portion of the proceeds. Marsha Blackburn, R-Tenn., added a provision barring the FCC from imposing network neutrality requirements on spectrum licensees, language strongly opposed by Senate Democrats.

Panel Republicans, who supported the bill along with Georgia Democrat John Barrow, said the legislation would allow for the expansion of mobile broadband, bolster the public safety network, create jobs, and help reduce the deficit. Democrats supported the provision for public safety use, but they wanted to allow the FCC to reserve some of the relinquished spectrum for unlicensed use. The draft bill also called for the network to be managed primarily by state broadband offices that would contract with private companies—language Democrats opposed. Henry Waxman, D-Calif., said "a profit-motivated private company could find ways to monetize the value of the license in its business dealings."

Senate Committee Action

The Senate Commerce, Science and Transportation Committee on June 8, 2011, approved a bill (S 911) by Chair John "Jay" Rockefeller, D-W.Va., by a vote of 21–4. Four Republicans voted no. The bill authorized the FCC to conduct the spectrum auctions and included language reallocating 10 MHz of the radio spectrum known as the "D block" to public safety. It also gave the FCC authority to conduct incentive auctions of commercial spectrum. Rockefeller said it would prevent communication failures like those that occurred on September 11, 2011, during the terrorist attacks in New York City and Washington, D.C., because first-responders could not communicate with each other.

"They were using conflicting radio equipment operating on different bandwidth and frequencies, calls were dropped, critical on-the-ground information was not relayed," Rockefeller said. His bill would allow some of the proceeds from the auctions to pay for the public safety network.

Jim DeMint, R-S.C., said he opposed giving away, rather than auctioning, the D block to the commercial sector and making network available for public safety during emergencies.

Among the amendments approved was one by Maria Cantwell, D-Wash., to ensure unlicensed spectrum in certain frequencies remained available.

Final Action

In December of that year, House and Senate aides worked to resolve differences between Rockefeller and Walden's measures. Major differences remained on the language designed to bolster a first-responder broadband network, as well as on the funding levels: Rockefeller's bill authorized $11.8 billion from future spectrum license auctions, while the House draft authorized about $5 billion. Differences also existed in language related to governance of the new network.

Ultimately, congressional leaders chose to add authorization for spectrum auctions to legislation on taxes, known as the Middle Class Tax Relief and Job Creation Act of 2011 (HR 3630—PL 112-96), which was signed on February 22, 2012.

The provisions added to the payroll tax-cut law included language authorizing the FCC to auction off wireless spectrum, with proceeds to be used to help pay for the tax cuts and unemployment benefits. It also promised a portion of the proceeds from the auctions to those television broadcasters who voluntarily give up wireless spectrum they were not using. The spectrum would be made available to wireless carriers looking to expand broadband services.

The legislation did not set limits on how the FCC could design the auctions but did say any new restrictions would have to go through an agency "notice and comment rulemaking" process. The legislation also included a provision to give public safety the 10 MHz of spectrum left over from a 700 MHz spectrum auction. It also permitted the use of unlicensed spectrum in the broadcast TV spectrum.

President Obama had requested indefinite FCC authority for spectrum auctions in its fiscal 2013 budget plan. Language in the final deal extended such authority until 2021. The Congressional Budget Office estimated it would generate $15 billion for the government over the next decade.

SATELLITE AND CABLE PROGRAMMING

With support from Congress and many in the industry, the FCC decided in a 5–0 vote in October 2012 to terminate rules from the 1992 Cable Act that required cable companies that produce and own TV programming to make it available on rival pay-TV platforms such as satellite and fiber-based video services offered by telephone companies. The rules had been established in the early years of the satellite broadcast industry when Congress wanted to ensure that cable operators that owned network programming would not refuse to sell that content to competitors.

Cable companies contended the rules were obsolete, particularly as satellite broadcasters DIRECTV and DISH Network had become established competitors in the industry. But satellite and telephone companies wanted to maintain the access rules, fearing that cable companies that also owned regional sports networks would refuse to sell programming on those channels.

Even before the FCC's action, Congress was debating eliminating the rules. Jim DeMint, R-S.C., who was expected to become the senior Republican on the Senate Commerce, Science, and Transportation Committee in the next Congress, had introduced legislation (S 2008) earlier in the year to repeal provisions of the 1992 law, saying the law was passed when few competitors to cable existed. But Sen. John Kerry, D-Mass., chair of the Communications, Technology, and Internet Subcommittee, contended the rules had fostered that competition among broadcast, cable, satellite, and online video providers. Senate Commerce Committee Chair John "Jay" Rockefeller, D-W.Va., warned that Congress might have to revisit the issue of program access.

Internet Gambling

Lobbyists pushing to legalize online gambling continued to face opposition from Republicans in Congress, but their position gained some strong support in 2011. The American Gaming Association, as well as big casino companies MGM and Caesars, joined in the effort under a lobbying group called Fair Play USA. Rep. Joe L. Barton, R-Texas, introduced legislation to overturn the 2006 law. *(Congress and the Nation Vol. XII, p. 423)*

Meanwhile, Barney Frank of Massachusetts, ranking Democrat on the House Financial Services Committee, and Barton worked together to try to convince the super committee on deficit reduction, set up under the Budget Control Act of 2011, to consider legalizing online gambling as a way to boost tax revenue and create jobs. Lawmakers interested in acting on the gaming issue felt further pressure when the Justice Department issued a memo in December 2011 that essentially cleared the way for states to legalize online poker and lotteries. The memo, written in response to questions from New York and Illinois about the legality of selling state lottery tickets online, said the 1961 Wire Act only applied to gambling on sporting events.

Senate Majority Leader Harry Reid, D-Nev., and Senate Minority Whip John Kyl, R-Ariz., in 2012 began crafting legislation to legalize online poker and off-track horse betting but outlaw other forms of online gaming. But the measure by that fall stalled as Reid and Kyl disagreed on how to move it. Reid had pushed Kyl and Sen. Dean Heller, R-Nev., a key backer, to help gather GOP votes to overcome a potential filibuster. But Kyl, author of the 2006 law, and Heller then suggested the House should go first. Barton said he assumed legislation would originate in the Senate.

Meanwhile, the National Governors Association (NGA) opposed such a move as several states, with permission granted in the Justice Department memo, began offering online gambling within their borders. In October 2012, the NGA sent a letter to House and Senate leaders requesting state input before they move on any online gaming legislation.

Internet Piracy

Halfway through the 112th Congress, protests by thousands of Internet-based companies, many of which blacked out their sites in a high-profile lobbying move on January 18, 2012, spurned efforts in Congress to pass legislation to restrict Internet piracy. Even the Gun Owners of America joined the protest, worried the bill might be used against them by gun control groups.

At the center of debate was a measure (HR 3261) introduced by House Judiciary Chair Lamar Smith, D-Texas, known as the Stop Online Piracy Act (SOPA), and a similar bill (S 968), called Preventing Real Online Threats to Economic Creativity and Theft of Intellectual Property Act or PIPA, introduced in the Senate by Judiciary Chair Patrick J. Leahy, D-Vt. The measures aimed to give the Justice Department and holders of intellectual property rights some legal tools to challenge foreign-based websites that infringe on copyrights to sell movies and music illegally—a practice commonly termed "piracy." Such legislation was advocated by record companies, the U.S. Chamber of Commerce, and Hollywood groups led by the Motion Picture Association that was headed by former senator Christopher Dodd, D-Conn.

Prominent Washington lobbyists and technology-sector trade organizations had been battling the measures since one such proposal had been introduced in the Senate in 2010. Since that time, other Hill priorities repeatedly shoved the issue lower on the agenda, and Sen. Ron Wyden, D-Ore., chair of the Finance Subcommittee on International Trade, Customers and Global Competitiveness, was a strong opponent of the measure.

Nevertheless, the Senate Judiciary Committee approved the bill by voice vote on May 26, 2011. Panel leaders then worked to try to address concerns on the legislation.

The House Judiciary Committee held a hearing on SOPA on November 16, and the social networking site Tumblr and many other websites posted messages protesting the legislation the day of that hearing. In December, the panel began considering Smith's bill and did not complete action, but had hopes of returning to it early the next year.

The January 18, 2012, protest came on the day of a hearing scheduled before House Oversight and Government Reform on a related issue of Internet domain-name blocking, which ultimately was cancelled even while the protest proceeded under the coordination of Fight for the Future, a nonprofit activist organization that claimed participation by more than 115,000 websites. While opponents generally agreed that Internet piracy was a problem, they argued that the measures could affect websites that do not engage in deliberate copyright infringement, give the government unwarranted censorship powers, and ultimately choke innovation and growth. Then questions arose about the definition of what constitutes an "infringing website" and about a provision to grant the Justice Department authority to seek court orders to bar search engines from steering web users to such sites.

Just a day before the protest, Senate Majority Leader Harry Reid, D-Nev., had vowed to move forward on a scheduled January 24 vote for cloture to end debate and proceed to the bill on the floor. But in the House, Smith halted plans to resume the committee markup of his bill, particularly as more GOP lawmakers, led by Government Reform Committee Chair Darrell Issa, R-Calif., expressed opposition.

Issa on January 18 offered a companion measure (HR 3782) to one (S 2029) introduced by Wyden in the Senate. Those proposals called on the International Trade Commission to move against foreign-based infringing sites, but Leahy and Smith opposed that idea. In the meantime, Leahy and Smith indicated they would be willing to drop language empowering the Justice Department to seek court orders to block domestic Internet users from accessing infringing foreign sites, and the Hollywood industry and others appeared ready to accept the move. But other provisions remained at the center of the disputes, and ultimately the legislation was abandoned, with supporters saying they would rethink how to draft a measure that would gain the support of the technology sector.

CHAPTER 7

Energy and Environment

Introduction 363

Chronology of Action on Energy and Environment 366

2009–2010 366

2011–2012 386

Energy and Environment

Barack Obama's election in 2008 appeared to promise a dramatic shift from the environmental and energy policies his predecessor, President George W. Bush. Whereas Bush had ties to the oil and gas industry, Obama spoke often of the need for more "green-collar" jobs and a greater reliance on emerging renewable and solar energy policies. He promised to begin combating climate change, which he characterized as one of the major challenges facing society, and put a greater stress on protecting and ensuring clean air and water.

As the 111th Congress began its work, Democratic lawmakers and the new president won a major victory in the winter of 2009. The economic stimulus package (HR 1—PL 111-5) contained tens of billions of dollars in initiatives designed to increase energy efficiency and boost renewable energy industries. These included provisions to make the electric grid more reliable, provide loan guarantees and grants for renewable energy generation and transmission, help Americans make their homes more energy-efficient, and develop technologies to reduce dependence on foreign oil.

Some Republicans warned that the provisions would interfere with the free market and plunge the government deeper into debt. But supporters said the proposals would not only put the United States on a more sustainable path but were also critical to helping the nation recover from the deep economic recession and compete globally. Underscoring the importance of clean energy to the economic stimulus, Obama signed the legislation in Denver in February after touring solar panels and meeting with the head of a locally based solar energy company. The legislation, he said, would help "transform the way we use energy."

The stimulus, however, represented the Democrats' high-water mark of the 111th Congress on energy and environmental issues. Part of the reason had to do with the economy; legislation that did not emphasize job creation or tighter scrutiny of the financial sector faced an uphill battle. In addition, the Democratic emphasis on the administration's top priority—health care—left limited time for other issues. But the reason also had to do with the most prominent issue on the environmental agenda: climate change. The notion of regulating greenhouse gases proved deeply unpopular with many in Congress, especially conservatives and those from states and districts with a strong reliance on the coal industry.

A deeply divided House narrowly passed legislation in June 2009 to cap greenhouse gas emissions. This marked the first time that either chamber had agreed to such an approach, and it took furious lobbying by Speaker Nancy Pelosi, D-Calif., and a Rose Garden speech and behind-the-scenes appeals by Obama. Even so, forty-four House Democrats, largely from conservative and rural districts, voted against the bill. Environmentalists would have lost more support had it not been for adroit maneuvering by Energy and Commerce Committee Chair Henry A. Waxman, D-Calif., who wooed

REFERENCES

Discussion of environmental and energy policy for the years 1945–1964 may be found in *Congress and the Nation Vol. I*, pp. 771–1095; for the years 1965–1968, *Congress and the Nation Vol. II*, pp. 463–528; for the years 1969–1972, *Congress and the Nation Vol. III*, pp. 745–849; for the years 1973–1976, *Congress and the Nation Vol. IV*, pp. 201–320; for the years 1977–1980, *Congress and the Nation Vol. V*, pp. 451–530, 533–597; for the years 1981–1984, *Congress and the Nation Vol. VI*, pp. 333–400, 403–482; for the years 1985–1988, *Congress and the Nation Vol. VII*, pp. 417–495; for the years 1989–1992, *Congress and the Nation Vol. VIII*, pp. 467–532; for the years 1993–1996, *Congress and the Nation Vol. IX*, pp. 401–476; for the years 1997–2001, *Congress and the Nation Vol. X*, pp. 341–414; for the years 2001–2004, *Congress and the Nation Vol. XI*, pp. 409–444; for the years 2005–2008, *Congress and the Nation Vol. XII*, pp. 443–505.

Outlays for Natural Resources and Environment

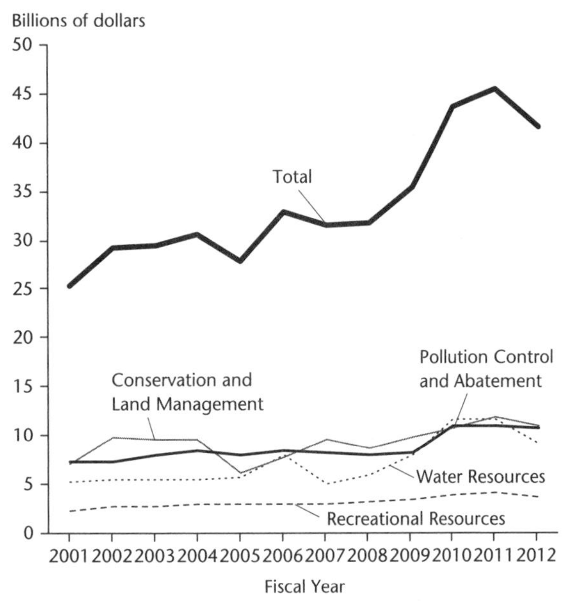

SOURCE: Office of Management and Budget, *Historical Tables, Budget of the United States Government: Fiscal Year 2013* (Washington, D.C.: U.S. Government Printing Office, 2012), Table 3.2.

NOTE: Total line includes some expenditures not shown separately.

farm-state Democrats with such last-minute provisions as putting the Agriculture Department, rather than the Environmental Protection Agency (EPA), in charge of special projects to reduce emissions in rural areas.

With cap-and-trade emerging as a potential midterm campaign issue and opposition mounting among Republicans and rural Democrats, the bill's momentum slowed in the Senate. Months elapsed before Environment and Public Works Chair Barbara Boxer, D-Calif., and Foreign Relations Chair John Kerry, D-Mass., introduced their climate change bill on September 30, and even then they left gaps to be filled based on negotiations. Boxer then pushed the bill through her committee over Republican objections to demonstrate progress in advance of international climate negotiations in Copenhagen, Denmark, in December, but she lost any real hope of a bipartisan agreement. Kerry opened negotiations with Lindsey Graham, R-S.C., and Joseph I. Lieberman, I-Conn., to try to reach a deal that would attract moderates and some Republicans. But as the health care debate reached a climax that left Congress bitterly divided, the climate bill lost all momentum in spring 2010.

Lawmakers similarly found themselves unable to advance energy legislation. In June 2009, the Senate Energy and Natural Resources Committee approved a bipartisan measure, seen as a component of the climate bill, that would have sharply increased electricity generated from renewable sources, opened vast new areas of the Gulf of Mexico to oil and gas drilling, and made it easier to find sites for new power transmission lines. But it died along with climate legislation. The following spring, the explosion of the Deepwater Horizon oil rig in the Gulf of Mexico spurred members of both parties to speak of the need for tougher oil drilling safety laws. Even though the House subsequently passed a bill to overhaul federal regulation of offshore drilling, differences over the scope and substance of the legislation led to the measure stalling in the Senate.

Instead of major legislative victories, Democrats had to take solace in such steps as boosting appropriations for key environmental programs and clearing a comprehensive public lands bill to designate more than two million acres of new wilderness areas and other protected lands.

The legislative landscape changed dramatically with the ascension of House Republicans to the majority in the 112th Congress following the 2010 midterm elections. Instead of seeking to take on climate change and boost funding for environmental programs, Democrats found themselves almost continually on the defensive.

Republicans viewed an overhaul of environmental regulations as critical for unleashing the potential of businesses and lifting the nation out of its economic malaise. To that end, the House passed a number of measures to relax federal oversight over activities ranging from power plant operations to pesticide use. Republicans also pressed for legislation to delay EPA regulations of greenhouse gases. But with Senate Democrats and the White House firmly opposed to such initiatives, lawmakers found themselves hopelessly stalemated.

Republicans also fell short of their goal of expanding domestic oil production. Amid concerns that few drilling permits had been issued since the Deepwater Horizon oil leak, the House passed a number of bills in both 2011 and 2012 to expand offshore drilling, open the Arctic National Wildlife Refuge to energy exploration and recovery activities, and require the Bureau of Land Management to begin issuing leases for oil shale under certain regulatory procedures. The House also voted to force the administration to take steps toward allowing more energy production on public lands and postponing implementation of new EPA regulations on air pollutants emitted by refineries. The measures, however, all died when the Senate declined to take them up.

A major flashpoint in the 112th Congress had to do with the proposed construction of the TransCanada Keystone XL pipeline from Canada to the Gulf of Mexico through the Great Plains. Republicans argued that the $7 billion, 1,700-mile pipeline would provide both a more secure source of oil to the United States and thousands of jobs for local workers. Environmental groups, however,

Outlays for Energy

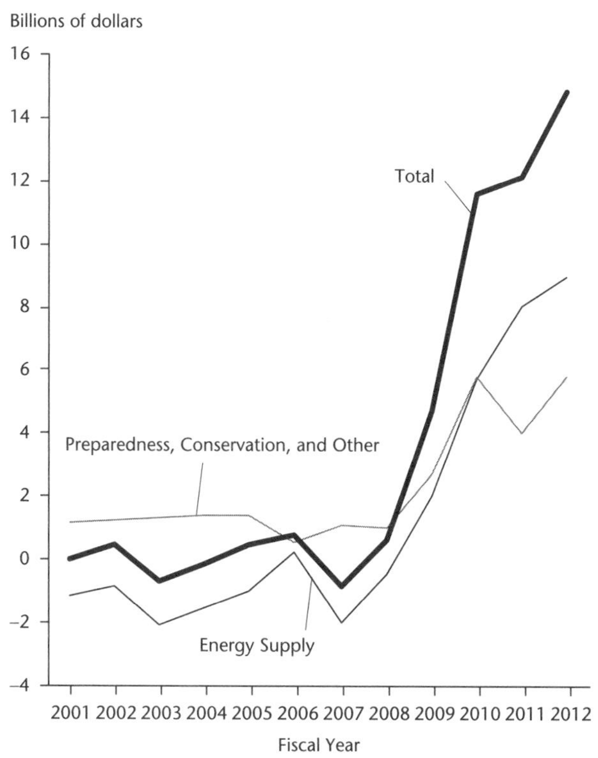

SOURCE: Office of Management and Budget, *Historical Tables, Budget of the United States Government: Fiscal Year 2013* (Washington, D.C.: U.S. Government Printing Office, 2012), Table 3.2.

allied with Midwestern farmers, landowners, and local activists, warned that a pipeline spill could contaminate the massive Ogallala Aquifer, a major source of irrigation and drinking water for the states in the region. The opponents also warned that extracting more oil from Canada's tar sands region would produce high levels of greenhouse gas emissions.

Republicans successfully added language in December 2011 to a one-year extension of the payroll tax cut that required the administration to decide on a permit for the Keystone XL pipeline within sixty days of the bill's enactment. *(Payroll tax action, p. 108)*

The following month, Obama rejected the permit application after the State Department said that the sixty-day window did not give officials enough time to complete the environmental review. Republicans in 2012 repeatedly returned to the issue, with the House adding language to a far-ranging surface transportation measure to try to get the pipeline approved. The Senate, however, refused to agree to the language.

With Democrats and Republicans so divided, the 112th Congress failed to clear any major stand-alone environmental or energy bills.

Conservatives, however, could claim modest victories, such as scaling back a handful of environmental regulations through the appropriations process and easing certain federal environmental requirements for transportation projects as part of a 2012 surface transportation bill. *(Surface transportation legislation, p. 340)*

President Barack Obama arrives March 22, 2012, to speak about the Keystone XL pipeline and his energy policies at the TransCanada Stillwater pipe yard in Cushing, Okla.

Source: AFP Photo/Mandel NGAN/AFP/GettyImages

Chronology of Action on Energy and Environment

2009–2010

Democrats failed to achieve their top environmental priority of the 111th Congress: clearing legislation to curb greenhouse gas emissions. The House narrowly passed legislation to combat global warming in June 2009, although a number of conservative Democrats joined almost all Republicans in opposing it. The biggest debate centered on the cap-and-trade model for reducing emissions, with supporters at odds over how soon to phase in stricter emissions caps. Lawmakers also disagreed over a number of other issues, including requirements that utilities provide more of their electricity from renewable sources.

Democrats on a deeply divided Senate Environment and Public Works Committee approved their version of the global warming bill in November 2009. But the cap-and-trade plan was fast losing momentum by the end of the year, facing intense opposition from Republicans and some Democrats while also competing with other White House priorities such as health care and Wall Street regulation.

A trio of senators—Democrat John F. Kerry of Massachusetts, Republican Lindsay Graham of South Carolina, and Independent Joseph I. Lieberman of Connecticut—sought to work across party lines to reach a compromise that could pass the Senate. But the talks fell apart in May 2010 when Graham walked away in a dispute over immigration legislation. The 2010 Gulf of Mexico oil spill complicated matters, which made it more difficult to use increased domestic offshore drilling to attract Republican votes. Although Kerry and Lieberman continued work on a scaled-back plan to cap only utilities emissions, they gave up before the midterm elections.

Congress also failed to advance a wide-ranging energy bill that was a separate component of the climate bill. The measure, which would sharply increase electricity generated from renewable sources, open vast new areas of the Gulf of Mexico to oil and gas drilling, and make it easier to find sites for new power transmission lines, won Senate Energy and Natural Resources Committee approval in June 2009 with bipartisan support after about two months of negotiations. But the measure failed to advance when the climate bill faded.

In the weeks after the April 20, 2010, explosion of the Deepwater Horizon oil rig in the Gulf of Mexico, members of both parties spoke of the need for tougher oil drilling safety laws. The House narrowly passed a bill in July 2010 to overhaul federal regulation of offshore drilling. But despite weeks of effort, Majority Leader Harry Reid, D-Nev., was unable to pass companion legislation in the Senate. Lawmakers differed sharply over both the scope and substance of the legislation, which focused on overhauling federal management of the outer continental shelf to address numerous legal, regulatory, and safety issues highlighted by the Gulf spill. The issue faded after the hole was plugged over the summer.

Despite such setbacks, Democrats could claim some major victories. Most notably, the 2009 economic stimulus legislation (HR 1—PL 111-5) contained tens of billions of dollars in initiatives designed to increase energy efficiency and boost renewable energy industries. These ranged from making the electric grid more reliable and efficient to providing loan guarantees and grants for renewable energy generation and transmission.

Congress in 2009 also cleared an omnibus federal lands bill that had long been delayed by procedural roadblocks. The legislation combined more than 150 measures to designate more than two million acres of new wilderness areas, along with wild and scenic rivers, historic sites, scenic trails, and other protected lands. Democrats also turned to spending bills to strengthen environmental protections, using the fiscal 2010 Interior-Environment bill—as well as the economic stimulus—to inject additional funds into the Environmental Protection Agency and Interior Department.

ENERGY, ENVIRONMENT LEADERSHIP

Department of Energy

President Barack Obama nominated Steven Chu, director of the Energy Department's Lawrence Berkeley National Laboratory and a Nobel laureate in physics, to head the Department of Energy. Chu's emphasis on technology and innovation to help solve energy and climate problems appealed to both environmentalists and leaders of the energy industry, and he enjoyed a reputation as bridging academia with commercial applications. At his confirmation hearing, he said he would put a greater focus at the Energy Department on global warming. While calling for investments in energy efficiency and renewable energy, he also presented himself as a pragmatist who believed the nation's energy needs would require new nuclear plants, continued reliance on coal-fired power plants, and oil and gas drilling.

Chu's qualifications drew praise from senators on both sides of the aisle. He was confirmed by voice vote on January 20, 2009.

Department of Interior

Obama's selection of Sen. Ken Salazar, D-Colo., as secretary of the Interior drew little controversy, although some environmentalists were wary of his perceived close ties with the coal and mining industries and some conservatives raised concerns about his views on oil shale development and drilling in environmentally sensitive areas. At his confirmation hearing before the Senate Energy and Natural Resources Committee, Salazar said his priorities would include reducing the nation's dependency on foreign oil, expanding the use of renewable energy, investing in new water conservation technologies, and modernizing the interstate electrical grid. Senate Republicans and Democrats alike praised the nomination. The Senate approved the nomination on voice vote on January 21, 2009.

Environmental Protection Agency

A chemical engineer by training, Lisa Jackson had been the New Jersey commissioner of environmental education before Obama tapped her to be his Environmental Protection Agency administrator. In her confirmation hearing before the Senate Environment and Public Works Committee, Jackson signaled an active approach toward environmental issues. She said she would serve Americans who suffered from "environmental negligence" such as the effects from untended Superfund sites or the government's botched response to Hurricane Katrina. Despite concerns by some conservatives, the Senate confirmed her on voice vote on January 23, 2009.

Climate Change

Creating a system to combat global warming was one of President Barack Obama's chief legislative aims, and he urged Congress to send him a bill in time for an international climate conference in Copenhagen in December 2009. Sweeping legislation squeaked through the House in June 2009, marking the first time that either chamber had passed a bill designed to curb greenhouse gas emissions. But companion legislation stalled in the Senate without making it to the floor for a vote. The highly controversial measure faced intense opposition from Republicans and a handful of Democrats, and the White House eventually put a greater emphasis on other priorities, such as Wall Street regulation.

The House-passed bill (HR 2454) called for a cap on greenhouse gas emissions at 17 percent of 2005 levels by 2050 and a system for buying and selling emissions credits. The bill also sought to encourage energy efficiency and spur the production and use of clean energy, including a requirement that electric utilities supply a percentage of their electricity from renewable sources, plus new subsidies and regulatory incentives for energy-related industries. Winning over enough moderate House Democrats to pass the bill required extensive concessions to members representing coal-producing, manufacturing, and farm states, plus intense lobbying by the White House. Even then, it took eight Republicans who broke with their party to provide a winning margin.

The Senate Energy and Natural Resources Committee approved an energy bill (S 1462) in June 2009 with provisions to increase electricity generated from renewable sources, open new areas of the Gulf of Mexico to drilling, and make it easier to find sites for new transmission lines. The measure was seen as one component of a comprehensive energy-climate bill. Before the summer recess, Senate Democratic leaders said they were on track to bring a global warming bill, together with the energy provisions, to the floor in the fall, with the goal of passing it in time for the Copenhagen conference. But Environment and Public Works Chair Barbara Boxer, D-Calif., and Foreign Relations Chair John Kerry, D-Mass., did not introduce their climate change bill (S 1733) until September 30, and they left gaps to be filled as negotiations progressed.

Boxer quickly pushed the bill through her committee, but at the cost of losing any semblance of partisan comity. By then, Kerry had stepped away from the bill, acknowledging that it had little chance of winning the sixty votes needed in the Senate to prevent a filibuster. Instead, he teamed up with Lindsey Graham, R-S.C., and Joseph I.

Lieberman, I-Conn., to begin drafting a bipartisan bill aimed at attracting moderate Democrats and some Republicans. But with the Senate deep in the health care debate and several committees yet to weigh in, further action was pushed into 2010, when the approach of midterm elections was likely to make passing a bill even more difficult.

ECONOMIC STIMULUS BILL BOOSTED ENERGY STRATEGY

Although Democrats failed to win enactment of major stand-alone energy legislation or a climate change bill, the 2009 economic stimulus legislation (HR 1—PL 111-5) contained sweeping provisions designed to increase energy efficiency and boost renewable energy industries. *(Economic stimulus legislation, p. 78)*

The House Energy and Commerce Committee approved much of the energy portion of the stimulus package on January 21 on a 34–17 vote. The measure included $54 billion for energy initiatives, such as making the electric grid more reliable and efficient and providing loan guarantees for renewable energy generation and transmission. The House Ways and Means Committee also approved energy provisions, including grants for wind, solar, and other projects, and a 30 percent investment tax credit for renewable energy technologies. The House passed the bill on January 28. Senate committees quickly followed and that chamber passed HR 1 on February 10. Reflecting the dire economic conditions throughout the United States, differences were quickly resolved and the bill sent to the president on February 13.

The energy title of the stimulus package was less controversial than other elements, and it largely survived legislative passage through the Senate and conference.

Republicans on the House committee offered amendments designed to tweak provisions. But they generally said they were comfortable with most of the plan's spending priorities, including weatherizing and retrofitting public buildings and low-income housing. Ranking Republican Joe L. Barton of Texas said of the provisions on such priorities as renewable energy, electricity transmission, and energy efficiency: "Those are all laudable goals, and if energy funds were spent right, they might yield some real results."

The final version of the stimulus bill, signed into law by President Barack Obama on February 17, contained close to $50 billion for energy programs.

Highlights included the following:

- $4.5 billion to modernize the electric grid.
- $5 billion for the Weatherization Assistance Program, helping low-income families make their homes more energy efficient.
- $3.2 billion in Energy Efficiency and Conservation Block Grants.
- $3.1 billion for state energy programs.
- $300 million for Energy Efficient Appliance Rebate Programs.
- $9.75 billion for the modernization of schools, including higher-education buildings.
- $4.5 billion to convert federal buildings to convert federal facilities to "High-Performance Green Buildings," along with an additional $400 million to establish an Office of Federal High-Performance Green Buildings.
- $3.6 billion to modernize Department of Defense facilities, including making them more energy efficient.
- $400 million research for the Advanced Research Projects Agency-Energy to develop technologies that reduce dependency on foreign oil, improve the energy efficiency of all economic sectors, and reduce greenhouse gas emissions.
- $2.5 billion for the Department of Energy's Office of Energy Efficiency and Renewable Energy, with specific subtotals directed for the development biomass and geothermal technologies.
- $6 billion for the development of advanced technologies that reduce air pollutants and the emission of greenhouse gases.
- $250 million for grants or loans for energy-saving retrofits and green investments to Section 8 housing owners.
- $1 billion for public housing agencies, including renovations and energy conservation retrofit investments.
- $2.4 billion in qualified energy conservation bonds to finance state, municipal, and tribal government programs, and initiatives designed to reduce greenhouse gas emissions.
- Tripling of tax credits to homeowners for residential energy-efficient improvements, up to $1,500 per household.
- 30 percent investment tax credit for the manufacture of "advanced energy property," including technology for the production of renewable energy, energy storage, energy conservation, efficient transmission and distribution of technology, and carbon capture and sequestration.
- Grants to businesses for specified energy systems placed in service during 2009 or 2010, including combined heat and power systems, geothermal heat pumps, fuel cells, and microturbines.
- Increase in monthly exclusion for employer-provided transit and vanpool benefits
- Modification of plug-in electric drive motor vehicle credits.

The biggest fight centered on the cap-and-trade model for reducing emissions, with moderates and environmentalists at odds over how soon to phase in stricter emissions caps. Another controversial question was which businesses or consumer groups should receive emissions permits, worth billions of dollars each year, to cushion them from the impact of higher energy costs. Supporters and opponents also disagreed over the potential impact on consumers' utilities bills and whether the legislation would create new "green" jobs or push existing jobs overseas. The requirement in the House bill that utilities provide more of their electricity from renewable sources worried southeastern lawmakers, who said their states lacked the wind and solar resources that could benefit other regions.

Rural Senate Democrats, led by Blanche Lincoln of Arkansas, chair of the Agriculture, Nutrition and Forestry Committee, raised questions about the bill's treatment of agriculture. Other senators were expected to try to include new incentives for nuclear power plants, which did not emit greenhouse gases but were unpopular with many environmentalists and would require huge government support. Several midwestern Democrats also conditioned their support on the inclusion of tariffs on imports from countries such as China and India that refused to reduce their emissions. The House bill included such a provision, but Obama opposed it, saying it would complicate global trade talks.

The Congressional Budget Office (CBO) and the Joint Committee on Taxation estimated that the House bill would result in a net reduction in the federal deficit of about $24 billion in fiscal years 2010 through 2019. Most of the revenue would come from auctioning off emissions allowances.

HIGHLIGHTS

The following are highlights of the House-passed bill:

Emissions caps. Beginning in 2012, the EPA would issue allowances that would effectively be permits to emit greenhouse gases. One allowance would equal 1 metric ton of carbon dioxide or an equivalent amount of another gas. The number of allowances would serve to cap emissions, bringing them down to 83 percent of 2005 emissions by 2020 and 17 percent by 2050. The EPA would distribute a percentage of the emissions allowances to polluters by formula, free of change, and the rest would be sold at auction. In 2012, more than three-quarters of the allowances would be distributed for free. By 2030, most allowances would be auctioned. An industry that exceeded its emissions cap would be subject to fines, with the money going to the EPA. Greenhouse gases would be defined as including carbon dioxide, methane, nitrous oxide, sulfur hexafluoride, and hydrofluorocarbons.

Emissions trading. A company could buy pollution allowances from another business in lieu of meeting its obligation to reduce emissions. The trades would have to be registered with the EPA, which would track the allowances and make the information public. Polluters could also "borrow" allowances from future years to cover current emissions. The Commodity Futures Trading Commission would have regulatory authority over new derivatives markets.

Emission offsets. Polluters could also offset part of their emissions through carbon sequestration and other projects that reduce greenhouse gas emissions. Like allowances, the offsets could be bought and sold. In an important concession to farm-state lawmakers, the Agriculture Department, rather than the EPA, would be given authority over offsetting projects in rural and agricultural areas.

Clean energy. Utilities would be required to meet a certain percentage of their load with electricity generated from renewable sources, such as wind and the sun, and from electricity savings resulting from greater efficiencies. The requirement would begin at 6 percent in 2012—double the level being achieved in 2009—and gradually rise to 20 percent in 2020. Allowances would also be available to companies that burned coal or petroleum coke and were developing technologies for carbon capture and storage, a technique that involved separating carbon dioxide from other gases emitted during the coal gasification process and storing it in geologic formations deep underground. The bill would allocate a percent of the allowances to companies investing in renewable-energy production and in the development of clean-vehicle technology. Technology to capture carbon dioxide existed, but storage was still in an experimental stage. Meeting the renewable-source goal—which would require an overhaul of the way electricity was generated, distributed, and sold—was viewed as the first major step in reducing greenhouse gas emissions and U.S. dependence on fossil fuels.

Energy efficiency. The bill would establish a national goal of increasing energy productivity by 2.5 percent per year from 2012 through 2030. By 2014, residential buildings would be required to use 30 percent less energy than comparable buildings built to standards established in 2006. New commercial buildings would have to use 50 percent less by 2015. New energy and fuel efficiency standards would be established for appliances, light fixtures, metropolitan transportation systems, government vehicle fleets, most government buildings, and many other uses.

HOUSE COMMITTEE ACTION

The House Energy and Commerce Committee approved the bill (HR 2454—H Rept 111-137, Part 1) by a vote of 33–25 on May 21, 2009, following four days of deliberation and several weeks of behind-the-scenes negotiations among Democrats with widely differing priorities. It marked the first time a House committee had approved comprehensive climate change legislation.

In action on some of the amendments, the committee:

- Rejected, 19–35, a Republican substitute that would have replaced the cap-and-trade program with a requirement that utilities lower greenhouse gas emissions relative to the amount of electricity generated. It would have expanded the bill's renewable-energy mandate to include nuclear power, hydropower, and clean-coal technology.

- Adopted by voice vote an amendment by Zack Space, D-Ohio, to clarify that the value of pollution credits allocated to electric utilities would be used to benefit ratepayers, not stockholders.
- Adopted by voice vote a proposal by G. K. Butterfield, D-N.C., and Baron P. Hill, D-Ind., to adjust a requirement for the EPA to set emissions standards for new vehicles and construction equipment. It would direct the agency to target large polluters from which the greatest reductions would be achievable.
- Adopted by voice vote amendments by Bruce Braley, D-Iowa, to provide loan guarantees for pipelines that would transport renewable fuels and by Jay Inslee, D-Wash., to authorize grants and a loan guarantee program for the adoption of high-capacity transmission technology.
- Rejected, 22–32, an amendment by Mike Rogers, R-Mich., to end the cap-and-trade program if it led to a loss of jobs in manufacturing industries. It was one of several GOP amendments that would have phased out key provisions of the bill if they were found to cause economic harm.

In response to concerns voiced in the committee, Chair Henry A. Waxman, D-Calif., said it would be premature to list specific agricultural projects that would be eligible for offsets before the EPA determined how to measure their effects on the environment. Waxman was the bill's sponsor.

Committee ranking Republican Joe L. Barton of Texas and other Republicans threatened to offer hundreds of amendments and use other procedural tactics to delay the bill. But after several days of stalling, they backed down when it became clear that Waxman was all but certain to win approval. Barton told Waxman that he did not agree with the bill but was "very much impressed with your ability in your first major test as chair to keep the committee functioning in a collegial way, which is no trivial accomplishment."

The bill largely skirted the issue of how the federal government might be able to site transmission lines to deliver renewable energy. However, Waxman said he would work on a floor amendment.

HOUSE FLOOR ACTION

The House on a **key vote of 219–212 (R 8–168; D 211–44)** passed the bill the evening of June 26, 2009, in the last legislative business before the July Fourth recess. The forty-four members of the Democratic Caucus who voted against the legislation were mostly from conservative and rural districts. *(2009 key votes, p. 751)*

The vote followed a day of furious lobbying by Speaker Nancy Pelosi, D-Calif., and other party leaders to win over wavering members, as well as a last-ditch effort by Minority Leader John A. Boehner, R-Ohio, to stall action with what amounted to a rare House equivalent of a filibuster. Using his privileges as a floor leader to circumvent the time limit for debate, Boehner spent about an hour quoting from a 300-page substitute amendment that contained numerous changes negotiated by Democratic leaders.

Urged by bill supporters to throw his popularity behind the legislation, Obama delivered a Rose Garden speech June 25 urging fence-sitters to support the bill, button-holed members at a White House luau for lawmakers that night, and made a round of telephone calls during the floor debate the next day. Republicans and business groups opposed to the climate change bill continued to argue that it would drive up costs to consumers and businesses and would cost American jobs. "The American people will remember this vote of this Congress," said Boehner, who vowed to make the legislation a campaign issue.

In the push to win the final votes, Waxman met with blocs of Democratic lawmakers to tweak and amend pieces of the bill. His changes were made automatically by the rule for floor debate, which was adopted, 217–205. The rule included provisions to woo farm-state members, reflecting an agreement between Waxman and Agriculture Chair Collin C. Peterson, D-Minn. Peterson said the changes picked up three or four votes for the bill. The provisions would:

- Put the Agriculture Department, rather than the EPA, in charge of special projects to reduce emissions in rural areas—for example, by planting trees on farmland.
- Redefine biomass to include most types of plant and wood production byproducts.
- Exempt agriculture and forestry entities, such as farms, from the bill's emissions caps.

Other changes made by the rule would:

- Exempt existing biodiesel plants from EPA renewable-fuels assessments.
- Impose tariffs on products from countries that had not adopted greenhouse gas emissions controls if the administration determined that other programs designed to mitigate the domestic impact had been insufficient. A presidential waiver would have to be approved by a joint resolution of Congress within ninety days.
- Give states the option, as an alternative to the requirement that electric utilities produce a certain percentage of electricity from renewable-energy sources, of requiring consumers to pay a fee with their electric bills that would be used by the state to promote the use of renewable-energy sources to generate electricity.
- Make vehicles fueled by natural gas eligible for clean-vehicle incentives and manufacturing incentives.
- Provide incentives to lenders and financial institutions to offer lower interest loans and other benefits to consumers who built, bought or remodeled homes or businesses to improve energy efficiency.

Before passing the bill, the House rejected, 172–256, a Republican substitute offered by J. Randy Forbes of Virginia to strike the text of the bill and replace it with provisions authorizing $24 billion for fiscal years 2010 through 2019 for the Energy Department to establish a grant program and prize system to reward researchers, businesses, universities, and certain individuals for work on sustainable-fuel and energy-efficient technologies. It also proposed a new commission to report recommendations to Congress for the United States to achieve 50 percent energy independence within ten years and 100 percent energy independence within twenty years.

SENATE ENERGY BILL

The Senate Energy and Natural Resources Committee approved a wide-ranging energy bill by a vote of 15–8 on June 17, with the support of ranking Republican Lisa Murkowski of Alaska and three other Republicans. The bill (S 1462—S Rept 111-48), which was marked up in pieces over two months, contained provisions that would sharply increase electricity generated from renewable sources, open vast new areas of the Gulf of Mexico to oil and gas drilling, and make it easier to site power transmission lines. The bill was viewed as a component of the climate legislation.

The bipartisan support reflected the compromises engineered during eleven markups over more than two months by Chair Jeff Bingaman, D-N.M., who won over Republicans by adding language to expand offshore drilling and weakening what was originally a stronger renewable-electricity mandate on utilities. The following are among the bill's central provisions:

Electricity standards. Fifteen percent of the nation's power would have to come from renewable sources, such as wind and the sun, by 2021, including up to 4 percent from energy savings that resulted from improved efficiency. That was a significant increase from the 3 percent that was required at the time, but it was lower than both the 25 percent sought by the White House and the 20 percent in Bingaman's initial draft and in the House bill. Reducing the standard to 15 percent enabled Bingaman to win support from several committee members whose states had limited wind and solar resources and who feared the higher standard would raise their utility costs. However, Bingaman and other Democrats said they would try to raise the requirement to 20 percent or 25 percent during Senate floor consideration.

The panel rejected by voice vote an amendment by Byron L. Dorgan, D-N.D., to raise the renewable standard to 20 percent. It also rejected, 9–13, a proposal by Murkowski and Jeff Sessions, R-Ala., to eliminate the electricity title from the bill.

Offshore drilling. The committee adopted, 13–10, a Dorgan amendment to allow drilling for oil and gas as close as forty-five miles off the west coast of Florida, as well as in the Destin Dome, a natural gas formation twenty-five miles off the coast of Pensacola. The proposal was designed to win GOP support, but it drew sharp opposition from Florida Democrat Bill Nelson, who threatened to filibuster the measure when it reached the Senate floor. Nelson said the provision violated an agreement to preserve a large buffer off Florida's beaches that was created to win support for a 2006 law (PL 109-432) that expanded drilling in the Gulf. (*Congress and the Nation Vol. XII, p. 471*)

The committee rejected, 10–13, an amendment by Mary L. Landrieu, D-La., to allow coastal states to receive a percentage of the royalties that oil companies paid for the expanded drilling. The 2006 drilling law allowed four Gulf states to share in offshore royalties. Most Republicans backed the Landrieu amendment, which would have advanced the GOP energy agenda by offering coastal states a financial incentive to support offshore drilling. Democrats, led by Bingaman, argued that offshore resources belong to the entire country and should be used for deficit reduction.

Offshore royalties. The committee adopted, 12–11, a Bingaman amendment to repeal a 2005 reduction in royalty payments on some offshore Gulf leases. The lower royalties had been authorized (PL 109-58) to encourage production, but by 2007 even the George W. Bush administration said the incentives were no longer needed in light of dramatic increases in oil and gas prices. (*Congress and the Nation Vol. XII, p. 446*)

Transmission lines. Under Bingaman's draft, the federal government would be empowered to locate new sites for thousands of miles of new electricity transmission lines, superseding state and local authorities. The committee rejected, 7–16, an amendment by Robert Menendez, D-N.J., to eliminate language that would permit the federal government to use eminent domain, if necessary, to overrule local authorities in choosing the location of new power lines. Bingaman said the amendment would "effectively neutralize the entire title," and would "elevate the NIMBY [not in my backyard] status" for siting high-priority transmission lines.

Nuclear energy. Provisions on nuclear energy focused on creating a national commission to find a solution to the country's nuclear waste problem, promoting research and development on advanced fuel-recycling processes, and ensuring that any advanced fuel-recycling facilities would be subject to licensing, regulation, and environmental requirements.

Republicans were largely unsuccessful in seeking to include incentives for nuclear power plants. Although nuclear was the only major power source that did not emit greenhouse gases, it remained unpopular with many environmentalists. The committee rejected, 10–13, an amendment by John McCain, R-Ariz., to include nuclear in the definition of renewable energy for the purposes of the electricity mandate. A McCain amendment to express the sense of the Senate that the federal government should move forward with plans and actions to store spent nuclear fuel at the Yucca Mountain, Nev., nuclear waste repository was also rejected, 10–13.

A Murkowski substitute amendment would have allowed the Energy Department to enter into cost-sharing agreements with the industry to design nuclear waste reprocessing facilities. "The amendment gives the public and nuclear industry the confidence it needs to move forward," she said. But it was rejected, 11–11.

Arctic National Wildlife Refuge. Murkowski sought to revive a decades-old GOP goal of permitting drilling in the Arctic National Wildlife Refuge, but with a new twist: drilling sideways, using a directional drill that would not disturb the pristine surface of the protected wilderness. "This kind of drilling would be siphoning, like a straw," she said. "The caribou don't know you're there; the native hunters don't know you're there. There can be no impact on the surface of the refuge or the wildlife that live there." The amendment failed, 10–13, but Bingaman acknowledged that the new technology could help keep the debate alive.

SENATE GLOBAL WARMING LEGISLATION

The Senate Environment and Public Works Committee approved its global warming bill (S 1733—S Rept 111-121) by a vote of 11–1 on November 5, 2009. As with the House measure (HR 2454), the bill proposed to cap emissions of carbon dioxide and other greenhouse gases and allow polluters to buy and sell government-issued emissions allowances. Republicans boycotted the session, saying they wanted to see a full EPA cost analysis. A preliminary EPA assessment said the bill's costs would be similar to those of the House climate provisions; the agency said it would take another four to five weeks to produce a more thorough assessment.

But Boxer was in a hurry to get the bill marked up before the international climate meeting in Copenhagen began December 7. Accusing Republicans of stalling, she used a technicality in the rules that allowed the panel to vote on a bill without anyone from the opposing party present as long as there were no amendments. Republicans were furious. "We have not been able to find a time when a bill has been marked up without minority participation," said James M. Inhofe of Oklahoma, the committee's ranking Republican.

Kerry and Boxer had filed the long-awaited bill on September 30, but it was full of blank spots and placeholders—including the crucial formula for distributing billions of dollars' worth of emissions allowances to coal and natural gas utilities and states, as well as for advanced vehicle technology development. They said it was an opening bid that would be substantially reshaped in the subsequent months in an effort to reach the sixty votes they would need on the floor. Boxer released a more detailed version before hearings in late October, but it still included placeholders.

The bill hewed closely to the outline of the House-passed measure. It followed a standard cap-and-trade model, requiring that polluters purchase allowances for each ton of greenhouse gas they emitted and creating a market in which allowances could be bought and sold. Like the House bill, it proposed an 83 percent reduction in emissions from 2005 levels by 2050. The Senate bill was more ambitious in the short term, however, setting a reduction target of 20 percent by 2020, compared with 17 percent in the House bill. Baucus and other coal state moderates worried that the 20 percent midrange target was too aggressive and would hurt their states.

Under both bills, most of the allowances would be given out in the early years, but eventually most would be auctioned. As in the House bill, the majority of permits would be given to electric utility customers and local electricity distribution companies to help defray their higher costs. In the early years, states would get about 10 percent of the permits to invest in renewable energy and efficiency.

SENATE BIPARTISAN BILL

Even as the Senate Environment and Public Works Committee's public deliberations were descending into partisan acrimony, Kerry was teaming up with Graham and Lieberman in talks aimed at constructing a bill that could draw support from both parties. The outline called for incentives to promote nuclear power and offshore drilling to draw Republicans, as well as funding for carbon sequestration technology to win over coal-state Democrats.

"The Kerry-Boxer bill is no longer on track," Murkowski said. "We've been talking a lot about starting over with a blank piece of paper, and if this allows for that, then that's a positive."

The effort got a boost in November with the cautious endorsement of the U.S. Chamber of Commerce, which had led opposition to other climate change legislation, including the House-passed bill. The chamber described the framework for compromise that Kerry and Graham laid out as "positive, practical and realistic." As recently as August, the Chamber had filed a petition questioning the scientific basis of the EPA finding that global warming endangered the public health. Several major corporations, including Apple, Inc., and Pacific Gas & Electric Co., quit the Chamber over its climate change stance, and Nike, Inc., resigned from the group's board.

Environmental Protection Agency Regulation

As lawmakers debated the issue, President Barack Obama's administration gradually stepped up the pressure on Congress by warning that, in the absence of legislation, the Environmental Protection Agency (EPA) was preparing to act on its own. Under a 2007 Supreme Court decision in *Massachusetts v. EPA* (549 U.S. 497), the agency was told to determine whether carbon dioxide and other greenhouse gases were pollutants that endangered public health and welfare and were therefore subject to regulation under the Clean Air Act Amendments (PL 101-549). *(Congress and the Nation Vol. VIII, p. 473)*

On April 17, 2009, the EPA issued a preliminary finding of endangerment. On September 15, the agency and the Transportation Department proposed vehicle emissions standards to combat global warming. On December 7, the opening day of the international climate control meeting in Copenhagen, the EPA issued its long-awaited finding that greenhouse gases qualified as dangerous pollutants under the Clean Air Act, paving the way for the agency to impose regulations. "After a thorough examination of the scientific evidence and careful consideration of public comments," the agency said in a statement, "the U.S. Environmental Protection Agency (EPA) announced today that greenhouse gases (GHGs) threaten the public health and welfare of the American people," adding that emissions from these gases "are the primary driver of climate change."

The endangerment finding covered emissions of six key greenhouse gases: carbon dioxide, methane, nitrous oxide, hydrofluorocarbons, perfluorocarbons, and sulfur hexafluoride. The EPA said that on-road vehicles contributed more than 23 percent of total gas emissions.

2010 LEGISLATIVE ACTION

Despite continued negotiations among industry, environmentalists, and senators from both parties, designed to reach a grand bargain to link caps on emissions to incentives to expand nuclear energy and offshore drilling, supporters never came close to the sixty votes necessary to move such a bill past a filibuster in the Senate.

Kerry, Lieberman, and Graham led an effort that targeted a handful of moderate Republicans, while working to address the concerns of Democrats who represented midwestern manufacturers and coal-producing states. With oil gushing into the Gulf of Mexico following the April 2010 explosion of an offshore-drilling rig, supporters of carbon caps saw the spill as a new opportunity to push for an overhaul.

The talks broke down in May 2010 when Graham walked away in a dispute over immigration legislation, and the 2010 Gulf oil spill made it tougher to sell the idea of increasing domestic offshore drilling, which was included to attract GOP support. Kerry and Lieberman continued negotiating with industry and environmentalists on a scaled-back plan to cap only utilities emissions, but they gave up before the midterm elections.

Postelection efforts to take up a stand-alone bill for renewable-energy standards failed to generate the sixty votes needed on the Senate floor.

The one Senate victory for those who favored taking action against climate change took place when the Senate in 2010 rejected a GOP resolution that would have stripped the EPA of its authority to regulate greenhouse gas emissions. On a **key vote of 47–53 (R 41–0; D 6–51; I 0–2)** on June 10, 2010, senators voted against proceeding on a resolution (S J Res 26) sponsored by Murkowski that would have overturned the EPA's finding that the gases are hazardous to human health. *(2010 key votes, p. 767)*

That "endangerment finding" triggered a requirement to regulate emissions under the Clean Air Act (PL 101-549). But Murkowski and other resolution backers said it was Congress's role to regulate gases that contribute to global warming. "This is a check on the EPA's regulatory ambitions," Murkowski said. Democrats painted the GOP argument as disingenuous, contending that many of those backing the resolution have resisted efforts to address global warming.

Lieberman said the resolution would reject a science-based finding that greenhouse gases endanger public health. "This looks an awful lot to me like trying to impose political judgments on scientific judgments—and that is wrong," he said.

Graham voted for the resolution, but he challenged colleagues to get serious about addressing climate change. "Carbon is bad—let's do something about it in a common-sense way," Graham said. "You don't have to believe in global warming to want to have clean air."

National Climate Service

A bill to create a national service to predict changes in climate was approved in 2009 by the House Science and Technology Committee as part of the Democrats' focus on global warming. In a nearly party-line vote, the panel on June 3 voted 24–12 to approve the measure (HR 2407). Republicans on the panel questioned the need for a National Climate Service and forced debate on a handful of amendments. One Republican, Bob Inglis of South Carolina, voted for the bill.

Ranking Republican Ralph M. Hall of Texas said the committee was rushing to create the office, which would be housed under the National Oceanic and Atmospheric Administration.

"We are well aware of drought forecasts and other such physical science products," he said in his opening remarks. "But we have also been told that climate products and services require the expertise and knowledge in a myriad of disciplines."

Chair Bart Gordon, D-Tenn., expressed confidence that the service would offer valuable and needed data on climate change. "We have built infrastructure, projected water availability, developed cropping systems and managed coastal resources, assuming a range of weather and climate is undergoing change," he said. "Without more specific information about the magnitude and direction of these changes, we will be ill-prepared to exploit new opportunities and to adapt to new challenges."

The panel rejected GOP amendments designed to create bureaucratic barriers to the immediate creation of a climate service and prevent climate "change" from being referenced in the bill. Pete Olson, R-Texas, who offered the latter amendment, said the bill as written would focus the office on causes of climate change, such as greenhouse gas emissions, instead of the environmental effects of that change.

Public Lands

Congress in 2009 cleared an omnibus federal lands bill that was long delayed by procedural roadblocks from opponents. The House cleared the bill (HR 146—PL 111-11) by agreeing to Senate amendments, 285–140, on March 25. The legislation combined more than 150 measures designating more than two million acres of new wilderness areas, along with wild and scenic rivers, historic sites, scenic trails, and other protected lands.

Although the bill's passage was never in doubt, Democrats were wary of Republican amendments, most likely on gun rights issues, that could be difficult votes for their caucus. They used procedural maneuvers to pass it by a simple majority vote, without allowing amendments or a last-minute motion to recommit the bill.

House Republicans complained bitterly about their inability to bring up amendments. One amendment the GOP wanted to offer concerned gun rights in national parks. Just before leaving office, the George W. Bush administration published a rule to allow loaded guns in the parks, reversing a long-standing policy that guns had to be concealed and stowed. But a federal judge placed an injunction on the rule after finding that the Interior Department had not conducted a proper analysis.

The measure authorized water rights settlements in western states, and it established new programs in the Interior Department on water reclamation and the effects of climate change on water availability. It authorized programs on ocean exploration, undersea research, and ocean acidification in the National Oceanic and Atmospheric Administration.

Some of the major new wilderness areas the bill designated were about 517,000 acres in Idaho's Owyhee-Bruneau Canyonlands; about 256,000 acres in Washington County, Utah, including in Zion National Park; and almost 250,000 acres in Rocky Mountain National Park, Colo.

The Senate had passed its first version of the measure (S 22) on January 15 by a vote of 73–21. It lumped together more than 160 public lands that had been introduced in the 110th Congress. Democrat Jeff Bingaman of New Mexico, chair of the Energy and Natural Resources Committee, called it "the most significant conservation legislation passed by the Senate in many years."

The measure also codified a National Landscape Conservation System that President Bill Clinton established by executive order. The goal was to improve management of already protected federal land. A number of Republicans said this would lead to new restrictions on land use, although supporters said that was not their intent.

The proposals were combined into a single bill to defeat objections by Tom Coburn, R-Okla., who complained that the legislation would authorize wasteful spending, block energy development on public lands, and infringe on property rights. He also said that Democratic leaders unfairly blocked Republicans from offering amendments. The way for passage was cleared January 14, when the Senate voted, 68–24, to invoke cloture, thereby limiting the remaining debate.

But the bill stalled in the House when backers fell two votes short of the two-thirds needed for passage under suspension of the rules. On that tally, on March 11, the vote was 282–144.

House leadership tried to work out a strategy for moving the package to the floor. Many of the bills combined in it had not been considered in committee or on the floor in the House, and it took time to assuage Democrats' concerns.

Leaders feared Republicans would try to bring up an amendment focused on a sensitive political topic, most likely related to gun rights. That would have forced moderate and conservative Democrats to take a difficult vote. To get around this problem, sponsors sought to amend the bill—in the motion to suspend the rules and pass the bill—with language proposed by Pennsylvania Democrat Jason Altmire. It clarified that nothing in the bill could restrict access for hunting, fishing, or trapping activities that are otherwise allowed by law, and also would not affect state authority to regulate these activities.

Striking again, the Senate called up HR 146, an unrelated battlefield preservation bill that passed the House on March 3, and substituted the text of its lands bill. It passed the measure, 77–20, on March 19. Senators killed five amendments from Coburn and adopted another intended to forestall criminal prosecution of casual park visitors who take stones containing fossils.

Because the House already passed the earlier version of HR 146, the measure was shielded from further amendments when it returned to that chamber.

Offshore Drilling

The House passed a bill in 2010 to overhaul federal regulation of offshore drilling, but despite weeks of effort, Majority Leader Harry Reid, D-Nev., was unable to pass companion legislation in the Senate.

In the weeks after the April 20 explosion of the Deepwater Horizon oil rig in the Gulf of Mexico, bipartisan sentiment ran high in Congress for tougher oil drilling safety laws. Democratic leaders in both chambers pulled together legislation from a flurry of bills that were introduced. But that sentiment yielded to bickering over both the scope and substance of the legislation. The House on July 30 voted, 209–193, to pass a bill (HR 3534—H Rept 111-582) to overhaul the regulation of offshore drilling, but partisan divisions and policy disputes within the Democratic Caucus stalled action in the Senate. The issue faded after the hole was plugged temporarily in July and permanently in September, and the legislation died at the end of the Congress.

Both the House-passed bill and a version developed by Senate Majority Leader Harry Reid, D-Nev., focused on overhauling federal management of the outer continental shelf to address numerous legal, regulatory, and safety issues highlighted by the Gulf spill. Both measures incorporated provisions from a flurry of bills that followed the explosion of the Deepwater Horizon rig. Republicans in both chambers protested that Democrats were using the crisis to push what GOP members called overly broad bills that included provisions unrelated to the spill. In the House, Republicans forced their Democratic colleagues to drop provisions that would have covered onshore energy projects.

The House-passed measure would have restructured the Interior Department agency formerly known as the Minerals Management Service, eliminated the existing $75 million cap on a company's liability for economic damages stemming from an oil spill, and imposed new safety requirements on the drilling industry. Although Republicans took part in the negotiations, only two voted for the bill.

In the Senate, Republicans and coal-state Democrats fended off efforts by John Kerry, D-Mass., and Joseph I. Lieberman, I-Conn., to use the legislation as a vehicle for imposing mandatory limits on greenhouse gas emissions. Opponents also protested provisions that would have required electric companies to generate more power from renewable energy sources. Senate liberals supported both provisions.

Reid scaled back his bill (S 3663) twice in an effort to win Senate passage before the August recess. He first removed the cap on greenhouse gases and then the renewable-energy standard.

The version he eventually produced included provisions from an offshore drilling overhaul (S 3516—S Rept 111-236) that had won bipartisan support in the chamber's Energy and Natural Resources Committee in June, as well as modest energy efficiency proposals. The bill would have codified an Obama administration reorganization of the Interior Department's oil oversight divisions, bolstered drilling safety requirements, increased penalties on operators who violate the law, and given the department more time to review drilling applications.

But Republicans, along with a handful of oil-state Democrats, were not willing to accept language eliminating the liability cap, which they argued would force independent producers out of business. Alternate proposals to let the president set liability caps on a project-by-project basis or allow the industry to pool its liability also drew opposition, and the measure was ultimately lost in the debate over tax and budget issues in the lame-duck session.

HOUSE ACTION

The House on July 30, 2010, passed a comprehensive offshore-drilling bill (HR 3534) by a largely party-line **key vote of 209–193 (R 2–154; D 207–39)** after Democratic leaders allowed caucus members from oil- and gas-producing states a vote on an amendment to ease a temporary moratorium on new deep-water drilling that the Obama administration had put in place in the aftermath of the explosion. *(2010 key votes, p. 767)*

Minutes before passage, the House adopted, 216–195, an amendment by Louisiana Democrat Charlie Melancon to exempt drillers from the moratorium if they demonstrated compliance with new safety requirements issued by the Interior Department. As many as thirty "oil patch" Democrats had signaled that they would oppose the bill because of concerns about the moratorium, which was thrown out by a federal court in June. The administration later issued a revised ban, sparking intense criticism from Republicans and industry-friendly Democrats, who said the job losses and other economic effects of the pause outweighed the risks from a second oil spill. (The administration lifted the moratorium in October, saying that new regulations had reduced the risks.)

On other amendments, the House:

- Adopted, 399–8, a proposal by Harry Teague, D-N.M., to allow companies to meet stringent new financial requirements for obtaining federal leases by pooling their resources. The approach was similar to a proposal under discussion in the Senate to allow the industry to collectively share the unlimited liability for economic damages that companies would face under both the House and Senate drilling overhauls. The unlimited-liability provision sparked considerable opposition from the industry, Republicans, and some Democrats, but the House Rules Committee did not allow votes on amendments that would have removed or altered the language in the House bill.
- Rejected, 166–239, a motion by Bill Cassidy, R-La., to return the bill to the Natural Resources Committee with instructions that it be reported back immediately with an amendment that would provide for termination of the moratorium.

Key provisions in the bill would have:

- Repealed the existing $75 million cap on liability for offshore oil spills.
- Abolished the Minerals Management Service and assigned its duties to three new regulatory and leasing agencies. The management service had been plagued by scandals in recent years, and congressional investigations reported that the agency was mismanaged.
- Created numerous safety regulations for offshore oil and gas development leases, including features designed to prevent well blowouts.
- Required all vessels engaged in oil drilling in the U.S. Exclusive Economic Zone to register in the United States.
- Repealed a law that had provided "royalty relief" for certain oil and natural gas producers. The bill barred issuing new leases to companies that held oil and gas leases on which no royalties were paid unless the company renegotiated the leases to

include royalty payments. It also prohibited the transfer or sale of such leases, unless the leases were similarly renegotiated.
- Created annual conservation fees for all oil and natural gas leases located on federal lands.

SENATE ACTION

After failing to reach agreement with Republicans to stage test votes on competing energy bills, Reid put off until after the August recess his effort to bring his offshore-drilling overhaul and energy bill (S 3663) to the floor.

Reid had trimmed the bill twice to win approval before the recess. First, he jettisoned a cap on greenhouse gas emissions. Next he dropped a renewable-energy standard that had broader support among Democrats but still raised regional issues. The legislation eventually included provisions from an offshore drilling overhaul that had won bipartisan support in committee, as well as modest proposals to promote electric and natural gas vehicles, energy efficiency retrofits for homes, and increased funding for the federal Land and Water Conservation Fund.

But Reid could not satisfy everyone. A provision to eliminate the $75 million liability cap was more than Republicans, along with a handful of oil-friendly Democrats, were willing to accept. Lifting the cap entirely, they argued, would force independent producers out of the business.

Meanwhile, a growing chorus of Democrats wanted to see a federal renewable-energy standard return to the mix, requiring utilities to generate an increasing percentage of electricity from renewable sources, such as wind and energy. John Kerry, D-Mass., and Joseph I. Lieberman, I-Conn., had pressed to include mandatory limits on greenhouse gas emissions, and a vocal group of liberals still wanted carbon controls. But the pair's climate push sparked not only opposition from Republicans but also grumbling from moderate Democrats from coal-dependent and manufacturing states, who wanted Reid to advance a narrower bill focused on the spill.

Reid never found a formula that would yield the sixty votes he needed to limit debate. That, plus the short period left before the end of the regular session, precluded further consideration of the bill.

Other Oil Production Legislation

Lawmakers considered a number of other bills related to oil production. These included the following.

OIL SPILL LIABILITY TRUST FUND

Lawmakers in 2010 cleared legislation to allow the president to withdraw more money from the Oil Spill Liability Trust Fund in response to the Gulf of Mexico accident. The measure passed both chambers without dissent.

The legislation removed limitations on the amount the administration could use from the fund for cleanup efforts for the Deepwater Horizon oil spill on the rig run by the giant oil company British Petroleum (BP). It allowed the president to take multiple advances of up to $100 million each from the fund, which held about $1.6 billion. Current law limited administration access to a total of $150 million during a fiscal year. Congress quickly sent the bill to the president in June 2010 after getting word that the available fiscal 2010 sum was expected to be exhausted as early as within a week.

Lawmakers agreed the Coast Guard should be given the funding. They also raised concerns that the bill did not stipulate that BP would be responsible for replenishing funding used to respond to the aftermath of the explosion of its rig. John L. Mica of Florida, ranking Republican on the House Transportation and Infrastructure Committee, said the fund should not be used as a "piggy bank" for BP or other responsible parties.

To support the trust fund, a pending tax break and social benefits measure (HR 4213) raised the current tax on oil companies. The House version increased the tax on a barrel of oil from 8 cents to 34 cents; the Senate's version increased the tax to 41 cents a barrel.

As passed by the Senate, a fiscal 2010 supplemental appropriations bill (HR 4899) contained the language of S 3473, but the stand-alone bill's backers did not want the removal of the cap to be held up by disagreements over the larger spending bill.

"BP is ultimately responsible for restoring this funding, but the Senate is acting properly to ensure the Coast Guard and other response agencies have what they need now to get the job done in the Gulf of Mexico," Sen. Thad Cochran of Mississippi, the top Republican on the Appropriations Committee, said in a statement.

The House voted 410–0 to clear the bill (S 3473—PL 111-191) on June 10, one day after the Senate passed it by voice vote.

SAFETY AND CLEANUP

Oil spill legislation advanced on July 21, 2010, as the House passed a pair of bills to promote safer deep-water drilling and provide a better response and cleanup for the next spill, but none cleared Congress.

One bill (HR 5716) overhauled the Ultra-Deepwater and Unconventional Natural Gas and Other Petroleum Resources Program, which was created in a wide-ranging 2005 energy law (PL 109-58) and aimed to promote research and development of deep-water oil and natural gas production. The other measure (HR 2693) more than doubled the authorized funding for the interagency Oil Pollution Research and Development Program, which was created by the 1990 Oil Pollution Act (PL 101-380).

The House passed both bills by voice vote.

The research and development bill required a greater focus on—and direct more money toward—safety and environmental protection. The program at the time received $50 million per year from fees on oil and gas leases. The bill altered how that money was spent:

- 35 percent for Energy Department research on safety, accident prevention, and environmental mitigation.
- 32.5 percent for researching "safe and environmentally responsible deepwater exploration and production."
- 25 percent set aside for unconventional onshore energy exploration and development.
- 7.5 percent allocated to small energy producers to improve output.

The bill also required that members from state regulatory agencies be included on the research program's advisory board and changed the name of the program to the Safer Oil and Natural Gas Drilling Technology Research and Development Program.

But even with these proposed changes, critics argued that the industry, not the public, should pay for research and development. President Obama had sought to eliminate the program, as did President George W. Bush. Two weeks early, the House Natural Resources Committee approved a bill (HR 3534) that to eliminate the program's funding.

Supporters countered that the program could lead to safer drilling technologies and could prevent another spill like the BP disaster.

The cleanup measure, introduced by California Democratic Rep. Lynn Woolsey, authorized $48 million annually for the interagency Oil Pollution Research and Development Program, to come out of the Oil Spill Liability Trust Fund.

Existing law authorized the program to receive $21 million each year from the trust fund. The bill's cost was estimated at $93 million from fiscal 2011 to fiscal 2015, according to the Congressional Budget Office.

The legislation also directed the interagency panel that oversaw the program to develop a national information clearinghouse of scientific information on preparedness, response, and restoration research. The panel also was required to submit to Congress a broad oil pollution research and technology plan, which would be updated once every five years.

"We have been slow to develop new technologies to prevent, mitigate, and clean up oil spills," Woolsey said after the Science and Technology Committee approved the bill. "The fact that we are responding to the BP oil spill with basically the same technology that we used with the Exxon *Valdez* spill twenty years ago pretty much says it all."

OIL SPILL RESPONSE

The Senate Commerce, Science and Transportation Committee gave voice vote approval on July 22, 2010, to a bill (S 3614), sponsored by Kay Bailey Hutchison of Texas, the committee's ranking Republican, to give the Coast Guard additional resources to prevent and respond to oil spills.

Hutchison's bill established a federal facility to train the Coast Guard to respond to oil spills and other hazardous-material releases. It also would provided training for state and local first-responders in response techniques and strategies as well as public affairs.

The panel agreed to an amendment by Sen. Tom Udall, D-N.M., to allow the facility to conduct modeling and simulations, along with research and testing efforts as the unamended bill had directed.

The bill also directed the Coast Guard to establish a National Strike Force to prepare for and respond to oil spills and other hazardous-material release events as well as district preparedness response teams.

The measure authorized funding for those efforts between fiscal 2010 and fiscal 2015 from funds appropriated for the Coast Guard to conduct research and testing. It also allowed the Coast Guard to make grants to academic institutions to conduct research and development for oil spill response equipment, technology and techniques.

Yucca Mountain Nuclear Waste

Congressional appropriators in 2009 and 2010 turned back efforts to direct funding for the unfinished nuclear waste repository at Yucca Mountain in Nevada.

President Barack Obama's administration in 2009 decided to pull the plug on the project, angering nuclear energy supporters in both parties in the process. However, supporters were given a reprieve in June 2010 when a Nuclear Regulatory Commission (NRC) panel ruled that the Energy Department did not have the authority to cancel the project.

In the fiscal 2010 Energy-Water spending bill (HR 3183—H Rept 111-278), lawmakers agreed to provide $197 million for Yucca Mountain. That amount would effectively cancel the project while allowing a federal license application to continue. The bill also would create an expert commission to recommend alternatives to the controversial facility. The Senate cleared the $34 billion measure on October 15, 2009.

Yucca Mountain remained a flash point in the fiscal 2011 appropriations bill, with lawmakers ultimately providing no funding for the facility. At the July 15, 2010, markup of the House Appropriations Energy-Water subcommittee, ranking Republican Rodney Frelinghuysen of New Jersey offered an amendment to direct $100 million in the bill to continue the licensing for Yucca Mountain. "I don't think Congress should subordinate its inclination to keep Yucca Mountain open," he said, noting that the House the previous year rejected by a wide margin a motion to strip all funding for the project.

However, Ed Pastor, D-Ariz., the acting chair of the subcommittee, said that Congress could appropriate funds to continue licensing if the full NRC upholds the decision. The Frelinghuysen amendment was rejected on a party-line vote, 6–10. Several related amendments also were rejected.

Senate appropriators also refused funds for the facility. "The president campaigned on the basis of shutting down that facility and has sent us a recommendation of zero funding," said Sen. Bryon Dorgan, D-N.D., chair of the Senate Energy-Water Appropriations Subcommittee. "We began that process last year, and this year zeroed it out."

At a July 22 Appropriations Committee markup of the Energy-Water bill (S 3635—S Rept 111-228), the panel rejected, 13–16, a proposal by Patty Murray, D-Wash., to restore $200 million to continue the Yucca licensing process. Murray said eliminating the money was a "serious mistake," calling the site the "best option for a nuclear repository."

Murray's effort pitted her against Majority Leader Harry Reid, D-Nev., who issued a statement applauding the panel's action.

Like most of the other fiscal 2011 appropriations bills, the Energy-Water measure stopped moving once it had been approved in different forms by the Senate Appropriations Committee and relevant House subcommittee. Programs under the bill were funded largely at fiscal 2010 levels through March 4, 2011, under a continuing resolution (HR 3082—PL 111-322).

Lead Pipes

Lawmakers in 2010 cleared a bill allowing for the expanded use of lead pipes but also establishing a more stringent definition for "lead free" pipes.

Under the bill, lead pipes and fixtures would be allowed for nonpotable services such as manufacturing, industrial processing, irrigation, outdoor watering, or other uses where the water is not expected to be used for human consumption. Lead would be permitted in pipes and fixtures such as toilets, bidets, urinals, tub fillers, and shower valves.

Existing law prohibited the presence of lead in pipes or fixtures used for the installation or repair of any public water system or any residential or nonresidential building that provides drinking water.

The measure, which was introduced in September by Barbara Boxer, D-Calif., chair of the Senate Environment and Public Works Committee, also modified the "lead free" definition for the wetted surface of pipes, pipe fitting, and other fixtures to reduce the allowable amount of lead to 0.25 percent of the weighted average lead content. At the time, the standard was 8 percent. It specified that this provision would take effect thirty-six months after enactment.

The House cleared the bill (S 3874—PL 111-380), 226–109, on December 17 after Senate passage by voice vote the previous day. President Obama signed the measure (the Reduction of Lead in Drinking Water Act) on January 4, 2011.

Air Pollution Grants

A Senate panel in 2010 approved legislation authorizing a grant program to help reduce air pollution in part of the chair's home state.

The Environment and Public Works Committee by voice vote on May 20 approved a bill (S 3373—S Rept 111-218) to authorize $20 million annually from fiscal 2011 through 2015 for the Environmental Protection Agency to provide grants to areas with extreme air pollution for replacing or retrofitting polluting vehicles or engines and for other activities that improve air quality. At the time, only the San Joaquin Valley, in Chair Barbara Boxer's state of California, had high enough pollution rates to qualify for the program.

The valley had failed continually to meet federally mandated ozone level limits and had a disproportionate number of residents with chronic illness such as asthma. "The people there are really impacted because they're in a valley, and they're in an economically hard-hit area," Boxer said. "And they want to retrofit their old dirty engines, and that's why they're looking to this."

Sen. James M. Inhofe of Oklahoma, the ranking Republican on the committee, raised objection to the fact that only the San Joaquin Valley would qualify. He also called the bill an unfunded mandate.

Algal Blooms

After first blocking what backers call a "life-or-death" bill, the House in 2010 voted to establish a federal strategy against harmful algal blooms. A similar measure won committee approval in the Senate but did not move to the floor.

The bill (HR 3650—H Rept 111-396), to authorize $205 million over five years for the program, passed the House, 251–103, on March 12. Some algal blooms release toxins that can be deadly to wildlife and humans who swim in contaminated water or consume shellfish from such water.

"I heard this a lot: 'Why are we coming back into session [on a Friday] to talk about algae?'" said Brian Baird, D-Wash., chair of the Science and Technology Subcommittee on Energy and Environment. "Well, I hope people can remember that if they eat shellfish with the poisoning, they can die."

The research program also would address hypoxia, or severe oxygen depletion, in seawater or freshwater. Harmful algal blooms can lead to hypoxia, and human activities, such as runoff of agricultural fertilizers heavy in nitrogen phosphorous, also can trigger it.

The bill came to the floor March 9 under suspension of the rules. But the vote tally, 263–142, fell seven short of the required two-thirds majority required under suspension of the rules.

Although the authorization stayed the same, the active dates for the bill were changed in the final bill to fiscal 2011–2015 instead of fiscal 2010–2014.

Opponents argued that the bill was too costly and could create an unfunded federal mandate for state and local governments.

The Congressional Budget Office in 2009 said the measure contained no unfunded mandates but estimated it would cost the federal government $153 million from 2010 through 2014 and $22 million thereafter.

Although the problem was usually described as one focused in coastal regions, algal blooms could be found in freshwater areas such as the Great Lakes. The blooms could grow dramatically as nutrients in water increased with changes in water quality, temperature, and sunlight, and the issue often took a toll on coastal ecosystems and economies.

Sen. Olympia J. Snowe, R-Maine, offered a similar measure (S 952—S Rept 111-125) that was reported out of the Senate Commerce, Science, and Transportation Committee on August 6, 2009, on a voice vote but never made it to the floor. That bill authorized $40 million annually from fiscal 2010 through 2014 for a program to research and control harmful algal blooms.

Recycling Electronic Products

The House and a Senate panel in 2009 approved legislation that sought ways to encourage more recycling of electronic products such as computers, mobile phones, and televisions.

The Senate bill (S 1397—S Rept 111-168), sponsored by Amy Klobuchar, D-Minn., authorized grants for programs aimed at researching ways to prevent improper disposal of electronic devices and mitigate the environmental effect of such waste. The Environment and Public Works Committee approved the measure by voice vote December 10.

The Environmental Protection Agency (EPA) estimated that two billion computers, television sets, wireless devices, printers, video game systems, and other devices had been sold since 1980. In 2005 alone, such devices generated two million tons of waste.

"There's a huge amount of work to be done," Klobuchar said, citing a Government Accountability Office report that found that "e-waste" sent to U.S. landfills and incinerators contained mercury, lead and other potentially harmful chemicals. Industry groups and consumer electronics retailers endorsed the legislation.

The bill authorized $18 million for fiscal 2011, $20 million for fiscal 2012, and $22 million for fiscal 2013 for EPA grants to improve electronics waste collection and boost state and national recycling programs. The grants also would fund research on separating hazardous materials from discarded electronics and designing devices that have a longer lifespan. The bill also authorized more than $15 million from fiscal 2011 through 2013 for National Science Foundation grants to universities that were developing curricula on reducing electronics waste and "green engineering."

The House passed its version of the bill (HR 1580) by voice vote in April.

Low-level Nuclear Waste

The House in 2009 voted overwhelmingly to block the importation of low-level nuclear waste. The Senate, however, did not take up the measure.

The bill (HR 515) would have amended the Atomic Energy Act (PL 85-177) to allow the Nuclear Regulatory Commission (NRC) to block the imports. The legislation, sponsored by Democrats Jim Matheson of Utah and Bart Gordon of Tennessee as well as Nebraska Republican Lee Terry, came in response to a plan proposed by Utah-based Energy Solutions, Inc., to import up to 20,000 tons of low-level radioactive waste from Italy, the largest amount ever imported to the United States for disposal. The NRC had been asked to allow the import but did not have the power to block the plan because it involved foreign waste.

Supporters of the legislation said U.S. disposal facilities should be reserved for domestic waste only, especially as the nation looked to expand its nuclear power use. But a number of Republicans said they favored relaxing regulatory restrictions on such imports. Republican Joe L. Barton of Texas, ranking member of the House Energy and Commerce Committee, said the measure "makes it impossible for some companies to do business" in the nuclear waste disposal field.

The committee's Energy and the Environment Subcommittee approved the legislation by voice vote on November 3.

The full committee approved it, 34–12, on November 19. The House passed the bill, 309–112, on December 2 under suspension of the rules.

The Senate did not act on a companion measure, S 232, introduced by Lamar Alexander, R-Tenn.

Formaldehyde Emissions

Congress in 2010 cleared legislation (S 1660—PL 111-199) to set standards for emissions of formaldehyde, a chemical commonly used in building materials and household products that the Environmental Protection Agency (EPA) has linked to serious health risks.

The measure created a national emissions standard for formaldehyde in domestic and imported composite wood products, the most common source of the chemical in homes, according to the EPA. The standards would be based on the California Air Resources Board regulations and would apply to both finished and unfinished products. "This legislation is pro-industry, pro-consumer, pro-environment and pro-public health," sponsor Amy Klobuchar, D-Minn., said in a statement.

Indoor pressed-wood products that often contain formaldehyde included particleboard, hardwood plywood paneling, and medium-density fiberboard, any of which could be used for subflooring, shelving, cabinetry, and furniture. At room temperature, the chemical let off an invisible gas, which could cause irritation of the eyes, nose, and throat; coughing and wheezing; fatigue; skin rash; and severe allergic reaction. The EPA had reported that formaldehyde also may cause cancer.

Under the bill, the EPA faced a July 1, 2013, deadline to issue new regulations and revise importation regulations concerning composite wood products. It also required the

EPA to submit a report to Congress on its progress in establishing the regulations within one year of the bill's enactment.

Certain windows, doors, and garage doors that contained a low percentage of composite wood products would be exempt.

By voice vote, the Senate passed the bill on June 14, 2010. The House cleared it on June 23, also on a voice vote. President Obama signed the measure (the Formaldehyde Standards for Composite Wood Products Act) on July 7, 2010.

Solar Energy Technology

The House in 2009 passed legislation bill (HR 3585—H Rept 111-302) that aimed to foster the continued development of solar energy technology. The Senate did not take up the measure.

The bill, sponsored by Gabrielle Giffords, D-Ariz., directed the secretary of energy to establish a Solar Technology Roadmap Committee tasked with creating a road map of solar technology needs and providing guidance for federal solar technology activities.

It authorized $2.3 billion over fiscal 2011 through 2015 and reauthorized certain solar research activities. Starting in 2013, it authorized the annual use of $3.5 million for daylight systems and direct solar light pipe technology and $2.5 million for solar air conditioning research and development.

The Science, Space, and Technology Committee approved the bill by voice vote on October 7. Ranking member Ralph M. Hall, R-Texas, said he and other committee Republicans supported solar energy, but could not support the bill's price tag.

The panel rejected an amendment from Paul Broun, R-Ga., that would have reduced the bill's authorization amounts to $200 million for each of fiscal years 2011 through 2013. A second Broun amendment, also turned down, would have removed requirements on when and where certain percentages of funds could be used, such as a requirement that 75 percent of funding for Energy Department solar technology research after 2014 support activities recommended by the Solar Technology Roadmap Committee.

The House, on a vote of 162–256, rejected an amendment by Broun that would have reduced the bill's annual authorization amounts to $250 million for 2011–2013.

Clean Water Act

The Senate Environment and Public Works Committee in 2009 approved legislation to broaden federal protections, which were limited by a pair of Supreme Court decisions, over the nation's bodies of water.

The bill (S 787—S Rept 361), approved 12–7 on June 18, altered the definition of water in the Clean Water Act (PL 80-845) to clarify the federal government's jurisdiction over all water sources. References to "navigable waters of the United States" would be replaced with the words "waters of the United States."

The measure was in response to Supreme Court rulings that precluded the EPA from using the Clean Water Act to regulate pollution in some wetlands because they were not considered navigable bodies of water. In both *Solid Waste Agency of Northern Cook County v. U.S. Army Corps of Engineers* (531 U.S. 159) in 2001 and *Rapanos v. United States* (547 U.S. 715) in 2006, the Supreme Court held that the phrase "navigable waters of the United States" included only permanent and continuously flowing bodies of water and did not apply to channels where water flows intermittently or that periodically provide drainage for rainfall.

The U.S. Chamber of Commerce, the American Farm Bureau Federation, and the National Association of Counties opposed the definition change, saying it would result in permitting delays and greater federal oversight of state and local decisions.

"If the term 'navigable' is removed, it is possible that ditches, pipes, streets, gutters, man-made ponds, drainage features, desert washes, and other features could be regulated," said Don Stapley, president of the counties association.

Bill sponsor Russ Feingold, D-Wis., said those concerns were unfounded. His said his bill would protect only the waters that were covered by law before the high court rulings and would preserve existing exemptions for farming, silviculture, and other activities.

Green Schools

The House passed a bill in 2009 to authorize billions of dollars for "green" school renovation and modernization projects. The bill (HR 2187—H Rept 111-106), which passed 275–155 on May 14, authorized $6.4 billion in fiscal 2010 for school construction projects and such funds as "necessary" through fiscal 2015.

The bill required that all funding by fiscal 2015 be used for projects that meet environmental friendliness standards.

Education and Labor Chair George Miller, D-Calif., said the bill would make critical investments while "breathing new life" into local economies. But most Republicans opposed the bill, contending that school construction historically had been a local responsibility. "States and local communities, not federal bureaucrats, have the primary responsibility to set public policy over education," said Howard P. "Buck" McKeon of California, the ranking Republican on the committee. "Federal law should reflect that."

The measure authorized $600 million from fiscal 2010 to fiscal 2015 specifically for schools in the Gulf Coast region, where many school buildings were destroyed or severely damaged by hurricanes Katrina and Rita in 2005.

Funds authorized under the bill were to be distributed following guidelines established under Title I of the Elementary and Secondary Education Act (PL 107-110), which directed federal funds to schools that serve low-income students.

The House Education and Labor Committee approved the bill, 31–14, on May 6.

Wastewater Treatment

The House in 2009 passed legislation authorizing $13.8 billion over five years in wastewater treatment grants and loans as part of a broader $19.6 billion package of water quality measures.

The bill was passed, 317–101, on March 12, after the House rejected a Republican amendment to strip language requiring contractors to pay prevailing wages. The legislation (HR 1262—HR Rept 111-026) was composed of five water quality bills that separately passed the House in the previous Congress.

Although the bill enjoyed solid bipartisan support, there was vigorous debate over an amendment by Connie Mack, R-Fla., to remove a provision applying the Davis-Bacon Act (PL 88-349) to projects receiving federal funding. The amendment was defeated, 140–284, with thirty-five Republicans joining Democrats in opposition.

Davis-Bacon, a Depression-era law that enjoys union backing and is a lightning rod for Republicans, requires contractors on federal projects to pay prevailing wages. The bill extended that requirement to state and local projects receiving funds through the Clean Water State Revolving Fund.

The bill reauthorized the Clean Water State Revolving Fund, which provided low-interest loans and grants to communities for building and maintaining wastewater treatment facilities for the first time in fifteen years. The measure provided $300 million each year through fiscal 2014 in state management assistance and $100 million in annual grants to nonprofit organizations to provide technical and management assistance in improving wastewater treatment systems in rural areas, small municipalities, and tribal communities.

As amended, the five-year authorization also included $500 million a year in grants for projects to prevent sewer overflows, $150 million a year to address Great Lakes watershed sediment contamination, and $50 million annually to provide grants for pilot programs testing such alternative methods for enhancing water supplies as wastewater reclamation and reuse.

Wind Energy

The House in 2009 passed a bill directing the Energy Department to create a wind energy demonstration program.

The bill (HR 3165—H Rept 111-248), passed by voice vote, authorized $200 million annually from fiscal 2010 through fiscal 2014 for a program to upgrade wind turbines and related technologies. The program was intended to promote efforts to optimize the design and adaptability of wind systems by developing larger, lighter, and more affordable blade materials. The program sought to reduce the cost of construction, generation, and maintenance of wind energy systems.

"As we continue to grow our dependency on wind power to meet this nation's energy needs, it is important, critically important, that we move forward aggressively with all efforts toward energy efficiency," said bill sponsor Paul Tonko, D-N.Y.

Energy Department Research Programs

The House on December 1, 2009, passed legislation that would promote research programs at the Energy Department to study gas turbines and hybrid automobiles. The bill (HR 3029—H Rept 111-343), sponsored by Paul Tonko, D-N.Y., would authorize $65 million annually for fiscal years 2011 through 2014 a research demonstration program on the efficiency of gas turbines used in combined-cycle power generation systems.

Members also passed a bill (HR 3246—H Rept 111-255), sponsored by Gary Peters, D-Mich., that would authorize $2.9 billion to establish an Energy Department research program on vehicle technologies. The House passed the measure on September 16 by a vote of 312–114.

The program would study technologies including the hybridization or full electrification of vehicle systems that could reduce petroleum use in cars. It would also direct the Energy secretary to appoint a full-time director to coordinate research of medium- to heavy-duty commercial and transit vehicle technologies.

Energy-efficient Home Improvements

Fighting off Republican arguments that it cost too much and may be unnecessary, the House in 2010 passed a $6 billion consumer rebate program for energy-efficient home improvements that had been touted by the Obama administration.

The House passed the bill (HR 5019—HR Rept 111-469), 246–161, on May 6 with the support of twelve Republicans.

"The result of this will be a concomitant reduction in energy bills," said Massachusetts Democrat Edward J. Markey, a leading backer of the rebate program, commonly called HomeStar or "cash for caulkers." It was modeled after the 2009 "cash for clunkers" program, which offered consumers money to trade in old cars and buy models with better energy efficiency. *(Cash for clunkers legislation, p. 321)*

The White House endorsed the new rebate measure, saying it "will create 'green' jobs in construction and manufacturing, help consumers lower their energy bills and reduce greenhouse gas emissions."

Republicans objected to the cost and questioned the demand for such retrofits. They won support for a provision that would terminate the program if it increases the deficit. It was agreed to as part of a motion to recommit to the Energy and Commerce Committee, 346–68.

Most Democrats supported the motion, which also required adding language to make households with incomes exceeding $250,000 ineligible, prohibit participating home repair contractors from hiring anyone convicted of sexual assault or child molestation, and disallow rebates for the installation or replacement of pool heaters.

The bill authorized about $6 billion for two years for HomeStar and required the Energy Department to manage the program. The measure also authorized $600 million over two years for a separate program that provided grants to states for assisting low-income households in replacing manufactured homes built before 1976.

The bill offered two levels of rebates. The first level, known as Silver Star, provided rebates of up to $1,500 for basic upgrades, such as replacing water heaters or adding insulation. Rebates would be capped at $3,000 per home. The second level, known as Gold Star, allowed consumers to receive a $3,000 rebate if they completed a home energy audit and made changes that cut energy costs by at least 20 percent.

Before agreeing to the motion to recommit, the House adopted several amendments to the bill by voice vote, including a manager's package offered by Henry Waxman, D-Calif. The manager's amendment, among other things, extended the time the Energy Department had to designate companies to manage the rebates to sixty days from thirty days after enactment. It required the department to ensure that each state had a sufficient number of such companies to process rebate applications.

In addition, the amendment required that companies handling rebates distribute federal funds to qualifying contractors or vendors within ten days of receiving funds, rather than the originally proposed thirty days.

It required contractors to agree to cooperate with quality assurance procedures on any work done through the rebate program, and it required random audits of completed home renovations to check compliance with the program.

Electric Grid Protection

The House passed legislation in 2010 to authorize the Federal Energy Regulatory Commission (FERC) to respond quickly to protect the nation's electric grid from threats, including cyber-attacks.

The bill (HR 5026—H Rept 111-493), sponsored by Edward J. Markey, D-Mass., authorized FERC to address imminent threats to the electric grid with emergency orders. It passed by voice vote on June 9. The measure allowed FERC to create a mechanism to allow owners, operators, or users of the bulk-power system to recover any "substantial costs" that were incurred as a result of complying with the emergency procedures in the event of a grid security threat.

The legislation also permitted FERC to issue emergency measures to protect critical electrical infrastructure if the president notified FERC of any imminent grid security threat. It also required that the president notify Congress of any imminent threat.

FERC was required to issue regulations that address the so-called Aurora vulnerability. Aurora was a 2006 analysis done by the Energy Department's Idaho National Laboratory that identified how intruders could hack into the control system infrastructure of the electric grid and initiate attacks that would lead to physical damage to its equipment.

Interior and Environment Funds

The fiscal 2010 spending bill for the Interior Department and environmental programs cleared easily on October 29, 2009, helped along by the addition of must-pass provisions to fund much of the federal government until December 18. President Barack Obama signed the legislation (HR 2996—PL 111-88) the next day. *(Omnibus appropriations, pp. 127, 129)*

The $32.3 billion bill consisted almost entirely of discretionary spending. The two chambers were only about $200 million apart on discretionary accounts, and conferees roughly split the difference, as they did on many of the spending bills.

The annual bill funded the Interior Department, the Environmental Protection Agency (EPA), and programs such as the Smithsonian Institution and the National Endowments for the Arts and Humanities. It also covered the Agriculture Department's Forest Service and the Department of Health and Human Services' Indian Health Service.

The $32.2 billion in the bill for discretionary programs was just $85 million less than Obama requested. It was $4.7 billion, or about 17 percent, more than the same programs received in the fiscal 2009 law. However, the economic stimulus law enacted in February (PL 111-5) steered an additional $11 billion in fiscal 2009 funds to programs that came under the Interior-Environment bill. Counting that money and a small amount for mandatory programs, the fiscal 2010 bill was a drop of $6.5 billion, or about 17 percent, below total fiscal 2009 funding. *(Stimulus bill, p. 78)*

The House passed a version of the bill in June with $32.3 billion in discretionary spending. The Senate bill, passed in September, called for $32.1 billion.

Rep. Jerry Lewis of California, the ranking Republican on the House Appropriations Committee, called the increased spending "irresponsible, especially in light of the fact that Congress must soon consider legislation to increase our national debt limit—this time to over $13 trillion." But Democrats maintained that more spending was required because of cuts in the programs under the George W. Bush administration. "This is a catch-up bill," said

Norm Dicks, D-Wash., chair of the House Interior-Environment Appropriations Subcommittee.

Money differences between the two bills were minimal. The main controversies were over policy issues such as whether to limit the EPA's ability to regulate carbon dioxide by finding that it contributed to global warming, exempt emissions from livestock feed yards, and exempt ships plying the Great Lakes.

With seven of the fiscal 2010 appropriations bills unfinished and the first temporary funding law (PL 111-68) about to expire, Democrats added a new continuing resolution to the conference report. The measure extended funding through December 18, mostly at 2009 levels, for departments and programs whose bills had not cleared. Republicans in both chambers criticized inclusion of the continuing resolution in the bill and chastised Democrats for not getting the regular fiscal 2010 spending bills finished on time. But there was little they could do: without a temporary extension, agencies funded by the seven unfinished spending bills could not operate.

HOUSE COMMITTEE ACTION

The House Appropriations Committee gave voice vote approval June 18 to a $32.4 billion bill that significantly boosted funding for environment-related agencies. The Interior-Environment Subcommittee, which drafted the bill, approved the measure by voice vote June 10.

Before approving the bill, the full committee added language to bar the transfer of detainees from the prison at Guantánamo Bay, Cuba, to U.S. territories. Of the total, $32.3 billion was for discretionary programs, close to the president's request and 17 percent more than regular fiscal 2009 discretionary funding. *(Guantánamo Bay, p. 314)*

The bill included:

- $11.1 billion for the Interior Department, an increase of about $920 million. The National Park Service was slated to get a $198 million increase to $2.7 billion, the Bureau of Land Management's funding would go up by $87 million to $1.1 billion, and the Fish and Wildlife Service would see a $190 million increase to $1.6 billion.
- $10.5 billion for the EPA, $2.9 billion more than the agency received in regular fiscal 2009 funding. This included a $2.2 billion increase for clean-water and drinking-water infrastructure funds, which would get $3.9 billion. Appropriators also included $475 million for the president's new program to battle pollution in the Great Lakes.
- $3.7 billion for wildfire management, $404 million more than regular fiscal 2009 spending.

During the full committee markup, the panel:

- Adopted by voice vote an amendment by Lewis to prohibit the transfer of prisoners held at Guantánamo Bay to Guam, American Samoa, the U.S. Virgin Islands, the Northern Mariana Islands, or Puerto Rico. Appropriations Chair David R. Obey, D-Wis., accepted the amendment, but he argued that the Interior bill was not the proper vehicle for the language.
- Rejected, 29–30, an amendment by Jo Ann Emerson, R-Mo., to bar the use of funds in the bill to implement an EPA proposal to include emissions from indirect land use changes in calculating greenhouse gas emissions from biofuels. Farmers opposed the EPA plan, saying it could weaken the view that biofuels such as ethanol are environmentally friendly alternatives to fossil fuels. Obey argued that the adoption of the detainee language already had made the bill controversial enough.
- Adopted, 31–27, an amendment by Tom Latham, R-Iowa, to prohibit the EPA from requiring livestock feedlots to report on methane emissions from their manure management programs. The EPA had issued a proposed rule in April to require all sectors of industry to monitor and report greenhouse gas emissions above a certain threshold.
- Adopted by voice vote an amendment by Todd Tiahrt, R-Kan., to bar the EPA from requiring permits under the Clean Air Act for emissions resulting from biological processes associated with livestock production.
- Adopted by voice vote an amendment by Mike Simpson, R-Idaho, to require the president to complete a report within 120 days on government-wide expenditures related to climate change.

HOUSE FLOOR ACTION

The House passed the $32.4 billion bill by a vote of 254–173 on June 26 with virtually no changes.

House Interior-Environment Appropriations Subcommittee Chair Dicks said there were "huge backlogs of work" in the National Park Service, Fish and Wildlife Service, and Bureau of Land Management. Simpson, the subcommittee's ranking Republican, said it would cost too much. "My major concern is the overall spending level in this bill, but in terms of what we spent it on, I have no problems with the way you're approaching this," he said.

Members rejected, 169–259, an amendment by Jim Jordan, R-Ohio, to reduce spending in the bill by $5.8 billion to match levels in fiscal 2008.

SENATE COMMITTEE ACTION

The Senate Appropriations Committee approved a $32.2 billion version of the bill, 30–0, on June 25. The measure included $32.1 billion in discretionary funds. There were mostly small differences between the House and Senate bills that scarcely showed up when the figures were rounded. These differences included:

- $11 billion for the Interior Department, $84 million less than in the House bill. Department funding

included $1.1 billion for the Bureau of Land Management, just $20 million more than in the House version; $1.6 billion for Fish and Wildlife, $30 million less, and $2.7 billion for the National Park Service, $22 million less.
- $10.2 billion for the EPA, $304 million below the House level.
- $3.6 billion for wildfire management, $93 million less than in the House version. An amendment by Sam Brownback, R-Kan., would have barred the EPA from requiring mandatory reporting of greenhouse gas emissions from manure management systems. Brownback said the requirement would be expensive and difficult to meet because feedlot operators "don't yet know how to measure or collect" the information. But he said his real fear was that it would lead to a "cow tax," meaning a tax on methane emitted by manure.

Dianne Feinstein, D-Calif., chair of the Interior-Environment Subcommittee, proposed a modification that would subject only large feedlots—those whose manure management systems emitted 25,000 tons or more of carbon dioxide equivalent per year—to any reporting requirements. Feinstein's amendment was adopted, 18–12; Brownback's modified amendment was then adopted by voice vote. Feinstein said the purpose was not to levy taxes but to know how much and what types of greenhouse gases were emitted in the United States to achieve meaningful climate change policy.

SENATE FLOOR ACTION

The Senate passed the $32.2 billion bill by a vote of 77–21 on September 24, after blocking a GOP effort to prevent the EPA from regulating greenhouse gas emissions.

In a debate that was seen as a preview of the coming fights in the Senate over climate change legislation, Democrats blocked an attempt by Lisa Murkowski of Alaska, the ranking Republican on the Energy and Natural Resources Committee, to offer an amendment that would have prohibited the EPA from using funds from the bill to regulate carbon dioxide emissions from stationary sources. Murkowski and colleagues said Congress needed to protect small businesses and family farms from being subjected to regulations meant for the big emitters. Feinstein took exception to the argument, saying that the amendment would exempt the large industrial plants that accounted for over half the country's greenhouse gas emissions.

Underlying the debate was an expectation that the EPA would issue a finding that emissions of carbon dioxide contribute to global warming, which is a danger to human health. That would trigger a requirement that the agency regulate greenhouse gas emissions under the 1990 Clean Air Act Amendments (PL 101-549). The Obama administration was using the threat of EPA regulation in an effort to push the Senate into acting on a climate change bill before a United Nations climate summit in Copenhagen in December. Republicans were looking for a way to preempt the White House push. *(Climate change, p. 367)*

Democrats also fended off several Republican amendments that were designed to rein in appointed presidential advisers sometimes referred to as "czars."

The Senate tabled (killed) by a vote of 57–41 an amendment by David Vitter, R-La., to bar the use of funds in the bill by the EPA or Interior Department to implement the policies of the president's adviser on energy and climate change. Vitter said he was taking aim not at Carol Browner, who occupied the position, but at the White House practice of appointing "czars," which he said was "an end run around the constitutional process" in which cabinet officials are confirmed by the Senate and appear regularly before Congress as part of its oversight process.

A related amendment by Susan Collins, R-Maine, to require regular reports and testimony to Congress by White House appointees with authority to oversee departments and agencies was ruled out of order as violating rules against legislating in spending bills.

In other action, the Senate:

- Tabled (killed), 64–34, a motion by John Ensign, R-Nev., to recommit the bill with instructions to freeze spending at fiscal 2009 levels.
- Adopted by voice vote an amendment by Tom Coburn, R-Okla., that would allow private property owners to opt out of any National Heritage Area.
- Tabled (killed), 79–19, a Coburn amendment to prevent the federal government from buying new land for national parks until it repaired existing facilities.
- Tabled (killed), 56–42, a motion by Vitter to recommit the bill to the committee to add language approving a George W. Bush administration five-year plan to drill for oil and gas in new areas off the U.S. coasts. The Obama administration was considering its own plan. Democrats agreed to hold a vote on the amendment to get Vitter to drop delaying tactics.
- Adopted, 85–11, an amendment by Mike Johanns, R-Neb., to bar funding in the bill from being distributed to the Association of Community Organizations for Reform Now (ACORN). The group had come under fire after the release of a video showing ACORN employees apparently advising a couple, posing as a prostitute and her pimp, about how to conceal their line of work, evade taxes, and handle undocumented, underage sex workers. Forty-five Democrats joined Republicans, who had long criticized the group, in voting for the amendment.

CONFERENCE AND FINAL ACTION

With the first continuing resolution set to expire October 31, Democratic leaders made the conference report on the Interior-Environment bill the vehicle for a new continuing resolution. The House adopted the conference report (H Rept 111-316) by a vote of 247–178 on October 29, and the Senate cleared the bill, 72–28, later the same day.

The two chambers were only about $200 million apart on discretionary spending, and conferees roughly split the difference. But a number of controversial policy issues also had to be resolved.

Great Lakes. The bill had been stalled while negotiators tried to resolve disputes over a plan by Obey and Transportation and Infrastructure Chair James L. Oberstar, D-Minn., to add language that would prevent the EPA from including cargo vessels on the Great Lakes from an upcoming regulation on ship emissions. Conferees included language exempting thirteen steam-powered ships on the Great Lakes. Environmental groups opposed the exemption, but Obey and Oberstar insisted that it be in the bill. Obey said the ships would "risk blowing up" if they switched fuel types to comply with the rule.

Manure emissions. Conferees agreed to bar the use of funds in the bill to require permits for greenhouse gas emissions from livestock producers or to require greenhouse gas emissions reporting from manure management systems. The House had agreed, 267–147, on October 27 to a nonbinding resolution instructing conferees to insist on the House provision exempting all manure management systems from having to report on greenhouse gas emissions.

Davis-Bacon. The bill included language that applied Davis-Bacon prevailing-wage requirements to the Clean Water and Drinking Water State Revolving Funds. Under the Davis-Bacon Act, workers on public projects must be paid no less than the local prevailing wages and benefits paid on similar projects.

Guantánamo detainees. The bill contained restrictions on transferring detainees held at Guantánamo Bay that mirrored most of the detainee provisions in the Homeland Security appropriations bill enacted October 28 (PL 111-83). Among other things, the Interior bill prohibited the release of detainees into the United States or its territories. It required detailed reports from the president before detainees could be brought to those locations for prosecution or transferred to other countries, and before the Guantánamo facility could be closed.

ACORN. Conferees included the Senate's provision prohibiting the distribution of funds in the bill to ACORN.

MAJOR PROVISIONS

Following are the major provisions of the Interior-Environment bill:

Interior Department. The department received $11 billion, which was $875 million, or nearly 9 percent, above the fiscal 2009 level, without economic stimulus funds. Counting about $2 billion in fiscal 2009 stimulus money, the department got 10 percent less than in the previous year. The amount for the department was virtually the same as Obama's request. Departmental funding included:

- $1.1 billion for the Bureau of Land Management, about 10 percent more than in fiscal 2009, not counting $305 million in stimulus funds. Most of the bureau's appropriation, $959 million, was for the management of public lands and resources.
- $2.7 billion for the National Park Service, a 9 percent increase over fiscal 2009, not counting $750 million from the stimulus bill. Most of the money, $2.3 billion, was for park operations.
- $1.6 billion for the Fish and Wildlife Service, 14 percent more than in fiscal 2009, excluding $280 million in stimulus funds.
- $2.6 billion for the Bureau of Indian Affairs, an increase of 10 percent over fiscal 2009, not counting $500 million from the stimulus law. Of the total, $2.3 billion was devoted to the operation of American Indian programs, such as schools, social services, education, employment development, law enforcement, and natural resources development.

Environmental Protection Agency. The EPA received $10.3 billion, a 35 percent increase over regular fiscal 2009 funding. The agency had received an additional $7.2 billion for fiscal 2009 under the stimulus law. Much of the fiscal 2010 increase was for wastewater and drinking-water improvements, which received $3.6 billion—$2 billion above regular fiscal 2009 funding. The bill applied the Davis-Bacon prevailing-wage requirements to the Clean Water and Drinking Water State Revolving Funds. The EPA's hazardous waste and toxic site cleanup programs received $1.5 billion, a $25 million increase over regular fiscal 2009 funding. Climate change programs got $385 million under the bill, a $155 million increase.

Forest Service. The agency, part of the Agriculture Department, received $5.3 billion. The amount was nearly 12 percent more than regular fiscal 2009 funding, excluding $1.4 billion in emergency funds that came mostly from the stimulus law.

Indian Health Service. Part of the Department of Health and Human Services, the agency received $4.1 billion, a 13 percent increase, not counting another $500 million provided in the stimulus law. It operated hospitals, health care centers, school health centers, and health stations serving American Indians.

Arts and Humanities. An array of other programs also received funds, including $761 million for the Smithsonian Institution, $168 million each for the National Endowment for the Arts and the National Endowment for the Humanities, and $167 million for the National Gallery of Art.

Wildfires. The bill also appropriated nearly $3.4 billion for preventing and fighting wildfires—$2.5 billion from the Forest Service accounts and $885 million from the Interior Department. A portion of the firefighting money was put into a new Federal Land Assistance, Management and Enhancement (FLAME) Fund, created under the bill to pay for emergency suppression of wildfires that covered at least 300 acres.

2011–2012

Flexing their newfound legislative muscle after winning control of the House in the 2010 midterm elections, Republicans repeatedly sought to roll back environmental regulations. The House passed a number of measures to relax federal oversight over activities ranging from greenhouse gas emissions to pesticide use, with conservatives saying that the legislation would spur business development, create jobs, and move the nation closer to energy independence. President Barack Obama's administration threatened to veto some of the measures. Although Republicans picked up a few House Democratic votes, the initiatives ran into a brick wall in the Democratic-controlled Senate.

Republicans also failed to realize their goal of expanding domestic oil production. Republicans and some Democrats were particularly concerned that few permits had been issued since the April 2010 Deepwater Horizon oil rig explosion and resulting spill in the Gulf of Mexico, even though the administration had lifted a temporary moratorium on permitting and lease sales. The House passed a number of bills in both 2011 and 2012 to expand offshore drilling, open the Arctic National Wildlife Refuge to energy exploration and recovery activities, and require the Bureau of Land Management to begin issuing leases for oil shale under certain regulatory procedures. Republicans also wanted the government to take steps toward more energy production on public lands and to postpone implementation of new EPA regulations on air pollutants emitted by refineries for at least six months. Although the GOP won House passage of such plans, the Senate declined to take them up.

The two chambers also found themselves repeatedly at odds over the issue of forcing President Obama to make a decision on whether to permit the construction of the TransCanada Keystone XL pipeline from Canada to Mexico. Republicans won a fleeting victory when they successfully added language in December 2011 to the one-year extension of the payroll tax cut that required the administration to decide on a permit for the Keystone XL pipeline within sixty days of the bill's enactment. The following month, Obama rejected the permit application after the State Department said that the sixty-day window did not give officials enough time to complete the environmental review. Republicans in 2012 repeatedly returned to the issue, with the House adding language to a far-ranging surface transportation measure in order to get the pipeline approved. The Senate, however, refused to agree to the language.

Due to the partisan differences, the 112th Congress failed to clear any major stand-alone environmental or energy bills.

Conservatives, however, could claim a modest victory in the surface transportation measure (HR 4348—PL 112-141) that Obama signed into law in July 2012. The bill included provisions to ease certain federal environmental requirements for transportation projects, allowing construction to proceed more quickly. The bill would also allow some projects to be exempted from environmental review requirements of the National Environmental Policy Act. *(Surface transportation legislation, p. 340)*

Environmental Protection Agency Regulations

Republicans vowed to use their newfound majority status in the House to push back against what they viewed as an overzealous Environmental Protection Agency (EPA) regulatory agenda—especially in controlling toxic emissions from power plants and other industrial sources.

In 2011, the House passed a bill to bar the EPA from regulating greenhouse gas emissions, as well as an assortment of other measures to limit the EPA's authority over environmental issues such as cross-state air pollution, industrial boiler emissions, and clean-water regulations. The Senate either did not take up most of the bills or rejected similar legislation. Restrictions on boiler emissions were included in a year-end payroll tax cut extension package (HR 3765—PL 112-78). *(Tax cut package, p. 108)*

GREENHOUSE GASES

With support from the dozens of freshman Republicans, many of them openly skeptical of human-made climate change, the House in April 2011 overwhelmingly passed a bill (HR 910) to bar regulation of greenhouse gases under the Clean Air Act (PL 101-549). The Senate, however, deadlocked on a similar measure the same week, effectively killing efforts in the 112th Congress to bar the rules from taking effect. The House continued to target the rules through the appropriations process, but those riders also fell away.

The fight was over regulations proposed by the EPA in January 2010 as the result of a 2007 Supreme Court ruling in which the justices found that carbon dioxide was a pollutant covered by the Clean Air Act. The court's ruling meant that the EPA had to conduct an assessment of whether the gas posed a threat to public health; in the resulting "endangerment finding," agency scientists found that carbon dioxide and five other greenhouse gases were the primary drivers of climate change and "threaten the public health and welfare of the American people." That triggered a lengthy and complex regulatory process for controlling emissions. Under EPA rules that took effect in January 2011, new or substantially modified major stationary sources of industrial pollution, such as power plants or refineries, were required to use the best available technology to reduce emissions.

TRANSPORTATION BILL EASES ENVIRONMENTAL REQUIREMENTS

A sweeping two-year transportation measure that President Barack Obama signed on July 6, 2012 (HR 4348—PL 112-141) eased certain federal environmental requirements and waived them in specified emergency situations in order to speed up the time actual construction began on highway projects. It required the Transportation Department to issue regulations specifying which types of projects could be granted "categorical exclusions," which would exempt them from environmental review requirements of the National Environmental Policy Act (NEPA; PL 91-190). However, Senate Democrats successfully turned back House-passed provisions that would have expedited approval of the controversial Keystone pipeline and expanded oil and gas drilling in new areas. *(Transportation legislation, p. 340)*

Under existing law, most highway projects and related transportation construction were subject to sometimes lengthy environmental reviews under NEPA. The new law exempted certain projects from NEPA, including the repair or reconstruction of transportation infrastructure damaged or destroyed by a natural disaster or similar emergency. It also created a two-phase contracting process that allowed preconstruction activities and land acquisition to occur prior to the completion of a NEPA review if it were determined that the action would not adversely affect the environment.

To expedite the process in cases where reviews were required by multiple agencies, it authorized the Transportation Department to designate a lead agency for a project's environmental review process. The lead agency could grant categorical exclusions for project components if a participating agency had previously granted an exclusion for a similar project. The Transportation Department was also authorized to establish review deadlines and to convene a meeting of project oversight bodies within thirty days of a public comment period to ensure that project deadlines were being met.

The measure authorized the Transportation Department to provide enhanced technical assistance to states to expedite the review process for complex projects. This assistance would become available in cases where a project had not received a decision allowing it to proceed within two years of its initial request.

Agencies were required to expedite their reviews or issue approved permits within a certain time period, or their budgets would be reduced. The measure also required the Transportation Department to survey the use of both categorical exclusions and state-level environmental reviews, and to issue regulations authorizing additional exclusions for projects that met certain criteria.

In addition, the Transportation Department was required, in consultation with relevant state agencies and other recipients of federal highway funds, to create a "project delivery initiative." The program would require the department to analyze and share best practices relating to timely highway project development, streamlined environmental reviews, and ways to expand eligibility for preconstruction activities such as land acquisition and planning. The program was to examine programmatic methods that would reduce the need for project-specific environmental reviews.

Critics argued that the Clean Air Act was not intended to regulate a ubiquitous gas such as carbon dioxide and that the rules would be detrimental to jobs in coal-mining states. Democrats portrayed Republicans as denying the science behind the EPA's climate change regulations.

House Action

The House passed HR 910 by a **key vote of 255–172 (R 236–0; D 19–172)** on April 7, 2011. The measure specified that the term "air pollutant" under the Clean Air Act did not include greenhouse gases, although a greenhouse gas could be regulated to address concerns other than climate change. The measure carved out an exception so that a carefully negotiated agreement between the Obama administration and automakers to reduce greenhouse gases from vehicles could proceed. However, those standards applied to vehicles from model years 2012 through 2016; the bill would have prevented federal and state authorities from setting standards for model years after that. *(2011 key votes, p. 785)*

"This legislation will remove the biggest regulatory threat to the American economy," the bill's sponsor, Energy and Commerce Chair Fred Upton, R-Mich., argued during House floor debate, pointing to the support of business groups such as the National Federation of Independent Business. "The EPA has gotten ahead of public opinion, and the Congress now has the responsibility to pull it back," said Transportation and Infrastructure ranking member Nick J. Rahall II of West Virginia, one of just nineteen Democrats—many representing districts with fossil fuel interests—who backed the legislation.

Democratic opponents of the measure said the bill would deter creators of clean energy jobs and would be bad for the economy and the nation's health. "We need to confront these realities, not put our heads in the sand," said Energy and Commerce ranking member Henry A. Waxman, D-Calif. "American families count on the Environmental Protection Agency to keep our air and water clean, but this bill has politicians overruling the experts." The House considered twelve Democratic amendments and adopted one, by Jerry McNerney of California, to clarify that voluntary programs to address climate change would be exempt from the bill's prohibitions.

The White House warned of a veto in a Statement of Administration Policy released the day before the vote, arguing that the measure would "harm Americans' health" and "undercut fuel efficiency standards that will save Americans money at the pump while decreasing our dependence on oil." It defended the EPA's "common-sense steps under the Clean Air Act to protect Americans from harmful air pollution."

The Energy and Commerce Committee had approved the bill, 34–19, on March 15 (H Rept 112-50), following voice vote approval by the panel's Energy and Power Subcommittee on March 10. Republicans sought to deflect the Democrats' efforts to focus the debate on science rather than economics, calling the measure a response to the merits of the EPA's regulations rather than an assessment of climate science.

Much of the debate was over whether, despite the carve-out, the bill would strip the EPA of its authority to enforce emissions standards for vehicles. Waxman charged that, by repealing the finding that carbon dioxide emissions posed a threat to human health, the bill would remove any basis the EPA had to enforce motor vehicle emissions standards. "The exception doesn't address the issue of whether those standards can survive legal challenge without the endangerment finding," Waxman said.

Senate Action

Minority Leader Mitch McConnell introduced an amendment to a small business bill (S 493) that was identical to the text of the House bill. The Kentucky Republican denounced the EPA regulations, saying they are detrimental to jobs in coal-mining states. But the Senate on April 6, 2011, rejected it on a **key vote of 50–50 (R 46–1; D 4–47; I 0–2)**. (A tie vote defeats a measure in any event, although under the rules in force, the amendment required sixty votes to pass.) *(2011 key votes, p. 785)*

INDUSTRIAL BOILERS

On October 13, 2011, the House passed a bill (HR 2250) to delay EPA emissions rules for boilers, solid-waste incinerators, and process heaters, by a vote of 275–142.

The Senate did not act on the measure, but the provisions were included in the year-end package that extended a payroll tax cut, federal unemployment benefits, and other programs. Both chambers cleared that bill by unanimous consent December 23, and President Barack Obama signed it the same day (HR 3765—PL 112-78).

The EPA proposed the rules—aimed at limiting emissions of mercury, cadmium, particulates, and other toxic air pollutants—in March 2011 in response to a 2007 order by the U.S. Court of Appeals for the D.C. Circuit. The court vacated an earlier version of the rules for wrongfully excluding industrial boilers from the definition of solid-waste incinerators.

The House Energy and Commerce Committee, which approved the bill, 36–14, on September 21 (H Rept 112-225), said in its report that the standards combined could affect as many as 200,000 individual facilities, including institutional facilities such as universities and hospitals, as well as industrial facilities such as garbage incinerators and chemical manufacturing plants. The bill required that the EPA repropose the rules and finalize them fifteen months after the bill's enactment. The agency would have to give regulated facilities at least five years to comply after the standards became effective. In setting a compliance date for the standards, the EPA would have to consider the cost of complying, health and environmental impacts other than air quality, and the effects on employment.

Republicans said that the boiler regulations would put thousands of jobs at risk in the affected facilities and that the delay was especially important given the shaky state of the economy. Democrats countered that the health benefits of the regulations outweighed the costs. According to the EPA's analysis of a version of the boiler rules issued in February, the standards would provide \$22 billion to \$54.5 billion in health benefits in 2014, at an annual implementation cost of about \$1.9 billion.

AIR POLLUTION

The EPA's ability to regulate air pollution across state borders would have been sharply restricted under a bill (HR 2401) that the House passed, 249–169, on September 23, 2011. But the Senate rejected the version (S J Res 27) offered by Rand Paul, R-Ky., by a vote of 41–56 on November 10.

Before passing the bill, the House voted 234–188 to adopt an amendment by Edward Whitfield, R-Ky., to delay federal cross-state air pollution rules until at least 2015. States would have to wait an additional three years to implement the rules. The standards were designed to control emissions of sulfur dioxide and nitrogen oxides in twenty-eight states that were blamed for poor air quality in downwind northeastern and mid-Atlantic states.

Under the amendment, the EPA would be barred from using modeled data to determine the impact of pollution on downwind states, which Administrator Lisa P. Jackson said would probably limit the agency's ability to issue a cross-border rule in the future. Air toxics standards for utilities would be delayed by at least two years, and power plants would have at least five years to comply with the rules once they were issued. The underlying measure also proposed the creation of a Cabinet-level committee to review the cumulative and incremental effects of a number of EPA regulations and actions.

The Energy and Commerce Committee approved it, 33–13, on July 12 (H Rept 112-208). During the floor debate, members adopted, 227–192, an amendment by Bob Latta, R-Ohio, directing the EPA to account for feasibility and cost when establishing national ambient-air-quality standards, effectively negating a 2001 U.S. Supreme Court decision that upheld the EPA's practice of considering only public health concerns when setting the standards.

The White House warned that the president's advisers would recommend he veto the bill.

WATER POLLUTION

Two of the House-passed EPA bills were aimed at limiting the agency's authority over water pollution. The first was legislation to block a pesticide regulation the EPA was required to issue under a court-ordered deadline. The second was a measure to restrict the agency's authority to preempt state water pollution plans with stricter rules.

Pesticides. The House voted, 292–130, on March 31, 2011, to pass a bill (HR 872) to prohibit the EPA administrator or a state from requiring a permit for the use of pesticides in or near navigable waters as long as the pesticides were registered under the Federal Insecticide, Fungicide and Rodenticide Act (PL 94-140). The bill had been approved by the Agriculture and Transportation and Infrastructure committees (H Rept 112-43, Parts 1 and 2).

The U.S. Court of Appeals for the Sixth Circuit ruled in 2009 that commercial pesticides were pollutants when used in, near, or on waterways to control mosquito larvae, weeds, and other pests. The court granted the EPA a two-year stay in issuing new permitting rules. The stay was supposed to end April 9, but the court had extended the deadline to October 31. The Justice Department decided not to appeal the ruling, which angered farm groups and their congressional allies.

On the other side of the Capitol, the Senate Agriculture, Nutrition, and Forestry Committee approved the bill by voice vote June 21, but the measure did not reach the Senate floor. In the absence of legislation, the EPA went ahead October 31 and issued a final rule on point source discharges from the application of pesticides to U.S. waters.

Clean water. The House voted, 239–184, on July 13, 2011, to pass a bill (HR 2018) to limit the EPA's ability to enforce new or revised clean water standards. The bill advanced on a mainly party-line vote, after Republicans fended off Democratic efforts to preserve a stronger role for the EPA.

The aim of the measure was to restrict the agency's authority under the Clean Water Act (PL 95-217) to reject state water pollution plans and enforce stricter standards. It came in response to EPA actions over the previous two years to stall mountaintop mining in Appalachia because of concerns that resulting debris contaminated streams.

House Transportation and Infrastructure Chair John L. Mica, R-Fla., and Rahall said the measure was desperately needed in Appalachian states where coal mining made up a significant portion of the local economy. GOP lawmakers argued that the bill would curb an overly aggressive EPA and restore the balance between states and the federal government on water quality regulation. Many in Congress argued that the long-standing system of "cooperative federalism" under the Clean Water Act gave states primary responsibility for water pollution control.

Although the measure garnered the backing of some Democrats, especially from Appalachia, many in the party caucus worried that the legislation would allow states to create their own standards, to the detriment of neighboring states that shared water resources. The White House issued a veto threat July 12, saying the bill would "significantly undermine the Clean Water Act and could adversely affect public health, the economy and the environment."

During the debate, the House:

- Rejected, 183–237, an amendment by Earl Blumenauer, D-Ore., to exclude from the bill's provisions waters that the EPA determined provided flood protection for communities, made up a fish and wildlife habitat that benefited the economy, or were for coastal recreation. Bob Gibbs, R-Ohio, said the Blumenauer proposal would exempt virtually all waters affected by the Clean Water Act, essentially gutting the bill—a charge that amendment cosponsor Peter A. DeFazio, D-Ore., embraced. "It would gut this bill, which deserves to be gutted," DeFazio said. "This bill is absurd."
- Rejected, 191–231, an amendment by Jared Polis, D-Colo., to exclude from the bill's provisions those permit-holders listed by the EPA as being in significant noncompliance with the Clean Water Act. Without his amendment, Polis said, the bill would give "our country's worst polluters . . . a get-out-of-jail-free card."
- Rejected, 181–240, an amendment by Gerald E. Connolly, D-Va., to exempt bodies of water where federal funds were spent for restoration projects, studies, or certain other programs.
- Rejected, 188–238, a Democratic motion to recommit the bill that would have added language to retain the EPA's authority over pollutants discharged into a source of public drinking water.

Members agreed to a few Democratic proposals, including one to require the EPA to report changes in the number of waterborne pathogenic microorganisms, toxic chemicals, or toxic metals in waters regulated by a state under the bill.

COAL ASH

In another attempt to restrict the EPA, the House passed a bill (HR 2273) on October 14, 2011, to establish a system of state-level regulation for coal combustion waste generated from electricity production and called on the EPA to defer to state regulators on the issue. The vote was 267–144.

The Energy and Commerce Committee reported the bill, 35–12, on July 13 (H Rept 112-226).

In 2009, coal-based power plants accounted for roughly half of U.S. electricity generation and resulted in the creation of 135 million tons of coal combustion waste, one of the largest waste streams generated in the United States. Under the bill, states that chose to establish coal waste management permitting programs would be required to notify the EPA and certify that they would meet baseline requirements. States could elect to institute programs at any time. For states that did not opt to create their own programs, or whose programs were deemed inadequate, the EPA would serve as the permitting authority. However, the EPA could not issue alternative coal ash regulations, nor could it sanction states that did not correct program deficiencies found by the federal agency. The bill proposed a set of minimum standards for the construction or lateral expansion of a coal waste containment unit and basic engineering standards for storage structures.

Coal waste was largely exempt from federal regulation, and most permitting for waste pools was handled at the state level. Following a December 2008 breach in a coal waste containment pool at a power plant at Kingston, Tenn., the EPA found that several state permitting systems were inadequate. The Kingston spill resulted in 1.1 billion gallons of liquid coal waste being released and required a cleanup estimated to cost $1.2 billion. The EPA recommended regulating coal waste as hazardous waste or focusing on the containment facilities by establishing national standards for new storage facilities and requirements for retrofitting existing waste pools. The final EPA regulations were not expected to be issued until 2012 at the earliest.

Industry groups were highly critical of the proposals, arguing that requiring retrofits of older existing facilities would cause many of them to close or increase the price of electricity. GOP leaders and industry groups also argued that the EPA had not actually demonstrated that state permitting programs were insufficient and that the agency needed to do so before taking any type of regulatory action. Environmental groups pointed to the contamination and cleanup costs of the Kingston spill as a primary reason for implementing more-stringent regulations.

During the floor debate, the House:

- Rejected, 171–236, a Waxman amendment to require that the state programs contain criteria to protect human health and the environment.
- Rejected, 164–241, an amendment by Bobby L. Rush, D-Ill., to allow the EPA to inspect coal waste containment units and enforce state guidelines if the agency determined that a state was in violation of the state permit program.
- Rejected, 173–231, an amendment by Edward J. Markey, D-Mass., to set a five-year deadline for bringing existing waste containment units into compliance with revised criteria for design, groundwater monitoring, and corrective action, with the possibility of a one-year extension.

Keystone Pipeline

Republicans in the 112th Congress won House passage of several bills to boost domestic oil resources, the most dramatic of which was aimed at forcing President Barack Obama to make a decision on whether to permit the construction of an oil pipeline from Canada to the Gulf of Mexico. A deadline for a decision on the TransCanada Keystone XL pipeline was enacted as part of year-end legislation that extended a payroll tax cut and several other expiring programs.

Three House-passed bills to expand offshore oil drilling were not taken up in the Senate.

2011 LEGISLATIVE ACTION

The House passed a one-year extension of the payroll tax cut in December 2011 (HR 3630—PL 112-96). The bill included a sweetener for Republicans: a provision to require the president to make a politically uncomfortable decision on the permit for the Keystone XL pipeline within sixty days of the bill's enactment.

Senate Majority Leader Harry Reid, D-Nev., and Minority Leader Mitch McConnell, R-Ky., transformed the bill itself into a short-term extension to allow time for negotiations on a longer-term payroll tax bill, but they retained the pipeline language. When House Republicans balked at the two-month extension shortly before the holidays, McConnell successfully pressed them to pass the measure, stressing the inclusion of the Keystone provisions. Obama signed a slightly modified version of the two-month bill on December 23, with the pipeline language intact (HR 3765—PL 112-78). *(Details, p. 108)*

The legislation required the president to approve the permit, unless he determined that the pipeline was not in the nation's interest. If the president took no action, the permit would be deemed approved after the sixty-day period. The measure specified that an August environmental-impact statement by the State Department, which issues permits for projects that cross international borders, was sufficient to satisfy requirements under environmental laws.

The bill required TransCanada to reconsider the route of the pipeline through environmentally sensitive areas in Nebraska and to coordinate with state authorities to conduct the review. If the route was altered, the president was required to approve the revision within ten days, or it would be deemed approved. The project was exempted from any future environmental-review requirements that might result from pipeline route modifications.

Republicans argued that the $7 billion, 1,700-mile pipeline would provide both a more secure source of oil to the United States and thousands of jobs for local workers. The issue was also attractive to the GOP because it put the president in a squeeze between two groups that were vital elements of his political base: environmentalists, who launched a national campaign to block construction of the pipeline, and labor unions, which saw it as a source of jobs.

Environmental groups joined forces with Midwestern farmers, landowners, local activists, and students who feared that a pipeline spill could contaminate the massive Ogallala Aquifer, a major source of irrigation and drinking water for the central Plains states. The opponents also warned that extracting more oil from Canada's tar sands region would produce high levels of greenhouse gas emissions—the equivalent, they claimed, of adding 5 million cars to U.S. highways.

The industry argued that the State Department had been reviewing the application since 2008 and that TransCanada had gone beyond federal requirements to ensure that the project would not harm Midwestern lands or water supplies. The Keystone XL project was part of a large network of pipelines proposed by TransCanada to link the company's Alberta facility to oil terminals in the Midwest and along the Texas coast. The first leg of the pipeline complex—Keystone 1—was completed in 2010 and was already carrying oil to refineries in the Midwest. During its first year of operations, the pipeline had more than a dozen leaks. The Keystone XL pipeline was slated to take a more direct path from Alberta through Nebraska's Sand Hills region and extend transmission to Port Arthur, Texas.

During the summer of 2011, the House passed a bill (HR 1938) to force the Obama administration to decide on the permit by no later than November 1. The bill passed, 279–147, on July 26. The White House issued a statement opposing the measure, saying it was unnecessary because the State Department was committed to deciding the pipeline's fate before the end of the year.

With no chance of defeating the bill, Democrats forced votes on numerous amendments that put Republicans on record on environmental issues. For example, during the debate, the House:

- Rejected, 164–260, an amendment by Peter Welch, D-Vt., to include in the bill's findings section the risks of building the pipeline through the Ogallala Aquifer.
- Rejected, 164–261, an amendment by Bobby L. Rush, D-Ill., to strike language in the bill stating that the pipeline would result in no significant change in greenhouse gas emissions.
- Rejected, 155–272, an amendment by Steve Cohen, D-Tenn., to strike language in the bill describing the pipeline's safety standards and replace it with language noting the leaks experienced by the first Keystone pipeline.
- Rejected, 168–260, an amendment by Colleen Hanabusa, D-Hawaii, to add language making approval of the pipeline permit conditional on certain federal agencies finding that TransCanada was prepared to respond to a "worst-case" oil spill scenario.

On November 10, the State Department announced it needed more time to review a yet-to-be-determined alternative route around the Sand Hills region, delaying a decision until early 2013, past the 2012 elections.

On December 13, House Republicans passed a package that included extensions of the payroll tax cut, unemployment benefits, and other programs—and the Keystone pipeline provisions. The pipeline requirement was added to woo conservatives who did not see the payroll tax bill as essential to economic growth. The House passed the bill, 234–193, on December 13. The Senate passed it, amended with the two-month compromise, 89–10, on December 17. The House passed the modified two-month bill (HR 3765) by unanimous consent December 23, and the Senate cleared the measure the same day, also by unanimous consent.

2012 LEGISLATIVE ACTION

On January 18, 2012, Obama rejected the Keystone XL permit application after the State Department said that the sixty-day window did not give officials enough time to complete the environmental review.

Republicans sharply criticized the decision. The House Energy and Commerce Committee approved a bill (HR 3548) on February 7 to shift permitting authority for the Keystone XL project from the State Department to the Federal Energy Regulatory Commission (FERC).

The Energy and Commerce bill granted FERC thirty days to approve a permit for the 1,700-mile-long pipeline stretching from Alberta to Texas refineries. The panel adopted an amendment by voice vote to specify that no presidential permits would be required and that FERC could not stipulate additional conditions.

Members rehashed familiar arguments over whether the Canadian tar sands pipeline would reduce U.S. dependence on foreign oil, given that the oil must be sold on the global market. Democrats also questioned the project's effect on private property based on testimony from Nebraska citizens who indicated that the company in charge of the pipeline had aggressively pursued access to private land.

The action came despite concerns expressed the previous month during testimony by FERC and State Department officials before the panel's Energy and Power Subcommittee. A senior FERC staff member said the legislation was vague in some key areas and would not give the agency enough time to act properly.

Jeffrey C. Wright, director of FERC's Office of Energy Projects, told the subcommittee on January 25 that the thirty-day decision requirement "does not allow sufficient time to build an adequate record to arrive at a defensible decision."

Assistant Secretary of State Kerri-Ann Jones also raised concerns at the hearing about the Terry bill. She said it creates "serious questions about existing legal authorities, questions the continuing force of much of the federal and all of the state and local environmental and land-use management authority over the pipeline, and overrides foreign policy and national security considerations . . . which are properly assessed by the State Department."

As part of a complicated strategy by House GOP leaders to win support for a comprehensive surface transportation bill, the House passed the Keystone language as well as provisions to expand shale gas exploration and offshore oil drilling. The bill (HR 3408) passed on February 16, 237–187. The following month, however, senators rejected several GOP amendments to approve Keystone as well as expand oil and gas drilling in new areas.

With House Republicans unable to agree on a long-term surface transportation authorization, and with the most recent short-term extension set to expire at the end of June, House Speaker John A. Boehner, R-Ohio, agreed to pass a new transportation bill (HR 4348)—another short-term extension—that could serve as a legislative vehicle for a conference on a multiyear bill. As a sweetener for House Republicans, the House bill included the Keystone XL pipeline provisions shifting the approval process to the FERC and providing for automatic approval of a permit if the agency did not act within thirty days of receiving it. The Keystone provisions became one of the last hurdles to negotiating a final transportation bill. In the end, the provisions were dropped in the face of strong Democratic opposition in both chambers.

Oil and Gas Production

The House in 2011 and 2012 passed several bills aimed at expanding offshore drilling and other sources of oil and gas production. Supporters said new exploration would create jobs and lead to energy independence. The White House issued statements opposing several of the bills, and the Senate did not pass the measures.

2011 LEGISLATIVE ACTION

Lease Sales

On May 5, the House passed the first of the bills, a measure (HR 1230—H Rept 112-68) requiring that the Interior Department conduct offshore oil and gas lease sales in two sections of the Gulf of Mexico and off the Virginia coast within a specified time period. The tally was 266–149, with thirty-three Democrats joining all but two Republicans in support.

GOP backers hailed the measure, sponsored by Natural Resources Chair Doc Hastings, R-Wash., as a jobs bill that would also boost energy production and eventually reduce fuel prices. Under existing law, a lease gave the lessee exclusive rights to energy development within a particular area of the outer continental shelf. To clear the path for the sales, the measure proposed to "deem" certain existing environmental-impact statements and plans as satisfactory in meeting the necessary environmental requirements.

The administration had suspended permitting and lease sales temporarily in response to the April 2010 Deepwater Horizon oil rig explosion and resulting spill in the Gulf of Mexico. It lifted the drilling moratorium in October but had issued only a handful of permits thereafter. The White House policy statement said the administration intended to hold all three Gulf lease sales in the bill by mid-2012. Democratic opponents insisted the measure would do nothing to ease gasoline prices and would ignore the lessons of the Deepwater Horizon disaster. In their dissent, they wrote that measure "'restarts' nothing, but would mandate that the lease sales go forward within unreasonable time limits and without proper environmental review."

Exploratory Drilling

The House passed the second bill (HR 1229—H Rept 112-67) by a vote of 263–163 on May 11. The measure proposed to give the Interior Department thirty days to approve an exploratory-drilling permit application; the department could extend the review by two fifteen-day periods for a total of sixty days. If the department did not rule on an application within the sixty-day period, it would be deemed approved. The department would be required to extend, for one year, leases that were nonproducing as of April 30, 2010, and certain leases suspended in response to the Deepwater Horizon spill. Civil actions could not be filed more than sixty days after final agency action on a drilling permit.

Outer Continental Shelf

On May 12, the House passed legislation (HR 1231—H Rept 112-69) to require the Interior Department to expand the area of the outer continental shelf that was available for oil and natural gas leasing and set a domestic oil and gas production goal. The vote was 243–179.

Opponents called the proposal an "amnesia act" that ignored the lessons of the Deepwater Horizon spill. Backers insisted it was a critical step in creating jobs and faulted the administration for ignoring the importance of fossil fuels to the economy. "In the Gulf there were 41,000 wells drilled without a spill," said Don Young, R-Alaska. "Add one spill and everybody thinks the world came to an end. . . . Not to let them drill, not to let them produce that oil, not to let them help America out, not to employ Americans—that's dead wrong."

The bill proposed to require Interior to make available for lease at least 50 percent of the unused acreage within each planning area in the outer continental shelf considered to have the largest undiscovered and technically recoverable oil and gas reserves. The department would be required to make available for lease any area estimated to contain more than 2.5 billion barrels of oil or 7.5 trillion cubic feet of natural gas. It also directed that the department determine a goal for oil and natural gas production as part of each five-year leasing plan, including an increase of no less than 3 million barrels of oil and no less than 10 billion cubic feet of natural gas per day by 2027.

2012 LEGISLATIVE ACTION

The House passed a package of Republican energy proposals (HR 3408) by a vote of 237–187 on February 16. The provisions had been incorporated into a four-year GOP surface transportation bill (HR 7) but, with the transportation measure drawing fire from some conservatives, Speaker John A. Boehner, R-Ohio, and other Republican leaders broke the energy package out for a separate vote. Although the energy bill passed, Boehner was not able to generate sufficient support to get the larger highway bill through the House.

HR 3408 consisted of four separate bills that the Natural Resources Committee had approved in February. It included provisions that:

- Required the Interior Department to make available for lease at least 50 percent of the unused acreage within outer continental shelf planning areas considered to have the largest undiscovered and technically recoverable oil and gas reserves, as well as any area estimated to contain more than 2.5 billion barrels of oil or 7.5 trillion cubic feet of natural gas. The Interior Department would be required to conduct sales of specific leases in mid-Atlantic/Virginia coastal areas, the central and eastern Gulf of Mexico, the western Gulf of Mexico, southern California, and the North Aleutian Basin near Alaska.
- Repealed the existing ban on energy exploration and recovery activities within Alaska National Wildlife Refuge and require the Interior Department to begin selling leases for 50,000 acres. The department could declare specified areas within the refuges as "special areas" and effectively withdraw their availability for lease.
- Transferred authority to approve the Keystone XL pipeline project from the State Department—which was involved because the pipeline crossed international borders—to FERC. If the agency did not act within thirty days of receiving an application, the permit would be approved automatically.
- Required the Bureau of Land Management to begin issuing leases for oil shale based on regulations issued in 2008 under President George W. Bush and make the existing environmental-impact statement sufficient to meet all additional review and legal requirements. The department would be required to hold lease sales for lands in Colorado, Utah, and Wyoming within 180 days of enactment. In addition to opening large amounts of public lands in those states for the production of shale oil, the 2008 regulations provided a temporary reduction in lease royalty rates.

Energy Measures

Returning to the issue, the House passed a package of six energy measures (HR 4480) on June 21 by a party-line vote of 248–163. Republicans said the bill would ease regulations and spur job growth while Democrats called it a massive giveaway to the oil and gas industries.

The legislation mandated an increase in oil and gas production equivalent to any amount released from the Strategic Petroleum Reserve. It also required that the Interior Department ensure that at least 25 percent of eligible federal land was available for leasing each year.

Among the bills folded into the package was one (HR 4471—H Rept 112-519) to postpone for at least six months implementation of new Environmental Protection Agency (EPA) regulations on air pollutants emitted by refineries. Also included were bills to require the Interior secretary to develop a plan for energy production on public lands (HR 4381—H Rept 112-530), bar the government from rescinding leases on federal lands for energy production (HR 4382—H Rept 112-531), streamline permitting (HR 4383—H Rept 112-528), establish a live Internet auction for Bureau of Land Management leases (HR 2752—H Rept 112-371), and hasten development of the National Petroleum Reserve-Alaska (HR 2150—H Rept 112-259).

The White House threatened to veto the measure, arguing that the bill "would undermine the nation's energy security."

Republicans criticized the Obama administration's handling of domestic energy development, including a June 2011 order to release thirty million barrels of oil from the Strategic Petroleum Reserve and a decision to place a temporary moratorium on drilling in the Gulf of Mexico, following the Deepwater Horizon oil spill in 2010. They argued that their bill would reduce U.S. dependence on foreign oil.

Democrats forced votes on numerous amendments aimed at putting Republicans on the spot. For example, the House:

- Rejected, 153–256, an amendment by Edward J. Markey of Massachusetts, ranking Democrat on the Natural Resources Committee, to prohibit oil and gas produced under new leases from being exported to foreign countries.
- Rejected, 164–249, an amendment by Henry A. Waxman, D-Calif., to bar the EPA from delaying finalization of any rules to establish standards for clean air and pollution reduction if the pollution was contributing to a number of specific conditions.
- Rejected, 174–244, a Gene Green, D-Texas, amendment to strike a provision to require the EPA to consider cost and feasibility when proposing modifications to air quality standards for ozone.
- Rejected, 190–233, an amendment by Gerald E. Connolly, D-Va., to undercut a provision that Democrats said would limit the legal standing of local communities to stop an energy lease or permit through a civil action.

- Rejected, 168–250, an amendment by Rush D. Holt, D-N.J., to require those who held certain leases in the Gulf of Mexico and received royalty relief under a 1994 law to renegotiate their leases before getting new leases in the Gulf.

Offshore Drilling

The House passed a bill (HR 6082—H Rept 112-615) on July 25, by a vote of 253–170, to replace an Obama administration offshore drilling plan with a GOP proposal to open new areas for oil and gas development, including waters off the California, South Carolina, mid-Atlantic, and Alaska coasts. The House then rebuffed, 164–261, an effort to pass another bill (HR 6168) that Republicans said reflected the president's plan.

The administration's offshore leasing plan, for 2012–2017, was finalized earlier in the year and made fifteen lease sales available—twelve in the Gulf of Mexico and three in waters surrounding Alaska. The administration said the plan covered 75 percent of the estimated undiscovered resources within the outer continental shelf

House Natural Resources Chair Doc Hastings, R-Wash., said the administration's plan would open fewer areas to drilling than any plan introduced since the amendments to the Outer Continental Shelf Lands Act (PL 83-212) went into effect in 1980. The GOP plan provided for twenty-nine lease sales in more geographically diverse areas—including the Eastern Gulf, the mid-Atlantic, the Santa Barbara Basin near California, and Alaska's North Aleutian Basin. Markey said the states opposed the offshore drilling. "The risk is too great to their beaches; the risk is too great to the fishing industries. They do not want it," Markey said.

The Republican plan also directed the Interior Department to conduct a limited "multilease sale" environmental review, effectively requiring a single environmental-impact statement for all the new leases not included in the Obama administration plan.

The White House threatened to veto the measure, saying it ignored the lessons of the 2010 Deepwater Horizon oil spill.

During the debate, the House:

- Adopted by voice vote an amendment by Laura Richardson, D-Calif., to require the Interior Department to consult with the governor and state legislature in California when deciding where to offer leases off that state's coast.
- Rejected, 158–262, a Markey amendment to prohibit export of oil and natural gas produced from the new leases.
- Rejected, 150–275, an amendment by Alcee L. Hastings, D-Fla., to require companies seeking leases to include in the application an assessment of how the drilling would affect climate change. During debate, Hastings said the amendment would harm the environment further by driving drilling to countries that had less-stringent laws than the United States.
- Rejected other Democratic amendments that would have required companies to pay royalties on existing leases before being eligible for new ones under the bill, added safety requirements, and required companies seeking leases to detail how the increased drilling would affect the price of gas.

Yucca Mountain Nuclear Waste

Congress did not provide any funding in fiscal year 2013 for the proposed repository for nuclear waste at Yucca Mountain in Nevada. Instead, members drafted report language directing the Department of Energy to spend up to $10 million in available funds to continue working toward a solution for nuclear waste disposal.

For much of 2012, the Senate and House laid out competing visions for Yucca Mountain. The Senate Appropriations Committee April 26 approved a $33.4 billion energy and water development spending bill (S 2465) to authorize the Energy Department to establish a pilot project for consolidating spent nuclear fuel at one or more interim storage sites. The vote was 28–1.

California Democrat Dianne Feinstein, chair of the Energy-Water Appropriations Subcommittee, called the provision, which she authored, "a small breakthrough to begin" alleviating the risks posed by the huge quantities of highly radioactive waste piling up at more than 100 reactors across the nation.

Under current law, such waste should be destined for Yucca Mountain, which Congress designated in 1987 as the national disposal site. It was supposed to start accepting waste from nuclear plants in 1998 but never opened its doors, in large part because of the opposition of Nevada and its powerful Democratic senator, Majority Leader Harry Reid. President Barack Obama's administration was attempting to shutter the facility to make good on a campaign pledge made to Nevada in 2008.

Consolidating the waste left orphaned by the dispute at interim storage facilities was among the major recommendations that a blue ribbon commission, tasked by Obama with laying out a new national disposal strategy, made early in 2012. Existing law barred such consolidation, which meant the commission's recommendation needed congressional approval.

But the Feinstein provision faced opposition in the House, where support for Yucca Mountain ran deep among appropriators.

The House Appropriations Committee approved its $32.1 billion energy-water spending measure on April 25 by a 28–1 vote, and the full House passed the bill (HR 5325) on June 6, 255–165. The version prohibited closing Yucca Mountain and appropriated $25 million to keep the site operational. "I believe, as many do in the House, that the administration's position to close the Yucca Mountain site runs counter to the letter and spirit of the Nuclear Waste Policy Act passed by the Congress," said Norm Dicks of Washington, the ranking Democrat on the Appropriations Committee.

A requirement that the Nuclear Regulatory Commission continue to license activities for the long-planned waste repository was added in an amendment by John Shimkus, R-Ill., that was adopted 326–81. The proposal included an additional $10 million to pay for Nuclear Regulatory Commission activities.

As with most other appropriations measures, the energy-water bill did not advance to the floor of the Senate but was instead rolled into a continuing resolution (H J Res. 117—PL 112-175).

Energy Projects Loans

In response to the controversy surrounding a government loan to a solar company that later went bankrupt, a House panel in 2011 approved legislation to narrow the federal government's loan authority for energy projects.

The bill (HR 2915), which the Natural Resources Committee approved 26–17 on October 5, repealed the $3.3 billion in borrowing authority granted to the Energy Department's Western Area Power Administration under the 2009 stimulus law (PL 111-5). The loans were to be used for building, planning, or maintaining the operation of new or upgraded electric-power transmission lines, with any remaining balance forgiven at the end of a project's useful life.

The legislative action came after the recent bankruptcy of solar-panel manufacturer Solyndra Inc., which received more than $500 million in federal loan guarantees and which President Barack Obama had touted as a successful example of government lending.

California Republican Tom McClintock, the bill's sponsor, said the lesson learned from Solyndra was that taxpayer dollars should not be put at "risk" in funding loans to similar power entities. But Rep. Edward J. Markey, D-Mass., argued that the legislation was a politically motivated attempt by Republicans to single out the renewable-energy industry.

The bill would exempt from the repeal three projects already approved by the Energy Department. Several Democratic members issued amendments to excuse other projects as well, including an amendment from Rush D. Holt, D-N.J., that would include the Colorado Highlands Wind Project.

McClintock argued that the amendments pertained to projects that did not have contracts and had not broken ground. Seven amendments seeking to exempt various projects were rejected.

Incandescent Light Bulbs

Republicans came up short in 2011 in an effort to permanently roll back energy-efficiency standards for incandescent light bulbs, although supporters managed to win support for a one-year delay.

The July 12 vote on HR 2417 to repeal the provision was 233–193, short of the two-thirds majority required for passage of measures considered under suspension of the rules, an expedited floor procedure usually reserved for noncontroversial legislation. Five Democrats voted for the measure; ten Republicans voted no. The bill repealed part of a 2007 energy law (PL 110-140) that created minimum efficiency standards for incandescent bulbs. It also eliminated $30 million in funding authority for Energy Department research, market assessments, and consumer education related to energy-efficient lighting.

But during consideration of the fiscal 2012 Energy-Water appropriations bill (HR 2345) on July 15, the House by voice vote adopted an amendment calling for a one-year delay in implementation of the standards, originally set for 2012.

The new standards were expected to lead to a phase-out of traditional light bulbs. Set to replace them were compact fluorescent lights (CFLs), light-emitting diodes (LEDs), and new styles of incandescent bulbs, many of which were halogen-based and used less power. But the price of the new bulbs, which could be many times that of the old incandescent products, sparked opposition to the regulation. "I'm not opposed to CFL lighting. I'm not opposed to the new incandescents," said Texas Republican Joe L. Barton, the bill's sponsor. "But I am opposed to telling my constituents that they have no choice at all."

Supporters of the standards contended that although the new bulbs were more expensive, they paid for themselves. "The light bulb efficiency standards alone will save Pennsylvania 3.7 billion kilowatt-hours of energy in a year," said Mike Doyle, D-Pa., during debate on HR 2417. "That means we'll save $465 million in Pennsylvania in just one year."

The light bulb standards were a source of tension among Republicans for a number of years. After the 2010 midterm elections, when Barton and Fred Upton of Michigan were both vying to chair the House Energy and Commerce Committee, Barton's backers used his support for repealing the light bulb standards to attack Upton's more moderate record. Upton, who ultimately won the committee chair position and pledged to revisit the issue, had worked with former representative Jane Harman, D-Calif., to write the standards.

Copper Mining

The House in 2011 endorsed a land exchange that would open part of southeastern Arizona to copper mining, despite protests from many Democrats about the project's possible effect on American Indian sites.

The legislation (HR 1904), which passed 235–186 on October 26 mainly along party lines, permitted a land swap between the federal government and Resolution Copper Mining, which was owned by subsidiaries of international mining giants Rio Tinto and BHP Billiton. Arizona lawmakers had tried since 2005 to move legislation to approve the exchange, but none of the bills passed.

Republicans praised the latest measure as a job creator in a pocket of the country with high unemployment, touting

Resolution Copper's claim that the project would create an estimated 3,700 jobs. Only eight Republicans voted no, while just seven Democrats voted yes.

The bill "is a perfect example of how safely and responsibly harnessing our resources will generate revenue and get our economy back on track," said Rep. Doc Hastings, R-Wash.

Democrats expressed concerns that the government was getting shortchanged by not receiving royalty payments for minerals extracted from the land. Royalties were not required under an 1872 mining statute that still applied. Some Democrats also worried that there had not been enough outreach to American Indian tribes about the land exchange.

The House rejected three Democratic amendments addressing those concerns. A proposal by Ben Ray Luján of New Mexico, which fell on a 189–233 vote, would have exempted all American Indian sacred and cultural sites from the exchange. An amendment by Edward J. Markey of Massachusetts, rejected 173–238, would have required that Resolution Copper pay an 8 percent royalty for all minerals produced in commercial quantities from land received in the conveyance. Lawmakers also defeated, 182–240, an amendment by Arizona's Raúl M. Grijalva that would have required Resolution Copper to locate its remote operations center in Superior, Ariz., and recruit and preferentially employ qualified state residents.

The House bill omitted compromise language drafted in the previous Congress by Sens. Jeff Bingaman, D-N.M., and John McCain, R-Ariz., that would have made the land exchange subject to approval by the agriculture secretary, in consultation with tribal governments.

Airlines and Carbon Emissions

The House in 2011 passed a bill to shield U.S. airlines from the pending carbon mandate from the European Union (EU), but the Senate took no action.

The bill (HR 2594), passed by voice vote October 24, prohibited U.S. airlines from complying with the carbon emissions trading rules that were to apply to airlines beginning in 2012. The EU system was intended to reduce emissions of pollutants that contributed to global warming. It capped emissions and required polluters to hold permits for each ton of carbon dioxide they emitted. Starting in 2012, the EU required airlines serving European airports to participate in the system.

House Transportation and Infrastructure Chair John L. Mica, R-Fla., called the EU requirements "an arbitrary and unjust violation of international law that disadvantages U.S. air carriers, threatens U.S. aviation jobs, and could close down direct travel from many central and western U.S. airports to Europe."

The airlines said the requirements violated international law. Environmental groups, however, lobbied against the House measure, arguing in part that the EU's carbon regulation is fair to all air carriers. They said the mandate would provide an economic incentive to reduce fuel consumption and to use more fuel-efficient aircraft. Some also contended that the bill could push the United States closer to a trade war with Europe.

Nuisance Dust

Legislation to bar the Environmental Protection Agency (EPA) for one year from revising standards on "nuisance dust" won House passage in 2011, but the Senate took no action.

House members voted 268–150 on December 8 to pass the bill (HR 1633), which was designed to prevent the EPA from using the Clean Air Act (PL 101-549) to regulate coarse particulates kicked up by farm operations. The EPA would, however, be allowed to regulate nuisance dust in cases where it was not regulated under state or local law and the benefits of regulation surpass the cost and potential economic effects on employment. The White House threatened to veto the bill.

Republicans said the legislation would provide regulatory certainty for farmers and rural citizens, while Democrats contended that the GOP was trying to regulate a threat that did not exist. EPA Administrator Lisa P. Jackson said she intended to propose no change to the air pollution standard for coarse particulates, which must be reviewed every five years. Such pollution likely caused adverse health effects due to its ability to travel to the lower regions of the respiratory tract, the EPA said.

Bill sponsor Kristi Noem, R-S.D., emphasized the legislation's focus on rural areas, saying in a floor speech that a "one-size-fits-all" air quality standard does not work when urban and rural locales experience different environmental realities. Democrats were concerned that the bill's provisions were written broadly enough to apply to dust generated from industrial activities such as open-pit mining.

Mike Johanns, R-Neb., spearheaded an effort in the Senate to prohibit regulation of farm dust. But after Jackson announced definitively in October that the EPA would not change its standards on coarse particulates, Johanns declared victory and ended his legislative push.

But Noem did not take Jackson's statement at face value. "At any minute, someone could bring litigation . . . that would change what the EPA's action is today," Noem said.

The Energy and Commerce Subcommittee on Energy and Power approved the bill (H Rept 112-317) November 3 in a 12–9 party-line vote.

Kentucky Republican Edward Whitfield, chair of the subcommittee, emphasized the heightened cost to farm and rural businessowners of more stringent EPA oversight. "This bill provides needed certainty that the agricultural sector and rural America will not be burdened with costly new EPA dust regulations," he said.

Democrats argued that Jackson had already addressed Republicans' concerns. Edward J. Markey, D-Mass., said the bill was solving an "imaginary problem."

California Water

Republican legislation designed to increase water access for central California farmers and consumers by limiting environmental regulation passed in the House in 2012 but did not advance further.

The measure (HR 1837), which passed 246–175 on February 29, would facilitate increased water access in the San Joaquin Valley for agricultural and municipal use and limit the enforcement or consideration of certain environmental rules and regulations. One Republican voted no, while ten Democrats backed the measure.

The bill's sponsor was Devin Nunes, R-Calif., who represented the heart of the valley in Fresno and Tulare counties.

Most Democrats said the bill would override the state's rights to manage its resources by overruling a California statute that required water contractors to meet certain environmental regulations, including some stipulated in the Endangered Species Act (PL 93-205).

California Democrat George Miller said the legislation was the "greatest pre-emption of state water rights in the history of this country," adding that the bill's main supporters were "heavily subsidized farmers."

Republicans charged that water deliveries to the region, especially to area farmers, had been unfairly limited because of environmental regulations protecting various fish species. "These are farmers that are seeing their families destroyed right now," California Republican Jeff Denham said. "They're certainly not special interests."

Democrats offered several amendments, all rejected by the House, to delay implementation until the Interior secretary certified that it would not cause harmful effects on residential and agricultural water supplies or negatively affect agriculture- or fishery-related jobs.

The bill would make changes to the environmental management law known as the Central Valley Project Improvement Act (PL 102-575) and would repeal provisions of the San Joaquin River settlement to boost water access for agricultural and municipal use. It also would limit enforcement or consideration of environmental rules under the landmark National Environmental Policy Act (PL 91-190) and the Endangered Species Act.

Among the bill's provisions was a proposal to require the Interior Department to increase the total water delivery capacity of the Central Valley Project. It would require the water resource management project to increase its annual water delivery capability by 800,000 acre-feet by the end of fiscal 2016. If necessary to meet that goal, the department would be required to end all nonmandatory water activities. An acre-foot is the volume of water that would cover one acre to a depth of one foot.

The Natural Resources Committee approved the bill (H Rept 112-403) on February 29 by a vote of 27–17.

The Obama administration said that it would veto the measure if Congress cleared it.

Hydropower

The House passed a bill in 2012 to encourage the development of small-scale hydropower facilities on federal property, despite Democratic opposition to a provision that would exempt such projects from environmental review.

Republicans said the legislation (HR 2842), passed 265–154 on March 7, would encourage the development of clean, renewable energy on canals and other human-made water conveyances managed by the Interior Department's Bureau of Reclamation. They said it would create jobs while cutting bureaucratic red tape.

In addition to exempting small-scale hydropower projects on federal canals and pipelines from environmental review, supporters said the measure would clarify the bureau's role in permitting such projects and would create a process for contracting the operations of the facilities to private or local entities.

Natural Resources Chair Doc Hastings, R-Wash., said the approval process mandated by the National Environmental Policy Act, or NEPA (PL 91-190), was unnecessary in such cases because the existing conduits had already been subject to environmental assessment. Republicans said the added review deterred companies from applying for permits to build such facilities.

Grace F. Napolitano of California led Democratic opposition to the measure as written, although she said she supported its "general premise." She said Republicans could not provide any examples of instances in which the environmental review process prevented a small-conduit hydropower project from moving forward. "It is not an obstacle—it is a tool used to facilitate coordination, cooperation and public input," Napolitano said.

Napolitano offered an amendment to strike the NEPA waiver language, but it was defeated 168–253.

The measure required the Interior Department to offer the lease of power privilege first to an irrigation district or relevant water-users' association.

The Natural Resources Committee approved the bill (H Rept 112-301) on October 5, 2011, by a vote of 30–12.

Clean Air Act

A House panel in 2012 approved Republican legislation to eliminate a key tenet of the Clean Air Act, drawing strong objections from Democrats who called for a transparent look at the law before such significant changes were made.

The Energy and Commerce Committee on May 17 approved, 28–13, a bill (HR 4471—H Rept 112-519) to create a new task force to study the cumulative economic effect of several Environmental Protection Agency (EPA) regulations. The legislation specifically delayed EPA's completion of new emissions and fuel standards, as well as ozone air quality standards under the Clean Air Act (CAA, PL 101-549), until the task force reported to Congress on the effect of those rules.

The bill sparked controversy over language that would essentially negate a 2001 Supreme Court decision that upheld the agency's practice of considering only public health concerns when setting national ambient air quality standards (NAAQS) for smog. Under the measure, the EPA would have to factor in feasibility and economic costs, including gas prices, when revising the standards.

Texas Democrat Gene Green, who sometimes voted with Republicans on environmental issues, offered an amendment to strike that language from the bill, the rest of which he said he supported. It was rejected, 18–28. "Let's don't pretend that this section isn't anything but a message," Green said, arguing that the air pollution law should be reopened only through separate legislation that was not linked to other issues.

Kentucky Republican Edward Whitfield maintained that the legislation was needed because the Supreme Court said the statute's language was "ambiguous" with respect to whether the EPA could consider costs when setting new or revised ozone-based air quality standards.

California Democrat Henry A. Waxman said Republicans were misinterpreting the opinion, which called sections of the law "ambiguous" with respect to its lack of explicit direction to account for costs when modifying the standards. But the justices unanimously agreed that the law, "interpreted in its statutory and historical context and with appreciation for its importance to the CAA as a whole, unambiguously bars cost considerations from the NAAQS-setting process and thus ends the matter for us, as well as the EPA."

Federal Lands

The House passed a bill in 2012 to ease dozens of environmental laws on federal lands in an attempt to promote recreational activity as well as to combat drug trafficking. The legislation, part of a wider effort by the GOP to relax federal environment and energy regulations, was not taken up in the Senate.

The House passed the bill (HR 2578) June 19 in a 232–188 vote, largely along party lines. Sixteen Democrats voted for the legislation, and nineteen Republicans opposed it.

The bill included language offered by Rob Bishop, R-Utah, to give U.S. Customs and Border Protection the authority to patrol as well as build roads, fences, and temporary offices on federal lands that lie within 100 miles of borders with Canada and Mexico. The areas would be exempt from certain environmental laws.

Bill supporters such as Bishop and Doc Hastings, R-Wash., chair of the Natural Resources panel, said many of the regulatory adjustments were necessary to maintain border security, spur local economic activity, and address regulatory overreach. They said environmental requirements currently hindered border enforcement actions. Waiving some of those requirements, they said, would facilitate the construction of border security infrastructure to combat violence related to drug smuggling.

The House adopted by voice vote a Bishop amendment to narrow to sixteen from thirty-six the list of laws from which the border patrol would be exempt. The measure would maintain the exemptions from the National Environmental Policy Act (PL 91-190) and the Endangered Species Act (PL 93-205), but would drop exemptions provided by the bill from the Clean Air Act (PL 101-549) and the Clean Water Act (PL 95-217).

Democrats said that border security issues should be dealt with separately as part of an overhaul of immigration laws. "To do so in a land management bill makes no sense," Jim Costa, D-Calif., said. "We should be taking up comprehensive immigration reform separate from land management bills." Homeland Security Secretary Janet Napolitano had said that waiving the environmental requirements would be "bad policy" and that it is not necessary for "immediate border control needs." Several environmental and conservation groups, including the Sierra Club and the League of Conservation Voters, also raised objections.

Bishop's amendment also clarified that federal land management agencies may not prohibit border patrol efforts aimed at preventing unlawful entries into the country by terrorists or illegal aliens.

Raúl M. Grijalva, D-Ariz., offered an amendment to strike Bishop's border security proposal. It was rejected, 177–247.

The measure also included the language from a separate bill (HR 3069) that, in an effort to protect endangered fish populations, would allow the hunting of sea lions near the Columbia River in the Pacific Northwest and a measure (HR 4094) to repeal restrictions on off-road vehicle use in North Carolina's Cape Hatteras Seashore Recreational Area.

The bill also included the text of a bill (HR 3065) to permit greater use of federal funds to establish public target-shooting ranges, as well as another (HR 4234) that would double the duration of grazing permits on federal lands.

The Obama administration said in a statement released June 18 that the bill would "disregard and shortchange public input on a range of community interests, including natural resource protections, and preclude agencies from considering less environmentally detrimental alternatives."

Mining on Public Lands

The House in 2012 passed a bill to expedite permits for mining critical minerals on public lands, dismissing objections from President Barack Obama and congressional Democrats that the bill would weaken environmental regulation and could cover virtually all hard-rock mining. The chamber on July 12 passed the measure (HR 4402) by a vote of 256–160. The Senate did not take up the measure.

Under the bill, mines on public lands that produced materials considered critical to national defense, energy infrastructure, and economic security and to supporting manufacturing, agriculture, and transportation infrastructure would be eligible for the concurrent environmental reviews that a March 2012 executive order provided for surface transportation, renewable-energy, and waterway projects.

Rare earth elements, a type of critical mineral, are important to commercial manufacturing and the defense industry and are used in such products as cell phones and satellite systems. The minerals were not mined domestically as of 2011, and the United States is almost entirely dependent on imports, with the bulk coming from China.

"We have the resources, but we simply made the permitting process so long, complicated, unpredictable that we've killed our supply and allowed other nations to control our future," said James Lankford, R-Okla.

Once an agreement is reached on a timeline with a "project proponent," the entire review process would have to be completed within thirty months unless the parties decide otherwise.

Permitting agencies would be allowed to determine that federal environmental review under the National Environmental Policy Act (PL 91-190) is not needed when their own or state review processes suffice. The bill also would set a sixty-day limit for filing civil actions against agency decisions.

Democrats maintained that the bill's definition of critical and strategic minerals was too broad and would subsequently cover virtually all mines, such as those for sand, gravel, gold, and coal. Edward J. Markey, D-Mass., said the bill was "chock full of giveaways" to the mining industry without addressing the absence of royalty payments for mining on public lands and argued that the move was part of a larger effort by House Republicans to benefit other energy industries, such as coal, timber, and oil.

The House rejected, 162–251, an amendment by Paul Tonko, D-N.Y., to narrow the bill's definition of critical and strategic minerals to what the National Research Council identified as critical minerals in a 2008 report, or to what the Interior secretary had identified as critical based on the report. The amendment would have excluded sand, gravel, and clay.

The House also adopted by voice vote an amendment by Chip Cravaack, R-Minn., to allow the bill to cover permit applications that have already been submitted.

The House rejected, 163–253, a proposal by Markey to require companies that mine for hard-rock minerals on federal lands to pay 12.5 percent in royalties to the federal government. The money would be directed to pay for lands reclamation at abandoned hard-rock mines.

The Natural Resources Committee approved the bill (H Rept 112-583, Part 1) on May 16, 24–12.

Chemical Safety Standards

Legislation to revise federal chemical safety standards won Senate committee approval in 2012, despite Republican complaints of a partisan approach. The Senate Environment and Public Works Committee approved the bill, 10–8, along party lines on July 25.

The measure (S 847—S Rept 112-264) required companies to disclose to the government test results proving that flame retardants and other chemical products are safe to keep on the market. The Environmental Protection Agency (EPA) was authorized to require the testing of any chemical substance and to impose restrictions on violators.

"This is a very important piece of legislation because [current law] is not strong enough, and we have people exposed to chemicals that are causing them harm," said Chair Barbara Boxer, D-Calif.

Republicans disagreed, arguing that while modernizing the Toxic Substances Control Act (PL 94-469) was crucial, Democrats abandoned bipartisanship in moving the legislation forward. "[S]imply introducing a partisan bill year in and year out has not and will not lead us to a bipartisan solution that modernizes TSCA," said ranking Republican James M. Inhofe of Oklahoma.

New Jersey Democrat Frank R. Lautenberg, the bill's sponsor, had sought for years to overhaul the act. Under existing law, the EPA could call for safety testing only after evidence surfaced demonstrating that a chemical is dangerous. The EPA's inventory listed more than 84,000 chemicals used in commerce, although just 200 had been subject to mandatory testing.

Republicans also said members did not have ample time to review an amendment by Lautenberg that would make several changes to the bill, including requiring the EPA to evaluate chemicals in stages and to rely on existing information before requiring companies to submit new information to the agency. The amendment was adopted by voice vote.

Coal Regulations

Capping two years of efforts to curb government rules in an effort to spur energy growth, House Republicans in 2012 advanced a package of measures to combat what they said was a "war on coal." by President Barack Obama's administration. The legislation was written to roll back fuel economy standards, bar regulation of greenhouse gas emissions, and cede authority over coal waste to the states.

In the final floor vote before leaving for the election recess, the House on September 21 voted 233–175 mostly along party lines for the combined legislation (HR 3409).

The House had already passed nearly all the bills in the package, but GOP leaders reprised their effort with an eye on Election Day to highlight their resistance to White House policies regarding coal. "The Obama administration has waged a war on coal—coal jobs and the small businesses in the mining supply chain and the low-cost energy that millions of Americans rely on," said Natural Resources Chair Doc Hastings, R-Wash.

Democrats said the perceived "war on coal" was a figment of GOP imagination. "The Republicans are saying that there is a war on coal, but the only battle coal is losing is in the free market to natural gas, to wind, and to solar," said Edward J. Markey of Massachusetts, the Natural Resources panel's ranking Democrat. "It's not a war; it's a revolution."

The Senate did not take up the bill, which was opposed by the Obama administration.

Although the White House finalized the fuel economy standards the previous month and touted it as one of its signature achievements, Republicans disagreed. Although the legislation would not affect tougher fuel economy standards slated to phase in through the 2016 model year, it would have had the effect of blocking stricter standards after 2017. The newly finalized rules mandating a national 54.5-miles-per-gallon average fuel economy standard by the 2025 model year incorporated an agreement among the Environmental Protection Agency (EPA), the National Highway Traffic Safety Administration, California's Air Resources Board, and a host of auto manufacturers.

The EPA estimated that motorists would save $1.7 trillion in fuel costs by 2025.

Another significant piece of the legislative package was a provision to give states primary regulatory authority over the waste produced by burning coal.

The House passed a bill (HR 2273) in October 2011 that would have allowed states to create permitting authorities to regulate coal ash while barring the EPA from issuing alternative rules.

Scott Slesinger, legislative director at the National Resources Defense Council, said the bill was flawed because it lacked deadlines and consequences should states decline to issue coal ash disposal permits.

But coal ash recyclers said the language would be a step in the right direction. "We are extremely pleased that members of both parties and both chambers have crafted such a thoughtful and positive solution to regulating fly ash disposal," said Kirk Benson, chief executive of Headwaters, the nation's largest coal ash recycling company, which was active in lobbying on the issue.

Hunting and Fishing

An otherwise popular bill designed to ease federal regulations on hunting and fishing died in the Senate at the end of the 112th Congress after a Republican insisted the legislation would raise taxes and violate the debt limit deal reached the previous August.

Senators on November 26 sustained a budgetary point of order against the bill (S 3525) in a mostly party-line 50–44 vote, with sixty votes required to override the motion. The chamber had voted, 84–12, on November 15 to invoke cloture.

Jeff Sessions, R-Ala., raised the point of order over a provision that would allow the Interior Department to increase the fee for duck stamps on hunting licenses, which raise revenue for conservation programs, and authorize $140 million over the following ten years. Sessions, who said he backed the measure overall, called the provision a new tax and said the fee would breach the spending caps in the 2011 debt limit deal (PL 112-25).

"Should we violate the Budget Control Act for a mere $14 million a year?" Sessions asked in floor remarks. "I don't think the average duck hunter would be concerned if we slowed down a little bit and sent this bill back to committee and had it paid for so we didn't violate the budget."

Although most federal lands were already open for recreational hunting and fishing, the bill (HR 4089), sponsored by Jeff Miller, R-Fla., who co-chaired the Congressional Sportsmen's Caucus, would codify such activities.

The measure applied to certain public lands, including federal wilderness areas, unless the Bureau of Land Management (BLM) or the U.S. Forest Service prohibited such activities for conservation, safety, national security, or energy and water supply purposes or to comply with federal or state law. According to the Congressional Budget Office, implementing the bill would cost $12 million over five years.

Democrats insisted that the measure was worthy of passage.

"The fact is, this is a responsible, bipartisan bill that will reduce the deficit by $5 million while expanding hunting and fishing opportunities for millions of Americans," said the bill's sponsor, Montana Democrat Jon Tester.

Barbara Boxer of California, the only Democrat to vote against waiving budget rules, said in a written statement that while she supported the bill generally, she was concerned about provisions that would broaden an exemption barring the use of environmental law to address threats from dangerous chemicals, including lead, in ammunition and fishing tackle.

The bill set aside 1.5 percent of the revenue paid into the Land and Water Conservation Fund for land purchases that improve access to remote federal lands for recreational hunting and fishing. It also authorized sales of federal land to private owners to raise money for such purchases.

The measure authorized permits to allow bow and crossbow hunters to traverse national parks when such routes provide the most direct access to hunting grounds.

The sportsmen's legislation combined twenty different bills, taking ideas from Democrats and Republicans, and was supported by nearly fifty conservation and other interest groups, from the National Wildlife Federation to the National Rifle Association, Tester said.

The House passed the measure, 274–146, on April 17, with thirty-nine Democrats voting for it and two Republicans voting no.

Rep. Raúl M. Grijalva, D-Ariz., said the bill was unnecessary because nearly 85 percent of federal lands were open for hunting, fishing, and shooting. "These activities have always been an essential part of the federal land management, and they always will be," Grijalva said.

But Democratic critics raised concerns that the bill would negatively affect local and state government cooperation with federal agencies, destroy wildlife habitats, and create a dangerous precedent allowing for the importation of trophies of endangered wildlife.

The House adopted by voice vote an amendment by House Natural Resources Chair Doc Hastings, R-Wash., to add shooting ranges to the list of valid uses of public land. It also would clarify that federal public land management officials are not required to consider the existence or availability of recreational fishing, hunting, or shooting facilities on nearby or adjacent public or private lands when planning or determining which federal lands are open for such activities.

Pipeline Safety

A bill to update federal safety standards for pipeline infrastructure was cleared without opposition in 2011.

The bill (HR 2845—PL 112-90), passed by voice vote in the House on December 12 and cleared by unanimous consent in the Senate on December 13, reflected the end result of bipartisan negotiations among leaders of the House Energy and Commerce and Transportation and Infrastructure committees and the Senate to respond to a number of high-profile pipeline accidents in recent years, including a California explosion and an oil spill in Michigan.

The measure reauthorized the Pipeline and Hazardous Materials Safety Administration through 2015 and codified a number of recommendations the National Transportation Safety Board made after the pipeline accidents. It limited some of the agency's regulatory authority.

The bill increased penalties for major violations to $175,000 per incident, up from the current $100,000 limit, and capped them at $1.8 million. It also permitted the Transportation Department to require the installation of automatic and remote-controlled shutoff valves on newly built or replaced transmission pipelines, but did not mandate them in existing pipelines.

Utilities and Environmental Regulations

Utility companies would have been allowed to violate certain environmental regulations without penalty during particular emergencies under legislation (HR 4273) that the House passed by voice vote on August 1, 2012.

Under the Federal Power Act (PL 66-280), the Energy Department could direct private utility companies to supply power in excess of their permitted operating capacity during emergency situations. Complying with those orders, however, could result in a temporary violation of environmental and zoning regulations. During a power outage in 2005, the Energy Department ordered a District of Columbia–area power company to maintain an adequate energy supply while other infrastructure was brought back online, forcing the company to break a National Ambient Air Quality Standard. Despite the order, the local environmental agency issued the utility company a citation.

The measure exempted utilities operating under an emergency order issued by the Energy Department from applicable federal or local environmental laws, as well as other ordinances that may be violated as a result of the order. The exemption extended to criminal or civil liability associated with such violations. "We should not punish generators who are simply following orders from the federal government," said the bill's sponsor, Texas Republican Pete Olson. "This bill will fix a clear conflict in federal laws," added Mike Doyle, D-Pa.

The Energy and Commerce Subcommittee on Energy and Power approved the measure (H Rept 112-586) by voice vote on June 7. However, John D. Dingell, D-Mich., said at the markup that he remained "concerned about unintended consequences that a waiver from all environmental laws could have."

Interior and Environmental Funds

Republicans repeatedly turned to the appropriations process to target the Environmental Protection Agency (EPA), which drew the ire of conservatives who accused the agency of pursuing an overly aggressive regulatory agenda. The agency managed to retain most of its regulatory powers but faced steep funding cuts.

FISCAL 2011

The EPA bore the brunt of the cuts made in the $29.6 billion Interior-Environment title of the bill, reversing increases that President Barack Obama's administration won in the 111th Congress. However, the agency emerged from the appropriations showdown with most of its regulatory powers intact.

All twelve fiscal year 2011 appropriations bills, including the Interior-Environment title, were left unfinished at the end of the 111th Congress. This gave the newly empowered Republican House its first opportunity to reduce government funding. The omnibus package signed by President Barack Obama on April 15, 2011 (HR 1473—PL 112-10), contained significant cuts throughout the federal government. *(Details, p. 150)*

Overall, programs funded through the Interior-Environment title were reduced by $2.6 billion, or 8 percent, from fiscal 2010. The total was $2.8 billion below

Obama's fiscal 2011 request but $1.8 billion more than would have been provided under a House-passed Republican bill (HR 1). Under the final spending package (PL 112-10), the EPA received $8.8 billion for fiscal 2011, a reduction of roughly $1.5 billion, or 17 percent, from fiscal 2010 levels and 58 percent of the total cuts in the title.

Still, the spending agreement offered the agency a reprieve from far deeper cuts included in the original House-passed bill, which would have reduced funding by $3.3 billion from fiscal 2010. It also omitted House riders targeting EPA policies, including greenhouse gas restrictions and other air and water regulations.

However, House Republican appropriators said funding for climate change programs was cut $49 million, or 13 percent, across the spending bill. About $1 billion of the cuts were absorbed by two popular water infrastructure programs: state revolving loan funds for clean water and for drinking water. The programs, which helped finance state and local water infrastructure improvements, received $2.5 billion. The bill included $1.1 billion in grants for state and tribal environmental programs and $2.8 billion for environmental programs and management. Science and technology programs got $815 million, while the superfund toxic-waste cleanup program received almost $1.3 billion.

Many Interior Department programs also experienced at least some funding reductions.

FISCAL 2012

Efforts by the House Republican majority to make deep cuts in spending for the Environmental Protection Agency (EPA) and to roll back a large number of environmental regulations failed during debate over fiscal 2012 appropriations, but the Interior-Environment spending bill still provided $2.1 billion less than requested.

The House began floor debate on the bill in late July but never got back to it after the August recess; Senate appropriators did not mark up a bill. Instead, the measure was packaged as part of a fiscal 2012 omnibus spending measure, which President Obama signed into law December 23 (HR 2055—PL 112-74). *(Details, p. 172)*

The Interior-Environment bill provided $29.2 billion, all but $55 million of which was discretionary spending. The discretionary total was $380 million, or 1 percent, less than provided in fiscal 2011 (PL 112-10) but $2.1 billion, or 7 percent, less than Obama requested. The EPA received $8.5 billion, compared with $7.1 billion in the House bill.

Most of the myriad policy riders the House had included to limit the EPA's regulatory authority were dropped in the final spending agreement. One of the remaining provisions delegated to the Interior Department, rather than the EPA, authority for issuing air pollution permits for offshore-drilling activities in the Arctic Ocean. Another provision exempted livestock producers from requirements for reporting greenhouse gas emissions. The bill cut $14 million from clean-air and climate research programs, $14 million from air regulatory programs, and $12 million from the EPA's regulatory development office. It also directed the president to report to Congress on how much the federal government spent on climate change programs in fiscal 2011.

MAJOR PROVISIONS

Major funding components of the bill included:

- $10.3 billion for the Interior Department, $310 million below fiscal 2011 spending and about $795 million less than requested. The bill prohibited individuals from filing lawsuits to prevent grazing on public lands until they exhausted all administrative hearings and appeals procedures. It also automatically renewed certain livestock grazing permits for public lands through fiscal 2013.
- $1.1 billion for the Bureau of Land Management, virtually the same as in fiscal 2011 and as requested by Obama. The conference agreement did not include an administration proposal to increase oil and gas leasing fees by $38 million.
- $2.6 billion for the National Park Service, virtually the same as in fiscal 2011 and about $310 million less than requested. Most of the funding—$2.2 billion—was for operating and maintaining existing national parks.
- $1.5 billion for the U.S. Fish and Wildlife Service, close to the fiscal 2011 level and about $220 million less than requested. The bulk of the agency's $1.2 billion in funding was for the management of critical habitat, fisheries, and endangered species.
- $2.5 billion for programs administered by the Bureau of Indian Affairs, including social services, education, employment development, law enforcement, and natural resources development. The total was a decrease of $60 million from fiscal 2011 and $35 million more than the administration's request.
- $8.5 billion for the Environmental Protection Agency, $220 million below fiscal 2011 spending and about $510 million less than requested. Funding included $2.7 billion for environmental programs, $2.5 billion for infrastructure assistance grants, and $1.2 billion for the Hazardous Substance Superfund. The bill provided $2.4 billion for the popular clean water and drinking water state revolving funds, which helped finance state and local water infrastructure improvements nationwide.
- $4.6 billion for the Forest Service, about the same as in fiscal 2011 and $330 million less than requested, for the Agriculture Department agency. The total included $1.7 billion for wild land fire suppression programs.
- $4.3 billion for the Indian Health Service, about $245 million more than in fiscal 2011 but $310 million less than requested. The health service was part of the Department of Health and Human Services.

- $146 million each, the requested amounts, for the National Endowment for the Arts and the National Endowment for the Humanities. The Smithsonian Institution received $812 million, $50 million less than requested.

HOUSE COMMITTEE ACTION

The House Appropriations Committee approved an Interior-Environment spending bill (HR 2584—H Rept 112-151) by a vote of 28–18 on July 12. The bill would have provided $27.5 billion, which was $2.1 billion, or 7 percent, below fiscal 2011 funding and $3.8 billion, or 12 percent, less than Obama requested, with the lion's share of the cuts coming from the EPA.

The Interior-Environment Subcommittee had approved a draft, 8–5, on July 7. Republicans on the full committee easily fended off attempts to remove a series of riders that Democrats denounced as an ideological onslaught on environmental programs. Republicans said the provisions addressed excessive spending and regulation by the EPA, which they called government overreach.

The bill included:

- $7.1 billion for the Environmental Protection Agency, a $1.5 billion cut from fiscal 2011 spending and $1.8 billion less than Obama requested. About $970 million of the proposed cuts came from the clean water and drinking water state revolving funds, which would have received $1.5 billion. The panel said in its report that the accounts had received $6 billion in the 2009 economic stimulus law (PL 111-5) and a 130 percent increase in funding in fiscal 2010. "Under the current allocation," the committee said, "these appropriations funds must inevitably shrink." The panel also urged authorizers to find mechanisms other than appropriated spending to fund the accounts.
- $9.9 billion for the Interior Department, $310 million below the previous year's funding and $795 million less than requested. Cuts were spread across most of the main bureaus.
- $4.5 billion for the Forest Service, close to the previous year's level and $470 million less than requested.
- $4.5 billion for the Indian Health Service, about $240 million more than in fiscal 2011 but $310 million below the request.
- $135 million each for the National Endowment for the Arts and the National Endowment for the Humanities, and $752 million for the Smithsonian.

Among the numerous policy riders that were later dropped, the bill included a one-year delay of EPA regulations on greenhouse gas emissions from stationary industrial sources. It would have prohibited the EPA from implementing a regulation governing cooling-water intake at power plants, regulating coal ash from power plants as hazardous waste, changing the definition of "navigable waters" under the Clean Water Act (PL 95-217), and expanding storm water discharge requirements. Although making permanent changes to statutes in spending bills was usually not allowed, the bill would have amended the Clean Air Act (PL 101-549) to require the EPA to rule on air quality permits for drilling in the outer continental shelf within six months of submission. The measure also contained numerous restrictions to agency water policies related to coal mining in Appalachia, while also exempting certain pesticide applications from the need for water permits.

Some of the proposed restrictions applied to the Interior Department. The bill would have blocked the Fish and Wildlife Service from using funds to pursue new listings under the Endangered Species Act (PL 93-205), prohibited the Office of Surface Mining from implementing guidance that limited where coal companies could dispose of mining waste, and rescinded a recent decision to extend a ban on uranium mining near the Grand Canyon, pending study of the environmental impact.

During the markup, the committee:

- Rejected, 19–28, an amendment by James P. Moran of Virginia, the ranking Democrat on the subcommittee, to strip what he called the twenty-five "worst" riders, including those on coal ash produced by power plants and on carbon dioxide emissions from stationary industrial sources.
- Rejected, 23–26, an effort to strike the uranium mining language.
- Rejected, 23–26, an amendment by Norm Dicks of Washington, the ranking Democrat on the full Appropriations Committee, to strike language that would have prohibited the Fish and Wildlife Service from listing new endangered species and habitats. "It seems that special interest riders have become, for some, the new earmarks," Dicks said.
- Adopted, 27–20, an amendment by Steve Austria, R-Ohio, to prohibit the EPA from regulating carbon dioxide emissions from new motor vehicles or their engines after model year 2016.

HOUSE FLOOR ACTION

The House began debate on the bill July 25 and worked slowly through amendments for four days before turning to the more pressing issue of increasing the debt limit. Republicans kept their bill largely intact, rejecting several Democratic amendments aimed at removing environment policy provisions. During the debate, the House:

- Adopted, 224–202, an amendment by Dicks striking the language that would have blocked the Fish and Wildlife Service from listing new species and habitats for protection. Moran cited environmental groups' influence as one factor in what was a surprise win for Democrats.

- Rejected, 174–250, an amendment by Dicks to strike language to prohibit judicial appeals for Interior Department decisions to remove gray wolves from the endangered species list in Wyoming and the Great Lakes region.

CONFERENCE AND FINAL ACTION

House and Senate appropriators negotiated a final version of the Interior-Environment measure as part of the nine-bill omnibus. Conferees filed the conference report on the package (H Rept 112-331) on December 15. The House adopted the report, 296–121 on December 16, and the Senate cleared the bill, 67–32, the following day.

CHAPTER 8

Agricultural Policy

Introduction 407

Chronology of Action on Agricultural Policy 409

2009–2010 409

2011–2012 414

Agricultural Policy

The four years of President Barack Obama's first term were unproductive with respect to agricultural legislation. Congress unsuccessfully attempted to pass a major five-year farm bill in 2012. Although the Senate approved the legislation in June 2012, it fell victim to political battles in the House and did not make it to the floor for a vote. Many farm-related programs were extended through October 1, 2013, as part of a last-minute deal, approved in January 2013.

The five-year bill was designed to replace the previous multiyear farm bill, which was set to expire on September 30, 2012, under the legislation passed in 2008 (PL 110-546). Even that bill became law only over two vetoes by President George W. Bush. *(Congress and the Nation Vol. XII, p. 514)*

One of the biggest sources of controversy in the 2012 farm bill involved the food stamp program, officially known as the Supplemental Nutrition Assistance Program (SNAP). At a time of escalating controversy over spending and budget deficits, some members, notably conservative Republicans, sought steep funding cuts in the program. Food stamp supporters argued that especially during tough economic times, the program's funding should not be slashed.

A new food safety law, signed by President Obama on January 4, 2011, was perhaps the most significant agriculture-related legislation enacted during this period. The law, PL 111-353, gave new authority to the Food and Drug Administration (FDA) to regulate food products. Among the FDA's new powers were the abilities to call for mandatory food recalls, to install a more effective system to track food and trace sources of food-borne illnesses, to inspect food facilities on the basis of risk, and to increase oversight of imported food.

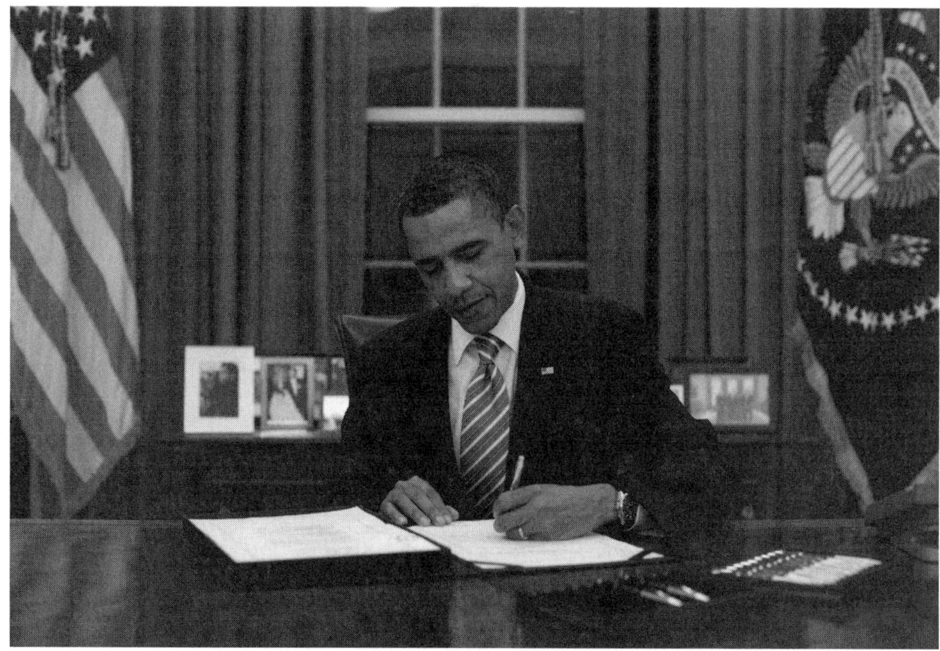

President Barack Obama signs HR 2751, the FDA Food Safety Modernization Act, in the Oval Office in Washington, D.C., on January 4, 2011.

Source: Pete Souza/The White House/Zumapress.com

Outlays for Agriculture

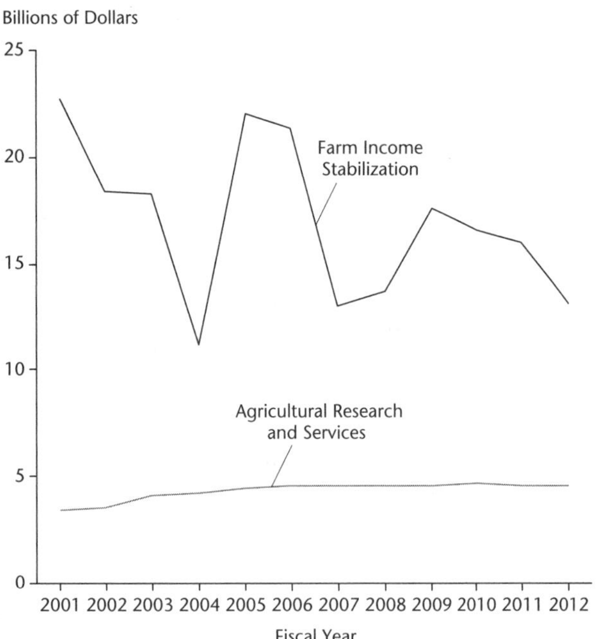

SOURCE: Office of Management and Budget, *Historical Tables, Budget of the United States Government: Fiscal Year 2013* (Washington, D.C.: U.S. Government Printing Office, 2012), Table 3.2.

REFERENCES

Discussion of agricultural policy for the years 1945–1964 may be found in *Congress and the Nation Vol. I*, pp. 665–767; for the years 1965–1968, *Congress and the Nation Vol. II*, pp. 555–597; for the years 1969–1972, *Congress and the Nation Vol. III*, pp. 331–352; for the years 1973–1976, *Congress and the Nation Vol. IV*, pp. 717–740; for the years 1977–1980, *Congress and the Nation Vol. V*, pp. 365–395; for the years 1981–1984, *Congress and the Nation Vol. VI*, pp. 485–516; for the years 1985–1988, *Congress and the Nation Vol. VII*, pp. 499–539; for the years 1989–1992, *Congress and the Nation Vol. VIII*, pp. 535–557; for the years 1993–1996, *Congress and the Nation Vol. IX*, pp. 479–505; for the years 1997–2000, *Congress and the Nation Vol. X*, pp. 417–431; for the years 2001–2004, *Congress and the Nation Vol. XI*, pp. 447–468; for the years 2005–2008, *Congress and the Nation Vol. XII*, pp. 509–528.

Chronology of Action on Agriculture

2009–2010

The 111th Congress was not a busy one for agricultural legislation, but lawmakers did manage to pass a major food safety measure that gave the Food and Drug Administration (FDA) increased regulatory powers over food production and safety. The bill was prompted in part by recent episodes of food-borne illnesses caused by various products including peanuts and spinach. The House passed HR 2749 on July 30, 2009, in what was seen as a big accomplishment for longtime Rep. John Dingell, D-Mich., who had attempted for two decades to get such a bill approved. The Senate, however, delayed floor consideration until 2010, ultimately passing its own bill, S 510, on November 30 of that year. The Senate bill ran into trouble when a constitutional challenge was raised over its inclusion of fees—a subject that is supposed to originate in the House rather than the Senate. In the end, both chambers passed HR 2751, in the same form.

In addition, lawmakers in 2009 passed a stand-alone agriculture appropriations bill for the first time in several years. The fiscal 2010 bill totaled $121.2 billion in spending, which included $23.4 billion in discretionary spending; most of the measure was mandatory spending.

Food Safety

A new food safety law (HR 2751—PL 111-353) giving the Food and Drug Administration (FDA) increased powers to regulate food products was generally considered the most important agriculture-related measure approved by the 111th Congress, encompassing the most sweeping change in federal food laws in seventy years. President Barack Obama signed the bill into law on January 4, 2011.

The legislation (the FDA Food Safety Modernization Act), estimated to cost $1.4 billion over fiscal years 2011–2015, required months to get through both houses, as sponsors had to overcome a series of obstacles. The focus on food safety was sparked by several well-publicized outbreaks of food-borne illnesses from products including spinach, jalapeño peppers, and peanuts. Indeed, food safety regulation picked up bipartisan support, in part because of these outbreaks, even though many Republicans were not in favor of additional federal regulations.

HOUSE ACTION

On June 10, 2009, the House Energy and Commerce's health subcommittee approved a food safety measure by voice vote. The bill, HR 2749, was sponsored by Rep. John Dingell, D-Mich., who had pushed for such a law for many years. The bill gave the FDA power to impose civil penalties and required food facilities that served U.S. customers to pay yearly fees and register with the agency. The monies generated from the fees were intended to help defray costs incurred by the bill's tougher inspection requirements. If a registered company faced a recall or reinspection, it would pay the costs. During consideration of the bill, Republicans expressed concern about some of the fees; as a result panel members approved changes that reduced the annual facility registration fee to $500 from $1,000 and limited fees to $175,000 per company per year. The bill's inspection schedule called for high-risk facilities to be checked every six to eighteen months, low-risk facilities every eighteen months to three years, and warehouses every three to four years.

On June 17, the House Energy and Commerce Committee approved the measure by voice vote. Among issues concerning Republicans were provisions giving the FDA authority to implement mandatory food quarantines and increasing the frequency of some food-facility inspections. But changes accepted by majority Democrats, approved by voice vote, loosened some requirements, giving the FDA more leeway on the inspection schedule.

The food safety bill reached the House floor in late July. Initially, it was brought up under rules requiring a two-thirds vote for passage, usually intended to expedite passage of noncontroversial legislation. But on July 29, it failed on a 280–150 vote.

AGRICULTURE LEADERSHIP

In December 2008, President-elect Barack Obama selected Tom Vilsack, the former Democratic governor of Iowa, as his agriculture secretary-designate. The two had briefly been rivals for the 2008 Democratic presidential nomination, but Vilsack had dropped out of the race in February 2007, citing fund-raising pressures. Subsequently, Vilsack threw his support behind Obama's main rival, Hillary Rodham Clinton, backing her in the important Iowa caucuses held in January 2008. But Obama defeated Clinton in the caucuses and went on to win the nomination. Vilsack then gave vigorous support to Obama.

At his confirmation hearings before the Senate Agriculture Committee on January 14, 2009, Vilsack pledged to implement the recently passed 2008 farm bill, promote renewable energy programs, improve the department's record on civil rights issues, and implement standards for junk food sold in schools. He was confirmed by voice vote January 20.

Vilsack, born December 13, 1950, in Pittsburgh, Pa., was adopted as an infant and grew up in Pittsburgh. After his graduation from Hamilton College and Albany Law School, he moved to Mount Pleasant, Iowa, the hometown of his wife, Christie, where he practiced law and became involved in politics. Before his election as governor, he served as mayor of Mount Pleasant and as a state senator.

Vilsack, the first Democrat elected Iowa governor in three decades, won the first of his two terms in 1998, in a come-from-behind victory that was seen as an upset. He won reelection in 2002 and was mentioned as a potential running mate for 2004 Democratic presidential nominee John Kerry. Vilsack had pledged to serve only two terms as governor and did not run for reelection in 2006. As governor, he was known for his support of corn-based ethanol production and biotechnology. Obama cited Vilsack's support for biotech and for renewable energy as key reasons for nominating him to the agriculture post.

Overall Vilsack received a favorable reception on Capitol Hill, yet some lawmakers expressed concern that given Vilsack's identification with a corn-producing state, he would not be as sympathetic toward the issues faced by farmers from other parts of the country, a worry that was heightened by the fact that Sen. Tom Harkin, another Iowa Democrat, chaired the Agriculture Committee.

Vilsack took over the Agriculture Department during a time of turmoil for the nation's farm economy. Like the economy as a whole, the agriculture sector was facing difficult conditions In his confirmation hearings, Vilsack noted that the overall economic downturn created more of a need for the food assistance programs run by the department.

The first four years of Vilsack's tenure as agriculture secretary were relatively low-key, but he did run into a controversy in July 2010, when a midlevel Agriculture Department official, Shirley Sherrod, who is African American, was forced to resign her job after a misleading video clip surfaced indicating a bias on Sherrod's part against a white farmer. It later emerged that Sherrod was actually using that example as part of a much longer set of remarks that demonstrated that she opposed racial bias. Vilsack publicly apologized to Sherrod, who had worked as rural development director in Georgia for the department, and offered her a new job with the department. After meeting with Vilsack in August, she declined the offer but said she might work with the department as a consultant. The entire episode proved embarrassing to Vilsack, the department, and President Obama.

During the first two years of Vilsack's stewardship at Agriculture, Democrats controlled both houses of Congress. In the next two years, following the 2010 midterm elections, Republicans took over the House. The Obama administration's relations with Congress, which already had been testy given the presence of a feisty GOP minority, became still more difficult with the advent of a sizeable group of Tea Party–backed conservative House GOP freshmen bent on cutting government spending. For example, as the House considered the 2012 multiyear farm bill, Vilsack expressed concern at the cuts that the House bill proposed, for example, to the food stamps. Many Democrats objected to the magnitude of the cuts, while some Republicans sought still steeper cuts, and the issue ultimately doomed the farm bill, as it would initially when the House brought it up again the following year.

Vilsack opted to stay on as agriculture secretary at the start of Obama's second term in 2013.

The bill was brought to the floor again the following day under rules requiring a simple majority vote. The House passed HR 2751 on a **key vote of 283–142 (R 54–122; D 229–20)** *(2009 key votes, p. 751)*

One important reason that the measure failed the first time involved jurisdictional issues. Members of the House Agriculture Committee were upset that the bill had not been referred to their panel, and, while committee Democrats were mollified by changes that exempted farms, livestock, poultry, and feed grain from most of the measure's provisions, the Republicans continued to deny support.

SENATE ACTION

After its approval by a comfortable margin in the House, the bill moved to the Senate where increasing food safety rules had even stronger bipartisan support. The Senate Health, Education, Labor, and Pensions Committee approved the Senate version of the bill, S 510, on November 18 by voice vote. But it would take another year for the Senate, busy with health care reform and other issues, to bring the food safety bill to the floor. Pressure to legislate, however, grew in August 2010 when more than 500 million eggs were recalled in the wake of a salmonella outbreak, adding to public concern over food safety.

Meanwhile, Sen. Tom Harkin, D-Iowa, chair of the Health, Education, Labor, and Pensions (HELP) Committee, and Sen. Mike Enzi, R-Wyo., the committee's ranking Republican, collaborated to line up support for the bill. Throughout 2010 senators continued negotiating on various issues that posed potential obstacles to Senate passage.

One key issue was an amendment sought by Sen. Dianne Feinstein, D-Calif., that would have put restrictions on the chemical bisphenol A (BPA) in plastic beverage and food containers, an idea opposed by the food industry. The House, in its bill, had called for the FDA to study the issue. In the end, Feinstein's proposal did not progress in the Senate, in part because of strong opposition from the chemical industry.

Another issue causing delays was a proposal to exempt small-scale producers whose customers were near their home base from the federal regulations. Sen. Jon Tester, D-Mont., a farmer, eventually won concessions that provided exemptions from some of the regulations. Tester's proposal was criticized by the liberal-leaning Center for Science in the Public Interest, which called it a threat to public health, and by the United Fresh Produce Association, an industry group that called for equal treatment for large and small producers. Under the compromise reached between Harkin and Enzi and Tester, exemptions would apply to small producers who sold within 275 miles and made less than $500,000 on average in sales, and if a food-borne illness struck, the FDA would be able to step in.

Sen. Tom Coburn, R-Okla., meanwhile, argued that the entire bill, at $1.4 billion, would cost too much and contained too much regulation.

The bill, however, easily passed the Senate on November 30 by a 73–25 vote, after two cloture votes. But another wrinkle developed when members of the House Ways and Means Committee argued that language in the bill dealing with permitting and inspection fees constituted revenue-raising, which under the Constitution was supposed to originate in the House and their committee, not in the Senate.

To get around this problem and avoid paths that opponents could use to scuttle the legislation, Senate leaders opted to put the language of its bill into the previously passed House bill, HR 2751, which the Senate endorsed by unanimous consent on December 19.

Coburn did not object. The House approved the measure (PL 111-353) on a vote of 215–144 on December 21, and President Obama signed it into law on January 4, 2011.

MAJOR PROVISIONS

Following are major provisions of the FDA Food Safety Modernization Act (PL 111-353):

Domestic Food Production

Records. Increased the FDA's ability to examine the records of food distributors, processors, and manufacturers under circumstances where the agency believed a problematic ingredient could be harmful or taint other ingredients in the factory.

Registration. Required food production facilities to register every two years with the FDA, allow FDA inspections, and give contact information for foreign partner facilities.

Prevention. Required facilities' owners and operators to create plans, accessible to the FDA, for preventive action, and work to lessen any "reasonably foreseeable" hazards. Also required corrective actions if the preventive actions did not succeed.

Safe produce. Directed the Department of Health and Human Services (HHS) to work with the Department of Agriculture to prepare new rules for the safe production and harvest of fruits and vegetables, including minimum standards for soil amendments, hygiene, packaging, temperature controls, animal encroachment, and water, and any hazards that might occur naturally.

Food tracking. Gave authority to the FDA to institute a new system for gathering information necessary in the event of a food-borne outbreak or distribution of contaminated food. Created pilot projects to find workable ways of quickly locating the recipients of contaminated food products.

Stepped-up inspections. Gave the FDA authority to increase inspections of high-risk domestic food facilities at least once in the five-year period and at least once every three years following. Required low-risk facilities to be inspected once in the seven-year period and once every five years after that.

Mandatory recalls. Gave the FDA authority to issue mandatory recalls of products already available that would cause death or serious health problems if there was no voluntary recall of the product. Allowed the FDA to force a facility to end production, distribution, holding, or selling of a contaminated or dangerous product if the facility failed to take voluntary action.

Food Imports and Foreign Facilities

FDA Inspection. Required the HHS to work with foreign governments for FDA inspection of food export production facilities, particularly emphasizing those facilities producing high-risk products as identified by the FDA or Department of Agriculture. Allowed the FDA to ban products from foreign governments or facilities that refused inspection from entering the United States. Required the FDA in the first year after enactment to inspect at least 600 registered foreign food export facilities. Provided that the number would double in each year for the following five years.

FDA offices. Required the HHS to consult with the Department of State and the Department of Homeland Security to create FDA offices abroad to help increase the enforcement and regulatory abilities of foreign governments regarding their domestic food industries.

Supplier verification. Required U.S. importers to set up a risk-based supplier verification scheme to ensure imported food was not adulterated or mislabeled. The FDA could deny U.S. entry to the products of any importer refusing to set up such a system.

Voluntary program. Established a new program to speed up the review and importation of food products from qualified importers. Specified that participation would be approved for importers whose products emerged from certified production facilities and met FDA standards.

Third-party certification. Directed the FDA to set up a system to recognize foreign government agencies and other third parties to inspect and certify facilities that produced food.

"Port shopping." Required the FDA to notify the Department of Homeland Security and U.S. Customs if an imported food product was turned back at a U.S. port to prevent the product from entering another port.

User Fees

Fee authority. Authorized the FDA to collect fees to cover the entire cost of implementing the law's new provisions, but set a limit on fees of $25 million a year.

User fees. Authorized the FDA to collect fees from domestic facilities subject to inspection or recalls.

Import fees. Required importers participating in the voluntary qualified program and those subject to reinspection to also pay fees.

Fiscal 2010 Agriculture Appropriations

Congress succeeded in 2009 in passing a fiscal year 2010 stand-alone agriculture appropriations bill (HR 2997—PL 111-80), the first such measure in several years.

The House Appropriations Agriculture subcommittee on June 11 approved the fiscal 2010 spending bill by voice vote. HR 2997 called for providing $20.4 billion to the Department of Agriculture, an increase of $2 billion over fiscal 2009; approximately $2.4 billion to the Food and Drug Administration (FDA), an increase of $299 million over the previous year; and $160.6 million to the Commodity Futures Trading Commission (CFTC), up $14.6 million over fiscal 2009. In total, the bill called for approximately $23 billion in discretionary spending, up $2.3 billion, or approximately 11 percent, from fiscal 2009. This increase, however, was less than President Obama had sought; his fiscal 2010 budget had asked for about $79 million more in agriculture spending than the subcommittee's bill provided.

Most of the bill consisted of mandatory spending, $100.8 billion, for such programs as food stamps, rural development, and farm subsidies.

The full House Appropriations Committee approved the draft spending bill June 18 by voice vote. Although observers had expected a contentious argument over Chinese poultry imports, that battle did not take place. Rep. Jack Kingston, R-Ga., the ranking Republican on the agriculture subcommittee, withdrew an amendment that would have ended a ban, which had been part of the spending bills since 2007, on imports of Chinese poultry. Agriculture subcommittee Chair Rep. Rosa DeLauro, D-Conn., who expressed concern over the safety of Chinese poultry, wanted the ban maintained.

The full House approved the $123.8 billion bill on July 9, on a 266–160 vote.

Meanwhile, the Senate moved ahead with its fiscal 2010 agriculture spending bill. The Senate Appropriations Committee approved the draft bill on July 7, on a 30–0 vote. The bill, S 1406, provided approximately $124 billion in overall agriculture-related funding, with approximately $23.1 billion of that in discretionary spending, an increase of about 12 percent in discretionary spending over the previous year.

The Senate version included a manager's amendment with language from Sen. Mark Pryor, D-Ark., which would permit the importation of Chinese poultry under certain conditions. Pryor sought to set up an inspection system under which the agriculture secretary would agree to audits of Chinese inspection systems, on-site reviews of slaughter and processing facilities, more reinspections at entry ports, and sharing of information with other countries accepting imports of Chinese poultry. The language was similar to that which Kingston had considered offering in the House version.

On August 4, the Senate passed its version of HR 2997 on a vote of 80–17. The bill's cost rose to $124.5 billion, including $23.7 billion in discretionary spending. During Senate debate on the measure, Sen. Tom Coburn, R-Okla., offered an amendment to cut the increase in discretionary spending to 2 percent. His proposal was rejected on a 32–65 vote.

Conferees faced some differences between the House and Senate versions of the bill. The figures for discretionary spending differed from one bill to the other. The Chinese poultry issue was expected to provoke debate.

Also at issue was the National Animal Identification System, a voluntary tracking program for poultry and livestock—meant to track disease—that many farmers and ranchers criticized. The Senate allotted $7.3 billion for the program, half of what the Obama budget had sought; the House cut funding for the program entirely.

In addition, the Senate bill included $350 million to raise dairy price supports, an important amount for Sen. Herb Kohl, D-Wis., the Senate Agriculture Appropriations Committee chairman, and Sen. Bernard Sanders, I-Vt., who originally had proposed including the money.

Conferees on September 30 approved a report that made some key compromises between the two bills. The report asked for $121.2 billion in overall spending, including $23.3 billion for discretionary programs.

On the Chinese poultry issue, House conferees agreed to the Senate position, under which the ban would be lifted if various inspections were made. Conferees agreed to allocate

$5.3 million to the National Animal Identification System, less than the Senate and the Obama administration had sought but an increase over the House's original plan to eliminate funding.

On the dairy issue, conferees adopted a compromise under which farmers would receive $290 million in direct payments and another $60 million would go to the Department of Agriculture for purchasing dairy products in order to reduce surpluses that hurt farmers' income.

Among other provisions in the conference report, the Women, Infants, and Children (WIC) program received $7.3 billion, an amount below what either chamber had passed or Obama had sought. The FDA received $2.4 billion.

Mandatory spending was $97.8 billion, an increase of about $10 billion over the previous year, including $58.3 billion for the Supplemental Nutrition Assistance Program (better known as food stamps), an increase of $4.3 billion over fiscal 2009. Child nutrition programs received $16.9 billion, an increase of $1.9 billion over the previous year.

The House approved the conference report on October 7 on a vote of 263–162, and the Senate followed the next day, voting 76–22 to clear the bill. President Obama signed the bill (the Agriculture, Rural Development, Food and Drug Administration, and Related Agencies Appropriations Act of 2010) on October 21, 2009.

MAJOR PROVISIONS

The major provisions of the fiscal 2010 agriculture appropriations bill provided the following spending amounts:

Farm programs. $30 billion for Agriculture Department farm programs, including $13.9 billion to reimburse the Commodity Credit Corporation, $350 million to help dairy farmers, and $7.5 billion for federal crop insurance.

Domestic food and nutrition. $82.8 billion for domestic food assistance programs, including $58.3 billion for food stamps (an extra $6.1 billion from the economic stimulus law boosted the food stamp total for fiscal 2010 to $64.4 billion), $16.9 billion for child nutrition programs, and $7.3 billion for the nutrition program for WIC.

Conservation. $1 billion for discretionary conservation programs.

Rural development. $3 billion for programs benefiting poor rural areas, and $24.4 billion for rural development loans.

Foreign food aid and exports. $2.1 billion for global food aid programs, including the Food for Peace Program, $187 million for maintaining and increasing foreign markets for U.S. farm products, and $210 million for an international nutrition effort.

Food and drug safety. $2.4 billion for the FDA, and $1 billion for the Food Safety and Inspection Service.

Commodity Futures Trading Commission. $169 million for the CFTC, an independent agency that regulates markets in futures contracts and options.

Black Farmers

Congress in 2010 approved legislation to provide additional funds to pay the costs relating to a long-standing legal issue regarding Black farmers who had missed a deadline to receive claims from a 1999 settlement involving discrimination by the Department of Agriculture.

In 1997, Black farmers who believed they were receiving unfair treatment from the Department of Agriculture had filed a class-action lawsuit, that resulted in a settlement two years later (*Pigford v. Glickman*, 185 F.R.D. 82, D.D.C., 1999).

The 1999 agreement gave claimants six months to seek a payment of $50,000, or, in some cases, more. Problems ensued when some of the farmers did not file claims within the specified period, and the deadline was extended.

Language was included in the 2008 farm bill allowing the farmers additional time, and Congress authorized $100 million to pay the claims. But the farmers sought more money, arguing that $100 million would not be enough.

In February 2010, when the Department of Agriculture reached a $1.2 billion settlement with Black farmers who had charged discrimination, the Obama administration asked Congress to fund the settlement. After months of stalled progress, the Senate on November 19 succeeded in approving the money, by voice vote, in a standalone bill. The House approved the bill on a 256–152 vote November 30, and President Obama signed it on December 8, 2010. The settlement (*In re Black Farmers Discrimination Litigation,* Case No. 08-mc-0511, D.D.C., known as *Pigford II*) was approved by Judge Paul Friedman on October 27, 2011.

The bill, HR 4783 (PL 111-291), also included among its provisions $3.4 billion to fund an unrelated settlement between American Indians. President Obama signed the measure—the Claims Resolution Act of 2010 (PL 111-291)—on December 8, 2010. *(Legal settlements details, p. 555)*

2011–2012

The 112th Congress, elected in 2010, failed to enact any major agriculture-related legislation.

After the 2010 midterm elections brought control of the House to the Republican Party, John Boehner of Ohio became the new Speaker. But as the new Congress began in 2011, Boehner had his hands full with a group of exceptionally conservative House freshmen, many of them elected with Tea Party support, whose main goal was to reduce the size of government. This objective often put them on a collision course with President Barack Obama, the Democratic-controlled Senate, and even some members of the GOP. This dynamic came into play when Congress attempted to pass a new farm bill to replace the one that President George W. Bush had signed into law in 2008. *(Congress and the Nation Vol. XII, p. 514)*

Working under a deadline—the 2008 farm law would expire on September 30, 2012—members of Congress faced a number of tough issues that ultimately became impossible to reconcile before the 112th Congress ended.

Hanging over all congressional activity was the economic crises that had begun in mid-2007, although it had been in the making for years before. It had left the nation still reeling with high unemployment, a crippled housing market, wobbly banks, and gloomy consumer attitudes.

Some parts of the economy were improving by 2011, especially in housing, but overall, lawmakers were working in an atmosphere of financial restraints that fit comfortably with small-government beliefs of many Republicans, who, now that they were in control of the House after four years in the minority, were in a position to push back against calls for more government spending.

The nation's huge farm programs, dating back to the New Deal periods in the 1930s, had become a target for an array of members of Congress, both liberal and conservative, although for different reasons.

Among the programs that became the most controversial as Congress debated a new farm bill was the food stamp program. Democrats generally argued that at a time of economic struggle when more people needed the program, it was more important than ever, while many conservative Republicans sought to make severe cuts in the program. Although lawmakers tried to broker compromises, those failed in the end.

Another issue that caused difficulties was what type of commodity program to offer. Although the bill eventually approved by the Senate featured a plan that resembled a type of insurance to protect farmers' actual *revenues,* the plan under consideration in the House instead opted for a price loss protection plan in which payments are made to farmers if *prices* fell below a certain level. In the end, the House leadership opted not to bring the farm bill to the floor. Instead, Congress approved a one-year extension to the 2008 farm bill.

Omnibus Farm Legislation

Lawmakers in the 112th Congress faced a deadline of September 30, 2012, to pass a new farm bill before the 2008 farm law expired on that date. But in an atmosphere of partisan tension, economic challenges, and election-year politics, members failed to revise and extend the law. The one-year extension of the 2008 legislation (PL 110-246) was passed by Congress as part of the end-of-year deal that avoided the looming budgetary changes that had become known as the "fiscal cliff." President Barack Obama signed the one-year extension (PL 112-240) on January 10, 2013. *(Congress and the Nation Vol. XII, p. 514)*

SENATE ACTION

The Senate Agriculture, Nutrition and Forestry Committee approved the Senate version of the farm bill (S 3240—S Rept 112-203) April 26, 2012, on a 16–5 vote. The draft bill, which reauthorized farm programs for five years, contained spending reductions of more than $23 billion over ten years. The bill changed the system under which direct payments totaling $5 billion annually went to cotton and grain growers. Instead, a "revenue protection plan" was substituted under which farmers with losses of at least 11 percent but no more than 21 percent would get direct payments and farmers with losses above 21 percent could seek crop insurance. In addition, the bill sought to end a 2002 countercyclical payment program designed to help farmers faced with commodity prices that fell below target levels. Twenty-three conservation programs were consolidated into thirteen programs, and stricter eligibility limits for food stamps, were established.

Senate Agriculture Chair Debbie Stabenow, D-Mich., and the committee's ranking Republican, Pat Roberts, Kan., had worked together in the months before the committee markup, hoping to win over as many factions in the agriculture interest world as possible. Nonetheless, during the markup, several southern senators, Republicans Thad Cochran of Mississippi, Saxby Chambliss of Georgia, and John Boozman of Arkansas, opposed the bill.

In June S 3240 went to the Senate floor, and various southerners voiced opposition, as they had done during the markup. Sen. Mary Landrieu, D-La., was among those charging that the new crop insurance approach to farm payments would benefit farmers in the Midwest, whose main crops include corn and soybeans, but would not provide adequate protection for southern farmers, whose main crops, peanuts, and rice, were more vulnerable to market fluctuations.

Meanwhile, urban and northeastern senators fought against the food stamp cuts and for increases in nutrition programs. Sen. Kirsten Gillibrand, D-N.Y., unsuccessfully fought the proposed cuts of $4.5 billion over ten years to the Supplemental Nutrition Assistance Program (SNAP), or food stamps, and proposed instead making similar spending reductions in federal subsidies to the crop insurance program. Spending on the food stamp program totaled almost $80 billion a year, more than half of the farm bill's mandatory spending.

On June 21, the Senate passed the farm bill on a **key vote of 64–35 (R 16–30; D 46–5; I 2–0)**. *(2012 key votes, p. 767)*

The Congressional Budget Office (CBO) estimated that the measure would cost about $969 billion over ten years, about $23.6 billion less than under the then-current farm law.

HOUSE ACTION

The House Agriculture Committee approved its version of farm legislation on July 11 on a 35–11 vote. The bill was reported on September 9 (HR 6083—H Rept 112-669). Twenty-two Republicans and thirteen Democrats backed the bill in the July action, while four conservative Republicans and seven liberal Democrats opposed it.

One major difference between the House and Senate bills involved food stamps, which took a much larger $16.1 billion reduction in the House version. The CBO projected that overall, the House bill would save $35 billion in mandatory programs over ten years, about $12 billion more than the comparable figure for the Senate bill.

Both amendments to restore the food stamp funding, backed by many Democrats, and those seeking to cut food stamps even more, backed by some Republicans, failed. Much of the debate centered on the estimated two to three million people who would lose their benefits under the proposed cuts. In total, about forty-five million people were eligible for food stamps at the time. Among those voicing criticism of the cuts was Secretary of Agriculture Tom Vilsack.

Another difference between the two bills involved farm payments. The House bill focused on a price loss protection plan, using target prices in the legislation to determine whether participating farmers would get payments. This plan was less controversial with southern farmers and lawmakers than the Senate approach that would have required farmers to buy crop insurance.

House Agriculture Committee Chairman Frank Lucas, R-Okla., wanted to get the bill to the House floor quickly, but GOP leaders were concerned about opposition to the measure by conservatives who contended that the measure's cost of more than $950 billion over ten years was too high.

FARM LAW EXTENDED

Getting any farm legislation approved proved elusive throughout 2012 until the deeply divided 112th Congress was just hours away from ending its term in the first days of 2013.

During the summer of 2012, farm legislation took on increased importance as a persistent severe drought plagued farmers, increasing pressure for congressional action. Instead of bringing up the five-year farm bill, however, House leaders considered bringing a one-year farm bill extension to the floor—an idea backed by Agriculture Chair Lucas—along with a disaster-relief package. But when GOP leaders realized they lacked the votes for even a one-year extension, they brought up the drought-relief measure alone. The bill had been referred to the Agriculture Committee but was brought directly to the floor on August 1. It sought to aid agriculture and livestock producers who were not covered by crop insurance but were hit by the drought or other natural disasters. On August 2, the House approved a $383 million package (HR 6233) on a 223–197 vote. Stabenow, meanwhile, had been urging the House to pass a five-year farm bill; the Senate did not act on the stand-alone drought measure.

House leaders remained reluctant to take the five-year farm bill to the floor, in part because of disagreements over the cuts to food stamps and controversy over the changes in farm payments. As a result, the 2008 farm bill expired on schedule, on September 30, 2012.

The next deadline was January 1, 2013. Without an extension at that point, a 1949 law would be triggered that agriculture experts said would send the entire farm system into price supports of a half-century earlier in vastly different agricultural conditions, leaving farmers unsure how to proceed in planning crops. In particular, dairy prices faced severe changes under a 1949 dairy support program that would have made milk prices jump to about $7 a gallon. Agriculture committee leaders from both chambers crafted a plan that would continue the 2008 law through 2013. But in the waning days of the 112th Congress, their work was superseded by a one-year farm bill extension proposed by Senate Minority Leader Mitch McConnell of Kentucky, working with Vice President Joseph R. Biden. Lawmakers in both the Senate and the House approved the proposal on January 1, extending parts of the 2008 farm bill for one year as part of the last-minute negotiations to avoid the fiscal cliff. *(Details, p. 185)*

CHAPTER 9

Health and Human Services

Introduction 419

Chronology of Action on Health 421

2009–2010 421

2011–2012 455

Chronology of Action on Human Services 465

2009–2010 465

2011–2012 468

Health and Human Services

President Barack Obama had more than a few difficulties with Congress in his first term, but perhaps his signature achievement was in enacting the Affordable Care Act, a major national health care overhaul. By providing government-sponsored health insurance to millions of Americans, some of whom could never afford it in the past, Obama succeeded where so many presidents and Congresses had failed in the past.

It wasn't pretty. In fact, it was downright ugly at times. But as Obama himself pointed out, the bill he signed on March 23, 2010 came "after almost a century of trying." It also came in the wake of notable failures from previous decades, the most recent being the one that befell President Bill Clinton in 1993 and 1994 and helped cost Clinton Democratic majorities in Congress for the remainder of his presidency. *(Clinton plan, Congress and the Nation Vol. IX, p. 513)*

Republicans rode doubts about even the successful health law to electoral victory, though, reclaiming the House in the 2010 elections. But Democrats retained control of the Senate, and thus they managed to fend off repeated GOP efforts throughout the 112th Congress (2011–2012) to repeal or otherwise undermine the nascent health law.

The Supreme Court also came to the law's defense. In a dramatic last-day decision in 2012, it upheld the measure's constitutionality on a 5–4 ruling, with Chief Justice John Roberts surprisingly casting the decisive vote to keep the law alive. *(Supreme Court decision, pp. 455, 586)*

OTHER HEALTH ISSUES

But while the health insurance overhaul claimed center stage during all four years of Obama's first term, Congress also managed to take care of some other health-related business, some of it significant.

For example, early in 2009, Congress for the first time approved legislation to give the Food and Drug Administration (FDA) the power to regulate tobacco products. Like the health care insurance overhaul, it was the culmination of a battle that had raged for decades and had pitted health advocates against powerful moneyed interests: growers, manufacturers, and sellers of tobacco products.

The Democratic-controlled 111th Congress, with a Democratic president, also managed in 2009 to do what its predecessor tried and failed to do: expand the Children's Health Insurance Program (CHIP). President George W. Bush had thwarted several attempts to allow more low- and moderate-income children into the popular program during his second term.

For the first time, Congress managed to reauthorize the Ryan White HIV/AIDS program in 2009 without the usual regional and urban-rural clashes that had slowed earlier renewal efforts. The program, first passed at the height of the nation's AIDS epidemic in 1990, provides funding to states and cities for services and medications for those with AIDS and HIV and for preventing the further spread of the virus.

One major health policy item Congress did not solve during the four years of Obama's first term, however, was to fix a continuing problem with the way doctors were paid under the Medicare program. A glitch created by a 1997

REFERENCES

Discussion of health policy for the years 1945–1964 may be found in *Congress and the Nation Vol. I*, pp. 1122–1194; for the years 1965–1968, *Congress and the Nation Vol. II*, pp. 665–707; for the years 1969–1972, *Congress and the Nation Vol. III*, pp. 551–580; for the years 1973–1976, *Congress and the Nation Vol. IV*, pp. 323–375; for the years 1977–1980, *Congress and the Nation Vol. V*, pp. 601–653; for the years 1981–1984, *Congress and the Nation Vol. VI*, pp. 521–556; for the years 1985–1988, *Congress and the Nation Vol. VII*, pp. 547–606; for the years 1989–1992, *Congress and the Nation Vol. VIII*, pp. 561–610; for the years 1993–1996, *Congress and the Nation Vol. IX*, pp. 513–569; for the years 1997–2000, *Congress and the Nation Vol. X*, pp. 429–503; for the years 2001–2004, *Congress and the Nation Vol. XI*, pp. 471–529; for the years 2005–2008, *Congress and the Nation Vol. XII*, pp. 531–578.

Ryan White's mother Jeanne White-Ginder (center) holds the Ryan White HIV/AIDS Treatment Extension Act of 2009 after being signed by President Barack Obama at the White House on October 30, 2009.
Source: AFP Photo/Jewel Samad

budget bill had ballooned to a more than $300 billion headache and created a need for Congress to pass five separate short-term bills in 2010 to prevent doctors from getting a 21 percent pay cut. A cut that large, lawmakers feared and doctors threatened, could have jeopardized seniors' ability to find doctors to care for them.

The 112th Congress also saw a major debate over the future of the Medicare and Medicaid programs. In 2011 and 2012 the GOP-led House, particularly under the leadership of Budget Chair Paul Ryan, R-Wis., voted budget resolutions

Outlays for Medicare and Medicaid

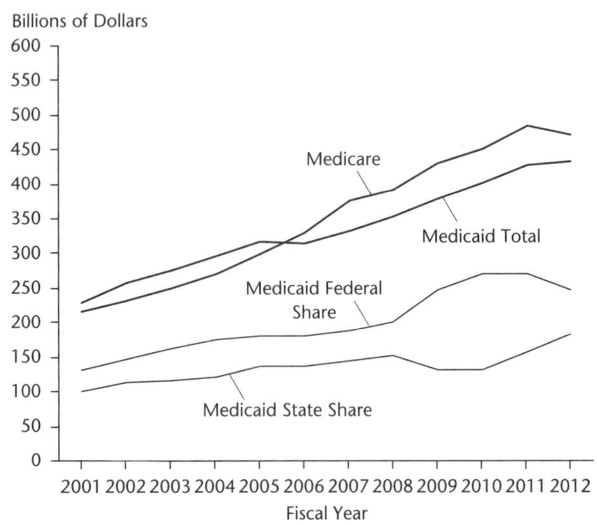

SOURCE: Medicare: Office of Management and Budget, *Historical Tables, Budget of the United States Government: Fiscal Year 2013* (Washington, D.C.; U.S. Government Printing Office, 2012), Table 8.5; Medicaid: Centers for Medicare and Medicaid Services, *2012 Actuarial Report on the Financial Outlook for Medicaid* (Washington, D.C., Department of Health and Human Services, 2012).

to dramatically limit future federal financial responsibility for the Medicare program and to turn more responsibility for Medicaid back to the states. But the Senate did not complete budget action in either year, so no legislation was considered either in committee or on either chamber's floor.

HUMAN SERVICES

There was little action on the human services front during Obama's first term. One major accomplishment, however, was a child nutrition bill passed in 2010.

First Lady Michelle Obama, who had made reducing childhood obesity a signature issue, was a major backer of the legislation, which for the first time gave the Department of Agriculture authority to set standards for food sold in school vending machines, snack stores, and à la carte lines, in addition to actual meals.

Chronology of Action on Health

2009–2010

The 111th Congress presented Democrats with a unique opportunity with both a president who had vowed to make a health care overhaul a top priority and big enough majorities in the House and Senate to make it happen, including a rare filibuster-proof sixty votes in the upper chamber.

Still, with an economy on the brink of falling into a depression, there were many voices urging the newly inaugurated President Barack Obama to turn his attentions elsewhere, and, indeed, he nearly did. But with so much groundwork having been laid in the previous Congress and so many major interest groups clamoring for a deal, in the end it proved too tempting not to at least try.

Yet in the end, the health insurance overhaul still proved nearly impossible, and the deal almost fell apart at several critical points, particularly after Republicans vowed early on to have no part in the venture. The fact that the measure ultimately became the first major health legislation to become law since the creation of Medicare nearly a half century earlier was a testament either to a nation finally ready to do something about the mess that many observers agreed the U.S. health system had become, or a political system that was sick and tired of trying and failing to do something about it.

Health Care Overhaul

The broadest expansion of health care coverage since the creation of Medicare in 1965 became law in March 2010, culminating nine months of dogged work by President Barack Obama and Democratic leaders in Congress. Obama, who had staked his presidency on the outcome, signed the legislation on March 23, two days after the House cleared it in a rare and dramatic Sunday evening vote (HR 3590—PL 111-148).

A hundred years after Theodore Roosevelt first proposed national health care, Obama, who had delayed a trip to Asia to be on hand, stressed the significance of the day. "Today, after almost a century of trying; today, after over a year of debate; today, after all the votes have been tallied, health insurance reform becomes law in the United States of America," he said.

John D. Dingell, D-Mich., the dean of the House, sat next to the president at the White House signing ceremony. Dingell's father, who was a member of the House of Representatives in the 1930s, was the first federal lawmaker to introduce a bill calling for universal health insurance. Several subsequent overhaul efforts—from a bid by President Harry S. Truman in the 1940s to President Bill Clinton's attempt in 1994—were unsuccessful. *(Clinton plan, Congress and the Nation Vol. IX, p. 513)*

The final legislation was the same as the bill the Senate had passed, with great difficulty, on Christmas Eve, 2009. Reluctant House Democrats were persuaded to clear it rather than negotiate a compromise that was certain to stall in the Senate, which had lost its sixty-vote filibuster-proof Democratic majority because of a special election in January.

The price for House Democrats' support was a second bill with modest changes that brought some provisions closer to those in the version the House had passed in November 2009. Lawmakers were able to use the budget reconciliation process for the second bill, which required only a simple majority and barred a filibuster in the Senate.

Among other things, the second bill increased subsidies to help uninsured individuals buy health coverage and increased certain taxes and fees to help pay for the expanded coverage. It also removed an embarrassing provision added in 2009 that helped secure the support of Ben Nelson, D-Neb., by providing special Medicaid funding for his state. Obama signed the second bill March 30 (HR 4872—PL 111-152).

Under the health care overhaul, as modified by the reconciliation bill, roughly 32 million uninsured Americans were expected to obtain health insurance coverage, mainly through subsidized private insurance policies or through expanded access to Medicaid, the joint federal-state health program for the poor.

The law required most Americans to have health coverage starting in 2014. States were required to create "American Health Benefit Exchanges," or marketplaces, where

Outlays for Health

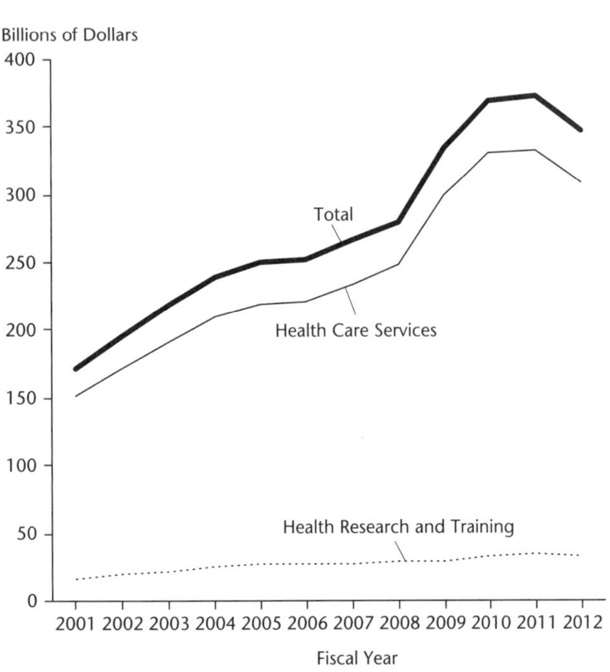

SOURCE: Office of Management and Budget, *Historical Tables, Budget of the United States Government: Fiscal Year 2013* (Washington, D.C.: U.S. Government Printing Office, 2012), Table 3.2.

NOTE: Total line includes some expenditures not shown separately.

uninsured individuals, families, and small businesses could shop for health plans. Families with incomes up to 400 percent of the federal poverty level could get federal subsidies to help pay for premiums and out-of-pocket expenses. Employers with fifty or more workers were required to pay fees to help cover the cost to the government of employees who received subsidized coverage through an exchange.

The law barred health insurance companies from denying coverage because of preexisting conditions, allowed parents to keep their children on their policies until age twenty-six, and phased out the prescription drug "doughnut hole," which required Medicare recipients to bear 100 percent of prescription drug costs above a certain level before costs were again shared between the patient and Medicare.

The cost of the combined bills—nearly $1 trillion over ten years—was offset mainly by a new Medicare hospital payroll tax on investment income of the wealthy, an excise tax on high-cost insurance plans, and reductions in Medicare payment rates. *(Provisions, pp. 436, 444)*

The legislation was entirely the work of Democrats. Republican leaders sought to block the bill at every stage, arguing that the vast majority of Americans rejected the makeover. No Republican voted for the final bill in either chamber. As a result, virtually all of the wooing, cajoling, and bargaining took place within the Democratic caucus.

That had largely been the story of the legislation from its beginnings in early 2009. Speaker Nancy Pelosi, D-Calif., and her leadership team managed to win House

HEALTH AND HUMAN SERVICES LEADERSHIP

Former Kansas governor Kathleen Sebelius was confirmed by the Senate on April 28, 2009, on a vote of 65–31, to become secretary of health and human services. The cabinet position was a critical one for President Barack Obama, who campaigned on reforming health care.

Sebelius, however, was not Obama's first choice to lead the sprawling department. The job was originally supposed to go to former Senate majority leader Tom Daschle, who was expected to play a central role negotiating the health overhaul. Daschle's nomination, however, was scuttled when, in early 2009, he was found to have failed to pay taxes on some of the income he had earned as a lobbyist after leaving the Senate following his defeat in the 2006 elections. With President Obama having already had to make amends for the tax problems of his Treasury nominee, Timothy Geithner, Daschle was ultimately forced to step aside. *(Obama cabinet members, p. 705)*

But while she was hardly as high-profile as Daschle when it came to health care, Sebelius was not without portfolio on the issue. Before becoming Kansas governor she had served as the state's insurance commissioner and was well known in health policy circles. What Sebelius proved unable to do, however, was play the role of top legislative negotiator, a vacuum that became clear as the legislation advanced through Congress.

Sebelius also caught her own share of controversy, most of it on reproductive health issues. In 2011, she overruled the Food and Drug Administration when it wanted to make the emergency contraceptive "morning after" pill available over-the-counter without age restrictions. Although Sebelius's decision was backed by President Obama, it was widely seen as a political one that overstepped the opinion of medical experts on the matter, and it would eventually be overturned by a federal judge.

On the other hand, Sebelius, a Roman Catholic, also tangled with the Catholic Church by accepting the recommendation of the Institute of Medicine in 2011 and requiring that most health insurance plans offer contraception as a no-copay covered benefit as part of their health insurance plans under the federal health overhaul. Religious groups and even some private firms sued over the requirement, charging that it violated their freedom of religion.

HEALTH CARE OVERHAUL: HOUSE VS. SENATE

Provision	Passed by the House (Hr 3962)	Passed by the Senate (HR 3590)
	Insurance Exchanges	
Marketplace where uninsured individuals and some small businesses could choose among insurance plans, with subsidies for eligible enrollees	National exchange, created and run by a new federal agency. Uninsured individuals and small businesses could purchase insurance from participating providers. States could create state-based exchanges if approved by Health and Human Services (HHS).	Create a system of state-run health insurance exchanges. If a state has not created an exchange by 2014, HHS will establish and run one in that state. Separate exchanges for small business. Groups of states could create regional exchanges if approved by HHS.
	Public Option	
Government-sponsored health insurance financed by premiums and offered as an alternative in the exchanges	Public option administered by HHS, financed through premiums. HHS would negotiate rates with providers that were no lower than Medicare rates and no higher than the average cost of private plans offered in the exchange. A new program would facilitate the creation of nonprofit, member-run co-ops to offer policies in the exchange.	No public option. Instead, the Office of Personnel Management (OPM) would administer a system of national health insurance plans. OPM would have to contract with at least two plans for each exchange, including one run by a nonprofit. A new program would foster the development of nonprofit insurers to offer policies in the exchanges.
	Individual Subsidies	
Tax credits to help pay premiums and out-of-pocket costs for policies purchased through an exchange	Premium and cost-sharing credits, on a sliding scale, for uninsured individuals and families with income up to 400 percent of the federal poverty level, or whose employer-sponsored plan costs more than 12 percent of their income. Out-of-pocket spending capped at $500 per individual and $10,000 per family for those with incomes between 133 percent and 150 percent of the poverty level.	Refundable premium credits for individuals and families with income of 100 percent to 400 percent of the poverty level, or whose employer-sponsored plan costs more than 9.8 percent of their income. Cost-sharing credits for those with incomes of 100 percent to 200 percent of the poverty level. Caps on out-of-pocket costs tied to income.
	Individual Mandate	
Most Americans required to obtain insurance coverage through employer plans, Medicare or Medicaid, or the new exchanges.	Enforced through 2.5 percent tax penalty on income above the level needed to file tax returns, up to the average cost of a policy on the exchange. Exemptions for those with too little income to file tax returns.	Enforced with tax penalty rising to $750 per person in 2016, up to a maximum of $2,250 per family or 2 percent of household income. Penalty indexed for inflation beginning in 2017. Exemptions for those with incomes below 100 percent of poverty level.
	Benefits Packages	
	All plans in the exchange must offer an "essential benefits" package as defined by the government. They could offer four types: Basic, Enhanced, Premium, and Premium Plus. Coverage would range from 70 percent (Basic) to 95 percent (Premium) of benefit costs. No cost sharing for preventive services under the Basic plan.	All plans in the exchange must offer an "essential benefits" package as defined by the government. They could offer four types: Bronze, Silver, Gold, and Platinum. Coverage would range from 60 percent (Bronze) to 90 percent (Platinum) of benefit costs. No cost sharing for preventive services. Separate catastrophic plan allowed.
	Small Business Subsidies	
Help for small businesses that provide health benefits	Tax credits for employers with fewer than twenty-five employees and average wages of less than $40,000.	Tax credits for employers with fewer than twenty-five employees and average waves of less than $50,000.
	Employer Mandate	
Penalty for employers who do not offer insurance benefits	Employers with annual payrolls above $500,000 required to offer coverage and pay 72.5 percent of individual premium or pay penalty of up to 8 percent of payroll.	No general penalty, but employers with more than fifty full-time workers that do not offer insurance and have at least one worker getting subsidized coverage on an exchange required to pay $750 penalty for each full-time employee.
	Medicaid	
Expanded eligibility	All individuals with income up to 150 percent of the federal poverty level eligible. HHS to pay 100 percent of costs for the added enrollees in 2014, and 91 percent of states' costs after that.	All individuals with income up to 133 percent of the federal poverty level eligible. HHS to pay 100 percent of costs for the added enrollees in 2014–2016, then share costs with states.

(Continued)

HEALTH CARE OVERHAUL: HOUSE VS. SENATE (Continued)

Provision	Passed by the House (Hr 3962)	Passed by the Senate (HR 3590)
	Insurance Requirements	
Regulations	No denial of coverage based on pre-existing conditions. Temporary high-risk pool created for citizens and legal immigrants who have been subject to such denials. No lifetime dollar limits on benefits. Insurers prohibited from rescinding policies, except in cases of fraud. Effective July 1, 2010.	Same.
Antitrust exemption	Elimination of most of the health insurance industry's exemption from federal antitrust law.	No provision.
Dependent coverage	Plans that cover dependents must allow parents to continue coverage for children up to age twenty-seven.	Plans that cover dependents must allow parents to continue coverage for children up to age twenty-six.
Medical loss ratio	Insurers required to spend 85 percent of premium revenue on medical claims or rebates.	Insurers required to spend 85 percent of premium revenue on medical claims or rebates in large-group market and 80 percent in small-group and individual markets.
	Prescription Drug Coverage	
Closing the gap, or "doughnut hole," in Medicare Part D prescription drug coverage	Gap reduced by $500 in 2010 and phased out by 2019, paid for by drug manufacturer rebates. Until 2019, drug manufacturers required to give a 50 percent discount on prescription drugs to enrollees while they are in the gap.	One-time $500 reduction in gap in 2010. Drug manufacturers required to give a 50 percent discount on prescription drugs while enrollee is in the coverage gap.
	Abortion	
Ban on federal funding	No use of funds under the act to purchase a plan on the exchange that covers elective abortion (that is, abortion in cases other than rape, incest, or danger to the woman's life). Individuals who receive federal subsidies would be required to buy separate polices with their own money to get coverage for elective abortions. No discrimination against providers based on whether they provide abortion services. No effect on federal or state abortion laws.	No use of federal funds to pay for elective abortion coverage. Each exchange required to offer one plan that does not cover elective abortion. Plans that offer such coverage must collect a separate payment from each enrollee, regardless of age or sex, for the portion of the plan cost attributable to the abortion coverage. No discrimination against providers based on whether they provide abortion services. No effect on federal or state abortion laws.
	Medical Malpractice	
	Incentive payments to states that enact laws to provide alternatives to traditional medical malpractice litigation, if the laws do not limit attorneys' fees or impose caps on damages.	Demonstration grants to develop alternatives to existing litigation laws. The alternatives must enhance patient safety and improve access to liability insurance.
	Coverage of Children	
Children's Health Insurance Program (CHIP)	No further funding for CHIP after fiscal 2013; shift children to the expanded Medicaid program or the exchange.	Increase in federal share of funding for CHIP. States required to maintain existing eligibility rules through 2019.
	Revenue	
Income tax surcharge	5.4 percent tax on income over $500,000 for individuals, $1 million for families.	None.
Excise tax on high-cost health insurance	None.	40 percent excise tax on insurers for costs of employer-sponsored plans in excess of $8,500 for individuals, $23,000 for families, indexed for inflation.
Medicare hospital insurance payroll tax	No change.	0.9 percent increase in Medicare Part A payroll tax rate for individuals earning more than $200,000; $250,000 for families.
Health industry fees, taxes	2.5 percent excise tax on sales of medical devices.	Annual fees on pharmaceutical, medical device, and insurance industries.

passage of a painstakingly negotiated overhaul bill by a vote of 220–215 on November 7. Majority Leader Harry Reid, D-Nev., kept the Senate in session for twenty-five straight days while he adjusted the Senate version to secure the votes of all sixty members of his caucus, the number needed to overcome a GOP filibuster. The vote to invoke cloture was 60–39; the bill passed early in the morning of December 24 by the same margin.

The only significant effort to write a bipartisan version took place in summer 2009 in informal negotiations among three Democrats and three Republicans on the Senate Finance Committee. Although the effort ultimately failed, the Senate bill reflected many of the compromises worked out in the talks and came closer than the House version to satisfying moderates.

Given the narrow margins of victory and the extensive bargaining that had gone into both bills, the notion of finding a compromise that could satisfy both chambers seemed nearly out of reach at the end of 2009.

Democrats' options narrowed further on January 19, 2010, when Republican Scott P. Brown was elected to the seat that had been held by Sen. Edward M. Kennedy, D-Mass., until his death in August 2009. Brown replaced Democrat Paul G. Kirk Jr., who had occupied the seat on an interim basis, leaving Reid one vote short of the crucial sixty-vote majority. *(Election, p. 30)*

After appearing on the brink of defeat several times, Democrats ultimately resorted to the two-bill strategy: having the House clear the Senate-passed bill, then passing a separate "corrections" bill that was sent to the Senate for final action. The fiscal 2010 budget resolution had made the reconciliation rules available for health care legislation.

Leaders also used the reconciliation package for another longtime Democratic goal: an overhaul of the student loan program. The provisions made the federal government the sole originator of the loans, which Democrats argued was less costly to taxpayers than subsidizing private student loans. *(Student loans, p. 476)*

Even in defeat, however, Republicans remained convinced that the legislation would be a disaster and that Democrats would pay at the polls in the 2010 midterm elections. "Mark my words, this legislation will reshape our nation, and Americans have already issued their verdict—they don't want it," said Minority Leader Mitch McConnell of Kentucky.

MAJOR HIGHLIGHTS

The following are major highlights of the health care overhaul as passed by the Senate, amended by the reconciliation bill, cleared by the House, and signed into law. *(Detailed provisions, p. 436)*

Exchanges. Unlike the House-passed bill, the final measure created a system of state-run exchanges where uninsured people could purchase health insurance coverage. The House version would have created a single national exchange run by a new federal agency.

Public option. Liberal Democrats in both chambers avidly supported the inclusion of a government-run insurance plan, or "public option," to compete with private plans in the exchanges. The House-passed bill included a public option, and Obama supported it, saying the competition was crucial to driving down insurance costs. But virtually all Republicans and some moderate Democrats rejected the idea, arguing that a government-sponsored plan would have unfair advantages over private competitors and that it would bring government bureaucrats into private health care decisions. Some warned that it was the first step toward "socialized medicine." Although many Senate Democrats favored a public option, they recognized that it would not pass in their chamber.

The final bill required the Office of Personnel Management (OPM) to contract with insurers to offer at least two multistate plans in each exchange. At least one plan had to be offered by a nonprofit group.

Subsidies. House Democrats had to settle for lower subsidies than they wanted for insurance purchased in the exchanges by low- and moderate-income individuals and families. The subsidies, which took the form of refundable tax credits, limited the portion of household income that a family had to spend on premiums and out-of-pocket expenses for those earning 133 percent to 400 percent of the federal poverty level. (Persons earning less generally qualified for Medicaid.)

However, the reconciliation bill made the subsidies more generous than they would have been under the Senate-passed version.

Abortion. The law restated long-standing federal law that barred the use of federal funds to cover abortions except to end pregnancies that resulted from rape or incest or that endangered the woman's life. Insurance plans that participated in an exchange and offered additional abortion coverage had to create separate accounts for premium payments for the abortion services. To get the additional coverage, an enrollee had to make two premium payments: one for regular benefits and one for the abortion services. The law did not preempt state abortion laws, and states could prohibit plans in their exchange from offering abortion coverage.

The House bill contained stricter abortion language, which Pelosi was forced to accept in 2009 as the price for getting critical votes from Democratic abortion foes. The House-passed measure would have barred the use of public funds to pay for abortions or for any health insurance plan that covered abortion in any program created by the bill. Plans offered on the exchanges could have included abortion coverage, but they would not have been eligible for government subsidies. To get abortion coverage, enrollees who received tax credits would have had to purchase separate, supplemental policies with their own money. Plans that offered abortion coverage on the exchange would have had to offer an identical plan that did not include the coverage. *(Abortion and the health law, pp. 432, 458)*

Individual mandate. The new law required that most Americans obtain basic health coverage starting in 2014 or pay a tax penalty that would be phased in over three years. The House bill would have set the penalty at 2.5 percent of household income above the tax filing threshold (at the time, $18,700 for a family). The original Senate-passed bill would have set a fine of $750 per year, up to a maximum of 2 percent of a family's income. The fee in the final, amended bill was $695 per year up to a maximum of 2.5 percent of household income.

Employer mandate. Unlike the House bill, the new law did not include a "play or pay" provision, which would have required employers with payrolls of $500,000 and above to offer health insurance or pay a penalty of up to 8 percent of their payroll. Instead, the final bill as modified required employers to pay a fee if they had employees who got subsidized insurance through an exchange; the fee was higher than in the original Senate-passed bill.

"Doughnut hole." Like the House-passed version, the final bill, as amended by the reconciliation measure, phased out the gap in Medicare Part D prescription drug coverage over ten years. It also provided a $500 reduction in the gap in 2010. The Senate bill would have provided only a one-time $500 reduction.

Revenue. In accepting the Senate bill, the House had to give up the chief source of revenue proposed in its legislation: a surtax on the income of top earners. Instead, the final bill included a modified version of a Senate provision that imposed an excise tax on insurers of high-cost employer-sponsored health plans, a cost that was likely to be passed on to the company and the employee. Labor leaders and many House Democrats opposed this tax on so-called Cadillac plans as unfair, saying it would hit workers in high-risk professions and union members who had negotiated generous benefits, often in lieu of higher wages.

The House proposal would have raised about twice as much revenue, but the Congressional Budget Office (CBO) said the Senate's excise tax would encourage consumers and employers to seek out lower-cost plans and eventually drive down health care costs.

The reconciliation bill scaled back the Senate-passed provision somewhat, delaying the effective date until 2018, rather than 2013. It also raised the threshold at which the tax would apply to $10,200 a year for individual health coverage and $27,500 for family coverage, up from $8,500 and $23,000 in the original Senate-passed bill.

Congress's Joint Committee on Taxation projected that the modified tax would raise $32 billion over ten years, down from the $148.9 billion estimated for the original Senate provision.

The reconciliation bill made up for the drop in revenue by expanding a Senate provision that increased the 1.45 percent Medicare payroll tax for hospital insurance by 0.9 percent for income above $200,000 for individuals and $250,000 for couples. The reconciliation bill added a 3.8 percent excise hospital insurance tax on investment income that exceeded those levels. The Joint Tax Committee estimated the ten-year revenue at $210.2 billion, up from $86.8 billion in the earlier Senate bill.

Medicaid. The new law expanded eligibility under state Medicaid programs to all individuals under age sixty-five, including parents and childless adults, with household incomes up to 133 percent of the federal poverty level, while keeping in place the Children's Health Insurance Program (CHIP). The House bill called for expanding Medicaid eligibility to those with household incomes up to 150 percent of the poverty level, while doing away with CHIP and shifting those children and families into health insurance exchanges or Medicaid. Under previous law, close to half of poor Americans did not have Medicaid coverage.

Deficit. The CBO estimated that the combined health care overhaul and reconciliation bill would reduce the deficit by a net $143 billion in the first decade after enactment. The projected reduction came largely through lowering anticipated Medicare costs by slowing the growth of payments to health care providers (mainly hospitals) and slashing payments to insurers who participated in the Medicare Advantage program. Under Medicare Advantage, an option strongly favored by Republicans, individuals who were eligible for Medicare could get their insurance from private companies rather than the federal government. Many Democrats contended that Medicare Advantage overpaid insurers for work the government could do just as well.

Hospitals had largely agreed to the cuts in anticipation of being able to provide less charity care because of the increase in people with health insurance. Insurers, however, strongly opposed the cuts.

ADMINISTRATIVE ACTION

Obama, who had made overhauling the American health care system a top priority in his presidential campaign, wasted no time calling on Congress to send him legislation that met two fundamental goals: putting the nation on a path to universal health care coverage and bringing down health care costs. The latter were threatening to swamp the federal budget. "The president has said to me on many occasions, personally, that this is an issue he will stake his presidency on," Tom Daschle, Obama's initial pick to head the Department of Health and Human Services (HHS), told reporters in March. "It doesn't get any more important to him."

But while Obama used his bully pulpit to try to rally support for the broad outlines of an overhaul, he left it largely to congressional leaders to work out the details. In part, the administration was determined to avoid repeating the failure of an overhaul proposed in 1993–1994 under President Bill Clinton. That plan's fate was seen as the product of a top-down, closed-door process. Also, Obama lost a crucial point man before the debate even began when Daschle stepped aside as the health and human services secretary nominee over tax questions. A former Senate majority leader, Daschle had close ties to Congress and expertise in health care that could not be replicated. *(HHS leadership, p. 422)*

Both Obama and congressional Democrats seriously underestimated the difficulty of assembling a bill that party members across the political spectrum would support, much less one that could meet Obama's goal of attracting at least some Republican votes. Despite weeks of work, Democrats left for the August recess in 2009 without having passed a bill in either chamber.

During the month-long break, Republicans launched a nationwide campaign to build opposition to what they called "Obamacare," saying it was nothing short of a government takeover of the health system. They charged that it would drive up health care costs, raise middle-class taxes, slash Medicare services, and force employers to cut jobs in the middle of the most severe recession in decades.

In town hall meetings, talk radio appearances, ad blitzes, and sometimes raucous rallies, conservatives raised the specter of Obama-backed cuts to Medicare and micromanagement of end-of-life decisions by government "death panels."

With virtually no chance of lining up Republican votes, Democratic leaders had to walk a fine line between moderates and liberals in their own party, negotiating for weeks to tailor provisions that could win enough votes to get a bill through their respective chambers. The task for Speaker Nancy Pelosi, D-Calif., was tough; it meant getting 218 of 258 Democrats. But it was far harder in the Senate, where Majority Leader Harry Reid, D-Nev., spent two months working to secure the sixty votes needed to get beyond GOP delaying tactics. The result was a twenty-five-day marathon that culminated in the December 24 vote.

"We are reshaping the nation. That's what we want to do. That's what we have to do," Reid said before the go-ahead vote in December. "With this vote we're rejecting a system in which one class of people can afford to stay healthy while another cannot. For the first time in American history, good health will not depend on wealth."

2009 LEGISLATIVE ACTION

Over a period that stretched from mid-June until mid-October, five committees—three in the House and two in the Senate—considered and approved versions of the health care legislation. Reid and Pelosi assembled their bills from the measures reported by their respective committees, selecting from among conflicting provisions and tweaking them again and again to corral votes.

The three House committees (Energy and Commerce, Ways and Means, and Education and Labor) worked from a 1,018-page bill (HR 3200) released by House Democratic leaders July 14. The proposal, the product of negotiations within the caucus, included a national health insurance exchange with a public insurance option; a requirement that individuals obtain coverage or pay fines, with exceptions and subsidies; and a "play or pay" proposal requiring that most large and midsize employers offer coverage or pay a substantial fine.

The Education and Labor and Ways and Means panels stuck largely to the leadership's provisions. But the Energy and Commerce Committee version contained compromises struck with members of the Blue Dog Coalition, a group of fiscally conservative Democrats.

The two Senate panels worked from separate scripts. The Health, Education, Labor, and Pensions (HELP) Committee draft reflected the views of liberals such as Chair Edward M. Kennedy, D-Mass., a longtime champion of universal health care. Kennedy, who was fighting brain cancer, could not be present for the debate, although he was in contact by telephone. He died in August.

By contrast, the bill that Finance Chair Max Baucus, D-Mont., brought to his panel was the product of months of bipartisan negotiations, though in the end, it did not win bipartisan support.

HOUSE WAYS AND MEANS COMMITTEE

The Ways and Means Committee approved its version of the House bill (HR 3200—H Rept 111-299, Part 2) by a vote of 23–18 on July 17 at the end of a sixteen-hour markup. Three Democrats joined all of the committee's Republicans to vote against the measure.

The committee, which was responsible for taxes and Medicare, wrote revenue provisions totaling $587 billion over ten years. Virtually all of the money came from a proposed income tax surcharge that was estimated to yield $544 billion over the ten years. The surtax would begin at 1 percent for modified adjusted gross incomes of $350,000 to $500,000, rising to a top rate of 5.4 percent for incomes above $1 million. The income thresholds would be indexed for inflation.

A delay in implementing a one-time modification of the way global companies allocated their interest expenses was projected to raise $26 billion over ten years. An additional $8.2 billion came from a proposed prohibition on the use of flexible health care accounts to pay for over-the-counter products.

Democrats turned back thirty-two GOP amendments, including efforts to eliminate the public option, drop the employer mandate, and delete the tax increases. Other GOP amendments would have allowed states to limit medical malpractice lawsuits, required members of Congress to enroll in the public plan, and prohibited plans offered in the exchange from including abortion coverage.

HOUSE EDUCATION AND LABOR COMMITTEE

The Education and Labor Committee met through the night of July 16–17 before approving an amended version of the bill (HR 3200—H Rept 111-298, Part 3), 26–22. Three Democrats sided with the Republicans against the bill. The panel, which had jurisdiction over a variety of health and worker issues, adopted twenty amendments, most of which expanded the scope of coverage and increased the number of people eligible to participate in the health insurance exchange.

As in Ways and Means, committee Democrats held off GOP attempts to strip key provisions from the bill, including the public insurance option and the requirement that employers offer health insurance or pay a fine. The committee also rejected two amendments by Mark Souder, R-Ind., to curtail abortion coverage in plans that participated in the exchange, including the public option.

The panel agreed to provide waivers from some of the bill's requirements for Hawaii's state-based health care system and for Tricare, the health care program for military families. Members agreed that both programs exceeded the standard likely to be set for the plans operating in the health insurance exchange.

The committee adopted several amendments designed to ease the bill's potential burden on small businesses, including a proposal by Duncan Hunter, R-Calif., to allow a waiver for employers who could show they would have to cut jobs to pay for health coverage for their workers.

Before approving the bill, the committee adopted by voice vote a 1,040-page substitute amendment by Chair George Miller, D-Calif., that included provisions to open the exchange to more small businesses and to families whose insurance premiums and out-of-pocket costs were more than 11 percent of their income.

HOUSE ENERGY AND COMMERCE COMMITTEE

The Energy and Commerce Committee approved its version of the bill (H Rept 111-299, Part 1) by a vote of 31–28 on July 31, after a grueling series of markups that began July 16. Two days before the vote, Chair Henry A. Waxman, D-Calif., reached a compromise with four members of the Blue Dog Coalition that broke a logjam and enabled him to get the bill out of committee. Waxman had halted the markup on July 21 after the moderates, led by Mike Ross of Arkansas, gave him a list of ten changes they wanted in the bill. The Blue Dogs had the votes to stop the bill in the committee, but Waxman's deal with them still upset some liberals who said they felt they were being held hostage by the moderates.

The compromise reduced the bill's cost by trimming eligibility for subsidies to help the uninsured buy coverage, making it easier for private insurers to compete with the government-run public plan and exempting more small businesses from the employer mandate.

In a series of amendments, the Blue Dogs won a requirement that the government-run insurance plan negotiate payments with health providers, instead of setting rates at the Medicare level plus 5 percent.

Liberals won changes that authorized HHS to negotiate Medicare drug prices, a step the pharmaceutical industry had long opposed, and required plans participating in the exchange to get government permission before increasing premiums faster than the rate of medical inflation.

SENATE HELP COMMITTEE

The Senate Health, Education, Labor, and Pensions (HELP) Committee approved its version of the bill (S 1679) on a 13–10 party-line vote July 15, completing a markup that had begun nearly a month before. Christopher J. Dodd, D-Conn., steered the measure through the committee in Kennedy's absence. Dodd said the panel considered almost 500 amendments and adopted nearly160 offered by Republicans.

The panel worked from pieces of a draft that Dodd said would be filled in along the way as agreements were reached on different issues. But angry Republicans asked how they could mark up a draft without knowing its full content, and they slowed the process by submitting more than 300 amendments.

The legislation, later introduced as S 1679, largely reflected the priorities of liberal Democrats and had many similarities with the House bill. It proposed state-based exchanges, or "gateways," and a government-run insurance option to compete with private plans in the exchange. HHS would negotiate rates with providers for the public plan and set premiums. The measure included an individual mandate with exemptions for those who could not afford coverage and a requirement that employers provide health benefits or pay a fine.

The HELP panel did not have jurisdiction over Medicare, Medicaid, or tax provisions, which were to come from the Finance Committee.

Democrats beat back Republican efforts to delete core provisions of the bill, such as a "play or pay" requirement that employers with more than twenty-five workers provide health insurance or pay a fee of $750 per worker per year. Supporters of the bill regarded the mandate as essential to improving access to health care. Republicans assailed the proposal, arguing that it would disproportionately hurt small businesses and could cause more layoffs at a time of high unemployment.

Republicans also sought to kill the government-run insurance option, saying it would have an unfair edge over private insurers and be run poorly. Democrats insisted that a public plan would drive down costs and introduce stability in a market abused by private insurers.

Republicans also challenged the scope of the proposed individual subsidies. Ranking Republican Michael B. Enzi of Wyoming argued that families with incomes at or below 400 percent of the poverty level—about $88,000 for a family of four and $43,000 for individuals at the time—"can and should be able to purchase their own health insurance."

Jeff Bingaman, D-N.M., said the subsidy would go only to families paying more than 12.5 percent of their incomes for health insurance premiums. Enzi offered an amendment to set the cutoff at 250 percent of the poverty level.

Like other strikes at the core of the bill, the amendment was rejected on a party-line vote.

SENATE FINANCE COMMITTEE

Senate Finance, the last committee to finish, approved its bill (S 1796—S Rept 111-89) by a vote of 14–9 on October 13, following seven days of debate and amendments. The panel, which had jurisdiction over changes to Medicare, Medicaid, and the tax code, was the only committee that came close to producing a bipartisan bill.

Baucus had spent four months in behind-the-scenes negotiations with Finance Committee members from both parties—mainly with a group dubbed the "Gang of Six," made up of two other Democrats and three Republicans. Their aim was to put together a draft that could win at least some GOP votes in committee and on the floor. Baucus was optimistic enough to schedule a formal markup of the bill for late June. Like his House counterparts, he had underestimated what a long road it would be.

Democrats in the group were Baucus, Kent Conrad of North Dakota, and Jeff Bingaman of New Mexico. The Republicans were Enzi, Charles E. Grassley of Iowa, and Olympia J. Snowe of Maine. The myriad topics of debate included how to expand Medicaid without busting state budgets, how to bring the bill's cost down, how tough to be with employers, and what to do about the public option. Sometimes the closed-door talks occurred daily. At times they were reportedly on the verge of a breakthrough; other times the talks were said to be near collapse.

Before the formal Finance Committee markup began on September 22, Baucus appeared ready to move on without lining up more support. "I'll find out who wants to support the mark and who doesn't," he said after a September 11 meeting in which the "Gang of Six" was unable to reach final agreement on a plan.

In the end, Snowe was the only Republican to vote for the committee bill, and she made it clear that she might not back the bill on the floor if it underwent changes. But the measure still reflected many of the group's compromises and was seen as the only version that had a chance on the Senate floor.

Baucus agreed to minor changes in the course of the markup, but he fended off attempts by liberal Democrats to significantly modify the bill. Republicans offered a slew of amendments aimed at gutting major features of the legislation or significantly scaling it back, as well as proposals on issues such as abortion and immigration that were important to social conservatives. But they were at a three-vote disadvantage on the panel and made little headway.

Committee Bill Highlights

Major highlights that distinguished the Senate Finance Committee bill from the versions produced by the other four committees included the following:

Public option. Instead of a government-sponsored insurance option, the bill proposed consumer-owned, nonprofit cooperatives that would offer health insurance and compete with private plans in state-run exchanges. Baucus was a strong supporter of the co-op plan, which was written mainly by panel colleague Kent Conrad. Baucus argued that there was no way to get a public option through the Senate.

Democrats John D. Rockefeller IV of West Virginia and Charles E. Schumer of New York tried unsuccessfully to add a government-run insurance option to the bill, and they vowed to try again on the floor. "This was the toughest terrain for us," Schumer said of the Finance Committee. "It's easier on the Senate floor, and then it gets easier still in conference."

The committee rejected, 8–15, a Rockefeller proposal for a public option that would pay doctors, hospitals, and other health care providers based on Medicare rates for the first two years and then negotiate pay rates after that. Five of the panel's thirteen Democrats voted no. Schumer offered a modification in which the government-run plan would negotiate rates from the outset. It was rejected, 10–13. "It is my genuine intent to create a public option that has no built-in legislative advantage over the private insurance market," Schumer said.

Although liberals failed to get a government-run insurance plan into the bill, they managed wins on some other coverage issues. Maria Cantwell, D-Wash., won a 12–11 vote to allow states to opt into a new federal "basic" health care plan for people who earned less than twice the poverty level but too much to qualify for Medicaid.

Employer mandate. Rather than requiring employers to provide health benefits or pay a fine, the Finance bill called for employers that did not offer health coverage to pay a fee for each employee who got subsidized insurance through an exchange.

Revenue. The main source of revenue in the Finance bill was a 40 percent excise tax on insurers of employer-sponsored policies for the portion of premiums that exceeded $8,000 for individuals and $21,000 for families. Other revenue provisions included a $2,500 limit on flexible health spending accounts and fees on the pharmaceutical, medical device, and health insurance industries. Republican attempts to eliminate the fees were unsuccessful.

In action on some of the other amendments, the committee:

- Adopted, 22–1, an amendment by Schumer and Snowe to provide an exemption from the bill's $750 penalty on those who did not obtain insurance for individuals who could not find health care costing less than 8 percent of their adjusted gross income. The hardship waiver in the chair's mark was set at 10 percent. "This is the major amendment on affordability," Schumer said. The amendment also provided for the $750 penalty to be phased in over a period of four years. "I would prefer to have no penalties, frankly," Snowe said.

OBAMA SPEAKS ON HEALTH CARE TO JOINT SESSION OF CONGRESS

On September 9, 2009, after acrimonious public battles during the August recess, President Barack Obama took the unusual step of going before a joint session of Congress to renew his call for a health care overhaul. Obama also addressed the nation in the nationally televised speech aimed at regaining control of the public debate and reassuring moderates in his own party.

"I am not the first president to take up this cause, but I am determined to be the last," he said, prodding Congress to finish its work.

Large parts of the speech were aimed at wavering Democrats who opposed the public option and were skeptical about government efforts to contain medical inflation. Obama repeated his support for a government-run insurance option, which he said would "provide a good deal for consumers" and "keep pressure on private insurers to keep their policies affordable." But for the first time, he signaled that he was open to alternatives.

In a reminder of the partisan hostility that had marked the August recess, Rep. Joe Wilson, R-S.C., stunned most members by yelling "you lie" when the president said his plan would not cover illegal immigrants. He later apologized for the breach of normal decorum.

In trying to reenergize his allies in Congress, he urged them to move forward quickly on legislation that would provide security and stability to individuals who already had coverage, extend coverage to those who did not, and slow the growth of health spending. He said his plan would cost $900 billion over ten years, all of which would be paid for. His comments on some key elements of the plan follow.

Individual mandate. "Individuals will be required to carry basic health insurance," but there would be "a hardship waiver for those who still can't afford coverage."

Employer mandate. "Businesses will be required to either offer their workers health care or chip in to help cover the cost of their workers." However, "95 percent of all small businesses . . . would be exempt from these requirements."

Insurance exchange. The plan includes "a new insurance exchange—a marketplace where individuals and small businesses will be able to shop for health insurance at competitive prices." However, "for those individuals and small businesses who still can't afford the lower-priced insurance available in the exchange, we'll provide tax credits, the size of which will be based on your need."

Public option. For the uninsured and small businesses, the plan would offer "a publicly sponsored insurance option, administered by the government just like Medicaid or Medicare." Obama said his guiding principle "is, and always has been, that consumers do better when there is choice and competition. That's how the market works." The public option "would have to be self-sufficient and rely on the premiums it collects." However, Obama added: "We should remain open to other ideas that accomplish our ultimate goal. . . . But I will not back down on the basic principle that if Americans can't find affordable coverage, we will provide you with a choice."

Preexisting conditions. "It will be against the law for insurance companies to deny you coverage because of a pre-existing condition." In addition, "they will no longer be able to place some arbitrary cap on the amount of coverage you can receive in a given year or in a lifetime. We will place a limit on how much can be charged for out-of-pocket expenses."

Malpractice. "I don't believe malpractice reform is a silver bullet, but I've talked to enough doctors to know that defensive medicine may be contributing to unnecessary costs. So I'm proposing that we move forward on a range of ideas about how to put patient safety first and let doctors focus on practicing medicine. I know that the Bush administration considered authorizing demonstration projects in individual states to test these ideas. I think it's a good idea, and I'm directing my secretary of Health and Human Services to move forward on this initiative today."

Paying for the plan. "I will not sign a plan that adds one dime to our deficits—either now or in the future. . . . And to prove that I'm serious, there will be a provision in this plan that requires us to come forward with more spending cuts if the savings we promised don't materialize."

- Rejected, 10–13, two abortion amendments by Orrin G. Hatch, R-Utah. One would have barred insurers that accepted subsidized premiums from providing abortion coverage, except in cases of rape, incest, or danger to the life of the woman. Individuals could use their own money to buy auxiliary policies covering the procedure. The second amendment would have prohibited federal and state governments from requiring doctors or hospitals to perform abortions. "The mark makes it clear that no federal funds will be used for abortion. None. None," Baucus said.
- Rejected, 10–13, several GOP immigration amendments, including a proposal by Jon Kyl of Arizona that would have required legal immigrants to reside in the United States for five years before being eligible for health tax credits. Opponents said it was unfair to require legal, permanent U.S. residents to obtain coverage and then deny them the federal subsidies that would help pay for it.
- Rejected, 9–14, a Hatch amendment to prevent the bill's changes to Medicare Advantage, a private insurance alternative for Medicare participants, unless

CBO certified that enrollees would not lose any benefits. The bill proposed a new competitive bidding program in Medicare Advantage, whose providers were paid, on average, about 13 percent more per customer than under traditional Medicare coverage. CBO said the provision would save the government about $123 billion over ten years, but might result in fewer Medicare Advantage plans and less generous benefits. Republicans created Medicare Advantage in the 2003 prescription drug law (PL 108-173) and were determined to save it. *(2003 Medicare drug law, Congress and the Nation Vol. XI, p. 496)*

- Rejected, 10–13, an amendment by Bill Nelson, D-Fla., to make Medicaid responsible for paying for low-income seniors' drugs. Under existing law, the payments were handled by Medicare. Medicaid generally got better prices for drugs than Medicare, and Democrats said the amendment would save $86 billion over ten years.

However, Baucus and two other Democrats voted against the amendment, which would have gutted a deal that Obama had struck with the pharmaceutical and biotechnology industry group PhRMA in exchange for the industry agreeing to contribute up to a maximum $80 billion to the health care overhaul over ten years. As part of the deal, PhRMA members agreed to provide 50 percent discounts to seniors who fell into the so-called doughnut hole gap in prescription drug coverage that forced many of them to pay full price for their drugs above annual thresholds.

The Finance Committee finished work on the bill October 1 but waited to vote until CBO delivered a cost analysis. The agency estimated that the bill would cost $829 billion over a decade and reduce the deficit by $81 billion over that period. It also would expand insurance coverage to 94 percent of Americans under age sixty-five, up from the 83 percent insured at the time.

HOUSE FLOOR ACTION

As planned, the House acted first, even though floor action was delayed weeks beyond what President Obama and congressional leaders would have liked.

In a rare Saturday session, the House on a **key vote of 220–215 (R 1–176; D 219–39)** on November 7 approved a version of the bill (HR 3962) that had been carefully calibrated over many weeks to secure a majority of Democrats. Pelosi and other Democratic leaders managed to win the support of all but thirty-nine Democrats. Freshman Rep. Anh "Joseph" Cao of Louisiana was the only Republican to vote for the overhaul on the floor of either chamber. *(2009 key votes, p. 751)*

Democrats hailed the vote as historic, with Pelosi likening the achievement to the creation of Medicare in 1965. "For generations, the American people have called for affordable, quality health care for their families. Today, that call will be answered," Pelosi said. Underscoring the historic nature of the occasion, House dean John D. Dingell, D-Mich., was in the Speaker's chair during debate on the rule for the bill. A longtime supporter of a national health insurance plan, Dingell had presided during the Medicare debate forty-four years before.

Republicans continued to hammer the Democrats and their bill. "The American people have spoken, and they've made it perfectly clear that the health care bill that's on the floor today, they want no part of," said Minority Leader John A. Boehner of Ohio. "We're going to do everything we can to try to stop this from becoming law."

Republicans frequently targeted Pelosi during the heated floor debate, while most Democrats credited the Speaker with leading them to victory. Before bringing the bill to the floor, Pelosi and her leadership team had blended the versions reported by the three committees, then negotiated with members, individually and in groups, turning periodically to the CBO to see whether they had cut the cost to $900 billion over ten years, the level Obama demanded. On October 29, they unveiled a 1,990-page bill in a ceremony on the West Front of the Capitol that was attended by a large retinue of House Democrats.

In a deal that outraged House liberals, Pelosi agreed to a demand by Bart Stupak, D-Mich., to add tougher antiabortion language. Stupak said that without his language, up to forty Democrats might vote against the bill. On the other hand, Diana DeGette of Colorado said the Democrats' 190-member Pro-Choice Caucus would not accept the language Stupak was circulating.

After trying in vain to draft provisions that would satisfy Democrats on both sides of the issue, Pelosi concluded that she had to allow Stupak to offer his amendment. It was adopted, 240–194, with sixty-four Democrats joining 176 Republicans to support it. The language stated that federal funds provided in the act could not be used for abortion services except in cases of rape, incest, or danger to the woman's life. Plans that received any subsidies under the bill could not cover abortion services. To get that coverage, enrollees would have to purchase a separate, supplemental policy with their own money.

Many abortion-rights backers unhappy over the outcome ultimately swallowed hard and voted for the amended bill.

Among other compromises, the bill:

- Preserved the public option that liberals favored, but required the government to negotiate rates with providers, rather than use Medicare rates, plus 5 percent, which was the method preferred by Pelosi and other liberals.
- Modified the income surtax to limit it to the very rich. Instead of phasing in the tax beginning with incomes of $350,000 as Ways and Means proposed, the bill called for a 5.4 percent tax on incomes of more than $1 million ($500,000 for individuals), not

ABORTION BECOMES AN ELEVENTH-HOUR ISSUE

Abortion restrictions emerged as a make-or-break issue for Democratic leaders as they worked to put the finishing touches on health care legislation in both chambers in the 111th Congress. *(112th Congress abortion controversies, p. 458)*

Democratic leaders and the White House insisted from the outset that the bills being debated would do nothing to alter existing law, which prohibited the use of taxpayer dollars to pay for abortions. However, antiabortion lawmakers from both parties demanded explicit language prohibiting funds appropriated in the bill from being used to cover any abortion services.

The final legislation did little to settle the debate. A postpassage executive order by President Barack Obama stipulating that nothing in the bill would permit public funding of abortion did win critical votes of some wavering antiabortion Democrats. But those on both sides of the issue continued to disagree over whether the measure expanded or contracted federal funding, however indirect, for abortion.

The controversy centered on what abortion coverage, if any, would be available in the insurance exchanges set up under the legislation. The final version of the bill signed into law created a system of state-run exchanges where individuals, small businesses, and uninsured people could purchase health insurance coverage.

Hyde Amendment

The starting point for all abortion discussions was the Hyde amendment, language added annually to the Labor–Health and Human Services–Education appropriations bill. Named after former Rep. Henry J. Hyde, R-Ill. (who was a representative from 1975–2007), who first attached the language to the spending bill in 1976, the amendment stated that none of the money being appropriated could be used to pay for abortions, or for health benefits that covered abortion, except to end a pregnancy that resulted from rape or incest or that threatened the woman's life. Democrats sought to avoid an abortion fight over the health care overhaul by having the legislation do no more or less than the status quo as reflected in the Hyde amendment.

House-Passed Bill

The health care overhaul bill (HR 3962) that Speaker Nancy Pelosi, D-Calif., brought to the House floor on November 7, 2009, reaffirmed existing law on abortion. It required that the government-sponsored insurance plan created in the bill cover abortions in cases of rape, incest, or danger to the woman's life. It did not prohibit the public plan provided for in the House legislation—which was not in the final bill—from covering elective abortions, so long as federal subsidies were not used to pay for the procedure. The bill also prohibited discrimination against health care providers or insurance plans based on whether they provided or covered abortion services.

But before the bill passed, the House adopted much more restrictive language. Pelosi accepted the changes, which angered liberals, in order to secure the votes of a number of antiabortion Democrats led by Bart Stupak of Michigan. Stupak's amendment, adopted **on a key vote of 240–194 (R 176–0; D 64–194),** explicitly barred the use of public funds to pay for abortions or for any health insurance plan that covered abortion in any program created by the bill. Plans offered on insurance exchanges set up under the bill could include abortion coverage, but they would not be eligible for government subsidies. To get abortion coverage, enrollees who received tax credits would have to purchase a separate, supplemental policy with their own money. Plans that offered abortion coverage on the exchange would also have to offer an identical plan that did not include the coverage. *(2009 key votes, p. 751)*

Senate-Passed Bill

The Senate health bill (HR 3590), passed in December, included abortion restrictions, but opponents criticized the provisions for not going as far as those in the House measure.

The initial version, filed by Majority Leader Harry Reid, D-Nev., on November 19, 2009, did not explicitly ban the use

indexed for inflation. The new revenue estimate dropped to $460.5 billion over ten years, compared with $544 billion in the committee bill.

- Added a 2.5 percent excise tax on certain medical devices to generate $20 billion over ten years. Another new provision barred paper makers from getting a cellulosic biofuels tax credit for a byproduct known as "black liquor." Most paper companies never expected to claim the credit, but it was counted as bringing in $23.9 billion over ten years.
- Included a new provision that would strip the health insurance industry of its antitrust exemption under the McCarran-Ferguson act.
- Further expanded eligibility for Medicaid by making it available to all individuals with incomes of up to 150 percent of the federal poverty level, rather than setting the cutoff at 133 percent as the committees had.
- Increased the subsidies that would help low-income people buy insurance in the exchanges.

of federal money to pay for abortions in all programs created by the bill, but Democratic leaders said that bill language reaffirming the Hyde amendment and existing regulations would prevent the programs from covering abortions.

Under Reid's amendment, insurance plans in the exchanges could offer abortion coverage, but enrollees would have to pay for it with their own money and the insurer would have to segregate money received as federal subsidies from the funds paid for abortion coverage. Each exchange would have to include one plan that covered elective abortion and one that did not. Abortion foes said that would be the first federal mandate for abortion coverage.

Nebraska Democrat Ben Nelson pressed Reid to substitute the Stupak language as the price of providing the critical sixtieth vote needed to get the bill through the Senate. Although Reid rejected the idea—the language could have been a bill killer in the Senate—he agreed to make changes. As passed, the bill required only that exchanges include a plan that did not cover elective abortion. It also required that every plan in the exchange that offered abortion coverage collect two checks from each enrollee: one for the regular premium, minus any subsidies, and the other to cover the value of abortion services.

The bill also included an antidiscrimination provision similar to the one in the House version.

The fight continued as the negotiations on the legislation neared a conclusion in early 2010, with antiabortion Democrats in the House again threatening to bring down the entire effort unless their demands were met.

Because Senate Democrats had lost their critical sixtieth vote with the election of Republican Scott P. Brown to fill the remaining term of the late Edward Kennedy in Massachusetts, the only way to get the health bill to the president's desk was to have the House pass the Senate bill in exactly the form the Senate had passed it. Some changes were to be made in an accompanying budget-reconciliation bill (HR 4872), but abortion was considered not "germane" to budget legislation. *(Details, p. 437)*

Meanwhile, antiabortion groups, led by the National Right to Life Committee, decried the Senate-passed bill as "the most pro-abortion single piece of legislation to reach the floor of either house of Congress since *Roe v. Wade*," and called the language added by Nelson "unacceptable."

Abortion-rights groups did not care for the Senate language, either. They worried that separating abortion coverage from other health benefits would undermine the coverage many women in the private sector already had—hardly the status quo sponsors said they were pursuing.

But the stakes ultimately got so high—abortion language or no health bill at all—that some antiabortion voices broke with the pack. First the Catholic Health Association endorsed the bill. Then a group representing nearly 60,000 nuns urged the House to vote for the Senate bill regardless, arguing that "despite false claims to the contrary, the Senate bill will not provide taxpayer funding for elective abortion," and that its support for pregnant women "is the real pro-life stance."

Finally, on March 21, 2010, literally hours before the House vote on the Senate bill, the White House announced a deal: President Barack Obama would issue an executive order after passage of the bill "that will reaffirm its consistency with long-standing restrictions on the use of federal funds for abortion," according to a White House statement.

The order said, in part: "The Act maintains current Hyde Amendment restrictions governing abortion policy and extends those restrictions to the newly-created health insurance exchanges."

The executive order was enough to win the votes of some, but not all, wavering antiabortion Democrats. But antiabortion groups did not forget. They campaigned hard against those who voted for the health law, and several were defeated in the November 2010 midterm elections. Stupak, who led the charge and ultimately voted for the health law, retired rather than seek election to a tenth term. Stupak had been receiving death threats, and a local Tea Party group was vowing a major campaign to see him unseated.

- Increased the maximum size at which small businesses would be exempt from the employer mandate.

SENATE FLOOR ACTION

The last, and most excruciating, phase of the 2009 health care debate came near the end of the year. The Senate stayed in session for twenty-five straight days and several snowstorms while Reid struggled to secure the sixty votes he needed to overcome GOP stalling tactics, and Minority Leader McConnell of Kentucky and other GOP leaders conducted all-out procedural warfare aimed at denying Democrats a victory before the end of the year.

Finally, at 7:05 A.M. on the day before Christmas, the Senate passed the bill 60–39 along strict party lines. The key vote on the issue came earlier when the Senate voted 60–40 to invoke cloture to end debate.

Reid had begun meeting with Baucus, Dodd, and administration officials—mainly White House Chief of Staff Rahm Emanuel and HHS Secretary Kathleen Sebelius—the day after the Finance Committee vote. It was the start of a two-month campaign to rally every member of the Democratic caucus—liberals, conservatives, and two independents, Joseph I. Lieberman of Connecticut and Bernard Sanders of Vermont.

On November 19, Reid unveiled a plan that represented his first crack at an intraparty compromise. In a convoluted procedure, he offered it as a substitute for the text of an unrelated tax bill (HR 3590) that became the vehicle for the Senate's health care overhaul. On November 21, Reid won a 60–39 vote to take up the bill, and the floor debate began.

In the meantime, Reid continued meeting with members of the caucus, sometimes one by one, piecing together a deal. His foremost problem remained what to do about the government-run insurance option. Democrats also continued to disagree over how to pay for the overhaul, what kind of subsidies to provide to low- and moderate-income uninsured Americans, and how far to go in pressing employers to provide coverage to their workers, to name just a few of the conflicts.

In an effort to reach an agreement, Obama called all the Senate Democrats to the White House for a pep talk on December 15 and arranged a series of conversations, in the Oval Office or by telephone, with wavering Democrats and even a few Republicans.

Two senators—Lieberman and Ben Nelson, D-Neb.—held out until the final weekend, securing major compromises. Reid assured Lieberman that the bill would include neither a government-sponsored insurance plan nor an opportunity for people ages fifty-five to sixty-four to "buy in" to some form of Medicare coverage. The Medicare expansion was backed by a group of liberal and centrist Democrats as an alternative to a public option. Nelson, the final holdout, won stricter abortion language that barred plans that received subsidized premiums from offering coverage for the procedure.

With his sixteenth vote in hand, Reid filed the rewritten legislation on Saturday, December 18, as a manager's amendment to his earlier substitute. McConnell responded by forcing the Senate clerks to read the 383-page document aloud.

The turning point came a little after 1 a.m. on. December 21, when Reid on the **key vote of 60–40 (R 0–40; D 58–0; I 2–0)** got the Senate to invoke cloture on the amendment, demonstrating conclusively that he had the votes to break the Republican filibuster. The Senate adopted the amendment, 60–39, the following day. Senators voted from their desks, a custom reserved for the most important matters. Ailing ninety-two-year-old Democrat Robert C. Byrd of West Virginia was brought to the floor in a wheelchair just as the tally began. Remaining through the end of the vote, Byrd stopped on his way to his desk to shake hands with Reid. *(2009 key votes, p. 751)*

Liberals were especially disappointed that Reid dropped the public option along with the Medicare buy-in plan. But they coalesced around the bill, saying it remained a historic rewrite of the nation's health system. "I think this bill has a lot in it that makes sense—among other things, insurance for 30 million poor Americans, insurance reform, disease prevention, primary health care expansion," Sanders said.

Republicans sat quiet and stone-faced after the vote, while Democrats smiled and talked among themselves. But McConnell made it clear that his caucus would continue to extract maximum pain from the Democrats, forcing two more cloture votes before the Senate could pass the bill. Republicans also insisted on the full thirty hours of debate permitted after each successful cloture vote, only agreeing on a shorter debate before the final vote to allow members to get home by Christmas.

Over the next three days, the Senate:

- Agreed, 60–39, on December 22 to invoke cloture, limiting debate on the original substitute amendment that Reid had filed in November.
- Adopted the substitute amendment, 60–39, on December 23.
- Agreed, 60–39, on December 23 to invoke cloture on the bill itself.
- Cast the final 60–39 vote passing the bill on December 24.

SENATE COMPROMISES

The CBO and the Joint Tax Committee estimated that the Senate plan would cost $871 billion over ten years. The following are a few of the dozens of changes Reid made over two months to corral the sixty votes:

Public option. Reid announced in late October that the bill he was working on would include a government-sponsored insurance option but that states could "opt out" and allow only private health plans in their exchange. But in statements that grew stronger as the fall progressed, Lieberman indicated that he would not vote for a bill that included any type of public option. His biggest concern, he said, was that taxpayers might be on the hook if the public plan ran into financial distress. On the other side of the issue, Sanders released a statement saying there were a "number of senators, including myself, who would not support final passage without a strong public option."

In the end, Reid chose an alternative suggested by moderates that replaced the public option with a system of national private insurance plans that would be administered by the OPM, which already managed health benefits for federal employees. The compromise also included the Finance Committee's proposal to assist in the creation of nonprofit, member-run co-ops in every state to offer alternatives to private insurance plans.

The decision to drop the public option reportedly went a long way toward securing the votes of a bloc of centrist Democrats.

Abortion. Encouraged by Stupak's victory in the House, abortion opponents campaigned for similar changes in the Senate bill.

On December 8, the Senate voted, 54–45, to table (or kill) an amendment by Nelson and Hatch to include the Stupak language. Reid, who personally opposed abortion, voted with most Democrats against the amendment, saying the bill left existing law in place and the amendment would exceed those standards.

But when Nelson became the last senator standing in the way of a sixty-vote majority, Reid had little choice but to make changes. Although the final bill did not contain Stupak's language, it explicitly barred the use of federal funds for abortion in any programs under the bill. Plans in an exchange that offered abortion coverage would have to collect separate payments for the portion of the plan cost attributable to the coverage. (Nelson also won favors for his state, including full federal financing for Nebraska's share of the cost of expanding Medicaid, a provision that came to be known as the "Cornhusker kickback.")

Revenue. Reid reduced the number of plans subject to the 40 percent excise tax by raising the threshold to plans that cost more than $8,500 for individuals and $23,000 for families, up from $8,000 and $21,000 under the Finance Committee version. Insurance plans for retirees, workers in high-risk jobs, and residents of high-cost states would have higher thresholds. The change reduced the expected revenue to $148.9 billion over ten years from about $205 billion under the Finance version.

Reid more than made up for the loss by adding a 0.9 percent increase in the Medicare hospital insurance payroll tax on wages above $200,000 for individuals and $250,000 for couples. The increase, which was not indexed for inflation, was estimated to raise $86.8 billion over ten years.

Annual fees on the pharmaceutical and medical device industries were reduced, offset by an increase in fees on the insurance industry.

Conrad had predicted months before on *Fox News Sunday* that the House would have to bend the Senate's way for any final agreement to get through Congress. "It is very clear that the final bill, to pass in the United States Senate, is going to have to be very close to the bill that has been negotiated here," Conrad said. "Otherwise, it will not get sixty votes."

2010 LEGISLATIVE ACTION

When Democrats began talking about a final bill in January 2010, Pelosi and other House Democratic leaders insisted they would not simply accept the Senate-passed version. They hoped to negotiate a compromise, attach it to the Senate bill, and send it to the other chamber to be cleared. But the math in the Senate ultimately made that impossible.

With Republican Scott Brown's victory in Massachusetts for the open seat following the death of Edward Kennedy, making changes that would require another Senate vote on the overhaul became a nonstarter, and hopes for completing the overhaul began to fade. Democrats appeared rattled, with some talking of declaring the bill dead and going back to the drawing board to find a compromise that could win at least some GOP support. Others advocated clearing the Senate bill with a subsequent bill to amend it, breaking out and clearing pieces that had bipartisan support, or dropping the issue and turning instead to job creation, which many rank-and-file Democrats said was a higher priority with midyear elections looming.

But Obama never seemed to consider backing away from his ambitious overhaul plan. He released a new proposal on February 22—essentially what a conference report might look like if lawmakers were able to write one—with compromises on key features of the House- and Senate-passed bills. Three days later, he held a televised health care forum that he said would give Republicans one more chance to join in completing the legislation. Predictably, each side reiterated its talking points, with Democrats calling Republicans obstinate and GOP leaders urging Obama to scrap his plan.

"Our view, with all respect, is that this is a car that can't be recalled or fixed and that we ought to start over," said Sen. Lamar Alexander, R-Tenn.

Having demonstrated that Republicans had no interest in the legislation, Obama gave up his longtime pledge to have a final health bill worked out in the open. Instead, he backed Democratic leaders' plan to bring the long battle to a climactic vote on the House floor without GOP support and to use reconciliation procedures to ease the process in the Senate.

"We cannot have another year-long debate about this," Obama said. "The question that I'm going to ask myself, and I ask of all of you, is: is there enough serious effort that in a month's time or a few weeks' time or six weeks' time we could actually resolve something? And if we can't, then I think we've got to go ahead and make some decisions, and then that's what elections are for."

Democratic leaders set in motion a timetable to get the overhaul to Obama by March 26, the start of Congress's spring recess, and Obama undertook a personal campaign to persuade wavering lawmakers from different groups within the Democratic caucus.

FINAL HOUSE FLOOR ACTION

Despite Obama's personal lobbying, House Democrats still remained wary of the Senate bill. Pelosi worked to limit defections among several factions, including liberals who were still unhappy over the lack of a public option, felt the subsidies for low-income families were insufficient, and opposed the tax on high-cost plans. Antiabortion Democrats threatened to vote against the bill if it did not include the stronger House language on abortion. Republicans added to Pelosi's headaches by urging moderates who voted for the original House bill to break with Obama, warning them they could pay a steep political price if they did not.

But on Sunday, March 21, with the Capitol grounds filled with demonstrators mostly protesting the bill,

Democratic leaders on a **key vote of 219–212 (R 0–178; 219–34),** cleared the Senate-passed health care overhaul, unchanged. *(2010 key votes, p. 767)*

Shortly afterward, the House passed the reconciliation bill (HR 4872), which carried modifications to the new health care law, by a vote of 220–211. A GOP motion to require the Budget Committee to report the bill back immediately after restoring the House language on abortion failed, 199–232.

Many House Democrats were nervous about clearing the overhaul before the Senate had signed off on the modifications. But the Senate parliamentarian ruled that a reconciliation bill could only change existing law, which left Democrats no choice but to send the overhaul to Obama first and trust that the Senate would clear the corrections measure.

Minority Leader John A. Boehner, R-Ohio, accused the Democrats of recklessly disregarding the will of the American people, who, he said, rejected the majority's ideas. "We have failed to listen to America, and we have failed to reflect the will of our constituents," he said. His voice rising, Boehner warned the Democratic majority: "In a democracy you can only ignore the will of the people for so long."

"Shame on each and every one of you who substitutes your will and your desires above those of your fellow countrymen," he added.

Democratic leaders, however, suggested that history was on their side when it came to social welfare legislation.

Alluding to other landmark pieces of legislation, Majority Leader Steny H. Hoyer, D-Md., said the attacks of Republicans and other opponents were as wrong as GOP attacks on Social Security and Medicare, enacted in 1935 and 1965. "Those slurs were false in 1935; they were false in 1965; and, ladies and gentlemen of this House, they are false in 2010," he said. He added, "This bill will stand in the same company—for the misguided outrage of its opposition and for its lasting accomplishment for the American people."

A group of antiabortion Democrats, led by Bart Stupak of Michigan, dropped their threats to scuttle the legislation only after Obama promised to issue an executive order stating that nothing in the health care overhaul would permit public funding of abortions. Obama issued the order March 24, but it did not satisfy some abortion foes. Stupak was among ten or so House Democrats who received threats after voting for the overhaul, and House leaders from both parties spoke out against the behavior. Pelosi warned members to take care that the rhetoric they used during floor debate did not inflame those who would use violence. Boehner said that "threats and violence should not be part of a political debate."

FINAL SENATE FLOOR ACTION

The Senate passed the reconciliation bill by a **key vote of 56–43 (R 0–40; D 54–3; I 2–0)** on March 25, with three Democrats and all Republicans senators opposed. Before passing the bill, the chamber spent most of three days on a series of forty-one GOP amendments. *(2010 key votes, p. 767)*

When the time for final passage arrived, Reid held a moment of silence in memory of Kennedy, who had fought for almost half a century in the Senate to provide universal health care. The chamber was so quiet that the whir of computers and electronic devices on the dais could be heard, as could the ambient noise outside the chamber.

Senators then cast their votes from their desks, a practice reserved for important occasions, with Vice President Joseph R. Biden Jr. holding the gavel in his role as president of the Senate.

Although Republicans won no significant changes to the bill, two minor provisions were dropped after the Senate parliamentarian ruled they were not germane. As a result, the measure was sent back to the House, which cleared it, 220–207, in the early evening of March 25.

Congress's work was done. The massive health care overhaul would henceforth be in the hands of federal agencies such as the Center for Medicare and Medicaid Services and the Office of Personnel Management, as well as the states, which would be called on to turn the myriad details of the new law into concrete rules and programs.

MAJOR PROVISIONS

The following are the major provisions of the landmark health care overhaul legislation—formally known as the Patient Protections and Affordable Care Act (PL 111-148) that President Barack Obama signed into law March 23, 2010, as amended by the reconciliation law (PL 111-152), signed March 30, 2010.

Expansion of Coverage

State-run exchanges. States were required to create "American Health Benefit Exchanges" by 2014 that offered a choice of health insurance plans to qualifying individuals and small businesses. The exchanges could be administered by either a governmental agency or a nonprofit entity established by the state. The law provided federal funding for states to create the exchanges but required that the exchanges be financially self-sustaining by 2015.

If a state did not create an exchange by January 1, 2014, the law required the Department of Health and Human Services (HHS) to create and operate one, either directly or through an agreement with a not-for-profit organization.

Health plans offered through the exchanges had to meet a number of requirements, including offering a "sufficient choice of providers" serving medically underserved communities, and meeting certain clinical access and quality standards. The details of the requirements were to be finalized in rulemaking by HHS.

The Office of Personnel Management (OPM) was directed to contract with health insurers so that at least two multistate plans were offered in each new state health insurance exchange. Insurers had to provide both individual and employer health plans, and one of the two in each exchange had to be run by a nonprofit organization. Also, each exchange had to have one plan that did not offer coverage of abortion services beyond the specifications of the Hyde amendment, which barred federal funding for abortion except in cases of rape or incest or when the pregnancy threatened the life of the woman.

Two or more states could enter into an agreement to operate multistate or regional exchanges, as long as HHS approved the arrangement and the exchanges covered a "distinct geographic area."

In addition, the law created a new Consumer Operated and Oriented Plan (CO-OP) program intended to encourage the development of nonprofit entities to provide health insurance coverage. The measure appropriated $6 billion for loans and grants to help finance the CO-OP program, which had to be awarded by July 1, 2013.

Eligibility for exchanges. Citizens and legal residents who were not incarcerated could obtain coverage through the new health insurance exchanges. Starting in 2014, employers with 100 or fewer employees could purchase coverage through the new state exchanges. Businesses with more than 100 employees could purchase health insurance through the exchanges beginning in 2017.

Individuals who applied for coverage in a state exchange had to be screened for eligibility for Medicaid, the federal-state health insurance program for low-income and disabled people, or for the federal-state Children's Health Insurance Program (CHIP) and be enrolled if eligible. Children who met income eligibility guidelines for CHIP but were unable to enroll because a state with budget constraints had frozen enrollment could receive tax credits to help pay premiums for health insurance through an exchange. Effective in fiscal 2016, states would have the option of transitioning CHIP-eligible children into a health insurance exchange, instead of CHIP, as long as HHS approved the transition.

"Essential benefits package." All qualified health benefits plans offered in the exchanges were required to provide coverage that met or exceeded the standards of an "essential benefits package." At a minimum, the essential benefits had to include outpatient services; emergency services; hospitalization; maternity and newborn care; mental health services, including behavioral health treatment; prescription drugs; laboratory services; preventive and wellness services; chronic disease management; rehabilitative services; and pediatric services, including dental and vision care.

Benefit structure. The new law created five tiers of health benefits to be offered in the health insurance exchanges. The Bronze Plan, which was the minimum level of health coverage available through the exchanges, covered 60 percent of the costs of the medical benefits provided. The Silver Plan covered 70 percent. The Gold Plan covered 80 percent. The Platinum Plan, which was the most generous health insurance coverage available through the exchanges, covered 90 percent of the costs of medical benefits. Finally, a Catastrophic Plan would be available to individuals age thirty or younger who were exempt from the law's requirement to purchase health insurance; it would cover only medically catastrophic events, such as injuries suffered in a major car accident, with the maximum amount of cost-sharing permitted under the law. The Catastrophic Plan was not available to employers.

"Basic Health Plan." States could create a "Basic Health Plan" that provided coverage to uninsured individuals with annual household incomes of 133 percent to 200 percent of the federal poverty level. The states would have to contract with private insurers to provide at least the essential benefits package.

Tax credits for lower-income households. Tax credits for part of the cost of premiums were available, starting in 2014, for those with household incomes of 100 percent to 400 percent of the federal poverty level (an annual income of $22,050 to $88,200 for a family of four, in 2011). Within each income bracket, the tax credits would be tied to the second lowest-cost Silver Plan in their area and determined on a sliding scale that limited the costs families had to pay for health insurance premiums to a percentage of their income, as follows:

- Households with incomes of 133 percent to 150 percent of the federal poverty level would pay 3 percent to 4 percent of their incomes for premiums.
- Those with incomes of 150 percent to 200 percent of the federal poverty level would pay 4 percent to 6.3 percent of their incomes.
- Those with incomes of 200 percent to 250 percent of the federal poverty level would pay 6.3 percent to 8.05 percent of their incomes.
- Those with incomes of 250 percent to 300 percent of the federal poverty level would pay 8.05 percent to 9.5 percent of their incomes.
- Those with incomes of 300 percent to 400 percent of the federal poverty level would pay 9.5 percent of their incomes for premiums.

Starting in 2015, the premium tax credits were to be adjusted to reflect year-to-year premium growth in the health plans.

The credits would be reduced if any member of a household was residing in the United States illegally. For example, if four people were supported by one income, and one family member was an illegal immigrant, the family income would be counted as supporting only three people.

The CBO projected that in 2015, the average federal premium tax credit would be $5,200 per household.

Limit on out-of-pocket costs. The percentage of a plan's cost that a low-income household would pay out of pocket was limited to:

- 6 percent for households with incomes of 100 percent to 150 percent of the federal poverty level.

- 13 percent for households with incomes of 150 percent to 200 percent of the federal poverty level.
- 27 percent for households with incomes of 200 percent to 250 percent of the federal poverty level.
- 30 percent for households with incomes of 250 percent to 400 percent of the federal poverty level.

Tax credits for small businesses. Starting in 2010, employers with twenty-five or fewer employees and annual average wages of less than $50,000 were eligible for new tax credits phased in over the course of several years. In tax years 2010 through 2013, qualifying small employers could receive a tax credit of 35 percent of the employer contribution to health insurance premiums, as long as the employer contributed at least 50 percent of the total premium costs. In tax years 2014 and after, the law provided a tax credit of 50 percent for qualified employers for the first two years in which they purchased health insurance through a state exchange, as long as they contributed at least 50 percent of the total premium costs.

Tax-exempt small businesses, such as religious organizations, that met all the other requirements were eligible for tax credits of up to 35 percent of their contributions to employees' premiums.

Abortion coverage. Health plans in a state exchange that covered abortion services beyond those allowed under the Hyde amendment were required to segregate payments for abortion coverage into separate accounts for those enrollees who received premium tax credits. To get the abortion coverage, an enrollee had to make two premium payments: one for regular benefits and one for abortion services. The enrollee could not receive federal tax credits for the premium for abortion services.

The law did not preempt state laws pertaining to abortion services, and states could choose to prohibit coverage of such services in the exchange. Health insurers in an exchange could not discriminate against health providers who were unwilling to provide abortion services or to refer patients to providers who did offer such services.

Temporary high-risk pool. Within ninety days of enactment, HHS was required to create a temporary, national high-risk insurance pool program to provide health care benefits to individuals who had preexisting conditions, until the health insurance exchanges created by the law were functioning in 2014. States that already had their own high-risk pools were required to continue operating them.

To be eligible for the high-risk pool, an individual could not be eligible for Medicare, Medicaid, or an employer-based plan, and could not have had insurance during the six-month period before applying. Illegal immigrants could not get coverage through the pool. The law appropriated $5 billion to pay claims and cover administrative costs of the high-risk pool that exceeded the premiums that were collected. If the funding in a given fiscal year was insufficient, HHS could make necessary adjustments.

Individual and Employer Requirements

Individual mandate. Starting in 2014, all citizens and legal residents were required to have "minimum essential coverage," defined as employer-sponsored coverage; government programs including Medicare, Medicaid, or CHIP; or coverage obtained through the new health insurance exchanges. In addition, individuals were allowed to obtain insurance outside the exchanges if the policies met "essential coverage" standards.

Those exempted from the requirements included illegal immigrants; individuals who were incarcerated; individuals who could not afford coverage, defined as those whose contributions to the cost of insurance were greater than 8 percent of their household incomes; individuals with household incomes of less than 100 percent of the federal poverty level ($10,830 per year for an individual or $22,050 for a family of four, at the time—2011), although people at this income level were entitled to coverage under Medicaid; members of American Indian tribes; individuals who were uninsured for a period of less than three continuous months; individuals for whom obtaining health insurance would create a "hardship," as determined by HHS; and those who belonged to certain religious groups with tenets that included conscientious objection to private or public insurance.

Individual penalties. Beginning in 2014, individuals who were required to obtain health insurance coverage and did not do so were subject to penalties, collected with their income tax returns. (Those who did not earn enough to file taxes were not subject to the penalties). The penalties were to be phased in over three years, reaching a maximum in 2016 of the greater of $695 per year or 2.5 percent of family income for each adult who did not have health insurance for more than three months in a given year. In 2014 the penalty was set at the greater of $95 per adult or 1 percent of family income. Family income was defined as income in excess of the tax filing thresholds ($10,000 for an individual and $20,000 for a family in 2013).

Employer penalties. The law did not require employers to offer health insurance benefits. But starting in 2014, employers with more than fifty workers that did not offer insurance, and that had at least one employee who received a federal premium tax credit to purchase insurance through an exchange, would be required to pay a $2,000 fee for each full-time employee, excluding the first thirty workers.

Employers with more than fifty workers that did offer health insurance benefits would be required to pay the lesser of $3,000 for each employee who received a premium credit or $2,000 per full-time employee, excluding the first thirty employees.

Employer vouchers. Starting in 2014, employers that offered health benefits had to offer vouchers to purchase insurance in the exchanges for low- and moderate-income employees who would have difficulty paying for the employer's health plan. Specifically, employers were required to offer vouchers to employees with incomes of up to 400 percent of the federal poverty level whose contribution to employer-sponsored insurance would constitute from 8 percent to 9.8 percent of their income.

Automatic enrollment in employer health plans. Employers with more than 200 employees were required to automatically enroll new, full-time employees in a health insurance plan (if one was offered) and to maintain the coverage each year unless an employee opted out. The law required employers to provide adequate notice so that employees could choose to opt out. This provision did not supersede any state law regarding automatic enrollment that was at least as stringent.

Medicaid Expansion

Medicaid eligibility. The law expanded eligibility under state Medicaid programs to all individuals with household incomes of up to 133 percent of the federal poverty level, effective in 2014. State Medicaid programs were required to cover qualified individuals who previously did not have to be covered, including those under age sixty-five, those who were not disabled, and adults without dependent children. The law prohibited states from changing their Medicaid programs in a way that set more restrictive standards, methodologies, or procedures than those that were in effect on the date of enactment——a so-called maintenance-of-effort requirement—through December 31, 2013.

Federal matching funds for Medicaid. The federal government was required to cover 100 percent of the state's cost of covering newly eligible people, including parents and childless adults, from 2014 through 2016. The percentage would drop to 95 percent in 2017, 94 percent in 2018, 93 percent in 2019, and 90 percent in 2020 and beyond. States that previously provided coverage to childless adults at 100 percent of the federal poverty level who continued to be enrolled in Medicaid would receive the same federal funding as states that did not previously provide such coverage.

Increased matching funds for Louisiana. Starting in 2011, the law provided an increase in federal Medicaid matching funds for Louisiana for continuing recovery efforts from major disasters, including Hurricane Katrina.

Medicaid income eligibility rules. Starting in 2014, the law required all states to use a uniform method to determine eligibility for Medicaid based on a household's modified gross income. States would no longer be permitted to disregard income or deduct certain types of income when determining eligibility, as many states did. However, states could continue to disregard or deduct income for applicants who were elderly, blind, or disabled. The law also prohibited states from imposing an asset test when determining eligibility for Medicaid, as many states did in the case of parents of poor children.

Federal matching funds for U.S. territories. The law provided an increase estimated at $7.3 billion for federal matching payments for Medicaid programs in the five U.S. territories in the period of fiscal 2014 through 2019 and increased caps on federal funding in the territories. It earmarked $925 million of the funds for Puerto Rico.

Medicaid reimbursements for primary care. Medicaid reimbursements for primary care services were increased in 2013 and 2014 to 100 percent of the Medicare payment rates for such services.

Children's Health Insurance Program

Federal matching funds. Starting in fiscal 2014, states were to receive an increase of 23 percentage points in their federal matching funds for CHIP, to a cap of 100 percent of the cost of a state's program. This provision effectively increased the minimum federal match for CHIP programs to 88 percent from the previous 65 percent, meaning that states would have to fund, at most, 12 percent of the cost of their programs.

Eligibility rules. States could not change their programs in a way that imposed more restrictive standards, methodologies, or procedures than were in effect June 16, 2009, through September 30, 2019.

Exchanges. Children who met income eligibility guidelines for CHIP but were unable to enroll because a state had frozen enrollment due to budget constraints were eligible for premium tax credits to obtain health insurance through the new exchanges starting in 2014. Children who received subsidized coverage through the exchanges were not eligible for coverage under CHIP. Children in an exchange could not switch to CHIP if the state reopened enrollment. Starting in fiscal 2016, states could transition children who were eligible for CHIP to receive coverage through one of the new health insurance exchanges instead, as long as HHS approved the transition.

New Health Insurance Regulations

Preexisting conditions. Starting in 2014, health insurers who offered group or individual coverage were prohibited from denying coverage because a potential enrollee had a preexisting condition. The law immediately prohibited insurers from denying coverage to children with preexisting conditions for newly issued plans, and as existing plans were renewed. Specifically, when determining eligibility for coverage, health insurers could not take into account health status, claims history, physical or mental medical conditions, genetic information, disability, or other factors determined by HHS.

Protection against coverage rescission. Starting in September 2010 (six months after enactment), health insurers were prohibited from rescinding group or individual coverage, unless there was clear and convincing evidence of fraud or intentional misrepresentation by an enrollee. If insurers did rescind coverage, they had to provide adequate prior notice to the affected enrollees.

Coverage of young adults. Starting in September 2010, health insurers who offered dependent coverage were required to continue coverage of children on their parents' plans, at the parents' discretion, until the children turned twenty-six. Group health plans that were operating before enactment had to cover these adult children only if the children did not have an offer of employer-sponsored insurance.

Lifetime spending limits. Starting in September 2010, health insurers were prohibited from setting lifetime limits on the dollar value of health care provided to an enrollee. Starting in 2014, insurers were barred from setting annual spending limits. Before 2014, insurers could set "reasonable" annual spending limits only if approved by the federal government.

Limit on deductibles. The law limited deductibles in employer-sponsored health plans in the small-group markets to $2,000 per year for individual coverage and $4,000 per year for family coverage, starting in 2014. These deductibles could be increased only if such an increase was offset through an amount "reasonably available" to an employee through a flexible spending arrangement.

Coverage of preventive care. The law required health insurers to cover certain preventive-care services without requiring any cost-sharing—meaning co-payments, co-insurance, or deductibles—by enrollees in individual or group plans. The services that had to be covered included vaccinations and screenings recommended by federal agencies. The law specifically stated that the recommendations issued in November 2009 by the federal Preventive Service Task Force on breast cancer screening and mammography did not apply, and that insurers, therefore, had to provide mammograms more frequently than called for in the guidelines. The task force had stated that women younger than fifty with no family history of breast cancer did not need to undergo mammograms, and that women fifty and older needed mammograms only once every two years. Previous guidelines had called for annual mammograms for women forty and older.

Premium reporting. Health insurers who offered coverage in the small- and large-group markets had to publicly report the percentage of premiums they spent for specific services, such as reimbursement for clinical services, efforts to promote quality of care, and administrative costs. Insurers were required to provide rebates to enrollees if the medical loss ratio—the portion of the premium that was spent on medical services as opposed to administrative expenses—for a given year was below 85 percent for large-group plans and 80 percent for small-group and individual-market plans. The provision was intended to limit insurers' administrative costs to 15 percent for large groups and 20 percent for small-group and individual coverage. The rebates began in 2011 and were in effect only until the health insurance exchanges were fully established.

Review of premium increases. Beginning in 2010, HHS was required to create a process, in conjunction with states, to review proposed premium increases of more than 10 percent by health insurers. Health insurers had to submit a justification for any premium increase before implementing it and place the information prominently on their websites. HHS was required to ensure public disclosure of the information. Starting in 2014, states were required to monitor premium increases inside and outside their insurance exchanges. States that met certain requirements could receive grants to assist them in reviewing and approving premium increases, where allowed by state law.

Changes in Medicare

Payment advisory commission. The law created an Independent Payment Advisory Board (IPAB) to draft legislative proposals to slow the growth rate in Medicare spending if spending exceeded a certain target rate. The Centers for Medicare and Medicaid Services (CMS) was required to project, on April 15, 2013, whether Medicare spending would exceed the projected growth in the Consumer Price Index that year. If so, the new fifteen-member board had to meet and submit recommendations to Congress and the president on how to slow Medicare's growth. The recommendations would be due January 15, 2014. Beginning in January 2018, recommendations would be required if the growth in Medicare spending was projected to exceed gross domestic product growth by more than 1 percent.

Board recommendations could include a reduction in reimbursements to Medicare Advantage plans or to prescription drug plans, or proposals to restructure Medicare payment mechanisms generally. Under Medicare Advantage, individuals who were eligible for Medicare got their insurance from private companies rather than the federal government. The board's targeted savings rate was 0.5 percent of projected total Medicare spending in 2015, 1 percent in 2016, 1.25 percent in 2017, and 1.5 percent in 2018 and beyond. The target rate could be less than the specified levels if so recommended by the chief actuary of CMS. The board recommendations could not include rationing care, changing benefits, changing eligibility rules, or requiring cost sharing, such as premiums and co-payments.

Once the commission submitted recommendations, Congress would have to consider the legislative proposals. If Congress did not act on a proposal by August 15 of the year it was submitted, CMS would be required to implement the commission's proposal.

Medicare drug benefit. The new law phased out the gap in Medicare drug coverage, known as the "doughnut hole," over ten years. Under previous law, after beneficiaries met their deductible for the year, the government covered 75 percent of their drug costs up to a set dollar amount. After that, the beneficiary entered the doughnut hole and was responsible for 100 percent of the costs up to a second dollar amount, known as the catastrophic threshold. The federal government was responsible for 95 percent of any remaining costs above the catastrophic limit for the rest of the year.

Under the new law, beneficiaries who fell into the doughnut hole in 2010 were eligible for a one-time $250 rebate. Starting in 2011, beneficiaries who fell into the coverage gap were eligible for a 50 percent discount on brand-name drugs. The discount would increase to 75 percent by 2020, with the government paying the rest of the cost of the drugs.

Medicare Advantage payments. Effective in 2011, the law froze federal payments to Medicare Advantage and then reformulated payments according to local costs. Under the new, phased-in formula, payments were to be allocated based on geographic variability of Medicare spending. Payments would start at 95 percent of traditional fee-for-service Medicare payments in areas that were in the top quartile of Medicare spending, and increase to 115 percent in areas in the lowest quartile. Starting in 2014, the amount that Medicare Advantage plans could spend on administrative costs was capped at 15 percent of the amount collected from premiums. If a plan spent more than that, it would be required to pay HHS a fine equal to the amount of funds spent on administrative costs that exceeded the cap.

"Market basket" updates. The law reduced the "market basket" inflation adjustments used to determine the reimbursement for certain services by Medicare providers. The new law incorporated adjustments based on gains in productivity into several market baskets used under Part A that did not previously incorporate such provisions. Such productivity adjustments were to be phased in during different years for different types of providers and would affect inpatient hospitals, long-term care hospitals, inpatient rehabilitation facilities, psychiatric hospitals, and outpatient hospitals. The formula was expected to reduce anticipated mandatory spending by an estimated $156.6 billion over ten years.

Disproportionate-share payments. The law reduced Medicare disproportionate-share hospital payments, federal payments to hospitals that treat a disproportionate share of low-income patients. Starting in fiscal 2014, the payments were reduced by 75 percent, and then increased based on both the percentage of the population that was uninsured in the area served by the hospital and the percentage of the hospital's care that went to uninsured patients.

Additional Medicare hospital payments. A total of $400 million was set aside from the Federal Hospital Insurance Trust Fund to cover additional Medicare payments in fiscal 2011 and 2012 to hospitals located in counties that were in the lowest quartile of per-capita Medicare spending for Part A and Part B (hospital services and physician services, respectively).

Center for Medicare and Medicaid Innovation. The law created a new Center for Medicare and Medicaid Innovation as part of CMS and provided $15 million over ten years for the center. The new center was directed to evaluate "innovative payment and service delivery models" that would reduce costs without negatively affecting the quality of care or the scope of benefits provided to enrollees. Models to be explored included: payment structured around patient-centered medical homes; contracting directly with groups of providers for care coordination; using comprehensive care plans for geriatric care; creating community-based health teams to support medical homes; and promoting greater access to outpatient services when possible.

Physician-owned hospitals. Effective in 2011, new physician-owned hospitals generally were prohibited from receiving Medicare reimbursements for patients who were referred by physicians with investment interests in the hospital. The law prohibited physician-owned hospitals from expanding, although hospitals could apply to the federal government to be exempted from the ban. The law permitted physician self-referrals to hospitals only if the hospital met certain criteria, including public disclosure of the financial interests of referring physicians and agreements with physicians governing investment in the hospitals.

Medicare Part B premiums. The new law froze the income levels used to calculate income-related premiums for Medicare Part B (physician and outpatient services) in 2011 through 2019 at levels set for 2010. Medicare Part B premiums were calculated on the basis of income levels, and upper-income beneficiaries paid premiums based on their annual income two years before the coverage year.

Reimbursement for hospital-acquired infections. Starting in fiscal 2015, reimbursements would be reduced by 1 percent for certain hospital-acquired conditions, to be determined by HHS.

Reimbursement for preventable readmission. A hospital's reimbursement rates would be reduced for what were considered to be preventable readmissions of Medicare beneficiaries. The provision was intended to give hospitals and health care providers incentives to allow for adequate medical follow-up to prevent multiple hospital readmissions for patients with chronic conditions. Starting in fiscal 2012, CMS would reduce payments by specified percentages, depending on the billing code, for preventable hospital readmissions. CMS was tasked with determining the number of hospital readmissions for a given condition that would be considered excessive and thus subject to reduced reimbursements. Within two years of enactment, a new CMS program would aid hospitals in reducing excessive readmissions.

Accountable Care Organizations. Starting in 2012, qualified health care providers were allowed to form groups, or Accountable Care Organizations, that were eligible for federal payments if they met certain quality standards. Eligibility criteria included having a leadership and administrative structure in place; demonstrating a willingness to take responsibility for the overall quality and cost of care of Medicare beneficiaries who were assigned to the group; and agreeing to contract with CMS for at least three years. The groups were required to submit data allowing CMS to evaluate the quality of care being provided.

Medicaid Cost Savings

Medicaid disproportionate-share payments. Federal matching Medicaid disproportionate-share payments—additional reimbursements for hospitals that served a disproportionate share of low-income individuals—would be reduced by $14.1 billion over the period of fiscal 2014 through 2019.

Medicaid prescription drug rebates. The law increased the rebate that Medicaid programs received for brand-name drugs by 23.1 percent starting in 2010. The discount included Medicaid managed-care plans run by private insurers. The law increased the Medicaid drug rebate for generic drugs to 13 percent of the average manufacturer price.

Acquired conditions. Effective July 1, 2011, the law prohibited federal funding to state Medicaid programs for certain acquired health care conditions, with the specific list up to HHS. Acquired health care conditions were those considered to be caused by health care providers, such as wrong-site surgery, or infections patients acquire in the hospital that could have been prevented with what was considered proper care.

Premium assistance. Starting in 2014, states were required to provide premium assistance to anyone eligible for Medicaid who had employer-sponsored coverage available if doing so was cost-effective for the state. The employer would have to contribute at least 40 percent of the cost of the health insurance premium. Under previous law, it was optional for states to provide premium assistance for employer-sponsored coverage for children and parents who were eligible for Medicaid, if it was cost-effective for the state.

Other Health Care Provisions

Long-term care. The law established a new national voluntary insurance program called Community Living Assistance Services and Support (CLASS) to assist adults with functional limitations in purchasing community living assistance services. It also established an infrastructure to address national needs, alleviate burdens on family caregivers, and address institutional bias.

HHS was required to develop at least three actuarially sound benefit plans as alternatives for designation as the CLASS Independence Benefit Plan. The premiums established in the first and subsequent years had to be based on actuarial analysis of the seventy-five-year costs to ensure solvency for that seventy-five-year period. Such plans would have to provide for payment of a cash benefit with an average of at least $50 per day, varying based on functional ability. The benefit would have to be paid either daily or weekly and could not be subject to lifetime or aggregate limits.

Once set, a monthly premium generally would remain the same as long as an individual was enrolled. The law provided exceptions to guarantee the program's solvency, but premium increases in those cases would not apply to those age sixty-five or older or to those who had paid premiums for at least twenty years.

Those age eighteen or older who received qualifying taxable wages and were actively employed were eligible for the program as long as they were not patients in a hospital, nursing home, care facility, or institution for mental diseases and were not receiving Medicaid.

Comparative-effectiveness research. The law created a nonprofit Patient-Centered Outcomes Research Institute to identify research priorities and conduct research to compare the effectiveness of medical treatments and technologies. The new institution replaced the Federal Coordinating Council that was created under the economic stimulus law (PL 111-5). The purpose of the institute was to assist patients, clinicians, purchasers, and policy makers in making informed health decisions. The law appropriated $210 million for the institute in fiscal 2010 through 2012, and $150 million in each of fiscal years 2013 through 2019. (*Stimulus legislation, p. 78*)

Biologic drug patents. The law created a process for the Food and Drug Administration (FDA) to receive and approve applications for biological products that were either similar to, or interchangeable with, a so-called reference product—a biological product that had already been approved. Biologic drugs were a new technology in which drug manufacturers used living cells to produce drug technology; previously, the FDA lacked statutory authority to approve generic versions of biologic drugs, known as biosimilars.

The law provided exclusivity for the first interchangeable product for certain periods and stipulated that a biosimilar product application could not be approved until twelve years after the date the reference product was first approved. It provided for an additional six months forreference products that had demonstrated benefits from pediatric studies. The FDA had to require labeling and packaging that uniquely identified the biosimilar product.

Community health centers. Funding was increased for community health centers that provided primary care services in areas where economic, geographic, or cultural barriers limited access to primary care. The law appropriated $1 billion in fiscal 2011, $1.2 billion in fiscal 2012, $1.5 billion in fiscal 2013, $2.2 billion in fiscal 2014, and $3.6 billion in fiscal 2015.

Medical malpractice. A new five-year demonstration program allowed states to evaluate alternatives to the existing medical liability tort system. HHS could award grants to states that developed pilot programs that allowed for the resolution of medical malpractice disputes and promoted a reduction of medical errors by encouraging the collection and analysis of relevant data. For instance, a state could propose a "no fault" dispute resolution process, in which all victims of certain errors would be compensated equally and health care providers would not be held at fault. States had to identify funding sources for any victim compensation. In addition, states were required to identify a "scope of jurisdiction" for the alternative system they were testing and notify patients who fell within that scope. The jurisdiction could be a geographic area, a health care system, a specific group of health care providers, or a specific specialization within medical practice.

Restaurant menu labeling. Chain restaurants and food vending machines with more than twenty outlets were required to list nutritional information for each available item, including the caloric content of each standard item, and provide an easily understood statement regarding the daily recommended intake of calories. Calorie labeling had to be placed near menu boards, drive-through window menus, and vending machines. The Agriculture Department was required to issue regulations regarding this provision within one year of enactment.

American Indian health. The law permanently reauthorized the Indian Health Care Improvement Act, which governed the provision of health care to American Indians and Alaska Natives through the HHS Indian Health Service. The law authorized programs aimed at increasing the recruitment and retention of health care professionals; expanded mental and behavioral health programs to address issues such as fetal alcohol spectrum disorders, child sexual abuse, and domestic violence; and authorized long-term care services. It required the Indian Health Service budget to account for medical inflation rates and population growth to address underfunding issues.

Sex education. The law provided grants of at least $250,000 per year for each state to conduct "Personal Responsibility Education Programs" to educate teenagers about "both abstinence and contraception for the prevention of pregnancy and sexually transmitted infections, including HIV/AIDS," as well as other life topics such as financial literacy and career skills.

Health insurance overhaul implementation fund. The law appropriated $1 billion to HHS for the administrative costs of implementing the law's provisions.

Revenue Provisions

Excise tax on high-cost health plans. The law established a 40 percent excise tax on high-cost insurance plans offered by employers. The tax, which would become effective in 2018, applied to the cost of premiums for medical coverage above designated thresholds: $10,200 for individuals and $27,500 for families. If medical costs rose faster than expected between 2010 and 2018, as measured by a formula set out in the law, the 2018 thresholds would be adjusted accordingly. The starting thresholds would increase from 2018 to 2019 by the Consumer Price Index (CPI) plus 1 percent, and by the CPI after that.

Several specified groups of taxpayers would get adjusted thresholds in an attempt to ensure that the tax targeted the highest-cost benefits. Thresholds would be increased to the extent that the age and gender characteristics of a company's workforce required higher premiums than would a more typical pool of employees. Thresholds would also be increased by an additional $1,650 for individuals and $3,450 for families for retirees who were not eligible for Medicare and for workers in high-risk professions, such as law enforcement, mining, construction, agriculture, and fishing.

Generally, the tax was to be paid by the insurance company or by the plan administrator for self-insured companies. The threshold amount was the sum of premiums and contributions to flexible spending arrangements, health savings accounts, and other similar mechanisms. Dental and vision benefits did not count toward the total.

The tax was expected to raise $32 billion in 2010 through 2019, the window set under the budget resolution, but because the tax did not begin until 2018, it was expected to bring in much more after that.

Additional Medicare hospital insurance tax. Effective in 2013, the law created a second tax bracket in the payroll levy used to finance Medicare. In addition to paying the existing 1.45 percent employee share of the Medicare tax, employees were required to pay an extra 0.9 percent on wages and self-employment income above $200,000 for individuals, and above $250,000 for married couples.

Also starting in 2013, individuals with adjusted gross income above $200,000 and married couples with adjusted gross income above $250,000 had to pay a new 3.8 percent Medicare tax on unearned income. That included capital gains, interest, dividends, annuities, royalties and rents, along with passive business investments. Active business income from sole proprietorships, S corporations, and partnerships was not subject to the tax. The tax applied to all of an individual's unearned income, but only to the extent that the total adjusted gross income exceeded the threshold. For example, an individual with $150,000 in unearned income out of a total of $250,000 in adjusted gross income would pay taxes on $50,000 of the unearned income, the amount by which adjusted gross income exceeded the $200,000 threshold.

Together, the two provisions were expected to raise $210.2 billion over ten years.

Pharmaceutical industry fee. The prescription drug industry as a whole was responsible for paying an annual fee, beginning with a total of $2.5 billion in 2011. The amount rose to $2.8 billion for 2012 and 2013; $3 billion for 2014, 2015, and 2016; $4 billion for 2017; $4.1 billion for 2018; but then declined to $2.8 billion beyond that. The government would divide the fees among pharmaceutical companies based on the value of the drugs they sold to certain government health care programs.

The fees were expected to raise $27 billion over ten years.

Medical device tax. A new 2.3 percent excise tax on medical devices, effective in 2013, applied to a wide range of devices, particularly those used in hospitals and doctors' offices. The tax did not apply to eyeglasses, contact lenses, and hearing aids; other items manufactured and sold at retail stores for individual use could also be exempted.

The tax was expected to generate $20 billion over ten years.

Health insurance industry fee. Starting in 2014, health insurance providers were required to pay an annual industrywide fee. The total annual fee was to begin at $8 billion in 2014, then rise to $11.3 billion for 2015 and 2016, $13.9 billion for 2017, and $14.3 billion for 2018. After that, the total would increase by the same percentage as health care premiums. The annual total would be divided among health insurers according to market share, based on each company's premiums as a percentage of those of the overall health insurance industry. The law provided a break for certain not-for-profit insurers and did not include any government entities or self-insuring employers.

The fees were projected to raise $60.1 billion over ten years.

Health spending account limits. Starting in 2011, people with health flexible spending arrangements, health savings accounts, health reimbursement accounts, and Archer medical savings accounts could not use the pretax money to pay for over-the-counter medication unless it was prescribed by a doctor. The provision was expected to raise $5 billion over ten years.

Penalties on nonmedical expenses. The law increased, to 20 percent from 10 percent, the tax penalty for people who used tax-advantaged health savings accounts and Archer medical savings accounts for nonhealth purposes, generating an estimated $1.4 billion over ten years.

Flexible spending caps. A statutory cap of $2,500 was placed on the amount of pretax dollars that a worker could set aside in a health flexible spending arrangement. The cap took effect in 2013, with annual adjustments after that based on the CPI. The change was expected to generate $13 billion.

Charitable hospitals. Nonprofit hospitals had to meet a new set of requirements to keep their tax exemptions. They had to conduct regular community health needs assessments and tell the Internal Revenue Service how they met the needs. They also had to establish written, publicized criteria for providing financial assistance to patients, and the law placed limits on their collections processes and fees.

Part D deduction elimination. A deduction that businesses received for providing prescription drug plans for their retirees was repealed. Previously, companies could get federal subsidies for offering the plans without counting the subsidies as income, then deduct the full cost of the plans, including the value of the subsidies. The change allowed companies to continue excluding subsidies from income but prohibited them from also deducting the subsidies. It was expected to generate $4.5 billion.

Itemized deduction. The law raised the threshold above which taxpayers could deduct medical expenses from 7.5 percent of adjusted gross income to 10 percent. The provision took effect in 2013, but for the first four years it did not apply to taxpayers who were age sixty-five and older or had a spouse in that age group. It was expected to raise $15.2 billion over ten years.

Executive compensation deductions. Health insurance companies faced new limits on their ability to deduct the compensation of their executives. The cap was $1 million for most companies, but it was $500,000 for health insurers. The provision took effect for payments made starting in 2013 for services provided anytime after 2009. Unlike most companies, health insurers were required to count any performance-based compensation and commissions toward the cap, and the limitation applied to all employees, directors and consultants, not just a small group of executives. It was projected to raise $600 million over ten years.

Blue Cross and Blue Shield. Blue Cross and Blue Shield health insurance plans had new restrictions starting in 2010. To keep a special 25 percent deduction for certain claims and an exception from the 20 percent reduction in deductions for certain premiums that for-profit companies faced, the Blue Cross and Blue Shield plans were required to have a medical loss ratio of at least 85 percent. The provision was expected to raise $400 million over ten years.

Tanning tax. A new 10 percent tax on indoor tanning services took effect in July 2010 and was expected to raise $2.7 billion over ten years.

Non-Health Revenue Provisions

"Black liquor." The law prevented paper companies from claiming a $1.01-per-gallon cellulosic biofuel tax credit for a manufacturing byproduct known as "black liquor." The substance was often used as fuel in the manufacturing process. The change was credited with raising $23.6 billion over ten years.

"Economic substance." The doctrine of "economic substance" that governed certain tax cases was put into statute. Under the legislation, business transactions had to have a substantial economic or business purpose and not be executed for tax purposes alone to qualify for tax benefits. Companies engaging in such transactions faced penalties of 20 percent to 40 percent if their maneuvers were disallowed. The change was expected to raise $4.5 billion over ten years.

Information reporting. A provision aimed at increasing tax compliance required that, effective in 2012, businesses report to the Internal Revenue Service aggregate payments to a single provider of goods or services if the payments totaled $600 or more in a calendar year. This expanded a previous requirement that similar payments to individuals be reported, and it included penalties for failure to file. The law was expected to generate $17.1 billion over ten years.

Corporate estimated taxes. Corporations faced a timing shift in their quarterly estimated taxes that affected revenue in 2014 only.

Other Revenue-related Provisions

Adoption credit. The law increased the maximum tax credit for adopting children by $1,000, to $13,170. The credit was made refundable, and the scheduled date for the expiration of the credit was delayed from the end of 2010 to the end of 2011. The exclusion for employer-provided adoption assistance underwent a similar change. The provision was expected to cost $1.2 billion over ten years.

W-2 reporting. Starting in 2011, employers had to report the cost of their employees' health coverage on their annual W-2 form.

Therapeutic discovery projects. Small companies could get a 50 percent tax credit for certain investments for medical research. Projects had to be certified by the HHS, address medical needs that were not being met, reduce long-term health care costs, or make a major advance in cancer treatment. The provision took effect for expenses made starting in 2009 and expired at the end of 2010. It was expected to cost $900 million.

Veterans' health study. By the end of 2012, the secretary of veterans affairs was required to produce a study on whether the fees and taxes on insurers, prescription drug manufacturers, and medical device makers were having an effect on the cost of veterans' medical care and access to drugs and devices.

Indian tribal governments exclusion. People receiving health care provided by the Indian Health Service or an American Indian tribe could exclude the value of those benefits from income.

Simple cafeteria plans for small businesses. Beginning in 2011, the law made it easier for small businesses to set up cafeteria plans for employees.

Children's Health Insurance Program (CHIP)

One of the Democrats' first acts in the 111th Congress was to clear a significant expansion of the state Children's Health Insurance Program (CHIP). The program provided health insurance to children in low-income families that were not poor enough to qualify for Medicaid but that could not afford private insurance. President Barack Obama signed the bill into law on February 4, 2009 (HR 2—PL 111-3).

The measure, which took effect April 1, reauthorized CHIP for four years and expanded it to cover an estimated 4.1 million previously uninsured children. It authorized $32.8 billion in mandatory funding over five years in addition to the approximately $5 billion already needed to maintain the joint state-federal program at existing levels. The extra cost was covered largely by an increase in the federal excise tax on cigarettes to $.62 per pack, which brought the tax to $1.01 per pack.

President George W. Bush had vetoed two versions of the legislation that were sent to him in 2007, arguing that the Democrats' plan was too costly and lacked sufficiently stringent income restrictions. Congress upheld both vetoes, the first in 2007 and the second in 2008. A temporary authorization enacted in December 2007 (PL 110-173) kept the program going through March 31, 2009. *(2007 bill, Congress and the Nation Vol. XII, p. 558)*

The program, formerly known as SCHIP (State Children's Health Insurance Program) was created with bipartisan support in 1997 (PL 105-33). It was financed by both the federal government and the states, which had some flexibility to set their own eligibility requirements. In 2006, twenty-six states set their eligibility thresholds at 200 percent of the poverty level, while fifteen states set it above 200 percent, and nine states set it below 200 percent. *(1997 law, Congress and the Nation Vol. X, p. 432)*

The 2007 bills would have expanded the program by $35 billion over five years, to $60 billion. Since then, however, the program's costs had risen and the revenue-raising power of the tobacco tax had shrunk, necessitating the shorter reauthorization.

Several changes made to the 2009 bill kept some previous Republican supporters from backing it. Among the most significant were the removal of a five-year waiting period for some new legal residents—specifically, pregnant women and children. The new law also set higher family income eligibility limits and less strict identity checks for enrollment. That had been a major source of contention during the Bush years. The Senate added a state option to provide dental insurance and offset the cost by bumping the cigarette tax increase to $.62 from $.61 in the earlier bills.

Although many Republicans criticized the expanded coverage, tax increase, and looser requirements for immigrants, Democrats hailed the program as a way to expand health care coverage and build momentum for a broader overhaul of the nation's health care system.

LEGISLATIVE ACTION

The House passed its bill (HR 2) by a vote of 289–139, on January 14, 2009. The measure differed only marginally from the two versions vetoed in 2007.

"This is far from health care reform, but it is a necessary start," said House Energy and Commerce Chair Henry A. Waxman, D-Calif., in a statement.

The bill called for an additional $35 billion for the program over four and a half years and relied on an increase of $.61 per pack in the federal cigarette tax and other tobacco tax increases to pay for most of the expansion. It also included new restrictions on referrals to specialty hospitals that were owned at least in part by physician-investors and specialized in one or two lucrative areas, such as cardiac care or orthopedics. Sponsors said reducing the number of medical procedures being performed at such hospitals would result in savings to the federal government.

Families with incomes of up to 300 percent of the poverty level—higher for states that already had waivers in place—would be eligible. Republicans wanted children and families with incomes below 200 percent of the federal poverty level to be covered before expanding to higher income levels.

"We are extremely concerned that any proposed expansion would include adults, illegal immigrants and those who already have private health insurance," House Minority

Whip Eric Cantor, R-Va., said in a statement. "Focusing on low-income children first would ensure the bipartisan agreement that this program deserves," he said.

SENATE COMMITTEE ACTION

The Senate Finance Committee approved a similar measure (S 275) by a vote of 12–7 on January 15. As introduced, the bill would have increased spending on CHIP by $31.5 billion over four and a half years, but committee changes raised the cost to $32.8 billion.

The panel eliminated the only major difference between the House and Senate bills when it added language by John D. Rockefeller IV, D-W.Va., to allow legal immigrants and new citizens into the program without the standard five-year waiting period. The panel adopted the amendment, 12–7.

One difference that remained was that the Senate bill did not include the provision in the House version imposing new restrictions on referrals to specialty hospitals.

The nearly five-hour markup turned contentious at points, with Republicans, including ranking member Charles E. Grassley of Iowa, charging that Democrats had shut them out of the process and betrayed compromises worked out in the 110th Congress. "It makes me damned disgusted," Grassley told the panel. "We had all sorts of cooperation. . . . Now it's kind of feeling like you're thrown overboard."

Grassley and other Republicans were upset about the elimination of the waiting period for immigrants and new citizens, looser citizenship and residency documentation requirements, changes to how the bill dealt with people who might transfer from private insurance to CHIP, and the bill's slightly looser provisions on income limits.

Rockefeller's amendment set off a lengthy immigration discussion and a slew of GOP amendments. Republicans said eliminating the waiting period would encourage illegal immigration.

John Ensign, R-Nev., also argued that if Congress eventually tackled immigration reform, it would suddenly add millions to the CHIP program as once-illegal immigrant children became legal and eligible. "If we cross the line here," he predicted, "we will be taking on a huge number of additional kids."

Republicans offered several amendments to require more stringent documentation of legal residency or citizenship. All failed, with the exception of a proposal by Grassley to require states to review the citizenship or legal residency status of enrollees when they rechecked their income levels. CHIP enrollees who lost their legal residency while still in the program would be dropped. The amendment was adopted by voice vote.

The committee also adopted by voice vote an amendment by Olympia J. Snowe, R-Maine, to give states the option of offering dental insurance to children who were privately insured but did not have dental coverage available.

A change in the Senate bill increased the enrollment targets required for states to receive bonus payments. The new bonus payments would kick in only after states exceeded target enrollment by 10 percent, instead of 3 percent.

SENATE FLOOR ACTION

The Senate passed HR 2, on a **key vote of 66–32 (R 9–32; D 55–0; I 2–0)**, on January 29, after amending it to reflect the Senate bill. Nine Republicans joined Democrats to support the measure. *(2009 key votes, p. 751)*

"Today, the Senate can keep all the children in CHIP covered . . . and we can reach more than four million more low-income, uninsured children," said Max Baucus, D-Mont., just before the vote.

Grassley, who voted "no," again bemoaned the changes as fracturing bipartisanship. He said he was given the bill as a "take it or leave it" proposition.

Despite some Republicans' objections, however, the floor action was a largely agreeable process. Democrats did not have to file cloture on the bill or take other procedural steps to get a vote on passage. The debate was more an exercise in patience, with Democrats letting Republicans offer amendments, then easily voting them down.

In action on some of the amendments offered, the Senate:

- Adopted, 55–43, a proposal by Jeff Bingaman, D-N.M., to eliminate a requirement that parents sign official government forms to enroll through the express-lane process.
- Rejected, 17–81, an amendment by Kay Bailey Hutchison, R-Texas, that would have given priority to states with higher numbers of uninsured children in receiving funds to boost CHIP enrollment.
- Tabled (or killed), 54–44, an amendment by Jim Bunning, R-Ky., to eliminate existing exceptions for states that covered children whose families' income was 300 percent or more of the federal poverty level. New York and New Jersey both had such exceptions. New Jersey Democrat Robert Menendez argued that his state's high cost of living made the exception necessary for families in the program.
- Rejected, 39–59, a proposal by Orrin G. Hatch, R-Utah, to change the definition of "child" to begin at the point of conception. The amendment triggered a minor argument over abortion.

FINAL ACTION

The House cleared the Senate-passed bill, on a **key vote of 290–135 (R 40–133; D 250–2),** on February 4. Forty Republicans voted for the bill, the same number as when it first passed the House on January 14. *(2009 key votes, p. 751)*

MAJOR PROVISIONS

The following are major provisions of PL 111-3:

Funding. The law authorized $10.6 billion in fiscal 2009, $12.5 billion in fiscal 2010, $13.5 billion in fiscal

2011, and $15 billion in fiscal 2012. For fiscal 2013, it authorized two semiannual allotments of $3 billion each: one for October 1 through March 31, and one for April 1 through September 30.

Enrollment expansion. To bring more children and pregnant women into CHIP, the new law:

- Gave states the option of using CHIP funds to insure legal immigrant children and pregnant women. Previously, legal immigrants could not enroll in CHIP or Medicaid for five years after entering the United States.
- Established a contingency fund for states that had funding shortfalls due to increased enrollment of low-income children. The annual amount for the fund was capped at 20 percent of the annual national allotment to states.
- Made states that covered children in families with incomes above 300 percent of the poverty level eligible for Medicaid federal matching payments for health coverage.
- Tied state allotments to the growth of existing and projected per capita health expenditures, indexed for inflation, and growth in the state's child population. States were given two years to spend their CHIP allotments.

State bonus payments. The law provided $3.2 billion for performance bonuses to states that exceeded enrollment targets for children. To be eligible, states also had to implement five of the following eight outreach and enrollment activities:

- Provide "presumptive eligibility" to cover children while a final determination of their eligibility was made.
- Provide twelve months of continuous eligibility for Medicaid and CHIP children.
- Eliminate an assets test.
- Eliminate an in-person interview requirement.
- Use a joint application for Medicaid and CHIP.
- Streamline the renewal process for CHIP enrollees.
- Implement an "express lane" policy that used income data and other eligibility information previously collected by public agencies to facilitate child enrollment in CHIP and Medicaid.
- Offer "premium assistance subsidies" to discourage people from transferring from employer-provided coverage to CHIP, a phenomenon known as "crowd out." The subsidies made up the difference between the employee's private insurance premium cost with out child coverage and with such coverage. It was available if the employer was paying 40 percent of the premium cost.

Program restrictions. The law:

- Barred the use of CHIP funds to enroll illegal immigrants.
- Prohibited states from covering new childless adults under CHIP, and required that all childless adults be removed from the program by October 1, 2010. States could request a one-year extension.
- Required states to verify enrollees' citizenship or nationality status, but allowed them to use matching Social Security data.

Other provisions. The measure also:

- Required states to include dental care in their CHIP coverage and allowed them to provide dental-only coverage to children who qualified for CHIP but were covered by other insurance that did not include dental care.
- Required states that included mental illness and substance abuse in their CHIP coverage to apply the same financial requirements and treatment limits that they did for physical illness.
- Required states to provide at least a thirty-day grace period for premium payments before terminating a child's coverage.

Tobacco tax. The law increased the federal excise taxes on tobacco products, raising what the Congressional Budget Office (CBO) estimated would be $71.4 billion through fiscal 2019. CBO also said the higher tobacco tax would reduce the number of smokers. It said a decline in smoking among pregnant women would "result in fewer low-birth-weight deliveries, including some funded by Medicaid," reducing federal spending for Medicaid by $200 million over the period of fiscal years 2009 through 2019.

The new excise taxes, which took effect on April 1, 2009, included:

- $1.01 per pack for most cigarettes, up from 39 cents per pack
- 52.8 percent of the manufacturer or importer's sale price for large cigars (those weighing more than three pounds per thousand) but no more than 40.26 cents per cigar. The previous rate was 20.7 percent of the manufacturer or importer's sales price, but not more than $48.75 per thousand.
- $1.51 per pound for snuff, up from 58.5 cents per pound.
- 50.33 cents per pound for chewing tobacco, up from 19.5 cents per pound.
- $2.831 per pound for pipe tobacco, from $1.0969 per pound.

The bill made manufacturers and importers of "processed tobacco" subject to the same requirements on permits, inventory, reporting, and record keeping as applied to manufacturers and importers of tobacco products, cigarette papers, and cigarette tubes.

The bill excluded the farming or growing of tobacco, as well as the handling of tobacco solely for sale, shipment, or delivery to a manufacturer of tobacco products or processed tobacco. The measure also broadened the authority of the Treasury Department to deny, suspend, or revoke tobacco permits.

Corporate tax payments. The law shifted some estimated tax payments by corporations with at least $1 billion in assets from the last quarter of fiscal 2012 to the first quarter of fiscal 2013. The shift had no long-term effect but offset the law's costs during a five-year period as required under pay-as-you-go rules.

Tobacco Regulation

A dozen years after tobacco company executives testified under oath on Capitol Hill that nicotine was not addictive, lawmakers in 2009 voted overwhelmingly to send President Barack Obama a landmark bill giving the Food and Drug Administration (FDA) broad authority to regulate tobacco products. Obama signed the measure into law on June 22, 2009 (HR 1256—PL 111-31).

"This bill has obviously been a long time coming," Obama said. "We've known for years, even decades, about the harmful, addictive and often deadly effects of tobacco products. . . . And after a decade of opposition, all of us are finally about to achieve the victory with this bill, a bill that truly defines change in Washington."

The bill empowered the FDA to regulate nicotine levels, bar flavor additives in tobacco products, and require tough new warning labels on cigarette packages and advertising.

The House passed similar legislation in the 110th Congress, but President George W. Bush threatened to veto the measure and tobacco-state opponents succeeded in stalling it in the Senate. Other efforts to regulate tobacco and cigarettes had failed over the previous two decades. *(2008 legislation, Congress and the Nation Vol. XII, p. 575)*

"Miracles still happen," Sen. Edward M. Kennedy, D-Mass., said in a statement. "The United States Senate has finally said 'no' to Big Tobacco." Kennedy was a longtime champion of the regulatory effort, and the final bill was virtually identical to a version he had introduced earlier in the year. But Kennedy was fighting brain cancer and could not be in Washington for the vote.

The nation's largest tobacco company, Philip Morris USA, backed the legislation, as it had in 2008, arguing that it would bring clear standards and predictability to the industry. But second-level tobacco companies such as Lorillard Tobacco Co. and R.J. Reynolds Tobacco Co. lobbied heavily against the measure, saying the advertising restrictions and other provisions would prevent small companies from increasing their sales and give Philip Morris a near-monopoly.

HOUSE COMMITTEE ACTION

Two House committees considered the bill:

Energy and Commerce. The Energy and Commerce Committee approved the bill (HR 1256—H Rept 111-58, Part 1) by a 39–13 vote on March 4. The legislation was nearly identical to the bill the House had passed in the 110th Congress.

"It has taken us far too long to get here," Committee Chair Henry A. Waxman, D-Calif., said in his opening remarks. "We came close last year. . . . I am hopeful this year will mark the end of this long road." Waxman had been a leading congressional crusader against tobacco for more than two decades, holding high-profile hearings, conducting investigations, acquiring documents and showing that manufacturers had long known of health hazards from tobacco.

Some Republican opponents argued that Democrats lacked the will and backing to make a more direct assault on tobacco use. Many said that FDA regulation of tobacco would overburden the agency, which was already being criticized for failure to adequately protect against food and drug problems. *(Food safety, p. 409)*

In action on some of the many amendments offered, the panel:

- Rejected, 14–31, an amendment by Michael C. Burgess, R-Texas, that would have allowed the FDA to ban nicotine entirely. Bill supporter Frank Pallone Jr., D-N.J., argued that an outright ban of tobacco products or nicotine "would be tantamount to a prohibition situation" that would drive sales and production underground."
- Rejected, 17–33, a substitute amendment by Steve Buyer, R-Ind., one of a half-dozen proposals he put forth, which would have created a separate agency within the Health and Human Services (HHS) Department to handle tobacco. It would not have placed smokeless tobacco products under the same regulations as cigarettes, as a way to get people to use those products instead.

Oversight and Government Reform. The Oversight and Government Reform Committee approved the bill (HR 1256—H Rept 111-58, Part 2) by voice vote March 18, after considering the provisions affecting the retirement savings program for federal employees. Large federal employee unions such as the American Federation of Government Employees supported the proposed changes in the bill, as did Committee Chair *Edolphus Towns,* D-N.Y.

The committee adopted by voice vote an amendment by ranking Republican Darrell Issa of California to exempt members of the military from the automatic enrollment.

HOUSE FLOOR ACTION

The House passed the bill April 2 by a vote of 298–112 after attaching the Thrift Savings Plan provisions, including the military exemption from automatic enrollment.

Members rejected, 142–284, a GOP alternative offered by Buyer that, like his committee proposals, would have created a new HHS agency to regulate tobacco.

Republicans said it defied common sense to ask the FDA, which approved products that were proven to be safe and effective, to regulate nicotine. "The last thing we should be doing is forcing the FDA to regulate an inherently dangerous product and carrying out a mission that is counter to its culture," Buyer said.

Waxman said the FDA was the government agency best qualified to regulate cigarettes and other tobacco products, given its combination of scientific expertise, regulatory experience, and public health focus.

SENATE ACTION

The Senate Health, Education, Labor and Pensions (HELP) Committee approved Kennedy's bill (S 982—no written report), 15–8, on May 20. The measure was nearly identical to the House version.

The panel gave voice vote approval to an amendment that required larger warnings on cigarette packages, with graphic images, and clarified that the FDA did not endorse the safety of cigarettes, a move designed to counter the critics' arguments that the bill would create an FDA endorsement of tobacco. The amendment was offered by Christopher J. Dodd, D-Conn., who was acting as chair in Kennedy's absence.

The committee rejected, 9–13, a substitute amendment by Richard M. Burr, R-N.C., that would have created a "Federal Tobacco Regulatory Agency" to regulate tobacco products, including marketing and advertising restrictions, instead of giving such authority to the FDA. The amendment also would have allowed easier market access for new products, including so-called reduced-risk products such as smokeless tobacco. It would not have allowed the FDA to force changes to tobacco products, but it would have required cigarette manufacturers to disclose the ingredients used to make their products.

Burr's amendment was drawn from a bill (S 579) he introduced with fellow North Carolinian Kay Hagan, the lone committee Democrat to vote against S 982. Burr and Hagan said the bill would harm the tobacco industry in North Carolina, home to R.J. Reynolds and Lorillard.

The Senate passed the bill on a **key vote of 79–17 (R 23–16; D 54–1; I 2–0),** on June 11, after substituting its own text. Hagan was the only Democrat to join sixteen Republicans in opposing the measure. *(2009 key votes, p. 751)*

Before its passage, the Senate had debated the bill over the course of two weeks, with supporters fending off amendments from tobacco-state senators and from other lawmakers trying to attach unrelated provisions.

Bill supporters, led by Dodd and Majority Whip Richard J. Durbin, D-Ill., called the legislation one of the most important steps Congress could take to improve public health. They reiterated that smoking was the Number One preventable cause of death in America, and stressed that the bill would help deter youth from smoking. "Every day that we don't act, 3,500 American kids will light up for the first time. . . . A thousand of those children will then become regular smokers, and addiction will begin," Durbin said.

As he had the previous year, Burr led the opposition on behalf of senators from tobacco-growing and -processing states. "No member can come to the floor and claim this is not a regulated product. It is the most regulated product sold in America today," Burr said of tobacco. But he acknowledged that oversight had been fragmented.

The Senate rejected, 36–60, an amendment by Burr to replace the text with a proposal to create a "tobacco harm re-education center" independent of the FDA.

Majority Leader Harry Reid, D-Nev., used a complicated series of cloture motions, each requiring sixty votes, to limit the debate, curtail amendments, and move the bill along. On June 2, the Senate voted, 84–11, to invoke cloture on proceeding to the bill. A second motion, adopted, 61–30, on June 8 limited debate on a substitute amendment by Dodd that reflected S 982. Finally, on June 10, the Senate voted, 67–30, to invoke cloture on the bill itself, clearing the way for passage the next day.

Lawmakers were unable to agree on a proposal by Byron L. Dorgan, D-N.D., to attach language to the FDA bill that would have allowed for the importation of prescription drugs. The idea was popular among Democrats, who argued that it would allow lower-cost pharmaceuticals into the country, but the pharmaceutical industry strongly opposed it and lobbied against it being added to the tobacco bill.

Michael B. Enzi, R-Wyo., an ardent antismoking activist, had opposed previous tobacco regulation legislation for not outlawing tobacco products altogether. This time, however, he supported the bill, saying it would help discourage smoking and also help millions exposed to secondhand smoke, as he experienced during childhood by parents who both died of smoking-related causes. But Enzi said he would monitor the FDA's use of its new authority and scrutinize the effectiveness of its efforts. "This is just one step toward the goal I know we all share, which is to reduce the public health toll of tobacco use," Enzi said.

Final House passage June 12 following the Senate action was even more lopsided than the original vote—seventy Republicans joined in the final tally to clear the bill and send it to the president, which passed on a **key vote of 307–97 (R 70–90; D 237–7).** *(2009 key votes, p. 751)*

MAJOR PROVISIONS

The legislation included the following major provisions:

New regulatory authority. The FDA was authorized to issue regulations restricting the sale, distribution, advertising, promotion, and use of tobacco products if doing so would be in the interest of public health. The bill established a Center for Tobacco Products within the FDA to handle the new regulations.

Nicotine. For the first time, the FDA was authorized to regulate nicotine levels and set product content standards to eliminate harmful ingredients. However, the FDA could not require companies to eliminate nicotine and could not ban tobacco products.

Warning labels. Cigarette and smokeless tobacco products were required to carry bigger, more explicit warning labels. The word "warning" had to appear in capital letters and be followed by one of several approved statements, such as "Tobacco smoke causes fatal lung disease in non-smokers" and "Smoking can kill you." The FDA also had the authority to require that advertisements for tobacco products carry the new warning. Tobacco manufacturers had to disclose the contents of tobacco smoke, although they did not have to do so directly on product packaging. Products intended for foreign distribution were exempted from the requirements.

Product information. Companies that manufactured or imported tobacco products were required to disclose information about the products to the FDA, including a list of all ingredients and additives; a description of nicotine content, delivery, and form; and a listing of all potentially harmful elements found in the tobacco product.

Flavor additives. Tobacco products could no longer include flavor additives, such as chocolate, grape, orange, and cherry, which were aimed at attracting underage smokers.

Product claims. The FDA could require prior approval of statements made on the label of a tobacco product and could prohibit unproven health claims. The terms "light," "mild," and "low tar" could no longer be used on labels or in advertising. Health advocates said the products did not in fact reduce harm from cigarettes, but rather led smokers to inhale more deeply or smoke more quickly to get their dosage of nicotine.

User fees. Producers and importers of tobacco products were required to pay user fees to help pay for the cost of administering the new FDA regulation. The bill authorized the appropriation of $85 million in fees in fiscal 2009, rising gradually to $712 million annually in fiscal 2019 and beyond.

Other revenue. Although user fees were the main source of funding in the bill, changes to the Thrift Savings Plan, a retirement program for federal employees similar to a 401(k) account, were projected to bring in $2.5 billion over ten years. The funds were needed to make up for a shortfall in excise tax revenue on cigarettes and other tobacco products that was expected to occur as a result of lower sales once the bill was enacted.

Under the bill, federal employees were automatically enrolled in the Thrift Savings Plan and also were given the option of opening a Roth-style investment retirement account. Roth accounts increased near-term revenues because investors paid taxes on the money before it was deposited and benefited from tax-free withdrawals on the investment and earnings later. Under traditional IRAs, taxes on the investment were deferred until the funds were withdrawn.

Penalties. Companies and others that violated the bill's restrictions were liable for penalties of up to $15,000 per violation, and up to $1 million for multiple violations handled at one time. Some violations carried higher fines.

Advisory committee. The bill directed the FDA to establish a twelve-person panel of physicians and other experts to advise the agency. Three members would come from the tobacco industry but would not have a vote.

Medicare Physician Payments

Again in the 111th Congress, lawmakers failed to fix a Medicare reimbursement problem that they had created in 1997. *(2012 legislation, p. 463)*

By missing a chance to revise the way physicians are paid in the Medicare program as part of the health overhaul, Congress ended up passing six separate short-term measures in 2009 and 2010 to avert deep cuts to doctor payments, with no long-term solution in sight. *(Health overhaul, p. 421)*

The reimbursement issue grew out of the 1997 Balanced Budget Act (PL 105-33), which created a statutory cost control formula known as the "sustainable growth rate" for calculating annual adjustments in the fees paid to physicians for their services to Medicare patients. Although in the early years doctors received healthy raises, beginning in 2002 the formula necessitated annual reductions in fee rates. Concerned that fewer doctors would be willing to see Medicare patients, lawmakers regularly passed legislation to prevent the scheduled cuts. As a result, only once had Congress allowed the reductions to take place. *(1997 law, Congress and the Nation Vol. X, p. 432)*

Still, most of the bills to prevent the cuts covered only a few months because the costs of a longer-term solution were unacceptable to many members at a time of widespread concern over the federal deficit. Even the short-term bills were so difficult to pass that three of them were signed after the previous law had expired and had to be made retroactive.

In 2008, Congress enacted a law (PL 110-275) over President George W. Bush's veto that canceled a scheduled 10.6 percent cut in Medicare physician payment rates, increased the rates slightly in 2008, and allowed a 1.1 percent increase in 2009. The estimated $94 billion cost over five years was offset mainly by reducing bonus payments to private plans under the Medicare Advantage program. *(2008 law, Congress and the Nation Vol. XII, p. 571)*

Democrats initially intended to fix the formula as part of the health overhaul effort. But that plan was dropped when it became clear it would add too much to the health bill's price tag. To maintain physician support for the health bill, the House passed a separate bill in November 2009 that would have replaced the cost control formula and ended the need for annual fixes.

It was already clear, however, that the Senate would not act on the bill before the end of the session. Democrat Debbie Stabenow of Michigan had introduced a similar bill with the backing of Majority Leader Harry Reid, D-Nev.

Like the House version, however, Stabenow's bill did not include offsets. Moderate Senate Democrats rebelled and joined Republicans to block Reid from bringing the bill to the floor. The vote, on a motion to invoke cloture, was one of Reid's biggest defeats of the year.

Reid had promised to take up Stabenow's bill after he and other Democratic leaders working on the health care overhaul bill decided not to include the doctors' pay increase in that measure. Leaving it out saved billions of dollars that could be used on other priorities in the bill. Republicans denounced the move as a transparent gimmick to keep the overhaul's ten-year price tag below $1 trillion.

After the cloture vote, Reid vowed to revisit the issue—a top priority for doctors and seniors—after the Senate finished its health care overhaul. But Senate Republicans blocked all but the most short-term reprieves for most of the rest of the year.

2009 LEGISLATIVE ACTION

In November 2009, the House passed a bill (HR 3961) that would have blocked the scheduled 21.2 percent fee reduction in 2010 and instead increased doctors' pay by about 1.2 percent. Beginning in 2011, it would have replaced the much-maligned "sustainable growth rate" cost control formula with a method closely tied to inflation, eliminating the need for the annual fixes.

The vote on HR 3961 was 243–183 on November 19, with all but one Republican opposed.

The Congressional Budget Office estimated that the bill would have required $209.6 billion in additional spending in fiscal years 2010 through 2019. Democrats said the spending was already taking place year by year as Congress canceled the scheduled cuts, and that replacing a broken law, rather than blocking it one year at a time, was not something that required offsets.

Republicans did not agree. They argued that the larger reimbursements would require vast new spending that would add to the deficit unless it was offset, and they succeeded in blocking a companion bill in the Senate.

The bill's sponsor, Michigan Democrat John D. Dingell, said scrapping the old formula would end "a budget gimmick that artificially reduces the deficit by assuming physician payments will be cut by 40 percent over the next several years."

The White House issued a statement supporting the House effort, warning that allowing a large cut in Medicare pay rates "could reduce access to physicians for Medicare beneficiaries throughout the country."

The rule for House debate automatically added the text of a separate House-passed pay-as-you-go (PAYGO) bill (HR 2920) requiring that future tax and mandatory spending legislation be budget-neutral. If it was not, automatic across-the-board spending cuts would be required. *(PAYGO, p. 142)*

The House Blue Dog Coalition, made up of fiscally conservative Democrats, had agreed to support four specific bills, including the doctors' pay fix, in exchange for language that would put the pay-as-you-go requirement into law.

But House passage was a mere formality. That's because Senate Democratic leaders had already lost a bid to advance companion legislation sponsored by Stabenow (S 1776) when thirteen members of their caucus joined all forty Republicans on October 21 to prevent the measure from coming to the floor. The Senate rejected, 47–53, Reid's motion to limit debate and proceed to the bill. Reid needed sixty votes to prevail.

Like the House bill, the Senate version would have blocked the 21.2 percent cut in physicians' reimbursement rates in 2010 and scrapped the 1997 formula in favor of a new budget "baseline" for calculating future pay rates. "We don't want to do this year by year anymore," Stabenow said.

Democrats argued, as they had in the House, that the $210 billion cost estimate was artificial because it assumed that, without the bill, physicians' pay rates would be cut.

Although Republicans opposed offsets for extending existing tax cuts, they argued that this was new spending and had to be paid for to avoid adding to the deficit. "All of us want to keep this cut from happening," Minority Leader Mitch McConnell, R-Ky., said of the impending pay reduction. "But the American people don't want us to borrow another cent to pay for it. And they don't want Democrats in Congress to pretend that this quarter of a trillion dollars isn't part of the cost of health care reform—because it is."

Democrat Kent Conrad of North Dakota, the chair of the Budget Committee, was among those who voted against cloture. "You can't just alter the baseline and say, all of a sudden, you don't have to pay for things," he said.

At the end of the 2009 session, with no resolution in sight and the cut still looming, Congress attached language to the fiscal 2010 defense appropriations bill (HR 3326—PL 111-118) that delayed the scheduled 21.2 percent pay cut for 2010 for two months, through February 28.

2010 LEGISLATIVE ACTION

In the absence of a longer-term solution, Congress kept the 2010 pay cuts at bay through a series of four short-term extensions of the provision enacted in December 2009. The fifth bill delayed cuts through 2011.

Extension through March 31

Unable to get Senate agreement on a large package of spending and tax-cut extensions, lawmakers cleared a quick one-month Medicare reimbursement bill in March that blocked the pay cut through March 31. It also extended federal unemployment benefits and a few other urgent expiring programs. President Barack Obama signed the measure on March 2 (HR 4691—PL 111-144). *(Unemployment benefits, p. 517)*

The House passed the short-term bill, which included no offsets, by voice vote February 25. But when the bill came to the Senate, Jim Bunning, R-Ky., mounted a one-man filibuster, insisting that Congress pay for the measure with unspent funds from the 2009 economic stimulus law (PL 111-5). As a result of the delay, Congress missed the February 28 cutoff date. Bunning relented on March 2, after getting a vote on a proposed offset; he lost 43–53 on a procedural vote.

The Senate then cleared the retroactive bill, 78–19.

Extension through May 31

Continued partisan wrangling in the Senate led to another brief lapse in the Medicare reimbursement provisions as well as in several other programs. Democrats and Republicans left in late March for their spring recess deadlocked over the bill, which was not signed until April 15 (HR 4851—PL 111-157). The measure delayed the Medicare rate cut for two more months, through May 31. Again, it was retroactive.

Other programs covered by the bill included federal unemployment insurance, health insurance premium subsidies for jobless workers, flood insurance, and small-business loan guarantees. *(Unemployment insurance, p. 517; flood insurance, p. 610)*

The House passed the bill by voice vote March 17, but several Senate Republicans, led by Tom Coburn of Oklahoma, refused to allow a vote in that chamber unless the bill's cost was fully offset.

After returning from the recess, Senate Democratic leaders tried again, rebuffing several amendments to pay for the bill. The Senate passed a slightly amended version of the bill by a vote of 59–38 on April 15, and the House cleared it, 289–112, later the same day.

Extension through November 30

After more efforts by Senate Democrats to pass a bill that would renew a number of expired tax provisions and social safety-net programs, including the Medicare "doc fix," the leadership pulled the measure and passed a stand-alone bill that postponed the deep cut in Medicare payments to physicians through November 30. Obama signed the retroactive bill on June 25 (HR 3962—PL 111-192).

The Senate had passed the measure by unanimous consent on June 18, and the House cleared it, 417–1, on June 24.

In response to calls from Senate moderates, the $6.4 billion cost of the bill was fully offset. It included provisions requiring certain pension plans to make extra contributions if they offered compensation in excess of $1 million to any employee, paid unusually high dividends, or engaged in extraordinary stock buybacks. The provision was estimated to raise about $2.1 billion over ten years. The bill also prohibited health care providers from submitting separate claims for certain outpatient services, saving an estimated $4.2 billion over ten years.

Extension through December 31

Lawmakers postponed the rate cut for the remainder of the year with another bill (HR 5712—PL 111-286). The Senate passed the bill by unanimous consent on November 18. The House cleared it by voice vote November 29. President Obama signed the bill on November 30, 2010.

The cost was estimated at $1 billion over ten years, and although the price tag was exempt under the pay-as-you-go law, deficit concerns had reached a point that only a fully funded bill was able to advance. The costs were offset by codifying a new Centers for Medicare and Medicaid Services policy that reduced Medicare payments for multiple therapy services provided to patients in one day.

Extension through 2011

As part of wrapping up the 2010 legislative year, lawmakers cleared a bill that blocked what would have been a 25 percent rate cut for the whole of 2011. President Barack Obama signed the measure into law on December 15, 2010 (HR 4994—PL 111-309).

The bill was the fifth so-called "doc fix" enacted during the 2010 congressional session. The estimated cost was $14.9 billion over ten years.

The legislation also extended several expiring Medicare programs, including protections for rural doctors and hospitals, adding $4.6 billion to the price tag.

The extensions were paid for mainly by changing a part of the health care overhaul that provided tax credits to help people with incomes between 100 percent and 400 percent of the federal poverty rate buy health insurance, beginning in 2014. Under the original law, recipients were required to pay back part of the subsidy—up to $250 for an individual or $400 for families—if they misstated their income or their income increased during the year. The bill replaced the repayment schedule with a sliding-scale structure, requiring smaller repayments at lower incomes and dramatically increasing the maximum amount for high earners.

It was the first time Congress had significantly altered a provision of the overhaul. (PL 111-148, PL 111-152). *(Health care legislation, p. 421)*

The measure was the result of a bipartisan compromise reached by Senate Finance Chair Max Baucus, D-Mont., and the panel's ranking Republican, Charles E. Grassley of Iowa.

The delays resulted largely from the fact that the issue became entangled in ongoing fighting over broader Democratic "jobs" bills, including the issue of offsetting the costs. A pay-as-you-go law enacted in February (PL 111-139) explicitly exempted legislation preventing the doctors' pay cut through 2011. However, Republicans still objected strongly to allowing a pay fix that added to the deficit. *(PAYGO, p. 142)*

Ryan White AIDS Act Reauthorization

The Ryan White HIV/AIDS Act—the primary source of federal assistance for low-income Americans with HIV and AIDS—was reauthorized for four years under legislation signed by President Barack Obama on October 30 (S 1793—PL 111-87). Unlike previous versions of the measure, the 2009 reauthorization of the program sailed through both Houses of Congress without any of the regional or political issues that had slowed earlier efforts.

The bill authorized a 5 percent funding increase for fiscal years 2010 through 2013 for grants and other activities. The programs were a last resort for those with the HIV virus or with full-blown AIDS who did not have adequate health insurance coverage or lacked the resources to pay for medicine and the other care they needed. It served an estimated 500,000 people a year.

The federal program was named for Ryan White, an Indiana teenager with hemophilia who contracted AIDS through a blood transfusion at age thirteen. He and his mother fought for his right to attend school, gaining international attention. He died on April 8, 1990, at the age of eighteen, just a few months before the Ryan White CARE (Comprehensive AIDS Resources Emergency) Act became law (PL 101-381). *(1990 law, Congress and the Nation Vol. VIII, p. 588)*

The popular law had been reauthorized three times since then with strong bipartisan support. The most recent authorization, enacted in 2006 (PL 109-415), was set to expire on September 30, 2009, but was continued for a month under the first stopgap funding bill of the year (PL 111-68). *(2006 reauthorization, Congress and the Nation Vol. XII, p. 546)*

The Ryan White Act provided grants and awards to states, metropolitan areas, and community organizations for core medical and support services. Most of the funding was distributed through formula grants based on the number of people in a city or state infected with HIV or diagnosed with AIDS. The rest was awarded on a competitive basis as supplemental grants to areas with the greatest need for AIDS-related services.

Nearly 40,000 new HIV/AIDS infections were reported annually, and according to the Centers for Disease Control and Prevention approximately 1.1 million Americans were living with the disease. At the end of 2007, the CDC estimated that 583,298 people had died of the disease.

The actual money for the program was discretionary spending provided through the annual appropriations process.

LEGISLATIVE HISTORY

House and Senate committees approved virtually identical versions of the 2009 reauthorization. The Senate Health, Education, Labor and Pensions Committee approved a bill (S 1793) sponsored by Chair Tom Harkin, D-Iowa, by voice vote September 30. The House Energy and Commerce Committee approved a companion bill (HR 379—H Rept 111-305) by voice vote October 15. The measure was sponsored by Frank Pallone Jr., D-N.J., chair of the panel's Health Subcommittee.

The Senate passed its version by voice vote October 19, and the House cleared it, 408–9, on October 21.

MAJOR PROVISIONS

The following are major provisions of PL 111-87:

Authorization. The bill authorized $2.6 billion for the program in fiscal 2010, $2.7 billion in fiscal 2011, $2.8 billion in fiscal 2012, and $3 billion in fiscal 2013.

Sunset. The bill dropped a sunset provision that previously required that the law be repealed on the date the reauthorization expired. The new law was retroactive to September 30.

Name-based reporting. By fiscal 2013, all states were required to submit name-based data on HIV cases. That gave states that were still using an older, code-based system three more years to completely convert their systems, although they were subject to penalties during that time.

Originally, most states sought to protect the privacy of AIDS patients by using a code-based system rather than recording their names. In the late 1990s, the CDC recommended that all states switch to a name-based system as a way to reduce duplication and provide a more accurate count. Under the 2006 reauthorization law, states that had not completed the switch were allowed to submit code-based HIV data for use in determining formula grants, but the number of cases they reported was reduced by 5 percent to account for potential duplication. Those states also were subject to a 5 percent cap on grant increases compared with the previous year. The 2009 law continued that system for two years. In fiscal 2012, the penalty was increased to 6 percent. In fiscal 2013, states would be allowed to submit only name-based data.

'Hold harmless' provision. The law continued a "hold harmless" provision from the 2006 reauthorization that protected states and metropolitan areas from large shifts in funding from one fiscal year to the next, which could destabilize their care system. The new law guaranteed that in 2010, grantees would receive at least 95 percent of what they got in 2009. In 2011 and 2012, they would get at least as much as they did in 2010. In 2013, they were guaranteed at least 92.5 percent of their fiscal 2012 funding.

National testing goal. The HHS secretary was required to set a new HIV/AIDS testing goal of five million tests per year by January 1, 2010, through federally supported HIV/AIDS prevention, treatment, and care programs.

Medicaid and Education Spending

Members of the House interrupted their August recess in 2010 to return to Washington and clear a $26.1 billion bill that provided funds to help state and local governments prevent layoffs of teachers and maintain Medicaid health coverage of the poor. President Barack Obama signed the bill into law the day it cleared (HR 1586—PL 111-226).

Speaker Nancy Pelosi, D-Calif., called the House back into session amid calls from state officials for quick action. New York governor David A. Paterson, a Democrat, warned that about thirty states had budgeted on the assumption that the federal funds would arrive.

Republicans criticized the legislation, saying it was essentially a Democratic election-year sop to teachers' unions. Democrats disagreed. "There's nothing in this bill that says that anyone has to belong to a union," responded Sen. Tom Harkin, D-Iowa, chair of the Health, Education, Labor and Pensions Committee.

However, it was not lost on Democrats that the assistance would resonate with many of their constituents.

Republicans also said that one of the prime offsets used to pay for the bill—changes to a number of foreign tax provisions—could harm the economic recovery by imposing new taxes on businesses. Major business groups opposed the tax proposals, saying they would make U.S. companies less competitive abroad. Democrats countered that the changes removed incentives for U.S. companies to locate their operations overseas.

Enactment was a victory, in particular, for liberal Democrat David R. Obey of Wisconsin, chair of the House Appropriations Committee, who was retiring at the end of the Congress and had made preventing planned teacher layoffs his top priority. The teacher aid was popular among House Democrats, 236 of whom had voted to add it to a war supplemental spending bill in July. The Senate, however, had killed the idea.

Still, many Democrats were unhappy that part of the bill was offset through an $11.9 billion reduction in funds for food stamp benefits and a $1.5 billion reduction in funds for renewable-energy programs.

The bill that Senate Majority Leader Harry Reid, D-Nev., used as a vehicle for the supplemental funding had several previous lives, including as a long-term authorization bill for the Federal Aviation Administration. *(FAA, p. 327)*

LEGISLATIVE ACTION

The Senate passed the bill August 5 on a **key vote of 61–39 (R 2–39; D 57–0; I 2–0)**, with Republicans Susan Collins and Olympia J. Snowe of Maine joining all fifty-nine members of the Democratic caucus. Passage was virtually assured after the Senate agreed, 61–38, the previous day to invoke cloture, limiting the length of the debate. *(2010 key votes, p. 767)*

The successful cloture vote in the Senate prompted Pelosi to call the House back. The chamber cleared the measure August 10 on a **key vote of 247–161 (R 2–158; D 245–3).** The Democratic majority extolled the measure for saving teachers and emergency personnel from layoffs while Republicans denounced it as a bailout that would do little about long-term economic problems. *(2010 key votes, p. 767)*

MAJOR PROVISIONS

The major provisions of the enacted bill:

Teachers. Appropriated $10 billion for a new Education Jobs Fund. It directed the Education Department to use the funds to provide aid to local school districts to prevent layoffs in elementary and secondary schools. Under a "maintenance of effort" requirement, states that received aid could not reduce their education funding in fiscal 2011. (*Details, p. 479*)

Medicaid. Appropriated $16.1 billion over two years to extend for six months, through June 30, 2011, an enhanced federal matching rate for state Medicaid programs. The 2009 economic stimulus law (PL 111-5) authorized the extra funding under the Federal Medical Assistance Percentage, but that provision was set to expire on December 31. (*Stimulus law, p. 78*)

The bill gave states a minimum federal match of 56.2 percent of the cost of their Medicaid programs for the first quarter of fiscal 2011, falling to 53.2 percent in the second quarter and 51.2 percent in the third.

Offsets. Covered the cost of the bill primarily through:

- Eliminating a 13.6 percent increase in food stamp benefits that was enacted in the stimulus law, as of March 31, 2014, reducing mandatory spending by $11.9 billion over ten years.
- Clarifying the calculation of rebates that drug companies were required to provide in order to participate in state Medicaid programs, reducing mandatory spending by $2 billion over ten years.
- Eliminating advance refundability of the earned-income tax credit after December 31, 2010, reducing mandatory spending by $900 million over ten years.
- Rescinding previously appropriated but unspent funds, including $2.3 billion from the economic stimulus law and $2.3 billion from the Defense Department, reducing spending by $2.8 billion over ten years.
- Closing a number of tax loopholes related to the foreign income of U.S.-based multinational corporations, increasing revenue by $9.8 billion over ten years.

2011–2012

The 112th Congress—at least the Republicans who took over the House in the 2010 elections—came roaring into Washington with one top priority: to repeal or somehow dismantle the Affordable Care Act that was enacted in early 2010 and was President Barack Obama's signature legislative victory.

Unfortunately for them, the Senate and the White House remained in control of the Democrats. Neither had any intention of letting his signature legislative achievement be rolled back, despite the 2010 elections setbacks. *(Elections, p. 30)*

That set off what would become largely two years of angry argument and occasional brinksmanship, on health care as well as many other issues. Little of legislative note was accomplished, with both sides mostly posturing for the next election, in 2012, when each side hoped to take enough control to effect still more changes.

Health Overhaul Repeal

With Republicans having ridden their opposition to the 2010 health care overhaul to a takeover of the House, they spent much of the 112th Congress trying—unsuccessfully—to keep their campaign pledge to overturn it.

Even with a smaller majority than it had in the previous Congress, the still Democratic-controlled Senate blocked more than thirty attempts by Republicans to repeal or scale

SUPREME COURT UPHOLDS HEALTH OVERHAUL

In a history-making decision, the Supreme Court ruled June 28, 2012, that President Barack Obama's signature 2010 health care law (PL 111-148, PL 111-152) could go forward largely as written, giving Democrats a reason to cheer and Republicans an issue they hoped would resonate with voters in the fall election. *(Health care law, p. 421; Court decision, p. 586)*

In a 5–4 opinion written by Chief Justice John G. Roberts Jr., the Court decided that the central part of the health care overhaul—the individual mandate that most Americans obtain health insurance or pay a penalty—could be enforced as a tax under Congress's constitutional powers and did not need to be struck down. Although agreeing with plaintiffs that the mandate would be unconstitutional under the commerce clause of the Constitution, the Court essentially chose to uphold the entire law with the mandate penalty treated as a tax.

"I think the real outcome of today's decision is to strengthen our resolve to make sure that this law is in fact repealed," House Speaker John A. Boehner, R-Ohio, said immediately after the court issued its ruling. "We're going to work every single day between now and Election Day, and the American people then will get an opportunity to make their decision on Election Day, because elections have consequences."

The Court's decision ended months of waiting in Washington and in state capitals, although some governors continued to place holds on plans to implement their part of the law until they knew the outcome of the presidential election. Throngs of people, including many activists on both sides of the issue as well as lawmakers, waited in front of the Supreme Court the morning the decision was to be announced, ready to cheer or protest the outcome, or just to witness history.

In writing the majority opinion, Roberts sided with the liberals on the bench, rather than his more typical alliance with other conservative justices. "The federal government does not have the power to order people to buy health insurance," Roberts wrote. "Section 5000A would therefore be unconstitutional if read as a command. The federal government does have the power to impose a tax on those without health insurance. Section 5000A is therefore constitutional because it can reasonably be read as a tax."

Many court observers had expected that Justice Anthony M. Kennedy, who wrote the dissent, would be the swing vote. Instead, it was Roberts, who was generally more conservative than Kennedy and was appointed to the Court in 2005 by President George W. Bush. Obama voted against Roberts's confirmation when he was an Illinois senator.

The decision did include some bad news for the law's supporters. The Court ruled that states could opt out of a provision in the law that significantly expanded the state-federal Medicaid health care program for the poor without losing all of their federal Medicaid funds. The law had included such a punishment for failure to participate.

But, overall, Democrats were pleased with the outcome of the case and called on Republicans to work with them to improve the law rather than continue to try to repeal it. Obama also suggested that there could be some targeted revisions.

"The highest court in the land has now spoken. We will continue to implement this law. And we'll work together to improve on it where we can," Obama said shortly after the Court's ruling. "But what we won't do, what the country can't afford to do, is refight the political battles of two years ago or go back to the way things were."

back the health law. Even piecemeal measures were mostly routinely shot down. *(Health care law enactment, p. 421)*

The only significant pieces of the law undone by lawmakers by the end of 2012 were a small tax-reporting requirement that had provoked complaints from many sides, and a long-term care bill that even the Obama administration had conceded was unworkable. *(Health law changes, box, below)*

The law also survived a near-death brush with the Supreme Court, which upheld its constitutionality on a 5–4 vote in June 2012. Chief Justice John G. Roberts Jr. cast a surprise vote with the majority to keep the law mostly intact. *(Supreme Court and health law, pp. 455, 586)*

As soon as Republicans took control of the House, Speaker John A. Boehner, R-Ohio, marked up a bill to repeal the overhaul as HR 2, a sign of its top priority. Despite a score from the nonpartisan Congressional Budget Office (CBO) that showed that repealing the overhaul (PL 111-148, PL 111-152) would cost $230 billion over ten years, the House passed the bill in January, with three Democrats joining all Republicans voting in favor.

Senate Majority Leader Harry Reid, D-Nev., denounced the effort as "partisan grandstanding," and President Obama pledged to veto any repeal bill that reached his desk. Senate Democrats in February unanimously defeated a repeal effort that was brought up as an amendment to an unrelated bill to reauthorize the Federal Aviation Administration. *(FAA legislation, p. 327)*

In February, House Republicans offered a series of repeal measures as part of a wish list of amendments to a

HEALTH LAW CHANGES

Although the vast majority of GOP-led efforts to alter the health overhaul law (PL 111-148, PL 111-152) were not successful, the 112th Congress did change or repeal a handful of provisions. In some cases it was to use funds to pay for other health care priorities; in other cases there were policy reasons to change the law.

Tax Reporting Requirement Repeal

The House passed a bill, 314–112, on March 3, 2011, (HR 4—PL 112-9) to repeal a tax-reporting requirement in the health care law that required businesses and owners of real estate to report to the Internal Revenue Service (IRS), on a Form 1099, payments of $600 or more made in a year to a single vendor. The goal of the program was to help the IRS identify unreported income. It was one of the revenue-raising provisions of the health overhaul law. *(Health law provisions, p. 436)*

The Senate cleared the bill, 87–12, on April 5, and President Obama signed it into law April 14.

Business groups including the U.S. Chamber of Commerce had lobbied hard to eliminate the requirement. Democrats eventually agreed, calling it a flaw that would have unintended consequences. The final hurdle was getting enough senators to agree on an offset for the $22 billion cost. The cleared bill ultimately took money from within the health care law by requiring some people to pay back a portion of the subsidies they received to join the state insurance exchanges if their income increased during the year.

Class Act Repeal

The Community Living Assistance Services and Supports (CLASS) Act, was one of the dying wishes of the late Sen. Edward Kennedy, D-Mass., at whose request it was included in the health law. It was one of the first comprehensive long-term care programs ever passed by the Congress

The CLASS program was designed to allow workers to pay into a fund that would provide a $50 daily cash benefit for long-term-care services delivered in community, rather than institutional, settings.

But there were doubts from the beginning about the financial sustainability of the program—particularly whether enough healthy people would sign up, or if only those who thought they might need the care would swamp the program. The Department of Health and Human Services (HHS) had worked for nineteen months to put a program in place that met the law's requirements of being voluntary, self-sustaining, and fiscally sound over seventy-five years, but the department announced October 14, 2011, that it did not see a way forward, and was suspending the program.

Meanwhile, Republicans were intent in wiping it off the books entirely.

The action began in the House, where the Energy and Commerce Committee approved a bill (HR 1173—H Rept 112-342, Part 1) on November 30 to repeal the suspended CLASS program. The panel's Subcommittee on Health had given voice vote approval to the measure November 15.

Democrats advocated using the existing framework to build a sustainable program and said that repealing the program without a replacement was irresponsible.

While calling the intent behind the program laudable, Republicans charged it had been used as a budgetary gimmick to allow passage of the overhaul. CBO estimated that the program, which was structured to collect premiums for five years before paying out benefits, would generate $70.2 billion over ten years.

continuing fiscal 2011 appropriations measure, but the bill quickly died in the face of Senate opposition. *(Fiscal 2011 appropriations, p. 150)*

Undaunted, Republicans then targeted individual pieces of the health care law that were unpopular or controversial, a tactic that won them the first significant change. In April—a little more than a year after the overhaul was signed into law—Congress cleared a bill to remove a requirement that businesses report all vendor payments of $600 a year or more to the Internal Revenue Service.

Republicans also worked to repeal a controversial long-term care program in the law after the administration announced in October 2011 that it could not see a way forward and would suspend the program's implementation. Republicans said the Community Living Assistance Services and Support (CLASS) program should be completely removed from the books and promoted House and Senate repeal bills. The House bill won committee approval but went no further in the first session. CLASS was finally removed from the books as part of the "fiscal cliff" legislation negotiated in literally the final hours of the Congress. *(CLASS, p. 456; fiscal cliff legislation, p. 185)*

A handful of other House GOP bills gained Democratic support, such as legislation to repeal an independent board tasked under the overhaul with making recommendations to limit Medicare spending growth. The House voted to repeal the Independent Payment Advisory Board (IPAB) in March 2012. But like most of the other House actions to undermine the health overhaul, the Senate did not act on the legislation.

Subcommittee Chair Joe Pitts, R-Pa., expressed sympathy for "millions of Americans" facing long-term-care cost concerns, but he said the CLASS program was not the solution. Republicans also maintained that the HHS secretary could face legal challenges if the program was not formally repealed. They cited a Congressional Research Service memo saying that by abandoning the program, the secretary would "appear to be committing a facial violation of the statutory requirement to designate such a plan."

On February 1, 2012, the House passed, 267–159, the bill approved by the committee the previous year (HR 1173—H Rept 112-342, Parts 1 and 2) to formally repeal CLASS.

Republicans argued that a formal repeal was necessary to prevent HHS from being in violation of the law when the HHS secretary did not comply with the legal requirement to designate a benefit plan by the following October. "That's not a very good example to set for the American people, to have the administration breaking the law," bill sponsor Charles Boustany Jr., R-La., said.

Democrats maintained that the CLASS program represented a significant step toward finding a long-term care solution and that moving forward with repeal ignores the problem. "I don't think it's perfect either," said Henry A. Waxman of California, the top Democrat on the Energy and Commerce Committee. "But the solution is to amend the program, to make it work—not just repeal it and leave nothing in its place."

News of the House action was met with cheers by Senate Republicans.

"If we're going to replace the president's health care bill with the kind of common-sense reforms the American people really want, repealing the CLASS Act is a good place to start," Senate Minority Leader Mitch McConnell, R-Ky., said after House passage. The Senate, however, did not take up a separate companion bill.

CLASS was, however, formally repealed as part of the year-end fiscal cliff law (HR 8—PL 112-240). *(Fiscal cliff action, p. 185)*

Consumer Owned and Oriented Plans: Co-Ops

The year-ending "fiscal cliff" legislation in 2012 (HR 8—PL 112-240) also prematurely ended another health program originally included in the health law by Senate Democrats. The health law had called for the creation of "Consumer Owned and Oriented Plans," or CO-OPs, that would compete alongside for-profit insurance companies in the health care exchanges.

Some senators had hoped the CO-OPs, which were to be run by consumer boards, might serve as a replacement for the government-run plans that failed to make it into the final version of the law. *(Health law passage, p. 421)*

About two dozen CO-OPs had already been funded under the health law, and they were allowed to continue under the provision in the fiscal cliff bill. But another forty or so had applications pending, and the legislation rescinded the remainder of the program's funding, leaving those applicants out of luck.

Other Changes

House Republicans had some success shifting funds from the health care law to pay for other critical bills. For example, Congress cleared a bill (PL 112-96) on February 17, 2012, that took funds from two provisions of the health care law to help offset the cost of a one-year extension of a cut in payroll taxes. The money came from the law's Prevention and Public Health Fund and from fixing a glitch in the law that gave some states extra Medicaid funding following a statewide disaster.

Although House Republicans were hammering away in Washington, GOP presidential nominee Mitt Romney vowed throughout his campaign that he would overturn what Republicans had dubbed "Obamacare." But Obama's clear victory in November showed the issue was not the effective cudgel they hoped it would be.

After the election, House Speaker John A. Boehner, R-Ohio, acknowledged that the health overhaul was "the law of the land" but said Republicans would continue to try to whittle it down.

2011 LEGISLATIVE ACTION

An emboldened House Republican majority laid down its first notable legislative marker January 19, 2011, on a **key vote of 245–189 (R 242–0; D 3–189)** passing a bill to repeal the health care overhaul law. Three Democrats—Dan Boren of Oklahoma, Mike McIntyre of North Carolina, and Mike Ross of Arkansas—joined the entire House GOP in backing the measure (HR 2). The only member not voting was Arizona Democrat Gabrielle Giffords, who was recovering from a gunshot wound suffered at a constituent event in her home state. *(2011 key votes, p. 785; Giffords shooting, p. 660)*

With the largely symbolic vote out of the way, House Republicans said they would take on the more difficult job of replacing the law. On January 20, the House adopted a resolution (H Res 9) in a 253–175 vote to set goals for the committees that would be involved. The resolution contained broad directives, including lowering health care premiums, overhauling the medical liability system, prohibiting federal funding of abortions, and providing people with preexisting conditions access to affordable health coverage.

In the end, committees held hearings, but there was no real effort to mark up or pass a replacement bill.

In a sign that they intended to thwart much of the ambitious House GOP agenda, Senate Democrats stuck together

ABORTION CONTINUES TO ROIL HEALTH LAW

Abortion, the issue that almost prevented the health overhaul from becoming law in 2010, continued to haunt legislators in the 112th Congress.

But while it was Democrats who did the hand-wringing during the drafting and passage of the law (PL 111-148, PL 111-152) in the 111th Congress, it was Republicans in the 112th Congress who continually tried to reopen the law to legislative alteration on the abortion issue.

Abortion became a focus for House Republicans in 2011 after attempts earlier in the year to fully repeal the health law foundered in the Senate. One bill, HR 358, would have put an outright ban, in legislation and not merely by executive order, on the use of any federal money to support abortion services.

Later in the year, and into 2012, lawmakers turned their attention to the part of the law that required health plans to provide preventive care with no copays—including, as it was interpreted by the Department of Health and Human Services, contraception. That brought a huge outcry from religious groups who complained that some forms of contraception approved by the Food and Drug Administration could be construed to cause very early abortions by blocking the implantation of fertilized eggs.

But no legislation managed to pass both houses and reach President Barack Obama's desk.

HR 358 Passes House

Language in the health care law required that insurance companies participating in health exchanges that offered plans with abortion coverage must keep the money clearly segregated so no federal dollars were used in support of abortion. Policyholders who wanted abortion as a covered benefit were required to use personal money to pay for that coverage.

In addition, just after passage of the law, President Obama signed an executive order affirming a ban against federal funding for abortion as part of a compromise struck with pro-life Democrats to get the health care overhaul passed. *(Details, p. 432)*

But Republicans argued that neither the language in the bill nor the executive order was sufficient to ensure that no federal funds would be used for abortion, and even stronger language needed to be passed anew.

During debate, conservatives argued that the bill would recognize public sentiment against public funding for abortion. "The vast majority of Americans do not support using their dollars in support of the abortion industry, and Americans should not be forced by the strong arm of the government to subsidize the abortion industry," said Rep. Jeff Fortenberry, R-Neb.

Those against the bill warned of dangerous health consequences if the legislation was enacted. "Today's bill will put the government in the middle of Americans' health choices and allow hospitals to refuse life-saving treatment to women," warned Rep. Joseph Crowley, D-N.Y.

But majority Republicans carried the day, with only two in dissent—Judy Biggert of Illinois and Richard Hanna of New York.

The House passed HR 358 on October 13, 2011, on a **key vote of 251–172 (R 236–2; D 15–170)**. *(2011 key votes, p. 785)*

to stop a similar effort that was offered as an amendment to the unrelated FAA bill (S 223). No Senate Democrat backed the proposal.

On a **key vote of 47–51 (R 47–0; D 0–50; I 0–1)**, senators declined to waive a budgetary point of order against an amendment offered by Minority Leader Mitch McConnell, R-Ky., that would have repealed the health care act. Under the rules, the motion to waive and keep the amendment alive required sixty affirmative votes. *(2011 key votes, p. 785)*

Much of the debate centered on the potential cost. Democrats cited the CBO in calling the amendment a "budget buster." McConnell called such arguments "preposterous." Republicans said only "budget gimmicks" made the overhaul law look like it would reduce the deficit.

With the stand-alone repeal effort effectively dead for the moment, House Republicans instead turned their attention to the ill-fated House omnibus appropriations bill (HR 1). On February 19, 2011, in a ninety-hour voting marathon, Republicans took a run at dozens of regulations and programs, including five roll-call votes on effectively repealing or gutting the health care law. During the debate, the House:

- Adopted, 239–187, an amendment by Denny Rehberg, R-Mont., to prohibit the use of funds provided for employees of the departments of Labor, HHS, or Education to implement the law.
- Adopted, 241–187, an amendment by Steve King, R-Iowa, to bar the use of funds to carry out provisions of the health care overhaul law.
- Adopted, 237–191, an amendment by King to bar the use of funds to pay any federal employee to carry out the law.
- Adopted, 246–182, an amendment by Jo Ann Emerson, R-Mo., to bar the IRS from using funds to implement or enforce the individual mandate under the law. The mandate required individuals and their

Contraceptive Coverage in the Senate

Meanwhile, the Senate, which had mostly avoided the debates over repealing or otherwise altering the health law, weighed in on the abortion issue, indirectly, when it voted in March 2012 to reject an effort to allow employers to opt out of offering women coverage of contraceptives if it conflicted with their religious or moral beliefs.

On March 1, 2012, as an amendment to an unrelated highway funding bill (S 1813), the Senate on a **key vote of 51–48 (R 1–45; D 48–3; I 2–0)** voted to table an amendment offered by Sen. Roy Blunt, R-Ky. *(2012 key votes, p. 803)*

Blunt's amendment was basically the text of a bill he had introduced the previous August when the Department of Health and Human Services first issued the requirement for most health plans to offer contraception as part of their preventive service benefits packages. The rules exempted actual houses of worship and organizations that employed generally only those of the same faith, but included hospitals and universities affiliated with religious institutions, much to the outrage of the Catholic Church.

The administration sought to soften the requirement in early 2012, after even some Democrats were taken aback at the furious backlash. It offered hospitals and universities sponsored by religious institutions, for example, the option of having their insurance company offer the coverage instead.

Although most Democrats were mollified, Republicans dismissed the modification as a "fig leaf" and vowed to continue pursuing legislation that would reverse the rule.

One of the rule's most vocal opponents, the United States Conference of Catholic Bishops, said in a statement that although details on how the change would work were pending, the lack of protection for some religious employers was "unacceptable and must be corrected."

During floor debate, Minority Leader Mitch McConnell of Kentucky sought to tie the issue to First Amendment rights for religious institutions. "Most of us probably assumed that if religious liberty were ever seriously challenged in this country, we could always expect a robust bipartisan defense of it at least from within the Congress itself," McConnell said. "Democrats have evidently decided that they'd rather defend a president of their own party, regardless of the impact of his policies."

But opponents of the measure contended the language was so vague—it allowed all employers, not just religious employers, to decline to offer any benefits that conflicted with their "religious beliefs or moral convictions"—that it could to open the door to denial of a wide range of benefits, such as routine vaccinations for children.

It would allow any employer or insurer to deny coverage for virtually any treatment, for virtually any reason," said Senate Majority Leader Harry Reid, D-Nev. Health and Human Services Secretary Kathleen Sebelius also pushed back against the amendment. "The Obama administration believes that decisions about medical care should be made by a woman and her doctor, not a woman and her boss," Sebelius said.

Despite a vow by House Speaker John A. Boehner, R-Ohio, to move a companion bill (HR 1179) in that chamber, however, no action was taken on the issue on the other side of the Capitol, either in committee or the floor, for the remainder of the Congress.

dependents to have "minimum essential coverage" beginning in 2014 or pay a penalty.

- Adopted, 241–184, an amendment by Cory Gardner, R-Colo., to bar the use of funds for any HHS employee to implement or provide guidance to the health insurance exchanges, which each state was required to establish as a marketplace where individuals could buy private health insurance.

The Senate later rejected HR 1; the fiscal 2011 spending bill that ultimately cleared did not contain any of the health-law related amendments that passed the House. *(2011 appropriations, p. 150)*

2012 LEGISLATIVE ACTION

The House's lone vote to repeal the law in its entirety in 2012 came in response to the Supreme Court's June 28 decision upholding it.

House Republicans reacted to the Supreme Court decision on a **key vote of 244–185 (R 239–0; D 5–185),** mostly along party lines, on July 11 to pass a bill (HR 6079) that would have repealed the health care overhaul. The Senate did not take up the measure. *(2012 key votes, p. 803)*

The Congressional Budget Office determined that the bill would add $109 billion to the deficit over the 2013–2022 period. Republicans disputed the agency's methodology and estimate.

"The Supreme Court, by virtue of determining that it's constitutional, does not make it [the bill] good public policy," David Dreier, R-Calif., said as members began five hours of floor debate.

Democrats dismissed the vote as political theater, blasting the GOP for not offering a replacement plan and for not keeping the spotlight on the struggling economy. "We have a repeal with no replacement, no alternative, no protection offered by my Republican colleagues," said Minority Whip Steny H. Hoyer, D-Md.

The White House said the president would veto the bill.

Despite the Senate's continued intransigence on the issue, though, House Republicans continued to pursue an agenda aimed at repealing, defunding, or otherwise trimming the law, mostly through amendments to unrelated bills, particularly appropriations measures. Other proposals were included as provisions in the spending bills reported by the House committee.

For example, during consideration of the Commerce-Justice-Science funding bill, the House voted 229–194 to adopt an amendment that would have barred the use of funds to pay for the entire health care overhaul.

The Financial Services bill approved by the House Appropriations Committee contained provisions to prohibit the transfer of funds between the IRS and the HHS Department to implement the overhaul. The panel adopted, 28–20, an amendment from Alan Nunnelee, R-Miss., to restrict federally administered plans in the state health insurance exchanges from using federal funds to pay for administrative costs associated with abortions. Senate appropriators voted along party lines, 14–16, to reject a companion amendment by Lindsey Graham, R-S.C.

The House Labor–Health and Services–Education funding bill proposed to rescind $1.6 billion for the Center for Medicare and Medicaid Innovation and $15 million for the Independent Payment Advisory Board. It proposed to block new discretionary funding for the health care overhaul in fiscal 2013. When the Senate Appropriations Committee considered the bill, it rejected, 14–16, an amendment by Ron Johnson, R-Wis., to cut off money for the Prevention and Public Health Fund created under the health care law.

All of these efforts were stymied in the Senate.

Lawmakers also took separate aim at some specific portions of the law. On March 22, the House passed, 223–181, a bill (HR 5—H Rept 112-39, Parts 1, 2, and 3) that would have abolished the Independent Payment Advisory Board created under the health care overhaul. The fifteen-member panel was charged with making cost-cutting recommendations if Medicare spending exceeded target growth rates. Critics called the board a "death panel," saying it might ration health care, although rationing was explicitly disallowed as part of the panel's charge. The bill also contained provisions to limit medical-malpractice suits.

The White House warned that the president's senior advisers would recommend a veto.

A second bill (HR 436—H Rept 112-514), passed by the House on a 270–146 vote June 7, would have repealed a 2.3 percent tax on medical devices that was designed, in part, to pay for the overhaul. The tax, scheduled to go into effect in 2013, covered a wide range of devices, particularly those used in hospitals and doctors' offices. To offset the $29 billion cost over ten years, the bill would have made those with subsidized coverage from state insurance exchanges created under the overhaul liable for any overpayments. The law capped the pay requirement for those with incomes of up to four times the poverty level.

The White House also issued a veto threat against that bill. Neither was considered by the Senate.

Food and Drug Administration User Fees

Congress easily cleared legislation allowing the Food and Drug Administration (FDA) to continue collecting the fees that supported the approval process for prescription drugs and medical devices. The bill also created two new user fee programs, one for generic drugs and the other for generic biologic drugs.

President Barack Obama signed the bill into law July 9 (S 3187—PL 112-144). The Congressional Budget Office said it would reduce the deficit by $311 million over ten years.

Approval from the FDA is a prerequisite for the manufacturers of prescription drugs and medical devices to market their products in the United States. In 1992, the agency for the first time was authorized to collect fees to finance its premarket reviews of drugs (PL 102-571). A similar fee authority for medical devices was authorized in 2003 (PL 107-250). *(1992 law, Congress and the Nation Vol. VIII, p. 603; 2003 law, Congress and the Nation Vol. XI, p. 482)*

The last bill renewing the FDA's user fee authority (PL 110-85), passed in 2007, was scheduled to expire October 1, 2012, and the agency had reached agreements with both medical-device manufacturers and prescription drug companies on fee and review program expansions, under which the FDA would be permitted to collect additional fees for generic drugs, biosimilar drugs, and devices. The term *biosimilar drugs* referred to biological products that were either similar to, or interchangeable with, a so-called reference product—a biological product that had already been approved. *(Congress and the Nation Vol. XII, p. 563)*

In exchange, the agency agreed to increase its capacity to review applications to reduce the backlog for generic drugs and various types of medical devices. The FDA also agreed to increase transparency when issuing regulations and facilitate the use of electronic applications.

The Senate and House passed similar versions of the five-year authorization bill by overwhelming majorities in the spring. In addition to the new user fee programs for generic drugs and biosimilars, the bills sought to expedite the availability of drugs meant to treat serious or life-threatening diseases.

Both bills also contained provisions to improve the safety of drug supply chains, address drug shortages, and permanently reauthorize programs that encouraged manufacturers to conduct studies on pediatric drugs.

The main differences concerned the regulation of medical devices, incentives for companies to create new antibiotics, and a tracking system in the Senate bill.

For years, the pharmaceutical industry and consumer safety advocates had pushed for federal programs to improve the safety of the drug supply chain, in part by tracking drugs to spot counterfeit or adulterated products that could endanger patients. But some groups representing businesses within the supply chain had balked at the requirements. On the other hand, some members of Congress saw the Senate proposal as not strong enough and feared it could preempt stronger state laws.

SENATE ACTION

The Senate passed its bipartisan five-year reauthorization measure (S 3187) by a vote of 96–1 on May 24, after turning back several proposed changes. The Health, Education, Labor, and Pensions Committee (HELP) had approved an earlier draft of the bill by voice vote April 25.

The Senate-passed measure was sponsored by committee Chair Tom Harkin, D-Iowa, and ranking Republican Michael B. Enzi of Wyoming.

The Senate bill authorized the FDA to halt clinical-device trials in cases where it was determined that the device posed too great a risk to the subject, permitted the FDA to modify device classifications, and codified the authority of the FDA to require postmarket analysis of devices as a condition of approval.

It also provided for the creation of a national drug-tracking and drug-tracing system. The "RxTec" provision would have required manufacturers to put a serial number on each individual unit of a product, such as a bottle of pills. When diversion or counterfeiting was suspected, regulators could verify a unit by the number. That pedigree also would allow products to be tracked at the lot level, which could include thousands of units.

The major amendments that were allowed on the floor required sixty votes for adoption under a bipartisan agreement. The Senate:

- Rejected, 28–67, an amendment by Jeff Bingaman, D-N.M., to get cheaper, generic drugs to the market faster by making "pay for delay" deals less attractive. Under such deals, the manufacturers of brand-name drugs paid competitors to wait to bring generic versions to the market. Bingaman proposed that companies that produced generic drugs be allowed to share some of the 180-day marketing exclusivity period given to the original generic patent holder if that holder entered into a delay deal.
- Rejected, 43–54, an amendment offered by John McCain, R-Ariz., with support from Sherrod Brown, D-Ohio, to allow the importation of lower-cost prescription drugs from approved pharmacies in Canada. McCain offered a similar amendment in the HELP markup but was rebuffed, 9–12. Advocates for patients and senators from both parties had long supported opening access to cheaper drugs. But critics of McCain's proposal suggested that the amendment would not provide proper control of the Canadian supply chain. The pharmaceutical industry—and the FDA—strongly opposed the idea, saying it could lead to an increase in counterfeit drugs. It successfully lobbied to keep a similar amendment from being added to the 2010 health care overhaul (PL 111-148, PL 111-152). *(Congress and the Nation Vol. XI, p. 508; health law, p. 421)*
- Rejected, 9–88, an amendment by Bernard Sanders, I-Vt., that would have ended a company's exclusive marketing rights if it were found guilty of fraud, including adulteration or illegal marketing of a particular drug. Sanders was the only senator to vote against the bill.
- Tabled, or killed, 77–20, an amendment by Majority Whip Richard J. Durbin, D-Ill., to require manufacturers of dietary supplements to register and share product information with the FDA. Under the amendment, not doing so would have resulted in the supplement being considered misbranded, and thus ineligible for sale.
- Tabled, 78–15, a proposal by Rand Paul, R-Ky., that would have barred the FDA from classifying and regulating food or dietary supplements as drugs, unless a federal court found that the product's health claims were false and misleading.

HOUSE ACTION

The House passed its bipartisan version of the legislation (HR 5651) on a 387–5 vote May 30. The Energy and Commerce Committee had approved it, 46–0, on May 10.

The House version incorporated an amendment by Fred Upton, R-Mich., the bill's sponsor, to shorten to 150 days from 180 days the FDA's timetable for making decisions to respond to citizen petitions requesting a stay on pending generic-drug applications, including those for generic biosimilars. Under existing law, there was no time limit on agency responses to petitions on biosimilars.

Notably, the House bill granted extended exclusivity rights to manufacturers of antibiotics for a wide range of treatments, as opposed to just treatments for life-threatening conditions. The House measure also included more stringent import restrictions in cases where foreign inspections were intentionally delayed or limited, and it limited the time the FDA had to respond to administrative complaints regarding the approval of generic drugs.

Although both Democrats and Republicans expressed support for the bill, Edward J. Markey, D-Mass., said the measure did not do enough to address the testing and safety of certain medical devices. "Today's bill is also a huge missed opportunity," he said, expressing concern about what he said was a federal "loophole" that required the FDA to clear medical devices that demonstrated their similarity to an earlier model.

FINAL ACTION

House and Senate negotiators signed off on the compromise legislation in mid-June, and the House agreed by voice vote June 20 to adopt the changes as an amendment to the Senate-passed bill. The Senate cleared the bill, 92–4, on June 26.

The agreement took elements from both bills, but certain provisions were left out of the final deal, including the national drug track-and-trace system.

The bill included the House language reducing the amount of time the FDA would have to make administrative decisions. The bill also set a 270-day time limit for the agency to respond to petitions related to generic-drug approval. Senate negotiators won a limitation on antibiotics that would qualify for an additional five years of marketing exclusivity, reserving the incentive for new products that treated serious or life-threatening conditions.

The leading industry group, the Pharmaceutical Research and Manufacturers of America, backed the agreement but noted the absence of any language addressing the tracking and tracing issue.

MAJOR PROVISIONS

Major provisions of PL 112-144 included:

Prescription drug user fees. Reauthorized the existing prescription user fee program through fiscal 2017. Fees were expected to total more than $700 million in fiscal 2013, with amounts increasing each subsequent year because of inflation, workload, and other adjustments.

Generic-drug user fees. Authorized the creation of a new user fee program to increase the capacity of the FDA to review generic-drug applications. Fees were expected to total roughly $1.5 billion over five years. In hopes of getting cheaper generic drugs to market more quickly, the measure also capped at 150 days, down from 180 days, the time the FDA had to review a citizen petition or a civil action seeking to halt FDA action related to approval of a generic-drug application. The FDA was required to issue a decision within 270 days on manufacturer petitions regarding denied generic and biosimilar applications.

Biosimilar user fees. Authorized the creation of four types of user fees for medical devices and biological products that were biologically similar to existing products and were approved under an expedited review process.

International supply chain. Increased the FDA's oversight of the global supply chain of prescription drugs and medical devices. The FDA was required to establish a system for uniquely identifying foreign drug producers in the same way that it maintained up-to-date information on domestic manufacturing facilities. The agency also was required to create a registry of commercial drug importers.

The measure authorized the FDA to inspect both domestic and foreign manufacturing facilities on a risk-based schedule, to share the information with foreign governments and to contract with third-party inspectors and reviewers. The agency could bar the entry of drugs into the United States if a foreign manufacturing facility purposely delayed or refused inspection. The FDA also could detain or destroy misbranded or adulterated products. The measure imposed a maximum twenty-year sentence for individuals found to have intentionally misbranded or adulterated prescription drugs or other medical products.

Pharmaceuticals for children. Permanently reauthorized the Best Pharmaceuticals for Children program, which was created in 1997 to encourage the development of safe prescription drugs for children. The program required manufacturers to conduct a pediatric assessment as part of the application to market a new active drug ingredient or drug regimen. The FDA could extend exclusive marketing periods for such drugs by six months in exchange for the pediatric assessments.

Drug shortage prevention. Required manufacturers of drugs that were deemed to be life-supporting or life-sustaining or used in the treatment of debilitating diseases or conditions to notify the FDA of any anticipated stoppage or disruption in manufacturing at least six months in advance. For controlled substances that might be subject to a shortage, the bill required the Drug Enforcement Administration to provide timely decisions regarding an increase in production quotas. Hospitals within a unified health system were allowed to repackage drugs into smaller amounts to extend supplies of drugs that might experience shortages.

Medical devices. Reauthorized the FDA user fee program for medical devices, which was expected to bring in about $500 million over five years. The legislation required the FDA to issue regulations to facilitate the creation of an identification system for medical devices.

Life-saving drugs. Required the FDA to create a process for the expedited approval of drugs that could treat "serious or life-threatening" diseases and that were shown to be substantially more effective than existing therapies. The measure also provided an incentive for the development of antibiotics to treat life-threatening conditions by giving the manufacturer a five-year window of marketing exclusivity.

Conflict of interest. Modified the FDA's conflict-of-interest policy by removing limits on recruitment eligibility and waivers granted to FDA advisory committee members who had potential conflicts of interest. However, the bill imposed disclosure requirements on FDA committee members regarding the type, nature, and magnitude of any financial holding that might represent a conflict of interest.

Scheduling of synthetic drugs. Required the addition of more than fifteen cannabimimetic agents (used to create synthetic marijuana) to the list of Schedule I controlled substances. It also added mephedrone and eleven synthetic stimulant and mephedrone derivative agents to the list.

Medicare Physician Payments

Like the five Congresses that preceded it, the 112th Congress proved unable to find a new way to reimburse physicians serving Medicare patients and put an end to repeated short-term "doc fix" patches.

Instead, Congress in 2011 and 2012 did largely what its predecessors did; continue to delay scheduled cuts while not actually solving the underlying problem.

During the two years lawmakers passed three separate bills, delaying cuts first for two months (January–February 2012), then for ten months (through December 2012). Then, during the very last hours of the 112th Congress in early January 2013, lawmakers extended the cuts for another twelve months, through the end of 2013, as part of omnibus legislation to avert the so-called "fiscal cliff." *(Fiscal cliff bill, p. 185)*

On December 23, 2011, President Barack Obama signed the two-month extension into law (HR 3765—PL 112-78). He signed the ten-month bill (HR 3630—PL 112-96) February 22. He signed the fiscal cliff bill (HR 8—PL 112-240) on January 2, 2013.

Before the action in the 112th Congress, the last patch had been enacted in December 2010 (HR 4994—PL 111-309). It extended through December 31, 2011.

Without congressional action in December 2011, physicians who saw Medicare patients would have been hit with a 27.4 percent reduction in their reimbursement rates beginning January 1, 2012.

The issue arose because the growth of health care provider costs continued to exceed the growth rate of the economy as a whole. Under the 1997 Balanced Budget Act (PL 105-33), a statutory cost control system known as the Sustainable Growth Rate formula provided a means to calculate annual adjustments in the fees paid to doctors under Medicare Part B. Beginning in 2002, escalating health care costs resulted in the formula requiring annual reductions in fee rates. *(PL 105-33, Congress and the Nation Vol. X, p. 432).*

But lawmakers, concerned that fewer doctors would be willing to serve Medicare patients, regularly passed legislation to prevent the scheduled cuts. Since the system was created, reimbursement rates had been cut just once, by 4.8 percent in 2002, while the cumulative potential cost to doctors of allowing the patch to expire had mounted.

Subcommittees of the House Energy and Commerce and Ways and Means committees held a number of hearings about how to replace the formula and solicited proposals from physician groups in 2011. Many of those plans centered on enacting a series of stable payments for five years and conducting demonstration projects during that time to find a new payment method. But the lawmakers avoided discussing how to pay for a permanent fix, which the Congressional Budget Office (CBO) said would cost roughly $300 billion over ten years.

Physician groups turned to the joint deficit reduction committee created by the August 2011 debt limit law (PL 112-25). They lobbied vigorously for the panel to resolve the matter, despite the fact that the committee's mandate was to find at least $1.2 trillion in savings. *(Deficit reduction committee, p. 168)*

In one of their proposals, deficit committee Democrats suggested using part of the expected savings from winding down the wars in Iraq and Afghanistan to help pay for a long-term resolution. But the committee was unable to come up with an overall deficit reduction plan by its November 23 deadline, leaving lawmakers with only a few weeks before the scheduled payment cuts were due to kick in once again.

House GOP leaders then sought to take care of the impending physician pay cuts as part of a year-end legislative package (HR 3630) that also contained extensions of the payroll tax cut and unemployment provisions.

But the bill hit an impasse in the Senate over proposed offsets, at which point the Senate passed a bipartisan version that extended the programs for two months. House Republicans blasted the Senate's short-term bill and instead insisted on a conference. That developed into a stalemate that dragged into the waning days of the year, leaving negotiators to consider a long-term extension in early January 2012.

Instead, Congress cleared a two-month extension of the three expiring programs, and President Obama signed the bill into law December 23.

2011 LEGISLATIVE ACTION

The House passed the extensions package (HR 3630) by a vote of 234–193 on December 13. The measure would have stopped the doctors' pay cuts for two years, with a 1 percent increase in payment rates each year at a cost of $38.9 billion over ten years, according to CBO.

Republicans proposed to pay for the package in part by cutting $8 billion over ten years from funding made available for state prevention and public health grants under the 2010 health care overhaul (PL 111-148, PL 111-152). Starting in 2017, the bill also proposed to increase Medicare Parts B and D premiums for high-income beneficiaries and lower the income threshold to increase the number of beneficiaries who would be subject to the increased rates.

The offsets were unacceptable to Senate Democrats, however.

With time running out before the holidays, the Senate passed the bill by unanimous consent December 17 after agreeing on a **key vote of 89–10 (R 39–7; D 49–2; I 1–1)** to amend it with a two-month extension of the doc fix, payroll tax cut, and unemployment benefits. The short-term deal had been negotiated by Majority Leader Harry Reid, D-Nev., and Minority Leader Mitch McConnell, R-Ky., to give lawmakers more time to reach agreement on a longer-term package. *(2011 key votes, p. 785)*

The bill continued the existing reimbursement rate for Medicare physicians during the two-month period. The cost of all the extensions in the bill was paid for by an increase in fees charged by Fannie Mae and Freddie Mac for guaranteeing housing loans. The two mortgage giants were operating under government conservatorship.

Shortly afterward, the senators left for the year, assuming that the House would clear the bipartisan compromise before going home.

House Republicans refused to go along with the short-term bill, raising the specter that all three programs would expire at the end of the year. After sharp criticism in the media and jabs from some Senate Republicans, House Speaker John A. Boehner, R-Ohio, did an about-face and informed his caucus in a conference call—members had already gone home for the holidays—that the House would clear the bill with a minor change to the payroll tax cut extension.

With a handful of members present, Boehner followed through on December 23, passing the slightly modified measure (HR 3765) by unanimous consent. The Senate cleared the bill the same day, also by unanimous consent. The doc fix provisions were unchanged, as were the offsets.

2012 LEGISLATIVE ACTION

Work on the February 2012 bill (HR 3630) originated in late 2011. The final version extended a payroll tax holiday and federal unemployment benefits, as well as blocked the reimbursement rate reduction through December 31. *(Payroll tax, pp. 79, 108; unemployment benefits, pp. 517, 535)*

The House adopted the conference report (H Rept 112-399) that provided the one-year delay by a vote of 293–132 on February 17.

The Senate cleared the bill, 60–36, later the same day. Although the payroll tax cut was not offset, the conferees paid for the doc fix and the unemployment extension with a sale of electromagnetic spectrum and an increase in the amount new federal employees had to contribute to their defined-benefit pensions.

With that settled, lawmakers began a series of hearings to look into possible replacements for the reimbursement system, focusing on innovations in the private sector. House and Senate panels investigated ways to repeal the current payment formula and move away from Medicare's fee-for-service system.

The Senate Finance Committee held a series of roundtable discussions with representatives from private insurers and groups representing physicians. The witnesses shared how they developed new physician payment models in the private sector. The House Energy and Commerce Committee, the House Ways and Means Committee, and the Senate Budget Committee also held hearings on how to replace the current payment formula.

But little legislation came from the efforts, and none received a hearing or a markup. The most substantial was a bill from the bipartisan House duo of Pennsylvania Democrat Allyson Y. Schwartz and Nevada Republican Joe Heck. The legislation would have repealed the existing formula and set up a five-year transition period during which the administration would test new payment models, from which doctors could choose.

Their bill paid for the cost of repealing the formula with a controversial offset: expected savings from winding down military operations in Iraq and Afghanistan. Although Democrats and several provider groups pushed for using that money, most Republicans maintained that it amounted to a budgetary gimmick.

Many assumed the payment rate patch would be included in part of a larger deficit reduction deal. But as January 1, 2013, approached with no deal in sight, House Energy and Commerce Chair Fred Upton, R-Mich., said he was working on a stand-alone bill to prevent the cuts.

Eventually, a one-year payment patch, through 2013, was included in the measure to avert the fiscal cliff (HR 8—PL 112-240). The provision, which kept payment rates steady through December 31, 2013, cost an estimated $25.2 billion, according to the CBO.

That cost was offset by adjustments to other Medicare providers, with hospitals bearing much of the burden. Recouping payments made to some hospitals for how they coded services under a certain payment system would save $10.5 billion, and extending lower Medicaid payments to hospitals that treat a high number of uninsured or low-income beneficiaries would save $4.2 billion.

Chronology of Action on Human Services

With health care taking center stage, human services had a much lower profile than usual in the 111th Congress, even with Democrats in the majority in both Houses.

Democrats, however, passed a major child nutrition bill in late 2010 that sought to address the nation's rising concerns about childhood obesity and how the federal government contributed to that problem through some of its agriculture and school feeding programs. The bill was a major priority for First Lady Michelle Obama, who lobbied vigorously for it.

2009–2010

Child Nutrition

The House cleared a Senate child nutrition bill in early December 2010 after House Democrats spent weeks rallying support, overcoming objections to funding offsets, and fending off a last-minute Republican attempt to derail the measure. President Barack Obama signed the measure into law on December 13 (S 3307—PL 111-296).

The bill boosted mandatory spending on child nutrition programs by $4.5 billion over ten years and, for the first time, gave the Agriculture Department the authority to set nutrition standards for foods sold in school vending machines, *à la carte* lines, and snack stores.

It also authorized the first increase in meal reimbursements to schools since 1973. The higher payment was tied to schools meeting new nutrition standards that promoted more fresh foods on school menus.

The legislation reauthorized school lunch, school breakfast, and after-school feeding programs, and the Special Supplemental Nutrition Program for Women, Infants, and Children (WIC), among others, through 2015. The programs had been operating with short-term extensions, the last of which was set to expire December 3 under a continuing resolution (PL 111-242) enacted September 30.

Participation in meal programs was expected to increase under a pilot program that allowed school districts to qualify low-income children for federally subsidized free and reduced-price meals using Medicaid enrollment information. Children could already qualify for subsidized meals if they received other forms of public assistance.

The cost was offset in part by moving up the end date for a temporary boost in food stamp benefits that was enacted in the 2009 stimulus law (PL 111-5), a plan that drew significant Democratic opposition. *(Stimulus law, p. 78)*

Some lawmakers also criticized a requirement that school districts put more nonfederal money into their meal accounts. State and school leaders said this would mean higher lunch fees for students who paid full price for their meals.

The White House issued a statement expressing strong support for the bill, although the new spending was less than half of the $10 billion the administration had requested.

REFERENCES

Discussion of human services policy for the years 1945–1964 may be found in *Congress and the Nation Vol. I*, pp. 1225–1331; for the years 1965–1968, *Congress and the Nation Vol. II*, pp. 745–778; for the years 1969–1972, *Congress and the Nation Vol. III*, pp. 605–633; for the years 1973–1976, *Congress and the Nation Vol. IV*, pp. 403–432; for the years 1977–1980, *Congress and the Nation Vol. V*, pp. 679–712; for the years 1981–1984, *Congress and the Nation Vol. VI*, pp. 581–612; for the years 1985–1988, *Congress and the Nation Vol. VII*, p. 607–632; for the years 1989–1992, *Congress and the Nation Vol. VIII*, pp. 611–624; for the years 1993–1996, *Congress and the Nation Vol. IX*, pp. 571–596; for the years 1997–2000, *Congress and the Nation Vol. X*, pp. 486–496; for the years 2001–2004, *Congress and the Nation Vol. XI*, pp. 520–529; for the years 2005–2008, *Congress and the Nation Vol. XII*, pp. 579–588.

Final House action on the bill was aided in part by an administration pledge to congressional leaders that it would help see that the food stamp program—officially the Supplemental Nutrition Assistance Program (SNAP)—received the necessary funding.

LEGISLATIVE ACTION

The Senate Agriculture, Nutrition, and Forestry Committee on March 24 gave voice vote approval to the $4.5 billion bill (S 3307—S Rept 111-178), despite some concerns over how to pay for it.

Senators from both parties applauded the increase proposed in the bill, which was sponsored by committee chair Blanche Lincoln, D-Ark. But they raised repeated concerns over the decision to pay for the boost in part by cutting $2.2 billion over ten years from the Environmental Quality Incentives Program (EQIP), a popular federal program that paid farmers to adopt conservation practices.

Lincoln called the program "critically important" and said she would work with other senators to identify alternate ways to pay for the bill. A coalition of environmental groups sent a letter to the committee March 23, urging senators to find offsets, stressing that the proposed reduction would cut the baseline amount for conservation funds, which would result in lower conservation funding in the next farm bill.

The committee rejected, 10–11, an amendment by Saxby Chambliss of Georgia, the panel's ranking Republican, that would have paid for the nutrition increase by instead cutting funds from the Conservation Stewardship Program, a separate Agriculture Department conservation program that he said had far fewer applicants.

The committee adopted a manager's package of amendments by voice vote, as well as:

- A proposal by John Thune, R-S.D., to ensure that funds in the bill were spent to research child hunger, obesity, and Type 2 diabetes on American Indian reservations.
- An amendment by Sherrod Brown, D-Ohio, to establish an organic-food school pilot program.
- Another Brown amendment to provide competitive grants to state agencies for summer food service programs.
- A plan by Debbie Stabenow, D-Mich., to require a study of best practices of states participating in a federal after-school supper program.

The Senate passed its bipartisan bill by unanimous consent on August 5. It was seen as a victory for Lincoln, who was locked in a tough reelection battle. Lincoln had warned that not acting before the August recess could endanger key policy changes to school lunch, school breakfast, after-school meals, and other nutrition programs, which were set to expire on September 30.

Outlays for Income Security

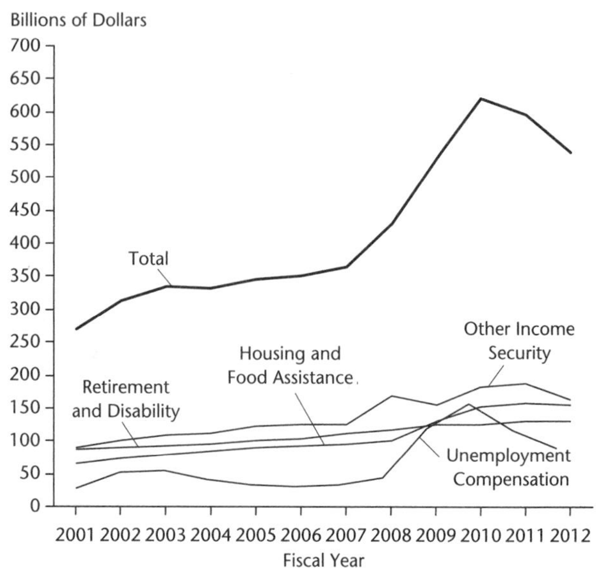

SOURCE: Office of Management and Budget, *Historical Tables, Budget of the United States Government: Fiscal Year 2013* (Washington, D.C.: U.S. Government Printing Office, 2012), Table 3.2.

Before the bill came to the floor, Lincoln and Chambliss reached an agreement that avoided tapping EQIP and instead offset the new spending with an early end to the boost in monthly food stamp benefits included in the stimulus package.

Advocacy groups opposed paying for the child nutrition bill with food stamp funds. "The bill, if enacted, will do far more harm than good," said Jim Weill, president of the Food Research and Action Center, who said the food stamp cuts would "increase hunger in America."

HOUSE ACTION

The House Education and Labor panel voted 32–13 on July 15 to approve a version of the legislation (HR 5504) that would have increased funding for school breakfast, lunch, and other nutrition programs by $8 billion over a decade without offsets.

Republicans insisted that the new spending be paid for. Chair George Miller, D-Calif., promised to work out offsets before the measure reached the floor.

Amendments adopted during the markup included:

- A manager's amendment by Miller, adopted 31–14, that reconciled some of the discrepancies between the House and Senate bills, including adding a provision that would provide for a nationwide expansion of an after-school meal program that existed in thirteen states and the District of Columbia. The amendment also added language to require the Agriculture Department to contract for an independent review of new ingredients in foods to be available for WIC.

- An amendment by Joe Courtney, D-Conn., adopted by voice vote, to require the Agriculture Department to purchase low-fat cheeses for the school breakfast and lunch programs. The need to help children stave off obesity had come into sharper focus as a result of a campaign spearheaded by First Lady Michelle Obama that emphasized exercise and healthy foods.

But it would take House Democratic leaders nearly the rest of the year—and the overcoming of several obstacles—before winning a 264–157 vote to clear the Senate bill on December 2.

Republicans were careful to express support for reauthorizing school meal programs, but they argued that the bill constituted an overreach by the federal government and complained that in clearing the Senate bill, Democrats were eliminating chances for House input.

Democratic leaders had to pull the bill from the floor temporarily December 1 after John Kline of Minnesota, ranking Republican on the Education and Labor Committee, introduced a motion to recommit the measure that seemed likely to succeed. Kline's motion would have dropped a provision that set a minimum price for paid school lunches and replaced it with language to bar institutions from receiving certain federal food funding if they had convicted sex offenders on staff or did not run background checks on child care staff.

Kline cited a bipartisan letter written by the National Governors Association earlier in the year saying the bill "would establish a federal mandate for every paid meal in every school in the country for the first time ever" and "destabilize" fair market prices for school meals.

To give members of their caucus political cover to vote against the motion, Democratic leaders brought a newly introduced bill (HR 6469) to the floor containing the background check language. The House passed that measure, 416–3, on December 2 and then rejected Kline's motion on the child nutrition bill, 200–221.

Majority Leader Steny H. Hoyer, D-Md., dismissed those charges. "The real purpose of this motion to recommit was to delay this bipartisan bill from being signed into law," he charged. Any change would have sent the bill back to the Senate, where it was expected to die, given the short time left on the legislative calendar.

Although Democrats came together to clear the legislation, conflict over the food stamp provisions had stalled the measure. More than 100 liberal lawmakers signed a letter in August calling on Speaker Nancy Pelosi, D-Calif., not to bring the bill to the floor with the offset.

But Democratic leaders stressed that this was their best chance to clear the bill, which would be unlikely to be taken up by the Republican-controlled House in the next Congress that resulted from GOP victories in the fall election. In addition, the White House weighed in with its promise to seek more money for the program.

"Quite frankly, if I did not believe that commitment to restore SNAP funding was real, I would have had a hard time voting for the underlying legislation," said Jim McGovern, D-Mass., co-author of the food stamp letter and co-chair of the House Hunger Caucus and the Congressional Hunger Center.

2011–2012

The 112th Congress was mostly dormant on the human services front, although appropriators did attempt to refight some of the unfinished battles left over from the landmark child nutrition bill enacted in the 111th Congress.

Nutrition Programs

The fiscal 2012 agriculture spending bill provided significantly more than House Republicans wanted for food and nutrition programs, blocked some school lunch nutrition standards, and liberalized a new means test for farm subsidies.

The measure was cleared as the vehicle for a three-bill "minibus" that President Barack Obama signed into law on November 18, 2011 (HR 2112—PL 112-55). *(Minibus, p. 170)*

The measure provided $137 billion for the Agriculture Department and Food and Drug Administration (FDA), including $19.8 billion in discretionary funding and $367 million in emergency spending for disaster relief. The discretionary amount was about $387 million, or 2 percent, below fiscal 2011 spending and $2.5 billion, or 11 percent, less than Obama requested. It was slightly less than the Senate proposed but $2.5 billion more than in the House-passed version.

Most of the funding in the bill—$116.8 billion—was for mandatory programs. Nearly $99 billion of it went to food and nutrition—including the Supplemental Nutrition Assistance Program (SNAP), known as food stamps, and child nutrition programs—an increase of $16 billion over fiscal 2011 and $6.6 billion more than the request. The House bill would have provided $8.6 billion less in mandatory food and nutrition funding.

Conferees included controversial policy language blocking the Agriculture Department from implementing proposed new standards that would have limited white potatoes and starchy vegetables in school meals. The deal began to roll back some of the authority the Agriculture Department gained under a 2010 law (PL 111-296) to set new standards for healthier school meals. Companies and trade associations trying to protect their shares of the $9.5 billion school food industry had been fighting the preliminary nutrition regulations since the Agriculture Department released them in January. Sen. Susan Collins, R-Maine, led the fight to preserve the role of white potatoes in school lunches. *(Child nutrition bill, p. 465)*

Nutrition advocates fared better in fending off cuts to the Women, Infants, and Children (WIC) nutrition program, which was paid for with discretionary funds. Democrats complained that cuts included in the version of the spending bill passed by the GOP-led House would have turned away 700,000 clients. Conferees agreed to fund the program at $6.6 billion, slightly less than the fiscal 2011 level of $6.7 billion but $570 million more than under the House bill.

Some of the additional money came from a $928 million reduction in mandatory funding for conservation programs that helped farmers and ranchers reduce runoff, prevent soil erosion, and provide habitats for wildlife.

Conferees protected funding for the FDA to carry out the 2010 food safety law (PL 111-353). They largely accepted the Senate's overall funding level of $2.5 billion for the FDA, excluding user fees, virtually the same as the amount provided in fiscal 2011. *(Food safety law, p. 409)*

The Agriculture Department's Food Safety Inspection Service, responsible for inspecting meat, poultry, and egg products, received close to the Senate level of a little more than $1 billion, about the same as in fiscal 2011. The House would have provided $972 million.

LEGISLATIVE ACTION

Versions of the bill had reached the House floor and been approved by the Senate Appropriations Committee before the measure was used to clear the three-bill minibus.

The House Appropriations Committee approved the Agriculture bill (HR 2112—H Rept 112-101) by voice vote May 31, proposing sharp cuts to nutrition programs, farm subsidies, and other spending. The Agriculture Subcommittee approved a draft of the measure by voice vote May 24.

The bill totaled $125.5 billion, with $17.3 billion in discretionary spending authority. The discretionary amount was roughly $2.9 billion, or 13 percent, below fiscal 2011 funding and $5.1 billion or 23 percent less than Obama had requested. The bill also included $108 billion for mandatory programs.

Republicans said the bill would allow agencies to do their work effectively while honoring the GOP commitment to fiscal restraint. Democrats pushed back with some success against deep cuts to a number of nutrition and food aid programs for those with low incomes.

The bill included:

- $24.5 billion for agriculture programs.
- $71.2 billion for food stamps.
- $18.8 billion for child nutrition.
- $6 billion for WIC.
- $1.4 billion for international food aid.
- $2.2 billion for the FDA.

During the markup, the committee:

- Adopted by voice vote an amendment by Rosa DeLauro, D-Conn., that shifted $147 million from a payment to Brazil in fiscal 2012 to boost the WIC account. The funding originally was provided for

Brazil's cotton industry to settle a World Trade Organization (WTO) dispute. Democrats had focused much of their ire on reductions to WIC, which was slated to receive a 12 percent cut from fiscal 2011 funding.

- Adopted by voice vote an amendment by Jeff Flake, R-Ariz., to lower from $750,000 to $250,000 per year the maximum adjusted gross income for a farmer to be eligible for subsidies under the direct-payment program. The program linked payments to a farm's past production levels, with the subsidy paid out regardless of market conditions.
- Adopted, 29–20, an amendment by Denny Rehberg, R-Mont., to bar funding for FDA rule-making activities or guidance unless the agriculture secretary based decisions on "hard science" rather than "cost and consumer behavior."
- Adopted, 24–21, language by James P. Moran, D-Va., prohibiting funding for Agriculture Department inspection of horse meat, which would effectively have prevented horse slaughter at U.S. meatpacking facilities.

HOUSE ACTION

The bill passed 217–203 on June 16 after two days of debate and votes on scores of amendments. Nineteen Republicans joined all Democrats in voting against it—the Democrats decrying what they said were draconian spending cuts, and the Republicans arguing the cuts were not deep enough.

During floor debate, the House:

- Adopted, 223–197, an amendment by Ron Kind, D-Wis., to block the $147 million annual payment to Brazil's cotton industry. Most Democrats voted for the amendment and most Republicans against, although the partisan division was not as strong as on the bill itself. "We are spending $147 million a year in order to bribe the Brazilian government so that they don't enforce the sanctions that they're entitled to now because of our unwillingness to reform our own cotton subsidy program," Kind said.
- Adopted by voice vote an amendment by Agriculture Subcommittee Chair Jack Kingston, R-Ga., to preserve the extra $147 million for WIC by shaving 0.78 percent in discretionary funding from each program in the first six titles of the bill to pay for it.
- Rejected two amendments to cut the bill's subsidies for upper-income farmers. Members defeated, 186–228, a proposal by Flake to reduce the existing $750,000 income threshold for farm subsidies under the direct-payment program to $250,000. An attempt by Earl Blumenauer, D-Ore., to reduce it to $125,000 was turned back, 154–262.

Republicans largely resisted attempts from their most conservative members to make deeper cuts. A majority of Republicans joined Democrats to turn back a number of proposals, including ones that would have trimmed millions for foreign food-aid programs, shaved 5 percent from every program in the bill, and slashed funds for an FDA smoking prevention initiative. "There comes a point in a budget exercise when you starve a program so much it just can't function," said the top Agriculture Subcommittee Democrat, Sam Farr of California. Kingston warned his caucus that taking out even bigger chunks would further embolden expected opposition from the Senate's Democratic majority.

SENATE ACTION

The Senate Appropriations Committee approved its bipartisan, $137 billion version of the bill (HR 2212—S Rept 112-73) by a vote of 28–2 on September 7. The measure included $20.1 billion in discretionary spending, 16 percent more than in the House measure and just 0.5 percent below fiscal 2011. The total included $266 billion in disaster relief.

The following were major components of the bill:

- $25 billion for agriculture programs.
- $80.4 billion for food stamps.
- $18.2 billion for child nutrition.
- $6.6 billion for WIC.
- $1.9 billion for international food aid.
- $2.5 billion for the FDA.

Lawmakers agreed to put off their amendments until the stand-alone bill reached the floor, but it never did.

Rather than considering the bill separately, the Senate made it the vehicle for the minibus. The Senate passed the three-bill package, 69–30, on November 1. Among the few changes made to the agriculture section, senators:

- Adopted, 58–41, an amendment by Kirsten Gillibrand, D-N.Y., to provide $110 million in additional funds for emergency conservation and watershed protection programs.
- Adopted, 84–15, an amendment by Tom Coburn, R-Okla., to prohibit direct payments to farmers who had an adjusted gross income of more than $1 million.
- Rejected, 45–55, an amendment by David Vitter, R-La., to allow individuals to reimport FDA-approved prescription drugs into the country from Canada.

CONFERENCE AND FINAL ACTION

By packaging the minibus in a conference report to HR 2112, appropriators avoided amendments on the House and Senate floors. The measure won bipartisan support in both chambers. The House adopted the conference report (H Rept 112-284), 298–121, on November 17, with the support of 165 Democrats and 133 Republicans. The Senate easily cleared the bill, 70–30, later the same day.

Conferees accepted an amendment by Coburn increasing the threshold for farmers or farm operations eligible for subsidies under the direct-payment program to those with adjusted gross incomes exceeding $1 million. Similar efforts to add restrictions fell short in the House. The amount was an increase from the $750,000 set in the 2008 farm law (PL 110-246).

The conference report also blocked the Agriculture Department from implementing proposed rules that the department said would "level the playing field" between livestock and poultry producers and the few big companies that controlled the industry practices. Most major livestock groups said the department's proposed rules went too far, and there was a bipartisan backlash from lawmakers from farm districts and states.

Negotiators also dropped a ban on the slaughter of horses for meat, which had been in the annual bill since 2006.

MAJOR PROVISIONS

The bill included the following major provisions:

- $25 billion for agriculture programs, $4.5 billion less than in fiscal 2011 and $465 million less than Obama requested.
- $80.4 billion for food stamps, a $15.2 billion increase over fiscal 2011 and $7.2 billion more than requested.
- $18.2 billion for child nutrition, $831 million more than in fiscal 2011 and $659 million less than requested.
- $6.6 billion for WIC, $115 million less than in fiscal 2011 and $772 million below the request.
- $1.8 billion for international food aid, slightly below the fiscal 2011 figure but $294 million less than requested.
- $2.5 billion for the FDA, excluding user fees, slightly above fiscal 2011 spending but $238 million below Obama's request.

CHAPTER 10

Education Policy

Introduction 473

Chronology of Action on Education Policy 476

2009–2010 476

2011–2012 483

Education Policy

The 2002 reauthorization of the Elementary and Secondary Education Act, known as the No Child Left Behind Act (PL 107-110), was controversial from the beginning but was enacted in a rare moment of bipartisan unity.

Strong leadership emerged on both sides of the aisle, most visibly with President George W. Bush and Ohio representative John A. Boehner on the Republican side and Sen. Edward M. Kennedy of Massachusetts and Rep. George Miller of California on the Democratic. Bush had run for the office promising to make education a priority, and GOP members were anxious to give him a victory. The involvement of Kennedy in the negotiations reassured otherwise skeptical Democrats. The measure got a final push when an atmosphere of bipartisanship and solidarity permeated both chambers after the September 11, 2001, terrorist attacks. (Congress completed action on No Child Left Behind in 2001; it was signed into law in 2002.)

Complaints about the new law, which for the first time tied federal education aid to improvements in students' test scores, emerged in short order—and across the political spectrum. But a clear path to fixing the measure proved elusive. While that rare moment existed in 2001 that allowed No Child Left Behind to become law, no such moment arrived after Barack Obama became president in 2009. He had other priorities, such as stimulating the faltering economy and overhauling health care. Kennedy, known for his ability to reach out to both parties and find compromise, died in August 2009.

As the health care debate took over Congress in late 2009 and early 2010, the party movement and the election in 2010 of conservative newcomers who regarded the law as a major intrusion on state and local prerogatives, saw compromise with Democrats on any subject become riskier for the Republican leadership.

In March 2011, President Obama challenged Congress to rewrite No Child Left Behind by the start of the fall school year. Senate Health, Education, Labor, and Pensions Committee Chair Tom Harkin, D-Iowa, pledged to have a bill through his committee by the end of April. His counterpart in the House, Education and the Workforce Committee Chair John Kline, R-Minn., also promised quick action. However, the deadlines came and went, and the first session of the 112th Congress ended without reauthorizing the law, which had expired in 2007. Little expectation existed that the job would be completed in 2012, during a presidential election year, and no meaningful progress was made. A hyperpartisan atmosphere, philosophical differences, and powerful stakeholder lobbying, for example, from teachers' unions, stymied congressional efforts.

EXECUTIVE ACTION

President Obama warned Congress that if it did not rewrite No Child Left Behind before the start of the 2011–2012 school year, he would begin taking executive action to relieve states and local school districts from the burdensome parts of the statute, such as requiring that students in every school be 100 percent proficient in math and reading by 2014. The plan was to offer states waivers that freed them from some mandates in the law on the condition that they put in force a series of new education policies that the administration favored. These were in line with the goals of the administration's new Race to the Top program that offered competitive federal grants to states that raised academic standards, improved measurements

REFERENCES

Discussion of education policy for the years 1945–1964 may be found in *Congress and the Nation Vol. I,* pp. 1195–1215; for the years 1965–1968, *Congress and the Nation Vol. II,* 709–733; for the years 1969–1972, *Congress and the Nation Vol. III,* pp. 581–604; for the years 1973–1976, *Congress and the Nation Vol. IV,* pp. 377–402; for the years 1977–1980, *Congress and the Nation Vol. V,* 655–677; for the years 1981–1984, *Congress and the Nation Vol. VI,* pp. 555–580; for the years 1985–1988, *Congress and the Nation Vol. VII,* pp. 647–663; for the years 1989–1992, *Congress and the Nation Vol. VIII,* pp. 641–660; for the years 1993–1996, *Congress and the Nation Vol. IX,* pp. 607–634; for the years 1997–2001, *Congress and the Nation Vol. X,* pp. 507–549; for the years 2001–2004, *Congress and the Nation Vol. XI,* pp. 537–552; for the years 2005–2008, *Congress and the Nation Vol. XII,* pp. 599–618.

Outlays for Education

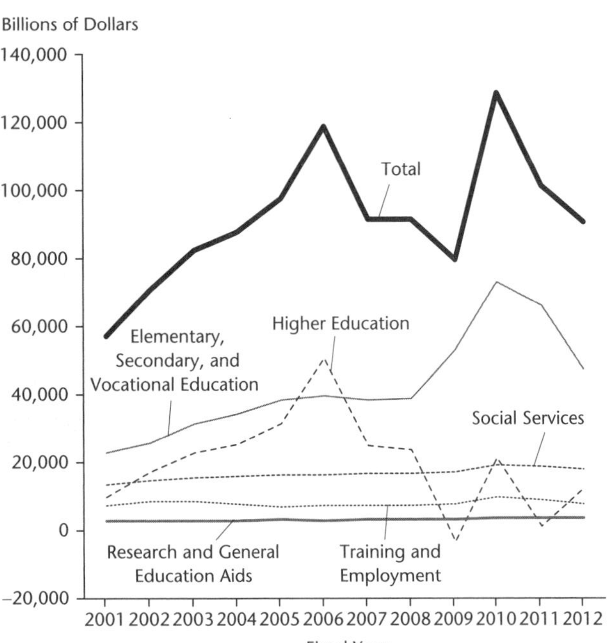

SOURCE: Office of Management and Budget, *Historical Tables, Budget of the United States Government: Fiscal Year 2013* (Washington, D.C.: U.S. Government Printing Office, 2012), Table 3.2.

NOTE: Total line includes expenditures not shown separately.

of student achievement and teacher quality, and turned around the lowest-performing schools.

The situation illustrated how paralysis in the legislative branch could create opportunities in the executive branch, in this case to move its agenda forward without waiting for a congressional seal of approval—and without having to compromise.

Education Secretary Arne Duncan liked to point out that the waivers were "Plan B." He said he would rather have Congress pass a robust reauthorization of No Child Left Behind. Those efforts were caught in partisan gridlock, however; and with teachers, principals, and school districts pleading for respite from the law's costly requirements, Obama in June 2011 gave Duncan the go-ahead to issue the conditional waivers.

From the moment the waivers were proposed, they were greeted warily by lawmakers on the left and right, teachers' unions, education policy experts, and the very school boards that were clamoring for regulatory relief. Republicans charged that conditional waivers were a backdoor way of forcing states to adopt policy changes the administration liked, while Democrats fretted that doling out waivers would take pressure off Congress to rewrite the law. Policy wonks and teachers' unions also did not understand how the administration could expect resource-strapped states and local school districts to implement new education initiatives, and school boards worried about the policy changes being too restrictive.

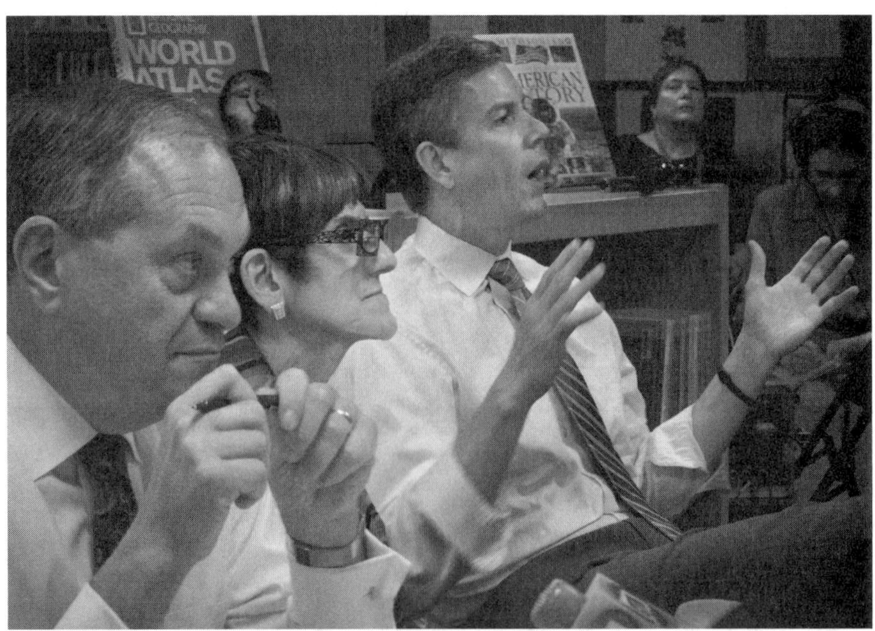

Mayor John DeStefano, Rep. Rosa DeLauro, and Education Secretary Arne Duncan (left to right) participate in a round table discussion on education reform on May 29, 2012, at Jepson School in New Haven, Conn.
Source: AP Photo/The New Haven Register, Melanie Stengel

By the end of 2012, the Department of Education had approved waivers for thirty-three states and the District of Columbia.

QUESTIONING THE SECRETARY'S AUTHORITY

While Democrats and teachers' groups eventually warmed to the idea of conditional waivers, House Republicans questioned Duncan's authority to issue them. A Congressional Research Service (CRS) analysis of the secretary's plan of action, requested by House education committee Chair Kline, appeared to back them up.

Waivers were nothing new, and the practice had never been challenged in court. The education secretary, the June 2011 CRS report said, had complete legal authority to issue a waiver from any part of No Child Left Behind whenever he wished. What was new and had no legal precedent, the report said, was the plan to condition the waivers on compliance with other requirements. "If the secretary did, as a condition of granting a waiver, require a grantee to take another action not currently required," CRS analysts wrote, "the likelihood of a successful legal challenge might increase," particularly if the Education Department "failed to sufficiently justify its rationale for imposing such conditions." The report went on to say: "Under such circumstances, a reviewing court could deem the conditional waiver to be arbitrary and capricious or in excess of the agency's statutory authority."

Duncan proved more willing than other cabinet secretaries to try to impose policy change by using the tools available to him. With Race to the Top, for example, he got forty-five states to adopt new standards, even though only eleven states and the District of Columbia won funding in the first round of awards. Some observed that Duncan was doing the same with the granting of conditional waivers, being aggressive and using creativity to achieve administration goals.

Sen. Lamar Alexander, R-Tenn., education secretary during the George H. W. Bush administration, introduced the State Innovation Pilot Act of 2011 (S 1568) that would prevent the education secretary from issuing conditional waivers. He said, "If by doing waivers, the secretary is trying to do through waivers what he couldn't do through Congress, I object." The bill was referred to the Senate Health, Education, Labor, and Pensions Committee but saw no further action.

With the partisan environment freezing the legislative pipeline and with the deep philosophical chasm between the House and Senate leadership, executive action was increasingly seen as the best chance for change in education policy, at least in the near-term future.

Chronology of Action on Education Policy

2009–2010

The most noteworthy action related to education policy taken by the 111th Congress was removing the federal government from the business of guaranteeing student loans offered by private lenders. Lawmakers also provided funding to state and local governments to avert teacher layoffs. A new competitive grant program called Race to the Top sought to improve and reform the educational system.

Federal Student Loans

Congress in 2010, as part of a budget reconciliation measure (HR 4872—PL 111-152) that was a "corrections" bill making limited modifications to the health care overhaul (HR 3590—PL 111-148), set out the most dramatic changes to federal student loan programs in a decade. The Student Aid and Fiscal Responsibility Act (SAFRA), part of the Health Care and Education Reconciliation Act of 2010, made the federal government the sole provider of student loans, cutting out the role of private companies as middlemen. Previously, the government had two programs: one that provided direct loans and another that guaranteed loans by private lenders. *(Budget reconciliation, p. 436; health care overhaul, p. 421)*

Eliminating the federal guarantees and subsidies that had enabled private lenders to keep interest rates low was expected to save about $61 billion in mandatory spending over ten years, according to the Congressional Budget Office (CBO). About 70 percent of the savings, or $42 billion, was dedicated to increased funding for Pell grants and other federal education programs. Another $10 billion was set aside for deficit reduction, and $9 billion went to help offset costs of the health care overhaul.

HR 4872 provided about 45 percent less funding for education programs than did a stand-alone student loan bill (HR 3221) that the House passed in 2009. The CBO estimated that HR 3221 would have reduced federal spending on student loans by $87 billion, of which $77 billion was directed to education programs. Since House passage of HR 3221, however, the CBO had reduced the projected net saving as more colleges and universities voluntarily enrolled in the federal lending program and costs associated with higher student eligibility and enrollment rose. Also, under HR 3221, all the net savings were to be used for education programs. Among other things, HR 4872 did not include $8 billion that HR 3221 would have devoted to competitive grants for early-childhood education, and it eliminated $7 billion for a program to improve graduation rates and upgrade facilities at two-year colleges.

BACKGROUND

The Federal Family Education Loan Program, which provided federal guarantees for private student loans, was created in 1965 (PL 89-329) under President Lyndon B. Johnson. The Direct Loan Program, established in 1993 (PL 103-66) under President Bill Clinton, provided federal student loans directly to borrowers. *(PL 89-329, Congress and the Nation Vol. II, p. 716; PL 103-66, Congress and the Nation Vol. IX, p. 625)*

Democrats and Republicans argued for years over which was the better approach. Democrats said direct loans were more reliable and efficient and saved billions of dollars that could better be used to expand programs for low-income students. Republicans called that a job-killing government takeover of a private industry.

After taking majority control of Congress in 2007, the Democrats began chipping away at the private student loan program. A 2007 law (PL 110-84) cut interest rates on subsidized student loans in half over four years. A 2008 law (PL 110-227) reauthorizing the 1965 Higher Education Act placed several new restrictions on private lenders. Another 2008 law (PL 110-350) temporarily allowed the government to buy private student loans and take other actions to ensure that students could still get college loans despite a freeze in the nation's credit markets. *(PL 110-84, Congress and the Nation Vol. XII, p. 612; PL 110-227, PL 110-350, Congress and the Nation Vol. XII, p. 615)*

EDUCATION LEADERSHIP

With bipartisan support, Arne Duncan was confirmed as secretary of education by the Senate on a voice vote January 20, 2009. He had served as chief executive officer of the Chicago Public Schools.

In testimony on January 13 before the Senate Health, Education, Labor, and Pensions Committee, Duncan pledged to make early childhood education and improving teacher quality his top priorities. He said that teachers needed more support through mentoring programs and career ladders. He also indicated that he would take a pragmatic approach in seeking to reauthorize the controversial 2002 No Child Left Behind Act (PL 107-110). He said that he believed the law was necessary to assess students based on their academic growth. *(No Child Left Behind, Congress and the Nation Vol. XI, p. 540)*

The National Education Association (NEA), unhappy with the Obama administration's education policy, directed its criticism at Duncan. In 2010, a resolution put forth—and quickly tabled—before the NEA Representative Assembly sought to encourage President Barack Obama to replace Duncan with "a person who is aligned with the interests of the NEA, its members, and especially the students it serves." The union was vocal in its opposition to, for example, the administration's support for charter schools and teacher evaluations based partly on student test scores.

Controversy arose when Duncan took part in a panel discussion about the use of education data alongside former Washington, D.C., chancellor of schools Michelle Rhee in February 2012, when the Education Department Office of Inspector General was conducting an investigation to determine whether, during Rhee's tenure, district schools had cheated to raise test scores. In his opening comment at the conference, Duncan said, "This is an amazing panel, so I'm thrilled to be part of it." Rhee, after resigning as chancellor in 2010, founded StudentsFirst, a nonprofit advocacy organization that supported school vouchers, charter schools, and teacher evaluation by student test scores and opposed tenure and teachers' unions.

Duncan did not have only detractors. Online interactive publisher Take Part noted in an August 1, 2012, article that "[m]any see him as a bridge builder between the Democratic Party's two sides—those who want to reform the system and the established teacher's union." It went on to say that "[s]ome supporters cite Duncan's achievements in making higher education more accountable and affordable," such as calling for expanding Pell grants, instituting income-based student loan repayment, and reporting of graduation, job placement, and student loan default rates by colleges and universities.

In mid-January 2013, Duncan announced that he would stay on as education secretary in Obama's second term.

LEGISLATIVE ACTION ON HR 3221

The House Education and Labor Committee approved the Student Aid and Fiscal Responsibility Act of 2009 (HR 3221) by 30–17 on July 21 and formally reported it (H Rept 111-232) on July 27. The full House passed the measure as a reconciliation bill, on a **key vote of 253–171 (R 6–167; D 247–4)** on September 17. Doing so gave the legislation protection from filibusters in the Senate, which meant that Democratic Senate leaders could bring up the measure without having to pull together the sixty votes required to overcome such delaying tactics. The use of the protective rules for the bill was sanctioned under the fiscal 2010 budget resolution (S Con Res 13), which called for reconciliation legislation that changed health care law and saved at least $1 billion from education programs. HR 3221 was referred to the Senate Committee on Health, Education, Labor, and Pensions but was put on hold until after the chamber finished its work on a health care overhaul. *(2009 key votes, p. 751)*

As passed by the House, HR 3221 was a close reflection of an Obama administration proposal to convert the private lending system to government loans and put the savings into investments in the Pell grant program, early-childhood education, community colleges, and deficit reduction.

House Education and Labor Committee Chair and bill sponsor George Miller, D-Calif., called the legislation the greatest investment in higher education since the GI bill. It would replace the Federal Family Education Loans program with direct government lending, saving billions in fees and subsidies. Critics accused Miller and other supporters of underreporting the cost of the bill, and they said the measure would destroy jobs. Many backed an alternative proposal by lending giant Sallie Mae that would have preserved the role of lenders in disbursing loans, saving what supporters said were an estimated 35,000 to 50,000 jobs. But that proposal also would have netted $13 billion less in savings, according to CBO, which would mean less money for the loans themselves.

During floor debate, the House adopted more than a dozen amendments, including proposals to prioritize funding for colleges in high-unemployment and distressed areas and to target special funding for dislocated workers and veterans. The House voted down three Republican proposals to limit or strike various sections of the bill. It also rejected, 165–265, on September 17, an amendment by Brett Guthrie, R-Ky., to preserve the existing subsidies for private lenders through 2014 and create a commission to develop a new private sector model for student lending. The House agreed 345–75 on September 17 to a motion by Darrell Issa, R-Calif., to recommit the bill to committee with instructions to report it back with language prohibiting the use of federal funds for the Association of Community Organizations for Reform Now (ACORN). ACORN had come under fire after the release of videos produced by conservative activists purporting to show ACORN employees providing illegal advice to actors posing as a pimp and a prostitute. Miller encouraged members to vote for the Issa motion to get the bill passed, noting that ACORN would receive no funding under the bill anyway.

The House-passed HR 3221 contained amendment to the Higher Education Act that would:

- Prohibit any new loans after June 30, 2010, under the Federal Family Education Loan program. All new federal student lending would come from the Direct Loan Program, which provided low-interest federal loans directly to the borrowers. Private lenders would still be permitted to service government-issued loans.
- Increase the maximum annual Pell grant scholarship to $5,500 in 2010, from $5,350 under existing law. Beginning in 2011, the maximum award would be automatically adjusted for inflation.
- Provide variable interest rates on subsidized student loans beginning in 2012. The rate would be capped at 6.8 percent and would be adjusted annually.
- Provide schools with $6 billion per year in lending authority for loans to low-income students under the Perkins Loan Program. Funding would be provided through the Direct Loan Program.
- Simplify the Free Application for Federal Student Aid.
- Provide $1 billion over seven years for grants for state initiatives to increase the number of disadvantaged children in early-learning programs and prepare more children for kindergarten.
- Provide $10 billion over ten years to upgrade programs at community colleges and construct and modernize facilities.
- Provide $2.1 billion per year for two years to renovate and modernize elementary and secondary schools.

LEGISLATIVE ACTION ON HR 4872

Like HR 3221, HR 4872 was a budget reconciliation bill. It was devoted primarily to modest changes to the health care package aimed at mollifying House Democrats who had to swallow the Senate-passed version of the health care bill, giving up many of their own priorities. While some Democratic senators balked at including the student loan provisions in the reconciliation bill, the plan provided needed offsets for the health care overhaul and was seen as attracting votes for that legislation in the House.

On March 21, 2010, the House passed HR 4872 by a vote of 220–211. The floor debate was a continuation of the months-long dispute over the health care overhaul legislation and made virtually no reference to the education provision. Dropped from the final House-passed version of the bill was language providing $8 billion in competitive grants to states to improve early education for children from birth to kindergarten. Also eliminated was $8.7 billion for the American Graduation Initiative, which was aimed at improving graduation rates and upgrading facilities at community colleges. Instead, $2 billion for the Trade Adjustment Assistance program originally authorized in the 2009 economic stimulus (HR 1—PL 111-5) was directed to schools. The House Budget Committee had reported HR 4872 (H Rept 111-443) on March 17. *(Economic stimulus, p. 78)*

On March 25, the Senate passed the reconciliation bill by 56–43. Roll calls were taken on March 24 on two education-related motions. Lamar Alexander, R-Tenn., offered a motion to waive the Budget Act and budget resolutions with respect to the Tom Harkin, D-Iowa, motion to table (kill) the Alexander motion to commit the bill to the Senate Health, Education, Labor, and Pensions Committee with instructions that it be reported back with changes that would reduce the student loan interest rate for the Direct Loan Program to 3.5 percent. The motion was rejected 58–41, because a three-fifths majority vote is required to waive the Budget Act. Harkin offered a motion to table (kill) an amendment by John Thune, R-S.D., to prevent enactment of provisions in the bill to place student loans under the direct lending program if any state experiences a job loss as a result of the provisions. The motion was agreed to, 55–43.

Although some Republican senators had vowed to impede the legislation with questions about whether portions of it truly constituted budget-related changes governed by the reconciliation rules, their appeals to the Senate parliamentarian were mainly in vain. The Senate dropped two minor education provisions after the parliamentarian ruled that they were out of order because they did not affect either mandatory spending or federal revenues. One of the provisions would have authorized the Education Department to provide additional mandatory funding in fiscal 2010 and subsequent fiscal years to cover the increased federal Pell grant amounts under the bill. The underlying bill, however, still appropriated additional Pell grant funds and indexed the funding to inflation. The other excised provision would have eliminated a requirement in existing law that the Education Department reduce Pell grant funding across the board if it was insufficient in a given year to provide the maximum grant level specified by law. The underlying bill effectively eliminated the requirement anyway by stipulating that a Pell grant awarded in a given year could not be smaller than the grant awarded the previous year.

The changes had little effect on the bill but forced it back to the House to be cleared. The House accepted the Senate changes by 220–207 on March 25.

MAJOR PROVISIONS

Following are major education provisions in HR 4872 (PL 111-152), signed into law on March 30, 2010:

Direct loans. Federal guarantees for private student loans under the Federal Family Education Loan Program were eliminated as of July 1, 2010, and the Direct Loan Program administered by the Department of Education was made the sole providers of the loans. Private lenders could continue servicing the loans under a competitive bidding system.

Pell grants. Funding was increased for the federal Pell grant program, the largest source of federal grants to low-income students attending college or other postsecondary programs. The legislation provided permanent mandatory budget authority, which was meant to supplement discretionary Pell grant funding and bring the maximum Pell grant award up to an annual level specified in the law. Overall, CBO estimated that the bill would increase mandatory spending for the Pell grant program by $36.1 billion over ten years.

Loan repayment. Income-based student loan payments were capped for new borrowers after July 1, 2014, at 10 percent of the borrower's net income, after adjustments for basic living costs, with the remaining balances forgiven after twenty years of repayment.

Minority-serving institutions. A program that provided $255 million per year in mandatory funding for historically black colleges and universities and minority-serving institutions was extended through 2019.

Community colleges. Community colleges were provided $500 million annually for fiscal years 2011 through 2014 to develop and improve educational or career training programs.

Low-income students. A total of $750 million was provided in fiscal years 2010 to 2014 for state grants to increase the number of low-income students prepared to enter and succeed in college and to manage their student loans.

Education Jobs Fund

Members of the House interrupted their August 2010 recess to return to Washington, D.C., and clear a $26.1 billion bill (HR 1586) that provided funds to help state and local governments prevent layoffs of teachers and maintain Medicaid health coverage of the poor. President Barack Obama signed the Education Jobs and Medicaid Funding bill into law (PL 111-226) on August 10. *(Medicaid funding, p. 453)*

Speaker Nancy Pelosi, D-Calif., brought the House back into session amid calls from state officials for quick action. Democratic New York governor David Paterson warned that about thirty states had budgeted on the assumption that the federal funds would arrive. Republicans criticized the legislation, saying it was essentially a Democratic election-year sop to teachers' unions. Democrats disagreed, arguing that nothing in the bill required anyone to be a union member. However, it was not lost on the Democrats that

E-READER ACCESSIBILITY

The Obama administration put colleges and universities on notice that if they supply or require electronic readers (e-readers) for students, the devices must be accessible to the blind. The Justice Department and the Education Department in June 2010 sent an open letter warning colleges and universities that e-readers that were not accessible could be classified as discriminatory under the Americans with Disabilities Act (PL 101-336). *(Americans with Disabilities Act, Congress and the Nation Vol. VIII, p. 743)*

Those who were blind or had impaired vision had difficulty operating popular e-readers such as Amazon's Kindle and Apple's iPad. In January 2010, Arizona State University reached a settlement with advocates for the blind not to renew a pilot program that distributed Kindles to some students. The Kindle, like the iPad, can read aloud the printed material it had stored, but the user first had to navigate through printed instructions and buttons. Amazon promised to make the Kindle fully accessible. Since the Arizona case, the Justice Department has resolved similar complaints from other schools, including Princeton University and Case Western Reserve.

Some lawmakers sought to require that electronics be more accessible, despite industry belief that the government should not be in the business of product design. The Twenty-first Century Communications and Video Accessibility Act of 2010 (S 3304—PL 111-260) was intended to ensure accessibility standards for Internet access and electronics. The legislation, sponsored by Sen. Mark Pryor, D-Ark., was reported from the Senate Commerce, Science, and Transportation Committee on August 3. The full Senate passed the measure by voice vote on August 5, and the House agreed by voice vote September 28 to pass S 3304 under suspension of the rules. The president signed the bill into law on October 28. The Commerce, Science, and Transportation Committee filed a written report (S Rept 111-386) on December 22. On July 26, 2010, a House companion measure (HR 3101), sponsored by Edward J. Markey, D-Mass., was reported by the House Energy and Commerce Committee (H Rept 111-563) and passed by the full House under suspension of the rules by 348–23.

the assistance would resonate with many of their constituents. Republicans also claimed that offsets in HR 1586 that made changes to foreign tax provisions could harm economic recovery in the United States by imposing new taxes on businesses, and Democrats were unhappy that the bill reduced funding for food stamp benefits and renewable-energy programs.

Enactment was a victory particularly for liberal Democrat David R. Obey of Wisconsin, chair of the House Appropriations Committee, who was retiring at the end of the 111th Congress and had made preventing planned teacher layoffs his top priority. The federal aid to prevent teacher layoffs was popular among Democrats, 236 of whom had voted to add it to a war supplemental spending bill (HR 4899—PL 111-212) on July 1, 2010. The Senate, however, killed the idea. *(War supplemental, p. 138)*

The House passed HR 1586 under suspension of the rules by 328–93 on March 19, 2009. The Senate passed an amended version by 93–0 on March 22, 2010. The House accepted the Senate changes and further amended the bill on March 25, 276–145. On August 4, the Senate agreed 61–38 to a motion to invoke cloture (thus limiting debate) on a motion by Majority Leader Harry Reid, D-Nev., to concur in the House changes with a substitute amendment, sponsored by Patty Murray, D-Wash., that would provide $36.1 billion for an extension of expanded Medicaid assistance to states and $10 billion in funding for states to create or retain teachers' jobs. (Three-fifths of the total Senate—that is, sixty senators—are required to invoke cloture.) Final Senate approval of the bill was virtually assured after the cloture vote. On August 5, the Senate agreed to the measure as modified, on a **key vote of 61–39 (R 2–39; D 57–0; I 2–0)**. The House cleared HR 1586 by a **key vote of 247–161 (R 2–158; D 245–3)** on August 10. *(2010 key votes, p. 767)*

The education-related provisions of HR 1586:

- Provided $10 billion for a new Education Jobs Fund, which offered aid to local school districts to prevent layoffs in elementary and secondary schools.
- Required the Education Department to allocate the funds within forty-five days of the bill's enactment to states that had submitted applications for funding. If a state government had not submitted an application within thirty days of enactment, the department could award funding directly to other agencies in the state.
- Stipulated that the funding could be used only for compensation, benefits, and other expenses directly related to retaining existing employees, recalling or rehiring former employees, or hiring new employees.
- Required that states receiving the funding maintain spending for education in fiscal 2011 at a level that was at least equal to spending for fiscal 2008 or, alternatively, allocate the same percentage of the overall state budget to education as they did in fiscal 2010.

Race to the Top

Included in the American Recovery and Reinvestment Act of 2009 (HR 1—PL 111-5), which President Barack Obama signed into law on February 17, 2009, was $4.4 billion for Race to the Top, a competitive grant program seeking to encourage and reward states that put forth proposals that best promised to accomplish four central goals: raising academic standards, improving data systems to measure student achievement and guide educators, ensuring teacher and principal quality, and turning around the lowest-performing schools.

The grants were made in two phases. Phase 1 applications were due on January 19, 2010; Phase 2, on June 1. States not ready to apply in time for the Phase 1 deadline could apply in Phase 2. Phase 1 awards were announced in April. States applying in Phase 1 that were not awarded a grant could reapply in Phase 2. Those states receiving grants in Phase 1 could not reapply for additional funds in Phase 2. Phase 2 awards were announced in September. All together, eighteen states and the District of Columbia were awarded Race to the Top grants in 2010.

Before the first applications were due, states began working to make themselves into attractive grant candidates. Several, for example, lifted caps on the number of permitted charter schools or eliminated barriers to using student performance data for teacher and principal evaluations. Such actions were evidence to Race to the Top supporters that the lure of federal money could be used to foster a healthy rivalry among states and successfully prod them into making changes in education policy along the way. With tight state budgets, the program offered an irresistible prize—potentially tens of millions or hundreds of millions of dollars, depending on the size of the state. Although teachers' union leaders were somewhat skeptical about the emphasis on competition, they were generally positive about the goals of the grant program.

During House floor consideration of a fiscal 2010 supplemental appropriations bill (HR 4899—PL 111-212) devoted primarily to paying for military operations in Iraq and Afghanistan, House Appropriations Committee Chair David R. Obey, D-Wis., offered and won approval of an amendment that included funding to enable school districts to avoid laying off teachers in the coming school year and to cover a shortfall in Pell grants for low-income students, among other things. To offset the added spending, Obey proposed rescinding $800 million in previously appropriated funds for education overhaul programs, including Race to the Top. The White House issued a statement expressing support for the extra funding for teachers and for Pell grants but warned of a potential veto if the proposed rescissions remained in the bill. A group of thirteen senators, led by Evan Bayh, D-Ind., sent a letter to Senate Appropriations Committee Chair Daniel K. Inouye, D-Hawaii, opposing the proposed rescissions. The full Senate refused to accept the domestic spending amendment added by the House, and the final bill did not contain the Obey language. *(War supplemental, p. 138)*

A 2011 assessment of Race to the Top by the Education Department found mixed results. *(112th Congress action, p. 492)*

D.C. School Vouchers

Congress, in omnibus fiscal 2009 appropriations legislation (HR 1105) that the president signed into law (PL 111-8) on March 11, 2009, required that the District of Columbia school voucher program be reauthorized by Congress and approved by the D.C. government to receive federal funding after the 2009–2010 academic year. As part of the omnibus fiscal 2010 appropriations bill (HR 3288) signed into law (PL 111-117) on December 16, 2009, Congress continued funding for the D.C. voucher program for private schools, but only for students already enrolled in the program and with new testing and evaluation requirements. *(HR 1105, p. 119; HR 3288, p. 127)*

In response to the District of Columbia's chronically underperforming public schools, Congress in 2003, in authorizing subsidies for low-income students in D.C. to attend private schools, created the nation's first federally funded private school voucher program (PL 108-199). The effort was conceived by congressional Republicans with the hope of turning the nation's capital into a laboratory for vouchers, which they believed would force public schools to compete for students and improve their academic performance. Democrats, however, tended to oppose taxpayer-funded vouchers, believing that voucher programs drained resources from already underfunded public schools. *(PL 108-199, Congress and the Nation Vol. XI, p. 549)*

Democrats contended that D.C.'s program was flawed by a lack of accountability at some of the schools that enrolled voucher recipients. Concerns were raised about hundreds of unaccounted-for vouchers and about inadequate safety inspections and teachers lacking college degrees. Voucher advocates and D.C. program supporters, meanwhile, saw the hand of one of the Democratic Party's most powerful interest groups at work—teachers' unions—and pointed to modest improvements in reading scores among voucher recipients as evidence that the program showed results. They maintained that concerns about how the program was administered were merely a pretext for eliminating the program altogether. The National Education Association and congressional Democrats were unimpressed by the evidence of improved reading, which they said was not seen in the lowest-achieving students from the worst schools. *(112th Congress action, p. 490)*

College Savings Accounts

By voice vote on April 20, 2010, the House agreed to suspend the rules and pass HR 4178, aimed at spurring contributions to college savings accounts by giving federal guarantees for cash deposits. The Deposit Restricted Qualified Tuition Program Act of 2010 would add a new option for contributing to tax-advantaged higher education savings accounts, known as Section 529 plans. The bill would allow the Federal Deposit Insurance Corporation (FDIC) to insure up to $250,000 in deposit-based college accounts.

Under existing law, the majority of 529 plans are security-based plans, with assets typically held in bonds and stock, and are not insured by the FDIC. As with asset-based accounts, cash contributions to deposit-based savings plans could be tax-exempt at the state level.

Bill sponsor Emanuel Cleaver II, D-Mo., said many families saw substantial declines in the value of their plans in the recession and were wary of putting more money into them.

The General Accountability Office (GAO) in 2012 issued an assessment of the program. *(GAO report, box, p. 487)*

Student Punishment

In 2010, the House took up legislation (HR 4247) that would for the first time set minimum federal standards for certain kinds of punishments in school. The Keep All Students Safe Act would allow restraints in some cases, such as when students or others are in danger. The legislation was intended for any school that accepted federal money—public, parochial, or private.

A May 2009 Government Accountability Office (GAO) report found hundreds of cases in which a student allegedly had been abused by an inappropriate use of seclusion or restraint, including some that had ended in death. The GAO report found that the practices were used disproportionately on students with disabilities. In half of the cases studied by the GAO, the school staff involved with the alleged abuse had continued working.

The House Education and Labor Committee approved HR 4247 by 34–10, with five Republicans joining all Democrats in voting for the measure, on February 4, 2010. The legislation was formally reported (H Rept 111-417) on February 23. Committee Chair and bill sponsor George Miller, D-Calif., had requested the GAO report.

Among the supporters of HR 4247 were the American Academy of Pediatrics and the American Federation of Teachers. Furthermore, widespread agreement existed that the practices targeted by the bill—physical restraint or seclusion of students in nonemergency situations, as well as the use of chemicals, without a doctor's prescription, to subdue a child—should be outlawed. Some specialized schools use such methods with students who have severe behavioral problems but usually within a program approved by the child's guardian and medical professionals and typically in emergency situations. The bill would provide exceptions for such cases.

Many Republicans said that the legislation had good intentions but amounted to an unnecessary expansion of federal power based on minimal research. They argued that the Department of Education had not regularly collected data on the use of restraint techniques in schools. Opponents of the legislation, including religious conservatives and advocates for private schools, objected that for the first time, federal rules would be imposed on private schools that had not entered into any agreement with the government. That is, they would be subject to regulation because the students they admitted were eligible for federal subsidies. Opponents also feared that HR 4247 was a slippery slope to future legislation that would require more intrusive rules, limiting the scope of the curriculum diversity that they said made private education desirable.

On March 3, 2010, the House passed HR 4247 by a 262–153 vote. As passed, the bill would direct the Department of Education to set standards that would prevent the use of mechanical, chemical, or physical restraints on students except in certain cases, such as when there was immediate danger to the student or others. It also would require that a sufficient number of school personnel be trained in crisis intervention and require schools to report use of restraint or seclusion to the student's parents on the day of the incident. Each state would be required to submit a plan within two years to show that its policies and procedures met the Department of Education's standards. States that failed to meet the standards could lose federal funding. The Education Department could award three-year grants to state educational agencies to help meet the department's standards. The bill would not affect either private schools that were not receiving federal funds or parents who home-schooled their children.

A companion measure (S 2860), sponsored by Christopher J. Dodd, D-Conn., was introduced in the Senate and was referred to the Senate Committee on Health, Education, Labor, and Pensions. It saw no further action.

College Campus Fire Safety

The House agreed by voice vote on May 19, 2010, to suspend the rules and pass HR 2136, which would establish a Department of Education program to provide grants to colleges to install sprinkler systems and other fire prevention technology in student housing. HR 2136 and a Senate companion measure (S 1791) were dubbed the Honorable Stephanie Tubbs Jones College Fire Prevention Act, named in honor of the late representative Stephanie Tubbs Jones, D-Ohio, who sponsored similar legislation in several Congresses before her death in 2008.

HR 2136, sponsored by Rep. Marcia L. Fudge, D-Ohio, would require recipients to provide an equal match on funds and to cap administrative expenses at 2 percent. It would set aside 10 percent of the funds annually for historically black schools, Hispanic-serving institutions, and tribally controlled colleges and universities serving Alaska Native and Native Hawaiian populations. Another 10 percent would be set aside for fraternities and sororities.

S 1791, sponsored by Sen. Sherrod Brown, D-Ohio, was referred to the Senate Health, Education, Labor, and Pensions Committee. It saw no further action.

2011–2012

The 112th Congress got little traction in its attempts to reauthorize the No Child Left Behind Act, a law that members along the entire political spectrum agreed needed changing. Lawmakers did roll back a scheduled student loan interest rate increase, authorize funding for a federal school voucher program in the District of Columbia, and keep the budget ax from falling heavily on the Pell grant program.

Elementary and Secondary Education Act

Efforts stalled to reauthorize the 2002 law (PL 107-110) dubbed the No Child Left Behind Act, which overhauled the 1965 Elementary and Secondary Education Act (ESEA; PL 89-10) and launched an ambitious effort to make schools accountable by requiring states to test student progress in reading, math, and science and to implement penalties for schools that did not meet specific targets. *(No Child Left Behind Act, Congress and the Nation Vol. XI, p. 540; 1965 law, Congress and the Nation Vol. II, p. 720)*

Discontent arose in the states, which charged that the law was too focused on punishing schools that did not meet testing goals and set an unrealistic target of 100 percent student proficiency by 2014. In July 2007, George Miller, D-Calif., then chair of the House Education and the Workforce Committee, announced that he intended to move a bill "making serious changes" to the law out of his committee and onto the House floor by September, when it would formally expire. But, when his panel released a four-hundred-page draft in August, Republicans argued that it moved too far away from standardized testing, and Democrats assailed the inclusion of grants to allow merit pay for teachers. The reauthorization date came and went, without progress.

The majority of complaints stemmed from the law's accountability system, which required states to meet a minimum level of proficiency, known as Adequate Yearly Progress (AYP), or else face sanctions. While education leaders widely praised the system's use of disaggregated data to identify gaps in achievement across student subgroups, such as children with limited English proficiency or disabilities, they criticized the formula that labeled a school as failing if it missed AYP in just one subgroup. According to the Education Department, one-third of the nation's schools did not make AYP in 2009. Schools with the fewest resources often were the ones facing penalties. For the most part, school officials were in consensus that the AYP system was not workable and presented a burden for states. More broadly, critics said that the law was too complicated, too restrictive, and destructive of academic achievement and morale.

Although everyone across the political spectrum seemed to want to change No Child Left Behind, no agreement emerged on an alternative. And, although leaders of both parties found common ground on a number of matters central to reworking the law—for example, replacing the AYP accountability system with a system that incorporated student growth, revamping teacher training and evaluation procedures, and giving states more flexibility to spend federal dollars—the law had become entangled with the larger ideological debate between the two parties over the role the federal government should play in overseeing elementary and secondary education.

Congress, however, considered several bills that sought to fix problems with the law in a piecemeal fashion. The four bills (HR 2445, HR 1891, HR 3989, HR 3990) were reported from the House Education and the Workforce Committee, and a draft bill (no number) emerged from the Senate Health, Education, Labor, and Pensions Committee. None of these measures saw further action. The full House did pass, in 2012, legislation (HR 2218) addressing charter schools. *(Charter schools, p. 491)*

HR 2445

HR 2445, approved 23–17 on July 13, 2011, by the House Education and Workforce Committee and formally reported (H Rept 112-180) on July 25, would provide states and school districts greater flexibility in how they use federal dollars, allowing them, for example, to shift funds governed by ESEA, including Title I grants for disadvantaged children, to programs they believed would boost student performance.

Democratic lawmakers and the Obama administration contended that the State and Local Funding Flexibility Act would result in districts shifting money away from low-income and minority students and English-language learners, undermining the intent of the 1965 law, which originated as part of the civil rights movement. Republicans said the measure would allow officials to direct money to the most effective programs and that administrators still would have to comply with civil rights requirements.

HR 1891

On June 14, 2011, the House Education and the Workforce Committee reported legislation (HR 1891—H Rept 112-106) that would repeal authorization for more than forty federal education programs—about half the programs under ESEA. Among those slated for the chopping block were at least a half-dozen literacy programs, including Even Start, which focuses on adult and family literacy. The committee had approved the bill on May 25 along party lines, 23–16. The Setting New Priorities in Education Spending Act sought to end programs that Republicans considered inefficient or ineffective. In their unified opposition, Democrats said that the bill would eliminate programs only for the sake of making cuts and without evaluating the effect their loss would have on students.

During markup, panel members offered more than a half-dozen amendments to preserve programs or services targeted for elimination, but only one of them was adopted. That proposal, sponsored by Todd R. Platts, R-Pa., would eliminate the bill's attempt to repeal the authorization for parental assistance and local family information centers. It was adopted by a vote of 20–19, with unanimous Democratic support and four Republicans crossing party lines to back it. Democrats offered several amendments to allow an expanded use of funds for certain categories of services targeted under the GOP plan, including literacy activities, counseling, and the development of teacher standards, instead of protecting specific programs.

HR 3989

HR 3989, approved by the House Education and the Workforce Committee by a vote of 23–16 on February 28, 2012, would eliminate the unpopular school accountability system AYP. The bill was formally reported (H Rept 112-458) on April 27.

The Student Success Act would not replace the federal system but would instead allow the states to develop their own school accountability standards. Democrats said that that would roll back decades of progress and be especially hurtful to low-income and minority students.

The measure also would scrap federal intervention requirements for low-performing schools and call on states to create their own requirements. Republicans argued that the existing models were too prescriptive, especially for rural school districts that had a difficult time recruiting teachers and principals.

Support for disadvantaged schools was a central element in winning Democrats' support for No Child Left Behind. "Access to a quality education is fundamental. . . . That's why Congress wrote Title I, to level the playing field," said Lynn Woolsey, D-Calif., referring to the funding that went to schools with high numbers or percentages of children from low-income families. HR 3989, she said, "guts these intentions and presumes that we no longer need to set aside funding for the least fortunate."

The committee gave voice-vote approval to a substitute amendment, offered by Chair John Kline, R-Minn., that would require states to set aside 3 percent of Title I money to provide competitive grants to school districts that wished to offer tutoring or public school choice to their students, including those in poor performing schools. The panel rejected, 16–23, an amendment by George Miller, the ranking Democrat, to maintain the law's requirements that states have standards and assessments for science and to require educational agencies to adopt college and college-ready standards. The amendment also sought to eliminate the GOP "funding flexibility" provisions that would allow funding for certain special-population programs to be spent in other areas.

HR 3990

On February 28, 2012, the House Education and the Workforce Committee, by a vote of 23–16, approved HR 3990, the Encouraging Innovation and Effective Teachers Act, which would require states to implement teacher evaluation systems based party on student test scores. The panel formally reported the bill (H Rept 112-459, Part 1) on April 27.

HR 3990 would require school districts to create their own evaluation systems within specific parameters. It also would consolidate teacher training programs into one block grant that states could use for a variety of teacher-focused initiatives, such as the implementation of performance-based pay systems. The legislation would eliminate more than seventy federal education programs, many of which had never been funded, and expand charter schools.

A substitute by Kline, approved by voice vote, would create an optional state set-aside of up to 3 percent so that states could award grants to go toward teacher or school leader preparation academies.

SENATE COMMITTEE ACTION

The Senate Health, Education, Labor, and Pensions Committee on October 20, 2011, approved a draft bill that would remove from existing law the much-criticized accountability system requiring all students to be proficient in math and reading by 2014 and instead would require states to adopt college and college-ready standards and develop accountability standards to receive federal funding. Three Republicans joined the Democrats in support of the legislation, 15–7.

Before the panel could begin marking up the proposal, Chair Tom Harkin, D-Iowa, and ranking member Michael B. Enzi, R-Wyo., had to reach an agreement to accommodate the concerns of Rand Paul, R-Ky., about the reauthorization process. Paul, who opposed all federal involvement in education, had employed a rarely used procedural tactic that would have forced the abandonment of the markup. He invoked a Senate rule that barred committees from meeting without unanimous consent beyond the first two hours of the chamber's day. On October 19, the committee met and worked through four of the 144 amendments filed before panel members received word that Paul was withholding consent, thereby stalling the markup. Paul was set to invoke the same rule the following day before reaching agreement with panel leaders. Under the agreement, the committee would hold an additional hearing before the bill reached the floor.

Paul offered an amendment that would repeal the No Child Left Behind Act and require federal education law to be implemented as if that legislation had never been enacted. The amendment was defeated 3–17. Also rejected was an amendment by Bernard Sanders, I-Vt., to require districts receiving aid under the bill to ensure that all teachers who had not completed preparation and obtained full state certification were closely monitored and overseen by a mentor teacher who had the proper credentials. The vote was 3–18.

The committee also spent considerable time debating an amendment offered by Lamar Alexander, R-Tenn., to address school intervention strategies. Under existing law, school districts must implement one of a handful of options in chronically failing schools that had been identified for restructuring. A major criticism of this system was that the law included an "other" option, which allowed districts to implement an intervention that they thought was suitable, often resulting in little change at struggling schools. The draft bill, in contrast, would require districts to implement one of six specified school improvement strategies for the bottom 5 percent of schools, with additional flexibility for rural schools. Under the Alexander amendment, states would be allowed to establish alternative school improvement strategies, with the education secretary's approval, for districts to select. Although several members voiced support for the amendment, arguing that it would provide additional flexibility, Harkin countered that up to 75 percent of schools chose the "other" option under current law, and he expressed concern about whether the state alternative would be rigorous and based on evidence. Despite Harkin's objections, the panel adopted the amendment 15–7. It was favored by the National Education Association, the nation's largest teachers' union.

ADMINISTRATION ACTION

In 2012, President Barack Obama announced that because Congress had not been able to rewrite No Child Left Behind, he would offer states relief from the law's most troublesome mandates, such as the requirement that all students be proficient in math and reading by 2014. In exchange, states would agree to make policy changes that meet goals along the lines of Obama's Race to the Top schools program. *(Race to the Top, pp. 480, 492)*

Federal Student Loans

Students and their families got a one-year reprieve from a scheduled increase in student loan interest rates as part of HR 4348, signed into law (PL 112-141) on July 6, 2012. The legislation extended the existing 3.4 percent rate through June 2013. Without congressional action, the rate would have reverted to 6.8 percent on July 1, 2012, affecting an estimated 7.4 million students with subsidized Stafford loans made to undergraduate students.

The interest rate fix was attached to a surface transportation authorization bill, know as Moving Ahead for Progress in the 21st Century Act or MAP-21. The House passed HR 4348 by 293–127 on April 18, 2012. The Senate passed an amended version by voice vote on April 24. The House agreed to the conference report (H Rept 112-557) by 373–52 on June 29, and the Senate followed suit by 74–19 on June 29, clearing the measure. *(Highway reauthorization, p. 340)*

President Barack Obama called for extending the student loan interest rate, which was enacted in 2007 (PL 110-84). According to the Education Department, for each year that Congress allowed the higher rate, the average student would pay an additional $1,000 in interest. Republicans initially resisted taking action, calling the idea a campaign ploy that would delay the problem a few more years. They argued that the interest rate break was never meant to be permanent. They also were emphatic that reducing the cost of college could not be accomplished solely at the federal level. They said increasing federal loans and grants allowed colleges to hike tuition because it put no pressure on them to lower costs. However, Republicans shifted their stance after 2012 GOP presidential candidate Mitt Romney agreed that Congress should keep the interest rate low. *(PL 110-84, Congress and the Nation Vol. XII, p. 612)*

The House April 27, 2012, on a **key vote of 215–195 (R 202–30; D 13–165,)** passed a bill (HR 4628) to extend the student loan interest rate break and to cover the approximately $6 billion cost by eliminating a fund in the 2010 health care overhaul (PL 111-148, PL 111-152) dedicated to prevention and public health. The Congressional Budget Office on April 26 had estimated a savings of $12 billion over ten years if the health care fund were repealed. House minority leader Nancy Pelosi, D-Calif., called the offset "an assault on women's health," noting that the fund covered breast and cervical cancer screenings, child immunizations, and initiatives to fight birth defects. Republicans countered that their proposed offset was reasonable and said that Democrats supported pulling $5 billion from the prevention fund earlier in 2012 to help pay for legislation (HR 3765—PL 112-78) to extend the payroll tax holiday and prevent a cut in Medicare payments to physicians. Speaker John A. Boehner, R-Ohio, called the health care fund a "slush fund." HR 4628, the Interest Rate Reduction Act, received only thirteen Democratic votes; all but thirty Republicans voted for it. The White House issued a veto threat on the measure because of the offset language. *(2012 key votes, p. 803; health care overhaul, p. 481; payroll tax cut, pp. 79, 108)*

In a party-line vote on May 8, 2012, the Senate voted 52–45 on a cloture motion, filed by Senate Majority Leader Harry Reid, D-Nev., to proceed to consideration of the Democrats' Stop the Student Loan Interest Rate Hike Act of 2012 (S 2343), which would extend the existing interest rate for one year and offset the cost by applying the 15.3 percent combined payroll tax on certain income earned by small businesses organized as S corporations that passed net income, losses, deductions, and credits through to shareholders for federal tax purposes. The tally fell short of the sixty votes needed to cut off debate. Reid switched his vote at the last minute to the prevailing side to preserve the right to reconsider the motion. Republicans were on board with the rate extension but objected to the corporate tax offset. The administration supported the legislation as one alternative but said that other options existed.

The Senate on May 24 turned back Democratic and Republican proposals to extend the interest rate break. Neither plan garnered the sixty affirmative votes needed to advance under a bipartisan agreement. The Senate first rejected, 34–62, a GOP-favored amendment to S 2343 to offset the cost by eliminating the preventive health care fund in the health care law. Ten Republicans voted "nay," along with a unified Democratic caucus. The amendment language matched that in other GOP-sponsored legislation (HR 4628, S 2366, also dubbed the Interest Rate Reduction Act). The Senate then rejected the Democratic-supported S 2343, which called for eliminating a tax preference for S corporations, on a near party-line 51–43 vote. Republicans said that ending the preference amounted to a tax increase on small business owners.

After days of political back-and-forth from key actors in the dispute, including the president, Senate Majority Leader Reid on June 7 advanced a possible solution to funding legislation that would preserve lower interest rates on federal student loans. In a letter to GOP leaders, he outlined two pension-related changes to cover the cost. The first would expand a change to employer pension funding contributions, generating approximately $9.5 billion, that the Senate had overwhelmingly endorsed in March 2012 as a way to offset part of the cost of its surface transportation bill. The second would increase the premiums paid by employers for the insurance provided by the Pension Benefit Guaranty Corp. (PBGC) to generate up to $8 billion. Spokespeople for Senate Minority Leader Mitch McConnell, R-Ky., and Speaker Boehner did not dismiss Reid's overture, indicating that agreement on an offset might be reached.

The first proposal would create a "stabilization range" for employers to compute their pension liabilities, similar to a provision in the Senate highway bill (S 1813), which passed 74–22 on March 14, 2012. Businesses would not have to put as much money into their defined benefit pension plans, freeing up more money to invest in their businesses and thus increasing their tax bills. Reid said there "has been bipartisan support" for this second proposal—increasing premiums paid by employers for the insurance provided by the PBGC. Employers were paying a flat-dollar premium of $35 per pension plan participant, as well as a variable premium equal to $9 for each $1,000 that the plan was underfunded.

The logjam was broken by a compromise reached by Reid and McConnell that paid for the one-year interest rate extension with the two pension-related changes proposed by Reid as well as a Republican proposal to cut the cost by reducing the amount of time that a student is eligible for an in-school interest subsidy. The idea of combining the deal with the transportation bill (HR 4348) grew out of the fact that the planned offsets exceeded the cost of the student loan extension and could help pay for the highway reauthorization.

In related action, S 365, signed into law (PL 112-25) on August 2, 2011, eliminated beginning on July 1, 2012, the ability of graduate and professional students to take out subsidized Stafford loans while they were in school, unless enrolled in a program leading up to a degree or certificate or a program necessary for a teaching credential. Furthermore, the Budget Control Act of 2011 provided that the current annual and cumulative loan limits for unsubsidized loans would be adjusted to permit students to borrow additional money in an unsubsidized loan program. The new law sunset the Education Department's authority to provide incentive payments for on-time repayment of student loans disbursed on or after July 1, 2012. It also explicitly prohibited the department from creating any incentives for on-time repayment of student loans. *(Budget Control Act of 2011, p. 160)*

Pell Grants

According to education experts, in the ongoing debate about debt reduction, the large increases required to sustain the Pell grant program for low-income college students made it particularly vulnerable. The Pell grant program is one of the federal government's largest education initiatives and was one of President Barack Obama's priorities. The program faced a shortfall each year because it was sustained only partly through mandatory spending. The rest of the money was subject to annual appropriations that usually did not fill the gap. With the difficult state of the economy, more people were qualifying for the grant and were going back to school to earn degrees, leaving the program strapped for cash.

At a June 29, 2011, news conference, Obama stressed the need to find "balanced" solutions to the government's fiscal woes that would protect priorities such as college scholarships. "Before we cut our children's education . . . I think it's only fair to ask an oil company or a corporate jet owner that has done so well to give up that tax break that no other business enjoys," he said. "If we do not have revenues, that means there are a bunch of kids out there who are not getting college scholarships."

But some Republicans said the program as structured was unsustainable. "Pell grants are the perfect example of promises that cannot be kept," House Budget Committee Chair Paul D. Ryan, R-Wis., wrote in his fiscal 2012 budget plan (H Con Res 34), which proposed restructuring the program and cutting it by $6 billion. Ryan's plan would overhaul the program, capping students' use of the grant at six years instead of nine. It also would shrink the number of eligible students by changing the aid formula to target only the neediest, instituting a maximum family income cap for eligibility in lieu of the existing formula, which was based on income as well as other factors, among them assets and household size, and eliminating eligibility for students enrolled less than half time.

529 PLANS FOR COLLEGE SAVINGS

The General Accountability Office (GAO) on December 12, 2012, issued a report on the college savings investment program known as 529 plans, concluding that they failed to spur much savings—except among relatively wealthy households. 529s got their name from section 529 of the Internal Revenue Code, which authorized state qualified tuition programs. *(111th Congress action, p. 481)*

Investments in 529 plans, which were managed by the states, grow tax-free as long as the money was used to pay for college. That resulted in a federal revenue loss of $1.6 billion in fiscal 2011.

When Congress created the program in 1996, via the Small Business Job Protection Act (PL 104-188), and expanded it in 2001, in the Economic Growth and Tax Relief Reconciliation Act of 2001 (PL 107-16), it was hoped that the plans would reduce the need for college loans. Instead, school loans grew to $914 billion, more than Americans owed to credit card companies. *(PL 104-188, Congress and the Nation Vol. IX, p. 100; PL 107-16, Congress and the Nation Vol. XI, p. 89)*

Total assets in the 529 plans were $167 billion in 2011, but tax savings were concentrated at the top of the income scale. The GAO said Federal Reserve data for 2010 showed that less than 3 percent of families had 529 plans or similar Coverdell plans. Even among families expecting to incur college costs, only 7 percent had 529 investments. Those who did had household assets worth $413,500 on average, about twenty-five times the national norm, and an average income of $142,400, compared with the median of $45,100.

The tax benefits of 529 savings also went overwhelmingly to the well-off. Those with incomes of $100,000 or less saw median savings of $561. By contrast, families with incomes higher than $150,000 got $3,132.

Many states and the District of Columbia also offered tax breaks to people who contributed to their college plans. For example, District residents could deduct up to $4,000 from their incomes when they calculate their local taxes if they put that much in the city's 529 plan.

The GAO said that lower-income families faced several barriers to using the plans. They had less disposable income to put aside, and they might not save because they overestimated the availability of financial aid, especially grants and scholarships. GAO found that most aid packages were not generous enough to pay for college without loans and a contribution from parents.

Chad Aldeman, senior policy analyst at Bellwether Educations partners, a nonprofit group that helped low-income students perform better in school, and former policy adviser to the Education Department, said Congress should consider eliminating the tax-preferred accounts and use the savings to send low-income students to college. By his calculation, the money lost to the tax break could pay for an additional 288,000 Pell grants.

Jon S. Fansmith, associate director of government relations at the American Council of Education, which represents the presidents and chancellors of accredited colleges and universities, responded to Ryan's proposal by saying, "Cuts for the max award is just the worst kind of policy. The people who are most impacted by that are people with the most need. For them, even $500 means everything."

The House passed H Con Res 34 on March 29, 2012, but the Senate on May 16 rejected a motion to invoke cloture and proceed to consideration of the measure, ending congressional action.

The fiscal 2011 omnibus appropriations legislation (HR 1473) provided $23 billion for Pell grants and maintained the maximum Pell grant for award year 2011–2012 at $5,550. It eliminated a program that allowed students to receive up to two Pell grants a year if they went to school year-round, a cut also proposed in the president's 2012 budget. HR 1473 was signed into law (PL 112-10) on April 15, 2011. *(Fiscal 2011 omnibus spending bill, p. 150)*

The fiscal 2012 omnibus spending measure (HR 2055) set the maximum Pell grant for which a student could be eligible during award year 2012–2013 at $4,860, and it changed some eligibility requirements to help pay for it. It lowered the income level that qualified a student to receive the maximum grant from $30,000 to $23,000; required a high school diploma or equivalent to receive a grant; limited grants to a maximum of twelve semesters, down from eighteen; and slightly adjusted the minimum award. The bill, which was signed into law (PL 112-74) on December 23, 2011, also temporarily eliminated the six-month grace period for new federal Stafford loans. *(Fiscal 2012 omnibus spending bill, p. 172)*

A fiscal 2013 continuing resolution (H J Res 117) funded federal education programs at fiscal 2012 levels through March 27, 2013. The legislation was signed into law (PL 112-175) on September 28, 2012. *(Fiscal 2013 continuing resolution, p. 180)*

Student Aid Rules

On February 28, 2012, the House by a vote of 303–114, passed HR 2117, which would rescind regulations that were part of a larger package of Education Department provisions designed to provide greater accountability for federal student aid spending under the Higher Education Act (PL 89-329). Under the 1965 law, colleges and universities that participated in federal student aid programs must be authorized to provide postsecondary education programs within the states where they were located. The law required aid to be distributed based on credit hours. HR 2117, the Protecting Academic Freedom in Higher Education Act, would rescind the Education Department's regulation defining credit hours and its rules on granting a college or university permission to operate within a state. *(PL 89-329, Congress and the Nation Vol. II, p. 716)*

Bill sponsor Virginia Foxx, R-N.C., said the regulations added several federal criteria to existing state authorization processes, which would complicate matters for academic institutions and add to the burdens of state governments. Proponents also said that the state authorization regulation could affect institutions' decisions to offer online education programs in some areas.

NEW RULES FOR FOR-PROFIT CAREER COLLEGES

Department of Education rules, effective on July 1, 2012, took aim at for-profit career colleges and certificate programs. The new rules were part of the federal government's crackdown on for-profit schools that promised more than they delivered and encouraged their students to take on unmanageable debt.

The final regulations, as explained in a Department of Education announcement on June 2, 2011, would require that occupational training programs, particularly for-profit career colleges, better prepare students for "gainful employment in a recognized occupation" or risk losing access to federal student aid. A program could claim it led to gainful employment if it met at least one of three conditions: "at least 35 percent of former students are repaying their loans (defined as reducing the loan balance by at least $1); the estimated annual loan payment of a typical graduate does not exceed 30 percent of his or her discretionary income; or the estimated annual loan payment of a typical graduate does not exceed 12 percent of his or her total earnings."

For-profit colleges waged a long campaign against the proposed regulations. The rules had another facet, though, that affected traditional colleges and universities, too. Those that recruited or taught students in other states through distance-learning programs had to show that they were authorized to operate in those states. If they could not, their online students would not be eligible for federal student aid. The Education Department rules on distance learning were designed to ensure proper state oversight of the for-profit colleges and trade schools, but they affected all schools. The House in 2012 moved to rescind these rules. *(Student aid rules, p. 487)*

Career colleges were familiar by their brand names, such as the University of Phoenix, Kaplan, DeVry University, and the ITT Technical Institute, as well as by their ticker symbols, such as APOL, for The Apollo Group, the parent company of the University of Phoenix. Typically, career-college campuses were satellite programs of larger parent companies that offered career-oriented certificates or degree programs, such as accounting, allied medical, and automotive technology.

Career colleges were a huge growth industry. By 2009, they enrolled more than three million students, representing more than 10 percent of the total market. Enrollment more than tripled in a decade, when the business of education underwent enormous change, with more emphasis on vocational programs. The downturn in the economy further pushed students who might have enrolled in traditional four-year institutions into career-oriented degree programs. However, according to a July 30, 2012, Senate Health, Education, Labor, and Pensions Committee report, growth was not confined to trade schools. The number of associate degrees conferred by for-profit schools increased by 77 percent and the number of bachelor's degrees awarded increased by 136 percent from 2004 to 2010.

The same report noted that, in 2010, the for-profit colleges included in the committee's investigation employed 35,202 recruiters but only 3,512 career service staff and 12,452 support service staff, an indication of their priorities. These schools were heavily dependent on tuition via federal loans, receiving $32 billion in 2009–2010—25 percent of the Education Department student aid program funds. Meanwhile, their students accounted for 47 percent of all federal student loan defaults. More than half a million students who were enrolled in a for-profit school certificate or degree program in 2008–2009 (of 54 percent of the total) left before finishing in mid-2010, and almost 300,000 two-year associate degree program enrollees (63 percent of total) had dropped out. The Senate committee report also said that, according to a National Center for Educational Statistics study, 23 percent of attendees of for-profit schools in 2008–2009 were unemployed.

The Education Department regulations were a response to numerous reports showing that some of these schools were looking out for their shareholders at the expense of students and taxpayers. For-profit colleges were shown to use deceptive come-ons to lure students, engage in a pattern of college personnel encouraging students to falsify financial aid forms, use high-pressure sales tactics, and make false claims about how much money students would earn and the sorts of jobs they could get.

Rep. George Miller, D-Calif., ranking minority member of the House Education and the Workforce Committee, said that the Education Department promulgated rules defining credit hour in response to its inspector general's findings that some higher education institutions were awarding more credits to get more student financial aid. Opponents said the regulations closed a loophole that could put taxpayer dollars at risk of waste, fraud, and abuse. Establishing a standard definition of a credit hour would ensure federal student aid is dispersed appropriately, they said, because the aid is awarded on the basis of credit hours.

The Education and the Workforce Committee approved HR 2117 by 27–11 on June 15, 2011, and formally reported it (H Rept 112-177) on July 22. The Senate took no action on the legislation.

New rules affecting for-profit career colleges were also part of the Education Department regulations package. *(Box, p. 488)*

Immigrant Student Visas

On a **key vote of 245–139 (R 218–5; D 27–134)**, the House on November 30, 2012, passed legislation (HR 6429) that would expand visa opportunities for skilled immigrant students. The bill would abolish the Diversity Visa Program, which allocated 55,000 permanent residency visas by lottery, and would redirect those visas to foreign graduates of U.S. universities with doctoral or master's degrees in science, technology, engineering, and math—known as the STEM fields—who committed to working in the United States for at least five years. Bill sponsor Rep. Lamar Smith, R-Texas, touted the legislation as a way to bolster employment. Democrats, however, said the STEM Jobs Act of 2012 did not do enough to address comprehensive immigration issues. *(2012 key votes, p. 803)*

The House had rejected HR 6429 on September 20, 2012, by 257–158 under suspension of the rules, which requires a two-thirds majority vote (277 in this case). The chamber's action followed a long and, at times, acrimonious effort to craft compromise legislation to loosen immigration laws. Under existing law, there was no specific immigration program or visa type for graduates in the specified fields, and many students waited several years before they were able to obtain permanent resident status. The business community, immigration advocates, and technology groups said that the system drove skilled foreign students back to their home countries. Many urged Congress to streamline a path to legal status. Although lawmakers generally agreed on the need for the STEM visas, bipartisan negotiations became embroiled in a broader immigration debate.

When the motion to pass HR 6429 under suspension of the rules was rejected, Democrats objected to the bill's elimination of the lottery and criticized the measure for not providing a path by which the family members of STEM graduates could obtain legal status. The House-passed version of HR 6429 retained language to eliminate the lottery but included provisions that would make it easier for family members to move to the United States while they awaited their own green cards. Under existing law, relatives of legal permanent residents had to wait for green cards in their home countries for up to two years. In the House-approved version of the legislation, spouses and children would have to wait one year. They would still be prohibited from working while they waited for green cards.

Many conservatives had called for abolishing the diversity program to control the number of new immigrants, saying the program invited fraud and posed a security risk. However, Democrats generally opposed eliminating diversity visas, which they said attracted immigrants from countries that otherwise might not send students to America. The Congressional Hispanic Caucus, Congressional Black Caucus, and Congressional Asian Pacific American Caucus joined in a "Dear Colleague" letter urging members to oppose HR 6429.

Rep. Zoe Lofgren of California, ranking Democrat on the House Judiciary Subcommittee on Immigration Policy and Enforcement, introduced HR 6412, the Attracting the Best and Brightest Act of 2012. It would grant 50,000 newly created green cards to STEM graduates while leaving the diversity visa program intact. Sen. Charles E. Schumer, D-N.Y., introduced the Benefits to Research and American Innovation through Nationality Statutes Act of 2012 or the BRAINS Act (S 3553), which was similar to Lofgren's. Neither bill emerged from committee.

Student Visa Mills

Under HR 3120, which the House passed by voice vote under suspension of the rules on August 1, 2012, academic institutions, including colleges, universities, and primary and secondary schools, would have to be fully accredited by an agency recognized by the Department of Education before admitting international students on what are known as F visas—a type of nonimmigrant student visa that allows international students to study in the United States. The House Judiciary Committee had reported the Student Visa Reform Act (H Rept 112-595) on July 12, 2012.

Under existing law, only English-language training programs that admitted foreign students on F visas had to be accredited. HR 3120 would permit the secretary of homeland security to waive accreditation requirements for a school that was otherwise in compliance with F visa standards and that made a good-faith effort to meet the requirements.

Bill sponsor Zoe Lofgren, D-Calif., said during floor debate on July 31 that the bill would stanch a trend known as "visa mills," in which illegitimate training organizations recruit foreign students, charge sizable fees, and provide unsubstantiated degrees. The proposed accreditation requirements would prevent illegitimate institutions from cheating students who legitimately wanted an education in the United States, she said. The bill was endorsed by House Judiciary Committee chairman Lamar Smith, R-Texas.

PHYSICAL EDUCATION REPORT, LEGISLATION

On February 29, 2012, the General Accountability Office (GAO) issued its first-ever report on school-based physical education (PE) and sports programs, which was requested by Senate Health, Education, Labor, and Pensions Committee Chair Tom Harkin, D-Iowa, and Rep. Mike McIntyre, D-N.C.

The GAO found that, although a greater percentage of the nation's schools required students to take PE courses, the percentage of schools able to offer gym classes at least three days a week was declining. Facing the need to make budget cuts, school districts often targeted PE. The GAO study reported that the estimated percentage of schools that required PE in the ninth grade increased from 13 percent in 2000 to 55 percent in 2006. However, cuts to school sports budgets reached $1.5 billion in the 2010–2011 school year and an estimated $2 billion in the 2009–2010 school year, according to Up2Us, a coalition of youth sports organizations.

Officials from one school district that the GAO visited said it had cut instruction time because of limited funding for instructors. Some schools, such as one in which the gym doubled as the cafeteria, lacked a dedicated space for PE, and school officials reported challenges in providing extracurricular sports because tight budgets complicated existing problems with transportation, facilities, and staffing. Booster clubs and community facilities mitigated some of the problems in attracting coaches or transporting students for practices or games. Some schools charged student fees for sports, which created a barrier for lower-income students. However, many schools, GAO found, waived these fees.

As First Lady Michelle Obama's Let's Move! campaign sought to show, physical activity was one way to help prevent or reduce childhood obesity, and also had academic and social benefits. Many children, the GAO reported, did not engage in the level of physical activity recommended by the Centers for Disease Control and Prevention. "Schools," the GAO said, "are uniquely positioned to provide students opportunities to increase physical activity through physical education . . . classes and involvement in sports teams."

A number of bills were introduced in the 112th Congress that sought to promote the health and welfare of children, in part by increasing the physical activity of youth, including HR 369 (Health Savings and Affordability Act of 2011), HR 422 (To Amend the Elementary and Secondary Education Act of 1965 to Ensure That Schools Have Physical Education Programs That Meet Minimum Requirements for Physical Education), HR 481 (Complete America's Great Trails Act of 2011), HR 709 (Urban Revitalization and Livable Communities Act), HR 1057 and S 576 (FIT Kids Act), HR 1090 and S 585 (Full-Service Community Schools Act of 2011), HR 1531 (Access to Complete Education Act), and HR 1780 (Safe and Complete Streets Act of 2011). None saw floor action.

D.C. School Vouchers

The first bill (HR 471) sponsored by Rep. John A. Boehner, R-Ohio, as Speaker was passed largely along party lines, 225–195, by the House on March 30, 2011. The Scholarships for Opportunity and Results Act (SOAR Act) would restore a federal school voucher program in Washington, D.C., authorizing $20 million annually for the D.C. Opportunity Scholarship Program from fiscal 2012 to fiscal 2016. The legislation subsequently was tacked onto a fiscal 2011 omnibus appropriations bill (HR 1473), which was signed into law (PL 112-10) on April 15, 2011. *(Omnibus appropriations bill, p. 150)*

The White House, teachers' unions, and D.C. officials opposed the voucher language. While HR 471 would apply only to the District, it sparked the traditional debate over private school vouchers. Republicans insisted that vouchers would allow parents to send their children to the best schools and hold poorly performing schools accountable. Democrats worried they would take money away from already cash-strapped public schools.

HR 471 would revive a five-year pilot program established by a fiscal 2004 omnibus appropriations package (PL 108-199), which gave nearly one thousand vouchers to D.C. students. When the program expired in 2009, it was not reauthorized, and the Obama administration sought to phase it out. As passed by the House, HR 471 authorized funding that would go toward scholarships for low-income residents to send their children to qualified private schools, including religious institutions. It also would authorize an additional $40 million annually to assist District public and charter schools. *(PL 108-199, Congress and the Nation Vol. XI, p. 549; 111th Congress action, p. 481)*

In the Committee of the Whole, the House rejected, 185–237, on March 30 a substitute amendment by Del. Eleanor Holmes Norton, D-D.C., that would terminate the voucher program and instead authorize $60 million annually over five years for the District's public and charter schools. Norton criticized GOP leaders for advancing the legislation without consulting local officials, such as D.C. Mayor Vincent C. Gray. Norton said that the program did not have sufficient support from District residents and that lawmakers had no right imposing their will on people they did not represent.

The House Oversight and Government Reform Committee had reported HR 471 (H Rept 112-36) on March 17. Hearings were held in the Senate Homeland Security and Governmental Affairs Committee on a companion measure (S 206), sponsored by Joseph I. Lieberman, I-Conn., but the bill saw no further action.

Charter Schools

By 365–54, the House on September 13, 2011, passed bipartisan legislation (HR 2218) that would expand successful charter school programs. The bill, sponsored by House Education and the Workforce Subcommittee on Early Childhood, Elementary, and Secondary Education chairman Duncan Hunter, R-Calif., was the first major measure to reach the House floor as part of a GOP effort to overhaul and reauthorize the No Child Left Behind Act (PL 107-110). The Senate, expected to consider the charter school issue as part of a broader Elementary and Secondary Education Act reauthorization instead of as a stand-alone bill, took no action on HR 2218. *(PL 107-110, Congress and the Nation Vol. XI, p. 540; Elementary and Secondary Education Act, p. 483)*

The House Committee on Education and the Workforce had approved the Empowering Parents through Quality Charter Schools Act by 34–5 on June 22 and formally reported it (H Rept 112-178) on July 22. Although the existing charter school program authorized funding for states to plan and start new schools, HR 2218 would specify that state educational agencies, state charter school boards, and state governors also could award subgrants for the replication and expansion of high-quality charter schools. Duncan highlighted a provision that would give priority to states without caps on the number of charter schools that could exist or the number of students that could attend them. More than 400,000 students were on charter school wait lists, he said, and the caps imposed in many states trapped students in low-performing schools. The bill would authorize $300 billion for fiscal 2012 and for each of the five years thereafter.

Overall, the committee-approved bill drew praise. Many Democrats, for example, liked that the legislation increased the accountability of charter schools. However, Rep. John F. Tierney, D-Mass., expressed concern about whether the programs would be accessible to all students on an equal basis. Also, the National School Boards Association in a June 21 letter made known its opposition to the bill, citing a study that found that only 17 percent of the charter schools across sixteen states were more effective than traditional public schools.

During floor consideration, the House on September 13 rejected, 195–220, an amendment by Rush D. Holt, D-N.J., that would encourage the education secretary to give priority to states that promote green school-building practices and certification under a grant program that helped finance charter school facilities. Education and the Workforce Chair John Kline, R-Minn., said that the amendment would weaken efforts at the state level to fund school construction and that it represented an inappropriate role for the federal government. The House September 13 also rejected, 43–374, an amendment by Steve King, R-Iowa, to eliminate a requirement that, to be considered high-quality, charter schools must increase achievement for students who were economically disadvantaged, were disabled, had limited English proficiency, and were from major racial and ethnic groups. King said the provision could preclude a school without one of the four categories of students from qualifying, but the committee's ranking minority member George Miller, D-Calif., called the idea "simply hokum." Kline joined Miller in opposing the King amendment.

Rural Schools

Congress in 2012, as part of the Moving Ahead for Progress in the 21st Century Act or MAP-21 (HR 4348—PL 112-141), reauthorized for one year two programs that fund rural schools and other local government services programs in areas with large amounts of federal land. Both programs were last reauthorized as part of the 2008 law that established the Troubled Asset Relief Program (PL 110-343). *(2008 action, Congress and the Nation Vol. XII, p. 154)*

Because the land covered by the programs was owned by the federal government, it could not be taxed to support local services. Advocates said the programs had to be preserved because the payments helped provide critical services such as education, police protection, and firefighting. The existing road- and school-funding law, known as Secure Rural Schools (PL 106-393), lapsed in September 2011. The rural schools program had ensured that counties receive funding based on historical timber sales, not actual sales. The other program, known as Payment in Lieu of Taxes, gave broader discretion for communities to spend the money, but much of it was used for highway construction. That program would expire at the end of fiscal 2012. *(PL 106-393, Congress and the Nation Vol. X, p. 399)*

Among the approximately $800 million in offsets needed to cover the cost of extending the programs was establishment of a new tax-reporting requirement on the sale of certain life insurance plans.

The Senate Environment and Public Works Committee reported its version of the legislation (S 1813—no written report) on February 6, 2012, and the full Senate passed it by 74–22 on March 14. The House passed HR 4348 by a vote of 293–127 on April 18, 2012; the Senate, by voice vote, April 24. On June 29, the conference report (H Rept 112-557) was adopted by the House 373–52 and by the Senate 74–19. President Obama signed the bill into law on July 6.

Antibullying and Gang Prevention

The House Judiciary Committee on July 9, 2012, formally reported HR 6019 (H Rept 112-582), to reauthorize and expand the use of grants to address occurrences of bullying, including cyberbullying, and for gang-prevention programs. The panel had ordered the

Juvenile Accountability Block Grant Reauthorization and the Bullying Prevention and Intervention Act of 2012 reported by voice vote on June 28.

Bill sponsor Sheila Jackson Lee, D-Texas, described HR 6019 as "a combination of bipartisan efforts" to address a growing "epidemic of bullying." Members on both sides of the aisle voiced support for the legislation, although several Democrats said that the authorization amount—$40 million annually to fund the grants from fiscal 2013 to fiscal 2017—was too low. Meanwhile, Rep. Steve King, R-Iowa, who supported the legislation, voiced concern that specific language in the bill could lead to the creation of additional, unnecessary federal programs that could be costly.

HR 6019 fared better than the Safe Schools Improvement Act of 2011 (HR 1648, S 506), which never got beyond committee consideration. The legislation would authorize funding for school districts to deal with bullying and require that they include antibullying language in their disciplinary policies. It was slow to garner GOP support, as conservatives believed, as they did with education as a whole, that state and local school districts were better than the federal government at fixing things.

The American Federation of Teachers and the National Education Association called on Congress to enact antibullying legislation. Once considered a schoolyard rite of passage, bullying became a civil rights issue for many students. Physical and mental bullying reportedly contributed to student suicides. The Department of Education in 2010 sent guidance to public schools and colleges emphasizing that school officials were required to investigate incidents of bullying, which could be considered discriminatory harassment under civil rights laws. On March 10, 2011, President Barack Obama and First Lady Michelle Obama hosted the first-ever White House Conference on Bullying Prevention. The day before, the Department of Health and Human Services, in collaboration with the Education Department and the Justice Department, launched a website called stopbullying.gov that provided information from various government agencies on what bullying and cyberbullying are, who is at risk, and how one can prevent and respond to bullying.

Adult Literacy

The House Education and the Workforce Committee on December 5, 2012, reported a bill (HR 4297—H Rept 112-699, Part 1) that would reauthorize the 1998 Workforce Investment Act (PL 105-220), which provided most of the federal funding for adult literacy and career development education. The Workforce Investment Improvement Act (WIA) of 2012, sponsored by Rep. Virginia Foxx, R-N.C., saw no further action. *(PL 105-220, Congress and the Nation Vol. X, p. 573)*

According to the National Research Council, more than ninety million adults in the United States in 2011, including more than thirty million who were unable to read beyond a fifth-grade level, were estimated to lack the literacy needed to navigate many aspects of modern life. People in this group faced an unemployment rate that hovered above 15 percent and were more likely to have children who struggled in school.

Title II of the WIA is the Adult Education and Family Literacy Act (AEFLA), which, as described in an August 10, 2012, Congressional Research Service report, "authorizes funds supporting programs related to basic education (that is, instruction at the secondary-school level and below) for individuals who are beyond school age, not enrolled in school, and lacking a high school diploma or equivalent. The program also funds educational services for English learners." HR 4297 would reauthorize AEFLA from fiscal 2012 through fiscal 2018 and sought to "emphasize the relationship between adult education and employment."

In related action, among several bills designed to make changes in federal education policy and rewrite the No Child Left Behind Act (PL 107-110) was legislation (HR 1891) that would repeal authorization for numerous federal education programs, including literacy programs. *(PL 107-110, Congress and the Nation Vol. XI, p. 540; Elementary and Secondary Education Act, p. 483)*

Race to the Top

In December 2011, the Department of Education issued a progress report on how well or, as it turned out in some cases, how poorly the winners of the Obama administration's Race to the Top education competition were implementing the changes they promised in exchange for bonus federal money. The grant program was established in 2009. *(111th Congress action, p. 480)*

In 2011, eleven states and the District of Columbia divvied up $4 billion as Race to the Top winners. In exchange for federal dollars, they pledged to improve schools and teaching by adopting various changes to their educational systems, such as implementing new standards and creating teacher evaluation systems based on student test scores. They were given four years to pull off their plans.

The Education Department reported that a majority of the states were making steady progress but that nearly all had experienced significant problems in hiring employees, contractors, and vendors to turn their plans into reality. States had the most trouble implementing new teacher evaluation systems, largely because those sometimes required renegotiating contracts with teachers' unions.

Specifically, Hawaii, New York, and Florida were targeted for their lack of progress in policy changes. In December 2011, the Education Department gave Hawaii "high risk" status and said that the state was in danger of losing its $75 million Race to the Top award. In a letter sent to Democratic Hawaii governor Neil Abercrombie, the department said that it was limiting access to Hawaii's remaining grant money, rejecting additional requests for changes and delays in its plan.

RESPECT PROJECT, STEM MASTERS

The Education Department in a February 15, 2012, announcement said that Education secretary Arne Duncan in a town hall meeting in Washington, D.C., to be held that day would launch the Recognizing Educational Success, Professional Excellence, and Collaborative Teaching (RESPECT) Project, envisioned as a teacher-led national conversation about the Obama administration's proposed competitive grant program to comprehensively reform the teaching profession, which would use the Race to the Top school improvement competition as a model. The White House requested $5 billion in its fiscal 2013 budget to kick-start efforts. *(Race to the Top, pp. 480, 492)*

Employing a grassroots strategy, teaching fellows at the Department of Education traveled around the country to meet with teachers and begin building support at the state level for the proposal. The administration said the goal was to collect teachers' feedback and give them a seat at the table, not to turn them into lobbyists. The blueprint for a new teacher workforce, Duncan and the teaching fellows maintained, would elevate the profession, putting it on par with medicine and law, to ultimately provide students with a better education.

The proposal was built on President Barack Obama's 2012 State of the Union address, during which he said: "Give [schools] the resources to keep good teachers on the job, and reward the best ones. In return, grant schools flexibility: To teach with creativity and passion; to stop teaching to the test; and to replace teachers who just aren't helping kids learn." The motivation behind the program stemmed in part from the embarrassing performance by U.S. high school students on international tests that placed them far behind students in other industrialized countries in reading, math, and science; the ballooning number of teacher preparation programs with low bars for entry or graduation compared with other parts of the world; and rapidly declining morale among teachers over state budget cuts and antiquated policies.

Under the RESPECT Project, students would no longer advance in lockstep, age-based grades but would instead progress through the system based on what they know and can do. The formulaic school day and year, originally based on an agrarian calendar, would be eliminated and redesigned based on students' needs. Teachers would have access to data measuring student learning and would be trained on how to use it to inform instruction hour to hour, day to day, and year to year.

Becoming a teacher would be much more difficult, with a new workforce recruited from the top tier of students in the country. They would be required to demonstrate subject area expertise, proficiency in improving student learning, and dispositions associated with successful teaching, such as perseverance and effective communication. In addition, teacher preparation programs would be required to track and publish data on how long their graduates stayed in the profession and how successful they were based on principals' evaluations and student learning.

Like aspiring doctors, graduates of teaching schools would enter a clinical residency for two to four years with a "master" teacher before getting their own classes. Starting salaries for teachers who completed their residency could be as high as $65,000, according to the plan. As teaching careers progress, salaries would increase faster and maximum salaries would be higher, so that master teachers could earn as much as $120,000 to $150,000 after about seven to ten years. While pay has usually been linked to years of service or professional credentials, the proposed salary structure would more reflect the quality of a teacher's work. Teacher evaluation would include an analysis of their responsibilities and accomplishments, measurements of student growth data, results from formal observations, self-evaluations, and feedback from students.

In related action, the White House on July 17, 2012, announced plans for the creation of the Science, Technology, Engineering, and Math (STEM) Master Teacher Corps as part of the RESPECT Project. The White House press release described STEM teachers as "classroom-based educators who are highly effective in improving learning outcomes for their students, model outstanding teaching, and share their practices and strategies with their professional colleagues to lead and guide improvements across education." STEM teachers would make a multiyear commitment to the corps and receive an annual $20,000 stipend in addition to their base salary.

The administration said that, to start, it would dedicate about $100 million of the Teacher Incentive Fund to support STEM teachers. The president's 2013 budget requested $1 billion for the corps. The program sought to recruit ten thousand teachers over four years, reaching 100,000 over ten years.

Although the department approved dozens of shifts in the timeline for improvements and had amended original plans, it repeatedly said it would hold all Race to the Top winners to their promises. Education secretary Arne Duncan said he would be willing to take money away from any state that did not follow through.

The fiscal 2012 omnibus appropriations bill (HR 2055), signed into law (PL 112-74) on December 23, 2011, provided $550 million for the Race to the Top education initiative, a cut of more than 20 percent from the fiscal 2011 level and nearly 40 percent below the administration request. Although the program suffered a substantial reduction in funding, Republicans were clear that it was among the Democratic-backed programs they would like to eliminate altogether. *(Fiscal 2012 omnibus spending bill, p. 172)*

A House subcommittee-approved fiscal 2013 draft bill to fund the departments of Labor, Health and Human Services (HHS), and Education would have blocked funding for Race to the Top. However, Congress did not complete action on a stand-alone labor-HHS-education appropriations bill. Instead, programs were funded at fiscal 2012 levels through March 27, 2013, under a continuing resolution signed into law on September 28, 2012 (H J Res 117—PL 112-175). *(Fiscal 2013 continuing resolution, p. 180)*

CHAPTER 11

Housing and Urban Aid

Introduction 497

Chronology of Action on Housing and Urban Aid 500

2009–2010 500

2011–2012 509

Housing and Urban Aid

A pillar of the American Dream is to have the freedom to pursue opportunities for prosperity and success. For the better part of a century, one representation of having achieved that slice of the dream was homeownership. The federal government played a central role in making residential loans cheaper and easier to get, as well encouraging people to buy houses in the first place. Over the decades, demands from consumers, lenders, and construction interests created a housing-industry complex with substantial political strength. However, in the aftermath of the housing bubble that burst in 2007, calls were made for a reexamination of the government's support for the residential real estate market and of the goal of homeownership itself.

BUILDUP AND FALLOUT

In the early twentieth century, before the federal government got heavily involved in the mortgage market, roughly 46 percent of American families owned their homes. By 2004, the homeownership rate reached an all-time high of 69.2 percent. The shift in federal policy started during the Great Depression, when Congress and the Franklin D. Roosevelt administration responded to a wave of foreclosures by establishing the Federal Housing Administration (FHA) to insure mortgages and Fannie Mae (then the National Mortgage Association of Washington; now the Federal National Mortgage Association) to stimulate lending by buying mortgages from lenders.

The FHA transformed the mortgage industry and made financing available and affordable for more people, by requiring relatively long terms and fixed rates for the loans it covered. Fannie Mae, which became a shareholder-owned company in the late 1960s, provided lenders with the cash they needed to originate more mortgages. Congress in 1970 created the Federal Home Loan Mortgage Corporation (Freddie Mac), as a private corporation, to provide additional liquidity and stability to the market.

As federal policy fueled borrowing and residential construction, homeownership became an entrenched goal. Eventually, people wanted bigger and bigger houses, and they were willing and able to go deeper into debt to get them. Because owning property could help low-income families build assets, expanding ownership became a political goal shared by Democrats and Republicans. By June 2002, during a speech in celebration of National Homeownership Month, President George W. Bush told employees of the Department of Housing and Urban Development, "It is essential that we make it easier for people to buy a home, not harder." He sought to push the ownership rate to about 75 percent. However, in the mid-2000s, many new owners began defaulting on loans they could no longer afford.

Many reasons could be cited for why the mortgage finance system and the entire economy reached a tipping point in the fall of 2008. Many experts contended that federal government policies were a principal cause. At the beginning of the 2000s, after the economic shocks caused by the September 11, 2001, terrorist attacks and the bursting of the bubble in technology stocks, the Federal Reserve kept interest rates consistently low. Federal regulation of loans, especially a new class of subprime mortgages aimed at borrowers with poor credit histories, was lax. In this environment, Fannie Mae and Freddie Mac bought up hundreds of billions of dollars of risky mortgages, feeding the market for them. When the subprime mortgage market crumbled, the companies faced enormous losses, were

REFERENCES

Discussion of housing and urban aid action for the years 1945–1964 may be found in *Congress and the Nation Vol. I,* pp. 459–515; for the years 1965–1968, *Congress and the Nation Vol. II,* 183–226; for the years 1969–1972, *Congress and the Nation Vol. III,* pp. 635–657; for the years 1973–1976, *Congress and the Nation Vol. IV,* pp. 471–502; for the years 1977–1980, *Congress and the Nation Vol. V,* 429–448; for the years 1981–1984, *Congress and the Nation Vol. VI,* pp. 629–639; for the years 1985–1988, *Congress and the Nation Vol. VII,* pp. 667–684; for the years 1989–1992, *Congress and the Nation Vol. VIII,* pp. 663–700; for the years 1993–1996, *Congress and the Nation Vol. IX,* pp. 637–650; for the years 1997–2001, *Congress and the Nation Vol. X,* pp. 553–567; for the years 2001–2004, *Congress and the Nation Vol. XI,* pp. 555–560; for the years 2005–2008, *Congress and the Nation Vol. XII,* pp. 621–648.

seized by the federal government, and were put under control of a new regulator, the Federal Housing Finance Agency. *(Financial crisis aftermath, p. 47; background to crisis, Congress and the Nation Vol. XII, p. 163)*

Even without the excesses that led to the financial crisis, experts said, a strong policy bias toward owner-occupied housing warped the economy and diverted resources from other types of investments. Investment in new housing and remodeling averaged about 4.8 percent of overall economic output since the beginning of recordkeeping in 1947. By the end of 2005, residential investment spending reached 6.3 percent of gross domestic product. This reflected, in part, a new reality driven by skyrocketing house prices: people began to see houses as a way to get rich instead of as a place to live. Evidence showed that federal policies disproportionately benefited the wealthy. In certain high-cost neighborhoods, borrowers with mortgages as large as $730,000 enjoyed relatively low interest rates because their loans qualified for purchase by Fannie Mae and Freddie Mac. Moreover, taxpayers who earned more than $100,000 claimed more than two-fifths of the billions of dollars in tax breaks for the mortgage interest deduction, which applied to loans as large as $1 million.

Meanwhile, for years, growth in the number of renters at all income levels far outpaced the construction of new rental units. As construction of residential homes was encouraged, both public housing and affordable apartments became scarcer. The federal government drew back from maintaining public housing, and an increasing number of squalid units were demolished. After the housing bubble burst, home prices saw a steep decline, creating a rising number of households with "negative equity," this is, people owed more on their mortgages than they could raise at a sale. Many owners walked away from their debts, wound up in foreclosure, or negotiated a short sale in which the lender accepted the sale price to pay off the loan.

Outlays for Community and Regional Development

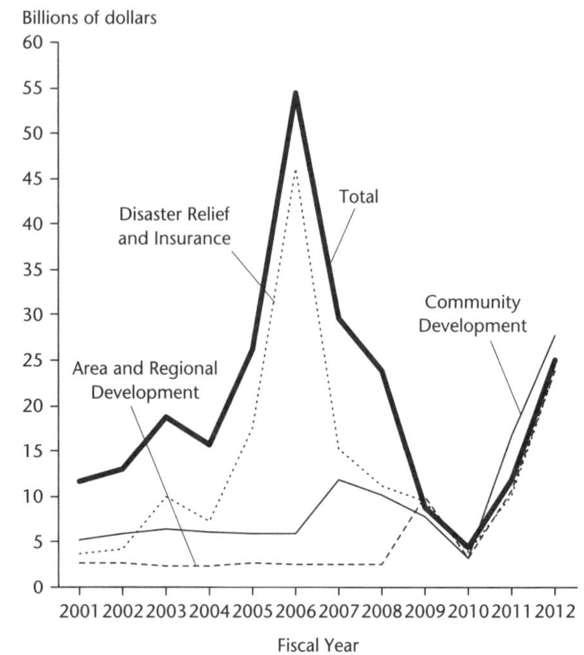

SOURCE: Office of Management and Budget, *Historical Tables, Budget of the United States Government: Fiscal Year 2013* (Washington, D.C.: U.S. Government Printing Office, 2012), Table 3.2.

They were unable or unwilling to purchase a house again and entered the rental market.

NEW DIRECTION?

Paradoxically, by the end of President Barack Obama's first term in early 2013, the slow but steady recovery of the housing market led to a legislative stasis, with little immediate pressure put on overhauling the system established after the housing market collapsed. However, lawmakers

Edward DeMarco, acting director of the Federal Housing Finance Agency (right) greets Sen. Tim Johnson, a Democrat from South Dakota and chair of the Senate Banking Committee, after testifying at a hearing on the housing market in Washington, D.C., on February 28, 2012. Sen. Richard Shelby, a Republican from Alabama and the committee's vice chair, questioned the fairness of a $25 billion mortgage servicing settlement, saying it "appears to come up short" for borrowers who wrongfully lost their homes.
Source: T. J. Kirkpatrick/Bloomberg via Getty Images

across the political spectrum were hard-pressed to endorse the existing system, in which the government underwrote 90 percent of new loans and taxpayers bore much of the risk.

Democrats warned that any move to pare back Uncle Sam's role in the home loan industry could easily raise borrowing costs for everyone. Strict Republican doctrine held that a new finance system had to be built entirely with private capital; nevertheless, with the rising specter of higher interest rates, some GOP lawmakers indicated a willingness to keep options open on the issue of government involvement in the mortgage market. The political fallout of entirely wiping out Fannie Mae and Freddie Mac and, more important, ending the market's government guarantee could be brutal, as lenders and borrowers would lose their cheapest and most stable loan product.

The administration favored a plan that called for a private finance system underpinned by a government-run catastrophic-reinsurance fund. Obama also proposed scaling back the mortgage interest deduction and denying it to the wealthiest taxpayers. The administration and Democrats in Congress began pushing for putting more federal dollars into affordable housing programs.

As events after the mid-2000s showed, housing in America was changing; the question was whether housing policy needed to change, too. As the number of renters increased, lawmakers and other government officials deliberated whether to steer policy to put rental housing on a more equivalent economic footing with homeownership. Determining the fate of Fannie Mae and Freddie Mac would force lawmakers to confront fundamental concerns about the government's role in the economy and the American dream of homeownership.

HOUSING LEADERSHIP

The Senate by voice vote on January 22, 2009, confirmed Shaun Donovan to be secretary of the Department of Housing and Urban Development (HUD). When he was tapped for the position, Donovan was director of the New York City Department of Housing Preservation and Development. He previously had served as deputy assistant secretary for multifamily housing during the Bill Clinton administration.

During his January 13 confirmation hearings before the Senate Banking, Housing, and Urban Affairs Committee, Donovan pledged to take a more aggressive and far-reaching approach to easing the foreclosure crisis that was at the center of the economic recession and promoting affordable housing. He enjoyed bipartisan support, with members of both parties praising his qualifications to lead HUD.

As HUD secretary, Donovan touted the National Mortgage Settlement, reached in February 2012 between the federal government, forty-nine state attorneys general, and the nation's five largest mortgage servicers, which provided that eligible borrowers could seek loan modifications, refinance their mortgage even though they owed more than their house was worth, and receive payments as compensation if they lost their homes to foreclosure during 2008–2011. Critics pointed out that relatively few borrowers obtained modification of the terms of their first mortgage—the only element of the agreement that could help borrowers keep their homes. They claimed that Donovan failed to demonstrate leadership by not holding banks accountable to the settlement's stated goal: saving families' homes from unnecessary foreclosure. The reality, however, was that nothing in the settlement precluded states from using the money in any manner they wished, helping homeowners or otherwise.

Secretary Donovan sought to link housing to jobs, transportation, and energy policies. He advocated, for example, that people receive estimates of energy consumption for a commute to work from a house they were considering buying, allowing them to assess the fuel costs of buying a particular home. Furthermore, he sought to incorporate economic and environmental sustainability requirements into HUD's competitive grant programs, including Leadership in Energy and Environmental Design (LEED), LEED for Neighborhood Development, and the Community Development Block Grant program. Donovan also established the Office of Sustainable Housing and Communities, which, according to the HUD website (http://hud.gov), would "work to coordinate federal housing and transportation investments with local land use decisions in order to reduce transportation costs for families, improve housing affordability, save energy, and increase access to housing and employment opportunities."

In the aftermath of 2012 Hurricane Sandy, President Barack Obama tapped Donovan to coordinate federal support of affected states as they set priorities and devised redevelopment plans. Locals welcomed the news of Donovan, who had personal as well as professional ties to New York, taking on the task. New York City Housing Development Corporation president Marc Jahr, quoted in the *New York Daily News* on December 2, 2012, said, "Shaun is not some bloodless bureaucrat who just sees a bunch of numbers on the page. He knows these numbers are infused with the everyday lives of real people." Donovan's tenure as "disaster czar" was not without controversy, however. For example, he upset residents when he said that there were a small number of areas devastated by the superstorm "where it may not make sense to rebuild at all."

Donovan remained at HUD after Obama was sworn in for a second term.

Chronology of Action on Housing and Urban Aid

2009–2010

In the aftermath of the housing market collapse, Congress helped alleviate some borrowers' worries by allowing easier access to mortgage modifications and by increasing federal deposit insurance coverage. Lawmakers also twice extended a tax credit for first-time homebuyers and created a credit for existing homeowners who bought a new home. Congress also called for a study of problematic drywall imported from China.

Mortgage Relief Assistance

Congress in 2009 cleared legislation (S 896—PL 111-22) that made it easier for troubled borrowers to seek mortgage modifications under the Hope for Homeowners program and extended, though December 31, 2013, an increase in deposit insurance coverage by the Federal Deposit Insurance Corporation (FDIC) and National Credit Union Administration (NCUA). The coverage limit had been raised from $100,000 to $250,000 in the 2008 financial industry bailout law (PL 110-343), but that increase was set to expire on December 31, 2009. *(PL 110-343, Congress and the Nation Vol. XII, p. 154)*

The Helping Families Save Their Homes Act of 2009 (S 896) also permanently boosted the FDIC's borrowing authority to $100 billion, from $30 billion, and would allow it to be temporarily raised to $500 billion for the FDIC and $30 billion for the NCUA through 2010 if deemed necessary by bank regulators. The measure eliminated a requirement that properties purchased under the Neighborhood Stabilization Program, a Housing and Urban Development Department (HUD) program, be bought at less than their appraised value. The program provided grants to buy foreclosed and abandoned projects.

In an effort to get more participation in the Hope for Homeowners program, a $300 billion initiative enacted in 2008 (PL 110-289), S 896 eased some eligibility requirements. The program attempted to aid homeowners on the brink of foreclosure by helping them refinance into thirty-year, fixed-rate mortgages insured by the Federal Housing Administration (FHA). The legislation changed the yearly insurance premiums that participating homeowners must pay to the FHA from 1.5 percent of the mortgage to "up to 1.5 percent," essentially giving the government the flexibility to lower the premiums. It also included a Senate provision that would authorize $2.2 billion to expand a program to provide federal funds for shelters, education, and other assistance for the homeless. *(PL 110-289, Congress and the Nation Vol. XII, p. 629)*

The costs of S 896 were offset by using $1.2 billion of the $700 billion authorized in PL 110-343.

HOUSE ACTION

On March 5, 2009, the House passed its version of mortgage relief legislation (HR 1106) on a **key vote of 234–191 (R 7–167; D 227–24)**. *(2009 key votes, p. 751)*

The bill's bankruptcy judge language, known as the "cramdown" provision, stirred up the most controversy. Lenders fiercely opposed the language, which would allow bankruptcy judges to reduce the principal owed on a primary residence mortgage and order other modifications in mortgage terms. The banking industry said such actions would force banks to raise interest rates for all borrowers summarily. The House on March 5 narrowly rejected, 211–218, an amendment offered by Tom Price, R-Ga., that would allow lenders to recover some or all of the amount of principal lost under a court-modified mortgage if a homeowner later sold the home at a profit.

For House Democrats, the vote marked at least a temporary victory in a long-running battle. The financial industry lobbied fiercely against the issue, and it appeared to gain traction the week of February 23, when Democratic leaders were forced to pull the bill from the floor amid last-minute concerns about whether it had enough votes to pass. A group of centrist and conservative Democrats—mainly from the New Democrat and "Blue Dog" coalitions—feared a backlash from constituents already wary of trillions of dollars in bank bailouts. Speaker Nancy Pelosi, D-Calif., who initially said the bill would be brought back to the floor unchanged, instead worked with dissidents to hammer out compromise language. The new wording would give bankruptcy judges the option to reduce interest rates before directly cutting the principal of a mortgage. It also would allow lenders to collect a portion of the profit if a home was sold within four years of modification.

At a Democratic caucus meeting, HUD secretary Shaun Donovan addressed the provision in the context of the administration's boarder mortgage aid plan. The procedure should be "considered a last resort," Donovan said, but it also was an important part of the White House's overall plan. The compromise language attempted to address the "last resort" calls by spelling out the specific steps a homeowner must take before considering bankruptcy. Republicans, however, much like the banking industry, argued that by stopping short of mandating that judges consider other options, the language did nothing to move reductions in principal to the bottom of modification options. For instance, some lawmakers wanted the option limited to subprime mortgages.

On March 5, before passing HR 1106, the House adopted by a vote of 263–164 an amendment sponsored by Zoe Lofgren, D-Calif., that would make individuals who can afford to repay their mortgages without judicial modification ineligible for loan relief, allow a bank to recover a higher percentage of funds if the homeowner sold the home for a profit, and require debtors to certify that they contacted a lender, provided proper statements, and sought an agreement on a qualified loan modification. It also would require bankruptcy courts to use FHA appraisal guidelines when the fair market value of a home was disputed and would allow courts to lower an individual's

PACE LOANS: PROPERTY-ASSISTED CLEAN ENERGY BORROWING

The idea behind property-assisted clean energy (PACE) loans was simple: let interested homeowners borrow money from their municipality for expensive improvements—for example, a $30,000 array of rooftop photovoltaic cells. Repayments for the loan would be tacked onto the property owner's local tax bill for the next twenty years or so. Ultimately, the homeowner would save on utility costs and the house would grow in value. The town would be participating in the desirable public purpose of boosting reliance on renewable energy, while attracting residents who wanted to be part of such an effort. Jobs would be created for the makers of solar panels and other innovations, as well as for those who installed them. Utilities would be freed from building new generating capacity. And homeowners could spread the payments across a longer period than a traditional loan might allow.

Led by states, cities, the Barack Obama administration, and others, fans of conservation, solar power, and other "green" initiatives thought PACE loans were a foolproof way to help families afford big investments that might not yield a full return through energy savings for many years. Proponents of this seemingly smart idea did not bank on mortgage companies objecting to loans that essentially amounted to tax liens. If a homeowner failed to pay the tax bill, two things could happen: the PACE loan could be declared in default, which could trigger an automatic default on the mortgage, and the municipality would have first claim on proceeds from any foreclosure action, because a tax lien on a house is senior to a mortgage loan. The result was a standoff between advocates of renewable energy at the household level and the realities of the market.

The Federal National Mortgage Association (Fannie Mae) and the Federal Home Loan Mortgage Corporation (Freddie Mac), with the blessing of their regulator, the Federal Housing Finance Agency, said they would not purchase loans on houses that were also tied to PACE loans. Because Fannie Mae and Freddie Mac set the standard for mortgage transactions, the market thus was essentially frozen for these houses. Furthermore, bank regulators cautioned lenders to be careful that municipalities were following appropriate underwriting standards, including an assessment that the loan was appropriate for the borrower and that the borrower had the ability to repay it. The saga of the PACE loans showed that, in the wake of the Great Recession, any financing plan that had not been thoroughly vetted and that even hinted at a threat to real estate was suspect.

A number of bills were introduced in the 111th Congress regarding PACE loans, but none made its way out of committee. HR 3836, titled "To authorize the Secretary of Energy to provide credit support to enhance the availability of private financing for clean energy technology deployment," was referred to the House Energy and Commerce Subcommittee on Energy and Environment. S 1574, the Clean Energy for Homes and Buildings Act of 2009, was referred to the Senate Energy and Natural Resources Committee. S 3642, the PACE Assessment Protection Act of 2010, was referred to the Senate Banking, Housing, and Urban Affairs Committee. HR 5766, titled "To ensure that the underwriting standards of Fannie Mae and Freddie Mac facilitate the use of property assessed clean energy programs to finance the installment of renewable energy and energy efficiency improvements," was referred to the House Financial Services Committee. HR 4155, the Property Assessed Clean Energy Tax Benefits Act of 2009, was referred to the House Ways and Means Committee.

HR 2599, introduced in the 112th Congress, also stalled. The PACE Assessment Protection Act of 2011 was referred to the House Financial Services Subcommittee on Capital Markets and Government Sponsored Enterprises and the Subcommittee on Insurance, Housing, and Community Opportunity.

interest rate instead of reducing mortgage principal. The House also adopted, 423–2, an amendment by Gary Peters, D-Mich., to allow a debtor whose home was in foreclosure to meet the credit counseling requirement by receiving counseling before or up to thirty days after the filing. Price offered a motion to recommit HR 1106 to the Judiciary Committee and the Financial Services Committee with instructions that the bill be reported back including language that would bar the use of funds from the Troubled Asset Relief Program, the Treasury Department's financial industry bailout, for foreclosure prevention or mitigation unless a plan for the use of the funds was submitted to Congress. The motion was rejected, 182–242.

The House-passed bill contained the language of four separate pieces of legislation, including the bankruptcy measure (HR 200—H Rept 111-19). HR 1106 also would give mortgage servicers who reworked terms a safe harbor from lawsuits if a homeowner defaulted on a revised loan or appeared likely to default. The legal shield, outlined in HR 788 (H Rept 111-13), would apply if the servicer believed that modifying a mortgage would produce more revenue than a foreclosure would have. Some mortgage servicers were reluctant to revise troubled loans without such protection, fearing that they could face suits from investors who held securities that were backed by the mortgages.

HR 1106 also contained language from HR 787 (H Rept 111-12) that would overhaul the Hope for Homeowners program, which originally was designed to aid up to 400,000 troubled homeowners. However, even its supporters deemed the program a failure, as relatively few persons sought to have their mortgages refinanced. Critics blamed high fees and minimal participation by lenders. HR 1106 would loosen eligibility requirements for the program; reduce the upfront fee from 3 percent to 2 percent of the purchase price of the property; and reduce the annual fee from 1.5 percent to 1 percent. It would place the HUD secretary in charge of the program and allow payments to servicers of up to $1,000 for each loan modification. Language from a fourth bill (HR 786—H Rept 111-18) would permanently increase the limit on deposits insured by the FDIC and the NCUA to $250,000 and index the limit to inflation starting in 2015. The FDIC's borrowing authority would increase to $100 billion from $30 billion, and the credit union agency's would grow to $6 billion from $100 million, to help them cope with a surge in bank and credit union failures.

SENATE ACTION

The Senate passed its version of the legislation (S 896) on May 6, 2009, by a vote of 91–5. The bill would ease requirements for the Hope for Homeowners program, increase the FDIC's borrowing authority from $30 billion to $100 billion, and continue through 2013 expanded FDIC insurance to cover bank accounts of up to $250,000.

The measure was largely noncontroversial. It had bipartisan support from the leaders of the Senate Banking, Housing, and Urban Affairs Committee, and business and consumer groups lobbied for its passage. However, several senators sought to amend the bill, with the most pivotal vote coming when the Senate on April 30 turned down a proposal to give bankruptcy judges the option of changing the terms of primary residence mortgages. The amendment by Richard J. Durbin, D-Ill., rejected on a **key vote of 45–51 (R 0–39; D 43–12; I 2–0)**, would allow judges to alter the interest rate, principal, or payment period on a mortgage—the cramdown process. Durbin blamed the defeat on lobbying by the banking industry. Throughout weeks of negotiations, a core group of moderate Democrats and Republicans had tried to limit the cramdown provision to subprime mortgages. But Durbin declined to move in that direction, which the industry pointed to as the reason for the amendment's failure. *(2009 key votes, p. 751)*

The Senate on May 6 adopted an amendment, sponsored by John Kerry, D-Mass., to let tenants in foreclosed buildings remain in their homes for the duration of their leases or for ninety days if they did not have a lease or if the property was sold to someone who planned to use it as a primary residence. The vote was 57–39.

FINAL ACTION

On May 19, the House agreed to suspend the rules and pass an amended version of S 896 by a vote of 367–54, with one member voting "present." The House made only technical or minor changes to the bill. For example, the Senate-passed version provided a safe harbor from liability for lenders and servicers if certain criteria were met during the loan modification process. The House clarified that this immunity would not apply in cases involving intentional fraud. The Senate agreed to the House changes by voice vote on May 19, clearing the measure.

The final legislation did not contain the cramdown language. President Obama signed PL 111-22 into law on May 20, 2009.

Mortgage Lender Regulation

The House passed a bill (HR 1728), by 300–114 on May 7, 2009, that would prohibit mortgage originators from steering consumers to residential loans the homebuyers clearly could not repay and that would require lenders to retain at least 5 percent of any mortgage sold to a third party. The House passed similar legislation in the 110th Congress. *(Earlier action, Congress and the Nation Vol. XII, p. 640)*

The primary purpose of the Mortgage Reform and Anti-Predatory Lending Act, according to House Financial Services Committee Chair Barney Frank, D-Mass., was to push the mortgage industry back toward more "plain vanilla" loans, particularly those with longer terms and fixed interest rates. That focus was a direct response to the crisis in subprime lending that was at the core of the economy's collapse and the recession that began in December 2007. *(2007–2009 U.S. economic crisis, Congress and the Nation Vol. XII, p. 163)*

Several central players in the debate, including the mortgage industry, supported in principle the 5 percent "skin in the game" language, but the mechanics of the requirement had not been worked out. Republicans and industry representatives strongly opposed the way the provision was written in the House-passed bill.

The Financial Services Committee had approved HR 1728 on April 29 by a vote of 49–21, with eight Republicans joining the Democrats in support. The bill's approval capped nearly two full days of work for the panel, as members approved twenty-four amendments and hammered out additional details, clarifications, and compromises. The measure was formally reported (H Rept 111-94) on May 4.

Many experts traced the problems in the housing market to a diffusion of responsibility that encouraged risky lending. Mortgages were typically taken off a bank's books after they were issued, converted to securities, and sold. The securities, in turn, were backed by insurance products known as credit default swaps. When loans were defaulted on, the financial system fell like dominoes, infecting the credit market and the wider economy. Although HR 1728 would require lenders to keep at least a 5 percent stake in any mortgages that were bundled into securities and sold to investors on the secondary market, the panel adopted an amendment on April 29 that would give federal banking agencies the authority to make exceptions or adjust the requirement. The amendment, adopted 67–1, would give regulators authority to apply the risk-retention provision to the securitizer of a loan.

Two key Republican amendments failed in committee. Scott Garrett, R-N.J., and Patrick T. McHenry, R-N.C., sponsored an amendment that would strike the risk-retention language and replace it with a study by banking agencies of ways for lenders to retain some responsibility for home loans. It was defeated by a vote of 27–43. Panel Republicans complained that a provision to apply legal liability to securitizers and others who assumed ownership of a mortgage would result in stunting the growth of a mortgage securitization market that they saw as vital to the rejuvenation of the economy. Ed Royce, R-Calif., offered an amendment that would shield such new owners of mortgages from liability. In promoting his amendment, Royce argued that HR 1728 would essentially "expose a broad number of financial institutions to legal action based on what instead occurred at the mortgage origination level." The amendment was defeated by voice vote.

Frank offered a manager's amendment, adopted by voice vote, requiring securitizers to retain access to all loans packaged and sold. Those who did not would be subject to punitive damages. The committee-approved bill also would prohibit any compensation structure that could cause a loan originator to steer applicants toward costlier mortgages; provide protections to tenants of property that was being foreclosed, including a ninety-day grace period before eviction; and create an Office of Housing Counseling within the Department of Housing and Urban Development.

Mortgage Insurance Premiums

On June 10, 2010, by a vote of 406–4, the House passed a bill (HR 5072) to allow the Federal Housing Administration (FHA) to raise the maximum annual mortgage insurance premium on loan guarantees, thus boosting dwindling reserves. The House Financial Services Committee had reported the FHA Reform Act of 2010 (H Rept 111-476) on May 6.

A surge in loan volume and rising defaults thinned the FHA's capital reserves, which by mid-2010 had dropped below the 2 percent threshold mandated by Congress. HR 5072 authorized the FHA to increase the mortgage insurance premiums it charged new borrowers by 1 percentage point.

Despite the bill's easy passage, Republicans seized on the opportunity to blast Democratic handling of mortgage giants Fannie Mae (Federal National Mortgage Association) and Freddie Mac (Federal Home Loan Mortgage Corporation), which were taken over by the federal government in 2008. Rep. Scott Garrett, R-N.J., said, "I find the debate over the problems with the FHA eerily similar to the debates we have had leading up to Fannie Mae and Freddie Mac." Garrett warned that as the FHA continued to insure more homes, it would be unable to recoup likely losses, which could lead to a bailout of the agency. *(2008 action, Congress and the Nation Vol. XII, pp. 139, 178)*

Financial Services Chair Barney Frank, D-Mass., countered that tying Fannie Mae's and Freddie Mac's troubles to those of the FHA was "a confusion of the reality" and blamed lawmakers who fought regulation of the subprime mortgage market for putting the government-sponsored enterprises in the position they found themselves in 2010.

In other Fannie Mae and Freddie Mac–related action, Congress in 2010, as part of the Continuing Appropriations and Surface Transportation Extensions Act (HR 3082—PL 111-322), allowed the two companies to continue to purchase or guarantee mortgages up to $729,750 in high-cost areas. *(Continuing resolution, p. 324)*

Homebuyer Tax Credit

Congress in 2009 twice extended and expanded a homebuyer tax credit that was created in 2008. Lawmakers extended the popular program through November 30, 2009, as part of a economic stimulus legislation (HR 1—PL 111-5). Weeks before the credit was set to expire, Congress acted again, clearing an unemployment compensation bill (HR 3548—PL 111-92) that contained another extension, pushing the credit into the spring 2010 buying season.

Supporters said that would be the last extension. *(Economic stimulus, p. 78; unemployment compensation, p. 517)*

Establishment of the credit, an incentive to homebuyers during the crisis in the housing market triggered by the collapse of subprime mortgages, was part of a wide-ranging 2008 mortgage finance bill (PL 110-289). The legislation provided a refundable tax credit of up to $7,500 for first-time homebuyers who purchased a home between April 9, 2008, and July 1, 2009. The credit was gradually phased out for taxpayers with adjusted gross incomes above $75,000 for individuals and $150,000 for couples filing jointly. The fact that it was refundable meant homebuyers who did not owe taxes because their incomes were too low could get the credit in the form of a check. The credit was effectively an interest-free loan. Borrowers were required to repay the government over fifteen years, or earlier if the homes were sold. *(PL 110-289, Congress and the Nation Vol. XII, p. 629)*

FIRST EXTENSION

HR 1, a $787.2 billion bill to boost the flagging economy extended the homebuyer tax credit through November 30 and increased the maximum amount to $8,000. In addition, those who bought homes after January 1 did not have to repay the government, unless the house was sold within three years. The Joint Committee on Taxation estimated that the provisions would cost $6.6 billion over eleven years.

The House passed the American Recovery and Reinvestment Act of 2009 on January 28 by a vote of 244–188. The Senate passed an amended version on February 10 by 61–37. The conference report (H Rept 111-16) was adopted in the House on February 13, by a vote of 246–183, with one member voting "present." The Senate followed suit the same day, voting 60–38, completing congressional action on the bill. President Obama signed HR 1 into law on that February 17, 2009.

An earlier House version of the legislation would have eliminated the repayment requirement for houses purchased after January 1, but it did not include an extension or an increase in the credit. That provision was projected to cost $2.6 billion over eleven years. The Senate version of the bill included a far more generous plan, drafted by Johnny Isakson, R-Ga. His amendment, which was adopted by voice vote, would have replaced the $7,500 for first-time homebuyers with a $15,000 tax credit for all individuals who bought homes within a year of the bill's enactment. Many lawmakers on both sides of the aisle were interested in expanding the credit beyond first-time buyers, but it was too expensive. The Senate provision was projected to cost $39.2 billion over eleven years.

SECOND EXTENSION

HR 3548, signed into law on November 6, extended the $8,000 credit to April 30, 2010, for first-time homebuyers who entered sales contracts by that date and closed within sixty days. Individuals could claim the credit for purchases in 2010 on their 2009 tax returns, which would mean they could get the money relatively quickly. The income cap for qualifying for the homeowner credit would be raised to $125,000 for individuals and $225,000 for married couples, up from $75,000 and $150,000, respectively. Homes sold for more than $800,000 would not be eligible for the credit. The measure also added a $6,500 credit for existing homeowners buying a new home, as long as they had lived in their homes for five consecutive years. The estimated cost was $10.8 billion over ten years.

Lawmakers, particularly Isakson, had pushed for a further extension and expansion of the homebuyer credit for months, citing weak home sales and arguing that propping up the housing sector would help speed economic recovery. In August, Isakson tried to add an expanded version of the credit to a bill (HR 3435) that put more money into the "cash for clunkers" auto trade-in program. The Senate on August 6 rejected a motion, 47–50, to waive the Budget Act with respect to a point of order against the Isakson amendment. Subsequently, the chair upheld the point of order and the amendment fell. The Senate action came in part because any change in the bill after the House left for the August recess would have killed the auto program. *(Cash for clunkers, p. 321)*

Prodded by Senate Majority Leader Harry Reid, D-Nev., whose home state was hit particularly hard by home foreclosures, lawmakers began negotiating in earnest when they returned in September. At the end of October, a bipartisan group of senators announced a deal to extend and expand the credit. The Senate added the provisions to the unemployment compensation bill, along with a provision that expanded the ability of money-losing companies to use current-year losses to offset up to five years of past profits for tax purposes, allowing them to claim refunds. Businesses from the manufacturing, retail, and financial services sectors lobbied hard for the expansion of the net operating loss carryback, which was previously limited to small businesses and allowed only two years of prior taxable profits to be offset. The provision was projected to cost $10.4 billion over ten years. Both the credit and the net operating loss provisions were offset by a multiyear delay in the effective date of a law (PL 108-357) that gave multinational corporations more flexibility in how they handled their interest expenses. *(PL 108-357, Congress and the Nation Vol. XI, p. 115)*

On September 22 the House passed HR 3548, the Unemployment Compensation Extension Act of 2009, by 331–83 under suspension of the rules. The Senate passed an amended version of the bill by a vote of 98–0 on November 4. The next day, the House agreed, 403–12, to suspend the rules and pass the Senate version, completing congressional action. *(Unemployment compensation legislation, p. 517)*

Senate Banking, Housing, and Urban Affairs Committee Chair Christopher J. Dodd, D-Conn., praised the expansion of the credit and predicted that it would be "a real job creator," boosting homebuilders, the real estate industry, and related businesses. The sentiment was echoed by House Speaker Nancy Pelosi, D-Calif., who said that the overall measure would not only help workers who had lost their jobs but also help stimulate the economy and create new jobs, especially with an expanded version of the homebuyer tax credit.

Senator Isakson stressed that the extension of the credit would be the last. "It would not be in the best interest of the United States or of this Senate to extend this credit," he said. "Part of the benefit of a tax credit is the scarcity or the urgency of its sunsetting."

Section 8 Voucher Program

The House Financial Services Committee on July 23, 2009, voted 41–24 to approve a bill (HR 3045) widening access to Section 8 public housing vouchers, under which qualifying low-income families could secure government rent subsidies. Demand for public housing options increased as a result of the recession that began in December 2007, but the supply did not keep pace. HR 3045 was formally reported (H Rept 111-227) on September 30.

PUBLIC HOUSING MARKET

For decades, cities across the nation bulldozed thousands of public housing units that had become magnets for crime and poverty and were too squalid for people to occupy. At the same time, federal policy emphasized Section 8 rental vouchers and public-private agreements that encouraged privately financed landlords to build affordable apartments. However, as such housing became increasingly scarce—and against a backdrop of high unemployment, record foreclosures, and tough credit—the dwindling stock of government-owned apartments was seen as a valuable resource that should be preserved.

The federal government as of 2010 owned approximately 1.1 million public housing units, which were home to low-income people and had years-long waiting lists. The problem was that many of the apartments were built in the 1950s, 1960s, and early 1970s and were increasingly becoming dilapidated. To continue to house low-income people, they needed an estimated $30 billion worth of critical repairs, from new roofs and heating systems to energy-efficient appliances. Mustering political support for low-income housing had always been difficult, which was why the backlog was so large. In an environment of tight budgets and partisan rancor, lawmakers were unlikely to appropriate enough money to pay for needed upgrades.

In the spring of 2010, the Obama administration proposed a startling solution: public housing operators, like homeowners everywhere, should be allowed to borrow against the equity accumulated in their crumbling buildings, potentially enabling them to come up with the cash from private lenders to finance rehabilitation all at once, instead of waiting for Congress to dole out a trickle of assistance. Far-reaching and unorthodox, the proposal was greeted with fierce debate over whether, for the first time, Washington, D.C., should allow private investors to gain an interest in public housing that existed to serve an inherently unprofitable purpose. Public housing was created because the marketplace would not serve the poorest citizens at rents they could afford. Meanwhile, the federal government never provided enough of a subsidy to keep the buildings in good repair. One thing all sides agreed on was that a new source of money was needed to keep the apartments from disappearing altogether. The question was how that should be accomplished.

Advocates said that preserving government-owned housing made sense from a financial and policy perspective, especially because so many billions of dollars had already been invested in these properties. A 2007 study commissioned by the Council of Large Public Housing Authorities estimated the cost of replacing existing developments, including land, at about $162 billion. Advocates also urged preservation because federal housing aid was not an entitlement and, therefore, fell far short of the need. Only about one in four families that received some sort of subsidy would qualify on the basis of income. Keeping public housing permanently in government hands, advocates said, would mean it would not be jeopardized by gentrification or other trends in the private market. Some worried about what would happen if housing authorities took on too much debt and the real estate fell into foreclosure and came under lenders' control. Interests ranging from housing authorities to low-income developers were concerned that a borrowing binge by public housing authorities could crowd out financing for other affordable apartment projects, estimates could understate the cost of repairs, and borrowing against equity might not cover maintenance at the worst projects. The administration was also criticized for proposing to cut the budget for capital maintenance on public housing to pay for the transition to the new system.

Despite the concerns and objections, many stakeholders acknowledged that borrowing in the private market could be the only way to save public housing because the mounting costs had gotten so huge. These interests cautioned, however, that it must be done right—with guarantees that properties would not transfer to private ownership in case of default.

The Section 8 Voucher Reform Act of 2009, sponsored by Rep. Maxine Waters, D-Calif., would alter the formula used to calculate wage eligibility, delineate tenant protections in cases of foreclosure or other landlord delinquency, and add 150,000 more vouchers to the available pool in fiscal 2010. The 111th Congress was the second Congress in a row in which Waters introduced the legislation, initially designed to counteract a 2004 rule change, instituted by the administration of George W. Bush, that decoupled the reimbursement rate on Section 8 vouchers from actual housing costs and instead tied it to older cost estimates without full adjustments for inflation, effectively reducing the stock of vouchers available. The Department of Housing and Urban Development (HUD) supervised Section 8 vouchers, but they were targeted and distributed to recipients by local public housing authorities. *(110th Congress action, Congress and the Nation Vol. XII, p. 644)*

The committee adopted, by voice vote, a manager's amendment, presented by Waters and Chair Barney Frank, D-Mass., to address the Housing Innovation Program, under which selected public housing agencies were authorized to experiment with programs designed to promote self-sufficiency, with the goal of moving people off Section 8 dependency. Republicans pushed to expand the program to more public housing agencies, but Democrats pushed back, arguing that kicking people off housing assistance could increase poverty and homelessness. They also said inadequate internal reviews meant that lawmakers did not know enough about what practices were successful to implement national standards. Under the manager's amendment, sixty housing agencies would be eligible for the program and the HUD secretary was instructed to authorize twenty more. In mid-2009, thirty-three public housing agencies had authorization to participate in the program.

A controversial amendment offered by Rep. Tom Price, R-Ga., and adopted 38–31, would bar any housing authority from restricting legal gun ownership. Thirteen Democrats voted for the measure; two Republicans opposed it. The amendment came in the wake of a 2008 Supreme Court ruling (*District of Columbia v. Heller,* 554 U.S. 570) that the Second Amendment protected an individual's right to bear arms. Although HUD did not have a specific policy concerning guns in public housing, several local agencies had banned them in an effort to reduce violent crime. Amendment opponents said the language would roll back decades of safety initiatives in the most dangerous urban housing projects. Bill supporters said they intended to remove the provision, but many Democrats favored the prohibition on gun bans. *(2008 Court case, Congress and the Nation Vol. XII, p. 769)*

Several Democrats also backed another Price amendment, which would require anyone applying for Section 8 vouchers to produce a photo identification (ID) that met the Real ID Act (PL 109-13) standard, such as a passport or other identification approved by the Department of Homeland Security. Opponents of the amendment, which was adopted 37–31, argued that the language, if intended to weed out illegal immigrants, was redundant, as undocumented immigrants were already prohibited from receiving public housing assistance. *(PL 109-13, Congress and the Nation Vol. XII, p. 234)*

Home Improvement Rebates

The House on May 6, 2010, passed by a vote of 246–161 a bill (HR 5019) to authorize $6 billion in fiscal 2010 and 2011 for Home Star, also known as "cash for caulkers," a consumer rebate program for energy-efficient home improvements. To be managed by the Energy Department, the program was modeled after the 2009 "cash for clunkers" program, which offered consumers money to trade in old cars and buy models with better energy efficiency. HR 5019 also authorized $600 million over two years for a separate program that provided grants to states for assisting low-income households in replacing manufactured homes built before 1976. *(Cash for clunkers, p. 321)*

The House Energy and Commerce Committee approved the Home Star Energy Retrofit Act of 2010 by a vote of 30–17 on April 15. Democrats argued that the program would assist in job creation in the construction sector. Supporters, viewing the program as a step toward energy conservation, said it could reduce America's dependence on foreign energy. Republicans criticized the $6 billion price tag and cast doubt on the Energy Department's ability to administer the program. Before approving the measure, the panel adopted by voice vote a substitute amendment offered by Chair Henry A. Waxman, D-Calif., and three other amendments by separate voice votes, calling for Department of Energy studies of the program, quicker disbursement of rebates, and incentives for low-income residents to participate in the program. HR 5019 was formally reported (H Rept 111-469, Part 1) on April 29.

The House-passed measure offered two levels of rebate. The first level, Silver Star, would provide rebates of up to $1,500 for basic upgrades, such as replacing water heaters or adding insulation. Rebates would be capped at $3,000 per home. The second level, Gold Star, would allow consumers to receive a $3,000 rebate if they completed a home energy audit and made changes that cut energy costs by at least 20 percent.

The House by voice vote adopted a manager's amendment, offered by Waxman, that would, among other things, extend the time the Energy Department would have to designate companies to manage the rebates from thirty to sixty days after enactment. It would require the department to ensure that each state had a sufficient number of such companies to process rebate applications. In addition, the amendment would require that companies handling rebates distribute federal funds to qualifying contractors or vendors within ten days of receiving funds, instead of the originally proposed thirty days. It would require contractors to agree to cooperate with quality assurance procedures on any work done through the rebate program, and it would require random audits of completed home renovations to check compliance with the program.

Republicans objected to the cost of the program and questioned the demand for retrofits. They won support for a provision that would terminate the program if it increased the deficit. It was agreed to, 346–68 on May 6, as part of a motion to recommit the bill to the Energy and Commerce Committee. Most Democrats supported the motion, which also required adding language to make households with incomes exceeding $250,000 ineligible, prohibit participating home repair contractors from hiring anyone convicted of sexual assault or child molestation, and disallow rebates for the installation or replacement of pool heaters.

The White House endorsed the new rebate measure, saying it would "create 'green' jobs in construction and manufacturing, help consumers lower their energy bills and reduce greenhouse gas emissions."

Covered Bonds

On July 28, 2010, the House Financial Services Committee ordered reported the United States Covered Bond Act (HR 5823—no written report), sponsored by Scott Garrett, R-N.J. Covered bonds are a method of finance used for two centuries in Europe that supporters saw as an ideologically friendly way to spur mortgage lending without direct government involvement. The legislation saw no further action.

Covered bonds built on one of the ways that banks found money: issuing debt to Wall Street investors. But they were not the typical bonds that banks and other companies sold every day, in which the firms essentially promised to repay the IOUs with interest. A bank issuing a covered bond backed it with a dedicated pool of mortgages, credit cards, or other loans that served as collateral.

Covered bonds had several perceived advantages over securitized loans that made the idea attractive to lawmakers. Collateral pools were often highly rated and fueled by the best mortgages, which made investors more willing to work with banks and, in turn, gave banks more money to lend to consumers. The collateral stayed on the bank's balance sheet, as opposed to being securitized (sliced up and sold to other institutions). Investors could track which homes and which borrowers were making good on their loans. If a loan in the pool was deteriorating, the bank would have to replace it with a better loan. That could make banks even more interested in ensuring that borrowers could repay their mortgages. Perhaps more important, covered bonds could reduce the industry's reliance on securitization. That practice won praise during the housing boom, which peaked in early 2006, for allowing banks to hand off their loans to investors but came under greater scrutiny during the financial crisis, which dated from late 2007. Critics said the process gave banks incentives to make bad loans and then spread them up and down Wall Street.

Garrett first introduced covered bonds legislation in July 2008, several months after investment bank Bear Stearns collapsed but before the worst of the recession and financial crisis hit. HR 5823 would not create a covered bonds market. In fact, two domestic banks (Washington Mutual and Bank of America) sold covered bonds in 2006. Garrett's proposal was more of an effort to clarify legalities for investors.

Federally insured banks were more likely candidates to issue these sorts of securities. Unlike small banks or uninsured mortgage lenders, the largest financial institutions had a massive portfolio of loans to choose from for inclusion in the covered bonds pool. But because banks were the ones issuing covered bonds, the Federal Deposit Insurance Corporation (FDIC) got involved—and that was when the industry said the market bogged down. Traditional bondholders were accustomed to their spot at the front line when a company crashed. They typically were repaid in full before any other creditors received a dime. The FDIC would probably repay covered bondholders as well, but those investors were not just interested in getting back all their money. They were often entities such as pension funds that invested for the long haul with funding strategies designed to pay out over years, even decades. The FDIC would upend all that if it were to seize collateral and provide covered bondholders a lump-sum repayment.

When Washington Mutual collapsed in 2008, the FDIC quickly sold the company's assets, including its covered bonds contracts, to J.P. Morgan Chase & Co., which continued to use them as a source of funding. However, Washington Mutual was the largest bank failure in history and the FDIC was prepared for it in advance. The agency might not always be able to replicate such a smooth transfer. Investors remained skittish about any mortgage-related asset, but observers said that, regarding covered bonds, what happened if a bank was taken over was the most significant hurdle. HR 5823 would ensure that the FDIC kept paying investors who bought covered bonds from a bank and narrowed the agency's ability to exercise discretion in the wake of a failure. The goal was to create a system in which a bank failure had no impact on investors who bought covered bonds.

The FDIC, which had powerful allies in Congress, was publicly supportive of efforts to improve the covered bonds market. However, the agency still wanted to retain as much discretion as possible over a failed bank. An agency official even raised doubts about whether the legislation was warranted. Instances still arose in which a loan was going south and the bank would rightly want to get rid of it. From the bank's vantage point, selling off that loan into securitization markets would make better sense. And, because the covered bonds market in the United States was largely untested, its success on a large scale was not a given. The biggest question remained whether a covered bonds market would make a tangible impact on the U.S. housing sector.

Drywall Safety

Congress in 2010, as part of the Dodd-Frank Wall Street Reform and Consumer Protection Act (HR 4173—PL 111-203), called on the secretary of housing and urban development, in consultation with the secretary of the Treasury, to conduct a study of the effect on residential mortgage loan foreclosures of the presence of drywall imported from China from 2004 to 2007 in residences subject to mortgage loans, as well as the availability of property insurance for residences with such drywall. *(PL 111-203, p. 88)*

During the housing boom in the early 2000s, a shortage of drywall—the gypsum plaster sandwiched in heavy construction paper that formed the interior walls of most American homes—forced builders, particularly in Florida and in areas of Louisiana and Mississippi that rebuilt after Hurricane Katrina, to import supplies from China. Some homeowners subsequently complained of a putrid odor, reminiscent of rotten eggs, which resulted in their spending thousands of dollars to replace their walls or, in some cases, finding new places to live.

S 739, sponsored by Bill Nelson, D-Fla., and Mary L. Landrieu, D-La., would instruct the Consumer Product Safety Commission (CPSC) to recall Chinese-made drywall, ask the CPSC to work with federal testing labs and the Environmental Protection Agency (EPA) to determine the level of hazard imposed by the drywall, and require the CPSC to issue an interim ban on imports of drywall until federal drywall safety standards were established. The Drywall Safety Act of 2009 was referred to the Senate Commerce, Science, and Transportation Committee but saw no further action. A companion measure (HR 1977), introduced by Robert Wexler, D-Fla., would require the CPSC to study drywall, to determine whether regulations concerning the composition of drywall were necessary, and to issue a ban on defective drywall with more than 5 percent organic compounds. The bill was referred to the House Energy and Commerce Subcommittee on Commerce, Trade, and Consumer Protection Committee.

The 112th Congress cleared drywall safety legislation. *(112th Congress action, p. 511)*

2011–2012

The House passed bills to terminate some federal mortgage aid programs and to establish minimum annual premiums for mortgage insurance offered by the Federal Housing Administration, but none was taken up for consideration by the Senate. Congress did clear legislation to curtail the sale of unsafe drywall for use in building construction.

Foreclosure Aid

The House in 2011 passed four GOP-backed measures (HR 830, HR 836, HR 839, HR 861) to end White House–supported federal mortgage aid programs. Republicans said the programs failed to produce promised results, only delayed the housing recovery, and were a waste of money. The Senate took no action on any of the measures, and President Barack Obama threatened to veto all of them. Congress in 2008 enacted housing finance legislation granting mortgage relief (PL 110-289) to protect overall market stability. *(110th Congress action, Congress and the Nation Vol. XII, p. 629)*

On March 10, HR 830—which passed by a vote of 256–171, with eighteen Democrats joining the Republican majority and one Republican voting "nay"—would end the Federal Housing Administration (FHA) Refinance Program, which was established to help homeowners who owed more than their homes were worth to refinance their loans. The FHA Refinance Program Termination Act would allow borrowers who were current on their mortgages to qualify for FHA-refinanced loans, provided that a lender or investor wrote off at least 10 percent of the unpaid mortgage principal. Republicans said that the program was ineffective and that the refinancing could be handled by the private sector.

The House Financial Services Committee had ordered HR 830 to be reported by a 33–22 vote on March 3 and formally reported the measure (H Rept 112-25) on March 7.

On March 11, HR 836—which passed by 242–177, with eight Democrats supporting it and two Republicans opposing it—would end a Department of Housing and Urban Development (HUD) program that provided emergency loans to unemployed homeowners facing foreclosure. The 2010 financial regulatory overhaul law (PL 111-203) provided $1 billion for the program and authorized HUD to make zero-interest emergency mortgage relief loan payments to unemployed homeowners facing foreclosure for up to twelve months. It also allowed HUD to extend those benefits for an additional year. The program was available to homeowners in Puerto Rico and the thirty-two states not designated as "hardest hit" states—those with unemployment rates at or above the national average or where home prices had declined more than 20 percent since the housing market downturn. *(Financial regulatory overhaul, p. 88)*

Republicans argued that loans provided through the HUD program increased a borrower's indebtedness, making the homeowner worse off, and they contended that the government could lose money as a result of the defaults. Democrats on the Financial Services Committee believed that the program should be continued, saying that it helped responsible homeowners who became unemployed. Along with bill sponsor Jeb Hensarling, R-Texas, Barney Frank of Massachusetts, the ranking Democrat on Financial Services, said that taxpayers should not bear the costs of the program. He said the largest financial institutions should be responsible for the cost of the program because they had caused the crisis.

The House Financial Services Committee had ordered the Emergency Mortgage Relief Program Termination Act to be reported by a vote of 33–22 on March 3 and formally reported it (H Rept 112-26) on March 7.

HR 861, passed on March 16 by a vote of 242–182, with five Democrats voting "aye" and two Republicans voting "nay," would end the Neighborhood Stabilization Program (NSP), which was created in 2008 and provided grants to states and local governments and nonprofit organizations to purchase and redevelop abandoned or foreclosed homes.

About $7 billion had been directed to the program, including allocations in the 2009 stimulus law (PL 111-5) and the 2010 financial regulatory overhaul. HR 861 would rescind $1 billion of unobligated funds authorized for the NSP. The House by voice vote March 16 adopted an amendment offered by Robert Hurt, R-Va., stipulating that all rescinded funds would go to deficit reduction. Frank warned that cities would be left without a way to deal with foreclosed or abandoned properties. *(Stimulus, p. 78)*

The House Financial Services Committee had ordered the NSP Termination Act reported, 31–24, on March 9 and formally reported it (H Rept 112-32) on March 11. A supplemental report (H Rept 112-32, Part 2) was filed on March 14.

HR 839, which was passed on March 29 by a vote of 252–170, with eighteen Democrats voting "aye" and one member voting "present," would terminate the Home Affordable Modification Program (HAMP), the Obama administration's flagship foreclosure prevention program.

Announced in February 2009, HAMP was designed to use money from the Troubled Asset Relief Program (PL 110-343) to give lenders incentives to renegotiate troubled loans with borrowers. More than 600,000 homeowners had worked out permanent mortgage modifications under the program, according to the Treasury Department. Republicans and government oversight agencies consistently criticized the program for being ineffective. At HAMP's inception, administration officials estimated that it would help up to four million at-risk homeowners avoid foreclosure by allowing those eligible to modify their mortgages.

Under the program, homeowners restructure their loans so that their monthly mortgage payments equal 31 percent of pretax gross income. *(PL 110-343, Congress and the Nation Vol. XII, p. 154)*

On March 9, the House Financial Services Committee had ordered the HAMP Termination Act of 2011 reported, 32–23, and formally reported it (H Rept 112-31) on March 11. The panel filed a supplemental report (H Rept 112-31, Part 2) on March 14.

The Senate Judiciary Committee on March 31, 2011, reported S 222 (no written report), aimed at helping homeowners facing foreclosure. The Limiting Investor and Homeowner Loss in Foreclosure Act, sponsored by Sheldon Whitehouse, D-R.I., would explicitly authorize bankruptcy courts to establish foreclosure mediation programs to facilitate negotiations between homeowners and lenders. The committee had approved the measure along party lines, 10–8.

Tom Coburn, R-Okla., argued against enacting the bankruptcy court bill without simultaneously ending HAMP. Whitehouse said he shared his colleague's frustration with HAMP but argued that a Coburn amendment to end the program fell outside the panel's jurisdiction and would unnecessarily broaden the scope of S 222. Whitehouse had criticized HAMP for not "producing anywhere near enough modification to stem the tide" and pointed to mediation programs as tools to help some homeowners. The Coburn amendment was tabled by voice vote.

Affordable Housing

On September 11, 2012, the House agreed by a vote of 402–7 to suspend the rules and pass HR 4264, to establish minimum annual premiums for mortgage insurance offered by the Federal Housing Administration (FHA). FHA insured more than $1 trillion worth of mortgages on more than seven million loans. The agency had been allowed, but was not required, to charge a premium.

The FHA Emergency Fiscal Solvency Act of 2012 would set a minimum annual premium of 0.55 percent of the remaining insured principal mortgage balance and allow a maximum of 2 percent. It also would bar lenders with high rates of early default or insurance claims from originating or underwriting FHA-insured loans. As originally written, the bill would cost an estimated $11 million from fiscal 2013 to 2017 to implement, according to the Congressional Budget Office. The House-passed amended version included offsets by redirecting $2.5 million annually from administrative contract expenses.

HR 4262 had been formally reported (H Rept 112-544) from the House Financial Services Committee on June 20, 2012.

In related action, the House Financial Services Subcommittee on Insurance, Housing, and Community Opportunity approved on February 7, 2012, an affordable housing draft bill that panel chairwoman Judy Biggert, R-Ill., said would modernize and overhaul the Section 8 housing assistance program to help local housing authorities put more low-income tenants on the path to self-sufficiency. The bill, dubbed the Affordable Housing and Self-Sufficiency Improvement Act of 2012, would require public housing agencies with more than 500 or more units to administer a family self-sufficiency program to develop local strategies to help voucher families obtain employment that would lead to economic independence.

Luis V. Gutierrez of Illinois, the ranking Democrat on the subcommittee, said he was concerned about a provision in the draft bill to increase the minimum payment on low-income housing units by nearly 40 percent, from the existing $50 to $69.45 a month. He offered, but later withdrew, an amendment to strike the provision. Gary G. Miller, R-Calif., said that the increase would adjust the minimum for inflation, which has not been increased since 1996.

The affordable housing draft bill was never formally introduced.

Fannie and Freddie Executive Pay

The House Financial Services Committee on January 17, 2012, reported a bill (HR 1221—H Rept 112-366, Part 1) to require the Federal Housing Finance Agency (FHFA) to suspend already-approved multimillion-dollar compensation packages for top executives at the Federal National Mortgage Association (Fannie Mae) and the Federal Home Loan Mortgage Corporation (Freddie Mac). The move would effectively limit their pay to the low- to mid-$200,000s, according to bill sponsor and committee Chair Spencer Bachus, R-Ala.

Existing pay packages of chief executive officers at the two agencies provided about $5 million in salary in addition to an annual bonus. Reports surfaced that ten executives at the two companies were set to receive more than $12 million in bonuses, provoking outcry from Democratic and Republican lawmakers alike. Barney Frank of Massachusetts, ranking Democrat on the Financial Services Committee, originally voted against the measure during a subcommittee markup but, in light of the news of the bonuses, changed his mind and voted for the bill during full committee consideration.

The measure's few opponents included Rep. Melvin Watts, D-N.C., who charged that slicing executive pay would have a negative effect on the companies in the future, undermining their ability to manage their assets.

During the mortgage crisis in 2008, the George W. Bush administration placed Fannie Mae and Freddie Mac under federal conservatorship. The agencies then used funds from the Treasury to cover losses related to bad loans made before the companies were seized.

FANNIE, FREDDIE, AND THE BAILOUT

Since the collapse of the Federal National Mortgage Association (Fannie Mae) and Federal Home Loan Mortgage Corporation (Freddie Mac) during the financial crisis and their takeover by the federal government in 2008, a funny thing happened: the two housing entities started making money again and, as a result, they began slowly paying off their debt to taxpayers with quarterly dividend payments. From the taxpayers' perspective, however, the two companies remained deep in the red.

In addition to the huge losses on their mortgage holdings, in the years immediately after the crisis, Fannie Mae and Freddie Mac sometimes had to borrow money from the Treasury to meet their dividend payment obligations. To stop that from occurring in the future, and to ensure that the companies did not exhaust their government lifeline, the Treasury Department in 2012 rewrote the terms of the 2008 mortgage industry bailout (PL 110-289). Fannie Mae and Freddie Mac would be required to pay all of their future profits as a dividend to the Treasury. In quarters when the companies did not report a profit, they would not be required to pay a dividend. *(2008 mortgage relief, Congress and the Nation Vol. XII, p. 629)*

Previously, Fannie Mae and Freddie Mac paid a 10 percent dividend to the Treasury, even when they made a relatively small profit. That produced a kind of vicious circle in which the two companies would borrow money over the course of the year to meet their total dividend obligations. Each time they required new injections from Treasury, the size of their dividend payment would also rise. At some level, that did not matter, as long as Treasury was providing unlimited aid to the two companies. However, at the end of 2012, Treasury had planned to put limitations on their lifelines, with Fannie Mae eligible for about $125 billion in remaining aid and Freddie Mac receiving up to $150 billion. Those caps meant that a long-term possibility existed, however remote, that they would use all their aid.

Treasury said the new terms would end "the circular practice" of the Treasury advancing money simply to allow the companies to pay dividends to the government, while also "providing greater market certainty regarding the financial strength" of Fannie Mae and Freddie Mac. The move also sent a signal to investors that the two companies would not be preserved in their existing form.

Drywall Safety

Congress in 2012 cleared legislation (HR 4212) to prevent the sale of unsafe drywall, to have the manufacturer of drywall readily identifiable, and to ensure that problem drywall removed from homes was not reused. President Barack Obama signed the Drywall Safety Act of 2012 into law (PL 112-266) on January 14, 2013.

Problems with drywall made in China—specifically, complaints of an unpleasant odor—surfaced in the mid-2000s, following an increased demand for the product because of the housing boom and the rebuilding in areas devastated by Hurricane Katrina in 2005. Congress in 2010 called for a study of the effect of the defective drywall on residential mortgage loan foreclosures. *(111th Congress action, p. 508)*

The House agreed by voice vote on September 19, 2012, to suspend the rules and pass HR 4212. The Senate passed an amended version by voice vote on December 21. The House agreed to the Senate changes under suspension of the rules, 378–37, on January 1, 2013.

As enacted, HR 4212 would require labels identifying gypsum board by manufacturer and month and year of production. It called on the Consumer Product Safety Commission (CPSC) to promulgate a rule limiting the sulfur content of drywall manufactured or imported for use in the United States. The CPSC also was instructed to revise its guidelines to specify that problem drywall removed from homes could not be reused or used as a component in the manufacture of new drywall. The law contained a sense of Congress section directing the secretary of commerce to insist that the government of the People's Republic of China meet with representatives of the companies that manufactured the drywall and of the U.S. government to seek a remedy for homeowners who had the problem drywall in their homes. Furthermore, it was the sense of Congress that the commerce secretary should insist that the Chinese government direct the drywall companies to submit to the rulings of the U.S. federal courts regarding homeowners' troubles with the problem drywall.

Government-Sponsored Enterprises

The House Financial Services Subcommittee on Capital Markets and Government Sponsored Enterprises by voice vote on July 12, 2011, approved three bills (HR 2439, HR 2440, HR 2462) to bar the creation of new versions of the Federal National Mortgage Association (Fannie Mae) and the Federal Home Loan Mortgage Corporation (Freddie Mac), limit federal contributions, and curb the companies' activities.

The federal government chartered Fannie Mae and Freddie Mac before they were sold to private investors. In September 2008, the two companies were taken over by the government as the housing sector collapsed and the firms absorbed huge losses. Although bipartisan consensus emerged on the need to overhaul the nation's housing finance system, Democrats and Republicans were at odds over the role the government-sponsored enterprises (GSEs) should play in the mortgage market. Most Republicans wanted to privatize the market, while Democrats said that some federal involvement was necessary.

The Removing GSEs Charters during Receivership Act of 2011 (HR 2439), sponsored by Steve Stivers, R-Ohio, prohibited the creation of any replica of Fannie Mae and Freddie Mac with a government charter and private stockholders. The subcommittee narrowly adopted, 18–14, an amendment offered by John Campbell, R-Calif., to hinge the revocation of the GSEs' charters on a determination by the Federal Housing Finance Agency that an alternate private secondary mortgage market existed.

The Market Transparency and Taxpayer Protection Act of 2011 (HR 2440), sponsored by Robert Hurt, R-Va., would require the GSEs to dispose of nonmission-related assets, including patents and valuable mortgage data, in hopes of further winding down the firms.

The Cap the GSE Bailout Act of 2011 (HR 2462), sponsored by Michael G. Fitzpatrick, R-Pa., would cap at $200 billion the amount of public funds Fannie Mae and Freddie Mac could receive while in government receivership.

In related action, the subcommittee on April 6, 2011, had voted 20–14 to forward to the full committee HR 1224, the GSE Portfolio Risk Reduction Act of 2011. The bill, sponsored by Jeb Hensarling, R-Texas, would cap the GSEs' maximum portfolio size at $700 billion and gradually reduce that cap to $250 billion over five years.

Homeless Children and Youth

The House Financial Services Subcommittee on Insurance, Housing, and Community Opportunity by voice vote February 7, 2012, approved the Homeless Children and Youth Act (HR 32), which would expand the Department of Housing and Urban Development definition of "homeless" to include all children and youth who were verified as homeless by other government agencies. The bill subsequently was referred to the House Education and the Workforce Subcommittee on Early Childhood, Elementary, and Secondary Education. It died upon adjournment of the 112th Congress.

CHAPTER 12

Labor and Pensions

Introduction	515
Chronology of Action on Labor and Persions	517
2009–2010	517
2011–2012	535

Labor and Pensions

President Obama entered office in 2009 amid a deep economic recession and immediately sought ways to provide relief for millions of unemployed workers, create new jobs, and launch retraining efforts. Those priorities became the underpinnings of the economic stimulus law that he and Democratic leaders ushered through Congress early that year. The stimulus law, signed on the heels of passage of a long-sought measure aimed at helping workers sue employers for wage discrimination, provided hope to labor unions—a traditional constituency of Democrats—that the party then controlling both the executive and legislative branches could move forward on a range of other priorities.

But Democrats' success on subsequent initiatives was more limited than labor had hoped because Congress faced continuing pressure to rein in the federal spending; Republicans, who took control of the House in the 112th session beginning in 2011, pushed back against high-priced proposals and sought to unravel what they viewed as cumbersome regulations throughout government, including labor rules.

The recession that began in 2007 ultimately was the longest since World War II. The unemployment rate was 7.8 percent in January 2009 and the same in December 2012, but the Bureau of Labor Statistics (BLS) reported a steep climb early in that four-year time period that peaked at close at 10.1 percent in October 2009.

The BLS also reported that the average length of time an individual was unemployed sharply increased between 2009 and 2012, from 19.8 weeks in January 2009 to 38.1 weeks in December 2012, reaching as high as nearly forty-one weeks in 2011. Unemployed individuals looked longer for work in 2011, compared with 2007, before giving up and leaving the labor force: 21.4 weeks versus 8.7 weeks, respectively.

Obama and Democrats pushed through Congress several extensions of unemployment benefits for those who continued to be unable to find jobs. They repeatedly beat back GOP attempts to offset the cost, estimated at about $30 billion annually, and eventually extended benefits up to ninety-nine weeks. Without the extension, unemployed workers would have been limited to a maximum of twenty-six weeks of aid. In the 112th Congress, Republicans trimmed down the long-term unemployment benefits in recognition that the economy was beginning to turn around.

Democrats also looked out for the long-term unemployed by including in the economic stimulus law a subsidy to help individuals and families cover premiums for health care under federal law, the Consolidated Omnibus Budget Reconciliation Act of 1985 (COBRA). Ultimately that subsidy became a victim of drawn-out negotiations on spending and was phased out even while other unemployment benefits continued. The stimulus law and subsequent extensions also continued aid to workers who either lost their jobs or faced reduced hours and wages as a result of trade agreements.

President Obama introduced a broad $447 billion package in September 2011 to address a range of further incentives to create jobs. Democrats made a brief attempt to pass the package as a whole, but ultimately had to settle for promoting a series of narrower bills. They pushed through a measure to provide hiring incentives for employers and

REFERENCES

Discussion of labor and pension policy for the years 1945–1964 may be found in *Congress and the Nation Vol. I,* pp. 565–657, 1220–1272, 1289–1320; for the years 1965–1968, *Congress and the Nation Vol. II,* pp. 601–622, 734–743, 745–778; for the years 1969–1972, *Congress and the Nation Vol. III,* pp. 605–621, 703–742; for the years 1973–1976, *Congress and the Nation Vol. IV,* pp. 403–432, 681–713; for the years 1977–1980, *Congress and the Nation Vol. V,* pp. 231–251, 399–425; for the years 1981–1984, *Congress and the Nation Vol. VI,* pp. 643–672; for the years 1985–1988, *Congress and the Nation Vol. VII,* pp. 687–709; for the years 1989–1992, *Congress and the Nation Vol. VIII,* pp. 703–738; for the years 1993–1996, *Congress and the Nation Vol. IX,* pp. 653–675; for the years 1997–2000, *Congress and the Nation Vol. X,* pp. 571–585; for the years 2001–2004, *Congress and the Nation Vol. XI,* pp. 563–578; for the years 2005–2008, *Congress and the Nation Vol. XII,* pp. 651–671.

Outlays for Social Security

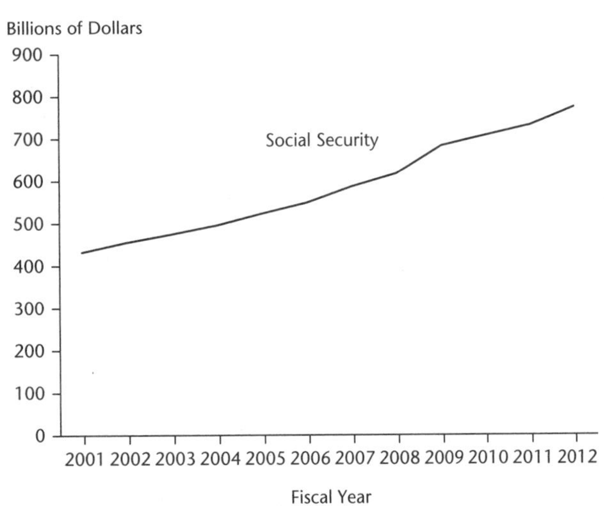

SOURCE: Office of Management and Budget, *Historical Tables, Budget of the United States Government: Fiscal Year 2013* (Washington, D.C.: U.S. Government Printing Office, 2012), Table 3.2.

NOTE: Total line includes expenditures not shown separately.

two other bills to send states money to stave off layoffs in education. (Funding for unemployment benefits also were part of the original package and addressed separately.)

On another front, Congress set restrictions on bonuses paid to executives of firms that had received funds from the financial services bailout of 2008, reacting to a public outrage that hundreds of thousands of workers were losing jobs in the wake of the financial meltdown of 2008, while high-level executives were reaping benefits paid for by the government.

Congress also pushed through a measure requiring a higher minimum wage for construction workers in Guam employed on projects for a U.S. marine relocation; however, lawmakers repeatedly delayed scheduled wage increases for workers in the U.S. territories of American Samoa and the Commonwealth of the Northern Mariana Islands. Issues in the debate over a minimum wage standard for home health care workers, a growing industry, were not resolved and were carried into the 113th Congress that opened in 2013.

Unions pushed for an increase in the minimum wage for all workers in the United States and reminded Obama of his 2008 campaign promise to propose such an increase. The president never made it part of his agenda during his first term in office, however. Although Democrats took some initial steps to propose an increase during the 112th Congress, they recognized Republicans would not support it and did not press the issue.

Organized labor groups remained frustrated on a number of other issues. When Republicans took majority control of the House in 2011, they sought to change a range of labor rules that governed, for example, how unions were organized. In addition, legislation regarding wage parity lawsuits did not clear Congress during Obama's first term.

Lawmakers did squeeze through a narrow measure mandating that new hires in the federal workforce pay more toward their pension premiums. Also, the growing costs of such entitlement programs as Social Security and Medicare continued to be the subject of political and budget debates as they had in previous years. Some discussions about slimming government costs focused on altering how the formula for the Consumer Price Index was used to set cost-of-living increases for Social Security payments, but no formal overhaul to the full entitlement program was proposed. *(CPI calculations, box, p. 542)*

Speaker of the House Nancy Pelosi signs the recently passed unemployment benefit extension legislation, as she is joined by members of the House Ways and Means Committee at an enrollment ceremony on Capitol Hill in Washington, D.C., on July 22, 2010. The House voted 272–152 to approve the legislation that will restore unemployment benefits to people who have been out of work for six months or more.
Source: Kevin Dietsch/UPI/Newscom

Chronology of Action on Labor and Pensions

2009–2010

In early 2009, Democratic leaders, emboldened by results of the election the previous fall in which their party won control of both the White House and Congress, were able to swiftly put into law President Barack Obama's economic stimulus plan. The legislation was estimated to cost $787 billion and included a range of provisions Democrats touted as job-creation measures, as well as benefits for the unemployed and underemployed.

Congress extended and expanded benefits programs for the jobless through the 111th Congress, but doing so was not easy as the Democratic leadership in both chambers battled with Republicans. Both parties recognized the need for such domestic programs, yet they differed on how to pay for them. The GOP argued that either offsets proposed in the bills to pay for them would smother economic progress or that the lack of offsets would increase the federal deficit. But Democrats said the measures fell under guidelines for emergency spending and therefore did not require offsets.

The stimulus measure also provided a subsidy to help the unemployed pay their premiums for continued health care under their former employer, and extended and expanded unemployment benefits for employees and firms whose jobs or business were affected by changes in international trade rules. *(Stimulus legislation, p. 78; trade rules, p. 199)*

The 111th Congress also saw long-awaited passage of the Lilly Ledbetter Act to help employees file wage discrimination suits, although Democrats were unable to pass a bill sought by organized labor that would place the burden of proof on employers involved in lawsuits alleging pay disparities between men and women.

Labor was encouraged about prospects for the rest of its agenda following passage of Obama's landmark health care reform package (HR 3590—PL 111-148) in March 2010. But a strengthened Tea Party movement, which wielded considerable power during the Republican primary and general elections that fall, maintained a vocal campaign to reduce government spending and blocked many of the proposals. *(Health care legislation, p. 421)*

By the end of the 111th Congress, the labor movement that had helped power Obama to the White House remained largely frustrated. Even labor's top priority of "card check" legislation to make it easier for workers to unionize did not clear Congress.

Unemployment Compensation

As the economic recession continued to deepen and the unemployment rate across the United States rose, Congress extended and expanded a 2008 program to provide federal unemployment benefits to workers.

The unemployment rate in January 2009 was 7.8 percent, and that rate continued to rise through the year, reaching 10.1 percent by October before dropping only slightly and remaining between 9.8 percent and 9.5 percent during most of 2010, according to the Bureau of Labor Statistics. *(Economic crisis background, p. 47)*

Beginning with the economic stimulus law in February 2009, Congress provided unemployment compensation programs to provide additional benefits to the millions of workers who could not find jobs in the hardest-hit states. Lawmakers further expanded the program and extended it five more times to continue to provide access to benefits for a growing number of unemployed. Lawmakers ultimately extended the benefits program to the end of 2011 as part of a contentious, year-end bargain between Republicans and President Obama that was focused primarily on tax cuts (HR 4853—PL 111-312). *(Tax legislation, p. 144)*

Passage of those extensions came amid fierce partisan debate. Republicans recognized support for unemployment benefits among their own constituents in the struggling economy, but they repeatedly called for budget

LABOR LEADERSHIP

Widely recognized as a progressive union advocate, former Democratic representative Hilda Solis of California, President Barack Obama's labor secretary during his first term, encountered challenges from Republicans both during her Senate confirmation process and later, as the GOP sought to bar a series of labor rules they charged would hurt businesses and further damage the economy.

"For the past eight years, the Department of Labor hasn't lived up to its role. That will change when Hilda Solis takes over," Obama vowed. But Republicans worked hard to bar major changes under her administration.

Solis, the first female Hispanic state senator in California, had successfully pressed to increase the state's minimum wage in the 1990s. After her election to the U.S. House of Representatives in 2000, she became the only member of Congress to sit on the board of American Rights at Work, a prolabor organization. She also backed labor protections in free-trade agreements and advocated training for workers to obtain jobs in environmental areas. She served four terms in the House, representing a predominantly Latino district.

Labor unions vigorously supported Obama's nomination of Solis. But she was an immediate target for Republicans owing to her work with American Rights at Work and her efforts in Congress to make it easier for unions to organize workers. During the Senate confirmation hearing in January 2009, Solis faced questions on several contentious issues, such as the Employee Free Choice Act and ergonomic rules that had been lifted during the administration of George W. Bush, Obama's predecessor. Republicans followed up with a series of written questions. When Republican lawmakers threatened to put a hold on the nomination, Obama appointed longtime Labor Department official Edward C. Hugler to serve as acting secretary.

Solis's written responses satisfied committee Republicans. Senators confirmed her nomination, 80–17, on February 24, 2009.

Labor leaders, however, became quickly disillusioned. Early in her tenure, she moved to strengthen enforcement of workplace safety rules, advocating legislation and hiring 250 additional inspectors for the Occupational Health and Safety Administration (OSHA). She also vowed to back a "card check" bill to help workers unionize by requiring employers to recognize a union as soon as a majority of workers signed cards saying they wanted a union, without a secret-ballot election. But Solis seemingly failed to play a prominent, or at least visible, role in addressing the issue of unemployment or in advancing union protections. She did not serve on the National Economic Council, as had President Bill Clinton's first labor secretary, Robert Reich.

Within the department, observers said, Solis worked to rally agency employees whose morale had sunk under the previous Republican administration. Solis told the *National Journal* in a September 2010 interview: "While Hilda may not be out there in the headlines or in the *Washington Post* or whatever, I think I am more effective when I am working behind the scenes and conducting the business I have to."

Solis faced increasing pressure to deal with unemployment and to address continuing questions about mine safety. She expressed hope for passage of stricter regulations governing mine and workplace safety following several industrial accidents, including an April 5, 2010, explosion that killed twenty-nine workers at a West Virginia mine. But proposed safety measures (HR 5663, S 3671) stalled during the 111th Congress among partisan wrangling and debates about the proper scope of the legislation.

Democrats renewed their calls for legislation in May 2011 after a West Virginia state investigation reported that lapses by Massey Energy, coupled with lax oversight by federal and state agencies, were responsible for the 2010 explosion. The Mine Safety and Health Administration also blamed weak regulations under a previous mine safety law (PL 109-236). Republicans, meanwhile, held the Labor Department responsible for the disaster and called on the agency to provide more responsible enforcement. Again, Solis was accused of adopting too low a profile on the issue.

She, along with other cabinet members, stepped out in front of the cameras a few times to advocate the president's broad job creation package in 2011. But conservative Republicans, with increasing numbers in the House and Senate, remained consistent foes of the administration's initiatives.

After Obama won reelection in 2012, Solis announced she would resign her position. She left the administration on January 22, 2013.

offsets to the cost and accused the White House and Democrats of uncontrolled spending.

The White House and Democrats on Capitol Hill in turn accused Republicans of being insensitive to the plight of millions of unemployed workers. Democrats increasingly called for Republicans to agree to partially offset the cost of unemployment benefits with a tax hike on the wealthy—a proposal GOP leaders strongly opposed. But Democrats also contended the benefits should qualify as emergency spending and therefore not be subject to statutory pay-as-you-go requirements.

BACKGROUND

Unemployed workers were eligible for up to twenty-six weeks of state compensation under a joint federal-state unemployment compensation (UC) program authorized by the Social Security Act of 1935. For individuals who exhausted those benefits and remained unemployed, the Supplemental Appropriations Act of 2008 (PL 110-252) included language that created a federal temporary program, called Emergency Unemployment Compensation 2008 (EUC08), which provided another thirteen weeks of federal benefits for individuals who had worked for twenty weeks before being laid off. State unemployment compensation agencies administered the EUC08 program along with regular unemployment compensation benefits. *(Congress and the Nation Vol. XII, p. 667)*

It was the eighth time since 1958 that Congress had created a temporary program to extend unemployment compensation during an economic slowdown, according to the Congressional Research Service (the temporary programs dated from 1958, 1961, 1972, 1975, 1982, 1991, and 2002).

As national unemployment rates continued to rise, from 5.6 percent in June 2008, when the measure was signed into law, to 6.5 percent in October 2008, Congress cleared a measure (PL 110-449) that November to extend the benefits. That law created two tiers of benefits. Under Tier I, the maximum number of weeks an individual was eligible for benefits was capped at twenty (with some individuals eligible for fewer weeks if their regular UC benefit entitlement at the state was less than twenty-six weeks). Once unemployed individuals had exhausted Tier I benefits, they were eligible for the second tier of benefits, which provided up to another thirteen weeks of compensation if the state's total unemployment rate was 6 percent or higher. *(Congress and the Nation Vol. XII, p. 668)*

Although the EUC08 was temporary, a separate program known as extended benefits (EB) was permanently authorized under the Federal-State Extended Unemployment Compensation Act of 1970 (PL 91-373). It provided for additional weeks of unemployment benefits: up to thirteen weeks during periods of unemployment and, at the option of each state, up to twenty weeks during periods of extremely high unemployment. The 2008 law allowed states to determine which benefit would be paid first—the EUC08 benefit or the EB benefit. The federal government financed half of the EB benefits while states funded the other half through their accounts in the Unemployment Trust Fund (UTF).

FIRST EXTENSION OF 2009: STIMULUS LEGISLATION (HR 1)

Before unemployment benefits provided in 2008 were phased out at the end of March 2009, Congress in February included in its economic stimulus law (HR 1—PL 111-5) language to extend the EUC08 program through December 31 and provide a Federal Additional Compensation (FAC) of $25 per week. The FAC was available for individuals who received benefits from other unemployment compensation programs, including the unemployment compensation program, the EUC08 program, Disaster Unemployment Assistance, or Trade Adjustment Assistance. The stimulus measure also suspended income taxation on the first $2,400 of unemployment benefits received in 2009.

The House passed HR 1 on January 28, 2009, by a partisan 244–188 vote with no Republicans supporting the bill and only eleven Democrats opposing it. It extended unemployment insurance from the end of March through December 31, 2009. On February 9, senators on a **key vote of 61–36 (R 3–36; D 56–0; I 2–0)** invoked cloture to end a filibuster against the legislation. The chamber passed the bill February 10 by a vote of 61–37. After differences in each chamber's version were resolved, the House adopted the conference report on February 13 by a **key vote of 246–183 (R 0–176; D 246–7)**. The Senate quickly cleared the conference report the same day by a 60–38 vote. President Obama signed the stimulus bill on February 17. *(2009 key votes, p. 751)*

Major Unemployment Compensation Provisions

- Extended the EUC08 program through December 2009.
- Provided temporary 100 percent federal financing of the extended benefits program.
- Authorized a temporary $25 per week FAC supplemental benefit.
- Specified that states did not owe or accrue interest, through December 2010, on federal loans for the payment of unemployment benefits.
- Provided for a transfer up to $7 billion from the federal unemployment account to state unemployment programs as "incentive payments" for changing certain state UC laws.
- Provided for a transfer of $500 million to the states for administering unemployment programs.
- Created an Emergency Contingency Fund (ECF) within the Temporary Assistance for Needy Families (TANF) block grant to states, Indian tribes, and the territories. States, Indian tribes, and the territories were reimbursed 80 percent of the costs of increased expenditures on direct aid to families.

FUNDING EXTENSION IN 2009 (HR 3357)

Until February 16, 2009, the EUC08 program had been financed with funds from the Unemployment Trust Fund. The stimulus law authorized the U.S. Treasury to cover 100 percent of the program as well as the $25 weekly supplemental benefit.

In July 2009, Congress cleared legislation (HR 3357—PL 111-46) that, among other things, provided open-ended appropriations for the Unemployment Trust Fund,

PERMANENT AND TEMPORARY UNEMPLOYMENT BENEFIT PROGRAMS

Permanent Unemployment Benefits Programs

Unemployment Compensation (UC) program authorized by Social Security Act of 1935. The federal-state program provided up to twenty-six weeks of unemployment benefits. (*Congress and the Nation Vol. I, p. 1290)*

Extended Benefits (EB) program, authorized under Federal-State Extended Unemployment Compensation Act of 1970 (PL 91-373). Provided for additional weeks of unemployment—up to thirteen weeks during periods of unemployment and up to twenty weeks during periods of high unemployment. *(Congress and the Nation Vol. III, p. 715)*

Temporary Benefits Programs of 2008

Supplemental Appropriations Act of 2008 (PL 110-252), signed into law in June 2008, created the Emergency Unemployment Compensation (EUC08) program. Provided for another thirteen weeks of unemployment benefits. *(Congress and the Nation Vol. XII, pp. 387, 667)*

Unemployment Compensation Extension Act of 2008 (PL 110-449) signed into law in October 2008, created two tiers of benefits under EUC08:

- Tier I: Maximum eligibility was capped at twenty weeks.
- Tier II: After Tier I benefits were exhausted, individuals were eligible for up to another thirteen weeks of benefits if they had worked in a state with a total unemployment rate of 6 percent or higher.

The law allowed states to determine which to pay first: EUC08 benefit or EB benefit. *(Congress and the Nation Vol. XII, p. 668)*

American Recovery and Reinvestment Act of 2009 (PL 111-5), signed into law in February 2009, extended expiration of EUC08 from March 2009 through December 31, 2009, provided a Federal Additional Compensation (FAC) of $25 per week, and suspended income taxation on the first $2,400 of unemployment benefits received in 2009. *(PL 111-5, pp. 78, 519)*

Worker, Homeownership and Business Assistance Act (PL 111-92), signed into law in November 2009, expanded the 2008 unemployment program, adding fourteen more weeks of benefits for the unemployed. *(PL 111-92, p. 521)*

It created the following tiers:

- A new Tier II that provided another fourteen weeks of benefits.
- A Tier III that offered another thirteen weeks of benefits in states with unemployment rates of at least 6 percent.
- A Tier IV that offered another six weeks of benefits in states with unemployment rates of at least 8.5 percent.

Fiscal 2010 Defense Appropriations Act (PL 111-118), signed into law December 2009, extended the benefits program to February 2010, including the $25 weekly benefit. *(PL 111-18, p. 521)*

Temporary Extension Act of 2010 (PL 111-144), signed March 2010, extended through April 5, 2010, the 2008 unemployment benefits program, the $25 FAC weekly supplement. Made benefits retroactive to February 28, 2010. *(PL 111-144, p. 522)*

Continuing Extension Act of 2010 (PL 111-157), signed April 2010, extended the EUC08 benefits to June 2, 2010. Extended COBRA subsidy (health benefits support) through May 31, after which point the subsidy ended. *(PL 111-157, p. 522)*

Unemployment Compensation Extension Act of 2010 (PL 111-205), signed July 2010, extended federal jobless benefits through November 30, 2010. It did not extend the $25 FAC benefit. *(PL 111-205, p. 523)*

The Tax Relief, Unemployment, Insurance Reauthorization, and Job Creation Act of 2010 (PL 111–312), signed into law December 2010, extended the EUC08 program until January 3, 2012. *(PL 111-312, p. 524)*

Temporary Payroll Tax Cut Continuation Act of 2011 (PL 112-78), signed December 2011, extended authorization for EUC08 program through the week ending on or before March 6, 2012. *(PL 112-78, p. 535)*

Middle Class Tax Relief and Job Creation Act of 2012 (PL 112-96), signed into law February 2011, extended the program through January 2, 2013. Reduced the maximum benefits from ninety-nine weeks to seventy-three weeks in states with unemployment rates above 9 percent, and sixty-three weeks in states with lower unemployment rates. *(PL 112-96, p. 536)*

American Taxpayer Relief Act of 2012 (PL 112-240), signed into law January 2013, extended the program through December 3, 2013. It maintained the four tiers of benefits and the reduced maximum weeks set by the previous extension. *(PL 112-240, p. 537)*

thus allowing states to continue to borrow federal funds to pay unemployment benefits. Congress had added $422 million to the fund in the fiscal 2009 omnibus spending law (PL 111-8), but almost all the money had been spent. (PL 111-46 also distributed funds to the federal Highway Trust Fund through the fiscal year and increased authority for the Federal Housing Administration's two main mortgage-assistance programs.)

The House passed the bill, 363–68, on July 29, and the Senate followed suit on July 30, voting 79–17. The president signed it into law on August 7.

BENEFITS EXPANSION IN 2009 (HR 3548)

As unemployment continued to rise, reaching 10.1 percent in October 2009, Congress expanded the 2008 extended unemployment compensation program in November, adding additional weeks of benefits for all states (PL 111-92). That measure created two more tiers of benefits, providing for up to another twenty weeks of benefits. The measure did not extend the expiration date in the stimulus.

On September 22, 2009, the House passed, 331–83, the Worker, Homeownership, and Business Assistance Act (HR 3548), which included language to create a third tier of EUC08 benefits. The primary purpose was to provide an additional thirteen weeks of benefits—for a total of forty-six weeks—for workers in states with an unemployment rate of 8.5 percent or higher. It included major provisions that:

- Authorized another year of 0.2 percent Federal Unemployment Tax Act surtax—about $14 per worker, paid by employers. (FUTA originally was enacted in 1939 to finance the national unemployment insurance program. The basic tax has been 6 percent on the first $7,000 employers paid to employees. The surtax of 0.2 percent was added in 1976.)
- Required employers to report the first day of earnings of a new worker to the National Directory of New Hires.
- Amended the Internal Revenue Code to permit states to reduce the federal income tax overpayment for individuals who owed a covered unemployment compensation debt regardless of whether the state recovering the funds and the state where the individual lived were the same.

On November 4, 2009, the Senate passed the House bill (HR 3548) by a vote of 98–0 after amending it to create another tier (a new Tier II) and adding a total of another fourteen weeks of benefits, regardless of a state's unemployment rate. It created a third tier offering another thirteen weeks of benefits in states with unemployment rate of at least 6 percent, and a fourth tier of another six weeks of benefits in states with unemployment rates of 8.5 percent or higher.

The measure also included provisions regarding eligibility for food stamp payments, assurance that railroad workers who have their own unemployment insurance system would receive about the same increase in benefits, and an authorization of the 0.2 percent FUTA surtax through 2010 and the first six months of 2011. (The tax expired on July 1, 2011.)

The House accepted the Senate version of HR 3548 on November 5, 2009, by a vote of 403–12. The president signed the bill into law (PL 111-92) on November 6.

BENEFITS EXTENSION TO FEBRUARY 2010 (HR 3326)

The House made several attempts to provide a long-term extension of unemployment benefits before attaching to a fiscal 2010 spending measure a short-term extension to February 28, 2010 (HR 3326—PL 111-118) while waiting for the Senate to complete work on a broad healthcare overhaul measure.

Tax extenders bill. In one unsuccessful attempt, the House on December 9, 2009, passed by a 241–181 vote a bill (HR 4213) that included language to extend unemployment insurance benefits. The language was wrapped in a package of extensions of popular tax provisions, paid for by restricting international tax evasion and hiking taxes on venture capitalists and investment fund managers. But the Senate, focused on the health care reform debate, did not take up the measure before tax provisions expired on December 31, 2009, forcing lawmakers to turn to short-term extensions of unemployment benefits.

Job creation legislation. A week later, on December 16, the House passed, 217–212, a bill, dubbed the Jobs for Main Street Act (HR 2847), that was aimed at stemming the unemployment rate. Among many provisions, it included $79 billion in assistance for families and small businesses that would come from general funds and be treated as emergency spending. It also included language to extend through June both supplemental federal unemployment benefits and eligibility for a 65 percent subsidy for laid-off workers to help pay federal COBRA premiums. (*HR 2847 action, p. 527*)

The rule for floor debate had added provisions enacting pay-as-you-go rules, requiring that any new entitlement spending or tax cuts not contribute to the deficit. Focused primarily on providing a tax incentive for employers to hire new workers, the bill became law (PL 111-147) on March 18, 2010. *(PL 111-147, P. 85)*

Defense appropriations bill. The defense appropriations bill (HR 3326), considered a "must-pass" bill, became a vehicle for several year-end measures that had not passed. After the Senate had approved an amended version of the spending bill in October 2009, the House passed the bill by a 395–34 vote on December 16, 2009. Included within the bill was an amendment to extend through February 28, 2010, certain provisions relating to emergency unemployment insurance benefits, including the extra $25 weekly benefit and 100 percent federal funding for the extended benefits program.

The Senate cleared the House-amended bill, 88–10, on December 19. The president signed it into law (PL 111-118) the same day.

EXTENSION TO APRIL 2010 (HR 4691)

In early March 2010, Congress cleared and the president signed the Temporary Extension Act of 2010 (HR 4691—PL 111-144), which extended three temporary unemployment provisions through the week ending on or before April 5, 2010: EUC08, the additional $25 supplemental weekly benefits, and 100 percent federal financing of the extended benefits program. The extension also made the benefits retroactive to February 28, 2010, to cover the brief gap in authorization before the latest extension was cleared.

The House passed HR 4691 by voice vote on February 25, with Democrats stating that the costs were emergency spending and therefore did not have to be offset.

Sen. Jim Bunning, R-Ky., who was not running for reelection, repeatedly barred the Senate from taking up the short-term reauthorization bill, holding a filibuster as he insisted that all programs be paid for with funds from the economic stimulus law.

Democrats charged Bunning with being insensitive, stating that millions of citizens hard hit by the recession would stop receiving unemployment checks. Bunning replied: "If we can't find $10 billion somewhere for a bill that everybody in this body supports, we will never pay for anything. So I continue my objection." Sen. Dick Durbin, D-Ill., stated on the floor: "The simple fact of the matter is that this is an emergency situation and should be treated as such."

Bunning finally relented on March 2, accepting Democratic leaders' offer to hold a vote on a proposal to pay for the bill by curbing paper manufacturers' ability to claim tax breaks for a wood byproduct called "black liquor." That proposal, considered as an amendment to the extension bill, was defeated, 43–53, on a procedural vote. The Senate then cleared the bill, 78–19, and Obama signed it into law the same day.

EXTENSION TO JUNE 2010 (HR 4851)

A similar battle caused a subsequent ten-day lapse in benefits before Congress on April 15 cleared the Continuing Extension Act of 2010 (HR 4851—PL 111-157) to extend benefits until the week ending on or before June 2, 2010.

Democrats had urged Republicans to sign onto the short-term measure to extend unemployment benefits through May 5 and extend COBRA health insurance subsidies and higher payments for physicians treating Medicare patients through April 30.

The House on March 17 agreed by voice vote to suspend the rules and pass a version of the bill providing a one-month extension and sent the legislation to the Senate.

In the Senate, the bill became a vehicle that the parties used to debate whether the spending, which most senators favored, was emergency in nature and thus did not require budget cuts to offset the amounts, or whether it was not a matter of emergency and therefore had to be paid for by cutting expenditures elsewhere.

Democrats continued to argue the funding was emergency spending in light of the recession, while Sen. Tom Coburn of Oklahoma led a group of Republicans who blocked a vote on the measure, complaining its costs were not fully offset and would add to the deficit.

"There's nobody on our side that doesn't want to extend the unemployment benefits. The difference is we want to extend them without hurting" future generations, Coburn stated. Before departing for the congressional spring break, Senate Majority Leader Harry Reid, D-Nev., filed a motion for cloture, to end debate and proceed to the bill, which the Senate would consider upon its return on April 12.

Reid's motion came after Republicans had repeatedly objected to attempts by Senate Democrats to first pass the measure by unanimous consent. Sen. Carl Levin, D-Mich., stated: "Here we are up against the wall of obstructionism again, while thousands of our constituents—people in every state—wonder what is it exactly that we're doing here that will deny the extension of unemployment benefits when we have a deep recession."

On April 12, the Senate voted 60–34 to limit debate and proceed to the bill. On April 14, senators voted 60–40 to waive a point of order that the plan violated pay-as-you-go budget rules. The Senate the following day passed the bill, with changes, by a vote of 59–38, after rebuffing GOP attempts to pay for the bill's cost.

The bill included provisions to extend unemployment benefits until June 2 (other programs under the extension—physician Medicare payments and a national flood insurance program, for example—were extended through the end of May). The measure also included back pay for workers furloughed because of a lapse in the Highway Trust Fund. Three Republicans voted for the bill: Olympia J. Snowe and Susan Collins of Maine and George V. Voinovich of Ohio.

The amended measure then went back to the House on April 15, where it was cleared a few hours later, by a vote of 289–112, after some further partisan sparring.

Democrats again accused Republicans of obstruction and insensitivity to the unemployed, while Republicans argued that Democrats were increasing the deficit while failing to lower the unemployment rate. "Those looking for work when there are no jobs available are waiting for action by this House. At long last the Senate has acted," said House Ways and Means Chair Sander M. Levin, D-Mich. "Those who talk about balancing budgets, who have not balanced them in the past, should not be now trying to do so on the backs of hundreds of thousands of unemployed in our beloved country," he said. Meanwhile, Rep. Kevin Brady, R-Texas, urged the House to reject the measure because costs were not offset.

The president signed the measure (PL 111-157) the same day.

The short-term extension was designed to give lawmakers time to resolve differences on the larger bill (HR 4213) to extend the programs until the end of 2010—a bill Democrats pushed as part of their "jobs agenda."

EXTENSION THROUGH NOVEMBER 2010 (HR 4213)

Congress cleared a measure (HR 4213—PL 111-205) on July 22, 2010, to extend through November 30, 2010, federal jobless benefits for those who had exhausted their six months of benefits. It also made the extension retroactive to June 2, when benefits again had expired. The legislation did not include the $25 weekly benefit.

The bill had changed many times since Charles B. Rangel, D-N.Y., who was chair of the House Ways and Means Committee at the time, introduced it December 7, 2009. The original version, which the House passed two days later, was devoted to extending expiring or expired tax provisions. The Senate then expanded the bill to include extension of unemployment and COBRA benefits, and later the measure began to serve as a catch-all for other lingering bills, including an adjustment to two highways programs, a summer jobs program for disadvantaged youth, and extensions for several expiring programs. At one point, new revenue provisions related to foreign tax credits and oil production taxes were attached as offsets, but these were later pulled as lawmakers considered those offsets for health care reform legislation. (COBRA included provisions that allow individuals and families who lose health care coverage to continue group health benefits for limited periods of time.)

Eventually leaders decided that the only way to extend unemployment compensation benefits, which eventually lapsed even while the unemployment rate continued to creep higher, was to separate it from the other contentious programs.

By June 2010, about 46 percent of unemployed individuals had been looking for work for more than twenty-six weeks, according to Department of Labor statistics. Some lawmakers proposed creating a fifth tier of EUC08 benefits offering additional weeks of compensation. In August, Sen. Debbie Stabenow, D-Mich., proposed a bill (S 3706) to create a Tier V offering twenty weeks of benefits for individuals who had worked in states with an average total unemployment rate of at least 7.5 percent, and Rep. Shelley Berkley, D-Nev., offered a similar proposal (HR 6091) in the House for workers in states with an unemployment rate of at least 10 percent. But neither measure saw action.

The Senate on March 10 passed by a 62–36 vote an expanded version of HR 4213. It approved language in a substitute amendment by Finance Chair Max Baucus, D-Mont., to extend federal unemployment benefits through December 31, 2010. Other provisions aimed to delay a cut in physicians' Medicare reimbursement rates, provide temporary help to states to cover Medicaid costs, extend some small-business loan and satellite TV programs, and provide tax break extensions. The Senate that day passed the bill after Reid twice obtained more than sixty votes to limit debate.

Among amendments adopted by the Senate was a proposal by Johnny Isakson, R-Ga., aimed at encouraging companies to continue their defined-benefit pension programs. The amendment gave employers two options to spread out their statutory pension obligations.

The House agreed on May 28 to hold two different votes on the Senate version of the bill, pulling out the Medicare physician payment for a separate vote. Later that day the House approved the Senate version by a vote of 215–204, including the unemployment benefits extension, after agreeing to shorten the extension by one month, through November 30, and to reduce its estimated cost.

Republicans continued to criticize the measure's impact on the deficit. Dave Camp of Michigan, ranking Republican on the Ways and Means Committee, criticized the bill as "more spending on the same failed policies and no net tax relief." Republicans also decried the maneuver to split the bill as evidence of "back-room deals" in which they were not included. But Rules Chair Louise M. Slaughter, D-N.Y., said negotiations were necessary to "do everything in our power to fund the necessary programs that protect unemployed Americans, help small business, enhance job creation efforts, and keep America on the road to economic recovery."

In order to obtain the necessary votes, Democratic leaders also reduced the package, which by that point had reached $200 billion during negotiations between Baucus and House Ways and Means Chair Sander M. Levin, D-Mich. They reduced the cost to $113 billion, eliminating from the bill an extension of the COBRA health insurance subsidies for jobless workers and an extension of extra federal Medicaid assistance to the states provided under the 2009 economic stimulus law. The House-passed version extended through November 30 the additional $25 weekly benefit and extended 100 percent federal funding for continued unemployment benefits.

Meanwhile, on July 1, 2010, the House passed, 270–153 a stand-alone bill (HR 5618) to extend the unemployment benefits through November 30 but did not extend the additional $25 weekly benefit.

For weeks, HR 4213 remained at a standstill in the Senate as Reid repeatedly failed to obtain the votes needed to limit debate. Reid ultimately pulled the bill from the floor June 24 after another cloture motion failed.

However, Senate Democrats then tried to combine a simple extension of federal unemployment benefits through November 30 with provisions to allow more homebuyers to qualify for a tax credit by extending a deadline for closing on a home purchase from June 30 to September 30. Again, Reid could not marshal the sixty votes necessary to end debate, this time losing by just one vote on June 30. (The homebuyer credit was then cleared in a separate bill, HR 5623.)

Republicans continued to demand offsets, while Democrats contended Congress had never made such a mandate during times of high unemployment. Eventually, Senate Democrats limited the legislation to unemployment provisions, dropping the extra $25 per week, and two key moderates—Maine Republicans Olympia J. Snowe and Susan Collins—agreed to support it. When Democrat Ben Nelson of Nebraska said he still would oppose the measure because the cost was not offset, Democrats waited until the late Sen. Robert C. Byrd's Democratic successor, Carte P. Goodwin, was sworn in July 21 to get the votes needed to win a 60–40 cloture vote.

The Senate then passed the bill 59–39 on July 21 after rejecting several Republican motions to offer amendments that were not in order. The House cleared the measure by a vote of 272–152 the following day.

On July 22, the president signed the bill, which included a provision to make the extension retroactive to June 2, thereby restoring unemployment aid to about 2.5 million people who had lost their benefits during the recent standoff. The final law (PL 111-205) was nearly identical to an unemployment measure (HR 5618) the House passed on July 1.

Major Provisions

- Extended, through November 30, 2010, expanded eligibility for unemployment insurance for laid-off workers.
- Extended, through November 30, 2010, the full 100 percent federal funding for expanded unemployment benefits under current law.
- Made extension of benefits retroactive to June 2.
- Permitted state unemployment programs to allow laid-off workers to remain eligible for extended unemployment benefits when they become newly eligible for state unemployment compensation, if switching to regular state benefits would reduce their unemployment benefits by either $100 or 25 percent.
- Stipulated that to be eligible for federal funding for unemployment benefits, states could not reduce their regular unemployment compensation programs below the levels in effect on June 2.
- Ended the additional $25 weekly benefit provided by the 2009 stimulus law (PL 111-5), which expired on June 2. Unemployed individuals who were receiving any type of unemployment benefit before May 29, 2010 (or May 30, 2010, in New York) continued to receive the weekly Federal Additional Compensation (FAC) until they had exhausted all unemployment benefits from all programs, or until December 11, 2010 (December 12, 2010, for New York), whichever date came first. Individuals who first began receiving unemployment compensation after May 29, 2010 (May 30 in New York) did not receive the FAC.

EXTENSION THROUGH 2011 (HR 4853)

As the year 2010 came to a close and unemployment benefits again lapsed, President Obama negotiated a controversial deal with Republicans: in exchange for their support for a thirteen-month extension of those benefits as well as an extension of the payroll tax cut, he would support continuing tax breaks for the highest-income brackets that were scheduled to expire at the end of the year. Congress then cleared the Tax Relief, Unemployment, Insurance Reauthorization, and Job Creation Act of 2010 (HR 4853—PL 111-312) that provided the fourth short-term renewal of federal benefits enacted in 2010 but did not change the structure of the program nor expand benefits.

In announcing the agreement before sending it to the Senate, Obama faced criticism from his party for relenting on tax breaks for the wealthy, which the Republicans strongly advocated. "I know there's some people in my own party and in the other party who would rather prolong this battle, even if we can't reach a compromise," Obama said. "But I'm not willing to let working families across this country become collateral damage for political warfare here in Washington. The American people didn't send us here to fight symbolic battles or win symbolic victories."

The Senate passed the bill 81–19 on December 15. The House cleared it 277–148 just after midnight December 17 and after a last-ditch attempt by liberals to derail the package. The president signed it that day. The law was retroactive to November 30 to cover the latest lapse in benefits coverage and extended authorization of the EUC08 program until January 3, 2012. It also continued the 100 percent federal financing of the extended benefits (EB) program until the week ending on or before January 4, 2012.

The law also extended the "look back trigger" of the EB program. Typically, benefits under that program could be triggered based on the unemployment rates of the previous two years (for instance, all states must pay up to thirteen weeks of benefits if the insured unemployment rate for the previous thirteen weeks is at least 5 percent and is 120 percent of the average of the rates for the same thirteen-week period in each of the previous two years). PL 111–312 allowed states to temporarily use calculations based on three years of unemployment rate data—meaning that states could continue their EB periods for a longer time.

Ultimately all of the unemployment extensions enacted in 2010 were treated as emergency spending and therefore not subject to budgetary requirements for offsets.

LAPSES IN UNEMPLOYMENT COMPENSATION

The program authorization lapsed four times: February 27 to March 2, 2010; April 3 to April 15, 2010; June 2 to July 22, 2010; and November 30 to December 17, 2010. Each of the lapses was addressed in each of the subsequent authorized extensions, which covered benefits retroactively.

COBRA Subsidy

Congress created within the economic stimulus law a short-term, 65 percent subsidy to help laid-off workers pay health insurance premiums under the Consolidated Omnibus Budget Reconciliation Act (COBRA), which allowed individuals to stay on their former health plan for eighteen months after losing their job but required them to pay the full premium. Democrats had hoped to extend the subsidy further, but it lapsed after May 31 when efforts were dropped amid a variety of negotiations with Republicans over what they contended were expensive jobs-related bills that were not offset by funding proposals. *(Stimulus legislation, p. 78)*

BACKGROUND

The Consolidated Omnibus Budget Reconciliation Act of 1985 (PL 99-272) included provisions requiring certain employers who offer health insurance to continue to make that coverage available for former employees under certain circumstances, including when their jobs are terminated or their work hours are reduced. Generally, COBRA coverage lasted eighteen months but could be longer under certain circumstances. Firms with twenty employees or fewer were exempt from the federal COBRA program (some states had programs for those small employers), as were federal, state, and local government employees, which were covered by other programs (such as the Federal Employees Health Benefits Program). *(COBRA legislation, Congress and the Nation Vol. VII, p. 44)*

The cost of COBRA premiums (the total cost of the insurance premiums previously paid by the employer and employee) could be hefty, and unemployed workers were expected to pay the full amount. In 2008, the average COBRA premium was about $400 per month for an individual and $1,078 a month for family coverage; average weekly unemployment benefits that year were about $297. That cost, COBRA advocates said, deterred many individuals from enrolling. In 2006, nearly six million people had COBRA coverage, according to the Urban Institute. A study by Hewitt Associates (a management consulting firm, which merged with Aon Corporation in 2010) indicated that the average COBRA enrollment among qualified individuals was about 19 percent before 2009.

2009 STIMULUS SUBSIDY

The 2009 economic stimulus law provided COBRA premium subsidies of 65 percent to help the unemployed afford health insurance coverage from their former employers. Employers were required to pay the subsidy, and they were reimbursed through a payroll tax credit. Individuals had to pay the other 35 percent.

The subsidy was available for up to nine months to persons who met certain requirements and were involuntarily laid off on or after September 1, 2008, and before January 1, 2010. (The House-passed version would have provided up to one year of assistance.) The subsidy also was made available to certain affected federal workers and workers covered under state COBRA laws targeting small firms. It was available to individuals whose modified adjusted gross income was no more than $125,000 for single filers or $250,000 for joint tax filers, and was phased out for higher-income individuals.

The subsidy was available for coverage beginning on or after the law was enacted (February 17, 2009) but would not retroactively cover COBRA premiums before enactment. The length of time individuals could be covered under COBRA remained the same (generally about eighteen months).

The stimulus law also created a special extended enrollment period for two groups of unemployed: individuals who did not opt for COBRA coverage when their jobs were terminated, and individuals who had chosen COBRA coverage after September 1, 2008, but dropped their coverage because they could not afford the premiums. In addition, it allowed employers to permit individuals to choose a different plan offered by the employer, within ninety days of their notification of the subsidy.

An estimated 51 percent of those who had been involuntarily terminated in February 2009 likely had employer-sponsored coverage before being laid off and were expected to benefit from the subsidies, according to the Congressional Research Service.

SUBSIDY EXTENSIONS

Congress extended the COBRA subsidy twice—first through a provision in a defense appropriations measure and then through an extension measure addressing several programs—before allowing it to expire.

Defense Spending Bill

In December 2009, Obama signed into law the fiscal 2010 defense spending bill (HR 3326—PL 111-118), which included a provision extending the subsidy another six months—for a total of fifteen months. The measure extended the subsidy to workers laid off between January and February 28, 2010, in addition to those laid off between September 1, 2008, and December 31, 2009, as authorized under the stimulus law.

On July 30, 2009, the House passed by a 400–30 vote a version of the bill that did not include provisions addressing COBRA. The Senate passed its version on October 6, 2009, by a 93–7 vote.

The House then took up an amendment to the bill, which included details of an informal agreement among House and Senate appropriators in lieu of a conference report. Among the provisions of that amendment was a six-month extension of the 65 percent federal subsidy of COBRA health insurance for the unemployed. It included provisions to allow for the payment of premiums retroactively and for refunds and credits for retroactive premium assistance eligibility. It designated the COBRA provisions as emergency spending that did not require compliance with pay-as-you-go rules. On December 16, 2009, the House passed the measure by voice vote, after Republicans had complained about use of the defense measure as a vehicle for clearing must-pass extensions. Two days later, on December 18 at 1 a.m., senators invoked cloture on the bill after Republicans had tried to stall the measure in order to waylay debate on the health care reform bill.

The Senate cleared the bill, 88–10, on December 19, 2009, and the president signed it into law the same day.

Temporary Extension Act of 2010

Congress then provided an extension through March 31, 2010, through the Temporary Extension Act of 2010 (HR 4691—PL 111-144), which the president signed March 2, 2010.

On February 25, 2010, the House passed HR 4691, which provided extensions for several programs, by voice vote. The measure included language to extend expanded unemployment benefits through April 5 as well as health insurance subsidies through March 31, along with other programs such as surface transportation programs, Medicare physician payments cuts, and satellite television transmission laws *(Legislative details, pp. 324, 450, 335).*

Senate Majority Leader Harry Reid, D-Nev., also offered a proposal that would, among other things, extend unemployment benefits through April 5 and a thirty-day extension of COBRA subsidies—for a total of sixteen months of assistance—for workers who lost their jobs between September 1, 2008 and March 31, 2010.

Senate action on HR 4691, however, was delayed as Sen. Jim Bunning, R-Ky., complained about what he considered unchecked spending. As the chamber became deadlocked, senators wavered between the short-term extension bill and a longer-term extension measure, HR 4213. But when jobless benefits expired February 28, lawmakers faced increasing pressure to pass some sort of extension. Negotiators ultimately convinced Bunning to end a filibuster, and the Senate passed HR 4691 by a vote of 78–19 on March 2, clearing it for the president.

In late March, the House and Senate departed for the spring recess without extending the federal COBRA subsidy that had been available for the previous year and was scheduled under the last extension to expire March 31. By April, an estimated fifteen million Americans were unemployed and some in Congress advocated extending as well as expanding COBRA subsidies by either providing more generous subsidies or making more people eligible. These discussions occurred even while lawmakers were wrapping up work on the health care overhaul that ultimately mandated new state health exchanges through which individuals could purchase health insurance (although those exchanges were not to take effect until 2014). *(Affordable Health Care Act, p. 421)*

Just before the recess, Sen. Barbara Boxer, D-Calif., introduced a bill (S 3182) to enable domestic partners, same-sex spouses, and extended family members of a covered worker to continue their own coverage under COBRA; the law at the time guaranteed coverage only for spouses and children. No action occurred on that bill.

Continuing Extension Act of 2010

On April 15, 2010, the president signed into law the Continuing Extension Act of 2010 (HR 4851—PL 111-157), providing another extension of the COBRA subsidy through May 31. The short-term extension was granted to buy time for House and Senate negotiators trying to reach a deal on the broader, longer-term extension measure, HR 4213.

On March 15, the House had passed by voice vote an initial version of the bill that included a provision to extend for one month, through April 30, 2010, several programs that had been set to expire at the end of that month, including unemployment insurance and the COBRA subsidy. Senate leaders attempted to take up the bill before the Spring recess, but Sen. Tom Coburn, R-Okla., blocked it as he called for offsets.

The Senate took up the bill April 15, amending it to provide a temporary extension of several programs through June 2 (although the COBRA subsidy extension was in effect until May 31) to give lawmakers more time to work on HR 4213. The bill therefore would extend for two months—for a total of eighteen months—COBRA premium subsidies that had expired at the start of April (the bill provided same for unemployment insurance benefits). The Senate on April 15 passed the amended bill with a vote of 59–38. The House took up the bill the same night, clearing it by a 289–112 vote. The president signed it the same night.

SUBSIDY ENDS

Debate that had started the previous year on providing a long-term extension for various tax cuts and unemployment benefits repeatedly stalled amid largely partisan arguments over costs and offsets. The House and Senate passed early versions of HR 4213 that included a provision to extend the COBRA subsidy, but in an effort to clear final hurdles on the measure and reduce costs, that provision was dropped and the subsidy allowed to expire.

In December 2009, the House passed, 241–181, a $31 billion package of tax cut extensions. By a vote of 62–36, the Senate passed the bill on March 10, 2010, after including a substitute amendment by Senate Finance Committee Chair Max Baucus, D-Mont., to extend long-term unemployment benefits and the COBRA subsidies for unemployed through December 31.

In May 2010, House Democrats unveiled a broader package extending a variety of tax break and unemployment benefit extensions that also included a continuation of the COBRA subsidy through December 2010. The package had been negotiated between House Ways and Means

Chair Sander M. Levin, D-Mich., and Senator Baucus. But its $200 billion price tag raised questions among even moderate and freshman House Democrats, along with Senate Republicans.

The House in May narrowly passed the tax extenders bill (HR 4213). But in working to scale back an original price tag of $200 billion to $113 billion for the measure, Democratic leaders—seeking to appease the fiscally conservative Blue Dog Coalition and several Democratic senators worried about the high price tag—shortened the extension of jobless benefits as originally included in the bill and dropped the COBRA subsidies.

As the Senate prepared to take up the tax and benefits bill in June, several Democrats, including Bob Casey of Pennsylvania, considered offering an amendment to restore the COBRA subsidy. Although Majority Whip Richard J. Durbin, D-Ill., agreed that Casey had a "good idea," he added, "But how do you pay for it?" The subsidy, and the overall measure, got caught up in debate over how to address growing federal deficit as midterm elections approached. With Republicans portraying the stimulus measure as uncontrolled spending, extending any of its provisions was considered politically risky.

The subsidy ended on May 31. Democrats continued to try to push for its renewal, but this was a hard sell on top of other unemployment benefits lawmakers continued to extend.

Job Creation and Protection

In 2009, in response to the continuing and increasingly serious economic recession, President Barack Obama and Democratic leaders on Capitol Hill initially sought to pass a broad $447 billion package of job-creation incentives, such as investments in infrastructure and funding for states to pay public workers, as well as spending for unemployment benefits. But ultimately the package had to be addressed piecemeal, in part because Republicans challenged high-priced spending legislation and objected to the offsets that included a surtax on income of persons earning over $1 million annually. *(Additional details on jobs bill, p. 85)*

Although debate on many of the pieces of the job-creation package was postponed until the next session of Congress, Congress did clear two bills to provide incentives for employers to hire new workers and funding to help states prevent layoffs of education employees. It also provided repeated extensions of unemployment benefits, health insurance subsidies, assistance to workers affected by trade agreements, and short-term authorization extensions of transportation and airline programs *(Economic crisis p. 47; economic and regulatory policy action, p. 88; Trade Adjustment Assistance, p. 200; unemployment benefits, p. 517; transportation legislation pp. 324, 327)*

In 2010, Congress cleared a measure (HR 2847—PL 111-147) to provide payroll tax relief for businesses that hired new workers between February 3, 2010, and January 1, 2011. The bill had bounced between the House and Senate in previous months as lawmakers reduced their requests for funding and added provisions to offset its costs, and was variously called the Jobs for Main Street Act and the Hiring Incentives to Restore Employment Act. *(Additional legislative details, p. 85)*

HOUSE ACTION

HR 2847 originally was a vehicle for appropriations for commerce, justice, and science agencies, but when negotiations on that spending measure stalled, the House replaced the bill's language with language aimed at creating jobs, calling it the Jobs for Main Street Act. The $154 billion included $48.3 billion in funding for infrastructure projects, $26.7 billion to state and local governments to help preserve public service jobs, and further assistance to families affected by the recession. It also extended unemployment insurance and COBRA premiums. The House passed the bill on December 16, 2009, by a vote of 217–212.

SENATE ACTION

Senate Finance Chair Max Baucus, D-Mont., and the committee's ranking Republican, Charles E. Grassley of Iowa, prepared an $85 billion counterproposal. But Senate Majority Leader Harry Reid, D-Nev., narrowed it even further, leaving only a few provisions. Senate Republicans called for funding offsets.

On February 24, 2010, the Senate passed its $15 billion version of the bill by a vote of 70–28. It was primarily focused on tax provisions and the exemptions of new hires from Social Security payroll taxes. (It also included extension of highway program authorization.)

FINAL ACTION

After the bill was returned to the House by the Senate, the House increased its funding requests slightly to $17.6 billion. Retained were provisions to provide tax incentives to businesses that hire or retain unemployed workers and to extend the highway authorization measure. The House also added a provision to replenish the Highway Trust Fund.

Another provision added by the House was to bar employers from using the payroll tax exemption on wages paid during the first calendar quarter of 2010. Instead, employers would have to use the first quarter tax as a credit against taxes imposed on the second calendar quarter of that year.

The House passed the measure on March 4, 2010, by a vote of 217–201. The Senate cleared the measure, 68–29, on March 17 and the president signed the legislation (PL 111-147) the next day. He hailed final passage of the bill. "It is the first of what I hope will be a series of jobs packages that help to continue to put people back to work," he said.

The final measure granted payroll tax forgiveness to employers who hire unemployed workers before December 31, 2010. Those workers had to start work after February 3,

2010, and before January 1, 2011, and had to certify they had worked for more than forty hours during the previous sixty-day period. The measure also:

- Barred employers from using the new exemption on wages paid during the first quarter of 2010; they had to use the first quarter tax as a credit against taxes imposed in the second quarter.
- Provided a business tax credit, increased by the lesser of $1,000 or 6.2 percent of the wages paid by the employer to each new employee who is retained for fifty-two consecutive weeks. Required that to be eligible for the credit, employers had to pay workers during the last twenty-six weeks of the year at least 80 percent of the wages they earned during the first half of the year.

Education Jobs Fund

In 2009 and 2010, Congress provided billions of dollars in aid to states to stave off teacher layoffs that had been threatened as local governments grappled with ways to reduce spending during the continued economic recession. Democrats' success required overcoming Republican objections that such measures were a giveaway to teachers' unions, particularly as the midterm elections approached.

Obama's 2009 economic stimulus plan (PL 111-5), cleared early in 2009, provided $4 billion to states to prevent teacher layoffs. *(Stimulus legislation, p. 78)*

After the Senate failed to move the president's broad jobs package, Democrats sought to pass separately those provisions targeting job protection for teachers, law enforcement officers, and emergency personnel. They ultimately narrowed their focus to provide protection for education jobs and sought several vehicles for such a provision before lawmakers ultimately cleared a bill in August 2010 in time to reduce expected layoffs. The final law (HR 1586—PL 111-226) provided $26.1 billion in aid to states, $10 billion of which funded efforts to create or retain education-related jobs.

Several groups had advocated providing additional federal funds to states to prevent budget cuts that would result in teacher layoffs. The Center on Budget and Policy Priorities reported that since the recession began, at least thirty-three states and the District of Columbia had cut funds for schools and various education programs. According to the National Education Association, without additional federal funds, an estimated 138,000 teachers would lose their jobs in the fall 2010. *(Education jobs fund legislative details, p. 479)*

Gender-Based Wage Discrimination

The election of Democratic President Barack Obama in 2008, along with a larger Democratic majority in the Senate, enabled long-sought passage of a measure to help workers contest wage discrimination, legislation known as the Lilly Ledbetter law. But Democrats were less successful with a bill to place the burden of proof on employers involved in lawsuits contending pay disparities between women and men.

BACKGROUND

The Lilly Ledbetter Fair Pay Act (S 181—PL 111-2) was the first major piece of legislation President Obama signed into law and allowed Democrats to claim an early victory. The measure amended the Civil Rights Act of 1964 to state that the statute of limitations in wage discrimination suits applied to each discriminatory paycheck, not just to the first instance of discrimination.

In May 2007, the Supreme Court ruled, 5–4, in *Ledbetter v. Goodyear Tire and Rubber Company* (550 U.S. 618) against longtime employee Lilly Ledbetter, who had discovered after almost twenty years that she had been paid less than men performing the same work. A federal jury awarded her back pay, but an appeals court later reversed that decision. The Supreme Court in its ruling stated that Ledbetter had failed to file her formal complaint within the 180-day period after the alleged discrimination first took place, as required by federal law. In her dissent, Supreme Court Justice Ruth Bader Ginsburg urged Congress to address the court's decision.

The House in 2007 had then passed a bill that was intended to reverse the Supreme Court's decision. But Republican opponents in the Senate contended the bill was an attempt to upend congressional intent behind the Civil Rights Act, which envisioned a statute of limitations for claims of discrimination, and the measure died. During the same 110th Congress, the House also passed a bill that aimed to shift the burden of proof in wage discrimination lawsuits from the employee to the employer. But Senate Republicans blocked it, contending it was duplicative of existing antidiscrimination standards and could subject businesses to frivolous lawsuits. *(Congress and the Nation Vol. XII, pp. 669, 670)*

HOUSE ACTION

On January 9, 2009, the House passed by a vote of 247–171 a bill (HR 11) introduced by George Miller, D-Calif., chair of the Education and Labor Committee, to reverse the 2007 Supreme Court decision.

Before passing that bill, the House had passed, 256–163, a bill (HR 12) introduced by Rosa DeLauro, D-Conn., to eliminate caps on compensatory and punitive damages in successful wage discrimination suits. It also sought to put the onus on employers to prove wage discrepancies between women and men doing the same jobs were the result of nondiscriminatory business considerations. Previously the employee filing the lawsuit had to prove the employer intended to discriminate. Another provision was intended to bar retaliation by employers against workers who shared their salary information with others.

Lawmakers then incorporated DeLauro's bill into Miller's measure before passing HR 11.

SENATE ACTION

The Senate passed a version (S 181) of the bill, introduced by Sen. Barbara Mikulski, D-Md., by a **key vote of 61–36 (D 54–0; R 5–36; I 2–0)** on January 22, 2009, after rejecting a series of Republican amendments. (*2009 key votes, p. 751*)

The Senate bill, unlike the House bill, was narrowly targeted to the statute-of-limitations issue. Republicans had again charged the legislation would invite numerous frivolous lawsuits. Senators rejected, 40–55, a substitute amendment by Kay Bailey Hutchison, R-Texas, that would have required charges to be filed within 180 days of when the employee had sufficient information to suspect discrimination.

FINAL ACTION

The House chose to vote on the narrower Senate bill and bar amendments on the floor, raising objections by Republicans who continued to argue that the legislation would invite a wave of lawsuits, hurt small businesses, and create disincentives to hire women. Bill supporters argued that without congressional action, it would remain difficult for employees to bring pay discrimination claims, and legitimate claims would never be adjudicated otherwise.

The House voted 250–177 on January 27 to clear the measure. Obama signed it into law on January 29. The measure stated that the protections of the Civil Rights Act of 1964, which barred employment discrimination based on race, color, religion, sex, or national origin—as well as the Age Discrimination in Employment Act, the Americans with Disabilities Act, and the Rehabilitation Act of 1973—extended to every paycheck or other compensation that resulted from past or present discriminatory pay practices.

Wage Parity

Democrats in 2010 tried to revive the second portion of the 2009 House-passed bill that had been dropped, which included language to put the burden of proof on employers involved in lawsuits contending pay disparities between women and men. But again efforts in the Senate failed.

The measure (HR 12), which the House passed in 2009 by a 256–163 vote, included language to amend the 1938 Fair Labor Standards Act (PL 75-718) to put the legal onus on employers to prove that any pay discrepancies between men and women were job-related. It also included language to permit workers to collect compensatory and punitive damages and to remove caps on such damages. It barred retaliation by employers against employees who shared salary information with their colleagues.

Senate Majority Leader Harry Reid, D-Nev., on September 13, 2010, offered a version of the wage parity bill (S 3772). But on November 17, the Senate rejected a motion to invoke cloture and end debate by a vote of 58–41, short of the sixty votes required.

Before the cloture vote, Sen. Barbara Mikulski, D-Md., said the measure "really gives women the tools to know what they are being paid." She said that, on average, a woman earned 77 cents for every dollar a man earned.

Michael B. Enzi, R-Wyo., responded that the comparison was skewed because more women than men choose part-time employment or lower-paying careers. He said the measure would have limited the defense that employers can use to respond to gender discrimination suits to "bona fide" factors such as training, experience, or educational background. He said that was a "trial lawyer bonanza sure to disadvantage all employers."

President Obama released a statement saying his administration would "continue to fight for a woman's right to equal pay for equal work."

Measures dubbed the Fair Pay Act (HR 2151, S 904) sought to go further by proposing to expand the Equal Pay Act, which is primarily focused on gender-based wage differences, to also protect racial and ethnic minorities. But no action occurred on the legislation, which was similar to measures that had been introduced repeatedly since the 103rd Congress.

Minimum Wage for U.S. Territory Workers

Discussions regarding the minimum wage during the 111th Congress primarily focused on wages of specific sectors or areas—namely workers in American Samoa and the Northern Mariana Islands, construction workers in Guam working on projects related to a U.S. marine relocation, and home health care aides.

Economic concerns among the industries in the U.S. territories of American Samoa and the Northern Mariana Islands—particularly in fishing—caused local businesses and leaders to push for a delay of scheduled minimum wage increases, and President Barack Obama and Congress responded by extending until 2012 the scheduled increases while local officials assessed the impact of the change.

A 2007 law (PL 110-28), which had raised the general minimum wage in the United States, set a schedule to incrementally raise the minimum wages in those territories. The first five-cent-per-hour increase was applied in July 2007 and additional increases were scheduled in each subsequent year until they reached the level of the U.S. minimum wage, which at the time was $7.25 per hour. That rate was expected to be reached in 2016 in American Samoa and 2015 in the Northern Mariana Islands.

In December 2009, President Obama signed into law the 2010 omnibus appropriations bill (HR 3288—PL 111-117), which included a provision added by the Senate to delay from May to September the yearly minimum wage hike for workers in those territories.

In April 2010 the Government Accountability Office (GAO) released a report indicating that employment in American Samoa had dropped between 2008 and 2009 and that local officials attributed the drop in large part to the wage increases mandated by the 2007 law. The GAO said the tuna industry had been deferring hires and reducing its workforce; Chicken of the Sea, a prominent national brand, in 2009 closed a tuna cannery there that had at one point employed nearly 2,000 people. Starkist, a competitor, continued to operate there but had raised labor cost concerns.

American Samoa's governor, Togiola Tulafono, requested the wage increase be delayed to "secure twelve months to review the problem and devise a response to the catastrophe of losing two-thirds of all private sector jobs in American Samoa."

LEGISLATIVE ACTION

In September 2010, Congress cleared a measure (HR 3940—PL 111-244) to again postpone the wage increases until 2012.

In 2009, Del. Madeleine Z. Bordallo, D-Guam, introduced HR 3940, which focused on authorizations for Interior Department grant and research assistance to United States territories for public education programs regarding the political status options for territories. The Committee on Natural Resources approved the bill on December 7, and the full House passed it by voice vote the same day.

The Senate Energy and Natural Resources Committee on September 28, 2010, discharged the bill to the floor by unanimous consent. On the floor, Sen. Dick Durbin, D-Ill., obtained unanimous consent approval for a substitute amendment that replaced the language with a "sense of the Congress" provision regarding political education, as well as a provision to delay the scheduled increase in the minimum wage in American Samoa and the Commonwealth of the Northern Mariana Islands. (A congressional "sense of" provision has no formal effect on public policy and has no force in law.) The bill also postponed until 2012 the minimum wage increases in American Samoa set for 2010 and 2011, and in the Commonwealth of the Northern Mariana Islands in 2011. This action pushed them from the September 20 deadline set in the law the president signed in December 2009.

The measure also required the GAO to assess the impact of minimum wage increases that had occurred and to submit subsequent reports by April 1, 2013, and every two years thereafter, until the minimum wage in those territories was equal to the federal minimum wage.

The Senate then passed the amended version of the measure by unanimous consent. The House passed the measure by a 385–5 vote on September 30, 2010, under suspension of the rules, clearing it for the president, who signed it into law the same day.

Minimum Wage for Guam Construction Workers

Congress cleared a measure in 2010 that called for construction workers on contract at a U.S. Marine base in Guam to be paid prevailing wages (HR 2647—PL 111-84).

The House Armed Services in June 2009 approved a $680.2 billion fiscal 2010 defense authorization measure that authorized more than $300 million funding for more than a dozen construction projects on Guam as the island prepared for a military buildup that included new facilities, training ranges, barracks, family housing, a headquarters, a hospital, motor pools, and other buildings for the 3rd Marine Expeditionary Forces and their families being relocated from Okinawa.

The measure included a provision by Neil Abercrombie, D-Hawaii, chair of the Air and Land Forces Subcommittee, that required all military construction on Guam to meet U.S. federal standards, directed the Labor Department to set a minimum wage standard for all construction workers on Guam, and stated that U.S. construction workers were to be provided additional notice about construction opportunities on Guam.

Abercrombie wrote in a July 13, 2009, letter to the *Washington Post*: "The Guam buildup will require up to 15,000 workers—many times the local workforce. . . . The alternative is to bring in foreign workers, for which the Guam government collects a bounty of $1,000 per head. However, this invites profiteering and would be a slap in the face of every qualified, unemployed American worker."

He said the measure would set wages at the same level as those for similar military construction in Hawaii, "because we believe that wages should be commensurate with the experience and skills the jobs demand." Abercrombie, a Democratic candidate for governor, was criticized for trying to protect a major portion of those military construction projects for Hawaii-based companies. The House in October 2009 passed the bill, which also included Abercrombie's provision to preserve 70 percent of those constructions jobs for American workers.

The Senate version of the bill (S 1390) did not include provisions on Guam wages and workers. Conferees then agreed to language calling on the Labor Department to set the minimum wage standard for the construction workers and to ensure U.S. workers were provided additional notice regarding opportunities on Guam.

In accordance with the final legislation (PL 111-84), the Labor Department on December 3, 2010, announced prevailing wage rates for those workers.

Executive Pay

Efforts to curb executive compensation quickly became a highly controversial issue at the start of the 111th Congress in 2009 when many of the country's biggest banks, which had received billions of dollars in financial assistance through the Troubled Asset Relief Program (TARP) passed in 2008 (PL 110-343), paid hefty bonuses to top employees. Financial institutions contended the bonuses helped them retain top talent, but lawmakers, particularly Democrats, contended the bonuses were inappropriate expenditures of taxpayer dollars. Public outcry worsened when it was reported that American International Group, Inc., which had received more than $180 billion in TARP funds, paid $165 million in retention bonuses in March 2009. *(TARP legislation, Congress and the Nation Vol. XII, pp. 154, 163)*

ECONOMIC STIMULUS BILL

The economic stimulus measure (HR 1—PL 111-5) that President Barack Obama signed into law February 17, 2009, included language amending the financial services bailout law of 2008 (PL 110-343) to set restrictions on the compensation of company executives during the period in which any bailout funds provided through TARP remained outstanding. *(Stimulus legislation, p. 78)*

The secretary of the Treasury was required to develop standards for executive compensation. In addition, the law created a Board Compensation Committee to review employee compensation plans. The law stated that any annual or other meeting of the shareholders of a recipient of TARP funds would have to allow a separate, nonbinding shareholder vote to approve compensation of executives.

During Senate debate on HR 1, senators adopted by voice vote an amendment by Sen. Claire McCaskill, D-Mo., to impose a $400,000 salary cap on officers and directors receiving funding from the financial bailout law. "These people just don't get it," she said on the floor regarding the company executives. "These people are idiots."

A week later, President Obama announced restrictions on executive compensation of recipients of TARP funds; he said such firms had to set a $500,000 salary cap on top executives, who also would not be eligible for bonuses above their base pay.

Senate Banking Chair Christopher J. Dodd, D-Conn., then won approval for an amendment barring bonuses and other incentives for top-paid executives at firms receiving bailout funds.

The final bill language negotiated between House and Senate conferees included provisions requiring TARP recipient companies to allow shareholders to have a nonbinding vote approving all executive compensation. It also set limits on executive compensation at companies that had received, or will receive, federal bailout funds through TARP.

MAJOR PROVISIONS

Following are the major provisions of the economic stimulus measure that dealt with executive pay (PL 111-5):

- Barred executives from receiving compensation based on "unnecessary and excessive risk" and false earning statements.
- Barred "golden parachute" payments that were usually made to executives terminated when a company experienced a change in control.
- Barred bonuses, retention awards, or inventive compensation while TARP funds are still outstanding.
- Outlined a scale by which executives at certain companies would be affected: the most highly compensated employee at each company that received at least $25 million in TARP funds; the top five most highly compensated employees at companies receiving between $25 million and $250 million; the five most highly compensated and the next ten most highly paid employees at companies receiving between $250 million and $500 million; and the five most highly compensated executives and the next twenty most highly paid employees at companies receiving more than $500 million.

Executive Bonuses

On March 19, the House quickly drafted and passed, 328–93, a bill (HR 1586) to set a 90 percent tax on retention bonuses that had been distributed. The measure would not affect bonus recipients who had adjusted gross incomes of less than $250,000 for couples and $125,000 for individuals or married people filing separately. Executives also could avoid the tax by waiving any right to the bonuses or returning the money by the end of the year. The rate was to apply only to bonuses received after January 1, 2009, as lawmakers were concerned about the constitutionality of making the law retroactive.

SENATE ACTION

HR 1586 as introduced did not move further, and was later used by the Senate as a vehicle for legislation to reauthorize the Federal Aviation Administration, and subsequently as a vehicle for Medicaid and education funds. *(Details, pp. 46, 140, 453, 479, 480)*

In the Senate, Finance Committee Chair Max Baucus, D-Mont., and ranking member Charles E. Grassley, R-Iowa, on March 19 introduced a measure (S 651) that specifically targeted AIG, and other companies that received federal bailout funds, as well as bonus recipients. That measure included language to place a 35 percent excise tax on AIG for its bonus costs and a 35 percent tax on the bonus income of recipients. It also sought to impose a 20 percent surtax on any deferred compensation of more than $1 million annually.

The bill would have applied to companies that had received federal bailout funds and in which the federal government had an equity stake—potentially affecting about 400 firms. It also would have applied to payments January 1, 2009, and later, until the bailout funds were repaid to the government. It would not have affected companies receiving less than $100 million in TARP funds and holding less than $500 million in total assets.

Republicans questioned the constitutionality of such a tax and action on legislation slowed. Senate Majority Leader Harry Reid, D-Nev., tried to bring the House bill on the floor for a vote, just hours after the full House passed it March 19. Minority Whip Jon Kyl, R-Ariz., insisted on more time to consider it.

President Barack Obama and some senators criticized the House bill as potentially unconstitutional and even bad policy. Further, House Majority Leader Steny Hoyer, D-Md., noted that several executives at AIG agreed to return their bonuses regardless, and momentum for a legislative remedy waned.

HOUSE ACTION

Meanwhile, the House Financial Services Committee took up and approved a bill (HR 1664) sponsored by Chair Barney Frank, D-Mass., that was designed to bar the payment of bonuses at all firms that received money from the financial bailout (PL 110-343). The bill also included language applying to mortgage giants Fannie Mae (the Federal National Mortgage Association) and Freddie Mac (the Federal Home Loan Mortgage Corporation). The measure would have retroactively inserted the language into the bailout law and into the law that had established the $300 billion "Hope for Homeowners" mortgage refinancing program (PL 110–289). *(Congress and the Nation Vol. XII, pp. 154, 158, 636)*

The House Judiciary Committee in March 2009 also approved by voice vote a measure (HR 1575) to use the bankruptcy code to go after the bonuses. But the House subsequently defeated the bill, on April 1, when leaders failed to get the two-thirds vote necessary for passage under suspension of the rules; the vote was 223–196. The bill would have treated the bonuses as fraudulent payments and authorized the attorney general to take steps to recover them in court. It would have applied only to employees at companies that had accepted at least $10 billion in financial bailout funds.

After defeating HR 1575, the House immediately turned to Frank's bill, HR 1664, which it passed by a vote of 247–171. But that measure did not move further amid concerns about its constitutionality.

Shareholder Oversight of Executive Pay

Lawmakers then approached the issue from another angle by ensuring that shareholders, as well as the SEC, had input on executive pay packages. Their proposals were signed into law in July 2010 (HR 4173—PL 111-203).

HOUSE ACTION

On July 30, 2009, the House Financial Services Committee approved by a vote of 40–28 a draft of a measure (HR 3269) by Frank that aimed to permit shareholders and regulators to have a greater say on executive pay packages. It became the first part of the Obama administration's financial regulatory overhaul. The panel approved the bill after adopting several amendments that narrowed its effect, including:

- By voice vote, a manager's amendment by Frank to permit regulators to curb only incentive-based payment plans, rather than all compensation.
- By voice vote, an amendment by Jeb Hensarling, R-Texas, to exempt from the measure financial institutions with assets of less than $1 billion.

Frank said the bill was intended to curb "incentive structures that give people a payoff for risk and no penalty for failed enterprises."

The House on July 31, 2009, passed the measure by a vote of 237–185. Under the bill, shareholders would get a nonbinding vote on executive compensation plans and federal regulators (the Securities and Exchange Commission) could restrict compensation practices deemed to threaten the health of a financial institution. House Republicans objected that the measure gave regulators broad authority to dictate pay at private companies.

Ultimately, language from the measure was incorporated in HR 4173, the Wall Street Reform and Consumer Protection Act, by the House before it passed the bill on December 11, 2009. That measure included language requiring all publicly traded companies to allow shareholders to participate in nonbinding votes on the compensation received by executives and certain compensation agreements between executives and an acquiring entity. It also required certain institutional investment managers to report at least yearly on how they voted regarding compensation. *(HR 4173 legislative action, p. 88)*

SENATE ACTION

Senate action was delayed by debate on health care overhaul legislation and a desire to work on more controversial aspects of the pending financial overhaul bill. Sen. Christopher J. Dodd, D-Conn., chair of the Banking, Housing, and Urban Affairs Committee, wanted to consider the plan as part of a broad financial industry regulations overhaul. On April 15, 2010, the Banking committee approved a draft version of Dodd's overhaul bill, which was formally introduced as S 3217 a few weeks later.

In May 2010, during the Senate's consideration of HR 4173, Reid blocked three proposed amendments. Among them was a proposal by Jim Webb, D-Va., to impose a tax on bonuses paid in 2009 to executives at financial institutions that received at least $5 billion from the financial services bailout program (PL 110–343).

The Senate then passed HR 4173 on May 20, 2010, by a vote of 59–39, after replacing the House bill with language from S 3217. That version retained language granting company shareholders more power over executive compensation by requiring that only shareholder-directed votes be included in the tally for advisory votes on pay.

FINAL ACTION

Conference negotiations, overseen by Frank, began on June 10. Leaders named twelve senators and thirty-one House members to the conference. The conference agreement retained a provision on executive compensation practices, providing shareholders of public corporations a nonbinding advisory vote on executive pay and "golden parachute" payments. It also gave the SEC authority to grant shareholders proxy access to nominate directors.

The House, by a 237–192 vote, agreed to the conference report for HR 4173, now titled the Dodd-Frank Wall Street Reform and Consumer Protection Act, on June 30, 2010. The Senate agreed to the conference report on July 15 by a 60–39 vote, and the president signed it into law on July 21, 2010 (PL 111–203).

Union Card Check

Organized labor groups hoped to get the 111th Congress to approve legislation to make it easier for unions to organize, but failed to do so. Their optimism was grounded in the election of Barack Obama, whose presidential candidacy in 2008 had been actively supported by labor unions, and in the strength of Democratic majorities in Congress.

The so-called "card check" legislation was a top priority for organized labor. But the sharp partisan divide in Congress—combined with a strong business lobbying force in opposition, a demand among centrist Democrats for a compromise, and wariness among lawmakers about expending political capital while working on difficult issues of health care and the economy—doomed the effort early in the 111th Congress.

Companion bills, called the Employee Free Choice Act (HR 1409, S 560), were introduced in the House and Senate in March 2009 by Rep. George Miller, D-Calif., chair of the Education and Labor Committee, and Sen. Edward M. Kennedy, D-Mass., chair of the Health, Education, Labor and Pensions Committee. The legislation would permit unions to organize a workplace by collecting the signatures of at least half of the employees.

Existing law permitted unions to form only via a secret ballot; the measure would permit employers to require a vote on unionization by a secret ballot even if a majority of workers requested the formation of a union by signing a card. The legislation also included language calling for binding arbitration a newly formed union could not quickly secure a contract with employees, and it would also have provided stiffer legal penalties for employers who tampered with union organizing efforts.

Organized labor, which in the first six months of 2009 gave $11 million to congressional campaigns—more money than any other interest group—contended the secret ballot permitted management to coerce workers to vote against union organization. But business lobbies, including the U.S. Chamber of Commerce and the National Association of Manufacturers, said the card check drives would encourage union representatives to intimidate workers.

The House had passed nearly identical legislation in 2007, but it had been blocked in the Senate. As a result, Miller said he wanted the Senate to act on the legislation first. *(Congress and the Nation Vol. XII, p. 668)*

Starbucks, Costco, and Whole Foods announced that March they were forming the Committee for a Level Playing Field to promote a proposal to guarantee unions worksite access to employees during nonwork hours and timely elections. Their plan did not include public sign-up and mandatory arbitration provisions.

Several key Democrats (Robert E. Andrews, D-N.J., chair of the Education and Labor Subcommittee of the House Health, Education, Labor, and Pensions Committee; Tom Harkin of Iowa, chair of the Senate Labor-HHS-Education Appropriations Subcommittee; and Miller) issued a joint statement March 22 saying the proposal was "not a serious attempt at labor law reform."

Meanwhile, several Republican senators said they were concerned about effects of the card check bill on small businesses and indicated they would oppose any version of the legislation. "The problem is that any kind of compromise on this can allow the bill to proceed and put it in front of a conference committee," said John Ensign, R-Nev. "That is dangerous."

With Republicans and several key Democrats leading forces from opposing sides of the spectrum, centrist Democrats were compelled to find a compromise. Sen. Mark Pryor of Arkansas, a moderate Democrat, said he repeatedly had been telling labor and the private sector to find a middle ground, and he commended the companies for making a "good faith effort." But meanwhile, many members were skeptical about pursuing the controversial subject while health care overhaul and financial service reform were still pending.

Democratic leaders were further discouraged when Sen. Arlen Specter, then a Pennsylvania Republican and typically prolabor, indicated he would not support a cloture motion to end debate and move to a vote on the bill on the Senate floor. His support was critical for Democrats to get the sixty-vote majority needed for cloture.

SENATE ACTION

Bill supporters were encouraged when Specter switched from the Republican to the Democratic Party in April, followed by his indication he would support cloture on a modified version of the bill. But he remained firm that he would oppose a card check provision allowing workers to form unions by petition, in addition to secret-ballot election, as well as its contract arbitration provisions.

In May, Harkin, with hope that Specter's stance was softening, huddled with some senators to find alternatives. By August, negotiators were indicating that the card check provision would be dropped, and Specter said he would support the bill. But following the death on August 25 of Sen. Edward Kennedy, D-Mass., from cancer, Harkin took the reins of the Health, Education, Labor, and Pensions (HELP) committee in September.

Dissension continued among moderate Democrats who were concerned the measure would end up costing jobs while the attention of many legislators, including the leadership, already was focusing heavily on legislation to create jobs. Matters worsened for prolabor Democrats in January 2010 when the party lost its sixty-vote majority—essential to end a filibuster—following the victory of Republican Scott Brown of Massachusetts to fill Kennedy's seat.

The legislation remained stalled through 2010, and the widespread GOP election victories that November left no prospect of passage in the 112th Congress.

Public Safety Workers

Senate Majority Leader Harry Reid, D-Nev., a former Capitol Police officer, made several attempts to push through a measure to grant bargaining rights to police and firefighters in states that did not allow such public safety workers to join unions. But Republicans blocked his attempts.

Michael B. Enzi, R-Wyo., vowed to oppose Reid's plan wherever it surfaced, arguing any such proposal should be considered by the Health, Education, Labor, and Pensions (HELP) Committee where he was ranking minority member. Enzi wanted to exempt small towns, allow states to opt out, and broaden restrictions on strikes by public safety workers.

Reid hoped to add his proposal as an amendment to a fiscal 2010 supplemental appropriations measure (HR 4899) in May 2010, but failed. That November, he introduced S 3991, which contained the language of his proposal. Senate Democrats reworked the bill to draw more support from their side of the aisle, including a provision sought by Mary L. Landrieu, D-La., to exempt sheriff's departments from the collective bargaining rights. But that led to opposition by the Fraternal Order of Police, which had been a critical backer of Reid's effort.

In December 2010, Senate Democrats failed to advance the bill. At the time, the Senate GOP conference refused to vote for cloture on any issue as it pushed for resolution on a deal to extend tax cuts and fund the federal government into 2011. It was another loss for organized labor in the 111th Congress. The vote on the motion to invoke cloture to end debate was 55–43, short of the sixty votes required.

Sen. Judd Gregg, R-N.H., had introduced a similar measure (S 1611) in August 2009, but it did not see action. Rep. Dale Kildee, D-Mich., had introduced a bill (HR 413) in January 2009 that did not get beyond a subcommittee hearing.

2011–2012

President Barack Obama and Democratic leaders in 2011 hoped to pass a wide-ranging package of what they called job creation incentives, along with unemployment assistance. But working with a Congress under divided control, in which conservative Republicans who had recaptured control of the House in the 2010 elections claimed a mandate to reduce government spending and regulation, they had to scale back plans.

The president presented his jobs proposal in September and Senate Democrats sought to move forward with it quickly but faced a Republican filibuster in October, primarily because of a proposed surtax on household income above $1 million to pay for the bill. Obama and several administration officials toured the country to promote the plan while Democratic leaders sought to advance it in pieces.

Congress cleared further extensions temporary of unemployment benefits as well as assistance for workers and businesses affected by trade liberalization, but after Democrats negotiating with House Republicans conceded to a slight reduction of those benefits.

Republicans blocked two other pieces of the job plan—a $35 billion package of state aid aimed at preventing layoffs of first-responders and educators) and a $60 billion measure to fund infrastructure and transportation projects. Ultimately, both chambers agreed to tax credits for companies that hire unemployed veterans and funding to help states minimize teacher layoffs.

Meanwhile, Republicans fought attempts to increase minimum wages. They tried, unsuccessfully, to block a labor rule to former employers to pay prevailing wages for immigrants working under H-2B visas. But both chambers did approve a measure to again delay a scheduled wage increase for workers in American Samoa. Republicans also sought to turn back new labor rules intended to provide a minimum wage increase for home health aides, a rule ultimately caught up in lawsuits. The House GOP also sought to turn back other labor rules governing union organization.

Republicans were more successful in clearing through Congress a law requiring an increase in pension contributions by new federal employees, and they began to launch efforts toward welfare reform.

Unemployment Compensation

During the 112th Congress, lawmakers three times extended supplemental unemployment benefits, ensuring coverage through 2013, even while the GOP continued to push for offsets. But Republicans, now controlling the House and with additional votes in the Senate, did win concessions to trim down the benefits and allow some to phase out. *(111th Congress unemployment benefits action, p. 517)*

Some legislators hoped legislation to extend unemployment benefits would be included in a package proposal expected from a joint committee on deficit reduction that was created under the Budget Control Act of 2011 (PL 112-25). But that committee never reached agreement by its November 23 deadline, setting the stage for a process, known as sequestration, that automatically began spending cuts and tax increases outlined in that 2011 law. *(PL 112-25, p. 160)*

The various tiers of unemployment benefits at that point provided as many as ninety-nine weeks of aid that were scheduled to expire on January 3, 2012. The House, now under GOP control, passed a bill (HR 3630) to reduce the ninety-nine-week eligibility and create certain new restrictions. But the Senate failed to reach agreement on it before the year ended. Congress instead cleared a two-month extension of benefits in late December and agreed to form a House-Senate conference committee in early 2012 to work out differences on a year-long extension.

The following year, Congress voted twice to continue supplemental federal benefits for the unemployed. The unemployment benefits extensions reduced the duration of long-term assistance from ninety-nine weeks to seventy-three weeks, and fewer weeks in states that had lower unemployment rates. Both extensions were included in broad packages extending deadlines for a range of programs.

BENEFITS EXTENSION TO MARCH 2012 (HR 3765)

Congress in late December 2011 approved a short-term extension of unemployment benefits into late winter 2012 but only after a convoluted series of steps that ultimately saw the Speaker of the House perform an about-face and abruptly give chamber endorsement to a Senate bill even after most of the representatives had left for the holidays.

It began on December 13, 2011, when the House passed by a 234–193 vote a bill (HR 3630) that primarily extended a Social Security payroll tax deduction but included language to extend expanded unemployment insurance benefits for another thirteen months, through January 31, 2013. It also aimed to reduce the length of benefits while requiring benefits recipients to show they were actively seeking work, meet certain minimum educational and reemployment training standards, and pass drug tests. However, a longer renewal and discussion of such requirements had to await short-term extensions that came later in December. *(Social Security payroll tax, p. 108)*

HR 3630 also included language requiring the president to act promptly on authorizing the construction of the controversial Keystone XL oil pipeline from Canada to the Gulf of Mexico. This provision was included to lure the votes of conservatives. *(Keystone pipeline, p. 390)*

In the Senate, Democrats were displeased with several features of the House bill, including its cost offsets and language ending the ninety-nine-week unemployment compensation eligibility. Majority Leader Harry Reid, D-Nev., and Minority Leader Mitch McConnell, R-Ky., worked on a two-month deal that they thought would enable lawmakers to avoid end-of-year pressures to resolve differences on the most controversial issues, particularly offsets.

The Senate adopted a substitute amendment to HR 3630 on December 17 by a **key vote of 89–10 (R 39–7; D 49–2; I 1–1),** replacing the House language with a two-month extension of the payroll tax cut and unemployment benefits, and delayed scheduled cuts to Medicare payment rates for physicians. The House responded December 20 by adopting, on a **key vote of 229–193 (R 229–7; D 0–186),** a motion to disagree with the Senate revisions and request a conference, thereby setting the stage for 2012 negotiations on HR 3630 that eventually led to final legislation on the array of issues in that bill. *(2011 key votes, p. 785)*

HR 3630, as revised in the Senate, continued existing unemployment compensation law through March 6, 2012, without the changes proposed by the House. It offset the cost of the extension with an increase in fees charged for loan guarantees by mortgage giants Fannie Mae and Freddie Mac, and retained the language urging Obama to act on the Keystone pipeline proposal. Shortly afterward, senators left for the year, assuming the House would immediately clear the measure.

However, House Republicans would not support the short-term extension, and Speaker John A. Boehner, R-Ohio, called for a House-Senate conference on the House's version. But he and his GOP colleagues were harshly criticized in the news media as all unemployment benefits threatened to lapse. Boehner then reversed position and told his members—most of whom already had left for the holidays—that the House would clear the Senate bill with a minor change to the payroll tax cut extension.

To do that, the House on December 23 passed a slightly modified measure (HR 3765) without objection, and the Senate cleared the bill the same day, by unanimous consent. On December 23, 2011, Obama signed HR 3765, the Temporary Payroll Tax Cut Continuation Act of 2011 (PL 112-78) that included provisions to extend the authorization for the EUC08 program through the week ending on or before March 6, 2012; the 100 percent federal financing of the Extended Benefits program until March 7, 2012; and the three-year look-back trigger option for the extended benefits program until the week ending on or before February 29, 2012. It also continued the availability of railroad extended unemployment benefits through February 29, 2012. (EUC08 stood for called Emergency Unemployment Compensation Act of 2008.) *(Background on unemployment compensation, p. 519)*

The bill did not include provisions that House Republicans sought to reduce jobless benefits from ninety-nine weeks to fifty-nine weeks, and it did not include provisions to impose conditions for eligibility such as drug testing, participation in state-run job placement programs, and mandatory education for those without a high school diploma. It also did not include language requiring reemployment demonstration projects in states.

EXTENSION THROUGH 2012 (HR 3630)

House and Senate conferees began meeting in January to negotiate differences in HR 3630, which both chambers had agreed to set aside while passing the two-month extension in another vehicle, HR 3765. Negotiations immediately came to a standstill when lawmakers could not agree to offsets for the bill that also included an extension of the payroll tax cut and an adjustment to the Medicare-physician payment rate.

In early February 2012, House GOP leaders indicated they would permit an extension of the payroll tax without offsets, essentially cutting in half the level of offsets needed and enabling conferees to reach agreement on the following issues:

- **Long-term extension**. Federal unemployment benefits, as well as a reduction in Social Security taxes for workers, were extended through January 2, 2013.
- **Number of benefits weeks**. The maximum number of benefits was reduced from ninety-nine weeks. In states where unemployment was higher than 9 percent, benefits were limited to seventy-three weeks (forty-seven weeks of federal benefits combined with twenty-six weeks of state benefits). In states where the unemployment rate was lower, benefits could last sixty-three weeks. The reduction was phased in through September.
- **Eligibility**. The measure required recipients to be actively seeking work and participating in reemployment training. The compromise retained the provision in the House bill allowing states to mandate drug testing of unemployment recipients who lost a job because of a failed drug test or who were searching for a job that required drug testing. It did not include House Republicans' proposal to require people receiving jobless benefits to pursue a high school equivalency degree.
- **Demonstration projects**. The Labor Department was authorized to enter into agreements with ten states to run demonstration projects aimed at expediting the reemployment of individuals receiving unemployment compensation.

The House adopted the conference report on HR 3630 (H Rept 112-399) by a **key vote of 293–132 (R 146–91; D 147–41)** on February 17. The Senate cleared the bill by a 60–36 vote the same day, and the president signed it into law on February 22, 2012 (PL 112-96). *(2012 key votes, p. 803)*

EXTENSION THROUGH 2013 (HR 8)

Benefits for the unemployed became a component of discussions regarding the "fiscal cliff"—automatic spending cuts and tax increases scheduled to take effect according to the Budget Control Act of 2011—that loomed over a lame duck session of Congress at the end of 2012. Republicans pushed back against President Obama's request to continue eligibility for unemployment benefits for another full year, but ultimately agreed to an extension in exchange for a continuation of the 2001 and 2003 payroll tax cuts enacted during the presidency of George W. Bush, both included in a final bill (HR 8, PL 112-240) that temporarily staved off the fiscal cliff.

But the bill kept the maximum number of weeks at seventy-three (and sixty-three weeks in states with lower unemployment) and continued the drug-testing authorization. The measure also extended through December 31, 2013, the availability of extended benefits to railroad workers.

The Senate passed an amended HR 8 on a **key vote of 89–8 (R 40–5; D 47–3; I 2–0)** on January 1, 2013, and the House cleared it on a **key vote of 257–167 (R 85–151; D 172–16)** the same day. The president signed it into law January 2 (PL 112-240). *(2012 key votes, p, 803; legislative action on HR 8 tax provisions, p. 185)*

Under provisions addressing unemployment insurance, PL 112-240:

- Extended long-term federal unemployment insurance benefits for laid-off workers through December 3, 2013.
- Maintained the benefit tiers as enacted under the previous benefit extension, PL 112-96, which reduced the maximum number of weeks an individual could receive unemployment benefits from ninety-nine weeks to seventy-three weeks, including forty-seven weeks of federal benefits on top of twenty-six weeks of state benefits.
- Retained the previous law's requirements for beneficiaries to show evidence of job search.
- Retained authorization for states to drug-test beneficiaries who had lost their jobs due to unlawful drug use.
- Extended through December 31, 2013, the extended unemployment benefits for railroad workers.
- Extended existing authorization of appropriations for federal aid to help states carry out re-employment services through fiscal 2014, at a rate of $85 per individual.

Labor Union Regulations

Rules governing union organization became a focus of the Republican Party in 2011—now with greater numbers in the Senate and a majority in the House—as it sought to roll back some of the Obama administration's regulatory powers across the board. On both sides of Capitol Hill, Republicans pushed regulatory overhaul as a primary feature of their own jobs agenda that they proposed as an alternative to President Barack Obama's jobs plan (S 1549) introduced in September. Among the GOP proposals were measures that sought to change the way workers could form unions and hold elections and to block National Labor Relation Board (NLRB) rules intended to make it easier for workers to join unions, permit what some called "micro unions," and require employers to post notices about labor rights.

The House passed two measures: one to bar the NLRB from interfering in a company's relocation decisions and another to bar a rule aimed to make it easier for workers to join unions. Both faced little prospects in the Democrat-controlled Senate and the latter rule became waylaid by legal challenges.

House conservatives remained undeterred in their efforts to roll back labor rules, even after Ohio voters that November, by a vote of 61 percent to 39 percent, repealed a new state law that curbed the bargaining power of the state's public-sector unions and their 350,000 members. Many political observers saw the vote as a rebuke to Republicans in other states—such as Wisconsin, Indiana, and Michigan—who had launched similar efforts and targeted pension cuts to help resolve state budget crises.

CHALLENGE TO LABOR RELATIONS BOARD

House Majority Leader Eric Cantor, R-Va., launched the party's efforts on regulatory overhaul with a bill (HR 2587), which the House quickly passed, to forbid the NLRB from interfering in a company's relocation decisions.

The measure, offered by freshman Tim Scott, R-S.C., was in reaction to the NLRB's April 20 complaint against airplane manufacturer Boeing Company. The complaint contended the company's decision to open a second production line for its 787 Dreamliner in South Carolina, a state that has a right-to-work law, was a retaliatory move against union workers in Washington State. Workers in Washington had gone on strike four times in the previous twenty-two years. As a remedy, the complaint sought an order mandating Boeing locate the second line in Washington.

But Republicans said the complaint, if successful, could create an environment hostile to job creation and send businesses the message not to locate in a union state to begin with. Democrats maintained that rushing the bill through would change labor law to benefit Boeing, whose request to dismiss the complaint had been turned down. They also said it would strip NLRB of its only remedy when companies cut or transfer jobs in violation of workers' rights and would make it easier to ship jobs overseas.

The House Education and the Workforce Committee on July 21 approved the bill (HR 2587) by a party-line vote of 23–16 to bar the NLRB from ordering an employer to restore, shut down, or relocate business operations. It would apply retroactively to any complaint that had not been resolved by the time the measure was enacted. On

September 15, 2011, the House passed the bill by a vote of 238–186, with seven Republicans voting no and eight Democrats supporting it.

During floor debate, Scott contended the NLRB's efforts were a perfect example of government overreach and would threaten 11,000 jobs that already had been created in his hometown of North Charleston. Republicans also said the NLRB's remedy could undermine the competitiveness of all right-to-work states. Democrats countered that the measure would permit companies to punish workers for exercising their rights and make it easier to ship jobs overseas.

In the Senate Minority Leader Mitch McConnell, R-Ky., called on Democrats to move a similar measure (S 1523) that Republican Lindsey Graham of South Carolina had introduced on September 8, 2011. Democrats contended Graham was trying to influence the ongoing Boeing case that needed to be decided within the judicial process.

Meanwhile, by December, Boeing and the union had reached a tentative collective-bargaining agreement that the union said could pave the way for its withdrawal of the complaint. GOP lawmakers were not willing to drop their challenge to NLRB authority, but it did not move further that session.

UNION ELECTION TIMELINE

The House passed a bill (HR 3094) to block a new NLRB rule that made it easier for workers to join unions but a similar effort in the Senate failed. The NLRB rule, proposed in June 2011 and published in the *Federal Register* on December 22, 2011, aimed to streamline the election process by permitting parties to file documents electronically and by setting deadlines for hearings. The NLRB, seeking to avoid delays on a union election often caused by lawsuits filed by employers, included in its rule a mandate that lawsuits on voter eligibility wait until after the vote.

Labor unions supported the rule, but Republicans said expediting elections was unfair to both employers and employees. House Education and Workforce Committee Chair John Kline, R-Minn., the bill's sponsor, contended that under the new rule, an election could occur "in as little as ten days." His bill sought to impose a thirty-five-day waiting period before a vote was held, permitting workers to learn more about the options. He said the bill aimed to eliminate a "barrage" of new NLRB rules imposed on businesses that made them reluctant to hire. "These regulations are very damaging to the economic recovery," Kline said. "We're trying to get Americans back to work."

George Miller of California, ranking Democrat of the Education and Workforce Committee, said, "Giving big corporations new powers to block workers' ability to bargain for a better life undermines our nation's ability to grow and strengthen the middle class."

The Education and the Workforce Committee approved Kline's measure on October 26, 2011, by a party-line vote of 23–16. The House passed HR 3094 by a 235–188 vote on November 30—the same day the labor board voted to proceed with a rule to postpone litigation related to a unionization vote until after the vote is taken. The House measure required the NLRB to wait at least fourteen days after certifying a unionization petition to hold a preelection hearing, and to wait at least thirty-five days after a successful preelection hearing to hold a unionization election.

The Senate did not take up the legislation, and the Appropriations Committee in June 2012 rebuffed GOP efforts to include in a fiscal 2013 spending bill for labor, health, and education a restriction of the NLRB's authority.

Earlier, the Senate on April 24 defeated a Republican-sponsored resolution (S J Res 36) aimed at blocking the NLRB rule to speed up union elections. During debate before the vote, Republicans maintained that the rule would result in "ambush elections" that would deny employers their First Amendment right to speak to their employees and try to persuade them not to vote for a union. Republicans also depicted the rule as the Obama administration's latest attempt to curry favor with unions, whose fundraising prowess was helping President Barack Obama as he campaigned for reelection.

Michael B. Enzi, R-Wyo., the resolution's sponsor, called the rule "reckless," adding: "It's kind of like Thelma and Louise driving off a cliff. I, for one, do not want to see the NLRB driving the economy off a cliff." Democrats, however, strongly supported the NLRB rule, saying it was a commonsense fix to ensure fair and timely elections. Sen. Tom Harkin, D-Iowa, called the resolution a "Republican assault on unions," adding that Republicans were using the new rule as an "election year political football." On a **key vote of 45–54 (R 45–1; D 0–51; I 0–2,** the Senate rejected Enzi's motion to proceed to consideration of S J Res 36. *(2012 key votes, p. 803)*

RULES ON EMPLOYER NOTICE

Several House Republicans, led by Kline, worked to roll back a separate NLRB rule mandating that employers post notices informing workers of their labor rights. They included in a House spending bill language to block the rule and filed statements supporting lawsuits by business groups against the rule. By the end of the session, the rules had been postponed indefinitely pending resolution of the lawsuits.

The proposed rule was announced in a December 22, 2010, *Federal Register* notice. The rule required employers to post prominently notices to inform employees of their right to self-organization; to form, join, or assist labor organizations; to bargain collectively; and to participate in other concerted activities for their mutual aid or protection. The notice also had to state that employees could refrain from engaging in such activities. A final rule was published in August 2011.

In October 2011, the NLRB postponed implementation of the rule until January 31, 2012, reportedly in response to a House Small Business Committee hearing during which lawmakers called the mandate overly onerous for businesses. Several business groups filed suit against the rule, and the NLRB postponed its implementation until April 30, 2012.

Kline and thirty-five other House Republicans filed amicus briefs in November 2011 in cases challenging the NLRB rule. One brief was filed with the U.S. District Court for the District of Columbia in response to suits filed by the National Association of Manufacturers and the National Right to Work Foundation. The other was with the U.S. District Court for the District of South Carolina Charleston Division in response to a suit by the U.S. Chamber of Commerce and the South Carolina chamber of commerce. In the briefs, the Republicans contended the National Labor Relations Act did not require employers to post notices, meaning Congress did not intend to impose such an obligation and that Congress intentionally limited the NLRB's jurisdiction over employers.

House Republicans also tried to target the rule in their fiscal 2012 spending bill for labor, health and human services, and education. That measure (HR 3070) included language barring funds from being used to implement or enforce that rule and other NLRB rulings. But that measure as drafted did not move forward.

On March 2, 2012, in *National Association of Manufacturers v. NLRB* (WL 691535, D.D.C), the District Court struck down some elements of the rule, but said the labor board did have the authority to require employers to post the notices and that it could consider an employer's "knowing and willful" failure to post the notice as unlawful. The plaintiff appealed that decision to the Court of Appeals for the District of Columbia. On April 13, in *Chamber of Commerce of the United States v. NLRB* (2:11-CV-02516-DCN, D.S.C), a separate District Court ruled the board did not have the authority to issue the rule. The D.C. Court of Appeals then granted an injunction, holding off the rule's implementation pending the appeal.

On April 17, the NLRB postponed implementation of the rule indefinitely, pending the resolution of several legal challenges.

Union Organizing Rules

Sen. Orrin G. Hatch, R-Utah, and Rep. Tim Scott, R-S.C., introduced companion bills in their chambers (S 1507 and HR 2810) in August 2011 to change the process by which workers could form and join a union. The measures called for secret-ballot elections to form a union and set a forty-day minimum waiting period between the day workers filed a petition to vote on a union and the day that vote was held. It required that unions be recertified every three years by a secret-ballot election. Employers could not voluntarily recognize a union.

The measures ran counter to Democrats' efforts to enable workers to form unions without holding elections. Under existing law, at least 30 percent of affected workers had to sign cards indicating their desire to join; then the NLRB held a secret-ballot election. A 2009 White House proposal called for workers to be able to join a union if half or more of them signed a card.

The legislation also aimed to make it harder for labor organizers to intimidate workers into joining unions by targeting a proposed NLRB rule change to speed up union elections once petitions had been filed. At the time, it took about fifty-eight days to organize an election, according to NLRB.

The legislation was not expected to have a chance of enactment during that session, and many Republicans hoped prospects for action would be better in the 113th Congress starting in 2013. Antiunion advocates joined the effort to promote the legislation, airing ads and making campaign donations.

Rail and Aviation Union Elections

Congress in 2011 included in a bill (HR 658—PL 112-95) reauthorizing federal aviation program provisions to alter a National Mediation Board (NMB) rule governing rail and aviation union elections.

In a May 11, 2010, notice in the *Federal Register*, the NMB announced a rule amending the Railway Labor Act to allow union certification where only a majority of the employees who actually vote in the election vote for certification. Previous rules required that a majority of all eligible airline workers vote in favor of union representation to gain union certification. The board said the change would "provide a more reliable measure/indicator of employee sentiment in representation disputes and provide employees with clear choices in representation matters."

The new standard essentially matched that applied by the National Labor Relations Board for elections under the National Labor Relations Act and would govern both railway and aviation union elections.

The House Transportation and Infrastructure Committee on February 16, 2011, approved its version of a Federal Aviation Administration (FAA) reauthorization bill (HR 658) that included a provision to nullify that rule. Before the panel approved the bill by a 34–25 vote, it rejected, 29–30, an amendment by Jerry F. Costello, D-Ill., that would have removed the provision nullifying the rule. *(FAA reauthorization, p. 349)*

House Transportation Committee Chair John L. Mica, R-Fla., said nullifying the rule on union elections would return union voting to a system that had worked well for seventy-five years. But Costello called the provision a "poison pill" that would keep the Senate from advancing the measure. Costello and Steve LaTourette, R-Ohio, made another attempt during House floor debate in April to remove the provision, and the White House threatened to veto any reauthorization bill that included a provision to reverse the ruling.

The Senate version of the FAA reauthorization did not include the provision, and it became a sticking point in negotiations between the two chambers that had to be resolved by party leaders. House Speaker John A. Boehner, R-Ohio, and Senate Majority Leader Harry Reid, D-Nev., ultimately agreed to leave in place the NMB rule but require that in any runoff election for which there are three or more options—including the option of not being represented by any union—and when none of the options receives a majority of votes, the board must arrange a second election between the options receiving the top votes. The measure also increased the threshold for elections, requiring that 50 percent—up from 25 percent—of eligible members of a bargaining unit must petition the board to call a new election.

The conference agreement also created a new dispute resolution process for FAA employees, requiring that when the FAA and one of its bargaining units do not reach agreement, they would have to go through the Federal Mediation and Conciliation Service to agree to an alternative dispute resolution procedure. If that was not successful, they would be subject to a binding arbitration by a three-person board.

The House passed the conference report on HR 658 on February 3, 2012 by a vote of 248–169. The Senate cleared the bill three days later by a vote of 75–20, and the president signed the measure (the FAA Modernization and Reform Act of 2012) into law on February 14.

TSA BARGAINING RIGHTS

Although the Senate in early 2011 considered its bill to reauthorize Federal Aviation Administration (FAA) projects and programs (S 223), the Obama administration announced on February 4 it would award collective bargaining rights to Transportation Security Administration (TSA) screeners. Sen. Roger Wicker, R-Miss., already had introduced an amendment to the FAA bill on the floor to block the administration from doing just that, but his proposal was rejected, 47–51. Under the law that created TSA (PL 107-71), the administration was allowed to extend collective bargaining rights to screeners.

The White House announcement came one week after it declared it would halt expansion of the Screening Partnership Program, which allowed some airports to use private contractors instead of government employees for screening duties. That move also angered Republicans who argued collective bargaining rights would limit TSA's flexibility to change employee assignments or workplace conditions for screeners to respond to shifting threats. But ranking Democrat Bennie Thompson of Mississippi said the move would boost workforce morale and thereby make the country safer.

NATIONAL LABOR RELATIONS ACT POWERS

In July 2012, Republicans pushed for passage of three bills to restrict the power granted to unions under the National Labor Relations Act of 1935 (PL 74-198), although none of them saw action. They included:

- HR 4385, to enable employers in unionized workplaces to offer raises and bonuses to workers outside of the process set forth in collective bargaining units.
- HR 972, to require all union elections to take place by secret ballot.
- HR 2335, to exempt American Indian tribes from many provisions of the NLRA.

Minimum Wage

In mid-2012, workers' advocates and labor unions urged Congress to raise the minimum wage from $7.25 per hour, which was set in 2009. Democrats had introduced several bills that session to boost the minimum wage, but Democrats did not push them in the face of likely rejection in the Republican House and a GOP filibuster in the Senate. *(2010 minimum wage actions, pp. 529–530)*

One measure (S 2252) was offered by Sen. Tom Harkin, D-Iowa, chair of the Health, Education, Labor, and Pensions Committee, in February to raise the wage by 85 cents a year for three years, then index it to inflation. Rep. Rosa DeLauro, D-Conn., introduced a similar bill in the House (HR 5727). Companion measures (HR 6211, S 3453) were introduced by House Education and the Workforce ranking member George Miller, D-Calif., and Harkin, to provide similar minimum wage increases.

Obama had promised during his 2008 campaign to raise the minimum wage to $9.50 an hour by 2011, but it was never presented as a priority during his first term.

Opponents of increasing the minimum wage said higher wages would drive employers out of business, while advocates of a wage hike said existing wages forced people to live on an annual salary that was about $7,000 below the poverty level. The last legislation increasing the level was cleared in 2007 and provided increases over three consecutive years. *(Congress and the Nation Vol. XII, pp. 661, 664)*

Meanwhile, the Labor Department projected many of the fastest-growing jobs as the economy began to recover would be low-wage occupations such as home health aide.

HOME HEALTH AIDES

Republicans briefly, and unsuccessfully, sought to block a proposed Labor Department rule that would guarantee overtime pay and minimum wages for home health care workers. The rule would alter a 1975 regulation that exempted "companionship services" from such requirements. President Bill Clinton (1993–2001) made a similar proposal late in his second term, but President George W. Bush (2001–2009) shelved it.

The original intent of the 1975 law had been to ease expenses for families seeking company for their homebound elderly or disabled relatives, but many advocates of the change said the provision was outdated and that most families hired workers from private agencies that used the exemption to lower labor costs.

When announcing the proposed rule in December 2011, Obama said the workers' low compensation "means that many home care workers are forced to rely on things like food stamps just to make ends meet. That's just wrong."

But Republicans raised concerns and the Education and Workforce Committee held a series of hearings on the proposal while industry lobbyists hoped Congress would block it.

"If finalized in its current form, the proposed rule would diminish the availability of in-home care," Reps. John Kline, R-Minn., chair of the Education and Workforce Committee, and Tim Walberg, R-Mich., chair of the Subcommittee on Workforce Protections, wrote in one of several letters to Labor Secretary Hilda L. Solis. Meanwhile, several members of the Congressional Labor and Working Families Caucus, including Rep. Linda Sanchez, D-Calif., wrote to Solis urging the rule be finalized.

In September 2011, Sanchez, co-chair of the caucus, introduced a bill (HR 2341) to eliminate the exemption of home health workers from minimum wage and maximum hour requirements of the Fair Labor Standards Act. Congress did not act on the proposal, but there was increasing focus on the Labor Department into the next session as it weighed comments on the proposed rule.

H-2B IMMIGRANTS

Before approving its fiscal 2013 spending bill (S 3295) for labor, health, and education in July 2012, the Senate Appropriations Committee adopted by a 19–11 vote an amendment by Richard C. Shelby, R-Ala., the ranking minority member on the Labor-HHS-Education appropriations subcommittee, to block two Labor Department rules governing temporary visas for nonagricultural workers. The rules, which had been finalized but not yet implemented, aimed to improve working conditions, increase the minimum wages for immigrants working under the H-2B visa, and set other visa requirements that business groups said were too onerous. One rule required H-2B employers to pay its H-2B workers prevailing wages.

Labor Secretary Hilda L. Solis said the rules aimed to prevent employers from taking advantage of guest workers, which resulted in driving down wages for American workers. The seafood, timber, landscaping, hotel, and other industries were heavily reliant on the visas to hire seasonal workers, and many such employers backed Shelby's amendment to block the rules.

Shelby, whose state was home to many seafood processors, called the rules "burdensome" and "misguided" because they would hike guest worker wages by more than 50 percent and thereby put many employers out of business. Five Democratic senators, including such representatives of seafood-producing states as Mary L. Landrieu of Louisiana and Barbara A. Mikulski of Maryland, were among the amendment's supporters.

The House draft bill for the fiscal 2013 spending bill for labor, health, and education contained similar language. That measure also included a provision to block a rule restricting the type of paid work that children could do on farms. In February, the Department of Labor pulled back on a draft child farm labor rule because of pressure from congressional Republicans.

In September 2012, as lawmakers sought to provide funds to continue government operations because Congress had not completed any of the spending bills, lawmakers took up a six-month continuing resolution that could not be amended and thereby did not provide lawmakers an opportunity to block the Labor rule.

AMERICAN SAMOA WORKERS

In July 2012 Congress cleared, and the president signed, a bill (S 2009—PL 112-149) to delay by three years the implementation of a scheduled minimum wage increase of fifty cents per hour for American Samoa workers.

The Senate passed the measure on December 16, 2011, by unanimous consent. The House on July 17, 2012, cleared it by a vote of 378–11. The measure delayed the increase until September 30, 2015, and called for subsequent increases to be calculated every three years, rather than annually.

The existing minimum wage had been scheduled to increase at the end of September, but the territorial government requested a delay because of economic concerns.

The bill set a $5.26 minimum wage for jobs in fish processing, the predominant industry on the island; $4.18 for garment manufacturing jobs, and $5.59 for shipping and transportation industry jobs. (The minimum wage on the mainland United States was $7.25 at that time.)

The measure also required the Energy Department to do radioactivity analysis of a nuclear testing debris storage facility on Runit Island, located on the Eniwetok Atoll in the Marshall Islands, where atomic devices had been tested decades earlier. It also permitted magistrate and territorial judges to be temporarily assigned to serve on courts of the South Pacific island nations (known as the Freely Associated States). *(2010 action, p. 529)*

Federal Worker Pension Contributions

In late 2011, Congress approved as part of a payroll tax-cut extension measure an increase in the amount of federal employee contributions to their pensions.

President Barack Obama that fall had recommended to the Joint Select Committee on Deficit Reduction a proposal to increase employee pension payments by 1.2 percent, but he asked that retirement totals remain the same.

The House took up a similar proposal and first attached it to a highway bill (HR 7) to offset costs, but later pulled it

COST OF LIVING CHANGES PROPOSED FOR SOCIAL SECURITY

Lawmakers seeking savings in the federal budget frequently scrutinized entitlements, including the cost of federal retirement benefits. During the 112th Congress, they briefly considered changing the method for calculating the Consumer Price Index (CPI) when determining the cost-of-living adjustments (COLAs) for Social Security, federal annuities, and military retiree pay. However, no action occurred before adjournment.

Federal policy analysts and lawmakers had long debated the value of changing the method of calculating CPI. Advocates of a switch to a method known as a "chained CPI" (see Calculating the CPI, in the following section) said the change would more accurately reflect consumer spending habits and produce savings to help reduce the federal deficit. Opponents, including federal employee unions and organizations representing seniors, argued it would only take more money out of seniors' pockets. They called for a calculation that would more accurately measure the spending habits of the elderly.

President Barack Obama's bipartisan fiscal commission in 2010 proposed the switch to the chained CPI, and Obama reportedly suggested it as an option during budget talks with House Republicans in the summer of 2011. A change to the CPI calculation was included in a proposal released on July 19, 2011, by the bipartisan "Gang of Six" that aimed to cut the deficit by $3.7 trillion over the following ten years. That proposal called for a shift to a chained CPI in 2012 for everything except Social Security income, which would move to a chained CPI starting in 2017. *(Fiscal commission, p. 142)*

But ultimately the idea was dropped because of considerable opposition from Social Security advocates who insisted that the program should not be considered in the context of deficit reduction because it was entirely self-financed and did not contribute to the deficit.

Calculating the CPI

Since 1972, Congress had enacted automatic Social Security COLAs based on the Bureau of Labor Standards (BLS) calculation of the consumer price index, called the CPI-W, that measures inflation experienced by urban wage earners and clerical workers, which accounted for about 32 percent of the population. That index measured changing prices of a full range of goods and services, called a "market basket," that population typically would purchase. (The BLS used another index, called the CPI-U, to index income tax brackets and poverty thresholds. That index was based on changing prices of the market basket for all urban residents (about 87 percent of the population).

In 1999, the CPI indexes grew more slowly because the BLS began accounting for consumers' changing buying habits as prices fluctuated among similar products (for example, buying fewer Gala apples but more Granny Smith apples when the prices changed). Some analysts preferred the calculation of the "chained" CPI-U that was based on an assumption that consumers changed their spending patterns across the board when prices changed. For example, consumers might buy less fuel when those costs rose but would buy more food.

---

from that bill and attached it to a payroll tax cut bill (HR 3630, PL 112-96) making its way through Congress.

Pension proposal. On February 7, 2012, the House Oversight and Government Reform Committee approved by a 22–16 vote a measure (HR 3813) to increase employee contributions to the Civil Service Retirement System (CSRS) and the Federal Employee Retirement System (FERS) by 1.5 percent of their salaries.

Under the measure, FERS employees would have to contribute a total 2.3 percent of their paycheck to their pensions, and lawmakers would have to contribute 2.8 percent. The bill also aimed to reduce total pensions for newly hired federal employees, who would have to pay 4 percent, and their pension calculation would be based on the average of their five highest salaries, rather than the current highest three.

Bill sponsor Dennis A. Ross, R-Fla., said, "It is clear that the taxpayers cannot afford to continue to maintain the current federal pension cost structure over the long term." The Congressional Budget Office (CBO) had released a report the previous month indicating that federal employee benefits were worth 48 percent more than those of private-sector employees. But ranking Democrat Elijah E. Cummings of Maryland said, "This legislation is a solution in search of a problem." The panel defeated by voice vote an amendment by Cummings that would have exempted from the changes those employees who made less than $30,000 annually.

Highway bill. Legislation enacted in July 2012 (PL 112-141) to reauthorize highway and transit programs included several funding maneuvers to provide a short-term infusion of money for the Highway Trust Fund. Those maneuvers included changes to pension rules.

The House-passed bill (HR 7) had included language from HR 3813 to increase employee contributions to the CSRS and FERS by 1.5 percent over three years, with the revenues directed to help pay for the highway bill. But lawmakers later decided to use that revenue to help pay for a payroll tax cut bill. *(Details below)*

Ultimately, the final measure provided for funding the highway trust fund via transfers from the general treasury

BLS statistics showed that the chained CPI-U, which the bureau had calculated since 1999, was rising about 0.3 percentage points more slowly each year than the CPI-W that was used for Social Security COLAs, but some economists said it was a more accurate measurement of inflation. A March 2011 Congressional Budget Office (CBO) report concluded that using a chained CPI-U to set Social Security COLAs would reduce federal expenditures by about $27 billion over five years and by $112 billion through 2021.

Opponents of the chained CPI method said it would underestimate inflation for seniors because of the costs of health care, particularly the rising out-of-pocket health care costs that were tending to rise faster than inflation. They argued, also, that the estimated 0.3 percent slower growth in the COLA for retirement benefits would compound over time, so that older or less affluent recipients would see the most significant cuts. In addition, the calculation process for the chained CPI took two years, meaning there would be an extensive lag time that would not accurately reflect current price fluctuation, opponents argued.

A CPI for Seniors

The BLS since 1988 had tracked an experimental index called the CPI-E, which accounted for the spending patterns of consumers aged sixty-two and older. That index tended to rise about 0.2 percent faster than the CPI-W, according to BLS statistics. That calculation tended to more heavily weight health care expenses and better estimate the cost of living for the disabled, the agency said. The CBO in its report also suggested policy makers might consider a chained version of the CPI-E, but it warned that "the impact of rising health care prices on the cost of someone's standard of living is problematic because it is difficult to accurately account for changes in the quality of health care."

Some policy experts suggested the BLS should increase its resources to create a more accurate CPI for the elderly that better analyzed their spending habits. They faulted the CPI-E because it was calculated based on the same shopping outlets and geographic areas as used in the regular CPI-U, for instance.

One-Time COLA Replacement

In 2010 and 2011, Social Security recipients were not granted a cost-of-living adjustment because inflation had not been high enough to trigger one, according to the Labor Department. Several Democrats proposed legislation (HR 5987 and S 3985) to grant Social Security recipients a one-time $250 payment (some recipients of federal disability payments also would have qualified). It mirrored a payment provided under the 2009 stimulus law.

The AARP, one of the nation's most influential lobbying groups for seniors, and other advocates for seniors strongly backed granting some form of relief in lieu of the regular COLA that was not provided. But critics, especially Republicans, said the $250 payment would cost about $14 billion and, in theory, was unnecessary. The measures were turned back in both chambers.

and the Leaking Underground Storage Tank Trust Fund, covering the cost of those transfers by changing the method by which businesses determine investment in employee-defined benefit pension plans, bringing in an estimated $94 billion over ten years. It also increased employer-paid insurance premiums paid to the Pension Benefit Guaranty Corporation, raising about $11.5 billion over ten years. *(Highway, transit reauthorization, p. 340)*

Payroll tax cut extension. Congressional leaders opted to use the pension change to help offset the costs of the tax-cut extension they were negotiating in February 2012 (HR 3630). That provision included language to increase by 2.3 percent the amount newly hired federal employees must contribute to their retirement accounts (it applied to those hired after 2012 and had fewer than five years of previous federal service).

Specifically, new employees would pay 3.1 percent of their basic salary toward the Federal Employees Retirement System (FERS), increased from 0.8 percent that employees were paying. Corresponding increases were made for those entering Central Intelligence Agency and Foreign Service pensions systems, as well as for pension contributions for new members of Congress and congressional employees. But retirement plans of current federal workers were untouched.

Democrats were angered that the conference agreement included the pension provision and threatened to vote against it. Sen. Benjamin Cardin, D-Md., one of the conferees, who represented a district in a state that was home to hundreds of federal workers, was a final holdout on the agreement because of the provisions. Ultimately, President Obama called Cardin to urge him to sign off on the agreement so it could go to the House and Senate for a vote. The conference agreement was agreed to in the House on February 17 by a vote of 293–132 and cleared by the Senate the same day by a vote of 60–36 (Cardin opposed it). The president signed the bill into law on February 22 (PL 112-96).

The agreement did not include House-passed provisions that would have frozen federal employee salaries for another year, based the pensions of new workers on the highest five years of salary rather than three years, modified the "multiplier" used in calculating pensions, or eliminated the FERS Annuity Supplement for individuals not subject to mandatory retirement.

Budget offsets. The House Committee on Oversight and Government Reform voted, 19–15, on April 26, 2012, to back a draft GOP proposal to require federal workers, lawmakers, and congressional aides to pay at least $82 billion in additional pension contributions over the next ten years.

Republicans said the plan would align federal employee pensions with those in the private sector, while Democrats called it an assault on federal workers.

The measure included language requiring federal employees to contribute another 5 percent of their pay to their pensions; congressional staffers would pay an additional 8.5 percent if they were enrolled in the Civil Service Retirement System (CSRS) and 7.5 percent if they were enrolled in the FERS. Lawmakers enrolled in either system would contribute another 8.5 percent.

The panel approved an amendment to allow federal employees to transfer payments for accumulated leave or unused vacation to their pensions under the Thrift Savings Funds.

The proposal aimed to help fulfill a requirement in the House-passed budget resolution (H Con Res 112) directing committees to find savings in domestic programs totaling $261.5 billion over the next ten years (the Oversight and Reform Committee's share was $78.9 billion)—part of a process intended to replace the automatic sequester that was to be triggered without reductions under the debt limit law (PL 112-25).

The proposal was included in the House GOP Sequester Replacement Reconciliation Act (HR 5652), which the House passed on May 10 by a vote of 218–199. It subsequently was included in another GOP sequester replacement proposal (HR 6684), which the House passed on December 20 by a 215–21 vote. Neither was taken up by the Senate.

Welfare Law Changes

With the increasing focus on jobs and unemployment, alongside long, drawn-out budget and deficit debates, Republicans began to call for reform of welfare laws, although they eventually decided the issue would have to wait until a future Congress convened.

The Republican push for welfare changes sharply increased after the Health and Human Services (HHS) Department announced in a July 12 memo that it would grant waivers to states to exempt them from the work requirements written into the 1996 bipartisan welfare legislation (PL 104-193) enacted during the Clinton administration. Republicans said the waivers would undermine the law's goal of weaning people off welfare and guiding them into the workforce. *(PL 104-93, Congress and the Nation Vol. IX, p. 578)*

HHS said the states, including some with Republican governors, such as Utah and Nevada, had requested the waiver because they needed more flexibility to help unemployed workers find jobs through the Temporary Assistance for Needy Families (TANF) program, which was created as part of the 1996 law.

That law replaced the old welfare program, which had authorized checks for eligible recipients, with block grants for the states. The grants required that states put pressure on recipients to find work. Under the law, states generally must enroll half of their participating families in job-training programs to qualify for the funding.

But according to the administration's memo, states wanted to launch their own pilot programs, on the grounds that "some TANF rules stifle innovation and focus attention on paperwork rather than helping parents find jobs."

On September 4, the Government Accountability Office issued a determination that the HHS proposal constituted federal rule making, and therefore would be subject to congressional consideration under the 1996 Congressional Review Act (PL 104-121). The law gave Congress the power to disapprove an executive branch regulation through enactment of a joint resolution within sixty days of receiving the proposal from the issuing agency.

On September 20, the House passed a resolution (H J Res118) by a 250–164 vote, mostly along party lines, to nullify the proposal. Democrats called the resolution vote an election-year ploy. Ways and Means ranking Democrat Sander M. Levin of Michigan said it would pave the way for a GOP attack on Obama's welfare policy.

Sen. Orrin Hatch, R-Utah, vowed to force a floor vote on his companion resolution (S J Res 50). He spoke on the floor in December and urged a vote even though, he said, he was "well aware that the vote on S J Res 50 would likely fall along party lines, and this is disappointing." The Senate did not act on the resolution.

CHAPTER 13

Law and Justice

Introduction 547

Chronology of Action on Law Enforcement 553

2009–2010 553

2011–2012 568

The Supreme Court 584

Law and Law Enforcement

Congressional consideration of law and justice issues during the first term of President Barack Obama fell largely into two categories. With the support of the White House, several significant pieces of legislation that had previously resisted legislative solution were cleared by Congress and signed by the president, either because they enjoyed bipartisan support or because Democrats, using their majorities in the 111th Congress during 2009–2010, were able to force them through. But other issues, particularly immigration, proved far too divisive to advance to Obama's desk, and they foreshadowed difficult partisan battles to come.

In 2009, Democrats muscled through two of their long-standing priorities. The first, in the opening weeks of the Obama administration, was a labor priority to make it easier for workers to file wage discrimination lawsuits against their employers. Months later, Democrats overcame the objections of many Republicans and cleared an expansion of federal hate crimes law to include crimes against people because of their sexual orientation, gender identity, or disability.

Despite their diminished numbers, conservatives also scored some victories. Republicans, joined by a number of Democrats, repeatedly blocked the administration's efforts to close the U.S. detainee facility at Guantánamo Bay, Cuba. Lawmakers attached provisions to several of the annual spending bills that placed restrictions on moving the prisoners and on shuttering the detention center. Republicans and pro–gun rights Democrats also came together successfully in 2009 to attach a provision to credit card legislation that would allow loaded firearms into national parks. The underlying bill was a priority for Obama, and he signed it into law.

Although the chambers were controlled by different parties in the 112th Congress, legislators in some ways became more productive on law and justice issues.

Lawmakers achieved a long-standing goal by clearing a bipartisan overhaul of federal patent law—an issue that had eluded resolution for years. They then managed a four-year extension of three provisions of the antiterrorism law known as the Patriot Act, despite the concerns of a number of lawmakers on the left and right. In the closing days of the 112th Congress, the House and Senate also worked to give an important victory to Obama and Senate Intelligence Chair Dianne Feinstein, D-Calif., by clearing a five-year renewal of the foreign intelligence law that allowed the federal government to wiretap foreigners in certain situations without obtaining a warrant first.

Although the deep differences between the two parties made headlines and stalled key pieces of Obama's agenda, Republicans and Democrats found themselves closely aligned on several significant matters. The House in the 111th Congress voted unanimously to impeach two federal judges charged with corruption. Although U.S. District Judge Samuel B. Kent resigned after being impeached in 2009, the other impeached judge, G. Thomas Porteous Jr. of the Eastern District of Louisiana, went to trial in the Senate in 2010. There senators voted overwhelmingly to convict him, making him just the eighth federal judge in history to be convicted by senators and forced out of office.

Lawmakers came together to take care of a significant piece of business in the lame duck session of 2010 that followed November elections by clearing legislation to pay for two federal legal settlements. This resolved decades-long

REFERENCES

Discussion of law enforcement policy for the years 1945–1964 may be found in *Congress and the Nation Vol. I*, pp. 1671–1676; for the years 1965–1968, *Congress and the Nation Vol. II*, pp. 309–334; for the years 1969–1972, *Congress and the Nation Vol. III*, pp. 255–286; for the years 1973–1976, *Congress and the Nation Vol. IV*, pp. 559–618; for the years 1977–1980, *Congress and the Nation Vol. V*, pp. 715–753; for the years 1981–1984, *Congress and the Nation Vol. VI*, pp. 675–709; for the years 1985–1988, *Congress and the Nation Vol. VII*, pp. 713–784; for the years 1989–1992, *Congress and the Nation Vol. VIII*, pp. 741–799; for the years 1993–1996, *Congress and the Nation Vol. IX*, pp. 679–758; for the years 1997–2000, *Congress and the Nation Vol. X*, pp. 589–683; for the years 2001–2004, *Congress and the Nation Vol. XI*, pp. 581–629; for the years 2005–2008, *Congress and the Nation Vol. XII*, pp. 675–726.

Outlays for Law Enforcement

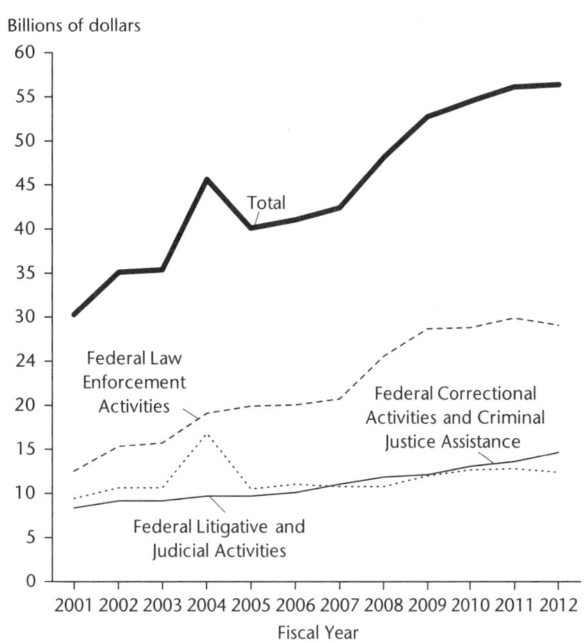

SOURCE: Office of Management and Budget, *Historical Tables, Budget of the United States Government: Fiscal Year 2013* (Washington, D.C.: U.S. Government Printing Office, 2012), Table 3.2.

challenges against the Interior Department by American Indians and against the Agriculture Department by Black farmers.

Lawmakers in both Congresses also cleared a number of relatively noncontroversial measures. These included making it a federal crime to sell videos featuring the graphic torture of live animals, outlawing caller identification or ID "spoofing" for fraudulent or other harmful purposes, making it more difficult to propagate Internet schemes that tricked consumers into signing up for unwanted services and membership clubs, and increasing the maximum monetary penalties for the theft of trade secrets

MAJOR ACCOMPLISHMENTS

Perhaps the most striking piece of law and justice legislation to be signed into law during Obama's first term was the overhaul of federal patent law. The 2011 legislation, a priority of big technology companies, marked an important breakthrough after years of inconclusive legislative debates over the issue.

The new law changed the procedures for issuing patents and for challenging the validity of patents once they were issued, with the aim of making the patent system faster and more efficient. It had bipartisan support as a means of fostering innovation and bolstering U.S. economic growth and global competitiveness, gaining additional momentum when supporters tied it to the drive to increase jobs, which was on the minds of members of both parties.

The version of the bill passed by the Senate would have let the U.S. Patent and Trademark Office keep and spend all the fees it took in from patent applicants, an issue that put the two chambers at odds over the bill. In the end, the Senate yielded and cleared the bill passed by the House, in the interest of finally getting the measure into law.

A bipartisan coalition in 2011 also succeeded in clearing an extension of three expiring provisions of the antiterrorism law known as the USA Patriot Act. The extended provisions allowed federal law enforcement officials to seek a court order to gain access to "any tangible thing" related to a terrorism investigation and to obtain "roving" wiretaps on terrorism suspects who used multiple communications devices or who repeatedly changed cell phone numbers or carriers. It also authorized officials to seek warrants to conduct surveillance on "lone wolf" terrorist suspects who could not be connected to specific terrorist groups or foreign nations.

The agreement came after lawmakers in 2009 and again in 2010 agreed to short-term extensions while they continued to debate the issue. The four-year extensions, strongly supported by the White House, finally came about after high-level negotiations among House Speaker John A. Boehner, R-Ohio; Senate Majority Leader Harry Reid, D-Nev.; and Senate Minority Leader Mitch McConnell, R-Ky.

Democrats could take satisfaction in a pair of legislative victories in 2009.

After coming up short in the four previous Congresses, Democrats finally succeeded in expanding federal hate crimes laws to include crimes committed against people because of their sexual orientation, gender identity, or disability. The legislation extended provisions of an existing law that made it a federal crime to use or threaten force against someone based on race, color, religion, or national origin. It also broadened the ability of the federal government to assist state and local law authorities in prosecuting hate crimes.

Supporters said the measure was needed to combat certain attacks based on bigotry. Many Republicans worried that it placed a higher value on some lives than on others. Opponents also argued that the statute could have a chilling effect on free speech.

The House passed a stand-alone hate crimes bill in April. Although the Senate did not act on the measure, Democratic leaders in that chamber managed to add the language as a floor amendment to the defense authorization bill. House and Senate conferees retained the language in the final bill, despite deep misgivings by Republican opponents.

Democrats also handed an important victory to organized labor in the opening weeks of the 111th Congress. They cleared legislation, known as the Lilly Ledbetter Fair Pay Act, to overturn a Supreme Court decision that had made it more difficult for workers to challenge wage discrimination.

The new law gave workers more time to file a lawsuit by applying the statute of limitations to each discriminatory

JUSTICE LEADERSHIP

President Barack Obama had a single attorney general for his entire first term: Eric H. Holder Jr. But Holder's tenure was not without controversy. He became the first attorney general in U.S. history to be held in contempt of Congress. The House's action was for failing to provide documents related to a gun-tracking program known as Operation Fast and Furious. *(Contempt action, p. 573)*

Lawmakers also faced an unusual legislative process for extending the tenure of FBI director Robert S. Mueller.

Attorney General

Holder, the first African American attorney general, had strong credentials for the post. He had served as a public corruption prosecutor and U.S. attorney before working as the second in command in the Justice Department in the final years of the administration of President Bill Clinton (1993–2001).

Obama's nomination of Holder in December 2008 drew some controversy. Republicans criticized Holder for a number of reasons, including his positions on national security and gun rights and his recommendations in controversial clemency decisions by Clinton. One of the most controversial involved his role in facilitating the pardon that Clinton had given to Marc Rich, a financier who had fled the United States to avoid prosecution. During a grueling seven-hour confirmation hearing before the Senate Judiciary Committee, Holder labeled waterboarding (a simulated drowning technique) as torture. He did not entirely rule out prosecution of officials from the administration of Obama's precedessor, George W. Bush, for their involvement in questioning detainees and conducting warrantless surveillance operations.

But Holder had support from a broad base of federal and state law enforcement groups as well as a bipartisan coalition of former Justice Department leaders. His experience and integrity were not questioned. On February 2, he won Senate approval, 75–21, with all the no votes coming from Republicans.

Federal Bureau of Investigation Director

With congressional blessing, FBI Director Robert S. Mueller III in 2011 won a two-year extension to his post in an unusual legislative process.

Nominated by President George W. Bush, Mueller took office just before the September 11, 2001, attacks and generated praise for his efforts to transform the FBI from an organization focused on fighting crime to one where antiterrorism became the priority. Obama in May 2011 said he wanted to keep Mueller in place for an additional two years to ensure continuity amid leadership transitions at other agencies.

The initial version of the legislation would have extended the term without a confirmation vote. It was sponsored by the chairs and ranking members of the Senate Judiciary and Intelligence committees

But some Republicans raised constitutional concerns. They pushed an alternative proposal to create a new, two-year term of service for the director. That approach would subject Mueller to another Senate confirmation process.

GOP senators warned that any actions taken by Mueller during an extended term could be subject to legal challenges and said their proposal would eliminate any doubt about his authority. Tom Coburn, R-Okla., who offered the amendment, cited testimony given to Senate Judiciary Committee from John C. Harrison, a University of Virginia law professor.

Harrison told the panel that the measure to extend Mueller's term would be an unconstitutional executive appointment by Congress, a power reserved solely for the president. To avoid potential legal challenges, Harrison said the legislation could be redrafted to create a new, two-year term. Judiciary Chair Patrick J. Leahy, D-Vt., and other Democrats were wary of that approach given the hurdles presented by the Senate confirmation process, and they said they did not think it was legally necessary.

Republicans warned that the constitutional concerns about the measure could be problematic, with Coburn saying it was a "big question" whether the underlying bill could get through the House.

To allow for the two-year extension, the Senate on July 21 passed legislation (S 1103—PL 112-24) by voice vote, thus allowing President Obama to renominate Mueller. The House cleared it by voice vote on July 25. Then the Senate on July 27 voted unanimously, 100–0, to confirm Mueller to serve until September 4, 2013.

Republican Charles E. Grassley of Iowa stressed that the Senate's actions should demonstrate that the extension of Mueller's term was an unusual case and involved rigorous congressional oversight. "Taken together, this process has established a historical record that we do not take this extension lightly and that any further, future extensions should have to go through no less than the same process," he said.

---

paycheck, rather than to the first instance of discrimination. Workers who won their claims in court can collect up to two years of back pay.

Republicans, who had blocked such legislation in the 110th Congress, contended that it would incite a rash of discrimination lawsuits. But Democrats said it was important during the recession to guarantee that women and minorities—who, according to census figures, were routinely paid less than white men in comparable positions—were not further burdened.

OTHER MAJOR LEGAL LEGISLATION CONSIDERED BY CONGRESS 2009–2013

In the four years of President Barack Obama's first term in office, from 2009 to 2013, Congress considered an array of legislation that touched on legal and law enforcement as well as on other high-profile national issues including national security, labor relations and discrimination, border security, campaign financing, and communications. The most prominent of these issues are discussed at greater length in different subject chapters in this volume. They are briefly summarized below.

Wage Discrimination

Lawmakers early in 2009 cleared legislation to make it easier for workers to challenge wage discrimination, in a major victory for advocates of workers rights. The House cleared the measure (S 181—PL 111-2), dubbed the Lilly Ledbetter Fair Pay Act, by a vote of 250–177 on January 27. President Obama signed it January 29. *(Details, p. 528)*

Ledbetter, who was a supervisor at a Goodyear Tire plant in Alabama, discovered after nearly twenty years that she had been paid less than men who were doing the same work. She sued, but the Supreme Court ruled 5–4 in 2007 that workers who believed they were victims of wage discrimination must file suit within 180 days of when the alleged bias first occurred. The legislation overturned that ruling.

Democrats said Ledbetter's plight was not unusual. Workers rarely knew what their colleagues were paid, and it could be years before they suspected they were the victims of illegal discrimination.

The 2009 legislation applied the statute of limitations to each discriminatory paycheck, rather than to the first instance of discrimination. Workers who win their claims in court can collect up to two years of back pay.

Republicans had long contended that the legislation—which they successfully blocked in the Senate during the 110th Congress—would incite a rash of discrimination lawsuits, calling it a "boondoggle" for trial lawyers. But Democrats said the legislation simply restored the law to what it was before the Supreme Court's decision.

Patriot Act

Three expiring provisions of the antiterrorism law, the USA Patriot Act, were extended for four years under legislation that cleared May 26, 2011. President Obama signed the legislation by autopen later the same day while on an official trip to Europe (S 990—PL 112-14). *(Details, p. 214)*

The extended provisions:

- Allowed federal law enforcement officials to seek a court order to gain access to "any tangible thing," including business and library records, related to a terrorism investigation.
- Allowed officials to obtain "roving" wiretaps on terrorism suspects who used multiple communications devices or who repeatedly changed cell phone numbers or carriers.
- Authorized officials to seek warrants to conduct surveillance on "lone wolf" terrorist suspects who could not be connected to specific terrorist groups or foreign nations.

The first two provisions were part of the Patriot Act (PL 107-56), which became law shortly after the September 11, 2001, terrorist attacks. The third was enacted in a 2004 overhaul of the intelligence community (PL 108-458). All three were originally set to expire after four years.

A pair of Patriot Act extension bills in 2006 (PL 109-177, PL 109-178) extended the provisions through the end of 2009.

Unable to agree on a long-term extension, lawmakers in December 2009 accepted a temporary plan (PL 111-118) that kept the provisions on the books for two additional months. When agreement still proved elusive, Congress cleared a bill (PL 111-141) in February 2010 that continued the provisions through February 28, 2011.

The short-term bills were intended to give Congress more time to develop a long-term solution. Many Republicans wanted to make the provisions permanent, while civil liberties groups and libertarians argued that they were too intrusive, particularly the ability to obtain broad authority to demand library, bookstore, and other business records. The Obama administration strongly supported the four-year extension.

Border Security

Despite disagreements over larger immigration issues, lawmakers in 2010 cleared a $600 million spending measure to strengthen patrol activity along the Mexican border with new personnel and equipment. After the House passed the measure (HR 6080—PL 111-230) by voice vote August 10, the Senate did the same two days later, clearing it for the president's signature later that day. *(Details, p. 212)*

The measure provided funds sought by the administration to send 1,500 new border patrol agents, two additional unmanned aerial drones, and millions of dollars in communications equipment to the border to help stem the flow of illegal immigrants and drugs. Its cost would be offset primarily through steep increases in visa fees for companies that rely on foreign workers for a large part of their workforce.

Campaign Finance

The House in 2010 passed a bill (HR 5175) to broaden campaign finance disclosure and reporting requirements. The bill passed on June 24 on a **key vote, 219–206 (R 2–170; D 217–36)**. However the bill died in the Senate. *(2010 key votes, p. 751; HR 5175 details, p. 678)*

After the Supreme Court's 5–4 ruling in January in *Citizens United v. Federal Election Commission*, 558 U.S. 310, which held that corporations have the same free-speech rights as individuals and can spend corporate money to sway election campaigns, Democrats mobilized to develop a legislative response.

A few days after the ruling, President Obama launched an unusually direct criticism of the decision during his State of the Union address—as several justices sat in the audience—saying it had been wrongly decided in favor of "powerful interests."

Congressional Democrats picked up that same populist critique as they introduced HR 5175 to tighten disclosure rules on campaign advertising by corporations, unions, and other independent groups and to prohibit foreign-controlled corporations or corporations receiving government assistance from making expenditures in political campaigns.

Republicans strongly opposed the measure, which they said would unconstitutionally curb free-speech rights and was designed mostly to improve Democrats' prospects in the midterm elections.

The bill's lead author was Chris Van Hollen of Maryland, who served as chair of the Democratic Congressional Campaign Committee. In seeking a majority to back the bill, Democrats angered advocacy groups and liberal lawmakers by amending the bill to exempt the National Rifle Association, which had threatened opposition, from certain disclosure requirements.

Foreign Intelligence Surveillance Act

In a victory for President Obama and Senate Intelligence Chair Dianne Feinstein, D-Calif., Congress cleared a five-year renewal of the foreign intelligence law in the final days of the session. Obama signed the measure December 30, 2012 (HR 5949—PL 112-238). *(Details, p.215)*

The bill extended through 2017 expiring provisions of a 2008 law (PL 110-261) that gave the intelligence community authority to conduct wiretaps of certain foreigners communicating with people in the United States without obtaining individual warrants.

The 2008 law, enacted after years of wrangling, was the result of efforts by President George W. Bush to persuade Congress to effectively authorize his warrantless wiretapping program. That statute was an update of the 1978 Foreign Intelligence Surveillance Act (FISA; PL 95-511).

The surveillance powers were set to expire at the end of 2012, and Obama administration intelligence officials made their renewal a priority. The director of national intelligence, Lt. Gen. James R. Clapper Jr., described the FISA law as an essential counterterrorism tool that was too vital to let lapse. But civil liberties groups and a number of liberal congressional Democrats decried the reauthorization, saying there was little information about the degree to which U.S. citizens' communications were being swept up under the program.

The 2008 FISA amendments act had come in response to a 2005 report that the National Security Agency had been secretly monitoring the international telephone calls and emails of U.S. residents without warrants. The secret program, authorized by an order signed by Bush in 2002, monitored thousands of U.S. citizens, permanent residents, tourists, and foreigners in the country in order to track possible links to al-Qaida.

The 2008 law empowered the attorney general and director of national intelligence to jointly authorize, for up to one year, investigations involving surveillance of targets who were not "U.S. persons" and who were "reasonably believed to be located outside the United States." It also authorized authorities to gather electronic communications and other data within the United States with respect to U.S. persons who were out of the country.

The statute allowed warrantless surveillance as long as it did not intentionally target U.S. persons or persons located within the United States, excluding foreign agents. Concerns over the use of these intelligence-gathering authorities led Congress to include a number of restrictions. Among them were a requirement that intelligence gathering be consistent with the Fourth Amendment and a prohibition on the intentional targeting of a U.S. person, directly or indirectly.

Balanced-Budget Amendment

The House and Senate in 2011 rejected proposals for a balanced-budget amendment to the Constitution. Legislation passed in August to increase the national debt limit (PL 112-25) required House and Senate votes on an amendment before the end of the year. But the decision by both chambers to turn a thumbs down on the amendment indicated waning support for the idea. *(Details, p. 167)*

The House rejected the proposal (H J Res 2) on November 18, 261–165, short of the two-thirds majority needed to send an amendment to the states for consideration. It marked the first time in sixteen years that the House went on record on the issue of constitutionally requiring the federal government to balance its budget. Unlike the last time, the measure was rejected. The Senate in December rejected its version of a constitutional amendment but the House's earlier vote killed the effort.

The proposal, put together by Republicans who now controlled the House following the 2010 midterm elections, would require that in every annual budget, total outlays not exceed total revenue unless a three-fifths majority in each chamber voted to allow it. The other exception would be if a congressional declaration of war was in effect, in which case a simple majority could waive the requirement.

PARTISAN BATTLES

Despite such legislative successes, liberals and conservatives found themselves increasingly at odds over a number of high-profile and politically combustible issues.

In one of his more visible legislative misses, Obama failed to persuade Congress to pass comprehensive immigration policy. The issue, which had also eluded President George W. Bush, was crowded out by other priorities in 2009 and early 2010, such as the economic stimulus, health care, and Wall Street regulations. When Democrats finally turned to immigration, it proved too divisive because of widespread opposition among Republicans and some Democrats to provide a path to citizenship for the roughly eleven million illegal immigrants in the nation.

Democrats in 2010 eventually focused on narrower measures, especially a plan to give undocumented adults under thirty the chance to obtain green cards and then citizenship if they met certain criteria. Supporters of the measure, known as the DREAM Act, contended that children should not be punished because of illegal acts by their parents. Opponents, however, criticized it for granting what they called "amnesty" to illegal immigrants. The bill passed the House in late 2010 and garnered the support of a narrow majority of senators. But Senate supporters failed to overcome a filibuster.

In the 112th Congress, Republicans and Democrats clashed sharply over reauthorizing a previously noncontroversial law, the Violence Against Women Act. Congress had twice previously given broad bipartisan backing to the 1994 act, which helped support the prevention and prosecution of domestic and sexual violence and provided state grants for services such as transitional housing and legal assistance. But this time the Republican-controlled House and the Democratic-controlled Senate passed notably different versions. Senate provisions to cover gay and lesbian victims and give American Indian authorities the power to prosecute non-Indians accused of abusing Indian women on tribal lands were not included in the House bill. Negotiations broke down with House Republicans saying they could not go to conference because the Senate-passed bill contained a little-noticed revenue provision, violating a House presumption that all revenue legislation had to start in the House.

Judicial nominations, not surprisingly, also proved to be a flash point. In the 111th Congress, the Senate confirmed Obama's two nominees to the Supreme Court—Sonya Sotomayor and Elena Kagan—despite the opposition of many Republicans. But in the 112th Congress, Republicans successfully filibustered two of Obama's nominees for appellate judgeships. These were the first successful filibusters of judicial nominees since a 2005 agreement that was meant to curtail filibusters except in extraordinary circumstances, and they provoked strong rebukes from Democrats who worried that they could presage increasingly divisive battles over the federal judiciary.

Taking aim at the administration, House Republicans in 2012 took the extraordinary step of voting to hold Attorney General Eric H. Holder Jr. in contempt of Congress for not providing lawmakers with subpoenaed documents related to a probe into a botched gun-tracking program known as Operation Fast and Furious. Never before in history had either chamber of Congress officially held an attorney general in contempt. The dispute continued when the House Oversight Committee subsequently filed a civil suit in the U.S. District Court for the District of Columbia to enforce the subpoena against Holder.

Law enforcement issues also became a focus of debate in the fiscal 2012 Commerce-Justice-Science appropriations bill. House Republicans sought to eliminate funding for the Community Oriented Policing Services (COPS) program, which provided grants for local police departments to hire officers. But senators successfully worked to restore much of the funding for COPS, as well as for other state and local law enforcement grants that faced deep cuts in the House.

Lawmakers engaged in partisan skirmishes over such political flashpoints and abortion and guns. House Republicans failed to win enactment of controversial measures that would have restricted abortions because of the sex of the fetus and allowed the transport of concealed handguns across state lines. Both the House and Senate also voted on a proposed balanced budget amendment to the Constitution. But supporters in both chambers fell short of the required two-thirds majority.

Chronology of Action on Law Enforcement

2009–2010

In firm control of both chambers, Democrats cleared a few long-standing priorities. In the first weeks of the Obama presidency, they won enactment of a prolabor bill to make it easier for workers to file wage discrimination lawsuits against their employers. Near the end of 2009, Congress cleared an expansion of federal hate crimes law to include crimes against people because of their sexual orientation, gender identity, or disability.

The following year, lawmakers cleared a longtime liberal priority to significantly narrow the sentencing disparity between crack and powder cocaine, although members of the Congressional Black Caucus worried that the bill did not go far enough.

The Senate also approved President Barack Obama's two nominees to the Supreme Court, Sonia Sotomayor and Elena Kagan. Although most Republicans opposed the nominations, both were confirmed with relatively little controversy. *(Confirmations, p. 585)*

Conservatives, for their part, scored a victory in 2009 when they successfully attached a provision to credit card legislation to allow loaded firearms into national parks. The underlying bill was a priority for President Obama, and he signed it into law. Republicans, joined by a number of Democrats, also blocked the administration's efforts to close the U.S. detainee facility at Guantánamo Bay, Cuba. Lawmakers attached provisions to several of the annual spending bills that placed restrictions on moving the prisoners and on shuttering the detention center.

Other issues, however, remained unresolved. Lawmakers failed to advance comprehensive immigration legislation, settling instead for a $600 million border security measure. They split over controversial provisions of the antiterrorism law known as the Patriot Act. Unable to bridge their differences, they temporarily extended the law and deferred the debate until 2011.

Members in both chambers advanced bills intended to protect journalists from being forced to reveal their sources to government officials. But they clashed over such details as how to define a journalist. Legislation to overhaul patent laws also divided lawmakers. The issue, which had proven difficult to resolve for years, hinged on how to change procedures for issuing patents and how to award damages in patent infringement cases.

Congress took care of a significant piece of business in the lame duck session of 2010 when it cleared legislation to pay for two federal legal settlements. This resolved decades-long challenges against the Interior Department by American Indians and against the Agriculture Department by Black farmers.

Lawmakers also cleared a number of relatively noncontroversial measures. These included making it a federal crime to sell videos featuring the graphic torture of live animals, outlawing caller identification (ID) "spoofing" for fraudulent or other harmful purposes, and making it more difficult to propagate Internet schemes that tricked consumers into signing up for unwanted services and membership clubs.

The House voted to impeach two federal judges. U.S. District Judge Samuel B. Kent, resigned after being impeached in 2009. But G. Thomas Porteous Jr. of the Eastern District of Louisian, went to trial in the Senate, where he became just the eighth federal judge in history to be convicted by senators and forced out of office.

Hate Crimes

After years of trying, Democrats in 2009 succeeded in expanding federal hate crimes laws to include crimes committed against people because of their sexual orientation, gender identity, or disability. The provisions became law as part of the fiscal 2010 defense authorization bill, which President Barack Obama signed into law October 28 (HR 2647—PL 111-84). *(Defense authorization, p. 273)*

Two horrendous murders from a decade earlier inspired the legislation: Matthew Shepard, a gay University of Wyoming college student, was tied to a fence and beaten to death in 1998, and James Byrd Jr., an African-American, was killed the same year in Texas by being dragged for several miles behind a pickup truck.

The hate crimes section of the law (Local Law Enforcement Hate Crimes Prevention Act of 2009) extended provisions of an existing law that made it a federal crime to use or threaten force against someone based on race, color, religion, or national origin. It also broadened the ability of the federal government to assist state and local law authorities in prosecuting hate crimes. Previously, the federal government could become involved only if a hate-motivated crime was connected with the victim's participation in one of six "federally protected activities," such as attending public schools, applying for a job, or serving on a jury. Under the new law, the Justice Department could aid state and local law enforcement agencies if a particular hate crime would be considered a violent crime under federal law or a felony under state law.

Republican critics said they opposed the hate crimes language because it placed a higher value on some lives than on others. Opponents also argued that the statute could have a chilling effect on free speech and expose religious leaders to prosecution because of the actions of people who heard their sermons. Supporters argued that the bill was needed to combat attacks in cases such as Shepard's and that fears about religious leaders' liability were unfounded.

The House passed a stand-alone hate crimes bill in April. Although the Senate did not act on the measure, Democratic leaders in that chamber managed to add the language as a floor amendment to the defense authorization bill. House and Senate conferees retained the language in the final bill.

Democrats had tried in the four previous Congresses to enact such an expansion of hate crimes laws. In almost a mirror image of 2009, the House passed a hate crimes bill in 2007, while in the Senate, Edward M. Kennedy, D-Mass., who had been fighting for the legislation for years, added it as a floor amendment to the fiscal 2008 defense authorization bill. However, a veto threat from President George W. Bush, combined with disaffection among many House Democrats because the bill authorized funds for the war in Iraq, led Senate Democrats to reluctantly drop the hate crimes provision in conference.

Both sides said strong support from the Obama administration and large Democratic majorities in both chambers were responsible for the changed outcome in 2009. Enactment was also a major victory for gay rights groups, which had been disappointed with the Obama administration's decision earlier in the year to defend a 1996 law barring federal recognition of same-sex marriages and for not moving more forcefully to repeal the military's "don't ask, don't tell" policy.

HOUSE ACTION

The House Judiciary Committee approved the stand-alone bill (HR 1913—H Rept 111-86, Parts 1 and 2) on a 15–12 party-line vote April 23, after a two-day debate and the defeat of more than a dozen Republican amendments.

Under the measure, violent crimes motivated by gender identity or sexual orientation in which fire, a gun, or a bomb was used would be punishable by a fine and up to ten years in prison. For several offenses, the bill would provide for up to a life sentence. Prosecutors would have to show a link to interstate commerce and receive permission from a senior Justice Department official before bringing charges.

Proponents of the measure argued that hate crimes had become more prevalent. According to FBI statistics, 118,000 hate crimes had been reported since 1991, and Northeastern University's Institute on Race and Justice estimated that more than 9,000 hate crimes occurred each year.

Committee Republicans objected to the bill on First Amendment grounds, saying it amounted to favoritism toward certain groups. "Every human being in the world deserves to be equally protected, no matter who they are or who they go to bed with," Republican Louie Gohmert of Texas, the ranking member on the Crime, Terrorism and Homeland Security Subcommittee, shouted in an impassioned speech opposing the measure.

GOP amendments rejected by the committee included proposals to add senior citizens, pregnant women, unborn children, and members of the armed forces to the list of protected groups. Other amendments would have made hate crimes punishable by the death penalty and prohibited the federal government from bringing hate crime charges unless the state had no law prohibiting such conduct.

Others were aimed at concerns that religious leaders could be targeted for prosecution. Robert C. Scott, D-Va., the chair of the panel's Crime, Terrorism and Homeland Security Subcommittee, said the bill included adequate protections for legitimate free speech and religious leaders, but he agreed to an amendment, added by voice vote, to clarify that the legislation would not affect constitutionally protected activities.

The House passed HR 1913 by a vote of 249–175 on April 29.

SENATE ACTION

The Senate agreed by voice vote July 16, 2009, to adopt a hate crimes amendment to the defense authorization bill, after the chamber, on a **key vote of 63–28 key vote (R 5–28; D 56–0; I 2–0)**, invoked cloture to halt debate on the proposal. The amendment was offered by Judiciary Chair Patrick J. Leahy, D-Vt. *(2009 key votes, p. 751)*

Before the cloture vote, the Senate:

- Rejected, 29–62, an amendment by Orrin G. Hatch, R-Utah, to require a study to compare the investigations, prosecutions, and sentencing in states that had differing laws regarding hate crimes. The hate crimes provisions could not have taken effect until the study was completed. "Until there is evidence that the state and local governments are not doing the job," Hatch said, "we shouldn't pass legislation like this." Leahy countered that Hatch's amendment "would in effect eviscerate the hate crimes legislation."

- Adopted, 78–13, an amendment by Sam Brownback, R-Kan., to prohibit the provisions of Leahy's amendment from being applied in a way that violated First Amendment rights or burdened any exercise of religion that was not intended to plan or incite violence against another individual.
- Adopted by voice vote a Leahy amendment also designed to ensure that First Amendment speech remained protected.

FINAL ACTION

The House adopted the conference report on the defense authorization bill (HR 2647—H Rept 111-288), which included the hate crimes language, by a vote of 281–146 on October 8. A total of 131 Republicans and fifteen Democrats voted against the measure. The Senate cleared the bill, 68–29, on October 22, after voting, 64–35, to limit debate.

The number of "yes" votes in the House was far less than the 360-plus that the annual defense measure had received in each of the previous two years, largely because of the inclusion of Leahy's amendment. Outraged members, mainly Republicans, either held their noses and voted for the conference report or, as in the case of Minority Leader John A. Boehner, R-Ohio, voted against it. "Frankly, I'm offended by it," Boehner said. "This is radical social policy that is being put on the defense authorization bill on the backs of our soldiers."

Two days earlier, the House had rejected, 178–234, a GOP motion that would have instructed the conferees to strip the language. Twenty-two Democrats voted for the motion.

The Democratic opponents came mostly from conservative midwestern and southern districts and included many of the caucus's most vulnerable or newest members. Social conservatives said Democrats from conservative districts who voted in favor of the conference report could be more vulnerable in the 2010 midterm elections.

Legal Settlements

Congress cleared legislation (HR 4783—PL 111-291) during the lame duck session in 2010 to pay for two federal legal settlements resolving decades-long challenges against the government by Black farmers and by American Indians. The measure (Claims Resolution Act of 2010) also extended funding through fiscal 2011 for the Temporary Assistance for Needy Families (TANF) program.

The bill approved a settlement in *Cobell v. Salazar* (573 F. 3d 808, D.C. Cir.), a long-running class-action lawsuit in which plaintiffs alleged that the Interior Department had mismanaged billions of dollars in grazing land, gas, oil, and other royalties owed to thousands of American Indians. It also appropriated funds for a settlement in a class-action suit, *Pigford v. Glickman* (185 F.R.D. 82, D.D.C.), in which Black farmers alleged that the Agriculture Department had exhibited racial bias in allocating farm loans and services.

After Congress missed a December 2009 deadline set by plaintiffs in the *Cobell* case, the two settlements were joined in the same legislation. The House included approval for the settlements in broader bills that provided supplementary war funding (PL 111-212) and extended unemployment benefits (PL 111-205), but the provisions were dropped in the Senate before the bills were enacted.

Although there was broad accord on the basic issues, Sen. Tom Coburn, R-Okla., blocked efforts to pass legislation in the weeks before the midterm elections, citing concerns about the bill's potential fiscal impact. An earlier effort to approve the accords was blocked by Sen. John Barrasso, R-Wyo., who sought to limit lawyers' fees in the *Cobell* case. Then, just before the Thanksgiving recess, the Senate passed a stand-alone bill to approve the two deals, as well as settlements dealing with American Indian water rights sought by Jon Kyl, R-Ariz.

The cost of the measure was offset with provisions to reduce erroneous payments of unemployment benefits, extend customs users fees, and rescind $562 million from the Women, Infants and Children program. The offsets satisfied Coburn that the bill would be budget neutral.

The House passed the legislation under suspension of the rules on March 10. The Senate made minor alterations and passed the legislation by unanimous consent on November 19. The House cleared the bill, 256–152, on November 30. The president signed the measure into law (PL 111-291) on December 8, 2010.

MAJOR PROVISIONS

American Indians. The legislation approved a December 2009 settlement reached by the Obama administration in the *Cobell v. Salazar* case and authorized $3.4 billion to implement the agreement. The royalty dispute stemmed from an 1887 law that distributed parcels of land to individual American Indians but did not allow them to control how the land was used. Instead, the properties were placed into trust accounts. The lead plaintiff in the lawsuit, Elouise Cobell, contended that the account holders were cheated out of their share of the revenue the government received for leasing the land. The funding included $1.4 billion to pay approximately 500,000 plaintiffs, and $2 billion to consolidate land holdings where the presence of multiple heirs had complicated the management of accounts. Money for the settlement came out of the Judgment Fund maintained by the Treasury Department, meaning that no further appropriation of funding was necessary.

Black farmers. The legislation appropriated $1.2 billion to implement a settlement reached in what had come to be called *Pigford II (In re Black Farmers Discrimination Litigation*, 08-mc-0511, D.D.C.). Under a settlement of the *Pigford v. Glickman* suit, approved by a federal district court judge in 1999, African Americans who farmed from 1981 through 1996 and who filed a complaint against the department by July 1, 1997, were eligible to seek monetary compensation from the government. The settlement was widely criticized because it left out tens of thousands of African American farmers who filed claims later than the 1997 cutoff date. The 2008 farm law (PL 110-246) authorized $100 million for the settlement of these claims. However, the law was inadequate to deal with the huge number of Black farmers who filed claims. In February 2010, the administration announced a settlement of the *Pigford II* claims and requested $1.2 billion to implement it.

Temporary Assistance for Needy Families. On March 10, 2010, the House by voice vote agreed to suspend the rules and pass HR 4783, which paired the settlements with extension of the basic federal welfare program known as Temporary Assistance for Needy Families (TANF). The Senate passed an amended version by voice vote on November 19. By a vote of 256–152 on November 30, the House agreed to a motion to accept the Senate changes, thus clearing the bill.

The legislation extended TANF through September 30, 2011, at fiscal 2010 levels. The bill also provided a six-month extension for a supplemental TANF grant program for states with high population growth or historically below-average welfare grants. The bill did not revive a TANF emergency fund, enacted as part of the 2009 economic stimulus law (PL 111-5), that enabled states to place adults with private employers and youth in summer jobs programs.

Immigration

Despite much discussion, the 111th Congress did not vote on comprehensive immigration policy. Lawmakers turned to narrower immigration bills but failed to clear them except for a $600 million border security bill.

President Barack Obama periodically pressed lawmakers to take up a comprehensive overhaul of the nation's immigration laws. Such a bill would have enhanced border security, provided a path to citizenship for the roughly eleven million illegal immigrants in the United States, and implemented safeguards against hiring undocumented workers. It would have been based in part on a bill that died in the Senate in 2007.

In 2009, however, the issue was crowded out of a packed legislative agenda. In 2010, proposals fell victim to partisan differences and discomfort among conservative Democrats.

The administration sent intermittent signals that it remained committed to an immigration overhaul as it sought to reassure Latino supporters who watched the issue fall behind other domestic priorities. Persistent calls to repair what was widely regarded as a broken system grew in urgency since passage of a contentious Arizona law giving local police new enforcement powers that critics said would lead to racial profiling of Hispanics.

In June 2009, lawmakers emerged from a meeting with President Obama with a promise to conclude debate on an immigration bill by January or February at the latest. But in August, Obama said he did not expect lawmakers to start acting on the bill until 2010—after completing work on health care, climate change, and a financial regulatory overhaul.

House Democrats indicated that they planned to hold off moving their bill until after the Senate acted. But Charles E. Schumer, D-N.Y., chair of the Senate Judiciary Subcommittee on Immigration, Refugees, and Border Security, missed a self-imposed Labor Day deadline for introducing a bill in that chamber, instead focusing on early 2010.

Homeland Security Secretary Janet Napolitano renewed the administration's commitment to working on the measure during a November speech at the Center for American Progress. "The hope is that when we get into the first part of 2010 that we will see legislation begin to move," she said.

But an anti-immigration message pushed by the Tea Party, a newly formed group of conservative activists who opposed the Obama administration's agenda, and other mainstream conservatives resonated widely, making it increasingly difficult to mobilize a political coalition to back immigration. The recession also sapped the appetite of many lawmakers to take up legislation aimed at immigrants, with about one out of ten American workers being unemployed. And as often happens in hard times, resentments flared over the notion that undocumented immigrants were taking scarce jobs away from Americans—even though such ideas were debunked by economists across the political spectrum.

The resulting inertia, coming after several failed efforts backed by former president George W. Bush, frustrated those who thought their moment had at long last arrived. "It's the history of being the bridesmaid and never the bride that seems to really be dogging the immigration issue," said Mary Giovagnoli, director of the Immigration Policy Center, a think tank that supported a comprehensive approach.

By the time Senate Democrats produced a blueprint for an overhaul and Robert Menendez, D-N.J., introduced a bill September 29, 2010, reflecting that blueprint, the moment had passed. Election year pressures and resistance by Republicans and conservative Democrats meant that lawmakers never took votes on the measure.

Instead, the focus turned to narrower bills including border security funding and border entry points and undocumented children. *(Legislative details, pp. 212, 219, below)*

Undocumented Children

With any chance for a broader immigration policy overhaul already dashed earlier in 2010, the Senate on December 18 rejected an effort by Democratic leaders to advance a targeted youth immigration bill. The action ended supporters' hopes of seeing the measure enacted in the 111th Congress.

In the rare Saturday session, the Senate on a **key vote of 55–41 (R 3–36; D 50–5; I 2–0)** failed to invoke cloture and move to an up-or-down vote on a House-passed measure (HR 5281). Just three Republicans—Richard G. Lugar of Indiana, Robert F. Bennett of Utah, and Lisa Murkowski of Alaska—supported cloture, an indication of the partisan division on the issue. Five Democrats opposed cloture. The House had passed that bill December 8 on a **key vote of 216–198 (R 8–160; D 208–38)** with only eight Republicans voting in favor. *(2010 key votes, p. 767)*

The bill, known as the DREAM Act, would give hundreds of thousands of undocumented adults under age thirty who had been in the United States for at least five years the chance to obtain green cards and then citizenship if they went to college or served in the armed forces for two years. Applicants would have to pay fees, meet certain requirements, and wait ten years before qualifying for the green card.

These young adults "live in the shadows and dream of greatness," said Senate Majority Whip Richard J. Durbin, D-Ill., a longtime supporter of the measure. "All they're asking for is a chance to serve this nation."

Durbin and other supporters argued that children should not be punished because of illegal acts by their parents and pointed to the numerous qualifications applicants would have to meet to benefit from the bill.

But critics denounced the legislation as granting what they called "amnesty" to illegal immigrants. This bill was "a reward for illegal activity," said Jeff Sessions of Alabama, the Judiciary Committee's ranking Republican, who spearheaded the opposition.

Some Senate Republicans also took aim at Democratic leaders' procedural handling of the legislation, noting that the latest version was not subject to committee action or floor amendments. "It deserves better than to be jammed through in the waning hours of a lame-duck session of Congress," said Judiciary panel member John Cornyn, R-Texas, in a statement.

Although a majority of senators wanted to proceed with the measure, the cloture vote showed that Senate conservatives from both parties were reluctant to go ahead with piecemeal legislation in the absence of a more comprehensive overhaul of immigration policy that included tougher measures to enforce border protection and to limit amnesty.

Some opponents said that whatever its merits—and there was debate even about that—the legislation just was not enough given the severity of the immigration situation.

"We're not going to pass the DREAM Act, or any other legalization program, until we secure our borders," said Lindsey Graham, R-S.C., who earlier in the year was working closely with Democrats on a broad, bipartisan bill. Other Republicans, such as Orrin G. Hatch of Utah, who had sponsored similar legislation nearly ten years earlier, have changed their positions on the issue in the face of public anger over illegal immigration and the economic downturn.

After House Judiciary Chair John Conyers Jr., D-Mich., argued for passage on the floor, panel Republican Robert W. Goodlatte of Virginia complained that more time was needed to explore the bill's possible ramifications. He said there had been no opportunity either in committee or on the floor to change the bill.

Goodlatte suggested that, especially in a lame duck session, it was time to shelve such legislation. "The American people have recently demonstrated their strong opposition to amnesty for millions of illegal immigrants," he said, "yet the DREAM Act offers amnesty to illegal immigrants who entered the U.S. before they were sixteen years old." He complained that the bill would allow the Department of Homeland Security to waive requirements because of undefined hardships, which he called "a very, very big loophole."

Impeachment of Federal Judges

The House impeached two federal judges during the 111th Congress. One judge, U.S. District Judge Samuel B. Kent, resigned after being impeached in 2009. The other, G. Thomas Porteous Jr. of the Eastern District of Louisiana, was subsequently convicted by the Senate and forced out of office.

Before 2009, the House had impeached only thirteen judges in its history. Seven were convicted by the Senate and removed from office, four were acquitted, and two resigned rather than face trial.

SAMUEL B. KENT

The House unanimously impeached Kent on June 19, 2009, on four separate counts. The judge had admitted that he gave false testimony to federal investigators looking into sexual misconduct complaints made by two female court employees.

Kent submitted a letter of resignation to the Senate on June 24, eliminating the need for a Senate trial.

The House Judiciary Committee voted, 29–0, on June 10 to approve four articles of impeachment against Kent, who had pleaded guilty to one count of obstruction of justice in February.

Kent was sentenced in May to thirty-three months in prison. He reported to a Massachusetts federal facility June 15.

The case against Kent grew out of complaints by two of his employees. In 2007, Cathy McBroom, Kent's case manager, filed a complaint alleging that Kent repeatedly initiated nonconsensual sexual contact ranging from unwanted hugs to groping and sexual assault. Donna Wilkerson, his secretary, later joined the complaint. Both women testified June 3 before a Judiciary Committee impeachment task force.

Two of the articles of impeachment outlined Kent's inappropriate sexual contact with McBroom and Wilkerson. The third and fourth focused on Kent's false statements and his guilty plea for obstruction of justice.

Federal authorities initially charged Kent with six counts of aggravated sexual abuse, abusive sexual contact, and obstruction of justice. In exchange for his guilty plea to obstruction of justice, prosecutors agreed to dismiss the five other charges.

At the time of his sentencing in May, Kent said he hoped to retain his pension and benefits while in prison, drawing bipartisan ire on Capitol Hill. At that time, he offered to resign effective June 2010, which would have allowed him to retain his salary—$174,000 per year—and benefits while in prison. House Judiciary Committee members angrily denounced that move and acted swiftly to advance the articles of impeachment.

After the House voted to impeach him, Kent revised his resignation to make it effective June 30, 2009.

G. THOMAS PORTEOUS JR.

For only the eighth time in its history, the Senate on December 8, 2010, removed a federal judge from the bench, voting to oust the sixty-three-year-old Porteous, of the Eastern District of Louisiana, after a year of investigation and a one-day trial. Porteous, who had been a federal trial judge since 1994, and a state judge before that, had been suspended from the bench for a period of two years beginning in September 2008.

The process of removing Porteous began with a January 21, 2010, vote of the House Judiciary Committee's special Task Force on Judicial Impeachment. The task force, by a 8–0 vote, approved a resolution (H Res 1031) recommending that the House impeach Porteous and present four articles to the Senate for trial.

In making its charges, the task force cited evidence that the judge "intentionally made material false statements and representations under penalty of perjury, engaged in a corrupt kickback scheme, solicited and accepted unlawful gifts, and intentionally misled the Senate during his confirmation proceedings."

Task Force Chair Adam B. Schiff, D-Calif., voiced strong support for Porteous's impeachment, arguing that his conduct was "incompatible with the trust and confidence placed in him as a federal judge" and "demonstrates his unfitness to serve." Committee ranking Republican Lamar Smith of Texas echoed that sentiment. "The American people deserve better from their federal judges," he said.

The House Judiciary Committee on January 27 voted, 24–0, to recommend the four articles of impeachment. The House on March 11 unanimously adopted each of the four articles of impeachment in separate votes.

In the one-day trial, the Senate convicted Porteous, on all four articles of impeachment and then voted to bar him from holding future federal office. He was convicted on charges of failing to recuse himself from a case despite having received money from lawyers involved, accepting gifts from bail bondsmen in exchange for official actions, falsifying and withholding information during a bankruptcy proceeding, and making false statements at his Senate confirmation hearing. On conviction, he also forfeited his pension.

Unlike the House, senators were unanimous only on the first of the four articles. A two-thirds majority was required to approve each charge.

Senators voted from their desks, rising to deliver their "guilty" or "not guilty" votes as Porteous and his attorneys looked on from the well of the chamber. The chair and ranking member of the House Task Force on Judicial Impeachment—Schiff and Republican Robert W. Goodlatte of Virginia, respectively—also looked on. The House members served as de facto prosecutors against Porteous.

Senators who voted "not guilty" on the second article—that Porteous set bails at levels allowing two bondsmen to collect substantial premiums in return for gifts to the judge—may have been persuaded by arguments from Porteous's attorney, Jonathan Turley. He said that allegations in that article charging Porteous with misconduct while he was a state judge should not be held against him. "In the history of this republic, no one has ever been removed from office on the basis of pre-federal conduct," Turley said.

Schiff rebutted Turley, saying that there was "serious consequence" to "[concluding] that judges cannot be impeached for prior misconduct, that confirmation is a safe harbor against all removal for all prior offenses."

Senators who voted "not guilty" on the second count included the chair and ranking member of the Senate panel charged with reporting the articles of impeachment to the full Senate—Democrat Claire McCaskill of Missouri and Republican Orrin G. Hatch of Utah.

"There were good legal reasons for not voting that far," Hatch said. Porteous was convicted on that article by just five votes.

But other Turley defenses failed to sway senators. On the allegation related to receiving money from lawyers and then failing to recuse himself from a case in which they appeared, Turley noted that the judge was a friend of the lawyers involved and argued that his acceptance of cash was a gift to help pay for his son's wedding.

"This was not a bribe, this was not a kickback. . . . It was a gift," Turley said. "Was it a dumb gift? Was it a gift he shouldn't have accepted? You bet. But the framers [of the Constitution] thought it was important to define things as they are."

Before voting on the impeachment articles, the Senate first unanimously dispensed with a defense motion that alleged that the House had improperly aggregated the impeachment articles. Porteous's lawyers argued that because a series of disparate allegations were lumped together in single articles, senators would have to vote for an impeachment article even if they do not believe Porteous was guilty of every charge.

After voting on the impeachment articles, the Senate approved an additional motion to bar Porteous from ever serving in another federal office, 94–2. Jeff Bingaman, D-N.M., and Joseph I. Lieberman, I-Conn., opposed that motion.

Rep. Alcee L. Hastings, D-Fla., who lost a seat on the federal bench after being convicted of impeachment charges, was able to run for Congress in 1992 because lawmakers never voted on barring him from future office.

Journalism Sources

Lawmakers in both chambers advanced bills in the 111th Congress intended to protect journalists from being forced to reveal their sources to government officials. But the proposals, although passing the House, never made it to the Senate floor.

Under the House version (HR 985) sponsored by Virginia Democrat Rick Boucher, reporters would be forced to divulge sources or other information to government officials only if a judge decided the information was critical to a criminal investigation, prosecution or defense, or was necessary to prevent bodily harm or death. The measure would allow the court to take into consideration potential harm to national security.

The measure included a more limited definition of journalist than past versions of the bill, said Robert W. Goodlatte, R-Va., one of the measure's cosponsors. The legislation would cover reporters, photographers, or bloggers who regularly publish news or information and earn a substantial portion of their livelihoods in the field of journalism, he said.

The House passed it by voice vote March 31, 2009, just six days after the Judiciary Committee approved the bill (H Rept 111-61), also by voice vote.

The House passed identical legislation, 398–21, in the previous Congress, but the measure stalled because the George W. Bush administration opposed the bill on national security grounds. President Barack Obama has said he generally supports the measure.

Supporters said the legislation was necessary to maintain government and corporate accountability. "Journalists serve as watchdogs bringing sensitive information to public scrutiny," Boucher said. He noted that thirty-four states and the District of Columbia had similar protections for journalists in state courts.

Although the measure had bipartisan support, Republican Lamar Smith of Texas said he opposed the bill because of its potential to impede law enforcement and intelligence gathering.

A companion bill (S 448) won approval in the Senate Judiciary Committee on December 10 by a vote of 14–15.

The bill, sponsored by Democrats Charles E. Schumer of New York and Arlen Specter of Pennsylvania, had been on the panel's agenda since April, but two Republican foes, Jon Kyl of Arizona and ranking member Jeff Sessions of Alabama, stalled it. But Schumer, Kyl, and panel Chair Patrick J. Leahy, D-Vt., reached an agreement allowing Kyl to offer eleven floor amendments and limit debate to two short statements, for and against.

The panel on December 10 adopted two Kyl amendments, one of which would bar journalists from invoking the privilege in cases regarding the destruction of critical infrastructure. The panel also adopted an amendment from Orrin Hatch, R-Utah, that would exclude child sexual abuse cases from protection.

But the most heated debate came at the end of the markup when Democrats Dianne Feinstein of California and Durbin offered an amendment that would narrow the definition of a journalist. Under a substitute amendment adopted in September, only persons who regularly gather, collect, write, record, and publish information in paper or electronic form were defined as journalists.

Feinstein and Durbin argued that the definition was too broad, encompassing everyone from white supremacists who blog to Senate press secretaries who prepare press releases. Their amendment, which would change the definition to cover any employee, contractor, or agent of an entity that disseminates news, was rejected, 8–11.

Firearms

FIREARMS ON FEDERAL LANDS

Lawmakers in 2009 cleared credit card legislation (HR 627—PL 111-24) with an amendment to allow visitors to national parks and wildlife refuges to carry loaded firearms. Previous federal policy had permitted guns in parks only if the weapons were stowed away or disassembled. *(Credit card legislation, p. 84)*

Sponsored by Sen. Tom Coburn, R-Okla., the provision was adopted by the Senate, 67–29, on May 12. The House concurred with this Senate amendment, 279–147, on May 20. The underlying bill seeking to prevent consumer credit card abuses by financial institutions was a priority for the Obama administration, and the president signed it with the gun amendment intact.

The provision applied if the gun was legally owned and possession complied with state law. Although there were often restrictions, all states except Illinois and Wisconsin had some form of a "concealed carry" law allowing for such possession.

Advocates on both sides squared off about the vote's ramifications. Daniel Vice, an attorney for the Brady Center to Prevent Gun Violence, painted a picture of armed tourists visiting the Liberty Bell or Statue of Liberty. But gun-rights groups countered that Americans had a right to carry guns for self-defense and argued that it made no sense to allow weapons to be carried everywhere in a state except a national park or wildlife refuge.

Rep. Spencer Bachus, R-Ala., said a citizen could carry a concealed gun in his state but violated federal law if he carried it into the Cahaba River National Wildlife Refuge.

"To me, it would be a violation of the Constitution and of our forefathers' intent if someone exercising his Second Amendment right were to suddenly cross a line, go into a national park and find himself facing a federal judge and a fine because of the uncertainty," Bachus said during House debate May 20.

Erich Pratt, a spokesperson for Gun Owners of America, also defended the new law. "People have been raped, murdered, attacked by wild animals," Pratt said. "Whether you're in national parks or Washington, D.C., it's just not right to tell people that you can't protect yourself, and we will punish you if you try to."

FIREARMS IN DISTRICT OF COLUMBIA

The Senate on February 26, 2009, during consideration of a District of Columbia voting rights bill (S 160), adopted on a **key vote of 62–36 (R 40–1; D 22–33; I 0–2)** a John Ensign, R-Nev., amendment that would bar the District from prohibiting firearms possession, repeal most of the city's registration laws, and repeal the D.C. requirement that firearms in homes be disassembled or secured with a trigger or other device. The amendment language was similar to that in a bill passed by the House in 2008. *(2009 key votes, p. 751; 2008 action, Congress and the Nation Vol. XII, p. 804)*

The vote was seen as a reflection of the strength of gun rights advocates. They prevailed even though Democrats held the majority in the Senate. Twenty-two Democrats joined all but one Republican to adopt the Ensign amendment to the District of Columbia Housing Voting Rights Act.

The amendment's adoption proved the death knell for the underlying voting rights legislation. *(D.C. representation, p. 648)*

Guantánamo Detainees

President Barack Obama's decision at the beginning of his presidency to order the closure of the U.S. detainee facility at Guantánamo Bay, Cuba, set off an intense debate in Congress over the fate of the detainees and the facility. Lawmakers in 2009 attached provisions to several of the annual spending bills that placed restrictions on moving the prisoners and on shuttering the detention center. *(Guantanamo detainees overview, p. 314)*

The executive order Obama issued to close Guantánamo was one of his first, but it proved politically impossible to implement in the 111th Congress.

Leading Republicans argued strongly against closing the Guantánamo facility and, during the first year of the Obama administration, repeatedly sought to block any attempt to bring detainees from the prison to the United States for any reason, including prosecution. "The right forum for bringing war criminals to justice is in military commissions at the secure facility we already have at Guantánamo. Not—I repeat, not—in civilian courts in U.S. communities," Minority Leader Mitch McConnell, R-Ky., said during a debate in November 2009.

Democrats agreed to a number of restrictions but held the line against provisions that would interfere with the Obama administration's ability to bring prisoners to the United States for trial. "We are not afraid of these guys," said Patrick J. Leahy, D-Vt., chair of the Senate Judiciary Committee. "They're murderers. They're criminals. Let's just prosecute them."

"Why," he continued, "would the Senate pass an amendment that suggests that our country and the brave men and women who staff these prisons cannot handle these prisoners, or that they are not up to the task?"

On May 28, 2010, the House adopted a motion on the defense authorization bill (HR 5136) on a **key vote of 282–131 (R 168–1; D 114–130)** to bar the transfer or release of any military detainees held at Guantánamo to the United States. *(2010 key votes, p. 767)*

Lawmakers attached detainee restrictions to the fiscal 2009 supplemental spending bill enacted in June (PL 111-32), and extended the restrictions through fiscal 2010 by including them in at least three of the annual spending bills: Interior-environment (PL 111-88), homeland security (PL 111-83) and Commerce-Justice-Science, which was enacted in the omnibus package (PL 111-117).

The spending bills generally barred the use of funds to release prisoners held at the Guantánamo facility into the United States or any U.S. territories. Detainees could not be transferred to the United States for prosecution or other legal proceedings until forty-five days after the president submitted a detailed report to Congress that included an assessment of risks that the transfer might pose and what the administration would do to mitigate that risk.

The governor of the state where the detainee was headed also had to be notified in advance.

Detainees could not be transferred to other countries until fifteen days after the president sent Congress the prisoners' names and the countries that would be receiving them, along with details on the potential risks to national security.

The president also had to send to Congress a report describing the disposition of each detainee still held at Guantánamo before the facility can be closed.

The issue became less contentious in the 2010 election year. Lawmakers again attached restrictions to appropriations bills. Few Democrats were comfortable addressing the issue, and staffers said privately that Democrats were divided over how strongly they could defend the administration.

DOCUMENTS ON DETAINEES

The House Judiciary Committee in 2009 rejected two attempts by Republicans to seek documents relating to the handing of detainees.

The committee on June 24 voted 13–12 along party lines to report unfavorably a resolution of inquiry related to the handling of detainees in Afghanistan. The committee's vote to report the resolution unfavorably effectively scuttled it.

The resolution (H Res 537) by Mike Rogers, R-Mich., would direct the attorney general and ask President Obama to turn over any documents or other material related to the Justice Department advising detainees imprisoned in Afghanistan of their procedural rights.

In a June 12 letter to Virginia Republican Frank R. Wolf, FBI Director Robert S. Mueller III said the FBI has given *Miranda* warnings to some detainees imprisoned in Afghanistan and elsewhere.

Mueller said the warnings, "modified to take into account the overseas location of the detainee," had been administered in cases in which the government thinks it eventually might want to try a particular detainee in a federal court.

Then on July 29, the committee voted along party lines to report unfavorably a resolution that would require the Justice Department to turn over records related to prisoners held at the U.S. detention facility at Guantánamo Bay, Cuba. The committee's 14–12 vote effectively scuttled the resolution (H Res 636).

The resolution would direct the attorney general to give the House information related to the transfer or release of detainees. The measure was introduced by Frank R. Wolf of Virginia, the top Republican on the Appropriations subcommittee that handles Justice Department funding. Wolf had accused Attorney General Eric H. Holder Jr. of stonewalling his requests for the records.

Wolf had been trying to get specific information from the Justice Department about individual detainees. He also posed several questions to Holder about the department's possible plans for moving Guantánamo detainees to the United States to stand trial. The response to several letters had not satisfied him.

Smuggling of Illegal Immigrants

The House passed a bill in 2009 to increase penalties on people who smuggled illegal immigrants into the United States but the Senate did not take it up. The bill (HR 1029), sponsored by Baron P. Hill, D-Ind., passed by voice vote March 31.

The legislation set a prison term of up to five years for each person knowingly brought into the United States or for transporting illegal immigrants within the country or harboring or encouraging them to enter. For so-called coyotes, who smuggle illegal immigrants for pay, the measure would set a prison sentence of three to ten years for each person smuggled for a first or second offense and a sentence of five to fifteen years for subsequent offenses. For smugglers who exposed their charges to dangers, including kidnapping and rape, the penalty would be up to twenty years per victim.

Smuggling of an immediate family member would result in a prison term of up to one year per person brought into the country. The bill instructed the homeland security secretary to check the identities of smugglers and their human cargo against the government's terrorist watch lists.

The legislation preserved a provision in existing law that allowed religious denominations to invite noncitizens to enter the country to perform religious duties, as long as they received no compensation other than basic living expenses.

Hill said the bill would help address a serious violation of U.S. border laws; more than 17,000 people came into the country through illegal trafficking last year, he said.

He sponsored a nearly identical measure in the 110th Congress that the House easily passed. But the Senate companion bill, sponsored by fellow Indiana Democrat Evan Bayh, never came to a vote in that chamber. *(Congress and the Nation Vol. IX, p. 717)*

Patent Law Overhaul

Long-stalled patent overhaul legislation was approved in 2009 by a Senate panel after lawmakers adopted a compromise approach to the contentious issue of how to award damages in patent infringement cases. The legislation did not advance further. *(2011 action, p. 568)*

The 15–4 vote on April 2 by the Judiciary Committee on the bill (S 515) was a major step forward for Chair Patrick J. Leahy, D-Vt., who had championed the legislation for years. Leahy saw it stall in the last Congress when he was unable to come to agreement with ranking Republican Arlen Specter of Pennsylvania.

This time, Specter and another key committee member, Dianne Feinstein, D-Calif., signed on to a compromise that defined judges as the gatekeepers in determining what evidence juries could hear in determining how to apportion damages. The compromise, approved by voice vote, also addressed postgrant review of patents, inequitable conduct by patent applicants, and venue rules for patent infringement cases.

Feinstein said the measure "heals" the split that has pitted a coalition of mostly big technology corporations against manufacturers, universities, and smaller technology companies. "The compromise on this bill actually gives the parties 90 percent of what they want," Feinstein said.

Language regarding inequitable conduct by patent applicants prompted Leahy's longtime Republican partner on the bill, Orrin G. Hatch of Utah, to vote against the bill. "This bill does not accomplish its original policy objectives and might not be good for the country," he said before he walked out of the markup.

Both Leahy and Feinstein said they hope to accommodate Hatch's objections.

COPS Authorization

The House passed legislation in 2009 to boost the funding authorization for a popular local law enforcement grant program. However, the Senate did not take up a related measure (S 167) by Herb Kohl, D-Wis.

Voting 342–78, the House passed HR 1139 on April 23. The bill, by Anthony Weiner, D-N.Y., authorized $1.8 billion per year for fiscal years 2009 through 2014 for the Community Oriented Policing Services (COPS) grant program, up from the previous authorization of $1.1 billion annually in fiscal years 2006 through 2009.

The program, authorized in 1994 (PL 103-322), provided grants to state, local, and tribal governments to hire additional law enforcement officers and prosecutors. It had helped to hire more than 117,000 officers, according to the Justice Department. In addition to funding for personnel, HR 1139 would authorize up to $350 million a year for grants to departments to obtain or upgrade equipment. It was reauthorized in 2002. *(Congress and the Nation Vol. IX, p. 684; Congress and the Nation Vol. XI, p.602)*

The Judiciary Committee on March 25 approved the bill (H Rept 111-78) by a vote of 17–7, after rejecting Republican attempts to decrease overall funding. Three Republicans voted in favor of the bill: J. Randy Forbes of Virginia, Ted Poe of Texas, and Tom Rooney of Florida.

Under a committee amendment by Adam B. Schiff, D-Calif., states would be allowed to use grants to hire forensic analysts and laboratory personnel. The measure would also require the Justice Department's inspector general to submit a report on the program to Congress.

Although the House passed a similar reauthorization with bipartisan support in the 110th Congress, several Republicans opposed the new version because of the cost. As introduced, the bill would have authorized $3.1 billion annually, but the Judiciary Committee reduced that figure as it considered the measure.

During the committee markup, Louie Gohmert, R-Texas, offered an amendment to reduce the funding in the measure to $1.2 billion—the same level as in the reauthorization attempt in the 110th Congress. The panel rejected the amendment, 9–16.

Penalties for Crack Cocaine

The House in 2010 cleared long-sought legislation that would significantly narrow the sentencing disparity between crack and powder cocaine despite misgivings from members of the Congressional Black Caucus that the bill did not go far enough.

The measure (S 1789—PL 111-220), which cleared by voice vote July 28, did not equalize the amount of each drug that triggered strict mandatory prison sentences, as advocacy groups and Black Caucus members had hoped to achieve. Nevertheless, they supported the bill as a pragmatic compromise with Republicans. Although the disparity had not been erased, said Majority Whip James E. Clyburn, D-S.C., "this will help to correct an enormous disparity in our criminal justice system."

Under existing law, drug-trafficking offenses had to involve 100 times as much powder cocaine as crack to trigger the same sentences. It took 500 grams of powder to spur a five-year sentence, but only five grams of crack resulted in the same term. The bill would set an 18-to-1 ratio for powder cocaine and crack in sentencing guidelines and would eliminate the mandatory minimum prison sentence for simple possession of crack, the only drug for which possession led to such sentences.

The lower trigger for crack disproportionately affected African Americans. According to a 2007 report by the U.S. Sentencing Commission, 82 percent of crack cocaine federal offenders in 2006 were African Americans.

The final wording of the legislation resulted from months of talks between its sponsor, Senate Majority Whip Richard J. Durbin, D-Ill., and Jeff Sessions of Alabama, ranking Republican on the Senate Judiciary Committee. But Sessions's counterpart on the House Judiciary Committee, Lamar Smith of Texas, spoke out strongly against the bill on the floor: "Reducing the penalties for crack cocaine could expose our neighborhoods to the same violence and addiction that caused Congress to act in the first place," he said.

The disparity between crack and powder cocaine sentencing dated to a 1986 law (PL 99-570), when Congress perceived crack to be more addictive. But Rep. Robert C. Scott, D-Va., said that the U.S. Sentencing Commission since then "has concluded there is no pharmacological difference."

Durbin had sought to eliminate the disparity but agreed to a compromise that would narrow it instead, in order to attract Republican support. The Senate then passed the measure passed by voice vote March 17.

Animal Crush Videos

Lawmakers in 2010 cleared legislation to make it a federal crime to sell videos featuring the graphic torture of live animals. The measure (HR 5566—PL 111-294) was cleared by the Senate by unanimous consent on November 19 after passage in the House four days earlier. The president signed the legislation (Animal Crush Video Prohibition Act of 2010) on December 9, 2010.

The bill (H Rept 111-549) was a response to a Supreme Court decision in April that struck down a 1999 law (PL 106-152) making it a federal crime to create, sell, or possess videos featuring animal cruelty for commercial gain. In *United States v. Stevens* (559 U.S. 460), the justices ruled, 8–1, that the categorical ban was too broad and violated free-speech rights.

In July, the House passed a version of the bill, 416–3, that would, like the 1999 statute, make illegal the sale and distribution of so-called "animal crush" videos and impose fines on offenders, who would face up to five years' imprisonment. However, House members subsequently agreed to Senate language that would impose fines and as much as seven years of confinement.

The measure would bar a person from knowingly creating an animal crush video if the person intended, or had reason to know, that the video would be distributed in interstate or foreign commerce. The legislation included exemptions for the depiction of veterinary or agricultural husbandry practices; hunting, trapping and fishing; the slaughter of food animals; and good-faith efforts to pass along a video to law enforcement agencies.

Internet Schemes

Lawmakers in 2010 cleared legislation (the Restore Online Shoppers' Confidence Act) designed to stop Internet schemes that tricked consumers into signing up for unwanted services and membership clubs. The measure (S 3386—PL 111-345) was passed by the Senate by unanimous consent November 30, then cleared by the House on a voice vote on December 15.

The legislation (S Rept 111-240) made it illegal for a merchant to disclose billing information to any post-transaction third-party seller for use in an Internet-based sale. It made it illegal to charge or attempt to charge a consumer for anything sold in a "negative option" feature—when a customer's silence or inaction on rejecting goods or services or canceling an agreement was interpreted as an offer of acceptance—unless the seller clearly disclosed all terms, obtained express purchaser consent before the charge, and enabled the purchaser to stop recurring charges.

The bill provided that a seller could be considered lawfully charging a consumer if the consumer could stop recurring charges through a simple process available over e-mail and the Internet. President Obama signed the bill into law on December 29, 2010.

Caller ID Spoofing

The House in 2010 cleared a measure (S 30—PL 111-331) to make it illegal to use caller identification (ID) "spoofing" for fraudulent or other harmful purposes. House members sent the bill (the Truth in Caller ID Act) to the president's desk by voice vote on December 15. President Obama signed it into law on December 22, 2010.

In addition to banning people from manipulating caller ID information for fraud through telecommunications or Internet phone services, the bill set maximum civil and criminal fines at $10,000 for each violation or $30,000 daily for continuing violations. The bill specified that it would not override existing imprisonment rules. Civil forfeitures would be capped at $1 million for single acts, and a two-year statute of limitations would apply.

Caller ID spoofing had been used to trick consumers and law enforcement agents and to conduct identify theft, according to a report on the measure by the Senate Commerce, Science and Transportation Committee (S Rept 111-96). In one instance, a caller who used spoofing to pose as a court official threatened a Michigan woman with arrest for missing jury duty and asked for her Social Security number.

The measure directed the Federal Communications Commission to issue regulations to implement the bill within six months of its enactment. The bill would provide exemptions for authorized law enforcement work and court orders.

The Senate passed the measure on February 23 by unanimous consent. The House passed similar legislation (HR 1258) on April 14, but that bill would not have set civil and criminal penalties. Another House-passed bill (HR 1110) would have set a maximum five-year prison term for individuals who provided false caller ID information to obtain anything of value.

Law Enforcement on Tribal Lands

Congress in 2010 cleared legislation (HR 725) authorizing and creating several programs within the Justice Department and the Bureau of Indian Affairs to bolster criminal justice proceedings on tribal lands.

Under existing law at the time of enactment of the Indian Arts and Crafts Amendment Act, tribal governments could not prosecute crimes committed on reservations by non-Indians and could sentence Indians to a maximum of one year in prison regardless of the offense. Tribal governments thus were forced to rely on federal agencies to prosecute crimes committed on their land by non-Indians as well as more serious crimes committed by Indians. However, critics said that the federal government gave short shrift to supporting Indian law enforcement.

The House Natural Resources Committee approved HR 725 by voice vote on December 16, 2009, and formally reported it (H Rept 111-397, Part 1) on January 15, 2010. By voice vote on January 19, the House agreed to suspend the rules and pass the bill. That narrower version of the bill would have allowed federal law enforcement officers to investigate only the production and sale of counterfeit American Indian arts and crafts products. The Senate by voice vote on June 23 passed an amended version of the bill that significantly expanded the scope of HR 725. The language was similar to that in a measure (S 797) sponsored by Senate Indian Affairs Committee chairman Byron L. Dorgan, D-N.D., who had long railed against the rising crime rate on tribal lands. The House agreed, on a vote of 326–92 on July 21, to suspend the rules and agreed to the Senate amendment, thus clearing the bill.

As signed into law (PL 111-211) on July 29, HR 735 allowed tribal courts to impose penalties of up to three years imprisonment or fines of up to $15,000 and aimed to foster greater law enforcement cooperation between the federal government and Indian tribes. It established an Office of Tribal Justice within the Justice Department to serve as a legal policy adviser and as a point of contact for Indian tribes. The legislation also created a Justice

Department position to coordinate with U.S. attorneys on prosecuting crimes committed on American Indian lands.

Railroad Mergers

Justice Department antitrust lawyers would be able to regulate railroad mergers and rate changes under similar bills approved in 2009 and 2010 by the Senate and House Judiciary Committees. But the bills were not taken up on the floor of either chamber.

The Senate measure (S 146—S Rept 111-9), sponsored by Herb Kohl, D-Wis., was approved 14–0 on March 5, 2009. It would eliminate a long-standing exemption to antitrust laws that allows railroads to gain approval from the Surface Transportation Board for rail mergers, acquisitions, and collective rate-making agreements.

Other transportation industries, such as trucking and aviation, were required to seek approval from the Justice Department. The legislation also would allow state attorneys general and individuals to sue to block mergers.

Kohl and other bill supporters said railroads had used the exemption to unfairly raise rates. Because of mergers, four Class I railroads—the large freight carriers—provided 90 percent of rail transportation, leaving some areas of the country with service from only one railroad. Supporters said that industries in these areas, known as captive shippers, had little choice but to pay the railroad's rate.

Although no one voted against the measure, five Republicans voted "present," including ranking Republican Arlen Specter of Pennsylvania. Specter said he had some concerns but would not hold up the bill. "I think that before we subject the railroads to significant changes, we ought to be sure it meshes with the [Surface Transportation Board]," Specter said, suggesting that Congress could consider legislation to speed up the complaint process rather than changing the regulatory structure.

The American Association of Railroads and other industry groups opposed the measure, arguing that changing the regulations would hamper economic growth.

The House Judiciary Committee on a voice vote approved a similar measure (HR 233—H Rept 111-669, Part 1), sponsored by Tammy Baldwin, D-Wis., on November 30, 2010.

Pricing Floors

The House and Senate Judiciary committees in the 111th Congress approved bills that would make it a violation of antitrust laws for retailers, wholesalers, and distributors to set pricing floors for their products. The bills were not taken up by the full House or Senate.

The bills were a response to a 2007 Supreme Court decision, *Leegin Creative Leather Products Inc. v. PSKS Inc.* (551 U.S. 877), in which the Court ruled that retail price maintenance was allowed. Sometimes called vertical price fixing, it referred to a practice whereby a producer set a minimum retail price at which a distributor could sell a product to a consumer. Since 1911, the Court had held that retail price maintenance was an antitrust violation. Although manufacturers were allowed to set a suggested retail price, they were prohibited from setting a minimum price.

The 2007 *Leegin* case, however, overturned that precedent. In a 5–4 decision, the Court ruled that retail price maintenance should be allowed because there were several reasonable economic reasons why a company might want to establish a pricing floor for its products.

The House measure (HR 3190—H Rept 111-676), reported by the committee on December 10, 2010, would restore the previous rule, allowing manufacturers to suggest prices but not mandate them. "Whenever retailers compete aggressively on price, the consumer unquestionably wins," Hank Johnson, D-Ga., said at the markup. Johnson, chair of the Courts and Competition Policy Subcommittee, said that since the 2007 case, manufacturers have implemented minimum prices on a variety of products, including baby goods, consumer electronics, and pet food. According to Johnson, the measure would not apply to manufacturers that wholly owned their retail franchises.

The Senate Judiciary Committee approved a similar bill (S 148—S Rept 111-227) on March 18 by voice vote and reported it July 17, 2010.

Missing Persons

A bill designed to make it easier for the public and law enforcement authorities to report and collect information about missing persons won voice vote passage in the House on February 23, 2010. But the Senate did not take it up.

The bill (HR 3695—H Rept 111-416) would authorize \$12.4 million over fiscal 2011–2015 for the Justice Department to maintain a pair of national missing persons databases. The databases, managed separately by the Federal Bureau of Investigation (FBI) and Justice Department, would be placed under the purview of the U.S. attorney general.

The legislation would require the FBI to send information from its database—accessible at the time only to law enforcement officials—to the publicly searchable Justice Department database.

Sponsor Christopher S. Murphy, D-Conn., said the bill was needed to make it easier for family members of missing persons and law enforcement officers to report and track information. "Billy's Law is an example of the vast legislative underbrush that happens here that changes lives," demonstrating "places where both parties work together to make this government work better," Murphy said.

The legislation was named for Billy Smolinski, a Connecticut man who had been missing since 2004. His mother, Janice, testified at a January 21 hearing of the House Judiciary Subcommittee on Crime, Terrorism and Homeland Security on the challenges her family faced in reporting and investigating her son's disappearance.

The Congressional Budget Office estimated that the bill would cost \$45 million over five years.

Haitian Children

The House in 2010 cleared a measure aimed at easing the adoption process for Haitian children admitted to the United States after the January 2010 earthquake in Haiti. The bill (HR 5283—PL 111-293) was cleared by voice vote December 1.

The measure authorized the Department of Homeland Security (DHS) to grant permanent U.S. residency to Haitian children brought to the United States as part of a humanitarian entry policy after the earthquake. It would then grant such a child adoption eligibility if he or she obtained permanent resident status before turning age eighteen and was adopted by a U.S. citizen.

The measure allowed applicants to request a status change up to three years after enactment and capped—at 1,400—the total number of requests for permanent residency that could be granted. It also prohibited any immigration benefits for biological parents of children whose status was adjusted under the measure.

After the earthquake, DHS implemented a policy to allow children from Haiti to enter the United States temporarily. The policy permitted the legal entry of children confirmed by Haiti as eligible for intercountry adoption and of children involved in adoption proceedings with prospective U.S. parents. Applications for legal entry under that policy were suspended April 15.

The Senate passed the measure by voice vote on August 4.

Social Security Lawsuits

Lawmakers in 2010 cleared a bill aimed at increasing legal representation for people who sue for overdue Social Security benefits. The House passed the bill, 412–6, on February 4, and the Senate cleared it by voice vote on February 22.

The measure (HR 4532—PL 111-142) made permanent a provision of existing Social Security law that provided for attorneys to receive a 25 percent fee from claimants' past-due benefits. Congress in 2004 first created the program that regulated withholding procedures for attorney fees (PL 108-203). But it was set to expire in 2010.

Witness Protection Programs

As reports mounted about violence toward witnesses in state and local criminal trials, the House in 2009 passed legislation that would grant more funds for witness protection programs. Members overwhelmingly voted for the bill (HR 1741—H Rept 111-138), 412–11, on June 9.

But the bill failed to advance to the Senate floor after winning approval in the Senate Judiciary Committee, 18–1, on February 25, 2010.

Rep. Elijah E. Cummings, D-Md., originally sponsored the bill in response to persistent witness intimidation that had stoked crime in his Baltimore district.

The legislation required the Justice Department to provide grants to state and local governments to establish or maintain witness protection and aid programs. It provided grants for witnesses in court proceedings involving a homicide, a violent felony, or a serious drug offense. Under existing law, state and local agencies had to reimburse the federal witness protection program for eligible nonfederal witnesses.

Before approving the bill, the Senate Judiciary committee adopted a substitute amendment by Charles E. Schumer, D-N.Y., to include grants for witnesses in proceedings involving gangs or organized crime.

The amendment also removed a provision that authorized $150 million over five years for the grants. Instead, it allowed using funds already authorized by an existing court security law (PL 110-177) that provided grants to states to protect witnesses and victims of crime.

Bankruptcy Judgeships

In a measure aimed at reducing bankruptcy courts' workload as filings increase amid rising unemployment and foreclosures, the House in 2010 passed a bill to authorize new judgeships. However the bill, after winning approval in the Senate Judiciary Committee on May 27, did not advance further.

The bill (HR 4506—H Rept 111-430), which passed 345–5 on March 12, created thirteen new positions, made permanent twenty-two temporary judgeships created in 1992 and 2005, and extended for five years the authorization on two other temporary positions. It increased the number of bankruptcy judges to 365.

Rep. Steve Cohen, D-Tenn., noted that bankruptcy proceedings increased 34.5 percent from fiscal 2008 to fiscal 2009. "A well-functioning bankruptcy system is absolutely essential to helping individuals and businesses weather our nation's current economic difficulties," he said.

Republicans supported the bill, but lamented the slow response to past efforts to increase bankruptcy judgeships in the Senate.

Although the House had acted favorably on judicial conference requests for judgeships several times, said Texas Republican Ted Poe, "our friends down the hallway, the Senate, has not acted."

TV Coverage of Court Proceedings

The Senate Judiciary Committee in 2010 approved a pair of measures aimed at opening federal court proceedings, including the Supreme Court, to television coverage. Neither measure was taken up by the full Senate.

One of the proposals approved April 29 was a bill (S 657) sponsored by Charles E. Grassley, R-Iowa, that would authorize U.S. appellate and district court judges to allow electronic media coverage of court proceedings. Under the bill, judges could allow the photographing, electronic recording, broadcasting, or televising of proceedings unless such coverage would violate due-process rights.

Grassley said the measure, approved 13–6, would "bring much-needed transparency to the judicial branch." Charles E. Schumer, D-N.Y., said courts should function under a presumption of openness, adding that the bill would give judges "a lot of latitude."

But opponents of district court coverage argued that cameras in a courtroom could influence proceedings, compromise witness security and privacy, lengthen trials, and drive up costs. District courts are the trial courts of the federal system. Sen. Dianne Feinstein, D-Calif., voiced strong opposition to televised trial court coverage, arguing that its risks outweigh its benefits. She said she was especially concerned about the bill's effect on witness intimidation.

She also contended that cameras could negatively affect the "demeanor of the court" and invite grandstanding. In contrast, Richard J. Durbin, D-Ill., argued that media coverage of judges could have the opposite effect, serving to "temper" any outrageous or extreme decisions.

Also on April 29, the panel approved, 13–6, a separate bill (S 446) that would require televising open Supreme Court proceedings unless a majority of justices agreed that due process would be violated.

Administrative Changes to Federal Courts

Lawmakers in 2010 cleared a bill to make a series of administrative changes to the federal court system. By voice vote May 18, the House cleared the measure (S 1782—PL 111-174). The Senate passed the bill by voice vote March 16.

Among the several administrative changes to criminal law, to protect confidential information, the bill permitted judgments to be filed separately from "statements of reasons," which a judge issued to explain the reasons for imposing a sentence.

Additionally, it clarified that pretrial officers could perform various pretrial services for juveniles who were awaiting trial. The change addressed concerns that existing law focused on adults, leaving the treatment of juveniles unclear.

It also changed the reporting schedule for criminal wiretap orders by requiring that reports be filed in January for orders that expired in the previous year, as well as any denials. Under existing law, such information had to be filed thirty days after an order or extension expired.

The bill increased and adjusted for inflation the threshold amount used to trigger reviews of the costs to hire expert witnesses and conduct investigations for indigent defendants.

Internet Gambling

A bill that would effectively repeal an online gambling ban and establish rules to govern Internet betting was approved in 2010 by the House Financial Services Committee. It did not advance further.

By 41–22, the panel on July 28 approved the bill (HR 2267—H Rept 11-656, Part 1) that would give the Treasury Department authority to set rules for the licensing of online gambling organizations. Seven Republicans voted in support of the bill, while four Democrats opposed the measure.

The bill, sponsored by Chair Barney Frank, D-Mass., would allow financial institutions to process bets for licensed Internet gambling, in effect repealing a provision of a 2006 port security law (PL 109-347) that barred banks and credit unions from doing so. *(Congress and the Nation Vol. XII, p. 423)*

Although online gambling was prohibited in the United States, millions of Americans were making online bets with offshore Internet operators who were not regulated. Frank's bill would require licensed Internet gambling operators to prohibit access by minors and residents of states where such gambling was not allowed. It would also require operators to enforce self-imposed bet limits and provide the option for self-exclusion to those who gamble compulsively.

Frank said the bill would not be considered on the House floor until it could be moved in tandem with a companion tax bill (HR 4976). That bill, sponsored by Rep. Jim McDermott, D-Wash., would impose a 2 percent federal tax on online gambling, raising an estimated $40 billion over ten years, in addition to up to $30 billion that states could choose to impose through their own taxes under the bill. However, lawmakers took no action on McDermott's measure.

Opponents of HR 2267 ranged from social conservatives, who objected to gambling on moral grounds, to college and professional sports leagues that worried the legislation could spur gambling on sports, despite the bill's prohibition on sports betting. Rep. Spencer Bachus of Alabama, the committee's top Republican and a critic of the bill, said he did not want children exposed to gambling before they were mature enough to appreciate its consequences.

As amended, the bill would prohibit Internet gambling licensees from accepting bets or wagers on sporting events, except for pari-mutuel racing, such as horse racing or greyhound racing, that is permitted by law.

Sex Tourism

In an attempt to stifle the "sex tourism" industry, the House in 2010 passed a bill that would require convicted sex offenders to report upcoming international travel. The Senate did not take it up.

The bill (HR 5138), passed by voice vote July 27, was intended to prevent predators from traveling abroad to abuse children. It would require convicted sex offenders to report international travel at least thirty days before leaving or arriving in the country and would establish a national center to collect the reports and notify officials in foreign countries about future travel. Failure to report upcoming travel would result in a fine, up to ten years in prison, or both.

Sponsored by Christopher H. Smith, R-N.J., the bill (H Rept 111—568, Part 1) was modeled on a measure from the mid-1990s, when Congress enacted legislation called Megan's Law (PL 104-145), which required law enforcement agencies to disclose information about registered sex offenders. The law followed the murder of seven-year-old Megan Kanka, who was raped and killed by a convicted sex offender who had been released after serving a maximum sentence. *(Congress and the Nation Vol. IX, p. 738)*

With the rise in tourism and the advent of the Internet, there was an upswing in sex offenders taking trips to countries with high rates of poverty and less-stringent enforcement of sex crime laws to partake in the child sex trade, according to the Justice Department.

Cyberstalking

The House in 2010 passed legislation aimed at expanding the scope of federal anti-stalking laws to cover cyberstalking. The Senate did not take action on the bill.

The bill (HR 5662), passed by voice vote July 27, would extend federal criminal laws to cover cyberstalking as well as physical stalking. Current laws focus on conventional acts of stalking, including following someone across state lines or making harassing phone calls. The legislation would cover electronic surveillance.

"No one can deny that the Internet is a remarkable tool capable of connecting billions of people throughout the world. Unfortunately, it has also proven to be an effective weapon for stalkers to prey on innocent people," said bill sponsor Loretta Sanchez, D-Calif.

The measure would allow for the prosecution of acts of stalking that were "reasonably expected" to cause another person serious emotional distress. Current law allowed for prosecution only if the victim demonstrated a reasonable fear of physical injury.

Under the measure, the U.S. attorney general would be required to annually evaluate federal, tribal, state, and local efforts to enforce stalking laws and identify the best practices for enforcement.

Although members of both parties voiced support for the legislation, California Republican Dan Lungren expressed concern that the bill had not been considered by the House Judiciary.

Apology for Slavery and Segregation

The Senate in 2009 adopted a resolution by voice vote June 17 offering a formal apology for slavery and the era of "separate but equal" Jim Crow laws that followed. The resolution (S Con Res 26), which lacked the force of law, stated that it did not authorize or support reparations, prompting criticism from Congressional Black Caucus members. The House adopted a similar resolution in 2008.

Roland W. Burris, D-Ill., the lone African American senator, acknowledged that the issue concerned him but praised the resolution nonetheless. "Words do matter. They matter a great deal," he said.

Such apologies were infrequent. Congress apologized for the World War II internment of Japanese-Americans. The Senate adopted apologies for the legacy of brutality against Native Americans and for the history of filibustering legislation designed to combat lynching of African Americans in the 19th and 20th centuries.

2011–2012

Although partisan differences in the 112th Congress prevented agreements on issues ranging from violence against women to judicial nominations, Republicans and Democrats found common ground on several high-profile bills.

Lawmakers achieved a long-standing goal by clearing a bipartisan overhaul of federal patent law. The 2011 legislation changed the procedures for issuing patents and for challenging the validity of patents once they were issued, with the aim of making the patent system faster and more efficient.

After considerable debate, Congress in 2011 also agreed to four-year extensions of three provisions of the antiterrorism law known as the Patriot Act. The provisions allowed federal law enforcement officials to seek a court order to gain access to "any tangible thing" related to a terrorism investigation, allowed them to obtain "roving" wiretaps on terrorism suspects who used multiple communications devices or who repeatedly changed cell phone numbers or carriers, and authorized them to seek warrants to conduct surveillance on "lone wolf" terrorist suspects who could not be connected to specific terrorist groups or foreign nations. Lawmakers in the closing days of the session gave a victory to President Barack Obama and Senate Intelligence Chair Dianne Feinstein, D-Calif., by clearing a five-year renewal of the law that gave the intelligence community authority to conduct wiretaps of certain foreigners communicating with people in the United States without obtaining individual warrants.

However, sharp partisan differences emerged on other issues. Lawmakers failed to clear a reauthorization of the Violence Against Women Act. Congress had twice previously given broad bipartisan backing to the 1994 act, which helped support the prevention and prosecution of domestic and sexual violence and provided state grants for services such as transitional housing and legal assistance. But this time the Republican-controlled House and the Democratic-controlled Senate passed sharply different versions. After months of arguing, the two chambers could not reach a compromise over provisions that would have expanded the law or made it stricter.

In an ominous sign for future court battles, Senate Republicans filibustered two of Obama's nominees for federal appellate judgeships. These were the first successful filibusters of judicial nominees since a 2005 agreement that was meant to curtail filibusters except in extraordinary circumstances, and they provoked strong rebukes from Democrats.

The increasingly acrimonious atmosphere in the nation's capital also contributed to the House taking the extraordinary action in 2012 of voting to hold Attorney General Eric H. Holder Jr. in contempt of Congress for not providing lawmakers with subpoenaed documents related to a probe into a botched gun-tracking program known as Operation Fast and Furious. It was the first time in history that either chamber of Congress had officially held an attorney general in contempt. The House Oversight Committee subsequently filed a civil suit in the U.S. District Court for the District of Columbia to enforce the subpoena against Holder.

House Republicans turned to the fiscal 2012 Commerce-Justice-Science bill to seek to eliminate funding for the Community Oriented Policing Services (COPS) program, which provided grants for local police departments to hire officers. But senators were able to restore much of the funding for COPS and for other state and local law enforcement grants that faced deep cuts in the House.

A number of conservative priorities stalled in the 112th Congress. These included a proposed balanced budget amendment to the Constitution, which fell short of the required two-thirds majority in both the House and Senate. Republicans also failed to win enactment of controversial measures that would have restricted certain abortions and allowed the transport of concealed handguns across state lines. *(Balanced-budget amendment, p. 167)*

Patent Law Overhaul

After an effort in congressional offices and committee rooms that spanned many years, Congress cleared and President Barack Obama signed bipartisan legislation to overhaul federal patent law (HR 1249—PL 112-29). The 2011 legislation changed the procedures for issuing patents and for challenging the validity of patents once they were issued, with the aim of making the patent system faster and more efficient.

It had broad support as a means of fostering innovation and bolstering U.S. economic growth and global competitiveness. The measure got an extra push when supporters tied it to the drive to increase jobs, which was on the minds of members of both parties.

The bill altered the basis for awarding patents from a "first to invent" principle to a "first inventor to file" system. In another major change, it allowed the U.S. Patent and Trademark Office (PTO) to set its own fees as a way of giving it the resources to clear out a mounting backlog of patent applications. However, the legislation did not give the patent office direct access to all the fees it collected, leaving appropriators with the power to decide how much of the revenue the office could keep.

The Senate-passed version of the bill would have let the office keep and spend all the fees it took in from patent applicants, an issue that put the two chambers at odds over the bill. In the end, the Senate gave up and cleared the House-passed bill, in the interest of finally getting the measure into law.

President Barack Obama addresses a crowd of students, teachers, business leaders, and members of Congress before signing the America Invents Act at Thomas Jefferson High School for Science and Technology in Alexandria, Va., on September 16, 2011. The act reforms patent law so as to give a patent to the first applicant rather than the first inventor.
Source: EPA/Chip Somodevilla/Pool

The legislation, originally sought by a group of big technology companies, had been in the works for years. The House passed a similar bill in 2007, but the Senate did not take it up.

Senate Judiciary Chair Patrick J. Leahy, D-Vt., and his House counterpart, Lamar Smith, R-Texas, teamed up early in the year on a final push for passage of the measure. Supporters—including the patent office itself, several industry and trade groups, and members of Congress—argued that problems within the patent legal framework were hindering innovation. They said that the current process sometimes resulted in abusive practices particular to patent litigation and in poor-quality patents, especially among those issued for "business methods."

The 1990s had seen a huge increase in the number of patents issued for business practices in a wide variety of areas, including e-commerce, insurance, banking, and tax compliance. The patent office lacked a sufficient number of examiners with expertise in the areas related to these patents. Advocates of the overhaul legislation argued that this had led to an increase in the number of lawsuits related to the infringement of business method patents.

MAJOR PROVISIONS

As enacted PL 112-29 contained the following major provisions.

First to file. Instituted the first-to-file system in place of the previous first-to-invent system for awarding patents. Under the new criteria, if more than one person claimed to have made an invention, the first to file received the patent. As under the previous law, the inventor had a one-year grace period to file for protection after first disclosing the invention or otherwise making it public. The first-to-invent system, used exclusively in the United States, could require the patent and trademark office to undertake a lengthy, costly process to referee disputes over who actually made an invention first.

Derivation proceeding. Created a new procedure to allow an inventor to challenge an earlier applicant's eligibility to receive a patent if the earlier applicant had derived the invention from information published by the inventor. As explained by the Congressional Research Service, "a first-inventor-to-file rule does not permit one individual to copy another's invention and then, by virtue of being the first to file a patent application, be entitled to a patent."

Post-grant review. Changed the process for granting a review of an already-issued patent. The bill replaced a procedure known as an *inter partes* reexamination—the Latin term meaning "between the parties"—with an *inter partes* review that expanded what was allowed as evidence in such hearings and placed the burden of proof on the party that was petitioning to have the patent revoked. To initiate such a review, the party had to have a "reasonable likelihood of success." The bill also created a new "postgrant review" that allowed a petitioner, including the patent office director, to challenge the validity of a patent based on any of the criteria for issuing patents. The provision was intended as a less costly alternative to litigation.

Fee authority. Allowed the patent and technology office to set and adjust its fees, a power that previously was exercised by Congress. Excess patent office revenue went to a reserve account for the agency's use, subject to appropriations.

Business methods. Created a special process for reviewing patents on business methods used in the financial services industry. The petitioner seeking a review had to have been sued or charged with infringement of the patent in question. The program was to sunset after ten years.

"Prior user" defense. Expanded a prior-user defense against claims of patent infringement to apply not just to business methods, as under the previous law, but to all inventions. Under the doctrine, an earlier user of an invention that was later patented by someone else could employ prior use as a defense against claims of infringement by the patent holder.

Tax strategies. Effectively eliminated the ability to seek patent protection for specific tax strategies, such as how to file returns and plan estates. The provision also applied to tax advice given to clients, but it did not apply to software that enabled individuals to file their own returns or assisted them in managing their finances.

SENATE COMMITTEE ACTION

The Senate Judiciary Committee approved Leahy's bill (S 23) by a vote of 15–0 on February 3. A bipartisan majority of the panel had backed similar legislation in the 111th Congress, but that measure never reached the Senate floor.

The bill included language changing the patent system to first-to-file, which supporters argued was simpler and would result in a less burdensome regulatory regime. But conservative activists opposed the change, saying, among other things, that it would hurt smaller inventors who did not have the legal resources to get their paperwork to the patent and trademark office first. They also opposed provisions to make it easier to challenge the validity of granted patents and cast the bill as an attack on the U.S. patent, a property right enshrined in the Constitution.

Leahy's bill included language to give the patent office power to set fees. The chair had made some changes to his bill before the markup to solidify bipartisan support on his panel, including incorporating a proposal to bar patents on tax strategies. The Senate panel made several additional changes aimed at garnering even more support for the bill.

The committee:

- Adopted by voice vote a Leahy amendment adding a provision to keep all patent cases in federal court and eliminate the ability of judges of the U.S. Court of Appeals for the Federal Circuit to maintain workstations outside the Washington, D.C., area.
- Adopted by voice vote an amendment by Dianne Feinstein, D-Calif., to remove changes to the criteria for "willful infringement" of a patent, a charge that could result in triple-damages awards under existing law. The proposed changes had been one of several sticking points in the 111th Congress.

SENATE FLOOR ACTION

The Senate passed the bill, 95–5, on March 8, after rejecting an attempt to eliminate the first-to-file provision and adding language to remove the patent office from the appropriations process. The White House issued a strong endorsement, calling the bill the "most significant patent reform in over half a century."

Senate passage led a group of big high-tech companies that had lobbied against the bill to shift their efforts to the House. The Coalition for Patent Fairness, a grouping that included Google, Inc., and Apple, Inc., had won some changes in the Senate committee, including the elimination of changes to the criteria for what constituted willful infringement. But the group still opposed replacing *inter partes* reexamination with an *inter partes* review process that had a higher threshold for postgrant patent challenges, as well as other provisions aimed at ensuring that such challenges were resolved quickly. The big tech companies worried about their legal exposure in patent infringement lawsuits filed by other companies, and they wanted challenging the validity of another company's patent to be kept as easy and open-ended as possible.

During a debate that extended over six days, the Senate:

- Adopted, 97–2, a bipartisan manager's amendment to allow the patent office to keep all the fees it collected. The amendment, by Leahy, was cosponsored by the Judiciary panel's top Republican, Charles E. Grassley of Iowa, and panel member Jon Kyl, R-Ariz., and reflected language advocated by Tom Coburn, R-Okla. The amendment also included a pilot program to review the validity of business method patents.
- Voted 87–13 to table (kill) an amendment by Feinstein that would have scrapped the first-to-file provisions. Leahy led critics of the amendment, citing opposition from the Obama administration and a host of outside stakeholders that were vital to advancing the bill. "This amendment would gut the reforms intended by the bill and be a poison pill to these legislative reform efforts," he said. "Supporters of the legislation, ranging from high-tech and life sciences companies to universities and small businesses . . . will not support a bill without those provisions." Amendment opponents also noted a series of protections already in the legislation for inventors, including the one-year grace period before an inventor had to file with the patent office after making public certain details of an invention.
- Adopted by voice vote an amendment by Jeff Bingaman, D-N.M., to require the patent office to publicly disclose the length of time between the start and the completion of reviews of challenged patents.

HOUSE COMMITTEE ACTION

The House Judiciary Committee approved a similar, bipartisan bill (HR 1249—H Rept 112-98, Part 1) by a vote of 32–3 on April 14. The bill included provisions to shift the basis for issuing patents to a first-to-file standard, alter mechanisms for challenging the validity of issued patents, and allow the patent and trademark office to set fees and keep all the revenue it collected, rather than being dependent on the appropriations process. It included new rules for *inter partes* review, as well as a postgrant review to allow disputes involving patent quality and scope to be settled.

During the markup, the committee:

- Rejected by voice vote an amendment by F. James Sensenbrenner Jr., R-Wis., to strike the first-to-file language. Like their Senate colleagues, supporters of the provision argued that it would provide greater certainty about patent ownership and put the United States in line with other nations.
- Adopted by voice vote an amendment by Melvin Watt, D-N.C., to sunset the patent office's fee-setting authority after six years.
- Adopted, 29–2, a manager's amendment by committee Chair Lamar Smith of Texas to extend the timeline in the bill for *inter partes* reviews of the validity of issued patents from nine months after service of a complaint to twelve months, and to raise the threshold for challenges to a "reasonable likelihood that the petitioner would prevail."
- Rejected, 8–21, a Zoe Lofgren, D-Calif., amendment to strike a provision that would have allowed patent owners to request a supplemental review of a patent to make corrections.
- But the committee adopted, 21–9, an amendment by Robert W. Goodlatte, R-Va., to bar the use of the supplemental review for cases revealed to involve fraud.

HOUSE FLOOR ACTION

The House passed the bill on a **key vote of 304–117 (R 168–67; D 136–50)** on June 23, 2011, after altering the committee bill to allow appropriators to retain control over patent office fees. The change came in a manager's amendment offered by Smith and adopted, 283–140. It was made at the insistence of Appropriations Chair Harold Rogers, R-Ky., and Budget Chair Paul D. Ryan, R-Wis. *(2011 key votes, p. 785)*

Previewing the reception the new fee language was likely to receive in the Senate, Coburn charged that since 1992, Congress had "pilfered nearly $1 billion in user fees dedicated to the Patent and Trademark Office and spent those dollars elsewhere."

Rogers promised that the appropriators would ensure that the patent office received all the revenue, but there was no comparable pledge from Senate appropriators, and Coburn was not mollified. "Unfortunately, the Appropriations Committee has a poor record of managing such accounts responsibly and honestly in this area and others," Coburn said.

During debate on the bill, the House also:

- Rejected, 129–295, an amendment by Sensenbrenner that would have struck the first-to-file language.
- Rejected, 105–316, an effort by John Conyers Jr., D-Mich., to delay the move to a first-to-file system until ninety days after a presidential finding that Japan and the European Union had adopted grace periods substantially similar to a one-year grace period provided in the bill.
- Rejected, 172–251, a motion by Brad Miller, D-N.C., to recommit the bill to the committee with instructions to report it back immediately with an amendment that would require the patent office to give priority to applications from small businesses that pledged to develop or manufacture their products in the United States.

FINAL ACTION

The Senate cleared the House bill on a **key vote of 89–9 (R 40–6; D 47–3; I 2–0)** on September 8, 2011. Bill supporters cautioned that any changes would necessitate further House action and could derail the measure. All amendments were rejected. *(2011 key votes, p. 785)*

During the debate, the Senate:

- Tabled, 50–48, a Coburn amendment to give the patent office the authority to spend all the fees it collected.
- Rejected, 13–85, an amendment by Maria Cantwell, D-Wash., to restore Senate language on a new process for reviewing the validity of financial-services-related business method patents. Cantwell said both chambers' provisions on the issue would benefit big banks but cautioned that the House version might go too far.
- Rejected, 47–51, a proposal by Jeff Sessions, R-Ala., to strip out a provision on a patent extension filing deadline sought by drug patent holders to compensate for delays caused by the Food and Drug Administration approval process.

Passage was advanced after the Senate voted 93–5 on September 6 to limit debate on a motion to take up the bill.

Violence Against Women Act

Both the House and Senate passed bills in the 112th Congress to reauthorize the Violence Against Women Act through 2017. But after months of arguing, the two chambers could not reach a compromise over provisions that would have expanded the law or made it stricter.

Congress twice had given broad bipartisan backing to the 1994 act (PL 103-322), but this time, the legislation fell prey to the same kind of partisan discord that sidetracked a number of other bills during the session. *(2000 reauthorization, Congress and the Nation Vol. X, pp. 629, 630)*

The law helped support the prevention and prosecution of domestic and sexual violence and provided state grants for services such as transitional housing and legal assistance. It also promoted a coordinated response by creating the Office of Violence Against Women in the Justice Department and bringing together victim advocates, law enforcement, courts, health care professionals, and faith leaders. Its last authorization (PL 109-162) expired in September 2012.

The Senate passed its five-year bill (S 1925), sponsored by Judiciary Chair Patrick J. Leahy, D-Vt., with sixty cosponsors, in April by a bipartisan vote. The legislation would have expanded protections significantly for an estimated thirty million people by including new provisions that would cover gay and lesbian victims, grant more visas to illegal immigrants who were victims of domestic violence, and give American Indian authorities the power to prosecute non-Indians accused of abusing Indian women on tribal lands.

The House bill (HR 4970), which passed narrowly in May on a largely party-line vote, included new visa application benchmarks for illegal immigrants who were victims of violent crime and assisted with law enforcement investigations. It did not have the Senate language on gender or on prosecution on tribal lands.

House Republicans said they could not go to conference on the Senate-passed bill because it contained a little-noticed revenue provision raising fees on certain kinds of immigrant visas. Under the House's long-standing interpretation of the Origination Clause of the Constitution, all revenue legislation had to start in the House, rendering the Senate bill effectively dead in the eyes of House leaders.

Speaker John A. Boehner, R-Ohio, called on the Senate either to remove the immigrant provision and pass its bill again or to take up the House-passed version and move to conference on it. Democrats called the constitutional objection an excuse intended to mask the House's more fundamental problems with the Senate bill.

Senate Democrats tried but failed to use a parliamentary maneuver to fix the constitutional problem by taking up unrelated House-passed revenue legislation and replacing it with the text of the Senate's domestic-violence reauthorization bill.

After the fall elections, Vice President Joseph R. Biden Jr. began working with House Majority Leader Eric Cantor, R-Va., to try to reach a compromise. In December, Republican representatives Darrell Issa of California and Tom Cole of Oklahoma introduced legislation (HR 6625) that contained the Senate provision regarding tribal lands.

Leahy called the move the compromise that would allow Congress to send a reauthorization bill to the president's desk, but the proposal met with some House GOP resistance and went no further.

SENATE COMMITTEE ACTION

In a partisan split over the issues of visa eligibility and sexual identity, the Senate Judiciary Committee approved its bill (S 1925—S Rept 112-153) by a vote of 10–8 on February 2, without the backing of any Republicans.

The party-line vote marked a shift: in 2000, Judiciary panel members voted 17–0 in support of a reauthorization measure.

Leahy made several changes to the bill in response to GOP objections, but they proved insufficient to win over Republican senators, including Charles E. Grassley of Iowa, the panel's ranking member. "I appreciate that [Leahy] deleted several troubling provisions from his original bill," Grassley said, pointing to the removal of language he said would have "watered down" a requirement that law enforcement vouch for a victim's willingness to help investigators or prosecutors respond to a crime in order to qualify for a special visa.

The U-visa program, which was capped at 10,000 per year, gave illegal immigrants who were the victims of violent crime in the United States an opportunity to gain legal status if they were, or were likely to be, helpful to law enforcement and government officials. Leahy's original bill would have loosened restrictions that specified which officials could sign off on the immigrant's cooperation.

Grassley also pushed for complete removal of language in the original bill that would have increased the 10,000-per-year cap on the number of visas made available. Instead, Leahy's amendment scaled back the underlying language to pair the existing cap with a proposal to allow unused visas from previous years to be transferred to future years.

On another front, Grassley took aim at Leahy's proposal to add the terms "gender identity" and "sexual orientation" to existing language that made grant money for victim services organizations conditional on their compliance with nondiscrimination practices. Grassley argued the change was "a solution in search of a problem," rejecting claims by backers of the proposal that victims were being denied services based on their sexual orientation or gender identity.

Grassley and other Republicans also objected to a provision to extend tribal authority. The Democratic majority said in the committee report on the bill that according to Census Bureau data, more than 50 percent of all Native American women were married to non-Indian men, and thousands of others were in intimate relationships with non-Indians, but tribes did not have the authority to prosecute non-Indians who abused Native American women on tribal lands.

SENATE FLOOR ACTION

The Senate passed the five-year reauthorization by a vote of 68–31 on April 26, after rejecting efforts by GOP opponents to narrow the measure's scope. Fifteen Republicans, including all the women in the caucus, joined all fifty-three members of the Democratic caucus in support of the expanded version.

During the debate, the Senate:

- Rejected, 37–62, a Republican substitute offered by Kay Bailey Hutchison of Texas that stuck more closely to existing law. Under a unanimous consent agreement, sixty votes were required for adoption of any amendments. The Senate had agreed to require a sixty-vote majority for adoption of the amendment.
- Rejected, 50–48, an amendment by John Cornyn, R-Texas, that would have directed the Justice Department to use more than 70 percent of the estimated

$100 million in funding for the rape kit testing program under a 2006 law (PL 109-105) for DNA tests and conduct audits to account for stored rape test kits. Cornyn and his allies charged that the department had used most of the funds to cover administrative costs and other expenses.

HOUSE COMMITTEE ACTION

The House Judiciary Committee approved its narrower version of the bill (HR 4970—H Rept 112-480, Part 1) by a vote of 17–15 on May 8 after a nearly eight-hour markup.

The measure, sponsored by Sandy Adams, R-Fla., left out new legal authority for American Indians on the grounds that the language could be unconstitutional, and omitted protections for gay and lesbian victims because many Republicans said there was no evidence such groups were being shut out of services. The House bill also did not include Senate language requiring that colleges and universities report campus incidents of domestic violence, dating violence, and stalking, which Adams said was outside the committee's jurisdiction.

Among provisions in the bill that Democrats found objectionable was a proposed change in the process under which battered immigrants could apply for legal-residency status. The bill included designated funding for analyzing untested rape kit DNA evidence from crime scenes.

During the markup, the committee:

- Adopted, 30–0, a proposal offered by Ted Poe, R-Texas, and revised by Melvin Watt, D-N.C., to drop requirements in the bill that applicants for U-visas report a crime within sixty days and that the crime still be prosecutable under the statute of limitations by the time law enforcement officials certified the victim's cooperation.
- Rejected, 10–15, an amendment by Sheila Jackson Lee, D-Texas, to strike additional requirements in the bill that the crime be under active investigation or prosecution and that the visa applicant help identify the accused if that information was unknown. The Jackson Lee proposal also would have dropped GOP language blocking U-visa recipients from gaining permanent residence.
- Rejected, 12–17, a proposal by Zoe Lofgren of California, the top Democrat on the Judiciary panel's immigration subcommittee, to provide for a nearly complete swap of the Senate-passed immigration language for that of the House bill.
- Rejected, 13–16, an amendment by Mike Quigley, D-Ill., to identify as an underserved population those who faced barriers to assistance because of their sexual orientation or gender identity. Reflecting the election-year implication of the issues, John Conyers Jr. of Michigan, the Judiciary Committee's ranking Democrat, declared that the legislation was part of a Republican "war on women," prompting jeers from several committee Republicans. Steve King, R-Iowa, referred to illegal immigrants as "undocumented Democrats," accusing Democrats of using the legislation to expand immigration law for political gains.

HOUSE FLOOR ACTION

The House passed the bill, on a 222–205 vote, on May 16, with twenty-three Republicans voting no and six Democrats supporting the bill. The rule for floor debate barred amendments.

The rule automatically made several changes, including dropping language that would have given immigration officials the option to interview an accused abuser when determining whether to grant permanent legal status to an immigrant victim without the involvement of the U.S. citizen or permanent-resident spouse. It also would have included a mechanism for victims to seek protection orders from federal courts related to domestic-violence offenses committed on tribal land.

Democrats argued the language would place burdens on victims, who would have to pay for legal counsel and travel to faraway courts. "The manager's amendment is a fig leaf meant to cover the simple truth that this bill rolls back existing law and fails to protect some of the most vulnerable victims of violence," Conyers said in a written statement.

Holder Held in Contempt of Congress

The House voted June 28, 2012, to hold Attorney General Eric H. Holder Jr. in contempt of Congress for not providing lawmakers with subpoenaed documents related to a probe into a botched gun-tracking program known as Operation Fast and Furious. It was the first time in history that either chamber of Congress had officially held an attorney general in contempt.

The vote marked a significant escalation in the political debate over the defunct "gun walking" operation, in which the Justice Department allowed some 2,000 assault rifles and other firearms to be transported from the United States into Mexico in an attempt to trace them to Mexican drug cartels. Some of the guns later turned up at crime scenes near the border, including a December 2010 incident in which a U.S. Border Patrol agent was killed.

The House Oversight and Government Reform Committee and its chair, Darrell Issa, R-Calif., had issued a wide-ranging subpoena in October 2011 seeking communications between Holder, others in the Justice Department, and White House officials relating to Fast and Furious. Of particular interest to Issa was a key category of documents concerning how the Justice Department came to withdraw a February 4, 2011, letter to Sen. Charles E. Grassley of Iowa, the top Republican on the Judiciary Committee, saying the Bureau of Alcohol, Tobacco, Firearms and Explosives (ATF), which was in charge of the operation, had not "knowingly allowed" the use of gun-walking tactics. Republicans demanded to know more about how Justice sent a letter with false information to Congress.

Holder told lawmakers in December 2011 that the operation had been "deeply flawed," but he said Justice Department officials did not know about or sanction the tactics. The department released documents detailing how the letter was drafted, showing that officials who actually wrote the letter based it on information that had been provided to them by lower-ranking officials.

HOUSE COMMITTEE ACTION

After months of negotiations, the Oversight Committee voted 23–17 along party lines June 20 to find Holder in contempt of Congress for withholding documents. The vote on the resolution (H Res 711—H Rept 112-546) came hours after President Barack Obama invoked executive privilege for the first time in his administration, saying release of the internal documents would impair the ability of the executive branch to deliberate "independently and effectively."

Speaker John A. Boehner, R-Ohio, and Majority Leader Eric Cantor, R-Va., called the assertion of executive privilege an "extraordinary step" and gave Holder a blunt ultimatum. "While we had hoped it would not come to this, unless the attorney general re-evaluates his choice and supplies the promised documents, the House will vote to hold him in contempt next week," they said in a statement. "If, however, Attorney General Holder produces these documents prior to the scheduled vote, we will give the Oversight Committee an opportunity to review [them] in hopes of resolving this issue."

Holder rejected GOP claims that the Justice Department had been unresponsive—the department subsequently said it had released 7,600 pages of documents—and accused Issa of turning aside efforts "to reach a reasonable accommodation." Democrats charged that Republicans were pursuing the issue to hurt Obama in an election year.

Grassley said the issue of executive privilege never came up when he, Issa, and other lawmakers met with Holder on June 19 in an unsuccessful attempt to avert the vote. "If it were a serious claim, the administration would have and should have raised it last night, if not much earlier," Grassley said in a statement the next day.

HOUSE FLOOR ACTION

The House adopted the contempt resolution June 28 by a vote of 255–67, with two Republicans against and seventeen Democrats in favor. The lopsided result reflected the fact that 108 Democrats, a majority of the caucus, declined to vote. Many caucus members instead walked out of the chamber and Capitol and down the House front steps. Republicans staged a similar walkout in 2008, when a Democratic House held two former aides to President George W. Bush, counsel Harriet Miers and Chief of Staff Joshua B. Bolten, in contempt for refusing to produce documents requested in connection with the firing of nine federal prosecutors. *(Miers and Bolten contempt, Congress and the Nation Vol. XII, p. 867)*

POSTSCRIPT

On June 29, one day after the House vote, the Justice Department stated that it would not pursue a criminal case against Holder because no crime had been committed. In a letter to Boehner, Deputy Attorney General James M. Cole noted that the president had asserted executive privilege and directed the attorney general not to supply certain documents in question. Not prosecuting under those circumstances, he wrote, was in line with long-standing standards used under administrations of both parties.

On August 13, the House Oversight Committee filed a civil suit in the U.S. District Court for the District of Columbia to enforce the subpoena against Holder. Boehner said in a statement that the Justice Department had been "stonewalling Congress" by ignoring the House's contempt order and therefore had left the House with "no choice but to take legal action so we can get to the bottom of the Fast and Furious operation."

Holder asked the court in October to throw out the suit, which was expected to last months if not years. Both sides in the dispute were able to claim some vindication in September, when the Justice Department released a report recommending that fourteen officials at the ATF be investigated further for their roles in the Fast and Furious operation.

The report, which Inspector General Michael E. Horowitz released September 19, resulted in the immediate departure of two officials: Kenneth Melson, the former acting director of ATF during the period in which the operation was in effect, and Jason Weinstein, a deputy assistant attorney general who was faulted for failing to stop questionable tactics from being employed in the operation.

Grassley and other Republicans said their concerns were validated by the inspector general's conclusion that senior department officials could have done more to avert the violence and murder.

According to the report, officials at the Justice Department's Criminal Division—who were not aware of the operation in advance—had approved wiretap applications without reading the details of those requests. Holder had always said senior department officials, including himself, had not been aware of the operation in advance, and that crucial claim was supported by the inspector general. Holder and congressional Democrats stressed that aspect of the report's findings and accused Republicans of leading a witch hunt against senior Justice Department officials.

Fiscal 2012 Appropriations

A prominent program for neighborhood policing that House Republicans had hoped to eliminate got a reprieve under the fiscal 2012 Commerce-Justice-Science appropriations bill. The measure cleared as part of a three-bill "minibus" that President Barack Obama signed into law on November 18, 2011 (HR 2112—PL 112-55).

The $60 billion legislation included $27.4 billion for the Justice Department. That was nearly flat compared with fiscal 2011 funding and $1.3 billion less than the president's request.

The House version would have eliminated funding for the Community Oriented Policing Services (COPS) program, which provided grants for local police departments to hire officers. Under the minibus, the COPS program got $199 million, still a 60 percent cut compared with fiscal 2011. The Senate panel had approved $256 million for the program.

The reduction from fiscal 2011 for the COPS program was part of a general cut in funds for state and local law enforcement grants, although, again, they were not as deep as House GOP appropriators proposed. The $2.2 billion in the bill for the grants was a 20 percent cut from fiscal 2011 funding.

However, several other federal law enforcement programs got more than in fiscal 2011. They included the FBI, which received a 2 percent increase, and the federal prison system, which got 4 percent more.

Policy language in the bill included House provisions that made permanent three firearms-related provisos, including one that required the destruction of identification information for approved firearms purchasers within twenty-four hours of notification that an individual passed a background check. It also modified language backed by the Senate that barred funds for operations similar to a botched Justice Department gun-tracking program known as Operation Fast and Furious, a sting operation on the Southwest border that resulted in a large number of guns remaining on the streets.

The measure forbade the use of funds—except for national background checks—for federal law enforcement to facilitate the transfer of operable guns to suspected drug cartel agents unless they were being continuously monitored. The bill did not include a House provision that would have blocked a requirement by the Bureau of Alcohol, Tobacco, Firearms and Explosives (ATF) that licensed dealers and pawnbrokers in New Mexico, Texas, California, and Arizona report bulk rifle sales.

LEGISLATIVE ACTION

Stand-alone versions of the bill were approved by the House and Senate Appropriations committees but did not reach the floor in either chamber.

The House Appropriations Committee gave voice-vote approval to a $57 billion Commerce-Justice-Science bill (HR 2596—H Rept 112-169) on July 13. It called for $26.3 billion for the Justice Department, including $1.7 billion for state and local law enforcement, but with no money for COPS or the State Criminal Alien Assistance Program, which helped with the costs associated with incarcerating undocumented immigrants who had committed crimes.

During the markup, the committee:

- Adopted, 28–19, a proposal by John Carter, R-Texas, to prohibit the use of funds in the bill to ban shotgun imports.
- Adopted, 25–16, a proposal by Denny Rehberg, R-Mont., to bar the ATF from requiring licensed firearm dealers to report to the agency on the bulk sales of rifles to a single buyer.
- Rejected, 22–25, a proposal by Chaka Fattah, D-Pa., to provide $35 million for COPS. "This is a program that's been vitally important to local communities in terms of hiring police officers," said Fattah, the ranking member on the Commerce-Justice-Science Subcommittee. Jack Kingston, R-Ga., noted that COPS was intended to be a five-year program. "This is how federal programs never die," he said.

The Senate Appropriations Committee approved its own funding bill (S 1572—S Rept 112-78) by a vote of 29–1 on September 15. The $59.5 billion bill called for $26.9 billion for the Justice Department, including $2.3 billion for state and local law enforcement. The bill proposed $200 million for COPS and $273 million for the State Criminal Alien Assistance Program. Those amounts were still below fiscal 2011 funding, bringing criticism from Democrats.

When the Senate took up the measure, it was as part of the three-bill minibus. The Senate passed the package, 69–30, on November 1.

During the floor debate on the justice section, the Senate:

- Adopted, 99–0, an amendment by John Cornyn, R-Texas, to generally bar the use of funds in the bill for Fast and Furious and similar "gun walking" programs.
- Rejected, 47–52, an amendment by Kelly Ayotte, R-N.H., to bar the use of Justice Department funds for civilian trials of suspects belonging to al Qaeda or its affiliates who had participated in planning attacks on the United States.
- By packaging the minibus in a conference report on the fiscal 2012 Agriculture spending bill (HR 2112), appropriators avoided amendments on the House or Senate floors. The measure won bipartisan support in both chambers. The House adopted the conference report (H Rept 112-284), 298–121, on November 17, with the support of 165 Democrats and 133 Republicans. The Senate easily cleared the bill, 70–30, later the same day.

Concealed Handguns

The House in 2011 passed a bill to allow permit holders to carry concealed handguns across state lines. The Senate did not take it up.

The bill (HR 822), which passed 272–154 on November 16, would allow those with a state permit to carry a concealed handgun into any state that allowed its residents to carry a concealed weapon, as long as the permit holder was not prohibited by federal law from having a firearm. In the United States, only Illinois and the District of Columbia did not provide concealed-carry permits. Forty-three Democrats voted for the bill.

Bill supporters say it would prevent concealed-carry permit holders from having to give up their rights when crossing state lines. The bill's sponsor, Rep. Cliff Stearns, R-Fla., said the existing system lacked uniformity, making it harder for permit holders to know if they are following the law. "Only the Congress can remedy this interstate muddle," Stearns said.

The legislation would require those carrying concealed handguns into a state to comply with that state's concealed-carry laws, except for regulations that determined who was eligible to have a firearm in the first place. Opponents took issue with that exception, arguing that it would encourage individuals to get permits from states with the most permissive laws and carry the handguns into states with stricter requirements. They noted varying state standards on such issues as background checks, training, age restrictions, and misdemeanor convictions. "Because any permit would suffice," said Rep. Jerrold Nadler, D-N.Y., "this bill would create a race to the bottom."

During debate, the House rejected Democratic efforts to subject those who carried a concealed handgun into another state to certain limits, including a proposal from Hank Johnson of Georgia that would have required out-of-state permit holders to meet firearm safety training standards set by the state they are entering. It was rejected, 144–281.

Also rejected, 147–274, was an amendment from Carolyn McCarthy, D-N.Y., to allow out-of-state individuals to carry a concealed handgun only into states that have enacted laws to allow such an act. "I don't want [eligibility] decisions imposed on the communities that I represent, and neither should anybody else," said McCarthy, who first ran for Congress seeking more gun control after a gunman killed her husband in 1993 on a commuter train.

The House Judiciary Committee approved the measure (H Rept 112-277) on October 25 by a vote of 19–11.

Appellate Judgeships

Amid considerable partisan tensions, Republicans in the 112th Congress filibustered the nominations of two appellate judicial nominees. The actions blocked the nominations of Goodwin Liu for the Ninth U.S. Circuit Court of Appeals and Caitlin J. Halligan for the U.S. Court of Appeals for the District of Columbia Circuit.

GOODWIN LIU

In the first successful filibuster against a judicial nominee since 2005, Senate Republicans in 2011 blocked the nomination of Liu to serve on a federal appeals court. The Senate on May 19 rejected, 52–43, a cloture motion on the nomination, falling short of the sixty votes needed.

Lisa Murkowski of Alaska was the only Republican to vote to limit debate; Ben Nelson of Nebraska was the only Democrat to break ranks with his party in opposition. Republican Orrin G. Hatch of Utah, a former chair of the Senate Judiciary Committee, voted present.

President Barack Obama in 2010 tapped Liu, a professor at the University of California at Berkeley, for a seat on the U.S. Circuit Court of Appeals for the Ninth Circuit. The San Francisco–based court heard federal appeals from nine western states and U.S. territories in the Pacific.

Majority Leader Harry Reid of Nevada and other supporters of Liu said that they found him within the judicial mainstream. They recalled the debate over the "nuclear option" to eliminate filibusters of judicial nominees that had been discussed in 2005, when Republicans controlled the Senate and the White House.

Judiciary Chair Patrick J. Leahy, D-Vt., said the vote marked the sixth time since Obama took office that Democrats had to seek cloture to overcome a Republican filibuster on a judicial nominee. "This is a far cry from when Republican senators were insisting just a few years ago that such filibusters of judicial nominees were unconstitutional," Leahy said.

Several Republican members of the 2005 "Gang of 14" that agreed to filibuster circuit court nominees only in exceptional cases voted against ending the debate on Liu. Gang of 14 member Lindsey Graham of South Carolina expressed particular concern about Liu's comments about current Associate Justice Samuel A. Alito Jr. "Goodwin Liu should run for elected office, not serve as a judge. Ideologues have their place, just not on the bench," said Graham. "This episode—along with his out-of-the-mainstream writings—requires me to take the extraordinary step of voting no on cloture."

In opposing the nomination, Jeff Sessions, R-Ala., seized on writings by Liu that seemed to indicate a view of the Constitution as an evolving document, including with respect to social welfare programs.

The Judiciary Committee had twice backed Liu in 2010. Without Senate floor consideration, the nomination was returned to the White House during the August 2010 recess and again at the end of the 111th Congress. The committee again approved the nomination in April on a 10–8 vote.

CAITLIN J. HALLIGAN

Republicans at the end of 2011 stopped a second appellate nominee. On December 6, the nomination of Halligan for the U.S. Court of Appeals for the District of Columbia Circuit, the most prominent federal appellate court, was blocked when a cloture motion on the nomination fell short on a **key vote of 54–45 (R 1–45; D 51–0; I 2–0)**. Sixty votes were required. Sen. Lisa Murkowski of Alaska was the only Republican to vote in favor of proceeding to a vote on the nomination. *(2011 key votes, p. 785)*

Reid said in a written statement, "I am concerned that today the Senate is backing away from the 2005 agreement that the minority would only block judicial nominees in extraordinary circumstances. Since Ms. Halligan's nomination clearly does not meet that standard, Republicans today lowered the bar for filibustering judicial nominees."

He accused GOP senators of putting "political gamesmanship" before qualifications.

But some Republicans argued that Halligan's record was the problem. "Halligan has an activist record," said the Judiciary Committee's ranking Republican, Charles E. Grassley of Iowa.

Democrats said the vote imperiled the 2005 agreement made by the "Gang of 14." This move, said Charles E. Schumer, D-N.Y., "declares the Gang of 14 agreement null and void" and risks "throwing the Senate into chaos" on judicial nominees. *(Gang of 14 agreement, Congress and the Nation Vol. XII, p. 820)*

Schumer and Leahy cited a statement from Gang of 14 member Lindsey Graham, a South Carolina Republican, that described extraordinary circumstances as those involving character or ethical concerns, not a judge's ideology. The Democrats argued that no extraordinary circumstances existed with respect to Halligan. By the 2005 standards, "this filibuster should be ended," Leahy said.

The White House also weighed in. "Today's vote dramatically lowers the bar used to justify a filibuster, which had required 'extraordinary circumstances,'" Obama said in a written statement. "The only extraordinary things about Ms. Halligan are her qualifications and her intellect."

GOP senators, however, contended that Halligan, who served as the solicitor general for New York, had taken an activist approach in her career.

Minority Leader Mitch McConnell, a Kentucky Republican, cited in particular a position she espoused on Second Amendment rights. She backed a legal argument that firearms manufacturers should be held liable for gun crimes committed by third parties.

McConnell also took issue with briefs that Halligan filed that argued that the president does not have the legal authority to detain, as enemy combatants, individuals associated with al Qaeda; that antiabortion protesters had engaged in extortion under federal law; and that the National Labor Relations Board should have the legal authority to grant back pay to illegal immigrants.

But Democrats refuted the accusation of judicial activism, contending that Halligan was not voicing her own views but simply representing clients. Schumer accused the GOP of advancing "gotcha arguments" that pulled snippets from her work on behalf of clients.

The Judiciary panel approved Halligan's nomination on a party-line vote in March.

The GOP filibuster of Halligan contributed to concerns by the end of the 112th Congress about the U.S. Circuit Court of Appeals for the District of Columbia. No new judges had been appointed since 2006. With three of the eleven seats vacant on a federal appeals court in Washington, it was becoming more difficult to contest the court's rulings. It took a majority of judges to agree to a full en banc review of a case, lengthening the odds for those challenging decisions.

The D.C. court was widely considered the most powerful of the thirteen circuit courts because it frequently hears challenges to rules made by executive branch agencies. With Congress entangled by legislative gridlock, rulemaking had taken on increasing importance, as had the legal battle over those rules.

Detention of Illegal Immigrants

Over the objections of Democrats complaining about federal overreach, a House panel in 2011 advanced a GOP measure aimed at blocking the release of dangerous immigrants into U.S. communities.

The bill (HR 1932—H Rept 112-255), approved by the Judiciary Committee in a 17–14 party-line vote on October 18, would allow the Department of Homeland Security to indefinitely detain certain immigrants awaiting deportation, including aggravated felons and violent criminals. Under the measure, detentions would be subject to review every six months.

The legislation would apply to any immigrant whose release into the community would threaten public safety and who was either an aggravated felon or a violent criminal likely to engage in future acts of violence. It also applied to immigrants who had highly contagious diseases that pose a threat to public safety, as well as to those whose release would threaten national security or have serious adverse foreign policy consequences.

The bill's supporters said it aimed to prevent the release of detained immigrants who were subject to deportation orders but who had not yet been removed from the United States because of an unwillingness by their home countries to facilitate their return. They argued that the measure targeted only dangerous individuals.

"Thousands of criminal immigrants ordered removed have been released," said Judiciary Chair Lamar Smith, R-Texas, the bill's sponsor. "This includes an immigrant who was implicated in a mob-related multiple homicide [and] an immigrant who shot a New York state trooper after being released."

But Democrats blasted the bill, calling it an attempt by Republicans to expand the government's ability to detain immigrants in the name of protecting American public safety. "Those are terrible cases, and the holes that they exposed in our system should be addressed," said Zoe Lofgren, D-Calif. "But this bill reaches far beyond dealing with these dangerous individuals."

Panel Democrats targeted a provision that would allow the indefinite detention throughout any removal proceedings of immigrants first arriving in the United States. Under the language, immigrants who are not eligible for admission into the country could remain in custody for as long as it took for a final order of removal to be issued.

Smith said the language was aimed at countering cases of asylum fraud, noting the difficulty of trying to remove immigrants if they are released before a final decision was made. But Democrats argued that the provision could unfairly affect asylum seekers and some returning permanent residents who pose no danger to public safety, subjecting them to lengthy detention without proper review of their cases.

Treatment of Suspected Terrorists

The House in 2011 adopted an amendment to a defense authorization bill that would require all foreign terrorist suspects subject to trial for attacking the United States, U.S. government, or personnel to be tried only by a military commission.

With a veto threat already looming over the House Armed Services Committee's version of the fiscal 2012 defense authorization bill (HR 1540), Republicans defied the White House and pushed through a floor amendment that would have strengthened terrorism-related language that was opposed publicly by the Obama administration. The language was adopted on May 26, 2011, on a **key vote of 246–173 (R 228–7; D 18–166).** *(2011 key votes, p. 785; treatment of Guantanamo prisoners, p. 314)*

The amendment, sponsored by Rep. Vern Buchanan, R-Fla., ultimately was stripped out of the bill during House-Senate conference negotiations in December.

But the nearly unanimous GOP support for the language—only seven Republicans cast "no" votes—underscored a strong political desire within the party to revisit the rules governing the prosecution of detainees a decade after the September 11 terrorist attacks.

Opponents charged that the floor amendment, which would have required the United States to consider all foreign terrorists to be enemy combatants and to prosecute them in military tribunals rather than civilian courts without any exceptions, was unconstitutional and would have dramatically limited the president's flexibility in handling detainees.

But supporters maintained that prosecuting a terrorism suspect in a military tribunal makes it easier to get a conviction, and also protects sensitive, classified information. Foreign terrorists, they said, should simply not be granted the same constitutional protections as U.S. citizens.

The Buchanan amendment complemented other detainee provisions in the committee-approved bill, including language that updated the 2001 law that authorized the war on terrorism (PL 107-40).

House Democrats and a small number of Republicans argued that the provision, which also drew a veto threat, would give the president nearly open-ended authority to wage war. Justin Amash, a Michigan Republican, led an effort to strip the language from the bill, but an amendment on the House floor that would have removed the provision was rejected, 187–234. However, like the Buchanan amendment, the language did not survive in the final conference report.

Prison Deaths

The House in 2011 passed legislation to reauthorize an expired law requiring reports on the details surrounding prisoner and law enforcement custody deaths. The bill (HR 2189) won passage on September 20, 398–18, under suspension of the rules, which requires two-thirds majority approval. But the measure (H Rept 112-198), after winning Senate Judiciary Committee approval by voice vote on November 17, did not advance further.

Enacted in 2000, the expired law (PL 106-297) directed the Justice Department to collect data on deaths that occurred while detainees were under arrest, incarcerated, or detained by law enforcement officials. *(Congress and the Nation Vol. X, p. 653)*

Democrat Robert C. Scott of Virginia, who had introduced reauthorization every Congress since the provision expired in 2006, said the reporting mandate would help policy makers "make informed judgments about the appropriate treatment of prisoners and develop ways to lower the prisoner death rate."

The Senate Judiciary Committee advanced similar legislation in the 110th Congress, but there was no floor consideration. In the 111th Congress, the panel never considered the House-passed measure.

Under the program, states that receive federal law enforcement assistance would be required to file quarterly reports to the U.S. attorney general detailing each deceased prisoner's name, gender, race, ethnicity, and age; the date, time, and location of death; the law enforcement agency involved; and a description of what happened.

According to the Justice Department's Bureau of Justice Statistics, almost 22,000 inmates died between 2001 and 2007 in state prisons. More than 80 percent of those deaths were caused by illnesses, and the number of illness-related deaths increased almost every year.

Abortion

A hotly debated measure that would criminalize the performance of abortions on the basis of the sex of the fetus received majority support in a House vote in 2012 but was defeated because a supermajority was required for passage.

The House on May 31 voted 246–168 to reject an effort to pass the bill (HR 3541) under suspension of the rules, an expedited procedure requiring a two-thirds majority. The legislation would impose criminal penalties for performing an abortion with the knowledge that it is being sought because of the sex of the fetus. Twenty Democrats voted for the bill, and seven Republicans opposed it.

Republican Trent Franks of Arizona, who sponsored the bill, said the decision of GOP leaders to bring up the measure under suspension of the rules "was something that we all agreed on." His home state in 2011 became the first in the nation to outlaw abortions based on the race or sex of the fetus. "This evil practice has now allowed thousands of little girls in America and millions of little girls across the world to be brutally dismembered.... simply because they were little girls, instead of little boys," Franks said during floor debate.

His bill would impose fines or a maximum five-year prison sentence, or both, on those who performed such abortions and those who transported women into the United States or across state lines, or who solicited or accepted payments, for such a procedure.

Along with most Democrats, the Obama administration expressed opposition to the measure. "The administration opposes gender discrimination in all forms, but the end result of this legislation would be to subject doctors to criminal prosecution if they fail to determine the motivations behind a very personal and private decision," Jamie Smith, White House deputy press secretary, said in a statement.

The Judiciary Committee on February 16 approved a broader version of the measure (H Rept 112-496) on a party-line vote, 20–13. Democratic critics called the bill a GOP attempt to chip away at women's reproductive rights. They argued that it would force doctors to become "mind readers" who must police their patients. The committee bill also contained provisions outlawing abortion based on the race of the unborn child. Opponents argued that such language did nothing to further civil rights and noted that higher rates of abortion among some communities of color were evidence not of racism but of the fact that such communities had been "historically underserved in the types of services that prevent unwanted pregnancies." The language concerning "race-selection abortion" was removed in an unsuccessful effort to gain support from Democrats.

Republican supporters of the measure pointed to countries such as India or China, where cultural and economic factors have led to numerous instances of abortion or abandonment when it was learned that a fetus is female. They argued that countries such as India had imposed bans to abate the rising practice of sex-based abortions, which might drive women to come to the United States to have the procedure performed.

"This issue of life is a divisive one in politics," said Florida Republican Sandy Adams. "But I think all Americans can agree that aborting babies because they are the wrong sex is just plain wrong. Let's put a stop to this egregious practice."

Democrat Jerrold Nadler of New York said such restrictions were not the solution to the problem, saying that Republicans had not supported legislation that would prevent unintended pregnancies in the first place.

Property Rights

The House in 2012 easily passed legislation to try to restore private property rights that bill supporters said were wrongly stripped away by a 2005 Supreme Court decision. But the Senate did not take up the measure.

The bill (HR 1433), which passed by voice vote February 28, would block states and localities receiving federal economic development funds from taking property for private economic development. Governments exercising such eminent domain powers would be prohibited from receiving the federal assistance for two years after a violation. The bill would allow the governments to reclaim their eligibility for the funds if they returned, replaced, or repaired wrongfully taken property.

In its ruling in *Kelo v. City of New London* (545 U.S. 469), the high Court held that a Connecticut city could exercise its power of eminent domain to force several homeowners to vacate their properties to make way for planned commercial development.

Bill sponsor F. James Sensenbrenner Jr., R-Wis., said the two-year funding ban would serve as "a strong disincentive" to states and localities to abuse eminent domain authority. Sensenbrenner was a senior member of the Judiciary Committee, which approved the bill (H Rept 112-401), 23–5, on January 24.

Sensenbrenner acknowledged that although several states had enacted varying measures to limit or bar the use of eminent domain, his bill would give all states the means to protect their private property from "exceedingly unsubstantiated claims of need."

Rep. John Conyers Jr., D-Mich., who opposed the bill, said Congress should leave the issue to the states on whether to exercise the power of eminent domain.

"Congress should not now come charging in after seven years of work and presume to sit as a national zoning board, relegating to our national government the right to decide which states have gotten the balance right and deciding which projects are or are not appropriate," Conyers said.

Attorneys' Fees

A House committee in 2011 endorsed a Republican bill to narrow the eligibility of individuals and organizations to receive payment for legal fees if they successfully sued the government. The Judiciary Committee approved the bill (HR 1996) in a 19–14 party-line vote November 17.

Under current law (PL 96-481), individuals whose net worth was $2 million or less and organizations worth $7 million or less could recover attorneys' fees of up to $125 per hour if they successfully sued the federal government.

Although the act was designed "to help small businesses and ordinary American taxpayers defend their rights in litigation against the federal government," said Chair Lamar Smith, R-Texas, its intended purposes was in doubt. Smith said attorneys' fees are being paid to certain frequent litigants, particularly 501(c)(3) organizations that also were exempt from the $7 million net worth limitation, for what he called ideologically driven lawsuits. "American taxpayers should not be forced to pay attorneys' fees and costs in some of these circumstances," Smith said.

Supporters of the measure argued that current law allowed well-financed environmental groups to push their political agendas at taxpayer expense.

The bill specified that litigants would need to have been directly affected because of medical costs, property damage, benefit denial, or lack of payment. It also removed an exemption currently in place for 501(c)(3) groups from a provision that disqualifies organizations worth more than $7 million. Under the bill, the same $7 million net-worth limitation that applied to other organizations would apply to 501(c)(3) groups.

The panel's top Democrat, John Conyers Jr. of Michigan, said the bill would block those trying to enforce food and highway safety as well as pollution protection issues from recovering attorneys' fees. Doing so would "harm all Americans and could serve as a de facto bar to the courthouse door for low-income citizens and all other parties that do not have access to free legal counsel," Conyers said.

Trade Secrets

The House on January 1, 2013, cleared a bill to increase the maximum monetary penalties for the theft of trade secrets. Under the bill (HR 6029—PL 112-269), which cleared by voice vote, those prosecuted for economic espionage would face fines of up to $5 million, as opposed to the existing $500,000 maximum.

The fines for organizations convicted of such activity were set at a maximum of $10 million, or three times the value of stolen information, whichever was greater. The Senate amended the bill (HR 6029) on December 19, 2012, to remove a provision that would have increased the possible prison term from fifteen to twenty years. The Senate then passed the measure by voice vote.

According to an October 2011 report from the Office of the National Counterintelligence Executive, foreign industrial espionage and the collection of economic data constituted a significant and growing threat to the prosperity and security of the United States. The report noted that China and Russia in particular were aggressive collectors of U.S. economic information and technology. These warnings were repeated in January 2012 by the director of national intelligence, who also said the United States needed to counter espionage by China and Russia.

Rep. Lamar Smith, R-Texas, the bill's sponsor, said Congress should "provide appropriate punishment" for criminals who targeted U.S. economic and security interests on behalf of foreign interests.

Holocaust Survivors

The House Foreign Affairs Committee in 2012 approved a bill to allow Holocaust survivors and their heirs to pursue claims against European insurance companies in U.S. courts. Enactment would have effectively reversed a 2003 Supreme Court decision.

The bill (HR 890), approved by voice vote on March 7, did not advance further.

The measure would affirm a right for Holocaust survivors and their beneficiaries to file civil suits in U.S. district courts to recover insurance policy proceeds that were purchased in Nazi Germany and other areas controlled by that regime during the World War II era.

Chair Ileana Ros-Lehtinen, R-Fla., called the bill a "long-overdue effort to see that justice is done." The measure was bipartisan, although critics said it infringed on separation of powers between the executive and legislative branches.

The International Commission on Holocaust Era Insurance Claims had identified policyholders and administered payment of Holocaust-era insurance benefits never honored by European companies after World War II. The commission, which closed in March 2007, had been created through an international collaboration among U.S. insurance regulators, Israel, Jewish organizations, and six European insurers in the 1990s.

The insurance commission processed 90,000 claims, awarding more than $300 million to more than 48,000 survivors and families.

After the commission closed, additional claimants sought reparations. But the executive branch encouraged the courts to dismiss such claims. The government said additional suits could damage cooperation between U.S. and European organizations regarding Holocaust victims in the future, since the insurance companies likely volunteered to participate in the insurance commission with the understanding that such suits would end at a defined point.

To help victims seeking claims, some states imposed disclosure requirements on Holocaust-era policies issued by insurance companies. But, siding with the executive branch, the Supreme Court, in *American Insurance Association v. Garamendi* (539 U.S. 396), barred them in 2003. The state laws infringed on executive foreign policy, the Court said.

The bill would have effectively overturned the Court's decision by prohibiting executive agreements reached by the federal government and such insurers from preempting state laws that imposed disclosure requirements on the companies.

Drug Traffickers

The Senate in 2012 cleared legislation to give more tools to federal law enforcement agencies to combat drug traffickers who used tunnels under the U.S.-Mexico border. The measure (HR 4119—PL 112-127) cleared by voice vote May 17 after passing the House one day earlier by a vote of 416–4.

The legislation would expand a 2006 law (PL 109-295) that criminalized the construction or financing of unauthorized cross-border tunnels used to smuggle drugs, weapons, illegal immigrants, or terrorists. It would subject tunnel smugglers and financiers to the same penalties imposed on those who construct the tunnels.

During House floor debate, sponsor Silvestre Reyes, D-Texas, said that while security along the U.S. southwest border had strengthened in recent years, it "has literally pushed drug cartels and transnational criminal organizations underground as they try to smuggle illicit drugs and people and other types of contraband."

"These are sophisticated, well-engineered and well-financed projects," Reyes added.

"That's why it is imperative that this legislation be passed." Lamar Smith, R-Texas, agreed, saying that reports of drug-smuggling tunnels had increased significantly in recent years. He called the tunnels an "unfortunate testament to the ingenuity of the Mexican drug cartels."

The bill would provide for criminal forfeiture of property used in tunneling activities and civil asset forfeiture of merchandise brought into the United States through a tunnel. It also would subject border tunnel offenses to money-laundering statutes.

The legislation would allow the Justice Department to seek a court order authorizing the use of surveillance to intercept wire, oral, or electronic communications to aid in the investigation of tunnel-smuggling activities. The president signed the Border Tunnel Prevention Act of 2012 into law on June 5, 2012.

Same-sex Couples

Senate committees in the 112th Congress approved two bills to advance rights of same-sex couples. But the bills were not taken up by the full Senate.

The first bill (S 598), which would have repealed the law that barred federal recognition of same-sex marriage, won approval from the Senate Judiciary Committee on a party-line, 10–8 vote on November 10, 2011. The bill would have stripped language from the 1996 statute (PL 104-199) known as the Defense of Marriage Act (DOMA) that directed the federal government to recognize marriages only between a man and a woman.

Sponsored by California Democrat Dianne Feinstein, the legislation would have allowed state-recognized same-sex marriages to be accepted for purposes of federal law as well.

Supporters of the repeal said DOMA denied same-sex couples equal protection under the law and blocked their access to more than 1,000 federal rights and benefits, such as Social Security spousal benefits, family-medical-leave protections, and certain tax deductions.

"DOMA is discriminatory and should be stricken in its entirety from federal law," said Feinstein. "This bill does that."

Republicans were quick to point out that a repeal of DOMA was unlikely to be taken up in the full Senate and was essentially a nonstarter in the other chamber. A Democratic repeal bill (HR 1116) had languished in the GOP-led House since its introduction in March by New York Democrat Jerrold Nadler, who attended the Senate markup.

In addition to granting federal recognition of same-sex marriage, the Senate bill would have repealed language that prohibits a state from being required to recognize any public act, record, or judicial proceeding of another state regarding the recognition of such marriages. GOP panel members argued against that change, saying it would force states without same-sex marriage laws to recognize such marriages from other states.

The second bill (S 1910—S Rept 112-257) would have made same-sex partners of federal employees eligible for benefits. It was approved by the Homeland Security and Governmental Affairs Committee by voice vote on May 16, 2012.

The measure would have made government workers in homosexual domestic partnerships eligible for the same health, long-term disability, retirement, and other benefits as those offered to heterosexual married couples.

The committee's vote came just a week after President Barack Obama endorsed same-sex marriage. But Chair Joseph I. Lieberman, I-Conn., the bill's sponsor, said the measure's advancement was not spurred by the president's comments. Lieberman, in fact, opposed legalized same-sex marriage.

Lieberman said extending the benefits to same-sex couples would cost about $70 million a year of the $400 billion the government spends on employee compensation.

The legislation would have subjected gay couples to the same financial disclosure and conflict-of-interest requirements as married couples. It would require them to file an affidavit with the Office of Personnel Management attesting to the legitimacy of the partnership and their intent to remain in that relationship.

Ranking Republican Susan Collins of Maine said the bill would allow the government to attract top talent. She argued that many young people—both gay and straight—cite benefits offered to or withheld from domestic partners as a sign of a good or bad employer. She said the bill would bring the government in line with almost 65 percent of Fortune 500 companies, which offer such benefits.

Although the legislation advanced by voice vote, Republicans Tom Coburn of Oklahoma, Ron Johnson of Wisconsin, and Jerry Moran of Kansas as well as Democrat Mark Pryor of Arkansas opposed it.

Child Pornography

The Senate in 2012 cleared a bill (HR 6063—PL 112-206) designed to combat online child pornography. The Senate cleared the measure by voice vote on November 26 after the House passed it by voice vote on August 1. The president signed the Child Protection Act of 2012 into law on December 7, 2012.

The bill (H Rept 112-638) increased penalties for the possession of child pornography and authorized $300 million for a five-year renewal of a task force program that helped state and local law enforcement agencies respond to cases of sexual exploitation of children online.

Continued expansion of online commerce and greater use of smart phones, digital cameras, and webcams made the production and exchange of child pornography easier. As a result, the possession of child pornography was estimated to be one of the fastest-growing crimes in the United States, according to the House Judiciary Committee.

The bill contained provisions that backers said were designed to safeguard victims and witnesses, including language to allow a federal court to issue a protective order for minor victims and witnesses who were being harassed or intimidated if they were likely to be deterred from testifying.

The bill imposed criminal penalties, including up to five years in prison, for violating the order. Under existing law, violators faced a contempt citation or fine.

In addition, the legislation gave the U.S. Marshals Service the authority to issue administrative subpoenas, which do not require approval by a court, in order to assist in locating sex offenders who fail to register their whereabouts.

Sponsor Lamar Smith, R-Texas, said during floor debate that the bill "ensures that paperwork does not stand in the way of apprehension of dangerous criminals." He added, "Narrow subpoena authority is critical to help take convicted sex offenders off the streets."

But Virginia Democrat Robert C. Scott said the bill would give the Marshals Service too much power. "There is already a comprehensive statutory scheme in place to assist judges and witnesses in proceedings," Scott said.

Highly Skilled Legal Immigrants

The House in 2011 advanced a measure that proponents said would foster economic growth by helping U.S. businesses hire highly skilled legal immigrants. The bipartisan bill (HR 3012), approved 389–15 on November 29, eliminated country-based caps on the number of employment visas issued annually and raised similar limits for immigrants sponsored by a spouse or relative in the United States. The Senate did not take up the measure.

Existing immigration law (PL 101-649) set a limit of 140,000 visas annually for employment-based legal permanent residents and specified that, each year, any given country be held to a numerical limit of 7 percent of total U.S. immigrant admissions. But the system was plagued by large backlogs, with some immigrants waiting decades to get work visas.

According to the nonpartisan National Foundation for American Policy, applicants from India faced a seventy-year wait for an employment-based visa because of restrictions limiting the number of visas issued by country of origin. A Chinese applicant had to wait about twenty years, and those from other countries faced waits of up to five years.

Supporters of the bill said lifting the country-based percentage cap would help ease the gridlock for countries with a large number of highly skilled applicants, such as India and China, by allowing those workers to move closer to the head of the line. The bill would not have increased the total annual admission numbers.

The Judiciary Committee approved the bill (H Rept 112-292) on October 27 by voice vote. Bill sponsor Jason Chaffetz, R-Utah, touted the legislation as "pro-growth, pro-jobs and pro-family." Judiciary Chair Lamar Smith, R-Texas, and Zoe Lofgren of California, the top Democrat on the panel's Immigration Subcommittee, also supported the bill.

"Because of these annual numerical caps on green cards and the fact that some countries have more of the skilled workers that American employers want, natives of these countries must often wait years longer for green cards than natives of other countries," Smith said at the mark-up. "Why should American employers who seek green cards for skilled foreign workers have to wait longer just because the workers are from India or China?"

Low-immigration Regions

Prompted by concerns over the possible falsification of credentials as well as the potential for terrorists to enter the country more easily, a House panel in 2011 approved Republican-sponsored legislation to eliminate a program that distributes visas to would-be immigrants from countries with low rates of immigration to the United States. Democrats said those concerns were overblown.

The Judiciary Committee approved the measure (HR 704—H Rept 112-275) along party lines, 19–11, on July 20. The program, created in 1990, was designed to allow citizens of countries within "low-immigration regions"—usually developed countries—to immigrate to the United States. Under the program, the State Department issues 55,000 such visas annually.

Republicans said the program was inherently flawed because its selected visa holders are chosen at random. "Basing our immigration system on the luck of the draw is not smart immigration policy," said Chair Lamar Smith, R-Texas. Citing testimony given by State Department officials during an April hearing on the issue, Republicans said applicants have been caught lying about their credentials because the program requires them to have a certain level of education or work experience.

Republicans also expressed concern that the program presents terrorists with easy access to the United States. "Each year, diversity visas are issued to individuals from countries listed as state sponsors of terrorism," Smith said.

Democrats said there was no proof that terrorists are more likely to enter the country via the diversity program than via any other immigration programs. "The truth is, this bill just seeks to reduce legal available avenues for people—to keep people from coming to this country," said Zoe Lofgren of California.

Elderly and Disabled Refugees

Federal aid for certain elderly and disabled refugees would have been reinstated under legislation passed by the Senate in 2011. The measure did not advance further.

The bill (S 1721), which passed by voice vote on October 17, would have revived for one year a program that provided Supplemental Security Income to certain refugees who were not eligible to become citizens. The program expired September 30.

Sen. Rand Paul, R-Ky., had placed a procedural hold on the measure, demanding an investigation into the program after two Iraqi refugees were arrested on terrorism charges in Bowling Green, Ky., that year.

New York Democrat Charles E. Schumer sponsored the legislation. He was the chair of the Senate Judiciary Subcommittee on Immigration, Refugees, and Border Security. As part of an agreement with Paul, Schumer was to hold an oversight hearing about refugee issues.

Schumer and Paul also agreed to request investigations from three inspectors general about a refugee program through which the two individuals from Iraq suspected of terrorist connections entered the United States. The terror suspects took up residence in Bowling Green, which prompted Paul's concern.

"Taxpayer-funded benefits to non-citizens is a luxury program afforded to refugees and managed so poorly that some of its beneficiaries have been found to be threats to the United States, as we saw earlier this year in Bowling Green," Paul said.

"This took longer than it should have, but we are glad to reach a bipartisan agreement to extend this assistance to disabled refugees," Schumer said in a statement.

The measure would be offset through a new $30 fee for Diversity Immigrant Visa applicants. That provision threatened to raise procedural questions in the House. In 2010, legislation that included a visa fee as an offset ran into a jurisdictional dispute, as the House turned back the Senate bill for possibly infringing on the House's constitutional obligation to originate revenue measures.

The Supreme Court, 2008–2012

President Barack Obama changed the face of the Supreme Court but not its generally conservative orientation by naming two women with liberal records in public life as justices during his first two years in office. The appointments of Sonia Sotomayor in 2009 and Elena Kagan in 2010 invigorated the Court's liberal wing, but a conservative bloc led by Chief Justice John G. Roberts Jr. continued to hold sway on most issues when Court was closely divided.

Despite the Court's conservative bent, Obama won the most important single case of his first term: a 5–4 decision upholding his health care reform law, the Patient Protection and Affordable Care Act. Roberts joined the four Democratic-appointed liberals in voting to uphold the law in the final decision of the 2011–2012 term. Roberts's four Republican-appointed conservative colleagues delivered a blistering dissent. *(Decision details, box, p. 586; legislative action, p. 421)*

The Sotomayor and Kagan appointments brought the number of female justices to three for the first time in the Court's history. Sotomayor, daughter of Puerto Rican parents, was also the first justice of Hispanic ancestry.

Sotomayor, a former federal appeals court judge, and Kagan, a former U.S. solicitor general and Harvard Law School dean, largely followed their predecessors—David H. Souter and John Paul Stevens, respectively—in voting along liberal lines in their early years on the Court.

The Court continued to have a working conservative majority on many of the most divisive issues as Roberts completed his seventh term. The Court clashed with the Obama administration on some issues, most notably in a decision in 2010 that allowed unlimited independent spending by corporations and labor unions in political campaigns.

Obama criticized the decision a few days later in his State of the Union address, with six of the justices seated just below him in the House chamber. Roberts later suggested that the justices' attendance at the annual address was "problematic," but he and several colleagues attended the sessions in 2011 and 2012.

Sotomayor and Kagan won Senate confirmation in contested votes divided along partisan lines. In their appearances before the Senate Judiciary Committee, Sotomayor and Kagan each promised to rule in cases without any ideological agenda. Democrats endorsed their qualifications, but Republican senators depicted both as likely to become liberal "activist" justices if confirmed. *(Confirmation details, box, p. 585)*

Once on the Court, Sotomayor and Kagan joined two other Democratic appointees—Ruth Bader Ginsburg and Stephen G. Breyer—in taking liberal positions on many issues, including civil litigation, civil rights, and criminal law. Roberts and three other Republican-appointed justices—Antonin Scalia, Clarence Thomas, and Samuel A. Alito Jr.—often sided with business interests in civil litigation cases and with law enforcement in criminal cases.

Justice Anthony M. Kennedy, the moderate conservative nominated by President Ronald Reagan in 1987, often held the balance of power between the conservative and liberal blocs. He joined the conservatives in striking down some campaign finance laws on free-speech grounds, limiting class action suits by workers and consumers, and making it somewhat harder for employers to adopt race-conscious affirmative action policies. But Kennedy sided with the liberal bloc in some 5–4 decisions, most notably

REFERENCES

Discussion of the Supreme Court for the years 1945–1964 may be found in *Congress and the Nation Vol. I*, pp. 1141–1454; for the years 1965–1968, *Congress and the Nation Vol. II*, pp. 335–340; for the years 1969–1972, *Congress and the Nation Vol. III*, pp. 289–327; for the years 1973–1976, *Congress and the Nation Vol. IV*, pp. 619–659; for the years 1977–1980, *Congress and the Nation Vol. V*, pp. 755–791; for the years 1981–1984, *Congress and the Nation Vol. VI*, pp. 711–768; for the years 1985–1988, *Congress and the Nation Vol. VII*, pp. 785–840; for the years 1989–1992, *Congress and the Nation Vol. VIII*, pp. 801–851; for the years 1993–1996, *Congress and the Nation Vol. IX*, pp. 759–799; for the years 1997–2001, *Congress and the Nation Vol. X*, pp. 684–729; for the years 2001–2005, *Congress and the Nation Vol. XI*, pp. 630–680; for the years 2005–2008, *Congress and the Nation Vol. XII*, pp. 727–737.

SUPREME COURT CONFIRMATIONS

President Barack Obama brought new diversity to the Supreme Court by filling vacancies with two women, including the Court's first Latina. But Sonia Sotomayor and Elena Kagan had to survive partisan confirmation battles in the Democratic-controlled Senate before taking their seats.

Sotomayor joined the Court in August 2009 after serving on the federal bench for seventeen years, first on the district court and then for twelve years on the Second U.S. Circuit Court of Appeals. Kagan had been a White House aide and dean of Harvard Law School before Obama appointed her as U.S. solicitor general in 2009. She joined the Court in 2009 as the first justice without previous judicial experience since William H. Rehnquist and Lewis F. Powell Jr. won confirmation in December 1971.

Along with Ruth Bader Ginsburg, Sotomayor and Kagan brought the number of female justices to three for the first time in history. The only other female justice previously was Sandra Day O'Connor, who served from August 1981 until she retired in January 2006. O'Connor and Ginsburg served together for just under twelve and one-half years, from 1993 to 2006.

Sotomayor, a graduate of Princeton University and Yale Law School, succeeded David H. Souter, who retired after completing his nineteenth term on the Court. Souter, who had become a reliable member of the liberal bloc, had long preferred life in his native New Hampshire to Washington.

Born in the Bronx in 1954, Sotomayor worked as an assistant district attorney and an attorney in a commercial litigation firm before President George H. W. Bush appointed her to the federal district court on the recommendation of Sen. Daniel Moynihan, a Democrat, as part of a power-sharing arrangement with the state's Republican senator, Alfonse D'Amato. President Bill Clinton elevated her to the Second Circuit in 1997.

Sotomayor was seen as a leading candidate for Souter's seat as soon as news of the retirement leaked. Obama was also seen as all but certain to name a woman for the seat. He personally interviewed four candidates—all of them women, including the future nominee Kagan—before settling on Sotomayor over Memorial Day weekend.

Democratic senators and liberal groups endorsed Sotomayor, but Senate Republicans and some conservative groups were critical. They focused on, among other issues, a speech in which Sotomayor had suggested "a wise Latina" would reach better decisions in some cases than "a white male." They also criticized her vote as a member of the three-judge panel that rejected a "reverse discrimination" suit by white firefighters against the city of New Haven, Conn. The Supreme Court ruled in favor of the firefighters in late June as Sotomayor's nomination was pending.

Appearing before the Senate Judiciary Committee, Sotomayor described her judicial philosophy as "simple: fidelity to the law" and apologized for the "misunderstanding" created by her "wise Latina" speech. Dividing along partisan lines, the committee voted on July 28 to recommend confirmation, 13–6, with only one Republican (South Carolina's Lindsey Graham) voting in favor. The Senate followed suit on August 6, with nine Republicans joining fifty-seven Democrats and two independents who caucused with Democrats in a **key vote of 68–31 (R 9–31; D 57–0; I 2–0).** She took the oath of office from Roberts two days later. *(2009 key votes, p. 751)*

Kagan was seen as the front-runner for the next seat after Stevens signaled his likely retirement in fall 2009 by hiring only a single law clerk for the next term instead of the full complement of four. As solicitor general, Kagan made her first-ever appellate court argument in September in what proved to be an unsuccessful defense of a major provision of the Bipartisan Campaign Reform Act. Out of five other cases she personally argued during the term, the government won three and lost one; one was dismissed without a ruling.

Born in New York City in 1960, Kagan graduated from Princeton University, earned a master's degree from Oxford University's Worcester College, and went on to Harvard Law School. She clerked for two liberal judges, including Supreme Court justice Thurgood Marshall, before teaching at the University of Chicago Law School and then serving in the Clinton White House. She left the White House for Harvard Law School, where she was named dean in 2003.

As dean, Kagan was credited with bridging divisions between liberal and conservative faculty members. She also supported a decision to limit military recruiters on campus because of the discriminatory "don't ask, don't tell" policy on gays and lesbians.

Stevens announced his intention to retire in April 2010. Obama again personally interviewed four candidates, including a female judge passed over in 2009 and two male judges, before deciding on Kagan in early May. In announcing the selection, Obama praised Kagan's "fair-mindedness and skill as a consensus-builder."

Appearing before the Senate Judiciary Committee on June 28, 2010, Kagan promised if confirmed to consider cases "impartially" and "modestly." Republican senators criticized her actions on the military recruiting issue as well as positions she took on abortion rights in the White House. They also cited a memo she wrote to Marshall saying she was "not sympathetic" to recognizing individual gun rights under the Second Amendment. Kagan noted that she wrote the memo twenty years before the Court recognized an individual right to possession of firearms in 2008.

The committee recommended Kagan's confirmation on July 20 by the same 13–6 vote as in Sotomayor's nomination, with Graham again the only senator to cross party lines. The Senate on a **key vote of 63–37 (R 5–36; D 56–1; I 2–0)** on August 5, 2010, confirmed Kagan with five Republicans voting for her and one Democrat voting no. She took the oath of office from Roberts two days later. *(2010 key votes, p. 767)* in a pair of rulings that limited criminal sentences for juvenile offenders and in a decision that required California to reduce the inmate population in the state's overcrowded prisons.

The Court continued to disappoint many people in the legal and academic communities with an historically low number of signed decisions. The Court issued sixty-four signed decisions in argued cases in the 2011–2012 term, the lowest number since the early 1950s.

In his confirmation hearing in September 2005, Roberts said he thought the Court could be deciding more cases. But the number fell to a then-record low of sixty-nine cases in Roberts's first term (2005–2006). The number reached a peak for the Roberts era of seventy-five cases in the 2010–2011 term.

Overall, the Court issued 277 signed decisions during the four terms. An unofficial compilation counted 110 unanimous decisions (40 percent) and 54 rulings decided by 5–4 votes (20 percent).

With the departure of Stevens and Souter, the Court had no Protestant justices for the first time in history. Six of the justices were Catholic: Roberts, Scalia, Kennedy, Thomas, Alito, and Sotomayor; three were Jewish: Ginsburg, Breyer, and Kagan.

ELECTION LAW

The Roberts Court's conservative majority stepped up its critical scrutiny of campaign finance laws by invalidating a major provision of a law restricting independent spending by corporations and labor unions in political campaigns. The broadly written 5–4 decision in *Citizens United v. Federal Election Commission* (2010), which overturned two Supreme Court precedents, cheered Republicans and conservative groups but produced a sharp dissent from liberal justices and strong criticism from Obama and other Democratic officials and groups.

In a second challenge to a major election-related law, the Court considered but backed away from striking down a central provision of the federal Voting Rights Act of 1965. The ruling in *Northwest Austin Municipal Utility District No. 1 v. Holder* (2009) questioned but left on the books the act's provision—section 5—that requires some

SUPREME COURT UPHOLDS HEALTH CARE LEGISLATION

President Barack Obama won a hard-fought political battle in Congress to enact his signature health care reform and then prevailed in another tense legal battle at the Supreme Court to keep the law mostly intact. *(Congressional action on health care, p. 421)*

Chief Justice John G. Roberts Jr. disappointed conservatives on and off the Court by casting the decisive vote to uphold the major provisions of the Patient Protection and Affordable Care Act. Roberts dramatically announced the Court's decision in the case, *National Federation of Independent Business v. Sebelius* (567 U.S. ___, 2012), on June 28, the final day of the 2011–2012 term, in an opinion that no other justice joined in toto.

Roberts joined with the four liberal justices—Ruth Bader Ginsburg, Stephen G. Breyer, and Obama's two appointees, Sonia Sotomayor and Elena Kagan—in upholding the act's central provision, which required virtually all Americans to have health insurance or pay a penalty. Roberts found the so-called individual mandate constitutional as an exercise of Congress's taxing power, but he rejected the Obama administration's principal argument supporting the mandate under Congress's power to regulate interstate commerce.

On a second issue, Roberts upheld the law's expanded eligibility for the joint federal-state Medicaid program but weakened the provision by reducing the potential penalty for states that refused to go along with the change. The vote to trim the provision was 7–2 with Breyer and Kagan joining Roberts and the four conservative justices: Antonin Scalia, Anthony M. Kennedy, Clarence Thomas, and Samuel A. Alito Jr.

The four conservatives filed a jointly authored opinion, announced by Kennedy, that said they would have ruled both the mandate and the Medicaid expansion unconstitutional and invalidated the law in its entirety. On the opposite side, Ginsburg wrote for the four liberals in defending the mandate under the Constitution's Commerce Clause; she and Sotomayor also said they would have upheld the Medicaid expansion as written, with states facing a possible loss of all Medicaid funds if they rejected the expanded coverage.

President Obama hailed the ruling as "a victory for people all over the country," but Republicans—including the then presumptive GOP nominee Mitt Romney—promptly stepped up calls to repeal the law. Obama's reelection in November took talk of repeal off the table.

The legal challenges began on the day Obama signed the bill into law, March 23, 2010, in a suit filed by the state of Florida and eventually joined by twenty-five other states. The National Federation of Independent Business (NFIB), an organization representing small and midsized businesses, filed a parallel suit two months later. Dozens of other suits were filed in federal courts around the country.

Ruling in the consolidated cases, U.S. District Court Judge Roger Vinson in Pensacola found the mandate exceeded Congress's power under either the Commerce Clause or the Necessary and Proper Clause. He went on to invalidate the entire law on the ground that the mandate could not be separated from the other provisions in the 2,700-page act. Vinson said, however, that the Medicaid expansion would states and localities with a history of racial discrimination in voting to get federal permission for any changes in election law or procedures.

On campaign finance, Roberts and Alito had provided decisive votes in their first years on the Court in two important cases for narrowing or striking down provisions of the Bipartisan Campaign Reform Act (BCRA), the 2003 law also known as the McCain-Feingold Act after its principal Senate sponsors. In its first decision, *Federal Election Commission v. Wisconsin Right to Life* (546 U.S. 410) in 2007, the Court significantly narrowed the scope of a BCRA provision limiting corporate or union spending on so-called "electioneering communications"—election-time broadcast advertising on political issues. In its second ruling, *Davis v. Federal Election Commission* (554 U.S. 724) in 2008, the Court struck down a provision easing contribution limits for candidates opposed by high-spending, self-financing opponents.

The BCRA provision on electioneering communications—section 203—prohibited labor unions and corporations, including incorporated nonprofit advocacy groups, from using their funds to pay for issue-related broadcast advertising shortly before a federal primary or general election. Corporations or unions were free, however, to form separate political action committees (PACs) to pay for such ads.

The law came under a new challenge in late 2007 in a suit by the conservative group Citizens United seeking permission from the Federal Election Commission (FEC) to distribute a documentary critical of Democratic presidential hopeful Hillary Clinton through video-on-demand services. Rejecting the challenge, a three-judge federal district court agreed with the FEC that the documentary fell within the ban because it amounted to "express advocacy" against Clinton's candidacy.

The Supreme Court agreed to hear Citizens United's appeal. In arguments in March 2009, Roberts and other conservative justices voiced strong doubts about the constitutionality of applying the law to the documentary. In a surprise move, however, the Court three months later asked for a second round of arguments. The order specifically directed lawyers to address the validity of two earlier

---

have been within Congress's power if not tied to the provision he ruled unconstitutional.

On appeal, the Eleventh U.S. Circuit Court of Appeals affirmed Vinson's ruling on the mandate, 2–1, but upheld the Medicaid provision and the rest of the law. Two other appeals courts, the Sixth and D.C. Circuits, upheld the act; the Fourth Circuit dismissed a legal challenge on the ground that it was barred by the Anti-Injunction Act, which generally bars lawsuits to block collection of federal taxes.

The Supreme Court agreed in November 2011 to hear appeals filed by all sides in the Florida litigation and scheduled an extraordinary six hours of arguments on March 26–28, 2012. Questions from the bench showed the justices sharply divided along conservative-liberal lines. Over the next three months, Court watchers and others came to expect a ruling to strike down the individual mandate and perhaps the entire law.

Roberts's delivery of the decision misled those in the courtroom and reporters who began filing stories within minutes after copies were distributed in the Court's Public Information Office. The individual mandate to purchase health insurance went beyond Congress's power under the Commerce Clause to regulate commerce, Roberts said. "Accepting the Government's theory would give Congress the same license to regulate what we do not do," he wrote. Without a "predicate," the mandate also went beyond the Necessary and Proper Clause, he wrote. After reading this far in the syllabus of the decision, two national news networks reported that the act had been struck down.

Continuing his opinion, however, Roberts said the mandate could be viewed as a tax penalty and upheld under Congress's taxing power. The provision, he said, "makes going without insurance just another thing the Government taxes, like buying gasoline or earning income." The four liberal justices joined this part of Roberts's opinion.

On the issue of the Medicaid expansion, Roberts acknowledged Congress's power to attach "appropriate conditions" to federal spending programs. But he said the threat to cut off all existing funds for states that refused to go along was unconstitutionally coercive. Severing that portion, however, did not affect the rest of the law, Roberts said. Breyer and Kagan joined this part of his opinion.

In their dissent, the conservative justices rejected the individual mandate under either Congress's commerce or taxing power. Roberts's "strained judicial interpretation" of the mandate as a tax penalty, they wrote, amounted to "judicial overreaching." On Medicaid, they stressed that seven justices found the provision as written coercive but rejected Roberts's solution to "rewrite" the provision.

In her opinion, Ginsburg said she would have upheld the individual mandate under the Commerce Clause and criticized Roberts's "crabbed reading" of the commerce power. On Medicaid, Ginsburg argued that Congress had always required states to comply with prescribed conditions in order to receive funds. But given Roberts's disposition of the issue, Ginsburg agreed the law could be upheld if the potential penalty for states was limited to loss of new funds.

rulings: *McConnell v. Federal Election Commission* (2003), which had upheld the BCRA provision; and *Austin v. Michigan Chamber of Commerce* (1990), which had upheld a state ban on independent campaign spending by corporations.

The Court's ruling, issued in January 2010 at the start of the election year, held the BCRA provision unconstitutional and explicitly overruled the two earlier decisions permitting bans on corporate political spending. "Government may not suppress political speech on the basis of the speaker's corporate identity," Kennedy wrote for the majority. "No sufficient governmental interest justifies limits on the political speech of nonprofit or for-profit corporations."

In an impassioned dissent joined by other liberals, Stevens criticized the majority for ruling more broadly than necessary to decide the case. He also argued that the majority had disregarded the dangers of "corporate domination of the airwaves" before an election. "While American democracy is imperfect," Stevens wrote, "few outside the majority of this Court would have thought its flaws included a dearth of corporate money in politics."

In a concurring opinion, Roberts defended the decision to issue a broad instead of narrow ruling. In his book *The Oath* (2012), author and legal journalist Jeffrey Toobin reported that Roberts had initially written a narrow decision in favor of *Citizens United*, but that Kennedy had successfully argued for a broader ruling.

On a secondary issue, the ruling rejected, on an 8–1 vote, *Citizens United*'s challenge to provisions requiring any entity that engages in "electioneering communications" to disclose donors who gave more than $1,000 and to include disclaimers specifying the individuals or groups responsible for the advertising. Thomas was the lone dissenter on the issue.

Republicans, including Senate GOP leader Michael McConnell, strongly praised the ruling as a vindication of First Amendment rights. McConnell had been the lead plaintiff in the earlier unsuccessful challenge to the law. Obama criticized the decision as inviting "a new stampede of special interest money." In his State of the Union address only five days later, Obama said the decision could allow unlimited spending by foreign corporations in U.S. campaigns. Alito could be seen mouthing the words, "Not true," in response. In fact, the ruling did not address provisions barring campaign spending by foreign corporations.

Two years after the decision, the Court made clear that the ruling applied to state as well as federal laws by overturning a Montana Supreme Court decision upholding a ban on corporate spending in state campaigns. The unsigned 5–4 decision in *American Tradition Partnership v. Bullock* (567 U. S. ___, 2012) said there was "no serious doubt" that the earlier ruling applied to the Montana law. The dissenters called for reconsidering the issue.

In another important campaign finance ruling, the Court rejected an Arizona law aimed at helping publicly financed candidates compete against higher spending, privately financed opponents. The 5–4 ruling in *Arizona Free Enterprise Club's Freedom Club PAC v. Bennett* (564 U.S. ___, 2012) struck down an Arizona law that gave publicly financed candidates as much as double the regular subsidy to help match higher spending by a privately financed candidate. Roberts said the scheme "substantially burdens" the free speech rights of privately financed candidates. Kagan led three other liberals in dissent.

The Court turned aside a First Amendment claim in a different context by upholding state laws requiring the disclosure of signers of referendum or initiative petitions. The 8–1 ruling in *Doe v. Reed* (561 U.S. ___, 2010) rejected a plea by organizers of a referendum in Washington to prevent application of the state's freedom of information law to petitions submitted to qualify the measure for the ballot. For the majority, Roberts said the law was "substantially related to the important interest of preserving the integrity of the electoral process," but he left the door open for signers to block disclosure if they could show a reasonable fear of harassment. In a lone dissent, Thomas said the state had "a less restrictive means" to protect the integrity of the process.

The Court took up a challenge to the Voting Rights Act's so-called preclearance provision in a test case brought by a small municipal utility district in Texas and financed by a group, the Project on Fair Representation, that opposed racial and ethnic preferences and classifications. As written, the law required six Deep South states (Alabama, Georgia, Louisiana, Mississippi, South Carolina, and Virginia) to obtain permission for any proposed voting or election law changes from either the U.S. Department of Justice or a three-judge federal court in Washington, D.C. The formula in the law was later amended to apply to three other states—Alaska, Arizona, and Texas—and portions of several others. Critics said the preclearance requirement was out of date in light of the dismantling of overt racial discrimination in voting in the jurisdictions covered.

A municipal utility district in suburban Austin with a population of about 3,600 challenged the law to avoid having to seek permission to move a voting precinct from a private garage to an elementary school. In arguments in late April 2009, conservative justices openly questioned the need for the law. However, in an anticlimactic decision, *Northwest Austin Municipal Utility District No. 1 v. Holder* (557 U.S. 193), the Court ended the term with a narrow 8–1 ruling that local jurisdictions, not just states, could invoke the law's "bailout" provision to gain exemption from the preclearance requirement.

In his opinion for the majority, Roberts said that progress in voting rights in the South helped raise "serious constitutional questions" about the continuing validity of the preclearance requirement. But he said the constitutional issue could be avoided by construing the bailout provision broadly to allow individual local jurisdictions to seek exemptions. In the lone dissent, Thomas said he would have ruled the preclearance requirement unconstitutional.

Critics continued to mount legal challenges to the law. The Court in November 2012 accepted one such case,

Shelby County v. Holder (570 U.S. ___), with a ruling due by the end of the term in June 2013.

In another Voting Rights Act case, the Court said that states have no obligation to create so-called "crossover voting districts" to enable minority voters to elect their preferred candidate with help from majority voters. The 5–4 ruling in *Bartlett v. Strickland* (556 U.S. 1, 2009), divided along conservative-liberal lines, represented a setback for traditional civil rights groups.

FIRST AMENDMENT

The Roberts Court supported free speech claims not only in campaign finance cases but also in most other First Amendment cases decided during the four-year period. The Court struck down a federal law prohibiting depictions of cruelty to animals, another federal measure criminalizing false claims of military awards, and a state law banning the sale or rental of violent video games to minors. In a closely watched media case, the Court also threw out penalties that the Federal Communications Commission imposed on two television networks for violating the agency's rules on broadcast indecency.

In church-state cases, the Court continued to ease somewhat the restrictions on government support for faith-based organizations and religious expression. In the most important of the decisions, conservative justices formed the 5–4 majority in blocking a challenge to an Arizona law that allowed state tax credits for private donations to scholarships for religious schools.

In striking down the two federal laws and the California video games measure, the Court rejected arguments for carving out new categories of speech outside the general protections of the First Amendment's Free Speech Clause. The 8–1 ruling in *United States v. Stevens* (2010) invalidated a 1999 law aimed at outlawing so-called crush videos—graphic depictions of the intentional killing of small animals marketed to people who found the videos sexually arousing. For the majority, Roberts said the law was unconstitutionally overbroad because, as written, it covered many forms of presumptively protected speech. Alito was the lone dissenter.

Two years later, the Court also struck down the federal Stolen Valor Act, which made it a crime to lie about having received military medals or honors. Writing for a four-justice plurality in *United States v. Alvarez* (567 U.S. ___, 2012), Kennedy said that false speech was not automatically outside First Amendment protection. He went on to find the law overly broad and to discount the government's claimed interest in protecting the integrity of military awards. Two justices—Breyer and Kagan—said a narrower law might be upheld, while Alito led three dissenters in voting to uphold the measure.

The video games decision, *Brown v. Entertainment Merchants Association* (564 U.S. ___, 2011), struck down on a 7–2 vote a California law passed in 2005 that prohibited the sale or rental of excessively violent video games to minors. For a five-justice majority, Scalia said that video games were protected speech and that the state had failed to prove a causal connection between violent games and harm to children. Alito and Roberts concurred separately, suggesting a narrower law could be upheld. Thomas and Breyer dissented.

In another prospeech ruling, the Court ruled that protests at military funerals are generally protected by the First Amendment. The 8–1 decision in *Snyder v. Phelps* (562 U.S. ___, 2009) threw out a $5 million damage award won by the father of a deceased service member whose funeral was picketed by members of the fundamentalist Westboro Baptist Church of Topeka, Kansas. Roberts acknowledged the "hurtful" impact of the demonstration but said the demonstration—aimed at protesting the moral climate in the United States—was entitled to "special" protection under the First Amendment. Alito was the lone dissenter.

The protracted litigation over the FCC's broadcast indecency policy ended with a partial victory for free-speech advocates. Acting under a stricter definition of indecency adopted in 2004, the FCC had penalized the Fox television networks for "fleeting expletives" on two music awards programs and ABC for brief nudity on a prime-time police drama. In 2009, the Court ruled, 5–4, that the FCC had adequate justification for the change in enforcement policy (*Federal Communications Commission v. Fox Television Stations,* 556 U.S. 502). On remand, a federal appeals court ruled the policy unconstitutional. When the case returned to the Supreme Court, the justices threw out the FCC sanctions on the narrow ground that the networks had no notice of the change in policy. The ruling in *Federal Communications Commission v. Fox Television Stations* (*Fox II*) (2012) left the constitutionality of the policy unresolved; Kennedy said it was up to the FCC to decide whether any changes were warranted.

The Court's only major ruling rejecting a free-speech claim came in a failed challenge by human rights groups to a federal law prohibiting "material support" to federally designated terrorist organizations abroad. The 6–3 decision in *Holder v. Humanitarian Law Project* (561 U.S. ___, 2010) rejected arguments to narrow the law to exempt training or assistance in advocacy and peaceful dispute resolution.

The Court broke no new ground doctrinally in church-state cases, but conservative justices appeared to continue to have the upper head in easing Establishment Clause restrictions on government policies. In one skirmish, the Court divided 5–4 along conservative-liberal lines in telling a federal judge to reconsider a decision that could have forced the removal of a Christian cross erected on public land as a memorial to World War I veterans. "The goal of avoiding governmental endorsement [of religion] does not require eradication of all religious symbols in the public realm," Kennedy wrote for the majority in *Salazar v. Buono* (559 U.S. 700, 2010).

Dividing along similar lines, the Court in 2011 rejected a taxpayer challenge to an Arizona law that allowed taxpayers to claim one-for-one tax credits for donations to organizations that provide scholarships to students attending religious schools. Writing for the majority in *Arizona Christian School Tuition Organization v. Winn* (563 U.S. ___, 2011), Kennedy said the provision did not amount to a direct religious tax subject to taxpayer challenge. The ruling left the door open to potential challenges later, but Kagan led liberal justices in arguing that the provision was equivalent to direct government support for religious organizations.

A year later, the Court was unanimous in recognizing a "ministerial exception" from employment discrimination laws for churches and other faith-based organizations. The ruling in *Hosanna-Tabor Evangelical Lutheran Church and School v. Equal Employment Opportunity Commission* (565 U.S. ___, 2012) rejected a suit brought by the Equal Employment Opportunity Commission (EEOC) on behalf of a former parochial school teacher who was fired after attempting to return from a disability leave. "The Establishment Clause prevents the Government from appointing ministers," Roberts wrote, "and the Free Exercise Clause prevents it from interfering with the freedom of religious groups to select their own."

In one setback for religious groups, the Court upheld the right of public universities to require school-based groups to be open to all students without regard to religious views or sexual orientation. The 5–4 ruling in *Christian Legal Society v. Martinez* (561 U.S. ___, 2010) allowed the University of California's Hastings College of Law to deny recognition to a Christian Legal Society chapter based on the organization's policy excluding homosexuals from membership. Ginsburg wrote for a majority that included Kennedy and three liberal justices; Alito wrote for four conservatives in dissent.

INDIVIDUAL RIGHTS

The Roberts Court's decisions on individual rights issues outside First Amendment areas reflected to some degree a conservative bent. The Court extended Second Amendment gun rights to state and local governments, made it harder for employers to adopt race-conscious hiring and promotion policies, and took a narrow view of personal privacy rights vis-à-vis government officials.

The Court also generally made it harder for plaintiffs to win civil suits against government officials by requiring greater specificity in allegations of misconduct at an early stage. The ruling extended to official misconduct suits procedural requirements set out in a decision two years earlier in an antitrust case.

Liberal groups counted one significant victory, however, when the Court struck down on federal preemption grounds some parts of an Arizona law cracking down on undocumented immigrants. The ruling in *Arizona v. United States* (567 U.S. ___, 2012) struck down on 5–3 or 6–2 votes provisions that created a state crime of failing to carry alien registration papers, penalized undocumented immigrants for seeking employment, and allowed warrantless searches of deportable aliens. But the decision upheld the law's most controversial provision, which directed state and local law enforcement officers to verify the immigration status of anyone arrested or stopped who was reasonably suspected of being in the country unlawfully. Kennedy wrote the opinion, which Roberts and three liberals joined in whole; Kagan was recused because she participated in the case as U.S. solicitor general.

The gun rights decision, *McDonald v. City of Chicago* (561 U.S. 3025, 2010), came two years after the Court interpreted the Second Amendment for the first time to establish a limited individual right to possession of firearms. Conservatives formed the majority in the 5–4 decision, *District of Columbia v. Heller* (554 U.S. 570, 2008), which struck down a virtually absolute ban on private possession of handguns in the nation's capital. Because Washington, D.C., is a federal jurisdiction, the ruling left open whether the Second Amendment also applied to state and local governments.

The issue reached the Court in a challenge to handgun bans in Chicago and Oak Park, a Chicago suburb. By a 5–4 vote divided along conservative-liberal lines, the Court held that the Second Amendment right is "fully applicable to the states." In a plurality opinion for four justices, Alito said the Second Amendment was incorporated against the states under the Fourteenth Amendment's Due Process Clause because it was "fundamental to *our* scheme of ordered liberty." Concurring separately, Thomas said he would have extended the amendment to the states instead under the Fourteenth Amendment's Privileges or Immunities Clause.

Writing for three dissenters, Breyer argued that extending the ruling would intrude on states' traditional police powers. The dissenters included the newest justice, Sotomayor, who had said in her confirmation hearing in 2009 that she would respect *Heller* as precedent. In a separate dissent, Stevens argued against incorporating the Second Amendment right because it is not "critical to leading a life of autonomy, dignity, or political equality."

The Court in *Heller* held only that the Second Amendment guaranteed the right to possess firearms for self-defense in the home. Following *Heller*, Alito said that the new ruling "does not imperil every law regulating firearms."

In another 5–4 decision divided along conservative-liberal lines, the Court limited the ability of government or private employers alike to adopt race-conscious employment policies in order to avoid or remedy liability for unintentional or so-called "disparate impact" discrimination. The ruling in *Ricci v. DeStefano* (557 U.S. 557, 2009) held that the city of New Haven, Connecticut, violated Title VII of the Civil Rights Act of 1964 by discarding the results of a firefighter promotion examination on the ground that white candidates significantly outperformed African Americans.

For the majority, Kennedy said that an employer can adopt discriminatory race-conscious policies only if it has "a strong basis in evidence" to fear disparate impact liability without such action. In a strong dissent, Ginsburg said the ruling would do "untold" damage to Congress's goal of promoting equal opportunity in the workplace. The decision overturned a ruling by a panel of the Second U.S. Circuit

Court of Appeals that included Sotomayor, the future Supreme Court nominee. Criticism of the appeals court ruling by conservatives figured in Republican senators' opposition to Sotomayor's nomination, which was pending at the time of the Supreme Court decision.

The Court in two separate cases refused to award damages to individuals subjected to strip searches by government officials even though it set some limits on the practice. In *Safford Unified School District #1 v. Redding* (557 U.S. 364, 2009), the Court ruled, 8–1, that school authorities cannot strip-search students without "specific suspicions" that students are hiding drugs or other potentially dangerous contraband in their underclothes. With two justices dissenting, however, the Court refused to hold the school authorities liable on the ground that the right had not been established at the time of the incident.

In the second ruling, the Court in *Florence v. Board of Chosen Freeholders of Burlington County* (566 U.S. ___, 2012) held that jail authorities can strip-search arrestees before admitting them to the general population of jails or prisons even if they are held for minor offenses. Kennedy based the 5–4 decision on jail officials' security needs; for the dissenters, Breyer said he would have barred strip-searches of minor offenders unless drugs or violence were involved.

In an unrelated case, the Court limited remedies against federal agencies for unauthorized disclosure of information in confidential government files. By a 5–3 vote, the Court in *Federal Aviation Administration v. Cooper* (566 U.S. ___, 2012) held that individuals bringing suit under the federal Privacy Act of 1974 are not entitled to damages for emotional or mental distress.

The Court used a federal civil rights suit against former attorney general John Ashcroft to tighten the pleading requirements for plaintiffs in official misconduct. The suit by Pakistani citizen Javaid Iqbal sought to hold some thirty-four officials, including Ashcroft and FBI Director Robert Mueller, liable for civil rights violations in his detention after the September 11, 2001, terrorist attacks on the United States.

The federal appeals court allowed the suit to proceed against all the defendants, but the Court ruled 5–4 in *Ashcroft v. Iqbal* (556 U.S. 662, 2009) that Ashcroft and Mueller were entitled to qualified immunity. Kennedy said that plaintiffs had to allege specific constitutional violations by each individual defendant to overcome a claim of qualified immunity; he based the ruling on a similar pleading requirement established in 2007 in an antitrust case, *Bell Atlantic Corp. v. Twombly* (550 U.S. 544). Souter, who wrote the *Twombly* decision, led the four dissenters.

In an important access-to-justice case, the Court limited somewhat attorney fee awards in federal civil rights cases. The 5–4 ruling in *Perdue v. Kenny A.* (559 U.S. ___, 2010) required reconsideration of a $10.5 million award to attorneys in a suit that overhauled Georgia's foster care system. Attorney fees should be raised above the prevailing rates, the Court said, only in "exceptional" cases and based on objective evidence reviewable on appeal.

CRIMINAL LAW AND PROCEDURE

Despite a generally conservative pro-law enforcement orientation, the Roberts Court favored criminal defendants in some of the most significant criminal law rulings of the four-year period. In closely divided rulings, the Court restricted life-without-parole sentences for juvenile offenders, protected the ability of defendants to cross-examine scientific evidence at trial, and strengthened the right to counsel in plea bargaining cases and other settings. Kennedy joined with liberal justices to create majorities in some of those rulings, while Scalia and Thomas cast the deciding votes in some of the others.

The Court remained unfavorable terrain, however, for defendants or inmates challenging procedures in death penalty cases. And Roberts and Alito authored opinions for the conservative majority that appeared to weaken enforcement of the exclusionary rule, which bars use of illegally obtained evidence in criminal trials. In a seminal, privacy-related ruling, however, the Court established some unspecified Fourth Amendment limits on the ability of police to use high-tech surveillance methods to track suspects in public places.

The juvenile sentencing decisions extended the logic of the Court's ruling in 2005, written by Kennedy, that barred the death penalty for juvenile offenders (*Roper v. Simmons,* 543 U.S. 551). In *Graham v. Florida* (560 U.S. ___, 2010), Kennedy quoted from his earlier decision in ruling that juvenile offenders could not be sentenced to life in prison without eligibility for parole for non-homicide offenses. In both cases, Kennedy joined four liberal justices to form the 5–4 majority.

Two years later, the Court in *Miller v. Alabama* (567 U.S. ___, 2012) somewhat similarly barred mandatory life-without-parole sentences for juveniles in homicide cases as a violation of the Eighth Amendment's Cruel and Unusual Punishments Clause. As the senior justice in the majority, Kennedy assigned the opinion to Kagan, the Court's newest justice. In her opinion, Kagan said that such sentences should be "uncommon." In dissenting opinions, conservative justices vigorously criticized each of the rulings as unwarranted intrusions on legislative prerogatives.

The Court extended another line of constitutionally based decisions in a ruling that strengthened the role of juries in imposing criminal fines. The ruling in *Southern Union Co. v. United States* (567 U.S. ___, 2012) required juries, instead of judges, to make factual findings needed to increase the fine imposed in a criminal case. The 6–3 decision, setting aside an $18 million fine in an environmental law case, applied precedents beginning with *Apprendi v. New Jersey* (530 U.S. 466, 2000) that limited judges' fact-finding roles in imposing prison terms. Scalia and Thomas, along with Roberts, joined liberal justices in the majority; Breyer led Kennedy and Alito in dissent.

In an important federal sentencing case, the Court voted 5–4 to apply a 2010 law reducing prison terms in crack cocaine cases retroactively to any defendants sentenced after enactment of the law even if the crimes occurred before passage (*Dorsey v. United States,* 567 U.S. ___, 2012). Rulings in other federal sentencing cases were mixed, but sentencing expert Douglas Berman of Ohio State University's Moritz College of Law said the Court appeared to be "much more pro-defendant" on those issues than most of the federal courts of appeals. In one other ruling, however, the Court upheld, on a 7–2 vote, a federal law allowing civil commitment of a mentally ill, dangerous sex offender after expiration of a federal prison sentence (*United States v. Comstock,* 560 U.S. 126, 2010).

Among rulings on substantive criminal law, the Court sharply limited federal prosecutors' use of a broadly written law making it a crime to use fraud to "deprive another of the intangible right of honest services." Unanimously, the Court held in *Skilling v. United States* (561 U.S. ___, 2010) that the honest-services provision applies only to bribery and other kickback schemes, not to more general white-collar offenses. The decision set aside the multiple-count conviction of former Enron chief executive Jeffrey Skilling for his role in financial misstatements that led to the energy trading company's bankruptcy.

The Court cited the right to confront witnesses established in the Sixth Amendment's Confrontation Clause in a precedential decision requiring prosecutors to use live witnesses instead of written reports to present scientific evidence such as drug tests in criminal trials. Scalia wrote for a 5–4 majority that included Thomas and three liberals in *Melendez-Diaz v. Massachusetts* (557 U.S. 305, 2009). Two years later, a similar majority extended the ruling to require testimony from a lab technician who performed the tests in question instead of a supervisor (*Bullcoming v. New Mexico,* 564 U.S. ___, 2011).

The Court somewhat weakened the requirement a year later by allowing a witness to compare a DNA profile that the witness prepared with a profile prepared by another laboratory without the other technician being called to testify (*Williams v. Illinois,* 566 U.S. ___, 2012). Dissenters in the 5–4 decision said the ruling contradicted the earlier cases.

Two rulings gave prisoners a limited opportunity in post-conviction challenges to force DNA testing of evidence used at trial. The Court in *District Attorney's Office v. Osborne* (557 U.S. 52, 2009) found no freestanding constitutional right to require such testing, but two years later ruled in *Skinner v. Switzer* (562 U.S. ___, 2011) that prisoners can invoke federal civil rights law to force reexamination of evidence. Three dissenters argued that the stricter limits of federal habeas corpus law applied.

In a setback for criminal defendants, the Court refused to strengthen protections against the use of suggestive identifications at trial. The 8–1 ruling in *Perry v. New Hampshire* (565 U.S. ___, 2012) allowed the exclusion of potentially dubious identifications only if police arranged the suggestive circumstances.

The Court broke new ground in ruling in companion cases that a defendant may be entitled to reopen plea bargaining based on ineffective assistance of counsel during the process. Kennedy led liberal justices in the companion 5–4 decisions. The ruling in *Lafler v. Cooper* (566 U.S. ___, 2012) required prosecutors to re-offer a favorable plea bargain that a defendant had rejected based on incorrect legal advice from his court-appointed lawyer. In *Missouri v. Frye* (566 U.S. ___, 2012), the Court similarly required reopening of a case because the defense lawyer had failed to communicate a favorable plea deal to the defendant. Scalia sharply criticized the rulings in dissenting opinions joined in whole or part by other conservatives.

In other cases, the Court was generally unreceptive to ineffective assistance claims raised by inmates in federal habeas corpus cases. Kennedy authored a pair of decisions released on the same day that faulted federal appeals courts for reopening cases after state courts had rejected attacks on defense counsel's performance at trial. In both rulings—*Harrington v. Richter* (562 U.S. ___, 2011) and *Premo v. Moore* (562 U.S. ___, 2011)—Kennedy criticized the lower courts for "failing to accord required deference" to state court decisions. In another significant ruling, the Court held that federal habeas courts cannot consider new evidence that was not part of the record in an inmate's state court proceeding (*Cullen v. Pinholster,* 563 U.S. ___, 2011).

The Court showed its conservative side most distinctly in successive decisions that somewhat weakened enforcement of the exclusionary rule. In *Herring v. United States* (555 U.S. 135, 2009), Roberts led the conservative bloc in a 5–4 decision that evidence need not be suppressed after an unconstitutional search unless the violation resulted from systemic errors or reckless or intentional disregard of Fourth Amendment rights. The defendant had been arrested and his truck searched on the basis of an outdated warrant that had not been removed from computerized records. Two years later, Alito wrote a 7–2 decision that evidence need not be excluded if police followed search procedures that the Supreme Court later ruled were improper (*United States v. Davis,* 564 U.S. ___, 2011).

Police and prosecutors did not fare well, however, in rulings on substantive search law. In the most significant decision, the Court ruled that the use of global positioning system (GPS) devices to track suspects amounts to a search subject to Fourth Amendment requirements. The ruling in *United States v. Jones* (565 U.S. ___, 2012) reversed the conviction of a suspected drug trafficker who was followed to a drug warehouse by means of a GPS device attached to his car. The ruling was unanimous, but the justices divided on the rationale. Scalia led a five-justice majority in finding a search based on the attachment of the device to the car; Alito wrote for himself and three liberal justices in finding that the lengthy surveillance violated the suspect's reasonable expectations of privacy. Alito argued that Scalia's approach failed to deal with surveillance accomplished without physical contact—for example, cell phone tracking.

In another ruling, the Court held that police can search a stopped vehicle if the driver and any passengers are outside the vehicle only for evidence related to the reason for the stop, not for other offenses (*Arizona v. Gant*, 556 U.S. 332, 2009). But the Court backed law enforcement in other cases, including a decision that allowed police to enter a home without a warrant after announcing their presence if necessary to prevent destruction of evidence (*Kentucky v. King*, 563 U.S. ___, 2011).

The Court in separate decisions gave police new discretion in interrogating suspects. The ruling in *Montejo v. Louisiana* (556 U.S. 778, 2009) overturned a 1986 precedent that had barred police from renewed questioning of a suspect once the suspect had invoked his right to counsel. A year later, the Court ruled that police can question a suspect after giving *Miranda* warnings unless the suspect makes an unequivocal invocation of his right to remain silent (*Berghuis v. Thompkins*, 560 U.S. 370, 2010). Both rulings came on 5–4 votes divided along conservative-liberal lines. Kennedy joined the liberal bloc, however, in a 5–4 decision requiring that the age of a juvenile suspect be considered in determining whether the juvenile is in custody and *Miranda* warnings are necessary before any interrogation (*J.D.B. v. North Carolina*, 564 U.S. ___, 2011).

The Court issued no major rulings on capital punishment during the period and applied its narrow view of federal habeas corpus in rejecting pleas by death row inmates to set aside their convictions or sentences. The Court in 2011 reinforced earlier decisions rejecting efforts by the Mexican government to block execution of Mexican nationals convicted and sentenced without having been advised before trial of their right to consular assistance under an international treaty signed by the United States. In *Leal Garcia v. Texas* (No. 11-5001, 2011), the Court divided 5–4 along conservative-liberal lines in denying a stay of execution to Humberto Leal Garcia because of unenacted legislation requiring federal court review in such cases. Leal was executed two hours after the Court refused to issue the stay.

BUSINESS LAW

Business interests generally fared well in cases before the Roberts Court, especially in various decisions that limited civil suits against companies by workers, consumers, or investors. The Court also often displayed an aversion to expansive government regulation, especially in environmental cases. *(See environmental law, below)*

In addition, it backed pleas from business groups in some cases to invoke federal preemption to supersede potentially stricter state regulation.

The Court sometimes cheered business groups in cases outside the traditional scope of business law—most notably, the campaign finance ruling that gave corporations and labor unions a First Amendment right to engage in independent political spending (*Citizens United v. Federal Election Commission*, 558 U.S. 310, 2010). Business executives and managers also stood to gain from an important criminal law decision, *Skilling v. United States* (2010), that limited the scope of a federal statute used to prosecute white-collar offenses.

Among traditional business-related cases, business groups celebrated in particular a decision that cut off a broad sex discrimination suit against Wal-Mart and made other expansive class actions harder to maintain in the future. The 5–4 decision in *Wal-Mart Stores v. Dukes* (564 U.S. ___, 2011) blocked a putative class action on behalf of an estimated 1.5 million women who had worked for the giant discount retailer.

The ruling, divided along conservative-liberal lines, sustained Wal-Mart's argument that the plaintiffs had failed to present sufficient evidence of common factual and legal issues in order to consolidate the claims as a class action. For the majority, Scalia said the evidence was "worlds away" from what would be needed to show a general policy of sex discrimination by Wal-Mart, the nation's largest private employer. For the dissenters, Ginsburg said the evidence indicated that "gender bias suffused Wal-Mart's company culture."

The justices were unanimous on a second issue, ruling that back pay is not available in a class action under the somewhat permissive procedures for seeking future injunctive relief (Rule 23(b)(2)). Instead, Scalia explained, back pay could be obtained under the class action rule (Rule 23(b)(3)) providing more procedural protection for individual plaintiffs and for defendants.

One month earlier, the Court had backed businesses by upholding companies' ability to enforce provisions in consumer contracts that bar class actions in arbitration proceedings. The 5–4 ruling in *AT&T Mobility v. Concepcion* (563 U.S. ___, 2011) was along the same conservative-liberal lines. For the majority, Scalia said that allowing class actions would undermine Congress's purpose in favoring arbitration where parties agree to resolve disputes outside the courts. Dissenters argued the ruling would make it harder for consumers to find lawyers willing to take on such cases.

The conservative majority had prevailed in two other arbitration cases the year before. In one ruling, the Court made it harder to challenge an arbitration clause on grounds of unconscionability (*Rent-A-Center West v. Jackson*, 561 U.S. ___, 2010). The other ruling barred classwide arbitration unless an agreement specifically envisioned use of the procedure (*Stolt-Nielsen v. Animal Feeds International*, 559 U.S. ___, 2010).

The Court also disfavored plaintiffs in the most important securities law case during the period, again divided along conservative-liberal lines. The ruling in *Janus Capital Group. v. First Derivative Traders* (564 U.S. ___, 2011) barred investors from holding mutual fund management advisers liable for misstatements made by the fund in its prospectuses. In another setback for investors, the Court barred securities fraud suits in regard to transactions outside the United States even if some elements of the fraud occurred in the United States (*Morrison v. National Australia Bank*, 561 U.S. ___, 2010). In a few cases, the Court did ease procedural rules for investors in securities-related cases—notably, in a ruling that allowed investors to proceed with a class action without proving that the defendant's alleged misstatements caused the investors' losses (*Erica P. John Fund v. Halliburton*, 563 U.S. ___, 2011).

The Court's rulings in employment law disputes were mixed. Employers won an important victory when the Court held, 5–4, that plaintiffs suing under the federal Age Discrimination in Employment Act (ADEA) must show that age was an essential "but-for" cause of an adverse employment action, not just a motivating factor (*Gross v. FBL Financial Services*, 557 U.S. ___, 2009).

Employees prevailed in some other discrimination cases. The Court broadened the anti-retaliation provision in the Civil Rights Act of 1964 by recognizing a claim for wrongful dismissal by an employee who made an allegation of discrimination not in a complaint of her own but during an investigation of another employee's allegation. The ruling in *Crawford v. Metropolitan Government of Nashville and Davidson County* (555 U.S. 271, 2009) came in a case against a government employer, but was seen as applicable to private employers too.

In another case, the Court allowed discrimination to be found on the basis of a supervisor's illegal motivation even if someone else made the personnel decision at issue (*Staub v. Proctor Hospital*, 562 U.S. ___, 2011).

The Court's rulings in federal preemption cases—a major interest for business groups—were also mixed. In the most important business victory, the Court blocked state court suits for false labeling against generic drug manufacturers. The 5–4 ruling in *PLIVA v. Mensing* (564 U.S. ___, 2011) relied in part on the federal law requirement that generic drug makers follow the labeling used on the brand-name equivalents. Two years earlier, however, the Court ruled, 6–3, that federal approval of a pharmaceutical warning label does not prevent state law claims based on inadequate warnings (*Wyeth v. Levine*, 555 U.S. 555, 2009). In the same year, the Court ruled that the federal cigarette labeling law did not block a state court suit by cigarette smokers charging tobacco companies with falsely claiming that "light" cigarettes deliver less tar and nicotine (*Altria Group v. Good*, 555 U.S. 70, 2009). Kennedy joined with the liberal bloc in the 5–4 decision.

In the most important setback for business, the Court refused to preempt an Arizona law imposing stiff penalties on companies for employing undocumented workers. The 5–3 ruling in *Chamber of Commerce v. Whiting* (563 U.S. ___, 2011), divided along conservative-liberal lines with Kagan recused, upheld a law allowing the state to suspend or revoke a business's operating license for repeat offenses of knowingly hiring illegal aliens.

Among other business-related areas, the Court took on a number of patent issues, with mixed results for patent-holders and patent-contesting rivals. In the most closely watched case, the Court opened the door somewhat to patents for business methods. The unanimous ruling in *Bilski v. Kappos* (561 U.S. ___, 2010) disallowed a patent for the business method at issue, but Kennedy's opinion for a five-justice majority allowed such patents as long as the business method was not "an abstract idea." Stevens wrote for four justices calling for a complete bar to business method patents.

ENVIRONMENTAL LAW

The Roberts Court dealt environmentalists a succession of blows as it sided with businesses or property owners on enforcement of federal water and air pollution laws. "The Court does seem to be bringing more common sense to environmental law," Robin Conrad, head of the U.S. Chamber of Commerce's National Chamber Litigation Center, remarked.

In the most important case, the Court unanimously rejected an effort by Northeastern states to sue electric utilities in federal court in an effort to force them to limit their carbon dioxide emissions. The ruling in *American Electric Power Co. v. Connecticut* (564 U.S. ___, 2011) held that the federal Clean Air Act gave the Environmental Protection Agency (EPA) authority to deal with the issue and displaced any public nuisance claim against the companies in federal court. The states had gone to federal court because the EPA had yet to issue regulations on the issue.

In a second victory for electric utilities, the Court ruled that the EPA can use cost-benefit analyses in deciding how to regulate the water intake systems that electric power plants use to cool the facilities. The 5–4 ruling in *Entergy Corp. v. Riverkeeper* (556 U.S. ___, 2009), divided along conservative-liberal lines, rejected environmental groups' argument that EPA had to require utilities to use the best technology available to minimize any adverse impact on aquatic life.

The *Riverkeeper* decision was one of five rulings that went against environmental groups during the 2008–2009 term. Among the other decisions, the Court somewhat eased liability for companies under the so-called Superfund Law governing cleanup of hazardous waste sites (*Burlington Northern and Santa Fe Railway v. United States*, 556 U.S. ___, 2009). It also allowed operators of an Alaskan gold mine to virtually fill a nearby lake with dredge material without meeting EPA pollution standards (*Coeur Alaska v. Southeast Alaska Conservation Council*, 557 U.S. ___, 2009). Ginsburg dissented alone in the Superfund decision; she led three dissenters in the Alaska case.

The Court also strengthened landowners' ability to challenge EPA enforcement orders. The unanimous ruling in *Sackett v. EPA* (566 U.S. ___, 2012) allowed an Idaho couple to go to federal court to challenge an EPA order blocking them from building on a residential lot near a protected wetland. The agency had argued that the law did not allow a preenforcement challenge, effectively requiring the Sacketts to risk a substantial penalty for violating the order in order to contest it.

CHAPTER 14

General Government

Introduction 597

Chronology of Action on General Government 600

2009–2010 600

2011–2012 621

General Government

Setting disaster aid policy not only proved to be a lesson in unintended consequences but also showed how politics can sidetrack the federal government in its role to help citizens.

As part of the 2011 debt reduction accord (S 365—PL 112-25), Congress broke away from a long-standing practice that made getting aid to regions hit by natural disasters a messy budgeting proposition and raised tensions as the federal debt soared. Formerly, Congress would stint on disaster spending by allocating an unrealistically low $1 billion to $2 billion annually for the Federal Emergency Management Agency (FEMA) Disaster Relief Fund, then supplementing that as needed later with new appropriations that were exempt from budget caps. Once the storms, floods, and forest fires did their damage, no real arguments were raised that the disaster spending was not needed, but the spending totals triggered bitter budget battles, making it tougher to clear any kind of appropriations measure, whether a regular annual spending bill or a disaster aid bill. *(S 365, p. 160)*

With the debt limit accord, conservatives saw a chance to stop the routine use of emergency supplemental appropriations legislation, which often became vehicles for unrelated or less urgent needs, by front-loading the process. They were joined in efforts to revamp disaster budgeting by Democratic senator Mary L. Landrieu of Louisiana, a champion for ending the "feast or famine" approach to this funding. FEMA had to put on hold applications for aid in ongoing recovery efforts from earlier disasters, including Hurricane Katrina in 2005, to conserve cash while waiting for Congress to supplement the Disaster Relief Fund. *(Hurricane Katrina, Congress and the Nation Vol. XII, p. 787)*

SUPERSTORM SANDY

The Disaster Relief Fund got a fresh infusion of $7.1 billion at the start of fiscal 2013 (October 1, 2012) and even had some leftover appropriations from the previous fiscal year. The funds, however, would be woefully inadequate when Superstorm Sandy hammered the Northeast in late October 2012.

Hurricane Sandy—dubbed "Superstorm Sandy" for its size and destructiveness—developed in the Caribbean and eventually traveled north, hitting the eastern seaboard as a posttropical cyclone with hurricane-force winds. In the United States, the states of New York and New Jersey experienced the most severe damage. New York City subway tunnels were flooded, about 100,000 homes on Long Island were damaged or destroyed, and the famed Jersey shore was torn up. Millions of people lost power, and gas shortages were evident throughout the region. More than 130 people died in the United States as a result of Sandy, making it the deadliest hurricane to hit the country since Katrina in 2005. The National Oceanic and Atmospheric Administration National Climate Data Center estimated the U.S. cost of Sandy to be $65 billion.

In the aftermath of the storm, what quickly came into focus was that an important downside existed to the new approach to disaster aid. Giving FEMA an adequate annual budget appeared to be fine for addressing the routine array of disasters—hurricanes, wildfires, and winter storms—that could be expected to hit in any given year. But it also diminished the urgency for Congress to provide a fresh injection of federal funds to address a true catastrophe.

REFERENCES

Discussion of general government action for the years 1945–1964 may be found in *Congress and the Nation Vol. I,* pp. 1455–1516; for the years 1965–1968, *Congress and the Nation Vol. II,* 655–660; for the years 1969–1972, *Congress and the Nation Vol. III,* pp. 435–468; for the years 1973–1976, *Congress and the Nation Vol. IV,* pp. 795–826; for the years 1977–1980, *Congress and the Nation Vol. V,* 817–870; for the years 1981–1984, *Congress and the Nation Vol. VI,* pp. 771–793; for the years 1985–1988, *Congress and the Nation Vol. VII,* pp. 843–867; for the years 1989–1992, *Congress and the Nation Vol. VIII,* pp. 855–909; for the years 1993–1996, *Congress and the Nation Vol. IX,* pp. 803–858; for the years 1997–2001, *Congress and the Nation Vol. X,* pp. 733–754; for the years 2001–2004, *Congress and the Nation Vol. XI,* pp. 683–701; for the years 2005–2008, *Congress and the Nation Vol. XII,* pp. 781–806.

Outlays for Science, Space, and General Government

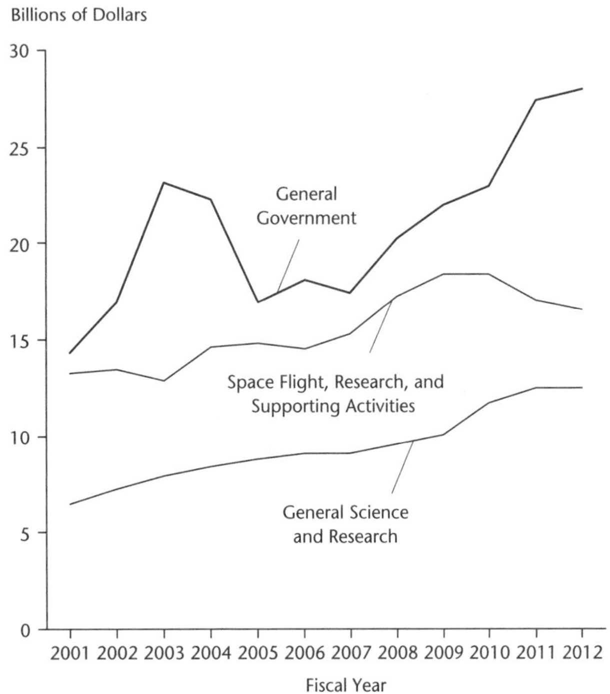

SOURCE: Office of Management and Budget, *Historical Tables, Budget of the United States Government: Fiscal Year 2013* (Washington, D.C.: U.S. Government Printing Office, 2012), Table 3.2.

With almost $4 billion remaining in the Disaster Relief Fund at the end of December 2012, House Speaker John A. Boehner, R-Ohio, decided to postpone consideration of Sandy recovery bills until the 113th Congress, removing a politically thorny question for conservatives who were trying at the time to address the major tax and spending issues that underlay the fiscal cliff (HR 8—PL 112-240). But Boehner's decision to put off consideration of a bill—and numerous officials laid the decision squarely on the Speaker—came at a cost to efforts to rebuild damaged parts of New York and New Jersey, officials said. That was because state and local officials and owners of small businesses needed to know how much federal help they would get before they could advance plans to rebuild damaged roads, buildings, public transit systems, and boardwalks. *(Fiscal cliff, p. 185)*

To New Jersey governor Chris Christie, a Republican, disaster funding was a simple matter of what the government did on behalf of its citizens. "This should not be something that's subject to politics," Christie said in criticizing Boehner and House Republicans. "This is a basic function of government." But conservatives argued that responsible planning also was basic to government functions.

POLITICAL DEBATE

The response to Katrina loomed over the often harsh political debate that flared up over Sandy aid. Christie contrasted the reaction by Congress to Katrina with the aftermath of Sandy. Katrina hit at the end of August 2005. By September 8 of that year, two emergency supplemental disaster appropriations measures had been enacted, providing about $62.6 billion in aid. For the Sandy recovery, the Senate passed its $60.4 billion recovery measure on December 28, 2012. However, many GOP senators maintained that the measure contained too much spending unrelated to Sandy, such as money for helping Alaskan fisheries and aiding western states in cleaning up after the summer's wildfires. The measure stalled.

President Barack Obama and New Jersey governor Chris Christie view Superstorm Sandy damage in Seaside Heights, N.J., from the helicopter on October 31, 2012. The storm carved a trail of devastation across New York City and New Jersey, killing dozens of people in several states and swamping miles of coastline.
Source: Doug Mills/AFP/Getty Images/Newscom

The Katrina request had come when Congress was far less concerned with federal spending and when a Republican presidential administration was taking hits for a weak response to the disaster. The nation was facing a much more manageable annual deficit of $318 billion for 2005, and the economy was growing strongly. By 2012, budget times were different. Also, environmental and climate-change advocates said that more pressing matters were at hand. They urged Congress to begin planning for more of the extreme weather seen in the United States in recent years. Less than two weeks before Sandy hit, German insurance giant Munich Re said a study of decades of claims found that the number of weather-related loss events nearly quintupled in North America during the past three decades, the most marked change of any region in the world.

Debate was ongoing about whether climate change had affected the weather, but even a top Republican congressional budget hawk said more should be done to prevent or minimize the damage from future catastrophes. "I think we need future disaster mitigation activities. We need studies," John McCain, R-Ariz., said on the Senate floor on December 18, 2012. "We are experiencing climate situations which we never anticipated. Certainly Hurricane Sandy was never anticipated by any of us." McCain objected, however, to such funding in a bill carrying an emergency designation, which exempted it from spending caps, and other Republicans were on the same path.

When Sen. Patrick J. Toomey, R-Pa., moved successfully to strip the emergency designation for $3.4 billion included in the Senate's Sandy package, he said, "This is not sandbags around someone's house who is in danger of a storm. That kind of infrastructure spending is the kind of spending we do routinely, but we plan for it and we budget it." However, Sandy exposed the weaknesses in the ability of political leaders to budget for the unforeseen.

Chronology of Action on General Government

2009–2010

Merit-based Pay Plan

Congress in 2009 terminated the National Security Personnel System (NSPS), a merit-based pay plan for the Department of Defense civilian workforce established in 2003 (PL 108-136). Action came on the fiscal 2010 defense authorization bill (HR 2647—PL 111-84). The repeal provision, offered by Carol Shea-Porter, D-N.H., was added to HR 2647 by the House Armed Services Committee during markup. The panel formally reported the National Defense Authorization Act (H Rept 111-166) on June 18, 2009. *(PL 108-136, Congress and the Nation Vol. XI p. 337; fiscal 2010 defense authorization, p. 273)*

At its inception, NSPS had wide support in Congress, coming on the heels of a recommendation in 2003 from a bipartisan commission that the General Schedule, the predominant pay scale—enacted in 1923—used for the civil service, was an impediment to government hiring efforts and should be dismantled. The commission recommended adoption of a system with pay flexibility.

The rigid, seniority-based pay scale set forth by the General Schedule had been criticized as not the best way to motivate a modern workforce and was seen as unfair by some. The George W. Bush administration had expressed concern about keeping top civilian Defense Department employees motivated, particularly in the aftermath of the 2001 terrorist attacks and invasion of Afghanistan. Also supporting the idea of overhauling federal worker pay were members of the administration of President Bill Clinton, including former Treasury secretary Robert E. Rubin and former health and human services secretary Donna E. Shalala. Federal employee unions, however, fought the merit-pay plan, saying it restricted union bargaining rights and could easily devolve into cronyism.

According to a *Federal Times* analysis, presented in an article entitled "Is DoD's New Pay System Fair?" dated August 11, 2008, "the first large-scale payout of performance-based pay raises and bonuses in January [2008] was riddled with inequalities." For example, white employees got higher average performance ratings, salary increases, and bonuses than those of other races and ethnicities. Those age forty and older and those under forty got similar performance ratings, but the former group got larger bonuses. Civilian employees at Defense Department agencies, such as the Defense Finance and Accounting Service and the Office of the Secretary of Defense, also received higher payouts overall than those in the Air Force, the Navy, and the Marine Corps.

Approximately 226,000 civilian Defense Department workers were covered by NSPS at the time that its dismantling was ordered. As a result, tens of thousands who were rewarded for their performance would be penalized for being too far ahead of the salaries in the General Schedule. If these workers stayed on the federal payroll, they would expect nominal raises while the seniority system caught up to their salaries under NSPS. The transfers out of the merit-pay system were to be completed by January 1, 2012.

Federal Worker Pay

As part of a fiscal 2011 continuing resolution (HR 3082—PL 111-322), Congress in 2010 imposed a freeze on pay for most federal civilian employees for two years, from January 1, 2011, to December 31, 2012. President Barack Obama signed the bill into law (PL 111-322) on December 22. *(Continuing resolution, p. 137)*

Also on December 22, the president issued a memorandum to the heads of executive department and agencies stating that he had signed HR 3082, which "freezes statutory pay adjustments for all executive branch pay schedules for a two-year period" and "generally prohibits executive departments and agencies from providing any base salary increases at all to senior executive or senior level employees, including performance-based increases." While law allowed agency heads to make some adjustments as an exercise of administrative discretion, the memorandum stated that "to ensure consistent treatment of executive branch employees and to promote the fiscal purpose of my [November 29, 2010, proposal to impose a two-year pay freeze], agency heads who had such discretion should not provide an upward adjustment in Federal employees' pay schedules or rates during the two-year period covered by the statutory pay freeze."

Executive Order 13561 (dated December 22, 2010) and Executive Order 13594 (dated December 19, 2011) stipulated the rates of basic pay or salaries of the statutory pay systems for federal employees pursuant to PL 111-322, effective January 1, 2011, and January 1, 2012, respectively.

Obama and the 112th Congress would extend the pay freeze for federal workers. *(112th Congress action, p. 621)*

Postal Service Retiree Benefit

Congress in 2009, as part of the fiscal 2010 legislative branch appropriations bill (HR 2918—PL 111-68), allowed the United States Postal Service (USPS) to reduce by $4 billion its contribution payments to the Postal Service Retiree Health Benefit Fund for fiscal year 2009. *(Fiscal 2010 appropriations, pp. 127, 128)*

The former cabinet-level Post Office Department was reorganized as an independent executive agency in 1971 under the Postal Reorganization Act (PL 91-375). Over the years, Congress placed constraints on the USPS, which, coupled with the migration of its customers to the Internet and a bad economy in recent years, left the agency in dire financial straits. The need for restructuring the Postal Service was evident, but the 111th Congress took no action. *(1971 reorganization, Congress and the Nation Vol. III, p. 441; 112th Congress action, p. 627)*

Little political support for taxpayer aid to the USPS was apparent, especially after the public outrage over government intervention in the banking and automobile industries and with the rising federal debt sparking calls for spending cuts and tax increases. During Senate debate on HR 2918, Judd Gregg, R-N.H., objected to the reprieve provision and raised a point of order. The Senate on September 30 voted 61–39 to waive the Budget Act with respect to points of order against the conference report (H Rept 111-265) on the bill.

Federal Teleworking

Congress in 2010 cleared legislation (HR 1722) to promote telecommuting for federal employees. The Telework Enhancement Act would require agencies to establish a policy permitting employees to telework as much as possible without diminishing performance. Teleworking allowed workers to perform their duties and responsibilities from home or at another worksite removed from their regular place of employment. Supporters claimed that teleworking would help mitigate congestion in high-traffic areas, reduce carbon emissions from vehicles, and improve the quality of life for all commuters.

The House Oversight and Government Reform Committee approved HR 1722 by voice vote on April 14, 2010, and formally reported it (H Rept 111-474) on May 4. Two days later, the House failed, by a vote of 268–147, to suspend the rules and pass the bill. (A two-thirds vote is required under suspension of the rules.) On May 14, before passing the measure by 290–131, the House adopted, 303–119, a motion offered by Darrell Issa of California, ranking Republican on Oversight and Government Reform, to recommit the legislation to committee to address concerns about the bill's costs.

The Congressional Budget Office (CBO) estimated that implementing the bill would increase administrative costs for federal agencies by $30 million from fiscal 2010 to fiscal 2015. In a letter to colleagues, bill sponsor John Sarbanes, D-Md., acknowledged the CBO estimate but said HR 1722 did not authorize any new appropriations and so was deficit-neutral. Republicans said that their support for the bill had always hinged on its being cost-free and that HR 1722 was not. Issa said that provision in the motion to recommit requiring agencies to certify to the Office of Personnel Management that the telework program would save money allowed House Republicans to ultimately support the measure.

The Senate passed an amended version of HR 1722 on September 29 by voice vote. Among the changes were those requiring that a mandatory written agreement between management and an employee outline the specific work arrangement; that each executive agency head provide an interactive training program; that the Office of Personnel Management offer policy guidance for pay and leave, agency closure, performance management, worksite, recruitment and retention, and employees with disabilities; and that the chief human capital officer of an agency, in consultation with its telework managing officer, submit an annual report on efforts to promote telework to the chair and vice chair of the Chief Human Capital Officers Council. On November 18 the House agreed, 254–152, to a motion by Stephen F. Lynch, D-Mass., to concur in the Senate changes, thus completing congressional action. The president signed the bill into law (PL 111-292) on December 9, 2010.

Whistleblower Protection

Both the Senate and the House passed the Whistleblower Protection Enhancement Act (S 372) in 2010, but the legislation died when differences were not resolved before adjournment. *(112th Congress action, p. 623)*

On July 29, 2009, the Senate Homeland Security and Governmental Affairs Committee approved a bill (S 372) sponsored by Daniel K. Akaka, D-Hawaii, by voice vote and formally reported it (S Rept 111-101) on December 3. The Senate passed the bill by voice vote on December 10, 2010, and the House passed an amended version, also by voice vote, on December 22. The House Oversight and Government Reform Committee held hearings in 2009 on a companion version (HR 1507), cosponsored by Chris Van Hollen, D-Md., and Todd R. Platts, R-Pa.

The House- and Senate-passed versions of S 372 differed in numerous ways. The Senate version provided that disclosure would not be excluded from whistleblower protections because the disclosure was made during the normal course of an employee's duties. The House extended that to stipulate an employee "with respect to whom another employee with authority took, failed to take, or threatened to take or fail to take a personnel action in reprisal for the disclosure." The Senate-passed bill would extend protections to any federal employee, current or prospective, for disclosures that the employee reasonably believed were evidence of censorship related to research, analysis, or technical information. The House went further, including disclosures that the employee believed were not specifically prohibited by law or were not specifically required to be kept classified in the interest of national defense or the conduct of foreign affairs.

The House dropped language amending the National Security Act of 1947 (PL 80-253) to establish within the Office of the Director of National Intelligence the Intelligence Community Whistleblower Protection Board and setting forth its composition, resources, and authority. The amended House version of the legislation dropped Senate language that would direct the Council of the Inspectors General on Integrity and Efficiency to study and report to Congress on security clearance revocations of federal employees at a select sample of agencies and on the appeals process at those agencies and at the Intelligence Community Whistleblower Protection Board. The House also jettisoned Senate provisions that amended the Inspector General Act of 1978 (PL 95-452) to allow a federal agency employee to report a concern to the inspector general of his agency and to require inspectors general to designate a whistleblower protection ombudsman. The House-passed bill also did not contain provisions, amending the Intelligence Reform and Terrorism Prevention Act of 2004 (PL 108-458), relating to security clearance. *(PL 80-253, Congress and the Nation Vol. I, p. 249; PL 95-452, Congress and the Nation Vol. V, p. 830; PL 108-458, Congress and the Nation Vol. XI, p. 263)*

President Barack Obama in his first inaugural address, delivered on January 20, 2009, pledged to "restore science to its rightful place" in the making of policy and in March 2009 issued a directive that agencies develop whistleblower protections for their scientists. However, some whistleblower advocates feared that the new rules would be insufficient and said that legislation was needed because court decisions had eroded existing protections.

While advocates trusted that Obama had the best interest of scientists at heart, they were concerned because the language of the Van Hollen–Platts bill was dropped from the final version of the economic stimulus package (HR 1—PL 111-5) after being adopted by voice vote on January 28, 2009, as an amendment by the House. Further complicating matters was Obama's statement, made during the signing ceremony of the legislation, about a provision aimed at punishing federal managers who interfered with whistleblowers. He said that the president had the right to control civil servants' communications with Congress that would reveal privileged or confidential information.

In related action, the Patient Protection and Affordable Care Act (HR 3590—PL 111-148) contained language that would make it easier for private parties to file federal lawsuits alleging that government contractors had defrauded the taxpayers. At issue was the Civil War–era False Claims Act, which was written to deter fraud against the government. It was changed in 1986 (PL 99-562) to encourage private parties to pursue claims on the government's behalf. They would receive a share of any damages awarded. Supporters said the legislation would help the government recover billions of dollars and deter wrongdoers. *(Health care overhaul, p. 421; PL 99-562, Congress and the Nation Vol. VII, p. 739)*

Whistleblowers who attempted to recover money were supposed to be the original source for the information upon which they filed suit. The courts strictly interpreted the law, for example, ruling against a whistleblower who obtained information under the Freedom of Information Act (PL 89-487). The change enacted by the health care law said that whistleblowers could pursue claims if they had knowledge of significant information independent of what had been publicly disclosed. Furthermore, the government would be the arbiter of whether such claims should go forward. Whistleblower advocates were pleased that the law made clear that all federal funds spent under the health care overhaul were subject to the Fair Claims Act. Some business lawyers believed the changes made a bad situation worse, creating a way for plaintiffs' lawyers to make money. *(PL 89-487, Congress and the Nation Vol. II, p. 643)*

Parental Leave for Federal Workers

The House passed a bill (HR 626) by a 258–154 vote on June 4, 2009, to amend the 1993 Family and Medical Leave Act (PL 103-3) to provide four weeks of regular pay for federal employees to deal with births, adoptions, and beginning foster care. A Senate companion measure (S 354) saw no action. *(1993 act, Congress and the Nation Vol. IX, p. 655)*

The House Oversight and Government Reform Committee had approved the Federal Employees Paid Parental Leave Act by voice vote on May 6 and formally reported it (H Rept 111-116, Part 1) on May 18.

Current law entitled all workers with at least a year of service at a company of fifty employees or more to twelve weeks of leave, though not necessarily paid, for parental care as well as to tend to the health of an ailing relative. HR 626 would not apply to Family and Medical Leave Act provisions that governed leave related to illness.

Many Republicans opposed the bill, arguing that the initiative would pose an undue burden on taxpayers during a recession. The Congressional Budget Office estimated that the legislation would cost $938 million from

2010 to 2014. Republicans criticized HR 626 as overly generous to federal workers, who already received more vacation benefits than the average worker. The House voted 157–258 on June 4 to reject an amendment, offered by bill opponent Darrell Issa, R-Calif., to require federal employees to use all accrued paid leave time before being eligible for an additional four weeks of paid leave.

Bill supporters argued that HR 626 was effectively cost-neutral—federal agencies were more likely to cover for absences from within rather than hire temporary labor—and potentially cost-beneficial as a means of retaining a trained workforce.

The House by voice vote June 4 adopted an amendment offered by Bobby Bright, D-Ala., guaranteeing that the time federal employees spent on active duty as members of the military reserves or National Guard be counted toward their leave eligibility. Also on June 4, before voting on final passage, the House rejected 171–241 a motion by Issa to recommit the bill to the House Oversight and Government Reform Committee with instructions to add a section entitled "Limitation."

The Senate did not take up the measure.

Federal Worker Software Sharing

On March 24, 2010, the House voted 408–13 (with one member voting "present") to suspend the rules and pass HR 4098, aimed at strengthening federal guidelines for software sharing among government employees. The Secure Federal File Sharing Act would require the Office of Management and Budget (OMB) to issue guidelines for federal employees and contractors using peer-to-peer file sharing, which allowed computer users to connect, search, and copy files without notifying the owner of the files. HR 4098 would prohibit government employees from using peer-to-peer software on federal computers and networks unless OMB authorized it.

The House Oversight and Government Reform Committee approved HR 4098 by voice vote on March 4 and formally reported it (H Rept 111-431) on March 11. Committee Chair Edolphus Towns, D-N.Y., said the panel's investigation into file sharing found child pornography, tax filings, medical records, and sensitive government information available over peer-to-peer networks, including the location of a United States Secret Service safe house for the first family and the electronic blueprint for *Marine One*, the president's helicopter.

California Republican Darrell Issa, ranking member of the committee, supported the bill, calling peer-to-peer networks "essentially spy software." He also said that the cost of implementing the legislation, which the Congressional Budget Office estimated at $10 million, would be worth protecting the privacy of Americans and the federal government.

A Senate companion measure (S 3484), sponsored by Claire McCaskill, D-Mo., was referred to the Senate Homeland Security and Governmental Affairs Committee but saw no further action.

Domestic Partner Benefits

The House Oversight and Government Reform Committee on January 22, 2010, and the Senate Homeland Security and Government Affairs Committee on December 17, 2010, formally reported the Domestic Partnership Benefits and Obligations Act (HR 2517—H Rept 111-400, Part 1, S 1102—S Rept 111-376). Neither version of the legislation saw floor action.

The House panel approved HR 2517 by a vote of 23–12, along party lines, on November 18, 2009. The bill would extend health care, vision, and dental coverage; disability benefits; family, medical, and emergency leave; long-term care insurance; and compensation for work injuries to domestic partners, who also could receive benefits from participation in the Thrift Savings Plan and the Federal Employees Retirement System.

Sponsored by Tammy Baldwin, D-Wis., the House measure would cover partners of employees in federal agencies, the White House, federal courts, and Congress. It would not apply to the military. The bill would define a domestic partner as an unmarried adult living with another unmarried adult of the same sex in a committed relationship who intended to live with the person indefinitely. Employees and their partners would have to submit a sworn affidavit. Before approving the bill, House Oversight and Government Reform adopted an amendment that would require the Government Accountability Office (GAO) to conduct a study on whether the benefit addition increased insurance premiums for federal employees, as well as the effect it would have on the government's recruitment and retention efforts.

Republicans opposed HR 2517, arguing that it represented an attack on the traditional definition of marriage. The panel rejected two GOP amendments dealing with the 1996 Defense of Marriage Act (PL 104-199), which declared that states did not have to recognize any same-sex marriage sanctioned by other states and defined marriage for the purpose of federal agencies as the legal union between a man and a woman. One, by Jim Jordan of Ohio, would have precluded anyone not considered under the law to be a "spouse"—a person married to someone of the opposite sex—from receiving benefits. The vote was 12–22. The other, by ranking member Darrell Issa of California, would have stated that nothing in the measure would supersede the 1996 law. The vote was 15–20. *(PL 104-199, Congress and the Nation Vol. IX, p. 746)*

During House Oversight and Government Reform Subcommittee on the Federal Workforce, Postal Service, and the District of Columbia consideration, subcommittee Chair Stephen F. Lynch, D-Mass., said that HR 2517 would help the federal government "catch up" with many private employers who already offered benefits to same-sex partners and would help with the government's recruitment, retention, and productivity, as well as boost employee morale. Panel Republicans turned the markup into a discussion about the definition of marriage and also painted the bill as discriminatory, saying it would treat one class of people differently, leaving out committed but unmarried heterosexual partners. The subcommittee had approved the bill on a party-line vote of 5–3 on July 30.

The Senate Homeland Security and Governmental Affairs Committee approved S 1102 on December 16, 2009, on a vote of 8–1, with Republican Robert F. Bennett of Utah the sole dissenter. Democrat Mark Pryor of Arkansas and four other Republicans on the panel indicated that they would have voted "no" if present; committee rules did not allow members to vote by proxy. Committee Chair Joseph I. Lieberman, I-Conn., and ranking Republican Susan Collins of Maine said the bill would likely need to be altered before it reached the floor to incorporate an offset to cover costs. The Office of Personnel Management estimated that S 1102 would cost about $63 million a year, Lieberman said.

The Senate committee–approved S 1102 was similar to the House committee–approved HR 2517. The Senate measure would extend several benefits to domestic partners, including health care, vision, and dental coverage; disability; family medical and emergency leave; long-term care insurance; and compensation for work injuries. Domestic partners also could receive benefits from participation in the thrift savings plan and the Federal Employees Retirement System. The bill would cover partners of employees of federal agencies, the White House, federal courts, and Congress. A domestic partner would be defined as an adult unmarried person who intended to live indefinitely with another adult unmarried person in a committed relationship. The Senate panel adopted an amendment that would require a GAO study on how the benefits would affect government recruitment and retention.

President Obama had issued a presidential memorandum on June 17, 2009, granting some benefits to same-sex partners of federal employees, but he said Congress had to change the law to extend other benefits, including health care coverage.

Community Service Programs

On April 21, 2009, President Barack Obama signed the Serve America Act (HR 1388—PL 111-13) amending the 1990 National and Community Service Act (PL 101-610) to expand the mission of the Corporation for National and Community Service (best known for its AmeriCorps program). HR 1388, a priority for the administration, authorized an estimated $5.7 billion over five years and sought to triple the number of Americans participating in national and community service programs. Push for passage of the bill took on new urgency with the declining health of the chief sponsor of the Senate version of the legislation (S 277), Edward M. Kennedy, D-Mass., a longtime champion of volunteer service. Kennedy died on August 25, 2009. *(1990 act, Congress and the Nation Vol. VIII, p. 616; AmeriCorps, Congress and the Nation Vol. IX, p. 623)*

In addition to reauthorizing the community service programs, the bill:

- Increased the education reward for participating in national volunteer programs from $4,725 to $5,350 and pegged it to the maximum Pell grant in the future.
- Created a new summer service program in which middle school and high school participants could receive $500 education awards for college.
- Established a clean energy corps, an education corps, a veterans corps, a healthy futures corps, and an opportunity corps with a goal of boosting financial literacy.
- Created one-year "encore fellowships" for those age fifty-five or older.
- Allowed participants older than fifty-five to transfer the education reward to their children, foster children, or grandchildren.

LEGISLATIVE ACTION

The House Education and Labor Committee approved HR 1388, sponsored by Carolyn McCarthy, D-N.Y., on March 11, in a 34–3 vote, and formally reported it on March 16 (H Rept 111-37). On March 18, before final passage of the measure by a vote of 321–105, the House adopted the following amendments: by 388–36, an amendment by Chellie Pingree, D-Maine, to add development of clean energy programs designed to meet the needs of rural communities to the list of approved Clean Energy Corps activities; by 261–168, an amendment by Dave Loebsack, D-Iowa, to authorize funding for the Corporation for National and Community Service to administer a new grant program called the Volunteer Generation Fund, to assist nonprofit, faith-based, and other civic organizations to develop and carry out volunteer programs; by 372–57, an amendment by Mary Jo Kilroy, D-Ohio, to allow the bill's grant funds to be used for volunteers in physical education classes at elementary and secondary schools and after-school programs, for student nutrition programs, and for food delivery, home legal and medical services, and transportation for the elderly; by 283–147, an amendment by Betsy Markey, D-Colo., to increase the authorization for operational grants to approved national service programs from $600 to $800 per full-time volunteer and from $800 to $1,000 per volunteer if the program supported at least 50 percent disadvantaged youth; and by 339–93, an amendment by Dina Titus, D-Nev., to create a National Service Reserve Corps to respond to national disasters and other emergencies and require corps volunteers to contribute at least ten hours annually.

Also on March 18, the House agreed, 318–105, to a motion by Virginia Foxx, R-N.C., to recommit the bill to the Education and Labor Committee with instructions to report it back immediately with language to bar participants in approved national service programs from attempting to influence legislation; organizing or engaging in protests, petitions, boycotts, or strikes; assisting, promoting, or deterring union organizing; or engaging in religious instruction.

The Senate Health, Education, Labor, and Pensions Committee by voice vote approved and then formally reported a companion measure (S 277—no written report) on March 18. During the markup, bill cosponsor Orrin G. Hatch of Utah encouraged fellow Republicans to support the legislation. On the floor March 23, the full Senate agreed, 74–14, to a motion to invoke cloture (thus limiting debate) on a motion by Majority Leader Harry Reid, D-Nev., to proceed to consideration of HR 1388. Three-fifths of the total Senate (sixty) was required to invoke cloture. The Senate on March 24 then agreed by voice vote to the motion to proceed to consideration of the measure. Over the next couple of days, members sought to attach extraneous language to HR 1388.

On March 25, the Senate rejected, 48–49, a motion by Michael D. Crapo, R-Idaho, to waive the Budget Act with respect to a Barbara A. Mikulski, D-Md., point of order against a Crapo amendment to a Mikulski substitute. (A three-fifths majority vote—sixty—of the total Senate was required to waive the Budget Act.) The Crapo amendment would increase the borrowing authority of the Federal Deposit Insurance Corporation (FDIC) from $30 billion to $100 billion and allow a temporary increase up to $500 billion if the FDIC board of directors, the Federal Reserve, and the Treasury secretary determined that it was necessary. The Mikulski substitute would reauthorize and expand Corporation for National and Community Service programs through fiscal 2014 and increase the education reward for full-time service volunteers. The chair subsequently upheld the point of order, and the amendment fell.

Also on March 25, the Senate agreed, 56–41, to motion by Mikulski to table (kill) an amendment by John Ensign, R-Nev., to an amendment by Max Baucus, D-Mont., to the Mikulski substitute. The Ensign amendment would clarify that certain crisis pregnancy centers and organizations that served battered women or victims of rape or incest would be eligible for a nonprofit capacity-building program. The Baucus amendment would authorize $5 million per year in additional funds over five years for a capacity-building program to provide training opportunities for small and midsize charities. The Baucus amendment subsequently was adopted by voice vote.

A Baucus amendment, adopted 56–41 on March 26, to the Mikulski substitute expressed the sense of the Senate that Congress should preserve the federal income tax deduction for charitable giving. The same day, the Senate rejected, 48–49, an amendment by John Thune, R-S.D., to the Mikulski substitute that would express the sense of the Senate that Congress would preserve the full federal income tax deduction for charitable giving. The Senate also agreed, 53–43, to a Mikulski motion to table (kill) an amendment by David Vitter, R-La., to the Mikulski substitute. The Vitter amendment would prohibit the Association of Community Organizations for Reform Now (ACORN)—which mounted a series of drives to register low-income voters and was faced with allegations of fraud from conservative interest groups and lawmakers—or any organizations affiliated with ACORN, from receiving assistance under the bill.

The Senate passed HR 1388, 79–19, on March 26, after agreeing by unanimous consent to raise the majority requirement for passage of the bill to sixty votes. Senator Kennedy, who had missed much of the session as he battled brain cancer, returned to vote on the legislation. He stood on the Senate floor throughout the roll call with his son, Rep. Patrick J. Kennedy, D-R.I., nearby. Afterward, he accepted prolonged applause from his Senate colleagues as they renamed the bill in his honor at the urging of Hatch, a longtime friend.

On March 31 the House agreed, 275–149, to a motion by George Miller, D-Calif., to concur in the Senate changes to the bill, thus clearing the measure for the president's signature.

The House had twice attempted to pass similar bills in the 110th Congress, but Republicans blocked the legislation both times. *(110th Congress action, Congress and the Nation Vol. XII, p. 802)*

NASA Reauthorization

A bill (S 3729) authorizing $58.4 billion for the National Aeronautics and Space Administration (NASA) for fiscal 2011 through 2013 was signed into law (PL 111-267) by President Barack Obama on October 11, 2010. It directed NASA to retain its shuttle-related workforce through fiscal 2011, but it also authorized the agency to foster the development of commercial capabilities in keeping with the Obama administration's push to shift the U.S. human spaceflight program toward commercial carriers. The National Aeronautics and Space Administration Authorization Act of 2010 directed NASA to contract with the National Academies in fiscal 2012 to conduct a study of the U.S. human spaceflight program. The last reauthorization, a one-year law, was enacted in 2008 (PL 110-422). *(2008 act, Congress and the Nation Vol. XII, p. 798)*

ADMINISTRATION PROPOSAL

President Obama initially provoked hostility in Congress when he sought to end NASA's Constellation human spaceflight program and to encourage commercial carriers instead. The Constellation program—which consisted of the *Ares* launch vehicles, the *Orion* crew vehicle, and systems needed to explore the moon's surface by 2020—was begun as part of President George W. Bush's plans to send astronauts to the space station, then to the moon, and ultimately to Mars and beyond.

Obama laid out his proposal for NASA in his fiscal 2011 budget, following the receipt of a report on the future of manned spaceflight from an independent committee that he had established in 2009. The panel, known as the Augustine Committee, concluded that the Constellation program had little chance of success under existing budget conditions. The committee also noted that NASA had siphoned funding from other important programs, such as robotic exploration and technology development, in an effort to keep the elements of the exploration program on track. In light of the International Space Station's value for research and international collaboration, the panel said that the administration should consider extending the life of the space station beyond 2015.

Obama's plan, released in February 2010, proposed a number of controversial changes, including canceling the Constellation program and making significant investments in the commercial space industry to develop a vehicle to transport crew to the space station. Citing the findings of the Augustine Committee, the president also called for aggressive investments in research and technology development and for restoring funds for NASA's earth science program, which used satellites to study the earth's climate, weather, and natural hazards. He sought a hiatus until 2015 in NASA's vehicle, launch, and launch-related activities and a decrease in the singular focus on the moon as a destination for exploration. He also agreed with the panel on extending the space station until 2020.

Following heavy public criticism, Obama adjusted his plan in April. He proposed that NASA develop a new heavy-lift rocket and a crew rescue vehicle for astronauts on the space station based on the crew capsule that had been under development in the Constellation program. The existing shuttle program had been scheduled to end after early 2011, making international partners dependent on Russia to service the space station during the five years before a new U.S. vehicle was expected to be ready.

LEGISLATIVE ACTION

The Senate Commerce, Science, and Transportation Committee by voice vote approved S 3729 on July 15, 2010, and formally reported it (S Rept 111-0278) on August 5. The measure had been worked out by a bipartisan group of senators in negotiations with the White House.

The bill preserved some rocket and capsule development at NASA but also authorized funding for the transition to commercial carriers. In its report accompanying S 3729, the committee explained the priority it placed on using elements of the Constellation program. It noted that NASA had already invested about $9 billion in the Constellation program and said that to cancel it outright would risk the loss of design and hardware, and could cost $2.5 billion in contract termination fees. Instead, it said, the committee's bill directed NASA "to maximize the use of recent investments and existing capabilities while still enabling the agency to develop substantial new technologies, commercial and international partnerships, and innovative approaches to meet its overall goal of ensuring long-term human presence and expansion in space." An administration official said the measure contained "the critical elements necessary for achieving the president's vision for NASA."

The House Science and Technology Committee approved a companion measure (HR 5781) by voice vote on July 22, 2010, and formally reported it (H Rept 111-576) on July 28. The bill directed NASA to restructure its space exploration program to include a government-owned, government-operated crew transportation system as well as the development of a heavy-lift launch vehicle. It required that the program use work already done on vehicles such as *Orion* and *Ares I,* and it called for NASA to phase in a new crew transportation system by the end of 2015 to minimize the coming gap in human spaceflight.

The bill hewed less closely than S 3729 to the administration's plan, including less for the transition to commercial carriers. HR 5781 would authorize $50 million in fiscal 2011 for crew development and $14 million for a cargo demonstration program, plus another $100 million for a new loan guarantee program for commercial carriers. The Senate committee-approved S 3729 included $300 million for commercial cargo development and $312 million for commercial crew development and related studies.

The House Science and Technology Committee rejected by voice vote an amendment offered by Suzanne M. Kosmas, D-Fla., to increase funding for crew development to $312 million and funding for commercial cargo to $300 million. But the House panel brought its bill closer to the Senate measure by approving, also by voice vote, a Kosmas amendment to add another flight for the retiring space shuttle fleet.

The full Senate passed S 3927 by voice vote on August 5, shortly before leaving for the August recess. While the House had not acted on HR 5781, the Senate measure, with bipartisan backing and the administration's support, was shaping up to be the vehicle for setting a new direction for NASA. (Provisions similar to those in S 3927 had been written into the Senate version of the fiscal 2011 Commerce-Justice-Science [C-J-S] appropriations bill [S 3636]. Both S 3636 and a House draft C-J-S spending bill subsequently stalled.) *(Fiscal 2011 appropriations, p. 150)*

With only a few weeks left before the new fiscal year was to begin on October 1, the split between the House and Senate on the pace of the proposed transition to commercial carriers remained unresolved. At that point, the question seemed likely to be settled by the appropriators in stopgap funding legislation that would not address policy changes. However, after weeks of negotiations between the House and Senate authorizers, the House agreed by a **key vote of 304–118 (R 119–54; D 185–64)** on September 29 to suspend the rules and pass S 3729, completing congressional action. *(2010 key votes, p. 767)*

Dissenters in the House continued to question bipartisan arguments that the bill would preserve NASA's human spaceflight activities and protect jobs. Gabrielle Giffords, D-Ariz., chair of the House Science and Technology Subcommittee on Space and Aeronautics, called the jobs argument a red herring and noted that the funding would actually be set by subsequent appropriations. She argued that the measure would authorize funds for companies that had not yet proven their ability to develop spacecraft to transport crew and cargo.

MAJOR PROVISIONS

Following are major provisions of S 3729 (PL 111-267):

Authorization. The bill authorized $19 billion in fiscal 2011, $19.5 billion in fiscal 2012, and $20 billion in fiscal 2013. The amounts were equal to those requested by the president.

Policy. The legislation reiterated previous congressional prescriptions that NASA have a balanced and adequately funded portfolio of programs in human spaceflight and exploration, aeronautics research and development, and scientific research. It also directed NASA to focus on designing and building elements of the manned space program within the amount budgeted instead of focusing on increasing performance, which the Augustine Committee said would be "a fundamental change from NASA's recent history with the Constellation program and a number of previous NASA launch initiatives."

Human spaceflight. The bill directed NASA to develop a new space launch system and continue work on a multipurpose crew vehicle as a follow-on to the shuttle and Constellation programs. The committee said that the legislation would provide a "government-owned and -operated capability" to support exploration missions and activities as well as crew and cargo delivery to the space station "as a backup, if necessary, to commercially developed" vehicles.

The measure included:

- $8.9 billion for the space station through fiscal 2013 and authority, with international partners, to support full utilization of the space station through at least 2020.
- $1.6 billion in fiscal 2011 to support space shuttle flight operations and allow one additional shuttle flight, which the Senate Commerce, Science, and Transportation Committee said could be essential to ensure the space station's sustainability.
- $6.9 billion toward development of a heavy-lift rocket, beginning in fiscal 2011, sooner than Obama had proposed, with a goal of having the core capabilities operational in 2016. NASA was directed to try to make use of existing assets and capabilities from the shuttle and Constellation programs.
- $3.9 billion over three years for a multipurpose crew vehicle that would be fully operational in 2016 and would make use of concept, designs, prototypes, and other materials developed for the *Orion* project.
- $1.6 billion for commercial development of space systems for manned crews and cargo.

Other priorities. The authorization also included $4.8 billion over three years for Earth sciences, $11 billion over three years for space science, $1.8 billion for aeronautics, and $1.4 billion for space technology.

America COMPETES Act Reauthorization

Congress in 2010 cleared a bill (HR 5116) that reauthorized the 2007 America COMPETES Act (Creating Opportunities to Meaningfully Promote Excellence in Technology, Education, and Science; PL 110-69), which

NASA AND CLIMATE CHANGE

The fiscal 2011 budget proposal that President Barack Obama sent to Congress in February 2010 declared that the mission of the National Aeronautics and Space Administration (NASA) included, along with space exploration and aeronautical research, "stewardship of the Earth." The language was in keeping with Obama's interest in climate change, as was the budget's proposed increase in spending for NASA's Earth and climate science work. *(NASA reauthorization, p. 605)*

NASA's mission statement had been revised in 2002 to include the task "to understand and protect our home planet." But, in 2006, amid a flap over whether people in the George W. Bush White House wanted to muzzle NASA climate scientists, the agency altered its mission to say that it sought "to pioneer the future in space exploration, scientific discovery and aeronautics research."

NASA spokesperson Doc Mirelson suggested that the mission statement was more like a company's brand identity and did not affect NASA's climate science missions. "I think what people felt politically about global warming or climate change didn't really affect most of the actual NASA missions that were flying or are still flying," Mirelson said. "Stewardship has never really been removed from the overall NASA mission."

A senior and veteran Democratic staff member at the Science, Commerce, and Transportation Committee, who was not permitted to speak publicly on the issue, said that the wording change was not surprising, given the difference between the two presidents: "In people's minds, NASA's actual activity didn't change that much." Somebody just made a political call to remove the wording, the aide said.

PLUTONIUM 238

President Barack Obama in his fiscal 2010 budget requested funding to resume production of plutonium 238, a highly radioactive substance that the National Aeronautics and Space Administration (NASA) said it needed to power the electronics on missions into space. The United States had not made the isotope since 1988, instead buying it from Russia under a 1992 agreement. Russia, however, had stopped making the plutonium, and the U.S. stockpile was dwindling, according to the Department of Energy (DOE). DOE had been responsible for making plutonium 238, and NASA was its primary consumer.

What made plutonium 238 somewhat controversial was that it is dangerous but very useful. A tiny amount produces enough heat to generate electricity in a radioisotope power system, like a battery that never needs recharging. That makes it ideal for equipment that could not be hooked to power lines or powered by solar cells, such as craft operating where solar power was lacking or unreliable.

Plutonium 238 is an isotope, or separate atomic form, of plutonium, which itself is created in nuclear reactors. NASA's original supply came as a byproduct of U.S. weapons production, although plutonium 238 was not suitable for weapons. Another isotope, plutonium 239, is used in weapons and power station reactors. Plutonium 238 also had been used to power intelligence equipment. Russia stipulated that it would sell plutonium 238 to the United States only if it was not used in military or intelligence applications.

The National Research Council, in a May 2009 report entitled "Radioisotope Power Systems: An Imperative for Maintaining U.S. Leadership in Space Exploration," urged restarting production as soon as possible to avoid disrupting NASA's plans for space exploration. The council estimated the total cost would be approximately $160 million over five to seven years. Obama asked Congress for $30 million in fiscal 2010 to begin the project, leading to production by 2016. Congress denied that request. However, it did provide $10 million in fiscal 2011 (PL 112-55) and $14.5 million in fiscal 2012 (PL 113-6) to restart production of plutonium 238.

was designed to improve U.S. economic competitiveness by providing funding for innovation and education. The three-year, $45.2 billion authorization for research programs at the National Science Foundation (NSF), the National Institute of Standards and Technology (NIST), and the Energy Department and for education and training in the fields of science, technology, engineering, and mathematics (STEM), was enacted after House Democrats were unable to advance a broader five-year measure. President Barack Obama signed HR 5116 into law (PL 111-358) on January 4, 2011. *(PL 110-69, Congress and the Nation Vol. XII, p. 617)*

LEGISLATIVE ACTION

The House Science and Technology Committee approved HR 5116 by voice vote on April 28, 2010, and formally reported it (H Rept 111-478, Part 1) on May 7. Panel Republicans objected mainly to the authorization levels, which they said were too high. The committee rejected several GOP amendments that would have reduced the authorization levels but adopted an amendment by committee Chair Bart Gordon, D-Tenn., to reduce authorizations across the board by about 10 percent.

The full House passed a five-year, $85.6 billion science programs reauthorization bill by a vote of 262–150 on May 28, after Democrats employed a rarely used parliamentary procedure to circumvent GOP maneuvering. HR 5116 appeared headed for passage in mid-May, when it was abruptly pulled from the House floor after Republicans successfully offered a motion to recommit. The motion, offered by Ralph M. Hall, R-Texas, required that the bill be revised to freeze the authorizations at fiscal 2010 levels for most programs, that the length be reduced from five years to three years, and that the authorization for the Department of Energy's Advanced Research Projects Agency (ARPA-E) be deleted. The motion also included language prohibiting the use of funds to pay the salaries of government employees who were disciplined for viewing pornography on their work computers. That provision was hard to oppose, and the motion was agreed to, 292–126, on May 13.

Republicans also stymied an effort on May 19—this one to pass a pared-back, three-year version of the bill (HR 5325)—by denying the leadership the two-thirds majority needed for passage under suspension of the rules. The vote was 261–148, twelve votes short. The $48 billion HR 5325 retained the anti-pornography language.

On May 28, Gordon brought the five-year version of HR 5116 back to the floor and employed a parliamentary procedure known as "dividing the question" to force nine votes on the GOP motion to recommit, allowing members to vote on each of the items separately. Lawmakers supported the antipornography language by a vote of 409–0 and rejected, 181–234, a provision that would have reduced the authorization's length by two years. They also rejected by voice votes amendments that would have struck from the bill a new manufacturing loan guarantee program and new multidisciplinary energy technology research centers, known as energy innovation hubs. The chamber also voted, 348–68, to prevent schools from receiving grants under the bill if they did not allow military recruiters on their campuses.

The Senate passed an amended version of HR 5116 by voice vote on December 17. The revised measure covered three years instead of five and carried a reduced price tag of $42.5 billion. It included language barring salary payments for employees convicted of a criminal offense involving pornography. It also required the Government Accountability Office to study the programs funded under the bill and report to Congress by spring 2013. Several provisions in the House-passed version were dropped, including the authorization for energy innovation hubs. The Senate-passed bill addressed agencies not in the House version. For example, it included policy provisions related to the National Aeronautics and Space Administration (NASA) and the National Oceanic and Atmospheric Administration (NOAA), and it authorized funds for certain Education Department programs.

The Senate Commerce, Science, and Transportation Committee had approved a three-year bill (S 3605) by voice vote on July 22, 2010, and formally reported it (no written report) on December 10. S 3605 would authorize funding for the NSF and NIST but not the Energy Department or the Education Department programs.

Supporters of HR 5116 were anxious to get the bill to the president's desk before the end of the year out of concern that Republicans' greater clout in the 112th Congress would mean cutbacks in spending on science. As a result, the House on December 21 agreed 228–130 to a motion by Gordon to accept the Senate changes, thus clearing the measure.

MAJOR PROVISIONS

As enacted, the America COMPETES Reauthorization Act (HR 5116—PL 111-358) included the following major provisions.

National Science Foundation. Authorized $23.5 billion for the NSF, an independent federal agency that was the major source of federal funding for math and science research in colleges and universities. The bill directed the NSF to:

- Create a program to award competitive grants to support fundamental research in colleges and universities leading to transformative advances in manufacturing technologies, processes, and enterprises, including research in nanotechnology, robotics, and advanced sensing and control techniques.
- Award grants to strengthen and expand scientific and technical education and training in advanced manufacturing, with the goal of helping to ensure a well-trained manufacturing workforce.
- Establish a National Center for Science and Engineering Statistics within the NSF to serve as a federal clearinghouse for the collection, interpretation, analysis, and dissemination of objective data on science, engineering, technology, and research and development.

National Institute of Standards and Technology. Authorized $2.9 billion over three years for NIST, an agency in the Commerce Department created to promote U.S. competitiveness by working with private industry to develop and apply technology, standards, and measures.

Energy Department. Authorized $16.9 billion over three years for programs in the department's Office of Science, including basic energy science, advanced scientific computing, and fusion energy research. The Office of Science was the largest supporter of basic research in the physical sciences in the country, providing more than 40 percent of total funding for such research.

- Authorized $918 million over three years for the department's ARPA-E, which was designed to fund projects that would reduce dependence on foreign energy imports, reduce energy consumption, and improve energy efficiency in all sectors of the economy.

Education Department. Authorized $225 million over three years for a program of competitive grants to help schools increase the number of teachers and students participating in international baccalaureate or advanced placement courses in high-need schools.

- Authorized $12 million over three years for the Teachers for a Competitive Tomorrow program directed to programs for bachelor's and master's degrees in the STEM fields or in critical foreign languages.

Commerce Department. Authorized $300 million over three years to award grants for the development of feasibility studies and plans for the construction of new science parks or the renovation or expansion of existing parks.

- Authorized $21 million over three years to enable the department to guarantee up to 80 percent of a loan used to finance the construction, expansion, or renovation of science parks.

Federal Science Programs

The House on June 8, 2009, passed two bills to enhance U.S. global competitiveness by expanding and coordinating science research and development programs.

HR 1709, passed by a vote of 353–39 under suspension of the rules, would mandate establishment of a committee to coordinate federal science, technology, engineering, and mathematics (STEM) education programs. Furthermore, the committee would establish and maintain an inventory of federally sponsored educational activities, to ensure that researchers and educators were fully informed about opportunities.

The House Science and Technology Committee approved the STEM Education Coordination Act by voice vote on April 29 and formally reported it (H Rept 111-130, Part 1) on June 2.

HR 1736, passed by a vote of 341–52 under suspension of the rules, would create a panel within the National Science and Technology Council to coordinate international science and technology cooperation across federal agencies. The House Science and Technology Committee approved the International Science and Technology Cooperation Act by voice vote on April 29 and formally reported it (H Rept 111-128) on May 21.

Related legislation (HR 2020), passed by the House by voice vote under suspension of the rules on May 12, 2009, would mandate periodic reviews of networking and information technology research. The bill would create an advisory committee on networking and information technology to evaluate and make recommendations on new large-scale research projects of national economic competitiveness or societal benefit. The House Science and Technology Committee approved the Networking and Information Technology Research and Development Act by voice vote on April 19 and formally reported it (H Rept 111-102) on May 12.

National Flood Insurance

The House in 2010 passed the Flood Insurance Reform Priorities Act (HR 5114) to reauthorize the National Flood Insurance Program through fiscal 2015. The bill then was referred to the Senate Banking, Housing, and Urban Affairs Committee, where it died upon adjournment of the 111th Congress. (2012 action, p. 627)

The program was established in 1968 (PL 90-448) in response to increasing federal government spending for disaster relief following a series of hurricanes that caused severe flooding in the 1960s. The program was supported by premium revenue until 2005, when Hurricanes Katrina, Rita, and Wilma devastated New Orleans, Louisiana, and other parts of the Gulf Coast and put it nearly $20 billion in the red. The program had received several short-term extensions since the last long-term reauthorization, enacted in 2004 (PL 108-264), expired in September 2008. The House and Senate each passed versions of a long-term bill in the 110th Congress, but disagreements over whether the government should offer multiple-peril policies that covered wind as well as flood damage helped sink the legislation. *(1968 act, Congress and the Nation Vol. II, p. 968; 2004 act, Congress and the Nation Vol. XI, p. 693; 109th Congress action, Congress and the Nation Vol. XII, pp. 791, 793; 110th Congress action, Congress and the Nation Vol. XII, p. 798)*

The Federal Emergency Management Agency (FEMA) administered the program and issued the rate maps that designated flood hazard areas, defined as those projected to have at least 1 percent chance of flooding in any given year. These maps ultimately determined where government flood insurance would be provided and what the insurance rates would be.

Gulf Coast lawmakers wanted to expand the program to cover wind damage. Proponents of making the change said that private insurers had refused to pay claims when property damage was caused by both wind and flood events, leaving the government to pay for the damages through disaster aid. The Obama administration, along with the U.S. Chamber of Commerce, opposed the change, saying that wind insurance was widely available both in the private market and through state insurance plans. They said that adding it to the legislation would increase the debt of an already overburdened federal program. Numerous environmental groups said it would encourage people to build in fragile coastal areas.

In related action, the House Financial Services Committee on April 27, 2010, approved, 39–26, and on July 13 formally reported HR 2555 (H Rept 111-534), the Homeowners' Defense Act. The legislation, a version of which had passed the House in 2007, would create a national catastrophic fund and would allow states to join a consortium to spread their disaster risk. The bill saw no further action.

LEGISLATIVE ACTION

The House Financial Services Committee approved HR 5114 by voice vote on April 27, 2010, and formally reported it (H Rept 111-495) on May 26. The full House passed the bill on July 15 by a lopsided vote of 329–90. The House-passed measure included provisions to:

- Increase the maximum coverage limit for flood insurance policies to $335,000 for residences, up from $250,000; $135,000 for the contents of a home, up from $100,000; and $670,000 for commercial property, up from $500,000.
- Allow flood insurance premiums to increase by up to 20 percent per year, instead of 10 percent, as allowed under existing law.
- Delay for five years a requirement that homeowners living in newly designated Special Flood Hazard Areas purchase flood insurance.
- Phase out subsidies for commercial and second homes built before 1974, the point at which flood insurance rate maps went into effect and premium subsidies were provided for property already in the flood zones. The phase-out would also apply to principal residences sold after enactment of the bill. It would not apply to multifamily rental properties or rentals that were a tenant's primary residence.
- Create a premium payment installment plan for low-income families, which would include families with an income level at or below 200 percent for the poverty level or that had no employed adult member.
- Authorize $250 million over five years for a new competitive grant program for local government agencies that conducted education and outreach to encourage homeowners to purchase flood insurance.

During floor debate, several lawmakers expressed frustration with a program they viewed as subsidizing reckless behavior. Jeb Hensarling, R-Texas, argued that constituents in districts like his, where flooding was not a major risk, had to pick up the tab for others.

Gene Taylor, D-Miss., questioned why an amendment he submitted to the Rules Committee to create an option for property owners to buy both wind and flood coverage was not made in order. Taylor's Gulf Coast home had been destroyed in Hurricane Katrina, and he later sued his insurance company for denying his wind-damage claim. Majority Leader Steny H. Hoyer, D-Md., announced that a Taylor-sponsored bill (HR 1264) containing similar provisions would be brought to the floor. [The House Financial Services Committee approved the Multiple Peril Insurance Act by 40–25 on April 27 and formally reported it (H Rept 111-551) on July 19. The House on July 22 passed the rule (H Res 1549) for floor consideration, but HR 1264 went no further.]

The House by voice vote on July 15 adopted an amendment by Adam H. Putnam, R-Fla., to require FEMA to report annually on use of the funds for the creation of the education and outreach program and the effectiveness of the grants. Members rejected, 191–229 on July 15, a motion by Hensarling to recommit HR 5114 to the House Financial Services Committee with instructions to immediately report back the bill without the education provisions.

SHORT-TERM EXTENSION

The federal flood insurance program was extended to September 30, 2011, after the House agreed to allow another year for negotiations. The Senate passed the National Flood Insurance Program Reextension Act (S 3814) by voice vote on September 21, 2010. The House agreed to suspend the rules and pass the bill by voice vote on September 23, completing congressional action. The president signed the measure into law (PL 111-250) on September 30.

The previous short-term extension, the National Flood Insurance Program Extension Act (HR 5569—PL 111-196), had kept the plan going through September 30, 2010. Senate Democrats Mary L. Landrieu of Louisiana and Bill Nelson of Florida had urged expedited passage of S 3814 to avoid disrupting the program. Existing policies would have remained in effect during a lapse, but providers could not underwrite new policies, causing delays in real estate transactions when flood insurance was a condition of obtaining a mortgage.

The House agreed by voice vote on June 23, 2010, to suspend the rules and pass HR 5569. The Senate passed the measure by voice vote on June 30, completing congressional action. The bill was signed into law on July 2.

The 112th Congress also acted to extend the program. *(112th Congress action, p. 627)*

Earthquake Hazard

The House on March 2, 2010, voted 335–50 to suspend the rules and pass HR 3820, to reauthorize a program aimed at coordinating research on ways to reduce the damage caused by earthquakes. The Natural Hazards Risk Reduction Act called for $905.7 million in funding for the National Earthquake Hazards Reduction Program through fiscal 2014. It also would authorize $136.7 million through fiscal 2014 for the National Windstorm Impact Reduction Program. The last reauthorization (PL 108-360), in 2004, had called for more than $880 million over five years for the two programs.

HR 3820 called for more research into improvement of buildings' resistance as well as preparedness education for local governments and communities. It also would fund efforts to reduce earthquake risk through grants and outreach. The House Science and Technology Committee had approved the bill by voice vote on October 21, 2009, and formally reported it (H Rept 111-424, Part 1) on February 26, 2010.

Established in 1977 (PL 95-124), the National Earthquake Hazards Reduction Program combined research efforts at the Federal Emergency Management Agency, the National Institute of Standards and Technology, the U.S. Geological Society, and the National Science Foundation. *(1977 law, Congress and the Nation Vol. V, p. 555)*

FEMA Independence

The House Transportation and Infrastructure Committee on April 13, 2010, reported a bill (HR 1174—H Rept 111-459, Part 1) to restore the independent, cabinet-level status of the Federal Emergency Management Agency (FEMA), which had been put under the Department of Homeland Security (DHS) in a 2002 law (PL 107-296). The issue had come up in the 109th Congress, during which the agency was retooled in the wake of its poor performance in the aftermath of 2005 Hurricane Katrina (PL 109-295). *(Department of Homeland Security, Congress and the Nation Vol. XI, p. 176; FEMA overhaul, Congress and the Nation Vol. XII, p. 236)*

The committee had approved the FEMA Independence Act by voice vote on November 5, 2009.

Committee Chair James L. Oberstar, D-Minn., who sponsored HR 1174, said the legislation would restore FEMA's "integrity and effectiveness." He said that FEMA was designed to be a "mobile, quick-response agency" but that could happen only if it were an independent organization with cabinet-level clout. Under the bill, the agency would be led by an administrator and a deputy administrator, both of whom would be appointed by the president and confirmed by the Senate. The agency head would be required to have extensive experience in emergency preparedness, response, recovery, and mitigation from hazards. One of the biggest criticisms leveled at FEMA after Katrina was that it had been led by someone who had minimal emergency management experience—Michael D. Brown.

The legislation faced bipartisan opposition from leaders of both the House Homeland Security Committee and the Senate Homeland Security and Governmental Affairs Committee, which also had jurisdiction. Objections were made to changing FEMA's mission while the retooling efforts were taking hold. Furthermore, Senate committee Chair Joseph I. Lieberman, I-Conn., and ranking Republican Susan Collins of Maine said in a joint statement issued November 5, 2009: "In May, the administration put to rest a long-simmering dispute about whether FEMA should be an independent agency when DHS Secretary Janet Napolitano announced the administration had no intention of cutting FEMA loose."

A Senate companion bill, the Federal Emergency Management Advancement Act (S 412) was sponsored by James M. Inhofe, R-Okla. The measure was referred to the Senate Homeland Security and Governmental Affairs Committee but saw no further action.

Government Agencies Efficiency

Congress in 2010 cleared a bill (HR 2142) aimed at strengthening the way federal government agencies do business. The Government Efficiency, Effectiveness, and Performance (GPRA) Modernization Act was signed into law (PL 111-352) on January 4, 2011.

The House Oversight and Government Reform Committee approved HR 2142 by voice vote on May 20, 2010, and formally reported it (H Rept 111-504) on June 14. The full House agreed by voice vote on June 16 to suspend the rules and pass the bill, which would require quarterly reviews of government programs to assess and improve their performance. The House-passed measure would require federal agencies to collaborate with the Office of Management and Budget (OMB) to identify goals related to each agency's mission. The quarterly reports would assess progress made toward achieving those goals. Semiannual reports would be required on existing performance goals.

Proponents of the measure in the House argued that periodic performance assessments helped Congress and the executive branch identify the most pressing policy and program issues and determine if changes were needed to increase a program's efficiency and effectiveness. The Blue Dog Coalition of fiscally conservative House Democrats advocated the measure as part of a plan for reducing government waste. The bill, which built on existing law (PL 103-62), included an emphasis on assessing similar programs and identifying potential opportunities for integrating federal functions. Republicans, however, voiced skepticism about HR 2142, contending that, to be complete, the bill had to follow through and cut duplicative programs. The conservative Republican Study Group issued a statement saying that the bill "does not contain an effective means in which to consolidate or eliminate ineffective programs at each agency." *(PL 103-62, Congress and the Nation Vol. IX, p. 814)*

The Senate Homeland Security and Governmental Affairs Committee approved HR 2142 by voice vote September 29 and formally reported it December 7. A written report (S Rept 111-372) was filed December 16, the same day the Senate passed an amended version of the bill by voice vote.

Bill sponsor Henry Cuellar, D-Texas, expressed his support for the Senate changes. On the House floor after Senate passage, he explained that the Senate amendments would require OMB to "develop a Federal Government performance plan that addresses program efforts across agencies. OMB is also required to work with agencies to develop federal program priority goals that cut across different agencies and measure progress toward meeting those goals. This will help agencies avoid duplicating efforts and become more efficient." Cuellar noted that Sen. Tom Coburn, R-Okla., was successful in adding language calling for "increasingly stringent requirements for agencies that do not meet performance goals, which can ultimately end up, for a nonperforming agency or program, with budget reduction or even elimination." The Senate also established the position of chief operating officer in the twenty-four biggest agencies.

The House on December 17 rejected a motion, 212–131, to suspend the rules and pass the amended HR 2142. (A two-thirds vote is required under suspension of the rules.) On December 21, the House approved, 216–129, a motion by Cuellar to agree to the Senate amendment, completing congressional action.

Cuellar reported that the Congressional Budget Office (CBO) estimated that implementation of the bill, with the Senate changes, would be $15 million a year. He noted that the measure did not contain any mandatory spending requirements and did not violate any pay-as-you-go requirements. House Oversight and Government Reform Committee Chair Edolphus Towns, D-N.Y., said money would be saved in the long run, pointing to a CBO assertion that the bill could lead to more effective management of government agencies, thus lowering their costs.

Improper Payments Elimination

Congress in 2010 cleared legislation (S 1508) to expand requirements for federal agencies to identify programs and activities susceptible to improper payments. The Improper Payments Elimination and Recovery Act, sponsored by Thomas R. Carper, D-Del., was signed by the president into law (PL 111-204) on July 22.

The Senate Homeland Security and Governmental Affairs Committee approved the bill by voice vote on July 29, 2009, and formally reported it (no written report) on June 15. The full Senate passed the bill by voice vote on June 23, 2010. The House agreed to suspend the rules and pass S 1508 by a vote of 414–0 on July 14, completing congressional action.

As enacted, the legislation required the head of each federal agency to review agency programs and activities every three years to determine whether these programs were susceptible to significant improper payments. "Significant" was defined as improper payments in the preceding fiscal year that exceeded $100 million or $10 million of all program and activity payments and 2.5 percent of program outlays; fiscal years before 2013, exceeded $100 million or $10 million of all program and activity payments and 1.5 percent of program outlays. Risk factors to be considered included whether the program or activity was new to the agency, how complex the program or activity was, the volume of payments made, whether major changes had recently been made in the program, the quality of personnel training, and deficiencies in auditing. Agency heads were required to conduct recovery audits for programs that expend $1 million or more annually if such audits were cost-effective.

On April 28, 2010, the House had agreed by voice vote to suspend the rules and pass a companion measure (HR 3393). In comparing HR 3393 with S 1508 on the House floor, Rep. Danny K. Davis, D-Ill., said the Senate bill strengthened the House version "by requiring recovery audit contractors to report the fraud they find and to conduct appropriate training on the means and methods to do so. S 1508 also requires the agencies to report to Congress and [the Office of Management and Budget] their actions and plans to address the recommendations they receive from the audit recovery contractors."

The Senate in 2012 sought to fortify PL 111-204 by further curbing overpayments and mispayments to contractors and program beneficiaries. *(112th Congress action, p. 634)*

Information Overclassification

Congress in 2010 cleared legislation (HR 553) aimed at reducing the overclassification of information and promoting the sharing of unclassified information. The president signed the Reducing Over-Classification Act into law (PL 111-258) on October 7, 2010.

The disclosure provisions of HR 553 would apply to agencies in addition to the Department of Homeland Security (DHS) that were involved in the classification process. The bill would clarify the authority of the director of national intelligence to share sensitive material with officials at other government agencies who had appropriate security clearance. It also would require government employees responsible for determining the classification of material to attend annual training on appropriate classification levels. It would provide employee incentives for appropriately classifying materials. The legislation also established the position of classified information advisory officer within DHS. Under the measure, the officer would help educate state and local officials and other stakeholders in how to appeal classification decisions that impeded information sharing.

The House agreed, by voice vote on February 3, 2009, to a motion to suspend the rules and pass the HR 553. The Senate Homeland Security and Governmental Affairs Committee approved the bill by voice vote on November 4 and formally reported it (S Rept 111-200) on May 27, 2010. The full Senate passed an amended version of the measure by voice vote on September 27, and the House agreed to a motion to suspend the rules and accept the Senate changes by voice vote on September 28, completing congressional action.

Plain Writing

In 2010, Congress cleared legislation (HR 946) to require federal agencies to use "plain writing" in any document providing information about government benefits or services or explaining how to comply with a government mandate. Plain writing, as opposed to plain language, would allow for some legal terminology, so long as it was understandable, supporters said. The Plain Writing Act also would give civil servants remedial training in writing and require agencies to set up websites where citizens could point out bad writing.

The House Oversight and Government Reform Committee approved HR 946, sponsored by Bruce Braley, D-Iowa, by voice vote on March 4, 2010, and formally reported it (H Rept 111-432) on March 11. The full House agreed to suspend the rules and pass the bill on March 17, by a vote of 386–33. The Senate passed an amended version by voice vote on September 27. The House on September 29 agreed, 341–82, to suspend the rules and accept the Senate changes, completing congressional action. President Barack Obama signed HR 946 into law (PL 111-274) on October 13, 2010.

The Senate Homeland Security and Governmental Affairs Committee approved a companion measure (S 574), sponsored by Daniel K. Akaka, D-Hawaii, by voice vote on April 1, 2009, and formally reported it (S Rept 111-102), on December 9, 2009.

In 1966, after reading one too many badly written documents at the Bureau of Land Management, an otherwise anonymous bureaucrat named John O'Hayre wrote a manifest: "Gobbledygook Has Gotta Go." It launched one of the first serious efforts to force the federal government out of its habit of making even simple documents unnecessarily complicated. President Richard Nixon demanded that the notoriously dense *Federal Register* be written in "layman's terms," and President Jimmy Carter in 1978 issued executive orders to make government regulations "easy to understand." Not much changed, however, and President Ronald Reagan let the issue drop, prompting a grassroots movement of agency writers to push for more formal attention on the matter. In 1998, President Bill Clinton signed a memorandum requiring that regulations issued by his administration use plain language. Taking a cue from O'Hayre, Clinton's vice president, Al Gore, handed out monthly "No Gobbledygook" awards to employees who untangled their prose. The movement flagged under President George W. Bush, who allowed agencies to take the lead on the issue.

The House in 2008 passed the Plain Language in Government Communications Act (HR 3548—H Rept 110-580), and a companion measure (S 2291—S Rept 110-412) was reported by the Senate Homeland Security and Governmental Affairs Committee. The plain-writing legislation was stymied in the 110th Congress by Sen. Robert F. Bennett, R-Utah, who said he worried that agencies such as the Federal Election Commission would not be able to use legal terminology when needed. Braley and Akaka accommodated Bennett by requiring in their legislation that agencies produce plain writing, instead of plain language.

Obama on January 18, 2011, issued Executive Order 13563 expanding on PL 111-274, which had omitted a requirement for plain writing in federal regulations. He said that regulations need to be "accessible, consistent, written in plain language and easy to understand."

Deceptive Use of "Census"

Congress in 2010 cleared a bill (HR 5148—PL 111-170) aimed at preventing deceptive use of the word "census" in nongovernmental direct mail.

Rep. Darrell Issa, R-Calif., introduced HR 5148, officially dubbed "To amend title 39, United States Code, to clarify the instances in which the term 'census' may appear on mailable matter," in response to a controversial fund-raising letter sent out by the Republican National Committee (RNC) in April 2010. Issa, ranking member of the House Oversight and Government Reform Committee, criticized the RNC for skirting a new law (HR 4621—PL 111-155) that barred use of the word "census" on the outside of nongovernmental mail without a clear disclaimer and return address. The RNC mailer included it on a document visible through a plastic window on the envelope. Action on HR 4621 had been prompted by similar RNC fund-raising letters sent in December 2009. HR 5148 would prohibit use of the word "census" in any way that was visible through the envelope or on a wrapper.

The House Oversight and Government Reform Committee by voice vote approved HR 4621, the Prevent Deceptive Census Look Alike Mailings Act, on March 4, 2010. The full House agreed, 416–0, on March 10 to suspend the rules and pass the bill. The Senate passed the measure by voice vote on March 26, completing congressional action. The president signed HR 4261 into law on April 7.

The House agreed by voice vote on April 28, 2010, to suspend the rules and pass HR 5148. The Senate passed the bill, unchanged, by voice vote on May 5. It was signed into law on May 24.

House passage of HR 5148 came just after top Democrats on the Oversight and Government Reform Committee asked the postmaster general to investigate whether the April RNC mailer violated PL 111-155. RNC spokesperson Doug Heye said that the mailing was in full compliance with the new statute and that any confusion stemmed from "vague or unclear legislative language." HR 4621, sponsored by Carolyn B. Maloney, D-N.Y., required any mailing with "census" marked on the envelope or outer wrapper to include the accurate name and return address of the entity sending the mailing. It also required any nongovernmental mailings that used the word to include a notice that the mailing was not affiliated with the federal government.

Immigration Status on Census

Action on the fiscal 2010 Commerce-Justice-Science appropriations bill (HR 2847) stalled in 2009 when Republican senators used the measure to try to block illegal immigrants from being counted in apportioning congressional seats.

David Vitter, R-La., offered an amendment to HR 2847, mandating that census takers ask people about their immigration status as part of the 2010 decennial census. The amendment made no mention of how the information would be used. However, Vitter and cosponsor Robert F. Bennett, R-Utah, made it clear that they sought to have the Census Bureau exclude counts of illegal immigrants in determining the next round of congressional reapportionment.

Groups that represented Latinos called the amendment a wrongheaded, intrusive approach that would drive immigrants away from the census and deny federal dollars to the localities in which they lived.

Another often cited problem was timing. Census experts said that adding any question at that point would throw the entire process into disarray, delay reapportionment, and come with an astronomical cost. Bennett, who sponsored a bill (S 1688) calling for the census questionnaire to require respondents to indicate citizenship status or lawful presence in the United States, scoffed at the idea that adding a question could be so disruptive. (The Fairness in Representation Act was referred to the Senate Homeland Security and Governmental Affairs Subcommittee on Federal Financial Management, Government Information, Federal Services, and International Security. It saw no further action.) Terri Ann Lowenthal, a census consultant, argued that if lawmakers wanted to change the questionnaire, they should have done so in 2007, when the Bureau of the Census presented the survey to members of Congress for changes, as required by law.

The Vitter amendment held up action on HR 2847 for more than three weeks, until November 5, when it was ruled nongermane after a point of order was raised against it and Majority Leader Harry Reid, D-Nev., was able to assemble the votes needed to invoke cloture (thus limiting debate). The vote on the motion was 60–39. Later the same day, the full Senate passed HR 2847. The bill subsequently was packaged into HR 3288, the Consolidated Appropriations Act, which was signed into law (PL 111-117) on December 16, 2009. *(Omnibus measure, p. 134)*

E-mail Records Protection

The House on March 17, 2010, by voice vote agreed to suspend the rules and pass HR 1387, to require the White House and federal agencies to save e-mail records electronically. The House Committee on Oversight and Government Reform had approved the Electronic Message Preservation Act, sponsored by Paul W. Hodes, D-N.H., by voice vote on March 10, 2009, and formally reported it (H Rept 111-406) on January 27, 2010.

Existing law required the executive branch to preserve certain electronic records, but HR 1387 would compel agencies and the White House to store e-mails electronically, instead of printing hard copies for storage. In addition to requiring the head of the National Archives and Records Administration to set new standards for storing federal and presidential e-mail records, the archives administration would be directed to certify that federal agencies and the White House were following the new requirements.

HR 1387 was nearly identical to a measure that the House passed in 2008 under a Democratic majority, despite a veto threat from President George W. Bush. *(2008 action, Congress and the Nation Vol. XII, p. 804)*

Cybersecurity Research

On February 4, 2010, the House passed by a vote of 422–5 a bill (HR 4061) intending to boost federal cybersecurity research. The House Science and Technology Committee had approved the Cybersecurity Enhancement Act by voice vote on November 18, 2009, and formally reported it (H Rept 111-405) on January 27, 2010. *(Computer networks cybersecurity, p. 217)*

HR 4061 would reauthorize and expand cybersecurity research programs at the National Science Foundation and the National Institute of Standards and Technology. The measure also would create a new cybersecurity scholarship program, require agencies to develop a strategic cybersecurity research plan, and establish a university-industry task force to explore public-private research partnerships. The legislation would authorize $639 million through fiscal 2014 and $320 million afterward.

A week before the House passed HR 4061, hackers vandalized forty-nine House websites after President Barack Obama's State of the Union Address. Those attacks prompted Speaker Nancy Pelosi, D-Calif., and Minority Leader John A. Boehner, R-Ohio, to request a review by the Office of the Chief Administrative Officer. The attacks on House members' websites were preceded by a high-profile cyber-intrusion against Google, which Director of National Intelligence Dennis C. Blair said, in an appearance before the Senate Intelligence Agency on February 2, 2010, was a "wake-up call to those who have not taken this problem seriously."

In related action, the Senate Homeland Security and Governmental Affairs Committee by voice vote approved S 3480, the Protecting Cyberspace as a National Asset Act, on June 24, 2010, and formally reported it (S Rept 111-368) on December 15. The bill, sponsored by Joseph I. Lieberman, I-Conn., would establish an Office of Cyberspace Policy in the Executive Office of the President, with the task of developing a national strategy to increase the security and resiliency of cyberspace.

Filing Federal Regulations

The House on June 16, 2009, agreed, 414–0, to suspend the rules and pass HR 2247, the Congressional Review Improvement Act. The measure would lift the requirement established by a 1996 law (PL 104-121) that government agencies send a copy of new rules to Congress and the Government Accountability Office (GAO). *(PL 104-121, Congress and the Nation Vol. IX, p. 76)*

The House Judiciary Committee had approved the bill by voice vote on May 20 and formally reported it (H Rept 111-150) on June 12. The Senate took no action.

The December 29, 2009, Congressional Research Service (CRS) report "Congressional Review Act: Rules Not Submitted to GAO and Congress" stated that, according to the GAO, twenty-eight agencies and cabinet departments had failed to file copies of 101 "substantive final rules" with the GAO in fiscal 2008. Among them was a Homeland Security Department rule that altered protocols for drug and alcohol testing in the transportation industry and an Interior Department rule designating critical habitats for the endangered guajón, a frog native to Puerto Rico. GAO officials told CRS investigator Curtis W. Copeland, author of the 2009 report, that five times in the past decade they had compared the log of rules received from federal agencies with a list of regulations published in the *Federal Register* and found a thousand rules missing.

Although failure to submit a copy of a new rule to Congress and the GAO seemed to some like a minor omission, others argued that opponents of rules or organizations subject to enforcement action could protest and sue to block rules that were not technically made final.

FDR Memorabilia

Congress in 2010 cleared legislation (S 692) that would pave the way for the public and historians to peer into the notes and other artifacts of a personal secretary to President Franklin D. Roosevelt (FDR).

If the papers were donated to the National Archives and Records Administration (NARA), S 692 would waive the government's claim to the Tully Archive, more than five thousand letters, documents, and other memorabilia related to the thirty-second president of the United States (1933–1945) and owned by his personal secretary, Grace Tully, at the time of her death in 1984.

The owner of the papers at the time S 692 was enacted, the Sun-Times Media Group, wanted to donate the archives to the Franklin D. Roosevelt Presidential Library and Museum in Hyde Park, N.Y. However, for the company to receive a full tax deduction, the federal government had to clarify that it had relinquished any claims it had made concerning the documents. NARA had previously asserted a claim on a portion, according to Stephen F. Lynch, D-Mass., chair of the House Oversight and Government Reform Subcommittee on Federal Workforce, Postal Service, and the District of Columbia.

The Senate Homeland Security and Governmental Affairs Committee approved S 692 by voice vote on May 20, 2009, and formally reported it (S Rept 111-87) on October 5. The Senate passed the bill by voice vote on October 14. The House passed the measure, unchanged, by voice vote under suspension of the rules on January 13, 2010, completing congressional action. President Barack Obama signed the legislation into law (PL 111-138) on February 1. The official title of the bill was: "A bill to provide that claims of the United States to certain documents relating to Franklin Delano Roosevelt shall be treated as waived and relinquished in certain circumstances."

Tully worked as the assistant to Missy LeHand, personal secretary to New York governor Roosevelt (1929–1932), and followed LeHand and FDR to the White House in 1933. After LeHand was incapacitated by a stroke in 1941, Tully assumed her position as personal secretary to the president. She was present in Warm Springs, Ga., when Roosevelt suffered his fatal stroke.

The Grace Tully Collection was opened for research at the FDR library in November 2010. It subsequently was completely digitized and posted online (www.fdrlibrary.marist.edu/archives/collections/tully.html) in spring 2011.

Presidential Records

The House on January 7, 2009, the House agreed, 359–58, to suspend the rules and pass HR 35, to codify the president's ability to choose whether to honor or reject his predecessors' requests for executive privilege. The Presidential Records Act Amendments would govern the right of the president to withhold certain information from other branches of government and the public. The Senate Homeland Security and Governmental Affairs Committee approved HR 35 by voice vote on April 1 and formally reported it (S Rept 111-21) on May 19. The measure saw no further action.

Presidents have issued conflicting executive orders on the subject. In 2001, George W. Bush issued an executive order requiring a sitting president to comply with his predecessors' requests to invoke executive privilege. Bush's order overturned one that Ronald Reagan had issued in 1989. Just one day into his term, Barack Obama issued an order revoking Bush's rule.

The Senate committee-approved version of HR 35 mirrored the language of President Obama's order and outlined a process for considering executive privilege claims. If the archivist of the United States made a determination to release previously undisclosed documents, the archivist would have to provide notice to the sitting president and the one under whom the documents were generated. After a review period, the sitting president would make the call on disclosing the information, although, if his decision conflicted with a former president's claim of privilege, the former chief executive could file suit. The bill also said that only a president could invoke executive privilege. Bush's executive order had given the vice president authority to assert the privilege over some White House records.

National Women's History Museum

On October 14, 2009, the House agreed by voice vote to suspend the rules and pass HR 1700, the National Women's History Museum Act. The bill, sponsored by Carolyn B. Maloney, D-N.Y., provided for the establishment of a National Women's History Museum in Washington, D.C.

Action stalled when two Republican senators—Tom Coburn of Oklahoma and Jim DeMint of South Carolina—held up the House-passed legislation after conservatives said the museum would glorify abortion. The project's organizers subsequently attempted to placate some critics by adding to their online museum the biographies of anti-abortion activist Ellen McCormack and Eagle Forum founder Phyllis Schlafly, whose organization had helped defeat the Equal Rights Amendment. *(Equal Rights Amendment, Congress and the Nation Vol. III, pp. 500, 504, 509; Vol. IV, p. 676; Vol. V, p. 798; Vol. VI, pp. 682, 697)*

The House Transportation and Infrastructure Committee approved HR 1700 by voice vote on September 24, 2009, and formally reported it (H Rept 111-295) on October 8. The Senate Environment and Public Works Committee approved the measure by voice vote on April 21, 2010, and formally reported it (S Rept 111-217) on June 28.

Companion legislation (S 2129), sponsored by Susan Collins, R-Maine, was approved by the Senate Environment and Public Works Committee by voice vote on April 21, 2010, and formally reported (S Rept 111-216) on June 28.

In the 112th Congress, the museum proposal became tied up with legislation to move the Federal Trade Commission. *(112th Congress action, p. 636)*

American-made U.S. Flags

The House by voice vote on September 30, 2010, agreed to suspend the rules and pass HR 2853, the All-American Flag Act. The bill would require federal agencies to buy only those American flags that had been fabricated entirely in the United States and from exclusively domestic materials. The measure also would require that all American flags bought by the federal government be made by legal U.S. residents.

Bruce Braley, D-Iowa, originally introduced the flag bill in 2008 and then reintroduced it in the 111th Congress. It was largely ignored until, in July 2010, Democrats put together their "Make It in America" list of bills to promote domestic manufacturing. The House Oversight and Government Reform Committee approved HR 2853 by voice vote on July 28 and formally reported it (H Rept 111-586) on September 14.

The legislation was referred to the Senate Homeland Security and Governmental Affairs Committee, but it saw no further action.

Apology to Native Americans

Tucked in the fiscal 2010 defense appropriations bill (HR 3326—PL 111-118), signed into law on December 19, 2009, was a long-sought formal apology to American Indians for decades of killings, mistreatment, and broken treaties.

The legislation stated: "The United States, acting through Congress—(1) recognizes the special legal and political relationship Indian tribes have with the United States and the solemn covenant with the land we share; (2) commends and honors Native Peoples for the thousands of years that they have stewarded and protected this land; (3) recognizes that there have been years of official depredations, ill-conceived policies, and the breaking of covenants by the Federal Government regarding Indian tribes; (4) apologizes on behalf of the people of the United States to all Native Peoples for the many instances of violence, maltreatment, and neglect inflicted on Native Peoples by citizens of the United States; (5) expresses its regret for the ramifications of former wrongs and its commitment to build on the positive relationships of the past and present to move toward a brighter future where all the people of this land live reconciled as brothers and sisters, and harmoniously steward and protect this land together; (6) urges the President to acknowledge the wrongs of the United States against Indian tribes in the history of the United States in order to bring healing to this land; and (7) commends the State governments that have begun reconciliation efforts with recognized Indian tribes located in their boundaries and encourages all State governments similarly to work toward reconciling relationships with Indian tribes within their boundaries."

Jacqueline Pata, executive director of the National Congress of American Indians and member of the Tlingit tribe of the Pacific Northwest, said tribes were more content with the apology than when it was first proposed in 2004 by Republican senator Sam Brownback of Kansas. Many were skeptical, however, given the disclaimer in HR 3326 that the contrition was not grounds for authorizing or settling claims against the United States. *(2004 action, Congress and the Nation Vol. XI, p. 701)*

Indian Health Service

Congress in 2010 reauthorized the Indian Health Service and other health programs aimed at American Indians.

The Senate Indian Affairs Committee by voice vote approved a bill (S 1790) on December 3, 2009, and formally reported it (no written report) on December 16. The Indian Health Care Improvement Reauthorization and Extension Act, sponsored by Byron L. Dorgan, D-N.D., would permanently reauthorize existing law (PL 94-437) that governed current Indian health care programs. The measure would authorize programs aimed at increasing the recruitment and retention of health care professionals. It would expand mental and behavioral health programs to address issues such as fetal alcohol spectrum disorders as well as child sexual abuse and domestic violence. *(PL 94-437, Congress and the Nation Vol. IV, p. 372)*

In addition, the legislation would authorize long-term care services, including hospice care, assisted living, long-term care, and home- and community-based care. It would provide incentives to use innovative facility construction methods, such as modular component construction and mobile health stations, in an effort to cut costs and improve access to services. It also would require that the Indian Health Service budget account for medical inflation rates and population growth, to combat underfunding of the Indian health system.

The language of the committee-approved S 1790, with minor changes, was included in the Patient Protection and Affordable Care Act (HR 3590—PL 111-148), signed into law on March 23, 2010. *(Health care overhaul, p. 421)*

On October 30, 2009, President Barack Obama had signed into law the fiscal 2010 appropriations bill for the Interior Department and environmental programs (HR 2996—PL 111-88), which contained the biggest spending increase for the Indian Health Service in twenty years—$4.1 billion. [Another $500,000 was provided in the economic stimulus law (HR 1—PL 111-5).] Also in 2009 Obama installed at the helm of the Indian Health Service the first American Indian woman to hold that position. Dr. Yvette Roubideaux was a member of the Rosebud Sioux Tribe in South Dakota. *(Fiscal 2010 interior appropriations, p. 129; economic stimulus, p. 78)*

Indian Tribes Recognition

On a vote of 240–179 taken June 3, 2009, the House passed HR 31, granting federal recognition to the Lumbee Tribe of North Carolina, which had been petitioning Congress since 1888 but had trouble documenting its claim to Indian heritage. The House Natural Resources Committee had approved the Lumbee Recognition Act by voice vote on April 22 and formally reported it (H Rept 111-103) on May 12. The Senate Indian Affairs Committee approved a companion measure (S 1735) by voice vote October 22, 2009, and reported it (S Rept 111-116) on January 20, 2010.

Also on June 3, the House by voice vote passed HR 1385, the Thomasina E. Jordan Indian Tribes of Virginia Federal Recognition Act. The bill would extend federal recognition to six tribes in Virginia: the Chickahominy Indian Tribe, the Chickahominy Indian Tribe–Eastern Division, the Upper Mattaponi Tribe, the Rappahannock

Tribe, Inc., the Monacan Indian Nation, and the Nansemond Indian Tribe. The House Natural Resources Committee approved HR 1385 by voice vote on April 22 and formally reported it (H Rept 111-104) on May 12. A companion measure (S 1178) was approved by voice vote by the Senate Indian Affairs Committee on October 22, 2009, and formally reported (S Rept 111-113) on December 23.

Congress had voted to acknowledge only seven of the many tribal entities that had sought legislation since 1978, when a formal, and rigorous, recognition process was established at the Interior Department. That process was created in part to remove Congress from the front line of having to decide remaining cases, which all had thorny questions involving tribes' locality, membership, and historicity that were not easy to answer even in the best of circumstances. To be recognized, tribes must prove that they met seven criteria, including that the predominant portion of the tribe was a distinct community that existed from historical times and that it had been continuously identified as an American Indian entity since 1900.

Some Indian groups also complained that the process took too long. Also, a complication of the success of Indian casinos was that some tribes opposed the recognition of others that could be business competitors.

Indian Casino Land

The Senate Indian Affairs Committee on December 17, 2009, by voice vote approved and on August 5, 2010, formally reported a bill (S 1703—S Rept 111-247) that would grant to all tribes, regardless of when they were recognized, the right to take land into trust. The measure, sponsored by Byron L. Dorgan, D-N.D., would effectively overrule the 2009 U.S. Supreme Court decision in *Carcieri v. Salazar* (555 U.S. 379), which held that the Interior secretary could not take land into trust for a specific Indian tribe because that tribe had not been under federal jurisdiction when the Indian Reorganization Act was enacted, on June 18, 1934.

The Court decision put a crimp in the ability of dozens of American Indian tribes to buy land for casinos and other economic development projects. It said that only those tribes recognized before 1934 were entitled to do so. Tribes recognized since then that wanted to buy real estate to add to their reservations were unable to do so unless they could prove that they should have been recognized before 1934, a process that tribes said was expensive and time-consuming.

The issue was crucial to the tribes because they did not have to abide by many state and local regulations on their reservations and, under some circumstances, could launch gambling ventures on them without state approval. That was not the case on land they owned that was not officially part of their reservation.

Matthew L. M. Fletcher, director of the Indigenous Law and Policy Center at Michigan State University College of Law, said that the Court decision was horribly unfair. "A lot of tribes recognized since 1934 were administratively terminated or went underground because of racism," he said. "They are in the most acute need for land." Some new tribes—such as the Mashpee Wampanoags, who won federal recognition in 2007—had no reservation at all. In order to build the casino they were planning in Fall River, on the border between Massachusetts and Rhode Island, they needed to take land into trust.

Tribes wanted it known, however, that the decision worried them for reasons beyond the impact on their gambling industry. In fact, the case was about real estate development. The Narragansett Tribe asserted that its housing development adjacent to a reservation in Rhode Island did not have to meet local building codes, especially since the Interior Department agreed in 1998 to take the land into trust. But Republican governor Donald L. Carcieri sued, contending that because the tribe was not recognized at the time of the 1934 law, it could not benefit from that statute. Two lower courts sided with the tribe, but in a 6–3 decision in February 2009 the Supreme Court sided with the governor.

The House Natural Resources Committee held hearings on two companion measures (HR 3697, HR 3742), but neither saw further action. Rep. Tom Cole, R-Okla., inserted language comparable with S 1703, officially dubbed "A bill to amend the Act of June 18, 1934, to reaffirm the authority of the Secretary of the Interior to take land into trust for Indian tribes," into the fiscal 2011 Interior Department appropriations House draft bill. Dorgan had expressed his desire to write the provisions into the Senate's version of that legislation. However, Senate Appropriations Committee Interior and Related Agencies Subcommittee Chair Dianne Feinstein, D-Calif., made it clear that she opposed a quick fix for the American Indians. California counties had sparred with tribes there over land use and gambling, and they preferred a broader rewrite of the 1934 law that would give local officials more power over the process.

Native Hawaiian Government

On February 23, 2010, the House voted 245–164 to pass a bill (HR 2314) that would allow native Hawaiians to create their own government. The Native Hawaiian Government Reorganization Act, sponsored by Neil Abercrombie, D-Hawaii, would provide sovereign immunity to a new governing entity yet to be established.

House passage of the measure came after Abercrombie made last-minute changes in an attempt to allay the concerns of Hawaii Republican governor Linda Lingle and state attorney general Mark Bennett. Abercrombie's substitute amendment would clarify that native Hawaiians would remain subject to state and federal laws and that the governing entity would be subject to state taxation and regulation when conducting commercial or business activities. However, the amendment, adopted 245–164 on February

23, did little to appease state officials. Lingle was still troubled by language that would provide authority to the native government before it began talks with the state about, among other issues, the new government's structure and its land policy. She also was concerned about provisions allowing that native government to operate free from state and federal rules.

The substitute amendment also clarified that lands would not be immediately transferred to the native Hawaiian governing entity and that property owned by the entity would not be immune from lawsuits brought by the state. But, as Lingle noted, it would provide for negotiations between the governing entity and the federal and state governments over land issues. The state was managing about 200,000 acres set aside in the 1920s for native Hawaiian use.

American Indian law would not apply to lands or land transfers in Hawaii, and the native government would not be allowed to conduct gaming activities. HR 2314 would require the Interior Department to oversee the new government's organization and an interim governing council, which would draft documents of the native government. Upon the Interior secretary's certification of the documents and election of governing officials, federal recognition would be extended.

Before adopting the Abercrombie substitute, the House rejected two amendments on February 23. The amendment offered by Doc Hastings, R-Wash., to the substitute amendment would require Hawaii voters to approve native Hawaiian governing entity documents before federal recognition was given. It was felled 163–241. The substitute would formally recognize native Hawaiians as a distinct indigenous group and outline a process for establishing a native Hawaiian governing entity. Arizona Republican Jeff Flake offered an amendment to the substitute that would clarify that nothing in HR 2314 could be interpreted to exempt a new native Hawaiian governing authority from complying with the Equal Protection Clause of the Fourteen Amendment of the U.S. Constitution. It was defeated 177–233.

The issue of granting native Hawaiians limited self-government raised broader philosophical questions about the federal government's relations with indigenous people. Washington, D.C., had been recognizing and dealing with hundreds of American Indian tribes, on a government-to-government basis, for more than two centuries. The Interior Department had a procedure and standards for federal recognition and dozens of laws and aid programs. Furthermore, many recognized tribes were allowed to open casinos or bingo halls. Native Hawaiians, however, being of mostly Polynesian descent, were not Indians and had no part in the long history of indigenous people on the mainland. Their monarch, Queen Liliuokalani, was overthrown in 1893, after an invasion by U.S. marines that helped confirm the grip of U.S. agricultural and other business interests on the islands, although others said the motive was a reaction by some natives to a ruler's attempt at democracy. In any event, Congress apologized in 1993 (PL 103-150).

The House Natural Resources Committee had approved HR 2314 by a vote of 26–13 on December 16, 2009, and formally reported it (H Rept 111-412) on February 22, 2010.

A Senate companion measure (S 1011), sponsored by Daniel K. Akaka, D-Hawaii, was reported (S Rept 111-162) on March 11, 2010. The Senate Indian Affairs Committee had approved the Native Hawaiian Government Reorganization Act by voice vote on December 17, 2009. The bill went no further in the Senate.

Puerto Rico Political Status

On April 29, 2010, the House passed a bill (HR 2499) that would authorize a vote by Puerto Ricans on whether to change the island's status. The tally was 223–169, with one member voting "present." The House Natural Resources Committee had approved the Puerto Rico Democracy Act by 30–8 on July 22, 2009, and formally reported it (H Rept 111-294) on October 8.

The measure, sponsored by Democrat Pedro R. Pierluisi, Puerto Rico's resident commissioner, would authorize the island's government to conduct a plebiscite to choose between retaining its status as a U.S. commonwealth or seeking a new status. If a majority supported a new status a second vote would offer four options: statehood, full independence, independence with a special association with the United States, or existing commonwealth status.

The choice to continue with commonwealth status was added on the House floor after opponents, including some Democrats of Puerto Rican descent and many Republicans, argued that the process established by the bill was tilted toward statehood. The amendment making the change, offered by Virginia Foxx, R-N.C., was adopted, 223–179, on April 29, 2010. Amendment foes, including Pierluisi, argued that commonwealth backers had the option of maintaining the status quo during the first plebiscite.

On April 29 the House voted on a number of other amendments to HR 2499. It adopted by a vote of 301–100 an amendment offered by Dan Burton, R-Ind., to require plebiscite ballots to be printed in English. The amendment also would require the Puerto Rico election commission to inform voters that if Puerto Rico retained its current political status or was admitted to statehood, the official language requirements of the federal government would apply. The House rejected two amendments offered by Luis V. Gutierrez, D-Ill.: to give voters an option to choose "none of the above" during the second stage of the plebiscite (164–236) and to require plebiscite ballots to be printed in Spanish, with ballots in English available on request (13–386). Three amendments offered by Nydia M. Velázquez, D-N.Y., were defeated: to make U.S. citizens of Puerto Rican descent eligible to vote in the plebiscites authorized by the bill (11–387); to authorize Puerto Rico to hold one plebiscite to choose between the four options and to authorize a runoff process between the two options that received the highest number of votes if no option received more than 50 percent of the vote (112–285); and to strike the text of the bill and insert language to express the sense of Congress that the government of Puerto Rico can hold a vote on whether to conduct a plebiscite to change its political status (171–223). Before passage, the House rejected, 194–198, a motion by Doc Hastings, R-Wash., to recommit the bill to the Natural Resources Committee with instructions that it be immediately reported back with an amendment that would redefine the Puerto Rican statehood option to specify that English would be the official language and state laws would have to permit residents to own and carry firearms.

HR 2499 brought out unusual divides. Gutierrez, who was of Puerto Rican descent, voted against the measure, while New York Democrat José E. Serrano, who was born in Puerto Rico, supported it. Some Republicans echoed the concerns over the process created by the bill, saying it would lead to statehood and a host of related complications. Other GOP members painted their support in simpler terms: Puerto Ricans would have a say in their own future.

Puerto Rico's status had been controversial since Spain ceded the island to the United States in 1898. Congress granted citizenship to Puerto Ricans in 1917, and Puerto Rico became a commonwealth in 1952. In a revolutionary act on March 1, 1954, four Puerto Rican nationalists, wishing to make known the island's struggle for independence from U.S. rule, opened fire from the gallery overlooking the floor of the U.S. House chamber. They were tried, convicted, and sentenced to prison. President Jimmy Carter in 1979 pardoned the four nationalists.

2011–2012

Federal Workforce Pensions

To offset the cost of payroll tax cut extension legislation (HR 3630—PL 112-96), lawmakers in 2012 made changes in federal workforce pensions. HR 3630, the Middle Class Tax Relief and Job Creation Act, increased by 2.3 percent (from 0.8 percent to 3.1 percent) the amount that federal employees who were hired after 2012 and who had fewer than five years of federal government service had to contribute to the Federal Employee Retirement System (FERS). New hires at the Central Intelligence Agency (CIA) and the Foreign Services also had to make larger payments into their pension systems. Current federal workers were not affected. Also not included in HR 3630 were provisions that stipulated a one-year freeze on federal employee salaries, based new worker pensions on their five highest salaries instead of three highest salaries, changed the multiplier used in calculating salaries, and dropped the FERS Annuity Supplement for employees who were not required to retire at a set age.

In related action, the House Oversight and Government Reform Committee approved HR 3813 by a vote of 22–16 on February 7, 2012, and formally reported it (H Rept 112-394, Part 1) on February 9. The Securing Annuities for Federal Employees Act was a GOP plan to require lawmakers and federal workers to increase substantially payments toward their retirement benefits. Republicans argued that the changes were a step toward aligning federal workforce pensions with those of state and local governments. Democrats argued that HR 3813 unfairly targeted government employees to balance the nation's books and constituted an assault on federal workers.

The bill, sponsored by Federal Workforce Subcommittee Chair Dennis A. Ross, R-Fla., would increase employee contributions to the Civil Service Retirement System (CSRS) and FERS by 1.5 percent of their salaries over a three-year period, starting in 2013. Employees enrolled in FERS were currently giving 0.8 percent to the fund. FERS, Democrats noted, already was completely funded. Furthermore, a 2010 law (PL 111-322) prohibited raises for federal employees and lawmakers for two years, and just a week before the Oversight and Government Reform Committee approved HR 3813, the House on February 1, 2012, passed a pay freeze extension through fiscal 2013 (HR 3835). *(PL 111-322, p. 600; HR 3835, this page)*

The committee-approved HR 3813 also would reduce total pensions for new federal employees hired since December 31, 2011, including lawmakers. They would be required to put 4 percent of their pay into federal retirement accounts, and their pension calculation would be based on the average of their five highest salaries, instead of the current highest three, and would be altered in other ways.

The panel by voice vote rejected an amendment offered by ranking Democrat Elijah E. Cummings of Maryland to exempt employees earning less than $30,000 annually from the changes.

The language of HR 3813 subsequently was included in and then dropped from HR 7, the American Energy and Infrastructure Act.

Republicans, seeking to make federal employee pensions comparable with those offered in the private sector, offered a draft proposal—adopted by the House Oversight and Government Reform Committee by a vote of 19–15 on April 26, 2012—requiring federal employees, members of Congress, and congressional aides to contribute at least an additional $82 billion to their pensions over the next ten years. Federal employees would contribute an additional 5 percent of their salaries; lawmakers enrolled in either CSRS or FERS, 8.5 percent; staffers enrolled in CSRS, 8.5 percent; and staffers enrolled in FERS, 7.5 percent. The committee also adopted an amendment that permitted federal workers to transfer payments of accumulated leave or unused vacation to pensions under the Thrift Savings Funds.

The GOP draft proposal also was intended to answer the call in the House-passed version of the budget resolution (H Con Res 112) for savings in domestic programs, to head off an automatic budget sequester (PL 112-25). The language later was included in two sequester replacement bills (HR 5652, HR 6684), both of which were passed by the House but were never considered by the Senate.

Federal Worker Pay

Budget concerns continued to keep civilian federal employees in the cold when it came to their compensation. The pay freeze was extended to December 31, 2013, and, because of the sequestration, federal workers were expected to become subject to de facto pay cuts—furloughs.

HR 3835. On February 1, 2012, the House agreed, 309–117, to suspend the rules and pass HR 3835, officially entitled "To extend the pay limitation for Members of Congress and Federal employees." The bill, sponsored by Sean P. Duffy, R-Wis., would hold the salaries of about 2.1 million federal employees to 2012 levels through 2013.

Before the vote on House passage, several Republicans touted a Congressional Budget Office (CBO) report that found that federal employees on average earned about 2 percent more than private-sector employees in comparable professions. Minority Whip Steny H. Hoyer, D-Md., who represented thousands of federal employees, led the opposition to HR 3835, saying it was a "clever" tactic meant for certain members to earn praise from constituents who favored using federal salaries to alleviate the government's financial distress.

HR 3835 was received in the Senate and referred to the Senate Homeland Security and Governmental Affairs Committee, but it saw no further action.

H J Res 117. As part of a fiscal 2013 continuing resolution (H J Res 117), Congress in 2012 extended the pay freeze for federal employees to March 27, 2013. President Barack Obama signed the measure into law (PL 112-175) on September 28, 2012. Earlier action (PL 111-322) had imposed a pay freeze through December 31, 2012. On December 21, 2012, Obama issued a memorandum instructing the heads of executive departments and agencies to continue the pay policy described in his December 22, 2010, memorandum. (*111th Congress action, p. 600*)

PL 113-6. On March 21, 2013, Congress cleared the Consolidated and Further Continuing Appropriations Act, which extended the pay freeze for most federal civilian employees until December 31, 2013. The president signed the measure into law (PL 113-6) on March 26.

The legislation superseded Executive Order 13635, issued December 27, 2012, in which the president set forth pay schedules showing a 0.5 percent increase. On April 5, 2013, Obama issued a memorandum instructing the heads of executive departments and agencies to continue the pay policy described in his December 22, 2010, and December 21, 2012, memorandums.

Sequestration. As a partial resolution of the fiscal cliff crisis, Congress cleared the American Taxpayer Relief Act (HR 8—PL 112-240) on January 1, 2013. A budget sequestration was set to begin on January 2, 2013, as stipulated by the Budget Control Act signed into law on August 2, 2011 (S 365—PL 112-25), but PL 112-240 extended the date for two months, to March 1, 2013. As a result of the sequester, federal workers were expected to be subject to involuntary unpaid time off, known as furloughs. (*Fiscal cliff, taxpayer relief, p. 185*)

Federal Employee Intelligence Leaks

Congress in 2011 included a provision in the fiscal 2011 intelligence authorization bill (HR 754—PL 112-18) seeking to limit leaks of classified information by federal workers. The language aimed to make it more difficult for government employees to leak information to the public, other governments, or rogue agents. The provision was included in response to incidents of government information appearing on the website WikiLeaks. *(Intelligence authorization, p. 250)*

HR 754 required the director of national intelligence to establish an insider threat detection program, an automated system that used networks, computer servers, routers, databases, website, and other methods of communications to detect prohibited transfers of information. The program was to reach full operating capacity by October 1, 2013.

The House Intelligence Committee approved HR 754 by a vote of 7–6 on March 10, 2011, and formally reported it (H Rept 112-72) on May 3. The full House passed the bill, 392–15, on May 13. The Senate passed it by voice vote on May 26, completing congressional action. On June 8 the president signed the measure into law. A Senate companion bill (S 719) was reported from the Senate Intelligence Committee (S Rept 112-12) on April 4, 2011.

Hatch Act Modernization

Congress in 2012 cleared legislation (S 2170) that would allow local and state employees, unless their salary was paid completely by the government, to seek partisan offices. It also would loosen mandatory minimum sentences for those violating the law. The Hatch Act Modernization Act was sponsored by Daniel K. Akaka, D-Hawaii.

The Senate Homeland Security and Governmental Affairs Committee approved S 2170 by voice vote on June 29 and on Sept. 13 formally reported it (S Rept 112-211). The Senate passed the bill by voice vote on Nov. 30. The House agreed by voice vote on Dec. 19 to suspend the rules and pass S 2170, completing congressional action. The measure was signed into law (PL 112-230) on December 28, 2012. A House companion bill (HR 4152), sponsored by Elijah E. Cummings, D-Md., was referred to the House Oversight and Government Reform Committee but saw no further action.

Congress in 1939 passed the Hatch Act to get rank-and-file federal workers out of partisan politics and, a year later, extended the act to cover state and local government workers whose pay included any federal money. The amendment, and the way it was interpreted over the decades, hobbled many would-be candidates and campaign workers with only the slenderest ties to Washington, D.C. Many said that the law was overreaching and needed an overhaul.

The Hatch Act was originally a Depression-era measure aimed at preventing government workers in positions of power from abusing their authority to influence elections. At the time, some evidence existed that Democratic Party bosses used Works Progress Administration (WPA) workers and others in campaigns, and the Hatch Act—named for Sen. Carl Hatch, a New Mexico Democrat—was heavily supported by Republicans. In 1993, after three tries, Congress amended the law (PL 103-94) to allow federal employees to actively participate in campaigns for federal offices. The debate since shifted to the law's effect on state and local government employees. *(1993 action, Congress and the Nation Vol. IX, p. 805)*

Supporters said S 2170 would save the U.S. Office of Special Counsel money, because 45 percent of its Hatch Act–related cases go toward investigating state and local candidates. Furthermore, backers of the bill said state and local governments, not the federal government, should regulate who can and cannot run for their particular offices.

Whistleblower Protection

Congress in 2012 cleared legislation (S 743) to expand whistleblower protections to federal employees who disclosed evidence of censorship related to research, analysis, or technical information. In the 111th Congress, both chambers passed different versions of a similar bill that were never reconciled. *(111th Congress action, p. 601)*

The Senate Homeland Security and Governmental Affairs Committee approved the Whistleblower Protection Enhancement Act, sponsored by Daniel K. Akaka, D-Hawaii, by voice vote on October 19, 2011, and formally reported it (S Rept 112-155) on April 19, 2012. The full Senate passed the bill by voice vote on May 8, 2012. The House passed an amended version by voice vote on September 28. The Senate agreed to the House changes by voice vote November 13, clearing the measure. It was signed into law (PL 112-199) on November 27.

As enacted, S 743 provided that a disclosure would not be excluded from whistleblower protections because the employee or an applicant for employment made the disclosure to a supervisor or another who took part in an activity that the person reasonably believed constituted gross mismanagement, gross waste of funds, abuse of authority, or a danger to public health or safety; because the information had previously been disclosed; because of the employee or applicant's motive for making the disclosure; because the disclosure was not made in writing; because the disclosure was made while the employee was off-duty; or because of the amount of time that had passed between the disclosure and the event in question. Furthermore, a disclosure was protected if it was made during the normal duties of an employee with respect to whom another person in a position of authority took, failed to take, or threatened to take or fail to take personnel action in reprisal. The legislation provided that substantial evidence could be used to rebut any presumptions made about a public officer's performance of duty. It also prohibited, as a personnel practice, the implementation or enforcement of any nondisclosure policy, form, or agreement that failed to spell out that its provisions were consistent with and do not supersede, conflict with, or alter employee obligations, rights, or liabilities stipulated by law or executive order relating to classified information, communications to Congress, reports to an inspector general, or any whistleblower protection.

Under certain circumstances, the Merit Systems Protection Board (MSPB) was authorized to require an agency where the prevailing party worked to pay reasonable attorney fees as well as compensatory damages. During the first two years of enactment, the legislation required that a petition to review an MSPB order or decision be filed in any court of appeals, not solely in the federal circuit, and allowed the court to grant a petition for judicial review.

S 743 extended whistleblower protections to employees of, and applicants for employment at, the Transportation Security Administration and to employees and prospective employees for disclosures that they reasonably believed were evidence of censorship related to research, analysis, or technical information. It stipulated that the Office of the Director of National Intelligence and the National Reconnaissance Office would be excluded from coverage of the 1989 Whistleblower Protection Act (PL 101-12). It also amended the 2002 Homeland Security Act (PL 107-296) so that a permissible use of independently obtained infrastructure information included disclosure of the information for whistleblower purposes. *(1989 law, Congress and the Nation Vol. VIII, p. 862; 2002 law, Congress and the Nation Vol. XI, p. 176)*

The legislation required the Government Accountability Office to report to Congress on the implementation of the new law, and it instructed the MSPB to cite the number and outcome of whistleblower cases in its annual program performance reports. The 1978 Inspector General Act (PL 95-452) was amended to require the inspector general of certain agencies to designate a whistleblower protection ombudsman. *(1978 law, Congress and the Nation Vol. V, p. 830)*

The House Oversight and Government Reform Committee approved a companion measure (HR 3289) by a vote of 35–0 on November 3, 2011, and formally reported it (H Rept 112-508, Part 1) on May 30, 2012.

Federal Employee Domestic Partnerships

Same-sex partners of federal employees would be eligible for benefits under a bill (S 1910) approved on a voice vote by the Senate Homeland Security and Governmental Affairs Committee on May 16, 2012, and formally reported (S Rept 112-257) on December 19. The Domestic Partnership Benefits and Obligations Act, sponsored by Joseph I. Lieberman, I-Conn., would make government workers in homosexual domestic partnerships eligible for the same health, long-term disability, retirement, and other benefits as those offered to heterosexual married couples. Lieberman said extending the benefits to same-sex couples would cost about $70 million a year.

S 1910 would subject gay couples to the same financial disclosure and conflict-of-interest requirements as married couples. It would require them to file an affidavit with the Office of Personnel Management attesting to the legitimacy of the partnership and their intent to remain in that relationship.

Susan Collins of Maine, ranking Republican on Homeland Security and Governmental Affairs, said the legislation would allow the government to attract top talent. She argued that many young people, both gay and straight, cited benefits offered to domestic partners as a sign of a good or bad employer. Collins also said that the bill would bring the federal government in line with almost 65 percent of Fortune 500 companies, which offered such benefits.

The committee's vote of approval came just a week after President Barack Obama endorsed same-sex marriage.

Tax Delinquents and Federal Work

The House on July 31, 2012, agreed by a vote of 263–114 to suspend the rules and pass HR 828, the Federal Employee Tax Accountability Act, sponsored by Jason Chaffetz, R-Utah. The bill would bar federal employees from keeping their jobs if they failed to pay taxes. The House Oversight and Government Reform Committee had approved the measure by voice vote on April 13, 2011, and formally reported it (H Rept 112-115) on June 23, 2011.

In a related action, the Oversight and Government Reform Committee approved HR 829, the Contracting and Tax Accountability Act, by voice vote on April 13, 2011. The bill, also sponsored by Chaffetz, would bar individuals and companies from receiving federal contracts or grants should they miss tax payments.

Both pieces of legislation would limit punishment to those with "seriously delinquent tax debt," defined as a debt that has forced the filing of a tax lien. Chair Darrell Issa, R-Calif., stressed that this definition would target only the most blatant offenders.

HR 829 received mostly bipartisan support. However, Gerald E. Connolly, D-Va., argued that the bill could adversely affect small businessowners—many of them minorities, veterans, and women—who might not realize that they had missed payments. His substitute amendment, rejected along party lines, would have put an additional step in place before contractors could be barred or suspended for delinquent tax debts.

Peace Corps Volunteer Protection

Congress in 2011 cleared legislation (S 1280) that supporters said would reduce the risk of sexual assault against Peace Corps volunteers and improve the U.S. government's response to such assaults. The Kate Puzey Peace Corps Volunteer Protection Act was sponsored by Johnny Isakson, R-Ga.

The Senate Foreign Relations Committee approved S 1280 by voice vote on July 26, 2011, and formally reported it (S Rept 112-82) on September 21. The Senate passed the bill by voice vote on September 26. The House agreed, 406–0, on November 1 to suspend the rules and pass the measure. The president signed S 1280 into law (PL 112-57) on November 21, 2011.

Over the years, hundreds of Peace Corps volunteers had been sexually assaulted in their host countries. Many alleged victims found that local authorities were reluctant to investigate or prosecute such crimes and that Peace Corps policies and procedures were inadequate to help them after the attacks. S 1280 would require training for Peace Corps volunteers in responding to, and reducing the risk of, sexual assault. It called for the establishment of sexual assault response teams made up of safety and security officers, medical staff, and a victim's advocate to respond to reports of sexual assault against a volunteer. House Foreign Affairs Committee Chair Ileana Ros-Lehtinen, R-Fla., said that the Peace Corps was an "institution that too often blamed the victim."

Kate Puzey was a Peace Corps volunteer who was murdered in Benin, Africa, on March 11, 2009. Puzey had informed the Peace Corps office in Cotonou of reports that teacher and Peace Corps volunteer Constant Bio, a host country national, was sexually abusing schoolchildren. Although she was promised anonymity, Puzey was killed shortly after Bio found out about her role in the matter and learned that he would be dismissed. Members of Puzey's family believed that the Peace Corps was not forthcoming about what happened and that the organization had failed to adequately protect her. The Peace Corps subsequently publicly apologized to Puzey's parents, and Bio was charged in her death.

National Flood Insurance

Congress in 2012 extended the National Flood Insurance Program for five years, through fiscal 2017. The flood insurance provisions were included in the conference report for a highway reauthorization bill (HR 4348—H Rept 112-557), which also extended lower student loan interest rates. On June 29, 2012, the House, 373–52, and the Senate, 74–19, adopted the conference report. The president signed Moving Ahead for Progress in the 21st Century (PL 112-141) on July 6. *(Highway reauthorization, p. 340; student loan interest rates, p. 485)*

Democratic senators Mark Pryor of Arkansas and Richard J. Durbin of Illinois, whose states border the Mississippi River, were opposed to language in HR 4348 that would require residents in a "residual risk area"—that is, behind or near flood levees—to buy flood insurance. Although they were unable to force a vote on an amendment to delete the requirement, which was not included in the original House bill, the provision was dropped hours before the package was voted on. Pryor and Durbin said that people who were already paying taxes to maintain the levees should not also be required to buy flood insurance.

Existing law required property owners in areas at high risk of flooding to purchase insurance. If the program were to lapse, buyers and homeowners would not be able to buy insurance or renew policies, preventing them from closing on mortgage and refinancing loans.

The flood insurance program was established in 1968 (PL 90-448) in response to increasing federal government spending for disaster relief. The program was intended to alleviate some of the public's financial burden, as the government would cover losses generated by floods in the form of disaster relief payments. By mid-2011, the program provided insurance against flood losses for an estimated 5.5 million homes at a reasonable price, which allowed for higher home prices than otherwise would be the case. The fund, run by the Federal Emergency Management Agency (FEMA), had historically been able to balance payouts with the money it brought in. However, claims payments for damages from hurricanes Katrina and Rita in 2005 put the program $18 million in debt. *(PL 90-448, Congress and the Nation Vol. II, p. 967)*

The flood insurance measure, as a stand-alone bill (S 1940), would revamp the program by phasing in higher premium rates and would make other tweaks to the program to try to make it solvent. The Senate Banking, Housing, and Urban Affairs Committee reported S 1940, entitled "An original bill to amend the National Flood Insurance Act of 1968, to restore the financial solvency of the flood insurance fund, and for other purposes," on December 5, 2011 (S Rept 112-98). Senators debated the bill on the floor in June 2012, but no final resolution was reached in the chamber.

The House on July 12, 2011, had passed, 406–22, its version of a five-year reauthorization bill (HR 1309) that included provisions that would allow temporary suspension of the mandatory purchase requirements for those in special flood hazard areas. It also would provide a five-year phase-in of flood insurance rates for newly mapped areas. The House Financial Services Committee by a vote of 54–0 had approved HR 1309, the Flood Insurance Reform Act, on May 13, 2011, and formally reported it (H Rept 112-102) on June 9.

Before enactment of HR 4348, Congress considered a short-term reauthorization, clearing legislation (HR 5740) that extended the flood insurance program through June 30, 2012. The National Flood Insurance Program Extension Act would allow homeowners to purchase private flood insurance to satisfy the program's mandatory flood insurance coverage requirements, as long as it met federal coverage requirements. The House agreed by a vote of 402–18 on May 17, 2012, to suspend the rules and pass HR 5740. The Senate passed an amended version by voice vote on May 24. The House by voice vote on May 30 agreed to suspend the rules and agree to the Senate changes, completing congressional action. President Barack Obama signed the bill into law (PL 112-123) on May 31, 2012. *(111th Congress action, p. 610)*

Senate Majority Leader Harry Reid, D-Nev., had asked on May 15, 2012, for unanimous consent to pass an extension bill (S 2344) that would go through December 31, 2012, but Tom Coburn, R-Okla., objected to the request and threatened to block all other flood insurance bills that did not deliver a major overhaul of the program. The Senate Banking, Housing, and Urban Affairs Subcommittee on Economic Policy held hearings on S 2344, but the measure, entitled "A bill to extend the National Flood Insurance Program until December 31, 2012," saw no further action.

Superstorm Sandy Disaster Relief

The Senate in 2012 used a fiscal 2011 continuing appropriations bill (HR 1) as a vehicle for providing Hurricane Sandy disaster relief. Also known as Superstorm Sandy, the October weather event was the largest Atlantic hurricane on record as measured by diameter and proved to be the most destructive hurricane of the 2012 Atlantic hurricane season. Although HR 1 got caught up in partisan politics and died upon adjournment, the 113th Congress in January 2013 cleared two related bills: one providing additional borrowing authority for the National Flood Insurance Program and another designating disaster relief funding to address damage from Sandy.

Propelled by conservative Republicans, the House on February 19, 2011, passed HR 1 by a 235–189 vote, with no Democratic support. The bill, which would fund the government for the remainder of fiscal 2011, provided discretionary funding authority well below President Barack Obama's budget request and the existing spending rate based on the continuing resolution in effect (PL 111-322). The Senate rejected, by 44–56 on March 9, the House-passed version of HR 1, with all Democrats voting against it.

The Senate subsequently passed an amended HR 1, by a vote of 62–32 on December 28, 2012, and also redubbed it the Disaster Relief Appropriations Act. The bill would provide $60.4 billion in disaster aid for communities affected by Sandy. During Senate floor consideration on December 21, Republicans succeeded in stripping the emergency designation from $3.4 billion intended for the Army Corps of Engineers to mitigate the effect of future storms. Without the designation, the money would count against the $1.1 trillion cap on the federal government's operating expenses, or discretionary spending, for fiscal 2013. Democrats said that the nation should not be forced to reduce other accounts to allow a robust response when catastrophe struck.

Five Republicans joined Democrats in the bid to prevent the reclassification of the spending—Roy Blunt of Missouri, Thad Cochran of Mississippi, Richard C. Shelby of Alabama, Olympia J. Snowe of Maine, and David Vitter of Louisiana. But even with their help, the 57–34 vote fell short of the sixty needed to waive the budget point of order that Patrick J. Toomey, R-Pa., had raised about the $3.4 billion. Toomey stated after the vote that he chose to target that particular account because it would fund long-term building work, which, he said, did not sound like emergency spending. He also said that his action was intended as an initial attack on the inclusion of such long-term measures in a disaster bill. Some Republicans, including Toomey, held firm in their effort to make the point that some of the costs of mitigation work in the bill be offset.

For days, Democratic and Republican leaders worked behind the scenes to come to an agreement that would let the measure proceed. In the end, more than twenty amendments were allowed, all with sixty-vote thresholds for adoption. During debate December 28, the Senate rejected many of the amendments, including an amendment by Tom Coburn, R-Okla., by a 44–51 vote, to reduce the federal cost requirements for rebuilding certain damaged maritime assets, such as harbors and locks, to 65 percent of the Army Corps of Engineers costs, instead of 90 percent; an amendment by Dan Coats, R-Ind., by a 41–54 vote, to reduce funding in the bill to $23.8 billion for communities hit by Superstorm Sandy; and an amendment by Rand Paul, R-Ky., by a 3–91 vote, to strip all the spending provisions of their emergency designation and rescind $9.0 billion in fiscal 2013 unobligated spending. The chamber did give voice vote approval to several amendments, including one from Coburn that would prohibit the distribution of supplemental funds to those with serious tax debts or to the deceased. Also adopted by voice vote was an amendment offered by Senate Judiciary Committee Chair Patrick J. Leahy, D-Vt., that would allow the transfer of previously appropriated foreign affairs funds to pay for increased security at U.S. embassies and other overseas posts. Lawmakers had been split along party lines on the need for Congress to boost funding for diplomatic security in the wake of the September 2012 attack on a U.S. facility in Benghazi, Libya.

When action shifted to the House, delaying the Sandy recovery bill was seen as strengthening the hand of conservatives who were seeking to reduce the cost of the bill, as the next major aid measure would almost certainly originate in the GOP-led House. In the waning days of the 112th Congress, while members of the New York and New Jersey delegations said they expected a vote on HR 1, Speaker John A. Boehner, R-Ohio, decided not to bring the measure to the floor. House Oversight and Government Reform Committee Chair Darrell Issa, R-Calif., said the Senate-passed bill would have been taken up by the House had it not provided too much money and resources to districts outside the area affected by the storm. This included, for example, funds for helping Alaskan fisheries and aiding western states in cleaning up after the summer 2012 wildfires. Bipartisan criticism was directed at the House leadership for putting off action on the disaster relief legislation.

In the new 113th Congress, the House on January 4, 2013, agreed, by 354–67, to suspend the rules and pass HR 41, to temporarily grant $9.7 billion in additional borrowing authority for the National Flood Insurance Program. The Senate passed the bill by voice vote the same day, completing congressional action. President Barack Obama signed the measure into law (PL 113-1) on January 6. A $50.5 billion supplemental appropriations bill (HR 152) that included assistance for victims of Sandy as well as funds for longer-term spending passed the House on a vote of 241–180 on January 15 and the Senate, 62–36, on January 28. It was signed into law (PL 113-2) on January 29.

FEMA Shelters

The House Transportation and Infrastructure Committee approved HR 2919 by voice vote on October 13, 2011, and formally reported it (H Rept 112-712) on December 20. The Community Shelter Protection Act, sponsored by Spencer Bachus, R-Ala., would prohibit the Federal Emergency Management Agency (FEMA) from requiring an elementary or secondary school covered by the 1988 Robert T. Stafford Disaster Relief and Emergency Assistance Act (PL 100-707) to reimburse FEMA for the market value of a covered temporary tornado shelter facility. *(1988 law, Congress and the Nation Vol. VII, p. 494)*

When FEMA shipped dozens of portable classrooms to Alabama schools that had been damaged by tornadoes in 2011, it offered to include a bonus: temporary storm shelters to protect the students while their regular schools were rebuilt. The shelters subsequently got caught in a political tug-of-war between the disaster agency, which wanted them returned later or paid for, and Alabama officials, who thought the shelters should be left as a gift. FEMA could tear down the shelters or disassemble and store them for future use if Alabama did not want to buy them.

FEMA, as a matter of policy, did not provide temporary storm shelters in its public assistance funding to storm-damaged schools. If schools wanted them, they had to pay for the shelters. The 2011 Alabama storms, however, were particularly destructive, killing 250 people and leaving a broad trail of destruction that was estimated to cost $1 billion for cleanup and rebuilding. FEMA was already paying 90 percent of damage costs not covered by insurance and, under a new policy, decided to cover most of the cost of temporary school shelters.

Under the new policy, FEMA split costs with schools that wanted shelters, then allowed the schools to use the shelters for however long it took to repair damaged school buildings. After that, the agency required that the schools either pay FEMA 75 percent of the shelters' market value or find a buyer for the shelters and then reimburse FEMA. If the schools could do neither, FEMA would appraise the buildings and the costs of either moving them or destroying them.

Constellation Space Program

Congress in 2011, in the fiscal 2011 omnibus appropriations bill (HR 1473—PL 112-10), effectively nullified a provision in the fiscal 2010 appropriations law (PL 111-117) that barred use of appropriated funds to terminate the Constellation space exploration program or to create new space exploration programs unless such activities were provided for in later appropriations laws. The National Aeronautics and Space Administration (NASA) said the language could hinder implementation of provisions of the 2010 NASA authorization law (PL 111-267) that effectively ended the Constellation program and directed NASA to develop a heavy-lift rocket and multipurpose crew vehicle as a follow-on to the space shuttle. *(PL 112-10, p. 150; PL 111-117, p. 127; PL 111-267, p. 605)*

Furthermore, HR 1473 barred NASA and the Office of Science and Technology Policy from using funds in the legislation to develop or carry out any program with China or any Chinese-owned company unless specifically authorized by law. That provision also prohibited the use of appropriated funds to host Chinese officials at NASA facilities.

Postal Service Overhaul

Despite agreement on both sides of the aisle that action was needed to change how the cash-strapped U.S. Postal Service operated, lawmakers in the 112th Congress were unable to reconcile their differences on overhaul legislation (S 1789, HR 2309). The last successful attempt to refashion the Postal Service was in 2006 (PL 109-435). *(2006 overhaul, Congress and the Nation Vol. XII, p. 784)*

BACKGROUND

As of 2011, the Postal Service serviced 151 million addresses per day, processing an average of 563 million pieces of mail. It maintained 32,000 retail offices, paid $1.9 billion in salaries every two weeks to about 555,000 career employees, and operated the largest civilian fleet in the world, with about 215,000 vehicles. However, the huge infrastructure was carrying less and less mail, with a decline of 20 percent from 2006 to 2010 largely because of the use of e-mail, electronic bill paying, and electronic greeting cards. The Postal Service also had crushing pension and benefit obligations it could not meet. It had borrowed $15 billion from the Treasury to stay afloat.

The Postal Service said it had experienced a net loss of $5.1 billion in fiscal 2011 and would have lost $10.6 billion if lawmakers had not included language in the fiscal 2012 omnibus appropriations package (HR 2055—PL 112-74) postponing payment of an annual $5.5 billion bill for future retiree health care benefits. The agency lost $15.9 billion in fiscal 2012 and defaulted in August 2012 on a $5.5 billion payment needed to cover future retiree health costs.

A number of lawmakers in both chambers backed the Postal Service's effort to recoup billions of dollars that the service said it had overpaid into the Civil Service Retirement System (CSRS) and its successor, the Federal Employee Retirement System (FERS), since the early 1970s. The agency argued that it had picked up $55 billion to $85 billion in expenses the federal government should have covered. It said it would use the funds to streamline operations and put itself on a path to fiscal solvency. Some lawmakers said it was Postal Service money. Others argued that the agency had agreed to the payment in the 1970s when it was given more independence. In mid-October 2011, the Government Accountability Office (GAO) recognized a small overpayment by the Postal Service to the FERS but rejected the far larger claim in CSRS funding. Lawmakers then shied away from the issue, focusing solely on refunding the GAO-recognized FERS overpayment, about $6.9 billion, to the agency.

Postmaster General Patrick R. Donahoe said the Postal Service needed to cut $22 billion in costs—more than a quarter of its fiscal 2010 operating expenses—by 2016. He wanted to achieve that goal by shuttering thousands of post offices and half the nation's mail-processing centers, slicing the workforce by 40 percent, streamlining services, and adjusting employee benefits. He also wanted the freedom to eliminate six-day-per-week delivery. However, although the service was an independent agency (it received almost no taxpayer funds for operating expenses), much of the way the Postal Service operated was set in law, and legislation was required before changes could be made. Adding to the difficulty, while many lawmakers thought the agency should behave as a business, voters saw it as a public service and reacted vociferously to any talk of closing post offices or shortening the delivery week.

HOUSE ACTION

The House Oversight and Government Reform Committee voted 22–18, mostly along party lines, on October 13, 2011, to approve a bill (HR 2309) that proposed a major restructuring of the Postal Service. The sponsors of the Postal Reform Act—Chair Darrell Issa, R-Calif., and Dennis A. Ross, R-Fla.—said the legislation would save billions of dollars annually. The measure, which was formally reported by the committee on January 17, 2012 (H Rept 112-363, Part 1), called for an oversight board to pursue cost reductions and a new advisory body to make financial recommendations, should the agency default for more than thirty days. The Postal Service could modify union contracts in some circumstances, close post offices with greater flexibility, and submit a proposal to the Postal Regulatory Commission to move to five-day delivery within six months of passage. If, two years after the advisory body was created, the Postal Service had an annual budget deficit of more than $2 billion, power over the agency would be transferred to the advisory body.

The House Rules Committee reported the bill (H Rept 112-363, Part 2) on March 29, 2012.

Issa warned that without an overhaul, the mail courier would turn into a "taxpayer-subsidized make-work program." But Democrats criticized the bill as an attack on federal workers. Under the bill, for example, the Postal Service could reconsider previously signed contracts and work agreements and forgo collective bargaining rights.

Democrats and Republicans offered more than two dozen amendments, the former mostly policy changes and the latter mostly small tweaks. Many Democratic amendments centered on reviving collective bargaining rights. The committee adopted by voice vote a Ross amendment striking a provision in the bill that would have waived a 1931 labor law (PL 71-798), known as the Davis-Bacon Act, for the Postal Service. Before the amendment, the bill would have exempted the agency from the federal workers' minimum wage law. Democrats argued that the bill still did not go far enough to protect federal workers.

The Oversight and Government Reform Subcommittee on Federal Workforce, U.S. Postal Service, and Labor Policy had approved the legislation, 8–5, along party lines

September 21, 2011. Gerald E. Connolly, D-Va., argued that the GOP-led committee's agenda was "to break the backs of the public employee unions." The subcommittee rejected, 5–8, an amendment by Danny K. Davis, D-Ill., to strike language barring employees above the retirement age from receiving federal workers' compensation. It also rejected, 5–8, an amendment by Stephen F. Lynch, D-Mass., to strike the underlying bill and, in its place, insert the text of legislation (HR 1351) to allow the Postal Service to recoup the money it believed it had overpaid into the two federal pension accounts.

The Issa and Ross bill did not address the overpayment issue. They and other Republicans disputed that there was any overpayment, arguing that the money had already been distributed to retirees according to a 1974 formula and that it could be "repaid" only through a taxpayer-funded initiative tantamount to a bailout.

SENATE ACTION

The Senate Homeland Security and Governmental Affairs Committee approved a bipartisan Postal Service bill (S 1789), 9–1, on November 9, 2011, and formally reported it (S Rept 112-143) on January 31, 2012. The legislation, the 21st Century Postal Service Act, was sponsored by panel Chair Joseph I. Lieberman, I-Conn. Under a key provision, the service could recoup about $7 billion in overpayments to the FERS. The Postal Service could use the refund to provide about 100,000 postal employees with incentives to retire or to otherwise leave the agency in return for buyouts of up to $25,000 each. The workforce reduction would allow the agency to save about $8 billion.

The measure proposed to reduce the Postal Service's annual advance payments for future retiree health care benefits by expanding the payments over a longer period of time. It also called for arbitration standards to require the consideration of the Postal Service's financial condition during contract disputes between unions and the agency and to give the service flexibility to brainstorm and create nonpostal products that could also bring in revenue.

Some panel Republicans said the bill did not give the Postal Service enough flexibility to downsize and consolidate. The bill included a two-year prohibition on the Postal Service's elimination of Saturday delivery, allowing it only as a last resort if the service could prove that the move was necessary to avoid insolvency.

During the markup, the committee rejected, 5–12, an amendment by John McCain, R-Ariz., to allow the agency to eliminate Saturday delivery immediately, and it adopted, 10–6, an amendment by Daniel K. Akaka, D-Hawaii, to strike a provision that would require postal retirees eligible for Medicare to enroll in that program, a change the Postal Service said would save $15 billion.

The full Senate passed S 1789 by a vote of 62–37 on April 25, 2012, after debating dozens of amendments, many of which were designed to guarantee that certain post offices and processing centers would remain open in lawmaker's individual states. Despite the postmaster general's warnings of financial collapse without more drastic changes, HR 1789 deferred other cost-saving measures. Democrats generally favored the bill, while most Republicans opposed it.

Under a unanimous consent agreement announced April 19, senators would consider amendments with a sixty-vote threshold. That would allow many members to offer changes but make it difficult for proposals subject to roll-call votes to be adopted. During the floor debate, the Senate:

- Adopted by voice vote on April 24 an amendment by Claire McCaskill, D-Mo., to prohibit the postmaster general from closing rural post offices for one year. After that, closures would be prohibited unless the Postal Service ensured that senior citizens and people with disabilities could still receive their prescription drugs in a timely fashion, local businesses would not suffer financial losses from the closure, and another post office was less than ten miles away.
- Rejected, 43–53, on April 25 an amendment by Joe Manchin III, D-W.Va., that would have strengthened the McCaskill language by barring the service from closing postal facilities for two years.
- Adopted by voice vote on April 24 an amendment by Richard J. Durbin, D-Ill., to bar the postmaster general from closing mail-processing centers if doing so would not benefit the service financially.
- Rejected, 43–56, on April 24 an amendment by Tom Udall, D-N.M., that would have struck a provision in the bill allowing Donahoe to eliminate Saturday delivery after a two-year waiting period.
- Rejected, 30–69, on April 24 an amendment by John McCain, R-Ariz., to insert part of the House postal overhaul measure that would speed up postal facility closures.
- Adopted by voice vote on April 25 an amendment by John D. Rockefeller IV, D-W.Va., to require any changes made to postal employee health benefits to offer comparable benefits with those offered by the federal government and include dental and vision insurance.
- Adopted by voice vote on April 25 an amendment by Jon Tester, D-Mont., to cap postal executives' pay.
- Adopted by voice vote on April 25 an amendment by Rand Paul, R-Texas, to limit the number of post offices in the Capitol to one in each chamber.
- Rejected, 46–53, in a strict party-line vote on April 25 an amendment by Jim DeMint, R-S.C., to bar the Postal Service's labor unions from using dues or other fees to contribute to any person, organization, or entity for purposes not "directly germane to the labor organization's collective bargaining or contract administration functions"—unless authorized annually in writing by those making the payments.

- Rejected, 46–53, in a near party-line vote on April 24 an Akaka amendment to substitute a government-wide workers' compensation overhaul included in the bill with a House-passed competing proposal (HR 2465).

Just before the amendment votes began April 24, Jeff Sessions, R-Ala., raised a point of order against S 1789, saying it violated the 2011 debt limit and deficit reduction law (PL 112-25). The Congressional Budget Office (CBO), he noted, said the legislation would cost $34 billion over the next decade. Homeland Security and Governmental Affairs Committee ranking Republican, as well as cosponsor of the bill, Susan Collins of Maine, argued that the CBO number was misleading. The chamber voted to waive Sessions's objection, 62–37.

FAILURE TO REACH A COMPROMISE

As the 112th Congress neared an end, key lawmakers and their staffs met more frequently to negotiate a compromise that would allow a Postal Service overhaul to be signed into law. In the end, however, they could not agree on a number of sticking points, particularly whether, or how aggressively, to eliminate Saturday delivery and to shutter post offices and mail-processing facilities, as well as on how the Postal Service should prefund health care costs for future retirees. While the Senate bill reconfigured the way in which the Postal Service set money aside in the hope it would be less onerous for the agency, the original House committee's bill stayed largely silent on the issue.

Republicans on the House committee took procedural measures in January 2012 to amend the bill to include new language allowing the Postal Service to take the money back in the event a formal calculation deemed it appropriate. But it was not enough to bridge the gap between the bills.

ALASKA BYPASS

Included in House legislation (HR 2309) to revamp the U.S. Postal Service was language to end the forty-year Alaska Bypass freight service. *(Postal Service overhaul, p. 627)*

According to a November 2011 report by the Postal Service's inspector general, the Bypass was a freight service primarily for merchants in Alaska towns that were inaccessible by road or cut off in winter. The system allowed Alaska shippers to bypass postal delivery altogether. While the report concluded that the "Alaska Bypass is not mail," the shipments included all the mail for isolated Alaskan communities, which was the reason the program was created in the first place.

The shipments had to be in pallets of at least one thousand pounds, for which shippers pay Parcel Post rates. Because the shipping rates for Alaska's airlines were set by the Transportation Department, not the Postal Service (an exception also made by Congress), the service said it lost money—$73 million in 2010 alone.

In designing HR 2309, House Oversight and Government Reform Committee Chair Darrell Issa, R-Calif., decided that, as a cost-saving measure, Alaska's special benefit should be eliminated. Alaska's congressional delegation, however, maintained that ending the practice would violate the federal government's promise of universal mail delivery. The members said that Issa's provision would require Alaskans' tax money to pay for mail deliveries that every other part of the country got for free. The Postal Service also said that the special deliveries were part of its universal mail service. The inspector general's report, though, concluded that the system was unfair to the Postal Service, whose only role in the Bypass was to pay the bills.

Mark Twain Commemorative Coin

Mark Twain said, "Suppose you were an idiot, and suppose you were a member of Congress; but I repeat myself." He likely would have gotten a kick out of watching legislation (HR 2453) authorizing a commemorative coin honoring the American author and humorist get snarled in a tiff over procedural issues. In the end, Congress in 2012 cleared the bill (PL 112-201) directing the Treasury secretary to mint and issue in 2016 $5 gold coins and $1 silver coins emblematic of the life and legacy of the man also known as Samuel L. Clemens. The Mark Twain Commemorative Coin Act also raised funds for several museums and educational projects having to do with Twain—including the Mark Twain House and Museum in Hartford, Conn., and the Mark Twain Project at the Bancroft Library at the University of California at Berkeley—through specified surcharges in the sale of the coins.

Legislation to authorize commemorative coins honoring American icons usually zip through Congress, but some deficit hawks wanted a reappraisal. They said that the federal government should quit giving part of the proceeds of coin sales to outside groups, no matter how civic-minded. They said that the federal government needed all such revenue to reduce the deficit, adding that the surcharges amounted to political favors that skirted existing bicameral bans on earmarks.

Since the development of a formal commemorative coin procedure in 1982, the U.S. Mint estimated that it had issued more than ninety such coins and raised more than $418 million for projects ranging from the Vietnam War Memorial to the Girl Scouts of America. The backlash against the coin program was spurred on by a June 1, 2012, *Chicago Tribune* report that a former girlfriend of Sen. Mark Steven Kirk, R-Ill., worked as a lobbyist for a firm that promoted several commemorative coins, including one for the March of Dimes (HR 3187—PL 112-209). Kirk was one of the original cosponsors of the bill.

Rep. Blaine Luetkemeyer, R-Mo., sponsor of the Twain measure, and other supporters defended the coins as a needed resource to recognize contributions of important individuals and groups in American history. They also emphasized that the program paid all of its own expenses. In 1996, Congress enacted a mandate that government costs be covered first before beneficiaries got their cut of net revenue.

On April 18, 2012, the House agreed by a vote of 408–4, with two members voting "present," to suspend the rules and pass HR 2453. The Senate passed an amended version of the bill by voice vote on September 22. The House on November 15 agreed, 370–19, to suspend the rules and accept the Senate changes, thus completing congressional action. The president signed the bill into law on December 4.

Contractors Withholding Rule

Congress in 2011 cleared legislation (HR 674) to repeal a withholding requirement for government payments to contractors. The measure also established programs aimed at decreasing unemployment among veterans. Sponsored by Wally Herger, R-Calif., the short title of that part of the bill was entitled VOW (Veterans Opportunity to Work) to Hire Heroes Act.

The House Ways and Means Committee approved HR 674 by voice vote on October 13, 2011, and formally reported it (H Rept 112-253) on October 18. The full House passed the measure by a vote of 405–16 on October 27. The bill would repeal the requirement that, starting in 2013, federal, state, and some local governments withhold 3 percent of payments to contractors. Supporters of repeal argued that continuing the withholding would crimp businesses' cash flow and lead to layoffs.

The Senate on November 10 passed, 95–0, an amended version of HR 674, which included language to boost veterans' employment. The Senate-passed bill would provide tax credits to companies that hired veterans with service-connected disabilities who had been unemployed for at least six months of the previous year. It would provide smaller tax credits to those that hired vets who were not disabled or had been unemployed for shorter periods. The measure would extend existing credits for hiring veterans through 2012 and could require the Department of Veterans Affairs (VA) to establish a retraining program by July 1, 2012.

The House agreed to suspend the rules and accept the Senate changes by 422–0 on November 16. As cleared, the measure also incorporated a bill (HR 2576), sponsored by Diane Black, R-Tenn., to modify an eligibility formula set to take effect in 2014 for health benefits such as Medicaid and subsidies to purchase health insurance. Under the 2010 health care overhaul (PL 111-148, PL 111-152), individuals would be allowed to exclude Social Security benefits from their income while calculating eligibility. The legislation would rescind that exclusion. To pay for the veterans' provisions, HR 674 would postpone scheduled decreases in fees charged to veterans obtaining VA-guaranteed mortgages until fiscal 2017. The Congressional Budget Office and Joint Committee on Taxation estimated that the bill would reduce the deficit by about $2 billion over ten years. *(Health care overhaul, p. 421)*

The House Ways and Means Committee approved HR 2576 by a vote of 23–12 on October 13, 2011, and formally reported it (H Rept 112-254) on October 18. The House passed the bill, entitled "To amend the Internal Revenue Code of 1986 to modify the calculation of modified adjusted gross income for purposes of determining eligibility for certain healthcare-related programs," by 262–157 on October 27, 2011.

President Obama signed the bill (PL 112-56) into law on November 21, 2011.

Small Business Federal Contracting

The House Small Business Committee in 2012 reported a number of bills (HR 3850, HR 3851, HR 3893, HR 3980, HR 4118, HR 4121) designed to overhaul small business federal contracting policies.

The panel approved the Government Efficiency through Small Business Contracting Act (HR 3850) by voice vote on March 7, 2012, and formally reported it (H Rept 112-720, Part 1) on December 21. The bill, sponsored by Sam Graves, R-Mo., would raise the federal small business contracting goal from 23 percent to 25 percent. It also would require the president to annually establish governmentwide goals for contracts awarded to certain types of small businesses, including those owned and controlled by service-disabled veterans, historically underutilized business zones (HUBZones), socially and economically disadvantaged individuals, and women. The bill would withhold bonuses of senior agency officials if small business contracting goals were not met. Ranking Democrat Nydia M. Velázquez of New York said that agencies had not achieved the initial goal of 23 percent, set by the 1997 Small Business Reauthorization Act (PL 105-135) because they lacked the resources to challenge many contracts to small firms.

Also sponsored by Graves, the Small Business Advocate Act (HR 3851) was approved by a vote of 11–7 on March 7, 2012, and was formally reported (H Rept 112-721, Part 1) on December 21. It would make the directorship of the Office of Small and Disadvantaged Business Utilization a senior executive position that would report directly and exclusively to agency heads.

HR 3893, the Subcontracting Transparency and Reliability Act, would place limitations on federal subcontracting. The measure, sponsored by Mick Mulvaney, R-S.C., would allow small businesses to team up with similar enterprises to compete for federal contracts and would require agencies to publish their insourcing processes. The Small Business Committee approved the bill by voice vote on March 7, 2012, and formally reported it (H Rept 112-731, Part 1) on December 27.

The panel also approved HR 3980 by voice vote on March 7, 2012. The Small Business Opportunity Act, sponsored by Jaime Herrera Beutler, R-Wash., would require small business advocates, called procurement center representatives, to participate in all stages of the federal contracting process and give them access to planning documents. Herrera Beutler said these advocates often were involved in only the last step of the contracting process, which limited their ability to alter or improve contracts. She also said that advocates often spent too much of their time training contracting personnel. HR 3980 would shift that responsibility to other employees so that advocates had more time for their primary tasks. The bill also would require some advocates to complete additional training; they were given five years to comply with those requirements. House Small Business formally reported the bill (H Rept 112-722) on December 21.

The House Small Business Committee approved HR 4118 by voice vote on March 7, 2012, and formally reported it (H Rept 112-726, Part 1) on December 21. The Small Business Procurement Improvement Act, sponsored by Mark S. Critz, D-Pa., would require federal agencies, to the maximum extent practical, to include small businesses in multiple-award contracts. The bill also would give the Small Business Administration a seat on the Federal Acquisition Regulatory Council.

HR 4121, the Early Stage Small Business Contracting Act, would give early stage small businesses the first opportunity on federal contracts worth from $3,000 to $75,000. Kurt Schrader, D-Ore., sponsored the legislation. The panel approved the bill by voice vote on March 7, 2012, and formally reported it (H Rept 112-727) on December 21.

Regulatory Oversight

On December 7, 2011, the House voted 241–184 to pass the Regulations from the Executive in Need of Scrutiny (REINS) Act (HR 10), which would prohibit major executive branch rules from taking effect without congressional approval. The Senate Homeland Security and Governmental Affairs Committee held hearings on a companion measure (S 299), sponsored by Rand Paul, R-Ky., but it saw no further action.

The House Judiciary Committee approved HR 10 along party lines, 22–14, on October 25, 2011, and formally reported it (H Rept 111-278, Part 1) on November 10. The measure would require federal agencies to submit to Congress a report with a proposed rule, and Congress then would have to pass a joint resolution of approval within seventy legislative days of receiving the report. The panel rebuffed several Democratic proposals that would exempt certain rules from requiring congressional approval, including an amendment by Hank Johnson, D-Ga., that would exempt any proposed rule that was determined to result in net job growth.

In a rare exercise of original jurisdiction, the House Rules Committee voted 7–3 on November 16 along party lines to approve an amended HR 10. The panel formally reported it (H Rept 111-278, Part 2) on November 18.

Republicans sought to constrain the federal prerogative, calling for an overhaul that included more oversight of agency rules that they believed killed jobs, smothered businesses, and stifled the economy. They contended that it was Congress's responsibility to oversee the regulation process because agencies could not be held accountable. Democrats said that blocking regulations would hinder and delay important executive branch actions that served the country. They argued that the measure would delay and complicate the rule-making process, potentially putting the safety and health of Americans at risk. They also said that HR 10 would be unworkable because it would require a busy Congress to approve dozens or even hundreds of rules. Louise M. Slaughter of New York, the ranking Democrat on the House Rules Committee, said the bill would infringe on the separation of powers, essentially prioritizing the legislature's power over the executive's. The White House expressed a similar uneasiness in a statement of administration policy: "This radical departure from the long-standing separation of powers between the executive and legislative branches would delay and, in many cases, thwart implementation of statutory mandates and execution of duly enacted laws."

As passed by the House, HR 10 stipulated that federal agency rules costing the economy at least $100 million or having "significant adverse" effects on consumer prices or businesses would require congressional ratification by joint resolution to enter full force. Republicans said it would free the economy from costly federal mandates, while Democrats said it would subject the executive branch to the partisan politicking of Congress. Under the existing system, agency regulations took effect unless Congress cleared and the president signed joint resolutions disapproving them.

On December 7, during floor debate on the HR 10, the House rejected a number of amendments. A Johnson amendment that would exempt rules that the Office of Management and Budget determined would result in net job creation from the bill's provisions was defeated 187–236. Rejected 183–238 was an amendment by Kurt Schrader, D-Ore., that would require agencies to submit a cost-benefit analysis when they submitted proposed major rules to Congress. It would require that federal agencies submit a list of the criteria they used to conduct cost-benefit analyses by January 1, 2013, or one year after the bill's enactment, whichever came later. An amendment by Carolyn McCarthy, D-N.Y., that would exempt rules related to food safety, workplace safety, consumer product safety, air quality, or water quality from the bill's provisions was rejected 177–246. Also defeated, 177–242, was an amendment by Sheila Jackson Lee, D-Texas, that would exempt rules issued by the Department of Homeland Security from the legislation's provisions. Gwen Moore, D-Wis., offered an amendment that would exempt rules related to veterans or veterans affairs from the bill's provisions. It was rejected 183–240. The House December 7 also rejected, 183–235, a motion by Rosa DeLauro, D-Conn., to recommit HR 10 to the Judiciary Committee with instructions that it be reported back immediately with an amendment that would exempt from the bill's provisions rules related to providing incentives for small businesses to hire veterans.

Several nonprofit organizations opposed the legislation, including the consumer watchdog group Public Citizen and the Natural Resources Defense Council.

Restrictions on Regulations

Mostly along party lines, the House voted 245–172 on July 26, 2012, to pass HR 4078, which Republicans said could help stimulate the economy. The Red Tape Reduction and Small Business Job Creation Act would bar significant government rules from taking effect until the jobless rate dropped to 6 percent.

The bill fulfilled GOP campaign pledges to try to scale back federal regulations. It would block the executive branch from writing new rules that cost more than $50 million until the unemployment rate dropped to or below 6 percent. For their part, Democrats contended that the measure would infringe on agencies' mandates to protect Americans from food poisoning, hazardous pollution, and defective products that could jeopardize consumer safety.

Republican leaders merged the bill, sponsored by Tim Griffin, R-Ark., with six other regulatory-related proposals, including HR 4607, which would bar an outgoing administration from writing significant regulations during lame-duck congressional sessions, so-called midnight rules. The Obama administration issued a veto threat against HR 4078.

A couple of clerical errors temporarily sidetracked the bill from House consideration. Democrats discovered that, as written, the HR 4078 would bar the creation of new regulations until employment—not unemployment—reached 6 percent. That forced the Rules Committee to meet again to correct the typo before sending the measure to the floor. Then, another error showed up in the correcting resolution, which referred to the first resolution by the wrong number. The chamber agreed by voice vote to amend the correcting resolution.

Democrats argued that government regulation is worth the expense, as it can save lives and prevent catastrophic injuries. Those safety nets, Democrats said, should not be contingent on the economy. Democrats unsuccessfully offered amendments to exempt various rules: an amendment by Alcee L. Hastings, D-Fla., to exempt regulatory proposals directed at maintaining or enhancing the safety of drinking water from the moratorium on "significant regulatory actions," rejected 188–231 on July 25; an amendment by Hank Johnson, D-Ga., to exempt consent decrees and settlement agreements pertaining to the health care overhaul from the bill's provisions to change the settlement process, rejected 159–259 on July 25; an amendment by Dennis J. Kucinich, D-Ohio, to exempt regulations designed to limit oil speculation from the moratorium on "significant regulatory actions," rejected 173–245 on July 25; an amendment by Peter Welch, D-Vt., to exempt regulations designed to increase or promote energy efficiency from the restrictions relating to consent decrees and settlement agreements, "significant regulatory actions," and midnight rules, rejected 174–242 on July 25; an amendment by Edward J. Markey, D-Mass., to exempt regulations to protect the public from extreme weather events, such as droughts, flooding, and catastrophic wildfires, from the restrictions on "significant regulatory actions" and midnight rules, rejected 177–240 on July 25; an amendment by Melvin Watt, D-N.C., to exempt regulations intended to increase efficiency within the patent and trademark process from the restrictions in the bill relating to consent decrees and settlement agreements, midnight rules, and "significant regulatory actions," rejected 177–244 on July 26; an amendment by Dave Loebsack, D-Iowa, to exempt regulations designed to lower fuel prices from the moratorium on "significant regulatory actions," rejected 177–238 on July 26; an amendment by Jerrold Nadler, D-N.Y., to exempt regulations related to nuclear power plant safety from the definition of "significant regulatory actions" and from provisions related to consent decrees, settlement agreements, and environmental review requirements, rejected 176–243 on July 26; an amendment by George Miller, D-Calif., to exempt regulations designed to prevent workplace injuries or deaths resulting from the ignition of flammable dust from the definition of "significant regulatory actions" and the restrictions on midnight rules, rejected 174–239 on July 26; and an amendment by Lynn Woolsey, D-Calif., to exempt regulations designed to reduce the number of electrocutions or fatalities resulting from working with high-voltage transmission and distribution lines from the definition of "significant regulatory actions" and the restrictions on midnight rules, rejected 178–236 on July 26.

Bill supporters said that HR 4078 allowed for the protection of health, safety, and national security when necessary, pointing to a provision in the bill that would allow the president to waive the moratorium by executive order in such circumstances. A congressional waiver also would allow lawmakers to override the moratorium for any rule. The GOP had long argued that regulations kill jobs and stunt economic growth.

The House Judiciary Committee approved HR 4078, 15–13, on March 20, 2012, and formally reported it (H Rept 112-461, Part 1) on April 27. The House Oversight and

Government Reform Committee approved the bill, 21–16, on April 26, 2012, and formally reported it (H Rept 112-461, Part 2) on July 20.

The House Oversight and Government Reform Committee by voice vote approved HR 4607, the Midnight Rule Relief Act, on April 26, 2012, and formally reported it (H Rept 112-513, Part 1) on June 1.

Federal Reserve Audit

The House in 2012 passed a bill (HR 459) to authorize an audit of the Federal Reserve System. The Federal Reserve Transparency Act would require the Government Accountability Office (GAO) to audit the Federal Reserve Board and its twelve regional banks and to report to Congress on any recommendations for action. The GAO would have one year to finish the audit. HR 459 also would require GAO, within six months of enactment, to audit the Federal Reserve System's review of the loan files of homeowners who were in foreclosure in 2009 and 2010.

HR 459 would allow government auditors to examine monetary policy deliberations, boosting oversight of an institution that bill sponsor Ron Paul, R-Texas, said had "presided over the near-complete destruction of the United States dollar." House Oversight and Government Reform Committee Chair Darrell Issa, R-Calif., stressed the need for Congress to conduct oversight of the Federal Reserve and said that existing law prohibited audits of more specific monetary policy operations and agreements with foreign banks. Most Democrats said the measure was about Paul's opposition to the Fed, not transparency. Oversight and Government Reform ranking member Elijah E. Cummings of Maryland said he was satisfied with provisions of the Dodd-Frank Wall Street Reform and Consumer Protection Act (PL 111-203) that gave the GAO greater power to conduct audits. Federal Reserve Chair Ben S. Bernanke argued forcefully against the bill, telling the House Financial Services Committee in June 2012 that the legislation would compromise the Fed's independence and create a "nightmare scenario." *(Dodd-Frank financial regulatory overhaul, p. 88)*

The House Oversight and Government Reform Committee by voice vote approved HR 459 on June 27, 2012, and formally reported it (H Rept 112-607, Part 1) on July 17. The full House agreed on July 25 to suspend the rules and pass the bill, 327–98.

Government Spending Accountability

The House in 2012 passed a bill (HR 4631) that would require federal agency heads to submit quarterly reports to Congress itemizing expenses for conferences for which the agency paid travel expenses. Joe Walsh, R-Ill., introduced the Government Spending Accountability Act after the General Services Administration (GSA) faced a backlash over a report by the agency's inspector general detailing lavish spending at a training conference in Las Vegas, Nev.

The House Oversight and Government Reform Committee approved the bill by voice vote on June 27, 2012, and formally reported it (H Rept 112-664) on September 11. The House agreed by voice vote on September 11 to suspend the rules and pass the bill.

During committee consideration of HR 4631, while Walsh and Chair Darrell Issa, R-Calif., detailed excesses such as entertainment by "mind readers" and catered meals at the GSA conference paid for with taxpayer dollars, Del. Eleanor Holmes Norton, D-D.C., said it was important to remember that the conference was an "outlier" and did not represent the behavior of most federal workers. On the House floor, Rush D. Holt, D-N.J., expressed his concerns about the impact the legislation would have on the ability of scientists employed by the federal government to travel to conferences and meetings, where they collaborate and communicate with scientists who worked outside the government.

As passed by the House, HR 4631 required each federal agency to post on its public website information about employee presentations at conferences, including the prepared text, and quarterly reports on each conference for which the agency paid travel expenses; set a limit of $500,000 for a single conference, allowing the limit to be waived in some cases; did not allow an agency to cover the travel expenses of more than fifty employees in the United States attending an international conference, unless the secretary of state deemed the additional employees' attendance as being in the national interest; limited agency travel expenses for fiscal 2013 to fiscal 2017 to 70 percent of aggregate travel expenses for fiscal 2010; required the Office of Management and Budget director to establish guidelines on what constituted travel expenses subject to the ceiling; and exempted military travel expenses from the limit.

OMB Performance Standards

On September 11, 2012, The House agreed by voice vote to suspend the rules and pass a bill (HR 538) requiring the Office of Management and Budget (OMB) to develop performance standards to ensure that federal agencies were proving high-quality customer service.

The legislation, sponsored by Henry Cuellar, D-Texas, would require agencies to collect information from their customers regarding the quality of services provided and to include such information in agency performance reports. In a 2011 survey, 31 percent of Americans were satisfied with agency customer service, while 79 percent said that the government could do a better job, according to the Federal Customer Experience Study.

The House Oversight and Government Reform Committee approved the Government Customer Service Improvement Act by voice vote on April 18, 2012, and formally reported it (H Rept 112-534) on June 15.

A Senate companion measure (S 3455), sponsored by Mark Warner, D-Va., was referred to the Senate Homeland

Security and Governmental Affairs Committee but saw no further action.

Improper Payments Elimination

By voice vote on August 1, 2012, the Senate passed a bill (S 1409) to expand a requirement for agencies to identify and stop payments made in error to contractors and program beneficiaries. The Senate Homeland Security and Governmental Affairs Committee approved the bill, sponsored by Thomas R. Carper, D-Del., by voice vote on October 19, 2011, and formally reported it (S Rept 112-181) on July 12, 2012.

The Improper Payments Elimination and Recovery Improvement Act would fortify an existing law (PL 111-204) to curb government overpayments and mispayments, including payments awarded to the wrong people and Social Security checks sent to dead people. Federal agencies in fiscal 2010 signed off on more than $125 billion in erroneous payments, according to an April 2011 Government Accountability Office study. The Office of Personnel Management in September 2011 reported that it had made $601 million in improper payments to deceased federal retirees over a span of five years. *(111th Congress action, p. 612)*

The bill would require the Office of Management and Budget to issue new rules to agencies that called for more consistent and complete estimates of overpayments. According to Carper, some departments, including the Defense Department, relied on contractors to self-report overpayments.

GAO Authority

The Senate Homeland Security and Governmental Affairs Committee by voice vote on October 19, 2011, approved a bill (S 237) that would clarify the authority of the Government Accountability Office (GAO) to obtain any federal agency records it needed to carry out investigations, evaluations, or audits. The legislation was formally reported (S Rept 112-159) on April 24, 2012. The Government Accountability Office Improvement Act was sponsored by Claire McCaskill, D-Mo.

The committee's ranking Republican, Susan Collins of Maine, expressed her outrage that federal agencies were refusing to give information to the GAO, citing the Health and Human Services Department's denial of GAO's request for access to the National Directory of New Hires.

Excess Public Properties

The House on February 7, 2012, by a vote of 259–164, passed a bill (HR 1734) that would establish a centralized process for the federal government to consolidate, sell, or exchange excess properties. The Civilian Property Realignment Act, sponsored by Jeff Denham, R-Calif., would not apply to military installations or properties excluded for national security reasons. A related measure approved by a Senate committee (S 2178), sponsored by Thomas R. Carper, D-Del., established a five-year pilot program to help agencies divest themselves of properties they did not need.

The appeal of doing something about unneeded federal property was bipartisan. It was a way of raising revenue, and thus reducing the deficit without raising taxes, and at the same time saving an estimated $1.7 billion that was spent annually to maintain surplus facilities. A government yard sale, though, might not be as easy or as profitable as some wished. Furthermore, the idea was not popular among some groups, such as advocates for the homeless, who had their own uses in mind for excess public property.

Some Democrats shied away from HR 1734 because it would exempt excess properties from environmental reviews and public comment periods before they were sold. The administration also was unhappy about that aspect of the legislation. It said, too, that the House bill would exempt too much surplus federal property from disposal. It would exempt not only military and other national security property but also "properties used in connection with federal programs for agricultural, recreational, and conservation purposes, including research in connection with the programs."

Groups that sought to aid the homeless complained that both HR 1734 and S 2178, in trying to simplify the property disposal process, would repeal a twenty-five-year-old rule requiring that suitable federal property be made available first to other federal agencies, then to those housing the homeless, and, finally, to state and local agencies. While some emphasized that the process of transferring federal property ownership had too many administrative hurdles, others pointed out that market reasons existed for the backlog of buildings. Many of the estimated 77,700 surplus federal properties had not been sold because no one wanted to buy them, because, for instance, they were far from population centers, they were contaminated, or they were too deteriorated.

The property problem was not new. Although the government disposed of hundreds of parcels of land and buildings each year, the inventory had been piling up for many decades. The Government Accountability Office (GAO) had been prodding Congress for ten years to streamline the disposal process because the extra properties cost so much to maintain. In 2004, President George W. Bush issued an executive order to develop a central database of properties, with a senior property officer designated within each agency and an interagency Federal Real Property Council to keep track of the process. President Barack Obama took up the issue in June 2010 with a memorandum setting a goal of $3 billion in savings from property disposal.

The GAO, however, expressed doubts about the government's property database. In a 2009 report the government auditors called it "inconsistent and unreliable." A June 2012 report was even harsher. At Carper's request, the GAO audited twenty-six surplus federal properties, comparing data that agencies had provided with the actual conditions of the buildings. The ninety-page report listed inaccuracies and wildly fluctuating estimates of the replacement costs of the properties or what they might get on the market. The GAO report concluded that the data were not reliable enough to support "sound decision making."

HR 1734 sought to address the problem by modeling on the Defense Department's Base Realignment and Closure (BRAC) program for military installations. The bill would create an independent Civilian Property Realignment Commission that would make recommendations to the president about federal properties to be consolidated, sold, exchanged, or redeveloped. It would authorize $62 million to implement the commission's recommendations. Once approved by the president, the recommendations would go to Congress. Unless lawmakers acted on a resolution of disapproval, the recommendations would have the force of law. The bill would require the commission to identify for sale at least five properties worth a total of at least $500 million within 180 days of enactment.

The House rejected, 191–230, an amendment by Gerald E. Connolly, D-Va., to give the General Services Administration (GSA) authority to exclude from transaction properties suitable for transferring to a state or municipality for use as a public park or recreation area. Bill sponsor Denham, who opposed the amendment, said it would give GSA veto authority over the president and Congress by allowing it to remove properties after recommendations were approved.

The House Transportation and Infrastructure Committee had approved HR 1734, 30–22, on October 13, 2011, and formally reported it (H Rept 112-384, Part 1) on February 1, 2012.

The Senate Homeland Security and Governmental Affairs Committee approved S 2178, the Federal Real Property Asset Management Reform Act, by voice vote on June 29, 2012, and formally reported it (S Rept 112-241) on November 27. The property council to be authorized by S 2178 at the Office of Management and Budget would develop guidelines and track agencies' progress in getting rid of property. The bill would direct 80 percent of the proceeds toward debt reduction, 18 percent to agencies for property management, and 2 percent to homeless assistance grants. The measure would negate a provision of housing law, the 1987 McKinney-Vento Homeless Assistance Act (PL 100-77), which required the government to review its surplus property to see if any was suitable for the homeless, then to allow state agencies and nonprofits time to apply for it. HR 1734 would require only smaller properties to be offered to the homeless "to the extent practicable." According to data kept by the Department of Health and Human Services, eighty-one properties containing about five hundred buildings had been conveyed to homeless-service providers. Carper argued that such limited use over almost a quarter of a century showed that the program was weak. Advocates for the homeless countered that the five hundred buildings served 2.4 million people. They also said that delays in the process were not the fault of McKinney-Vento but of the GSA. *(1987 act, Congress and the Nation Vol. VII, p. 677)*

American Community Survey

On May 9, 2012, during consideration of the fiscal 2013 Commerce-Justice-Science appropriations bill (HR 5326), the House voted largely along party lines, 232–190, to adopt an amendment by Daniel Webster, R-Fla., to bar use of funds in the legislation for conducting the Commerce Department's American Community Survey (ACS). The House, by 247–163 on May 10, passed HR 5326 (H Rept 112-463) with the Webster language, but the bill stalled in the Senate. The Commerce-Justice-Science fiscal 2013 spending subsequently was covered in continuing appropriations bills, but the ACS provision was not included. *(Continuing appropriations, p. 170)*

The U.S. Bureau of the Census had developed the ACS over many years. According to government agencies and businesses, it provided information about demographic trends on the national, state, and local level. Business was one of the drivers behind the launch of the survey. It wanted a more detailed picture of the American population than any that had emerged from the ten-year census, and its efforts led to the 2005 launch of the ACS. For example, an inquiry about indoor plumbing is part of a larger set of questions about housing trends, answers to which could be used by government agencies to target resources and by retailers to target sales. The government used data about plumbing facilities to allocate federal housing subsidies to local governments, helping Americans gain access to safe and decent housing. To assess the quality of housing stock in neighborhoods throughout the country, the Department of Housing and Urban Development used that information.

The survey became a key data point for a new political environment, one that measured the value of government activities in different ways and signaled that agencies that seemed to be beyond politics had to justify their actions. Some of the questions on the ACS used to be collected on the long form of the decennial census. The ACS collects detailed demographic data from a sample of about two million people annually. It helped determine how more than $400 billion in government funds was distributed throughout the country. For businesses, the survey provided a trove of information about changes in economic activity and demographics and served as a resource for companies making fundamental decisions about investment, marketing, and hiring. Just as the ten-year census documented the shift of the American population from a rural to an urban and then a suburban setting, the more detailed ACS tracked recent changes in household sizes and commuting patterns as well as shifts that affected government priorities and corporate decisions on where to locate stores and what to put on the shelves.

However, after winning a House majority in 2010 on a wave of Tea Party support, some Republicans touting lean government clashed with the party's traditional allies in industry, including companies that saw federal programs giving them a leg up in business efficiency and global competition. To this new generation of conservative lawmakers, the survey, which asked personal questions about individuals' income and family structure, was a warning sign of an overreaching and out-of-control federal government. A strain of distrust of the census had long existed, and in recent years conservative criticism of the ACS had been rampant on the Internet. An amendment by Ted Poe, R-Texas, to HR 5326, which would prohibit penalizing people who refused to respond to the survey, was adopted by voice vote on May 9, 2012. Poe went on record saying that the ACS was intrusive and asking whether the government had a right to ask certain questions.

Webster went a step further, calling the survey unconstitutional. However, the power to conduct a decennial census was specified in the U.S. Constitution—Article I, Section 2, part of what is commonly called the Enumeration clause—and it served in part to apportion representation in the U.S. House of Representatives. The courts had consistently determined that more-elaborate survey questions were constitutional. As recently as 2002, the Supreme Court declined a petition to hear a case questioning the 2000 census.

After adoption of the Poe and Webster amendments, business advocates began to take action, telling lawmakers that they depended on the ACS for sales forecasting, small business lending, opening new facilities, and more.

Sen. Rand Paul, R-Ky., introduced a bill in the Senate (S 3079) to make the survey voluntary. It saw no further action.

FTC and the National Gallery

A Republican effort to oust the Federal Trade Commission (FTC) from its downtown Washington, D.C., headquarters so that the majestic building it occupied could become an annex for the National Gallery of Art, just across Constitution Avenue, stalled in the 112th Congress. The House Transportation and Infrastructure Committee approved HR 690 by voice vote on February 16, 2011. However, the Federal Trade Commission and National Gallery of Art Facility Consolidation, Savings, and Efficiency Act, sponsored by committee Chair John L. Mica, R-Fla., saw no further action.

Mica said that HR 690 could save taxpayers between a quarter-million and a half-million dollars because the FTC staff could be consolidated in one building. (It currently occupied three buildings and proposed to lease a fourth.) And the gallery said it would raise $200 million from private money to renovate the current FTC building. Opponents said that the government should not give away such prime real estate, which, if sold, could bring in a swath of cash. Some argued that the plan could cost the government money. According to the Congressional Budget Office, the FTC building would need renovation and repair before the National Gallery could use it. Critics also worried that the FTC would demand a new headquarters, and a new building meant even more money.

The National Gallery, which occupied a half-mile of frontage along the National Mall with two galleries and a garden, favored the proposal. The FTC was not willing to give up its prime location without a fight, though. The FTC headquarters, built in the late 1930s at roughly the same time as the National Gallery's main building was going up, was called the Apex Building because it was situated at the eastern point of the Federal Triangle, looking down on Pennsylvania Avenue and Constitution Avenue. In a stiff letter to Mica's committee, the five FTC commissioners wrote, "Forcing the FTC out of its federally owned headquarters would displace our agency from a building that it has continuously occupied since it was designed and built for us over seventy years ago." They went on to write that the move would cost taxpayers money if, for example, the agency had to do any remodeling.

In need of momentum on HR 690, Mica turned to a well-worn tactic of combining a stalled bill with another idea that might be more popular. Mica thus offered HR 2844, the National Women's History Museum and Federal Facilities Consolidation and Efficiency Act. The bill, approved by the House Transportation and Infrastructure Committee by voice vote on September 8, 2011, put the FTC proposal together with a plan to establish in Washington a museum dedicated to women's history. Construction of a National Women's History Museum had become a pet project for actress Meryl Streep, which helped focus public attention on the proposal. Furthermore, the idea appeared to have a bipartisan green light, as the House in 2009 had passed a bill to create such a museum. *(111th Congress action, p. 616)*

CHAPTER 15

Inside Congress

Introduction 639

Chronology of Action on Congress: Members and Procedures 642

2009–2010 644

2011–2012 661

Chronology of Action on Congress: Election Issues 677

2009–2010 677

2011–2012 681

Chronology of Action on Congress: Pay and Benefits 683

2009–2010 683

2011–2012 685

Inside Congress

Entrenched partisanship was reflected in members' inability to find common ground on issues and to fashion legislative solutions to the nation's problems. It also served to change the way Congress as an institution has functioned.

CONFERENCE COMMITTEES

An increasingly rare sound on Capitol Hill was that of a gavel being brought down to convene a conference committee. Such temporary panels, which since the eighteenth century were used to resolve differences between the House and Senate on the most complex and contentious legislative details, had all but disappeared from Congress over the past few decades. Since the time of Republican rule in the mid-1990s and persisting under the Democrats, conference committees—which played such an important role historically as to be dubbed the "third house of Congress"—took a back seat to out-of-view dealmaking by a handful of leaders or the "ping-ponging" of competing versions of a bill across the Rotunda.

The result, advocates of open government said, was that the public lost a valuable window into the normally opaque process of lawmaking, a loss that bred public cynicism about Congress. Committee chairs said their ability to fine-tune their legislative handiwork was usurped by congressional leaders. Rank-and-file members on those committees essentially were shut out altogether, thus undermining their ability to serve the needs of their constituents. A thoughtful, deliberative process gave way to a hurried approach, which, some said, violated the intent of the drafters of the U.S. Constitution.

In an era of stultifying partisanship, when the minority party's default setting was to try to derail whatever the majority wanted and the majority had little incentive to award the opposition a forum for doing so, lawmakers found it easier to cut a deal in private than to negotiate a position in conference committees.

FILIBUSTERS AND THE SIXTY-VOTE THRESHOLD

Traditionally, a filibuster involved one or more senators gaining control of the floor and then talking for hours and using other tactics to halt the proceedings, often in an attempt to persuade senators to agree to make changes in impending legislation, kill a bill, or derail a presidential nomination. In recent times, the mere threat of a filibuster usually was enough to get Senate leaders to alter their plans or to move to invoke cloture (end debate), which required a three-fifths vote of the membership (sixty if there were no vacancies).

In the 2000s, when the minority members of one party in the Senate filibustered judicial nominees put forth by a president who was of the opposing party, discussion arose of executing an arcane parliamentary move, dubbed the "nuclear option," that would require a simple majority to end debate. Despite the threats to make such a rule change, the repercussions of which—for good or ill—were unknown, these filibusters remained a common tactic.

Perhaps counterintuitively, the rise of the routine filibuster and the emergence of the increasingly used self-imposed sixty-vote requirement for getting almost anything done in the Senate strengthened the hand of senators in many legislative deliberations, allowing them to present their House counterparts with a credible "take it or leave it" ultimatum based on simple political math. Either the House accepted the Senate's version of a contentious provision or it risked

REFERENCES

Discussion of congressional action for the years 1945–1964 may be found in *Congress and the Nation Vol. I,* pp. 1407–1431; for the years 1965–1968, *Congress and the Nation Vol. II,* pp. 893–924; for the years 1969–1972, *Congress and the Nation Vol. III,* pp. 353–433; for the years 1973–1976, *Congress and the Nation Vol. IV,* pp. 743–794; for the years 1977–1980, *Congress and the Nation Vol. V,* pp. 873–953; for the years 1981–1984, *Congress and the Nation Vol. VI,* pp. 797–840; for the years 1985–1988, *Congress and the Nation Vol. VII,* pp. 871–910; for the years 1989–1992, *Congress and the Nation Vol. VIII,* pp. 913–988; for the years 1993–1996, *Congress and the Nation Vol. IX,* pp. 861–925; for the years 1997–2001, *Congress and the Nation Vol. X,* pp. 757–794; for the years 2001–2004, *Congress and the Nation Vol. XI,* pp. 705–742; for the years 2005–2008, *Congress and the Nation Vol. XII,* pp. 809–850.

Empty seats line the Republican side of the dais as Chair Max Baucus, D-Mont., speaks during the Senate Finance "mock" markup, which he adjourned without proceeding on draft measures to implement pending trade agreements with Colombia, South Korea, and Panama. Senate Finance Republicans boycotted the markup, denying the panel a quorum to consider the long-stalled trade deals.
Source: Photo by Scott J. Ferrell/Congressional Quarterly/Getty Images

ending up with nothing, because only the Senate's language proved it could attract the supermajority that would be required to enact a compromise bill. The effectiveness of that practical argument diminished the use of language written by the House.

The same dynamic gave additional policy-making sway to the less-populated states, because they wielded an outsized share of influence in the Senate. That was because each state had two senators, no matter how many people lived there, and House seats were assigned on the basis of population. Most Democratic senators hailed from the more populous states, prompting increasing hand-wringing among liberals about the fact that conservative small-state senators held so much sway in that chamber.

SECRET HOLDS

A "hold" was shorthand for a notice to the majority or minority leader that a senator planned to object to bringing up a particular bill or nomination—strong power in an institution where unanimous consent was the standard practice. Holds were supposed to be disclosed after six days, although that was not written into Senate rules. In fact, holds were not part of the formal rules at all, and the anonymity of holds often meant an indefinite period of secrecy. Several attempts were made to limit holds after they became popular in the 1970s, but senators were reluctant to give up a tactic that offered them leverage with the White House—especially when its occupant was of the other party—and colleagues on the other side of an issue.

The most ironclad way to ban secret holds would be to change Senate rules, which could take sixty-seven votes. That meant the opposition would need only thirty-three votes to stop any effort to end the practice.

LIVE QUORUMS

Partisanship in the Senate was so bitter it spread even to rare live quorum calls, in which senators voted on whether to dispatch the Sergeant at Arms to round up enough senators (fifty-one of them, usually) to make a quorum. In years past, senators routinely voted "aye," because the very act of showing up to vote created a quorum on the floor. Since Democrats took control of the Senate in 2007, though, Republicans increasingly took to voting "no" as a means of protest and to preserve their attendance records.

SUSPENDING SENATE RULES

In an effort to embarrass Democratic senators by making them cast politically difficult votes, Republicans revived a rarely used procedural maneuver in which they moved to suspend Senate rules to offer amendments to a bill after cloture was imposed and debate limited.

Although the House routinely agreed to suspend the rules (as a way of quickly passing noncontroversial legislation), the Senate seldom did. Senate Republicans would know that they did not have the votes to overcome the prohibition against offering amendments that were not germane to the underlying legislation once cloture was invoked. They just wanted Democrats to have to choose whether to vote against something that might sound popular back home.

ANTI-EARMARKS

Some House Republicans began using the annual appropriations process to push provisions that would block future federal spending on projects they opposed. The tactic was unusual and looked much like an earmark—except in reverse. Instead of adding spending for a specific project, they tried to take it away.

Such amendments were a new feature in the spending debate that began when Republicans banned earmarks after they gained control of the House in 2011. Federal money was still used to finance local projects, but much of the power to secure targeted appropriations was taken out of the hands of individual lawmakers, who had to seek new ways to influence spending. For decades, lawmakers had included policy riders on appropriations bills to broadly block spending on programs they opposed, particularly when it came to hot-button social issues. While the maneuver to block funding for local projects was not unprecedented, it was uncommon and was being used more publicly, with most of the language proposed through floor amendments.

Chronology of Action on Congress: Members and Procedures

2009–2010

The 111th Congress opened amidst controversy over who would take the seat vacated by Democratic senator Barack Obama, president-elect of the United States. The sought-after position went to former Illinois state comptroller and attorney general Roland W. Burris, who also got a Senate Ethics Committee investigation into how he landed it. Democratic governor Rod R. Blagojevich, who made the appointment, ended up in jail for trying to sell the seat.

The House meted out one of its harshest punishments to a longtime member when it censured Charles B. Rangel, D-N.Y. Rangel lost the chair of the House Ways and Means Committee, but the voters in his district kept the popular representative in the House.

Organization: 111th Congress

The 111th Congress convened at noon on January 6, 2009. No major changes were made in the House or Senate leadership, as the Democrats kept their majority in both chambers.

SENATE

On the one hand, the Senate appeared little changed, with all top-tier majority and minority leaders as well as most committee chairs and ranking members continuing in their posts. On the other hand, the chamber marked the end of an era with the passing of the longest-serving U.S. senator, Robert C. Byrd, Democrat of West Virginia.

Majority Leadership

The Senate Democratic caucus met on November 18, 2008, to select the majority leadership. Democrats reelected Majority Leader Harry Reid of Nevada, Majority Whip Richard J. Durbin of Illinois, Democratic Caucus Vice Chair Charles E. Schumer of New York, Democratic Caucus Secretary Patty Murray of Washington, and Democratic Policy Committee Chair Byron L. Dorgan of North Dakota.

Robert Menendez of New Jersey succeeded Schumer as Democratic Senatorial Campaign Committee chair.

Robert Byrd retained his post as president pro tempore until his death on June 28, 2010. Daniel K. Inouye of Hawaii succeeded him.

Minority Leadership

Republicans on November 18, 2008, reelected Minority Leader Mitch McConnell of Kentucky, Minority Whip Jon Kyl of Arizona, and Republican Conference Chair Lamar Alexander of Tennessee.

John Cornyn of Texas succeeded John Ensign of Nevada as chair of the National Republican Senatorial Committee. Cornyn avoided a potential contest when Norm Coleman dropped his bid to focus on a recount in his Senate race in Minnesota. Coleman would go on to lose his seat to Democrat Al Franken. John Thune of South Dakota succeeded Cornyn as Republican Conference vice chair. *(Coleman election contest, Congress and the Nation Vol. XII, pp. 35, 40)*

Ensign became chair of the Republican Policy Committee, assuming the post vacated by Kay Bailey Hutchison of Texas. John Thune of South Dakota took over as Policy Committee head after Ensign resigned the post in June 2009 amidst an ethics investigation. *(Ensign ethics probe, p. 651)*

Committees

As the Democrats maintained their majority status, most committee chairs stayed in the same hands. Some shuffling around did take place, however.

Retaining their chairs were Carl Levin of Michigan at Armed Services; Christopher J. Dodd of Connecticut at Banking, Housing, and Urban Affairs; Kent Conrad of North Dakota at Budget; Jeff Bingaman of New Mexico at Energy and Natural Resources; Barbara Boxer of California

GIFFORDS ASSASSINATION ATTEMPT

Rep. Gabrielle Giffords, a three-term Arizona Democrat, was severely wounded in the head January 8, 2011, outside a supermarket in Tucson during a single-shooter rampage. She survived the assassination attempt. The shooting was the first serious physical assault on a sitting member of Congress since the November 1978 killing of Rep. Leo J. Ryan, D-Calif., on an airstrip in Guyana just before the Jonestown massacre. *(Ryan assassination, Congress and the Nation Vol. V, p. 912)*

Giffords was the target of the attack, which began when a gunman approached and started shooting in her direction about ten minutes after she began addressing constituents at the outdoor event. In August 2009, a protester was removed from a similar community event hosted by Giffords when a gun the protester was carrying fell on the floor. Her Tucson office was vandalized after the 2010 passage of the health care overhaul (HR 3590—PL 111-148, HR 4872—PL 111-152), which she supported. *(Health care overhaul, p. 421)*

The Tucson attack took the lives of Giffords staffer Gabriel Zimmerman, U.S. District Judge John M. Roll, and four others, including a nine-year-old girl. Thirteen others were injured. Bystanders on the scene subdued the shooter, twenty-two-year-old former college student Jared Lee Loughner, and he subsequently was arrested. Loughner, diagnosed as paranoid schizophrenic, pleaded guilty on August 7, 2012, to nineteen counts—including the attempted assassination of Giffords—and, thus, was spared the death penalty. He was sentenced on November 8 to life in prison.

On the day of the shooting, Speaker John A. Boehner, R-Ohio, was the first prominent official to react publicly to the news, suggesting that, whatever its political differences, the House for the time stood unified. "An attack on one who serves is an attack on all who serve," he said. In a solemn House chamber on January 12, 2011, Boehner choked back tears as he launched a daylong tribute for Giffords and other victims. The House adopted by voice vote a resolution (H Res 32) honoring the victims. It was entitled: "Expressing the sense of the House of Representatives with respect to the tragic shooting in Tucson, Arizona, on January 8, 2011."

Hours after the House action, President Barack Obama spoke at a memorial service in Tucson, stressing the need for civility in political debate. "At a time when our discourse has become so sharply polarized, at a time when we are far too eager to lay the blame for all that ails the world at the feet of those who happen to think differently than we do," the president said, "it's important for us to pause for a moment and make sure that we're talking with each other in a way that heals, not in a way that wounds."

Responding to the attack on Giffords, lawmakers discussed measures to increase their own security and limit the ability of people to carry guns near federal officials. A few Democrats called on Congress to work on gun control legislation. Rep. Jane Harman, D-Calif., expressed support for legislation being developed to bar the type of high-capacity ammunition magazine used by the Tucson gunman. Such clips had been banned as part of an assault weapons law (PL 103-322) that expired in 2004. *(Assault weapons ban, Congress and the Nation Vol. IX, p. 683; Congress and the Nation Vol. XI, p. 615)*

While Giffords's recovery was described as remarkable, she announced on January 22, 2012, that she would resign from Congress to focus on continuing her physical rehabilitation. On January 25, she formally submitted her resignation on the House floor, where she was greeted with a standing ovation and a bipartisan, heroine's tribute.

at Environment and Public Works; Max Baucus of Montana at Finance; Byron L. Dorgan of North Dakota at Indian Affairs; Patrick J. Leahy of Vermont at Judiciary; Herb Kohl of Wisconsin at Special Aging; and Daniel K. Akaka of Hawaii at Veterans' Affairs.

Tom Harkin of Iowa relinquished the top position on the Agriculture, Nutrition, and Forestry Committee to Blanche Lincoln of Arkansas when he assumed the helm of Health, Education, Labor, and Pensions. He succeeded Edward M. Kennedy of Massachusetts, who died on August 25, 2009.

Daniel Inouye gave up the chair of Commerce, Science, and Transportation and took on leadership of the Appropriations Committee, succeeding Robert Byrd. John D. Rockefeller IV of West Virginia succeeded Inouye on Commerce. Rockefeller handed off the top spot on Select Intelligence to Dianne Feinstein of California. Charles Schumer succeeded Feinstein as chair of Rules and Administration.

John Kerry of Massachusetts became chair of the Foreign Relations Committee, upon Joseph R. Biden Jr.'s resignation from Congress to become vice president of the United States. Leading the Small Business and Entrepreneurship Committee instead of Kerry was Mary L. Landrieu of Louisiana.

Barbara Boxer of California had been designated the acting chair of the Senate Ethics Committee during the 110th Congress, after sitting chair Tim Johnson of South Dakota fell ill. Boxer took full charge of the panel in the 111th Congress.

Controversy arose over whether Joseph I. Lieberman of Connecticut, an Independent, would retain the chair of the Homeland Security and Governmental Reform Committee. The Democratic caucus on November 18, 2008, voted, 42–13, to allow Lieberman, who had actively supported Republican candidate John McCain over Democratic

CAPITOL HILL DRESS CODE

Capitol Hill's notoriously conservative dress code was showing signs of relaxing a bit, perhaps a reflection of the informality of the times, perhaps spurred on by First Lady Michelle Obama's notable sleeveless attire at her husband's first speech to a joint session of Congress.

No hard-and-fast Capitol dress code existed beyond the elaborate requirements imposed on congressional pages, the teenagers who did the bidding of senators and representatives. Those rules even specified the materials for their clothing: "navy blue wool or acrylic jackets; dark gray slacks; a uniform tie; a white, long-sleeved, permanent press dress shirt; solid black shoes and socks." The official House rules said nothing about sleeves for members of Congress or journalists in or near the chamber—or much of anything else. According to Rule 1, Clause 2, men were required to wear a coat and tie on the floor, and women had to wear "appropriate attire," which was not defined. Senate rules mentioned nothing about clothing. Asked for guidance about interpreting the word "appropriate," Drew Hammill, a spokesperson for House Speaker Nancy Pelosi, D-Calif., said she "encourages anyone on the House floor or in the Speaker's Lobby to use common sense and good judgment."

Over the decades, despite a general conservatism in dress and decorum—striped pants and cutaway coats did not disappear from the Senate until World War II—Congress allowed some license around the edges. After he first arrived as a House member in 1987, Ben Nighthorse Campbell of Colorado persuaded Speaker Jim Wright, D-Texas, to permit him to wear neckerchiefs and bolos. (Campbell, a Democrat who switched to the GOP as a senator in the 1990s, argued that his chronic neck pain made traditional ties uncomfortable.) Cynthia McKinney, a Georgia Democrat, often wore her gold-colored tennis shoes to the House floor. The House rule against hats on the floor, though, prevailed even against New York Democrat Bella S. Abzug and her trademark broad-brimmed hats in the 1970s.

By 2009, the clothing standards seemed to have eased even more. Although women in the past were told to leave the Speaker's Lobby if they were wearing a sleeveless dress or blouse, House doorkeepers no longer even noticed them. An exposed midriff did prove too much, though. A female reporter was sent out of the Speaker's Lobby for wearing pants that bared her midriff, but the House Press Gallery fashioned a belt for her and she was able to return, having met the unwritten standards of decorum.

candidate Barack Obama in the 2008 White House race, to keep his gavel. Lieberman had split with the Democratic Party repeatedly on Iraq policy and incurred the wrath of many Democrats for stumping for McCain as well as criticizing Obama at the Republican National Convention and on the campaign trail. The Democratic nominee for vice president in 2000, Lieberman was reelected to the Senate as an independent in 2006 after losing the Democratic primary. Initially, Reid offered Lieberman the chair of a lesser committee if he would give up the Homeland Security position. But Lieberman rejected that proposal and even signaled that he might join the Republican caucus if Democrats pushed him too hard. Democratic lawmakers agreed that Lieberman's vote on domestic issues would be far too valuable in the 111th Congress to risk completely alienating him. In what was essentially a slap on the wrist, the Connecticut independent did lose his spot on the Environmental and Public Works Committee, which meant he was stripped of a subcommittee chair.

Most Republicans kept their ranking member status, with some exceptions.

Remaining as the top GOP committee member were Saxby Chambliss of Georgia at Agriculture, Nutrition, and Forestry; Thad Cochran of Mississippi at Appropriations; John McCain of Arizona at Armed Services; Richard C. Shelby of Alabama at Banking, Housing, and Urban Affairs; Judd Gregg of New Hampshire at Budget; James M. Inhofe of Oklahoma at Environment and Public Works; Charles E. Grassley of Iowa at Finance; Richard G. Lugar of Indiana at Foreign Relations; Michael B. Enzi of Wyoming at Health, Education, Labor, and Pensions; Susan Collins of Maine at Homeland Security and Governmental Affairs; Robert J. Bennett of Utah at Rules and Administration; Christopher S. Bond of Missouri at Select Intelligence; and Olympia J. Snowe of Maine at Small Business and Entrepreneurship.

Ted Stevens of Alaska resigned as ranking member of the Commerce, Science, and Transportation Committee after being indicted on federal charges of making false statements. Kay Bailey Hutchison of Texas took Stevens's slot on the panel. Pete V. Domenici of New Mexico did not seek reelection in 2008, leaving open the ranking membership on Energy and Natural Resources. It was filled by Lisa Murkowski of Alaska.

John Barrasso of Wyoming became ranking member of the Indian Affairs Committee, when Larry Craig of Idaho gave up the spot after public disclosure of his guilty plea to a misdemeanor charge of disorderly conduct in a men's restroom at the Minneapolis–St. Paul International Airport. Craig also relinquished the ranking member position on Veterans' Affairs, which was taken up by Richard M. Burr of North Carolina.

Arlen Specter of Pennsylvania was ranking member of the Judiciary Committee in the 110th Congress and kept

SIGN-ON LETTERS

A common tactic for a lawmaker hoping to heighten his appeal to the White House or Capitol Hill leaders was to persuade as many colleagues as possible, and in person, to put their signatures on a letter. But this traditional form of persuasion, known as the sign-on letter, became streamlined for the twenty-first century with the use of powerful computer servers.

With the use of this technology, once a lawmaker agreed to sign a letter that sounded the alarm about something the president was considering or exhorted congressional leaders to get a certain bill off the back burner, the permission—and, in some cases, a facsimile of the actual signature—could be gathered and applied electronically. To save time and labor, an image file of a lawmaker's signature, or frank, could be e-mailed to any other congressional office, where it could be arranged in alphabetical or seniority order at the end of a sign-on letter. The "e-dear colleague" system allowed for electronic correspondence among members, with no pen-on-paper signature needed.

Although this kind of thing had already become prevalent in the business world, Congress continued to jealously guard its electronic privacy and prerogatives, resulting in a quirky process as technology evolved. For example, some lawmakers took to the new system wholeheartedly while others whose offices were dependent on their wireless handheld devices nevertheless decreed that they would respond to constituent e-mail only by "snail mail." Meanwhile, a handful eschewed the autopen for an actual signature on each of the thousands of individual letters written each year (even though those were almost always forgeries of the member's handwriting).

that position when the 111th Congress convened. However, on April 28, 2009, he announced that he was switching membership to the Democratic Party. (He would go on to be defeated in the May 18, 2010, Democratic primary.) Jeff Sessions of Alabama succeeded Specter on Judiciary.

Mel Martinez of Florida became the top Republican on the Special Aging Committee. The post had been held in the 110th Congress by Gordon H. Smith of Oregon, who was defeated in his 2008 reelection bid. Bob Corker of Tennessee took the slot after Martinez resigned his Senate seat on September 9, 2009.

Johnny Isakson of Georgia became vice chair of the Senate Ethics Committee, succeeding John Cornyn of Texas.

HOUSE

The top three Democratic leaders—including Nancy Pelosi of California, the first woman to hold the position of Speaker since its advent in 1789—remained the same, while Minority Leader John A. Boehner, R-Ohio, found himself head of a team that was more conservative than the outgoing roster of GOP leaders, after embracing members of the Republican Study Committee for top spots.

Majority Leadership

Democrat Nancy Pelosi was easily reelected to the post of Speaker on January 6, 2009, by a vote of 255–174, defeating Republican John Boehner. The House Democratic caucus on November 18, 2008, had reelected Pelosi, as well as Majority Leader Steny H. Hoyer of Maryland and Majority Whip James E. Clyburn of South Carolina, by acclamation. None faced opposition.

John B. Larson of Connecticut also was unopposed in his move up from vice chair of the caucus to the chair's slot, replacing Rahm Emanuel of Illinois, who left to serve as White House chief of staff in the Obama administration.

Chris Van Hollen of Maryland continued to chair the Democratic Congressional Campaign Committee, the House Democrats' national campaign arm. Van Hollen also took on the job as assistant to the Speaker, with special responsibility as liaison to the Obama White House. That position had been held by Xavier Becerra of California, who bested Marcy Kaptur of Ohio for vice chair of the caucus in the only contested race among Democrats.

Minority Leadership

Boehner won a second term as minority leader at a meeting of House Republicans on November 19, 2008. He defeated Dan Lungren of California on a secret ballot. Eric Cantor of Virginia succeeded Roy Blunt of Missouri as minority whip, and Mike Pence of Indiana replaced Adam H. Putnam of Florida as House Republican Conference chair. Both Cantor and Pence were unopposed and had Boehner's backing.

Thaddeus McCotter of Michigan kept his post as House Republican Policy Committee chair, defeating challenger and committee vice chair Michael C. Burgess of Texas. Pete Sessions of Texas replaced Tom Cole of Oklahoma as chair of the National Republican Congressional Committee. Cole declined to seek another term. Sessions was unopposed and had Boehner's support.

Committees

The Democrats continued to hold the committee chairs, which saw little turnover from the previous Congress.

Continuing their service as committee heads were Collin C. Peterson of Minnesota at Agriculture; David R. Obey of Wisconsin at Appropriations; Ike Skelton of Missouri at

HARRY REID'S REMARKS ABOUT OBAMA

Senate colleagues from both sides of the aisle declined to take issue with comments revealed in 2010 that Majority Leader Harry Reid, D-Nev., had made during the 2008 campaign about Democratic presidential candidate Barack Obama's race. Obama's mother was Caucasian and his father was black.

Reid had described Obama, then an Illinois senator, as "light-skinned" and "with no Negro dialect, unless he wanted to have one." Reid, who publicly supported Obama's campaign only after it became apparent he would be the party's nominee, was quoted making those observations in a book about the presidential campaign, *Game Change,* by Mark Halperin and John Heilemann, released in January 12, 2010.

Reid characterized his comments as "a poor choice of words" that he deeply regretted. He called the president to apologize after disclosure of the remarks touched off a firestorm of criticism. Obama said he accepted the apology "without question, because I've known him for years, I've seen the passionate leadership he's shown on issues of social justice, and I know what's in his heart."

Minority Leader Mitch McConnell, R-Ky., declined to say January 12 whether he agreed with other top Republicans—notably Republican National Committee Chair Michael Steele and National Republican Senatorial Committee Chair John Cornyn of Texas—who had called for Reid to relinquish his post as Democratic leader. Asked twice whether he agreed that Reid should step aside as majority leader, McConnell gave the same answer: "I think that's an issue for the Democratic Conference." Reid's Democratic colleagues for the most part publicly supported him.

Steele, Cornyn, and others accused Reid and the Democrats of hypocrisy because Reid in 2002 called for Senate Majority Leader Trent Lott, R-Miss., to surrender his leadership post after Lott made controversial comments at a one hundredth birthday party for Sen. Strom Thurmond, R-S.C. Lott said the nation would have been better off had Thurmond won his 1948 presidential bid on a segregationist platform. Lott stepped down when it became clear he did not have support among his GOP colleagues to retain the post.

Armed Services; John M. Spratt Jr. of South Carolina at Budget; George Miller of California at Education and Labor (renamed from Education and the Workforce); Barney Frank of Massachusetts at Financial Services; Bennie Thompson of Mississippi at Homeland Security; John Conyers Jr. of Michigan at Judiciary; Nick J. Rahall II of West Virginia at Natural Resources; Louise M. Slaughter of New York at Rules; Bart Gordon of Tennessee at Science and Technology; Silvestre Reyes of Texas at Select Intelligence; Edward J. Markey of Massachusetts at Select Energy Independence and Global Warming; Nydia M. Velázquez of New York at Small Business; James L. Oberstar of Minnesota at Transportation and Infrastructure; and Bob Filner of California at Veterans' Affairs.

An unusual battle ensued for leadership of the Energy and Commerce Committee. By a vote of 137–122 on November 20, 2008, by the House Democratic caucus, John D. Dingell of Michigan was deposed as chair, handing the powerful panel's gavel to Henry A. Waxman of California. Dingell, who was the longest-serving member of the House (and would become the longest-serving member of Congress on June 7, 2013), had been the chair or ranking Democrat of the committee since 1981. Waxman had earned a towering reputation in the House and was allied with House Speaker Pelosi. He touted a theme of change and, after the balloting, expressed his great respect for Dingell. Dingell, in turn, acknowledged the political winds of the day, congratulated Waxman, and pledged to work closely with him on the panel. Some members cautioned that challenging the seniority system traditionally used by the Democratic Party to select committee chairs and ranking members could prove disruptive in the future.

With Waxman going to Energy and Commerce, he gave up chair of the Oversight and Government Reform Committee. He was succeeded by Edolphus Towns of New York.

In the 110th Congress, Robert A. Brady of Pennsylvania assumed the chair of House Administration following the death of Juanita Millender-McDonald on April 22, 2007. He continued to hold the post in the 111th Congress. Another passing—Tom Lantos of California on February 11, 2008—left open the top spot on the House Foreign Affairs Committee during the 110th Congress. It was taken by Howard L. Berman of California, who continued as chair in the 111th Congress. Zoe Lofgren of California became chair of the House Committee on Standards of Official Conduct. Her predecessor was Stephanie Tubbs Jones of Oklahoma, who died on August 20, 2008.

Sander M. Levin of Michigan took over as chair of the Ways and Means Committee on March 4, 2010, when Charles B. Rangel of New York stepped aside amidst an investigation into alleged ethics violations. *(Rangel ethics probe, p. 657)*

While most ranking members stayed at their posts, vacancies created a number of openings for Republicans.

The ranking member carryovers were Jerry Lewis of California at Appropriations; Paul D. Ryan of Wisconsin at Budget; Joe L. Barton of Texas at Energy and Commerce;

Spencer Bachus of Alabama at Financial Services; Peter T. King of New York at Homeland Security; Ileana Ros-Lehtinen of Florida at Foreign Affairs; Lamar Smith of Texas at Judiciary; David Dreier of California at Rules; Ralph M. Hall of Texas at Science and Technology; Peter Hoekstra of Michigan at Select Intelligence; F. James Sensenbrenner Jr. of Wisconsin at Select Energy Independence and Global Warming; John L. Mica of Florida at Transportation and Infrastructure; and Steve Buyer of Indiana at Veterans' Affairs.

John M. McHugh of New York became ranking member of the Armed Service Committee, succeeding Duncan Hunter of California, who in 2008 did not seek reelection to the House. Hunter made an unsuccessful run for the Republican Party nomination for president. McHugh left Congress on September 21, 2009, to become secretary of the army. Howard P. "Buck" McKeon of California took the top GOP spot on the panel. Meanwhile, he relinquished the comparable position on the Education and the Workforce Committee. John Kline of Minnesota succeeded him there.

Darrell Issa of California became the ranking member of the Oversight and Government Reform Committee. His predecessor, Thomas M. Davis III of Virginia, had resigned from the House on November 24, 2008. Sam Graves of Missouri assumed the top Republican post on the Small Business Committee. His predecessor, Steve Chabot of Ohio, lost his 2008 reelection bid. Jim McCrery of Louisiana decided not to run for reelection in 2008. His ranking member position on the Ways and Means Committee was filled by Dave Camp of Michigan.

Frank D. Lucas of Oklahoma succeeded Robert W. Goodlatte of Virginia as ranking member of the Agriculture Committee. Dan Lungren of California succeeded Vernon L. Ehlers of Michigan as the top Republican on the House Administration Committee. Doc Hastings of Washington succeeded Don Young of Alaska as ranking member of the Natural Resources Committee. Hastings was succeeded as ranking member by Jo Bonner of Alabama on the Standards of Official Conduct Committee.

Rules

The House on January 6, 2009, adopted a package (H Res 5) setting the chamber's rules for operation. The party-line 242–181 vote came after Republicans angrily accused the Democratic majority of rolling back attempts to make the lawmaking process more transparent and members more accountable. Democrats maintained that the new rules would make the House function more effectively.

Several significant rules changes were made:

- Elimination of the six-year term limit for committee chairs, established in 1995 when Republicans took control of the House.
- Restrictions on the minority's ability to order a bill reported back to committee. Under the new rules, the bills can no longer be reported back "promptly," a vague term that has meant "never" in practice. Now, any vote to recommit an amended bill must include instructions that it be returned to the floor "forthwith," meaning the House must vote on the amended bill within minutes.
- Rescission of a rule adopted in the 110th Congress that barred holding votes open with the intent of changing the outcome. *(110th Congress action, Congress and the Nation Vol. XII, p. 830)*
- Permission to attach an emergency designation to entitlement spending bills that exempted those measures from pay-as-you-go mandates. A bill that did not meet pay-as-you-go requirements could be linked procedurally with another piece of legislation that did have offsets. Legislation could receive an emergency designation "if such provisions are necessary to respond to an act of war, an act of terrorism, a natural disaster, or a period of sustained low economic growth."
- Nullification, for the purposes of the 111th Congress, of the requirement in the 2003 prescription drug law (PL 108-173) that if 45 percent or more of Medicare's funding comes from general tax revenues for two years in a row, the president must submit—and Congress debate—legislation to slow spending. *(2003 law, Congress and the Nation Vol. XI, p. 496)*

H Res 5 also authorized the House Judiciary Committee to continue its lawsuit against current and former White House advisers regarding the investigation into the firing of nine U.S. attorneys. The authorization would allow the committee to reissue subpoenas to White House chief of staff Joshua B. Bolten and former White House counsel Harriet Miers to testify and produce documents related to the 2006 firings. The subpoenas issued in 2007 expired at the end of the 110th Congress. *(Fired U.S. attorneys, Congress and the Nation Vol. XII, p. 721)*

Another change closed a loophole that allowed lame-duck members, delegates, and the resident commissioner to directly negotiate future employment or compensation without public disclosure. All members would have to file with the House ethics committee reports of any employment negotiations or agreements.

Burris Appointment

Before an appointment had even been made, controversy arose over filling the seat vacated by Democratic senator Barack Obama of Illinois, who had resigned on November 16, 2008, after winning the presidential election. On December 9, Illinois governor Rod R. Blagojevich was arrested on federal corruption charges, including essentially trying to sell the Senate appointment to the highest bidder. In a December 10 letter to the governor, which was signed by all members of the Senate Democratic caucus, Majority Leader Harry Reid, D-Nev., insisted that Blagojevich resign as governor and refrain from naming anyone to the vacant seat, saying that "any appointment by you would raise serious questions." Reid told the governor that, if he ignored the request, the Senate would determine whether the appointee should be seated according to its authority under Clause 1 of Article I, Section 5 of the U.S. Constitution. Although Blagojevich did make an appointment and the appointee did experience a delay in being sworn in, events played out differently than Reid anticipated.

Illinois Secretary of State Jesse White registered Blagojevich's appointment of Roland W. Burris, former Illinois state comptroller and attorney general, in the state's official records on December 31 but declined to sign the U.S. Senate's certification form. The secretary of the Senate on January 5, 2009, rejected Burris's certification of appointment as invalid, stating that the Senate's rules require that both the state's governor and secretary of state certify the appointment. Reid and Majority Whip Richard J. Durbin, D-Ill., agreed, and the next day Burris was denied entry into the chamber to be administered the oath of office. Reid, Durbin, and Burris then determined a path for Burris to be seated: get White's signature, testify at Blagojevich's impeachment proceedings in the Illinois Legislature, and be subject to a Senate Rules and Administration Committee review of the legality of the appointment.

The Illinois Supreme Court on January 9 ruled that White's registration of the appointment was sufficient, that the state was not obligated to use the "recommended" Senate certification form, and that Burris could submit a certified copy of the appointment registration instead. During a news conference Durbin said that, despite the court ruling, Senate rules demanded the secretary of state's signature on the governor's appointment paperwork. White produced a separate document affirming that he had registered Burris's appointment and that his signature on the certification form was not required to make the appointment credentials legal. He said that he "could not and would not in good conscience sign my name to any appointment made by Gov. Rod Blagojevich." The secretary of the Senate on January 12 deemed that the new credentials met the requirements of the chamber's rules and, thus, were valid. The Senate leadership, meanwhile, signaled a softening of its hard-line position by dropping its demand for an investigation by the Rules panel. Burris was sworn in January 15. In November 2009 the Senate Ethics Committee, while saying Burris did not violate the law, admonished him for being less than candid about the controversial circumstances surrounding his appointment. *(Burris ethics probe, p. 652)*

D.C. Representation

Legislation (HR 157, S 160) to give the District of Columbia a full voting member of Congress fell victim in 2010 to objections from Democrats who opposed language that would have killed many of the District's gun control laws and from Republicans who opposed the way Utah would be given an additional House seat. The legislation provided that the seat would go to Utah until the next reapportionment. The state barely lost out getting an additional seat after the 2000 census. The District of Columbia House Voting Rights Act would have brought the total House membership to 437 and the total electoral college membership to 539 (adding one for Utah; D.C. already had three votes).

The chief dispute over the legislation itself concerned its constitutionality. Most Republicans argued that the District was not a state and that, under the U.S. Constitution, only states could elect members to the House. Supporters countered that the Constitution's District Clause gave Congress sweeping authority to decide all matters related to the District of Columbia, including voting representation. The Constitution permitted the House to set its ratio of representation up to a maximum of one House member for every thirty thousand residents. Each state was guaranteed at least one representative. After all but one of the thirteen censuses conducted between 1790 and 1910, the House expanded (the exception was the 1840s). A dispute over census figures forestalled the 1920 reapportionment, though, and the Reapportionment Act of 1929 set the membership at 435. But it could be changed with another statute. The average number of people in each House district has grown steadily since then—to about 280,000 in 1929 and almost 700,000 by 2009. But district populations varied widely.

The District was represented in Congress by one nonvoting delegate, as were American Samoa, Guam, Northern Mariana Islands, and the Virgin Islands. Puerto Rico was represented by a nonvoting resident commissioner.

Democrats in the 111th Congress renewed their effort to provide full voting representation to Washington, D.C., hoping that expanded majorities in both chambers and a Democrat in the White House would ease the path to enactment. The Senate had been the obstacle in 2007, the last time Democrats tried to get the legislation through Congress, but many Republican opponents had been defeated in 2008 or retired at the end of the 110th Congress, replaced by Democrats who were more supportive. The plan to pair the D.C. seat with the Utah seat was designed to maximize political support, as the District was overwhelmingly Democratic and Utah was heavily Republican. *(2007 action, Congress and the Nation Vol. XII, p. 836)*

SENATE COMMITTEE ACTION

The Senate Homeland Security and Governmental Affairs Committee approved S 160, sponsored by Chair Joseph I. Lieberman, I-Conn., by a vote of 11–1 on February 11, 2009. John McCain, R-Ariz., was the only "no" vote. The bill was formally reported (no written report) on February 12.

The bill proposed adding a seat for Utah by carving out a fourth congressional district in the state. The panel gave voice vote approval to an amendment by Lieberman to clarify that, starting with the 113th Congress, the new House seat would be apportioned based on 2010 census figures and would not automatically be awarded to Utah. McCain's opposition was based on his concern that Arizona, also a fast-growing state, would be shortchanged by the awarding of a new House seat to Utah, which he called "patently unfair." The senator's position put him at odds with Lieberman, who had campaigned for the Republican when he ran for president in 2008.

Spirited debate ensued over the validity of using legislation, instead of a constitutional amendment, to give the District voting representation. Susan Collins of Maine, the panel's ranking Republican, said that while she "concluded the constitutionality of this legislation is a close call . . . the question is best resolved by the courts and not by this committee."

SENATE FLOOR ACTION

The Senate passed S 160, 61–37, on February 26, after both overcoming a constitutional challenge and adding the gun language that set up a major conflict with the House. Lieberman, who managed the floor debate, said D.C. citizens had "the wholly unsought-after distinction of being the only residents of a democratically ruled national capital in the world who have no say in how their nation is governed. It is really astounding." Minority Whip Jon Kyl, R-Ariz., countered that the District did not need full representation because its residents had done well by its House delegate.

The bill survived a critical test when senators rejected, 36–62 on February 25, a constitutional point of order lodged by McCain. McCain argued that S 160 violated Article I, Section 2, of the Constitution, which stated that the House "shall be composed of members chosen every second year by the people of the several states." Robert C. Byrd, D-W.Va., spoke in favor of McCain's challenge, saying that the legislation circumvented the Constitution. Advocates of the bill argued that Article I, Section 8, granting Congress power "to exercise exclusive legislation in all cases whatsoever, over such District," trumped the first section.

The Senate on February 26 voted, 62–36, to adopt an amendment offered by John Ensign, R-Nev., to repeal the District's restrictions on semiautomatic weapons, bar the city's registration requirements for most guns, and drop criminal penalties for possessing an unregistered firearm in the District. Twenty-two Democrats—most of them from western or conservative-leaning states—voted for the amendment, which was aimed at codifying the 2008 U.S. Supreme Court ruling in *District of Columbia v. Heller* (554 U.S. 570) that struck down a District of Columbia gun ownership ban and declared for the first time that the Second Amendment included an individual right to bear arms. *(Court ruling, Congress and the Nation Vol. XII, p. 769)*

Majority Whip Richard J. Durbin, D-Ill., called the Ensign amendment "one of the most extreme pieces of legislation on the issue of guns" that he had seen. "I believe the amendment is reckless. I believe it is irresponsible," said Dianne Feinstein, D-Calif. "I believe it will lead to more weapons and more violence on the streets of our nation's capital." Ensign dismissed the criticism, saying, "Will law-abiding citizens be able to protect themselves in their own homes? That is what this amendment is attempting to do: to say to citizens living in the District of Columbia, 'We will protect your rights.'"

In other action, the Senate on February 26 rejected, 30–67, an amendment by Kyl to return all nonfederal land in the District to Maryland, provided that Maryland agreed to take back the land and that the provision in the Twenty-third Amendment giving the District three votes in the electoral college was repealed. The Senate on February 25 rejected, 7–91, a substitute amendment by Tom Coburn, R-Okla., that would have replaced the bill's text with language stating that District residents would not have to pay individual federal income taxes. The proposal was aimed at refuting the District's slogan: "Taxation without representation."

HOUSE COMMITTEE ACTION

The House Judiciary Committee approved a companion bill (HR 157) by a vote of 20–12 on February 25, the day before the Senate floor vote on S 160. Unlike the Senate measure, the House bill proposed an at-large seat for Utah instead of a new fourth district. Like the Senate bill, HR 157 requested expedited judicial review if the legislation was challenged in court, which it surely would be.

During the markup, the committee rejected, 9–19, an amendment by F. James Sensenbrenner Jr., R-Wis., that would have brought the legislation more in line with the Senate bill by requiring Utah to create a fourth House district. It also defeated, 12–20, an amendment by Darrell Issa, R-Calif., to strike the provision that would create an additional House seat for Utah. Republican Jason Chaffetz of Utah supported the amendment, arguing that his state should wait until the next census for another shot at a seat. Also rejected, 15–15, was an amendment by the panel's ranking Republican, Lamar Smith of Texas, to specify that members of the House would have legal standing to mount a court challenge. "The Democratic majority is pursuing a constitutionally suspect bill when constitutional alternatives are available," Smith argued. Opponents of HR 157 said that the bill was unconstitutional and that it would take years of litigation before D.C. would see a representative.

The panel adopted, 24–5, a Jerrold Nadler, D-N.Y., substitute amendment that, among other things, included a request for expedited judicial review if the legislation was challenged in court.

The bill, sponsored by Del. Eleanor Holmes Norton, D-D.C., was formally reported (H Rept 111-22) on March 2.

STALLED ACTION

House Majority Leader Steny H. Hoyer, D-Md., a longtime advocate of District voting rights, said on June 9 that the D.C. representation legislation likely would not come to the floor in 2009. A deadlock had formed over the Senate-passed language that would strip many of the District's gun ownership restrictions. Part of the problem was that District leaders disagreed over whether to accept the gun provision. Some members of the D.C. Council and Democratic mayor Adrian M. Fenty indicated that it might be worthwhile to proceed with the bill, even with the gun language. However, Norton strongly opposed the idea. Senate Majority Leader Harry Reid of Nevada, who as with many other moderate and conservative Democrats voted for the gun amendment to S 160, expressed his hope that the District legislation would be revived.

Hoyer on April 14, 2010, laid the groundwork for House floor action on the D.C. voting rights legislation. He was said to be nearing agreement with Norton on a plan for moving forward with a version of HR 157 that would incorporate language aimed at weakening or stripping gun restrictions in the District. Hoyer said he thought gun law changes had no place in the bill, but he led efforts to find a way to break the stalemate.

In a quick reversal, Hoyer on April 20 said he was "profoundly disappointed" that the bill was likely dead for the year, with its supporters unable to overcome opposition to it. Some D.C. Council members voiced their opposition to gutting local gun laws, and the *Washington Post* on April 18 ran an editorial against the plan. Furthermore, Sen. Orrin G. Hatch, R-Utah, said he would filibuster the House version of the bill because it added an at-large House seat to Utah's three existing three districts. He preferred that Utah's new seat be carved out of existing districts, as stipulated in the Senate-passed bill.

Senate Appointments

On August 6, 2009, the House Judiciary Committee approved by voice vote a joint resolution (S J Res 7) proposing a constitutional amendment to bar governors from appointing senators. The measure, sponsored by Russ Feingold, D-Wis., was officially entitled "A joint resolution proposing an amendment to the Constitution of the United States relative to the election of Senators."

At its markup for S J Res 7 on July 30, the Judiciary Subcommittee on the Constitution did not muster the quorum necessary to approve the proposal. Subcommittee Chair Feingold said the joint resolution would be "polled out" of the subcommittee, whereby individual senators would give consent to move it forward. Although several subcommittee members, including ranking Republican Tom Coburn of Oklahoma and Democrat Benjamin L. Cardin of Maryland, raised concerns about the proposal, no one signaled they would stand in the way of moving it to the full committee.

Feingold's proposal would amend the Constitution by barring gubernatorial appointments and requiring states to hold special elections to fill Senate vacancies. Feingold said that "the right to elect one's representatives is a bedrock principle of our democracy, and it is time to unambiguously reaffirm it in the Constitution."

Recent controversy about gubernatorial appointments surfaced when embattled Illinois governor Rod R. Blagojevich named Democrat Roland W. Burris to the Senate seat vacated by Barack Obama, who had been elected president. *(Burris appointment, p. 647)*

Pocket Veto

On January 13, 2010, the House voted, 143–245, to sustain President Barack Obama's December 30, 2009, veto of a stopgap spending measure (H J Res 64) that was rendered unnecessary after the fiscal 2010 defense appropriations bill (HR 3326—PL 111-118) became law on December 19. In scheduling the vote, which fell well short of the two-thirds required to override, House leaders never intended to succeed but wanted to preserve their position on the president's pocket veto power—when a president killed a bill by declining to sign it while Congress was not in session and could not receive the returned measure. *(Defense appropriations, p. 133)*

In his veto statement, Obama said he was using his pocket veto authority by withholding his signature while Congress was out of session. He also returned the measure to the clerk of the House with a memorandum of disapproval, which was the process used for a regular veto. The January 13 bipartisan vote served as the latest round in a long-running constitutional dispute. Constitutional scholars were divided on whether a pocket veto was valid when the House and Senate were in recess or during the period between the two sessions of a Congress as long as the chambers made arrangements to receive messages from the White House. *(Veto text, p. 915)*

House Appropriations Committee chair David R. Obey, D-Wis., urged members to sustain the president's veto and said the vote was needed to send a message that, in this case, the House did not recognize a pocket veto and considered the president's action to be a regular veto.

Online Disclosure of Expenditures

The Senate, by voice vote on July 6, 2009, adopted an amendment by Tom Coburn, R-Okla., to the fiscal 2010 legislative branch appropriations bill (HR 2918—PL 111-68) to require the online disclosure of Senate expenditures. Coburn said his amendment, which was included in the final version of the legislation signed into law on October 1, would provide more transparency. *(Legislative branch appropriations, p. 128)*

House Speaker Nancy Pelosi, D-Calif., on June 3, 2009, in a letter to the House chief administrative officer had ordered expense reports for House offices to be posted online "at the earliest date."

Architect of the Capitol

The president's role in nominating the head of the agency that maintained and developed the Capitol complex would be eliminated under legislation (HR 2843) passed by the House by voice vote under suspension of the rules on February 3, 2010. The House Administration Committee had approved the bill by voice vote on November 4, 2009, and formally reported it (H Rept 111-372, Part 1) on December 10.

The Architect of the Capitol Appointment Act, sponsored by Debbie Wasserman Schultz, D-Fla., would provide for joint appointment of the architect of the Capitol by congressional leaders. Under existing law, the architect was nominated by the president, who chose from recommendations made by congressional leaders, and was confirmed by the Senate for a ten-year term. HR 2843 would provide for appointment of the architect by the top congressional leaders from both parties and the chairs and ranking members of House and Senate committees with jurisdiction over the agency.

Wasserman Schultz said the legislation was necessary to eliminate delays in appointing the architect. An acting architect had been in control of the agency since February 2007, and the Capitol complex, at the time the House passed HR 2843, faced more than $1 billion in deferred maintenance requests.

In related action, the Senate by voice vote on July 6, 2009, adopted a Jim DeMint, R-S.C., amendment to the fiscal 2010 legislative branch appropriations bill (HR 2918—PL 111-68) directing the architect of the Capitol to engrave the Pledge of Allegiance and the phrase "In God We Trust" at the Capitol Visitor Center. Neither the House-passed nor the final version of the legislation included the language. *(Legislative branch appropriations, p. 128)*

U.S.-made Goods in the Capitol

The House agreed, by a vote of 371–36 on September 15, 2010, to suspend the rules and pass HR 2039, the Congressional Made in America Promise Act. The bill, sponsored by Marcy Kaptur, D-Ohio, would specify that the Buy American Act (PL 72-428)—a 1933 law covering federal agencies—would also apply to the legislative branch.

The Buy American Act required that unmanufactured goods for public use be mined or produced in the United States and that manufactured goods for public use be made in the United States with "substantially" domestic components. The law did not apply if agencies decided that purchasing certain domestic goods would not be in the public interest or would be too costly. It also exempted goods that could not be produced domestically in sufficient quantities or quality, items used abroad, and contracts in which the amount was less than or equal to a micro-purchase threshold (purchases under $3,000). In addition to setting these requirements for the legislative branch, HR 2039 would establish stricter rules for products bearing official congressional insignias.

A Senate companion measure (S 4019), sponsored by Bob Casey, D-Pa., was referred to the Senate Homeland Security and Governmental Affairs Committee and died upon adjournment.

Ethics Probes

The House, for the first time since 1983, imposed the punishment of censure on one of its own—the amiable chair of the powerful House Ways and Means Committee, Charles B. Rangel, D-N.Y. Although the litany of wrongdoing was lengthy, Rangel maintained that the evidence against him showed no corruption and no acts for personal gain. In addition to Rangel, there were a number of other ethics probes during the 111th Congress.

SEN. JOHN ENSIGN

On June 16, 2009, Sen. John Ensign, R-Nev., disclosed that he had had an affair from December 2007 to August 2008 with Cynthia Hampton, his campaign treasurer, who was married to Douglas Hampton, one of his Senate aides. The watchdog group Citizens for Responsibility and Ethics in Washington (CREW) filed a complaint with the Senate Ethics Committee, raising questions about Ensign's dismissal of Cynthia Hampton and alleged severance payments made to her and her husband—$96,000 paid by Ensign's parents, which Ensign said was a gift. Ensign resigned as chair of the Republican Policy Committee on June 17.

In a letter dated June 11, sent to Fox News on June 15, and made public June 19, Douglas Hampton wrote: "The actions of Senator Ensign have ruined our lives and careers and left my family in shambles." He went on to say: "I need justice, help and restitution for what Senator Ensign has done to me and my family." In response, Ensign's office issued a statement claiming that "within the past month, Doug Hampton's legal counsel made exorbitant demands for cash and other financial benefits on behalf of his client."

During an appearance on the ABC News program *Nightline*, Douglas Hampton on November 23 said that after he left Ensign's staff, the Nevada senator offered him a new career as a lobbyist and helped him line up clients who sought access to Ensign. It was a felony for former Senate staffers to lobby senators within a year of their departure from employment on Capitol Hill.

The news organization Politico on January 19, 2010, reported that the Justice Department and the Federal Bureau of Investigation were looking into whether any criminal violations had occurred in connection with the extramarital affair. The local CBS affiliate in Las Vegas, Nevada—*8 News*

Now—reported on May 6 that Senate Ethics Committee attorneys were in town that week interviewing witnesses in the Ensign case and that Justice Department criminal investigators had interviewed witnesses there in April. Politico reported on July 23 that Sen. Tom Coburn, R-Okla., a friend and roommate of Ensign's who had tried to persuade him to stop the affair, was cooperating with the Justice Department and had turned over e-mails to federal authorities. Sources close to the investigation, Politico reported, indicated that the focus seemed to be on the relationship between Ensign and Douglas Hampton and whether they broke federal lobbying law. *(Coburn ethics probe, p. 672)*

The Federal Election Commission on November 10 dismissed a complaint lodged by CREW against Ensign over the $96,000 payment. On December 1, Ensign's attorney said he had been told by the Justice Department that it had "no plans" to bring charges against the senator regarding Hampton's lobbying. When the 111th Congress adjourned, the Senate Ethics Committee investigation was ongoing. *(112th Congress action, p. 671)*

SEN. MARY L. LANDRIEU

In November 2009 the Senate Ethics Committee dismissed a complaint by Citizens for Responsibility and Ethics in Washington (CREW), filed in January 2008, against Mary L. Landrieu of Louisiana, questioning a $2 million earmark for Voyager Expanded Learning that she secured in 2001, when she was the ranking Democrat on the District of Columbia Appropriations Subcommittee. The money was for a program to build literacy among the District's kindergarteners and first-graders. CREW contended that Landrieu wrote the earmark four days after receiving $30,000 in campaign contributions from the company's executives and their relatives. In a November 6, 2009, letter to CREW's executive director, the committee said it "intends no further action with respect to your complaint" and "considers the matter closed."

SEN. RONALD W. BURRIS

In a November 20, 2009, letter of qualified admonition, the Senate Ethics Committee concluded that Ronald W. Burris, D-Ill., had misled investigators and senators and inappropriately lobbied Illinois governor Rod R. Blagojevich for the Senate seat vacated by Barack Obama in November 2008 after his election as president. The panel found no evidence that Burris violated the law, but it said his actions nonetheless reflected unfavorably on the Senate. *(Burris appointment, p. 647)*

The panel began its investigation soon after Burris took office on January 15, 2009. He was appointed December 30, 2008, weeks after Blagojevich was arrested on federal charges of soliciting bribes and conspiracy to commit mail fraud in a wide-ranging "pay-to-play" scandal. Burris swore at a January 2009 hearing of the Illinois House Impeachment Committee that he had not spoken to anyone associated with the governor about the seat. But in an affidavit released February 14, Burris acknowledged speaking repeatedly with Blagojevich's brother Robert about fund-raising. He said under oath that he attended a June 27, 2008, fund-raiser for Blagojevich, where he told two people he was interested in filling Obama's seat if Obama won the presidency. The governor's brother then called Burris three times to ask for fund-raising assistance, according to the affidavit. But Burris insisted that he did not raise money for Blagojevich after the June 27 event. The Ethics Committee letter said: "[You] should have known that you were providing incorrect, inconsistent, misleading or incomplete information to the public, the Senate and those conducting legitimate inquiries into your appointment." The committee found that, during a wiretapped November 13, 2008, phone call with Blagojevich's brother, Burris pleaded for the Senate appointment and indicated he would help raise money for the governor. The call, "while not rising to the level of an explicit quid pro quo, was inappropriate," the committee said.

Burris did not run for election to a full six-year term in the Senate in 2010.

SENS. CHRISTOPHER J. DODD AND KENT CONRAD

The Senate Ethics Committee in 2009 dropped yearlong probes of Banking, Housing, and Urban Affairs Committee Chair Christopher J. Dodd, D-Conn., and Budget Committee Chair Kent Conrad, D-N.D.

Citizens for Responsibility and Ethics in Washington had filed a complaint with the committee on June 13, 2008, after an article in *Condé Nast's Portfolio* magazine said Dodd and Conrad benefited from a special loan program at Countrywide Financial Corp. in which certain points, fees, and borrowing rules were waived for officials. Both Dodd and Conrad said they did not know they were given special interest rates and loan terms because they were senators, as suggested by an e-mail obtained by *Portfolio*.

Conrad told the Ethics Committee about the article just before it was published on June 12. He said he gave $10,700—the value of the benefit he said he received—to the charity Habitat for Humanity. He also said he paid off the $32,000 left on the mortgage on a Bismarck, N.D., apartment house. Dodd said he would have rejected the loan if he had thought that being in Countrywide's VIP program—known as Friends of Angelo and started by Countrywide chief executive Angelo Mozilo—would get him special treatment.

In letters to Dodd and Conrad dated August 7, 2009, the committee dismissed the complaint against the two senators, saying that while it found "no substantial credible evidence" that their actions violated Senate rules, they "should have exercised more vigilance in [their] dealings with Countrywide to avoid the appearance" that they received "preferential treatment" because they were in the Senate. In the investigations, the committee reviewed eighteen thousand documents and interviewed witnesses. It found that while the VIP program offered quicker and more efficient loan processing, the discounts "were not the best deals that were available at Countrywide or in the marketplace at large."

REP. JESSE L. JACKSON JR.

Rep. Jesse L. Jackson Jr., D-Ill., confirmed in a statement April 8, 2009, that the Office of Congressional Ethics, a quasi-independent panel created in 2008 by the House, had launched a review of his conduct as it related to the federal probe of former Illinois governor Rod R. Blagojevich. He was not accused of any wrongdoing. *(Office of Congressional Ethics, Congress and the Nation Vol. XII, p. 837)*

Blagojevich was indicted April 2, 2009, on sixteen felony charges, including allegations that he sought to use his power to appoint a successor to the Senate seat vacated by Barack Obama, who was elected president of the United States in 2008, for personal and political gain. Jackson was widely mentioned as a possible appointee before the governor's arrest in December 2008. According to the federal charges, Blagojevich talked about a Senate candidate's associate offering to raise $1.5 million in campaign funds in exchange for the appointment. Several media organizations identified Jackson as that candidate. At a December 10 news conference, Jackson said that neither he nor anyone acting on his behalf had offered the governor anything in return for an appointment. Jackson's brother Jonathan attended a December 6 fund-raiser for Friends of Blagojevich, according to media reports. *(Burris appointment, p. 647)*

The Office of Congressional Ethics would not confirm or deny the launching of a probe. FOX Chicago News reported on November 17, 2010, that a House ethics committee probe of Jackson was put on hold pending a Justice Department investigation. *(112th Congress action, p. 675)*

REP. JANE HARMAN

According to the *Washington Post,* the House ethics committee on June 9, 2009, approved subpoenas to the Justice Department, National Security Agency, and Federal Bureau of Investigation (FBI) for "certain intercepted communications" related to Rep. Jane Harman, D-Calif. The Justice Department declared Harman "neither a subject nor a target" of a criminal investigation.

Harman was heard on a 2005 wiretap telling a suspected Israeli agent that she would lobby the Justice Department to reduce espionage-related charges against two former officials of the American Israel Public Affairs Committee, the most powerful pro-Israel organization in Washington, D.C. In return, the Israeli agent pledged to help lobby for Harman to become chair of the House Intelligence Committee.

Two former senior national security officials, one who had read a transcript of the wiretap and another who was briefed on its contents, said Justice Department officials decided sufficient evidence existed to initiate an FBI investigation of Harman. However, Attorney General Alberto R. Gonzalez aborted the plan, saying that he needed Harman's help defending the George W. Bush administration's warrantless wiretapping program. Gonzalez intervened, according to the two officials, as the *New York Times* was about to disclose the program.

On April 21, 2009, Harman said that she "never contacted the Department of Justice, the White House or anyone else to seek favorable treatment regarding the national security cases on which I was briefed, or any other cases." She also asked Attorney General Eric H. Holder Jr. "to release any transcripts that he has that involve wiretaps of me."

House Select Intelligence Committee chair Silvestre Reyes, D-Texas, instructed the panel's staff to begin an inquiry into the wiretap. In fall 2006, after Democrats won control of Congress, Reyes had been chosen over Harman to lead the committee. On the wiretap, according to the official who read the transcript, Harman was heard lamenting to the suspected Israeli agent how the tactics of a major California donor—Haim Saban, who made a fortune from his Mighty Morphin Power Rangers—to use the threat of withholding political contributions to Speaker Nancy Pelosi, D-Calif., to win Harman the gavel badly backfired. Pelosi said April 22 that Harman, who had been the ranking Democrat on the intelligence panel for two terms, was passed over strictly because of term limits and that the wiretap had nothing to do with Reyes's selection as chair.

Harman resigned from Congress on February 28, 2011, to become president and director of the Woodrow Wilson International Center for Scholars.

REP. JOE WILSON

The House on September 15, 2009, voted largely along party lines, 240–179, to adopt a resolution of disapproval (H Res 744) against Joe Wilson, R-S.C., for his conduct in shouting "You lie!" while President Barack Obama was addressing a joint session of Congress. Seven Republicans, including institutionalists who felt Wilson's breach of decorum toward a visitor in the House required reprimand, voted to adopt the resolution. Twelve Democrats voted against the measure; five voted "present."

The short resolution stated that Wilson "interrupted" the president's address to Congress on September 9 and that "the conduct of the Representative from South Carolina was a breach of decorum and degraded the proceedings of the joint session, to the discredit of the House." It stated that the House "disapproves" of Wilson's behavior. Wilson's outburst came as Obama said it was not true that illegal immigrants would get coverage under Democrats' health care reform proposals. The House Rules Committee had released a summary of guidelines for floor debate noting that members are prohibited from calling the president "a liar," but the resolution did not address the substance of Wilson's remarks.

During the hour-long debate, Republicans accused the majority of playing politics. Wilson was lauded for apologizing to Obama within hours of the speech. Democrats argued that not responding to Wilson's behavior would be tantamount to consent. Rep. Gerald E. Connolly, D-Va., added: "The other side doesn't get the symbolism of a conservative white Republican, from South Carolina of all places, screaming at the first African-American president that he's a liar." Wilson denied any racial intent in his comment.

REP. SAM GRAVES

The House Committee on Standards of Official Conduct released a report on October 29, 2009, and ended its investigation of Rep. Sam Graves, R-Mo., finding no ethical violations. Graves, a member of the Small Business Committee, had invited Brooks Hurst, a friend and business partner of his wife, Lesley, to testify at a committee hearing on renewable fuels but failed to mention that his wife and Hurst were investors in a renewable fuels plant.

The Office of Congressional Ethics had referred the case to the ethics panel, after it found "substantial reason to believe that an appearance of conflict of interest was created." However, the ethics committee report said that neither it nor the office found evidence that the hearing or Hurst's testimony "resulted in any action that could benefit" Graves, his wife, or Hurst.

REP. ALAN B. MOLLOHAN

The U.S. Attorney's Office for the District of Columbia announced that a four-year Justice Department investigation of Rep. Alan B. Mollohan, D-W.Va., ended January 21, 2010, but declined to provide details. The inquiry began after the National Legal and Policy Center, a conservative watchdog group, filed a complaint on February 28, 2006, alleging that he had misreported his personal assets on congressional financial disclosure forms. The *New York Times* on April 7, 2006, reported on earmarks that Mollohan procured for five West Virginia nonprofit groups run by friends and campaign contributors, some of whom participated in real estate deals with him. Mollohan, who on April 21, 2006, stepped down as ranking Democrat on the House Committee on Standards of Official Conduct, denied any wrongdoing.

Although the Justice Department had terminated its probe, it remained unclear whether the House Committee on Standards of Official Conduct would conduct its own review of Mollohan. According to a confidential ethics document leaked in October 2009, the ethics committee appeared to be conducting its own investigation. That document indicated the Justice Department had requested that the panel defer its probe for an unspecified period of time. The ethics committee never confirmed the authenticity of that leaked document or that it was ever investigating Mollohan.

REP. PETE STARK

In clearing Rep. Pete Stark, D-Calif., on January 28, 2010, of wrongdoing involving a Maryland property tax credit, the House Committee on Standards of Official Conduct criticized the work of the Office of Congressional Ethics that had brought the case to its attention.

The office alleged that Stark, a senior member of the Ways and Means Committee, had violated Maryland law and House ethics rules by intentionally filing a false application for a property tax credit for a home in Anne Arundel County. In its report, the committee said he did not file a false application and did not receive the tax credit as a result of filing an application for it. "Representative Stark did not seek out the Maryland property tax credit," the committee wrote. "The State of Maryland required every homeowner in Maryland to fill out a form to determine their eligibility for the tax credit."

The report accused the office of conducting "an inadequate review, the result of which was to subject Representative Stark to unfounded criminal allegations." The panel also said that the office treated Stark inconsistently with the way it treated other members in similar situations whose cases were "properly dismissed." The office had terminated inquiries into other lawmakers without recommending a formal probe.

REP. ERIC MASSA

A senior member of Rep. Eric Massa's staff filed a complaint with the House ethics committee on February 8, 2010, that the New York Democrat made sexual advances toward and harassed a junior male staffer. Massa denied any wrongdoing but admitted to using "salty language" and engaging in improper physical contact with his staff. Citing health reasons and the ongoing ethics investigation, Massa on March 5 announced that he would resign from the House on March 8. In a March 7 radio address, Massa claimed that White House Chief of Staff Rahm Emanuel had orchestrated the ethics probe to intimidate him because he opposed the Obama administration's health care reform proposal.

Because Massa no longer was a member, he was not subject to House discipline. However, House Republicans sought to force the ethics committee to examine the circumstances leading to its investigation of Massa. On March 11, Minority Leader John A. Boehner, R-Ohio, offered a privilege resolution (H Res 1164) demanding that the ethics panel look into whether Democratic leaders knew about allegations of sexual harassment against Massa. Boehner's resolution cited numerous reports that the staff of Speaker Nancy Pelosi, D-Calif., had been notified of accusations regarding Massa's behavior as early as October 2009. Pelosi acknowledged that her staff had heard a "rumor" about Massa but decided not to brief her. The House agreed, 402–1 on March 11, to a motion to refer the resolution to the House Committee on

Standards of Official Conduct. Majority Leader Steny H. Hoyer, D-Md., said in February that his aides had been alerted to allegations against Massa. Hoyer's staff directed Massa's aides to report the matter to the ethics panel. If they did not do so, Hoyer's staff told the aides, Hoyer would do it himself.

In April the ethics committee established an investigatory subcommittee to review whether members, House officers, or aides had knowledge about Massa's alleged activities and what they had done about reporting or disclosing those allegations. The allegations and the response to them "are serious and warrant a full and complete investigation," Chair Zoe Lofgren, D-Calif., and ranking Republican Jo Bonner of Alabama said in a joint statement issued April 21.

The *Washington Post* reported on April 22 that the public integrity section of the Justice Department and the public corruption unit of the U.S. Attorney's Office for the District of Columbia were jointly investigating potential abuses of public office by Massa. The preliminary inquiry centered on a $40,000 payment Massa's campaign made on March 4, just a few days before he resigned his seat, to his chief of staff, Joe Racalto, and a $31,896 payment the campaign made on March 3 to renew a car lease for a vehicle for Massa to use during the campaign. Massa claimed that he did not authorize the $40,000 payment and that Racalto had lied to the campaign comptroller in saying that Massa had approved the fee. Racalto said that he was owed the money for ongoing political work. He subsequently filed a sexual harassment complaint himself against Massa.

On July 14, 2011, the House Committee on Ethics voted to reauthorize the investigative subcommittee for the 112th Congress.

REPS. YVETTE D. CLARKE, CAROLYN CHEEKS KILPATRICK, DONALD M. PAYNE, BENNIE THOMPSON, AND DEL. DONNA M. C. CHRISTENSEN

On February 25, 2010, the House ethics committee admonished Rep. Charles B. Rangel, D-N.Y., for taking trips to conferences in the Caribbean in violation of House rules. The same ethics investigatory subcommittee, created on June 25, 2009, also looked into the travel of Yvette D. Clarke, D-N.Y., Carolyn Cheeks Kilpatrick, D-Mich., Donald M. Payne, D-N.J., Bennie Thompson, D-Miss., and Del. Donna M. C. Christensen, D-V.I. The five were exonerated of wrongdoing. *(Rangel ethics probe, p. 657)*

Under a 2007 rules change put in place by Democrats, House members were prohibited from taking trips lasting more than two days that were paid for by lobbyists or by entities that employed lobbyists, other than colleges and universities. The lawmakers had traveled to a beach resort and casino in St. Maarten for a three-day conference in November 2008 that was sponsored by the New York Carib News Foundation, which is affiliated with a newspaper aimed at New York's Caribbean immigrant community. The National Legal and Policy Center, a conservative group, said the conference also was underwritten by several companies including Pfizer, Citigroup, and IBM Corp.

Despite some lawmakers' claims that the ethics panel had preapproved the trips in question, the subcommittee was instructed to "conduct a complete inquiry into allegations that have arisen regarding sponsorship of travel in 2007 and 2008." While Clarke, Kilpatrick, Payne, Thompson, and Christensen had traveled with Rangel, the subcommittee determined that they did not know about the corporate funding.

REPS. JOHN P. MURTHA, PETER J. VISCLOSKY, JAMES P. MORAN, MARCY KAPTUR, NORM DICKS, C. W. BILL YOUNG, AND TODD TIAHRT

Seven Democratic members of the House Appropriations Committee—Defense Subcommittee Chair John P. Murtha of Pennsylvania, Energy-Water Subcommittee Chair Peter J. Visclosky of Indiana, James P. Moran of Virginia, Marcy Kaptur of Ohio, Norm Dicks of Washington, C. W. Bill Young of Florida, and Todd Tiahrt of Kansas—were cleared by the House Committee on Standards of Official Conduct on February 26, 2010, of having had improper ties to the PMA Group, a lobbying organization. At issue was whether the lawmakers exchanged earmarks for campaign contributions from PMA, which closed in 2009 after being raided by the Federal Bureau of Investigation (FBI) in 2008 amid allegations of improper donations. PMA and its clients had lavished millions of dollars on lawmakers' campaigns over the past two decades, and the firm was extremely successful in obtaining earmarks for its clients from members who received donations.

However, in its report, the ethics panel said that "simply because a member sponsors an earmark for an entity that also happens to be a campaign contributor . . . does not support a claim that a member's actions are being influenced by campaign contributions." The committee determined that "earmarks were evaluated based upon criteria independent of campaign contributions."

The ethics panel began its investigation into PMA in spring 2009. On June 3, the House agreed, 270–134, to a motion by Jim McGovern, D-Mass., to refer the Steny H. Hoyer, D-Md., privileged resolution (H Res 500) to the House ethics committee. H Res 500 would require the committee to report to the House, within forty-five days of the resolution's adoption, on actions it took concerning any misconduct of members and employees of the House in connection with the PMA Group. The committee, however, never formally responded beyond issuing a statement that it was looking into the matter. In December 2009, the Office of Congressional Ethics (OCE) recommended to the ethics committee that it dismiss the inquiries into Dicks, Kaptur, Moran, Murtha (who had died February 8, 2009), and Young. It also suggested further review into the actions of Tiahrt and Visclosky.

The ethics panel report noted that Tiahrt and Visclosky were singled out by OCE only because they chose not to be interviewed. OCE took that to be a lack of cooperation, even though both members provided investigators with evidence, the ethics report stated. The OCE probe of Tiahrt appeared to center on an earmark he never sought. A federal grand jury in June 2009 had subpoenaed records from Visclosky's congressional and campaign offices, as well as those of several employees. Visclosky subsequently recused himself from managing the fiscal 2010 energy-water appropriations bill (HR 3183). *(Energy-Water appropriations, p. 128)*

The ethics report concluded that PMA had "employed 'strong-arm' tactics," threatening retaliation against members who did not support earmarks. However, the committee found that members were unaware of the pressure that PMA was putting on clients.

REP. NATHAN DEAL

The Office of Congressional Ethics set a precedent on March 26, 2010, when it released an investigative report critical of Georgia Republican Nathan Deal, who had resigned on March 21—presumably figuring he could thereby avoid just such a disclosure. The 138-page report concluded that Deal appeared to have used his congressional office in trying to persuade Georgia officials (unsuccessfully) to continue an inspection program for wrecked and repaired vehicles that benefited his family's auto salvage business. The office board also found that Deal might have reported as investment dividends what was actually a salary he drew from the business, which would violate a House limit on outside earned income.

Deal was furious at the disclosure, which threatened his campaign for the July 20 Republican gubernatorial nomination in Georgia. He said the report's release was a "politically motivated witch hunt," even though the board had an equal number of Democrats and Republicans and was acting on a complaint that followed a story on Deal's business in the *Atlanta Journal-Constitution* several months earlier.

The Office of Congressional Ethics has no real authority except to refer cases to the House ethics committee and to make public its findings at the appropriate time. The office's role was different from that of the ethics panel, which did not accept complaints from the public and disclosed only what it chose to. It had been known to open and close an investigation without saying anything publicly. When Deal resigned from Congress, the ethics committee probe ended. Seemingly unwilling to be outmaneuvered, the office board voted unanimously to release its findings.

Deal was elected governor of Georgia in 2010.

REP. LAURA RICHARDSON

On July 1, 2010, the Committee on Standards of Official Conduct cleared Rep. Laura Richardson, D-Calif., of violating House rules by having failed to report information on her financial disclosure forms concerning whether she had received gifts or preferential treatment related to her home in Sacramento. The house had been foreclosed upon, sold, and subsequently returned to her in 2008. The committee opened its investigation upon a referral from the Office of Congressional Ethics.

The ethics panel referred Richardson's mortgage broker, Washington Mutual Bank, to the Justice Department for mortgage fraud.

Richardson faced other ethics charges in the 112th Congress. *(112th Congress action, p. 674)*

REP. MAXINE WATERS

The House Committee on Standards of Official Conduct announced August 2, 2010, that Rep. Maxine Waters, D-Calif., would face a public trial on alleged ethics violations. However, the trial was postponed indefinitely on November 19 after the discovery of undisclosed new evidence. The allegations against Waters, who chaired the Financial Services Subcommittee on Housing and Community Opportunity, focused on whether she broke House rules in seeking federal help for OneUnited Bank, a Los Angeles institution where her husband, Sidney Williams, was a board member from 2004 through 2008 and owned between $250,000 and $500,000 in stock in 2007. *(112th Congress action, p. 674)*

The Waters case stemmed from a probe begun by the Office of Congressional Ethics. The evidence that the office gathered was turned over in July 2009 to the ethics committee, which formed a four-member investigative subcommittee to look into the matter. In the spring of 2010 it agreed to release a report that criticized Waters's conduct in the case but did not recommend any sanctions. The committee's chief counsel and staff director at the time, however, advised that the panel could not publish a report that criticized a member without giving the lawmaker a chance to respond in a hearing. The investigative subcommittee instead on June 15 adopted a Statement of Alleged Violation that described three possible counts of misconduct against Waters. She held a news conference and disclosed information about the matter that was subject to a nondisclosure agreement. Ethics committee chair Zoe Lofgren, D-Calif., advised Waters in writing to adhere to the agreement.

The investigative subcommittee on July 28 formally transmitted its Statement of Alleged Violation to the full ethics committee, which on August 2 announced that the subcommittee had found substantial reason to believe that Waters violated House rules or federal law, triggering the formation of an adjudicatory subcommittee to hold a trial. Waters denounced the charges against her in an August 2 statement. "I have not violated any House rules," she said. "Therefore, I simply will not be forced to admit to something I did not do, and instead have chosen to respond to charges . . . in a public hearing. . . . The accusations against me stem from work I have done throughout my decades of

> **RANGEL: COUNTS AND CONVICTIONS**
>
> Acting on recommendations from the Committee on Standards of Official Conduct, the House censured Charles B. Rangel, D-N.Y., on December 2, 2010, for eleven violations of House rules. Rangel was originally charged with thirteen counts, but an eight-member bipartisan ethics subcommittee narrowed them to eleven after deadlocking on count 3 and merging counts 4 and 5 because they were so similar. The following are the eleven counts on which Rangel was found guilty.
>
> 1. Solicitation and gift ban violation. Rangel sought contributions to the Charles B. Rangel Center for Public Service at the City College of New York using congressional resources.
> 2. Government code of ethics violation. Rangel solicited donations for the center from individuals with whom he had professional relationships.
> 4. and 5. Violation of postal and franking laws. Rangel solicited center donations using congressional stationery and the frank.
> 6. House office building commission regulations violation. Rangel used congressional office space as the "home base" for seeking funds for the center.
> 7. Purpose law and member's congressional handbook violation. House resources were used to solicit for the center and were paid out of the Member's Representational Allowance.
> 8. Letterhead rule violation. Congressional letterhead was used to solicit donations for the center.
> 9. Ethics in Government Act and House Rule 26 violation. Rangel filed incomplete and inaccurate financial disclosure statements.
> 10. Government code of ethics violation. Rangel accepted use of a rent-controlled residential apartment in New York for office space.
> 11. Government code of ethics violation. Rental income related to Rangel's Dominican Republic vacation home was unreported.
> 12. Violation of code of conduct—spirit and letter of House rules. Rangel violated "the spirit and letter of the Rules of the House."
> 13. Violation of code of conduct—conduct reflecting discreditably on the House. Rangel violated the rule that a member "shall behave at all times in a manner that shall reflect creditably on the House."

public service as an advocate for minority communities and businesses in California and nationally."

The investigatory subcommittee reported that when the banking system was on the verge of collapse in September 2008, Waters approached Treasury Secretary Henry M. Paulson Jr. to arrange a meeting between Treasury officials and representatives of the National Bankers Association, a trade group for minority-owned banks. Waters did not attend the meeting. According to the report, at the meeting, OneUnited executives pressed for federal assistance to compensate for the bank's losses stemming from the federal takeover of the Federal National Mortgage Association (Fannie Mae) and the Federal Home Loan Mortgage Corporation (Freddie Mac). OneUnited subsequently received $12 million through the Troubled Asset Relief Program (TARP; PL 110-343). The report said Waters might have violated House rules by having a conflict of interest in pushing the meetings and then allowing monetary compensation through her husband's stock holding to accrue to her interest. *(TARP, p. 62)*

For her part, Waters said she had made one phone call on behalf of the bankers association and did not receive any material benefit. Waters said she never advocated specifically for OneUnited but sought the meeting for the National Bankers Association, the umbrella group for minority-owned banks.

The ethics committee on August 9 released a ten-page statement of its findings, accusing Waters of violating three rules: requiring that House members "behave at all times in a manner that shall reflect creditably on the House," prohibiting the use of their influence for personal benefit, and forbidding the granting of favors.

Less than two weeks before the November 29 scheduled start of the trial, the ethics committee said that new information had been uncovered requiring more investigation and the trial was postponed. Leaked documents later revealed that the panel's staff director at the time questioned whether the investigation was compromised by staff members who had improperly discussed the merits of the case with lawmakers who would sit in judgment of Waters. Subsequently, two of the lead staff attorneys on the case were placed on administrative leave.

Waters charged that the committee broke its own rules on a series of technical matters. More seriously, she alleged that leaked information, ex parte communication, and subpoenas that were issued based on incomplete facts had compromised her right to a fair trial.

REP. CHARLES B. RANGEL

After two years of investigation, an indictment, and an aborted trial in which he declined to take part, Rep. Charles B. Rangel, D-N.Y., was censured for ethics violations on December 2, 2010, on a bipartisan 333–79 vote. Six of the eleven counts related to Rangel's efforts to secure donations for the Charles B. Rangel Center for Public Service at the City College of New York. Other violations pertained to inaccurate reporting of personal income, failure to pay all his taxes, and use of a rent-controlled apartment for office space. The House also found Rangel guilty of breaching the "spirit and letter of the Rules of the House" and bringing discredit to the House. Censure was the harshest sanction, short of expulsion, for rule-breakers in Congress. The House had not imposed censure since 1983, when Reps. Gerry E. Studds, D-Mass., and Daniel B. Crane, R-Ill., were both censured for having sexual relations with congressional pages. *(Counts, box, p. this page 1983 action, Congress and the Nation Vol. VI, p. 813)*

Rangel's troubles began in July 2008 when the *New York Times* reported on his leases on four rent-stabilized apartments in Harlem. More disclosures followed, the most serious of which was that he failed to report and pay federal and state taxes on $75,000 in rental income on a villa he owned in the Dominican Republic. The House on July 31 tabled (killed) a motion by Minority Leader John A. Boehner, R-Ohio, to censure Rangel. The House Committee on Standards of Official Conduct in September 2008 formed a subcommittee to launch an investigation into the allegations. Rangel, who denied any wrongdoing, had requested a formal inquiry. The House on September 18 agreed to table a Boehner resolution to remove Rangel as chair of the House Ways and Means Committee. *(2008 action, Congress and the Nation Vol. XII, p. 843)*

The ethics committee met February 10, 2009, for the first time in the 111th Congress and issued a statement saying it had voted to reauthorize the investigative subcommittee that was begun in the 110th Congress to review Rangel's conduct. The closed-door decision came hours before the House agreed, on a partisan 242–157 vote, to a motion by Joseph Crowley, D-N.Y., to table (kill) a John Carter, R-Texas, privileged resolution (H Res 143) to remove Rangel from the Ways and Means chair. The investigative subcommittee's probe was expanded in October 2009 to include an examination of $500,000 in previously unreported assets that Rangel disclosed when he amended his financial disclosure statements in August. The House on October 7 agreed, 246–153, to a Crowley motion to refer to the House Committee on Standards of Official Conduct a privileged resolution (H Res 805) offered by Carter, to remove Rangel as Ways and Means chair until the ethics probe was complete. The effect of the vote was to kill the resolution. However, signs were that Democratic support for Rangel was beginning to erode, as six Democrats voted "present." In the February vote to remove Rangel, Democrats were united in opposition.

By October 2009, the subcommittee said it had held more than thirty closed-door meetings, issued 150 subpoenas, interviewed about thirty-five witnesses, produced twenty-one hundred pages of transcripts, and pored over twelve thousand pages of documents.

On February 25, 2010, the House ethics committee offered its first punishment, admonishing Rangel for improperly accepting Caribbean trips from corporations in violation of gift rules. This was the result of a separate investigation that was opened in June 2009. The ethics panel said it had approved the trips—to Antigua and Barbuda in 2007 and to St. Maarten in 2008—based on "false and misleading information." The trips were to attend the Carib News Foundation Multi-National Business Conferences, which were underwritten, the committee determined, in part by corporations. The panel found that Rangel had violated the House gift rule for accepting payments or reimbursements for the trips because his aides were aware of the impermissible funding. Rangel said he was unaware that private funds helped pay for the trips when he made them. The ethics committee also admonished one of its own former aides for her role in approving the trips. The committee required Rangel to repay the cost of travel but exonerated five other House Democrats—Reps. Yvette D. Clarke of New York, Carolyn Cheeks Kilpatrick of Michigan, Donald M. Payne of New Jersey, and Bennie Thompson of Mississippi, and Del. Donna M. C. Christensen of the Virgin Islands—who had also participated in the trips but, according to the committee, were unaware of the corporate funding. *(Clarke, Kilpatrick, Payne, Thompson, and Christensen, p. 654)*

On March 3, as Republicans were mounting an offensive against him, Rangel gave up the coveted chair of the Ways and Means Committee. John Carter was set to introduce a privileged resolution calling for Rangel to vacate the chair, and many influential Democrats indicated that they were prepared to vote with Republicans on the issue.

A bipartisan investigatory subcommittee of the ethics panel on July 29 approved a thirteen-count Statement of Alleged Violations. The allegations centered on four areas: "1) solicitations and donations to the Rangel Center for Public Service at the City College of New York; 2) errors and omissions on [Rangel's] financial disclosure statements; 3) use of a rent-stabilized residential apartment by [Rangel's] campaign committees; and 4) failure to report and pay taxes on rental income on [Rangel's] Punta Cana beach villa" in the Dominican Republic. The panel said that Rangel had solicited donations for the center from corporations and foundations that had "business and interests before the House," creating "an appearance of impropriety." The subcommittee also said that Rangel had violated House rules by soliciting potential donors using his official House staff and letterhead.

The subcommittee's formal announcement came after lengthy private talks between Rangel's lawyers and the panel's attorneys failed to reach a settlement. In the absence of a deal, the case was set to move to the trial phase in September. At the public trial, Rangel would have the opportunity to present his defense to the subcommittee, which could send the case to the full ten-member ethics committee only if a majority agreed. The full panel would decide what sanctions to recommend.

On August 10, the embattled Rangel took to the House floor for more than a half-hour to defend himself and appeal for a quick opportunity to clear his name. Rangel acknowledged that some of his fellow Democrats wanted him to quit, to spare them the issue of his ethics problems in their upcoming midterm election campaigns. He went on to apologize to the House and said, "I'm not asking for leniency. I am asking for exposure of the facts." He also said that "if I can't get my dignity back here, then fire your best shot on getting rid of me through expulsion."

Democrats decided to postpone the trial until after the general election. Rangel easily won a twenty-first term on November 2.

An adjudicatory subcommittee set up by the ethics panel for Rangel's case on November 15 approved thirteen identical motions for summary judgment, one for each of the thirteen charges, determining that no dispute existed with the material fact of each charge. The subcommittee's approval of the summary charges cut short what many experts expected to be a several-day trial, complete with opening and closing statements, live witnesses, and hundreds of pieces of evidence. Instead, panel members agreed to a closed-door session.

The subcommittee planned to hold a trial before voting, but Rangel unexpectedly announced at the start of the hearing that he would not participate in the proceedings without a lawyer. Representing himself, he requested that the ethics panel postpone the hearing so he could secure the means to hire an attorney. He said that he had lost his counsel nearly a month before in the face of mounting legal costs of more than $2 million. The panel met briefly behind closed doors to consider, and ultimately reject, Rangel's request, saying that it had repeatedly provided Rangel with guidance on how to cover his legal bills. In light of Rangel's decision to let the hearing continue without his participation, Blake Chisam, the staff director and chief counsel for the full committee, recommended that the subcommittee waive the trial portion and proceed right to the votes on the charges. He added that Rangel had not contested any of the evidence or witness testimony that the ethics committee told him it would introduce.

On November 16 the adjudicatory subcommittee found Rangel guilty on eleven of the thirteen counts, setting the stage for the full ethics panel to decide on sanctions. Two of the counts were considered so similar that they were combined. The panel voted unanimously to convict Rangel of that combined charge, as well as nine other charges. The subcommittee voted, 7–1, to find Rangel guilty of violating a broad House rule that "members shall behave at all times in a manner that reflects creditably on the House." Members rejected, 4–4, the remaining charge that Rangel violated a House gift rule. Rangel held the record for having been charged with the highest number of counts of misconduct of any other member of the House.

The full committee on November 18 voted, 9–1, to recommend that the House censure the veteran lawmaker. House ethics committee Chair Zoe Lofgren, D-Calif., was blunt in her assessment. "We found his actions an accumulation of actions that reflected poorly on the institution of the House and, thereby, brought discredit to the House," she said. In deciding on punishment, members took into consideration advice from Chisam, who served as the de facto prosecutor against Rangel in the proceedings. Rangel returned to the hearing room before the committee went into closed session to deliberate. In a statement and in answers to questions from committee members, Rangel did not deny his "irresponsible behavior" and apologized for putting his colleagues in the "awkward situation" of having to judge him. He also expressed his frustration that witnesses had not been invited to testify, witnesses who could shed light on his behavior. For instance, he said, witnesses would have shown that the City University of New York approached him to lend his name to the public policy center it hoped to establish, not the other way around. As members sought to parse through the information to determine a verdict, they pushed Chisam to elaborate on whether any of Rangel's ethics violations showed evidence of corruption or personal gain. Chisam said the findings suggested no evidence of either. But some Republican members of the panel had strong words about the need to impose a harsh punishment nonetheless.

Rangel's supporters tried to lighten the sentence to a written reprimand, a sanction that carried less stigma and would not have required Rangel's presence in the chamber after the vote. The House rejected the proposal, offered by Rep. G. K. Butterfield, D-N.C., by 146–267 on December 2. The vote against a lesser sanction split Democrats but was predominantly a party-line affair for Republicans. Rangel distributed a two-page document to lawmakers titled "10 Reasons Why Charles B. Rangel Should Not Receive Censure." In it, he drew comparisons between what he perceived as truly censure-worthy actions and his own, which he called "sloppy, or even stupid" but not rooted in corruption or the promise of personal gain. Addressing his peers before the censure vote, Rangel apologized for his actions and again implored members on both sides of the aisle to vote with compassion.

Immediately after the censure vote, Rangel stood in the well of the House while his longtime friend and confidante, Speaker Nancy Pelosi, D-Calif., delivered an oral rebuke. Although the censure resolution did not strip Rangel of any powers in Congress, it did order him to pay unpaid taxes on income received from his property in the Dominican Republic and to provide proof of payment to the ethics committee. After Pelosi's reading of the resolution, Rangel spoke again to his colleagues: "I want to make sure that this body knows it never entered my mind to enrich myself or do violence" to the integrity of the House. He went on to say: "I know in my heart that . . . I am going to be judged by my life . . . [and] my contributions to society." He ended his remarks with a line from his autobiography about his good fortune since being wounded in the Korean War. "Compared to where I've been, I haven't had a bad day since," he said. He left the House floor to applause, receiving hugs from some members.

FORMER MEMBERS

William J. Jefferson

Former representative William J. Jefferson, D-La., was convicted on August 5, 2009, of bribery, wire fraud, money laundering, and racketeering in a case stemming from business deals he had brokered in West Africa. A federal jury in Alexandria, Va., convicted him on eleven of sixteen counts. Jefferson was acquitted of one count each of obstruction of justice and violation of the Foreign Corrupt Practices Act (PL 105-366) and three counts of concocting a scheme to commit wire fraud. Several of those charges were incorporated into other counts. He was sentenced to thirteen years in prison on November 13.

On August 7, 2007, the House Committee on Standards of Official Conduct had suspended its investigation of Jefferson in response to a request from prosecutors who thought its probe could interfere with the criminal case. Jefferson lost his 2008 reelection bid. *(Background, Congress and the Nation Vol. XII, p. 841)*

The U.S. Court of Appeals for the Fourth Circuit on March 26, 2012, upheld Jefferson's conviction on ten of the eleven counts, vacating the count involving alleged wire fraud. His attorneys made what experts called a novel legal argument: that Jefferson's actions were not covered by public corruption laws because he had arranged and conducted the trips on his own time. The three-judge panel, which ruled unanimously in the representative's case, wrote: "An absurd result would occur if we were to deem Jefferson's illicit actions as outside the purview of the bribery statute." During oral arguments in 2011, the appellate judges asked Jefferson's legal team whether legal statutes were the sole guide to official behavior.

The U.S. Supreme Court on November 26 without comment declined to hear Jefferson's bribery conviction appeal.

Tom DeLay

Former House majority leader Tom DeLay, R-Texas, who was the subject of three House ethics committee probes during his tenure in the House (1985–2006), was convicted after nineteen hours of deliberation by a jury in Austin, Texas, on November 24, 2010, of money laundering and conspiracy to money launder. He faced a possible sentence to life in prison. On January 10, 2011, he was sentenced to three years in prison and ten years of probation. The Texas Third Court of Appeals in a 2–1 ruling on September 19, 2013, overturned DeLay's conviction, citing insufficient evidence. *(DeLay ethics probes, Congress and the Nation Vol. X, p. 773; Congress and the Nation Vol. XI, p. 721; Congress and the Nation Vol. XII, p. 822)*

The Justice Department informed DeLay on August 16, 2010, that investigators had dropped the probe into his ties to disgraced lobbyist Jack Abramoff, who in 2006 had pleaded guilty to federal charges of conspiracy, mail fraud, and tax evasion. DeLay stated that he had no regrets about his relationship with Abramoff, including traveling on junkets.

2011–2012

Americans in the 2010 elections decided to opt for divided government, giving the Republicans the House while keeping the Senate in Democratic hands.

Ethics watchdog organizations for years warned of the danger that members of Congress or their aides might enrich themselves through savvy investments based on confidential information they acquired while on the job. The approach of the 2012 elections, record low public approval ratings, and a critical news report about stock trading by congressional leaders combined to spur a bipartisan rush for legislation. The result was the Stop Trading on Congressional Knowledge (STOCK) Act.

Organization: 112th Congress

The 112th Congress convened at noon on January 5, 2011. Republicans, for the first time in four years, assumed the majority in the House.

SENATE

The state of the leadership was largely status quo in the Senate, where Democrats remained in the majority.

Majority Leadership

Senate Democrats on November 16, 2010, picked their leaders, and several names were the same as in the previous Congress: Majority Leader Harry Reid of Nevada, Majority Whip Richard J. Durbin of Illinois, Democratic Caucus Vice Chair Charles E. Schumer of New York, and Democratic Caucus Secretary Patty Murray of Washington.

Schumer also took on the post of Democratic Policy Committee chair, succeeding Byron L. Dorgan of North Dakota. Dorgan did not run for reelection to the Senate in 2010. Murray also became chair of the Democratic Senatorial Campaign Committee, succeeding Robert Menendez of New Jersey.

HOUSE TRANSITION TEAM

Formal political transitions from one party to another, with teams of aides, policy experts, and budgets, were a relatively recent phenomenon. Only in 1963 did Congress write into law a process for presidential transitions and provide the tax money to pay for it. Before that, the parties themselves footed the bills.

When Republicans won control of the House of Representatives in 1994, for the first time in forty years, incoming Speaker Newt Gingrich of Georgia thought it was necessary, or politically advantageous, to have a formal transition, with a ten-member team of his colleagues to deliberate the details. In the process, he was able to borrow something of the aura of a presidential change of command. Nancy Pelosi, D-Calif., went in the opposite direction when she became Speaker after the 2006 midterm elections. Her team consisted only of Rep. Michael E. Capuano of Massachusetts. As a result of the 2010 midterm elections, House Republicans returned to power after just four years, but they set up a formal transition team, plus an office. Where Gingrich had his team of ten, incoming House Speaker John A. Boehner of Ohio appointed twenty-two.

Though a transition team handled many managerial details, it could serve as a window into the new House administration. Gingrich's transition team was half freshmen, a message that he wanted new people with new ideas in charge. Jim Nussle of Iowa, who was the chair of Gingrich's transition team, said the new Speaker was sending "a signal that a group of new faces, of reformers, so to speak, was going to come in and shake it up."

Despite the zeal of the Tea Party movement, Boehner's transition team was made up more of institutionalists—a cross-section of his power base in Congress. He appointed just four freshmen to the transition team, demonstrating that he did not envision a Gingrich-style revolution in the House. Of those four, Adam Kinzinger of Illinois, was an Air Force veteran of Iraq and Afghanistan, which was an important symbolic move if nothing else, as 24 percent of the incoming House freshmen in the 111th Congress had seen military service, double the percentage in the last midterm election in 2006.

Boehner somewhat balanced the shortage of freshmen on the team by saying that one new member would be invited to sit in at the leadership table and that the number of freshmen on the Republican Steering Committee, which made committee assignments, would be doubled from one to two. More broadly, Boehner's transition team represented three areas of the country where the GOP was strongest—the South (though Florida had no one on the transition team), the Midwest, and the West—and completely excluded the Northeast. Twelve of the twenty-two team members came from just five states: California, Michigan, Ohio, Texas, and Utah. Most of the team members were Boehner loyalists and lawmakers who would chair committees or hold leadership jobs.

By unanimous consent, Patrick J. Leahy of Vermont was elected president pro tempore following the death of Daniel K. Inouye of Hawaii on December 17, 2012.

Minority Leadership

On November 16, 2010, Republicans approved by acclamation the continuation of their leadership: Minority Leader Mitch McConnell of Kentucky, Minority Whip Jon Kyl of Arizona, and Republican Conference Chair Lamar Alexander of Tennessee.

John Thune of South Dakota stayed on as Policy Committee chair. He was elected, on December 13, 2011, as Republican Conference chair, after Alexander announced that he would step down from the post in January 2012. Alexander cited his belief that he could work better to foster consensus in the Senate outside of the leadership structure. Taking Thune's role as Policy Committee chair was John Barrasso of Wyoming, who was serving as the vice chair of the Senate Republican Conference.

John Cornyn of Texas remained as chair of the National Republican Senatorial Committee.

Committees

Most of those who chaired Senate committees in the 111th Congress retained their positions in the 112th Congress: Daniel Inouye at Appropriations; Carl Levin of Michigan at Armed Services; Kent Conrad of North Dakota at Budget; John D. Rockefeller IV of West Virginia at Commerce, Science, and Transportation; Jeff Bingaman of New Mexico at Energy and Natural Resources; Barbara Boxer of California at Environment and Public Works as well as Select Ethics; Max Baucus of Montana at Finance; John Kerry of Massachusetts at Foreign Relations; Tom Harkin of Iowa at Health, Education, Labor, and Pensions; Joseph I. Lieberman of Connecticut at Homeland Security and Governmental Affairs; Patrick Leahy at Judiciary; Charles Schumer at Rules and Administration; Dianne Feinstein of California at Select Intelligence; Mary L. Landrieu of Louisiana at Small Business and Entrepreneurship; and Herb Kohl of Wisconsin at Special Aging.

With Blanche Lincoln of Arkansas losing her 2010 reelection bid, Debbie Stabenow of Michigan took the helm at Agriculture, Nutrition, and Forestry. Christopher J. Dodd, who chaired the Banking, Housing, and Urban Affairs Committee, decided to retire from Congress; Tim Johnson of South Dakota succeeded him as Banking chair. Also retiring at the end of the 111th Congress was Indian Affairs Committee chair Byron L. Dorgan of North Dakota. He was succeeded on the panel by Daniel K. Akaka of Hawaii. Akaka, who had been chair of the Veterans' Affairs Committee, was, in turn, succeeded by Patty Murray of Washington on that panel.

Keeping their ranking member spots were Thad Cochran of Mississippi at Appropriations; John McCain of Arizona at Armed Services; Richard C. Shelby of Alabama at Banking, Housing, and Urban Affairs; Kay Bailey Hutchison of Texas at Commerce, Science, and Transportation; Lisa Murkowski of Alaska at Energy and Natural Resources; James M. Inhofe of Oklahoma at Environment and Public Works; Richard G. Lugar of Indiana at Foreign Relations; Michael B. Enzi of Wyoming at Health, Education, Labor, and Pensions; Susan Collins of Maine at Homeland Security and Governmental Affairs; John Barrasso of Wyoming at Indian Affairs; Johnny Isakson of Georgia at Select Ethics; Olympia J. Snowe of Maine at Small Business and Entrepreneurship; Bob Corker of Tennessee at Special Aging; and Richard M. Burr of North Carolina at Veterans' Affairs.

Christopher S. Bond of Missouri, who did not seek reelection in 2010, was succeeded by Saxby Chambliss of Georgia as ranking member on the Select Intelligence Committee. Chambliss gave up his top GOP spot on Agriculture, Nutrition, and Forestry and was succeeded by Pat Roberts of Kansas. Also choosing not to run for reelection was Judd Gregg of New Hampshire. Filling his spot as ranking member on the Budget Committee was Jeff Sessions of Alabama. Sessions was succeeded by Charles E. Grassley of Iowa as ranking member on Judiciary. Grassley exited the ranking position on Finance. Orrin G. Hatch of Utah took his place.

The Utah State Republican Convention in 2010 denied Robert F. Bennett a place on the primary ballot, and he left the Senate at the end of the 111th Congress. Bennett was succeeded as ranking member on Rules and Administration by Lamar Alexander.

Rules

The Senate on January 27, 2011, took action on a number of proposed rules changes. It voted 92–4 on S Res 28, to limit the practice of secret holds used to anonymously block legislation and nominations, clearing a sixty-vote threshold needed for approval under an agreement. The four "nay" votes came from Jim DeMint, R-S.C.; Mike Lee, R-Utah; and Rand Paul, R-Ky.—all members of the new Senate Tea Party caucus—plus John Ensign, R-Nev. The change in the holds procedure required disclosure of the identity of a senator within two days of the time the senator notified his or her party leader of an intent to place a hold, down from the existing six days after a hold was announced. If the senator did not step forward publicly, the hold would be attributed to that member's party leader.

Also adopted, 81–15, was a standing order (S Res 29) to prevent senators from forcing the reading of legislation or an amendment if the text had been available for seventy-two hours. That change also required sixty votes for approval.

Majority Leader Reid and Minority Leader McConnell made a two-part gentlemen's agreement: majority Democrats would allow Republicans to offer more amendments to legislation and, in return, Republicans vowed not to use filibusters to block legislation from coming to the Senate floor, even though a measure (S Res 10) calling explicitly for that change was rejected, 44–51.

The Senate turned back two other filibuster-related resolutions. S Res 8, defeated 12–84, would have reduced the number of votes needed to overcome filibusters. S Res 21, defeated 46–49, would have forced senators to talk continuously on the floor if they wanted to filibuster legislation or a nomination.

Reid and McConnell also said that in the 112th and 113th Congresses neither would use parliamentary force to change Senate rules through a simple majority vote, a promise that would require all significant rules changes to garner the support of two-thirds of senators present and voting. The agreement meant that as long as either Reid or McConnell was majority leader, the chamber would not resort to the so-called constitutional or nuclear option, invoking a procedural maneuver using a simple majority to approve a change in certain procedures and rules. (However, Reid would adopt a change to this for certain presidential nominations in the 114th Congress.)

The Senate on June 29, 2011, by a vote of 89–8, adopted S Res 116, which made changes in the Senate rules to establish a section of the executive calendar to expedite approximately 250 nominees, mainly for part-time advisory and oversight boards and commissions.

On October 6, 2011, during consideration of a China currency bill (S 1619), Republicans tried to bring up amendments that had no relationship to the legislation, so Reid made a countermove that set a new precedent about the rights of the minority and effectively changed the Senate rules through a simple majority vote—something that was supposed to take at least three-fifths and often two-thirds of senators. The change limited the amendments that could be considered once the Senate voted to invoke cloture and brought debate on a bill to a close, a step that required sixty votes. Under Reid's precedent, it would be against the rules to seek the sixty-seven votes needed to suspend the rules and bring up an amendment that was nongermane, or unrelated, to the bill in question after a successful cloture vote.

Republicans on October 6 attempted to force Democrats to cast symbolic votes on a variety of topics, filing a series of motions to suspend the rule against considering nongermane amendments after cloture on S 1619 had been invoked, 62–38. Reid called the ploy "filibuster by amendment" and said the practice could end up delaying the bill indefinitely. He then set up his own defeat on a motion to uphold a ruling of the chair against his effort to change the rules. By losing, on a **key vote of 48–51 (R 47–0; D 1–49; I 0–2)**, Reid won and the ruling fell. *(2011 key votes, p. 785)*

HOUSE

Republicans took over the majority in the House for the first time since the 109th Congress (2005–2007).

Majority Leadership

The final tally of the January 5, 2011, roll call for Speaker was 241 votes for Republican John A. Boehner of Ohio and 173 votes for Democrat Nancy Pelosi of California. There were also eighteen votes for other Democrats, and one member voted "present"—these were protest votes and demonstrated that Pelosi had fence mending to do within the Democratic caucus in light of the party's disappointing performance in the 2010 midterm elections. Heath Shuler of North Carolina drew eleven votes, John Lewis of Georgia got two votes, and five were cast for others, including Steny H. Hoyer of Maryland.

The House Republican Caucus had nominated Boehner as Speaker, as expected and without opposition, at a meeting November 17, 2010. It also chose Eric Cantor of Virginia as majority leader and Kevin McCarthy of California as majority whip.

Tom Price of Georgia succeeded Thaddeus McCotter of Michigan as House Republican Policy Committee chair. Pete Sessions of Texas retained his post as chair of the National Republican Congressional Committee.

Minority Leadership

During a meeting of the House Democratic Caucus on November 17, 2010, Speaker Pelosi was forced to beat back an open challenge by Blue Dog Coalition member Heath Shuler in her bid to return to the minority leader position she held before the Democrats took control of the House in 2007. Although she won the caucus nomination handily, 150–43, the fact that the vote even took place indicated the depths of soul-searching in the caucus after Democrats were ousted from the majority in the midterm elections. Earlier in the day, Peter A. DeFazio of Oregon sought to delay the leadership votes until December, so that the caucus could have more time to think about the Democratic losses at the polls. That effort was turned back, 129–68, on a secret ballot.

Majority Whip James E. Clyburn of South Carolina, who had the support of the Congressional Black Caucus, announced that he would challenge Majority Leader Steny Hoyer for minority whip. However, Pelosi brokered a deal whereby Hoyer would become minority whip and Clyburn would assume a new, third-ranking leadership post designated as assistant leader. Clyburn, an African American, was satisfied that, by taking the position created for him, the party's House leadership would continue to reflect the makeup of its diverse membership.

John B. Larson of Connecticut was returned as chair of the Democratic Caucus. Steve Israel of New York succeeded Chris Van Hollen of Maryland as chair of the Democratic Congressional Campaign Committee (DCCC). Van Hollen decided not to run for reelection as DCCC chair, instead successfully pursing the ranking member spot on the House Budget Committee.

Committees

Each House committee got a new chair and ranking member, as Democrats lost the majority to the Republicans in the 2010 elections. House Republicans stuck to their party rules, passing over candidates for committee chairs who had sought term-limit waivers to take gavels. The GOP had adopted a rule in 1995 limiting a lawmaker to six consecutive years as a chair or ranking member of a committee. Thus, Republicans picked Harold Rogers of Kentucky to chair the Appropriations Committee and Fred Upton of Michigan to lead the Energy and Commerce Committee. They were chosen over Jerry Lewis of California, the sitting ranking member of Appropriations, and Joe L. Barton of Texas, ranking member of Energy and Commerce, both of whom had argued that their experience and track record were more important than the term-limits rule.

Spencer Bachus of Alabama, instead of Ed Royce of California, was selected to lead Financial Services and Ralph M. Hall of Texas, instead of Dana Rohrabacher of California, was chosen to chair Science, Space, and Technology (renamed from Science and Technology). Cliff Stearns of Florida, a candidate for the Energy and Commerce gavel, did not challenge Jeff Miller of Florida for chair of Veterans' Affairs.

In the following cases, the person who became chair had been the ranking member: Frank D. Lucas of Oklahoma at Agriculture; Howard C. "Buck" McKeon of California at Armed Services; Paul D. Ryan of Wisconsin at Budget; John Kline of Minnesota at Education and Labor; Darrell Issa of California at Oversight and Government Reform; Peter T. King of New York at Homeland Security; Ileana Ros-Lehtinen of Florida at Foreign Affairs; Lamar Smith of Texas at Judiciary; Doc Hastings of Washington at Natural Resources; David Dreier of California at Rules; Sam Graves of Missouri at Small Business; John L. Mica of Florida at Transportation and Infrastructure; and David Camp of Michigan at Ways and Means.

Dan Lungren of California was selected to chair the House Administration Committee. Mike Rogers of Michigan was picked over William M. "Mac" Thornberry of Texas for chair of the Select Intelligence Committee. Jo Bonner of Alabama was chosen to head the Ethics Committee (renamed from the Standards of Official Conduct Committee).

In many instances, the Democratic committee chair from the 111th Congress became the ranking member in the 112th Congress: Collin C. Peterson of Minnesota at Agriculture; George Miller of California at Education and Labor; Henry A. Waxman of California at Energy and Commerce; Barney Frank of Massachusetts at Financial Services; Bennie Thompson of Mississippi at Homeland Security; Howard L. Berman of California at Foreign Affairs; John Conyers Jr. of Michigan at Judiciary; Louise M. Slaughter of New York at Rules; Nydia M. Velázquez of New York at Small Business; Bob Filner of California at Veterans' Affairs; and Sander M. Levin of Michigan at Ways and Means.

Norm Dicks of Washington took the top Democratic spot on the Appropriations Committee. David R. Obey of Wisconsin, who chaired the panel in the 111th Congress, did not seek reelection to Congress in 2010. Also not seeking reelection was Bart Gordon of Tennessee. Eddie Bernice Johnson of Texas became ranking member of the Science, Space, and Technology Committee; Gordon was chair of its forerunner, Science and Technology. Losing at the polls was Ike Skelton of Missouri, who headed the Armed Services Committee, and John M. Spratt Jr., chair of the Budget Committee. Taking the ranking member spot in the 112th Congress on Armed Services was Adam Smith of Washington and on Budget was Chris Van Hollen of Maryland. Smith faced challenges from Loretta Sanchez of California and Silvestre Reyes of Texas. After Reyes finished third on the first ballot, Smith beat Sanchez, 28–23, for the backing of the Democratic Steering and Policy Committee. Nick J. Rahall II of West Virginia, who had been chair of the Natural Resources Committee, became ranking member of the Transportation and Infrastructure Committee. James L. Oberstar had chaired Transportation and Infrastructure in the 111th Congress, but he was defeated in his reelection bid. Edward J. Markey of Massachusetts became ranking member on Natural Resources.

Edolphus Towns of New York, who had been chair of the Oversight and Government Reform Committee, took himself out of the running for ranking member on the panel in the 112th Congress. Speaker Pelosi and the White House reportedly did not support his candidacy for the post, as they wanted someone more aggressive to go up against incoming GOP chair Issa. The Steering Committee subsequently chose Elijah E. Cummings of Maryland as ranking member, bypassing Carolyn Maloney of New York, the senior Democrat on the panel.

Robert A. Brady of Pennsylvania became ranking member at House Administration, where he had served as chair in the 111th Congress. C. A. Dutch Ruppersberger of Maryland was designated as ranking member at Select Intelligence. He became the first Democratic freshman to be appointed to the Intelligence panel. Linda T. Sánchez of California was picked as ranking member on the Ethics Committee.

The House Select Committee on Energy Independence and Global Warming, established in 2007, was dismantled by the GOP-controlled House in January 2011, at the beginning of the 112th Congress.

Rules

In taking control of the House, the new Republican majority changed a number of House rules, chiefly to expedite the handling of budget-related matters. The changes aimed to promote GOP priorities for cutting federal spending and reducing the deficit. The rules package (H Res 5) was adopted, 238–191, on January 5, 2011.

A new "cut-as-you-go" rule made it out of order to consider a bill or joint resolution that would have the net effect of increasing mandatory spending. The rule replaced the "pay-as-you-go" rule, instituted by Democrats, which applied to both mandatory spending increases and tax cuts and allowed increases or mandatory spending reductions to be used to offset each other.

The new rules package also eliminated the so-called Gephardt rule that had permitted automatic House passage, without a vote, of a measure to increase the debt limit if both the House and Senate adopted a budget resolution. The procedure, named after former majority and minority leader Richard A. Gephardt, D-Mo., had sent the debt bill automatically to the Senate and allowed House members to advance the legislation without having to cast a politically uncomfortable vote on it.

Perhaps the most controversial change effectively required the House Budget Committee chair to set spending parameters for the remainder of fiscal 2011, instead of having the limits set in a House-adopted budget resolution. Some budget analysts were alarmed that the typically months-long budget process was reduced to a leadership decision. Republicans countered that Democrats were at fault for not adopting a fiscal 2011 budget resolution in 2010, when they controlled the House.

The new rules called for a spending-cut "lockbox," which applied to floor amendments that made cuts to appropriations bills. Cuts would go to a special account in an effort to make it easier to reduce the overall size of spending bills. Eliminated was a requirement that appropriators fund highway and transit projects at levels set in the surface transportation authorization. Without the requirement, cutting such spending on the House floor would be easier.

In a move foreshadowed in the Republicans' 2010 preelection Pledge to America, the new rules required members, when they introduced a bill or joint resolution, to provide a statement that specifically cited the constitutional authority to enact such legislation. The package barred consideration of a bill or joint resolution that had not been reported by a committee if it had not been available online for at least three business days. Committees would be required to post their rules online; provide three-day notice for markups; webcast all hearings and markups when technically possible; and post roll call votes within forty-eight hours and text of adopted amendments within twenty-four hours after markup.

In addition, the changes struck a rule established by Democrats that had allowed the five House delegates and the resident commissioner to vote on the floor during consideration of measures in the Committee of the Whole. The new majority also reinstated the six-year limit on committee chairs, which had been repealed by Democrats in the 110th Congress. *(110th Congress action on rules, Congress and the Nation Vol. XII, p. 830)*

The Select Intelligence Oversight Subcommittee of the House Appropriations Committee was discontinued. The House Committee on Standards of Official Conduct was renamed the Committee on Ethics.

When the House Republican Conference met on December 8, 2010, members included in the new GOP rules package a ban on votes on commemorative resolutions, such as those that honored sports teams, in an effort to make time on the House floor more productive. The conference sidelined a proposal by Todd Akin of Missouri to create a new select committee to examine ways to cut government spending, after Republican leaders said they were exploring strategies to slash spending without amending the conference rules. A proposal by Steve King of Iowa to codify and make public the structure of the Republican Steering Committee failed on a voice vote. The existing GOP rules package contained information on what the Steering Committee did, but its structure was undefined and typically changed from one Congress to the next.

On January 6, the House, by a vote of 408–13, approved a resolution (H Res 22) to cut roughly 5 percent from members' expense accounts, as well as from committee and leadership budgets.

In their intraparty rules deliberation, House Democrats rejected a resolution, offered by Melvin Watts of North Carolina, to amend party rules to stop chairs and ranking members of most committees from also serving as chair or ranking member of a subcommittee.

STOCK Act

In the aftermath of a November 13, 2011, story on the CBS program *60 Minutes* suggesting that members of Congress might have used knowledge gained in the course of their duties to profit in the stock market, Congress in 2012 cleared the Stop Trading on Congressional Knowledge Act (S 2038), know as the STOCK Act. President Barack Obama signed the measure into law on April 4 (PL 112-105).

Initially drafted as a bill to state explicitly that Securities and Exchange Commission (SEC) rules banning insider trading applied to members of Congress, the legislation grew into a rewrite of financial disclosure requirements that applied not only to lawmakers and congressional staff but also to officials and senior staff throughout the government. Those covered by the bill were required to report any stock or securities transaction within forty-five days, with the information made available to the public.

Although existing law did not exempt members of Congress or federal officials from the prohibition against insider trading, lawmakers generally were not considered to have a confidential or fiduciary relationship with the source of the information they received, raising questions as to whether they met the legal definition of an "insider." The new law clarified that they did.

BACKGROUND

In the aftermath of the Watergate scandal in the 1970s, lawmakers passed the Ethics in Government Act of 1978 (PL 95-521), mandating disclosure requirements for top government officials. Under that law, the federal government had two types of disclosure requirements for employees: public and confidential. *(PL 95-521, Congress and the Nation Vol. V, pp. 824, 891)*

As of 2012, about 28,000 higher-level employees leading government agencies disclosed their personal financial information each year to their agencies, to be made public. The Office of Government Ethics launched a website in 2012 that listed the public financial information of about one thousand presidential appointees subject to Senate confirmation. An additional 364,000 midlevel employees annually file financial information to their agencies' oversight entities under a confidential system. Those disclosures, although scrutinized internally for conflicts of interest, were not made public.

Congress's effect on financial markets through appropriations decisions, tax incentives, deficit reduction steps, and other actions stoked a voracious appetite on Wall Street for up-to-the-second information about Capitol Hill. It also sparked questions about whether more restrictions should be placed on the use of financially beneficial information by lawmakers and their staffs.

Experts disagreed on whether insider trading legislation was needed. Some argued that current ethics rules in the two chambers and an SEC requirement for "trust and confidence" in the handling of sensitive information by business employees, lawmakers, and other individuals was an effective ban on insider trading on Capitol Hill. Critics said that members should be able to make routine investments and have it suffice to file complete disclosure reports. An argument also was made that an explicit legislative ban would deter potential congressional candidates from running. Some authorities, meanwhile, pushed for simple language to clearly state that lawmakers and staff had a legal, fiduciary responsibility—as well as a mandate under ethics rules and SEC regulations—not to trade on inside or confidential information.

Some members grumbled that S 2038 was largely a public relations exercise responding to the *60 Minutes* report suggesting that House Speaker John A. Boehner, R-Ohio, House Minority Leader Nancy Pelosi, D-Calif., and other lawmakers were cashing in on nonpublic information. The allegations were "all news to me," said House Rules Committee Chair David Dreier, R-Calif. "And I'm not a new kid on the block," the sixteen-term veteran added.

SENATE ACTION

On December 14, 2011, the Senate Homeland Security and Governmental Affairs Committee approved, 7–2, a draft bill to prohibit members of Congress and aides from using nonpublic information for personal gain or to tip off others. S 2038, sponsored by committee chair Joseph I. Lieberman, I-Conn., was ordered reported on January 26, 2012. The panel did not file a report (S Rept 112-244) until December 3.

The full Senate passed the bill by a vote of 96–3 on February 2, 2012, after significantly expanding the scope of the original measure. As introduced, the measure contained the core provisions of the final legislation, clarifying that existing prohibitions on insider trading on nonpublic information applied to lawmakers and congressional staff. It required that lawmakers and congressional aides who already filed annual financial disclosure statements report stock and bond transactions within thirty days of the transaction, with the information posted on a website.

During floor consideration on February 2, the Senate adopted, 58–41, an amendment by Banking, Housing, and Urban Affairs ranking Republican Richard C. Shelby of Alabama to extend the reporting provisions to executive branch officials and staff. The amendment also prohibited executive branch appointees and staff from holding positions that gave them oversight, rule-making, or loan- or grant-making abilities over industries or companies in which they or their spouses had a significant interest.

Also adopted, 60–39, was an amendment by Charles E. Grassley, R-Iowa, to require political intelligence consultants to register in a manner similar to lobbyists for their activities on Capitol Hill. Political intelligence consultants collected information about legislative and executive branch activities through direct contact with lawmakers and aides and sold the information to financial services companies and other interested parties. The amendment carved out a specific exemption for journalists providing information to the public. The Senate adopted by voice vote an amendment by California Democrat Barbara Boxer, chair of the Select Ethics Committee, and Georgia Republican Johnny Isakson, the panel's vice chair, to require increased disclosure on home mortgages from lawmakers and their spouses. Also by voice vote, the Senate adopted an amendment by Patrick J. Leahy, D-Vt., and John Cornyn, R-Texas, to strengthen criminal penalties in some public corruption cases.

The Leahy-Cornyn amendment incorporated language from a bill (S 401), the Corruption Prosecution Improvements Act, approved by voice vote and reported (no written report) on July 28, 2011, by the Senate Judiciary Committee. The House Judiciary Committee on December 1, 2011, approved by a vote of 30–0 and on September 21, 2012, reported (H Rept 112-688) similar legislation (HR 2572). The measures were introduced in response to a 2010 Supreme Court ruling in *Skilling v. United States* that sponsors said made it difficult for prosecutors to pursue cases involving public officials acting in their own financial self-interest and against the best interests of the public. The Court partially struck down the convictions of Jeffrey Skilling, the former Enron chief executive officer, for "honest services fraud." In an opinion written by Justice Ruth Bader Ginsburg, the Court held that the fraud statute had been interpreted too broadly by lower courts and limited such fraud to bribery and kickbacks. The Justice Department supported the Leahy-Cornyn language.

Also on February 2, the Senate rejected, 26–73, an amendment by Sherrod Brown, D-Ohio, to require that lawmakers either divest or place in blind trusts stock and security holdings in industries over which they had jurisdiction through their work.

HOUSE ACTION

The House passed, 417–2, a version of the bill that had been revised by Majority Leader Eric Cantor, R-Va. The nearly unanimous support masked widespread divisions and unusual procedural maneuvering. Cantor amended the bill and then brought it to the floor February 9 under suspension of the rules, a procedure requiring a two-thirds majority and prohibiting amendments.

Cantor made virtually no changes in core parts of the Senate-passed version clarifying that current SEC prohibitions on insider trading on nonpublic information be extended to lawmakers and congressional staff, plus top executive branch officials. All would be required to report stock and bond transactions shortly after they took place, and the information would be publicly available on a website. Both the Senate- and House-passed versions of the legislation directed congressional ethics committees to issue guidance underscoring that lawmakers and congressional staff cannot use confidential information for "private profit."

Cantor's changes called for additional requirements for coverage of employees outside Congress. Another House change required stock and bond transactions to be reported within forty-five days of the transaction; the Senate version called for thirty days. Cantor also added a provision to bar covered officials from participating in initial public offerings (IPOs) on a favored basis. That change was designed to call attention to claims in the *60 Minutes* report that Pelosi and her husband had participated in an IPO related to Visa at a time when major legislation affecting the credit card companies was making its way through the House. In the segment, Pelosi denied any wrongdoing. Cantor's version also would repeal an existing requirement that lawmakers and congressional candidates file printed campaign disclosure statements with state election officers. The provision would not affect requirements for electronic filings.

Critics focused on two sections of S 2038 that Cantor dropped: the Grassley amendment on political intelligence consultants and the Leahy-Cornyn amendment on strengthened penalties in public corruption cases. House Republicans who succeeded in removing the Grassley language voiced reservations that the Senate-passed version of the bill was a redundant citation of existing law and that it could jeopardize First Amendment rights of individuals seeking to contact lawmakers. Grassley decried the decision to drop his provision. "It's astonishing and extremely disappointing that the House would fulfill Wall Street's wishes by killing this provision," he said. "The Senate clearly voted to try to shed light on an industry that's behind the scenes."

Expressing the views of a number of Republicans, John Carter of Texas, secretary of the House Republican Conference and a former local judge, said the Leahy-Cornyn provision, and perhaps other parts of the Senate-passed bill, would "walk over people's rights." Leahy said, "If we are serious about restoring faith in government and addressing the kinds of egregious misconduct that we have witnessed in recent years in high-profile public corruption cases, Congress must act now to enact serious anti-corruption legislation. The House Republicans' version of the STOCK Act misses that opportunity."

Louise M. Slaughter, D-N.Y., the lead sponsor of a House congressional insider trading bill (HR 1148) that had drawn broad bipartisan backing, objected that GOP leaders had changed the legislation behind closed doors and then used the suspension procedure to jam it through the House. She objected particularly to dropping the Grassley provision. Slaughter, along with Pelosi, decided to move S 2038 forward with the hope that it would go to conference committee. Both Grassley and Leahy joined in calling for a conference.

FINAL ACTION

The rapid push to move the legislation began with Obama's January 24, 2012, State of the Union address, during which he called the measure "an important step to rebuild the trust between Washington and the American people." Senate Majority Leader Harry Reid, D-Nev., decided not to have the two chambers work out the differences in a conference, saying there was not enough time before a scheduled two-week congressional recess in April. A conference had the potential to generate weeks or even months of additional debate. Lawmakers were eager to get the measure on the books to show they were determined to act quickly in response to the allegations. Also, Reid, along with Minority Leader Mitch McConnell, R-Ky., opposed the Grassley amendment, and accepting the House bill allowed them to drop it without further debate.

The Senate cleared the bill by unanimous consent March 22, after earlier voting 96–3 to invoke cloture and close debate on Reid's motion to agree to the House version.

MAJOR PROVISIONS

Following are the major provisions of S 2038 (PL 112-105):

Insider trading. Stated that insider trading provisions of securities law and regulations contained no exemption for members and employees of Congress, or for officials and staff of the executive and judicial branches, and clarified that these individuals were subject to the ban on trading based on nonpublic knowledge gained as a result of their federal positions.

- Directed the House and Senate to issue rules requiring adherence to the prohibitions. The executive branch's Office of Government Ethics and the Judicial Conference were required to issue similar guidance.

- Prohibited lawmakers and senior employees in all three branches who were subject to financial reporting requirements under the Ethics in Government Act of 1978 from participating in an initial public offering of stock except when the IPO was generally available to any member of the public.

Disclosure. In an effort to increase transparency in financial disclosure reporting, the bill required members of Congress and government employees subject to the ethics act to report, within forty-five days, transactions of stocks or securities. The new reporting did not apply to certain publicly traded mutual funds and other widely held investments. Previously, transactions had to be reported annually.

- Required both the legislative and executive branches to develop online filing systems for the disclosure forms and make them available to the public on the Internet.

Home mortgages. Required that lawmakers, the president and vice president, and government officials subject to Senate confirmation publicly disclose the terms of their home mortgages. A number of lawmakers in previous years had been found to have received preferential treatment in terms of lower interest rates through a VIP program administered by the since-defunct Countrywide Home Loans company. Those members stated they never asked for special treatment, never gave any favor to Countrywide, and were unaware of a list of special clients.

Other provisions. Expanded the types of crimes for which members of Congress would lose their congressional pension benefits, including insider trading, and denied them benefits even if the crime was committed while they were subsequently serving in another elected office. Previous law denied congressional retirement benefits to members convicted of bribery, perjury, conspiracy, or other related crimes in the course of carrying out their official duties.

- Required the Government Accountability Office, with the Congressional Research Service, to submit a report on the role of "political intelligence" in financial markets, but did not regulate political intelligence consultants.
- Prohibited payment of bonuses to executives of the Federal National Mortgage Association (Fannie Mae) and the Federal Home Loan Mortgage Corporation (Freddie Mac) during the conservatorship of those enterprises.
- Extended to anyone required to file a financial disclosure statement under the Ethics in Government Act a prohibition on entering into negotiations or having an agreement concerning future employment or compensation unless the employee filed a statement disclosing the negotiation or agreement. The bill also required individuals who filed such statements to recuse themselves whenever there was a real or apparent conflict of interest. Previously, such rules applied only to members of Congress.

Senate Confirmations

Congress in 2012 cleared legislation (S 679) that reduced the number of executive branch nominations that required Senate confirmation. The Presidential Appointment Efficiency and Streamlining Act would eliminate the confirmation requirement for about 170 executive posts, including nominations to boards and commissions for the National Science Foundation, the National Council on Disability, and the National Museum and Library Services Board. It eliminated confirmation requirements for individuals whose immediate superiors were subject to confirmation. The bill also would create a working group to revise the vetting process for nominees by reducing duplicative paperwork requirements.

S 679 was a housekeeping measure of sorts, intended to streamline Senate operations. Supporters said the move would allow senators to devote more attention to the other one thousand or so executive branch civilian positions that required confirmation. The past fifty years had seen a steady growth in the number of presidential appointees facing Senate confirmation, according to the Congressional Research Service. When President John F. Kennedy took office in 1961, the Senate had about 850 nominees to confirm; by the time Obama was sitting in the Oval Office in 2009, there were about 1,215.

Backed by leaders from both parties, the measure's supporters touted it as a way to speed the process for confirming nominees to upper-level positions. But critics argued that the proposal would give the White House too much power over appointments and weaken the Senate's role in the process. They also said that more attention should be paid to the use of recess appointments to fill vacancies with controversial nominees.

The Senate Homeland Security and Governmental Affairs Committee approved S 679 by voice vote on April 13, 2011, and formally reported it on June 13. The committee filed a report (S Rept 112-24) on June 21. The Senate passed the bill, 79–20, on June 29. Under a unanimous consent agreement, sixty votes were required to pass the bill.

During debate on S 679, Ohio Republican Rob Portman, who earlier in his career was confirmed as U.S. trade representative and Office of Management and Budget director, succeeded in convincing his colleagues that many potential appointees want the prestige that came with Senate confirmation. By voice vote on June 29, the Senate adopted a Portman amendment that would retain confirmation for top financial officers at several departments and agencies. The amendment also would continue to require confirmation of the comptrollers of the Army, Air

Force, and Navy. A manager's amendment, adopted June 28 by voice vote, would retain Senate confirmation for at least eleven assistant secretaries responsible for legislative and intergovernmental affairs, including those at the departments of Defense, State, and the Treasury.

On July 31, 2012, the House agreed, 261–116, to suspend the rules and pass S 679, clearing the measure. The president signed the bill into law (PL 112-166) on August 10, 2012.

House Office of General Counsel

Members of the House Appropriations Committee in 2011 and 2012 bickered over whether the House Office of General Counsel should pay a private law firm to defend the Defense of Marriage Act (DOMA; PL 104-199), which defined marriage as the union of a man and a woman. Rep. Michael M. Honda, D-Calif., offered an unsuccessful amendment to the fiscal 2012 legislative branch appropriations bill (PL 112-74) that would have required the General Accountability Office (GAO) to complete a study on best contracting practices to highlight the dispute. The activities of the Office of General Counsel were directed by the Bipartisan Legal Advisory Group (BLAG), which was made up of the Speaker, the majority and minority leaders, and the majority and minority whips. *(DOMA, Congress and the Nation Vol. IX, p. 746; PL 112-74, p. 172)*

Section 3 of DOMA, by describing a heterosexual couple in a recognized marriage, essentially codified the nonrecognition of same-sex marriage. The Obama administration defended the law in court until 2011, when it concluded that Section 3 was unconstitutional—a violation of the Equal Protection Clause of the Fifth Amendment. In response, Speaker John A. Boehner, R-Ohio, convened a meeting of BLAG, which on a partisan 3–2 vote March 9, 2011, directed the Office of General Counsel to defend DOMA in court, in place of the Department of Justice. The Office of General Counsel then engaged the services of a private law firm to argue the case.

On May 12, 2011, during a House Legislative Branch Appropriations Subcommittee hearing, ranking member Honda sought a clarification for how the GOP leadership planned to pay for the law firm to defend DOMA. As Honda explained in a press release dated the same day, House Administration Committee Chair Dan Lungren, R-Calif., and House general counsel Kerry Kircher, at the direction of Speaker Boehner, "signed a $500,000 contract with the private law firm Bancroft PLLC for legal services to assist the House in defending DOMA. While the contract states that 'the General Counsel agrees to pay the Contractor for all contractual services,' Mr. Kircher said at the hearing that he was told by the House Republican leadership that funds will not come out of the Office of General Counsel's budget. The Chief Administrative Officer . . . Dan Strodel, who would ultimately write the checks to Bancroft PLLC on behalf of the House, said that he too had no knowledge of where the money would come from."

Honda, in his press release, raised another issue: "Is this a case where an overzealous House Speaker committed $500,000 of the American people's tax dollars to push a partisan and political agenda without having a funding source already in place? If so, do Speaker Boehner's actions violate the Antideficiency Act, which prohibits involving the government in any obligation to pay money before funds have been appropriated for that purpose[?]"

The GAO on July 6, 2011, responded to an inquiry about the contract from Ander Crenshaw, R-Fla., chair of the House Appropriations Subcommittee on the Legislative Branch. The GAO concluded that, when the contract was signed, "the House Office of General Counsel incurred an obligation of $500,000 against its appropriation for salaries and expenses. The House Chief Administrative Office has advised us that there was an adequate unobligated balance to satisfy the obligation. We conclude, therefore, that the House General Counsel did not violate the Antideficiency Act. . . . In addition, because of the statutory authorities to transfer appropriations of the House of Representatives, the House may transfer amounts to the Office of General Counsel's appropriation, as needed, in order to avoid Antideficiency Act violations."

On December 7, 2012, the Supreme Court agreed to hear *United States v. Windsor* (570 U.S. 12), a case in which Edith Windsor, upon the death of her same-sex spouse, who left her estate to Windsor, challenged DOMA when barred from being able to claim the federal tax exemption for surviving spouses. The Court asked the parties arguing the case to address the issue of whether BLAG had standing; that is, whether it had a direct interest in the case, not a mere general interest.

The House on January 3, 2013, adopted a rule authorizing BLAG to defend DOMA, stating "the Bipartisan Legal Advisory Group continues to speak for, and articulate the institutional position of, the House in all litigation matters in which it appears." On June 26, the Court ruled 5–4 in *Windsor* that Section 3 of DOMA was unconstitutional. Justice Anthony M. Kennedy, writing for the majority, recognized that "BLAG's sharp adversarial presentation of the issues satisfies the prudential concerns that otherwise might counsel against hearing an appeal from a decision with which the principal parties agree"—that is, the Department of Justice and Windsor. He went on to say that the Court "need not decide whether BLAG would have standing to challenge" a lower court's ruling. In his dissent, Justice Samuel A. Alito Jr. stated that BLAG was authorized to act on behalf of the House and that it had standing because "the House of Representatives was a necessary party to DOMA's passage." He went on to say that "in the narrow category of cases in which a court strikes down an Act of Congress and the Executive declines to defend the Act, Congress both has standing to defend the undefended statute and is a proper party to do so."

On July 18, 2013, in light of the Supreme Court ruling in *Windsor* and after having spent about $3 million of taxpayer money defending DOMA, the Bipartisan Legal Advisory Group announced that it would cease defending the law in court.

Going Green at the Capitol

House Republicans in the 112th Congress successfully thwarted efforts to make the U.S. Capitol more "green" by barring use of funds for polystyrene containers in House dining facilities. The House, on July 22, 2011, during floor consideration of HR 2551, the fiscal 2012 legislative branch appropriations bill, rejected, by 179–234, an amendment by James P. Moran, D-Va., to bar the use of funds in HR 2551 to purchase polystyrene containers, which resemble Styrofoam, for use in House food-service facilities. *(HR 2551, p. 175)*

During conference consideration of HR 2055, a fiscal 2012 omnibus appropriations measure, the GOP scored a victory in retaining language barring the implementation of new lighting efficiency rules that Republicans said were a privacy intrusion. The House adopted the conference report (H Rept 112-331) by a vote of 296–121 on December 16, 2011. The Senate followed suit, by a vote of 67–32, on December 17, completing congressional action. President Barack Obama signed the bill into law (PL 112-74) on December 23.

Moran again offered his polystyrene containers amendment to the fiscal 2013 legislative branch appropriations bill (HR 5882), and again the House turned it back. The 178–229 vote came on June 8, 2012.

In the 110th Congress, Speaker Nancy Pelosi, D-Calif., endorsed the Green the Capitol initiative, which sought to reduce the environmental waste caused by House operations. Funding for the project was included in a fiscal 2008 omnibus appropriations measure (PL 110-161). Pelosi was spurring on in part by a Lawrence Berkeley National Laboratory calculation that the House emitted the same amount of greenhouse gases as do 17,200 cars in a single year, mostly due to its electricity bill. As part of the program, energy-efficient LED lights were installed in the House chamber's ceiling. The new, dimmable lights used 78 percent less energy than the old lights, and they also generated less heat and lasted much longer, according to Pelosi's office. *(110th Congress action, Congress and the Nation Vol. VII, p. 112)*

Printing Bills and Resolutions

The House on January 18, 2011, agreed to suspend the rules and pass HR 292, the Stop the OverPrinting (STOP) Act, sponsored by Christopher Lee, R-N.Y. The bill would prohibit Congress from printing hundreds of paper copies of bills and resolutions for distribution to individual members. They would have to read the bills online or ask for a printed copy.

Republicans said this step would save $7 million a year, plus a significant amount of paper. Existing law required the Government Printing Office to run off hundreds of copies of bills and resolutions for House and Senate clerks and document rooms, as well as for distribution to bill sponsors. With close to 14,000 pieces of legislation introduced last year alone, that added up to nearly 2.8 million paper copies, according to House Speaker John A. Boehner, R-Ohio.

The House-passed HR 292 would curtail only paper copies for members' offices; they would get bills electronically. Although the measure would not stop members from printing their own copies, Lee and other lawmakers said their colleagues seemed increasingly willing to shift to a paperless world.

Pocket Edition Constitution

The House by voice vote on February 1, 2012, and the Senate by voice vote on July 26 passed H Con Res 90, entitled "Authorizing the printing of the 25th edition of the pocket version of the United States Constitution." The official pocket edition of the Constitution was a longtime popular perquisite for members who, for example, would hand them out to school groups or brandish them in debate. The publication became a target, however, when House Republicans, newly in the majority in the 112th Congress, set about cutting expenses, including the biennial printing of compact versions of the Constitution.

The concurrent resolution called for printing the lesser of 235,500 copies of the document (220,500 for the House, 10,000 for the Senate, and 5,000 for the Joint Committee on Printing) or as many copies as could be produced and printed at a cost not exceeding $114,849. The 235,500 figure represented less than half the number of copies available in the 111th Congress. Some senior senators objected to the size of the reduction and noted that House members would get most of the copies. The resolution would halve the House allotment and cut the Senate allotment by 90 percent. Joint Committee on Printing Chair Gregg Harper, R-Miss., denied that House Republicans were trying to insult the Senate. He suggested that the two chambers could share copies or refer constituents to other sources.

The compact versions of the Constitution first gained popularity in 1937, when Congress celebrated the 150th anniversary of the document's adoption. Congress began printing its own pocket editions after the Constitution's bicentennial celebration in 1987.

A concurrent resolution is nonbinding; that is, it does not become law.

Ethics Probes

Two promising up-and-comers from opposite ends of the political spectrum were felled in the 112th Congress. Sen. John Ensign, R-Nev., a social conservative with presidential

SEXUAL MISADVENTURES LED TO RESIGNATIONS

An extramarital affair and ill-advised uses of the Internet proved the downfall for lawmakers in the 111th and 112th Congresses. Rep. Mark Souder, R-Ind., gave up his seat in 2010; Christopher Lee, R-N.Y., and Anthony Weiner, D-N.Y., in 2011. Reps. Eric Massa, D-N.Y., and David Wu, D-Ore., and Sen. John Ensign, R-Nev., also left Congress following revelations of sexual misadventures, but their cases involved other issues that prompted calls for ethics investigations. *(Massa ethics probe, p. 654; Ensign ethics probe, pp. 651, 671; Wu ethics probe, p. 673)*

Souder, a social conservative who said that religion drove his views on policies, resigned May 21, 2010, after admitting to an affair. In a May 18 statement, he said: "I sinned against God, my wife and my family by having a mutual relationship with a part-time member of my staff. In the poisonous environment of Washington, D.C., any personal failing is seized upon, often twisted, for political gain. I am resigning rather than to put my family through that painful, drawn-out process." Souder's extramarital affair came to light two weeks after he was renominated with a 48 percent plurality against three GOP challengers.

Lee abruptly resigned February 9, 2011, after allegations that the married lawmaker had pursued a date with a woman on the Craigslist website and sent her a revealing photo of himself. The Gawker website published a series of e-mails purportedly between Lee and a woman he met on Craigslist and posted a photo that Lee had taken of himself shirtless that was sent electronically to the woman.

Weiner on June 16, 2011, ended a three-week drama over his sordid online behavior by saying he would resign from Congress. Weiner expressed sorrow and said that while "I had hoped to continue the work . . . unfortunately the distraction I have created has made that impossible." The scandal, which revolved around the married lawmaker's online relationships with at least six women, quickly became a national spectacle. Photographs of Weiner's genitals were leaked, as were photographs of a scantily clad Weiner flexing in the mirror of the House gym. He initially said he intended to send a photo of himself as a joke to a woman but accidentally posted it to Twitter. He said he panicked, took down the photo, and claimed that his personal Twitter account had been hacked. In a rambling press conference on June 6, he admitted that he had lied to his family, the media, and his colleagues. Weiner's resignation was effective June 21.

ambitions, admitted to an extramarital affair and allegedly was involved with helping a former aide—and husband of his paramour—break federal lobbying law. Rep. Jesse L. Jackson Jr., D-Ill., a liberal and son of civil rights activist Jesse Jackson, was diagnosed with bipolar disorder and, after resigning his seat, admitted to violating federal campaign law.

SEN. JOHN ENSIGN

Mired in a sex scandal and dogged by a Senate Ethics Committee investigation, Sen. John Ensign, R-Nev., on April 21, 2011, announced that he would resign from Congress on May 3. Ensign said in a statement: "While I stand behind my firm belief that I have not violated any law, rule, or standard of conduct of the Senate, and I have fought to prove this publicly, I will not continue to subject my family, my constituents or the Senate to any further rounds of investigation, depositions, drawn out proceedings or especially public hearing." Ensign had said on March 7 that he would not seek reelection in 2012. *(111th Congress action, p. 651)*

The Senate Ethics Committee on February 1, 2011, had announced that it was appointing a special counsel—Carol Elder Bruce—to investigate whether Ensign violated Senate ethics rules as well as federal law in the aftermath of his extramarital affair. Ensign in June 2009 had disclosed the relationship with his campaign treasurer, Cynthia Hampton, who was married to his Senate aide, Douglas Hampton. At issue was a $96,000 payment that Ensign's parents gave to the Hamptons (the couple called it severance; Ensign, a gift) and the circumstances of Douglas Hampton working as a lobbyist before the one-year cooling-off period had passed. Caught up in the probe was Ensign's friend and colleague Sen. Tom Coburn, R-Okla. *(Coburn ethics probe, p. 672)*

Ethics Committee Chair Barbara Boxer, D-Calif., took to the Senate floor on May 12, 2011, less than two weeks after Ensign resigned his seat, to discuss Bruce's findings. The panel had voted the day before to release the special counsel's seventy-five-page report. Boxer described the conclusions reached as being "so disturbing that [the special counsel] believed that had Senator Ensign not resigned, and had we been able to proceed to that adjudicatory phase, the evidence of Senator Ensign's wrongdoing would have been substantial enough to warrant the consideration of expulsion, the harshest penalty available to the Ethics Committee and the Senate." The committee, its staff, and the special counsel, according to Boxer, deposed or interviewed seventy-two witnesses, issued thirty-two subpoenas for documents, and reviewed more than half a million documents in the Ensign case.

Boxer cited eight findings in which Bruce found "substantial credible evidence" that Ensign acted illegally or in violation of Senate rules: (1) conspired to violate Douglas Hampton's postemployment contact ban; (2) aided and abetted Hampton's violations of the contact ban; (3) made false and misleading statements to the Federal Election Commission regarding the $96,000 payment to the Hamptons; (4) violated federal campaign laws with the payment to the Hamptons; (5) violated a law and a Senate rule prohibiting unofficial office accounts; (6) permitted spoliation of documents and engaged in potential obstruction of justice; (7) discriminated on the basis of gender; and (8) engaged in improper conduct reflecting on the Senate, including violating his own office policies, written in a manual.

In a rare move, the Ethics Committee asked the Justice Department to investigate Ensign. The last time the committee referred a case involving a sitting or former member to federal investigators was in 1995.

In related action, Douglas Hampton on March 24, 2011, was indicted on seven counts for violating the one-year lobbying ban. He subsequently reached a plea agreement with federal prosecutors and on June 7, 2012, pled guilty to a single misdemeanor charge of lobbying the Senate in violation of the law.

SEN. DAVID VITTER

The Senate Ethics Committee on March 29, 2012, dismissed a complaint filed by Citizens for Responsibility and Ethics in Washington (CREW) against Sen. David Vitter, R-La., who threatened to block legislation (S J Res 3) providing a salary increase for Interior Secretary Ken Salazar until Salazar increased deepwater oil and gas drilling permits for exploratory wells in the Gulf of Mexico. CREW alleged that Vitter's actions were bribery and that he violated Senate rules. Offering anything of value to a public official with the intent of influencing an official act constituted bribery according to federal statute.

Efforts to increase Salazar's salary came as a result of his being subject to the U.S. Constitution's Ineligibility Clause when he became Interior secretary. On May 23, 2011, Vitter sent Salazar a letter stating: "I was asked to support legislation in the Senate to grant you a nearly $20,000 salary increase. Given the completely unsatisfactory pace of your department's issuance of new deepwater exploratory permits in the Gulf, I cannot possibly give my assent. . . . [W]hen the rate of permits issued for *new* deepwater exploratory wells reaches pre-moratorium levels (so 6 per month), I will end my efforts to block your salary increase." *(Ineligibility clause, p. 684)*

Upon concluding its investigation, the ethics panel, in a letter to Vitter, said that "[w]hile the committee found that there was no substantial credible evidence that you violated the law or Senate rules, it did conclude that it is inappropriate to condition support for a Secretary's personal salary increase directly on his or her performance of a specific official act." The committee said it would not take further action because "no clear Senate guidance addressing such conduct" existed. However, the letter stated that the panel would issue a new guidance, "which makes it clear that going forward such actions will be viewed by the Committee as improper conduct reflecting discreditably on the Senate."

Vitter, in response to the committee, remained defiant. In a statement he said: "I'm glad that I killed Ken Salazar's salary increase—he has completely failed us on energy policy. And I'll absolutely place a hold on any raise for him in the future."

The ethics committee in 2008 had dismissed another CREW complaint regarding Vitter's ties to a Washington, D.C., prostitution ring. *(Details, Congress and the Nation Vol. XII, p. 840)*

SEN. TOM COBURN

Sen. Tom Coburn, R-Okla., received a Public Letter of Qualified Admonition on May 25, 2012, from the Senate Ethics Committee for discussing official business with Douglas Hampton, a former aide to Sen. John Ensign, R-Nev., during his one-year cooling-off period. The contact came after Hampton became an industry lobbyist. Ensign had had an affair with Hampton's wife, Cynthia.

Coburn and Ensign had both lived in a dormitory in Washington, D.C., maintained by the religious organization known as The Family. Coburn, who was a physician and an ordained deacon, learned of Ensign's extramarital affair before it became public knowledge and tried to get Ensign to stop it. He also counseled Hampton.

The committee concluded that because Coburn had known Hampton when he worked in Ensign's office, the lawmaker was aware that when Hampton contacted him, it fell within the one-year period during which former Senate staffers were prohibited from lobbying their former employer. The panel wrote: "While the Committee did not find that your conduct constituted actionable violations of criminal law, it determined that you did not meet the . . . higher standards expected of a U.S. Senator." Coburn's office called the admonition "gratuitous," considering that he cooperated fully in the probe.

The Senate Ethics Committee, in its May 2011 report on Ensign, stated that Coburn was involved in an effort to negotiate a financial settlement to cover up the affair. Ensign resigned in 2011 as the committee was investigating his financial relationship with the Hamptons. *(Ensign ethics probe, pp. 651, 671)*

REPS. JOSEPH CROWLEY, TOM PRICE, AND JOHN CAMPBELL

In a report issued January 26, 2011, the House Committee on Ethics dismissed allegations of campaign finance violations against Joseph Crowley, D-N.Y., Tom Price, R-Ga., and John Campbell, R-Calif. The Office of Congressional Ethics in 2010 had transmitted its findings to the ethics panel, alleging that the three representatives' fund-raising activities in December 2009, when the House was considering the Dodd-Frank Wall Street Reform and Consumer Protection Act of 2009 (H 4173—PL 111-203), created the appearance of special treatment or access to campaign donors or the appearance that campaign contributions were linked to their official actions. *(Dodd-Frank, p. 88)*

The ethics committee concluded that the members' "fundraising activities raised no appearance of impropriety. Nor did [the members] violate any law or other applicable standard of conduct in connection with their fundraising activities." It said their activities "were no different from any routine fundraising event held by any other House Member."

REP. DAVID WU

House minority leader Nancy Pelosi, D-Calif., on July 25, 2011, made a formal request to the House Ethics Committee to determine whether Rep. David Wu, D-Ore., had violated House rules, following allegations that he had engaged in sexual misconduct with the eighteen-year-old daughter of his high school friend. The next day, Wu, the first person of full Chinese ancestry to serve in Congress, announced that he would resign from Congress. His resignation was effective August 3.

The Oregonian had reported on July 22 that a recent high school graduate had called Wu's office in the spring and left a voice mail message accusing the lawmaker of sexually assaulting her. Wu acknowledged the sexual encounter, which took place over Thanksgiving weekend in 2010, but insisted it was consensual. Also in his initial response to the allegations, Wu said that he would not resign, but that he would not seek reelection in 2012. The woman did not contact the police at the time of the incident, and no criminal charges were filed.

Wu had a history of exhibiting erratic behavior, but his staffers said the situation had escalated around the 2010 midterm campaign. For example, according to a February 18, 2011, article in *The Oregonian,* his staffers said he "delivered a belligerent and rambling 19-minute monologue to Washington County Democrats" on October 27, tried to get Health and Human Services Secretary Kathleen Sebelius to talk to his children on his cell phone during a fund-raiser on October 29, and that same day used his influence as a member of Congress to gain access to a restricted area at the Portland International Airport, where he solicited votes from passengers. After Wu sent his staff a picture of himself dressed as a tiger for Halloween, staff members on October 30 "checked for available hospital beds." While Wu admittedly was having a tough time—his marriage had recently broken up, his reelection campaign was hard fought, and so on—his staffers said his behavior "was not an ordinary response to stress." They tried twice to conduct an intervention, to get the lawmaker professional help, but to no avail. After Wu won reelection, at least six staffers left his employment, including his chief of staff and communications director. House leaders in February and March 2011 continued to express support for Wu, in light of his acknowledgment of mental health problems and his assertion that he was getting mental health treatment, which included undergoing therapy and taking medication.

The Oregonian had reported on October 12, 2004, that in the summer of 1976 Wu allegedly tried to force a woman, a fellow student at Stanford University, to have sex. At the time, Wu said what happened was consensual but later described his behavior as "inexcusable." He was disciplined by Stanford and saw a counselor. The woman did not press charges.

REP. DON YOUNG

The House ethics committee on December 20, 2011, announced its findings that Rep. Don Young, R-Alaska, did not violate any provision of the Code of Official Conduct or any law, rule, regulation, or other standard of conduct with respect to the receipt of twelve $5,000 contributions to the lawmaker's legal expense trust fund.

According to the Office of Congressional Ethics (OCE), which on October 13, 2011, had sent a referral to the ethics panel regarding the contributions, the same individuals who owned and operated the twelve corporations each contributed $5,000 to the fund. The OCE determined that if the contributions came from a single source, then they could have exceeded the annual $5,000 limit stipulated in the House rules and committee regulations.

The ethics committee found that the twelve corporations were owned by Gary Chouest, his wife, and his five children, or some combination thereof, and that each company was a distinct legal entity. Because the companies were separate legal entities, each with a unique tax identification number, and because contributions from multiple entities owned by the same individual or group of individuals were permissible, the committee dismissed the allegations in the OCE referral.

On March 19, 2013, the House Ethics Committee announced that it had formed investigatory subcommittees to look into allegations that Young and Rep. Robert E. Andrews, D-N.J., had violated chamber rules by misusing campaign funds and making false statements. The Federal Bureau of Investigation had referred Young's case to the committee, which began reviewing it in the 111th Congress.

REP. ALCEE L. HASTINGS

U.S. District Court Judge Barbara Rothstein on February 14, 2012, dismissed a sexual harassment lawsuit against Rep. Alcee L. Hastings, D-Fla. A second lawsuit filed under the 1995 Congressional Accountability Act (PL 104-1) and a House Ethics Committee investigation over the charges were ongoing. *(1995 law, Congress and the Nation Vol. IX, p. 890)*

The lawsuit was filed in March 2011 by the conservative watchdog group Judicial Watch on behalf of Winsome Packer, who worked as a staff representative for the U.S. Commission on Security and Cooperation in Vienna, Austria. Packer alleged that commission chair Hastings sexually harassed her between January 2008 and February 2010. In the lawsuit, she said that she was "particularly vulnerable to such threats because she was a Republican working for a Democratically controlled commission." The suit claimed that Hastings pressured her to let him stay with her in Vienna, to give him gifts, and to make contributions to his reelection campaign. It also alleged that he made inappropriate remarks to Parker, including asking her, while they were in the company of other people, what kind of underwear she had on. Furthermore, the lawsuit alleged that Hastings and a commission aide, Fred Turner, sought to retaliate against her when she tried to report the allegations. Hastings vehemently denied all the charges.

The court's action dismissed the claims against Hastings and Turner as individuals, but the commission continued to face charges based on the allegations against the two men.

The Office of Congressional Ethics began investigating Hastings after the lawsuit was filed in 2011. The House Ethics Committee announced January 11, 2012, that it needed more time to investigate the allegations against the lawmaker, and it released a report that contained details of the claims made by Packer. Hastings criticized the report for not considering Parker's motive in bringing the lawsuit, as she was in the process of promoting a self-published novel.

Hastings in 1989 lost his U.S. district court judgeship after being convicted on eight articles of impeachment. The bulk of the charges stemmed from a 1983 trial for bribery. A jury acquitted him in that case. *(Impeachment, Congress and the Nation Vol. VIII, p. 775; Congress and the Nation Vol. VII, p. 768)*

REP. VERN BUCHANAN

The House Committee on Ethics on July 10, 2012, cleared Rep. Vern Buchanan, R-Fla., of charges that he violated chamber rules by intentionally misleading Congress about his finances. The committee said it found "no evidence that the errors were knowing or willful," and it "unanimously determined that the errors were not substantially different from the hundreds or thousands of errors corrected by amendment by the requirement of the Committee every year." The Office of Congressional Ethics (OCE) had forwarded its findings in the matter to the Ethics Committee in November 2011.

As described by *The Hill* on July 10, the committee was "still probing a separate series of charges that Buchanan attempted to procure a false affidavit from a witness testifying [before the Federal Election Commission (FEC)] about allegations of a straw-donor scheme." Citing a CNN source, the Huffington Post had reported on June 23, 2012, that Buchanan "is facing allegations that he tried to steal money from car dealerships he owned to use for his own political campaigns. He is also being accused of attempting to silence a witness—former business partner Sam Kazran—to the alleged finance fraud." The OCE had referred these concerns to the Ethics Committee in February 2012. Reports surfaced in 2013 that the Justice Department also was looking into the matter.

The FEC on January 17, 2012, had released documents showing that it had voted 5–0 to close its investigation into Buchanan, regarding political donations made to his campaign, because of questions about the reliability of key witnesses in the case.

REP. LAURA RICHARDSON

On August 2, 2012, the House adopted by voice vote a resolution (H Res 755) to concur in the House Committee on Ethics recommendation that Rep. Laura Richardson, D-Calif., be reprimanded and fined after the panel found that she had likely broken federal law and House rules by requiring her congressional staff to work on her reelection campaign. Richardson lost her reelection bid in November.

The panel's unflinching report, which was accompanied by the release of its investigatory findings, portrayed a lawmaker who unapologetically misused official resources and abused congressional staffers for personal gain. The committee said that, as part of the negotiated resolution, Richardson agreed to admit to the misdeeds listed in the report and to waive all rights in the matter with respect to House or committee rules. In a written statement, Richardson said she "takes this matter with the utmost seriousness and takes full responsibility for her actions."

The subcommittee probing Richardson "unanimously concluded that there was substantial reason to believe" she broke federal law, House rules, and the Code of Ethics for Government Service, Ethics Chair Jo Bonner, R-Ala., and ranking Democrat Linda T. Sánchez of California said in a joint statement. Richardson, the investigative subcommittee found, engaged in misconduct by "improperly using House resources for campaign, personal and nonofficial purposes; by requiring or compelling her official staff to perform campaign work; and by obstructing the investigation of the committee." She also altered and destroyed evidence during the probe, deliberately failed to hand over subpoenaed documents, and attempted to improperly influence witnesses.

As part of her agreement, Richardson would pay a $10,000 fine by December 1, 2012. In addition, the committee urged her to prohibit current government staffers from working on her 2012 reelection bid. Richardson ran in a redrawn Southern California district east of Los Angeles against fellow Democratic Rep. Janice Hahn. Richardson lost the November 6 race.

The House ethics committee in 2010 had examined an unorthodox financial transaction that allowed Richardson to repurchase a home that had fallen into foreclosure. *(111th Congress action, p. 656)*

REP. MAXINE WATERS

The House Committee on Ethics on September 21, 2012, cleared Rep. Maxine Waters, D-Calif., of wrongdoing following an inquiry that spanned three years and spurred allegations that the committee had mishandled the case. Those concerns had led to the hiring of an outside counsel. Waters's grandson and chief of staff, Mikael Moore, received a letter of reproval in the conflict-of-interest case, which centered on whether the Waterses had improperly intervened with Treasury Department officials on behalf of a bank in which her husband had a financial stake. *(111th Congress action, p. 656)*

The case began in the independent Office of Congressional Ethics, which in April 2009 reviewed allegations that Waters had asked Treasury Department officials to meet with representatives from the National Bankers Association. The ethics office focused on the group's discussion of assisting OneUnited Bank, given that Waters's husband had a financial stake in the institution and previously had served on its board. In August 2010, the ethics committee announced it had found Waters in violation of three House rules. In mid-November, a scheduled public trial was indefinitely postponed.

On July 18, 2011, the news organization Politico published internal committee documents that showed the delay was due in part to the belief by the committee staff director at the time that internal communications probably had compromised the committee's investigation. Waters said the exchanges were evidence that her due process rights had been violated and said that the committee's case against her should be dropped.

Before deciding whether it could proceed, the committee on July 20 voted unanimously to hire former Justice Department prosecutor and trial lawyer Billy Martin as an outside counsel to examine whether panel members and staffers had acted in ways that improperly affected the Waters case. During the course of carrying out Martin's task, approximately 100,000 pages of documents were reviewed and more than two dozen interviews were conducted. In February 2012, six committee members who had worked on the Waters probe voluntarily recused themselves at Martin's recommendation, and alternates were appointed to take their places.

Acting Chair Robert W. Goodlatte, R-Va., and ranking member John Yarmuth, D-Ky., told Waters in a June 6 letter, accompanied by a brief public statement, that Martin concluded that the committee had not violated the lawmaker's constitutional rights during her disciplinary proceedings, which amounted to the "notice and opportunity to be heard." Although Goodlatte and Yarmuth acknowledged that a former aide probably had broken rules by leaking confidential information, and that one had made racially insensitive remarks (it was not clear whether it was the same individual), the stand-in committee members unanimously decided that the behavior amounted to minor infractions that did not compromise the integrity of the proceedings, which the committee could resume.

On the same day that the Ethics Committee dismissed all charges of misconduct against Waters, September 21, 2012, it convened a rare public hearing to settle the question of whether to issue a letter of reproval to Mikael Moore, who was being charged with using Waters's office to intervene on behalf of the bank.

In clearing Waters, the panel cited evidence that she explicitly instructed Moore not to get involved with the bank and even approached Financial Services Committee Chair Barney Frank, D-Mass., to report the possible conflict of interest. Moore maintained that the committee, in its own findings, determined that the chronology of events was unknown, and because of that, it was not possible to say for sure whether Moore knowingly ignored Waters's instructions. He also said that the two e-mails cited as some proof of misconduct were not substantial enough to warrant hard evidence against him. But earlier testimony and correspondence suggested that Moore did know, or at least should have known, that it was against House rules to pursue legislation on behalf of an organization in which the member he was working for had a stake.

REP. JESSE L. JACKSON JR.

Rep. Jesse L. Jackson Jr. resigned from Congress on November 21, 2012, shortly after winning his reelection bid and on the heels of reports that he was in negotiations with federal prosecutors about alleged misuse of campaign funds. Any plea agreement reportedly would have required Jackson to resign from the House. The federal probe was unrelated to a House Ethics Committee review of Jackson over the attempts by Gov. Rod R. Blagojevich, D-Ill., to sell the Senate seat vacated when Barack Obama became president.

The House ethics panel voted October 13, 2011, to end the deferral of its probe of alleged ethics violations by Jackson, after the Justice Department withdrew the request for the panel to suspend its investigation. Jackson was accused of offering to raise money in 2008 for Blagojevich in exchange for a Senate appointment. Blagojevich ultimately appointed former state comptroller Roland W. Burris to the seat. A jury in June 2011 found Blagojevich guilty of numerous corruption charges, but Jackson claimed innocence, contending that he was not part of the Blagojevich scheme. *(Jackson ethics probe, 111th Congress, p. 653; Burris appointment, p. 647)*

When the ethics panel announced on December 2, 2011, that it would continue its investigation of Jackson, it also mentioned the results of a review of the case by the Office of Congressional Ethics, which found "probable cause" that Jackson had directed a third party to offer raise money for Blagojevich in exchange for appointing Jackson to the Senate or that Jackson knew this third party would make such an offer after Jackson had told him to advocate on his behalf with the governor. Jackson responded in a statement: "I have said from the beginning that I publicly and transparently sought to have the governor of Illinois appoint me to fulfill the final two years of then-Senator Barack Obama's term in the U.S. Senate. I did nothing illegal, unethical or inappropriate in that pursuit."

Amid reports of declining health and mounting legal troubles, Jackson was largely absent from the public eye and from Capitol Hill beginning June 10, 2012, when he took a medical leave of absence from the House, citing exhaustion. His office announced on July 11 that he was being treated for a mood disorder. It became public on August 13 that Jackson suffered from bipolar disorder. Meanwhile, multiple reports said that he was under investigation by federal prosecutors in Washington, D.C., over improper use of campaign money for personal use.

On February 20, 2013, Jackson pleaded guilty to one count of wire and mail fraud in connection with having spent $750,000 in campaign funds on personal items. The same day, Jackson's wife, Sandra, pleaded guilty to filing false joint federal income tax returns. The prosecution did not say what had launched the probe into Jackson's campaign funds but noted that it did not come out of the House ethics committee investigation into Jackson and Blagojevich. On August 14, Jackson was sentenced to thirty months in prison as well as three years of supervised release. His wife received a sentence of one year in prison and twelve months of supervised release.

REP. SHELLEY BERKLEY

The House Committee on Ethics on December 20, 2012, announced that it had found that Rep. Shelley Berkley, D-Nev., broke House rules, laws, and standards of conduct related to conflicts of interest when her office assisted her husband's medical practice with the Department of Veterans Affairs, Medicare, and Medicaid claims. At the same time, it cleared her for actions she took to save a kidney transplant program at a hospital where her husband's medical practice had a lucrative contract.

An investigative subcommittee did not recommend that Berkley be sanctioned and could not reach a consensus on whether a formal letter of reproval should be written. The committee agreed with the subcommittee's recommendation that the release of the investigatory report should serve as a reproval. It also noted that she had fully cooperated with the probe.

The committee's report noted that, between April 2008 and December 2010, Berkley's husband, Dr. Lawrence Lehrner, contacted her office four times on behalf of Kidney Specialists of Southern Nevada to discuss payments his practice was due from the Veterans Affairs Department, Medicare, and Medicaid. On two occasions, Berkley and her staff sought to address those issues. "Because such actions caused 'compensation to accrue to the beneficial interest' of Representative Berkley, the Committee finds that they violated [House rules]," the committee's report said.

The investigative subcommittee handling the case noted that no evidence existed that Berkley took action with the intent to enrich herself, and it said that she had a legitimate concern that government programs should expediently reimburse medical providers and that the sort of assistance she provided her husband's practice was similar to what she provided to other physicians.

The original complaint was filed by the Nevada Republican Party after a story appeared in the *New York Times* on September 5, 2011, on Berkley's actions in Congress vis-à-vis the business interests of her husband.

Chronology of Action on Congress: Election Issues

2009–2010

Congress reacted swiftly to the 2010 U.S. Supreme Court ruling in *Citizens United v. Federal Election Commission* (558 U.S. 310), which struck down provisions of the 2002 Bipartisan Campaign Reform Act (commonly known as McCain-Feingold, after its congressional sponsors) prohibiting corporations and unions from making independent political expenditures. However, with deep divides between the parties, no legislation to soften or reverse the decision cleared.

After alleged misadventures by the Association of Community Organizers for Reform Now (ACORN) were secretly videotaped and made public, various congressional efforts were made to stop federal funds from going to the group, which for years had conducted well-publicized voter registration drives. Despite largely being exonerated of wrongdoing, ACORN disbanded as a result of the scandal.

CITIZENS UNITED RULING

The U.S. Supreme Court on January 21, 2010, handed down a decision in *Citizens United v. Federal Election Commission,* ruling that corporations have the same rights to political speech as individuals and, by extension, the same First Amendment right to spend money to influence elections. Critics, including President Barack Obama and many congressional Democrats, said the 5–4 decision not only swept away decades of campaign finance law but also effectively opened the floodgates for corporations to all but buy elections by swamping the airwaves with advertising for their preferred candidates or against those they opposed. *(Court case, pp. 584, 586)*

The ruling involved a caustic documentary, *Hillary: The Movie,* produced during Hillary Rodham Clinton's 2008 presidential campaign by Citizens United, a conservative nonprofit corporation. The Federal Election Commission (FEC) ruled that because the movie took a position against a particular candidate, it was effectively a campaign ad and would have to comply with existing campaign law. By siding with Citizens United, the Supreme Court effectively voided part of the 2002 Bipartisan Campaign Reform Act (PL 107-155)—often called "McCain-Feingold" after its Senate sponsors, Republican John McCain of Arizona and Democrat Russ Feingold of Wisconsin—and overturned a 1990 precedent (*Austin v. Michigan State Chamber of* Commerce, 494 U.S. 652) that permitted bans on direct spending by corporations on ads that promoted or disparaged individual candidates. *(McCain-Feingold, Congress and the Nation Vol. XI, p. 730; 1990 case, Congress and the Nation Vol. VIII, pp. 829, 955)*

Conservatives hailed the decision in *Citizens United,* which also applied to labor unions and nonprofit organizations, as a victory for free speech. "When government seeks to use its full power, including the criminal law, to command where a person may get his or her information or what distrusted source he or she may not hear, it uses censorship to control thought," Justice Anthony M. Kennedy wrote for the majority.

For critics, the silver lining could be that eight justices also upheld existing regulations that were intended to make clear just who was paying for campaign advertising and other forms of political speech. And because the law the justices considered was an absolute ban on corporate and union spending, the decision theoretically left room for more tailored restrictions.

Campaign Finance

Democrats in 2010 tried without success to limit the impact of a Supreme Court ruling that opened the door for corporations and labor unions to directly fund campaign advertising. The House passed a bill (HR 5175) that would have required increased financial disclosure and disclaimers, but Republicans blocked a similar measure in the Senate (S 3628). *(112th Congress action, p. 681)*

The legislation was a response to a January 21, 2010, Supreme Court ruling in *Citizens United v. Federal Election Commission* (558 U.S. 310) that struck down laws that prevented corporations, unions, and certain other interest groups, including so-called 527 political advocacy groups, from spending their own funds for advertising that called for the election or defeat of a candidate. The Court decided 5–4 that those laws violated the right to free speech under the First Amendment, effectively ruling that corporations had the same free-speech rights as individuals. The decision applied to advertising expenditures that were not coordinated with a political campaign. Corporations were still barred from contributing directly to a campaign. *(Citizens United ruling, box, p. 677; Court ruling, p. 586)*

Democrats warned that the ruling could allow wealthy businesses to buy elections by pouring money into campaign ads and drowning out the voices of less well-funded grassroots groups. President Barack Obama took the controversial step of chiding the Supreme Court justices for the decision as they sat before him during his 2010 State of the Union address. But, from the start, a large coalition of business groups, led by the U.S. Chamber of Commerce, opposed the legislation as an infringement on the right of free speech, and they had strong Republican backing.

HOUSE COMMITTEE ACTION

The House Administration Committee approved HR 5175 by voice vote on May 20, 2010, and formally reported it (H Rept 111-492, Part 1) on May 25.

The Democracy Is Strengthened by Casting Light on Spending in Elections (DISCLOSE) Act, drafted by Chris Van Hollen, D-Md., would create new disclaimer requirements, including a "stand by your ad" provision under which individuals or groups funding an ad would have to identify themselves. Organizations would be required to provide the identities of donors who gave at least $600 in a year for campaign-related activities. The bill required that chief executives appear in ads funded by their organizations and included a ban on election-related spending by companies that received federal aid or had significant foreign ownership or large government contracts.

The bill also would prohibit companies that received assistance under the Troubled Asset Relief Program (TARP; PL 110-343) from making political expenditures until they have repaid the government. *(TARP, p. 60, 62, 75)*

During the markup, the committee adopted by voice vote an amendment by Zoe Lofgren, D-Calif., to exempt from the ban businesses whose government contracts were less than $1 million. The concern, she said, was undue influence by large corporations. The panel rejected 3–5, along party lines, an amendment by the panel's ranking Republican, Dan Lungren of California, to prohibit labor unions that had representational contracts with the government from making election expenditures. The amendment was part of an unsuccessful effort by Republicans to apply the election-financing prohibitions to labor unions in the same fashion that they would apply to corporations.

Obama said he supported the legislation because it would "shine an unprecedented light on corporate spending in political campaigns so that the American people can clearly see who is trying to influence campaigns for public office."

HOUSE FLOOR ACTION

The House on June 24 passed a modified version of HR 5175, after extensive prodding by Democratic leaders. The **key vote of 219–206 (R 2–170; D 217–36)** came after the House adopted a rule for floor debate that created a controversial carve-out exempting the National Rifle Association (NRA) and certain other tax-exempt nonprofit organizations from the bill's reporting and disclaimer requirements. Several interest groups—including the NRA, the National Right to Life Committee, and the U.S. Chamber of Commerce—had raised concerns over the committee-approved version of the bill, arguing that the reporting and disclaimer provisions were too onerous. *(2010 key votes, p. 803)*

In response, lawmakers announced plans June 14 to exempt nonprofit tax-exempt groups with more than one million dues-paying members in the United States that had been in existence for at least ten years and received no more than 15 percent of their funding from corporations or unions. The NRA accepted the language, but progressive Democrats and members of the Congressional Black Caucus—along with groups such as the Brady Campaign to Prevent Gun Violence and the U.S. Public Interest Research Group—objected, saying there should not be exemptions for special interest groups. Fiscally conservative Blue Dog Democrats supported the NRA exemption but voiced concern about taking a politically difficult vote on a bill that might never be considered in the Senate. Most Republicans continued to oppose the measure, as did a coalition of hundreds of groups, including the U.S. Chamber of Commerce, the National Association of Manufacturers, and Planned Parenthood Federation of America.

As House leaders worked to garner votes, Senate majority leader Harry Reid, D-Nev., and Sen. Charles E. Schumer, D-N.Y., sent a letter to Speaker Nancy Pelosi, D-Calif., pledging that the Senate would consider the legislation soon, "so it could be signed by the president in time to take effect for the 2010 elections." Schumer was the sponsor of the companion bill, S 3628.

A new agreement was released June 23 that reduced the threshold for the exemption to organizations with more than 500,000 dues-paying members, which included the Sierra Club among other groups. That change was included in the rule.

During the floor debate on June 24, the House adopted, 274–152, an amendment by Patrick J. Murphy, D-Pa., to require sponsors of political advertisements to disclose their locations and adopted by voice vote an amendment by Dennis J. Kucinich, D-Ohio, to clarify that the provisions of the bill would apply to companies with federal leases to drill for oil and gas in the outer continental shelf. The same day, it rejected, by 57–369, an amendment by Steve King, R-Iowa, that would have exempted contributions made beginning in 2009 from the existing law on federal campaign contributions and, by 208–217, a motion by Lungren to send the bill back to committee with instructions to add language that would have banned contributions by lobbyists whose clients included individuals or governments that repeatedly supported acts of international terrorism. It also would have prohibited the use of campaign funds for political robocalls to those on the national "do not call" list.

SENATE FLOOR ACTION

The Senate voted 57–41 on July 27 to reject an effort to end a GOP filibuster on a motion to proceed to S 3628. No Republicans backed the cloture motion, which needed sixty votes. All Democrats voted for it except Reid, who voted "no" to have the option of again calling up the bill.

As with the House bill, Schumer's measure sought to promote transparency by requiring chief executives to appear in ads funded by their organizations. It also would have banned election-related spending by companies that received federal aid, those with large government contracts, or those with more than 20 percent foreign ownership.

Schumer made several changes to the bill in an unsuccessful effort to defuse GOP arguments that it would give unions an unfair advantage and to try to win over either of Maine's two moderate Republican senators, Olympia J. Snowe and Susan Collins.

He removed a provision that would have required businesses, unions, and other groups to disclose transfers of $10,000 or more to, from, or between their affiliates. He also struck two provisions that were in the House version: one to prevent oil and gas companies that drilled in the outer continental shelf from funding political advertisements, and another to require organizations to disclose their location in TV and radio ads.

But Republicans remained unified in opposing the bill. Minority Leader Mitch McConnell of Kentucky called it a "monstrosity" whose sole purpose was to give Democrats an election-year advantage. Schumer said he would "keep fighting and fighting" for passage, but when Reid tried to proceed to the bill in September, Republicans united once again to defeat a motion to invoke cloture. The **key vote of 59–39 (R 0–39; D 57–0; I 2–0)** on September 23, 2010, effectively rendered the legislation dead. Republicans stuck together in part because of concerns about protecting the rights of the minority party to offer amendments to legislation on the floor, although Schumer said that if the bill reached the floor, Democrats would amend it to make it effective in 2011 and would "welcome Republican amendments." *(2010 key votes, p. 767)*

During lengthy debate September 22, Democrats again criticized the Supreme Court for its decision in *Citizens United*. Speaking at a fund-raiser that same day, Obama pressed Democratic donors to support the party to counter independent expenditure groups backing GOP candidates. "None of them will disclose who is paying for these ads. They are spending tens of millions of dollars against Democratic candidates without telling the American people where that flood of money is coming from," he said.

Republicans remained unconvinced. "There are many concerns I have with this legislation," Snowe said in a statement, "including the continued unequal treatment of unions and corporations, and I continue to believe this bill would not withstand constitutional scrutiny due to the overly burdensome federal mandates it would impose upon free speech."

In its last action on S 3628, the Senate on September 23 rejected, 59–39, a motion to invoke cloture on the motion to proceed to consideration of the bill. (A cloture motion requires sixty votes to succeed.) Both S 3628 and HR 5175 died upon adjournment.

Shareholder Approval of Campaign Spending

The House Financial Services Committee on July 29, 2010, approved, 35–28, and on September 22 reported the Shareholder Protection Act (HR 4790—H Rept 111-620, Part 1), which would require shareholder approval of expenditures on elections and would make boards of directors vote on expenditures of more than $50,000. The bill, sponsored by Michael E. Capuano, D-Mass., saw no further action. A related Senate measure (S 3004), sponsored by Sherrod Brown, D-Ohio, was described by the Congressional Research Service as amending "the Securities Exchange Act of 1934 [PL 73-291] to require issuers of securities to disclose to their shareholders electioneering communications they have made or in which they have participated" and requiring "an issuer to obtain prior approval by majority vote of all shareholders before making or participating in any electioneering communication." The Citizens Right to Know Act was referred to the Senate Banking, Housing, and Urban Affairs Committee and died upon adjournment.

Both HR 4790 and S 3004 had the backing of a new coalition of campaign finance activists, investment firms, and shareholder groups. Among them were the Center for Political Accountability, which sponsored scores of related shareholder resolutions and persuaded nearly half of the one hundred largest U.S. firms to disclose voluntarily their political spending; the Interfaith Center on Corporate Responsibility, a coalition of approximately three hundred faith-based institutional investors; and the Social Investment Forum, which represented nearly four hundred investment professionals and organizations.

Defunding ACORN

Efforts in both the House and Senate in the 111th Congress to defund the Association of Community Organizers for Reform Now (ACORN) proved moot when the organization disbanded. According to ACORN's website, it was "the nation's largest community organization of low and moderate-income families, working together for social justice and stronger communities. From 1970 to its end in 2010, ACORN had grown to more than 175,000 member families, organized in 850 neighborhood chapters in 75 cities across the U.S. and in cities in Canada, the Dominican Republic and Peru." Republicans had long set their sights against the ACORN, referring, for example, to its voter registration drives, which it had conducted since the 1980s, as "voter fraud." The group claimed to have registered approximately 1.3 million voters in key swing states that went for Barack Obama, the Democratic presidential candidate, in 2008.

The tipping point came after the April 2009 release of a videotape made with a hidden camera by a team of conservative activists of ACORN employees apparently advising a couple, a female prostitute accompanied by a man, about how to conceal their line of work, evade taxes, and handle undocumented, underage sex workers. Republicans quickly moved to rein in government assistance to the group. The office of House Minority Leader John A. Boehner, R-Ohio, reported that ACORN had received $53 million in federal funds since 1994. The organization also received support from private donations.

The Defund ACORN Act (HR 357), sponsored by Boehner, and the Protect Taxpayers from ACORN Act (S 1687), sponsored by Mike Johanns, R-Neb., would prohibit any federal agreement being awarded and any federal funds being provided to ACORN. Also, federal employees and contractors could not promote ACORN or any ACORN-related affiliate. Neither bill saw congressional action. Both chambers, however, did attach ACORN defunding language to other various pieces of legislation. For example, on September 14, 2009, the Senate adopted, 83–7, an amendment by Johanns to the fiscal 2010 Transportation and Housing and Urban Development appropriations measure (HR 3288) that would bar ACORN from getting any money that the bill would spend on low-income housing programs. Forty-nine Democrats and thirty-three Republicans voted for the measure. The Senate by a vote of 85–11 on September 17 adopted a Johanns amendment to the fiscal 2010 Interior appropriations bill (HR 2996) that would bar funds in the bill from being provided to ACORN. Forty-five Democrats and Independent Joseph I. Lieberman of Connecticut joined thirty-nine Republicans in support of the amendment. Hours before the Senate vote, the House voted, 345–75, to agreed to a procedural motion by Darrell Issa, R-Calif., to add language to a student loan bill (HR 3221) requiring that no federal funds be directed to ACORN. On the vote, 172 Democrats joined the 173 Republicans backing the move. The Senate by voice vote on November 5 adopted a Johanns amendment to HR 2847, a fiscal 2010 Commerce-Justice-Science appropriations bill, prohibiting the use of funds for ACORN. *(Fiscal 2010 appropriations, p. 137; student loans, p. 476)*

Trade groups for government contractors subsequently pointed out that the language added to HR 3221 to penalize ACORN could apply more broadly. It would deny federal contracts to any organization that was indicted on charges of violating a campaign finance law, that had a state corporate charter revoked, or that filed a fraudulent form with a state or federal regulatory agency. Companies employing individuals indicted for campaign finance violations also would be subject to the ban. Trade groups said that that sounded like a denial of due process. Of particular concern was that the Issa provision would punish companies for the unauthorized actions of employees and deny contracts to companies accused of wrongdoing at the state level.

Shortly before ACORN closed its doors, the General Accountability Office (GAO) on June 14, 2010, issued a preliminary report, created upon direction of the Consolidated Appropriations Act (HR 3288—PL 111-117), indicating that ACORN did not misuse the more than $40 million in federal funds it received between 2005 and 2009. The GAO, however, did find five cases in which ACORN employees pleaded guilty to charges of voter fraud. *(PL 111-117, p. 127)*

Conservative activist James O'Keefe, who was the man in the ACORN videotape, earned a reputation for surreptitiously videotaping staged encounters and then editing them to show bad behavior, including a 2011 recording of National Public Radio executives. He was arrested on January 26, 2010, along with three other men, for trying to tamper with phones in the New Orleans office of Sen. Mary L. Landrieu, D-La.

2011–2012

Republicans were instrumental in stopping a campaign finance bill in the Senate and were successful in passing legislation in the House to abolish the Presidential Election Campaign Fund. Spared the chopping block was the Election Assistance Commission.

Campaign Finance

Senate Republicans in 2012 twice blocked legislation (S 3369) to require greater disclosure of campaign contributions. Democrats said the Democracy Is Strengthened by Casting Light on Spending in Elections (DISCLOSE) Act would bring greater transparency, and Republicans said it would infringe on First Amendment rights and could threaten the safety of donors. *(111th Congress action, p. 678)*

S 3369, which was sponsored by Sheldon Whitehouse, D-R.I., would require groups to disclose all expenditures of $10,000 or more on election-related communications, as well as the names of individual and corporate contributors that gave $10,000 or more to fund such efforts. An exemption would be provided for segregated accounts set up by groups that contributed to operations besides election-related independent campaigns. Lawmakers on July 17 rejected a procedural motion that would have allowed the Senate to take up S 3369. The 53–45 vote was strictly along party lines. Sixty votes were needed to invoke cloture and, thus, proceed to the measure. The vote came one day after the Senate rejected the initial cloture motion, 51–44. Senate majority leader Harry Reid, D-Nev., had filed a motion to reconsider that vote, which allowed the Senate to vote again.

Complaints emerged from both ends of the political spectrum about the tone of the 2012 congressional and presidential campaigns, but the parties sharply disagreed about whether S 3369 would change it. After the initial vote on July 16, Democrats seized on the opportunity to draw an election-year distinction between themselves and Republicans on campaign finance disclosures. They stayed past midnight—about seven hours after the vote was held—to denounce Republicans' unwillingness to allow the bill to move forward. Supporters of the measure blamed anonymous contributors to nonprofit groups with "patriotic-sounding names" for negative campaign ads. But Republicans said that the legislation would violate the First Amendment, expose wealthy donors to threats of harm and intimidation, and allow unions to "fly below the regulatory radar." Sen. Saxby Chambliss, R-Ga., charged that union members could give large numbers of small donations that would fall below the threshold for mandatory

CAMPAIGN ADS ON PUBLIC TV

In an April 12, 2012, decision, a panel for the U.S. Court of Appeals for the Ninth Circuit ruled 2–1 in favor of the ban on commercial ads on public TV and radio stations but declared that issue and political ads were protected by the First Amendment. The ban on political and issue advertising is "a content-based restriction on speech, and this restriction in particular burdens speech on issues of public importance and political speech," Circuit judge Carlos Bea wrote for the majority.

The government argued that for-profit and political ads would harm public broadcasting by diluting its educational mission, encouraging mass market programming, and making public broadcasting indistinguishable from commercial media. In a dissent, Judge Richard Paez agreed. "For almost 60 years, noncommercial public broadcasters have been effectively insulated from the lure of paid advertising," he wrote. "The court's judgment will disrupt this policy and could jeopardize the future of public broadcasting."

The case involved the Minority Television Project, an independent public broadcaster that aired close to two thousand ads over a three-year period for Chevrolet, State Farm, and other for-profit companies on KMTP-TV in San Francisco, Calif. In 2002, the Federal Communications Commission imposed a $10,000 fine on the group for violating the ad rules. The broadcaster sued, arguing that the federal ban violated the First Amendment. A trial court upheld the ban, but the Ninth Circuit panel disagreed.

The nation's more than thirteen hundred public TV and radio stations have operated essentially commercial-free since Congress created the Corporation for Public Broadcasting in 1967 (PL 90-129). In 1981, Congress allowed stations to raise private money through underwriting announcements and sponsorships, but the law specifically barred political or public issues ads, as well as ads on behalf of for-profit entities (PL 97-35). *(1967 law, Congress and the Nation Vol. II, p. 297; 1981 law, Congress and the Nation Vol. VI, p. 264)*

Republicans had argued for decades that public broadcasting should raise more money through advertising and not get public funding. Public broadcasters typically get about 15 percent of their funding from the federally supported Corporation for Public Broadcasting and collect the rest from grants and through audience pledge drives.

A federal appeals court in San Francisco on November 21 said it voted to grant the federal government's request for a rehearing of the appeals court ruling before an eleven-judge panel. The hearing was scheduled for March 2013.

disclosure. The bill, thus, would favor unions over the private sector. Whitehouse disagreed, saying the $10,000 threshold for reporting contributions would apply to all groups and individuals.

Backers of the legislation said negative ads were "drowning out the voices of regular American families who wish to participate in elections," Whitehouse said. He went on: "Campaigns are no longer waged by candidates and parties fighting over ideas; they are now waged by shadowy political attack groups posing as social welfare organizations." Whitehouse said anonymous spending made up 1 percent of outside spending in 2006, before the Supreme Court's ruling in *Citizens United v. Federal Election Commission* (558 U.S. 310) in 2010 ended restrictions on direct independent campaign expenditures by corporations, unions, and other outside groups. In 2010, anonymous spending constituted about 44 percent of campaign contributions, he said, suggesting those previously limited by spending limits were taking advantage of the changes. Reid said the existing system allowed for a small group of individuals to influence national politics disproportionately. (Citizens United *ruling, box, p. 677; Court case, p. 586)*

The Obama administration supported S 3369, saying in a statement of administration policy that it would "equip Americans with the tools to know who is attempting to influence the nation's elections."

Presidential Election Campaign Fund

In a symbolic attack by majority Republicans on the federal deficit, the House on January 26, 2011, by a vote of 239–160 passed a bill (HR 359) to end the Presidential Election Campaign Fund. The Congressional Budget Office estimated that the move, which would eliminate the $3 checkoff for public campaigns on 1040 tax forms, would reduce spending by $617 million over ten years. The official title of HR 359, which was sponsored by Tom Cole, R-Okla., was "To reduce Federal spending and the deficit by terminating taxpayer financing of presidential election campaigns and party conventions."

The fund had been set up after the Watergate scandal and provided matching funds for presidential primary candidates and grants for general election candidates who complied with spending and contribution limits (PL 92-178). The system also provided money to each major party for its national convention. According to the Federal Election Commission, every presidential election cycle since 1976 had been financed, at least in part, with public funds. In the 2008 election cycle nearly $136 million was spent, including almost $30 million for the party conventions. Democratic presidential nominee Barack Obama, however, opted out for his 2008 general election campaign—the first major-party presidential candidate to do so in the program's history, and a point emphasized by bill supporters. According to Republicans, taxpayer participation in the system declined from 28.7 percent in 1980 to 7.3 percent in 2009, revealing, in their view, general agreement among the public that the system had not worked. *(PL 92-178, Congress and the Nation Vol. III, p. 410)*

During floor consideration of HR 359 on January 26, the House adopted, 396–7, an amendment offered by Gary Peters, D-Mich., to specify that funds returned to the Treasury could be used only for reducing the deficit. As originally written, the measure directed the Treasury Department to transfer all amounts remaining in the fund after the date of enactment to the Treasury's general fund. The House rejected, 173–228, a motion to recommit offered by Tim Walz, D-Minn., that would have preserved the fund and required disclosure of foreign countries, companies, or individuals donating to campaigns, as well as donors spending more than $100,000 on those contests.

A statement of administration policy released January 25 expressed strong opposition to the bill, calling for the public financing system to be "fixed rather than dismantled." To that end, Reps. David E. Price, D-N.C., and Chris Van Hollen, D-Md., introduced a bill (HR 414) that would make a number of changes, including lifting spending limits, altering matching rates for small contributions, and requiring increased disclosures. It also would increase the amount of the checkoff to $10 per individual and eliminate public funding for national party conventions. HR 414 was referred to the House Administration Committee and the House Ways and Means Committee but saw no further action.

Election Assistance Commission

On June 22, 2011, the House rejected on a strict party-line vote of 235–187 a motion to suspend the rules and pass HR 672, which would eliminate the Election Assistance Commission. The vote fell short of the two-thirds majority needed under suspension of the rules. The House Administration Committee had approved the Election Support Consolidation and Efficiency Act by voice vote on May 25 and formally reported it (H Rept 112-100, Part 1) on June 2.

Established in 2002 as part of a law to overhaul federal elections (PL 107-252), the commission served as a national clearinghouse of election information and oversaw voting system testing and certification. Democrats maintained that it ensured that elections across the country were administered with integrity and that its dismantling could result in disenfranchisement. The House GOP majority said the commission was ineffective and wasted money. Sponsor Gregg Harper, R-Miss., and other bill advocates argued that the commission had outlived its usefulness. After developing guidance to meet the requirements of the 2002 law, the agency, they contended, no longer made meaningful contributions to the voter experience. It also faced lawsuits regarding its hiring practices. Harper added that terminating the commission and transferring some of its functions to the Federal Election Commission would save nearly $14 million annually. *(2002 law, Congress and the Nation Vol. XI, p. 726)*

Chronology of Action on Congress: Pay and Benefits

2009–2010

Lawmakers decided to forgo their annual automatic cost-of-living increases, keeping their salaries at 2009 levels.

A senator who objected to Interior Department policies successfully blocked a salary increase for the department secretary, a former senator whose pay was subject to the Ineligibility Clause.

Congressional Pay

Amidst a struggling economy and high unemployment, members of the 111th Congress in both 2009 and 2010 froze their salaries for the next year, that is, for 2010 and 2011, respectively. Thus, lawmakers' compensation was set at what they earned in 2009, which was a 2.8 percent increase from what they had received in 2008. Rank-and-file members earned $174,000 per year, and party leaders earned more: Speaker of the House, $223,500; House majority leader, House minority leader, Senate majority leader, Senate minority leader, and Senate president pro tempore, $193,400.

Under the terms of the Ethics Reform Act of 1989 (PL 101-194), lawmakers would receive an automatic cost-of-living increase unless they acted to stop it. The annual increases were based on a formula calculated by the Bureau of Labor Statistics, which took into consideration changes in private industry wages and salaries. *(1989 law, Congress and the Nation Vol. VIII, p. 920)*

2009 LEGISLATIVE ACTION

Congress implemented the 2010 pay freeze as part of the fiscal 2009 omnibus appropriations law (HR 1105—PL 111-8). The rule (H Res 184) for House floor consideration of HR 1105 had included an amendment to eliminate the cost-of-living increase for members of Congress that was scheduled to take effect automatically in January 2010. *(Omnibus appropriations, p. 119)*

In the Senate, Majority Leader Harry Reid, D-Nev., struck a deal with Sen. David Vitter, R-La., that allowed the chamber to pass a bill (S 620), by voice vote on March 17, 2009, that would eliminate automatic annual pay raises for members of Congress. The legislation, dubbed "A bill to repeal the provision of law that provides automatic pay adjustments for Members of Congress," would require lawmakers to vote on whether to give themselves an annual pay increase, repealing a provision of PL 101-194 that automatically enacts a congressional pay raise each year.

The majority leader's successful bid to revive the pay raise legislation marked an end to several rounds of sparring between Reid and Vitter over the issue, which gained attention as the economy declined. The dispute began when Vitter sought to force a vote March 10 on an amendment to HR 1105 that not only would have canceled the automatic pay adjustments but also would have sent the omnibus back to the House, thereby delaying, and potentially jeopardizing, its passage. The Senate narrowly tabled, or killed, Vitter's amendment by a vote of 52–45, after Vitter objected to the passage of a similar stand-alone bill (S 542) sponsored by Reid. Vitter accused Reid of offering that measure solely to drain support from his amendment.

2010 LEGISLATIVE ACTION

On May 14, 2010, President Barack Obama signed into law a bill (HR 5146—PL 111-165) that continued for another year the pay freeze that Congress instituted for 2010 as part of PL 111-8. Obama's fiscal 2011 budget had contained a $2 million increase for lawmakers' salaries and administrative expenses.

The House voted 402–15 on April 27 to suspend the rules and pass the bill, entitled "To provide that Members of Congress shall not receive a cost of living adjustment in pay during fiscal year 2011." The Senate passed the measure by voice vote the next day, completing congressional action. The Senate had passed similar legislation (S 3244) by voice vote on April 22.

Absent Congress's action to block it, most members would have received a $1,600 raise for 2011. *(Member pay, 112th Congress action, p. 685)*

Ineligibility Clause

The Ineligibility Clause, also known as the Emoluments Clause, of the U.S. Constitution (Article I, Section 6, Clause 2) prohibited members of Congress, during their terms in office, from taking jobs they voted to create or from benefiting from pay—emoluments—they voted to increase. For example, when President Barack Obama nominated Hillary Rodham Clinton to be secretary of state in 2009, some conservatives argued that she was ineligible because, as a senator from New York, she had voted for a cost-of-living pay hike for federal officials, including cabinet members, an increase from which she would benefit.

For more than a century, presidents had found the Ineligibility Clause a hindrance to their cabinet selections, and the favorite workaround in recent decades was devised by President Richard Nixon to have Sen. William Saxbe as his attorney general. In the so-called Saxbe fix, when a lawmaker was appointed to a federal post after having voted to raise the job's salary, his starting pay was rolled back to where it was before he cast the vote and it stayed there until the term of office for which he was elected expired. Clinton, for instance, was not eligible for a pay raise until the beginning of 2013, when her Senate term would have expired.

For Interior Secretary Ken Salazar, who was a senator from Colorado before joining the Obama cabinet in 2009, the situation got intense. Legislation (S J Res 3), entitled "A joint resolution ensuring that the compensation and other emoluments attached to the office of Secretary of the Interior are those which were in effect on January 1, 2005," was passed by voice vote in the Senate on January 6, 2009; a motion to suspend the rules and pass the joint resolution was agreed to by voice vote in the House on January 7; and the president signed the measure into law (PL 111-1) on January 16. Salazar's Senate term would have expired at the start of 2011, which meant he was eligible for a raise to the level of most other cabinet members in 2011. However, Louisiana senator David Vitter, a Republican, blocked legislation providing for the raise, promising to maintain his hold until Salazar approved more oil drilling leases in the Gulf of Mexico.

Salazar wrote Majority Leader Harry Reid of Nevada on May 24, 2011, accusing Vitter of attempted coercion and asking that his pay raise be dropped. Reid said it was "wrong for Sen. Vitter to try to get something in return for moving forward on a matter that the Senate has considered routine for more than a century." Citizens for Responsibility and Ethics in Washington on June 21, 2011, filed a complaint with the Senate Ethics Committee, asking that Vitter be investigated for bribery. *(Vitter ethics probe, p. 672)*

Debate was ongoing over whether the Saxbe fix was constitutional, which has never been tested.

2011–2012

Members of Congress continued to keep the cap on their salaries, but they managed to protect themselves from sequestration cuts.

Congressional Pay

Members' salaries remained fixed at the 2009 level in 2011 and 2012. *(111th Congress action, p. 683)*

In 2010, Congress froze lawmakers' pay for 2011 (PL 111-65). In addition, a fiscal 2011 continuing appropriations resolution (PL 111-322) stipulated that no adjustment would be made in the General Schedule (GS) base pay for federal workers before December 31, 2012. According to a September 24, 2013, Congressional Research Service (CRS) report entitled "Salaries of Members of Congress: Recent Actions and Historical Tables," that action effectively froze lawmakers' salaries, too, because "the percentage adjustment in Member pay may not exceed the percentage adjustment in the base pay of GS employees. . . . If not limited by GS pay, Member pay could have been adjusted by 1.3% in 2012." *(PL 111-322, p. 137; federal worker pay, pp. 621, 622)*

The fiscal 2013 continuing appropriations resolution (H J Res 117—PL 112-175), which was signed into law on September 28, 2012, extended the GS pay rate freeze for federal workers and, by extension, continued the freeze on lawmakers' salaries.

The American Taxpayer Relief Act of 2012 (HR 8—PL 112-240) provided that members would receive no adjustment in their salaries in fiscal 2013. The president signed the bill into law on January 2, 2013. *(PL 112-240, p. 185)*

Members' Pay and Sequestration

While the 2011 Budget Control Act (S 365—PL 112-25) provided automatic, across-the-board spending cuts if certain specified discretionary spending caps were not met—which resulted, for example, in the reduction of congressional office budgets and the furloughing of congressional staffers—the pay of members of Congress was unaffected. How that happened was unclear or, as the *Washington Post* on March 6, 2013, described the situation, it was "a mystery with conflicting explanations that led deep into a rabbit hole of federal budgeting arcana." *(PL 112-25, p. 160)*

Some news organizations, including CNN, claimed that the Twenty-seventh Amendment protected members' salaries from the sequester. The so-called Madison amendment, proposed as part of the Bill of Rights in 1789 but not ratified until 1992, prohibited midterm changes in congressional pay. That is, an increase or decrease in salary could take effect only after an intervening election had taken place. The amendment was meant to restrain sitting members from setting their own salaries. (The courts have ruled that the amendment does not affect the annual cost-of-living adjustment made to congressional pay.) However, President Barack Obama signed S 365 into law on August 2, 2011, and the 2012 elections were held before the sequestration took effect in 2013. *(Madison amendment, Congress and the Nation Vol. VIII, p. 972)*

Pursuant to the 2012 Sequestration Transparency Act (HR 5872—PL 112-155), signed into law on August 7, 2012, the Office of Management and Budget (OMB) was to prepare a report on the sequestration to be submitted to Congress. In its report, OMB said that congressional salaries were exempt from PL 112-25, but it provided no explanation for why.

The newspaper *The Hill* on April 2, 2013, explained that the reason members' pay was spared the ax could be found in the 1985 Balanced Budget and Emergency Deficit Control Act (PL 99-177), popularly known as the Gramm-Rudman-Hollings anti-deficit law. The automatic cuts mechanism provided for in PL 112-25 were implemented according to the system of spending sequesters enacted as part of PL 99-177. Subject to the cuts were federal accounts; that is, appropriations made by Congress. However, members' pay was provided through a permanent appropriations account. Thus, according to *The Hill*, OMB did not apply the sequester to congressional pay. *(PL 99-177, Congress and the Nation Vol. VII, p. 44)*

Online Advertising

During consideration of the fiscal 2013 legislative branch appropriations measure (HR 5882), the House by a vote of 148–261 on June 8, 2012, rejected an amendment, offered by Jeff Flake, R-Ariz., that would bar the use of funds in the bill for members, committees, and leadership offices to purchase online advertising on websites outside of their own official sites.

The House Appropriations Committee on May 31 had rejected by voice vote a Flake amendment to HR 5882 barring lawmakers from using their member representational allowances—which covered salaries, travel funds, and other office expenses—to pay to promote their events or activities online. During markup of the legislation, panel leaders said the amendment could reduce members' ability to communicate with constituents, as Internet ads could increase traffic to their websites. Flake warned of the potential for abuse with online advertising.

Disclaimers in Mailings

During House Appropriations Committee markup of the fiscal 2013 legislative branch appropriations bill (HR 5882), panel members rejected by voice vote an amendment offered by Jeff Flake, R-Ariz. to require members to insert into leaflets sent to constituents disclaimers that detailed how much members spent on the mailing campaigns.

Existing law required members to notify readers that mail was "prepared, published and mailed at taxpayers' expense" in at least 7-point type in a "prominent place" on envelopes or wrappers.

CHAPTER 16

The Obama Presidency

The Presidency of Barack Obama, 2009–2012

Few presidents have assumed office with higher expectations and greater challenges than Barack Obama. His place in history as the nation's first African American leader, his soaring rhetoric, and his campaign built on a vision of hope and change gave many Americans the belief that something existential had taken place—that perhaps the nation had finally moved past both its troubled racial past and seemingly endless cycle of partisan stalemates into a different and perhaps more harmonious and productive era. The national enthusiasm was such that the crowd for Obama's inauguration on January 20, 2009, was believed to set a record attendance for any event in the nation's capital, with an estimated 1.8 million people witnessing the proceedings.

Such enthusiasm was important, given that the nation faced a unique set of difficulties that would challenge any leader, let alone one whose national experience amounted to just four years in the Senate. The United States was engaged in dual wars in Iraq and Afghanistan, the economy was at its weakest than at any time since the Great Depression in the 1930s, and the soaring national debt hampered a strong federal response. Perhaps to tamp down expectations, Obama delivered a somewhat muted inaugural address, acknowledging the difficulties of the times while reassuring Americans that better times lay ahead. "That we are in the midst of crisis is now well understood," he said. "Our nation is at war, against a far-reaching network of violence and hatred. Our economy is badly weakened, a consequence of greed and irresponsibility on the part of some, but also our collective failure to make hard choices and prepare the nation for a new age. . . . Less measurable but no less profound is a sapping of confidence across our land—a nagging fear that America's decline is inevitable, and that the next generation must lower its sights." The challenges, he added, "will not be met easily or in a short span of time. But know this, America—they will be met." *(Address text, p. 877)*

As if to underscore the difficulties, the very administration of the oath of office by Chief Justice John Roberts was fumbled by the two men in the recitation of the words. Roberts administered it a second time in the White House the following day, a precaution designed to forestall any constitutional challenges.

The events on inauguration day seemed to foreshadow much of Obama's first term: great excitement (and controversy) over ambitious plans that ran headlong into the difficult details of legislating and administering. At the end of his first term, in 2012, the president could take satisfaction in a number of significant achievements. His administration helped steady the economy through a number of bold initiatives to aid the banking and automotive sectors and steer hundreds of billions of dollars to companies and workers. It won passage of a massive health care bill designed to extend health insurance to most Americans. It improved the nation's reputation overseas—so much so that Obama won the Nobel Peace Prize after just nine months in office despite questions over what he had accomplished to have earned such recognition so early in his term. The administration also extricated the United States from war in Iraq, oversaw the tracking down and killing of terrorist leader Osama bin Laden, severely disrupted the Al Qaeda network with targeted drone attacks and other tactics, and waged a successful bombing campaign that ended the regime of Muammar Gaddafi in Libya.

In other ways, Obama fell short. Faced with congressional opposition, he failed to fulfill several of his campaign promises, particularly when it came to limiting emissions of carbon dioxide and other greenhouse gases blamed for climate change, and overhauling the nation's immigration laws. Still, few presidents could point to so many first-term accomplishments.

Yet virtually every one of Obama's victories came with major caveats. Although the unemployment rate gradually declined after peaking late in Obama's first year, it was no lower at 7.8 percent when he won reelection in 2012 than when he was inaugurated. Similarly, the nation's gross domestic product grew after a devastating drop in late 2008, but the increases were in fits and starts, averaging no more than a couple of percentage points per quarter from 2009 to 2012. As a result, the economy remained fragile during his entire first term, leaving Obama and his fellow Democrats vulnerable to charges that their often-expensive policies were doing little good for working Americans.

President Barack Obama looks at the Nobel Peace Prize medal at the Norwegian Nobel Institute in Oslo, Norway, on December 10, 2009.
Source: Official White House Photo by Pete Souza

In addition, the success of the health care overhaul remained in doubt as Obama's first term wound down. Implementation of the law, which barely withstood legal challenges, was slowed by opposition from a number of Republican governors while failing to excite much enthusiasm among many Americans who would need to participate in state insurance exchanges to make the system work as planned. In addition, many Americans remained skeptical or deeply opposed to the requirement that every person buy health insurance or pay a penalty.

Implementation of another major Obama initiative, overhauling Wall Street regulations, also moved slowly because of uncertainties over the new law.

For all of Obama's foreign policy successes, the world remained almost as dangerous when he took the oath of office in January 2013 after winning reelection in 2012 as when he began his first term. A surge of troops in Afghanistan appeared to have done little to quell violence in that country; Iran was believed to be closer to success in development of a nuclear weapon; North Korea—already in possession of nuclear capability—remained a major threat; little if any progress could be discerned in relations between Israel and its neighbors; and the European Union was struggling to contain potentially crippling financial defaults by member countries. The continued threats to America came into tragic focus on September 11, 2012, when a heavily armed group attacked the American diplomatic mission at Benghazi, Libya, killing four people including U.S. Ambassador J. Christopher Stevens.

But perhaps Obama's greatest setback had to do with his failure to win over even a small number of congressional Republicans for most of his top priorities. The continued economic weakness, among other factors, enabled Republicans to retake control of the House and bolster their Senate minority in the 2010 midterm elections. Although Obama won a few surprising victories in the lame duck session after the election—including an extension of unemployment insurance, ratification of a new nuclear treaty with Russia, and the end of the military's "don't ask, don't tell" policy that barred openly gay, lesbian, and bisexual people from serving—the new Republican majority essentially ended any prospect of Obama winning passage of another major legislative initiative. Instead, the president was forced on the defensive, trying to protect his priorities from steep budget cuts that were instituted by House Republicans, many of whom were influenced by the rock-ribbed, antispending philosophy of the Tea Party.

Indeed, the second half of the Obama administration, at least in terms of domestic policy, looked diametrically different than the first two years: instead of advancing historically significant initiatives to reshape the American economy and expand the reach of the federal government, the president focused his energies on trying to persuade Congress to lift the debt ceiling cap and forestall spending cuts of tens of billions of dollars. For their part, the Republicans were hardly subtle in their disdain for Obama. Shortly before the 2010 midterm elections, Senate Minority Leader Mitch McConnell of Kentucky said bluntly, "The single most important thing we want to achieve is for President Obama to be a one-term president."

The conflict also spilled over into the confirmation process and escalated dramatically during the traditional period for the 2011–2012 winter recess. Congress did not officially go into recess because Republicans wanted to block the appointment of Ohio attorney general Richard Cordray as director of the newly created Consumer Financial Protection Bureau. Although Obama had made fewer than thirty recess appointments before January 2012 (George W. Bush, in contrast, made 171 recess appointments during his two terms), the White House claimed authority to appoint Cordray and others while Congress remained in *pro forma* sessions. The action touched off a legal battle that continued into the beginning of Obama's second term. Obama also struggled to fill vacant district and appellate court federal judgeships, although his two Supreme Court nominees in 2009 and 2010 won approval without full-scale battles. The problem with judgeships was twofold: the president moved slowly to make nominations (in part, perhaps, because of Republicans not recommending nominees in states where they held both Senate seats), while Republicans used delaying tactics to block some of those who had been nominated. There were seventy-seven vacant judgeships in January 2013 as opposed to fifty-three in January 2009.

In retrospect, Obama's strengths and weaknesses as chief executive were telegraphed by his two biggest legislative victories: the economic stimulus and an overhaul of the health care system.

In his first month in office, Obama won enactment of the sweeping American Recovery and Reinvestment Act of 2009, an approximately $800 billion measure designed to apply Keynesian economics of government spending to stimulate the economy, with an emphasis on funding Democratic priorities such as renewable energy. Determined to win Republican votes, the White House had targeted the $800 billion figure both because that appeared to be the limit of what was politically achievable and because analysts hoped that would be sufficient to inject the economy with the jolt needed to restore it back to health. Indeed, two Obama staffers drafted a memo before the inauguration that estimated that a generic stimulus measure of $775 billion could help keep the nation's unemployment rate to no more than 8 percent. Unfortunately, the economy was in far worse shape than the administration or many independent experts realized; for example, the nation's gross domestic product had dropped in the fourth quarter of 2008 by almost 9 percent even though the initial government estimates that were available to the new administration indicated a much less drastic decline of 3.8 percent. As a result, unemployment kept climbing to a peak of more than 10 percent late in 2009 and was much higher in some hard-hit states. That gave ammunition to critics who said the stimulus fell short of its goals—both those on the right who said it was a costly mistake that exacerbated the deficit and those on the left who said the president should have been bolder. Although the stimulus in fact almost certainly helped stop the economy's free fall, it left Obama still contending with a high jobless rate while becoming increasingly handcuffed by the nation's worsening debt.

Nevertheless, Obama in the middle of 2009 made the politically risky decision to focus on health care instead of job creation. This would fulfill his campaign promise of instituting a system of universal health care and enable Democrats to achieve what had become perhaps the party's number-one priority. But the battle over health care, while ultimately won, drastically weakened Obama's political standing while producing a complex new insurance system that left Americans divided and analysts uncertain over its merits.

The president made a series of missteps, beginning with the nomination of former Senate Majority Leader Tom Daschle, D-S.D., to head the Department of Health and Human Services and serve as the administration's point person on the issue. The White House chose to disregard Daschle's past lobbying activities, even though they seemed to violate its high ethical standards. But the strategy backfired when Daschle withdrew amid criticism of those activities and, more seriously, a series of tax problems, leaving Obama without a key Washington insider to oversee the legislative debate. Second, the president left most of the health care measure's details up to Congress. This meant that a multitude of House and Senate committees crafted often conflicting plans, stalling forward movement and giving critics more time to assail individual provisions. In addition, he made little effort to sell the plan to the public, seemingly unaware that falling popular support endangered both his top priority and his party. Senate Democrats lost their filibuster-proof majority at the beginning of 2010 when voters in heavily Democratic Massachusetts, apparently reacting to the health care proposal and a relatively weak Democratic candidate, elevated Republican Scott Brown in a special election to an open seat previously held by Sen. Edward Kennedy, who had died. Perhaps most critically, Obama assumed that he could win some Republican support for a plan that drew heavily from the GOP's own ideas in the 1990s and the system that Republican governor Mitt Romney had put in place in Massachusetts. Instead, the president faced unrelenting opposition from Republicans who worried that the federal government was overreaching and who also sensed a political opening. Even though Obama signed the measure into law in April 2010, his administration never entirely regained its footing.

In addition to the tactical errors, the economic stimulus and health care bills also revealed one of the most baffling aspects of Obama's presidency: his ability to be cautious and bold almost simultaneously. The stimulus was an enormous initiative, roughly equal to the amount of money the nation spent in the wars in Iraq and Afghanistan under Bush. Yet it was also far smaller than met the eye, splintering the cash in three ways: tax cuts and credits, financial assistance to state budgets, and infrastructure and investment. The stimulus did not showcase any major projects, as the Hoover Dam had done when it was built between 1931 and 1936 in the midst of the Great Depression, and it failed to capture the public imagination.

With health care, Obama would not go as far as many Democrats who favored a government-run system, preferring the less dramatic step of expanding coverage by private insurers. But after a series of political setbacks caused some of his aides to advise scaling back the legislation, he insisting on sticking with the entire plan. The stories he was hearing of young mothers who had cancer and lacked health insurance, just like his own mother, stiffened his resolve. Describing a meeting with a Wisconsin mother, he told a top White House aide: "She's terrified that she's going to die and leave her family bankrupt," he said. "So you know, this fight is worth it. We have to keep going."

But Obama avoided other contentious issues, such as gun control. He waited until the 2012 election before endorsing gay marriage, safely after polls showed the public warming to the point of view. He conceded ground to Republicans in negotiations over budget cuts, signing bills to impose deep cuts in spending instead of the balanced approach he favored that could also include tax increases. Overseas, he responded to civil war in Libya by sending in American bombers despite considerable criticism (and without seeking congressional approval). But he took little action when civil war broke out in Syria in early 2011. When he ran for reelection, he eschewed the big ideas and promises of change from his 2008 campaign, instead focusing on waves of negative ads against Republican nominee Mitt Romney, the former Massachusetts governor.

To some extent, the president's difficulties were of his own making. Far from the stereotype of the back-slapping pol, Obama appeared disinterested in building strong bonds with other public figures. In a 2009 meeting with House Republicans, he bluntly rebuked Rep. Eric Cantor of Virginia, the Republican whip at the time. "Elections have consequences," the president said. "And, Eric, I won." His chilly relationship with House Republican leader John A. Boehner of Ohio scuttled what little chance there was of a deficit-cutting "grand bargain" of tax hikes and spending cuts once Republicans took the House. Under the headline "Obama: The Loner President," a 2011 profile in the *Washington Post* began: "Beyond the economy, the wars and the polls, President Obama has a problem: people. This president endures with little joy the small talk and back-slapping of retail politics, rarely spends more than a few minutes on a rope line, refuses to coddle even his biggest donors." Not only did he eschew small talk, Obama sometimes came across in negotiations as scolding those with other views.

Oddly, despite his considerable oratorical skills, the president often failed to communicate effectively outside the Beltway. Rather than whip up public support for his positions, as had such successful predecessors as Ronald Reagan and Bill Clinton, he often seemed oddly listless, content to let Congress drive the message while failing to spotlight his victories. Even though the stimulus lowered taxes for working Americans, White House aides lamented how many voters instead attributed their higher paychecks to raises from their employers. Obama also risked appearing out of touch during moments of crisis—not because he was disengaged but rather because he did not want to make pronouncements before knowing all the facts. To some extent, this was an outgrowth of the "no-drama Obama" persona that helped steady his presidential campaign. Although the style could project confident leadership, it also could leave Americans impatient or baffled. "Whether things seem to be going very well or very badly around him—whether he is announcing the death of Osama bin Laden or his latest compromise in the face of Republican opposition in Congress—Obama always presents the same dispassionate face," wrote James Fallows in a detailed 2012 analysis in *The Atlantic*.

In the end, though, the American public never entirely lost faith in the president. Even when his approval ratings dropped into the low 40 percentiles, polls showed that most Americans blamed former president Bush, rather than Obama, for the nation's ills. The same ironclad GOP resistance to Obama's proposals turned off many voters, who began viewing GOP intransigence in Congress as a larger problem than any shortcomings that the president might have. Apart from the ongoing economic weakness, Obama did not give voters many reasons to oppose him. His first term was largely free of scandal and his cabinet was remarkably stable. *(Cabinet members, p. 705)*

Obama may not have been a beloved president, but he seemed a competent one. His reelection victory meant he would get the opportunity to demonstrate whether he had learned from the mistakes of his first term. He would be able to oversee implementation of the new health care law and focus on returning to priorities of his first term that had died in Congress, especially immigration and climate change, while perhaps pursuing a landmark deficit reduction package with Republicans, who still controlled the House. He also would begin his second term free of at least some of the pressures that had dogged him when he had taken the oath of office for the first time with the nation facing two wars overseas and a plummeting economy at home. Perhaps with that in mind, Obama in his victory speech after winning reelection said, "Our economy is recovering. A decade of war is ending. . . . In the coming weeks and months, I am looking forward to reaching out and working with leaders of both parties to meet the challenges we can only solve together. . . . We've got more work to do."

Domestic Policy

Obama began his presidency with a dual focus when it came to domestic policy: restoring economic health and fulfilling the long-time Democratic goal of universal health care coverage. His priorities, a sharp break from the outgoing Bush administration, emphasized a combination of major infrastructure projects, assistance to lower- and middle-income Americans, and tax cuts that were more targeted toward the middle class as a way to kick-start the ailing economy and create new jobs. Even as conservatives warned that he was plunging the nation deeper into debt, the Obama administration made no secret that its economic recovery plan was also designed to reshape federal priorities and focus on programs long favored by Democrats, such as clean energy and education. As the new White House Chief of Staff Rahm Emanuel famously said: "You never let a serious crisis go to waste."

Even before he was sworn in, Obama went to Capitol Hill on January 6, 2009, and urged lawmakers of both parties to set aside their differences to pass a massive stimulus plan designed to inject about $800 billion into the economy. "The economy is very sick," he told them. "The situation is getting worse. . . . We have to act and act now to break the momentum of this recession."

Two weeks later, in his inaugural address, the new president laid out a broad plan to heal the economy by focusing on traditional Democratic priorities, ranging from infrastructure spending to education and renewable energy. He declared: "The state of the economy calls for action, bold and swift, and we will act—not only to create new jobs, but to lay a new foundation for growth. We will build the roads and bridges, the electric grids and digital lines that feed our commerce and bind us together. We will restore science to its rightful place, and wield technology's wonders to raise health care's quality and lower its cost. We will harness the sun and the winds and the soil to fuel our cars and run our factories. And we will transform our schools and colleges and universities to meet the demands of a new age."

With solid Democratic majorities in both chambers and widespread public support for action on the economy, Obama was well-positioned to get his way. But victory would not come without a struggle. Critics on both the left and right found much to criticize about the economic stimulus. Liberals complained that the plan would fail to inject enough money into the economy and focused too much on tax cuts; conservatives viewed it as an enormous boondoggle that emphasized potentially wasteful government spending over tax cuts and would plunge future generations into depth. In addition, economists were split over the extent to which the plan would help the economy, and many were not persuaded that it would keep unemployment to no more than 8 percent, as projected by a memo by Obama advisors. Despite the pressing need to help the badly ailing economy, Obama's stimulus plan picked up no Republican votes in the House and just three in the Senate that were needed to overcome a possible filibuster by the GOP (three-fifths of the total Senate, or sixty senators, are usually required to invoke cloture to end a filibuster) and those GOP votes only after scaling back funding for education and health care, among other provisions.

Still, the final product was an impressive victory for the new president in the first month of his administration. It stopped the free fall in job losses and helped launch the beginnings of a fragile economic recovery, although unemployment numbers would continue to increase for several months. In all likelihood, the economy would have been in even worse shape without the stimulus. A 2011 Congressional Budget Office report concluded that the stimulus helped to cushion the nation's economic fall, increasing the number of people with jobs in 2010 by 1.8 million to 5.2 million. The measure also moved the nation decisively in a direction favored by the White House, advancing policies on middle-class tax cuts, education, and health care for which Obama had campaigned. By authorizing $90 billion for a range of clean energy programs ranging from electric vehicles to wind farms, the stimulus was also the largest energy bill in history. But the legislation came with a political cost, leaving Obama vulnerable to charges of running up the deficit without making a noticeable dent in the deep recession. In many ways, the legislation would encapsulate the first two years of his presidency: working with Democratic majorities to advance measures that, while signaling a change of direction, often seemed to deliver far less than originally promised.

As difficult as the stimulus package was to get through Congress, it was just a warm-up for the epic battle over health care. Providing Americans with near-universal health care coverage had been a goal for Democratic presidents since Harry S. Truman in the 1940s, and Obama's top priority was to finally win enactment. The year-long battle over the issue consumed Congress, distracted Obama from other priorities such as worsening unemployment, and contributed to a steep decline in his poll numbers and those of his party. Far more than the stimulus, the health care overhaul exposed Obama to criticism from both the right (which accused him of unconstitutionally expanding the reach of the federal government) and the left (which worried that he was compromising away core principles such as a government-run insurance program). Political analysts warned he was badly blundering by failing to stay focused on the economy, which was a far greater concern for voters than an overhaul of the health care system. Some leading Democrats, including Chief of Staff Emanuel, wondered if Obama should scale back his plans and settle for incremental steps on health care rather than sweeping change. Voters in liberal Massachusetts made their feelings known in a stunning rebuke of Democrats in January 2010, narrowly electing Brown to fill Kennedy's seat. Even though Massachusetts was one of the most Democratic states in the country, an exit poll conducted by a Republican firm, Fabrizio, McLaughlin & Associates, concluded that 42 percent of Bay State voters cast their ballots to block health care.

Despite such setbacks, Obama dug in. In a January 2010 interview, he told *ABC World News* that pressing ahead with health care was more important than winning a second term. "I'd rather be a really good one-term president than a mediocre two-term president," he said. "I will not slow down in terms of going after the big problems that this country faces. . . . I don't want to look back on my time here and say to myself all I was interested in was nurturing my own popularity."

Even after Congress finally cleared the massive health care bill in March 2010, controversy lingered. Democrats had expected Americans to begin supporting the bill when they became more familiar with certain provisions, such as the requirement that insurance companies provide coverage to anyone regardless of preexisting conditions. Instead, polls showed that Americans remained almost evenly divided over the law. The hostility toward the new law, which detractors dubbed "Obamacare," was not just an academic matter; analysts warned that its ultimate effectiveness would be determined partly by the extent to which Americans would be willing to sign up for the new health insurance exchanges rather than opting to forego insurance and pay a penalty to the Internal Revenue Service. With so many Americans opposed to the law, the prospects for winning large-scale compliance were deeply uncertain. In a sign of the entrenched opposition to the expansive bill, a number of Republican governors or legislatures declined to take steps to set up health-care exchanges, as called for in the legislation. Some attorney generals across the nation took legal action, filing lawsuits in the federal courts that threatened to accomplish what Republican lawmakers could not: prevent enactment of the health care law on the grounds that it was unconstitutional. Until the Supreme Court upheld the central thrust of the health care law in June 2012, its future was left uncertain, thereby slowing efforts to implement key provisions of the law.

Obama himself, cognizant of the scars left by the bruising health care battle, said little about the issue after enactment. Republicans, however, repeatedly invoked Obamacare in the midterm elections of 2010, characterizing it as a prime example of government overreach into the private lives of citizens. Although the new law itself may not have been the main cause of the Election Day rout that brought Republicans into power in the House and closer to parity in the Senate, political strategists in both parties felt it played a role. Obama had appeared to leave his party vulnerable by deemphasizing the economy. Health-care reform "had an impact because the number one issue on Tuesday, by far, was the economy, and by focusing so much attention and resources and political capital on health care, Democrats were not perceived as focused on jobs and the economy," Democratic pollster Fred Yang told the *Washington Post*.

BANKS, CARS, AND CLIMATE CHANGE

Although he still enjoyed Democratic majorities in 2009–2010, Obama pressed ahead on three other key priorities: stabilizing the economy, overhauling bank regulation, and limiting carbon emissions in order to address climate change. On the economy and banks, the administration made some headway, although not as much as its supporters may have wished. On climate change, the White House was handed a ringing defeat.

TARP AND AUTO COMPANY BAILOUTS

When he took over the presidency, Obama inherited a controversial policy begun the previous fall under President Bush to shore up the financial sector. The $700 billion Troubled Asset Relief Program (TARP) aimed to strengthen banks and other financial institutions by buying assets and equity. Obama had supported TARP as a senator. But he broadened it after taking office, using the program's funds to increase lending among small businesses, help homeowners refinance their homes, and create programs to steer funds to those states that were hit hardest by the housing crisis. *(TARP background, p. 62; Congress and the Nation Vol. XII, pp. 154, 163)*

In the face of some criticism, Obama also used TARP funds to bail out struggling automaker General Motors. Although the president said that he did not want to run a car company and would not interfere with daily operations, the bailout plan led to the ouster of GM chief executive officer Rick Wagoner Jr. in March 2009, closed numerous GM dealerships, and, in exchange for concessions from the United Auto Workers, provided the union with a significant stake in the company. Controversial though these actions were, they were ultimately seen as critical for nursing the bankrupt automaker back to financial health. The company's CEO announced in April 2010 that the government loans were repaid. Seven months later, the company again went public in a successful stock offering.

The bailout of GM as well as a program to strengthen Chrysler (together totaling about $80 billion) shored up Obama's political standing in critical battleground states such as Ohio and Michigan and would ultimately play an important role in his successful reelection campaign. In the final weeks before the 2012 presidential election, Republican nominee Mitt Romney, who criticized the bailouts, ran ads suggesting that the two automakers were planning to ship jobs overseas. Both GM and Chrysler vigorously disputed the ads. Obama wound up carrying the two states by clear margins. *(2012 elections, pp. 35, 702; GM, Chrysler aid, p. 63)*

BANK STRESS TESTS

A centerpiece of the Obama administration's policy to nurse the financial sector back to health was to administer "stress tests" to the nation's largest banks. The policy, unveiled in February 2009 as part of the administration's policy to provide banks with more government support, aimed to determine whether banks could survive a protracted slump, even if unemployment exceeded 10 percent and housing prices continued a sharp drop.

Markets were initially roiled when Treasury Secretary Timothy Geithner announced the plan. But the twelve-week period of waiting for stress test results gave banks an important window in which to dispose of troubled assets, issue debt without government assistance, and take other steps to firm up their financial strength. The first round of test results, announced in spring 2009, began restoring some confidence in the financial sector. The Federal Reserve concluded in a somewhat reassuring analysis that banks had continued to strengthen but were not yet healed. Some ten of the nation's nineteen biggest banks needed a total of $75 billion in new capital to withstand losses in case the economy worsened, according to the tests.

Some critics raised concerns at the time that the tests were not rigorous enough and failed to take into account the full extent of the nation's ongoing economic slump. However, by spring 2010, additional infusions of government funds helped larger banks stage an impressive recovery, even though some regional banks continued to struggle. Investors began feeling more confident. The program had succeeded, at least to some extent, in providing critical transparency about the underlying health of many financial firms at a time when investors were deeply concerned about vulnerability in the banking sector. Financial experts generally gave the administration high marks for its approach. Comptroller of the Currency John Dugan lauded the policy, calling it "the most significant and successful policy proposal of the new administration to address the banking crisis."

By the 2012 presidential elections, Obama could plausibly say that the government's loans to banks had generated a profit for taxpayers. As of October 2012, of the $245.2 billion of TARP funds that went to banks, the government had taken back $266.7 billion—about $21.5 billion more than the initial investment. Although not all banks were able to repay 100 percent of the loans, most of them did, and the government profit resulted from interest on the loans, as well as dividends and other revenue sources. In fact, the bank bailout produced a better taxpayer return than other TARP programs. Overall, the Treasury Department reported in March 2013 that the federal government had spent a total of $418 billion of TARP funds through 2012 and gained back all but $55.5 billion.

WALL STREET REFORM

Even as the administration worked to stabilize the financial sector, it also proposed a sweeping overhaul of financial regulations to prevent another crisis from occurring. "It is an indisputable fact that one of the most significant contributors to our economic downturn was an unraveling of major financial institutions and the lack of adequate regulatory structures to prevent abuse and excess," Obama said in June 2009 as he unveiled his much-anticipated blueprint for regulatory reform. "A regulatory regime basically crafted in the wake of a 20th century economic crisis—the Great Depression—was overwhelmed by the speed, scope, and sophistication of a 21st century global economy."

The financial legislation was Obama's third major legislative priority, after the stimulus and health care plans. Although he won congressional approval in 2010 after protracted legislative battles, it was an uneasy victory. House Republicans repeatedly, if unsuccessfully, attempted to roll back key provisions. During the 2012 presidential election, Romney pledged to repeal the entire law if elected. Prominent business organizations lambasted the act, with the American Bankers Association terming it as "a tsunami of new rules and restrictions for traditional banks that had nothing to do with causing the financial crisis in the first place." Although Obama had sought at times to court key business leaders, the financial regulatory overhaul undercut those efforts and likely hurt Democrats in the 2010 elections.

Liberals and consumer groups also were disappointed and felt the new law fell short of what was needed. It did not attempt to alter the fundamental shape of Wall Street, despite widespread concerns over the sector's practices. It did not include far-reaching steps espoused by reformers, such as breaking up megabanks, banning the trade of certain derivatives, and setting clear limits on executive pay. It also did not significantly streamline the federal regulatory process.

Still, the final product tracked closely with Obama's June 2009 proposal. Although it did not restrict trading or limit executive pay, it mandated oversight of the vast market for derivatives, which had helped set off the crisis, and it gave shareholders more say on how corporate executives are paid. The government gained more authority to seize and wind down struggling financial firms, such as Lehman Brothers. It set up a council of federal regulators to monitor threats to the financial system. One of its most discussed provisions established an independent consumer bureau within the Federal Reserve to protect borrowers against abuses by mortgage and credit card companies and some other lenders.

Analysts warned that the law would only be as effective as the regulators who sought to enforce it—a point that Obama conceded when he signed it in July 2010. "For these new rules to be effective, regulators will have to be vigilant," he said. "We also may need to make adjustments along the way as our financial system adapts to these changes. And no law can force anybody to be responsible; it is still incumbent on those on Wall Street to heed the lessons of this crisis in how they conduct business."

The administration, however, moved slowly on implementation. As of November 2012, regulators had missed 61 percent of their deadlines, according to a law firm, Davis Polk, that tracked the law. Part of the reason was that the law allocated a number of key decisions to regulators. Prominent among these was the so-called Volcker rule, named after its chief proponent, former Federal Reserve Chair Paul Volcker, that focused on preventing banks from making speculative bets but included provisions that were left open to interpretation. As a result of disagreement over that and other rules, the ultimate effectiveness of the law remained very much in question as the end of Obama's first term.

CLIMATE CHANGE AND OTHER ENVIRONMENTAL ISSUES

If the administration could take credit for at least limited success in taking on the financial sector, it could make no such claim when it came to the politically contentious issue of global warming. Obama had warned during his 2008 campaign that emissions of greenhouse gases such as carbon dioxide posed a grave, long-term threat to society by warming the planet, and he repeatedly returned to the subject in his first year of office. "The threat from climate change is serious, it is urgent, and it is growing," Obama said in a September 2009 speech to the United Nations. "Our generation's response to this challenge will be judged by history, for if we fail to meet it—boldly, swiftly, and together—we risk consigning future generations to an irreversible catastrophe." Emphasizing the issue in meetings with world leaders, Obama went so far as to take a high-stakes trip to Copenhagen, Denmark, in December 2009 during international talks over greenhouse gas emissions in a largely unsuccessful attempt to strike a global agreement.

Despite his stated commitment to the issue, the president could not win enactment of a broad measure designed to cut greenhouse gas emissions even at a time when Democrats controlled both chambers of Congress. Obama and his congressional allies won a largely Pyrrhic victory in June 2009 when Democrats in the House narrowly passed legislation to limit emissions of heat-trapping gases through a cap-and-trade system. To win passage of the deeply contentious plan, Obama personally lobbied numerous wavering lawmakers in the days leading up to the vote. Politically, however, the vote proved costly for the Democrats. The business community sharply opposed the bill. Republicans successfully framed it as a tax on energy and lambasted vulnerable Democrats in the 2010 elections. Although the legislation marked the first time that a chamber of Congress passed a measure to address climate change, environmentalists found themselves deeply divided, concerned that the legislation fell far short of what was needed to avert the most worrisome effects of global warming.

As Obama turned his attention elsewhere, to the health care and financial overhaul measures, the climate bill stalled. Given the intense industry opposition and reluctance of Senate Democrats facing difficult reelection battles, especially in coal-producing states, it was not clear whether a stronger White House focus on the legislation could have made a difference. Nevertheless, environmentalists complained vigorously that Obama, by failing to rally public support and pressing senators to take it up, had missed a rare opportunity. The issue haunted Democrats in the midterm elections, as Republicans hammered them for trying to raise the price of energy. Obama, sensing this was a no-win issue, stopped highlighting climate change in his speeches.

With environmental initiatives stalled in Congress, Obama used his executive powers to tackle climate change and air pollution. One day after the 2010 elections, with any legislation to regulate greenhouse gas emissions clearly doomed, Obama defiantly told reporters that there was more than one way of "skinning a cat." His administration took a series of steps applauded by environmentalists, such as imposing the first-ever limits on carbon dioxide emissions from power plants, using the auto bailout to tighten auto fuel-efficiency standards, and steering billions of dollars toward clean-energy projects. Using authority from the Clean Air Act, the White House also placed limits on several types of air pollutants. Business groups and conservatives criticized the moves as heavy-handed. The House in 2012 passed legislation to block several of Obama's regulations, but the bill stalled in the Democratic-controlled Senate.

The administration, however, broke with its environmental allies in certain cases. Most notably, Obama in September 2011 decided to defer an Environmental Protection Agency (EPA) proposal to limit ozone emissions that were linked to smog, contending that it would hurt the economy. Two months later, the administration announced it would hold off on a decision on the controversial Keystone XL oil pipeline, which was to run from Canada through the Great Plains to Texas, with the State Department saying it would review alternate routes to avoid the environmentally sensitive Sand Hills region of Nebraska. The announcement meant that any decision would be postponed until after the 2012 election, which angered business interests but also left environmentalists uneasy. Environmentalists were also disappointed that Obama failed to put a greater focus on creating new wilderness areas or even, like Clinton, drawing on his executive authority under the 1906 Antiquities Act to protect wild areas by creating national monuments.

EDUCATION

Obama worked largely with the states, rather than Congress, to initiate significant changes of public education. His goals were to narrow the gap between low-income and more affluent students, increase high school graduation rates and better prepare students for competition in the global marketplace. Although Congress did not revamp "No Child Left Behind," the standards-based education law signed by President George W. Bush, the Obama administration effectively revised it by excusing states from its requirements if they instead adopted certain measures that promoted competition and accountability. As additional incentive, the administration also leveraged $4.3 billion in education stimulus money to create a series of grants called "Race to the Top." Cash-strapped states that competed for the dollars had to adopt certain administration-backed policies, such as using student test scores to evaluate teachers and turning to specific benchmarks such as rigorous academic standards. Most states agreed to compete. In some cases, the administration was able to exert influence even in noncompliant states. For example, after Texas governor Rick Perry said his state would not compete in Race to the Top, the administration unveiled a new program to allow districts to compete for certain grants regardless of in which states they were located.

Under Obama's approach, teachers who had high ratings that were linked to student achievement would get a boost in pay, while those with poor ratings could lose their jobs. In most states, schoolchildren had to meet common standards regardless of where they lived in the country. Whether these changes would lead to improved education remained uncertain because of a lack of research. Some critics, including unions, worried that Obama's approach could overemphasize testing while moving focus away from classes in the arts and similar subjects. Others noted that it was leading to a confusing set of state guidelines as opposed to the national approach espoused in No Child

Left Behind. But few questioned that the administration was remarkably successful at using its resources to influence state policies and advance its education agenda.

The administration also worked with Congress to remove banks from the federal student loan program. As part of the 2010 health care reform bill, lawmakers agreed to end the long-standing practice of subsidizing banks that provided student loans. Instead Obama achieved a centerpiece of his education agenda by enabling students to get their federal student loans directly from the federal government. Part of the savings from this change went toward expanding Pell Grants to lower-income students and to other programs to help relieve lower-income graduates of potentially crushing debt. In order to win passage, however, the administration had to sacrifice a plan to spend $8 billion on early childhood education and give up most of the "American Graduation Initiative" that would have provided federal support for community colleges.

BUDGET BATTLES: 2011–2012

After the 2010 midterm elections, Obama pulled back from the ambitious agenda of his first two years. During much of the 112th Congress, the White House played defense, parrying efforts by the Republican-led House to undercut or even repeal the health care and financial overhaul measures. Many of the largest Washington battles focused on the budget. In a sharp reversal from the first two years of the Obama administration, in which a Democratic-controlled Congress focused on spurring the economy through spending increases and tax cuts that helped drive up the budget deficit, the fiscal conservatives who drove the House agenda insisted on focusing on deficit reduction. Annual deficits were exceeding $1 trillion, a level that was widely viewed as unsustainable. The GOP prescription for spending cuts ran headlong into opposition with Obama, who favored reducing the budget deficit through a dual approach of tax increases and spending cuts. Another significant difference was that Obama, unlike his Republican adversaries, wanted to nurture the economy back to health before tackling the massive deficits.

Obama had taken a seemingly inconsistent approach toward the budget in his first couple of years in office. In 2010, for example, he signed "PAYGO" rules that required Congress to find funds to offset any tax cuts or spending increases. He also imposed a three-year spending freeze on discretionary spending and created a bipartisan National Commission on Fiscal Responsibility and Reform to make recommendations for reducing the deficit and reining in spending on entitlements. At the same time, he exasperated conservatives by continuing to press for targeting spending and tax cuts in order to stimulate the economy. He also declined to champion the package of spending cuts and tax hikes that were recommended by a bipartisan commission that he created, headed by former Republican senator Alan Simpson of Wyoming and Clinton White House chief of staff Erskine Bowles.

When Republicans took back the House in 2010, they inherited a fiscally chaotic situation of soaring deficits and no clear spending blueprints. Democrats had left themselves in a vulnerable position by failing to pass a fiscal 2011 budget before losing their House majority. In spring 2011, the Republicans insisted on tens of billions of dollars in cuts as the price for keeping the government funded through the end of the fiscal year. With a government shutdown looming and some 800,000 workers facing potential furloughs, Obama and congressional leaders agreed on $37.8 billion in cuts for the rest of the fiscal year. That figure was far less than the $61 billion passed by the House, but it nevertheless served as a potent sign of the increasing clout of fiscal conservatives. Reluctant though Obama was to make deep cuts, he appeared to have limited negotiating room. Even though a government shutdown could disrupt the fledgling economic recovery, the Tea Party conservatives who constituted a large part of the House caucus appeared to be willing to risk economic havoc to rein in government programs.

The budget returned to the fore in summer 2011 as the nation approached its limit for borrowing more money. Republicans refused to lift the $14.3 trillion debt ceiling without substantial spending cuts. Sensing an opening to bring the deficit under control, the White House engaged congressional leaders in negotiations over striking a "grand bargain" that would reduce the debt by as much as $4 trillion over ten years through a combination of tax increases and spending cuts, including reining in the costs of entitlements. The negotiations generally followed the contours of the Simpson-Bowles recommendations. Although winning agreement on a grand bargain became a top administration priority, the on-again, off-again talks broke off just days before the Treasury feared hitting its borrowing limit. Obama and Boehner exchanged bitter recriminations, with administration officials accusing Boehner of reneging on a deal that would have included higher taxes and Boehner saying the president went back on his word. Relations between the president and the Speaker, which were always chilly, appeared to hit a low point when both held dueling press conferences on July 22 accusing the other of negotiating in bad faith. Obama appeared visibly irked that Boehner could not seem to get his caucus to agree to what he viewed as a reasonable package that would have largely achieved GOP goals of deficit reduction. "I've been left at the altar now a couple of times," he told reporters.

Although there was plenty of blame to go around, the collapse of the talks represented one of several instances in which Obama appeared to antagonize congressional leaders even as he was trying to win them over. Republican staffers complained that during White House talks, Obama adopted a stern, lecturing tone about the need to raise taxes. Press accounts also depicted Obama as negotiating inconsistently, moving between offers of $800 billion to $1.2 trillion in tax cuts—although some of that movement may have had to do with the need to accommodate demands by Democratic congressional leaders. For his part, Obama confronted the unyielding resistance of the Republican rank-and-file to any kind of tax increase, even when that increase would help the government's bottom line.

In the end, Obama had to abandon a grand bargain compromise. Instead, he accepted a last-minute deal that, in exchange for an increase in the debt ceiling of more than $1 trillion, imposed nearly $1 trillion in spending cuts over ten years but did not raise taxes. Trying to focus on the positive, Obama hailed the agreement as "an important first step" in getting the budget deficit under control. Speaking in the White House Rose Garden after senators approved the deal, he added that the deal avoided "cutting too sharply while the economy is still fragile." From Obama's point of view, he had staved off a potentially devastating government default while creating a new bipartisan legislative "supercommittee" that could pave the way toward the long-elusive grand bargain. Nevertheless, liberals criticized the president for failing to hold the line against Republican demands. The spectacle of the nation on the edge of a government default while the administration and Congress could not come to terms on a debt ceiling increase rattled the economy and shook confidence in the American political system. Standard & Poor's went so far as to downgrade the nation's credit rating from AAA to AA+ for the first time in the firm's history. The showdown, analysts felt, slowed down economic growth just when it seemed the nation was ready to rise out of the persistent recession.

With a temporary ceasefire in the budget battles and a presidential election year looming, Obama tried to change the political narrative from budget reduction to the economy. The nation's unemployment rate remained stuck at about 9 percent. Most polls showed that Obama's approval ratings were upside down, with fewer than 45 percent of Americans approving of the job he was doing and about 50 percent disapproving—the result, analysts believed, of the weak economy and continuing gridlock in Washington. As he shifted into campaign mode, Obama appealed to the Democratic base, positioning himself as a champion of the middle class. "You say you're the party of tax cuts? Well then, prove you'll fight just as hard for tax cuts for middle-class families as you do for oil companies and the most affluent Americans," Obama said rhetorically to his Republican foes at a raucous Labor Day rally in Detroit. "We're going to see if congressional Republicans will put country before party."

Although Obama was successful during the presidential campaign in painting the GOP as favoring the rich, he could do little to alter the budget trajectory in Washington. The legislative supercommittee created by the debt ceiling agreement could not meet its mandate of identifying at least $1.2 trillion in savings over the next decade. As a result, the government faced the specter of deep, across-the-board budget cuts of more than $100 billion split evenly between defense and nondefense programs. Those cuts were set to kick in at the beginning of January 1, 2013—the same moment when the Bush-era tax cuts were set to expire. The combination of events, which became known as the fiscal cliff, threatened to plunge the country back into a recession.

If there was ever a moment when Obama appeared to hold the upper hand, this was it. Inaction would mean a massive tax hike, including a return to Clinton-era higher rates on upper income tax brackets that were anathema to the GOP. In addition, the political timing seemed opportune for a grand bargain, with a lame duck Congress not needing to face the voters again for two years. Once again, Obama tried to win agreement for a major agreement, and once again he failed. The president, fresh from his reelection victory and sailing high in the polls, was reduced to urging Republicans to "take the deal." But Boehner and McConnell said Obama's proposed $2 trillion in deficit reduction relied too much on revenue instead of spending cuts. In the end, political leaders struck a last-minute agreement on New Year's Eve, brokered by McConnell and Biden, that effectively raised taxes on upper-income Americans by $600 billion over ten years, far less than the $1.6 trillion that Obama had originally proposed. The deal would also make most of the Bush tax cuts permanent while ending the payroll tax holiday that had helped stimulate the economy for the previous two years. Some analysts on the left worried that the president had failed to take advantage of the expiring tax cuts to force larger revenue increases. Robert B. Reich, the former labor secretary, told the *New York Times* that Obama is "still the same President Obama who wants a deal above all else and seems willing to compromise on even the most basic principle."

But Obama, while falling short of his goal of a grand bargain, could take solace in a number of Democratic priorities that were included in the legislation. These included an extension of unemployment benefits for two million Americans; renewed tax credits for child care, college tuition, and renewable energy production; an increase in capital gains taxes; and phased-out deductions for the wealthy. However, the president failed to win an increase in the debt ceiling limit, and he succeeded in staving off the imposition of automatic spending cuts for just a couple of months. As a result, Obama began his second term facing the prospect of continuing budget battles with Congress.

Foreign Policy

Obama set out to establish a fundamentally different approach to foreign policy from that taken by George W. Bush. The Bush doctrine was predicated on a clear principle: if the United States felt threatened by a nation, it should attack before the other nation could cause harm. When he ran for president in 2008, Obama repeatedly stressed the importance of talking with adversaries and using diplomacy before resorting to force. "Strong nations and strong leaders talk to their enemies," he maintained.

Although Republicans scorned that approach, Obama came to office fully prepared to initiate it. "Our security emanates from the justness of our cause; the force of our example; the tempering qualities of humility and restraint," he proclaimed in his inaugural address.

Obama received plaudits from many in the international community for his focus on preventing nuclear proliferation, his use of international bodies such as the United Nations to pursue foreign policy goals, and his outreach to the Islamic world. He delivered a highly regarded address in Cairo, Egypt, in June 2009, urging improved relations and understanding between Islamic nations and the West. Just four months later, Obama was unexpectedly awarded the 2009 Nobel Peace Prize. The Nobel Committee hailed his "extraordinary efforts to strengthen international diplomacy and cooperation between peoples," although committee chair Thorbjørn Jagland conceded that some people might find the award premature. Critics, in fact, wondered if the prize was more about repudiating Bush's policies than endorsing Obama's. In his acceptance speech, Obama acknowledged the controversy that the award had generated, saying, "I am at the beginning, and not the end, of my labors on the world stage." He added: "But perhaps the most profound issue surrounding my receipt of this prize is the fact that I am the commander-in-chief of a nation in the midst of two wars."

Indeed, for all of Obama's emphasis on diplomacy, he did not hesitate to use force in a number of situations. He had inherited wars in Iraq and Afghanistan, as well as tense relations with a number of Islamic countries and North Korea. Terrorist attacks remained a constant concern. Instead of a total break with the Bush administration's approach, Obama continued the war in Iraq for longer than he had pledged in his presidential campaign while seeking to bring stability to that country. He also diverted additional troops to Afghanistan, launched a controversial and ultimately successful bombing campaign in Libya, and greatly expanded the use of military drones in war zones. In perhaps his most clear-cut success in the battle against terror, he issued a high-risk order in November 2011 to send Navy Seals into Pakistan for a surprise raid that succeeded in killing Osama bin Laden, the al Qaeda leader who ordered the 2001 terrorist attacks against the United States.

Obama's diplomatic record received mixed reviews. The reduced influence of the United States came into focus when the president flew to Copenhagen in December 2009, making a highly visible but largely unsuccessful effort to persuade the international community to reach consensus on reducing emissions of greenhouse gases. Throughout Obama's term, he repeatedly labeled Iran as a major threat and imposed sanctions against the country but failed to persuade Iranian leaders to drop their nuclear programs, which he and other world leaders believed were intended to produce nuclear weapons. Although his Cairo speech spurred hopes that Obama might be able to build momentum toward a lasting Middle East peace and he initially pushed to restart peace talks between the Israelis and Palestinians, he backed off when those efforts failed in fall 2010. On the other hand, the administration worked hard to improve relations with China and was largely successful, in part by welcoming its ascendancy while pursuing discussion on discrete topics, such as currency and pollution. The United States also worked assiduously to build stronger ties to several of China's neighbors. It encouraged the European Union to address its debt crisis while working to insulate the United States from its potential impacts.

WARS IN IRAQ AND AFGHANISTAN

The most pressing foreign policy imperative for Obama when he took office was overseeing the wars in Iraq and Afghanistan.

Iraq

As senator, he had sharply criticized Bush's use of force and voted against military action in Iraq. When running for president, Obama pledged to withdraw one to two brigades a month and wind down all military action within sixteen months. However, extricating the United States from Iraq proved difficult. Saying that the country should be as "careful getting out of Iraq as we were careless getting into it," Obama largely followed a plan set up late in the Bush administration for a gradual draw down. The number of troops declined from 140,000 when Obama took office to about 50,000 in August 2010, when Obama announced that combat operations in Iraq had ended. U.S. and Iraqi officials, concerned over the possibility of spiraling violence without the presence of the United States, then spent months in fruitless negotiations over whether remaining U.S. troops would have immunity from prosecution in Iraqi courts. No such deal could be reached, and the United States ultimately withdrew its troops at the end of 2011, as called for in a 2008 agreement that had been negotiated under Bush. In announcing the end of the controversial war, Obama in October 2011 praised the men and women who fought rather than the mission itself. The troops, he said, would leave "with their heads held high, proud of their success, and knowing that the American people stand united in our support for our troops."

Members of Congress were divided over the withdrawal, with Democrats generally supportive and Republicans worrying that it was premature. The nation had spent about $800 billion during eight years of fighting, and some 4,500 U.S. troops lost their lives. Several leading Republicans warned that the withdrawal could leave Iraq unstable with ramifications across the Middle East. "I fear this decision has set in motion events that will come back to haunt our country," said Sen. Lindsay Graham, R-S.C. Indeed, violence in Iraq, including sectarian killing, increased in late 2012. But U.S. military officials and independent analysts toward the end of Obama's first term expressed guarded optimism, saying Iraqi security forces were doing a good job in maintaining order.

Afghanistan

Although Obama opposed the war in Iraq from the onset and focused on ending it, he supported military action in Afghanistan as critical to the fight against terror. Accordingly, one of his early actions was to shift troops from Iraq into Afghanistan and pursue the battle against the Taliban and their al Qaeda allies more vigorously than his predecessor.

Early in 2009, Obama sent 21,000 additional troops in Afghanistan, bringing the total to about 68,000, while announcing that he would develop a new strategy for that country and neighboring Pakistan. It took the president many months, however, to formulate that strategy. In December 2009, he announced in a speech at West Point that the United States would send an additional 30,000 troops into Afghanistan, along with increased funds and civilian activities, in a bid to stabilize the country. Withdrawal of the troops would begin within eighteen months, he said.

Generals and top administration officials had been divided over policy in Afghanistan leading up to Obama's announcement. The president had studied the situation intensely for three months and met with his national security team at least ten times before making his decision. Gen. Stanley McChrystal pressed for a buildup of 40,000 troops who would remain for a number of years; Vice President Joseph R. Biden Jr. opposed additional troops and recommended a greater focus on Afghanistan's nuclear-armed neighbor, Pakistan, instead. In the end, Obama chose a middle path. He reasoned that a quick jolt of U.S. force would be sufficient to change the situation on the ground and enable Afghanistan's civilian government to take charge, even though there were widespread concerns about corruption and inefficiency in the government of Afghan President Hamid Karzai. Toward the end of his first term, he would recall his decision on deploying more troops to Afghanistan as the most difficult of his presidency. "Any time you send our brave men and women into battle, you know that not everyone will come home safely, and that necessarily weighs heavily on you," Obama said in a 2012 chat with the website Reddit.

Obama's complex approach to Afghanistan sparked criticism almost immediately. Republicans in particular warned that the pledge to begin drawing down troops in 2011 would serve as a virtual invitation to Taliban fighters to hold out until the Americans began leaving. Some experts questioned whether Afghan troops could be trained by the time of the withdrawal and warned that the influx of American troops could spark a backlash in Afghanistan that would fuel the insurgency. Many wondered whether Pakistan could be viewed as a reliable ally and could prevent Taliban fighters from finding safe havens in its land.

Although the withdrawal proceeded on schedule in 2011, those questions were not fully resolved by the end of Obama's first term. Despite some significant setbacks, the surge succeeded in dividing Taliban fighters and largely confining violence to remote areas of the country, at least temporarily. North Atlantic Treaty Organization (NATO) leaders in 2012 signed off on Obama's exit strategy, which called for an end to combat operations the following year and the withdrawal of the U.S.-led international military force by the end of 2014. However, violence continued to rage in parts of the country, with both Afghans and the remaining U.S. troops frequently targeted. If there was progress in quelling the insurgency, it was difficult to measure. The senior combat leader in Afghanistan, Gen. John Allen, said in 2012 that insurgent violence in southern Afghanistan was down 3 percent over 2011 levels, but he admitted it was not "statistically significant." Still, the U.S. military continued to provide assistance to Afghan security forces to help them take the lead in eventually safeguarding the country.

Although the war against the Taliban failed to deliver a clear-cut victory, the Obama administration could claim success in disrupting al Qaeda and its allies. An aggressive expansion in the use of drones over Afghanistan and Pakistan killed a number of terrorist leaders and left al Qaeda severely weakened. However, the drone strikes and other military operations proved intensely controversial, especially because a number of the strikes targeted civilians by mistake. U.N. officials, friendly foreign governments, and human rights activists criticized the secretive drone program on legal, moral, and practical grounds. Some military and intelligence experts warned that the drone strikes could undermine efforts to battle extremism by alienating local populations. The Obama administration pledged to work more closely with Congress to add transparency to the drone program and develop a legal framework for it.

ARAB SPRING: EGYPT, LIBYA, SYRIA

The so-called Arab Spring, a series of both nonviolent and violent uprisings across the Middle East that targeted entrenched regimes, provided Obama with an opening to influence the future direction of the region. The uprisings began in December 2010 in Tunisia and spread to Algeria, Egypt, Yemen, and other countries. The president determined to take a different path than in 2009, when he had largely ignored widespread street protests in Iran and said he did not want to be seen as interfering in Iranian domestic politics. By the time the Arab Spring broke out, Obama felt the United States must set a moral example, calling for the ouster of dictators—even those who had helped advance U.S. interests.

The first major test for his policy occurred in January 2011 with the outbreak of large-scale demonstrations in Egypt calling for the resignation of Egyptian president Hosni Mubarak, a long-time U.S. ally. On February 1, Mubarak announced that he would not run for reelection but would not step down. In a tense phone call shortly after, Obama urged the Egyptian ruler to resign. When Mubarak refused, Obama gave national televised remarks in which he said that an "orderly transition must be meaningful, it must be peaceful, and it must begin now." In urging the Egyptian leader to step down immediately, Obama overrode the advice of senior State Department and Pentagon officials who had worked with Egypt's autocratic but pro-American leader for decades. Just eleven days after Obama urged Mubarak to heed the demonstrators, the Egyptian president, beset by mounting domestic opposition, left office.

Obama's decision to side with the protesters, however, failed to win the United States much goodwill with either the Arab people or their governments. Egypt subsequently entered a period of political turmoil that culminated in the election of a government dominated by the Muslim Brotherhood, an Islamist organization with a longtime record of hostility to Israel and the West. The change in government raised questions about Egypt's long-term relationship with Israel and the United States. Obama also found himself unable or unwilling to stand up to some other Arab leaders. When Saudi Arabia unleashed tanks against prodemocracy demonstrators in Bahrain, Obama raised few objections.

In contrast, Obama scored a clear-cut foreign policy success when uprisings spread to Libya. He moved cautiously at first, speaking out against the violence that began in February 2011 in the city of Benghazi but not immediately calling for the removal of Libyan leader Muammar Gaddafi. As the fighting increased, the president successfully worked on a resolution by the U.N. security council calling for a no-fly zone over the war-torn country. Moving decisively, the administration imposed sanctions on Libya, called for Gaddafi to step down, and then worked with NATO allies and several Arab countries to launch a bombing campaign with NATO allies in support of rebel forces. The White House did not ask for congressional authorization.

Obama defended the military action, saying it was necessary to stop what he termed a looming genocide in the Libyan city of Benghazi. "I refused to wait for the images of slaughter and mass graves before taking action," he said on March 28. At the same time, he ruled out sending in ground troops because that could splinter international support.

With his actions on Libya, the president distinguished his approach from the often unilateral one of his predecessor. Obama made it clear that he was willing to act unilaterally when it was necessary to defend the nation and its core interests. But in other cases, when the safety of Americans was not directly threatened but where action could be justified—such as in instances of genocide, humanitarian relief, regional security, or economic interests—Obama believed the United States should coordinate its actions with other countries. Aaron David Miller, a State Department Middle East peace negotiator during the Clinton administration, characterized Obama's doctrine as trying to do the right thing so long as the risks were relatively low and the United States would not have to go it alone. "If we can, if there's a moral case, if we have allies, and if we can transition out and not get stuck, we'll move to help," Miller said. "The Obama doctrine is the 'hedge your bets and make sure you have a way out' doctrine. He learned from Afghanistan and Iraq."

The president's actions sparked criticism from both Republicans and Democrats. Some accused him of acting too aggressively and getting America involved in hostilities in another Muslim country without an exit strategy. Others accused him of acting too timidly by ruling out ground troops and by ceding U.S. leadership to a multinational coalition. Many lawmakers in both parties complained that he was violating the War Powers Act by failing to consult with Congress. The administration argued that it did not need authorization from Congress, saying the War Powers Act did not apply to Libya because the bombing campaign fell short of full-blown hostilities. The House delivered a stern rebuke in June, voting 123–295 against a resolution that would have authorized the mission in Libya. But on a narrower vote, 180–238, House members rejected a proposal to cut off funding for it.

In the end, Obama largely won vindication after rebels killed Gaddafi on October 20 and took control of the country. "I think the administration deserves great credit," said Sen. John McCain, R-Ariz., who had favored more decisive military action. "Obviously, I had different ideas on the tactical side, but the world is a better place."

Obama, however, moved much more cautiously when civil war broke out in Syria early in 2011, pitting the brutal regime of President Bashar al-Assad against rebel factions, some of which had ties to terrorist groups. After several months of escalating violence, Obama, in coordination with Western allies, announced the imposition of sanctions against Syria and the freezing of the nation's assets. He also called for Assad to step down in August. At the same time, however, he said that the Syrian people must control their own destiny without interference from abroad.

As Obama's first term wound down at the end of 2012, he announced that the United States would recognize the recently organized National Coalition for Syrian Revolutionary and Opposition Forces as the "legitimate representatives of the Syrian people." In doing so, he was following the lead of other governments, including Great Britain, France, Turkey, and the Arab Gulf states. But the president remained cautious, as the administration also branded the Al-Nusra Front, one of the most effective of the rebel groups fighting the Assad regime, as an Islamist terrorist organization linked to al Qaeda. With the Syrian situation unresolved, and other threats still percolating—especially in Iran, whose government was believed to be in pursuit of a nuclear weapon—Obama entered his second term with the United States facing a number of difficult challenges.

Reelection Campaign

In winning reelection on November 6, 2012, Barack Obama became the first Democratic president to win back-to-back victories with more than 50 percent of the vote since Franklin D. Roosevelt in 1940 and 1944. He also was the first president of either party since Roosevelt to win reelection with an unemployment rate above 7.5 percent (it hovered at about 7.9 percent in the weeks before Election Day). Although the 51–47 percent victory over former Massachusetts Governor Mitt Romney marked a clear-cut win, it fell short of Obama's 7-point margin over Sen. John McCain, R-Ariz., in 2008. The reelection margin in the electoral college was more lopsided: 332–206. The victory also gave Obama a second chance at cementing his legacy after an up-and-down first term in which congressional Republicans came together to sink much of his agenda and the Democratic Party was sharply repudiated by voters in the midterm elections of 2010.

Mindful of the divisions in the country and continued weakness of the economy, Obama gave a somewhat muted victory speech. "As it has for more than two centuries, progress will come in fits and starts. It's not always a straight line," he said, adding: "Whether I earned your vote or not, I have listened to you, I have learned from you, and you've made me a better president."

Obama's victory could be traced to several factors: he ran a more sophisticated campaign; the economy, although weak, was slowly improving; a broad coalition of women, minority, and younger voters appeared to prefer Democratic policies; Romney made a series of tactical errors; and the late October devastation by Superstorm Sandy on the East Coast enabled Obama to dominate the news cycle for several days as he pledged assistance to stricken areas. Obama also enjoyed the advantages of incumbency. In fact, his victory marked the third time in a row that a sitting president had won reelection. The only other time that there were three consecutive two-term presidencies occurred in the early nineteenth century, with Thomas Jefferson, James Madison, and James Monroe each winning reelection.

But it was not an easy contest. The campaign lacked the soaring rhetoric of hope and change that marked Obama's historic victory in 2008. Obama won less by appealing to the idealistic yearnings of Americans then by going on the attack early against Romney and by conducting a remarkable, precinct-by-precinct ground game that turned out as many supporters as possible. The campaign also seized relentlessly on every Romney miscue, including videotaped remarks in which the former governor bluntly criticized the "47 percent" of Americans who rely on government assistance.

Obama set the tactical tone of the campaign early when, on April 4, 2011, he announced his reelection bid via e-mail and a web video sent to supporters. "Today, we are filing papers to launch our 2012 campaign," Obama wrote in the e-mail. "We're doing this now because the politics we believe in does not start with expensive TV ads or extravaganzas, but with you—with people organizing block-by-block, talking to neighbors, co-workers, and friends." The video, which featured voters instead of the president, appeared to be a tacit acknowledgment that many of his supporters had been disappointed by the uneven pace of change and the compromises Obama has made in the previous two-and-half years. Reaching out to independent voters who were less than thrilled with Obama's record, the video featured a voter from North Carolina who said, "I don't agree with Obama on everything, but I respect him and I trust him."

At the time, Obama's job approval rating was about 45 percent with about an equal number disapproving, according to Gallup. The unemployment rate was hovering at about 9 percent, an improvement over its peak of more than 10 percent in the fall of 2009 but still potentially fatal territory for a president seeking reelection. In addition, Obama had failed to deliver on promises such as addressing immigration and climate change, the tone in Washington remained poisonous despite his pledge to change it, and his signature achievement of health care reform divided the electorate and remained vulnerable to legal and political challenges.

Yet Obama began his campaign with two critical advantages. He had a vast fund-raising network that would draw in more than $1 billion, a mark that had never before been achieved. And if he and fellow Democrats were failing to gain much traction with voters, Republicans seemed to be in even worse shape. Voters continued to blame Bush more than Obama for the economic downturn, and they distrusted Republicans on a variety of key issues. Further boosting Obama, Republicans had a weak field of candidates that included highly polarizing figures such as Rep. Michele Bachmann of Minnesota and former senator Rick Santorum of Pennsylvania; more mainstream candidates such as Minnesota governor Tim Pawlenty and Texas governor Rick Perry, who failed to gain any traction with voters; and candidates who, while polling strongly at times, were ultimately judged as unready for the job, such as former House Speaker Newt Gingrich of Georgia and business executive Herman Cain. Although Romney was distrusted by the party's conservative base, he also had the best-funded and best-organized campaign. He more than held his own in a series of primary debates and outlasted the rest of the field.

By the time Romney secured the nomination in the spring of 2012, the prospects for a Republican victory were beginning to sag. Romney had been bloodied during the primaries by a series of attacks that questioned his principles and criticized his actions as a principal of Bain Capital, a controversial asset management company that specialized in buying underperforming corporations with hopes of turning them around and making a profit. The economy was continuing to slowly strengthen, with the unemployment rate at just more than 8 percent. Obama had shored up his national security credentials thanks to a string of highly visible victories in 2011 that included the slaying of

Osama bin Laden and the successful campaign against the government of Moammar Ghaddafi in Libya. Polls in the spring of 2012 indicated a competitive race, with most showing Obama in the lead by a few percentage points but falling short of the critical 50 percent mark.

The Obama campaign strengthened its position in the spring and early summer by unleashing a merciless series of negative ads against Romney, attempting to define the former governor before he could introduce himself to the general electorate. Tens of millions of dollars worth of attack ads hammered Romney for sending jobs overseas, refusing to release his tax returns, and espousing policies that would cut taxes for himself and other wealthy Americans at the expense of the middle class. By focusing on Romney, the attacks deflected attention from Obama's handling of the economy and instead framed the Republican as a high-risk alternative. "That was the key strategic calculation," said political scientist George Edwards of Texas A&M University. "Romney wanted a referendum on Obama's performance, but Obama made it a choice between two people." The attacks worked; by July, Obama led in virtually every poll. However, his margin generally was in the precarious range of low- to midsingle digits, and he still failed to crack 50 percent in most surveys.

For its part, the Romney campaign and its Republican allies were hardly silent. They attacked Obama on any number of issues, including mishandling the economy and health care, alleged cronyism, and planning to do away with work requirements for welfare recipients. As the campaign grew increasingly negative, fact-checkers found a number of ads on both sides to be blatantly false.

By the time election season reached full swing in early September, many political analysts believed that Romney was running out of opportunities to turn around the race. He had not achieved much of a bounce in the polls following the Republican convention in Tampa, and his choice of House Budget Chair Paul Ryan of Wisconsin to be his running mate failed to excite voters. His attacks did not seem to be altering voter perceptions of Obama. For his part, the incumbent seemed to be running out the clock. The president was content to give a workmanlike but uninspiring acceptance speech at the Democratic convention in Charlotte, acknowledging the difficult challenges while laying out a long-term blueprint for strengthening the nation. "I won't pretend the path I'm offering is quick or easy; I never have," Obama said. "You didn't elect me to tell you what you wanted to hear. You elected me to tell you the truth. And the truth is, it will take more than a few years for us to solve challenges that have built up over decades."

Part of the reason for the Obama campaign's confidence had to do with the his approaching a virtual lock on the electoral college. Most of the contested states, such as Pennsylvania, Virginia, Iowa, Wisconsin, Colorado, and especially the pivotal battleground of Ohio, were leaning in the president's direction. The reasons varied from state to state; Ohio, for example, favored Obama because of the General Motors and Chrysler bailouts, while Colorado seemed favorable partly because of the growing number of Hispanic voters. At the same time, the Obama campaign had engineered a remarkable apparatus to turn out voters. It would register about 1.8 million voters in the main battleground states and make more than 125 million personal phone calls and door knocks. Although the Romney campaign could roughly match Obama's in terms of funding, it lagged in terms of targeting and turning out supporters. Despite their difficult position, Romney's aides believed that the polls were overstating Obama's strength by overestimating such variables as minority turnout. They felt, erroneously, their candidate had the upper hand.

Two events in September and early October threatened to change the trajectory of the race. On September 11, the American diplomatic mission in Benghazi, Libya, came under attack by a heavily armed group. Four people were killed, including U.S. Ambassador J. Christopher Stevens. The deaths forced the Obama administration to defend its handling of the situation in the face of criticism, largely from Republicans, that it failed to take proper steps to secure the consulate site and then provided misleading information about the attack. But the event failed to put much of a dent in Obama's reelection prospects.

On October 3, however, Obama stumbled badly in the first presidential debate in Denver. He appeared detached and weary, especially compared with an energized Romney. The debate was viewed by more than sixty-seven million Americans, and polls showed that they overwhelmingly believed Romney had won. Over the next three weeks, Romney pulled into a virtual tie with Obama in national polls, although Obama held a slight edge in polls of battleground states.

The debate served as a wakeup call to the Obama campaign. The incumbent came out swinging the next day, questioning Romney's honesty. "Gov. Romney may dance around his positions, but if you want to be president, you owe the American people the truth," Obama said in an energetic appearance in Denver. The campaign launched an ad campaign that hit Romney for failing to be straightforward with voters over how his tax plan would affect them. Obama also performed much more strongly in the second and third presidential debates, as did Biden in the vice presidential debate. For his part, Romney failed to effectively take advantage of Obama's weak first debate performance. After stressing his conservative credentials for much of the campaign, he began to tack toward the political center—a move, some analysts felt, that came too little and too late. The Romney campaign was also knocked off stride by the release of a video that showed him criticizing the 47 percent of Americans who took government assistance. Trying to close the gap in Ohio, the campaign then launched a controversial ad campaign alleging that General Motors and Chrysler had plans to lay off U.S. workers. Executives with the automakers heatedly denied the allegations.

In perhaps the final blow to the Romney campaign, Superstorm Sandy came ashore in New Jersey and New York on October 29, causing devastating flooding, knocking out power to millions, and ultimately costing an estimated $70 billion or more in damages. The storm diverted attention from the presidential campaign during a critical period when Romney needed to make up ground. It also placed a media spotlight on Obama, who toured storm-ravaged areas and pledged relief. New Jersey governor Chris Christie, a Republican and leading Romney supporter, strongly praised Obama's response. When attention turned back to the presidential race, Romney found himself on the defensive over a 2011 proposal to eliminate the Federal Emergency Management Agency. Some Republicans felt that Romney would have won had it not been for Sandy. Polls, however, suggested that Obama held a narrow but steady lead before the storm, and many analysts felt that Romney's fate was already sealed.

Although Obama was weakened by a frail economy and difficult first term, he won every state he had carried in 2008 except Indiana and North Carolina, besting Romney in virtually all the key battlegrounds. Pollsters who pored over the results concluded that his victory was attributable in large part to the nation's shifting demographics. Minorities cast 28 percent of the vote and supported Obama overwhelmingly, amid concerns that Republican policies were anti-immigrant and favored the wealthy. Hispanics, for example, voted for Obama by a nearly three-to-one margin. The president captured just 39 percent of the white vote, down from 43 percent in 2008. But that was enough to ensure his reelection.

Appointments

Obama created a remarkably diverse cabinet in his first term. It included a record three Asian Americans, the first African American attorney general, two Hispanic Americans, and four women. It also featured an impressive array of highly accomplished intellectuals, many with advanced degrees and many years of experience in their fields and one, Energy Secretary Steven Chu, who was the first Nobel laureate to be named to a cabinet. Obama also seemed unafraid to pick political rivals. These included Secretary of State Hillary Clinton, who finished a close second to Obama in the 2008 Democratic primaries, and several of her supporters who, like Clinton, campaigned for Obama in the general election. Obama's cabinet also included two Republicans, Defense Secretary Robert M. Gates and Transportation Secretary Ray LaHood.

Most of Obama's picks sailed through the confirmation process with strong bipartisan support. However, several were slowed by questions about taxes, and a few—especially Labor Secretary Hilda Solis—drew some criticism from Republicans concerned that they were too far to the left. Nominees for two departments, Health and Human Services and Commerce, were forced to withdraw over ethical questions or tax issues. Once confirmed, Obama's cabinet proved remarkably durable. Just two of the secretaries left during the president's first term: Gates, a holdover from the Bush administration who had ruled out serving for all four years, and Commerce Secretary Gary Locke, who was named ambassador to China.

SECRETARY OF STATE

Obama surprised many by picking a powerful rival within the Democratic Party, New York senator and former first lady Hillary Clinton, for secretary of state. The two had clashed repeatedly during the bitter and close campaign for the Democratic nomination, with Obama criticizing Clinton's foreign policy credentials. But after Obama clinched the nomination, Clinton hit the campaign trail for him.

Obama broached the issue of the secretary of state appointment when meeting with Clinton days after the election. Although not without risk, the selection could provide Obama with considerable benefits. In addition to placing a high-profile figure at the top of his cabinet, choosing Clinton would show that he could reach beyond his political circle. Some commentators even likened it to a "team of rivals" like that assembled by President Abraham Lincoln during the Civil War. The selection would also presumably sideline Clinton from criticizing Obama or potentially challenging him in 2012.

Clinton needed a couple of weeks to consider the offer. She was seen as a prime candidate to move up in Senate leadership. But there were no immediate opportunities, and it remained highly uncertain whether she would ever achieve the position of majority leader. She also had not ruled out running for president in 2016, and it was uncertain how a cabinet position would affect that. Finally, she needed to consider her husband, former President Bill Clinton, whose financial and other overseas activities could potentially violate conflict-of-interest rules for a cabinet member. In the end, she accepted the offer. As she expressed it later, "I finally began thinking, look, if I had won and I had called him, I would have wanted him to say yes. And, you know, I'm pretty old-fashioned, and it's just who I am. So at the end of the day, when your president asks you to serve, you say yes, if you can." On December 1, 2008, Obama formally announced that Clinton would be his nominee for secretary of state. Bill Clinton agreed to various conditions and restrictions on his fund-raising and other activities for the Clinton Presidential Center and the Clinton Global Initiative.

Hillary Clinton had become a hugely popular public figure, and the nomination was generally greeted warmly by senators in both parties. At her confirmation hearings, Clinton stressed the importance of a multifaceted approach to foreign policy. "We must use what has been called 'smart power,' the full range of tools at our disposal—diplomatic, economic, military, political, legal and cultural—picking

PRESIDENT BARACK OBAMA'S CABINET

Following is a list of cabinet officers who served in the administration of President Barack Obama during his first term in office between January 20, 2009, and January 20, 2013. Dates given are for actual service in office, beginning with the cabinet officers' swearing-in date, which often varies from date of confirmation by the Senate. Some cabinet members remained in office into Obama's second term. Officials who left during 2013 are noted. Only heads of the major departments are listed; offices that have been designated as cabinet-level are not included.

Department head	Dates of service
Secretary of State	
Hillary Rodham Clinton	January 21, 2009–February 1, 2013
Secretary of the Treasury	
Timothy Geithner	January 26, 2009–January 25, 2013
Secretary of Defense	
Robert M. Gates	December 18, 2006–July 1, 2011[1]
Leon Panetta	July 1, 2011–February 27, 2013
Attorney General	
Eric Holder Jr.	February 3, 2009–
Secretary of the Interior	
Ken S. Salazar	January 20, 2009–April 12, 2013
Secretary of Agriculture	
Thomas J. Vilsack	January 21, 2009–
Secretary of Commerce	
Gary Locke	March 26, 2009–August 1, 2011
Rebecca Blank (acting)	August 1, 2011–October 21, 2011
John Bryson	October 21, 2011–June 11, 2012
Rebecca Blank (acting)	June 11, 2012–June 1, 2013

Department head	Dates of service
Secretary of Labor	
Hilda L. Solis	February 24, 2009–January 22, 2013
Secretary of Health and Human Services	
Kathleen Sebelius	April 8, 2009–
Secretary of Education	
Arne Duncan	January 21, 2009–
Secretary of Housing and Urban Development	
Shaun Donovan	January 26, 2009–
Secretary of Transportation	
Ray LaHood	January 23, 2009–July 2, 2013
Secretary of Energy	
Steven Chu	January 21, 2009–April 22, 2013
Secretary of Veterans Affairs	
Eric K. Shinseki	January 21, 2009–
Secretary of Homeland Security	
Michael Chertoff	February 15, 2005–January 21, 2009[2]
Janet Napolitano	January 21, 2009–September 6, 2013

[1]Gates served as defense secretary in the administration of George W. Bush, President Obama's predecessor. Obama retained him as defense secretary when his administration began in January 2009. Gates did not require reconfirmation by the Senate.

[2]Chertoff, who held the post in President Bush's administration, remained in office until the day after Obama was inaugurated to expedite transition to the new administration.

the right tool or combination of tools for each situation," she said. "With smart power, diplomacy will be the vanguard of our foreign policy." The Senate Foreign Relations Committee approved the nomination on January 15 by a vote of 16–1, with David Vitter, R-La., casting the only dissenting vote. The Senate confirmed her on January 21, 94–2, with only Republicans Vitter and Jim DeMint of South Carolina voting no.

DEPARTMENT OF DEFENSE

Obama announced that he would retain Defense Secretary Gates in December 2008. The highly regarded administrator had assumed the office at the end of 2006 under former President Bush. Obama's announcement ensured a degree of continuity in the nation's military policy at a time of wars in both Iraq and Afghanistan, and it also fulfilled a campaign pledge by Obama to include Republicans in his cabinet. The reappointment of Gates, who enjoyed good relations with both Republicans and Democrats, received bipartisan praise. Gates let it be known at the time that he would not serve during the entire administration. He announced in August 2010 that he would step down in 2011, thereby avoiding confirmation hearings over his successor being held during the 2012 election year.

To fill the position, Obama announced on April 28, 2011, that he would nominate Leon Panetta, the director of the Central Intelligence Agency (CIA). Like Gates, Panetta had a strong reputation among both parties as an able administrator even though his background as former chair of the House Budget Committee was more political. Senators of both parties praised his leadership of the CIA and particularly his role in tracking down Osama bin Laden, who was killed in May 2011. The Senate approved the nomination on a 100–0 vote on June 21, 2011. In addition with being charged with overseeing the drawdown of troops from Afghanistan, one of Panetta's first major acts as defense secretary was to jointly certify with the chairman of the Joint Chiefs of Staff that the military was prepared to repeal its controversial "don't ask, don't tell" policy for gay members of the military.

DEPARTMENT OF THE TREASURY

With the nation facing its most dangerous economic crisis since the Great Depression, Obama nominated Timothy Geithner, president of the New York Federal Reserve Bank, for Treasury secretary. The post was expected to be among the most important in the new administration as Geithner would lead the administration's efforts to guide the nation's weakened financial sector back to the health.

The nomination was not initially regarded as particularly controversial. Geithner enjoyed a strong reputation for his financial expertise, steady leadership during the early days of the financial crisis, and ability to get along with members of both parties. "Having served in senior roles at Treasury, the IMF and the New York Fed, Tim Geithner offers not just extensive experience shaping economic policy and managing financial markets, but an unparalleled understanding of our current economic crisis, in all of its depth, complexity and urgency," Obama said in announcing the nomination. "Tim will waste no time getting up to speed. He will start his first day on the job with a unique insight into the failures of today's markets—and a clear vision of the steps we must take to revive them."

Some critics of the bailouts for large Wall Street firms, however, criticized the nomination because of Geithner's central role in engineering them. Then it was revealed that Geithner had a series of tax problems. The Internal Revenue Service (IRS) in 2006 had found that he failed to pay self-employment taxes in 2003 and 2004 for income related to his work for the International Monetary Fund (IMF). Geithner had paid $16,732 in back taxes, plus interest. After Obama decided to tap him as Treasury secretary, however, the presidential transition team discovered additional tax issues, including the fact that he had not paid self-employment taxes for 2001 and 2002 even after the IRS pointed out his failure to pay those taxes in 2003 and 2004. Although Geithner was no longer required to pay the taxes, he voluntarily wrote a check to the IRS for another $25,970. Other, smaller problems were discovered, such as Geithner claiming a tax deduction for summer camp for his children.

Geithner apologized for the errors at his confirmation hearings, calling them "careless mistakes" but unintentional. Obama stood by his nominee, saying that similar mistakes were commonly made by people working for international organizations because of the complexities in the tax code. Still, the revelations unleashed a storm of criticism, with influential Republican senators saying the person who would oversee the IRS had to set a better example of paying his own taxes. "Can this system operate with integrity if all parts of it reports to someone who was unable to meet his own obligations over a long period of time and did so only as a condition of his nomination?" asked Sen. Charles E. Grassley, R-Iowa, the ranking member of the Finance Committee. He ultimately voted against the nomination.

The Finance Committee delayed its confirmation hearing by a week, dashing Obama's hope to have Geithner in place when his administration took charge. But, although some senators questioned how Geithner could have underpaid his taxes by accident, the nomination never seemed in danger. The Senate was under great pressure to move quickly given the magnitude of the economic threat facing the nation. Overcoming opposition by Republicans and a few Democrats, Geithner was confirmed, 60–34, on January 26.

DEPARTMENT OF JUSTICE

Eric H. Holder Jr., one of the most credentialed lawyers ever to fill the position of attorney general, had served as a public corruption prosecutor and U.S. attorney before operating as the second in comment in the Justice Department in the final years of the Clinton administration. He served as senior legal advisor to Obama during the presidential campaign. Holder would also be the first African American attorney general.

Still, Obama's nomination of Holder in December 2008 was not without controversy. Republicans criticized Holder for a number of reasons, including his positions on national security and gun rights and his recommendations in controversial clemency decisions by Bill Clinton. Perhaps Holder's greatest vulnerability was his role in facilitating the pardon that Clinton had given to Marc Rich, a financier who had fled the United States to avoid prosecution on federal tax evasion charges. During a grueling seven-hour confirmation hearing, Holder was grilled by the Senate Judiciary Committee over his views on interrogating suspected terrorists. Asked about the technique known as waterboarding, which simulates drowning, Holder declared that it constitutes torture, in violation of the Geneva Conventions. To the dismay of Republicans, he did not entirely rule out prosecution of Bush administration officials for their involvement in questioning detainees and conducting warrantless surveillance operations. His views on gun registration also concerned conservatives, some of whom said his position would mean that a person could not give a gun to someone else without involving the government.

But Holder had support from a broad base of federal and state law enforcement groups as well as a bipartisan coalition of former Justice Department leaders. Even his Republican critics did not question his experience or integrity. On February 2, he won Senate approval, 75–21, with all the no votes coming from Republicans.

DEPARTMENT OF HEALTH AND HUMAN SERVICES

Given that Obama's top legislative priority was winning passage of a comprehensive health care bill, the president wanted to fill the position of Secretary of Health and Human Services (HHS) with a widely respected Washington insider. Unfortunately for the president, the HHS position wound up being the last cabinet position to be confirmed in April 2009. Obama's first choice, former Senate Majority Leader Thomas Daschle, D-S.D., was nominated on December 11, 2008, but withdrew after questions were raised about his taxes. The position ultimately went to Kansas governor Kathleen Sebelius, who successfully endured a difficult confirmation process. In the interim, the health department was overseen by an acting secretary, Charles E. Johnson, who had served in the Bush administration.

Obama's announcement of Daschle's nomination underscored the new administration's emphasis on health care legislation. As a former majority leader turned lobbyist with a focus on health care issues, Daschle had almost unrivaled expertise on guiding difficult proposals through Congress. An early supporter of Obama and a key member of the transition team, he had even been considered for the position of chief of staff, which ultimately went instead to Rep. Rahm Emmanuel, D-Ill. The White House envisioned Daschle as handling a broad portfolio, overseeing the Department of Health and Human Services as well as shepherding the health care bill through Congress. "He knows how to build consensus across the aisle," President-elect Obama said in a press conference announcing the nomination. "And he has the trust of folks from every angle of this issue: doctors, nurses and patients; workers and businesses; hospitals and consumer groups—all of whom will have a seat at the table as we work on this vital issue."

But the nomination ran into trouble after reports surfaced that Daschle, who had made millions in lobbying after leaving the Senate in 2005, had failed to fully pay his taxes on those activities. He was forced to file amended tax returns and pay more than $140,000 in back taxes and interest for 2005–2007 for a number of errors that included failing to report $15,000 in charitable donations, unreported use of a limousine and driver, and more than $80,000 in unreported income from consulting. Daschle failed to assuage Republican concerns at a closed-door meeting of the Senate Finance Committee at the beginning of February. Republicans pointed out that Daschle should have known better given that he sat on the Senate's tax-writing committee. Sen. John Ensign, R-Nev., said Daschle's explanation for not paying his taxes "had holes in it."

The nomination also came under fire over concerns about Daschle's extensive ties to the health care industry and other powerful Washington interests. Obama had pledged "a new era of openness in our country" and signed executive orders barring lobbyists who joined the administration from working on matters that they had lobbied on during the first two years. The White House contended that the restriction did not apply to Daschle, who was not a registered lobbyist, but critics pointed out that he had made millions of dollars advancing the interests of powerful business organizations.

Although a group of Democratic senators released a statement supporting the nomination, Daschle announced on February 3, 2009, that he was withdrawing his name from consideration. Obama praised his friend and political ally while taking responsibility for the politically embarrassing episode. "I think I screwed up. And I take responsibility for it and we're going to make sure we fix it so it doesn't happen again," the president said in an interview shortly after Daschle's withdrawal. "Ultimately, I campaigned on changing Washington and bottom-up politics. And I don't want to send a message to the American people that there are two sets of standards—one for powerful people and one for ordinary folks who are working every day and paying their taxes."

The Daschle incident was particularly damaging to the administration. In addition to the political embarrassment, it set back efforts on health care reform just as the White House was gearing up an all-out push on the issue and cost Obama his right-hand man on the issue. It also came just hours after Obama's pick to the new post of chief performance officer, Nancy Killefer, resigned over tax issues.

On March 2, Obama announced the nomination of Kansas governor Kathleen Sebelius for the HHS post. Sebelius, who had previously served as state insurance commissioner, enjoyed a reputation for reaching across the aisle in her solidly Republican home state. Although she was not experienced with health care legislation on the scale that the White House would undertake, she had overseen the addition of tens of thousands of low-income children to state health programs in Kansas. A Roman Catholic, Sebelius had endured scorching criticism for vetoing a bill that would have required doctors who perform late-term abortions to report a reason for the procedure. After the veto, the archbishop of Kansas City asked Sebelius to stop taking communion.

Sebelius, as it turned out, also had tax issues. She and her husband had to pay more than $7,000 in back taxes and interest after discovering what she characterized as "unintentional errors" in their returns for 2005–2007. Although senators regarded that as a minor issue, her confirmation vote kept getting pushed back amid concerns over her support for abortion rights and the administration's plan for overhauling the health care system. But Democrats pressed the issue when an outbreak of the swine flu in the United States and other countries evoked concerns of a public health emergency. Despite continuing opposition from most Republicans, the Senate approved the confirmation, 65–31, on April 28.

DEPARTMENT OF ENERGY

Obama's selection of Steven Chu to head the Department of Energy broke ground in two ways. Chu, a Nobel physics laureate, was the first person selected to a cabinet post after winning a Nobel Prize, and he was also the first Asian American to head the Department of Energy. Chu had been director of the Energy Department's Lawrence Berkeley National Laboratory in California since 2004. An advocate for renewable energy research, he believed it critical to find scientific solutions to climate change. His emphasis on technology and innovation to help solve energy and climate problems appealed to both environmentalists and leaders of the energy industry, and he enjoyed a reputation as the rare academic with an interest in the commercial side. At his confirmation hearing, he said he would put a greater focus at the Energy Department on climate change. Although calling for investments in energy efficiency and renewable energy, he also presented himself as a pragmatist who believed the nation's energy needs would require new nuclear plants, continued reliance on coal-fired power plants, and oil and gas drilling. His qualifications drew praise from senators on both sides of the aisle. He was confirmed by voice vote on January 20, 2009.

DEPARTMENT OF COMMERCE

The position of secretary of Commerce proved more difficult than most for Obama to fill. His first two choices withdrew before Obama settled on former Washington governor Gary Locke in February 2009. His second commerce secretary, business executive John Bryson, survived a difficult confirmation process in 2011 and then resigned a year later because of health reasons. Bryson was succeeded by the deputy secretary, Rebecca Blank, who served without Senate confirmation.

Obama's initial pick for the position, announced on December 3, 2008, appeared to be a strong nominee. Bill Richardson, governor of New Mexico, was a popular politician with strong business ties who had served as energy secretary and U.N. ambassador in the Clinton administration. He ran for president in 2008, then threw his support to Obama after withdrawing. He would have been a high-profile Hispanic member of the Obama administration. But Richardson withdrew on January 4, 2009, because of an ongoing federal investigation of some of his political donors. The investigation, which had begun over the summer and heated up around the time of Richardson's nomination, focused on whether Richardson's office urged a state agency to hire a California firm as a result of generous contributions from the company and its president to political action committees established by the governor. Richardson maintained his innocence. But the probe could take months and, given the legal questions, Senate confirmation of Richardson's nomination was far from a sure thing. The withdrawal raised questions about how closely the Obama transition team had vetted Richardson.

On February 3, Obama announced the surprising nomination of Sen. Judd Gregg, R-N.H., to be commerce secretary. The pick sparked political concerns among Republicans because the Senate seat would have been filled by the state's governor, John Lynch, a Democrat. That would have given Democrats a filibuster-proof margin of sixty seats in the Senate, assuming that Democrat Al Franken would be declared the victor in a close and disputed Minnesota contest (as eventually happened). Both Obama and Gregg gave assurances that the cabinet post would not be used as an attempt to increase the Democrats' margin in the Senate. Nevertheless, Gregg withdrew his nomination on February 12, saying he "made a mistake." He cited fundamental disagreements with the administration over both its economic stimulus package and its plans to have the next census director report to senior White House officials as well as the commerce secretary. The withdrawal embarrassed the administration at a politically sensitive time when it was trying to win congressional approval over the stimulus program.

Playing it safe, Obama then announced the nomination of Locke on February 25. Locke, the first Chinese American to be elected governor, enjoyed a strait-laced reputation and had considerable expertise on trade issues. His nomination continued Obama's emphasis on diversity and reaching out to former rivals. The governor had been an early supporter of Clinton in the Democratic presidential race, serving as a co-chair of her campaign in his state. Locke breezed through the confirmation process, reassuring senators that the 2010 census process would remain in the Commerce Department and would be handled in a professional manner. He was confirmed on a voice vote on March 4, 2009.

After nominating Locke as the new U.S. ambassador to China, Obama announced on May 31, 2011, that Bryson would be his pick for the next Commerce secretary. Bryson, a California energy and utility executive, would add a business outlook to the cabinet. Obama also lauded Bryson's support of clean energy initiatives. However, Republicans and some Democrats became concerned about some of Bryson's environmental positions, including favorable comments that the nominee had made in 2009 about legislation to limit carbon emissions in order to slow climate change. Bryson had also helped found a major environmental advocacy group, the Natural Resources Defense Council, in the early 1970s.

In his confirmation hearings, Republicans as well as Sen. Jay Rockefeller of West Virginia wanted assurances that Bryson would not set back coal or other traditional energy industries. Bryson emphasized that his focus as commerce secretary would be on jobs, not the environment. He added that he would work to simplify the tax code and eliminate unnecessary regulations in order to help businesses. His business background and emphasis on job creation won over most senators. Bryson also picked up the support of influential business groups, including the Business Roundtable. But confirmation was delayed for months when Senate Republicans threatened to block the confirmation until Obama submitted long-delayed trade agreements with Colombia, Panama, and South Korea for congressional approval. In addition, Sen. James M. Inhofe of Oklahoma, the ranking Republican on the Environment and Public Works Committee, put a hold on the nomination because of Bryson's environmental views. After Congress passed the trade agreements and the hold was lifted, the Senate voted, 74–26, to confirm Bryson on October 20.

However, Bryson resigned on June 21, 2012, following his involvement in a pair of car accidents after apparently suffering a seizure. Blank then served as acting secretary for the remainder of Obama's first term .

DEPARTMENT OF EDUCATION

Obama announced his pick of Chicago schools executive Arne Duncan on December 16, 2008, to be his secretary of education. In making the announcement at Dodge Renaissance Academy, a Chicago elementary school, the president warned that the nation's education system was on an unsustainable path. Citing poor test scores, high dropout rates, and the expense of college, Obama said, "We cannot continue on like this. It is morally unacceptable for our children and economically untenable for America."

Two years younger than the president-elect, Duncan had grown up in Chicago's Hyde Park neighborhood, and the two men were longtime friends. Duncan had been chief executive of Chicago public schools, the nation's third-largest school district, since 2001. He had worked with the Chicago Teachers Union to establish a performance-based pay program and supported the expansion of charter schools. During his tenure in Chicago, he maintained ties both with teachers unions, who were concerned about high-stakes testing and linking merit pay to test scores, and with reformers who advocated tougher standards to reformers. At Duncan's confirmation hearing, members of the Senate Health, Education, Labor and Pensions Committee praised him for pursuing a number of measures to boost achievement in the diverse and high-poverty Chicago schools during his seven years as chief executive. He promised to pursue Obama's agenda of expanding preschool, making college more accessible and affordable, and helping to overhaul the 2002 No Child Left Behind law. The Senate confirmed him by voice vote on January 21, 2009.

DEPARTMENT OF HOUSING AND URBAN AFFAIRS

At a time of falling housing values and soaring foreclosures, Obama turned to the New York City housing commissioner, Shaun Donovan, to be his secretary of housing and urban development. Donovan would work with an economic team led by Treasury Secretary Geithner and Larry Summers, chair of Obama's National Economic Council. In naming Donovan as his pick during his Saturday radio address on December 13, Obama stressed the importance of a fresh approach to housing. "We need to approach the old challenge of affordable housing with new energy, new ideas, and a new, efficient style of leadership," he said. Donovan, who had worked for the Department of Housing and Urban Development in the Clinton administration, had a national reputation for curtailing low-income foreclosures, developing affordable housing, and managing the nation's largest housing plan. As New York Mayor Michael Bloomberg's top aide for housing, Donovan kept foreclosures to a minimum in the city's low- and moderate-income homeownership plan, with just five of 17,000 participating homes falling. He oversaw the creation of the $200 million New York Acquisition Fund, a collaboration involving the city, foundations, and financial institutions that aimed to help small developers and nonprofit groups compete for land in the private market.

Donovan was well regarded by a range of housing interests, including low-income housing and homeless advocates, public officials, developers, and financiers. At his confirmation hearing, members of the Senate Banking Committee urged him to be more aggressive than his predecessors in fighting home foreclosures and shaping responses toward the economic crisis. Senators from both parties praised his extensive resume, including two graduate degrees from Harvard. "He's far more qualified than I was," said Sen. Mel Martinez, R-Fla., who served as President Bush's first housing secretary. The Senate on January 22 approved the nomination by voice vote.

DEPARTMENT OF TRANSPORTATION

Obama turned to a retiring Republican representative, Ray LaHood of Illinois, to head the Transportation Department. The president-elect had said repeatedly that he wanted to include several Republicans in prominent positions in his administration to move beyond partisan bickering, and LaHood would be the second Republican in his cabinet with Defense Secretary Gates. LaHood had little experience with transportation issues. But work on the Appropriations Committee was viewed as preparing him for the large amount of spending that Obama wished to undertake on infrastructure projects as part of an economic stimulus package. As a member of the House, LaHood enjoyed a generally centrist and pragmatic reputation. After Obama won election to the Senate, the two men forged a close relationship as LaHood became a key player on the House Appropriations Committee on behalf of their home state. But the Republican strongly backed Sen. John McCain, R-Ariz., in the presidential election.

LaHood was greeted warmly by members of the Senate Commerce and Transportation Committee at his confirmation hearing, receiving praise from members of both parties. He stressed the importance of making labor peace with air traffic controllers, modernizing the Federal Aviation Administration, and playing an important role on the economic stimulus package. He also promised to seek full financing for Amtrak. Although some environmentalists worried that LaHood did not care about issues such as sprawl and climate change, he coasted through the confirmation process and was confirmed on a voice vote on January 23.

DEPARTMENT OF HOMELAND SECURITY

On December 1, 2008, Obama announced Arizona governor Janet Napolitano as his pick for secretary of homeland security. Napolitano, a rising star among Democratic women, had gained national attention for her work on border security efforts and her opposition to President Bush's plan to build a 700-mile fence. An expert on law enforcement, she had served as a U.S. attorney and Arizona attorney general before her gubernatorial election in 2002. "She knows firsthand the need to have a partner in Washington that works well with state and local governments," Obama said in announcing the appointment. "She understands as well as anyone the danger of an unsecure border." Napolitano, however, faced major challenges with the ongoing threat of terrorism, a difficult war on illegal drugs that were being smuggled across the U.S. border, and rising illegal immigration rates. Warmly greeted at her confirmation hearing, Napolitano won Senate approval on a voice vote on January 20.

DEPARTMENT OF INTERIOR

Sen. Ken Salazar, D-Colo., was nominated to be secretary of the Interior on December 19, 2008. Although some in the environmental community were wary of his perceived close ties with the coal and mining industries and some conservatives raised concerns about his views on oil shale development and drilling in environmentally sensitive areas, the nomination stirred little controversy. At his confirmation hearing before the Senate Energy and Natural Resources Committee, Salazar said his priorities would include reducing the nation's dependency on foreign oil, expanding the use of renewable energy, investing in new water conservation technologies, and modernizing the interstate electrical grid. He also stressed the importance of making policy based on scientific findings. Senate Republicans and Democrats alike praised the nomination. The Senate approved the nomination on voice vote on January 21, 2009.

DEPARTMENT OF VETERANS AFFAIRS

To head the Department of Veterans Affairs, Obama tapped retired Army General Eric K. Shinseki. The four-star general had been army chief of staff when, in 2003, he publicly disputed the Bush administration's optimistic estimates for the number of troops needed to maintain the postwar peace in Iraq, saying "something on the order of several hundred thousand soldiers" could be necessary. Although his remarks irritated Defense Secretary Donald H. Rumsfeld at the time, his prediction proved largely prescient.

That controversy over, Obama's announcement of Shinseki's nomination on December 7, 2008, was greeted warmly by military leaders and veterans advocates. As someone who had twice received the Purple Heart for wounds sustained in Vietnam, Shinseki was viewed as someone who understood the needs of veterans, as well as how to run a large bureaucracy. At a difficult time for the department in the wake of two wars and the many physical and emotional scars borne by veterans, Skinseki pledged at his confirmation hearing to streamline the disability claims system, use new information technologies to improve the delivery of benefits and services, and focus on unemployed and homeless veterans. He also said the nation needed to more effectively fulfill its promise to take care of wounded veterans, those "bearing scars of battle, some visible and many others invisible," a reference not only to those with physical wounds but also to those suffering from posttraumatic stress and traumatic brain injuries.

Shinseki was a Japanese American who, like Obama, was born in Hawaii. His nomination received praise from both Republicans and Democrats, and he was confirmed by voice vote on January 20.

DEPARTMENT OF LABOR

In a foreshadowing of partisan battles over labor issues, confirmation of Obama's nominee for labor secretary, Rep. Hilda Solis, D-Calif., stalled for more than a month over conservative concerns before the Senate approved her by a wide margin. Obama announced the nomination of Solis on December 19, 2008, to overwhelming approval by labor unions. The first female Hispanic state senator in California, Solis had successfully pressed to increase the state's minimum wage in the 1990s. After her election to the House, she became the only member of Congress to sit on the board of American Rights at Work, a prolabor organization, and she shared the concerns of organized labor about free-trade agreements. Solis also advocated the development of jobs in environmental areas such as renewable energy. She had supported Clinton in the 2008 Democratic primaries but then forged a close relationship with Obama.

The nomination came under scrutiny because of Republican concerns over her support of the Employee Free Choice Act, which would make it much easier for unions to organize workers. Republicans also questioned her work with American Rights at Work, a prolabor group for which Solis served as an unpaid treasurer. Some lawmakers wondered whether her position on a board that organization officials said met only annually amounted to a lobbying role, but Solis disagreed. In her January 9, 2009, confirmation hearing before the Senate Health, Education, Labor, and Pensions Committee, Solis refused to be pinned down on several contentious issues, such as the Employee Free Choice Act and ergonomic rules that had been lifted during the Bush administration. The issues led to weeks of written questions and answers between Solis and GOP members of the committee. Amid threats by some Republican lawmakers to put a hold on the nomination, Obama appointed longtime Labor Department official Edward C. Hugler to serve as acting secretary.

Solis's written responses satisfied committee Republicans. But the committee delayed its vote for a week amid news that Solis's husband, Sam Sayyad, had recently paid $6,400 in outstanding state and local tax liens for his auto repair business. Solis and Sayyad filed separate taxes, and the White House maintained that Solis should not be penalized for any mistakes that her husband may have made. Senators agreed, confirming her, 80–17, on February 24.

DEPARTMENT OF AGRICULTURE

Obama turned to a one-time political rival, former Iowa governor Tom Vilsack, for agriculture secretary. Vilsack had briefly run for president, before dropping out and endorsing Clinton while criticizing Obama for his lack of experience. After Obama won the nomination, however, Vilsack campaigned vigorously for him.

Vilsack's nomination came at a challenging time for the agricultural industry, because of both the recession and the contentious debate over plans to expand the use of ethanol and other biofuels to reduce the nation's dependence on foreign oil. Vilsack, like Obama, was an enthusiastic proponent of renewable energy and of combating global warming. In his confirmation hearing, he pledged to pursue the development of biofuels, promote locally grown fruits and vegetables, and explore additional ways of increasing farmers' incomes such as expanding the use of wind turbines and encouraging organic farming.

The nomination was generally greeted warmly by the agricultural industry, although some worried that he might be too close to ethanol interests. Republicans and Democrats alike praised Vilsack. He won Senate approval on a voice vote on January 21, 2009.

SUPREME COURT NOMINATIONS

Obama made two successful nominations to the Supreme Court: Sonia Sotomayor in 2009 and Elena Kagan in 2010. He became the first president in history to place two women on the Court. Although neither nomination set off full-scale political battles, they both sparked considerable debate in the Senate, with most Republicans ultimately voting no. The appointments did not change the Court's political balance, as the left-leaning women replaced two members of the court's liberal wing. However, the Court went from being dominated by appointees by Republican presidents (7–2) to one that was more equally balanced between the parties (five justices appointed by Republican presidents vs. four justices appointed by Democrats). *(Supreme Court analysis, p. 584)*

Sonia Sotomayor

The Senate approved the nomination of fifty-five-year-old Sotomayor on a largely party-line vote of 68–31 on August 6, 2009. The vote came ten weeks after the White House formally submitted the nomination.

Obama's first opportunity to shape the Supreme Court arose when Associate Justice David Souter announced on May 1, 2009, that he would step down from his seat. Souter had been named to the Court by President George H. W. Bush and was thought at the time to be a reliably conservative vote. But he soon began to side with the Court's liberal wing. Although the opening gave Obama little room to move the Court to the left, it did provide him the opportunity to make the Court more diverse. There had never been a Hispanic justice, and eight of the nine justices were male.

The Obama administration began preparing for a possible Supreme Court opening shortly after the election, with White House counsel Greg Craig identifying potential nominees. It took the White House just a week after Souter's announcement to finalize a short list of leading candidates, reportedly headed by Sotomayor, a judge with the Second Circuit Court of Appeals; Judge Diane Pamela Wood of the Seventh Circuit; and Solicitor General Elena Kagan. Other candidates were believed to include Homeland Security Secretary Janet Napolitano, California Supreme Court Justice Carlos Moreno, Michigan Governor Jennifer Granholm, Georgia Supreme Court Chief Justice Leah Ward Sears, Judge Merrick B. Garland of the U.S. Court of Appeals for the District of Columbia, and Judge Ruben Castillo of the Federal District Court for the Northern District in Illinois. Obama winnowed the list to four women: Sotomayor, Wood, Kagan, and Napolitano. He conducted one-hour, private interviews with them on May 19 and May 21, and announced his decision, with Sotomayor at his side in the White House, on May 26.

Obama stressed Sotomayor's "extraordinary journey" from being raised by Puerto Rican parents in a Bronx housing project to the Ivy League and then to a successful career as prosecutor, corporate litigator, and federal district judge before joining the United States Court of Appeals for the Second Circuit a decade earlier. Standing by Obama's side in the East Room of the White House, Sotomayor said her life experiences helped inform her jurisprudence. "This wealth of experiences, personal and professional, have helped me appreciate the variety of perspectives that present themselves in every case that I hear," she said.

Even before the nomination was announced, Obama had set off alarms in conservative circles by saying he wanted a nominee with "empathy," which some interpreted as opening the door to a justice who would seek to impose personal views from the bench. Sotomayor was viewed as the most controversial of the finalists, and conservatives quickly mobilized in opposition. Raising questions about the nominee's past comments about how her sex and ethnicity shaped her decisions, and emphasizing the role of appeals courts in making policy, they warned that she would likely be a judicial activist. They especially seized on a comment that Sotomayor had made in a 2001 lecture about the role that her background had played in her judicial approach: "I would hope that a wise Latina woman with the richness of her experiences would more often than not reach a better conclusion than a white male who hasn't lived that life." The nominee's defenders, however, said the comment was being taken out of context. Republicans also questioned Sotomayor's opinions in cases involving Second Amendment rights, property rights, and a racial discrimination claim that had been filed by a group of white firefights in New Haven, Conn. The National Rifle Association, which had previously stayed out of Supreme Court confirmation battles, was so concerned that Sotomayor would be hostile to gun rights that it said it would include the confirmation vote on its scorecard of senators for the 2010 election.

But Republicans from the start faced two major obstacles in blocking the nomination: They risked antagonizing Hispanic voters if they sought to stop her, and they lacked the needed votes in the Senate. Republicans took great pains to emphasize that their opposition to Sotomayor did not mean they were anti-Hispanic, and they stressed their support for previous Hispanic nominees, such as Miguel Estrada, an appellate court pick by George W. Bush who had been blocked by Democrats. But they could not overcome their numerical deficit. Unable to rally the public against Sotomayor's voting record and faced with her compelling life story, they failed to erode solid Democratic backing for the nominee. In a triumph for Obama, no Democrat opposed her, and nine of the forty Senate Republicans broke ranks to vote for her.

Elena Kagan

Obama nominated Kagan, the U.S. solicitor general, to the Supreme Court on May 10, 2010, to fill the seat of retiring Justice John Paul Stevens. The senior member of the Court's liberal wing, Stevens had been appointed by President Gerald R. Ford but gradually broke from his Republican roots and assumed a more left-leaning approach to the law. The Senate, divided largely along party lines, confirmed Kagan by a 63–37 vote on August 5.

A runner-up when Obama nominated Sotomayor to the Court, Kagan was considered the clear front-runner for the new opening. Obama interviewed three other candidates who were all federal appeals court judges: Merrick B. Garland of Washington, Diane P. Wood of Chicago, and Sidney R. Thomas of Montana. But he knew Kagan best and was impressed with both her legal knowledge and her capacity to persuade others—an important skill on a Court divided closely between conservatives and liberals. At fifty, she was also the youngest of the finalists and therefore more likely to influence the Court for decades. In addition, she has won seven Republican votes the year before when confirmed as solicitor general and so appeared to be in a good position to again win at least a small amount of support from Republicans. By nominating Kagan, Obama could claim a middle ground; she appeared more liberal than Garland but not as far to the left as Wood.

At the East Room ceremony announcing the nomination, Obama praised Kagan for appreciating the law's tangible impacts. "That understanding of law, not as an intellectual exercise or words on a page, but as it affects the lives of ordinary people, has animated every step of Elena's career," he said. For her part, Kagan said the Court serves the country "by upholding the rule of law and by enabling all Americans, regardless of their background or their beliefs, to get a fair hearing and an equal chance at justice."

From the beginning, Kagan faced criticism for both her political views and her judicial inexperience. She was a highly accomplished lawyer who, after serving as a legal advisor in the Clinton White House, became the first woman dean of Harvard Law School and then the first woman solicitor general. But she had never served as a judge, and it had been nearly forty years since a new Supreme Court justice had lacked that experience. Conservative critics questioned whether she was truly qualified. They were hamstrung by a lack of a judicial paper trail that could have fueled attacks, although they repeatedly criticized her for briefly barring military recruiters from a campus facility on the grounds that the ban on openly gay people serving in the military violated the school's antidiscrimination policy. They also worried that her record in two Democratic administrations indicated that she might reach decisions based on political leanings. For their part, liberals were concerned about her support for strong executive power and her outreach to conservatives as law school dean, although they quickly lined up behind her.

As with Sotomayor, the nomination failed to ignite an all-out war and Republicans lacked the muscle to block the nomination. In the end, five Republicans supported Kagan; just one Democrat, Ben Nelson of Nebraska, opposed her. The relatively close vote indicated the extent to which debates over judicial nominees were becoming increasingly polarized.

Appendix

Glossary of Congressional Terms 715

The Legislative Process in Brief 745

Key Votes, 2009–2012 749

Congress and Its Members 823

The Presidency 875

Political Charts 917

Public Laws 949

Glossary of Congressional Terms

AA—*(See Administrative Assistant.)*

Absence of a Quorum—Absence of the required number of members to conduct business in a house or a committee. When a quorum call or roll-call vote in a house establishes that a quorum is not present, no debate or other business is permitted except a motion to adjourn or motions to request or compel the attendance of absent members, if necessary by arresting them.

Absolute Majority—A vote requiring approval by a majority of all members of a chamber rather than a majority of members present and voting. Also referred to as constitutional majority.

Account—Organizational units used in the federal budget primarily for recording spending and revenue transactions.

Act—(1) A bill passed in identical form by the House and Senate and signed into law by the president or enacted over the president's veto. A bill also becomes an act without the president's signature if it is unsigned but not returned to Congress within ten days (Sundays excepted) and if Congress has not adjourned within that period. (2) Also, the technical term for a bill passed by at least one house and engrossed.

Ad Hoc Select Committee—A temporary committee formed for a special purpose or to deal with a specific subject. Conference committees are ad hoc joint committees. A House rule adopted in 1975 authorizes the Speaker to refer measures to special ad hoc committees, appointed by the Speaker with the approval of the House. *(See and compare Select or Special Committee.)*

Adjourn—A motion to adjourn is a formal motion to end a day's session or meeting of a house or a committee. A motion to adjourn usually has no conditions attached to it, but it sometimes may specify the day or time for reconvening or make reconvening subject to the call of the chamber's presiding officer or the committee's chair. In both houses, a motion to adjourn is of the highest privilege, takes precedence over all other motions, is not debatable, and must be put to an immediate vote. Adjournment of a chamber ends its legislative day. For this reason, the House or Senate sometimes adjourns for only a brief period of time, during the course of a day's session. The House does not permit a motion to adjourn after it has resolved into the Committee of the Whole or when the previous question has been ordered on a measure to final passage without an intervening motion.

Adjourn for More Than Three Days—Under Article I, Section 5, of the Constitution, neither house may adjourn for more than three days without the approval of the other. The necessary approval is given in a concurrent resolution to which both houses have agreed.

Adjournment *Sine Die*—Final adjournment of an annual or two-year session of Congress; literally, adjournment without a day. The two houses must agree to a privileged concurrent resolution for such an adjournment. A *sine die* adjournment precludes Congress from meeting again until the next constitutionally fixed date of a session (January 3 of the following year) unless Congress determines otherwise by law or the president calls it into special session. Article II, Section 3, of the Constitution authorizes the president to adjourn both houses until such time as the president thinks proper when the two houses cannot agree to a time of adjournment. No president, however, has ever exercised this authority.

Adjournment to a Day (and Time) Certain—An adjournment that fixes the next date and time of meeting for one or both houses. It does not end an annual session of Congress.

Administration Bill—A bill drafted in the executive office of the president or in an executive department or agency to implement part of the president's program. An administration bill is introduced in Congress by a member who supports it or as a courtesy to the administration.

Administrative Assistant (AA)—The title formerly given to a member's chief aide, political advisor, and head of office staff. Today, the title most commonly used for such an individual is chief of staff. The administrative assistant often represents the member at meetings with visitors or officials when the member is unable (or unwilling) to attend.

Adoption—The usual parliamentary term for approval of a conference report. It is also commonly applied to amendments.

Advance Appropriation—In an appropriation act for a particular fiscal year, an appropriation that does not become available for spending or obligation until a subsequent fiscal year. The amount of the advance appropriation is counted as part of the budget for the fiscal year in which it becomes available for obligation.

Advance Funding—A mechanism whereby statutory language may allow budget authority for a fiscal year to be increased, and obligations to be incurred, with an offsetting decrease in the budget authority available in the succeeding fiscal year. If not used, the budget authority remains available for obligation in the succeeding fiscal year. Advance funding is sometimes used to provide contingency funding of a few benefit programs.

Adverse Report—A committee report recommending against approval of a measure or some other matter. Committees usually pigeonhole measures they oppose instead of reporting them adversely, but they may be required to report them by a statutory rule, chamber rule, or an instruction from their parent body.

Advice and Consent—The Senate's constitutional role in consenting to or rejecting the president's nominations to executive branch and judicial offices and treaties with other nations. Confirmation of nominees requires a simple majority vote of senators present and voting. Treaties must be approved by a two-thirds majority of those present and voting.

Aisle—The center aisle of each chamber. When facing the presiding officer, Republicans usually sit to the right of the aisle, Democrats to the left. When members speak of "my side of the aisle" or "this side," either literally or metaphorically, they are referring to their party.

Amendment—A formal proposal to alter the text of a bill, resolution, amendment, motion, treaty, or some other text. Technically, it is a motion. An amendment may strike out (eliminate) part of a text, insert new text, or strike out and insert—that is, replace all or part of the text with new text. The texts of amendments considered on the floor are printed in full in the *Congressional Record.*

Amendment in the Nature of a Substitute—Usually, an amendment to replace the entire text of a measure. It strikes out everything after the enacting clause of a bill or resolving clause of a resolution and inserts a version that may be somewhat, substantially, or entirely different. When a committee adopts extensive amendments to a measure, the panel often incorporates them into such an amendment. Occasionally, the term is applied to an amendment that replaces a major portion of a measure's text.

Amendment Tree—A diagram showing the number and types of amendments that the rules and practices of a house permit to be offered to a measure before any of the amendments is voted on. It shows the relationship of one amendment to the others, and it may also indicate the degree of each amendment, whether it is a perfecting or substitute amendment, the order in which amendments may be offered, and the order in which they are put to a vote. The same type of diagram can be used to display an actual amendment situation.

Amendments between the Houses—This is a method for reconciling differences between the House and Senate versions of a measure by passing the measure with successive amendments back and forth between the two chambers until both chambers have agreed to identical language.

Annual Authorization—Legislation that authorizes appropriations for a single fiscal year and usually for a specific amount. Under the rules of the authorization-appropriation process, an annually authorized agency or program must be reauthorized each year if it is to receive appropriations for that year. Sometimes Congress fails to enact the reauthorization (or authorization) but nevertheless provides appropriations to continue (or fund) the program, circumventing the rules by one means or another. *(See also Authorization.)*

Appeal—A member's formal challenge of a ruling or decision by the presiding officer or committee or subcommittee chair. On appeal, a house or a committee or subcommittee may overturn the ruling by majority vote. The right of appeal ensures the body against arbitrary control by the chair. Appeals are rarely made in the House and are even more rarely successful. Rulings are more frequently appealed in the Senate and occasionally overturned, in part because its presiding officer may not be of the same party or disposition as the Senate majority.

Apportionment—The action, after each decennial census, of allocating the number of seats in the House of Representatives to each state. By law, the total number of House members (not counting delegates and a resident commissioner) is fixed at 435. The number allotted to each state is based approximately on its proportion of the nation's total population. Because the Constitution guarantees each state one representative no matter how small its population, exact proportional distribution is virtually impossible. The mathematical formula currently used to determine the apportionment is called the Method of Equal Proportions. *(See Method of Equal Proportions.)*

Appropriated Entitlement—An entitlement program, such as veterans' pensions, that is funded through annual appropriations rather than by a permanent appropriation. Because such an entitlement law requires the government to provide eligible recipients the benefits to which they are entitled, whatever the cost, Congress must appropriate the necessary funds.

Appropriation—(1) Legislative language that permits a federal agency to incur obligations and make payments from the Treasury for specified purposes, usually during a specified period of time. (2) The specific amount of money made available by such language. The Constitution prohibits payments from the Treasury except "in Consequence of Appropriations made by Law." With some exceptions, the rules of both houses forbid consideration of appropriations for purposes that are unauthorized in law or of appropriation amounts larger than those authorized in law. The House of Representatives claims the exclusive right to originate appropriation bills—a claim the Senate denies in theory but accepts in practice. *(See General Appropriation Bill.)*

At-Large—Elected by and representing an entire state instead of a district within a state. The term usually refers to a representative rather than to a senator. *(See Apportionment; Congressional District; Redistricting.)*

August Adjournment—A congressional adjournment during the month of August in odd-numbered years, required by the Legislative Reorganization Act of 1970. (In practice, Congress typically adjourns as well during August in even-numbered years.) The law instructs the two houses to adjourn for a period of at least thirty days before the second day after Labor Day, unless Congress provides otherwise or if, on July 31, a state of war exists by congressional declaration.

Authorization—(1) A statutory provision that establishes or continues a federal agency, activity, or program for a fixed or indefinite period of time. It may also establish policies and restrictions and deal with organizational and administrative matters. (2) A statutory provision, as described in (1), may also, explicitly or implicitly, authorize congressional action to provide appropriations for an agency, activity, or program. The appropriations may be authorized for one year, several years, or an indefinite period of time, and the authorization may be for a specific amount of money or an indefinite amount ("such sums as may be necessary"). Authorizations of specific amounts are construed as ceilings on the amounts that subsequently may be appropriated in an appropriation bill, but not as minimums; either house may appropriate lesser amounts or nothing at all.

Authorization-Appropriation Process—The two-stage procedural system that the rules of each house require for establishing and funding federal agencies and programs: first, enactment of authorizing legislation that creates or continues an agency or program; second, enactment of appropriations legislation that provides funds for the authorized agency or program. *(See Appropriation; Authorization.)*

Automatic Roll Call—Under a House rule, the automatic ordering of the yeas and nays when a quorum is not present on a voice or division vote and a member objects to the vote on that ground. It is not permitted in the Committee of the Whole.

Backdoor Spending Authority—Authority to incur obligations that evades the normal congressional appropriations process because it is provided in legislation other than appropriation acts. The most common forms are borrowing authority, contract authority, and entitlement authority. *(See Borrowing Authority; Contract Authority; Entitlement Program; Spending Authority.)*

Baseline—A projection of the levels of federal spending, revenues, and the resulting budgetary surpluses or deficits for the upcoming and subsequent fiscal years, taking into account laws enacted to date and assuming no new policy decisions. It provides a benchmark for measuring the budgetary effects of proposed changes in federal revenues or spending, assuming certain economic conditions.

Bells—A system of electric signals and lights that informs members of activities in each chamber. The type of activity taking place is indicated by the number of signals and the interval between them. When the signals are sounded, a corresponding number of lights are lit around the perimeter of many clocks in House or Senate offices and corridors.

Bicameral—Consisting of two houses or chambers. Congress is a bicameral legislature whose two houses have an equal role in enacting legislation. In other national bicameral legislatures, one house may be significantly more powerful than the other. Most state legislatures are bicameral.

Bigger Bite Amendment—An amendment that substantively changes a portion of a text including language that had previously been amended. Normally, language that has been amended may not be amended again. However, a part of a sentence that has been changed by amendment, for example, may be changed again by an amendment that amends a "bigger bite" of the text—that is, by an amendment that also substantively changes the unamended parts of the sentence or the entire section or title in which the previously amended language appears. The biggest possible bite is an amendment in the nature of a substitute that amends the entire text of a measure. Once adopted, therefore, such an amendment ends the amending process. *(See Amendment in the Nature of a Substitute.)*

Bill—The term for the chief vehicle Congress uses for enacting laws. Bills that originate in the House of Representatives are designated as "H.R." and are followed by a number assigned in the order in which the bills are introduced during a two-year Congress. Bills in the Senate are similarly designated except they begin with an "S." Any bill that has not passed both houses of Congress in identical form at the end of a two-year Congress dies; its proponents must introduce a bill again in the next Congress to seek its consideration. A bill becomes a law if passed in identical language by both houses and signed by the president, or passed over the president's veto, or if the president fails to sign it within ten days after receiving it while Congress is in session.

Bill of Attainder—An act of a legislature finding a person guilty of treason or a felony. The Constitution prohibits the passage of such a bill by the U.S. Congress or any state legislature.

Bills and Resolutions Introduced—Members formally present measures to their respective houses by delivering them to a clerk in the chamber when their house is in session. Both houses permit any number of members to join in introducing a bill or resolution. The first member listed on the measure is the sponsor; the other members listed are its cosponsors. *(See Hopper.)*

Bills and Resolutions Referred—After a bill or resolution is introduced, it is normally sent to one or more committees that have jurisdiction over its subject, as defined by House and Senate rules and precedents. A Senate measure is usually referred to the committee with jurisdiction over the predominant subject of its text, but it may be sent to two or more committees by unanimous consent or on a motion offered jointly by the majority and minority leaders. In the House, a rule requires the Speaker to refer a measure to the committee that has primary jurisdiction. The Speaker is also authorized to refer measures to additional committees with subject jurisdiction over one or more of a bill's provisions under House rules and to impose time limits on such referrals.

Bipartisan Committee—A committee with an equal number of members from each political party. The House Committee on Ethics and the Senate Select Committee on Ethics are the only bipartisan permanent full committees.

Borrowing Authority—Statutory authority permitting a federal agency, such as the Export-Import Bank, to borrow money from the public or the Treasury to finance its operations. It is a form of backdoor spending. To bring such spending under the control of the congressional appropriation process, the Congressional Budget Act requires that new borrowing authority is effective only to the extent and in such amounts as are provided in appropriations acts. *(See Backdoor Spending Authority.)*

Budget—A detailed statement of actual or anticipated revenues and expenditures during an accounting period. For the national government, the period is the federal fiscal year (October 1 to September 30). The budget usually refers to the president's budget submission to Congress early each calendar year. The president's budget estimates federal government income and spending for the upcoming fiscal year and contains detailed recommendations for appropriation, revenue, and other legislation. Congress is not required to accept or even vote directly on the president's proposals, and it often revises the president's budget extensively. *(See Fiscal Year.)*

Budget Act—Common name for the Congressional Budget and Impoundment Control Act of 1974, which established the basic procedures of the current congressional budget process; created the House and Senate Budget Committees; and enacted procedures for reconciliation, deferrals, and rescissions. *(See Budget*

Process; Congressional Budget and Impoundment Control Act of 1974; Deferral; Impoundment; Reconciliation; Rescission. See also Gramm-Rudman-Hollings Act of 1985.)

Budget and Accounting Act of 1921—The law that, for the first time, authorized the president to submit to Congress an annual budget for the entire federal government. Before passage of the act, most federal agencies sent their budget requests to the appropriate congressional committees without review by the president. Also established the Bureau of the Budget, forerunner of today's Office of Management and Budget. *(See also Budget; Office of Management and Budget.)*

Budget Authority—Generally, the amount of money that may be spent or obligated by a government agency or for a government program or activity. Technically, it is statutory authority to enter into obligations that normally result in outlays. The main forms of budget authority are appropriations, borrowing authority, and contract authority. It also includes authority to obligate and expend the proceeds of offsetting receipts and collections (that is, proceeds treated not as revenue but as negative budget authority). Congress may make budget authority available for only one year, several years, or an indefinite period, and it may specify definite or indefinite amounts. *(See Appropriation; Borrowing Authority; Contract Authority; Obligation; Outlays.)*

Budget Control Act—PL 112-25, legislation enacted in the 112th Congress, to provide for an increase in the statutory limit on the public debt in conjunction with other measures to reduce the budget deficit, including the creation of a Joint Select Committee on Deficit Reduction. The committee failed to report recommendations, thereby triggering automatic spending reductions.

Budget Enforcement Act of 1990—An act that revised the sequestration process established by the Gramm-Rudman-Hollings Act of 1985, replaced the earlier act's fixed deficit targets with adjustable ones, established discretionary spending limits for fiscal years 1991 through 1995, instituted pay-as-you-go rules to enforce deficit neutrality on revenue and mandatory spending legislation, and reformed the budget and accounting rules for federal credit activities. Unlike the Gramm-Rudman-Hollings Act, the 1990 act emphasized restraints on legislated changes in taxes and spending instead of fixed deficit limits. *(See Gramm-Rudman-Hollings Act of 1985.)*

Budget Enforcement Act of 1997—An act that revised and updated the provisions of the Budget Enforcement Act of 1990, including by extending the discretionary spending caps and pay-as-you-go rules through 2002. *(See Budget Enforcement Act of 1990.)*

Budget Process—(1) In Congress, the procedural system it uses to approve an annual concurrent resolution on the budget that sets goals for aggregate and functional categories of federal expenditures, revenues, and the surplus or deficit for an upcoming fiscal year; and to implement those goals in spending, revenue, and, if necessary, reconciliation and debt-limit legislation. (2) In the executive branch, the process of formulating the president's annual budget, submitting it to Congress, defending it before congressional committees, implementing subsequent budget-related legislation, impounding or sequestering expenditures as permitted by law, auditing and evaluating programs, and compiling final budget data. The Budget and Accounting Act of 1921 and the Congressional Budget and Impoundment Control Act of 1974 established the basic elements of the current budget process. Major revisions were enacted in the Gramm-Rudman-Hollings Act of 1985, the Budget Enforcement Act of 1990, and the Budget Enforcement Act of 1997. *(See individual entries for the laws named in this entry.)*

Budget Resolution—A concurrent resolution in which Congress establishes or revises its version of the federal budget's broad financial features for the upcoming fiscal year and several additional fiscal years. As with other concurrent resolutions, it does not have the force of law, but it provides the framework within which Congress subsequently considers revenue, spending, and other budget-implementing legislation. The framework consists of two basic elements: (1) aggregate budget amounts (total revenues, new budget authority, outlays, loan obligations and loan guarantee commitments, deficit or surplus, and debt limit); and (2) subdivisions of the relevant aggregate amounts among the functional categories of the budget. Although it does not allocate funds to specific programs or accounts, the Budget Committees' reports accompanying the resolution often discuss the major program assumptions underlying the functional amounts. These assumptions are not binding. *(See Budget Authority; Debt Limit; Federal Debt; Function or Functional Category; Outlays.)*

By Request—A designation indicating that a member has introduced a measure on behalf of the president, an executive agency, or a private individual or organization. Members introduce such measures as a courtesy because neither the president nor any person other than a member of Congress may introduce legislation. The term, which appears next to the sponsor's name, implies that the member who introduced the measure does not necessarily endorse it. A House rule dealing with by-request introductions dates from 1888, but the practice goes back to the earliest history of Congress.

Byrd Rule—The popular name of an amendment to the Congressional Budget Act that bars the inclusion of extraneous matter in any reconciliation legislation considered in the Senate. The ban is enforced by points of order sustained by the presiding officer. The provision defines different categories of extraneous matter, but it also permits certain exceptions. Its chief sponsor was Sen. Robert C. Byrd, D-W.Va.

Calendar—A list of measures or other matters (most of them favorably reported by committees) that are eligible for floor consideration. The House has four calendars; the Senate has two. A place on a calendar does not guarantee consideration. Each house decides which measures and matters it will take up, when, and in what order, in accordance with political considerations, rules, and practices.

Call Up—To bring a measure or report to the floor for immediate consideration.

Casework—Assistance to constituents who seek help in dealing with federal and local government agencies. Constituent service is a high priority in most members' offices.

Caucus—(1) A common term for the official organization of each party in each house. (2) The official title of the organization of House Democrats. House and Senate Republicans and Senate Democrats call their organizations "conferences." (3) A term for an informal group of members who share legislative interests, such as the Black Caucus, Hispanic Caucus, and Children's Caucus. These groups in the House are formally called Congressional Member Organizations and were formerly called Legislative Service Organizations. *(See Party Caucus.)*

Censure—The strongest formal condemnation of a member for misconduct short of expulsion. A house usually adopts a resolution of censure to express its condemnation, after which the presiding officer reads its rebuke aloud to the member in the presence of his or her colleagues.

Chairman—The presiding officer of a committee, a subcommittee, or a task force. Increasingly, the term chairwoman is used, reflecting the growing number of women in Congress who have gained seniority, or simply "chair." At meetings, the chair preserves order, enforces the rules, recognizes members to speak or offer motions, and puts questions to a vote. The chair of a committee or subcommittee usually appoints its staff and sets its agenda, subject to the panel's veto. The presiding officer in the House or Senate may be referred to as the chair.

Chamber—The Capitol room in which a house of Congress normally holds its sessions. The chamber of the House of Representatives, officially called the Hall of the House, is considerably larger than that of the Senate because it must accommodate 435 representatives, five delegates, and one resident commissioner. Unlike the Senate chamber, members have no desks or assigned seats. In both chambers, the floor slopes downward to the well in front of the presiding officer's raised desk. A chamber is often referred to as "the floor," as when members are said to be on or going to the floor. Those expressions usually imply that the member's house is in session. *(See Floor.)*

Christmas Tree Bill—Jargon for a bill adorned with amendments, many of them unrelated to the bill's subject, that provide benefits for interest groups, specific states, congressional districts, companies, and individuals.

Classes of Senators—A class under the Constitution consists of the thirty-three or thirty-four senators elected to a six-year term in the same general election. Because the terms of approximately one-third of the senators expire every two years, there are three classes.

Clean Bill—After a House committee extensively amends a bill, it often assembles its amendments and what is left of the bill into a new measure that one or more of its members introduce as a "clean bill." The revised measure is assigned a new number, reported to the House, and placed on the appropriate calendar.

Clerk of the House—An officer of the House of Representatives responsible principally for administrative support of the legislative process in the House. The clerk is invariably the choice of the majority party.

Cloakrooms—Two rooms with access to the rear of each chamber's floor, one for each party's members, where members may confer privately, sit quietly, or have a snack. The presiding officer sometimes urges members who are conversing too loudly on the floor to retire to their cloakrooms. *(See Chamber.)*

Closed Hearing—A hearing closed to the public and the media; a hearing conducted "in executive session" is a closed hearing. A House committee may close a hearing only if it determines that disclosure of the testimony to be taken would endanger national security, violate any law, or tend to defame, degrade, or incriminate any person. The Senate has a similar rule. Both houses require roll-call votes in open session to close a hearing.

Closed Rule—A special rule reported from the House Rules Committee that prohibits amendments to a measure or that only permits amendments offered by the reporting committee. *(See Rule.)*

Cloture—A Senate procedure that limits further consideration of a pending proposal to thirty hours to end a filibuster. Sixteen senators must first sign and submit a cloture petition to the presiding officer. One hour after the Senate meets on the second calendar day thereafter, the chair puts the motion to a yea-and-nay vote following a live quorum call. If three-fifths of all senators (sixty if there are no vacancies) vote for the motion to invoke cloture, the Senate must take final action on the cloture proposal by the end of the thirty hours of consideration and may consider no other business until it takes that action. Cloture on a proposal to amend the Senate's standing rules requires approval by two-thirds of the senators present and voting. *(See Nuclear Option.)*

Code of Official Conduct—A House rule that bans certain actions by House members, officers, and employees; requires them to conduct themselves in ways that "reflect creditably" on the House; and orders them to adhere to the spirit and the letter of House rules and those of its committees. The code's provisions govern the receipt of outside compensation, gifts, and honoraria, and the use of campaign funds; prohibit members from using their clerk-hire allowance to pay anyone who does not perform duties commensurate with that pay; forbid discrimination in members' hiring or treatment of employees on the grounds of race, color, religion, sex, disability, age, or national origin; restrict members convicted of a crime who might be punished by imprisonment of two or more years from participating in committee business or voting on the floor until exonerated or reelected; and restrict employees' contact with federal agencies on matters in which they have a significant financial interest. The Senate's rules contain some similar prohibitions.

College of Cardinals—A popular term for the subcommittee chairs of the appropriations committees, reflecting their influence over appropriation measures.

Colloquy—A discussion between members to put a mutual understanding about the intent of a measure or amendment on the record. The discussion may be scripted in advance.

Comity—The practice of maintaining mutual courtesy and civility between the two houses in their dealings with each other and in members' speeches on the floor. Although the practice is largely governed by long-established customs, a House rule explicitly cautions its members not to characterize any Senate action or inaction, refer to individual senators except under certain circumstances, or quote from Senate proceedings except to make legislative history on a measure. The Senate has no rule on the subject but references to the House have been held out of order on several occasions. Generally the houses do not interfere with each other's appropriations in the legislative branch appropriations bill, although minor conflicts sometimes occur. A refusal to receive a message from the other house has also been held to violate the practice of comity.

Committee—A panel of members elected or appointed to perform some service or function for its parent body. Congress has four types of committees: standing, special or select, joint, and, in the House, a Committee of the Whole. Committees conduct investigations, make studies, issue reports and recommendations, and, in the case of standing committees, review and prepare measures on their assigned subjects for action by their respective houses. Most committees divide their work among several subcommittees. With rare exceptions, the majority party in a house holds a majority of the seats on its committees, and their chairs are also from that party. *(See Committee of the Whole.)*

Committee Jurisdiction—The legislative subjects and other functions assigned to a committee by rule, precedent, resolution, or statute. A committee's title usually indicates the general scope of its jurisdiction but often fails to mention other significant subjects assigned to it.

Committee of the Whole—Common name of the Committee of the Whole House on the State of the Union, a committee consisting of all members of the House of Representatives. Measures from the Union Calendar must be considered in the Committee of the Whole before the House completes action on them; the committee often considers other major bills as well. A quorum of the committee is 100, and it meets in the House chamber under a chair appointed by the Speaker. Procedures in the Committee of the Whole expedite consideration of legislation because of its smaller quorum requirement, its ban on certain motions, and its five-minute rule for debate on amendments. The Senate does not use a Committee of the Whole.

Committee Ratios—The ratios of majority to minority party members on committees. By custom, the ratios of most committees reflect party strength in their respective houses.

Committee Report on a Measure—A document submitted by a committee to report a measure to its parent chamber. Customarily, the report explains the measure's purpose, describes provisions and any amendments recommended by the committee, and presents arguments for its approval. House and Senate rules prescribe the content of their committees' reports. The House requires its committees to write a report on legislation reported to the House, the Senate does not. *(See Cordon Rule; Ramseyer Rule.)*

Committee Staff—Employees who assist the majority or minority party members of a committee. Most committees hire separate majority and minority party staffs, but they instead may hire nonpartisan staff, either professional and administrative staff or only administrative staff. Senate rules state that a committee's staff must reflect the relative number of its majority and minority party committee members, and the rules guarantee the minority at least one-third of the funds available for hiring partisan staff. In the House, each committee is authorized thirty professional staff, and the minority members of most committees may select up to ten of these staff (subject to full committee approval). Under House rules, the minority party is to be "treated fairly" in the apportionment of any additional staff resources. Each House committee determines the portion of its additional staff that it allocates to the minority; some committees allocate one-third, and others allot less. *(See Staff Director.)*

Committee Veto—A procedure that requires an executive department or agency to submit certain proposed policies, programs, or action to designated committees for review before implementing them. Before 1983, when the Supreme Court declared that a legislative veto was unconstitutional, these provisions permitted committees to veto the proposals. Language is still included in committee reports requiring agencies to seek committee approval before taking a specified action or type of action. Agencies usually take the pragmatic approach of trying to reach a consensus with a committee before carrying out an action, especially when an appropriations committee is involved. *(See Legislative Veto.)*

Concur—To agree to an amendment of the other house, either by adopting a motion to concur in that amendment or a motion to concur with an amendment to that amendment. After both houses have agreed to the same version of an amendment, neither house may amend it further, nor may any subsequent conference change it or delete it from the measure. Concurrence by one house in all amendments of the other house completes action on the measure; no vote is then necessary on the measure as a whole because both houses previously passed it.

Concurrent Resolution—A resolution that requires approval by both houses but does not need the president's signature and therefore cannot have the force of law. Concurrent resolutions deal with the prerogatives or internal affairs of Congress as a whole. Designated "H. Con. Res." in the House and "S. Con. Res." in the Senate, they are numbered consecutively in each house in their order of introduction during a two-year Congress. *(See, for example, Budget Resolution.)*

Conferees—A common title for managers, the members from each house appointed to a conference committee. The Senate usually authorizes its presiding officer to appoint its conferees. The Speaker appoints House conferees and under a rule adopted in 1993 can remove conferees "at any time after an original appointment" and also appoint additional conferees at any time. Conferees are expected to support the positions of their houses despite their personal views, but in practice this is not always the case. The party ratios of conferees generally reflect the ratios in their houses. Each house may appoint as many conferees as it pleases. House conferees often outnumber their Senate colleagues; however, each house has only one vote in a conference, so the size of its delegation is immaterial. *(See Conference; Conference Committee; Conference Report.)*

Conference—(1) A formal meeting or series of meetings between members representing each house to reconcile House and Senate differences on a measure (occasionally several measures). Because one house cannot require the other to agree to its proposals, the conference usually reaches agreement by compromise. When a conference completes action on a measure, or as much action as appears possible, it sends its recommendations to both houses in the form of a conference report, accompanied by an explanatory statement. (2) The official title of the organization of all Democrats or Republicans in the Senate and of all Republicans in the House of Representatives. *(See Conferees; Conference Committee; Conference Report; Party Caucus.)*

Conference Committee—A temporary joint committee formed for the purpose of resolving differences between the houses on a measure. Major and controversial legislation may require conference committee action. Voting in a conference committee is not by individuals but within the House and Senate delegations. Consequently, a conference committee report requires the support of a majority of the conferees from each house. Both houses require that conference committees open their meetings to the public. The Senate's rule permits the committee to close its meetings if a majority of conferees in each delegation agree by a roll-call vote. The House rule permits closed meetings only if the House authorizes them to do so on a roll-call vote. Otherwise, there are no congressional rules governing the organization of, or procedure in, a conference committee. The committee chooses its chair, but on measures that go to conference regularly, such as general appropriation bills, the chairmanship traditionally rotates between the houses. *(See Conferees; Conference; Conference Report.)*

Conference Report—A document submitted to both houses that contains a conference committee's agreements for resolving their differences on a measure. It must be signed by a majority of the conferees from each house separately and must be accompanied by an explanatory statement. Both houses prohibit amendments to a conference report and require it to be accepted or rejected in its entirety, although specific disagreements may be presented to a chamber in a manner allowing the chamber to agree to its conferees recommendation. *(See Conferees; Conference; Conference Committee; Recommit a Conference Report.)*

Congress—(1) The national legislature of the United States, consisting of the House of Representatives and the Senate. (2) The national legislature in office during a two-year period. Congresses are numbered sequentially; thus, the 1st Congress of 1789–1791 and the 113th Congress of 2013–2015. Before implementation of the Twentieth Amendment in 1935, the two-year period began on the first Monday in December of odd-numbered years. Since then it has extended from January of an odd-numbered year through noon on January 3 of the next odd-numbered year. A Congress usually holds two annual sessions, but some have had three sessions and the pre-1935 67th Congress had four. When a Congress expires, measures die if they have not yet been enacted.

Congressional Accountability Act of 1995 (CAA)—An act applying eleven labor, workplace, and civil rights laws to the legislative branch and establishing procedures and remedies for legislative branch employees with grievances in violation of these laws. The following laws are covered by the CAA: Fair Labor Standards Act of 1938; Title VII of the Civil Rights Act of 1964; Americans with Disabilities Act of 1990; Age Discrimination in Employment Act of 1967; Family and Medical Leave Act of 1993; Occupational Safety and Health Act of 1970; Chapter 71 of Title 5, *U.S. Code* (relating to federal service labor-management relations); Employee Polygraph Protection Act of 1988; Worker Adjustment and Retraining Notification Act; Rehabilitation Act of 1973; and Chapter 43 of Title 38, *U.S. Code* (relating to veterans' employment and reemployment).

Congressional Budget and Impoundment Control Act of 1974—The law that established the basic elements of the congressional budget process, the House and Senate Budget Committees, the Congressional Budget Office, and the procedures for congressional review of impoundments in the form of rescissions and deferrals proposed by the president. The budget process consists of procedures for coordinating congressional revenue and spending decisions made in separate tax, appropriations, and legislative measures. The impoundment provisions were intended to give Congress greater control over executive branch actions that delay or prevent the spending of funds provided by Congress. *(See Budget Process; Budget Resolution; Congressional Budget Office; Deferral; Impoundment; Rescission.)*

Congressional Budget Office (CBO)—A congressional support agency created by the Congressional Budget and Impoundment Control Act of 1974 to provide nonpartisan budgetary information and analysis to Congress and its committees. CBO acts as a scorekeeper when Congress is voting on the federal budget, tracking bills' compliance with overall budget goals. The agency also estimates what proposed legislation would cost over a five-year period. CBO works most closely with the House and Senate Budget Committees.

Congressional Directory—The official who's who of Congress, usually published during the first session of a two-year Congress. Contains statistical and other information on past Congresses and the current one as well as rosters of executive branch officials, foreign ambassadors, and other individuals.

Congressional District—The geographical area represented by a single member of the House of Representatives. For states with only one representative, the entire state is a congressional district. After the reapportionment from the 2010 census, seven states had only one representative each: Alaska, Delaware, Montana, North Dakota, South Dakota, Vermont, and Wyoming. *(See Apportionment; Gerrymandering; Redistricting.)*

Congressional Record—The daily, printed, and substantially verbatim account of proceedings in both the House and Senate chambers. Extraneous materials submitted by members appear in a section titled "Extensions of Remarks." A "Daily Digest" appendix contains highlights of the day's floor and committee action plus a list of committee meetings and floor agendas for the next day's session.

Although the official reporters of each house take down every word spoken during the proceedings, members are permitted to edit and "revise and extend" their remarks before they are printed. In the Senate section, all speeches, articles, and other material submitted by senators but not actually spoken or read on the floor are set off by large black dots, called bullets. However, bullets do not appear when a senator reads part of a speech and inserts the rest. In the House section, undelivered speeches and materials are printed in a distinctive typeface. The term "permanent *Record*" refers to the bound volumes of the daily *Records* of an entire session of Congress, which are repaginated so that page numbers run consecutively through a whole session of Congress. *(See also* Journal.*)*

Congressional Research Service (CRS)—Established in 1914, a department of the Library of Congress whose staff provide nonpartisan, objective analysis and information on virtually any subject to committees, members, and staff of Congress. Originally the Legislative Reference Service, it is the oldest congressional support agency, except for the Library of Congress.

Congressional Support Agencies—A term often applied to three agencies in the legislative branch that provide nonpartisan information and analysis to committees and members of Congress: the Congressional Budget Office (CBO), the Congressional Research Service (CRS) of the Library of Congress, and the Government Accountability Office (GAO)—previously called the General Accounting Office. The Library of Congress also supports Congress in many ways, but provides numerous services to the public and to specialized users, including copyright and book cataloguing. *(See Congressional Budget Office; Congressional Research Service; Government Accountability Office.)*

Congressional Terms of Office—A term normally begins on January 3 of the year following a general election and runs two years for representatives and six years for senators. A representative chosen in a special election to fill a vacancy is sworn in for the remainder of the predecessor's term. An individual appointed or elected to fill a Senate vacancy usually serves until the next general election or until the end of the predecessor's term, whichever comes first.

Constitutional Option—*(See Nuclear Option.)*

Constitutional Rules—Constitutional provisions that prescribe procedures for Congress. In addition to certain types of votes required in particular situations, these provisions include the following: (1) the House chooses its Speaker, the Senate its president pro tempore, and both houses their officers; (2) each house requires a majority quorum to conduct business; (3) less than a majority may adjourn from day to day and compel the attendance of absent members; (4) neither house may adjourn for more than three days without the consent of the other; (5) each house must keep a journal; (6) the yeas and nays are ordered when supported by one-fifth of the members present; (7) all revenue-raising bills must originate in the House, but the Senate may propose amendments to them. The Constitution also sets out the procedure in the House for electing a president, the procedure in the Senate for electing a vice president, the procedure for filling a vacancy in the office of vice president, and the procedure for overriding a presidential veto.

Constitutional Votes—Constitutional provisions that require certain votes or voting methods in specific situations. They include (1) the yeas and nays at the desire of one-fifth of the members present; (2) a two-thirds vote by the yeas and nays to override a veto; (3) a two-thirds vote by one house to expel one of its members and by both houses to propose a constitutional amendment; (4) a two-thirds vote of senators present to convict someone whom the House has impeached and to consent to ratification of treaties; (5) a two-thirds vote in each house to remove political disabilities from persons who have engaged in insurrection or rebellion or given aid or comfort to the enemies of the United States; (6) a majority vote in each house to fill a vacancy in the office of vice president; (7) a majority vote of all states to elect a president in the House of Representatives when no candidate receives a majority of the electoral votes; (8) a majority vote of all senators when the Senate elects a vice president under the same circumstances; and (9) the casting vote of the vice president in case of tie votes in the Senate.

Contempt of Congress—Willful obstruction of the proper functions of Congress. Most frequently, it is a refusal to obey a subpoena to appear and testify before a committee or to produce documents demanded by it. Such obstruction is a misdemeanor and persons cited for contempt are subject to prosecution in federal courts. A house cites an individual for contempt by agreeing to a privileged resolution to that effect reported by a committee. The presiding officer then refers the matter to a U.S. attorney for prosecution.

Continuing Body—A characterization of the Senate on the theory that it continues from Congress to Congress and has existed continuously since it first convened in 1789. The rationale for the theory is that under the system of staggered six-year terms for senators, the terms of only about one-third of them expire after each Congress and, therefore, a quorum of the Senate is always in office. Consequently, under this theory, the Senate, unlike the House, has not adopted its rules at the beginning of each Congress because those rules continue from one Congress to the next. Under Senate rules, a two-thirds vote of the senators present and voting is needed to invoke cloture against a filibuster of a proposed rules change.

Continuing Resolution (CR)—A joint resolution that provides funds to continue the operation of federal agencies and programs at the beginning of a new fiscal year if their annual appropriation bills have not yet been enacted; also called continuing appropriations. Continuing resolutions are enacted shortly before or after the new fiscal year begins and usually make funds available for a specified period. Additional resolutions may be needed after the first expires. Some continuing resolutions have provided appropriations for an entire fiscal year. Continuing resolutions for specific periods customarily fix a rate at which agencies may incur obligations based either on the previous year's appropriations, the president's budget request, or the amount as specified in the agency's regular annual appropriation bill if that bill has already been passed by one or both houses. In the House, continuing resolutions are privileged after September 15. *(See Appropriation; Privilege.)*

Contract Authority—Statutory authority permitting an agency to enter into contracts or incur other obligations even though it has not received an appropriation to pay for them. Congress must eventually fund them because the government is legally liable for such payments. The Congressional Budget Act of

1974 requires, with a few exceptions, that new contract authority may not be used unless provided for in advance by an appropriation act. *(See Backdoor Spending Authority.)*

Cordon Rule—A Senate rule that requires a committee report to show changes the reported measure would make in current law. The rule was named after its sponsor, Sen. Guy Cordon, R-Ore. The House's analogous rule is called the Ramseyer rule. *(See Committee Report on a Measure; Ramseyer Rule.)*

Correcting Recorded Votes—The rules of both houses prohibit members from changing their votes after a vote result has been announced. Nevertheless, the Senate permits its members to withdraw or change their votes, by unanimous consent, immediately after the announcement. In rare instances, senators have been granted unanimous consent to change their votes several days or weeks after the announcement. Votes tallied by the electronic voting system in the House may not be changed. But when a vote actually given is not recorded during an oral call of the roll, a member may demand a correction as a matter of right. On all other alleged errors in a recorded vote, the Speaker determines whether the circumstances justify a change. Occasionally, members merely announce that they were incorrectly recorded; announcements can occur hours, days, or even months after the vote and appear in the *Congressional Record.*

Cosponsor—A member who has joined one or more other members to sponsor a measure. Joining on the day of introduction qualifies the member as an original sponsor.

Credit Authority—Authority granted to an agency to incur direct loan obligations or to make loan guarantee commitments. The Congressional Budget Act of 1974 bans congressional consideration of credit authority legislation unless the extent of that authority is made subject to provisions in appropriation acts.

C-SPAN—Cable-Satellite Public Affairs Network, which provides live, gavel-to-gavel coverage of Senate floor proceedings on one cable television channel and coverage of House floor proceedings on another channel. C-SPAN also televises selected committee hearings of both houses. Each house also transmits its televised proceedings directly to congressional offices.

Current Services Estimates—Executive branch estimates of the anticipated costs of federal programs and operations for the next and future fiscal years at existing levels of service and assuming no new initiatives or changes in existing law. The president submits these estimates to Congress with the annual budget and includes an explanation of the underlying economic and policy assumptions on which they are based, such as anticipated rates of inflation, real economic growth, and unemployment, plus program caseloads and pay increases.

Custody of the Papers—Possession of an engrossed measure and certain related basic documents that the two houses produce as they pass and then try to resolve their differences over the measure.

Dean—Within a state's delegation in the House of Representatives, the member with the longest continuous service; also the longest-serving member of the House.

Debate—In congressional parlance, speeches delivered during consideration of a measure, motion, or other matter, as distinguished from speeches in other parliamentary situations, such as one-minute and special order speeches when no business is pending. Virtually all debate in the House of Representatives is under some kind of time limitation. Most debate in the Senate is unlimited; that is, a senator, once recognized, may speak for as long as he or she chooses, unless the Senate invokes cloture or agrees by unanimous consent to limit debate time.

Debt Limit—The maximum amount of outstanding federal public debt permitted by law. The limit (or ceiling) covers virtually all debt incurred by the government except agency debt. A congressional budget resolution sets forth the new debt limit that may be required under its provisions. *(See Budget Resolution; Federal Debt; Public Debt.)*

Deferral—An impoundment of funds for a specific period of time that may not extend beyond the fiscal year in which it is proposed. Under the Impoundment Control Act of 1974, the president must notify Congress that he is deferring the spending or obligation of funds provided by law for a project or activity. Congress can disapprove the deferral by legislation. *(See Congressional Budget and Impoundment Control Act of 1974.)*

Deficit—The amount by which the government's outlays exceed its budget receipts for a given fiscal year. Both the president's budget and congressional budget resolutions provide estimates of the deficit or surplus for the upcoming and several future fiscal years. *(See Budget Resolution.)*

Degrees of Amendment—Designations that indicate the relationships of amendments to the text of a measure and to each other. In general, an amendment offered directly to the text of a measure is an amendment in the first degree, and an amendment to that amendment is an amendment in the second degree. Both houses normally prohibit amendments in the third degree—that is, an amendment to an amendment to an amendment. *(See Amendment; Amendment Tree.)*

Delegate—A nonvoting member of the House of Representatives elected to a two-year term from the District of Columbia, the territory of Guam, the territory of the Virgin Islands, the territory of American Samoa, or the territory of the Northern Marianas. By law, delegates may not vote in the full House but they may participate in debate, offer motions (except to reconsider), and serve and vote on standing and select committees. On their committees, delegates possess the same powers and privileges as other members and the Speaker may appoint them to appropriate conference committees and select committees. Delegates are given an office budget according to the same formulas as representatives. *(See also Resident Commissioner from Puerto Rico.)*

Denounce—A formal action that condemns a member for misbehavior; considered by some experts to be equivalent to censure. *(See Censure.)*

Dilatory Tactics—Procedural actions intended to delay or prevent action by a house or a committee. They include, among others, offering numerous motions, demanding quorum calls and recorded votes at every opportunity, making numerous points of order and parliamentary inquiries, and speaking as long as the applicable rules permit. The Senate rules permit a battery of dilatory tactics, especially lengthy speeches, except under cloture or a unanimous consent agreement. In the House, possible dilatory tactics are more limited. Speeches are always subject to time limits and debate-ending motions. Moreover, a House rule instructs the Speaker not to entertain dilatory motions and lets the Speaker decide whether a motion is dilatory. However, the Speaker may not override the constitutional right of a member to demand the yeas and nays and in practice usually waits for a point of order before exercising that authority. *(See Cloture.)*

Discharge a Committee—Remove a measure from a committee to which it has been referred in order to make it available for floor consideration. Noncontroversial measures are often discharged by unanimous consent. However, because congressional committees have no obligation to report measures referred to them, each house has procedures to extract measures from committees.

District and State Offices—Representatives maintain one or more offices in their districts for the purpose of assisting and communicating with constituents. The costs of maintaining these offices are paid from members' official allowances. Senators can use the official expense allowance to rent offices in their home state, subject to a funding formula based on their state's population and other factors.

District Work Period—The House term for a congressional recess during which members may visit their districts and conduct constituency business.

Division Vote—A vote in which the chair first counts those in favor of a proposition and then those opposed to it, with no record made of how each member voted. In the Senate, the chair may count raised hands or ask senators to stand, whereas the House requires members to stand; hence, often called a standing vote. Committees in both houses ordinarily use a show of hands. A division usually occurs after a voice vote and may be demanded by any member or ordered by the chair if there is any doubt about the outcome of the voice vote. The demand for a division can also come before a voice vote. In the Senate, the demand must come before the result of a voice vote is announced. It may be made after a voice vote announcement in the House, but only if no intervening business has transpired and only if the member was standing and seeking recognition at the time of the announcement. A demand for the yeas and nays or, in the House, for a recorded vote takes precedence over a demand for a division vote.

Earmark—A set-aside within a measure, committee report, or conference report for a specific purpose. *(See Pork or Pork Barrel Legislation.)*

Effective Dates—Provisions of an act that specify when the entire act or individual provisions in it become effective as law. Most acts become effective on the date of enactment, but it is sometimes necessary or desirable to delay the effective dates of some provisions or to make them effective retroactively.

Electronic Voting—Since 1973 the House has used an electronic voting system to record the yeas and nays and to conduct recorded votes. Members vote by inserting their voting cards in one of the boxes at several locations in the chamber. They are given at least fifteen minutes to vote. However, when several votes occur immediately after each other, the Speaker or chair of the Committee of the Whole may reduce the voting time to five minutes (or less in some circumstances) on the second and subsequent votes. The Speaker or chair routinely allows additional time on each vote but may close a vote at any time after the minimum time has expired. Members can change their votes at any time before the Speaker announces the result. The House also uses the electronic system for quorum calls. While a vote is in progress, a large panel above the Speaker's desk displays how each member has voted. Smaller panels on either side of the chamber display running totals of the votes and the time remaining. The Senate does not have electronic voting.

Enacting Clause—The opening language of each bill, stating "Be it enacted by the Senate and House of Representatives of the United States of America in Congress assembled. . . . " This language gives legal force to measures approved by Congress and signed by the president or enacted over the president's veto. A successful motion to strike it from a bill kills the entire measure.

Engrossed Bill—The official copy of a bill or joint resolution as passed by one chamber, including the text as amended by floor action, and certified by the clerk of the House or the secretary of the Senate (as appropriate). Amendments by one house to a measure or amendments of the other also are engrossed. House engrossed documents are printed on blue paper; the Senate's are printed on white paper.

Enrolled Bill—The final official copy of a bill or joint resolution passed in identical form by both houses. An enrolled bill usually is printed on parchment. After it is certified by the chief officer of the house in which it originated and signed by the House Speaker and the Senate president pro tempore, the measure is sent to the White House for the president's signature.

Entitlement Program—A federal program under which individuals, businesses, or units of government that meet the requirements or qualifications established by law are entitled to receive certain payments if they seek such payments. Major examples include Social Security, Medicare, Medicaid, unemployment insurance, and military and federal civilian pensions. Congress cannot control their expenditures by refusing to appropriate the sums necessary to fund them because the government is legally obligated to pay eligible recipients the amounts to which the law entitles them. *(See Backdoor Spending Authority.)*

Equality of the Houses—A component of the Constitution's emphasis on checks and balances under which each house is given essentially equal status in the enactment of legislation and in the relations and negotiations between the two houses. Although the House of Representatives initiates revenue and appropriation measures, the Senate has the right to amend them. Either house may initiate any other type of legislation, and neither can force the other to agree to, or even act on, its measures. Moreover, each house has a potential veto over the other because legislation requires agreement by both. Similarly, in a conference to resolve their differences on a measure, each house casts one vote, as determined by a majority of its conferees. In other national bicameral legislatures, the powers of one house may be markedly greater than those of the other.

Ethics Rules—Several rules or standing orders in each house that mandate certain standards of conduct for members and congressional employees in finance, employment, franking, and other areas. The Senate Select Committee on Ethics and the House Committee on Ethics investigate alleged violations of conduct and recommend appropriate actions to their respective houses.

Exclusive Committee—(1) Under the rules of the Republican Conference and House Democratic Caucus, a standing committee whose members usually cannot serve on any other standing committee. As of 2013 the Appropriations, Energy and Commerce (for Democrats beginning service in the 105th Congress), Financial Services (for Democrats beginning in the 109th Congress), Ways and Means, and Rules committees were designated as exclusive committees. The parties may choose to ignore or waive their rule for specific members. (2) Under the rules of the two-party conferences in the Senate, a standing committee whose members may not simultaneously serve on any other exclusive committee.

Executive Calendar—The Senate's calendar for executive business, that is, treaties and nominations. The calendar numbers indicate the order in which items were referred to the calendar but have no bearing on when or if the Senate will consider them. The Senate, by motion or unanimous consent, resolves itself into executive session to consider items on the executive calendar. The Senate's legislative calendar is the Calendar of General Orders, and is referred to colloquially as the Senate Calendar. *(See Executive Session; Nomination; Resolution of Ratification.)*

Executive Document—A document, usually a treaty, sent by the president to the Senate for approval. It is referred to a committee in the same manner as other measures. Resolutions to ratify treaties have their own "treaty document" numbers. For example, the first treaty submitted in the 113th Congress was "Treaty Document 113-1," a treaty on fishery resources in the South Pacific Ocean. *(See Ratification; Resolution of Ratification; Treaty.)*

Executive Order—A document signed by the president that has a policy-making or legislative impact on the management of the federal government's operations. Members of Congress have challenged some executive orders on the grounds that they usurped the authority of the legislative branch. Although the Supreme Court has ruled that a particular order exceeded the president's authority, it has upheld others as falling within the president's general constitutional powers. An executive order might also be explicitly or implicitly authorized by law.

Executive Privilege—The assertion that presidents have the right to withhold certain information from Congress. Presidents have based their claim on (1) the constitutional separation of powers; (2) the need for secrecy in military and diplomatic affairs; (3) the need to protect individuals from unfavorable publicity; (4) the need to safeguard the confidential exchange of ideas in the executive branch; and (5) the need to protect individuals who provide confidential advice to the president.

Executive Session—(1) A Senate meeting devoted to the consideration of treaties or nominations. Normally, the Senate meets in legislative session; it resolves itself into executive session, by motion or by unanimous consent, to deal with its executive business. It also keeps a separate *Journal* for executive sessions. Executive sessions are usually open to the public, but the Senate may choose to close them. (Closed committee meetings in the House and Senate are also referred to as executive sessions.) *(See Executive Calendar.)*

Expulsion—A member's removal from office by a two-thirds vote of his or her chamber; the supermajority is required by the Constitution. It is the most severe and most rarely used sanction a house can invoke against a member. Although the Constitution provides no explicit grounds for expulsion, the courts have ruled that it may be applied only for misconduct during a member's term of office, not for conduct before the member's election. Generally, neither house will consider expulsion of a member convicted of a crime until the judicial processes have been exhausted. At that stage, members sometimes resign rather than face expulsion. In 1977 the House adopted a rule urging members convicted of certain crimes to voluntarily abstain from voting or participating in other legislative business.

Extensions of Remarks—An appendix to the daily *Congressional Record* that consists primarily of miscellaneous material submitted by members. It often includes members' statements not delivered on the floor, newspaper articles and editorials, praise for a member's constituents, and noteworthy letters received by a member, among other material. Representatives supply the bulk of this material; senators submit little. "Extensions of Remarks" pages are separately numbered, and each number is preceded by the letter "E." Materials may be placed in the Extensions of Remarks section only by unanimous consent. *(See* Congressional Record.*)*

Fast Track—Also called expedited procedures, this refers to any set of procedures applicable to a specific piece or specific subject of legislation. A fast track set of procedures circumvents or speeds up all or part of the legislative process to ensure or better ensure that a congressional decision is reached. Rulemaking statutes may prescribe expedited procedures for designated measures, such as statutes granting trade promotion authority to the president.

Federal Debt—The total amount of monies borrowed and not yet repaid by the federal government. Federal debt consists of public debt and agency debt. Public debt is the portion of the federal debt borrowed by the Treasury or the Federal Financing Bank directly from the public or from another federal fund or account. For example, the Treasury regularly borrows money from the Social Security trust fund. Public debt accounts for about 99 percent of the federal debt. Agency debt refers to the debt incurred by federal agencies such as the Export-Import Bank but excluding the Treasury and the Federal Financing Bank, which are authorized by law to borrow funds from the public or from another government fund or account. *(See Debt Limit; Public Debt.)*

Filibuster—The use of time-consuming debate and parliamentary tactics by one member or a group of members to delay, modify, or defeat proposed legislation or rules changes. Filibusters are also sometimes used to delay urgently needed measures to force the body to consider other legislation. The Senate's rules permitting unlimited debate and the extraordinary majority it requires to invoke cloture make filibustering particularly effective in that chamber. Under the restrictive debate and other rules of the House, filibusters in that body are short-lived and infrequently attempted. *(See Cloture.)*

Fiscal Year—The federal government's annual accounting period. It begins October 1 and ends on the following September 30. A fiscal year is designated by the calendar year in which it ends and is often referred to as FY. Thus, fiscal year 2014 began October 1, 2013, ended September 30, 2014, and is called FY14. In theory, Congress is supposed to complete action on all budgetary measures applying to a fiscal year before that year begins. It rarely does so. *(See Budget.)*

Five-Minute Rule—A House rule that limits debate on an amendment offered in the Committee of the Whole to five minutes for its sponsor and five minutes for an opponent. In practice, the committee routinely permits longer debate by three devices: offering pro forma amendments, each debatable for five minutes; unanimous consent for a member to speak longer than five minutes; and special rule. Consequently, debate on an amendment could continue for hours or, more commonly today, be limited to ten or twenty minutes, with the amendment's proponent and an opponent each controlling half the time and yielding parcels of it to colleagues. In the absence of a special rule or unanimous consent, however, at any time after the first ten minutes, the committee may shut off debate immediately or by a specified time, either by unanimous consent or by majority vote on a nondebatable motion. *(See Committee of the Whole; Pro Forma Amendment; Rule.)*

Floor—The level of the House or Senate chamber where members sit and the houses conduct their business. When members are attending a meeting of their house they are said to be on the floor. Floor action refers to the procedural actions taken during floor consideration such as deciding on motions, taking up measures, amending them, and voting. *(See Chamber.)*

Floor Manager—A majority party member responsible for guiding a measure through its floor consideration in a house and for devising the political and procedural strategies that might be required to get it passed. The presiding officer gives the floor manager priority recognition to debate, offer amendments, oppose amendments, and make crucial procedural motions. The minority party member is referred to as the minority floor manager.

Frank—Informally, members' legal right to send official mail postage free under their signatures; often called the franking privilege. Technically, it is the autographic or facsimile signature used on envelopes instead of stamps that permits members and certain congressional officers to send their official mail free of charge. The franking privilege has been authorized by law since the first Congress, except for a few months in 1873. Congress reimburses the U.S. Postal Service for the franked mail it handles.

Function *or* Functional Category—A broad category of national need and spending of budgetary significance. A category provides an accounting method for allocating and keeping track of budgetary resources and expenditures for that function because it includes all budget accounts related to the function's subject or purpose such as agriculture, administration of justice, commerce and housing, and energy. Functions do not necessarily correspond with appropriations acts or with the budgets of individual agencies. As of 2013 there were twenty functional categories, each divided into a number of subfunctions. *(See Budget Resolution.)*

Gag Rule—A pejorative term for any type of special rule reported by the House Rules Committee that proposes to prohibit amendments to a measure or only permits amendments offered by the reporting committee.

Galleries—The balconies overlooking each chamber from which the public, news media, staff, and others may observe floor proceedings.

General Appropriation Bill—A term applied to each of the annual bills that provide funds for most federal agencies and programs and also to the supplemental appropriation bills that contain appropriations for more than one agency or program. *(See Appropriation.)*

Germaneness—The requirement that an amendment be closely related—in terms of subject or purpose, for example—to the text it proposes to amend. A House rule requires that all amendments be germane. In the Senate, only amendments offered to general appropriation bills and budget measures or proposed under cloture must be germane. Germaneness rules can be waived by suspension of the rules in both houses, by unanimous consent agreements in the Senate, and by special rules from the Rules Committee in the House. Moreover, presiding officers usually do not enforce germaneness rules on their own initiative; therefore, a nongermane amendment can be adopted if no member raises a point of order against it. Under cloture in the Senate, however, the chair may take the initiative to rule amendments out of order as not being germane, without a point of order being made. All House debate must be germane except during general debate in the Committee of the Whole, but special rules invariably require that such debate be "confined to the bill." The Senate requires germane debate only during the first three hours of each daily session. Under the precedents of both houses, an amendment can be relevant but not necessarily germane. A crucial factor in determining germaneness in the House is how the subject of a measure or matter is defined. For example, the subject of a measure authorizing construction of a naval vessel is defined as being the construction of a single vessel; therefore, an amendment to authorize an additional vessel is not germane.

Gerrymandering—The manipulation of legislative district boundaries to benefit a particular party, politician, or minority group. The term originated in 1812 when the Massachusetts legislature redrew the lines of state legislative districts to favor the party of Gov. Elbridge Gerry, and some critics said one district resembled a salamander. *(See also Congressional District; Redistricting.)*

Government Accountability Office (GAO)—A congressional support agency, often referred to as the investigative arm of Congress. It evaluates and audits federal agencies and programs in the United States and abroad on its initiative or at the request of congressional committees or members. The office, created in 1921, was called the General Accounting Office until 2004.

Gramm-Rudman-Hollings Act of 1985—Common name for the Balanced Budget and Emergency Deficit Control Act of 1985, which established new budget procedures intended to balance the federal budget by fiscal year 1991. (The timetable subsequently was extended and then deleted.) The act's chief sponsors were senators Phil Gramm, R-Texas, Warren Rudman, R-N.H., and Ernest Hollings, D-S.C.

Grandfather Clause—A provision in a measure, law, or rule that exempts an individual, entity, or a defined category of individuals or entities from complying with a new policy or restriction. For example, a bill that would raise taxes on persons who reach the age of sixty-five after a certain date inherently grandfathers out those who are sixty-five before that date. Similarly, a Senate rule limiting senators to two major committee assignments also grandfathers some senators who were sitting on a third major committee before a specified date.

Grants-in-Aid—Payments by the federal government to state and local governments to help provide for assistance programs or public services.

Hearing—Committee or subcommittee meetings to receive testimony on proposed legislation or for oversight purposes. Relatively few bills are important enough to justify formal hearings. Witnesses often include experts, government officials, spokespersons for interested groups, officials of the Government Accountability Office, and members of Congress.

Hold-Harmless Clause—In legislation providing a new formula for allocating federal funds, a clause to ensure that recipients of those funds do not receive less in a future year than they did in the current year if the new formula would result in a reduction for them. Similar to a grandfather clause, it has been used most frequently to soften the impact of sudden reductions in federal grants. *(See Grandfather Clause.)*

Hold—A senator's request that his or her party leaders delay or halt floor consideration of certain legislation or presidential nominations. The majority leader usually honors a hold for a reasonable period of time, especially if its purpose is to assure the senator that the matter will not be called up during his or her absence or to give the senator time to gather necessary information.

Hold (or Have) the Floor—A member's right to speak without interruption, unless he or she violates a rule, after recognition by the presiding officer. At the member's discretion, he or she may yield to another member for a question in the Senate or for a question or statement in the House, but may reclaim the floor at any time.

Hopper—A box on the clerk's desk in the House chamber into which members deposit bills and resolutions to introduce them. In House jargon, to drop a bill in the hopper is to introduce it.

Hour Rule—A House rule that permits members, when recognized, to hold the floor in debate for no more than one hour each. A member recognized for one hour typically yields one-half of the time to an opposing member. In the instance of debate on a special rule, the majority party member customarily yields one-half the time to a minority member. Although the hour rule also applies to general debate in the Committee of the Whole, special rules routinely vary the length of time for such debate and its control to fit the circumstances of particular measures. *(See Rule, second definition.)*

House as in Committee of the Whole—A hybrid combination of procedures from the general rules of the House and from the rules of the Committee of the Whole, seen infrequently today and most often only when the House considers a private bill. *(See Private Bill.)*

House Calendar—The calendar reserved for all public bills and resolutions that do not raise revenue or directly or indirectly appropriate money or property when they are favorably reported by House committees.

House Manual—A commonly used title for the compilation of the rules of the House of Representatives, the Constitution, *Jefferson's Manual,* and rulemaking statutes, published in each Congress. Its official title is *Constitution, Jefferson's Manual, and Rules of the House of Representatives.*

House of Representatives—The house of Congress in which states are represented roughly in proportion to their populations, but every state is guaranteed at least one representative. By law, the number of voting representatives is fixed at 435. Five delegates and one resident commissioner also serve in the House; they may vote in their committees but not on the House floor. Although the House and Senate have equal legislative power, the Constitution gives the House sole authority to originate revenue measures. The House also claims the right to originate appropriation measures, a claim the Senate disputes in theory but concedes in practice. The House has the sole power to impeach (only the Senate convicts, however) and elects the president when no candidate has received a majority of the electoral votes. The House is sometimes referred to as the lower body. *(See Delegate; Lower Body; Representative; Resident Commissioner from Puerto Rico; Senate.)*

Immunity—(1) Members' constitutional protection from lawsuits and arrest in connection with their legislative duties. They may not be tried for libel or slander for anything they say on the floor of a house or in committee. Nor may they be arrested while attending sessions of their houses or when traveling to or from sessions of Congress, except when charged with treason, a felony, or a breach of the peace. (2) In the case of a witness before a committee, a grant of protection from prosecution based on that person's testimony to the committee. It is used to compel witnesses to testify who would otherwise refuse to do so on the constitutional ground of possible self-incrimination. Under such a grant, none of a witness's testimony may be used against him or her in a court proceeding except in a prosecution for perjury or for giving a false statement to Congress. *(See also Contempt of Congress.)*

Impeachment—The first step to remove the president, the vice president, Supreme Court justices, or other federal civil officers from office and possibly to disqualify them from any future federal office "of honor, Trust or Profit." An impeachment is a formal charge of treason, bribery, or "other high Crimes and Misdemeanors." The House has the sole power of impeachment and the Senate the sole power of trying the charges and convicting. The House impeaches by a simple majority vote; conviction requires a two-thirds vote of all senators present.

Impeachment Trial, Removal, and Disqualification—The Senate conducts an impeachment trial under a separate set of twenty-six rules that appears in the *Senate Manual.* Under the Constitution, the chief justice of the Supreme Court presides over the impeachment trial of the president, but the vice president, the president pro tempore, or any other senator may preside over the impeachment trial of another official.

The Constitution requires senators to take an oath for an impeachment trial. During the trial, senators may not engage in colloquies or participate in arguments, but they may submit questions in writing to House managers or defense counsel. After the trial concludes, the Senate votes separately on each article of impeachment without debate unless the Senate orders the doors closed for private discussions. During deliberations senators may speak no more than once on a question, not for more than ten minutes on an interlocutory question and not more than fifteen minutes on the final question. These rules may be set aside by unanimous consent or suspended on motion by a two-thirds vote.

The Senate's impeachment trial of President Bill Clinton in 1999 was only the second such trial involving a president (the first being the impeachment trial of President Andrew Johnson in 1868). It continued for five weeks, with the Senate voting not to convict on the two impeachment articles.

Senate impeachment rules allow the Senate, at its discretion, to name a committee to hear evidence and conduct the trial, with all senators thereafter voting on the charges. The impeachment trials of three federal judges were conducted this way, and the Supreme Court upheld the validity of these rules in *Nixon v. United States* (506 U.S. 224, 1993).

An official convicted on impeachment charges is removed from office immediately. However, the convicted official is not barred from holding a federal office in the future unless the Senate, after its conviction vote, also approves a resolution disqualifying the convicted official from future office. For example, federal judge Alcee L. Hastings was impeached and convicted in 1989, but the Senate did not vote to bar him from office in the future. In 1992 Hastings was elected to the House of Representatives, and no challenge was raised against seating him when he took the oath of office in 1993.

Impoundment—An executive branch action or inaction that delays or withholds the expenditure or obligation of budget authority provided by law. The Impoundment Control Act of 1974 classifies impoundments as either deferrals or rescissions, requires the president to notify Congress about all such actions, and gives Congress authority to approve or reject them. *(See Congressional Budget and Impoundment Control Act of 1974; Deferral; Rescission.)*

Inspector General in the House of Representatives—A position established with the passage of the House Administrative Reform Resolution of 1992. The duties of the office have been revised several times and are now contained in House Rule II. The inspector general (IG), who is subject to the policy direction and oversight of the Committee on House Administration, is appointed for a Congress jointly by the Speaker and the majority and minority leaders of the House. The IG communicates the results of audits to the House officers or officials who were the subjects of the audits and suggests appropriate corrective measures. The IG submits a report of each audit to the Speaker, the majority and minority leaders, and the chair and ranking minority member of the House Administration Committee; notifies these five members in the case of any financial irregularity discovered; and reports to the Committee on Ethics on possible violations of House rules or any applicable law by any House member, officer, or employee. The IG's office also has certain duties to audit various financial operations of the House that had previously been performed by the Government Accountability Office.

Instruct Conferees—A formal action by a house urging its conferees to uphold a particular position on a measure in conference. The instruction may be to insist on certain provisions in the measure as passed by that house or to accept a provision in the version passed by the other house. Instructions to conferees are not binding because the primary responsibility of conferees is to reach agreement on a measure and neither house can compel the other to accept particular provisions or positions.

Investigative Power—The authority of Congress and its committees to pursue investigations, upheld by the Supreme Court but limited to matters related to, and in furtherance of, a legitimate task of the Congress. Standing committees in both houses are permanently authorized to investigate matters within their jurisdictions. Major investigations are sometimes conducted by temporary select, special, or joint committees established by resolutions for that purpose.

Some rules of the House provide certain safeguards for witnesses and others during investigative hearings. These permit counsel to accompany witnesses, require that each witness receive a copy of the committee's rules, and order the committee to go into closed session if it believes the testimony to be heard might defame, degrade, or incriminate any person. The committee may subsequently decide to hear such testimony in open session. There are no Senate rules of this kind.

Item Veto—Item veto authority, which is available in some form to most state governors, allows governors to eliminate or reduce items in legislative measures presented for their signature without vetoing the entire measure, and sign the rest into law. A similar authority was briefly granted to the U.S. president under the Line Item Veto Act of 1996. According to the majority opinion of the Supreme Court in its 1998 decision *Clinton v. City of New York* (524 U.S. 417) overturning that law, a constitutional amendment would be necessary to give the president such veto authority. *(See Line Item; Line Item Veto Act of 1996.)*

Jefferson's Manual—Short title of *Jefferson's Manual of Parliamentary Practice,* prepared by Thomas Jefferson for his guidance when he was president of the Senate from 1797 to 1801. Although it reflects English parliamentary practice in his day, many procedures in both houses of Congress are still rooted in its precepts. Under a House rule adopted in 1837, the manual's provisions govern House procedures when applicable and when they are not inconsistent with its standing rules and orders. The Senate, however, has never officially acknowledged it as a direct authority for its legislative procedure.

Johnson Rule—A policy instituted in 1953 under which all Democratic senators are assigned to one major committee before any Democrat is assigned to two. The Johnson Rule is named after its author, Sen. Lyndon B. Johnson, D-Texas, then the Senate's Democratic leader. Senate Republicans adopted a similar policy soon thereafter.

Joint Committee—A committee composed of members selected from each house. The functions of contemporary joint committees involve investigation, research, or oversight of agencies or activities closely related to congressional work, although they might have regulatory authority over a legislative branch agency or function. Permanent joint committees, created by statute, are sometimes called standing joint committees. Only four joint committees existed as of 2013: Joint Economic, Joint Taxation, Joint Library, and Joint Printing. None has authority to report legislation.

Joint Explanatory Statement—This is a statement appended to a conference report that explains in plain English the conference agreement and the intent of the conferees.

Joint Resolution—A legislative measure that Congress uses for special purposes based on tradition. Similar to a bill, a joint resolution has the force of law when passed by both houses and either approved by the president or passed over the president's veto. Unlike a bill, a joint resolution enacted into law is not called an act; it retains its original title. Most often, joint resolutions deal with such relatively limited matters as the correction of errors in existing law, a single appropriation, or the establishment of permanent joint committees. They are also used for important matters such as declaring war or providing continuing appropriations and to carry out fast-track procedures included by Congress in some statutes. Joint resolutions, in addition, are used to propose constitutional amendments, which are submitted to the states for ratification when approved by a two-thirds vote in each house of Congress; these joint resolutions do not require the president's signature and become effective only when ratified by three-fourths of the states. The House designates joint resolutions as "H. J. Res." and the Senate as "S. J. Res." Each house numbers its joint resolutions consecutively in the order of introduction during a two-year Congress. Unless passed by both chambers in identical form before the end of a two-year Congress, joint resolutions die with the Congress's *sine die* adjournment. *(See Bill; Continuing Resolution; Fast Track.)*

Joint Session—Informally, any combined meeting of the Senate and the House. Technically, a joint session is a combined meeting to count the electoral votes for president and vice president or to hear a presidential address, such as the State of the Union message; any other formal combined gathering of both houses is a joint meeting. Joint sessions are authorized by concurrent resolutions and are held in the House chamber, because of its larger seating capacity. Although the president of the Senate and the Speaker sit side by side at the Speaker's desk during combined meetings, the former presides over the electoral count and the latter presides on all other occasions and introduces the president or other guest speaker. The president and other guests may address a joint session or meeting only by invitation.

Joint Sponsorship—Two or more members sponsoring the same measure.

Journal—The official record of House or Senate actions, including every motion offered, every vote cast, amendments agreed to, quorum calls, and so forth. Unlike the *Congressional Record,* it does not provide reports of speeches, debates, statements, and other items. The Constitution requires each house to maintain a *Journal* and to publish it periodically. *(See* Congressional Record.*)*

Junket—A derisive term for a member's trip at government expense, especially abroad, on official business but, it is often alleged, for pleasure.

Killer Amendment—An amendment that, if agreed to, might lead to the defeat of the measure it amends, either in the house in which the amendment is offered or at some later stage of the legislative process. Also called a poison-pill amendment. Members sometimes deliberately offer or vote for such an amendment in the expectation that it will undermine support for the measure in Congress or increase the likelihood that the president will veto it.

King of the Mountain (or Hill Rule)—*(See Queen of the Hill Rule.)*

LA—*(See Legislative Assistant.)*

Lame Duck—Jargon for a member who has not been reelected, or did not seek reelection, and is serving the balance of his or her term.

Lame Duck Session—A session of a Congress held after the election for the succeeding Congress, so-called after the lame duck members still serving.

Last Train Out—Colloquial name for last must-pass bill of a session of Congress.

Law—An act of Congress (in the form of a bill or joint resolution, the latter of which is not a constitutional amendment) that has been signed by the president, passed over the president's veto, or allowed by the president to become law without his signature.

Lay on the Table—A motion to dispose of a pending proposition immediately, finally, and adversely; that is, to kill it without a direct vote on its substance. Often simply called a motion to table, it is not debatable and is adopted by majority vote or without objection. It is a highly privileged motion, taking precedence over all others except the motion to adjourn in the House and all but three additional motions in the Senate. It can kill a bill or resolution, an amendment, another motion, an appeal, or virtually any other matter.

Tabling an amendment also tables the measure to which the amendment is pending in the House, but not in the Senate. The House does not allow the motion against the motion to recommit, in the Committee of the Whole, and in some other situations. In the Senate it is the only permissible motion that immediately ends debate on a proposition, but only to kill it.

(The) Leadership—Usually, a reference to the majority and minority leaders of the Senate or to the Speaker and minority leader of the House. The term sometimes includes the majority leader in the House and the majority and minority whips in each house and, at other times, other party officials as well.

Legislation—(1) A synonym for legislative measures: bills and joint resolutions. (2) Provisions in such measures or in substantive amendments offered to them. (3) In some contexts, provisions that change existing substantive or authorizing law, rather than provisions that make appropriations.

Legislation on an Appropriation Bill—A common reference to provisions changing existing law that appear in, or are offered as amendments to, a general appropriation bill. A House rule prohibits the inclusion of such provisions in general appropriation bills unless they retrench expenditures. An analogous Senate rule permits points of order against amendments to a general appropriation bill that propose general legislation. In both chambers, such prohibitions may be waived by procedures such as special rules in the House, by failure of any member to make a point of order against such a provision, or by other means. *(See Authorization-Appropriation Process.)*

Legislative Assistant (LA)—A member's staff person responsible for monitoring and preparing legislation on particular subjects and for advising the member on them; commonly referred to as an LA. Today, members' offices typically employ a legislative director (LD) to oversee an office's LAs.

Legislative Day—The day that begins when a house meets after an adjournment and ends when it next adjourns. Because the House of Representatives normally adjourns at the end of a daily session, its legislative and calendar days usually coincide. The Senate, however, might recess at the end of a daily session, and its legislative day may extend over several calendar days or longer. Among other uses, this technicality permits the Senate to continue for procedural purposes on the same day or to save time by circumventing its morning hour, a procedure required at the beginning of every legislative day.

Legislative History—(1) A chronological list of actions taken on a measure during its progress through the legislative process. (2) The official documents relating to a measure, the entries in the *Journals* of the two houses on that measure, and the *Congressional Record* text of its consideration in both houses. The documents include all committee reports and the conference report and joint explanatory statement, if any. Courts and affected federal agencies might study a measure's legislative history for congressional intent about its purpose and interpretation.

Legislative Process—(1) Narrowly, the stages in the enactment of a law from introduction to final disposition. An introduced measure that becomes law typically travels through reference to committee; committee and subcommittee consideration; committee report to the chamber; floor consideration and amendment; passage; engrossment; messaging to the other house; similar steps in that house, including floor amendment of the measure; return of the measure to the first house; consideration of amendments between the houses or a conference to resolve their differences; approval of the conference report by both houses; enrollment; approval by the president or override of the president's veto; and deposit with the Archivist of the United States. (2) Broadly, the political, lobbying, and other factors that affect or influence the process of enacting laws.

Legislative Veto—A procedure, declared unconstitutional in 1983, that allowed Congress or one of its houses to nullify certain actions of the president, executive branch agencies, or independent agencies. Sometimes called congressional vetoes or congressional disapprovals. Following the Supreme Court's 1983 decision in *Immigration and Naturalization Service v. Chadha* (462 U.S. 919), Congress amended several legislative veto statutes to require enactment of joint resolutions, which are subject to presidential veto, for nullifying executive branch actions. Alternately, Congress may include in a statute a provision requiring congressional approval of a proposed executive action before its implementation. *(See Committee Veto.)*

Limitation on a General Appropriation Bill—Language that prohibits expenditures for part of an authorized purpose from funds provided in a general appropriation bill. Precedents require that the language be phrased in the negative: that none of the funds provided in a pending appropriation bill shall be used for a specified authorized activity. Limitations in general appropriation bills are permitted on the grounds that Congress can refuse to fund authorized programs and, therefore, can refuse to fund any part of them as long as the prohibition does not change existing law. House precedents have established that a limitation does not change existing law if it does not impose additional duties or burdens on executive branch officials, interfere with their discretionary authority, or require them to make judgments or determinations not required by existing law. The proliferation of limitation amendments in the 1970s and early 1980s prompted the House to adopt a rule in 1983 making it more difficult for members to offer them. The rule bans such amendments during the reading of an appropriation bill for amendment, unless they are specifically authorized in existing law. Other limitations may be offered after the reading, but the Committee of the Whole can foreclose them by adopting a motion to rise and report the bill back to the House. In 1995 the rule was amended to allow the motion to rise and report to be made only by the majority leader or his or her designee. The House Appropriations Committee, however, can include limitation provisions in the bills it reports.

Line Item—An amount in an appropriation measure. It can refer to a single appropriation account or to separate amounts within the account. In the congressional budget process, the term usually refers to assumptions about the funding of particular programs or accounts that underlie the broad functional amounts in a budget resolution. These assumptions are discussed in the reports accompanying each resolution and are not binding.

Line Item Veto Act of 1996—A law, in effect only from January 1997 until June 1998, that granted the president authority intended to be functionally equivalent to an item veto, by amending the Impoundment Control Act to incorporate an approach known as enhanced rescission. Key provisions established a new procedure that permitted the president to cancel amounts of new discretionary appropriations (budget authority), new items of direct spending (entitlements), or certain limited tax benefits. It also required the president to notify Congress of the cancellation in a special message within five calendar days after signing the measure. The cancellation would become permanent unless legislation disapproving it was enacted within thirty days. On June 25, 1998, in *Clinton v. City of New York* (524 U.S. 417) the Supreme Court held the Line Item Veto Act unconstitutional, on the grounds that its cancellation provisions violated the presentment clause in Article I, clause 7, of the Constitution. *(See Item Veto; Line Item.)*

Line-Item Veto—*(See Item Veto; Line Item Veto Act of 1996.)*

Live Pair—A voluntary and informal agreement between two members on opposite sides of an issue, one of whom is absent for a recorded vote, under which the member who is present withholds or withdraws his or her vote to offset the failure to vote by the member who is absent. Usually the member in attendance announces that he or she has a live pair, states how each would have voted, and votes "present." In the House, under a rules change enacted in the 106th Congress, a live pair is only permitted on the rare occasions when electronic voting is not used.

Live Quorum—In the Senate, a quorum call to which senators are expected to respond. Senators usually suggest the absence of a quorum, not to force a quorum to appear, but to provide a pause in the proceedings during which senators can engage in private discussions or wait for a senator to come to the floor (a "dead quorum"). A senator desiring a live quorum usually announces his or her intention, giving fair warning that there will be an objection to any unanimous consent request that the quorum call be dispensed with before it is completed.

Loan Guarantee—A statutory commitment by the federal government to pay part or all of a loan's principal or interest or both to a lender or the holder of a security in case the borrower defaults.

Lobby—To try to persuade members of Congress to propose, pass, modify, or defeat proposed legislation or to change or repeal existing laws. Lobbyists attempt to promote their preferences or those of a group, organization, or industry. Originally the term referred to persons frequenting the lobbies or corridors of legislative chambers in order to speak to lawmakers. In a general sense, lobbying includes not only direct contact with members but also indirect attempts to influence them, such as writing to them or persuading others to write or visit them, attempting to mold public opinion toward a desired legislative goal by various means, and contributing or arranging for contributions to members' election campaigns. The right to lobby stems from the First Amendment to the Constitution, which bans laws that abridge the right of the people to petition the government for a redress of grievances.

Lobbying Disclosure Act of 1995—The principal statute requiring disclosure of—and also, to a degree, circumscribing—the activities of lobbyists. In general, it requires lobbyists who spend more than 20 percent of their time on lobbying activities to register and make semiannual reports of their activities to the clerk of the House and the secretary of the Senate, although the law provides for a number of exemptions. Among the statute's prohibitions, lobbyists are not allowed to make contributions to the legal defense fund of a member or high government official or to reimburse for official travel. Civil penalties for failure to comply may include fines. The act does not include grassroots lobbying in its definition of lobbying activities.

The act amended several other lobby laws, notably the Foreign Agents Registration Act (FARA), so that lobbyists can submit a single filing. The 1995 act repealed the 1946 Federal Regulation of Lobbying Act.

Logrolling—Jargon for a legislative tactic or bargaining strategy in which members try to build support for their legislation by promising to support legislation desired by other members or by accepting amendments they hope will induce their colleagues to vote for their bill.

Lower Body—A way to refer to the House of Representatives, which is sometimes considered pejorative by House members. One source of this designation is the design of the capitol in colonial Williamsburg. The House of Burgesses met in a chamber on the ground floor of the capitol; the Council met in a chamber on the second floor above the Burgesses's chamber.

Mace—The symbol of the authority of the House and entrusted to the office of the House sergeant at arms. Under the direction of the Speaker, the sergeant at arms is responsible for preserving order on the House floor by holding up the mace in front of an unruly member, or by carrying the mace up and down the aisles to quell boisterous behavior. When the House is in session, the mace sits on a pedestal at the Speaker's right; when the House is in Committee of the Whole, it is moved to a lower pedestal. The mace is forty-six inches high and consists of thirteen ebony rods bound in silver and topped by a silver globe with a silver eagle, wings outstretched, perched on it.

Majority Leader—The majority party's chief floor strategist, elected by that party's caucus, sometimes called floor leader. In the Senate, the majority leader develops the party's political and procedural strategy, usually in collaboration with other party officials and committee chairs, and serves as his or her party's principal spokesperson. The majority leader negotiates the Senate's agenda and committee ratios with the minority leader and usually calls up measures for floor action. The chamber traditionally concedes to the majority leader the right to determine the days on which it will meet and the hours at which it will convene and adjourn. In the House, the majority leader is the Speaker's deputy and possibly heir apparent, helps plan the floor agenda, leads the party's legislative strategy, and often speaks for the party leadership in debate. *(See (The) Leadership.)*

Majority Staff—*(See Committee Staff.)*

Managers—(1) The official title of members appointed to a conference committee, commonly called conferees. The ranking majority and minority managers for each house also manage floor consideration of the committee's conference report. (2) The members who manage the initial floor consideration of a measure. (3) The official title of House members appointed to present impeachment articles to the Senate and to act as prosecutors on behalf of the House during the Senate trial of the impeached person. *(See Conferees; Floor Manager; Impeachment Trial, Removal, and Disqualification.)*

Mandatory Appropriations—Amounts that Congress must appropriate annually because it has no discretion over them unless it first amends existing substantive law. Certain entitlement programs, for example, require annual appropriations. *(See Appropriated Entitlement.)*

Markup—A meeting or series of meetings by a committee or subcommittee during which members mark up a measure by offering, debating, and voting on amendments to it.

Means-Tested Programs—Programs that provide benefits or services to low-income individuals who meet a test of need. Most are entitlement programs, such as Medicaid, food stamps, and

Supplementary Security Income. A few—for example, subsidized housing and various social services—are funded through discretionary appropriations.

Members' Allowances—Official expenses that are paid for or for which members are reimbursed by their houses. Among these are the costs of office space in their home states or districts; office equipment and supplies; postage-free mailings (the franking privilege); a set number of trips to and from home states or districts, as well as travel elsewhere on official business; telephone and other telecommunications services; and staff salaries. Other cost items are not allocated to individual members, such as the cost of offices in the congressional office buildings in Washington, D.C., or staff overhead such as health insurance, life insurance, and retirement.

Member's Staff—The personal staff to which a member is entitled. The House sets a maximum number of staff and a monetary allowance equal for each representative. The Senate does not set a maximum staff level, but it does set a monetary allowance for each senator based on the population of a senator's state. In each house, the staff allowance is included with office expense allowances and other allowances such as travel and mail in a consolidated allowance. Representatives and senators can generally spend as much money in their consolidated allowances for staff, office expenses, or other allowable expenses, as long as they do not exceed the monetary value of the consolidated allowance. This provides members with flexibility in operating their offices.

Method of Equal Proportions—The mathematical formula used since 1950 to determine how the 435 seats in the House of Representatives should be distributed among the fifty states in the apportionment following each decennial census. It minimizes as much as possible the proportional difference between the average district population in any two states. Because the Constitution guarantees each state at least one representative, fifty seats are automatically apportioned. The formula calculates priority numbers for each state, assigns the first of the 385 remaining seats to the state with the highest priority number, the second to the state with the next highest number, and so on until all seats are distributed. *(See Apportionment.)*

Midterm Elections—The general elections for members of Congress that occur in November of the second year in a presidential term.

Minority Leader—The minority party's leader and chief, strategist and spokesperson, elected by the party caucus; sometimes called minority floor leader. With the assistance of other party officials and the ranking minority members of committees, the minority leader devises the party's political and procedural strategy. *(See (The) Leadership.)*

Minority Staff—*(See Committee Staff.)*

Modified Rule—A special rule from the House Rules Committee that permits only certain amendments to be offered to a measure during its floor consideration or that bans certain specified amendments or amendments on certain subjects. Also referred to as a structured rule or a restrictive rule. *(See Rule, second definition.)*

Morning Business—In the Senate, routine business that is to be transacted at the beginning of the morning hour. The business consists, first, of laying before the Senate, and referring to committees, matters such as messages from the president and the House, federal agency reports, and unreferred petitions, memorials, bills, and joint resolutions. Next, senators may present additional petitions and memorials. Then committees may present their reports, after which senators may introduce bills and resolutions. Finally, resolutions coming over from a previous day are taken up for consideration. In practice, the Senate adopts standing orders that permit senators to introduce measures and file reports at any time, but only if there has been a morning business period on that day. Because the Senate often remains in the same legislative day for several days, it orders a morning business period almost every calendar day for the convenience of senators who wish to introduce measures or make reports. *(See Legislative Day; Morning Hour.)*

Morning Hour—A two-hour period at the beginning of a new legislative day during which the Senate is supposed to conduct routine business, call the calendar on Mondays, and deal with other matters described in a Senate rule. In practice, the morning hour rarely, if ever, occurs because the Senate today typically agrees to a period for morning business for its next meeting in a unanimous consent agreement at the end of a daily session. If the Senate recesses at the end of day rather than adjourns, the rule requiring morning hour does not apply when the Senate next meets. The Senate's rules reserve the first hour of the morning for morning business. After the completion of morning business, or at the end of the first hour, the rules permit a motion to proceed to the consideration of a measure on the calendar out of its regular order (except on Mondays). Because that normally debatable motion is not debatable if offered during the morning hour, the majority leader may, but rarely does, use this procedure in anticipating a filibuster on the motion to proceed. If the Senate agrees to the motion, it can consider the measure until the end of the morning hour, and if there is no unfinished business from the previous day the Senate can continue considering it after the morning hour. But if there is unfinished business, a motion to continue consideration is necessary, and that motion is debatable. *(See Legislative Day; Morning Business.)*

Motion—A formal proposal for a procedural action, such as to consider, to amend, to lay on the table, to reconsider, to recess, or to adjourn. It has been estimated that at least eighty-five motions are possible under various circumstances in the House of Representatives, somewhat fewer in the Senate. Not all motions are created equal; some are privileged or preferential and enjoy priority over others. Some motions are debatable, amendable, or divisible, while others are not.

Multiple and Sequential Referrals—The practice of referring a measure to two or more committees for joint consideration (multiple referral) or successively to several committees in sequence (sequential referral). A measure may also be divided into several parts, with each referred to a different committee or to several committees sequentially (split referral). In theory this gives all committees that have jurisdiction over parts of a measure the opportunity to consider and report on them.

Before 1975, House precedents banned such referrals. A 1975 rule required the Speaker to make concurrent and sequential referrals "to the maximum extent feasible." On sequential referrals, the

Speaker could set deadlines for reporting the measure. The Speaker ruled that this provision authorized him to discharge a committee from further consideration of a measure and place it on the appropriate calendar of the House if the committee failed to meet the Speaker's deadline. In 1995 joint referrals were prohibited. Measures are referred to a primary committee and also may be referred, either additionally or sequentially, to one or more other committees, but usually only for consideration of portions of the measure that fall within the jurisdiction of each of those other committees. In 2003 the Speaker was authorized to not designate a primary committee under "extraordinary circumstances."

In the Senate, before 1977 joint and sequential referrals were permitted only by unanimous consent. In that year, a rule authorized a privileged motion for such a referral if offered jointly by the majority and minority leaders. Debate on the motion and all amendments to it is limited to two hours. The motion may set deadlines for reporting and provide for discharging the committees involved if they fail to meet the deadlines. To date, this procedure has never been invoked; multiple referrals in the Senate, if made, continue to be made by unanimous consent.

Multiyear Appropriation—An appropriation that remains available for spending or obligation for more than one fiscal year; the exact period of time is specified in the act making the appropriation. *(See Appropriation.)*

Multiyear Authorization—(1) Legislation that authorizes the existence or continuation of an agency, program, or activity for more than one fiscal year. (2) Legislation that authorizes appropriations for an agency, program, or activity for more than one fiscal year. *(See Authorization.)*

Nomination—A proposed presidential appointment to a federal office submitted to the Senate for confirmation. Approval is by majority vote. The Constitution explicitly requires Senate confirmation for ambassadors, consuls, "public Ministers" (department heads), and Supreme Court justices. By law, other federal judges, all military promotions of officers, and many high-level civilian officials must be confirmed by the Senate. *(See Executive Calendar.)*

Nuclear Option—A popular name for a parliamentary maneuver to interpret Senate rules to allow the Senate to limit debate on most nominations by a simple majority rather than the sixty votes that had previously been required. The Senate invoked this option in 2013. Also referred to as the constitutional option.

Oath of Office—On taking office, members of Congress must swear or affirm that they will "support and defend the Constitution . . . against all enemies, foreign and domestic," that they will "bear true faith and allegiance" to the Constitution, that they take the obligation "freely, without any mental reservation or purpose of evasion," and that they will "well and faithfully discharge the duties" of their office. The oath is required by the Constitution, and the wording is prescribed by a statute. All House members must take the oath at the beginning of each new Congress. Usually, the member with the longest continuous service in the House swears in the Speaker, who then swears in the other members. The president of the Senate (the vice president of the United States) or a surrogate administers the oath to newly elected or reelected senators.

Obligation—A binding agreement by a government agency to pay for goods, products, services, studies, and so on, either immediately or in the future. When an agency enters into such an agreement, it incurs an obligation. As the agency makes the required payments, it liquidates the obligation. Appropriation laws usually make funds available for obligation for one or more fiscal years but do not require agencies to spend their funds during those specific years. The actual outlays can occur years after the appropriation is obligated, as with a contract for construction of a submarine may provide for payment to be made when it is delivered in the future. Such obligated funds are often said to be "in the pipeline." Under these circumstances, an agency's outlays in a particular year can come from appropriations obligated in previous years as well as from its current-year appropriation. Consequently, the money Congress appropriates for a fiscal year does not equal the total amount of appropriated money the government will actually spend in that year. *(See Budget Authority; Outlays.)*

Off-Budget Entities—Specific federal entities whose budget authority, outlays, and receipts are excluded by law from the calculation of budget totals, although they are part of government spending and income. As of 2005 these included the Social Security trust funds (Federal Old-Age and Survivors Insurance Fund and the Federal Disability Insurance Trust Fund) and the Postal Service. Government-sponsored enterprises are also excluded from the budget because they are considered private rather than public organizations.

Office of Management and Budget (OMB)—A unit in the Executive Office of the President, reconstituted in 1990 from the former Bureau of the Budget. The Office of Management and Budget (OMB) assists the president in preparing the budget and in formulating the government's fiscal program. The OMB also plays a central role in supervising and controlling implementation of the budget, pursuant to provisions in appropriations laws and other statutes. In addition to these budgetary functions, the OMB has various management duties, including those performed through its three statutory offices: Federal Financial Management, Federal Procurement Policy, and Information and Regulatory Affairs.

Officers of Congress—The Constitution refers to the Speaker of the House and the president of the Senate as officers and declares that each house "shall chuse" its "other Officers," but it does not name them or indicate how they should be selected. A House rule refers to its clerk, sergeant at arms, and chaplain as officers. Officers are not named in the Senate's rules, but *Riddick's Senate Procedure* lists the president pro tempore, secretary of the Senate, sergeant at arms, chaplain, and the secretaries for the majority and minority parties as officers. A few appointed officials are sometimes referred to as officers, including the parliamentarians and the legislative counsels. The House elects its officers by resolution at the beginning of each Congress. The Senate also elects its officers, but once elected, Senate officers serve from Congress to Congress until their successors are chosen, following a change in party control or an individual officer's death or retirement. *(See Clerk of the House; Parliamentarian; President Pro Tempore; Secretary of the Senate; Sergeant at Arms; Speaker.)*

Official Objectors—House members who screen measures on the Private Calendar and decide whether or not to object to the consideration of any one or more of them. *(See Private Bill.)*

Omnibus Bill—A measure that combines the provisions of several disparate subjects into a single and often lengthy bill. Omnibus appropriations bills have become commonplace in recent years.

One-Minute Speeches—Addresses by House members that can be on any subject but are limited to one minute. They are usually permitted at the beginning of a daily session after the chaplain's prayer, the pledge of allegiance, and approval of the *Journal*, although they may be permitted at other times, such as at the conclusion of legislative business. They are a customary practice, not a right granted by rule. Consequently, recognition for one-minute speeches requires unanimous consent and is entirely within the Speaker's discretion. The Speaker sometimes does not permit them when the House has a heavy legislative schedule, or he limits or postpones them until a later time of the day.

Open Rule—A special rule from the House Rules Committee that permits members to offer as many floor amendments as they wish as long as the amendments are germane and do not violate other House rules. *(See Rule, second definition.)*

Order of Business (House)—The sequence of events prescribed by a House rule during the meeting of the House on a new legislative day, also called the general order of business. The sequence consists of (1) the chaplain's prayer; (2) reading and approval of the *Journal;* (3) the pledge of allegiance; (4) correction of the reference of public bills to committee; (5) disposal of business on the Speaker's table; (6) unfinished business; (7) the morning hour call of committees and consideration of their bills; (8) motions to go into Committee of the Whole; and (9) orders of the day. In practice, the House never fully complies with this rule. Instead, the items of business that follow the pledge of allegiance are supplanted by any special orders of business that are in order on that day (for example, conference reports; the discharge or private calendars; or motions to suspend the rules) and by other privileged business (for example, general appropriation bills and special rules) or measures made in order by special rules or unanimous consent. The regular order of business is also modified by unanimous consent practices and orders that govern recognition for one-minute speeches (which date from 1937) and for morning-hour debates, begun in 1994. By this combination of an order of business with privileged interruptions, the House gives precedence to certain categories of important legislation, brings to the floor other major legislation from its calendars in any order it chooses, and provides expeditious processing for minor and noncontroversial measures.

Order of Business (Senate)—The sequence of events at the beginning of a new legislative day, as prescribed by Senate rules and standing orders. The sequence consists of (1) the chaplain's prayer; (2) the pledge of allegiance; (3) the designation of a temporary presiding officer if any; (4) *Journal* reading and approval; (5) recognition of the majority and minority leaders or their designees under the standing order adopted by unanimous consent at the beginning of each Congress; (6) morning business in the morning hour; (7) call of the calendar during the morning hour (largely obsolete); and (8) unfinished business from the previous session day.

Organization of Congress—The actions each house takes at the beginning of a Congress that are necessary to its operations. These include swearing in newly elected members, notifying the president that a quorum of each house is present, making committee assignments, and fixing the hour for daily meetings. Because the House of Representatives is not a continuing body, it must also elect its Speaker and other officers and adopt its rules.

Original Bill—(1) A measure drafted by a committee and introduced by its chair or another designated member when the committee reports the measure to its house. Unlike a clean bill, it is not referred back to the committee after introduction. The Senate permits all its legislative committees to report original bills. In the House, this authority is referred to in the rules as the "right to report at any time," and five committees (Appropriations, Budget, House Administration, Rules, and Ethics) have such authority under circumstances specified in House Rule XIII, clause 5.

(2) In the House, special rules reported by the Rules Committee often propose that an amendment in the nature of a substitute be considered as an original bill for purposes of amendment, meaning that the substitute, as with a bill, may be amended in two degrees. Without that requirement, the substitute may only be amended in one further degree. In the Senate, an amendment in the nature of a substitute automatically is open to two degrees of amendment, as is the original text of the bill, if the substitute is offered when no other amendment is pending.

Original Jurisdiction—The authority of certain committees to originate a measure and report it to the chamber. For example, general appropriation bills reported by the House Appropriations Committee are original bills, and special rules reported by the House Rules Committee are original resolutions.

Other Body—A commonly used reference to a chamber by a member of the other chamber. Congressional comity discourages members from directly naming the other chamber during debate.

Outlays—Amounts of government spending. They consist of payments, usually by check or in cash, to liquidate obligations incurred in prior fiscal years as well as in the current year, including the net lending of funds under budget authority. In federal budget accounting, net outlays are calculated by subtracting the amounts of refunds and various kinds of reimbursements to the government from actual spending. *(See Budget Authority; Obligation.)*

Override a Veto—Congressional enactment of a measure over the president's veto. A veto override requires a recorded two-thirds vote of those voting in each house, a quorum being present. Because the president must return the vetoed measure to its house of origin, that house votes first, but neither house is required to attempt an override, whether immediately or at all. If an override attempt fails in the house of origin, the veto stands and the measure dies.

Oversight—Congressional review of the way in which federal agencies implement laws to ensure that they are carrying out the intent of Congress and to inquire into the efficiency of the implementation and the effectiveness of the law. The Legislative Reorganization Act of 1946 defined oversight as the function of exercising continuous watchfulness over the execution of the laws by the executive branch.

Parliamentarian—The official advisor to the presiding officer in each house on questions of procedure. The parliamentarian and his or her assistants also answer procedural questions from members and congressional staff, refer measures to committees on behalf of the presiding officer, and maintain compilations of the precedents. The House parliamentarian revises the House Manual at the beginning of every Congress and usually reviews special rules before the Rules Committee reports them to the House. Either a parliamentarian or an assistant is always present and near the podium during sessions of each house.

Party Caucus—Generic term for each party's official organization in each house. Only House Democrats officially call their organization a caucus. House and Senate Republicans and Senate Democrats call their organizations conferences. The party caucuses elect their leaders, approve committee assignments and chairmanships (or ranking minority members if the party is in the minority), establish party committees and study groups, and discuss party and legislative policies. On rare occasions, they have stripped members of committee seniority or expelled them from the caucus for party disloyalty. *(See Caucus.)*

Pay-as-You-Go (PAYGO)—A provision first instituted under the Budget Enforcement Act of 1990 that applies to legislation enacted before October 1, 2002. It requires that the cumulative effect of legislation concerning either revenues or direct spending should not result in a net negative impact on the budget. If legislation does provide for an increase in spending or decrease in revenues, that effect is supposed to be offset by legislated spending reductions or revenue increases. If Congress fails to enact the appropriate offsets, the act requires presidential sequestration of sufficient offsetting amounts in specific direct spending accounts. Congress and the president can circumvent this requirement if both agree that an emergency requires a particular action or if a law is enacted declaring that deteriorated economic circumstances make it necessary to suspend the requirement.

Permanent Appropriation—An appropriation that remains continuously available, without current action or renewal by Congress, under the terms of a previously enacted authorization or appropriation law. One such appropriation provides for payment of interest on the public debt and another the salaries of members of Congress. *(See Appropriation.)*

Permanent Authorization—An authorization without a time limit. It usually does not specify any limit on the funds that may be appropriated for the agency, program, or activity that it authorizes, leaving such amounts to the discretion of the appropriations committees and the two houses. *(See Authorization.)*

Personally Obnoxious (or Objectionable)—A characterization a senator sometimes applies to a president's nominee for a federal office in that senator's state to justify his or her opposition to the nomination.

Pocket Veto—The indirect veto of a bill as a result of the president withholding approval of it until after Congress has adjourned *sine die*. A bill the president does not sign but does not formally veto while Congress is in session automatically becomes a law ten days (excluding Sundays) after it is received. But if Congress adjourns its annual session during that ten-day period the measure dies even if the president does not formally veto it.

Point of Order—A parliamentary term used in committee and on the floor to object to an alleged violation of a rule and to demand that the chair enforce the rule. The point of order immediately halts the proceedings until the chair decides whether the contention is valid. In some instances, a member may be able to reserve a point of order, hear the proponent's argument, and then insist on or withdraw the point of order. If the point of order is insisted on, the chair must rule.

Pork or Pork Barrel Legislation—Pejorative terms for federal appropriations, bills, or policies that provide funds to benefit a legislator's district or state, with the implication that the legislator presses for enactment of such benefits to ingratiate himself or herself with constituents rather than on the basis of an impartial, objective assessment of need or merit. The terms are often applied to such benefits as new parks, federal office buildings, dams, canals, bridges, roads, water projects, sewage treatment plants, and public works of any kind, as well as demonstration projects, research grants, and relocation of government facilities. Funds released by the president for various kinds of benefits or government contracts approved by him allegedly for political purposes are also sometimes referred to as pork. *(See Earmark.)*

Postcloture Filibuster—A filibuster conducted after the Senate invokes cloture. It employs an array of procedural tactics rather than lengthy speeches to delay final action. The Senate curtailed the post-cloture filibuster's effectiveness by closing a variety of loopholes in the cloture rule in 1979 and 1986. *(See Cloture.)*

Power of the Purse—A reference to the constitutional power Congress has over legislation to raise revenue and appropriate monies from the Treasury. Article I, Section 8, states that Congress "shall have Power To lay and collect Taxes, Duties, Imposts and Excises, [and] to pay the Debts." Section 9 declares: "No Money shall be drawn from the Treasury, but in Consequence of Appropriations made by Law."

Preamble—Introductory language describing the reasons for and intent of a measure, sometimes called a whereas clause. It occasionally appears in joint, concurrent, and simple resolutions but rarely in bills.

Precedent—A previous ruling on a parliamentary matter or a long-standing practice or custom of a house. Precedents serve to control arbitrary rulings and serve as the common law of a house.

President of the Senate—One constitutional role of the vice president is serving as the president of the Senate, its presiding officer. The Constitution permits the vice president to cast a vote in the Senate only to break a tie, but the vice president is not required to do so.

President Pro Tempore—Under the Constitution, an officer elected by the Senate to preside over it during the absence of the vice president of the United States. Often referred to as the "pro tem," this senator is usually the member of the majority party with the longest continuous service in the chamber and may also be, by virtue of seniority, a committee chair. When attending to committee and other duties, the president pro tempore appoints other, usually junior, senators to preside.

Presiding Officer—In a formal meeting, the individual authorized to maintain order and decorum, recognize members to speak or offer motions, and apply and interpret the chamber's rules, precedents, and practices. The Speaker of the House and the president of the Senate are the chief presiding officers in their respective houses.

Previous Question—A nondebatable motion that, when agreed to by majority vote, cuts off further debate, prevents the offering of additional amendments, and brings the pending matter to an immediate vote. A decision to order the previous question is a decision saying that the debate and amending process are completed and the body is ready to move to a final vote on the main proposition. A special rule in the House may by its provisions allow some specified business despite a provision in the special rule ordering the previous question. It is a major debate-limiting device in the House; it is not permitted in the Committee of the Whole in the House or in the Senate.

Private Bill—A bill that applies to one or more specified persons, corporations, institutions, or other entities, usually to grant relief when no other legal remedy is available to them. Many private bills deal with claims against the federal government, immigration and naturalization cases, and land titles.

Private Calendar—The title for a calendar in the House reserved for private bills and resolutions favorably reported by committees.

Private Law—A private bill enacted into law. Private laws are numbered separately but in the same fashion as public laws. *(See Public Law.)*

Privilege—An attribute of a motion, measure, report, question, or proposition that gives it priority status for consideration. Privileged motions and motions to bring up privileged questions are not debatable.

Privilege of the Floor—In addition to the members of a house, certain individuals are admitted to its floor while it is in session. The rules of the two houses differ somewhat but both extend the privilege to the president and vice president, Supreme Court justices, cabinet members, state governors, former members of that house, members of the other house, certain officers and officials of Congress, certain staff of that house in the discharge of official duties, and the chamber's former parliamentarians. They also allow access to a limited number of committee and members' staff when their presence is necessary.

Pro Forma Amendment—In the House, an amendment that ostensibly proposes to change a measure or another amendment by moving "to strike the last word" or "to strike the requisite number of words." A member offers it not to make any actual change in the measure or amendment but only to obtain time for debate. *(See Five-Minute Rule.)*

Pro Tem—A common reference to the president pro tempore of the Senate or, occasionally, to a Speaker pro tempore. *(See President Pro Tempore; Speaker Pro Tempore.)*

Procedures—The methods of conducting business in a deliberative body. The procedures of each house are governed first by applicable provisions of the Constitution, and then by its standing rules and orders, precedents, traditional practices, and any statutory rules that apply to it. The authority of the houses to adopt rules in addition to those specified in the Constitution is derived from Article I, Section 5, clause 2 of the Constitution, which states: "Each House may determine the Rules of its Proceedings. . . . " By rule, the House of Representatives also follows the procedures in *Jefferson's Manual* that are not inconsistent with its standing rules and orders. Many Senate procedures also conform with Jefferson's provisions, but by practice rather than by rule. At the beginning of each Congress, the House uses procedures in general parliamentary law until it adopts its standing rules. *(See Rule, first definition.)*

Proxy Voting—The practice of permitting a member to cast the vote of an absent colleague in addition to his or her own vote. Proxy voting is prohibited on the floors of the House and Senate, but the Senate permits its committees to authorize proxy voting, and most do. In 1995, House rules were changed to prohibit proxy voting in committee.

Public Bill—A bill dealing with general legislative matters having national applicability or applying to the federal government or to a class of persons, groups, or organizations.

Public Debt—Federal government debt incurred by the Treasury or the Federal Financing Bank by the sale of securities to the public or borrowings from a federal fund or account. *(See Debt Limit; Federal Debt.)*

Public Law—A public bill or joint resolution enacted into law. It is cited by the letters "PL" followed by a hyphenated number. The digits before the hyphen indicate the number of the Congress in which it was enacted; the digits after the hyphen indicate its position in the numerical sequence of public measures that became law during that Congress. For example, the Budget Enforcement Act of 1990 became PL 101-508 because it was the 508th measure in that sequence for the 101st Congress. This system of numbering began in the late 1950s; before that, the number of the Congress in which a law was enacted was not part of the law's numerical designation. *(See also Private Law.)*

Qualification (of Members)—The Constitution requires members of the House of Representatives to be twenty-five years of age at the time their terms begin. They must have been citizens of the United States for seven years before that date and, when elected, must be "Inhabitant[s]" of the state from which they were elected. There is no constitutional requirement that they reside in the districts they represent. Senators are required to be thirty years of age at the time their terms begin. They must have been citizens of the United States for nine years before that date and, when elected, must be "Inhabitant[s]" of the states in which they were elected. The "Inhabitant" qualification is broadly interpreted, and in modern times a candidate's declaration of state residence has generally been accepted as meeting the constitutional requirement.

Queen of the Hill Rule—A special rule from the House Rules Committee that permits votes on a series of amendments, especially complete substitutes for a measure, in a specified order, but directs that the amendment receiving the greatest number of votes shall be the winning one. This kind of rule permits the House to vote directly on a variety of alternatives to a measure. In doing so, it sets aside the precedent that once an amendment has been adopted, no further amendments may be offered to the text it has amended. Under an earlier practice that took root in the 1970s, the Rules Committee reported "king of the hill" rules under which there also could be votes on a series of amendments, again in a specified order. If more than one of the amendments was adopted under this kind of rule, it was the last amendment to receive a majority vote that was considered as having been finally adopted, whether or not it had received the greatest number of votes. *(See Rule, second definition.)*

Quorum—The minimum number of members required to be present for the transaction of business. Under the Constitution, a quorum in each house is a majority of its members: 218 in the House and 51 in the Senate when there are no vacancies. By House rule, a quorum in the Committee of the Whole is 100. In practice, both houses usually assume a quorum is present even if it is not, unless a member makes a point of no quorum in the House or a live quorum or vote exposes the absence of a quorum in the Senate. Consequently, each house transacts much of its business, and even passes bills, when only a few members are present. For House and Senate committees, chamber rules allow a minimum quorum of one-third of a committee's members to conduct many types of business. *(See Live Quorum.)*

Quorum Call—A procedure for determining whether a quorum is present in a chamber. In the Senate, a clerk calls the roll (roster) of senators. The House usually employs its electronic voting system. *(See Quorum.)*

Ramseyer Rule—A House rule that requires a committee's report on a bill or joint resolution to show the changes the measure, and any committee amendments to it, would make in existing law. The rule requires the report to present the text of any statutory provision that would be repealed and a comparative print showing, through typographical devices such as stricken-through type or italics, other changes that would be made in existing law. The rule, adopted in 1929, was named after its sponsor, Rep. Christian W. Ramseyer, R-Iowa. The Senate's analogous rule is called the Cordon Rule. *(See Committee Report on a Measure; Cordon Rule.)*

Rank or Ranking—A member's position on the list of his or her party's members on a committee or subcommittee. When first assigned to a committee, a member is usually placed at the bottom of the list, then moves up as those above leave the committee. On subcommittees, however, a member's rank may not have anything to do with the length of his or her service on it.

Ranking Member—(1) A reference to the minority member with the highest ranking on a committee or subcommittee. (2) A reference to the majority member next in rank to the chair or to the highest ranking majority member present at a committee or subcommittee meeting.

Ratification—(1) The president's formal act of promulgating a treaty after the Senate has approved it. The resolution of ratification agreed to by the Senate is the procedural vehicle by which the Senate gives its consent to ratification. (2) A state legislature's (or state convention's) act in approving a proposed constitutional amendment. Such an amendment becomes effective when ratified by three-fourths of the states. *(See Executive Document; Ratification; Resolution of Ratification; Treaty.)*

Reapportionment—*(See Apportionment.)*

Recess—(1) A temporary interruption or suspension of a meeting of a chamber or committee. Unlike an adjournment, a recess does not end a legislative day. Because the Senate might recess from one calendar day to another, its legislative day may extend over several calendar days or longer. (2) A period of adjournment for more than three days to a day certain.

Recess Appointment—A presidential appointment to a vacant federal position made after the Senate has adjourned *sine die*. Presidents have also argued that a recess appointment is possible when the Senate has adjourned or recessed for more than thirty days and for shorter periods, including times of recess when the Senate is conducting pro forma sessions. If the president submits the recess appointee's nomination during the next session of the Senate, that individual can continue to serve until the end of the session even though the Senate might have rejected the nomination.

Recommit—To send a measure back to the committee that reported it; sometimes called a straight motion to recommit to distinguish it from a motion to recommit with instructions. A successful motion to recommit kills the measure. A motion to recommit with instructions is normally an attempt to amend a measure. In the House, the rules provide that minority will have a motion to commit or recommit a measure with or without instructions before a vote on final passage of the measure. The motion to recommit in the Senate may be offered during the amending process. *(See Recommit with Instructions.)*

Recommit a Conference Report—To return a conference report to the conference committee for renegotiation of some or all of its agreements. A motion to recommit may be offered with or without instructions. Once one chamber has approved a conference report, a motion to recommit is no longer possible since that vote dissolved the conference. *(See Conference Report.)*

Recommit with Instructions—To send a measure back to a committee with instructions to take some action on it, usually to amend it as provided in the instructions. In the House, the instructions must be written so that the measure remains on the House floor and does not literally return to committee. *(See Recommit.)*

Reconciliation—A procedure for changing existing revenue and spending laws to bring total federal revenues and spending within the limits established in a budget resolution. This procedure is triggered by the inclusion of reconciliation instructions directed at specific committees in a budget resolution. Congress has applied reconciliation chiefly to revenues and mandatory spending programs, especially entitlements. Discretionary spending is controlled through annual appropriation bills. *(See Budget Process; Budget Resolution.)*

Reconsider—A practice that gives a chamber an opportunity to review its action on any proposition. Any member who voted on the prevailing side can ask to reconsider the vote, creating, in effect, the opportunity for another vote on the same proposition. In practice, a proposition's proponents typically engage in a scripted dialogue where one member moves that the vote be reconsidered and a second member moves to lay that motion on the table, and the presiding officer then states that the motion to table has been agreed to. Invoking this procedure may create the anomalous situation of an opponent of a measure changing his or her "no" vote to a "yea" vote (or a proponent changing a "yea" vote to a "no" vote) to force a new vote. Not all votes on propositions may be reconsidered.

Recorded Vote—(1) Generally, any vote in which members are recorded by name for or against a measure; also called a record vote or roll-call vote. The only recorded vote in the Senate is a vote by the yeas and nays and is commonly called a roll-call vote. (2) Technically, a recorded vote is one demanded in the House of Representatives and supported by at least one-fifth of a quorum (forty-four members) in the House sitting as the House or at least twenty-five members in the Committee of the Whole.

Redistricting—The redrawing of congressional district boundaries within a state after a decennial census. Redistricting may be required to equalize district populations or to accommodate an increase or decrease in the number of a state's House seats that might have resulted from the decennial apportionment. While redistricting was traditionally a responsibility of state legislatures, and still is in most states, some states use commissions instead of or as a complement to the role of their state legislatures, and courts have become active players, sometimes imposing their own district maps on a state. *(See Apportionment; Congressional District; Gerrymandering.)*

Referral—The assignment of a measure to one or more committees for consideration; also called reference in the Senate. *(See Multiple and Sequential Referrals.)*

Report—(1) As a verb, a committee is said to report when it submits a measure or other document to its parent chamber. (2) A clerk is said to report when he or she reads a measure's title, text, or the text of an amendment to the body at the direction of the chair. (3) As a noun, a committee document that accompanies a reported measure. It describes the measure, the committee's views on it, its costs, and the changes it proposes to make in existing law; it also includes certain impact statements. (4) A committee document submitted to its parent chamber that describes the results of an investigation or other study or provides information it is required to provide by rule or law. *(See Committee Report.)*

Representative—An elected and duly sworn member of the House of Representatives who is entitled to vote in the chamber. The Constitution requires that a representative be at least twenty-five years old, a citizen of the United States for at least seven years, and an inhabitant of the state from which he or she is elected. Customarily, members reside in the districts they represent. Representatives are elected in even-numbered years to two-year terms that begin the following January. Representatives may also be elected in special elections to fill a vacancy created by a death or resignation; they then serve until the next general election.

Reprimand—A formal condemnation of a member for misbehavior, considered a milder reproof than censure. The House of Representatives first used it in 1976. The Senate first used it in 1991. *(See also Censure.)*

Rescission—A provision of law that repeals previously enacted budget authority in whole or in part. Under the Impoundment Control Act of 1974, the president can impound such funds by sending a message to Congress requesting one or more rescissions and the reasons for doing so. If Congress does not pass a rescission bill for the programs requested by the president within forty-five days of continuous session after receiving the message, the president must make the funds available for obligation and expenditure. If the president does not, the comptroller general of the United States is authorized to bring suit to compel the release of those funds. A rescission bill may rescind all, part, or none of an amount proposed by the president, and may rescind funds the president has not impounded. *(See Congressional Budget and Impoundment Control Act of 1974; Deferral; Impoundment.)*

Reserve the Right to Object—A member's declaration that the member may object to a unanimous consent request. It provides an alternative to silence (acquiescence to the request) or to objecting, instead allowing the member making the reservation to clarify the requester's purpose, suggest an amendment to the request, express views, or undertake another purpose. The member reserving the right to object must ultimately withdraw the reservation, allowing the unanimous consent request to take effect, or object. *(See Unanimous Consent.)*

Resident Commissioner from Puerto Rico—A nonvoting member of the House of Representatives, elected to a four-year term. The resident commissioner has the same status and privileges as delegates. As with the delegates, the resident commissioner may not vote in the House but may do so in committee. *(See Delegate.)*

Resolution—(1) A simple resolution; that is, a nonlegislative measure effective only in the house in which it is proposed and not requiring concurrence by the other chamber or approval by the president. Simple resolutions are designated "H. Res." in the House and "S. Res." in the Senate. Simple resolutions express nonbinding opinions on policies or issues or deal with the internal affairs or prerogatives of a house. (2) Any type of resolution: simple, concurrent, or joint. *(See Concurrent Resolution; Joint Resolution.)*

Resolution of Inquiry—A resolution usually simple rather than concurrent calling on the president or the head of an executive agency to provide specific information or papers to one or both houses.

Resolution of Ratification—The Senate vehicle for consenting to ratification of a treaty. The constitutionally mandated vote of two-thirds of the senators present and voting applies to the adoption of this resolution. However, it may also contain amendments, reservations, declarations, or understandings that the Senate had previously added to it by majority vote. *(See Executive Document; Ratification; Treaty.)*

Revenue Legislation—Measures that levy new taxes or tariffs or change existing ones. Under Article I, Section 7, clause 1 of the Constitution, the House of Representatives originates federal revenue measures, but the Senate can propose amendments to them. The House Ways and Means Committee and the Senate Finance Committee have jurisdiction over such measures, with a few minor exceptions. *(See Budget Resolution.)*

Revise and Extend One's Remarks—A unanimous consent request to publish in the *Congressional Record* a statement a member did not deliver on the floor, a longer statement than the one made on the floor, or miscellaneous extraneous material. *(See* Congressional Record.*)*

Revolving Fund—A trust fund or account, the income of which remains available to finance its continuing operations without any fiscal year limitation.

Rider—Congressional slang for an amendment unrelated or extraneous to the subject matter of the measure to which it is attached. Riders may contain proposals that are less likely to become law on their own merits as separate bills, either because of opposition in the committee of jurisdiction, resistance in the other house, or the probability of a presidential veto.

Roll Call—A call of the roll to determine whether a quorum is present, to establish a quorum, or to vote on a question. Usually, the House uses its electronic voting system for a roll call. The Senate does not have an electronic voting system; its roll is always called by a clerk.

Rule—(1) A permanent regulation that a house adopts to govern its conduct of business, its procedures, its internal organization, behavior of its members, regulation of its facilities, duties of an officer, or some other subject it chooses to govern in that form. (2) In the House, a privileged simple resolution reported by the Rules Committee that provides methods and conditions for floor consideration of a measure or several measures.

Rule Twenty-Two—A common reference to the Senate's cloture rule, which is contained in Senate Rule Twenty-Two. *(See Cloture.)*

Second-Degree Amendment—An amendment to an amendment in the first degree. *(See Degrees of Amendment.)*

Secretary of the Senate—The chief financial, administrative, and legislative officer of the Senate. Elected by resolution or order of the Senate, the secretary is invariably the candidate of the majority party and usually chosen by the majority leader. In the absence of the vice president and pending the election of a president pro tempore, the secretary presides over the Senate. The secretary is subject to policy direction and oversight by the Senate Committee on Rules and Administration. The secretary manages a wide range of functions that support the administrative operations of the Senate as an organization as well as those functions necessary to its legislative process, including record keeping, document management, certifications, housekeeping services, administration of oaths, and lobbyist registrations. The secretary is responsible for accounting for all funds appropriated to the Senate and conducts audits of Senate financial activities.

Section—A subdivision of a bill or statute. By law, a section must be numbered and, as nearly as possible, contain "a single proposition of enactment."

Select or Special Committee—A committee established by a resolution in either house for a special purpose and, usually, for a limited time. Most select and special committees are assigned specific investigations or studies but are not authorized to report measures to their chambers. A select or special committee might, however, be given legislative authority in the resolution establishing it. Legislative authority allows legislation to be referred to the select or special committee, and provides the committee with authority to report measures to its parent chamber. *(See Ad Hoc Select Committee.)*

Senate—The house of Congress in which each state is represented by two senators; each senator has one vote. Article V of the Constitution declares that "No State, without its Consent, shall be deprived of its equal Suffrage in the Senate." The Constitution also gives the Senate equal legislative power with the House of Representatives. Although the Senate is prohibited from originating revenue measures, and as a matter of practice it does not originate appropriation measures, it can amend both. Only the Senate can give or withhold consent to treaties and nominations from the president. It also acts as a court to try impeachments by the House and elects the vice president when no candidate receives a majority of the electoral votes. It is often referred to as "the upper body," but not by members of the House. *(See House of Representatives; Lower Body.)*

Senate Manual—The compilation of the Senate's standing rules and orders and the laws and other regulations that apply to the Senate.

Senator—A duly sworn elected or appointed member of the Senate. The Constitution requires that a senator be at least thirty years old, a citizen of the United States for at least nine years, and an inhabitant of the state from which he or she is elected. Senators are usually elected in even-numbered years to six-year terms that begin the following January; one-third of the Senate—known as a class—is subject to election every two years. When a vacancy occurs before the end of a term, the state governor follows state law on appointing a replacement or calling a special election to fill the position until a successor is chosen at the state's next general election to serve the remainder of the term. Until the Seventeenth Amendment was ratified in 1913, senators were chosen by their state legislatures.

Senatorial Courtesy—The Senate's practice of declining to confirm a presidential nominee for an office in the state of a senator of the president's party unless that senator approves.

Seniority—The priority, precedence, or status accorded members according to the length of their continuous service in a house or on a committee.

Seniority Loss—A type of punishment that reduces a member's seniority on his or her committees, including the loss of chairmanships. Party caucuses in both houses have occasionally imposed such punishment on their members, for example, for publicly supporting candidates of the other party.

Seniority Rule—The customary practice, rather than a rule, of assigning the chairmanship of a committee to the majority party member who has served on the committee for the longest continuous period of time.

Seniority System—A collection of long-standing customary practices under which members with longer continuous service than their colleagues in their house or on their committees receive various kinds of preferential treatment. Although some of the practices are no longer as rigidly observed as in the past, they still pervade the organization and procedures of Congress.

Sequestration—A procedure for canceling budgetary resources—that is, money available for obligation or spending—to enforce budget limitations established in law. Sequestered funds are no longer available for obligation or expenditure.

Sergeant at Arms—The officer in each house responsible for maintaining order, security, and decorum in its wing of the Capitol, including the chamber and its galleries. Although elected by their respective houses, both sergeants at arms are invariably the candidates of the majority party.

Session—(1) The annual series of meetings of a Congress. Under the Constitution, Congress must assemble at least once a year at noon on January 3 unless it appoints a different day by law. (2) The special meetings of Congress or of one house convened by the president, called a special session. (3) A house is said to be in session during the period of a day when it is meeting.

Severability (or Separability) Clause—Language stating that if any particular provisions of a measure are declared invalid by the courts the remaining provisions shall remain in effect.

Sine Die—Without fixing a day for a future meeting. An adjournment *sine die* signifies the end of an annual or special session of Congress.

Slip Law—The first official publication of a measure that has become law. It is published separately in unbound, single-sheet form or pamphlet form. A slip law usually is available two or three days after the date of the law's enactment. *(See Statutes at Large;* U.S. Code.*)*

Speaker—The presiding officer of the House of Representatives and the leader of its majority party. The Speaker is selected by the majority party and formally elected by the House at the beginning of each Congress. Although the Constitution does not require the Speaker to be a member of the House, in fact, all Speakers have been members.

Speaker Pro Tempore—A member of the House who is designated as the temporary presiding officer by the Speaker or elected by the House to that position during the Speaker's absence.

Speaker's Vote—The Speaker is not required to vote, and the Speaker's name is not called on a roll-call vote unless so requested. The Speaker might vote either to create a tie vote, and thereby defeat a proposal, or to break a tie in favor of a proposal. Occasionally, the Speaker votes to emphasize the importance of a matter.

Special Rule—*(See Rule, second definition.)*

Special Session—A session of Congress convened by the president, under his constitutional authority, after Congress has adjourned *sine die* at the end of a regular session. *(See Adjournment* Sine Die*; Session.)*

Spending Authority—The technical term for backdoor spending. The Congressional Budget Act of 1974 defines it as borrowing authority, contract authority, and entitlement authority for which appropriation acts do not provide budget authority in advance. Under the Budget Act, legislation that provides new spending authority may not be considered unless it provides that the authority shall be effective only to the extent or in such amounts as provided in an appropriation act. *(See Backdoor Spending Authority; Borrowing Authority; Contract Authority; Entitlement Program.)*

Spending Cap—The statutory limit for a fiscal year on the amount of new budget authority and outlays allowed for discretionary spending. The Budget Enforcement Act of 1997 required a sequester if the cap was exceeded. *(See Sequester.)*

Split Referral—A measure divided into two or more parts, with each part referred to a different committee. *(See Multiple and Sequential Referrals; Referral.)*

Sponsor—The principal proponent and introducer of a measure or an amendment.

Staff Director—The most frequently used title for the head of staff of a committee or subcommittee. On some committees, that person is called chief of staff, clerk, chief clerk, chief counsel, general counsel, or executive director. The head of a committee's minority staff is usually called minority staff director. *(See Committee Staff.)*

Standing Committee—A permanent committee established by a House or Senate standing rule or standing order. The rule also describes the subject areas on which the committee may report bills and resolutions and conduct oversight. Most introduced measures are referred to one or more standing committees according to their jurisdictions.

Standing Order—A continuing regulation or directive that has the force and effect of a rule but is not incorporated into the standing rules. The Senate's numerous standing orders, such as its standing rules, continue from Congress to Congress unless changed or the order states otherwise. The House uses relatively few standing orders, and those it adopts expire at the end of a session of Congress.

Standing Rules—The rules of the Senate that continue from one Congress to the next and the rules of the House of Representatives that it adopts at the beginning of each new Congress.

Standing Vote—An alternative and informal term for a division vote, during which members in favor of a proposal and then members opposed stand and are counted by the chair. *(See Division Vote.)*

Star Print—A reprint of a bill, resolution, amendment, or committee report correcting technical or substantive errors in a previous printing; so called because of the small black star that appears on the front page or cover.

State of the Union Message—A presidential message to Congress under the constitutional directive that the president shall "from time to time give to the Congress Information of the State of the Union, and recommend to their Consideration such Measures as he shall judge necessary and expedient." Customarily, the president sends an annual State of the Union message to Congress, usually late in January, presenting it in person in an address to a joint session.

Statutes at Large—A chronological arrangement of the laws enacted in each session of Congress. Though indexed, the laws are not arranged by subject matter, nor is there an indication of how they affect or change previously enacted laws. The volumes are numbered by Congress, and the laws are cited by their volume and page number. The Gramm-Rudman-Hollings Act, for example, appears as 99 Stat. 1037. *(See Slip Law;* U.S. Code.*)*

Straw Vote Prohibition—Under a House precedent, a member who has the floor during debate may not conduct a straw vote or otherwise ask for a show of support for a proposition. Only the chair may put a question to a vote.

Strike from the *Record*—Expunge objectionable remarks from the *Congressional Record,* after a member's words have been taken down on a point of order.

Strike the Last Word—*(See Pro Forma Amendment.)*

Subcommittee—A panel of committee members assigned a portion of the committee's jurisdiction or other functions. On legislative committees, subcommittees hold hearings, mark up legislation, and report measures to their full committee for further action; they cannot report directly to the chamber. A subcommittee's party composition usually reflects the ratio on its parent committee.

Subpoena Power—The authority granted to committees by the rules of their respective houses to issue legal orders requiring individuals to appear and testify, or to produce documents pertinent to the committee's functions, or both. Persons who do not comply with subpoenas can be cited for contempt of Congress and prosecuted.

Subsidy—Generally, a payment or benefit made by the federal government for which no current repayment is required. Subsidy payments may be designed to support the conduct of an economic enterprise or activity, such as ship operations, or to support certain market prices, as in the case of farm subsidies.

Sunset Legislation—A term sometimes applied to laws authorizing the existence of agencies or programs that expire annually or at the end of some other specified period of time. One of the purposes of setting specific expiration dates for agencies and programs is to encourage the committees with jurisdiction over them to determine whether they should be continued or terminated. *(See Authorization.)*

Sunshine Rules—Rules requiring open committee hearings and business meetings, including markup sessions, in both houses, and also open conference committee meetings. However, all may be closed under certain circumstances and using certain procedures required by the rules. *(See Closed Hearing.)*

Supermajority—A term sometimes used for a vote on a matter that requires approval by more than a simple majority of those members present and voting; also referred to as extraordinary majority. *(See Constitutional Votes; Suspension of the Rules (House).)*

Supplemental Appropriation Bill—A measure providing appropriations for use in the current fiscal year, in addition to those already provided in annual general appropriation bills. Supplemental appropriations are often for unforeseen emergencies. *(See Appropriation.)*

Suspension of the Rules (House)—An expeditious procedure for passing relatively noncontroversial or emergency measures by a two-thirds vote of those members voting, a quorum being present.

Suspension of the Rules (Senate)—A procedure to set aside one or more of the Senate's rules; it is used infrequently.

Task Force—A title sometimes given to a panel of members assigned to a special project, study, or investigation. A task force might be convened by leadership, a party caucus or conference, or a committee. Ordinarily, these groups do not have authority to report measures to their respective houses.

Tax Expenditure—Loosely, a tax exemption or advantage, sometimes called an incentive or loophole; technically, a loss of governmental tax revenue attributable to some provision of federal tax laws that allows a special exclusion, exemption, or deduction from gross income or that provides a special credit, preferential tax rate, or deferral of tax liability.

Televised Proceedings—Television and radio coverage of the floor proceedings of the House of Representatives have been available since 1979 and of the Senate since 1986. They are broadcast over a coaxial cable system to all congressional offices and to some congressional agencies on channels reserved for that purpose. Coverage is also available free of charge to commercial and public television and radio broadcasters. C-SPAN carries gavel-to-gavel coverage of both houses. *(See C-SPAN.)*

Third Reading—A required reading to a chamber of a bill or joint resolution by title only before the vote on passage. In modern practice, it has merely become a pro forma step.

Third-Degree Amendment—An amendment to a second-degree amendment. Both houses prohibit such amendments. *(See Degrees of Amendment.)*

Three-Day Rule—(1) In the House, a measure cannot be considered until the third calendar day on which the committee report has been available. (2) In the House, a conference report cannot be considered until the third calendar day on which its text has been available in the *Congressional Record.* (3) In the House, a general appropriation bill cannot be considered until the third calendar day on which printed hearings on the bill have been available. (4) In the Senate, when a committee votes to report a measure, a committee member is entitled to three calendar days within which to submit separate views for inclusion in the committee report. (In House committees, a member is entitled to two calendar days for this purpose, after the day on which the committee votes to report.) (5) In both houses, a majority of a committee's members may call a special meeting of the committee if its chair fails to do so within three calendar days after three or more of the members, acting jointly, formally request such a meeting. In calculating such periods, the House omits holiday and weekend days on which it does not meet. The Senate makes no such exclusion.

Tie Vote—When the votes for and against a proposition are equal, it loses. The president of the Senate—the constitutional role of the vice president—may cast a vote only to break a tie. Because the Speaker is invariably a member of the House, the Speaker is entitled to vote but usually does not. The Speaker may choose to do so to break, or create, a tie vote.

Title—(1) A major subdivision of a bill or act, designated by a roman numeral and usually containing legislative provisions on the same general subject. Titles are sometimes divided into subtitles as well as sections. (2) The official name of a bill or act, also called a caption or long title. (3) Some bills also have short titles that appear in the sentence immediately following the enacting clause. (4) Popular titles are the unofficial names given to some bills or acts by common usage. For example, the Balanced Budget and Emergency Deficit Control Act of 1985 (short title) is almost invariably referred to as Gramm-Rudman (popular title). In other cases, significant legislation is popularly referred to by its title number *(see definition (1) above)*. For example, the federal legislation that requires equality of funding for women's and men's sports in educational institutions that receive federal funds is popularly called Title IX.

Track System—An occasional Senate practice that expedites legislation by dividing a day's session into two or more specific time periods, commonly called tracks, each reserved for consideration of a different measure.

Transfer Payment—A federal government payment to which individuals or organizations are entitled under law and for which no goods or services are required in return. Payments include welfare and Social Security benefits, unemployment insurance, government pensions, and veterans benefits.

Treaty—A formal document containing an agreement between two or more sovereign nations. The Constitution authorizes the president to make treaties, but the president must submit them to the Senate for its approval by a two-thirds vote of the senators present. Under the Senate's rules, that vote actually occurs on a resolution of ratification. Although the Constitution does not give the House a direct role in approving treaties, that body has sometimes insisted that a revenue treaty is an invasion of its prerogatives. In any case, the House may significantly affect the application of a treaty by its equal role in enacting legislation to implement the treaty. *(See Executive Document; Ratification; Resolution of Ratification.)*

Trust Funds—Special accounts in the Treasury that receive earmarked taxes or other kinds of revenue collections, such as user fees, and from which payments are made for special purposes or to recipients who meet the requirements of the trust funds as established by law. Of the more than 150 federal government trust funds, several finance major entitlement programs, such as Social Security, Medicare, and retired federal employees' pensions. Others fund infrastructure construction and improvements, such as highways and airports.

Unanimous Consent—Without an objection by any member. A unanimous consent request asks permission, explicitly or implicitly, to set aside one or more rules. Both houses and their committees frequently use such requests to expedite their proceedings. If all members are silent, consent is given. If any member objects, unanimous consent is denied. *(See Reserve the Right to Object.)*

Uncontrollable Expenditures—A frequently used term for federal expenditures that are mandatory under existing law and therefore cannot be controlled by the president or Congress without a change in the existing law. Uncontrollable expenditures include spending required under entitlement programs and also fixed costs, such as interest on the public debt and outlays to pay for prior-year obligations. In recent years, uncontrollables have accounted for approximately three-quarters of federal spending in each fiscal year.

Unfunded Mandate—Generally, any provision in federal law or regulation that imposes a duty or obligation on a state or local government or private sector entity without providing the necessary funds to comply. The Unfunded Mandates Reform Act of 1995 amended the Congressional Budget Act of 1974 to provide a mechanism for the control of new unfunded mandates.

Union Calendar—A calendar of the House of Representatives for bills and resolutions favorably reported by committees that raise revenue or directly or indirectly appropriate money or property. In addition to appropriation bills, measures that authorize expenditures are also placed on this calendar. The calendar's full title is the Calendar of the Committee of the Whole House on the State of the Union.

Upper Body—A common reference to the Senate, but not used by members of the House. *(See Lower Body.)*

U.S. Code—Popular title for the *United States Code: Containing the General and Permanent Laws of the United States in Force on*. . . .It is a consolidation and partial codification of the general and permanent laws of the United States arranged by subject under fifty titles. The first six titles deal with general or political subjects, the other forty-four with subjects ranging from agriculture to war, alphabetically arranged. A supplement is published after each session of Congress, and the entire *Code* is revised every six years. *(See Slip Law; Statutes at Large.)*

User Fee—A fee charged to users of goods or services provided by the federal government. When Congress levies or authorizes such fees, it determines whether the revenues should go into the general collections of the Treasury or be available for expenditure by the agency that provides the goods or services.

Veto—The president's disapproval of a legislative measure passed by Congress. The president returns the measure to the house in which it originated without his signature but with a veto message stating his objections to it. When Congress is in session, the president must veto a bill within ten days, excluding Sundays, after the president has received it; otherwise it becomes law without his signature. The ten-day clock begins to run at midnight following his receipt of the bill. *(See Override a Veto; Pocket Veto.)*

Voice Vote—A method of voting in which members who favor a question answer "aye" in chorus, after which those opposed answer "no" in chorus, and the chair decides which position prevails.

Voting—Members vote in three ways on the floor: (1) by shouting "aye" or "no" on voice votes in the House; (2) by standing for or against on division votes; and (3) on recorded votes (including the yeas and nays), by answering "aye" or "no" when their names are called or, in the House, by recording their votes through the electronic voting system. In the Senate, members do not shout their position on voice votes; rather, the majority's position is presumed to prevail unless there is a request for a roll-call vote.

War Powers Resolution of 1973—An act that requires the president "in every possible instance" to consult Congress before committing U.S. forces to ongoing or imminent hostilities. If the president commits forces to a combat situation without congressional consultation, the president must notify Congress within forty-eight hours. Unless Congress declares war or otherwise authorizes the operation to continue, the forces must be withdrawn within sixty or ninety days, depending on certain conditions. No president has ever acknowledged the constitutionality of the resolution.

Well—The sunken, level, open space between members' seats and the podium at the front of each chamber. House members usually address their chamber from their party's lectern in the well on its side of the aisle or from their party's two tables among the House seats. Senators usually speak at their assigned desks.

Whip—The majority or minority party member in each house who acts as assistant leader, helps plan and marshal support for party strategies, encourages party discipline, and advises his or her leader on how colleagues intend to vote on the floor.

Yeas and Nays—A vote in which members usually respond "aye" or "no" (despite the official title of the vote) on a question when their names are called in alphabetical order. In the House, such votes are conducted by electronic device. The Constitution requires the yeas and nays when a demand for it is supported by one-fifth of the members present, and it also requires an automatic yea-and-nay vote on overriding a veto. Senate precedents assume the presence of a quorum and therefore require the support of at least one-fifth of a quorum, a minimum of eleven members with the present membership of 100. If a live quorum or vote has exposed the absence of a quorum, the yeas and nays will be ordered with the support of one-fifth of those present.

The Legislative Process in Brief

Note: *Parliamentary terms used below are defined in the glossary.*

INTRODUCTION OF BILLS

A House member (including the resident commissioner of Puerto Rico and nonvoting delegates of the District of Columbia, Guam, the Virgin Islands, and American Samoa) may introduce any one of several types of bills and resolutions at any time the House is in session by handing it to the clerk of the House or placing it in a box called the hopper. A senator usually introduces a measure by presenting it, along with a formal statement, to a clerk at the presiding officer's desk.

As the usual next step in either the House or the Senate, the bill is numbered, referred to the appropriate committee (or, in the House, committees), labeled with the sponsor's name and sent to the Government Printing Office so that copies can be made for subsequent study and action. House and Senate bills may be jointly sponsored and carry several lawmakers' names. Print and electronic versions of the bill are available to the public. A bill written in the executive branch and proposed as an administration measure usually is introduced by the chair of the congressional committee that has jurisdiction, as a courtesy to the White House.

Bills—Prefixed with "H.R." in the House, "S." in the Senate, followed by a number. Used as the form for most legislation, whether general or special, public or private.

Joint Resolutions—Designated "H. J. Res." or "S. J. Res." Subject to the same procedure as bills, with the exception of a joint resolution proposing an amendment to the Constitution. The latter must be approved by two-thirds of both houses and is thereupon sent directly to the archivist of the United States at the National Archives and Records Administration for submission to the states for ratification instead of being presented to the president for his approval.

Concurrent Resolutions—Designated "H. Con. Res." or "S. Con. Res." Used for matters affecting the operations of both houses. These resolutions do not become law.

Resolutions—Designated "H. Res." or "S. Res." Used for a matter concerning the operation of either house alone and adopted only by the chamber in which it originates.

COMMITTEE ACTION

With few exceptions, bills are referred to the appropriate standing committees. The job of referral formally is the responsibility of the Speaker of the House and the presiding officer of the Senate, but this task usually is carried out on their behalf by the parliamentarians of the House and Senate. Precedent, statute, and the jurisdictional mandates of the committees as set forth in the rules of the House and Senate determine which committees receive what kinds of bills. Bills are technically considered "read for the first time" when referred to House committees. Bills are read twice before being referred to Senate committees.

When a bill reaches a committee it is placed on the committee's calendar. Failure of a committee to act on a bill is equivalent to killing it and most fall by the legislative roadside. The measure can be withdrawn from the committee's purview by a discharge petition signed by a majority of the House membership on House bills. Both the House and Senate discharge bills from committees by unanimous consent, with the cooperation of committees. Other discharge options are available in both chambers.

The first committee action taken on a bill may be a request for comment on it by interested agencies of the government. The committee chair may assign the bill to a subcommittee for study and hearings, or it may be considered by the full committee. Hearings may be public, closed (executive session) or both. A subcommittee, after marking up a bill (considering amendments to it), reports to the full committee its recommendations for action and any proposed amendments.

The full committee then marks up and votes on its recommendation to the House or Senate. This procedure is called "ordering a bill reported." Occasionally a committee may order a bill reported unfavorably, especially if it must report a measure pursuant to a rule, rulemaking law, or chamber order. Most of the time a report, submitted by the chair of the committee to the House or Senate, calls for favorable action on the measure since the committee can effectively "kill" a bill by simply failing to take any action.

When the bill is reported, the committee chair instructs the staff to prepare a written report. The report describes the purposes and scope of the bill, explains the committee revisions, notes proposed changes in existing law and, usually, includes the views of the executive branch agencies consulted. Often committee members opposing a measure issue dissenting minority statements that are included in the report.

Usually, the committee "marks up" or proposes amendments to the bill. If they are substantial and the measure is complicated, the committee may order a "clean bill" introduced, which will embody the proposed amendments. The original bill then is put aside and the clean bill, with a new number, is reported to the floor.

The chamber must approve, alter, or reject the committee amendments before the bill itself can be put to a vote.

FLOOR ACTION

After a bill is reported back to the house where it originated, it is placed on the calendar.

There are four legislative calendars in the House, issued in one cumulative document titled *Calendars of the United States House of Representatives and History of Legislation*. The House calendars are:

The Union Calendar to which are referred bills raising revenues, general appropriations bills, and any measures directly or indirectly appropriating money or property. It is the Calendar of the Committee of the Whole House on the state of the Union.

The House Calendar to which are referred bills of public character not raising revenue or appropriating money.

The Private Calendar to which are referred bills for relief in the nature of claims against the United States or private immigration bills that may be passed without debate when the Private Calendar is called the first and third Tuesdays of each month.

The Discharge Calendar to which are referred motions to discharge committees when the necessary signatures are signed to a discharge petition.

There is only one legislative calendar in the Senate and one "executive calendar" for treaties and nominations submitted to the Senate.

Debate

A bill is brought to debate by varying procedures. In the Senate the majority leader, often in consultation with the minority leader and others, schedules the bills that will be taken up for debate. If it is widely supported by senators it can be taken up in the Senate either by unanimous consent or by a motion agreed to by majority vote.

Senate debate is unlimited, unless it is limited by unanimous consent, rule, rulemaking law, or supermajority vote. Typically, the Senate attempts to invoke cloture to limit debate, which requires a three-fifths vote of all senators. If invoked, debate may continue for only another thirty hours. To invoke cloture on a proposed change to Senate rules, a two-thirds vote of all senators is required.

In the House, precedence is granted to a bill if a special rule is obtained from the Rules Committee. A request for a special rule usually is made by the chair of the committee that favorably reported the bill, after consultation with the majority party leadership. The request is considered by the Rules Committee in the same fashion that other committees consider legislative measures. The committee proposes a simple resolution (H. Res.) providing for the consideration of the bill. The Rules Committee reports the resolution to the House where it is debated and voted on in the same fashion as regular bills.

The resolutions providing special rules are important because they specify how long the bill may be debated and whether it may be amended from the floor. If floor amendments are banned, the bill is considered under a "closed rule."

When a bill is debated under an "open rule," germane amendments may be offered from the floor. A "structured rule" has become the most commonly used form of rule. In the resolution reported by the Rules Committee, those amendments that may be offered are listed and the duration of debate on each prescribed. Committee amendments always are taken up first but may be changed, as may all amendments up to the second degree, if permitted by the rule; that is, an amendment to an amendment to an amendment is not in order.

Duration of debate in the House depends on whether the bill is under discussion by the House proper or before the House when it is sitting as the Committee of the Whole House on the state of the Union. In the former, the amount of time for debate occurs under the one-hour rule, which allows members to hold the floor for one hour each. In practice, the member first recognized to speak moves the previous question after an hour, which the House almost always approves and which ends further debate. In the Committee of the Whole the amount of time specified in the special rule for general debate is equally divided between proponents and opponents. At the end of general debate, the bill is often read section by section for amendment if it is considered under an open rule. Debate on an amendment is limited to five minutes for each side; this is called the "five-minute rule." In practice, amendments under an open rule are regularly debated more than ten minutes, with members gaining the floor by offering pro forma amendments or obtaining unanimous consent to speak longer than five minutes.

The House considers almost all important bills within a parliamentary framework known as the Committee of the Whole. It is not a committee as the word usually is understood; it is the full House meeting under another name for the purpose of speeding action on legislation. Technically, the House sits as the Committee of the Whole when it considers any tax measure or bill dealing with public appropriations or authorizations. Upon adoption of a special rule, the Speaker declares the House resolved into the Committee of the Whole and appoints a member of the majority party to serve as the chair. Instead of the required quorum of 218 for the House, the rules of that chamber permit the Committee of the Whole to meet when a quorum of 100 members is present on the floor and to amend and act on bills. When the Committee of the Whole has concluded consideration of a bill for amendment, it "rises," the Speaker returns as the presiding officer of the House, and the member appointed chair of the Committee of the Whole reports the action of the committee and its recommendations.

The Committee of the Whole cannot pass a bill; instead it reports the measure to the full House with whatever amendments it has adopted. Before the vote on final passage, the minority under House rules is guaranteed one attempt to kill or change the bill. This attempt is called the motion to recommit. A motion to recommit with no additional language is an attempt to get a majority to vote to kill the bill. A motion to recommit with instructions is an attempt to get a majority to adopt the amendatory language that comprises the instructions. These motions rarely succeed. After this vote, the House votes to pass or reject the bill. Amendments adopted in the Committee of the Whole may be put to a second vote in the full House.

Votes

Voting on bills may occur repeatedly before they are finally approved or rejected. The House votes on the rule for the bill and on various amendments to the bill. Voting on amendments often is a more illuminating test of a bill's support than is the final tally. Sometimes members approve final passage of bills after vigorously supporting amendments that, if adopted, would have scuttled the legislation.

The Senate has three different methods of voting: an untabulated voice vote, a standing vote (called a division), and a recorded roll call to which members answer "yea" or "nay" when their names are called. The House also employs voice and standing votes, but since January 1973 yeas and nays have been recorded by an electronic voting device, eliminating the need for time-consuming roll calls.

After amendments to a bill have been voted upon and, in the House, the motion to recommit disposed of, it is "read for the third time." The final vote is taken and is followed by a pro forma motion to reconsider, which is laid on the table. With that, the bill has been formally passed by the chamber.

ACTION IN SECOND CHAMBER

After a bill is passed it is sent to the other chamber. This body may then take one of several steps. It may pass the bill as is—accepting the other chamber's language. It may send the bill to committee for scrutiny or alteration, or reject the entire bill, advising the other house of its actions. Or it simply may ignore the bill submitted while it continues work on its version of the proposed legislation. Frequently, one chamber may approve a version of a bill that is greatly at variance with the version already passed by the other house, and then substitute its contents for the language of the other, retaining only the latter's bill number.

This graphic shows the most typical way in which proposed legislation is enacted into law. There are more complicated, as well as simpler, routes, and most bills never become law. The process is illustrated with two hypothetical bills, House bill No. 1 (H.R.1) and Senate bill No. 2 (S.2). Bills must be passed by both houses in identical form before they can be sent to the president. The path of H.R.1 is traced by a black line, that of S.2 by a gray line. In practice, most bills begin as similar proposals in both houses.

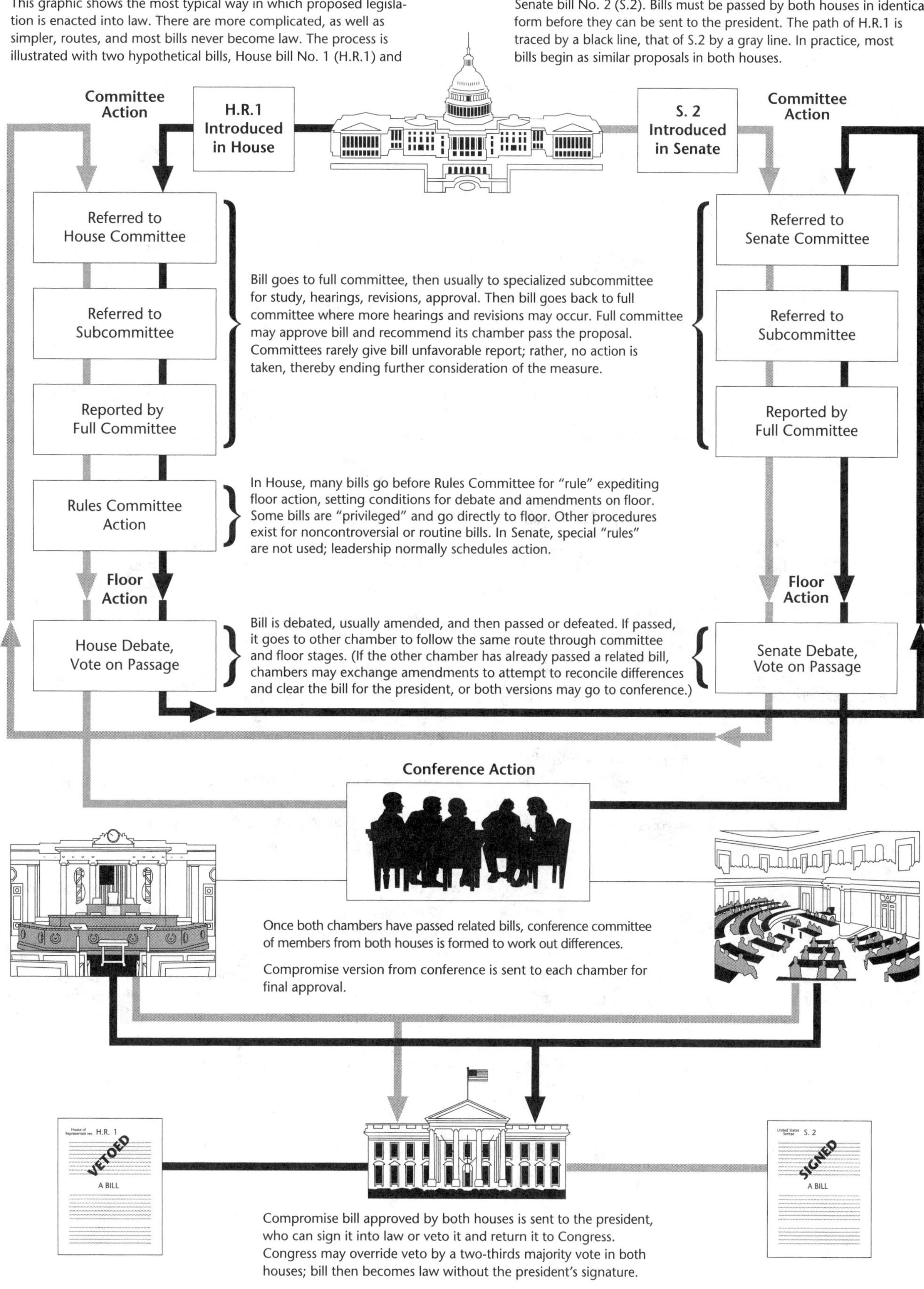

Committee Action
H.R.1 Introduced in House
S. 2 Introduced in Senate
Committee Action
Referred to House Committee
Referred to Senate Committee
Referred to Subcommittee
Bill goes to full committee, then usually to specialized subcommittee for study, hearings, revisions, approval. Then bill goes back to full committee where more hearings and revisions may occur. Full committee may approve bill and recommend its chamber pass the proposal. Committees rarely give bill unfavorable report; rather, no action is taken, thereby ending further consideration of the measure.
Referred to Subcommittee
Reported by Full Committee
Reported by Full Committee
Rules Committee Action
In House, many bills go before Rules Committee for "rule" expediting floor action, setting conditions for debate and amendments on floor. Some bills are "privileged" and go directly to floor. Other procedures exist for noncontroversial or routine bills. In Senate, special "rules" are not used; leadership normally schedules action.
Floor Action
Floor Action
House Debate, Vote on Passage
Bill is debated, usually amended, and then passed or defeated. If passed, it goes to other chamber to follow the same route through committee and floor stages. (If the other chamber has already passed a related bill, chambers may exchange amendments to attempt to reconcile differences and clear the bill for the president, or both versions may go to conference.)
Senate Debate, Vote on Passage
Conference Action
Once both chambers have passed related bills, conference committee of members from both houses is formed to work out differences.
Compromise version from conference is sent to each chamber for final approval.
H.R. 1
VETOED
A BILL
S. 2
SIGNED
A BILL
Compromise bill approved by both houses is sent to the president, who can sign it into law or veto it and return it to Congress. Congress may override veto by a two-thirds majority vote in both houses; bill then becomes law without the president's signature.

Often the second chamber makes only minor changes. If these are readily agreed to by the other house, the bill then is routed to the president. Large or small differences between each chamber's version of a bill are commonly dealt with today by amendments between the houses, whereby the first chamber considers the changes of the second chamber, and may accept those changes, clearing the bill for the president, or respond with additional changes. The second chamber then considers the first chamber's additional changes and may accept them, clearing the bill for the president, or respond with additional changes. This exchange of amendments may continue until differences are resolved. If the opposite chamber significantly alters the bill submitted to it, or the houses are not able to reach agreement through an exchange of amendments, the measure may be "sent to conference." The chamber that has possession of the "papers" (engrossed bill, engrossed amendments, messages of transmittal) requests a conference and the other chamber may agree to it. If the second chamber does not agree, the bill dies unless subsequent parliamentary actions take place.

CONFERENCE ACTION

A conference works out conflicting House and Senate versions of a legislative bill. The conferees include senior members from the committees that managed the legislation who are appointed by the presiding officers of the two houses. Under this arrangement the conferees of one house have the duty of trying to maintain their chamber's position in the face of amending actions by the conferees (also referred to as "managers") of the other house.

The number of conferees from each chamber may vary from single to double or even triple digits depending on the length or complexity of the bill and the number of committees involved. But a majority vote controls the action of each group so that a large representation does not give one chamber a voting advantage over the other chamber's conferees.

Theoretically, conferees are not allowed to write new legislation in some parliamentary circumstances in reconciling the two versions before them, but this curb sometimes is bypassed. Many bills have been put into acceptable compromise form only after new language was provided by the conferees. Frequently the ironing out of difficulties takes days or even weeks. Conferences on complex and controversial bills sometimes are particularly drawn out.

As a conference proceeds, conferees reconcile differences between the versions, but generally they grant concessions only insofar as they remain sure that the chamber they represent will accept the compromises. Occasionally, uncertainty over how either house will react, or the positive refusal of a chamber to back down on a disputed amendment, results in an impasse, and the bill dies in conference even though each version was approved by its sponsoring chamber.

When the conferees have reached agreement, they prepare a conference report embodying their recommendations (compromises in the form of legislative text) and a joint explanatory statement. The report, in document form, must be submitted to each house. The conference report must be approved by each house. Consequently, approval of the report is approval of the compromise bill. In the order of voting on conference reports, the chamber that asked for a conference yields to the other chamber the opportunity to vote first.

FINAL ACTION

After a bill has been passed by both the House and Senate in identical form, all of the original papers are sent to the enrolling clerk of the chamber in which the bill originated. The clerk then prepares an enrolled bill, which is printed on parchment paper.

When this bill has been certified as correct by the secretary of the Senate or the clerk of the House, depending on which chamber originated the bill, it is signed first (no matter whether it originated in the Senate or House) by the Speaker of the House and then by the president of the Senate. It is next sent to the White House to await action.

If the president approves the bill, he signs it, dates it, and usually writes the word "approved" on the document. If he does not sign it within ten days (Sundays excepted) and Congress is in session, the bill becomes law without his signature, an extremely rare event.

If Congress adjourns *sine die* at the end of the second session the president can pocket veto a bill and it dies without Congress having the opportunity to override. While presidents have sought to pocket veto bills after the adjournment of the first session of a Congress, they and Congress have engaged in additional procedures surrounding these vetoes that have left it unclear whether or not constitutional authority for pocket vetoes exists in an intersession adjournment.

A president vetoes a bill by refusing to sign it and, before the ten-day period expires, returning it to Congress with a message stating his reasons. The message is sent to the chamber that originated the bill. If no action is taken on the message, the bill dies. Congress, however, can attempt to override the president's veto and enact the bill, "the objections of the president to the contrary notwithstanding." Overriding a veto requires a two-thirds vote of those present in each chamber, who must number a quorum and vote by roll call.

If the president's veto is overridden by a two-thirds vote in both houses, the bill becomes law. Otherwise it is dead.

When bills are passed finally and signed, or passed over a veto, they are given law numbers in numerical order as they become law. There are two series of numbers, one for public and one for private laws, starting at the number "1" for each two-year term of Congress. They are then identified by law number and by Congress—for example, Private Law 1, 112th Congress (or Private Law 112-1); Public Law 75, 113th Congress (or P.L. 113-75).

Key Votes

2009 Key Votes 751

2010 Key Votes 767

2011 Key Votes 785

2012 Key Votes 803

Each year *Congressional Quarterly* editors select a series of key votes on major issues, and CQ Press reproduces those votes here with permission. An issue is judged by the extent to which it represents one or more of the following:

- A matter of major controversy.
- A test of presidential or political power.
- A decision of potentially great impact on the nation and lives of Americans.

For each series of related votes on an issue only one key vote is usually chosen. This vote is the roll call in the House or Senate that in the opinion of *Congressional Quarterly* editors was the most important in determining the outcome.

Senate

1. RELEASE OF TARP FUNDING

Senate rejection of a joint resolution to prevent the release of the second half of the $700 billion included in the 2008 financial industry bailout law.

In a solid opening win for the Obama administration before it even took office, the Senate on January 15 easily voted down a measure that would have withheld the remaining half of the funds in the Troubled Asset Relief Program (TARP).

The chamber voted down the resolution of disapproval by a vote of 42–52 after a week of intense lobbying from the Obama team as it began its efforts to address the nation's financial troubles growing from a burst housing bubble that plunged the nation into a deep recession in late 2007.

It was a crucial first victory for an administration that would shortly thereafter begin the push for economic stimulus legislation approaching $800 billion.

The outcome remained in doubt until the afternoon of the vote. Just a few hours before the roll call took place, leaders on both sides of the aisle received a letter from President-elect Barack Obama providing more details about the conditions he proposed attaching to the remaining $350 billion of bailout money. (The other half had been used by Obama's predecessor, George W. Bush.) Several senators credited other parts of the letter with tipping the scales for the vote. Obama also proposed directing a minimum of $50 billion toward foreclosure mitigation, increased transparency in the financial system and stronger reporting requirements for companies receiving bailout funds.

Senate rejection of S J Res 5 on January 15, 42–52: R 33–6; D 8–45; I 1–1. *(Vote 1, p. 755)*

2. WAGE DISCRIMINATION

Senate passage of legislation designed to expand the ability of victims of wage discrimination to seek remedies in court.

The vote was an early victory for the newly enlarged Democratic majority in the Senate on the way to enactment of legislation designed to reverse a 2007 Supreme Court ruling that supporters said made recovery in wage discrimination suits more difficult.

Democrats advocated legislation after the Supreme Court ruled against Lilly Ledbetter, an Alabama tire plant employee who discovered she had been paid less than her male colleagues. The measure was designed to ensure that the statute of limitations begins with the date of the most recent paycheck for which a disparity exists, rather than at the time the discrimination began, which is often years earlier.

Sponsors brought the measure to the Senate floor in January 2009 in a stronger position than a year earlier, when they could not find enough votes to invoke cloture or overcome a potential veto by President George W. Bush.

Republican resistance changed with the election of Obama, and Democrats moved quickly for an early labor victory. Hoping to advance the bill in the early months of the new administration, Senate Democrats bypassed committee consideration and took up a narrower version than that passed by the House two weeks earlier.

Republicans abandoned efforts to hold up the bill after Democrats agreed to a series of votes on GOP amendments, including one designed to start the clock running on the statute of limitations at the point at which a plaintiff "should be expected to have enough information" to realize that he or she was the victim of employment discrimination.

Democrats easily defeated those amendments, and five Republicans—including all four women in the GOP caucus—joined with Democrats to vote in favor of the underlying bill.

The House subsequently cleared the Senate bill, and it became the first piece of substantive legislation signed by President Obama.

Senate passage of S 181 (PL 111-2) on January 22, 61–36: R 5–36; D 54–0; I 2–0. *(Vote 2, p. 755)*

3. CHILDREN'S HEALTH INSURANCE PROGRAM

Passage of a bill to expand the Children's Health Insurance Program.

Although a handful of Republicans joined Democrats to move forward with one of the majority party's most important domestic priorities, notable were some of the Senate Republicans who voted against the $32.8 billion expansion of health care coverage to 4.1 million previously uninsured children.

Several supporters of the policy in previous Congresses, notably Finance Committee ranking GOP member Charles E. Grassley of Iowa, declined to vote in favor of the measure this time, saying Democrats had gone beyond the deal made in the past Congress to expand the program. In all, nine Republicans voted for the bill, with Grassley and Orrin G. Hatch of Utah the notable exceptions among previous backers.

The Senate passage vote set up the House's vote to clear the bill for the president a week later.

Senate passage of HR 2 (PL 111-3) on January 29, 66–32: R 9–32; D 55–0; I 2–0. *(Vote 3, p. 755)*

4. ECONOMIC STIMULUS COMPROMISE

Approval of a motion to invoke cloture and thus limit debate on the economic stimulus bill (HR 1).

The vote illustrated the limits that Senate Democratic leaders would have in moving forward on the party's agenda, as moderates were able to scale back the size of the package for it to proceed.

While the Democrats gained seats in the 2008 elections, with GOP threats to filibuster major initiatives, sixty votes were needed to move most legislation, a reality on display with this vote.

Senate Democratic leaders brought to the floor a bill with an eleven-year cost of more than $900 billion, but moderates in both parties balked at the expense as well as some specific provisions.

A group led by Ben Nelson, D-Neb., and Susan Collins, R-Maine, which sometimes grew to as many as twenty centrist senators, began meeting to come up with ways to change the legislation. Nelson and Collins, primarily, then began meeting with Senate Democratic leaders and White House officials to come up with a compromise.

In order to get the needed sixty votes to shut off a filibuster, Senate leaders agreed to cut the bill's spending down to $838.1 billion, primarily by scaling back funds for state governments and school construction. Some Democratic senators were not happy with the compromise, but for leaders it was the price to pay for the votes.

Eventually, three Republicans—Collins, Arlen Specter of Pennsylvania, and Olympia J. Snowe of Maine—joined all Democrats to shut off debate and move the bill forward.

In April, Specter switched parties, citing the harsh reaction among Republican voters to his role in the stimulus debate as a factor in his decision.

Senate approval of a motion to invoke cloture February 9, 61–36: R 3–36; D 56–0; I 2–0. *(Vote 4, p. 755)*

5. GUN CONTROLS

Amendment to a District of Columbia voting rights bill with language that would bar the District from prohibiting firearms possession and repeal the city's registration laws.

The vote demonstrated the continued power of gun rights advocates, despite lopsided Democratic majorities in the Senate and House as well as a Democratic administration. Offered by Sen. John Ensign, R-Nev., the amendment was one of several initiatives by Republicans during 2009 to strengthen gun rights.

Most Senate Republicans opposed legislation to grant full House representation to residents of the capital city. The underlying bill, by independent Joseph I. Lieberman of Connecticut, added a House member with full voting rights from the staunchly Democratic city, and, in a balance of partisan interests, another seat from conservative state of Utah.

The amendment, unrelated to voting rights, barred the District from prohibiting firearms possession, repealed most District firearms registration mandates, and repealed the city's requirement that firearms in homes had to be disassembled or secured with a trigger lock or other device. The bill was similar to legislation the House overwhelmingly passed in 2008.

Nearly two dozen Democrats—mostly from the South and West, where gun control is unpopular—joined all but one Republican in adopting the amendment.

The success of the amendment also ended action on D.C. voting rights legislation in the House, which was scheduled to consider its version the week after the Senate acted. House Democratic leaders pulled the measure after moderate and conservative Democrats teamed with Republicans to push for a vote on a gun amendment.

Senate adoption of a gun rights amendment to a D.C. voting rights bill (S 160) on February 26, 62–36: R 40–1; D 22–33; I 0–2. *(Vote 5, p. 755)*

6. DISCRETIONARY SPENDING LIMIT

Rejection of an amendment to the Senate budget resolution (S Con Res 13) to freeze nondefense discretionary spending for two years.

In bringing the vote to the floor, Senate Republicans tried to draw a clear contrast with Democrats over discretionary spending.

Sen. Jeff Sessions, R-Ala., offered the amendment during debate on the fiscal 2010 budget resolution as Republicans attempted to portray Democrats as profligate. He and other Republicans argued that the recently enacted $787 billion economic stimulus bill had showered domestic agencies and programs with funding and that deficit concerns should be heeded during debate on the budget.

But Democrats dismissed the GOP premise, saying many agencies had not received adequate resources during the George W. Bush administration and needed more funding.

The amendment adjusted the totals in the budget resolution to set nondefense discretionary spending at fiscal 2009 levels for fiscal 2010 and fiscal 2011, then increase them by 1 percent in fiscal 2012 through fiscal 2014. Its only real effect would have been in fiscal 2010 because Congress writes a new budget resolution each year.

The amendment drew the support of one Democrat: Evan Bayh of Indiana. Among Republicans, it was rejected by Susan Collins of Maine and Mel Martinez of Florida.

Senate rejection of the amendment to S Con Res 13 on April 1, 40–58: R 39–2; D 1–54; I 0–2. *(Vote 6, p. 755)*

7. MORTGAGE LOAN MODIFICATION

Rejection of an amendment to a foreclosure relief bill (S 896) to allow bankruptcy judges to write down the principal and interest rates of certain mortgages on primary homes if the homeowner and creditor had not been able to reach agreement on an acceptable loan modification.

The Senate vote on a procedure its critics called judicial cramdown demonstrated the extent to which Congress was attempting to use government powers in an attempt to stem home foreclosures.

Practically cursing at a lobbying juggernaut that he "frankly can't match," Richard J. Durbin, D-Ill., watched as his amendment to give bankruptcy judges the option of changing the terms of a mortgage fell to a united Republican caucus and a few steadfast Democrats.

Even with the support of the Obama administration, the Senate defeated the amendment, which Durbin tried to attach to a broader housing bill. Twelve Democrats joined Republicans to defeat the measure. The House had already passed a bill that included the provision.

Durbin blamed the defeat on the lobbying efforts of the banking industry, widely considered to be politically weakened after six months of federal bailouts and economic crisis. But the Senate vote demonstrated that the industry remained a potent lobbying force.

Senate rejection of the amendment to S 896 on April 30, 45–51: R 0–39; D 43–12; I 2–0. *(Vote 7, p. 755)*

8. CREDIT CARD REGULATION

Senate passage of legislation to impose restrictions on lending practices of credit card companies, including barring retroactive increases in annual percentage interest rates and requiring companies to give at least forty-five days' notice before increasing such rates.

In a rare moment of bipartisanship on a major issue during the session, the vote was a successful compromise on legislation designed to protect consumers from arbitrary increases in credit card interest rates and fees.

The top Democrat and Republican on the Senate Banking, Housing and Urban Affairs Committee—Chair Christopher J. Dodd of Connecticut and ranking Republican Richard C. Shelby of Alabama—reached a deal in May that cleared the way for passage. They agreed on substitute language to a House-passed bill after lengthy discussions and a final weekend of legislative drafting staff members.

The compromise allowed for easy passage by the Senate. The issue was propelled by consumer anger, along with almost-daily calls from the Obama administration for Congress to act.

Senate passage of HR 627 on May 19, 90–5: R 35–4; D 53–1; I 2–0. *(Vote 8, p. 755)*

9. TOBACCO REGULATION

Senate passage of legislation giving the Food and Drug Administration (FDA) the authority to regulate tobacco.

The vote, uniting all but one Senate Democrat with many Republicans against a handful of tobacco-state lawmakers who fought the bill, highlighted a strengthened influence among health advocates and the weakened state of the tobacco industry.

Led by Richard M. Burr, R-N.C., and Kay Hagan, D-N.C., the opposition did not have the numbers to block a longtime priority for Democrats and Republicans, who saw the legislation as a major public health win. The bill (HR 1256) gave the FDA the right to regulate the marketing, advertising, and content of cigarettes. The regulation was funded with user fees on tobacco products.

Its biggest champion, Edward M. Kennedy, D-Mass. (1962–2009), was absent from the vote, however, because of his battle with brain cancer, which claimed his life later in the year. But broad support for the legislation, even from traditional Kennedy political foes such as John Cornyn, R-Texas, ensured its passage and eventual enactment (PL 111-31).

Senate passage of HR 1256 on June 11, 79–17: R 23–16; D 54–1; I 2–0. *(Vote 9, p. 755)*

10. HATE CRIMES EXPANSION

Senate vote to invoke cloture, and thus limit debate, on an amendment to the fiscal 2010 defense authorization measure aimed at expanding federal hate crimes law to cover crimes based on sexual orientation, gender identity, or disability.

Backers of legislation to expand hate crimes law, which had been sought for years by gay rights and civil rights groups, had folded it into the annual defense authorization measure previously to try to get it enacted. In 2007, a similar hate crimes expansion was dropped from the conference report on the fiscal 2008 authorization bill at the insistence of the House.

Most Senate Republicans opposed the attachment of the hate crimes language—as an amendment by Judiciary Chair Patrick J. Leahy, D-Vt.—to the defense authorization bill. South Carolina Republican Jim DeMint criticized Senate Democrats for engineering a vote on the provisions "in the middle of a defense authorization debate which should be bipartisan, should be focused on the defense of our country, a clear constitutional responsibility."

Senate Armed Services Chair Carl Levin, D-Mich., defended the effort to attach the crime measure to the defense bill. "This bill is an available vehicle for an important subject. We've done this before on this bill," Levin said. "And one other thing that I feel keenly about as chairman of the Armed Services Committee: This bill embodies values of diversity and freedom that our men and women in uniform fight to defend."

With the House in Democratic hands and the Obama administration strongly supporting the hate crimes bill, senators cast their votes late at night July 16 knowing that if the provisions were written into the underlying measure in the Senate, there was a very good chance they would survive in the enacted legislation. Five Republicans joined fifty-six Democrats and two independents in voting to invoke cloture on the amendment. The Senate then adopted the amendment by unanimous consent. The underlying bill was later cleared and signed into law.

Senate approval of the motion to invoke cloture July 16, 63–28: R 5–28; D 56–0; I 2–0. *(Vote 10, p. 755)*

11. F-22 FUNDING

Adoption of an amendment to the fiscal 2010 defense authorization bill (S 1390) that terminated production of the F-22 Raptor fighter jet.

The vote was a significant victory for President Obama, who had threatened to veto legislation that approved the purchase of additional F-22s. He argued that the Air Force had already purchased enough of the planes, when combined with other weapons, to combat likely threats in the future. While a broad swath of the Senate disagreed with him on that point, enough senators reversed themselves on this vote to give the White House the win.

Obama exerted considerable lobbying resources to gain those reversals and achieve a rarity: Congress terminating a major defense industrial program, no less one that had survived repeated attempts on its life in previous Congresses.

The amendment, by Armed Services Chair Carl Levin, D-Mich., and ranking Republican John McCain of Arizona, took $1.8 billion that the panel's bill had dedicated to buy seven F-22s and instead dispersed it to various broad spending categories within the bill. The outcome of the vote was unclear even as balloting neared. Most Republicans were wary of ending production of a premier weapon in a period of uncertain security. Many Democrats, particularly those with jobs in their states reliant on the project, agreed.

But a critical group of senators from both parties, most of whom had no direct interest in the program, sided with the president out of loyalty or because they thought his decision was correct. Among the group were some Republicans who typically voted against the president on security issues, such as Jon Kyl of Arizona, and a Democrat, John Kerry, in whose state of Massachusetts some of the F-22 work is done.

Another important factor was the decision by the F-22's lead contractor, Lockheed Martin Corp., not to lobby publicly for the F-22 against the president's wishes.

After the vote, defense appropriators who had supported continued production of the F-22 relented and said they would not fund it because the Senate had spoken. When the House and Senate conference committee met to resolve differences on the defense authorization bill, the House conferees, whose bill had backed more F-22 production, backed away.

Senate adoption of the amendment to S 1390 on July 21, 58–40: R 15–25; D 42–14; I 1–1. *(Vote 11, p. 755)*

12. CONFIRMATION OF SONIA SOTOMAYOR

Senate vote to confirm Sonia Sotomayor as an associate justice of the Supreme Court.

The vote enabled Sotomayor to replace David H. Souter on the Supreme Court and become the first Hispanic and third female associate justice. It demonstrated the strength of the sixty-vote Senate Democratic caucus in preventing successful GOP filibusters of judicial nominations.

The outcome had been foretold for weeks. Besides the Democrats' solid majority in the Senate, Sotomayor's quietly competent performance during her Senate Judiciary Committee confirmation hearing in July had ensured her eventual confirmation.

The nominee had effectively rebutted GOP attacks against her and given Republican opponents nothing they could use to build momentum for a rejection of her candidacy. Jeff Sessions of Alabama, ranking Republican on the panel, ended any suspense about an attempt at a filibuster on the last day of the confirmation hearing. "I will not support and I don't think any member of this side will support a filibuster or any attempt to block a vote on your nomination," Sessions told Sotomayor.

The most inflammatory rhetoric during the floor debate came on its first day, when Oklahoma Republican James M. Inhofe branded as "racist" Sotomayor's much-debated past comment that a "wise Latina" judge often could reach a better conclusion than a white male counterpart.

Senate Judiciary Chair Patrick J. Leahy, D-Vt., cast Sotomayor's nomination as akin to the evolution of civil rights and voting rights in American history and major legislation pertaining to those rights that was enacted during the 1960s.

By the time the Senate gathered August 6 to vote on the nomination, it was easy to predict the final tally, because every Republican had already announced how he or she would vote.

Unlike activity in the chamber on most Senate votes, senators sat at their desks through the roll call, rising to cast their votes as their names were called. Nearly every senator participated.

Confirmation of Sotomayor on August 6, 68–31: R 9–31; D 57–0; I 2–0. *(Vote 12, p. 755)*

13. HEALTH CARE OVERHAUL/CLOTURE

Senate cloture vote to shut off debate on a health care overhaul bill (HR 3590) to introduce fundamental changes in national health care delivery and insurance coverage.

The vote mirrored the partisan gridlock that marked the first session of the 111th Congress, as the Senate by the narrowest possible margin removed the final obstacle to passage of the historic legislation. Majority Leader Harry Reid, D-Nev., needed the votes of all sixty members of the Democratic caucus (including two independents), as all forty Republicans voted no.

The bill included mandates on employers, establishment of insurance "exchanges" to serve as marketplaces where the uninsured could buy coverage, and, to pay for its implementation, new taxes on drug companies, medical device makers, insurance companies, and wealthy individuals.

But it also contained a number of compromises, without which Reid might not have won sixty votes. It barred direct or indirect federal support of abortions, a prohibition that secured the vote of the last remaining Democratic holdout, Ben Nelson of Nebraska. In another concession to Independent Joseph I. Lieberman of Connecticut, a "public option" alternative from a group of ten liberal and centrist Democrats was dropped from the bill.

Three days later, the Senate passed the underlying bill, 60–39. The only change from the cloture vote was the absence of Jim Bunning, R-Ky.

Senate approval of cloture on HR 3590 on December 21, 60–40: R 0–40; D 58–0; I 2–0. *(Vote 13, p. 755)*

1. S J Res 5. Release of TARP Funding. Passage of the joint resolution to prevent the release of the second half of the $700 billion provided under the 2008 financial industry bailout law known as the Troubled Asset Relief Program. Rejected 42–52: R 33–6; D 8–45; I 1–1. January 15, 2009.

2. S 181. Wage Discrimination. Passage of the bill to amend the 1964 Civil Rights Act to clarify time limits for workers to file employment discrimination lawsuits. The legislation allowed workers who allege discrimination based on race, gender, national origin, religion, age, or disability to file charges of pay discrimination within 180 days of the last received paycheck affected by the alleged discriminatory decision. The bill provided that the statute of limitations would be renewed with each act of discrimination. Passed 61–36: R 5–36; D 54–0; I 2–0. (By unanimous consent, the Senate agreed to raise the majority requirement for passage of the bill to 59 votes.) January 22, 2009.

3. HR 2. Children's Health Insurance Program. Passage of the bill to reauthorize the State Children's Health Insurance Program for four and a half years and increase funding by $32.8 billion. The federal tax on cigarettes was increased to 62 cents per pack and taxes on other tobacco products were raised to offset the cost of the expansion. The legislation limited program eligibility to families earning three times the federal poverty level or less and required states to phase out coverage of childless adults. Passed 66–32: R 9–32; D 55–0; I 2–0. January 29, 2009.

4. HR 1. Economic Stimulus Compromise. Motion to invoke cloture (thus limiting debate) on the Reid, D-Nev., amendment to provide approximately $838 billion in tax cuts and additional spending to stimulate the economy, including a provision to prevent the alternative minimum tax from applying to more taxpayers in 2009. The legislation provided funds for a state fiscal stabilization fund; authorized a one-time payment to seniors, disabled veterans, and persons who receive disability payments; expanded bonus depreciation for 2009; increased weekly unemployment benefits; and provided an additional twenty weeks of unemployment benefits (an additional thirty-three weeks in states with high unemployment rates). It also suspended federal income tax on the first $2,400 of unemployment benefits for 2009, expanded a homeownership tax credit by up to $15,000, and allowed the credit for purchases of a primary residence. Motion agreed to 61–36: R 3–36; D 56–0; I 2–0. Three-fifths of the total Senate (sixty) is required to invoke cloture. February 9, 2009.

5. S160. Gun Controls. Ensign, R-Nev., amendment to prevent the District of Columbia from prohibiting an individual from possessing firearms, and to repeal District laws barring possession of semiautomatic firearms. The amendment repealed the District's mandates for firearm registration and the requirement that firearms be disassembled or secured with a trigger lock in the home. Adopted 62–36: R 40–1; D 22–33; I 0–2. February 26, 2009.

6. S Con Res 13. Discretionary Spending Limit. Sessions, R-Ala., amendment to the fiscal 2010 budget resolution to set nondefense discretionary spending at fiscal 2009 levels for fiscal 2010 and 2011, and allow it to increase by 1 percent annually in fiscal 2012 through 2014. Rejected 40–58: R 39–2; D 1–54; I 0–2. A "nay" was a vote in support of the president's position. April 1, 2009.

7. S 896. Mortgage Loan Modification. Durbin, D-Ill., amendment to allow bankruptcy judges to write down the principal and interest rates of certain mortgages on primary homes if the homeowner and creditor have not been able to reach agreement on a modification of the loan. The amendment applied to borrowers who were at least sixty days delinquent on payments for loans originated before January 1, 2009, and set the maximum value of loans that qualified at $729,000. Rejected 45–51: R 0–39; D 43–12; I 2–0. (By unanimous consent, the Senate agreed to raise the majority requirement for adoption of the amendment to sixty votes.) April 30, 2009.

8. HR 627. Credit Card Regulation. Passage of the bill to impose restrictions on credit card company lending practices, including restricting when companies could increase the annual percentage interest rate retroactively on existing balances, requiring companies to give at least forty-five days' notice before increasing an annual percentage rate or changing an open-ended contract, and restricting companies from computing interest charges based on balances from more than one billing cycle. Passed 90–5: R 35–4; D 53–1; I 2–0. A "yea" was a vote in support of the president's position. May 19, 2009.

9. HR1256. Tobacco Regulation. Passage of the bill to allow the Food and Drug Administration (FDA) to regulate the manufacture, sale, and promotion of tobacco products. The legislation required new and larger labels warning consumers of the health risks associated with tobacco products, and clarified that the FDA did not endorse the safety of such products. The bill established standards for tobacco products marketed as lower in health risks, and allowed the FDA to regulate the amount of nicotine but not ban any class of tobacco products or eliminate nicotine levels completely. Passed 79–17: R 23–16; D 54–1; I 2–0. A "yea" was a vote in support of the president's position. June 11, 2009.

10. S 1390. Hate Crimes Expansion. Motion to invoke cloture (thus limiting debate) on the Leahy, D-Vt., amendment to the fiscal 2010 defense authorization bill to expand federal hate crimes law to cover crimes based on sexual orientation, gender identity, or disability. Motion agreed to 63–28: R 5–28; D 56–0; I 2–0. Three-fifths of the total Senate (sixty) is required to invoke cloture. (Subsequently, the Leahy amendment was adopted by voice vote.) July 16, 2009.

11. S 1390. F-22 Funding. Levin, D-Mich., amendment to the fiscal 2010 defense authorization bill to strike $1.8 billion for the procurement of F-22A aircraft, shifting funding instead to operations and maintenance by $350 million for the Army, $100 million for the Navy, $250 million for the Air Force, and $150 million defense-wide. The amendment also increased the authorization for military personnel by $400 million and general Defense Department activities by $500 million. Adopted 58–40: R 15–25; D 42–14; I 1–1. A "yea" was a vote in support of the president's position. July 21, 2009.

12. Confirmation of Sonia Sotomayor. Confirmation of President Obama's nomination of Sonia Sotomayor of New York to be an associate justice of the U.S. Supreme Court. Confirmed 68–31: R 9–31; D 57–0; I 2–0. A "yea" was a vote in support of the president's position. August 6, 2009.

13. HR 3590. Health Care Overhaul/Cloture. Motion to invoke cloture (thus limiting debate) on the Reid, D-Nev., substitute amendment to create a system of national private insurance plans known as exchanges to be supervised by the Office of Personnel Management. The amendment removed a provision in the substitute to create a public health insurance option. The amendment increased the percentage of revenue that insurers covering employees of large businesses must spend on medical claims, and further expanded Medicaid coverage. It also required every exchange to offer at least one plan that did not cover abortion and laid out a financial structure for insurance plans to cover abortion if they do not use federal subsidies to pay for the procedure. Motion agreed to 60–40: R 0–40; D 58–0; I 2–0. Three-fifths of the total Senate (sixty) is required to invoke cloture. A "yea" was a vote in support of the president's position. December 21, 2009.

KEY

	Republican	Democrat	**Independent**
Y	Voted for (yea)	–	Announced against
#	Paired for	P	Voted "present"
+	Announced for	C	Voted "present" to avoid possible conflict of interest
N	Voted against (nay)		
X	Paired against	?	Did not vote or otherwise make a position known

Senate Key Votes	1	2	3	4	5	6	7	8	9	10	11	12	13
ALABAMA													
Shelby	Y	N	N	N	Y	Y	N	Y	Y	N	Y	N	N
Sessions	Y	N	N	N	Y	Y	?	Y	Y	N	N	N	N
ALASKA													
Murkowski	Y	Y	Y	N	Y	Y	N	Y	Y	Y	N	N	N
Begich	N	Y	Y	Y	Y	N	Y	Y	Y	Y	N	Y	Y
ARIZONA													
McCain	Y	N	N	N	Y	Y	N	Y	Y	N	Y	N	N
Kyl	N	N	N	N	Y	Y	N	N	N	N	Y	N	N
ARKANSAS													
Lincoln	Y	Y	Y	Y	Y	N	N	Y	Y	Y	Y	Y	Y
Pryor	N	Y	Y	Y	Y	N	N	Y	Y	Y	Y	Y	Y
CALIFORNIA													
Feinstein	N	Y	Y	Y	N	N	Y	Y	Y	Y	N	Y	Y
Boxer	N	Y	Y	Y	N	N	Y	Y	Y	Y	N	Y	Y
COLORADO													
Udall	N	Y	Y	Y	Y	N	Y	Y	Y	Y	Y	Y	Y
Salazar[1]	N												
Bennet[1]		Y	Y	Y	Y	N	N	Y	Y	Y	Y	Y	Y
CONNECTICUT													
Dodd	N	Y	Y	Y	N	N	Y	Y	Y	Y	N	Y	Y
Lieberman	N	Y	Y	Y	N	N	Y	Y	Y	Y	N	Y	Y
DELAWARE													
Biden[2]	N												
Carper	N	Y	Y	Y	N	N	N	Y	Y	Y	Y	Y	Y
Kaufman[2]		Y	Y	Y	N	N	Y	Y	Y	Y	Y	Y	Y
FLORIDA													
Nelson	N	Y	Y	Y	N	N	Y	Y	Y	Y	Y	Y	Y
Martinez[3]	Y	N	Y	N	Y	N	N	Y	Y	?	N	Y	
LeMieux[3]													N
GEORGIA													
Chambliss	Y	N	N	N	Y	Y	N	Y	N	N	N	N	N
Isakson	Y	N	N	N	Y	Y	N	Y	N	N	N	N	N
HAWAII													
Inouye	N	Y	Y	Y	N	N	Y	Y	Y	Y	N	Y	Y
Akaka	N	Y	Y	Y	N	N	Y	Y	Y	Y	N	Y	Y
IDAHO													
Crapo	Y	N	N	N	Y	Y	N	Y	Y	N	N	N	N
Risch	Y	N	N	N	Y	Y	N	Y	Y	N	N	N	N
ILLINOIS													
Durbin	N	Y	Y	Y	N	N	Y	Y	Y	Y	Y	Y	Y
Burris	N	Y	Y	Y	N	N	Y	Y	Y	Y	Y	Y	Y
INDIANA													
Lugar	N	N	Y	N	N	Y	N	Y	Y	Y	Y	Y	N
Bayh	Y	Y	Y	Y	Y	Y	Y	Y	Y	Y	Y	Y	Y
IOWA													
Grassley	Y	N	N	N	Y	Y	N	Y	Y	N	N	N	N
Harkin	N	Y	Y	Y	N	N	Y	Y	Y	Y	Y	Y	Y
KANSAS													
Brownback	Y	N	N	N	Y	Y	N	Y	N	N	N	N	N
Roberts	Y	N	N	N	Y	Y	N	Y	N	N	N	N	N
KENTUCKY													
McConnell	Y	N	N	N	Y	Y	N	Y	N	N	N	N	N
Bunning	+	N	N	N	Y	Y	N	Y	N	?	N	N	N
LOUISIANA													
Landrieu	N	Y	Y	Y	Y	N	N	Y	Y	Y	Y	Y	Y
Vitter	Y	N	N	N	Y	Y	N	Y	Y	N	N	N	N
MAINE													
Snowe	N	Y	Y	Y	Y	Y	N	Y	Y	Y	N	Y	N
Collins	Y	Y	Y	Y	Y	N	N	Y	Y	Y	N	Y	N
MARYLAND													
Mikulski	N	Y	Y	Y	N	N	Y	Y	Y	Y	?	Y	Y
Cardin	N	Y	Y	Y	N	N	Y	Y	Y	Y	Y	Y	Y
MASSACHUSETTS													
Kennedy[4]	X	?	?	Y	?	?	?	?	?	?	?	?	
Kirk[4]													Y
Kerry	N	Y	Y	Y	N	N	Y	Y	Y	Y	Y	Y	Y
MICHIGAN													
Levin	N	Y	Y	Y	N	N	Y	Y	Y	Y	Y	Y	Y
Stabenow	N	Y	Y	Y	N	N	Y	Y	Y	Y	Y	Y	Y
MINNESOTA													
Klobuchar	N	Y	Y	Y	N	N	Y	Y	Y	Y	Y	Y	Y
Franken[5]										Y	Y	Y	Y
MISSISSIPPI													
Cochran	Y	N	N	N	Y	Y	N	Y	Y	N	N	N	N
Wicker	Y	N	N	N	Y	Y	N	Y	Y	N	N	N	N
MISSOURI													
Bond	Y	N	N	N	Y	Y	N	Y	–	?	Y	Y	N
McCaskill	N	Y	Y	Y	Y	N	Y	Y	Y	Y	Y	Y	Y
MONTANA													
Baucus	N	Y	Y	Y	Y	N	N	Y	Y	Y	N	Y	Y
Tester	#	Y	Y	Y	Y	N	N	Y	Y	Y	N	Y	Y
NEBRASKA													
Nelson	Y	Y	Y	Y	Y	N	N	Y	Y	Y	Y	Y	Y
Johanns	Y	N	N	N	Y	Y	N	Y	Y	N	N	N	N
NEVADA													
Reid	N	Y	Y	Y	Y	N	Y	Y	Y	Y	Y	Y	Y
Ensign	Y	N	N	N	Y	Y	N	+	N	N	Y	N	N
NEW HAMPSHIRE													
Gregg	N	N	N	?	Y	Y	N	Y	Y	?	Y	Y	N
Shaheen	Y	Y	Y	Y	N	N	Y	Y	Y	Y	N	Y	Y
NEW JERSEY													
Lautenberg	N	Y	Y	Y	N	N	Y	Y	Y	Y	Y	Y	Y
Menendez	N	Y	Y	Y	N	N	Y	Y	Y	Y	Y	Y	Y

[1]Sen. Michael Bennet, D-Colo., was sworn in January 22, 2009, to fill the seat vacated by fellow Democrat Ken Salazar, who resigned January 20, 2009, to become secretary of Interior. The first key vote for which Bennet was eligible was vote 2; the last key vote for which Salazar was eligible was vote 1.

[2]Sen. Ted Kaufman, D-Del., was sworn in January 16, 2009, to fill the seat vacated by fellow Democrat Joseph R. Biden Jr., who resigned January 15, 2009, to become vice president. The first key vote for which Kaufman was eligible was vote 2; the last vote for which Biden was eligible was vote 1.

[3]Sen. George LeMieux, R-Fla., was sworn in September 10, 2009, to fill the seat vacated by fellow Republican Mel Martinez, who resigned September 9, 2009. The first key vote for which LeMieux was eligible was vote 13; the last vote for which Martinez was eligible was vote 12.

[4]Sen. Paul G. Kirk Jr., D-Mass., was sworn in September 25, 2009, to fill the seat vacated by fellow Democrat Edward M. Kennedy, who died August 25, 2009. The first key vote for which Kirk was eligible was vote 13; the last key vote for which Kennedy was eligible was vote 12.

[5]Sen. Al Franken, D-Minn., was sworn in July 7, 2009, after he was certified the winner of that state's contested election. The first key vote for which he was eligible was vote 10.

Senate Key Votes	1	2	3	4	5	6	7	8	9	10	11	12	13
NEW MEXICO													
Bingaman	N	Y	Y	Y	N	N	Y	Y	Y	Y	N	Y	Y
Udall	N	Y	Y	Y	Y	N	Y	Y	Y	Y	N	Y	Y
NEW YORK													
Schumer	N	Y	Y	Y	N	N	Y	Y	Y	Y	Y	Y	Y
Clinton[6]	N												
Gillibrand[6]			Y	Y	N	N	Y	Y	Y	Y	Y	Y	Y
NORTH CAROLINA													
Burr	Y	N	N	N	Y	Y	N	Y	N	N	N	N	N
Hagan	N	Y	Y	Y	Y	N	Y	Y	N	Y	Y	Y	Y
NORTH DAKOTA													
Conrad	N	Y	Y	Y	Y	N	Y	Y	Y	Y	Y	Y	Y
Dorgan	Y	Y	Y	Y	Y	N	N	Y	Y	Y	Y	Y	Y
OHIO													
Voinovich	N	N	N	N	Y	Y	N	Y	Y	Y	Y	Y	N
Brown	X	Y	Y	Y	N	N	Y	Y	Y	Y	Y	Y	Y
OKLAHOMA													
Inhofe	Y	N	N	N	Y	Y	N	Y	N	N	N	N	N
Coburn	Y	N	N	N	Y	Y	N	Y	N	N	Y	N	N
OREGON													
Wyden	Y	Y	Y	Y	N	N	Y	Y	Y	Y	Y	Y	Y
Merkley	N	Y	Y	Y	N	N	Y	Y	Y	Y	Y	Y	Y
PENNSYLVANIA													
Specter[7]	Y	Y	Y	Y	Y	Y	N	Y	Y	Y	Y	Y	Y
Casey	N	Y	Y	Y	Y	N	Y	Y	Y	Y	Y	Y	Y
RHODE ISLAND													
Reed	N	Y	Y	Y	N	N	Y	Y	Y	Y	Y	Y	Y
Whitehouse	N	Y	Y	Y	N	N	Y	Y	Y	Y	Y	Y	Y
SOUTH CAROLINA													
Graham	Y	N	N	N	Y	Y	N	Y	N	?	Y	Y	N
DeMint	Y	N	N	N	Y	Y	N	Y	N	N	Y	N	N
SOUTH DAKOTA													
Johnson	N	Y	Y	Y	Y	N	N	N	Y	Y	Y	Y	Y
Thune	Y	N	N	N	Y	Y	N	N	Y	N	N	N	N
TENNESSEE													
Alexander	N	N	Y	N	Y	Y	N	N	N	?	Y	Y	N
Corker	Y	N	Y	N	Y	Y	N	Y	Y	?	Y	N	N
TEXAS													
Hutchison	Y	Y	Y	N	Y	Y	N	Y	Y	N	N	N	N
Cornyn	Y	N	N	–	Y	Y	N	Y	Y	N	N	N	N
UTAH													
Hatch	#	N	N	N	Y	Y	N	Y	N	N	N	N	N
Bennett	Y	N	N	N	Y	Y	N	N	N	N	N	N	N
VERMONT													
Leahy	N	Y	Y	Y	N	N	Y	Y	Y	Y	Y	Y	Y
Sanders	Y	Y	Y	Y	N	N	Y	Y	Y	Y	Y	Y	Y
VIRGINIA													
Webb	N	Y	Y	Y	Y	N	Y	Y	Y	Y	Y	Y	Y
Warner	N	Y	Y	Y	Y	N	Y	Y	Y	Y	Y	Y	Y
WASHINGTON													
Murray	N	Y	Y	Y	N	N	Y	Y	Y	Y	N	Y	Y
Cantwell	Y	Y	Y	Y	N	N	Y	Y	Y	Y	N	Y	Y
WEST VIRGINIA													
Byrd	N	Y	Y	Y	Y	N	N	?	?	?	N	Y	Y
Rockefeller	N	Y	Y	Y	N	N	?	+	Y	Y	Y	Y	Y
WISCONSIN													
Kohl	N	Y	Y	Y	N	N	Y	Y	Y	Y	Y	Y	Y
Feingold	Y	Y	Y	Y	Y	N	Y	Y	Y	Y	Y	Y	Y
WYOMING													
Enzi	Y	N	N	N	Y	Y	N	Y	Y	N	Y	N	N
Barrasso	Y	N	N	N	Y	Y	N	Y	Y	N	Y	N	N

[6]Sen. Kirsten Gillibrand, D-N.Y., was sworn in January 27, 2009, to fill the seat vacated by fellow Democrat Hillary Rodham Clinton, who resigned January 21, 2009, to become secretary of state. The first key vote for which Gillibrand was eligible was vote 3; the last vote for which Clinton was eligible was vote 1.

[7]Sen. Arlen Specter of Pennsylvania switched party affiliation from Republican to Democrat, effective April 30, 2009. The first key vote he cast as a Democrat was vote 7.

House

1. CHILDREN'S HEALTH INSURANCE PROGRAM

House vote to clear for the president an expansion of the Children's Health Insurance Program (CHIP).

The vote was a landmark for Democrats in their new status controlling both the White House and Congress, allowing them to boast of their first victory among several major social policy programs that had been stymied by President George W. Bush in the previous eight years.

The bill provided $32.8 billion in extra funding over four and one-half years for CHIP. Lawmakers estimated at the time that it would allow coverage of an additional 4.1 million children. The program covered about 7 million in 2008. Following easy Senate passage of the bill, only two House Democrats voted against it, and forty House Republicans voted for it. President Obama signed the bill into law (PL 111-3) the same day.

The House cleared the legislation, HR 2, on February 4, 290–135: R 40–133; D 250–2. *(Vote 1, p. 762)*

2. ECONOMIC STIMULUS CONFERENCE REPORT

House passage of a $787 billion bill to help stimulate the economy through a combination of spending and tax cuts.

Enactment of the bill was an early and major legislative victory for President Obama, although the economy and high jobless numbers continued to dog the new administration during its first year in office.

Obama took office with the economy in severe recession and some politicians and economists warning of a possible second Great Depression. Against this backdrop, the presidential transition team and congressional Democratic leaders got to work quickly after the election on assembling the package, and it was signed into law less than a month after the new president was sworn in.

But the path to enactment was bumpy, and the effort required was an indicator of the political dynamic that played out over the rest of the year. There was little bipartisan support for the legislation. No House Republicans voted for the conference report, and only three Senate Republicans did—one of whom, Arlen Specter of Pennsylvania, soon switched parties. The other two were Maine Republicans, Olympia J. Snowe and Susan Collins.

At first both parties expressed support for working together on the package, but, as happened on subsequent legislation, Democratic and GOP leaders quickly drew battle lines with Republicans believing they had little to gain by compromising with Obama.

In another indicator of what was to come for the year, Senate moderates such as Ben Nelson, D-Neb., were also able to flex their dealmaking muscles, knowing that party leaders needed sixty votes to end GOP filibuster attempts.

The role Senate moderates played was particularly irksome to House Democrats, who argued that Senate leaders watered down the bill by cutting back on such things as school construction funds to placate a few senators. Similar tensions played out in other legislative battles, especially health care overhaul that became the most controversial legislation of Obama's first term.

With regard to the stimulus, Senate Majority Leader Harry Reid, D-Nev., had little choice but to make compromises with a group led by Nelson and Collins, and House Democrats agreed to support a compromise to get something quickly into law. On the final vote only seven House Democrats voted against the bill.

House adoption of the conference report on HR 1 on February 13, 246–183: R 0–176; D 246–7. *(Vote 2, p. 762)*

3. MORTGAGE LOAN MODIFICATION

House passage of legislation to allow bankruptcy judges to write down the principal and interest rates of existing loans to a home's current market value for individuals whose mortgages were larger than the value of their homes or who met other requirements.

For House Democrats, the vote marked at least a temporary victory in a long-running battle. The financial industry had lobbied fiercely against the proposal, popularly known as cramdown legislation because it forced financial institution to take significant losses on mortgages. The industry appeared to gain enough traction in February to block the populist-driven momentum when Democratic leaders were forced to pull the bill (HR 1106) from the floor amid last-minute concerns about whether enough votes were available to pass it.

A group of centrist and conservative Democrats—mainly from the New Democrat and "Blue Dog" coalitions—had expressed concern that there would be a backlash from constituents already wary of trillions of dollars in bank bailouts.

Speaker Nancy Pelosi, D-Calif., who initially said the bill would be brought back to the floor unchanged, instead worked with dissidents to hammer out compromise language. The bill was put back onto the House floor—and passed—on March 5. But the difficulty Democratic leaders had getting their own members on board turned out to be a prescient glimpse into the difficulties the legislation and its bankruptcy provision would eventually face in the Senate, where the bankruptcy language was rejected.

House passage of HR 1106 on March 5, 234–191: R 7–167; D 227–24. *(Vote 3, p. 762)*

4. TOBACCO REGULATION

House vote to clear for the president a bill authorizing the Food and Drug Administration (FDA) to regulate tobacco products.

The vote was the first time that Congress granted the FDA the power to regulate tobacco products, demonstrating the muscle of the Democrats' expanded congressional majority.

House and Senate Democrats had tried to pass the tobacco legislation for years, but the House had traditionally been an obstacle until the 2006 midterm elections, which gave Democrats control of the chamber. The bill (HR 1256) gave the FDA the power to regulate the marketing, advertising, and content of cigarettes. Funding for the legislation came from user fees on tobacco products.

After Senate passage, the House cleared it overwhelmingly, with seventy Republicans joining almost all Democrats.

Some House Republicans who had opposed the bill maintained that it was essentially a new tax and that the FDA was the wrong agency to regulate tobacco. But many joined with Democrats to pass the legislation because of its potential public health effects, a sign of the diminished influence of the tobacco industry on Congress.

House cleared HR 1256 for the president on June 12, 307–97: R 70–90; D 237–7. *(Vote 4, p. 762)*

5. RULE TO LIMIT FLOOR AMENDMENTS ON AN APPROPRIATIONS BILL

Adoption of a rule governing debate on the fiscal 2010 Commerce-Justice-Science appropriations bill that restricted the number of amendments to the bill that could be offered.

This vote signaled a decision by House Democrats to fight back against what they regarded as Republican efforts to disrupt the appropriations process on the first of the twelve regular spending bills to come to the floor. GOP lawmakers had initially tried to offer 103 amendments to the relatively noncontroversial Commerce-Justice-Science measure.

After debate had already begun on the bill June 16, the Democrats returned to the Rules Committee and obtained a new rule for floor debate that allowed only thirty-three amendments.

House Majority Leader Steny H. Hoyer, D-Md., said that the leadership was concerned that Republicans would offer scores of amendments to all the appropriations measures to delay action. "We would like to proceed in a fashion that is reasonable and that provides for opportunities for amendments to be offered," Hoyer said. "But we also believe it is our responsibility to ensure that the appropriations process is completed."

The new, restrictive rule was adopted June 17, and action on amendments to the bill proceeded for a time. But Republicans eventually used parliamentary procedures to disrupt floor action, forcing fifty-three separate roll-call votes on June 18, a modern record. The spending bill was passed that evening by a 259–157 vote, with twenty-four Republicans voting in favor. Democrats used restrictive rules to keep the appropriations process moving for the rest of the year.

House adoption of H Res 552 on June 17, 221–201: R 0–174; D 221–27. *(Vote 5, p. 762)*

6. CLIMATE CHANGE

House passage of a bill to create a cap-and-trade system to limit emissions of greenhouse gases that cause global warming, and to require electric utilities to produce a percentage of their power from renewable sources such as wind, solar, and geothermal.

In a dramatic vote that turned on the defection of eight Republicans who provided the slender margin of victory, the House passed legislation designed to address global warming by capping emissions of greenhouse gases and boosting the production of electricity from renewable sources. The vote marked the first time either chamber of Congress had passed an emissions cap, and it handed President Obama a hard-fought victory on one of his legislative priorities.

The legislation capped greenhouse gas emissions at 17 percent below existing levels by 2020, 42 percent below current levels by 2030, and 83 percent below current levels by 2050. Utilities, refineries, and factories were required to hold government-issued emissions allowances, but the credits could be traded as commodities in the marketplace. Utilities were required to generate a growing share of electricity from renewable sources while improving efficiency.

The bill that came to the floor was the product of months of negotiations between Energy and Commerce Chair Henry A. Waxman, D-Calif., and moderate Democrats from industrial, rural, and coal-producing districts, who feared that a cap on carbon emissions could harm their states' economies. In his efforts to win votes, Waxman agreed to concessions that included slowing the phase-in of emissions caps, providing some free emissions allowances to hard-hit industries and allowing farmers to earn money for agricultural practices that offset carbon emissions.

Even with the concessions, the fate of the bill remained in doubt in the hours leading up to the vote. Waxman and Democratic leaders spent the last twenty-four hours furiously lobbying fence-sitters. The White House also stepped in, calling on senior advisers Carol Browner, Rahm Emanuel, and David Axelrod to press members for support, while Obama met with wavering Democrats. The night before the vote, Obama took advantage of a Hawaiian-style luau at the White House for lawmakers and their families to lobby undecided members.

Waxman's 300-page substitute amendment, incorporating a host of new provisions to win over a crucial handful of moderate Democrats, was filed in the early hours of June 26.

When the bill came to the floor that day, Minority Leader John A. Boehner, R-Ohio, mounted a last-ditch attempt to stall it with what amounted to a House equivalent of a filibuster. Using his unlimited leadership time to circumvent the time limit for debate, Boehner spent about an hour going almost line by line through the substitute amendment, questioning individual provisions.

The legislation passed, 219–212, with forty-four Democrats voting against the bill and eight Republican for it, votes that tipped the balance. While Boehner and Majority Leader Steny H. Hoyer, D-Md., were at odds on the merits of the bill, both agreed on its significance. Hoyer called the measure "historic," while Boehner described it as the "most profound piece of legislation to come to this floor in 100 years."

A similar measure (S 1733) stalled in the Senate, but bipartisan talks were aimed at devising a compromise bill that could come to the floor in the first half of 2010.

House passage of HR 2454 on June 26, 219–212: R 8–168; D 211–44. *(Vote 6, p. 762)*

7. FOOD SAFETY

Passage of a comprehensive food safety bill, after a string of food-borne illnesses shook the public's confidence and left key industry players searching for ways to reassure consumers.

Passage of the bill was the first major food safety legislation in decades. Deaths from tainted spinach, jalapeño peppers, and peanuts—all regulated by the Food and Drug Administration (FDA)—provided the impetus for lawmakers to pass the Food Safety Enhancement Act (HR 2749). The Centers for Disease Control and Prevention estimated that each year food pathogens sicken 76 million people, sending 325,000 to the hospital and killing 5,000.

The bill had strong bipartisan support, despite fears expressed by GOP leaders and some farm-state Democrats that the legislation would impose burdensome regulations on small farms and food production operations.

Opponents said they still had concerns despite concessions by Michigan Democrat John D. Dingell, the second-ranking Democrat on the Energy and Commerce Committee. Dingell, who shepherded the bill through the House, negotiated with Agriculture Committee Chair Collin C. Peterson, D-Minn., to exempt livestock, poultry, and feed grain producers from most new FDA rules and continue regulation by the U.S. Agriculture Department.

Peterson won the concessions after threatening to have his committee issue an unfavorable recommendation on the bill—a symbolic act because his panel did not have jurisdiction but problematic if Democrats wanted to maintain a largely unified front on the bill.

Dingell also compromised on annual registration or user fees for food facilities to satisfy GOP objections. Fees were reduced to $500 per facility, from $1,000, with fees for companies with multiple facilities not to exceed $175,000.

House passage of HR 2749 on July 30, 283–142: R 54–122; D 229–20. *(Vote 7, p. 762)*

8. CASH FOR CLUNKERS

Passage of legislation to replenish a federal fund that offered as much as $4,500 to car owners who traded in fuel-inefficient vehicles for newer, more fuel-efficient vehicles.

With unusual alacrity, the House voted to replenish, with $2 billion, a popular auto trade-in program that nearly ran out of money only a week after it was implemented by the Transportation Department. The vote, taken just before the House recessed for August, demonstrated Democrats' continued support for the domestic auto industry and their pleasant surprise with an economic measure that actually stimulated quick demand—but also put on display Republican concerns that the government was picking winners and losers in its economic interventions of the past two years.

Designed to bolster the struggling auto industry while taking gas-guzzling vehicles off of the road, the program—known as "cash for clunkers"—was enacted as part of a war supplemental funding bill (PL 111-32) and implemented by the Transportation Department in late July.

The program offered up to $4,500 in cash rebates to help people who traded in cars or SUVs with a combined fuel economy of eighteen miles per gallon or less to buy newer, more fuel-efficient vehicles. Congress appropriated $1 billion for the program, which was set to expire November 1, or whenever the money ran out. Unlike some other economic measures enacted since the recession started, the program, touted by automakers and car dealers, fueled a huge consumer response, rapidly depleting the funds. Without action, funding appeared set to run out during the summer break.

After the Transportation Department notified congressional leaders July 30 that the funding was almost gone, Appropriations Chair David R. Obey, D-Wis., quickly wrote legislation adding $2 billion to the program, designed to take it into the autumn as lawmakers prepared to leave town for the August recess. The funding was offset by taking $2 billion from Title 17 renewable-energy loan guarantees, which Democrats promised to replenish later. House leaders brought the bill to the House floor July 31, under suspension of the rules.

Even some skeptics of the program acknowledged its success, though conservatives called it an unfair handout to the auto industry. "'Cash for clunkers' is another example of the government picking winners and losers and enshrines us as a bailout nation," said Rep. Jeb Hensarling, R-Texas.

The Senate followed suit, clearing the bill the next week.

House passage of HR 3435 on July 31, 316–109: R 77–95, D 239–14. *(Vote 8, p. 762)*

9. STUDENT LOAN OVERHAUL

Passage of legislation to establish the government as the sole provider of student loans and provide billions of dollars in savings toward various scholarship and education programs.

With this vote, the House took the first step toward a significant overhaul of the provision of student loans, one that would remove private companies from originating loans but preserve their role as servicers.

The bill passed by the House largely reflected the proposal put forth by the Obama administration to convert the private lending system to government loans and put the savings into education programs such as Pell grants, early-childhood education, and community colleges.

But Democrats first had to defeat a series of amendments offered by Republicans, who said the bill overestimated the likely savings and threatened to wipe out tens of thousands of jobs. Republicans proposed preserving existing subsidies for private lenders through 2014 and creating a commission to develop a new private sector model for student lending.

In order to ease passage, bill sponsor George Miller, D-Calif., chair of the Education and Labor Committee, encouraged members to vote for a GOP motion to recommit the bill to committee with instructions to report it back with language prohibiting the use of federal funds for the Association of Community Organizations for Reform Now (ACORN). Miller said ACORN would not receive funding under the bill, anyway. ACORN was a controversial organization that came under sharp criticism after release of a video showing ACORN employees apparently advising a couple, posing as a prostitute and her pimp, about how to conceal their line of work, evade taxes, and handle undocumented, underage sex workers.

The House passed the legislation as a reconciliation bill, leaving the option open in the Senate of avoiding a filibuster. But the Senate did not take up the measure at all in 2009.

House passage of HR 3221 on September 17, 253–171: R 6–167; D 247–4. *(Vote 9, p. 762)*

10. ABORTION FUNDING

Adoption in the House of an amendment to restrict insurance coverage for abortions to help secure enough votes to pass under underlying legislation on health care overhaul.

House Democratic leaders allowed a vote on this amendment, sponsored by Bart Stupak, D-Mich., to allow antiabortion members of their caucus a vote on the highly controversial issue that threatened to undermine President Obama's signature proposal to reform the nation's health care system.

With the vote, antiabortion House Democrats and Republicans showed they were a force to be reckoned with, even though the Democratic majority was made up mostly of prochoice members.

Lawmakers on either side of the abortion issue had observed an uneasy truce for years, essentially agreeing not to alter longstanding federal policy that prevents taxpayer dollars from being used to pay for the procedure. That truce ended during debate on Democratic health care overhaul legislation, leading to what abortion opponents considered the most important vote on the issue in more than a decade.

As the health care legislation was developed, Democrats had struggled to maintain the principle that taxpayer dollars would not pay for abortions. The bill created a new subsidy program to help people buy health insurance and also offered a new government-run insurance plan as an alternative to private insurance. In what liberals considered a compromise, the bill included language requiring insurance plans as well as the government alternative that covering abortions to pay for the procedure using only revenue from premiums paid by their customers, not federal subsidies. But many abortion opponents, including the influential U.S. Conference of Catholic Bishops, considered that language nothing more than an accounting gimmick; the bill, they said, would lead to a huge increase in elective abortions.

Democrats won the House majority beginning in 2009 in large part by seeking candidates in 2006 and 2008 who could win conservative districts. These candidates were often opposed to abortion. On the health care bill, liberals reaped the sour fruits of the party's electoral strategy.

A group of about forty antiabortion Democrats led by Stupak told Democratic leaders they would not support the health care bill unless it included greater restrictions on abortion coverage. In a key point of dispute, Stupak and his allies demanded that the government, or public, option be forbidden from covering abortions altogether, arguing that by definition it would be a government program such as Medicaid, the entitlement for the poor.

By law, Medicaid covers only abortions that result from rape or incest, or when a pregnancy threatens a woman's life. Democratic leaders negotiated directly with Stupak and the Catholic bishops up until hours before the vote, trying to find a compromise. In the end, they failed and instead agreed to allow a vote on a Stupak amendment that abortion rights supporters opposed.

House adoption of the Stupak amendment November 7, 240–194: R 176–0; D 64–194. *(Vote 10, p. 762)*

11. HEALTH CARE OVERHAUL

The House passed far-reaching health care legislation aimed at insuring most Americans and paid for with a controversial combination of reductions in Medicare spending, tax increases, and a mandate that all citizens purchase health insurance.

Although many votes in Congress are described as historic, the House's passage of health care overhaul legislation, both sides agreed, deserved the moniker. With the arguable exception of Medicare in 1965, never before had a chamber of Congress passed legislation that would so dramatically restructure the health care system; according to the Congressional Budget Office, the overhaul bill would ensure access to affordable health insurance for nearly every American.

Despite its lofty aims, Democrats had considerable trouble securing the votes for the bill, their top domestic priority of the year. Moderates and liberals in the caucus had clashed for months over controversial issues in the legislation, including a government-run insurance plan called the "public option," insurance coverage for abortion, and whether the bill would sufficiently slow the rise of health care costs.

Democratic leaders did not secure support for the bill until the evening before the vote, when they agreed to allow a group of antiabortion Democrats led by Michigan's Bart Stupak to offer an amendment restricting coverage for the procedure. The amendment was adopted, angering abortion rights supporters but securing passage of the legislation.

In a surprise, Democrats also won the support of a single Republican—freshman Anh "Joseph" Cao of Louisiana. Cao defeated Democrat William J. Jefferson (1991–2009) in 2008 after Jefferson came under criminal investigation for accepting bribes (he was later convicted and imprisoned). His district overwhelmingly supported President Obama's election, and Cao said Obama had promised additional federal assistance in the area's ongoing recovery from Hurricane Katrina in exchange for his vote.

In the vote's signature scene, Minority Whip Eric Cantor, R-Va., aware of Cao's possible defection, sat next to him as the roll was called, quietly lobbying him to stick with his party. Cao voted only after it became clear Democrats would win regardless.

House passage of HR 3962 on November 7, 220–215: R 1–176; D 219–39. *(Vote 11, p. 762)*

1. HR 2. Children's Health Insurance Program. Waxman, D-Calif., motion to concur in the Senate amendment to the bill to reauthorize the State Children's Health Insurance Program over four and a half years and increase funding by $32.8 billion and, to offset the cost of the expansion, increase the federal tax on cigarettes by sixty-two cents per pack and raise taxes on other tobacco products. HR 2 limited program eligibility to families earning three times the federal poverty level or less and required states to phase out coverage of childless adults. Motion agreed to 290–135: R 40–133; D 250–2. February 4, 2009. The vote cleared the bill for the president.

2. HR 1. Economic Stimulus Conference Report. Adoption of the conference report on the bill to provide an estimated $787.2 billion in tax cuts and spending increases to stimulate economic activity. The legislation also prevented the alternative minimum tax from applying to millions of additional taxpayers in 2009 and increased the ceiling on federal borrowing by $789 billion to $12.1 trillion. Tax provisions included extending existing accelerated depreciation allowances for businesses, suspending taxes on the first $2,400 of unemployment benefits for 2009, and expanding a number of individual tax credits. Mandatory spending increases included an extension of unemployment and welfare benefits, Medicaid payments to states, and grants for health information technology. Discretionary spending included grants for state and local schools and funds for public housing, transportation, and nutrition assistance. Adopted 246–183: R 0–176; D 246–7. A "yea" was a vote in support of the president's position. February 13, 2009. The vote sent the conference agreement to the Senate for consideration.

3. HR 1106. Mortgage Loans Modification. Passage of the bill to allow bankruptcy judges to write down the principal and interest rates of loans issued before the bill's enactment to a home's current market value for individuals whose mortgages are larger than the value of their homes or who met other requirements. The legislation allowed the government to reimburse mortgage lenders for reduced principal, interest rates, or fees if the mortgage was guaranteed by the Federal Housing Administration, the Veterans Affairs Department, or other federal mortgage guarantors. It also increased, to $250,000, Federal Deposit Insurance Corporation and National Credit Union Administration deposit insurance coverage on individual bank accounts, and indexed the coverage to inflation from 2015 forward. Passed 234–191: R 7–167; D 227–24. March 5, 2009.

4. HR 1256. Tobacco Regulation. Waxman, D-Calif., motion to concur in the Senate amendment to the bill that provided the Food and Drug Administration (FDA) authority to regulate the manufacture, sale, and promotion of tobacco products, to require larger labels warning consumers of the health risks associated with tobacco products, and to clarify that the FDA does not endorse the safety of such products. The legislation required tobacco manufacturers and importers to pay quarterly user fees to help cover the cost of the regulation. Motion agreed to 307–97: R 70–90; D 237–7. A "yea" was a vote in support of the president's position. June 12, 2009. The vote cleared the bill for the president.

5. HR 2847. Rule Governing Floor Debate on an Appropriations Bill. Adoption of the rule (H Res 552) to provide for further House floor consideration of legislation to appropriate $64.4 billion in fiscal 2010 for the departments of Commerce and Justice and other federal agencies, including the National Aeronautics and Space Administration and the National Science Foundation. The rule was written by the Democratic majority after Republicans used a series of roll-call votes to delay action, which Democrats considered an effort to disrupt the appropriations process. The rule, which was used for other funding bills later in the year, limited the number of amendments that could be offered. Adopted 221–201: R 0–174; D 221–27. June 17, 2009.

6. HR 2454. Climate Change. Passage of the bill to create a cap-and-trade system to limit greenhouse gas emissions and to establish new requirements for electric utilities. The legislation set emissions limits at 17 percent below existing levels in 2020, expanding to 83 percent in 2050, and required utilities to produce 15 percent of the nation's electricity from renewable sources by 2020. Passed 219–212: R 8–168; D 211–44. A "yea" was a vote in support of the president's position. June 26, 2009.

7. HR 2749. Food Safety. Passage of the bill to revise food safety laws, including establishing a risk-based inspection schedule for food facilities and imposing criminal and civil penalties for violations. The legislation required facilities that serve U.S. customers to register with the Food and Drug Administration and pay a registration fee, but exempted farms, grocery stores, and restaurants. Passed 283–142: R 54–122; D 229–20. A "yea" was a vote in support of the president's position. July 30, 2009.

8. HR 3435. Cash for Clunkers Auto Program. Obey, D-Wis., motion to suspend the rules and pass the bill to provide $2 billion for the "cash for clunkers" vehicle trade-in program, which offered vouchers worth up to $4,500 toward the purchase of new vehicles to consumers who traded in their older, less fuel-efficient models. Motion agreed to 316–109: R 77–95; D 239–14. A two-thirds majority of those present and voting (284 in this case) was required for passage under suspension of the rules. A "yea" was a vote in support of the president's position. July 31, 2009.

9. HR 3221. Student Loan Overhaul. Passage of the bill to terminate the authority of the Federal Family Education Loan program to make or insure new loans after June 30, 2010, and direct the federal government to originate student loans. The legislation established a competitive bidding process for entities to service the loans, and modified several education programs, including increasing funding for Pell grants, early-childhood education, and community colleges. Passed 253–171: R 6–167; D 247–4. A "yea" was a vote in support of the president's position. September 17, 2009.

10. HR 3962. Health Care Overhaul/Abortion Funding. Stupak, D-Mich., amendment to bar the use of federal funds authorized in the legislation to pay for abortion or to cover any part of the costs of any health plan that includes abortion coverage, unless the pregnancy is the result of rape or incest or would endanger the woman's life, thereby requiring individuals with subsidized policies who wanted abortion coverage to purchase it separately with their own money. Adopted 240–194: R 176–0; D 64–194. November 7, 2009.

11. HR 3962. Health Care Overhaul. Passage of the bill to overhaul the nation's health insurance system and require most individuals to buy health insurance by 2013. The legislation established federal health insurance exchanges, including a government-run option to allow individuals without coverage to purchase insurance. The legislation imposed an excise tax on persons who did not obtain coverage but provided hardship waivers. Employers were required to offer health insurance or contribute to a fund for coverage, with penalties for noncompliance up to 8 percent of their payrolls. The legislation authorized tax credits to certain small businesses that offered coverage and provided subsidies to low-income individuals, excluding illegal immigrants. Passed 220–215: R 1–176; D 219–39. A "yea" was a vote in support of the president's position. November 7, 2009.

KEY

Republican		Democrat	**Independent**
Y	Voted for (yea)	–	Announced against
#	Paired for	P	Voted "present"
+	Announced for	C	Voted "present" to avoid possible conflict of interest
N	Voted against (nay)		
X	Paired against	?	Did not vote or otherwise make a position known

House Key Votes	1	2	3	4	5	6	7	8	9	10	11
ALABAMA											
1 *Bonner*	N	N	N	N	N	N	N	N	N	Y	N
2 Bright	N	N	N	N	N	N	N	Y	Y	Y	N
3 *Rogers*	Y	N	N	Y	N	N	N	Y	N	Y	N
4 *Aderholt*	?	N	N	N	N	N	N	Y	N	Y	N
5 Griffith	Y	N	N	Y	Y	N	N	Y	Y	Y	N
6 *Bachus*	N	N	N	Y	N	N	N	Y	N	Y	N
7 Davis	Y	Y	Y	Y	?	N	Y	Y	Y	Y	N
ALASKA											
AL *Young*	Y	N	N	Y	N	N	N	N	N	Y	N
ARIZONA											
1 Kirkpatrick	Y	Y	Y	N	Y	N	Y	N	Y	N	Y
2 *Franks*	N	N	N	N	N	N	N	N	N	Y	N
3 *Shadegg*	N	N	N	N	N	N	N	N	N	P	N
4 Pastor	Y	Y	Y	Y	Y	Y	Y	Y	Y	N	Y
5 Mitchell	Y	Y	Y	Y	N	N	Y	N	Y	N	Y
6 *Flake*	?	N	N	N	N	?	N	N	N	Y	N
7 Grijalva	Y	Y	Y	Y	Y	Y	Y	Y	Y	N	Y
8 Giffords	Y	Y	Y	Y	Y	Y	Y	N	Y	N	Y
ARKANSAS											
1 Berry	Y	Y	N	Y	Y	N	Y	Y	Y	Y	Y
2 Snyder	Y	Y	Y	Y	Y	Y	Y	Y	Y	Y	Y
3 *Boozman*	N	N	N	N	N	N	N	N	N	Y	N
4 Ross	Y	Y	Y	Y	Y	N	Y	Y	Y	Y	N
CALIFORNIA											
1 Thompson	Y	Y	Y	Y	N	Y	Y	Y	Y	N	Y
2 *Herger*	N	N	N	N	N	N	N	N	N	Y	N
3 *Lungren*	N	N	N	Y	N	N	N	N	N	Y	N
4 *McClintock*	N	N	N	N	N	N	N	N	N	Y	N
5 Matsui	Y	Y	Y	Y	Y	Y	Y	Y	Y	N	Y
6 Woolsey	Y	Y	Y	Y	N	Y	N	Y	Y	N	Y
7 Miller, George	Y	Y	Y	Y	N	Y	Y	Y	Y	N	Y
8 Pelosi[1]	Y	Y	Y	Y		Y			Y	N	Y
9 Lee	Y	Y	Y	Y	Y	Y	Y	Y	Y	N	Y
10 Tauscher[2]	Y	Y	Y	Y	Y	Y					
10 Garamendi[2]										N	Y
11 McNerney	Y	Y	Y	Y	Y	Y	Y	Y	Y	N	Y
12 Speier	Y	Y	Y	Y	N	Y	Y	Y	Y	N	Y
13 Stark	?	Y	?	Y	Y	N	Y	Y	Y	N	Y
14 Eshoo	Y	Y	Y	?	N	Y	Y	Y	Y	N	Y
15 Honda	Y	Y	Y	Y	N	Y	Y	Y	Y	N	Y
16 Lofgren	Y	Y	Y	Y	Y	Y	Y	Y	Y	N	Y
17 Farr	Y	Y	Y	Y	N	Y	Y	Y	Y	N	Y
18 Cardoza	Y	Y	Y	Y	Y	Y	Y	Y	Y	Y	Y
19 *Radanovich*	N	N	N	N	N	N	N	N	?	Y	N
20 Costa	Y	Y	Y	Y	Y	N	Y	Y	?	Y	Y
21 *Nunes*	N	N	N	?	N	N	N	N	–	Y	N
22 *McCarthy*	N	N	N	Y	N	N	N	N	N	Y	N
23 Capps	Y	Y	Y	Y	N	Y	Y	Y	Y	N	Y
24 *Gallegly*	N	N	N	?	N	N	N	N	N	Y	N
25 *McKeon*	N	N	N	Y	N	N	N	Y	N	Y	N
26 *Dreier*	N	N	N	Y	N	N	N	Y	N	Y	N
27 Sherman	Y	Y	Y	Y	Y	Y	Y	Y	Y	N	Y
28 Berman	Y	Y	Y	Y	Y	Y	Y	Y	Y	N	Y
29 Schiff	Y	Y	Y	Y	Y	Y	Y	Y	Y	N	Y
30 Waxman	Y	Y	Y	Y	Y	Y	Y	Y	Y	N	Y

House Key Votes	1	2	3	4	5	6	7	8	9	10	11
31 Becerra	Y	Y	Y	Y	Y	Y	Y	Y	Y	N	Y
32 Solis[3]	Y	Y									
32 Chu[3]							Y	Y	Y	N	Y
33 Watson	Y	Y	Y	Y	Y	Y	Y	Y	Y	N	Y
34 Roybal-Allard	Y	Y	Y	Y	Y	Y	Y	Y	Y	N	Y
35 Waters	Y	Y	Y	Y	N	Y	Y	Y	Y	N	Y
36 Harman	Y	Y	Y	Y	?	Y	Y	Y	Y	N	Y
37 Richardson	Y	Y	Y	Y	Y	Y	Y	Y	Y	N	Y
38 Napolitano	Y	Y	Y	Y	Y	Y	Y	Y	Y	N	Y
39 Sanchez, Linda	Y	Y	Y	Y	Y	Y	Y	Y	Y	N	Y
40 *Royce*	N	N	N	N	N	N	N	N	N	Y	N
41 *Lewis*	N	N	N	N	N	N	N	N	N	Y	N
42 *Miller, Gary*	N	N	?	?	N	N	N	Y	N	Y	N
43 Baca	Y	Y	Y	?	Y	Y	Y	Y	Y	Y	Y
44 *Calvert*	N	N	N	N	N	N	N	Y	N	Y	N
45 *Bono Mack*	Y	N	N	Y	N	Y	N	Y	N	Y	N
46 *Rohrabacher*	N	N	N	N	N	N	N	N	N	Y	N
47 Sanchez, Loretta	Y	Y	Y	?	Y	Y	?	Y	Y	N	Y
48 *Campbell*	–	–	N	N	N	N	N	Y	N	Y	N
49 *Issa*	N	N	N	N	N	N	N	Y	N	Y	N
50 *Bilbray*	N	N	N	Y	N	N	N	Y	N	Y	N
51 Filner	Y	Y	Y	Y	Y	Y	Y	Y	Y	N	Y
52 *Hunter*	N	N	N	N	N	N	N	N	N	Y	N
53 Davis	Y	Y	Y	Y	Y	Y	Y	Y	Y	N	Y
COLORADO											
1 DeGette	Y	Y	Y	Y	Y	Y	Y	Y	Y	N	Y
2 Polis	Y	Y	Y	Y	Y	Y	Y	N	Y	N	Y
3 Salazar	Y	Y	Y	Y	Y	N	?	?	Y	Y	Y
4 Markey	Y	Y	N	Y	Y	Y	N	Y	Y	N	N
5 *Lamborn*	N	N	N	N	N	N	N	N	N	Y	N
6 *Coffman*	N	N	-	N	N	N	N	N	N	Y	N
7 Perlmutter	Y	Y	Y	Y	Y	Y	Y	Y	Y	N	Y
CONNECTICUT											
1 Larson	Y	Y	Y	Y	+	Y	Y	Y	Y	N	Y
2 Courtney	Y	Y	Y	Y	Y	Y	Y	Y	Y	N	Y
3 DeLauro	Y	Y	Y	Y	Y	Y	Y	Y	Y	N	Y
4 Himes	Y	Y	Y	Y	Y	Y	Y	Y	Y	N	Y
5 Murphy	Y	Y	Y	Y	Y	Y	Y	Y	Y	N	Y
DELAWARE											
AL *Castle*	Y	N	Y	Y	N	Y	Y	Y	N	Y	N
FLORIDA											
1 *Miller*	N	N	N	N	N	N	N	N	N	Y	N
2 Boyd	Y	Y	Y	Y	Y	Y	Y	N	N	N	N
3 Brown	Y	Y	Y	?	Y	Y	Y	Y	Y	N	Y
4 *Crenshaw*	N	N	N	Y	N	N	Y	N	N	Y	N
5 *Brown-Waite*	N	N	N	Y	N	N	Y	Y	N	Y	N
6 *Stearns*	N	N	N	Y	N	N	N	Y	N	Y	N
7 *Mica*	N	N	N	N	N	N	N	N	N	Y	N
8 Grayson	Y	Y	Y	Y	Y	Y	+	Y	Y	N	Y
9 *Bilirakis*	N	N	N	Y	N	N	Y	N	N	Y	N
10 *Young*	Y	N	N	Y	?	N	Y	Y	N	Y	N
11 Castor	Y	Y	Y	Y	Y	Y	Y	Y	Y	N	Y
12 *Putnam*	N	N	N	Y	N	N	Y	Y	N	Y	N
13 *Buchanan*	Y	N	N	?	N	N	Y	P	Y	Y	N
14 *Mack*	N	N	N	N	N	N	N	N	N	Y	N
15 *Posey*	N	N	N	N	N	N	N	N	N	Y	N
16 *Rooney*	N	N	N	N	N	N	N	N	N	Y	N
17 Meek	Y	Y	Y	Y	N	Y	Y	Y	Y	N	Y
18 *Ros-Lehtinen*	Y	N	Y	Y	N	N	Y	Y	Y	Y	N
19 Wexler	Y	Y	Y	Y	Y	Y	Y	Y	Y	N	Y
20 Wasserman Schultz	Y	Y	Y	Y	Y	Y	Y	Y	Y	N	Y
21 *Diaz-Balart, L.*	Y	N	Y	N	N	N	Y	Y	N	Y	N
22 Klein	Y	Y	Y	Y	N	Y	Y	Y	Y	N	Y
23 Hastings	Y	Y	Y	Y	Y	?	Y	Y	Y	N	Y
24 Kosmas	Y	Y	Y	Y	N	Y	Y	Y	Y	N	N
25 *Diaz-Balart, M.*	Y	N	Y	N	N	N	Y	Y	N	Y	N

[1]The Speaker votes only at her discretion.

[2]Rep. John Garamendi, D-Calif., was sworn in November 5, 2009, to fill the seat vacated by fellow Democrat Ellen O. Tauscher, who resigned June 26, 2009, to become an undersecretary of state. The first key vote for which Garamendi was eligible was vote 10; the last key vote for which Tauscher was eligible was vote 6.

[3]Rep. Judy Chu, D-Calif., was sworn in July 14, 2009, to fill the seat vacated by fellow Democrat Hilda L. Solis, who resigned February 24, 2009, to become secretary of labor. The first key vote for which Chu was eligible was vote 7; the last key vote for which Solis was eligible was vote 2.

KEY

Republican Democrat **Independent**

Y	Voted for (yea)	–	Announced against
#	Paired for	P	Voted "present"
+	Announced for	C	Voted "present" to avoid possible conflict of interest
N	Voted against (nay)		
X	Paired against	?	Did not vote or otherwise make a position known

House Key Votes	1	2	3	4	5	6	7	8	9	10	11
GEORGIA											
1 *Kingston*	N	N	N	N	N	N	N	Y	N	Y	N
2 Bishop	Y	Y	Y	Y	Y	Y	Y	Y	Y	Y	Y
3 *Westmoreland*	N	N	N	N	N	N	N	N	N	Y	N
4 Johnson	Y	Y	Y	Y	Y	Y	Y	Y	Y	N	Y
5 Lewis	Y	Y	Y	?	?	Y	Y	Y	Y	N	Y
6 *Price*	N	N	N	N	N	N	N	N	N	Y	N
7 *Linder*	N	N	N	N	N	N	?	?	N	Y	N
8 Marshall	N	Y	Y	Y	Y	N	N	N	Y	Y	N
9 *Deal*	N	N	N	?	N	N	Y	P	N	Y	N
10 *Broun*	N	N	N	N	N	N	N	N	N	Y	N
11 *Gingrey*	N	N	N	?	N	N	Y	Y	N	Y	N
12 Barrow	Y	Y	Y	Y	Y	N	Y	Y	Y	Y	N
13 Scott	Y	Y	Y	Y	Y	Y	Y	Y	Y	N	Y
HAWAII											
1 Abercrombie	Y	Y	Y	Y	Y	Y	Y	Y		N	Y
2 Hirono	Y	Y	Y	Y	Y	Y	Y	Y	Y	N	Y
IDAHO											
1 Minnick	Y	N	Y	Y	N	N	N	Y	Y	N	N
2 *Simpson*	Y	N	N	Y	N	N	N	Y	N	Y	N
ILLINOIS											
1 Rush	Y	Y	Y	Y	Y	Y	Y	Y	Y	N	Y
2 Jackson	Y	Y	Y	Y	Y	Y	Y	Y	Y	N	Y
3 Lipinski	Y	P	Y	Y	Y	Y	Y	Y	Y	Y	Y
4 Gutierrez	Y	Y	Y	Y	Y	Y	Y	Y	Y	N	Y
5 Quigley[4]				Y	Y	Y	Y	Y	Y	N	Y
6 *Roskam*	N	N	N	Y	N	N	Y	N	N	Y	N
7 Davis	Y	Y	Y	Y	Y	Y	Y	Y	Y	N	Y
8 Bean	+	Y	Y	Y	Y	Y	Y	Y	Y	N	Y
9 Schakowsky	Y	Y	Y	Y	Y	Y	Y	Y	Y	N	Y
10 *Kirk*	Y	N	N	Y	N	Y	Y	Y	N	Y	N
11 Halvorson	Y	Y	Y	Y	Y	Y	Y	Y	Y	N	Y
12 Costello	Y	Y	Y	Y	Y	N	Y	Y	Y	Y	Y
13 *Biggert*	N	N	N	Y	N	N	Y	Y	N	Y	N
14 Foster	Y	Y	Y	Y	Y	N	Y	Y	Y	N	Y
15 *Johnson*	N	N	N	Y	N	N	N	N	Y	Y	N
16 *Manzullo*	N	N	N	Y	N	N	N	Y	N	Y	N
17 Hare	Y	Y	Y	Y	Y	Y	Y	Y	Y	N	Y
18 *Schock*	N	N	N	Y	N	N	N	N	N	Y	N
19 *Shimkus*	N	N	N	Y	N	N	Y	Y	N	Y	N
INDIANA											
1 Visclosky	Y	Y	Y	Y	Y	N	Y	Y	Y	N	Y
2 Donnelly	Y	Y	Y	Y	N	N	Y	Y	Y	Y	Y
3 *Souder*	N	N	N	N	N	N	N	Y	N	Y	N
4 *Buyer*	N	N	N	N	N	N	Y	Y	N	Y	N
5 *Burton*	N	N	N	Y	N	N	N	Y	N	Y	N
6 *Pence*	N	N	N	N	N	N	N	N	N	Y	N
7 Carson	Y	Y	Y	Y	Y	Y	Y	Y	Y	N	Y
8 Ellsworth	Y	Y	N	Y	Y	N	Y	Y	Y	Y	Y
9 Hill	Y	Y	N	Y	N	Y	Y	Y	Y	Y	Y
IOWA											
1 Braley	Y	Y	Y	Y	Y	Y	Y	Y	Y	N	Y
2 Loebsack	Y	Y	Y	Y	Y	Y	Y	Y	Y	N	Y
3 Boswell	Y	Y	Y	Y	Y	Y	Y	Y	Y	N	Y
4 *Latham*	N	N	N	N	N	N	N	Y	N	Y	N
5 *King*	N	N	N	N	N	N	N	N	N	Y	N
KANSAS											
1 *Moran*	Y	N	N	N	N	N	N	N	N	Y	N
2 *Jenkins*	N	N	N	N	N	N	N	N	N	Y	N
3 Moore	Y	Y	Y	Y	Y	Y	Y	Y	Y	N	Y
4 *Tiahrt*	N	N	N	N	N	N	N	Y	N	Y	N
KENTUCKY											
1 *Whitfield*	N	N	N	N	N	N	Y	N	N	Y	N
2 *Guthrie*	N	N	N	N	N	N	Y	Y	N	Y	N
3 Yarmuth	Y	Y	Y	Y	Y	Y	Y	Y	Y	N	Y
4 *Davis*	N	N	N	N	N	N	N	Y	N	Y	N
5 *Rogers*	N	N	N	N	N	N	Y	N	N	Y	N
6 Chandler	Y	Y	Y	Y	Y	Y	Y	Y	Y	Y	N
LOUISIANA											
1 *Scalise*	N	N	N	N	N	N	Y	N	N	Y	N
2 *Cao*	Y	N	?	Y	N	N	Y	Y	Y	Y	Y
3 Melancon	Y	Y	?	Y	Y	N	Y	Y	Y	Y	N
4 *Fleming*	N	N	N	Y	N	N	N	N	N	Y	N
5 *Alexander*	N	N	N	N	?	N	N	N	N	Y	N
6 *Cassidy*	N	N	N	Y	N	N	N	Y	N	Y	N
7 *Boustany*	N	N	N	N	N	N	N	Y	N	Y	N
MAINE											
1 Pingree	Y	Y	Y	Y	Y	Y	N	Y	Y	N	Y
2 Midland	Y	Y	Y	Y	Y	Y	Y	Y	Y	Y	Y
MARYLAND											
1 Kratovil	Y	Y	N	Y	N	Y	N	Y	Y	N	N
2 Ruppersberger	Y	Y	Y	?	Y	Y	Y	Y	Y	N	Y
3 Sarbanes	Y	Y	Y	Y	Y	Y	Y	Y	Y	N	Y
4 Edwards	Y	Y	Y	Y	Y	Y	Y	Y	Y	N	Y
5 Hoyer	Y	Y	Y	Y	Y	Y	Y	Y	Y	N	Y
6 *Bartlett*	N	N	N	Y	N	N	N	N	N	Y	N
7 Cummings	Y	Y	Y	Y	Y	Y	Y	Y	Y	N	Y
8 Van Hollen	Y	Y	Y	Y	Y	Y	Y	Y	Y	N	Y
MASSACHUSETTS											
1 Olver	Y	Y	Y	Y	Y	Y	Y	Y	Y	N	Y
2 Neal	Y	Y	Y	Y	Y	Y	Y	Y	Y	Y	Y
3 McGovern	Y	Y	Y	Y	Y	Y	Y	Y	Y	N	Y
4 Frank	Y	Y	Y	Y	Y	Y	Y	Y	?	N	Y
5 Tsongas	Y	Y	Y	Y	Y	Y	Y	Y	Y	N	Y
6 Tierney	Y	Y	Y	Y	Y	Y	Y	N	Y	N	Y
7 Markey	Y	Y	Y	Y	Y	Y	Y	Y	Y	N	Y
8 Capuano	Y	Y	Y	Y	Y	Y	Y	Y	Y	N	Y
9 Lynch	Y	Y	Y	Y	Y	Y	Y	Y	Y	Y	Y
10 Delahunt	Y	Y	Y	Y	Y	Y	Y	Y	Y	N	Y
MICHIGAN											
1 Stupak	Y	Y	N	Y	Y	Y	Y	Y	Y	Y	Y
2 *Hoekstra*	N	N	N	N	N	N	N	Y	N	Y	N
3 *Ehlers*	Y	N	–	?	N	N	Y	Y	N	Y	N
4 *Camp*	N	N	N	Y	N	N	Y	Y	N	Y	N
5 Kildee	Y	Y	Y	Y	Y	Y	Y	Y	Y	Y	Y
6 *Upton*	Y	N	N	Y	N	N	Y	Y	N	Y	N
7 Schauer	Y	Y	Y	Y	Y	Y	Y	Y	Y	N	Y
8 *Rogers*	N	N	N	?	N	N	Y	Y	N	Y	N
9 Peters	Y	Y	Y	Y	Y	Y	Y	Y	Y	N	Y
10 *Miller*	Y	N	N	Y	N	N	Y	Y	N	Y	N
11 *McCotter*	Y	N	N	N	N	N	Y	Y	N	Y	N
12 Levin	Y	Y	Y	Y	Y	Y	Y	Y	Y	N	Y
13 Kilpatrick	Y	Y	Y	Y	Y	Y	Y	Y	Y	N	Y
14 Conyers	Y	Y	Y	Y	N	Y	Y	Y	+	N	Y
15 Dingell	Y	Y	Y	Y	Y	Y	Y	Y	Y	N	Y
MINNESOTA											
1 Walz	Y	Y	Y	Y	Y	Y	Y	Y	Y	N	Y
2 *Kline*	N	N	N	?	N	N	Y	Y	N	Y	N
3 *Paulsen*	Y	N	N	Y	N	N	Y	N	N	Y	N

[4]Rep. Mike Quigley, D-Ill, was sworn in July 16, 2009, to fill the seat vacated by fellow Democrat Rahm Emanuel, D-Ill., who resigned January 2, 2009, to become President Obama's chief of staff. The first key vote for which Quigley was eligible was vote 4; Emanuel was not eligible for any key votes in 2009.

House Key Votes	1	2	3	4	5	6	7	8	9	10	11
4 McCollum	Y	Y	Y	Y	Y	Y	Y	Y	Y	N	Y
5 Ellison	Y	Y	Y	Y	Y	Y	Y	Y	Y	N	Y
6 *Bachmann*	N	N	N	N	?	N	Y	N	N	Y	N
7 Peterson	Y	N	Y	Y	?	Y	Y	N	Y	Y	N
8 *Oberstar*	Y	Y	Y	Y	Y	Y	Y	Y	Y	Y	Y
MISSISSIPPI											
1 Childers	Y	Y	N	?	Y	N	N	Y	Y	Y	N
2 Thompson	Y	Y	Y	Y	Y	Y	Y	Y	Y	N	Y
3 *Harper*	N	N	N	Y	N	N	N	?	N	Y	N
4 Taylor	Y	N	N	Y	Y	N	Y	Y	Y	Y	N
MISSOURI											
1 Clay	Y	Y	Y	Y	Y	Y	Y	Y	Y	N	Y
2 *Akin*	N	N	N	N	N	N	–	N	N	Y	N
3 Carnahan	Y	Y	Y	Y	Y	Y	Y	Y	Y	N	Y
4 Skelton	Y	Y	Y	Y	Y	Y	Y	Y	Y	Y	N
5 Cleaver	Y	Y	Y	Y	Y	Y	Y	Y	Y	N	Y
6 *Graves*	N	N	N	N	N	N	N	N	N	Y	N
7 *Blunt*	N	N	N	?	N	N	N	Y	N	Y	N
8 *Emerson*	Y	N	N	Y	N	N	N	Y	N	Y	N
9 *Luetkemeyer*	N	N	N	–	N	N	N	N	N	Y	N
MONTANA											
AL *Rehberg*	Y	N	N	Y	N	N	N	Y	N	Y	N
NEBRASKA											
1 Fortenberry	N	N	N	Y	N	N	Y	N	N	Y	N
2 Terry	N	N	N	Y	N	N	Y	Y	N	Y	N
3 Smith	N	N	N	N	N	N	N	N	N	Y	N
NEVADA											
1 Berkley	Y	Y	Y	Y	Y	Y	Y	Y	Y	N	Y
2 *Heller*	N	N	N	N	N	N	N	N	N	Y	N
3 Titus	Y	Y	Y	Y	Y	Y	Y	Y	Y	N	Y
NEW HAMPSHIRE											
1 Shea-Porter	Y	Y	Y	Y	Y	Y	Y	Y	Y	N	Y
2 Hodes	Y	Y	Y	Y	Y	Y	Y	Y	Y	N	Y
NEW JERSEY											
1 Andrews	Y	Y	Y	Y	Y	Y	Y	Y	Y	N	Y
2 *LoBiondo*	Y	N	N	Y	N	Y	Y	Y	N	Y	N
3 Adler	Y	Y	Y	+	?	Y	+	Y	Y	N	N
4 *Smith*	Y	N	N	Y	N	Y	Y	Y	N	Y	N
5 *Garrett*	N	N	N	N	N	N	N	N	N	Y	N
6 Pallone	Y	Y	Y	Y	Y	Y	Y	Y	Y	N	Y
7 *Lance*	Y	N	N	Y	N	Y	Y	Y	N	Y	N
8 Pascrell	Y	Y	Y	Y	Y	Y	Y	Y	Y	N	Y
9 Rothman	Y	Y	Y	Y	Y	Y	Y	Y	Y	N	Y
10 Payne	Y	Y	Y	Y	Y	Y	Y	Y	Y	N	Y
11 *Frelinghuysen*	Y	N	N	Y	N	N	Y	N	N	Y	N
12 Holt	Y	Y	Y	+	Y	Y	Y	Y	Y	N	Y
13 Sires	Y	Y	Y	Y	Y	Y	Y	Y	Y	N	Y
NEW MEXICO											
1 Heinrich	Y	Y	Y	Y	Y	Y	N	Y	Y	N	Y
2 Teague	Y	Y	N	Y	Y	Y	N	Y	Y	Y	N
3 Lujan	Y	Y	Y	Y	Y	Y	N	Y	Y	N	Y
NEW YORK											
1 Bishop	Y	Y	Y	Y	Y	Y	Y	Y	Y	N	Y
2 Israel	Y	Y	Y	Y	Y	Y	Y	Y	Y	N	Y
3 *King*	Y	N	N	Y	N	N	Y	Y	N	Y	N
4 McCarthy	Y	Y	Y	Y	Y	Y	?	+	Y	N	Y
5 Ackerman	Y	Y	Y	?	Y	Y	Y	Y	Y	N	Y
6 Meeks	Y	Y	Y	Y	Y	Y	Y	Y	Y	N	Y
7 Crowley	Y	Y	Y	Y	Y	Y	Y	Y	Y	N	Y
8 Nadler	Y	Y	Y	Y	Y	Y	Y	Y	Y	N	Y
9 Weiner	Y	Y	Y	Y	Y	Y	Y	Y	Y	N	Y
10 Towns	Y	Y	Y	Y	Y	Y	Y	Y	Y	N	Y
11 Clarke	Y	Y	Y	Y	Y	Y	Y	Y	Y	N	Y
12 Velazquez	Y	Y	Y	Y	Y	Y	Y	Y	Y	N	Y
13 McMahon	Y	Y	Y	Y	Y	Y	Y	Y	N	N	N
14 Maloney	Y	Y	Y	Y	Y	Y	Y	Y	Y	N	Y
15 Rangel	Y	Y	Y	Y	Y	Y	Y	Y	Y	N	Y
16 Serrano	Y	Y	Y	Y	Y	Y	Y	Y	Y	N	Y
17 Engel	Y	Y	Y	Y	Y	Y	Y	Y	Y	N	Y
18 Lowey	Y	Y	Y	Y	Y	Y	Y	Y	Y	N	Y
19 Hall	Y	Y	Y	Y	Y	Y	Y	Y	Y	N	Y
20 Murphy[5]				Y	N	Y	Y	N	Y	N	N
21 Tonko	Y	Y	Y	Y	Y	Y	Y	Y	Y	N	Y
22 Hinchey	Y	Y	Y	Y	Y	Y	N	Y	Y	N	Y
23 *McHugh*[6]	Y	N	Y	N	N	Y	Y	Y	?		
23 Owens[6]										N	Y
24 Arcuri	Y	Y	N	Y	N	N	N	Y	Y	N	Y
25 Maffei	Y	Y	Y	Y	Y	Y	Y	Y	Y	N	Y
26 *Lee*	Y	–	N	Y	N	N	Y	Y	N	Y	N
27 Higgins	Y	Y	Y	Y	Y	Y	Y	Y	Y	N	Y
28 Slaughter	Y	Y	Y	Y	Y	Y	Y	Y	Y	N	Y
29 Massa	Y	Y	N	Y	Y	N	N	Y	Y	N	N
NORTH CAROLINA											
1 Butterfield	Y	Y	Y	Y	Y	Y	Y	Y	Y	N	Y
2 Etheridge	Y	Y	Y	Y	Y	Y	Y	Y	Y	Y	Y
3 *Jones*	N	N	Y	?	N	N	N	Y	N	Y	N
4 Price	Y	Y	Y	Y	Y	Y	Y	Y	Y	N	Y
5 *Foxx*	N	N	N	N	N	N	N	N	N	Y	N
6 *Coble*	N	N	N	N	N	N	N	Y	N	Y	N
7 McIntyre	Y	Y	Y	N	Y	N	Y	Y	Y	Y	N
8 Kissell	?	Y	N	N	Y	N	Y	Y	Y	N	N
9 *Myrick*	N	N	N	N	N	N	Y	N	N	Y	N
10 *McHenry*	N	N	N	N	N	N	N	N	N	Y	N
11 Shuler	Y	N	Y	N	N	Y	N	Y	Y	Y	N
12 Watt	Y	Y	Y	Y	Y	Y	Y	Y	Y	N	Y
13 Miller	Y	Y	Y	Y	Y	Y	Y	Y	Y	N	Y
NORTH DAKOTA											
AL Pomeroy	Y	Y	Y	Y	Y	N	Y	Y	Y	Y	Y
OHIO											
1 Driehaus	Y	Y	Y	Y	Y	Y	Y	Y	Y	Y	Y
2 *Schmidt*	N	N	N	N	N	N	N	N	N	Y	N
3 *Turner*	Y	N	Y	Y	N	N	Y	Y	N	Y	N
4 *Jordan*	N	N	N	N	N	N	N	N	N	Y	N
5 *Latta*	N	N	N	N	N	N	N	N	N	Y	N
6 Wilson	Y	Y	Y	?	Y	N	Y	Y	Y	Y	Y
7 *Austria*	Y	N	N	Y	N	N	N	Y	N	Y	N
8 *Boehner*	N	N	N	N	N	N	N	N	N	Y	N
9 Kaptur	Y	Y	Y	Y	Y	Y	Y	Y	Y	Y	Y
10 Kucinich	Y	Y	Y	Y	Y	N	Y	Y	Y	N	N
11 Fudge	Y	Y	Y	Y	Y	Y	Y	Y	Y	N	Y
12 *Tiberi*	Y	N	N	Y	N	N	Y	Y	N	Y	N
13 Sutton	Y	Y	Y	Y	Y	Y	Y	Y	Y	N	Y
14 *LaTourette*	Y	N	N	Y	N	N	Y	Y	N	Y	N
15 Kilroy	Y	Y	Y	Y	Y	Y	Y	Y	Y	N	Y
16 Boccieri	Y	Y	Y	Y	Y	Y	Y	Y	Y	Y	N
17 Ryan	Y	Y	Y	Y	Y	Y	Y	Y	Y	Y	Y
18 Space	Y	Y	Y	Y	Y	Y	Y	Y	Y	Y	Y
OKLAHOMA											
1 *Sullivan*	N	N	N	?	?	–	N	N	N	Y	N
2 Boren	Y	Y	N	Y	Y	N	Y	Y	Y	Y	N
3 *Lucas*	N	N	N	N	N	N	N	N	N	Y	N
4 *Cole*	N	N	N	N	N	N	N	N	N	Y	N
5 *Fallin*	N	N	N	Y	N	N	N	N	N	Y	N
OREGON											
1 Wu	Y	Y	Y	Y	N	Y	Y	Y	Y	N	Y
2 *Walden*	N	N	N	Y	N	N	Y	Y	N	Y	N
3 Blumenauer	Y	Y	Y	Y	N	Y	Y	N	Y	N	Y
4 DeFazio	Y	N	Y	Y	N	N	Y	Y	Y	N	Y
5 Schrader	Y	Y	Y	Y	Y	Y	Y	N	Y	N	Y
PENNSYLVANIA											
1 Brady	Y	Y	Y	Y	Y	Y	Y	Y	Y	N	Y

[5]Rep. Scott Murphy, D-N.Y., was sworn in April 29, 2009, to fill the seat of fellow Democrat Kirsten Gillibrand, who resigned January 26, 2009, after being appointed to replace Sen. Hillary Rodham Clinton, who resigned January 21, 2009, to become secretary of state. The first key vote for which Murphy was eligible was vote 4; Gillibrand was not eligible for any key vote in 2009.

[6]Rep. Bill Owens, D-N.Y., was sworn in November 6, 2009, to fill the seat vacated by Republican John M. McHugh, who resigned September 21, 2009, to become secretary of the army. The first key vote for which Owens was eligible was vote 10; the last key vote for which McHugh was eligible was vote 9.

KEY

Republican | Democrat | **Independent**

Y	Voted for (yea)	–	Announced against
#	Paired for	P	Voted "present"
+	Announced for	C	Voted "present" to avoid possible conflict of interest
N	Voted against (nay)		
X	Paired against	?	Did not vote or otherwise make a position known

House Key Votes	1	2	3	4	5	6	7	8	9	10	11
2 Fattah	Y	Y	Y	Y	Y	Y	Y	Y	Y	N	Y
3 Dahlkemper	Y	Y	N	Y	Y	N	Y	Y	Y	Y	Y
4 Altmire	Y	Y	Y	Y	Y	N	Y	Y	Y	Y	N
5 *Thompson*	Y	N	N	N	N	N	N	Y	N	Y	N
6 *Gerlach*	Y	N	N	Y	N	N	Y	Y	N	Y	N
7 Sestak	Y	Y	Y	Y	Y	Y	Y	Y	Y	N	Y
8 Murphy, P.	Y	Y	Y	Y	Y	Y	Y	Y	Y	N	Y
9 *Shuster*	N	N	N	N	N	N	N	Y	N	Y	N
10 Carney	Y	Y	N	Y	N	N	Y	Y	Y	Y	Y
11 Kanjorski	Y	Y	Y	Y	Y	Y	Y	Y	N	Y	Y
12 Murtha	Y	Y	Y	Y	Y	Y	?	Y	Y	Y	Y
13 Schwartz	Y	Y	Y	Y	Y	Y	Y	Y	Y	N	Y
14 Doyle	Y	Y	Y	Y	Y	Y	Y	Y	Y	Y	Y
15 *Dent*	Y	N	N	Y	N	N	Y	N	N	Y	N
16 *Pitts*	N	N	N	N	N	N	N	Y	N	Y	N
17 Holden	Y	Y	N	Y	Y	N	Y	Y	Y	Y	N
18 *Murphy, T.*	Y	N	N	Y	N	N	Y	Y	N	Y	N
19 *Platts*	Y	N	N	Y	N	N	Y	Y	Y	Y	N
RHODE ISLAND											
1 Kennedy	Y	Y	Y	?	?	Y	Y	Y	Y	N	Y
2 Langevin	Y	Y	Y	Y	Y	Y	Y	Y	Y	Y	Y
SOUTH CAROLINA											
1 *Brown*	N	N	N	Y	N	N	N	N	N	Y	N
2 *Wilson*	N	N	N	N	N	N	N	N	N	Y	N
3 *Barrett*	N	N	N	–	N	N	N	N	?	Y	N
4 *Inglis*	N	N	N	N	N	N	N	N	N	Y	N
5 Spratt	Y	Y	Y	Y	Y	Y	Y	Y	Y	Y	Y
6 Clyburn	Y	?	Y	Y	Y	Y	Y	Y	Y	N	Y
SOUTH DAKOTA											
AL Herseth Sandlin	Y	Y	Y	Y	Y	N	Y	N	N	N	N
TENNESSEE											
1 *Roe*	N	N	N	N	N	N	N	Y	N	Y	N
2 *Duncan*	N	N	N	Y	N	N	N	Y	N	Y	N
3 *Wamp*	–	N	N	Y	N	N	N	Y	N	Y	N
4 Davis	Y	Y	N	N	Y	N	N	Y	Y	Y	N
5 Cooper	Y	Y	Y	Y	Y	Y	Y	Y	Y	Y	Y
6 Gordon	Y	Y	N	Y	Y	Y	Y	Y	Y	Y	N
7 *Blackburn*	N	N	N	?	N	N	N	N	N	Y	N
8 Tanner	Y	Y	Y	Y	Y	N	Y	Y	?	Y	N
9 Cohen	Y	Y	Y	Y	Y	Y	Y	Y	Y	N	Y
TEXAS											
1 *Gohmert*	N	N	N	?	N	N	N	?	N	Y	N
2 *Poe*	?	N	N	Y	N	N	N	Y	N	Y	N
3 *Johnson, S.*	N	N	N	N	N	N	N	N	N	Y	N
4 *Hall*	N	N	N	Y	N	N	N	Y	N	Y	N
5 *Hensarling*	N	N	N	N	N	N	N	N	N	Y	N
6 *Barton*	N	N	N	N	N	N	Y	Y	N	Y	N
7 *Culberson*	N	N	N	N	N	N	N	N	N	Y	N
8 *Brady*	N	N	N	Y	N	N	N	N	N	Y	N
9 Green, A.	Y	Y	Y	Y	Y	Y	Y	Y	Y	N	Y
10 *McCaul*	N	N	N	Y	N	N	N	?	N	Y	N

House Key Votes	1	2	3	4	5	6	7	8	9	10	11
11 *Conaway*	N	N	N	N	N	N	N	N	N	Y	N
12 *Granger*	N	N	N	Y	N	N	N	N	N	Y	N
13 *Thornberry*	N	N	N	N	N	N	N	N	N	Y	N
14 *Paul*	N	N	N	N	N	N	N	N	?	Y	N
15 Hinojosa	Y	Y	Y	Y	Y	Y	Y	Y	Y	N	Y
16 Reyes	Y	Y	Y	Y	Y	Y	Y	Y	Y	Y	Y
17 Edwards	Y	Y	N	Y	Y	N	Y	Y	Y	N	N
18 Jackson Lee	Y	Y	Y	Y	Y	Y	Y	Y	Y	N	Y
19 *Neugebauer*	N	N	N	N	N	N	N	N	N	Y	N
20 Gonzalez	Y	Y	Y	Y	Y	Y	Y	Y	Y	N	Y
21 *Smith*	N	N	N	Y	N	N	N	N	N	Y	N
22 *Olson*	N	N	N	N	N	N	N	N	N	Y	N
23 Rodriguez	Y	Y	Y	Y	Y	N	Y	Y	Y	Y	Y
24 *Marchant*	N	N	N	?	N	N	N	Y	N	Y	N
25 Doggett	Y	Y	Y	Y	Y	Y	Y	N	Y	N	Y
26 *Burgess*	N	N	N	N	N	N	Y	N	N	Y	N
27 Ortiz	Y	Y	Y	Y	Y	N	Y	Y	Y	Y	Y
28 Cuellar	Y	Y	Y	Y	Y	Y	Y	Y	Y	Y	Y
29 Green, G.	Y	Y	Y	Y	Y	Y	Y	Y	Y	N	Y
30 Johnson, E.	Y	Y	Y	Y	Y	Y	Y	Y	Y	N	Y
31 *Carter*	N	N	N	N	N	N	N	N	N	Y	N
32 *Sessions*	N	N	N	N	N	N	N	N	N	Y	N
UTAH											
1 *Bishop*	N	N	N	N	N	N	N	N	N	Y	N
2 Matheson	Y	Y	N	Y	Y	N	Y	Y	Y	Y	N
3 *Chaffetz*	N	N	N	N	N	N	N	N	N	Y	N
VERMONT											
AL Welch	Y	Y	Y	Y	Y	Y	N	Y	Y	N	Y
VIRGINIA											
1 *Wittman*	N	N	N	Y	N	N	N	N	N	Y	N
2 Nye	Y	Y	Y	Y	Y	N	Y	Y	Y	N	N
3 Scott	Y	Y	Y	Y	Y	Y	Y	Y	Y	N	Y
4 *Forbes*	N	N	N	N	N	N	N	N	N	Y	N
5 Perriello	Y	Y	?	N	N	Y	N	Y	Y	Y	Y
6 *Goodlatte*	N	N	N	N	N	N	N	N	N	Y	N
7 *Cantor*	N	N	N	Y	N	N	N	N	N	Y	N
8 Moran	Y	Y	Y	Y	Y	Y	Y	Y	Y	N	Y
9 Boucher	Y	Y	N	Y	Y	Y	Y	Y	Y	N	N
10 *Wolf*	Y	N	N	Y	N	N	Y	N	N	Y	N
11 Connolly	Y	Y	Y	Y	Y	Y	Y	Y	Y	N	Y
WASHINGTON											
1 Inslee	Y	Y	Y	Y	Y	Y	Y	Y	Y	N	Y
2 Larsen	Y	Y	Y	Y	Y	Y	Y	Y	Y	N	Y
3 Baird	Y	Y	Y	Y	Y	Y	Y	N	Y	N	N
4 *Hastings*	N	N	N	?	N	N	N	N	N	Y	N
5 *McMorris-Rogers*	N	N	N	Y	N	N	N	N	N	Y	N
6 Dicks	Y	Y	Y	Y	Y	Y	Y	Y	Y	N	Y
7 McDermott	Y	Y	Y	Y	Y	Y	Y	Y	Y	N	Y
8 *Reichert*	Y	N	N	Y	N	Y	Y	Y	N	Y	N
9 Smith	Y	Y	Y	Y	Y	Y	Y	Y	Y	N	Y
WEST VIRGINIA											
1 Mollohan	Y	Y	Y	Y	Y	N	Y	Y	Y	Y	Y
2 *Capito*	Y	N	N	Y	N	N	Y	Y	N	Y	N
3 Rahall	Y	Y	Y	Y	Y	N	Y	Y	Y	Y	Y
WISCONSIN											
1 *Ryan*	N	N	N	N	N	N	N	N	N	Y	N
2 Baldwin	Y	Y	Y	Y	Y	Y	Y	Y	Y	N	Y
3 Kind	Y	Y	N	Y	Y	Y	N	Y	Y	N	Y
4 Moore	Y	Y	Y	Y	Y	Y	Y	Y	Y	N	Y
5 *Sensenbrenner*	N	N	N	N	N	N	N	N	N	Y	N
6 *Petri*	Y	N	N	N	N	N	N	Y	Y	Y	N
7 Obey	Y	Y	Y	Y	Y	Y	Y	Y	Y	Y	Y
8 Kagen	Y	Y	Y	Y	Y	Y	Y	Y	Y	N	Y
WYOMING											
AL *Lummis*	N	N	N	N	N	N	N	N	N	Y	N

Senate

1. DEBT LIMIT AND FISCAL TASK FORCE

Defeat of a proposal to established a bipartisan task force to address government long-term debt and deficit issues.

Senate Budget Chair Kent Conrad, D-N.D., and ranking member Judd Gregg, R-N.H., began pushing for a vote on their proposal to create a debt commission late in the first session of the 111th Congress. A compromise worked out just before the Senate adjourned in December 2009 gave them almost a month to build bipartisan support for their plan.

But many members from both parties were uneasy about a provision that would have required Congress to hold straight up-or-down votes—without amendments—on any recommendation supported by a supermajority on the panel. The amendment became a key test of whether lawmakers would commit to such a vote: The vote showed an unwillingness to force themselves to go on the record for or against a yet-to-be-determined deficit-cutting plan. That occurred even as they were preparing to increase the nation's statutory debt limit by $1.9 trillion to $14.3 trillion. The deficit panel amendment was offered to the debt limit legislation.

Eleven months later, an eighteen-member bipartisan debt commission created by President Barack Obama released recommendations to cut domestic and defense spending by hundreds of billions of dollars, overhaul the tax system by lowering rates and eliminating popular deductions, raise the retirement age for Social Security, and make other changes in entitlement programs. In a compromise with Conrad and Gregg, Democratic leaders in the House and Senate had agreed informally to hold votes on the panel's plan if fourteen of the eighteen members endorsed it. But the commission vote on the recommendations was three shy of that threshold, and lawmakers never had to record a position on those proposals.

Senate rejected the Conrad, D-N.D., amendment to H J Res 45 on January 26, 53-46: R 16-23; D 36-22; I 1-1. By unanimous consent, the Senate agreed to raise the majority requirement for adoption of the amendment to sixty votes. *(Vote 1, p. 772)*

2. CONFIRMATION OF BEN S. BERNANKE

Confirmation of Ben S. Bernanke for a second four-year term as chair of the Federal Reserve.

The first time Bernanke was nominated to be Federal Reserve (Fed) chair, the Senate confirmed him by a unanimous consent agreement and without a roll call. But four years later, senators used this vote to express frustrations with the Obama administration over national economic conditions and the cost of keeping the financial system functioning.

Although the Senate confirmed Bernanke for a second term by a comfortable margin, thirty senators voted "no." It was the most votes ever cast against a nominee for Fed chair and almost double the sixteen "no" votes recorded against Paul A. Volcker in 1983, when he was up for a second term after pushing interest rates into double digits to combat significant inflation.

The bipartisan group of senators who objected to Bernanke's second term—eleven Democrats, eighteen Republicans, and one independent—foreshadowed difficulties the Fed faced later in the year when Congress debated restricting the central bank's powers during consideration of an overhaul of financial services regulations. Yet, just as with Bernanke's confirmation, lawmakers opted to leave the Fed's authority intact and in some ways enhanced it.

Bernanke had led the central bank in pumping trillions of dollars into banks and other threatened enterprises and had pressed for enactment of the $700 billion bailout fund in 2008 known as the Troubled Asset Relief Program.

But Bernanke was attacked by liberal lawmakers for ignoring the needs of middle-class and poor Americans and for having spent lavishly to shore up Wall Street, while conservatives objected to the scope of the Fed's intervention in markets and financial institutions. The central bank was singled out by lawmakers at both ends of the ideological spectrum for having contributed to the financial crisis.

Obama in August 2009 had announced his intention to keep Bernanke at the Fed, five months before the chair's term was up, to reassure skittish investors fearful of a change in monetary policy. The Senate Banking Committee did not act on the nomination until mid-December. Even then, seven lawmakers—one Democrat and six Republicans—voted against sending it to the floor, a sign that confirmation would not be simple.

The White House stepped up a lobbying campaign as the nomination headed for a vote in late January, portraying the vote as a test of the nation's financial stability. Senate leaders assured lawmakers they would have other opportunities down the road to express their anger and to insist on greater transparency and accountability at the Fed.

Senate confirmed Bernanke on January 28, 70-30: R 22-18; D 47-11; I 1-1. *(Vote 2, p. 772)*

3. HEALTH CARE BILL CHANGES

Passage of a budget reconciliation bill that modified pending health care overhaul legislation, and revised federal student loan programs.

The vote on the reconciliation bill (HR 4872) was the final piece of the complex health care overhaul puzzle. It was a way to make good on promises offered to liberal Democrats in the House who supported the health care legislation but wanted more generous subsidies for the uninsured.

The bill made numerous changes to the health care bill (HR 3590) that the Senate had passed December 24, 2009. It increased subsidies to help uninsured people buy health coverage beginning in 2014 and boosted certain taxes and fees to help pay for the expanded coverage. In action unrelated to health care, it also made the federal government the sole originator of college student loans and increased the maximum Pell grant for low-income students.

The vote on the health care bill alterations served two purposes: It gave members who thought the subsidies in the underlying bill were too low an opportunity to expand them, and it allowed senators to reaffirm their support for the overhaul itself.

The bill was part of a delicate agreement put together by Democratic leaders and the White House. Many House Democrats had been reluctant to support the Senate health care bill, demanding leaders' assurances that they would push the second measure through Congress. Democratic leaders gave those assurances, then chose to use a fast-track budget reconciliation process, which does not require sixty votes in the Senate, to move the companion bill. Had the reconciliation bill been defeated in the Senate, the deal almost certainly would have disintegrated. The Senate passed it, 56–43.

Three Democratic senators did join Republicans in voting against passage of the secondary legislation, even though they had supported the underlying bill: Ben Nelson of Nebraska and Mark Pryor and Blanche Lincoln of Arkansas.

During the debate, Republicans did everything they could to disrupt the process. Senate leaders had to navigate through a lengthy process in which Republicans offered numerous amendments after the end of debate time. The GOP strategy was to win a public opinion war on and make Democrats take politically tough votes.

Democrats defeated amendment after amendment, hoping to avoid having to send the bill back to the House for one last vote. But their hopes were dashed when the Senate parliamentarian upheld a GOP challenge to two minor provisions dealing with higher education grants. The House then passed the secondary bill.

Senate passed HR 4872 on March 25, 56–43: R 0–40; D 54–3; I 2–0. *(Vote 3, p. 772)*

4. DISCRETIONARY SPENDING CAPS

Rejection of a motion to place a spending cap on appropriations.

Although Jeff Sessions, R-Ala., and Claire McCaskill, D-Mo., never mustered the sixty votes necessary to win adoption of an amendment to limit government spending, their efforts helped shape the appropriations debate in Congress.

The Senate voted four times from January to June on their joint offering to cap spending at $1.1 trillion annually through fiscal 2014.

The 57–41 vote on June 9 was the closest they came. Still, sixteen Democrats joined them, rejecting their leadership's entreaties. McCaskill said she considered it a victory that so many of her Democratic colleagues "withstood the pressure of leadership trying to convince people to jump ship."

Despite the votes to reject it, Minority Leader Mitch McConnell, R-Ky., gave the Sessions-McCaskill proposal a prominent role in the debate on fiscal 2011 spending. He and other Republicans announced at a Senate Appropriations Committee markup in July that they would not vote for any bill that spent more than the Sessions-McCaskill number.

Senate Appropriations Chair Daniel K. Inouye, D-Hawaii, pushed for a slightly larger cap, but he eventually relented and began writing spending bills that would come in under the $1.1 trillion limit.

Senate rejected a motion to waive the Budget Act on the Sessions, R-Ala., amendment to HR 4213 on June 9, 57–41: R 40–0; D 16–40; I 1–1. Three-fifths of the total Senate (sixty) is required to waive the Budget Act. *(Vote 4, p. 772)*

5. GREENHOUSE GAS REGULATION

Rejection of a resolution to strip the Environmental Protection Agency (EPA) of its authority to regulate greenhouse gases under the federal Clean Air Act.

Although the vote on the resolution by Lisa Murkowski, R-Alaska, to prevent EPA action on greenhouse gases was unsuccessful, it marked a shift by environmentalists and their political allies from offense to defense in the fight over controlling gases that were believed to contribute to climate change.

Murkowski's resolution was filed under the Congressional Review Act (PL 104-121), which allowed lawmakers to cast an up-or-down vote on an agency's regulations before they took effect. It would have negated an EPA finding that greenhouse gas emissions posed a public health threat. That finding, which stemmed from a 2007 Supreme Court decision, triggered a requirement for the agency to regulate emissions.

For months, President Obama held out the prospect of EPA regulation of greenhouse gas emissions to pressure Congress to enact a "cap and trade" law that would restrict overall emissions of carbon dioxide and other gases that contribute to global warming and would establish a market for trading government-issued pollution allowances. The House passed a cap-and-trade bill in June 2009, but efforts to assemble a bipartisan bill in the Senate fell apart the following spring. That meant EPA regulation was no longer a fallback plan for the administration, but rather an imminent reality.

The outcome of the vote was uncertain. Solid Republican support was expected, but the positions of several moderate Democrats were unknown. When ballots were cast, just six Democrats voted with a unanimous GOP caucus in favor of the resolution.

Even if the resolution had succeeded in the Senate, it was unlikely to get through the House, and if it did, it faced a certain presidential veto. Still, Senate adoption would have been a symbolic setback for the administration.

Senate rejected a motion to proceed on S J Res 26 on June 10, 47–53: R 41–0; D 6–51; I 0–2. *(Vote 5, p. 772)*

6. FINANCIAL REGULATORY OVERHAUL

Completing action on and sending to the president an overhaul of federal regulation of the financial services industry.

The Senate's final action on this bill (HR 4173) resulted in the most extensive changes in financial regulation since the Great Depression and gave President Obama his second major legislative accomplishment, coming three months after his health care overhaul cleared Congress.

The legislation granted financial industry regulators broad new authority and created agencies to oversee consumer lending and to determine whether changing financial conditions were a threat to the economy. The Federal Deposit Insurance Corporation was given new powers to take over and wind down huge financial companies on the verge of collapse. Trading in derivatives, the complex instruments that were behind the collapse of financial companies such as insurance giant American International Group Inc. came under close regulatory scrutiny, mostly for the first time.

The vote on a House-Senate conference report on HR 4173 showed a united Democratic caucus in favor of setting new standards for industry. Republicans, on the other hand, were consistent in their stance that the bill gave the government too much power and could damage an already-weak economy.

In the early preparation of the Senate bill, Banking Committee Chair Christopher J. Dodd, D-Conn., had hoped to reach an agreement with his panel's ranking member, Alabama Republican

Richard C. Shelby. Talks broke down over expanding consumer protections and government powers to dismantle failed financial institutions.

The White House pushed Democrats to take a firm position on consumer protections, urging the creation of a powerful new regulator that could restrict or ban financial products it deemed abusive or predatory. Administration officials also demanded tough regulations for the over-the-counter financial derivatives market.

The House passed its version of the bill in December 2009 with no Republican support; only three GOP House members backed the conference report. But in the final Senate vote, Democrats won the support of three New England Republicans: Scott P. Brown of Massachusetts and Susan Collins and Olympia J. Snowe of Maine. Because adoption of a conference report in the Senate required only a simple majority report, their votes were not critical to clearing the bill. But their backing was crucial earlier in the day on two procedural votes requiring sixty votes.

Democrat Russ Feingold of Wisconsin, concerned that the legislation did not go far enough in regulating the banks, voted with the minority on the procedural votes as well as on clearing the package. That defection, plus the vacancy left by the June death of Democrat Robert C. Byrd of West Virginia, left no room to spare for supporters.

Senate cleared HR 4173 by adopting a conference report on the bill July 15, 60–39: R 3–38; D 55–1; I 2–0. *(Vote 6, p. 772)*

7. MEDICAID AND EDUCATION ASSISTANCE

Passage of legislation (HR 1586) to provide state and local governments with funds to avert layoffs of teachers and other public employees, and to extend increased Medicaid reimbursements for states.

One of the most significant divides of 2010 was between persons who believed in more government spending to foster economic recovery and those who contended that government was spending enough already. That division was seen in a Senate vote in August on a domestic spending bill to provide $10 billion to avert teacher layoffs and $16.1 billion to extend increased Medicaid reimbursements to states for six months.

Democrats, who had to rely on the votes of Maine Republicans Susan Collins and Olympia J. Snowe to obtain cloture and end a filibuster on the bill, said the measure would boost the economy and protect vulnerable state and local government jobs. Most Republicans criticized it as an election year gambit by Democrats to assuage teachers' unions, among their biggest campaign supporters.

The Senate previously had turned back the education funding when the House attached it to a $58.8 billion fiscal 2010 supplemental appropriations measure to pay for the wars in Afghanistan and Iraq, as well as other priorities.

The effort to pass the stand-alone bill was led by Majority Leader Harry Reid, D-Nev., and Patty Murray, D-Wash., who faced difficult reelection challenges.

Offsets to pay for the bill, a potpourri of spending rescissions and revenue-raisers, drew criticism from a number of sources. Republicans disliked provisions that targeted use of foreign tax credits by multinational corporations. Supporters of the food stamp program opposed reductions starting in 2014 to extra benefits that had been provided under the 2009 economic stimulus package. In addition, the bill rescinded $1.5 billion in stimulus funds for an Energy Department program backed by many Democrats, including House Speaker Nancy Pelosi, D-Calif.

Senate passed HR 1586 on August 5, 61–39: R 2–39; D 57–0; I 2–0. *(Vote 7, p. 772)*

8. CONFIRMATION OF ELENA KAGAN

Confirmation of Elena Kagan as an associate justice of the Supreme Court.

With this vote, the Senate gave U.S. Solicitor General Elena Kagan a seat on the Supreme Court, replacing Associate Justice John Paul Stevens, who retired in June 2010.

Five Republicans supported her confirmation, but that was four fewer than President Obama's first nominee to the high court, Sonia Sotomayor, had received a year earlier, demonstrating an increasing reluctance among senators to back nominees selected by presidents of the opposing party.

There was little doubt about the outcome of the vote, given the sizable Democratic majority and Kagan's competent and occasionally humorous performance before the Senate Judiciary Committee. Any concerns about possible drama on the Senate floor were eliminated on the last day of Kagan's testimony, when Republicans conceded that her confirmation was all but inevitable and said a filibuster would be unrealistic.

Jeff Sessions of Alabama, the top Republican on the committee, led the opposition to Kagan, citing her lack of prior experience as a judge and her work history as a lawyer and domestic policy adviser in Bill Clinton's White House.

In the days before the vote, five Republicans who had voted for Sotomayor announced plans to vote for Kagan. The first was Lindsey Graham of South Carolina, the only one of the seven Republicans on the Judiciary Committee to support her. He was joined by four who also had voted the previous year for Kagan's nomination to be solicitor general: Richard G. Lugar of Indiana; Susan Collins and Olympia J. Snowe of Maine; and Judd Gregg of New Hampshire.

On the Democratic side, the only surprise came the week before the vote, when Ben Nelson of Nebraska announced that he intended to vote against Kagan. He became the first Democrat to vote against a nominee of his president's own party since Abe Fortas's failed elevation to chief justice in 1968.

Senate confirmed Kagan on August 5, 63–37: R 5–36; D 56–1; I 2–0. *(Vote 8, p. 772)*

9. CAMPAIGN FINANCE DISCLOSURE

Refusal to invoke cloture to halt a filibuster and to proceed to a bill to broaden campaign finance disclosure and reporting.

Senate Democratic leaders fell just short of the sixty votes needed to invoke cloture on a far-reaching campaign finance disclosure bill backed by the White House as Republicans stood firm in opposition for the second time in two months to effectively kill the measure. The bill (S 3628) was a response to a Supreme Court decision handed down eight months earlier.

In *Citizens United v. Federal Election Commission* (558 U.S. 310, 2010), the court held that corporations had the same free-speech rights as individuals and could spend their own funds to influence elections. The decision was sharply criticized by Democrats, including President Obama, who charged that the 5–4 majority had sided with "powerful interests" over average Americans and would unleash a flood of donations aimed at swaying elections.

The measure, which would have set new disclosure requirements and spending limits on foreign companies or those receiving federal assistance, first reached the Senate floor in July, one month after the House passed its version (HR 5175). Republicans united against the bill, which they said unconstitutionally impinged on free speech and gave preferential treatment to unions.

In the first vote, after Democrats fell short of the sixty votes needed to stop debate, Majority Leader Harry Reid, D-Nev., changed his vote to "nay" in order to leave open the possibility of reconsideration. In an effort to attract the single Republican vote they needed the second time around, sponsors proposed amending the measure to delay implementation until January 2011. But that was not enough to win over any of the three New England Republicans identified as the most likely GOP supporters: Susan Collins and Olympia J. Snowe of Maine, and Scott P. Brown of Massachusetts.

Senate rejected a motion to invoke cloture to proceed to S 3628 on September 23, 59–39: R 0–39; D 57–0; I 2–0. Three-fifths of the total Senate (sixty) is required to invoke cloture. *(Vote 9, p. 772)*

10. TAX CUT EXTENSIONS

Successful cloture motion to end debate and allows a vote on passage of a bill to extend income tax cuts for two years and set a new rate and threshold for estate taxes.

When President Obama announced December 6, 2009, that he had reached a compromise with Republicans to extend 2001 and 2003 George W. Bush–era tax cuts—including those for the wealthiest Americans—many congressional Democrats were openly angry. The most vocal resentment came from House Democrats, especially from the liberal wing of the party.

The next day, Obama dispatched Vice President Joseph R. Biden Jr. to the Senate, rather than the House, even though reaction there had been much more restrained.

Less than a week later, the Senate gave such overwhelming support to a bill to enact Obama's proposal that the House had little choice but to go along with it. In a Senate where the search for sixty votes dominated strategy all year on almost any piece of legislation or nomination, the 83–15 vote to advance the president's initiative essentially signaled that the deal had been sealed, and House Democrats would look irresponsible if they chose to fight back.

Immediately after the Senate agreed to invoke cloture and limit debate on the bill (HR 4853), talk in the House shifted from a demand by Democrats to not bring up the measure to how it could reach the floor, possibly with changes to its estate tax provisions. The Senate's slightly narrower 81–19 vote to pass the bill two days later all but ensured that the measure could not be changed.

When the House took up the bill December 16, Democrats in that chamber had to settle for a separate, guaranteed-to-fail vote on an amendment to increase the estate tax rate for upper-income people (rejected 194–233), before clearing the bill ten days after Obama asked for it.

Senate agreed to invoke cloture on a motion to limit debate on HR 4853 on December 13, 83–15: R 37–5; D 45–9; I 1–1. *(Vote 10, p. 772)*

11. IMMIGRATION POLICY

Refusal to invoke cloture to limit debate on a bill to allow legal status for some undocumented children of illegal immigrants.

Immigration policy at the end of the 111th Congress was left largely where it had been at the beginning: in a state of uncertainty. Nothing captured that situation better than the end-of-the-session Senate vote to reject cloture on the bill known as the DREAM Act.

The legislation was drafted narrowly to provide a path for legal status for adults younger than thirty who were brought illegally to the United States before turning sixteen. Those who met the age eligibility and finished two years of college or military service would be eligible to apply for permanent residency and ultimately for citizenship.

The 55–41 vote demonstrated that a majority of senators wanted to move on the legislation. But it did not meet the sixty-vote threshold needed to invoke cloture. The vote showed that Senate conservatives from both parties were reluctant to go ahead with piecemeal legislation in the absence of a more comprehensive overhaul of immigration policy that included tougher measures to enforce border protection and limit amnesty.

Some opponents said that whatever its merits the legislation just was not enough given the severity of the immigration problems.

Senate rejected a motion to invoke cloture on HR 5281 on December 18, 55–41: R 3–36; D 50–5; I 2–0. Three-fifths of the total Senate (sixty) is required to invoke cloture. *(Vote 11, p. 772)*

12. "DON'T ASK, DON'T TELL" REPEAL

Clearing for the president a repeal of the law banning openly gay people from serving in the military.

The Senate vote was a significant victory for President Obama, who had fought to repeal the ban. The president argued that asking servicemembers who put their lives on the line to lie about who they are was anathema to the honor and integrity embodied by the uniformed services. A number of GOP senators argued against repeal, saying a time of war was the wrong moment to introduce such a change into an already-stressed force. But an internal Pentagon study released in early December on how to implement the change appeared to swing enough Republican votes to secure passage.

Repeal of the 1993 law was always expected to face its most significant challenge in the Senate. But the effort gained momentum after Adm. Mike Mullen, chair of the Joint Chiefs of Staff, spoke passionately before the Senate Armed Services Committee early in the year about the necessity of such a change. After Defense Secretary Robert M. Gates launched a study on how to implement the change, Democrat Carl Levin of Michigan, chair of the Armed Services panel, indicated he would incorporate repeal language into the fiscal 2011 defense authorization bill.

In September, Senate Republicans blocked consideration of the authorization bill, primarily because of the repeal language. As a result, Joseph I. Lieberman, I-Conn., and Susan Collins, R-Maine, quickly filed a stand-alone repeal bill. Rep. Patrick J. Murphy, D-Pa., and House Majority Leader Steny H. Hoyer, D-Md., filed a similar measure, which the House passed December 15.

The House bill was sent to the Senate in the form of a message, enabling Majority Leader Harry Reid, D-Nev., to bring it up without a procedural vote that would have required sixty votes. At that point, a few Republican senators indicated they had been swayed by the results of the internal study. Others, such as John McCain of Arizona and Lindsey Graham of South Carolina, continued to oppose the measure. Graham called the bill a partisan measure that "poisoned the water."

Senate cleared, through a motion to concur, HR 2965 on December 18, 65–31: R 8–31; D 55–0; I 2–0. *(Vote 12, p. 772)*

13. START TREATY RATIFICATION

Approval of ratification of a strategic arms reduction treaty with Russia.

In its last major vote of the 111th Congress, the Senate handed President Obama an important victory when thirteen Republicans joined all fifty-eight members of the Democratic caucus in voting to approve ratification of the newest arms accord with Russia, known as New START (Treaty Doc 111-5).

Although the treaty did not earn the resounding support that past bilateral arms treaties enjoyed in the Senate, Democrats secured more than enough GOP support to reach the two-thirds vote threshold necessary to approve ratification.

Entering the final week of the lame duck session, it remained uncertain whether the Senate would approve ratification of New START. Democrats needed at least nine Republicans to guarantee ratification, but only four had publicly confirmed their support, and the Senate's two top Republicans—Minority Leader Mitch McConnell of Kentucky and Minority Whip Jon Kyl of Arizona—announced they would vote against ratification.

It soon became clear, however, that the Obama administration was making headway with its weeks-long lobbying push. After a closed Senate session on the treaty during the afternoon of December 20, a series of support statements from Republicans brought to ten the number of GOP senators prepared to approve ratification of New START. When the actual vote occurred, Republicans Thad Cochran of Mississippi, Judd Gregg of New Hampshire, and Mike Johanns of Nebraska joined them in support.

As notable as the Republican supporters were those in opposition, especially Kyl, John McCain of Arizona, and Lindsey Graham of South Carolina, in addition to McConnell.

The administration spent more than a year wooing Kyl, the GOP's point man on the treaty, and was stunned when he announced in November that he did not believe there would be sufficient time in the lame duck session for a proper debate on New START. Kyl's stance was initially seen as the death knell for a vote on the accord in 2010, but Democrats' persistent and ultimately successful effort to peel off Republicans without his blessing left Kyl with weakened authority.

Senate adopted the resolution of ratification of Treaty Doc 111-5 on December 22, 71–26: R 13–26; D 56–0; I 2–0. A two-thirds majority of those present and voting (sixty-five in this case) is required for adoption of resolutions of ratification. *(Vote 13, p. 772)*

1. H J Res 45. Debt Limit and Fiscal Task Force. Conrad, D-N.D., amendment to establish a bipartisan fiscal task force with the authority to propose debt and deficit reduction policies. The resolution authorized the task force to transmit proposals in legislative language that would be considered under expedited floor procedures, could not be amended, and required a three-fifths majority vote in both chambers. Rejected 53–46: R 16–23; D 36–22; I 1–1. (By unanimous consent, the Senate agreed to raise the majority required for adoption of the Conrad amendment to sixty votes.) A "yea" was a vote in support of the president's position. January 26, 2010.

2. Confirmation of Ben S. Bernanke. Confirmation of President Obama's nomination of Ben S. Bernanke of New Jersey for a second four-year term as chair of the Board of Governors of the Federal Reserve System. Confirmed 70–30: R 22–18; D 47–11; I 1–1. A "yea" was a vote in support of the president's position. January 28, 2010.

3. HR 4872. Health Care Bill Changes. Passage of the bill to make changes to the 2010 health care overhaul law, revise student loan programs, and include revenue-raising provisions. The legislation increased federal subsidies to help low- and moderate-income families purchase coverage through new health insurance exchanges, phased out the coverage gap for Medicare prescription drug enrollees, and adjusted the federal matching funds for Medicaid. It also delayed a tax on high-cost health plans and reduced the reach of the tax, and modified a Medicare payroll tax for high-income taxpayers. In education provisions the bill made the federal government the sole originator of federal student loans and directed the monetary savings generated to education programs, including Pell grants. Passed 56–43: R 0–40; D 54–3; I 2–0. A "yea" was a vote in support of the president's position. March 25, 2010.

4. HR 4213. Discretionary Spending Caps. Sessions, R-Ala., motion to waive the Budget Act and budget resolutions on a point of order against a Sessions amendment to reestablish discretionary spending limits for fiscal years 2011, 2012, and 2013 equal to the levels for defense and nondefense spending in the fiscal 2010 budget resolution. Motion rejected 57–41: R 40–0; D 16–40; I 1–1. A three-fifths majority vote (sixty) of the total Senate was required to waive the Budget Act. June 9, 2010.

5. S J Res 26. Greenhouse Gas Regulation. Murkowski, R-Alaska, motion to proceed to consideration of a joint resolution of congressional disapproval of an Environmental Protection Agency finding that greenhouse gases qualify as dangerous pollutants under the Clean Air Act. Motion rejected 47–53: R 41–0; D 6–51; I 0–2. A "nay" was a vote in support of the president's position. June 10, 2010.

6. HR 4173. Financial Regulatory Overhaul. Adoption of the conference report on the bill to overhaul the regulation of the financial services industry. The legislation created new regulatory mechanisms to assess risks posed by large financial institutions and to facilitate the orderly dissolution of failing businesses that posed a threat to the economy. It created a new federal agency to oversee consumer financial products, brought the derivatives market under significant federal regulation for the first time, and gave company shareholders and regulators a larger say on executive-pay packages. Adopted (cleared for the president) 60–39: R 3–38; D 55–1; I 2–0. A "yea" was a vote in support of the president's position. July 15, 2010.

7. HR 1586. Medicaid and Education Assistance. Reid, D-Nev., motion to concur in a House amendment with a Murray, D-Wash., substitute amendment to provide $16.1 billion to extend increased Medicaid assistance to states and $10 billion in funding for states to create or retain teachers' jobs, with costs offset by changing foreign tax provisions, ending increased food stamp benefits beginning in April 2014, and rescinding previously enacted spending. Motion agreed to 61–39: R 2–39; D 57–0; I 2–0. A "yea" was a vote in support of the president's position. August 5, 2010.

8. Confirmation of Elena Kagan. Confirmation of President Obama's nomination of Elena Kagan of Massachusetts to be an associate justice of the Supreme Court. Confirmed 63–37: R 5–36; D 56–1; I 2–0. A "yea" was a vote in support of the president's position. August 5, 2010.

9. S 3628. Campaign Finance Disclosure. Reid, D-Nev., motion to invoke cloture (thus limiting debate) on a motion to proceed to consideration of a bill requiring corporations and unions to disclose in their campaign advertising the chief donors who paid for the ad. Motion rejected 59–39: R 0–39; D 57–0; I 2–0. Three-fifths of the total Senate (sixty) was required to invoke cloture. A "yea" was a vote in support of the president's position. September 23, 2010.

10. HR 4853. Tax Cut Extensions. Reid (D-Nev.) motion to invoke cloture (thus limiting debate) on a proposal to extend the 2001 and 2003 tax cuts for taxpayers for two years, reinstitute the estate tax at a 35 percent rate on the value of estates in excess of $5 million, and continue expanded unemployment insurance benefits for thirteen months. Motion agreed to 83–15: R 37–5; D 45–9; I 1–1. Three-fifths of the total Senate (sixty) was required to invoke cloture. December 13, 2010.

11. HR 5281. Immigration Policy. Reid (D-Nev.) motion to invoke cloture (thus limiting debate) on an amendment to allow the Homeland Security Department to grant conditional nonimmigrant status to the undocumented children of illegal immigrants if they met certain requirements, including having been in the United States continuously for more than five years, having been younger than sixteen when they entered the country, and having been admitted to a U.S. college or university or enlisted in the military. The proposal allowed an eligible individual, after paying certain fees, to apply for legal permanent status after ten years. Motion rejected 55–41: R 3–36; D 50–5; I 2–0. Three-fifths of the total Senate (sixty) was required to invoke cloture. A "yea" was a vote in support of the president's position. December 18, 2010.

12. HR 2965. "Don't Ask, Don't Tell" Repeal. Reid, D-Nev., motion to concur in a House amendment to allow repeal of the "don't ask, don't tell" policy, which prohibited military service by openly gay men and women after certain requirements were met, including a certification by the president, the Secretary of Defense, and the chair of the Joint Chiefs of Staff that the repeal was consistent with military readiness and effectiveness. Motion agreed to (clearing the bill for the president) 65–31: R 8–31; D 55–0; I 2–0. A "yea" was a vote in support of the president's position. December 18, 2010.

13. Treaty Doc 111-5. START Treaty Ratification. Adoption of the resolution of ratification for the New Strategic Arms Reduction Treaty (START) with Russia. The treaty restricted each country to a maximum of 1,550 deployed nuclear warheads, a reduction of about 30 percent. The resolution of ratification stated that the April 2010 unilateral statement by Russia on missile defense did not impose any legal obligation on the United States. Adopted (thereby consenting to ratification) 71–26: R 13–26; D 56–0; I 2–0. A two-thirds majority of those present and voting (sixty-five in this case) was required for adoption of resolutions of ratification. A "yea" was a vote in support of the president's position. December 22, 2010.

KEY

Republican | Democrat | **Independent**

Y	Voted for (yea)	–	Announced against
#	Paired for	P	Voted "present"
+	Announced for	C	Voted "present" to avoid possible conflict of interest
N	Voted against (nay)		
X	Paired against	?	Did not vote or otherwise make a position known

Senate Key Votes	1	2	3	4	5	6	7	8	9	10	11	12	13
ALABAMA													
Shelby	N	N	N	Y	Y	N	N	N	N	Y	N	N	N
Sessions	N	N	N	Y	Y	N	N	N	N	N	N	N	N
ALASKA													
Murkowski	?	Y	N	Y	Y	N	N	N	?	Y	Y	Y	Y
Begich	Y	N	Y	Y	N	Y	Y	Y	Y	Y	Y	Y	Y
ARIZONA													
McCain	N	N	N	Y	Y	N	N	N	N	Y	N	N	N
Kyl	N	Y	N	Y	Y	N	N	N	N	Y	N	N	N
ARKANSAS													
Lincoln	Y	Y	N	Y	Y	Y	Y	Y	Y	Y	Y	Y	Y
Pryor	Y	Y	N	N	Y	Y	Y	Y	Y	Y	N	Y	Y
CALIFORNIA													
Feinstein	Y	Y	Y	N	N	Y	Y	Y	Y	Y	Y	Y	Y
Boxer	Y	N	Y	N	N	Y	Y	Y	Y	Y	Y	Y	Y
COLORADO													
Udall	Y	Y	Y	Y	N	Y	Y	Y	Y	N	Y	Y	Y
Bennet	Y	Y	Y	Y	N	Y	Y	Y	Y	Y	Y	Y	Y
CONNECTICUT													
Dodd	N	Y	Y	N	N	Y	Y	Y	Y	Y	Y	Y	Y
Lieberman	Y	Y	Y	Y	N	Y	Y	Y	Y	Y	Y	Y	Y
DELAWARE													
Carper	Y	Y	Y	Y	N	Y	Y	Y	Y	Y	Y	Y	Y
Kaufman[1]	Y	N	Y	N	N	Y	Y	Y	Y				
Coons[1]										Y	Y	Y	Y
FLORIDA													
Nelson	Y	Y	Y	Y	N	Y	Y	Y	Y	Y	Y	Y	Y
LeMieux	Y	N	N	Y	Y	N	N	N	N	Y	N	N	N
GEORGIA													
Chambliss	Y	Y	N	Y	Y	N	N	N	N	Y	N	N	N
Isakson	Y	Y	?	Y	Y	N	N	N	N	Y	N	N	Y
HAWAII													
Inouye	N	Y	Y	N	N	Y	Y	Y	Y	Y	Y	Y	Y
Akaka	N	Y	Y	N	N	Y	Y	Y	Y	Y	Y	Y	Y
IDAHO													
Crapo	N	N	N	Y	Y	N	N	N	N	Y	N	N	N
Risch	N	N	N	Y	Y	N	N	N	N	Y	N	N	N
ILLINOIS													
Durbin	Y	Y	Y	N	N	Y	Y	Y	Y	Y	Y	Y	Y
Burris	N	Y	Y	N	N	Y	Y	Y	Y				
Kirk										Y	N	Y	N
INDIANA													
Lugar	Y	Y	N	Y	Y	N	N	Y	N	Y	Y	N	Y
Bayh	Y	Y	Y	Y	Y	Y	Y	Y	Y	Y	Y	Y	Y
IOWA													
Grassley	N	N	N	Y	Y	N	N	N	N	Y	N	N	N
Harkin	N	N	Y	N	N	Y	Y	Y	Y	Y	Y	Y	Y

Senate Key Votes	1	2	3	4	5	6	7	8	9	10	11	12	13
KANSAS													
Brownback	N	N	N	Y	Y	N	N	N	N	Y	N	N	?
Roberts	N	N	N	?	Y	N	N	N	N	Y	N	N	N
KENTUCKY													
McConnell	N	Y	N	Y	Y	N	N	N	N	Y	N	N	N
Bunning	N	N	N	Y	Y	N	N	N	N	Y	–	–	?
LOUISIANA													
Landrieu	Y	Y	Y	N	Y	Y	Y	Y	Y	Y	Y	Y	Y
Vitter	Y	N	N	Y	Y	N	N	N	N	Y	N	N	N
MAINE													
Snowe	N	Y	N	Y	Y	Y	Y	Y	N	Y	N	Y	Y
Collins	Y	Y	N	Y	Y	Y	Y	Y	N	Y	N	Y	Y
MARYLAND													
Mikulski	N	Y	Y	N	N	Y	Y	Y	Y	Y	Y	Y	Y
Cardin	N	Y	Y	N	N	Y	Y	Y	Y	Y	Y	Y	Y
MASSACHUSETTS													
Kerry	Y	Y	Y	N	N	Y	Y	Y	Y	Y	Y	Y	Y
Kirk[2]	N	Y											
Brown[2]			N	Y	Y	Y	N	N	N	Y	N	Y	Y
MICHIGAN													
Levin	Y	Y	Y	N	N	Y	Y	Y	Y	N	Y	Y	Y
Stabenow	N	Y	Y	N	N	Y	Y	Y	Y	Y	Y	Y	Y
MINNESOTA													
Klobuchar	Y	Y	Y	Y	N	Y	Y	Y	Y	Y	Y	Y	Y
Franken	Y	N	Y	N	N	Y	Y	Y	Y	Y	Y	Y	Y
MISSISSIPPI													
Cochran	N	Y	N	Y	Y	N	N	N	N	Y	N	N	Y
Wicker	Y	N	N	Y	Y	N	N	N	N	Y	N	N	N
MISSOURI													
Bond	Y	Y	N	Y	Y	N	N	N	N	Y	N	N	?
McCaskill	Y	Y	Y	Y	N	Y	Y	Y	Y	Y	Y	Y	Y
MONTANA													
Baucus	N	Y	Y	N	N	Y	Y	Y	Y	Y	N	Y	Y
Tester	Y	Y	Y	N	N	Y	Y	Y	Y	Y	N	Y	Y
NEBRASKA													
Nelson	Y	Y	N	Y	Y	Y	Y	N	Y	Y	N	Y	Y
Johanns	Y	Y	N	Y	Y	N	N	N	N	Y	N	N	Y
NEVADA													
Reid	Y	Y	Y	N	N	Y	Y	Y	Y	Y	Y	Y	Y
Ensign	N	N	N	Y	Y	N	N	N	N	N	N	Y	N
NEW HAMPSHIRE													
Gregg	Y	Y	N	Y	Y	N	N	Y	N	Y	?	?	Y
Shaheen	Y	Y	Y	Y	N	Y	Y	Y	Y	Y	Y	Y	Y
NEW JERSEY													
Lautenberg	N	Y	Y	N	N	Y	Y	Y	Y	N	Y	Y	Y
Menendez	Y	Y	Y	N	N	Y	Y	Y	Y	Y	Y	Y	Y
NEW MEXICO													
Bingaman	Y	Y	Y	N	N	Y	Y	Y	Y	N	Y	Y	Y
Udall	N	Y	Y	N	N	Y	Y	Y	Y	Y	Y	Y	Y
NEW YORK													
Schumer	Y	Y	Y	N	N	Y	Y	Y	Y	Y	Y	Y	Y
Gillibrand	Y	Y	Y	N	N	Y	Y	Y	Y	N	Y	Y	Y
NORTH CAROLINA													
Burr	N	Y	N	Y	Y	N	N	N	N	Y	N	Y	N
Hagan	Y	Y	Y	Y	N	Y	Y	Y	Y	N	N	Y	Y

[1]Sen. Chris Coons, D-Del., was sworn in November 15, 2010, to replace fellow Democrat Ted Kaufman, appointed January 15, 2009, to temporarily fill the vacancy created by Democrat Joseph R. Biden Jr., who resigned to become vice president. The first key vote for which Coons was eligible was vote 10; the last key vote for which Kaufman was eligible was vote 9.

[2]Sen. Scott P. Brown, R-Mass., was sworn in February 4, 2010, to replace Democrat Paul G. Kirk Jr., who was appointed September 24, 2009, to temporarily fill the vacancy created by Democrat Edward M. Kennedy, who died August 25, 2009. The first key vote for which Brown was eligible was vote 3; the last key vote for which Kirk was eligible was vote 2.

Senate Key Votes	1	2	3	4	5	6	7	8	9	10	11	12	13
NORTH DAKOTA													
Conrad	Y	Y	Y	N	N	Y	Y	Y	Y	Y	Y	Y	Y
Dorgan	Y	N	Y	N	N	Y	Y	Y	Y	Y	Y	Y	Y
OHIO													
Voinovich	Y	Y	N	Y	Y	N	N	N	N	N	N	Y	Y
Brown	N	Y	Y	N	N	Y	Y	Y	Y	N	Y	Y	Y
OKLAHOMA													
Inhofe	N	N	N	Y	Y	N	N	N	N	Y	N	N	N
Coburn	N	Y	N	Y	Y	N	N	N	N	N	N	N	N
OREGON													
Wyden	Y	Y	Y	N	N	Y	Y	Y	Y	?	Y	Y	Y
Merkley	N	N	Y	N	N	Y	Y	Y	Y	?	Y	Y	Y
PENNSYLVANIA													
Specter	N	N	Y	N	N	Y	Y	Y	Y	Y	Y	Y	Y
Casey	N	Y	Y	Y	N	Y	Y	Y	Y	Y	Y	Y	Y
RHODE ISLAND													
Reed	N	Y	Y	N	N	Y	Y	Y	Y	Y	Y	Y	Y
Whitehouse	N	N	Y	N	N	Y	Y	Y	Y	Y	Y	Y	Y
SOUTH CAROLINA													
Graham	Y	Y	N	Y	Y	N	N	Y	N	Y	N	N	N
DeMint	N	N	N	Y	Y	N	N	N	N	N	N	N	N
SOUTH DAKOTA													
Johnson	Y	Y	Y	N	N	Y	Y	Y	Y	Y	Y	Y	Y
Thune	N	N	N	Y	Y	N	N	N	N	Y	N	N	N
TENNESSEE													
Alexander	Y	Y	N	Y	Y	N	N	N	N	Y	N	N	Y
Corker	Y	Y	N	Y	Y	N	N	N	N	Y	N	N	Y
TEXAS													
Hutchison	N	N	N	Y	Y	N	N	N	?	Y	N	N	N
Cornyn	Y	N	N	Y	Y	N	N	N	N	Y	N	N	N

Senate Key Votes	1	2	3	4	5	6	7	8	9	10	11	12	13
UTAH													
Hatch	N	Y	N	Y	Y	N	N	N	N	Y	–	–	N
Bennett	N	Y	N	Y	Y	N	N	N	N	Y	Y	N	Y
VERMONT													
Leahy	Y	Y	Y	N	N	Y	Y	Y	Y	N	Y	Y	Y
Sanders	N	N	Y	N	N	Y	Y	Y	Y	N	Y	Y	Y
VIRGINIA													
Webb	Y	Y	Y	Y	N	Y	Y	Y	Y	Y	Y	Y	Y
Warner	Y	Y	Y	Y	N	Y	Y	Y	Y	Y	Y	Y	Y
WASHINGTON													
Murray	N	Y	Y	N	N	Y	Y	Y	Y	Y	Y	Y	Y
Cantwell	N	N	Y	Y	N	Y	Y	Y	Y	Y	Y	Y	Y
WEST VIRGINIA													
Byrd[3]	N	Y	Y	?	N								
Rockefeller	N	Y	Y	N	Y	Y	Y	Y	Y	Y	Y	Y	Y
Goodwin[3]							Y	Y	Y				
Manchin[4]										Y	–	?	Y
WISCONSIN													
Kohl	Y	Y	Y	N	N	Y	Y	Y	Y	Y	Y	Y	Y
Feingold	Y	N	Y	N	N	N	Y	Y	Y	N	Y	Y	Y
WYOMING													
Enzi	Y	Y	N	Y	Y	N	N	N	N	Y	N	N	N
Barrasso	N	Y	N	Y	Y	N	N	N	N	Y	N	N	N

[3] Sen. Carte P. Goodwin, D-W.Va., was appointed July 16, 2010 to temporarily fill the vacancy created by Democrat Robert C. Byrd, who died June 28, 2010. The last key vote for which Byrd voted was vote 5; the first key vote for which Goodwin was eligible was vote 7.

[4] Sen. Joe Manchin III, D-W.Va., was sworn in November 15, 2010, to replace fellow Democrat Carte P. Goodwin, who was appointed July 16, 2010, to temporarily fill the vacancy created by Democrat Robert C. Byrd, who died June 28, 2010. The first key vote for which Manchin was eligible was vote 10; Goodwin was eligible for key votes 7 through 9; the last key vote for which Byrd voted was vote 5.

House

1. HEALTH CARE OVERHAUL

Clearing a bill to overhaul health care insurance coverage by requiring individuals to buy insurance, requiring employers with more than fifty workers to provide coverage, creating state-run marketplaces for consumers to buy insurance and prohibiting insurance companies from denying care to people with preexisting conditions.

The overhaul was the largest revision of federal health policy since the enactment of Medicare in 1965. It was the product of negotiations between the House and Senate over the previous nine months, but those talks were mostly among Democrats; some wanted more-generous subsidies to help people buy insurance, and others were concerned that the measure would cost the government too much.

As such, the 219–212 vote was a reflection of members' views on the size and role of government in the American health care system. No Republicans voted for the legislation (HR 3590) and thirty-four Democrats, mostly moderates and members of the fiscally conservative Blue Dog Coalition, joined all 178 Republicans in voting against it.

During the floor debate, Republicans characterized the measure as one that expanded government's role to the point of socialized medicine. Democrats argued that it was necessary to prevent insurance companies from discriminating against people with preexisting conditions and to get uninsured Americans coverage they needed.

Conservative Democrats were opposed on cost considerations. Some Democrats wanted the legislation to prohibit the use of federal funds to cover abortions.

Given the Democratic defections, the vote was a measure of the abilities of Speaker Nancy Pelosi, D-Calif., and her leadership team to persuade wavering members to get on board.

Many liberal Democrats had hoped that a more-liberal health care bill passed in November 2009 would be blended with one passed by the Senate on December 24 of that year. But when the Democrats lost a Senate seat with the election of Massachusetts Republican Scott P. Brown, it became clear that the Senate measure would have to be the operative one. The measure offered less-generous subsidies to help individuals buy insurance than many Democrats wanted, and it contained a number of special provisions criticized as sweetheart deals designed to win senators' votes.

House cleared HR 3590 on March 21, 219–212: R 0–178; D 219–34. *(Vote 1, p. 779)*

2. FUNDING FOR F-35 ALTERNATIVE ENGINE

Defeat of an amendment to the fiscal 2011 defense authorization bill to eliminate funding for the F-35 Joint Strike Fighter alternative engine.

The normal tendency of members of Congress to protect defense funding that often benefited manufacturing plants in their districts was fully in operation on a May 27 vote to defeat an amendment to the defense authorization bill to eliminate funding for General Electric's alternative engine for the F-35 Joint Strike Fighter. Congress had funded the alternative engine for fourteen years.

President Obama and Defense Secretary Robert M. Gates argued that spending an additional $2.9 billion to complete development of the F35 engine program over the next six years was unnecessary. General Electric and its proponents disputed the $2.9 billion figure, saying they believed it could be about $1 billion less.

Proponents of a second engine to complement and compete with the base Pratt & Whitney–built F135 engine said a second engine would save enough over the life of the program to pay for itself. They also argued nonmonetary benefits to having a competitive engine, such as improved contractor responsiveness and engine reliability.

The House Armed Services Committee proposed authorizing $485 million for alternative-engine development and included language to prohibit the Pentagon from spending 25 percent of its F-35 budget until all alternative-engine funds had been obligated.

On the day the House turned back the amendment to drop the funding, the White House threatened a veto.

The House vote took on even greater significance when, on the same day, the Senate Armed Services Committee reported a defense authorization bill that heeded the president's veto threat and did not include the funding authorization.

In July, the House Defense Appropriations Subcommittee included $450 million for the alternative engine in deference to the House vote in May. Funding for the engine was left out of a Senate Appropriations Committee draft in September. With time running out on the session, Congress cleared a trimmed-down defense authorization that neither endorsed nor blocked spending for the alternative engine. A continuing resolution cleared in December funded the program at the fiscal 2010 level until early March. Congress had appropriated $465 million for the F136 engine in fiscal 2010, $35 million of which was for procurement.

House rejected the Pingree, D-Maine, amendment to HR 5136 on May 27, 193–231: R 57–116; D 136–115. *(Vote 2, p. 779)*

3. REPEAL OF "DON'T ASK, DON'T TELL" POLICY

Adoption of an amendment to the 2011 defense authorization bill to repeal the law that banned openly gay people from serving in the military.

The House's May 27 vote in favor of repeal was a landmark decision by lawmakers after years of debate within the military and the nation about the "don't ask, don't tell" policy.

Adoption of the amendment was the initial House attempt to repeal the 1993 law that barred openly gay people from serving in the military, and forbade their commanders to ask about sexual orientation. Many who voted against repealing the law were simply opposed to openly gay people serving in the military. But others were undecided, or at least wanted to first hear the results of a Pentagon review of the matter that did not come until December 1.

Until just days before the spring vote, Pentagon senior civilian and uniformed leaders argued that Congress should wait for the department's review. But on May 24, the White House, Pentagon, and congressional repeal advocates agreed on the provision that later was incorporated into the House and Senate defense authorization bills.

The compromise came from language added to the amendment stipulating that the repeal would not occur before completion of the Pentagon review, nor before the White House and Defense Department certified that repeal would not harm the military.

House adopted the Murphy, D-Pa., amendment to HR 5136 on May 27, 234–194: R 5–168; D 229–26. *(Vote 3, p. 779)*

4. GUANTÁNAMO BASE CLOSING

Adoption of a motion to bar the transfer or release of any military detainees held at Guantánamo Bay, Cuba, to the United States.

With a significant number of Democrats joining Republicans, the House sent a strong signal of opposition to President Obama's plans to close the detention facility at Guantánamo Bay. The vote was on a procedural issue—a motion to recommit the defense authorization bill to committee—but the meaning was clear: The House was trying to bar the Obama administration from funding the transfer or release of Guantánamo detainees into the United States. The language was included in the final agreement on the defense authorization bill.

Closing the facility had been one of the top national security priorities of the Obama administration, which argued that Guantánamo served as a recruitment tool for terrorist organizations. But Congress had grown leery of alternatives favored by the president and had stymied his Guantánamo agenda.

House agreed to a motion to recommit HR 5136 on May 28, 282–131: R 168–1; D 114–130. *(Vote 4, p. 779)*

5. CAMPAIGN FINANCE DISCLOSURE

Passage of a bill to broaden campaign finance disclosure and reporting requirements.

After a 5-4 Supreme Court ruling in January in *Citizens United v. Federal Election Commission* (558 U.S. 310, 2010), which held that corporations had the same free-speech rights as individuals and could spend corporate money to sway election campaigns, Democrats mobilized to develop a legislative response.

A few days after the ruling, President Obama made an unusually direct criticism of the decision during his State of the Union address—as several justices sat in the audience—saying it had been wrongly decided in favor of "powerful interests."

Congressional Democrats voiced the same populist critique in introducing this bill to tighten disclosure rules on campaign advertising by corporations, unions, and other independent groups and to prohibit foreign-controlled corporations or corporations receiving government assistance from making expenditures in political campaigns.

Republicans strongly opposed the measure, which they said would unconstitutionally curb free-speech rights and was designed mostly to improve Democrats' prospects in the midterm elections.

The House vote was the high-water mark for the measure, which died in the Senate.

House passed HR 5175 on June 24, 219-206: R 2–170; D 217–36. *(Vote 5, p. 779)*

6. FINANCIAL REGULATORY OVERHAUL

Adoption of the conference report on financial regulatory overhaul.

Having used their majority to push through a major remake of the health care system in early 2010, Democrats forged ahead in their efforts on another major sector of the economy: financial services.

The House had passed a financial regulation bill at the end of 2009 and the Senate in May 2010. The 2010 key votes, in both houses, on the legislation came on the compromise bill that emerged from a conference committee.

But partisan tensions had been mounting through 2009 into 2010 over legislation, fueled by a lagging economic recovery and the increasingly strident cries from a voting bloc that became known as the Tea Party, which was pressing GOP members, in particular, to oppose more and larger government.

The result was a mostly party-line vote on an issue—banking regulation—that had historically been developed in a more bipartisan way.

Conferees made some changes to the legislation, but the overall intent was the same: to create new regulatory mechanisms to deal with the risks posed by large financial companies, establish a new federal agency to oversee consumer financial products, and force most banks and other financial institutions to hold more capital to protect against future upheaval.

House adoption of the conference report on HR 4173 on June 30, 237–192: R 3–173; D 234–19. *(Vote 6, p. 779)*

7. FUNDING FOR AFGHANISTAN WAR

Rejection of an amendment to the fiscal 2010 supplemental spending bill to force withdrawal of U.S. troops from Afghanistan.

President Obama's request for $33.5 billion in supplemental funding to support his Afghanistan surge strategy of sending additional troops to the war zone split House Democrats into two camps. It became clear just how deeply divided the party was in the early summer, when ninety-three Democrats voted in favor of an amendment that instead would have used supplemental spending to pay for the withdrawal of U.S. troops.

That proposal was rejected, 100–321, but the vote demonstrated to administration officials that they needed significant House GOP support for the new strategy, which was set to place 30,000 additional U.S. forces in Afghanistan to counter Taliban gains.

On July 27, the House voted, 308–114, to clear the spending measure and support the president's strategy, but only 148 of 250 Democrats supported the measure, while 160 of 172 Republicans backed the bill.

In a statement issued the day of the debate, the White House warned of a veto if the amendment prevailed.

House rejected a motion to concur in the Senate amendments to HR 4899 with a Barbara Lee, D-Calif., amendment on withdrawal from Afghanistan July 1, 100–321: R 7–164; D 93–157. *(Vote 7, p. 779)*

8. SUPPLEMENTAL APPROPRIATIONS: WAR FUNDING

Clearing a bill to provide $58.8 billion in emergency spending to fund the nation's war efforts.

Senate appropriators prevailed on this measure, insisting that the bill stick mostly to its intended purpose of ensuring that the wars in Iraq and Afghanistan were funded through the rest of the fiscal year. The House had amended the legislation with an extra $22.8 billion in domestic-spending provisions, but the Senate refused to allow the measure to expand.

With the August recess approaching—and the chance to return home to campaign for the midterm elections—House Democratic leaders conceded defeat and scheduled another vote on the Senate's original work, this time under suspension of the rules, avoiding any further attempts to amend it.

The 308–114 vote showed that the appetite for attaching as many projects as possible onto a critical spending bill had diminished as the Tea Party cry for reducing the deficit grew louder. More than 100 Democrats—including Appropriations Chair David R. Obey, D-Wis.—voted in protest against the leadership's handling of the measure. Overwhelming Republican support ended up making the difference in clearing the bill.

Obey's dogged persistence did pay off eventually, as another measure passed in August to provide $10 billion for schools and Medicaid assistance for states.

House cleared HR 4899 on July 27, 308–114: R 160–12; D 148–102. The bill was considered under suspension of the rules, thereby requiring a two-thirds majority of those present and voting (282 in this case) for passage. *(Vote 8, p. 779)*

9. OFFSHORE OIL DRILLING REGULATIONS

Passage of a bill to revise federal oversight of offshore drilling and lift a $75 million cap on liability for offshore oil spills.

Congressional hearings after the April 20 explosion of a British Petroleum (BP) drilling rig, called Deepwater Horizon, in the Gulf of Mexico exposed serious weaknesses in the regulation of offshore drilling and shortcomings by the agency that was supposed to be policing operations. The disaster killed eleven workers and caused the worst oil spill in U.S. history.

Congress's main legislative response came in the House, which passed a bill designed to split the duties of the troubled Minerals Management Service among three agencies, establish new safety requirements for offshore oil and gas development, and lift the $75 million cap on liability for a spill.

House leaders took the bill to the floor just before the August recess, as the magnitude of the spill was sinking in with an angry public and weeks before oil giant BP was able to cap the ruptured well. But while bipartisan sentiment for a tough legislative response initially ran high, by the eve of the vote, prospects for passage were in doubt.

Stubbornly high national unemployment was compounded in the Gulf region by the spill, which crippled both the energy and fishing industries. As many as thirty "oil patch" Democrats threatened to join Republicans in opposing the bill over concerns about the Obama administration's temporary ban on new deep-water drilling.

But enough Democrats were kept on board with an amendment by Democrats Charlie Melancon of Louisiana and Travis W. Childers of Mississippi to exempt drillers from the moratorium if they demonstrate compliance with new Interior Department safety requirements. The House also adopted an amendment to let companies pool their resources to meet tough new financial requirements under the bill for obtaining federal leases. Democrats dropped unrelated environmental provisions.

The concessions did not satisfy Republicans—who also complained that the bill was loaded with provisions unrelated to the spill—but it allowed Democrats to pass the legislation with just sixteen votes to spare. All but two Republicans voted against passage, but only thirty-nine Democrats defected. However, the Senate never took up the House bill or its own companion legislation.

House passed HR 3534 on July 30, 209–193: R 2–154; D 207–39. *(Vote 9, p. 779)*

10. MEDICAID AND EDUCATION ASSISTANCE

Clearing a bill aimed at preventing layoffs of teachers and other public employees and boosting Medicaid reimbursement to states.

The vote to clear a scaled-back bill (HR 1586) that provided $10 billion to create or retain education-related jobs and $16.1 billion to extend increased Medicaid aid to states was a small victory for Democratic leaders, who for months had been unable to deliver on promises of more ambitious help.

After intense lobbying from governors, states, teachers, and public employees unions, Democrats voted for the legislation despite concerns about some of the offsets, including an $11.9 billion cut from increased food stamps benefits starting in April 2014 and a $1.5 billion reduction in appropriated funds for an Energy Department renewable-energy program.

Republicans objected to another round of government spending and characterized the bill as a political payoff to unions.

House Appropriations Chair David R. Obey, D-Wis., who championed the measure, criticized Senate Republicans for delays in moving it forward. The Senate had previously turned back the $10 billion in education funding, which Obey had attached to a $58.8 billion fiscal 2010 supplemental appropriations measure to fund the wars in Afghanistan and Iraq.

House cleared HR 1586 on August 10, 247–161: R 2–158; D 245–3. *(Vote 10, p. 779)*

11. CHINESE CURRENCY VALUATION

Passage of a bill intended to encourage China to raise the value of its currency by giving the Commerce Department power to impose duties on products deemed to be unfairly subsidized by Chinese currency policy.

Taken just before lawmakers left town for the final 2010 election campaign stretch, this unexpectedly bipartisan House vote demonstrated a deep level of public and congressional unease with China's trade practices, and to some degree with the inability of the White House to remedy the situation.

The vote came amid growing frustration with China's refusal to allow its currency, the yuan, to appreciate against the dollar—a tactic that Beijing had long used to help its exporters—in the face of complaints from the Obama administration. To some observers, the vote strengthened the White House's hand in currency negotiations with Beijing, reflecting the long-standing "good cop, bad cop" dynamics of the issue, with Congress applying public pressure while the administration toed a more diplomatic line.

With the election approaching, rank-and-file Democrats made clear that they wanted an opportunity to vote on the legislation, and the Ways and Means Committee quickly revised an earlier version of the bill, addressing concerns that it would violate World Trade Organization rules. Some lawmakers viewed the vote as a signal to China to stop undervaluing the yuan; others used it to voice frustration with the administration's approach.

The bill split the business community. Many large corporations worried it would spark a trade war with China, while many small and midsize manufacturers backed it.

Despite opposition from GOP leaders, the bill won the support of ninety-nine Republicans, a majority of the caucus, including Dave Camp of Michigan, the ranking member of Ways and Means. Organized labor strongly backed the bill.

Despite strong bipartisan support for currency legislation in the Senate, the issue cooled somewhat after the election. A crowded lame duck calendar thwarted efforts to schedule a vote on the issue.

House passed HR 2378 on September 29, 348–79: R 99–74; D 249–5. *(Vote 11, p. 779)*

12. INTELLIGENCE AUTHORIZATION

Clearing the fiscal 2010 intelligence authorization bill.

This vote sent legislation to President Obama that became the first intelligence authorization law in six years. The measure required the executive branch to more broadly disclose information to Congress about the most sensitive intelligence activities. It also reestablished the main legislative method by which the House and Senate Select Intelligence panels exerted authority over spy agencies.

Although there was some question of how effective the legislation would be in compelling administration disclosures about its intelligence operations, the new set of rules gave the congressional Intelligence committees a potential lever they did not have before. Under previous law, only a limited number of members, made up of party leaders in both chambers and on the two Intelligence committees, received briefings on findings in covert actions.

The new rules required that the entire membership of the Intelligence panels receive notification when a briefing occurred, along with a general description of the subject.

Although the Senate moved the bill to the House by voice vote, House Republicans were less enthusiastic than their Senate counterparts. The bill excluded several House GOP proposals included in earlier versions of the legislation, such as a provision to forbid officials from reading *Miranda* rights to terrorism suspects.

House cleared HR 2701 on September 29, 244–181: R 1–172; D 243–9. *(Vote 12, p. 779)*

13. NASA AUTHORIZATION

Clearing a reauthorization of the National Aeronautics and Space Administration (NASA) programs and changes to the federal focus on manned space missions.

The vote in the House was a test of President Obama's ability to win congressional backing for his proposal to make fundamental changes to the government's approach to manned spaceflight.

The president proposed ending the agency's manned spaceflight program, known as Constellation, which was begun during the George W. Bush administration to develop vehicles to send astronauts to the moon and Mars. Instead, Obama sought to emphasize development of commercial carriers for both astronauts and cargo, in a departure from the approach to space exploration that NASA had followed since the Mercury flights of the 1960s.

The House and Senate authorizing committees approved legislation that differed from Obama's proposal. The White House worked closely with the Senate, whose bill more closely followed Obama's proposal. The Senate bill authorized significantly more funding to support the development of commercial space transportation systems, although it added one more shuttle flight than previously authorized in an attempt to mollify skeptics of the new approach.

With the two chambers unable to resolve their differences, Senate Democrats persuaded their House counterparts to vote on the Senate-passed bill so the space agency would have some direction from Congress as fiscal 2011 began.

On the day of the vote, Florida Democrat Bill Nelson, the lead senator in the effort, spent a lot of time on the House floor and in the corridors near the chamber lobbying his counterparts to vote to clear the Senate bill.

House cleared S 3729 on September 29, 304–118: R 119–54; D 185–64. The bill was considered under suspension of the rules, thereby requiring a two-thirds majority of those present and voting (282 in this case) for passage. *(Vote 13, p. 779)*

14. IMMIGRATION POLICY

Passage of a bill to allow legal status for some undocumented children of illegal immigrants.

Although the legislation was stripped down from a more ambitious proposal to overhaul federal immigration policy, in order to strengthen its prospects in the Senate, passage made it the first significant immigration-related bill to advance in the House in several years.

The measure, known as the DREAM Act, would have applied to adults younger than thirty who immigrated illegally to the United States before turning sixteen and who had been in the country for at least five years. It would have granted conditional legal status—and after ten years, permanent residency—to qualifying young adults who completed at least two years of college or military service. Under the bill, those permanent residents would have been eligible to apply for naturalization after three years.

The nearly party-line vote reflected the deep partisan divisions over immigration policy in general and the bill specifically. Even though Democrats won the vote, it was for naught as the Senate rejected cloture on the bill in the last few days of the 111th Congress.

House passed HR 5281 on December 8, 216–198: R 8–160; D 208–38. *(Vote 14, p. 779)*

15. TAX CUT EXTENSIONS

Clearing legislation extending income tax cuts for two years and setting a new rate and threshold for estate taxes.

The evolution of the tax-cut legislation and the subsequent votes on it were a measure of the degree to which lawmakers had come to accept the postelection political dynamics. Many did, but some, particularly House liberals, did not.

The deal came about after the White House, recognizing Republican ascendancy, negotiated directly with Senate Republicans. Liberal Democrats in both chambers were left out of the talks, making them as angry about the process as they were about the substance.

In the resulting deal, Democrats were asked to give up their hopes for an end to the tax cuts for the wealthiest Americans and to swallow a reinstatement of the estate tax at GOP-preferred rates of 35 percent on estates of more than $5 million.

Republicans, on the other hand, were being asked to agree with their leaders on several concessions to the White House, including a one-year payroll tax cut and a thirteen-month extension of federal unemployment benefits. Neither of those provisions was offset by spending cuts, as many Republicans had demanded.

For members in the liberal and conservative wings of their respective parties, the vote was a reflection of their willingness to move away from their ideological base and come to the center. Liberals in the House erupted in anger over the deal, and Democrats even approved a caucus resolution December 9 disapproving of it, threatening to scuttle the package when it eventually came to the floor for a final vote.

They focused their anger on the estate tax provisions and the extension of lower income tax rates for wealthy taxpayers.

The Senate passed the package overwhelmingly December 15. The House cleared the measure December 17, just after midnight, ending a frenzied month of postelection bargaining and averting a substantial rise in tax rates that would have taken effect January 1.

House cleared HR 4853 on December 17, 277–148: R 138–36; D 139–112. *(Vote 15, p. 779)*

1. HR 3590. Health Care Overhaul. Spratt, D-S.C., motion to concur in the Senate amendment to the bill to overhaul the nation's health insurance system and require most individuals to buy health insurance by 2014. The legislation created a system of private insurance plans and state-run marketplaces for the insurance, and imposed fines on persons who did not obtain coverage. Employers with more than fifty workers were required to provide coverage or pay a fine if any employee obtained a subsidized plan on the exchange. With some exceptions, the legislation barred use of federal funds to pay for abortions in the new programs. Insurance companies were prohibited from denying coverage based on pre-existing medical conditions beginning in 2014 and could not drop coverage of people who become ill. Motion agreed to, clearing the bill for the president, 219–212: R 0–178; D 219–34. A "yea" was a vote in support of the president's position. March 21, 2010.

2. HR 5136. Funding for F-35 Alternative Engine. Pingree, D-Maine, amendment to strike funds authorized for the F-35 alternative-engine program, contained in the fiscal 2011 defense authorization bill. Rejected 193–231: R 57–116; D 136–115. A "yea" was a vote in support of the president's position. May 27, 2010.

3. HR 5136. Repeal of "Don't Ask, Don't Tell" Policy. Murphy, D-Pa., amendment to the fiscal 2011 defense authorization bill to repeal the "don't ask, don't tell" policy on military service by openly gay men and women, to take effect sixty days after certification by the Secretary of Defense, chair of the Joint Chiefs, and the president that repeal is consistent with the standards of military readiness, military effectiveness, unit cohesion, and recruiting. Adopted 234–194: R 5–168; D 229–26. A "yea" was a vote in support of the president's position. May 27, 2010.

4. HR 5136. Guantánamo Base Closing. Forbes, R-Va., motion to recommit the legislation, the fiscal 2011 defense authorization bill, to the Armed Services Committee with instructions that it be reported back immediately with an amendment to prohibit the use of funds authorized in the bill to transfer or release individuals detained at the U.S. facility at Guantánamo Bay, Cuba, into the United States or its territories. Motion agreed to 282–131: R 168–1; D 114–130. A "nay" was a vote in support of the president's position. May 28, 2010.

5. HR 5175. Campaign Finance Disclosure. Passage of the bill to establish new reporting requirements for corporations, unions, and other interest groups for campaign-related activities, including prohibiting corporations that are foreign-controlled or have received a specified amount of government assistance from making expenditures in political campaigns. Exempted from some identification disclosure rules certain charitable organizations as well as organizations at least ten years old, have at least 500,000 dues-paying members, have members in each state, and receive no more than 15 percent of their funding from corporations and unions. Passed 219–206: R 2–170; D 217–36. A "yea" was a vote in support of the president's position. June 24, 2010.

6. HR 4173. Financial regulatory overhaul. Adoption of the conference report on the bill to overhaul the regulation of the financial services industry. The measure created a new regulatory mechanism to assess risks posed by large financial institutions and facilitate the orderly dissolution of failing firms that posed a threat to the economy. The bill also created a new federal agency to oversee consumer financial products, brought the derivatives market under broadened federal regulation, and gave company shareholders and regulators a larger say on executive-pay packages. Adopted (and sent to the Senate) 237–192: R 3–173; D 234–19. A "yea" was a vote in support of the president's position. June 30, 2010.

7. HR 4899. Funding for Afghanistan War. Lee, D-Calif., amendment to limit the use of military funding for Afghanistan to activities relating to the safe withdrawal of U.S. troops and protection of civilian and military personnel in the country. Motion rejected 100–321: R 7–164; D 93–157. A "nay" was a vote in support of the president's position. July 1, 2010.

8. HR 4899. Supplemental Appropriations. Obey, D-Wis., motion to concur in the Senate amendment to the bill to provide $58.8 billion in supplemental funds for fiscal 2010. The total included $33.5 billion for the Defense Department for the addition of 30,000 troops in Afghanistan, $3.6 billion for Afghan and Iraqi security forces, and $4.9 billion for Defense Department procurement. It also provided $162 million in funds related to the oil spill in the Gulf of Mexico resulting from a blowout on a drilling rig known as Deepwater Horizon. It also provided $5.1 billion for the Federal Emergency Management Agency to pay for costs of past disasters and $13.4 billion in mandatory funds to compensate Vietnam War veterans exposed to Agent Orange. Motion agreed to (clearing the bill for the president) 308–114: R 160–12; D 148–102. The action was considered under suspension of the rules, which requires a two-thirds majority of those present and voting (282 in this case) for approval. A "yea" was a vote in support of the president's position. July 27, 2010.

9. HR 3534. Offshore Oil Drilling Regulations. Passage of the bill to repeal the current $75 million cap on liability for offshore oil spills, and to abolish the agency formerly known as the Minerals Management Service in the Interior Department and assign its responsibilities to three new agencies in the department. The bill created numerous new safety regulations for leases for offshore oil and gas development, including features designed to prevent well blowouts. It also required some holders of leases to renegotiate royalty payments disputed by industry. The legislation prevented oil companies from shifting oil spill cleanup costs to taxpayers in the event one of its subsidiaries declared bankruptcy. Passed 209–193: R 2–154; D 207–39. July 30, 2010.

10. HR 1586. Medicaid and Education Assistance. Obey, D-Wis., motion to concur in a Senate amendment to the bill providing $16.1 billion to extend increased Medicaid assistance to states and $10 billion in funding for states to create or retain teachers' jobs, with costs offset by changing foreign tax provisions, ending increased food stamp benefits beginning in April 2014, and rescinding previously enacted spending. Motion agreed to (clearing the bill for the president) 247–161: R 2–158; D 245–3. A "yea" was a vote in support of the president's position. August 10, 2010.

11. HR 2378. Chinese Currency Valuation. Passage of the bill to permit the Commerce Department to impose duties on imported goods if it finds that a foreign government has undervalued its currency. Passed 348–79: R 99–74; D 249–5. September 29, 2010.

12. HR 2701. Intelligence Authorization. Reyes, D-Texas, motion to concur in the Senate amendment to the bill to authorize intelligence programs for fiscal 2010. The bill expanded disclosure requirements and congressional oversight of intelligence agencies and required the director of national intelligence to allow access for Government Accountability Office personnel to audit certain intelligence agencies. Motion agreed to (clearing the bill for the president) 244–181: R 1–172; D 243–9. September 29, 2010.

13. S 3729. NASA Authorization. Gordon, D-Tenn., motion to suspend the rules and pass the bill to authorize $58.4 billion for the National Aeronautics and Space Administration (NASA) for fiscal 2011 through 2013, including $1.6 billion for commercial crew and cargo systems development, $6.9 billion for a NASA space launch system, $3.9 billion for a crew vehicle, and $1.6 billion for space shuttle flight operations. The bill allowed for one additional shuttle flight, supported using the International Space Station through at least 2020, and authorized $8.9 billion for the station. Motion agreed to (clearing the bill for the president) 304–118: R 119–54; D 185–64. A two-thirds majority of those present and voting (282 in this case) is required for passage under suspension of the rules. September 29, 2010.

14. **HR 5281. Immigration Policy.** Conyers, D-Mich., motion to concur in Senate amendments to the bill with a House amendment adding language to allow the Homeland Security Department to grant conditional nonimmigrant status to undocumented children of illegal immigrants if they met certain requirements, including having been in the United States continuously for more than five years, been younger than sixteen when they entered the country, and been admitted to a U.S. college or university or enlisted in the military. Provided that qualifying individuals would be eligible to apply for permanent legal status after ten years. Motion agreed to 216–198: R 8–160; D 208–38. A "yea" was a vote in support of the president's position. December 8, 2010.

15. **HR 4853. Tax Cut Extensions.** Levin, D-Mich., motion to concur in the Senate amendment to extend 2001 and 2003 tax reductions for taxpayers for two years, revive the lapsed estate tax, and set the tax rate at 35 percent on the value of estates in excess of $5 million for 2011 and 2012. The legislation also continued expanded unemployment insurance benefits for thirteen months and cut the employee portion of the Social Security tax by 2 percentage points. Motion agreed to (clearing the bill for the president) 277–148: R 138–36; D 139–112. A "yea" was a vote in support of the president's position. December 17, 2010.

KEY

Republican Democrat **Independent**

Y	Voted for (yea)	–	Announced against
#	Paired for	P	Voted "present"
+	Announced for	C	Voted "present" to avoid possible conflict of interest
N	Voted against (nay)	?	Did not vote or otherwise make a position known
X	Paired against		

House Key Votes	1	2	3	4	5	6	7	8	9	10	11	12	13	14	15
ALABAMA															
1 *Bonner*	N	N	N	Y	N	N	N	Y	N	N	Y	N	Y	N	Y
2 Bright	N	N	N	Y	N	N	N	Y	N	N	Y	Y	Y	N	Y
3 *Rogers*	N	N	N	Y	N	N	N	Y	N	N	Y	N	Y	N	N
4 *Aderholt*	N	N	N	Y	N	N	N	Y	N	N	Y	N	Y	N	Y
5 *Griffith*	N	Y	N	Y	N	N	?	Y	?	N	Y	N	Y	?	Y
6 *Bachus*	N	N	N	Y	N	N	N	Y	N	N	Y	N	Y	N	Y
7 Davis	N	?	?	?	Y	Y	N	Y	N	Y	Y	Y	Y	Y	Y
ALASKA															
AL *Young*	N	N	N	Y	N	?	?	Y	N	?	Y	N	N	N	Y
ARIZONA															
1 Kirkpatrick	Y	Y	Y	Y	Y	N	N	Y	N	Y	Y	Y	Y	?	Y
2 *Franks*	N	N	N	Y	N	N	N	Y	N	N	N	N	Y	N	N
3 *Shadegg*	N	Y	N	Y	N	N	N	Y	?	N	N	N	Y	N	N
4 Pastor	Y	Y	Y	N	Y	Y	Y	Y	Y	Y	Y	Y	Y	Y	Y
5 Mitchell	Y	Y	Y	Y	N	N	N	Y	N	Y	N	Y	Y	Y	Y
6 *Flake*	N	Y	N	Y	N	N	N	N	N	N	N	N	N	N	N
7 Grijalva	Y	Y	Y	N	Y	Y	Y	N	Y	Y	Y	Y	N	Y	N
8 Giffords	Y	Y	Y	Y	Y	Y	N	Y	Y	Y	Y	Y	N	Y	Y
ARKANSAS															
1 Berry	N	Y	N	N	Y	N	N	Y	?	?	Y	Y	N	?	?
2 Snyder	Y	N	Y	N	Y	Y	N	Y	Y	?	N	Y	N	Y	Y
3 *Boozman*	N	N	N	Y	N	N	N	Y	N	N	Y	N	Y	N	Y
4 Ross	N	Y	N	Y	Y	N	N	Y	N	Y	Y	Y	Y	N	Y
CALIFORNIA															
1 Thompson	Y	Y	Y	N	Y	Y	N	N	Y	Y	Y	Y	Y	Y	N
2 *Herger*	N	Y	N	Y	N	N	N	Y	N	N	N	N	N	N	Y
3 *Lungren*	N	N	N	Y	N	N	N	Y	N	?	Y	N	Y	N	Y
4 *McClintock*	N	Y	N	Y	N	N	N	Y	N	N	N	N	Y	N	Y
5 Matsui	Y	Y	Y	N	Y	Y	Y	N	Y	Y	Y	Y	Y	Y	N
6 Woolsey	Y	P	Y	N	Y	+	+	N	Y	Y	Y	Y	N	Y	N
7 Miller, George	Y	Y	Y	N	Y	Y	Y	N	Y	Y	Y	Y	Y	Y	N
8 Pelosi[1]	Y		Y		Y	Y			Y	Y	Y			Y	
9 Lee	Y	Y	Y	N	Y	Y	Y	N	Y	Y	Y	N	N	Y	N
10 Garamendi	Y	N	Y	Y	Y	Y	Y	N	Y	Y	Y	Y	Y	Y	N
11 McNerney	Y	N	Y	Y	Y	Y	N	Y	Y	Y	Y	Y	Y	Y	Y
12 Speier	Y	Y	Y	N	Y	Y	Y	N	Y	?	Y	Y	Y	Y	N
13 Stark	Y	Y	Y	N	Y	Y	Y	N	Y	Y	Y	N	N	Y	N
14 Eshoo	Y	Y	Y	N	Y	Y	N	N	Y	Y	Y	Y	Y	Y	N
15 Honda	Y	Y	Y	N	Y	Y	Y	N	Y	Y	Y	Y	Y	Y	N
16 Lofgren	Y	Y	Y	N	Y	Y	Y	N	Y	Y	Y	Y	Y	Y	N
17 Farr	Y	Y	Y	N	Y	Y	Y	N	Y	Y	Y	Y	Y	Y	N
18 Cardoza	Y	Y	Y	Y	Y	Y	N	Y	Y	Y	Y	Y	Y	Y	Y
19 *Radanovich*	N	N	N	Y	N	N	?	Y	?	?	?	?	?	?	Y
20 Costa	Y	Y	Y	Y	Y	Y	N	Y	N	Y	Y	Y	Y	Y	Y
21 *Nunes*	N	N	N	Y	N	N	N	Y	?	N	N	N	Y	N	Y
22 *McCarthy*	N	N	N	Y	N	N	N	Y	?	N	N	N	Y	N	Y
23 Capps	Y	Y	Y	N	Y	Y	N	Y	Y	Y	Y	Y	Y	Y	Y
24 *Gallegly*	N	N	N	Y	N	N	N	Y	N	N	Y	N	Y	N	Y
25 *McKeon*	N	N	N	Y	N	N	N	Y	?	N	Y	N	Y	N	Y
26 *Dreier*	N	N	N	Y	N	N	N	Y	N	N	N	N	Y	N	Y
27 Sherman	Y	Y	Y	N	Y	Y	N	Y	Y	Y	Y	Y	Y	Y	Y
28 Berman	Y	Y	Y	?	Y	Y	N	Y	Y	Y	Y	Y	N	Y	Y
29 Schiff	Y	Y	Y	N	Y	Y	N	Y	Y	Y	Y	Y	Y	?	Y
30 Waxman	Y	Y	Y	N	Y	Y	Y	N	Y	Y	Y	N	N	Y	Y
31 Becerra	Y	Y	Y	N	Y	Y	Y	N	Y	Y	Y	Y	Y	Y	N
32 Chu	Y	N	Y	N	Y	Y	Y	N	Y	Y	Y	Y	Y	Y	N
33 Watson	Y	N	Y	N	Y	Y	?	?	?	Y	Y	N	Y	Y	N
34 Roybal-Allard	Y	N	Y	N	Y	Y	N	Y	Y	Y	Y	Y	Y	Y	N
35 Waters	Y	P	Y	N	N	Y	Y	N	Y	Y	Y	Y	Y	Y	N
36 Harman	Y	Y	Y	N	Y	Y	Y	Y	Y	Y	Y	Y	Y	Y	Y
37 Richardson	Y	N	Y	Y	Y	Y	Y	N	Y	Y	Y	?	?	Y	Y
38 Napolitano	Y	Y	Y	N	Y	Y	Y	N	Y	Y	Y	Y	Y	Y	N
39 Sanchez, Linda	Y	Y	Y	N	Y	Y	Y	N	Y	Y	Y	Y	Y	Y	N
40 *Royce*	N	N	N	Y	N	N	N	Y	N	N	Y	N	Y	N	Y
41 *Lewis*	N	N	N	Y	N	N	N	Y	N	N	N	N	Y	N	Y
42 *Miller, Gary*	N	N	N	Y	N	N	N	Y	P	?	N	N	Y	N	Y
43 Baca	Y	N	Y	Y	Y	Y	N	Y	Y	Y	Y	Y	Y	Y	Y
44 *Calvert*	N	N	N	Y	N	N	N	Y	N	N	Y	N	Y	N	Y
45 *Bono Mack*	N	N	N	Y	N	N	N	Y	N	N	N	N	Y	N	Y
46 *Rohrabacher*	N	Y	N	Y	N	N	Y	N	N	N	Y	N	Y	N	Y
47 Sanchez, Loretta	Y	N	Y	N	Y	Y	Y	N	Y	Y	Y	Y	Y	Y	N
48 *Campbell*	N	Y	N	Y	N	N	Y	N	?	N	N	N	Y	N	N
49 *Issa*	N	N	N	Y	N	N	N	Y	N	N	N	N	Y	N	Y
50 *Bilbray*	N	N	N	Y	N	N	N	Y	N	N	Y	N	N	?	Y
51 Filner	Y	Y	Y	N	Y	Y	Y	N	Y	Y	Y	Y	Y	Y	N
52 *Hunter*	N	N	N	Y	N	N	N	Y	N	N	Y	N	Y	N	Y
53 Davis	Y	N	Y	N	Y	Y	N	Y	Y	Y	Y	Y	Y	Y	Y
COLORADO															
1 DeGette	Y	Y	Y	N	Y	Y	Y	Y	Y	?	Y	Y	Y	Y	N
2 Polis	Y	Y	Y	N	Y	Y	Y	N	Y	Y	N	Y	Y	Y	Y
3 Salazar	Y	Y	Y	Y	Y	Y	N	Y	N	Y	Y	Y	Y	Y	Y
4 Markey	Y	Y	Y	Y	Y	Y	N	Y	Y	Y	Y	Y	Y	Y	Y
5 *Lamborn*	N	N	N	Y	N	N	N	Y	N	N	N	N	Y	N	N
6 *Coffman*	N	Y	N	Y	N	N	N	Y	N	N	Y	N	Y	N	Y
7 Perlmutter	Y	Y	Y	N	Y	Y	N	Y	?	Y	Y	Y	Y	Y	N
CONNECTICUT															
1 Larson	Y	Y	Y	N	Y	Y	Y	N	Y	Y	Y	Y	Y	Y	N
2 Courtney	Y	Y	Y	Y	Y	Y	N	Y	Y	Y	Y	Y	N	Y	Y
3 DeLauro	Y	Y	Y	N	Y	Y	Y	N	Y	Y	Y	Y	Y	Y	N
4 Himes	Y	Y	Y	N	Y	Y	N	Y	+	Y	Y	Y	Y	Y	Y
5 Murphy	Y	Y	Y	N	Y	Y	N	N	Y	Y	Y	Y	Y	Y	N
DELAWARE															
AL *Castle*	N	N	N	Y	Y	Y	N	Y	N	Y	Y	N	N	Y	Y
FLORIDA															
1 *Miller*	N	Y	N	Y	N	N	N	Y	N	N	Y	N	Y	N	Y
2 Boyd	Y	Y	Y	Y	N	Y	N	Y	Y	Y	Y	Y	Y	Y	N
3 Brown	Y	Y	Y	Y	Y	Y	N	N	Y	Y	Y	Y	Y	Y	N
4 *Crenshaw*	N	N	N	Y	N	N	N	Y	N	N	Y	N	Y	N	Y
5 *Brown-Waite*	N	?	?	?	N	N	N	Y	N	N	Y	N	Y	N	Y
6 *Stearns*	N	Y	N	Y	N	N	N	Y	N	N	Y	N	Y	N	Y
7 *Mica*	N	N	N	Y	N	N	N	Y	N	N	Y	N	Y	N	Y
8 Grayson	Y	Y	Y	Y	Y	Y	Y	–	Y	Y	Y	Y	Y	Y	N
9 *Bilirakis*	N	N	N	Y	N	N	N	Y	N	N	Y	N	Y	N	N
10 *Young*	N	N	N	Y	N	N	N	?	?	?	?	?	?	N	?
11 Castor	Y	Y	Y	Y	Y	Y	N	N	Y	Y	Y	Y	Y	Y	Y
12 *Putnam*	N	N	N	Y	N	N	N	Y	N	N	Y	N	Y	N	Y
13 *Buchanan*	N	Y	N	Y	N	N	N	Y	N	?	N	N	Y	N	Y
14 *Mack*	N	Y	N	Y	N	N	N	Y	N	N	N	N	N	N	N
15 *Posey*	N	Y	N	Y	N	N	N	Y	N	N	Y	N	Y	N	Y
16 *Rooney*	N	Y	N	Y	N	N	N	Y	N	?	Y	N	Y	N	Y
17 Meek	Y	Y	Y	Y	Y	Y	N	?	Y	?	Y	Y	Y	Y	Y
18 *Ros-Lehtinen*	N	N	Y	Y	N	N	N	Y	N	N	Y	N	Y	Y	Y
19 Deutch[2]		Y	Y	N	Y	Y	N	Y	Y	Y	Y	Y	Y	Y	Y
20 Wasserman Schultz	Y	N	Y	N	Y	Y	N	Y	Y	Y	Y	Y	Y	Y	Y
21 *Diaz-Balart, L.*	N	N	N	Y	N	N	N	Y	N	?	Y	N	Y	Y	Y
22 Klein	Y	Y	Y	Y	Y	Y	N	Y	Y	Y	Y	Y	Y	Y	Y
23 Hastings	Y	?	?	?	N	Y	Y	N	Y	Y	Y	Y	Y	Y	N
24 Kosmas	Y	Y	Y	Y	Y	Y	N	Y	Y	Y	Y	Y	Y	Y	Y
25 *Diaz-Balart, M.*	N	N	N	Y	N	N	N	Y	N	N	Y	N	Y	Y	Y

[1]The Speaker votes only at her discretion.

[2]Rep. Ted Deutch, D-Fla., was sworn in April 15, 2010, to fill the seat vacated by the January 3 resignation of Democrat Robert Wexler. The first key vote for which Deutch was eligible was vote 2; Wexler did not cast a key vote in 2010.

KEY

Republican Democrat **Independent**

Y	Voted for (yea)	–	Announced against
#	Paired for	P	Voted "present"
+	Announced for	C	Voted "present" to avoid possible conflict of interest
N	Voted against (nay)		
X	Paired against	?	Did not vote or otherwise make a position known

House Key Votes	1	2	3	4	5	6	7	8	9	10	11	12	13	14	15
GEORGIA															
1 *Kingston*	N	N	N	Y	N	N	N	Y	N	N	N	N	N	N	N
2 Bishop	Y	Y	N	Y	N	Y	N	Y	Y	Y	Y	Y	Y	Y	Y
3 *Westmoreland*	N	Y	N	Y	N	N	N	Y	N	N	Y	N	N	N	Y
4 Johnson	Y	Y	Y	Y	Y	Y	N	N	Y	Y	Y	Y	Y	Y	Y
5 Lewis	Y	Y	Y	N	Y	Y	Y	N	Y	Y	Y	Y	N	Y	N
6 *Price*	N	N	N	Y	N	N	N	Y	N	N	N	N	N	N	Y
7 *Linder*	N	Y	N	?	N	N	N	N	?	?	N	N	Y	N	N
8 Marshall	N	N	N	Y	N	Y	N	Y	N	Y	Y	Y	Y	?	Y
9 *Graves*[3]					N	N	N	Y	N	N	N	N	N	N	N
10 *Broun*	N	Y	N	Y	N	N	N	N	N	?	N	N	Y	N	N
11 *Gingrey*	N	Y	N	Y	N	N	N	N	N	?	Y	N	Y	?	N
12 Barrow	N	Y	Y	Y	N	Y	N	Y	Y	Y	Y	Y	N	N	Y
13 Scott	Y	N	Y	N	Y	Y	N	Y	Y	Y	Y	Y	Y	Y	Y
HAWAII															
1 *Djou*[4]		N	Y	Y	N	N	N	Y	N	N	N	Y	Y	Y	Y
2 Hirono	Y	Y	Y	N	Y	Y	Y	N	Y	Y	Y	Y	N	Y	N
IDAHO															
1 Minnick	N	Y	Y	Y	N	Y	N	Y	Y	Y	Y	Y	Y	Y	Y
2 *Simpson*	N	N	N	Y	N	N	N	Y	N	N	Y	N	N	N	N
ILLINOIS															
1 Rush	Y	Y	Y	N	N	Y	Y	N	Y	Y	Y	Y	Y	Y	N
2 Jackson	Y	Y	Y	Y	Y	Y	Y	N	Y	Y	Y	Y	N	Y	N
3 Lipinski	N	N	N	Y	Y	Y	N	Y	Y	Y	Y	Y	Y	N	Y
4 Gutierrez	Y	N	Y	N	Y	Y	Y	N	Y	Y	Y	Y	Y	Y	Y
5 Quigley	Y	Y	Y	N	Y	Y	Y	N	Y	Y	Y	Y	Y	Y	Y
6 *Roskam*	N	N	N	Y	N	N	N	Y	N	?	Y	N	N	N	Y
7 Davis	Y	Y	Y	N	N	Y	Y	N	Y	Y	Y	Y	Y	Y	Y
8 Bean	Y	Y	Y	Y	N	Y	N	Y	Y	Y	Y	Y	N	Y	Y
9 Schakowsky	Y	N	Y	N	Y	Y	Y	N	Y	Y	Y	Y	Y	Y	Y
10 *Kirk*[5]	N	Y	N	Y	N	N	N	Y	N	N	Y	N	Y		
11 Halvorson	Y	N	Y	Y	Y	Y	N	Y	N	Y	Y	Y	Y	Y	Y
12 Costello	Y	N	N	Y	Y	Y	Y	N	Y	Y	Y	Y	Y	N	N
13 *Biggert*	N	N	Y	Y	N	N	N	Y	N	N	Y	N	Y	N	Y
14 Foster	Y	N	Y	Y	Y	Y	N	Y	Y	Y	Y	Y	Y	Y	Y
15 *Johnson*	N	Y	N	Y	N	N	Y	N	Y	N	Y	N	N	N	Y
16 *Manzullo*	N	N	N	Y	N	N	N	Y	N	N	Y	N	Y	N	Y
17 Hare	Y	Y	Y	N	Y	Y	N	Y	Y	Y	Y	Y	Y	Y	Y
18 *Schock*	N	N	N	Y	N	N	N	Y	N	N	Y	N	Y	N	Y
19 *Shimkus*	N	N	N	Y	N	N	N	Y	N	N	Y	N	N	N	Y
INDIANA															
1 Visclosky	Y	N	Y	Y	+	Y	N	Y	Y	Y	Y	Y	N	N	N
2 Donnelly	Y	N	N	Y	N	Y	N	Y	N	Y	Y	Y	Y	N	Y
3 *Souder*[6]	N														
Stutzman[6]														–	Y
4 *Buyer*	N	N	N	Y	N	N	N	Y	?	N	?	N	Y	?	Y
5 *Burton*	N	N	N	Y	N	N	N	Y	N	N	Y	N	Y	N	Y
6 *Pence*	N	N	N	Y	–	N	N	Y	N	N	N	N	Y	N	N
7 Carson	Y	N	Y	Y	Y	Y	N	?	Y	Y	Y	Y	Y	Y	Y
8 Ellsworth	Y	N	Y	Y	Y	Y	N	Y	N	Y	Y	Y	Y	N	Y
9 Hill	Y	N	Y	Y	N	Y	N	Y	Y	Y	Y	Y	N	Y	Y
IOWA															
1 Braley	Y	Y	Y	N	Y	Y	N	Y	Y	Y	Y	Y	Y	Y	N
2 Loebsack	Y	N	Y	N	Y	Y	N	Y	Y	Y	Y	Y	Y	Y	Y
3 Boswell	Y	N	Y	Y	Y	Y	N	Y	Y	Y	Y	Y	N	Y	Y
4 *Latham*	N	N	N	Y	N	N	N	Y	N	N	N	N	Y	N	Y
5 *King*	N	N	N	Y	N	N	N	Y	N	N	N	N	Y	N	N
KANSAS															
1 *Moran*	N	Y	N	Y	N	N	N	?	?	N	Y	N	Y	N	N
2 *Jenkins*	N	Y	N	Y	N	N	N	Y	N	N	N	N	Y	N	Y
3 Moore	Y	N	Y	Y	Y	Y	N	Y	Y	Y	Y	Y	Y	Y	Y
4 *Tiahrt*	N	Y	N	Y	N	N	N	?	?	N	N	N	Y	N	Y
KENTUCKY															
1 *Whitfield*	N	N	N	Y	N	N	N	Y	N	N	Y	N	Y	N	Y
2 *Guthrie*	N	N	N	Y	N	N	N	Y	N	N	Y	N	Y	N	Y
3 Yarmuth	Y	N	Y	N	Y	Y	Y	Y	Y	Y	Y	Y	N	Y	N
4 *Davis*	N	–	–	+	N	N	N	Y	–	N	Y	N	Y	N	Y
5 *Rogers*	N	N	N	Y	N	N	N	Y	N	N	Y	N	Y	N	Y
6 Chandler	N	N	Y	Y	Y	N	N	Y	Y	Y	Y	Y	N	N	Y
LOUISIANA															
1 *Scalise*	N	N	N	Y	N	N	N	Y	N	N	N	N	Y	N	Y
2 Cao	N	N	Y	Y	Y	Y	N	Y	N	Y	Y	N	Y	Y	Y
3 Melancon	N	?	?	?	Y	Y	N	Y	Y	Y	Y	Y	Y	Y	N
4 *Fleming*	N	N	N	Y	N	N	N	Y	N	N	N	N	Y	N	N
5 *Alexander*	N	N	N	Y	N	N	N	Y	N	N	N	N	Y	N	Y
6 *Cassidy*	N	Y	N	Y	N	N	N	Y	N	N	Y	N	Y	N	Y
7 *Boustany*	N	Y	N	Y	N	N	N	Y	N	?	N	N	Y	N	Y
MAINE															
1 Pingree	Y	Y	Y	N	Y	Y	Y	N	Y	Y	Y	Y	N	Y	N
2 Michaud	Y	Y	Y	N	Y	Y	Y	N	Y	Y	Y	Y	N	Y	N
MARYLAND															
1 Kratovil	N	Y	Y	Y	N	Y	N	Y	Y	Y	Y	Y	Y	N	Y
2 Ruppersberger	Y	N	Y	Y	Y	Y	N	Y	Y	Y	Y	Y	Y	Y	Y
3 Sarbanes	Y	N	Y	N	Y	Y	N	Y	Y	Y	Y	Y	Y	Y	Y
4 Edwards	Y	Y	Y	N	N	Y	Y	N	Y	Y	Y	Y	N	Y	N
5 Hoyer	Y	Y	Y	N	Y	Y	N	Y	Y	Y	Y	Y	Y	Y	Y
6 *Bartlett*	N	N	N	Y	N	N	N	Y	N	N	N	N	Y	N	Y
7 Cummings	Y	Y	Y	N	Y	Y	Y	N	Y	Y	Y	Y	Y	Y	N
8 Van Hollen	Y	Y	Y	N	Y	Y	N	Y	Y	Y	Y	Y	Y	Y	N
MASSACHUSETTS															
1 Olver	Y	Y	Y	N	Y	Y	Y	N	Y	Y	Y	Y	Y	Y	N
2 Neal	Y	Y	Y	N	Y	Y	Y	N	Y	Y	Y	Y	Y	Y	N
3 McGovern	Y	N	Y	N	Y	Y	Y	N	Y	Y	Y	Y	N	Y	N
4 Frank	Y	N	Y	N	Y	Y	Y	N	Y	Y	Y	Y	N	Y	N
5 Tsongas	Y	N	Y	N	Y	Y	Y	N	Y	Y	Y	Y	Y	Y	Y
6 Tierney	Y	N	Y	N	Y	Y	Y	N	Y	Y	Y	Y	N	Y	N
7 Markey	Y	N	Y	N	Y	Y	Y	N	Y	Y	Y	Y	Y	Y	N
8 Capuano	Y	N	Y	N	Y	Y	Y	N	Y	Y	Y	N	N	Y	N
9 Lynch	N	N	Y	Y	Y	Y	N	Y	Y	Y	Y	Y	N	Y	N
10 Delahunt	Y	N	Y	?	Y	Y	Y	N	?	Y	?	?	?	?	Y
MICHIGAN															
1 Stupak	Y	Y	Y	–	Y	Y	Y	N	Y	Y	Y	Y	Y	N	N
2 *Hoekstra*	N	Y	N	Y	?	N	?	Y	?	N	Y	N	N	N	N
3 *Ehlers*	N	N	N	Y	N	N	N	N	Y	N	Y	N	N	Y	Y
4 *Camp*	N	Y	N	Y	N	N	N	Y	N	N	Y	N	N	N	Y
5 Kildee	Y	N	Y	N	Y	Y	N	Y	Y	Y	Y	Y	Y	Y	Y
6 *Upton*	N	Y	N	Y	N	N	N	Y	N	N	Y	N	N	N	Y
7 Schauer	Y	N	Y	Y	Y	Y	N	Y	Y	Y	Y	Y	Y	Y	Y
8 *Rogers*	N	N	N	Y	N	N	N	Y	?	N	Y	N	N	N	Y

[3]Rep. Tom Graves, R-Ga., was sworn in June 14, 2010, to fill the seat vacated by Republican Nathan Deal, who resigned March 21 to run for governor. The first key vote for which Graves was eligible was vote 5; Deal did not cast a key vote in 2010.

[4]Rep. Charles K. Djou, R-Hawaii, was sworn in May 25 to fill the seat vacated by Democrat Neil Abercrombie, who resigned February 28 to run for governor. The first key vote for which Djou was eligible was vote 2; Abercrombie did not cast a key vote in 2010.

[5]Rep. Mark Steven Kirk, R-Ill., resigned November 29, 2010, to assume the Senate seat he won in a November 2 special election. The last key vote for which Kirk was eligible was vote 13.

[6]Rep. Marlin Stutzman, R-Ind., was sworn in November 16, 2010, to fill the vacancy created by the May 21 resignation of Republican Mark Souder. The first key vote for which Stutzman was eligible was vote 14; the last key vote for which Souder was eligible was vote 1.

House Key Votes	1	2	3	4	5	6	7	8	9	10	11	12	13	14	15
9 Peters	Y	N	Y	Y	Y	Y	N	Y	Y	Y	Y	Y	Y	Y	Y
10 *Miller*	N	N	N	Y	N	N	N	Y	N	N	Y	N	N	N	Y
11 *McCotter*	N	N	N	Y	N	N	N	Y	N	N	Y	N	N	N	N
12 Levin	Y	N	Y	N	Y	Y	N	Y	Y	Y	Y	Y	Y	Y	Y
13 Kilpatrick	Y	N	Y	N	N	Y	N	N	+	Y	Y	Y	Y	?	N
14 Conyers	Y	Y	Y	N	Y	Y	?	N	Y	Y	Y	Y	N	Y	N
15 Dingell	Y	N	Y	N	Y	Y	N	Y	Y	Y	Y	Y	Y	Y	Y
MINNESOTA															
1 Walz	Y	Y	Y	Y	Y	Y	N	Y	Y	Y	Y	Y	N	Y	Y
2 *Kline*	N	N	N	Y	N	N	N	Y	N	N	N	N	Y	N	Y
3 *Paulsen*	N	N	N	Y	N	N	N	Y	N	N	N	N	N	N	Y
4 McCollum	Y	Y	Y	N	Y	Y	Y	N	Y	Y	Y	Y	Y	Y	N
5 Ellison	Y	Y	Y	N	Y	Y	Y	N	Y	Y	Y	Y	Y	Y	N
6 *Bachmann*	N	N	N	Y	N	N	N	Y	N	N	N	N	Y	N	N
7 Peterson	N	Y	N	Y	N	Y	N	Y	N	Y	Y	Y	Y	N	Y
8 Oberstar	Y	Y	Y	N	Y	Y	Y	N	Y	Y	Y	Y	N	Y	Y
MISSISSIPPI															
1 Childers	N	N	N	Y	N	N	N	Y	N	Y	Y	Y	N	N	Y
2 Thompson	Y	N	Y	N	N	Y	Y	N	Y	Y	Y	Y	N	Y	N
3 *Harper*	N	N	N	Y	N	N	N	Y	N	N	Y	N	Y	N	Y
4 Taylor	N	N	N	Y	N	?	N	Y	Y	N	Y	Y	Y	N	N
MISSOURI															
1 Clay	Y	N	Y	N	Y	Y	Y	N	Y	Y	Y	Y	N	Y	Y
2 *Akin*	N	N	N	Y	N	N	N	+	–	N	Y	N	Y	N	Y
3 Carnahan	Y	Y	Y	Y	Y	Y	N	Y	Y	Y	Y	Y	Y	Y	Y
4 Skelton	N	N	N	Y	Y	N	N	Y	N	Y	Y	Y	Y	Y	Y
5 Cleaver	Y	N	Y	N	Y	Y	Y	N	Y	Y	Y	Y	Y	Y	N
6 *Graves*	N	–	–	+	N	N	N	+	N	N	Y	?	?	N	Y
7 *Blunt*	N	N	N	Y	?	N	N	Y	?	?	?	?	?	?	Y
8 *Emerson*	N	N	N	Y	N	N	N	Y	N	N	Y	N	N	N	Y
9 *Luetkemeyer*	N	N	N	Y	N	N	N	Y	N	N	Y	N	Y	N	Y
MONTANA															
AL *Rehberg*	N	Y	N	Y	N	N	N	Y	N	N	Y	N	Y	N	N
NEBRASKA															
1 *Fortenberry*	N	N	N	Y	N	N	N	Y	N	N	Y	N	Y	N	N
2 *Terry*	N	N	N	Y	N	N	N	Y	N	N	Y	N	N	N	Y
3 *Smith*	N	N	N	Y	N	N	N	Y	N	N	N	N	Y	N	Y
NEVADA															
1 Berkley	Y	Y	Y	Y	Y	Y	N	Y	Y	Y	Y	Y	Y	Y	Y
2 *Heller*	N	N	N	Y	N	N	N	+	N	N	N	N	N	N	Y
3 Titus	Y	Y	Y	Y	Y	Y	N	Y	N	Y	Y	Y	Y	Y	Y
NEW HAMPSHIRE															
1 Shea-Porter	Y	N	Y	Y	Y	Y	N	N	Y	Y	Y	Y	N	Y	N
2 Hodes	Y	Y	Y	Y	Y	Y	N	Y	Y	Y	Y	Y	N	Y	Y
NEW JERSEY															
1 Andrews	Y	N	Y	Y	Y	Y	N	Y	Y	Y	Y	Y	N	Y	Y
2 *LoBiondo*	N	N	N	Y	N	N	N	Y	N	N	Y	N	Y	N	Y
3 Adler	N	N	Y	Y	Y	Y	N	Y	Y	Y	Y	Y	N	Y	Y
4 *Smith*	N	N	N	Y	N	N	N	Y	N	N	Y	N	Y	N	Y
5 *Garrett*	N	Y	N	Y	N	N	N	Y	N	N	N	N	N	N	N
6 Pallone	Y	Y	Y	N	Y	Y	Y	N	Y	Y	Y	Y	Y	Y	Y
7 *Lance*	N	Y	N	Y	N	N	N	Y	N	N	N	N	N	N	Y
8 Pascrell	Y	Y	Y	N	Y	Y	N	Y	Y	Y	Y	Y	Y	Y	Y
9 Rothman	Y	N	Y	N	?	Y	N	Y	Y	Y	Y	Y	Y	Y	Y
10 Payne	Y	N	Y	N	N	Y	Y	N	Y	Y	Y	Y	N	Y	N
11 *Frelinghuysen*	N	N	N	Y	N	N	N	Y	N	N	N	N	N	N	Y
12 Holt	Y	Y	Y	N	Y	Y	Y	N	Y	Y	Y	Y	N	Y	N
13 Sires	Y	N	Y	Y	Y	Y	Y	Y	Y	Y	Y	Y	Y	Y	Y
NEW MEXICO															
1 Heinrich	Y	Y	Y	N	Y	Y	N	Y	Y	Y	Y	Y	Y	Y	N
2 Teague	N	Y	Y	Y	Y	Y	N	Y	N	Y	Y	Y	Y	Y	Y
3 Luján	Y	Y	Y	N	Y	Y	N	Y	Y	Y	Y	Y	Y	Y	N
NEW YORK															
1 Bishop	Y	Y	Y	Y	Y	Y	N	Y	Y	Y	Y	Y	Y	Y	Y
2 Israel	Y	N	Y	Y	Y	Y	N	Y	Y	Y	Y	Y	N	Y	Y
3 *King*	N	Y	N	?	N	N	N	Y	N	N	N	N	Y	N	Y
4 McCarthy	Y	N	Y	N	N	Y	N	Y	Y	Y	Y	Y	Y	Y	+
5 Ackerman	Y	N	Y	?	Y	Y	N	Y	Y	Y	Y	Y	Y	Y	N
6 Meeks	Y	Y	Y	N	Y	Y	N	N	Y	Y	Y	Y	Y	Y	Y

House Key Votes	1	2	3	4	5	6	7	8	9	10	11	12	13	14	15
7 Crowley	Y	N	Y	N	Y	Y	Y	N	Y	Y	Y	Y	N	Y	Y
8 Nadler	Y	Y	Y	N	Y	Y	Y	N	Y	Y	Y	Y	Y	Y	N
9 Weiner	Y	N	Y	N	Y	Y	Y	N	Y	Y	Y	Y	Y	Y	N
10 Towns	Y	Y	Y	N	Y	Y	Y	N	Y	Y	Y	Y	Y	Y	N
11 Clarke	Y	N	Y	N	N	Y	Y	N	Y	Y	Y	Y	N	Y	N
12 Velázquez	Y	N	Y	N	Y	Y	Y	N	Y	Y	Y	Y	Y	Y	N
13 McMahon	N	N	Y	Y	Y	Y	N	Y	N	Y	Y	Y	+	Y	Y
14 Maloney	Y	Y	Y	Y	Y	Y	Y	N	Y	Y	Y	Y	Y	Y	Y
15 Rangel	Y	N	Y	N	Y	Y	Y	N	Y	Y	Y	Y	Y	Y	N
16 Serrano	Y	N	Y	N	Y	Y	Y	N	Y	Y	Y	Y	Y	Y	N
17 Engel	Y	N	Y	Y	Y	Y	N	Y	Y	Y	Y	Y	N	Y	N
18 Lowey	Y	Y	Y	Y	Y	Y	N	Y	Y	Y	Y	Y	Y	Y	Y
19 Hall	Y	Y	Y	Y	Y	Y	N	Y	Y	Y	Y	Y	Y	Y	Y
20 Murphy	Y	N	Y	Y	Y	Y	N	Y	Y	Y	Y	Y	N	Y	Y
21 Tonko	Y	N	Y	Y	Y	Y	Y	N	Y	Y	Y	Y	Y	Y	N
22 Hinchey	Y	Y	Y	N	Y	Y	Y	N	Y	Y	Y	Y	N	Y	N
23 Owens	Y	Y	Y	Y	N	N	N	Y	Y	Y	Y	Y	N	N	Y
24 Arcuri	N	N	Y	Y	Y	Y	N	Y	Y	Y	Y	Y	Y	N	Y
25 Maffei	Y	N	Y	Y	Y	Y	N	Y	Y	Y	Y	Y	N	Y	Y
26 *Lee*	N	Y	N	Y	N	N	N	Y	N	N	Y	N	Y	N	Y
27 Higgins	Y	N	Y	Y	Y	Y	N	Y	Y	Y	Y	Y	Y	N	Y
28 Slaughter	Y	P	Y	?	Y	Y	Y	N	Y	Y	Y	Y	Y	Y	N
29 *Reed*[7]														N	Y
NORTH CAROLINA															
1 Butterfield	Y	N	Y	N	N	Y	N	Y	Y	Y	Y	Y	N	Y	N
2 Etheridge	Y	N	N	Y	Y	Y	N	Y	Y	Y	Y	Y	?	Y	Y
3 *Jones*	N	Y	N	?	N	Y	Y	N	N	?	Y	N	N	N	Y
4 Price	Y	N	Y	N	Y	Y	N	Y	Y	Y	Y	Y	Y	Y	Y
5 *Foxx*	N	N	N	Y	N	N	N	Y	N	N	Y	N	Y	N	N
6 *Coble*	N	N	N	Y	N	N	N	Y	N	N	Y	N	N	N	Y
7 McIntyre	N	N	N	Y	N	N	N	Y	Y	Y	Y	Y	Y	N	Y
8 Kissell	N	N	Y	Y	Y	Y	N	Y	Y	Y	Y	Y	Y	N	Y
9 *Myrick*	N	N	N	Y	N	N	N	Y	N	N	Y	N	N	N	Y
10 *McHenry*	N	N	N	Y	N	N	N	Y	N	N	Y	N	Y	N	Y
11 Shuler	N	N	N	?	Y	Y	N	Y	Y	Y	Y	Y	Y	N	Y
12 Watt	Y	Y	Y	N	N	Y	Y	N	Y	Y	Y	Y	N	Y	Y
13 Miller	Y	N	Y	Y	Y	Y	N	Y	Y	Y	Y	Y	N	Y	N
NORTH DAKOTA															
AL Pomeroy	Y	N	N	Y	Y	Y	N	Y	N	Y	Y	Y	Y	Y	N
OHIO															
1 Driehaus	Y	N	Y	Y	Y	Y	N	Y	Y	Y	Y	Y	Y	Y	Y
2 *Schmidt*	N	N	N	Y	N	N	N	Y	N	N	N	N	N	N	N
3 *Turner*	N	N	N	Y	N	N	N	Y	N	N	Y	N	N	N	Y
4 *Jordan*	N	N	N	Y	N	N	N	Y	N	N	N	N	N	N	N
5 *Latta*	N	N	N	+	N	N	N	Y	N	N	N	N	N	N	Y
6 Wilson	Y	N	Y	Y	Y	Y	N	Y	N	Y	Y	Y	Y	N	Y
7 *Austria*	N	N	N	Y	N	N	N	Y	N	N	Y	N	N	N	Y
8 *Boehner*	N	N	N	Y	N	N	N	Y	N	N	N	N	N	N	Y
9 Kaptur	Y	N	Y	N	Y	N	N	N	Y	Y	Y	Y	Y	N	N
10 Kucinich	Y	N	Y	N	Y	Y	Y	N	Y	Y	Y	N	N	Y	Y
11 Fudge	Y	N	Y	N	N	Y	Y	N	Y	Y	Y	Y	Y	Y	N
12 *Tiberi*	N	N	N	Y	N	N	N	Y	N	N	Y	N	N	N	Y
13 Sutton	Y	N	Y	Y	Y	Y	N	Y	Y	Y	Y	Y	Y	Y	Y
14 *LaTourette*	N	N	N	Y	N	N	N	Y	N	?	Y	N	N	N	Y
15 Kilroy	Y	N	Y	N	Y	Y	N	Y	Y	Y	Y	Y	N	Y	N
16 Boccieri	Y	N	Y	Y	Y	Y	N	Y	N	Y	Y	Y	Y	N	Y
17 Ryan	Y	N	Y	Y	Y	Y	N	Y	Y	Y	Y	Y	Y	Y	Y
18 Space	N	N	Y	Y	Y	Y	N	Y	N	Y	Y	Y	Y	N	Y
OKLAHOMA															
1 *Sullivan*	N	Y	N	Y	N	N	N	Y	N	N	N	N	N	N	N
2 Boren	N	+	–	+	N	N	N	Y	N	Y	Y	Y	Y	N	Y
3 *Lucas*	N	N	N	Y	N	N	N	Y	N	N	Y	N	Y	N	Y
4 *Cole*	N	Y	N	Y	N	N	N	Y	N	N	Y	N	Y	N	Y
5 *Fallin*	N	N	N	Y	N	N	N	Y	N	N	?	?	?	?	Y
OREGON															
1 Wu	Y	Y	Y	N	Y	Y	N	N	Y	Y	Y	N	N	?	N
2 *Walden*	N	Y	N	Y	N	N	N	Y	N	N	N	N	N	N	Y

[7]Rep. Tom Reed, R-N.Y., was sworn in November 18, 2010, to fill the vacancy created by the March 8 resignation of Democrat Eric Massa. The first key vote for which Reed was eligible was vote 14; Massa did not cast a key vote in 2010.

House Key Votes	1	2	3	4	5	6	7	8	9	10	11	12	13	14	15
3 Blumenauer	Y	Y	Y	N	Y	Y	Y	N	Y	Y	Y	Y	Y	Y	N
4 Defazio	Y	Y	Y	N	Y	Y	Y	N	Y	Y	Y	Y	N	Y	N
5 Schrader	Y	Y	Y	Y	Y	Y	Y	N	Y	Y	Y	Y	Y	N	N
PENNSYLVANIA															
1 Brady	Y	N	Y	N	Y	Y	N	Y	Y	Y	Y	Y	Y	Y	Y
2 Fattah	Y	Y	Y	N	Y	Y	N	N	Y	Y	Y	Y	Y	Y	Y
3 Dahlkemper	Y	N	Y	Y	N	Y	N	Y	Y	Y	Y	Y	N	N	N
4 Altmire	N	Y	Y	Y	Y	Y	N	Y	Y	Y	Y	Y	Y	N	Y
5 *Thompson*	N	Y	N	Y	N	N	N	Y	N	N	Y	N	Y	N	Y
6 *Gerlach*	N	N	N	Y	N	N	N	Y	N	N	Y	N	Y	N	Y
7 Sestak	Y	N	Y	N	Y	Y	N	Y	Y	Y	Y	Y	Y	Y	Y
8 Murphy, P.	Y	Y	Y	Y	Y	Y	N	Y	Y	Y	Y	Y	Y	N	Y
9 *Shuster*	N	N	N	Y	N	N	N	Y	N	N	Y	N	N	N	Y
10 Carney	Y	Y	N	Y	Y	Y	N	Y	?	Y	Y	N	Y	N	Y
11 Kanjorski	Y	N	Y	Y	Y	Y	N	Y	Y	Y	Y	Y	Y	N	N
12 Critz[8]		N	N	Y	N	N	N	Y	Y	Y	Y	Y	Y	N	Y
13 Schwartz	Y	Y	Y	Y	Y	Y	N	Y	Y	Y	Y	Y	Y	Y	Y
14 Doyle	Y	Y	Y	N	Y	Y	Y	N	Y	Y	Y	Y	Y	Y	Y
15 *Dent*	N	Y	N	Y	N	N	N	Y	N	N	Y	N	Y	N	Y
16 *Pitts*	N	N	N	Y	N	N	N	Y	N	N	Y	N	Y	N	Y
17 Holden	N	Y	Y	Y	N	Y	N	Y	N	Y	Y	Y	Y	N	Y
18 *Murphy, T.*	N	N	N	Y	N	N	N	Y	N	N	Y	N	Y	N	Y
19 *Platts*	N	N	N	Y	N	N	N	Y	N	N	Y	N	Y	N	Y
RHODE ISLAND															
1 Kennedy	Y	N	Y	N	Y	Y	Y	Y	Y	Y	Y	Y	Y	Y	Y
2 Langevin	Y	N	Y	Y	Y	Y	N	Y	Y	Y	Y	Y	Y	Y	Y
SOUTH CAROLINA															
1 *Brown*	N	N	N	Y	?	N	N	Y	?	N	Y	N	Y	N	?
2 *Wilson*	N	N	N	Y	N	N	N	Y	N	N	Y	N	N	N	N
3 *Barrett*	N	N	N	Y	?	N	N	Y	–	N	Y	N	N	N	Y
4 *Inglis*	N	N	N	Y	N	N	N	Y	N	N	Y	N	N	Y	Y
5 Spratt	Y	N	N	Y	Y	Y	N	Y	Y	Y	Y	Y	Y	Y	Y
6 Clyburn	Y	N	Y	N	Y	Y	N	Y	Y	Y	Y	Y	Y	Y	N
SOUTH DAKOTA															
AL Herseth Sandlin	N	Y	Y	Y	N	Y	N	Y	N	Y	Y	Y	Y	Y	Y
TENNESSEE															
1 *Roe*	N	Y	N	Y	N	N	N	Y	N	N	Y	N	Y	N	Y
2 *Duncan*	N	Y	N	Y	N	N	Y	N	N	N	Y	N	N	N	Y
3 *Wamp*	N	Y	N	Y	?	?	?	Y	?	?	Y	N	Y	N	?
4 Davis	N	Y	N	Y	N	N	N	Y	N	Y	Y	Y	Y	Y	Y
5 Cooper	Y	Y	Y	Y	Y	N	N	Y	N	N	Y	Y	Y	Y	N
6 Gordon	Y	Y	Y	Y	Y	Y	N	Y	Y	Y	Y	Y	Y	Y	Y
7 *Blackburn*	N	Y	N	Y	N	N	N	Y	N	N	N	N	N	N	Y
8 Tanner	N	Y	N	Y	Y	Y	N	Y	N	?	Y	Y	N	Y	N
9 Cohen	Y	Y	Y	N	Y	Y	Y	N	Y	Y	Y	Y	N	+	N
TEXAS															
1 *Gohmert*	N	Y	N	Y	N	N	N	Y	N	N	N	N	Y	N	N
2 *Poe*	N	N	N	Y	N	N	N	Y	N	N	N	N	Y	N	N
3 *Johnson, S.*	N	Y	N	Y	N	N	?	Y	?	N	N	N	Y	N	Y
4 *Hall*	N	N	N	Y	N	N	N	Y	N	N	N	N	Y	N	Y
5 *Hensarling*	N	Y	N	Y	N	N	N	Y	N	N	N	N	N	N	Y
6 *Barton*	N	Y	N	Y	N	N	N	Y	N	N	N	N	Y	N	N
7 *Culberson*	N	N	N	Y	N	N	N	Y	N	N	N	N	Y	N	Y
8 *Brady*	N	Y	N	Y	N	N	N	Y	N	N	N	N	Y	N	Y
9 Green, A	Y	Y	Y	N	Y	Y	N	Y	Y	Y	Y	Y	Y	Y	Y
10 *McCaul*	N	N	N	Y	N	N	N	Y	N	N	N	N	Y	N	Y
11 *Conaway*	N	N	N	Y	N	N	N	Y	N	N	N	N	Y	N	Y
12 *Granger*	N	Y	N	Y	N	N	N	Y	N	N	N	N	Y	–	+
13 *Thornberry*	N	N	N	Y	N	N	N	Y	N	N	N	N	Y	N	Y
14 *Paul*	N	Y	Y	N	N	N	Y	N	N	N	N	N	N	N	Y
15 Hinojosa	Y	N	Y	Y	Y	Y	Y	Y	N	?	Y	Y	?	Y	Y
16 Reyes	Y	Y	Y	Y	Y	Y	N	Y	?	Y	Y	Y	Y	Y	N
17 Edwards	N	Y	N	Y	Y	N	N	Y	N	Y	Y	Y	Y	Y	Y
18 Jackson Lee	Y	Y	Y	N	Y	Y	Y	N	N	Y	Y	Y	Y	Y	N
19 *Neugebauer*	N	Y	N	Y	N	N	N	Y	N	?	N	N	Y	N	Y
20 Gonzalez	Y	Y	Y	Y	Y	Y	N	Y	N	Y	Y	Y	Y	Y	Y
21 *Smith*	N	N	N	Y	N	N	N	Y	N	N	N	N	Y	N	Y
22 *Olson*	N	N	N	Y	N	N	N	Y	N	N	N	N	Y	N	Y
23 Rodriguez	Y	Y	Y	Y	Y	Y	?	Y	N	Y	Y	Y	Y	Y	N
24 *Marchant*	N	N	N	Y	N	N	N	Y	N	N	N	N	Y	–	–
25 Doggett	Y	Y	Y	N	Y	Y	N	N	Y	Y	Y	Y	Y	Y	N
26 *Burgess*	N	Y	N	Y	N	N	N	Y	N	N	Y	N	Y	N	N
27 Ortiz	Y	Y	N	Y	Y	Y	N	Y	N	Y	Y	Y	Y	Y	N
28 Cuellar	Y	Y	Y	Y	Y	N	N	Y	N	Y	N	Y	Y	Y	Y
29 Green, G	Y	Y	N	Y	Y	Y	N	Y	N	Y	Y	Y	Y	Y	N
30 Johnson, E	Y	Y	Y	N	Y	Y	N	N	Y	Y	Y	Y	Y	Y	?
31 *Carter*	N	N	N	Y	N	N	N	Y	N	N	N	N	Y	N	Y
32 *Sessions*	N	N	N	Y	N	N	N	Y	N	N	N	N	Y	N	Y
UTAH															
1 *Bishop*	N	N	N	Y	N	N	N	Y	N	N	Y	N	Y	N	Y
2 Matheson	N	N	Y	Y	Y	Y	N	Y	N	Y	Y	Y	Y	N	Y
3 *Chaffetz*	N	Y	N	Y	N	N	Y	N	N	N	N	N	Y	N	N
VERMONT															
AL Welch	Y	N	Y	N	Y	Y	Y	N	Y	Y	Y	N	Y	Y	N
VIRGINIA															
1 *Wittman*	N	N	N	Y	N	N	N	Y	N	N	Y	N	Y	N	Y
2 Nye	N	N	Y	Y	N	Y	N	Y	N	Y	Y	Y	Y	N	Y
3 Scott	Y	N	Y	N	Y	Y	Y	N	Y	Y	Y	Y	Y	Y	N
4 *Forbes*	N	N	N	Y	N	N	N	Y	N	N	Y	N	Y	N	N
5 Perriello	Y	N	Y	Y	Y	N	N	Y	N	Y	Y	Y	Y	Y	Y
6 *Goodlatte*	N	N	N	Y	N	N	N	Y	N	N	Y	N	N	N	Y
7 *Cantor*	N	N	N	Y	N	N	N	Y	N	N	N	N	Y	N	Y
8 Moran	Y	N	Y	N	Y	Y	N	N	Y	Y	Y	Y	Y	Y	N
9 Boucher	N	N	N	Y	Y	N	N	Y	N	Y	Y	Y	Y	N	Y
10 *Wolf*	N	N	N	Y	N	N	N	Y	N	N	Y	N	Y	N	N
11 Connolly	Y	N	Y	Y	Y	Y	N	Y	Y	Y	Y	Y	Y	Y	Y
WASHINGTON															
1 Inslee	Y	Y	Y	N	Y	Y	Y	N	Y	Y	Y	Y	Y	Y	N
2 Larsen	Y	N	Y	N	Y	Y	N	Y	Y	Y	N	Y	Y	Y	Y
3 Baird	Y	Y	Y	N	Y	Y	N	Y	Y	Y	Y	Y	N	N	N
4 *Hastings*	N	N	N	Y	N	N	N	Y	N	N	N	N	Y	N	Y
5 *McMorris Rodgers*	N	N	N	Y	N	N	N	Y	N	N	N	N	Y	–	Y
6 Dicks	Y	Y	Y	N	Y	Y	N	Y	Y	Y	Y	Y	Y	Y	Y
7 McDermott	Y	Y	Y	N	Y	Y	Y	N	Y	Y	Y	Y	N	Y	N
8 *Reichert*	N	N	N	Y	N	N	N	Y	N	N	N	N	Y	N	Y
9 Smith	Y	N	Y	N	Y	Y	N	Y	Y	Y	Y	Y	N	Y	N
WEST VIRGINIA															
1 Mollohan	Y	N	Y	N	Y	Y	N	Y	Y	Y	Y	Y	Y	?	Y
2 *Capito*	N	Y	N	Y	N	N	?	Y	N	N	Y	N	Y	N	Y
3 Rahall	Y	Y	N	Y	Y	Y	N	Y	Y	Y	Y	Y	Y	N	Y
WISCONSIN															
1 *Ryan*	N	+	–	+	N	N	N	Y	N	N	N	N	N	N	Y
2 Baldwin	Y	Y	Y	N	Y	Y	Y	N	Y	Y	Y	Y	N	Y	N
3 Kind	Y	Y	Y	Y	Y	Y	N	Y	Y	Y	Y	Y	Y	Y	N
4 Moore	Y	Y	Y	N	Y	Y	Y	N	Y	Y	Y	Y	N	Y	N
5 *Sensenbrenner*	N	Y	N	Y	N	N	N	Y	N	N	Y	N	N	N	Y
6 *Petri*	N	Y	N	Y	N	N	N	Y	N	N	Y	N	N	N	Y
7 Obey	Y	Y	Y	N	Y	Y	Y	N	?	Y	Y	Y	Y	Y	N
8 Kagen	Y	Y	Y	N	Y	Y	Y	N	Y	Y	Y	Y	N	Y	N
WYOMING															
AL *Lummis*	N	N	N	Y	N	N	N	Y	N	N	N	N	N	N	Y
DELEGATES															
Faleomavaega (A.S.)	Y	Y													
Norton (D.C.)	N	Y													
Bordallo (Guam)	N	Y													
Sablan (N. Marianas)	?	?													
Pierluisi (P.R.)	?	?													
Christensen (V.I.)	Y	Y													

[8]Rep. Mark Critz, D-Pa., was sworn in May 20, 2010, to fill the seat vacated by the February 8 death of fellow Democrat John P. Murtha, D-Pa. The first key vote for which Critz was eligible was vote 286; Murtha did not cast a key vote in 2010.

Senate

1. REPEAL OF HEALTH CARE OVERHAUL

Rejection of a procedural motion to allow a vote on an amendment repealing the 2010 health care law.

After the House January 19 passed its health care repeal along party lines, Senate Republicans were eager to try also, especially after gaining seven seats in the 2010 elections, in which the new law was a big campaign issue.

However, Democrats still controlled the Senate. Although Majority Leader Harry Reid, D-Nev., wanted to avoid bringing the repeal to the floor, he knew Republicans could make procedural moves to tie up the Senate until the issue was put to a vote. In a deal with Minority Leader Mitch McConnell, R-Ky., Reid agreed to allow amendments to legislation on the floor, including nongermane ones, in return for a Republican agreement to forgo filibusters on motions to proceed.

The vehicle in this case was a bill to authorize the Federal Aviation Administration (S 223). McConnell offered an amendment with language identical to the repeal bill (HR 2) passed by the House. Senate Budget Chair Kent Conrad, D-N.D., made a point of order against the McConnell amendment, arguing that it violated the Budget Act because a repeal would add to the deficit. McConnell then moved to waive the Budget Act, saying that "only in Washington could you argue with a straight face that starting a new multitrillion dollar entitlement program is going to save money."

Although the vote was on waiving the Budget Act, it was widely viewed as a measure of senators' position on repeal. In addition, the vote made clear that the health care law remained a strictly partisan issue. Although the law was unpopular with many voters, Republicans were unable to convince any Democrats to support repeal.

As in the House, the Senate vote fell along party lines, with all forty-seven Republicans voting in favor and all fifty Democrats who were present voting against, along with Vermont independent Bernard Sanders. Virginia Democrat Mark Warner and Connecticut independent Joseph I. Lieberman did not vote.

Senate rejected the McConnell motion to waive the Budget Act with respect to health care repeal on February 2, 47–51: R 47–0; D 0–50; I 0–1. *(Vote 1, p. 790)*

2. GREENHOUSE GAS REGULATIONS

Rejection of an amendment to bar Environmental Protection Agency (EPA) regulation of greenhouse gases under the Clean Air Act.

With the House preparing to take up legislation in early April designed to bar the EPA from regulating greenhouse gases, Senate Minority Leader Mitch McConnell, R-Ky., saw an opportunity to seize the momentum and offer the text of the House bill on the Senate floor as an amendment to an unrelated small-business bill (S 493). The vote would put senators on record on an issue that many believed was the most important environmental concern of the day.

But Majority Leader Harry Reid, D-Nev., was prepared to deal with the vote, which was a potential trap for a handful of moderate Democrats facing tough reelection bids in 2012. To stem Democratic defections, Reid lined up three competing amendments that also would have limited EPA authority under the Clean Air Act to restrict emissions. McConnell criticized the narrowly tailored amendments as an effort to provide political cover for vulnerable Democrats with ailing home-state industries. The first contained agricultural exemptions along with new restrictions on the EPA's authority to allow states to enact stronger fuel economy standards.

Another was a proposal that would have permanently exempted small businesses and some farms from greenhouse gas regulation. A third plan would have delayed the EPA's regulations for two years, a pause that sponsor John D. Rockefeller IV, D-W.Va., said would allow time for development of clean-coal technology. All three were easily rejected.

By the time senators got around to voting on the McConnell amendment, Reid's gambit had paid off. Just four Democrats—Mary L. Landrieu of Louisiana, Joe Manchin III of West Virginia, Ben Nelson of Nebraska, and Mark Pryor of Arkansas—joined Republicans in backing McConnell's amendment. With one Republican, Maine's Susan Collins, voting no, the chamber deadlocked on McConnell's amendment on a 50–50 vote.

Under a unanimous consent agreement, sixty votes were required to adopt any of the amendments. But the tie vote on McConnell's proposal dealt EPA critics a significant defeat by denying them even a simple majority against the agency's regulatory scheme. While the House easily passed its measure a day later, the vote on McConnell's amendment demonstrated that the Senate would not go along with rolling back EPA emissions regulations, effectively ending any serious prospect for legislation to block the rules in the 112th Congress.

Senate rejected an amendment to a small-business research bill (S 493) to block the EPA from regulating carbon dioxide and other greenhouse gases under the Clean Air Act on April 6, 50–50: R 46–1; D 4–47; I 0–2. (Sixty votes were required for adoption.) *(Vote 2, p. 790)*

3. BUDGET RESOLUTION

Senate rejection of consideration of the House GOP budget resolution to specify significant spending reductions over a decade, impose new budgetary controls, and endorse a future change in Medicare from an open-ended entitlement into a more limited, voucher-type of program.

The Senate's rejection of the House budget resolution, although not a surprise, underscored the inability of conservative Republicans to wrest most of the substantive changes they sought from a divided Congress and previewed a yearlong conflict between the two chambers on tax and spending issues.

Five Senate Republicans, four of them moderates and the fifth a freshman who said the House proposal was not aggressive enough, joined every voting Senate Democrat and independent in opposing the measure.

The fiscal 2012 budget resolution, written by House Budget Chair Paul D. Ryan, R-Wis., proposed holding nonsecurity discretionary spending below fiscal 2008 levels for five years and cutting overall anticipated spending by $5.8 trillion over a decade. The plan called for replacing Medicare's open-ended, fee-for-service system with a premium support model, in which seniors and the disabled would receive an annual stipend to buy government-approved, private insurance plans of their choice, beginning in 2022. The open-ended Medicaid program would be replaced with block grants to states, which would be given more authority to shape the health care program for the poor.

While the House adopted the budget on a party-line vote, the Senate's rejection demonstrated the Democratic majority's unwillingness to agree to spending cuts of the magnitude demanded by the House GOP and foreshadowed conflicts to come.

Senate rejected a motion to proceed to H Con Res 34 on May 25, 40–57: R 40–5; D 0–50; I 0–2. *(Vote 3, p. 790)*

4. PATRIOT ACT EXTENSION

Passage of a bill to extend three expiring provisions of the antiterrorism law known as the Patriot Act.

At odds over the length of an extension for several expiring antiterrorism authorities, under pressure from the Obama administration to act swiftly, and facing resistance from critics of federal government power, the House and Senate came together at the last minute to renew three provisions of the 2001 law known as the Patriot Act.

After reaching a compromise with the House over the extension, the Senate overcame a floor bid to modify it from a newly elected Republican opponent of the statute and voted overwhelmingly on the day the provisions were set to expire to send the extension to the House.

The Senate Judiciary chair, Vermont Democrat Patrick J. Leahy, had wanted a two-year extension. The House Judiciary chair, Texas Republican Lamar Smith, sought a six-year extension. The final bill split the difference at four years.

The provisions that the Senate voted to extend permitted the government to seek court orders for roving wiretaps on suspects who use multiple devices or modes of communication, to seek access to "any tangible thing" deemed related to a terrorism investigation, and to request warrants to conduct surveillance of "lone wolf" foreign terrorism suspects who may not be connected to a larger terrorist group.

But with the deadline nearing, Rand Paul, a Kentucky Republican and Patriot Act opponent, sought to amend the bill. The main obstacle to passage was a Paul amendment to bar government investigators from using the Patriot Act's "business record" provision to obtain the background forms that gun buyers fill out when they purchase firearms from licensed gun dealers. The Senate voted to table, and thus kill, the amendment by a vote of 85–10. By a vote of 91–4, the Senate also tabled another Paul amendment to restrict the collection of suspicious-activity reports to those requested by law enforcement. The Senate then voted to send the extension bill to the House.

Senate passed S 990 on May 26, 72–23: R 41–4; D 30–18; I 1–1. *(Vote 4, p. 790)*

5. DEBT LIMIT AGREEMENT

Clearing for the president a compromise debt limit was negotiated largely between the White House and Senate Republicans.

By voting to raise the $14.3 trillion ceiling on Treasury borrowing the Senate ended weeks of high-stakes confrontation that left all sides politically damaged, yet ensured that the government would not risk a potentially catastrophic default on its obligations. The vote followed House passage the day before, and came hours before the Treasury was scheduled to run out of borrowing authority.

Senate support for the increase was never in question, although a few Senate conservatives raised doubts that the danger of default was all that great and many joined with House Republicans in advocating use of the debt ceiling as a bargaining chip for spending cuts. In fact, throughout months of negotiations, Senate Republicans sought to pin the threat of a default on their House colleagues even as they insisted that their party was united on the issue.

Senate Minority Leader Mitch McConnell, R-Ky., introduced a "Plan B" proposal midway through the talks that was designed to place the political burden of raising the debt ceiling on the president and end the debate. But McConnell played a central role in engineering the eventual deal and the solidly bipartisan final vote, in which a majority of Republicans voted "yes." Senate Majority Leader Harry Reid, D-Nev., also helped structure the package, particularly the statutory discretionary spending caps that were to take effect upon enactment, and the creation of a special House-Senate committee to negotiate $1.2 trillion in budgetary savings.

The deal, which traded a long-term debt ceiling increase for two rounds of spending cuts, and none of the tax increases that Democrats had insisted upon, left many Senate Democrats angry. Vice President Joseph R. Biden Jr. came to Capitol Hill to lobby Democrats in both chambers the day of the House vote. Yet, while nineteen Republicans voted no, only six Senate Democrats opposed the bill because few wanted to be seen as favoring a default. Still, before the vote, Reid defended the negotiating process on the Senate floor, which was seen as a clear sign of the toll that the protracted debt ceiling fight took on both parties.

Senate cleared S 365 on August 2, 74–26: R 28–19; D 45–6; I 1–1 *(Vote 5, p. 790)*

6. PATENT LAW OVERHAUL

Clearing for the president a major rewrite of patent law, including changes to U.S. Patent and Trademark Office procedures.

The vote in the Senate cleared major bipartisan legislation that was the product of a year-long effort on Capitol Hill. The Senate was both the first and last chamber to vote in 2011 on legislation to revamp patent laws. In March, senators voted 95–5 to pass their version of the bill. That vote tally helped fuel a House effort on companion legislation that Judiciary Chair Lamar Smith, R-Texas, had written in consultation with Senate Judiciary Chair Patrick J. Leahy, D-Vt.

The House passed its bill (HR 1249) in June, after supporters worked through several difficult policy debates. The final House product was somewhat different from the Senate bill, particularly regarding whether patent office funding would continue to be handled through the regular appropriations process. But Leahy and other Senate proponents, along with the Obama administration, threw their support behind the House bill as the only chance to get patent overhaul legislation signed into law.

Leahy and his allies stuck together to defeat several amendments proposed to the House bill on the Senate floor. Adoption of any would have required another House vote, probably dooming legislation for the year. The Senate cleared the House bill on September 8, 89–9: R 40–6; D 47–3; I 2–0. *(Vote 6, p. 790)*

7. EMERGENCY DISASTER RELIEF AND MYANMAR TRADE

Adoption of an amendment to provide $6.9 billion for emergency disaster relief.

The vote was one of the rare moments in 2011 when majority Senate Democrats were able to attract enough GOP support to obtain sixty votes to advance a controversial measure.

By late summer, the federal response to a number of natural disasters, including floods, fires, and Hurricane Irene, had nearly depleted funding for such calamities. Although House GOP leaders favored some offsets to the proposal to replenish the funds, Senate Majority Leader Harry Reid, D-Nev., and his caucus pushed for no offsets because the funding was in response to an emergency.

In mid-September, Reid set up a vote on an amendment on an unrelated bill (H J Res 66) that would reflect the political power of majority Democrats and a small group of GOP senators who were willing to fund the relief without offsets.

In the pivotal vote, an amendment to the bill calling for $6.9 billion in immediate aid with no offsets and requiring sixty votes for adoption, Reid was able to attract the votes of 10 Republicans to go along with a united Democratic front. Before the vote, Reid took pains to thank Republicans, noting that "the cooperation we have had this week by both Democrats and Republicans has been extremely important." It marked one of the high points of the year for Senate comity.

Much of the GOP support came from moderates such as Olympia J. Snowe and Susan Collins of Maine and Scott P. Brown of Massachusetts, although a few conservatives, including Patrick J. Toomey of Pennsylvania and David Vitter of Louisiana, whose states experienced considerable damage from natural disasters, joined the majority.

Senate adopted an amendment to H J Res 66 on September 15, 62–37: R 10–37; D 50–0; I 2–0. (Sixty votes were needed.) *(Vote 7, p. 790)*

8. GERMANENESS OF SENATE AMENDMENTS

Rejection of a motion to sustain a ruling that overrode a point of order. In so doing, the Senate established a precedent that by a simple majority, it could vote to effectively change a procedural rule. The change prevented senators from offering motions permitting the consideration of nongermane amendments after cloture has been invoked.

A long-running feud between Senate Democrats and Republicans over the slow pace of legislative action came to an explosive and dramatic head October 6, when Majority Leader Harry Reid used a variation of the so-called nuclear option to establish by a simple majority vote a precedent that effectively changed a Senate procedural rule. The nuclear option phrase had come into use earlier in debates over changing Senate rules to restrict or end the filibuster by a simple majority vote.

The October 6 vote demonstrating raw political power within the Senate, Democrats stopped Republicans from using motions to suspend the rules to get around a prohibition against senators offering nongermane amendments after cloture has been invoked.

A frustrated Reid had pressed to curb the delaying tactics, which Republicans were using to force symbolic votes on issues the minority considered politically advantageous. The majority leader asserted that the practice threatened to render cloture procedures meaningless and leave the Senate tied up in procedural knots. Minority Leader Mitch McConnell sharply criticized Reid's move, saying it trampled the Senate's storied minority rights and would turn "the Senate into the House."

Senate leaders worked out a deal at the start of the 112th Congress to curtail the use of secret holds for blocking bills and other delaying tactics, while rejecting limits on the use of the Senate's procedures to filibuster legislation. Reid of Nevada and McConnell of Kentucky forged a gentleman's agreement under which Democrats would allow Republicans to offer amendments to bills. But months of squabbling and political maneuvering by both sides over spending and the nation's borrowing authority had left nerves frayed.

The clash came as the Senate was nearing the final stages of debate on a measure to establish sanctions for Chinese currency manipulation. The Senate had voted to limit debate on the measure, but Republicans continued trying to force Democrats to cast symbolic votes on a number of topics, including a piece of President Obama's original job creation proposal that Democrats wanted to revise.

Reid said he and McConnell reached a preliminary agreement to hold votes on seven GOP motions, but the Republican leader said Reid swapped out one of them without reaching an agreement to do so. McConnell demanded that Reid allow Republicans to vote on the amendments they wanted and said Reid should not dictate the content of the minority party's amendments. At issue was an amendment by Nebraska Republican Mike Johanns regarding potential regulation of dust produced by agriculture operations.

Reid's capacity to endure further delays appeared to run out. He raised a point of order that postcloture motions to suspend the germaneness rule were a prohibited dilatory tactic. The chair, after conferring with the parliamentarian, overruled Reid's objection. But Senate Democrats defeated with a simple majority a motion to sustain the chair's ruling, so the ruling fell. Democrat Ben Nelson of Nebraska sided with Republicans, arguing against changes in Senate procedures without hearings.

Senate defeated a motion to sustain the ruling of the chair on Reid's point of order on October 6, 48–51: R 47–0; D 1–49; I 0–2. *(Vote 8, p. 790)*

9. COLOMBIA TRADE AGREEMENT

Clearing for the president a bill to implement a trade agreement with Colombia.

Over the objections of most Democrats and their allies in organized labor, the Senate sent to President Obama a trade pact with Colombia. The vote reflected a delicate balance of political power in which free-trade advocates and opponents each got at least some of what they wanted.

Obama had criticized the Bush-era trade deal in his 2008 presidential campaign because of the Latin American nation's history of violence against union organizers. After negotiating an agreement with Colombia to protect labor activists, Obama changed his mind and supported the measure, along with separate trade pacts with Panama and South Korea.

Senate Majority Leader Harry Reid, a Nevada Democrat, brought the Colombia measure to the floor, even though a majority of his caucus opposed it, as part of a deal that required Republicans in both chambers to accept an extension of economic benefits for U.S. workers who had been displaced by foreign competition.

Congress cleared all four bills October 12.

The Colombia trade deal eliminated tariffs on more than 80 percent of Colombia-bound exports of industrial and consumer goods. Colombia, Bolivia, Ecuador, and Peru already received duty-free treatment on many of their U.S.-bound exports because of trade preferences for the Andean nations.

The Bush administration had negotiated the Colombia pact in 2006, and Colombia's legislature approved it in 2007. Bush sent it to Congress in April 2008, ignoring the strong opposition of the Democrats who controlled both chambers. Within two days, the House voted to change its rules and revoke expedited treatment for the Colombia bill, casting it into limbo.

Democrats argued that Colombia had a long history of violence by paramilitary forces that had killed hundreds of activists seeking to improve workers' rights. To address the concern, Obama signed an "action plan" in April 2011 with Colombian President Juan Manuel Santos. Under its terms, Colombia agreed to pass laws to protect labor organizers and carry out the prosecution of individuals charged with violence against labor leaders. But many Democrats remained skeptical.

Senate cleared HR 3078 on October 12, 66–33: R 44–2; D 21–30; I 1–1. *(Vote 9, p. 790)*

10. TREATMENT OF SUSPECTED TERRORISTS

Adoption of an amendment to the fiscal 2012 defense authorization bill to clarify that the measure would not affect existing law relating to the detention of U.S. citizens and lawful residents.

Senate consideration of the annual defense authorization bill exposed striking differences among top Democratic lawmakers over detainees when traditional allies battled publicly and passionately over new policy provisions the Armed Services Committee had written into the measure.

The overwhelming vote in favor of a compromise amendment on the issue from California Democrat Dianne Feinstein broke a logjam and paved the way for eventual passage of the legislation. The vote was a bipartisan resolution, for the time being, of the detainee controversy.

During several days of floor debate, Feinstein, chair of the Select Committee on Intelligence; Vermont Democrat Patrick J. Leahy, chair of the Judiciary Committee; and other top Democrats tried to strike, or at least revise, several detainee policies in the bill they believed would dramatically rewrite existing law.

They were met, however, with stiff resistance from Armed Services Chair Carl Levin, D-Mich., who steadfastly supported the language in his bill that provoked a White House veto threat and had solid GOP backing.

At stake over two days of debate was an effort to further define the management and handling of suspects taken in the war on terrorism. But Democrats failed in their efforts to change the bill until Feinstein and Levin struck a last-minute deal just before the Senate voted to approve the measure.

The new language, intended to pacify opponents who charged that the measure would indefinitely expose U.S. citizens accused of terrorist activities to the military's control, stated that the bill would not affect existing law relating to the detention of U.S. citizens and lawful residents. The language, which was endorsed on a 99–1 vote, effectively left it to the Supreme Court to decide. The only no vote came from Jon Kyl, R-Ariz.

Senate adopted the Feinstein amendment to S 1867 on December 1, 99–1: R 46–1; D 51–0; I 2–0. *(Vote 10, p. 790)*

11. HALLIGAN JUDICIAL NOMINATION

Rejection of an effort to limit debate on the nomination of Caitlin J. Halligan to the D.C. Circuit Court of Appeals, thereby blocking her confirmation.

The vote by Senate Republicans to block a prominent judicial nomination challenged presidential power and marked a departure from a bipartisan agreement put together in the George W. Bush administration.

In 2005, the Senate was brought to a standstill over the minority party's use of the filibuster to effectively create a sixty-vote-majority requirement for appeals court judges nominated by a president from the opposite party. The impasse was broken when seven senators from each party promised to oppose such tactics except in "extraordinary circumstances," which were not further defined. In almost all circumstances, these senators said, nominations that made it as far as the floor deserved an "up-or-down" vote with a simple-majority threshold.

The agreement by the so-called Gang of 14 created a lasting cease-fire, as minority Democrats did not mount filibusters against Bush's picks for the rest of the 109th Congress. After taking the majority in 2007, Democrats used the traditional methods at their disposal to block Bush's most conservative choices, either denying them hearings or rejecting them in committee. In the first two years of Obama's presidency, the minority Republicans made only one sustained effort to block a judicial nominee.

The situation changed in 2010, however. Republicans twice formed nearly unified blocs that prevented invoking of cloture on Obama appeals court choices, blocking their confirmations. The first vote, in May, did not come as a surprise: Conservatives asserted from the outset that Goodwin Liu's legal writings as a professor at the University of California at Berkeley were far outside the legal mainstream, unduly harsh toward both of Bush's successful Supreme Court picks, and indicative of an inappropriate interest in judicial activism.

But the second, in December, was both unexpected and more consequential because it signaled that the GOP was willing to abandon the six-year truce and set aside the precedent set by the Gang of 14. If maintained, that could limit Obama's power to shape the judiciary, while also reviving partisan congressional battles that were thought settled.

Halligan was nominated to one of three vacancies on the eleven-seat D.C. Circuit, generally considered the second most powerful federal court. Several Republicans, including senior Judiciary Committee member Charles E. Grassley of Iowa, made clear their preference was to keep those seats empty at least through 2012, thereby sustaining a 5–3 majority on the court for judges nominated by Republicans.

In public, the GOP leadership asserted that Halligan's record, especially as solicitor general of New York from 2001 through 2006, revealed her as a liberal activist. They took particular issue with an argument, made on the state's behalf, that firearms manufacturers should be held liable for crimes committed with the guns they made. They also criticized her legal positions on immigration, abortion, and terrorism cases. Democrats countered that it would be bad precedent to block a nominee based on positions taken at the behest of either government or corporate clients.

Among those opposing Halligan on the key vote were all four of the Republicans still in Congress from the Gang of 14: John McCain of Arizona, Lindsey Graham of South Carolina, and

Olympia J. Snowe and Susan Collins of Maine. The only Republican who voted with the Democrats was Alaska's Lisa Murkowski, who said she opposed confirmation but did not think the "extraordinary circumstances" standard for a filibuster had been met. Utah's Orrin G. Hatch, the GOP chair of the Judiciary Committee in 2003 and 2004, voted "present."

Senate rejected cloture on the Halligan nomination on December 6, 54–45: R 1–45; D 51–0; I 2–0. *(Vote 11, p. 790)*

12. PAYROLL TAX CUT EXTENSION, DOCTOR REIMBURSEMENT, UNEMPLOYMENT BENEFITS

Adoption of a bipartisan substitute to provide a two-month extension of the expiring payroll tax cut to allow time for further negotiations, along with a two-month extension of benefits for long-term jobless workers and continued Medicare reimbursement rates for doctors.

At the end of a year in which they consistently felt outmaneuvered by House Republicans in economic policy negotiations, Senate Democrats decided to press their case by insisting on a twelve-month extension of the expiring Social Security payroll tax cut enacted at the end of 2010 and a similar extension of expiring jobless benefits for workers who have been unemployed for more than half a year. President Obama made this a centerpiece of his jobs proposal to Congress in September, and Senate Democrats upped the ante by proposing to offset the cost with a surtax on household incomes higher than $1 million.

Democrats pushed the payroll tax cut in several forms over the fall. But the surtax, while popular with a majority of the public, did not have enough support in the Senate to overcome a Republican filibuster.

Meantime, the House, which was at first dismissive of the payroll tax cut extension, passed a bill in mid-December to renew the payroll tax cut and other expiring provisions for a full year after adding language to require the president to act promptly on authorizing the construction of the controversial Keystone XL oil pipeline from Canada to the Gulf of Mexico. The House bill's cost was to be offset with spending cuts anathema to Democrats. Senate Democrats were unwilling to consider the House-passed bill's offsets, as well as some of its other provisions. House Speaker John A. Boehner, R-Ohio, told Senate Majority Leader Harry Reid, D-Nev., and Minority Leader Mitch McConnell, R-Ky., to decide between themselves how to proceed.

The two Senate leaders decided that a short-term extension was the best approach to give themselves an opportunity away from end-of-year pressures to resolve their differences, particularly on offsets. The compromise preserved the Social Security tax rate paid by workers at 4.2 percent, down from the pre-2011 rate of 6.2 percent, through February 2012 and continued existing law on long-term jobless benefits and Medicare reimbursements for two months as well. In an effort to stave off GOP defections in both chambers, the two-month extension retained the Keystone pipeline language.

Senate adopted a substitute amendment to HR 3630 on December 17, 89–10: R 39–7; D 49–2; I 1–1. *(Vote 12, p. 790)*

1. **S 223. Repeal of Health Care Overhaul.** McConnell, R-Ky., motion to waive the Budget Act and budget resolutions with respect to the Conrad, D-N.D., point of order against the McConnell amendment to repeal the 2010 health care overhaul, which requires most individuals to buy health insurance by 2014, makes changes to government health care programs and sets new requirements for health insurers. The amendment restored provisions of law amended or repealed by the health care overhaul and repealed certain provisions of the health care reconciliation law. Motion rejected 47–51: R 47–0; D 0–50; I 0–1. A three-fifths majority vote (sixty) of the total Senate is required to waive the Budget Act. A "nay" was a vote in support of the president's position. February 2, 2011.

2. **S 493 Greenhouse Gas Regulations.** McConnell, R-Ky., amendment to block the Environmental Protection Agency from regulating carbon dioxide and other greenhouse gases under the Clean Air Act. Rejected 50–50: R 46–1; D 4–47; I 0–2. (By unanimous consent, the Senate agreed to require sixty votes for adoption of the amendment.) A "nay" was a vote in support of the president's position. April 6, 2011.

3. **H Con Res 34. Budget Resolution.** Reid, D-Nev., motion to proceed to the concurrent resolution, passed by the House, to allow $2.9 trillion in new budget authority for fiscal 2012 and to specify significant spending reductions over a decade, impose new budgetary controls, and endorse future changes in Medicare from an open-ended entitlement into a more limited, voucher-type of program. Motion rejected 40–57: R 40–5; D 0–50; I 0–2. May 25, 2011.

4. **S 990. Patriot Act Extension.** Reid, D-Nev., motion to extend through June 1, 2015, three provisions of the antiterrorism law known as the Patriot Act allowing the government to seek court orders for roving wiretaps on suspects who use multiple devices or modes of communication, to request access to "any tangible thing" deemed related to a terrorism investigation, and to seek warrants to conduct surveillance of "lone wolf" foreign terrorist suspects who may not be connected to a larger terrorist group. Motion agreed to 72–23: R 41–4; D 30–18; I 1–1. A "yea" was a vote in support of the president's position. May 26, 2011.

5. **S 365. Debt Limit Agreement.** Reid, D-Nev., motion to concur in the House amendment to the bill to provide a process to reduce the federal government deficit by up to $2.4 trillion, and allow the president to raise the debt limit immediately by $400 billion, with an additional $500 billion subject to a resolution of disapproval. The legislation set discretionary spending caps to reduce the deficit by $917 billion in fiscal 2012 through 2021 and establish a firewall between security and nonsecurity spending for fiscal 2012 and 2013. It also established a bipartisan, bicameral committee to recommend reductions in the deficit by $1.5 trillion. It also required across-the-board cuts in nonexempt discretionary and mandatory accounts by up to $1.2 trillion over fiscal 2013 through 2021 if committee reductions totaling $1.2 trillion were not enacted. The measure required Congress to vote on a balanced-budget constitutional amendment by the end of 2011. Motion agreed to (clearing the bill for the president) 74–26: R 28–19; D 45–6; I 1–1. (By unanimous consent, the Senate agreed to raise the majority requirement for the motion to concur to sixty votes.) A "yea" was a vote in support of the president's position. August 2, 2011.

6. **HR 1249. Patent Law Overhaul.** Passage of the bill to overhaul the U.S. patent system, changing how patents are awarded, reviewed, and challenged. The legislation changed the basis for awarding patents from a "first to invent" to a "first inventor to file" standard, and altered the process for challenging the validity of issued patents through the U.S. Patent and Trademark Office review proceedings as well as authorizing a reexamination of certain previously issued business method patents. Passed (clearing the bill for the president) 89–9: R 40–6; D 47–3; I 2–0. A "yea" was a vote in support of the president's position. September 8, 2011.

7. **H J Res 66. Emergency Disaster Relief and Myanmar Trade.** Reid, D-Nev., amendment to provide $6.9 billion for disaster relief, including $5.1 billion to replenish the Federal Emergency Management Agency's Disaster Relief Fund, of which $500 million would be available in fiscal 2011, $266 million would be for emergency programs administered by the Agriculture Department, and more than $1.3 billion would be for the Army Corps of Engineers. The amendment also renewed trade restrictions on Myanmar. Adopted 62–37: R 10–37; D 50–0; I 2–0. (By unanimous consent, the Senate agreed to raise the majority requirement for adoption of the Reid amendment to sixty votes). September 15, 2011.

8. **S 1619. Germaneness of Senate Amendments.** Judgment of the Senate to affirm the ruling of the chair against a point of order against suspending Rule 22 to permit consideration of the Coburn, R-Okla., amendment on the grounds that the motion was "dilatory." By the vote the Senate established a precedent that by a simple majority it could vote to effectively change a procedural rule. The change prevented senators from offering motions permitting the consideration of nongermane amendments after cloture has been invoked. The Coburn amendment prohibited appropriations of foreign aid to nations owning more than $10 billion in U.S. debt and rescinded some funds already appropriated to such countries for fiscal 2012. Ruling of the chair rejected 48–51: R 47–0; D 1–49; I 0–2. The ruling of the chair did not stand and the point of order was sustained. October 6, 2011.

9. **HR 3078. Colombia Trade Agreement.** Passage of the bill to implement a trade agreement between the United States and Colombia. The agreement reduced most tariffs and duties on goods traded between the two countries, reduced barriers to trade in services, increased protections for intellectual property, and required Colombia to take steps to strengthen its labor and environmental enforcement standards. Passed (clearing the bill for the president) 66–33: R 44–2; D 21–30; I 1–1. A "yea" was a vote in support of the president's position. October 12, 2011.

10. **S 1867. Treatment of Suspected Terrorists.** Feinstein, D-Calif., amendment to clarify that the legislation under consideration, the fiscal 2012 defense authorization bill, would not affect current law on the question of holding citizens in military detention if taken into custody within the United States. Adopted 99–1: R 46–1; D 51–0; I 2–0. December 1, 2011.

11. **Halligan Judicial Nomination.** Motion to invoke cloture (thus limiting debate) on President Obama's nomination of Caitlin Joan Halligan of New York to be a judge for the U.S. Court of Appeals in the District of Columbia Circuit. Motion rejected 54–45: R 1–45; D 51–0; I 2–0. (Sixty votes were required for cloture.) A "yea" was a vote in support of the president's position. December 6, 2011.

12. **HR 3630. Payroll Tax Cuts, Doctor Reimbursements, Unemployment Benefits.** Reid, D-Nev., and McConnell, R-Ky., amendment to extend through February 2012 the 4.2 percent employee payroll tax rate, existing Medicare payment rates to doctors, and workers' eligibility for certain expanded unemployment benefits. The cost was to be offset through an increase in loan fees levied by government-backed mortgage lenders Fannie Mae and Freddie Mac for guaranteeing loans purchased in the secondary mortgage market. Adopted 89–10: R 39–7; D 49–2; I 1–1. (By unanimous consent, the Senate agreed to raise the majority requirement for adoption of the Reid-McConnell amendment to sixty votes). December 17, 2011.

KEY

Republican		Democrat	**Independent**
Y	Voted for (yea)	–	Announced against
#	Paired for	P	Voted "present"
+	Announced for	C	Voted "present" to avoid possible conflict of interest
N	Voted against (nay)		
X	Paired against	?	Did not vote or otherwise make a position known

Senate Key Votes	1	2	3	4	5	6	7	8	9	10	11	12
ALABAMA												
Shelby	Y	Y	Y	Y	N	Y	N	Y	Y	Y	N	N
Sessions	Y	Y	Y	Y	N	Y	N	Y	Y	Y	N	N
ALASKA												
Murkowski	Y	Y	N	N	Y	Y	Y	Y	Y	Y	Y	Y
Begich	N	N	N	N	Y	Y	Y	N	N	Y	Y	Y
ARIZONA												
McCain	Y	Y	Y	Y	Y	N	N	Y	Y	Y	N	Y
Kyl	Y	Y	Y	Y	Y	Y	N	Y	Y	N	N	Y
ARKANSAS												
Pryor	N	Y	N	Y	Y	Y	Y	N	Y	Y	Y	Y
Boozman	Y	Y	Y	Y	Y	Y	N	Y	Y	Y	N	Y
CALIFORNIA												
Feinstein	N	N	N	Y	Y	Y	Y	N	Y	Y	Y	Y
Boxer	N	N	N	Y	Y	N	Y	?	N	Y	Y	Y
COLORADO												
Udall	N	N	N	N	Y	Y	Y	N	Y	Y	Y	Y
Bennet	N	N	N	Y	Y	Y	Y	N	Y	Y	Y	Y
CONNECTICUT												
Lieberman		N	N	Y	Y	Y	Y	N	Y	Y	Y	Y
Blumenthal	N	N	N	?	Y	Y	Y	N	N	Y	Y	Y
DELAWARE												
Carper	N	N	N	Y	Y	Y	Y	N	Y	Y	Y	Y
Coons	N	N	N	N	Y	Y	Y	N	N	Y	Y	Y
FLORIDA												
Nelson	N	N	N	Y	Y	Y	Y	N	Y	Y	Y	Y
Rubio	Y	Y	Y	?	N	–	Y	Y	Y	Y	N	Y
GEORGIA												
Chambliss	Y	Y	Y	Y	N	Y	N	Y	Y	Y	N	Y
Isakson	Y	Y	Y	Y	Y	Y	N	Y	Y	Y	N	Y
HAWAII												
Inouye	N	N	N	Y	Y	Y	Y	N	Y	Y	Y	Y
Akaka	N	N	N	N	Y	Y	Y	N	N	Y	Y	Y
IDAHO												
Crapo	Y	Y	Y	Y	Y	Y	N	Y	Y	Y	N	Y
Risch	Y	Y	Y	Y	Y	Y	N	Y	Y	Y	N	Y
ILLINOIS												
Durbin	N	N	N	N	Y	Y	Y	N	N	Y	Y	Y
Kirk	Y	Y	Y	Y	Y	Y	N	Y	Y	Y	N	N
INDIANA												
Lugar	Y	Y	Y	Y	Y	Y	N	Y	Y	Y	N	Y
Coats	Y	Y	Y	Y	N	Y	N	Y	Y	Y	N	Y
IOWA												
Grassley	Y	Y	Y	Y	N	Y	N	Y	Y	Y	N	Y
Harkin	N	N	N	N	N	Y	Y	N	N	Y	Y	Y
KANSAS												
Roberts	Y	Y	?	?	Y	Y	N	Y	Y	Y	N	Y
Moran	Y	Y	Y	Y	N	Y	N	Y	Y	Y	N	N
KENTUCKY												
McConnell	Y	Y	Y	Y	Y	Y	N	Y	Y	Y	N	Y
Paul	Y	Y	N	N	N	N	N	Y	Y	Y	N	?
LOUISIANA												
Landrieu	N	Y	N	Y	Y	Y	Y	N	Y	Y	Y	Y
Vitter	Y	Y	Y	Y	N	Y	Y	Y	Y	Y	N	Y
MAINE												
Snowe	Y	Y	N	Y	Y	Y	Y	Y	N	Y	N	Y
Collins	Y	N	N	Y	Y	Y	Y	Y	N	Y	N	Y
MARYLAND												
Mikulski	N	N	N	Y	Y	Y	Y	N	N	Y	Y	Y
Cardin	N	N	N	Y	Y	Y	Y	N	N	Y	Y	Y
MASSACHUSETTS												
Kerry	N	N	N	Y	Y	Y	Y	N	Y	Y	Y	Y
Brown	Y	Y	N	Y	Y	Y	Y	Y	Y	Y	N	Y
MICHIGAN												
Levin	N	N	N	Y	Y	Y	Y	N	N	Y	Y	Y
Stabenow	N	N	N	Y	Y	Y	Y	N	N	Y	Y	Y
MINNESOTA												
Klobuchar	N	N	N	Y	Y	Y	Y	N	N	Y	Y	Y
Franken	N	N	N	N	Y	Y	Y	N	N	Y	Y	Y
MISSISSIPPI												
Cochran	Y	Y	Y	Y	Y	Y	N	Y	Y	Y	N	Y
Wicker	Y	Y	Y	Y	Y	Y	N	Y	Y	Y	N	Y
MISSOURI												
McCaskill	N	N	N	Y	Y	N	Y	N	N	Y	Y	Y
Blunt	Y	Y	Y	Y	Y	Y	Y	Y	Y	Y	N	Y
MONTANA												
Baucus	N	N	N	N	Y	Y	Y	N	Y	Y	Y	Y
Tester	N	N	N	N	Y	Y	Y	N	N	Y	Y	Y
NEBRASKA												
Nelson	N	Y	N	Y	N	Y	Y	Y	Y	Y	Y	Y
Johanns	Y	Y	Y	Y	Y	Y	N	Y	Y	Y	N	Y
NEVADA												
Reid	N	N	N	Y	Y	Y	Y	N	N	Y	Y	Y
Ensign[1]	Y	Y										
Heller[1]			Y	N	N	Y	Y	Y	Y	Y	N	Y
NEW HAMPSHIRE												
Shaheen	N	N	N	Y	Y	Y	Y	N	Y	Y	Y	Y
Ayotte	Y	Y	Y	Y	N	Y	N	Y	Y	Y	N	Y
NEW JERSEY												
Lautenberg	N	N	N	N	N	Y	Y	N	N	Y	Y	Y
Menendez	N	N	N	?	N	Y	Y	N	N	Y	Y	Y
NEW MEXICO												
Bingaman	N	N	N	N	Y	Y	Y	N	Y	Y	Y	Y
Udall	N	N	N	N	Y	Y	Y	N	N	Y	Y	Y
NEW YORK												
Schumer	N	N		+	Y	Y	Y	N	N	Y	Y	Y
Gillibrand	N	N	N	Y	N	Y	Y	N	N	Y	Y	Y
NORTH CAROLINA												
Burr	Y	Y	Y	Y	Y	Y	N	Y	Y	Y	N	Y
Hagan	N	N	N	Y	Y	Y	Y	N	N	Y	Y	Y
NORTH DAKOTA												
Conrad	N	N	N	Y	Y	Y	Y	N	Y	Y	Y	Y
Hoeven	Y	Y	Y	Y	Y	Y	Y	Y	Y	Y	N	Y
OHIO												
Brown	N	N	N	N	Y	Y	Y	N	N	Y	Y	Y
Portman	Y	Y	Y	Y	Y	Y	N	Y	Y	Y	N	Y
OKLAHOMA												
Inhofe	Y	Y	Y	Y	N	Y	N	Y	Y	Y	N	Y
Coburn	Y	Y	Y	Y	N	N	N	Y	?	Y	N	Y

[1]Sen. Dean Heller, R-Nev., was sworn in May 9, 2011, to fill the vacancy created by the May 3 resignation of fellow Republican John Ensign. The first vote for which Heller was eligible was vote 3; the last vote for which Ensign was eligible was vote 2.

Senate Key Votes	1	2	3	4	5	6	7	8	9	10	11	12
OREGON												
Wyden	N	N	N	N	Y	Y	Y	N	Y	Y	Y	Y
Merkley	N	N	N	N	N	Y	Y	N	N	Y	Y	Y
PENNSYLVANIA												
Casey	N	N	N	Y	Y	Y	Y	N	N	Y	Y	Y
Toomey	Y	Y	Y	Y	N	Y	Y	Y	Y	Y	N	Y
RHODE ISLAND												
Reed	N	N	N	Y	Y	Y	Y	N	N	Y	Y	Y
Whitehouse	N	N	N	Y	Y	Y	Y	N	N	Y	Y	Y
SOUTH CAROLINA												
Graham	Y	Y	Y	Y	N	Y	N	Y	Y	Y	N	Y
DeMint	Y	Y	Y	Y	N	N	N	Y	Y	Y	N	N
SOUTH DAKOTA												
Johnson	N	N	N	Y	Y	Y	Y	N	Y	Y	Y	Y
Thune	Y	Y	Y	Y	Y	Y	N	Y	Y	Y	N	Y
TENNESSEE												
Alexander	Y	Y	Y	Y	Y	Y	N	Y	Y	Y	N	Y
Corker	Y	Y	Y	Y	Y	Y	N	Y	Y	Y	N	N
TEXAS												
Hutchison	Y	Y	?	Y	Y	Y	N	Y	Y	Y	N	Y
Cornyn	Y	Y	Y	Y	Y	Y	N	Y	Y	Y	N	Y

Senate Key Votes	1	2	3	4	5	6	7	8	9	10	11	12
UTAH												
Hatch	Y	Y	Y	Y	N	Y	N	Y	Y	Y	P	Y
Lee	Y	Y	Y	N	N	N	N	Y	Y	Y	N	Y
VERMONT												
Leahy	N	N	N	N	Y	Y	Y	N	Y	Y	Y	N
Sanders	N	N	N	N	N	Y	Y	N	N	Y	Y	N
VIRGINIA												
Webb	N	N	N	Y	Y	Y	Y	N	Y	Y	Y	Y
Warner	–	N	N	Y	Y	Y	Y	N	Y	Y	Y	Y
WASHINGTON												
Murray	N	N	N	N	Y	Y	Y	N	Y	Y	Y	Y
Cantwell	N	N	N	N	Y	N	Y	N	Y	Y	Y	Y
WEST VIRGINIA												
Rockefeller	N	N	N	Y	Y	?	Y	N	N	Y	Y	Y
Manchin	N	Y	N	Y	Y	Y	Y	N	N	Y	Y	N
WISCONSIN												
Kohl	N	N	N	Y	Y	Y	?	N	N	Y	Y	Y
Johnson	Y	Y	Y	Y	N	N	N	Y	Y	Y	N	N
WYOMING												
Enzi	Y	Y	Y	Y	Y	Y	N	Y	Y	Y	N	Y
Barrasso	Y	Y	Y	Y	Y	Y	N	Y	Y	Y	N	Y

House

1. REPEAL OF HEALTH CARE OVERHAUL

Repeal of the health care overhaul law passed by Democrats in the previous Congress.

Newly empowered House Republicans rolled into Washington determined to undo the Democrats' signature initiative of the previous year: the new law designed to expand health care coverage in the United States, including a mandate that everyone have insurance. Republicans' promises to repeal the law were central to the party's 2010 campaign platform, as they portrayed the overhaul as a huge government overreach and repeated the "Obamacare" label in an effort to associate the law closely with the president. Many believed it helped them win.

They lost some momentum as the start of the 112th Congress was delayed after the January 8 mass shooting and assassination attempt against Rep. Gabrielle Giffords, D-Ariz., which seriously injured her and twelve others and killed six people. But newly elected House Speaker John A. Boehner of Ohio moved ahead, setting the vote for the following week with two days of debate. The discussion was civil, but the passion was clear on both sides.

Republicans claimed the law would push the nation to bankruptcy. Democrats charged that Republicans were putting insurance companies' interests ahead of ordinary people, saying health care represents the most fundamental American values.

The result was no surprise when the roll-call vote was called January 19, but it put members, especially the new Republican majority, on record regarding the controversial law. Every House Republican voted for the repeal, and all but three Democrats voted against it. The Democrats supporting it were Dan Boren of Oklahoma, Mike McIntyre of North Carolina, and Mike Ross of Arkansas. The only member not voting was Giffords.

House passed HR 2 on January 19, 245–189: R 242–0; D 3–189. *(Vote 1, p. 798)*

2. FUNDING FOR F-35 ALTERNATIVE ENGINE

Adoption of an amendment to strip from a fiscal 2011 spending bill money to continue developing a second type of engine for the Joint Strike Fighter.

Reversing years of consistent support, the February vote marked the first time a chamber of Congress had blocked funding for an alternative engine for the next-generation F-35 Joint Strike Fighter. Less than a year earlier the House rejected a proposal to stop funding the engine. The change was widely attributed to the infusion of fiscal conservatives into the House in 2011, joined by liberal Democrats long opposed to the second engine.

More than fifteen years earlier the government began funding a second type of engine for the new fighter jet that would become known as the F-35 under the belief that having two companies competing would lower prices, improve quality, and provide insurance against technical design failures that would undermine the program.

Congress backed the program repeatedly even when the Pentagon and the White House urged lawmakers not to fund it. Both presidents George W. Bush and Barack Obama contended that the benefits of having two manufacturers were not as clear as advocates said and that spending the several billion dollars needed to finishing developing the second engine was not an appropriate use of tax dollars.

In the face of such opposition, a multimillion-dollar lobbying and advertising campaign was waged by both the maker of the primary engine, Pratt & Whitney, and the firm developing the alternative engine, General Electric Co. (GE). Obama stepped up the pressure in 2011 by threatening to veto any measure that funded the second engine.

The House amendment by Tom Rooney, R-Fla., stripped $450 million in research and development funds from a spending bill. Nearly two-thirds of Democrats supported Rooney. Republicans split but the key to his victory was support from more than half the freshman Republicans.

The Senate later killed the House spending bill. But when the two chambers voted in April on the fiscal 2011 spending measure that ultimately became law, neither Appropriations Committee recommended funding the engine. The vote on the Rooney amendment sent such a clear signal that the Pentagon did not even wait for that April vote before announcing in late March that it was terminating the GE program.

After the loss of federal funding, GE said it would pay for development itself but the program came to an end in December when the company said it would no longer continue support. The company cited uncertainty about future purchases of F-35s amid the budget crisis.

House adopted the Rooney, R-Fla., amendment to HR 1 on February 16, 233–198: R 110–130; D 123–68. *(Vote 2, p. 798)*

3. GREENHOUSE GAS REGULATION

Passage of legislation to amend the Clean Air Act to prevent the Environmental Protection Agency (EPA) from regulating greenhouse gases.

The House vote in April on legislation (HR 910) to block new EPA rules struck at the core of the Obama administration's effort to curb greenhouse gas emissions that many scientists believed were warming the planet, while also making good on Republican pledges to unravel what they called the White House's "job-killing" regulatory agenda. Less than two years after a Democratic-controlled House passed legislation to cap greenhouse gas emissions, the 2011 vote provided the new Republican majority an opportunity to reverse policy direction on global warming.

The bill, sponsored by House Energy and Commerce Chair Fred Upton, R-Mich., prevented the government from addressing climate change through the regulation of carbon dioxide and other greenhouse gases under the federal Clean Air Act. Almost all Republican lawmakers, along with some Democrats from coal-dependent states, supported the measure, maintaining that Congress never intended for the law to be used to regulate greenhouse gases and that the statute was ill-equipped for reducing ubiquitous pollution such as carbon dioxide. They said the new rules would impose new costs on utilities and other industrial polluters, hurting consumers and killing jobs. Opponents, led by former Energy and Commerce Committee Chair Henry A. Waxman, D-Calif., contended the bill would damage the economy by deterring the creation of clean-energy jobs. However, a substantial number of House Republicans were skeptical about the science of global warming.

The House vote was largely symbolic because one day earlier the Senate had rejected similar language, but it provided a launch for a continuing GOP campaign throughout the year against a variety of environmental regulations.

House passed HR 910 on April 7, 255–172: R 236–0; D 19–172. *(Vote 3, p. 798)*

4. BUDGET RESOLUTION

Adoption of House Republicans' fiscal 2012 budget resolution, which specified significant spending cuts over a decade, imposed new budgetary controls, and endorsed a future change in Medicare from an open-ended entitlement into a more limited, voucher-like program.

The party-line House vote in April to adopt the budget resolution for fiscal 2011 was the high point for the year in Republican efforts to reduce the scope and cost of government. The resolution, a blueprint written by House Budget Chair Paul D. Ryan, R-Wis., represented the most ambitious elements of Republican fiscal policy. Those included holding nonsecurity discretionary spending below fiscal 2008 levels for five years, cutting overall anticipated spending by $5.8 trillion over a decade, and fundamentally restructuring health care entitlement programs.

Conservatives argued that the spending and tax blueprint was necessary to preserve Medicare and Medicaid for the future. Liberals responded that the proposal was an abrogation of a long-standing federal commitment to ensure that older Americans and the poor have access to health care. However, the changes endorsed by the budget blueprint would have required separate legislation to take effect.

The plan was adopted with overwhelming support from House Republicans. Only four House GOP lawmakers joined a united Democratic caucus in opposing it. Because Ryan's budget faced solid Democratic opposition in the Senate, it had no chance of being the instrument for setting fiscal policy on Capitol Hill. The wide gulf between Republicans and Democrats over the budget plan also foreshadowed a conflict that would unfold repeatedly in the following months as the two parties battled over spending, taxes, and the debt limit.

House adopted H Con Res 34 on April 15, 235–193: R 235–4; D 0–189. *(Vote 4, p. 798)*

5. PROSECUTION OF SUSPECTED TERRORISTS

Adoption of an amendment to a defense authorization bill to require all foreign terrorist suspects subject to trial for attacking the United States, U.S. government, or personnel be tried only by a military commission.

With a veto threat already looming over the House Armed Services Committee's version of the fiscal 2012 defense authorization bill (HR 1540), Republicans defied the White House and pushed through a floor amendment to strengthen terrorism-related language that was already opposed publicly by the Obama administration. The amendment, sponsored by Rep. Vern Buchanan, R-Fla., ultimately was dropped from the bill during House-Senate conference negotiations in December.

But the nearly unanimous GOP support for the language—only seven Republicans cast "no" votes—underscored a strong political desire within the party to revisit rules governing the prosecution of detainees a decade after the September 11 terrorist attacks.

Opponents charged that the floor amendment, which required the United States to consider all foreign terrorists to be enemy combatants and to prosecute them in military tribunals rather than civilian courts without any exceptions, was unconstitutional and would dramatically limit the president's flexibility in handling detainees.

Supporters maintained that prosecuting a terrorism suspect in a military tribunal made it easier to get a conviction, and also protected sensitive, classified information. Foreign terrorists, they said, should not be granted the same constitutional protections as U.S. citizens. The amendment complemented other detainee provisions in the committee bill.

House Democrats and a small number of Republicans contended that the committee's action gave the president nearly open-ended authority to wage war. Justin Amash, a Michigan Republican, led an effort to strip committee language from the bill but lost in a House vote of 187–234. However, like the Buchanan amendment, the language was not included in the final conference report.

House adopted the detainee amendment to HR 1540 on May 26, 246–173: R 228–7; D 18–166. *(Vote 5, p. 798)*

6. PATRIOT ACT EXTENSION

Clearing for the president a bill to extend three expiring provisions of the antiterrorism law known as the Patriot Act.

Hours before several provisions of the Patriot Act were scheduled to expire, the House cleared a measure May 26 to extend some of the Obama administration's antiterrorism authorities for four years. The House vote for a long-term extension came three months after the chamber had unexpectedly rejected a shorter extension.

The extension followed White House warnings that antiterrorism investigations could be jeopardized if the authorities expired.

The provisions allowed the government to seek court orders for roving wiretaps on suspects who use multiple devices or modes of communication, to request access to "any tangible thing" deemed related to a terrorism investigation, and to seek warrants to conduct surveillance of "lone wolf" foreign terrorist suspects who may not be connected to a larger terrorist group.

In February, House GOP leaders sought extension through December under suspension-of-the-rules procedures requiring a two-thirds majority for passage but fell seven votes short, 277–148. Democrats concerned about civil liberties combined with GOP conservatives wary of federal government power to defeat the bill. In May House leaders used a procedure requiring only a simple majority and barring amendments.

Thirty-one House Republicans voted against the four-year extension bill. But their opposition did not prevent the legislation from going to the president, who signed the measure hours later on a trip to Europe, reflecting of the importance the administration placed on extension.

House cleared S 990 on May 26, 250–153: R 196–31; D 54–122. *(Vote 6, p. 798)*

7. LIMITATION ON FORCES IN LIBYA

Adoption of a resolution demanding the president report to Congress on the details and rationale for the use of U.S. forces in combat operations in Libya and banning the use of ground troops as part of the operation.

In early June, House Speaker John A. Boehner, R-Ohio, took the unusual step of introducing his own resolution related to U.S. military operations in Libya to fend off passage of a tougher measure. Instead of demanding that all troops withdraw by June 15, as called for in a rival resolution by Dennis J. Kucinich, D-Ohio, Boehner's measure gave the White House two weeks to justify its strategy on Libya and requested a long list of documents to back up that justification.

The vote on the measure was the closest either chamber came to condemning the Obama administration's decision to participate in the North Atlantic Treaty Organization (NATO) operation to help oust Libyan strongman Muammar el-Gaddafi. There was widespread consternation among members over the White House's lack of formal consultation with Congress before or during the engagement.

Surprised by the depth of support for the Kucinich measure within the Republicans' ranks, GOP leaders delayed the vote until the end of the week, then quickly pulled together their rival proposal. The resolution criticized the president for failing to "provide Congress with a compelling rationale based upon United States national security interests for current U.S. military activities regarding Libya." It also stated that the president should not deploy ground troops in the North African country but stopped short of declaring the administration in violation of the 1973 War Powers Resolution governing the president's warmaking authority, or calling for the administration to halt its participation in the operation.

House Adopted H Res 292 on June 3, 268–145: R 223–10; D 45–135. *(Vote 7, p. 798)*

8. PATENT LAW OVERHAUL

Passage of a major revision of patent law, including changes to U.S. Patent and Trademark Office procedures.

The House vote gave momentum to a rare bipartisan effort on major legislation in the 112th Congress. After years of trying to write a bill to make numerous changes to U.S. patent law, the Republican and Democratic chairs of the House and Senate Judiciary committees began the year determined to clear the measure.

Texas Republican Rep. Lamar Smith and Vermont Democratic Sen. Patrick J. Leahy dropped some contentious language that had stalled the bill in previous congresses, such as provisions on calculating damage awards in patent infringement lawsuits. They compromised on other aspects of the bill, such as creating a new process for reviewing patents.

But the chances for the bill in the House were thrown into doubt after Appropriations and Budget Committee chairs opposed provisions allowing the patent office to keep and spend all its fees. Republicans Harold Rogers of Kentucky and Paul D. Ryan of Wisconsin argued that appropriators should maintain control of that spending.

Smith brokered a deal with Rogers and Ryan to leave the funding control with appropriators and included new language before the House took up the bill. Those changes, in turn, became a major point of contention, prompting some Democratic supporters of the measure to oppose it because of the funding language changes.

House Republican leaders, worried that Democratic and Republican opponents might muster enough votes to defeat legislation GOP leaders were touting as a job-creation bill, postponed planned action on the legislation June 22 to shore up support.

Before passing the bill, the House voted, 283–140, to adopt Smith's changes, with Democrats joining Republicans to form a majority. Supporters then defeated several other amendments but adopted one—on calculating the deadline for patent application extensions—in a contentious revote before passing the legislation.

House passed HR 1249 on June 23, 304–117: R 168–67; D 136–50. *(Vote 8, p. 798)*

9. EXTENSION OF FEDERAL AVIATION ADMINISTRATION PROGRAMS

Passage of a bill to extend the authorization for the Federal Aviation Administration (FAA).

As summer wound to a close, Congress was faced with doing what had previously been a routine exercise: Extending for a short period an expiring stopgap authorization for the FAA. House Republicans, frustrated by the glacial pace of negotiations on a longer-term reauthorization bill, attached a policy rider to the extension that was tailored to anger and provoke the Senate.

The vote on the bill (HR 2553) was a show of force by the new House Republican majority because the rider eliminated subsidies for a handful of airports that receive funding under the Essential Air Service program, which paid airlines a subsidy to keep regular service to small airports that would otherwise be unprofitable to serve. The list of airports to be cut included those in states represented by key Senate Democratic negotiators on the long-term FAA bill: Commerce, Science and Transportation Chair John D. Rockefeller IV of West Virginia, Finance Chair Max Baucus of Montana, and Majority Leader Harry Reid of Nevada. Rep. Tom Petri, R-Wis., criticized Essential Air Service as an "air limousine service."

The House passed the measure largely along party lines, and as expected, Senate Democrats refused to bring the measure to the floor. Their efforts to pass an extension were blocked by Republican senators.

The standoff ended up throwing the FAA into a two-week partial shutdown that caused the furlough of more than 3,500 employees and halted hundreds of airport construction projects. At a moment of widespread public dissatisfaction with Congress, the shutdown left both parties with black eyes. Congress departed for a summer recess with the issue unresolved.

The impasse was settled eventually when the Senate cleared the House bill by unanimous consent with the understanding that Transportation Secretary Ray LaHood would use his authority to waive cuts in Essential Air Service subsidies to the affected small airports.

House passed HR 2553 on July 20, 243–177: R 230–6; D 13–171. *(Vote 9, p. 798)*

10. DEBT LIMIT AGREEMENT

Passage of a compromise debt limit increase that was negotiated largely between the White House and Senate Republicans.

The August 1 House vote to raise the $14.3 trillion debt ceiling for the federal government capped months of political brinkmanship that consumed Capitol Hill and brought the federal government within hours of a default and unable to pay its bills. The vote was widely seen as a victory for House Republicans' yearlong effort to force deep cuts in federal spending, even though many conservatives objected to its terms.

It was neither the first time during the year, nor the last, when Speaker John A. Boehner, R-Ohio, would ask members of the House Republican Conference to accept a deal because it was the best they could get.

Leaders from both parties and Obama administration officials began anticipating the critical vote early in 2011. When it became clear that the Treasury Department would reach the statutory cap on its borrowing authority, and that Congress would be asked to raise the ceiling, the new House Republican majority signaled it would demand vigorous steps to reduce the budget deficit and slow the growth of the debt as the price for an increase. Some conservatives from both chambers contended that a refusal to raise the debt ceiling could be managed without catastrophic economic consequences, an assertion the Treasury strongly rejected.

Months of bipartisan talks led by Vice President Joseph R. Biden Jr. collapsed when Republican negotiators walked out over Democratic insistence that any deficit deal include tax increases. Talks led by President Obama at the White House also broke down.

Worried that a default would ruin the Republican Party's long-term prospects, Senate Minority Leader Mitch McConnell, R-Ky., soon proposed a fallback plan to guarantee a long-term debt ceiling increase without any spending cuts, but forced a series of symbolic votes on it throughout 2011 and 2012, in effect putting the political burden of raising the debt limit on the White House. Yet House GOP leaders warned that their restive freshmen were a wild card, unlikely to support an agreement deal that did not include major cuts.

With his credibility on the line, Boehner acceded to the demands of conservatives and successfully pushed two GOP debt ceiling plans linked to spending cuts and a balanced-budget constitutional amendment through the House, the second only after hours of late-night wrangling with recalcitrant rank-and-file members. Republicans sought to call Obama's bluff and force him to accept a short-term debt ceiling increase, with a second tranche of borrowing authority contingent on additional spending cuts. Yet after it became clear that Boehner's second bill was dead in the Senate, McConnell stepped in, engineering an eleventh-hour deal with Obama by phone.

After hours of negotiations, Republicans accepted Obama's demand that the debt ceiling be raised through the 2012 election, albeit with a series of intervening, largely symbolic votes. In return, discretionary spending would be limited by statutory spending caps through fiscal 2021, resulting in almost $1 trillion in projected savings. At the heart of the deal was a powerful trigger mechanism designed to force an additional $1.2 trillion in automatic spending cuts, unless Congress passed an alternative plan for that amount of deficit savings that was to be proposed by a special, House-Senate committee. The compromise set up guaranteed House and Senate votes, by year's end, on a balanced-budget constitutional amendment.

The deal appeared to secure sufficient support in both chambers, as both sides came to understand the consequences of a default. The threat to defense spending from the automatic cut mechanism sparked a last-minute push-back from Republicans on the House Armed Services Committee, but Boehner was able to quiet the worries by warning that the Pentagon might do worse if negotiations continued. The House then passed the bill, on August 1, by a wide margin, with most Republicans and half of the Democrats voting "yes."

House passed S 365 on August 1, 269–161: R 174–66; D 95–95. *(Vote 10, p. 798)*

11. TRADE LIBERALIZATION AGREEMENTS

Adoption of a rule to consider bills to implement trade agreements with Colombia, South Korea, and Panama, and to revive Trade Adjustment Assistance for U.S. workers.

Congress settled unfinished business from the George W. Bush administration and provided the biggest anomaly in a year of partisan stalemates by clearing free-trade agreements with Colombia (HR 3078), Panama (HR 3079), and South Korea (HR 3080) by lopsided majorities.

The House prepared the way for passage on a 281–128 vote that showed how months of negotiations among the Obama administration, trade partners, business interests, and labor unions yielded a balance on an issue that split both parties. The rule bringing the bills to the floor also set the stage for the House to send President Obama one of his priorities, an extension of aid to workers displaced by foreign trade, which many Republicans opposed.

The following day, all four bills passed by wide margins. The trade deals went back to the Senate for quick final approval, while the bill extending Trade Adjustment Assistance (HR 2832) headed for the president's signature.

Both the White House and Republicans said that the pacts will help create jobs by promoting U.S. exports, with Obama predicting a $13 billion boost.

Bush had negotiated the trade deals in 2006 and 2007. Obama campaigned against them in 2008, but in office he set about negotiating revisions to make them more acceptable. His officials reached a new deal on auto tariffs with South Korea, an agreement with Colombia to tamp down violence, and a side deal with Panama to reduce tax avoidance. The administration also demanded an expanded version of Trade Adjustment Assistance to accompany the trade deals.

House adopted the rule for consideration of trade agreements and aid to displaced workers October 11, 281–128: R 232–1; D 49–127. *(Vote 11, p. 798)*

12. ABORTION FUNDING RESTRICTIONS

Passage of a bill to ban the use of federal money for abortion services.

After a flurry of attention in the spring among newly empowered House Republicans toward repealing the health care law, the issue waned on the GOP priority list. There were, however, a few focused attempts to turn back elements of the health care overhaul, and none drew more fire than the question of abortion funding.

One bill (HR 358) would have put an outright ban, in legislation and not merely executive order, on the use of any federal money to support abortion services. Although the measure stood little chance in the Senate, the vote represented an attempt to shift more power on regulating abortion to the legislature.

The language in the health care law required that companies that receive federal money and offer insurance plans with abortion coverage must keep the money clearly segregated so no federal dollars are used in support of plans providing abortion coverage. Policyholders must use personal money to pay for their abortion coverage. In addition, President Obama signed an executive order affirming a ban against federal funding for abortion as part of a compromise struck with prolife Democrats to get the health care overhaul passed.

Obama's executive order never sat well with many conservatives. The bill would have amended the health care law to say that no federal money could be used to support any insurance plan that included coverage for abortion services, and it included an exemption in cases of rape, incest, or danger to a woman's life.

The central issue on the vote on HR 358 was about whether to extend the principle of the Hyde amendment to the new health care law. The Hyde amendment, named after former Rep. Henry J. Hyde, R-Ill., prohibited federal spending on abortion and was regularly added to legislation. Given the history of the Hyde amendment as the baseline expectation for prolife members of the House, HR 358 gave a clear picture of the strength of that contingent in the House of 2011.

House passed HR 358 on October 13, 251–172: R 236–2; D 15–170. *(Vote 12. p. 798)*

13. BALANCED-BUDGET CONSTITUTIONAL AMENDMENT

Rejection of a joint resolution proposing a constitutional amendment that would require a balanced budget.

For the first time in sixteen years the House went on record on the issue of constitutionally requiring the federal government to balance its budget, but unlike the earlier vote in 2011 the measure was rejected. Nonetheless, the vote demonstrated a marked change in House members' attitude about mandating a balanced budget. As part of the complex deal in August to raise the debt ceiling, amendment supporters won a requirement that each chamber take an up-or-down vote on the issue before the end of the year.

With their House majority, Republicans advanced to the floor a constitutional amendment to require that in every annual budget, total outlays not exceed total revenue unless a three-fifths majority in each chamber voted to allow it. The other exception would be if a congressional declaration of war was in effect, in which case a simply majority could waive the requirement.

During two days of debate preceding the vote, the chamber split generally along party lines. Each side spent time blaming the other for annual deficits approaching $1 trillion. Democrats pointed to GOP tax cuts and war funding, while Republicans said runaway entitlement spending had gotten out of control.

Democratic opponents predicted grave consequences if forced cuts materialized. A constitutional amendment would jeopardize Social Security and Medicare, said Jerrold Nadler, D-N.Y., who cited the inability of the joint deficit reduction committee to reach agreement on savings as evidence that courts would end up enforcing the cuts because of an indecisive Congress.

In the vote, although backers attracted support from more than two dozen mostly moderate Democrats, they fell short of the two-thirds requirement by twenty-three votes, killing the amendment's prospects for the session.

In an anticlimax, the Senate on December 14 turned down two versions of the amendment (S J Res 10 and S J Res 24).

House rejected H J Res 2 on November 18, 261–165: R 236–4; D 25–161. (A two-thirds majority is required to advance a constitutional amendment. *(Vote 13, p. 798)*

14. PAYROLL TAX CUT EXTENSION

Adoption of a motion to disagree with the Senate amendment to the payroll tax cut bill and to request a House-Senate conference to resolve differences.

All year long, Speaker John A. Boehner, R-Ohio, struggled to get the Tea Party–aligned members of the House Republican Conference to accept compromises on economic policies they did not like. In mid-December, when he told Senate Majority Leader Harry Reid, D-Nev., and Minority Leader Mitch McConnell, R-Ky., to make a deal to extend the expiring Social Security payroll tax cut, Boehner probably did not know that he would have to contend yet again with a rebellious caucus. Nor did he probably anticipate that in the end he would have to unilaterally overrule his unhappy troops.

The House had been for some time unwilling to consider the payroll tax cut extension, which was a centerpiece of the jobs package President Obama presented in September to a joint session of Congress. However, public support was strong to retain the worker share of the Social Security tax at 4.2 percent, down from the pre-2011 rate of 6.2 percent. As a result, in December the House passed a bill (HR 3630) to renew the payroll tax cut, to extend some but not all expiring benefits for some long-term unemployed workers and to continue current Medicare reimbursement rates for physicians. In addition, the House bill required the president to act promptly on the controversial Keystone XL oil pipeline from Canada to the Gulf of Mexico. It also paid for the cost with a mix of fee increases and spending cuts, including a pay freeze for federal workers through 2013.

Senate Democrats quickly denounced the House measure, and Reid and McConnell set about trying to negotiate a compromise that all sides might accept. McConnell said he kept Boehner informed of their progress, and Boehner had indicated before the Senate voted that he would bring to a vote whatever McConnell and Reid devised.

But when Reid and McConnell settled on a two-month extension of the payroll tax cut, jobless benefits, and Medicare reimbursements, rank-and-file House Republicans, including some of Boehner's fellow House GOP leaders, revolted.

They were not even placated by the inclusion of the Keystone pipeline language in the two-month compromise. Nor at first did the Senate's overwhelming bipartisan support for the short-term extension faze the House GOP.

Boehner was forced to back away from scheduling an up-or-down vote on the Senate language, and instead the House voted on a motion to disagree with the Senate amendment and request that a conference committee convene to continue the negotiations. House Republicans insisted that a two-month extension amounted to an abrogation of Congress's duty to provide tax certainty for Americans and demanded that the Senate come back into session to work on a yearlong deal instead.

Boehner and his conferees even met—alone—to emphasize that the Senate was already gone from Washington. But public sentiment clearly had turned against the House, and even most Senate Republicans who spoke out, including McConnell, urged the House to accept the short-term deal.

Three days after the initial House vote, Boehner gave in. On a conference call, he informed his fellow House GOP lawmakers, most of whom were out of town, that their gambit had not worked, and this time he did not allow any dissenting comments in the call. The following morning, both chambers passed by unanimous consent a slightly modified version of the Senate's two-month extension. The only shred of a victory that the House GOP could claim on the back-and-forth with the Senate is that a conference committee still had to negotiate the yearlong extension that many Republicans never wanted in the first place.

House adopted the motion to disagree with the Senate amendment and request a conference on HR 3630 on December 20, 229–193: R 229–7; D 0–186. *(Vote 14, p. 798)*

1. HR 2. Repeal of Health Care Overhaul. Passage of the bill to repeal the 2010 health care overhaul, which required most individuals to buy health insurance by 2014, made changes to government health care programs, and set new requirements for health insurers. Passed 245–189: R 242–0; D 3–189. A "nay" was a vote in support of the president's position. January 19, 2011.

2. HR 1. Funding for F-35 Alternative Engine. Rooney, R-Fla., amendment to reduce funding for Army and Air Force research, development, testing, and evaluation by $450 million, with the aim of reducing funding by that amount for the F-35 Joint Strike Fighter alternative engine. Adopted 233–198: R 110–130; D 123–68. A "yea" was a vote in support of the president's position. February 16, 2011.

3. HR 910. Greenhouse Gas Regulation. Passage of the bill to prohibit the Environmental Protection Agency (EPA) from regulating greenhouse gases in any effort to address climate change by amending the Clean Air Act to strike specific elements from the definition of "air pollutant," unless regulation of those chemicals is not used in an attempt to address climate change. Passed 255–172: R 236–0; D 19–172. A "nay" was a vote in support of the president's position. April 7, 2011.

4. H Con Res 34. Budget Resolution. Adoption of the concurrent resolution to allow $2.9 trillion in new budget authority for fiscal 2012, including up to $1.0 trillion in nonemergency discretionary spending. The resolution called for $659 billion in security spending and $360 billion in nonsecurity spending and converting the federal share of Medicaid to a block grant to states. It also called for converting Medicare for persons currently younger than fifty-five into a system in which the government would pay private insurance companies directly for each enrollee. It also assumed consolidating the current six tax brackets and cutting the corporate tax rate and the top individual tax rate to 25 percent. Adopted 235–193: R 235–4; D 0–189. April 15, 2011.

5. HR 1540. Prosecution of Suspected Terrorists. Buchanan, R-Fla., amendment to require all foreign terrorism suspects who are accused of attacking the United States, its government, or its personnel, and who are subject to trial for that offense, to be tried only by a military commission. Adopted 246–173: R 228–7; D 18–166. A "nay" was a vote in support of the president's position. May 26, 2011.

6. S 990. Patriot Act Extension. Smith, R-Texas, motion to concur in a Senate amendment to extend through June 1, 2015, three provisions of the antiterrorism law known as the Patriot Act. The provisions allowed the government to seek court orders for roving wiretaps on suspects who use multiple devices or modes of communication, to request access to "any tangible thing" deemed related to a terrorism investigation, and to seek warrants to conduct surveillance of "lone wolf" foreign terrorist suspects who may not be connected to a larger terrorist group. Motion agreed to (clearing the bill for the president) 250–153: R 196–31; D 54–122. A "yea" was a vote in support of the president's position. May 26, 2011.

7. H Res 292. Limitation on Forces in Libya. Adoption of the resolution to direct the administration to transmit certain documents to the House and direct the president to transmit a report within fourteen days containing information about the military activity in Libya. The resolution stated that the armed forces should be used exclusively to defend and advance U.S. national security interests, that the president did not provide a "compelling rationale" to Congress regarding the action in Libya, and that the president should not deploy ground forces in Libya other than to rescue a member of the armed forces in imminent danger. Adopted 268–145: R 223–10; D 45–135. June 3, 2011.

8. HR 1249. Patent Law Overhaul. Passage of the bill to overhaul the U.S. patent system, changing how patents are awarded, reviewed, and challenged. The legislation changed the basis for awarding patents from a "first to invent" to a "first inventor to file" standard. It also altered the process for challenging the validity of issued patents through the U.S. Patent and Trademark Office review proceedings, as well as authorized a reexamination of certain previously issued business method patents. Passed 304–117: R 168–67; D 136–50. A "yea" was a vote in support of the president's position. June 23, 2011.

9. HR 2553. Extension of Federal Aviation Administration Programs. Passage of legislation to reauthorize the Federal Aviation Administration through September 16, 2011. The legislation required that communities be at least ninety miles from a hub airport, up from seventy miles, in order to receive benefits from the Essential Air Service program. Passed 243–177: R 230–6; D 13–171. July 20, 2011.

10. S 365. Debt Limit Agreement. Passage of the bill to provide a process to reduce the federal deficit by up to $2.4 trillion. The measure allowed the president to raise the debt limit immediately by $400 billion, with an additional $500 billion subject to a resolution of disapproval in Congress. The bill set discretionary spending caps to reduce the deficit by $917 billion in fiscal 2012 through 2021 and establish a firewall between security and nonsecurity spending for fiscal 2012 and 2013. It established a bipartisan, bicameral committee tasked with making recommendations to reduce the deficit by $1.5 trillion, and required Congress to vote on a balanced-budget constitutional amendment by the end of 2011. Passed 269–161: R 174–66; D 95–95. A "yea" was a vote in support of the president's position. August 1, 2011.

11. HR 3078, HR 3079, HR 3080. Trade Liberalization Agreements. Adoption of the rule (H Res 425) to provide for House floor consideration of bills to implement trade agreements with Colombia (HR 3078), Panama (HR 3079), and South Korea (HR 3080). It also provided for consideration of the Senate amendment to a bill (HR 2832) to extend Trade Adjustment Assistance programs and the Generalized System of Preferences. Adopted 281–128: R 232–1; D 49–127. October 11, 2011.

12. HR 358. Abortion Funding Restrictions. Passage of the bill to bar the use of federal funds to purchase insurance plans that cover abortion services. The bill required that insurance companies offering plans on state exchanges that cover abortion services also offer identical plans that do not cover abortion services. It also barred federal agencies and state or local entities that receive funding under the health care overhaul, passed in 2010, from discriminating against health care entities that refuse to provide abortions or training related to abortions. Passed 251–172: R 236–2; D 15–170. A "nay" was a vote in support of the president's position. October 13, 2011.

13. H J Res 2. Balanced-budget Constitutional Amendment. Smith, R-Texas, motion to suspend the rules and pass the joint resolution proposing a constitutional amendment to require a federal government balanced budget starting in fiscal 2018 or the second fiscal year after ratification by three-fourths of the states, whichever was later. Under the proposal, three-fifths of the entire House and Senate would be required to approve deficit spending or an increase in the public debt limit. A simple majority could waive the requirement in times of congressionally declared war or in the face of a serious military threat. Motion rejected 261–165: R 236–4; D 25–161. A two-thirds majority of those present and voting (284 in this case) is required for passage under suspension of the rules and to pass a joint resolution proposing an amendment to the Constitution. A "nay" was a vote in support of the president's position. November 18, 2011.

14. HR 3630. Payroll Tax Cut Extension. Camp, R-Mich., motion to disagree with the Senate amendments to extend the 4.2 percent employee payroll tax rate, Medicare payment rates for doctors, and workers' eligibility for certain expanded unemployment benefits through February 2012, and to request a conference on the bill (HR 3630). Motion agreed to 229–193: R 229–7; D 0–186. December 20, 2011.

KEY

Republican		Democrat		**Independent**
Y	Voted for (yea)	–	Announced against	
#	Paired for	P	Voted "present"	
+	Announced for	C	Voted "present" to avoid possible conflict of interest	
N	Voted against (nay)			
X	Paired against	?	Did not vote or otherwise make a position known	

House Key Votes		1	2	3	4	5	6	7	8	9	10	11	12	13	14
ALABAMA															
1	*Bonner*	Y	N	Y	Y	Y	Y	Y	Y	Y	Y	Y	Y	Y	Y
2	*Roby*	Y	Y	Y	Y	Y	Y	Y	Y	Y	N	Y	Y	Y	Y
3	*Rogers*	Y	N	Y	Y	Y	Y	Y	Y	Y	Y	Y	Y	Y	Y
4	*Aderholt*	Y	N	Y	Y	Y	Y	Y	N	Y	Y	Y	Y	Y	Y
5	*Brooks*	Y	N	Y	Y	Y	Y	Y	N	Y	N	Y	Y	Y	Y
6	*Bachus*	Y	N	Y	Y	Y	Y	Y	Y	Y	Y	Y	Y	Y	Y
7	Sewell	N	N	Y	N	N	Y	N	Y	Y	Y	Y	N	N	N
ALASKA															
AL	*Young*	Y	N	?	Y	Y	N	Y	Y	?	Y	Y	Y	Y	Y
ARIZONA															
1	*Gosar*	Y	Y	Y	Y	Y	Y	Y	N	Y	Y	Y	Y	Y	Y
2	*Franks*	Y	N	Y	Y	Y	Y	Y	N	Y	N	Y	Y	Y	Y
3	*Quayle*	Y	Y	Y	Y	Y	Y	Y	Y	Y	N	Y	Y	Y	Y
4	Pastor	N	Y	N	N	N	N	N	N	N	N	N	N	N	N
5	*Schweikert*	Y	Y	Y	Y	Y	Y	N	Y	Y	N	Y	Y	Y	Y
6	*Flake*	Y	Y	Y	Y	?	?	N	N	Y	N	Y	Y	Y	N
7	Grijalva	N	Y	N	N	N	N	N	N	N	N	?	N	N	N
8	Giffords	?	?	?	?	?	?	?	?	?	Y	?	?	?	?
ARKANSAS															
1	*Crawford*	Y	Y	Y	Y	Y	Y	Y	Y	Y	Y	Y	Y	Y	Y
2	*Griffin*	Y	Y	Y	Y	Y	Y	Y	Y	Y	Y	Y	Y	Y	Y
3	*Womack*	Y	Y	Y	Y	Y	Y	Y	Y	Y	Y	Y	Y	Y	Y
4	Ross	Y	Y	Y	N	Y	Y	Y	Y	N	Y	Y	Y	Y	N
CALIFORNIA															
1	Thompson	N	Y	N	N	N	N	N	Y	N	Y	Y	N	N	N
2	*Herger*	Y	Y	Y	Y	Y	Y	Y	Y	Y	Y	Y	Y	Y	Y
3	*Lungren*	Y	Y	Y	Y	Y	Y	Y	N	Y	Y	Y	Y	Y	Y
4	*McClintock*	Y	Y	Y	Y	Y	N	Y	N	Y	N	Y	Y	Y	Y
5	Matsui	N	Y	N	N	N	N	N	N	N	N	Y	N	N	N
6	Woolsey	N	Y	N	N	N	N	N	N	N	N	N	N	N	–
7	Miller, George	N	Y	N	N	N	–	+	N	N	N	N	N	N	N
8	Pelosi	N	Y	N	N	N	N	N	N	?	Y	N	N	N	N
9	Lee	N	Y	N	N	N	N	N	N	N	N	N	N	N	N
10	Garamendi	N	Y	N	N	N	N	Y	N	N	Y	N	N	N	N
11	McNerney	N	N	N	N	N	N	Y	N	N	N	N	N	N	N
12	Speier	N	Y	N	N	N	N	N	Y	N	Y	N	N	N	N
13	Stark	N	Y	N	N	N	N	Y	N	N	N	N	N	N	N
14	Eshoo	N	Y	N	N	N	N	N	N	N	Y	Y	N	N	N
15	Honda	N	Y	N	N	N	N	N	N	N	N	N	N	N	N
16	Lofgren	N	Y	N	N	N	N	?	N	Y	N	Y	N	N	N
17	Farr	N	Y	N	N	N	N	N	N	N	N	Y	N	N	N
18	Cardoza	N	Y	N	N	Y	Y	N	Y	N	N	Y	N	Y	N
19	*Denham*	Y	Y	Y	Y	Y	Y	Y	N	Y	Y	Y	Y	Y	Y
20	Costa	N	Y	Y	N	Y	Y	N	Y	N	Y	Y	N	Y	N
21	*Nunes*	Y	N	Y	Y	Y	Y	Y	Y	Y	N	Y	Y	?	Y
22	*McCarthy*	Y	N	Y	Y	Y	Y	Y	Y	Y	Y	Y	Y	Y	Y
23	Capps	N	Y	N	N	N	N	N	Y	N	Y	N	N	N	N
24	*Gallegly*	Y	N	Y	Y	Y	Y	Y	Y	Y	Y	Y	Y	Y	Y
25	*McKeon*	Y	N	Y	Y	Y	?	Y	Y	Y	Y	Y	Y	Y	Y
26	*Dreier*	Y	N	Y	Y	Y	Y	Y	Y	Y	Y	Y	Y	N	Y
27	Sherman	N	Y	N	N	N	N	N	N	N	Y	N	N	N	N
28	Berman	N	Y	N	N	N	?	N	Y	N	Y	Y	N	N	N
29	Schiff	N	Y	N	N	N	Y	N	N	N	Y	Y	N	N	N
30	Waxman	N	Y	N	N	N	N	N	N	N	N	N	N	N	N
31	Becerra	N	Y	N	N	N	–	N	Y	N	N	N	N	N	N
32	Chu	N	N	N	N	N	N	N	Y	N	N	N	N	N	N
33	Bass	N	Y	N	N	N	N	N	Y	N	Y	Y	N	–	N
34	Roybal-Allard	N	N	N	N	N	N	N	Y	N	N	N	N	N	N
35	Waters	N	Y	N	N	N	N	P	N	N	N	N	N	N	N
36	Harman[1]	N	Y												
36	Hahn[1]									N	N	N	N	N	N
37	Richardson	N	N	N	N	N	N	Y	Y	N	N	–	N	N	N
38	Napolitano	N	Y	N	N	N	N	N	+	N	N	–	N	–	N
39	Sanchez, Linda	N	Y	N	N	N	N	N	Y	N	N	?	N	N	N
40	*Royce*	Y	Y	Y	Y	Y	Y	Y	N	Y	Y	Y	Y	Y	Y
41	*Lewis*	Y	N	Y	Y	Y	Y	Y	Y	Y	Y	Y	Y	Y	Y
42	*Miller, Gary*	Y	N	Y	Y	Y	Y	Y	Y	Y	Y	Y	Y	Y	Y
43	Baca	N	Y	N	N	N	?	N	Y	N	+	N	N	N	N
44	*Calvert*	Y	N	Y	Y	Y	Y	Y	Y	Y	Y	Y	Y	Y	Y
45	*Bono Mack*	Y	N	Y	Y	Y	?	Y	Y	Y	Y	Y	Y	Y	Y
46	*Rohrabacher*	Y	Y	Y	Y	Y	N	Y	N	Y	Y	Y	Y	Y	Y
47	Sanchez, Loretta	N	N	N	N	Y	?	N	N	N	Y	N	N	N	N
48	*Campbell*	Y	Y	Y	Y	Y	N	N	Y	Y	Y	Y	Y	Y	Y
49	*Issa*	Y	N	Y	Y	Y	Y	Y	Y	Y	Y	Y	Y	Y	Y
50	*Bilbray*	Y	N	Y	Y	Y	Y	Y	Y	Y	Y	Y	Y	Y	Y
51	Filner	N	Y	N	N	–	–	N	N	N	N	N	N	–	–
52	*Hunter*	Y	N	Y	Y	Y	Y	Y	N	Y	N	Y	Y	Y	Y
53	Davis	N	Y	N	N	N	Y	N	Y	N	Y	Y	N	N	N
COLORADO															
1	DeGette	N	Y	N	N	N	N	N	N	N	N	N	N	N	N
2	Polis	N	Y	N	N	N	N	–	–	Y	Y	?	?	N	N
3	*Tipton*	Y	Y	Y	Y	Y	N	Y	Y	Y	N	Y	Y	Y	Y
4	*Gardner*	Y	Y	Y	Y	Y	Y	Y	Y	Y	Y	Y	Y	Y	Y
5	*Lamborn*	Y	N	Y	Y	Y	Y	Y	N	Y	N	Y	Y	Y	Y
6	Coffman	Y	Y	Y	Y	Y	Y	Y	N	Y	Y	Y	Y	Y	Y
7	Perlmutter	N	Y	N	N	N	N	N	Y	N	Y	?	N	N	N
CONNECTICUT															
1	Larson	N	Y	N	N	N	N	N	Y	N	N	N	N	N	N
2	Courtney	N	Y	N	N	N	N	N	Y	N	Y	N	N	N	N
3	DeLauro	N	Y	N	N	N	N	N	Y	N	N	N	N	N	N
4	Himes	N	Y	N	N	N	N	Y	Y	N	Y	Y	N	N	N
5	Murphy	N	Y	N	N	N	N	N	Y	N	N	N	N	N	N
DELAWARE															
AL	Carney	N	N	N	N	N	Y	N	Y	Y	Y	Y	N	N	N
FLORIDA															
1	*Miller*	Y	Y	Y	Y	Y	Y	+	N	Y	Y	Y	Y	Y	Y
2	*Southerland*	Y	Y	Y	Y	Y	Y	Y	N	Y	N	Y	Y	Y	Y
3	Brown	N	Y	N	N	N	Y	N	Y	N	N	?	?	N	N
4	*Crenshaw*	Y	N	Y	Y	Y	Y	Y	Y	Y	Y	Y	Y	Y	Y
5	*Nugent*	Y	N	Y	Y	Y	Y	Y	Y	Y	Y	Y	Y	Y	Y
6	*Stearns*	Y	Y	Y	Y	Y	Y	Y	Y	Y	N	Y	Y	Y	Y
7	*Mica*	Y	Y	Y	Y	Y	Y	Y	Y	Y	Y	Y	Y	Y	Y
8	*Webster*	Y	Y	Y	Y	Y	Y	Y	N	Y	Y	Y	Y	Y	Y
9	*Bilirakis*	Y	N	+	Y	Y	Y	Y	N	Y	Y	Y	Y	Y	Y
10	*Young*	Y	N	Y	Y	Y	Y	Y	N	Y	Y	Y	Y	Y	Y
11	Castor	N	Y	N	N	N	?	Y	Y	?	Y	Y	N	N	N
12	*Ross*	Y	N	Y	Y	Y	Y	Y	Y	Y	N	Y	Y	Y	Y
13	*Buchanan*	Y	Y	Y	Y	Y	?	Y	Y	Y	Y	Y	Y	Y	?
14	*Mack*	Y	Y	Y	Y	Y	N	Y	N	Y	N	Y	Y	Y	Y
15	*Posey*	Y	Y	Y	Y	Y	N	Y	N	Y	N	Y	Y	Y	Y
16	*Rooney*	Y	Y	Y	Y	Y	Y	Y	Y	Y	Y	Y	Y	Y	Y
17	*Wilson*	N	Y	N	N	N	N	N	Y	N	Y	?	?	N	N
18	*Ros-Lehtinen*	Y	N	Y	Y	Y	Y	Y	Y	Y	Y	Y	Y	Y	Y
19	*Deutch*	N	Y	N	N	N	Y	N	Y	N	Y	Y	N	?	N
20	*Wasserman Schultz*	N	N	N	N	N	Y	N	Y	N	Y	?	N	N	N
21	*Diaz-Balart*	Y	N	Y	Y	Y	Y	Y	Y	Y	Y	Y	Y	Y	?
22	*West*	Y	Y	Y	Y	Y	N	N	N	Y	Y	Y	Y	Y	Y
23	*Hastings*	N	Y	N	N	N	N	N	Y	N	N	Y	N	N	N
24	*Adams*	Y	Y	Y	Y	Y	Y	Y	Y	Y	Y	Y	Y	Y	Y
25	*Rivera*	Y	N	Y	Y	Y	Y	Y	Y	Y	Y	Y	Y	Y	Y

[1]Rep. Janice Hahn, D-Calif., was sworn in July 19, 2011, to fill the vacancy created by the February 28 resignation of fellow Democrat Jane Harman. The first key vote for which Hahn was eligible was vote 9; the last key vote for which Harman was eligible was vote 2.

KEY

	Republican		Democrat		**Independent**
Y	Voted for (yea)	–	Announced against		
#	Paired for	P	Voted "present"		
+	Announced for	C	Voted "present" to avoid possible conflict of interest		
N	Voted against (nay)				
X	Paired against	?	Did not vote or otherwise make a position known		

House Key Votes		1	2	3	4	5	6	7	8	9	10	11	12	13	14
GEORGIA															
1	*Kingston*	Y	N	Y	Y	Y	Y	Y	N	Y	N	Y	Y	Y	Y
2	Bishop	N	Y	Y	N	N	Y	Y	Y	N	Y	Y	Y	Y	N
3	*Westmoreland*	Y	Y	Y	Y	Y	Y	Y	Y	Y	N	Y	Y	Y	Y
4	Johnson	N	Y	N	N	N	N	?	Y	N	Y	Y	N	N	N
5	Lewis	N	Y	N	N	N	N	N	Y	N	N	N	N	N	N
6	*Price*	Y	N	Y	Y	Y	Y	Y	Y	Y	Y	Y	Y	Y	Y
7	*Woodall*	Y	N	Y	Y	Y	N	Y	Y	Y	Y	Y	Y	Y	Y
8	*Scott, A.*	Y	Y	Y	Y	Y	Y	Y	N	Y	N	Y	Y	Y	Y
9	*Graves*	Y	Y	Y	Y	Y	N	Y	N	Y	N	Y	Y	Y	Y
10	*Broun*	Y	Y	Y	Y	Y	N	Y	N	Y	N	Y	Y	Y	Y
11	*Gingrey*	Y	Y	Y	Y	Y	Y	Y	+	Y	N	Y	Y	Y	Y
12	Barrow	N	Y	Y	N	Y	Y	Y	Y	Y	Y	N	N	Y	N
13	Scott, D.	N	N	N	N	N	Y	N	Y	N	Y	N	N	N	N
HAWAII															
1	Hanabusa	N	Y	N	N	N	N	Y	Y	N	Y	Y	N	N	N
2	Hirono	N	Y	N	N	N	N	N	N	N	Y	Y	N	N	N
IDAHO															
1	*Labrador*	Y	Y	Y	Y	Y	N	Y	Y	Y	N	Y	Y	Y	Y
2	*Simpson*	Y	N	Y	Y	Y	Y	Y	Y	Y	Y	Y	Y	Y	Y
ILLINOIS															
1	Rush	N	N	N	N	N	N	?	N	N	Y	Y	N	N	N
2	Jackson	N	Y	N	N	–	–	N	Y	N	N	Y	N	N	N
3	Lipinski	N	N	N	N	Y	Y	Y	N	N	Y	N	Y	Y	N
4	Gutierrez	N	N	N	N	N	N	N	Y	N	Y	Y	N	N	N
5	Quigley	N	Y	N	N	N	Y	N	Y	N	Y	N	N	N	N
6	*Roskam*	Y	N	Y	Y	Y	Y	Y	Y	Y	Y	Y	Y	Y	Y
7	Davis	N	Y	N	N	N	N	N	Y	N	Y	N	N	N	N
8	Walsh	Y	Y	Y	Y	Y	Y	N	Y	Y	N	?	Y	Y	Y
9	Schakowsky	N	Y	N	N	N	N	N	Y	N	N	N	N	N	N
10	*Dold*	Y	Y	Y	Y	N	Y	Y	Y	Y	Y	Y	Y	Y	Y
11	*Kinzinger*	Y	N	Y	Y	Y	Y	Y	Y	Y	Y	Y	Y	Y	Y
12	*Costello*	N	N	Y	N	Y	N	Y	N	N	Y	N	Y	Y	N
13	*Biggert*	Y	N	Y	Y	Y	Y	Y	Y	Y	Y	Y	N	Y	Y
14	*Hultgren*	Y	N	Y	Y	Y	Y	Y	N	Y	N	Y	Y	Y	Y
15	*Johnson*	Y	Y	Y	Y	Y	N	N	Y	Y	N	Y	Y	Y	N
16	*Manzullo*	Y	N	Y	Y	Y	N	Y	N	Y	Y	Y	Y	Y	Y
17	*Schilling*	Y	N	Y	Y	Y	Y	Y	N	Y	Y	Y	Y	Y	Y
18	*Schock*	Y	Y	Y	Y	Y	Y	Y	N	Y	Y	Y	Y	Y	Y
19	*Shimkus*	Y	N	Y	Y	Y	Y	Y	Y	Y	Y	Y	Y	Y	Y
INDIANA															
1	Visclosky	N	N	N	N	N	N	Y	N	N	N	–	N	N	N
2	Donnelly	N	N	Y	N	Y	Y	N	Y	Y	Y	N	Y	Y	N
3	*Stutzman*	Y	N	Y	Y	Y	Y	Y	Y	Y	N	Y	Y	Y	Y
4	*Rokita*	Y	N	Y	Y	Y	N	Y	Y	Y	N	Y	Y	Y	Y
5	*Burton*	Y	N	Y	Y	Y	Y	Y	N	Y	N	?	Y	Y	Y
6	*Pence*	Y	N	Y	Y	Y	Y	Y	Y	Y	Y	?	Y	Y	Y
7	*Carson*	N	N	N	N	N	N	N	Y	Y	N	N	N	N	N
8	*Bucshon*	Y	N	Y	Y	Y	Y	Y	Y	Y	Y	Y	Y	Y	Y
9	*Young*	Y	N	Y	Y	Y	Y	Y	Y	Y	Y	Y	Y	Y	Y
IOWA															
1	Braley	N	Y	N	N	N	N	Y	Y	N	N	N	N	N	N
2	Loebsack	N	N	N	N	N	N	Y	Y	N	N	N	N	Y	N

House Key Votes		1	2	3	4	5	6	7	8	9	10	11	12	13	14
3	Boswell	N	N	Y	N	N	Y	Y	Y	N	N	N	N	Y	N
4	*Latham*	Y	N	Y	Y	Y	Y	Y	Y	Y	N	Y	Y	Y	Y
5	*King*	Y	N	Y	Y	Y	Y	Y	N	Y	N	Y	Y	Y	Y
KANSAS															
1	*Huelskamp*	Y	Y	Y	Y	Y	+	N	N	Y	N	Y	Y	Y	Y
2	*Jenkins*	Y	Y	Y	Y	Y	Y	Y	Y	Y	Y	Y	Y	Y	Y
3	*Yoder*	Y	Y	Y	Y	Y	Y	Y	Y	Y	N	Y	Y	Y	Y
4	*Pompeo*	Y	Y	Y	Y	Y	+	Y	Y	Y	Y	Y	Y	Y	Y
KENTUCKY															
1	*Whitfield*	Y	N	Y	Y	Y	Y	Y	Y	Y	Y	Y	Y	Y	Y
2	*Guthrie*	Y	N	Y	Y	Y	Y	+	Y	Y	Y	Y	Y	Y	Y
3	*Yarmuth*	N	N	N	N	N	N	Y	Y	N	N	N	N	N	N
4	*Davis*	Y	N	Y	Y	Y	Y	Y	N	Y	N	Y	Y	Y	Y
5	*Rogers*	Y	N	Y	Y	Y	Y	Y	Y	Y	Y	Y	Y	Y	Y
6	Chandler	N	N	Y	N	Y	Y	Y	Y	N	Y	N	N	Y	N
LOUISIANA															
1	*Scalise*	Y	N	Y	Y	Y	Y	Y	Y	Y	N	Y	Y	Y	Y
2	Richmond	N	N	N	N	N	N	N	Y	N	Y	N	N	N	N
3	*Landry*	Y	Y	Y	Y	Y	Y	Y	N	Y	N	Y	Y	Y	Y
4	*Fleming*	Y	N	Y	Y	Y	Y	Y	Y	Y	N	Y	Y	Y	Y
5	*Alexander*	Y	N	Y	Y	Y	Y	Y	Y	Y	Y	Y	Y	Y	Y
6	*Cassidy*	Y	Y	Y	Y	Y	Y	Y	Y	Y	Y	Y	Y	Y	Y
7	*Boustany*	Y	Y	Y	Y	?	+	Y	Y	Y	Y	Y	Y	Y	Y
MAINE															
1	Pingree	N	Y	N	N	N	N	Y	N	N	N	N	N	N	N
2	Michaud	N	Y	N	N	N	N	Y	Y	N	Y	N	N	N	N
MARYLAND															
1	*Harris*	Y	Y	Y	Y	Y	N	Y	Y	Y	N	Y	Y	Y	Y
2	Ruppersberger	N	N	N	N	N	Y	N	Y	N	Y	N	N	N	N
3	Sarbanes	N	N	N	N	N	N	N	Y	N	N	N	N	N	N
4	Edwards	N	Y	N	N	N	N	N	N	N	N	N	N	N	N
5	Hoyer	N	Y	N	N	N	Y	?	Y	?	Y	Y	N	N	N
6	*Bartlett*	Y	N	Y	Y	Y	N	Y	N	Y	Y	Y	Y	Y	Y
7	Cummings	N	Y	N	N	N	N	N	Y	N	N	N	N	N	N
8	Van Hollen	N	Y	N	N	N	N	N	Y	N	Y	N	N	N	N
MASSACHUSETTS															
1	Olver	N	Y	N	?	?	?	N	Y	N	N	N	N	?	?
2	Neal	N	Y	N	N	N	N	?	Y	N	N	N	N	N	N
3	McGovern	N	N	N	N	N	N	N	Y	N	N	N	N	N	N
4	Frank	N	Y	N	N	N	N	N	Y	N	N	?	N	N	N
5	Tsongas	N	N	N	N	N	Y	Y	N	N	Y	N	N	N	N
6	Tierney	N	N	N	N	N	N	N	Y	N	N	N	N	N	N
7	Markey	N	N	N	N	N	N	N	N	N	N	N	N	N	N
8	Capuano	N	N	N	N	N	N	N	Y	–	N	N	N	N	N
9	Lynch	N	Y	N	N	N	N	Y	Y	N	Y	N	N	N	N
10	Keating	N	N	N	N	N	Y	N	Y	N	Y	N	N	N	N
MICHIGAN															
1	*Benishek*	Y	Y	Y	Y	Y	Y	Y	N	Y	Y	Y	Y	Y	Y
2	*Huizenga*	Y	Y	Y	Y	Y	Y	Y	Y	Y	Y	Y	Y	Y	Y
3	*Amash*	Y	Y	Y	Y	N	N	Y	N	N	N	Y	Y	N	Y
4	*Camp*	Y	Y	Y	Y	Y	Y	Y	Y	Y	Y	Y	?	Y	Y
5	*Kildee*	N	N	N	N	N	N	N	N	N	Y	N	N	N	N
6	*Upton*	Y	Y	Y	Y	Y	Y	Y	Y	Y	Y	Y	Y	Y	Y
7	*Walberg*	Y	N	Y	Y	Y	Y	Y	Y	Y	Y	Y	Y	Y	Y
8	*Rogers*	Y	N	Y	Y	Y	Y	Y	Y	Y	Y	Y	Y	Y	Y
9	*Peters*	N	N	N	N	N	Y	Y	Y	N	N	N	N	N	N
10	*Miller*	Y	Y	Y	Y	Y	Y	Y	Y	Y	Y	Y	Y	Y	Y
11	McCotter	Y	N	Y	Y	Y	Y	?	N	Y	Y	Y	Y	Y	Y
12	Levin	N	N	N	N	N	Y	N	Y	N	Y	Y	N	N	N
13	Clarke	N	N	N	N	N	N	Y	N	N	N	N	N	N	N
14	Conyers	N	Y	N	N	N	–	N	N	N	N	N	N	N	N
15	Dingell	N	N	N	N	?	?	N	Y	N	Y	Y	N	N	N
MINNESOTA															
1	Walz	N	Y	N	N	N	N	Y	Y	N	Y	N	N	N	N
2	*Kline*	Y	N	Y	Y	Y	Y	Y	Y	Y	Y	Y	Y	Y	Y
3	*Paulsen*	Y	Y	Y	Y	Y	Y	Y	Y	Y	Y	Y	Y	Y	Y
4	McCollum	N	Y	N	N	N	N	N	Y	N	N	N	N	N	N
5	Ellison	N	Y	N	N	N	N	N	Y	–	N	N	N	N	N
6	*Bachmann*	Y	N	Y	Y	Y	Y	Y	N	?	N	?	?	Y	?
7	*Peterson*	N	Y	Y	N	N	Y	Y	Y	N	Y	Y	Y	Y	N
8	*Cravaack*	Y	N	Y	Y	Y	Y	Y	N	Y	N	Y	Y	Y	Y

House Key Votes	1	2	3	4	5	6	7	8	9	10	11	12	13	14
MISSISSIPPI														
1 *Nunnelee*	Y	N	Y	Y	Y	Y	Y	N	Y	Y	?	Y	Y	Y
2 *Thompson*	N	N	N	N	N	N	N	Y	N	N	N	N	N	N
3 *Harper*	Y	N	Y	Y	Y	Y	Y	Y	Y	Y	Y	Y	Y	Y
4 *Palazzo*	Y	N	Y	Y	Y	Y	Y	Y	Y	Y	Y	Y	Y	Y
MISSOURI														
1 Clay	N	Y	N	N	N	N	N	Y	N	Y	N	N	N	N
2 *Akin*	Y	N	Y	Y	Y	?	Y	N	Y	N	Y	Y	Y	Y
3 Carnahan	N	Y	N	N	N	N	N	Y	N	Y	N	N	N	N
4 *Hartzler*	Y	N	Y	Y	Y	Y	Y	N	Y	N	Y	Y	Y	Y
5 Cleaver	N	N	N	N	N	N	N	Y	N	N	N	N	N	N
6 *Graves*	Y	Y	Y	Y	Y	Y	Y	Y	Y	Y	+	Y	Y	Y
7 *Long*	Y	Y	Y	Y	+	+	Y	Y	Y	Y	Y	Y	Y	Y
8 *Emerson*	Y	N	Y	Y	Y	Y	Y	N	Y	Y	Y	Y	Y	Y
9 *Luetkemeyer*	Y	N	Y	Y	Y	Y	Y	Y	Y	Y	Y	Y	Y	Y
MONTANA														
AL *Rehberg*	Y	Y	Y	N	Y	N	Y	N	N	N	Y	Y	Y	Y
NEBRASKA														
1 *Fortenberry*	Y	N	Y	Y	Y	Y	Y	N	Y	Y	Y	Y	Y	Y
2 *Terry*	Y	N	Y	Y	Y	Y	Y	N	Y	Y	Y	Y	Y	Y
3 *Smith*	Y	N	Y	Y	Y	Y	Y	N	Y	Y	Y	Y	Y	Y
NEVADA														
1 Berkley	N	N	N	N	N	Y	N	Y	N	Y	N	N	N	N
2 *Heller*[2]	Y	N	Y	Y										
2 *Amodei*[2]											Y	Y	Y	Y
3 *Heck*	Y	N	Y	Y	Y	Y	Y	Y	Y	Y	Y	Y	Y	Y
NEW HAMPSHIRE														
1 *Guinta*	Y	N	Y	Y	Y	Y	Y	Y	Y	Y	Y	Y	Y	Y
2 *Bass*	Y	N	Y	Y	Y	Y	+	Y	Y	Y	Y	Y	Y	N
NEW JERSEY														
1 *Andrews*	N	N	N	N	N	Y	N	N	N	Y	N	N	N	N
2 *LoBiondo*	Y	N	Y	Y	Y	Y	Y	Y	Y	Y	Y	Y	Y	Y
3 *Runyan*	Y	N	Y	Y	Y	Y	Y	Y	?	Y	Y	Y	Y	Y
4 *Smith*	Y	N	Y	Y	Y	Y	Y	Y	Y	Y	Y	Y	Y	Y
5 *Garrett*	Y	Y	Y	Y	Y	Y	Y	N	Y	N	Y	Y	Y	Y
6 Pallone	N	Y	N	N	N	N	Y	Y	N	N	N	N	N	N
7 *Lance*	Y	Y	Y	Y	Y	Y	Y	Y	Y	Y	Y	Y	Y	Y
8 Pascrell	N	Y	N	N	N	Y	Y	Y	N	Y	N	N	N	N
9 Rothman	N	N	N	N	N	Y	N	Y	N	Y	N	N	N	N
10 Payne	N	Y	N	N	?	N	N	N	?	N	N	N	N	N
11 *Frelinghuysen*	Y	N	+	Y	Y	Y	?	Y	Y	Y	Y	Y	Y	Y
12 Holt	N	Y	N	N	N	N	N	Y	N	N	N	N	N	N
13 Sires	N	Y	N	N	N	?	N	Y	N	Y	Y	N	N	N
NEW MEXICO														
1 Heinrich	N	Y	N	N	N	N	N	Y	N	Y	N	N	N	N
2 *Pearce*	Y	Y	Y	Y	Y	Y	N	N	Y	N	Y	Y	Y	Y
3 Lujan	N	Y	N	N	N	N	N	N	N	N	N	N	N	N
NEW YORK														
1 Bishop	N	Y	N	N	N	Y	N	Y	N	Y	N	N	N	N
2 Israel	N	N	N	N	N	Y	N	Y	N	Y	N	N	N	N
3 *King*	Y	Y	Y	Y	Y	Y	Y	Y	Y	Y	Y	Y	Y	Y
4 McCarthy	N	Y	N	N	?	?	Y	Y	N	Y	N	N	N	N
5 Ackerman	N	Y	N	N	N	N	N	Y	N	N	N	N	N	N
6 Meeks	N	Y	N	?	N	N	N	?	N	Y	Y	N	N	N
7 Crowley	N	N	N	N	N	N	N	Y	N	N	N	N	N	N
8 Nadler	N	Y	N	N	N	N	N	Y	N	N	N	N	N	N
9 Weiner[3]	N	Y	N	N	N	N	N							
9 Turner[3]											Y	Y	Y	Y
10 Towns	N	Y	N	N	N	N	N	Y	N	N	N	N	N	N
11 Clarke	N	N	N	N	N	N	N	Y	N	N	N	N	N	N
12 Velazquez	N	Y	N	N	N	N	N	N	N	N	N	N	N	N
13 *Grimm*	Y	N	Y	Y	Y	Y	Y	Y	Y	Y	Y	Y	Y	Y
14 Maloney	N	Y	N	N	N	N	N	Y	N	N	N	N	N	N
15 Rangel	N	Y	N	N	N	N	N	?	N	N	Y	N	N	N
16 Serrano	N	N	N	N	N	N	N	Y	N	N	N	N	N	N
17 Engel	N	N	N	N	N	N	N	Y	N	N	N	N	N	N
18 Lowey	N	Y	N	N	N	Y	N	Y	N	Y	N	N	N	N
19 *Hayworth*	Y	Y	Y	Y	Y	Y	Y	Y	Y	Y	Y	Y	Y	Y
20 *Gibson*	Y	Y	Y	Y	Y	N	Y	N	Y	Y	Y	Y	Y	N
21 Tonko	N	N	N	N	N	N	Y	Y	N	N	N	N	N	N
22 Hinchey	N	N	N	N	N	N	N	N	?	?	?	N	N	N
23 Owens	N	Y	N	N	Y	?	Y	Y	Y	Y	Y	N	N	N
24 *Hanna*	Y	N	Y	Y	Y	N	Y	Y	Y	Y	Y	N	Y	Y
25 *Buerkle*	Y	Y	Y	Y	Y	Y	Y	N	Y	N	Y	Y	Y	Y
26 Lee[4]	Y													
26 Hochul[4]							Y	Y	Y	Y	N	N	Y	N
27 Higgins	N	N	N	N	N	Y	Y	Y	N	Y	N	N	N	N
28 Slaughter	N	N	N	N	N	N	N	N	N	N	N	–	N	N
29 *Reed*	Y	Y	Y	Y	Y	Y	Y	Y	Y	Y	Y	Y	Y	Y
NORTH CAROLINA														
1 Butterfield	N	Y	N	N	N	Y	N	Y	N	N	Y	N	N	N
2 *Ellmers*	Y	Y	Y	Y	Y	Y	Y	Y	Y	Y	Y	Y	Y	Y
3 *Jones*	Y	Y	Y	N	N	N	N	N	Y	N	N	Y	Y	N
4 Price	N	N	N	N	N	N	N	Y	N	N	N	N	N	N
5 *Foxx*	Y	N	Y	Y	Y	Y	Y	Y	Y	Y	Y	Y	Y	Y
6 *Coble*	Y	Y	Y	Y	Y	Y	Y	Y	Y	Y	Y	Y	Y	?
7 McIntyre	Y	N	Y	N	Y	Y	Y	Y	Y	N	N	Y	Y	N
8 Kissell	N	N	N	N	N	Y	N	Y	Y	N	N	N	Y	N
9 *Myrick*	Y	N	Y	Y	Y	?	?	Y	Y	Y	Y	Y	Y	Y
10 *McHenry*	Y	N	Y	Y	Y	Y	Y	Y	Y	Y	Y	Y	Y	Y
11 Shuler	N	N	N	N	Y	Y	?	Y	N	Y	N	Y	Y	N
12 Watt	N	P	N	N	N	N	N	Y	N	N	N	N	N	N
13 Miller	N	N	N	N	N	Y	N	Y	N	N	N	N	N	N
NORTH DAKOTA														
AL *Berg*	Y	N	Y	Y	Y	Y	Y	?	Y	Y	Y	Y	Y	Y
OHIO														
1 *Chabot*	Y	N	Y	Y	Y	Y	Y	Y	Y	Y	Y	Y	Y	Y
2 *Schmidt*	Y	N	Y	Y	Y	Y	Y	Y	Y	Y	Y	Y	Y	Y
3 *Turner*	Y	N	Y	Y	Y	Y	Y	N	Y	N	Y	Y	Y	Y
4 *Jordan*	Y	N	Y	Y	Y	Y	Y	Y	Y	N	Y	Y	Y	Y
5 *Latta*	Y	N	Y	Y	Y	Y	Y	Y	Y	Y	Y	Y	Y	Y
6 *Johnson*	Y	N	Y	Y	Y	Y	Y	Y	Y	Y	Y	Y	Y	Y
7 *Austria*	Y	N	Y	Y	Y	Y	Y	Y	Y	Y	Y	Y	Y	Y
8 *Boehner*[5]	Y									Y			Y	
9 Kaptur	N	N	N	N	N	N	?	N	N	N	N	N	N	N
10 Kucinich	N	N	N	N	N	N	Y	N	N	N	N	N	N	N
11 Fudge	N	N	N	N	N	N	N	Y	N	N	N	N	N	N
12 *Tiberi*	Y	N	Y	Y	Y	Y	Y	Y	Y	Y	Y	Y	Y	Y
13 Sutton	N	N	N	N	N	N	N	N	N	N	N	N	N	N
14 *LaTourette*	Y	N	Y	Y	Y	Y	Y	Y	Y	Y	Y	Y	Y	Y
15 *Stivers*	Y	N	Y	Y	Y	Y	Y	?	Y	Y	Y	Y	Y	Y
16 *Renacci*	Y	N	Y	Y	Y	Y	Y	Y	Y	Y	Y	Y	Y	Y
17 Ryan	N	N	N	N	N	N	N	N	N	N	N	N	N	N
18 *Gibbs*	Y	N	Y	Y	Y	Y	Y	Y	Y	Y	Y	Y	Y	Y
OKLAHOMA														
1 Sullivan	Y	Y	Y	Y	Y	?	Y	Y	Y	Y	Y	Y	Y	Y
2 Boren	Y	Y	Y	N	Y	Y	Y	Y	Y	Y	Y	Y	Y	N
3 *Lucas*	Y	N	Y	Y	Y	Y	Y	Y	Y	Y	Y	Y	Y	Y
4 *Cole*	Y	Y	Y	Y	Y	Y	Y	Y	Y	Y	Y	Y	Y	Y
5 *Lankford*	Y	Y	Y	Y	Y	Y	Y	Y	Y	Y	Y	Y	Y	Y
OREGON														
1 Wu[6]	N	Y	N	N	N	N	Y	Y	N	Y				
2 *Walden*	Y	Y	Y	Y	Y	Y	Y	Y	Y	Y	Y	Y	Y	Y
3 *Blumenauer*	N	Y	N	N	N	N	N	Y	–	N	Y	N	N	N
4 DeFazio	N	Y	N	N	N	N	Y	N	N	N	N	N	Y	N
5 Schrader	N	Y	Y	N	N	N	Y	Y	N	Y	Y	N	N	?

[2]Rep. Mark Amodei, R-Nev., was sworn in September 15, 2011, to fill the vacancy created by fellow Republican Dean Heller, who resigned May 9 to become a senator. The first key vote for which Amodei was eligible was vote 11; the last key vote for which Heller was eligible was vote 4.

[3]Rep. Bob Turner, R-N.Y., was sworn in September 15, 2011, to fill the vacancy created by the June 22 resignation of Democrat Anthony Weiner. The first key vote for which Turner was eligible was vote 11; the last key vote for which Weiner was eligible was vote 7.

[4]Rep. Kathy Hochul, D-N.Y., was sworn in June 1, 2011, to fill the vacancy created by the February 16 resignation of Republican Christopher Lee. The first key vote for which Hochul was eligible was vote 7; the only key vote for which Lee was eligible was vote 1.

[5]The Speaker votes only at his discretion.

[6]Rep. David Wu, D-Ore., resigned August 3, 2011. The last key vote for which he was eligible was vote 10. His successor did not cast a key vote in 2011.

KEY

Republican Democrat **Independent**

Y	Voted for (yea)	–	Announced against
#	Paired for	P	Voted "present"
+	Announced for	C	Voted "present" to avoid possible conflict of interest
N	Voted against (nay)		
X	Paired against	?	Did not vote or otherwise make a position known

House Key Votes		1	2	3	4	5	6	7	8	9	10	11	12	13	14
PENNSYLVANIA															
1	Brady	N	Y	N	N	N	N	N	N	N	Y	N	N	N	N
2	Fattah	N	Y	N	N	?	N	N	Y	N	Y	N	N	N	N
3	*Kelly*	Y	N	Y	Y	Y	Y	Y	Y	Y	Y	Y	Y	Y	Y
4	Altmire	N	Y	Y	N	Y	Y	Y	Y	N	Y	N	Y	Y	N
5	*Thompson*	Y	Y	Y	Y	Y	Y	Y	N	N	Y	Y	Y	Y	Y
6	*Gerlach*	Y	N	Y	Y	Y	Y	Y	Y	Y	Y	Y	Y	Y	Y
7	*Meehan*	Y	Y	Y	Y	N	Y	Y	Y	Y	Y	Y	Y	Y	Y
8	*Fitzpatrick*	Y	Y	Y	Y	Y	N	Y	Y	Y	Y	Y	Y	Y	Y
9	*Shuster*	Y	N	Y	Y	Y	Y	Y	Y	Y	Y	Y	Y	Y	Y
10	*Marino*	Y	N	Y	Y	Y	Y	Y	Y	Y	Y	Y	Y	Y	Y
11	*Barletta*	Y	N	Y	Y	Y	Y	Y	Y	Y	Y	Y	Y	Y	Y
12	Critz	N	N	Y	N	N	Y	N	Y	N	Y	N	Y	N	N
13	Schwartz	N	Y	N	N	N	Y	?	Y	N	Y	Y	N	N	N
14	Doyle	N	Y	N	N	N	N	N	Y	N	N	N	N	N	N
15	*Dent*	Y	Y	Y	Y	Y	Y	Y	Y	Y	Y	Y	Y	Y	Y
16	*Pitts*	Y	N	Y	Y	Y	Y	Y	?	Y	Y	Y	Y	Y	Y
17	Holden	N	Y	Y	N	Y	Y	N	?	N	Y	N	Y	Y	N
18	*Murphy*	Y	N	Y	Y	Y	Y	Y	Y	Y	Y	Y	Y	Y	Y
19	*Platts*	Y	Y	Y	Y	Y	Y	Y	Y	Y	Y	Y	Y	Y	Y
RHODE ISLAND															
1	Cicilline	N	Y	N	N	N	N	N	Y	N	Y	N	N	N	N
2	Langevin	N	Y	N	N	N	Y	N	Y	N	Y	N	N	N	N
SOUTH CAROLINA															
1	*Scott*	Y	Y	Y	Y	Y	Y	Y	Y	Y	N	Y	Y	Y	Y
2	*Wilson*	Y	N	Y	Y	Y	Y	Y	Y	Y	N	Y	Y	Y	Y
3	*Duncan*	Y	Y	Y	Y	Y	N	Y	N	Y	N	Y	Y	Y	Y
4	*Gowdy*	Y	N	Y	Y	Y	Y	Y	Y	Y	N	Y	Y	Y	Y
5	*Mulvaney*	Y	N	Y	Y	Y	Y	Y	Y	Y	N	Y	Y	Y	Y
6	Clyburn	N	N	N	N	N	N	N	Y	N	Y	N	N	N	N
SOUTH DAKOTA															
AL	*Noem*	Y	Y	Y	Y	Y	Y	Y	Y	Y	Y	Y	Y	Y	Y
TENNESSEE															
1	*Roe*	Y	Y	Y	Y	Y	N	Y	Y	Y	Y	Y	Y	Y	Y
2	*Duncan*	Y	Y	Y	Y	Y	N	Y	N	Y	Y	Y	Y	Y	Y
3	*Fleischmann*	Y	Y	Y	Y	Y	Y	Y	Y	Y	N	Y	Y	Y	Y
4	*DesJarlais*	Y	N	Y	Y	Y	Y	Y	Y	Y	N	Y	Y	Y	Y
5	Cooper	N	Y	N	N	Y	Y	N	Y	N	Y	Y	N	Y	N
6	*Black*	Y	N	Y	Y	Y	Y	Y	Y	Y	Y	Y	Y	Y	Y
7	*Blackburn*	Y	Y	Y	Y	Y	Y	Y	Y	Y	Y	Y	Y	Y	Y
8	*Fincher*	Y	Y	Y	Y	Y	Y	Y	Y	Y	Y	Y	Y	Y	Y
9	Cohen	N	Y	N	N	N	N	N	Y	N	N	N	N	N	N
TEXAS															
1	*Gohmert*	Y	Y	Y	Y	Y	Y	N	N	Y	N	Y	Y	N	Y
2	*Poe*	Y	Y	Y	Y	Y	Y	Y	Y	Y	N	Y	Y	Y	Y
3	*Johnson, S.*	Y	Y	Y	Y	Y	Y	Y	Y	Y	Y	Y	Y	Y	Y
4	*Hall*	Y	Y	Y	Y	Y	Y	Y	Y	Y	N	Y	Y	Y	Y
5	*Hensarling*	Y	Y	Y	Y	Y	Y	Y	Y	Y	Y	Y	Y	Y	Y
6	*Barton*	Y	Y	Y	Y	Y	Y	Y	Y	Y	Y	Y	Y	Y	Y
7	*Culberson*	Y	Y	Y	Y	Y	Y	Y	Y	Y	Y	Y	Y	Y	Y
8	*Brady*	Y	Y	Y	Y	Y	Y	Y	Y	Y	Y	Y	Y	Y	Y
9	Green, A.	N	Y	N	N	N	N	N	Y	N	N	N	N	N	N
10	*McCaul*	Y	N	Y	Y	Y	Y	Y	Y	Y	Y	Y	Y	Y	Y
11	*Conaway*	Y	N	Y	Y	Y	Y	Y	Y	Y	Y	Y	Y	Y	Y
12	*Granger*	Y	Y	Y	Y	Y	Y	Y	Y	Y	Y	?	Y	Y	Y
13	*Thornberry*	Y	N	Y	Y	Y	Y	Y	Y	Y	Y	Y	Y	Y	Y
14	*Paul*	Y	Y	Y	N	N	N	Y	N	N	N	?	?	?	?
15	Hinojosa	N	Y	N	N	N	Y	N	Y	N	Y	?	N	N	N
16	*Reyes*	N	Y	N	N	N	Y	N	Y	N	N	N	?	N	N
17	Flores	Y	Y	Y	Y	Y	Y	Y	Y	Y	Y	Y	Y	Y	Y
18	Jackson Lee	N	N	N	N	N	N	N	Y	N	Y	N	N	N	N
19	*Neugebauer*	Y	Y	Y	Y	Y	Y	Y	Y	Y	N	Y	Y	Y	Y
20	Gonzalez	N	Y	N	N	N	N	N	N	N	N	N	?	N	N
21	*Smith*	Y	N	Y	Y	Y	Y	Y	Y	Y	Y	Y	Y	Y	Y
22	*Olson*	Y	N	Y	Y	Y	Y	Y	Y	Y	Y	Y	Y	Y	Y
23	*Canseco*	Y	Y	Y	Y	Y	Y	Y	Y	Y	Y	Y	Y	Y	Y
24	*Marchant*	Y	Y	Y	Y	Y	Y	Y	N	Y	Y	Y	Y	Y	Y
25	*Doggett*	N	Y	N	N	N	N	Y	Y	N	Y	N	N	N	N
26	*Burgess*	Y	Y	?	Y	Y	Y	Y	N	Y	Y	Y	Y	Y	Y
27	*Farenthold*	Y	Y	Y	Y	Y	Y	Y	Y	Y	Y	Y	Y	Y	Y
28	Cuellar	N	Y	Y	N	N	Y	Y	Y	N	Y	Y	Y	Y	N
29	Green, G.	N	Y	N	N	Y	–	Y	N	N	Y	–	N	N	N
30	Johnson, E.	N	Y	N	N	N	Y	N	Y	N	Y	Y	N	N	?
31	*Carter*	Y	Y	Y	Y	Y	Y	Y	Y	Y	Y	Y	Y	Y	Y
32	*Sessions*	Y	N	Y	Y	Y	Y	Y	Y	Y	Y	Y	Y	Y	Y
UTAH															
1	*Bishop*	Y	N	Y	Y	Y	N	Y	N	Y	N	Y	Y	Y	Y
2	Matheson	N	Y	Y	N	Y	Y	Y	Y	Y	Y	Y	Y	Y	N
3	*Chaffetz*	Y	N	Y	Y	Y	N	Y	N	Y	N	Y	Y	Y	Y
VERMONT															
AL	Welch	N	N	N	N	N	N	N	Y	N	N	N	N	N	N
VIRGINIA															
1	*Wittman*	Y	N	Y	Y	Y	Y	Y	Y	Y	Y	Y	Y	Y	Y
2	*Rigell*	Y	N	Y	Y	Y	Y	Y	Y	Y	Y	Y	Y	Y	Y
3	Scott	N	N	N	N	N	N	N	Y	N	N	N	N	N	N
4	*Forbes*	Y	N	Y	Y	Y	Y	Y	Y	Y	N	Y	Y	Y	Y
5	*Hurt*	Y	N	Y	Y	Y	Y	Y	Y	Y	Y	Y	Y	Y	Y
6	*Goodlatte*	Y	N	Y	Y	Y	Y	Y	Y	Y	Y	Y	Y	Y	Y
7	*Cantor*	Y	N	Y	Y	Y	Y	Y	Y	Y	Y	Y	Y	Y	Y
8	Moran	N	N	N	N	N	N	N	Y	N	N	Y	N	N	N
9	*Griffith*	Y	N	Y	Y	Y	N	Y	Y	Y	N	Y	Y	Y	Y
10	*Wolf*	Y	N	Y	Y	Y	Y	Y	N	Y	Y	Y	Y	Y	N
11	Connolly	N	N	N	N	N	N	Y	Y	N	Y	Y	N	N	N
WASHINGTON															
1	Inslee	N	Y	N	N	N	N	N	Y	N	Y	Y	N	Y	N
2	Larsen	N	N	N	N	N	N	N	Y	N	Y	Y	N	N	N
3	*Herrera Beutler*	Y	N	Y	Y	Y	N	Y	Y	Y	Y	Y	Y	Y	N
4	*Hastings*	Y	N	Y	Y	?	?	Y	Y	Y	Y	Y	Y	Y	Y
5	*McMorris Rodgers*	Y	N	Y	Y	Y	Y	Y	Y	Y	Y	Y	Y	Y	Y
6	Dicks	N	Y	N	N	N	Y	N	Y	N	Y	Y	N	N	N
7	McDermott	N	Y	N	N	N	N	N	Y	N	N	Y	N	N	N
8	*Reichert*	Y	N	Y	?	Y	Y	Y	Y	Y	Y	Y	Y	Y	Y
9	Smith	N	N	N	N	N	Y	N	Y	N	N	Y	N	N	N
WEST VIRGINIA															
1	*McKinley*	Y	Y	Y	N	Y	Y	Y	Y	N	Y	Y	Y	Y	Y
2	*Capito*	Y	Y	Y	Y	N	Y	Y	Y	Y	Y	Y	Y	Y	Y
3	Rahall	N	N	Y	N	N	Y	N	Y	N	Y	N	Y	N	N
WISCONSIN															
1	*Ryan*	Y	Y	Y	Y	Y	Y	Y	Y	Y	Y	Y	Y	N	Y
2	Baldwin	N	Y	N	N	N	N	N	N	N	N	N	N	N	N
3	Kind	N	Y	N	N	N	Y	N	N	N	Y	?	N	Y	N
4	Moore	N	Y	N	N	N	N	?	N	N	+	N	N	N	N
5	*Sensenbrenner*	Y	Y	Y	Y	Y	Y	Y	N	N	Y	Y	Y	Y	Y
6	*Petri*	Y	Y	Y	Y	N	Y	Y	N	Y	Y	Y	Y	Y	Y
7	*Duffy*	Y	Y	Y	Y	Y	Y	Y	Y	Y	Y	Y	Y	Y	Y
8	*Ribble*	Y	Y	Y	Y	Y	Y	Y	Y	Y	Y	Y	Y	Y	Y
WYOMING															
AL	*Lummis*	Y	Y	Y	Y	Y	Y	Y	N	Y	Y	Y	Y	Y	Y

Senate

1. RELIGIOUS EXEMPTIONS FOR HEALTH CARE

Rejection of an amendment to allow health insurance plans to deny coverage for provisions of medical services that were in conflict with the plan sponsor or employer's religious beliefs.

The narrow vote against the amendment from Missouri Republican Roy Blunt effectively doused Republicans' plans to continue fighting an Obama administration rule requiring insurance coverage of contraceptive services without sharing costs. It also served as one of the few times in 2012 that the Senate directly voted on modifying the 2010 health care overhaul. By opposing the amendment, Senate Democrats showed they would continue to defend the law.

For weeks in early 2012, Republicans' opposition to the rule gained headlines and national attention. The debate tapped into several contentious areas: the health care law, women's health issues, and religious freedom.

GOP leaders maintained that the rule would violate religious freedoms of employers that did not qualify as religious institutions, which are exempt from its requirements. Supporters, meanwhile, defended it as necessary to protect women's health and as an important part of the health care law's coverage of preventive services.

In early February, House Speaker John A. Boehner, R-Ohio, made a rare floor speech pledging to undo the rule and put the Energy and Commerce Committee in charge of finding a legislative way to reverse it.

Blunt introduced a proposal that would allow health plans to deny coverage for services that are against the plan sponsor or employer's religious beliefs, similar to a House measure from Rep. Jeff Fortenberry, R-Neb. Blunt offered his measure as an amendment to a highway funding bill February 9, but Senate Majority Leader Harry Reid, D-Nev., blocked it.

The next day, the administration clarified its rule to say that religiously affiliated hospitals, charities, and other institutions would not have to pay for coverage of contraception and that their insurance plans would offer it directly to employees instead.

Republicans, however, vowed to fight on, saying the modification was insufficient. A few days later, Reid changed his tune and said he would allow the vote on the Blunt amendment.

The Senate turned back the amendment 51–48 on March 1, with Maine Republican Olympia J. Snowe joining most Democrats in opposition and three Democrats—Bob Casey of Pennsylvania, Ben Nelson of Nebraska, and Joe Manchin III of West Virginia—supporting it.

Following that vote, the contraception issue lost momentum. House leaders never brought legislation on the controversial subject to the floor or held a committee markup on the issue. Fortenberry acknowledged in March that progress had stalled, although he still pushed for action on his bill.

By May, a senior Senate leadership aide was urging Republicans to stay away from the contraception fight. GOP leaders let the issue drop, and the debate since moved to several legal challenges.

Senate agreed to a motion to table the Blunt, R-Mo., amendment to the Reid, D-Nev., amendment to S 1813 on March 1, 51–48: R 1–45; D 48–3; I 2–0. *(Vote 1, p. 809)*

2. KEYSTONE XL PIPELINE

Rejection of an amendment to the surface transportation authorization bill to require immediate federal approval of the Keystone XL oil pipeline from Canada without further executive branch review.

President Barack Obama survived a test of his power in March when the Senate narrowly defeated an attempt to strip him of authority to review the Keystone XL pipeline project. While a majority of senators supported the proposal by North Dakota Republican John Hoeven, the 56–42 vote fell short of a sixty-vote threshold set by unanimous consent.

The vote had more of a political than a practical impact on the project, since TransCanada, the company developing the pipeline between Canada's tar sands and Gulf Coast refineries, was trying at the time to map a new route that would skirt environmentally sensitive areas in Nebraska. Citing Nebraska's concerns, Obama had deferred a decision until after the election.

Republicans were determined not to let the president duck the politically tough decision. A GOP-backed rider on a payroll tax cut law enacted late in 2011 required the government to make a final decision on the pipeline by February 21, 2012. Obama rejected the application, saying the deadline was unrealistic, although he invited the project developer to reapply when it had completed its revised plan. Hoeven's amendment was designed to reverse that decision by allowing TransCanada to begin construction without waiting for Nebraska to approve the new route—and without further review by the State Department, which must approve such projects crossing the U.S. border.

Hoeven's amendment put Obama in a difficult position. A coalition of business and labor groups was pressing him to sign off on the project because it would create jobs. But the president faced furious opposition from environmental groups important to his reelection. The groups contended that expanding oil production in Alberta's vast tar sands would accelerate global warming.

The outcome of the vote remained uncertain as debate on the amendment began. The Senate rejected, with a 33–65 vote, Oregon Democrat Ron Wyden's competing proposal to set a ninety-day deadline for a presidential decision and to bar the export of any oil transported through the pipeline. The focus turned to whether Hoeven could attract enough Democrats to reach the sixty-vote threshold.

Hoeven, a former governor of a state in the midst of an oil and natural gas boom, said on the Senate floor that the vote offered a "clear choice" between energy security and continued reliance on oil from unstable parts of the world. In response to assertions that the amendment would improperly usurp executive authority, Hoeven secured an opinion from the nonpartisan Congressional Research Service that affirmed Congress's constitutional authority to approve the project.

Eleven Democrats joined all forty-five Republican senators present in voting for the amendment. Democratic supporters of the measure included senators from states that produce fossil fuels, such as Finance Chair Max Baucus of Montana and Budget Chair Kent Conrad of North Dakota, as well as some from Republican-leaning Southern states, such as Kay Hagan of North Carolina and Mark Pryor of Arkansas.

The vote still left supporters of the amendment four votes shy of what they needed. Keystone remained a political talking point as the 2012 political campaign unfolded, but the Senate showdown in March marked the last serious legislative attempt to challenge Obama's authority to decide the issue.

Senate rejected the Keystone pipeline amendment to a surface transportation authorization (S 1813) on March 8, 56–42: R 45–0; D 11–40; I 0–2. *(Vote 2, p. 809)*

3. SMALL-BUSINESS STARTUPS

Passage of legislation to loosen securities regulations on smaller businesses to encourage capital formation and foster job growth.

The Senate's lopsided vote to pass bipartisan House legislation to ease financial rules for companies with the hope of spurring job creation belied the misgivings of a number of lawmakers and took place only after the Senate rejected attempts by Democrats to add protection for consumers.

Securities experts and regulators worried that by raising the threshold for federal regulation of companies—for instance, by allowing them to sell $50 million in stock, rather than $5 million, before having to register with the Securities and Exchange Commission (SEC)—and lifting other regulations for small companies, Congress would leave investors vulnerable to fraud.

President Obama's endorsement of the legislation, though, made it difficult for congressional Democrats to head off or amend the bill. In September 2011, Obama had urged Congress to "cut away the red tape that prevents too many rapidly growing startup companies from raising capital and going public."

The bill that the House passed, 390–23, on March 8 with Obama's blessing, was actually a bundle of several measures designed to ease regulation and help smaller companies raise capital. Assembled by House Majority Leader Eric Cantor of Virginia and called the Jumpstart Our Business Startups Act, or JOBS Act, it included new language to raise the threshold for the number of shareholders a company or bank could have before triggering an SEC registration. It also included provisions to allow certain companies to sell shares to the public without complying with some audit requirements in the 2002 financial regulation bill known as the Sarbanes-Oxley law.

The Senate initially balked at the bill. Democratic leaders in the Senate promised to introduce their version, which they said would also help smaller companies raise capital but would include enhanced protections for consumers.

However, a few days later, Senate Democrats reversed course and decided not to advance their own bill, largely because of the overwhelming vote for passage in the House and the president's support for the measure. Still, some Senate Democrats, including Jack Reed of Rhode Island, Carl Levin of Michigan, and Jeff Merkley of Oregon, sought to delay the measure in hopes of making changes.

The Senate then passed the amended bill with unanimous GOP backing and an almost even division among Democrats. That paved the way for the House to clear the bill for Obama's signature the following week.

Senate passed HR 3606 on March 22, 73–26: R 46–0; D 26–25; I 1–1. *(Vote 3, p. 809)*

4. UNION ELECTION RULES

Rejection of a Republican effort to block a federal rule speeding up union elections.

In a year that otherwise saw little action on labor legislation, this Senate vote served as an important election season statement from both parties on the issue of union organizing. Republicans used the vote to try to protect businesses and bash the Obama administration, while Democrats sided with their labor union allies.

The April 24 Senate vote was on a Republican-sponsored resolution aimed at blocking a National Labor Relations Board (NLRB) rule that would speed up union elections by postponing voter eligibility lawsuits until after the workers' vote. According to the NLRB, employers could stall a unionization vote for months by filing such lawsuits.

During debate before the vote, Republicans maintained that the rule would result in "ambush elections" that would deny employers their First Amendment right to speak to their employees and try to persuade them not to vote for a union. Republicans also depicted the rule as the Obama administration's latest attempt to curry favor with unions, whose fund-raising prowess was helping President Obama as he campaigned for reelection.

The NLRB "seems hell-bent on changing processes across the board more for a political reason than a substantive reason," Lindsey Graham, R-S.C., said during floor debate. Michael B. Enzi, R-Wyo., the resolution's sponsor, called the rule "reckless," adding: "It's kind of like Thelma and Louise driving off a cliff. I, for one, do not want to see the NLRB driving the economy off a cliff."

Democrats, however, strongly supported the NLRB rule, saying it was a common-sense fix to ensure fair and timely elections. Tom Harkin, D-Iowa, called the resolution a "Republican assault on unions," adding that Republicans were using the new rule as an "election year political football."

The White House threatened to veto the resolution if it got that far, saying in a statement that it was "committed to supporting the right of workers to join and participate in a union and bargain for fair wages, benefits and a safe workplace." The resolution "attacks these bedrock values," the statement said.

Interest groups heavily lobbied senators in advance of the vote. On one side were business groups, including the U.S. Chamber of Commerce and the National Retail Federation; on the other were unions, including the AFL-CIO.

The Senate rejected the resolution by a simple majority, 45–54. Lisa Murkowski of Alaska was the only Republican to vote no. The House did not take up its companion resolution.

The NLRB rule went into effect on April 30, but business groups challenged it in court. In May, a federal judge at the U.S. District Court for the District of Columbia ruled the NLRB's action invalid because only two board members voted on the rule and at least three were needed for a quorum.

Senate rejected S J Res 36 on April 24, 45–54: R 45–1; D 0–51; I 0–2. *(Vote 4, p. 809)*

5. FISCAL 2013 BUDGET RESOLUTION

Rejection of a motion to take up a fiscal 2013 budget resolution adopted by the House that called for significant spending cuts over a decade, new budgetary controls, and a future change in how Medicare provides health care for seniors.

The Senate Democratic majority's rejection of the fiscal 2013 budget blueprint written by House Republicans, a near replay of events a year earlier, reinforced the stark differences between the two parties' fiscal policies and signaled that Congress would once again be unable to agree on an annual budget resolution.

With Democratic leaders refusing for a third year in a row to bring any budget resolution to the floor, Republicans charged that, once again, Democrats were afraid to lay out their own spending plans. Budget Chair Kent Conrad, D-N.D., said a budget resolution was unnecessary because the 2011 debt limit law set the annual discretionary spending cap that a budget resolution would normally provide.

All Democrats and the Senate's two independents voted against taking up the House budget resolution, mirroring the united opposition to it among House Democrats. Five Senate Republicans voted against consideration of the House proposal.

Dubbed "The Path to Prosperity," the fiscal 2013 budget resolution (H Con Res 112) written by House Budget Chair and eventual GOP vice presidential nominee Paul D. Ryan, R-Wis., proposed a discretionary spending limit of $1.028 trillion, $19 billion below the $1.047 trillion cap in the debt limit law. That discrepancy in the two caps resulted in the House and Senate proceeding on different appropriations tracks, with the Senate marking up bills at the higher limit and the House sticking with its lower cap. The House eventually acceded to the $1.047 trillion limit in a six-month stopgap funding measure that was passed to fund the government operations through March 27, 2013.

The Ryan budget proposed to reduce spending by $4 trillion over a decade, in part by converting Medicaid to a block grant. A proposed Medicare change would give seniors the option of taking subsidies for private insurance rather than the traditional fee-for-service program beginning in 2023. The premium support proposal was based on a plan crafted by Ryan and Oregon Democratic Sen. Ron Wyden. Wyden, however, denounced the plan as differing from his concept in important respects.

Senate rejected a motion to proceed to H Con Res 112 on May 16, 41–58: R 41–5; D 0–51; I 0–2. *(Vote 5, p. 809)*

6. FARM BILL REAUTHORIZATION

Passage of a five-year reauthorization of farm and nutrition programs.

Some groups had privately begun doubting Congress could produce a five-year farm bill in 2012 before Senate Agriculture Chair Debbie Stabenow moved her bill to the floor in June. It was an unusual action because the House Agriculture Committee traditionally has been the first to write the bill that sets policy for agriculture, nutrition, conservation, rural development, and other areas.

But Stabenow, D-Mich., hoped to build pressure for action in the House with a bipartisan vote in her chamber. She said her House counterpart, Frank D. Lucas, R-Okla., faced an unfavorable environment for taking the lead in writing a farm bill.

In April, Stabenow and the committee's ranking Republican, Pat Roberts of Kansas, took less than five hours to move the bill (S 3240) through the panel despite opposition from several members from the South. The southerners said the legislation's new insurance-like revenue protection plan disproportionately favored Midwest growers. To fund the plan partially, Stabenow and Roberts shifted much of the $5 billion a year in annual direct payments to the new revenue plan. The legislation created a separate program for cotton farmers to address a World Trade Organization ruling that the United States needed to change its cotton subsidy program to comply with trade rules. In that ruling, Brazil won the right to impose more than $800 million in retaliatory import taxes against U.S. industries such as automobiles and financial services.

On the floor, the bill idled after cloture was invoked June 7. Over the course of six days, Stabenow and Roberts were largely able to defeat amendments on changes to the sugar program and the Supplemental Nutrition Assistance Program (SNAP) they thought could stall the bill in the Senate or cause problems in negotiations with the House on a compromise measure.

The Senate passed the bill June 21 on a 64–35 vote. Forty-six Democrats and sixteen Republicans voted for the legislation, while thirty Republicans and five Democrats voted against it.

Even with Stabenow's and Roberts's efforts, though, the measure turned out to be the only long-term reauthorization of farm programs to pass a chamber. The House Agriculture Committee approved its bill (HR 6083) in July, but Republican leaders kept the bill off the floor. Conservatives said the proposed level of cuts to SNAP was not enough and Democrats said it was too high. As a result, House leaders knew they could not get enough support for the measure to pass. Lawmakers settled January 1 on a one-year extension of the 2008 law, which had been allowed to expire in September, a rare occurrence in farm bill history.

Senate passed S 3240 on June 21, 64–35: R 16–30; D 46–5; I 2–0. *(Vote 6, p. 809)*

7. CYBERSECURITY STANDARDS

Rejection of a motion to end debate on a bill that would create cybersecurity standards for industry.

The vote was a rebuff to the Obama administration and Senate Democratic leaders, who had made the cybersecurity legislation a top national-security priority, and a sign of the power of business groups such as the U.S. Chamber of Commerce that shared ideological common ground with the majority of Senate Republicans on the issue. Although both sides acknowledged the dire nature of the threat, they became deadlocked over the proper role of the government in defending computer networks from attack; the disagreement doomed congressional action on cybersecurity.

At the beginning of 2012, a group of mostly Senate Democrats working at the behest of Senate Majority Leader Harry Reid, D-Nev., produced a bill to create mandatory security standards for the nation's most vital digital infrastructure that was owned by the private sector. The White House endorsed the legislation, but once business groups came out in opposition to the bill, calling it inflexible and expensive, its authors were forced to modify it toward a more voluntary approach where businesses would receive incentives such as liability protection for adopting security standards.

That change was enough to clear the path to floor debate. But while the Obama administration accepted the altered measure, it was not enough to win over Republicans and business lobbyists, who contended that the voluntary standards could become mandatory in practice and that the incentives were not enough in exchange. Although the two sides worked privately to find a compromise, they could not, and in the meantime a large stack of amendments piled up, some of them unrelated to cybersecurity.

Republicans filibustered the bill without an agreement on amendments, and while a handful of GOP senators voted to invoke cloture August 2, Democrats fell short of the sixty votes needed to move forward and blamed business lobbying for the bill's demise.

Republicans said the Senate could have taken up a House-passed bill that was centered on fostering information sharing between businesses and the federal government about cybersecurity threats. The bill had come out of the House with some Democratic support. But backers of the failed Senate bill, which also contained information-sharing provisions, said any legislation without security standards for industry was inadequate. Although Reid made a second attempt to end debate on the bill in November, it was never expected to succeed; the vote in August sealed the fate of cybersecurity legislation for the year.

Senate rejected a motion to invoke cloture on S 3414 on August 2, 52–46: R 5–40; D 45–6; I 2–0. *(Vote 7, p. 809)*

8. GUANTÁNAMO BAY DETAINEES

Approval of an amendment to the fiscal 2013 defense authorization bill blocking transfer of Guantánamo Bay detainees to the United States.

The vote exemplified major reasons President Obama was unable to close the Guantánamo Bay Naval Base detention center in Cuba. Even a Senate controlled by his own party was willing to restrict Obama's actions on the methods with which he could move detainees out of the facility. The amendment attracted significant Democratic support, despite Armed Services Chair Carl Levin, D-Mich., labeling it "veto bait."

If Obama was to close Guantánamo, which he said was a symbol that served as a terrorist recruitment tool in the Arab world, he needed to be able to either transfer detainees to other countries or conduct trials that freed or convicted them but keep them elsewhere during their sentences. The amendment to the defense authorization bill offered by Kelly Ayotte, R-N.H., blocked several of those options, such as trial in federal court or detention in a domestic prison.

Ayotte said it was too dangerous to have ex-Guantánamo detainees on U.S. soil and that the Guantánamo facility was ample for U.S. needs. But many Democrats said there were already terrorists kept safely in U.S. prisons and that Ayotte's amendment would place too many restrictions on the executive branch.

However, nine Democrats still voted for the amendment, along with every Republican present and one independent, Joseph I. Lieberman of Connecticut, giving it more than enough votes to succeed.

Republicans had used debate over Guantánamo to portray Democrats as soft on national security, and Democrats who lack safe seats and emphasize national security issues or represent states that lean right tended to vote with Republicans on the issue. A similar but more restrictive amendment was adopted to the defense authorization measure in the House. It mandated that all detainee trials be conducted at Guantánamo. Both the Ayotte amendment and the House amendment were left out of the final version of the bill to avoid a threatened White House veto.

Senate adopted the Ayotte amendment to the fiscal 2013 defense authorization bill (S 3254) on November 29, 54–41: R 44–0; D 9–40; I 1–1. *(Vote 8, p. 809)*

9. IRAN SANCTIONS

Adoption of an amendment to the fiscal 2013 defense authorization bill to blacklist Iran's energy and shipping sectors.

The White House succeeded in watering down Congress's latest Iran sanctions initiative. But lawmakers demonstrated their determination to press for a tougher policy toward Iran by forcing a reluctant administration to accept another round of sanctions. A Senate amendment containing the new sanctions was adopted without a dissenting vote. The latest measure, attached to the annual defense authorization bill, was intended to put additional economic pressure on Tehran as it considered a new round of diplomatic negotiations on its nuclear program.

Sens. Robert Menendez, D-N.J., and Mark S. Kirk, R-Ill., who sponsored the amendment to the defense bill, initially considered restrictions that would have effectively imposed an international trade embargo by requiring all countries to reduce nonpetroleum sales to Iran significantly. The senators also wanted to force other countries to freeze Iranian foreign currency reserves.

The administration warned that such moves could cause a diplomatic backlash. With the help of several influential senators—Armed Services Chair Carl Levin, D-Mich., the manager of the defense bill; Foreign Relations Chair John Kerry, D-Mass.; and Banking Chair Tim Johnson, D-S.D.—the White House persuaded Kirk and Menendez to delete or dilute some of their toughest language. The measure barred all transactions with Tehran's energy, shipping, and shipbuilding sectors and its ports, as well as sales to Iran of metals including graphite, aluminum, steel, and metallurgical coal that are used in those sectors and in other manufacturing.

The legislation continued to allow countries to buy oil from Iran if they demonstrated every 180 days that they had significantly reduced their purchases or for 120 days if a nation "faced exceptional circumstances that prevented it from significantly reducing purchases."

The Senate provisions survived almost entirely intact in the final version of the defense authorization bill.

Much of the new sanctions language came from proposals left out of legislation that President Obama reluctantly signed into law in August. That law expanded sanctions targeting financial institutions, including Iran's Central Bank, that Tehran used to facilitate its oil trade and maintain its economy.

Senate adopted the Menendez amendment to S 3254, November 30, 94–0: R 43–0; D 49–0; I 2–0. *(Vote 9, p. 809)*

10. INTERNATIONAL TREATY ON DISABILITY RIGHTS

Refusal to ratify a multilateral treaty that sought to bring foreign disabilities rights laws up to U.S. standards.

Although outnumbered, conservative Republicans in the Senate, backed by outside groups such as Heritage Action, retained enough voting power to prevent ratification of a popular multilateral treaty modeled on the Americans with Disabilities Act (ADA) that the Senate passed two decades earlier with just eight dissenting votes.

Thirty-eight Republicans voted against the U.N. Convention on the Rights of Persons with Disabilities, enough to deny the treaty the two-thirds majority necessary for ratification. The dissenters said the treaty was unnecessary, and that it might compromise U.S. sovereignty, with international tribunals intruding in domestic policy on issues such as child care and abortion.

As the Senate prepared for debate after Thanksgiving, one Republican critic, Mike Lee of Utah, said opponents had the votes to block the treaty. Even the presence on the floor of eighty-nine-year-old former Sen. Robert Dole, the Kansas Republican who pushed the ADA through the Senate in 1990, did not change the outcome. Senate Foreign Relations Chair John Kerry of Massachusetts, who shepherded the bill through his committee by a 13–6 vote, declared it "one of the saddest days I've seen in almost twenty-eight years in the Senate."

The treaty was written to bring other countries up to U.S. standards on the treatment of persons with disabilities. It had been widely supported by disability rights groups and veterans organizations, as well as former officials from both Republican and Democratic administrations. Republican Sens. John McCain of Arizona and John Barrasso of Wyoming were prominent backers.

But Heritage Action, an advocacy arm of the Heritage Foundation, warned senators that it would keep score of those who backed the treaty. Many Republicans, in fact, had signed a letter to Majority Leader Harry Reid, D-Nev., that they would oppose any treaty taken up during the lame duck-session of Congress that followed the November election.

Just one of the thirty-six GOP senators who signed that letter, Scott P. Brown of Massachusetts, voted for the disability treaty.

Senate rejected ratification of Treaty Doc 112-7 on December 4, 61–38: R 8–38; D 51–0; I 2–0. *(Vote 10, p. 809)*

11. U.S.-RUSSIA TRADE RELATIONS

Passage of legislation to establish permanent normal trade relations with Russia and Moldova. The bill also provided sanctions against individuals involved in human rights violations in Russia.

The historic vote to lift Cold War–era trade restrictions on Russia, after nearly four decades, was an important victory for U.S. business and the Obama administration, which had begun lobbying Congress to take the step soon after the World Trade Organization (WTO) approved Russia's membership in December 2011.

For U.S. businesses to take full advantage of the lowered trade barriers that came with Russia's joining the WTO, the United States had to establish permanent normal trade relations and lift the 1974 sanctions known as Jackson-Vanik, which had targeted communist countries that restricted Jewish emigration.

Although the step had broad support, relations with Russia remained sensitive on Capitol Hill. Senate leaders wanted to wait for the House to act, and House leaders were wary of bringing the bill to the floor before the November elections for fear it might make lawmakers look soft on Russian President Vladimir V. Putin.

To win the backing of lawmakers concerned about human rights violations during Putin's tenure, the administration agreed to support attaching provisions to the legislation that would sanction human rights violators. The Senate Foreign Relations and Senate Finance committees approved language to target such violators anywhere in the world and named the provision for attorney and anticorruption activist Sergei Magnitsky, who died while in Russian police custody.

Proponents of the bill, who argued that it would boost U.S. exports and create jobs, had hoped it would pass before or shortly after Russia formally joined the WTO in August 2012.

Early in the lame duck session, the House took up the measure and passed it easily. The bill included human rights provisions that differed from that backed by the Senate committees, imposing sanctions on only human rights violators who were tied to the Magnitsky case.

Despite concerns from Sen. Benjamin L. Cardin, a Maryland Democrat, and other human rights advocates, the Senate took up the measure a few weeks later. The Senate then passed the bill without trying to amend it, and it was cleared for the president's signature with overwhelming bipartisan support.

Senate passed HR 6156 on December 6, 92–4: R 46–0; D 45–3; I 1–1. *(Vote 11, p. 809)*

12. SUPERSTORM SANDY EMERGENCY RELIEF

Passage of a $60.4 billion supplemental emergency aid package for mid-Atlantic communities damaged by Superstorm Sandy in late October 2012.

In seventeen of the twenty-two budget years from fiscal 1989 through 2010, lawmakers appropriated supplemental funds to help communities hit by natural disasters, according to the Congressional Research Service.

But the willingness to shell out extra money for disaster relief decreased significantly in recent years before 2012, for several reasons. First, Congress had greatly increased its initial appropriations for the Disaster Relief Fund in the hope of being able to avoid emergency appropriations bills. More important, however, was a growing anti-spending sentiment, especially in the House, that no longer accepted extra appropriations without offsetting cuts in other programs.

Robert B. Aderholt, R-Ala., chair of the House Homeland Security Appropriations Subcommittee, said in mid-2012 that funding disaster relief through supplementals "is simply an irresponsible gimmick," as it puts spending outside of budget caps.

With this type of sentiment gaining strength, Congress essentially ignored devastation in 2012 from an active tornado season, wildfires in Colorado, and intense summer thunderstorms from the Midwest to the mid-Atlantic. But when a superstorm named Sandy struck the East Coast, destroying homes and businesses from Delaware to Connecticut, lawmakers were hard-pressed to look the other way. Governors and mayors demanded federal assistance, and President Obama promised $60 billion.

As a result, even though such legislation usually starts in the House, the Senate took the lead, using a House-passed appropriations bill from 2011. After two weeks of debate on the $60.4 billion recovery package, the Senate passed it before leaving town for the Christmas holidays.

Nevertheless, passage was not as simple as Democratic leaders had hoped. Patrick J. Toomey, a Pennsylvania Republican, succeeded in stripping the emergency designation from $3.4 billion to be provided for longer-term Army Corps of Engineers projects intended to better protect communities from future storms. Barbara A. Mikulski, a Maryland Democrat, called this a "dangerous precedent" and noted that cuts would be needed elsewhere in the federal budget to make up for the Army Corps spending. Toomey argued that such spending for longer-term projects should be provided through the regular appropriations process.

Democrats did reject a perhaps bigger threat in an alternative by Dan Coats, R-Ind. His $23.8 billion measure addressed immediate community needs from the storm and had a better chance for House passage. But four Republicans joined Democrats to reject Coats's alternative.

On the final vote, a dozen Republicans joined Democrats in the 62–32 margin to pass the Sandy recovery bill, with much

GOP support coming from members from hurricane-prone Gulf Coast states.

The solid vote and bipartisan outcome was seen as a message to House leaders that the supplemental money was needed. Speaker John A. Boehner of Ohio tried to ignore that message, and chose to conclude the 112th Congress without taking up the Senate disaster aid bill. But a loud, public, and immediate uproar from northeastern Republicans, particularly Rep. Peter T. King of New York and Gov. Chris Christie of New Jersey, led the speaker to retreat quickly. Boehner scheduled a vote on January 4, the second day of the 113th Congress, on flood insurance provisions of the Senate bill, and another on January 15, on disaster relief money. The flood insurance bill (HR 41) passed the House 354–67, and the Senate cleared it by unanimous consent the same day. The House passed the funding portion (HR 152) by a narrower 241–180 vote, carried by Democratic support. It too soon cleared Congress.

Senate passed HR 1 on December 28, 62–32: R 12–32; D 48–0; I 2–0. *(Vote 12, p. 809)*

13. TAX RATES EXTENSIONS

Passage of bill to extend a number of tax cuts while increasing taxes on high-income earners.

After talks broke down for the last time between President Obama and House Speaker John A. Boehner, it was left to the Senate to take a lead role in averting the full brunt of the fiscal cliff. The eventual compromise was largely crafted by Senate Minority Leader Mitch McConnell, R-Ky., and Vice President Joseph R. Biden Jr. after negotiations between McConnell and Senate Majority Leader Harry Reid, D-Nev., also reached a dead end.

The bill allowed, for the first time in two decades, the top marginal tax rate to rise on family income of more than $450,000 while permanently extending tax rates on income below that threshold. The top tax rates on capital gains, dividends, and large estates also were allowed to go up.

To satisfy the constitutional requirement that revenue measures originate in the House, the Senate voted on the McConnell-Biden measure as a substitute amendment to a House-passed tax bill. The order of events was considered important because House Republicans were never going to vote for a tax increase, or even allow a bill to come to the floor, unless the Senate acted first. Once an agreement had been reached at the leadership level, the Senate vote was a formality. In the early morning hours of January 1, 2013, the legislation was passed 89–8, with even some staunch conservatives such as Patrick J. Toomey, R-Pa., and Jeff Sessions, R-Ala., voting "yea" because they saw the legislation as the only way to avoid a broader tax increase.

The lopsided vote made it even more difficult for House leaders to stall on the bill. Hours later, after a day of closed-door strategy meetings and vote counting, GOP leaders allowed a vote on the Senate-passed bill, and allowed the measure to clear without a majority of the majority Republicans supporting it.

Senate passed HR 8 on January 1, 2013, 89–8: R 40–5; D 47–3; I 2–0. *(Vote 13, p. 809)*

1. S 1813. Religious Exemptions for Health Care. Murray, D-Wash., motion to table (kill) the Blunt, R-Mo., amendment to allow health insurance plans to deny coverage for medical services that run counter to the plan sponsor's or employer's religious beliefs, and to establish a private right of legal action for enforcement of the coverage exemptions. The underlying legislation to which Blunt sought to attach his amendment reauthorized federal highway programs for two years. Motion agreed to 51–48: R 1–45; D 48–3; I 2–0. A "yea" was a vote in support of the president's position. March 1, 2012.

2. S 1813. Keystone XL Pipeline. Hoeven, R-N.D., amendment to provide for approval of the Keystone XL pipeline between Canada and the United States by requiring that the route for the pipeline in Nebraska be submitted by the state of Nebraska. Rejected 56–42: R 45–0; D 11–40; I 0–2. (By unanimous consent, the Senate agreed to raise the majority requirement for adoption of the Hoeven amendment to sixty votes.) A "nay" was a vote in support of the president's position. March 8, 2012.

3. HR 3606. Small-Business Startups. Passage of the bill to define "emerging growth companies" and exempt them from certain independent auditing requirements. The legislation increased from $5 million to $50 million the annual public offering threshold for companies to be exempt from full Securities and Exchange Commission (SEC) filing requirements, raised the number of shareholders that would trigger mandatory SEC registration from 750 to 2,000, raised to 2,000 the number of shareholders that would trigger a requirement for SEC registration for a bank, and lifted an SEC ban that prevented small, privately held companies from using advertisements to solicit investors and allow companies to sell up to $1 million worth of securities. Passed 73–26: R 46–0; D 26–25; I 1–1. A "yea" was a vote in support of the president's position. March 22, 2012.

4. S J Res 36. Union Election Rules. Enzi, R-Wyo., motion to proceed to the joint resolution to disapprove of a National Labor Relations Board rule regarding union elections. Motion rejected 45–54: R 45–1; D 0–51; I 0–2. A "nay" was a vote in support of the president's position. April 24, 2012.

5. H Con Res 112. Fiscal 2013 Budget Resolution. Conrad, D-N.D., motion to proceed to the concurrent resolution to allow $2.8 trillion in new budget authority for fiscal 2013, not including off-budget accounts. Motion rejected 41–58: R 41–5; D 0–51; I 0–2. May 16, 2012.

6. S 3240. Farm Programs. Passage of the bill to reauthorize federal farm and nutrition programs for five years, including crop subsidies, food stamps, conservation, rural development, and foreign food aid programs, for a total projected cost of roughly $969 billion over the following decade. The legislation reauthorized the Supplemental Nutrition Assistance Program, and eliminated direct and countercyclical payments and replaced them with a new supplemental coverage option to allow producers to purchase additional crop insurance coverage. The legislation also barred any person with a nonfarm adjusted gross income of more than $750,000 from commodity program payments, capped at $50,000 under existing law, pending a study to determine the impact on costs. Passed 64–35: R 16–30; D 46–5; I 2–0. (By unanimous consent, the Senate agreed to raise the majority requirement for passage of the bill to 60 votes.) A "yea" was a vote in support of the president's position. June 21, 2012.

7. S 3414. Cybersecurity Standards. Motion to invoke cloture (thus limiting debate) on legislation to create voluntary security standards for vital digital infrastructure. Three-fifths of the total Senate (sixty) is required to invoke cloture. Motion rejected 52–46: R 5–40; D 45–6; I 2–0. A "yea" was a vote in support of the president's position. August 2, 2012.

8. S 3254. Guantánamo Bay Detainees. Ayotte, R-N.H., amendment to the fiscal 2013 defense authorization bill to prohibit the transfer of detainees from Guantánamo Bay, Cuba, military facilities to the United States. Adopted 54–41: R 44–0; D 9–40; I 1–1. A "nay" was a vote in support of the president's position. November 29, 2012.

9. S 3254. Iran Sanctions. Menendez, D-N.J., amendment to the fiscal 2013 defense authorization bill to bar all transactions with Iran's energy, shipping, and shipbuilding sectors and its ports, and to ban the sale to Iran of certain metals, including graphite, aluminum, steel, and metallurgical coal. Adopted 94–0: R 43–0; D 49–0; I 2–0. November 30, 2012.

10. Treaty Doc 112-7. International Treaty on Disability Rights. Adoption of the resolution of ratification of the Convention on the Rights of Persons with Disabilities (Treaty Doc 112-7), which established global standards for the treatment of people with disabilities. The resolution stated that current U.S. law fulfills or exceeds the obligations of the treaty. Rejected 61–38: R 8–38; D 51–0; I 2–0. (A two-thirds majority of senators present and voting, sixty-six in this case, is required for adoption of resolutions of ratification.) A "yea" was a vote in support of the president's position. December 4, 2012.

11. HR 6156. U.S.-Russian Trade Relations. Passage of the bill to establish permanent normal trade relations with Russia and Moldova and to end Jackson-Vanik restrictions on both economies. Passed (clearing the legislation for the president) 92–4: R 46–0; D 45–3; I 1–1. A "yea" was a vote in support of the president's position. December 6, 2012.

12. HR 1. Superstorm Sandy Emergency Relief. Passage of the bill to provide $60.4 billion in emergency spending for communities hit by Superstorm Sandy in October 2012, including an additional $9.7 billion in borrowing authority for the National Flood Insurance Program, $13 billion for mitigation projects, $11.5 billion for the Federal Emergency Management Agency's Disaster Relief Fund, and $10.8 billion to the Federal Transit Administration to rebuild public transit systems. Passed 62–32: R 12–32; D 48–0; I 2–0. A "yea" was a vote in support of the president's position. December 28, 2012.

13. HR 8. Tax Rates Extensions. Passage of the bill to extend the 2001 and 2003 tax rates for individual income below $400,000 and joint-filer income below $450,000. The legislation increased rates for income above those thresholds to 39.6 percent from 35 percent, and permanently extended tax rates on dividends and capital gains for individual income below $400,000 and joint-filer income below $450,000 but allowed rates for taxpayers above those thresholds to rise to 20 percent. The legislation also permanently altered the alternative minimum tax to account for inflation, extended unemployment insurance through 2013, blocked scheduled cuts to Medicare physician payment rates, extended for five years tax credits included in the 2009 stimulus law including the child tax credit and the earned income tax credit, and allowed the 2 percent payroll tax holiday to expire. Passed 89–8: R 40–5; D 47–3; I 2–0. (By unanimous consent, the Senate agreed to raise the majority requirement for passage of the bill to sixty votes.) A "yea" was a vote in support of the president's position. January 1, 2013, in the session that began and the *Congressional Record* dated December 31, 2012.

KEY

Republican	Democrat	**Independent**

Y	Voted for (yea)	–	Announced against
#	Paired for	P	Voted "present"
+	Announced for	C	Voted "present" to avoid possible conflict of interest
N	Voted against (nay)		
X	Paired against	?	Did not vote or otherwise make a position known

Senate Key Votes	1	2	3	4	5	6	7	8	9	10	11	12	13
ALABAMA													
Shelby	N	Y	Y	Y	Y	N	N	Y	Y	N	Y	Y	N
Sessions	N	Y	Y	Y	Y	N	N	Y	Y	N	Y	N	Y
ALASKA													
Murkowski	N	Y	Y	N	Y	N	N	Y	Y	Y	Y	Y	Y
Begich	Y	Y	N	N	N	Y	Y	N	Y	Y	Y	Y	Y
ARIZONA													
McCain	N	Y	Y	Y	Y	N	N	Y	Y	Y	Y	N	Y
Kyl	N	Y	Y	Y	Y	N	N	Y	Y	N	Y	N	Y
ARKANSAS													
Pryor	Y	Y	Y	N	N	N	N	Y	Y	Y	Y	Y	Y
Boozman	N	Y	Y	Y	Y	N	N	Y	Y	N	Y	N	Y
CALIFORNIA													
Feinstein	Y	N	N	N	N	Y	Y	N	Y	Y	Y	Y	Y
Boxer	Y	N	N	N	N	Y	Y	N	Y	Y	Y	?	Y
COLORADO													
Udall	Y	N	Y	N	N	Y	Y	N	Y	Y	Y	Y	Y
Bennet	Y	N	Y	N	N	Y	Y	N	Y	Y	Y	Y	N
CONNECTICUT													
Lieberman	Y	N	Y	N	N	Y	Y	Y	Y	Y	Y	Y	Y
Blumenthal	Y	N	N	N	N	Y	Y	N	Y	Y	Y	Y	Y
DELAWARE													
Carper	Y	N	Y	N	N	Y	Y	N	Y	Y	Y	Y	N
Coons	Y	N	Y	N	N	Y	Y	N	Y	Y	Y	Y	Y
FLORIDA													
Nelson	Y	N	Y	N	N	Y	Y	N	Y	Y	Y	Y	Y
Rubio	N	Y	Y	Y	Y	N	?	Y	Y	N	Y	N	N
GEORGIA													
Chambliss	N	Y	Y	Y	Y	N	N	Y	Y	N	Y	N	Y
Isakson	N	Y	Y	Y	Y	N	N	Y	Y	N	Y	N	Y
HAWAII													
Inouye[1]	Y	N	Y	N	N	Y	Y	Y	Y	Y	?		
Schatz[1]												Y	Y
Akaka	Y	N	N	N	N	Y	Y	N	Y	Y	Y	Y	Y
IDAHO													
Crapo	N	Y	Y	Y	Y	N	N	Y	Y	N	Y	N	Y
Risch	N	Y	Y	Y	Y	N	N	Y	Y	N	Y	?	Y
ILLINOIS													
Durbin	Y	N	N	N	N	Y	Y	N	Y	Y	Y	Y	Y
Kirk	?	?	?	?	?	?	?	?	?	?	?	?	?
INDIANA													
Lugar	N	Y	Y	Y	Y	Y	Y	Y	Y	Y	Y	Y	Y
Coats	N	Y	Y	Y	Y	Y	Y	Y	Y	N	Y	N	Y
IOWA													
Grassley	N	Y	Y	Y	Y	Y	N	Y	Y	N	Y	N	N
Harkin	Y	N	N	N	N	Y	Y	N	Y	Y	Y	Y	N

Senate Key Votes	1	2	3	4	5	6	7	8	9	10	11	12	13
KANSAS													
Roberts	N	Y	Y	Y	Y	Y	N	Y	Y	N	Y	N	Y
Moran	N	Y	Y	Y	Y	Y	N	Y	Y	N	Y	N	Y
KENTUCKY													
McConnell	N	Y	Y	Y	Y	N	N	Y	Y	N	Y	N	Y
Paul	N	Y	Y	Y	N	N	N	Y	Y	N	Y	N	N
LOUISIANA													
Landrieu	Y	Y	N	N	N	N	Y	Y	Y	Y	Y	Y	Y
Vitter	N	Y	Y	Y	Y	N	N	Y	Y	N	Y	Y	Y
MAINE													
Snowe	Y	Y	Y	Y	N	Y	Y	Y	Y	Y	Y	Y	Y
Collins	N	Y	Y	Y	N	Y	Y	Y	Y	Y	Y	Y	Y
MARYLAND													
Mikulski	Y	N	N	N	N	Y	Y	N	Y	Y	Y	Y	Y
Cardin	Y	N	N	N	N	Y	Y	N	Y	Y	Y	Y	Y
MASSACHUSETTS													
Kerry	Y	N	Y	N	N	Y	Y	N	Y	Y	Y	Y	Y
Brown	N	Y	Y	Y	N	Y	Y	Y	Y	Y	Y	Y	Y
MICHIGAN													
Levin	Y	N	N	N	N	Y	Y	N	Y	Y	N	Y	Y
Stabenow	Y	N	Y	N	N	Y	Y	Y	Y	Y	Y	Y	Y
MINNESOTA													
Klobuchar	Y	N	Y	N	N	Y	Y	N	Y	Y	Y	Y	Y
Franken	Y	N	N	N	N	Y	Y	N	Y	Y	Y	Y	Y
MISSISSIPPI													
Cochran	N	Y	Y	Y	Y	N	N	Y	Y	N	Y	Y	Y
Wicker	N	Y	Y	Y	Y	N	N	Y	Y	N	Y	Y	Y
MISSOURI													
McCaskill	Y	Y	Y	N	N	Y	Y	N	Y	Y	Y	Y	Y
Blunt	N	Y	Y	Y	Y	Y	N	Y	Y	N	Y	N	Y
MONTANA													
Baucus	Y	Y	N	N	N	Y	N	Y	Y	Y	Y	Y	Y
Tester	Y	Y	Y	N	N	Y	N	N	Y	Y	Y	Y	Y
NEBRASKA													
Nelson	N	N	Y	N	N	Y	Y	Y	Y	Y	Y	Y	Y
Johanns	N	Y	Y	Y	Y	Y	N	Y	Y	N	Y	N	Y
NEVADA													
Reid	Y	N	Y	N	N	Y	N	N	Y	Y	Y	Y	Y
Heller	N	Y	Y	Y	N	N	N	?	+	N	Y	Y	Y
NEW HAMPSHIRE													
Shaheen	Y	N	Y	N	N	Y	Y	N	Y	Y	Y	Y	Y
Ayotte	N	Y	Y	Y	Y	N	N	Y	Y	Y	Y	N	Y
NEW JERSEY													
Lautenberg	Y	N	N	N	N	N	Y	N	Y	Y	Y	?	?
Menendez	Y	N	Y	N	N	Y	Y	N	Y	Y	Y	Y	Y
NEW MEXICO													
Bingaman	Y	N	Y	N	N	Y	Y	N	Y	Y	Y	Y	Y
Udall	Y	N	N	N	N	Y	Y	N	Y	Y	Y	Y	Y
NEW YORK													
Schumer	Y	N	Y	N	N	Y	Y	N	Y	Y	Y	Y	Y
Gillibrand	Y	N	N	N	N	Y	Y	N	Y	Y	Y	Y	Y
NORTH CAROLINA													
Burr	N	Y	Y	Y	Y	N	N	Y	Y	N	Y	N	Y
Hagan	Y	Y	Y	N	N	Y	Y	Y	Y	Y	Y	Y	Y
NORTH DAKOTA													
Conrad	Y	Y	N	N	N	Y	Y	N	Y	Y	+	Y	Y
Hoeven	N	Y	Y	Y	Y	Y	N	Y	Y	N	Y	Y	Y
OHIO													
Brown	Y	N	N	N	N	Y	Y	N	Y	Y	Y	Y	Y
Portman	N	Y	Y	Y	Y	N	N	Y	Y	N	Y	N	Y

[1]Brian Schatz, D-Hawaii, was sworn in December 27, 2012, to fill the vacancy created by the December 17 death of fellow Democrat Daniel K. Inouye. The first key vote for which Schatz was eligible was vote 12; the last key vote for which Inouye was eligible was vote 11.

Senate Key Votes	1	2	3	4	5	6	7	8	9	10	11	12	13
OKLAHOMA													
Inhofe	N	Y	Y	Y	Y	N	N	Y	Y	N	Y	N	Y
Coburn	N	Y	Y	Y	Y	N	N	Y	Y	N	Y	N	Y
OREGON													
Wyden	Y	N	Y	N	N	Y	N	?	?	Y	Y	Y	Y
Merkley	Y	N	N	N	N	Y	N	N	Y	Y	Y	Y	Y
PENNSYLVANIA													
Casey	N	Y	Y	N	N	Y	Y	N	Y	Y	Y	Y	Y
Toomey	N	Y	Y	Y	Y	N	N	Y	Y	N	Y	N	Y
RHODE ISLAND													
Reed	Y	N	N	N	N	N	Y	N	Y	Y	N	Y	Y
Whitehouse	Y	N	N	N	N	N	Y	N	Y	Y	N	Y	Y
SOUTH CAROLINA													
Graham	N	Y	Y	Y	Y	N	N	Y	Y	N	Y	N	Y
DeMint	N	Y	Y	Y	Y	N	N	?	Y	N	Y	?	?
SOUTH DAKOTA													
Johnson	Y	N	Y	N	N	Y	Y	N	Y	Y	Y	Y	Y
Thune	N	?	Y	Y	Y	Y	N	Y	Y	N	Y	N	Y
TENNESSEE													
Alexander	N	Y	Y	Y	Y	Y	N	Y	+	N	Y	N	Y
Corker	N	Y	Y	Y	Y	N	N	Y	Y	N	Y	N	Y
TEXAS													
Hutchison	N	Y	Y	Y	Y	Y	N	Y	Y	N	Y	Y	Y
Cornyn	N	Y	Y	Y	Y	N	N	Y	Y	N	Y	N	Y

Senate Key Votes	1	2	3	4	5	6	7	8	9	10	11	12	13
UTAH													
Hatch	N	Y	Y	Y	Y	N	N	Y	?	N	Y	N	Y
Lee	N	Y	Y	Y	Y	N	N	Y	Y	N	Y	N	N
VERMONT													
Leahy	Y	N	N	N	N	Y	Y	N	Y	Y	Y	Y	Y
Sanders	Y	N	N	N	N	Y	Y	N	Y	Y	N	Y	Y
VIRGINIA													
Webb	Y	Y	N	N	N	Y	Y	Y	Y	Y	Y	Y	Y
Warner	Y	N	Y	N	N	Y	Y	N	Y	Y	Y	?	Y
WASHINGTON													
Murray	Y	N	N	N	N	Y	Y	N	Y	Y	Y	Y	Y
Cantwell	Y	N	Y	N	N	Y	Y	N	Y	Y	Y	Y	Y
WEST VIRGINIA													
Rockefeller	Y	N	N	N	N	Y	Y	?	?	Y	?	Y	Y
Manchin	N	Y	Y	N	N	Y	Y	Y	Y	Y	Y	Y	Y
WISCONSIN													
Kohl	Y	N	Y	N	N	Y	Y	N	Y	Y	Y	Y	Y
Johnson	N	Y	Y	Y	Y	N	N	Y	Y	N	Y	N	Y
WYOMING													
Enzi	N	Y	Y	Y	Y	Y	N	Y	Y	N	Y	N	Y
Barrasso	N	Y	Y	Y	Y	Y	N	Y	Y	Y	Y	N	Y

House

1. TEMPORARY PAYROLL TAX CUT

Passage of legislation to extend a Social Security payroll tax cut, unemployment benefits, and Medicare payments to physicians.

After months of twists and turns, the House cleared the way in February for an extension of the payroll tax cut through the end of 2012, reducing the tax burden for the vast majority of households during a period of tepid economic growth.

The vote came relatively quickly and easily once House Republican leaders abandoned their demand that the cost of the tax cut be offset by spending cuts, a harbinger of the political dynamic later in the year that dogged action on fiscal-cliff and Superstorm Sandy legislation.

Before then, House and Senate leaders had been involved in protracted negotiations, highlighted by a short-term extension of the tax break and other temporary policies at the end of 2011. A 2 percentage point reduction in the 6.2 percent Social Security payroll tax on employees was first enacted in late 2010 as a response to the lingering recession.

Lawmakers attempted to resolve their differences in the new year through a House-Senate conference committee. The panel, led by Republican House Ways and Means Chair Dave Camp of Michigan, featured civil discussions but saw little progress until Republicans made their crucial concession. Even then, lawmakers still needed to pay for an extension of long-term unemployment benefits and a Medicare fix to prevent payment cuts to doctors. One solution, a reduction in contributions to federal worker pensions, angered some Democrats, particularly those from Maryland where many constituents would be affected, but not enough to derail the bill.

By the end, many Republicans were eager to move on from the payroll tax debate. The push for a deficit-neutral bill had come largely from House Republican freshmen, who disliked the tax break for its associations with stimulus spending and President Obama. Nevertheless, Republican leaders came to realize that a fight over the payroll tax cut was not helping them politically, as Democrats relentlessly attacked them for obstructing tax relief for low- and middle-income families.

The final House vote on the payroll tax cut extension was 293–132. Among Republicans, the split was 146–91 in a solid but less-than-enthusiastic show of support for House Speaker John A. Boehner of Ohio.

After the Senate cleared the bill and President Obama signed it, the themes of the payroll tax cut debate lingered through the November elections, with Republicans fighting against the impression that they cared more about the rich than the middle class. However, the tax cut was not renewed at the end of the year, as Democrats decided to fight for other priorities.

House passed HR 3630 on February 17, 293–132: R 146–91; D 147–41. *(Vote 1, p. 817)*

2. SMALL-BUSINESS STARTUPS

Passage of legislation to loosen securities regulations on smaller businesses in order to attract capital and foster job growth.

The vote was the culmination of a months-long bipartisan push to ease financial regulations for some companies in the hope of spurring job creation. In a rare instance of agreement, congressional Republicans and the Obama administration concurred to boost the sluggish economy, and the vote showed the power of such an agreement.

Business leaders long maintained that certain Securities and Exchange Commission (SEC) rules should be relaxed to better reflect changing investment practices and to reduce regulatory costs for smaller companies. In September 2011, President Obama joined that chorus when he urged Congress to "cut away the red tape that prevents too many rapidly growing startup companies from raising capital and going public."

In November 2011, the House passed several measures intended to do just that. One bill exempted registration with the SEC for companies that plan to sell $50 million in shares as part of a public offering, up from the existing threshold of $5 million. Another lifted an SEC ban on small, privately held companies using advertisements to solicit investors. A third bill permitted companies to employ "crowd-funding," or the use of social media and the Internet, to raise capital from the public without having to register with the SEC.

Although some senators introduced companion measures, the broader deregulation effort largely fell off the radar until House Majority Leader Eric Cantor of Virginia bundled these bills together, as well as a few others, into a single piece of legislation. The bill, named the Jumpstart Our Business Startups Act, or JOBS Act, included new provisions to raise the threshold for the number of shareholders a company or bank could have before triggering an SEC registration. It also included provisions to allow certain companies to sell shares to the public without complying with some audit requirements in 2002 financial legislation known as the Sarbanes-Oxley law.

On March 8, with Obama's endorsement, the House passed the measure 390–23. The Senate initially balked at the bill, which top securities experts and regulators had warned would leave the typical investor vulnerable to fraud. With Obama behind the legislation, though, the pressure on the Senate to act was enormous. Several attempts to add consumer protections were defeated; the lone amendment adopted, offered by Oregon Democrat Jeff Merkley, required individuals acting as crowd-funding intermediaries to register with the SEC.

The Senate then passed the amended bill, sending it back to the House, where it was quickly cleared.

House cleared HR 3606 on March 27, 380–41: R 235–0; D 145–41. *(Vote 2, p. 817)*

3. FISCAL 2013 BUDGET RESOLUTION

Adoption of a fiscal 2013 budget resolution written by House Republicans that called for significant spending cuts over a decade, new budgetary controls, and a transition of Medicare from a fee-for-service entitlement to a premium support program for private-insurance coverage.

The House and Senate once again were unable to agree on a budget resolution for fiscal 2013. The House's adoption of a blueprint written by Budget Committee Chair and GOP vice presidential nominee Paul D. Ryan of Wisconsin demonstrated both the stark partisan divide in the chamber and the determination of some Republicans to make deeper spending cuts than those required under terms of a 2011 deal to increase the federal debt limit.

House leaders had to work harder to round up Republican votes for their fiscal 2013 budget resolution than they did for the fiscal 2012 version. Although the tax and spending blueprint differed little from the previous year's offering, it did not call for spending cuts deep enough for some conservatives. No Democrat voted for the plan.

Dubbed "The Path to Prosperity" for the second consecutive year, the budget resolution (H Con Res 112) included a higher discretionary spending limit, $1.0 trillion, than many conservatives favored. That figure represented a middle ground between a smaller figure favored by conservatives and the discretionary limit imposed by the debt limit law. The plan was projected to reduce spending by $4 trillion over a decade. It assumed an overhaul of Medicare and Medicaid and simplification of the tax code.

The resolution would have led to a balanced budget by 2040. Some conservatives wanted a plan for achieving that goal in ten years.

By the time the House voted, most GOP conservatives accepted the discretionary cap, although some did so grudgingly. Six more Republicans voted against the budget resolution, however, than had opposed the fiscal 2012 version. The Republican dissenters included Budget Committee members Justin Amash of Michigan and Tim Huelskamp of Kansas, who were removed from the panel for the 113th Congress in a signal to others not to abandon the party on important votes.

The proposed Medicare rewrite was not particularly controversial among Republicans. The plan borrowed from a bipartisan measure offered by Ryan and Oregon Democratic Sen. Ron Wyden. Unlike the House's fiscal 2012 budget resolution, the Ryan-Wyden proposal in the fiscal 2013 version gave seniors the option of choosing traditional Medicare or private health care coverage plans starting in 2023.

Another provision that enjoyed widespread support among Republicans was a reconciliation instruction directing House committees to find at least $261 billion in ten-year savings from mandatory programs as an alternative to most of the $109 billion in automatic spending cuts that were then scheduled to begin January 2, 2013, under the debt limit law.

Because Ryan's budget faced solid Democratic opposition in the Senate, it once again had no chance of becoming a template for fiscal policy.

House adopted H Con Res 112 on March 29, 228–191: R 228–10; D 0–181. *(Vote 3, p. 817)*

4. STUDENT LOAN INTEREST RATES

Passage of a bill to provide a one-year reprieve from a scheduled increase in student-loan interest rates.

With President Obama traveling the country in spring 2012 to chastise Republicans for not renewing a 3.4 percent interest rate for subsidized college loans, House GOP leaders hastily responded with a remedy typical in the hyper-partisan age of 2012: a one-year extension of the interest rate, but with the estimated $6 billion cost to be paid for with money from the president's health care program. That, of course, was anathema to Obama who called the bill a "politically motivated proposal and not a serious response" and said he would veto it if it reached him.

The subsequent maneuvering led to a House vote that illustrated not only the almost routine opposition Obama faced in the midst of a presidential campaign, but also the fissures within each party. The GOP bill lost thirty Republican votes and would have failed had not thirteen Democrats voted for it.

Congress had addressed the rising cost of college in a 2007 law that, among other things, started lowering the interest rate for subsidized Stafford Loans made to undergraduate students, to 3.4 percent from 6.8 percent. Because of the cost, though, the special rate was set to expire July 1, 2012. On that date, the rate would immediately revert to 6.8 percent.

Obama called for the lower rate to be extended. Republicans initially resisted, calling the idea a campaign ploy, but they shifted their stance after GOP presidential candidate Mitt Romney, a month away from wrapping up the nomination, agreed that Congress should preserve the low rate.

The problem was how to cover the budgetary cost. The House Republican bill drew money from the Prevention and Public Health Fund created by the 2010 health care law, which provided money for programs designed to prevent tobacco use, obesity, heart disease, strokes, and cancer. Judy Biggert, R-Ill., the bill's sponsor, said the money for disease prevention was "nothing more than an open-ended fund that has no clear oversight or purpose." Other Republicans called it a slush fund for Health and Human Services Secretary Kathleen Sebelius.

Democrats who voted with Republicans on the bill included Collin C. Peterson of Minnesota, who had opposed Obama's health care overhaul, and his fellow Minnesotan Tim Walz, who issued a statement afterward in which he wrote, "While I strongly disagree with how this bill is paid for, I will not let politics get in the way of keeping college affordable." Democrat Timothy H. Bishop of New York explained to constituents that he expected the offsets in the bill to be changed in conference.

Some Democrats responded with a separate bill (HR 4816) to pay for the one-year loan rate extension by ending tax subsidies for oil and gas companies.

By the time the House Republican bill passed on April 27, the battle had already moved to the Senate, where a compromise was eventually worked out to extend the low interest rate for a year and to pay for it by changing two provisions of pension law and by shortening the time period for which students are eligible for the subsidized loans. Because these offsets raised more money than the loan bill cost, the language was added to a highway and transit authorization bill that was passed in late June.

House passed HR 4628 on April 27, 215–195: R 202–30; D 13–165. *(Vote 4, p. 817)*

5. INDEFINITE DETENTION OF TERRORISM SUSPECTS

Rejection of an amendment to the defense authorization bill to ban indefinite detention of terrorism suspects captured in the United States.

When the House debated the fiscal 2013 defense authorization bill, its members had to decide between competing amendments on the detention of terrorism suspects. The split in the votes illustrated divisions over the issue of the Guantánamo Bay, Cuba, detention facility and over civil liberties in general, particularly within the Tea Party movement. One, offered by Louie Gohmert, R-Tex., was adopted, and a version of it became law. The other, by Adam Smith, D-Wash., and Justin Amash, R-Mich., was more ambitious in scope and drew a more politically diverse group of supporters, but ultimately it was rejected.

The Smith amendment brought together not only unlikely allies such as Smith and Amash but also groups as far apart as the liberal American Civil Liberties Union and the conservative

Young Americans for Liberty. The amendment would have banned indefinite detention of suspected terrorists without charge or trial if they were apprehended within the United States, something the Obama administration says it would never do. A similar amendment was offered to the Senate version of the bill and adopted on the floor, but it was left out of the final conference agreement.

The Smith amendment also split Tea Party Republicans, some of whom backed it because they considered indefinite detention an example of government overreach. Others favored the Gohmert amendment, which stated broadly that Americans detained in the United States on terrorism charges are entitled to all constitutional protections. Backers of the Smith amendment decried the Gohmert amendment as a do-nothing smokescreen that just restated rights already guaranteed. Republican leaders, though, rallied their troops behind it as an alternative to the Smith amendment. They also whipped up opposition to the Smith amendment by arguing that it would allow not just Americans, but also foreign suspects the right to a trial in civilian courts that does not now exist in law.

The Gohmert amendment, in modified form, appeared in the final conference agreement on the defense authorization measure.

House rejected the Smith amendment to HR 4310 on May 18, 182–238: R 19–219; D 163–19. *(Vote 5, p. 817)*

6. HOLDER CONTEMPT RESOLUTION

Adoption of a resolution citing Attorney General Eric H. Holder Jr. for contempt of Congress.

The House made history June 28, when it held Holder in contempt of Congress; it was the first time the nation's top law enforcement officer had faced that sanction.

Republicans brought the resolution (H Res 711) to the floor after Holder refused to provide documents sought by the House Oversight and Government Reform Committee pertaining to a law enforcement operation known as "Fast and Furious," in which the Justice Department lost track of thousands of guns it had hoped to trace to drug cartels in Mexico. Two of those guns were later discovered at the murder scene of a U.S. Border Patrol agent in Arizona, prompting Republicans to launch a months-long investigation into the operation and the Justice Department's handling of it.

Holder previously had testified about the operation before the Oversight panel and turned over thousands of pages of documents to its investigators, but he stopped short of providing everything the committee had sought. Instead, he invoked executive privilege before a committee hearing June 20, arguing that the documents he was withholding could legally be shielded from congressional review. That prompted a contempt vote along party lines in the Oversight panel, with the full House following eight days later.

On the floor, all but two Republicans supported the contempt resolution, and nearly half of the House Democratic Caucus boycotted the vote, underscoring the intensely partisan nature of the resolution, which passed 255–67. Republicans accused Holder of ignoring congressional oversight powers, while Democrats defended him and said that the GOP had set up the vote to gain an advantage in a presidential election year. The National Rifle Association, which had long called on Holder to resign over the Fast and Furious scandal, scored the vote and gave lower marks to lawmakers who voted against the resolution.

Legally, the contempt resolution had little effect. Holder remained in office, while the House was suing him in federal court, hoping to obtain the documents it sought through a judicial order. The case was pending in U.S. District Court in the District of Columbia at the end of the year.

House passed H Res 711 on June 28, 255–67: R 238–2; D 17–65. *(Vote 6, p. 817)*

7. HEALTH CARE OVERHAUL REPEAL

Passage of a bill to repeal the 2010 health care law.

In the lead-up to the Supreme Court's ruling on the 2010 health care law, House Republicans said they would move to repeal whatever was left if the justices did not strike down the overhaul in its entirety. So once the high court announced its decision largely upholding the law, GOP leaders scheduled a vote on full repeal.

The symbolic response was a way to reiterate Republicans' commitment to undoing the overhaul and put lawmakers on the record once again before the November election. House Republicans had passed in January 2011 a measure (HR 2) to repeal the law, with support from three Democrats, but that bill never advanced in the Democrat-led Senate.

In its June 28 decision, the Supreme Court ruled that the law's requirement that most individuals maintain health coverage or pay a penalty falls under Congress's taxing power, and Republicans seized on the tax label as a new line of attack. They also maintained, as the House began consideration of the bill July 10, that the overhaul stifles job growth and raises health care costs.

But Democrats criticized the GOP for not offering its own proposal to replace the law and slammed the vote as a waste of time and political theater.

When the House passed the legislation July 11, five Democrats joined a unified Republican caucus in support of repeal: Dan Boren of Oklahoma, Mike McIntyre of North Carolina, and Mike Ross of Arkansas—the three Democrats who voted for the 2011 repeal bill—as well as Larry Kissell of North Carolina and Jim Matheson of Utah.

As expected, the Senate never took up the bill or anything similar to it, and the effort died with the end of the 112th Congress.

House passed HR 6079 on July 11, 244–185: R 239–0; D 5–185. *(Vote 7, p. 817)*

8. U.S.-RUSSIA TRADE RELATIONS

Passage of legislation to establish permanent normal trade relations with Russia and Moldova. The bill also provided sanctions against individuals involved in human rights violations in Russia.

Efforts by business groups and the Obama administration to persuade Congress to normalize trade relations permanently with Russia began a year earlier, after the World Trade Organization (WTO) agreed to accept Russian membership. The step was a requirement for the United States to be able to take full advantage of the lower trade barriers that came with Russia joining the WTO.

Mindful of China's poor trade record even after it was granted permanent normal trade relations with the United States, though, many lawmakers were initially reluctant to normalize trade relations with Russia. To do so would mean certifying that Russia was in full compliance with the Jackson-Vanik amendment, a Cold War measure prohibiting normal trade with any communist country that restricted emigration. In reality, since 1992 successive presidents had waived the restrictions of Jackson-Vanik and allowed normal trade with Russia, although only Congress could lift the law formally.

Human rights advocates in Congress also opposed improving trade ties with Russia without new methods to counteract the sorts of human rights violations that Russian President Vladimir V. Putin had been accused of and that had grown in number since Putin won a third term as president, earlier in 2012.

In order to win support from these and other lawmakers, the Obama administration agreed to borrow human rights provisions from bills that were approved in June by the Senate Foreign Relations and House Foreign Affairs committees and add them to the trade measure. They were named for attorney and anticorruption activist Sergei Magnitsky, who died while in Russian police custody. The House language sanctioned all Russian human rights violators and in particular those tied to the Magnitsky case, while the Senate version was more expansive, potentially targeting human rights violators anywhere in the world. The final legislation followed the House's version.

Those moves won the support of top lawmakers in both parties and cleared the way for legislative progress. Both the House Ways and Means and Senate Finance committees approved bills in July, with virtually no opposition.

Proponents of lifting Jackson-Vanik had hoped to pass the bill before, or shortly after, Russia joined the WTO. But congressional leaders were initially wary of bringing the measure to the floor. Organized labor had expressed some opposition to the bill, which might have siphoned off Democratic votes. Meanwhile, House GOP leaders did not want to force their incumbents to take a vote shortly before the 2012 elections that might make them appear soft on Putin.

After Congress returned from the elections, the obstacles to the bill appeared to melt away in the lame duck session. Bearing the limited human rights provisions, the bill breezed through the House with the support of nearly all Republicans and the vast majority of Democrats. House passage set up the Senate's vote to clear the bill for the president only a few weeks later.

House passed HR 6156 on November 16, 365–43: R 227–6; D 138–37. *(Vote 8, p. 817)*

9. STEM VISA PROGRAM

Passage of a bill to create a visa program for foreign graduates of U.S. colleges and universities in high-tech fields.

Less than a month after Latino voters helped President Obama win a second term, backing him over GOP challenger Mitt Romney by a nearly three-to-one margin, House Republicans set up a floor vote on a measure they said showed their willingness to work with Democrats on immigration, and perhaps win over some of those Latino voters.

In fact, the vote on the bill, which was to provide 55,000 additional green cards for highly skilled foreign-born graduates of U.S. universities, laid down initial markers for an immigration debate that continued throughout the year.

After the election, Speaker John A. Boehner of Ohio and other House Republicans made clear that they prefer an incremental, "step-by-step" approach to immigration that could involve a series of small immigration bills, such as the high-tech visa legislation. The Obama administration and many congressional Democrats wanted a comprehensive overhaul of immigration law.

That is why the White House said it opposed the House's high-tech visa bill, even though the administration generally backed the bill's underlying goal of admitting skilled workers. "The administration," explained a White House statement, "does not support narrowly tailored proposals that do not meet the president's long-term objectives with respect to comprehensive immigration reform."

The so-called STEM bill, referring to the science, technology, engineering, and mathematics specialists the measure was to benefit, had been seen as an area of potential compromise in the tricky political terrain of immigration. Both parties had expressed support for the idea, and the sponsor, Rep. Lamar Smith, R-Tex., had negotiated with Sen. Charles E. Schumer, D-N.Y., for months in an effort to find common ground.

When it came time to vote, though, the House measure failed to attract the support of Democrats, who said the Republican legislation pitted one group of immigrants against another by creating the additional visas for STEM workers by eliminating a separate "diversity" visa program that offers green cards through a lottery system. Democrats also maintained that the bill did not do enough to keep families together throughout the immigration process and said that it would decrease overall immigration levels, since the number of high-tech visas available under the measure would have exceeded the number of beneficiaries.

The House passed the bill on a largely party-line vote, with Republicans accusing Democrats of blocking a broadly popular measure they said would have benefited businesses and boosted job creation. The Senate did not take up the issue before the end of the session.

House passed HR 6429 on November 30, 245–139: R 218–5; D 27–134. *(Vote 9, p. 817)*

10. SEQUESTER REPLACEMENT

Passage of legislation to replace the across-the-board spending sequester with a reduction in discretionary appropriations caps and $300 billion in other savings over ten years.

With conservative Republicans balking at the attempt by Speaker John A. Boehner of Ohio to avert economic damage from the fiscal cliff by raising income taxes on people making more than $1 million a year, GOP party leaders offered a last-minute budgetary sweetener to help ease passage of the tax measure.

Boehner had hoped his tax bill would win support from a majority of his caucus and show the White House and congressional Democrats that Republicans were closing ranks against all but the smallest, most targeted tax increases. Democrats were pushing to raise taxes on households making $250,000 or more.

Despite Boehner's public statements that the tax bill would pass, conservatives remained unconvinced, objecting that the measure did not include any spending cuts. House leaders proposed the separate spending-reduction bill (HR 6684) at the last minute, during a Rules Committee meeting the night before the tax measure was to come to the floor. Although the goal was to win votes for the tax measure, the vote on the spending measure provided stark evidence not only of the deep partisan divide in the chamber but also of the difficulties Boehner had in rallying his caucus.

Angry Democrats staged a walkout of the December 19 Rules panel meeting, accusing Republicans of forcing the spending bill to the floor right before the holiday recess in order to appease conservatives and to pressure Senate Democrats. The bill made it through the committee with only Republican votes.

The new measure was modeled on legislation that passed the House in May on a close vote, 218–199. The measure replaced the $98 billion automatic spending cut scheduled to start in January 2013 with a $19 billion reduction in spending caps and a $300 billion cut in entitlement spending over ten years. The automatic cuts under the sequester had been required as part of an August 2011 spending deal that raised the debt ceiling, but both parties had since tried to find ways to forestall them.

On December 20, House leaders called up the spending bill before considering the tax proposal. The sequester-replacement measure passed even more narrowly than before, 215–209, with twenty-one Republicans joining all Democrats in voting against it. More important, the spending measure did little to build GOP enthusiasm for Boehner's tax increase and, as a result, did not succeed in its original purpose. After spending hours trying to whip up conservative votes for the tax measure, House leaders admitted defeat and pulled that bill from the floor.

House passed HR 6684 on December 20, 215–209: R 215–21; D 0–188. *(Vote 10, p. 817)*

11. TAX RATES EXTENSION

Passage of legislation to extend most income tax rates set in 2001 and 2003 while allowing taxes for top-bracket taxpayers to rise.

Concluding a long battle over the extension of the George W. Bush administration's tax cuts, the Republican-controlled House voted to allow an income tax increase that many in the GOP opposed. While most expiring tax cuts were extended at a huge cost, an increased rate for top-bracket taxpayers provided a victory for President Obama as he prepared to begin his second term.

The vote settled some of the most urgent tax issues that loomed over Congress and the administration in recent years, but it pushed into the next Congress a broader tax overhaul that Republicans and Democrats alike said was needed.

Obama had long supported extending income tax rates on earnings up to $250,000 for couples while allowing tax rates to revert to Clinton administration levels for those above that threshold. After Obama's reelection, it was clear that Republicans, who had staunchly resisted any tax increase, would have to give ground. House Speaker John A. Boehner, R-Ohio, said after the election that he would go along with up to $800 billion in new revenue, although the money, he said, should come from the curtailment of tax breaks rather than from tax rate increases.

Boehner and Obama resumed the fiscal negotiations they had pursued but ultimately abandoned during the 2011 debt limit debate. The goal for the renewed talks was to reach an agreement that would reduce the deficit by approximately $2 billion over ten years. The two leaders came close in terms of spending and revenue targets but, once again, could not agree on specifics.

Boehner decided to advance a Plan B approach, which would have increased the tax rate only on income above $1 million. But the Speaker abandoned that proposal when it appeared that a majority of Republicans would vote against it. After that embarrassment, Boehner left it to Senate leaders to negotiate a compromise.

A deal was struck between Senate Minority Leader Mitch McConnell, R-Ky., and White House negotiators, led by Vice President Joseph R. Biden Jr., to increase the top tax rate from 35 percent to 39.6 percent on joint income above $450,000. The resulting legislation also delayed automatic spending cuts for two months, extended benefits for the long-term unemployed for a year, kept farm programs operating through fiscal 2013, and deferred for a year a scheduled cut in Medicare payments to doctors.

The bill (HR 8) was passed on a bipartisan vote in the Senate, but House Republicans were a tougher sell. After considering a plan to amend the bill and send it back to the Senate, Republican leaders found enough GOP votes to clear the measure, with the support of House Democrats.

Although Democrats wondered whether they could have gotten a better deal by driving a harder bargain, Republicans emerged from the fight angry, somewhat disorganized, and eager to cut spending in future budget battles.

House cleared HR 8 on January 1, 2013, 257–167: R 85–151; D 172–16. *(Vote 11, p. 817)*

1. HR 3630. Temporary Payroll Tax Cut. Adoption of the conference report on the bill to extend the 4.2 percent employee payroll tax rate through 2012, renew long-term unemployment benefits into January 2013, and preserve Medicare reimbursement rates for physicians through 2012, thereby preventing a scheduled 27.4 percent payment cut. Adopted (and sent to the Senate) 293–132: R 146–91; D 147–41. A "yea" was a vote in support of the president's position. February 17, 2012.

2. HR 3606. Small-Business Startups. Bachus, R-Ala., motion to suspend the rules and concur in the Senate amendment to the bill to define "emerging-growth companies" and exempt them from certain independent auditing requirements, to increase from $5 million to $50 million the annual public-offering threshold for companies to be exempt from full Securities and Exchange Commission (SEC) filing requirements, and to raise the number of shareholders that would trigger mandatory SEC registration from 750 to 2,000. The legislation also lifted an SEC ban that prevented small, privately held companies from using advertisements to solicit investors and to allow companies to sell up to $1 million worth of securities without registering with the SEC. Motion agreed to (clearing the bill for the president) 380–41: R 235–0; D 145–41. A "yea" was a vote in support of the president's position. March 27, 2012.

3. H Con Res 112. Fiscal 2013 Budget Resolution. Adoption of the concurrent resolution to provide $2.8 trillion in new budget authority for fiscal 2013, not including off-budget accounts. The resolution called for limiting discretionary appropriations to $1.0 trillion in 2013, and for major cuts in nondefense discretionary and mandatory spending over the following ten years. It also assumed significant future savings by restructuring Medicare into a "premium support" system beginning in 2023, converting Medicaid and the food stamp program into block grants to states, and repealing the 2010 health care overhaul. It also called for an overhaul of the tax code, including repeal of the alternative minimum tax, consolidation of the six existing individual income tax brackets consolidated into two, elimination or reduction of tax credits and deductions, and changes in corporate taxation to reduce the top rate from 35 percent to 25 percent. Adopted 228–191: R 228–10; D 0–181. March 29, 2012.

4. HR 4628. Student Loan Interest Rates. Passage of the bill to extend for one year, through June 30, 2013, the 3.4 percent interest rate for federally subsidized undergraduate student loans, and to offset costs by repealing the Prevention and Public Health Fund established by the health care overhaul. Passed 215–195: R 202–30; D 13–165. A "nay" was a vote in support of the president's position. April 27, 2012.

5. HR 4310. Indefinite Detention of Terrorist Suspects. Smith, D-Wash., amendment to strike language from the fiscal 2013 defense authorization bill to provide the authority to transfer individuals captured within the United States, territories, or other locations to military authorities and prevent the indefinite detention of such individuals at Guantánamo Bay detention facility, Cuba. Rejected 182–238: R 19–219; D 163–19. May 18, 2012.

6. H Res 711. Holder Contempt Resolution. Adoption of the resolution citing Attorney General Eric H. Holder Jr. for contempt of Congress for refusing to comply with the subpoena issued by the House Oversight and Government Reform Committee to provide documents to the committee regarding the "Operation Fast and Furious" gun-tracking program. Adopted 255–67: R 238–2; D 17–65. A "nay" was a vote in support of the president's position. June 28, 2012.

7. HR 6079. Repeal of Health Care Overhaul. Passage of the bill to repeal the 2010 health care overhaul, which required most individuals to buy health insurance by 2014, made changes to government health care programs, and set new requirements for health insurers. Passed 244–185: R 239–0; D 5–185. A "nay" was a vote in support of the president's position. July 11, 2012.

8. HR 6156. U.S.-Russia Trade Relations. Passage of the bill to establish permanent normal trade relations with Russia and Moldova and end Jackson-Vanik restrictions on both economies, and to provide sanctions against people involved in human rights violations in Russia. Passed 365–43: R 227–6; D 138–37. A "yea" was a vote in support of the president's position. November 16, 2012.

9. HR 6429. STEM Visa Program. Passage of the bill to create a new visa program under which foreign students earning advanced degrees in science, technology, engineering, or mathematics at eligible U.S. colleges and universities could remain in the United States to work in those fields. The bill eliminated the Diversity Visa Program and reallocated 55,000 visas to the new STEM visa program. Passed 245–139: R 218–5; D 27–134. A "nay" was a vote in support of the president's position. November 30, 2012.

10. HR 6684. Sequester Replacement. Passage of the bill to cancel the automatic cuts from discretionary programs set to occur in January 2013 and replace the sequester with a $19 billion reduction in the discretionary cap for fiscal 2013 and savings from mandatory programs totaling more than $300 billion over ten years. It also eliminated the separate cap on defense spending for the year to allow for higher spending levels. Passed 215–209: R 215–21; D 0–188. A "nay" was a vote in support of the president's position. December 20, 2012.

11. HR 8. Tax Rates Extension. Camp, R-Mich., motion to concur in the Senate amendments to the bill to permanently extend the 2001 and 2003 tax rates for individual income below $400,000 and joint-filer income below $450,000 and to allow rates for income above those thresholds to rise from 35 percent to 39.6 percent. In addition, the legislation permanently extended the tax rates on dividends and capital gains for individual income below $400,000 and joint-filer income below $450,000 while allowing rates for the dividends and capital gains taxes to rise to 20 percent for income above those thresholds. The measure delayed the automatic, across-the-board cuts known as sequester for two months. The measure also taxed individual estates valued at more than $5 million and joint estates valued at more than $10 million at 40 percent, and permanently altered the alternative minimum tax to account for inflation. Unemployment insurance was extended through 2013. The bill also blocked scheduled cuts to Medicare physician payment rates and extended for five years tax credits included in the 2009 stimulus law, including the child tax credit and the earned income tax credit. It also allowed the 2 percent payroll tax holiday to expire. Motion agreed to (clearing the bill for the president) 257–167: R 85–151; D 172–16. A "yea" was a vote in support of the president's position. January 1, 2013.

KEY

Republican Democrat **Independent**

Y	Voted for (yea)	–	Announced against
#	Paired for	P	Voted "present"
+	Announced for	C	Voted "present" to avoid possible conflict of interest
N	Voted against (nay)		
X	Paired against	?	Did not vote or otherwise make a position known

House Key Votes		1	2	3	4	5	6	7	8	9	10	11
ALABAMA												
1	*Bonner*	N	Y	Y	Y	N	Y	?	Y	?	Y	N
2	*Roby*	N	Y	Y	Y	N	Y	Y	Y	Y	Y	N
3	*Rogers*	N	Y	Y	Y	?	Y	Y	Y	Y	Y	N
4	*Aderholt*	N	Y	Y	Y	N	Y	Y	Y	Y	Y	N
5	*Brooks*	N	Y	Y	Y	N	Y	Y	Y	Y	Y	N
6	*Bachus*	N	Y	Y	Y	N	Y	Y	Y	Y	Y	N
7	Sewell	Y	Y	N	N	N	?	N	Y	N	N	Y
ALASKA												
AL	*Young*	Y	Y	Y	Y	N	Y	Y	Y	?	Y	Y
ARIZONA												
1	*Gosar*	?	Y	Y	N	?	Y	Y	Y	Y	Y	N
2	*Franks*	N	Y	Y	N	N	Y	Y	Y	Y	Y	N
3	*Quayle*	N	Y	Y	N	N	Y	Y	Y	Y	Y	N
4	Pastor	Y	N	N	N	Y	N	N	Y	N	N	Y
5	*Schweikert*	Y	Y	Y	N	N	Y	Y	Y	?	N	N
6	*Flake*	N	Y	Y	N	N	Y	Y	Y	Y	Y	N
7	Grijalva	Y	N	N	N	Y	?	N	N	N	N	Y
8	Barber[1]						N	N	Y	+	N	Y
ARKANSAS												
1	*Crawford*	Y	Y	Y	Y	N	Y	Y	Y	Y	Y	N
2	Griffin	Y	Y	Y	Y	N	Y	Y	Y	Y	Y	N
3	*Womack*	Y	Y	Y	Y	N	Y	Y	Y	Y	Y	Y
4	Ross	Y	Y	N	N	N	Y	Y	Y	Y	N	Y
CALIFORNIA												
1	Thompson	N	Y	N	N	Y	N	N	Y	N	N	Y
2	*Herger*	Y	Y	Y	Y	N	Y	Y	Y	+	Y	Y
3	*Lungren*	Y	Y	Y	Y	N	Y	Y	Y	Y	Y	Y
4	McClintock	N	Y	Y	N	Y	Y	Y	Y	?	Y	N
5	Matsui	Y	Y	N	N	Y	?	N	Y	N	N	Y
6	Woolsey	N	N	N	N	Y	?	N	–	N	N	?
7	Miller, George	Y	N	N	N	Y	N	N	?	N	N	Y
8	Pelosi	Y	Y	?	N	Y	?	N	Y	N	N	Y
9	Lee	N	N	N	N	Y	?	N	N	N	N	Y
10	Garamendi	Y	Y	N	N	Y	?	N	Y	Y	N	Y
11	McNerney	Y	Y	N	N	Y	N	N	Y	Y	N	Y
12	Speier	Y	Y	N	N	?	N	N	Y	?	N	Y
13	Stark	Y	N	N	N	Y	?	N	N	?	?	?
14	Eshoo	Y	Y	N	N	Y	N	N	Y	N	N	Y
15	Honda	Y	Y	N	N	Y	?	N	Y	N	N	Y
16	Lofgren	Y	Y	N	N	Y	N	N	N	N	N	Y
17	Farr	N	Y	N	?	Y	N	N	Y	N	N	Y
18	Cardoza[2]	N	Y	N	?	?	?	N				
19	*Denham*	Y	Y	Y	Y	N	Y	Y	Y	N	Y	Y
20	Costa	Y	Y	N	+	N	?	N	Y	N	N	Y
21	*Nunes*	Y	Y	Y	?	N	Y	Y	Y	Y	Y	N
22	*McCarthy*	Y	Y	Y	Y	N	Y	Y	Y	Y	Y	N
23	Capps	Y	Y	N	N	Y	N	N	Y	N	N	Y
24	*Gallegly*	N	Y	Y	Y	N	Y	Y	?	?	Y	Y
25	*McKeon*	Y	Y	Y	Y	N	Y	Y	Y	Y	Y	Y
26	*Dreier*	Y	Y	Y	Y	N	Y	Y	Y	Y	Y	Y
27	Sherman	Y	Y	N	N	Y	N	N	Y	N	N	Y
28	Berman	Y	N	N	N	Y	N	N	Y	?	N	Y
29	Schiff	Y	Y	N	N	Y	?	N	Y	N	N	Y
30	Waxman	Y	N	N	N	Y	N	N	Y	N	N	Y
31	Becerra	Y	N	N	N	Y	?	N	Y	N	N	N
32	Chu	Y	Y	N	N	Y	?	N	N	Y	N	Y
33	Bass	Y	Y	N	N	Y	?	N	Y	N	N	Y
34	Roybal-Allard	Y	Y	N	N	Y	?	N	Y	–	N	Y
35	Waters	Y	Y	N	N	Y	?	N	N	N	N	Y
36	Hahn	Y	Y	N	N	Y	?	N	N	N	N	Y
37	Richardson	Y	Y	N	N	Y	?	N	Y	?	N	Y
38	Napolitano	Y	N	N	N	Y	?	N	N	N	N	Y
39	Sanchez, Linda	Y	Y	N	N	Y	?	N	Y	N	N	Y
40	*Royce*	N	Y	Y	Y	N	Y	Y	Y	Y	Y	Y
41	*Lewis*	Y	Y	Y	Y	N	?	Y	Y	Y	Y	?
42	*Miller, Gary*	Y	Y	Y	Y	N	Y	Y	Y	Y	Y	Y
43	Baca	Y	Y	N	N	Y	?	N	N	N	N	Y
44	*Calvert*	Y	Y	Y	Y	N	Y	Y	Y	Y	Y	Y
45	*Bono Mack*	?	Y	Y	Y	N	Y	Y	Y	Y	Y	Y
46	*Rohrabacher*	N	Y	Y	Y	N	Y	Y	Y	Y	Y	N
47	Sanchez, Loretta	Y	Y	N	N	?	N	N	Y	N	N	Y
48	*Campbell*	?	Y	Y	Y	N	Y	Y	Y	N	Y	N
49	*Issa*	Y	Y	Y	Y	N	Y	Y	Y	Y	Y	N
50	*Bilbray*	Y	Y	Y	Y	N	Y	Y	Y	?	Y	Y
51	Filner[3]	N	N	–	–	+	?	N	?	–		
52	Hunter	Y	Y	Y	Y	N	Y	Y	Y	Y	Y	N
53	Davis	Y	Y	N	N	Y	?	N	Y	N	N	Y
COLORADO												
1	DeGette	Y	Y	N	N	Y	?	N	Y	?	N	Y
2	Polis	Y	Y	N	N	Y	?	N	Y	N	N	Y
3	*Tipton*	Y	Y	Y	Y	Y	Y	Y	Y	Y	Y	N
4	*Gardner*	N	Y	Y	Y	N	Y	Y	Y	Y	Y	N
5	Lamborn	N	Y	Y	N	N	Y	Y	Y	Y	Y	N
6	*Coffman*	Y	Y	Y	Y	N	Y	Y	Y	Y	Y	N
7	Perlmutter	Y	Y	N	N	Y	N	N	Y	N	N	Y
CONNECTICUT												
1	Larson	Y	Y	N	N	Y	?	N	Y	N	N	Y
2	Courtney	Y	Y	N	N	Y	N	N	Y	N	N	Y
3	DeLauro	Y	Y	N	N	Y	N	N	N	N	N	N
4	Himes	Y	Y	N	N	Y	N	N	Y	Y	N	Y
5	Murphy	Y	Y	N	N	Y	N	N	Y	?	N	Y
DELAWARE												
AL	Carney	Y	Y	N	N	Y	?	N	Y	Y	N	Y
FLORIDA												
1	*Miller*	N	Y	Y	N	N	Y	Y	Y	Y	Y	N
2	*Southerland*	Y	Y	Y	Y	N	Y	Y	Y	Y	Y	N
3	Brown	+	Y	N	N	Y	?	N	Y	N	N	Y
4	*Crenshaw*	Y	Y	Y	Y	N	Y	Y	Y	Y	Y	Y
5	*Nugent*	N	Y	Y	Y	N	Y	Y	Y	Y	Y	N
6	*Stearns*	Y	Y	Y	Y	N	Y	Y	Y	Y	Y	N
7	*Mica*	N	Y	Y	Y	N	Y	Y	Y	Y	Y	N
8	*Webster*	Y	Y	Y	Y	N	Y	Y	Y	Y	Y	N
9	*Bilirakis*	Y	Y	Y	Y	N	Y	Y	Y	Y	Y	N
10	*Young*	Y	Y	Y	Y	N	Y	Y	Y	Y	Y	Y
11	Castor	Y	Y	N	N	Y	?	N	Y	N	N	Y
12	*Ross*	N	Y	Y	Y	N	Y	Y	Y	Y	Y	N
13	*Buchanan*	Y	Y	Y	Y	N	Y	Y	Y	Y	Y	Y
14	*Mack*	Y	?	?	Y	N	Y	Y	Y	Y	Y	N
15	*Posey*	N	Y	Y	Y	N	Y	Y	Y	Y	Y	N
16	*Rooney*	Y	Y	Y	Y	N	Y	Y	Y	Y	Y	N
17	Wilson	N	Y	N	N	Y	?	N	N	N	N	Y
18	*Ros-Lehtinen*	Y	Y	Y	Y	N	Y	Y	Y	Y	Y	Y
19	Deutch	Y	N	N	N	Y	N	N	Y	N	N	Y
20	Wasserman Schultz	Y	Y	N	N	Y	N	N	Y	N	N	Y
21	*Diaz-Balart*	Y	+	Y	Y	N	Y	Y	Y	Y	Y	Y

[1]Ron Barber, D-Ariz., was sworn in June 19, 2012, to fill the vacancy created by the January 25 resignation of fellow Democrat Gabrielle Giffords. The first key vote for which Barber was eligible was vote 6; Giffords did not cast a key vote in 2012.

[2]Dennis Cardoza, D-Calif., resigned August 15, 2012. The last key vote for which he was eligible was vote 7. His seat was left vacant for the remainder of the session.

[3]Bob Filner, D-Calif., resigned December 3, 2012. The last key vote for which he was eligible was vote 9. His seat was left vacant for the remainder of the session.

House Key Votes		1	2	3	4	5	6	7	8	9	10	11
22	*West*	N	Y	Y	Y	N	Y	Y	Y	Y	Y	N
23	Hastings	N	Y	N	N	Y	?	N	Y	?	N	Y
24	*Adams*	N	Y	Y	Y	N	Y	Y	Y	Y	Y	N
25	*Rivera*	Y	Y	Y	Y	N	Y	Y	Y	Y	?	N
GEORGIA												
1	*Kingston*	N	Y	Y	?	N	Y	Y	Y	Y	Y	N
2	Bishop	Y	Y	N	N	N	?	N	?	N	N	Y
3	*Westmoreland*	Y	Y	Y	N	N	Y	Y	Y	Y	Y	N
4	Johnson	N	N	N	N	Y	?	N	Y	N	N	Y
5	Lewis	Y	Y	N	N	Y	?	N	Y	?	N	?
6	*Price*	Y	Y	Y	N	N	Y	Y	Y	Y	Y	N
7	*Woodall*	N	Y	Y	N	N	Y	Y	Y	Y	Y	N
8	*Scott, A.*	N	Y	Y	Y	N	Y	Y	Y	Y	Y	N
9	*Graves*	N	Y	Y	N	N	Y	Y	Y	Y	Y	N
10	*Broun*	N	Y	?	N	Y	Y	Y	Y	Y	N	N
11	*Gingrey*	N	Y	Y	Y	N	Y	Y	Y	Y	Y	N
12	Barrow	Y	Y	N	Y	N	Y	N	Y	Y	N	N
13	Scott, D.	Y	Y	N	N	Y	?	N	Y	N	N	Y
HAWAII												
1	Hanabusa	Y	Y	N	N	Y	?	N	Y	N	N	Y
2	Hirono	Y	Y	N	?	Y	N	N	Y	N	N	Y
IDAHO												
1	*Labrador*	N	Y	Y	N	Y	Y	Y	Y	Y	N	N
2	*Simpson*	N	Y	Y	Y	N	Y	Y	Y	+	Y	Y
ILLINOIS												
1	Rush	Y	Y	N	N	Y	?	N	?	?	N	Y
2	Jackson[4]	Y	?	?	N	Y	?	?	?			
3	Lipinski	Y	Y	N	Y	N	P	N	N	Y	N	Y
4	Gutierrez	N	Y	N	N	Y	?	N	Y	N	N	Y
5	Quigley	Y	Y	N	N	Y	N	N	Y	N	N	Y
6	*Roskam*	Y	Y	Y	Y	N	Y	Y	Y	Y	Y	N
7	Davis, D.	N	Y	N	N	Y	?	N	Y	N	N	Y
8	*Walsh*	Y	Y	Y	N	N	Y	Y	Y	Y	N	N
9	Schakowsky	Y	N	N	N	Y	–	N	Y	N	N	Y
10	*Dold*	Y	Y	Y	Y	N	Y	Y	Y	Y	Y	Y
11	*Kinzinger*	Y	Y	Y	Y	N	Y	Y	Y	Y	Y	Y
12	Costello	N	Y	N	N	?	N	N	?	?	?	Y
13	*Biggert*	Y	Y	Y	Y	N	Y	Y	Y	Y	Y	Y
14	*Hultgren*	Y	Y	Y	Y	N	Y	Y	Y	Y	Y	N
15	*Johnson*	N	Y	Y	Y	Y	Y	Y	Y	Y	N	Y
16	*Manzullo*	Y	Y	Y	Y	N	Y	Y	Y	+	Y	Y
17	*Schilling*	Y	Y	Y	Y	N	Y	Y	Y	Y	Y	N
18	*Schock*	Y	Y	Y	Y	N	Y	Y	Y	Y	Y	Y
19	*Shimkus*	Y	Y	Y	Y	Y	Y	Y	Y	Y	Y	Y
INDIANA												
1	Visclosky	N	N	N	N	Y	N	N	N	-	N	N
2	Donnelly	Y	Y	N	Y	N	Y	N	Y	Y	N	Y
3	*Stutzman*	Y	Y	Y	Y	N	Y	Y	Y	Y	Y	N
4	*Rokita*	N	Y	Y	Y	N	Y	Y	Y	Y	Y	N
5	*Burton*	N	Y	Y	Y	N	Y	Y	Y	?	Y	?
6	*Pence*	Y	Y	Y	Y	N	Y	Y	+	–	Y	N
7	Carson	Y	Y	N	N	Y	?	N	Y	N	N	Y
8	*Bucshon*	Y	Y	Y	Y	N	Y	Y	Y	Y	Y	N
9	*Young*	Y	Y	Y	Y	N	Y	Y	Y	Y	Y	N
IOWA												
1	Braley	Y	Y	N	N	Y	N	N	Y	N	N	Y
2	Loebsack	Y	Y	N	N	Y	N	N	Y	N	N	Y
3	Boswell	Y	Y	N	N	Y	Y	N	Y	Y	N	Y
4	*Latham*	Y	Y	Y	Y	N	Y	Y	Y	Y	Y	N
5	*King*	N	Y	Y	Y	N	Y	Y	Y	Y	Y	N
KANSAS												
1	*Huelskamp*	Y	Y	N	N	Y	Y	Y	Y	Y	N	N
2	*Jenkins*	Y	Y	Y	?	N	Y	Y	Y	Y	Y	N
3	*Yoder*	Y	Y	Y	Y	N	Y	Y	Y	Y	Y	N
4	*Pompeo*	N	Y	Y	Y	N	Y	Y	Y	Y	Y	N
KENTUCKY												
1	*Whitfield*	N	Y	N	Y	N	Y	Y	Y	Y	N	N
2	*Guthrie*	Y	Y	Y	Y	N	Y	Y	Y	Y	Y	N
3	Yarmuth	Y	Y	N	N	Y	?	N	?	N	N	Y
4	*Davis*[5]	Y	Y	Y	+	N	Y	Y				
4	*Massie*[5]								Y	Y	N	N
5	*Rogers*	Y	Y	Y	Y	N	Y	Y	Y	Y	Y	Y
6	Chandler	Y	Y	N	N	N	Y	N	Y	?	N	Y
LOUISIANA												
1	*Scalise*	Y	Y	Y	Y	N	Y	Y	Y	Y	Y	N
2	Richmond	Y	Y	N	N	Y	?	N	Y	N	N	Y
3	*Landry*	N	?	Y	Y	N	Y	Y	Y	Y	N	N
4	*Fleming*	N	Y	Y	Y	N	Y	Y	Y	Y	Y	N
5	*Alexander*	Y	Y	Y	Y	N	Y	Y	Y	Y	Y	Y
6	*Cassidy*	N	Y	Y	?	N	Y	Y	Y	Y	N	N
7	*Boustany*	N	Y	Y	Y	N	Y	Y	Y	Y	Y	N
MAINE												
1	Pingree	N	N	?	N	Y	?	N	N	N	N	Y
2	Michaud	Y	Y	N	N	Y	N	N	Y	Y	N	Y
MARYLAND												
1	*Harris*	N	Y	Y	Y	N	Y	Y	Y	Y	Y	N
2	Ruppersberger	Y	Y	N	N	N	?	N	Y	Y	N	Y
3	Sarbanes	N	N	N	N	Y	?	N	Y	N	N	Y
4	Edwards	N	N	N	N	Y	?	N	Y	–	N	Y
5	Hoyer	N	Y	N	N	Y	?	N	Y	N	N	Y
6	*Bartlett*	Y	Y	Y	Y	Y	Y	Y	?	Y	Y	N
7	Cummings	N	N	N	N	Y	?	N	Y	N	N	Y
8	Van Hollen	N	Y	N	N	Y	?	N	Y	N	N	Y
MASSACHUSETTS												
1	Olver	Y	N	N	N	Y	?	N	Y	N	N	Y
2	Neal	Y	?	N	N	Y	?	N	Y	N	N	Y
3	McGovern	Y	Y	N	N	Y	?	N	Y	N	N	Y
4	Frank	Y	Y	N	N	Y	?	N	Y	N	N	Y
5	Tsongas	Y	Y	N	N	Y	N	N	Y	N	N	Y
6	Tierney	Y	N	N	N	Y	N	N	N	N	N	Y
7	Markey	Y	N	N	N	Y	?	N	Y	N	N	Y
8	Capuano	N	N	N	N	Y	?	N	N	N	N	Y
9	Lynch	N	Y	N	N	Y	N	N	Y	N	N	Y
10	Keating	Y	Y	N	N	Y	?	N	N	N	N	Y
MICHIGAN												
1	*Benishek*	Y	Y	Y	Y	N	Y	Y	Y	Y	Y	Y
2	*Huizenga*	Y	Y	Y	N	N	Y	Y	Y	Y	Y	N
3	*Amash*	N	Y	N	N	Y	Y	Y	Y	Y	N	N
4	*Camp*	Y	Y	Y	?	N	Y	Y	Y	Y	Y	Y
5	Kildee	Y	N	N	N	Y	?	N	N	N	N	Y
6	*Upton*	Y	Y	Y	Y	N	Y	Y	N	Y	Y	Y
7	*Walberg*	N	Y	Y	N	N	Y	Y	Y	Y	Y	N
8	*Rogers*	Y	Y	Y	Y	N	Y	Y	N	Y	Y	Y
9	Peters	Y	Y	N	N	Y	?	N	Y	N	N	Y
10	*Miller*	Y	Y	Y	Y	N	Y	Y	Y	Y	Y	Y
11	*McCotter*[6]	N	Y	Y	Y	N	Y					
11	Curson[6]								Y	N	N	Y
12	Levin	Y	Y	N	N	N	?	N	Y	N	N	Y
13	Clarke	Y	Y	N	N	Y	?	N	N	N	N	Y
14	Conyers	Y	Y	N	N	Y	?	N	Y	N	N	Y
15	Dingell	Y	N	N	N	Y	N	N	Y	N	N	Y
MINNESOTA												
1	Walz	Y	Y	N	Y	Y	Y	N	Y	N	N	Y
2	*Kline*	Y	Y	Y	Y	N	Y	Y	Y	Y	Y	Y
3	*Paulsen*	Y	Y	Y	Y	N	Y	Y	Y	Y	Y	N
4	McCollum	Y	N	N	N	Y	?	N	N	N	N	Y
5	Ellison	N	Y	N	N	N	?	N	Y	N	N	Y
6	*Bachmann*	N	Y	Y	Y	N	Y	Y	Y	Y	Y	N
7	Peterson	N	Y	N	Y	N	Y	N	Y	Y	N	N
8	*Cravaack*	Y	Y	Y	Y	N	Y	Y	Y	Y	Y	N

[4]Jesse L. Jackson Jr., D-Ill., resigned November 21, 2012. The last key vote for which he was eligible was vote 8. His seat was left vacant for the remainder of the session.

[5]Thomas Massie, R-Ky., was sworn in November 6, 2012, to fill the vacancy created by the July 31 resignation of fellow Republican Geoff Davis. The first key vote for which Massie was eligible was vote 8; the last key vote for which Davis was eligible was vote 7.

[6]David A. Curson, D-Mich., was sworn in November 6, 2012, to fill the vacancy created by the July 6 resignation of Republican Thaddeus McCotter. The first key vote for which Curson was eligible was vote 8. The last key vote for which McCotter was eligible was vote 6.

KEY

	Republican		Democrat	**Independent**
Y	Voted for (yea)	–	Announced against	
#	Paired for	P	Voted "present"	
+	Announced for	C	Voted "present" to avoid possible conflict of interest	
N	Voted against (nay)			
X	Paired against	?	Did not vote or otherwise make a position known	

House Key Votes		1	2	3	4	5	6	7	8	9	10	11
MISSISSIPPI												
1	*Nunnelee*	Y	Y	Y	Y	N	Y	Y	Y	Y	Y	N
2	Thompson	Y	Y	N	N	Y	?	N	N	N	N	Y
3	*Harper*	Y	Y	Y	Y	N	Y	Y	Y	Y	Y	N
4	*Palazzo*	Y	Y	Y	Y	N	Y	Y	Y	Y	Y	N
MISSOURI												
1	Clay	N	N	N	N	?	?	N	Y	N	N	Y
2	*Akin*	N	+	Y	Y	N	Y	Y	Y	?	Y	N
3	Carnahan	Y	Y	N	N	Y	?	N	Y	?	N	Y
4	*Hartzler*	Y	Y	Y	Y	N	Y	Y	Y	Y	Y	N
5	Cleaver	N	Y	N	N	Y	?	N	Y	N	N	Y
6	*Graves*	N	Y	Y	Y	N	Y	Y	Y	Y	Y	–
7	*Long*	Y	Y	Y	Y	N	Y	Y	Y	Y	Y	N
8	*Emerson*	Y	Y	Y	Y	N	Y	Y	Y	Y	Y	Y
9	*Luetkemeyer*	Y	Y	Y	Y	N	Y	Y	Y	Y	Y	Y
MONTANA												
AL	*Rehberg*	Y	Y	N	Y	Y	Y	Y	Y	Y	Y	N
NEBRASKA												
1	*Fortenberry*	N	Y	Y	Y	N	Y	Y	Y	Y	Y	Y
2	*Terry*	N	Y	Y	Y	N	Y	Y	Y	Y	Y	N
3	*Smith*	Y	Y	Y	Y	N	Y	Y	Y	Y	Y	N
NEVADA												
1	Berkley	Y	Y	N	N	Y	N	N	Y	N	N	Y
2	*Amodei*	Y	Y	Y	Y	?	Y	Y	Y	Y	Y	N
3	*Heck*	Y	Y	Y	Y	N	Y	Y	Y	Y	Y	Y
NEW HAMPSHIRE												
1	*Guinta*	Y	Y	Y	Y	N	Y	Y	Y	Y	Y	N
2	*Bass*	Y	Y	Y	Y	N	Y	Y	Y	Y	Y	Y
NEW JERSEY												
1	Andrews	Y	Y	N	N	Y	?	N	Y	N	N	Y
2	*LoBiondo*	Y	Y	Y	Y	N	Y	Y	N	Y	N	Y
3	*Runyan*	Y	Y	Y	Y	N	Y	Y	Y	Y	Y	Y
4	*Smith*	Y	Y	Y	Y	N	Y	Y	Y	Y	Y	Y
5	*Garrett*	N	Y	Y	N	N	Y	Y	Y	Y	Y	N
6	Pallone	Y	Y	N	N	Y	?	N	N	N	N	Y
7	*Lance*	Y	Y	Y	Y	N	Y	Y	Y	Y	Y	Y
8	Pascrell	Y	Y	N	N	+	?	N	Y	N	N	Y
9	Rothman	Y	Y	N	N	Y	N	N	?	?	N	Y
10	Payne[7]	?							Y	N	N	Y
11	*Frelinghuysen*	Y	Y	Y	Y	N	Y	Y	Y	+	Y	Y
12	Holt	Y	N	N	N	Y	N	N	?	N	N	Y
13	Sires	Y	Y	N	?	Y	?	N	Y	N	N	Y
NEW MEXICO												
1	Heinrich	Y	Y	N	N	Y	N	N	?	N	N	Y
2	*Pearce*	N	Y	Y	Y	N	Y	Y	Y	Y	Y	N
3	Lujan	Y	Y	N	N	Y	N	N	Y	N	N	Y
NEW YORK												
1	Bishop	Y	Y	N	Y	Y	N	N	Y	N	N	Y
2	Israel	Y	Y	N	N	Y	?	N	Y	N	N	Y
3	*King*	Y	Y	Y	Y	N	Y	Y	Y	Y	Y	Y
4	McCarthy	Y	Y	N	N	N	?	N	Y	N	N	Y
5	Ackerman	N	Y	N	N	Y	?	N	Y	N	N	Y
6	Meeks	Y	Y	?	N	Y	?	N	Y	N	N	Y
7	Crowley	Y	Y	N	N	Y	?	N	Y	N	N	Y
8	Nadler	Y	N	N	N	Y	N	N	N	N	N	Y
9	*Turner*	Y	Y	Y	Y	N	Y	Y	Y	Y	Y	Y
10	Towns	Y	Y	N	?	Y	?	N	?	?	N	Y
11	Clarke	N	N	N	N	Y	?	N	N	N	N	Y
12	Velazquez	Y	Y	N	N	Y	?	N	N	–	N	Y
13	*Grimm*	Y	Y	Y	Y	N	Y	Y	Y	Y	Y	Y
14	Maloney, C.	Y	Y	N	N	Y	?	N	?	N	N	Y
15	Rangel	?	?	?	?	Y	?	N	Y	N	N	Y
16	Serrano	Y	Y	N	N	Y	?	N	N	N	N	Y
17	Engel	Y	?	N	N	Y	?	N	Y	N	N	Y
18	Lowey	Y	Y	N	N	Y	?	N	Y	N	N	Y
19	*Hayworth*	Y	Y	Y	Y	N	Y	Y	Y	Y	Y	Y
20	*Gibson*	Y	Y	N	Y	Y	Y	Y	Y	Y	N	Y
21	Tonko	Y	Y	N	N	Y	?	N	Y	Y	N	Y
22	Hinchey	Y	N	?	N	Y	?	N	N	N	N	Y
23	Owens	Y	Y	N	Y	N	Y	N	Y	–	N	Y
24	*Hanna*	Y	Y	Y	Y	N	Y	Y	Y	Y	Y	Y
25	*Buerkle*	N	Y	Y	Y	N	Y	Y	Y	Y	Y	-
26	Hochul	Y	Y	N	Y	Y	Y	N	Y	Y	N	Y
27	Higgins	Y	Y	N	Y	Y	N	N	Y	N	N	Y
28	Slaughter	Y	Y	N	–	+	N	N	Y	–	N	Y
29	*Reed*	Y	Y	Y	Y	N	Y	Y	Y	Y	Y	Y
NORTH CAROLINA												
1	Butterfield	Y	Y	N	N	Y	?	N	Y	N	N	Y
2	*Ellmers*	Y	Y	Y	Y	N	Y	Y	Y	Y	Y	N
3	*Jones*	Y	Y	N	Y	Y	Y	Y	N	N	N	N
4	Price	Y	Y	N	N	Y	?	N	Y	N	N	Y
5	Foxx	N	Y	Y	N	N	Y	Y	Y	Y	Y	N
6	*Coble*	Y	Y	Y	N	N	Y	Y	Y	Y	Y	Y
7	McIntyre	Y	Y	N	Y	N	Y	Y	Y	Y	N	N
8	Kissell	Y	Y	N	Y	N	Y	Y	Y	Y	N	Y
9	*Myrick*	Y	Y	Y	Y	N	Y	Y	Y	Y	Y	N
10	*McHenry*	Y	Y	Y	?	N	Y	Y	Y	Y	Y	N
11	Shuler	?	Y	N	N	Y	N	N	?	?	N	Y
12	Watt	Y	Y	?	N	Y	?	N	Y	?	N	Y
13	Miller	Y	Y	N	N	Y	N	N	Y	N	N	N
NORTH DAKOTA												
AL	*Berg*	Y	Y	Y	Y	N	Y	Y	Y	Y	Y	N
OHIO												
1	*Chabot*	N	Y	Y	Y	N	Y	Y	Y	Y	Y	N
2	*Schmidt*	N	Y	Y	Y	N	Y	Y	Y	?	Y	N
3	Turner	Y	Y	Y	Y	N	Y	Y	Y	Y	Y	N
4	*Jordan*	N	Y	Y	Y	N	Y	Y	Y	Y	Y	N
5	*Latta*	Y	Y	Y	Y	N	Y	Y	Y	Y	Y	Y
6	*Johnson*	Y	Y	Y	Y	N	Y	Y	Y	Y	Y	Y
7	*Austria*	Y	Y	Y	Y	N	Y	Y	Y	Y	Y	N
8	*Boehner*[8]				Y							Y
9	Kaptur	Y	Y	N	N	Y	?	N	N	N	N	Y
10	Kucinich	Y	N	N	N	Y	?	N	N	N	N	Y
11	Fudge	N	N	N	N	Y	?	N	N	N	N	Y
12	*Tiberi*	Y	Y	Y	Y	N	Y	Y	Y	Y	Y	Y
13	Sutton	Y	Y	N	N	Y	N	N	N	?	N	Y
14	*LaTourette*	Y	Y	Y	Y	N	N	Y	N	Y	Y	Y
15	*Stivers*	Y	Y	Y	Y	N	Y	Y	Y	Y	Y	Y
16	*Renacci*	Y	Y	Y	Y	N	Y	Y	Y	Y	Y	N
17	Ryan	N	Y	N	N	Y	N	N	N	N	N	Y
18	*Gibbs*	Y	Y	Y	Y	N	Y	Y	Y	Y	Y	N
OKLAHOMA												
1	*Sullivan*	N	Y	Y	Y	N	Y	Y	?	Y	Y	Y
2	Boren	Y	Y	N	Y	N	Y	Y	?	?	N	Y
3	*Lucas*	Y	Y	Y	Y	N	Y	Y	Y	Y	Y	Y
4	*Cole*	Y	Y	Y	Y	N	Y	Y	Y	Y	Y	Y
5	*Lankford*	N	Y	Y	Y	N	Y	Y	Y	Y	Y	N

[7]Donald M. Payne Jr., D-N.J., was sworn in November 15, 2012, to fill the vacancy created by the March 6 death of his father, fellow Democrat Donald M. Payne. The first key vote for which Payne Jr. was eligible was vote 8; the only key vote for which the elder Payne was eligible was vote 1 but he did not cast a ballot then and did not later state a position on the issue in vote 1.

[8]The Speaker votes only at his discretion.

House Key Votes		1	2	3	4	5	6	7	8	9	10	11
OREGON												
1	Bonamici	Y	Y	N	N	Y	N	N	Y	N	N	Y
2	*Walden*	Y	Y	Y	Y	N	Y	Y	Y	Y	Y	Y
3	Blumenauer	Y	Y	N	?	Y	N	N	Y	Y	N	N
4	DeFazio	N	Y	N	N	Y	N	N	N	Y	N	N
5	Schrader	N	Y	N	N	Y	N	N	Y	Y	N	N
PENNSYLVANIA												
1	Brady	Y	N	N	N	Y	?	N	?	N	N	Y
2	Fattah	Y	Y	N	N	Y	?	N	Y	?	N	Y
3	*Kelly*	Y	Y	Y	Y	N	Y	Y	Y	Y	Y	Y
4	Altmire	Y	Y	N	N	Y	Y	N	Y	Y	N	Y
5	*Thompson*	Y	Y	Y	Y	N	Y	Y	Y	Y	Y	Y
6	*Gerlach*	Y	Y	Y	Y	N	Y	Y	Y	Y	Y	Y
7	*Meehan*	Y	Y	Y	Y	N	Y	Y	Y	Y	Y	Y
8	*Fitzpatrick*	Y	Y	Y	Y	N	Y	Y	?	Y	N	Y
9	*Shuster*	Y	Y	Y	Y	N	Y	Y	Y	Y	Y	Y
10	*Marino*	Y	Y	Y	?	N	Y	Y	Y	Y	Y	Y
11	*Barletta*	Y	Y	Y	Y	N	Y	Y	Y	N	Y	Y
12	Critz	Y	Y	N	N	Y	Y	N	Y	N	N	Y
13	Schwartz	Y	Y	N	N	Y	N	N	Y	+	N	Y
14	Doyle	Y	N	N	N	Y	?	N	N	N	N	Y
15	*Dent*	Y	Y	Y	Y	N	Y	Y	Y	Y	Y	Y
16	*Pitts*	Y	Y	Y	Y	N	Y	Y	Y	Y	Y	Y
17	Holden	Y	N	N	?	Y	N	N	?	N	N	Y
18	*Murphy*	Y	Y	Y	N	N	Y	Y	Y	Y	Y	Y
19	*Platts*	Y	Y	N	Y	N	Y	Y	Y	Y	N	Y
RHODE ISLAND												
1	Cicilline	Y	Y	N	N	Y	?	N	N	N	N	Y
2	Langevin	Y	Y	N	N	Y	N	N	Y	N	N	Y
SOUTH CAROLINA												
1	*Scott*	Y	Y	Y	Y	N	Y	Y	Y	Y	Y	N
2	*Wilson*	N	Y	Y	N	N	Y	Y	Y	Y	Y	N
3	*Duncan*	N	Y	Y	N	N	Y	Y	Y	Y	Y	N
4	*Gowdy*	N	Y	Y	N	N	Y	Y	Y	Y	Y	N
5	*Mulvaney*	N	Y	Y	N	N	Y	Y	Y	Y	Y	N
6	Clyburn	Y	Y	N	N	Y	?	N	Y	N	N	Y
SOUTH DAKOTA												
AL	*Noem*	N	Y	Y	Y	N	Y	Y	Y	Y	Y	Y
TENNESSEE												
1	*Roe*	N	Y	Y	Y	N	Y	Y	Y	Y	Y	N
2	*Duncan*	N	Y	N	Y	Y	Y	Y	Y	Y	N	N
3	*Fleischmann*	Y	Y	Y	Y	N	Y	Y	Y	Y	Y	N
4	*DesJarlais*	N	Y	Y	Y	N	Y	Y	Y	Y	Y	N
5	Cooper	N	Y	N	N	Y	N	N	Y	Y	N	N
6	*Black*	N	Y	Y	N	N	Y	Y	Y	+	Y	N
7	*Blackburn*	N	Y	Y	Y	N	Y	Y	Y	Y	Y	N
8	*Fincher*	Y	Y	Y	N	N	Y	Y	Y	Y	Y	N
9	Cohen	Y	N	N	N	Y	N	N	Y	Y	N	Y
TEXAS												
1	*Gohmert*	N	Y	Y	Y	N	Y	Y	Y	Y	N	N
2	*Poe*	N	Y	Y	Y	N	Y	Y	Y	Y	Y	N
3	*Johnson, S.*	Y	Y	Y	Y	N	Y	Y	Y	Y	?	N
4	*Hall*	N	Y	Y	Y	N	Y	Y	Y	Y	Y	N
5	*Hensarling*	Y	Y	Y	Y	N	Y	Y	Y	Y	Y	N
6	*Barton*	N	Y	N	Y	N	Y	Y	Y	Y	Y	N
7	*Culberson*	Y	Y	Y	Y	N	Y	Y	Y	?	?	N
8	*Brady*	Y	Y	Y	Y	N	Y	Y	Y	Y	Y	Y
9	Green, A.	Y	Y	N	N	Y	?	N	Y	N	N	Y
10	*McCaul*	Y	Y	Y	Y	N	Y	Y	Y	Y	Y	N
11	*Conaway*	Y	Y	Y	Y	N	Y	Y	Y	Y	Y	N
12	*Granger*	N	Y	Y	Y	N	Y	Y	Y	Y	Y	N
13	*Thornberry*	N	Y	Y	Y	N	Y	Y	Y	Y	Y	Y
14	*Paul*	?	Y	?	?	Y	Y	Y	N	Y	N	?
15	Hinojosa	Y	Y	N	?	Y	?	N	Y	N	N	Y
16	Reyes	N	Y	N	N	Y	?	N	Y	?	?	Y
17	*Flores*	Y	?	Y	Y	N	Y	Y	Y	Y	Y	N
18	Jackson Lee	Y	Y	N	N	Y	?	N	+	N	N	Y
19	*Neugebauer*	N	Y	Y	N	N	Y	Y	Y	Y	Y	N
20	Gonzalez	Y	Y	N	N	Y	?	N	Y	N	N	Y
21	*Smith*	Y	Y	Y	Y	N	Y	Y	Y	?	Y	Y
22	*Olson*	N	Y	Y	Y	N	Y	Y	Y	Y	Y	N
23	*Canseco*	Y	Y	Y	+	N	Y	Y	Y	Y	Y	N
24	*Marchant*	Y	?	Y	Y	N	Y	Y	Y	Y	Y	N
25	Doggett	Y	Y	N	N	Y	N	N	Y	N	N	Y
26	*Burgess*	N	Y	Y	Y	N	Y	Y	Y	Y	Y	N
27	*Farenthold*	N	Y	Y	Y	N	Y	Y	Y	Y	Y	N
28	Cuellar	Y	Y	N	N	N	N	N	Y	Y	N	Y
29	Green, G.	Y	N	N	N	Y	N	N	N	N	N	Y
30	Johnson, E.	N	N	N	N	Y	?	N	Y	N	N	Y
31	*Carter*	N	Y	Y	Y	N	Y	Y	Y	Y	Y	N
32	*Sessions*	N	Y	Y	Y	N	Y	Y	Y	Y	Y	Y
UTAH												
1	*Bishop*	N	Y	Y	Y	Y	Y	Y	Y	Y	P	N
2	Matheson	Y	Y	N	Y	N	Y	Y	Y	Y	N	N
3	*Chaffetz*	N	Y	Y	Y	N	Y	Y	Y	Y	Y	N
VERMONT												
AL	Welch	N	Y	N	N	Y	N	N	Y	N	N	Y
VIRGINIA												
1	*Wittman*	Y	Y	Y	Y	N	Y	Y	Y	Y	Y	N
2	*Rigell*	Y	Y	Y	Y	N	N	Y	Y	Y	Y	N
3	Scott	N	N	N	N	Y	?	N	Y	N	N	N
4	*Forbes*	N	Y	Y	Y	N	Y	Y	?	Y	Y	N
5	*Hurt*	Y	Y	Y	Y	N	Y	Y	Y	Y	Y	N
6	*Goodlatte*	N	Y	Y	Y	N	Y	Y	Y	Y	Y	N
7	*Cantor*	Y	Y	Y	Y	N	Y	Y	Y	Y	Y	N
8	Moran	N	Y	N	N	Y	N	N	Y	Y	N	N
9	*Griffith*	N	Y	Y	Y	Y	Y	Y	Y	Y	Y	N
10	*Wolf*	N	Y	Y	Y	N	Y	Y	?	Y	N	N
11	Connolly	N	Y	N	N	Y	N	N	Y	N	N	Y
WASHINGTON												
1	Inslee[9]	Y										
1	DelBene[9]								Y	N	N	Y
2	Larsen	Y	Y	N	N	Y	N	N	Y	N	N	Y
3	Herrera Beutler	Y	Y	Y	Y	N	Y	Y	Y	Y	N	Y
4	*Hastings*	Y	Y	Y	Y	N	Y	Y	Y	N	Y	Y
5	*McMorris Rodgers*	Y	Y	Y	Y	N	Y	Y	Y	Y	Y	Y
6	Dicks	Y	Y	?	N	Y	N	N	Y	N	N	Y
7	McDermott	N	N	N	N	Y	N	N	Y	N	N	N
8	*Reichert*	Y	Y	Y	Y	N	Y	Y	Y	Y	Y	Y
9	Smith	N	Y	N	N	Y	N	N	Y	–	N	N
WEST VIRGINIA												
1	*McKinley*	N	Y	N	Y	N	Y	Y	Y	Y	Y	N
2	*Capito*	Y	Y	Y	Y	N	Y	Y	Y	Y	Y	N
3	Rahall	Y	Y	N	N	Y	Y	N	N	N	N	Y
WISCONSIN												
1	*Ryan*	N	Y	Y	Y	N	Y	Y	Y	Y	Y	Y
2	Baldwin	Y	Y	N	N	Y	N	N	Y	?	N	Y
3	Kind	N	Y	N	N	Y	Y	N	Y	Y	N	Y
4	Moore	Y	Y	N	N	Y	?	N	Y	N	N	Y
5	*Sensenbrenner*	N	Y	Y	Y	Y	Y	Y	Y	Y	Y	N
6	*Petri*	N	Y	Y	Y	Y	Y	Y	Y	Y	Y	N
7	*Duffy*	Y	Y	Y	Y	N	Y	Y	Y	Y	Y	N
8	*Ribble*	Y	Y	Y	Y	Y	Y	Y	Y	Y	Y	Y
WYOMING												
AL	*Lummis*	N	Y	Y	Y	N	Y	Y	Y	Y	Y	N

[9]Suzan DelBene, D-Wash., was sworn in November 6, 2012, to fill the vacancy created by the March 20 resignation of fellow Democrat Jay Inslee. The first key vote for which DelBene was eligible was vote 8; the only key vote for which Inslee was eligible was vote 1.

Congress and Its Members

Senate Membership in the 111th Congress 825

House Membership in the 111th Congress 826

Membership Changes, 111th and 112th Congresses 829

Senate Membership in the 112th Congress 831

House Membership in the 112th Congress 832

Members of Congress, 2009–2013 835

Congressional Leadership and Committees, 111th and 112th Congresses 843

Postelection Sessions 857

Senate Cloture Votes, 1917–2012 860

Attempted and Successful Cloture Votes, 1919–2013 871

House Discharge Petitions since 1931 872

Congressional Reapportionment, 1789–2010 873

Senate Membership in the 111th Congress

Membership at the beginning of Congress in January 2009: Democrats 57; Republicans 41; Independents 2. Changes during the 2009–2011 period are noted.

Alabama
Richard C. Shelby (R)
Jeff Sessions (R)

Alaska
Mark Begich (D)
Lisa Murkowski (R)

Arizona
John McCain (R)
Jon Kyl (R)

Arkansas
Blanche Lincoln (D)
Mark Pryor (D)

California
Dianne Feinstein (D)
Barbara Boxer (D)

Colorado
Mark Udall (D)
Ken Salazar (D)[1]
Michael F. Bennett (D)

Connecticut
Christopher J. Dodd (D)
Joseph I. Lieberman (I)

Delaware
Joseph R. Biden Jr. (D)[2]
Ted Kaufman (D)
Christopher Coons (D)
Thomas R. Carper (D)

Florida
Bill Nelson (D)
Mel Martinez (R)[3]
George LeMieux (R)

Georgia
Saxby Chambliss (R)
Johnny Isakson (R)

Hawaii
Daniel K. Inouye (D)
Daniel K. Akaka (D)

Idaho
Jim Risch (R)
Michael D. Crapo (R)

Illinois
Richard J. Durbin (D)
Roland W. Burris (D)[4]
Mark Kirk (R)

Indiana
Richard G. Lugar (R)
Evan Bayh (D)

Iowa
Charles E. Grassley (R)
Tom Harkin (D)

Kansas
Sam Brownback (R)
Pat Roberts (R)

Kentucky
Mitch McConnell (R)
Jim Bunning (R)

Louisiana
Mary L. Landrieu (D)
David Vitter (R)

Maine
Olympia J. Snowe (R)
Susan Collins (R)

Maryland
Barbara A. Mikulski (D)
Benjamin L. Cardin (D)

Massachusetts
Edward M. Kennedy (D)[5]
Paul Kirk (D)
Scott P. Brown (R)
John F. Kerry (D)

Michigan
Carl Levin (D)
Deborah Stabenow (D)

Minnesota
Al Franken (D)
Amy Klobuchar (D)

Mississippi
Thad Cochran (R)
Roger Wicker (R)

Missouri
Christopher S. Bond (R)
Claire McCaskill (D)

Montana
Max Baucus (D)
Jon Tester (D)

Nebraska
Mike Johanns (R)
Ben Nelson (D)

Nevada
Harry Reid (D)
John Ensign (R)

New Hampshire
Judd Gregg (R)
Jeanne Shaheen (D)

New Jersey
Frank R. Lautenberg (D)
Robert Menendez (D)

New Mexico
Tom Udall (D)
Jeff Bingaman (D)

New York
Charles E. Schumer (D)
Hillary Rodham Clinton (D)[6]
Kirsten E. Gillibrand (D)

North Carolina
Kay Hagan (D)
Robert M. Burr (R)

North Dakota
Kent Conrad (D)
Byron L. Dorgan (D)

Ohio
George V. Voinovich (R)
Sherrod Brown (D)

Oklahoma
James M. Inhofe (R)
Tom Coburn (R)

Oregon
Ron Wyden (D)
Jeff Merkley (D)

Pennsylvania
Arlen Specter (R)
Robert P. Casey Jr. (D)

Rhode Island
Jack Reed (D)
Sheldon Whitehouse (D)

South Carolina
Lindsey Graham (R)
Jim DeMint (R)

South Dakota
Tim Johnson (D)
John Thune (R)

Tennessee
Lamar Alexander (R)
Bob Corker (R)

Texas
Kay Bailey Hutchison (R)
John Cornyn (R)

Utah
Orrin G. Hatch (R)
Robert F. Bennett (R)

Vermont
Patrick J. Leahy (D)
Bernard Sanders (I)

Virginia
Mark Warner (D)
Jim Webb (D)

Washington
Patty Murray (D)
Maria Cantwell (D)

West Virginia
Robert C. Byrd (D)[7]
Carte Goodwin (D)
Joe Manchin III (D)
John D. Rockefeller IV (D)

Wisconsin
Herb Kohl (D)
Russell D. Feingold (D)

Wyoming
John Barrasso (R)
Michael B. Enzi (R)

1. Salazar resigned January 20, 2009, to become secretary of the Interior. Bennet was appointed to fill the vacancy and was sworn in January 22, 2009. Bennet was elected to a full term in November 2010.
2. Biden resigned January 15, 2009, following his election as vice president. Kaufman was appointed to fill the vacancy, and was sworn in January 16, 2009. He served until the general elections in November 2010 but did not seek election to complete Biden's term, which ran through 2014. Kaufman was succeeded by Coons, who was sworn in November 15, 2010, after winning the seat in the 2010 elections.
3. Martinez resigned September 9, 2009. LeMieux was appointed to fill the seat. He was sworn in September 19, 2009.
4. Burris was appointed to fill a vacancy created when Barack Obama resigned November 16, 2008, following his election as president of the United States. Burris was sworn in January 15, 2009, and served until November 29, 2010. In November Kirk won a special election to fill the remainder of the term in the 111th Congress and the regular election for a six-year term starting in 2011.
5. Kennedy died August 25, 2009. Kirk was appointed to fill the vacancy and was sworn in September 25, 2009. Brown won a special election on January 19, 2010, to fill the remainder of Kennedy's term for the 111th Congress and all of the 112th Congress. He was sworn in February 4, 2010.
6. Clinton resigned January 21, 2009, to become secretary of state. House member Gillibrand was appointed to fill the vacancy and was sworn in January 27, 2009. In November 2010 she won a full six-year term.
7. Byrd died June 28, 2010. Goodwin was appointed to fill the vacancy and was sworn in on July 20, 2010. Manchin won a special election in November 2010 to fill the remaining two years of Byrd's term. He was sworn in November 15, 2010.

House Membership in the 111th Congress

Membership at the beginning of the Congress in January 2009: D 236; R 199. Changes during the 2009–2011 period are noted.

Alabama

1. Jo Bonner (R)
2. Bobby N. Bright (D)
3. Mike D. Rogers (R)
4. Robert B. Aderholt (R)
5. Parker Griffith (R)[1]
6. Spencer Bachus (R)
7. Artur Davis (D)

Alaska

AL Don Young (R)

Arizona

1. Ann Kirkpatrick (D)
2. Trent Franks (R)
3. John Shadegg (R)
4. Ed Pastor (D)
5. Harry E. Mitchell (D)
6. Jeff Flake (R)
7. Raúl M. Grijalva (D)
8. Gabrielle Giffords (D)

Arkansas

1. Marion Berry (D)
2. Vic Snyder (D)
3. John Boozman (R)
4. Mike Ross (D)

California

1. Mike Thompson (D)
2. Wally Herger (R)
3. Dan Lungren (R)
4. Tom McClintock (R)
5. Doris Matsui (D)
6. Lynn Woolsey (D)
7. George Miller (D)
8. Nancy Pelosi (D)
9. Barbara Lee (D)
10. Ellen O. Tauscher (D)
    (resigned June 26, 2009)
    John Garamendi (D)
    (sworn in Nov. 3, 2009)
11. Jerry McNerney (D)
12. Jackie Speier (D)
13. Pete Stark (D)
14. Anna G. Eshoo (D)
15. Michael M. Honda (D)
16. Zoe Lofgren (D)
17. Sam Farr (D)
18. Dennis Cardoza (D)
19. George Radanovich (R)
20. Jim Costa (D)
21. Devin Nunes (R)
22. Kevin McCarthy
23. Lois Capps (D)
24. Elton Gallegly (R)
25. Howard P. "Buck" McKeon (R)
26. David Dreier (R)
27. Brad Sherman (D)
28. Howard L. Berman (D)
29. Adam B. Schiff (D)
30. Henry A. Waxman (D)
31. Xavier Becerra (D)
32. Hilda L. Solis (D)
    (resigned Feb. 24, 2009)
    Judy Chu (D)
    (sworn in July 14, 2009)
33. Diane Watson (D)
34. Lucille Roybal-Allard
35. Maxine Waters (D)
36. Jane Harman (D)
37. Laura Richardson (D)
38. Grace F. Napolitano (D)
39. Linda T. Sánchez (D)
40. Ed Royce (R)
41. Jerry Lewis (R)
42. Gary G. Miller (R)
43. Joe Baca (D)
44. Ken Calvert (R)
45. Mary Bono Mack (R)
46. Dana Rohrabacher (R)
47. Loretta Sanchez (D)
48. John Campbell (R)
49. Darrell Issa (R)
50. Brian P. Bilbray (R)
51. Bob Filner (D)
52. Duncan Hunter (R)
53. Susan A. Davis (D)

Colorado

1. Diana DeGette (D)
2. Jared Polis (D)
3. John Salazar (D)
4. Betsy Markey (D)
5. Doug Lamborn (R)
6. Mike Coffman (R)
7. Ed Perlmutter (D)

Connecticut

1. John B. Larson (D)
2. Joe Courtney (D)
3. Rosa DeLauro (D)
4. Jim Himes (D)
5. Christopher S. Murphy (D)

Delaware

AL Michael N. Castle (R)

Florida

1. Jeff Miller (R)
2. Allen Boyd (D)
3. Corrine Brown (D)
4. Ander Crenshaw (R)
5. Ginny Brown-Waite (R)
6. Cliff Stearns (R)
7. John L. Mica (R)
8. Alan Grayson (D)
9. Gus Bilirakis (R)
10. C. W. Bill Young (R)
11. Kathy Castor (D)
12. Adam H. Putnam (R)
13. Vern Buchanan (R)
14. Connie Mack (R)
15. Bill Posey (R)
16. Tom Rooney (R)
17. Kendrick B. Meek (D)
18. Ileana Ros-Lehtinen (R)
19. Robert Wexler (D)
    (resigned Jan. 4, 2010)
    Ted Deutch (D)
    (sworn in April 13, 2010)
20. Debbie Wasserman Schultz (D)
21. Lincoln Diaz-Balart (R)
22. Ron Klein (D)
23. Alcee L. Hastings (D)
24. Suzanne Kosmas (D)
25. Mario Diaz-Balart (R)

Georgia

1. Jack Kingston (R)
2. Sanford D. Bishop Jr. (D)
3. Lynn Westmoreland (R)
4. Hank Johnson (D)
5. John Lewis (D)
6. Tom Price (R)
7. John Linder (R)
8. Jim Marshall (D)
9. Nathan Deal (R)
    (resigned March 21, 2010)
    Tom Graves (R)
    (sworn in June 8, 2010)
10. Paul Broun (R)
11. Phil Gingrey (R)
12. John Barrow (D)
13. David Scott (D)

Hawaii

1. Neil Abercrombie (D)
    (resigned Feb. 28, 2010)
    Charles K. Djou (R)
    (sworn in May 22, 2010)
2. Mazie K. Hirono (D)

Idaho

1. Walt Minnick (D)
2. Mike Simpson (R)

Illinois

1. Bobby L. Rush (D)
2. Jesse L. Jackson Jr. (D)
3. Daniel Lipinski (D)
4. Luis V. Gutierrez (D)
5. Mike Quigley (D)
    (sworn in April 7, 2009)
6. Peter Roskam (R)
7. Danny K. Davis (D)
8. Melissa Bean (D)
9. Jan Schakowsky (D)
10. Mark Steven Kirk (R)
11. Debbie Halvorson (D)
12. Jerry F. Costello (D)
13. Judy Biggert (R)
14. Bill Foster (D)
15. Timothy V. Johnson (R)
16. Donald Manzullo (R)
17. Phil Hare (D)
18. Aaron Schock (R)
19. John Shimkus (R)

Indiana

1. Peter J. Visclosky (D)
2. Joe Donnelly (D)
3. Mark Souder (R)
    (resigned May 21, 2010)
4. Marlin Stutzman (R)
    (sworn in Nov. 2, 2010)
5. Steve Buyer (R)
6. Dan Burton (R)
7. Mike Pence (R)
8. André Carson (D)
9. Brad Ellsworth (D)
10. Baron P. Hill (D)

Iowa

1. Bruce Braley (D)
2. Dave Loebsack (D)
3. Leonard L. Boswell (D)
4. Tom Latham (R)
5. Steve King (R)

Kansas

1. Jerry Moran (R)
2. Lynn Jenkins (R)
3. Dennis Moore (D)
4. Todd Tiahrt (R)

Kentucky

1. Ed Whitfield (R)
2. Brett Guthrie (R)
3. John Yarmuth (D)
4. Geoff Davis (R)
5. Harold Rogers (R)
6. Ben Chandler (D)

Louisiana

1. Steve Scalise (R)
2. Anh "Joseph" Cao (R)
3. Charlie Melancon (D)
4. John Fleming (R)
5. Rodney Alexander (R)
6. Bill Cassidy (R)
7. Charles Boustany Jr. (R)

Maine

1. Chellie Pingree (D)
2. Michael H. Michaud (D)

Maryland

1. Frank Kratovil Jr. (D)
2. C. A. Dutch Ruppersberger (D)
3. John Sarbanes (D)
4. Donna Edwards (D)
5. Steny H. Hoyer (D)
6. Roscoe G. Bartlett (R)
7. Elijah E. Cummings (D)
8. Chris Van Hollen (D)

Massachusetts
1. John W. Olver (D)
2. Richard E. Neal (D)
3. Jim McGovern (D)
4. Barney Frank (D)
5. Niki Tsongas (D)
6. John F. Tierney (D)
7. Edward J. Markey (D)
8. Michael E. Capuano (D)
9. Stephen F. Lynch (D)
10. Bill Delahunt (D)

Michigan
1. Bart Stupak (D)
2. Peter Hoekstra (R)
3. Vernon J. Ehlers (R)
4. Dave Camp (R)
5. Dale E. Kildee (D)
6. Fred Upton (R)
7. Mark Schauer (D)
8. Mike Rogers (R)
9. Gary Peters (D)
10. Candice S. Miller (R)
11. Thaddeus McCotter (R)
12. Sander M. Levin (D)
13. Carolyn Cheeks Kilpatrick (D)
14. John Conyers Jr. (D)
15. John D. Dingell (D)

Minnesota
1. Tim Walz (D)
2. John Kline (R)
3. Erik Paulsen (R)
4. Betty McCollum (D)
5. Keith Ellison (D)
6. Michele Bachmann (R)
7. Collin C. Peterson (D)
8. James L. Oberstar (D)

Mississippi
1. Travis W. Childers (D)
2. Bennie Thompson (D)
3. Gregg Harper (R)
4. Gene Taylor (D)

Missouri
1. William Lacy Clay (D)
2. Todd Akin (R)
3. Russ Carnahan (D)
4. Ike Skelton (D)
5. Emanuel Cleaver II (D)
6. Sam Graves (R)
7. Roy Blunt (R)
8. Jo Ann Emerson (R)
9. Blaine Luetkemeyer (R)

Montana
AL Denny Rehberg (R)

Nebraska
1. Jeff Fortenberry (R)
2. Lee Terry (R)
3. Adrian Smith (R)

Nevada
1. Shelley Berkley (D)
2. Dean Heller (R)
3. Dina Titus (D)

New Hampshire
1. Carol Shea-Porter (D)
2. Paul W. Hodes (D)

New Jersey
1. Robert E. Andrews (D)
2. Frank A. LoBiondo (R)
3. John Adler (D)
4. Christopher H. Smith (R)
5. Scott Garrett (R)
6. Frank Pallone Jr. (D)
7. Leonard Lance (R)
8. Bill Pascrell Jr. (D)
9. Steven R. Rothman (D)
10. Donald M. Payne (D)
11. Rodney Frelinghuysen (R)
12. Rush D. Holt (D)
13. Albio Sires (D)

New Mexico
1. Martin Heinrich (D)
2. Harry Teague (D)
3. Ben Ray Luján (D)

New York
1. Timothy H. Bishop (D)
2. Steve Israel (D)
3. Peter T. King (R)
4. Carolyn McCarthy (D)
5. Gary L. Ackerman (D)
6. Gregory W. Meeks (D)
7. Joseph Crowley (D)
8. Jerrold Nadler (D)
9. Anthony Weiner (D)
10. Edolphus Towns (D)
11. Yvette D. Clarke (D)
12. Nydia M. Velázquez (D)
13. Michael E. McMahon (D)
14. Carolyn B. Maloney (D)
15. Charles B. Rangel (D)
16. José E. Serrano (D)
17. Eliot L. Engel (D)
18. Nita M. Lowey (D)
19. John Hall (D)
20. Kirsten Gillibrand (D) *(resigned Jan. 26, 2009)*
    Scott Murphy (D) *(sworn in March 31, 2009)*
21. Paul Tonko (D)
22. Maurice D. Hinchey (D)
23. John M. McHugh (R) *(resigned Sep. 21, 2009)*
    William L. Owens (D) *(sworn in Nov. 3, 2009)*
24. Michael Arcuri (D)
25. Dan Maffei (D)
26. Christopher Lee (R)
27. Brian Higgins (D)
28. Louise M. Slaughter (D)
29. Eric J. J. Massa (D) *(resigned March 8, 2010)*
    Thomas W. Reed II (R) *(sworn in Nov. 2, 2010)*

North Carolina
1. G. K. Butterfield (D)
2. Bob Etheridge (D)
3. Walter B. Jones (R)
4. David E. Price (D)
5. Virginia Foxx (R)
6. Howard Coble (R)
7. Mike McIntyre (D)
8. Larry Kissell (D)
9. Sue Myrick (R)
10. Patrick T. McHenry (R)
11. Heath Shuler (D)
12. Melvin Watt (D)
13. Brad Miller (D)

North Dakota
AL Earl Pomeroy (D)

Ohio
1. Steve Driehaus (D)
2. Jean Schmidt (R)
3. Michael R. Turner (R)
4. Jim Jordan (R)
5. Bob Latta (R)
6. Charlie Wilson (D)
7. Steve Austria (R)
8. John A. Boehner (R)
9. Marcy Kaptur (D)
10. Dennis J. Kucinich (D)
11. Marcia L. Fudge (D)
12. Pat Tiberi (R)
13. Betty Sutton (D)
14. Steven C. LaTourette (R)
15. Mary Jo Kilroy (D)
16. John Boccieri (D)
17. Tim Ryan (D)
18. Zack Space (D)

Oklahoma
1. John Sullivan (R)
2. Dan Boren (D)
3. Frank D. Lucas (R)
4. Tom Cole (R)
5. Mary Fallin (R)

Oregon
1. David Wu (D)
2. Greg Walden (R)
3. Earl Blumenauer (D)
4. Peter A. DeFazio (D)
5. Kurt Schrader (D)

Pennsylvania
1. Robert A. Brady (D)
2. Chaka Fattah (D)
3. Kathy Dahlkemper (D)
4. Jason Altmire (D)
5. Glenn Thompson (R)
6. Jim Gerlach (R)
7. Joe Sestak (D)
8. Patrick J. Murphy (D)
9. Bill Shuster (R)
10. Christopher Carney (D)
11. Paul E. Kanjorski (D)
12. John P. Murtha Jr. (D) *(died Feb. 8, 2010)*
    Mark S. Critz (D) *(sworn in May 18, 2010)*
13. Allyson Y. Schwartz (D)
14. Mike Doyle (D)
15. Charlie Dent (R)
16. Joe Pitts (R)
17. Tim Holden (D)
18. Tim Murphy (R)
19. Todd R. Platts (R)

Rhode Island
1. Patrick J. Kennedy (D)
2. Jim Langevin (D)

South Carolina
1. Henry E. Brown Jr. (R)
2. Joe Wilson (R)
3. J. Gresham Barrett (R)
4. Bob Inglis (R)
5. John M. Spratt Jr. (D)
6. James E. Clyburn (D)

South Dakota
AL Stephanie Herseth Sandlin (D)

Tennessee
1. Phil Roe (R)
2. John J. "Jimmy" Duncan Jr. (R)
3. Zach Wamp (R)
4. Lincoln Davis (D)
5. Jim Cooper (D)
6. Bart Gordon (D)
7. Marsha Blackburn (R)
8. John Tanner (D)
9. Steve Cohen (D)

Texas
1. Louie Gohmert (R)
2. Ted Poe (R)
3. Sam Johnson (R)
4. Ralph M. Hall (R)
5. Jeb Hensarling (R)
6. Joe L. Barton (R)
7. John Culberson (R)
8. Kevin Brady (R)
9. Al Green (D)
10. Michael McCaul (R)
11. K. Michael Conaway (R)
12. Kay Granger (R)
13. William M. "Mac" Thornberry (R)
14. Ron Paul (R)
15. Rubén Hinojosa (D)
16. Silvestre Reyes (D)
17. Chet Edwards (D)
18. Sheila Jackson Lee (D)
19. Randy Neugebauer (R)
20. Charlie Gonzalez (D)
21. Lamar Smith (R)
22. Pete Olson (R)
23. Ciro D. Rodriguez (D)
24. Kenny Marchant (R)
25. Lloyd Doggett (D)
26. Michael C. Burgess (R)
27. Solomon P. Ortiz (D)
28. Henry Cuellar (D)
29. Gene Green (D)
30. Eddie Bernice Johnson (D)
31. John Carter (R)
32. Pete Sessions (R)

Utah
1. Rob Bishop (R)
2. Jim Matheson (D)
3. Jason Chaffetz (R)

Vermont
AL Peter Welch (D)

Virginia
1. Rob Wittman (R)
2. Glenn Nye (D)
3. Robert C. Scott (D)
4. J. Randy Forbes (R)
5. Tom Perriello (D)
6. Robert W. Goodlatte (R)
7. Eric Cantor (R)
8. James P. Moran (D)
9. Rick Boucher (D)
10. Frank R. Wolf (R)
11. Gerald E. Connolly (D)

Washington
1. Jay Inslee (D)
2. Rick Larsen (D)
3. Brian Baird (D)
4. Doc Hastings (R)
5. Cathy McMorris Rodgers (R)
6. Norm Dicks (D)
7. Jim McDermott (D)
8. Dave Reichert (R)
9. Adam Smith (D)

West Virginia
1. Alan B. Mollohan (D)
2. Shelley Moore Capito (R)
3. Nick J. Rahall II (D)

Wisconsin
1. Paul D. Ryan (R)
2. Tammy Baldwin (D)
3. Ron Kind (D)
4. Gwen Moore (D)
5. F. James Sensenbrenner Jr. (R)
6. Tom Petri (R)
7. David R. Obey (D)
8. Steve Kagen (D)

Wyoming
AL Cynthia M. Lummis (R)

NOTE: Changes that occurred during 2009 and 2010 are noted following the names of individuals who did not serve their full terms. Members of the 111th Congress also included delegates Eni F. H. Faleomavaega, D-American Samoa; Eleanor Holmes Norton, D-District of Columbia; Madeleine Z. Bordallo, D-Guam; Gregorio Kilili Camacho Sablan, D-Northern Mariana Islands; Donna M. C. Christian, D-Virgin Islands; and resident commissioner Pedro Pierluisi, D-Puerto Rico. AL—At Large.

1. Griffith switched from Democrat to Republican on December 22, 2009.

Membership Changes, 111th and 112th Congresses

111th Congress

Member/party	*Died*	*Resigned*	*Switched party*	*Successor*	*Elected*	*Sworn in*
Senate						
Ken Salazar, D-Colo.[1]		1/20/2009		Michael F. Bennett, D		1/22/2009
Joseph R. Biden Jr., D-Del.[2]		1/15/2009		Ted Kaufmann, D		1/16/2009
Ted Kaufman, D-Del.[3]				Christopher Coons, D	11/2/2010	11/15/2010
Hillary Rodham Clinton, D-N.Y.[4]		1/21/2009		Kirsten E. Gillibrand, D		1/27/2009
Edward M. Kennedy, D-Mass.	8/25/2009			Paul Kirk, D		9/25/2009
Paul Kirk, D-Mass.[5]		2/4/2010		Scott P. Brown, R[6]	1/19/2010	2/4/2010
Arlen Specter, D-Pa.			4/30/2009			
Mel Martinez, R-Fla.[7]		9/9/2009		George LeMieux, R		9/10/2009
Roland W. Burris, D-Ill.[8]		11/29/2010		Mark Kirk, R[8]	11/2/2010	11/29/2010
Robert C. Byrd, D-W.Va.[9]	6/28/2010			Carte Goodwin, D[9]		7/20/2010
Joe Manchin, III D-W.Va.[9]					11/2/2010	11/15/2010
House						
Rahm Emanuel, D-Ill.[10]		1/2/2009		Mike Quigley, D	4/7/2009	4/7/2009
Kirsten E. Gillibrand, D-N.Y.[11]		1/26/2009		Scott Murphy, D	3/31/2009	3/31/2009
Hilda L. Solis, D-Calif.[12]		2/24/2009		Judy Chu, D	7/14/2009	7/14/2009
Ellen O. Tauscher, D-Calif.[13]		6/26/2009		John Garamendi, D	11/3/2009	11/3/2009
John M. McHugh, R-N.Y.[14]		9/21/2009		Bill Owens, D	11/3/2009	11/3/2009
Parker Griffith, R-Ala.			12/22/2009			
Robert Wexler, D-Fla.[15]		1/3/2010		Ted Deutch, D	4/13/2010	4/13/2010
Nathan Deal, R-Ga.[16]		3/21/2010		Tom Graves, R	6/8/2010	6/8/2010
Neil Abercrombie, D-Hawaii[17]		2/28/2010		Charles Djou, R	5/22/2010	5/22/2010
Mark Souder, R-Ind.[18]		5/21/2010		Marlin A. Stutzman, R	11/2/2010	11/2/2010
Eric J. J. Massa, D-N.Y.[19]		3/8/2010		Thomas W. Reed II, R	11/2/2010	11/2/2010
John P. Murtha, D-Pa.	2/8/2010			Mark S. Critz, D	5/18/2010	5/18/2010

112th Congress

Member/party	*Died*	*Resigned*	*Switched party*	*Successor*	*Elected*	*Sworn in*
Senate						
John Ensign, R-Nev.[20]		5/3/2011		Dean Heller, R		5/9/2011
Daniel K. Inouye, D-Hawaii	12/17/2012			Brian Schatz, D		12/27/2012
House						
Jane Harman, D-Calif.[21]		2/28/2011		Janice Hahn, D	7/12/2011	7/12/2011
Dean Heller, R-Nev.[22]		5/9/2011		Mark Amodei, R	9/13/2011	9/13/2011
Anthony Weiner, D-N.Y.[23]		7/21/2011		Robert L. Turner, R	9/13/2011	9/13/2011
Christopher John Lee, R-N.Y.[24]		2/9/2011		Kathy Hochul, D	5/24/2011	5/24/2011
David Wu, R-Ore.[25]		8/3/2011		Suzanne Bonamici, D	1/31/2012	1/31/2012
Gabrielle Giffords, D-Ariz.[26]		1/25/2012		Ron Barber, D	6/12/2012	6/12/2012
Donald M. Payne, D-N.J.	3/6/2012			Donald M. Payne Jr., D	11/6/2012	11/6/2012
Jay Inslee, D-Wash.[27]		3/20/2012		Suzan Del Bene, D	11/6/2012	11/6/2012
Geoff Davis, R-Ky.[28]		7/31/2012		Thomas Massie, R	11/6/2012	11/6/2012
Thaddeus McCotter, R-Mich.[29]		7/6/2012		David Curson, D	11/6/2012	11/6/2012
Dennis Cardoza, D-Calif.[30]		8/15/2012				
Jesse Jackson Jr., D-Ill.		11/21/2012[31]				
Bob Filner, D-Calif.[32]		12/3/2012				

1. Salazar resigned to become secretary of the Interior in President Barack Obama's cabinet.

2. Biden resigned following his election in 2008 as vice president.

3. Kaufman was appointed to fill the seat vacated by Biden. He served until the general election in 2010 but did not seek reelection for the remainder of Biden's term, which ran through 2014.

4. Clinton resigned to become secretary of state in President Obama's cabinet.

5. Kirk was appointed to fill the vacancy created by the death of Kennedy. He served until a special election was held on January 19, 2010, to fill the vacancy. Kirk was not a candidate in that election.

6. Brown was elected in a special election held January 19, 2010, to fill the vacancy created by the death of Kennedy in 2009. His predecessor, Kirk, was not a candidate in the special election.

7. News organizations reported that Martinez resigned to become a Washington lobbyist and to join a private firm.

8. Burris was appointed by the then-Illinois governor to fill a vacancy created when Barack Obama (who had two years left on his six-year term) resigned November 16, 2008, following his election as president. However, because of controversy surrounding the appointment, Burris did not take his seat until January 15, 2009, eleven days after the new Congress convened. Burris served until the November 2010 elections. Kirk won a special election to fill the remainder of the term in the 111th Congress and the regular election for a six-year term starting in 2011.
9. Goodwin was appointed to fill the vacancy created by the death of Byrd but was not a candidate in November 2010 to fill the unexpired portion of Byrd's term. Manchin won a special election, held with the 2010 regular election, to fill the remainder of the term.
10. Emanuel resigned to become White House chief of staff for President Obama.
11. Gillibrand resigned her House seat to accept appointment to the Senate to fill the vacancy created by the resignation of Clinton, who resigned to become secretary of state.
12. Solis resigned to become secretary of labor in President Obama's cabinet.
13. Tauscher resigned to become undersecretary of state for arms control and international security.
14. McHugh resigned to become secretary of the army.
15. Wexler resigned to become president of the Center for Middle East Peace.
16. Deal resigned to focus on his campaign for governor of Georgia.
17. Abercrombie resigned to focus on his campaign for governor of Hawaii.
18. Souder resigned after admitting to an affair with a part-time staff member.
19. Massa resigned in connection with an ethics investigation into charges that he sexually harassed male staffers.
20. Ensign resigned in the midst of a Senate Ethics Committee investigation into his affair with a female staff member and the propriety of monetary payments to the staffer's family.
21. Harman resigned to become president of the Woodrow Wilson International Center for Politics, in Washington, D.C.
22. Heller resigned after being appointed to fill the remainder of the term of Ensign, who had resigned his seat.
23. Weiner resigned after admitting to numerous "sexting" tweets.
24. Lee resigned after a "beefcake" photo of the married representative appeared on the Internet.
25. Wu resigned following accusations of "aggressive and unwanted sexual behavior" with a female teenager.
26. Giffords resigned to focus on regaining her health after being severely wounded by gunshots while meeting with constituents in her district.
27. Inslee resigned to focus on his campaign for governor of Washington.
28. Davis resigned, citing a "family health" issue as the reason.
29. McCotter resigned after disclosure that many signatures on his petition to qualify for a primary election were invalid.
30. Cardoza resigned, citing "family concerns" as the reason. His seat was left vacant for the remainder of the congressional term.
31. Jackson resigned citing health problems including bipolar disorder and depression. In October federal prosecutors and FBI agents announced an investigation of Jackson involving alleged financial improprieties including misuse of congressional funds. Jackson acknowledged he was under investigation by the House Ethics Committee. A special election to fill the vacancy was schedule for April 9, 2013. Kelly won that election.
32. Filner was not a candidate for reelection to the House in 2012. Rather he ran for mayor of San Diego, a contest he won in November.

Senate Membership in the 112th Congress

Membership at the beginning of Congress in 2011: Democrats 51; Republicans 47; Independents 2. Changes that occurred during the two year period are noted.

Alabama
Richard C. Shelby (R)
Jeff Sessions (R)

Alaska
Mark Begich (D)
Lisa Murkowski (R)

Arizona
John McCain (R)
Jon Kyl (R)

Arkansas
John Boozman (R)
Mark Pryor (D)

California
Dianne Feinstein (D)
Barbara Boxer (D)

Colorado
Mark Udall (D)
Michael F. Bennet (D)

Connecticut
Richard Blumenthal (D)
Joseph I. Lieberman (I)

Delaware
Christopher A. Coons (D)
Thomas R. Carper (D)

Florida
Bill Nelson (D)
Marco Rubio (R)

Georgia
Saxby Chambliss (R)
Johnny Isakson (R)

Hawaii
Daniel K. Inouye (D)[1]
Brian Schatz (D)
Daniel K. Akaka (D)

Idaho
Jim Risch (R)
Michael D. Crapo (R)

Illinois
Richard J. Durbin (D)
Mark S. Kirk (R)

Indiana
Richard G. Lugar (R)
Dan Coats (R)

Iowa
Charles E. Grassley (R)
Tom Harkin (D)

Kansas
Jerry Moran (R)
Pat Roberts (R)

Kentucky
Mitch McConnell (R)
Rand Paul (R)

Louisiana
Mary L. Landrieu (D)
David Vitter (R)

Maine
Olympia J. Snowe (R)
Susan Collins (R)

Maryland
Barbara A. Mikulski (D)
Benjamin L. Cardin (D)

Massachusetts
Scott P. Brown (R)
John F. Kerry (D)

Michigan
Carl Levin (D)
Deborah Stabenow (D)

Minnesota
Al Franken (D)
Amy Klobuchar (D)

Mississippi
Thad Cochran (R)
Roger Wicker (R)

Missouri
Roy Blunt (R)
Claire McCaskill (D)

Montana
Max Baucus (D)
Jon Tester (D)

Nebraska
Mike Johanns (R)
Ben Nelson (D)

Nevada
Harry Reid (D)
John Ensign (R)[2]
Dean Heller (R)

New Hampshire
Jeanne Shaheen (D)
Kelly Ayotte (R)

New Jersey
Frank R. Lautenberg (D)
Robert Menendez (D)

New Mexico
Tom Udall (D)
Jeff Bingaman (D)

New York
Charles E. Schumer (D)
Kirsten E. Gillibrand (D)

North Carolina
Kay Hagan (D)
Robert M. Burr (R)

North Dakota
Kent Conrad (D)
John Hoeven (R)

Ohio
Rob Portman (R)
Sherrod Brown (D)

Oklahoma
James M. Inhofe (R)
Tom Coburn (R)

Oregon
Ron Wyden (D)
Jeff Merkley (D)

Pennsylvania
Patrick J. Toomey (R)
Robert P. Casey Jr. (D)

Rhode Island
Jack Reed (D)
Sheldon Whitehouse (D)

South Carolina
Lindsey Graham (R)
Jim DeMint (R)

South Dakota
Tim Johnson (D)
John Thune (R)

Tennessee
Lamar Alexander (R)
Bob Corker (R)

Texas
Kay Bailey Hutchison (R)
John Cornyn (R)

Utah
Orrin G. Hatch (R)
Mike Lee (R)

Vermont
Patrick J. Leahy (D)
Bernard Sanders (I)

Virginia
Mark Warner (D)
Jim Webb (D)

Washington
Patty Murray (D)
Maria Cantwell (D)

West Virginia
Joe Manchin (D)
John D. Rockefeller IV (D)

Wisconsin
Herb Kohl (D)
Ron Johnson (R)

Wyoming
John Barrasso (R)
Michael B. Enzi (R)

1. Inouye died December 17, 2012. Schatz was appointed by Hawaii's governor to succeed him.

2. Ensign resigned on May 3, 2011, while under investigation by the Senate Ethics Committee involving charges he improperly covered up an extramarital affair with a former staff member. Heller, a House member from Nevada, was appointed to fill the vacancy and was sworn in May 9, 2011.

House Membership in the 112th Congress

Membership at the beginning of Congress in January 2011: Republicans 242; Democrats 193. Changes during the 2011–2012 period are noted.

Alabama

1. Jo Bonner (R)
2. Martha Roby (R)
3. Mike D. Rogers (R)
4. Robert B. Aderholt (R)
5. Mo Brooks (R)
6. Spencer Bachus (R)
7. Terri A. Sewell (D)

Alaska

AL Don Young (R)

Arizona

1. Paul Gosar (R)
2. Trent Franks (R)
3. Ben Quayle (R)
4. Ed Pastor
5. David Schweikert (R)
6. Jeff Flake (R)
7. Raúl M. Grijalva (D)
8. Gabrielle Giffords (D) *(resigned Jan. 25, 2012)*
   Ron Barber (D) *(sworn in June 12, 2012)*

Arkansas

1. Rick Crawford (R)
2. Tim Griffin (R)
3. Steve Womack (R)
4. Mike Ross (D)

California

1. Mike Thompson (D)
2. Wally Herger (R)
3. Dan Lungren (R)
4. Tom McClintock (R)
5. Doris Matsui (D)
6. Lynn Woolsey (D)
7. George Miller (D)
8. Nancy Pelosi (D)
9. Barbara Lee (D)
10. John Garamendi (D)
11. Jerry McNerney (D)
12. Jackie Speier (D)
13. Pete Stark (D)
14. Anna G. Eshoo (D)
15. Michael M. Honda (D)
16. Zoe Lofgren (D)
17. Sam Farr (D)
18. Dennis Cardoza (D) *(resigned Aug. 15, 2012)*[1]
19. Jeff Denham (R)
20. Jim Costa (D)
21. Devin Nunes (R)
22. Kevin McCarthy (R)
23. Lois Capps (D)
24. Elton Gallegly (R)
25. Howard P. "Buck" McKeon (R)
26. David Dreier (R)
27. Brad Sherman (D)
28. Howard L. Berman (D)
29. Adam B. Schiff (D)
30. Henry A. Waxman (D)
31. Xavier Becerra (D)
32. Judy Chu (D)
33. Karen Bass (D)
34. Lucille Roybal-Allard (D)
35. Maxine Waters (D)
36. Jane Harman (D) *(resigned Feb. 28, 2011)*
   Janice Hahn (D) *(sworn in July 12, 2011)*
37. Laura Richardson (D)
38. Grace F. Napolitano (D)
39. Linda T. Sánchez (D)
40. Ed Royce (R)
41. Jerry Lewis (R)
42. Gary G. Miller (R)
43. Joe Baca (D)
44. Ken Calvert (R)
45. Mary Bono Mack (R)
46. Dana Rohrabacher (R)
47. Loretta Sanchez (D)
48. John Campbell (R)
49. Darrell Issa (R)
50. Brian P. Bilbray (R)
51. Bob Filner (D) *(resigned Dec. 3, 2012)*[1]
52. Duncan Hunter (R)
53. Susan A. Davis (D)

Colorado

1. Diana DeGette (D)
2. Jared Polis (D)
3. Scott Tipton (R)
4. Cory Gardner (R)
5. Doug Lamborn (R)
6. Mike Coffman (R)
7. Ed Perlmutter (D)

Connecticut

1. John B. Larson (D)
2. Joe Courtney (D)
3. Rosa DeLauro (D)
4. Jim Himes (D)
5. Christopher S. Murphy (D)

Delaware

AL John Carney (D)

Florida

1. Jeff Miller (R)
2. Steve Southerland (R)
3. Corrine Brown (D)
4. Ander Crenshaw (R)
5. Richard Nugent (R)
6. Cliff Stearns (R)
7. John L. Mica (R)
8. Daniel Webster (R)
9. Gus Bilirakis (R)
10. C. W. Bill Young (R)
11. Kathy Castor (D)
12. Dennis Ross (R)
13. Vern Buchanan (R)
14. Connie Mack (R)
15. Bill Posey (R)
16. Tom Rooney (R)
17. Frederica Wilson (D)
18. Ileana Ros-Lehtinen (R)
19. Ted Deutch (D)
20. Debbie Wasserman Schultz (D)
21. Mario Diaz-Balart (R)
22. Allen West (R)
23. Alcee L. Hastings (D)
24. Sandy Adams (R)
25. David Rivera (R)

Georgia

1. Jack Kingston (R)
2. Sanford D. Bishop Jr. (D)
3. Lynn Westmoreland (R)
4. Hank Johnson (D)
5. John Lewis (D)
6. Tom Price (R)
7. Rob Woodall (R)
8. Austin Scott (R)
9. Tom Graves (R)
10. Paul Broun (R)
11. Phil Gingrey (R)
12. John Barrow (D)
13. David Scott (D)

Hawaii

1. Colleen Hanabusa (D)
2. Mazie K. Hirono (D)

Idaho

1. Raúl R. Labrador (R)
2. Mike Simpson (R)

Illinois

1. Bobby L. Rush (D)
2. Jesse L. Jackson Jr. (D) *(resigned Nov. 21, 2012)*[1]
3. Daniel Lipinski (D)
4. Luis V. Gutierrez (D)
5. Mike Quigley (D)
6. Peter Roskam (R)
7. Danny K. Davis (D)
8. Joe Walsh (R)
9. Jan Schakowsky (D)
10. Robert Dold (R)
11. Adam Kinzinger (R)
12. Jerry F. Costello (D)
13. Judy Biggert (R)
14. Randy Hultgren (R)
15. Timothy V. Johnson (R)
16. Donald Manzullo (R)
17. Bobby Schilling (R)
18. Aaron Schock (R)
19. John Shimkus (R)

Indiana

1. Peter J. Visclosky (D)
2. Joe Donnelly (D)
3. Marlin Stutzman (R)
4. Todd Rokita (R)
5. Dan Burton (R)
6. Mike Pence (R)
7. André Carson (D)
8. Larry Bucshon (R)
9. Todd Young (R)

Iowa

1. Bruce Braley (D)
2. Dave Loebsack (D)
3. Leonard L. Boswell (D)
4. Tom Latham (R)
5. Steve King (R)

Kansas

1. Tim Huelskamp (R)
2. Lynn Jenkins (R)
3. Kevin Yoder (R)
4. Mike Pompeo (R)

Kentucky

1. Ed Whitfield (R)
2. Brett Guthrie (R)
3. John Yarmuth (D)
4. Geoff Davis (R) *(resigned July 31, 2012)*
   Thomas Massie (R) *(sworn in Nov. 6, 2012)*
5. Harold Rogers (R)
6. Ben Chandler (D)

Louisiana

1. Steve Scalise (R)
2. Cedric Richmond (D)
3. Jeff Landry (R)
4. John Fleming (R)
5. Rodney Alexander (R)
6. Bill Cassidy (R)
7. Charles Boustany Jr. (R)

Maine

1. Chellie Pingree (D)
2. Michael H. Michaud (D)

Maryland

1. Andy Harris (R)
2. C. A. Dutch Ruppersberger (D)
3. John Sarbanes (D)
4. Donna Edwards (D)
5. Steny H. Hoyer (D)
6. Roscoe G. Bartlett (R)

7. Elijah E. Cummings (D)
8. Chris Van Hollen (D)

Massachusetts
1. John W. Olver (D)
2. Richard E. Neal (D)
3. Jim McGovern (D)
4. Barney Frank (D)
5. Niki Tsongas (D)
6. John F. Tierney (D)
7. Edward J. Markey (D)
8. Michael E. Capuano (D)
9. Stephen F. Lynch (D)
10. William Keating (D)

Michigan
1. Dan Benishek (R)
2. Bill Huizenga (R)
3. Justin Amash (R)
4. Dave Camp (R)
5. Dale E. Kildee (D)
6. Fred Upton (R)
7. Tim Walberg (R)
8. Mike Rogers (R)
9. Gary Peters (D)
10. Candice S. Miller (R)
11. Thaddeus McCotter (R) *(resigned July 6, 2012)* David Curson (D) *(sworn in Nov. 6, 2012)*
12. Sander M. Levin (D)
13. Hansen Clarke (D)
14. John Conyers Jr. (D)
15. John D. Dingell (D)

Minnesota
1. Tim Walz (D)
2. John Kline (R)
3. Erik Paulsen (R)
4. Betty McCollum (D)
5. Keith Ellison (D)
6. Michele Bachmann (R)
7. Collin C. Peterson (D)
8. Chip Cravaack (R)

Mississippi
1. Alan Nunnelee (R)
2. Bennie Thompson (D)
3. Gregg Harper (R)
4. Steven Palazzzo (R)

Missouri
1. William Lacy Clay (D)
2. Todd Akin (R)
3. Russ Carnahan (D)
4. Vicky Hartzler (R)
5. Emanuel Cleaver II (D)
6. Sam Graves (R)
7. Billy Long (R)
8. Jo Ann Emerson (R)
9. Blaine Luetkemeyer (R)

Montana
AL Denny Rehberg (R)

Nebraska
1. Jeff Fortenberry (R)
2. Lee Terry (R)
3. Adrian Smith (R)

Nevada
1. Shelley Berkley (D)
2. Dean Heller (R) *(resigned May 9, 2011)* Mark Amodei (R) *(sworn in Sep. 12, 2011)*
3. Joe Heck (R)

New Hampshire
1. Frank Guinta (R)
2. Charles Bass (R)

New Jersey
1. Robert E. Andrews (D)
2. Frank A. LoBiondo (R)
3. Jon Runyan (R)
4. Christopher H. Smith (R)
5. Scott Garrett (R)
6. Frank Pallone Jr. (D)
7. Leonard Lance (R)
8. Bill Pascrell Jr. (D)
9. Steven R. Rothman (D)
10. Donald M. Payne (D) *(died March 6, 2012)* Donald M. Payne Jr. (D) *(sworn in Nov. 6, 2012)*
11. Rodney Frelinghuysen (R)
12. Rush D. Holt (D)
13. Albio Sires (D)

New Mexico
1. Martin Heinrich (D)
2. Steve Pearce (R)
3. Ben Ray Luján (D)

New York
1. Timothy H. Bishop (D)
2. Steve Israel (D)
3. Peter T. King (R)
4. Carolyn McCarthy (D)
5. Gary L. Ackerman (D)
6. Gregory W. Meeks (D)
7. Joseph Crowley (D)
8. Jerrold Nadler (D)
9. Anthony Weiner (D) *(resigned June 22, 2011)* Robert L. Turner (R) *(sworn in Sep. 13, 2011)*
10. Edolphus Towns (D)
11. Yvette D. Clarke (D)
12. Nydia M. Velázquez (D)
13. Michael Grimm (R)
14. Carolyn B. Maloney (D)
15. Charles B. Rangel (D)
16. José E. Serrano (D)
17. Eliot L. Engel (D)
18. Nita M. Lowey (D)
19. Nan Hayworth (R)
20. Chris Gibson (R)
21. Paul Tonko (D)
22. Maurice D. Hinchey (D)
23. Bill Owens (D)
24. Richard Hanna (D)
25. Ann Marie Buerkle (R)
26. Christopher Lee (R) *(resigned Feb. 9, 2011)* Kathy Hochul (D) *(sworn in May 24, 2011)*
27. Brian Higgins (D)
28. Louise M. Slaughter (D)
29. Tom Reed (R)

North Carolina
1. G. K. Butterfield (D)
2. Renee Ellmers (R)
3. Walter B. Jones (R)
4. David E. Price (D)
5. Virginia Foxx (R)
6. Howard Coble (R)
7. Mike Lungren (D)
8. Larry Kissell (D)
9. Sue Myrick (R)
10. Patrick T. McHenry (R)
11. Heath Shuler (D)
12. Melvin Watt (D)
13. Brad Miller (D)

North Dakota
AL Rick Berg (R)

Ohio
1. Steve Chabot (R)
2. Jean Schmidt (R)
3. Michael R. Turner (R)
4. Jim Jordan (R)
5. Bob Latta (R)
6. Bill Johnson (R)
7. Steve Austria (R)
8. John A. Boehner (R)
9. Marcy Kaptur (D)
10. Dennis J. Kucinich (D)
11. Marcia L. Fudge (D)
12. Pat Tiberi (R)
13. Betty Sutton (D)
14. Steven C. LaTourette (R)
15. Steve Stivers (R)
16. Jim Renacci (R)
17. Tim Ryan (D)
18. Bob Gibbs (R)

Oklahoma
1. John Sullivan (R)
2. Dan Boren (D)
3. Frank D. Lucas (R)
4. Tom Cole (R)
5. James Lankford (R)

Oregon
1. David Wu (D) *(resigned Aug. 3, 2011)* Suzanne Bonamici (D) *(sworn in Jan. 31, 2012)*
2. Greg Walden (R)
3. Earl Blumenauer (D)
4. Peter A. DeFazio (D)
5. Kurt Schrader (D)

Pennsylvania
1. Robert A. Brady (D)
2. Chaka Fattah (D)
3. Mike Kelly (R)
4. Jason Altmire (D)
5. Glenn Thompson (R)
6. Jim Gerlach (R)
7. Pat Meehan (R)
8. Michael G. Fitzpatrick (R)
9. Bill Shuster (R)
10. Tom Marino (R)
11. Lou Barletta (R)
12. Mark Critz (D)
13. Allyson Y. Schwartz (D)
14. Mike Doyle (D)
15. Charlie Dent (R)
16. Joe Pitts (R)
17. Tim Holden (D)
18. Tim Murphy (R)
19. Todd R. Platts (R)

Rhode Island
1. David Cicilline (D)
2. Jim Langevin (D)

South Carolina
1. Tim Scott (R)
2. Joe Wilson (R)
3. Jeff Duncan (R)
4. Trey Gowdy (R)
5. Mick Mulvaney (R)
6. James E. Clyburn (D)

South Dakota
AL Kristi Noem (R)

Tennessee
1. Phil Roe (R)
2. John J. "Jimmy" Duncan Jr. (R)
3. Chuck Fleischmann (R)
4. Scott DesJarlais (R)
5. Jim Cooper (D)
6. Diane Black (R)
7. Marsha Blackburn (R)
8. Stephen Fincher (R)
9. Steve Cohen (D)

Texas
1. Louie Gohmert (R)
2. Ted Poe (R)
3. Sam Johnson (R)
4. Ralph M. Hall (R)
5. Jeb Hensarling (R)
6. Joe L. Barton (R)
7. John Culberson (R)
8. Kevin Brady (R)
9. Al Green (D)
10. Michael McCaul (R)
11. K. Michael Conaway (R)
12. Kay Granger (R)
13. William M. "Mac" Thornberry (R)

14. Ron Paul (R)
15. Rubén Hinojosa (D)
16. Silvestre Reyes (D)
17. Bill Flores (R)
18. Sheila Jackson Lee (D)
19. Randy Neugebauer (R)
20. Charlie Gonzalez (D)
21. Lamar Smith (R)
22. Pete Olson (R)
23. Francisco "Quico" Canseco (R)
24. Kenny Marchant (R)
25. Lloyd Doggett (D)
26. Michael C. Burgess (R)
27. Blake Farenthold (R)
28. Henry Cuellar (D)
29. Gene Green (D)
30. Eddie Bernice Johnson (D)
31. John Carter (R)
32. Pete Sessions (R)

Utah

1. Rob Bishop (R)
2. Jim Matheson (D)
3. Jason Chaffetz (R)

Vermont

AL Peter Welch (D)

Virginia

1. Rob Wittman (R)
2. Scott Rigell (R)
3. Robert C. Scott (D)
4. J. Randy Forbes (R)
5. Robert Hurt (R)
6. Robert W. Goodlatte (R)
7. Eric Cantor (R)
8. James P. Moran (D)
9. Morgan Griffith (R)
10. Frank R. Wolf (R)
11. Gerald E. Connolly (D)

Washington

1. Jay Inslee (D) *(resigned March 20, 2012)*
   Susan K. DelBene (D) *(sworn in Nov. 6, 2012)*
2. Rick Larsen (D)
3. Jaime Herrera (R)
4. Doc Hastings (R)
5. Cathy McMorris Rodgers (R)
6. Norm Dicks (D)
7. Jim McDermott (D)
8. Dave Reichert (R)
9. Adam Smith (D)

West Virginia

1. David McKinley (R)
2. Shelley Moore Capito (R)
3. Nick J. Rahall II (D)

Wisconsin

1. Paul D. Ryan (R)
2. Tammy Baldwin (D)
3. Ron Kind (D)
4. Gwen Moore (D)
5. F. James Sensenbrenner Jr. (R)
6. Tom Petri (R)
7. Sean P. Duffy (R)
8. Reid Ribble (R)

Wyoming

AL Cynthia M. Lummis (R)

NOTE: Changes that occurred during 2011 and 2012 are noted following the names of individuals who did not serve their full terms. Members of the 112th Congress also included delegates Eni F. H. Faleomavaega, D-American Samoa; Eleanor Holmes Norton, D-District of Columbia; Madeleine Z. Bordallo, D-Guam; Gregorio Kilili Camacho Sablan, D-Northern Mariana Islands; Donna M. C. Christian, D-Virgin Islands; and resident commissioner Pedro Pierluisi, D-Puerto Rico. AL—At Large.

1. Seat left vacant for remainder of term.

Members of Congress, 2009–2013

The names in this list include, alphabetically, senators, representatives, resident commissioners, and territorial delegates who served in the 111th and 112th Congresses—from January 3, 2009, to January 3, 2013.

The material is organized as follows: name; party, state (of service); date of birth; date of death (if applicable); congressional service; service as president, vice president, governor, Speaker of the House, president pro tempore of the Senate, majority leader, minority leader.

If the member changed parties during his or her congressional service, the party designation appearing after the member's name is that which applied at the end of such service and further information is included in the entry.

Dates of service are inclusive, starting in year of service and ending when service ends. Where the service date is left open, the member continued to serve after the 112th Congress.

Under the Constitution, terms of service since 1934 have been from January 3 to January 3. In actual practice, members have been sworn in on other dates at the beginning of a Congress. The exact date is shown (where available) if a member began or ended his or her service in midterm.

The major sources for the following list were *Congressional Quarterly's Biographical Directory of the American Congress 1774–1996*; *America Votes* series; the *CQ Almanac*; *American Political Leaders 1789–2005*; *CQ Weekly* magazine and online database and the Biographical Directory of the United States Congress available at bioguide.congress.gov.

In the list, D stands for Democrat; R, Republican; and I, Independent.

A

Abercrombie, Neil (D-Hawaii) June 26, 1938– ; House September 23, 1986–1987, 1991–February 28, 2010; Gov. 2010– .

Ackerman, Gary L. (D-N.Y.) November 19, 1942– ; House March 1, 1983–2013.

Adams, Sandy (R-Fla.) December 14, 1956– ; House 2011–2013.

Aderholt, Robert (R-Ala.) July 22, 1965– ; House 1997– .

Adler, John H. (D-N.J.) August 3, 1942–April 4, 2011; House 2009–2011.

Akaka, Daniel K. (D-Hawaii) September 11, 1924– ; House 1977–May 15, 1990; Senate May 16, 1990–2013.

Akin, Todd (R-Mo.) July 5, 1947– ; House 2001–2013.

Alexander, Lamar (R-Tenn.) July 3, 1940– ; Senate 2003– ; Gov. 1979–1987.

Alexander, Rodney (R-La.) December 5, 1946– ; House 2003– (2003–August 9, 2004 Democrat).

Altmire, Jason (D-Pa.) March 7, 1968– ; House 2007–2013.

Amash, Justin (R-Mich.) April 18, 1980– ; House 2011– .

Amodei, Mark (R-Nev.) June 12, 1958– ; House September 13, 2011– .

Andrews, Robert E. (D-N.J.) August 4, 1957– ; House 1990– .

Arcuri, Michel (D-N.Y.) June 11, 1959– ; House 2007–2011.

Austria, Steve (D-Ohio) October 12, 1958– ; House 2009–2013.

Ayotte, Kelly (R-N.H.) June 27, 1968– ; Senate 2011– .

B

Baca, Joe (D-Calif.) January 23, 1947– ; House November 16, 1999–2013.

Bachmann, Michele (R-Minn.) April 6, 1956– ; House 2007– .

Bachus, Spencer (R-Ala.) 28, 1947– ; House 1993– .

Baird, Brian (D-Wash.) March 7, 1956– ; House 1999–2011.

Baldwin, Tammy (D-Wis.) February 11, 1962– ; House 1999–2013; Senate 2013– .

Barber, Ron (D-Ariz.) August 25, 1945– ; House June 12, 2012– .

Barletta, Lou (R-Pa.) January 28, 1956– ; House 2011– .

Barrasso, John (R-Wyo.) July 21, 1952– ; Senate June 25, 2007– .

Barrett, J. Gresham (R-S.C.) February 14, 1961– ; House 2003–2011.

Barrow, John (D-Ga.) October 31 1955– ; House 2005– .

Bartlett, Roscoe G. (R-Md.) June 3, 1926– ; House 1993– .

Barton, Joe L. (R-Texas) September 15, 1949– ; House 1985– .

Bass, Charles (R-N.H.) January 8, 1952– ; House 1995–2007; 2011–2013.

Bass, Karen (D-Calif.) October 3, 1953– ; House 2011– .

Baucus, Max (D-Mont.) December 11, 1941– ; House 1975–December 14, 1978; Senate December 15, 1978– .

Bayh, Evan (D-Ind.) December 26, 1955– ; Senate 1999–2011; Gov. 1989–1997.

Bean, Melissa (D-Ill.) January 22, 1962– ; House 2005–2011.

Beauprez, Bob (R-Colo.) September 22, 1948– ; House 2003–2007.

Becerra, Xavier (D-Calif.) January 26, 1958– ; House 1993– .

Begich, Mark (D-Alaska) March 30, 1962– ; Senate 2009– .

Bennet, Michael F. (D-Colo.) November 28, 1964– ; Senate January 22, 2009– .

Bennett, Robert F. (R-Utah) September 18, 1933– ; Senate 1993–2011.

Berg, Rick (R-N.D.) August 15, 1959– ; House 2011–2013.

Berkley, Shelley (D-Nev.) January 21, 1951– ; House 1999–2013.

Berman, Howard L. (D-Calif.) April 15, 1941– ; House 1983–2013.

Benishek, Dan (R-Mich.) April 20, 1952– ; House 2011– .

Berry, Marion (D-Ark.) August 27, 1942– ; House 1997–2011.

Biden, Joseph R. Jr. (D-Del.) November 20, 1942– ; Senate 1973–January 15, 2009; vice president 2009– .

Biggert, Judy (R-Ill.) August 15, 1937– ; House 1999–2013.

Bilbray, Brian P. (R-Calif.) January 28, 1951– ; House 1955–2001; June 6, 2006–2013.

Bilirakis, Gus (R-Fla.) February 8, 1963– ; House 2007– .

Bingaman, Jeff (D-N.M.) October 3, 1943– ; Senate 1983–2013.

Bishop, Rob (R-Utah) July 13, 1951– ; House 2003– .

Bishop, Sanford D. Jr. (D-Ga.) February 4, 1947– ; House 1993– .

Bishop, Timothy H. (D-N.Y.) June 1, 1950– ; House 2003– .

Black, Diane (R-Tenn.) January 16, 1951– ; House 2011– .

Blackburn, Marsha (R-Tenn.) June 6, 1952– ; House 2003– .

Blumenauer, Earl (D-Ore.) August 16, 1949– ; House May 30, 1996– .

Blumenthal, Richard (D-Conn.) February 13, 1946– ; Senate 2011– .

Blunt, Roy (R-Mo.) January 10, 1950– ; House 1997–2011; Senate 2011– .

Boccieri, John (D-Ohio) October 5, 1969– ; House 2009–2011.

Boehner, John A. (R-Ohio) November 17, 1949– ; House 1991– ; House majority leader 2006–2007; minority leader 2007–2011; Speaker 2011– .

Bonamici, Suzanne (D-Ore.) October 14, 1954– ; House January 31, 2012– .

Bond, Christopher S. (R-Mo.) March 6, 1939– ; Senate 1987–2011.

Bonner, Jo (R-Ala.) November 19, 1959– ; House 2003– .

Bono-Mack, Mary (R-Calif.) October 24, 1961; House April 21, 1998–2013.

Boozman, John (R-Ark.) December 10, 1950– ; House November 29, 2001–2011; Senate 2011– .

Bordallo, Madeleine Z. (D-Guam) May 31, 1933– ; House (Delegate) 2003– .

Boren, Dan (D-Okla.) August 2, 1973– ; House 2005–2013.

Boswell, Leonard L. (D-Iowa) January 10, 1934– ; House 1997–2013.

Boucher, Rick (D-Va.) August 1, 1946– ; House 1983–2011.

Boustany, Charles Jr. (R-La.) February 21, 1956– ; House 2005– .

Boxer, Barbara (D-Calif.) November 11, 1940– ; House 1983–1993; Senate 1993– .

Boyd, Allen (D-Fla.) June 6, 1945– ; House 1997–2011.

Brady, Kevin (R-Texas) April 11, 1955– ; House 1997– .

Brady, Robert A. (D-Pa.) April 7, 1945– ; House May 28, 1998– .

Braley, Bruce (D-Iowa) October 30, 1957– ; House 2007– .

Bright, Bobby (D-Ala.) July 21, 1952– ; House 2009–2011.

Brooks, Mo (R-Ala.) April 29, 1954– ; House 2011– .

Broun, Paul (D-Ga.) May 14, 1946– ; House July 17, 2007– .

Brown, Corrine (D-Fla.) November 11, 1946– ; House 1993– .

Brown, Henry E. Jr. (R-S.C.) December 20, 1935– ; House 2001–2011.

Brown, Scott (R-Mass.) September 12, 1959– ; Senate February 4, 2010–2013.

Brown, Sherrod (D-Ohio) November 9, 1952– ; House 1993–2007; Senate 2007– .

Brownback, Sam (R-Kan.) September 12, 1956– ; House 1995–November 6, 1996; Senate November 27, 1996–2011; Gov 2011– .

Brown-Waite, Ginny (R-Fla.) October 5, 1943– ; House 2003–2011.

Buchanan, Vern (R-Fla.) May 8, 1951– ; House 2007– .

Bucshon, Larry (R-Ind.) May 31, 1962– ; House 2011– .

Buerkle, Ann Marie (R-N.Y.) May 8, 1951– ; House 2011–2013.

Bunning, Jim (R-Ky.) October 23, 1931– ; House 1987–1999; Senate 1999–2011.

Burgess, Michael (R-Texas) December 23, 1950– ; House 2003– .

Burns, Conrad (R-Mont.) January 25, 1935– ; Senate 1989–2007.

Burr, Richard M. (R-N.C.) November 30, 1955– ; House 1995–2005; Senate 2005– .

Burris, Roland W. (D-Ill.) August 3, 1937– ; Senate January 15, 2009–November 29, 2010.

Burton, Dan (R-Ind.) June 21, 1938– ; House 1983– .

Butterfield, G. K. (D-N.C.) April 27, 1947– ; House July 21, 2004– .

Buyer, Steve (R-Ind.) November 26, 1958– ; House 1993–2011; Gov. 1971–1975.

Byrd, Robert C. (D-W.Va.) November 20, 1917–June 28, 2010; House 1953–1959; Senate 1959– ; Senate minority leader, 1981–1987; Senate majority leader 1977–1981, 1987–1989; pres. pro tempore 1989–1995, June 6, 2001–2003, 2007–June 28, 2010.

C

Calvert, Ken (R-Calif.) June 8, 1953– ; House 1993– .

Camp, Dave (R-Mich.) July 9, 1953– ; House 1991– .

Campbell, John (R-Calif.) July 19, 1955– ; House December 7, 2005– .

Canseco, Francisco "Quico" (R-Texas) July 30, 1949– ; House 2011–2013.

Cantor, Eric I. (R-Va.) June 6, 1963– ; House 2001– .

Cantwell, Maria (D-Wash.) October 13, 1958– ; House 1993–1994; Senate 2001– .

Cao, Anh "Joseph" Quang (R-La.) March 13, 1967– ; House 2009–2011.

Capito, Shelley Moore (R-W.Va.) November 26, 1953– ; Houses 2001– .

Capps, Lois D. (D-Calif.) January 10, 1938– ; House March 17, 1998– .

Capuano, Michael D. (D-Mass.) January 9, 1952– ; House 1999– .

Cardin, Benjamin L. (D-Md.) October 5, 1943– ; House 1987–2007; Senate 2007– .

Cardoza, Dennis (D-Calif.) March 31, 1959– ; House 2003–August 15, 2012.

Carnahan, Russ (D-Mo.) July 10, 1958– ; House 2005–2013.

Carney, Christopher (D-Pa.) March 2, 1959– ; House 2007–2011.

Carney, John (D-Del.) May 20, 1956– ; House 2011– .

Carper, Thomas R. (D-Del.) January 23, 1947– ; House 1983–1993; Senate 2001– ; Gov. 1993–2001.

Carson, Andre (D-Ind.) October 16, 1974– ; House March 13, 2008– .

Carter, John (R-Texas) November 6, 1941– ; House 2003– .

Casey, Robert P. Jr. (D-Pa.) April 13, 1960– ; Senate 2007– .

Cassidy, Bill (R-La.) September 27, 1957– ; House 2009– .

Castle, Michael N. (R-Del.) July 2, 1939– ; House 1993–2011.

Castor, Kathy (D-Fla.) August 20, 1966– ; House 2007– .

Chabot, Steve (R-Ohio) January 22, 1953– ; House 1995–2009; 2011– .

Chaffetz, Jason (R-Utah) March 26, 1967– ; House 2009– .

Chambliss, Saxby (R-Ga.) November 10, 1943– ; House 1995–2003; Senate 2003– .

Chandler, Ben (D-Ky.) September 12, 1959– ; House February 17, 2004–2013.

Childers, Travis W. (D-Miss.) March 29, 1958– ; House May 21, 2008–2011.

Christensen, Donna M. C. (D-Virgin Is.) September 19, 1945– ; House (Delegate) 1997– .

Chu, Judy (D-Calif.) July 7, 1953– ; House July 14, 2009– .

Cicilline, David (D-R.I.) July 15, 1961– ; House 2011– .

Clark, Yvette D. (D-N.Y.) November 21, 1964– ; House 2007– .

Clarke, Hansen (R-Mich.) March 2, 1957– ; House 2011–2013.

Clay, William Lacy Jr. (D-Mo.) July 27, 1956– ; House 2001– .

Cleaver, Emanuel, II (D-Mo.) October 26, 1944– ; House 2005– .

Clinton, Hillary Rodham (D-N.Y.) (wife of President Bill Clinton) October 26, 1947– ; First Lady 1993–2001; Senate 2001–January 21, 2009.

Clyburn, James E. (D-S.C.) July 21, 1940– ; House 1993– .

Coats, Dan (R-Ind.) May 16, 1943– ; House 1981–1989; Senate 1989–1999; 2011– .

Coble, Howard (R-N.C.) March 18, 1931– ; House 1985– .

Cochran, Thad, (R-Miss.) December 7, 1937– ; House 1973–December 26, 1978; Senate December 27, 1978– .

Coffman, Mike (R-Colo.) March 29, 1955– ; House 2009– .

Cohen, Steve (D-Tenn.) May 24, 1959– ; House 2007– .

Cole, Tom (R-Okla.) April 28, 1949– ; House 2003– .

Collins, Susan (R-Maine) December 7, 1952– ; Senate 1997– .

Conaway, K. Michael (R-Texas) June 11, 1948– ; House 2005– .

Connolly, Gerald E. (D-Va.) March 30, 1950– ; House 2009– .

Conrad, Kent (D-N.D.) March 12, 1948– ; Senate 1987–December 14, 1992, December 14, 1992–2013.

Conyers, John Jr. (D-Mich.) May 16, 1929– ; House 1965– .

Coons, Christopher A. (D-Del.) September 9, 1963– ; Senate November 15, 2010– ;

Cooper, Jim (D-Tenn.) June 19, 1954– ; House 1983–1995; 2003– .

Corker, Bob (R-Tenn.) August 24, 1952– ; Senate 2007– .

Cornyn, John (R-Texas) February 2, 1952– ; Senate December 2, 2002– .

Costa, Jim (D-Calif.) April 13, 1952– ; House 2005– .

Costello, Jerry F. (D-Ill.) September 25, 1949– ; House August 11, 1988–2013.

Courtney, Joe (D-Conn.) April 6, 1953– ; House 2007– .

Cramer, Robert E. "Bud" (D-Ala.) August 22, 1947– ; House 1991– .

Crapo, Michael D. (R-Idaho) May 20, 1951– ; House 1993–1999; Senate 1999– .

Cravaack, Chip (R-Minn.) December 29, 1954– ; House 2011–2013.

Crawford, Rick (R-Ark.) January 22, 1966– ; House 2011– .

Crenshaw, Ander (R-Fla.) September 1, 1944– ; House 2001– .

Critz, Mark S. (D-Pa.) January 5, 1962– ; House May 18, 2010–2013.

Crowley, Joseph (D-N.Y.) March 16, 1962– ; House 1999– .
Cuellar, Henry (D-Texas) September 19, 1955– ; House 2005– .
Culberson, John (R-Texas) August 24, 1956– ; House 2001– .
Cummings, Elijah E. (D-Md.) January 18, 1951– ; House April 25, 1996– .
Curson, David (D-Mich.) November 4, 1948– ; House November 6, 2012–2013.

D

Dahlkemper, Kathleen A. (D-Pa.) December 10, 1957– ; House 2009–2011.
Davis, Artur (D-Ala.) Oct, 9, 1957– ; House 2003–2011.
Davis, Danny K. (D-Ill.) September 6, 1941– ; House 1997– .
Davis, Geoff (R-Ky.) October 26, 1958– ; House 2005–July 31, 2012.
Davis, Lincoln (D-Tenn.) September 13, 1943– ; House 2003–2011.
Davis, Susan A. (D-Calif.) April 13, 1944– ; House 2001– .
Deal, Nathan (R-Ga.) August 25, 1942– ; House 1993–March 21, 2010 (1993–April 10, 1995, Democrat). Gov. 2011– .
DeFazio, Peter A. (D-Ore.) May 27, 1947– ; House 1987– .
DeGette, Diana (D-Colo.) July 29, 1957– ; House 1997– .
Delahunt, William (D-Mass.) July 18, 1941– ; House 1997–2011.
DeLauro, Rosa (D-Conn.) March 2, 1943– ; House 1991– .
DelBene, Suzan K. (D-Wash.) February 17, 1962– ; House November 6, 2012– .
DeMint, Jim (R-S.C.) September 2, 1951– ; House 1999–2005; Senate 2005– .
Denham, Jeff (R-Calif.) July 29, 1967– ; House 2011– .
Dent, Charlie (R-Pa.) May 24, 1960– ; House 2005– .
DesJarlais, Scott (R-Tenn.) February 21, 1964– ; House 2011– .
Deutch, Ted (D-Fla.) May 7, 1966– ; House April 13, 2010– .
Diaz-Balart, Lincoln (R-Fla.) August 13, 1954– ; House 1993–2011.
Diaz-Balart, Mario (R-Fla.) September 25, 1961– ; House 2003– .
Dicks, Norm (D-Wash.) December 16, 1940– ; House 1977–2013.
Dingell, John D. (D-Mich.) July 8, 1926– ; House December 13, 1955– .
Djou, Charles (R-Hawaii) August 9, 1970– ; House May 22, 2010–2011.
Dodd, Christopher J. (D-Conn.) May 27, 1944– ; House 1975–1981; Senate 1981–2011.
Doggett, Lloyd (D-Texas) October 6, 1946– ; House 1995– .
Dold, Robert (R-Ill.) June 23, 1969– ; House 2011–2013.
Donnelly, Joe (D-Ind.) September 29, 1959– ; House 2007–2013; Senate 2013– .
Dorgan, Byron L. (D-N.D.) May 14, 1942– ; House 1981–December 14, 1992; Senate December 15, 1992–2011.
Doyle, Mike (D-Pa.) August 5, 1953– ; House 1995– .
Dreier, David (R-Calif.) July 5, 1952– ; House 1981–2013.
Driehaus, Steve (D-Ohio) June 24, 1966– ; House 2009–2011.
Duffy, Sean P. (R-Wis.) October 3, 1971– ; House 2011.
Duncan, Jeff (R-S.C.) January 27, 1966– ; House 2011– .
Duncan, John J. "Jimmy" Jr. (R-Tenn.) July 21, 1947– ; House 1988– .
Durbin, Richard J. (D-Ill.) November 21, 1944– ; House 1983–1997; Senate 1997– .

E

Edwards, Chet (D-Texas) November 24, 1951– ; House 1991–2011.
Edwards, Donna F. (D-Md.) June 28, 1958; House June 17, 2008– .
Ehlers, Vernon J. (R-Mich.) February 6. 1934– ; House January 25, 1994–2011.
Ellison, Keith (D-Minn.) February 6, 1984– ; House 2007– .
Ellmers, Renee (R-N.C.) February 9, 1964– ; House 2011– .
Ellsworth, Brad (D-Ind.) September 11, 1958– ; House 2007–2011.
Emerson, Jo Ann (R-Mo.) September 16, 1950– ; House November 5, 1996– . (Elected as an Independent in a 1996 special election following the death of her husband, Rep. Bill Emerson, because the filing date had passed but ran as a Republican in the general election and thereafter.)
Engel, Eliot L. (D-N.Y.) February 18, 1947– ; House 1989– .
Ensign, John (R-Nev.) March 25, 1958– ; House 1995–1999; Senate 2001–May 3, 2011.
Enzi, Michael B. (R-Wyo.) February 1, 1944– ; Senate 1997– .
Eshoo, Anna G. (D-Calif.) December 13, 1942– ; House 1993– .
Etheridge, Bob (D-N.C.) August 7, 1941– ; House 1997–2011.

F

Faleomavaega, Eni F. H. (D-Am. Samoa) August 15, 1943– ; House (Delegate) 1989– .
Fallin, Mary (R-Okla.) December 9, 1954– ; House 2007–2011. Gov. 2011– .
Farenthold, Blake (R-Texas) December 12, 1962– ; House 2011– .
Farr, Sam (D-Calif.) July 4, 1941– ; House June 16, 1993– .
Fattah, Chaka (D-Pa.) November 21, 1956– ; House 1995– .
Feeney, Tom (R-Fla.) May 21, 1958– ; House 2003– .
Feingold, Russell D. (D-Wis.) March 2, 1953– ; Senate 1993–2011.
Feinstein, Dianne (D-Calif.) June 22, 1933– ; Senate November 10, 1992– .
Filner, Bob (D-Calif.) September 4, 1942– ; House 1993–December 3, 2012.
Fincher, Stephen (R-Tenn.) February 7, 1973– ; House 2011– .
Fitzpatrick, Michel G. (R-Pa.) June 28, 1963– ; House 2005–2007; 2011– .
Flake, Jeff (R-Ariz.) December 31, 1962– ; House 2001–2013; Senate 2013– .
Fleischmann, Chuck (R-Tenn.) October 11, 1962– ; House 2011– .
Fleming, John (R-La.) July 5, 1951– ; House 2009– .
Flores, Bill (R-Texas) February 25, 1954– ; House 2011– .
Forbes, J. Randy (R-Va.) February 17, 1952– ; House June 26, 2001– .
Ford, Harold E. Jr. (D-Tenn.) May 11, 1970– ; House 1997–2007.
Fortenberry, Jeff (R-Neb.) December 27, 1960– ; House 2005– .
Fortuno, Luis (R-P.R.) October 31, 1960– ; House (Resident Commissioner) 2005– .
Foster, Bill (D-Ill.) March 7, 1955– ; House March 11, 2008–2011; 2013– .
Foxx, Virginia (R-N.C.) June 29, 1943– ; House 2005– .
Frank, Barney (D-Mass.) March 31, 1940– ; House 1981–2013.
Franken, Al (D-Minn.) May 21, 1951– ; Senate July 7, 2009– .
Franks, Trent (R-Ariz.) June 19, 1957– ; House 2003– .
Frelinghuysen, Rodney (R-N.J.) April 29, 1946– ; House 1995– .
Fudge, Marcia L. (D-Ohio) October 29, 1952; House November19, 2008– .

G

Gallegly, Elton (R-Calif.) March 7, 1944– ; House 1987–2013.
Garamendi, John (D-Calif.) January 24, 1945– ; House November 3, 2009– .
Gardner, Cory (R-Colo.) August 27, 1974– ; House 2011– .
Garrett, Scott (R-N.J.) July 9, 1959– ; House 2003– .
Gerlach, Jim (R-Pa.) February 25, 1955– ; House 2003– .
Gibbs, Bob (R-Ohio) June 14, 1954– ; House 2011– .
Gibson, Chris (R-N.Y.) May 13, 1964– ; House 2011– .
Giffords, Gabrielle (D-Ariz.) June 8, 1970– ; House 2007–January 25, 2012.
Gillibrand, Kirsten (D-N.Y.) December 9, 1966– ; House 2007–January 26, 2009; Senate January 27, 2009– .
Gingrey, Phil (R-Ga.) July 10, 1942– ; House 2003– .
Gohmert, Louie (R-Texas) August 18, 1953– ; House 2005– .
Gonzalez, Charlie (D-Texas) May 5, 1945– ; House 1999–2013.
Goodlatte, Robert W. (R-Va.) September 22, 1952– ; House 1993– .
Goodwin, Carte (D-W.Va.) February 27, 1974– ; Senate July 16, 2010–November 15, 2010.
Gordon, Bart (D-Tenn.) January 24, 1949– ; House 1985–2011.
Gosar, Paul (R-Ariz.) November 22, 1958– ; House 2011– .

Gowdy, Trey (R-S.C.) August 22, 1964– ; House 2011– .
Graham, Lindsey (R-S.C.) July 9, 1955– ; House 1995–2003; Senate 2003– .
Granger, Kay (R-Texas) January 18, 1943– ; House 1997– .
Grassley, Charles E. (R-Iowa) September 17, 1933– ; House 1975–1981; Senate 1981– .
Graves, Sam (R-Mo.) November 7, 1963– ; House 2001– .
Graves, Tom (R-Ga.) February 3, 1970– ; House June 8, 2010– .
Grayson, Alan (D-Fla.) March 13, 1958– ; House 2009–2011; 2013– .
Green, Al (D-Texas) September 1, 1947– ; House 2005– .
Green, Gene (D-Texas) October 17, 1947– ; House 1993– .
Green, Mark (R-Wis.) June 1, 1960– ; House 1999–2007.
Gregg, Judd (R-N.H.) February 14, 1947– ; Senate 1993–2011.
Griffin, Tim (R-Ark.) August 21, 1968– ; House 2011– .
Griffith, Morgan (R-Va.) March 15, 1958– ; House 2011– .
Griffith, Parker (R-Ala.) August 6, 1942– ; House 2009–2011 (2005–December 22, 2009 Democrat).
Grijalva, Raül M. (D-Ariz.) February 19, 1948– ; House 2003– .
Grimm, Michael (R-N.Y.) February 7, 1970– ; House 2011– .
Guinta, Frank (R-N.H.) September 26, 1970– ; House 2011–2013.
Guthrie, Brett (R-Ky.) February 18, 1964– ; House 2009– .
Gutierrez, Luis V. (D-Ill.) December 10, 1954– ; House 1993– .

H

Hagan, Kay (D-N.C.) May 26, 1953– ; Senate 2009– .
Hahn, Janice (D-Calif.) March 30, 1952– ; House July 12, 2011– .
Hall, John (D-N.Y.) July 23, 1938– ; House 2007–2011.
Hall, Ralph M. (R-Texas) May 3, 1923– ; House 1981– (1981–January 5, 2004 Democrat).
Halvorson, Deborah L. (D-Ill.) March 1, 1958– ; House 2009–2011.
Hanabusa, Colleen (D-Hawaii) May 4, 1951– ; House 2011– .
Hanna, Richard (R-N.Y.) January 25, 1951– ; House 2011–2013.
Hare, Phil (D-Ill.) February 21, 1949– ; House 2007–2011.
Harkin, Tom (D-Iowa) November 19, 1939– ; House 1975–1985; Senate 1985– .
Harman, Jane (D-Calif.) June 28, 1945– ; House 1993–1999; 2001–February 28, 2011.
Harper, Gregg (R-Miss.) June 1, 1956– ; House 2009– .
Harris, Andy (R-Md.) January 25, 1957– ; House 2011– .
Hartzler, Vicky (R-Mo.) October 13, 1960– ; House 2011– .
Hastings, Alcee L. (D-Fla.) September 5, 1936– ; House 1993– .
Hastings, Richard "Doc" (R-Wash.) February 7, 1941– ; House 1995– .
Hatch, Orrin G. (R-Utah) March 22, 1934– ; Senate 1977– .
Hayes, Robin (R-N.C.) August 14, 1945– ; House 1999– .
Hayworth, Nan (R-N.Y.) December 14, 1959– ; House 2011–2013.
Heck, Joe (R-Nev.) October 30, 1961– ; House 2011– .
Heinrich, Martin (D-N.M.) October 17, 1971-; House 2009–2013; Senate 2013– .
Heller, Dean (R-Nev.) May 10, 1960– ; House 2007–May 9, 2011; Senate May 9, 2011– .
Hensarling, Jeb (R-Texas) May 29, 1957– ; House 2003– .
Herger, Wally (R-Calif.) May 20, 1945– ; House 1987–2013.
Herrera Beutler, Jamie (R-Wash.) November 3, 1978– ; House 2011– .
Herseth Sandlin, Stephanie (D-S.D.) December 3, 1970– ; House June 1, 2004–2011.
Hill, Baron P. (D-Ind.) June 23, 1953– ; House 2007–2011.
Himes, James (D-Conn.) July 5, 1966– ; House 2009– .
Hinchey, Maurice D. (D-N.Y.) October 27, 1938– ; House 1993–2013.
Hinojosa, Ruben (D-Texas) August 20, 1940– ; House 1997– .
Hirono, Mazie K. (D-Hawaii) November 3, 1947– ; House 2007–2013; Senate 2013– .
Hochul, Kathy (D-N.Y.) August 27, 1958; House May 24, 2011–2013.
Hodes, Paul W. (D-N.H.) March 21, 1951– ; House 2007–2011.
Hoekstra, Peter (R-Mich.) October 30, 1953– ; House 1993–2011.
Hoeven, John (R-N.D.) March 13, 1957– ; Senate 2011– ; Gov. 2000–2010.
Holden, Tim (D-Pa.) March 5, 1957– ; House 1993–2013.
Holt, Rush D. (D-N.J.) October 15, 1948– ; House 1999– .
Honda, Mike (D-Calif.) June 27, 1941– ; House 2001– .
Hoyer, Steny H. (D-Md.) June 14, 1939– ; House June 3, 1981– . House majority leader 2007–2011; minority leader 2011– .
Huelskamp, Tim (R-Kan.) November 11, 1968– ; House 2011– .
Huizenga, Bill (R-Mich.) January 21, 1969– ; House 2011– .
Hultgren, Randy (R-Ill.) March 1, 1966– ; House 2011– .
Hunter, Duncan Duane (R-Calif.) December 7, 1974– ; House 2009– .
Hurt, Robert (R-Va.) June 16, 1969– ; House 2011– .
Hutchison, Kay Bailey (R-Texas) July 22, 1943– ; Senate June 14, 1993–2013.

I

Inglis, Bob (R-S.C.) October 11, 1959– ; House 1993–1999; 2005–2011.
Inhofe, James M. (R-Okla.) November 17, 1934– ; House 1987–November 15, 1994; Senate November 17, 1994– .
Inouye, Daniel K. (D-Hawaii) September 7, 1924–December 17, 2012; House August 21, 1959–1963; Senate 1963–December 17, 2012.
Inslee, Jay (D-Wash.) February 9, 1951– ; House 1993–1995; 1999–March 20, 2012. Gov. 2013– .
Isakson, Johnny (R-Ga.) December 28, 1944– ; House February 25, 1999–2005; Senate 2005– .
Israel, Steven (D-N.Y.) May 30, 1958– ; House 2001– .
Issa, Darrell (R-Calif.) November 1, 1953– ; House 2001– .

J

Jackson, Jesse Jr. (D-Ill.) March 11, 1965– ; House December 12, 1995–November 21, 2012.
Jackson-Lee, Sheila (D-Texas) January 12, 1950– ; House 1995– .
Jenkins, Lynn (R-Kan.) June 10, 1963– ; House 2009– .
Johanns, Mike (R-Neb.) June 18, 1950– ; Senate 2009– ; Gov. 1999–2005.
Johnson, Bill (R-Ohio) November 10, 1954– ; House 2011– .
Johnson, Eddie Bernice (D-Texas) December 3, 1935– ; House 1993– .
Johnson, Hank (D-Ga.) October 2, 1954– ; House 2007– .
Johnson, Ron (R-Wis.) April 8, 1955– ; Senate 2011– .
Johnson, Sam (R-Texas) October 11, 1930– ; House May 22, 1991– .
Johnson, Tim (D-S.D.) December 28, 1946– ; House 1987–1997; Senate 1997– .
Johnson, Timothy V. (R-Ill.) July 23, 1946– ; House 2001–2013.
Jones, Walter B. Jr. (R-N.C.) February 10, 1943– ; House 1995– .
Jordan, Jim (R-Ohio) February 17, 1964– ; House 2007– .

K

Kagen, Steve (D-Wis.) December 12, 1949– ; House 2007–2011.
Kanjorski, Paul E. (D-Pa.) April 2, 1937– ; House 1985–2011.
Kaptur, Marcy (D-Ohio) June 17, 1946– ; House 1983– .
Kaufman, Ted (D-Del.) March 15, 1939– ; Senate January 16, 2009–November 15, 2010.
Keating, William (D-Mass.) September 6, 1952– ; House 2011– .
Keller, Richard "Ric" (R-Fla.) September 5, 1964– ; House 2001– .
Kelly, Mike (R-Pa.) May 10, 1948– ; House 2011– .
Kelly, Sue W. (R-N.Y.) September 26, 1936– ; House 1995–2007.
Kennedy, Edward M. February 22, 1932–August 25, 2009; Senate November 7, 1962–August 25, 2009.

Kennedy, Mark (R-Minn.) April 11, 1957– ; House 2001–2007.

Kennedy, Patrick J. (D-R.I.) July 14, 1967– ; House 1995–2011.

Kerry, John (D-Mass.) December 11, 1943– ; Senate 1985– .

Kildee, Dale E. (D-Mich.) September 16, 1929– ; House 1977–2013.

Kilpatrick, Carolyn Cheeks (D-Mich.) June 25, 1945– ; House 1997–2011.

Kilroy, Mary Jo (D-Ohio) April 30, 1949– ; House 2009–2011.

Kind, Ron (D-Wis.) March 16, 1963– ; House 1997– .

King, Peter T. (R-N.Y.) April 5, 1944– ; House 1993– .

King, Steve (R-Iowa) May 28, 1949– ; House 2003– .

Kingston, Jack (R-Ga.) April 24, 1955– ; House 1993– .

Kinzinger, Adam (R-Ill.) February 27, 1978– ; House 2011– .

Kirk, Mark Steven (R-Ill.) September 15, 1959– ; House 2001–November 29, 2010; Senate November 29, 2010– .

Kirk, Paul (D-Mass.) January 18, 1938– ; Senate September 25, 2009–February 4, 2010.

Kirkpatrick, Ann (D-Ariz.) March 24, 1950– ; House 2009–2011; 2013– .

Kissell, Larry (D-N.C.) January 31, 1951– ; House 2009–2013

Klein, Ron (D-Fla.) July 10, 1957– ; House 2007–2011.

Kline, John (R-Minn.) September 6, 1947– ; House 2003– .

Klobuchar, Amy (D-Minn.) May 25, 1960– ; Senate 2007– .

Knollenberg, Joe (R-Mich.) November 28, 1933– ; House 1993– .

Kohl, Herb (D-Wis.) February 7, 1935– ; Senate 1989–2013.

Kosmas, Suzanne M. (D-Fla.) February 25, 1944– ; House 2009–2011.

Kratovil, Frank Jr. (D-Md.) May 29, 1968– ; House 2009–2011.

Kucinich, Dennis J. (D-Ohio) October 8, 1946– ; House 1997–2013.

Kyl, Jon (R-Ariz.) April 25, 1942– ; House 1987–1995; Senate 1995–2013.

L

Labrador, Raul R. (R-Idaho) December 8, 1967– ; House 2011– .

LaHood, Ray (R-Ill.) December 6, 1945– ; House 1995–2009.

Lamborn, Doug (R-Colo.) May 24, 1954– ; House 2007– .

Lampson, Nick (D-Texas) February 14, 1945– ; House 1997–2005; 2007– .

Lance, Leonard (R-N.J.) June 25, 1952– ; House 2009– .

Landrieu, Mary L. (D-La.) November 23, 1955– ; Senate 1997– .

Landry, Jeff (R-La.) December 23, 1970– ; House 2011– .

Langevin, Jim (D-R.I.) April 22, 1964– ; House 2001– .

Lankford, James (R-Okla.) March 4, 1968– ; House 2011– .

Larsen, Rick (D-Wash.) June 15, 1965– ; House 2001– .

Larson, John B. (D-Conn.) July 22, 1948– ; House 1999– .

Latham, Tom (R-Iowa) July 14, 1948– ; House 1995– .

LaTourette, Steven C. (R-Ohio) July 22, 1954– ; House 1995–2013.

Latta, Bob (R-Ohio) April 18, 1956– ; House December 13, 2007– .

Lautenberg, Frank R. (D-N.J.) January 23, 1924– ; Senate December 27, 1982–2001; 2003– .

Leahy, Patrick J. (D-Vt.) March 31, 1940– ; Senate 1975– .

Lee, Barbara (D-Calif.) July 16, 1946– ; House April 21, 1998– .

Lee, Christopher (R-N.Y.) April 1, 1964– ; House 2009–February 9, 2011.

Lee, Mike (R-Utah) June 4, 1971– ; Senate 2011– .

LeMieux, George (R-Fla.) May 21, 1969– ; Senate September 10, 2009–2011.

Levin, Carl (D-Mich.) June 28, 1934– ; Senate 1979– .

Levin, Sander M. (D-Mich.) September 6, 1931– ; House 1983– .

Lewis, Jerry (R-Calif.) October 21, 1934– ; House 1979–2013.

Lewis, John (D-Ga.) February 21, 1940– ; House 1987– .

Lieberman, Joseph I. (I-Conn.) February 24, 1942– ; Senate 1989–2013 (Democrat 1989–2006.)

Lincoln, Blanche Lambert (D-Ark.) September 30, 1960– ; House 1993–1997; Senate 1999–2011.

Linder, John (R-Ga.) September 9, 1942– ; House 1993–2011.

Lipinski, Dan (D-Ill.) July 15, 1966– ; House 2005– .

LoBiondo, Frank A. (R-N.J.) May 12, 1946– ; House 1995– .

Loebsack, Dave (D-Iowa) December 23, 1952– ; House 2007– .

Lofgren, Zoe (D-Calif.) December 21, 1947– ; House 1995– .

Long, Billy (R-Mo.) August 11, 1955– ; House 2011– .

Lowey, Nita M. (D-N.Y.) July 5, 1937– ; House 1989– .

Lucas, Frank D. (R-Okla.) January 6, 1960– ; House May 17, 1994– .

Luetkemeyer, Blaine (R-Mo.) May 7, 1952– ; House 2009– .

Lugar, Richard G. (R-Ind.) April 4, 1932– ; Senate 1977–2013.

Lujan, Ben Ray Jr. (D-N.M.) June 7, 1972– ; House 2009.

Lummis, Cynthia M. (R-Wyo.) September 10, 1954– ; House 2009– .

Lungren, Dan (R-Calif.) September 22, 1946– ; House 1979–1989; 2005–2013.

Lynch, Stephen F. (D-Mass.) March 31, 1955– ; House October 23, 2001– .

M

Mack, Connie, IV (R-Fla,) August 12, 1967– ; House 2005–2013.

Maffei, Daniel B. (D-N.Y.) July 4, 1968– ; House 2009–2011; 2013– .

Mahoney, Tim (D-Fla.) August 15, 1956– ; House 2007– .

Maloney, Carolyn B. (D-N.Y.) February 19, 1948– ; House 1993– .

Manchin, Joe III (D-W.Va.) August 24, 1947– ; Senate November 15, 2010– .

Manzullo, Donald (R-Ill.) March 24, 1944– ; House 1993–2013.

Marchant, Kenny (R-Calif.) February 23. 1951– ; House 2005– .

Marino, Thomas A. (R-Pa.) August 15, 1952– ; House 2011– .

Markey, Edward J. (D-Mass.) July 11, 1946– ; House November 2, 1976– .

Markey, Betsy (D-Colo.) April 27, 1956– ; House 2009–2011.

Marshall, Jim (R-Ga.) March 31, 1948– ; House 2003–2011.

Martinez, Mel (R-Fla.) October 23, 1946– ; Senate 2005–September 9, 2009.

Massa, Eric (D-N.Y.) September 16, 1949– ; House 2009–March 8, 2010.

Massie, Thomas (R-Ky.) Jan 13, 1971– ; House November 6, 2012– .

Matheson, Jim (D-Utah) March 21, 1960– ; House 2001– .

Matsui, Doris (D-Calif.) September 25, 1944– ; House March 10, 2005– .

McCain, John (R-Ariz.) August 29, 1936– ; House 1983–1987; Senate 1987– .

McCarthy, Carolyn (D-N.Y.) January 5, 1944– ; House 1997– .

McCarthy, Kevin (R-Calif.) January 26, 1965– ; House 2007– .

McCaskill, Claire (D-Mo.) July 24, 1953– ; Senate 2007– .

McCaul, Michael (R-Texas) January 14, 1962– ; House 2005– .

McClintock, Tom (R-Calif.) July 19, 1956– ; House 2009– .

McCollum, Betty (D-Minn.) July 12, 1954– ; House 2001– .

McConnell, Mitch (R-Ky.) February 20, 1942– ; Senate 1985– .

McCotter, Thaddeus (R-Mich.) August 22, 1965– ; House 2003–July 6, 2012.

McDermott, Jim (D-Wash.) December 28, 1936– ; House 1989– .

McGovern, James (D-Mass.) November 20, 1959– ; House 1997– .

McHenry, Patrick T. (R-N.C.) October 22, 1975– ; House 2005– .

McHugh, John M. (R-N.Y.) September 29, 1948– ; House 1993–September 21, 2009.

McIntyre, Mike (D-N.C.) August 6, 1956– ; House 1997– .

McKeon, Howard P. "Buck" (R-Calif.) September 9, 1939– ; House 1993– .

McKinley, David B. (R-W.Va.) March 28, 1947– ; House 2011– .

McMahon, Michael E. (D-N.Y.) September 12, 1957– ; House 2009–2011.

McMorris, Cathy (R-Wash.) May 22, 1969– ; House 2005– .
McNerney, Jerry (D-Calif.) June 18, 1951– ; House 2007– .
Meehan, Patrick (R-Pa.) October 20, 1955– ; House 2011– .
Meek, Kendrick (D-Fla.) September 6, 1966– ; House 2003–2011.
Meeks, Gregory W. (D-N.Y.) September 25, 1953– ; House February 5, 1998– .
Melancon, Charlie (D-La.) October 3, 1947– ; House 2005–2011.
Menendez, Robert (D-N.J.) January 1, 1954– ; House 1993–January 16, 2006; Senate January 18, 2006– .
Merkley, Jeff (D-Ore.) October 24, 1956– ; Senate 2009– .
Mica, John L. (R-Fla.) January 27, 1943– ; House 1993– .
Michaud, Michael H. (D-Maine) January 18, 1955– ; House 2003– .
Mikulski, Barbara A. (D-Md.) July 20, 1936– ; House 1977–1987; Senate 1987– .
Miller, Brad (D-N.C.) May 19, 1953– ; House 2003–2013.
Miller, Candice S. (R-Mich.) May 7, 1954– ; House 2003– .
Miller, Gary (R-Calif.) October 16, 1948– ; House 1999– .
Miller, George (D-Calif.) May 17, 1945– ; House 1975– .
Miller, Jeff (R-Fla.) June 27, 1959– ; House October 23, 2001– .
Minnick, Walt (D-Idaho) September 20, 1942– ; House 2009–2011.
Mitchell, Harry E. (D-Ariz.) July 18, 1940– ; House 2007–2011.
Mollohan, Alan B. (D-W.Va.) May 14, 1943– ; House 1983–2011.
Moore, Dennis (D-Kan.) November 8, 1945– ; House 1999–2011.
Moore, Gwen (D-Wis.) April 18, 1951– ; House 2005– .
Moran, James P. (D-Va.) May 16, 1945– ; House 1991– .
Moran, Jerry (R-Kan.) May 29, 1954– ; House 1997–2011; Senate 2011– .
Mulvaney, Mick (R-S.C.) July 21, 1967– ; House 2011– .
Murkowski, Lisa (R-Alaska) May 22, 1957– ; Senate January 7, 2003– .
Murphy, Christopher S. (D-Conn.) April 20, 1947– ; House 2007–2013; Senate 2013– .
Murphy, Patrick J. (D-Pa.) October 19, 1973– ; House 2007–2011.
Murphy, Scott (D-N.Y.) January 26, 1970– ; House March 31, 2009–2011.
Murphy, Tim (R-Pa.) September 11, 1952– ; House 2003– .
Murray, Patty (D-Wash.) October 11, 1950– ; Senate 1993– .
Murtha, John P. (D-Pa.) June 17, 1932–February 8, 2010; House February 5, 1974–February 8, 2010.
Musgrave, Marilyn (R-Colo.) January 27, 1949– ; House 2003– .
Myrick, Sue (R-N.C.) August 1, 1941– ; House 1995–2013.

N

Nadler, Jerrold (D-N.Y.) June 13, 1947– ; House November 4, 1992– .
Napolitano, Grace Flores (D-Calif.) December 4, 1936– ; House 1999– .
Neal, Richard E. (D-Mass.) February 14, 1949– ; House 1989– .
Nelson, Ben (D-Neb.) May 17, 1941– ; Senate 2001–2013; Gov. 1991–1999.
Nelson, Bill (D-Fla.) September 29, 1942– ; House 1979–1991; Senate 2001– .
Neugebauer, Randy (R-Texas) December 24, 1949– ; House June 5, 2003– .
Noem, Kristi (R-S.D.) November 30, 1971– ; House 2011– .
Norton, Eleanor Holmes (D-D.C.) June 13, 1937– ; House (Delegate) 1991– .
Nugent, Richard (R-Fla.) May 26, 1951– ; House 2011– .
Nunes, Devin (R-Calif.) October 1, 1973– ; House 2003– .
Nunnelee, Alan (R-Miss.) October 9, 1958– ; House 2011– .
Nye, Glenn (D-Va.) September 9, 1974– ; House 2009–2011.

O

Oberstar, James L. (D-Minn.) September 10, 1934– ; House 1975–2011.
Obey, David R. (D-Wis.) October 3, 1938– ; House April 1, 1969–2011.
Olson, Pete (R-Texas) December 9, 1962– ; House 2009– .
Olver, John W. (D-Mass.) September 3, 1936– ; House June 18, 1991–2013.
Ortiz, Solomon P. (D-Texas) June 3, 1937– ; House 1983–2011.
Osborne, Tom (R-Neb.) February 23, 1937– ; House 2001–2007.
Otter, C. L. "Butch" (R-Idaho) May 3, 1942– ; House 2001–2007. Gov. 2007– .
Owens, William (D-N.Y.) January 29, 1949– ; House November 3, 2009– .
Oxley, Michael G. (R-Ohio) February 11, 1944– ; House June 25, 1981–2007.

P

Palazzo, Steven (R-Miss.) February 21, 1970– ; House 2011– .
Pallone, Frank Jr. (D-N.J.) October 30, 1951– ; House November 8, 1988– .
Pascrell, Bill Jr. (D-N.J.) January 25, 1937– ; House 1997– .
Pastor, Ed (D-Ariz.) June 28, 1943– ; House October 3, 1991– .
Paul, Rand (R-Ky.) January 7, 1963– ; Senate 2011– .
Paul, Ron (R-Texas) August 20, 1935– ; House 1976–1977; 1979–1985; 1997–2013.
Paulsen, Erik (D-Minn.) May 14, 1965– ; House 2009– .
Payne, Donald M. (D-N.J.) July 16, 1934–March 6, 2012; House 1989–March 6, 2012.
Payne, Donald M. Jr. (D-N.J.) December 17, 1958– ; House November 6, 2012– .
Pearce, Stevan (R-N.M.) August 24, 1947– ; House 2003–2009; 2011– .
Pelosi, Nancy (D-Calif.) March 26, 1940; House June 9, 1987– ; House minority leader 2003–2007; Speaker 2007–2011; minority leader 2011– .
Pence, Mike (R-Ind.) June 7, 1959– ; House 2001–2013.
Perlmutter, Ed (D-Colo.) May 1, 1953– ; House 2007– .
Perriello, Thomas S. P. (D-Va.) October 9, 1974– ; House 2009–2011.
Peters, Gary (D-Mich.) December 1, 1958– ; House 2009– .
Peterson, Collin C. (D-Minn.) June 29, 1944– ; House 1991– .
Petri, Thomas E. (R-Wis.) May 28, 1940– ; House April 3, 1979– .
Pingree, Chellie (D-Maine) April 2, 1955– ; House 2009– .
Pitts, Joseph R. (R-Pa.) October 10, 1939– ; House 1997– .
Platts, Todd (R-Pa.) March 5, 1962– ; House 2001–2013.
Poe, Ted (R-Texas) September 10, 1948– ; House 2005– .
Polis, Jared (D-Colo.) May 12, 1975– ; Senate 2009– .
Pomeroy, Earl (D-N.D.) September 2, 1952– ; House 1993–2011.
Pompeo, Mike (R-Kan.) December 30, 1963– ; House 2011– .
Porter, Jon (R-Nev.) May 16, 1955– ; House 2003– .
Portman, Rob (R-Ohio) December 19, 1955– ; House May 5, 1993–April 29, 2005; Senate 2011– .
Posey, Bill (R-Fla.) December 19, 1947– ; House 2009– .
Price, David (D-N.C.) August 17, 1940– ; House 1987–1995, 1997– .
Pryor, Mark (D-Ark.) January 10, 1963– ; Senate 2003– .
Putnam, Adam (R-Fla.) July 31, 1974– ; House 2001–2011.

Q

Quayle, Ben (R-Ariz.) November 3, 1976–: House 2011–2013.
Quigley, Mike (D-N.Y.) October 17, 1958– ; House April 7, 2009– .

R

Radanovich, George P. (R-Calif.) June 20, 1955– ; House 1995–2011.
Rahall, Nick J. II (D-W.Va.) May 20, 1949– ; House 1977– .
Rangel, Charles B. (D-N.Y.) June 11, 1930– ; House 1971– .
Reed, Jack (D-R.I.) November 12, 1949– ; House 1991–1997; Senate 1997– .
Reed, Thomas W. II (R-N.Y.) November 18, 1971– ; House November 2, 2010– .
Rehberg, Denny (R-Mont.) October 5, 1955– ; House 2001–2013.
Reichert, Dave (R-Wash.) August 29, 1950– ; House 2005– .
Reid, Harry (D-Nev.) December 2, 1939– ; House 1983–1987; Senate 1987– ; Senate

minority leader 2005–2007; majority leader 2007– .

Renacci, Jim (R-Ohio) December 3, 1938– ; House 2011– .

Reyes, Silvestre (D-Texas) November 10, 1944– ; House 1997–2013.

Ribble, Reid (R-Wis.) April 5, 1966– ; House 2011– .

Richardson, Laura (D-Calif.) April 14, 1962– ; House August 21, 2007–2013.

Richmond, Cedric L. (D-La.) September 13, 1973– ; House 2011– .

Rigell, Scott (R-Va.) May 28, 1960– ; House 2011– .

Risch, James (R-Idaho) May 3, 1943; Senate 2009– ; Gov. 2007–2009.

Rivera, David (R-Fla.) September 15, 1965– ; House 2011–2013.

Roberts, Pat (R-Kan.) April 20, 1936– ; House 1981–1997; Senate 1997– .

Roby, Martha (R-Ala.) July 27, 1976– ; House 2011– .

Rockefeller, John D. IV (D-W.Va.) June 18, 1937– ; Senate January 15, 1985– ; Gov. 1977–1985.

Rodriguez, Ciro D. (D-Texas) December 9, 1946– ; House April 17, 1997–2005; 2007–2011.

Roe, David P. (R-Tenn.) July 21, 1945-; House 2009– .

Rogers, Harold (R-Ky.) December 31, 1937– ; House 1981– .

Rogers, Mike (R-Mich.) June 2, 1963– ; House 2001– .

Rogers, Mike D. (R-Ala.) July 16, 1958– ; House 2003– .

Rohrabacher, Dana (R-Calif.) June 21, 1947– ; House 1989– .

Rokita, Todd (R-Ind.) Feb, 9, 1970– ; House 2011– .

Rooney, Thomas (R-Fla.) November 21, 1970– ; House 2009– .

Roskam, Peter (R-Ill.) September 13, 1961– ; House 2007– .

Ros-Lehtinen, Ileana (R-Fla.) July 15, 1952– ; House 1989– .

Ross, Dennis (R-Fla.) October 18, 1959– ; House 2011– .

Ross, Mike (D-Ark.) August 2, 1961– ; House 2001–2013.

Rothman, Steven R. (D-N.J.) October 14, 1952– ; House 1997–2013.

Roybal-Allard, Lucille (D-Calif.) June 12, 1941– ; House 1993– .

Royce, Ed (R-Calif.) October 12, 1951– ; House 1993– .

Rubio, Marco (R-Fla.) May 28, 1971– ; Senate 2011– .

Runyan, Jon (R-N.J.) November 27, 1973– ; House 2011– .

Ruppersberger, C. A. Dutch (D-Md.) January 31, 1946– ; House 2003– .

Rush, Bobby L. (D-Ill.) November 23, 1946– ; House 1993– .

Ryan, Paul D. (R-Wis.) January 29, 1970– ; House 1999– .

Ryan, Tim (D-Ohio) July 16, 1973– ; House 2003– .

S

Salazar, John (D-Colo.) July 21, 1953– ; House 2005–2011

Salazar, Ken (D-Colo.) March 2, 1955– ; Senate 2007–January 20, 2009.

Sali, Bill (R-Idaho) February 17, 1954– ; House 2007– .

Sanchez, Linda T. (D-Calif.) January 28, 1969– ; House 2003– .

Sanchez, Loretta (D-Calif.) January 7, 1960– ; House 1997– .

Sanders, Bernard (I-Vt.) September 8, 1941– ; House 1991–2007; Senate 2007– .

Sarbanes, John (D-Md.) May 22, 1961– ; House 2007– .

Scalise, Steve (R-La.) October 6, 1965– ; House May 3, 2008– .

Schakowsky, Janice D. "Jan" (D-Ill.) May 26, 1944– ; House 1999– .

Schatz, Brian (D-Hawaii) October 20, 1972– ; Senate December 27, 2012– .

Schauer, Mark (D-Mich.) October 2, 1961– ; House 2009–2011.

Schiff, Adam (D-Calif.) June 22, 1960– ; House 2001– .

Schilling, Bobby (R-Ill.) January 23, 1964– ; House 2011–2013.

Schmidt, Jean (R-Ohio) November 29, 1951; House September 6, 2005–2013.

Schock, Aaron (R-Ill.) May 28, 1981– ; House 2009– .

Schrader, Kurt (D-Ore.) October 19, 1951– ; House 2009– .

Schumer, Charles E. (D-N.Y.) November 23, 1950– ; House 1981–1999; Senate 1999– .

Schwartz, Allyson Y. (D-Pa.) October 3, 1948– ; House 2005– .

Schweikert, David (R-Ariz.) March 3, 1962– ; House 2011– .

Scott, Austin (R-Ga.) December 10, 1969– ; House 2011– .

Scott, David (D-Ga.) June 27, 1946– ; House 2003– .

Scott, Robert C. (D-Va.) April 30, 1947– ; House 1993– .

Scott, Tim (R-S.C.) September 19, 1965– ; House 2011– .

Sensenbrenner, F. James Jr. (R-Wis.) June 14, 1943– ; House 1979– .

Serrano, Jose E. (D-N.Y.) October 24, 1943– ; House March 28, 1990– .

Sessions, Jeff (R-Ala.) December 24, 1946– ; Senate 1997– .

Sessions, Pete (R-Texas) March 22, 1955– ; House 1997– .

Sestak, Joe (D-Pa.) December 12, 1951– ; House 2007–2011.

Sewell, Terri A. (D-Ala.) January 1, 1965– ; House 2011– .

Shadegg, John (R-Ariz.) October 22, 1949– ; House 1995–2011.

Shaheen, Jeanne (D-N.H.) January 28, 1947– ; Senate 2009– ; Gov. 1997–2003.

Shea-Porter, Carol (D-N.H.) December 2, 1952– ; House 2007–2011; 2013– .

Shelby, Richard C. (R-Ala.) May 6, 1934– ; House 1979–1987; Senate 1987– (1979–November 19, 1994, Democrat).

Sherman, Brad (D-Calif.) October 24, 1954– ; House 1997– .

Shimkus, John M. (R-Ill.) February 21, 1958– ; House 1997– .

Shuler, Heath (D-N.C.) December 31, 1971– ; House 2007–2013.

Shuster, Bill (R-Pa.) January 10, 1961– ; House May 17, 2001– .

Simpson, Mike (R-Idaho) September 8, 1950– ; House 1999– .

Sires, Albio (D-N.J.) January 26, 1951– ; House November 13, 2006– .

Skelton, Ike (D-Mo.) December 20, 1931– ; House 1977–2011.

Slaughter, Louise M. (D-N.Y.) August 14, 1929– ; House 1987– .

Smith, Adam (D-Wash.) June 15, 1965– ; House 1997– .

Smith, Adrian (R-Neb.) December 19, 1970– ; House 2007– .

Smith, Christopher H. (R-N.J.) March 4, 1953– ; House 1981– .

Smith, Lamar (R-Texas) November 19, 1947– ; House 1987– .

Snowe, Olympia J. (wife of John R. McKernan Jr.) (R-Maine) February 21, 1947– ; House 1979–1995; Senate 1995–2013.

Snyder, Vic (D-Ark.) September 27, 1947– ; House 1997–2011.

Solis, Hilda L. (D-Calif.) October 20, 1957– ; House 2001–February 24, 2009.

Souder, Mark (R-Ind.) July 18, 1950– ; House 1995–May 21, 2010.

Southerland, Steve (R-Fla.) October 10, 1965– ; House 2011– .

Space, Zack (D-Ohio) January 27, 1961– ; House 2005–2011.

Specter, Arlen (D-Pa.) February 12, 1930–October 14, 2012; Senate 1981–2011 (1981–April 30, 2009 Republican)

Speier, Jackie (D-Calif.) May 14, 1950; House April 10, 2008– .

Spratt, John M. Jr. (D-S.C.) November 1, 1942– ; House 1983–2011.

Stabenow, Debbie (D-Mich.) April 29, 1950– ; House 1997–2001; Senate 2001– .

Stark, Fortney "Pete" (D-Calif.) November 11, 1931– ; House 1973–2013.

Stearns, Clifford B. (R-Fla.) April 16, 1941– ; House 1989–2013.

Stivers, Steve (R-Ohio) March 24, 1965– ; House 2011– .

Stupak, Bart (D-Mich.) February 29, 1952– ; House 1993–2011.

Stutzman, Marlin (R-Ind.) August 31, 1976– ; House November 2, 2010– .

Sullivan, John (R-Okla.) January 1, 1965– ; House February 27, 2002–2013.

Sutton, Betty (D-Ohio) July 31, 1963– ; House 2007–2013.

T

Tanner, John (D-Tenn.) September 22, 1944– ; House 1989–2011.

Tauscher, Ellen O. (D-Calif.) November 15, 1951– ; House 1997–June 26, 2009.

Taylor, Gene (D-Miss.) September 17, 1953– ; House October 24, 1989–2011.

Teague, Harry (D-N.M.) June 29, 1949– ; House 2009–2011.

Terry, Lee (R-Neb.) January 29, 1962– ; House 1999– .

Tester, Jon (D-Mont.) August 21, 1956– ; Senate 2007– .

Thompson, Bennie (D-Miss.) January 28, 1948– ; House April 20, 1993– .

Thompson, Glenn (R-Pa.) July 27, 1959– ; House 2009– .

Thompson, Mike (D-Calif.) January 24, 1951– ; House 1999– .

Thornberry, William M. "Mac" (R-Texas) July 15, 1958– ; House 1995– .

Thune, John (R-S.D.) January 7, 1961– ; House 1997–2003; Senate 2005– .

Tiahrt, Todd (R-Kan.) June 15, 1951– ; House 1995–2011.

Tiberi, Pat (R-Ohio) October 21, 1962– ; House 2001– .

Tierney, John F. (D-Mass.) September 18, 1951– ; House 1997– .

Tipton, Scott (R-Colo.) November 9, 1956– ; House 2011– .

Titus, Dina (D-Nev.) May 23, 1950– ; House 2009–2011; 2013– .

Tonko, Paul (D-N.Y.) June 18, 1949– ; House 2009– .

Toomey, Patrick J. (R-Pa.) November 17, 1961– ; House 1999–2005; Senate 2011– .

Towns, Edolphus (D-N.Y.) July 21, 1934– ; House 1983–2013.

Tsongas, Niki (D-Mass.) April 26, 1946– ; House October 16, 2007– .

Turner, Michael R. (R-Ohio) January 11, 1960– ; House 2003– .

Turner, Robert L. (R-N.Y.) May 2, 1941– ; House September 13, 2011–2013.

U

Udall, Mark (D-Colo.) July 18, 1950– ; House 1999–2009; Senate 2009– .

Udall, Tom (D-N.M.) May 18, 1948– ; House 1999–2009; Senate 2009– .

Upton, Fred (R-Mich.) April 23, 1953– ; House 1987– .

V

Van Hollen, Chris (D-Md.) January 10, 1959– ; House 2003– .

Velázquez, Nydia M. (D-N.Y.) March 22, 1953– ; House 1993– .

Visclosky, Peter J. (D-Ind.) August 13, 1949– ; House 1985– .

Vitter, David (R-La.) May 3, 1961– ; House June 8, 1999–2005; Senate 2005– .

Voinovich, George V. (R-Ohio) July 15, 1936– ; Senate 1999–2011; Gov. 1991–1998.

W

Walberg, Tim (R-Mich.) April 12, 1951– ; House 2007–2009; 2011– .

Walden, Greg (R-Ore.) January 10, 1957– ; House 1999– .

Walsh, Joe (R-Ill.) December 27, 1961– ; House 2011–2013

Walz, Tim (D-Minn.) April 6, 1964– ; House 2007– .

Wamp, Zach (R-Tenn.) October 28, 1957– ; House 1995–2011.

Warner, Mark (D-Va.) December 15, 1954– ; Senate 2009 –; Gov. 2002–2006.

Wasserman Schultz, Debbie (D-Fla.) September 27, 1966– ; House 2005– .

Waters, Maxine (D-Calif.) August 15, 1938– ; House 1991– .

Watson, Diane (D-Calif.) November 12, 1933– ; House June 7, 2001–2011.

Watt, Melvin (D-N.C.) August 26, 1945– ; House 1993– .

Waxman, Henry A. (D-Calif.) September 12, 1939– ; House 1975– .

Webb, Jim (D-Va.) February 9, 1946– ; Senate 2007–2013.

Webster, Daniel (R-Fla.) April 27, 1949– ; House 2011– .

Weiner, Anthony (D-N.Y.) September 4, 1964– ; House 1999–June 22, 2011.

Welch, Peter (D-Vt.) May 2, 1947– ; House 2007– .

West, Allen B. (R-Fla.) February 7, 1961– ; House 2011–2013.

Westmoreland, Lynn (R-Ga.) April 2, 1950– ; House 2005– .

Wexler, Robert (D-Fla.) January 2, 1961– ; House 1997–January 4, 2010.

Whitehouse, Sheldon (D-R.I.) October 20, 1955– ; Senate 2007– .

Whitfield, Edward (R-Ky.) May 25, 1943– ; House 1995– .

Wicker, Roger (R-Miss.) July 5, 1951– ; House 1995–December 31, 2007; Senate December 31, 2007– .

Wilson, Charlie (D-Ohio) January 18, 1943– ; House 2007–2011.

Wilson, Frederica S. (D-Fla.) November 5, 1942– ; House 2011– .

Wilson, Joe (R-S.C.) July 31, 1947– ; House December 19, 2001– .

Wittman, Rob (R-Va.) February 3, 1959– ; House December 11, 2007– .

Wolf, Frank R. (R-Va.) January 30, 1939– ; House 1981– .

Womack, Steve (R-Ark.) February 18, 1957– ; House 2011– .

Woodall, Rob (R-Ga.) February 11, 1970– ; House 2011– .

Woolsey, Lynn (D-Calif.) November 3, 1937– ; House 1993–2013.

Wu, David (R-Ore.) April 8, 1955– ; House 1999–August 3, 2011.

Wyden, Ron (D-Ore.) May 3, 1949– ; House 1981–February 5, 1996; Senate February 6, 1996– .

Y

Yarmuth, John (D-Ky.) Nov 4, 1947– ; House 2007– .

Yoder, Kevin (R-Kan.) January 8, 1976– ; House 2011– .

Young, C. W. "Bill" (R-Fla.) December 16, 1930– ; House 1971– .

Young, Don (R-Alaska) June 9, 1933– ; House March 6, 1973– .

Young, Todd (R-Ind.) August 24, 1972– ; House 2011– .

Congressional Leadership and Committees, 111th and 112th Congresses

Senate Leadership

President Pro Tempore, 111th Congress: Robert C. Byrd, W. Va.; Daniel K. Inouye, Hawaii

President Pro Tempore, 112th Congress: Daniel K. Inouye, Hawaii; Patrick J. Leahy, Vt.

Democratic Leaders

Majority Floor Leader 111th Congress and 112th Congress: Harry M. Reid, Nev.

Assistant Floor Leader 111th Congress and 112th Congress: Richard J. Durbin, Ill.

Chief Deputy Whip 111th Congress and 112th Congress: Barbara Boxer, Calif.

Republican Leaders

Minority Floor Leader 111th Congress and 112th Congress: Mitch McConnell, Ky.

Minority Whip 111th Congress and 112th Congress: Jon Kyl, Ariz.

Senate Political Committees

Democratic Policy Committee—Byron L. Dorgan, N.D., chair (111th Congress and 112th Congress).

Democratic Senatorial Campaign Committee—Robert Menendez, N.J., chair (111th Congress and 112th Congress).

Democratic Steering and Outreach Committee—Debbie Stabenow, Mich., chair (111th Congress and 112th Congress).

Democratic Communications Center—Harry Reid, Nev., chair (111th Congress and 112th Congress).

National Republican Senatorial Committee—John Cornyn, Texas, chair (111th Congress and 112th Congress).

Republican Conference—Lamar Alexander, Tenn., chair (111th Congress and 112th Congress).

Republican Policy Committee—John Ensign, Nev., chair (111th Congress); John Thune, S.D. chair (112th Congress).

House Leadership

Speaker of the House:

Nancy Pelosi, D, Calif. 111th Congress
John A. Boehner, R, Ohio, 112th Congress

Democratic Leaders 111th Congress:

Steny H. Hoyer, Md., Majority Leader
James E. Clyburn, S.C., Majority Whip
John Lewis, Ga., Senior Chief Deputy Majority Whip

Democratic Leaders 112th Congress:

Nancy Pelosi, Calif., Minority Leader
Steny H. Hoyer, Md., Minority Whip
James E. Clyburn, S.C., Assistant Leader

Republican Leaders 111th Congress:

John A. Boehner, Ohio, Minority Leader
Eric I. Cantor, Va., Minority Whip

Republican Leaders 112th Congress:

Eric I. Cantor, Va., Majority Leader
Kevin McCarthy, Calif., Majority Whip
Peter Roskam, Ill., Chief Deputy Whip

Political Committees

Democratic Congressional Campaign Committee—Chris Van Hollen, Md., chair (111th Congress); Steve Israel, N.Y., chair (112th Congress).

Democratic Steering and Policy Committees—Nancy Pelosi, Calif., co-chair (both committees); Rosa L. DeLauro, Conn., co-chair (Steering, 111th Congress); and George Mill, Calif., co-chair (Policy, 111th Congress). Committee reorganized in 112th Congress.

Democratic Caucus—John B. Larson, Conn., chair (112th Congress).

Democratic Steering and Outreach Committee—Mark Begich, Ark., chair (112th Congress).

National Republican Congressional Committee—Pete Sessions, Texas (111th Congress and 112th Congress).

Republican Conference—Mike Pence, Ind. (111th Congress); John Hensarling, Texas (112th Congress).

Republican Policy Committee—Thaddeus McCotter, Mich., chair (111th Congress); Tom Price, Ga., chair (112th Congress).

Republican Steering Committee—John A. Boehner, Ohio (111th Congress and 112th Congress).

Congressional Committees

Following is a list of House and Senate leaders and congressional committees and subcommittees for the 111th and 112th Congresses. The committee listings are as of the beginning of both congresses. Some changes, usually because of resignations or death, occurred later. The House listings are divided between the 111th Congress and the 112th Congress because Republicans won control of the House in the 2010 elections; Democrats controlled the House for the 111th Congress. Democrats controlled the Senate in both congresses.

Committee jurisdictions, party ratios, committee chairs and the dates of their service in that capacity, ranking minority members (in italics), and subcommittee chairs are included. Political and joint committees also are listed.

Senate Committees

AGRICULTURE, NUTRITION, AND FORESTRY

Agriculture in general; animal industry and diseases; crop insurance and soil conservation; farm credit and farm security; food from fresh waters; food stamp programs; forestry in general; home economics; human nutrition; inspection of livestock, meat, and agricultural products; pests and pesticides; plant industry, soils, and agricultural engineering; rural development, rural electrification, and watersheds; school nutrition programs.

D 12–R 9 *(111th Congress)*

Blanche L. Lincoln, Ark.
Saxby Chambliss, Ga.

Domestic and Foreign Marketing, Inspection, and Plan and Animal Health—Kirsten E. Gillibrand, N.Y.

Energy, Science, and Technology—Michael F. Bennett, Col
Hunger, Nutrition, and Family Farms—Sherrod Brown, Ohio.
Nutrition and Food Assistance, Sustainable and Organic Agriculture, and General Legislation—Production, Income Protection, and Price Support—Robert P. Casey Jr., Pa.
Rural Revitalization, Conservation, Forestry, and Credit—Debbie Stabenow, Mich.

D 11–R 10 *(112th Congress)*

Debbie Stabenow, Mich.
Pat Roberts, Kan.

Livestock, Dairy, Poultry, Marketing, and Agriculture Security—Kirsten E. Gillibrand, N.Y.
Conservation, Forestry, and Natural Resources—Michael F. Bennett, Colo
Jobs, Rural Economic Growth, and Energy Innovation—Sherrod Brown, Ohio.
Nutrition and Food Assistance, Sustainable and Organic Agriculture, and General Legislation—Commodities, Markets, Trade, and Risk Management—Ben Nelson, Neb.
Nutrition, Specialty Crops, Food and Agricultural Research—Robert P. Casey Jr., Pa.

APPROPRIATIONS

Appropriation of revenue; rescission of appropriations; new spending authority under the Congressional Budget Act.

D 18–R 12 *(111th Congress)*

Daniel K. Inouye, Hawaii
Thd Cochran, Miss.

Agriculture, Rural Development, Food and Drug Administration—Herb Kohl, Wis.
Commerce, Justice, Science—Barbara Mikulski, Md.
Defense—Daniel K. Inouye, Hawaii
Energy and Water Development—Bryon L. Dorgan, N.D.
Financial Services and General Government—Richard J. Durbin, Ill.
Homeland Security—Robert C. Byrd, W.Va.
Interior and Environment—Diane Feinstein, Calif.
Labor, Health and Human Services, Education—Tom Harkin, Iowa
Legislative Branch—Ben Nelson, Neb.
Military Construction, Veterans Affairs—Tim Johnson, S.D.
State, Foreign Operations, and Related Programs—Patrick J. Leahy, Vt.
Transportation, Housing, and Urban Development—Patty Murray, Wash.

D 16–R 14 *(112th Congress)*

Daniel K. Inouye, Hawaii
That Cochran, Miss.

Agriculture, Rural Development, Food and Drug Administration—Herb Kohl, Wis.
Commerce, Justice, Science—Barbara Mikulski, Md.
Defense—Daniel K. Inouye, Hawaii
Energy and Water Development—Diane Feinstein, Calif.
Financial Services and General Government—Richard J. Durbin, Ill.
Homeland Security—Mary Landrieu, La.
Interior and Environment—Harry Reid, Nev.
Labor, Health and Human Services, Education—Tom Harkin, Iowa
Legislative Branch—Ben Nelson, Neb.
Military Construction, Veterans Affaires—Tim Johnson, S.D.
State, Foreign Operations, and Related Programs—Patrick J. Leahy, Vt.
Transportation, Housing, and Urban Development—Patty Murray, Wash.

ARMED SERVICES

Defense and defense policy generally; aeronautical and space activities peculiar to or primarily associated with the development of weapons systems or military operations; maintenance and operation of the Panama Canal, including the Canal Zone; military research and development; national security aspects of nuclear energy; naval petroleum reserves (except Alaska); armed forces generally; Selective Service System; strategic and critical materials.

D 15–R 11 *(111th Congress)*

Carl Levin, Mich.
John McCain, Ariz.

Airland Forces— Joseph I. Lieberman, Conn.
Emerging Threats and Capabilities—Bill Nelson, Fla.
Personnel—Jim Webb, Va.
Readiness and Management Support—Evan Bayh, Ind.
Seapower—Harry Reid, Nev.
Strategic Forces—Ben Nelson, Neb.

D 14–R 12 *(112th Congress)*

Carl Levin, Mich.
John McCain, Ariz.

Airland Forces—Joseph I. Lieberman, Conn.
Emerging Threats and Capabilities—Kay R. Hagan, N.C.
Personnel—Jim Webb, Va.
Readiness and Management Support—Claire McCaskill, Mo.
Seapower—Jack Reid, R.I.
Strategic Forces—Ben Nelson, Neb.

BANKING, HOUSING, AND URBAN AFFAIRS

Banks, banking, and financial institutions; price controls; deposit insurance; economic stabilization and growth; defense production; export and foreign trade promotion; export controls; federal monetary policy, including Federal Reserve System; financial aid to commerce and industry; issuance and redemption of notes; money and credit, including currency and coinage; nursing home construction; public and private housing, including veterans' housing; renegotiation of government contracts; urban development and mass transit; international economic policy.

D 13–R 10 *(111th Congress)*

Christopher J. Dodd, Conn.
Richard C. Shelby, Ala.

Economic Policy—Sherrod Brown, Ohio
Financial Institutions—Tim Johnson, S.D.
Housing, Transportation, and Community Development—Robert Menendez, N.J.
Security and International Trade and Finance—Evan Bayh
Securities, Insurance, and Investment—Jack Reed

D 12–R 10 *(112th Congress)*

Tim Johnson, S.D.
Richard C. Shelby, Ala.

Economic Policy—Jon Tester, Mont.
Financial Institutions and Consumer Protection—Sherrod Brown, Ohio
Housing, Transportation, and Community Development—Robert Menendez, N.J.
Security and International Trade and Finance—Mark R. Warner, Va.
Securities, Insurance, and Investment—Jack Reed, R.I.

BUDGET

Federal budget generally; concurrent budget resolutions; Congressional Budget Office.

D 13–R 10 *(111th Congress)*

Kent Conrad, N.D.
Judd Gregg, N.H.

D 13–R 10 *(112th Congress)*

Kent Conrad, N.D.
Jeff Sessions, Ala.

No standing subcommittees.

COMMERCE, SCIENCE, AND TRANSPORTATION

Interstate commerce and transportation generally; Coast Guard; coastal zone management; communications; highway safety; inland waterways, except construction; marine fisheries; Merchant Marine and navigation; nonmilitary aeronautical and space sciences; oceans, weather, and atmospheric activities; interoceanic canals generally; regulation of consumer products and services; science, engineering, and technology research, development and policy; sports; standards and measurement; transportation and commerce aspects of outer continental shelf lands.

D 14–R 11 *(111th Congress)*

John D. Rockefeller IV, W.Va.
Kay Bailey Hutchison, Texas

Aviation Operations, Safety, and Security—Byron L. Dorgan, N.D.
Communications and Technology—John F. Kerry, Mass.
Competiveness, Innovation, and Export Promotion—Amy Klobuchar, Minn.
Consumer Protection, Product Safety and Insurance—Mark L. Pryor, Ark.
Oceans, Atmosphere, Fisheries, and Coast Guard—Maria Cantwell, Wash.
Science and Space—Bill Nelson, Fla.
Surface Transportation and Merchant Marine—Frank R. Lautenberg, N.J.

D 13–R 12 *(112th Congress)*

John D. Rockefeller IV, W.Va.
Kay Bailey Hutchison, Texas

Aviation Operations, Safety, and Security—Maria Cantwell, Wash.
Communications, Technology, and the Internet—John F. Kerry, Mass.
Competiveness, Innovation, and Export Promotion—Amy Klobuchar, Minn.
Consumer Protection, Product Safety and Insurance—Mark L. Pryor, Ark.
Oceans, Atmosphere, Fisheries, and Coast Guard—Mark Begich, Alaska
Science and Space—Bill Nelson, Fla.
Surface Transportation and Merchant Marine Infrastructure, Safety, and Security—Frank R. Lautenberg, N.J.

ENERGY AND NATURAL RESOURCES

Energy policy, regulation, conservation, research, and development; coal; energy-related aspects of deep-water ports; hydroelectric power, irrigation, and reclamation; mines, mining, and minerals generally; national parks, recreation areas, wilderness areas, wild and scenic rivers, historic sites, military parks, and battlefields; naval petroleum reserves in Alaska; nonmilitary development of nuclear energy; oil and gas production and distribution; public lands and forests; solar energy systems; territorial possessions of the United States.

D 13–R 10 *(111th Congress)*

Jeff Bingaman, N.M.
Lisa Murkowski, Alaska

Energy—Maria Cantwell, Wash.
Public Lands and Forests—Ron Wyden, Ore.
National Parks—Mark Udall, Colo.
Water and Power—Debbie Stabenow, Mich.

D 12–R 10 *(112th Congress)*

Jeff Bingaman, N.M.
Lisa Murkowski, Alaska

Energy—Maria Cantwell, Wash.
Public Lands and Forests— Ron Wyden, Ore.
National Parks—Mark Udall, Colo.
Water and Power—Jeanne Shaheen, N.H.

ENVIRONMENT AND PUBLIC WORKS

Environmental policy, research, and development; air, water, and noise pollution; construction and maintenance of highways; environmental aspects of outer continental shelf lands; environmental effects of toxic substances other than pesticides; fisheries and wildlife; flood control and improvements of rivers and harbors; nonmilitary environmental regulation and control of nuclear energy; ocean dumping; public buildings and grounds;

public works, bridges, and dams; regional economic development; solid waste disposal and recycling; water resources.

D 12–R 7 *(111th Congress)*

Barbara Boxer, Calif.
James M. Inhofe. Okla.

Children's Health—Amy Klobuchar, Minn.
Clean Air and Nuclear Safety—Thomas R. Carper, Del.
Green Jobs and the New Economy—Bernard Sanders, Vt.
Oversight—Sheldon Whitehouse, R.I.
Superfund, Toxics and Environmental Health—Frank R. Lautenberg, N.J.
Transportation and Infrastructure—Max Baucus, Mont.
Water and Wildlife—Benjamin L. Cardin, Md.

D 10–R 8 *(112th Congress)*

Barbara Boxer, Calif.
James M. Inhofe. Okla.

Children's Health and Environmental Responsibility—Tom Udall, N.M.
Clean Air and Nuclear Safety—Thomas R. Carper, Del.
Green Jobs and the New Economy—Bernard Sanders, Vt.
Oversight—Sheldon Whitehouse, R.I.
Superfund, Toxics and Environmental Health—Frank R. Lautenberg, N.J.
Transportation and Infrastructure—Max Baucus, Mont.
Water and Wildlife—Benjamin L. Cardin, Md.

FINANCE

Revenue measures generally; taxes; tariffs and import quotas; reciprocal trade agreements; customs; revenue sharing; federal debt limit; Social Security; health programs financed by taxes or trust funds.

D 13–R 10 *(111th Congress)*

Max Baucus, Mont.
Charles E. Grassley, Iowa

Energy, Natural Resources, and Infrastructure—Jeff Bingaman, N.M.
Health Care—John D. Rockefeller IV, W.Va.
International Trade, Customs, and Global Competitiveness—Ron Wyden, Ore.
Social Security, Pensions, and Family Policy—Blanche Lincoln, Ark.
Taxation, IRS Oversight, and Long-term Growth—Kent Conrad, N.D.

D 13–R 11 *(112th Congress)*

Max Baucus, Mont.
Orrin G. Hatch, Utah

Energy, Natural Resources, and Infrastructure—Jeff Bingaman, N.M.
Fiscal Responsibility and Economic Growth—Bill Nelson, Fla.
Health Care—John D. Rockefeller IV, W.Va.
International Trade, Customs, and Global Competitiveness—Ron Wyden, Ore.
Social Security, Pensions, and Family Policy—Debbie Stabenow, Mich.
Taxation and IRS Oversight—Kent Conrad, N.D.

FOREIGN RELATIONS

Relations of the United States with foreign nations generally; treaties; foreign economic, military, technical, and humanitarian assistance; foreign loans; diplomatic service; International Red Cross; international aspects of nuclear energy; International Monetary Fund; intervention abroad and declarations of war; foreign trade; national security; oceans and international environmental and scientific affairs; protection of U.S. citizens abroad; United Nations; World Bank and other development assistance organizations.

D 11–R 8 *(111th Congress)*

John F. Kerry, Mass.
Richard G. Lugar, Ind.

African Affairs—Russell D. Feingold, Wis.
East Asian and Pacific Affairs—Jim Webb, Va.
European Affairs—Jeanne Shaheen, N.H.
International Development and Foreign Assistance, Economic Affairs and International Environmental Protection—Robert Menendez, N.J.
International Operations and Organizations, Human Rights, Democracy, Global Women's Issues—Barbara Boxer, Calif.
Near Eastern and South and Central Asian Affairs—Robert P. Casey Jr., Pa.
Western Hemisphere, Peace Corps, and Global Narcotics Affairs—Christopher J. Dodd, Conn.

D 10–R 9 *(112th Congress)*

John F. Kerry, Mass.
Richard G. Lugar, Ind.

African Affairs—Christopher A. Coons, Del.
East Asian and Pacific Affairs—Jim Webb, Va.
European Affairs—Jeanne Shaheen, N.H.
International Development and Foreign Assistance, Economic Affairs and International Environmental Protection—Benjamin L. Cardin, Md.
International Operations and Organizations, Human Rights, Democracy, Global Women's Issues—Barbara Boxer, Calif.
Near Eastern and South and Central Asian Affairs—Robert P. Casey Jr., Pa.
Western Hemisphere, Peace Corps, and Global Narcotics Affairs—Robert Menendez, N.J.

HEALTH, EDUCATION, LABOR, AND PENSIONS

Education, labor, health, and public welfare in general; aging; arts and humanities; biomedical research and development; child labor; convict labor; domestic activities of the Red Cross; equal employment opportunity; handicapped people; labor standards and statistics; mediation and arbitration of labor disputes; occupational safety and health; private pensions; public health; railway labor and retirement; regulation of foreign laborers; student loans; wages and hours; agricultural colleges; Gallaudet University; Howard University; St. Elizabeth's Hospital in Washington, D.C.

D 13–R 10 *(111th Congress)*

Tom Harkin, Iowa
Michael B Enzi, Wyo.

Children and Families—Christopher J. Dodd, Conn.
Employment and Workplace Safety—Patty Murray, Wash.
Retirement and Aging—Barbara Mikulski, Md.

D 12–R 10 *(112th Congress)*

Tom Harkin, Iowa
Michael B Enzi, Wyo.

Children and Families—Barbara Mikulski, Md.
Employment and Workplace Safety—Patty Murray, Wash.
Primary Health and Aging—Bernard Sanders, Vt.

HOMELAND SECURITY AND GOVERNMENTAL AFFAIRS

Homeland Security Department except the Coast Guard, Transportation Security Administration, Federal Law Enforcement Training Center, Secret Service, Citizenship and Immigration Service, immigration and commercial functions of Customs and Border Protection and Immigration and Customs Enforcement, and customs revenue functions; Archives of the United States; budget and accounting measures; census and statistics; federal civil service; congressional organization; intergovernmental relations; government information; District of Columbia; organization and management of nuclear export policy; executive branch organization and reorganization; Postal Service; efficiency, economy, and effectiveness of government.

D 10–R 7 *(111th Congress)*

Joseph I. Lieberman, Conn.
Susan M Collins, Maine

Contracting Oversight—Claire McCaskill, Mo.
Disaster Recovery—Mary L. Landrieu, La.
State, Local, and Private Sector Preparedness and Integration—Mark Pryor, Ark.
Permanent Subcommittee on Investigations—Carl Levin, Mich.
Federal Financial Management, Government Information, Federal Services, and International Security—Thomas R. Carper, Del.
Oversight of Government Management, the Federal Workforce, and the District of Columbia—Daniel K. Akaka, Hawaii

D 9–R 8 *(112th Congress)*

Joseph I. Lieberman, Conn.
Susan M Collins, Maine

Contracting Oversight—Claire McCaskill, Mo.
Disaster Recovery and International Affairs—Mark Pryor, Ark.
Permanent Subcommittee on Investigations—Carl Levin, Mich.
Federal Financial Management, Government Information, Federal Services, and International Security—Thomas R. Carper, Del.
Oversight of Government Management, the Federal Workforce, and the District of Columbia—Daniel K. Akaka, Hawaii

INDIAN AFFAIRS

Problems and opportunities of Native Americans, including Native American land management and trust responsibilities, education, health, special services, loan programs, and claims against the United States.

D 9–R 6 *(111th Congress)*

Byron Dorgan, N.D.
John Barrasso, Wyo.

D 8–R 6 *(112th Congress)*

Daniel Akaka, Hawaii
John Barrasso, Wyo.

No standing subcommittees.

JUDICIARY

Civil and criminal judicial proceedings in general; national penitentiaries; bankruptcy, mutiny, espionage, and counterfeiting; civil liberties; constitutional amendments; apportionment of representatives; government information; immigration and naturalization; interstate compacts in general; claims against the United States; patents, copyrights, and trademarks; monopolies and unlawful restraints of trade; holidays and celebrations; revision and codification of the statutes of the United States; state and territorial boundary lines.

D 12–R 7 *(111th Congress)*

Patrick J. Leahy, Vt.
Jeff Sessions, Ala.

Administrative Oversight and the Courts—Sheldon Whitehouse, R.I.
Antitrust, Competition Policy, Consumer Rights—Herb Kohl, Wis.
Crime and Drugs—Arlen Specter, Pa.
Human Rights and the Law—Richard J. Durbin, Ill.
Immigration, Refugees, and Border Security—Charles E. Schumer, N.Y.
Terrorism and Homeland Security—Benjamin L. Cardin, Md.
The Constitution—Russell D. Feingold, Wis.

D 10–R 8 *(112th Congress)*

Patrick J. Leahy, Vt.
Charles E. Grassley, Iowa

Administrative Oversight and the Courts—Amy Klobuchar, Wis.

Antitrust, Competition Policy, Consumer Rights—Herb Kohl, Wis.

Constitution, Civil Rights, and Human Rights—Richard J. Durbin, Ill.

Crime and Terrorism—Sheldon Whitehouse, R.I.

Immigration, Refugees, and Border Security—Charles E. Schumer, N.Y.

Privacy, Technology, and the Law—Al Franken, Minn.

RULES AND ADMINISTRATION

Senate rules and regulations; Senate administration in general; corrupt practices; qualifications of senators; contested elections; federal elections in general; Government Printing Office; *Congressional Record*; meetings of Congress and attendance of members; presidential succession; the Capitol, congressional office buildings, the Library of Congress, the Smithsonian Institution, and the Botanic Garden; purchase of books and manuscripts and erection of monuments to the memory of individuals.

D 11–R 8 *(111th Congress)*

Charles E. Schumer N.Y.
Robert F. Bennett, Utah

D 10–R 8 *(112th Congress)*

Charles E. Schumer, N.Y.
Lamar Alexander, Tenn.

No standing subcommittees.

SELECT ETHICS

Studies and investigates standards and conduct of Senate members and employees and may recommend remedial action.

D 3–R 3 *(111th Congress)*

Barbara Boxer, Calif.
Johnny Isakson, Ga.

D 3–R 3 *(112th Congress)*
Barbara Boxer, Calif.
Johnny Isakson, Ga.

No standing subcommittees.

SELECT INTELLIGENCE

Legislative and budgetary authority over the Central Intelligence Agency, the Defense Intelligence Agency, the National Security Agency, and intelligence activities of the Federal Bureau of Investigation, and other components of the federal intelligence community.

D 8–R 7 *(111th Congress)*

Dianne Feinstein, Calif.
Chrishtopher S. Bond, Mo.

D 8–R 7 *(112th Congress)*

Dianne Feinstein, Calif.
Saxby Chambliss, Ga.

No standing subcommittees.

SMALL BUSINESS AND ENTREPRENEURSHIP

Problems of small business; Small Business Administration.

D 11–R 8 *(111th Congress)*

Mary L. Landrieu, La.
Olympia J. Snowe, Maine

D 10–R 9 *(112th Congress)*

Mary L. Landrieu, La.
Olympia J. Snowe, Maine

No standing subcommittees.

SPECIAL AGING

Problems and opportunities of older people including health, income, employment, housing, and care and assistance. Reports findings and makes recommendations to the Senate but cannot report legislation.

D 13–R 8 *(111th Congress)*

Herb Kohl, Wis.
Bob Corker, Tenn.

D 11–R 10 *(112th Congress)*

Herb Kohl, Wis.
Bob Corker, Tenn.

No standing subcommittees.

VETERANS' AFFAIRS

Veterans' measures in general; compensation; life insurance issued by the government on account of service in the armed forces; national cemeteries; pensions; readjustment benefits; veterans' hospitals, medical care and treatment; vocational rehabilitation and education; soldiers' and sailors' civil relief.

D 10–R 5 *(111th Congress)*

Daniel A. Akaka, Hawaii
Richard Burr, N.C.

D 8–R 7 *(112th Congress)*

Patty Murray, Wash.
Richard Burr, N.C.

No standing subcommittees.

House Committees

AGRICULTURE

Agriculture generally; forestry in general, and forest reserves other than those created from the public domain; adulteration of seeds, insect pests, and protection of birds and animals in forest reserves; agricultural and industrial chemistry; agricultural colleges and experiment stations; agricultural economics and research; agricultural education extension services;

agricultural production and marketing and stabilization of prices of agricultural products, and commodities (not including distribution outside the United States); animal industry and diseases of animals; commodities exchanges; crop insurance and soil conservation; dairy industry; entomology and plant quarantine; extension of farm credit and farm security; inspection of livestock, poultry, meat products, seafood and seafood products; human nutrition and home economics; plant industry, soils, and agricultural engineering; rural electrification; rural development; water conservation related to activities of the Department of Agriculture.

D 28–R 18 *(111th Congress)*

Collin C. Peterson, Minn.
Frank D. Lucas, Okla.

Conservation, Credit, Energy, and Research—Tim Holden, Pa.

Department Operations, Oversight, Nutrition and Forestry—Joe Baca, Calif.

General Farm Commodities and Risk Management—Leonard L. Boswell, Iowa

Horticulture and Organic Agriculture—Dennis A. Cardoza, Calif.

Livestock, Dairy, and Poultry—David Scott, Ga.

Rural Development, Biotechnology, Specialty Crops, and Foreign Agriculture—Mike McIntyre, N.C.

R 26–D 20 *(112th Congress)*

Fred D. Lucas, Okla.
Collin C. Peterson, Minn.

Conservation, Energy, and Forestry—Glenn Thompson, Pa.

Department Operations, Oversight, and Credit—Jeff Fortenberry, Neb.

General Farm Commodities and Risk Management—K. Michael Conaway, Texas

Livestock, Dairy, and Poultry—Tom Rooney, Fla.

Nutrition and Horticulture—Jean Schmidt, Fla.

Rural Development, Research, Biotechnology, and Foreign Agriculture-Timothy V. Johnson, Ill.

APPROPRIATIONS

Appropriation of the revenue for the support of the government; rescissions of appropriations contained in appropriation acts; transfers of unexpended balances; new spending authority under the Congressional Budget Act.

D 37–R 23 *(111th Congress)*

David R. Obey, Wis.
Jerry Lewis, Calif.

Agriculture, Rural Development, Food and Drug Administration—Rosa L. DeLauro, Conn.

Commerce, Justice, Science and Related Agencies—Alan B. Mollohan, W.Va.

Defense—Norman D. Dicks, Wash.

Energy and Water Development—Peter J. Visclosky, Ind.

Financial Services and General Government—Jose E. Serrano, N.Y.

Homeland Security—David E. Price, N.C.

Interior, Environment, and Related Agencies—James P. Moran, Va.

Labor, Health and Human Services, Education and Related Agencies—David R. Obey, Wis.

Legislative Branch—Debbie Wasserman Schultz, Fla.

Military Construction, Veterans Affairs, and Related Agencies—Chet Edwards, Texas

State, Foreign Operations, and Related Agencies—Nita M. Lowery, N.Y.

Transportation, Housing and Urban Development, and Related Agencies—John W. Olver, Mass.

R 29–D 21 *(112th Congress)*

Harold Rogers, Ky.
Norman D. Dicks, Wash.

Agriculture, Rural Development, Food and Drug Administration and Related Agencies—Jack Kingston, Ga.

Commerce, Justice, Science and Related Agencies—Frank R. Wolf, Va.

Defense—C. W. Bill Young, Fla.

Energy and Water Development and Related Agencies—Rodney P. Frelinghuysen, N.J.

Financial Services and General Government—Jo Ann Emerson, Mo.

Homeland Security—Robert B. Aderholt, Ala.

Interior, Environment, and Related Agencies—Michael K. Simpson, Idaho

Labor, Health and Human Services, Education, and Related Agencies—Denny Rehberg, Mont.

Legislative Branch—Ander Crenshaw, Fla.

Military Construction, Veterans Affairs, and Related Agencies—John Abney Culberson, Texas

State, Foreign Operations, and Related Agencies—Kay Granger, Texas

Transportation, Housing and Urban Development, and Related Agencies—Tom Latham, Iowa

ARMED SERVICES

Ammunition depots; forts; arsenals; Army, Navy, and Air Force reservations and establishments; common defense generally; conservation, development, and use of naval petroleum and oil shale reserves; Department of Defense generally, including the Departments of the Army, Navy, and Air Force generally; interoceanic canals generally; including measures relating to the maintenance, operation, and administration of interoceanic canals; Merchant Marine Academy, and state maritime academies; military applications of nuclear energy; tactical intelligence and intelligence related activities of the Department of Defense; national security aspects of merchant marine, including financial assistance for the construction and operation of vessels, the maintenance of the U.S. shipbuilding and ship repair industrial base, cabotage, cargo preference, and merchant marine officers and seamen as these matters relate to the national security; pay, promotion, retirement, and other benefits and privileges of members of the armed forces; scientific research and development in support of the armed services; selective service; size and composition of the Army, Navy, Marine Corps, and Air Force; soldiers' and sailors' homes; strategic and critical materials necessary for the common defense.

D 37–R 25 *(111th Congress)*

Ike Skelton, Mo.
Howard P. "Buck" McKeon, Calif.

Air and Land Forces—Adam Smith, Wash.
Readiness—Solomon P. Ortiz, Texas
Terrorism, Unconventional Threats and Capabilities—Loretta Sanchez, Calif.
Military Personnel—Susan A. Davis, Calif.
Strategic Forces—James R. Langevin, R.I.
Seapower and Expeditionary Forces—Gene Taylor, Miss.
Oversight and Investigations—Vic Snyder, Ariz.

R 35–D 27 *(112th Congress)*

Howard P. "Buck" McKeon, Calif.
Adam Smith, Wash.

Emerging Threats and Capabilities—Mac Thornberry, Texas
Military Personnel—Joe Wilson, S.C.
Oversight and Investigations—Robert J. Wittman, Va.
Readiness—J. Randy Forbes, Va.
Seapower and Projection Forces—W. Todd Akin, Mo.
Strategic Forces—Michael R. Turner, Ohio
Tactical Air and Land Forces—Roscoe G. Bartlett, Md.

BUDGET

Congressional budget process generally; concurrent budget resolutions; measures relating to special controls over the federal budget; Congressional Budget Office.

D 24–R 15 *(111th Congress)*

John M. Spratt Jr., S.C.
Paul D. Ryan, Wis.

R 22–D 16 *(112th Congress)*

Paul D. Ryan, Wis.
Chris Van Hollen, Md.

No standing subcommittees.

EDUCATION AND LABOR *(111TH CONGRESS)*/EDUCATION AND THE WORKFORCE *(112TH CONGRESS)*

Measures relating to education or labor generally; child labor; Columbia Institution for the Deaf, Dumb, and Blind; Howard University; Freedmen's Hospital; convict labor and the entry of goods made by convicts into interstate commerce; food programs for children in schools; labor standards and statistics; mediation and arbitration of labor disputes; regulation or prevention of importation of foreign laborers under contract; U.S. Employees' Compensation Commission; vocational rehabilitation; wages and hours of labor; welfare of miners; work incentive programs.

D 30–R 19 *(111th Congress)*

George Miller, Calif.
John Kline, Minn.

Early Childhood, Elementary and Secondary Education—Dale E. Kildee, Mich.
Healthy Families and Communities—Carolyn McCarthy, N.Y.
Higher Education, Lifelong Learning, and Competitiveness—Ruben Hinojosa, Texas
Workforce Protections—Lynn C. Woolsey, Calif.
Health, Employment, Labor and Pensions—Robert E. Andrews, N.J.

R 23–D 17 *(112th Congress)*

John Kline, Minn.
George Miller, Calif.

Early Childhood, Elementary and Secondary Education—Duncan Hunter, Calif.
Workforce Protections—Tim Walberg, Mich.
Higher Education and Workforce Training—Virginia Foxx, N.C.
Health, Employment, Labor, and Pensions—David P. Roe, Tenn.

ENERGY AND COMMERCE

Interstate and foreign commerce generally; biomedical research and development; consumer affairs and consumer protection; health and health facilities, except health care supported by payroll deductions; interstate energy compacts; measures relating to the exploration, production, storage, supply, marketing, pricing, and regulation of energy resources, including all fossil fuels, solar energy, and other unconventional or renewable energy resources; measures relating to the conservation of energy resources; measures relating to energy information generally; measures relating to (1) the generation and marketing of power (except by federally chartered or federal regional power marketing authorities), (2) the reliability and interstate transmission of, and ratemaking for, all power, and (3) the siting of generation facilities, except the installation of interconnections between government water power projects; measures relating to general management of the Department of Energy, and the management and all functions of the Federal Energy Regulatory Commission; national energy policy generally; public health and quarantine; regulation of the domestic nuclear energy industry, including regulation of research and development reactors and nuclear regulatory research; regulation of interstate and foreign communications; travel and tourism; nuclear and other energy.

D 36–R 23 *(111th Congress)*

Henry A. Waxman, Calif.
Joe Barton, Texas

Commerce, Trade, and Consumer Protection—Bobby L. Rush, Ill.
Energy and Environment—Edward J. Markey, Mass.
Health—Frank Pallone Jr., N.J.
Oversight and Investigations—Bart Stupak, Mich.

Communications, Technology, and the Internet—Rick Boucher, Va.

R 31–D 23 *(112th Congress)*

Fred Upton, Mich.
Henry A. Waxman, Calif.

Commerce, Manufacturing, and Trade—Mary Bono Mack, Calif.
Communications and Technology—Greg Walden, Ore.
Energy and Power—Ed Whitfield, Ky.
Environment and the Economy—John Shimkus, Ill.
Health—Joseph R. Pitts, Pa.
Oversight and Investigations—Cliff Stearns, Fla.

ETHICS (STANDARDS OF OFFICIAL CONDUCT IN 111TH CONGRESS)

R 5–D 5 *(112th Congress)*

Jo Bonner, Ala.
Linda T. Sánchez, Calif.

FINANCIAL SERVICES

Banks and banking, including deposit insurance and federal monetary policy; economic stabilization, defense production, renegotiation, and control of the price of commodities, rents, and services; financial aid to commerce and industry (other than transportation); insurance generally; international finance; international financial and monetary organizations; money and credit, including currency and the issuance of notes and redemption thereof; gold and silver, including the coinage thereof; valuation and revaluation of the dollar; public and private housing; securities and exchanges; and urban development.

D 42–R 29 *(111th Congress)*

Barney Frank, Mass.
Spencer Bachus, Ala.

Capital Markets, Insurance, and Government-Sponsored Enterprises—Paul E. Kanjorski, Pa.
Financial Institutions and Consumer Credit—Luis V. Gutiérrez, Ill.
Housing and Community Opportunity—Maxine Waters, Calif.
Domestic Monetary Policy and Technology—Melvin L. Watt, N.C.
International Monetary Policy and Trade—Gregory W. Meeks, N.Y.
Oversight and Investigations—Dennis Moore, Kan.

R 34–D 27 *(112th Congress)*

Spencer Baucus, Ala.
Barney Frank, Mass.

Capital Markets and Government Sponsored Enterprises—Scott Garrett, N.J.
Domestic Monetary Policy, and Technology—Ron Paul, Texas
Financial Institutions and Consumer Credit—Shelley Moore Capito, W.Va.
Insurance, Housing and Community Opportunity—Judy Biggert, Ill.
International Monetary Policy and Trade—Gary G. Miller, Calif.
Oversight and Investigations—Randy Neugebauer, Texas

FOREIGN AFFAIRS

Relations of the United States with foreign nations generally; acquisition of land and buildings for embassies and legations in foreign countries; establishment of boundary lines between the United States and foreign nations; export controls, including nonproliferation of nuclear technology and nuclear hardware; foreign loans; international commodity agreements (other than those involving sugar), including all agreements for cooperation in the export of nuclear technology and nuclear hardware; international conferences and congresses; international education; intervention abroad and declarations of war; measures relating to the diplomatic service; measures to foster commercial intercourse with foreign nations and to safeguard American business interests abroad; measures relating to international economic policy; neutrality; protection of American citizens abroad and expatriation; American National Red Cross; trading with the enemy; U.N. organizations.

D 28–R 19 *(111th Congress)*

Howard L. Berman, Calif.
Ileana Ros-Lehtinen, Fla.

Africa and Global Health—Donald M. Payne, N.J.
Asia, the Pacific, and Global Environment—Eni F. H. Faleomavaega, American Samoa
Europe—Bill Delahunt, Mass.
International Organizations, Human Rights, and Oversight—Russ Carnahan, Mo.
Middle East and South Asia—Gary Ackerman, N.Y.
Terrorism, Nonproliferation, and Trade—Brad Sherman, Calif.
Western Hemisphere—Eliot Engel, N.Y.

R 26–D 20 *(112th Congress)*

Ileana Ros-Lehtinen, Fla.
Howard L. Berman, Calif.

Africa, Global Health, and Human Rights—Christopher H. Smith, N.J.
Asia and the Pacific—Donald A. Manzullo, Ill.
Europe and Eurasia—Dan Burton, Ind.
Middle East and South Asia—Steve Chabot, Ohio
Oversight and Investigations—Dana Rohrabacher, Calif.
Terrorism, Nonproliferation, and Trade—Edward R. Royce, Calif.
Western Hemisphere—Connie Mack, Fla.

HOMELAND SECURITY

Overall homeland security policy; organization and administration of the Department of Homeland Security; functions of the

Department of Homeland Security; border and port security (except immigration policy and non-border enforcement); customs (except customs revenue); integration, analysis, and dissemination of homeland security information; domestic preparedness for and collective response to terrorism; research and development; transportation security.

D 21–R 13 *(111th Congress)*

Bennie G. Thompson, Miss.
Peter T. King, N.Y.

Intelligence, Information Sharing, and Terrorism Risk Assessment—Jane Harman, Calif.
Transportation Security and Infrastructure Protection—Sheila Jackson Lee, Texas
Border, Maritime, and Global Counterterrorism—Henry Cuellar, Texas
Management, Investigations, and Oversight—Christopher P. Carney, Pa.
Emerging Threats, Cybersecurity, and Science and Technology—Yvette D. Clark, N.Y.
Emergency Communications, Preparedness, and Response—Laura Richardson, Calif.

R 19–D 14 *(112th Congress)*

Peter T. King, N.Y.
Bernie G. Thompson, Miss.

Cybersecurity, Infrastructure Protection, and Security—Daniel E. Lungren, Calif.
Transportation Security—Mike Rogers, Ala.
Oversight, Investigations, and Management—Michael T. McCall, Texas
Emergency Preparedness, Response, and Communication—Gus M. Bilirakis, Fla.
Border and Maritime Security—Candice S. Miller, Mich.
Counterterrorism and Intelligence—Patrick Meehan, Pa.

HOUSE ADMINISTRATION

Accounts of the House generally; assignment of office space for members and committees; disposition of useless executive papers; matters relating to the election of the president, vice president, or members of Congress; corrupt practices; contested elections; credentials and qualifications; federal elections generally; appropriations from accounts for committee salaries and expenses (except for the Committee on Appropriations), House Information Systems, and allowances and expenses of members, House officers, and administrative offices of the House; auditing and settling of all such accounts; expenditure of such accounts; employment of persons by the House, including clerks for members and committees, and reporters of debates; Library of Congress and the House Library; statuary and pictures; acceptance or purchase of works of art for the Capitol; the Botanic Garden; management of the Library of Congress; purchase of books and manuscripts; Smithsonian Institution and the incorporation of similar institutions; Franking Commission; printing and correction of the *Congressional Record*; services to the House, including the House restaurant, parking facilities, and administration of the House office buildings and of the House wing of the Capitol; travel of members of the House; raising, reporting, and use of campaign contributions for candidates for office of representative in the House of Representatives, of delegate, and of resident commissioner to the United States from Puerto Rico; compensation, retirement and other benefits of the members, officers, and employees of the Congress.

D 6–R 3 *(111th Congress)*

Robert A. Brady, Pa.
Daniel E. Lungren, Calif.

Capitol Security—Michael E. Capuano, Mass.
Elections—Zoe Lofgren, Calif.

R 6–D 3 *(112th Congress)*

Daniel E. Lungren, Calif.
Robert A. Brady, Pa.

Elections—Gregg Harper, Miss.
Oversight—Phil Gingrey, Ga.

JUDICIARY

The judiciary and judicial proceedings, civil and criminal; administrative practice and procedure; apportionment of representatives; bankruptcy, mutiny, espionage, and counterfeiting; civil liberties; constitutional amendments; federal courts and judges, and local courts in the territories and possessions; immigration and naturalization; interstate compacts, generally; measures relating to claims against the United States; meetings of Congress, attendance of members and their acceptance of incompatible offices; national penitentiaries; patents, the Patent Office, copyrights, and trademarks; presidential succession; protection of trade and commerce against unlawful restraints and monopolies; revision and codification of the Statutes of the United States; state and territorial boundaries; subversive activities affecting the internal security of the United States.

D 24–R 16 *(111th Congress)*

John Conyers Jr., Mich.
Lamar Smith, Texas

Courts and Competition Policy—Henry C. "Hank" Johnson Jr., Ga.
Crime, Terrorism, and Homeland Security—Robert B. "Bobby" Scott, Va.
Immigration, Citizenship, Refugees, Border Security, and International Law—Zoe Lofgren, Calif.
Constitution, Civil Rights, and Civil Liberties—Jerrold Nadler, N.Y.
Commercial and Administrative Law—Steve Cohen, Tenn.

R 23–D 16 *(112th Congress)*

Lamar Smith, Texas
John Conyers Jr., Mich.

Courts, Commercial and Administrative Law—Howard Coble, N.C.
Constitution—Trent Franks, Ariz.

Intellectual Property, Competition, and the Internet—Bob Goodlatte, Va.

Crime, Terrorism, and Homeland Security—F. James Sensenbrenner Jr., Wis.

Immigration Policy and Enforcement—Elton Gallegly, Calif.

NATURAL RESOURCES

Public lands generally, including entry, easements, and grazing; mining interests generally; fisheries and wildlife, including research, restoration, refuges, and conservation; forest reserves and national parks created from the public domain; forfeiture of land grants and alien ownership, including alien ownership of mineral lands; Geological Survey; international fishing agreements; interstate compacts relating to apportionment of waters for irrigation purposes; irrigation and reclamation, including water supply for reclamation projects, and easements of public lands for irrigation projects, and acquisition of private lands when necessary to complete irrigation projects; measures relating to the care and management of Indians, including the care and allotment of Native American lands and general and special measures relating to claims that are paid out of Native American funds; measures relating generally to the insular possessions of the United States, except those affecting the revenue and appropriations; military parks and battlefields, national cemeteries administered by the secretary of the interior, parks within the District of Columbia, and the erection of monuments to the memory of individuals; mineral land laws and claims and entries thereunder; mineral resources of the public lands; mining schools and experimental stations; marine affairs (including coastal zone management), except for measures relating to oil and other pollution of navigable waters; oceanography; petroleum conservation on the public lands and conservation of the radium supply in the United States; preservation of prehistoric ruins and objects of interest on the public domain; relations of the United States with the Native Americans and the Native American tribes; disposition of oil transported by the Trans-Alaska Oil Pipeline.

D 29–R 20 *(111th Congress)*

Nick J. Rahall II, W.Va
Doc Hastings, Wash.

National Parks, Forests, and Public Lands—Raul M. Grijalva, Ariz.

Insular Affairs, Oceans, and Wildlife— Madeleine Z. Bordallo, Guam

Energy and Mineral Resources—Jim Costa, Calif.

Water and Power— Grace F. Napolitano, Calif.

R 27–D 21 *(112th Congress)*

Doc Hastings, Wash.
Edward J. Markey, Mass.

Energy and Mineral Resources—Doug Lamborn, Colo.

Fisheries, Wildlife, Oceans, and Insular Affairs—John Fleming, La.

Indian and Alaska Native Affairs—Don Young, Alaska

National Parks, Forests, and Public Lands—Rob Bishop, Utah

Water and Power—Tom McClintock, Calif.

OVERSIGHT AND GOVERNMENT REFORM

Civil service, including intergovernmental personnel; the status of officers and employees of the United States, including their compensation, classification, and retirement; measures relating to the municipal affairs of the District of Columbia in general, other than appropriations; federal paperwork reduction; budget and accounting measures, generally; holidays and celebrations; overall economy, efficiency, and management of government operations and activities, including federal procurement; National Archives; population and demography generally, including the census; Postal Service generally, including the transportation of mail; public information and records; relationship of the federal government to the states and municipalities generally; reorganizations in the executive branch of the government.

D 25–R 16 *(111th Congress)*

Edolphus Downs, N.Y.
Darrell E. Issa, Calif.

National Security and Foreign Affairs—John F. Tierney, Mass.

Government Management, Organization, and Procurement—Diane E. Watson, Calif.

Information Policy, Census, and National Archives—William Lacy Clay, Mo.

Federal Workforce, Postal Service, and the District of Columbia—Stephen F. Lynch, Mass.

Domestic Policy—Dennis J. Kucinich, Ohio

R 23–D 17 *(112th Congress)*

Darrell E. Issa, Calif.
Elijah J. Cummings, Md.

Federal Workforce, U.S. Postal Service, and Labor Policy—Dennis A. Ross, Fla.

Government Organization, Efficiency, and Financial Management—Todd Russell Platts, Pa.

Health Care, District of Columbia, Census, and National Archives—Trey Gowdy, S.C.

National Security, Homeland Defense, and Foreign Operations—Jason Chaffetz, Utah

Regulatory Affairs, Stimulus Oversight, and Government Spending—Jim Jordan, Ohio

TARP, Financial Services, and Bailouts of Public and Private Programs—Patrick T. McHenry, N.C.

Technology, Information Policy, Intergovernmental Relations, and Procurement Reform—James Lankford, Okla.

RULES

Rules and joint rules (other than rules or joint rules relating to the Code of Official Conduct), and order of business of the House; recesses and final adjournments of Congress.

D 9–R 4 *(111th Congress)*

Louise M. Slaughter, N.Y.
David Dreier, Calif.

Legislative and Budget Process—Alcee L. Hastings, Fla.

Rules and Organization of the House—James P. McGovern, Mass.

D 9–R 4 *(112th Congress)*

David Dreier, Calif.
Louise M. Slaughter, N.Y.

Legislative and Budget Process—Pete Sessions, Texas.
Rules and Organization of the House—Richard B. Nugent, Fla.

SCIENCE AND TECHNOLOGY *(111TH CONGRESS)*/SCIENCE, SPACE, AND TECHNOLOGY *(112TH CONGRESS)*

All energy research, development, and demonstration, and projects thereof, and all federally owned or operated nonmilitary energy laboratories; astronautical research and development, including resources, personnel, equipment, and facilities; civil aviation research and development; environmental research and development; marine research; measures relating to the commercial application of energy technology; National Institute of Standards and Technology, standardization of weights and measures and the metric system; National Aeronautics and Space Administration; National Space Council; National Science Foundation; National Weather Service; outer space, including exploration and control thereof; science scholarships; scientific research, development, and demonstration, and projects thereof.

D 27–R 17 *(111th Congress)*

Bart Gordon, Tenn.
Ralph M. Hall, Texas

Energy and Environment—Brian Baird, Wash.
Technology and Innovation—David Wu., Ore.
Research and Science Education—Daniel Lipinski, Ill.
Space and Aeronautics—Gabrielle Giffords, Ariz.
Investigations and Oversight—Brad Miller, N.C.

R 23–D 17 *(112th Congress)*

Ralph M. Hall, Texas
Eddie Bernice Johnson, Texas

Energy and Environment—Andy Harris, Md.
Investigations and Oversight—Paul C. Broun, Ga.
Research and Science Education—Mo Brooks, Ala.
Space and Aeronautics—Steven M. Palazzo, Miss.
Technology and Innovation—Benjamin Quayle, Ariz.

SELECT INTELLIGENCE

Legislative and budgetary authority over the National Security Agency and the director of central intelligence, the Defense Intelligence Agency, the National Security Agency, intelligence activities of the Federal Bureau of Investigation, and other components of the federal intelligence community.

D 13–R 9 *(111th Congress)*

Silvestre Reyes, Texas
Peter Hoekstra, Mich.

Terrorism, Human Intelligence, Analysis and Counterintelligence—Mike Thompson, Calif.
Intelligence Community Management—Anna G. Eshoo, Calif.
Technical and Tactical Intelligence—C. A. Dutch Ruppersberger, Md.
Oversight and Investigations— Janice D. Schakowsky, Ill.

R 12–D 8 *(112th Congress)*

Mike Rogers, Mich.
C. A. Dutch Ruppersberger, Md.

Terrorism, Human Intelligence, Analysis and Counterintelligence—Sue Wilkins Myrick, N.C.
Technical and Tactical Intelligence—Joseph J. Heck, Nev.
Oversight and Investigations—Lynn A. Westmoreland, Ga.

SMALL BUSINESS

Assistance to and protection of small business, including financial aid, regulatory flexibility, and paperwork reduction; participation of small business enterprises in federal procurement and government contracts.

D 17–R 12 *(111th Congress)*

Nydia M. Velazquez, N.Y.
Sam Graves, Mo.

Regulations and Healthcare—Kathleen A. Dahlkemper, Pa.
Finance and Tax—Kurt Schrader, Ore.
Rural Development, Entrepreneurship, and Trade—Heath Shuler, N.C.
Contracting and Technology—Glenn C. Nye, Va.
Investigations and Oversight—Jason Altmire, Pa.

R 15–D 11 *(112th Congress)*

Sam Graves, Mo.
Nydia M. Velazquez, N.Y.

Agriculture, Energy, and Trade—Scott Tipton, Colo.
Contracting and Workforce—Mick Mulvaney, S.C.
Economic Growth, Tax, and Capital Access—Joe Walsh, Ill.
Healthcare and Technology—Renee Ellmers, N.C.
Investigation, Oversight, and Regulations—Mike Coffman, Colo.

STANDARDS OF OFFICIAL CONDUCT *(ETHICS IN 112TH CONGRESS)*

Measures relating to the Code of Official Conduct.

D 5–R 5 *(111th Congress)*

Zoe Lofgren, Calif.
Jo Bonner, Ala.

D 5–R 5 *(112th Congress)*

Jo Bonner, Ala.
Linda T. Sanchez, Calif.

TRANSPORTATION AND INFRASTRUCTURE

Transportation, including civil aviation, railroads, water transportation, transportation safety (except automobile safety), transportation infrastructure, transportation labor, and railroad retirement and unemployment (except revenue measures); water power; the Coast Guard; federal management of emergencies and natural disasters; flood control and improvement of waterways; inspection of merchant marine vessels; navigation and related laws; rules and international arrangements to prevent collisions at sea; measures, other than appropriations, that relate to construction, maintenance and safety of roads; buildings and grounds of the Botanic Gardens, the Library of Congress, and the Smithsonian Institution and other government buildings within the District of Columbia; post offices, customhouses, federal courthouses, and merchant marine, except for national security aspects; pollution of navigable waters; and bridges and dams and related transportation regulatory agencies.

D 45–R 30 *(111th Congress)*

James L. Oberstar, Minn.
John L. Mica, Fla.

Aviation—Jerry F. Costello, Ill.
Coast Guard and Maritime Transportation—Elijah E. Cummings, Md.
Economic Development, Public Buildings, and Emergency Management—Eleanor Holmes Norton, D.C.
Highways and Transit—Peter A. DeFazio, Ore.
Railroads, Pipelines, and Hazardous Materials—Corrine Brown, Fla.
Water Resources and Environment—Eddie Bernice Johnson, Texas

R 33–D 26 *(112th Congress)*

John L. Mica, Fla.
Nick J. Rahall, W.Va.

Aviation—Thomas E. Petri, Wis.
Coast Guard and Maritime Transportation—Frank A. LoBiondo, N.J.
Economic Development, Public Buildings, and Emergency Management—Jeff Denham, Calif.
Highways and Transit—John J. Duncan Jr., Tenn.
Railroads, Pipelines, and Hazardous Materials—Bill Shuster, Pa.
Water Resources and Environment—Bob Gibbs, Ohio

VETERANS' AFFAIRS

Veterans' measures generally; cemeteries of the United States in which veterans of any war or conflict are or may be buried, whether in the United States or abroad, except cemeteries administered by the secretary of the Interior; compensation, vocational rehabilitation, and education of veterans; life insurance issued by the government on account of service in the armed forces; pensions of all the wars of the United States, readjustment of service personnel to civil life; soldiers' and sailors' civil relief; veterans' hospitals, medical care, and treatment of veterans.

D 18–R 11 *(111th Congress)*

Bob Filner, Calif.
Steve Buyer, Ind.

Disability Benefits and Memorial Affairs—John J. Hall, N.Y.
Economic Opportunity—Stephanie Herseth Sandlin, S.D.
Health—Michael H. Michaud, Maine.
Oversight and Investigations—Harry E. Mitchell, Ariz.

R 15–D 11 *(112th Congress)*

Jeff Miller, Fla.
Bob Filner, Calif.

Disability Assistance and Memorial Affairs—Jon Runyan, N.J.
Economic Opportunity—Marlin A. Stutzman, N.J.
Health—Ann Marie Buerkle, N.Y.
Oversight and Investigations—Bill Johnson, Ohio

WAYS AND MEANS

Revenue measures generally; reciprocal trade agreements; customs, collection districts, and ports of entry and delivery; revenue measures relating to the insular possessions; bonded debt of the United States; deposit of public moneys; transportation of dutiable goods; tax-exempt foundations and charitable trusts; national Social Security, except (1) health care and facilities programs that are supported from general revenues as opposed to payroll deductions and (2) work incentive programs.

D 26–R 15 *(111th Congress)*

Sander M. Levin, Mich.
Dave Camp, Mich.

Trade—John S. Tanner, Tenn.
Oversight—John Lewis, Ga.
Health—Fortney Pete Stark, Calif.
Social Security—Earl Pomeroy, N.D .
Income Security and Family Support—Jim McDermott, Wash.
Select Revenue Measures—Richard E. Neal, Mass.

R 22–D 15 *(112th Congress)*

Dave Camp, Mich.
Sander M. Levin, Mich.

Health—Wally Herger, Calif.
Human Resources—Geoff Davis, Ky.
Oversight—Charles S. Boustany Jr., La.
Select Revenue Measures—Patrick J. Tiberi, Ohio
Social Security—Sam Johnson, Texas
Trade—Kevin Brady, Texas

SELECT COMMITTEE ON ENERGY INDEPENDENCE AND GLOBAL WARMING

D 9–R 6 *(111th Congress)*

Edward J. Markey, Mass.
F. James Sensenbrenner Jr., Wis.

(Committee did not exist in the 112th Congress)

Joint Committees

Joint committees are set up to examine specific questions and are established by public law. Membership is drawn from both chambers and both parties. When a senator serves as chairman, the vice chairman usually is a representative, and vice versa. The chairmanship traditionally rotates from one chamber to the other at the beginning of each Congress. However, the Committee on Taxation chairmanship rotates at the start of each session with the House having the chair in the first session and the Senate in the second session. In the alternate sessions the House and Senate members have the vice chair.

ECONOMIC

Studies and investigates all recommendations in the president's annual Economic Report to Congress. Reports findings and recommendations to the House and Senate.

Rep. Carolyn B. Maloney, D-N.Y., chair (111th Congress)
Sen. Charles E. Schumer, D-N.Y., vice chair (111th Congress)
Sen. Robert P. Casey Jr., D-Pa, chair (112th Congress)
Rep. Kevin Brady, R-Texas, vice chair (112th Congress)

No standing subcommittees.

LIBRARY

Management and expansion of the Library of Congress; receipt of gifts for the benefit of the library; development and maintenance of the Botanic Garden; placement of statues and other works of art in the Capitol.

Rep. Robert A. Brady, D-Pa., chair (111th Congress)
Sen. Charles E. Schumer, D-N.Y., vice chair (111th Congress)
Sen. Charles E. Schumer, D-N.Y., chair (112th Congress)
Rep. Gregg Harper, R-Miss., vice chair (112th Congress)

No standing subcommittees.

PRINTING

Probes inefficiency and waste in the printing, binding, and distribution of federal government publications. Oversees arrangement and style of the *Congressional Record.*

Sen. Charles E. Schumer, D-N.Y., chair (111th Congress)
Rep. Robert A. Brady, D-Pa., vice chair (111th Congress)
Rep. Gregg Harper, R-Miss. Chair (112th Congress)
Sen. Charles E. Schumer, D-N.Y., vice chair (112th Congress)

No standing subcommittees.

TAXATION

Operation, effects, and administration of the federal system of internal revenue taxes; measures and methods for simplification of taxation.

Sen. Max Baucus, D-Mont. (111th Congress)
Rep. Sander M. Levin, D-Mich. (111th Congress)
Sen. Max Baucus, D-Mont. (112th Congress)
Rep. Dave Camp, R-Mich. (112th Congress)

No standing subcommittees.

Postelection Sessions

A postelection session of Congress often is labeled a lame duck session. It takes place after an election for the next Congress but before the official end of the current Congress. As a result members who participate in the lame duck session are from the existing, or current, Congress, not from the Congress that will convene as a result of the just-held elections.

Lame duck sessions in the modern sense began in 1935 after the Twentieth Amendment to the Constitution was ratified in 1933. This amendment specified that regular congressional sessions would begin on January 3 of each year unless Congress passed a law designating a different date. Also, terms of members of Congress begin and end on January 3 of odd-numbered years, regardless of the date that a Congress officially ends its session. Originally the Constitution specified much later starting dates in recognition of the difficulty of travel in the early years of the nation, but those dates meant that lame duck sessions occurred in the second session of every Congress. In the modern sense, post-1935, a lame duck session is any meeting of Congress after election day in even-numbered years but before the following January 3.

Between 1935 and 2013, Congress held nineteen lame-duck sessions.

1941. The 76th Congress actually had adjourned in 1939 but President Franklin D. Roosevelt called the legislators into special session—technically, the third session of that Congress–to deal with the threat of war in Europe. However, little of substance was accomplished during the lame duck session.

1942. By this year the United States was at war with Germany, Japan, and Italy but little was done during the period as legislators decided to leave many major decisions to the next Congress. Congress did approve bills on overtime pay for government workers and to provide for the military draft of eighteen and nineteen-year-old men.

1944. World War II was well along by this time, which meant Congress faced a host of exceptionally important issues including postwar universal military training, continuing the war effort, Social Security taxes, a rivers and harbors bill, and various post-war reconstruction matters. But, like the previous several lame duck sessions, legislators decided to postpone most actions until the new Congress convened in 1945.

1948. The 1948 postelection session of the 80th Congress lasted only two hours. Both chambers swore in new members, approved several minor resolutions, and received last-minute reports from committees. In addition to final floor action, several committees resumed work. The most active was the House Un-American Activities Committee, which continued its investigation of alleged communist espionage in the federal government.

1950. After the 1950 elections, President Harry S. Truman sent a "must" agenda to the lame duck session of the 81st Congress. The president's list included supplemental defense appropriations, an excess profits tax, aid to Yugoslavia, a three-month extension of federal rent controls, and statehood for Hawaii and Alaska. During a marathon session that lasted until only a few hours before its successor took over, the 81st Congress acted on all of the president's legislative items except the statehood bills, which were blocked by a Senate filibuster.

1954. Only one chamber of the 83rd Congress convened after the 1954 elections. The Senate returned November 8 to hold what has been called a "censure session," a continuing investigation into the conduct of Sen. Joseph R. McCarthy, R-Wis. (1947–1957). By a 67–22 roll call, the Senate December 2 voted to "condemn" McCarthy for his behavior. In other postelection floor action, the Senate passed a series of miscellaneous and administrative resolutions and swore in new members.

1970. President Richard Nixon criticized the lame duck Congress as one that had "seemingly lost the capacity to decide and the will to act." Filibusters and intense controversy contributed to inaction on the president's request for trade legislation and welfare reform. Congress nevertheless claimed some substantive results during the session, which ended January 2, 1971. Several major appropriations bills were cleared for presidential signature. Congress also approved foreign aid to Cambodia, provided interim funding for the supersonic transport (SST) plane, and repealed the Tonkin Gulf Resolution that had been used as a basis for American military involvement in Vietnam.

1974. In a session that ran from November 18 to December 20, 1974, the 93rd Congress cleared several important bills for presidential signature, including a mass transit bill, a Labor-Health, Education and Welfare appropriations bill, and a foreign assistance package. A House-Senate conference committee reached agreement on a major strip-mining bill but President Gerald R. Ford vetoed it. Congress approved the nomination of Nelson A. Rockefeller as vice president. It also overrode presidential vetoes of two bills: one broadening the Freedom of Information Act, a

Congressional Lame Duck Sessions

Year	*Congress*	*Dates*
1941	76th	Adjourned January 3, 1941*
1942	77th	Adjourned December 16, 1942*
1944	78th	November 14, 1944–December 19, 1944
1948	80th	December 31, 1948 (two-hour session)
1950	81st	November 27, 1950–January 2, 1951
1954	83rd	November 8, 1954–December 2, 1954
1970	91st	November 16, 1970–January 2, 1971 (Senate)
1974	93rd	November 18, 1974–December 20, 1974
1980	96th	November 12, 1980–December 16, 1980
1982	97th	November 29, 1982–December 23, 1982 (Senate)
		November 29, 1982–December 21, 1982 (House)
1994	103rd	November 29, 1994 (House)
		November 30, 1994–December 1, 1994 (Senate)
1998	105th	December 17, 1998–December 19, 1998 (House)
2000	106th	November 13, 2000–December 15, 2000 (House)
		November 14, 2000–December 15, 2000
2002	107th	Adjourned November 20, 2002 (Senate)*
		Adjourned November 22, 2002 (House)*
2004	108th	November 16, 2004–December 7, 2004 (House)
		November 16, 2004–December 8, 2004 (Senate)
2006	109th	November 13, 2006–December 8, 2006 (House)
		November 13, 2006–December 8, 2006 (Senate)
2008	110th	November 19, 2008–December 10, 2008 (House)
		November 17, 2008–December 11, 2008 (Senate)
2010	111th	November 15, 2010–December 22, 2010 (House)
		November 15, 2010–December 22, 2010 (Senate)
2012	112th	November 13, 2012–January 3, 2013 (House)
		November 13, 2012–January 2, 2013 (Senate)**

* Congress stayed in session.

** The Senate did not adjourn *sine die*.

second authorizing educational benefits for Korean War and Vietnam-era veterans.

1980. The lame duck session of the 96th Congress was productive, at least until December 5, the original adjournment date set by congressional leaders. By that date a budget had been approved, along with a budget reconciliation measure. Ten regular appropriations bills had cleared, though one subsequently was vetoed. Congress had approved two major environmental measures—an Alaskan lands bill and toxic waste "superfund" legislation—as well as a three-year extension of general revenue sharing.

After December 5, however, the legislative pace slowed noticeably. Action on a continuing appropriations resolution for those departments and agencies whose regular funding had not been cleared was delayed, first by a filibuster on a fair housing bill and later by more than 100 "Christmas tree" amendments, including a $10,000-a-year pay raise for members. After the conference report failed in the Senate and twice was rewritten, the bill was shorn of virtually all its "ornaments" and finally cleared by both chambers on December 16.

1982. Despite the reluctance of congressional leaders, President Ronald Reagan urged the convening of a postelection session at the end of the 97th Congress, principally to pass remaining appropriations bills. Rising unemployment—and Democratic election gains in the House—made job creation efforts the focus of the lame duck Congress, however. Overriding the objections of Republican conservatives, Congress passed Reagan-backed legislation raising the federal gasoline tax from 4 cents to 9 cents a gallon to pay for highway repairs and mass transit. Supporters said the legislation would help alleviate unemployment by creating 300,000 jobs.

Congress eventually cleared four additional appropriations bills, packaging the remaining six in a continuing appropriations resolution that also included a pay raise for House members. Conferees dropped funding for emergency jobs programs to avert a threatened veto of the resolution. The lame duck session also was highlighted by Congress's refusal to fund production and procurement of the first five MX intercontinental missiles. This was the first time in recent history that either house of Congress had denied a president's request to fund production of a strategic weapon.

1994. Congress reconvened to reconsider, and ultimately approve, the Uruguay Round pact strengthening the General Agreement on Tariffs and Trade (GATT). The bill had been submitted September 27, 1994, by President Bill Clinton under fast-track rules for trade legislation, which allowed each chamber only an up-or-down vote on the bill without amendments. But the rules also allowed every chairman with jurisdiction to take up to forty-five days to review the bill. Sen. Ernest F. Hollings, D-S.C., demanded his forty-five days, forcing the Senate leadership to schedule a two-day lame duck session. Clinton asked the House to approve the bill before the October adjournment but the Democratic leadership delayed consideration. The House reconvened for a one-day session November 29 and passed the GATT bill by a wide margin. Following a twenty-hour debate November 30 and December 1, the Senate gave overwhelming approval to the bill.

1998. The House reconvened in December for a remarkable and historic event: to vote on the impeachment of a president. After a tumultuous political year, House Republicans pushed through articles of impeachment for what they believed was President Clinton's lying under oath. The event was characterized by a year-long political chasm between House Republicans, who led the effort for impeachment, and Democrats in both chambers. It also was characterized by charges of sexual misconduct involving Clinton and release of a controversial and in places graphic report about sexual conduct of the president that Republicans defended as necessary to prove their case. The report was prepared by an independent prosecutor. In the short time the House was in session it voted—largely along party lines in favor of impeachment charges, which would be tried, and rejected, by the Senate early in the following year.

2000. Congress returned after the 2000 elections largely to complete action on appropriations measures that had remained unfinished as President Clinton continued to wrestle with his Republican adversaries in Congress over spending priorities. Partisan fighting over spending and taxes had been one of the principal matters that divided the White House and Capitol Hill during the latter years of Clinton's presidency. The year 2000 was no exception as Congress was unable to avert its annual pileup of appropriations bills at the end of the session. The pileup was exacerbated in 2000 because of the controversial presidential elections that were not decided until a Supreme Court decision in December awarding contested Florida electoral votes to Republican George W. Bush. With the GOP about to reclaim the White House, party members in Congress suddenly had new leverage in the final bargaining over appropriations. The lame duck session lumbered into mid-December when an omnibus package was used to close the books on four spending bills and move other unrelated legislation.

2004. Congress came back after Republicans scored impressive gains in the fall elections that returned Bush to the White House and increased GOP control of both chambers of Congress. The additional votes meant the GOP was strongly positioned to push Bush's legislative program in the 109th Congress. But before they could get there important legislative matters remained for the 108th Congress. The most important was a sweeping overhaul of the U.S. intelligence community, Congress's last major act of the year. It came only at the prodding of the independent, bipartisan National Commission on Terrorist Attacks Upon the United States—better known as the 9/11 commission—and the powerful lobbying of some of the victims' families of those attacks. In addition, all but four of the appropriations bills had been left hanging when Congress went out of the elections break. Congress bundled the other nine into an omnibus bill during the lame duck session and cleared it on November 20.

2006. Legislators returned after the 2006 midterm elections to a wholly new playing field because Democrats had recaptured control of both chambers, although the Senate by a one-vote margin. The principal agenda for the postelection session was completion of appropriations bills, only two of which (defense and homeland security) had been completed. A continuing resolution keeping the government operating was set to expire November 17. Dealing with several expiring tax benefits also was on the list of actions needed. But much of the plan never got going as Democrats decided to fund the government until February 15, 2007, through additional continuing resolutions, thereby leaving all the other regular appropriation bills to die. But some work was done. A package of tax benefits was completed in connection with a trade package. Perhaps most significantly, Congress approved a bill allowing President Bush to negotiate a nuclear power agreement with India, one of the president's most significant foreign policy accomplishments. The Senate also confirmed Robert M. Gates as defense secretary to replace Donald Rumsfeld.

2008. The main focus of attention in the postelection session was the continuing financial crisis in the United States and worldwide, but the elections, like those two years earlier, had put a new cast on events. In the elections, Democrats had improved their margin in the House and significantly increased it in the Senate and had won the presidential contest when Barack Obama defeated John McCain by a comfortable 53–47 percentage margin. This meant that governmental activity to stave off an economic collapse that many economists thought would rival the Great Depression of the 1930s was left to coordination of action between the outgoing Bush administration and the new Obama administration. Congress, which had passed a $700 billion package of aid for the financial services industry before the election, was left with little to do. One major effort failed: with the nation's three principal auto-manufacturers facing bankruptcy, Congress considered providing $14 billion in loans to the companies from an existing program. The House passed the bill but the Senate did not go along. As a result, Bush later provided $13.4 billion in loans to the automakers from the funds previously approved to save the financial services industry.

2010. The 111th Congress turned out to be one of the odder two-year periods because of the amount of significant, and highly controversial, legislation that became law. Earlier in the year, Democrats forced through a far-reaching health care reform bill; later in the summer, they passed a financial regulation overhaul that grew from the vast economic collapse that started in 2008. These actions alone would have made the 111th Congress exceptionally notable, and hardly required a lame duck session.

But one was to occur anyway and it too turned out to be significant. The postelection session was unusual because it came after an election in which Democrats, previously riding high with their successes, took a beating when Republicans surged back to recapture the House majority. Even President Obama acknowledged his party had taken a "shellacking" in the election. Although little was expected in the session after the voting, Congress extended income and estate taxes, approved a conditional repeal of the ban on gays in the military, and approved ratification of a nuclear arms treaty with Russia. The tax legislation also included a year-long extension of extra benefits for long-term unemployed persons. Congress also approved a food safety bill and worked out funding to keep the government operating into 2012.

2012. For the eighth time in a row, going back to the 105th Congress in 1998, legislators in 2012 returned after the national elections—in which the political divisions in Washington were largely repeated—to deal with tangled issues that the divisions had blocked from resolution before the voting took place. But unlike the lame duck session two years earlier, only the most pressing issues were addressed, and then only—as many observers noted—by kicking cans down the road.

The issues, mainly taxes and spending, were so intractable that the 112th Congress went past New Year's Eve right up to the January 3 deadline when the Constitution decreed it had to end. It was the first time in forty-two years that Congress slid past the turn of the calendar and evening celebrations.

In fact, there was little to celebrate in legislative terms. The legislators struck a deal on the looming deadline that had come to be called the fiscal cliff, which at the end of 2012 would have sent tax rates for all Americans back to levels last seen more than a decade earlier. The "cliff" described not only the expiration of an array of earlier tax cuts that were put in place as temporary but also an existing law that would force across-the-board spending cuts of some $109 billion, starting January 2, 2013.

The deal that emerged permanently extended the existing reduced tax rates for most taxpayers, while allowing rates on higher earners (above $400,000 for individuals and $450,000 for couples) to rise. A long-standing fight over federal estate taxes was settled, and a permanent "patch" was included for the alternative minimum tax to limit that levy from reaching into middle class incomes. The bill also extended long-term unemployment benefits for another year.

On the other hand, the across-the-board cuts, known as a sequester, were only delayed until March 1, 2013. Backers of the extension said it would give Congress time to work out a compromise. But Congress did not, and the forced cuts began then.

The 112th Congress did end, with the House adjourning a few minutes before the required session's end and the Senate merely allowing the clock to run out. Traditionally, at the end of a Congress, leaders make a ceremonial telephone call to the president and then hold news conferences about their accomplishments. None of that occurred for the 112th.

Senate Cloture Votes, 1917–2012

The filibuster, identified by the public primarily as nonstop speech, has been an enshrined Senate tradition throughout the chamber's history but became a focus of increasing criticism in the twentieth century as a device to thwart majority decisions. It was not until 1917 that the Senate adopted a rule, known as cloture, that allowed a majority—albeit a supermajority—to end a filibuster and bring a measure to a vote. The number of votes required to invoke cloture has varied over the years, standing at sixty in 2012 if there are no Senate vacancies. (The actual rules required a three-fifths majority of members to invoke cloture; the Senate has 100 members.)

Even with the rule in place, however, the number of filibusters and attempts to invoke cloture was limited until the 92nd Congress in 1971–1973. From that time on, and especially after 2000, cloture attempts expanded greatly as the character of the Senate changed from what one scholar called "communitarian" and deliberative to individualistic, increasingly partisan, and media-driven. This pattern was seen during the 1990s also. In both decades, deep-seated partisan divisions in Congress led both parties to try whatever tools worked to block the initiatives or judicial or executive appointments of the other.

In the ten Congresses during the twenty years from 1971 to 1991 cloture was attempted no less than thirteen times in each two-year period, and on the average twenty-five times each Congress. As dramatic as that growth was, it paled against the expansion in the following eleven Congresses from 1991 through 2012. During those eleven Congresses from the 102nd through the 112th cloture votes were taken an average of nearly sixty-three times for each two-year period.

During this two decade period cloture was typically used more for political and legislative maneuvering than to consider far-reaching national issues. For example, senators might start or threaten a filibuster to gain leverage for a matter completely unrelated to the legislation before the Senate. In one instance during President Barack Obama's first term, his nomination to head a new consumer protection bureau was blocked by a filibuster even through most senators agreed the nominee was qualified. The opposition to him centered, rather, on Republican demands that the bureau as enacted in a previous Congress be restricted in ways that reflected their unhappiness with the agency's powers.

The filibuster also was used increasingly in this period to thwart the choices of both Republican and Democratic presidents for positions in the federal judiciary, as each party saw control of the courts as core, nonnegotiable interests of their political bases.

CHANGES IN THE RULE

The Senate's ultimate check on the filibuster is the provision for cloture, or limitation of debate, contained in Rule 22 of its Standing Rules. The original Rule 22 was adopted in 1917 following a furor over the "talking to death" of a proposal by President Woodrow Wilson for arming American merchant ships before the United States entered World War I. The new cloture rule required the votes of two-thirds of all the senators present and voting to invoke cloture. In 1949, during a parliamentary skirmish preceding scheduled consideration of a Fair Employment Practices Commission bill, the requirement was raised to two-thirds of the entire Senate membership.

A revision of the rule in 1959 provided for limitation of debate by a vote of two-thirds of the senators present and voting, two days after a cloture petition was submitted by sixteen senators. If cloture was adopted by the Senate, further debate was limited to one hour for each senator on the bill itself and on all amendments affecting it. No new amendments could be offered except by unanimous consent. Amendments that were not germane to the pending business and dilatory motions were out of order. The rule applied both to regular legislation and to motions to change the Standing Rules.

Rule 22 was revised significantly in 1975 by lowering the vote needed for cloture to three-fifths of the Senate membership (sixty if there were no vacancies). That revision applied to any matter except proposed rules changes, for which the old requirement of a two-thirds majority of senators present and voting still applied.

In a further revision of the rule, the Senate in 1979 limited postcloture delaying tactics by providing that once cloture was invoked, a final vote had to be taken after no more than 100 hours of debate. All time spent on quorum calls, roll-call votes and other parliamentary procedures was to be included in the 100-hour limit.

When the Senate decided to televise its floor proceedings in 1986, it further tightened up the time on postcloture debate. Rule 22 was revised to reduce to thirty hours, from 100, the time allowed for debate, procedural moves and roll-call votes after the Senate had invoked cloture to end a filibuster.

Following is a list of the 988 cloture votes taken between 1917, when Senate Rule 22 was adopted, and the end of 2012. Those in **bold type**, 440, were successful; 548 votes, 55.5 percent, were not. *(Table of votes in each Congress, p. 871)*

Issue	*Date*	*Vote*	*Yeas needed*
Versailles Treaty	November 15, 1919	78–16	63
Emergency tariff	February 2, 1921	36–35	48
Tariff bill	July 7, 1922	45–35	54
World Court	January 25, 1926	68–26	63
Migratory birds	June 1, 1926	46–33	53
Branch banking	February 15, 1927	65–18	56
Disabled officers	February 26, 1927	51–36	58
Colorado River	February 26, 1927	32–59	61
D.C. buildings	February 28, 1927	52–31	56
Prohibition Bureau	February 28, 1927	55–27	55
Banking Act	January 19, 1933	58–30	59
Antilynching	January 27, 1938	37–51	59
Antilynching	February 16, 1938	42–46	59
Antipoll tax	November 23, 1942	37–41	52
Antipoll tax	May 15, 1944	36–44	54
Fair Employment Practices Commission	February 9, 1946	48–36	56
British loan	May 7, 1946	41–41	55

Issue	*Date*	*Vote*	*Yeas needed*
Labor disputes	May 25, 194	63–77	54
Antipoll tax	July 31, 1946	39–33	48
Fair Employment	May 19, 1950	52–32	64
Fair Employment	July 12, 1950	55–33	64
Atomic Energy Act	July 26, 1954	44–42	64
Civil Rights Act	March 10, 1960	42–53	64
Amend Rule 22	September 19, 1961	37–43	54
Literacy tests	May 9, 1962	43–53	64
Literacy tests	May 14, 1962	42–52	63
Comsat Act	August 14, 1962	63–27	60
Amend Rule 22	February 7, 1963	54–42	64
Civil Rights Act	June 10, 1964	71–29	67
Legislative reapportionment	September 10, 1964	30–63	62
Voting Rights Act	May 25, 1965	70–30	67
Right-to-work repeal	October 11, 1965	45–47	62
Right-to-work repeal	February 8, 1966	51–48	66
Right-to-work repeal	February 10, 1966	50–49	66
Civil Rights Act	September 14, 1966	54–42	64
Civil Rights Act	September 19, 1966	52–41	62
D.C. Home Rule	October 10, 1966	41–37	52
Amend Rule 22	January 24, 1967	53–46	66
Open Housing	February 20, 1968	55–37	62
Open Housing	February 26, 1968	56–36	62
Open Housing	March 1, 1968	59–35	63
Open Housing	March 4, 1968	65–32	65
Fortas nomination	October 1, 1968	45–43	59
Amend Rule 22	January 16, 1969	51–47	66
Amend Rule 22	January 28, 1969	50–42	62
Electoral College	September 17, 1970	54–36	60
Electoral College	September 29, 1970	53–34	58
Supersonic transport	December 19, 1970	43–48	61
Supersonic transport	December 22, 1970	42–44	58
Amend Rule 22	February 18, 1971	48–37	57
Amend Rule 22	February 23, 1971	50–36	58
Amend Rule 22	March 2, 1971	48–36	56
Amend Rule 22	March 9, 1971	55–39	63
Military Draft	June 23, 1971	65–27	62
Lockheed loan	July 26, 1971	42–47	60
Lockheed loan	July 28, 1971	59–39	66
Lockheed loan	July 30, 1971	53–37	60
Military Draft	September 21, 1971	61–30	61
Rehnquist nomination	December 10, 1971	52–42	63
Equal job opportunity	February 1, 1972	48–37	57
Equal job opportunity	February 3, 1972	53–35	59
Equal job opportunity	February 22, 1972	71–23	63
U.S.-Soviet arms pact	September 14, 1972	76–15	61
Consumer Agency	September 29, 1972	47–29	51
Consumer Agency	October 3, 1972	55–32	58
Consumer Agency	October 5, 1972	52–30	55
School busing	October 10, 1972	45–37	55
School busing	October 11, 1972	49–39	59
School busing	October 12, 1972	49–38	58
Voter registration	April 30, 1973	56–31	58
Voter registration	May 3, 1973	60–34	63
Voter registration	May 9, 1973	67–32	66
Public campaign financing	December 2, 1973	47–33	54
Public campaign financing	December 3, 1973	49–39	59
Rhodesian chrome ore	December 11, 1973	59–35	63
Rhodesian chrome ore	December 13, 1973	62–33	64
Legal services program	December 13, 1973	60–36	64
Legal services program	December 14, 1973	56–29	57
Rhodesian chrome ore	December 18, 1973	63–26	60
Legal services program	January 30, 1974	68–29	65
Genocide Treaty	February 5, 1974	55–36	61
Genocide Treaty	February 6, 1974	55–38	62

Issue	*Date*	*Vote*	*Yeas needed*
Government pay raise	March 6, 1974	67–31	66
Public campaign financing	April 4, 1974	60–36	64
Public campaign financing	April 9, 1974	64–30	63
Public debt ceiling	June 19, 1974	50–43	62
Public debt ceiling	June 19, 1974	45–48	62
Public debt ceiling	June 26, 1974	48–50	66
Consumer Agency	July 30, 1974	56–42	66
Consumer Agency	August 1, 1974	59–39	66
Consumer Agency	August 20, 1974	59–35	63
Consumer Agency	September 19, 1974	64–34	66
Export-Import Bank	December 3, 1974	51–39	60
Export-Import Bank	December 4, 1974	48–44	62
Trade reform	December 13, 1974	71–19	60
Fiscal 1975 supplemental funds	December 14, 1974	56–27	56
Export-Import Bank	December 14, 1974	49–35	56
Export-Import Bank	December 16, 1974	54–34	59
Social services programs	December 17, 1974	70–23	62
Tax law changes	December 17, 1974	67–25	62
Rail Reorganization Act	February 26, 1975	86–8	63
Amend Rule 22	March 5, 1975	73–21	63
Amend Rule 22	March 7, 1975	73–21	63
Tax reduction	March 20, 1975	59–38	60
Tax reduction	March 21, 1975	83–13	60
Consumer Advocacy Agency	May 13, 1975	71–27	60
Senate staffing	June 11, 1975	77–19	64
New Hampshire Senate seat	June 24, 1975	57–39	60
New Hampshire Senate seat	June 25, 1975	56–41	60
New Hampshire Senate seat	June 26, 1975	54–40	60
New Hampshire Senate seat	July 8, 1975	57–38	60
New Hampshire Senate seat	July 9, 1975	57–38	60
New Hampshire Senate seat	July 10, 1975	54–38	60
Voting Rights Act	July 21, 1975	72–19	60
Voting Rights Act	July 23, 1975	76–20	60
Oil price decontrol	July 30, 1975	54–38	60
Anti-school busing amendments	September 23, 1975	46–48	60
Anti-school busing amendments	September 24, 1975	64–33	60
Common-site picketing	November 11, 1975	66–30	60
Common-site picketing	November 14, 1975	58–31	60
Common-site picketing	November 18, 1975	62–37	60
Rail reorganization	December 4, 1975	61–27	60
New York City aid	December 5, 1975	70–27	60
Rice Production Act	February 3, 1976	70–19	60
Antitrust amendments	June 3, 1976	67–22	60
Antitrust amendments	August 31, 1976	63–27	60
Civil rights attorneys' fees	September 23, 1976	63–26	60
Draft resisters pardons	January 24, 1977	53–43	60
Campaign financing	July 29, 1977	49–45	60
Campaign financing	August 1, 1977	47–46	60
Campaign financing	August 2, 1977	52–46	60
Natural gas pricing	September 26, 1977	77–17	60
Labor Law revision	June 7, 1978	42–47	60
Labor Law revision	June 8, 1978	49–41	60
Labor Law revision	June 13, 1978	54–43	60
Labor Law revision	June 14, 1978	58–41	60
Labor Law revision	June 15, 1978	58–39	60
Labor Law revision	June 22, 1978	53–45	60
Revenue Act of 1978	October 9, 1978	62–28	60
Energy taxes	October 14, 1978	71–13	60
Windfall profits tax	December 12, 1979	53–46	60
Windfall profits tax	December 13, 1979	56–40	60
Windfall profits tax	December 14, 1979	56–39	60
Windfall profits tax	December 17, 1979	84–14	60
Lubbers nomination	April 21, 1980	46–60	60

Issue	*Date*	*Vote*	*Yeas needed*
Lubbers nomination	April 22, 1980	62–34	60
Rights of institutionalized	April 28, 1980	44–39	60
Rights of institutionalized	April 29, 1980	56–34	60
Rights of institutionalized	April 30, 1980	53–35	60
Rights of institutionalized	May 1, 1980	60–34	60
Bottlers' antitrust immunity	May 15, 1980	86–6	60
Draft registration funding	June 10, 1980	62–32	60
Zimmerman nomination	August 1, 1980	51–35	60
Zimmerman nomination	August 4, 1980	45–31	60
Zimmerman nomination	August 5, 1980	63–31	60
Alaska lands	August 18, 1980	63–25	60
Vessel tonnage/strip mining	August 21, 1980	61–32	60
Fair Housing amendments	December 3, 1980	51–39	60
Fair Housing amendments	December 4, 1980	62–32	60
Fair Housing amendments	December 9, 1980	54–43	60
Breyer nomination	December 9, 1980	68–28	60
Justice Department authorization	July 10, 1981	38–48	60
Justice Department authorization	July 13, 1981	54–32	60
Justice Department authorization	July 29, 1981	59–37	60
Justice Department authorization	September 10, 1981	57–33	60
Justice Department authorization	September 16, 1981	61–36	60
Justice Department authorization	December 10, 1981	64–35	60
State, Justice, Commerce, Judiciary funds	December 11, 1981	59–35	60
Justice Department authorization	February 9, 1982	63–33	60
Broadcast Senate proceedings	April 20, 1982	47–51	60
Criminal Code Reform Act	April 27, 1982	45–46	60
1982 supplemental funds	May 27, 1982	95–2	60
Voting Rights Act	June 15, 1982	86–8	60
Debt limit increase	September 9, 1982	41–47	60
Debt limit increase	September 13, 1982	45–35	60
Debt limit increase	September 15, 1982	50–44	60
Debt limit increase	September 20, 1982	50–39	60
Debt limit increase	September 21, 1982	53–47	60
Debt limit increase	September 22, 1982	54–46	60
Debt limit increase	September 23, 1982	53–45	60
Antitrust Equal Enforcement Act	December 2, 1982	38–58	60
Antitrust Equal Enforcement Act	December 2, 1982	44–51	60
Transportation Assistance Act	December 13, 1982	75–13	60
Transportation Assistance Act	December 16, 1982	48–50	60
Transportation Assistance Act	December 16, 1982	5–93	60
Transportation Assistance Act	December 19, 1982	89–5	60
Transportation Assistance Act	December 20, 1982	87–8	60
Transportation Assistance Act	December 23, 1982	81–5	60
Jobs funding/interest withholding	March 16, 1983	50–48	60
Jobs funding/interest withholding	March 16, 1983	59–39	60
International trade/interest withholding	April 19, 1983	34–53	60
International trade /interest withholding	April 19, 1983	39–59	60
Defense authorizations, 1984	July 21, 1983	55–41	60
Radio broadcasting to Cuba	August 3, 1983	62–33	60
National Gas Policy Act	November 3, 1983	86–7	60
Capital punishment	February 9, 1984	65–26	60
Hydroelectric power plants	July 30, 1984	60–28	60
Wilkinson nomination	July 31, 1984	57–39	60
Agriculture funds, fiscal 1985	August 6, 1984	54–31	60
Agriculture funds, fiscal 1985	August 8, 1984	68–30	60
Wilkinson nomination	August 9, 1984	65–32	60
Financial Services Act	September 10, 1984	89–3	60
Financial Services Act	September 13, 1984	92–6	60
Broadcasting of Senate proceedings	September 18, 1984	73–26	60
Broadcasting of Senate proceedings	September 21, 1984	37–44	60
Surface Transportation Act	September 24, 1984	70–12	60
Continuing funds	September 29, 1984	92–4	60
Anti-apartheid	July 10, 1985	88–8	60
Line-item veto	July 18, 1985	57–42	60
Line-item veto	July 23, 1985	57–41	60
Line-item veto	July 24, 1985	58–40	60
Anti-apartheid	September 9, 1985	53–34	60
Anti-apartheid	September 11, 1985	57–41	60
Anti-apartheid	September 12, 1985	11–88	60
Debt limit/balanced budget	October 6, 1985	57–38	64
Debt limit/balanced budget	October 9, 1985[1]	53–39	62
Conrail sale	January 23, 1986	90–7	60
Conrail sale	January 30, 1986	70–27	60
Fitzwater nomination	March 18, 1986	64–33	60
Washington airports transfer	March 21, 1986	50–39	60
Washington airports transfer	March 25, 1986	66–32	60
Hobbs Act amendments	April 16, 1986	44–54	60
Defense authorization, fiscal 1987	August 6, 1986	53–46	60
Aid to Nicaraguan contras	August 13, 1986	59–40	60
South Africa sanctions	August 13, 1986	89–11	60
Aid to Nicaraguan contras	August 13, 1986	62–37	60
Rehnquist nomination	September 17, 1986	68–31	60
Product liability reform	September 25, 1986	97–1	60
Omnibus drug bill	October 15, 1986	58–38	60
Immigration reform	October 17, 1986	69–21	60
Contra aid moratorium	March 23, 1987	46–45	60
Contra aid moratorium	March 24, 1987	50–50	60
Contra aid moratorium	March 25, 1987	54–46	60
Relief for the homeless	April 9, 1987	68–29	60
Defense authorization, fiscal 1988	May 15, 1987	52–36	60
Defense authorization, fiscal 1988	May 19, 1987	58–41	60
Defense authorization, fiscal 1988	May 20, 1987	59–39	60
Campaign finance	June 9, 1987	52–47	60
Campaign finance	June 16, 1987	49–46	60
Campaign finance	June 17, 1987	51–47	60
Campaign finance	June 18, 1987	50–47	60
Campaign finance	June 19, 1987	45–43	60
Kuwaiti tanker reflagging	July 9, 1987	57–42	60
Kuwaiti tanker reflagging	July 14, 1987	53–40	60
Kuwaiti tanker reflagging	July 15, 1987	54–44	60
Wells nomination	September 9, 1987	65–24	60
Campaign finance	September 10, 1987	53–42	60
Campaign finance	September 15, 1987	51–44	60
Kuwaiti tanker escort	October 1, 1987	54–45	60
Defense authorization, fiscal 1988	October 1, 1987	41–58	60
Verity nomination	October 13, 1987	85–8	60
War powers compliance	October 20, 1987	67–28	60
Nuclear waste depository	November 10, 1987	87–0	60
Campaign finance	February 26, 1988	53–41	60

Issue	*Date*	*Vote*	*Yeas needed*
Polygraph protection	March 3, 1988	77–19	60
Intelligence oversight	March 15, 1988	73–18	60
Risk notification	March 23, 1988	33–59	60
Risk notification	March 24, 1988	2–93	60
Risk notification	March 28, 1988	41–44	60
Risk notification	March 29, 1988	42–52	60
Campaign spending limitations	April 21, 1988	52–42	60
Campaign spending limitations	April 22, 1988	53–37	60
Immigration legalization program extension	April 28, 1988	40–56	60
Drug-related killings death penalty	June 9, 1988	70–26	60
Great Smoky Mountain Wilderness Act	June 20, 1988	49–35	60
Great Smoky Mountain Wilderness Act	June 21, 1988	54–42	60
Plant-closing notification	June 29, 1988	58–39	60
Plant-closing notification	July 6, 1988	88–5	60
Textile import quotas	September 7, 1988	68–29	60
Minimum wage restoration	September 22, 1988	53–43	60
Minimum wage restoration	September 23, 1988	56–35	60
Parental and medical leave	October 3, 1988	85–6	60
Parental and medical leave	October 7, 1988	50–46	60
Defense authorization, fiscal 1990	August 2, 1989	84–13	60
Airline smoking ban	September 14, 1989	77–21	60
Eastern Airlines strike commission	October 3, 1989	61–36	60
Nicaraguan election aid	October 13, 1989	52–42	60
Nicaraguan election aid	October 17, 1989	74–25	60
Eastern Airlines strike commission	October 26, 1989	62–38	60
Capital gains tax cut	November 14, 1989	51–47	60
Capital gains tax cut	November 15, 1989	51–47	60
Government pay-and-ethics package	November 17, 1989	90–9	60
Armenian genocide day	February 22, 1990	49–49	60
Armenian genocide day	February 27, 1990	48–51	60
Hatch Act revisions	May 1, 1990	70–28	60
AIDS emergency relief	May 15, 1990	95–3	60
Chemical weapons sanctions	May 17, 1990	87–4	60
Omnibus crime package	June 5, 1990	54–37	60
Omnibus crime package	June 7, 1990	57–37	60
Air travel rights for the blind	June 12, 1990	56–44	60
Civil Rights Act of 1990	July 17, 1990	62–38	60
Defense authorization, fiscal1991	August 3, 1990	58–41	60
Motor Vehicle Fuel Efficiency Act	September 14, 1990	68–28	60
Motor Vehicle Fuel Efficiency Act	September 25, 1990	57–42	60
Title X family planning amendments	September 26, 1990	50–46	60
National motor-voter registration	September 26, 1990	55–42	60
Foreign operations funds, fiscal 1991	October 12, 1990	51–38	60
Vertical price fixing	May 7, 1991	61–37	60
Vertical price fixing	May 8, 1991	63–35	60
Crime bill	June 28, 1991	41–58	60
Crime bill	July 10, 1991	56–43	60
Crime bill	July 10, 1991	71–27	60
National motor-voter registration	July 18, 1991	57–41	60
VA-HUD funds, fiscal 1992	July 18, 1991	57–40	60

Issue	*Date*	*Vote*	*Yeas needed*
National motor-voter registration	July 18, 1991	59–40	60
Foreign aid authorization	July 24, 1991	87–10	60
Foreign aid authorization	July 25, 1991	52–44	60
Foreign aid authorization	July 25, 1991	63–33	60
Extended unemployment benefits	July 29, 1991	96–1	60
Defense authorization, fiscal 1992	August 2, 1991	58–40	60
Interior funds, fiscal 1992	September 19, 1991	55–41	60
Federal Facility Compliance Act	October 17, 1991	85–14	60
Civil Rights Act	October 22, 1991	93–4	60
National energy policy	November 1, 1991	50–44	60
Banking reform	November 13, 1991	76–19	60
Iranian hostage release investigation	November 22, 1991	51–43	60
Crime conference report	November 27, 1991	49–38	60
School improvement bill	January 21, 1992	93–0	60
National energy strategy	February 4, 1992	90–5	60
Joint ventures antitrust	February 25, 1992	98–0	60
Lumbee Tribe recognition	February 27, 1992	58–39	60
Public Broadcasting Corp.	March 3, 1992	87–7	60
Crime bill	March 19, 1992	54–43	60
Defense/domestic spending walls	March 26, 1992	50–48	60
Fetal tissue research	March 31, 1992	98–2	60
Motor-voter registration	May 7, 1992	61–38	60
Motor-voter registration	May 12, 1992	58–40	60
Drug abuse mental health	June 9, 1992	84–9	60
Striker replacement	June 11, 1992	55–41	60
Striker replacement	June 16, 1992	57–42	60
Balanced budget amendment	June 30, 1992	56–39	60
Balanced budget amendment	July 1, 1992	56–39	60
National energy strategy	July 23, 1992	58–33	60
National energy strategy	July 28, 1992	93–3	60
Carnes nomination	September 9, 1992	66–30	60
Product liability	September 10, 1992	57–39	60
Product liability	September 10, 1992	58–38	60
School improvement bill	September 15, 1992	85–6	60
Labor, HHS, education funds	September 16, 1992	56–38	60
START treaty	September 29, 1992	87–6	60
School improvement bill	October 2, 1992	59–40	60
Crime bill	October 2, 1992	55–43	60
Fetal tissue research	October 2, 1992	85–12	60
National energy strategy	October 8, 1992	84–8	60
Tax bill	October 8, 1992	80–10	60
Motor-voter registration	March 5, 1993	52–36	60
Motor-voter registration	March 9, 1993	62–38	60
Motor-voter registration	March 16, 1993	59–41	60
Stimulus package	April 2, 1993	55–43	60
Stimulus package	April 3, 1993	52–37	60
Stimulus package	April 5, 1993	49–29	60
Stimulus package	April 21, 1993	56–43	60
Motor-voter registration	May 11, 1993	63–37	60
Campaign finance	June 10, 1993	53–41	60
Campaign finance	June 15, 1993	52–45	60
Campaign finance	June 16, 1993	62–37	60
National service	July 29, 1993	59–41	60
Dellinger nomination	October 7, 1993	59–39	60
Interior funds	October 21, 1993	53–41	60
Interior funds	October 26, 1993	51–45	60
Interior funds	October 28, 1993	54–44	60
State Department nominations	November 3, 1993	58–42	60
Brady bill (gun controls)	November 19, 1993	57–42	60

Issue	*Date*	*Vote*	*Yeas needed*
Napolitano nomination	November 19, 1993	72–26	60
Brady bill (gun controls)	November 19, 1993	57–41	60
Competitiveness bill	March 15, 1994	56–42	60
Federal worker retirement buyout	March 24, 1994	58–41	60
Federal worker retirement buyout	March 24, 1994	63–36	60
Education goals 2000	March 26, 1994	62–23	60
Shearer nomination	May 24, 1994	63–35	60
Brown nomination	May 24, 1994	54–44	60
Brown nomination	May 25, 1994	56–42	60
Product liability	June 28, 1994	54–44	60
Product liability	June 29, 1994	57–41	60
Striker replacement	July 12, 1994	53–47	60
Striker replacement	July 13, 1994	53–46	60
Crime bill	August 25, 1994	61–38	60
Campaign finance	September 22, 1994	96–2	60
California desert protection	September 23, 1994	73–20	60
Campaign finance	September 27, 1994	57–43	60
Campaign finance	September 30, 1994	52–46	66[2]
Tigert nomination	October 3, 1994	63–32	65[3]
Sarokin nomination	October 4, 1994	85–12	60
Elementary and secondary education	October 5, 1994	75–24	60
Lobbying disclosure/gift ban	October 6, 1994	52–46	60
Lobbying disclosure/gift ban	October 7, 1994	55–42	60
California desert protection	October 8, 1994	68–23	60
Unfunded mandates	January 19, 1995	54–44	60
Balanced-budget amendment	February 16, 1995	57–42	60
Striker replacement	March 15, 1995	58–39	60
Health insurance tax deduction	April 3, 1995	83–0	60
Supplemental funds and rescissions	April 6, 1995	56–44	60
Product liability	May 4, 1995	46–53	60
Product liability	May 4, 1995	47–52	60
Product liability	May 8, 1995	43–49	60
Product liability	May 9, 1995	60–38	60
Interstate waste	May 12, 1995	50–47	60
Telecommunications	June 14, 1995	89–11	60
Foster nomination	June 21, 1995	57–43	60
Foster nomination	June 22, 1995	57–43	60
Regulatory overhaul	July 17, 1995	48–46	60
Regulatory overhaul	July 18, 1995	53–47	60
Regulatory overhaul	July 20, 1995	58–40	60
State Department authorization	August 1, 1995	55–45	60
State Department authorization	August 1, 1995	55–45	60
Cuba sanctions	October 12, 1995	56–37	60
Cuba sanctions	October 17, 1995	59–36	60
Cuba sanctions	October 18, 1995	98–0	60
Farm bill	February 1, 1996	53–45	60
Farm bill	February 6, 1996	59–34	60
District of Columbia funds	February 27, 1996	54–44	60
District of Columbia funds	February 29, 1996	52–42	60
District of Columbia funds	March 5, 1996	53–43	60
District of Columbia funds	March 12, 1996	56–44	60
Whitewater committee extension	March 12, 1996	53–47	60
Whitewater committee extension	March 13, 1996	53–47	60
Whitewater committee extension	March 14, 1996	51–46	60
Product liability	March 20, 1996	60–40	60
Whitewater committee extension	March 20, 1996	53–47	60
Whitewater committee extension	March 21, 1996	52–46	60
Presidio Park management	March 27, 1996	51–49	60
Presidio Park management	March 28, 1996	55–45	60
Whitewater committee extension	April 16, 1996	51–46	60
Term limits constitutional amendment	April 23, 1996	58–42	60
Immigration revision	April 29, 1996	91–0	60
Immigration revision	May 2, 1996	100–0	60
White House Travel Office reimbursement	May 7, 1996	52–44	60
White House Travel Office reimbursement	May 8, 1996	53–45	60
White House Travel Office reimbursement	May 9, 1996	52–44	60
White House Travel Office reimbursement	May 14, 1996	54–43	60
Missile defense	June 4, 1996	53–46	60
Campaign finance overhaul	June 25, 1996	54–46	60
Defense authorization	June 26, 1996	52–46	60
Defense authorization	June 28, 1996	53–43	60
Right-to-work legislation	July 10, 1996	31–68	60
Nuclear waste storage	July 16, 1996	65–34	60
FAA reauthorization	October 3, 1996	6–31	60
Volunteer liability limitation	April 29, 1997	53–46	60
Volunteer liability limitation	April 30, 1997	55–44	60
Supplemental funds	May 7, 1997	100–0	60
Compensatory time, flexible credit	May 15, 1997	53–47	60
Compensatory time, flexible credit	June 4, 1997	51–47	60
Defense authorization, fiscal 1998	July 8, 1997	46–45	60
Klein nomination	July 14, 1997	78–11	60
FDA overhaul	September 5, 1997	89–5	60
FDA overhaul	September 16, 1997	94–4	60
District of Columbia funds, fiscal 1998	September 30, 1997	58–41	60
Campaign finance reform	October 7, 1997	52–48	60
Campaign finance reform	October 7, 1997	53–47	60
District of Columbia funds	October 7, 1997	99 –1	60
Campaign finance reform	October 8, 1997	52–47	60
Campaign finance reform	October 9, 1997	52–47	60
Campaign finance reform	October 9, 1997	51–48	60
Highway and Transit reauthorization	October 23, 1997	48–52	60
Highway and Transit reauthorization	October 23, 1997	48–50	60
Highway and Transit reauthorization	October 24, 1997	43–49	60
Highway and Transit reauthorization	October 28, 1997	52–48	60
Education savings accounts	October 31, 1997	56–41	60
Defense authorization, fiscal 1998	October 31, 1997	93–2	60
Education savings accounts	November 4, 1997	56–44	60
Fast track trade procedures	November 4, 1997	69–31	60
Satcher confirmation	February 10, 1998	75–23	60
Human cloning research ban	February 11, 1998	42–54	60
Restrict political use of union dues	February 26, 1998	51–48	60
Restrict political use of union dues	February 26, 1998	45–54	60

Issue	Date	Vote	Yeas needed
Highway and mass transit programs	March 11, 1998	96-3	60
Education savings accounts	March 17, 1998	74-24	60
Expand education savings accounts	March 19, 1998	55-44	60
Expand education savings accounts	March 26, 1998	58-42	60
U.S. antimissile defense policy	May 13, 1998	59-41	60
Create nuclear waste storage in Nevada	June 2, 1998	56-39	60
Set federal policies to curb smoking	June 9, 1998	42-56	62
Set federal policies to curb smoking	June 10, 1998	43-55	60
Set federal policies to curb smoking	June 11, 1998	43-56	60
Set federal policies to curb smoking	June 17, 1998	57-42	60
Limit product liability suits	July 7, 1998	71-24	60
Limit product liability punitive damages	July 9, 1998	51-47	60
U.S. court review, local zoning decisions	July 13, 1998	52-42	60
Legislative branch funds, fiscal 1999	July 21, 1998	83-16	60
U.S. missile defense policy	September 9, 1998	59-41	60
Consumer bankruptcy laws	September 9, 1998	99-1	60
Campaign finance reform	September 10, 1998	52-48	60
Parental consent abortion bill	September 11, 1998	97-0	60
Limit union organizing	September 14, 1998	52-42	60
Evading parental consent abortion laws	September 22, 1998	54-45	60
Limit presidential appointment powers	September 24, 1998	96-1	60
Limit presidential appointment powers	September 28, 1998	53-38	60
Internet sales taxes	September 29, 1998	89-6	60
Banking regulation revision	October 5, 1998	93-0	60
Ban Internet sales taxes for two years	October 7, 1998	94-4	60
Waive federal education spending rules	March 8, 1999	54-41	60
Waive federal education spending rules	March 9, 1999	55-39	60
Authorize $11.4 billion for new teachers	March 10, 1999	44-55	60
Special education funding	March 10, 1999	55-44	60
U.S. troops in Kosovo	March 23, 1999	55-44	60
Social Security "lockbox," debt limit	April 22, 1999	54-45	60
Y2K liability limits	April 26, 1999	94-0	60
Y2K liability limits	April 29, 1999	52-47	60
Social Security "lockbox," debt limit	April 30, 1999	49-44	60
2K liability limits	May 18, 1999	53-45	60
Social Security "lockbox" debt limit	June 15, 1999	53-46	60
Steel, oil, gas loan guarantee	June 15, 1999	70-29	60
Social Security "lockbox"	June 16, 1999	55-44	60
Steel import quotas	June 22, 1999	42-57	60
Agriculture funds, fiscal 2000	June 28, 1999	50-37	60
Transportation funds, fiscal 2000	June 28, 1999	49-40	60
Commerce, State, Justice funds, fiscal 2000	June 28, 1999	49-39	60
Foreign operations funds, fiscal 2000	June 28, 1999	49-41	60
Budget procedures	July 1, 1999	99-1	60
Social Security "lockbox," debt limit	July 16, 1999	52-43	60
Intelligence authorization, fiscal 2000	July 20, 1999	99-0	60
Juvenile justice programs	July 28, 1999	77-22	60
Agriculture funds/milk marketing	August 4, 1999	53-47	60
Transportation funds, fiscal 2000	September 9, 1999	49-49	60
Puerto Rican nationalists clemency	September 13, 1999	93-0	60
Oil royalty valuation system	September 13, 1999	54-40	60
Bankruptcy law revision	September 21, 1999	53-45	60
Stewart nomination	September 21, 1999	55-44	60
Oil royalty valuation system	September 23, 1999	62-39	60
Agriculture funds, fiscal 2000	October 12, 1999	79-20	60
Campaign finance soft money ban	October 19, 1999	52-48	60
Campaign finance soft money, union dues	October 19, 1999	53-47	60
Trade with Sub-Saharan Africa	October 26, 1999	91-8	60
Sub-Saharan African, Caribbean trade	October 29, 1999	45-46	60
Sub-Saharan African, Caribbean trade	November 2, 1999	74-23	60
Omnibus funds, fiscal 2000	November 19, 1999	87-9	60
Nuclear waste storage	February 2, 2000	94-3	60
Berzon nomination	March 8, 2000	86-13	60
Paez nomination	March 8, 2000	85-14	60
Flag desecration amendment	March 29, 2000	100-0	60
Federal gas tax suspension	March 30, 2000	86-11	60
Federal gas tax suspension	April 11, 2000	43-56	60
Marriage penalty tax	April 13, 2000	53-45	60
Marriage penalty tax	April 13, 2000	53-45	60
Victims rights	April 25, 2000	82-12	60
Marriage penalty tax	April 27, 2000	51-44	60
African trade agreement	May 11, 2000	76-18	60
Estate tax repeal	July 11, 2000	99-1	60
Treasury funds, fiscal 2001	July 26, 2000	97-0	60
Intelligence authorization, fiscal 2001	July 26, 2000	96-1	60
Energy, water funds, fiscal 2001	July 27, 2000	100-0	60
Trade with China	July 27, 2000	86-12	60
High technology visas	September 19, 2000	97-1	60
High technology visas	September 26, 2000	94-3	60
High technology visas	September 28, 2000	92-3	60
Interior funds, fiscal 2001	October 5, 2000	89-8	60
Bankruptcy law revision	November 1, 2000	53-30	60
Bankruptcy law revision	December 5, 2000	67-31	60
Bankruptcy law revision	March 14, 2001	80-19	60
ESEA reauthorization	May 1, 2001	96-3	60
Bankruptcy law revision	July 12, 2001	88-10	60
Bankruptcy law revision	July 17, 2001	88-10	60
Mexican trucks access to U.S.	July 26, 2001	70-30	60
Mexican trucks in U.S.	July 27, 2001	57-27	60
Supplemental farm funds	July 30, 2001	95-2	60
Transportation/Mexican trucks in U.S.	August 2, 2001	100-0	60
Supplemental farm funds	August 3, 2001	49-48	60
Defense/energy funds authorization	October 2, 2001	100-0	60
Federal airport security	October 9, 2001	97-0	60

Issue	Date	Vote	Yeas needed
Aviation workers assistance	October 11, 2001	56–44	60
Foreign operations funds	October 15, 2001	50–46	60
Foreign operations funds	October 23, 2001	50–47	60
Safety officers collective bargaining rights	November 6, 2001	56–44	60
Pension contribution limits	November 29, 2001	96–4	60
Energy policies/human cloning	December 3, 2001	1–94	60
Railroad retirement pension board	December 3, 2001	81–15	60
Farm policy revisions	December 5, 2001	73–26	60
Farm policy revisions	December 13, 2001	53–45	60
Farm policy revisions	December 18, 2001	54–43	60
Farm policy revisions	December 19. 2001	54–43	60
Tax bill/unemployment benefits	February 6, 2002	56–39	60
Business tax cut/unemployment benefits	February 6, 2002	48–47	60
Election procedures requirements	March 1, 2002	49–39	60
Election procedures requirements	March 4, 2002	51–44	60
Campaign finance revisions	March 20, 2002	68–32	60
Energy policy bill	April 10, 2002	48–50	60
Energy bill/ANWR drilling	April 18, 2002	36–64	60
Energy bill/ANWR drilling	April 18, 2002	46–54	60
Energy policy bill	April 23, 2002	86–13	60
Andean duty-free trade	April 29, 2002	69–21	60
Andean trade/steelworkers health insurance	May 21, 2002	56–40	60
Andean duty-free trade	May 22, 2002	68–29	60
Supplemental funds, fiscal 2002	June 6, 2002	87–10	60
Hate crimes definitions	June 11, 2002	54–43	60
Terrorism insurance	June 18, 2002	65–31	60
Defense authorization, fiscal 2003	June 26, 2002	98–0	60
Accounting industry reform	July 12, 2002	91–2	60
Smith appeals court nomination	July 15, 2002	94–3	60
Drug patents	July 17, 2002	99–0	60
Clifton appeals court nomination	July 18, 2002	97–1	60
Carmona surgeon general nomination	July 23, 2002	98–0	60
Gibbons appeals court nomination	July 26, 2002	89–0	60
Drug patents	July 31, 2002	66–33	60
Trade promotion authority	August 1, 2002	64–32	60
Interior funds, fiscal 2002/farm disaster aid	September 17, 2002	50–49	60
Homeland security department	September 19, 2002	50–49	60
Interior funds, fiscal 2002/farm disaster aid	September 23, 2002	49–46	60
Interior funds, fiscal 2002/farm disaster aid	September 25, 2002	51–47	60
Homeland security department	September 25, 2002	49–49	60
Homeland security department	September 26, 2002	50–49	60
Homeland security/worker union rights	September 26, 2002	44–53	60
Homeland security/worker union rights	October 1, 2002	45–52	60
Justice department reauthorization	October 3, 2002	93–5	60
Use of force against Iraq	October 3, 2002	95–1	60
Use of force against Iraq	October 10, 2002	75–25	60

Issue	Date	Vote	Yeas needed
Homeland security/worker union rights	November 13, 2002	89–8	60
Homeland security department	November 15, 2002	65–29	60
Homeland security department	November 19, 2002	83–16	60
Terrorism insurance	November 19, 2002	85–12	60
Estrada appeals court nomination	March 6, 2003	55–44	60
Estrada appeals court nomination	March 13, 2003	55–42	60
Estrada appeals court nomination	March 18, 2003	55–45	60
Estrada appeals court nomination	April 2, 2003	55–44	60
Owen appeals court nomination	May 1, 2003	52–44	60
Estrada appeals court nomination	May 5, 2003	52–39	60
Estrada appeals court nomination	May 8, 2003	54–43	60
Owen appeals court nomination	May 8, 2003	52–45	60
Medical malpractice award caps	July 9, 2003	49–48	60
Owen appeals court nomination	July 29, 2003	53–43	60
Estrada appeals court nomination	July 30, 2003	55–43	60
Pryor appeals court nomination	July 31, 2003	53–44	60
Class action lawsuits	October 22, 2003	59–39	60
Pickering appeals court nomination	October 30, 2003	54–43	60
Pryor appeals court nomination	November 6, 2003	51–43	60
Owen appeals court nomination	November 14, 2003	53–42	60
Kuhl appeals court nomination	November 14, 2003	53–43	60
Brown appeals court nomination	November 14, 2003	53–43	60
FAA authorization	November 17, 2003	45–43	60
Dorr agriculture undersecretary nomination	November 18, 2003	57–39	60
Dorr Commodity Credit Corp. nomination	November 18, 2003	57–39	60
Energy policy bill conference report	November 21, 2003	57–40	60
Medicare prescription drug bill	November 24, 2003	70–29	60
Omnibus appropriations, fiscal 2004	January 20, 2004	48–45	60
Omnibus appropriations, fiscal 2004	January 22, 2004	61–32	60
Highway funding	February 2, 2004	75–11	60
Highway funding	February 12, 2004	86–11	60
Medical malpractice lawsuit caps	February 24, 2004	48–45	60
Gun liability lawsuits	February 25, 2004	75–22	60
Corporate tax changes	March 24, 2004	51–47	60
Welfare reauthorization	April 1, 2004	51–47	60
Medical malpractice lawsuit caps	April 7, 2004	49–48	60
Corporate tax changes	April 7, 2004	50–47	60
Asbestos claims fund	April 22, 2004	50–47	60
Internet tax moratorium	April 26, 2004	74–11	60
Internet tax/ethanol	April 29, 2004	40–59	60
Internet tax/energy policy	April 29, 2004	55–43	60
Internet tax moratorium	April 29, 2004	64–34	60
Corporate tax changes	May 11, 2004	90–8	60
Class action lawsuits	July 8, 2004	44–43	60
Same-sex marriage amendment	July 14, 2004	48–50	60

Issue	*Date*	*Vote*	*Yeas needed*
Myers appeals court nomination	July 20, 2004	53–44	60
Saad appeals court nomination	July 22, 2004	52–46	60
Griffin appeals court nomination	July 22, 2004	54–44	60
McKeague appeals court nomination	July 22, 2004	53–44	60
Intelligence operations overhaul	October 5, 2004	85–10	60
Senate intelligence oversight	October 8, 2004	88–3	60
Corporate tax changes	October 10, 2004	66–14	60
Tariffs and trade bill	November 19, 2004	88–5	60
Bankruptcy overhaul	March 8, 2005	69–31	60
Foreign workers temporary U.S. status	April 19, 2005	21–77	60
Agricultural workers in U.S. illegally	April 19, 2005	53–45	60
Seasonal workers exemption	April 19, 2005	83–17	60
Iraq, Afghanistan war funding	April 19, 2005	100–0	60
Surface transportation reauthorization	April 26, 2005	94–6	60
Johnson EPA administrator nomination	April 28, 2005	61–37	60
Surface transportation reauthorization	May 12, 2005	92–7	60
Owen appeals court nomination	May 24, 2005	81–18	60
Bolton United Nations nomination	May 26, 2005	56–42	60
Brown appeals court nomination	June 7, 2005	65–32	60
Pryor appeals court nomination	June 8, 2005	67–32	60
Bolton United Nations nomination	June 20, 2005	54–38	60
Energy policy overhaul	June 23, 2005	92–4	60
Defense authorization	July 26, 2005	50–48	60
Gun liability limitations	July 26, 2005	66–32	60
Defense appropriations	October 5, 2005	95–4	60
Labor-HHS-Education appropriations	October 27, 2005	97–0	60
Patriot Act reauthorization	December 16, 2005	52–47	60
Defense appropriations	December 21, 2005	56–44	60
Alito Supreme Court nomination	January 30, 2006	72–25	60
Asbestos trust fund	February 7, 2006	98–1	60
Patriot Act reauthorization	February 16, 2006	96–3	60
Patriot Act reauthorization	February 28, 2006	69–30	60
Patriot Act reauthorization	March 1, 2006	84–15	60
Low income home energy assistance	March 7, 2006	75–25	60
Lobbying overhaul	March 9, 2006	51–47	60
Lobbying overhaul	March 28, 2006	81–16	60
Immigration overhaul	April 6, 2006	39–60	60
Immigration overhaul	April 6, 2006	38–60	60
Immigration overhaul	April 7, 2006	36–62	60
Flory Defense Department nomination	April 7, 2006	52–41	60
Iraq, Afghanistan war funding	May 2, 2006	92–4	60
Medical malpractice	May 8, 2006	48–42	60
Medical malpractice	May 8, 2006	49–44	60
Small business health plans	May 9, 2006	96–2	60
Small business health plans	May 11, 2006	55–43	60
Immigration overhaul	May 24, 2006	73–25	60
Kavanaugh appeals court nomination	May 25, 2006	67–30	60

Issue	*Date*	*Vote*	*Yeas needed*
Interior secretary nomination	May 26, 2006	85–8	60
Same-sex marriage ban amendment	June 7, 2006	49–48	60
Estate tax repeal	June 8, 2006	57–41	60
Native Hawaiians policy	June 8, 2006	56–41	60
Defense authorization	June 22, 2006	98–1	60
Gulf of Mexico offshore drilling	July 26, 2006	86–12	60
Gulf of Mexico offshore drilling	July 31, 2006	72–23	60
Tax package and minimum wage	August 3, 2006	56–42	60
Port security overhaul	September 14, 2006	98–0	60
U.S.-Mexican border fence	September 20, 2006	94–0	60
U.S.-Mexican border fence	September 28, 2006	71–28	60
Abortion parental notification	September 29, 2006	57–42	60
FDA commissioner nomination	December 7, 2006	89–6	60
Jordan appeals court nomination	December 8, 2006	93–0	60
Tax and trade package	December 9, 2006	78–10	60
Ethics and lobbying overhaul	January 16 2007	95–2	60
Ethics and lobbying overhaul	January 17, 2007	51–46	60
Minimum wage increase	January 24, 2007	49–48	60
Minimum wage increase	January 24, 2007	54–43	60
Minimum wage increase	January 30, 2007	87–10	60
Minimum wage increase	January 31, 2007	88–8	60
U.S. troop levels in Iraq	February 1, 2007	0–97	60
U.S. troop levels in Iraq	February 5, 2007	49–47	60
Continuing appropriations fiscal 2007	February 13, 2007	71–26	60
Iraq war troop surge	February 17, 2007	56–34	60
September 11 commission recommendations	February 27, 2007	97–0	60
September 11 commission recommendations	March 9, 2007	46–49	60
September 11 commission recommendations	March 9, 2007	69–26	60
Iraq mission	March 14, 2007	89–9	60
Supplemental appropriations fiscal 2007	March 28, 2007	97–0	60
Intelligence authorization fiscal 2007	April 12, 2007	94–3	60
Intelligence authorization fiscal 2007	April 16, 2007	41–40	60
Intelligence authorization fiscal 2007	April 17, 2007	50–45	60
Medicare prescription drug negotiations	April 18, 2007	55–42	60
Court security	April 18, 2007	93–3	60
FDA overhaul	May 3, 2007	63–28	60
FDA overhaul	May 7, 2007	82–8	60
Water projects authorization	May 10, 2007	89–7	60
Iraq troop withdrawal by March 31, 2008	May 16, 2007	29–67	60
Withholding Iraq economic aid	May 16, 2007	52–44	60
Sense of Senate on Iraq funding	May 16, 2007	87–9	60
Sense of Senate on Iraq mission	May 17, 2007	94–1	60
Immigration overhaul	May 21, 2007	69–23	60
Immigration overhaul	June 7, 200	33–63	60
Immigration overhaul	June 7, 2007	34–61	60

Issue	Date	Vote	Yeas needed
Immigration overhaul	June 7, 2007	45–50	60
No confidence: Attorney General Gonzales	June 11, 2007	53–38	60
Energy policy	June 11, 2007	91–0	60
Energy policy	June 21, 2007	57–36	60
Energy policy	June 21, 2007	61–32	60
Energy policy	June 21, 2007	62–32	60
Employee union formation	June 26, 2007	51–48	60
Immigration overhaul	June 26, 2007	64–35	60
Immigration overhaul	June 28, 2007	46–53	60
Defense authorization fiscal 2008	July 11, 2007	56–41	60
Defense authorization fiscal 2008	July 17, 2007	52–47	60
Small business tax breaks	July 30, 2007	80–0	60
Ethics and lobbying overhaul	August 2, 2007	80–17	60
District of Columbia voting rights	September 18, 2007	57–42	60
Defense authorization fiscal 2008	September 19, 2007	56–43	60
Defense authorization fiscal 2008	September 27, 2007	60–39	60
Children's health insurance	September 27, 2007	69–30	60
Defense authorization fiscal 2008	September 27, 2007	89–6	60
Southwick appeals court nomination	October 24, 2007	62–35	60
Immigrant education	October 24, 2007	52–44	60
Amtrak reauthorization	October 30, 2007	79–13	60
Children's health insurance	October 31, 2007	62–33	60
Children's health insurance	November 1, 2007	65–30	60
Iraq war appropriations	November 16, 2007	45–53	60
Iraq war appropriations/troop withdrawal	November 16, 2007	53–45	60
Farm bill reauthorization	November 16, 2007	55–42	60
Alternative minimum tax	December 6, 2007	46–48	60
Energy policy	December 7, 2007	53–42	60
Energy policy/CAFE standards	December 13, 2007	59–40	60
Farm bill reauthorization	December 13, 2007	78–12	60
Foreign intelligence surveillance	December 17, 2007	76–10	60
Omnibus appropriations fiscal 2008	December 18, 2007	44–51	60
Foreign intelligence surveillance	January 28, 2008	48–45	60
Foreign intelligence surveillance	January 28, 2008	48–45	60
Economic stimulus	February 4, 2008	80–4	60
Economic stimulus	February 6, 2008	58–41	60
Foreign intelligence surveillance	February 12, 2008	69–29	60
Intelligence authorization fiscal 2008	February 13, 2008	92–4	60
Indian health care reauthorization	February 25, 2008	85–2	60
U.S. troop deployments in Iraq	February 26, 2008	70–24	60
Report on al Qaeda	February 27, 2008	89–3	60
Renewable energy	February 28. 2008	48–46	60
Consumer Product Safety Commission	March 3, 2008	86–1	60
Renewable energy	April 1, 2008	94–1	60
Renewable energy/mortgage relief	April 8, 2008	92–6	60
Surface Transportation law corrections	April 14, 2008	93–1	60
Surface transportation corrections	April 17, 2008	90–2	60

Issue	Date	Vote	Yeas needed
Veterans benefits expansion	April 22, 2008	94–0	60
Wage discrimination	April 23, 2008	56–42	60
FAA reauthorization	April 28, 2008	88–0	60
FAA reauthorization	May 6, 2008	49–42	60
National flood insurance	May 6, 2008	90–1	60
Public safety workers organizing rights	May 13, 2008	69–29	60
Climate change trading system	June 2, 2008	74–14	60
Climate change trading system	June 6, 2008	48–36	60
Energy and oil company taxes	June 10, 2008	51–43	60
Tax reduction extensions	June 10, 2008	50–44	60
Medicare physician payments	June 12, 2008	54–39	60
Tax reduction extensions	June 17, 2008	52–44	60
Mortgage relief	June 24, 2008	83–9	60
Foreign intelligence surveillance	June 25, 2008	80–15	60
Medicare physician payments	June 26, 2008	58–40	60
Mortgage relief	July 7, 2008	76–10	60
Foreign intelligence surveillance	July 9, 2008	72–26	60
Medicare physician payments	July 9, 2008	69–30	60
Mortgage relief	July 10, 2008	84–12	60
HIV/AIDS program reauthorization	July 11, 2008	65–3	60
Energy futures speculation	July 22, 2008	94–0	60
Energy futures speculation	July 25, 2008	50–43	60
Mortgage relief	July 25, 2008	80–13	60
Low-income energy assistance	July 26, 2008	50–35	60
Omnibus domestic and foreign policy bills	July 28, 2008	52–40	60
Tax cuts extensions	July 29, 2008	53–43	60
Media shield	July 30, 2008	51–43	60
Tax reduction extensions	July 30, 2008	51–43	60
Defense authorization fiscal 2009	July 31, 2008	51–39	60
Defense authorization fiscal 2009	September 8, 2008	83–0	60
Defense authorization fiscal 2009	September 16, 2008	61–32	60
Continuing appropriations	September 27, 2008	83–12	60
Railroad safety/Amtrak authorization	September 29, 2008	69–17	60
Unemployment benefits extension	November 20, 2008	89–6	60
Automobile industry loans	December 11, 2008	52–35	60
Public lands designations	January 11, 2009	66–12	60
Public lands designations	January 14, 2009	68–24	60
Wage discrimination/Lilly Ledbetter Act	January 15, 2009	72–23	60
Economic stimulus legislation	February 9, 2009	61–36	60
District of Columbia House membership	February 24, 2009	62–34	60
Omnibus appropriations fiscal 2009	March 10, 2009	62–35	60
Public lands historic sites	March 16, 2009	73–21	60
National Service Programs authorization	March 23, 2009	74–14	60
Hill nomination as Iraq ambassador	April 20, 2009	73–17	60
Expand federal fraud laws	April 27, 2009	84–4	60
Hayes nomination as Interior secretary	May 13, 2009	57–39	60
Credit card company regulation	May 19, 2009	92–2	60
Supplemental appropriations fiscal 2009	May 21, 2009	94–1	60
Tobacco regulation by FDA	June 2, 2009	84–11	60

Issue	*Date*	*Vote*	*Yeas needed*
Tobacco regulation by FDA	June 8, 2009	61–30	60
Tobacco regulation by FDA	June 10, 2009	67–30	60
Foreign tourism promotion office	June 16, 2009	90–3	60
Foreign tourism promotion office	June 16, 2009	53–34	60
Koh State Department nomination	June 24. 2009	65–31	60
Groves nomination as Census director	July 13, 2009	76–15	60
Expanding federal hate crime laws	July 16, 2009	63–28	60
Agriculture appropriations fiscal 2010	August 3, 2009	83–11	60
Foreign tourism promotion office	September 8, 2009	80–19	60
Sunstein nomination to OMB office	September 9, 2009	63–35	60
State, Justice, Commerce appropriations fiscal 2010	October 13, 2009	56–38	60
Energy, water appropriations fiscal 2010	October 14, 2009	79–17	60
Medicare doctor reimbursements	October 21, 2009	47–53	60
Defense funding authorization fiscal 2010	October 22, 2009	64–35	60
Unemployment benefits extension	October 27, 2009	87–13	60
Unemployment benefits extension	November 2, 2009	85–2	60
Unemployment benefits extension	November 4, 2009	97–1	60
State, Justice, Commerce appropriations fiscal 2010	November 5, 2009	60–39	60
Hamilton circuit court nomination	November 17, 2009	70–29	60
Health care overhaul, homeowners tax	November 21, 2009	60–39	60
Omnibus appropriations fiscal 2010	December 12, 2009	60–34	60
Defense appropriations fiscal 2010	December 18, 2009	63–33	60
Health care overhaul	December 21, 2009	60–40	60
Health care overhaul	December 22, 2009	60–39	60
Health care overhaul	December 23, 2009	60–39	60
Bernanke Federal Reserve nomination	January 28, 2010	77–23	60
Smith Labor Dept. solicitor nomination	February 1, 2010	60–32	60
Johnson GSA administrator nomination	February 4, 2010	82–16	60
Becker nomination Labor Relations Board	February 9, 2010	52–33	60
Jobs package; payroll tax holiday	February 22, 2010	62–30	60
Travel promotion, Capitol police	February 25, 2010	76–20	60
Keenan appeals court nomination	March 2, 2010	99–0	60
Extend tax cut, unemployment benefits	March 9, 2010	66–34	60
Extend tax cuts, unemployment benefits	March 10, 2010	66–33	60
Business taxes, highway extension	March 15, 2010	61–30	60

Issue	*Date*	*Vote*	*Yeas needed*
Short-term program extension	April 12, 2010	60–34	60
Short-term program extensions	April 15, 2010	60–38	60
Brainard Treasury nomination	April 19, 2010	84–10	60
Financial regulatory overhaul	April 26, 2010	57–41	60
Financial regulatory overhaul	April 27, 2010	57–41	60
Financial regulatory overhaul	April 28, 2010	56–42	60
Financial regulatory overhaul	May 19, 2010	57–42	60
Financial regulatory overhaul	May 20, 2010	60–40	60
Supplemental appropriations fiscal 2010	May 27, 2010	69–29	60
Tax cut extension, unemployment benefits	June 17, 2010	56–40	60
Tax cut extension, unemployment benefits	June 24, 2010	57–41	60
Small business taxes and lending fund	June 29, 2010	66–33	60
Tax extension and unemployment benefits	June 30, 2010	58–38	60
Financial regulatory overhaul	July 15, 2010	60–38	60
Unemployment benefits extension	July 20, 2010	60–40	60
Small business lending fund	July 22, 2010	60–37	60
Supplemental appropriations fiscal 2010	July 22, 2010	46–51	60
Campaign finance disclosure	July 27, 2010	57–41	60
Small business taxes and lending fund	July 29, 2010	58–42	60
Medicaid and education assistance	August 4, 2010	61–38	60
Health care overhaul law amendments	September 14, 2010	46–52	60
Health care overhaul law amendments	September 14, 2010	56–42	60
Small business taxes and lending fund	September 14, 2010	61–37	60
Small business taxes and lending fund	September 16, 2010	61–38	60
"Don't ask, don't tell" policy repeal	September 21, 2010	56–43	60
Campaign finance disclosure	September 23, 2010	59–39	60
Social Security tax cut for corporations	September 28, 2010	53–45	60
Continuing appropriations fiscal 2010 and 2011	September 28, 2010	84–14	60
Wage discrimination	November 17, 2010	58–4	60
Food safety overhaul, FDA enforcement	November 17, 2010	74–25	60
Food safety overhaul, FDA enforcement	November 29, 2010	69–26	60
Tax rate extensions	December 4, 2010	53–36	60
Tax rate extensions	December 4, 2010	53–37	60
Social Security single payment	December 8, 2010	53–45	60
Public safety workers collective bargaining	December 8, 2010	55–43	60
Health, compensation fund first-responders	December 9, 2010	57–42	60
"Don't ask, don't tell" policy repeal	December 9, 2010	57–40	60
Tax rate extensions	December 13, 2010	83–15	60
Immigration policy revisions	December 18, 2010	55–41	60
"Don't ask, don't tell" policy repeal	December 18, 2010	63–33	60

Issue	*Date*	*Vote*	*Yeas needed*
Continuing appropriations fiscal 2011	December 21, 2010	82–14	60
New START agreement with Russia	December 21, 2010	67–28	60
FAA reauthorization	February 17, 2011	96–2	60
Patent law overhaul	March 7, 2011	87–3	60
Small business research	March 14, 2011	84–12	60
Small business research	May 4, 2011	52–44	60
McConnell judicial nomination	May 4, 2011	63–33	60
Cole Justice Department nomination	May 9, 2011	50–40	60
Liu judicial nomination	May 19, 2011	52–43	60
Patriot Act extension	May 23, 2011	74–8	60
Patriot Act extension	May 26, 2011	79–18	60
Ethanol tax provisions	June 14, 2011	40–59	60
Economic development reauthorization	June 21, 2011	49–51	60
Millionaires' taxes sense of Senate	July 7, 2011	74–22	60
Millionaires' taxes sense of Senate	July 13, 2011	51–49	60
Military constructions, VA funding	July 13, 2011	89–11	60
Military constructions, VA funding	July 14, 2011	71–26	60
Debt limit increase	July 31, 2011	50–49	60
Patent law overhaul	September 6, 2011	93–5	60
Myanmar sanctions	September 12, 2011	53–33	60
Myanmar sanctions	September 13, 2011	61–38	60
Trade preferences	September 19, 2011	84–8	60
Short-term continuing appropriations	September 26, 2011	54–35	60
Currency misalignment/China	October 3, 2011	79–19	60
Currency misalignment/China	October 6, 2011	62–38	60
Job creation	October 11, 2011	50–49	60
Public employee jobs funding	October 20, 2011	50–50	60
Tax withholding payments repeal	October 20, 2011	57–43	60
Agriculture, CJS, Housing appropriations	October 20, 2011	82–16	60
Tax withholding payments repeal	November 7, 2011	94–1	60
Energy, State, Treasury appropriations	November 10, 2011	81–14	60
Defense funding authorization	November 30, 2011	88–12	60
Halligan judicial nomination	December 6, 2011	54–45	60
Cordray consumer agency nomination	December 8, 2011	53–45	60
Eisen ambassador nomination	December 12, 2011	70–16	60
Aponte ambassador nomination	December 12, 2011	49–37	60
Congressional insider-trading ban	January 30, 2012	93–2	60
Surface transportation reauthorization	February 9, 2012	85–11	60
Jordan judicial nomination	February 13, 2012	89–5	60
Surface transportation reauthorization	February 17, 2012	54–42	60
Surface transportation reauthorization	March 6, 2012	52–44	60
Small business auditing, SEC oversight	March 20, 2012	54–45	60
Small business auditing, SEC oversight	March 20, 2012	55–44	60
Small business auditing, SEC oversight	March 21, 2012	76–22	60
Congressional insider-trading ban	March 22, 2012	96–3	60
Oil and gas tax breaks repeal	March 26, 2012	92–4	60
Postal Service overhaul	March 27, 2012	51–46	60
Oil and gas tax breaks repeal	March 29, 2012	51–47	60
Millionaires minimum tax	April 16, 2012	51–45	60
Postal Service overhaul	April 17, 2012	74–22	60
Student loan interest rate extension	May 8, 2012	52–45	60
Outlaw wage discrimination by gender	June 5, 2012	52–47	60
Farm, food, nutrition reauthorizations	June 7, 2012	90–8	60
Aponte ambassador nomination	June 14, 2012	62–37	60
Hurwitz judicial nomination	June 11, 2012	60–31	60
Flood insurance reauthorization	June 21, 2012	96–2	60
FDA user fees reauthorization	June 25, 2012	89–3	60
Small business tax cuts	July 10, 2012	80–14	60
Small business tax cuts	July 12, 2012	57–41	60
Small business tax cuts	July 12, 2012	53–44	60
Campaign finance disclosure	July 16, 2012	51–44	60
Campaign finance disclosure	July 17, 2012	53–45	60
U.S. jobs outsourcing tax credits	July 19, 2012	56–42	60
Cybersecurity standards	July 26, 2012	84–11	60
Bacharach judicial nomination	July 30, 2012	56–34	60
Cybersecurity standards	August 2, 2012	52–46	60
Veterans job trainings	September 11, 2012	95–1	60
Continuing appropriations fiscal 2013	September 19, 2012	76–22	60
Continuing appropriations fiscal 2013	September 21, 2012	62–30	60
Hunting access on U.S. lands	September 21, 2012	84–7	60
Cybersecurity standards	November 14, 2012	51–47	60
Hunting access on U.S. lands	November 15, 2012	84–12	60
Defense authorization fiscal 2013	December 3, 2012	93–0	60
Extend FDIC insurance	December 11, 2012	76–20	60
Disaster supplement, Superstorm Sandy	December 21, 2012	91–1	60

1. Vote was taken after midnight in the session that began October 8, 1985.

2. Because the bill would have changed Senate rules, two-thirds of those present and voting were required to invoke cloture: sixty-six in this case instead of the usual sixty.

3. Because the bill would have changed Senate rules, two-thirds of those present and voting were required to invoke cloture: sixty-five in this case instead of the usual sixty.

Attempted and Successful Cloture Votes, 1919–2013

Congress		First session		Second session		Total	
		Attempted	*Successful*	*Attempted*	*Successful*	*Attempted*	*Successful*
66th	(1919–1921)	2	1	0	0	2	1
67th	(1921–1923)	1	0	0	0	1	0
68th	(1923–1925)	0	0	0	0	0	0
69th	(1925–1927)	2	1	5	2	7	3
70th	(1927–1929)	0	0	0	0	0	0
71st	(1929–1931)	0	0	0	0	0	0
72nd	(1931–1933)	1	0	0	0	1	0
73rd	(1933–1935)	0	0	0	0	0	0
74th	(1935–1937)	0	0	0	0	0	0
75th	(1937–1939)	0	0	2	0	2	0
76th	(1939–1941)	0	0	0	0	0	0
77th	(1941–1943)	0	0	1	0	1	0
78th	(1943–1945)	0	0	1	0	1	0
79th	(1945–1947)	0	0	4	0	4	0
80th	(1947–1949)	0	0	0	0	0	0
81st	(1949–1951)	0	0	2	0	2	0
82nd	(1951–1953)	0	0	0	0	0	0
83rd	(1953–1955)	0	0	1	0	1	0
84th	(1955–1957)	0	0	0	0	0	0
85th	(1957–1959)	0	0	0	0	0	0
86th	(1959–1961)	0	0	1	0	1	0
87th	(1961–1963)	1	0	3	1	4	1
88th	(1963–1965)	1	0	2	1	3	1
89th	(1965–1967)	2	1	5	0	7	1
90th	(1967–1969)	1	0	5	1	6	1
91st	(1969–1971)	2	0	4	0	6	0
92nd	(1971–1973)	10	2	10	2	20	4
93rd	(1973–1975)	10	2	21	7	31	9
94th	(1975–1977)	23	13	4	4	27	17
95th	(1977–1979)	5	1	8	2	13	3
96th	(1979–1981)	4	1	17	9	21	10
97th	(1981–1983)	7	2	20	7	27	9
98th	(1983–1985)	7	2	12	9	19	11
99th	(1985–1987)	9	1	14	9	23	10
100th	(1987–1989)	23	5	20	6	43	11[1]
101st	(1989–1991)	9	6	15	5	24	11
102nd	(1991–1993)	20	9	28	14	48	23
103rd	(1993–1995)	20	4	22	10	42	14[2]
104th	(1995–1997)	21	4	29	5	50	9
105th	(1997–1999)	24	7	29	11	53	18
106th	(1999–2001)	36	11	22	17	58	28
107th	(2001–2003)	22	12	39	22	61	34
108th	(2003–2005)	23	1	26	11	49	12
109th	(2005–2007)	21	13	33	21	54	34
110th	(2007–2009)	62	31	50	30	112	61
111th	(2009–2011)	39	35	52	28	91	63
112th	(2011–2013)	34	19	39	22	73	41
Totals		442	184	546	256	988	440

NOTE: The number of votes required to invoke cloture was changed March 7, 1975, from two-thirds of those present and voting, to three-fifths of the total Senate membership, as Rule XXII of the standing rules of the Senate was amended.

1. The Senate Historical Office records twelve successful votes. One of the twelve, taken on July 16, 1987, and related to Kuwaiti tanker flagging, is recorded by the Office as having been by unanimous consent. For this table, the eleven votes were all by roll call.

2. The Senate Historical Office records forty-six attempted cloture votes for the 100th Congress. However, five of those votes, all on nominations, were taken together with one roll call. For this table, CQ Press treats the five as a single vote, giving a total of forty-two.

SOURCES: *Congress and the Nation*, selected volumes (Washington, D.C.: CQ Press, selected years); *CQ Almanac*, selected volumes (Washington, D.C.: Congressional Quarterly, selected years); Richard S. Beth, Congressional Research Service, Library of Congress; www.senate.gov/reference.

House Discharge Petitions since 1931

The discharge petition is a little-used but dramatic House device that enables a majority of representatives to bring to the floor legislation blocked in committee. The following table shows the frequency with which the discharge petition has been used since the present discharge procedure was adopted in 1931 through 2012.

Although the procedure is rarely used and even more rarely successful, it may on occasion indirectly succeed by prompting a legislative committee, the Rules Committee, or the leadership to act on a measure and thereby avoid the discharge.

Congress		*Discharge petitions*	Discharge motion		*Committee discharged*	Underlying measure[3]	
			Entered[1]	*Called up*[2]		*Passed House*	*Received final approval*[4]
72nd	(1931–1933)	12	5	5	1	1	–
73rd	(1933–1935)	31	6	1	1	1	–
74th	(1935–1937)	33	3	2	2	–	–
75th	(1937–1939)	43	4	4	3[5]	2	1
76th	(1939–1941)	37[5]	2	2	2	2	–
77th	(1941–1943)	15	1	1	1	1	–
78th	(1943–1945)	21	3	3	3	3	1[6]
79th	(1945–1947)	35	3	1	1	1	–
80th	(1947–1949)	20	1	1	1	1	–
81st	(1949–1951)	34	3	1	1	1	–
82nd	(1951–1953)	14	–	–	–	–	–
83rd	(1953–1955)	10	1	1	1	1	–
84th	(1955–1957)	6	–	–	–	–	–
85th	(1957–1959)	7	1	1	1	1	–
86th	(1959–1961)	7	1	1	1	1	1
87th	(1961–1963)	6	–	–	–	–	–
88th	(1963–1965)	5	–	–	–	–	–
89th	(1965–1967)	6	1	1	1	1	–
90th	(1967–1969)	4	–	–	–	–	–
91st	(1969–1971)	12	1	1	1	1	–
92nd	(1971–1973)	15	1	1	1	–	–
93rd	(1973–1975)	10	–	–	–	–	–
94th	(1975–1977)	15	–	–	–	–	–
95th	(1977–1979)	11	–	–	–	–	–
96th	(1979–1981)	14	2	1	1	–	–
97th	(1981–1983)	24	1	–	–	–	–
98th	(1983–1985)	13	1	–	–	–	–
99th	(1985–1987)	10	1	–	–	–	–
100th	(1987–1989)	5[8]	–	–	–	–	–
101st	(1989–1991)	8	1	–	–	–	–
102nd	(1991–1993)	8	1[9]	1[9]	1[9]	–	–
103rd	(1993–1995)	26	2[9]	2[9]	2[9]	1	1[6]
104th	(1995–1997)	15	–	–	–	–	–
105th	(1997–1999)	8	–	–	–	–	–
106th	(1999–2001)	11	–	–	–	–	–
107th	(2001–2003)	12	1	–	–	–	–
108th	(2003–2005)	16	–	–	–	–	–
109th	(2005–2007)	18	–	–	–	–	–
110th	(2007–2009)	18	–	–	–	–	–
111th	(2009–2011)	13	–	–	–	–	–
112th	(2011–2013)	6	–	–	–	–	–
Totals		634	47	31	26	19	4

1. A discharge motion is "entered" when the petition receives a sufficient number of member signatures for it to be entered on the Calendar of Motions to Discharge Committees. This number was 145 in the 72nd and 73rd Congresses, 219 in the 86th and 87th Congresses, and 218 for all other Congresses in the table.
2. A discharge motion may be offered on the floor on any second or fourth Monday falling at least seven legislative days after the discharge petition is entered. Each day on which the House convenes is usually a legislative day.
3. A discharge petition may be filed to bring to the floor either a substantive measure in committee or a "special rule" from the Committee on Rules providing for House consideration of such a measure that is either in committee or previously reported. The last two columns of this table reflect action on the underlying, substantive measure, not on the special rule, if any, on which discharge was directly sought.
4. Includes bills and joint resolutions becoming law; constitutional amendments submitted to the states for ratification; resolutions agreed to by the House; and concurrent resolutions finally agreed to by both chambers.
5. During this Congress, the Rules Committee was discharged from a special rule for consideration of one measure, and the measure was taken up but then recommitted. Subsequently, the Rules Committee was discharged from a second special rule for consideration of the measure. This measure accordingly appears twice under "Committee discharged" and earlier columns, but only once under "Passed House" and subsequently.
6. Resolution attempting to change House Rules.
7. Includes one petition entered with respect to a special rule on a measure and another on the same measure directly.
8. Includes one petition filed on a special rule for considering two measures.
9. Includes one measure in the 102nd Congress and two in the 103rd from which the committee was discharged, and which were brought to the floor, by unanimous consent after the discharge petition was entered.

SOURCE: Richard S. Beth, "The Discharge Rule in the House: Recent Use in Historical Context," Congressional Research Service, Library of Congress, September 15, 1997; update provided by CRS, September 1999, April 2000, December 2005. Clerk of the House, March 2010, http://clerk.house.gov/art_history/house_history/index.html.

Congressional Reapportionment, 1789–2010

	Constitution										*Year of Census*[1]												
	(1789)[2]	*1790*	*1800*	*1810*	*1820*	*1830*	*1840*	*1850*	*1860*	*1870*	*1880*	*1890*	*1900*	*1910*	*1930*[3]	*1940*	*1950*	*1960*	*1970*	*1980*	*1990*	*2000*	*2010*
Alabama				1[4]	3	5	7	7	6	8	8	9	9	10	9	9	9	8	7	7	7	7	7
Alaska																	1[4]	1	1	1	1	1	1
Arizona														1[4]	1	2	2	3	4	5	6	8	9
Arkansas						1[4]	1	2	3	4	5	6	7	7	7	7	6	4	4	4	4	4	4
California							2[4]	2	3	4	6	7	8	11	20	23	30	38	43	45	52	53	53
Colorado										1[4]	1	2	3	4	4	4	4	4	5	6	6	7	7
Conn.	5	7	7	7	6	6	4	4	4	4	4	4	5	5	6	6	6	6	6	6	6	5	5
Delaware	1	1	1	2	1	1	1	1	1	1	1	1	1	1	1	1	1	1	1	1	1	1	1
Florida							1[4]	1	1	2	2	2	3	4	5	6	8	12	15	19	23	25	27
Georgia	3	2	4	6	7	9	8	8	7	9	10	11	11	12	10	10	10	10	10	10	11	13	14
Hawaii																	1[4]	2	2	2	2	2	2
Idaho											1[4]	1	1	2	2	2	2	2	2	2	2	2	2
Illinois				1[4]	1	3	7	9	14	19	20	22	25	27	27	26	25	24	24	22	20	19	18
Indiana				1[4]	3	7	10	11	11	13	13	13	13	13	12	11	11	11	11	10	10	9	9
Iowa							2[4]	2	6	9	11	11	11	11	9	8	8	7	6	6	5	5	4
Kansas									1	3	7	8	8	8	7	6	6	5	5	5	4	4	4
Kentucky		2	6	10	12	13	10	10	9	10	11	11	11	11	9	9	8	7	7	7	6	6	6
Louisiana				1[4]	3	3	4	4	5	6	6	6	7	8	8	8	8	8	8	8	7	7	6
Maine				7[4]	7	8	7	6	5	5	4	4	4	4	3	3	3	2	2	2	2	2	2
Maryland	6	8	9	9	9	8	6	6	5	6	6	6	6	6	6	6	7	8	8	8	8	8	8
Massachusetts	8	14	17	13[5]	13	12	10	11	10	11	12	13	14	16	15	14	14	12	12	11	10	10	9
Michigan						1[4]	3	4	6	9	11	12	12	13	17	17	18	19	19	18	16	15	14
Minnesota								2[4]	2	3	5	7	9	10	9	9	9	8	8	8	8	8	8
Mississippi				1[4]	1	2	4	5	5	6	7	7	8	8	7	7	6	5	5	5	5	4	4
Missouri					1	2	5	7	9	13	14	15	16	16	13	13	11	10	10	9	9	9	8
Montana											14	1	1	2	2	2	2	2	2	2	1	1	1
Nebraska									1[4]	1	3	6	6	6	5	4	4	3	3	3	3	3	3
Nevada									1[4]	1	1	1	1	1	1	1	1	1	1	2	2	3	4
New Hampshire	3	4	5	6	6	5	4	3	3	3	2	2	2	2	2	2	2	2	2	2	2	2	2
New Jersey	4	5	6	6	6	6	5	5	5	7	7	8	10	12	14	14	14	15	15	14	13	13	12
New Mexico														1[4]	1	2	2	2	2	3	3	3	3
New York	6	10	17	27	34	40	34	33	31	33	34	34	37	43	45	45	43	41	39	34	31	29	27
North Carolina	5	10	12	13	13	13	9	8	7	8	9	9	10	10	11	12	12	11	11	11	12	13	13
North Dakota											1[4]	1	2	3	2	2	2	2	1	1	1	1	1
Ohio			1[4]	6	14	19	21	21	19	20	21	21	21	22	24	23	23	24	23	21	19	18	16
Oklahoma													5[4]	8	9	8	6	6	6	6	6	5	5
Oregon								1[4]	1	1	1	2	2	3	3	4	4	4	4	5	5	5	5
Pennsylvania	8	13	18	23	26	28	24	25	24	27	28	30	32	36	34	33	30	27	25	23	21	19	18
Rhode Island	1	2	2	2	2	2	2	2	2	2	2	2	2	3	2	2	2	2	2	2	2	2	2
South Carolina	5	6	8	9	9	9	7	6	4	5	7	7	7	7	6	6	6	6	6	6	6	6	7
South Dakota											2[4]	2	2	3	2	2	2	2	2	1	1	1	1
Tennessee		1[4]	3	6	9	13	11	10	8	10	10	10	10	10	9	10	9	9	8	9	9	9	9
Texas							2[4]	2	4	6	11	13	16	18	21	21	22	23	24	27	30	32	36
Utah												1[4]	1	2	2	2	2	2	2	3	3	3	4
Vermont		2	4	6	5	5	4	3	3	3	2	2	2	2	1	1	1	1	1	1	1	1	1
Virginia	10	19	22	23	22	21	15	13	11	9	10	10	10	10	9	9	10	10	10	10	11	11	11
Washington											1[4]	2	3	5	6	6	7	7	7	8	9	9	10
West Virginia										3	4	4	5	6	6	6	6	5	4	4	3	3	3
Wisconsin							2[4]	3	6	8	9	10	11	11	10	10	10	10	9	9	9	8	8
Wyoming											1[4]	1	1	1	1	1	1	1	1	1	1	1	1
Total	65	106	142	186	213	242	232	237	243	293	332	357	391	435	435	435	437[6]	435	435	435	435	435	435

1. Apportionment effective with congressional election two years after census.

2. Original apportionment made in Constitution, pending first census.

3. No apportionment was made in 1920.

4. These figures are not based on any census, but indicate the provisional representation accorded newly admitted states by Congress, pending the next census.

5. Twenty members were assigned to Massachusetts, but seven of these were credited to Maine when that area became a state.

6. Normally 435, but temporarily increased two seats by Congress when Alaska and Hawaii became states.

SOURCES: *Biographical Directory of the American Congress* and Bureau of the Census.

The Presidency

Selected Texts 877

Votes and Veto Messages 915

President Obama's First Inaugural Address

Following is the White House transcript of the inaugural address of Barack Obama, the nation's forty-fourth president, delivered on January 20, 2009.

My fellow citizens: I stand here today humbled by the task before us, grateful for the trust you've bestowed, mindful of the sacrifices borne by our ancestors.

I thank President Bush for his service to our nation, as well as the generosity and cooperation he has shown throughout this transition.

Forty-four Americans have now taken the presidential oath. The words have been spoken during rising tides of prosperity and the still waters of peace. Yet, every so often, the oath is taken amidst gathering clouds and raging storms. At these moments, America has carried on not simply because of the skill or vision of those in high office, but because we, the people, have remained faithful to the ideals of our forebears and true to our founding documents.

So it has been; so it must be with this generation of Americans.

That we are in the midst of crisis is now well understood. Our nation is at war against a far-reaching network of violence and hatred. Our economy is badly weakened, a consequence of greed and irresponsibility on the part of some, but also our collective failure to make hard choices and prepare the nation for a new age. Homes have been lost, jobs shed, businesses shuttered. Our health care is too costly, our schools fail too many—and each day brings further evidence that the ways we use energy strengthen our adversaries and threaten our planet.

These are the indicators of crisis, subject to data and statistics. Less measurable, but no less profound, is a sapping of confidence across our land; a nagging fear that America's decline is inevitable, that the next generation must lower its sights.

Today I say to you that the challenges we face are real. They are serious and they are many. They will not be met easily or in a short span of time. But know this America: They will be met.

On this day, we gather because we have chosen hope over fear, unity of purpose over conflict and discord. On this day, we come to proclaim an end to the petty grievances and false promises, the recriminations and worn-out dogmas that for far too long have strangled our politics. We remain a young nation. But in the words of Scripture, the time has come to "set aside childish things." The time has come to reaffirm our enduring spirit, to choose our better history, to carry forward that precious gift, that noble idea passed on from generation to generation: the God-given promise that all are equal, all are free and all deserve a chance to pursue their full measure of happiness.

OUR JOURNEY

In reaffirming the greatness of our nation, we understand that greatness is never a given. It must be earned. Our journey has never been one of shortcuts or settling for less. It has not been the path for the fainthearted, for those that prefer leisure over work, or seek only the pleasures of riches and fame. Rather, it has been the risk-takers, the doers, the makers of things—some celebrated, but more often men and women obscure in their labor—who have carried us up the long rugged path toward prosperity and freedom.

For us, they packed up their few worldly possessions and traveled across oceans in search of a new life. For us, they toiled in sweatshops, and settled the West, endured the lash of the whip, and plowed the hard earth. For us, they fought and died in places like Concord and Gettysburg, Normandy and Khe Sahn.

Time and again these men and women struggled and sacrificed and worked till their hands were raw so that we might live a better life. They saw America as bigger than the sum of our individual ambitions, greater than all the differences of birth or wealth or faction.

This is the journey we continue today. We remain the most prosperous, powerful nation on Earth. Our workers are no less productive than when this crisis began. Our minds are no less inventive, our goods and services no less needed than they were last week, or last month, or last year. Our capacity remains undiminished. But our time of standing pat, of protecting narrow interests and putting off unpleasant decisions—that time has surely passed. Starting today, we must pick ourselves up, dust ourselves off and begin again the work of remaking America.

WORK TO BE DONE

For everywhere we look, there is work to be done. The state of our economy calls for action, bold and swift. And we will act, not only to create new jobs, but to lay a new foundation for growth. We will build the roads and bridges, the electric grids and digital lines that feed our commerce and bind us together. We'll restore science to its rightful place and wield technology's wonders to raise health care's quality and lower its cost. We will harness the sun and the winds and the soil to fuel our cars and run our factories. And we will transform our schools and colleges and universities to meet the demands of a new age. All this we can do. All this we will do.

Now, there are some who question the scale of our ambitions, who suggest that our system cannot tolerate too many big plans. Their memories are short, for they have forgotten what this country has already done, what free men and women can achieve when imagination is joined to common purpose, and necessity to courage. What the cynics fail to understand is that the ground has shifted beneath them, that the stale political arguments that have consumed us for so long no longer apply.

The question we ask today is not whether our government is too big or too small, but whether it works—whether it helps families find jobs at a decent wage, care they can afford, a retirement that is dignified. Where the answer is yes, we intend to move forward. Where the answer is no, programs will end. And those of us who manage the public's dollars will be held to account, to spend wisely, reform bad habits and do our business in the light of day, because only then can we restore the vital trust between a people and their government.

Nor is the question before us whether the market is a force for good or ill. Its power to generate wealth and expand freedom is unmatched. But this crisis has reminded us that without a watchful eye, the market can spin out of control. The nation cannot prosper long when it favors only the prosperous. The success of our economy has always depended not just on the size of our gross domestic product, but on the reach of our prosperity, on the ability to extend opportunity to every willing heart—not out of charity, but because it is the surest route to our common good.

A FRIEND OF EACH NATION

As for our common defense, we reject as false the choice between our safety and our ideals. Our Founding Fathers, faced with perils that we can scarcely imagine, drafted a charter to assure the rule of law and the rights of man—a charter expanded by the blood of generations. Those ideals still light the world, and we will not give them up for expedience's sake.

And so, to all the other peoples and governments who are watching today, from the grandest capitals to the small village where my father was born, know that America is a friend of each nation, and every man, woman and child who seeks a future of peace and dignity. And we are ready to lead once more.

Recall that earlier generations faced down fascism and communism not just with missiles and tanks, but with sturdy alliances and enduring convictions. They understood that our power alone cannot protect us, nor does it entitle us to do as we please. Instead they knew that our power grows through its prudent use; our security emanates from the justness of our cause, the force of our example, the tempering qualities of humility and restraint.

We are the keepers of this legacy. Guided by these principles once more, we can meet those new threats that demand even greater effort, even greater cooperation and understanding between nations. We will begin to responsibly leave Iraq to its people and forge a hard-earned peace in Afghanistan. With old friends and former foes, we'll work tirelessly to lessen the nuclear threat and roll back the specter of a warming planet.

We will not apologize for our way of life, nor will we waver in its defense. And for those who seek to advance their aims by inducing terror and slaughtering innocents, we say to you now that our spirit is stronger and cannot be broken—you cannot outlast us, and we will defeat you.

For we know that our patchwork heritage is a strength, not a weakness. We are a nation of Christians and Muslims, Jews and Hindus, and non-believers. We are shaped by every language and culture, drawn from every end of this Earth, and because we have tasted the bitter swill of civil war and segregation, and emerged from that dark chapter stronger and more united, we cannot help but believe that the old hatreds shall someday pass, that the lines of tribe shall soon dissolve, that as the world grows smaller, our common humanity shall reveal itself, and that America must play its role in ushering in a new era of peace.

To the Muslim world, we seek a new way forward, based on mutual interest and mutual respect. To those leaders around the globe who seek to sow conflict or blame their society's ills on the West, know that your people will judge you on what you can build, not what you destroy.

To those who cling to power through corruption and deceit and the silencing of dissent, know that you are on the wrong side of history, but that we will extend a hand if you are willing to unclench your fist.

To the people of poor nations, we pledge to work alongside you to make your farms flourish and let clean waters flow, to nourish starved bodies and feed hungry minds. And to those nations like ours that enjoy relative plenty, we say we can no longer afford indifference to the suffering outside our borders, nor can we consume the world's resources without regard to effect. For the world has changed, and we must change with it.

THE SPIRIT OF SERVICE

As we consider the role that unfolds before us, we remember with humble gratitude those brave Americans who at this very hour patrol far-off deserts and distant mountains. They have something to tell us, just as the fallen heroes who lie in Arlington whisper through the ages.

We honor them not only because they are the guardians of our liberty, but because they embody the spirit of service—a willingness to find meaning in something greater than themselves.

And yet at this moment, a moment that will define a generation, it is precisely this spirit that must inhabit us all. For as much as government can do, and must do, it is ultimately the faith and determination of the American people upon which this nation relies. It is the kindness to take in a stranger when the levees break, the selflessness of workers who would rather cut their hours than see a friend lose their job, which sees us through our darkest hours. It is the firefighter's courage to storm a stairway filled with smoke, but also a parent's willingness to nurture a child that finally decides our fate.

Our challenges may be new. The instruments with which we meet them may be new. But those values upon which our success depends—honesty and hard work, courage and fair play, tolerance and curiosity, loyalty and patriotism—these things are old. These things are true. They have been the quiet force of progress throughout our history.

What is demanded, then, is a return to these truths. What is required of us now is a new era of responsibility—a recognition on the part of every American that we have duties to ourselves, our nation and the world, duties that we do not grudgingly accept, but rather seize gladly, firm in the knowledge that there is nothing so satisfying to the spirit, so defining of our character than giving our all to a difficult task.

This is the price and the promise of citizenship. This is the source of our confidence—the knowledge that God calls on us to shape an uncertain destiny. This is the meaning of our liberty and our creed, why men and women and children of every race and every faith can join in celebration across this magnificent mall, and why a man whose father less than 60 years ago might not have been served in a local restaurant can now stand before you to take a most sacred oath.

THE WINTER OF OUR HARDSHIP

So let us mark this day with remembrance of who we are and how far we have traveled. In the year of America's birth, in the coldest of months, a small band of patriots huddled by dying campfires on the shores of an icy river. The capital was abandoned. The enemy was advancing. The snow was stained with blood. At the moment when the outcome of our revolution was most in doubt, the father of our nation ordered these words to be read to the people:

"Let it be told to the future world, that in the depth of winter, when nothing but hope and virtue could survive . . . that the city and the country, alarmed at one common danger, came forth to meet [it]."

America, in the face of our common dangers, in this winter of our hardship, let us remember these timeless words. With hope and virtue, let us brave once more the icy currents and endure what storms may come. Let it be said by our children's children that when we were tested we refused to let this journey end, that we did not turn back nor did we falter, and with eyes fixed on the horizon and God's grace upon us, we carried forth that great gift of freedom and delivered it safely to future generations.

Thank you. God bless you. And God bless the United States of America.

President Obama on the State of Economy

Following is the White House transcript of President Obama's address delivered to a joint session of Congress on February 24, 2009.

Madame Speaker, Mr. Vice President, Members of Congress, and the first lady of the United States:

I've come here tonight not only to address the distinguished men and women in this great chamber, but to speak frankly and directly to the men and women who sent us here.

I know that for many Americans watching right now, the state of our economy is a concern that rises above all others. And rightly so. If you haven't been personally affected by this recession, you probably know someone who has—a friend, a neighbor, a member of your family. You don't need to hear another list of statistics to know that our economy is in crisis, because you live it every day. It's the worry you wake up with and the source of sleepless nights. It's the job you thought you'd retire from but now have lost, the business you built your dreams upon that's now hanging by a thread, the college acceptance letter your child had to put back in the envelope. The impact of this recession is real, and it is everywhere.

But while our economy may be weakened and our confidence shaken, though we are living through difficult and uncertain times, tonight I want every American to know this:

We will rebuild, we will recover, and the United States of America will emerge stronger than before.

The weight of this crisis will not determine the destiny of this nation. The answers to our problems don't lie beyond our reach. They exist in our laboratories and universities, in our fields and our factories, in the imaginations of our entrepreneurs and the pride of the hardest-working people on Earth. Those qualities that have made America the greatest force of progress and prosperity in human history we still possess in ample measure. What is required now is for this country to pull together, confront boldly the challenges we face and take responsibility for our future once more.

Now, if we're honest with ourselves, we'll admit that for too long, we have not always met these responsibilities—as a government or as a people. I say this not to lay blame or look backwards, but because it is only by understanding how we arrived at this moment that we'll be able to lift ourselves out of this predicament.

The fact is, our economy did not fall into decline overnight. Nor did all of our problems begin when the housing market collapsed or the stock market sank. We have known for decades that our survival depends on finding new sources of energy. Yet we import more oil today than ever before. The cost of health care eats up more and more of our savings each year, yet we keep delaying reform. Our children will compete for jobs in a global economy that too many of our schools do not prepare them for. And though all these challenges went unsolved, we still managed to spend more money and pile up more debt, both as individuals and through our government, than ever before.

In other words, we have lived through an era where, too often, short-term gains were prized over long-term prosperity; where we failed to look beyond the next payment, the next quarter or the next election. A surplus became an excuse to transfer wealth to the wealthy instead of an opportunity to invest in our future. Regulations were gutted for the sake of a quick profit at the expense of a healthy market. People bought homes they knew they couldn't afford from banks and lenders who pushed those bad loans anyway. And all the while, critical debates and difficult decisions were put off for some other time on some other day.

Well that day of reckoning has arrived, and the time to take charge of our future is here.

Now is the time to act boldly and wisely—to not only revive this economy, but to build a new foundation for lasting prosperity. Now is the time to jump-start job creation, restart lending and invest in areas like energy, health care and education that will grow our economy, even as we make hard choices to bring our deficit down. That is what my economic agenda is designed to do, and that's what I'd like to talk to you about tonight.

It's an agenda that begins with jobs.

STIMULUS PACKAGE

As soon as I took office, I asked this Congress to send me a recovery plan by Presidents Day that would put people back to work and put money in their pockets. Not because I believe in bigger government—I don't. Not because I'm not mindful of the massive debt we've inherited—I am. I called for action because the failure to do so would have cost more jobs and caused more hardships. In fact, a failure to act would have worsened our long-term deficit by ensuring weak economic growth for years. That's why I pushed for quick action. And tonight, I am grateful that this Congress delivered and pleased to say that the American Recovery and Reinvestment Act is now law.

Over the next two years, this plan will save or create 3.5 million jobs. More than 90 percent of these jobs will be in the private sector—jobs rebuilding our roads and bridges, constructing wind turbines and solar panels, laying broadband and expanding mass transit.

Because of this plan, there are teachers who can now keep their jobs and educate our kids. Health care professionals can continue caring for our sick. There are 57 police officers who are still on the streets of Minneapolis tonight because this plan prevented the layoffs their department was about to make.

Because of this plan, 95 percent of the working households in America will receive a tax cut—a tax cut that you will see in your paychecks beginning on April 1st.

Because of this plan, families who are struggling to pay tuition costs will receive a $2,500 tax credit for all four years of college. And Americans who have lost their jobs in this recession will be able to receive extended unemployment benefits and continued health care coverage to help them weather this storm.

I know there are some in this chamber and watching at home who are skeptical of whether this plan will work. I understand that skepticism. Here in Washington, we've all seen how quickly good intentions can turn into broken promises and wasteful spending. And with a plan of this scale comes enormous responsibility to get it right.

That is why I have asked Vice President Biden to lead a tough, unprecedented oversight effort—because nobody messes with

Joe. I have told each member of my Cabinet as well as mayors and governors across the country that they will be held accountable by me and the American people for every dollar they spend. I have appointed a proven and aggressive inspector general to ferret out any and all cases of waste and fraud. And we have created a new Web site called recovery.gov so that every American can find out how and where their money is being spent.

CREDIT AND HOUSING

So the recovery plan we passed is the first step in getting our economy back on track. But it is just the first step. Because even if we manage this plan flawlessly, there will be no real recovery unless we clean up the credit crisis that has severely weakened our financial system.

I want to speak plainly and candidly about this issue tonight, because every American should know that it directly affects you and your family's well-being. You should also know that the money you've deposited in banks across the country is safe; your insurance is secure; and you can rely on the continued operation of our financial system. That is not the source of concern.

The concern is that if we do not restart lending in this country, our recovery will be choked off before it even begins.

You see, the flow of credit is the lifeblood of our economy. The ability to get a loan is how you finance the purchase of everything from a home to a car to a college education, how stores stock their shelves, farms buy equipment and businesses make payroll.

But credit has stopped flowing the way it should. Too many bad loans from the housing crisis have made their way onto the books of too many banks. With so much debt and so little confidence, these banks are now fearful of lending out any more money to households, to businesses or to each other. When there is no lending, families can't afford to buy homes or cars. So businesses are forced to make layoffs. Our economy suffers even more, and credit dries up even further.

That is why this administration is moving swiftly and aggressively to break this destructive cycle, restore confidence and restart lending.

We will do so in several ways. First, we are creating a new lending fund that represents the largest effort ever to help provide auto loans, college loans and small-business loans to the consumers and entrepreneurs who keep this economy running.

Second, we have launched a housing plan that will help responsible families facing the threat of foreclosure lower their monthly payments and refinance their mortgages. It's a plan that won't help speculators or that neighbor down the street who bought a house he could never hope to afford, but it will help millions of Americans who are struggling with declining home values—Americans who will now be able to take advantage of the lower interest rates that this plan has already helped bring about. In fact, the average family who refinances today can save nearly $2,000 per year on their mortgage.

Third, we will act with the full force of the federal government to ensure that the major banks that Americans depend on have enough confidence and enough money to lend even in more difficult times. And when we learn that a major bank has serious problems, we will hold accountable those responsible, force the necessary adjustments, provide the support to clean up their balance sheets and ensure the continuity of a strong, viable institution that can serve our people and our economy.

I understand that on any given day, Wall Street may be more comforted by an approach that gives banks bailouts with no strings attached and that holds nobody accountable for their reckless decisions. But such an approach won't solve the problem. And our goal is to quicken the day when we restart lending to the American people and American business and end this crisis once and for all.

I intend to hold these banks fully accountable for the assistance they receive, and this time, they will have to clearly demonstrate how taxpayer dollars result in more lending for the American taxpayer. This time, CEOs won't be able to use taxpayer money to pad their paychecks or buy fancy drapes or disappear on a private jet. Those days are over.

Still, this plan will require significant resources from the federal government—and yes, probably more than we've already set aside. But while the cost of action will be great, I can assure you that the cost of inaction will be far greater, for it could result in an economy that sputters along for not months or years, but perhaps a decade. That would be worse for our deficit, worse for business, worse for you and worse for the next generation. And I refuse to let that happen.

I understand that when the last administration asked this Congress to provide assistance for struggling banks, Democrats and Republicans alike were infuriated by the mismanagement and results that followed. So were the American taxpayers. So was I.

So I know how unpopular it is to be seen as helping banks right now, especially when everyone is suffering in part from their bad decisions. I promise you—I get it.

But I also know that in a time of crisis, we cannot afford to govern out of anger or yield to the politics of the moment. My job—our job—is to solve the problem. Our job is to govern with a sense of responsibility. I will not spend a single penny for the purpose of rewarding a single Wall Street executive, but I will do whatever it takes to help the small business that can't pay its workers or the family that has saved and still can't get a mortgage.

That's what this is about. It's not about helping banks—it's about helping people. Because when credit is available again, that young family can finally buy a new home. And then some company will hire workers to build it. And then those workers will have money to spend, and if they can get a loan, too, maybe they'll finally buy that car or open their own business. Investors will return to the market, and American families will see their retirement secured once more. Slowly, but surely, confidence will return, and our economy will recover.

So I ask this Congress to join me in doing whatever proves necessary. Because we cannot consign our nation to an open-ended recession. And to ensure that a crisis of this magnitude never happens again, I ask Congress to move quickly on legislation that will finally reform our outdated regulatory system. It is time to put in place tough new common-sense rules of the road so that our financial market rewards drive and innovation, and punishes shortcuts and abuse.

The recovery plan and the financial stability plan are the immediate steps we're taking to revive our economy in the short term. But the only way to fully restore America's economic strength is to make the long-term investments that will lead to new jobs, new industries and a renewed ability to compete with the rest of the world. The only way this century will be another American century is if we confront at last the price of our dependence on oil and the high cost of health care, the schools that aren't preparing our children, and the mountain of debt they stand to inherit. That is our responsibility.

BUDGET PROPOSAL

In the next few days, I will submit a budget to Congress. So often, we have come to view these documents as simply numbers on a page or laundry lists of programs. I see this document differently. I see it as a vision for America—as a blueprint for our future.

My budget does not attempt to solve every problem or address every issue. It reflects the stark reality of what we've inherited: a trillion-dollar deficit, a financial crisis and a costly recession.

Given these realities, everyone in this chamber—Democrats and Republicans—will have to sacrifice some worthy priorities for which there are no dollars. And that includes me.

But that does not mean we can afford to ignore our long-term challenges. I reject the view that says our problems will simply take care of themselves, that says government has no role in laying the foundation for our common prosperity.

For history tells a different story. History reminds us that at every moment of economic upheaval and transformation, this nation has responded with bold action and big ideas. In the midst of civil war, we laid railroad tracks from one coast to another that spurred commerce and industry. From the turmoil of the Industrial Revolution came a system of public high schools that prepared our citizens for a new age. In the wake of war and depression, the GI Bill sent a generation to college and created the largest middle class in history. And a twilight struggle for freedom led to a nation of highways, an American on the moon and an explosion of technology that still shapes our world.

In each case, government didn't supplant private enterprise; it catalyzed private enterprise. It created the conditions for thousands of entrepreneurs and new businesses to adapt and to thrive.

We are a nation that has seen promise amid peril and claimed opportunity from ordeal. Now we must be that nation again. That is why, even as it cuts back on the programs we don't need, the budget I submit will invest in the three areas that are absolutely critical to our economic future: energy, health care and education.

ENERGY

It begins with energy.

We know the country that harnesses the power of clean, renewable energy will lead the 21st century. And yet, it is China that has launched the largest effort in history to make their economy energy efficient. We invented solar technology, but we've fallen behind countries like Germany and Japan in producing it. New plug-in hybrids roll off our assembly lines, but they will run on batteries made in Korea.

Well, I do not accept a future where the jobs and industries of tomorrow take root beyond our borders—and I know you don't either. It is time for America to lead again.

Thanks to our recovery plan, we will double this nation's supply of renewable energy in the next three years. We have also made the largest investment in basic research funding in American history—an investment that will spur not only new discoveries in energy, but breakthroughs in medicine, science and technology.

We will soon lay down thousands of miles of power lines that can carry new energy to cities and towns across this country. And we will put Americans to work making our homes and buildings more efficient so that we can save billions of dollars on our energy bills.

But to truly transform our economy, protect our security, and save our planet from the ravages of climate change, we need to ultimately make clean, renewable energy the profitable kind of energy. So I ask this Congress to send me legislation that places a market-based cap on carbon pollution and drives the production of more renewable energy in America. And to support that innovation, we will invest $15 billion a year to develop technologies like wind power and solar power, advanced biofuels, clean coal, and more fuel-efficient cars and trucks built right here in America.

As for our auto industry, everyone recognizes that years of bad decision-making and a global recession have pushed our automakers to the brink. We should not, and will not, protect them from their own bad practices. But we are committed to the goal of a retooled, reimagined auto industry that can compete and win. Millions of jobs depend on it. Scores of communities depend on it. And I believe the nation that invented the automobile cannot walk away from it.

None of this will come without cost, nor will it be easy. But this is America. We don't do what's easy. We do what is necessary to move this country forward.

HEALTH CARE

For that same reason, we must also address the crushing cost of health care.

This is a cost that now causes a bankruptcy in America every 30 seconds. By the end of the year, it could cause 1.5 million Americans to lose their homes. In the last eight years, premiums have grown four times faster than wages. And in each of these years, 1 million more Americans have lost their health insurance. It is one of the major reasons why small businesses close their doors and corporations ship jobs overseas. And it's one of the largest and fastest-growing parts of our budget.

Given these facts, we can no longer afford to put health care reform on hold.

Already, we have done more to advance the cause of health care reform in the last 30 days than we have in the last decade. When it was days old, this Congress passed a law to provide and protect health insurance for 11 million American children whose parents work full time. Our recovery plan will invest in electronic health records and new technology that will reduce errors, bring down costs, ensure privacy and save lives. It will launch a new effort to conquer a disease that has touched the life of nearly every American by seeking a cure for cancer in our time. And it makes the largest investment ever in preventive care, because that is one of the best ways to keep our people healthy and our costs under control.

This budget builds on these reforms. It includes a historic commitment to comprehensive health care reform—a down payment on the principle that we must have quality, affordable health care for every American. It's a commitment that's paid for in part by efficiencies in our system that are long overdue. And it's a step we must take if we hope to bring down our deficit in the years to come.

Now, there will be many different opinions and ideas about how to achieve reform, and that is why I'm bringing together businesses and workers, doctors and health care providers, Democrats and Republicans to begin work on this issue next week.

I suffer no illusions that this will be an easy process. It will be hard. But I also know that nearly a century after Teddy Roosevelt first called for reform, the cost of our health care has weighed down our economy and the conscience of our nation long enough. So let there be no doubt: Health care reform cannot wait; it must not wait; and it will not wait another year.

EDUCATION

The third challenge we must address is the urgent need to expand the promise of education in America.

In a global economy where the most valuable skill you can sell is your knowledge, a good education is no longer just a pathway to opportunity—it is a prerequisite.

Right now, three-quarters of the fastest-growing occupations require more than a high school diploma. And yet, just over half of our citizens have that level of education. We have one of the highest high school dropout rates of any industrialized nation. And half of the students who begin college never finish.

This is a prescription for economic decline, because we know the countries that out-teach us today will out-compete us tomorrow. That is why it will be the goal of this administration to ensure that every child has access to a complete and competitive education—from the day they are born to the day they begin a career.

Already, we have made a historic investment in education through the economic recovery plan. We have dramatically expanded early childhood education and will continue to improve its quality, because we know that the most formative learning comes in those first years of life. We have made college affordable for nearly 7 million more students. And we have provided the resources necessary to prevent painful cuts and teacher layoffs that would set back our children's progress.

But we know that our schools don't just need more resources. They need more reform. That is why this budget creates new incentives for teacher performance, pathways for advancement and rewards for success. We'll invest in innovative programs that are already helping schools meet high standards and close achievement gaps. And we will expand our commitment to charter schools.

It is our responsibility as lawmakers and educators to make this system work. But it is the responsibility of every citizen to participate in it. And so tonight, I ask every American to commit to at least one year or more of higher education or career training. This can be community college or a four-year school, vocational training or an apprenticeship. But whatever the training may be, every American will need to get more than a high school diploma. And dropping out of high school is no longer an option. It's not just quitting on yourself, it's quitting on your country—and this country needs and values the talents of every American. That is why we will provide the support necessary for you to complete college and meet a new goal: By 2020, America will once again have the highest proportion of college graduates in the world.

I know that the price of tuition is higher than ever, which is why if you are willing to volunteer in your neighborhood or give back to your community or serve your country, we will make sure that you can afford a higher education. And to encourage a renewed spirit of national service for this and future generations, I ask this Congress to send me the bipartisan legislation that bears the name of Sen. Orrin Hatch, as well as an American who has never stopped asking what he can do for his country, Sen. Edward Kennedy.

These education policies will open the doors of opportunity for our children. But it is up to us to ensure they walk through them. In the end, there is no program or policy that can substitute for a mother or father who will attend those parent-teacher conferences, or help with homework after dinner, or turn off the TV, put away the video games and read to their child. I speak to you not just as a president but as a father when I say that responsibility for our children's education must begin at home.

DEBT AND DEFICIT

There is, of course, another responsibility we have to our children. And that is the responsibility to ensure that we do not pass on to them a debt they cannot pay. With the deficit we inherited, the cost of the crisis we face and the long-term challenges we must meet, it has never been more important to ensure that as our economy recovers, we do what it takes to bring this deficit down.

I'm proud that we passed the recovery plan free of earmarks, and I want to pass a budget next year that ensures that each dollar we spend reflects only our most important national priorities.

Yesterday, I held a fiscal summit where I pledged to cut the deficit in half by the end of my first term in office. My administration has also begun to go line by line through the federal budget in order to eliminate wasteful and ineffective programs. As you can imagine, this is a process that will take some time. But we're starting with the biggest lines. We have already identified $2 trillion in savings over the next decade.

In this budget, we will end education programs that don't work and end direct payments to large agribusinesses that don't need them. We'll eliminate the no-bid contracts that have wasted billions in Iraq and reform our defense budget so that we're not paying for Cold War–era weapons systems we don't use. We will root out the waste, fraud and abuse in our Medicare program that doesn't make our seniors any healthier, and we will restore a sense of fairness and balance to our tax code by finally ending the tax breaks for corporations that ship our jobs overseas.

In order to save our children from a future of debt, we will also end the tax breaks for the wealthiest 2 percent of Americans. But let me be perfectly clear, because I know you'll hear the same old claims that rolling back these tax breaks means a massive tax increase on the American people: If your family earns less than $250,000 a year, you will not see your taxes increased a single dime. I repeat: not one single dime. In fact, the recovery plan provides a tax cut—that's right, a tax cut—for 95 percent of working families. And these checks are on the way.

To preserve our long-term fiscal health, we must also address the growing costs in Medicare and Social Security. Comprehensive health care reform is the best way to strengthen Medicare for years to come. And we must also begin a conversation on how to do the same for Social Security, while creating tax-free universal savings accounts for all Americans.

Finally, because we're also suffering from a deficit of trust, I am committed to restoring a sense of honesty and accountability to our budget. That is why this budget looks ahead 10 years and accounts for spending that was left out under the old rules—and for the first time, that includes the full cost of fighting in Iraq and Afghanistan. For seven years, we have been a nation at war. No longer will we hide its price.

IRAQ AND AFGHANISTAN

We are now carefully reviewing our policies in both wars, and I will soon announce a way forward in Iraq that leaves Iraq to its people and responsibly ends this war.

And with our friends and allies, we will forge a new and comprehensive strategy for Afghanistan and Pakistan to defeat al Qaeda and combat extremism, because I will not allow terrorists to plot against the American people from safe havens half a world away.

As we meet here tonight, our men and women in uniform stand watch abroad, and more are readying to deploy. To each and every one of them and to the families who bear the quiet burden of their absence, Americans are united in sending one message: We honor your service; we are inspired by your sacrifice; and you have our unyielding support. To relieve the strain on our forces, my budget increases the number of our soldiers and Marines. And to keep our sacred trust with those who serve, we will raise their pay and give our veterans the expanded health care and benefits that they have earned.

To overcome extremism, we must also be vigilant in upholding the values our troops defend—because there is no force in the world more powerful than the example of America. That is why I have ordered the closing of the detention center at Guantánamo Bay, and will seek swift and certain justice for captured terrorists—because living our values doesn't make us weaker, it makes us safer and it makes us stronger. And that is why I can stand here tonight and say without exception or equivocation that the United States of America does not torture.

In words and deeds, we are showing the world that a new era of engagement has begun. For we know that America cannot meet the threats of this century alone, but the world cannot meet them without America. We cannot shun the negotiating table, nor ignore the foes or forces that could do us harm. We are instead called to move forward with the sense of confidence and candor that serious times demand.

To seek progress toward a secure and lasting peace between Israel and her neighbors, we have appointed an envoy to sustain our effort. To meet the challenges of the 21st century—from terrorism to nuclear proliferation, from pandemic disease to cyber threats to crushing poverty—we will strengthen old alliances, forge new ones and use all elements of our national power.

And to respond to an economic crisis that is global in scope, we are working with the nations of the G-20 to restore confidence in our financial system, avoid the possibility of escalating protectionism and spur demand for American goods in markets across the globe. For the world depends on us to have a strong economy, just as our economy depends on the strength of the world's.

As we stand at this crossroads of history, the eyes of all people in all nations are once again upon us—watching to see what we do with this moment, waiting for us to lead.

"EXTRAORDINARY TIMES"

Those of us gathered here tonight have been called to govern in extraordinary times. It is a tremendous burden, but also a great privilege—one that has been entrusted to few generations of Americans. For in our hands lies the ability to shape our world for good or for ill.

I know that it is easy to lose sight of this truth—to become cynical and doubtful, consumed with the petty and the trivial.

But in my life, I have also learned that hope is found in unlikely places, that inspiration often comes not from those with the most power or celebrity, but from the dreams and aspirations of Americans who are anything but ordinary.

I think about Leonard Abess, the bank president from Miami who reportedly cashed out of his company, took a $60 million bonus, and gave it out to all 399 people who worked for him, plus another 72 who used to work for him. He didn't tell anyone, but when the local newspaper found out, he simply said, "I knew some of these people since I was 7 years old. I didn't feel right getting the money myself."

I think about Greensburg, Kan., a town that was completely destroyed by a tornado but is being rebuilt by its residents as a global example of how clean energy can power an entire community—how it can bring jobs and businesses to a place where piles of bricks and rubble once lay. "The tragedy was terrible," said one of the men who helped them rebuild. "But the folks here know that it also provided an incredible opportunity."

And I think about Ty'Sheoma Bethea, the young girl from that school I visited in Dillon, S.C.—a place where the ceilings leak, the paint peels off the walls and they have to stop teaching six times a day because the train barrels by their classroom. She has been told that her school is hopeless, but the other day after class she went to the public library and typed up a letter to the people sitting in this room. She even asked her principal for the money to buy a stamp. The letter asks us for help, and says, "We are just students trying to become lawyers, doctors, congressmen like yourself and one day president, so we can make a change to not just the state of South Carolina but also the world. We are not quitters."

We are not quitters.

These words and these stories tell us something about the spirit of the people who sent us here. They tell us that even in the most trying times, amid the most difficult circumstances, there is a generosity, a resilience, a decency, and a determination that perseveres, a willingness to take responsibility for our future and for posterity.

Their resolve must be our inspiration. Their concerns must be our cause. And we must show them and all our people that we are equal to the task before us.

I know that we haven't agreed on every issue thus far, and there are surely times in the future when we will part ways. But I also know that every American who is sitting here tonight loves this country and wants it to succeed. That must be the starting point for every debate we have in the coming months, and where we return after those debates are done. That is the foundation on which the American people expect us to build common ground.

And if we do—if we come together and lift this nation from the depths of this crisis, if we put our people back to work and restart the engine of our prosperity, if we confront without fear the challenges of our time and summon that enduring spirit of an America that does not quit—then someday years from now our children can tell their children that this was the time when we performed, in the words that are carved into this very chamber, "something worthy to be remembered." Thank you, God bless you, and may God bless the United States of America.

President Obama's Address at Cairo University in Egypt

Following is the White House's transcript of President Obama's address, aimed principally at the Muslim world, delivered at Cairo University in Cairo, Egypt, on June 4, 2009.

Thank you very much. Good afternoon. I am honored to be in the timeless city of Cairo, and to be hosted by two remarkable institutions. For over a thousand years, Al-Azhar has stood as a beacon of Islamic learning; and for over a century, Cairo University has been a source of Egypt's advancement. And together, you represent the harmony between tradition and progress. I'm grateful for your hospitality, and the hospitality of the people of Egypt. And I'm also proud to carry with me the goodwill of the American people, and a greeting of peace from Muslim communities in my country: Assalaamu alaykum.

We meet at a time of great tension between the United States and Muslims around the world—tension rooted in historical forces that go beyond any current policy debate. The relationship between Islam and the West includes centuries of coexistence and cooperation, but also conflict and religious wars. More recently, tension has been fed by colonialism that denied rights and opportunities to many Muslims, and a Cold War in which Muslim-majority countries were too often treated as proxies without regard to their own aspirations. Moreover, the sweeping change brought by modernity and globalization led many Muslims to view the West as hostile to the traditions of Islam.

Violent extremists have exploited these tensions in a small but potent minority of Muslims. The attacks of September 11, 2001, and the continued efforts of these extremists to engage in violence against civilians has led some in my country to view Islam as inevitably hostile not only to America and Western countries, but also to human rights. All this has bred more fear and more mistrust.

So long as our relationship is defined by our differences, we will empower those who sow hatred rather than peace, those who promote conflict rather than the cooperation that can help all of our people achieve justice and prosperity. And this cycle of suspicion and discord must end.

I've come here to Cairo to seek a new beginning between the United States and Muslims around the world, one based on mutual interest and mutual respect, and one based upon the truth that America and Islam are not exclusive and need not be in competition. Instead, they overlap, and share common principles—principles of justice and progress; tolerance and the dignity of all human beings.

I do so recognizing that change cannot happen overnight. I know there's been a lot of publicity about this speech, but no single speech can eradicate years of mistrust, nor can I answer in the time that I have this afternoon all the complex questions that brought us to this point. But I am convinced that in order to move forward, we must say openly to each other the things we hold in our hearts and that too often are said only behind closed doors. There must be a sustained effort to listen to each other; to learn from each other; to respect one another; and to seek common ground. As the Holy Koran tells us, "Be conscious of God and speak always the truth." That is what I will try to do today—to speak the truth as best I can, humbled by the task before us, and firm in my belief that the interests we share as human beings are far more powerful than the forces that drive us apart.

Now part of this conviction is rooted in my own experience. I'm a Christian, but my father came from a Kenyan family that includes generations of Muslims. As a boy, I spent several years in Indonesia and heard the call of the azaan at the break of dawn and at the fall of dusk. As a young man, I worked in Chicago communities where many found dignity and peace in their Muslim faith.

As a student of history, I also know civilization's debt to Islam. It was Islam—at places like Al-Azhar—that carried the light of learning through so many centuries, paving the way for Europe's Renaissance and Enlightenment. It was innovation in Muslim communities—it was innovation in Muslim communities that developed the order of algebra; our magnetic compass and tools of navigation; our mastery of pens and printing; our understanding of how disease spreads and how it can be healed. Islamic culture has given us majestic arches and soaring spires; timeless poetry and cherished music; elegant calligraphy and places of peaceful contemplation. And throughout history, Islam has demonstrated through words and deeds the possibilities of religious tolerance and racial equality.

I also know that Islam has always been a part of America's story. The first nation to recognize my country was Morocco. In signing the Treaty of Tripoli in 1796, our second President, John Adams, wrote, "The United States has in itself no character of enmity against the laws, religion or tranquility of Muslims." And since our founding, American Muslims have enriched the United States. They have fought in our wars, they have served in our government, they have stood for civil rights, they have started businesses, they have taught at our universities, they've excelled in our sports arenas, they've won Nobel Prizes, built our tallest building, and lit the Olympic Torch. And when the first Muslim American was recently elected to Congress, he took the oath to defend our Constitution using the same Holy Koran that one of our Founding Fathers—Thomas Jefferson—kept in his personal library.

So I have known Islam on three continents before coming to the region where it was first revealed. That experience guides my conviction that partnership between America and Islam must be based on what Islam is, not what it isn't. And I consider it part of my responsibility as President of the United States to fight against negative stereotypes of Islam wherever they appear.

But that same principle must apply to Muslim perceptions of America. Just as Muslims do not fit a crude stereotype, America is not the crude stereotype of a self-interested empire. The United States has been one of the greatest sources of progress that the world has ever known. We were born out of revolution against an empire. We were founded upon the ideal that all are created equal, and we have shed blood and struggled for centuries to give meaning to those words—within our borders, and around the world. We are shaped by every culture, drawn from every end of the Earth, and dedicated to a simple concept: E pluribus unum—"Out of many, one."

Now, much has been made of the fact that an African American with the name Barack Hussein Obama could be elected President. But my personal story is not so unique. The dream of opportunity for all people has not come true for everyone in America, but its promise exists for all who come to our shores—and that includes nearly 7 million American Muslims in our country today who, by the way, enjoy incomes and educational levels that are higher than the American average.

Moreover, freedom in America is indivisible from the freedom to practice one's religion. That is why there is a mosque in every state in our union, and over 1,200 mosques within our borders. That's why the United States government has gone to court to protect the right of women and girls to wear the hijab and to punish those who would deny it.

So let there be no doubt: Islam is a part of America. And I believe that America holds within her the truth that regardless of race, religion, or station in life, all of us share common aspirations—to live in peace and security; to get an education and to work with dignity; to love our families, our communities, and our God. These things we share. This is the hope of all humanity.

Of course, recognizing our common humanity is only the beginning of our task. Words alone cannot meet the needs of our people. These needs will be met only if we act boldly in the years ahead; and if we understand that the challenges we face are shared, and our failure to meet them will hurt us all.

For we have learned from recent experience that when a financial system weakens in one country, prosperity is hurt everywhere. When a new flu infects one human being, all are at risk. When one nation pursues a nuclear weapon, the risk of nuclear attack rises for all nations. When violent extremists operate in one stretch of mountains, people are endangered across an ocean. When innocents in Bosnia and Darfur are slaughtered, that is a stain on our collective conscience. That is what it means to share this world in the 21st century. That is the responsibility we have to one another as human beings.

And this is a difficult responsibility to embrace. For human history has often been a record of nations and tribes—and, yes, religions—subjugating one another in pursuit of their own interests. Yet in this new age, such attitudes are self-defeating. Given our interdependence, any world order that elevates one nation or group of people over another will inevitably fail. So whatever we think of the past, we must not be prisoners to it. Our problems must be dealt with through partnership; our progress must be shared.

Now, that does not mean we should ignore sources of tension. Indeed, it suggests the opposite: We must face these tensions squarely. And so in that spirit, let me speak as clearly and as plainly as I can about some specific issues that I believe we must finally confront together.

The first issue that we have to confront is violent extremism in all of its forms.

In Ankara, I made clear that America is not—and never will be—at war with Islam. We will, however, relentlessly confront violent extremists who pose a grave threat to our security—because we reject the same thing that people of all faiths reject: the killing of innocent men, women, and children. And it is my first duty as President to protect the American people.

The situation in Afghanistan demonstrates America's goals, and our need to work together. Over seven years ago, the United States pursued al Qaeda and the Taliban with broad international support. We did not go by choice; we went because of necessity. I'm aware that there's still some who would question or even justify the events of 9/11. But let us be clear: Al Qaeda killed nearly 3,000 people on that day. The victims were innocent men, women and children from America and many other nations who had done nothing to harm anybody. And yet al Qaeda chose to ruthlessly murder these people, claimed credit for the attack, and even now states their determination to kill on a massive scale. They have affiliates in many countries and are trying to expand their reach. These are not opinions to be debated; these are facts to be dealt with.

Now, make no mistake: We do not want to keep our troops in Afghanistan. We see no military—we seek no military bases there. It is agonizing for America to lose our young men and women. It is costly and politically difficult to continue this conflict. We would gladly bring every single one of our troops home if we could be confident that there were not violent extremists in Afghanistan and now Pakistan determined to kill as many Americans as they possibly can. But that is not yet the case.

And that's why we're partnering with a coalition of 46 countries. And despite the costs involved, America's commitment will not weaken. Indeed, none of us should tolerate these extremists. They have killed in many countries. They have killed people of different faiths—but more than any other, they have killed Muslims. Their actions are irreconcilable with the rights of human beings, the progress of nations, and with Islam. The Holy Koran teaches that whoever kills an innocent is as—it is as if he has killed all mankind. And the Holy Koran also says whoever saves a person, it is as if he has saved all mankind. The enduring faith of over a billion people is so much bigger than the narrow hatred of a few. Islam is not part of the problem in combating violent extremism—it is an important part of promoting peace.

Now, we also know that military power alone is not going to solve the problems in Afghanistan and Pakistan. That's why we plan to invest $1.5 billion each year over the next five years to partner with Pakistanis to build schools and hospitals, roads and businesses, and hundreds of millions to help those who've been displaced. That's why we are providing more than $2.8 billion to help Afghans develop their economy and deliver services that people depend on.

Let me also address the issue of Iraq. Unlike Afghanistan, Iraq was a war of choice that provoked strong differences in my country and around the world. Although I believe that the Iraqi people are ultimately better off without the tyranny of Saddam Hussein, I also believe that events in Iraq have reminded America of the need to use diplomacy and build international consensus to resolve our problems whenever possible. Indeed, we can recall the words of Thomas Jefferson, who said: "I hope that our wisdom will grow with our power, and teach us that the less we use our power the greater it will be."

Today, America has a dual responsibility: to help Iraq forge a better future—and to leave Iraq to Iraqis. And I have made it clear to the Iraqi people that we pursue no bases, and no claim on their territory or resources. Iraq's sovereignty is its own. And that's why I ordered the removal of our combat brigades by next August. That is why we will honor our agreement with Iraq's democratically elected government to remove combat troops from Iraqi cities by July, and to remove all of our troops from Iraq by 2012. We will help Iraq train its security forces and develop its economy. But we will support a secure and united Iraq as a partner, and never as a patron.

And finally, just as America can never tolerate violence by extremists, we must never alter or forget our principles. Nine-eleven was an enormous trauma to our country. The fear and anger that it provoked was understandable, but in some cases, it led us to act contrary to our traditions and our ideals. We are taking concrete actions to change course. I have unequivocally prohibited the use of torture by the United States, and I have ordered the prison at Guantánamo Bay closed by early next year.

So America will defend itself, respectful of the sovereignty of nations and the rule of law. And we will do so in partnership with Muslim communities which are also threatened. The sooner the extremists are isolated and unwelcome in Muslim communities, the sooner we will all be safer.

The second major source of tension that we need to discuss is the situation between Israelis, Palestinians and the Arab world.

America's strong bonds with Israel are well known. This bond is unbreakable. It is based upon cultural and historical ties, and the recognition that the aspiration for a Jewish homeland is rooted in a tragic history that cannot be denied.

Around the world, the Jewish people were persecuted for centuries, and anti-Semitism in Europe culminated in an unprecedented Holocaust. Tomorrow, I will visit Buchenwald, which was part of a network of camps where Jews were enslaved, tortured, shot and gassed to death by the Third Reich. Six million Jews were killed—more than the entire Jewish population of Israel today. Denying that fact is baseless, it is ignorant, and it is hateful. Threatening Israel with destruction—or repeating vile stereotypes about Jews—is deeply wrong, and only serves to evoke in the minds of Israelis this most painful of memories while preventing the peace that the people of this region deserve.

On the other hand, it is also undeniable that the Palestinian people—Muslims and Christians—have suffered in pursuit of a homeland. For more than 60 years they've endured the pain of dislocation. Many wait in refugee camps in the West Bank, Gaza, and neighboring lands for a life of peace and security that they have never been able to lead. They endure the daily humiliations—large and small—that come with occupation. So let there be no doubt: The situation for the Palestinian people is intolerable. And America will not turn our backs on the legitimate Palestinian aspiration for dignity, opportunity, and a state of their own.

For decades then, there has been a stalemate: two peoples with legitimate aspirations, each with a painful history that makes compromise elusive. It's easy to point fingers—for Palestinians to point to the displacement brought about by Israel's founding, and for Israelis to point to the constant hostility and attacks throughout its history from within its borders as well as beyond. But if we see this conflict only from one side or the other, then we will be blind to the truth: The only resolution is for the aspirations of both sides to be met through two states, where Israelis and Palestinians each live in peace and security.

That is in Israel's interest, Palestine's interest, America's interest, and the world's interest. And that is why I intend to personally pursue this outcome with all the patience and dedication that the task requires. The obligations—the obligations that the parties have agreed to under the road map are clear. For peace to come, it is time for them—and all of us—to live up to our responsibilities.

Palestinians must abandon violence. Resistance through violence and killing is wrong and it does not succeed. For centuries, black people in America suffered the lash of the whip as slaves and the humiliation of segregation. But it was not violence that won full and equal rights. It was a peaceful and determined insistence upon the ideals at the center of America's founding. This same story can be told by people from South Africa to South Asia; from Eastern Europe to Indonesia. It's a story with a simple truth: that violence is a dead end. It is a sign neither of courage nor power to shoot rockets at sleeping children, or to blow up old women on a bus. That's not how moral authority is claimed; that's how it is surrendered.

Now is the time for Palestinians to focus on what they can build. The Palestinian Authority must develop its capacity to govern, with institutions that serve the needs of its people. Hamas does have support among some Palestinians, but they also have to recognize they have responsibilities. To play a role in fulfilling Palestinian aspirations, to unify the Palestinian people, Hamas must put an end to violence, recognize past agreements, recognize Israel's right to exist.

At the same time, Israelis must acknowledge that just as Israel's right to exist cannot be denied, neither can Palestine's. The United States does not accept the legitimacy of continued Israeli settlements. This construction violates previous agreements and undermines efforts to achieve peace. It is time for these settlements to stop.

And Israel must also live up to its obligation to ensure that Palestinians can live and work and develop their society. Just as it devastates Palestinian families, the continuing humanitarian crisis in Gaza does not serve Israel's security; neither does the continuing lack of opportunity in the West Bank. Progress in the daily lives of the Palestinian people must be a critical part of a road to peace, and Israel must take concrete steps to enable such progress.

And finally, the Arab states must recognize that the Arab Peace Initiative was an important beginning, but not the end of their responsibilities. The Arab-Israeli conflict should no longer be used to distract the people of Arab nations from other problems. Instead, it must be a cause for action to help the Palestinian people develop the institutions that will sustain their state, to recognize Israel's legitimacy, and to choose progress over a self-defeating focus on the past.

America will align our policies with those who pursue peace, and we will say in public what we say in private to Israelis and Palestinians and Arabs. We cannot impose peace. But privately, many Muslims recognize that Israel will not go away. Likewise, many Israelis recognize the need for a Palestinian state. It is time for us to act on what everyone knows to be true.

Too many tears have been shed. Too much blood has been shed. All of us have a responsibility to work for the day when the mothers of Israelis and Palestinians can see their children grow up without fear; when the Holy Land of the three great faiths is the place of peace that God intended it to be; when Jerusalem is a secure and lasting home for Jews and Christians and Muslims, and a place for all of the children of Abraham to mingle peacefully together as in the story of Isra—as in the story of Isra, when Moses, Jesus, and Mohammed, peace be upon them, joined in prayer.

The third source of tension is our shared interest in the rights and responsibilities of nations on nuclear weapons.

This issue has been a source of tension between the United States and the Islamic Republic of Iran. For many years, Iran has defined itself in part by its opposition to my country, and there is in fact a tumultuous history between us. In the middle of the Cold War, the United States played a role in the overthrow of a democratically elected Iranian government. Since the Islamic Revolution, Iran has played a role in acts of hostage-taking and violence against U.S. troops and civilians. This history is well known. Rather than remain trapped in the past, I've made it clear to Iran's leaders and people that my country is prepared to move forward. The question now is not what Iran is against, but rather what future it wants to build.

I recognize it will be hard to overcome decades of mistrust, but we will proceed with courage, rectitude, and resolve. There will be many issues to discuss between our two countries, and we are willing to move forward without preconditions on the basis of mutual respect. But it is clear to all concerned that when it comes to nuclear weapons, we have reached a decisive point. This is not simply about America's interests. It's about preventing a nuclear arms race in the Middle East that could lead this region and the world down a hugely dangerous path.

I understand those who protest that some countries have weapons that others do not. No single nation should pick and choose which nation holds nuclear weapons. And that's why I strongly reaffirmed America's commitment to seek a world in which no nations hold nuclear weapons. And any nation—including Iran—should have the right to access peaceful nuclear power if it complies with its responsibilities under the nuclear Non-Proliferation Treaty. That commitment is at the core of the treaty, and it must be kept for all who fully abide by it. And I'm hopeful that all countries in the region can share in this goal.

The fourth issue that I will address is democracy.

I know—I know there has been controversy about the promotion of democracy in recent years, and much of this controversy is connected to the war in Iraq. So let me be clear: No system of government can or should be imposed by one nation by any other.

That does not lessen my commitment, however, to governments that reflect the will of the people. Each nation gives life to this principle in its own way, grounded in the traditions of its own people. America does not presume to know what is best for everyone, just as we would not presume to pick the outcome of a peaceful election. But I do have an unyielding belief that all people yearn for certain things: the ability to speak your mind and have a say in how you are governed; confidence in the rule of law and the equal administration of justice; government that is transparent and doesn't steal from the people; the freedom to live as you choose. These are not just American ideas; they are human rights. And that is why we will support them everywhere.

Now, there is no straight line to realize this promise. But this much is clear: Governments that protect these rights are ultimately more stable, successful and secure. Suppressing ideas never succeeds in making them go away. America respects the right of all peaceful and law-abiding voices to be heard around the world, even if we disagree with them. And we will welcome all elected, peaceful governments—provided they govern with respect for all their people.

This last point is important because there are some who advocate for democracy only when they're out of power; once in power, they are ruthless in suppressing the rights of others. So no matter where it takes hold, government of the people and by the people sets a single standard for all who would hold power: You must maintain your power through consent, not coercion; you must respect the rights of minorities, and participate with a spirit of tolerance and compromise; you must place the interests of your people and the legitimate workings of the political process above your party. Without these ingredients, elections alone do not make true democracy.

The fifth issue that we must address together is religious freedom.

Islam has a proud tradition of tolerance. We see it in the history of Andalusia and Cordoba during the Inquisition. I saw it firsthand as a child in Indonesia, where devout Christians worshiped freely in an overwhelmingly Muslim country. That is the spirit we need today. People in every country should be free to choose and live their faith based upon the persuasion of the mind and the heart and the soul. This tolerance is essential for religion to thrive, but it's being challenged in many different ways.

Among some Muslims, there's a disturbing tendency to measure one's own faith by the rejection of somebody else's faith. The richness of religious diversity must be upheld—whether it is for Maronites in Lebanon or the Copts in Egypt. And if we are being honest, fault lines must be closed among Muslims, as well, as the divisions between Sunni and Shia have led to tragic violence, particularly in Iraq.

Freedom of religion is central to the ability of peoples to live together. We must always examine the ways in which we protect it. For instance, in the United States, rules on charitable giving have made it harder for Muslims to fulfill their religious obligation. That's why I'm committed to working with American Muslims to ensure that they can fulfill zakat.

Likewise, it is important for Western countries to avoid impeding Muslim citizens from practicing religion as they see fit—for instance, by dictating what clothes a Muslim woman should wear. We can't disguise hostility towards any religion behind the pretence of liberalism.

In fact, faith should bring us together. And that's why we're forging service projects in America to bring together Christians, Muslims, and Jews. That's why we welcome efforts like Saudi Arabian King Abdullah's interfaith dialogue and Turkey's leadership in the Alliance of Civilizations. Around the world, we can turn dialogue into interfaith service, so bridges between peoples lead to action—whether it is combating malaria in Africa, or providing relief after a natural disaster.

The sixth issue—the sixth issue that I want to address is women's rights. I know—I know—and you can tell from this audience, that there is a healthy debate about this issue. I reject the view of some in the West that a woman who chooses to cover her hair is somehow less equal, but I do believe that a woman who is denied an education is denied equality. And it is no coincidence that countries where women are well educated are far more likely to be prosperous.

Now, let me be clear: Issues of women's equality are by no means simply an issue for Islam. In Turkey, Pakistan, Bangladesh, Indonesia, we've seen Muslim-majority countries elect a woman to lead. Meanwhile, the struggle for women's equality continues in many aspects of American life, and in countries around the world.

I am convinced that our daughters can contribute just as much to society as our sons. Our common prosperity will be advanced by allowing all humanity—men and women—to reach their full potential. I do not believe that women must make the same choices as men in order to be equal, and I respect those women who choose to live their lives in traditional roles. But it should be their choice. And that is why the United States will partner with any Muslim-majority country to support expanded literacy for girls, and to help young women pursue employment through micro-financing that helps people live their dreams.

Finally, I want to discuss economic development and opportunity.

I know that for many, the face of globalization is contradictory. The Internet and television can bring knowledge and information, but also offensive sexuality and mindless violence into the home. Trade can bring new wealth and opportunities, but also huge disruptions and change in communities. In all nations—including America—this change can bring fear. Fear that because of modernity we lose control over our economic choices, our politics, and most importantly our identities—those things we most cherish about our communities, our families, our traditions, and our faith.

But I also know that human progress cannot be denied. There need not be contradictions between development and tradition. Countries like Japan and South Korea grew their economies enormously while maintaining distinct cultures. The same is true for the astonishing progress within Muslim-majority countries from Kuala Lumpur to Dubai. In ancient times and in our times, Muslim communities have been at the forefront of innovation and education.

And this is important because no development strategy can be based only upon what comes out of the ground, nor can it be sustained while young people are out of work. Many Gulf states have enjoyed great wealth as a consequence of oil, and some are beginning to focus it on broader development. But all of us must recognize that education and innovation will be the currency of the 21st century—and in too many Muslim communities, there remains underinvestment in these areas. I'm emphasizing such investment within my own country. And while America in the past has focused on oil and gas when it comes to this part of the world, we now seek a broader engagement.

On education, we will expand exchange programs, and increase scholarships, like the one that brought my father to America. At the same time, we will encourage more Americans to study in Muslim communities. And we will match promising Muslim students with internships in America; invest in online learning for teachers and children around the world; and create a new online network, so a young person in Kansas can communicate instantly with a young person in Cairo.

On economic development, we will create a new corps of business volunteers to partner with counterparts in Muslim-majority countries. And I will host a Summit on Entrepreneurship this year to identify how we can deepen ties between business leaders, foundations and social entrepreneurs in the United States and Muslim communities around the world.

On science and technology, we will launch a new fund to support technological development in Muslim-majority countries, and to help transfer ideas to the marketplace so they can create more jobs. We'll open centers of scientific excellence in Africa, the Middle East and Southeast Asia, and appoint new science envoys to collaborate on programs that develop new sources of energy, create green jobs, digitize records, clean water, grow new crops. Today I'm announcing a new global effort with the Organization of the Islamic Conference to eradicate polio. And we will also expand partnerships with Muslim communities to promote child and maternal health.

All these things must be done in partnership. Americans are ready to join with citizens and governments; community organizations, religious leaders, and businesses in Muslim communities around the world to help our people pursue a better life.

The issues that I have described will not be easy to address. But we have a responsibility to join together on behalf of the world that we seek—a world where extremists no longer threaten our people, and American troops have come home; a world where Israelis and Palestinians are each secure in a state of their own, and nuclear energy is used for peaceful purposes; a world where governments serve their citizens, and the rights of all God's children are respected. Those are mutual interests. That is the world we seek. But we can only achieve it together.

I know there are many—Muslim and non-Muslim—who question whether we can forge this new beginning. Some are eager to stoke the flames of division, and to stand in the way of progress. Some suggest that it isn't worth the effort—that we are fated to disagree, and civilizations are doomed to clash. Many more are simply skeptical that real change can occur. There's so much fear, so much mistrust that has built up over the years. But if we choose to be bound by the past, we will never move forward. And I want to particularly say this to young people of every faith, in every country—you, more than anyone, have the ability to reimagine the world, to remake this world.

All of us share this world for but a brief moment in time. The question is whether we spend that time focused on what pushes us apart, or whether we commit ourselves to an effort—a sustained effort—to find common ground, to focus on the future we seek for our children, and to respect the dignity of all human beings.

It's easier to start wars than to end them. It's easier to blame others than to look inward. It's easier to see what is different about someone than to find the things we share. But we should choose the right path, not just the easy path. There's one rule that lies at the heart of every religion—that we do unto others as we would have them do unto us. This truth transcends nations and peoples—a belief that isn't new; that isn't black or white or brown; that isn't Christian or Muslim or Jew. It's a belief that pulsed in the cradle of civilization, and that still beats in the hearts of billions around the world. It's a faith in other people, and it's what brought me here today.

We have the power to make the world we seek, but only if we have the courage to make a new beginning, keeping in mind what has been written.

The Holy Koran tells us: "O mankind! We have created you male and a female; and we have made you into nations and tribes so that you may know one another."

The Talmud tells us: "The whole of the Torah is for the purpose of promoting peace."

The Holy Bible tells us: "Blessed are the peacemakers, for they shall be called sons of God."

The people of the world can live together in peace. We know that is God's vision. Now that must be our work here on Earth.

Thank you. And may God's peace be upon you. Thank you very much. Thank you.

President Obama's Address on Accepting the Nobel Peace Prize

Following is the White House transcript of President Obama's address in Oslo, Norway, on acceptance of the Nobel Peace Prize, delivered on December 10, 2009.

Your Majesties, Your Royal Highnesses, distinguished members of the Norwegian Nobel Committee, citizens of America, and citizens of the world:

I receive this honor with deep gratitude and great humility. It is an award that speaks to our highest aspirations—that for all the cruelty and hardship of our world, we are not mere prisoners of fate. Our actions matter, and can bend history in the direction of justice.

And yet I would be remiss if I did not acknowledge the considerable controversy that your generous decision has generated. In part, this is because I am at the beginning, and not the end, of my labors on the world stage. Compared to some of the giants of history who've received this prize—Schweitzer and King; Marshall and Mandela—my accomplishments are slight. And then there are the men and women around the world who have been jailed and beaten in the pursuit of justice; those who toil in humanitarian organizations to relieve suffering; the unrecognized millions whose quiet acts of courage and compassion inspire even the most hardened cynics. I cannot argue with those who find these men and women—some known, some obscure to all but those they help—to be far more deserving of this honor than I.

But perhaps the most profound issue surrounding my receipt of this prize is the fact that I am the Commander-in-Chief of the military of a nation in the midst of two wars. One of these wars is winding down. The other is a conflict that America did not seek; one in which we are joined by 42 other countries—including Norway—in an effort to defend ourselves and all nations from further attacks.

Still, we are at war, and I'm responsible for the deployment of thousands of young Americans to battle in a distant land. Some will kill, and some will be killed. And so I come here with an acute sense of the costs of armed conflict—filled with difficult questions about the relationship between war and peace, and our effort to replace one with the other.

Now these questions are not new. War, in one form or another, appeared with the first man. At the dawn of history, its morality was not questioned; it was simply a fact, like drought or disease—the manner in which tribes and then civilizations sought power and settled their differences.

And over time, as codes of law sought to control violence within groups, so did philosophers and clerics and statesmen seek to regulate the destructive power of war. The concept of a "just war" emerged, suggesting that war is justified only when certain conditions were met: if it is waged as a last resort or in self-defense; if the force used is proportional; and if, whenever possible, civilians are spared from violence.

Of course, we know that for most of history, this concept of "just war" was rarely observed. The capacity of human beings to think up new ways to kill one another proved inexhaustible, as did our capacity to exempt from mercy those who look different or pray to a different God. Wars between armies gave way to wars between nations—total wars in which the distinction between combatant and civilian became blurred. In the span of 30 years, such carnage would twice engulf this continent. And while it's hard to conceive of a cause more just than the defeat of the Third Reich and the Axis powers, World War II was a conflict in which the total number of civilians who died exceeded the number of soldiers who perished.

In the wake of such destruction, and with the advent of the nuclear age, it became clear to victor and vanquished alike that the world needed institutions to prevent another world war. And so, a quarter century after the United States Senate rejected the League of Nations—an idea for which Woodrow Wilson received this prize—America led the world in constructing an architecture to keep the peace: a Marshall Plan and a United Nations, mechanisms to govern the waging of war, treaties to protect human rights, prevent genocide, restrict the most dangerous weapons.

In many ways, these efforts succeeded. Yes, terrible wars have been fought, and atrocities committed. But there has been no Third World War. The Cold War ended with jubilant crowds dismantling a wall. Commerce has stitched much of the world together. Billions have been lifted from poverty. The ideals of liberty and self-determination, equality and the rule of law have haltingly advanced. We are the heirs of the fortitude and foresight of generations past, and it is a legacy for which my own country is rightfully proud.

And yet, a decade into a new century, this old architecture is buckling under the weight of new threats. The world may no longer shudder at the prospect of war between two nuclear superpowers, but proliferation may increase the risk of catastrophe. Terrorism has long been a tactic, but modern technology allows a few small men with outsized rage to murder innocents on a horrific scale.

Moreover, wars between nations have increasingly given way to wars within nations. The resurgence of ethnic or sectarian conflicts; the growth of secessionist movements, insurgencies, and failed states—all these things have increasingly trapped civilians in unending chaos. In today's wars, many more civilians are killed than soldiers; the seeds of future conflict are sown, economies are wrecked, civil societies torn asunder, refugees amassed, children scarred.

I do not bring with me today a definitive solution to the problems of war. What I do know is that meeting these challenges will require the same vision, hard work, and persistence of those men and women who acted so boldly decades ago. And it will require us to think in new ways about the notions of just war and the imperatives of a just peace.

We must begin by acknowledging the hard truth: We will not eradicate violent conflict in our lifetimes. There will be times when nations—acting individually or in concert—will find the use of force not only necessary but morally justified.

I make this statement mindful of what Martin Luther King Jr. said in this same ceremony years ago: "Violence never brings permanent peace. It solves no social problem: it merely creates new and more complicated ones." As someone who stands here as a direct consequence of Dr. King's life work, I am living testimony to the moral force of non-violence. I know there's nothing weak—nothing passive—nothing naïve—in the creed and lives of Gandhi and King.

But as a head of state sworn to protect and defend my nation, I cannot be guided by their examples alone. I face the world as it is, and cannot stand idle in the face of threats to the American people. For make no mistake: Evil does exist in the world. A non-violent movement could not have halted Hitler's armies. Negotiations cannot convince al Qaeda's leaders to lay down their arms. To say that force may sometimes be necessary is not a call to cynicism—it is a recognition of history; the imperfections of man and the limits of reason.

I raise this point, I begin with this point because in many countries there is a deep ambivalence about military action today, no matter what the cause. And at times, this is joined by a reflexive suspicion of America, the world's sole military superpower.

But the world must remember that it was not simply international institutions—not just treaties and declarations—that brought stability to a post–World War II world. Whatever mistakes we have made, the plain fact is this: The United States of America has helped underwrite global security for more than six decades with the blood of our citizens and the strength of our arms. The service and sacrifice of our men and women in uniform has promoted peace and prosperity from Germany to Korea, and enabled democracy to take hold in places like the Balkans. We have borne this burden not because we seek to impose our will. We have done so out of enlightened self-interest—because we seek a better future for our children and grandchildren, and we believe that their lives will be better if others' children and grandchildren can live in freedom and prosperity.

So yes, the instruments of war do have a role to play in preserving the peace. And yet this truth must coexist with another—that no matter how justified, war promises human tragedy. The soldier's courage and sacrifice is full of glory, expressing devotion to country, to cause, to comrades in arms. But war itself is never glorious, and we must never trumpet it as such.

So part of our challenge is reconciling these two seemingly irreconcilable truths—that war is sometimes necessary, and war at some level is an expression of human folly. Concretely, we must direct our effort to the task that President Kennedy called for long ago. "Let us focus," he said, "on a more practical, more attainable peace, based not on a sudden revolution in human nature but on a gradual evolution in human institutions." A gradual evolution of human institutions.

What might this evolution look like? What might these practical steps be?

To begin with, I believe that all nations—strong and weak alike—must adhere to standards that govern the use of force. I—like any head of state—reserve the right to act unilaterally if necessary to defend my nation. Nevertheless, I am convinced that adhering to standards, international standards, strengthens those who do, and isolates and weakens those who don't.

The world rallied around America after the 9/11 attacks, and continues to support our efforts in Afghanistan, because of the horror of those senseless attacks and the recognized principle of self-defense. Likewise, the world recognized the need to confront Saddam Hussein when he invaded Kuwait—a consensus that sent a clear message to all about the cost of aggression.

Furthermore, America—in fact, no nation—can insist that others follow the rules of the road if we refuse to follow them ourselves. For when we don't, our actions appear arbitrary and undercut the legitimacy of future interventions, no matter how justified.

And this becomes particularly important when the purpose of military action extends beyond self-defense or the defense of one nation against an aggressor. More and more, we all confront difficult questions about how to prevent the slaughter of civilians by their own government, or to stop a civil war whose violence and suffering can engulf an entire region.

I believe that force can be justified on humanitarian grounds, as it was in the Balkans, or in other places that have been scarred by war. Inaction tears at our conscience and can lead to more costly intervention later. That's why all responsible nations must embrace the role that militaries with a clear mandate can play to keep the peace.

America's commitment to global security will never waver. But in a world in which threats are more diffuse, and missions more complex, America cannot act alone. America alone cannot secure the peace. This is true in Afghanistan. This is true in failed states like Somalia, where terrorism and piracy is joined by famine and human suffering. And sadly, it will continue to be true in unstable regions for years to come.

The leaders and soldiers of NATO countries, and other friends and allies, demonstrate this truth through the capacity and courage they've shown in Afghanistan. But in many countries, there is a disconnect between the efforts of those who serve and the ambivalence of the broader public. I understand why war is not popular, but I also know this: The belief that peace is desirable is rarely enough to achieve it. Peace requires responsibility. Peace entails sacrifice. That's why NATO continues to be indispensable. That's why we must strengthen U.N. and regional peacekeeping, and not leave the task to a few countries. That's why we honor those who return home from peacekeeping and training abroad to Oslo and Rome; to Ottawa and Sydney; to Dhaka and Kigali—we honor them not as makers of war, but of wagers—but as wagers of peace.

Let me make one final point about the use of force. Even as we make difficult decisions about going to war, we must also think clearly about how we fight it. The Nobel Committee recognized this truth in awarding its first prize for peace to Henry Dunant—the founder of the Red Cross, and a driving force behind the Geneva Conventions.

Where force is necessary, we have a moral and strategic interest in binding ourselves to certain rules of conduct. And even as we confront a vicious adversary that abides by no rules, I believe the United States of America must remain a standard bearer in the conduct of war. That is what makes us different from those whom we fight. That is a source of our strength. That is why I prohibited torture. That is why I ordered the prison at Guantánamo Bay closed. And that is why I have reaffirmed America's commitment to abide by the Geneva Conventions. We lose ourselves when we compromise the very ideals that we fight to defend. And we honor—we honor those ideals by upholding them not when it's easy, but when it is hard.

I have spoken at some length to the question that must weigh on our minds and our hearts as we choose to wage war. But let me now turn to our effort to avoid such tragic choices, and speak of three ways that we can build a just and lasting peace.

First, in dealing with those nations that break rules and laws, I believe that we must develop alternatives to violence that are tough enough to actually change behavior—for if we want a lasting peace, then the words of the international community must mean something. Those regimes that break the rules must be held accountable. Sanctions must exact a real price. Intransigence must be met with increased pressure—and such pressure exists only when the world stands together as one.

One urgent example is the effort to prevent the spread of nuclear weapons, and to seek a world without them. In the middle of the last century, nations agreed to be bound by a treaty whose bargain is clear: All will have access to peaceful nuclear power; those without nuclear weapons will forsake them; and those with nuclear weapons will work towards disarmament. I am committed to upholding this treaty. It is a centerpiece of my foreign policy. And I'm working with President Medvedev to reduce America and Russia's nuclear stockpiles.

But it is also incumbent upon all of us to insist that nations like Iran and North Korea do not game the system. Those who claim to respect international law cannot avert their eyes when those laws are flouted. Those who care for their own security cannot ignore the danger of an arms race in the Middle East or East Asia. Those who seek peace cannot stand idly by as nations arm themselves for nuclear war.

The same principle applies to those who violate international laws by brutalizing their own people. When there is genocide in Darfur, systematic rape in Congo, repression in Burma—there must be consequences. Yes, there will be engagement; yes, there will be diplomacy—but there must be consequences when those things fail. And the closer we stand together, the less likely we will be faced with the choice between armed intervention and complicity in oppression.

This brings me to a second point—the nature of the peace that we seek. For peace is not merely the absence of visible conflict. Only a just peace based on the inherent rights and dignity of every individual can truly be lasting.

It was this insight that drove drafters of the Universal Declaration of Human Rights after the Second World War. In the wake of devastation, they recognized that if human rights are not protected, peace is a hollow promise.

And yet too often, these words are ignored. For some countries, the failure to uphold human rights is excused by the false suggestion that these are somehow Western principles, foreign to local cultures or stages of a nation's development. And within America, there has long been a tension between those who describe themselves as realists or idealists—a tension that suggests a stark choice between the narrow pursuit of interests or an endless campaign to impose our values around the world.

I reject these choices. I believe that peace is unstable where citizens are denied the right to speak freely or worship as they please; choose their own leaders or assemble without fear. Pent-up grievances fester, and the suppression of tribal and religious identity can lead to violence. We also know that the opposite is true. Only when Europe became free did it finally find peace. America has never fought a war against a democracy, and our closest friends are governments that protect the rights of their citizens. No matter how callously defined, neither America's interests—nor the world's—are served by the denial of human aspirations.

So even as we respect the unique culture and traditions of different countries, America will always be a voice for those aspirations that are universal. We will bear witness to the quiet dignity of reformers like Aung Sang Suu Kyi; to the bravery of Zimbabweans who cast their ballots in the face of beatings; to the hundreds of thousands who have marched silently through the streets of Iran. It is telling that the leaders of these governments fear the aspirations of their own people more than the power of any other nation. And it is the responsibility of all free people and free nations to make clear that these movements—these movements of hope and history—they have us on their side.

Let me also say this: The promotion of human rights cannot be about exhortation alone. At times, it must be coupled with painstaking diplomacy. I know that engagement with repressive regimes lacks the satisfying purity of indignation. But I also know that sanctions without outreach—condemnation without discussion—can carry forward only a crippling status quo. No repressive regime can move down a new path unless it has the choice of an open door.

In light of the Cultural Revolution's horrors, Nixon's meeting with Mao appeared inexcusable—and yet it surely helped set China on a path where millions of its citizens have been lifted from poverty and connected to open societies. Pope John Paul's engagement with Poland created space not just for the Catholic Church, but for labor leaders like Lech Walesa. Ronald Reagan's efforts on arms control and embrace of perestroika not only improved relations with the Soviet Union, but empowered dissidents throughout Eastern Europe. There's no simple formula here. But we must try as best we can to balance isolation and engagement, pressure and incentives, so that human rights and dignity are advanced over time.

Third, a just peace includes not only civil and political rights—it must encompass economic security and opportunity. For true peace is not just freedom from fear, but freedom from want.

It is undoubtedly true that development rarely takes root without security; it is also true that security does not exist where human beings do not have access to enough food, or clean water, or the medicine and shelter they need to survive. It does not exist where children can't aspire to a decent education or a job that supports a family. The absence of hope can rot a society from within.

And that's why helping farmers feed their own people—or nations educate their children and care for the sick—is not mere charity. It's also why the world must come together to confront climate change. There is little scientific dispute that if we do nothing, we will face more drought, more famine, more mass displacement—all of which will fuel more conflict for decades. For this reason, it is not merely scientists and environmental activists who call for swift and forceful action—it's military leaders in my own country and others who understand our common security hangs in the balance.

Agreements among nations. Strong institutions. Support for human rights. Investments in development. All these are vital ingredients in bringing about the evolution that President Kennedy spoke about. And yet, I do not believe that we will have the will, the determination, the staying power, to complete this work without something more—and that's the continued expansion of our moral imagination; an insistence that there's something irreducible that we all share.

As the world grows smaller, you might think it would be easier for human beings to recognize how similar we are; to understand that we're all basically seeking the same things; that we all hope for the chance to live out our lives with some measure of happiness and fulfillment for ourselves and our families.

And yet somehow, given the dizzying pace of globalization, the cultural leveling of modernity, it perhaps comes as no surprise that people fear the loss of what they cherish in their particular identities—their race, their tribe, and perhaps most powerfully their religion. In some places, this fear has led to conflict. At times, it even feels like we're moving backwards. We see it in the Middle East, as the conflict between Arabs and Jews seems to harden. We see it in nations that are torn asunder by tribal lines.

And most dangerously, we see it in the way that religion is used to justify the murder of innocents by those who have distorted and defiled the great religion of Islam, and who attacked my country from Afghanistan. These extremists are not the first to kill in the name of God; the cruelties of the Crusades are amply recorded. But they remind us that no Holy War can ever be a just war. For if you truly believe that you are carrying out divine will, then there is no need for restraint—no need to spare the pregnant mother, or the medic, or the Red Cross worker, or even a person of one's own faith. Such a warped view of religion is not just incompatible with the concept of peace, but I believe it's incompatible with the very purpose of faith—for the one rule that lies at the heart of every major religion is that we do unto others as we would have them do unto us.

Adhering to this law of love has always been the core struggle of human nature. For we are fallible. We make mistakes, and fall victim to the temptations of pride, and power, and sometimes evil. Even those of us with the best of intentions will at times fail to right the wrongs before us.

But we do not have to think that human nature is perfect for us to still believe that the human condition can be perfected. We do not have to live in an idealized world to still reach for those ideals that will make it a better place. The non-violence practiced by men like Gandhi and King may not have been practical or possible in every circumstance, but the love that they preached—their fundamental faith in human progress—that must always be the North Star that guides us on our journey.

For if we lose that faith—if we dismiss it as silly or naïve; if we divorce it from the decisions that we make on issues of war and peace—then we lose what's best about humanity. We lose our sense of possibility. We lose our moral compass.

Like generations have before us, we must reject that future. As Dr. King said at this occasion so many years ago, "I refuse to accept despair as the final response to the ambiguities of history. I refuse to accept the idea that the 'isness' of man's present condition makes him morally incapable of reaching up for the eternal 'oughtness' that forever confronts him."

Let us reach for the world that ought to be—that spark of the divine that still stirs within each of our souls.

Somewhere today, in the here and now, in the world as it is, a soldier sees he's outgunned, but stands firm to keep the peace. Somewhere today, in this world, a young protestor awaits the brutality of her government, but has the courage to march on. Somewhere today, a mother facing punishing poverty still takes the time to teach her child, scrapes together what few coins she has to send that child to school—because she believes that a cruel world still has a place for that child's dreams.

Let us live by their example. We can acknowledge that oppression will always be with us, and still strive for justice. We can admit the intractability of depravation, and still strive for dignity. Clear-eyed, we can understand that there will be war, and still strive for peace. We can do that—for that is the story of human progress; that's the hope of all the world; and at this moment of challenge, that must be our work here on Earth.

Thank you very much.

President Obama's Address on Climate Change

Following is the White House's transcript of President Obama's address at the morning plenary session of the United Nations Climate Change Conference, in Copenhagen, Denmark, delivered on December 18, 2009.

Good morning. It is an honor for me to join this distinguished group of leaders from nations around the world. We come here in Copenhagen because climate change poses a grave and growing danger to our people. All of you would not be here unless you—like me—were convinced that this danger is real. This is not fiction, it is science. Unchecked, climate change will pose unacceptable risks to our security, our economies, and our planet. This much we know.

The question, then, before us is no longer the nature of the challenge—the question is our capacity to meet it. For while the reality of climate change is not in doubt, I have to be honest, as the world watches us today, I think our ability to take collective action is in doubt right now, and it hangs in the balance.

I believe we can act boldly, and decisively, in the face of a common threat. That's why I come here today—not to talk, but to act.

Now, as the world's largest economy and as the world's second largest emitter, America bears our responsibility to address climate change, and we intend to meet that responsibility. That's why we've renewed our leadership within international climate change negotiations. That's why we've worked with other nations to phase out fossil fuel subsidies. That's why we've taken bold action at home—by making historic investments in renewable energy; by putting our people to work increasing efficiency in our homes and buildings; and by pursuing comprehensive legislation to transform to a clean energy economy.

These mitigation actions are ambitious, and we are taking them not simply to meet global responsibilities. We are convinced, as some of you may be convinced, that changing the way we produce and use energy is essential to America's economic future—that it will create millions of new jobs, power new industries, keep us competitive, and spark new innovation. We're convinced, for our own self-interest, that the way we use energy, changing it to a more efficient fashion, is essential to our national security, because it helps to reduce our dependence on foreign oil, and helps us deal with some of the dangers posed by climate change.

So I want this plenary session to understand, America is going to continue on this course of action to mitigate our emissions and to move towards a clean energy economy, no matter what happens here in Copenhagen. We think it is good for us, as well as good for the world. But we also believe that we will all be stronger, all be safer, all be more secure if we act together. That's why it is in our mutual interest to achieve a global accord in which we agree to certain steps, and to hold each other accountable to certain commitments.

After months of talk, after two weeks of negotiations, after innumerable side meetings, bilateral meetings, endless hours of discussion among negotiators, I believe that the pieces of that accord should now be clear.

First, all major economies must put forward decisive national actions that will reduce their emissions, and begin to turn the corner on climate change. I'm pleased that many of us have already done so. Almost all the major economies have put forward legitimate targets, significant targets, ambitious targets. And I'm confident that America will fulfill the commitments that we have made: cutting our emissions in the range of 17 percent by 2020, and by more than 80 percent by 2050 in line with final legislation.

Second, we must have a mechanism to review whether we are keeping our commitments, and exchange this information in a transparent manner. These measures need not be intrusive, or infringe upon sovereignty. They must, however, ensure that an accord is credible, and that we're living up to our obligations. Without such accountability, any agreement would be empty words on a page.

I don't know how you have an international agreement where we all are not sharing information and ensuring that we are meeting our commitments. That doesn't make sense. It would be a hollow victory.

Number three, we must have financing that helps developing countries adapt, particularly the least developed and most vulnerable countries to climate change. America will be a part of fast-start funding that will ramp up to $10 billion by 2012. And yesterday, Secretary Hillary Clinton, my Secretary of State, made it clear that we will engage in a global effort to mobilize $100 billion in financing by 2020, if—and only if—it is part of a broader accord that I have just described.

Mitigation. Transparency. Financing. It's a clear formula—one that embraces the principle of common but differentiated responses and respective capabilities. And it adds up to a significant accord—one that takes us farther than we have ever gone before as an international community.

I just want to say to this plenary session that we are running short on time. And at this point, the question is whether we will move forward together or split apart, whether we prefer posturing to action. I'm sure that many consider this an imperfect framework that I just described. No country will get everything that it wants. There are those developing countries that want aid with no strings attached, and no obligations with respect to transparency. They think that the most advanced nations should pay a higher price; I understand that. There are those advanced nations who think that developing countries either cannot absorb this assistance, or that will not be held accountable effectively, and that the world's fastest-growing emitters should bear a greater share of the burden.

We know the fault lines because we've been imprisoned by them for years. These international discussions have essentially taken place now for almost two decades, and we have very little to show for it other than an increased acceleration of the climate change phenomenon. The time for talk is over. This is the bottom line: We can embrace this accord, take a substantial step forward, continue to refine it and build upon its foundation. We can do that, and everyone who is in this room will be part of a historic endeavor—one that makes life better for our children and our grandchildren.

Or we can choose delay, falling back into the same divisions that have stood in the way of action for years. And we will be back having the same stale arguments month after month, year after year, perhaps decade after decade, all while the danger of climate change grows until it is irreversible.

Ladies and gentlemen, there is no time to waste. America has made our choice. We have charted our course. We have made our commitments. We will do what we say. Now I believe it's the time for the nations and the people of the world to come together behind a common purpose.

We are ready to get this done today—but there has to be movement on all sides to recognize that it is better for us to act than to talk; it's better for us to choose action over inaction; the future over the past—and with courage and faith, I believe that we can meet our responsibility to our people, and the future of our planet.

Thank you very much.

President Obama's 2010 State of the Union Address

Following is the White House transcript of President Obama's State of the Union address, delivered to a joint session of Congress on January 27, 2010.

Madame Speaker, Vice President Biden, members of Congress, distinguished guests, and fellow Americans:

Our Constitution declares that from time to time, the President shall give to Congress information about the state of our union. For 220 years, our leaders have fulfilled this duty. They've done so during periods of prosperity and tranquility. And they've done so in the midst of war and depression; at moments of great strife and great struggle.

It's tempting to look back on these moments and assume that our progress was inevitable—that America was always destined to succeed. But when the Union was turned back at Bull Run, and the Allies first landed at Omaha Beach, victory was very much in doubt. When the market crashed on Black Tuesday, and civil rights marchers were beaten on Bloody Sunday, the future was anything but certain. These were the times that tested the courage of our convictions, and the strength of our union. And despite all our divisions and disagreements, our hesitations and our fears, America prevailed because we chose to move forward as one nation, as one people.

Again, we are tested. And again, we must answer history's call.

One year ago, I took office amid two wars, an economy rocked by a severe recession, a financial system on the verge of collapse, and a government deeply in debt. Experts from across the political spectrum warned that if we did not act, we might face a second depression. So we acted—immediately and aggressively. And one year later, the worst of the storm has passed.

But the devastation remains. One in 10 Americans still cannot find work. Many businesses have shuttered. Home values have declined. Small towns and rural communities have been hit especially hard. And for those who'd already known poverty, life has become that much harder.

This recession has also compounded the burdens that America's families have been dealing with for decades—the burden of working harder and longer for less, of being unable to save enough to retire or help kids with college.

So I know the anxieties that are out there right now. They're not new. These struggles are the reason I ran for president. These struggles are what I've witnessed for years in places like Elkhart, Ind., Galesburg, Ill. I hear about them in the letters that I read each night. The toughest to read are those written by children—asking why they have to move from their home, asking when their mom or dad will be able to go back to work.

For these Americans and so many others, change has not come fast enough. Some are frustrated; some are angry. They don't understand why it seems like bad behavior on Wall Street is rewarded, but hard work on Main Street isn't; or why Washington has been unable or unwilling to solve any of our problems. They're tired of the partisanship and the shouting and the pettiness. They know we can't afford it. Not now.

So we face big and difficult challenges. And what the American people hope—what they deserve—is for all of us, Democrats and Republicans, to work through our differences, to overcome the numbing weight of our politics. For while the people who sent us here have different backgrounds, different stories, different beliefs, the anxieties they face are the same. The aspirations they hold are shared: a job that pays the bills; a chance to get ahead; most of all, the ability to give their children a better life.

You know what else they share? They share a stubborn resilience in the face of adversity. After one of the most difficult years in our history, they remain busy building cars and teaching kids, starting businesses and going back to school. They're coaching Little League and helping their neighbors. One woman wrote to me and said, "We are strained but hopeful, struggling but encouraged."

It's because of this spirit—this great decency and great strength—that I have never been more hopeful about America's future than I am tonight. Despite our hardships, our union is strong. We do not give up. We do not quit. We do not allow fear or division to break our spirit. In this new decade, it's time the American people get a government that matches their decency, that embodies their strength.

And tonight, tonight I'd like to talk about how together we can deliver on that promise.

REVIVING THE ECONOMY

It begins with our economy.

Our most urgent task upon taking office was to shore up the same banks that helped cause this crisis. It was not easy to do. And if there's one thing that has unified Democrats and Republicans, and everybody in between, it's that we all hated the bank bailout. I hated it—I hated it. You hated it. It was about as popular as a root canal.

But when I ran for president, I promised I wouldn't just do what was popular—I would do what was necessary. And if we had allowed the meltdown of the financial system, unemployment might be double what it is today. More businesses would certainly have closed. More homes would have surely been lost.

So I supported the last administration's efforts to create the financial rescue program. And when we took that program over, we made it more transparent and more accountable. And as a result, the markets are now stabilized, and we've recovered most of the money we spent on the banks. Most, but not all.

To recover the rest, I've proposed a fee on the biggest banks. Now, I know Wall Street isn't keen on this idea. But if these firms can afford to hand out big bonuses again, they can afford a modest fee to pay back the taxpayers who rescued them in their time of need.

Now, as we stabilized the financial system, we also took steps to get our economy growing again, save as many jobs as possible and help Americans who had become unemployed.

That's why we extended or increased unemployment benefits for more than 18 million Americans, made health insurance 65 percent cheaper for families who get their coverage through COBRA, and passed 25 different tax cuts.

Now, let me repeat: We cut taxes. We cut taxes for 95 percent of working families. We cut taxes for small businesses. We cut taxes for first-time homebuyers. We cut taxes for parents trying to care for their children. We cut taxes for 8 million Americans paying for college.

I thought I'd get some applause on that one.

As a result, millions of Americans had more to spend on gas and food and other necessities, all of which helped businesses keep more workers. And we haven't raised income taxes by a single dime on a single person. Not a single dime.

Because of the steps we took, there are about 2 million Americans working right now who would otherwise be unemployed. Two hundred thousand work in construction and clean energy; 300,000 are teachers and other education workers. Tens of thousands are cops, firefighters, correctional officers, first-responders. And we're on track to add another 1½ million jobs to this total by the end of the year.

The plan that has made all of this possible, from the tax cuts to the jobs, is the Recovery Act. That's right—the Recovery Act, also known as the stimulus bill. Economists on the left and the right say this bill has helped save jobs and avert disaster. But you don't have to take their word for it. Talk to the small business in Phoenix that will triple its workforce because of the Recovery Act. Talk to the window manufacturer in Philadelphia who said he used to be skeptical about the Recovery Act, until he had to add two more work shifts just because of the business it created. Talk to the single teacher raising two kids who was told by her principal in the last week of school that because of the Recovery Act, she wouldn't be laid off after all.

There are stories like this all across America. And after two years of recession, the economy is growing again. Retirement funds have started to gain back some of their value. Businesses are beginning to invest again, and slowly some are starting to hire again.

But I realize that for every success story, there are other stories, of men and women who wake up with the anguish of not knowing where their next paycheck will come from; who send out résumés week after week and hear nothing in response. That is why jobs must be our number one focus in 2010, and that's why I'm calling for a new jobs bill tonight.

Now, the true engine of job creation in this country will always be America's businesses. But government can create the conditions necessary for businesses to expand and hire more workers.

SMALL BUSINESSES

We should start where most new jobs do—in small businesses, companies that begin when—companies that begin when an entrepreneur—when an entrepreneur takes a chance on a dream, or a worker decides it's time she became her own boss. Through sheer grit and determination, these companies have weathered the recession and they're ready to grow. But when you talk to small-business owners in places like Allentown, Pa., or Elyria, Ohio, you find out that even though banks on Wall Street are lending again, they're mostly lending to bigger companies. Financing remains difficult for small-business owners across the country, even those that are making a profit.

So tonight, I'm proposing that we take $30 billion of the money Wall Street banks have repaid and use it to help community banks give small businesses the credit they need to stay afloat. I'm also proposing a new small-business tax credit—one that will go to over 1 million small businesses who hire new workers or raise wages. While we're at it, let's also eliminate all capital gains taxes on small-business investment, and provide a tax incentive for all large businesses and all small businesses to invest in new plants and equipment.

Next, we can put Americans to work today building the infrastructure of tomorrow. From the first railroads to the Interstate Highway System, our nation has always been built to compete. There's no reason Europe or China should have the fastest trains, or the new factories that manufacture clean-energy products.

Tomorrow, I'll visit Tampa, Fla., where workers will soon break ground on a new high-speed railroad funded by the Recovery Act. There are projects like that all across this country that will create jobs and help move our nation's goods, services and information.

We should put more Americans to work building clean-energy facilities and give rebates to Americans who make their homes more energy efficient, which supports clean-energy jobs. And to encourage these and other businesses to stay within our borders, it is time to finally slash the tax breaks for companies that ship our jobs overseas, and give those tax breaks to companies that create jobs right here in the United States of America.

Now, the House has passed a jobs bill that includes some of these steps. As the first order of business this year, I urge the Senate to do the same, and I know they will. They will. People are out of work. They're hurting. They need our help. And I want a jobs bill on my desk without delay.

But the truth is, these steps won't make up for the 7 million jobs that we've lost over the last two years. The only way to move to full employment is to lay a new foundation for long-term economic growth, and finally address the problems that America's families have confronted for years.

We can't afford another so-called economic "expansion" like the one from the last decade—what some call the "lost decade"—where jobs grew more slowly than during any prior expansion; where the income of the average American household declined while the cost of health care and tuition reached record highs; where prosperity was built on a housing bubble and financial speculation.

FINANCIAL REGULATIONS

From the day I took office, I've been told that addressing our larger challenges is too ambitious; such an effort would be too contentious. I've been told that our political system is too gridlocked and that we should just put things on hold for a while.

For those who make these claims, I have one simple question: How long should we wait? How long should America put its future on hold?

You see, Washington has been telling us to wait for decades, even as the problems have grown worse. Meanwhile, China is not waiting to revamp its economy. Germany is not waiting. India is not waiting. These nations—they're not standing still. These nations aren't playing for second place. They're putting more emphasis on math and science. They're rebuilding their infrastructure. They're making serious investments in clean energy because they want those jobs. Well, I do not accept second place for the United States of America.

As hard as it may be, as uncomfortable and contentious as the debates may become, it's time to get serious about fixing the problems that are hampering our growth.

Now, one place to start is serious financial reform. Look, I am not interested in punishing banks. I'm interested in protecting our economy. A strong, healthy financial market makes it possible for businesses to access credit and create new jobs. It channels the savings of families into investments that raise incomes. But that can only happen if we guard against the same recklessness that nearly brought down our entire economy.

We need to make sure consumers and middle-class families have the information they need to make financial decisions. We can't allow financial institutions, including those that take your deposits, to take risks that threaten the whole economy.

Now, the House has already passed financial reform with many of these changes. And the lobbyists are trying to kill it. But we cannot let them win this fight. And if the bill that ends up on my desk does not meet the test of real reform, I will send it back until we get it right. We've got to get it right.

Next, we need to encourage American innovation. Last year, we made the largest investment in basic research funding in history—an investment that could lead to the world's cheapest solar cells or treatment that kills cancer cells but leaves healthy ones untouched. And no area is more ripe for such innovation than energy. You can see the results of last year's investments in clean energy—in the North Carolina company that will create 1,200 jobs nationwide helping to make advanced batteries; or in the California business that will put a thousand people to work making solar panels.

But to create more of these clean-energy jobs, we need more production, more efficiency, more incentives. And that means building a new generation of safe, clean nuclear power plants in this country. It means making tough decisions about opening new offshore areas for oil and gas development. It means continued investment in advanced biofuels and clean-coal technologies. And, yes, it means passing a comprehensive energy and climate bill with incentives that will finally make clean energy the profitable kind of energy in America.

I am grateful to the House for passing such a bill last year. And this year I'm eager to help advance the bipartisan effort in the Senate.

I know there have been questions about whether we can afford such changes in a tough economy. I know that there are those who disagree with the overwhelming scientific evidence on climate change. But here's the thing—even if you doubt the evidence, providing incentives for energy efficiency and clean energy are the right thing to do for our future, because the nation that leads the clean-energy economy will be the nation that leads the global economy. And America must be that nation.

Third, we need to export more of our goods, because the more products we make and sell to other countries, the more jobs we support right here in America. So tonight, we set a new goal: We will double our exports over the next five years, an increase that will support 2 million jobs in America. To help meet this goal, we're launching a National Export Initiative that will help farmers and small businesses increase their exports, and reform export controls consistent with national security.

We have to seek new markets aggressively, just as our competitors are. If America sits on the sidelines while other nations sign trade deals, we will lose the chance to create jobs on our shores. But realizing those benefits also means enforcing those agreements so our trading partners play by the rules. And that's why we'll continue to shape a Doha trade agreement that opens global markets, and why we will strengthen our trade relations in Asia and with key partners like South Korea and Panama and Colombia.

Fourth, we need to invest in the skills and education of our people.

EDUCATIONAL SUCCESS

Now, this year, we've broken through the stalemate between left and right by launching a national competition to improve our schools. And the idea here is simple: Instead of rewarding failure, we only reward success. Instead of funding the status quo, we only invest in reform—reform that raises student achievement, inspires students to excel in math and science, and turns around failing schools that steal the future of too many young Americans, from rural communities to the inner city. In the 21st century, the best anti-poverty program around is a world-class education. And in this country, the success of our children cannot depend more on where they live than on their potential.

When we renew the Elementary and Secondary Education Act, we will work with Congress to expand these reforms to all 50 states. Still, in this economy, a high school diploma no longer guarantees a good job. That's why I urge the Senate to follow the House and pass a bill that will revitalize our community colleges, which are a career pathway to the children of so many working families.

To make college more affordable, this bill will finally end the unwarranted taxpayer subsidies that go to banks for student loans. Instead, let's take that money and give families a $10,000 tax credit for four years of college and increase Pell grants. And let's tell another 1 million students that when they graduate, they will be required to pay only 10 percent of their income on student loans, and all of their debt will be forgiven after 20 years—and forgiven after 10 years if they choose a career in public service, because in the United States of America, no one should go broke because they chose to go to college.

And by the way, it's time for colleges and universities to get serious about cutting their own costs, because they, too, have a responsibility to help solve this problem.

Now, the price of college tuition is just one of the burdens facing the middle class. That's why last year I asked Vice President

Biden to chair a task force on middle-class families. That's why we're nearly doubling the child care tax credit, and making it easier to save for retirement by giving access to every worker a retirement account and expanding the tax credit for those who start a nest egg. That's why we're working to lift the value of a family's single largest investment—their home. The steps we took last year to shore up the housing market have allowed millions of Americans to take out new loans and save an average of $1,500 on mortgage payments.

This year, we will step up refinancing so that homeowners can move into more affordable mortgages. And it is precisely to relieve the burden on middle-class families that we still need health insurance reform. Yes, we do.

Now, let's clear a few things up. I didn't choose to tackle this issue to get some legislative victory under my belt. And by now it should be fairly obvious that I didn't take on health care because it was good politics. I took on health care because of the stories I've heard from Americans with pre-existing conditions whose lives depend on getting coverage; patients who've been denied coverage; families—even those with insurance—who are just one illness away from financial ruin.

After nearly a century of trying—Democratic administrations, Republican administrations—we are closer than ever to bringing more security to the lives of so many Americans. The approach we've taken would protect every American from the worst practices of the insurance industry. It would give small businesses and uninsured Americans a chance to choose an affordable health care plan in a competitive market. It would require every insurance plan to cover preventive care.

And by the way, I want to acknowledge our first lady, Michelle Obama, who this year is creating a national movement to tackle the epidemic of childhood obesity and make kids healthier. Thank you. She gets embarrassed.

Our approach would preserve the right of Americans who have insurance to keep their doctor and their plan. It would reduce costs and premiums for millions of families and businesses. And according to the Congressional Budget Office—the independent organization that both parties have cited as the official scorekeeper for Congress—our approach would bring down the deficit by as much as $1 trillion over the next two decades.

Still, this is a complex issue, and the longer it was debated, the more skeptical people became. I take my share of the blame for not explaining it more clearly to the American people. And I know that with all the lobbying and horse-trading, the process left most Americans wondering, "What's in it for me?"

But I also know this problem is not going away. By the time I'm finished speaking tonight, more Americans will have lost their health insurance. Millions will lose it this year. Our deficit will grow. Premiums will go up. Patients will be denied the care they need. Small-business owners will continue to drop coverage altogether. I will not walk away from these Americans, and neither should the people in this chamber.

So, as temperatures cool, I want everyone to take another look at the plan we've proposed. There's a reason why many doctors, nurses, and health care experts who know our system best consider this approach a vast improvement over the status quo. But if anyone from either party has a better approach that will bring down premiums, bring down the deficit, cover the uninsured, strengthen Medicare for seniors and stop insurance company abuses, let me know. Let me know. Let me know. I'm eager to see it.

Here's what I ask Congress, though: Don't walk away from reform. Not now. Not when we are so close. Let us find a way to come together and finish the job for the American people. Let's get it done. Let's get it done.

FACING THE DEBT

Now, even as health care reform would reduce our deficit, it's not enough to dig us out of a massive fiscal hole in which we find ourselves. It's a challenge that makes all others that much harder to solve, and one that's been subject to a lot of political posturing. So let me start the discussion of government spending by setting the record straight.

At the beginning of the last decade, the year 2000, America had a budget surplus of over $200 billion. By the time I took office, we had a one-year deficit of over $1 trillion and projected deficits of $8 trillion over the next decade. Most of this was the result of not paying for two wars, two tax cuts and an expensive prescription drug program. On top of that, the effects of the recession put a $3 trillion hole in our budget. All this was before I walked in the door.

Now—just stating the facts. Now, if we had taken office in ordinary times, I would have liked nothing more than to start bringing down the deficit. But we took office amid a crisis. And our efforts to prevent a second depression have added another $1 trillion to our national debt. That, too, is a fact.

I'm absolutely convinced that was the right thing to do. But families across the country are tightening their belts and making tough decisions. The federal government should do the same. So tonight, I'm proposing specific steps to pay for the trillion dollars that it took to rescue the economy last year.

Starting in 2011, we are prepared to freeze government spending for three years. Spending related to our national security, Medicare, Medicaid and Social Security will not be affected. But all other discretionary government programs will. Like any cash-strapped family, we will work within a budget to invest in what we need and sacrifice what we don't. And if I have to enforce this discipline by veto, I will.

We will continue to go through the budget, line by line, page by page, to eliminate programs that we can't afford and don't work. We've already identified $20 billion in savings for next year. To help working families, we'll extend our middle-class tax cuts. But at a time of record deficits, we will not continue tax cuts for oil companies, for investment fund managers, and for those making over $250,000 a year. We just can't afford it.

Now, even after paying for what we spent on my watch, we'll still face the massive deficit we had when I took office. More importantly, the cost of Medicare, Medicaid and Social Security will continue to skyrocket. That's why I've called for a bipartisan fiscal commission, modeled on a proposal by Republican Judd Gregg and Democrat Kent Conrad. This can't be one of those Washington gimmicks that lets us pretend we solved a problem. The commission will have to provide a specific set of solutions by a certain deadline.

Now, yesterday the Senate blocked a bill that would have created this commission. So I'll issue an executive order that will allow us to go forward, because I refuse to pass this problem on to another generation of Americans. And when the vote comes tomorrow, the Senate should restore the pay-as-you-go law that was a big reason for why we had record surpluses in the 1990s.

Now, I know that some in my own party will argue that we can't address the deficit or freeze government spending when so many are still hurting. And I agree—which is why this freeze won't take effect until next year, when the economy is stronger. That's how budgeting works. But understand—understand, if we don't take meaningful steps to rein in our debt, it could damage our markets, increase the cost of borrowing, and jeopardize our recovery—all of which would have an even worse effect on our job growth and family incomes.

From some on the right, I expect we'll hear a different argument—that if we just make fewer investments in our people, extend tax cuts including those for the wealthier Americans, eliminate more regulations, maintain the status quo on health care, our deficits will go away. The problem is, that's what we did for eight years. That's what helped us into this crisis. It's what helped lead to these deficits. We can't do it again.

Rather than fight the same tired battles that have dominated Washington for decades, it's time to try something new. Let's invest in our people without leaving them a mountain of debt. Let's meet our responsibility to the citizens who sent us here. Let's try common sense. A novel concept.

"A DEFICIT OF TRUST"

To do that, we have to recognize that we face more than a deficit of dollars right now. We face a deficit of trust—deep and corrosive doubts about how Washington works that have been growing for years. To close that credibility gap we have to take action on both ends of Pennsylvania Avenue—to end the outsized influence of lobbyists; to do our work openly; to give our people the government they deserve.

That's what I came to Washington to do. That's why—for the first time in history—my administration posts our White House visitors online. That's why we've excluded lobbyists from policy-making jobs or seats on federal boards and commissions.

But we can't stop there. It's time to require lobbyists to disclose each contact they make on behalf of a client with my administration or with Congress. It's time to put strict limits on the contributions that lobbyists give to candidates for federal office.

With all due deference to separation of powers, last week the Supreme Court reversed a century of law that I believe will open the floodgates for special interests—including foreign corporations—to spend without limit in our elections. I don't think American elections should be bankrolled by America's most powerful interests, or worse, by foreign entities. They should be decided by the American people. And I'd urge Democrats and Republicans to pass a bill that helps to correct some of these problems.

I'm also calling on Congress to continue down the path of earmark reform. Democrats and Republicans. Democrats and Republicans. You've trimmed some of this spending; you've embraced some meaningful change. But restoring the public trust demands more. For example, some members of Congress post some earmark requests online. Tonight, I'm calling on Congress to publish all earmark requests on a single website before there's a vote, so that the American people can see how their money is being spent.

Of course, none of these reforms will even happen if we don't also reform how we work with one another. Now, I'm not naïve. I never thought that the mere fact of my election would usher in peace and harmony and some post-partisan era. I knew that both parties have fed divisions that are deeply entrenched. And on some issues, there are simply philosophical differences that will always cause us to part ways. These disagreements, about the role of government in our lives, about our national priorities and our national security, they've been taking place for over 200 years. They're the very essence of our democracy.

CHANGING POLITICS

But what frustrates the American people is a Washington where every day is Election Day. We can't wage a perpetual campaign where the only goal is to see who can get the most embarrassing headlines about the other side—a belief that if you lose, I win. Neither party should delay or obstruct every single bill just because they can. The confirmation of—I'm speaking to both parties now—the confirmation of well-qualified public servants shouldn't be held hostage to the pet projects or grudges of a few individual senators.

Washington may think that saying anything about the other side, no matter how false, no matter how malicious, is just part of the game. But it's precisely such politics that has stopped either party from helping the American people. Worse yet, it's sowing further division among our citizens, further distrust in our government.

So, no, I will not give up on trying to change the tone of our politics. I know it's an election year. And after last week, it's clear that campaign fever has come even earlier than usual. But we still need to govern.

To Democrats, I would remind you that we still have the largest majority in decades, and the people expect us to solve problems, not run for the hills. And if the Republican leadership is going to insist that 60 votes in the Senate are required to do any business at all in this town—a supermajority—then the responsibility to govern is now yours as well. Just saying no to everything may be good short-term politics, but it's not leadership. We were sent here to serve our citizens, not our ambitions. So let's show the American people that we can do it together.

This week, I'll be addressing a meeting of the House Republicans. I'd like to begin monthly meetings with both Democratic and Republican leadership. I know you can't wait.

IRAQ AND AFGHANISTAN WARS

Throughout our history, no issue has united this country more than our security. Sadly, some of the unity we felt after 9/11 has dissipated. We can argue all we want about who's to blame for this, but I'm not interested in relitigating the past. I know that all of us love this country. All of us are committed to its defense. So let's put aside the schoolyard taunts about who's tough. Let's reject the false choice between protecting our people and upholding our values. Let's leave behind the fear and division, and do what it takes to defend our nation and forge a more hopeful future—for America and for the world.

That's the work we began last year. Since the day I took office, we've renewed our focus on the terrorists who threaten our nation. We've made substantial investments in our homeland security and disrupted plots that threatened to take American lives. We are filling unacceptable gaps revealed by the failed Christmas attack with better airline security and swifter action on our intelligence. We've prohibited torture and strengthened partnerships from the Pacific to South Asia to the Arabian Peninsula. And in the past year, hundreds of al Qaeda's fighters and affiliates, including many senior leaders, have been captured or killed—far more than in 2008.

And in Afghanistan, we're increasing our troops and training Afghan security forces so they can begin to take the lead in July of 2011, and our troops can begin to come home. We will reward good governance, work to reduce corruption, and support the rights of all Afghans—men and women alike. We're joined by allies and partners who have increased their own commitments and who will come together tomorrow in London to reaffirm our common purpose. There will be difficult days ahead. But I am absolutely confident we will succeed.

As we take the fight to al Qaeda, we are responsibly leaving Iraq to its people. As a candidate, I promised that I would end this war, and that is what I am doing as president. We will have all of our combat troops out of Iraq by the end of this August. We will support the Iraqi government—we will support the Iraqi government as they hold elections, and we will continue to partner with the Iraqi people to promote regional peace and prosperity. But make no mistake: This war is ending, and all of our troops are coming home.

Tonight, all of our men and women in uniform—in Iraq, in Afghanistan, and around the world—they have to know that we—that they have our respect, our gratitude, our full support. And just as they must have the resources they need in war, we all have a responsibility to support them when they come home. That's why we made the largest increase in investments for veterans in decades last year. That's why we're building a 21st century VA. And that's why Michelle has joined with Jill Biden to forge a national commitment to support military families.

NUCLEAR THREATS

Now, even as we prosecute two wars, we're also confronting perhaps the greatest danger to the American people—the threat of nuclear weapons. I've embraced the vision of John F. Kennedy and Ronald Reagan through a strategy that reverses the spread of these weapons and seeks a world without them. To reduce our stockpiles and launchers, while ensuring our deterrent, the United States and Russia are completing negotiations on the farthest-reaching arms control treaty in nearly two decades. And at April's Nuclear Security Summit, we will bring 44 nations together here in Washington, D.C., behind a clear goal: securing all vulnerable nuclear materials around the world in four years, so that they never fall into the hands of terrorists.

Now, these diplomatic efforts have also strengthened our hand in dealing with those nations that insist on violating international agreements in pursuit of nuclear weapons. That's why North Korea now faces increased isolation and stronger sanctions—sanctions that are being vigorously enforced. That's why the international community is more united and the Islamic Republic of Iran is more isolated. And as Iran's leaders continue to ignore their obligations, there should be no doubt: They, too, will face growing consequences. That is a promise.

That's the leadership that we are providing—engagement that advances the common security and prosperity of all people. We're working through the G-20 to sustain a lasting global recovery. We're working with Muslim communities around the world to promote science and education and innovation. We have gone from a bystander to a leader in the fight against climate change. We're helping developing countries to feed themselves, and continuing the fight against HIV/AIDS. And we are launching a new initiative that will give us the capacity to respond faster and more effectively to bioterrorism or an infectious disease—a plan that will counter threats at home and strengthen public health abroad.

As we have for over 60 years, America takes these actions because our destiny is connected to those beyond our shores. But we also do it because it is right. That's why, as we meet here tonight, over 10,000 Americans are working with many nations to help the people of Haiti recover and rebuild. That's why we stand with the girl who yearns to go to school in Afghanistan; why we support the human rights of the women marching through the streets of Iran; why we advocate for the young man denied a job by corruption in Guinea. For America must always stand on the side of freedom and human dignity. Always.

EQUAL RIGHTS

Abroad, America's greatest source of strength has always been our ideals. The same is true at home. We find unity in our incredible diversity, drawing on the promise enshrined in our Constitution: the notion that we're all created equal; that no matter who you are or what you look like, if you abide by the law you should be protected by it; if you adhere to our common values you should be treated no different than anyone else.

We must continually renew this promise. My administration has a Civil Rights Division that is once again prosecuting civil rights violations and employment discrimination. We finally strengthened our laws to protect against crimes driven by hate. This year, I will work with Congress and our military to finally repeal the law that denies gay Americans the right to serve the country they love because of who they are. It's the right thing to do.

We're going to crack down on violations of equal-pay laws—so that women get equal pay for an equal day's work. And we should continue the work of fixing our broken immigration system—to secure our borders and enforce our laws, and ensure that everyone who plays by the rules can contribute to our economy and enrich our nation.

A SPIRIT OF OPTIMISM

In the end, it's our ideals, our values that built America—values that allowed us to forge a nation made up of immigrants from every corner of the globe, values that drive our citizens still. Every day, Americans meet their responsibilities to their families and their employers. Time and again, they lend a hand to their neighbors and give back to their country. They take pride in their labor and are generous in spirit. These aren't Republican values or Democratic values that they're living by, business values or labor values. They're American values.

Unfortunately, too many of our citizens have lost faith that our biggest institutions—our corporations, our media, and, yes, our government—still reflect these same values. Each of these institutions are full of honorable men and women doing important work that helps our country prosper. But each time a CEO rewards himself for failure, or a banker puts the rest of us at risk for his own selfish gain, people's doubts grow. Each time lobbyists game the system or politicians tear each other down instead of lifting this country up, we lose faith. The more that TV pundits reduce serious debates to silly arguments, big issues into sound bites, our citizens turn away.

No wonder there's so much cynicism out there. No wonder there's so much disappointment.

I campaigned on the promise of change—change we can believe in, the slogan went. And right now, I know there are many Americans who aren't sure if they still believe we can change—or that I can deliver it.

But remember this—I never suggested that change would be easy, or that I could do it alone. Democracy in a nation of 300 million people can be noisy and messy and complicated. And when you try to do big things and make big changes, it stirs passions and controversy. That's just how it is.

Those of us in public office can respond to this reality by playing it safe and avoid telling hard truths and pointing fingers. We can do what's necessary to keep our poll numbers high and get through the next election instead of doing what's best for the next generation.

But I also know this: If people had made that decision 50 years ago, or 100 years ago, or 200 years ago, we wouldn't be here tonight. The only reason we are here is because generations of Americans were unafraid to do what was hard; to do what was needed even when success was uncertain; to do what it took to keep the dream of this nation alive for their children and their grandchildren.

Our administration has had some political setbacks this year, and some of them were deserved. But I wake up every day knowing that they are nothing compared to the setbacks that families all across this country have faced this year. And what keeps me going—what keeps me fighting—is that despite all these setbacks, that spirit of determination and optimism, that fundamental decency that has always been at the core of the American people, that lives on.

It lives on in the struggling small-business owner who wrote to me of his company, "None of us," he said, ". . . are willing to consider, even slightly, that we might fail."

It lives on in the woman who said that even though she and her neighbors have felt the pain of recession, "We are strong. We are resilient. We are American."

It lives on in the 8-year-old boy in Louisiana who just sent me his allowance and asked if I would give it to the people of Haiti.

And it lives on in all the Americans who've dropped everything to go someplace they've never been and pull people they've never known from the rubble, prompting chants of "U.S.A.! U.S.A.! U.S.A!" when another life was saved.

The spirit that has sustained this nation for more than two centuries lives on in you, its people. We have finished a difficult year. We have come through a difficult decade. But a new year has come. A new decade stretches before us. We don't quit. I don't quit. Let's seize this moment—to start anew, to carry the dream forward, and to strengthen our union once more.

Thank you. God bless you. And God bless the United States of America.

President Obama's 2011 State of the Union Address

Following is the White House transcript of President Obama's State of the Union address, delivered to a joint session of Congress on January 25, 2011.

Mr. Speaker, Mr. Vice President, members of Congress, distinguished guests, and fellow Americans:

Tonight I want to begin by congratulating the men and women of the 112th Congress, as well as your new Speaker, John Boehner. And as we mark this occasion, we're also mindful of the empty chair in this chamber, and we pray for the health of our colleague—and our friend—Gabby Giffords.

It's no secret that those of us here tonight have had our differences over the last two years. The debates have been contentious; we have fought fiercely for our beliefs. And that's a good thing. That's what a robust democracy demands. That's what helps set us apart as a nation.

But there's a reason the tragedy in Tucson gave us pause. Amid all the noise and passion and rancor of our public debate, Tucson reminded us that no matter who we are or where we come from, each of us is a part of something greater—something more consequential than party or political preference.

We are part of the American family. We believe that in a country where every race and faith and point of view can be found, we are still bound together as one people; that we share common hopes and a common creed; that the dreams of a little girl in Tucson are not so different than those of our own children, and that they all deserve the chance to be fulfilled.

That, too, is what sets us apart as a nation.

Now, by itself, this simple recognition won't usher in a new era of cooperation. What comes of this moment is up to us. What comes of this moment will be determined not by whether we can sit together tonight, but whether we can work together tomorrow.

I believe we can. And I believe we must. That's what the people who sent us here expect of us. With their votes, they've determined that governing will now be a shared responsibility between parties. New laws will only pass with support from Democrats and Republicans. We will move forward together, or not at all—for the challenges we face are bigger than party and bigger than politics.

At stake right now is not who wins the next election—after all, we just had an election. At stake is whether new jobs and industries take root in this country or somewhere else. It's whether the hard work and industry of our people is rewarded. It's whether we sustain the leadership that has made America not just a place on a map but the light to the world.

We are poised for progress. Two years after the worst recession most of us have ever known, the stock market has come roaring back. Corporate profits are up. The economy is growing again.

But we have never measured progress by these yardsticks alone. We measure progress by the success of our people. By the jobs they can find and the quality of life those jobs offer. By the prospects of a small-business owner who dreams of turning a good idea into a thriving enterprise. By the opportunities for a better life that we pass on to our children.

That's the project the American people want us to work on. Together.

We did that in December. Thanks to the tax cuts we passed, Americans' paychecks are a little bigger today. Every business can write off the full cost of new investments that they make this year. And these steps, taken by Democrats and Republicans, will grow the economy and add to the more than 1 million private sector jobs created last year.

But we have to do more. These steps we've taken over the last two years may have broken the back of this recession, but to win the future, we'll need to take on challenges that have been decades in the making.

"THE WORLD HAS CHANGED"

Many people watching tonight can probably remember a time when finding a good job meant showing up at a nearby factory or a business downtown. You didn't always need a degree, and your competition was pretty much limited to your neighbors. If you worked hard, chances are you'd have a job for life, with a decent paycheck and good benefits and the occasional promotion. Maybe you'd even have the pride of seeing your kids work at the same company.

That world has changed. And for many, the change has been painful. I've seen it in the shuttered windows of once-booming factories and the vacant storefronts on once-busy Main Streets. I've heard it in the frustrations of Americans who've seen their paychecks dwindle or their jobs disappear—proud men and women who feel like the rules have been changed in the middle of the game.

They're right. The rules have changed. In a single generation, revolutions in technology have transformed the way we live, work and do business. Steel mills that once needed 1,000 workers can now do the same work with 100. Today, just about any company can set up shop, hire workers and sell their products wherever there's an Internet connection.

Meanwhile, nations like China and India realized that with some changes of their own, they could compete in this new world. And so they started educating their children earlier and longer, with greater emphasis on math and science. They're investing in research and new technologies. Just recently, China became the home to the world's largest private solar research facility and the world's fastest computer.

So, yes, the world has changed. The competition for jobs is real. But this shouldn't discourage us. It should challenge us. Remember: For all the hits we've taken these last few years, for all the naysayers predicting our decline, America still has the largest, most prosperous economy in the world. No workers—no workers are more productive than ours. No country has more successful companies, or grants more patents to inventors and entrepreneurs. We're the home to the world's best colleges and universities, where more students come to study than any place on Earth.

What's more, we are the first nation to be founded for the sake of an idea—the idea that each of us deserves the chance to shape our own destiny. That's why centuries of pioneers and immigrants have risked everything to come here. It's why our students don't just memorize equations but answer questions like "What do you think of that idea? What would you change about the world? What do you want to be when you grow up?"

The future is ours to win. But to get there, we can't just stand still. As Robert Kennedy told us, "The future is not a gift. It is an achievement." Sustaining the American Dream has never been about standing pat. It has required each generation to sacrifice, and struggle, and meet the demands of a new age.

And now it's our turn. We know what it takes to compete for the jobs and industries of our time. We need to out-innovate, out-educate and outbuild the rest of the world. We have to make America the best place on Earth to do business. We need to take responsibility for our deficit and reform our government. That's how our people will prosper. That's how we'll win the future. And tonight, I'd like to talk about how we get there.

STEP ONE: REINVENT OURSELVES

The first step in winning the future is encouraging American innovation. None of us can predict with certainty what the next big industry will be or where the new jobs will come from. Thirty years ago, we couldn't know that something called the Internet would lead to an economic revolution. What we can do—what America does better than anyone else—is spark the creativity and imagination of our people. We're the nation that put cars in driveways and computers in offices, the nation of Edison and the Wright brothers, of Google and Facebook. In America, innovation doesn't just change our lives. It is how we make our living.

Our free-enterprise system is what drives innovation. But because it's not always profitable for companies to invest in basic research, throughout our history, our government has provided cutting-edge scientists and inventors with the support that they need. That's what planted the seeds for the Internet. That's what helped make possible things like computer chips and GPS. Just think of all the good jobs—from manufacturing to retail—that have come from these breakthroughs.

Half a century ago, when the Soviets beat us into space with the launch of a satellite called Sputnik, we had no idea how we would beat them to the moon. The science wasn't even there yet. NASA didn't exist. But after investing in better research and education, we didn't just surpass the Soviets; we unleashed a wave of innovation that created new industries and millions of new jobs.

This is our generation's Sputnik moment. Two years ago, I said that we needed to reach a level of research and development we haven't seen since the height of the Space Race. And in a few weeks, I will be sending a budget to Congress that helps us meet that goal. We'll invest in biomedical research, information technology, and especially clean-energy technology—an investment that will strengthen our security, protect our planet and create countless new jobs for our people.

Already, we're seeing the promise of renewable energy. Robert and Gary Allen are brothers who run a small Michigan roofing company. After September 11, they volunteered their best roofers to help repair the Pentagon. But half of their factory went unused, and the recession hit them hard. Today, with the help of a government loan, that empty space is being used to manufacture solar shingles that are being sold all across the country. In Robert's words, "We reinvented ourselves."

That's what Americans have done for over 200 years: reinvented ourselves. And to spur on more success stories like the Allen brothers, we've begun to reinvent our energy policy. We're not just handing out money. We're issuing a challenge. We're telling America's scientists and engineers that if they assemble teams of the best minds in their fields and focus on the hardest problems in clean energy, we'll fund the Apollo projects of our time.

At the California Institute of Technology, they're developing a way to turn sunlight and water into fuel for our cars. At Oak Ridge National Laboratory, they're using supercomputers to get a lot more power out of our nuclear facilities. With more research and incentives, we can break our dependence on oil with biofuels and become the first country to have a million electric vehicles on the road by 2015.

We need to get behind this innovation. And to help pay for it, I'm asking Congress to eliminate the billions in taxpayer dollars we currently give to oil companies. I don't know if—I don't know if you've noticed, but they're doing just fine on their own. So instead of subsidizing yesterday's energy, let's invest in tomorrow's.

Now, clean-energy breakthroughs will only translate into clean-energy jobs if businesses know there will be a market for what they're selling. So tonight, I challenge you to join me in setting a new goal: By 2035, 80 percent of America's electricity will come from clean energy sources.

Some folks want wind and solar. Others want nuclear, clean coal and natural gas. To meet this goal, we will need them all—and I urge Democrats and Republicans to work together to make it happen.

STEP TWO: EDUCATION ENRICHES

Maintaining our leadership in research and technology is crucial to America's success. But if we want to win the future—if we want innovation to produce jobs in America and not overseas—then we also have to win the race to educate our kids.

Think about it. Over the next 10 years, nearly half of all new jobs will require education that goes beyond a high school education. And yet, as many as a quarter of our students aren't even finishing high school. The quality of our math and science education lags behind many other nations. America has fallen to ninth in the proportion of young people with a college degree. And so the question is whether all of us—as citizens, and as parents—are willing to do what's necessary to give every child a chance to succeed.

That responsibility begins not in our classrooms but in our homes and communities. It's family that first instills the love of learning in a child. Only parents can make sure the TV is turned off and homework gets done. We need to teach our kids that it's not just the winner of the Super Bowl who deserves to be celebrated, but the winner of the science fair. We need to teach them that success is not a function of fame or PR but of hard work and discipline.

Our schools share this responsibility. When a child walks into a classroom, it should be a place of high expectations and high performance. But too many schools don't meet this test. That's why instead of just pouring money into a system that's not working, we launched a competition called Race to the Top. To all 50 states, we said, "If you show us the most innovative plans to improve teacher quality and student achievement, we'll show you the money."

Race to the Top is the most meaningful reform of our public schools in a generation. For less than 1 percent of what we spend on education each year, it has led over 40 states to raise their standards for teaching and learning. And these standards were developed, by the way, not by Washington but by Republican and Democratic governors throughout the country. And Race to the Top should be the approach we follow this year as we replace No Child Left Behind with a law that's more flexible and focused on what's best for our kids.

You see, we know what's possible from our children when reform isn't just a top-down mandate but the work of local teachers and principals, school boards and communities. Take a school like Bruce Randolph in Denver. Three years ago, it was rated one of the worst schools in Colorado—located on turf between two rival gangs. But last May, 97 percent of the seniors received their diploma. Most will be the first in their families to go to college. And after the first year of the school's transformation, the principal who made it possible wiped away tears when a student said, "Thank you, Ms. Waters, for showing that we are smart and we can make it." That's what good schools can do, and we want good schools all across the country.

Let's also remember that after parents, the biggest impact on a child's success comes from the man or woman at the front of the classroom. In South Korea, teachers are known as "nation builders." Here in America, it's time we treated the people who educate our children with the same level of respect. We want to reward good teachers and stop making excuses for bad ones. And over the next 10 years, with so many baby boomers retiring from our classrooms, we want to prepare 100,000 new teachers in the fields of science and technology and engineering and math.

In fact, to every young person listening tonight who's contemplating their career choice: If you want to make a difference in the life of our nation, if you want to make a difference in the life of a child, become a teacher. Your country needs you.

Of course, the education race doesn't end with a high school diploma. To compete, higher education must be within the reach of every American. That's why we've ended the unwarranted taxpayer subsidies that went to banks, and used the savings to make college affordable for millions of students. And this year, I ask Congress to go further, and make permanent our tuition tax credit—worth $10,000 for four years of college. It's the right thing to do.

Because people need to be able to train for new jobs and careers in today's fast-changing economy, we're also revitalizing America's community colleges. Last month, I saw the promise of these schools at Forsyth Tech in North Carolina. Many of the students there used to work in the surrounding factories that have since left town. One mother of two, a woman named Kathy Proctor, had worked in the furniture industry since she was 18 years old. And she told me she's earning her degree in biotechnology now, at 55 years old, not just because the furniture jobs are gone, but because she wants to inspire her children to pursue their dreams, too. As Kathy said, "I hope it tells them to never give up."

If we take these steps—if we raise expectations for every child and give them the best possible chance at an education, from the day they are born until the last job they take—we will reach the goal that I set two years ago: By the end of the decade, America will once again have the highest proportion of college graduates in the world.

One last point about education. Today, there are hundreds of thousands of students excelling in our schools who are not American citizens. Some are the children of undocumented workers, who had nothing to do with the actions of their parents. They grew up as Americans and pledge allegiance to our flag, and yet they live every day with the threat of deportation. Others come here from abroad to study in our colleges and universities. But as soon as they obtain advanced degrees, we send them back home to compete against us. It makes no sense.

Now, I strongly believe that we should take on, once and for all, the issue of illegal immigration. And I am prepared to work with Republicans and Democrats to protect our borders, enforce our laws and address the millions of undocumented workers who are now living in the shadows. I know that debate will be difficult. I know it will take time. But tonight, let's agree to make that effort. And let's stop expelling talented, responsible young people who could be staffing our research labs or starting a new business, who could be further enriching this nation.

STEP THREE: REDUCE BARRIERS

The third step in winning the future is rebuilding America. To attract new businesses to our shores, we need the fastest, most reliable ways to move people, goods and information—from high-speed rail to high-speed Internet.

Our infrastructure used to be the best, but our lead has slipped. South Korean homes now have greater Internet access than we do. Countries in Europe and Russia invest more in their roads and railways than we do. China is building faster trains and newer airports. Meanwhile, when our own engineers graded our nation's infrastructure, they gave us a "D."

We have to do better. America is the nation that built the transcontinental railroad, brought electricity to rural communities, constructed the Interstate Highway System. The jobs created by these projects didn't just come from laying down track or pavement. They came from businesses that opened near a town's new train station or the new offramp.

So over the last two years, we've begun rebuilding for the 21st century, a project that has meant thousands of good jobs for the hard-hit construction industry. And tonight, I'm proposing that we redouble those efforts.

We'll put more Americans to work repairing crumbling roads and bridges. We'll make sure this is fully paid for, attract private investment and pick projects based [on] what's best for the economy, not politicians.

Within 25 years, our goal is to give 80 percent of Americans access to high-speed rail. This could allow you to go places in half the time it takes to travel by car. For some trips, it will be faster than flying—without the pat-down. As we speak, routes in California and the Midwest are already under way.

Within the next five years, we'll make it possible for businesses to deploy the next generation of high-speed wireless coverage to 98 percent of all Americans. This isn't just about—this isn't about faster Internet or fewer dropped calls. It's about connecting every part of America to the digital age. It's about a rural community in Iowa or Alabama where farmers and small-business owners will be able to sell their products all over the world. It's about a firefighter who can download the design of a burning building onto a handheld device; a student who can take classes with a digital textbook; or a patient who can have face-to-face video chats with her doctor.

All these investments—in innovation, education and infrastructure—will make America a better place to do business and create jobs. But to help our companies compete, we also have to knock down barriers that stand in the way of their success.

For example, over the years, a parade of lobbyists has rigged the tax code to benefit particular companies and industries. Those with accountants or lawyers to work the system can end up paying no taxes at all. But all the rest are hit with one of the highest corporate tax rates in the world. It makes no sense, and it has to change.

So tonight, I'm asking Democrats and Republicans to simplify the system. Get rid of the loopholes. Level the playing field. And use the savings to lower the corporate tax rate for the first time in 25 years—without adding to our deficit. It can be done.

To help businesses sell more products abroad, we set a goal of doubling our exports by 2014—because the more we export, the more jobs we create here at home. Already, our exports are up. Recently, we signed agreements with India and China that will support more than 250,000 jobs here in the United States. And last month, we finalized a trade agreement with South Korea that will support at least 70,000 American jobs. This agreement has unprecedented support from business and labor, Democrats and Republicans—and I ask this Congress to pass it as soon as possible.

Now, before I took office, I made it clear that we would enforce our trade agreements, and that I would only sign deals that keep faith with American workers and promote American jobs. That's what we did with Korea, and that's what I intend to do as we pursue agreements with Panama and Colombia and continue our Asia-Pacific and global trade talks.

To reduce barriers to growth and investment, I've ordered a review of government regulations. When we find rules that put an unnecessary burden on businesses, we will fix them. But I will not hesitate to create or enforce common-sense safeguards to protect the American people. That's what we've done in this country for more than a century. It's why our food is safe to eat, our water is safe to drink and our air is safe to breathe. It's why we have speed limits and child labor laws. It's why last year, we put in place consumer protections against hidden fees and penalties by credit card companies and new rules to prevent another financial crisis. And it's why we passed reform that finally prevents the health insurance industry from exploiting patients.

Now, I have heard rumors that a few of you still have concerns about our new health care law. So let me be the first to say that anything can be improved. If you have ideas about how to improve this law by making care better or more affordable, I am eager to work with you. We can start right now by correcting a flaw in the legislation that has placed an unnecessary bookkeeping burden on small businesses.

What I'm not willing to do—what I'm not willing to do is go back to the days when insurance companies could deny someone coverage because of a pre-existing condition.

I'm not willing to tell James Howard, a brain cancer patient from Texas, that his treatment might not be covered. I'm not willing to tell Jim Houser, a small-business man from Oregon, that he has to go back to paying $5,000 more to cover his employees. As we speak, this law is making prescription drugs cheaper for seniors and giving uninsured students a chance to stay on their patients'—parents' coverage.

So I say to this chamber tonight, instead of re-fighting the battles of the last two years, let's fix what needs fixing, and let's move forward.

FINAL STEP: CONFRONTING DEBT

Now, the final critical step in winning the future is to make sure we aren't buried under a mountain of debt.

We are living with a legacy of deficit spending that began almost a decade ago. And in the wake of the financial crisis, some of that was necessary to keep credit flowing, save jobs and put money in people's pockets.

But now that the worst of the recession is over, we have to confront the fact that our government spends more than it takes in. That is not sustainable. Every day, families sacrifice to live within their means. They deserve a government that does the same.

So tonight, I am proposing that starting this year, we freeze annual domestic spending for the next five years. Now, this would reduce the deficit by more than $400 billion over the next decade, and will bring discretionary spending to the lowest share of our economy since Dwight Eisenhower was president.

This freeze will require painful cuts. Already, we've frozen the salaries of hardworking federal employees for the next two years. I've proposed cuts to things I care deeply about, like community action programs. The secretary of Defense has also agreed to cut tens of billions of dollars in spending that he and his generals believe our military can do without.

I recognize that some in this chamber have already proposed deeper cuts, and I'm willing to eliminate whatever we can honestly afford to do without. But let's make sure that we're not doing it on the backs of our most vulnerable citizens. And let's make sure that what we're cutting is really excess weight. Cutting the deficit by gutting our investments in innovation and education is like lightening an overloaded airplane by removing its engine. It may make you feel like you're flying high at first, but it won't take long before you feel the impact.

Now, most of the cuts and savings I've proposed only address annual domestic spending, which represents a little more than 12 percent of our budget. To make further progress, we have to stop pretending that cutting this kind of spending alone will be enough. It won't.

The bipartisan fiscal commission I created last year made this crystal clear. I don't agree with all their proposals, but they made important progress. And their conclusion is that the only way to tackle our deficit is to cut excessive spending wherever we find it—in domestic spending, defense spending, health care spending, and spending through tax breaks and loopholes.

This means further reducing health care costs, including programs like Medicare and Medicaid, which are the single biggest contributor to our long-term deficit. The health insurance law we passed last year will slow these rising costs, which is part of the reason that nonpartisan economists have said that repealing the health care law would add a quarter of a trillion dollars to our deficit. Still, I'm willing to look at other ideas to bring down costs, including one that Republicans suggested last year—medical malpractice reform to rein in frivolous lawsuits.

To put us on solid ground, we should also find a bipartisan solution to strengthen Social Security for future generations. We must do it without putting at risk current retirees, the most vulnerable, or people with disabilities; without slashing benefits for future generations; and without subjecting Americans' guaranteed retirement income to the whims of the stock market.

And if we truly care about our deficit, we simply can't afford a permanent extension of the tax cuts for the wealthiest 2 percent of Americans. Before we take money away from our schools or scholarships away from our students, we should ask millionaires to give up their tax break. It's not a matter of punishing their success. It's about promoting America's success.

In fact, the best thing we could do on taxes for all Americans is to simplify the individual tax code. This will be a tough job, but members of both parties have expressed an interest in doing this, and I am prepared to join them.

So now is the time to act. Now is the time for both sides and both houses of Congress—Democrats and Republicans—to forge a principled compromise that gets the job done. If we make the hard choices now to rein in our deficits, we can make the investments we need to win the future.

GOING FURTHER: REORGANIZE

Let me take this one step further. We shouldn't just give our people a government that's more affordable. We should give them a government that's more competent and more efficient. We can't win the future with a government of the past.

We live and do business in the Information Age, but the last major reorganization of the government happened in the age of black-and-white TV. There are 12 different agencies that deal with exports. There are at least five different agencies that deal with housing policy. Then there's my favorite example: The Interior Department is in charge of salmon while they're in fresh water, but the Commerce Department handles them when they're in saltwater. I hear it gets even more complicated once they're smoked.

Now, we've made great strides over the last two years in using technology and getting rid of waste. Veterans can now download their electronic medical records with a click of the mouse. We're selling acres of federal office space that hasn't been used in years, and we'll cut through red tape to get rid of more. But we need to think bigger. In the coming months, my administration will develop a proposal to merge, consolidate and reorganize the federal government in a way that best serves the goal of a more competitive America. I will submit that proposal to Congress for a vote—and we will push to get it passed.

In the coming year, we'll also work to rebuild people's faith in the institution of government. Because you deserve to know exactly how and where your tax dollars are being spent, you'll be able to go to a website and get that information for the very first time in history. Because you deserve to know when your elected officials are meeting with lobbyists, I ask Congress to do what the White House has already done—put that information online. And because the American people deserve to know that special interests aren't larding up legislation with pet projects, both parties in Congress should know this: If a bill comes to my desk with earmarks inside, I will veto it. I will veto it.

The 21st century government that's open and competent. A government that lives within its means. An economy that's driven by new skills and new ideas. Our success in this new and changing world will require reform, responsibility and innovation. It will also require us to approach that world with a new level of engagement in our foreign affairs.

SHINING LIGHT ACROSS BORDERS

Just as jobs and businesses can now race across borders, so can new threats and new challenges. No single wall separates East and West. No one rival superpower is aligned against us.

And so we must defeat determined enemies, wherever they are, and build coalitions that cut across lines of region and race and religion. And America's moral example must always shine for all who yearn for freedom and justice and dignity. And because we've begun this work, tonight we can say that American leadership has been renewed and America's standing has been restored.

Look to Iraq, where nearly 100,000 of our brave men and women have left with their heads held high. American combat patrols have ended, violence is down and a new government has been formed. This year, our civilians will forge a lasting partnership with the Iraqi people, while we finish the job of bringing our troops out of Iraq. America's commitment has been kept. The Iraq War is coming to an end.

Of course, as we speak, al Qaeda and their affiliates continue to plan attacks against us. Thanks to our intelligence and law enforcement professionals, we're disrupting plots and securing our cities and skies. And as extremists try to inspire acts of violence within our borders, we are responding with the strength of our communities, with respect for the rule of law and with the conviction that American Muslims are a part of our American family.

We've also taken the fight to al Qaeda and their allies abroad. In Afghanistan, our troops have taken Taliban strongholds and trained Afghan security forces. Our purpose is clear: By preventing the Taliban from re-establishing a stranglehold over the Afghan people, we will deny al Qaeda the safe haven that served as a launching pad for 9/11.

Thanks to our heroic troops and civilians, fewer Afghans are under the control of the insurgency. There will be tough fighting ahead, and the Afghan government will need to deliver better governance. But we are strengthening the capacity of the Afghan people and building an enduring partnership with them. This year, we will work with nearly 50 countries to begin a transition to an Afghan lead. And this July, we will begin to bring our troops home.

In Pakistan, al Qaeda's leadership is under more pressure than at any point since 2001. Their leaders and operatives are being removed from the battlefield. Their safe havens are shrinking. And we've sent a message from the Afghan border to the Arabian Peninsula to all parts of the globe: We will not relent, we will not waver, and we will defeat you.

POWER WITH A PURPOSE

American leadership can also be seen in the effort to secure the worst weapons of war. Because Republicans and Democrats approved the New START treaty, far fewer nuclear weapons and launchers will be deployed. Because we rallied the world, nuclear materials are being locked down on every continent so they never fall into the hands of terrorists.

Because of a diplomatic effort to insist that Iran meet its obligations, the Iranian government now faces tougher sanctions, tighter sanctions than ever before. And on the Korean Peninsula, we stand with our ally South Korea and insist that North Korea keeps its commitment to abandon nuclear weapons.

This is just a part of how we're shaping a world that favors peace and prosperity. With our European allies, we revitalized NATO and increased our cooperation on everything from counterterrorism to missile defense. We've reset our relationship with Russia, strengthened Asian alliances, built new partnerships with nations like India.

This March, I will travel to Brazil, Chile and El Salvador to forge new alliances across the Americas. Around the globe, we're standing with those who take responsibility—helping farmers grow more food, supporting doctors who care for the sick and combating the corruption that can rot a society and rob people of opportunity.

Recent events have shown us that what sets us apart must not just be our power—it must also be the purpose behind it. In south Sudan—with our assistance—the people were finally able to vote for independence after years of war. Thousands lined up before dawn. People danced in the streets. One man who lost four of his brothers at war summed up the scene around him: "This was a battlefield for most of my life," he said. "Now we want to be free."

And we saw that same desire to be free in Tunisia, where the will of the people proved more powerful than the writ of a dictator. And tonight, let us be clear: The United States of America stands with the people of Tunisia and supports the democratic aspirations of all people.

We must never forget that the things we've struggled for, and fought for, live in the hearts of people everywhere. And we must always remember that the Americans who have borne the greatest burden in this struggle are the men and women who serve our country.

Tonight, let us speak with one voice in reaffirming that our nation is united in support of our troops and their families. Let us serve them as well as they've served us—by giving them the equipment they need, by providing them with the care and benefits that they have earned, and by enlisting our veterans in the great task of building our own nation.

Our troops come from every corner of this country—they're black, white, Latino, Asian, Native American. They are Christian and Hindu, Jewish and Muslim. And, yes, we know that some of them are gay. Starting this year, no American will be forbidden from serving the country they love because of who they love. And with that change, I call on all our college campuses to open their doors to our military recruiters and ROTC. It is time to leave behind the divisive battles of the past. It is time to move forward as one nation.

WE'VE ALWAYS DARED TO DREAM

We should have no illusions about the work ahead of us. Reforming our schools, changing the way we use energy, reducing our deficit—none of this will be easy. All of it will take time. And it will be harder because we will argue about everything. The costs. The details. The letter of every law.

Of course, some countries don't have this problem. If the central government wants a railroad, they build a railroad, no matter how many homes get bulldozed. If they don't want a bad story in the newspaper, it doesn't get written.

And yet, as contentious and frustrating and messy as our democracy can sometimes be, I know there isn't a person here who would trade places with any other nation on Earth.

We may have differences in policy, but we all believe in the rights enshrined in our Constitution. We may have different opinions, but we believe in the same promise that says this is a place where you can make it if you try. We may have different backgrounds, but we believe in the same dream that says this is a country where anything is possible. No matter who you are. No matter where you come from.

That dream is why I can stand here before you tonight. That dream is why a working-class kid from Scranton can sit behind me. That dream is why someone who began by sweeping the floors of his father's Cincinnati bar can preside as Speaker of the House in the greatest nation on Earth.

That dream—that American Dream—is what drove the Allen Brothers to reinvent their roofing company for a new era. It's what drove those students at Forsyth Tech to learn a new skill and work towards the future. And that dream is the story of a small-business owner named Brandon Fisher.

Brandon started a company in Berlin, Pa., that specializes in a new kind of drilling technology. And one day last summer, he saw the news that halfway across the world, 33 men were trapped in a Chilean mine, and no one knew how to save them.

But Brandon thought his company could help. And so he designed a rescue that would come to be known as Plan B. His employees worked around the clock to manufacture the necessary drilling equipment. And Brandon left for Chile.

Along with others, he began drilling a 2,000-foot hole into the ground, working three or four-hour–three or four days at a time without any sleep. Thirty-seven days later, Plan B succeeded, and the miners were rescued. But because he didn't want all of the attention, Brandon wasn't there when the miners emerged. He'd already gone back home, back to work on his next project.

And later, one of his employees said of the rescue, "We proved that Center Rock is a little company, but we do big things."

We do big things.

From the earliest days of our founding, America has been the story of ordinary people who dare to dream. That's how we win the future.

We're a nation that says, "I might not have a lot of money, but I have this great idea for a new company." "I might not come from a family of college graduates, but I will be the first to get my degree." "I might not know those people in trouble, but I think I can help them, and I need to try." "I'm not sure how we'll reach that better place beyond the horizon, but I know we'll get there. I know we will."

We do big things.

The idea of America endures. Our destiny remains our choice. And tonight, more than two centuries later, it's because of our people that our future is hopeful, our journey goes forward and the state of our union is strong.

Thank you. God bless you, and may God bless the United States of America.

President Obama's Statement on Death of Osama bin Laden

Following is the White House transcript of President Obama's televised address on May 2, 2011, informing the nation of the death of al Qaeda leader Osama bin Laden.

Good evening. Tonight, I can report to the American people and to the world that the United States has conducted an operation that killed Osama bin Laden, the leader of al Qaeda and a terrorist who's responsible for the murder of thousands of innocent men, women and children.

It was nearly 10 years ago that a bright September day was darkened by the worst attack on the American people in our history. The images of 9/11 are seared into our national memory—hijacked planes cutting through a cloudless September sky; the Twin Towers collapsing to the ground; black smoke billowing up from the Pentagon; the wreckage of Flight 93 in Shanksville, Pa., where the actions of heroic citizens saved even more heartbreak and destruction.

And yet we know that the worst images are those that were unseen to the world. The empty seat at the dinner table. Children who were forced to grow up without their mother or their father. Parents who would never know the feeling of their child's embrace. Nearly 3,000 citizens taken from us, leaving a gaping hole in our hearts.

On September 11, 2001, in our time of grief, the American people came together. We offered our neighbors a hand, and we offered the wounded our blood. We reaffirmed our ties to each other and our love of community and country. On that day, no matter where we came from, what God we prayed to, or what race or ethnicity we were, we were united as one American family.

We were also united in our resolve to protect our nation and to bring those who committed this vicious attack to justice. We quickly learned that the 9/11 attacks were carried out by al Qaeda—an organization headed by Osama bin Laden—which had openly declared war on the United States and was committed to killing innocents in our country and around the globe. And so we went to war against al Qaeda to protect our citizens, our friends and our allies.

Over the last 10 years, thanks to the tireless and heroic work of our military and our counterterrorism professionals, we've made great strides in that effort. We've disrupted terrorist attacks and strengthened our homeland defense. In Afghanistan, we removed the Taliban government, which had given bin Laden and al Qaeda safe haven and support. And around the globe, we worked with our friends and allies to capture or kill scores of al Qaeda terrorists, including several who were a part of the 9/11 plot.

Yet Osama bin Laden avoided capture and escaped across the Afghan border into Pakistan. Meanwhile, al Qaeda continued to operate from along that border and operate through its affiliates across the world.

And so shortly after taking office, I directed Leon Panetta, the director of the CIA, to make the killing or capture of bin Laden the top priority of our war against al Qaeda, even as we continued our broader efforts to disrupt, dismantle, and defeat his network.

Then, last August, after years of painstaking work by our intelligence community, I was briefed on a possible lead to bin Laden. It was far from certain, and it took many months to run this thread to ground. I met repeatedly with my national security team as we developed more information about the possibility that we had located bin Laden hiding within a compound deep inside of Pakistan. And finally, last week, I determined that we had enough intelligence to take action, and authorized an operation to get Osama bin Laden and bring him to justice.

Today, at my direction, the United States launched a targeted operation against that compound in Abbottabad, Pakistan. A small team of Americans carried out the operation with extraordinary courage and capability. No Americans were harmed. They took care to avoid civilian casualties. After a firefight, they killed Osama bin Laden and took custody of his body.

A LEADER AND SYMBOL

For over two decades, bin Laden has been al Qaeda's leader and symbol, and has continued to plot attacks against our country and our friends and allies. The death of bin Laden marks the most significant achievement to date in our nation's effort to defeat al Qaeda.

Yet his death does not mark the end of our effort. There's no doubt that al Qaeda will continue to pursue attacks against us. We must—and we will—remain vigilant at home and abroad.

As we do, we must also reaffirm that the United States is not—and never will be—at war with Islam. I've made clear, just as President Bush did shortly after 9/11, that our war is not against Islam. Bin Laden was not a Muslim leader; he was a mass murderer of Muslims. Indeed, al Qaeda has slaughtered scores of Muslims in many countries, including our own. So his demise should be welcomed by all who believe in peace and human dignity.

Over the years, I've repeatedly made clear that we would take action within Pakistan if we knew where bin Laden was. That is what we've done. But it's important to note that our counterterrorism cooperation with Pakistan helped lead us to bin Laden and the compound where he was hiding. Indeed, bin Laden had declared war against Pakistan as well, and ordered attacks against the Pakistani people.

Tonight, I called President Zardari, and my team has also spoken with their Pakistani counterparts. They agree that this is a good and historic day for both of our nations. And going forward, it is essential that Pakistan continue to join us in the fight against al Qaeda and its affiliates.

THE COSTS OF WAR

The American people did not choose this fight. It came to our shores and started with the senseless slaughter of our citizens. After nearly 10 years of service, struggle and sacrifice, we know well the costs of war. These efforts weigh on me every time I, as commander in chief, have to sign a letter to a family that has lost a loved one, or look into the eyes of a service-member who's been gravely wounded.

So Americans understand the costs of war. Yet as a country, we will never tolerate our security being threatened, nor stand idly by when our people have been killed. We will be relentless in defense of our citizens and our friends and allies. We will be true to the values that make us who we are. And on nights like this one, we can say to those families who have lost loved ones to al Qaeda's terror: Justice has been done.

Tonight, we give thanks to the countless intelligence and counterterrorism professionals who've worked tirelessly to achieve this outcome. The American people do not see their work, nor know their names. But tonight, they feel the satisfaction of their work and the result of their pursuit of justice.

We give thanks for the men who carried out this operation, for they exemplify the professionalism, patriotism and unparalleled courage of those who serve our country. And they are part of a generation that has borne the heaviest share of the burden since that September day.

Finally, let me say to the families who lost loved ones on 9/11 that we have never forgotten your loss, nor wavered in our commitment to see that we do whatever it takes to prevent another attack on our shores.

And tonight, let us think back to the sense of unity that prevailed on 9/11. I know that it has, at times, frayed. Yet today's achievement is a testament to the greatness of our country and the determination of the American people.

The cause of securing our country is not complete. But tonight, we are once again reminded that America can do whatever we set our mind to. That is the story of our history, whether it's the pursuit of prosperity for our people or the struggle for equality for all our citizens, our commitment to stand up for our values abroad and our sacrifices to make the world a safer place.

Let us remember that we can do these things not just because of wealth or power, but because of who we are: one nation, under God, indivisible, with liberty and justice for all.

Thank you. May God bless you. And may God bless the United States of America.

President Obama's 2012 State of the Union Address

Following is the transcript of President Barack Obama's State of the Union address, delivered to a joint session of Congress on January 24, 2012.

Mr. Speaker, Mr. Vice President, members of Congress, distinguished guests and fellow Americans, last month I went to Andrews Air Force Base and welcomed home some of our last troops to serve in Iraq. Together, we offered a final, proud salute to the colors under which more than a million of our fellow citizens fought, and several thousand gave their lives.

We gather tonight knowing that this generation of heroes has made the United States safer and more respected around the world.

For the first time in nine years, there are no Americans fighting in Iraq.

For the first time in two decades, Osama bin Laden is not a threat to this country.

Most of al Qaida's top lieutenants have been defeated. The Taliban's momentum has been broken. And some troops in Afghanistan have begun to come home.

These achievements are a testament to the courage, selflessness and teamwork of America's armed forces. At a time when too many of our institutions have let us down, they exceed all expectations. They're not consumed with personal ambition. They don't obsess over their differences. They focus on the mission at hand. They work together.

Imagine what we could accomplish if we followed their example.

Think about the America within our reach: a country that leads the world in educating its people; an America that attracts a new generation of high-tech manufacturing and high-paying jobs; a future where we're in control of our own energy and our security and prosperity aren't so tied to unstable parts of the world. An economy built to last, where hard work pays off and responsibility is rewarded.

We can do this. I know we can, because we've done it before. At the end of World War II, when another generation of heroes returned home from combat, they built the strongest economy and middle class the world has ever known.

My grandfather, a veteran of Patton's army, got the chance to go to college on the GI Bill. My grandmother, who worked on a bomber assembly line, was part of a workforce that turned out the best products on earth.

The two of them shared the optimism of a nation that had triumphed over a depression and fascism. They understood they were part of something larger, that they were contributing to a story of success that every American had a chance to share: the basic American promise that if you worked hard, you could do well enough to raise a family, own a home, send your kids to college and put a little away for retirement.

The defining issue of our time is how to keep that promise alive. No challenge is more urgent. No debate is more important. We can either settle for a country where a shrinking number of people do really well, while a growing number of Americans barely get by, or we can restore an economy where everyone gets a fair shot, and everyone does their fair share, and everyone plays by the same set of rules.

What's at stake aren't Democratic values or Republican values, but American values. And we have to reclaim them.

"IT WAS IRRESPONSIBLE"

Let's remember how we got here. Long before the recession, jobs and manufacturing began leaving our shores. Technology made businesses more efficient, but also made some jobs obsolete. Folks at the top saw their incomes rise like never before, but most hard-working Americans struggled with costs that were growing, paychecks that weren't and personal debt that kept piling up.

In 2008, the house of cards collapsed. We learned that mortgages had been sold to people who couldn't afford or understand them. Banks had made huge bets and bonuses with other people's money. Regulators had looked the other way or didn't have the authority to stop the bad behavior.

It was wrong. It was irresponsible. And it plunged our economy into a crisis that put millions out of work, saddled us with more debt, and left innocent, hard-working Americans holding the bag.

In the six months before I took office, we lost nearly 4 million jobs. And we lost another 4 million before our policies were in full effect. Those are the facts.

But so are these. In the last 22 months, businesses have created more than 3 million jobs.

Last year, they created the most jobs since 2005. American manufacturers are hiring again, creating jobs for the first time since the late 1990s. Together, we've agreed to cut the deficit by more than $2 trillion. And we've put in place new rules to hold Wall Street accountable, so a crisis like this never happens again.

The state of our union is getting stronger, and we've come too far to turn back now.

As long as I'm president, I will work with anyone in this chamber to build on this momentum. But I intend to fight obstruction with action, and I will oppose any effort to return to the very same policies that brought on this economic crisis in the first place.

No, we will not go back to an economy weakened by outsourcing, bad debt and phony financial profits. Tonight, I want to speak about how we move forward and lay out a blueprint for an economy that's built to last, an economy built on American manufacturing, American energy, skills for American workers and a renewal of American values.

This blueprint begins with American manufacturing.

On the day I took office, our auto industry was on the verge of collapse. Some even said we should let it die. With a million jobs at stake, I refused to let that happen.

In exchange for help, we demanded responsibility. We got workers and automakers to settle their differences. We got the industry to retool and restructure. Today, General Motors is back on top as the world's No. 1 automaker.

Chrysler has grown faster in the U.S. than any major car company. Ford is investing billions in U.S. plants and factories. And together, the entire industry added nearly 160,000 jobs.

We bet on American workers. We bet on American ingenuity. And tonight, the American auto industry is back.

What's happening in Detroit can happen in other industries. It can happen in Cleveland and Pittsburgh and Raleigh. We can't bring every job back that's left our shore. But right now, it's getting more expensive to do business in places like China. Meanwhile, America is more productive.

A few weeks ago, the CEO of Master Lock told me that it now makes business sense for him to bring jobs back home.

Today, for the first time in 15 years, Master Lock's unionized plant in Milwaukee is running at full capacity.

So we have a huge opportunity at this moment to bring manufacturing back. But we have to seize it. Tonight, my message to business leaders is simple: Ask yourselves what you can do to bring jobs back to your country, and your country will do everything we can to help you succeed.

We should start with our tax code. Right now, companies get tax breaks for moving jobs and profits overseas. Meanwhile, companies that choose to stay in America get hit with one of the highest tax rates in the world. It makes no sense, and everyone knows it.

So let's change it. First, if you're a business that wants to outsource jobs, you shouldn't get a tax deduction for doing it.

That money should be used to cover moving expenses for companies like Master Lock that decide to bring jobs home.

Second, no American company should be able to avoid paying its fair share of taxes by moving jobs and profits overseas.

From now on, every multinational company should have to pay a basic minimum tax. And every penny should go towards lowering taxes for companies that choose to stay here and hire here in America.

Third, if you're an American manufacturer, you should get a bigger tax cut. If you're a high-tech manufacturer, we should double the tax deduction you get for making your products here. And if you want to relocate in a community that was hit hard when a factory left town, you should get help financing a new plant, equipment or training for new workers.

TAX OVERHAUL IS NEEDED

So my message—my message is simple. It is time to stop rewarding businesses that ship jobs overseas and start rewarding companies that create jobs right here in America. Send me these tax reforms, and I will sign them right away.

We're also making it easier for American businesses to sell products all over the world. Two years ago, I set a goal of doubling U.S. exports over five years. With the bipartisan trade agreements we signed into law, we're on track to meet that goal ahead of schedule.

And soon there will be millions of new customers for American goods in Panama, Colombia and South Korea. Soon, there will be new cars on the streets of Seoul imported from Detroit, and Toledo, and Chicago.

I will go anywhere in the world to open new markets for American products. And I will not stand by when our competitors don't play by the rules. We've brought trade cases against China at nearly twice the rate as the last administration, and it's made a difference.

Over a thousand Americans are working today because we stopped a surge in Chinese tires. But we need to do more. It's not right when another country lets our movies, music and software be pirated. It's not fair when foreign manufacturers have a leg up on ours only because they're heavily subsidized.

UNIT TO ENFORCE FAIR TRADE

Tonight, I'm announcing the creation of a Trade Enforcement Unit that will be charged with investigating unfair trading practices in countries like China.

There will be more inspections—there will be more inspections to prevent counterfeit or unsafe goods from crossing our borders. And this Congress should make sure that no foreign company has an advantage over American manufacturing when it comes to accessing financing or new markets like Russia. Our workers are the most productive on earth, and if the playing field is level, I promise you: America will always win.

I also hear from many business leaders who want to hire in the United States but can't find workers with the right skills. Growing industries in science and technology have twice as many openings as we have workers who can do the job. Think about that: openings at a time when millions of Americans are looking for work.

It's inexcusable. And we know how to fix it.

Jackie Bray is a single mom from North Carolina who was laid off from her job as a mechanic. Then Siemens opened a gas turbine factory in Charlotte and formed a partnership with Central Piedmont Community College. The company helped the college design courses in laser and robotics training. It paid Jackie's tuition, then hired her to help operate their plant.

I want every American looking for work to have the same opportunity as Jackie did. Join me in a national commitment to train 2 million Americans with skills that will lead directly to a job.

My administration has already lined up more companies that want to help. Model partnerships between businesses like Siemens and community colleges in places like Charlotte, and Orlando, and Louisville are up and running. Now you need to give more community colleges the resources they need to become community career centers, places that teach people skills that businesses are looking for right now, from data management to high-tech manufacturing.

And I want to cut through the maze of confusing training programs so that from now on people like Jackie have one program, one website and one place to go for all the information and help that they need. It is time to turn our unemployment system into a re-employment system that puts people to work.

These reforms will help people get jobs that are open today. But to prepare for the jobs of tomorrow, our commitment to skills and education has to start earlier.

For less than 1 percent of what our nation spends on education each year, we've convinced nearly every state in the country to raise their standards for teaching and learning, the first time that's happened in a generation.

But challenges remain. And we know how to solve them.

At a time when other countries are doubling down on education, tight budgets have forced states to lay off thousands of teachers. We know a good teacher can increase the lifetime income of a classroom by over $250,000. A great teacher can offer an escape from poverty to the child who dreams beyond his circumstance.

Every person in this chamber can point to a teacher who changed the trajectory of their lives. Most teachers work tirelessly, with modest pay, sometimes digging into their own pocket for school supplies, just to make a difference.

Teachers matter. So instead of bashing them, or defending the status quo, let's offer schools a deal. Give them the resources to keep good teachers on the job, and reward the best ones. And in return, grant schools flexibility: to teach with creativity and passion, to stop teaching to the test, and to replace teachers who just aren't helping kids learn. That's a bargain worth making.

We also know that when students don't walk away from their education, more of them walk the stage to get their diploma. When students are not allowed to drop out, they do better. So tonight, I am proposing that every state—every state—requires that all students stay in high school until they graduate or turn 18.

When kids do graduate, the most daunting challenge can be the cost of college. At a time when Americans owe more in tuition debt than credit card debt, this Congress needs to stop the interest rates on student loans from doubling in July.

Extend the tuition tax credit we started that saves millions of middle-class families thousands of dollars. And give more young people the chance to earn their way through college by doubling the number of work-study jobs in the next five years.

Of course, it's not enough for us to increase student aid. We can't just keep subsidizing skyrocketing tuition. We'll run out of money. States also need to do their part, by making higher education a higher priority in their budgets. And colleges and universities have to do their part by working to keep costs down.

Now, recently, I spoke with a group of college presidents who've done just that. Some schools redesign courses to help students finish more quickly. Some use better technology. The point is, it's possible.

So let me put colleges and universities on notice: If you can't stop tuition from going up, the funding you get from taxpayers will go down. Higher education can't be a luxury. It is an economic imperative that every family in America should be able to afford.

And let's also remember that hundreds of thousands of talented, hard-working students in this country face another challenge: the fact that they aren't yet American citizens. Many were brought here as small children, are American through and through, yet they live every day with the threat of deportation. Others came more recently, to study business and science and engineering, but as soon as they get their degree, we send them home to invent new products and create new jobs somewhere else. That doesn't make sense.

I believe as strongly as ever that we should take on illegal immigration. That's why my administration has put more boots on the border than ever before. That's why there are fewer illegal crossings than when I took office.

The opponents of action are out of excuses. We should be working on comprehensive immigration reform right now.

But if election year politics keeps Congress from acting on a comprehensive plan, let's at least agree to stop expelling responsible young people who want to staff our labs, start new businesses, defend this country. Send me a law that gives them the chance to earn their citizenship; I will sign it right away.

You see, an economy built to last is one where we encourage the talent and ingenuity of every person in this country. That means women should earn equal pay for equal work.

It means we should support everyone who's willing to work and every risk taker and entrepreneur who aspires to become the next Steve Jobs.

After all, innovation is what America has always been about. Most new jobs are created in startups and small businesses. So let's pass an agenda that helps them succeed. Tear down regulations that prevent aspiring entrepreneurs from getting the financing to grow.

Expand tax relief to small businesses that are raising wages and creating good jobs. Both parties agree on these ideas. So put them in a bill, and get it on my desk this year.

Innovation also demands basic research. Today, the discoveries taking place in our federally financed labs and universities could lead to new treatments that kill cancer cells but leave healthy ones untouched, new lightweight vests for cops and soldiers that can stop any bullet.

Don't gut these investments in our budget. Don't let other countries win the race for the future. Support the same kind of research and innovation that led to the computer chip and the Internet, to new American jobs and new American industries.

And nowhere is the promise of innovation greater than in American-made energy. Over the last three years, we've opened millions of new acres for oil and gas exploration. And tonight, I'm directing my administration to open more than 75 percent of our potential offshore oil and gas resources.

Right now—right now, American oil production is the highest that it's been in eight years. That's right, eight years. Not only that, last year, we relied less on foreign oil than in any of the past 16 years.

But with only 2 percent of the world's oil reserves, oil isn't enough. This country needs an all-out, all-of-the-above strategy that develops every available source of American energy. A strategy that's cleaner, cheaper and full of new jobs.

We have a supply of natural gas that can last America nearly 100 years.

And my administration will take every possible action to safely develop this energy. Experts believe this will support more than 600,000 jobs by the end of the decade. And I'm requiring all companies that drill for gas on public lands to disclose the chemicals they use, because America will develop this resource without putting the health and safety of our citizens at risk.

The development of natural gas will create jobs and power trucks and factories that are cleaner and cheaper, proving that we don't have to choose between our environment and our economy.

And, by the way, it was public research dollars over the course of 30 years that helped develop the technologies to extract all this natural gas out of shale rock, reminding us that government support is critical in helping businesses get new energy ideas off the ground. Now, what's true for natural gas is just as true for clean energy. In three years, our partnership with the private sector has already positioned America to be the world's leading manufacturer of high-tech batteries. Because of federal investments, renewable-energy use has nearly doubled, and thousands of Americans have jobs because of it.

When Bryan Ritterby was laid off from his job making furniture, he said he worried that, at 55, no one would give him a second chance. But he found work at Energetx, a wind turbine manufacturer in Michigan. Before the recession, the factory only made luxury yachts. Today, it's hiring workers like Bryan, who said, "I'm proud to be working in the industry of the future."

Our experience with shale gas, our experience with natural gas, shows us that the payoffs on these public investments don't always come right away. Some technologies don't pan out; some companies fail. But I will not walk away from the promise of clean energy. I will not walk away from workers like Bryan.

I will not cede the wind or solar or battery industry to China or Germany because we refuse to make the same commitment here. We've subsidized oil companies for a century. That's long enough.

It's time to end the taxpayer giveaways to an industry that rarely has been more profitable and double down on a clean-energy industry that never has been more promising. Pass clean-energy tax credits. Create these jobs.

We can also spur energy innovation with new incentives. The differences in this chamber may be too deep right now to pass a comprehensive plan to fight climate change, but there's no reason why Congress shouldn't at least set a clean-energy standard that creates a market for innovation.

So far, you haven't acted. Well, tonight, I will.

I'm directing my administration to allow the development of clean energy on enough public land to power 3 million homes. And I'm proud to announce that the Department of Defense, working with us—the world's largest consumer of energy—will make one of the largest commitments to clean energy in history, with the Navy purchasing enough capacity to power a quarter of a million homes a year.

Of course, the easiest way to save money is to waste less energy. So here's a proposal: Help manufacturers eliminate energy waste in their factories and give businesses incentives to upgrade their buildings. Their energy bills will be $100 billion lower over the next decade, and America will have less pollution, more manufacturing, more jobs for construction workers who need them.

Send me a bill that creates these jobs.

Building this new energy future should be just one part of a broader agenda to repair America's infrastructure. So much of America needs to be rebuilt. We've got crumbling roads and bridges, a power grid that wastes too much energy, an incomplete high-speed broadband network that prevents a small-business owner in rural America from selling her products all over the world.

ORDER TO CLEAR RED TAPE

During the Great Depression, America built the Hoover Dam and the Golden Gate Bridge. After World War II, we connected our states with a system of highways. Democratic and Republican administrations invested in great projects that benefited everybody, from the workers who built them to the businesses that still use them today.

In the next few weeks, I will sign an executive order clearing away the red tape that slows down too many construction projects. But you need to fund these projects. Take the money we're no longer spending at war, use half of it to pay down our debt, and use the rest to do some nation building right here at home.

There's never been a better time to build, especially since the construction industry was one of the hardest hit when the housing bubble burst. Of course, construction workers weren't the only ones who were hurt. So were millions of innocent Americans who've seen their home values decline. And while government can't fix the problem on its own, responsible homeowners shouldn't have to sit and wait for the housing market to hit bottom to get some relief.

And that's why I'm sending this Congress a plan that gives every responsible homeowner the chance to save about $3,000 a year on their mortgage by refinancing at historically low rates. No more red tape. No more runaround from the banks. A small fee on the largest financial institutions will ensure that it won't add to the deficit and will give those banks that were rescued by taxpayers a chance to repay a deficit of trust.

Let's never forget: Millions of Americans who work hard and play by the rules every day deserve a government and a financial system that do the same. It's time to apply the same rules from top to bottom: no bailouts, no handouts and no cop-outs. An America built to last insists on responsibility from everybody.

We've all paid the price for lenders who sold mortgages to people who couldn't afford them and buyers who knew they couldn't afford them. That's why we need smart regulations to prevent irresponsible behavior.

Rules to prevent financial fraud, or toxic dumping, or faulty medical devices, these don't destroy the free market. They make the free market work better.

Now, there's no question that some regulations are outdated, unnecessary or too costly. In fact, I've approved fewer regulations in the first three years of my presidency than my Republican predecessor did in his.

I've ordered every federal agency to eliminate rules that don't make sense. We've already announced over 500 reforms, and just a fraction of them will save business and citizens more than $10 billion over the next five years.

We got rid of one rule from 40 years ago that could have forced some dairy farmers to spend $10,000 a year proving that they could contain a spill, because milk was somehow classified as an oil. With a rule like that, I guess it was worth crying over spilled milk.

Now, I'm confident a farmer can contain a milk spill without a federal agency looking over his shoulder. Absolutely.

But I will not back down from making sure an oil company can contain the kind of oil spill we saw in the gulf two years ago.

I will not back down from protecting our kids from mercury poisoning or making sure that our food is safe and our water is clean. I will not go back to the days when health insurance companies had unchecked power to cancel your policy, deny your coverage or charge women differently from men.

And I will not go back to the days when Wall Street was allowed to play by its own set of rules. The new rules we passed restore what should be any financial system's core purpose: getting funding to entrepreneurs with the best ideas, and getting loans to responsible families who want to buy a home, or start a business, or send their kids to college.

So if you are a big bank or financial institution, you're no longer allowed to make risky bets with your customers' deposits. You're required to write out a living will that details exactly how you'll pay the bills if you fail, because the rest of us are not bailing you out ever again.

And if you're a mortgage lender or a payday lender or a credit card company, the days of signing people up for products they can't afford with confusing forms and deceptive practices, those days are over. Today, American consumers finally have a watchdog in Richard Cordray, with one job: to look out for them.

CRACK DOWN ON FRAUD

We'll also establish a Financial Crimes Unit of highly trained investigators to crack down on large-scale fraud and protect people's investments. Some financial firms violate major antifraud laws because there's no real penalty for being a repeat offender. That's bad for consumers, and it's bad for the vast majority of bankers and financial-service professionals who do the right thing. So pass legislation that makes the penalties for fraud count.

And tonight, I'm asking my attorney general to create a special unit of federal prosecutors and leading state attorneys general to expand our investigations into the abusive lending and packaging of risky mortgages that led to the housing crisis. This new unit will hold accountable those who broke the law, speed assistance to homeowners and help turn the page on an era of recklessness that hurt so many Americans.

Now, a return to the American values of fair play and shared responsibility will help protect our people and our economy. But it should also guide us as we look to pay down our debt and invest in our future.

Right now, our most immediate priority is stopping a tax hike on 160 million working Americans while the recovery is still fragile.

People cannot afford losing $40 out of each paycheck this year. There are plenty of ways to get this done. So let's agree right here, right now: No side issues. No drama. Pass the payroll tax cut without delay. Let's get it done.

When it comes to the deficit, we've already agreed to more than $2 trillion in cuts and savings. But we need to do more, and that means making choices.

Right now, we're poised to spend nearly $1 trillion more on what was supposed to be a temporary tax break for the wealthiest 2 percent of Americans. Right now, because of loopholes and shelters in the tax code, a quarter of all millionaires pay lower tax rates than millions of middle-class households.

Right now, Warren Buffett pays a lower tax rate than his secretary.

Do we want to keep these tax cuts for the wealthiest Americans? Or do we want to keep our investments in everything else, like education and medical research, a strong military, and care for our veterans? Because if we're serious about paying down our debt, we can't do both.

FOLLOW THE BUFFETT RULE

The American people know what the right choice is. So do I. As I told the speaker this summer, I'm prepared to make more reforms that rein in the long-term costs of Medicare and Medicaid and strengthen Social Security, so long as those programs remain a guarantee of security for seniors.

But in return, we need to change our tax code so that people like me, and an awful lot of members of Congress, pay our fair share of taxes.

Tax reform should follow the Buffett rule: If you make more than a million dollars a year, you should not pay less than 30 percent in taxes.

And my Republican friend Tom Coburn is right: Washington should stop subsidizing millionaires.

In fact, if you're earning a million dollars a year, you shouldn't get special tax subsidies or deductions. On the other hand, if you make under $250,000 a year—like 98 percent of American families—your taxes shouldn't go up. You're the ones struggling with rising costs and stagnant wages.

You're the ones who need relief.

Now, you can call this class warfare all you want. But asking a billionaire to pay at least as much as his secretary in taxes? Most Americans would call that common sense.

We don't begrudge financial success in this country. We admire it. When Americans talk about folks like me paying my fair share of taxes, it's not because they envy the rich. It's because they understand that when I get a tax break I don't need and the country can't afford, it either adds to the deficit or somebody else has to make up the difference, like a senior on a fixed income, or a student trying to get through school, or a family trying to make ends meet.

That's not right. Americans know that's not right. They know that this generation's success is only possible because past generations felt a responsibility to each other, and to the future of their country, and they know our way of life will only endure if we feel that same sense of shared responsibility. That's how we'll reduce our deficit. That's an America built to last.

Now, I recognize that people watching tonight have differing views about taxes and debt, energy and health care. But no matter what party they belong to, I bet most Americans are thinking the same thing right about now: Nothing will get done in Washington this year, or next year, or maybe even the year after that, because Washington is broken. Can you blame them for feeling a little cynical?

The greatest blow to our confidence in our economy last year didn't come from events beyond our control. It came from a debate in Washington over whether the United States would pay its bills or not. Who benefited from that fiasco?

"DEFICIT OF TRUST"

I've talked tonight about the deficit of trust between Main Street and Wall Street. But the divide between this city and the rest of the country is at least as bad, and it seems to get worse every year.

Now, some of this has to do with the corrosive influence of money in politics. So together, let's take some steps to fix that. Send me a bill that bans insider trading by members of Congress; I will sign it tomorrow.

Let's limit any elected official from owning stocks in industries they impact. Let's make sure people who bundle campaign contributions for Congress can't lobby Congress, and vice versa, an idea that has bipartisan support, at least outside of Washington.

Some of what's broken has to do with the way Congress does its business these days. A simple majority is no longer enough to get anything—even routine business—passed through the Senate.

Neither party has been blameless in these tactics. Now both parties should put an end to it.

For starters, I ask the Senate to pass a simple rule, that all judicial and public service nominations receive a simple up-or-down vote within 90 days.

The executive branch also needs to change. Too often, it's inefficient, outdated and remote.

That's why I've asked this Congress to grant me the authority to consolidate the federal bureaucracy so that our government is leaner, quicker and more responsive to the needs of the American people.

Finally, none of this can happen unless we also lower the temperature in this town. We need to end the notion that the two parties must be locked in a perpetual campaign of mutual destruction, that politics is about clinging to rigid ideologies instead of building consensus around common-sense ideas.

I'm a Democrat. But I believe what Republican Abraham Lincoln believed, that government should do for people only what they cannot do better by themselves, and no more.

That's why my education reform offers more competition and more control for schools and states. That's why we're getting rid of regulations that don't work. That's why our health care law relies on a reformed private market, not a government program.

On the other hand, even my Republican friends who complain the most about government spending have supported federally financed roads, and clean-energy projects, and federal offices for the folks back home.

The point is, we should all want a smarter, more effective government. And while we may not be able to bridge our biggest philosophical differences this year, we can make real progress.

With or without this Congress, I will keep taking actions that help the economy grow. But I can do a whole lot more with your help, because when we act together, there's nothing the United States of America can't achieve.

That's the lesson we've learned from our actions abroad over the last few years. Ending the Iraq War has allowed us to strike decisive blows against our enemies.

From Pakistan to Yemen, the al Qaida operatives who remain are scrambling, knowing that they can't escape the reach of the United States of America.

From this position of strength, we've begun to wind down the war in Afghanistan. Ten thousand of our troops have come home. Twenty-three thousand more will leave by the end of this summer. This transition to Afghan lead will continue, and we will build an enduring partnership with Afghanistan, so that it is never again a source of attacks against America.

As the tide of war recedes, a wave of change has washed across the Middle East and North Africa, from Tunis to Cairo, from Sana'a to Tripoli.

A year ago, Qaddafi was one of the world's longest-serving dictators, a murderer with American blood on his hands. Today, he is gone.

And in Syria, I have no doubt that the Assad regime will soon discover that the forces of change cannot be reversed and that human dignity cannot be denied.

ADVOCATING FOR VALUES

How this incredible transformation will end remains uncertain, but we have a huge stake in the outcome. And while it's ultimately up to the people of the region to decide their fate, we will advocate for those values that have served our own country so well. We will stand against violence and intimidation. We will stand for the rights and dignity of all human beings; men and women; Christians, Muslims and Jews. We will support policies that lead to strong and stable democracies and open markets, because tyranny is no match for liberty.

And we will safeguard America's own security against those who threaten our citizens, our friends and our interests. Look at Iran. Through the power of our diplomacy, a world that was once divided about how to deal with Iran's nuclear program now stands as one. The regime is more isolated than ever before. Its leaders are faced with crippling sanctions. And as long as they shirk their responsibilities, this pressure will not relent.

Let there be no doubt: America is determined to prevent Iran from getting a nuclear weapon, and I will take no options off the table to achieve that goal.

But a peaceful resolution of this issue is still possible, and far better. And if Iran changes course and meets its obligations, it can rejoin the community of nations.

The renewal of American leadership can be felt across the globe. Our oldest alliances in Europe and Asia are stronger than ever. Our ties to the Americas are deeper. Our iron-clad commitment—and I mean iron-clad—to Israel's security has meant the closest military cooperation between our two countries in history.

We've made it clear that America is a Pacific power, and a new beginning in Burma has lit a new hope.

From the coalitions we've built to secure nuclear materials to the missions we've led against hunger and disease, from the blows we've dealt our enemies to the enduring power of our moral example, America is back. Anyone who tells you otherwise, anyone who tells you that America is in decline or that our influence has waned, doesn't know what they're talking about.

That's not the message we get from leaders around the world who are eager to work with us. That's not how people feel from Tokyo to Berlin, from Cape Town to Rio, where opinions of America are higher than they've been in years.

Yes, the world is changing. No, we can't control every event. But America remains the one indispensable nation in world affairs. And as long as I'm president, I intend to keep it that way.

That's why, working with our military leaders, I've proposed a new defense strategy that ensures we maintain the finest military in the world, while saving nearly half a trillion dollars in our budget. To stay one step ahead of our adversaries, I've already sent this Congress legislation that will secure our country from the growing danger of cyberthreats.

Above all, our freedom endures because of the men and women in uniform who defend it.

As they come home, we must serve them as well as they've served us. That includes giving them the care and the benefits they have earned, which is why we've increased annual VA spending every year I've been president.

And it means enlisting our veterans in the work of rebuilding our nation. With the bipartisan support of this Congress, we're providing new tax credits to companies that hire vets. Michelle and Jill Biden have worked with American businesses to secure a pledge of 135,000 jobs for veterans and their families. And tonight, I'm proposing a Veterans Job Corps that will help our communities hire veterans as cops and firefighters, so that America is as strong as those who defend her.

Which brings me back to where I began. Those of us who've been sent here to serve can learn a thing or two from the service of our troops. When you put on that uniform, it doesn't matter if you're black or white, Asian, Latino, Native American, conservative, liberal, rich, poor, gay, straight. When you're marching into battle, you look out for the person next to you, or the mission fails. When you're in the thick of the fight, you rise or fall as one unit, serving one nation, leaving no one behind.

A PROUD MOMENT

You know, one of my proudest possessions is the flag that the SEAL team took with them on the mission to get bin Laden. On it are each of their names. Some may be Democrats; some may be Republicans. But that doesn't matter. Just like it didn't matter that day in the Situation Room, when I sat next to Bob Gates, a man who was George Bush's defense secretary, and Hillary Clinton, a woman who ran against me for president.

All that mattered that day was the mission. No one thought about politics. No one thought about themselves.

One of the young men involved in the raid later told me that he didn't deserve credit for the mission. It only succeeded, he said, because every single member of that unit did their job: the pilot who landed the helicopter that spun out of control; the translator who kept others from entering the compound; the troops who separated the women and children from the fight; the SEALs who charged up the stairs. More than that, the mission only succeeded because every member of that unit trusted each other, because you can't charge up those stairs into darkness and danger unless you know that there's somebody behind you watching your back.

So it is with America. Each time I look at that flag, I'm reminded that our destiny is stitched together like those 50 stars and those 13 stripes. No one built this country on their own. This nation is great because we built it together. This nation is great because we worked as a team. This nation is great because we get each other's backs. And if we hold fast to that truth, in this moment of trial, there is no challenge too great, no mission too hard. As long as we're joined in common purpose, as long as we maintain our common resolve, our journey moves forward, and our future is hopeful, and the state of our union will always be strong.

Thank you, God bless you, and may God bless the United States of America.

President Obama's Statement on Winning Reelection in 2012

Following is the transcript of the speech President Barack Obama gave to supporters in Chicago on November 6, 2012, after winning reelection.

Thank you. Thank you. Thank you so much.

Tonight, more than 200 years after a former colony won the right to determine its own destiny, the task of perfecting our union moves forward.

It moves forward because of you. It moves forward because you reaffirmed the spirit that has triumphed over war and depression, the spirit that has lifted this country from the depths of despair to the great heights of hope, the belief that while each of us will pursue our own individual dreams, we are an American family and we rise or fall together as one nation and as one people.

Tonight, in this election, you, the American people, reminded us that while our road has been hard, while our journey has been long, we have picked ourselves up, we have fought our way back, and we know in our hearts that for the United States of America the best is yet to come.

I want to thank every American who participated in this election, whether you voted for the very first time or waited in line for a very long time. By the way, we have to fix that. Whether you pounded the pavement or picked up the phone. Whether you held an Obama sign or a Romney sign, you made your voice heard and you made a difference.

I just spoke with Gov. Romney, and I congratulated him and Paul Ryan on a hard-fought campaign.

We may have battled fiercely, but it's only because we love this country deeply and we care so strongly about its future. From George to Lenore to their son Mitt, the Romney family has chosen to give back to America through public service, and that is the legacy that we honor and applaud tonight.

In the weeks ahead, I also look forward to sitting down with Gov. Romney to talk about where we can work together to move this country forward.

I want to thank my friend and partner of the last four years, America's happy warrior, the best vice president anybody could ever hope for, Joe Biden.

And I wouldn't be the man I am today without the woman who agreed to marry me 20 years ago.

Let me say this publicly: Michelle, I have never loved you more. I have never been prouder to watch the rest of America fall in love with you, too, as our nation's first lady.

Sasha and Malia, before our very eyes you're growing up to become two strong, smart beautiful young women, just like your mom.

And I'm so proud of you guys. But I will say that, for now, one dog's probably enough.

To the best campaign team and volunteers in the history of politics. The best. The best ever. Some of you were new this time around, and some of you have been at my side since the very beginning.

But all of you are family. No matter what you do or where you go from here, you will carry the memory of the history we made together, and you will have the lifelong appreciation of a grateful president. Thank you for believing all the way, through every hill, through every valley.

You lifted me up the whole way, and I will always be grateful for everything that you've done and all the incredible work that you put in.

I know that political campaigns can sometimes seem small, even silly. And that provides plenty of fodder for the cynics that tell us that politics is nothing more than a contest of egos or the domain of special interests. But if you ever get the chance to talk to folks who turned out at our rallies and crowded along a rope line in a high school gym, or saw folks working late in a campaign office in some tiny county far away from home, you'll discover something else.

You'll hear the determination in the voice of a young field organizer who's working his way through college and wants to make sure every child has that same opportunity.

You'll hear the pride in the voice of a volunteer who's going door to door because her brother was finally hired when the local auto plant added another shift.

You'll hear the deep patriotism in the voice of a military spouse who's working the phones late at night to make sure that no one who fights for this country ever has to fight for a job or a roof over their head when they come home.

That's why we do this. That's what politics can be. That's why elections matter. It's not small, it's big. It's important. Democracy in a nation of 300 million can be noisy and messy and complicated. We have our own opinions. Each of us has deeply held beliefs. And when we go through tough times, when we make big decisions as a country, it necessarily stirs passions, stirs up controversy.

That won't change after tonight, and it shouldn't. These arguments we have are a mark of our liberty. We can never forget that, as we speak. People in distant nations are risking their lives right now just for a chance to argue about the issues that matter, the chance to cast their ballots like we did today.

But despite all our differences, most of us share certain hopes for America's future. We want our kids to grow up in a country where they have access to the best schools and the best teachers.

A country that lives up to its legacy as the global leader in technology and discovery and innovation, with all the good jobs and new businesses that follow.

We want our children to live in an America that isn't burdened by debt, that isn't weakened by inequality, that isn't threatened by the destructive power of a warming planet.

We want to pass on a country that's safe and respected and admired around the world, a nation that is defended by the strongest military on earth and the best troops this world has ever known.

But also a country that moves with confidence beyond this time of war, to shape a peace that is built on the promise of freedom and dignity for every human being. We believe in a generous America, in a compassionate America, in a tolerant America, open to the dreams of an immigrant's daughter who studies in our schools and pledges to our flag.

To the young boy on the south side of Chicago who sees a life beyond the nearest street corner.

To the furniture worker's child in North Carolina who wants to become a doctor or a scientist, an engineer or an entrepreneur, a diplomat or even a president—that's the future we hope for. That's the vision we share. That's where we need to go—forward.

That's where we need to go.

Now, we will disagree, sometimes fiercely, about how to get there. As it has for more than two centuries, progress will come in fits and starts. It's not always a straight line. It's not always a smooth path.

By itself, the recognition that we have common hopes and dreams won't end all the gridlock or solve all our problems or substitute for the painstaking work of building consensus and making the difficult compromises needed to move this country forward. But that common bond is where we must begin.

Our economy is recovering. A decade of war is ending. A long campaign is now over.

And whether I earned your vote or not, I have listened to you, I have learned from you, and you've made me a better president. And with your stories and your struggles, I return to the White House more determined and more inspired than ever about the work there is to do and the future that lies ahead.

Tonight, you voted for action, not politics as usual.

You elected us to focus on your jobs, not ours. And in the coming weeks and months, I am looking forward to reaching out and working with leaders of both parties to meet the challenges we can only solve together. Reducing our deficit. Reforming our tax code. Fixing our immigration system. Freeing ourselves from foreign oil. We've got more work to do.

But that doesn't mean your work is done. The role of citizens in our democracy does not end with your vote. America's never been about what can be done for us. It's about what can be done by us together through the hard and frustrating, but necessary, work of self-government. That's the principle we were founded on.

This country has more wealth than any nation, but that's not what makes us rich. We have the most powerful military in history, but that's not what makes us strong. Our university, our culture are all the envy of the world, but that's not what keeps the world coming to our shores.

What makes America exceptional are the bonds that hold together the most diverse nation on earth; the belief that our destiny is shared, that this country only works when we accept certain obligations to one another and to future generations. The freedom which so many Americans have fought for and died for come with responsibilities as well as rights. And among those are love and charity and duty and patriotism. That's what makes America great.

I am hopeful tonight, because I've seen the spirit at work in America. I've seen it in the family business whose owners would rather cut their own pay than lay off their neighbors, and in the workers who would rather cut back their hours than see a friend lose a job.

I've seen it in the soldiers who re-enlist after losing a limb and in those SEALs who charged up the stairs into darkness and danger because they knew there was a buddy behind them watching their back.

I've seen it on the shores of New Jersey and New York, where leaders from every party and level of government have swept aside their differences to help a community rebuild from the wreckage of a terrible storm.

And I saw just the other day, in Mentor, Ohio, where a father told the story of his 8-year-old daughter, whose long battle with leukemia nearly cost their family everything had it not been for health care reform passing just a few months before the insurance company was about to stop paying for her care.

I had an opportunity to not just talk to the father, but meet this incredible daughter of his. And when he spoke to the crowd listening to that father's story, every parent in that room had tears in their eyes, because we knew that little girl could be our own.

And I know that every American wants her future to be just as bright. That's who we are. That's the country I'm so proud to lead as your president.

And tonight, despite all the hardship we've been through, despite all the frustrations of Washington, I've never been more hopeful about our future.

I have never been more hopeful about America. And I ask you to sustain that hope. I'm not talking about blind optimism, the kind of hope that just ignores the enormity of the tasks ahead or the roadblocks that stand in our path. I'm not talking about the wishful idealism that allows us to just sit on the sidelines or shirk from a fight.

I have always believed that hope is that stubborn thing inside us that insists, despite all the evidence to the contrary, that something better awaits us so long as we have the courage to keep reaching, to keep working, to keep fighting.

America, I believe we can build on the progress we've made and continue to fight for new jobs and new opportunity and new security for the middle class. I believe we can keep the promise of our founders, the idea that if you're willing to work hard, it doesn't matter who you are or where you come from or what you look like or who you love. It doesn't matter whether you're black or white or Hispanic or Asian or Native American or young or old or rich or poor, able, disabled, gay or straight, you can make it here in America if you're willing to try.

I believe we can seize this future together because we are not as divided as our politics suggests. We're not as cynical as the pundits believe. We are greater than the sum of our individual ambitions, and we remain more than a collection of red states and blue states. We are and forever will be the United States of America.

And together with your help and God's grace we will continue our journey forward and remind the world just why it is that we live in the greatest nation on Earth.

Thank you, America. God bless you. God bless these United States.

Presidential Vetoes, 2009–2012

President Barack Obama vetoed only two bills during his first term in office, neither involving major legislation. The first, in 2009, was on a short-term continuing appropriations resolution for defense spending that had been made moot by approval of defense funding a few days earlier. The second veto, in 2010, was on a bill requiring state and federal courts to recognize notarization actions done by a licensed notary in a different state. He indicated sympathy to the purpose of facilitating interstate commerce and pledged to work with Congress on revised legislation.

The two vetoes were the fewest of any president, by far, since Dwight D. Eisenhower began his presidential term in 1953. *(See table, below)*

Obama's predecessor, President George W. Bush, did not veto any legislation during his first four years in office, from 2001 through 2004. He was the first president since John Quincy Adams in the 1820s to go through a full term without issuing a veto. Both Obama and Bush were able to avoid first-term vetoes because their parties controlled both houses of Congress. But Bush's second term was quite different with Democrats in control of Congress for two of the four years: he cast twelve votes from 2005 through 2008. *(Congress and the Nation Vol. XII, p. 1039)*

By contrast, presidents from Eisenhower to Clinton issued many vetoes. Eisenhower, faced with a Democratic Congress throughout his eight years in the White House, vetoed many more than any of his successors. But only two were overridden. President Bill Clinton, similarly faced a Republican Congress for six of his eight years in office; he issued thirty-seven vetoes with also only two overridden.

Grover Cleveland issued the most vetoes in one term, 414. Franklin D. Roosevelt, who served as president for three full terms and into a fourth, vetoed the most measures, 635. Seven presidents before Bush vetoed no bills.

Following is a list of bills vetoed by President Barack Obama during his first term, 2009–2013, and his messages to Congress on the vetoes.

2009

1. H.J. Res 64 (Continuing appropriations, defense, fiscal 2010)
Vetoed Dec. 30, 2009
House sustained veto Jan. 13, 2010: 143–245.

2010

1. HR 3808 (Requiring interstate recognition of notarizations)
Vetoed Oct. 8, 2010
House sustained veto Nov. 17, 2010: 185–235.

President Obama's Veto of Continuing Defense Appropriations for Fiscal 2010

Following is the text of President Obama's Dec. 30, 2009, veto message on H.J. Res 64, making continuing defense appropriations for fiscal 2010. (Story, p. 133)

President	*Congress vetoes*	*Regular vetoes*	*Pocket vetoes*	*Total*	*Overridden*
Dwight D. Eisenhower	83rd–86th	73	108	181	2
John F. Kennedy	87th–88th	12	9	21	0
Lyndon B. Johnson	88th–90th	16	14	30	0
Richard M. Nixon	91st–93rd	26	17	43	7
Gerald R. Ford	93rd–94th	48	18	66	12
Jimmy Carter	95th–96th	13	18	31	2
Ronald Reagan	97th–100th	39	39	78	9
George H. W. Bush[1]	101st–102nd	29	15	44	1
Bill Clinton[2]	103rd–106th	36	1	37	2
George W. Bush	107th–108th	12	0	12	4
Barack Obama	109th–110th	2	0	2	0

[1]President George H. W. Bush attempted to pocket veto two bills during recess periods. Congress considered the two bills enacted into law because of the president's failure to return the legislation. The bills are not counted as pocket vetoes in this table.

[2]Does not include line-item vetoes, which were permitted under a 1996 law that was struck down by the Supreme Court.

To the House of Representatives

The enactment of H.R. 3326 (Department of Defense Appropriations Act, 2010, Public Law 111-118), which was signed into law on December 19, 2009, has rendered the enactment of H.J. Res. 64 (Continuing Appropriations, FY 2010) unnecessary. Accordingly, I am withholding my approval from the bill. (The Pocket Veto Case, 279 U.S. 655 (1929)).

To leave no doubt that the bill is being vetoed as unnecessary legislation, in addition to withholding my signature, I am also returning H.J. Res. 64 to the Clerk of the House of Representatives, along with this Memorandum of Disapproval.

BARACK OBAMA
THE WHITE HOUSE
Dec. 30, 2009

President Obama's Veto of Notarization Legislation

Following is the text of President Obama's Oct. 8, 2010, veto message on HR 3808, requiring state and federal courts to recognize notarizations affecting interstate commerce done by a notary acting in another state.

To the House of Representatives

It is necessary to have further deliberations about the possible unintended impact of H.R. 3808, the "Interstate Recognition of Notarizations Act of 2010," on consumer protections, including those for mortgages, before the bill can be finalized. Accordingly, I am withholding my approval of this bill. (The Pocket Veto Case, 279 U.S. 655 (1929).

The authors of this bill no doubt had the best intentions in mind when trying to remove impediments to interstate commerce. My Administration will work with them and other leaders in Congress to explore the best ways to achieve this goal going forward.

To leave no doubt that the bill is being vetoed, in addition to withholding my signature, I am returning H.R. 3808 to the Clerk of the House of Representatives, along with this Memorandum of Disapproval.

BARACK OBAMA
THE WHITE HOUSE
Oct. 8, 2010

Political Charts

Summary of Presidential Elections, 1789–2012 919

Victorious Party in Presidential Races, 1860–2012 922

2008 Presidential Election 924

2008 Electoral Votes and Map 925

2012 Presidential Election 926

2012 Electoral Votes and Map 927

Distribution of House Seats and Electoral Votes 928

Party Affiliations in Congress and the Presidency, 1789–2015 929

111th Congress Special Elections, 2009 Gubernatorial Elections 931

2010 Election Returns for Governor, Senate, and House 932

112th Congress Special Elections, 2011 Gubernatorial Elections 941

2012 Election Returns for Governor, Senate, and House 942

Results of House Elections, 1928–2012 950

Governors, 2009–2013 956

Summary of Presidential Elections, 1789–2012

Year	No. of states	Candidates	Party	Electoral vote	Popular vote
1789[1]	10	**George Washington**	**F**	**69**	—[2]
		John Adams	F	34	
1792[1]	15	**George Washington**	**F**	**132**	—[2]
		John Adams	F	77	
1796[1]	16	**John Adams**	**F**	**71**	—[2]
		Thomas Jefferson	D-R	68	
1800[1]	16	**Thomas Jefferson**	**D-R**	**73**	—[2]
		Aaron Burr	D-R	73	
		John Adams	F	65	
		Charles Cotesworth Pinckney	F	64	
1804	17	**Thomas Jefferson**	**D-R**	**162**	—[2]
		George Clinton			
		Charles Cotesworth Pinckney	F	64	
		Rufus King			
1808	17	**James Madison**	**D-R**	**122**	—[2]
		George Clinton			
		Charles Cotesworth Pinckney	F	64	
		Rufus King			
1812	18	**James Madison**	**D-R**	**128**	—[2]
		Elbridge Gerry			
		George Clinton	F	89	
		Jared Ingersoll			
1816	19	**James Monroe**	**D-R**	**183**	—[2]
		Daniel D. Tompkins			
		Rufus King	F	34	
		John Howard			
1820	24	**James Monroe**	**D-R**	**231**[3]	—[2]
		Daniel D. Tompkins			
1824[4]	24	**John Quincy Adams**	**D-R**	**99**	**113,122 (30.9%)**
		John C. Calhoun			
		Andrew Jackson	D-R	84	151,271 (41.3%)
		Nathan Sanford			
1828	24	**Andrew Jackson**	**D-R**	**178**	**642,553 (56.0%)**
		John C. Calhoun			
		John Quincy Adams	N-R	83	500,897 (43.6%)
		Richard Rush			
1832[5]	24	**Andrew Jackson**	**D**	**219**	**701,780 (54.2%)**
		Martin Van Buren			
		Henry Clay	N-R	49	484,205 (37.4%)
		John Sergeant			
1836[6]	26	Martin Van Buren	**D**	**170**	**764,176 (50.8%)**
		Richard M. Johnson			
		William Henry Harrison	W	73	550,816 (36.6%)
		Francis Granger			
1840	26	**William Henry Harrison**	**W**	**234**	**1,275,390 (52.9%)**
		John Tyler			
		Martin Van Buren	D	60	1,128,854 (46.8%)
		Richard M. Johnson			
1844	26	**James K. Polk**	**D**	**170**	**1,339,494 (49.5%)**
		George M. Dallas			
		Henry Clay	W	105	1,300,004 (48.1%)
		Theodore Frelinghuysen			
1848	30	**Zachary Taylor**	**W**	**163**	**1,361,393 (47.3%)**
		Millard Fillmore			
		Lewis Cass	D	127	1,223,460 (42.5%)
		William O. Butler			
1852	31	**Franklin Pierce**	**D**	**254**	**1,607,510 (50.8%)**
		William R. King			
		Winfield Scott	W	42	1,386,942 (43.9%)
		William A. Graham			
1856[7]	31	**James Buchanan**	**D**	**174**	**1,836,072 (45.3%)**
		John C. Breckinridge			
		John C. Fremont	R	114	1,342,345 (33.1%)
		William L. Dayton			
1860[8]	33	**Abraham Lincoln**	**R**	**180**	**1,865,908 (39.8%)**
		Hannibal Hamlin			
		Stephen A. Douglas	D	12	1,380,202 (29.5%)
		Herschel V. Johnson			
1864[9]	36	**Abraham Lincoln**	**R**	**212**	**2,218,388 (55.0%)**
		Andrew Johnson			
		George B. McClellan	D	21	1,812,807 (45.0%)
		George H. Pendleton			
1868[10]	37	Ulysses S. Grant	R	214	3,013,650 (52.7%)
		Schuyler Colfax			
		Horatio Seymour	D	80	2,708,744 (47.3%)
		Francis P. Blair Jr.			
1872	37	**Ulysses S. Grant**	**R**	**286**	**3,598,235 (55.6%)**
		Henry Wilson			
		Horace Greeley	D	—[11]	2,834,761 (43.8%)
		Benjamin Gratz Brown			
1876	38	**Rutherford B. Hayes**	**R**	**185**	**4,034,311 (47.9%)**
		William A. Wheeler			
		Samuel J. Tilden	D	184	4,288,546 (51.0%)
		Thomas A. Hendricks			
1880	38	**James A. Garfield**	**R**	**214**	**4,446,158 (48.3%)**
		Chester A. Arthur			
		Winfield S. Hancock	D	155	4,444,260 (48.2%)
		William H. English			
1884	38	**Grover Cleveland**	**D**	**219**	**4,874,621 (48.5%)**
		Thomas A. Hendricks			
		James G. Blaine	R	182	4,848,936 (48.2%)
		John A. Logan			
1888	38	**Benjamin Harrison**	**R**	**233**	**5,443,892 (47.8%)**
		Levi P. Morton			

Year	No. of states	Candidates	Party	Electoral vote	Popular vote
		Grover Cleveland	D	168	5,534,488 (48.6%)
		Allen G. Thurman			
1892[12]	44	**Grover Cleveland**	**D**	**277**	**5,551,883 (46.1%)**
		Adlai E. Stevenson			
		Benjamin Harrison	R	145	5,179,244 (43.0%)
		Whitelaw Reid			
1896	45	**William McKinley**	**R**	**271**	**7,108,480 (51.0%)**
		Garret A. Hobart			
		William J. Bryan	D	176	6,511,495 (46.7%)
		Arthur Sewall			
1900	45	**William McKinley**	**R**	**292**	**7,218,039 (51.7%)**
		Theodore Roosevelt			
		William J. Bryan	D	155	6,358,345 (45.5%)
		Adlai E. Stevenson			
1904	45	**Theodore Roosevelt**	**R**	**336**	**7,626,593 (56.4%)**
		Charles W. Fairbanks			
		Alton B. Parker	D	140	5,028,898 (37.6%)
		Henry G. Davis			
1908	46	**William Howard Taft**	**R**	**321**	**7,676,258 (51.6%)**
		James S. Sherman			
		William J. Bryan	D	162	6,406,801 (43.0%)
		John W. Kern			
1912[13]	48	**Woodrow Wilson**	**D**	**435**	**6,293,152 (41.8%)**
		Thomas R. Marshall			
		William Howard Taft	R	8	3,486,333 (23.2%)
		James S. Sherman			
1916	48	**Woodrow Wilson**	**D**	**277**	**9,126,300 (49.2%)**
		Thomas R. Marshall			
		Charles E. Hughes	R	254	8,546,789 (46.1%)
		Charles W. Fairbanks			
1920	48	**Warren G. Harding**	**R**	**404**	**16,133,314 (60.3%)**
		Calvin Coolidge			
		James M. Cox	D	127	9,140,884 (34.2%)
		Franklin D. Roosevelt			
1924[14]	48	**Calvin Coolidge**	**R**	**382**	**15,717,553 (54.1%)**
		Charles G. Dawes			
		John W. Davis	D	136	8,386,169 (28.8%)
		Charles W. Bryan			
1928	48	**Herbert C. Hoover**	**R**	**444**	**21,411,991 (58.2%)**
		Charles Curtis			
		Alfred E. Smith	D	87	15,000,185 (40.8%)
		Joseph T. Robinson			
1932	48	**Franklin D. Roosevelt**	**D**	**472**	**22,825,016 (57.4%)**
		John N. Garner			
		Herbert C. Hoover	R	59	15,758,397 (39.6%)
		Charles Curtis			
1936	48	**Franklin D. Roosevelt**	**D**	**523**	**27,747,636 (60.8%)**
		John N. Garner			
		Alfred M. Landon	R	8	16,679,543 (36.5%)
		Frank Knox			
1940	48	**Franklin D. Roosevelt**	**D**	**449**	**27,263,448 (54.7%)**
		Henry A. Wallace			
		Wendell L. Willkie	R	82	22,336,260 (44.8%)
		Charles L. McNary			
1944	48	**Franklin D. Roosevelt**	**D**	**432**	**25,611,936 (53.4%)**
		Harry S. Truman			
		Thomas E. Dewey	R	99	22,013,372 (45.9%)
		John W. Bricker			
1948[15]	48	**Harry S. Truman**	**D**	**303**	**24,105,587 (49.5%)**
		Alben W. Barkley			
		Thomas E. Dewey	R	198	21,970,017 (45.1%)
		Earl Warren			
1952	48	**Dwight D. Eisenhower**	**R**	**442**	**33,936,137 (55.1%)**
		Richard M. Nixon			
		Adlai E. Stevenson II	D	89	27,314,649 (44.4%)
		John J. Sparkman			
1956[16]	48	**Dwight D. Eisenhower**	**R**	**457**	**35,585,245 (57.4%)**
		Richard M. Nixon			
		Adlai E. Stevenson II	D	73	26,030,172 (42.0%)
		Estes Kefauver			
1960[17]	50	**John F. Kennedy**	**D**	**303**	**34,221,344 (49.7%)**
		Lyndon B. Johnson			
		Richard Nixon	R	219	34,106,671 (49.5%)
		Henry Cabot Lodge			
1964	50*	**Lyndon B. Johnson**	**D**	**486**	**43,126,584 (61.1%)**
		Hubert H. Humphrey			
		Barry Goldwater	R	52	27,177,838 (38.5%)
		William E. Miller			
1968[18]	50*	**Richard Nixon**	**R**	**301**	**31,785,148 (43.4%)**
		Spiro T. Agnew			
		Hubert H. Humphrey	D	191	31,274,503 (42.7%)
		Edmund S. Muskie			
1972[19]	50*	**Richard Nixon**	**R**	**520**	**47,170,179 (60.7%)**
		Spiro T. Agnew			
		George McGovern	D	17	29,171,791 (37.5%)
		Sargent Shriver			
1976[20]	50*	**Jimmy Carter**	**D**	**297**	**40,830,763 (50.1%)**
		Walter F. Mondale			
		Gerald R. Ford	R	240	39,147,793 (48.0%)
		Robert Dole			
1980	50*	**Ronald Reagan**	**R**	**489**	**43,904,153 (50.7%)**
		George H. W. Bush			
		Jimmy Carter	D	49	35,483,883 (41.0%)
		Walter F. Mondale			
1984	50*	**Ronald Reagan**	**R**	**525**	**54,455,074(58.8%)**
		George H. W. Bush			
		Walter F. Mondale	D	13	37,577,137 (40.6%)
		Geraldine Ferraro			

Year	No. of states	Candidates	Party	Electoral vote	Popular vote
1988[21]	50*	**George H. W. Bush**	**R**	**426**	**48,881,278 (53.4%)**
		Dan Quayle			
		Michael S. Dukakis	D	111	41,805,374 (45.6%)
		Lloyd Bentsen			
1992	50*	**Bill Clinton**	**D**	**370**	**44,908,233 (43.0%)**
		Al Gore			
		George H. W. Bush	R	168	39,102,282 (37.4%)
		Dan Quayle			
1996	50*	**Bill Clinton**	**D**	**379**	**47,402,357 (49.2%)**
		Al Gore			
		Bob Dole	R	159	39,198,755 (40.7%)
		Jack Kemp			
2000[22]	50*	**George W. Bush**	R	271	50,455,156 (47.9%)
		Richard B. Cheney			
		Al Gore	D	266	50,992,335 (48.4%)
		Joseph I. Lieberman			
2004[23]	50*	**George W. Bush**	**R**	**286**	**62,040,610 (50.7%)**
		Richard B. Cheney			
		John Kerry	D	251	59,028,439 (48.3%)
		John Edwards			
2008[24]	50*	**Barack Obama**	**D**	**365**	**69,498,516 (52.9%)**
		Joseph R. Biden Jr.			
		John McCain	R	173	59,948,323 (45.7%)
		Sarah Palin			
2012	50*	**Barack Obama**	**D**	**332**	**65,915,796 (51.1%)**
		Joseph R. Biden Jr.			
		Mitt Romney	R	206	60,933,500 (47.2%)
		Paul Ryan			

SOURCE: Harold W. Stanley and Richard G. Niemi, *Vital Statistics on American Politics,* 5th ed. (Washington, D.C.: CQ Press, 1995), Table 3-13; Richard M. Scammon, Alice V. McGillivray, and Rhodes Cook, *America Votes 24, 30* (Washington, D.C.: Sage/CQ Press, 2009, 2013).

NOTE: Bold indicates victors. In the elections of 1789, 1792, 1796, and 1800, each candidate ran for the office of president. The candidate with the second-highest number of electoral votes became vice president. For elections after 1800, italic indicates vice presidential candidates. D—Democratic; DR—Democratic-Republican; F—Federalist; NR—National Republican; R—Republican; W—Whig.

1. Elections of 1789–1800 were held under rules that did not allow separate voting for president and vice president.
2. Popular vote returns are not shown before 1824 because consistent, reliable data are not available.
3. Monroe ran unopposed. One electoral vote was cast for John Adams and Richard Stockton, who were not candidates.
4. 1824: All four candidates represented Democratic-Republican factions. William H. Crawford received 41 electoral votes, and Henry Clay received 37 votes. Since no candidate received a majority, the election was decided (in Adams's favor) by the House of Representatives.
5. 1832: Two electoral votes were not cast.
6. 1836: Other Whig candidates receiving electoral votes were Hugh L. White, who received 26 votes, and Daniel Webster, who received 14 votes.
7. 1856: Millard Fillmore, Whig-American, received 8 electoral votes.
8. 1860: John C. Breckinridge, Southern Democrat, received 72 electoral votes. John Bell, Constitutional Union, received 39 electoral votes.
9. 1864: Because of the Civil War, 81 electoral votes were not cast.
10. 1868: Because of Reconstruction, 23 electoral votes were not cast.
11. 1872: Horace Greeley, Democrat, died after the election. In the electoral college, Democratic electoral votes went to Thomas Hendricks, 42 votes; Benjamin Gratz Brown, 18 votes; Charles J. Jenkins, 2 votes; and David Davis, 1 vote. Seventeen electoral votes were not cast.
12. 1892: James B. Weaver, People's Party, received 22 electoral votes.
13. 1912: Theodore Roosevelt, Progressive Party, received 86 electoral votes.
14. 1924: Robert M. La Follette, Progressive Party, received 13 electoral votes.
15. 1948: J. Strom Thurmond, States' Rights Party, received 39 electoral votes.
16. 1956: Walter B. Jones, Democrat, received 1 electoral vote.
17. 1960: Harry Flood Byrd, Democrat, received 15 electoral votes.
18. 1968: George C. Wallace, American Independent Party, received 46 electoral votes.
19. 1972: John Hospers, Libertarian Party, received 1 electoral vote.
20. 1976: Ronald Reagan, Republican, received 1 electoral vote.
21. 1988: Lloyd Bentsen, the Democratic vice-presidential nominee, received 1 electoral vote for president.
22. 2000: One District of Columbia elector did not vote.
23. 2004: A Democratic elector in Minnesota cast a vote for Edwards rather than Kerry.
24. 2008: Nebraska split its five electoral votes, with four going to John McCain and one to Barack Obama. Nebraska is one of two states, along with Maine, that splits electoral votes between congressional districts. Nebraska has three. The winner of each district receives that district's vote; the statewide winner receives the other two. The 2008 election was the first time that split electoral vote occurred in either state.

*Fifty states plus the District of Columbia.

Victorious Party in Presidential Races, 1860–2012

State	1860	1864	1868	1872	1876	1880	1884	1888	1892	1896	1900	1904	1908	1912	1916	1920	1924	1928	1932	1936
Alabama	SD	[2]	R	R	D	D	D	D	D	D	D	D	D	D	D	D	D	D	D	D
Alaska																				
Arizona														D	D	R	R	R	D	D
Arkansas	SD	[2]	R	[4]	D	D	D	D	D	D	D	D	D	D	D	D	D	D	D	D
California	R	R	R	R	R	D[6]	R	R	D[7]	R[12]	R	R	R	PR	D	R	R	R	D	D
Colorado					R	R	R	R	PP	D	D	R	D	D	D	R	R	R	D	D
Connecticut	R	R	R	R	D	R	D	D	D	R	R	R	R	D	R	R	R	R	R	D
Delaware	SD	D	D	R	D	D	D	D	D	R	R	R	R	D	R	R	R	R	R	D
Dist. of Columbia																				
Florida	SD	[2]	R	R	R	D	D	D	D	D	D	D	D	D	D	D	D	R	D	D
Georgia	SD	[2]	D	D[5]	D	D	D	D	D	D	D	D	D	D	D	D	D	D	D	D
Hawaii																				
Idaho									PP	D	D	R	R	D	D	R	R	R	D	D
Illinois	R	R	R	R	R	R	R	R	D	R	R	R	R	D	R	R	R	R	D	D
Indiana	R	R	R	R	D	R	D	R	D	R	R	R	R	D	R	R	R	R	D	D
Iowa	R	R	R	R	R	R	R	R	R	R	R	R	R	D	R	R	R	R	D	D
Kansas		R	R	R	R	R	R	R	PP	D	R	R	R	D	D	R	R	R	R	R
Kentucky	CU	D	D	D	D	D	D	D	D	R[13]	D	D	D	D	D	D	R	R	D	D
Louisiana	SD	[2]	D	[4]	R	D	D	D	D	D	D	D	D	D	D	D	D	D	D	D
Maine	R	R	R	R	R	R	R	R	R	R	R	R	R	D	R	R	R	R	R	R
Maryland	SD	R	D	D	D	D	D	D	D	R	R	D[14]	D[15]	D	D	R	R	R	D	D
Massachusetts	R	R	R	R	R	R	R	R	R	R	R	R	R	D	R	R	R	D	D	D
Michigan	R	R	R	R	R	R	R	R	R[8]	R	R	R	R	PR	R	R	R	R	D	D
Minnesota	R	R	R	R	R	R	R	R	R	R	R	R	R	PR	R	R	R	R	D	D
Mississippi	SD	[2]	[3]	R	D	D	D	D	D	D	D	D	D	D	D	D	D	D	D	D
Missouri	D	R	R	D	D	D	D	D	D	D	D	R	R	D	D	R	R	R	D	D
Montana									R	D	D	R	R	D	D	R	R	R	D	D
Nebraska			R	R	R	R	R	R	R	D	R	R	D	D	D	R	R	R	D	D
Nevada		R	R	R	R	R	D	R	PP	D	D	R	D	D	D	R	R	R	D	D
New Hampshire	R	R	R	R	R	R	R	R	R	R	R	R	R	D	D	R	R	R	R	D
New Jersey	R[1]	D	D	R	D	D	D	D	D	R	R	R	R	D	R	R	R	R	D	D
New Mexico														D	D	R	R	R	D	D
New York	R	R	D	R	D	R	D	R	D	R	R	R	R	D	R	R	R	R	D	D
North Carolina	SD	[2]	R	R	D	D	D	D	D	D	D	D	D	D	D	D	D	R	D	D
North Dakota									[9]	R	R	R	R	D	D	R	R	R	D	D
Ohio	R	R	R	R	R	R	R	R	R[10]	R	R	R	R	D	D	R	R	R	D	D
Oklahoma													D	D	D	R	D	R	D	D
Oregon	R	R	D	R	R	R	R	R	R[11]	R	R	R	R	D	R	R	R	R	D	D
Pennsylvania	R	R	R	R	R	R	R	R	R	R	R	R	R	PR	R	R	R	R	R	D
Rhode Island	R	R	R	R	R	R	R	R	R	R	R	R	R	D	R	R	R	D	D	D
South Carolina	SD	[2]	R	R	D	D	D	D	D	D	D	D	D	D	D	D	D	D	D	D
South Dakota									R	D	R	R	R	PR	R	R	R	R	D	D
Tennessee	CU	[2]	R	D	D	D	D	D	D	D	D	D	D	D	D	R	D	R	D	D
Texas	SD	[2]	[3]	D	D	D	D	D	D	D	D	D					D	R	D	D
Utah											D	R	R	R	D	R	R	R	D	D
Vermont	R	R	R	R	R	R	R	R	R	R	R	R	R	R	R	R	R	R	R	R
Virginia	CU	[2]	[3]	R	D	D	D	D	D	D	D	D	D	D	D	D	D	R	D	D
Washington									R	D	R	R	R	PR	D	R	R	R	D	D
West Virginia		R	R	R	D	D	D	D	D	R	R	R	R	D	R[16]	R	R	R	D	D
Wisconsin	R	R	R	R	R	R	R	R	D	R	R	R	R	D	R	R	PR	R	D	D
Wyoming									R	D	R	R	R	D	D	R	R	R	D	D
Winning Party	R	R	R	R	R	R	D	R	D	R	R	R	R	D	D	R	R	R	D	D

NOTE: With the exception of the District of Columbia, blanks indicate states not yet admitted to the Union. The District of Columbia received the presidential vote in 1961. AI—American Independent Party; CU—Constitutional Union Party; D—Democratic Party; PP—People's Party; PR—Progressive (Bull Moose) Party; R—Republican Party; SD—Southern Democratic Party; SR—States' Rights Democratic Party.

1. Four electors voted Republican; three, Democratic.

2. Confederate states did not vote in 1864.

3. Did not vote in 1868.

4. Votes were not counted.

5. Three votes for Greeley not counted.

6. Five electors voted Democratic; one, Republican.

7. Eight electors voted Democratic; one, Republican.

8. Nine electors voted Republican; five, Democratic.

9. One vote each for Democratic, Republican, and People's parties.

10. Twenty-two electors voted Republican; one, Democratic.

11. Three electors voted Republican; one, People's Party.

12. Eight electors voted Republican; one, Democratic.

1940	*1944*	*1948*	*1952*	*1956*	*1960*	*1964*	*1968*	*1972*	*1976*	*1980*	*1984*	*1988*	*1992*	*1996*	*2000*	*2004*	*2008*	*2012*	*Dems*	*Reps*	*Other*
D	D	SR	D	D[18]	D[19]	R	AI	R	D	R	R	R	R	R	R	R	R	R	22	13	3
					R	D	R	R	R	R	R	R	R	R	R	R	R	R	1	13	0
D	D	D	R	R	R	R	R	R	R	R	R	R	R	D	R	R	R	R	8	18	0
D	D	D	D	D	D	D	AI	R	R	R	R	R	D	D	R	R	R	R	26	9	2
D	D	D	R	R	R	D	R	R	R	R	R	R	D	D	D	D	D	D	15	23	1
R	R	D	R	R	R	D	R	R	R	R	R	R	D	R	R	R	D	D	12	22	1
D	D	R	R	R	D	D	D	R	R	R	R	R	D	D	D	D	D	D	17	22	0
D	D	R	R	R	D	D	R	R	D	R	R	R	D	D	D	D	D	D	20	18	1
						D	D	D	D	D	D	D	D	D	D[26]	D	D	D	13	0	0
D	D	D	R	R	R	D	R	R	D	R	R	R	R	D	R	R	D	D	22	15	1
D	D	D	D	D	D	R	AI	R	D	D	R	R	D	R	R	R	R	R	27	9	2
					D	D	D	R	D	D	R	D	D	D	D	D	D	D	12	2	0
D	D	D	R	R	R	D	R	R	R	R	R	R	R	R	R	R	R	R	10	20	1
D	D	D	R	R	D	D	R	R	R	R	R	R	D	D	D	D	D	D	15	24	0
R	R	R	R	R	R	D	R	R	R	R	R	R	R	R	R	R	D	R	8	31	0
R	R	D	R	R	R	D	R	R	R	R	R	D	D	D	D	R	D	D	11	28	0
R	R	R	R	R	R	D	R	R	R	R	R	R	R	R	R	R	R	R	6	31	1
D	D	D	D	R	R	D	R	R	D	R	R	R	D	D	R	R	R	R	24	14	1
D	D	SR	D	R	D	R	AI	R	D	R	R	R	D	D	R	R	R	R	23	11	3
R	R	R	R	R	R	D	D	R	R	R	R	R	D	D	D	D	D	D	9	30	0
D	D	R	R	R	D	D	D	R	D	D	R	R	D	D	D	D	D	D	26	12	1
D	D	D	R	R	D	D	D	D	D	R	R	D	D	D	D	D	D	D	19	20	0
R	D	R	R	R	D	D	D	R	R	R	R	R	D	D	D	D	D	D	12	26	1
D	D	D	R	R	D	D	D	R	D	D	D	D	D	D	D	D[27]	D	D	18	20	1
D	D	SR	D	D	[20]	R	AI	R	D	R	R	R	R	R	R	R	R	R	21	12	4
D	D	D	R	D	D	D	R	R	D	R	R	R	D	D	R	R	R	R	22	17	0
D	D	D	R	R	R	D	R	R	R	R	R	R	D	R	R	R	R	R	11	20	0
R	R	R	R	R	D	R	R	R	R	R	R	R	R	R	R	R	R[28]	R	7	30	0
D	D	D	R	R	D	D	R	R	R	R	R	R	D	D	R	R	D	D	17	20	1
D	D	R	R	R	R	D	R	R	R	R	R	R	D	D	R	D	D	D	11	28	0
D	D	R	R	R	D	D	R	R	R	R	R	R	D	D	D	D	D	D	20	19	0
D	D	D	R	R	D	D	R	R	R	R	R	R	D	D	D	R	D	D	14	12	0
D	D	R	R	R	D	D	D	R	D	R	R	D	D	D	D	D	D	D	20	19	0
D	D	D	D	D	D	D	R[22]	R	D	R	R	R	R	R	R	R	D	R	24	13	1
R	R	R	R	R	R	D	R	R	R	R	R	R	R	R	R	R	R	R	5	25	1
D	R	D	R	R	R	D	R	R	D	R	R	R	D	D	R	R	D	D	12	27	0
D	D	D	R	R	R[21]	D	R	R	R	R	R	R	R	R	R	R	R	R	10	17	0
D	D	R	R	R	R	D	R	R	R	R	R	D	D	D	D	D	D	D	14	25	0
D	D	R	R	R	D	D	D	R	D	R	R	R	D	D	D	D	D	D	13	25	1
D	D	D	R	R	D	D	D	R	D	D	R	D	D	D	D	D	D	D	19	20	0
D	D	SR	D	D	D	R	R	R	D	R	R	R	R	R	R	R	R	R	21	15	2
R	R	R	R	R	R	D	R	R	R	R	R	R	R	R	R	R	R	R	4	26	1
D	D	D[17]	R	R	R	D	R	R	D	R	R	R	D	D	R	R	R	R	22	15	1
D	D	D	R	R	D	D	D	R	D	R	R	R	R	R	R	R	R	R	23	13	1
D	D	D	R	R	R	D	R	R	R	R	R	R	R	R	R	R	R	R	8	22	0
R	R	R	R	R	R	D	R	R	R	R	R	R	D	D	D	D	D	D	7	32	0
D	D	D	R	D	D	D	D	R[23]	R	R	R	R	R	R	R	R	D	D	21	15	1
D	D	D	R	R	R	D	D	R	R[24]	R	R	D	D	D	D	D	D	D	16	14	1
D	D	D	D	R	D	D	D	R	D	D	R	D[25]	D	D	R	R	R	R	20	18	0
D	R	D	R	R	R	D	R	R	D	R	R	D	D	D	D	D	D	D	15	23	1
D	R	D	R	R	R	D	R	R	R	R	R	R	R	R	R	R	R	R	8	23	0
D	D	D	R	R	D	D	R	R	D	R	R	R	D	D	R	R	D	D	16	23	0

13. Twelve electors voted Republican; one, Democratic.

14. Seven electors voted Democratic; one, Republican.

15. Six electors voted Democratic; two, Republican.

16. Seven electors voted Republican; one, Democratic.

17. Eleven electors voted Democratic; one, States' Rights.

18. One elector voted for Walter B. Jones.

19. Six of eleven electors voted for Harry F. Byrd.

20. Eight independent electors voted for Byrd.

21. One vote cast for Byrd.

22. Twelve electors voted Republican; one, American Independent.

23. One elector voted Libertarian.

24. One elector voted for Ronald Reagan.

25. One elector voted for Lloyd Bentsen.

26. One elector did not vote.

27. One elector voted for John Edwards.

28. Obama won the vote of one elector.

2008 Presidential Election

State	Total vote	Barack Obama (Democrat)		John McCain (Republican)		Other		Dem.-Rep.	
		Votes	%	Votes	%	Votes	%	Plurality	
Alabama	2,099,819	813,479	38.7	1,266,546	60.3	19,794	0.9	453,067	R
Alaska	326,197	123,594	37.9	193,841	59.4	8,762	2.7	70,247	R
Arizona	2,293,475	1,034,707	45.1	1,230,111	53.6	28,657	1.2	195,404	R
Arkansas	1,086,617	422,310	38.9	638,017	58.7	26,290	2.4	215,707	R
California	13,561,900	8,274,473	61.0	5,011,781	37.0	275,646	2.0	3,262,692	D
Colorado	2,401,462	1,288,633	53.7	1,073,629	44.7	39,200	1.6	215,004	D
Connecticut	1,646,797	977,772	60.6	629,428	38.2	19,597	1.1	368,344	D
Delaware	412,412	255,459	61.9	152,374	36.9	4,579	1.1	103,085	D
Florida	8,390,744	4,282,074	51.0	4,045,624	48.2	63,046	0.8	236,450	D
Georgia	3,924,486	1,844,123	47.0	2,048,759	52.2	31,604	0.8	204,636	R
Hawaii	453,568	325,871	71.8	120,566	26.6	7,131	1.6	205,305	D
Idaho	655,122	236,440	36.1	403,012	61.5	15,670	2.4	166,572	R
Illinois	5,522,371	3,419,348	61.9	2,031,179	36.8	71,844	1.3	1,388,169	D
Indiana	2,751,054	1,374,039	49.9	1,345,648	48.9	31,367	1.1	28,391	D
Iowa	1,537,123	828,940	53.9	682,379	44.4	25,804	1.7	146,561	D
Kansas	1,235,872	514,765	41.7	699,655	56.6	21,452	1.7	184,890	R
Kentucky	1,826,620	751,985	41.2	1,048,462	57.4	26,173	1.4	296,477	R
Louisiana	1,960,761	782,989	39.9	1,148,275	58.6	29,497	1.5	365,286	R
Maine	731,163	421,923	57.7	295,273	40.4	13,967	1.9	126,650	D
Maryland	2,631,596	1,629,467	61.9	959,862	36.5	42,267	1.6	669,605	D
Massachusetts	3,080,985	1,904,097	61.8	1,108,854	36.0	68,034	2.2	795,243	D
Michigan	5,001,766	2,872,579	57.4	2,048,639	41.0	80,548	1.6	823,940	D
Minnesota	2,910,369	1,573,354	54.1	1,275,409	43.8	61,606	2.1	297,945	D
Mississippi	1,289,865	554,662	43.0	724,597	56.2	10,606	0.8	169,935	R
Missouri	2,925,205	1,441,911	49.3	1,445,814	49.4	37,480	1.3	3,903	R
Montana	490,302	231,667	47.3	242,763	49.5	15,872	3.2	11,096	R
Nebraska	801,281	333,319	41.6	452,979	56.5	14,983	1.9	119,660	R
Nevada	967,848	533,736	55.1	412,827	42.7	21,285	2.2	120,909	D
New Hampshire	710,970	384,826	54.1	316,534	44.5	9,610	1.4	68,292	D
New Jersey	3,868,237	2,215,422	57.3	1,613,207	41.7	39,608	1.0	602,215	D
New Mexico	830,158	472,422	56.9	346,832	41.8	10,904	1.3	125,590	D
New York	7,640,931	4,804,945	62.9	2,752,771	36.0	83,215	1.1	2,052,174	D
North Carolina	4,310,789	2,142,651	49.7	2,128,474	49.4	39,664	0.9	14,177	D
North Dakota	316,621	141,278	44.6	168,601	53.3	6,742	2.1	27,323	R
Ohio	5,708,350	2,940,044	51.5	2,677,820	46.9	90,486	1.6	262,224	D
Oklahoma	1,462,661	502,496	34.4	960,165	65.6	0	—	457,669	R
Oregon	1,827,864	1,037,291	56.7	738,475	40.4	52,098	2.9	298,816	D
Pennsylvania	6,013,272	3,276,363	54.5	2,655,885	44.2	81,024	1.0	620,478	D
Rhode Island	471,766	296,571	62.9	165,391	35.1	9,804	1.7	131,180	D
South Carolina	1,920,969	862,449	44.9	1,034,896	53.9	23,624	1.2	172,447	R
South Dakota	381,975	170,924	44.7	203,054	53.2	7,997	2.1	32,130	R
Tennessee	2,599,749	1,087,437	41.8	1,479,178	56.9	33,134	1.3	391,741	R
Texas	8,077,795	3,528,633	43.7	4,479,328	55.5	69,834	0.9	950,695	R
Utah	952,370	327,670	34.4	596,030	62.6	28,670	3.0	268,360	R
Vermont	325,046	219,262	67.5	98,974	30.4	6,810	2.1	120,288	D
Virginia	3,723,260	1,959,532	52.6	1,725,005	46.3	38,723	1.0	234,527	D
Washington	3,036,878	1,750,848	57.7	1,229,216	40.5	56,814	1.9	521,632	D
West Virginia	713,451	303,857	42.6	397,466	55.7	12,128	1.7	93,609	R
Wisconsin	2,983,417	1,677,211	56.2	1,262,393	42.3	43,813	1.5	414,818	D
Wyoming	254,658	82,868	32.5	164,958	64.8	6,832	2.7	82,090	R
District of Columbia	265,853	245,800	92.5	17,367	6.5	2,686	1.0	228,433	D
Totals	131,313,820	69,498,516	52.9	59,948,323	45.7	1,866,981	1.4	9,550,193	D

2008 Electoral Votes and Map

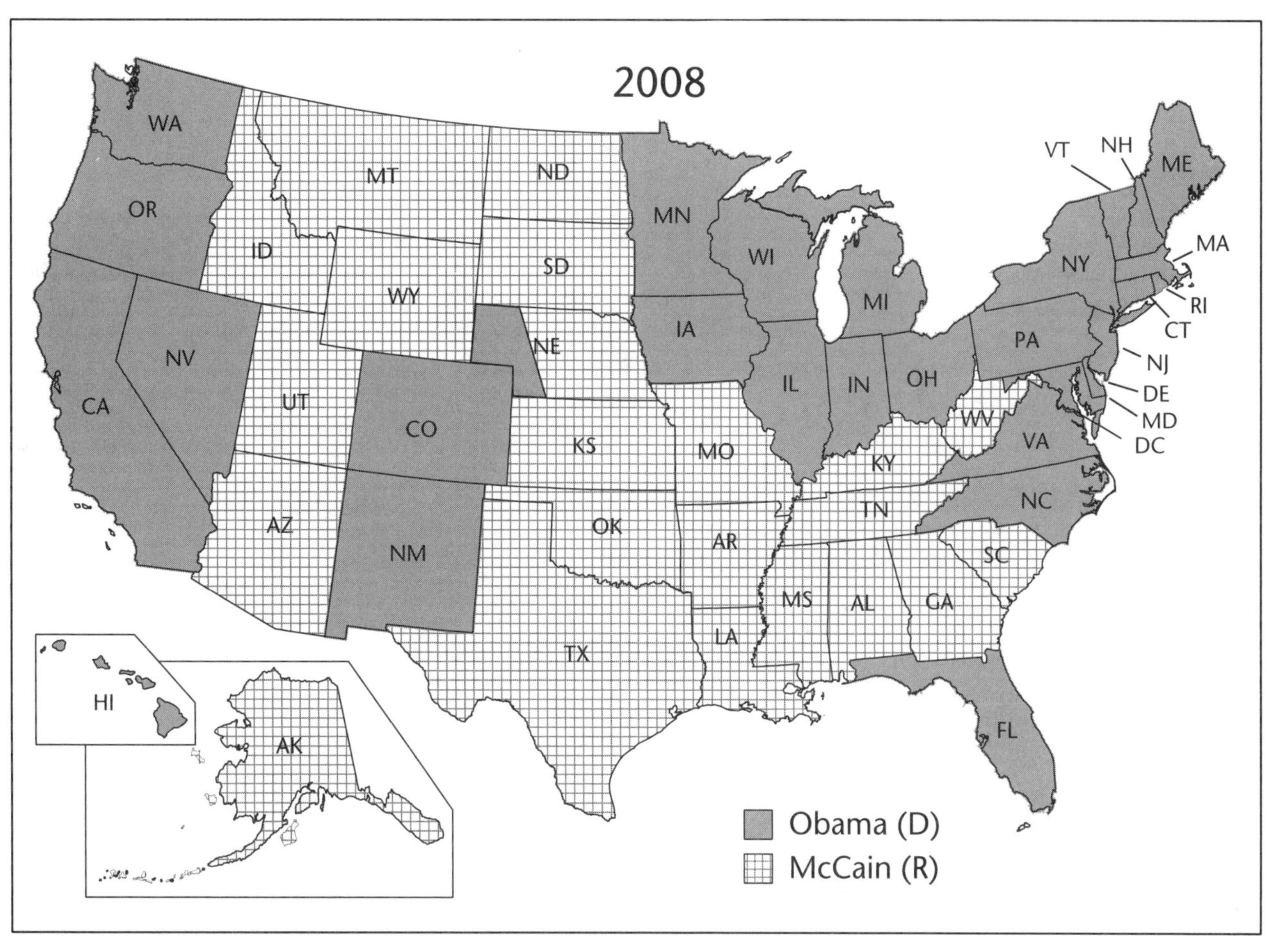

States	*Electoral votes*	*Obama*	*McCain*
Alabama	(9)	–	9
Alaska	(3)	–	3
Arizona	(10)	–	10
Arkansas	(6)	–	6
California	(55)	55	–
Colorado	(9)	9	–
Connecticut	(7)	7	–
Delaware	(3)	3	–
District of Columbia	(3)	3	–
Florida	(27)	27	–
Georgia	(15)	–	15
Hawaii	(4)	4	–
Idaho	(4)	–	4
Illinois	(21)	21	–
Indiana	(11)	11	–
Iowa	(7)	7	–
Kansas	(6)	–	6
Kentucky	(8)	–	8
Louisiana	(9)	–	9
Maine	(4)	4	–
Maryland	(10)	10	–
Massachusetts	(12)	12	–
Michigan	(17)	17	–
Minnesota	(10)	10	–
Mississippi	(6)	–	6
Missouri	(11)	–	11
Montana	(3)	–	3
Nebraska[1]	(5)	1	4
Nevada	(5)	5	–
New Hampshire	(4)	4	–
New Jersey	(15)	15	–
New Mexico	(5)	5	–
New York	(31)	31	–
North Carolina	(15)	15	–
North Dakota	(3)	–	3
Ohio	(20)	20	–
Oklahoma	(7)	–	7
Oregon	(7)	7	–
Pennsylvania	(21)	21	–
Rhode Island	(4)	4	–
South Carolina	(8)	–	8
South Dakota	(3)	–	3
Tennessee	(11)	–	11
Texas	(34)	–	34
Utah	(5)	–	5
Vermont	(3)	3	–
Virginia	(13)	13	–
Washington	(11)	11	–
West Virginia	(5)	–	5
Wisconsin	(10)	10	–
Wyoming	(3)	–	3
Totals	(538)	365	173

1. Barack Obama won one electoral vote. Nebraska divides three of its five votes by the winner in a congressional districts; the other two go to the statewide winner.

2012 Presidential Election

State	Total vote	Barack Obama (Democrat) Votes	%	Mitt Romney (Republican) Votes	%	Other Votes	%		Dem-Rep. Plurality
Alabama	2,074,338	759,696	38.4	1,255,925	60.6	22,717	1.1	R	460,229
Alaska	300,495	122,640	40.8	164,676	54.8	13,179	4.4	R	42,036
Arizona	2,299,254	1,025,232	44.6	1,233,654	53.6	40,368	1.8	R	208,422
Arkansas	1,069,468	394,409	36.9	647,744	60.6	27,315	2.6	R	253,335
California	13,038,547	7,854,285	60.2	4,839,958	37.1	344,304	2.6	D	3,014,327
Colorado	2,569,522	1,323,102	51.5	1,185,243	46.1	61,177	2.4	D	137,858
Connecticut	1,558,960	905,083	58.1	634,892	40.7	18,985	1.2	D	270,191
Delaware	413,921	242,584	58.6	165,484	40.0	5,822	1.4	D	77,100
Florida	8,474,179	4,237,756	50.0	4,163,447	49.1	72,976	0.9	D	74,309
Georgia	3,900,050	1,773,827	45.5	2,078,688	53.3	47,535	1.2	R	304,861
Hawaii	434,697	306,658	70.5	121,015	27.8	7,024	1.6	D	185,643
Idaho	652,346	212,787	32.6	420,911	64.5	18,648	2.9	R	208,124
Illinois	5,242,014	3,019,512	57.6	2,135,216	40.7	87,286	1.7	D	884,286
Indiana	2,624,534	1,152,887	43.9	1,420,543	54.1	51,104	2.0	R	267,656
Iowa	1,582,180	822,544	52.0	730,617	46.2	29,019	1.8	D	91,927
Kansas	1,159,971	440,726	38.0	692,634	59.7	26,611	2.3	R	251,908
Kentucky	1,797,212	679,370	37.8	1,087,190	60.5	30,652	1.7	R	407,820
Louisiana	1,994,065	809,141	40.6	1,152,262	57.8	32,662	1.6	R	343,121
Maine	713,180	401,306	56.3	292,276	41.0	19,598	2.8	D	109,030
Maryland	2,707,327	1,677,844	62.0	971,869	35.9	57,614	2.1	D	705,975
Massachusetts	3,167,767	1,921,290	60.7	1,188,314	37.5	58,163	1.8	D	732,976
Michigan	4,730,961	2,564,569	54.2	2,115,256	44.7	51,136	1.1	D	449,313
Minnesota	2,936,561	1,546,167	52.7	1,320,225	45.0	70,169	2.4	D	225,942
Mississippi	1,285,584	562,949	43.8	710,746	55.3	11,889	0.9	R	147,797
Missouri	2,757,323	1,223,323	44.4	1,482,440	53.8	51,087	1.9	R	258,644
Montana	484,048	201,839	41.7	267,928	55.4	14,281	3.0	R	66,089
Nebraska	794,379	302,081	38.0	475,064	59.8	17,234	2.2	R	172,983
Nevada	1,014,918	531,373	52.4	463,567	45.7	19,978	2.0	D	67,806
New Hampshire	710,972	369,561	52.0	329,918	46.4	11,493	1.6	D	39,643
New Jersey	3,640,292	2,125,101	58.4	1,477,568	40.6	37,623	1.0	D	647,533
New Mexico	783,757	415,335	53.0	335,788	42.8	32,635	4.2	D	79,547
New York	7,081,159	4,480,244	63.3	2,489,569	35.2	104,910	1.5	D	1,990,675
North Carolina	4,505,372	2,178,391	48.4	2,270,395	50.4	56,586	1.3	R	92,004
North Dakota	322,627	124,966	58.3	188,320	58.3	9,646	3.0	R	63,354
Ohio	5,580,840	2,827,710	50.7	2,661,433	47.7	91,697	1.6	D	166,277
Oklahoma	1,334,872	443,547	33.2	891,325	66.8	–	–	R	447,778
Oregon	1,789,270	970,488	54.2	754,175	42.1	64,607	3.6	D	216,313
Pennsylvania	5,753,670	2,990,274	52.0	2,680,434	46.6	82,962	1.4	D	309,840
Rhode Island	446,049	279,677	62.7	157,204	35.2	9,168	2.1	D	122,473
South Carolina	1,964,118	865,941	44.1	1,071,645	54.6	26,532	1.4	R	205,704
South Dakota	363,815	145,039	39.9	210,610	57.9	8,166	2.2	R	65,571
Tennessee	2,458,577	960,709	39.1	1,462,330	59.5	35,538	1.5	R	501,621
Texas	7,993,851	3,308,124	41.4	4,569,843	57.2	115,884	1.5	R	1,261,719
Utah	1,017,440	251,813	24.8	740,600	72.8	25,027	2.5	R	488,787
Vermont	299,290	199,239	66.6	92,698	31.0	7,353	2.5	D	106,541
Virginia	3,854,489	1,971,820	51.2	1,822,522	47.3	60,147	1.6	D	149,298
Washington	3,125,516	1,755,369	56.2	1,290,670	41.3	79,450	2.5	D	464,726
West Virginia	670,438	238,269	35.5	417,655	62.3	14,514	2.2	R	179,386
Wisconsin	3,068,434	1,620,985	52.8	1,407,966	45.9	39,483	1.3	D	213,019
Wyoming	249,061	69,286	27.8	170,962	68.6	8,813	3.5	R	101,676
District of Columbia	293,764	267,070	90.9	21,371	7.3	5,313	1.8	D	245,689
Totals	129,085,474	65,915,796	51.1	60,933,500	47.2	2,236,178	1.7	D	4,738,804

NOTE: Percentages are of the total vote.

2012 Electoral Votes and Map

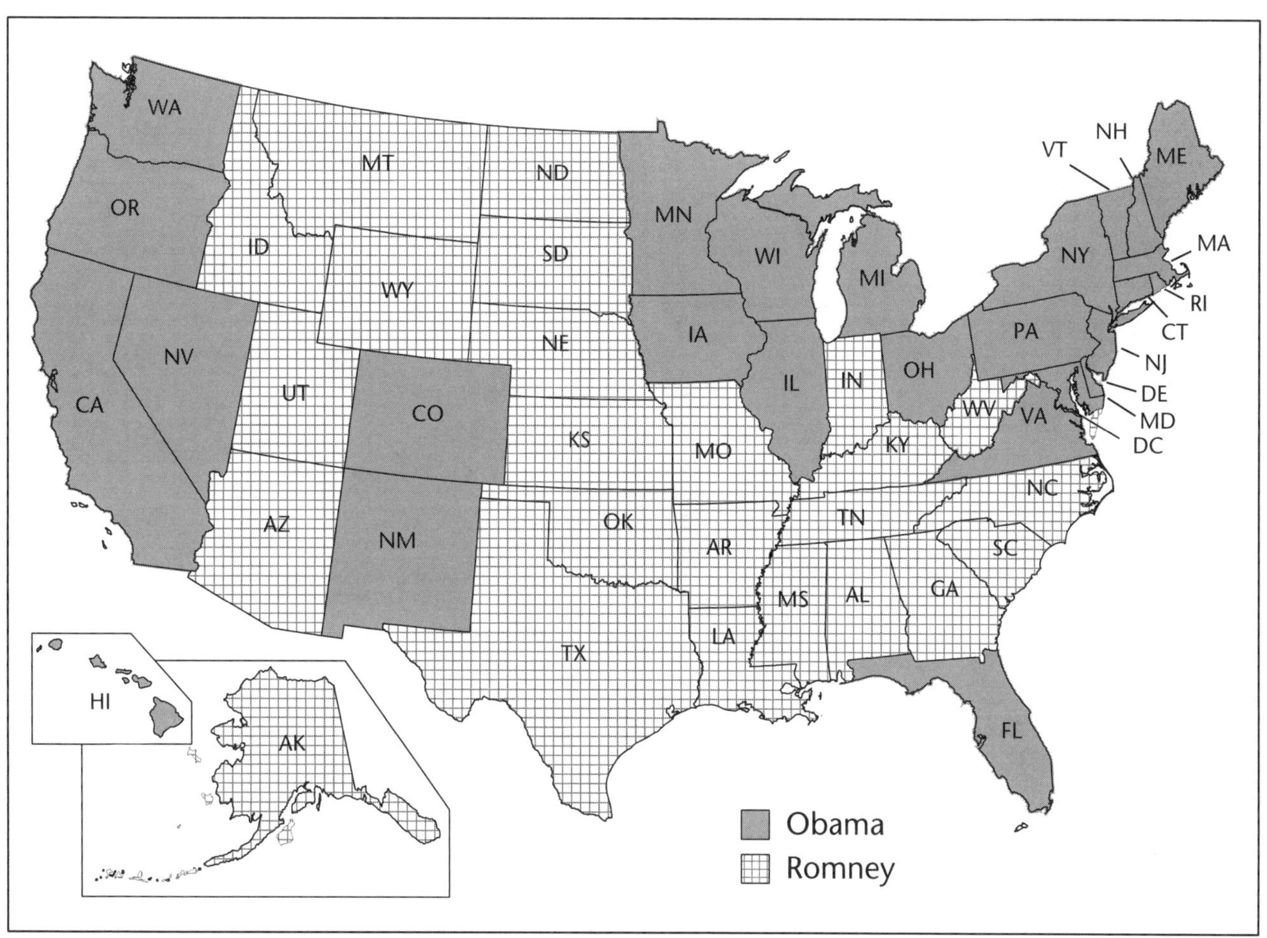

States	Electoral votes	Obama	Romney
Alabama	9	–	9
Alaska	3	–	3
Arizona	11	–	11
Arkansas	6	–	6
California	55	55	–
Colorado	9	9	–
Connecticut	7	7	–
Delaware	3	3	–
District of Columbia	3	3	–
Florida	29	29	–
Georgia	16	–	16
Hawaii	4	4	–
Idaho	4	–	4
Illinois	20	20	–
Indiana	11	–	11
Iowa	6	6	–
Kansas	6	–	6
Kentucky	8	–	8
Louisiana	8	–	8
Maine	4	4	–
Maryland	10	10	–
Massachusetts	11	11	–
Michigan	16	16	–
Minnesota	10	10	–
Mississippi	6	–	6
Missouri	10	–	10
Montana	3	–	3
Nebraska	5	–	5
Nevada	6	6	–
New Hampshire	4	4	–
New Jersey	14	14	–
New Mexico	5	5	–
New York	29	29	–
North Carolina	15	–	15
North Dakota	3	–	3
Ohio	18	18	–
Oklahoma	7	–	7
Oregon	7	7	–
Pennsylvania	20	20	–
Rhode Island	4	4	–
South Carolina	9	–	9
South Dakota	3	–	3
Tennessee	11	–	11
Texas	38	–	38
Utah	6	–	6
Vermont	3	3	–
Virginia	13	13	–
Washington	12	12	–
West Virginia	5	–	5
Wisconsin	10	10	–
Wyoming	3	–	3
Totals	538	332	206

Distribution of House Seats and Electoral Votes

State	*U.S. House Seats* 1963–1973	1970 Census changes	1973–1983	1980 Census changes	1983–1993	1990 Census changes	1993–2003	2000 Census changes	2003–2013	2010 Census changes	2013–2023	*Electoral Votes* 1952, 1956, 1960	1964, 1968	1972, 1976, 1980	1984, 1988	1992, 1996, 2000	2004, 2008	2012, 2016, 2020
Alabama	8	−1	7	—	7	—	7	—	7	—	7	11	10	9	9	9	9	9
Alaska	1	—	1	—	1	—	1	—	1	—	1	3	3	3	3	3	3	3
Arizona	3	+1	4	+1	5	+1	6	+2	8	+1	9	4	5	6	7	8	10	11
Arkansas	4	—	4	—	4	—	4	—	4	—	4	8	6	6	6	6	6	6
California	38	+5	43	+2	45	+7	52	+1	53	—	53	32	40	45	47	54	55	55
Colorado	4	+1	5	+1	6	—	6	+1	7	—	7	6	6	7	8	8	9	9
Connecticut	6	—	6	—	6	—	6	−1	5	—	5	8	8	8	8	8	7	7
Delaware	1	—	1	—	1	—	1	—	1	—	1	3	3	3	3	3	3	3
Dist. of Col.	—	—	—	—	—	—	—	—	—	—	—	—	3	3	3	3	3	3
Florida	12	+3	15	+4	19	+4	23	+2	25	+2	27	10	14	17	21	25	27	29
Georgia	10	—	10	—	10	+1	11	+2	13	+1	14	12	12	12	12	13	15	16
Hawaii	2	—	2	—	2	—	2	—	2	—	2	3	4	4	4	4	4	4
Idaho	2	—	2	—	2	—	2	—	2	—	2	4	4	4	4	4	4	4
Illinois	24	—	24	−2	22	−2	20	−1	19	−1	18	27	26	26	24	22	21	20
Indiana	11	—	11	−1	10	—	10	−1	9	—	9	13	13	13	12	12	11	11
Iowa	7	−1	6	—	6	−1	5	—	5	−1	4	10	9	8	8	7	7	6
Kansas	5	—	5	—	5	−1	4	—	4	—	4	8	7	7	7	6	6	6
Kentucky	7	—	7	—	7	−1	6	—	6	—	6	10	9	9	9	8	8	8
Louisiana	8	—	8	—	8	−1	7	—	7	−1	6	10	10	10	10	9	9	8
Maine	2	—	2	—	2	—	2	—	2	—	2	5	4	4	4	4	4	4
Maryland	8	—	8	—	8	—	8	—	8	—	8	9	10	10	10	10	10	10
Massachusetts	12	—	12	−1	11	−1	10	—	10	−1	9	16	14	14	13	12	12	11
Michigan	19	—	19	−1	18	−2	16	−1	15	−1	14	20	21	21	20	18	17	16
Minnesota	8	—	8	—	8	—	8	—	8	—	8	11	10	10	10	10	10	10
Mississippi	5	—	5	—	5	—	5	−1	4	—	4	8	7	7	7	7	6	6
Missouri	10	—	10	−1	9	—	9	—	9	−1	8	13	12	12	11	11	11	10
Montana	2	—	2	—	2	−1	1	—	1	—	1	4	4	4	4	3	3	3
Nebraska	3	—	3	—	3	—	3	—	3	—	3	6	5	5	5	5	5	5
Nevada	1	—	1	+1	2	—	2	+1	3	+1	4	3	3	3	4	4	5	6
New Hampshire	2	—	2	—	2	—	2	—	2	—	2	4	4	4	4	4	4	4
New Jersey	15	—	15	−1	14	−1	13	—	13	−1	12	16	17	17	16	15	15	14
New Mexico	2	—	2	+1	3	—	3	—	3	—	3	4	4	4	5	5	5	5
New York	41	−2	39	−5	34	−3	31	−2	29	−2	27	45	43	41	36	33	31	29
North Carolina	11	—	11	—	11	+1	12	+1	13	—	13	14	13	13	13	14	15	15
North Dakota	2	−1	1	—	1	—	1	—	1	—	1	4	4	3	3	3	3	3
Ohio	24	−1	23	−2	21	−2	19	−1	18	−2	16	25	26	25	23	21	20	18
Oklahoma	6	—	6	—	6	—	6	−1	5	—	5	8	8	8	8	8	7	7
Oregon	4	—	4	+1	5	—	5	—	5	—	5	6	6	6	7	7	7	7
Pennsylvania	27	−2	25	−2	23	−2	21	−2	19	−1	18	32	29	27	25	23	21	20
Rhode Island	2	—	2	—	2	—	2	—	2	—	2	4	4	4	4	4	4	4
South Carolina	6	—	6	—	6	—	6	—	6	+1	7	8	8	8	8	8	8	9
South Dakota	2	—	2	−1	1	—	1	—	1	—	1	4	4	4	3	3	3	3
Tennessee	9	−1	8	+1	9	—	9	—	9	—	9	11	11	10	11	11	11	11
Texas	23	+1	24	+3	27	+3	30	+2	32	+4	36	24	25	26	29	32	34	38
Utah	2	—	2	+1	3	—	3	—	3	+1	4	4	4	4	5	5	5	6
Vermont	1	—	1	—	1	—	1	—	1	—	1	3	3	3	3	3	3	3
Virginia	10	—	10	—	10	+1	11	—	11	—	11	12	12	12	12	13	13	13
Washington	7	—	7	+1	8	+1	9	—	9	+1	10	9	9	9	10	11	11	12
West Virginia	5	−1	4	—	4	−1	3	—	3	—	3	8	7	6	6	5	5	5
Wisconsin	10	−1	9	—	9	—	9	−1	8	—	8	12	12	11	11	11	10	10
Wyoming	1	—	1	—	1	—	1	—	1	—	1	3	3	3	3	3	3	3

NOTE: Table was constructed by CQ Press editors based on the censuses of 1950, 1960, 1970, 1980, 1990, 2000, and 2010.

Party Affiliations in Congress and the Presidency, 1789–2015

Year	Congress	House		Senate		President
		Majority party	*Principal minority party*	*Majority party*	*Principal minority party*	
1789–1791	1st	AD-38	Op-26	AD-17	Op-9	F (Washington)
1791–1793	2nd	F-37	DR-33	F-16	DR-13	F (Washington)
1793–1795	3rd	DR-57	F-48	F-17	DR-13	F (Washington)
1795–1797	4th	F-54	DR-52	F-19	DR-13	F (Washington)
1797–1799	5th	F-58	DR-48	F-20	DR-12	F (J. Adams)
1799–1801	6th	F-64	DR-42	F-19	DR-13	F (J. Adams)
1801–1803	7th	DR-69	F-36	DR-18	F-13	DR (Jefferson)
1803–1805	8th	DR-102	F-39	DR-25	F-9	DR (Jefferson)
1805–1807	9th	DR-116	F-25	DR-27	F-7	DR (Jefferson)
1807–1809	10th	DR-118	F-24	DR-28	F-6	DR (Jefferson)
1809–1811	11th	DR-94	F-48	DR-28	F-6	DR (Madison)
1811–1813	12th	DR-108	F-36	DR-30	F-6	DR (Madison)
1813–1815	13th	DR-112	F-68	DR-27	F-9	DR (Madison)
1815–1817	14th	DR-117	F-65	DR-25	F-11	DR (Madison)
1817–1819	15th	DR-141	F-42	DR-34	F-10	DR (Monroe)
1819–1821	16th	DR-156	F-27	DR-35	F-7	DR (Monroe)
1821–1823	17th	DR-158	F-25	DR-44	F-4	DR (Monroe)
1823–1825	18th	DR-187	F-26	DR-44	F-4	DR (Monroe)
1825–1827	19th	AD-105	J-97	AD-26	J-20	DR (J. Q. Adams)
1827–1829	20th	J-119	AD-94	J-28	AD-20	DR (J. Q. Adams)
1829–1831	21st	D-139	NR-74	D-26	NR-22	DR (Jackson)
1831–1833	22nd	D-141	NR-58	D-25	NR-21	D (Jackson)
1833–1835	23rd	D-147	AM-53	D-20	NR-20	D (Jackson)
1835–1837	24th	D-145	W-98	D-27	W-25	D (Jackson)
1837–1839	25th	D-108	W-107	D-30	W-18	D (Van Buren)
1839–1841	26th	D-124	W-118	D-28	W-22	D (Van Buren)
1841–1843	27th	W-133	D-102	W-28	D-22	W (W. Harrison); W (Tyler)
1843–1845	28th	D-142	W-79	W-28	D-25	W (Tyler)
1845–1847	29th	D-143	W-77	D-31	W-25	D (Polk)
1847–1849	30th	W-115	D-108	D-36	W-21	D (Polk)
1849–1851	31st	D-112	W-109	D-35	W-25	W (Taylor); W (Fillmore)
1851–1853	32nd	D-140	W-88	D-35	W-24	W (Fillmore)
1853–1855	33rd	D-159	W-71	D-38	W-22	D (Pierce)
1855–1857	34th	R-108	D-83	D-40	R-15	D (Pierce)
1857–1859	35th	D-118	R-92	D-36	R-20	D (Buchanan)
1859–1861	36th	R-114	D-92	D-36	R-26	D (Buchanan)
1861–1863	37th	R-105	D-43	R-31	D-10	R (Lincoln)
1863–1865	38th	R-102	D-75	R-36	D-9	R (Lincoln)
1865–1867	39th	U-149	D-42	U-42	D-10	R (Lincoln); R (A. Johnson)
1867–1869	40th	R-143	D-49	R-42	D-11	R (A. Johnson)
1869–1871	41st	R-149	D-63	R-56	D-11	R (Grant)
1871–1873	42nd	R-134	D-104	R-52	D-17	R (Grant)
1873–1875	43rd	R-194	D-92	R-49	D-19	R (Grant)
1875–1877	44th	D-169	R-109	R-45	D-29	R (Grant)
1877–1879	45th	D-153	R-140	R-39	D-36	R (Hayes)
1879–1881	46th	D-149	R-130	D-42	R-33	R (Hayes)
1881–1883	47th	R-147	D-135	R-37	D-37	R (Garfield); R (Arthur)
1883–1885	48th	D-197	R-118	R-38	D-36	R (Arthur)
1885–1887	49th	D-183	R-140	R-43	D-34	D (Cleveland)
1887–1889	50th	D-169	R-152	R-39	D-37	D (Cleveland)
1889–1891	51st	R-166	D-159	R-39	D-37	R (B. Harrison)
1891–1893	52nd	D-235	R-88	R-47	D-39	R (B. Harrison)
1893–1895	53rd	D-218	R-127	D-44	R-38	D (Cleveland)
1895–1897	54th	R-244	D-105	R-43	D-39	D (Cleveland)
1897–1899	55th	R-204	D-113	R-47	D-34	R (McKinley)
1899–1901	56th	R-185	D-163	R-53	D-26	R (McKinley)
1901–1903	57th	R-197	D-151	R-55	D-31	R (McKinley); R (T. Roosevelt)
1903–1905	58th	R-208	D-178	R-57	D-33	R (T. Roosevelt)
1905–1907	59th	R-250	D-136	R-57	D-33	R (T. Roosevelt)
1907–1909	60th	R-222	D-164	R-61	D-31	R (T. Roosevelt)

(Continued)

(Continued)

Year	Congress	*House* Majority party	*House* Principal minority party	*Senate* Majority party	*Senate* Principal minority party	President
1909–1911	61st	R-219	D-172	R-61	D-32	R (Taft)
1911–1913	62nd	D-228	R-161	R-51	D-41	R (Taft)
1913–1915	63rd	D-291	R-127	D-51	R-44	D (Wilson)
1915–1917	64th	D-230	R-196	D-56	R-40	D (Wilson)
1917–1919	65th	D-216	R-210	D-53	R-42	D (Wilson)
1919–1921	66th	R-240	D-190	R-49	D-47	D (Wilson)
1921–1923	67th	R-301	D-131	R-59	D-37	R (Harding)
1923–1925	68th	R-225	D-205	R-51	D-43	R (Harding); R (Coolidge)
1925–1927	69th	R-247	D-183	R-56	D-39	R (Coolidge)
1927–1929	70th	R-237	D-195	R-49	D-46	R (Coolidge)
1929–1931	71st	R-267	D-167	R-56	D-39	R (Hoover)
1931–1933	72nd	D-220	R-214	R-48	D-47	R (Hoover)
1933–1935	73rd	D-310	R-117	D-60	R-35	D (F. Roosevelt)
1935–1937	74th	D-319	R-103	D-69	R-25	D (F. Roosevelt)
1937–1939	75th	D-331	R-89	D-76	R-16	D (F. Roosevelt)
1939–1941	76th	D-261	R-164	D-69	R-23	D (F. Roosevelt)
1941–1943	77th	D-268	R-162	D-66	R-28	D (F. Roosevelt)
1943–1945	78th	D-218	R-208	D-58	R-37	D (F. Roosevelt)
1945–1947	79th	D-242	R-190	D-56	R-38	D (F. Roosevelt); D (Truman)
1947–1949	80th	R-245	D-188	R-51	D-45	D (Truman)
1949–1951	81st	D-263	R-171	D-54	R-42	D (Truman)
1951–1953	82nd	D-234	R-199	D-49	R-47	D (Truman)
1953–1955	83rd	R-221	D-211	R-48	D-47	R (Eisenhower)
1955–1957	84th	D-232	R-203	D-48	R-47	R (Eisenhower)
1957–1959	85th	D-233	R-200	D-49	R-47	R (Eisenhower)
1959–1961	86th	D-283	R-153	D-64	R-34	R (Eisenhower)
1961–1963	87th	D-263	R-174	D-65	R-35	D (Kennedy)
1963–1965	88th	D-258	R-177	D-67	R-33	D (Kennedy); D (L. Johnson)
1965–1967	89th	D-295	R-140	D-68	R-32	D (L. Johnson)
1967–1969	90th	D-247	R-187	D-64	R-36	D (L. Johnson)
1969–1971	91st	D-243	R-192	D-57	R-43	R (Nixon)
1971–1973	92nd	D-254	R-180	D-54	R-44	R (Nixon)
1973–1975	93rd	D-239	R-192	D-56	R-42	R (Nixon); R (Ford)
1975–1977	94th	D-291	R-144	D-60	R-37	R (Ford)
1977–1979	95th	D-292	R-143	D-61	R-38	D (Carter)
1979–1981	96th	D-276	R-157	D-58	R-41	D (Carter)
1981–1983	97th	D-243	R-192	R-53	D-46	R (Reagan)
1983–1985	98th	D-269	R-165	R-54	D-46	R (Reagan)
1985–1987	99th	D-252	R-182	R-53	D-47	R (Reagan)
1987–1989	100th	D-258	R-177	D-55	R-45	R (Reagan)
1989–1991	101st	D-259	R-174	D-55	R-45	R (G. H.W. Bush)
1991–1993	102nd	D-267	R-167	D-56	R-44	R (G. H.W. Bush)
1993–1995	103rd	D-258	R-176	D-57	R-43	D (Clinton)
1995–1997	104th	R-230	D-204	R-53	D-47	D (Clinton)
1997–1999	105th	R-227	D-207	R-55	D-45	D (Clinton)
1999–2001	106th	R-222	D-211	R-55	D-45	D (Clinton)
2001–2003	107th	R-221	D-212	R-50	D-50	R (G.W. Bush)
2003–2005	108th	R-229	D-205	R-51	D-48	R (G.W. Bush)
2005–2007	109th	R-232	D-202	R-55	D-44	R (G.W. Bush)
2007–2009	110th	D-233	R-202	D-49*	R-49	R (G.W. Bush)
2009–2011	111th	D-236	R-199	D-57*	R-41	D (Obama)
2011–2013	112th	R-242	D-193	D-51*	R-47	D (Obama)
2013–2015	113th	R-234	D-201	D-53*	R-45	D (Obama)

SOURCE: U.S. Bureau of the Census, *Historical Statistics of the United States, Colonial Times to 1970* (Washington, D.C.: Government Printing Office, 1975); and U.S. Congress, Joint Committee on Printing, *Official Congressional Directory* (Washington, D.C.: Government Printing Office, 1967–); and *America Votes 26–30* (Washington, D.C,: CQ Press, 2007, 2009, 2011, 2013).

NOTE: Figures are for the beginning of the first session of each Congress. AD—Administration; AM—Anti-Masonic; D—Democratic; DR—Democratic-Republican; F—Federalist; J—Jacksonian; NR—National Republican; Op—Opposition; R—Republican; U—Unionist; W—Whig.

*The 110th Congress had two independent senators who caucused with the Democrats, giving them control of the chamber that otherwise would have been in Republican control because the vice president at the time was Republican, allowing him to cast a deciding vote in case of a tie. The 111th Congress, 112th Congress, and 113th Congress (when in convened in January 2013) also had two independent senators who caucused with Democrats, thereby increasing their majority in the chamber.

111th Congress Special Elections, 2009 Gubernatorial Elections

Special House Elections, 111th Congress

	Vote total	*Percent*
New York 20th CD–March 31, 2009		
Scott Murphy (D)	80,833	50.2
Jim Tedisco (R)	80,107	49.8
Illinois 5th CD–April 7, 2009		
Mike Quigley (D)	30,561	61.9
Rosanna Pulido (R)	10,662	24.2
Matt Reichel (Green)	2,911	6.6
California 32nd CD–July 14, 2009		
Judy Chu (D)	16,194	61.9
Betty Chu (R)	8,630	33.0
Christopher M. Agrella (Libertarian)	1,356	5.2
California 10th CD–November 3, 2009		
John Garamendi (D)	72,817	52.8
David Hammer (R)	59,017	42.8
New York 23rd CD–November 3, 2009		
William Owens (D)	73,137	48.3
Douglas L. Hoffman (Conservative)	69,553	46.0
Dede Scozzafava (R)	8,582	5.7

	Vote total	*Percent*
Florida 19th CD–April 13, 2010		
Ted Deutch (D)	43,269	62.1
Edward Lynch (R)	24,549	35.2
Pennsylvania 12th CD–May 18, 2010		
Mark S. Critz (D)	72,218	52.6
Tim Burns (R)	61,722	45.0
Hawaii 1st CD–May 22, 2010		
Charles Djou (R)	67,610	39.7
Colleen Hanabusa (D)	52,802	31.0
Ed Case (D)	47,391	27.8
Georgia 9th CD–June 8, 2010		
Tom Graves (R)	22,694	56.4
Lee Hawkins (D)	17,509	43.6
Indiana 3rd CD–November 2, 2010		
Marin A. Stutzman (R)	115,415	62.7
Thomas Hayhurst (D)	60,880	33.1
New York 29th CD–November 2, 2010		
Thomas W. Reed II (R)	105,907	56.7
Matthew C. Zeller (D)	80,480	43.1

Special Senate Elections, 111th Congress

	Vote total	*Percent*
Massachusetts–January 19, 2010		
Scott P. Brown (R)	1,168,178	51.9
Martha Coakley (D)	1,060,861	47.1
Illinois–November 2, 2010		
Mark Steven Kirk (R)[1]	1,677,729	47.3
Alexander Giannoulias (D)	1,641,486	46.3

1. This was a special election to fill the remainder of the term of Barack Obama. It was held in conjunction with the election for a full six-year Senate term. Kirk also defeated Giannoulias in the general election vote. *(See Membership Changes, p. 829; and 2010 election returns, p. 932)*

2009 Gubernatorial Elections

	Vote total	*Percent*
New Jersey		
Chris Christie (R)	1,174,445	48.5
Jon Corzine (D)	1,807,731	44.9
Virginia		
Robert F. McDonnell (R)	1,163,651	58.6
R. Creigh Deeds (D)	818,950	41.3

NOTE: Vote totals are included for all candidates listed on the ballot who received 5 percent or more of the total vote.

2010 Elections Returns for Governor, Senate, and House

Following are the official vote returns for the gubernatorial, Senate, and House contests based on figures supplied by the fifty state election boards.

Vote totals are included for all candidates listed on the ballot who received 5 percent or more of the total vote. For candidates who received under 5 percent, consult *America Votes 29* (2009–2010), published by CQ Press/Sage. The percent column shows the percentage of the total vote cast.

An asterisk (*) indicates an incumbent.

An "X" denotes candidates without major part opposition; no votes were tallied.

An AL indicates an at-large member of Congress in a state with a single congressional district.

Alabama

		Vote total	Percent
Governor			
	Robert Bentley (R)	860,472	57.6
	Ron Sparks (D)	625,710	41.9
Senate			
	Richard C. Shelby (R)*	968,181	65.2
	William G. Barnes (D)	515,619	34.7
House			
1	Jo Bonner (R)*	129,063	82.6
	David Walter (CNSTP)	26,357	16.9
2	Martha Roby (R)	111,645	51.0
	Bobby Bright (D)*	106,865	48.8
3	Mike D. Rogers (R)*	117,736	59.4
	Steve Segrest (D)	80,204	40.5
4	Robert B. Aderholt (R)*	167,714	98.8
5	Mo Brooks (R)	131,109	57.9
	Steve Raby (D)	95,192	42.1
6	Spencer Bachus (R)*	205,288	98.0
7	Terri A. Sewell (D)	136,696	72.4
	Don Chamberlain (R)	51,890	27.5

Alaska

		Vote total	Percent
Governor			
	Sean Parnell (R)	151,318	59.1
	Ethan Berkowitz (D)	96,519	37.7
Senate			
	Lisa Murkowski (WRI)*	101,091	39.6
	Joe Miller (R)	90,839	35.3
	Scott T. McAdams (D)	60,045	23.3
House			
AL	Don Young (R)*	175,384	69.0
	Harry T. Crawford Jr. (D)	77,606	30.5

Arizona

		Vote total	Percent
Governor			
	Jan Brewer (R)*	938,934	54.3
	Terry Goddard (D)	733,935	42.5
Senate			
	John McCain (R)*	1,005,615	58.9
	Rodney Glassman (D)	592,011	34.6
House			
1	Paul Gosar (R)	112,816	49.7
	Ann Kirkpatrick (D)*	99,233	43.7
	Nicole Patti (LIBERT)	14,869	6.6
2	Trent Franks (R)*	173,173	64.9
	John Thrasher (D)	82,891	31.1
3	Ben Quayle (R)	108,689	58.9
	Jon Hulburd (D)	85,610	41.1
	Michael Shoen (LIBERT)	10,478	4.6
4	Ed Pastor (D)*	61,524	66.9
	Janet Contreras (R)	25,300	27.5
5	David Schweikert (R)	110,374	52.0
	Harry E. Mitchell (D)*	91,749	43.2
6	Jeff Flake (R)*	165,649	66.4
	Rebecca Schneider (D)	72,615	29.1
7	Raúl M. Grijalva (D)*	79,935	50.2
	Ruth McClung (R)	70,385	44.2
8	Gabrielle Giffords (D)*	138,280	48.8
	Jesse Kelly (R)	134,124	47.3

Arkansas

		Vote total	Percent
Governor			
	Mike Beebe (D)*	503,336	64.4
	Jim Keet (R)	262,784	33.6
Senate			
	John Boozman (R)	451,618	57.9
	Blanche Lincoln (D)*	288,156	36.9
House			
1	Rick Crawford (R)	93,224	51.8
	Chad Causey (D)	78,267	43.5
2	Tim Griffin (R)	122,091	57.9
	Joyce Elliott (D)	80,687	38.3
3	Steve Womack (R)	148,581	72.4
	David Whitaker (D)	56,542	27.6
4	Mike Ross (D)*	102,479	57.5
	Beth Anne Rankin (R)	71,526	40.2

California

		Vote total	Percent
Governor			
	Jerry Brown (D)	5,428,149	53.8
	Meg Whitman (R)	4,127,391	40.9
Senate			
	Barbara Boxer (D)*	5,218,137	52.2
	Carly Fiorina (R)	4,217,386	42.2
House			
1	Mike Thompson (D)*	147,307	62.8
	Loren Hanks (R)	72,803	31.0
2	Wally Herger (R)*	130,837	57.1
	Jim Reed (D)	98,092	42.8
3	Dan Lungren (R)*	131,169	50.1
	Ami Bera (D)	113,128	43.2
4	Tom McClintock (R)*	186,397	61.3
	Clint Curtis (D)	95,653	31.4
	Benjamin Emery (GREEN)	22,179	7.3
5	Doris Matsui (D)*	124,220	72.0
	Paul A. Smith (R)	43,577	25.3
6	Lynn Woolsey (D)*	172,216	65.9
	Jim Judd (R)	77,361	29.6
7	George Miller (D)*	122,118	68.3
	Rick Tubbs (R)	56,798	31.7
8	Nancy Pelosi (D)*	167,957	80.1
	John Dennis (R)	31,711	15.1
9	Barbara Lee (D)*	180,400	84.3
	Gerald Hashimoto (R)	23,054	10.8
10	John Garamendi (D)*	137,578	58.8
	Gary Clift (R)	88,512	37.9
11	Jerry McNerney (D)*	115,361	48.0
	David Harmer (R)	112,703	46.9
	David Christensen (AMI)	12,439	5.2
12	Jackie Speier (D)*	152,044	75.6
	Mike Moloney (R)	44,475	22.1

Abbreviations for Party Designations

AC	American Constitution	L	Liberal
AMI	American Independent	LIBERT	Libertarian
C	Conservative	MDE	Moderate
CNSTP	Constitution	NPA	No Party Affiliation
D	Democratic	R	Republican
GREEN	Green	REF	Reform
I	Independent	WRI	Write-in
INDC	Independence		

		Vote total	Percent
13	Pete Stark (D)*	118,278	72.0
	Forest Baker (R)	45,575	27.7
14	Anna G. Eshoo (D)*	151,217	69.1
	Dave Chapman (R)	60,917	27.8
15	Michael M. Honda (D)*	126,147	67.6
	Scott Kirkland (R)	60,468	32.4
16	Zoe Lofgren (D)*	105,841	67.8
	Daniel Sahagun (R)	37,913	24.3
	Edward Gonzalez (LIBERT)	12,304	7.9
17	Sam Farr (D)*	118,734	66.6
	Jeff Taylor (R)	53,176	29.8
18	Dennis Cardoza (D)	72,853	58.5
	Michael Clare Berryhill Sr. (R)	51,716	41.5
19	Jeff Denham (R)	128,394	64.6
	Loraine Goodwin (D)	69,912	35.1
20	Jim Costa (D)*	46,247	51.7
	Andy Vidak (R)	43,197	48.3
21	Devin Nunes (R)*	135,979	100.0
22	Kevin McCarthy (R)*	173,490	98.8
23	Lois Capps (D)*	111,768	57.8
	Tom Watson (R)	72,744	37.6
24	Elton Gallegly (R)*	144,055	59.9
	Timothy J. Allison (D)	96,279	40.1
25	Howard P. "Buck" McKeon (R)*	118,308	61.8
	Jackie Conaway (D)	73,028	38.2
26	David Dreier (R)*	112,774	54.1
	Russ Warner (D)	76,093	36.5
	David L. Miller (AMI)	12,784	6.1
27	Brad Sherman (D)*	102,927	65.2
	Mark Reed (R)	55,056	34.8
28	Howard L. Berman (D)*	88,385	69.5
	Merlin Froyd (R)	28,493	22.4
	Carlos A. Rodriguez (LIBERT)	10,229	8.0
29	Adam B. Schiff (D)*	104,374	64.8
	John P. Colbert (R)	51,534	32.0
30	Henry A. Waxman (D)*	153,663	64.6
	Charles E. Wilkerson (R)	75,948	31.9
31	Xavier Becerra (D)*	76,363	83.8
	Stephen C. Smith (R)	14,740	16.2
32	Judy Chu (D)*	77,759	71.0
	Edward "Ed" Schmerling (R)	31,697	29.0
33	Karen Bass (D)	131,990	86.1
	James L. Andion (R)	21,342	13.9
34	Lucille Roybal-Allard (D)*	69,382	77.2
	Wayne Miller (R)	20,457	22.8
35	Maxine Waters (D)*	98,131	79.3
	K. Bruce Brown (R)	25,561	20.7
36	Jane Harman (D)*	114,489	59.6
	Mattie Fein (R)	66,706	34.7
	Herb Peters (LIBERT)	10,840	5.6
37	Laura Richardson (D)*	85,799	68.4
	Star Parker (R)	29,159	23.2
	Nicholas Dibs (I)	10,560	8.4
38	Grace F. Napolitano (D)*	85,459	73.4
	Robert Vaughn (R)	30,883	26.5
39	Linda T. Sánchez (D)*	81,590	63.3
	Larry S. Andre (R)	42,037	32.6
40	Ed Royce (R)*	119,455	66.8
	Christina Avalos (D)	59,400	33.2
41	Jerry Lewis (R)*	127,857	63.2
	Pat Meagher (D)	74,394	36.8
42	Gary G. Miller (R)*	127,161	62.2
	Michael Williamson (D)	65,122	31.9
	Mark Lambert (LIBERT)	12,115	5.9
43	Joe Baca (D)*	70,026	65.5
	Scott Folkens (R)	36,890	34.5
44	Ken Calvert (R)*	107,482	55.6
	Bill Hedrick (D)	85,784	44.4
45	Mary Bono Mack (R)*	106,472	51.5
	Steve Pougnet (D)	87,141	42.1
	Bill Lussenheide (AMI)	13,188	6.4
46	Dana Rohrabacher (R)*	139,822	62.2
	Ken Arnold (D)	84,940	37.8
47	Loretta Sanchez (D)*	50,832	53.0
	Van Tran (R)	37,679	39.3
	Cecilia "Ceci" Iglesias (I)	7,443	7.8
48	John Campbell (R)*	145,481	59.9
	Beth Krom (D)	88,465	36.4
49	Darrell Issa (R)*	119,088	62.8
	Howard Katz (D)	59,714	31.5
50	Brian P. Bilbray (R)*	142,247	56.6
	Francine Busby (D)	97,818	39.0
51	Bob Filner (D)*	86,423	60.0
	Nick Popaditch (R)	57,488	39.9
52	Duncan Hunter (R)*	139,460	63.1
	Ray Lutz (D)	70,870	32.1
53	Susan A. Davis (D)*	104,800	62.3
	Michael Crimmins (R)	57,230	34.0

Colorado

		Vote total	Percent
Governor			
	John W. Hickenlooper (D)	912,436	51.0
	Tom Tancredo (AC)	651,232	36.4
	Dan Maes (R)	199,792	11.1
Senate			
	Michael Bennet (D)*	851,685	48.0
	Ken Buck (R)	824,789	46.4
House			
1	Diana DeGette (D)*	140,073	67.4
	Mike Fallon (R)	59,747	28.8
2	Jared Polis (D)*	148,768	57.4
	Stephen Bailey (R)	98,194	37.9
3	Scott Tipton (R)	131,227	52.0
	John Salazar (D)*	121,114	48.0
4	Cory Gardner (R)	138,634	52.5
	Betsy Markey (D)*	109,249	41.4
5	Doug Lamborn (R)*	152,829	65.8
	Kevin Bradley (D)	68,039	29.3
6	Mike Coffman (R)*	217,400	65.7
	John Flerlage (D)	104,159	31.5
7	Ed Perlmutter (D)*	112,667	53.4
	Ryan Frazier (R)	88,026	41.8

Connecticut

		Vote total	Percent
Governor			
	Dannel P. Malloy (D)	567,278	49.5
	Tom Foley (R)	560,874	49.0
Senate			
	Richard Blumenthal (D)	636,040	55.2
	Linda McMahon (R)	498,341	43.2
House			
1	John B. Larson (D)*	138,440	61.2
	Ann Brickley (R)	84,076	37.2
2	Joe Courtney (D)*	147,748	59.9
	Janet Peckinpaugh (R)	95,671	38.8
3	Rosa DeLauro (D)*	143,565	65.1
	Jerry Labriola Jr. (R)	74,107	33.6
4	Jim Himes (D)*	115,351	53.1
	Dan Debicella (R)	102,030	46.9
5	Christopher S. Murphy (D)*	122,879	54.1
	Sam Caligiuri (R)	104,402	45.9

Delaware

		Vote total	Percent
Senate			
	Chris Coons (D)	174,012	56.6
	Christine O'Donnell (R)	123,053	40.0
House			
AL	John Carney (D)	173,543	56.8
	Glen Urquhart (R)	125,442	41.0

Florida

		Vote total	Percent
Governor			
	Rick Scott (R)	2,619,335	48.9
	Alex Sink (D)	2,557,785	47.7
Senate			
	Marco Rubio (R)	2,645,743	48.9
	Charlie Crist (I)	1,607,549	29.7
	Kendrick B. Meek (D)	1,092,936	20.2
House			
1	Jeff Miller (R)*	170,821	80.0
	Joe Cantrell (No party affiliation)	23,250	10.9
	John Krause (No party affiliation)	18,253	8.5
2	Steve Southerland II (R)	136,371	53.6
	Allen Boyd (D)	105,211	41.4
3	Corrine Brown (D)*	94,744	63.0
	Michael "Mike" Yost (R)	50,932	33.9
4	Ander Crenshaw (R)*	178,238	77.2
	Troy Dwayne Stanley (No party affiliation)	52,540	22.8
5	Rich Nugent (R)	208,815	67.4
	James Piccillo (D)	100,858	32.6
6	Cliff Stearns (R)*	179,349	71.5
	Steve Schonberg (No party affiliation)	71,632	28.5
7	John L. Mica (R)*	185,470	69.0
	Heather Beaven (D)	83,206	31.0
8	Daniel Webster (R)	123,586	56.1
	Alan Grayson (D)*	84,167	38.2

		Vote total	Percent
9	Gus Bilirakis (R)*	165,433	71.4
	Anita de Palma (D)	66,158	28.6
10	C.W. Bill Young (R)*	137,943	65.9
	Charlie Justice (D)	71,313	34.1
11	Kathy Castor (D)*	91,328	59.6
	Mike Prendergast (R)	61,817	40.4
12	Dennis A. Ross (R)	102,704	48.1
	Lori Edwards (D)	87,769	41.1
	Randy Wilkinson (TEA)	22,857	10.7
13	Vern Buchanan (R)*	183,811	68.9
	James T. Golden (D)	83,123	31.1
14	Connie Mack (R)*	188,341	68.6
	James Lloyd Roach (D)	74,525	27.1
15	Bill Posey (R)*	157,079	64.7
	Shannon Roberts (D)	85,595	35.3
16	Tom Rooney (R)*	162,285	66.8
	Jim Horn (D)	80,327	33.1
17	Frederica S. Wilson (D)	106,361	86.2
	Roderick D. Vereen (No party affiliation)	17,009	13.8
18	Ileana Ros-Lehtinen (R)*	102,360	68.9
	Rolando A. Banciella (D)	46,235	31.1
19	Ted Deutch (D)*	132,098	62.6
	Joe Budd (R)	78,733	37.3
20	Debbie Wasserman Schultz (D)*	100,787	60.1
	Karen Harrington (R)	63,845	38.1
	Stanley Blumenthal (No party affiliation)	1,663	1.0
21	Mario Diaz-Balart (R)*	X	X
22	Allen B. West (R)	118,890	54.4
	Ron Klein (D)*	99,804	45.6
23	Alcee L. Hastings (D)*	100,066	79.1
	Bernard Sansaricq (R)	26,414	20.9
24	Sandra Adams (R)	146,129	59.6
	Suzanne M. Kosmas (D)*	98,787	40.3
25	David Rivera (R)	74,859	52.1
	Joe Garcia (D)	61,138	42.6

Note: In Florida in a district where a candidate had no opposition, including write-ins, no vote was taken.

Georgia

Governor

		Vote total	Percent
	Nathan Deal (R)	1,365,832	53.0
	Roy Barnes (D)	1,107,011	43.0

Senate

		Vote total	Percent
	Johnny Isakson (R)*	1,489,904	58.3
	Michael Thurmond (D)	996,516	39.0

House

		Vote total	Percent
1	Jack Kingston (R)*	117,270	71.6
	Oscar L. Harris II (D)	46,449	28.4
2	Sanford D. Bishop Jr. (D)*	86,520	51.4
	Mike Keown (R)	81,673	48.6
3	Lynn Westmoreland (R)*	168,304	69.5
	Frank Saunders (D)	73,932	30.5
4	Hank Johnson Jr. (D)*	131,760	74.7
	Lisbeth "Liz" Carter (R)	44,707	25.3
5	John Lewis (D)*	130,782	73.7
	Fenn Little (R)	46,622	26.3
6	Tom Price (R)*	198,100	99.9
7	Rob Woodall (R)	160,898	67.1
	Doug Heckman (D)	78,996	32.9
8	Austin Scott (R)	102,770	52.7
	Jim Marshall (D)*	92,250	47.3
9	Tom Graves (R)*	173,512	100.0
10	Paul Broun (R)*	138,062	67.4
	Russell Edwards (D)	66,905	32.6
11	Phil Gingrey (R)*	163,515	100.0
12	John Barrow (D)*	92,459	56.6
	Raymond McKinney (R)	70,938	43.4
13	David Scott (D)*	140,294	69.4
	Mike Crane (R)	61,771	30.6

Hawaii

Governor

		Vote total	Percent
	Neil Abercrombie (D)	222,724	58.2
	Duke Aiona (R)	157,311	41.1

Senate

		Vote total	Percent
	Daniel K. Inouye (D)	277,228	74.8
	Cam Cavasso (R)	79,939	21.6

House

		Vote total	Percent
1	Colleen Hanabusa (D)	94,140	53.2
	Charles K. Djou (R)*	82,723	46.8
2	Mazie K. Hirono (D)*	132,290	72.2
	John W. Willoughby (R)	46,404	25.3

Idaho

Governor

		Vote total	Percent
	C. L. "Butch" Otter (R)*	267,483	59.1
	Keith Allred (D)	148,680	32.8

Senate

		Vote total	Percent
	Michael D. Crapo (R)*	319,953	71.2
	P. Tom Sullivan (D)	112,057	24.9

House

		Vote total	Percent
1	Raúl R. Labrador (R)	126,231	51.0
	Walt Minnick (D)*	102,135	41.3
	Dave Olson (I)	14,365	5.8
2	Mike Simpson (R)*	137,468	68.8
	Mike Crawford (D)	48,749	24.4
	Brian Schad (I)	13,500	6.8

Illinois

Governor

		Vote total	Percent
	Pat Quinn (D)*	1,745,219	46.8
	Bill Brady (R)	1,713,385	45.9

Senate

		Vote total	Percent
	Mark Steven Kirk (R)*	1,778,698	48.0
	Alexi Giannoulias (D)	1,719,478	46.4

House

		Vote total	Percent
1	Bobby L. Rush (D)*	148,170	80.4
	Raymond G. Wardingley (R)	29,253	15.9
2	Jesse Jackson Jr. (D)*	150,666	80.5
	Isaac C. Hayes (R)	25,883	13.8
	Anthony W. Williams (GREEN)	10,564	5.6
3	Daniel Lipinski (D)*	116,120	69.7
	Michael A. Bendas (R)	40,479	24.3
	Laurel Lambert Schmidt (GREEN)	10,028	6.0
4	Luis V. Gutierrez (D)*	63,273	77.4
	Israel Vasquez (R)	11,711	14.3
	Robert J. Burns (GREEN)	6,808	8.3
5	Mike Quigley (D)*	108,360	70.6
	David Ratowitz (R)	38,935	25.4
6	Peter Roskam (R)*	114,456	63.6
	Benjamin S. Lowe (D)	65,379	36.4
7	Danny K. Davis (D)*	149,846	81.5
	Mark M. Weiman (R)	29,575	16.1
8	Joe Walsh (R)	98,115	48.5
	Melissa Bean (D)*	97,825	48.3
9	Jan Schakowsky (D)*	117,553	66.3
	Joel Barry Pollak (R)	55,182	31.1
10	Robert Dold (R)	109,941	51.1
	Dan Seals (D)	105,290	48.9
11	Adam Kinzinger (R)	129,108	57.3
	Debbie Halvorson (D)*	96,019	42.6
12	Jerry F. Costello (D)*	121,272	59.8
	Teri Newman (R)	74,046	36.5
13	Judy Biggert (R)*	152,132	63.8
	Scott Harper (D)	86,281	36.2
14	Randy Hultgren (R)	112,369	51.3
	Bill Foster (D)*	98,645	45.0
15	Timothy V. Johnson (R)*	136,915	64.3
	David Gill (D)	75,948	35.7
16	Donald Manzullo (R)*	138,299	65.0
	George W. Gaulrapp (D)	66,037	31.0
17	Bobby Schilling (R)	104,583	52.6
	Phil Hare (D)*	85,454	43.0
18	Aaron Schock (R)*	152,868	69.1
	Deirdre Hirner (D)	57,046	25.8
	Sheldon Schafer (GREEN)	11,256	5.1
19	John Shimkus (R)*	166,166	71.2
	Tim Bagwell (D)	67,132	28.8

Indiana

Senate

		Vote total	Percent
	Dan Coats (R)*	952,116	54.6
	Brad Ellsworth (D)	697,775	40.0
	Rebecca Sink-Burris (LIBERT)	94,330	5.4

House

		Vote total	Percent
1	Peter J. Visclosky (D)*	99,387	58.6
	Mark Leyva (R)	65,558	38.6
2	Joe Donnelly (D)*	91,341	48.2
	Jackie Walorski (R)	88,803	46.8
	Mark Vogel (LIBERT)	9,447	5.0
3	Marlin Stutzman (R)	116,140	62.8
	Thomas Hayhurst (D)	61,267	33.1
4	Todd Rokita (R)	138,732	68.6
	David Sanders (D)	53,167	26.3
	John Duncan (LIBERT)	10,423	5.2

		Vote total	Percent
5	Dan Burton (R)*	146,899	62.1
	Tim Crawford (D)	60,024	25.4
	Richard Reid (LIBERT)	18,266	7.7
6	Mike Pence (R)*	126,027	66.6
	Barry A. Welsh (D)	56,647	29.9
7	André Carson (D)*	86,011	58.9
	Marvin B. Scott (R)	55,213	37.8
8	Larry Bucshon (R)	117,259	57.5
	Trent Van Haaften (D)	76,265	37.4
	John Cunningham (LIBERT)	10,240	5.0
9	Todd Young (R)	118,040	52.3
	Baron P. Hill (D)*	95,353	42.3
	Greg Knott (LIBERT)	12,070	5.4

Iowa

Governor

		Vote total	Percent
	Terry E. Branstad (R)*	592,494	52.8
	Chet Culver (D)	484,789	43.2

Senate

		Vote total	Percent
	Charles E. Grassley (R)*	718,215	64.4
	Roxanne Conlin (D)	371,686	33.3

House

		Vote total	Percent
1	Bruce Braley (D)*	104,428	49.5
	Benjamin Lange (R)	100,219	47.5
2	Dave Loebsack (D)*	115,839	51.0
	Mariannette Miller-Meeks (R)	104,319	45.9
3	Leonard L. Boswell (D)*	122,147	50.7
	Brad Zaun (R)	111,925	46.5
4	Tom Latham (R)*	152,588	65.6
	Bill Maske (D)	74,300	32.0
5	Steve King (R)*	128,363	65.7
	Matthew Campbell (D)	63,160	32.4

Kansas

Governor

		Vote total	Percent
	Sam Brownback (R)	530,760	63.3
	Tom Holland (D)	270,166	32.2

Senate

		Vote total	Percent
	Jerry Moran (R)	587,175	70.1
	Lisa Johnston (D)	220,971	26.4

House

		Vote total	Percent
1	Tim Huelskamp (R)	142,281	73.8
	Alan Jilka (D)	44,068	22.8
2	Lynn Jenkins (R)*	130,034	63.1
	Cheryl Hudspeth (D)	66,588	32.3
3	Kevin Yoder (R)	136,246	58.4
	Stephene Moore (D)	90,193	38.7
4	Mike Pompeo (R)	119,575	58.8
	Raj Goyle (D)	74,143	36.4

Kentucky

Senate

		Vote total	Percent
	Rand Paul (R)	755,411	55.7
	Jack Conway (D)	599,843	44.2

House

		Vote total	Percent
1	Edward Whitfield (R)*	153,519	71.2
	Charles Kendall Hatchett (D)	61,960	28.8
2	Brett Guthrie (R)*	155,906	67.9
	Ed Marksberry (D)	73,749	32.1
3	John Yarmuth (D)*	139,940	54.7
	Todd Lally (R)	112,627	44.0
4	Geoff Davis (R)*	151,774	69.5
	John William Waltz (D)	66,675	30.5
5	Harold Rogers (R)*	151,019	77.4
	Jim Holbert (D)	44,034	22.6
6	Ben Chandler (D)*	119,812	50.1
	Andy Barr (R)	119,165	49.8

Louisiana

Senate

		Vote total	Percent
	David Vitter (R)*	715,415	56.6
	Charlie Melancon (D)	476,572	37.7

House

		Vote total	Percent
1	Steve Scalise (R)*	157,182	78.5
	Myron Katz (D)	38,416	19.2
2	Cedric L. Richmond (D)	83,705	64.6
	Anh "Joseph" Cao (R)*	43,378	33.5
3	Jeff Landry (R)	108,963	63.8
	Ravi Sangisetty (D)	61,914	36.2
4	John Fleming (R)*	105,223	62.3
	David Melville (D)	54,609	32.4
	Artis "Doc" Cash (I)	8,962	5.3
5	Rodney Alexander (R)*	122,033	78.6
	Tom Gibbs (No party affiliation)	33,279	21.4
6	Bill Cassidy (R)*	138,607	65.6
	Merritt E. McDonald Sr. (D)	72,577	34.4
7	Charles Boustany Jr. (R)	X	X

Maine

Governor

		Vote total	Percent
	Paul R. LePage (R)	218,065	38.1
	Eliot Cutler (I)	208,270	36.4
	Libby Mitchell (D)	109,387	19.1
	Shawn Moody (I)	28,756	5.0

House

		Vote total	Percent
1	Chellie Pingree (D)*	169,114	56.8
	Dean Scontras (R)	128,501	43.2
2	Michael H. Michaud (D)*	147,042	55.1
	Jason J. Levesque (R)	119,669	44.9

Maryland

Governor

		Vote total	Percent
	Martin O'Malley (D)*	1,044,961	56.2
	Robert L. Ehrlich Jr. (R)	776,319	41.8

Senate

		Vote total	Percent
	Barbara A. Mikulski (D)*	1,140,531	62.2
	Eric Wargotz (R)	655,666	35.8

House

		Vote total	Percent
1	Andy Harris (R)	155,118	54.1
	Frank Kratovil Jr. (D)*	120,400	42.0
2	C.A. Ruppersberger (D)*	134,133	64.2
	Marcelo Cardarelli (R)	69,523	33.3
3	John Sarbanes (D)*	147,448	61.1
	Jim Wilhelm (R)	86,947	36.0
4	Donna Edwards (D)*	160,228	83.4
	Robert Broadus (R)	31,467	16.4
5	Steny H. Hoyer (D)*	155,110	64.3
	Charles J. Lollar (R)	83,575	34.6
6	Roscoe G. Bartlett (R)*	148,820	61.4
	Andrew James Duck (D)	80,455	33.2
7	Elijah E. Cummings (D)*	152,669	75.2
	Frank Mirabile Jr. (R)	46,375	22.8
8	Chris Van Hollen (D)*	153,613	73.3
	Michael Philips (R)	52,421	25.0

Massachusetts

Governor

		Vote total	Percent
	Deval Patrick (D)*	1,112,283	48.4
	Charlie Baker (R)	964,866	42.0
	Tim Cahill (I)	184,395	8.0

House

		Vote total	Percent
1	John W. Olver (D)*	128,011	60.0
	William J. Gunn (R)	74,418	34.9
	Michael Engel (I)	10,880	5.1
2	Richard E. Neal (D)*	122,751	57.3
	Tom Wesley (R)	91,209	42.6
3	Jim McGovern (D)*	122,708	56.5
	Marty Lamb (R)	85,124	39.2
	Patrick Barron (I)	9,388	4.3
4	Barney Frank (D)*	126,194	53.9
	Sean Bielat (R)	101,517	43.4
5	Niki Tsongas (D)*	122,858	54.8
	Jon Golnik (R)	94,646	42.2
6	John F. Tierney (D)*	142,732	56.8
	Bill John Hudak Jr. (R)	107,930	43.0
7	Edward J. Markey (D)*	145,696	66.4
	Gerry Dembrowski (R)	73,467	33.5
8	Michael E. Capuano (D)*	134,974	98.0
9	Stephen F. Lynch (D)*	157,071	68.3
	Vernon Harrison (R)	59,965	26.1
	Phil Dunkelbarger (I)	12,572	5.5
10	William Keating (D)	132,743	46.9
	Jeff Perry (R)	120,029	42.4
	Maryanne Lewis (I)	16,705	5.9

Michigan

Governor

		Vote total	Percent
	Rick Snyder (R)	1,874,834	58.1
	Virg Bernero (D)	1,287,320	39.9

House

		Vote total	Percent
1	Dan Benishek (R)*	120,523	51.9
	Gary McDowell (D)	94,824	40.9
2	Bill Huizenga (R)	148,864	65.3
	Fred Johnson (D)	72,118	31.6
3	Justin Amash (R)	133,714	59.7
	Pat Miles (D)	83,953	37.5
4	Dave Camp (R)*	148,531	66.2
	Jerry M. Campbell (D)	68,458	30.5
5	Dale E. Kildee (D)*	107,286	53.0
	John Kupiec (R)	89,680	44.3
6	Fred Upton (R)*	123,142	62.0
	Don Cooney (D)	66,729	33.6
7	Tim Walberg (R)	113,185	50.2
	Mark Schauer (D)*	102,402	45.4
8	Mike Rogers (R)*	156,931	64.1
	Lance Enderle (D)	84,069	34.3

		Vote total	Percent
9	Gary Peters (D)*	125,730	49.8
	Rocky Raczkowski (R)	119,325	47.2
10	Candice S. Miller (R)*	168,364	72.0
	Henry Yanez (D)	58,530	25.0
11	Thaddeus McCotter (R)*	141,224	59.3
	Natalie Mosher (D)	91,710	38.5
12	Sander M. Levin (D)*	124,671	61.1
	Don Volaric (R)	71,372	35.0
13	Hansen Clarke (D)	100,885	79.4
	John Hauler (R)	23,462	18.5
14	John Conyers Jr. (D)*	115,511	76.8
	Don Ukrainec (R)	29,902	19.9
15	John D. Dingell (D)*	118,336	56.8
	Rob Steele (R)	83,488	40.1

Minnesota

Governor

		Vote total	Percent
	Mark Dayton (D)	919,232	43.6
	Tom Emmer (R)	910,462	43.2
	Tom Horner (INDC)	251,487	11.9

House

		Vote total	Percent
1	Tim Walz (D)*	122,365	49.3
	Randy Demmer (R)	109,242	44.0
	Steven Wilson (INDC)	13,242	5.3
2	John Kline (R)*	181,341	63.3
	Shelley Madore (D)	104,809	36.6
3	Erik Paulsen (R)*	161,177	58.8
	Jim Meffert (D)	100,240	36.6
4	Betty McCollum (D)*	136,746	59.1
	Teresa Collett (R)	80,141	34.6
	Steve Carlson (INDC)	14,207	6.1
5	Keith Ellison (D)*	154,833	67.7
	Joel Demos (R)	55,222	24.1
6	Michele Bachmann (R)*	159,476	52.5
	Tarryl Clark (D)	120,846	39.8
	Bob Anderson (INDC)	17,698	5.8
7	Collin C. Peterson (D)*	133,096	55.2
	Lee Byberg (R)	90,652	37.6
8	Chip Cravaack (R)	133,490	48.2
	James Oberstar (D)*	129,091	46.6

Mississippi

House

		Vote total	Percent
1	Alan Nunnelee (R)	121,074	55.3
	Travis W. Childers (D)*	89,388	40.8
2	Bennie Thompson (D)*	105,327	61.5
	William "Bill" Marcy (R)	64,499	37.6
3	Gregg Harper (R)*	132,393	68.0
	Joel L. Gill (D)	60,737	31.2
4	Steven M. Palazzo (R)	105,613	51.9
	Gene Taylor (D)*	95,243	46.8

Missouri

Senate

		Vote total	Percent
	Roy Blunt (R)	1,054,160	54.2
	Robin Carnahan (D)	789,736	40.6

House

		Vote total	Percent
1	William Lacy Clay (D)*	135,907	73.6
	Robyn Hamlin (R)	43,649	23.6
2	Todd Akin (R)*	180,481	67.9
	Arthur Lieber (D)	77,467	29.2
3	Russ Carnahan (D)*	99,398	48.9
	Ed Martin (R)	94,757	46.7
4	Vicky Hartzler (R)	113,489	50.4
	Ike Skelton (D)*	101,532	45.1
5	Emanuel Cleaver II (D)*	102,076	53.3
	Jacob Turk (R)	84,578	44.2
6	Sam Graves (R)*	154,103	69.4
	Clint Hylton (D)	67,762	30.5
7	Billy Long (R)	141,010	63.4
	Scott Eckersley (D)	67,545	30.4
	Kevin Craig (LIBERT)	13,866	6.2
8	Jo Ann Emerson (R)*	128,499	65.6
	Tommy Sowers (D)	56,377	28.8
9	Blaine Luetkemeyer (R)*	162,724	77.4
	Christopher W. Dwyer (LIBERT)	46,817	22.3

Montana

House

		Vote total	Percent
AL	Denny Rehberg (R)*	217,696	60.4
	Dennis McDonald (D)	121,954	33.8
	Mike Fellows (LIBERT)	20,691	5.7

Nebraska

Governor

		Vote total	Percent
	Dave Heineman (R)*	360,645	73.9
	Mike Meister (D)	127,343	26.1

House

		Vote total	Percent
1	Jeff Fortenberry (R)*	116,871	71.3
	Ivy Harper (D)	47,106	28.7
2	Lee Terry (R)*	93,840	60.8
	Tom White (D)	60,486	39.2
3	Adrian Smith (R)*	117,275	70.1
	Rebekah Davis (D)	29,932	17.9
	Dan Hill (I)	20,036	12.0

Nevada

Governor

		Vote total	Percent
	Brian Sandoval (R)	382,350	53.4
	Rory Reid (D)	298,171	41.6

Senate

		Vote total	Percent
	Harry Reid (D)*	362,785	50.3
	Sharron Angle (R)	321,361	44.5

House

		Vote total	Percent
1	Shelley Berkley (D)*	103,246	61.7
	Kenneth Wegner (R)	58,995	35.3
2	Dean Heller (R)*	169,458	63.3
	Nancy Price (D)	87,421	32.7
3	Joe Heck (R)	128,916	48.1
	Dina Titus (D)*	127,168	47.5
	Barry Michaels (I)	6,473	2.4

New Hampshire

Governor

		Vote total	Percent
	John Lynch (D)*	240,346	52.6
	John A. Stephen (R)	205,616	45.0

Senate

		Vote total	Percent
	Kelly Ayotte (R)	273,218	60.0
	Paul W. Hodes (D)	167,545	36.8

House

		Vote total	Percent
1	Frank Guinta (R)	121,655	54.0
	Carol Shea-Porter (D)*	95,503	42.4
2	Charles Bass (R)	108,610	48.3
	Ann McLane Kuster (D)	105,060	46.8

New Jersey

House

		Vote total	Percent
1	Robert E. Andrews (D)*	106,334	63.2
	Dale M. Glading (R)	58,562	34.8
2	Frank A. LoBiondo (R)*	109,460	65.5
	Gary Stein (D)	51,690	30.9
3	Jon Runyan (R)	110,215	50.0
	John Adler (D)*	104,252	47.3
4	Christopher H. Smith (R)*	129,752	69.4
	Howard Kleinhendler (D)	52,118	27.9
5	Scott Garrett (R)*	124,030	64.9
	Tod Theise (D)	62,634	32.8
6	Frank Pallone Jr. (D)*	81,933	54.7
	Anna C. Little (R)	65,413	43.7
7	Leonard Lance (R)*	105,084	59.4
	Ed Potosnak (D)	71,902	40.6
8	Bill Pascrell Jr. (D)*	88,478	62.7
	Roland Straten (R)	51,023	36.1
9	Steven R. Rothman (D)*	83,564	60.7
	Michael Agosta (R)	52,082	37.8
10	Donald M. Payne (D)*	95,299	85.2
	Michael J. Alonso (R)	14,357	12.8
11	Rodney Frelinghuysen (R)*	122,149	67.2
	Douglas Herbert (D)	55,472	30.5
12	Rush D. Holt (D)*	108,214	53.0
	Scott Sipprelle (R)	93,634	45.9
13	Albio Sires (D)*	62,840	74.1
	Henrietta Dwyer (R)	19,538	23.0

New Mexico

Governor

		Vote total	Percent
	Susana Martinez (R)	321,219	53.3
	Diane Denish (D)	280,614	46.5

House

		Vote total	Percent
1	Martin Heinrich (D)*	112,707	51.9
	Jon Barela (R)	105,543	48.1
2	Steve Pearce (R)	94,053	55.4
	Harry Teague (D)*	75,709	44.6
3	Ben Ray Luján (D)*	120,057	57.0
	Tom Mullins (R)	90,621	43.0

New York

Governor

		Vote total	Percent
	Andrew M. Cuomo (D)	2,911,721	62.5
	Carl P. Paladino (R)	1,548,184	33.2

		Vote total	Percent
Senate			
	Charles E. Schumer (D)*	3,047,880	66.3
	Jay Townsend (R)	1,480,423	32.2
	Kirsten Gillibrand (D)*	2,837,684	62.9
	Joseph J. DioGuardi (R)	1,582,693	35.1
House			
1	Timothy H. Bishop (D)*	98,316	50.1
	Randy Altschuler (R)	97,723	49.8
2	Steve Israel (D)*	94,594	56.3
	John Gomez (R)	72,029	42.9
3	Peter T. King (R)*	131,674	71.9
	Howard A. Kudler (D)	51,346	28.0
4	Carolyn McCarthy (D)*	94,483	53.6
	Fran Becker (R)	81,718	46.4
5	Gary L. Ackerman (D)*	72,239	63.0
	James Milano (R)	41,493	36.2
6	Gregory W. Meeks (D)*	85,096	87.7
	Asher Taub (R)	11,826	12.2
7	Joseph Crowley (D)*	71,247	80.5
	Ken Reynolds (R)	16,145	18.2
8	Jerrold Nadler (D)*	98,839	75.5
	Susan Kone (R)	31,996	24.4
9	Anthony Weiner (D)*	67,011	60.8
	Bob Turner (R)	43,129	39.1
10	Edolphus Towns (D)*	95,485	91.1
	Diana Muniz (R)	7,419	7.1
11	Yvette D. Clarke (D)*	104,297	90.5
	Hugh C. Carr (R)	10,858	9.4
12	Nydia M. Velázquez (D)*	68,624	93.8
	Alice Gaffney (C)	4,482	6.1
13	Michael G. Grimm (R)	65,024	51.3
	Michael E. McMahon (D)*	60,773	47.9
14	Carolyn B. Maloney (D)*	107,327	75.0
	Ryan Brumberg (R)	32,065	22.4
15	Charles B. Rangel (D)*	91,225	80.2
	Michel Faulkner (R)	11,754	10.3
	Craig Schley (INDC)	7,803	6.9
16	Jose E. Serrano (D)*	61,642	95.7
17	Eliot L. Engel (D)*	95,346	72.8
	Anthony Mele (R)	29,792	22.8
18	Nita M. Lowey (D)*	104,836	63.4
	Jim Russell (R)	70,413	37.8
19	Nan Hayworth (R)	109,956	52.6
	John Hall (D)*	98,766	47.2
20	Chris Gibson (R)	130,178	54.8
	Scott Murphy (D)*	107,075	47.2
21	Paul Tonko (D)*	124,889	59.2
	Theodore J. Danz Jr. (R)	85,752	40.7
22	Maurice D. Hinchey (D)*	98,661	52.6
	George K. Phillips (R)	88,687	47.3
23	Bill Owens (D)*	82,232	47.5
	Matt Doheny (R)	80,237	46.4
	Doug Hoffman (C)	10,507	6.1
24	Richard Hanna (R)	101,599	53.0
	Michael Arcuri (D)*	89,809	46.8
25	Ann Marie Buerkle (R)	104,602	50.1
	Dan Maffei (D)*	103,954	49.8
26	Christopher Lee (R)*	151,449	73.6
	Philip A. Fedele (D)	54,307	26.4
27	Brian Higgins (D)*	119,085	60.9
	Leonard A. Roberto (R)	76,320	39.1
28	Louise M. Slaughter (D)*	102,514	64.9
	Jill A. Rowland (R)	55,392	35.1
29	Tom Reed (R)	112,314	56.5
	Matthew Zeller (D)	86,099	43.3

North Carolina

		Vote total	Percent
Senate			
	Richard M. Burr (R)*	1,458,046	54.8
	Elaine Marshall (D)	1,145,074	43.0
House			
1	G.K. Butterfield (D)*	103,294	59.3
	Ashley Woolard (R)	70,867	40.7
2	Renee Ellmers (R)	93,876	49.5
	Bob Etheridge (D)*	92,393	48.7
3	Walter B. Jones (R)*	143,225	71.9
	Johnny Rouse (D)	51,317	25.7
4	David E. Price (D)*	155,384	57.2
	William "B.J." Lawson (R)	116,448	42.8
5	Virginia Foxx (R)*	140,525	65.9
	Billy Kennedy (D)	72,762	34.1
6	Howard Coble (R)*	156,252	75.2
	Sam Turner (D)	51,507	24.8
7	Mike McIntyre (D)*	113,957	53.7
	Ilario Pantano (R)	98,328	46.3
8	Larry Kissell (D)*	88,776	53.0
	Harold Johnson (R)	73,129	43.7
9	Sue Myrick (R)*	158,790	69.0
	Jeff Doctor (D)	71,450	31.0
10	Patrick T. McHenry (R)*	130,813	71.2
	Jeff Gregory (D)	52,972	28.8
11	Heath Shuler (D)*	131,225	54.3
	Jeff Miller (R)	110,246	45.7
12	Melvin Watt (D)*	103,495	63.9
	Greg Dority (R)	55,315	34.1
13	Brad Miller (D)*	116,103	55.5
	William Randall (R)	93,099	44.5

North Dakota

		Vote total	Percent
Senate			
	John Hoeven (R)	181,689	76.1
	Tracy Potter (D)	52,955	22.2
House			
AL	Rick Berg (R)	129,802	54.7
	Earl Pomeroy (D)*	106,542	44.9

Ohio

		Vote total	Percent
Governor			
	John R. Kasich (R)	1,889,186	49.0
	Ted Strickland (D)*	1,812,047	47.0
Senate			
	Rob Portman (R)	2,168,742	56.8
	Lee Fisher (D)	1,503,297	39.4
House			
1	Steve Chabot (R)	103,770	51.5
	Steve Driehaus (D)*	92,672	46.0
2	Jean Schmidt (R)*	139,027	58.4
	Surya Yalamanchili (D)	82,431	34.7
	Marc Johnston (LIBERT)	16,259	6.8
3	Michael R. Turner (R)*	152,629	68.1
	Joe Roberts (D)	71,455	31.9
4	Jim Jordan (R)*	146,029	71.5
	Doug Litt (D)	50,533	24.7
5	Bob Latta (R)*	140,703	67.8
	Caleb Finkenbiner (D)	54,919	26.5
	Brian L. Smith (LIBERT)	11,831	5.7
6	Bill Johnson (R)	103,170	50.2
	Charlie Wilson (D)*	92,823	45.2
7	Steve Austria (R)*	135,721	62.2
	William R. Conner (D)	70,400	32.2
8	John A. Boehner (R)*	142,731	65.6
	Justin A. Coussoule (D)	65,883	30.3
9	Marcy Kaptur (D)*	121,819	59.4
	Rich Iott (R)	83,423	40.6
10	Dennis J. Kucinich (D)*	101,343	53.0
	Peter Corrigan (R)	83,809	43.9
11	Marcia L. Fudge (D)*	139,693	82.9
	Thomas Pekarek (R)	28,754	17.1
12	Pat Tiberi (R)*	150,163	55.8
	Paula Brooks (D)	110,307	41.0
13	Betty Sutton (D)*	118,806	55.7
	Tom Ganley (R)	94,367	44.3
14	Steven C. LaTourette (R)*	149,878	64.9
	Bill O'Neill (D)	72,604	31.4
15	Steve Stivers (R)	119,471	54.2
	Mary Jo Kilroy (D)*	91,077	41.3
16	James B. Renacci (R)	114,652	52.1
	John Boccieri (D)*	90,833	41.3
	Jeffrey J. Blevins (LIBERT)	14,585	6.6
17	Tim Ryan (D)*	102,758	53.9
	Jim Graham (R)	57,352	30.1
	James A. Traficant Jr. (I)	30,556	16.0
18	Bob Gibbs (R)	107,426	53.9
	Zack Space (D)*	80,756	40.5
	Lindsey Sutton (CNSTP)	11,246	5.6

Oklahoma

		Vote total	Percent
Governor			
	Mary Fallin (R)	625,506	60.4
	Jari Askins (D)	409,261	39.6
Senate			
	Tom Coburn (R)*	718,482	70.6
	Jim Rogers (D)	265,814	26.1

		Vote total	Percent
House			
1	John Sullivan (R)*	151,173	76.8
	Angelia O'Dell (I)	45,656	23.2
2	Dan Boren (D)*	108,203	56.5
	Charles Thompson (R)	83,226	43.5
3	Frank D. Lucas (R)*	161,927	78.0
	Frankie Robbins (D)	45,689	22.0
4	Tom Cole (R)*	X	X
5	James Lankford (R)	123,236	62.5
	Billy Coyle (D)	68,074	34.5

Oregon

		Vote total	Percent
Governor			
	John Kitzhaber (D)	716,525	49.3
	Chris Dudley (R)	694,287	47.8
Senate			
	Ron Wyden (D)*	825,507	57.2
	Jim Huffman (R)	566,199	39.2
House			
1	David Wu (D)*	160,357	54.7
	Rob Cornilles (R)	122,858	41.9
2	Greg Walden (R)*	206,245	73.9
	Joyce B. Segers (D)	72,173	25.9
3	Earl Blumenauer (D)*	193,104	70.0
	Delia Lopez (R)	67,714	24.6
4	Peter A. DeFazio (D)*	162,416	54.5
	Art Robinson (R)	129,877	43.6
5	Kurt Schrader (D)*	145,319	51.2
	Scott Bruun (R)	130,313	46.0

Pennsylvania

		Vote total	Percent
Governor			
	Tom Corbett (R)	2,172,763	54.5
	Dan Onorato (D)	1,814,788	45.5
Senate			
	Patrick J. Toomey (R)	2,028,945	51.0
	Joe Sestak (D)	1,948,716	49.0
House			
1	Robert A. Brady (D)*	149,944	100.0
2	Chaka Fattah (D)*	182,800	89.3
	Rick Hellberg (R)	21,907	10.7
3	Mike Kelly (R)	111,909	55.7
	Kathy Dahlkemper (D)*	88,924	44.3
4	Jason Altmire (D)*	120,827	50.8
	Keith Rothfus (R)	116,958	49.2
5	Glenn Thompson (R)*	127,427	68.7
	Michael Pipe (D)	52,375	28.2
6	Jim Gerlach (R)*	133,770	57.1
	Manan Trivedi (D)	100,493	42.9
7	Patrick Meehan (R)	137,825	54.9
	Bryan Lentz (D)	110,314	44.0
8	Michael G. Fitzpatrick (R)	130,759	53.5
	Patrick J. Murphy (D)*	113,547	46.5
9	Bill Shuster (R)*	141,904	73.1
	Tom Conners (D)	52,322	26.9
10	Tom Marino (R)	110,599	55.2
	Christopher Carney (D)*	89,846	44.8
11	Lou Barletta (R)	102,179	54.7
	Paul E. Kanjorski (D)*	84,618	45.3
12	Mark Critz (D)*	94,056	50.8
	Tim Burns (R)	91,170	49.2
13	Allyson Y. Schwartz (D)*	118,710	56.3
	Dee Adcock (R)	91,987	43.7
14	Mike Doyle (D)*	122,073	68.8
	Melissa Haluszczak (R)	49,997	28.2
15	Charlie Dent (R)*	109,534	53.5
	John Callahan (D)	79,766	39.0
	Jake Towne (I)	15,248	7.4
16	Joe Pitts (R)*	134,113	65.4
	Lois K. Herr (D)	70,994	34.6
17	Tim Holden (D)*	118,486	55.5
	Dave Argall (R)	95,000	44.5
18	Tim Murphy (R)*	161,888	67.3
	Dan Connolly (D)	78,558	32.7
19	Todd R. Platts (R)*	165,219	71.9
	Ryan S. Sanders (D)	53,549	23.3

Rhode Island

		Vote total	Percent
Governor			
	Lincoln Chafee (I)	123,571	36.1
	John F. Robitaille (R)	114,911	33.6
	Frank T. Caprio (D)	78,896	23.0
	Kenneth Block (MDE)	22,146	6.5
House			
1	David Cicilline (D)	81,269	50.6
	John Loughlin (R)	71,542	44.6
2	Jim Langevin (D)*	104,442	59.9
	Mark Zaccaria (R)	55,409	31.8
	John O. Matson (I)	14,584	8.4

South Carolina

		Vote total	Percent
Governor			
	Nikki R. Haley (R)	690,525	51.4
	Vincent Sheheen (D)	630,534	46.9
Senate			
	Jim DeMint (R)*	810,771	61.5
	Alvin M. Greene (D)	364,598	27.6
	Tom Clements (GREEN)	121,472	9.2
House			
1	Tim Scott (R)	152,755	65.4
	Ben Frasier (D)	67,008	28.7
2	Joe Wilson (R)*	138,861	53.5
	Rob Miller (D)	113,625	43.8
3	Jeff Duncan (R)	126,235	62.5
	Jane Dyer (D)	73,095	36.2
4	Trey Gowdy (R)	137,586	63.4
	Paul Corden (D)	62,438	28.8
	Dave Edwards (CNSTP)	11,059	5.1
5	Mick Mulvaney (R)	125,834	55.1
	John M. Spratt Jr. (D)*	102,296	44.8
6	James E. Clyburn (D)*	125,459	62.9
	Jim Pratt (R)	72,661	36.4

South Dakota

		Vote total	Percent
Governor			
	Dennis Daugaard (R)	195,046	61.5
	Scott Heidepriem (D)	122,037	38.5
Senate			
	John Thune (R)*	227,947	100.0
House			
AL	Kristi Noem (R)	153,703	48.1
	Stephanie Herseth Sandlin (D)*	146,589	45.9
	B. Thomas Marking (I)	19,134	6.0

Tennessee

		Vote total	Percent
Governor			
	Bill Haslam (R)	1,041,545	65.0
	Mike McWherter (D)	529,851	33.1
House			
1	Phil Roe (R)*	123,006	80.8
	Michael Edward Clark (D)	26,045	17.1
2	John J. Duncan Jr. (R)*	141,796	81.8
	Dave Hancock (D)	25,400	14.6
3	Chuck Fleischmann (R)	92,032	56.8
	John Wolfe Jr. (D)	45,387	28.0
	Savas T. Kyriakidis (I)	17,077	10.5
4	Scott DesJarlais (R)	103,969	57.1
	Lincoln Davis (D)*	70,254	38.6
5	Jim Cooper (D)*	99,162	56.2
	David Hall (R)	74,204	42.1
6	Diane Black (R)	128,517	67.3
	Brett Carter (D)	56,145	29.4
7	Marsha Blackburn (R)*	158,916	72.4
	Greg Rabidoux (D)	54,347	24.8
8	Stephen Fincher (R)	98,759	59.0
	Roy Herron (D)	64,960	38.8
9	Steve Cohen (D)*	99,827	74.0
	Charlotte Bergmann (R)	33,879	25.1

Texas

		Vote total	Percent
Governor			
	Rick Perry (R)*	2,737,481	55.0
	William H. White (D)	2,106,395	42.3
House			
1	Louie Gohmert (R)*	129,398	89.7
	Charles Parkes (LIBERT)	14,811	10.3
2	Ted Poe (R)*	130,020	88.6
	David W. Smith (LIBERT)	16,711	11.4
3	Sam Johnson (R)*	101,180	66.3
	John Lingenfelder (D)	47,848	31.3
4	Ralph M. Hall (R)*	136,338	73.2
	VaLinda Hathcox (D)	40,975	22.0
5	Jeb Hensarling (R)*	106,742	70.5
	Tom Berry (D)	41,649	27.5
6	Joe L. Barton (R)*	107,140	65.9
	David E. Cozad (D)	50,717	31.2
7	John Culberson (R)*	143,655	81.4
	Bob Townsend (LIBERT)	31,704	18.0

		Vote total	Percent
8	Kevin Brady (R)*	161,417	80.3
	Kent Hargett (D)	34,694	17.2
9	Al Green (D)*	80,107	75.7
	Steve Mueller (R)	24,201	22.9
10	Michael McCaul (R)*	144,980	64.7
	Ted Ankrum (D)	74,086	33.0
11	K. Michael Conaway (R)*	125,581	80.8
	James Quillian (D)	23,989	15.4
12	Kay Granger (R)*	109,882	71.9
	Tracey Smith (D)	38,434	25.1
13	William M. Thornberry (R)*	113,201	87.0
	Keith Dyer (I)	11,192	8.6
14	Ron Paul (R)*	140,623	76.0
	Robert Pruett (D)	44,431	24.0
15	Rubén Hinojosa (D)*	53,546	55.7
	Eddie Zamora (R)	39,964	41.6
16	Silvestre Reyes (D)*	49,301	58.1
	Tim Besco (R)	31,051	36.6
	Bill Collins (LIBERT)	4,319	5.1
17	Bill Flores (R)	106,696	61.8
	Chet Edwards (D)*	63,138	36.6
18	Sheila Jackson Lee (D)*	85,108	70.2
	John Faulk (R)	33,067	27.3
19	Randy Neugebauer (R)*	106,059	77.8
	Andy Wilson (D)	25,984	19.1
20	Charlie Gonzalez (D)*	58,645	63.6
	Clayton Trotter (R)	31,757	34.4
21	Lamar Smith (R)*	162,924	68.9
	Lainey Melnick (D)	65,927	27.9
22	Pete Olson (R)*	140,537	67.5
	Kesha Rogers (D)	62,082	29.8
23	Francisco "Quico" Canseco (R)	74,853	49.4
	Ciro Rodriguez (D)*	67,348	44.4
24	Kenny Marchant (R)*	100,078	81.6
	David Sparks (LIBERT)	22,609	18.4
25	Lloyd Doggett (D)*	99,967	52.8
	Donna Campbell (R)	84,849	44.8
26	Michael C. Burgess (R)*	120,984	67.0
	Neil L. Durrance (D)	55,385	30.7
27	Blake Farenthold (R)	51,001	47.8
	Solomon P. Ortiz (D)*	50,226	47.1
	Edward C. Mishou (LIBERT)	5,372	5.0
28	Henry Cuellar (D)*	62,773	56.3
	Bryan Underwood (R)	46,740	42.0
29	Gene Green (D)*	43,257	64.6
	Roy Morales (R)	22,825	34.1
30	Eddie Bernice Johnson (D*)	86,322	75.7
	Stephen E. Broden (R)	24,668	21.6
31	John Carter (R)*	126,384	82.5
	Bill Oliver (LIBERT)	26,735	17.5
32	Pete Sessions (R)*	79,433	62.6
	Grier Raggio (D)	44,258	34.9

Utah

		Vote total	Percent
Governor			
	Gary R. Herbert (R)*	412,151	64.1
	Peter Corroon (D)	205,246	31.9
Senate			
	Mike Lee (R)	390,179	61.6
	Sam F. Granato (D)	207,685	32.8
House			
1	Rob Bishop (R)*	135,247	69.2
	Morgan E. Bowen (D)	46,765	23.9
2	Jim Matheson (D)*	127,151	50.5
	Morgan Philpot (R)	116,001	46.1
3	Jason Chaffetz (R)*	139,721	72.3
	Karen Hyer (D)	44,320	22.9

Vermont

		Vote total	Percent
Governor			
	Peter Shumlin (D)	119,543	49.5
	Brian E. Dubie (R)	115,212	47.7
Senate			
	Patrick J. Leahy (D)*	151,281	64.3
	Len Britton (R)	72,699	30.9
House			
AL	Peter Welch (D)*	154,006	64.6
	Paul D. Beaudry (R)	76,403	32.0

Virginia

		Vote total	Percent
House			
1	Rob Wittman (R)*	135,564	63.9
	Krystal M. Ball (D)	73,824	34.8
2	Scott Rigell (R)	88,340	53.1
	Glenn Nye (D)*	70,591	42.4
3	Robert C. Scott (D)	114,754	70.0
	C.L. Smith Jr. (R)	44,553	27.2
4	J. Randy Forbes (R)*	123,659	62.3
	Wynne LeGrow (D)	74,298	37.4
5	Robert Hurt (R)	119,560	50.8
	Tom Perriello (D)*	110,562	47.0
6	Robert W. Goodlatte (R)*	127,487	76.3
	Jeffrey W. Vanke (I)	21,649	13.0
	Stuart M. Bain (LIBERT)	15,309	9.2
7	Eric Cantor (R)*	138,209	59.2
	Rick E. Waugh Jr. (D)	79,616	34.1
	Floyd C. Bayne (GREEN)	15,164	6.5
8	James P. Moran (D)*	116,404	61.0
	J. Patrick Murray (R)	71,145	37.3
9	Morgan Griffith (R)	95,726	51.2
	Rick Boucher (D)*	86,743	46.4
10	Frank R. Wolf (R)*	131,116	62.9
	Jeffrey R. Barnett (D)	72,604	34.8
11	Gerald E. Connolly (D)*	111,720	49.2
	Keith Fimian (R)	110,739	48.8

Washington

		Vote total	Percent
Senate			
	Patty Murray (D)*	1,314,930	52.4
	Dino Rossi (R)	1,196,164	47.6
House			
1	Jay Inslee (D)*	172,642	57.7
	James Watkins (R)	126,737	42.3
2	Rick Larsen (D)*	155,241	51.1
	John Koster (R)	148,722	48.9
3	Jaime Herrera Beutler (R)	152,799	53.0
	Denny Heck (D)	135,654	47.0
4	Doc Hastings (R)*	156,726	67.6
	Jay Clough (D)	74,973	32.4
5	Cathy McMorris Rodgers (R)*	177,235	63.7
	Daryl Romeyn (D)	101,146	36.3
6	Norm Dicks (D)*	151,873	58.0
	Doug Cloud (R)	109,800	42.0
7	Jim McDermott (D)*	232,649	83.0
	Bob Jeffers-Schroder (I)	47,741	17.0
8	Dave Reichert (R)	161,296	52.0
	Suzan DelBene (D)	148,581	48.0
9	Adam Smith (D)*	123,743	54.8
	Richard Muri (R)	101,851	45.1

West Virginia

		Vote total	Percent
Senate			
	Joe Manchin III (D)	283,358	53.5
	John Raese (R)	230,013	43.4
House			
1	David B. McKinley (R)	90,660	50.4
	Mike Oliverio (D)	89,220	49.6
2	Shelley Moore Capito (R)*	126,814	68.5
	Virginia Lynch Graf (D)	55,001	29.7
3	Nick J. Rahall II (D)*	83,636	56.0
	Elliott E. Maynard (R)	65,611	44.0

Wisconsin

		Vote total	Percent
Governor			
	Scott Walker (R)	1,128,941	52.2
	Tom Barrett (D)	1,004,303	46.5
Senate			
	Ron Johnson (R)	1,125,999	51.9
	Russ Feingold (D)*	1,020,958	47.0
House			
1	Paul D. Ryan (R)*	179,819	68.2
	John Heckenlively (D)	79,363	30.1

		Vote total	Percent
2	Tammy Baldwin (D)*	191,164	61.8
	Chad Lee (R)	118,099	38.2
3	Ron Kind (D)*	126,380	50.3
	Dan Kapanke (R)	116,838	46.5
4	Gwen Moore (D)*	143,559	69.0
	Dan Sebring (R)	61,543	29.6
5	James Sensenbrenner Jr. (R)*	229,642	69.3
	Todd P. Kolosso (D)	90,634	27.4
6	Tom Petri (R)*	183,271	70.7
	Joseph C. Kallas (D)	75,926	29.3
7	Sean P. Duffy (R)	132,551	52.1
	Julie Lassa (D)	113,018	44.4
8	Reid Ribble (R)	143,998	54.8
	Steve Kagen (D)*	118,646	45.1

Wyoming

		Vote total	Percent
Governor			
	Matt Mead (R)	123,780	65.7
	Leslie Petersen (D)	43,240	22.9
House			
AL	Cynthia M. Lummis (R)*	131,661	70.4
	David Wendt (D)	45,768	24.5

112th Congress Special Elections, 2011 Gubernatorial Elections

Special House Elections, 112th Congress

	Vote Total	Percent
Arizona 8th CD–June 12, 2012		
Ron Barber (D)	111,204	52.0
Jesse Kelly (R)	96,465	45.2
California 36th CD–July 12, 2011		
Janice Hahn (D)	47,000	55.0
Craig Huey (R)	38,624	45.0
Kentucky 4th CD–November 6, 2012		
Thomas Massie (R)	174,092	60.0
William R. Adkins (D)	106,598	36.7
Michigan 11th CD–November 6, 2012		
David Curson (D)	159,258	48.4
Kerry Bentivolio (R)	151,736	46.1
Nevada 2nd CD-September 13, 2011		
Mark Amodei (R)	74,976	58.0
Kate Marshall (D)	46,669	36.1
New Jersey 10th CD–November 6, 2012		
Donald M. Payne Jr. (D)	166,413	97.4
New York 9th CD–September 13, 2011		
Robert L. Turner (R)	37,342	52.4
David I. Weprin (D)	33,656	47.3
New York 26th CD–May 24, 2011		
Kathy Hochul (D)	52,713	47.3
Jane Corwin (R)	47,187	42.4
Jack Davis (Tea Party)	10,029	9.0
Oregon 1st CD–January 31, 2012		
Suzanne Bonamici (D)	113,404	53.8
Rob Cornillis (R)	83,396	39.6
Washington 1st CD–November 6, 2012		
Suzan DelBene (D)	141,591	60.4
John Koster (R)	141,591	39.8

Special Senate Elections, 112th Congress

None

2011 Gubernatorial Elections

	Vote Total	Percent
Kentucky–November 8, 2011		
Steven L. Beshear (D)	464,245	55.7
David Lynn Williams (R)	294,034	35.3
Louisiana–October 22, 2011		
Bobby Jindal (R)	673,239	65.8
Tara Hollis (D)*	288,181	28.2
Mississippi–November 8, 2011		
Phil Bryant (R)	544,851	61.0
Johnny L. Dupree (D)	348,617	39.0

NOTE: Most vote totals are included for all candidates listed on the ballot who received 5 percent or more of the total vote. In the 2011 Louisiana gubernatorial race there were four Democratic candidates on the ballot. The vote total is the combined total for all four candidates. Tara Hollis received 182,925 votes for 17 percent of the total vote. None of the other three candidates received more than 5 percent of the vote.

2012 Election Returns for Governor, Senate, and House

Following are the official vote returns for the gubernatorial, Senate, and House contests based on figures supplied by the fifty state election boards.

Vote totals are included for all candidates listed on the ballot who received 5 percent or more of the total vote. For candidates who received under 5 percent, consult *America Votes 30* (2011–2012), published by CQ Press/Sage. The percent column shows the percentage of the total vote cast.

An asterisk (*) indicates an incumbent. Congressional redistricting following the 2010 census forced some incumbents into the same district. Those are noted with an asterisk (*) by both names.

An "X" denotes candidates without major part opposition; no votes were tallied.

An AL indicates an at-large member of Congress in a state with a single congressional district.

Alabama

House

		Vote total	Percent
1	Jo Bonner (R)*	196,374	97.9
2	Martha Roby (R)*	180,591	63.6
	Therese Ford (D)	103,092	36.3
3	Mike D. Rogers (R)*	175,306	64.0
	John Andrew Harris (D)	98,141	35.8
4	Robert B. Aderholt (R)*	199,071	74.0
	Daniel H. Boman (D)	69,706	25.9
5	Mo Brooks (R)*	189,185	64.9
	Charlie L. Holley (D)	101,772	34.9
6	Spencer Bachus (R)*	219,262	71.2
	Penny H. Bailey (D)	88,267	28.6
7	Terri A. Sewell (D)*	232,520	75.8
	Don Chamberlain (R)	73,835	24.1

Alaska

House

		Vote total	Percent
AL	Don Young (R)*	185,296	63.9
	Sharon M. Cissna (D)	82,927	28.6
	Jim C. McDermott (LIBERT)	15,028	5.2

Arizona

Senate

		Vote total	Percent
	Jeff Flake (R)	1,104,457	49.2
	Richard Carmona (D)	1,036,542	46.2

House

		Vote total	Percent
1	Ann Kirkpatrick (D)	122,7749	48.8
	Jonathan Paton (R)	113,594	45.2
	Kim Allen (LIBERT)	15,227	6.1
2	Ron Barber (D)*	147,338	50.4
	Martha E. McSally (R)	144,884	49.6
3	Raul M. Grijalva (D)*	98,468	58.4
	Gabriela Saucedo Mercer (R)	62,663	37.1
4	Paul Gosar (R)*	162,907	66.8
	Johnnie Robinson (D)	69,154	28.4
5	Matt Salmon (R)	183,470	67.2
	Spencer Morgan (D)	89,589	32.8
6	David Schweikert (R)*	179,706	61.3
	Matt Jette (D)	97,666	33.3
7	Ed Pastor (D)*	104,489	81.7
	Joe Cobb (LIBERT)	23,338	18.3
8	Trent Franks (R)*	172,809	63.3
	Gene Scharer (D)	95,635	35.1
9	Kyrsten Sinema (D)	121,881	48.7
	Vernon B. Parker(R)	111,630	44.6
	Powell Gammill (LIBERT)	16,620	6.6

Arkansas

House

		Vote total	Percent
1	Rick Crawford (R)*	138,800	56.2
	Scott Ellington (D)	96,601	39.1
2	Tim Griffin (R)*	158,175	55.2
	Herb Rule (D)	113,156	39.5
3	Steve Womack (R)*	186,467	75.9
	Rebekah Kennedy (GREEN)	39,318	16.0
	David Pangrac (LIBERT)	19,875	8.1
4	Tom Cotton (R)	154,149	59.5
	Gene Jeffress (D)	95,013	36.7

California

Senate

		Vote total	Percent
	Dianne Feinstein (D)*	7,864,624	62.5
	Elizabeth Emken (R)	4,713,887	37.5

House

		Vote total	Percent
1	Doug LaMalfa (R)	168,827	57.4
	Jim Reed (D)	125,386	42.6
2	Jared Huffman (D)	226,216	71.2
	Daniel W. Roberts (R)	91,310	28.8
3	John Garamendi (D)*	126,882	54.2
	Kim Dolbow Vann (R)	107,086	45.8
4	Tom McClintock (R)*	197,803	61.1
	Jack Uppal (D)	125,885	38.9
5	Mike Thompson (D)*	202,872	74.5
	Randy Loftin (R)	69,545	25.5
6	Doris Matsui (D)*	160,667	75.0
	Joseph McCray Sr. (R)	53,406	24.9
7	Ami Bera (D)	141,241	51.7
	Dan Lungren (R)*	132,050	48.3
8	Paul Cook (R) *	103,093	57.4
	Gregg Imus (R)	76,551	42.6
9	Jerry McNerney (D)*	118,373	55.6
	Ricky Gill (R)	94,704	44.4
10	Jeff Denham (R)*	110,265	52.7
	Jose M. Hernandez (D)	98,934	47.3
11	George Miller (D)*	200,743	69.7
	Virginia Fuller (R)	87,136	30.3
12	Nancy Pelosi (D)	253,709	85.1
	John Dennis (R)	44,478	14.9
13	Barbara Lee (D)*	250,436	86.8
	Marilyn M. Singleton (No party affiliation)	38,146	13.2
14	Jackie Speier (D)*	203,828	78.9
	Deborah "Debbie" Bacigalupi (R)	54,455	21.1
15	Eric Swalwell (D)	120,388	52.1
	Pete Stark (D)*	110,646	47.9
16	Jim Costa (D)*	84,649	57.4
	Brian Daniel Whelan (R)	62,801	42.6
17	Michael M. Honda (D)*	159,392	73.5
	Evelyn Li (R)	57,336	26.5
18	Anna G. Eshoo (D)*	212,831	70.5
	Dave Chapman (R)	89,103	29.5
19	Zoe Lofgren (D)*	162,300	73.2
	Robert Murray (R)	59,313	26.8
20	Sam Farr (D)*	172,996	74.1
	Jeff Taylor (R)	60,566	25.9
21	David Valadao (R)	67,164	57.8
	John Hernandez (D)	49,119	42.2
22	Devin Nunes (R)*	132,386	61.9
	Otto Lee (D)	81,555	38.1
23	Kevin McCarthy (R)*	158,161	73.2

Abbreviatio ns for party designation

C	Conservative	INDC	Independence
CNSTP	Constitution	LIBERT	Libertarian
D	Democratic	R	Republican
GREEN	Green	REF	Reform
I	Independent		

District	Candidate	Vote total	Percent
	Terry Phillips (No party affiliation)	57,842	26.8
24	Lois Capps (D)*	156,749	55.1
	Abel Maldonado (R)	127,746	44.9
25	Howard "Buck" McKeon (R)*	129,593	54.8
	Lee C. Rogers (D)	106,982	45.2
26	Julia Brownley (D)	139,072	52.7
	Tony Strickland (R)	124,863	47.3
27	Judy Chu (D)*	154,191	64.0
	Jack Orswell (R)	86,817	36.0
28	Adam B. Schiff (D)*	188,703	76.5
	Phil Jennerjahn (R)	58,008	23.5
29	Tony Cardenas (D)	111,287	74.0
	David R. Hernandez Jr. (No party affiliation)	38,994	25.9
30	Brad Sherman (D)*	149,456	60.3
	Howard L. Berman (D)*	98,395	39.7
31	Gary G. Miller (R)*	88,964	55.2
	Robert Dutton (R)	72,255	44.8
32	Grace F. Napolitano (D)*	124,903	65.7
	David L. Miller (R)	65,208	34.3
33	Henry A. Waxman (D)*	171,860	54.0
	Bill Bloomfield (No party affiliation)	146,660	46.0
34	Xavier Becerra (D)*	120,367	85.6
	Stephen C. Smith (R)	20,223	14.4
35	Gloria McLeod (D)	79,698	55.9
	Joe Baca (D)*	62,982	44.1
36	Raul Ruiz (D)	110,189	52.9
	Mary Bono Mack (R)*	97,953	47.1
37	Karen Bass (D)*	207,039	86.4
	Morgan Osborne (R)	32,541	13.6
38	Linda T. Sanchez (D)*	145,280	67.5
	Benjamin Campos (R)	69,807	32.5
39	Ed Royce (R)*	145,607	57.8
	Jay Chen (D)	106,360	42.2
40	Lucille Roybal-Allard (D)*	73,940	58.9
	David Sanchez (D)	51,613	41.1
41	Mark Takano (D)	103,578	59.0
	John F. Tavaglione (R)	72,074	41.0
42	Ken Calvert (R)*	130,245	60.6
	Michael Williamson (D)	84,702	39.4
43	Maxine Waters (D)*	143,123	71.2
	Bob Flores (D)	57,771	28.8
44	Janice Hahn (D)*	99,909	60.2
	Laura Richardson (D)*	65,989	39.8
45	John Campbell (R)*	171,417	58.5
	Sukhee Kang (D)	121,814	41.5
46	Loretta Sanchez (D)*	95,694	63.9
	Jerry Hayden (R)	54,121	36.1
47	Alan Lowenthal (D)	130,093	56.6
	Gary DeLong (R)	99,919	43.4
48	Dana Rohrabacher (R)*	177,144	61.0
	Ron Varasteh (D)	113,358	39.0
49	Darrell Issa (R)*	159,725	58.2
	Jerry Tetalman (D)	114,893	41.8
50	Duncan Hunter (R)*	174,838	67.7
	David B. Secor (D)	83,455	32.3
51	Juan C. Vargas (D)	113,934	71.5
	Michael Crimmins (R)	45,464	28.5
52	Scott Peters (D)	151,451	51.2
	Brian P. Bilbray (R)*	144,459	48.8
53	Susan A. Davis (D)*	164,825	61.4
	Nick Popaditch (R)	103,482	38.6

Colorado

House

District	Candidate	Vote total	Percent
1	Diana DeGette (D)*	237,579	68.2
	Danny Stroud (R)	93,217	26.8
2	Jared Polis (D)*	234,758	55.7
	Kevin Lundberg (R)	162,639	38.6
3	Scott Tipton (R)*	185,291	53.4
	Sal Pace (D)	142,920	41.1
4	Cory Gardner (R)*	200,006	58.4
	Brandon Shaffer (D)	125,800	36.7
5	Doug Lamborn (R)*	199,639	65.0
	Dave Anderson (No party affiliation)	53,318	17.4
	Jim Pirtle (LIBERT)	22,778	7.4
	Misha Luzov (GREEN)	18,284	6.0
6	Mike Coffman (R)*	163,938	47.8
	Joe Miklosi (D)	156,937	45.8
7	Ed Perlmutter (D)*	182,460	53.5
	Joe Coors (R)	139,066	40.8

Connecticut

Senate

Candidate	Vote total	Percent
Christopher S. Murphy (D)	828,761	54.8
Linda McMahon (R)	651,089	43.1

House

District	Candidate	Vote total	Percent
1	John B. Larson (D)*	206,973	69.7
	John Henry Decker (R)	82,321	27.7
2	Joe Courtney (D)*	204,708	68.2
	Paul M. Formica (R)	88,103	29.4
3	Rosa DeLauro (D)*	217,573	74.7
	Wayne Winsley (R)	73,726	25.3
4	Jim Himes (D)*	175,929	60.0
	Steve Obsitnik (R)	117,503	40.0
5	Elizabeth Esty (D)	146,098	51.3
	Andrew Roraback (R)	138,637	48.7

Delaware

Governor

Candidate	Vote total	Percent
Jack Markell (D)*	275,993	69.3
Jeffrey E. Cragg (R)	113,793	28.6

Senate

Candidate	Vote total	Percent
Thomas R. Carper (D)	265,415	66.4
Kevin Wade (R)	115,700	29.0

House

District	Candidate	Vote total	Percent
AL	John Carney (D)*	249,933	64.4
	Thomas H. Kovach (R)	129,757	33.4

Florida

Senate

Candidate	Vote total	Percent
Bill Nelson (D)	4,523,451	55.2
Connie Mack (R)	3,458,267	42.2

House

District	Candidate	Vote total	Percent
1	Jeff Miller (R)*	238,440	69.6
	Jim Bryan (D)	92,961	27.1
2	Steve Southerland (R)*	175,856	52.7
	Al Lawson (D)	157,634	47.2
3	Ted Yoho (R)	204,331	64.7
	J. R. Gaillot (D)	102,468	32.5
4	Ander Crenshaw (R)*	239,988	76.1
	Jim Klauder (No party affiliation)	75,236	23.9
5	Corrine Brown (D)*	190,472	70.8
	LeAnne Kolb (R)	70,700	26.3
6	Ron DeSantis (R)	195,962	57.2
	Heather Beaven (D)	146,489	42.8
7	John L. Mica (R)*	185,518	58.7
	Jason H. Kendall (D)	130,479	41.3
8	Bill Posey (R)*	205,432	58.9
	Shannon Roberts (D)	130,870	37.5
9	Alan Grayson (D)	164,891	62.5
	Todd Long (R)	98,856	37.5
10	Daniel Webster (R)*	164,649	51.7
	Val B. Demings (D)	153,574	48.2
11	Rich Nugent (R)*	218,360	64.5
	H. David Werder (D)	120,303	35.5
12	Gus Bilirakis (R)*	209,604	63.5
	Jonathan Michael Snow (D)	108,770	32.9
13	C.W. Bill Young (R)*	189,605	57.6
	Jessica Ehrlich (D)	139,742	42.4
14	Kathy Castor (D)*	197,121	70.2
	Evelio 'EJ' Otero (R)	83,480	29.8
15	Dennis A. Ross (R)*	X	X
16	Vern Buchanan (R)*	187,147	53.6
	Keith Fitzgerald (D)	161,929	46.4
17	Tom Rooney (R)*	165,488	58.6
	William Bronson (D)	116,766	41.4
18	Patrick Murphy (D)	166,257	50.3
	Allen B. West (R)*	164,353	49.7
19	Trey Radel (R)	189,833	62.0
	Jim Roach (D)	109,746	35.8
20	Alcee L. Hastings (D)*	214,727	87.9
	Randall Terry (No party affiliation)	29,553	12.1
21	Ted Deutch (D)*	221,263	77.8
	W. Michael Trout (No party affiliation)	37,776	13.3
	Cesar Henao (No party affiliation)	25,361	8.9
22	Lois Frankel (D)	171,021	54.6
	Adam Hasner (R)	142,050	45.4
23	Debbie Wasserman Schultz (D)*	174,205	63.2
	Karen Harrington (R)	98,096	35.6
24	Frederica S. Wilson (D)*	X	X

		Vote total	Percent
25	Mario Diaz-Balart (R)*	151,466	75.6
	Stanley Blumenthal (No party affiliation)	31,664	15.8
	Voteforeddie.com (No party affiliation)	17,099	8.5
26	Joe Garcia (D)	135,694	53.6
	David Rivera (R)*	108,820	43.0
27	Ileana Ros-Lehtinen (R)*	138,488	60.2
	Manny Yevancey (D)	85,020	36.9

Georgia

House

		Vote total	Percent
1	Jack Kingston (R)*	157,181	63.0
	Lesli Rae Messinger (D)	92,399	37.0
2	Sanford D. Bishop Jr. (D)*	162,751	63.8
	John House (R)	92,410	36.2
3	Lynn Westmoreland (R)*	232,380	100.0
4	Hank Johnson (D)*	208,861	73.6
	J. Chris Vaughn (R)	75,041	26.4
5	John Lewis (D)*	234,330	84.4
	Howard Stopeck (R)	43,335	15.6
6	Tom Price (R)*	189,669	64.5
	Jeff Kazanow (D)	104,365	35.5
7	Rob Woodall (R)*	156,689	62.2
	Steve Reilly (D)	95,377	37.8
8	Austin Scott (R)*	197,789	100.0
9	Doug Collins (R)	192,101	76.2
	Jody Cooley (D)	60,052	23.8
10	Paul Broun (R)*	211,065	100.0
11	Phil Gingrey (R)*	196,968	68.6
	Patrick Thompson (D)	90,353	31.4
12	John Barrow (D)*	139,148	53.7
	Lee Anderson (R)	119,973	46.3
13	David Scott (D)*	201,988	71.7
	S. Malik (R)	79,550	28.3
14	Tom Graves (R)*	159,947	73.0
	Daniel "Danny" Grant (D)	59,245	27.0

Hawaii

Senate

		Vote total	Percent
	Mazie K. Hirono (D)	269,489	62.6
	Linda Lingle (R)	160,994	37.4

House

		Vote total	Percent
1	Colleen Hanabusa (D)*	116,505	54.6
	Charles K. Djou (R)	96,824	45.4
2	Tulsi Gabbard (D)*	168,503	80.5
	Kawika Crowley (R)	40,707	19.5

Idaho

House

		Vote total	Percent
1	Raul R. Labrador (R)*	199,402	63.0
	Jimmy Farris (D)	97,450	30.8
2	Mike Simpson (R)*	207,412	65.2
	Nicole LeFavour (D)	110,847	34.8

Illinois

House

		Vote total	Percent
1	Bobby L. Rush (D)*	236,854	73.8
	Donald E. Peloquin (R)	83,989	26.2
2	Jesse L. Jackson Jr. (D)*	188,303	63.2
	Brian Woodworth (R)	69,115	23.2
	Marcus Lewis (I)	40,006	13.4
3	Daniel Lipinski (D)*	168,738	68.5
	Richard L. Grabowski (R)	77,653	31.5
4	Luis V. Gutierrez (D)*	133,226	83.0
	Hector Concepcion (R)	27,279	17.0
5	Mike Quigley (D)*	177,729	65.7
	Dan Schmitt (R)	77,289	28.6
	Nancy Wade (GREEN)	15,359	5.7
6	Peter Roskam (R)*	193,138	59.2
	Leslie Coolidge (D)	132,991	40.8
7	Danny K. Davis (D)*	242,439	84.6
	Rita Zak (R)	31,466	11.0
8	Tammy Duckworth (D)	123,206	54.7
	Joe Walsh (R)*	101,860	45.3
9	Jan Schakowsky (D)*	194,869	66.3
	Timothy C. Wolfe (R)	98,924	33.7
10	Brad Schneider (D)	133,890	50.6
	Robert Dold (R)*	130,564	49.4
11	Bill Foster (D)	148,928	58.6
	Judy Biggert (R)*	105,348	41.4
12	Bill Enyart (D)	157,000	51.6
	Jason Plummer (R)	129,902	42.7
	Paula Bradshaw (GREEN)	17,045	5.6
13	Rodney Davis (R)	137,034	46.5
	David Gill (D)	136,032	46.2
	John Hartman (I)	21,319	7.2
14	Randy Hultgren (R)*	177,603	58.8
	Dennis Anderson (D)	124,351	41.2
15	John Shimkus (R)*	205,775	68.6
	Angela Michael (D)	94,162	31.4
16	Adam Kinzinger (R)*	181,789	61.8
	Wanda Rohl (D)	112,301	38.2
17	Cheri Bustos (D)	153,519	53.3
	Bobby Schilling (R)*	134,623	46.7
18	Aaron Schock (R)*	244,467	74.2
	Steve Waterworth (D)	85,164	25.8

Indiana

Governor

		Vote total	Percent
	Mike Pence (R)	1,275,424	49.5
	John R. Gregg (D)	1,200,016	46.6

Senate

		Vote total	Percent
	Joe Donnelly (D)	1,281,181	50.0
	Richard E. Mourdock (R)	1,133,621	44.3
	Andy Horning (LIBERT)	145,282	5.7

House

		Vote total	Percent
1	Peter J. Visclosky (D)*	187,743	67.3
	Joel Phelps (R)	91,291	32.7
2	Jackie Walorski (R)*	134,033	49.0
	Brendan Mullen (D)	130,113	47.6
3	Marlin Stutzman (R)*	187,872	67.0
	Kevin R. Boyd (D)	92,363	33.0
4	Todd Rokita (R)*	168,688	62.0
	Tara E. Nelson (D)	93,015	34.2
5	Susan W. Brooks (R)*	194,570	58.4
	Scott Reske (D)	125,347	37.6
6	Luke Messer (R)*	162,613	59.1
	Bradley T. Bookout (D)	96,678	35.1
	Rex Bell (LIBERT)	15,962	5.8
7	André Carson (D)*	162,122	62.8
	Carlos A. May (R)	95,828	37.2
8	Larry Bucshon (R)*	151,533	53.4
	Dave Crooks (D)	122,325	43.1
9	Todd Young (R)*	165,332	55.4
	Shelli Yoder (D)	132,848	44.6

Iowa

House

		Vote total	Percent
1	Bruce Braley (D)*	222,422	56.9
	Benjamin Lange (R)	162,465	41.6
2	Dave Loebsack (D)*	211,863	55.6
	John Archer (R)	161,977	42.5
3	Tom Latham (R)*	202,000	52.2
	Leonard L. Boswell (D)*	168,632	43.6
4	Steve King (R)*	200,063	52.9
	Christie Vilsack (D)	169,470	44.8

Kansas

House

		Vote total	Percent
1	Tim Huelskamp (R)*	211,337	100.0
2	Lynn Jenkins (R)*	167,463	57.0
	Tobias Schlingensiepen (D)	113,735	38.7
3	Kevin Yoder (R)*	201,087	68.4
	Joel Balam (LIBERT)	92,675	31.5
4	Mike Pompeo (R)*	161,094	62.2
	Robert Leon Tillman (D)	81,770	31.6
	Thomas Jefferson (LIBERT)	16,058	6.2

Kentucky

House

		Vote total	Percent
1	Edward Whitfield (R)*	199,956	69.6
	Charles Kendall Hatchett (D)	87,199	30.4
2	Brett Guthrie (R)*	181,508	64.3
	David Lynn Williams (D)	89,541	31.7
3	John Yarmuth (D)*	206,385	64.0
	Brooks Wicker (R)	111,452	34.5
4	Thomas Massie (R)	186,036	62.1
	William R. "Bill" Adkins (D)	104,734	35.0
5	Harold Rogers (R)*	195,408	77.9
	Kenneth Stepp (D)	55,447	22.1
6	Andy Barr (R)	153,222	50.6
	Ben Chandler (D)*	141,438	46.7

Louisiana

House

		Vote total	Percent
1	Steve Scalise (R)*	193,496	66.6
	M. V. "Vinny" Mendoza (D)	61,703	21.2
	Gary King (R)	24,844	8.6

		Vote total	Percent
2	Cedric L. Richmond (D)*	158,501	55.2
	Gary Landrieu (D)	71,916	25.0
	Dwayne Bailey (R)	38,801	13.5
3[1]	Charles Boustany Jr. (R)*	58,820	60.9
	Jeff Landry (R)*	37,767	39.1
4	John Fleming (R)*	187,894	75.3
	Randall Lord (LIBERT)	61,637	24.7
5	Rodney Alexander (R)*	202,536	77.8
	Ron Ceasar (No party affiliation)	37,486	14.4
	Clay Steven Grant (LIBERT)	20,194	7.8
6	Bill Cassidy (R)*	243,553	79.4
	Rufus Holt Craig Jr. (LIBERT)	32,185	10.5
	Richard "RPT" Torregano (No party affiliation)	30,975	10.1

Maine

Senate

		Vote total	Percent
	Angus King (I)	370,580	52.9
	Charlie Summers (R)	215,399	30.7
	Cynthia Ann Dill (D)	92,900	13.3

House

		Vote total	Percent
1	Chellie Pingree (D)*	236,363	64.8
	Jonathan T. E. Courtney (R)	128,440	35.2
2	Michael H. Michaud (D)*	191,456	58.2
	Kevin L. Raye (R)	137,542	41.8

Maryland

Senate

		Vote total	Percent
	Benjamin L. Cardin (D)*	1,474,028	56.0
	Daniel John Bongino (R)	693,291	26.3
	S. Rob Sobhani (Unaffiliated)	430,934	16.4

House

		Vote total	Percent
1	Andy Harris (R)*	214,204	63.4
	Wendy Rosen (D)	92,812	27.5
2	C. A. Dutch Ruppersberger (D)*	194,088	65.6
	Nancy C. Jacobs (R)	92,071	31.1
3	John Sarbanes (D)*	213,747	66.8
	Eric Delano Knowles (R)	94,549	29.6
4	Donna Edwards (D)*	240,385	77.2
	Faith M. Loudon (R)	64,560	20.7
5	Steny H. Hoyer (D)*	236,618	69.2
	Tony O'Donnell (R)	95,271	27.9
6	John Delaney (D)	181,921	58.8
	Roscoe G. Bartlett (R)*	117,313	37.9
7	Elijah E. Cummings (D)*	247,770	76.5
	Frank Mirabile Jr. (R)	67,405	20.8
8	Chris Van Hollen (D)*	217,531	63.4
	Kenneth R. Timmerman (R)	113,033	32.9

Massachusetts

Senate

		Vote total	Percent
	Elizabeth Warren (D)	1,696,346	53.7
	Scott P. Brown (R)*	1,458,048	46.2

House

		Vote total	Percent
1	Richard E. Neal (D)*	261,936	98.4
2	Jim McGovern (D)	259,257	98.4
3	Niki Tsongas (D)*	212,119	65.9
	Jon Golnik (R)	109,372	34.0
4	Joseph P. Kennedy III (D)	221,303	61.1
	Sean Bielat (R)	129,936	35.9
5	Edward J. Markey (D)*	257,490	75.5
	Thomas P. Tierney (R)	82,944	24.3
6	John F. Tierney (D)*	180,942	48.3
	Richard Tisei (R)	176,612	47.1
7	Michael E. Capuano (D)*	210,794	83.4
	Karla Romero (I)	41,199	16.3
8	Stephen F. Lynch (D)*	263,999	76.1
	Joe Selvaggi (R)	82,242	23.7
9	William Keating (D)*	212,754	58.7
	Christopher Sheldon (R)	116,531	32.2
	Daniel S. Botelho (I)	32,655	9.0

Michigan

Senate

		Vote total	Percent
	Debbie Stabenow (D)	2,735,826	58.8
	Peter Hoekstra (R)	1,767,386	38.0

House

		Vote total	Percent
1	Dan Benishek (R)*	167,060	48.1
	Gary McDowell (D)	165,179	47.6
2	Bill Huizenga (R)*	194,653	61.2
	Willie German Jr. (D)	108,973	34.2
3	Justin Amash (R)*	171,675	52.6
	Steve Pestka (D)	144,108	44.2
4	Dave Camp (R)*	197,386	63.1
	Debra Freidell Wirth (D)	104,996	33.6
5	Dan Kildee (D)	214,531	65.0
	Jim Slezak (R)	103,931	31.5
6	Fred Upton (R)*	174,955	54.6
	Mike O'Brien (D)	136,563	42.6
7	Tim Walberg (R)*	169,668	53.3
	Kurt Richard Haskell (D)	136,849	43.0
8	Mike Rogers (R)*	202,217	58.6
	Lance Enderle (D)	128,657	37.3
9	Sander M. Levin (D)*	208,846	61.9
	Don Volaric (R)	114,760	34.0
10	Candice S. Miller (R)*	226,075	68.8
	Chuck Stadler (D)	97,734	29.7
11	Kerry Bentivolio (R)	181,788	50.8
	Syed S. Taj (D)	158,879	44.4
12	John D. Dingell (D)*	216,884	67.9
	Cynthia Kallgren (R)	92,472	29.0
13	John Conyers Jr. (D)*	235,336	82.8
	Harry T. Sawicki (R)	38,769	13.6
14	Gary Peters (D)*	270,450	82.3
	John Hauler (R)	51,395	15.6

Minnesota

Senate

		Vote total	Percent
	Amy Klobuchar (D)*	1,854,595	65.2
	Kurt Bills (R)	867,974	30.5

House

		Vote total	Percent
1	Tim Walz (D)*	193,211	57.5
	Allen Quist (R)	142,164	42.3
2	John Kline (R)*	193,587	54.0
	Mike Obermueller (D)	164,338	45.8
3	Erik Paulsen (R)*	222,335	58.1
	Brian Barnes (D)	159,937	41.8
4	Betty McCollum (D)*	216,685	62.3
	Tony Hernandez (R)	109,659	31.5
	Steve Carlson (INDC)	21,135	6.1
5	Keith Ellison (D)*	262,102	74.5
	Chris Fields (R)	88,753	25.2
6	Michele Bachmann (R)*	179,240	50.5
	Jim Graves (D)	174,944	49.3
7	Collin C. Peterson (D)*	197,791	60.4
	Lee Byberg (R)	114,151	34.8
8	Rick Nolan (D)	191,976	54.3
	Chip Cravaack (R)*	160,520	45.4

Mississippi

Senate

		Vote total	Percent
	Roger Wicker (R)*	709,626	57.2
	Albert N. Gore Jr. (D)	503,467	40.6

House

		Vote total	Percent
1	Alan Nunnelee (R)*	186,760	60.4
	Brad Morris (D)	114,076	36.9
2	Bennie Thompson (D)*	214,978	67.1
	Bill Marcy (R)	99,160	31.0
3	Gregg Harper (R)*	234,717	80.0
	John "Luke" Pannell (REF)	58,605	20.0
4	Steven M. Palazzo (R)*	182,998	64.1
	Matt Moore (D)	82,344	28.8
	Ron Williams (LIBERT)	17,982	6.3

Missouri

Governor

		Vote total	Percent
	Jay Nixon (D)	1,494,056	54.8
	David "Dave" Spence (R)	1,160,265	42.5

Senate

		Vote total	Percent
	Claire McCaskill (D)	1,494,125	54.8
	Todd Akin (R)	1,066,159	39.1
	Jonathan Dine (LIBERT)	165,468	6.1

House

		Vote total	Percent
1	William Lacy Clay (D)*	267,927	78.7
	Robyn Hamlin (R)	60,832	17.9
2	Ann Wagner (R)	236,971	60.1
	Glenn Koenen (D)	146,272	37.1
3	Blaine Luetkemeyer (R)*	214,843	63.5
	Eric C. Mayer (D)	111,189	32.9
4	Vicky Hartzler (R)*	192,237	60.3
	Teresa Hensley (D)	113,120	35.5
5	Emanuel Cleaver II (D)*	200,290	60.5
	Jacob Turk (R)	122,149	36.9

	Candidate	Vote total	Percent
6	Sam Graves (R)*	216,906	65.0
	Kyle Yarber (D)	108,503	32.5
7	Billy Long (R)*	203,565	63.9
	Jim Evans (D)	98,498	30.9
	Kevin Craig (LIBERT)	16,668	5.2
8	Jo Ann Emerson (R)*	216,083	71.9
	Jack Rushin (D)	73,755	24.6

Montana

Governor

	Candidate	Vote total	Percent
	Steve Bullock (D)	236,450	48.9
	Rick Hill (R)	228,879	47.3

Senate

	Candidate	Vote total	Percent
	Jon Tester (D)*	236,123	48.6
	Denny Rehberg (R)	218,051	44.9
	Dan Cox (LIBERT)	31,892	6.6

House

	Candidate	Vote total	Percent
AL	Steve Daines (R)	255,468	53.2
	Kim Gillan (D)	204,939	42.7

Nebraska

Senate

	Candidate	Vote total	Percent
	Deb Fischer (R)	455,593	57.8
	Bob Kerrey (D)	332,979	42.2

House

	Candidate	Vote total	Percent
1	Jeff Fortenberry (R)*	174,889	68.3
	Korey L. Reiman (D)	81,206	31.7
2	Lee Terry (R)*	133,964	50.8
	John W. Ewing Jr. (D)	129,767	49.2
3	Adrian Smith (R)*	187,423	74.2
	Mark Sullivan (D)	65,266	25.8

Nevada

Senate

	Candidate	Vote total	Percent
	Dean Heller (R)*	457,656	45.9
	Shelley Berkley (D)	446,080	44.7

House

	Candidate	Vote total	Percent
1	Dina Titus (D)	113,967	63.6
	Chris Edwards (R)	56,521	31.5
2	Mark Amodei (R)*	162,213	57.6
	Samuel Koepnick (D)	102,019	36.2
3	Joe Heck (R)*	137,244	50.4
	John Oceguera (D)	116,823	42.9
4	Steven Horsford (D)*	120,501	50.1
	Danny Tarkanian (R)	101,261	42.1

New Hampshire

Governor

	Candidate	Vote total	Percent
	Maggie Hassan (D)	378,934	54.6
	Ovide M. Lamontagne (R)	295,026	42.5

House

	Candidate	Vote total	Percent
1	Carol Shea-Porter (D)	171,650	49.8
	Frank Guinta (R)*	158,659	46.0
2	Ann McLane Kuster (D)	169,275	50.2
	Charles Bass (R)*	152,977	45.4

New Jersey

Senate

	Candidate	Vote total	Percent
	Robert Menendez (D)*	1,985,783	58.8
	Joseph M. Kyrillos (R)	1,329,405	39.4

House

	Candidate	Vote total	Percent
1	Robert E. Andrews (D)*	210,470	68.2
	Gregory W. Horton (R)	92,459	30.0
2	Frank A. LoBiondo (R)*	166,677	57.7
	Cassandra Shober (D)	116,462	40.3
3	Jon Runyan (R)*	174,257	53.7
	Shelley Adler (D)	145,509	44.8
4	Christopher H. Smith (R)*	195,146	63.7
	Brian P. Froelich (D)	107,992	35.3
5	Scott Garrett (R)*	167,503	55.0
	Adam Gussen (D)	130,102	42.7
6	Frank Pallone Jr. (D)*	151,782	63.3
	Anna C. Little (R)	84,360	35.2
7	Leonard Lance (R)*	175,704	57.2
	Upendra J. Chivukula (D)	123,090	40.1
8	Albio Sires (D)*	130,857	78.0
	Maria Karczewski (R)	31,767	18.9
9	Bill Pascrell Jr. (D)*	162,834	74.0
	Shmuley Boteach (R)	55,094	25.0
10	Donald M. Payne Jr. (D)	201,435	87.6
	Brian C. Kelemen (R)	24,271	10.6
11	Rodney Frelinghuysen (R)*	182,239	58.8
	John Arvanites (D)	123,935	40.0
12	Rush D. Holt (D)*	189,938	69.2
	Eric A. Beck (R)	80,907	29.5

New Mexico

Senate

	Candidate	Vote total	Percent
	Martin Heinrich (D)	395,717	51.0
	Heather A. Wilson (R)	351,259	45.3

House

	Candidate	Vote total	Percent
1	Michelle Lujan Grisham (D)	162,924	59.1
	Janice E. Arnold-Jones (R)	112,473	40.8
2	Steve Pearce (R)*	133,180	59.1
	Evelyn Madrid Erhard (D)	92,162	40.9
3	Ben Ray Lujan (D)*	167,103	63.1
	Jefferson L. Byrd (R)	97,616	36.9

New York

Senate

	Candidate	Vote total	Percent
	Kirsten Gillibrand (D)*	4,822,330	72.2
	Wendy Long (R)	1,758,702	26.4

House

	Candidate	Vote total	Percent
1	Timothy H. Bishop (D)*	146,179	52.4
	Randy Altschuler (R)	131,304	47.6
2	Peter T. King (R)*	142,309	58.7
	Vivianne C. Falcone (D)	100,545	41.3
3	Steve Israel (D)*	157,880	57.8
	Stephen A. Labate (R)	113,203	41.5
4	Carolyn McCarthy (D)*	163,955	61.8
	Fran Becker (R)	85,693	32.3
	Frank Scaturro (CNSTP)	15,603	5.9
5	Gregory W. Meeks (D)*	167,836	89.7
	Allan W. Jennings Jr. (R)	17,875	9.6
6	Grace Meng (D)	111,501	67.9
	Daniel J. Halloran (R)	50,846	31.0
7	Nydia M. Velazquez (D)*	143,930	94.8
	James Murray (C)	7,971	5.2
8	Hakeem Jeffries (D)	184,039	90.2
	Alan S. Bellone (R)	17,650	8.6
9	Yvette D. Clarke (D)*	186,141	87.3
	Daniel J. Cavanagh (R)	24,164	11.3
10	Jerrold Nadler (D)*	165,743	80.8
	Michael W. Chan (R)	39,413	19.2
11	Michael G. Grimm (R)*	103,118	52.2
	Mark S. Murphy (D)	92,428	46.8
12	Carolyn B. Maloney (D)*	194,370	80.6
	Christopher R. Wight (R)	46,481	19.4
13	Charles B. Rangel (D)*	175,016	90.8
	Craig Schley (R)	12,147	6.3
14	Joseph Crowley (D)*	120,761	83.2
	William F. Gibbons Jr. (R)	21,755	15.0
15	José E. Serrano (D)*	152,661	97.2
16	Eliot L. Engel (D)*	179,562	75.9
	Joseph McLaughlin (R)	53,935	22.8
17	Nita M. Lowey (D)*	171,417	64.4
	Joe Carvin (R)	91,899	34.5
18	Sean Patrick Maloney (D)	143,845	51.9
	Nan Hayworth (R)*	133,049	48.0
19	Chris Gibson (R)*	150,245	52.8
	Julian Schreibman (D)	134,295	47.1
20	Paul Tonko (D)*	203,401	68.4
	Robert J. Dieterich (R)	93,778	31.6
21	Bill Owens (D)*	126,631	50.2
	Matt Doheny (R)	121,646	48.2
22	Richard Hanna (R)*	157,941	60.7
	Dan Lamb (D)	102,080	39.3
23	Tom Reed (R)*	137,669	51.9
	Nate Shinagawa (D)	127,535	48.1
24	Dan Maffei (D)	143,044	48.9
	Ann Marie Buerkle (R)*	127,054	43.4
	Ursula E. Rozum (GREEN)	22,670	7.7
25	Louise M. Slaughter (D)*	179,810	57.4
	Maggie Brooks (R)	133,389	42.6
26	Brian Higgins (D)*	212,588	74.8
	Michael H. Madigan (R)	71,666	25.2
27	Chris Collins (R)	161,220	50.8
	Kathy Hochul (D)*	156,219	49.2

North Carolina

Governor

	Candidate	Vote total	Percent
	Pat McCrory (R)	2,440,707	54.6
	Walter H. Dalton (D)	1,931,580	43.2

House

		Vote total	*Percent*
1	G. K. Butterfield (D)*	254,644	75.3
	Pete DiLauro (R)	77,288	22.9
2	Renee Ellmers (R)*	174,066	55.9
	Steve Wilkins (D)	128,973	41.4
3	Walter B. Jones (R)*	195,571	63.1
	Erik Anderson (D)	114,314	36.9
4	David E. Price (D)*	259,534	74.5
	Tim D'Annunzio (R)	88,951	25.5
5	Virginia Foxx (R)*	200,945	57.5
	Elisabeth Motsinger (D)	148,252	42.5
6	Howard Coble (R)*	222,116	60.9
	Tony Foriest (D)	142,467	39.1
7	Mike McIntyre (D)*	168,695	50.1
	David Rouzer (R)	168,041	49.9
8	Richard Hudson (R)	160,695	53.2
	Larry Kissell (D)*	137,139	45.4
9	Robert Pittenger (R)	194,537	51.8
	Jennifer Roberts (D)	171,503	45.6
10	Patrick T. McHenry (R)*	190,826	57.0
	Patsy Keever (D)	144,023	43.0
11	Mark Meadows (R)	190,319	57.4
	Hayden Rogers (D)	141,107	42.6
12	Melvin Watt (D)*	247,591	79.6
	Jack Brosch (R)	63,317	20.4
13	George Holding (R)	210,495	56.8
	Charles Malone (D)	160,115	43.2

North Dakota

Governor

		Vote total	Percent
	Jack Dalrymple (R)*	200,525	63.1
	Ryan M. Taylor (D)	109,047	34.3

Senate

		Vote total	Percent
	Heidi Heitkamp (D)	161,337	50.2
	Rick Berg (R)	158,282	49.3

House

		Vote total	Percent
AL	Kevin Cramer (R)	173,433	54.9
	Pam Gulleson (D)	131,869	41.7

Ohio

Senate

		Vote total	Percent
	Sherrod Brown (D)*	2,762,757	50.7
	Josh Mandel (R)	2,435,740	44.7

House

		Vote total	Percent
1	Steve Chabot (R)*	201,907	57.7
	Jeff Sinnard (D)	131,490	37.6
2	Brad Wenstrup (R)	194,299	58.6
	William R. Smith (D)	137,082	41.4
3	Joyce Beatty (D)	201,921	68.3
	Chris Long (R)	77,903	26.3
4	Jim Jordan (R)*	182,643	58.4
	Jim Slone (D)	114,214	36.5
	Chris Kalla (LIBERT)	16,141	5.2
5	Bob Latta (R)*	201,514	57.3
	Angela Zimmann (D)	137,806	39.2
6	Bill Johnson (R)*	164,536	53.2
	Charlie Wilson (D)	144,444	46.7
7	Bob Gibbs (R)*	178,104	56.4
	Joyce R. Healy-Abrams (D)	137,708	43.6
8	John A. Boehner (R)*	246,380	99.2
9	Marcy Kaptur (D)*	217,775	73.0
	Samuel J. Wurzelbacher (R)	68,666	23.0
10	Michael R. Turner (R)*	208,201	59.5
	Sharen Swartz Neuhardt (D)	131,097	37.5
11	Marcia L. Fudge (D)*	258,359	100.0
12	Pat Tiberi (R)*	233,874	63.5
	Jim Reese (D)	134,605	36.5
13	Tim Ryan (D)*	235,492	72.8
	Marisha G. Agana (R)	88,120	27.2
14	David Joyce (R)	183,660	54.0
	Dale Virgil Blanchard (D)	131,638	38.7
15	Steve Stivers (R)*	205,277	61.6
	Pat Lang (D)	128,188	38.4
16	James B. Renacci (R)*	185,167	52.0
	Betty Sutton (D)*	170,604	48.0

Oklahoma

House

		Vote total	Percent
1	Jim Bridenstine (R)	181,084	63.5
	John Olson (D)	91,421	32.0
2	Markwayne Mullin (R)	143,701	57.3
	Rob Wallace (D)	96,081	38.3
3	Frank D. Lucas (R)*	201,744	75.3
	Timothy Ray Murray (D)	53,472	20.0
4	Tom Cole (R)*	176,740	67.9
	Donna Marie Bebo (D)	71,846	27.6
5	James Lankford (R)*	153,603	58.7
	Tom Guild (D)	97,504	37.3

Oregon

House

		Vote total	Percent
1	Suzanne Bonamici (D)*	197,845	59.6
	Delinda Morgan (R)	109,699	33.0
2	Greg Walden (R)*	228,043	68.6
	Joyce B. Segers (D)	96,741	29.1
3	Earl Blumenauer (D)*	264,979	74.5
	Ronald Green (R)	70,325	19.8
4	Peter A. DeFazio (D)*	212,866	59.1
	Art Robinson (R)	140,549	39.0
5	Kurt Schrader (D)*	177,229	54.0
	Fred Thompson (R)	139,223	42.4

Pennsylvania

Senate

		Vote total	Percent
	Bob Casey (D)*	3,021,364	53.7
	Tom Smith (R)	2,509,132	44.6

House

		Vote total	Percent
1	Robert A. Brady (D)*	235,394	84.9
	John J. Featherman (R)	41,708	15.0
2	Chaka Fattah (D)*	318,176	89.3
	Robert Mansfield Jr. (R)	33,381	9.4
3	Mike Kelly (R)*	165,826	54.8
	Missa Eaton (D)	123,933	41.0
4	Scott Perry (R)	181,603	59.7
	Harry Perkinson (D)	104,643	34.4
5	Glenn Thompson (R)*	177,740	62.9
	Charles Dumas (D)	104,725	37.1
6	Jim Gerlach (R)*	191,725	57.1
	Manan Trivedi (D)	143,803	42.9
7	Patrick Meehan (R)*	209,942	59.4
	George Badey (D)	143,509	40.6
8	Michael G. Fitzpatrick (R)	199,379	56.6
	Kathy Boockvar (D)	152,859	43.4
9	Bill Shuster (R)*	169,177	61.7
	Karen Ramsburg (D)	105,128	38.3
10	Tom Marino (R)*	179,563	65.6
	Philip Scollo (D)	94,227	34.4
11	Lou Barletta (R)*	166,967	58.5
	Gene Stilp (D)	118,231	41.5
12	Keith Rothfus (R)	175,352	51.7
	Mark Critz (D)*	163,589	48.3
13	Allyson Y. Schwartz (D)	209,901	69.1
	Joseph Rooney (R)	93,918	30.9
14	Mike Doyle (D)*	251,932	76.9
	Hans Lessmann (R)	75,702	23.1
15	Charlie Dent (R)*	168,960	56.8
	Rick Daugherty (D)	128,764	43.2
16	Joe Pitts (R)*	156,192	54.8
	Aryanna Strader (D)	111,185	39.0
17	Matt Cartwright (D)	161,393	60.3
	Laureen Cummings (R)	106,208	39.7
18	Tim Murphy (R)*	216,727	64.0
	Larry Maggi (D)	122,146	36.0

Rhode Island

Senate

		Vote total	Percent
	Sheldon Whitehouse (D)*	271,034	64.8
	B. Barrett Hinckley (R)	146,222	35.0

House

		Vote total	Percent
1	David Cicilline (D)*	108,612	53.0
	Brendan Doherty (R)	83,737	40.8
	David S. Vogel (I)	12,504	6.1
2	Jim Langevin (D)*	124,067	55.7
	Michael G. Riley (R)	78,189	35.1
	Abel G. Collins (I)	20,212	9.1

South Carolina

House

		Vote total	Percent
1	Tim Scott (R)*	179,908	62.0
	Bobbie Rose (D)	103,557	35.7
2	Joe Wilson (R)*	196,116	96.3
3	Jeff Duncan (R)*	169,512	66.5
	Brian Ryan Doyle (D)	84,735	33.3
4	Trey Gowdy (R)*	173,201	64.9
	Deb Morrow (D)	89,964	33.7
5	Mick Mulvaney (R)*	154,324	55.5
	Joyce Knott (D)	123,443	44.4
6	James E. Clyburn (D)*	218,717	93.6
	Nammu Y. Muhammad (GREEN)	12,920	5.5

		Vote total	Percent
7	Tom Rice (R)	153,068	55.5
	Gloria Bromell Tinubu (D)	122,389	44.4

South Dakota

House

		Vote total	Percent
AL	Kristi Noem (R)*	207,640	57.4
	Matt Varilek (D)	153,789	42.6

Tennessee

Senate

		Vote total	Percent
	Bob Corker (R)*	1,506,443	64.9
	Mark E. Clayton (D)	705,882	30.4

House

		Vote total	Percent
1	Phil Roe (R)*	182,252	76.0
	Alan Woodruff (D)	47,663	19.9
2	John J. Duncan Jr. (R)*	196,894	74.4
	Troy Goodale (D)	54,522	20.6
3	Chuck Fleischmann (R)*	157,830	61.4
	Mary M. Headrick (D)	91,094	35.5
4	Scott DesJarlais (R)*	128,568	55.8
	Eric Stewart (D)	102,022	44.2
5	Jim Cooper (D)*	171,621	65.2
	Brad Staats (R)	86,240	32.8
6	Diane Black (R)*	184,383	76.4
	Scott Beasley (I)	34,766	14.4
	Pat Riley (GREEN)	21,633	9.0
7	Marsha Blackburn (R)*	182,730	71.0
	Credo Amouzouvik (D)	61,679	24.0
8	Stephen Fincher (R)*	190,923	68.3
	Timothy D. Dixon (D)	79,490	28.4
9	Steve Cohen (D)*	188,422	75.1
	George S. Flinn Jr. (R)	59,742	23.8

Texas

Senate

		Vote total	Percent
	Ted Cruz (R)	4,440,137	56.5
	Paul Sadler (D)	3,194,927	40.6

House

		Vote total	Percent
1	Louie Gohmert (R)*	178,322	71.4
	Shirley J. McKellar (D)	67,222	26.9
2	Ted Poe (R)*	159,664	64.8
	Jim Dougherty (D)	80,512	32.7
3	Sam Johnson (R)*	187,180	100
4	Ralph M. Hall (R)*	182,679	73.0
	VaLinda Hathcox (D)	60,214	24.0
5	Jeb Hensarling (R)*	134,091	64.4
	Linda S. Mrosko (D)	69,178	33.2
6	Joe L. Barton (R)*	145,019	58.0
	Kenneth Sanders (D)	98,053	39.2
7	John Culberson (R)*	142,793	60.8
	James Cargas (D)	85,553	36.4
8	Kevin Brady (R)*	194,043	77.3
	Neil Burns (D)	51,051	20.3
9	Al Green (D)*	144,075	78.5
	Steve Mueller (R)	36,139	19.7
10	Michael McCaul (R)*	159,783	60.5
	Tawana W. Cadien (D)	95,710	36.2
11	K. Michael Conaway (R)	177,742	78.6
	Jim Riley (D)	41,970	18.6
12	Kay Granger (R)*	175,649	70.9
	Dave Robinson (D)	66,080	26.7
13	Mac Thornberry (R)*	187,775	91.0
	John Robert Deek (LIBERT)	12,701	6.2
14	Randy Weber (R)	131,460	53.5
	Nick Lampson (D)	109,697	44.6
15	Rubén Hinojosa (D)*	89,296	60.9
	Dale A. Brueggemann (R)	54,056	36.9
16	Beto O'Rourke (D)	101,403	65.4
	Barbara Carrasco (R)	51,043	32.9
17	Bill Flores (R)*	143,284	79.9
	Ben Easton (LIBERT)	35,978	20.1
18	Sheila Jackson Lee (D)*	146,223	75.0
	Sean Seibert (R)	44,015	22.6
19	Randy Neugebauer (R)*	163,239	85.0
	Richard "Chip" Peterson (LIBERT)	28,824	15.0
20	Joaquin Castro (D)	119,032	63.9
	David Rosa (R)	62,376	33.5
21	Lamar Smith (R)*	187,015	60.5
	Candace E. Duval (D)	109,326	35.4
22	Pete Olson (R)*	160,668	64.0
	Kesha Rogers (D)	80,203	32.0
23	Pete Gallego (D)	96,676	50.3
	Francisco "Quico" Canseco (R)*	87,547	45.6
24	Kenny Marchant (R)*	148,586	61.0
	Tim Rusk (D)	87,645	36.0
25	Roger Williams (R)	154,245	58.4
	Elaine M. Henderson (D)	98,827	37.4
26	Michael C. Burgess (R)*	176,642	68.3
	David Sanchez (D)	74,237	28.7
27	Blake Farenthold (R)*	120,684	56.8
	Rose Meza Harrison (D)	83,395	39.2
28	Henry Cuellar (D)*	112,456	67.9
	William R. Hayward (R)	49,309	29.8
29	Gene Green (D)*	86,053	90.0
	James Stanczak (LIBERT)	4,996	5.2
30	Eddie Bernice Johnson (D)*	171,059	78.8
	Travis Washington Jr. (R)	41,222	19.0
31	John Carter (R)*	145,348	61.3
	Stephen Wyman (D)	82,977	35.0
32	Pete Sessions (R)*	146,653	58.3
	Katherine Savers McGovern (D)	99,288	39.5
33	Marc Veasey (D)	85,114	72.5
	Chuck Bradley (R)	30,252	25.8
34	Filemon Vela (D)	89,606	61.9
	Jessica Puente-Bradshaw (R)	52,448	36.2
35	Lloyd Doggett (D)*	105,626	63.9
	Susan Narvaiz (R)	52,894	32.0
36	Steve Stockman (R)	165,405	70.7
	Max Martin (D)	62,143	26.6

Utah

Governor

		Vote total	Percent
	Gary R. Herbert (R)*	688,592	68.4
	Peter Cooke (D)	277,622	27.6

Senate

		Vote total	Percent
	Orrin G. Hatch (R)*	657,608	65.3
	Scott N. Howell (D)	301,873	30.0

House

		Vote total	Percent
1	Rob Bishop (R)*	175,487	71.5
	Donna M. McAleer (D)	60,611	24.7
2	Chris Stewart (R)	154,523	62.2
	Jay Seegmiller (D)	83,176	33.5
3	Jason Chaffetz (R)*	198,828	76.6
	Soren Simonsen (D)	60,719	23.4
4	Jim Matheson (D)*	119,803	48.8
	Mia Love (R)	119,035	48.5

Vermont

Governor

		Vote total	Percent
	Peter Shumlin (D)*	170,598	57.8
	Randy Brock (R)	110,940	37.6

Senate

		Vote total	Percent
	Bernard Sanders (I)	209,053	71.0
	John MacGovern (R)	73,198	24.9

House

		Vote total	Percent
AL	Peter Welch (D)*	208,600	71.9
	Mark Donka (R)	67,543	23.3

Virginia

Senate

		Vote total	Percent
	Tim Kaine (D)	2,010,067	52.9
	George Allen (R)	1,785,542	47.0

House

		Vote total	Percent
1	Rob Wittman (R)*	200,845	56.3
	Adam M. Cook (D)	147,036	41.2
2	Scott Rigell (R)*	166,231	53.8
	Paul Hirschbiel (D)	142,548	46.1
3	Robert C. Scott (D)*	259,199	81.3
	Dean L. Longo (R)	58,931	18.5
4	J. Randy Forbes (R)*	199,292	56.9
	Ella P. Ward (D)	150,190	42.9
5	Robert Hurt (R)*	193,009	55.4
	John Wade Douglass (D)	149,214	42.9
6	Robert W. Goodlatte (R)*	211,278	65.2
	Andrew B. Schmookler (D)	111,949	34.6
7	Eric Cantor (R)*	222,983	58.4
	E. Wayne Powell (D)	158,012	41.4
8	James P. Moran (D)*	226,847	64.6
	J. Patrick Murray (R)	107,370	30.6
9	Morgan Griffith (R)*	184,882	61.3
	Anthony J. Flaccavento (D)	116,400	38.6

		Vote total	Percent
10	Frank R. Wolf (R)*	214,038	58.4
	Kristin A. Cabral (D)	142,024	38.8
11	Gerald E. Connolly (D)*	202,606	61.0
	Chris S. Perkins (R)	117,902	35.5

Washington

		Vote total	Percent
Governor			
	Jay Inslee (D)	1,582,802	51.5
	Rob McKenna (R)	1,488,245	48.5
Senate			
	Maria Cantwell (D)*	1,855,493	60.4
	Michael Baumgartner (R)	1,213,924	39.5
House			
1	Suzan DelBene (D)	177,025	53.9
	John Koster (R)	151,187	46.1
2	Rick Larsen (D)*	184,826	61.1
	Dan Matthews (R)	117,465	38.9
3	Jaime Herrera Beutler (R)*	177,446	60.4
	Jon T. Haugen (D)	116,438	39.6
4	Doc Hastings (R)*	154,749	66.2
	Mary Baechler (D)	78,940	33.8
5	Cathy McMorris Rodgers (R)*	191,066	61.9
	Rich Cowan (D)	117,512	38.1
6	Derek Kilmer (D)	186,661	59.0
	Bill Driscoll (R)	129,725	41.0
7	Jim McDermott (D)*	298,368	79.6
	Ron Bemis (R)	76,212	20.3
8	Dave Reichert (R)*	180,204	59.6
	Karen Porterfield (D)	121,886	40.3
9	Adam Smith (D)*	192,034	71.6
	James Postma (R)	76,105	28.4
10	Denny Heck (D)	163,036	58.6
	Richard "Dick" Muri (R)	115,381	41.4

West Virginia

		Vote total	Percent
Governor			
	Earl Ray Tomblin (D)*	335,468	50.5
	Bill Maloney (R)	303,291	45.6
Senate			
	Joe Manchin III (D)*	399,908	60.6
	John Raese (R)	240,787	36.5
House			
1	David B. McKinley (R)*	133,809	62.5
	Sue Thorn (D)	80,342	37.5
2	Shelley Moore Capito (R)*	158,206	69.8
	Howard Swint (D)	68,560	30.2
3	Nick J. Rahall II (D)*	108,199	54.0
	Rick Snuffer (R)	92,238	46.0

Wisconsin

		Vote total	Percent
Senate			
	Tammy Baldwin (D)	1,547,104	51.4
	Tommy G. Thompson (R)	1,380,126	45.9
House			
1	Paul D. Ryan (R)*	200,423	54.9
	Rob Zerban (D)	158,414	43.4
2	Mark Pocan (D)	265,422	67.9
	Chad Lee (R)	124,683	31.9
3	Ron Kind (D)*	217,712	64.1
	Ray Boland (R)	121,713	35.8
4	Gwen Moore (D)*	235,257	72.2
	Dan Sebring (R)	80,787	24.8
5	Jim Sensenbrenner (R)*	250,335	67.7
	Dave Heaster (D)	118,478	32.0
6	Tom Petri (R)*	223,460	62.1
	Joseph C. Kallas (D)	135,921	37.8
7	Sean P. Duffy (R)*	201,720	56.1
	Pat Kreitlow (D)	157,524	43.8
8	Reid Ribble (R)*	198,874	55.9
	Jamie Wall (D)	156,287	44.0

Wyoming

		Vote total	Percent
Senate			
	John Barrasso (R)*	185,250	75.6
	Tim Chesnut (D)	53,019	21.7
House			
AL	Cynthia M. Lummis (R)*	166,452	68.9
	Chris Henrichsen (D)	57,573	23.8

1. Results are from December 12, 2012, runoff. Neither candidate had received a 50 percent majority in the November election.

Results of House Elections, 1928–2012

	1928	*1930*	*1932*	*1934*	*1936*	*1938*	*1940*	*1942*	*1944*	*1946*	*1948*	*1950*	*1952*	*1954*	*1956*	*1958*	*1960*	*1962*	*1964*	*1966*	*1968*	*1970*
Totals																						
Democrats	165	217	313	322	334	262	268	222	242	188	263	235	213	232	234	283	263	259	295	248	243	255
Republicans	269	217	117	103	88	169	162	209	191	246	171	199	221	203	201	153	174	176	140	187	192	180
Alabama																						
Democrats	10	10	9[1]	9	9	9	9	9	9	9	9	9	9	9	9	9	9	8[1]	3	5	5	5
Republicans	0	0	0	0	0	0	0	0	0	0	0	0	0	0	0	0	0	0	5	3	3	3
Alaska																						
Democrats	—	—	—	—	—	—	—	—	—	—	—	—	—	—	—	1	1	1	1	0	0	1
Republicans	—	—	—	—	—	—	—	—	—	—	—	—	—	—	—	0	0	0	0	1	1	0
Arizona																						
Democrats	1	1	1	1	1	1	1	2[2]	2	2	2	2	1	1	1	1	1	2[2]	2	1	1	1
Republicans	0	0	0	0	0	0	0	0	0	0	0	0	1	1	1	1	1	1	1	2	2	2
Arkansas																						
Democrats	7	7	7	7	7	7	7	7	7	7	7	7	6[1]	6	6	6	6	4[1]	4	3	3	3
Republicans	0	0	0	0	0	0	0	0	0	0	0	0	0	0	0	0	0	0	0	1	1	1
California																						
Democrats	1	1	11[2]	13	15	12	11	12[2]	16	9	10	10	11[2]	11	13	16	16	25[2,3]	23	21	21	20
Republicans	10	10	9	7	4	8	9	11	7	14	13	13	19	19	17	14	14	13	15	17	17	18
Colorado																						
Democrats	1	1	4	4	4	4	2	1	0	1	3	2	2	2	2	3	2	2	4	3	3	2
Republicans	3	3	0	0	0	0	2	3	4	3	1	2	2	2	2	1	2	2	0	1	1	2
Connecticut																						
Democrats	0	2	2[2]	4	6	2	6	0	4	0	3	2	1	1	0	6	4	5	6	5	4	3
Republicans	5	3	4	2	0	4	0	6	2	6	3	4	5	5	6	0	2	1	0	1	2	2
Delaware																						
Democrats	0	0	1	0	1	0	1	0	1	0	0	0	0	1	0	1	1	1	1	0	0	0
Republicans	1	1	0	1	0	1	0	1	0	1	1	0	1	0	0	0	0	0	0	1	1	1
Florida																						
Democrats	4	4	5[2]	5	5	5	5	6[2]	6	6	6	6	8[2]	7	7	7	7	10[2]	10	9	9	9
Republicans	0	0	0	0	0	0	0	0	0	0	0	0	0	1	1	1	1	2	2	3	3	3
Georgia																						
Democrats	12	12	10[1]	10	10	10	10	10	10	10	10	10	10	10	10	10	10	10	9	8	8	8
Republicans	0	0	0	0	0	0	0	0	0	0	0	0	0	0	0	0	0	0	1	2	2	2
Hawaii																						
Democrats	—	—	—	—	—	—	—	—	—	—	—	—	—	—	—	—	1	2[2]	2	2	2	2
Republicans	—	—	—	—	—	—	—	—	—	—	—	—	—	—	—	—	0	0	0	0	0	0
Idaho																						
Democrats	0	0	2	2	2	1	1	1	1	0	1	0	1	1	1	1	2	2	1	0	0	0
Republicans	2	2	0	0	0	1	1	1	1	2	1	2	1	1	1	1	0	0	1	2	2	2
Illinois																						
Democrats	6	13[4]	19	21	21	17	11	7[1]	11	6	12	8	9[1]	12	11	14	14	12[1]	13	12	12	12
Republicans	21	14	8	6	6	10	16	19	15	20	14	18	16	13	14	11	11	12	11	12	12	12
Indiana																						
Democrats	3	9	12[1]	11	11	5	4	2[1]	2	2	7	2	1	2	2	8	4[4]	4	6	5	4	5
Republicans	10	4	0	1	1	7	8	9	9	9	4	9	10	9	9	3	7	7	5	6	7	6
Iowa																						
Democrats	0	1	6[1]	6	5	2	2	0[1]	0	0	0	0	0	0	1	4	2	1[1]	6	2	2	2
Republicans	11	10	3	3	4	7	7	8	8	8	8	8	8	8	7	4	6	6	1	5	5	5
Kansas																						
Democrats	1	1	3[1]	3	2	1	1	0[1]	0	0	0	0	1	0	1	3	1	0[1]	0	0	0	1
Republicans	7	7	4	4	5	6	6	6	6	6	6	6	5	6	5	3	5	5	5	5	5	4
Kentucky																						
Democrats	2	9	9[1]	8	8	8	8	8	8	6	7	7	6[1]	6	6	7	7	5[1]	6	4	4	5
Republicans	9	2	0	1	1	1	1	1	1	3	2	2	2	2	2	1	1	2	1	3	3	2
Louisiana																						
Democrats	8	8	8	8	8	8	8	8	8	8	8	8	8	8	8	8	8	8	8	8	8	8
Republicans	0	0	0	0	0	0	0	0	0	0	0	0	0	0	0	0	0	0	0	0	0	0
Maine																						
Democrats	0	0	2[1]	2	0	0	0	0	0	0	0	0	0	0	1	2	0	0[1]	1	2	2	2
Republicans	4	4	1	1	3	3	3	3	3	3	3	3	3	3	2	1	3	2	1	0	0	0

1. State lost seats due to reapportionment.

2. State gained seats due to reapportionment.

3. Alaska 1972, California 1962, and Louisiana 1972: national and state totals reflect the reelection of a Democrat who died before the election but whose name remained on the ballot.

	1972	*1974*	*1976*	*1978*	*1980*	*1982*	*1984*	*1986*	*1988*	*1990*	*1992*	*1994*	*1996*	*1998*	*2000*	*2002*	*2004*	*2006*	*2008*	*2010*	*2012*
Totals																					
Democrats	243	291	292	277	243	269	253	258	260	267	258	204	207	211	212	205	202	233	255	193	201
Republicans	192	144	143	158	192	166	182	177	175	167	176	230	227	223	221	229	232	202	180	242	234
Alabama																					
Democrats	4[1]	4	4	4	4	5	5	5	5	5	4	4	2	2	2	2	2	2	3	1	1
Republicans	3	3	3	3	3	2	2	2	2	2	3	3	5	5	5	5	5	5	4	6	6
Alaska																					
Democrats	1[3]	0	0	0	0	0	0	0	0	0	0	0	0	0	0	0	0	0	0	0	0
Republicans	0	1	1	1	1	1	1	1	1	1	1	1	1	1	1	1	1	1	1	1	1
Arizona																					
Democrats	1[2]	1	2	2	2	2[2]	1	1	1	1	3[2]	1	1	1	1	2	2	4	3	3	5[2]
Republicans	3	3	2	2	2	3	4	4	4	4	3	5	5	5	5	6	6	4	5	5	4
Arkansas																					
Democrats	3	3	3	2	2	2	3	3	3	3	2	2	2	2	3	3	3	3	3	1	0
Republicans	1	1	1	2	2	2	1	1	1	1	2	2	2	2	1	1	1	1	1	3	4
California																					
Democrats	23[2]	28	29	26	22	28[2]	27	27	27	26	30[2]	27	29	28	32	33	33	34	34	34	38
Republicans	20	15	14	17	21	17	18	18	18	19	22	25	23	24	20	20	20	19	19	19	15
Colorado																					
Democrats	2[2]	3	3	3	3	3[2]	2	3	3	3	2	2	2	2	2	2	3	4	5	3	3
Republicans	3	2	2	2	2	3	4	3	3	3	4	4	4	4	4	5	4	3	2	4	4
Connecticut																					
Democrats	3	4	4	5	4	4	3	3	3	3	3	3	4	4	3	2	2	4	5	5	5
Republicans	3	2	2	1	2	2	3	3	3	3	3	3	2	2	3	3	3	1	0	0	0
Delaware																					
Democrats	0	0	0	0	0	1	1	1	1	1	0	0	0	0	0	0	0	0	0	1	1
Republicans	1	1	1	1	1	0	0	0	0	0	1	1	1	1	1	1	1	1	1	0	0
Florida																					
Democrats	11[2]	10	10	12	11	13[2]	12	12	10	9	10[2]	8	8	8	8	7	7	9	10	6	10[2]
Republicans	4	5	5	3	4	6	7	7	9	10	13	15	15	15	15	18	18	16	15	19	17
Georgia																					
Democrats	9	10	10	9	9	9	8	8	9	9	7[2]	4	3	3	3	5	6	7	6	5	5[2]
Republicans	1	0	0	1	1	1	2	2	1	1	4	7	8	8	8	8	7	6	7	8	9
Hawaii																					
Democrats	2	2	2	2	2	2	2	1	1	2	2	2	2	2	2	2	2	2	2	2	2
Republicans	0	0	0	0	0	0	0	1	1	0	0	0	0	0	0	0	0	0	0	0	0
Idaho																					
Democrats	0	0	0	0	0	0	1	1	1	2	1	0	0	0	0	0	0	2	1	0	0
Republicans	2	2	2	2	2	2	1	1	1	0	1	2	2	2	2	2	2	0	1	2	2
Illinois																					
Democrats	10	13	12	11	10	12[1]	13	13	14	15	12[1]	10	10	10	10	9	10	10	12	8	12[1]
Republicans	14	11	12	13	14	10	9	9	8	7	8	10	10	10	10	10	9	9	7	11	6[8]
Indiana																					
Democrats	4	9	8	7	6	5[1]	5[4]	6	6	8	7	4	4	4	4	3	2	5	5	3	2
Republicans	7	2	3	4	5	5	5	4	4	2	3	6	6	6	6	6	7	4	4	6	7
Iowa																					
Democrats	3[1]	5	4	3	3	3	2	2	2	2	1[1]	0	1	1	1	1	1	3	3	3	2[1]
Republicans	3	1	2	3	3	3	4	4	4	4	4	5	4	4	4	4	4	2	2	2	2
Kansas																					
Democrats	1	1	2	1	1	2	2	2	2	2	2[1]	0	0	1	1	1	1	2	1	0	0
Republicans	4	4	3	4	4	3	3	3	3	3	2	4	4	3	3	3	3	2	3	4	4
Kentucky																					
Democrats	5	5	5	4	4	4	4	4	4	4	4[1]	2	1	1	1	1	1	2	2	2	1
Republicans	2	2	2	3	3	3	3	3	3	3	2	4	5	5	5	5	5	4	4	4	5
Louisiana																					
Democrats	7[3]	6[5]	6	5	6	6	6	5	4	4	4[1]	4	2	2	2	3	2	2	1	1	1[1]
Republicans	1	2	2	3	2	2	2	3	4	4	3	3	5	5	5	4	5	5	6	6	5
Maine																					
Democrats	1	0	0	0	0	0	0	1	1	1	1	1	2	2	2	2	2	2	2	2	2
Republicans	1	2	2	2	2	2	2	1	1	1	1	1	0	0	0	0	0	0	0	0	0

4. Illinois 1930, Indiana 1960 and 1984, and New Hampshire 1936: national and state totals reflect the final outcome of a contested election in which a Republican was first certified the winner, but the House decided to seat the Democrat.

5. Louisiana 1974: national and state totals reflect the final outcome of a contested election in which no winner was declared, followed by a special election won by the Republican.

	1928	1930	1932	1934	1936	1938	1940	1942	1944	1946	1948	1950	1952	1954	1956	1958	1960	1962	1964	1966	1968	1970
Maryland																						
Democrats	4	6	6	6	6	6	6	4	5	4	4	3	3[2]	4	4	7	6	6[2]	6	5	4	5
Republicans	2	0	0	0	0	0	0	2	1	2	2	3	4	3	3	0	1	2	2	3	4	3
Massachusetts																						
Democrats	3	4	5[1]	7	5	5	6	4[1]	4	5	4	6	6	7	7	8	8	7[1]	7	7	7	8
Republicans	13	12	10	8	10	10	9	10	10	9	8	8	8	7	7	6	6	5	5	5	5	4
Michigan																						
Democrats	0	0	10[2]	6	8	5	6	5	6	3	5	5	5[2]	7	6	7	7	8[2]	12	7	7	7
Republicans	13	13	7	11	9	12	11	12	11	14	12	12	13	11	12	11	11	11	7	12	12	12
Minnesota																						
Democrats	0	0	1[1]	1	1	1	0	0	2	1	4	4	4	5	5	4	3	4[1]	4	3	3	4
Republicans	9	9	3	5	3	7	8	8	7	8	5	5	5	4	4	5	6	4	4	5	5	4
Mississippi																						
Democrats	8	8	7[1]	7	7	7	7	7	7	7	7	7	6[1]	6	6	6	6	5[1]	4	5	5	5
Republicans	0	0	0	0	0	0	0	0	0	0	0	0	0	0	0	0	0	0	1	0	0	0
Missouri																						
Democrats	6	12	13[1]	12	12	12	10	5	7	4	12	10	7	9	10	10	9	8[1]	8	8	9	9
Republicans	10	4	0	1	1	1	3	8	6	9	1	3	4	2	1	1	2	2	2	2	1	1
Montana																						
Democrats	1	1	2	2	2	1	1	2	1	1	1	1	1	1	2	2	1	1	1	1	1	1
Republicans	1	1	0	0	0	1	1	0	1	1	1	1	1	1	0	0	1	1	1	1	1	1
Nebraska																						
Democrats	2	4	5[1]	4	4	2	2	0[1]	0	0	1	0	0	0	0	2	0	0[1]	1	0	0	0
Republicans	4	2	0	1	1	3	3	4	4	4	3	4	4	4	4	2	4	3	2	3	3	3
Nevada																						
Democrats	0	0	1	1	1	1	1	1	1	0	1	1	0	0	1	1	1	1	1	1	1	1
Republicans	1	1	0	0	0	0	0	0	0	1	0	0	1	1	0	0	0	0	0	0	0	0
New Hampshire																						
Democrats	0	0	1	1	1[4]	0	0	0	0	0	0	0	0	0	0	0	0	0	1	0	0	0
Republicans	2	2	1	1	1	2	2	2	2	2	2	2	2	2	2	2	2	2	1	2	2	2
New Jersey																						
Democrats	2	3	4[2]	4	7	3	4	3	2	2	5	5	5	6	4	5	6	7[2]	11	9	9	9
Republicans	10	9	10	10	7	11	10	11	12	12	9	9	9	8	10	9	8	8	4	6	6	6
New Mexico																						
Democrats	0	1	1	1	1	1	1	2[2]	2	2	2	2	2	2	2	2	2	2	2	2	0	1
Republicans	1	0	0	0	0	0	0	0	0	0	0	0	0	0	0	0	0	0	0	0	2	1
New York																						
Democrats	23	23	29[2]	29	29	25	25	23	22	16	24	23	16[1]	17	17	19	22	20[1]	27	26	26	24
Republicans	20	20	16	16	16	19	19	21	22	28	20	22	27	26	26	24	21	21	14	15	15	17
North Carolina																						
Democrats	8	10	11[2]	11	11	11	11	12[2]	12	12	12	12	11	11	11	11	11	9[1]	9	8	7	7
Republicans	2	0	0	0	0	0	0	0	0	0	0	0	1	1	1	1	1	2	2	3	4	4
North Dakota																						
Democrats	0	0	0[1]	0	0	0	0	0	0	0	0	0	0	0	0	1	0	0	1	0	0	1
Republicans	3	3	2	2	2	2	2	2	2	2	2	2	2	2	2	1	2	2	1	2	2	1
Ohio																						
Democrats	3	9	18[2]	18	22	9	12	3[1]	6	4	12	7	6	6	6	9	7	6[2]	10	5	6	7
Republicans	19	13	6	6	2	15	12	20	17	19	11	15	16	17	17	14	16	18	14	19	18	17
Oklahoma																						
Democrats	5	7	9[2]	9	9	9	8	7[1]	6	6	8	6	5[1]	5	5	5	5	5	5	4	4	4
Republicans	3	1	0	0	0	0	1	1	2	2	0	2	1	1	1	1	1	1	1	2	2	2
Oregon																						
Democrats	0	1	2	1	2	1	1	0[2]	0	0	0	0	0	1	3	3	2	3	3	2	2	2
Republicans	3	2	1	2	1	2	2	4	4	4	4	4	4	3	1	1	2	1	1	2	2	2
Pennsylvania																						
Democrats	1	3	11[1]	23	27	15	19	14[1]	15	5	16	13	11[1]	14	13	16	14	13[1]	15	14	14	14
Republicans	35	33	23	11	7	9	15	19	18	28	19	20	19	16	17	14	16	14	12	13	13	13
Rhode Island																						
Democrats	1	1	2[1]	2	2	0	2	2	2	2	2	2	2	2	2	2	2	2	2	2	2	2
Republicans	2	2	0	0	0	2	0	0	0	0	0	0	0	0	0	0	0	0	0	0	0	0
South Carolina																						
Democrats	7	7	6[1]	6	6	6	6	6	6	6	6	6	6	6	6	6	6	6	6	5	5	5
Republicans	0	0	0	0	0	0	0	0	0	0	0	0	0	0	0	0	0	0	0	1	1	1
South Dakota																						
Democrats	0	0	2[1]	2	1	0	0	0	0	0	0	0	0	0	1	1	0	0	0	0	0	2
Republicans	3	3	0	0	1	2	2	2	2	2	2	2	2	2	1	1	2	2	2	2	2	0

6. Massachusetts 1972 and Pennsylvania 1980: national and state Democratic totals reflect the election of an Independent candidate who previously announced he would serve as a Democrat.

7. Texas 1928: national and state totals reflect the final outcome of a contested election in which a Democrat was at first certified the winner, but the House decided to seat the Republican.

	1972	*1974*	*1976*	*1978*	*1980*	*1982*	*1984*	*1986*	*1988*	*1990*	*1992*	*1994*	*1996*	*1998*	*2000*	*2002*	*2004*	*2006*	*2008*	*2010*	*2012*
Maryland																					
Democrats	4	5	5	6	7	7	6	6	6	5	4	4	4	4	4	6	6	6	7	6	7
Republicans	4	3	3	2	1	1	2	2	2	3	4	4	4	4	4	2	2	2	1	2	1
Massachusetts																					
Democrats	9[6]	10	10	10	10	10[1]	10	10	10	10	8[1]	8	10	10	10	10	10	10	10	10	9
Republicans	3	2	2	2	2	1	1	1	1	1	2	2	0	0	0	0	0	0	0	0	0
Michigan																					
Democrats	7	12	11	13	12	12[1]	11	11	11	11	10[1]	9	10	10	9	6	6	6	8	6	5[1]
Republicans	12	7	8	6	7	6	7	7	7	7	6	7	6	6	7	9	9	9	7	9	9
Minnesota																					
Democrats	4	5	5	4	3	5	5	5	5	6	6	6	6	6	5	4	4	5	5	4	5
Republicans	4	3	3	4	5	3	3	3	3	2	2	2	2	2	3	4	4	3	3	4	3
Mississippi																					
Democrats	3	3	3	3	3	3	3	4	4	5	5	4	2	3	3	2	2	2	3	1	1
Republicans	2	2	2	2	2	2	2	1	1	0	0	1	3	2	2	2	2	2	1	3	3
Missouri																					
Democrats	9	9	8	8	6	6[1]	6	5	5	6	6	6	5	5	4	4	4	4	4	3	2[1]
Republicans	1	1	2	2	4	3	3	4	4	3	3	3	4	4	5	5	5	5	5	6	6
Montana																					
Democrats	1	2	1	1	1	1	1	1	1	1	1[1]	1	1	0	0	0	0	0	0	0	0
Republicans	1	0	1	1	1	1	1	1	1	1	0	0	0	1	1	1	1	1	1	1	1
Nebraska																					
Democrats	0	0	1	1	0	0	0	0	1	1	1	0	0	0	0	0	0	0	0	0	0
Republicans	3	3	2	2	3	3	3	3	2	2	2	3	3	3	3	3	3	3	3	3	3
Nevada																					
Democrats	0	1	1	1	1	1[2]	1	1	1	1	1	0	0	1	1	1	1	1	2	1	2
Republicans	1	0	0	0	0	1	1	1	1	1	1	2	2	1	1	2	2	2	1	2	2
New Hampshire																					
Democrats	0	1	1	1	1	1	0	0	0	1	1	0	0	0	0	0	0	2	2	0	2
Republicans	2	1	1	1	1	1	2	2	2	1	1	2	2	2	2	2	2	0	0	2	0
New Jersey																					
Democrats	8	12	11	10	8	9[1]	8	8	8	8	7[1]	5	6	7	7	7	7	7	8	7	6[1]
Republicans	7	3	4	5	7	5	6	6	6	6	6	8	7	6	6	6	6	6	5	6	6
New Mexico																					
Democrats	1	1	1	1	0	1[2]	1	1	1	1	1	1	1	1	1	1	1	1	3	2	2
Republicans	1	1	1	1	2	2	2	2	2	2	2	2	2	2	2	2	2	2	0	1	1
New York																					
Democrats	22[1]	27	28	26	22	20[1]	19	20	21	21	18[1]	17	18	18	19	19	20	23	26	21	21[1]
Republicans	17	12	11	13	17	14	15	14	13	13	13	14	13	13	12	10	9	6	3	8	6
North Carolina																					
Democrats	7	9	9	9	7	9	6	8	8	7	8[2]	4	6	5	5	6	6	7	8	7	4
Republicans	4	2	2	2	4	2	5	3	3	4	4	8	6	7	7	7	7	6	5	6	9
North Dakota																					
Democrats	0[1]	0	0	0	1	1	1	1	1	1	1	1	1	1	1	1	1	1	1	0	0
Republicans	1	1	1	1	0	0	0	0	0	0	0	0	0	0	0	0	0	0	0	1	1
Ohio																					
Democrats	7[1]	8	10	10	11	10[1]	11	11	11	11	10[1]	6	8	8	8	6	6	7	10	5	4[1]
Republicans	16	15	13	13	12	11	10	10	10	10	9	13	11	11	11	12	12	11	8	13	12
Oklahoma																					
Democrats	5	6	5	5	5	5	5	4	4	4	4	1	0	0	1	1	1	1	1	1	0
Republicans	1	0	1	1	1	1	1	2	2	2	2	5	6	6	5	4	4	4	4	4	5
Oregon																					
Democrats	2	4	4	4	3	3[2]	3	3	3	4	4	3	4	4	4	4	4	4	4	4	4
Republicans	2	0	0	0	1	2	2	2	2	1	1	2	1	1	1	1	1	1	1	1	1
Pennsylvania																					
Democrats	13[1]	14	17	15	13[6]	13[1]	13	12	12	11	11[1]	11	11	11	10	7	7	11	12	7	5[1]
Republicans	12	11	8	10	12	10	10	11	11	12	10	10	10	10	11	12	12	8	7	12	13
Rhode Island																					
Democrats	2	2	2	2	1	1	1	1	0	1	1	2	2	2	2	2	2	2	2	2	2
Republicans	0	0	0	0	1	1	1	1	2	1	1	0	0	0	0	0	0	0	0	0	0
South Carolina																					
Democrats	4	5	5	4	2	3	3	4	4	4	3	2	2	2	2	2	2	2	2	1	1[2]
Republicans	2	1	1	2	4	3	3	2	2	2	3	4	4	4	4	4	4	4	4	5	6
South Dakota																					
Democrats	1	0	0	1	1	1[1]	1	1	1	1	1	1	0	0	0	0	1	1	1	0	0
Republicans	1	2	2	1	1	0	0	0	0	0	0	0	1	1	1	1	0	0	0	1	1

8. At the time of the 2012 elections, Illinois had 18 House seats divided between 12 Democrats and 6 Republicans. However, following the election one Democrat—Jesse Jackson Jr.—resigned his seat, citing health and other issues. A special election to fill the vacancy was scheduled in 2013. For purposes of this table, that contest has been assigned to Democrats because Jackson's seat in Chicago is one of the safest Democratic seats in the nation. If a Democrat wins, as expected, the Illinois ratio of Democrats to Republicans will be 12 to 6.

	1928	1930	1932	1934	1936	1938	1940	1942	1944	1946	1948	1950	1952	1954	1956	1958	1960	1962	1964	1966	1968	1970
Tennessee																						
Democrats	8	8	7[1]	7	7	7	7	8[2]	8	8	8	8	7[1]	7	7	7	7	6	6	5	5	5
Republicans	2	2	2	2	2	2	2	2	2	2	2	2	2	2	2	2	2	3	3	4	4	4
Texas																						
Democrats	17	17	21[2]	21	21	21	21	21	21	21	21	21	22[2]	21	21	21	21	21[2]	23	21	20	20
Republicans	1[7]	1	0	0	0	0	0	0	0	0	0	0	0	1	1	1	1	2	0	2	3	3
Utah																						
Democrats	0	0	2	2	2	2	2	2	2	1	2	2	0	0	0	1	2	0	1	0	0	1
Republicans	2	2	0	0	0	0	0	0	0	1	0	0	2	2	2	1	0	2	1	2	2	1
Vermont																						
Democrats	0	0	0[1]	0	0	0	0	0	0	0	0	0	0	0	0	1	0	0	0	0	0	0
Republicans	2	2	1	1	1	1	1	1	1	1	1	1	1	1	1	0	1	1	1	1	1	1
Virginia																						
Democrats	8	9	9[1]	9	9	9	9	9	9	9	9	9	7[2]	8	8	8	8	8	8	6	5	4
Republicans	2	1	0	0	0	0	0	0	0	0	0	0	3	2	2	2	2	2	2	4	5	6
Washington																						
Democrats	1	1	6[2]	6	6	6	6	3	4	1	2	2	1[2]	1	1	1	2	1	5	5	5	6
Republicans	4	4	0	0	0	0	0	3	2	5	4	4	6	6	6	6	5	6	2	2	2	1
West Virginia																						
Democrats	1	2	6	6	6	5	6	3	5	2	6	6	5	6	4	5	5	4[1]	4	4	5	5
Republicans	5	4	0	0	0	1	0	3	1	4	0	0	1	0	2	1	1	1	1	1	0	0
Wisconsin																						
Democrats	0	1	5[1]	3	3	0	1	3	2	0	2	1	1	3	3	5	4	4	5	3	3	5
Republicans	11	10	5	0	0	8	6	5	7	10	8	9	9	7	7	5	6	6	5	7	7	5
Wyoming																						
Democrats	0	0	0	1	1	0	1	0	0	0	0	0	0	0	0	0	0	1	0	0	1	1
Republicans	1	1	1	0	0	1	0	1	1	1	1	1	1	1	1	1	1	1	0	1	1	0

NOTE: State totals reflect the number of Democrats and Republicans in each House delegation at the start of each Congress. The above totals do not include "other" representatives elected as independent or third-party candidates. Those numbers are California: Progressive 1936 (1). (No formal party. The representative became a Democrat in 1938.) Minnesota: Farmer-Labor 1928–1930 (1), 1932 (5), 1934 (3), 1936 (5), 1938–1942 (1). (Merged with D in 1944.) New York: American Labor 1938–1948 (1). (Party disbanded after 1954.) Ohio: Independent 1950–1952 (1). (Defeated by Democrat in 1954.) Wisconsin: Progressive 1934 (7), 1936–1938 (2), 1940 (3), 1942 (2) and 1944 (1). (Disbanded after 1944. The last Progressive became a Republican in 1946.) Vermont: Independent 1990–2000 (1). Virginia: Independent 2000 (1). National totals: 1928–1930 (1), 1932 (5), 1934 (10), 1936 (13), 1938 (4), 1940 (5), 1942 (4), 1944 (2), 1946–1952 (1), 1990–1998 (1), and 2000 (2).

	1972	*1974*	*1976*	*1978*	*1980*	*1982*	*1984*	*1986*	*1988*	*1990*	*1992*	*1994*	*1996*	*1998*	*2000*	*2002*	*2004*	*2006*	*2008*	*2010*	*2012*
Tennessee																					
Democrats	3[1]	5	5	5	5	6[2]	6	6	6	6	6	4	4	4	4	5	5	5	5	2	2
Republicans	5	3	3	3	3	3	3	3	3	3	3	5	5	5	5	4	4	4	4	7	7
Texas																					
Democrats	20[2]	21	22	20	19	22[2]	17	17	19	19	21[2]	19	17	17	17	17	11	13	12	9	12[2]
Republicans	4	3	2	4	5	5	10	10	8	8	9	11	13	13	13	15	21	19	20	23	24
Utah																					
Democrats	2	2	1	1	0	0[2]	0	1	1	2	2	1	0	0	1	1	1	1	1	1	1[2]
Republicans	0	0	1	1	2	3	3	2	2	1	1	2	3	3	2	2	2	2	2	2	3
Vermont																					
Democrats	0	0	0	0	0	0	0	0	0	0	0	0	0	0	0	0	0	1	1	1	1
Republicans	1	1	1	1	1	1	1	1	1	0	0	0	0	0	0	0	0	0	0	0	0
Virginia																					
Democrats	3	5	4	4	1	4	4	5	5	6	7[2]	6	6	6	4	3	3	3	6	3	3
Republicans	7	5	6	6	9	6	6	5	5	4	4	5	5	5	6	8	8	8	5	8	8
Washington																					
Democrats	6	6	6	6	5	5[2]	5	5	5	5	8[2]	2	3	5	6	6	6	6	6	5	6[2]
Republicans	1	1	1	1	2	3	3	3	3	3	1	7	6	4	3	3	3	3	3	4	4
West Virginia																					
Democrats	4[1]	4	4	4	2	4	4	4	4	4	3[1]	3	3	3	2	2	2	2	2	1	1
Republicans	0	0	0	0	2	0	0	0	0	0	0	0	0	0	1	1	1	1	1	2	2
Wisconsin																					
Democrats	5[1]	7	7	6	5	5	5	5	5	4	4	3	5	4	5	4	4	5	5	3	3
Republicans	4	2	2	3	4	4	4	4	4	5	5	6	4	5	4	4	4	3	3	5	5
Wyoming																					
Democrats	1	1	0	0	0	0	0	0	0	0	0	0	0	0	0	0	0	0	0	0	0
Republicans	0	0	0	1	1	1	1	1	1	1	1	1	1	1	1	1	1	1	1	1	1

Governors, 2009–2013

Following is a list of governors who served during the period of President Barack Obama's first term, 2009–2013. All governors serve four-year terms except those representing New Hampshire and Vermont; they serve two-year terms. Party designations appear in parentheses following the governor's name. The following abbreviations were used: (D) Democrat; (R) Republican.

	Dates of Service
Alabama	
Bob Riley (R)	January 20, 2003–January 17, 2011
Robert Bentley (R)	January 17, 2011–
Alaska	
Sarah H. Palin (R)	December 4, 2006–July 26, 2009
Sean R. Parnell (R)	July 26, 2009–
Arizona	
Janet Napolitano (D)	January 6, 2003–January 21, 2009
Jan Brewer (R)	January 21, 2009–
Arkansas	
Mike Beebe (D)	July 9, 2007–
California	
Arnold Schwarzenegger (R)	November 17, 2003–January 3, 2011
Edmund G. Brown Jr. (D)	January 3, 2011–
Colorado	
Bill Ritter Jr. (D)	January 9, 2007–January 11, 2011
John Hickenlooper (D)	January 11, 2011–
Connecticut	
M. Jodi Rell (R)	July 1, 2004–January 5, 2011
Dan Malloy (D)	January 5, 2011–
Delaware	
Ruth Ann Miner (D)	January 3, 2001–January 20, 2009
Jack A. Markell (D)	January 20, 2009–
Florida	
Charlie Crist (R)	January 2, 2007–January 4, 2011
Rick Scott (R)	January 4, 2011–
Georgia	
Sonny Perdue (R)	January 13, 2003–January 10, 2011
John Nathan Deal (R)	January 10, 2011–
Hawaii	
Linda Lingle (R)	December 2, 2002–December 6, 2010
Neil Abercrombie (D)	December 6, 2010–
Idaho	
C. L. "Butch" Otter (R)	January 1, 2007–
Illinois	
Rod R. Blagojevich (D)	January 13, 2003–January 29, 2009
Pat Quinn (D)	January 29, 2009–
Indiana	
Mitchell E. Daniels Jr. (R)	January 10, 2005–January 14, 2013
Mike Pence (R)	January 14, 2013–
Iowa	
Chet Culver (D)	January 12, 2007–January 14, 2011
Terry E. Branstad (R)	January 14, 2011–

	Dates of Service
Kansas	
Kathleen Sebelius (D)	January 13, 2003–April 28, 2009
Mark Parkinson (D)	April 28, 2009–January 10, 2011
Sam Brownback (R)	January 10, 2011–
Kentucky	
Steven L. Beshear (D)	December 11, 2007–
Louisiana	
Bobby Jindal (R)	January 14, 2008–
Maine	
John E. Baldacci (D)	January 8, 2003–January 5, 2011
Paul R. LePage (R)	January 5, 2011–
Maryland	
Martin O'Malley (D)	January 17, 2007–
Massachusetts	
Deval Patrick (D)	January 4, 2007–
Michigan	
Jennifer Granholm (D)	January 1, 2003–January 1, 2011
Rick Snyder (R)	January 1, 2011–
Minnesota	
Tim Pawlenty (R)	January 6, 2003–January 3, 2011
Mark Dayton (D)	January 3, 2011–
Mississippi	
Haley Barbour (D)	January 13, 2004–January 10, 2012
Phil Bryant (R)	January 10, 2012–
Missouri	
Jeremiah W. "Jay" Nixon (D)	January 12, 2009–
Montana	
Brian Schweitzer (D)	January 3, 2005–
Nebraska	
Dave Heineman (R)	January 20, 2005–
Nevada	
Jim Gibbons (R)	January 1, 2007–January 3, 2011
Brian Sandoval (R)	January 3, 2011–
New Hampshire	
John Lynch (D)	January 6, 2005–January 3, 2013
Maggie Hassan (D)	January 3, 2013–
New Jersey	
Jon Corzine (D)	November 17, 2006–January 19, 2010
Chris Christie (R)	January 19, 2010–
New Mexico	
William "Bill" Richardson (D)	January 1, 2003–January 1, 2011
Susana Martinez (R)	January 1, 2011–

	Dates of Service
New York	
David Paterson (D)	March 17, 2008–December 31, 2010
Andrew Cuomo (D)	January 1, 2011–
North Carolina	
Beverly Perdue (D)	January 10, 2009–January 5, 2013
Pat McCrory (R)	January 5, 2013–
North Dakota	
John Hoeven (R)	December 15, 2000–December 7, 2010
Jack Dalrymple (R)	December 7, 2010–
Ohio	
Ted Strickland (D)	January 8, 2007–January 10, 2011
John R. Kasich (R)	January 10, 2011–
Oklahoma	
Brad Henry (D)	January 13, 2003–January 10, 2011
Mary Fallin (R)	January 10, 2011–
Oregon	
Ted Kulongoski (D)	January 13, 2003–January 10, 2011
John Kitzhaber (D)	January 10, 2011–
Pennsylvania	
Edward G. Rendell (D)	January 21, 2003–January 18, 2011
Tom Corbett (R)	January 18, 2011–
Rhode Island	
Don Carcieri (R)	January 7, 2003–January 4, 2011
Lincoln D. Chafee (D)	January 4, 2011–
South Carolina	
Mark Sanford (R)	January 15, 2003–January 12, 2011
Nikki R. Haley (R)	January 12, 2011–
South Dakota	
M. Michael Rounds (R)	January 7, 2003–January 8, 2011
Dennis Daugaard (R)	January 8, 2011–

	Dates of Service
Tennessee	
Phil Bredesen (D)	January 18, 2003–January 15, 2011
Bill Haslam (R)	January 15, 2011–
Texas	
Rick Perry (R)	December 21, 2000–
Utah	
Jon M. Huntsman Jr. (R)	January 3, 2005–August 11, 2009
Gary R. Herbert (R)	August 11, 2009–
Vermont	
James H. Douglas (R)	January 9, 2003–January 6, 2011
Peter Shumlin (D)	January 6, 2011–
Virginia	
Timothy M. Kaine (D)	January 14, 2006–January 16, 2010
Robert F. McDonnell (R)	January 16, 2010–
Washington	
Christine Gregoire (D)	January 12, 2005–January 16, 2013
Jay Inslee (D)	January 16, 2013–
West Virginia	
Joe Manchin III (D)	January 17, 2005–November 15, 2010
Earl Ray Tomblin (D)	November 14, 2010–
Wisconsin	
James E. Doyle (D)	January 6, 2003–January 3, 2011
Scott Walker (R)	January 3, 2011–
Wyoming	
David Freudenthal (D)	January 6, 2003–January 3, 2011
Matt Mead (R)	January 3, 2011–

Public Laws 2009–2012

111th Congress 2009–2011 961

112th Congress 2011–2012 985

Public Laws 2009–2012

Following are public laws passed by the 111th Congress and 112th Congress and signed by the president.

111th Congress 2009–2011

PL 111-1 (S J Res 3) Ensure that the compensation and other emoluments attached to the office of secretary of the Interior are those that were in effect on January 1, 2005. Introduced by Reid, D-Nev., January 6, 2009. Senate passed January 6. House passed, under suspension of the rules, January 7. President George W. Bush signed January 16, 2009.

PL 111-2 (S 181) Amend Title VII of the Civil Rights Act of 1964 and the Age Discrimination in Employment Act of 1967, modify the operation of the Americans with Disabilities Act of 1990 and the Rehabilitation Act of 1973, and clarify that a discriminatory compensation decision or other practice that is unlawful under such acts occurs each time compensation is paid pursuant to the discriminatory compensation decision or other practice. Introduced by Mikulski, D-Md., January 8, 2009. Senate passed January 22. House passed January 27. President Barack Obama signed January 29, 2009.

PL 111-3 (HR 2) Amend Title XXI of the Social Security Act to extend and improve the Children's Health Insurance Program. Introduced by Pallone, D-N.J., January 13, 2009. House passed January 4. Senate passed, amended, January 29. House agreed to Senate amendment February 4. President signed February 4, 2009.

PL 111-4 (S 352) Delay the deadline for the transition from analog to digital television broadcasting. Introduced by Rockefeller, D-W.Va., January 29, 2009. Senate passed January 29. House passed February 4. President signed February 11, 2009.

PL 111-5 (HR 1) Make supplemental appropriations for job preservation and creation, infrastructure investment, energy efficiency and science, assistance to the unemployed, and state and local fiscal stabilization for fiscal year 2009. Introduced by Obey, D-Wis., January 26, 2009. House passed, amended, January 28. Senate passed, amended, February 10. Conference report filed in the House February 12 (H Rept 111-16). House agreed to the conference report February 13. Senate agreed to the conference report February 13. President signed February 17, 2009.

PL 111-6 (H J Res 38) Make further continuing appropriations for fiscal year 2009. Introduced by Obey, D-Wis., March 6, 2009. House passed March 6. Senate passed March 6. President signed March 6, 2009.

PL 111-7 (S 234) Designate the facility of the U.S. Postal Service located at 2105 East Cook St. in Springfield, Ill., as the "Colonel John H. Wilson Jr. Post Office Building." Introduced by Durbin, D-Ill., January 14, 2009. House Homeland Security and Governmental Affairs reported February 11 (no written report). Senate passed February 12. House passed, under suspension of the rules, February 24. President signed March 9, 2009.

PL 111-8 (HR 1105) Make omnibus appropriations for fiscal year 2009. Introduced by Obey, D-Wis., February 23, 2009. House passed, amended, February 25. Senate passed March 10. President signed March 11, 2009.

PL 111-9 (HR 1127) Extend certain immigration programs. Introduced by Lofgren, D-Calif., February 23, 2009. House passed, under suspension of the rules, March 4. Senate passed March 11. President signed March 20, 2009.

PL 111-10 (HR 1541) Provide for an additional temporary extension of programs under the Small Business Act and the Small Business Investment Act of 1958. Introduced by Velázquez, D-N.Y., March 17, 2009. House passed, under suspension of the rules, March 17. Senate passed March 17. President signed March 20, 2009.

PL 111-11 (HR 146) Designate certain lands as components of the National Wilderness Preservation System, and authorize certain programs and activities in the Department of the Interior and the Department of Agriculture. Introduced by Holt, D-N.J., January 6, 2009. House passed, amended, under suspension of the rules, March 3. Senate passed, amended, March 19. House agreed to Senate amendments March 25. President signed March 30, 3009.

PL 111-12 (HR 1512) Amend the Internal Revenue Code of 1986 to extend the funding and expenditure authority of the Airport and Airway Trust Fund, and amend Title 49, U.S. Code, to extend authorizations for the airport improvement program. Introduced by Rangel, D-N.Y., March 16, 2009. House passed, under suspension of the rules, March 18. Senate passed March 18. President signed March 30, 2009.

PL 111-13 (HR 1388) Reauthorize and reform the national service laws. Introduced by McCarthy, D-N.Y., March 9, 2009. House Education and Labor reported, amended, March 16 (H Rept 111-37). House passed, amended, March 18. Senate passed, amended, March 26. House agreed to Senate amendments March 31. President signed April 21, 2009.

PL 111-14 (S 520) Designate the U.S. courthouse under construction at 327 South Church St., Rockford, Ill., as the "Stanley J. Roszkowski United States Courthouse." Introduced by Durbin, D-Ill., March 3, 2009. Senate passed March 3. House passed, under suspension of the rules, March 25. President signed April 23, 2009.

PL 111-15 (S 383) Amend the Emergency Economic Stabilization Act of 2008 (division A of Public Law 110-343) to provide the special inspector general with additional authorities and responsibilities. Introduced by McCaskill, D-Mo., February 4, 2009. Senate passed February 4. House Financial Services reported March 19 (H Rept 111-41, Part 1). House Oversight and Government Reform discharged. House passed, under suspension of the rules, March 25. President signed April 24, 2009.

PL 111-16 (HR 1626) Make technical amendments to laws containing time periods affecting judicial proceedings. Introduced by Johnson, D-Ga., March 19, 2009. House passed, under suspension of the rules, April 22. Senate passed April 27. President signed May 7, 2009.

PL 111-17 (S J Res 8) Provide for the appointment of David M. Rubenstein as a citizen regent of the Board of Regents of the Smithsonian Institution. Introduced by Leahy, D-Vt., February 10, 2009. Senate Rules and Administration discharged. Senate passed March 17. House passed, under suspension of the rules, April 22. President signed May 7, 2009.

PL 111-18 (S 39) Repeal section 10(f) of Public Law 93-531, commonly known as the "Bennett Freeze." Introduced by McCain, R-Ariz., January 6, 2009. Senate Indian Affairs discharged. Senate passed March 12. House passed, under suspension of the rules, April 21. President signed May 8, 2009.

PL 111-19 (HR 586) Direct the Librarian of Congress and the secretary of the Smithsonian Institution to carry out a joint project at the Library of Congress and the National Museum of African American History and Culture to collect video and audio recordings of personal histories and testimonials of individuals who participated in the civil rights movement. Introduced by McCarthy, D-N.Y., January 15, 2009. House passed, under suspension of the rules, April 22. Senate passed April 24. President signed May 12, 2009.

PL 111-20 (S 735) Ensure that states receive adoption incentive payments for fiscal 2008 in accordance with the Fostering Connections to Success and Increasing Adoptions Act of 2008. Introduced by Baucus, D-Mont., March 30, 2009. Senate Finance discharged. Senate passed April 3. House passed, under suspension of the rules, April 29. President signed May 15, 2009.

PL 111-21 (S 386) Strengthen the investigation and prosecution of mortgage fraud, securities fraud, financial institution fraud and other types of fraud related to federal assistance and relief programs, and for the recovery of funds lost to these frauds. Introduced by Leahy, D-Vt., February 5, 2009. Senate Judiciary reported, amended, March 23 (S Rept 111-10). Senate passed, amended, April 28. House passed, with amendments, under suspension of the rules, May 6. Senate agreed to House amendments, with amendment, May 14. House agreed to Senate amendment to House amendments, under suspension of the rules, May 18. President signed May 20, 2009.

PL 111-22 (S 896) Prevent mortgage foreclosures and enhance mortgage credit availability. Introduced by Dodd, D-Conn., April 24, 2009. Senate passed, amended, May 6. House passed, amended, under suspension of the rules, May 19. Senate agreed to House amendment May 19. President signed May 20, 2009.

PL 111-23 (S 454) Improve the organization and procedures of the Department of Defense for the acquisition of major weapon systems. Introduced by Levin, D-Mich., February 23, 2009. Senate Armed Services reported, amended, April 2 (no written report). Senate passed, amended, May 7. House passed, amended, May 13. Conference report filed in the House May 20 (H Rept 111-124). Senate agreed to the conference report May 20. House agreed to the conference report May 21. President signed May 22, 2009.

PL 111-24 (HR 627) Amend the Truth in Lending Act to establish fair and transparent practices relating to the extension of credit under an open-end consumer credit plan. Introduced by Maloney, D-N.Y., January 22, 2009. House Financial Services reported, amended, April 27 (H Rept 111-88). House passed, amended, April 30. Senate passed, with amendment, May 19. House agreed to Senate amendment May 20. President signed May 22, 2009.

PL 111-25 (HR 131) Establish the Ronald Reagan Centennial Commission. Introduced by Gallegly, R-Calif., January 6, 2009. House passed, amended, under suspension of the rules, March 9. Senate passed May 19. President signed June 2, 2009.

PL 111-26 (HR 663) Designate the facility of the U.S. Postal Service located at 12877 Broad St. in Sparta, Ga., as the "Yvonne Ingram-Ephraim Post Office Building." Introduced by Barrow, D-Ga., January 23, 2009. House passed, under suspension of the rules, February 13. Senate Homeland Security and Governmental Affairs reported May 20 (no written report). Senate passed May 21. President signed June 19, 2009.

PL 111-27 (HR 918) Designate the facility of the U.S. Postal Service located at 300 East 3rd St. in Jamestown, N.Y., as the "Stan Lundine Post Office Building." Introduced by Higgins, D-N.Y., February 9, 2009. House passed, under suspension of the rules, March 23. Senate Homeland Security and Governmental Affairs reported March 20 (no written report). Senate passed May 21. President signed June 19, 2009.

PL 111-28 (HR 1284) Designate the facility of the U.S. Postal Service located at 103 West Main St. in McLain, Miss., as the "Maj. Ed W. Freeman Post Office." Introduced by Taylor, D-Miss., March 3, 2009. House passed, under suspension of the rules, March 16. Senate Homeland Security and Governmental Affairs reported May 20 (no written report). Senate passed May 21. President signed June 19, 2009.

PL 111-29 (HR 1595) Designate the facility of the U.S. Postal Service located at 3245 Latta Road in Rochester, N.Y., as the "Brian K. Schramm Post Office Building." Introduced by Lee, R-N.Y., March 18, 2009. House passed, under suspension of the rules, April 28. Senate Homeland Security and Governmental Affairs reported May 20 (no written report). Senate passed May 21. President signed June 19, 2009.

PL 111-30 (HR 2675) Amend Title II of the Antitrust Criminal Penalty Enhancement and Reform Act of 2004 to extend the operation of the title for a one-year period ending June 22, 2010. Introduced by Johnson, D-Ga., June 3, 2009. House passed, under suspension of the rules, June 9. Senate passed June 17. President signed June 19, 2009.

PL 111-31 (HR 1256) Protect public health by providing the Food and Drug Administration with certain authority to regulate tobacco products. Introduced by Waxman, D-Calif., March 3, 2009. House Energy and Commerce reported March 26 (H Rept 111-58, Part 1). House Oversight and Government Reform reported, amended, March 26 (H Rept 111-58, Part 2). House passed, amended, April 2. Senate passed, amended, June 11. House agreed to Senate amendment June 12. President signed June 22, 2009.

PL 111-32 (HR 2346) Make supplemental appropriations for fiscal year 2009. Introduced by Obey, D-Wis., May 12, 2009. House Appropriations reported May 12 (H Rept 111-105). House passed, amended, May 14. Senate passed, amended, May 21. Conference report filed in the House June 12 (H Rept 111-151). House agreed to conference report June 16. Senate agreed to conference report June 18. President signed June 24, 2009.

PL 111-33 (H J Res 40) Honor the achievements and contributions of Native Americans to the United States. Introduced by Baca, D-Calif., March 12, 2009. House passed, amended, under suspension of the rules, June 2. Senate passed June 9. President signed June 26, 2009.

PL 111-34 (HR 813) Designate the federal building and U.S. courthouse located at 306 East Main St. in Elizabeth City, N.C., as the "J. Herbert W. Small Federal Building and United States Courthouse." Introduced by Butterfield, D-N.C., February 3, 2009. House Transportation and Infrastructure reported March 10 (H Rept 111-27). House passed, under suspension of the rules, March 10. Senate Environment and Public Works reported June 11 (no written report). Senate passed June 17. President signed June 30, 2009.

PL 111-35 (HR 837) Designate the federal building located at 799 United Nations Plaza in New York City as the "Ronald H. Brown United States Mission to the United Nations Building." Introduced by Rangel, D-N.Y., February 3, 2009. House Transportation and Infrastructure reported March 10 (H Rept 111-28). House passed, under suspension of the rules, March 10. Senate Environment and Public Works reported June 11 (no written report). Senate passed June 17. President signed June 30, 2009.

PL 111-36 (HR 2344) Amend Section 114 of Title 17, U.S. Code, to provide for agreements for the reproduction and performance of sound recordings by webcasters. Introduced by Inslee, D-Wash., May 12, 2009. House Judiciary reported June 8 (H Rept 111-139). House passed, under suspension of the rules, June 9. Senate passed June 17. President signed June 30, 2009.

PL 111-37 (S 407) Increase, effective as of December 1, 2009, the rates of compensation for veterans with service-connected disabilities and the rates of dependency and indemnity compensation for the survivors of certain disabled veterans. Introduced by Akaka, D-Hawaii, February 10, 2009. Senate Veterans' Affairs reported, amended, June 4 (S Rept 111-24). Senate passed, amended, June 10. House passed, under suspension of the rules, June 23. President signed June 30, 2009.

PL 111-38 (S 615) Provide additional personnel authority for the special inspector general for Afghanistan reconstruction. Introduced by Collins, R-Maine, March 17, 2009. Senate Homeland Security and Governmental Affairs reported April 29 (S Rept 111-15). Senate passed April 30. House passed, under suspension of the rules, June 15. President signed June 30, 2009.

PL 111-39 (HR 1777) Make technical corrections to the Higher Education Act of 1965. Introduced by Miller, D-Calif., March 30, 2009. House passed, under suspension of the rules, March 30. Senate Health, Education, Labor and Pensions discharged. Senate passed, amended, June 23. House agreed to Senate amendment, under suspension of the rules, June 23. President signed July 1, 2009.

PL 111-40 (S 614) Award a Congressional Gold Medal to the Women Airforce Service Pilots. Introduced by Hutchison, R-Texas, March 17, 2009. Senate Banking, Housing and Urban Affairs discharged. Senate passed, amended, May 20. House passed, under suspension of the rules, June 16. President signed July 1, 2009.

PL 111-41 (HR 2632) Amend Title 4, U.S. Code, to encourage the display of the U.S. flag on National Korean War Veterans Armistice Day. Introduced by Rangel, D-N.Y., May 21, 2009. House passed, under suspension of the rules, July 21. Senate passed July 24. President signed July 27, 2009.

PL 111-42 (H J Res 56) Approving the renewal of import restrictions contained in the Burmese Freedom and Democracy Act of 2003. Introduced by Crowley, D-N.Y., June 4, 2009. House passed, amended, under suspension of the rules, July 21. Senate passed July 23. President signed July 28, 2009.

PL 111-43 (S 1513) Provide for an additional temporary extension of programs under the Small Business Act and the Small Business Investment Act of 1958. Introduced by Landrieu, D-La., July 24, 2009. Senate passed July 24. House passed, under suspension of the rules, July 29. President signed July 31, 2009.

PL 111-44 (HR 2245) Authorize the president, on the occasion of the 40th anniversary of the first lunar landing by humans in 1969, to award gold medals on behalf of the U.S. Congress to Neil A. Armstrong, the first human to walk on the moon; Edwin E. "Buzz" Aldrin Jr., pilot of the lunar module and second person to walk on the moon; Michael Collins, pilot of their Apollo 11 mission's command module; and John Herschel Glenn Jr., the first American to orbit the Earth. Introduced by Grayson, D-Fla., May 5, 2009. House passed, under suspension of the rules, July 20. Senate passed July 21. President signed August 7, 2009.

PL 111-45 (HR 3114) Authorize the director of the U.S. Patent and Trademark Office to use funds made available under the Trademark Act of 1946 for patent operations in order to avoid furloughs and reductions in force. Introduced by Conyers, D-Mich., July 7, 2009. House passed, under suspension of the rules, July 7. Senate passed July 16. President signed August 7, 2009.

PL 111-46 (HR 3357) Restore sums to the Highway Trust Fund. Introduced by Rangel, D-N.Y., July 28, 2009. House passed, amended, under suspension of the rules, July 29. Senate passed July 30. President signed August 7, 2009.

PL 111-47 (HR 3435) Make supplemental appropriations for fiscal 2009 for the Consumer Assistance to Recycle and Save Program. Introduced by Obey, D-Wis., July 31, 2009. House passed, under suspension of the rules, July 31. Senate passed August 6. President signed August 7, 2009.

PL 111-48 (HR 838) Provide for the conveyance of a parcel of land held by the Bureau of Prisons of the Department of Justice in Dade County, Fla., to facilitate the construction of a new educational facility that includes a secure parking area for the Bureau of Prisons. Introduced by Ros-Lehtinen, R-Fla., February 3, 2009. House passed, amended, under suspension of the rules, March 31. Senate Judiciary discharged. Senate passed July 28. President signed August 12, 2009.

PL 111-49 (S 1107) Amend Title 28, U.S. Code, to provide for a limited six-month period for federal judges to opt into the Judicial Survivors' Annuities System and begin contributing toward an annuity for their spouses and dependent children upon their deaths. Introduced by Durbin, D-Ill., May 20, 2009. Senate Judiciary reported June 25, 2009 (no written report). Senate passed July 10. House Judiciary discharged. House passed July 29. President signed August 12, 2009.

PL 111-50 (HR 774) Designate the facility of the U.S. Postal Service located at 46-02 21st St. in Long Island City, N.Y., as the "Geraldine Ferraro Post Office Building." Introduced by Maloney, D-N.Y., January 28, 2009. House passed, under suspension of the rules, May 5. Senate Homeland Security and Governmental Affairs reported July 30 (no written report). Senate passed August 4. President signed August 19, 2009.

PL 111-51 (HR 987) Designate the facility of the U.S. Postal Service located at 601 8th St. in Freedom, Pa., as the "John Scott Challis Jr. Post Office." Introduced by Altmire, D-Pa., February 11, 2009. House passed, under suspension of the rules, March 16. Senate Homeland Security and Governmental Affairs reported July 30 (no written report). Senate passed August 4. President signed August 19, 2009.

PL 111-52 (HR 1271) Designate the facility of the U.S. Postal Service located at 2351 West Atlantic Blvd. in Pompano Beach, Fla., as the "Elijah Pat Larkins Post Office Building." Introduced by Hastings, D-Fla., March 3, 2009. House passed, under suspension of the rules, May 5. Senate Homeland Security and Governmental Affairs reported July 30 (no written report). Senate passed August 4. President signed August 19, 2009.

PL 111-53 (HR 1275) Direct the exchange of certain land in Grand, San Juan and Uintah counties, Utah. Introduced by Matheson, D-Utah, March 3, 3009. House Natural Resources reported, amended, June 23 (H Rept 111-179). House passed, amended, under suspension of the rules, July 8. Senate Energy and Natural Resources reported August 4 (S Rept 111-67). Senate passed August 5. President signed August 19, 2009.

PL 111-54 (HR 1397) Designate the facility of the U.S. Postal Service located at 41 Purdy Ave. in Rye, N.Y., as the "Caroline O'Day Post Office Building." Introduced by Lowey, D-N.Y., March 9, 2009. House passed, under suspension of the rules, May 5. Senate Homeland Security and Governmental Affairs reported July 30 (no written report). Senate passed August 4. President signed August 19, 2009.

PL 111-55 (HR 2090) Designate the facility of the U.S. Postal Service located at 431 State St. in Ogdensburg, N.Y., as the "Frederic Remington Post Office Building." Introduced by McHugh, R-N.Y., April 23, 2009. House passed, under suspension of the rules, June 3. Senate Homeland Security and Governmental Affairs reported July 30 (no written report). Senate passed August 4. President signed August 19, 2009.

PL 111-56 (HR 2162) Designate the facility of the U.S. Postal Service located at 123 11th Ave. South in Nampa, Idaho, as the "Herbert A. Littleton Postal Station." Introduced by Minnick, D-Idaho, April 29, 2009. House passed, under suspension of the rules, May 13. Senate Homeland Security and Governmental Affairs reported July 30 (no written report). Senate passed August 4. President signed August 19, 2009.

PL 111-57 (HR 2325) Designate the facility of the U.S. Postal Service located at 1300 Matamoros St. in Laredo, Texas, as the "Laredo Veterans Post Office." Introduced by Cuellar, D-Texas, May 7, 2009. House passed, under suspension of the rules, June 15. Senate Homeland Security and Governmental Affairs reported July 30 (no written report). Senate passed August 4. President signed August 19, 2009.

PL 111-58 (HR 2422) Designate the facility of the U.S. Postal Service located at 2300 Scenic Drive in Georgetown, Texas, as the "Kile G. West Post Office Building." Introduced by Carter, R-Texas, May 14, 2009. House passed, under suspension of the rules, June 15. Senate Homeland Security and Governmental Affairs reported July 30 (no written report). Senate passed August 4. President signed August 19, 2009.

PL 111-59 (HR 2470) Designate the facility of the U.S. Postal Service located at 19190 Cochran Blvd. in Port Charlotte, Fla., as the "Lt. Cmdr. Roy H. Boehm Post Office Building." Introduced by Rooney, R-Fla., May 18, 2009. House passed, under suspension of the rules, June 16. Senate Homeland Security and Governmental Affairs reported July 30 (no written report). Senate passed August 4. President signed August 19, 2009.

PL 111-60 (HR 2938) Extend the deadline for commencement of construction of the Melvin Price Dam Hydroelectric Project in Illinois. Introduced by Costello, D-Ill., June 18, 2009. House passed, under suspension of the rules, July 22. Senate Energy and Natural Resources reported August 4 (S Rept 111-68). Senate passed August 5. President signed August 19, 2009.

PL 111-61 (H J Res 44) Recognize the service, sacrifice, honor and professionalism of the noncommissioned officers of the U.S. Army. Introduced by Skelton, D-Mo., April 29, 2009. House passed, under suspension of the rules, July 28. Senate Armed Services discharged. Senate passed August 4. President signed August 19, 2009.

PL 111-62 (S J Res 19) Grant the consent and approval of Congress to amendments made by Maryland, Virginia and the District of Columbia to the Washington Metropolitan Area Transit Regulation Compact. Introduced by Cardin, D-Md. Senate passed July 28. House Judiciary discharged. House passed July 31. President signed August 19, 2009.

PL 111-63 (HR 3325) Amend Title XI of the Social Security Act to reauthorize for one year the Work Incentives Planning and Assistance program and the Protection and Advocacy for Beneficiaries of Social Security program. Introduced by Tanner, D-Tenn., July 24, 2009. House passed, under suspension of the rules, July 28. Senate Finance discharged. Senate passed August 6. President signed September 18, 2009.

PL 111-64 (S J Res 9) Provide for the appointment of France A. Cordova as a citizen regent of the Board of Regents of the Smithsonian Institution. Introduced by Leahy, D-Vt., February 10, 2009. Senate Rules and Administration discharged. Senate passed March 17. House passed, under suspension of the rules, September 9. President signed September 18, 2009.

PL 111-65 (HR 1243) Provide for the award of a gold medal on behalf of Congress to Arnold Palmer in recognition of his service to the nation in promoting excellence and good sportsmanship in golf. Introduced by Baca, D-Calif., March 2, 2009. House passed, under suspension of the rules, April 28. Senate Banking, Housing and Urban Affairs discharged. Senate passed September 9. President signed September 30, 2009.

PL 111-66 (HR 3614) Provide for an additional temporary extension of programs under the Small Business Act and the Small Business Investment Act of 1958. Introduced by Velázquez, D-N.Y., September 22, 2009. House passed, under suspension of the rules, September 23. Senate passed, amended, September 25. House agreed to Senate amendment, under suspension of the rules, September 29. President signed September 30, 2009.

PL 111-67 (S 1677) Reauthorize the Defense Production Act of 1950. Introduced by Dodd, D-Conn., September 16, 2009. Senate passed September 16. House passed, under suspension of the rules, September 23. President signed September 30, 2009.

PL 111-68 (HR 2918) Make appropriations for the Legislative Branch for fiscal year 2010. Introduced by Wasserman Schultz, D-Fla., June 17, 2009. House Appropriations Committee reported June 17 (H Rept 111-160). House passed, amended, June 19. Senate passed, amended, July 6. Conference report filed in the House September 24 (H Rept 111-265). House agreed to the conference report September 25. Senate agreed to the conference report September 30. President signed October 1, 2009.

PL 111-69 (HR 3607) Amend the Internal Revenue Code of 1986 to extend the funding and expenditure authority of the Airport and Airway Trust Fund, and amend Title 49 of the U.S. Code, to extend authorizations for the airport-improvement program. Introduced by Oberstar, D-Minn., September 21, 2009. House passed, under suspension of the rules, September 23. Senate passed September 24. President signed October 1, 2009.

PL 111-70 (HR 2131) Amend the Foreign Affairs Reform and Restructuring Act of 1998 to reauthorize the United States Advisory Commission on Public Diplomacy. Introduced by Watson, D-Calif., April 27, 2009. House passed, under suspension of the rules, September 23. Senate Foreign Relations Committee discharged. Senate passed September 29. President signed October 9, 2009.

PL 111-71 (HR 3593) Amend the United States International Broadcasting Act of 1994 to extend the operation of Radio Free Asia by one year. Introduced by Royce, R-Calif., September 17, 2009. House passed, under suspension of the rules, September 23. Senate Foreign Relations Committee discharged. Senate passed September 29. President signed October 9, 2009.

PL 111-72 (HR 3663) Amend Title XVIII of the Social Security Act to delay the date on which the accreditation requirement under Medicare applies to pharmacies that are suppliers of durable medical equipment. Introduced by Space, D-Ohio, September 29, 2009. House passed, under suspension of the rules, September 30. Senate passed October 5. President signed October 13, 2009.

PL 111-73 (S 1707) Authorize economic and security assistance for Pakistan for fiscal 2010 through 2014. Introduced by Kerry, D-Mass., September 24, 2009. Senate passed September 24. House passed, under suspension of the rules, September 30. President signed October 15, 2009.

PL 111-74 (HR 1687) Designate the federally occupied building located at McKinley Avenue and Third Street Southwest in Canton, Ohio, as the "Ralph Regula Federal Building and United States Courthouse." Introduced by Boccieri, D-Ohio, March 24, 2009. House Transportation and Infrastructure reported, amended, June 8 (H Rept 111-140). House passed, under suspension of the rules, June 11. Senate Environment and Public Works discharged. Senate passed September 24, 2009. President signed October 19, 2009.

PL 111-75 (HR 2053) Designate the U.S. courthouse located at 525 Magoffin Ave. in El Paso, Texas, as the "Albert Armendariz Sr. United States Courthouse." Introduced by Reyes, D-Texas, April 22, 2009. House Transportation and Infrastructure reported July 31 (H Rept 111-241). House passed, under suspension of the rules, September 9. Senate Environment and Public Works discharged. Senate passed September 24. President signed October 19, 2009.

PL 111-76 (HR 2121) Authorize the General Services administrator to convey a parcel of real property in Galveston, Texas, to the Galveston Historical Foundation. Introduced by Paul, R-Texas, April 27, 2009. House Transportation and Infrastructure reported, amended, September 8 (H Rept 111-246). House passed, under suspension of the rules, September 9. Senate Environment and Public Works discharged. Senate passed September 24. President signed October 19, 2009.

PL 111-77 (HR 2498) Designate the federal building located at 844 North Rush St. in Chicago as the "William O. Lipinski Federal Building." Introduced by Oberstar, D-Minn., May 19, 2009. House Transportation and Infrastructure reported July 20 (H Rept 111-213). House passed, under suspension of the rules, September 9. Senate Environment and Public Works discharged. Senate passed September 24. President signed October 19, 2009.

PL 111-78 (HR 2913) Designate the U.S. courthouse located at 301 Simonton St. in Key West, Fla., as the "Sidney M. Aronovitz United States Courthouse." Introduced by Ros-Lehtinen, R-Fla., June 17, 2009. House Transportation and Infrastructure reported July 31 (H Rept 111-240). House passed July 31. Senate Environment and Public Works discharged. Senate passed September 24. President signed October 19, 2009.

PL 111-79 (S 1289) Revise Title 18 of the U.S. Code. Introduced by Whitehouse, D-R.I., June 18, 2009. Senate Judiciary discharged. Senate passed July 10. House passed, under suspension of the rules, September 30. President signed October 19, 2009.

PL 111-80 (HR 2997) Make appropriations for Agriculture, Rural Development, the Food and Drug Administration, and related agencies for fiscal year 2010. Introduced by DeLauro, D-Conn., June 23, 2009. House Appropriations reported June 23 (H Rept 111-181). House passed July 9. Senate passed, amended, August 4. Conference report filed in the House September 30 (H Rept 111-279). House agreed to the conference report October 7. Senate agreed to the conference report October 8. President signed October 21, 2009.

PL 111-81 (HR 1016) Amend Title 38, U.S. Code, to provide advance appropriations authority for certain accounts of the Department of Veterans Affairs. Introduced by Filner, D-Calif., February 12, 2009. House Veterans' Affairs reported, amended, June 19 (H Rept 111-171). House passed, amended, under suspension of the rules, June 23. Senate passed, amended, August 6. House agreed to Senate amendment, with an amendment, October 8. Senate agreed to House amendment to Senate amendment October 13. President signed October 22, 2009.

PL 111-82 (S 1717) Authorize major medical facility leases for the Department of Veterans Affairs for fiscal year 2010. Introduced by Akaka, D-Hawaii, September 25, 2009. Senate passed September 25. House passed, under suspension of the rules, October 7. President signed October 26, 2009.

PL 111-83 (HR 2892) Make appropriations for the Department of Homeland Security for fiscal year 2010. Introduced by Price, D-N.C., June 15, 2009. House Appropriations reported June 16 (H Rept 111-157). House passed June 24. Senate passed, amended, July 9. Conference report filed in the House on October 13 (H Rept 111-298). House agreed to the conference report October 15. Senate agreed to the conference report October 20. President signed October 28, 2009.

PL 111-84 (HR 2647) Authorize appropriations for fiscal year 2010 for military activities of the Department of Defense, to prescribe military personnel strengths for fiscal year 2010. Introduced by Skelton, D-Mo., June 2, 2009. House Armed Services reported, amended, June 18 (H Rept 111-16). Supplemental report filed by House Armed Services June 23 (H Rept 111-166, Part 2). House passed June 25. Senate passed, amended, July 23. Conference report filed in the House on October 7 (H Rept 111-288). House agreed to the conference report October 8. Senate agreed to the conference report October 22. President signed October 28, 2009.

PL 111-85 (HR 3183) Make appropriations for energy and water development and related agencies for fiscal year 2010. Introduced by Pastor, D-Ariz., July 13, 2009. House Appropriations reported July 13 (H Rept 111-203). House passed July 17. Senate passed, with an amendment, July 29. Conference report filed in the House on September 30 (H Rept 111-278). House agreed to the conference report October 1. Senate agreed to the conference report October 5. President signed October 28, 2009.

PL 111-86 (HR 621) Require the secretary of the Treasury to mint coins in commemoration of the centennial of the establishment of the Girl Scouts of the United States of America. Introduced by Kingston, R-Ga., January 21, 2009. House passed, under suspension of the rules, October 13. Senate passed October 19. President signed October 29, 2009.

PL 111-87 (S 1793) Amend title XXVI of the Public Health Service Act to revise and extend the program for providing life-saving care for those with HIV/AIDS. Introduced by Harkin, D-Iowa, October 15, 2009. Senate Health, Education, Labor and Pensions reported October 15 (no written report). Senate passed, with amendments, October 19. House passed, under suspension of the rules, October 21. President signed October 30, 2009.

PL 111-88 (HR 2996) Make appropriations for the Department of Interior, the environment, and related agencies for fiscal year 2010. Introduced by Dicks, D-Wash., June 23, 2009. House Appropriations reported June 23 (H Rept 111-180). House passed June 26. Senate Appropriations reported, amended, July 7 (S Rept 111-38). Conference report filed in the House October 28 (H Rept 111-316). House agreed to the conference report October 29. Senate agreed to the conference report October 29. President signed October 30, 2009.

PL 111-89 (S 1929) Provide for an additional temporary extension of programs under the Small Business Act and the Small Business Investment Act of 1958. Introduced by Landrieu, D-La., October 26, 2009. Senate passed October 26. House passed, amended, under suspension of the rules, October 28. Senate agreed to the House amendment October 29. President signed October 30, 2009.

PL 111-90 (S 1818) Amend the Morris K. Udall Scholarship and Excellence in National Environmental and Native American Public Policy Act of 1992 to honor the legacy of Stewart L. Udall. Introduced by Bingaman, D-N.M., October 20, 2009. Senate passed October 20. House passed, under suspension of the rules, October 21. President signed November 3, 2009.

PL 111-91 (HR 1209) Require the secretary of the Treasury to mint coins in recognition and celebration of the establishment in 1861 of the Medal of Honor, America's highest award for valor in action against an enemy force; to honor the American military men and women who have been recipients of the Medal of Honor; and to promote awareness of what the Medal of Honor represents and how ordinary Americans, through courage, sacrifice, selfless service and patriotism, can challenge fate and change the course of history. Introduced by Carney, D-Pa., February 26, 2009. House passed, under suspension of the rules, May 14. Senate Banking, Housing and Urban Affairs discharged. Senate passed October 22. President signed November 6, 2009.

PL 111-92 (HR 3548) Amend the Supplemental Appropriations Act of 2008 to provide for the temporary availability of certain additional emergency unemployment compensation. Introduced by McDermott, D-Wash., September 10, 2009. House passed, amended, under suspension of the rules, September 22. Senate passed, amended, November 4. House agreed to the Senate amendment, under suspension of the rules, November 5. President signed November 6, 2009.

PL 111-93 (HR 3606) Amend the Truth in Lending Act to make a technical correction to an amendment made by the Credit CARD Act of 2009. Introduced by Welch, D-Vt., September 17, 2009. House passed, under suspension of the rules, October 13. Senate passed October 29. President signed November 6, 2009.

PL 111-94 (H J Res 26) Proclaim Casimir Pulaski to be an honorary citizen of the United States posthumously. Introduced by Kucinich, D-Ohio, March 2, 2009. House passed, under suspension of the rules, October 8. Senate Judiciary discharged. Senate passed October 22. President signed November 6, 2009.

PL 111-95 (S 832) Amend Title 36, U.S. Code, to grant a federal charter to the Military Officers Association of America. Introduced by Nelson, D-Fla., April 20, 2009. Senate Judiciary discharged. Senate passed September 24. House passed October 27. President signed November 6, 2009.

PL 111-96 (S 1694) Allow funding for the interoperable emergency communications grant program established under the Digital Television Transition and Public Safety Act of 2005 to remain available until expended through fiscal 2012. Introduced by Rockefeller, D-W.Va., September 22, 2009. Senate Commerce, Science and Transportation discharged. Senate passed October 14. House passed, under suspension of the rules, October 28. President signed November 6, 2009.

PL 111-97 (S 475) Amend the Servicemembers Civil Relief Act to guarantee the equity of spouses of military personnel with regard to matters of residency. Introduced by Burr, R-N.C., February 25, 2009. Senate Veterans' Affairs reported July 15 (S Rept 111-46). Senate passed August 4. House passed, under suspension of the rules, November 2. President signed November 11, 2009.

PL 111-98 (S 509) Authorize a major medical facility project at the Department of Veterans Affairs Medical Center, Walla Walla, Wash. Introduced by Murray, D-Wash., March 2, 2009. Senate Veterans' Affairs discharged. Senate passed July 15. House passed, under suspension of the rules, November 2. President signed November 11, 2009.

PL 111-99 (HR 955) Designate the facility of the U.S. Postal Service located at 10355 Northeast Valley Road in Rollingbay, Wash., as the "John 'Bud' Hawk Post Office." Introduced by Inslee, D-Wash., February 10, 2009. House passed, under suspension of the rules, March 17. Senate Homeland Security and Governmental Affairs reported November 4 (no written report). Senate passed November 9. President signed November 30, 2009.

PL 111-100 (HR 1516) Designate the facility of the U.S. Postal Service located at 37926 Church St. in Dade City, Fla., as the "Sgt. Marcus Mathes Post Office." Introduced by Brown-Waite, R-Fla., March 16, 2009. House passed, under suspension of the rules, April 21. Senate Homeland Security and Governmental Affairs reported November 4 (no written report). Senate passed November 9. President signed November 30, 2009.

PL 111-101 (HR 1713) Name the South Central Agricultural Research Laboratory of the Department of Agriculture in Lane, Okla., and the facility of the U.S. Postal Service located at 310 N. Perry St., in Bennington, Okla., in honor of former Rep. Wes Watkins, D-Okla. (1977–91) and R-Okla. (1997–2003). Introduced by Boren, D-Okla., March 25, 2009. House passed, under suspension of the rules, September 16. Senate Homeland Security and Governmental Affairs reported November 4 (no written report). Senate passed November 9. President signed November 30, 2009.

PL 111-102 (HR 2004) Designate the facility of the U.S. Postal Service located at 4282 Beach St. in Akron, Mich., as the "Akron Veterans Memorial Post Office." Introduced by Kildee, D-Mich., April 21, 2009. House passed, under suspension of the rules, September 8. Senate Homeland Security and Governmental Affairs reported November 4 (no written report). Senate passed November 9. President signed November 30, 2009.

PL 111-103 (HR 2215) Designate the facility of the U.S. Postal Service located at 140 Merriman Road in Garden City, Mich., as the "John J. Shivnen Post Office Building." Introduced by McCotter, R-Mich., April 30, 2009. House passed, under suspension of the rules, September 23. Senate Homeland Security and Governmental Affairs reported November 4 (no written report). Senate passed November 9. President signed November 30, 2009.

PL 111-104 (HR 2760) Designate the facility of the U.S. Postal Service located at 1615 N. Wilcox Ave. in Los Angeles as the "Johnny Grant Hollywood Post Office Building." Introduced by Watson, D-Calif., June 8, 2009. House passed, under suspension of the rules, September 8. Senate Homeland Security and Governmental Affairs reported November 4 (no written report). Senate passed November 9. President signed November 30, 2009.

PL 111-105 (HR 2972) Designate the facility of the U.S. Postal Service located at 115 W. Edward St. in Erath, La., as the "Conrad DeRouen Jr. Post Office." Introduced by Boustany, R-La., June 19, 2009. House passed, under suspension of the rules, July 22. Senate Homeland Security and Governmental Affairs reported November 4 (no written report). Senate passed November 9. President signed November 30, 2009.

PL 111-106 (HR 3119) Designate the facility of the U.S. Postal Service located at 867 Stockton St. in San Francisco as the "Lim Poon Lee Post Office." Introduced by Pelosi, D-Calif., July 7, 2009. House passed, under suspension of the rules, July 22. Senate Homeland Security and Governmental Affairs reported November 4 (no written report). Senate passed November 9. President signed November 30, 2009.

PL 111-107 (HR 3386) Designate the facility of the U.S. Postal Service located at 1165 Second Ave. in Des Moines, Iowa, as the "Iraq and Afghanistan Veterans Memorial Post Office." Introduced by Boswell, D-Iowa, July 29, 2009. House passed, under suspension of the rules, September 15. Senate Homeland Security and Governmental Affairs reported November 4 (no written report). Senate passed November 9. President signed November 30, 2009.

PL 111-108 (HR 3547) Designate the facility of the U.S. Postal Service located at 936 South 250 East in Provo, Utah, as the "Rex E. Lee Post Office Building." Introduced by Chaffetz, R-Utah, September 10, 2009. House passed, under suspension of the rules, October 7. Senate Homeland Security and Governmental Affairs reported November 4 (no written report). Senate passed November 9. President signed November 30, 2009.

PL 111-109 (S 748) Redesignate the facility of the U.S. Postal Service located at 2777 Logan Ave. in San Diego as the "Cesar E. Chavez Post Office." Introduced by Boxer, D-Calif., March 31, 2009. Senate Homeland Security and Governmental Affairs reported July 30 (no written report). Senate passed August 4. House passed, under suspension of the rules, November 5. President signed November 30, 2009.

PL 111-110 (S 1211) Designate the facility of the U.S. Postal Service located at 60 School St. in Orchard Park, N.Y., as the "Jack F. Kemp Post Office Building." Introduced by Schumer, D-N.Y., June 9, 2009. Senate Homeland Security and Governmental Affairs reported July 30 (no written report). Senate passed August 4. House passed, under suspension of the rules, November 6. President signed November 30, 2009.

PL 111-111 (S 1314) Designate the facility of the U.S. Postal Service located at 630 NE Killingsworth Ave. in Portland, Ore., as the "Dr. Martin Luther King Jr. Post Office." Introduced by Wyden, D-Ore., June 22, 2009. Senate Homeland Security and Governmental Affairs reported July 30 (no written report). Senate passed August 4. House passed, under suspension of the rules, November 16. President signed November 30, 2009.

PL 111-112 (S 1825) Extend the authority for test programs on relocation expenses for federal employees. Introduced by Lieberman, I-Conn., October 21, 2009. Senate Homeland Security and Governmental Affairs reported November 4 (no written report). Senate passed November 9. House passed, under suspension of the rules, November 16. President signed November 30, 2009.

PL 111-113 (S 1599) Amend Title 36, U.S. Code, to include in the federal charter of the Reserve Officers Association leadership positions newly added in its constitution and bylaws. Introduced by Leahy, D-Vt., August 6, 2009. Senate Armed Services discharged. Senate Judiciary reported September 10 (no written report). Senate passed September 24. House passed, under suspension of the rules, November 19. President signed December 14, 2009.

PL 111-114 (S 1860) Permit each current member of the board of directors of the Office of Compliance to serve for three terms. Introduced by Lieberman, I-Conn., October 22, 2009. Senate Homeland Security and Governmental Affairs reported November 4 (no written report). Senate passed November 5. House Administration discharged. House passed November 19. President signed December 14, 2009.

PL 111-115 (HR 4218) Amend Titles II and XVI of the Social Security Act to prohibit retroactive payments to individuals during periods in which they are prisoners, fugitive felons, or probation or parole violators. Introduced by Tanner, D-Tenn., December 8, 2009. House passed, under suspension of the rules, December 8. Senate passed December 10. President signed December 15, 2009.

PL 111-116 (HR 4217) Amend the Internal Revenue Code of 1986 to extend the funding and expenditure authority of the Airport and Airway Trust Fund, and to amend Title 49, U.S. Code, to extend authorizations for the airport-improvement program. Introduced by Rangel, D-N.Y., December 8, 2009. House passed, under suspension of the rules, December 8. Senate passed December 10. President signed December 16, 2009.

PL 111-117 (HR 3288) Make appropriations for the departments of Transportation and Housing and Urban Development for fiscal year 2010, subsequently amended with an omnibus package providing fiscal 2010 funding for departments and agencies covered by five unfinished spending bills. Introduced by Olver, D-Mass., July 22, 2009. House Appropriations reported July 22 (H Rept 111-218). House passed July 23. Senate Appropriations reported, amended, August 5 (S Rept 111-69). Senate passed, amended, September 17. Conference report filed in the House on December 8 (H Rept 111-366). House agreed to the conference report December 10. Senate agreed to the conference report December 13. President signed December 16, 2009.

PL 111-118 (HR 3326) Make appropriations for the Department of Defense for fiscal year 2010. Introduced by Murtha, D-Pa., July 24, 2009. House Appropriations reported July 24 (H Rept 111-230). House passed July 30. Senate Appropriations reported, amended, September 10 (S Rept 111-74). Senate passed October 6. House agreed to the Senate amendment, with an amendment, December 16. Senate concurred in the House amendment to the Senate amendment December 19. President signed December 19, 2009.

PL 111-119 (S 1422) Amend the Family and Medical Leave Act of 1993 to clarify the eligibility requirements with respect to airline flight crews. Introduced by Murray, D-Wash., July 9, 2009. Senate Health, Education, Labor and Pensions discharged. Senate passed November 10. House passed, under suspension of the rules, December 2. President signed December 21, 2009.

PL 111-120 (HR 4165) Extend through December 31, 2010, the authority of the secretary of the Army to accept and expend funds contributed by nonfederal public entities to expedite the processing of permits. Introduced by Larsen, D-Wash., December 1, 2009. House passed, under suspension of the rules, December 8. Senate passed December 10. President signed December 22, 2009.

PL 111-121 (H J Res 62) Appoint the day for convening the second session of the 111th Congress. Introduced by Hoyer, D-Md., December 11, 2009. House passed, under suspension of the rules, December 11. Senate passed December 14. President signed December 22, 2009.

PL 111-122 (S 1472) Establish a section within the Criminal Division of the Department of Justice to enforce human rights laws and to make technical and conforming amendments to criminal and immigration laws pertaining to human rights violations. Introduced by Durbin, D-Ill., July 20, 2009. Senate Judiciary reported November 6 (no written report). Senate passed, amended, November 21. House passed, under suspension of the rules, December 15. President signed December 22, 2009.

PL 111-123 (HR 4314) Permit continued financing of government operations by increasing the limit on the public debt. Introduced by Rangel, D-N.Y., December 15, 2009. House passed December 16. Senate passed December 24. President signed December 28, 2009.

PL 111-124 (HR 4284) Extend the Generalized System of Preferences and the Andean Trade Preference Act. Introduced by Rangel, D-N.Y., December 11, 2009. House passed, under suspension of the rules, December 14. Senate passed December 22. President signed December 28, 2009.

PL 111-125 (HR 3819) Extend the commercial space transportation liability regime. Introduced by Gordon, D-Tenn., October 15, 2009. House passed, under suspension of the rules, October 20. Senate Commerce, Science and Transportation reported December 22 (no written report). Senate passed December 23. President signed December 28, 2009.

PL 111-126 (HR 4462) Accelerate the income tax benefits for charitable cash contributions for the relief of victims of the earthquake in Haiti. Introduced by Rangel, D-N.Y., on January 19, 2010. House passed, under suspension of the rules, January 20. Senate passed January 21. President signed January 22, 2010.

PL 111-127 (S 2949) Amend Section 1113 of the Social Security Act to provide authority for increased fiscal 2010 payments for temporary assistance to U.S. citizens returned from foreign countries and to provide necessary funding to avoid shortfalls in the Medicare cost-sharing program for low-income qualifying individuals. Introduced by Baucus, D-Mont., on January 25, 2010. Senate passed January 25. House passed, under suspension of the rules, January 26. President signed January 27, 2010.

PL 111-128 (HR 1817) Designate the facility of the U.S. Postal Service located at 116 N. West St. in Somerville, Tenn., as the "John S. Wilder Post Office Building." Introduced by Blackburn, R-Tenn., on March 31, 2009. House passed, under suspension of the rules, June 4. Senate Homeland Security and Governmental Affairs reported December 17 (no written report). Senate passed December 21. President signed January 29, 2010.

PL 111-129 (HR 2877) Designate the facility of the U.S. Postal Service located at 76 Brookside Ave. in Chester, N.Y., as the "1st Lt. Louis Allen Post Office." Introduced by Hall, D-N.Y., on June 15, 2009. House passed, under suspension of the rules, October 13. Senate Homeland Security and Governmental Affairs reported December 17 (no written report). Senate passed December 21. President signed January 29, 2010.

PL 111-130 (HR 3072) Designate the facility of the U.S. Postal Service located at 9810 Halls Ferry Road in St. Louis as the "Coach Jodie Bailey Post Office Building." Introduced by Clay, D-Mo., on June 26, 2009. House passed, under suspension of the rules, July 29. Senate Homeland Security and Governmental Affairs reported December 17 (no written report). Senate passed December 21. President signed January 29, 2010.

PL 111-131 (HR 3319) Designate the facility of the U.S. Postal Service located at 440 S. Gulling St. in Portola, Calif., as the "Army Spc. Jeremiah Paul McCleery Post Office Building." Introduced by McClintock, R-Calif., July 23, 2009. House passed, under suspension of the rules, October 20. Senate Homeland Security and Governmental Affairs reported December 17 (no written report). Senate passed December 21. President signed January 29, 2010.

PL 111-132 (HR 3539) Designate the facility of the U.S. Postal Service located at 427 Harrison Ave. in Harrison, N.J., as the "Patricia D. McGinty Juhl Post Office Building." Introduced by Sires, D-N.J., on September 8, 2009. House passed, under suspension of the rules, November 16. Senate Homeland Security and Governmental Affairs reported December 17 (no written report). Senate passed December 21. President signed January 29, 2010.

PL 111-133 (HR 3667) Designate the facility of the U.S. Postal Service located at 16555 Springs St. in White Springs, Fla., as the "Clyde L. Hillhouse Post Office Building." Introduced by Crenshaw, R-Fla., on September 29, 2009. House passed, under suspension of the rules, December 1. Senate Homeland Security and Governmental Affairs reported December 17 (no written report). Senate passed December 21. President signed January 29, 2010.

PL 111-134 (HR 3767) Designate the facility of the U.S. Postal Service located at 170 N. Main St. in Smithfield, Utah, as the "W. Hazen Hillyard Post Office Building." Introduced by Bishop, R-Utah, on October 8, 2009. House passed, under suspension of the rules, November 16. Senate Homeland Security and Governmental Affairs reported December 17 (no written report). Senate passed December 21. President signed January 29, 2010.

PL 111-135 (HR 3788) Designate the facility of the U.S. Postal Service located at 3900 Darrow Road in Stow, Ohio, as the "Cpl. Joseph A. Tomci Post Office Building." Introduced by LaTourette, R-Ohio, on October 13, 2009. House passed, under suspension of the rules, November 6. Senate Homeland Security and Governmental Affairs reported December 17 (no written report). Senate passed December 21. President signed January 29, 2010.

PL 111-136 (HR 4508) Provide for an additional temporary extension of programs under the Small Business Act and the Small Business Investment Act of 1958. Introduced by Velázquez, D-N.Y., on January 26, 2010. House passed, under suspension of the rules, January 27. Senate passed January 28. President signed January 29, 2010.

PL 111-137 (HR 1377) Amend Title 38 of the U.S. Code to expand veteran eligibility for reimbursement by the Department of Veterans Affairs for emergency treatment furnished in a non-department facility, introduced by Filner, D-Calif., on March 6, 2009. House Veterans' Affairs reported, amended, March 26 (H Rept 111-55). House passed, under suspension of the rules, March 30. Senate Veterans' Affairs discharged December 18. Senate passed December 18. President signed February 1, 2010.

PL 111-138 (S 692) Provide that claims of the United States to certain documents relating to Franklin D. Roosevelt shall be treated as waived and relinquished in certain circumstances. Introduced by Schumer, D-N.Y., on March 25, 2009. Senate Homeland Security and Governmental Affairs reported October 5 (S Rept 111-87). Senate passed October 14. House passed, under suspension of the rules, January 13, 2010. President signed February 1, 2010.

PL 111-139 (H J Res 45) Increase the statutory limit on the public debt. Introduced April 29, 2009. House passed April 29. Senate Finance discharged. Senate passed, amended, January 28, 2010. House adopted Senate amendments February 4. President signed February 12, 2010.

PL 111-140 (HR 730) Strengthen efforts by the Department of Homeland Security to develop nuclear forensics capabilities to permit attribution of the source of nuclear material. Introduced by Schiff, D-Calif., on January 27, 2009. House passed, under suspension of the rules, March 24. Senate Homeland Security and Governmental Affairs reported December 17 (no written report). Senate passed, amended, December 23. House agreed to Senate amendment, under suspension of the rules, January 21, 2010. President signed February 16, 2010.

PL 111-141 (HR 3961) Extend expiring provisions of the USA PATRIOT Improvement and Reauthorization Act of 2005 and the Intelligence Reform and Terrorism Prevention Act of 2004 until February 28, 2011. Introduced by Dingell, D-Mich., on October 29, 2009. House passed November 19. Senate passed, amended, February 24, 2010. House agreed to Senate amendments February 25. President signed February 27, 2010.

PL 111-142 (HR 4532) Provide for permanent extension of the attorney-fee-withholding procedures under Title II of the Social Security Act to Title XVI of the act, and provide for permanent extension of such procedures under Titles II and XVI of the act to qualified nonattorney representatives. Introduced by Tanner, D-Tenn., on January 27, 2010. House passed, under suspension of the rules, February 4. Senate passed February 22. President signed February 27, 2010.

PL 111-143 (S 2950) Extend the pilot program for volunteer groups to obtain criminal history background checks. Introduced by Schumer, D-N.Y., on January 25, 2010. Senate passed January 25. House passed, under suspension of the rules, February 4. President signed March 1, 2010.

PL 111-144 (HR 4691) Provide a temporary extension of extended federal unemployment payments, federal insurance subsidies to jobless workers and other programs. Introduced by Rangel, D-N.Y., on February 25, 2010. House passed, under suspension of the rules, February 25. Senate passed March 2. President signed March 2, 2010.

PL 111-145 (HR 1299) Make technical corrections to the laws affecting certain administrative authorities of the U.S. Capitol Police. Introduced by Brady, D-Pa., on March 4, 2009. House Administration reported March 30 (H Rept 111-66). House passed, under suspension of the rules, March 31. Senate Rules and Administration discharged. Senate passed, amended, October 29. House agreed to Senate amendment, with an amendment, November 16. Senate agreed to House amendment to Senate amendment February 25, 2010. President signed March 4, 2010.

PL 111-146 (S 2968) Make certain technical and conforming amendments to the Lanham Act. Introduced by Leahy, D-Vt., on January 28, 2010. Senate passed January 28. House passed, under suspension of the rules, March 3. President signed March 17, 2010.

PL 111-147 (HR 2847) Provide incentives for hiring and retaining employees and extend certain surface transportation programs. Introduced by Mollohan, D-W.Va., on June 12, 2009. House Appropriations reported June 12 (H Rept 111-149). House passed June 18. Senate Appropriations reported, amended, June 25 (S Rept 111-34). Senate passed, amended, November 5. House agreed to Senate amendment, with an amendment, December 16. Senate agreed to House amendment to Senate amendment, with an amendment, February 24, 2010. House agreed to Senate amendment to House amendment, with an amendment, March 4. Senate agreed to House amendment to Senate amendment to House amendment to Senate amendment March 17. President signed March 18, 2010.

PL 111-148 (HR 3590) Patient Protection and Affordable Care Act. Introduced by Rangel, D-N.Y., on September 17, 2009. House passed, under suspension of the rules, October 8. Senate passed, amended, December 24. House agreed to Senate amendments March 21, 2010. President signed March 23, 2010.

PL 111-149 (HR 3433) Amend the North American Wetlands Conservation Act to establish requirements regarding payment of the nonfederal share of the costs of wetlands conservation projects in Canada funded under that act. Introduced by Wittman, R-Va., on July 30, 2009. House Natural Resources reported October 9 (H Rept 111-296). House passed, under suspension of the rules, October 13. Senate Environment and Public Works reported March 5, 2010 (S Rept 111-158). Senate passed March 9. President signed March 25, 2010.

PL 111-150 (HR 4938) Permit the use of previously appropriated funds to extend the Small Business Loan Guarantee Program. Introduced by Serrano, D-N.Y., on March 25, 2010. House passed, under suspension of the rules, March 25. Senate passed March 25. President signed March 26, 2010.

PL 111-151 (S 3186) Reauthorize the Satellite Home Viewer Extension and Reauthorization Act of 2004 through April 30, 2010. Introduced by Rockefeller, D-W.Va., on March 25, 2010. Senate passed March 25. House passed March 25. President signed March 26, 2010.

PL 111-152 (HR 4872) Provide for reconciliation pursuant to Title II of the concurrent resolution on the fiscal 2010 budget (S Con Res 13). Introduced by Spratt, D-S.C., on March 17, 2010. House Budget reported March 17 (H Rept 111-443). House passed March 21. Senate passed, amended, March 25. House agreed to Senate amendments March 25. President signed March 30, 2010.

PL 111-153 (HR 4957) Extend the funding and expenditure authority of the Airport and Airway Trust Fund, and extend authorizations for the airport improvement program. Introduced by Richardson, D-Calif., on March 25, 2010. House Transportation discharged. House Ways and Means discharged. House passed March 25. Senate passed March 26. President signed March 31, 2010.

PL 111-154 (S 1147) Prevent tobacco smuggling and ensure the collection of all tobacco taxes. Introduced by Kohl, D-Wis., on May 21, 2009. Senate Judiciary reported, amended, November 19 (no written report). Senate passed, amended, March 11, 2010. House passed, under suspension of the rules, March 17. President signed March 31, 2010.

PL 111-155 (HR 4621) Protect the integrity of the constitutionally mandated U.S. census and prohibit deceptive mail practices that attempt to exploit the decennial census. Introduced by Maloney, D-N.Y., on February 9, 2010. House passed, amended, under suspension of the rules, March 10. Senate Homeland Security and Governmental affairs discharged. Senate passed March 26. President signed April 7, 2010.

PL 111-156 (H J Res 80) Recognize and honor the Blinded Veterans Association on its 65th anniversary of representing blinded veterans and their families. Introduced by Halvorson, D-Ill., on March 4, 2010. House passed, under suspension of the rules, March 23. Senate passed March 26. President signed April 7, 2010.

PL 111-157 (HR 4851) Provide a temporary extension of federal unemployment benefits, COBRA subsidies and other programs. Introduced by Levin, D-Mich., on March 16, 2010. House passed, amended, under suspension of the rules, March 17. Senate passed, amended, April 15. House agreed to Senate amendment, April 15. President signed April 15, 2010.

PL 111-158 (HR 4573) Urge the secretary of the Treasury to instruct the U.S. executive directors at the International Monetary

Fund, the World Bank, the Inter-American Development Bank, and other multilateral development institutions to seek the cancellation of Haiti's debts to such institutions. Introduced by Waters, D-Calif., February 2, 2010. House passed, amended, under suspension of the rules, March 10. Senate passed, amended, March 26. House agreed to Senate amendments, under suspension of the rules, April 14. President signed April 26, 2010.

PL 111-159 (HR 4887) Amend the Internal Revenue Code of 1986 to ensure that health coverage provided by the Department of Defense is treated as minimal essential coverage. Introduced by Skelton, D-Mo., on March 19, 2010. House passed, amended, under suspension of the rules, March 20. Senate Finance discharged. Senate passed April 12. President signed April 26, 2010.

PL 111-160 (S J Res 25) Grant the consent and approval of Congress to amendments made by the State of Maryland, the Commonwealth of Virginia, and the District of Columbia to the Washington Metropolitan Area Transit Regulation Compact. Introduced by Cardin, D-Md., on December 24, 2009. Senate Judiciary discharged. Senate passed January 21, 2010. House passed, under suspension of the rules, April 14. President signed April 26, 2010.

PL 111-161 (HR 5147) Extend the funding and expenditure authority of the Airport and Airway Trust Fund and extend authorizations for the airport improvement program. Introduced by Oberstar, D-Minn., on April 27, 2010. House passed, under suspension of the rules, April 28. Senate passed April 28. President signed April 30, 2010.

PL 111-162 (S 3253) Provide for an additional temporary extension of programs under the Small Business Act and the Small Business Investment Act of 1958. Introduced by Landrieu, D-La., on April 22, 2010. Senate passed April 22. House passed, under suspension of the rules, April 27. President signed April 30, 2010.

PL 111-163 (S 1963) Amend Title 38, U.S. Code, to provide assistance to the caregivers of veterans and improve the provision of health care to veterans. Introduced by Akaka, D-Hawaii, on October 28, 2009. Senate passed November 19. House passed, amended, under suspension of the rules, April 21, 2010. Senate agreed to House amendment April 22. President signed May 5, 2010.

PL 111-164 (HR 4360) Designate the Department of Veterans Affairs blind rehabilitation center in Long Beach, Calif., as the "Major Charles Robert Soltes Jr., O.D. Department of Veterans Affairs Blind Rehabilitation Center." Introduced by Campbell, R-Calif., on December 16, 2009. House passed, under suspension of the rules, March 25, 2010. Senate Veterans' Affairs discharged. Senate passed April 19. President signed May 7, 2010.

PL 111-165 (HR 5146) Provide that members of Congress shall not receive a cost-of-living adjustment in pay for fiscal 2011. Introduced by Mitchell, D-Ariz., on April 27, 2010. House passed, under suspension of the rules, April 27. Senate passed April 28. President signed May 14, 2010.

PL 111-166 (HR 3714) Amend the Foreign Assistance Act of 1961 to include information in the Annual Country Reports on Human Rights Practices about press freedom in foreign countries. Introduced by Schiff, D-Calif., on October 1, 2009. House passed, amended, under suspension of the rules, December 16. Senate Foreign Relations discharged. Senate passed April 29, 2010. President signed May 17, 2010.

PL 111-167 (HR 1121) Authorize a land exchange to acquire lands for the Blue Ridge Parkway from the town of Blowing Rock, N.C. Introduced by Foxx, R-Va., on February 23, 2009. House Natural Resources reported, amended, July 24 (H Rept 111-227). House passed, amended, under suspension of the rules, July 27. Senate Energy and Natural Resources reported March 2, 2010 (S Rept 111-147). Senate passed May 7. President signed May 24, 2010.

PL 111-168 (HR 1442) Provide for the sale of the federal government's reversionary interest in approximately sixty acres of land in Salt Lake City originally conveyed to the Mount Olivet Cemetery Association under the Act of January 23, 1909. Introduced by Matheson, D-Utah, on March 11, 2009. House Natural Resources reported, amended, July 10 (H Rept 111-198). House passed, amended, under suspension of the rules, July 16. Senate Energy and Natural Resources reported March 2, 2010 (S Rept 111-150). Senate passed May 7. President signed May 24, 2010.

PL 111-169 (HR 2802) Provide for an extension of the legislative authority of the Adams Memorial Foundation to establish a commemorative work honoring President John Adams. Introduced by Delahunt, D-Mass., on June 10, 2009. House Natural Resources reported, amended, September 21 (H Rept 111-261). House passed, amended, under suspension of the rules, September 22. Senate Energy and Natural Resources reported March 2, 2010 (S Rept 111-155). Senate passed May 7. President signed May 24, 2010.

PL 111-170 (HR 5148) Amend Title 39, U.S. Code, to clarify the instances in which the term "census" may appear on mailable matter. Introduced by Issa, R-Calif., on April 27, 2010. House passed, under suspension of the rules, April 28. Senate Homeland Security and Governmental Affairs discharged. Senate passed May 5. President signed May 24, 2010.

PL 111-171 (HR 5160) Extend the Caribbean Basin Economic Recovery Act and provide customs support services to Haiti. Introduced by Rangel, D-N.Y., on April 28, 2010. House passed, amended, under suspension of the rules, May 5. Senate passed May 6. President signed May 24, 2010.

PL 111-172 (S 1067) Support stabilization and lasting peace in northern Uganda and areas affected by the Lord's Resistance Army. Introduced by Feingold, D-Wis., on May 19, 2009. Senate Foreign Relations reported, amended, December 15 (S Rept 111-108). Senate passed, amended, March 10, 2010. House passed, under suspension of the rules, May 12. President signed May 24, 2010.

PL 111-173 (HR 5014) Clarify the definition of health care provided by the secretary of Veterans Affairs that constitutes minimum essential coverage. Introduced by Filner, D-Calif., on April 14, 2010. House passed, amended, under suspension of the rules, May 12. Senate passed May 18. President signed May 27, 2010.

PL 111-174 (S 1782) Provide improvements for the operations of the federal courts. Introduced by Whitehouse, D-R.I., on October 14, 2009. Senate Judiciary discharged. Senate passed

March 16, 2010. House passed, under suspension of the rules, May 18. President signed May 27, 2010.

PL 111-175 (S 3333) Extend the statutory license for secondary transmissions of television broadcast signals under Title 17, U.S. Code. Introduced by Leahy, D-Vt., on May 7, 2010. Senate passed May 7. House passed, under suspension of the rules, May 12. President signed May 27, 2010.

PL 111-176 (HR 5128) Designate the U.S. Department of Interior Building in Washington, D.C., as the "Stewart Lee Udall Department of the Interior Building." Introduced by Heinrich, D-N.M., on April 22, 2010. House Transportation reported, amended, May 18 (H Rept 111-485). House passed, amended, under suspension of the rules, May 20. Senate passed May 25. President signed June 8, 2010.

PL 111-177 (HR 5139) Extend immunities provided in the International Organizations Immunities Act to the Office of the High Representative and the International Civilian Office in Kosovo. Introduced by Berman, D-Calif., on April 26, 2010. House passed, amended, under suspension of the rules, May 19. Senate passed May 20. President signed June 8, 2010.

PL 111-178 (HR 2711) Provide transportation of the dependents, remains, and effects of certain federal employees who die as a result of injuries sustained in the performance of official duties. Introduced by Rogers, R-Mich., on June 4, 2009. House Oversight and Government Reform reported, amended, September 29 (H Rept 111-274). House passed, amended, under suspension of the rules, December 8. Senate Homeland Security and Governmental Affairs reported December 17 (no written report). Senate passed, amended, May 14, 2010. House agreed to Senate amendments, under suspension of the rules, May 25. President signed June 9, 2010.

PL 111-179 (HR 3250) Designate the facility of the U.S. Postal Service located at 1210 West Main St. in Riverhead, N.Y., as the "Private First Class Garfield M. Langhorn Post Office Building." Introduced by Bishop, D-N.Y., on July 17, 2009. House passed, under suspension of the rules, January 21, 2010. Senate Homeland Security and Governmental Affairs reported May 18 (no written report). Senate passed May 25. President signed June 9, 2010.

PL 111-180 (HR 3634) Designate the facility of the U.S. Postal Service located at 109 Main St. in Swifton, Ark., as the "George Kell Post Office." Introduced by Berry, D-Ark., on September 23, 2009. House passed, under suspension of the rules, December 2. Senate Homeland Security and Governmental Affairs reported May 18, 2010 (no written report). Senate passed May 25. President signed June 9, 2010.

PL 111-181 (HR 3892) Designate the facility of the U.S. Postal Service located at 101 West Highway 64 Bypass in Roper, N.C., as the "E. V. Wilkins Post Office." Introduced by Butterfield, D-N.C., on October 21, 2009. House passed, under suspension of the rules, January 13, 2010. Senate Homeland Security and Governmental Affairs reported May 18 (no written report). Senate passed May 25. President signed June 9, 2010.

PL 111-182 (HR 4017) Designate the facility of the U.S. Postal Service located at 43 Maple Ave. in Shrewsbury, Mass., as the "Ann Marie Blute Post Office." Introduced by McGovern, D-Mass., on November 4, 2009. House passed, under suspension of the rules, December 10. Senate Homeland Security and Governmental Affairs reported May 18, 2010 (no written report). Senate passed May 25. President signed June 9, 2010.

PL 111-183 (HR 4095) Designate the facility of the U.S. Postal Service located at 9727 Antioch Road in Overland Park, Kan., as the "Congresswoman Jan Meyers Post Office Building." Introduced by Moore, D-Kan., on November 17, 2009. House passed, under suspension of the rules, January 20, 2010. Senate Homeland Security and Governmental Affairs reported May 18 (no written report). Senate passed May 25. President signed June 9, 2010.

PL 111-184 (HR 4139) Designate the facility of the U.S. Postal Service located at 7464 Highway 503 in Hickory, Miss., as the "Sgt. Matthew L. Ingram Post Office." Introduced by Harper, R-Miss., on November 19, 2009. House passed, under suspension of the rules, January 13, 2010. Senate Homeland Security and Governmental Affairs reported May 18 (no written report). Senate passed May 25. President signed June 9, 2010.

PL 111-185 (HR 4214) Designate the facility of the U.S. Postal Service located at 45300 Portola Ave. in Palm Desert, Calif., as the "Roy Wilson Post Office." Introduced by Bono Mack, R-Calif., on December 7, 2009. House passed, under suspension of the rules, March 18, 2010. Senate Homeland Security and Governmental Affairs reported May 18 (no written report). Senate passed May 25. President signed June 9, 2010.

PL 111-186 (HR 4238) Designate the facility of the U.S. Postal Service located at 930 39th Ave. in Greeley, Colo., as the "W.D. Farr Post Office Building." Introduced by Markey, D-Colo., on December 8, 2009. House passed, under suspension of the rules, February 22, 2010. Senate Homeland Security and Governmental Affairs reported May 18 (no written report). Senate passed May 25. President signed June 9, 2010.

PL 111-187 (HR 4425) Designate the facility of the U.S. Postal Service located at 2-116th St. in North Troy, N.Y., as the "Martin G. 'Marty' Mahar Post Office." Introduced by Tonko, D-N.Y., on January 12, 2010. House passed, under suspension of the rules, February 22. Senate Homeland Security and Governmental Affairs reported May 18 (no written report). Senate passed May 25. President signed June 9, 2010.

PL 111-188 (HR 4547) Designate the facility of the U.S. Postal Service located at 119 Station Road in Cheyney, Pa., as the "Capt. Luther H. Smith, U.S. Army Air Forces Post Office." Introduced by Sestak, D-Pa., on January 27, 2010. House passed, under suspension of the rules, March 9. Senate Homeland Security and Governmental Affairs reported May 18 (no written report). Senate passed May 25. President signed June 9, 2010.

PL 111-189 (HR 4628) Designate the facility of the U.S. Postal Service located at 216 Westwood Ave. in Westwood, N.J., as the "Sgt. Christopher R. Hrbek Post Office Building." Introduced by Garrett, R-N.J., on February 22, 2010. House passed, under suspension of the rules, March 16. Senate Homeland Security and Governmental Affairs reported May 18 (no written report). Senate passed May 25. President signed June 9, 2010.

PL 111-190 (HR 5330) Extend certain provisions of the Antitrust Criminal Penalty Enhancement and Reform Act of 2004. Introduced by Johnson, D-Ga., on May 18, 2010. House passed, amended, under suspension of the rules, May 24. Senate passed May 27. President signed June 9, 2010.

PL 111-191 (S 3473) Amend the Oil Pollution Act of 1990 to authorize advances from the Oil Spill Liability Trust Fund for the Deepwater Horizon oil spill. Introduced by Reid, D-Nev., on June 9, 2010. Senate passed June 9. House passed, under suspension of the rules, June 10. President signed June 15, 2010.

PL 111-192 (HR 3962) Prevent a Medicare payment cut to physicians and provide a payment increase in 2010. Introduced by Dingell, D-Mich., on October 29, 2009. House passed, amended, November 7. Senate passed, amended, June 18, 2010. House agreed to Senate amendments to the House amendment, under suspension of the rules, June 24. President signed June 25, 2010.

PL 111-193 (HR 3951) Designate the facility of the U.S. Postal Service located at 2000 Louisiana Ave. in New Orleans as the "Roy Rondeno Sr. Post Office Building." Introduced by Cao, R-La., on October 28, 2009. House passed, under suspension of the rules, December 9. Senate Homeland Security and Governmental Affairs reported June 14, 2010 (no written report). Senate passed June 15. President signed June 28, 2010.

PL 111-194 (S J Res 33) Provide for the reconsideration and revision of the proposed constitution of the U.S. Virgin Islands to correct provisions inconsistent with the U.S. Constitution and federal law. Introduced by Bingaman, D-N.M., on June 17, 2010. Senate passed June 17. House passed, under suspension of the rules, June 29. President signed June 30, 2010.

PL 111-195 (HR 2194) Amend the Iran Sanctions Act of 1996 to enhance U.S. diplomatic efforts with respect to Iran by expanding economic sanctions against Iran. Introduced by Berman, D-Calif., on April 30, 2009. House Foreign Affairs reported, amended, November 19 (H Rept 111-342, Part 1). House Financial Services discharged. House Oversight and Government Reform discharged. House Ways and Means discharged. House passed, amended, under suspension of the rules, December 15. Senate Banking, Housing, and Urban Affairs discharged. Senate passed, amended, March 11, 2010. Conference report filed in the House on June 23 (H Rept 111-512). Senate agreed to conference report June 24. House agreed to conference report, under suspension of the rules, June 24. President signed July 1, 2010.

PL 111-196 (HR 5569) Extend the National Flood Insurance Program until September 30, 2010. Introduced by Waters, D-Calif., on June 22, 2010. House passed, under suspension of the rules, June 23. Senate passed June 30. President signed July 2, 2010.

PL 111-197 (HR 5611) Amend the Internal Revenue Code of 1986 to extend the funding and expenditure authority of the Airport and Airway Trust Fund, and amend Title 49, U.S. Code, to extend authorizations for the airport improvement program. Introduced by Levin, D-Mich., on June 28, 2010. House passed, under suspension of the rules, June 29. Senate passed June 30. President signed July 2, 2010.

PL 111-198 (HR 5623) Amend the Internal Revenue Code of 1986 to extend the homebuyer tax credit to homes purchased by October 1, 2010. Introduced by Dahlkemper, D-Pa., on June 29, 2010. House passed, amended, under suspension of the rules, June 29. Senate passed June 30. President signed July 2, 2010.

PL 111-199 (S 1660) Amend the Toxic Substances Control Act to reduce the emissions of formaldehyde from composite wood products. Introduced by Klobuchar, D-Minn., on September 10, 2009. Senate Environment and Public Works reported, amended, April 19, 2010 (S Rept 111-169). Senate passed, amended, June 14. House passed, under suspension of the rules, June 23. President signed July 7, 2010.

PL 111-200 (S 2865) Reauthorize the Congressional Award Act. Introduced by Lieberman, I-Conn., on December 10, 2009. Senate Homeland Security and Governmental Affairs reported March 15, 2010 (S Rept 111-163). Senate passed March 17. House passed, under suspension of the rules, June 23. President signed July 7, 2010.

PL 111-201 (S J Res 32) Recognize the 60th anniversary of the outbreak of the Korean War and reaffirm the United States-Korea alliance. Introduced by Burr, R-N.C., on June 16, 2010. Senate passed June 16. House passed, under suspension of the rules, June 23. President signed July 7, 2010.

PL 111-202 (S 3104) Permanently authorize Radio Free Asia. Introduced by Lugar, R-Ind., on March 11, 2010. Senate Foreign Relations reported, amended, June 22 (S Rept 111-214). Senate passed, amended, June 25. House passed, under suspension of the rules, June 30. President signed July 13, 2010.

PL 111-203 (HR 4173) Provide for financial regulatory reform, protect consumers and investors, enhance federal understanding of insurance issues, and regulate the over-the-counter derivatives markets. Introduced by Frank, D-Mass., on December 2, 2009. House passed, amended, December 11. Senate Banking, Housing and Urban Affairs discharged. Senate passed, amended, May 20, 2010. Conference report filed in the House on June 29 (H Rept 111-517). House agreed to conference report June 30. Senate agreed to conference report July 15. President signed July 21, 2010.

PL 111-204 (S 1508) Amend the Improper Payments Information Act of 2002 to reduce improper payments by federal agencies. Introduced by Carper, D-Del., on July 23, 2009. Senate Homeland Security and Governmental Affairs reported, amended, June 15, 2010 (no written report). Senate passed, amended, June 23. House passed, under suspension of the rules, July 14. President signed July 22, 2010.

PL 111-205 (HR 4213) Amend the Internal Revenue Code of 1986 to extend certain expiring provisions. Introduced by Rangel, D-N.Y., on December 7, 2009. House passed December 9. Senate Finance discharged. Senate passed, amended, March 10, 2010. House agreed to Senate amendment, with amendments, May 28. Senate agreed to House amendment to Senate amendment, with amendment, July 1. House agreed to Senate amendment to House amendment to Senate amendment July 22. President signed July 22, 2010.

PL 111-206 (HR 689) Exchange administrative jurisdiction of certain federal lands between the Forest Service and the Bureau of Land Management. Introduced by Herger, R-Calif., on January 26, 2009. House Natural Resources reported, amended, May 14 (H Rept 111-108). House passed, amended, under suspension of the rules, June 2. Senate Energy and Natural Resources reported, amended, March 2, 2010 (S Rept 111-145). Senate passed, amended, May 7. House agreed to Senate amendment, under suspension of the rules, July 13. President signed July 27, 2010.

PL 111-207 (HR 3360) Amend Title 46, U.S. Code, to establish requirements to ensure the security and safety of passengers and crew on cruise vessels. Introduced by Matsui, D-Calif., on July 28, 2009. House Transportation and Infrastructure reported November 7 (H Rept 111-332). House passed, amended, under suspension of the rules, November 17. Senate passed, amended, June 10, 2010. House agreed to Senate amendment, under suspension of the rules, June 30. President signed July 27, 2010.

PL 111-208 (HR 4840) Designate the facility of the U.S. Postal Service located at 1981 Cleveland Ave. in Columbus, Ohio, as the "Clarence D. Lumpkin Post Office." Introduced by Tiberi, R-Ohio, on March 12, 2010. House passed, under suspension of the rules, March 21. Senate Homeland Security and Governmental Affairs reported, amended, May 18 (no written report). Senate passed, amended, May 25. House agreed to Senate amendment, under suspension of the rules, July 14. President signed July 27, 2010.

PL 111-209 (HR 5502) Amend the effective date of the gift card provisions of the Credit Card Accountability Responsibility and Disclosure Act of 2009. Introduced by Maffei, D-N.Y., on June 10, 2010. House passed, under suspension of the rules, June 14. Senate Banking, Housing and Urban Affairs discharged. Senate passed July 13. President signed July 27, 2010.

PL 111-210 (H J Res 83) Approve the renewal of import restrictions contained in the Burmese Freedom and Democracy Act of 2003. Introduced by Crowley, D-N.Y., on May 11, 2010. House passed, amended, under suspension of the rules, July 14. Senate passed July 22. President signed July 27, 2010.

PL 111-211 (HR 725) Protect American Indian arts and crafts through the improvement of applicable criminal proceedings. Introduced by Pastor, D-Ariz., on January 27, 2009. House Natural Resources reported January 15, 2010 (H Rept 111-397, Part 1). House Judiciary discharged. House passed, amended, under suspension of the rules, January 19. Senate passed, amended, June 23. House agreed to Senate amendment, under suspension of the rules, July 21. President signed July 29, 2010.

PL 111-212 (HR 4899) Make emergency supplemental appropriations for operations in Iraq and Afghanistan and for other purposes for the fiscal year ending September 30, 2010. Introduced by Obey, D-Wis., on March 21, 2010. House passed March 24. Senate Appropriations reported, amended, May 14 (S Rept 111-188). Senate passed, amended, May 27. House agreed to Senate amendment, with amendments July 1. Senate disagreed to House amendment to Senate amendment July 22. House receded and concurred in Senate amendment, under suspension of the rules, July 27. President signed July 29, 2010.

PL 111-213 (HR 5610) Provide a technical adjustment with respect to funding for independent living centers under the Rehabilitation Act of 1973. Introduced by Miller, D-Calif., on June 28, 2010. House passed, amended, under suspension of the rules, June 30. Senate Health, Education, Labor and Pensions discharged. Senate passed, amended, July 27. House agreed to Senate amendment, under suspension of the rules, July 28. President signed July 29, 2010.

PL 111-214 (HR 5849) Provide for an additional temporary extension of programs under the Small Business Act and the Small Business Investment Act of 1958. Introduced by Velázquez, D-N.Y., on July 26, 2010. House passed, under suspension of the rules, July 27. Senate passed July 27. President signed July 30, 2010.

PL 111-215 (S 3372) Modify the date on which the EPA administrator and applicable states may require permits for discharges from certain vessels. Introduced by Boxer, D-Calif., on May 13, 2010. Senate Environment and Public Works reported June 18 (S Rept 111-209). Senate passed July 14. House passed, under suspension of the rules, July 29. President signed July 30, 2010.

PL 111-216 (HR 5900) Amend the Internal Revenue Code of 1986 to extend the funding and expenditure authority of the Airport and Airway Trust Fund; amend Title 49, U.S. Code, to extend airport improvement program project grant authority; and improve airline safety. Introduced by Oberstar, D-Minn., on July 28, 2010. House passed, under suspension of the rules, July 29. Senate passed July 30. President signed August 1, 2010.

PL 111-217 (HR 4861) Designate the facility of the U.S. Postal Service located at 1343 West Irving Park Road in Chicago as the "Steve Goodman Post Office Building." Introduced by Quigley, D-Ill., on March 16, 2010. House passed, under suspension of the rules, April 26. Senate Homeland Security and Governmental Affairs reported June 29 (no written report). Senate passed July 14. President signed August 3, 2010.

PL 111-218 (HR 5051) Designate the facility of the U.S. Postal Service located at 23 Genesee St. in Hornell, N.Y., as the "Zachary Smith Post Office Building." Introduced by Crowley, D-N.Y., on April 15, 2010. House passed, under suspension of the rules, May 11. Senate Homeland Security and Governmental Affairs reported June 29 (no written report). Senate passed July 14. President signed August 3, 2010.

PL 111-219 (HR 5099) Designate the facility of the U.S. Postal Service located at 15 South Main St. in Sharon, Mass., as the "Michael C. Rothberg Post Office." Introduced by Frank, D-Mass., on April 21, 2010. House passed, under suspension of the rules, May 19. Senate Homeland Security and Governmental Affairs reported June 29 (no written report). Senate passed July 14. President signed August 3, 2010.

PL 111-220 (S 1789) Reduce the disparity in sentencing guidelines between powder and crack cocaine for federal drug offenses. Introduced by Durbin, D-Ill., on October 15, 2009. Senate Judiciary reported, amended, March 15, 2010 (no written report). Senate passed, amended, March 17. House passed, under suspension of the rules, July 28. President signed August 3, 2010.

PL 111-221 (HR 4684) Require the secretary of the Treasury to strike medals in commemoration of the 10th anniversary of the September 11, 2001, terrorist attacks and the establishment of the National September 11 Memorial & Museum at the World

Trade Center. Introduced by Nadler, D-N.Y., on February 24, 2010. House passed, amended, under suspension of the rules, July 20. Senate passed July 22. President signed August 6, 2010.

PL 111-222 (S 1053) Amend the National Law Enforcement Museum Act to delay the termination date. Introduced by Murkowski, R-Alaska, on May 14, 2009. Senate Energy and Natural Resources reported March 2, 2010 (S Rept 111-137). Senate passed May 7. House passed, under suspension of the rules, July 21. President signed August 6, 2010.

PL 111-223 (HR 2765) Amend Title 28, U.S. Code, to prohibit recognition and enforcement of foreign defamation judgments and certain foreign judgments against the providers of interactive computer services. Introduced by Cohen, D-Tenn., on June 9, 2009. House Judiciary reported June 15 (H Rept 111-154). House passed, amended, under suspension of the rules, June 15. Senate Judiciary reported, amended, July 14, 2010 (S Rept 111-224). Senate passed, amended, July 19. House agreed to Senate amendment, under suspension of the rules, July 27. President signed August 10, 2010.

PL 111-224 (HR 5874) Make supplemental appropriations for the U.S. Patent and Trademark Office for the fiscal year ending September 30, 2010. Introduced by Mollohan, D-W.Va., on July 27, 2010. House passed, under suspension of the rules, July 28. Senate passed July 29. President signed August 10, 2010.

PL 111-225 (S 1749) Amend Title 18, U.S. Code, to prohibit the possession or use of cell phones and similar wireless devices by federal prisoners. Introduced by Feinstein, D-Calif., on October 5, 2009. Senate Judiciary reported, amended, February 2, 2010 (no written report). Senate passed, amended, April 13. House passed, amended, under suspension of the rules, July 20. Senate agreed to House amendment July 28. President signed August 10, 2010.

PL 111-226 (HR 1586) To provide Medicaid and education funding for states and localities. Introduced by Rangel, D-N.Y., as tax bill on March 18, 2009. House passed, under suspension of the rules, March 19. Senate passed, amended, as Federal Aviation Administration authorization, March 22, 2010. House agreed to Senate amendment, with amendment, March 25. Senate agreed to House amendment to Senate amendment, with amendment, as state Medicaid and education funding August 5. House agreed to Senate amendment to House amendment to Senate amendment August 10. President signed August 10, 2010.

PL 111-227 (HR 4380) Amend the Harmonized Tariff Schedule of the United States to modify temporarily certain rates of duty. Introduced by Levin, D-Mich., on December 16, 2009. House passed, amended, under suspension of the rules, July 21, 2010. Senate passed July 27. President signed August 11, 2010.

PL 111-228 (HR 5872) Provide adequate commitment authority for fiscal year 2010 for guaranteed loans that are obligations of the General and Special Risk Insurance Funds of the Department of Housing and Urban Development. Introduced by Frank, D-Mass., on July 27, 2010. House passed, amended, under suspension of the rules, July 28. Senate Banking, Housing and Urban Affairs discharged. Senate passed August 4. President signed August 11, 2010.

PL 111-229 (HR 5981) Increase the flexibility of the secretary of Housing and Urban Development on the amount of premiums charged for FHA single-family housing mortgage insurance. Introduced by Frank, D-Mass., on July 30, 2010. House passed, under suspension of the rules, July 30. Senate Banking, Housing and Urban Affairs discharged. Senate passed August 4. President signed August 11, 2010.

PL 111-230 (HR 6080) Make emergency supplemental appropriations for border security for the fiscal year ending September 30, 2010. Introduced by Price, D-N.C., on August 9, 2010. House passed, under suspension of the rules, August 10. Senate passed August 12. President signed August 13, 2010.

PL 111-231 (HR 511) Authorize the secretary of agriculture to terminate certain easements held by the secretary on land owned by the village of Caseyville, Ill., and terminate associated contractual arrangements with the village. Introduced by Costello, D-Ill., on January 14, 2009. House Agriculture reported September 10 (H Rept 111-253). House passed, under suspension of the rules, September 15. Senate Agriculture, Nutrition, and Forestry reported December 16 (no written report). Senate passed August 5, 2010. President signed August 16, 2010.

PL 111-232 (HR 2097) Require the secretary of the Treasury to mint coins in commemoration of the bicentennial of the writing of "The Star-Spangled Banner." Introduced by Ruppersberger, D-Md., on April 23, 2009. House passed, under suspension of the rules, September 9. Senate Banking, Housing and Urban Affairs discharged. Senate passed August 2, 2010. President signed August 16, 2010.

PL 111-233 (HR 3509) Reauthorize state agricultural mediation programs under Title V of the Agricultural Credit Act of 1987. Introduced by Peterson, D-Minn., on July 31, 2009. House passed, under suspension of the rules, March 18, 2010. Senate Agriculture, Nutrition, and Forestry discharged. Senate passed August 5. President signed August 16, 2010.

PL 111-234 (HR 4275) Designate the annex building under construction for the Elbert P. Tuttle U.S. Court of Appeals Building in Atlanta as the "John C. Godbold Federal Building." Introduced by Lewis, D-Ga., on December 10, 2009. House Transportation and Infrastructure reported, amended, March 18, 2010 (H Rept 111-444). House passed, amended, under suspension of the rules, April 14. Senate Environment and Public Works reported June 15 (no written report). Senate passed August 5. President signed August 16, 2010.

PL 111-235 (HR 5278) Designate the facility of the U.S. Postal Service located at 405 West Second St. in Dixon, Ill., as the "President Ronald W. Reagan Post Office Building." Introduced by Foster, D-Ill., on May 12, 2010. House passed, under suspension of the rules, June 9. Senate Homeland Security and Governmental Affairs reported July 28 (no written report). Senate passed July 30. President signed August 16, 2010.

PL 111-236 (HR 5395) Designate the facility of the U.S. Postal Service located at 151 North Maitland Ave. in Maitland, Fla., as the "Paula Hawkins Post Office Building." Introduced by Mica, R-Fla., on May 25, 2010. House passed, under suspension of the rules, June 30. Senate Homeland Security and Governmental

Affairs reported July 28 (no written report). Senate passed July 30. President signed August 16, 2010.

PL 111-237 (HR 5552) Amend the Internal Revenue Code of 1986 to require that the manufacturers' excise tax on recreational equipment be paid quarterly and provide for the assessment by the secretary of the Treasury of certain criminal restitution. Introduced by Kind, D-Wis., on June 17, 2010. House passed, amended, under suspension of the rules, June 29. Senate passed August 5. President signed August 16, 2010.

PL 111-238 (HR 6102) Amend the National Defense Authorization Act for fiscal year 2010 to extend the authority of the secretary of the Navy to enter into multiyear contracts for F/A-18E, F/A-18F, and EA-18G aircraft. Introduced by Taylor, D-Miss., on August 10, 2010. House passed, under suspension of the rules, September 14. Senate passed September 16. President signed September 27, 2010.

PL 111-239 (S 3656) Amend the Agricultural Marketing Act of 1946 to improve the reporting on sales of livestock and dairy products. Introduced by Lincoln, D-Ark., on July 27, 2010. Senate Agriculture, Nutrition and Forestry reported August 5 (no written report). Senate passed August 5. House passed, under suspension of the rules, September 15. President signed September 27, 2010.

PL 111-240 (HR 5297) Create the Small Business Lending Fund to increase the availability of credit for small businesses and amend the Internal Revenue Code of 1986 to provide tax incentives for small-business job creation. Introduced by Frank, D-Mass., on May 13, 2010. House Financial Services reported, amended, May 27 (H Rept 111-499). House passed, amended, June 17. Senate passed, amended, September 16. House agreed to Senate amendment September 23. President signed September 27, 2010.

PL 111-241 (HR 1454) Provide for the issuance of a multinational species conservation funds semipostal stamp. Introduced by Brown, R-S.C., on March 12, 2009. House Natural Resources reported, amended, December 7 (H Rept 111-358, Part 1). House Oversight and Government Reform discharged. House passed, amended, under suspension of the rules, December 7. Senate Homeland Security and Governmental Affairs reported, amended, July 27, 2010 (S Rept 111-234). Senate passed, amended, July 29. House agreed to Senate amendment, under suspension of the rules, September 22. President signed September 30, 2010.

PL 111-242 (HR 3081) Make continuing appropriations for fiscal year 2011. Introduced by Lowey, D-N.Y., on June 26, 2009, as fiscal 2010 Foreign Operations bill. House Appropriations reported June 26 (H Rept 111-187). House passed, amended, July 9. Senate passed, amended, as continuing resolution, September 29, 2010. House agreed to Senate amendment September 30. President signed September 30, 2010.

PL 111-243 (HR 3562) Designate the federally occupied building at 1220 Echelon Parkway in Jackson, Miss., as the "James Chaney, Andrew Goodman, Michael Schwerner and Roy K. Moore Federal Building." Introduced by Thompson, D-Miss., on September 14, 2009. House Transportation and Infrastructure reported, amended, February 22, 2010 (H Rept 111-414). House passed, amended, under suspension of the rules, March 24. Senate Environment and Public Works reported, amended, July 26 (no written report). Senate passed, amended, August 5. House agreed to Senate amendment, under suspension of the rules, September 16. President signed September 30, 2010.

PL 111-244 (HR 3940) Clarify the availability of existing funds for political status education in the territory of Guam. Introduced by Bordallo, D-Guam, on October 27, 2009. House Natural Resources reported, amended, December 7 (H Rept 111-357). House passed, amended, under suspension of the rules, December 7. Senate Energy and Natural Resources discharged. Senate passed, amended, September 28, 2010. House agreed to Senate amendment, under suspension of the rules, September 30. President signed September 30, 2010.

PL 111-245 (HR 3978) Amend the Homeland Security Act of 2002 to authorize the secretary of Homeland Security to accept and use gifts for otherwise authorized activities of the Center for Domestic Preparedness that are related to preparedness for a response to terrorism. Introduced by Rogers, R-Ala., on November 2, 2009. House Homeland Security reported December 15 (H Rept 111-376). House passed, under suspension of the rules, December 15. Senate Homeland Security and Governmental Affairs reported, amended, August 2, 2010 (no written report). Senate passed, amended, August 5. House agreed to Senate amendment, under suspension of the rules, September 15. President signed September 30, 2010.

PL 111-246 (HR 4505) Enable the secretary of veterans affairs to allow state homes to furnish nursing-home care to parents who had at least one child die while serving in the Armed Forces. Introduced by Thornberry, R-Texas, on January 26, 2010. House passed, under suspension of the rules, June 30. Senate Veterans' Affairs discharged. Senate passed September 20. President signed September 30, 2010.

PL 111-247 (HR 4667) Increase, effective December 1, 2010, the rates of compensation for veterans with service-connected disabilities and the rates of dependency and indemnity compensation for the survivors of certain disabled veterans. Introduced by Perriello, D-Va., on February 23, 2010. House Veterans' Affairs reported March 22 (H Rept 111-452). House passed, under suspension of the rules, March 22. Senate Veterans' Affairs discharged. Senate passed September 22. President signed September 30, 2010.

PL 111-248 (HR 5682) Improve the operation of certain facilities and programs of the House of Representatives. Introduced by Brady, D-Pa., on July 1, 2010. House Administration reported July 27 (H Rept 111-569). House passed, amended, under suspension of the rules, July 27. Senate Rules and Administration discharged. Senate passed September 22. President signed September 30, 2010.

PL 111-249 (HR 6190) Amend the Internal Revenue Code of 1986 to extend the funding and expenditure authority of the Airport and Airway Trust Fund and amend Title 49, U.S. Code, to extend the airport improvement program. Introduced by Levin, D-Mich., on September 23, 2010. House passed, under suspension of the rules, September 23. Senate passed September 24. President signed September 30, 2010.

PL 111-250 (S 3814) Extend the National Flood Insurance Program until September 30, 2011. Introduced by Vitter, R-La., on September 21, 2010. Senate passed September 21. House passed, under suspension of the rules, September 23. President signed September 30, 2010.

PL 111-251 (S 3839) Provide for an additional temporary extension of programs under the Small Business Act and the Small Business Investment Act of 1958. Introduced by Landrieu, D-La., on September 24, 2010. Senate passed September 24. House passed, under suspension of the rules, September 28. President signed September 30, 2010.

PL 111-252 (HR 1517) Allow certain U.S. Customs and Border Protection employees who serve under an overseas limited appointment for at least two years, and whose service is rated fully successful or higher throughout that time, to be converted to a permanent appointment in the competitive service. Introduced by Engel, D-N.Y., on March 16, 2009. House Homeland Security reported, amended, December 14 (H Rept 111-373, Part 1). House Oversight and Government Reform discharged. House passed, amended, under suspension of the rules, December 15. Senate Homeland Security and Governmental Affairs reported, amended, August 5, 2010 (S Rept 111-248). Senate passed, amended, August 5. House agreed to Senate amendment, under suspension of the rules, September 23. President signed October 5, 2010.

PL 111-253 (S 846) Award a congressional gold medal to Dr. Muhammad Yunus in recognition of his contributions to the fight against global poverty. Introduced by Durbin, D-Ill., on April 21, 2009. Senate Banking, Housing and Urban Affairs discharged. Senate passed October 13. House passed, under suspension of the rules, September 23, 2010. President signed October 5, 2010.

PL 111-254 (S 1055) Grant the congressional gold medal, collectively, to the 100th Infantry Battalion and the 442nd Regimental Combat Team, U.S. Army, in recognition of their dedicated service during World War II. Introduced by Boxer, D-Calif., on May 14, 2009. Senate Banking, Housing and Urban Affairs discharged. Senate passed, amended, August 2, 2010. House passed, under suspension of the rules, September 23. President signed October 5, 2010.

PL 111-255 (S 1674) Provide for an exclusion under the Supplemental Security Income program and the Medicaid program for compensation provided to individuals who participate in clinical trials for rare diseases or conditions. Introduced by Wyden, D-Ore., on September 15, 2009. Senate Finance discharged. Senate passed August 5, 2010. House passed, under suspension of the rules, September 23. President signed October 5, 2010.

PL 111-256 (S 2781) Change references in federal law from "mental retardation" to "intellectual disability" and change references from a "mentally retarded" individual to an individual with an "intellectual disability." Introduced by Mikulski, D-Md., on November 17, 2009. Senate Health, Education, Labor and Pensions reported, amended, August 3, 2010 (S Rept 111-244). Senate passed, amended, August 5. House passed, under suspension of the rules, September 22. President signed October 5, 2010.

PL 111-257 (S 3717) Amend the Securities Exchange Act of 1934, the Investment Company Act of 1940, and the Investment Advisers Act of 1940 to provide for certain disclosures under Section 552, Title 5, U.S. Code (commonly referred to as the Freedom of Information Act). Introduced by Leahy, D-Vt., on August 5, 2010. Senate Judiciary reported September 16 (no written report). Senate passed September 21. House passed, under suspension of the rules, September 23. President signed October 5, 2010.

PL 111-258 (HR 553) Require the secretary of Homeland Security to develop a strategy to prevent the overclassification of homeland security and other information and to promote the sharing of unclassified homeland security and other information. Introduced by Harman, D-Calif., on January 15, 2009. House passed, under suspension of the rules, February 3. Senate Homeland Security and Governmental Affairs reported, amended, May 27, 2010. (S Rept 111-200). Senate passed, amended, September 27. House agreed to Senate amendment, under suspension of the rules, September 28. President signed October 7, 2010.

PL 111-259 (HR 2701) Authorize appropriations for fiscal year 2010 for intelligence and intelligence-related activities of the U.S. government, the Community Management Account and the Central Intelligence Agency Retirement and Disability System. Introduced by Reyes, D-Texas, on June 4, 2009. House Select Intelligence reported, amended, June 26 (H Rept 111-186). House passed, amended, February 26, 2010. Senate passed, amended, September 27. House agreed to Senate amendment September 29. President signed October 7, 2010.

PL 111-260 (S 3304) Increase the access of persons with disabilities to modern communications. Introduced by Pryor, D-Ark., on May 4, 2010. Senate Commerce, Science and Transportation reported, amended, August 3 (no written report). Senate passed, amended, August 5. House passed, under suspension of the rules, September 28. President signed October 8, 2010.

PL 111-261 (HR 714) Authorize the secretary of the Interior to lease certain lands in the Virgin Islands National Park. Introduced by Christensen, D-V.I., on January 27, 2009. House passed, under suspension of the rules, February 23. Senate Energy and Natural Resources reported, amended, March 2, 2010 (S Rept 111-146). Senate passed, amended, May 13. House agreed to Senate amendment, under suspension of the rules, September 28. President signed October 8, 2010.

PL 111-262 (HR 1177) Require the secretary of the Treasury to mint coins in recognition of five U.S. Army five-star generals: George Marshall, Douglas MacArthur, Dwight D. Eisenhower, Henry "Hap" Arnold, and Omar Bradley, all alumni of the U.S. Army Command and General Staff College, Fort Leavenworth, Kan., to coincide with the celebration of the 132nd Anniversary of the founding of the U.S. Army Command and General Staff College. Introduced by Moore, D-Kan., on February 25, 2009. House passed, amended, under suspension of the rules, May 20, 2010. Senate Banking, Housing and Urban Affairs discharged. Senate passed September 28. President signed October 8, 2010.

PL 111-263 (S 2868) Provide increased access to the federal supply schedule of the General Services Administration to the

American Red Cross, other qualified organizations, and state and local governments. Introduced by Lieberman, I-Conn., on December 10, 2009. Senate Homeland Security and Governmental Affairs reported May 17, 2010 (S Rept 111-192). Senate passed May 24. House Oversight and Government Reform reported, amended, September 14 (H Rept 111-587). House passed, amended, under suspension of the rules, September 15. Senate agreed to House amendment September 27. President signed October 8, 2010.

PL 111-264 (S 3751) Amend the Stem Cell Therapeutic and Research Act of 2005 to revise the National Cord Blood Inventory Program. Introduced by Hatch, R-Utah, on August 5, 2010. Senate Health, Education, Labor and Pensions reported, amended, September 23 (no written report). Senate passed September 28. House passed, under suspension of the rules, September 30. President signed October 8, 2010.

PL 111-265 (S 3828) Make technical corrections in the 21st Century Communications and Video Accessibility Act of 2010 and the amendments made by that act. Introduced by Pryor, D-Ark., on September 22, 2010. Senate passed September 22. House passed, under suspension of the rules, September 28. President signed October 8, 2010.

PL 111-266 (S 3847) Implement certain defense trade cooperation treaties. Introduced by Kerry, D-Mass., on September 27, 2010. Senate passed September 27. House passed, under suspension of the rules, September 28. President signed October 8, 2010.

PL 111-267 (S 3729) Authorize the programs of the National Aeronautics and Space Administration for fiscal years 2011 through 2013. Introduced by Rockefeller, D-W.Va., on August 5, 2010. Senate Commerce, Science and Transportation reported August 5 (S Rept 111-278). Senate passed, amended, August 5. House passed, under suspension of the rules, September 29. President signed October 11, 2010.

PL 111-268 (HR 2923) Enhance the ability to combat methamphetamine. Introduced by Gordon, D-Tenn., on June 17, 2009. House Energy and Commerce reported September 22, 2010 (H Rept 111-615, Part 1). House Judiciary discharged. House passed, amended, under suspension of the rules, September 22. Senate passed September 27. President signed October 12, 2010.

PL 111-269 (HR 3553) Exclude from consideration as income under the Native American Housing Assistance and Self-Determination Act of 1996 amounts received by a family from the Department of Veterans Affairs for service-related disabilities of a member of the family. Introduced by Kirkpatrick, D-Ariz., on September 10, 2009. House passed, under suspension of the rules, April 20, 2010. Senate Indian Affairs reported September 22 (S Rept 111-299). Senate passed September 27. President signed October 12, 2010.

PL 111-270 (HR 3689) Provide for an extension of the legislative authority of the Vietnam Veterans Memorial Fund Inc. to establish a Vietnam Veterans Memorial visitor center. Introduced by Rahall, D-W.Va., on October 1, 2009. House passed, under suspension of the rules, October 13. Senate Energy and Natural Resources reported May 24, 2010 (S Rept 111-198). Senate passed September 28. President signed October 12, 2010.

PL 111-271 (HR 3980) Provide for identifying and eliminating redundant reporting requirements and developing meaningful performance metrics for homeland security preparedness grants. Introduced by Cuellar, D-Texas, on November 2, 2009. House Homeland Security reported December 1 (H Rept 111-346). House passed, amended, under suspension of the rules, December 2. Senate Homeland Security and Governmental Affairs reported, amended, September 16, 2010 (S Rept 111-291). Senate passed, amended, September 22. House agreed to Senate amendment, under suspension of the rules, September 28. President signed October 12, 2010.

PL 111-272 (S 1132) Amend Title 18, U.S. Code, to improve the provisions relating to the carrying of concealed weapons by law enforcement officers. Introduced by Leahy, D-Vt., on May 21, 2009. Senate Judiciary reported, amended, March 11, 2010 (S Rept 111-233). Senate passed, amended, May 13. House passed, under suspension of the rules, September 29. President signed October 12, 2010.

PL 111-273 (S 3397) Amend the Controlled Substances Act to provide for take-back disposal of controlled substances in certain instances. Introduced by Klobuchar, D-Minn., on May 24, 2010. Senate Judiciary reported, amended, July 29 (no written report). Senate passed, amended, August 3. House passed, amended, under suspension of the rules, September 29. Senate agreed to House amendment September 29. President signed October 12, 2010.

PL 111-274 (HR 946) Enhance citizen access to government information and services by establishing that government documents issued to the public must be written in language the public can understand and use. Introduced by Braley, D-Iowa, on February 10, 2009. House Oversight and Government Reform reported, amended, March 11, 2010 (H Rept 111-432). House passed, amended, under suspension of the rules, March 17. Senate passed, amended, September 27. House agreed to Senate amendment, under suspension of the rules, September 29. President signed October 13, 2010.

PL 111-275 (HR 3219) Amend Title 38, U.S. Code, to make certain improvements in the laws administered by the secretary of Veterans Affairs relating to insurance and health care. Introduced by Filner, D-Calif., on July 15, 2009. House Veterans' Affairs reported July 23 (H Rept 111-223). Passed House, amended, under suspension of the rules, July 27. Senate Veterans' Affairs discharged. Senate passed, amended, September 28, 2010. House agreed to Senate amendment, under suspension of the rules, September 29. President signed October 13, 2010.

PL 111-276 (HR 4543) Designate the facility of the U.S. Postal Service located at 4285 Payne Ave. in San Jose, Calif., as the "Anthony J. Cortese Post Office Building." Introduced by Lofgren, D-Calif., on January 27, 2010. House passed, under suspension of the rules, April 26. Senate Homeland Security and Governmental Affairs reported September 29 (no written report). Senate passed September 29. President signed October 13, 2010.

PL 111-277 (HR 5341) Designate the facility of the U.S. Postal Service located at 100 Orndorf Drive in Brighton, Mich., as the "Joyce Rogers Post Office Building." Introduced by Dingell, D-Mich., on May 19, 2010. House passed, under suspension of the rules, July 22. Senate Homeland Security and Governmental Affairs reported September 29 (no written report). Senate passed September 29. President signed October 13, 2010.

PL 111-278 (HR 5390) Designate the facility of the U.S. Postal Service located at 13301 Smith Road in Cleveland as the "David John Donafee Post Office Building." Introduced by Kucinich, D-Ohio, on May 25, 2010. House passed, under suspension of the rules, July 14. Senate Homeland Security and Governmental Affairs reported September 29 (no written report). Senate passed September 29. President signed October 13, 2010.

PL 111-279 (HR 5450) Designate the facility of the U.S. Postal Service located at 3894 Crenshaw Blvd. in Los Angeles as the "Tom Bradley Post Office Building." Introduced by Watson, D-Calif., on May 27, 2010. House passed, under suspension of the rules, July 14, 2010. Senate Homeland Security and Governmental Affairs reported September 29 (no written report). Senate passed September 29. President signed October 13, 2010.

PL 111-280 (HR 6200) Amend Part A of Title XI of the Social Security Act to provide for a one-year extension of the authorizations for the Work Incentives Planning and Assistance program and the Protection and Advocacy for Beneficiaries of Social Security program. Introduced by Pomeroy, D-N.D., on September 23, 2010. House passed, under suspension of the rules, September 28. Senate passed September 29. President signed October 13, 2010.

PL 111-281 (HR 3619) Authorize appropriations for the Coast Guard for fiscal year 2011. Introduced by Oberstar, D-Minn., on September 22, 2009. House Transportation and Infrastructure reported, amended, October 16 (H Rept 111-303, Part 1). House Homeland Security discharged. House passed, amended, October 23. Senate passed, amended, May 7, 2010. House agreed to Senate amendment, with amendment, September 28. Senate agreed to House amendment to Senate amendment, with amendment, September 29. House agreed to Senate amendment to House amendment to Senate amendment September 30. President signed October 15, 2010.

PL 111-282 (S 1510) Transfer statutory entitlements to pay and hours of work authorized by the District of Columbia Code for current members of the U.S. Secret Service Uniformed Division to the U.S. Code. Introduced by Lieberman, I-Conn., on July 23, 2009. Senate Homeland Security and Governmental Affairs reported October 5 (S Rept 111-86). Senate passed October 13. House passed, amended, under suspension of the rules, June 28, 2010. Senate agreed to House amendment, with amendment, September 27. House agreed to Senate amendment to House amendment September 30. President signed October 15, 2010.

PL 111-283 (S 3196) Amend the Presidential Transition Act of 1963 to provide that certain transition services shall be available to eligible candidates before the general election. Introduced by Kaufman, D-Del., on April 13, 2010. Senate Homeland Security and Governmental Affairs reported August 2 (S Rept 111-239). Senate passed, amended, September 24. House passed, under suspension of the rules, September 30. President signed October 15, 2010.

PL 111-284 (S 3802) Designate a mountain and icefield in the state of Alaska as "Mount Stevens" and the "Ted Stevens Icefield," respectively. Introduced by Murkowski, R-Alaska, on September 20, 2010. Senate Energy and Natural Resources discharged. Senate passed, amended, September 27. House Natural Resources discharged. House passed September 30. President signed October 18, 2010.

PL 111-285 (S 3774) Extend the deadline for Social Services Block Grant expenditure of supplemental funds appropriated following disasters occurring in 2008. Introduced by Cornyn, R-Texas, on September 14, 2010. Senate passed, amended, September 29. House passed, under suspension of the rules, November 18. President signed November 24, 2010.

PL 111-286 (HR 5712) Provide for certain clarifications and extensions under Medicare, Medicaid and the Children's Health Insurance Program. Introduced by Levin, D-Mich., on July 13, 2010. House passed, under suspension of the rules, August 14. Senate passed, amended, November 29. House agreed to Senate amendments, under suspension of the rules, November 29. President signed November 30, 2010.

PL 111-287 (S 1376) Restore immunization and sibling age exemptions for children adopted by U.S. citizens under the Hague Convention on Intercountry Adoption to allow their admission into the United States. Introduced by Klobuchar, D-Minn., on June 25, 2009. Senate Judiciary reported, amended, July 14, 2010 (S Rept 111-220). Senate passed, amended, July 21. House passed, under suspension of the rules, November 15. President signed November 30, 2010.

PL 111-288 (S 3567) Designate the facility of the U.S. Postal Service located at 100 Broadway in Lynbrook, N.Y., as the "Navy Corpsman Jeffrey L. Wiener Post Office Building." Introduced by Schumer, D-N.Y., on July 12, 2010. Senate Homeland and Governmental Affairs reported July 28 (no written report). Senate passed July 30. House passed, under suspension of the rules, November 16. President signed November 30, 2010.

PL 111-289 (S J Res 40) Appoint the day for the convening of the first session of the 112th Congress. Introduced by Reid, D-Nev., on November 15, 2010. Senate passed November 15. House passed November 17. President signed November 30, 2010.

PL 111-290 (H J Res 101) Making further continuing appropriations for fiscal year 2011. Introduced by Obey, D-Wis., on November 30, 2010. House passed December 1. Senate passed December 2. President signed December 4, 2010.

PL 111-291 (HR 4783) Provide for final settlement of claims against the government regarding the allocation of farm loans and services and by American Indians regarding government-run trust funds. Introduced by Levin, D-Mich., on March 9, 2010, to accelerate the income tax benefits for charitable cash contributions for victims of the earthquake in Chile, and to extend the period from which such contributions for victims of the earthquake in Haiti could be accelerated. House passed, under suspension of the rules, March 10. Senate passed, amended, November 19. House agreed to Senate amendments, November 30. President signed December 8, 2010.

PL 111-292 (HR 1722) Develop a program that allows employees at executive branch agencies to telework at least 20 percent of the hours worked in every two administrative workweeks. Introduced by Sarbanes, D-Md., on March 25, 2009. House Oversight and Government Reform reported, amended, May 4, 2010 (H Rept 111-474). House passed, amended, July 14. Senate passed, with an amendment, September 29. House agreed to Senate amendment November 18. President signed December 9, 2011.

PL 111-293 (HR 5283) Provide for adjustment of status for certain Haitian orphans paroled into the United States after the earthquake of January 12, 2010. Introduced by Fortenberry, R-Neb., on May 12, 2010. House passed, amended, under suspension of the rules, July 20. Senate passed, with an amendment, August 4. House agreed to Senate amendment, under suspension of the rules, December 1. President signed December 9, 2010.

PL 111-294 (HR 5566) Amend Title 18, U.S. Code, to prohibit interstate commerce in animal "crush" videos. Introduced by Gallegly, R-Calif., on June 22, 2010. House Judiciary reported July 19 (H Rept 111-549). House passed, under suspension of the rules, July 21. Senate passed, with an amendment, September 28. House agreed to the Senate amendment, with an amendment, November 15. Senate agreed to House amendment November 19. President signed December 9, 2010.

PL 111-295 (S 3689) Clarify, improve and correct the laws relating to copyrights. Introduced by Leahy, D-Vt., on August 2, 2010. Senate passed August 2. House passed, amended, November 15. Senate agreed to House amendments, under suspension of the rules, November 19. President signed December 9, 2010.

PL 111-296 (S 3307) Reauthorize child nutrition programs. Introduced by Lincoln, D-Ark., on May 5, 2010. Senate Agriculture, Nutrition and Forestry reported (S Rept 111-178). Senate passed August 5. House passed December 2. President signed December 13, 2010.

PL 111-297 (HR 4387) Designate the federal building located at 100 North Palafox St. in Pensacola, Fla., as the "Winston E. Arnow Federal Building." Introduced by Miller, R-Fla., on December 16, 2009. House Transportation reported September 20, 2010 (H Rept 111-610). House passed, under suspension of the rules, September 28. Senate Environment and Public Works reported November 30 (no written report). Senate passed December 1. President signed December 14, 2010.

PL 111-298 (HR 5651) Designate the federal building and U.S. courthouse located at 515 9th St. in Rapid City, S.D., as the "Andrew W. Bogue Federal Building and United States Courthouse." Introduced by Herseth Sandlin, D-S.D., on June 30, 2010. House Transportation and Infrastructure reported September 14 (H Rept 111-590). House passed, under suspension of the rules, September 15. Senate Environment and Public Works reported November 30 (no written report). Senate passed December 1. President signed December 14, 2010.

PL 111-299 (HR 5706) Designate the building occupied by the Government Printing Office located at 31451 East United Ave. in Pueblo, Colo., as the "Frank Evans Government Printing Office Building." Introduced by Salazar, D-Colo., on July 1, 2010. House Transportation and Infrastructure reported, amended, September 14 (H Rept 111-591). House passed, under suspension of the rules, September 15. Senate Environment and Public Works reported November 30 (no written report). Senate passed December 1. President signed December 14, 2010.

PL 111-300 (HR 5758) Designate the facility of the U.S. Postal Service located at 2 Government Center in Fall River, Mass., as the "Sgt. Robert Barrett Post Office Building." Introduced by Frank, D-Mass., on July 15, 2010. House passed, under suspension of the rules, November 17. Senate Homeland Security and Governmental Affairs reported December 1 (no written report). Senate passed December 2. President signed December 14, 2010.

PL 111-301 (HR 5773) Designate the federal building located at 6401 Security Blvd. in Baltimore as the "Robert M. Ball Federal Building." Introduced by Cummings, D-Md., on July 19, 2010. House Transportation and Infrastructure reported, amended, September 14 (H Rept 111-592). House passed, under suspension of the rules, September 15. Senate Environment and Public Works reported November 30 (no written report). Senate passed December 1. President signed December 14, 2010.

PL 111-302 (HR 6162) Provide research and development authority for alternative coinage materials to the secretary of the Treasury, increase congressional oversight over coin production, and ensure the continuity of certain numismatic items. Introduced by Watt, D-N.C., on September 22, 2010. House passed September 29. Senate passed November 30. President signed December 14, 2010.

PL 111-303 (HR 6166) Authorize the production of palladium bullion coins to provide affordable opportunities for investments in precious metals. Introduced by Rehberg, R-Mont., on September 22, 2010. House passed September 29. Senate passed November 30. President signed December 14, 2010.

PL 111-304 (HR 6237) Designate the facility of the U.S. Postal Service located at 1351 2nd St. in Napa, Calif., the "Tom Kongsgaard Post Office Building." Introduced by Thompson, D-Calif., on September 28, 2010. House passed, amended, under suspension of the rules, November 16. Senate Homeland Security and Governmental Affairs reported December 1 (no written report). Senate passed December 2. President signed December 14, 2010.

PL 111-305 (HR 6387) Designate the facility of the U.S. Postal Service located at 337 West Clark St. in Eureka, Calif., as the "Sam Sacco Post Office Building." Introduced by Thompson, D-Calif., on September 29, 2010. House passed, amended, under suspension of the rules, November 16. Senate Homeland Security and Governmental Affairs reported December 1 (no written report). Senate passed December 2. President signed December 14, 2010.

PL 111-306 (S 1338) Require English language programs for foreign students entering the United States to study English be accredited by an agency recognized by the Education secretary. Introduced by Carper, D-Del., on June 24, 2009. Senate passed September 27, 2010. House passed, under suspension of the rules, December 1. President signed December 14, 2010.

PL 111-307 (S 1421) Amend Section 42, Title 18, of the U.S. Code to prohibit the importation and shipment of certain species of carp. Introduced by Levin, D-Mich., on July 9, 2009.

Senate Environment and Public Works reported May 5, 2010 (S Rept 111-181). Senate passed November 17. House passed, under suspension of the rules, December 1. President signed December 14, 2010.

PL 111-308 (S 3250) Provide for the training of federal building personnel. Introduced by Carper, D-Del., on April 22, 2010. Senate Environment and Public Works reported June 21 (S Rept 111-212). Senate passed July 20. House passed, under suspension of the rules, December 1. President signed December 14, 2010.

PL 111-309 (HR 4994) Extend certain expiring provisions of the Medicare and Medicaid programs. Introduced by Lewis, D-Ga., on April 13, 2010, as a bill to revise certain tax provisions. House passed, amended, under suspension of the rules, April 14. Senate passed, amended, December 8. House agreed to Senate amendments, under suspension of the rules, December 9. President signed December 15, 2010.

PL 111-310 (HR 6118) Designate the facility of the U.S. Postal Service located at 2 Massachusetts Ave. NE in Washington, D.C., as the "Dorothy I. Height Post Office." Introduced by Norton, D-D.C., on September 14, 2010. House passed, amended, under suspension of the rules, September 30. Senate Homeland Security reported December 1 (no written report). Senate passed December 2. President signed December 15, 2010.

PL 111-311 (S 2847) Regulate the audio volume of commercials. Introduced by Whitehouse, D-R.I., on December 8, 2009. Senate Commerce, Science, and Transportation reported, amended, September 28, 2010 (no written report). Senate passed, with an amendment, September 29. House passed, under suspension of the rules, December 2. President signed December 15, 2010.

PL 111-312 (HR 4853) Extend tax cuts, investment incentives, and unemployment insurance, revive the estate tax, and cut the employee portion of the Social Security tax. Introduced by Oberstar, D-Minn., on March 16, 2010, as a bill to extend Federal Aviation Administration programs. House passed, under suspension of the rules, March 17. Senate passed, amended, September 23. House agreed to Senate amendments, amended, December 2. Senate agreed to House amendments, amended, December 15. House agreed to Senate amendments, December 16. President signed December 17, 2010.

PL 111-313 (HR 2480) Improve the accuracy of fur product labeling. Introduced by Moran, D-Va., on May 19, 2009. House Energy and Commerce reported, amended, July 27, 2010 (H Rept 111-571). House passed, under suspension of the rules, July 28. Senate passed December 7. President signed December 18, 2010.

PL 111-314 (HR 3237) Codify certain existing laws relating to national and commercial space programs as Title 51, U.S. Code, "National and Commercial Space Programs." Introduced by Conyers, D-Mich., on July 16, 2009. House Judiciary reported November 2 (H Rept 111-325). House passed, under suspension of the rules, January 13, 2010. Senate Judiciary reported May 10 (no written report). Senate passed December 3. President signed December 18, 2010.

PL 111-315 (HR 6184) Amend the Water Resources Development Act of 2000 to extend and modify the program allowing the secretary of the Army to accept and expend funds contributed by nonfederal public entities to expedite the evaluation of permits. Introduced by Larsen, D-Wash., on September 22, 2010. House passed, amended, under suspension of the rules, December 1. Senate passed December 7. President signed December 18, 2010.

PL 111-316 (HR 6399) Improve certain administrative operations of the Office of the Architect of the Capitol. Introduced by Brady, D-Pa., on November 15, 2010. House passed, under suspension of the rules, November 16. Senate passed December 4. President signed December 18, 2010.

PL 111-317 (H J Res 105) Make further continuing appropriations for fiscal year 2011. Introduced by Obey, D-Wis., on December 17, 2010. House passed December 17. Senate passed December 17. President signed December 18, 2010.

PL 111-318 (S 3789) Limit access to Social Security account numbers. Introduced by Feinstein, D-Calif., on September 15, 2010. Senate passed September 28. House passed, under suspension of the rules, December 8. President signed December 18, 2010.

PL 111-319 (S 3987) Amend the Fair Credit Reporting Act with respect to the applicability of identity theft guidelines to creditors. Introduced by Thune, R-S.D., on November 30, 2010. Senate passed November 30. House passed, under suspension of the rules, December 7. President signed December 18, 2010.

PL 111-320 (S 3817) Reauthorize and amend the Child Abuse Prevention and Treatment Act, the Family Violence Prevention and Services Act, the Child Abuse Prevention and Treatment and Adoption Reform Act of 1978, and the Abandoned Infants Assistance Act of 1988. Introduced by Dodd, D-Conn., on September 22, 2010. Senate Health, Education, Labor and Pensions reported December 2 (no written report). Senate passed, amended, December 3. House passed, with an amendment, under suspension of the rules, December 8. Senate agreed to House amendment December 10. President signed December 20, 2010.

PL 111-321 (HR 2965) Repeal the statutory elements of the military's "don't ask, don't tell" policy. Introduced by Altmire, D-Pa., on June 19, 2009, as a bill to enhance small-business research and innovation. House Small Business reported, amended, June 26 (H Rept 111-190, Part 1). House Science and Technology reported, amended, July 7 (H Rept 111-190, Part 2). House passed July 8. Senate passed, with an amendment, July 13. House agreed to Senate amendment, with an amendment, December 15, 2010. Senate agreed to the House amendment, December 18. President signed December 22, 2010.

PL 111-322 (HR 3082) Make further continuing appropriations for fiscal year 2011 and extend surface transportation programs. Introduced by Edwards, D-Texas, on June 26, 2009, as a bill to provide appropriations for military construction, the Department of Veterans Affairs, and related agencies for the fiscal year ending September 30, 2010. House Appropriations reported June 26 (H Rept 111-188). House passed July 10. Senate passed, with an amendment, November 17. House agreed to Senate amendment, with an amendment, December 8, 2010. Senate agreed to the House amendment, with an amendment, December 21. House agreed to Senate amendment December 21. President signed December 22, 2010.

PL 111-323 (HR 1061) Place certain land into trust for the Hoh Indian Tribe. Introduced by Dicks, D-Wash., on February 13, 2009. House Natural Resources reported, amended, October 21 (H Rept 111-306). House passed, under suspension of the rules, June 8, 2010. Senate passed, amended, September 29. House agreed to Senate amendments, under suspension of the rules, December 14. President signed December 22, 2010.

PL 111-324 (HR 2941) Reauthorize and enhance Johanna's Law to increase public awareness and knowledge with respect to gynecologic cancers. Introduced by DeLauro, D-Conn., on June 18, 2009. House Energy and Commerce reported, amended, September 28, 2010 (H Rept 111-635). House passed, under suspension of the rules, September 30. Senate Health, Education, Labor and Pensions reported, amended, December 6 (no written report). Senate passed, amended, December 10. House agreed to Senate amendment, under suspension of the rules, December 16. President signed December 22, 2010.

PL 111-325 (HR 4337) Amend the Internal Revenue Code of 1986 to modify certain rules applicable to regulated investment companies. Introduced by Rangel, D-N.Y., on December 16, 2009. House passed, amended, under suspension of the rules, September 28, 2010. Senate passed, with an amendment, December 8. House agreed to Senate amendment, under suspension of the rules, December 15. President signed December 22, 2010.

PL 111-326 (HR 5591) Designate the airport traffic control tower located at Spokane International Airport in Spokane, Wash., as the "Ray Daves Airport Traffic Control Tower." Introduced by McMorris Rodgers, R-Wash., on June 24, 2010. House Transportation and Infrastructure reported, amended, September 20 (H Rept 111-611). House passed, under suspension of the rules, September 28. Senate passed December 9. President signed December 22, 2010.

PL 111-327 (HR 6198) Amend Title 11 of the U.S. Code to make technical corrections to bankruptcy law. Introduced by Conyers, D-Mich., on September 23, 2010. House passed, amended, under suspension of the rules, September 28. Senate passed, with an amendment, November 19. House agreed to the Senate amendment, under suspension of the rules, December 16. President signed December 22, 2010.

PL 111-328 (HR 6278) Amend the National Children's Island Act of 1995 to expand allowable uses for Kingman and Heritage islands by the District of Columbia. Introduced by Norton, D-D.C., on September 29, 2010. House passed, under suspension of the rules, November 16. Senate passed December 13. President signed December 22.

PL 111-329 (HR 6473) Amend the Internal Revenue Code of 1986 to extend the funding and expenditure authority of the Airport and Airway Trust Fund and to amend Title 49, U.S. Code, to extend the airport improvement program. Introduced by Oberstar, D-Minn., on December 2, 2010. House passed, under suspension of the rules, December 2. Senate passed December 18. President signed December 22, 2010.

PL 111-330 (HR 6516) Make technical corrections to provisions of law enacted by the Coast Guard Authorization Act of 2010. Introduced by Oberstar, D-Minn., on December 13, 2010. House passed, under suspension of the rules, December 14. Senate passed December 15. President signed December 22, 2010.

PL 111-331 (S 30) Amend the Communications Act of 1934 to prohibit manipulation of caller identification information. Introduced by Nelson, D-Fla., on January 7, 2009. Senate Commerce, Science and Transportation reported November 2 (S Rept 111-96). Senate passed, amended, February 23, 2010. House passed, under suspension of the rules, December 15. President signed December 22, 2010.

PL 111-332 (S 1275) Establish a National Foundation on Physical Fitness and Sports to carry out activities to support and supplement the mission of the President's Council on Physical Fitness and Sports. Introduced by Warner, D-Va., on June 16, 2009. Senate Health, Education, Labor and Pensions reported, amended, December 7, 2010 (no written report). Senate passed December 9. House passed, under suspension of the rules, December 14. President signed December 22, 2010.

PL 111-333 (S 1405) Redesignate the Longfellow National Historic Site in Cambridge, Mass., as the "Longfellow House-Washington's Headquarters National Historic Site." Introduced by Kennedy, D-Mass., on July 7, 2009. Senate Energy and Natural Resources reported March 2, 2010 (S Rept 111-141). Senate passed May 7. House passed, under suspension of the rules, December 14. President signed December 22, 2010.

PL 111-334 (S 1448) Amend the Act of August 9, 1955, to authorize the Coquille Indian Tribe; the Confederated Tribes of Siletz Indians; the Confederated Tribes of the Coos, Lower Umpqua and Siuslaw; the Klamath Tribes; and the Burns Paiute Tribe to obtain 99-year lease authority for trust land. Introduced by Merkley, D-Ore., on July 14, 2009. Senate Indian Affairs reported August 3, 2010 (S Rept 111-245). Senate passed September 22. House passed, under suspension of the rules, December 14. President signed December 22, 2010.

PL 111-335 (S 1609) Authorize a single fisheries cooperative for the Bering Sea Aleutian Islands longline catcher processor subsector. Introduced by Cantwell, D-Wash., on August 6, 2009. Senate Commerce, Science and Transportation reported August 5, 2010 (S Rept 111-250). Senate passed November 18. House passed, under suspension of the rules, December 14. President signed December 22, 2010.

PL 111-336 (S 2906) Amend the Act of August 9, 1955, to modify a provision relating to leases involving certain American Indian tribes. Introduced by Cantwell, D-Wash., on December 18, 2009. Senate Indian Affairs reported, amended, August 3, 2010 (S Rept 111-246). Senate passed September 22. House passed, under suspension of the rules, December 14. President signed December 22, 2010.

PL 111-337 (S 3199) Amend the Public Health Service Act regarding early detection, diagnosis, and treatment of hearing loss. Introduced by Snowe, R-Maine, on April 14, 2010. Senate Health, Education, Labor and Pensions reported, amended, December 6 (no written report). Senate passed December 7. House passed, under suspension of the rules, December 15. President signed December 22, 2010.

PL 111-338 (S 3794) Amend Chapter 5, Title 40, of the U.S. Code to include organizations whose memberships comprise "substantially veterans" as recipient organizations for the donation of federal surplus personal property through state agencies. Introduced by Leahy, D-Vt., on September 16, 2010. Senate Homeland Security and Governmental Affairs reported, amended, September 29 (no written report). Senate passed September 29. House passed, under suspension of the rules, December 14. President signed December 22, 2010.

PL 111-339 (S 3860) Require reports on the management of Arlington National Cemetery. Introduced by McCaskill, D-Mo., on September 28, 2010. Senate passed December 4. House passed, under suspension of the rules, December 16. President signed December 22, 2010.

PL 111-340 (S 3984) Amend and extend the Museum and Library Services Act. Introduced by Reed, D-R.I., on November 29, 2010. Senate Health, Education, Labor and Pensions reported December 3 (no written report). Senate passed December 7. House passed, under suspension of the rules, December 14. President signed December 22, 2010.

PL 111-341 (S 3998) Extend the Child Safety Pilot Program. Introduced by Schumer, D-N.Y., on December 1, 2010. Senate passed December 1. House passed, under suspension of the rules, December 8. President signed December 22, 2010.

PL 111-342 (S 4005) Amend Title 28 of the U.S. Code to prevent the proceeds or instrumentalities of foreign crime located in the United States from being shielded from foreign forfeiture proceedings. Introduced by Whitehouse, D-R.I., on December 2, 2010. Senate passed December 15. House passed, under suspension of the rules, December 16. President signed December 22, 2010.

PL 111-343 (HR 6398) Require the Federal Deposit Insurance Corporation to fully insure interest on Lawyers Trust Accounts. Introduced by Doggett, D-Texas, on November 15, 2010. House passed, amended, under suspension of the rules, November 30. Senate passed December 22. President signed December 29, 2010.

PL 111-344 (HR 6517) Extend Trade Adjustment Assistance and certain trade preference programs and amend the Harmonized Tariff Schedule of the United States to modify temporarily certain rates of duty. Introduced by Levin, D-Mich., on December 13, 2010. House passed, amended, under suspension of the rules, December 15. Senate passed, with an amendment, December 22. House agreed to the Senate amendment December 22. President signed December 29, 2010.

PL 111-345 (S 3386) Protect consumers from certain aggressive sales tactics on the Internet. Introduced by Rockefeller, D-W.Va., on May 19, 2010. Senate Commerce, Science and Transportation reported, amended, August 2 (S Rept 111-240). Senate passed, amended, November 30. House passed, under suspension of the rules, December 15. President signed December 29, 2010.

PL 111-346 (S 4058) Extend certain expiring provisions that provide enhanced protections for servicemembers relating to mortgages and mortgage foreclosure. Introduced by Kerry, D-Mass., on December 22, 2010. Senate passed December 22. House passed December 22. President signed December 29, 2010.

PL 111-347 (HR 847) Amend the Public Health Service Act to extend and improve protections and services to individuals directly affected by the September 11, 2001, terrorist attack in New York City. Introduced by Maloney, D-N.Y., on February 4, 2009. House Energy and Commerce reported, amended, July 22, 2010 (H Rept 111-560, Part 1). House Judiciary reported, amended, July 22 (H Rept 111-560, Part 2). House passed September 29. Senate passed, amended, December 22. House agreed to Senate amendment December 22. President signed January 2, 2011.

PL 111-348 (HR 81) Amend the High Seas Driftnet Fishing Moratorium Protection Act and the Magnuson-Stevens Fishery Conservation and Management Act to improve the conservation of sharks. Introduced by Bordallo, D-Guam, on January 6, 2009. House passed, under suspension of the rules, March 2. Senate passed, amended, December 20, 2010. House agreed to Senate amendment, under suspension of the rules, December 21. President signed January 4, 2011.

PL 111-349 (HR 628) Establish a pilot program in certain U.S. district courts to encourage enhancement of expertise in patent cases among district judges. Introduced by Issa, R-Calif., on January 22, 2009. House passed, under suspension of the rules, March 17. Senate passed, amended, December 13, 2010. House agreed to Senate amendment, under suspension of the rules, December 17. President signed January 4, 2011.

PL 111-350 (HR 1107) Enact certain laws relating to public contracts as Title 41, U.S. Code, "Public Contracts." Introduced by Conyers, D-Mich., on February 23, 2009. House Judiciary reported March 23 (H Rept 111-42). House passed, under suspension of the rules, May 6. Senate passed, amended, December 2, 2010. House agreed to Senate amendments, under suspension of the rules, December 17. President signed January 4, 2011.

PL 111-351 (HR 1746) Amend the Robert T. Stafford Disaster Relief and Emergency Assistance Act to reauthorize the predisaster mitigation program of the Federal Emergency Management Agency. Introduced by Oberstar, D-Minn., on March 26, 2009. House Transportation and Infrastructure reported April 23 (H Rept 111-83). House passed, under suspension of the rules, April 27. Senate passed, amended, December 20, 2010. House agreed to Senate amendment, under suspension of the rules, December 21. President signed January 4, 2011.

PL 111-352 (HR 2142) Require quarterly performance assessments of government programs for the purpose of assessing agency performance and improvement, and establish agency performance improvement officers and the Performance Improvement Council. Introduced by Cuellar, D-Texas, on April 28, 2009. House Oversight and Government Reform reported June 14, 2010 (H Rept 111-504). House passed, under suspension of the rules, June 16. Senate Homeland Security and Governmental Affairs reported, amended, December 16 (S Rept 111-372). Senate passed, amended, December 16. House agreed to Senate amendment December 21. President signed January 4, 2011.

PL 111-353 (HR 2751) Amend the Federal Food, Drug, and Cosmetic Act with respect to the safety of the food supply. Introduced by Sutton, D-Ohio, on June 8, 2009, as a bill to accelerate motor fuel savings nationwide and provide incentives to registered owners of high-polluting automobiles to replace them with new fuel efficient and less-polluting cars. House passed, under suspension of the rules, June 9. Senate passed, amended, December 19, 2010. House agreed to Senate amendments December 21. President signed January 4, 2011.

PL 111-354 (HR 4445) Amend Public Law 95-232 to repeal a restriction on treating certain lands held in trust for American Indian pueblos in New Mexico as Indian country. Introduced by Heinrich, D-N.M., on January 13, 2010. House Natural Resources reported, amended, June 28 (H Rept 111-515). House passed, under suspension of the rules, June 30. Senate Indian Affairs reported December 20 (S Rept 111-379). Senate passed December 21. President signed January 4, 2011.

PL 111-355 (HR 4602) Designate the facility of the U.S. Postal Service located at 1332 Sharon Copley Road in Sharon Center, Ohio, as the "Emil Bolas Post Office." Introduced by Boccieri, D-Ohio, on February 4, 2010. House passed, under suspension of the rules, September 30. Senate passed December 16. President signed January 4, 2011.

PL 111-356 (HR 4748) Amend the Office of National Drug Control Policy Reauthorization Act of 2006 to require a northern-border counternarcotics strategy. Introduced by Owens, D-N.Y., on March 3, 2010. House passed, under suspension of the rules, July 27. Senate passed, amended, December 20. House agreed to Senate amendment, under suspension of the rules, December 21. President signed January 4, 2011.

PL 111-357 (HR 4973) Amend the Fish and Wildlife Act of 1956 to reauthorize volunteer programs and community partnerships for national wildlife refuges. Introduced by Kratovil, D-Md., on March 25, 2010. House Natural Resources reported, amended, July 13 (H Rept 111-531). House passed, under suspension of the rules, July 13. Senate Environment and Public Works reported December 14 (S Rept 111-366). Senate passed December 17. President signed January 4, 2011.

PL 111-358 (HR 5116) Invest in innovation through research and development to improve U.S. competitiveness. Introduced by Gordon, D-Tenn., on April 22, 2010. House Science and Technology reported, amended, May 7 (H Rept 111-478). House passed May 28. Senate passed, amended, December 17. House agreed to Senate amendment December 21. President signed January 4, 2011.

PL 111-359 (HR 5133) Designate the facility of the U.S. Postal Service located at 331 First St. in Carlstadt, N.J., as the "Staff Sgt. Frank T. Carvill and Lance Cpl. Michael A. Schwarz Post Office Building." Introduced by Rothman, D-N.J., on April 22, 2010. House passed, under suspension of the rules, June 9. Senate passed December 16. President signed January 4, 2011.

PL 111-360 (HR 5470) Exempt from certain energy efficiency standards under the Energy Policy and Conservation Act external power supplies for certain security or life-safety alarms and surveillance system components. Introduced by Pallone, D-N.J., on May 28, 2010. House passed, under suspension of the rules, December 8. Senate passed December 21. President signed January 4, 2011.

PL 111-361 (HR 5605) Designate the facility of the U.S. Postal Service located at 47 East Fayette St. in Uniontown, Pa., as the "George C. Marshall Post Office." Introduced by Critz, D-Pa., on June 25, 2010. House passed, under suspension of the rules, September 30. Senate passed December 16. President signed January 4, 2011.

PL 111-362 (HR 5606) Designate the facility of the U.S. Postal Service located at 47 South Seventh St. in Indiana, Pa., as the "James M. 'Jimmy' Stewart Post Office Building." Introduced by Critz, D-Pa., on June 25, 2010. House passed, under suspension of the rules, September 30. Senate passed December 16. President signed January 4, 2011.

PL 111-363 (HR 5655) Designate the Little River Branch facility of the U.S. Postal Service located at 140 Northeast 84th St. in Miami as the "Jesse J. McCrary Jr. Post Office." Introduced by Meek, D-Fla., on June 30, 2010. House passed, under suspension of the rules, November 16. Senate passed December 16. President signed January 4, 2011.

PL 111-364 (HR 5809) Amend the Energy Policy Act of 2005 to reauthorize and modify provisions relating to the diesel emissions reduction program. Introduced by Inslee, D-Wash., on July 21, 2010. House Energy and Commerce reported, amended, September 22 (H Rept 111-618). House passed, under suspension of the rules, September 22. Senate passed, amended, December 16. House agreed to Senate amendments, under suspension of the rules, December 21. President signed January 4, 2011.

PL 111-365 (HR 5877) Designate the facility of the U.S. Postal Service located at 655 Centre St. in Jamaica Plain, Mass., as the "Lance Cpl. Alexander Scott Arredondo, U.S. Marine Corps Post Office Building." Introduced by Capuano, D-Mass., on July 27, 2010. House passed, under suspension of the rules, November 29. Senate passed December 16. President signed January 4, 2011.

PL 111-366 (HR 5901) Amend the Internal Revenue Code of 1986 to authorize the tax court to appoint employees. Introduced by Crowley, D-N.Y., on July 28, 2010. House passed, under suspension of the rules, July 30. Senate passed, amended, December 17. House agreed to Senate amendments December 22. President signed January 4, 2011.

PL 111-367 (HR 6392) Designate the facility of the U.S. Postal Service located at 5003 Westfields Blvd. in Centreville, Va., as the "Col. George Juskalian Post Office Building." Introduced by Wolf, R-Va., on September 29, 2010. House passed, under suspension of the rules, November 29. Senate passed December 16. President signed January 4, 2011.

PL 111-368 (HR 6400) Designate the facility of the U.S. Postal Service located at 111 North Sixth St. in St. Louis as the "Earl Wilson Jr. Post Office." Introduced by Clay, D-Mo., on November 15, 2010. House passed, under suspension of the rules, December 7. Senate passed December 16. President signed January 4, 2011.

PL 111-369 (HR 6412) Amend Title 28, U.S. Code, to require the attorney general to share criminal records with state sentencing commissions. Introduced by Scott, D-Va., on November 16, 2010. House passed, under suspension of the rules, December 9. Senate passed December 20. President signed January 4, 2011.

PL 111-370 (HR 6510) Direct the administrator of general services to convey a parcel of real property in Houston to the Military Museum of Texas. Introduced by Jackson Lee, D-Texas, on December 9, 2010. House passed, under suspension of the rules, December 14. Senate passed December 18. President signed January 4, 2011.

PL 111-371 (HR 6533) Implement the recommendations of the Federal Communications Commission report to Congress regarding low-power FM service. Introduced by Doyle, D-Pa., on December 16, 2010. House passed, under suspension of the rules, December 17. Senate passed December 18. President signed January 4, 2011.

PL 111-372 (S 118) Amend Section 202 of the Housing Act of 1959 to improve the program for supportive housing for the elderly. Introduced by Kohl, D-Wis., on January 6, 2009. Senate Banking, Housing and Urban Affairs reported, amended, November 30, 2010 (no written report). Senate passed December 18. House passed, under suspension of the rules, December 21. President signed January 4, 2011.

PL 111-373 (S 841) Direct the secretary of Transportation to study and establish a motor vehicle safety standard that provides for a means of alerting blind and other pedestrians of motor vehicle operation. Introduced by Kerry, D-Mass., on April 21, 2009. Senate passed, amended, December 9, 2010. House passed, under suspension of the rules, December 16. President signed January 4, 2011.

PL 111-374 (S 1481) Amend Section 811 of the Cranston-Gonzalez National Affordable Housing Act to improve the program for supportive housing for persons with disabilities. Introduced by Menendez, D-N.J., on July 21, 2009. Senate Banking, Housing and Urban Affairs reported, amended, December 14, 2010 (no written report). Senate passed December 17. House passed, under suspension of the rules, December 21. President signed January 4, 2011.

PL 111-375 (S 3036) Establish the National Alzheimer's Project. Introduced by Bayh, D-Ind., on February 24, 2010. Senate Health, Education, Labor and Pensions reported, amended, December 6 (no written report). Senate passed, amended, December 8. House passed, under suspension of the rules, December 15. President signed January 4, 2011.

PL 111-376 (S 3243) Require U.S. Customs and Border Protection to administer polygraph examinations to all applicants for law enforcement positions with the agency and to require it to initiate all periodic background reinvestigations of certain law enforcement personnel. Introduced by Pryor, D-Ark., on April 21, 2010. Senate Homeland Security and Governmental Affairs reported, amended, September 27 (S Rept 111-338). Senate passed, amended, September 28. House passed, under suspension of the rules, December 21. President signed January 4, 2011.

PL 111-377 (S 3447) Amend Title 38, U.S. Code, to improve educational assistance for veterans who served in the Armed Forces after September 11, 2001. Introduced by Akaka, D-Hawaii, on May 27, 2010. Senate Veterans' Affairs reported, amended, October 26 (S Rept 111-346). Senate passed December 13. House passed, under suspension of the rules, December 16. President signed January 4, 2011.

PL 111-378 (S 3481) Amend the Federal Water Pollution Control Act to clarify federal responsibility for stormwater pollution. Introduced by Cardin, D-Md., on June 10, 2010. Senate Environment and Public Works reported December 17 (no written report). Senate passed, amended, December 21. House passed, under suspension of the rules, December 22. President signed January 4, 2011.

PL 111-379 (S 3592) Designate the facility of the U.S. Postal Service located at 100 Commerce Drive in Tyrone, Ga., as the "1st Lt. Robert Wilson Collins Post Office Building." Introduced by Chambliss, R-Ga., on July 15, 2010. Senate passed December 16. House passed, under suspension of the rules, December 21. President signed January 4, 2011.

PL 111-380 (S 3874) Amend the Safe Drinking Water Act to reduce lead in drinking water. Introduced by Boxer, D-Calif., on September 29, 2010. Senate Environment and Public Works reported December 16 (no written report). Senate passed December 16. House passed, under suspension of the rules, December 17. President signed January 4, 2011.

PL 111-381 (S 3903) Authorize leases of up to 99 years for lands held in trust for Ohkay Owingeh Pueblo. Introduced by Udall, D-N.M., on September 29, 2010. Senate Indian Affairs reported, amended, December 16 (S Rept 111-371). Senate passed December 21. House passed December 22. President signed January 4, 2011.

PL 111-382 (S 4036) Clarify the National Credit Union Administration authority to make stabilization fund expenditures without borrowing from the Treasury. Introduced by Dodd, D-Conn., on December 16, 2010. Senate passed December 16. House passed December 22. President signed January 4, 2011.

PL 111-383 (HR 6523) Authorize appropriations for fiscal year 2011 for military activities of the Department of Defense, for military construction, and for defense activities of the Energy Department. Introduced by Skelton, D-Mo., on December 15, 2010. House passed, under suspension of the rules, December 17. Senate passed, amended, December 22. House agreed to Senate amendment December 22. President signed January 7, 2011.

112th Congress 2011–2012

PL 112-1 (HR 366) Provide for an additional temporary extension of programs under the Small Business Act and the Small Business Investment Act of 1958. Introduced by Graves, R-Mo., on January 20, 2011. House passed, under suspension of the rules, January 25. Senate passed January 26. President signed January 31, 2011.

PL 112-2 (S 188) Designate the U.S. courthouse under construction at 98 West First St. in Yuma, Ariz., as the "John M. Roll United States Courthouse." Introduced by McCain, R-Ariz., on January 26, 2011. Senate passed February 1. House passed, under suspension of the rules, February 9. President signed February 17, 2011.

PL 112-3 (HR 514) Extend expiring provisions of the USA PATRIOT Improvement and Reauthorization Act of 2005 and

Intelligence Reform and Terrorism Prevention Act of 2004 relating to access to business records, individual terrorists as agents of foreign powers, and roving wiretaps until December 8, 2011. Introduced by Sensenbrenner, R-Wis., on January 26, 2011. House passed February 14. Senate passed, amended, February 15. House agreed to the Senate amendment February 17. President signed February 25, 2011.

PL 112-4 (H J Res 44) Make further continuing appropriations for fiscal 2011. Introduced by Rogers, R-Ky., on February 28, 2011. House passed March 1. Senate passed March 2. President signed March 2, 2011.

PL 112-5 (HR 662) Provide an extension of federal aid programs for highways, highway safety, motor carrier safety, transit, and others funded out of the Highway Trust Fund pending enactment of a multiyear reauthorization. Introduced by Mica, R-Fla., on February 11, 2011. House Transportation and Infrastructure reported February 28 (H Rept 112-18). House passed March 2. Senate passed March 3. President signed March 4, 2011.

PL 112-6 (H J Res 48) Make further continuing appropriations for fiscal year 2011. Introduced by Rogers, R-Ky., on March 11, 2011. House passed March 15. Senate passed March 17. President signed March 18, 2011.

PL 112-7 (HR 1079) Amend the Internal Revenue Code of 1986 to extend the funding and expenditure authority of the Airport and Airway Trust Fund and amend Title 49 of the U.S. Code to extend the airport improvement program. Introduced by Mica, R-Fla., on March 15, 2011. House Transportation and Infrastructure reported March 29 (H Rept 112-41). House passed, under suspension of the rules, March 29. Senate passed March 29. President signed March 31, 2011.

PL 112-8 (HR 1363) Make appropriations for the Defense Department for the fiscal year ending September 30, 2011. Introduced by Rogers, R-Ky., on April 4, 2011. House passed April 7. Senate passed, amended, April 8. House agreed to the Senate amendment April 9. President signed April 9, 2011.

PL 112-9 (HR 4) Repeal the requirement for reporting information to the IRS for vendors to whom businesses pay more than $600 in a year. Introduced by Lungren, R-Calif., on January 12, 2011. House Ways and Means reported February 22 (H Rept 112-15). House passed March 3. Senate passed April 5. President signed April 14, 2011.

PL 112-10 (HR 1473) Make appropriations for the Defense Department and the other departments and agencies of the government for the fiscal year ending September 30, 2011. Introduced by Rogers, R-Ky., on April 11, 2011. House passed April 14. Senate passed April 14. President signed April 15, 2011.

PL 112-11 (S 307) Designate the federal building and U.S. courthouse located at 217 West King St. in Martinsburg, W.Va., as the "W. Craig Broadwater Federal Building and United States Courthouse." Introduced by Rockefeller, D-W.Va., on February 8, 2011. Senate passed February 17. House Transportation and Infrastructure reported April 12 (H Rept 112-59). House passed, under suspension of the rules, April 12. President signed April 25, 2011.

PL 112-12 (S J Res 8) Provide for the appointment of Stephen M. Case as a citizen regent of the Board of Regents of the Smithsonian Institution. Introduced by Leahy, D-Vt., on February 28, 2011. Senate passed March 15. House passed April 12. President signed April 25, 2011.

PL 112-13 (HR 1308) Amend the Ronald Reagan Centennial Commission Act to extend the termination date for the commission. Introduced by Gallegly, R-Calif., on April 1, 2011. House passed, under suspension of the rules, April 12. Senate passed April 14. President signed May 12, 2011.

PL 112-14 (S 990) Provide for an additional temporary extension of programs under the Small Business Act and the Small Business Investment Act of 1958. Introduced by Landrieu, D-La., on May 12, 2011. Senate passed, amended, May 19. House passed, amended, May 24. Senate agreed to House amendment, with an amendment, May 26. House agreed to Senate amendment to the House amendment, May 26. President signed May 26, 2011.

PL 112-15 (HR 793) Designate the facility of the U.S. Postal Service located at 12781 Sir Francis Drake Blvd. in Inverness, Calif., as the "Spc. Jake Robert Velloza Post Office." Introduced by Woolsey, D-Calif., on February 17, 2011. House passed, under suspension of the rules, March 14. Senate Homeland Security and Governmental Affairs reported May 12 (no written report). Senate passed May 16. President signed May 31, 2011.

PL 112-16 (HR 1893) Amend the Internal Revenue Code of 1986 to extend the funding and expenditure authority of the Airport and Airway Trust Fund and amend Title 49 of the U.S. Code to extend the airport improvement program. Introduced by Mica, R-Fla., on May 13, 2011. House passed, under suspension of the rules, May 23. Senate passed May 24. President signed May 31, 2011.

PL 112-17 (S 1082) Provide for an additional temporary extension of programs under the Small Business Act and the Small Business Investment Act of 1958. Introduced by Landrieu, D-La., on May 26, 2011. Senate passed May 26. House passed, under suspension of the rules, May 31. President signed June 1, 2011.

PL 112-18 (HR 754) Authorize appropriations for fiscal 2011 for intelligence and intelligence-related activities of the U.S. government, the Community Management Account, and the Central Intelligence Agency Retirement and Disability System. Introduced by Rogers, R-Mich., on February 17, 2011. House Select Intelligence reported, amended, May 3 (H Rept 112-72). House passed May 13. Senate passed May 26. President signed June 1, 2011.

PL 112-19 (S J Res 7) Provide for the reappointment of Shirley Ann Jackson as a citizen regent of the Board of Regents of the Smithsonian Institution. Introduced by Leahy, D-Vt., on February 28, 2011. Senate passed March 15. House passed June 16. President signed June 24, 2011.

PL 112-20 (S J Res 9) Provide for the reappointment of Robert P. Kogod as a citizen regent of the Board of Regents of the Smithsonian Institution. Introduced by Leahy, D-Vt., on February 28, 2011. Senate passed March 15. House passed March 16. President signed June 24, 2011.

PL 112-21 (HR 2279) Amend the Internal Revenue Code of 1986 to extend the funding and expenditure authority of the Airport and Airway Trust Fund, and amend Title 49 of the U.S. Code to extend the airport improvement program. Introduced by Mica, R-Fla., on June 22, 2011. House passed June 24. Senate passed June 27. President signed June 29, 2011.

PL 112-22 (S 349) Designate the facility of the U.S. Postal Service located at 4865 Tallmadge Road in Rootstown, Ohio, as the "Marine Sgt. Jeremy E. Murray Post Office." Introduced by Brown, D-Ohio, on February 15, 2011. Senate Homeland Security and Governmental Affairs reported May 12 (no written report). Senate passed May 16. House passed June 21. President signed June 29, 2011.

PL 112-23 (S 655) Designate the facility of the U.S. Postal Service located at 95 Dogwood St. in Cary, Miss., as the "Spencer Byrd Powers Jr. Post Office." Introduced by Cochran, R-Miss., on March 28, 2011. Senate Homeland Security and Governmental Affairs reported May 12 (no written report). Senate passed May 16. House passed June 21. President signed June 29, 2011.

PL 112-24 (S 1103) Extend the term of the incumbent director of the FBI. Introduced by Leahy, D-Vt., on May 26, 2011. Senate Judiciary reported June 16 (S Rept 112-23). Senate passed, amended, July 21. House passed, under suspension of the rules, July 25. President signed July 26, 2011.

PL 112-25 (S 365) Provide for a mechanism to raise the federal debt ceiling and take deficit reduction measures. Introduced by Harkin, D-Iowa, on February 16, 2011, as a bill to make a technical amendment to the Education Science Reform Act of 2002. Senate Health, Education, Labor and Pensions reported February 16 (no written report). Senate passed February 17. House passed, amended with debt and deficit provisions, August 1. Senate agreed to the House amendments August 2. President signed August 2, 2011.

PL 112-26 (HR 1383) Temporarily preserve higher rates for tuition and fees for programs of education at nonpublic institutions of higher learning pursued by individuals enrolled in the Post-9/11 Educational Assistance Program of the Department of Veterans Affairs before the enactment of the Post-9/11 Veterans Educational Assistance Improvements Act of 2010. Introduced by Miller, R-Fla., on April 6, 2011. House Veterans' Affairs reported, amended, May 20 (H Rept 112-81). House passed, under suspension of the rules, May 23. Senate passed, amended, July 21. House agreed to Senate amendments, under suspension of the rules, July 26. President signed August 3, 2011.

PL 112-27 (HR 2553) Amend the Internal Revenue Code of 1986 to extend the funding and expenditure authority of the Airport and Airway Trust Fund, and amend Title 49 of the U.S. Code, to extend the airport improvement program. Introduced by Mica, R-Fla., on July 15, 2011. House passed July 20. Senate passed August 5. President signed August 5, 2011.

PL 112-28 (HR 2715) Provide the Consumer Product Safety Commission with greater authority and discretion in enforcing consumer product safety laws. Introduced by Bono Mack, R-Calif., on August 1, 2011. House passed, under suspension of the rules, August 1. Senate passed August 1. President signed August 12, 2011.

PL 112-29 (HR 1249) Provide for patent overhaul. Introduced by Smith, R-Texas, on March 30, 2011. House Judiciary reported June 1 (H Rept 112-98, Part 1). House passed June 23. Senate passed September 8. President signed September 16, 2011.

PL 112-30 (HR 2887) Provide a temporary extension of surface and air transportation programs. Introduced by Mica, R-Fla., on September 12, 2011. House passed, under suspension of the rules, September 13. Senate passed September 15. President signed September 16, 2011.

PL 112-31 (S 846) Designate the U.S. courthouse located at 80 Lafayette St. in Jefferson City, Mo., as the "Christopher S. Bond U.S. Courthouse." Introduced by Blunt, R-Mo., on April 14, 2011. Senate Environment and Public Works reported July 22 (no written report). Senate passed July 26. House passed, under suspension of the rules, September 21. President signed September 23, 2011.

PL 112-32 (HR 2005) Reauthorize the Combating Autism Act of 2006. Introduced by Smith, R-N.J., on May 26, 2011. House passed, under suspension of the rules, September 20. Senate passed September 26. President signed September 30, 2011.

PL 112-33 (HR 2017) Make continuing appropriations for fiscal 2012. Introduced by Aderholt, R-Ala., on May 26, 2011. House Appropriations reported May 26 (H Rept 112-91). House passed June 2. Senate Appropriations reported September 7 (S Rept 112-74). Senate passed, amended, September 26. House agreed to Senate amendments September 29. President signed September 30, 2011.

PL 112-34 (HR 2883) Amend part B of Title IV of the Social Security Act to extend the child and family services program through fiscal 2016. Introduced by Davis, R-Ky., on September 12, 2011. House Ways and Means reported September 19 (H Rept 112-210). House Budget discharged. House passed, under suspension of the rules, September 21. Senate passed September 22. President signed September 30, 2011.

PL 112-35 (HR 2943) Extend the program of block grants to states for Temporary Assistance to Needy Families and related programs through December 31, 2011. Introduced by Davis, R-Ky., on September 15, 2011. House passed, under suspension of the rules, September 21. Senate passed September 23. President signed September 30, 2011.

PL 112-36 (HR 2608) Make continuing appropriations for fiscal 2012. Introduced by Graves, R-Mo., on July 21, 2011. House passed, under suspension of the rules, July 26. Senate passed, amended, July 28. House agreed to Senate amendment, with an amendment, September 23. Senate agreed to House amendment to Senate amendment, with an amendment, September 26. House agreed to Senate amendment to House amendment to Senate amendment, October 4. President signed October 5, 2011.

PL 112-37 (HR 2646) Authorize certain major Department of Veterans Affairs (VA) medical facility projects and leases, extend certain expiring provisions of law, and modify certain authorities of the VA secretary. Introduced by Johnson, R-Ohio, on July 26, 2011. House Veterans' Affairs reported September 15 (H Rept 112-209). House passed, under suspension of the rules, September 20. Senate passed September 23. President signed October 5, 2011.

PL 112-38 (HR 771) Designate the facility of the U.S. Postal Service located at 1081 Elbel Road in Schertz, Texas, as the "Schertz Veterans Post Office." Introduced by Cuellar, D-Texas, on February 17, 2011. House passed, under suspension of the rules, June 21. Senate Homeland Security and Governmental Affairs discharged. Senate passed October 4. President signed October 12, 2011.

PL 112-39 (HR 1632) Designate the facility of the U.S. Postal Service located at 5014 Gary Ave. in Lubbock, Texas, as the "Sgt. Chris Davis Post Office." Introduced by Neugebauer, R-Texas, on April 15, 2011. House passed, under suspension of the rules, June 21. Senate Homeland Security and Governmental Affairs discharged. Senate passed October 4. President signed October 12, 2011.

PL 112-40 (HR 2832) Extend the Generalized System of Preferences. Introduced by Camp, R-Mich., on September 2, 2011. House passed, under suspension of the rules, September 7. Senate passed, amended to include an extension of Trade Adjustment Assistance, September 22. House agreed to Senate amendment October 12. President signed October 21, 2011.

PL 112-41 (HR 3080) Implement the U.S.-Korea Free Trade Agreement. Introduced by Cantor, R-Va., on October 3, 2011. House Ways and Means reported October 6 (H Rept 112-239). House passed October 12. Senate passed October 12. President signed October 21, 2011.

PL 112-42 (HR 3078) Implement the U.S.-Colombia Free Trade Agreement. Introduced by Cantor, R-Va., on October 3, 2011. House Ways and Means reported October 6 (H Rept 112-237). House passed October 12. Senate passed October 12. President signed October 21, 2011.

PL 112-43 (HR 3079) Implement the U.S.-Panama Free Trade Agreement. Introduced by Cantor, R-Va., on October 3, 2011. House Ways and Means reported October 6 (H Rept 112-238). House passed October 12. Senate passed October 12. President signed October 21, 2011.

PL 112-44 (HR 2944) Provide for the continued performance of the functions of the U.S. Parole Commission. Introduced by Smith, R-Texas, on September 15, 2011. House passed, under suspension of the rules, September 20. Senate passed, amended, October 6. House agreed to Senate amendment October 12. President signed October 21, 2011.

PL 112-45 (HR 489) Clarify the jurisdiction of the secretary of the Interior with respect to the C. C. Cragin Dam and Reservoir. Introduced by Gosar, R-Ariz., on January 26, 2011. House Natural Resources reported July 20 (H Rept 112-160). House passed, under suspension of the rules, October 3. Senate passed October 18. President signed November 7, 2011.

PL 112-46 (HR 765) Amend the National Forest Ski Area Permit Act of 1986 to clarify the authority of the secretary of Agriculture regarding additional recreational uses of National Forest System land that is subject to ski area permits. Introduced by Bishop, R-Utah, February 17, 2011. House Natural Resources reported July 20 (H Rept 112-164). House passed, under suspension of the rules, October 3. Senate passed October 18. President signed November 7, 2011.

PL 112-47 (HR 1843) Designate the facility of the U.S. Postal Service located at 489 Army Drive in Barrigada, Guam, as the "John Pangelinan Gerber Post Office Building." Introduced by Bordallo, D-Guam, on May 11, 2011. House passed, under suspension of the rules, July 30. Senate Homeland Security and Governmental Affairs reported October 19 (no written report). Senate passed October 20. President signed November 7, 2011.

PL 112-48 (HR 1975) Designate the facility of the U.S. Postal Service located at 281 East Colorado Blvd. in Pasadena, Calif., as the "1st Lt. Oliver Goodall Post Office Building." Introduced by Schiff, D-Calif., on May 24, 2011. House passed, under suspension of the rules, July 30. Senate Homeland Security and Governmental Affairs reported October 19 (no written report). Senate passed October 20. President signed November 7, 2011.

PL 112-49 (HR 2062) Designate the facility of the U.S. Postal Service located at 45 Meetinghouse Lane in Sagamore Beach, Mass., as the "Matthew A. Pucino Post Office." Introduced by Keating, D-Mass., on May 31, 2011. House passed, under suspension of the rules, July 30. Senate Homeland Security and Governmental Affairs reported October 19 (no written report). Senate passed October 20. President signed November 7, 2011.

PL 112-50 (HR 2149) Designate the facility of the U.S. Postal Service located at 4354 Pahoa Ave. in Honolulu as the "Cecil L. Heftel Post Office Building." Introduced by Hanabusa, D-Hawaii, on June 13, 2011. House passed, under suspension of the rules, July 28. Senate Homeland Security and Governmental Affairs reported October 19 (no written report). Senate passed October 20. President signed November 7, 2011.

PL 112-51 (HR 368) Amend Title 28, U.S. Code, to clarify and improve certain provisions relating to the removal of litigation against federal officers or agencies to federal courts. Introduced by Johnson, D-Ga., on January 20, 2011. House Judiciary reported February 28 (H Rept 112-17, Part 1). House Budget discharged. House passed, under suspension of the rules, February 28. Senate Judiciary reported October 17 (no written report). Senate passed October 31. President signed November 9, 2011.

PL 112-52 (HR 818) Direct the secretary of the Interior to allow for prepayment of repayment contracts between the United States and the Uintah Water Conservancy District. Introduced by Matheson, D-Utah, on February 18, 2011. House Natural Resources reported October 14 (H Rept 112-247). House passed, under suspension of the rules, October 24. Senate passed November 3. President signed November 4, 2011.

PL 112-53 (S 894) Amend Title 38, U.S. Code, to provide for an increase, effective December 1, 2011, in the rates of compensation for veterans with service-connected disabilities and the rates of dependency and indemnity compensation for the survivors of certain disabled veterans. Introduced by Murray, D-Wash., on May 5, 2011. Senate Veterans' Affairs reported August 1 (S Rept 112-44). Senate passed October 19. House passed, under suspension of the rules, November 2. President signed November 9, 2011.

PL 112-54 (S 1487) Authorize the secretary of homeland security, in coordination with the secretary of state, to establish a program to issue Asia-Pacific Economic Cooperation Business Travel Cards. Introduced by Cantwell, D-Wash., August 2, 2011. Senate

Homeland Security and Governmental Affairs reported November 3 (S Rept 112-92). Senate passed, amended, November 3. House passed November 4. President signed November 12, 2011.

PL 112-55 (HR 2112) Make consolidated appropriations for the Departments of Agriculture, Commerce, Justice, Transportation, and Housing and Urban Development and for related programs for the fiscal year ending September 30, 2012. Introduced by Kingston, R-Ga., on June 3, 2011. House Appropriations reported June 3 (H Rept 112-101). House passed June 16. Senate Appropriations reported September 7 (S Rept 112-73). Senate passed, amended, November 1. Conference report filed in the House November 14 (H Rept 112-284). House agreed to the conference report November 17. Senate agreed to the conference report November 17. President signed November 18, 2011.

PL 112-56 (HR 674) Amend the Internal Revenue Code of 1986 to repeal the imposition of 3 percent withholding on certain payments made to vendors by government entities and to modify the calculation of modified adjusted gross income for the purposes of determining eligibility for certain programs related to health care. Introduced by Herger, R-Calif., on February 11, 2011. House Ways and Means reported October 18 (H Rept 112-253). House passed October 27. Senate passed, amended, November 10. House agreed to Senate amendment November 16. President signed November 21, 2011.

PL 112-57 (S 1280) Amend the Peace Corps Act to require training in responding to, and reducing the risk of, sexual assault; the development of a sexual-assault policy; the establishment of an Office of Victim Advocacy; and the establishment of a Sexual Assault Advisory Council. Introduced by Isakson, R-Ga., on June 27, 2011. Senate Foreign Relations reported September 21 (S Rept 112-82). Senate passed, amended, September 26. House passed, under suspension of the rules, November 1. President signed November 21, 2011.

PL 112-58 (HR 398) Amend the Immigration and Nationality Act to toll, during active-duty service abroad in the Armed Forces, the periods of time to file a petition and appear for an interview to remove the conditional basis for permanent-resident status. Introduced by Lofgren, D-Calif., on January 24, 2011. House Judiciary reported July 8 (H Rept 112-141, Part 1). House Budget discharged. House passed, under suspension of the rules, August 1. Senate Judiciary discharged. Senate passed November 10. President signed November 23, 2011.

PL 112-59 (HR 2447) Grant the Congressional Gold Medal to the Montford Point Marines. Introduced by Brown, D-Fla., on July 7, 2011. House passed, under suspension of the rules, October 25. Senate Banking, Housing and Urban Affairs discharged. Senate passed November 9. President signed November 23, 2011.

PL 112-60 (S 1412) Designate the facility of the U.S. Postal Service located at 462 Washington St., Woburn, Mass., as the "Officer John Maguire Post Office." Introduced by Kerry, D-Mass., on July 25, 2011. Senate Homeland Security and Governmental Affairs reported October 19 (no written report). Senate passed October 20. House passed, under suspension of the rules, November 14. President signed November 23, 2011.

PL 112-61 (HR 3321) Facilitate the hosting in the United States of the 34th America's Cup by authorizing certain eligible vessels to participate in activities related to the competition. Introduced by Herger, R-Calif., on November 2, 2011. House passed, under suspension of the rules, November 4. Senate passed, amended, November 17. House agreed to Senate amendment, November 18. President signed November 29, 2011.

PL 112-62 (S 1637) Clarify appeal time limits in civil actions to which U.S. officers or employees are parties. Introduced by Klobuchar, D-Minn., on October 3, 2011. Senate Judiciary reported October 17 (no written report). Senate passed October 31. House passed November 18. President signed November 29, 2011.

PL 112-63 (HR 394) Amend Title 28, U.S. Code, to clarify the jurisdiction of the federal courts. Introduced by Smith, R-Texas, on January 24, 2011. House Judiciary reported February 11 (H Rept 112-10). House passed, under suspension of the rules, February 28. Senate Judiciary reported October 17 (no written report). Senate passed, amended, October 31. House agreed to Senate amendment, with an amendment, November 18. Senate agreed to House amendment to Senate amendment, November 30. President signed December 2, 2011.

PL 112-64 (HR 2192) Extend, for an additional four-year period, an exemption from the application of the means test presumption of abuse under Chapter 7 for qualifying members of reserve components of the Armed Forces and members of the National Guard who, after September 11, 2001, are called to active duty or to perform a homeland defense activity for not less than ninety days. Introduced by Cohen, D-Tenn., on June 15, 2011. House Judiciary reported October 18 (H Rept 112-256). House passed, under suspension of the rules, November 29. Senate passed December 1. President signed December 13, 2011.

PL 112-65 (S 1541) Revise the federal charter for the Blue Star Mothers of America, Inc., to reflect a change in eligibility requirements for membership. Introduced by Bennett, D-Colo., on September 12, 2011. Senate Judiciary discharged. Senate passed November 18. House passed, under suspension of the rules, December 6. President signed December 8, 2011.

PL 112-66 (S 1639) Amend Title 36, U.S. Code, to authorize the American Legion under its federal charter to provide guidance and leadership to the individual departments and posts of the American Legion. Introduced by Tester, D-Mont., on October 3, 2011. Senate Judiciary discharged. Senate passed October 6. House passed, under suspension of the rules, December 6. President signed December 13, 2011.

PL 112-67 (H J Res 94) Make further continuing appropriations for fiscal 2012. Introduced by Rogers, R-Ky., on December 16, 2011. House passed December 16. Senate passed December 16. President signed December 16, 2011.

PL 112-68 (H J Res 95) Make further continuing appropriations for fiscal 2012. Introduced by Rogers, R-Ky., on December 16, 2011. House passed December 16. Senate passed December 17. President signed December 17, 2011.

PL 112-69 (S 535) Authorize the secretary of the Interior to lease certain lands within Fort Pulaski National Monument in

Georgia. Introduced by Isakson, R-Ga., on March 9, 2011. Senate Energy and Natural Resources reported August 30 (S Rept 112-59). Senate passed November 2. House Natural Resources reported December 1 (H Rept 112-298). House passed, under suspension of the rules, December 7. President signed December 19, 2011.

PL 112-70 (S 683) Provide for the conveyance of certain parcels of land to the town of Mantua, Utah. Introduced by Lee, R-Utah, on March 30, 2011. Senate Energy and Natural Resources reported August 30 (S Rept 112-60). Senate passed, amended, November 2. House passed, under suspension of the rules, December 7. President signed December 19, 2011.

PL 112-71 (S J Res 22) Grant the consent of Congress to an amendment to the compact between the states of Missouri and Illinois providing that bonds issued by the Bi-State Development Agency may mature in no more than forty years. Introduced by McCaskill, D-Mo., on June 28, 2011. Senate Judiciary discharged. Senate passed September 26. House passed, amended, under suspension of the rules, December 6. Senate agreed to House amendment December 8. President signed December 19, 2011.

PL 112-72 (HR 470) Further allocate and expand the availability of hydroelectric power generated at Hoover Dam. Introduced by Heck, R-Nev., on January 26, 2011. House Natural Resources reported July 20 (H Rept 112-159, Part 1). House Budget discharged. House passed, amended, under suspension of the rules, October 3. Senate passed October 18. President signed December 20, 2011.

PL 112-73 (HR 2061) Authorize the presentation of a U.S. flag on behalf of federal civilian employees who die of injuries incurred in connection with their employment. Introduced by Hanna, R-N.Y., on May 31, 2011. House Oversight and Government Reform reported July 18 (H Rept 112-149). House passed, amended, under suspension of the rules, November 2. Senate Homeland Security and Governmental Affairs discharged. Senate passed December 8. President signed December 20, 2011.

PL 112-74 (HR 2055) Make appropriations for military construction, the Department of Veterans Affairs, and related agencies for the fiscal year ending September 30, 2012. Introduced by Culberson, R-Texas, on May 31, 2011. House Appropriations reported May 31 (H Rept 112-94). House passed June 14. Senate Appropriations reported June 30 (S Rept 112-29). Senate passed, amended, July 20. Conference report—which added appropriations for the departments of Defense, Treasury, Energy, Homeland Security, Interior, Labor, Health and Human Services, Education and State, as well as the legislative branch and related agencies—filed in the House on December 15 (H Rept 112-331). House agreed to the conference report December 16. Senate agreed to the conference report December 17. President signed December 21, 2011.

PL 112-75 (HR 2867) Reauthorize the International Religious Freedom Act of 1998. Introduced by Wolf, R-Va., on September 8, 2011. House passed, under suspension of the rules, September 15. Senate Foreign Relations discharged. Senate passed, amended, December 13. House agreed to Senate amendments, under suspension of the rules, December 16. President signed December 23, 2011.

PL 112-76 (HR 3421) Award Congressional Gold Medals in honor of the men and women who perished as a result of the terrorist attacks on the United States on September 11, 2001. Introduced by Shuster, R-Pa., on November 14, 2011. House passed, under suspension of the rules, December 14. Senate passed December 15. President signed December 23, 2011.

PL 112-77 (HR 3672) Make appropriations for disaster relief for the fiscal year ending September 30, 2012. Introduced by Rogers, R-Ky., on December 14, 2011. House passed, under suspension of the rules, December 16. Senate passed December 17. President signed December 23, 2011.

PL 112-78 (HR 3765) Extend the payroll tax holiday, unemployment compensation, and Medicare physician payments, and provide for the consideration of the Keystone XL pipeline. Introduced by Camp, R-Mich., on December 23, 2011. House Ways and Means, Energy and Commerce, Transportation, Natural Resources, Foreign Affairs, Financial Services and Budget discharged. House passed December 23. Senate passed December 23. President signed December 23, 2011.

PL 112-79 (S 278) Provide for the exchange of certain land located in the Arapaho-Roosevelt National Forests in the state of Colorado. Introduced by Udall, D-Colo., on February 3, 2011. Senate Energy and Natural Resources reported August 30 (S Rept 112-51). Senate passed November 2. House passed, amended, under suspension of the rules, December 16. Senate agreed to House amendment December 17. President signed December 23, 2011.

PL 112-80 (S 384) Amend Title 39, U.S. Code, to extend the authority of the U.S. Postal Service to issue a stamp to raise money for breast cancer research. Introduced by Feinstein, D-Calif., on February 17, 2011. Senate Homeland Security and Governmental Affairs reported November 29 (S Rept 112-97). Senate passed December 5. House passed, under suspension of the rules, December 13. President signed December 23, 2011.

PL 112-81 (HR 1540) Authorize appropriations for fiscal 2012 for military activities of the Defense Department, for military construction and for defense activities of the Department of Energy and to prescribe military personnel strengths. Introduced by McKeon, R-Calif., on April 14, 2011. House Armed Services reported May 17 (H Rept 112-78). House passed, amended, May 26. Senate Armed Services discharged December 1. Senate passed, amended, December 1. Conference report filed in the House (H Rept 112-329). House agreed to the conference report December 14. Senate agreed to the conference report December 15. President signed December 31, 2011.

PL 112-82 (HR 515) Reauthorize the Belarus Democracy Act of 2004. Introduced by Smith, R-N.J., on January 26, 2011. House passed, under suspension of the rules, July 6. Senate Foreign Relations discharged. Senate passed, amended, December 14. House agreed to Senate amendments, under suspension of the rules, December 20. President signed January 3, 2012.

PL 112-83 (HR 789) Designate the facility of the U.S. Postal Service located at 20 Main St. in Little Ferry, N.J., as the "Sgt. Matthew J. Fenton Post Office." Introduced by Rothman, D-N.J., on February 17, 2011. House passed, under suspension of the rules, July 29. Senate Homeland Security and Governmental Affairs reported December 15 (no written report). Senate passed December 17. President signed January 3, 2012.

PL 112-84 (HR 1059) Protect the safety of judges by extending the authority of the Judicial Conference to redact sensitive information contained in their financial-disclosure reports. Introduced by Conyers, D-Mich., on March 14, 2011. House Judiciary reported July 29 (H Rept 112-189). House passed, under suspension of the rules, September 12. Senate Homeland Security and Governmental Affairs reported, amended, November 15 (no written report). Senate passed, amended, November 17. House agreed to Senate amendment December 20. President signed January 3, 2012.

PL 112-85 (HR 1264) Designate the property between the U.S. federal courthouse and the Ed Jones Building located at 109 South Highland Ave. in Jackson, Tenn., as the "M. D. Anderson Plaza" and authorize the placement of a historical identification marker on the grounds recognizing the achievements and philanthropy of M. D. Anderson. Introduced by Fincher, R-Tenn., on March 30, 2011. House Transportation and Infrastructure reported December 12 (H Rept 112-325). House passed, under suspension of the rules, December 14. Senate passed December 17. President signed January 3, 2012.

PL 112-86 (HR 1801) Amend Title 49, U.S. Code, to provide for expedited security screenings for members of the Armed Forces. Introduced by Cravaack, R-Minn., on May 10, 2011. House Homeland Security reported November 4 (H Rept 112-271). House passed, amended, under suspension of the rules, November 29. Senate Commerce, Science and Transportation discharged. Senate passed, amended, December 12. House agreed to Senate amendment, under suspension of the rules, December 20. President signed January 3, 2012.

PL 112-87 (HR 1892) Authorize appropriations for fiscal 2012 for intelligence and intelligence-related activities of the U.S. government, the Community Management Account, and the Central Intelligence Agency Retirement and Disability System. Introduced by Rogers, R-Mich., on May 13, 2011. House Intelligence reported September 2 (H Rept 112-197). House passed September 9. Senate passed, amended, December 14. House agreed to Senate amendment, under suspension of the rules, December 16. President signed January 3, 2012.

PL 112-88 (HR 2056) Instruct the inspector general of the Federal Deposit Insurance Corporation to study the impact of failures of insured depository institutions. Introduced by Westmoreland, R-Ga., on May 31, 2011. House Financial Services reported July 26 (H Rept 112-182). House passed, under suspension of the rules, July 28. Senate Banking, Housing and Urban Affairs discharged. Senate passed, amended, November 17. House agreed to Senate amendments, under suspension of the rules, December 20. President signed January 3, 2012.

PL 112-89 (HR 2422) Designate the facility of the U.S. Postal Service located at 45 Bay St., Suite 2, in Staten Island, N.Y., as the "Sgt. Angel Mendez Post Office." Introduced by Grimm, R-N.Y., on July 6, 2011. House passed, under suspension of the rules, November 14. Senate Homeland Security and Governmental Affairs reported December 15 (no written report). Senate passed December 17. President signed January 3, 2012.

PL 112-90 (HR 2845) Amend Title 49, U.S. Code, to provide for enhanced safety and environmental protection in pipeline transportation and provide for enhanced reliability in the transportation of the nation's energy products by pipeline. Introduced by Shuster, R-Pa., on September 7, 2011. House Transportation and Infrastructure reported December 1 (H Rept 112-297, Part 1). House Energy and Commerce discharged. House passed, amended, under suspension of the rules, December 12. Senate passed December 13. President signed January 3, 2012.

PL 112-91 (HR 3800) Extend funding and expenditure authority of the Airport and Airway Trust Fund and amend Title 49, U.S. Code, to extend authorizations for the airport improvement program. Introduced by Mica, R-Fla., on January 23, 2012. House passed, under suspension of the rules, January 24. Senate passed January 26. President signed January 31, 2012.

PL 112-92 (HR 3237) Clarify the scope of coverage of the Scholarships for Opportunity and Results Act. Introduced by Gowdy, R-S.C., on October 18, 2011. House Oversight and Government Reform reported December 6 (H Rept 112-315). House passed, under suspension of the rules, December 6. Senate Health, Education, Labor and Pensions discharged. Senate passed January 23, 2012. President signed February 1, 2012.

PL 112-93 (HR 3801) Amend the Tariff Act of 1930 to clarify the definition of aircraft and the offenses penalized under aviation smuggling provisions. Introduced by Giffords, D-Ariz., on January 23, 2012. House passed, under suspension of the rules, January 25. Senate passed January 26. President signed February 10, 2012.

PL 112-94 (HR 588) Redesignate the Noxubee National Wildlife Refuge as the Sam D. Hamilton Noxubee National Wildlife Refuge. Introduced by Harper, R-Miss., on February 9, 2011. House Natural Resources reported November 10 (H Rept 112-279). House passed, under suspension of the rules, November 14. Senate Environment and Public Works discharged. Senate passed February 1, 2012. President signed February 14, 2012.

PL 112-95 (HR 658) Amend Title 49, U.S. Code, to authorize appropriations for the Federal Aviation Administration for fiscal 2011 through 2014. Introduced by Mica, R-Fla., on February 11, 2011. House Transportation reported March 10 (H Rept 112-29, Part 1) and filed supplemental report March 16 (H Rept 112-29, Part 2). House Science, Space and Technology and House Judiciary discharged. House passed April 1. Senate passed April 7. Conference report filed February 1, 2012 (H Rept 112-381). House agreed to the conference report February 3. Senate agreed to the conference report February 6. President signed February 14, 2012.

PL 112-96 (HR 3630) Extend payroll tax deduction, extend and revise federal unemployment benefits, and prevent a reduction in pay rates for doctors serving Medicare patients. Introduced by Camp, R-Mich., on December 9, 2011. House passed December 13. Senate passed, amended, December 17. Conference report filed February 16, 2012 (H Rept 112-399). House agreed to conference report February 17. Senate agreed to conference report February 17. President signed February 22, 2012.

PL 112-97 (HR 1162) Provide tsunami and flood protection to the Quileute Indian Tribe. Introduced by Dicks, D-Wash., on March 17, 2011. House Natural Resources reported February 3, 2012 (H Rept 112-387). House passed, under suspension of the rules, February 6. Senate passed February 13. President signed February 27, 2012.

PL 112-98 (HR 347) Correct and simplify the drafting of section 1752, relating to restricted buildings or grounds, of Title 18, U.S. Code. Introduced by Rooney, R-Fla., on January 19, 2011. House Judiciary reported February 11 (H Rept 112-9). House passed, under suspension of the rules, February 28. Senate Judiciary reported November 17 (no written report). Senate passed, amended, February 6, 2012. House agreed to Senate amendment February 27. President signed March 8, 2012.

PL 112-99 (HR 4105) Apply the countervailing-duty provisions of the Tariff Act of 1930 to nonmarket-economy countries. Introduced by Camp, R-Mich., on February 29, 2012. House passed, under suspension of the rules, March 6. Senate passed March 7. President signed March 13, 2012.

PL 112-100 (S 1134) Authorize the St. Croix River Crossing Project. Introduced by Klobuchar, D-Minn., on May 26, 2011. Senate Energy and Natural Resources reported December 16 (S Rept 112-124). Senate passed January 23, 2012. House passed, under suspension of the rules, on March 1. President signed March 14, 2012.

PL 112-101 (S 1710) Designate the U.S. courthouse located at 222 West 7th Ave., Anchorage, Alaska, as the James M. Fitzgerald United States Courthouse. Introduced by Begich, D-Alaska, on October 13, 2011. Senate Environment and Public Works. Senate passed December 17. House passed, under suspension of the rules, March 5, 2012. President signed March 14, 2012.

PL 112-102 (HR 4281) Provide an extension of federal-aid highway, highway safety, motor carrier safety, transit, and other programs funded out of the Highway Trust Fund pending enactment of a multiyear law reauthorizing such programs. Introduced by Mica, R-Fla., on March 28, 2012. House passed March 29. Senate passed March 29. President signed March 30, 2012.

PL 112-103 (HR 473) Provide for the conveyance of approximately 140 acres of land in the Ouachita National Forest in Oklahoma to the Indian Nations Council Inc. of the Boy Scouts of America. Introduced by Boren, D-Okla., on January 26, 2011. Reported by the House Natural Resources September 23 (H Rept 112-218). House passed, under suspension of the rules, October 3. Senate Agriculture, Nutrition and Forestry discharged. Senate passed March 15, 2012. President signed April 2, 2012.

PL 112-104 (HR 886) Require the secretary of the Treasury to mint coins in commemoration of the 225th anniversary of the establishment of the nation's first federal law enforcement agency, the U.S. Marshals Service. Introduced by Womack, R-Ark., on March 2, 2011. House passed, under suspension of the rules, December 15. Senate Banking, Housing and Urban Affairs discharged. Senate passed, amended, March 15, 2012. House agreed to Senate amendment, under suspension of the rules, March 21. President signed April 2, 2012.

PL 112-105 (S 2038) Prohibit members and employees of Congress from using nonpublic information derived from their official positions for personal benefit. Introduced by Lieberman, I-Conn., on January 26, 2012. Senate Homeland Security and Governmental Affairs reported January 26 (no written report). Senate passed, amended, February 2. House passed, amended, under suspension of the rules, February 9. Senate agreed to House amendment March 22. President signed April 4, 2012.

PL 112-106 (HR 3606) Increase U.S. job creation and economic growth by improving access to the public capital markets for emerging growth companies. Introduced by Fincher, R-Tenn., on December 8, 2011. House Financial Services reported, amended, on March 1, 2012 (H Rept 112-406). House passed March 8. Senate passed, amended, March 22. House agreed to Senate amendment, under suspension of the rules, March 27. President signed April 5, 2012.

PL 112-107 (HR 298) Designate the facility of the U.S. Postal Service located at 500 E. Whitestone Blvd. in Cedar Park, Texas, as the "Army Spc. Matthew Troy Morris Post Office Building." Introduced by Carter, R-Texas, on January 18, 2011. House passed, under suspension of the rules, November 14. Senate Homeland Security and Governmental Affairs reported April 25, 2012 (no written report). Senate passed April 26. President signed May 15, 2012.

PL 112-108 (HR 1423) Designate the facility of the U.S. Postal Service located at 115 Fourth Ave. SW in Ardmore, Okla., as the "Spc. Micheal E. Phillips Post Office." Introduced by Cole, R-Okla., on April 7, 2011. House passed, under suspension of the rules, May 2. Senate Homeland Security and Governmental Affairs reported April 25, 2012 (no written report). Senate passed April 26. President signed May 15, 2012.

PL 112-109 (HR 2079) Designate the facility of the U.S. Postal Service located at 10 Main St. in East Rockaway, N.Y., as the "John J. Cook Post Office." Introduced by McCarthy, D-N.Y., on June 1, 2011. House passed February 15, 2012. Senate Homeland Security and Governmental Affairs reported April 25 (no written report). Senate passed April 26. President signed May 15, 2012.

PL 112-110 (HR 2213) Designate the facility of the U.S. Postal Service located at 801 W. Eastport St. in Iuka, Miss., as the "Sgt. Jason W. Vaughn Post Office." Introduced by Nunnelee, R-Miss., on June 16, 2011. House passed, under suspension of the rules, July 29. Senate Homeland Security and Governmental Affairs reported April 25, 2012 (no written report). Senate passed April 26. President signed May 15, 2012.

PL 112-111 (HR 2244) Designate the facility of the U.S. Postal Service located at 67 Castle St. in Geneva, N.Y., as the "Cpl. Steven Blaine Riccione Post Office." Introduced by Hanna, R-N.Y., on June 21, 2011. House passed, under suspension of the rules, July 29. Senate Homeland Security and Governmental Affairs reported April 25, 2012 (no written report). Senate passed April 26. President signed May 15, 2012.

PL 112-112 (HR 2660) Designate the facility of the U.S. Postal Service located at 122 N. Holderrieth Blvd. in Tomball, Texas, as the "Tomball Veterans Post Office." Introduced by McCaul, R-Texas, on July 26, 2011. House passed, under suspension of the rules, November 11. Senate Homeland Security and Governmental Affairs reported April 25, 2012 (no written report). Senate passed April 26. President signed May 15, 2012.

PL 112-113 (HR 2668) Designate the station of the U.S. Border Patrol located at 2136 S. Naco Highway in Bisbee, Ariz., as the "Brian A. Terry Border Patrol Station." Introduced by Issa, R-Calif., on July 27, 2011. House Transportation and Infrastructure reported December 12 (H Rept 112-326). House passed, under suspension of the rules, December 14. Senate Homeland Security and Governmental Affairs reported May 7, 2012 (no written report). Senate passed May 8. President signed May 15, 2012.

PL 112-114 (HR 2767) Designate the facility of the U.S. Postal Service located at 8 W. Silver St. in Westfield, Mass., as the "William T. Trant Post Office Building." Introduced by Olver, D-Mass., on August 1, 2011. House passed, under suspension of the rules, December 13. Senate Homeland Security and Governmental Affairs reported April 25, 2012 (no written report). Senate passed April 26. President signed May 15, 2012.

PL 112-115 (HR 3004) Designate the facility of the U.S. Postal Service located at 260 California Dr. in Yountville, Calif., as the "Pfc. Alejandro R. Ruiz Post Office Building." Introduced by Thompson, D-Calif., on September 21, 2011. House passed, under suspension of the rules, November 16. Senate Homeland Security and Governmental Affairs reported April 25, 2012 (no written report). Senate passed April 26. President signed May 15, 2012.

PL 112-116 (HR 3246) Designate the facility of the U.S. Postal Service located at 15455 Manchester Rd. in Ballwin, Mo., as the "Spc. Peter J. Navarro Post Office Building." Introduced by Akin, R-Mo., on October 24, 2011. House passed, under suspension of the rules, December 13. Senate Homeland Security and Governmental Affairs reported April 25, 2012 (no written report). Senate passed April 26. President signed May 15, 2012.

PL 112-117 (HR 3247) Designate the facility of the U.S. Postal Service located at 1100 Town and Country Commons in Chesterfield, Mo., as the "Lance Cpl. Matthew P. Pathenos Post Office Building." Introduced by Akin, R-Mo., on October 24, 2011. House passed, under suspension of the rules, February 15, 2012. Senate Homeland Security and Governmental Affairs reported April 25, 2012 (no written report). Senate passed April 26. President signed May 15, 2012.

PL 112-118 (HR 3248) Designate the facility of the U.S. Postal Service located at 112 S. Fifth St. in Saint Charles, Mo., as the "Lance Cpl. Drew W. Weaver Post Office Building." Introduced by Akin, R-Mo., on October 24, 2011. House passed, under suspension of the rules, February 15, 2012. Senate Homeland Security and Governmental Affairs reported April 25 (no written report). Senate passed April 26. President signed May 15, 2012.

PL 112-119 (S 1302) Authorize the administrator of General Services to convey a parcel of real property in Tracy, Calif., to the City of Tracy. Introduced by Boxer, D-Calif., on June 29, 2011. Senate Environment and Public Works reported July 28 (S Rept 112-40). Senate passed August 2. House passed, under suspension of the rules, May 7, 2012. President signed May 15, 2012.

PL 112-120 (HR 4045) Modify the Department of Defense Program Guidance relating to the award of Post-Deployment/Mobilization Respite Absence administrative absence days to members of the reserves. Introduced by Kline, R-Minn., on February 15, 2012. House passed, under suspension of the rules, May 15. Senate passed May 17. President signed May 25, 2012.

PL 112-121 (HR 4967) Prevent the termination of the temporary office of bankruptcy judges in certain judicial districts. Introduced by Smith, R-Texas, on April 27, 2012. House Judiciary discharged. House passed May 9. Senate passed May 10. President signed May 25, 2012.

PL 112-122 (HR 2072) Reauthorize the Export-Import Bank of the United States. Introduced by Miller, R-Calif., on June 1, 2011. House Financial Services reported, amended, September 8 (H Rept 112-201). House passed, under suspension of the rules, May 9, 2012. Senate passed May 14. President signed May 30, 2012.

PL 112-123 (HR 5740) Extend the National Flood Insurance Program. Introduced by Biggert, R-Ill., on May 15, 2012. House passed, under suspension of the rules, May 17. Senate passed, amended, May 24. House agreed to Senate amendment, under suspension of the rules, May 30. President signed May 31, 2012.

PL 112-124 (HR 2415) Designate the facility of the U.S. Postal Service located at 11 Dock St. in Pittston, Pa., as the "Trooper Joshua D. Miller Post Office Building." Introduced by Barletta, R-Pa., on July 6, 2011. House passed, under suspension of the rules, November 16. Senate Homeland Security and Governmental Affairs reported May 16, 2012 (no written report). Senate passed May 17. President signed June 5, 2012.

PL 112-125 (HR 3220) Designate the facility of the U.S. Postal Service located at 170 Evergreen Square SW in Pine City, Minn., as the "Master Sgt. Daniel L. Fedder Post Office." Introduced by Cravaack, R-Minn., on October 14, 2011. House passed, under suspension of the rules, December 12. Senate Homeland Security and Governmental Affairs reported May 16, 2012 (no written report). Senate passed May 17. President signed June 5, 2012.

PL 112-126 (HR 3413) Designate the facility of the U.S. Postal Service located at 1449 West Ave. in Bronx, N.Y., as the "Pvt. Isaac T. Cortes Post Office." Introduced by Crowley, D-N.Y., on November 14, 2011. House passed, under suspension of the rules, March 5, 2012. Senate Homeland Security and Governmental Affairs reported May 16 (no written report). Senate passed May 17. President signed June 5, 2012.

PL 112-127 (HR 4119) Reduce the trafficking of drugs and prevent human smuggling across the southwest border by deterring the construction and use of border tunnels. Introduced by Reyes, D-Texas, on March 1, 2012. House Judiciary reported March 21 (H Rept 112-418, Part 1). House Ways and Means discharged. House Homeland Security discharged. House passed, under suspension of the rules, May 16. Senate passed May 17. President signed June 5, 2012.

PL 112-128 (HR 4849) Direct the secretary of the Interior to issue commercial-use authorizations to commercial stock operators for operations in designated wilderness within the Sequoia and Kings Canyon national parks. Introduced by Nunes, R-Calif., on April 26, 2012. House Natural Resources discharged. House passed April 27. Senate passed, amended, May 17. House agreed to Senate amendment May 18. President signed June 5, 2012.

PL 112-129 (HR 2947) Provide for the release of the reversionary interest held by the United States in certain land conveyed by the United States in 1950 for the establishment of an airport in Cook County, Minn. Introduced by Cravaack, R-Minn., on September 15, 2011. House Natural Resources reported April 16,

2012 (H Rept 112-441). House passed, under suspension of the rules, April 24. Senate Energy and Natural Resources discharged. Senate Agriculture, Nutrition and Forestry discharged. Senate passed May 24. President signed June 8, 2012.

PL 112-130 (HR 3992) Allow otherwise eligible Israeli nationals to receive E-2 nonimmigrant visas if similarly situated U.S. nationals are eligible for similar nonimmigrant status in Israel. Introduced by Berman, D-Calif., on February 9, 2012. House Judiciary reported March 8 (H Rept 112-410). House passed, under suspension of the rules, March 19. Senate Judiciary discharged. Senate passed May 24. President signed June 8, 2012.

PL 112-131 (HR 4097) Amend the John F. Kennedy Center Act to authorize appropriations for the John F. Kennedy Center for the Performing Arts. Introduced by Mica, R-Fla., on February 28, 2012. House Transportation and Infrastructure reported April 27 (H Rept 112-457). House passed, under suspension of the rules, May 7. Senate passed May 23. President signed June 8, 2012.

PL 112-132 (S 3261) Allow the chief of the Forest Service to award certain contracts for large air tankers. Introduced by Wyden, D-Ore., on June 4, 2012. Senate Agriculture, Nutrition and Forestry discharged. Senate passed June 7. House Agriculture discharged. House passed June 8. President signed June 13, 2012.

PL 112-133 (S 292) Resolve the claims of the Bering Straits Native Corporation and the state of Alaska to land adjacent to Salmon Lake and provide for the conveyance to the Bering Straits Native Corporation of certain other public land in partial satisfaction of the land entitlement of the corporation under the Alaska Native Claims Settlement Act. Introduced by Murkowski, R-Alaska, on February 4, 2011. Senate Energy and Natural Resources reported, amended, August 30 (S Rept 112-52). Senate passed, amended, October 18. House Natural Resources reported April 16, 2012 (H Rept 112-428). House passed, under suspension of the rules, June 6. President signed June 15, 2012.

PL 112-134 (S 363) Authorize the secretary of commerce to convey property of the National Oceanic and Atmospheric Administration to the City of Pascagoula, Miss. Introduced by Wicker, R-Miss., on February 16, 2011. Senate Commerce, Science and Transportation reported November 8 (no written report). Senate passed, amended, November 10. Senate Commerce, Science and Transportation reported January 26, 2012 (S Rept 112-133). House Natural Resources reported May 30 (H Rept 112-502). House passed, under suspension of the rules, June 6. President signed June 15, 2012.

PL 112-135 (HR 5883) Make a technical correction in Public Law 112-108. Introduced by Cole, R-Okla., on June 1, 2012. House Oversight and Government Reform discharged June 5. House passed June 5. Senate passed June 7. President signed June 21, 2012.

PL 112-136 (HR 5890) Correct a technical error in Public Law 112-122. Introduced by Dold, R-Ill., on June 5, 2012. House Financial Services discharged. House passed June 5. Senate passed June 7. President signed June 21, 2012.

PL 112-137 (S 404) Modify a land grant patent issued by the secretary of the Interior. Introduced by Levin, D-Mich., on February 17, 2011. Senate Energy and Natural Resources reported August 30 (S Rept 112-56). Senate passed October 18. House Natural Resources reported April 16, 2012 (H Rept 112-433). House passed, under suspension of the rules, June 18. President signed June 27, 2012.

PL 112-138 (S 684) Provide for the conveyance of certain parcels of land to the town of Alta, Utah. Introduced by Lee, R-Utah, on March 30, 2011. Senate Energy and Natural Resources reported, amended, August 30 (S Rept 112-61). Senate passed, amended, November 2. House Natural Resources reported April 16, 2012 (H Rept 112-434). House passed, under suspension of the rules, June 18. President signed June 27, 2012.

PL 112-139 (S 997) Authorize the secretary of the Interior to extend a water contract between the United States and the East Bench Irrigation District. Introduced by Tester, D-Mont., on May 12, 2011. Senate Energy and Natural Resources reported August 30 (S Rept 112-65). Senate passed November 2. House Natural Resources reported June 15, 2012 (H Rept 112-527). House passed, under suspension of the rules, June 18. President signed June 27, 2012.

PL 112-140 (HR 6064) Provide an extension of federal-aid highway, highway safety, motor carrier safety, transit, and other programs funded out of the Highway Trust Fund pending enactment of a multiyear law reauthorizing such programs. Introduced by Mica, R-Fla., on June 29, 2012. House Transportation discharged. House passed June 29. Senate passed June 29. President signed June 29, 2012.

PL 112-141 (HR 4348) Authorize funds for federal-aid highways, highway safety programs, and transit programs. Introduced by Mica, R-Fla., on April 16, 2012. House passed April 18. Senate passed, amended, April 24. Conference report filed June 28 (H Rept 112-557). House agreed to conference report June 29. Senate agreed to conference report June 29. President signed July 6, 2012.

PL 112-142 (HR 33) Amend the Securities Act of 1933 to specify when certain securities issued in connection with church plans are treated as exempted securities for purposes of that act. Introduced by Biggert, R-Ill., on January 5, 2011. House Financial Services reported, amended, July 1 (H Rept 112-131). House passed, under suspension of the rules, July 18. Senate Banking, Housing and Urban Affairs discharged. Senate passed June 21, 2012. President signed July 9, 2012.

PL 112-143 (HR 2297) Promote the development of the Southwest waterfront in the District of Columbia. Introduced by Norton, D-D.C., on June 22, 2011. House passed, amended, under suspension of the rules, December 6. Senate Homeland Security and Governmental Affairs reported March 29, 2012 (S Rept 112-154). Senate passed, amended, March 29. House agreed to Senate amendment under suspension of the rules, June 26. President signed July 9, 2012.

PL 112-144 (S 3187) Amend the federal Food, Drug and Cosmetic Act to revise and extend the user fee programs for prescription drugs and medical devices and to establish user fee programs for generic drugs and biosimilars. Introduced by Harkin, D-Iowa, on May 15, 2012. Senate passed, amended, May 24. House passed, amended, under suspension of the rules,

June 20. Senate agreed to House amendment June 26. President signed July 9, 2012.

PL 112-145 (HR 3902) Amend the District of Columbia Home Rule Act to revise the timing of special elections for local office in the District of Columbia. Introduced by Norton, D-D.C., on February 6, 2012. House passed, amended, under suspension of the rules, February 29. Senate Homeland Security and Governmental Affairs reported July 12 (no written report). Senate passed July 12. Senate Homeland Security and Governmental Affairs reported July 16 (S Rept 112-186). President signed July 18, 2012.

PL 112-146 (S 2061) Provide for an exchange of land between the Department of Homeland Security and the South Carolina State Ports Authority. Introduced by Graham, R-S.C., on February 1, 2012. Senate Homeland Security and Governmental Affairs reported May 24 (S Rept 112-171). Senate passed, amended, June 5. House passed, under suspension of the rules, July 9. President signed July 18, 2012.

PL 112-147 (HR 4155) Direct the head of each federal department and agency to treat relevant military training as sufficient to satisfy training or certification requirements for federal licenses. Introduced by Denham, R-Calif., on March 7, 2012. House Oversight and Government Reform reported, amended, July 9 (H Rept 112-585). House passed, under suspension of the rules, July 9. Senate passed July 11. President signed July 23, 2012.

PL 112-148 (HR 3001) Award a Congressional Gold Medal to Raoul Wallenberg in recognition of his achievements and heroic actions during the Holocaust. Introduced by Meeks, D-N.Y., on September 21, 2011. House passed, under suspension of the rules, April 16, 2012. Senate passed July 11. President signed July 26, 2012.

PL 112-149 (S 2009) Improve the administration of programs in the insular areas. Introduced by Bingaman, D-N.M., on December 16, 2011. Senate passed December 16. House passed, on motion to suspend the rules, July 17, 2012. President signed July 26, 2012.

PL 112-150 (S 2165) Enhance strategic cooperation between the United States and Israel. Introduced by Boxer, D-Calif., on March 6, 2012. Senate Foreign Relations reported, amended, June 27 (S Rept 112-179). Senate passed, amended, June 29. House passed, under suspension of the rules, July 17. President signed July 27, 2012.

PL 112-151 (HR 205) Provide for Indian tribes to enter into certain leases without prior express approval from the secretary of the Interior. Introduced by Heinrich, D-N.M., on January 6, 2011. House Natural Resources reported, amended, April 16, 2012 (H Rept 112-427). House passed, under suspension of the rules, May 15. Senate Indian Affairs discharged. Senate passed July 17. President signed July 30, 2012.

PL 112-152 (HR 2527) To require the secretary of the Treasury to mint coins in recognition and celebration of the National Baseball Hall of Fame. Introduced by Hanna, R-N.Y., on July 14, 2011. House passed, amended, under suspension of the rules, October 26. Senate Banking, Housing and Urban Affairs discharged. Senate passed, amended, July 12, 2012. House agreed to Senate amendment July 19. President signed August 3, 2012.

PL 112-153 (S 1335) Amend title 49, U.S. Code, to provide rights for pilots. Introduced by Inhofe, R-Okla., on July 6, 2011. Senate Commerce, Science and Transportation discharged. Senate passed, amended, June 29, 2012. House passed, under suspension of the rules, July 23. President signed August 3, 2012.

PL 112-154 (HR 1627) Furnish hospital care and medical services to veterans who were stationed at Camp Lejeune, N.C., while the water was contaminated, to improve the provision of housing assistance to veterans and their families. Introduced by Miller, R-Fla., on April 15, 2011. House Veterans' Affairs reported, amended, May 20 (H Rept 112-84, Part 1). House Armed Services discharged. House passed, under suspension of the rules, May 23. Senate Veterans' Affairs discharged. Senate passed, amended, July 18, 2012. House agreed to the Senate amendments, under suspension of the rules, July 31. President signed August 6, 2012.

PL 112-155 (HR 5872) Require the president to provide a report detailing the sequester required by the Budget Control Act of 2011 on January 2, 2013. Introduced by Hensarling, R-Texas, on May 31, 2012. House Budget reported, amended, July 2 (H Rept 112-577). House passed, under suspension of the rules, July 18. Senate passed July 25. President signed August 7, 2012.

PL 112-156 (HR 1369) Designate the facility of the U.S. Postal Service located at 1021 Pennsylvania Ave. in Hartshorne, Okla., as the "Warren Lindley Post Office." Introduced by Boren, D-Okla., on April 5, 2011. House passed, under suspension of the rules, July 23, 2012. Senate Homeland Security and Governmental Affairs discharged. Senate passed August 1. President signed August 10, 2012.

PL 112-157 (HR 1560) Amend the Ysleta del Sur Pueblo and Alabama and Coushatta Indian Tribes of Texas Restoration Act to allow the Ysleta del Sur Pueblo Tribe to determine blood quantum requirement for membership in that tribe. Introduced by Reyes, D-Texas, on April 14, 2011. House Natural Resources reported September 23 (H Rept 112-222). House passed, under suspension of the rules, December 7. Senate Indian Affairs reported July 31, 2012 (no written report). Senate passed August 1. President signed August 10, 2012.

PL 112-158 (HR 1905) Strengthen Iran sanctions laws for the purpose of compelling Iran to abandon its pursuit of nuclear weapons and other threatening activities. Introduced by Ros-Lehtinen, R-Fla., on May 13, 2011. House passed, under suspension of the rules, December 14. Senate Foreign Relations discharged. Senate passed, amended, May 21, 2012. House agreed to Senate amendment with amendment August 1. Senate agreed to House amendment to Senate amendment August 1. President signed August 10, 2012.

PL 112-159 (HR 3276) Designate the facility of the U.S. Postal Service located at 2810 E. Hillsborough Ave. in Tampa, Fla., as the "Rev. Abe Brown Post Office Building." Introduced by Castor, D-Fla., on October 27, 2011. House passed, under suspension of the rules, June 28, 2012. Senate Homeland Security and Governmental Affairs discharged. Senate passed August 1. President signed August 10, 2012.

PL 112-160 (HR 3412) Designate the facility of the U.S. Postal Service located at 1421 Veterans Memorial Drive in Abbeville, La., as the "Sgt. Richard Franklin Abshire Post Office Building." Introduced by Boustany, R-La., on November 14, 2011. House passed, under suspension of the rules, June 28, 2012. Senate Homeland Security and Governmental Affairs discharged. Senate passed August 1. President signed August 10, 2012.

PL 112-161 (HR 3501) Designate the facility of the U.S. Postal Service located at 125 Kerr Ave. in Rome City, Ind., as the "Spc. Nicholas Scott Hartge Post Office." Introduced by Stutzman, R-Ind., on November 18, 2011. House passed, under suspension of the rules, June 28, 2012. Senate Homeland Security and Governmental Affairs discharged. Senate passed August 1. President signed August 10, 2012.

PL 112-162 (HR 3772) Designate the facility of the U.S. Postal Service located at 150 South Union St. in Canton, Miss., as the "1st Sgt. Landres Cheeks Post Office Building." Introduced by Thompson, D-Miss., on January 13, 2012. House passed, under suspension of the rules, June 28. Senate Homeland Security and Governmental Affairs discharged. Senate passed August 1. President signed August 10, 2012.

PL 112-163 (HR 5986) Amend the African Growth and Opportunity Act to extend the third-country fabric program and to add South Sudan to the list of countries eligible for designation under that act, to make technical corrections to the Harmonized Tariff Schedule of the United States relating to the textile and apparel rules of origin for the Dominican Republic–Central America–United States Free Trade Agreement, to approve the renewal of import restrictions contained in the Burmese Freedom and Democracy Act of 2003. Introduced by Camp, R-Mich., on June 21, 2012. House passed, under suspension of the rules, August 2. Senate passed August 2. President signed August 10, 2012.

PL 112-164 (S 270) Direct the secretary of the Interior to convey certain federal land to Deschutes County, Ore. Introduced by Wyden, D-Ore., on February 3, 2011. Senate Energy and Natural Resources reported August 30 (S Rept 112-49). Senate passed, amended, October 18. House Natural Resources reported July 9, 2012 (H Rept 112-581). House passed, under suspension of the rules, August 1. President signed August 10, 2012.

PL 112-165 (S 271) Require the secretary of Agriculture to enter into a property conveyance with the city of Wallowa, Ore. Introduced by Wyden, D-Ore., on February 3, 2011. Senate Energy and Natural Resources reported, amended, August 30 (S Rept 112-50). Senate passed, amended, November 2. House Natural Resources reported April 16, 2012 (H Rept 112-432). House passed, under suspension of the rules, August 1. President signed August 10, 2012.

PL 112-166 (S 679) Reduce the number of executive positions subject to Senate confirmation. Introduced by Schumer, D-N.Y., on March 30, 2011. Senate Homeland Security and Governmental Affairs reported, amended, June 13 (S Rept 112-24). Senate passed June 29. House passed, under suspension of the rules, July 31, 2012. President signed August 10, 2012.

PL 112-167 (S 739) A bill to authorize the Architect of the Capitol to establish battery-recharging stations for privately owned vehicles in parking areas under the jurisdiction of the Senate at no net cost to the federal government. Introduced by Levin, D-Mich., on April 6, 2011. Senate Rules reported May 12 (no written report). Senate passed, amended, May 24, 2012. House passed August 2. President signed August 10, 2012.

PL 112-168 (S 1959) Require a report on the designation of the Haqqani Network as a foreign terrorist organization. Introduced by Burr, R-N.C., on December 7, 2011. Senate Foreign Relations discharged. Senate passed, amended, December 17. House passed, under suspension of the rules, July 17, 2012. Senate agreed to House amendment July 26. President signed August 10, 2012.

PL 112-169 (S 3363) Provide for the use of National Infantry Museum and Soldier Center Commemorative Coin surcharges. Introduced by Chambliss, R-Ga., on June 29, 2012. Senate passed June 29. House passed August 1. President signed August 10, 2012.

PL 112-170 (HR 1402) To authorize the Architect of the Capitol to establish battery-recharging stations for privately owned vehicles in parking areas under the jurisdiction of the House of Representatives at no net cost to the federal government. Introduced by Kildee, D-Mich., on April 6, 2011. House Administration reported, amended, July 26, 2012 (H Rept 112-625). House passed August 2. Senate passed August 2. President signed August 16, 2012.

PL 112-171 (HR 3670) To require the Transportation Security Administration to comply with the Uniformed Services Employment and Reemployment Rights Act. Introduced by Walz, D-Minn., on December 14, 2011. House Veterans' Affairs reported May 18, 2012 (H Rept 112-487, Part 1). House passed, under suspension of the rules, May 30. Senate Commerce, Science and Transportation discharged. Senate passed August 2. President signed August 16, 2012.

PL 112-172 (HR 4240) Reauthorize the North Korean Human Rights Act of 2004. Introduced by Ros-Lehtinen, R-Fla., on March 22, 2012. House passed, under suspension of the rules, May 15. Senate Foreign Relations reported July 18 (no written report). Senate passed August 2. President signed August 16, 2012.

PL 112-173 (S 3510) Prevent harm to the national security or endangering the military officers and civilian employees to whom Internet publication of certain information applies. Introduced by Reid, D-Nev., on August 2, 2012. Senate passed August 2. House passed August 2. President signed August 16, 2012.

PL 112-174 (HR 6336) Direct the Joint Committee on the Library to accept a statue depicting Frederick Douglass from the District of Columbia and to provide for the permanent display of the statue in Emancipation Hall of the U.S. Capitol. Introduced by Lungren, R-Calif., on August 2, 2012. House passed, under suspension of the rules, September 10. Senate passed September 12. President signed September 20, 2012.

PL 112-175 (H J Res 117) Make continuing appropriations for fiscal 2013. Introduced by Rogers, R-Ky., on September 10, 2012. House passed September 13. Senate passed September 22. President signed September 28, 2012.

PL 112-176 (S 3245) Extend by three years the authorization of the EB-5 Regional Center Program, the E-Verify Program, the Special Immigrant Non-Minister Religious Worker Program, and the Conrad State 30 J-1 Visa Waiver Program. Introduced by Leahy, D-Vt., on May 24, 2012. Senate Judiciary discharged August 2. Senate passed, amended, August 2. House passed, under suspension of the rules, September 13. President signed September 28, 2012.

PL 112-177 (S 3552) Reauthorize the Federal Insecticide, Fungicide and Rodenticide Act. Introduced by Stabenow, D-Mich., on September 13, 2012. Senate passed September 13. House passed September 14. President signed September 28, 2012.

PL 112-178 (S 3625) Change the effective date for the Internet publication of certain information to prevent harm to the national security or endangering the military officers and civilian employees to whom the publication requirement applies. Introduced by Lieberman, I-Conn., on September 22, 2012. Senate passed September 22. House passed September 28. President signed September 28, 2012.

PL 112-179 (HR 1272) Provide for the use and distribution of the funds awarded to the Minnesota Chippewa Tribe, et al., by the U.S. Court of Federal Claims in Docket Numbers 19 and 188. Introduced by Peterson, D-Minn., on March 30, 2011. House Natural Resources reported, amended, May 30, 2012 (H Rept 112-501). House passed, under suspension of the rules, June 18. Senate Indian Affairs reported August 1 (no written report). Senate passed September 22. President signed October 5, 2012.

PL 112-180 (HR 1791) Designate the U.S. courthouse under construction at 101 South U.S. Route 1 in Fort Pierce, Fla., as the "Alto Lee Adams Sr. U.S. Courthouse." Introduced by Rooney, R-Fla., on May 5, 2011. House Transportation and Infrastructure reported November 14 (H Rept 112-282). House passed, under suspension of the rules, November 16. Senate Homeland Security and Governmental Affairs discharged. Senate Environment and Public Works reported July 10 (no written report). Senate passed September 22, 2012. President signed October 5, 2012.

PL 112-181 (HR 2139) Require the secretary of the Treasury to mint coins in commemoration of the centennial of the establishment of Lions Clubs International. Introduced by Roskam, R-Ill., on June 3, 2011. House passed, under suspension of the rules, September 10, 2012. Senate passed September 22. President signed October 5, 2012.

PL 112-182 (HR 2240) Authorize the exchange of land or interest in land between Lowell National Historical Park and the city of Lowell in the Commonwealth of Massachusetts. Introduced by Tsongas, D-Mass., on June 16, 2011. House Natural Resources reported April 19, 2012 (H Rept 112-450). House passed, under suspension of the rules, April 26. Senate passed September 22. President signed October 5, 2012.

PL 112-183 (HR 2706) Prohibit the sale of billfish. Introduced by Miller, R-Fla., on July 29, 2011. House Natural Resources reported, amended, September 10, 2012 (H Rept 112-656). House passed, under suspension of the rules, September 10. Senate passed September 22. President signed October 5, 2012.

PL 112-184 (HR 3556) Designate the new U.S. courthouse in Buffalo, N.Y., as the "Robert H. Jackson U.S. Courthouse." Introduced by Higgins, D-N.Y., on December 2, 2011. House Transportation and Infrastructure reported April 27, 2012 (H Rept 112-456). House passed, under suspension of the rules, July 23. Senate passed September 22. President signed October 5, 2012.

PL 112-185 (HR 4158) Confirm full ownership rights for certain U.S. astronauts to artifacts from the astronauts' space missions. Introduced by Hall, R-Texas, on March 7, 2012. House passed, under suspension of the rules, September 19. Senate passed September 22. President signed October 5, 2012.

PL 112-186 (HR 4223) Amend title 18, U.S. Code, to prohibit theft of medical products. Introduced by Sensenbrenner, R-Wis., on March 20, 2012. House Judiciary reported, amended, June 25, 2012 (H Rept 112-549). House passed, under suspension of the rules, June 26. Senate Judiciary discharged. Senate passed September 22. President signed October 5, 2012.

PL 112-187 (HR 4347) Designate the U.S. courthouse at 709 W. Ninth St. in Juneau, Alaska, as the "Robert Boochever U.S. Courthouse." Introduced by Young, R-Alaska, on March 30, 2012. House Transportation and Infrastructure reported July 19 (H Rept 112-614). House passed, under suspension of the rules, July 23. Senate passed September 22. President signed October 5, 2012.

PL 112-188 (HR 5512) Amend title 28, U.S. Code, to realign divisions within two judicial districts. Introduced by Thompson, D-Miss., on May 7, 2012. House Judiciary reported May 29 (H Rept 112-497). House passed, under suspension of the rules, May 30. Senate Judiciary discharged. Senate passed September 22. President signed October 5, 2012.

PL 112-189 (HR 6189) Eliminate unnecessary reporting requirements for unfunded programs under the Office of Justice Programs. Introduced by Conyers, D-Mich., on July 25, 2012. House Judiciary reported September 10 (H Rept 112-648). House passed, under suspension of the rules, September 11. Senate Judiciary discharged. Senate passed September 22. President signed October 5, 2012.

PL 112-190 (HR 6215) Amend the Trademark Act of 1946 to correct an error in the provisions relating to remedies for dilution. Introduced by Smith, R-Texas, on July 26, 2012. House Judiciary reported September 10 (H Rept 112-647). House passed, under suspension of the rules, September 11. Senate Judiciary discharged. Senate passed September 22. President signed October 5, 2012.

PL 112-191 (HR 6375) Authorize certain Department of Veterans Affairs major medical facility projects to amend title 38, U.S. Code, to extend certain authorities of the secretary of Veterans Affairs. Introduced by Miller, R-Fla., on September 11, 2012. House passed, under suspension of the rules, September 19. Senate passed September 22. President signed October 5, 2012.

PL 112-192 (HR 6431) Provide flexibility with respect to U.S. support for assistance provided by international financial institutions for Burma. Introduced by Royce, R-Calif., on September 19, 2012. House passed, under suspension of the rules, September 19. Senate passed September 22. President signed October 5, 2012.

PL 112-193 (HR 6433) Make corrections with respect to Food and Drug Administration user fees. Introduced by Upton, R-Mich., on September 19, 2012. House Energy discharged. House passed September 19, 2012. Senate passed September 22. President signed October 5, 2012.

PL 112-194 (S 300) Prevent abuse of government charge cards. Introduced by Grassley, R-Iowa, on February 8, 2011. Senate Homeland Security and Governmental Affairs reported, amended, July 18 (S 112-37). Senate passed, amended, July 22, 2011. House Oversight and Government Reform reported January 27 (H Rept 112-376, Part 1). House Armed Services discharged. House passed, under suspension of the rules, August 1. Senate agreed to House amendment September 22. President signed October 5, 2012.

PL 112-195 (S 710) Amend the Solid Waste Disposal Act to direct the administrator of the Environmental Protection Agency to establish a hazardous-waste electronic-manifest system. Introduced by Thune, R-S.D., on March 31, 2011. Senate passed August 2, 2011. House Energy and Commerce reported September 10, 2012 (H Rept 112-654). House passed, amended, under suspension of the rules, September 11. Senate agreed to House amendment September 22. President signed October 5, 2012.

PL 112-196 (S 3624) Amend Section 31311 of Title 49, U.S. Code, to permit states to issue commercial driver's licenses to members of the Armed Forces whose duty station is located in the state. Introduced by Snowe, R-Maine, on September 22, 2012. Senate passed September 22. Transportation discharged. House passed September 28. President signed October 19, 2012.

PL 112-197 (HR 2606) Authorize the secretary of the Interior to allow the construction and operation of natural-gas pipeline facilities in the Gateway National Recreation Area. Introduced by Grimm, R-N.Y., on July 21, 2011. House Natural Resources reported, amended, January 3, 2012 (H Rept 112-373). House passed, under suspension of the rules, February 7. Senate Energy and Natural Resources discharged. Senate passed September 22. House agreed to Senate amendment November 14. President signed November 27, 2012.

PL 112-198 (HR 4114) Increase, effective December 1, 2012, the rates of compensation for veterans with service-connected disabilities and the rates of dependency and indemnity compensation for the survivors of certain disabled veterans. Introduced by Runyan, R-N.J., on February 29, 2012. House Veterans' Affairs reported May 18 (H Rept 112-486). House passed, under suspension of the rules, July 9. Senate Veterans' Affairs discharged. Senate passed November 13. President signed November 27, 2012.

PL 112-199 (S 743) Amend Chapter 23 of Title 5, U.S. Code, to clarify the disclosures of information protected from prohibited personnel practices; to require a statement in nondisclosure policies, forms, and agreements that such policies, forms, and agreements conform with certain disclosure protections; and to provide certain authority for the Special Counsel. Introduced by Akaka, D-Hawaii, on April 6, 2011. Senate Homeland Security and Governmental Affairs reported April 19, 2012 (S Rept 112-155). Senate passed, amended May 8. House Oversight and Government discharged. House Select Intelligence discharged. House Homeland Security discharged. House passed, under suspension of the rules, September 28. Senate agreed to House amendment November 13. President signed November 27, 2012.

PL 112-200 (S 1956) Prohibit operators of civil aircraft of the United States from participating in the European Union's emissions-trading scheme. Introduced by Thune, R-S.D., on December 7, 2011. Senate Commerce, Science and Transportation reported, amended, August 2, 2012 (S Rept 112-195). Senate passed, amended, September 22. House passed, under suspension of the rules, November 13. President signed November 27, 2012.

PL 112-201 (HR 2453) Require the secretary of the Treasury to mint coins in commemoration of Mark Twain. Introduced by Luetkemeyer, R-Mo., on July 7, 2011. House passed, under suspension of the rules, April 18, 2012. Senate Banking, Housing and Urban Affairs discharged. Senate passed, amended, September 22. House agreed to Senate amendments, under suspension of the rules, November 15. President signed December 4, 2012.

PL 112-202 (HR 6118) Amend Section 353 of the Public Health Service Act with respect to suspension, revocation, and limitation of laboratory certification. Introduced by Grimm, R-N.Y., on July 12, 2012. House passed, under suspension of the rules, September 19. Senate passed November 14. President signed December 4, 2012.

PL 112-203 (HR 6131) Extend the Undertaking Spam, Spyware, and Fraud Enforcement With Enforcers Beyond Borders Act of 2006. Introduced by Bono Mack, R-Calif., on July 17, 2012. House Energy and Commerce reported September 10 (H Rept 112-653). House passed, under suspension of the rules, September 11. Senate passed November 14. President signed December 4, 2012.

PL 112-204 (HR 6570) Amend the American Recovery and Reinvestment Act of 2009 and the Emergency Economic Stabilization Act of 2008 to consolidate certain CBO reporting requirements. Introduced by Garrett, R-N.J., on October 12, 2012. House passed, under suspension of the rules, November 14. Senate passed November 15. President signed December 4, 2012.

PL 112-205 (HR 915) Establish a Border Enforcement Security Task Force program to enhance border security by fostering coordinated efforts among federal, state, and local border and law enforcement officials to protect U.S. border cities and communities from transnational crime, including violence associated with drug trafficking, arms smuggling, illegal-alien trafficking and smuggling, violence, and kidnapping along and across the international borders of the United States. Introduced by Cuellar, D-Texas, on March 3, 2011. House Homeland Security reported, amended November 4 (H Rept 112-268). House passed, under suspension of the rules, May 30, 2012. Senate Homeland Security and Governmental Affairs reported, amended, August 28 (S Rept 112-206). Senate passed, amended, September 22. House agreed to the Senate amendment, under suspension of the rules, November 27. President signed December 7, 2012.

PL 112-206 (HR 6063) Amend Title 18, U.S. Code, with respect to child pornography and child exploitation offenses. Introduced by Smith, R-Texas, on June 29, 2012. House Judiciary reported, amended, July 31 (H Rept 112-638). House passed, under suspension of the rules, August 1. Senate Judiciary discharged. Senate passed November 26. President signed December 7, 2012.

PL 112-207 (HR 6634) Change the effective date for the Internet publication of certain financial-disclosure forms. Introduced by Cantor, R-Va., on December 5, 2012. Oversight and Government discharged. House Administration discharged. House passed December 5. Senate passed December 6. President signed December 7, 2012.

PL 112-208 (HR 6156) Authorize the extension of nondiscriminatory treatment (normal-trade-relations treatment) to products of the Russian Federation and Moldova and require reports on the compliance of the Russian Federation with its obligations as a member of the World Trade Organization. Introduced by Camp, R-Mich., on July 19, 2012. House Ways and Means reported July 31 (H Rept 112-632). House passed November 16. Senate passed December 6. President signed December 14, 2012.

PL 112-209 (HR 3187) Require the secretary of the Treasury to mint coins in recognition and celebration of the 75th anniversary of the establishment of the March of Dimes Foundation. Introduced by Dold, R-Ill., on October 13, 2011. House passed, under suspension of the rules, August 1, 2012. Senate passed December 10. President signed December 18, 2012.

PL 112-210 (HR 6582) Allow for innovations and alternative technologies that meet or exceed desired energy efficiency goals and to make technical corrections to existing federal energy efficiency laws to allow American manufacturers to remain competitive. Introduced by Aderholt, R-Ala., on November 2, 2012. House passed, under suspension of the rules, December 4. Senate passed December 6. President signed December 12, 2012.

PL 112-211 (S 3486) Implement the provisions of the Hague Agreement and the Patent Law Treaty. Introduced by Leahy, D-Vt., on August 2, 2012. Senate Judiciary reported, amended, September 20, 2012 (no written report). Senate passed, amended, September 22. House passed, under suspension of the rules, December 5. President signed December 10, 2012.

PL 112-212 (HR 2467) Take certain federal lands in Mono County, Calif., into trust for the benefit of the Bridgeport Indian Colony. Introduced by McKeon, R-Calif., on July 8, 2011. House Natural Resources reported, amended, July 19, 2012 (H Rept 112-611). House passed, under suspension of the rules, July 23. Senate Indian Affairs reported September 21 (no written report). Senate passed December 11. President signed December 20, 2012.

PL 112-213 (HR 2838) Authorize appropriations for the Coast Guard for fiscal 2013 and 2014. Introduced by Lobiondo, R-N.J., on September 2, 2011. House Transportation and Infrastructure reported, amended, October 3 (H Rept 112-229). House passed November 15. Senate Commerce, Science and Transportation discharged. Senate passed, amended, September 22, 2012. House agreed to Senate amendments, with an amendment, December 5. Senate agreed to House amendment December 12. President signed December 20, 2012.

PL 112-214 (HR 3319) Allow the Pascua Yaqui Tribe to determine the requirements for membership in that tribe. Introduced by Grijalva, D-Ariz., on November 2, 2011. House Natural Resources reported, amended, September 18, 2012 (H Rept 112-675). House passed, under suspension of the rules, September 19. Senate Indian Affairs discharged. Senate passed December 11. President signed December 20, 2012.

PL 112-215 (HR 4014) Amend the Federal Deposit Insurance Act with respect to information provided to the Bureau of Consumer Financial Protection. Introduced by Huizenga, R-Mich., on February 13, 2012. House Financial Services reported March 20 (H Rept 112-417). House passed, under suspension of the rules, March 26. Senate passed December 11. President signed December 20, 2012.

PL 112-216 (HR 4367) Amend the Electronic Fund Transfer Act to limit the fee disclosure requirement for an automatic-teller machine to the screen of that machine. Introduced by Luetkemeyer, R-Mo., on April 17, 2012. House Financial Services reported June 29 (H Rept 112-576). House passed, under suspension of the rules, July 9. Senate passed December 11. President signed December 20, 2012.

PL 112-217 (S 1998) Obtain an unqualified audit opinion and improve financial accountability and management at the Department of Homeland Security. Introduced by Brown, R-Mass., on December 15, 2011. Senate Homeland Security and Governmental Affairs reported, amended, November 2, 2012 (S Rept 112-230). Senate passed, amended, November 28. House passed, under suspension of the rules, December 12. President signed December 20, 2012.

PL 112-218 (S 3542) Authorize the assistant secretary of Homeland Security (Transportation Security Administration) to modify screening requirements for checked baggage arriving from preclearance airports. Introduced by Klobuchar, D-Minn., on September 13, 2012. Senate Commerce, Science and Transportation discharged. Senate passed, amended, November 29. House passed, under suspension of the rules, December 12. President signed December 20, 2012.

PL 112-219 (HR 3477) Designate the facility of the U.S. Postal Service located at 133 Hare Road in Crosby, Texas, as the "Army 1st Sgt. David McNerney Post Office Building." Introduced by Poe, R-Texas, on November 8, 2011. House passed, under suspension of the rules, July 3, 2012. Senate Homeland Security and Governmental Affairs discharged. Senate passed December 19. President signed December 28, 2012.

PL 112-220 (HR 3783) Provide for a comprehensive strategy to counter Iran's growing hostile presence and activity in the Western Hemisphere. Introduced by Duncan, R-S.C., on January 18, 2012. House passed, under suspension of the rules, September 19. Senate passed, amended, December 12. House agreed to Senate amendment, under suspension of the rules, December 18. President signed December 28, 2012.

PL 112-221 (HR 3870) Designate the facility of the U.S. Postal Service located at 6083 Highway 36 West in Rose Bud, Ark., as the "Nicky 'Nick' Daniel Bacon Post Office." Introduced by Griffin, R-Ark., on February 1, 2012. House passed, under suspension of the rules, July 23. Senate Homeland Security and Governmental Affairs discharged. Senate passed December 19. President signed December 28, 2012.

PL 112-222 (HR 3912) Designate the facility of the U.S. Postal Service located at 110 Mastic Road in Mastic Beach, N.Y., as the

"Brig. Gen. Nathaniel Woodhull Post Office Building." Introduced by Bishop, D-N.Y., on February 7, 2012. House passed, under suspension of the rules, November 28. Senate Homeland Security and Governmental Affairs discharged. Senate passed December 19. President signed December 28, 2012.

PL 112-223 (HR 5738) Designate the facility of the U.S. Postal Service located at 15285 Samohin Drive in Macomb, Mich., as the "Lance Cpl. Anthony A. DiLisio Clinton-Macomb Carrier Annex." Introduced by Miller, R-Mich., on May 11, 2012. House passed, under suspension of the rules, November 28. Senate Homeland Security and Governmental Affairs discharged. Senate passed December 19. President signed December 28, 2012.

PL 112-224 (HR 5837) Designate the facility of the U.S. Postal Service located at 26 East Genesee St. in Baldwinsville, N.Y., as the "Cpl. Kyle Schneider Post Office Building." Introduced by Buerkle, R-N.Y., on May 18, 2012. House passed, under suspension of the rules, July 23. Senate Homeland Security and Governmental Affairs discharged. Senate passed December 19. President signed December 28, 2012.

PL 112-225 (HR 5954) Designate the facility of the U.S. Postal Service located at 320 7th St. in Ellwood City, Pa., as the "Sgt. Leslie H. Sabo Jr. Post Office Building." Introduced by Altmire, D-Pa., on June 18, 2012. House passed, under suspension of the rules, November 28. Senate Homeland Security and Governmental Affairs discharged. Senate passed December 19. President signed December 28, 2012.

PL 112-226 (HR 6116) Amend the Revised Organic Act of the Virgin Islands to provide for direct review by the U.S. Supreme Court of decisions of the Virgin Islands Supreme Court. Introduced by Christensen, D-V.I., on July 12, 2012. House passed, under suspension of the rules, November 14. Senate Judiciary discharged. Senate passed December 13. President signed December 28, 2012.

PL 112-227 (HR 6223) Amend Section 1059(e) of the National Defense Authorization Act for Fiscal Year 2006 to clarify that a period of employment abroad by the Chief of Mission or U.S. Armed Forces as a translator or an interpreter or in a security-related position in an executive or managerial capacity is to be counted as a period of residence and physical presence in the United States for the purposes of qualifying for naturalization. Introduced by Dent, R-Pa., on July 26, 2012. House passed, under suspension of the rules, December 5. Senate passed December 17. President signed December 28, 2012.

PL 112-228 (H J Res 122) Establish the date for the counting of electoral votes for president and vice president cast by the electors in December 2012. Introduced by Denham, R-Calif., on December 18, 2012. House passed December 18. Senate passed December 18. President signed December 28, 2012.

PL 112-229 (S 1379) Amend Title 11, District of Columbia Official Code, to revise certain administrative authorities of the D.C. courts and to authorize the D.C. Public Defender Service to provide professional liability insurance for officers and employees of the service for claims relating to services furnished within the scope of employment with the Service. Introduced by Akaka, D-Hawaii, on July 18, 2011. Senate Homeland Security and Governmental Affairs reported, amended, June 25, 2012 (S Rept 112-178). Senate passed, amended, July 9. House passed, under suspension of the rules, December 13. President signed December 28, 2012.

PL 112-230 (S 2170) Amend the provisions of Title 5, U.S. Code, which are commonly referred to as the "Hatch Act," to scale back the provision forbidding certain state and local employees from seeking elective office, to clarify the application of certain provisions to the District of Columbia, and to modify the penalties that may be imposed for certain violations under Subchapter III of Chapter 73 of that title. Introduced by Akaka, D-Hawaii, on March 7, 2012. Senate Homeland Security and Governmental Affairs reported, amended, September 13 (S Rept 112-211). Senate passed, amended, November 30. House passed, under suspension of the rules, December 19. President signed December 28, 2012.

PL 112-231 (S 2367) Strike the word "lunatic" from federal law. Introduced by Conrad, D-N.D., on April 25, 2012. Senate Banking, Housing and Urban Affairs discharged. Senate passed May 23. House passed, under suspension of the rules, December 5. President signed December 28, 2012.

PL 112-232 (S 3193) Make technical corrections to the legal description of certain land to be held in trust for the Barona Band of Mission Indians. Introduced by Feinstein, D-Calif., on May 16, 2012. Senate Indian Affairs reported August 28 (S Rept 112-207). Senate passed, amended, September 22. House Natural Resources reported December 17 (H Rept 112-702). House passed, under suspension of the rules, December 17. President signed December 28, 2012.

PL 112-233 (S 3311) Designate the U.S. courthouse located at 2601 Second Ave. North in Billings, Mont., as the "James F. Battin U.S. Courthouse." Introduced by Baucus, D-Mont., on June 19, 2012. Senate Environment and Public Works reported July 10 (no written report). Senate passed September 22. House passed, under suspension of the rules, December 19. President signed December 28, 2012.

PL 112-234 (S 3315) Repeal or modify certain mandates of the Government Accountability Office. Introduced by Carper, D-Del., on June 20, 2012. Senate Homeland Security and Governmental Affairs reported, amended, September 19 (S Rept 112-219). Senate passed, amended, September 22. House passed, under suspension of the rules, December 13. President signed December 28, 2012.

PL 112-235 (S 3564) Extend the Public Interest Declassification Act of 2000 until 2014. Introduced by Lieberman, I-Conn., on September 19, 2012. Senate Homeland Security and Governmental Affairs discharged. Senate passed, amended, December 11. House passed, under suspension of the rules, December 19. President signed December 28, 2012.

PL 112-236 (S 3642) Clarify the scope of the Economic Espionage Act of 1996. Introduced by Leahy, D-Vt., on November 27, 2012. Senate passed November 27. House passed, under suspension of the rules, December 18. President signed December 28, 2012.

PL 112-237 (S 3687) Amend the Federal Water Pollution Control Act to reauthorize the Lake Pontchartrain Basin Restoration

Program, to designate certain federal buildings. Introduced by Boxer, D-Calif., on December 17, 2012. Senate passed December 17. House Transportation, Judiciary and Natural Resources discharged. House passed December 18. President signed December 28, 2012.

PL 112-238 (HR 5949) Extend the FISA Amendments Act of 2008 for five years. Introduced by Smith, R-Texas, on June 15, 2012. House Judiciary reported, amended, August 2 (H Rept 112-645, Part 1). House Select Intelligence reported, amended, August 2 (H Rept 112-645, Part 2). House passed September 12. Senate passed December 28. President signed December 30, 2012.

PL 112-239 (HR 4310) Authorize appropriations for fiscal 2013 for military activities of the Department of Defense, for military construction and for defense activities of the Department of Energy, to prescribe military personnel strengths for such fiscal year. Introduced by McKeon, R-Calif., on March 29, 2012. House Armed Services reported, amended, May 11 (H Rept 112-479). House passed May 18. Senate Armed Services discharged. Senate passed, amended, December 4. Senate passed, amended, December 12. House agreed to conference report December 20. Senate agreed to conference report December 21. President signed January 2, 2013.

PL 112-240 (HR 8) Permanently extend the 2001 and 2003 tax rates for individual income less than $400,000 and joint-filer income less than $450,000. Introduced by Camp, R-Mich., on July 24, 2012. House passed August 1. Senate passed January 1, 2013. House agreed to the Senate amendments January 1. President signed January 2, 2013.

PL 112-241 (HR 1339) Designate the City of Salem, Mass., as the birthplace of the National Guard of the United States. Introduced by Tierney, D-Mass., on April 1, 2011. House passed, amended, under suspension of the rules, March 28, 2012. Senate Armed Services discharged. Senate passed December 21. President signed January 10, 2013.

PL 112-242 (HR 1845) Provide a demonstration project providing Medicare coverage for in-home administration of intravenous immune globulin and amend Title XVIII of the Social Security Act with respect to the application of Medicare secondary-payer rules for certain claims. Introduced by Brady, R-Texas, on May 11, 2011. House passed, under suspension of the rules, December 19. Senate passed December 21. President signed January 10, 2013.

PL 112-243 (HR 2338) Designate the facility of the U.S. Postal Service located at 600 Florida Ave. in Cocoa, Fla., as the "Harry T. and Harriette Moore Post Office." Introduced by Posey, R-Fla., on June 23, 2011. House passed, under suspension of the rules, November 28, 2012. Senate Homeland Security and Governmental Affairs discharged. Senate passed December 27. President signed January 10, 2013.

PL 112-244 (HR 3263) Authorize the secretary of the Interior to allow the storage and conveyance of nonproject water at the Norman project in Oklahoma. Introduced by Cole, R-Okla., on October 26, 2011. House Natural Resources reported April 16, 2012 (H Rept 112-442). House passed, under suspension of the rules, June 5. Senate passed December 30. President signed January 10, 2013.

PL 112-245 (HR 3641) Establish Pinnacles National Park in the state of California as a unit of the National Park System. Introduced by Farr, D-Calif., on December 13, 2011. House Natural Resources reported, amended, July 26, 2012 (H Rept 112-626). House passed, amended, under suspension of the rules, July 31. Senate passed December 30. President signed January 10, 2013.

PL 112-246 (HR 3869) Designate the facility of the U.S. Postal Service located at 600 E. Capitol Ave. in Little Rock, Ark., as the "Sidney 'Sid' Sanders McMath Post Office Building." Introduced by Griffin, R-Ark., on February 1, 2012. House passed, under suspension of the rules, December 20. Senate passed December 27. President signed January 10, 2013.

PL 112-247 (HR 3892) Designate the facility of the U.S. Postal Service located at 8771 Auburn Folsom Road in Roseville, Calif., as the "Lance Cpl. Victor A. Dew Post Office." Introduced by McClintock, R-Calif., on February 2, 2012. House passed, amended, under suspension of the rules, November 28. Senate Homeland Security and Governmental Affairs discharged. Senate passed December 27. President signed January 10, 2013.

PL 112-248 (HR 4053) Intensify efforts to identify, prevent and recover payment error, waste, fraud and abuse within federal spending. Introduced by Towns, D-N.Y., on February 16, 2012. House Oversight and Government Reform reported, amended, November 30 (H Rept 112-698). House passed, amended, under suspension of the rules, December 13. Senate passed December 20. President signed January 10, 2013.

PL 112-249 (HR 4057) Amend Title 38, U.S. Code, to direct the secretary of Veterans Affairs to develop a comprehensive policy to improve outreach and transparency to veterans and members of the Armed Forces through the provision of information on institutions of higher learning. Introduced by Bilirakis, R-Fla., on February 16, 2012. House Veterans' Affairs reported, amended, September 10 (H Rept 112-646). House passed, amended, under suspension of the rules, September 11. Senate Veterans' Affairs discharged. Senate passed, amended, December 19. House agreed to Senate amendment, under suspension of the rules, December 30. President signed January 10, 2013.

PL 112-250 (HR 4073) Authorize the secretary of Agriculture to accept the quitclaim, disclaimer, and relinquishment of a railroad right of way within and adjacent to Pike National Forest in El Paso County, Colo., originally granted to the Mount Manitou Park and Incline Railway Co. pursuant to the Act of March 3, 1875. Introduced by Lamborn, R-Colo., on February 17, 2012. House Natural Resources reported, amended, July 17 (H Rept 112-599). House passed, amended, under suspension of the rules, August 1. Senate passed December 30. President signed January 10, 2013.

PL 112-251 (HR 4389) Designate the facility of the U.S. Postal Service located at 19 E. Merced St. in Fowler, Calif., as the "Cecil E. Bolt Post Office." Introduced by Costa, D-Calif., on April 18, 2012. House passed, under suspension of the rules, December 20. Senate passed December 27. President signed January 10, 2013.

PL 112-252 (HR 5859) Repeal an obsolete provision in Title 49, U.S. Code, requiring motor vehicle insurance cost reporting.

Introduced by Harper, R-Miss., on May 30, 2012. House Energy and Commerce reported, amended, July 10 (H Rept 112-591). House passed, amended, under suspension of the rules, July 23. Senate Commerce, Science and Transportation discharged. Senate passed December 21. President signed January 10, 2013.

PL 112-253 (HR 6014) Authorize the attorney general to award grants for states to implement collection processes for arrestee DNA. Introduced by Schiff, D-Calif., on June 21, 2012. House passed, amended, under suspension of the rules, December 18. Senate passed December 28. President signed January 10, 2013.

PL 112-254 (HR 6260) Designate the facility of the U.S. Postal Service located at 211 Hope St. in Mountain View, Calif., as the "Lt. Kenneth M. Ballard Memorial Post Office." Introduced by Eshoo, D-Calif., on August 1, 2012. House passed, under suspension of the rules, December 20. Senate passed December 27. President signed January 10, 2013.

PL 112-255 (HR 6379) Designate the facility of the U.S. Postal Service located at 6239 Savannah Highway in Ravenel, S.C., as the "Rep. Curtis B. Inabinett Sr. Post Office." Introduced by Clyburn, D-S.C., on September 12, 2012. House passed, under suspension of the rules, December 20. Senate passed December 27. President signed January 10, 2013.

PL 112-256 (HR 6587) Designate the facility of the U.S. Postal Service located at 225 Simi Village Drive in Simi Valley, Calif., as the "Postal Inspector Terry Asbury Post Office Building." Introduced by Gallegly, R-Calif., on November 13, 2012. House passed, under suspension of the rules, December 20. Senate passed December 27. President signed January 10, 2013.

PL 112-257 (HR 6620) Amend Title 18, U.S. Code, to eliminate certain limitations on the length of Secret Service protection for former presidents and for the children of former presidents. Introduced by Gowdy, R-S.C., on November 30, 2012. House passed, under suspension of the rules, December 5. Senate Judiciary discharged. Senate passed December 28. President signed January 10, 2013.

PL 112-258 (HR 6671) Amend Section 2710 of Title 18, U.S. Code, to clarify that a videotape service provider may obtain a consumer's informed, written consent on an ongoing basis and that consent may be obtained through the Internet. Introduced by Goodlatte, R-Va., on December 17, 2012. House passed, under suspension of the rules, December 18. Senate passed December 20. President signed January 10, 2013.

PL 112-259 (S 925) Designate a mountain peak in Mono County, Calif., as "Mount Andrea Lawrence" in honor of the renowned conservationist, three-time Olympian, and former member of the Mono County Board of Supervisors who passed away in 2009. Introduced by Boxer, D-Calif., on May 9, 2011. Senate Energy and Natural Resources discharged. Senate passed October 18. House Natural Resources reported May 30, 2012 (H Rept 112-506). House passed, under suspension of the rules, December 20. President signed January 10, 2013.

PL 112-260 (S 3202) Amend Title 38, U.S. Code, to ensure that deceased veterans with no known next of kin can receive a dignified burial. Introduced by Murray, D-Wash., on May 17, 2012. Senate Veterans' Affairs discharged. Senate passed, amended, December 19. House passed, under suspension of the rules, December 30. President signed January 10, 2013.

PL 112-261 (S 3666) Amend the Animal Welfare Act to modify the definition of "exhibitor." Introduced by Vitter, R-La., on December 6, 2012. Senate Veterans' Affairs discharged. Senate passed, amended, December 19. House passed, under suspension of the rules, December 30. President signed January 10, 2013.

PL 112-262 (S J Res 49) Provide for the appointment of Barbara Barrett as a citizen regent of the Board of Regents of the Smithsonian Institution. Introduced by Leahy, D-Vt., on August 1, 2012. Senate passed August 1. House Administration discharged. House passed December 20. President signed January 10, 2013.

PL 112-263 (HR 443) Provide for the conveyance of certain property from the United States to the Maniilaq Association located in Kotzebue, Alaska. Introduced by Young, R-Alaska, on January 25, 2011. House Natural Resources reported, amended, December 8. (H Rept 112-318, Part 1). Energy and Commerce discharged December 8. House passed, amended, under suspension of the rules, December 15. Senate Indian Affairs reported, December 13, 2012 (S Rept 112-250). Senate passed, amended, December 20. House agreed to Senate amendment, under suspension of the rules, January 1, 2013. President signed January 14, 2013.

PL 112-264 (HR 1464) Express the sense of Congress regarding North Korean children and the children of one North Korean parent and to require the Department of State to regularly brief appropriate congressional committees on efforts to advocate for and develop a strategy to provide assistance in the best interest of these children. Introduced by Royce, R-Calif., on April 8, 2011. House passed, under suspension of the rules, September 11, 2012. Senate Foreign Relations discharged. Senate passed, amended, December 28. House agreed to the Senate amendments January 1, 2013. President signed January 14, 2013.

PL 112-265 (HR 2076) Amend Title 28, U.S. Code, to clarify the statutory authority for the Justice Department's long-standing practice of providing investigatory assistance on request of state and local authorities with respect to certain serious violent crimes. Introduced by Gowdy, R-S.C., on June 1, 2011. House Judiciary reported, amended, January 29, 2012 (H Rept 112-186). House passed, amended, under suspension of the rules, September 12. Senate Judiciary reported, amended, November 17 (no written report). Senate passed, amended, December 17. House agreed to the Senate amendment, under suspension of the rules, January 1, 2013. President signed January 14, 2013.

PL 112-266 (HR 4212) Prevent the introduction into commerce of unsafe drywall, ensure that the manufacturer of drywall is readily identifiable, and ensure that problematic drywall removed from homes is not reused. Introduced by Rigell, R-Va., on March 19, 2012. House passed, amended, under suspension of the rules, September 19. Senate Commerce, Science and Transportation discharged. Senate passed, amended, December 21. House agreed to the Senate amendment, under suspension of the rules, January 1, 2013. President signed January 14, 2013.

PL 112-267 (HR 4365) Amend Title 5, U.S. Code, to make clear that accounts in the Thrift Savings Fund are subject to certain federal tax levies. Introduced by Buerkle, R-N.Y., on April 17, 2012. House Oversight and Government Reform reported, amended, July 30 (H Rept 112-630). House passed, amended, under suspension of the rules, August 1. Senate Homeland Security and Governmental Affairs discharged. Senate passed January 1, 2013. President signed January 14, 2013.

PL 112-268 (HR 4606) Authorize the issuance of right-of-way permits for natural-gas pipelines in Glacier National Park. Introduced by Rehberg, R-Mont., on April 24, 2012. House Natural Resources reported, amended, July 26 (H Rept 112-627). House passed, amended, under suspension of the rules, December 17. Senate passed January 2, 2013. President signed January 14, 2013.

PL 112-269 (HR 6029) Amend Title 18, U.S. Code, to provide for increased penalties for foreign and economic espionage. Introduced by Smith, R-Texas, on June 27, 2012. House Judiciary reported July 19 (H Rept 112-610). House passed, under suspension of the rules, August 1. Senate passed, amended, December 19. House agreed to the Senate amendment, under suspension of the rules, January 1, 2013. President signed January 14, 2013.

PL 112-270 (HR 6060) Amend Public Law 106-392 to maintain annual base funding for the Upper Colorado and San Juan fish recovery programs through fiscal 2019. Introduced by Bishop, R-Utah, on June 29, 2012. House Natural Resources reported September 14 (H Rept 112-672). House passed, under suspension of the rules, September 19. Senate Energy and Natural Resources discharged. Senate passed January 1, 2013. President signed January 14, 2013.

PL 112-271 (HR 6328) Amend Title 49, U.S. Code, to direct the assistant secretary of Homeland Security (Transportation Security Administration) to transfer unclaimed clothing recovered at airport security checkpoints to local veterans organizations and other local charitable organizations. Introduced by Hochul, D-N.Y., on August 2, 2012. House passed, under suspension of the rules, November 27. Senate passed, amended, December 11. House agreed to Senate amendment, under suspension of the rules, January 1, 2013. President signed January 14, 2013.

PL 112-272 (HR 6364) Establish a commission to ensure a suitable observance of the centennial of World War I and to provide for the designation of memorials to the service of members of the U.S. Armed Forces in World War I. Introduced by Poe, R-Texas, on September 10, 2012. House Natural Resources reported, amended, December 12 (H Rept 112-701, Part 1). House passed, amended, under suspension of the rules, December 12. Senate passed, amended, December 21. House agreed to Senate amendment, December 31. President signed January 14, 2013.

PL 112-273 (HR 6586) Extend the application of certain space launch liability provisions through 2014. Introduced by Palazzo, R-Miss., on November 9, 2012. House passed, under suspension of the rules, November 13. Senate passed, amended, January 1, 2013. House agreed to the Senate amendment January 2. President signed January 14, 2013.

PL 112-274 (HR 6621) Correct and improve certain provisions of the Leahy-Smith America Invents Act and Title 35, U.S. Code. Introduced by Smith, R-Texas, on November 30, 2012. House passed, amended, under suspension of the rules, December 18. Senate passed, amended, December 28. House agreed to Senate amendment, under suspension of the rules, January 1, 2013. President signed January 14, 2013.

PL 112-275 (HR 6655) Establish a commission to develop a national strategy and recommendations for reducing fatalities resulting from child abuse and neglect. Introduced by Doggett, D-Texas, on December 13, 2012. House passed, under suspension of the rules, December 19. Senate Health, Education, Labor and Pensions discharged January 2, 2013. Senate Finance discharged January 2. Senate passed January 2. President signed January 14, 2013.

PL 112-276 (S 3331) Provide for universal intercountry adoption accreditation standards. Introduced by Kerry, D-Mass., on June 21, 2012. Senate Foreign Relations reported November 13 (S Rept 112-234). Senate passed, amended, December 5. House passed, under suspension of the rules, January 1, 2013. President signed January 14, 2013.

PL 112-277 (S 3454) Authorize appropriations for fiscal 2013 for intelligence and intelligence-related activities of the U.S. government, the Office of the Director of National Intelligence, and the Central Intelligence Agency Retirement and Disability System. Introduced by Feinstein, D-Calif., on July 30, 2012. Senate Select Intelligence reported July 30 (S Rept 112-192). Senate passed, amended, December 28. House passed, under suspension of the rules, December 31. President signed January 14, 2013.

PL 112-278 (S 3472) Amend the Family Educational Rights and Privacy Act of 1974. Introduced by Landrieu, D-La., on August 1, 2012. Senate Health, Education, Labor and Pensions discharged. Senate passed, amended, December 17. House passed, under suspension of the rules, January 1, 2013. President signed January 14, 2013.

PL 112-279 (S 3630) Designate the facility of the U.S. Postal Service located at 218 N. Milwaukee St. in Waterford, Wis., as the "Capt. Rhett W. Schiller Post Office." Introduced by Johnson, R-Wis., on November 14, 2012. Senate Homeland Security and Governmental Affairs discharged. Senate passed December 19. House passed, under suspension of the rules, January 1, 2013. President signed January 14, 2013.

PL 112-280 (S 3662) Designate the facility of the U.S. Postal Service located at 6 Nichols St. in Westminster, Mass., as the "Lt. Ryan Patrick Jones Post Office Building." Introduced by Brown, R-Mass., on December 5, 2012. Senate Homeland Security and Governmental Affairs discharged. Senate passed December 19. House passed, under suspension of the rules, January 1, 2013. President signed January 14, 2013.

PL 112-281 (S 3677) Make a technical correction to the Flood Disaster Protection Act of 1973. Introduced by Johnson, D-S.D., on December 12, 2012. Senate passed December 12. Financial Services discharged January 1, 2013. House passed January 1. President signed January 14, 2013.

PL 112-282 (S J Res 44) Grant the consent of Congress to the State and Province Emergency Management Assistance Memorandum of Understanding. Introduced by Kohl, D-Wis., on June 14, 2012. Senate Judiciary reported August 2 (no written report). Senate passed September 13. House passed, under suspension of the rules, January 1, 2013. President signed January 14, 2013.

PL 112-283 (S 2318) Authorize the secretary of state to pay a reward to combat transnational organized crime and for information concerning foreign nationals wanted by international criminal tribunals. Introduced by Kerry, D-Mass., on April 19, 2012. Senate Foreign Relations reported, amended, November 13 (S Rept 112-232). Senate passed, amended, December 19. House passed, under suspension of the rules, January 1, 2013. President signed January 15, 2013.

Index to Legislation by Public Law Number

The following index is a supplement to the primary index for the volume. It is organized by the public law number for legislation enacted by the 111th Congress and the 112th Congress between 2009 and 2013. Congress in recent years has approved many bills on different subjects using a single piece of legislation. This index will help a reader who knows a public law number locate material in different parts of the volume. For example, PL 111-5 below included provisions on economic stimulus, education, homebuyer assistance, unemployment compensation, and executive pay.

Legislation	*Public law Number*	*Number Page*
Ineligibility Clause	111-1	684
Employment wage-gender discrimination	111-2	528
Children's Health Insurance Program (CHIP)	111-3	445
Economic stimulus	111-5	61, 76, 78, 114, 386, 478
Race to the Top	111-5	480
Homebuyer tax credit	111-5	79, 503
Unemployment compensation extension 2009	111-5	519
Executive pay	111-5	530
Fiscal 2009 omnibus appropriations	111-8	114, 119
Fiscal 2009 State-foreign operations funding	111-8	232
District of Columbia school vouchers	111-8	481
Congressional pay freeze 2010	111-8	683
Public lands	111-11	374
Community service programs	111-13	604
Mortgage relief assistance	111-22	76, 79, 500
Defense acquisition rules	111-23	267
Credit card restrictions	111-24	84
Firearms on federal lands	111-24	559
Patent law overhaul	111-29	561, 568
Tobacco regulation	111-31	448
Fiscal 2009 second supplemental appropriations	111-32	76, 122, 233
Fiscal 2009 war supplemental	111-32	269
Cash for clunkers	111-32	79, 321
Highway trust fund money	111-46	324
Unemployment compensation funding extension through 2009	111-46	519
Cash for clunkers program extension	111-47	79, 321, 324
Congressional pay freeze 2011	111-65	112
Fiscal 2010 legislative branch appropriations/continuing resolution	111-68	114, 128
Chemical plant security	111-68	212
Surface transportation authorization	111-68	326
Postal service retiree benefit	111-68	601
Online disclosure of Senate expenditures	111-68	650
FAA reauthorization	111-69	331
Pakistan aid authorization	111-73	236
Fiscal 2010 agriculture appropriations	111-80	128, 412
Veterans health programs	111-81	280
Fiscal 2010 homeland security appropriations	111-83	129, 209
Chemical plant security	111-83	212
Fiscal 2010 defense authorization	111-84	273
Minimum wage: Guam construction workers	111-84	530
Hate crimes	111-84	553
Merit-based pay plan	111-84	600
Fiscal 2010 energy, water appropriations	111-85	128
Strategic Petroleum Reserve oil sources	111-85	241
Ryan White AIDS reauthorization	111-87	452
Fiscal 2010 Interior, environment appropriations; continuing resolution	111-88	114, 129
Surface transportation authorization	111-88	326
Fiscal 2010 Interior and environment Funds	111-88	382
Homebuyer tax credit	111-92	79, 503
Unemployment compensation benefits expansion, 2009	111-92	76, 521
FAA reauthorization extension	111-116	331
Fiscal 2010 omnibus appropriations	111-117	127, 130
Export-Import credits for Iran suppliers	111-117	241
Fiscal 2010 State-foreign operations funding	111-117	243
Fiscal 2010 military construction appropriations	111-117	284
District of Columbia school vouchers	111-117	127, 243, 481
Minimum wage in U.S. territories	111-117	529
Fiscal 2010 defense appropriations	111-118	133
Patriot Act two-month extension at end of 2009	111-118	208
Fiscal 2010 defense appropriations	111-118	280
Surface transportation authorization	111-118	326
Medicare physician payments through February 28, 2010	111-118	450, 451
Unemployment compensation extension to February 28, 2010	111-118	521
COBRA subsidy first extension	111-118	525
Apology to native Americans	111-118	617
Debt ceiling increase, 2009	111-123	114, 134
Franklin Delano Roosevelt memorabilia	111-138	615
Debt ceiling increase, 2010	111-139	141

Legislation	*Public law Number*	*Number Page*
Budget enforcement rules: PAYGO	111-139	114, 142
Patriot Act one year extension through February 28, 2011	111-141	208
Social Security lawsuits	111-142	565
Medicare physician payments through March 31, 2010	111-144	450,451
Unemployment compensation extension to April 2010	111-144	522
COBRA subsidy second extension	111-144	526
Surface transportation authorization	111-147	327
Job creation and protection	111-147	76, 85, 527
Health care overhaul	111-148	421
Indian health service	111-148	617
Health care law changes	111-152	421, 436, 476
Federal student loans	111-152	476, 479
Medicare physician payments through May 31, 2010	111-157	450, 452
Unemployment compensation extension to June 2010	111-157	522
COBRA subsidy third extension	111-157	526
FAA reauthorization extension	111-161	331
Deceptive use of Census	111-170	614
Administrative changes to federal courts	111-174	566
Satellite and cable programming	111-175	335
Oil Spill Liability Trust Fund	111-191	376
Medicare physician payments through November 30, 2010	111-192	450, 452
Iran sanctions	111-195	238
FAA reauthorization extension	111-197	331
Formaldehyde emissions	111-199	379
TARP program terminated	111-203	78
Financial regulation overhaul	111-203	62, 68, 76, 88, 105
Drywall safety	111-203	508
Shareholder, SEC oversight of executive pay	111-203	98, 532
Improper payments elimination	111-204	612, 634
Unemployment compensation extension to November 30, 2010	111-205	523
Law enforcement on tribal lands	111-211	563
Fiscal 2010 war supplemental appropriations	111-212	138, 286
FAA reauthorization extension	111-216	332
Airline safety, pilot training	111-216	332
Penalties for crack cocaine	111-220	562
Teachers, Medicaid supplemental appropriations	111-226	76, 140
Medical, education spending	111-226	76, 453
Education jobs fund	111-226	76, 479, 480
Border security supplemental appropriations	111-230	139
Border security funding	111-230	212
Small business assistance	111-240	76, 102
Fiscal 2011 appropriations first continuing resolution	111-242	138
FAA reauthorization extension	111-249	332
Information over-classification	111-258	613
Fiscal 2010 intelligence authorization	111-259	245
E-reader accessibility	111-260	479
NASA reauthorization	111-267	605
Plain writing	111-274	613
Medicare physician payments through December 31, 2010	111-286	450, 452
Fiscal 2011 appropriations two week continuing resolution	111-290	138
Legal settlements: American Indians, black farmers	111-291	413, 555
Temporary Assistance for Needy Families TANF	111-291	556
Federal teleworking	111-292	601
Haitian children	111-293	565
Animal crush videos	111-294	562
Child nutrition	111-296	465
Medicare physician payments extension through 2011	111-309	450, 452
Employee payroll tax cut	111-312	77, 108
Bush-era tax cuts extended	111-312	66, 76, 114, 144
Estate taxes	111-312	146
Tax breaks extension	111-312	66, 76, 147
Unemployment compensation extension through 2011	111-312	76, 524
'Don't Ask, Don't Tell' repeal	111-321	289
Fiscal 2011 appropriations extension to March 4, 2011	111-322	138
State Department authorization bill	111-322	241
Yucca Mountain nuclear waste	111-322	377
Fannie, Freddie mortgage guarantees	111-322	503
Federal worker pay freeze	111-322	600
FAA reauthorization extension	111-329	332
Caller ID spoofing	111-331	563
Trade preference extensions	111-334	194
Internet schemes	111-345	563
Government agencies efficiency	111-352	612
Food Safety	111-353	409
America COMPETES Act reauthorization	111-358	607
Lead pipes	111-380	378
Fiscal 2011 defense authorization	111-383	291
Surface transportation authorization	112-2	344
Fiscal 2011 appropriations continuing resolution to March 18, 2011	112-4	151
Fiscal 2011 appropriations continuing resolution to April 8, 2011	112-6	121, 151
Fiscal 2011 appropriations continuing resolution to April 15, 2011	112-8	151, 152
Tax reporting requirement	112-9	169, 456
Health law reporting requirement repeal	112-9	169, 456
Fiscal 2011 omnibus appropriations	112-10	115, 150, 152
Fiscal 2011 State-foreign operations funding	112-10	248, 249
Fiscal 2011 defense appropriations	112-10	295, 296
Fiscal 2011 military construction-VA appropriations	112-10	297
Fiscal 2011 Interior and environmental funds	112-10	401
Pell college grants	112-10	486
District of Columbia school vouchers	112-10	481
Constellation space program	112-10	626
Patriot Act extension	112-14	214
FAA reauthorization extension	112-16	351
Fiscal 2011 intelligence authorization	112-18	250
Federal employee intelligence leaks	112-18	622
FAA reauthorization extension	112-21	351
Debt limit increase, Budget Control Act	112-25	115, 160
Balanced budget amendment	112-25	167
Stafford loan limits	112-25	486
Unsubsidized college loan limits	112-25	486
FAA reauthorization extension	112-27	351
Fiscal 2012 appropriations continuing resolutions	112-33	115, 168, 170

Legislation	Public law Number	Number Page
Fiscal 2012 appropriations continuing resolutions	112-36	115, 168
Trade Adjustment Assistance-GPS extension	112-40	77, 199
Korea trade pact	112-41	196
Trade preference extensions	112-42	194
Colombia trade pact	112-42	197
Panama trade pact	112-43	198
Fiscal 2012 appropriations continuing resolution	112-55	115, 168, 170
Fiscal 2012 'Minibus' appropriations; COPS program	112-55	115, 170, 575
Nutrition program	112-55	468
Fiscal 2012 appropriations: Commerce-Justice-science	112-55	572
Job creation legislation	112-56	106
Contractor tax withholding repeal	112-56	106, 169, 630
Peace Corps volunteer protection	112-57	624
Fiscal 2012 appropriations continuing resolutions	112-67	168, 170
Fiscal 2012 appropriations continuing resolutions	112-68	168, 170
Fiscal 2012 omnibus appropriations	112-74	116, 172, 670
Fiscal 2012 State-foreign operations funding	112-74	252
Fiscal 2012 defense appropriations	112-74	304
Fiscal 2012 Interior and environmental funding	112-74	402
Pell college grants maximum grant level	112-74	487
Race to the Top funding	112-74	492, 494
Disaster assistance funding	112-77	176
Employee payroll tax cut	112-78	77, 108,
Industrial boilers regulation	112-78	388
Keystone pipeline	112-78	390
Medical physician payments to March 2012	112-78	463
Unemployment compensation extension to March 2012	112-78	77, 535
Iran Central Bank, financial institutions	112-81	241
Fiscal 2012 defense authorization	112-81	299
Pipeline safety	112-90	401
FAA reauthorization extension	112-91	351
FAA reauthorization	112-95	349
Rail and aviation union elections	112-95	539
Keystone pipeline	112-96	390
Medicare physician payments through 2012	112-96	463
Unemployment compensation extension through 2012	112-96	77, 536
Pension rules	112-96	542
Federal workforce pensions	112-96	621
STOCK Act for members of Congress	112-105	665
Small business regulation eased	112-106	110

Legislation	Public law Number	Number Page
Export-Import bank reauthorization	112-122	200
Drug traffickers	112-127	580
Surface transportation authorization	112-141	340
Environmental regulation on transportation	112-141	386
Federal student loans	112-141	485
Rural schools	112-141	491
National Flood Insurance	112-141	610, 624
Food and Drug Administration user fees	112-144	460
Minimum wages: American Samoa workers	112-149	541
Iran sanctions	112-158	255
Trade measures package	112-163	200
Senate confirmations	112-166	669
Fiscal 2013 appropriations continuing resolution	112-175	115, 180
Fiscal 2013 appropriations roundup	112-175	181
Fiscal 2013 State-foreign operations funding	112-175	258
Fiscal 2013 defense appropriations	112-175	312
Race to the Top funding	112-175	492, 494
Federal worker pay freeze	112-175	621, 622
Congressional pay freeze 2012	112-175	685
Mark Twain commemorative coin	112-201	629
Child pornography	112-206	581
Russian trade normalization	112-208	201
Coast Guard reauthorization	112-213	218
Privileged information clarification	112-215	105
Hatch Act modernization	112-230	622
FISA extension	112-238	215
Iran sanctions	112-239	257
Fiscal 2013 defense authorization	112-239	307
Fiscal cliff	112-240	67, 77, 115, 185
Trade adjustment assistance extension	112-240	199
Farm legislation extension	112-240	414
Health care: tax reporting, CLASS Act repeal	112-240	456
Consumer owned and oriented plans repeal	112-240	457
Medicare physician payments through 2013	112-240	464
Unemployment compensation extension through 2013	112-240	77, 537
Federal worker pay/sequestration	112-240	77, 622
Congressional pay freeze 2013	112-240	685
Drywall safety	112-266	511
Trade secrets	112-269	580
Fiscal 2013 intelligence authorization	112-277	254
Superstorm Sandy supplemental funding	113-1	189, 625, 626
Superstorm Sandy supplemental funding	113-2	189, 625, 626
Federal worker pay	113-6	622

Index

Abbas, Mahmoud, 228
ABC World News, 693
Abdulmutallab, Umar Farouk, 207 (box)
Abercrombie, Neil (D-Hawaii), 492
  minimum wage, 530
  Native Hawaiian government, 618
Abortion, 578–579
  Affordable Care Act, 4–5, 8, 424 (box), 425, 430, 431, 432 (box), 434–435, 438, 458 (box)
  appropriations
    FY 2010, 131
    FY 2011, 152
  Hyde amendment, 432–433 (box)
  Mexico City policy, 131, 176, 185, 244, 248, 252, 253, 258
  for military service members, 308, 310–311
  rape and funding for, 131, 432 (box)
  United Nations Population Fund, 176, 185, 252
  See also Birth control
Abramoff, Jack, 660
Abrams tanks, 312
Abstinence-only sex education, 132, 175
Abu Ghraib prison, 235 (box)
Abzug, Bella S. (D-N.Y.), 644 (box)
Accountable Care Organizations, 441
Ackerman, Gary (D-N.Y.), 851
ACLU. *See* American Civil Liberties Union (ACLU)
ACORN. *See* Association of Community Organizers for Reform Now (ACORN)
Acquired immunodeficiency syndrome. *See* AIDS/HIV
ADA. *See* Americans with Disabilities Act (ADA)
Adams, Sandy (R-Fla.)
  abortion, 579
  Violence Against Women Act, 573
ADEA (Age Discrimination in Employment Act). *See* Age Discrimination in Employment Act (ADEA)
Adelson, Sheldon, 36
Aderholt, Robert B. (R-Ala.), 339, 849
Administration Committee (House). *See* House Administration Committee
Adolescents and youth
  Affordable Care Act, 424 (box), 439–440
  antibullying and gang prevention, 491–492
  homeless, 512
  "morning after" pill access, 422 (box)
  sex education, 443
  teen pregnancy prevention, 131
Adoption credit, 444
Adult Education and Family Literacy Act (AEFLA), 492
Advanced Research Projects Agency-Energy (ARPA-E), 153
Advertising
  cigarettes, 450
  drug companies, 461
  online, 685
  prescription drugs, 461
  tobacco, 450
Aegis cruisers, 182
Affordable Care Act, 3, 15, 34, 44, 419
  Accountable Care Organizations, 441
  administrative action, 426–427
  American Health Benefit Exchanges, 421–422
  benefits
    abortion, 4–5, 8, 424 (box), 425, 430, 431, 432 (box), 434–435, 438, 458 (box)
    automatic enrollment in employer health plans, 439
    Basic Health Plan, 437
    benefit structure, 437
    contraception coverage, 422 (box), 459 (box)
    essential benefits package, 437
  biologic drug patents, 442
  Center for Medicare and Medicaid Innovation, 184, 441
  charitable hospitals, 444
  Children's Health Insurance Program, 424 (box), 426, 437, 439
  CLASS act, 442
    repeal, 456–457 (box), 457
  community health centers, 442
  comparative-effectiveness research, 442
  coverage
    preventive care, 440
    of young adults, 424 (box), 439–440
  deficit impact, 426, 430 (box)
  disproportionate-share payments, 441
  employers
    mandate, 426, 429, 430 (box)
    penalties, 438
    vouchers, 438–439
  executive compensation deductions, 444
  fees
    health insurance industry, 443–444
    pharmaceutical industry, 443
  flexible spending caps, 444
  health insurance overhaul implementation fund, 443
  Indian tribal governments exclusion, 445
  individual mandate, 423 (box), 426, 430 (box), 438, 455 (box), 456
    penalties, 438

legislative action
2009, 427
2010, 435
final House floor action, 435–436
final Senate floor action, 436
House Education and Labor Committee, 427–428
House Energy and Commerce Committee, 428
House floor action, 431–433
House *vs.* Senate provisions, 423–424 (box)
House Ways and Means Committee, 427
Indian Health Care Improvement Act, 443
Senate compromises, 434–435
Senate Finance Committee, 429–431
Senate floor action, 433–434
Senate HELP panel, 428–429
limits
on deductibles, 424 (box), 440
health spending account, 444
lifetime spending, 424 (box), 440
on out-of-pocket costs, 437–438
long-term care, 442
major highlights, 425–426
major provisions, 436–444
market basket updates, 441
Medicaid expansion, 20, 421, 423 (box), 426, 439, 441–442
medical malpractice, 424 (box), 430 (box), 442
Medicare, 422, 434, 440–441
additional hospital insurance tax, 443
Part B premiums, 441
Part D deduction elimination, 444
non-health revenue provisions, 444–445
passage of, 19–20
penalties on nonmedical expenses, 444
physician-owned hospitals, 441
preexisting conditions, 422, 424 (box), 430 (box), 439
premiums
increases review, 440
reporting, 440
protection against coverage recession, 439
public option, 425, 429, 430 (box), 434
reimbursement
for hospital-acquired infections, 441
for preventable readmission, 441
repeal efforts, 455–460
restaurant menu labeling, 443
Scott Brown and, 19
sex education, 443
small businesses, 422, 423 (box), 438
simple cafeteria plans, 445
state-run exchanges, 421–422, 430 (box), 436–437
subsidies, 422, 423 (box), 425, 432
taxes, 426, 429, 435, 443
credits for lower-income households, 437
credits for small businesses, 438
high-cost health plans, 443
itemized deductions, 444
medical devices, 424 (box), 432, 443
reporting requirement repeal, 456 (box)
surcharge, 20, 424 (box)
temporary high-risk pool, 438
therapeutic discovery projects, 445
upheld by Supreme Court, 586–587
W-2 reporting, 445
See also Health insurance
Afghanistan, 10, 225, 244, 249
Afghanistan Infrastructure Fund, 153, 304, 310
Afghanistan Security Forces Fund, 153, 310
foreign aid to, 131, 233, 270
nonhumanitarian aid, 248
Obama's policy toward, 229–231, 700
Afghanistan war, 263–264, 300
appropriations
FY 2009, 16, 122
FY 2010, 133, 138–139, 279
FY 2011, 138, 153
FY 2013, 182, 184
Commander's Emergency Response Program, 153, 284, 295, 304, 307
congressional action, 2009-2011, 231
insider attacks, 230–231, 312
2009 surge, 229–230, 249, 264, 700
U.S. casualties, 236 (box)
use-of-force law, 300
AFL-CIO. *See* American Federation of Labor-Congress of Industrial Organizations (AFL-CIO)
African Americans
farmers, 413
members of Congress
1947-2011, 32 (table)
Roland Burris (D-Ill.), 17, 26, 648, 650, 652, 675
presidential election of 2008, 3
unemployment rate, 52
See also Congressional Black Caucus
African Growth and Opportunity Act, 200–201
Afridi, Shakil, 231
Age Discrimination in Employment Act (ADEA), 529, 594
Agency for International Development. *See* U.S. Agency for International Development (USAID)
Agent Orange, 139, 288
Agius, Marcus, 72
Agricultural policy, 407
Agriculture, Nutrition, and Forestry Committee, Senate, 643, 644
ranking members and chairs, 662
Agriculture, Nutrition and Forestry Committee, 414
Agriculture and farming
Bush veto, 407
cap-and-trade system and, 16, 369
foreign trade pacts, 197, 198
policy, 407–415
subsidies, 413, 469
Agriculture Committee, House, 647, 848–849
ranking members and chairs, 645, 664
Agriculture Committee, Senate, 843–844
Agriculture Department, U.S. (USDA)
appointments, 711
appropriations
FY 2010, 128, 129
FY 2011, 152–153
FY 2012, 170–171
FY 2013, 182
assistance to black farmers, 413

child nutrition standards, 420, 465–467, 468
Commodity Futures Trading Commission (*See* Commodity Futures Trading Commission (CFTC))
leadership, 410
restaurant menu labeling, 443
Ahmadinejad, Mahmoud, 238
AID. *See* U.S. Agency for International Development (USAID)
AIDS. *See* HIV/AIDS
AIDS/HIV
appropriations, 2011, 154, 155
global funding, 248
name-based reporting, 453
national testing goal, 453
needle exchange programs and, 132
Ryan White HIV/AIDS Act, 419, 420 (figure), 452–453
AIG. *See* American International Group (AIG)
Aircraft, military. *See specific aircraft*
Air Force, U.S.
appropriations, FY 2013, 182–183
F-35 alternative engine, 266
F-22 cancellation, 265–266
Global Hawk surveillance drones, 182, 310, 312
retired aircraft, 312
Selfridge Air National Guard Base, 311
Airlines. *See* Air transportation
Air National Guard
reserve aircraft, 312
Selfridge Base, 311
Air pollution, 175, 378
Clean Air Act, 107, 384, 387, 397–398, 594, 696
greenhouse gas emissions, 5, 151, 175, 363–364, 386–387
cap-and-trade model for reducing, 369
Clean Air Act Amendments, 372–373
Green the Capitol initiative, 670
regulation, 5, 151, 175
Airport and Airway Extension Act of 2010, 331–332
Airport Improvement Program (AIP), 331
Air security
airports, 154
no-fly list, 211, 316
pilot training and, 332
Air transportation
Airport and Airway Extension Act of 2010, 331–332
Federal Aviation Administration (*See* Federal Aviation Administration (FAA))
Rail and Aviation Union Elections, 539
security (*See* Air security)
travel documents, 244
Akaka, Daniel K. (D-Hawaii), 847, 848
Hatch Act, 622
Native Hawaiian government, 619
plain writing, 614
Postal Service, 628
Veterans' Affairs Committee, 643, 662
whistleblower protection, 601, 623
Akin, Todd (R-Mo.), 41, 850
2012 defense authorization, 299
government spending committee, 665
military marriage, 300
Alaska
Arctic National Wildlife Refuge, 372
bypass, 629
missile defense program in, 311
Al-Assad, Bashar, 224, 224 (figure), 701
Aldeman, Chad, college savings plans, 487 (box)
Alexander, Lamar (R-Tenn.), 5 (table)
Affordable Care Act, 435
committees, 843, 848
education, 475, 478, 485
New START treaty, 291
Republican Conference Chair, 642, 662
Rules and Administration Committee, 662
Alexander, Rodney (R-La.), 18
Algal blooms, 378
Algeria, 700
Ali, Ben, 223
Aliens. *See* Illegal immigrants
Alito, Samuel A., Jr., 669
appellate judgeships, 576
appointment of, 586, 587, 589, 590, 591, 592
Allen, Geroge (R-Va.), 41
Ally Financial, 64, 69
Al-Maliki, Nouri, 234 (box)
Al-Nusra Front, 701
Al Qaeda, 229, 231, 234 (box), 248, 251, 300, 301, 302, 310, 315, 689, 699
Alternative fuels and vehicles, biofuels, 308, 311
Alternative minimum tax (AMT), 127, 146, 187
budget resolution adjustment, 80–81, 82, 83, 124
exemptions, 136
National Commission on Fiscal Responsibility and Reform recommendations, 144
Altmire, Jason (D-Pa.), 854
Amash, Justin (R-Mich.), 300, 309
terrorists, 578
Amendments. *See* Constitution, U.S.
America COMPETES Act reauthorization, 607–609
American Association of Railroads, 564
American Bankers Association, 92, 695
American Civil Liberties Union (ACLU), 216, 309
American Community Survey, 635–636
American Crossroads, 36
American Energy and Infrastructure Financing Act, 341–342
American Federation of Government Employees, 448
American Federation of Labor-Congress of Industrial Organizations (AFL-CIO), 107
Russian trade normalization and, 201
American Federation of Teachers, antibullying and gang prevention law, 492
American Gaming Association, 339
American Graduation Initiative, 478, 697
American Health Benefit Exchanges, 421–422, 436
American Indians. *See* Native Americans
American International Group (AIG), 48, 60, 63, 65, 89, 94
American Jobs Act, 49
American-made U.S. flags, 616–617
American Opportunity Tax Credit, 80, 83
American Recovery and Reinvestment Act of 2009, 47, 61, 66, 480, 504, 520, 691
American Rights at Work, 711

American Samoa, 648
  workers, 541
Americans with Disabilities Act (ADA), 259, 479 (box), 529
American Taxpayer Relief Act of 2012, 67, 520, 622, 684
AMLF. *See* Asset-Backed Commercial Paper Money Market Mutual Fund Liquidity Facility
Amodei, Mark (R-Nev.), 30
AMT. *See* Alternative minimum tax (AMT)
Amtrak, 133, 325, 341, 710
Andean Trade Preference Act, 194 (box), 197, 198
Andrews, Robert E. (D-N.J.), 850
  ethics probe, 673
  F-35 engine, 300
Angle, Sharon, 24–25
Animals
  crush videos, 562–563
  Endangered Species Act, 397, 403
  Fish and Wildlife Service, 383
  hunting and fishing regulations, 400–401
Antibullying and gang prevention, 491–492
Antideficiency Act, 669
Antiquities Act of 1906, 696
Antitrust law and Affordable Care Act, 424 (box)
ANWR. *See* Arctic National Wildlife Refuge (ANWR)
Appellate judgeships, 576–577
Appointments. *See* Nominations and confirmations
Appropriations
  bridge funding, 122
  budget actions
    FY 2009, 16, 34–35, 78–84, 269–273
    FY 2009–2010, 16, 34–35, 78–84, 79–80
    FY 2010, 123–126, 123–133, 127–133, 138–139, 245–248, 286–289
    FY 2011, 27–29, 134–138, 150–156, 248, 250–251
    FY 2012, 9–10, 29, 31–32, 165–167, 250–254, 574–575
    intelligence authorization (FY 2010), 245–248
    "minibus" (FY 2012), 170–172
    omnibus (FY 2009), 119–112
    omnibus (FY 2012), 172–176
    roundup (FY 2013), 181–185
    war supplemental (FY 2009), 122–123, 269–273
    war supplemental (FY 2010), 138–139, 286–289
  defined, 120
  disaster aid, 10, 33
  education (*See* Education)
  foreign aid (*See* Foreign aid)
  military, 16, 138–139
    vetoed, 915
  Pell grants, 487
  Race to the Top, 494
  veto (*See* Line-item veto)
  See also Budget, U.S.
Appropriations Committee, House, 646, 849
  budget actions
    FY 2009, 121, 122
    FY 2010, 80, 126, 128, 210, 243
    FY 2011, 136–137
    FY 2012, 159–160
    FY 2013, 179–180
  operating budget, 155, 159–160
  ranking members and chairs, 645, 664
  reconciliation bill, 2013, 180
  State-Foreign Operations subcommittee, 233
Appropriations Committee, Senate, 541, 644
  alternative minimum tax adjustment, 80–81
  budget actions
    FY 2009, 121–122
    FY 2010, 126, 128, 210–211, 243
    FY 2011, 136
    FY 2012, 160
    FY 2013, 180
  ranking members and chairs, 643, 662
Arab Spring, 223–224, 249, 700–701
Architect of the Capitol, 155, 184, 651
Arctic National Wildlife Refuge (ANWR), 372
Argentina, 60
Arleigh Burke-class destroyers, 283, 303, 306, 312
Armed Services. *See* Defense Department, U.S. (DOD); Military personnel; Veterans; *specific services and branches*
Armed Services Committee, House, 578, 647, 849–850
  defense authorizations
    FY 2012, 299–300
    FY 2013, 308–310
  Leon Panetta nomination, 274 (box)
  New START treaty, 291
  ranking members and chairs, 645–646, 662, 664
Armed Services Committee, Senate, 644, 844
  defense authorization
    FY 2012, 300–301
    FY 2013, 310–311
  New START treaty, 291
  ranking members and chairs, 642, 662
  2010 war supplemental, 288
Army, U.S.
  authorizations for force levels
    FY 2009, 16
    FY 2011, 294
    FY 2012, 303
  Engineers Corp. (*See* Army Corps of Engineers, U.S.)
  Future Combat System (FCS) (*See* Future Combat Systems)
  Ground Combat Vehicle, 294, 303, 307
Army Corps of Engineers, U.S.
  appropriations
    FY 2010, 128
    FY 2011, 153
    FY 2012, 170, 176
    FY 2013, 183
  economic stimulus, 80
  future storms mitigation, 625–626
  water projects, 128
Army National Guard. *See* National Guard
Ashcroft, John, 591
Asia, foreign policy pivot toward, 228
  See also specific countries
Asia-Pacific Economic Cooperation summit, 192
Assault weapons. *See* Guns and gun control
Asset-Backed Commercial Paper Money Market Mutual Fund Liquidity Facility, 57
Asset Guarantee Program, 63
Association of Community Organizers for Reform Now (ACORN), 384, 385, 677
  defunding, 680

Association of Public Television Stations, 336
ATF (Bureau of Alcohol, Tobacco, Firearms and Explosives), 573, 575
Atlanta Journal-Constitution, 656
Atlantic, The, 692
Attorney general, 315, 549
  Eric J. Holder, Jr., 285, 315, 705 (box)
    nomination by Obama, 706–707
Attorneys fees, 579–580
Auburn University, 71
Augustine Committee, 606
Aurora, 54
Austin v. Michigan State Chamber of Commerce, 677 (box)
Austria, Steve (R-Ohio), 403
Auto industry
  bailout, 694
    overview, 63–64
    TARP, 48, 61, 63–64
  biofuels, 308, 311
  Cash for Clunkers program and, 64, 79, 122, 272
  foreign trade pacts, 196–197, 198
  motor fuel excise tax, 133
Aviation. *See* Air transportation
Aviation Safety Whistleblower Investigation Office, 332
Ayotte, Kelly (R-N.H.), 301
  fiscal 2012 appropriations, 575

Baca, Joe (D-Calif.), 849
Bachmann, Michele (R-Minn.), 37, 162
  presidential campaign, 702
Bachus, Spencer (R-Ala.), 77, 89
  committees, 851
  Fannie and Freddie executive pay, 510
  FEMA shelters, 626
  Financial Services Committee, 647, 664
  firearms, 560
  Internet gambling, 566
Bagram Air Base, 276
Bahrain, 298, 701
Bailout: An Inside Account of How Washington Abandoned Main Street While Rescuing Wall Street, 65
Bain Capital, 49
Bair, Sheila, 68
  on JP Morgan Chase, 72
Baird, Brian (D-Wash.), 378, 854
Baker, James A., III, 290
Balanced Budget Act of 1997, 49, 450, 463
Balanced-budget amendment, 167–168, 551
Balanced Budget and Emergency Deficit Control Act, 685
Baldwin, Tammy (D-Wis.), 41
  domestic partner benefits, 603
Ballot initiatives, 44
Bancroft PLLC, 669
Bank for International Settlements, 70
Bank Holding Company Act, 95
Banking, Housing, and Urban Affairs Committee, Senate, 85, 625, 644, 844–845
  Dodd-Frank Act, 90
  Iran sanctions, 256
  ranking members and chairs, 642, 662
Bank of America, 54, 62–63, 65
Bank of England, 72
Bank of Kunlun, 256
Bankruptcy
  Chrysler, 64
  Dodd-Frank Act and, 93
  General Motors, 63–64
  judgeships, 565
  personal, 500–501
Banks and banking
  American Bankers Association, 92, 695
  bailouts, 6, 14, 47, 48, 62–63, 74
  concentration limits, 95
  credit cards, 14
  debit card fees, 99
  deleveraging, 52–53
  Dodd-Frank legislation, 68–69
  Export-Import Bank
    Iran sanctions, 240
    reauthorization, 200
  JP Morgan Chase losses and, 71–72
  LIBOR scandal and, 72
  Obama's policy, 694
  payment, clearing, settlement procedures, 95
  profits, 54
  proprietary trading by, 69, 95
  regulation, 15–16, 20, 68–69
  stress tests, 69–70, 694–695
  Troubled Assets Relief Program (TARP), 6, 14, 47, 48, 60–61, 62–63, 74, 75–78
  winding down of failing, 93
  See also Business and industry; Commerce; Economic policy
Barber, Ron (D-Ariz.), 43
Barbour, Haley, 30
Barclays, 72
Barofsky, Neil, 65
Barrasso, John (R-Wyo.)
  committees, 847
  2010 defense appropriations, 282
  disability rights, 259
  Indian Affairs Committee, 644, 662
  legal settlements, 555
  Senate Republican Conference, 662
Barrett, Tom, 44
Barth, James, 71
Bartlett, Roscoe G. (R-Md.), 850
  federal contractors, 309
Barton, Joe L. (R-Texas), 850
  Energy and Commerce Committee, 646, 664
Barton Joe L. (R-Tex.), 370
Basel Accords III, 70
Base realignment and closure (BRAC)
  defense authorization
    FY 2010, 280
    FY 2011, 294
    FY 2012, 304
    FY 2013, 308, 312
  excess public properties, 2012, 635
  military construction appropriation, FY 2010, 285
Basic Health Plan, Affordable Care Act, 437
Bass, Charles (R-N.H.), 43

Battered women. *See* Domestic violence
Baucus, Max (D-Mont.), 86, 102, 195 (box), 640 (figure)
  Affordable Care Act, 427, 429, 430, 433
  2012 budget negotiations, 161
  Children's Health Insurance Program, 446
  committees, 846, 851, 856
  community service programs, 605
  Congressional deficit committee, 168
  executive bonuses, 531
  Finance Committee, 662
  foreign trade agreements, 193, 196, 199
  Medicare payments to physicians, 452
  National Commission on Fiscal Responsibility and Reform, 143
  unemployment compensation, 523, 526, 527
Baucus, Sen. Max (D-Mont), 326
Bayh, Evan (D-Ind.), 844, 845
  education, 480
  F-35 fighter, 277
  illegal immigrants, 561
BCRA (Bipartisan Campaign Reform Act), 585, 587
Bea, Carlos, 681 (box)
Becerra, Xavier (D-Calif.), 143, 645
  Congressional deficit committee, 168
Begich, Mark (D-Ark.), 843
Benghazi attack, 224, 249, 690
Bennett, Michael (D-Colo.), 17, 23, 24
  committees, 844
  Native Hawaiian government, 618
Bennett, Robert F. (R-Utah), 662, 848
  domestic partner benefits, 604
  immigration status on census, 614
  plain writing, 614
  Rules and Administration Committee, 644
  undocumented children, 557
Bentivolio, Kerry (R-Mich.), 44
Bentsen, Lloyd, 921 (table)
Berg, Rick (R-N.D.), 41
  nuclear weapons, 313
Berkley, Shelley (D-Nev.), 41
  ethics probe, 676
  unemployment compensation, 523
Berman, Douglas, 592
Berman, Howard L. (D-Calif.), 36, 43, 335–336
  committees, 851
  Foreign Affairs Committee, 646, 664
  Iran sanctions, 238, 239
  Pakistan aid, 236–237
  State Department reauthorization, 241, 242
Bernanke, Ben S., 48, 56, 60
  criticisms of, 59
  on the debt ceiling, 161
  Dodd-Frank Act and, 91
  Federal Reserve audit, 633
  fiscal cliff, 113
  on the "fiscal cliff," 66–67
  on global recession, 55
  on quantitative easing, 58
  second term, 86 (box)
Beshear, Steve, 30
Best Pharmaceuticals for Children program, 462
Biden, Joseph R., Jr., vice president, 8, 22, 698
  Affordable Care Act, 436
  Afghanistan war, 700
  budget negotiations (2011), 113, 151
  budget negotiations (2012), 35
  debt limit negotiations (2011), 161
  extension of Bush tax cuts, 145
  fiscal cliff, 188–189
  New START treaty, 289
  pay-as-you-go rules, 141
  presidential campaign (2012) and, 38
  resignation from Senate, 17, 643
  tax increases, 113
  Violence Against Women Act, 572
Biggert, Judy (R-Ill.), 851
  Affordable Care Act, 458 (box)
  affordable housing, 510
Bilirakis, Gus M. (R-Fla.), 852
Bingaman, Jeff (D-N.M.), 342, 371, 845, 846
  Affordable Care Act, 428–429
  Children's Health Insurance Program, 446
  copper mining, 396
  Energy and Natural Resources Committee, 642, 662
  generic drugs, 461
  impeachment of Federal judges, 559
Bin Laden, Osama
  death of, 10, 185, 215, 231, 251, 258, 300, 311, 689, 699, 706, 905–906
  2012 presidential election and, 703
Biofuels, 308, 311
Biologic drug patents, 442
Biosimilar drugs, 461, 462
Bipartisan bill, 582
Bipartisan Campaign Reform Act (BCRA), 585, 587
Bipartisan Legal Advisory Group (BLAG), 669–670
Birth control
  abstinence education, 132, 175
  Affordable Care Act, 422 (box), 459 (box)
  family planning funding, 243
  international family planning programs, 176, 185, 245
  "morning after" pill, 422 (box)
  See also Abortion
Bishop, Rob (R-Utah), 275, 853
  federal lands bill, 398
Black, Diane (R-Tenn.), 630
Black farmers, 555–556
"Black liquor," 444
BLAG. *See* Bipartisan Legal Advisory Group (BLAG)
Blagojevich, Rod R., 17, 647–648, 650, 652, 653, 675
Blair, Dennis C., 227 (box)
  cybersecurity research, 615
Blank, Rebecca, 705 (box)
Bloomberg, Michael, 709
Bloomfield, Bill, 36
Blue Chip Consensus, 126, 136, 179
Blue Cross/Blue Shield, 444
Blue Dog Coalition, 14, 21, 86, 87, 90, 612
  Affordable Care Act, 428
  budget negotiations (2011), 139
  debt ceiling increase, 134

Democracy Is Strengthened by Casting Light on Spending in Elections (DISCLOSE) Act, 678
Medicare payments to physicians, 451
pay-as-you go rules, 126–127
Speaker Pelosi and, 663
war supplemental (2010), 287
Blumenauer, Earl (D-Ore.), 390, 469
Blunt, Roy (R-Mo.), 645
Affordable Care Act, 459 (box)
Hurricane Sandy, 625
Board Compensation Committee, 531
Boehner, John A. (R-Ohio), 5 (table), 8, 151
ACORN defunding, 680
Affordable Care Act, 436, 455 (box), 456, 458, 459 (box)
budget negotiations (2009), 82
budget negotiations (2010), 10, 123
budget negotiations (2011), 27–29, 113, 151
budget negotiations (2012), 35, 172
Charles Rangel ethics probe, 658
climate change legislation filibuster, 370
committees, 843
continuing resolutions (2012), 170
cybersecurity research, 615
debt limit negotiations (2011), 160–167
Defense of Marriage Act, 669
education, 473, 490
emissions filibuster, 370
Eric Massa ethics probe, 654, 655
fiscal cliff, 187–188
Giffords shooting, 643 (box)
Hastert rule and, 29 (box), 31
hate crimes, 555
health care, 485
Holder held in contempt of Congress, 574
Hurricane Sandy, 189–190, 598, 626
infrastructure spending, 341–342
job creation legislation, 106
on Keystone Pipeline, 345
law and law enforcement, 548
Medicare payments to physicians, 464
minority leader, 645
National Commission on Fiscal Responsibility and Reform, 143
National Mediation Board (NMB) ruling, 355
negotiations with Obama, 692, 697
omnibus appropriations (2011), 150
Patriot Act, 215
payroll tax cut, 109
on the 2012 presidential election, 40
Speaker of the House, 21, 24, 27, 663, 843
STOCK Act, 666
Stop the OverPrinting (STOP) Act, 670
transition team, 661 (box)
transportation bill (HR 4348), 392, 393
unemployment compensation, 536
unions, 540
use of force in Libya, 250
Violence Against Women Act, 572
Boeing Co., 200
Boeing Company, 537–538
Boiling Mad: Inside the Tea Party America, 7
Bolten, Joshua B., 647
Holder held in contempt of Congress, 574
Bombings. *See* Terrorism and counterterrorism
Bonamici, Suzanne (D-Ore.), 43
Bond, Christopher S. (R-Mo.), 662, 848
defense appropriations (2010), 282
Select Intelligence Committee, 644
Bonds. *See* Stocks, bond, and securities
Bonner, Jo (R-Ala.), 851, 854
Ethics Committee, 664, 674
Standards of Official Conduct Committee, 647
Bono Mack, Mary (R-Calif.), 851
Bonuses, 516, 531–532
Boozman, John (R-Ark.), 25
Bordallo, Madeleine Z. (D-Guam), 853
minimum wage, 530
Border security, 205, 550
appropriations
FY 2009, 122
FY 2010, 139–140, 212–213
FY 2011, 154
bill (2010), 206–207
Southwest border fence, 129, 208, 211
See also Homeland security
Boren, Dan (D-Okla.), 458
Boswell, Leonar L. (D-Iowa), 849
Boucher, Rick (D-Va.), 333, 335, 336
committees, 851
journalism sources, 559
Boustany, Charles S. (R-La.), 457 (box), 855
Bowles, Erskine, 143, 697
Boxer, Barbara (D-Calif.), 25
chemical safety standards, 399
committees, 843, 846, 848
Environment and Public Works Committee, 368–370, 642–643, 662
Ethics Committee, 643
Highway Trust Fund extension, 326
hunting and fishing, 400
hunting and fishing regulations, 400–401
John Ensign ethics probe, 671
lead-free pipes, 378
unemployment compensation, 526
Boycotts. *See* Foreign trade and business, sanctions
BRAC. *See* Base realignment and closure (BRAC)
Bradley Fighting Vehicle, 312
Brady, Kevin (R-Texas)
committees, 855, 856
unemployment compensation, 522
Brady, Robert A. (D-Pa.), 852, 856
House Administration Committee, 646, 664
Brady Campaign to Prevent Gun Violence, 678
Brady Center to Prevent Gun Violence, 559
Braley, Bruce (D-Iowa), 370
American-made U.S. flags, 616
plain writing, 613, 614
Brazil, 60, 468
Bretton Woods Agreement Act, 101

Breyer, Stephen G.
  Affordable Care Act, 587 (box)
  liberal positions, 584, 586, 591
  Stolen Valor Act, 589
Bright, Bobby (D-Ala.), 603
British Bankers Association, 72
British Petroleum, 288
  See also Gulf of Mexico oil spill
Broadband access, 334–335
Broadband Technology Opportunities program, 325, 333
Broadcasting
  campaign ads on, 681 (box)
  coverage of TARP, 65
  John Ensign, 651
  Obama interviews, 693
  public, appropriations, 2011, 155
  satellite and cable programming, 335–337
  See also Federal Communications Commission (FCC)
Broadcasting, television
  campaign ads on public, 681 (box)
  satellite and cable programming, 335–337
Brokers and brokerages. *See* Stocks, bond, and securities
Bronze Plan, Affordable Care Act, 437
Brooks, Mo (R-Ala.), 18, 854
Broun, Paul (R-Ga.), 380, 854
Brown, Corrine (D-Fla.), 855
Brown, Jerry, 25
Brown, Michael D., 611
Brown, Scott P. (R-Mass.), 6, 18, 19, 26, 40
  Affordable Care Act, 425, 433 (box), 435
  disability rights, 259
  Dodd-Frank Act, 90, 91, 92
  "don't ask, don't tell," 289
  election of, 693
  unions, 534
Brown, Sherrod (D-Ohio), 41, 81, 844, 845
  child nutrition bill, 466
  college campus fire safety, 482
  importation of prescription drugs, 461
  Shareholder Protection Act, 679
  STOCK Act, 667
Brownback, Sam (R-Kan.), 244, 384
  hate crimes, 555
  Mexico City policy, 248
  Native Americans, 617
Browner, Carol, 384
Bruce, Carol Elder, 671
Brueuer, Lanny A., 72
Bryant, Paul, 30
Bryson, John E., 323, 705 (box), 709
Buchanan, Vern (R-Fla.), 300
  ethics probe, 674
  terrorists, 578
Buchwald, Naomi Rice, 72
Buck, Ken, 24
Budget, U.S.
  action chronology, 111–118
    2009-2010, 78–84, 114, 119–148
    2011-2012, 114–116, 149–190
    2013, 116
  appropriations
    FY 2009, 16, 34–35, 78–84
    FY 2009-2010, 16, 34–35, 78–84
    FY 2010, 123–133
    FY 2011, 27–29, 134–138, 248, 250–251
    FY 2012, 9–10, 29, 31–32, 165–167, 250–251, 252–254
    intelligence authorization (FY 2010), 245–248
    "minibus" (FY 2012), 170–172
    omnibus (FY 2009), 119–112
    omnibus (FY 2012), 172–176
    roundup (FY 2013), 181–185
    war supplemental (FY 2009), 122–123, 269–273
    war supplemental (FY 2010), 138–139, 286–289
  authority, 120
  balanced budget amendment, 167–168, 551
  Budget Control Act of 2011, 160, 168, 177, 179–182, 188, 263, 312, 486, 535, 537, 622
  budget enforcement resolution, 137
  continuing resolutions
    FY 2010, 128
    FY 2011, 113, 137–138, 151
    FY 2012, 168–170
    FY 2013, 180–181
    short-term, 138
  cuts
    FY 2010, 66–67
    FY 2011, 135–136
    lockbox, 665
  debt ceiling, 16, 19, 28, 84, 119, 698
    2009 increase, 134
    2010 increase, 112, 141
    2012 negotiations, 160–167
  deficit, 23, 66, 74, 75, 80, 112, 117, 698
    Affordable Care Act, 426
    FY 2010, 124–125
    FY 2011, 136
    FY 2013, 178
    Gramm-Rudman-Hollings anti-deficit law, 685
  discretionary spending
    caps, 2012-2021, 166
    defined, 120
    FY 2010, 123–124, 126, 128–130, 133
  earmarks, 640–641
  education (*See* Education)
  emergency spending, 120
  enforcement rules, 126–127, 142
  entitlement programs, 9
  federal debt levels, 117, 160
    1990-2013, 124 (table)
    2010, 124–125
  federal receipts, 1988-2012, 118 (table)
  fiscal 1993-2012, 117 (table)
  foreign aid (*See* Foreign aid)
  Gephardt rule, 134
  glossary, 120
  Joint Select Committee on Deficit Reduction, 166–167
  mandatory spending
    defined, 120
    FY 2010, 128

National Commission on Fiscal Responsibility and Reform, 142–144, 697
Obama's requests, 697–698
FY 2009, 122
FY 2010, 125–126
FY 2011, 112, 135–136
FY 2012, 157–159
FY 2013, 177–180
outlays, 120
pay-as-you-go rules, 126–127, 141, 142, 697
reconciliation, 120, 476
FY 2013, 180
resolutions
defined, 120
FY 2010, 122–126
FY 2011, 134–137
FY 2013, 177–180
revenues, 120
sequestration, 29, 113, 116–117, 120, 177, 186, 189, 263, 685
congressional pay and, 685
veto (*See* Line-item veto)
See also Appropriations; Congressional Budget Office (CBO); Management and Budget, Office of (OMB); Treasury Department, U.S.
Budget Committee, House, 646, 706, 850
ranking members and chairs, 646, 662, 664
Budget Committee, Senate, 134, 644, 845
ranking members and chairs, 642, 662
Budget Control Act of 2011, 160, 168, 177, 179–182, 188, 263, 312, 486, 535, 537, 622
Buerkle, Ann Marie (R-N.Y.), 42, 855
Build America bond program, 83, 87
Bullock, Steve (D-Mont.), 44
Bullying Prevention and Intervention Act of 2012, 491–492
Bunning, Jim (R-Ky.), 86 (box)
Children's Health Insurance Program, 446
Medicare payments to physicians, 451
unemployment compensation, 522, 526
Bureau of Alcohol, Tobacco, Firearms and Explosives (ATF), 573, 575
Bureau of Consumer Financial Protection, 69
Burgess, Michael C. (R-Texas), 645
Republican Policy Committee, 645
tobacco regulation, 448
Burns, William J., 226 (box)
Burr, Richard (R-N.C.), 848
"don't ask, don't tell," 289
tobacco regulation, 449
Veterans' Affairs Committee, 644, 662
Burris, Roland W. (D-Ill.), 17, 26, 648, 650, 652, 675
slavery and segregation, 567
Burton, Dan (R-Ind.), 851
Puerto Rico political status, 619
State Department reauthorization, 242
Burwell, Sylvia Mathews, 49
Bush, George H. W., president, 226 (box), 711, 921 (table)
Bush, George W., president, 13, 22
antiterrorism efforts, 216
appointments made by, 9
Children's Health Insurance Program, 445
discretionary budget request, 2009, 125
doctrine, 698
economic crisis of 2007-2008 and, 48, 60–61, 75
e-mail records protection, 615
excess public properties, 634
farm bill (2008), 414
F-22 fighter, 266
Foreign Intelligence Surveillance Act, 551
Guantánamo Bay, Cuba, 314
hate crimes, 554
Holder held in contempt of Congress, 574
housing, 497
immigration, 556
Iraq and Afghanistan wars and, 10, 225, 232
journalism sources, 559
justice leadership, 549
Medicare physician payment rates, 450
merit-based pay plan, 600
military buildup by, 263
military commissions act, 316
minimum wage, 540
NASA, 605–606, 607
No Child Left Behind, 473, 696–697
partisan battles, 4, 552
plain writing, 613
presidential records, 616
Robert M. Gates, defense secretary, 264, 267, 274 (box)
spending cuts in environmental programs, 382–383
tax cuts under, 7, 9, 35, 66–67, 112, 124, 135–136, 144–146, 698
ties to oil and gas industries, 363
trade agreements, 193, 196
Troubled Assets Relief Program (TARP), 6, 14, 62
unemployment compensation, 537
vetoes by, 407, 915
wiretapping, 206
Business and industry
economic development (*See* Economic policy)
executive compensation, 65, 84, 98
health insurance deduction, 444
lobbying issues (*See* Lobbyists and lobbying)
Patriot Act and business records, 214, 215
Shareholder Protection Act, 679–680
Small Business Administration (*See* Small Business Administration (SBA))
taxes (*See* Business taxes)
venture capital, 147–148
See also Banks and banking; Commerce; Small business
Business law, 593–594
Business taxes
budget action, 2009-2010, 83, 87
business retention credit, 87
corporate estimated taxes and Affordable Care Act, 444
investment expensing, 87
National Commission on Fiscal Responsibility and Reform recommendations, 144
proposal (2013), 178
small business, 169, 438
Small Business Jobs Act of 2010, 103
Butterfield, G. K. (D-N.C.), 370, 659
Buy American Act, 651

Buyer, Steve (R-Ind.), 647, 855
  tobacco regulation, 448
Byrd, James, Jr., 553
Byrd, Robert C. (D-W.Va.), 5 (table), 10, 20, 26, 30, 91, 642
  Affordable Care Act, 434
  committees, 643, 843, 844
  D.C. representation, 649
  unemployment compensation, 524

Cable Act of 1992, 337
Cain, Herman, 37, 702
Cairo University, Egypt, 883–888
California
  gubernatorial elections, 25
  missile defense program, 311
  redistricting in, 36, 43
  water, 397
  wildfires, 139, 288
Caller ID spoofing, 563
Camp, Dave (R-Mich.), 110
  committees, 855, 856
  foreign trade agreements, 196, 199
  National Commission on Fiscal Responsibility and Reform, 143
  unemployment compensation, 523
  Ways and Means Committee, 647, 664
Campaign finance, 19, 550–551
  Citizens United v. Federal Election Commission, 36, 677, 678, 682
  Democracy Is Strengthened by Casting Light on Spending in Elections (DISCLOSE) Act, 677–679, 681
  Federal Election Commission (*See* Federal Election Commission (FEC))
  Shareholder Protection Act, 679–680
  See also Congressional elections
Campbell, Ben Nighthorse (D/R-Colo.), 644 (box)
Campbell, John (R-Calif.), 672–673
  government-sponsored enterprises, 512
Cantor, Eric (R-Va.), 5 (table), 21, 692
  budget negotiations (2012), 161
  Children's Health Insurance Program, 445–446
  committees, 843
  Export-Import Bank reauthorization, 200
  Holder held in contempt of Congress, 574
  Jumpstart Our Business Startups Act, 110
  labor union regulations, 537–538
  majority leader, 663
  minority whip, 645
  STOCK Act, 667
  Violence Against Women Act, 572
Cantwell, Maria (D-Wash.), 90, 845
  Affordable Care Act, 429
  Export-Import Bank reauthorization, 200
  Patent law, 571
Cao, Anh "Joseph" (R-La.), 24
  Affordable Care Act, 431
Cap-and-trade system, 15, 16, 124, 125, 126
Capital gains, 146, 189
Capital Purchase Program, 62–63
Capito, Shelley Moore (R-W.Va.), 851
Capitol Architect. *See* Architect of the Capitol
Capitol Building, U.S.
  Architect of the Capitol, 155, 184, 651
  Green the Capital initiative, 670
Capitol Police, 128, 155, 175
Capuano, Michael (D-Mass.), 661 (box)
  Shareholder Protection Act, 679
Carbon dioxide emissions
  airlines and, 396
  cap-and-trade system, 15, 16, 124, 125, 126
  EPA authority to regulate, 130
  greenhouse gas emissions, 5, 151, 175, 363–364
    cap-and-trade model for reducing, 369
    Clean Air Act Amendments, 372–373
    Green the Capitol initiative, 670
    HR 2454, 367–x
    regulation, 5, 151, 175
Carcieri, Donald L., 618
Cardin, Benjamin L. (D-Md.), 543
  committees, 846, 847
  D.C. representation, 650
Cardoza, Dennis A. (D-Calif.), 849
Carib News Foundation Multi-National Business Conferences, 658
Carnahan, Russ (D-Mo.), 851
Carney, Christopher P. (D-Pa.), 852
Carney, Jay, 302
Carper, Thomas R. (D-Del.)
  committees, 846, 847
  excess public properties, 634, 635
  improper payments, 612, 634
Carter, Jimmy, president
  plain writing, 613
  Puerto Rico political status, 620
Carter, John (R-Texas), 658
  fiscal 2012 appropriations, 575
  STOCK Act, 667
Cartwright, James, 275 (box), 288
Casey, Robert P. (D-Pa.)
  committees, 844, 846, 856
  unemployment compensation, 527
  U.S.-made goods in the Capitol, 651
Cash for Clunkers, 64, 79, 122, 272
  background, 321–322
Castillo, Ruben, 711
Castle, Michael N. (R-Del.), 24
  State Department reauthorization, 242
Catastrophic Plan, Affordable Care Act, 437
Catholic Church, 422 (box), 459 (box)
Catholic Health Association, 433 (box)
CBO. *See* Congressional Budget Office (CBO)
C-17 cargo planes, 281, 282, 283
C-27 cargo planes, 312
C-130 cargo planes, 312
CDBG. *See* Community Development Block Grants (CDBG)
CDC. *See* Centers for Disease Control and Prevention (CDC)
CEA. *See* Council of Economic Advisers (CEA)
Censuring of members of Congress, 22, 642, 658, 659
Census Bureau, U.S.
  appropriations
    FY 2010, 130
    FY 2011, 153

illegal immigrants, 614
Native American women, 572
Center for American Progress, 556
Center for Medicare and Medicaid Innovation, 184, 441, 460
Center for Middle East Peace and Economic Cooperation, 26
Center for Political Accountability, 679–680
Center for Science in the Public Interest, 411
Centers for Disease Control and Prevention (CDC), 155, 453
Centers for Medicare and Medicaid Services (CMS), 440
Central America, 201
Central Bank of Iran, 257, 301
Central Intelligence Agency (CIA), 274 (box)
Afghanistan insider attacks and, 230
appropriations
FY 2010, 133, 246, 280
FY 2013, 254
FY 2011 and 2012, 251
Benghazi attack and, 226 (box)
Center on Climate Change, 282
David Petraeus, 274–275 (box)
Leon Panetta as director of, 227 (box), 706
See also Intelligence activities and agencies
Central Valley Project Improvement Act (PL 102-575), 397
CFPB. *See* Consumer Financial Protection Bureau (CFPB)
CFTC. *See* Commodity Futures Trading Commission (CFTC)
Chabot, Steve (R-Ohio), 647, 851
Chafee, Lincoln, 25
Chaffetz, Jason (R-Utah)
committees, 853
D.C. representation, 649
tax delinquents and Federal work, 624
Chamber of Commerce, U.S., 107, 161
Affordable Care Act, 456 (box)
cybersecurity bill, 218
Democracy Is Strengthened by Casting Light on Spending in Elections (DISCLOSE) Act, 678
Export-Import Bank reauthorization, 200
opposes solar energy technology, 380
Russian trade normalization, 201
tax reporting requirement, 169
Chambliss, Saxby (R-Ga.), 91, 227 (box)
Agriculture, Nutrition, and Forestry Committee, 644
budget negotiations (2012), 161
child nutrition bill, 466
committees, 848
Democracy Is Strengthened by Casting Light on Spending in Elections (DISCLOSE) Act, 681
Foreign Intelligence Surveillance Act, 217
intelligence authorization (2013), 255
Select Intelligence Committee, 662
war supplemental (2009), 271
Charities and non-profit organizations, 444
Charter schools, 477 (box), 480, 484, 490, 491, 709, 882
Chávez, Hugo, 239
Chemical plant security, 207, 208, 212
Cheney, Dick, vice president, 18, 921 (table)
Chertoff, Michael, 705 (box)
Chicago, Illinois, 709
Child nutrition, 420, 465–467
See also Food assistance programs; Women, Infants, and Children (WIC) program
Child pornography, 581–582
Child Protection Act, 581–582
Children
adolescents and youth (*See* Adolescents and youth)
adoption, 444
Affordable Care Act, 424 (box), 439–440
antibullying and gang prevention, 491–492
child tax credit, 80, 83, 124, 136, 146
global health and, 245, 248
homeless, 512
obesity, 420, 465–467
pharmaceuticals for, 462
undocumented, 556
See also Education
Children's Health Insurance Program (CHIP), 445–448
Affordable Care Act, 424 (box), 426, 437, 439
enrollment expansion, 447
expansion, 14–15, 419
final action, 446
funding, 446–447
legislative action, 445–446
major provisions, 446–448
Senate committee action, 446
Senate floor action, 446
state bonus payments, 447
tobacco tax, 445, 447–448
Child welfare and social services
Head Start (*See* Head Start)
Women, Infants and Children (WIC) program (*See* Women, Infants, and Children (WIC) program)
China, 51
Bank of Kunlun sanctions, 256
currency revaluation, 191
cybersecurity, 217
foreign policy toward, 228
NASA and, 153, 171
trade with, 192, 193–194
CHIP. *See* Children's Health Insurance Program (CHIP)
Choice Neighborhoods, 185
Chouest, Gary, 673
Christensen, Donna M. C. (D-V.I.), 655, 658
Christie, Chris, 18, 38, 39, 190, 598, 704
Christopher, Warren, 226 (box)
Chrysler Corporation, 703
bailout, 61, 63–64, 76
bankrupcty, 64
Chrysler Financial, 65
franchise dealerships, 131
Chu, Steven, 367, 704, 705 (box), 708
Church, Frank (D-Idaho), 216
Churches and religious groups and Affordable Care Act
abortion coverage, 433 (box)
contraceptive coverage, 422 (box), 459 (box)
CIA. *See* Central Intelligence Agency (CIA)
Cicilline, David (D-R.I.), 43
nuclear weapons, 313
Cigarettes. *See* Tobacco
Circuit Court of Appeals, U.S., 122
Citibank, 54
Cities, Securing the Cities initiative, 210
See also State and local government

Citigroup, 62–63, 65, 69, 195
Citizens for Responsibility and Ethics in Washington (CREW), 651, 652, 672, 684
Citizens Right to Know Act, 679
Citizens United v. Federal Election Commission, 36, 677, 678, 682
Civilian Property Realignment Act of 2013, 634
Civilian Property Realignment Commission, 635
Civil Rights
  ACLU, 216, 309
  disabled persons (*See* Disabled persons)
  discrimination (*See* Discrimination)
  homosexuals (*See* Homosexuals)
  individual rights, 590–591
Civil Rights Act (1964), 25, 528, 529, 590, 594
Civil service. *See* Federal employees
Civil Service Retirement System (CSRS), 542, 544, 621, 627
Civil War-era False Claims Act, 602
Claims Resolution Act of 2010, 413
Clapper, James R., Jr., 215, 216, 227 (box), 551
Clarke, Yvette D. (D-N.Y.), 655, 658, 852
CLASS. *See* Community Living Assistance Services and Support (CLASS)
Clawson, Patrick, 239
Clay, William Lacy (D-Mo.), 853
Clean Air Act, 107, 387, 594, 696
  amendments, 384
  task force to delay standards, 397–398
Clean Energy Corps, 604
Clean Water Act, 173, 184, 380
Clean Water and Drinking Water State Revolving Funds, 184, 381, 385
Cleaver, Emauel (D-Mo.), 481
Cleveland, Grover, president, 915
Climate. *See* Global climate change
Clinton, Bill, president, 49, 226 (box), 227 (box), 265, 692
  Elena Kagan, 712
  Eric Holder, 707
  extension of Bush tax cuts, 145
  F-22 fighters, 266
  health care overhaul, 421, 426
  Iran sanctions, 238
  justice leadership, 549
  merit-based pay plan, 600
  minimum wage, 540
  National Commission on Fiscal Responsibility and Reform, 143
  nomination of Sotomayor by, 585
  plain writing, 613
  vetoes by, 915
Clinton, Hillary Rodham (D-N.Y.), 587
  presidential campaign, 18
Clinton, Hillary Rodham (Secretary of State), 17, 26, 49, 226 (box), 270
  appointment, 704–705
  Benghazi attack, 224, 249
  ineligibility clause, 684
  New START treaty, 290
  same-sex partner benefits, 242
Clinton Global Initiative, 704
Clinton Presidential Center, 704
Cloture. *See* Filibusters and cloture votes
Club for Growth, 200
Clyburn, James E. (D-S.C.), 5 (table), 22, 663
  2012 budget negotiations, 161
  cocaine penalties, 562
  committees, 843
  Congressional deficit committee, 168
  majority whip, 645
CMS. *See* Centers for Medicare and Medicaid Services (CMS)
Coakley, Martha, 19
Coal, 399, 708
  Ken Salazar, 710
Coalition for Patent Fairness, 570
Coast Guard, U.S.
  appropriations
    FY 2010, 129, 211
    FY 2011, 154
  disaster response, 205
  Loran-C program, 210, 211
  reauthorization bill, 2012, 207, 214, 218–219, 298 (box)
Coats, Dan (T-Ind.), Hurricane Sandy, 626
Coble, Howard (R-N.C.), 852
COBRA (Consolidated Omnibus Budget Reconciliation Act) (1985), 525–527
Coburn, Tom (R-Okla.), 129, 384, 412
  2012 budget negotiations, 161
  D.C. representation, 649, 650
  2010 defense appropriations, 282
  efficiency of government agencies, 612
  ethics probe, 672
  firearms, 559
  foreclosure aid, 510
  Hurricane Sandy, 625–626
  John Ensign and, 652
  justice leadership, 549
  legal settlements, 555
  Medicare payments to physicians, 452
  National Commission on Fiscal Responsibility and Reform, 143
  national flood insurance, 625
  National Women's History Museum, 616
  nutrition bill, 469, 470
  online disclosure of expenditures, 650
  Patent law, 570
  same-sex couples, 581
  unemployment compensation, 522, 526
Cochran, Thad (R-Miss.), 271, 282, 376
  Appropriations Committee, 644, 662
  Hurricane Sandy, 625
Code Pink, 66 (figure)
Coffman, Mike (R-Colo.), 854
  federal contractors, 309–310
  F-35 engine, 300
Cohan, William D., 59
Cohen, Steve (D-Tenn.), 852
  Afghanistan Infrastructure Fund, 313
  bankruptcy judgeships, 565
  2010 war supplemental, 287
Cole, James M., Holder held in contempt of Congress, 574
Cole, Tom (R-Okla.), 305
  Indian casino land, 618
  National Republican Congressional Committee, 645

Presidential Election Campaign Fund, 682
Violence Against Women Act, 572
Coleman, Norm (R-Minn.), 17, 642
Collective bargaining and federal contractors, 309
College campus fire safety, 482
Colleges and Universities. *See* Higher education; Student aid
College savings accounts, 481, 487(box)
Collins, Susan (R-Maine), 81, 384
committees, 847
D.C. representation, 649
Dodd-Frank Act, 90, 91, 92
domestic partner benefits, 604
"don't ask, don't tell," 288–289, 293
Federal employee domestic partnerships, 623
Homeland Security Committee, 644, 662
Loran-C program, 210
Medicaid and education spending bill, 2010, 454
National Women's History Museum, 616
nutrition bill, 468
Postal Service, 629
same-sex couples, 581
unemployment compensation, 522, 524
war supplemental (2010), 288–289
Colombia, 74
foreign aid to, 233
intellectual property, 197
trade agreements, 193, 194 (box), 195, 197–198
Colorado, 703
Commander's Emergency Response Program, 153, 284, 295, 304, 307
Commerce, 319–359
action chronology
FY 2009-2010, 321–339
FY 2011-2012, 340–359
air transportation (*See* Air transportation; Federal Aviation Administration (FAA))
Internet gambling, 566
background, 338
House action, 338
112th Congress work on, 357–358
Senate action, 338–339
Internet piracy, 358–359
notarization legislation, 339, 915–916
satellite and cable programming, 335–337
Surface Transportation Authorization, 324–327, 340–344
See also Banks and banking; Business and industry
Commerce, Science, and Transportation Committee, Senate, 330, 342, 479 (box), 563, 606, 644, 845
ranking members and chairs, 643, 662
Commerce Department, U.S., 609
appointments, 708–709
appropriations
FY 2009, 127
FY 2010, 130–131
FY 2011, 152–153
FY 2012, 171–172
FY 2013, 182
leadership, 323
Commercial Paper Funding Facility, 57
Committee for a Level Playing Field, 533
Commodity Futures Trading Commission (CFTC), 68
appropriations
FY 2011, 154
FY 2013, 182, 183
Dodd-Frank Act and, 91, 104–105
Financial Stability Oversight Council and, 92
LIBOR scandal and, 72
MF Global and, 71
Communications
broadcast (*See* Broadcasting)
Federal Communications Commission (FCC), 144, 563
broadband access, 356
Broadband Technology Opportunities Program, 333
Internet piracy, 357–359
leadership, 323
Lifeline program, 335
National Broadband Plan, 334–335
net neutrality, 355–356
Open Internet Advisory Committee, 334
Open Internet Order, 334
overhaul, 354–355
satellite and cable programming, 357–358
Spectrum Auction, 356–357
Internet (*See* Internet)
new media, 4, 152
print (*See* Print media and publishing)
social media, 110
television (*See* Television)
wiretaps (*See* Wiretapping)
Communications, Technology and the Internet subcommittee, 333–334
Community Development Block Grants (CDBG), 156, 185
Community Development Capital Initiative, 63
Community health centers, 442
Community Living Assistance Services and Support (CLASS), 442, 456–457 (box)
Community Oriented Policing Services (COPS) program, 153, 171, 552, 561–562, 568, 575
Community service programs, 604–605
Community Shelter Protection Act of 2011, 626
Comparative-effectiveness research, Affordable Care Act, 442
Compensation, executive, 65
Conaway, K. Michael (R-Texas), 849
Concealed handguns, 575–576
Conditional education waivers, 473–475
Conference committees, Congressional, 639
Confirmations. *See* Nominations and confirmations
Conflict of interest, FDA policy on, 463
Congress, members of, 835–842
2009-2013, 835–842
House, 826–828, 832–834
Senate, 825, 831
age structure of, 9 (table)
censuring of, 22, 642, 658, 659
changes, 111th and 112th Congresses, 829–830
disclaimers in mailings, 685
dress code, 644 (box)
fundraising, 672–673 (*See also* Campaign finance)
incumbents reelected, defeated, or retired, 1946-2012, 12 (table)
keys votes (*See* Congressional votes)

leadership
2009-2013, 5 (table)
and committees, 111th and 112th Congresses, 642–647, 661–665, 843–856
online advertising by, 685
partisanship among, 4
party affiliations, 1789-2015, 929–930
pay and benefits (*See* Congressional pay and benefits)
sexual harassment lawsuits against, 673–674
sign-on letters, 645 (box)
STOCK Act and, 665–668
Congress, U.S.
action chronology
2009-2010, 321–339, 366–385, 409–413, 414–415, 642–660
2011-2012, 340–359, 386–403, 414–415, 661–676
committee organization
111th Congress, 642–645
112th Congress, 664
conference committees, 639
distribution of house seats and electoral votes, 928
earmarks, 640–641
economic and financial regulation policy actions, 76–77 (box)
filibusters (*See* Filibusters and cloture votes)
Holder in contempt of, 573–574
lame duck sessions, 7, 9, 22, 138, 857–859
leadership and committees, 843–856
111th Congress, 642–660
112th Congress, 661–665
legislative process in brief, 745–748
live quorums, 640
major legislation considered by during 2009-2013, 550–551
number of public laws enacted, 1975-2012, 15 (box)
operating budgets, 128, 155, 175, 184
organization
111th Congress, 642–647
112th Congress, 661–665
partisanship in, 4, 7, 7 (table), 8–9
reapportionment, 1789-2010, 873
redistricting, 4, 10
rules suspension, 640
secret holds, 640
session overview
111th Congress, 13–26
112th Congress, 27–44
session statistics (boxes)
2009, 13
2010, 19
2011, 28
2012, 31
special elections, 6, 30, 941
terminology, 715–743
viewed as dysfunctional, 4
Congressional Black Caucus, 14, 553, 562, 567, 663
2010 budget resolution, 126
debt ceiling negotiations, 2012, and, 160
Democracy Is Strengthened by Casting Light on Spending in Elections (DISCLOSE) Act, 678
jobs creation bill, 2010, and, 87
2010 war supplemental, 287
Congressional Budget Office (CBO), 67, 143, 542, 601
Affordable Care Act, 426, 431, 456
appropriations
FY 2010, 128
FY 2011, 155
budget analyses
FY 2010, 124, 125, 126
FY 2011, 135, 152
FY 2012, 157–158, 166
FY 2013, 178–179, 189
defense acquisition rules, 268
estimated net cost of TARP programs, 78
Presidential Election Campaign Fund, 682
State Department reauthorization, 241
student aid, 476
Congressional committees, *Appropriations Committee, For internal affairs of a specific committee, Senate). For committee action on a bill. See The topic of the legislation;* individual committee name (e.g.
Congressional elections
2009, 17–18
special elections, 18, 19
2010, 6–7, 22–23
special elections, 26
incumbents in, 12 (table)
See also Campaign finance
Congressional ethics probes
Alan B. Mollohan (D-W.Va.), 654
Bennie Thompson (D-Miss.), 655
C. W. Bill Young (R-Fla.), 655–656
Carolyn Cheeks Kilpatrick (D-Mich.), 655
Charles Rangel (D-N.Y.), 22, 642, 646, 655, 657–659
Christopher Dodd (D-Conn.), 652–653
Donald M. Payne (D-N.J.), 655
Donna M. C. Christensen (D-V.I.), 655
Eric Massa (D-N.Y.), 654–655
James P. Moran (D-Va.), 655–656
Jane Harman (D-Calif.), 653
Jesse L. Jackson, Jr. (D-Ill.), 653
Joe Wilson (R-S.C.), 653–654
John Ensign (R-Nev.), 651–652, 670–672
John P. Murtha (D-Pa.), 655–656
Kent Conrad (D-N.D.), 652–653
Laura Richards (D-Calif.), 656
Marcy Kaptur (D-Ohio), 655–656
Mary Landrieu (D-La.), 652
Maxine Waters (D-Calif.), 656–657
Nathan Deal (R-Ga.), 656
Norman D. Dicks (D-Wash.), 655–656
Peter J. Visclosky (D-Ind.), 655–656
Pete Stark (D-Calif.), 654
Sam Graves (R-Mo.), 654
sexual misadventures and resignation, 671 (box)
Todd Tiahrt (R-Kan.), 655–656
Tom DeLay (R-Texas), 660
William J. Jefferson (D-La.), 660
Yvette D. Clarke (D-N.Y.), 655

Congressional Made in America Promise Act, 651
Congressional pay and benefits, 121, 155
ineligibility clause, 684
legislative action
2009, 683
2010, 683–684
2011-2012, 685
sequestration and, 685
Congressional Progressive Caucus, 14
Congressional Research Service (CRS), 235 (box), 299, 341–342
conditional education waivers, 475
STOCK Act, 668
Congressional Review Act of 1996, 544
"Congressional Review Act Rules Not Submitted to GAO and Congress," 615
Congressional Review Improvement Act of 2008, 615
Congressional votes, 3
D.C. representation, 648–650
Hastert rule and, 29 (box), 31
key votes
2009, 13–17, 477, 500, 501, 751–766
2010, 19–22, 480, 767–784
2011, 785–802
2012, 485, 489, 803–821
recorded vote totals, 21 (table)
by region, 43 (table)
rule changes, 16, 860
See also Filibusters and cloture votes
Connolly, Gerald E. (D-Va.), 393, 654
excess public properties, 635
Postal Service, 628
tax delinquents and Federal work, 624
Conrad, Kent (D-N.D.), 23
Affordable Care Act, 429, 435
Budget Committee, 642, 662
budget negotiations (2010), 123, 126
budget negotiations (2011), 135
budget negotiations (2012), 161, 163
budget negotiations (2013), 180
committees, 845, 846
debt ceiling increase, 134, 141
debt commission bill, 127
ethics probe, 652–653
Medicare payments to physicians, 451
National Commission on Fiscal Responsibility and Reform, 143
pay-as-you go rules, 127
Conrad, Robert, 594
Conservative Club for Growth, 18
Consolidated and Further Continuing Appropriations Act of 2013, 622
Consolidated Appropriations Act, 680
Consolidated Omnibus Budget Reconciliation Act (COBRA), 83, 133, 525–527
Constellation space program, 605, 606, 607, 626–627
Constitution, U.S.
Fifth Amendment, Equal Protection Clause, 669
First Amendment
Affordable Care Act contraceptive coverage, 459 (box)
campaign ads on public tv, 681 (box)
Ineligibility Clause, 672, 684
pocket edition, 670
Twenty-seventh Amendment, 685
Consumer Confidence Index, 51
Consumer Financial Protection Bureau (CFPB), 9, 88–89, 96–97, 154, 174
derivatives regulation, 97–98
Financial Stability Oversight Council and, 92, 97
Richard Cordray and, 104, 105–106, 690
Consumer Operated and Oriented Plan (CO-OP), 437, 457 (box)
Consumer Price Index (CPI), 187, 188, 443, 542–543
Medicare spending, 440
Consumer Product Safety Commission (CPSC), 511
drywall safety, 508
Consumer protection
Bureau of Consumer Financial Protection and, 69
credit cards (*See* Credit cards)
financial (*See* Consumer Financial Protection Board (CFPB))
Financial Insurance Office and, 98–99
mortgage
predatory lending, 100–101
robo-signing, 54
Continuing Appropriations and Surface Transportation Extensions Act, 503
Continuing Extension Act of 2010, 520, 522, 526
Continuing resolutions (CR)
FY 2010, 128
FY 2011, 113, 137–138, 151
FY 2012, 168–170
FY 2013, 180–181
short-term, 138
Contraception. *See* Birth control
Contracting and Tax Accountability Act of 2011, 624
Contractors withholding rule, 630
Conway, Jack, 24
Conyers, John, Jr. (D-Mich.)
attorneys fees, 580
committees, 852
Foreign Intelligence Surveillance Act, 216
intelligence authorization (2013), 254–255
Judiciary Committee, 646, 664
Libya, 300
Patent law, 571
Patriot Act, 206, 209
property rights, 579
undocumented children, 557
use-of-force law, 300
Violence Against Women Act, 573
Cook, Rhodes, 39–40
Coons, Chris (D-Del.), 24
Foreign Intelligence Surveillance Act, 217
Copeland, Curtis W., 615
Copper mining, 395–396
Copper mining, 395–396
COPS (Community Oriented Policing Services) program, 552, 561–562
Copyright Office, compulsory statutory license, satellite providers, 336
Cordray, Richard, 9, 69, 104, 105–106, 690

Corker, Bob (R-Tenn.), 90, 848
  Iran sanctions, 239
  New START treaty, 290
  Special Aging Committee, 645, 662
"Cornhusker kickback," 435
Cornilles, Rob, 43
Cornyn, John (R-Texas), 843
  Ethics Committee, 645
  fiscal 2012 appropriations, 575
  Harry Reid's remarks about Obama, 646 (box)
  Hillary Clinton nomination as Secretary of State and, 226 (box)
  National Republican Senatorial Committee ranking members and chairs, 642, 662
  Patriot Act, 209
  STOCK Act, 666
  undocumented children, 557
  Violence Against Women Act, 572–573
Corporation for National and Community Service, 604
Corporation for Public Broadcasting, 155
Corps of Engineers. *See* Army Corps of Engineers, U.S.
Corruption Prosecution Improvements Act, 666
Corwin, Jane, 30
Corzine, Jon, 18
  MF Global and, 70–71
Costa, Jim (D-Calif.), 853
  federal lands bill, 398
Costello, Jerry F. (D-Ill.), 855
  unions, 539
Cost-of-living adjustments (COLAs), 542–543
Cote, Dave, 143
Council of Economic Advisers (CEA), 49
Countrywide Financial Corp., 652–653, 668
Courtney, Joe (D-Conn.), 467
Court proceedings
  Courts and Competition Policy Subcommittee, 564
  TV coverage of, 565–566
  See also Supreme Court
Coverdell plans, 487(box)
Covert agents, 248
CPI (Consumer Price Index), 542–543
CR. *See* Continuing resolutions (CR)
Crack cocaine, penalties for, 562
Craig, Greg, 711
Craig, Larry (R-Idaho), 644
Crane, Daniel B. (R-Ill.), 658
Crapo, Michael D. (R-Idaho), 143
  2012 budget negotiations, 161
  community service programs, 605
Cravaack, Chip (R-Minn.), 399
Credit cards, 14, 15, 65
  Bureau of Consumer Financial Protection and, 69
  disclosure requirements, 85
  protections for young consumers, 85
  rates and fees, 84–85
Credit default swaps, 60–61, 76
Credit market programs, TARP, 64–65
Credit rating agencies, 99–100
Crenshaw, Ander (R-Fla.), 849
  Defense of Marriage Act, 669
Crime and criminals
  Community Oriented Policing Services (COPS) program, 153, 171, 552, 561–562, 568, 575
  criminal law and procedure, 591–593
  hate-crimes laws, 277
  Miranda warnings, 247, 279
Crist, Charlie, 18
Critz, Mark S. (D-Pa.), 26, 43
  small business Federal contracting, 631
Crossroads Grassroots Policy Strategies, 36
Crowd-funding, 110
Crowley, Joseph (D-N.Y.), 658
  Affordable Care Act, 458 (box)
  ethics probe, 672–673
CRS. *See* Congressional Research Service (CRS)
Cruel and Unusual Punishments Clause, 591
CSRS (Civil Service Retirement System), 542, 544, 621, 627
C-17 transport planes, 295
Cuba, 174
  See also Guantánamo Bay, Cuba
Cuellar, Henry (D-Texas)
  committees, 852
  efficiency of government agencies, 612
  2013 intelligence authorization, 255
  OMB performance standards, 633
Culberson, John Abney (R-Texas)
  budget negotiations (2010), 244
  committees, 849
Culver, Chet, 25
Cummings, Elijah E. (D-Md.), 853, 855
  Federal Reserve audit, 633
  Federal worker pension contributions, 542, 621
  Hatch Act, 622
  Oversight and Government Reform Committee, 664
  witness protection programs, 565
Cuomo, Andrew, 25
Currency Reform for Fair Trade Act, 193
Curson, David (D-Mich.), 44
Customs and Border Protection Agency, 206
  border entry points, 219
  budget bill, 2010, 211, 213
Cut-as-you-go rules, 664–665
Cybersecurity, 207, 214, 217–218, 298 (box)
  Director of National Intelligence and, 248
  research, 615
Cybersecurity Enhancement Act (2009), 615
Cyberstalking, 567
Czech Republic, 277, 278, 293

Daggett, Christopher, 18
Dahlkemper, Kathleen A. (D-Pa.), 854
Dairy products. *See* Milk and dairy products
Daley, William, 49
Dalton, Walter, 44
D'Amato, Alfonse, 585
Daniels, Mitch, 44
Darin, Roger, 72
Daschle, Tom (D-S.D.), 691
  Affordable Care Act, 422 (box), 426–427
  tax problems, 707

David-Bacon Act, 627
Davis, Danny K. (D-Ill.)
  improper payments, 613
  Postal Service, 628
Davis, Geoff (R-Ky.), 44, 855
Davis, Gray, 44
Davis, Jack, 30
Davis, Susan A. (D-Calif.), 850
Davis, Thomas M., III (R-Va.), 647
Davis-Bacon Act, 381
  Clean Water and Drinking Water State Revolving Funds, 385
  wage rules, 326
Davis Polk law firm, 695
DDG-51 *Arleigh Burke*-class destroyers, 283, 303, 306, 312
DDG-1000 combat ship, 278
Deal, Nathan (R-Ga.), 26
  ethics probe, 656
Debit card fees, 99
Debt, federal. *See* Budget, U.S.
Deceptive use of "census," 614
Deeds, Creigh, 18
Deepwater Horizon spill, 392, 393
DeFazio, Peter A. (D-Ore.), 326, 390, 663, 855
Defense Department, U.S. (DOD)
  aircraft and weapons (*See specific types*)
  appointments, 706
  appropriations, recissions
    FY 2009, 122
    FY 2010, 123–124, 133, 280–284, 287–288, 520
    FY 2011, 140, 152, 295, 296–297
    FY 2012, 172–173, 175–176, 252, 304–307
    FY 2013, 182–183, 307–312, 312–313
    FY 2010 military construction, 284–285
  authorizations
    FY 2010, 273–280
    FY 2011, 291–295
    FY 2012, 299–304
    FY 2013, 307–312
  defense policy (*See* Defense policy)
  intelligence funding
    FY 2010, 133, 245–248
    FY 2013, 254–255
    FY 2011 and 2012, 250–251
  missile defense programs (*See* Missile defense)
  Overseas Contingency Operations (OCO), 252, 284, 294–295, 304, 307, 312
  prisoner abuse photos, 122
  war supplementals
    FY 2009, 122–123, 269–273
    FY 2010, 138–139, 286–289
Defense of Marriage Act (DOMA), 182, 289, 313, 581, 603
  House Office of General Counsel, 669–670
Defense policy, 263–316
  action chronology, 267–295
    2011–2012, 296–313
  defense acquisition rules, 267–269
  Guantánamo Bay, Cuba (*See* Guantánamo Bay, Cuba)
  Joint Chiefs of Staff, 22, 275 (box)
    Afghanistan war insider attacks, 230
  outlays, 2001-2012, 264 (figure)
  Strategic Arms Reduction Treaty (START), 7, 22, 138, 152, 232, 289–291
Deficit. *See* Budget, U.S.
Deficit Reduction, Joint Select Committee on, 166–167, 168, 541
Deflation, 51
Defund ACORN Act, 680
DeGette, Diana (D-Colo.), 431
Delahunt, Bill (D-Mass.)
  committees, 851
  State Department reauthorization, 242
DeLauro, Rosa L. (D-Conn.), 843, 849
  gender-based wage discrimination, 528
  minimum wage, 540
  nutrition bill, 468
  regulatory oversight, 632
DeLay, Tom (R-Texas), 660
DelBene, Suzan (D-Wash.), 44
Delta Air Lines Inc., 200
DeMint, Jim (R-S.C.), 122, 332
  Architect of the Capitol, 651
  border fence, 211
  Hillary Clinton nomination as Secretary of State and, 226 (box), 705
  National Women's History Museum, 616
  Postal Service, 628
  Senate rules, 662
  war supplemental (2009), 271
Democracy Is Strengthened by Casting Light on Spending in Elections (DISCLOSE) Act, 677–679, 681
Democratic Caucus, 642, 645, 661, 663, 843
Democratic Communications Center, 843
Democratic Congressional Campaign Committee, 645, 663, 843
Democratic National Committee, 18
Democratic Party
  Affordable Care Act and, 15, 19–20
  'Blue Dog" Democrats (*See* Blue Dog Coalition)
  independent voters and, 23
  key votes (*See* Congressional votes)
  leadership (*See* Congress, U.S.)
  modern partisanship and, 4
  state elections
    2010, 25
    2012, 44
  switches, 18
Democratic Policy Committee, 642, 661, 843
Democratic Republic of the Congo, 101
Democratic Senatorial Campaign Committee, 642, 661, 843
Democratic Steering and Outreach Committee, 843
Democratic Steering and Policy Committees, 843
Dempsey, Martin, 275 (box)
Denham, Jeff (R-Calif.), 634, 635, 855
Deposit Restricted Qualified Tuition Program Act of 2010, 481
Derivatives, financial, 89, 92, 97, 104–105
Detainees, Guantánamo Bay, Cuba, 10, 211, 560–561
  appropriations
    FY 2009, 122
    FY 2010, 129
    FY 2013, 307–308
  Director of National Intelligence and, 248
  immigration benefits, 316

Miranda warnings for, 247, 279
no-fly list, 316
photos, 272
prosecution of, 285, 315
Red Cross access to, 276, 279
release of, 266, 278, 279, 292, 299
restrictions on transferring, 129, 130, 173, 210, 243–244, 271, 292, 301, 307, 314–316
Deutch, Ted (D-Fla.), 26
DHS. *See* Homeland Security Department, U.S. (DHS)
Diamond, Bob, 72
Dicks, Norman D. (D-Wash.), 394, 403
Appropriations Committee, 664
2013 budget negotiations, 181
committees, 849
environmental spending cuts, 382–383
ethics probe, 655–656
Dietary supplements, 461
Digital piracy, 320
Dill, Cynthia, 41
Dimon, Jamie, 71–72
Dingell, John D. (D-Mich.), 646
Affordable Care Act, 421, 431
FCC overhaul, 355
Federal Power Act, 401
Food Safety Modernization Act, 409
Medicare payments to physicians, 451
utility regulation, 401
Direct Loan Program, 476, 478, 479
Direct student loans, 479
Disabled persons
Americans with Disabilities Act (ADA), 259, 479 (box), 529
disability insurance outlays, 2001-2012, 466 (figure)
disability rights, 258–259
e-reader accessibility, 479 (box)
refugees, 583
Disaster relief, 10, 33
appropriations
FY 2010, 288
FY 2011, 139, 154
FY 2012, 170, 176
FY 2013, 189–190, 625
Army Corps of Engineers, U.S.
appropriations
economic stimulus, 80
FY 2010, 128
FY 2011, 153
FY 2012, 170, 176
FY 2013, 183
future storms mitigation, 625–626
water projects, 128
DISCLOSE Act. *See* Democracy Is Strengthened by Casting Light on Spending in Elections (DISCLOSE) Act
Disclosure, stock/securities, 668
Discretionary spending
caps, 2012-2021, 166
defined, 120
National Commission on Fiscal Responsibility and Reform recommendations, 143
proposed cuts, FY 2011, 135
Discrimination
Defense of Marriage Act, 182, 289, 313
House Office of General Counsel, 669–670
hate-crimes laws, 277
sexual orientation, 242, 264–265, 267, 288–289, 291, 299–300
DISH Network, 336, 337
Disproportionate-share payments, Affordable Care Act, 441–442
Distance-learning programs, 488 (box)
District of Columbia, 5, 648–650
firearms in, 560
Housing Voting Rights Act, 560
school vouchers, 121, 481, 490–491
District of Columbia v. Heller, 649
Diversity Visa Program, 489
Djou, Charles K. (D-Hawaii), 24, 26
DLA Piper, 18
DNI. *See* Office of the Director of National Intelligence (DNI)
DOD. *See* Defense Department, U.S. (DOD)
Dodd, Christopher J. (D-Conn.), 20, 68, 88, 482
Affordable Care Act, 428, 433
Banking, Housing, and Urban Affairs Committee, 642, 662
committees, 844, 846, 847
credit card regulations, 84
ethics probe, 652–653
executive pay, 531, 532
homebuyer tax credit, 504–505
Iran sanctions, 238, 239
tobacco regulation, 449
Dodd-Frank Wall Street Reform and Consumer Protection Act, 48, 68–69, 173–174, 508, 532, 533, 633
attempts to weaken, 104–105
Consumer Financial Protection Bureau (CFPB), 9, 88–89, 96–97
credit rating agencies, 99–100
debit card fees, 99
ethics probes, 672–673
executive compensation, 98
Federal Insurance Office, 98
Federal Reserve powers, 89, 93–94
final action, 91–92
Financial Stability Oversight Council, 69, 88, 92
hedge fund registration, 98
highlights, 88–89
House action, 89–90
investor protections, 101
liability and bankruptcy of failing institutions, 93
major provisions, 92–101
Office of Financial Research, 93
offsets, 89, 99
regulation of derivatives, 89
Senate action, 90–91
systemic risks management, 88
DOE. *See* Education Department, U.S. (DOE)
Doha Round, 192
Dold, Robert (R-Ill.), 43
Dole, Bob, 921 (table)
DOMA. *See* Defense of Marriage Act (DOMA)

Domenici, Pete V. (R-N.M.), 644
Domestic Nuclear Detection Office, 210
Domestic partner benefits, 603–604
  Domestic Partnership Benefits and Obligations Act (2013), 623
Domestic policy, 692–698
  See also Budget, U.S.; Economic policy
Domestic violence, 33
Dominican Republic, 201
Donahoe, Patrick R., 627
Donilon, Tom, 226 (box), 228
Donovan, Shaun, 499 (box), 501, 705 (box), 709
"Don't ask, don't tell" policy, 264–265, 267, 288–289, 291, 293, 299–300
Dorgan, Byron L. (D-N.D.), 5 (table), 371, 378
  committees, 843, 844, 845, 847
  Democratic Policy Committee ranking members and chairs, 642, 661
  Indian Affairs Committee, 643, 662
  Indian casino land, 618
  Indian health service, 617
  law enforcement on tribal lands, 563
  tobacco regulation, 449
Doyle, Mike (D-Pa.), 395
  Federal Power Act (PL 66-280), 401
Draghi, Mario, 55
DREAM (Development, Relief, and Education for Alien Minors) Act, 7, 552, 557
Dreier, David (R-Calif.), 168
  Affordable Care Act, 460
  committees, 647, 664, 853, 854
  STOCK Act, 666
Drew, Ina R., 71
Drones, Global Hawk, 182, 310, 312
Drugs and pharmaceutical industry
  Affordable Care Act, 428, 430–431, 442, 443
  biologic drug patents, 442
  biosimilar, 461, 462
  for children, 462
  classification of food or dietary supplements as drugs, 461
  drug approval process, 33, 461, 463
  drug shortage prevention, 462
  FDA user fees, 460–463
  generic, 461, 462
  importation of prescription, 461, 462
  life-saving drugs, 463
  marketing rights, 461
  medical devices tax, 424 (box)
  Medicare
    coverage gap, 424 (box), 426, 440–441
    Part D, 444
  scheduling of synthetic drugs, 463
  See also Food and Drug Administration (FDA)
Drug trafficking, 580–581
  U.S.-Mexico border, 212, 292
Drywall Safety Act of 2012, 511
Duckworht, Tammy (D-Ill.), 36
Due Process Clause, 590
Duffy, Sean P. (R-Wisc.), 621
Dugan, John, 695
Dukakis, Michael S., 921 (table)
Duncan, Arne, 705 (box), 709
  conditional education waivers, 474
  confirmation as secretary of education, 477 (box)
  RESPECT Project, 495 (box)
Duncan, John J., Jr. (R-Tenn.), 855
DuPree, Johnny, 30
Durbin, Richard J. (D-Ill.), 5 (table), 22
  Ben S. Bernanke and, 86 (box)
  budget negotiations (2012), 161, 172
  cocaine penalties, 562
  committees, 843, 844, 847, 848
  D.C. representation, 649
  dietary supplements, 461
  Foreign Intelligence Surveillance Act, 217
  Guantánamo Bay, Cuba, 315
  home loans and mortgages, 502
  majority whip, 642, 661
  minimum wage, 530
  National Commission on Fiscal Responsibility and Reform, 143
  national flood insurance, 624
  opposition to Roland Burris, 18
  Patriot Act, 209
  Postal Service, 628
  Roland W. Burris appointment, 648
  tobacco regulation, 449
  TV coverage of court proceedings, 566
  undocumented children, 557
  unemployment compensation, 527
  2009 war supplemental, 271
Dust, nuisance, 396

EA-18G Growler planes, 303, 306, 312
Eagleburger, Lawrence, 226 (box), 290
Early Head Start, 82
Early Stage Small Business Contracting Act, 631
Earmarks, 640–641
  border security bill, 2010, 212
  112th Congress ban on, 341–342
Earned-income tax credit (EITC), 80, 83
Earthquake hazard, 611
Eastwood, Clint, 38
EB (Extended Benefits) program, 520
ECB. *See* European Central Bank (ECB)
Ecology. *See* Environmental protection
Economic assistance. *See* Foreign aid
Economic Club of New York, 161
Economic crisis (2007-2008)
  bank collapses, 507
  deleveraging and, 52–53
  early recovery, 51
  Federal Reserve and, 48–49
  global impact, 55, 58–60
  household wealth and, 51
  housing bubbles, 497–498
  housing bubbles and, 53–54
  output gap, 51
  slow recovery from, 54–55
  supplemental unemployment benefits and, 79 (box)

Timothy F. Geithner and, 48
U.S. Treasury and, 48
See also Dodd-Frank Wall Street Reform and Consumer Protection Act; Troubled Assets Relief Program (TARP)
Economic Growth and Tax Relief Reconciliation Act of 2001, 487(box)
Economic policy, 47–202
American Recovery and Reinvestment Act of 2009 and, 61, 531
banks and banking (*See* Banks and banking)
budget (*See* Budget, U.S.)
Cash for Clunkers, 64, 74, 122, 272
economic growth and inflation, 1996-2012, 50 (table), 51
economic stimulus packages, 14
2009, 47, 61, 66, 78–84, 691, 692–693
2010, 74
environmental protection (*See* Environmental protection)
executive leadership, 48–49, 692–693
fiscal cliff and, 66–67, 113, 149
foreign trade (*See* Foreign trade and business)
jobs creation bill, 2010, 85–87
legislative chronology
2009-2010, 75–103, 119–148
2011-2012, 104–110
Obama's address on the state of the economy, 2009, 879–883
See also Troubled Assets Relief Program (TARP)
Economic Policy Institute, 193
Economics, Joint Committee on, 856
Economic stimulus packages, 319, 325, 353, 366
energy programs in, 368
Federal Reserve, 2008-2013, 53
2009, 47, 61, 66, 78–84
2010, 74
unused money, 99
"Economic substance," 444
Economic Support Fund program, 233
Ecuador, 194 (box)
Education
action chronology
2009-2010, 476–482
2011-2012, 483–494
adult literacy, 492
American Graduation Initiative, 478, 697
Build America bond program, 83
Chicago, Illinois, 709
distance-learning programs, 488 (box)
Elementary and Secondary Education Act of 1965, 483, 491
financial aid, 474, 476, 480–481, 484, 485
leadership for, 477 (box)
policy, 473–494
Race to the Top program, 175, 287, 473–474, 480–481, 492–494, 696
school voucher program, Washington, D.C., 121
sex, 132, 175, 443
spending bill, 2010, 453–454
State Fiscal Stabilization Fund, 82
STEM Education Coordination Act, 609–610
STEM Jobs Act of 2012, 489
STEM (Science, Technology, Engineering, and Math) Master Teacher Corps, 495 (box)
stimulus package of 2010 and, 74
student punishment, 481–482
teacher layoffs, 139
voucher program, Washington D.C., 121, 481, 490–491
See also Education Department, U.S. (DOE); Head Start; Higher education; Schools
Educational loans. *See* Student aid
Education and Labor Committee, House
Student Aid and Fiscal Responsibility Act of 2009, 477
student punishment, 481
Education and Labor/Education and the Workforce Committee, House, 647, 850
Affordable Care Act, 427–428
child nutrition bill, 466
ranking members and chairs, 646, 664
Education and Workforce Committee, House, 483, 538, 541
adult literacy, 492
charter schools, 491
homeless children, 512
school accountability, 484
student aid, 489
Education Department, U.S. (DOE), 609
appointments, 709
appropriations
FY 2010, 131
FY 2011, 139–140, 155
FY 2012, 175
FY 2013, 184
bullying and gang prevention, 492
conditional waivers, 475
disability rights, 479 (box)
Education Jobs Fund, 454
fire safety on college campuses, 482
Office of Inspector General, 477 (box)
Pell grants, 478
rules for student aid, 488
student punishment, 482
See also Education
Education Jobs and Medicaid Funding bill, 479–480
Education Jobs Fund, 454, 528
Edwards, Chet (D-Texas), 849
Edwards, George, 703
Egypt, 249, 250
Arab Spring, 223, 224, 700–701
foreign aid to, 233, 245, 252, 254
Obama's address at Cairo University, 883–888
Ehlers, Vernon L. (R-Mich.), 647
Eighth Amendment, 591
Eisenhower, Dwight D., president, 915
EITC. *See* Earned-income tax credit (EITC)
Elaf Islamic Bank, 256
Elderly persons
Affordable Care Act, 430–431
Medicare (*See* Medicare)
refugees, 583
Social Security (*See* Social Security)
Special Aging Committee, 643, 645, 662, 848
Election Assistance Commission, 682
Elections
action chronology
2009-2010, 677–680
2011-2012, 681–682

ballot initiatives, 44
campaign ads on public tv, 681 (box)
Congressional, 17–18, 23–26, 30, 40–44
2010, 932–940
2012, 941–949
lame duck sessions, 7, 9, 22, 857–859
reapportionment, 1789-2010, 873
distributions of house seats and electoral votes, 928
gubernatorial, 18, 25, 44, 932–940, 942–949
law, 586–587
money in, 36
presidential
Presidential Election Campaign Fund, 154, 682
1789-2012 summary, 919–921
2008, 3, 643–644, 702, 924, 925
2012, 9–12, 35–40, 702–704, 926, 927
Presidential Election Campaign Fund, 154
by region, 2000-2012, 43 (table)
results of House, 1928-2012, 950–955
special, 6, 30, 43–44, 931, 941
state, 25, 44
voter fraud, 680
See also Campaign finance
Electric grid protection, 382
Electronic products recycling, 379
Elementary and Secondary Education Act of 1965, 483, 491
Ellmers, Renee (R-N.C.), 854
E-mail records protection, 614–615
Emanuel, Rahm, 17, 645, 654, 693
Affordable Care Act, 433
Embryos, human, 131
Emergency contraceptive, 422 (box)
Emergency Economic Stabilization Act of 2008, 60, 62
See also Troubled Assets Relief Program (TARP)
Emergency Homeowners Relief Fund, 101
Emergency preparedness. *See* Disaster relief; Federal Emergency Management Agency (FEMA)
Emergency spending, 120
Emergency Unemployment Compensation program, 519
Emerson, Jo Ann (R-Mo.), 383, 849
Affordable Care Act, 459
Employee benefits
health insurance (*See* Affordable Care Act; Health insurance)
pensions and retirement income (*See* Pensions and retirement income)
Trade Adjustment Assistance Act, 199–200
unemployment compensation (*See* Unemployment compensation)
Employee Free Choice Act, 533, 711
Employers and Affordable Care Act
automatic enrollment, 439
employer notice rules, 538–539
mandate, 423 (box), 426, 429, 430 (box)
penalties, 438
vouchers, 438–439
Employment
contractor tax withholding repeal, 169
economic development (*See* Economic policy)
E-Verify system, 129, 210
'green' jobs, 507
Lilly Ledbetter Fair Pay Act (2009), 517, 528, 548, 550
pensions, 486
preparation for, 488 (box)
sex discrimination (*See* Sex discrimination)
STEM jobs, 489
unemployment (*See* Unemployment)
unemployment compensation (*See* Unemployment compensation)
Encouraging Innovation and Effective Teachers Act of 2012, 484
Endangered Species Act, 397, 403
End users, 105
Energy and Commerce Committee, House, 80, 334, 646, 850–851
Affordable Care Act, 427, 428
on Communications, Technology, and the Internet, 336
home improvement rebates, 506
ranking members and chairs, 646, 664
tobacco regulation, 448
Energy and Natural Resources Committee, Senate, 364, 371, 644, 710, 845
ranking members and chairs, 642, 662
Energy Department, U.S. (DOE), 608, 609
appointments, 708
appropriations
FY 2009, 121, 128
FY 2010, 124
FY 2012, 173
FY 2013, 183
"cash for clunkers," 506
energy-efficient home improvements, 381–382
Federal Power Act (PL 66-280), 401
Idaho National Laboratory, 382
leadership, 367
nuclear programs, 278–279, 294, 303–304, 307
Office of Science, 121
research programs, 381
See also Energy policy
Energy Independence and Global Warming Committee, House, 646, 647, 664, 855
Energy policy, 363–404
action chronology
FY 2009-2010, 366–385
FY 2011-2012, 386–404
climate change, 364
domestic oil production, 364
electric grid protection, 382
energy-efficient home improvements, 381–382
energy production credit, 83
Green the Capitol initiative, 670
incandescent light bulbs, 395
Low Income Home Energy Assistance Program, 138
oil drilling safety laws, 364
renewable-energy programs, 125, 183
TransCanada Keystone XL pipeline, 364–365
Weather Assistance Program, 82
wind, 381
Engel, Eliot (D-N.Y.), 851
England. *See* Great Britain
Enron, 666
Ensign, John (R-Nev.), 30, 384
Children's Health Insurance Program, 446
D.C. representation, 649

"don't ask, don't tell," 289
ethics probe, 651–652, 670–672
Republican Policy Committee, 642
Senate rules, 662
sexual misadventures and resignation, 671 (box)
Tom Daschle, 707
Entitlement programs, 9, 161–162
National Commission on Fiscal Responsibility and Reform, 142–144, 697
See also Social Security; Welfare and social services
Environment. *See* Environmental protection; Environmental Protection Agency (EPA)
Environmental protection
algal blooms, 378
Clean Air Act, 107, 384, 387, 397–398, 594, 696
Clean Water Act, 173, 184, 380
Clean Water and Drinking Water State Revolving Funds, 184, 381, 385
environmental law, 594
foreign trade agreements, 197, 198
greenhouse emissions, 5, 151, 175
green schools, 380–381
lead pipes, 378
nuclear waste cleanup, 173, 183
Obama policy, 695–696
outlays for natural resources, 364 (figur)
recycling electronic products, 379
Environmental Protection Agency (EPA), 82, 107, 594, 696
air pollution, 388–389
air pollution grants, 378
algal blooms, 378
appropriations
FY 2010, 129–130
FY 2011, 27, 152, 154
FY 2012, 174–175
FY 2013, 183–184
carbon dioxide regulation authority, 130
chemical safety standards bill, 399
coal
ash, 389–390
regulations, 399–400
drywall safety, 508
formaldehyde emissions, 379–380
low-level nuclear waste, 379
nuisance dust, 396
oil spill response, 377
pesticides, 390
refinery pollutant, 393
Environmental Quality Incentives Program (EQIP), 466
Environment and Public Works Committee, Senate, 342, 491, 644, 709, 845–846
chemical safety standards, 399
global warming bill, 372
National Women's History Museum, 616
ranking members and chairs, 642–643, 662
Enzi, Michael B. (R-Wyo.), 411, 847
Affordable Care Act, 428
education, 484
FDA user fees, 461
Health, Education, Labor, and Pensions Committee, 644, 662
labor union regulations, 538
public safety workers, 534
tobacco regulation, 449
wage parity, 529
EPA. *See* Environmental Protection Agency (EPA)
Equal Protection Clause, Fifth Amendment, 669
Equal Rights Amendment, 616
E-reader accessibility, 479 (box)
Erickson, Erick, 152
Eshoo, Anna G. (D-Calif.), 336
committees, 854
2011 defense authorization, 292
Essential benefits package, Affordable Care Act, 437
Establishment Clause, First Amendment, 590
Estate taxes, 146–147
Estrada, Miguel, 712
Ethics Committee, House, 851, 854
ethics probes
Alan B. Mollohan (D-W.Va.), 654
Alcee L. Hastings (D-Fla.), 673–674
Bennie Thompson (D-Miss.), 655
C. W. Bill Young (R-Fla.), 655–656
Carolyn Cheeks Kilpatrick (D-Mich.), 655
Charles Rangel (D-N.Y.), 22, 642, 646, 655, 657–659
Christopher Dodd (D-Conn.), 652–653
David Wu (D-Ore.), 673
Donald M. Payne (D-N.J.), 655
Donna M. C. Christensen (D-V.I.), 655
Don Young (R-Alaska), 673
Eric Massa (D-N.Y.), 654–655
James P. Moran (D-Va.), 655–656
Jane Harman (D-Calif.), 653
Jesse L. Jackson, Jr. (D-Ill.), 653, 675–676
Joe Wilson (R-S.C.), 653–654
John Campbell (R-Calif.), 672–673
John P. Murtha (D-Pa.), 655–656
Joseph Crowley (D-N.Y.), 672–673
Kent Conrad (D-N.D.), 652–653
Laura Richardson (D-Calif.), 656, 674
Marcy Kaptur (D-Ohio), 655–656
Mary Landrieu (D-La.), 652
Maxine Waters (D-Calif.), 656–657, 674–675
Nathan Deal (R-Ga.), 656
Norman D. Dicks (D-Wash.), 655–656
Peter J. Visclosky (D-Ind.), 655–656
Pete Stark (D-Calif.), 654
Sam Graves (R-Mo.), 654
sexual misadventures and resignation, 671 (box)
Shelley Berkley (D-Nev.), 676
Todd Tiahrt (R-Kan.), 655–656
Tom DeLay (R-Texas), 660
Tom Price (R-Ga.), 672–673
Vern Buchanan (R-Fla.), 674
William J. Jefferson (D-La.), 660
Yvette D. Clarke (D-N.Y.), 655
ranking members and chairs, 662, 664
See also Standards of Official Conduct Committee, House
Ethics Committee, Senate, 645, 662, 848
ethics probes
David Vitter (R-La.), 672, 684
John Ensign, 671–672

Roland W. Burris (D-Ill.), 17
Tom Coburn (R-Okla.), 672
ranking members and chairs, 643
See also Congressional ethics probes
Ethics in Goverment Act, 668
Ethics Reform Act of 1989, 683
EURIBOR, 72
Europe
bank stress tests, 70
economic crisis of 2007-2008, 51, 55
European Union (EU), 192
Iran sanctions and, 238
See also specific countries
European Banking Authority, 70
European Central Bank (ECB), 55, 70
European Union (EU), 192
E-Verify system, 129, 210
Excess public properties, 634–635
Executive bonuses, 531–532
Executive branch
party affiliations, 1789-2015, 929–930
See Federal government (general); *specific agencies and departments*
Executive compensation, 65, 84, 98
health insurance deductions, 444
Executive in Need of Scrutiny (REINS) Act, 631
Executive pay, 530–533
Export-Import Bank
Iran sanctions, 240, 241
reauthorization, 200
Extended Benefits (EB) program, 520

FAA. *See* Federal Aviation Administration (FAA)
F/A-18 aircraft, 278, 293–294, 303, 306
Fabrizio, McLaughlin & Associates, 693
FAC (Federal Additional Compensation), 519
Facebook, 4, 6
F/A-18 E/F Super Hornet planes, 312
Fair Claims Act of 2012, 602
Fair Labor Standards Act of 1938, 529, 541
Faleomavaega, Eni F. H. (D-Am. Samoa), 851
Fallows, James, 692
Family and Medical Leave Act (1993), 602–603
Family Education Loan Program, 476, 477–478, 479
Family planning. *See* Birth control
Fannie Mae. *See* Federal National Mortgage Association (Fannie Mae)
Fansmith, Jon S., 487
F-22A Raptor Fighter, 306
Farm Credit System, 101
Farms and farming. *See* Agriculture and farming
Farr, Sam (D-Calif.), 469
Fast-track rules, 196
Fattah, Chaka (D-Pa.), 575
FBI. *See* Federal Bureau of Investigation (FBI)
FCC. *See* Federal Communications Commission (FCC)
FDA. *See* Food and Drug Administration (FDA)
FDIC. *See* Federal Deposit Insurance Corporation (FDIC)
FEC. *See* Federal Election Commission (FEC)
Federal Additional Compensation (FAC), 519
Federal Aviation Administration (FAA), 10–11, 539, 540, 710
Airport Improvement Grant, 325
budget outlays, 33
Extension Act, 327–332
airline safety and pilot training, 332
reauthorization, 139, 327–328, 340, 349–354
final House action, 331
House Committee Action, 328–329
House floor action, 329–330
senate approval, 330–331
short-term extensions, 331–332
shutdown, 319–320
Federal Bureau of Investigation (FBI), 549
appropriations
FY 2010, 246
FY 2012, 171
FY 2013, 254
MF Global and, 70–71
Patriot Act, 208
wiretapping, 205
Federal Communications Commission (FCC), 144, 563
broadband access, 356
Broadband Technology Opportunities Program, 333
Internet piracy, 357–359
leadership, 323
Lifeline program, 335
National Broadband Plan, 334–335
net neturality, 355–356
Open Internet Advisory Committee, 334
Open Internet Order, 334
overhaul, 354–355
satellite and cable programming, 357–358
Spectrum Auction, 356–357
Federal contractors
collective bargaining, 309
performing functions of civilian employees, 309–310
Federal courts, administrative changes to, 566
Federal debt and deficit. *See* Budget, U.S.
Federal Deposit Insurance Corporation (FDIC), 20, 54, 605
Asset Guarantee Program and, 63
borrowing authority, 500, 502
covered bonds, 507
deposit-based college accounts, 481
Dodd-Frank Act and, 68, 69, 88, 91, 93–96
Financial Stability Oversight Council and, 92
increase in deposit insurance, 500, 502
JP Morgan Chase and, 72
orderly liquidation of failing financial institutions, 93
short term guarantees, 96
Federal Election Commission (FEC), 36, 652, 674
Citizens United v. Federal Election Commission, 36, 677, 678, 682
Presidential Election Campaign Fund, 154, 682
Federal Emergency Management Agency (FEMA), 29, 597, 610, 611–612, 624–625, 626
appropriations
FY 2010, 129, 210, 211–212, 288
FY 2011, 139, 154
FY 2012, 174
FY 2013, 190

Disaster Relief Fund, 154, 176, 597
disaster response, 205
National Flood Insurance Program, 190
Superstorm Sandy, 704
Federal Employee Retirement System (FERS), 133, 448, 450, 542, 543, 621, 627
Federal employees
American Federation of Government Employees, 448
contractors (*See* Federal contractors)
domestic partnerships, 623
federal worker pension contributions, 543
Foreign Service, 241, 242, 250
intelligence leaks, 622
parental leave for, 602–603
pay for, 600–601, 621–622
pension contributions, 541–544, 621
retirement, 133, 448, 450, 542, 543, 621, 627
software sharing, 603
tax delinquent, 624
teleworking, 601
Thrift Savings Plan, 448, 450
tobacco regulation, 448
whistleblowers, 251, 601, 623
Federal Employee Tax Accountability Act of 2013, 624
Federal Energy Regulatory Commission (FERC), 382
Federal Facilities Consolidation and Efficiency Act (2011), 636
Federal government (general)
budget (*See* Budget, U.S.)
Census Bureau, 130, 153
sequestration, 29, 113, 116–117, 120, 177, 186, 189, 685
congressional pay and, 685
Federal Highway Trust Fund, 32, 87, 133, 172, 185, 319, 324, 326, 340, 342, 527
Federal Home Loan Mortgage Corporation (Freddie Mac), 48, 53, 67–68, 108, 138, 497–499, 532
bailout, 511 (box)
Dodd-Frank Act and, 91
executive pay, 510
limiting, 511–512
PACE loans, 501 (box)
STOCK Act, 668
Federal Housing Administration (FHA)
appropriations, FY 2011, 138
establishment of, 497
insurance premiums, 500
mortgage insurance, 503
Refinance Program, 509
Federal Housing Finance Agency, 53–54, 497–498
Financial Stability Oversight Council and, 92
Federal Insecticide, Fungicide and Rodenticide Act, 390
Federal Insurance Office, 98–99
Federal judges, impeachment of, 557–559
Federal lands, 374, 398, 485
Federal Land Assistance, Management, and Enhancement (FLAME) Fund, 385
firearms on, 559–560
Federal Mediation and Conciliation Service, 540
Federal Medical Assistance Percentage, 141
Federal National Mortgage Association (Fannie Mae), 48, 53, 67–68, 108, 532
appropriations, 138
Dodd-Frank Act and, 91
STOCK Act, 668
Federal National Mortgage Association (Fannie Mae)
bailout, 511 (box)
economic crisis, 497–499
executive pay, 510
limiting, 511–512
PACE loans, 501 (box)
Federal Railroad Administration, 325
Federal Real Property Asset Management Reform Act (2012), 635
Federal Real Property Council, 634
Federal Register, 538
Federal regulations filing, 615
Federal Reserve Act, 95
Federal Reserve Bank, 47, 48, 143
actions during the financial crisis and recession, 56–59, 60
audit, 633
bank stress tests, 69–70
Ben S. Bernanke and, 48–49, 86 (box)
crisis programs, 56–57
criticisms of, 59
deleveraging and, 52
Dodd-Frank Act and, 89, 93–94
Financial Stability Oversight Council and, 92
housing bubble and, 53–54
large-scale asset purchases, 57–58
leadership, 48–49, 54
results of crisis actions by, 58–59
stimulus, 2008-2013, 53
Federal Reserve Transparency Act of 2009, 633
Federal science programs, 609–610
Federal-State Extended Unemployment Compensation Act of 1970, 519
Federal teleworking, 601
Federal Trade Commission and National Gallery of Art Facility Consolidation, Savings, and Efficiency Act of 2011, 636
Federal Transit Administration, 325
Feinberg, Richard, 65
Feingold, Russ (D-Wis.), 20, 23, 25, 41
Bipartisan Campaign Reform Act, 677 (box)
committees, 846, 847
D.C. representation, 650
Dodd-Frank Act, 90, 92
Patriot Act, 209
sponsors solar energy technology bill, 380
Feinstein, Dianne (D-Calif.), 227 (box)
BPA restrictions, 411
committees, 844, 848
D.C. representation, 649
defense authorization (2012), 301
defense authorization (2013), 311
detainees photos, 272
detention of U.S. citizens, 311
feedlot modification, 384
Foreign Intelligence Surveillance Act, 215, 217, 551
Indian casino land, 618
2013 intelligence authorization, 255

journalism sources, 559
law and law enforcement, 568
Patent law, 561, 570
Patriot Act, 209
same-sex couples, 581
Select Intelligence Committee, 643, 662
TV coverage of court proceedings, 566
on Yucca Mountain bill, 394
FEMA. *See* Federal Emergency Management Agency (FEMA)
Fenty, Adrian M., 650
FERS (Federal Employee Retirement System), 542, 543, 621, 627
F-18 fighter, 276
FHA Reform Act of 2010, 503
Fifth Amendment, U.S., Equal Protection Clause, 669
Fighter planes. *See specific aircraft*
Filibusters and cloture votes, 4, 6, 639–640
Affordable Care Act, 15, 425
Dodd-Frank Act, 90
"don't ask, don't tell," 288–289
Education Jobs and Medicaid Funding bill, 479–480
exemptions rules, 136
FY 2010, 129
FY 2010 war supplemental, 139
rules, 663
Senate cloture votes, 1917-2013, 860–871
See also Congressional votes
Filner, Bob (D-Calif.), 855
Veterans Affairs Committee, 646, 664
Finance
banking (*See* Banks and banking)
budget (*See* Budget, U.S.)
economic policy (*See* Economic policy)
interest rates, 1996-2012, 50 (table)
Finance Committee, Senate, 644, 846
Affordable Care Act, 429–431
Children's Health Insurance Program, 446
ranking members and chairs, 643, 662
Russian trade normalization, 201
Financial aid to students. *See* Student aid
Financial crisis. *See* Economic crisis (2007-2008)
Financial crisis responsibility fee, 136
Financial derivatives, 89, 92, 97, 104–105
Financial institutions
regulatory changes under Dodd-Frank Act, 94–95
winding down of failing, 93
See also Banks and banking
Financial regulation policy, 20, 104–105, 695
See also Dodd-Frank Wall Street Reform and Consumer Protection Act; Troubled Assets Relief Program (TARP)
Financial Services Committee, House, 105, 338, 647, 851
covered bonds, 507
Fannie Mae and Freddie Mac, 511–512
homeless children, 512
mortgage lender regulation, 503
ranking members and chairs, 646, 664
Section 8 vouchers, 505
Shareholder Protection Act, 679–680
Subcommittee on Oversight and Investigations, 71
Financial Services Roundtable, 161
Financial Stability Oversight Council, 69, 88, 92, 97
Financial Times, 192, 228
Firearms. *See* Guns and gun control
First Amendment, U.S. Constitution, 589–590
Affordable Care Act contraceptive coverage, 459 (box)
campaign ads on public tv, 681 (box)
establishment clause, 590
FISA. *See* Foreign Intelligence Surveillance Act (FISA)
Fiscal cliff, 66–67, 113, 149, 185–186, 263, 537
background, 186
bill major provisions, 189
early skirmishing, 186–187
McConnell-Biden compromise, 188–189
postelection positioning, 187
private talks between Obama, Boehner, 187–188
See also Budget, U.S.; Economic crisis (2007-2008)
Fiscal year, 120
Fish and Wildlife Service, 383
Fitzpatrick, Michael G. (R-Pa.), 512
F-35 Joint Strike Fighter, 22, 266, 273, 276, 300–301, 302
appropriations
FY 2010, 133, 281–283
FY 2011, 151, 153, 292, 294
FY 2012, 173, 302–303, 306
FY 2013, 312
engine, 266, 277, 292, 295, 299, 300
termination, 297
Flags, American made, 616–617
Flake, Jeff (R-Ariz.), 300
disclaimers in mailings bill, 685
Native Hawaiian government, 619
nutrition bill, 469
online advertising bill, 685
Pakistan Counterinsurgency Fund, 304
Fleming, John (R-La.), 853
Fletcher, Matthew L.M., 618
Flood Insurance Reform Act of 2011, 625
Flood Insurance Reform Priorities Act of 2010, 610
Floods, 139, 153, 288
insurance, 190, 610–611, 625–626
Flu, pandemic, 270, 272
FOIA. *See* Freedom of Information Act (FOIA)
Food, Conservation, and Energy Act of 2008, 102
Food and Drug Administration (FDA)
appropriations
FY 2010, 128
FY 2012, 171
FY 2013, 182
approval process for prescription drugs, 33
biologic drug patents, 442
conflict of interest policy, 463
emergency contraceptive, 422 (box)
medical devices review, 461
regulating food products, 407, 409
scheduling of synthetic drugs, 463
tobacco regulation, 15, 419, 448–450
user fees, 460–463
See also Drugs and pharmaceutical industry
Food and nutrition
bill, 2012, 468–470
child nutrition bill, 420, 465–467
classification of food or dietary supplements as drugs, 461
dietary supplements, 461

food safety, 22, 138, 152, 171, 196
Food Safety Modernization Act, 411–412
restaurant menu labeling, 443
Senate committees, 843–844
Food assistance programs
Supplemental Nutrition Assistance Program (SNAP), 33, 61, 82, 141, 171, 407, 413, 466–467, 468
Women's, Infants, and Children's (WIC) program, 128, 152, 171, 413
See also Welfare and social services
Food Research and Action Center, 466
Food Safety and Inspection Service, 152
Food stamps. *See* Supplemental Nutrition Assistance Program (SNAP)
Forbes, J. Randy (R-Va.), 276, 850
COPS, 562
detainee release, 292
Forbes, Michael P. (R-N.Y.), 18
Ford, Gerald R., president, 712
Ford Motor Company, 63, 196
Foreclosures, 53–54
TARP programs for, 64
Foreign Affairs Committee, House, 647, 851
Iran sanctions, 239
Pakistan aid, 236
ranking members and chairs, 646, 664
Foreign aid
Afghanistan (*See* Afghanistan)
appropriations
FY 2010, 156
FY 2011, 156
FY 2012, 176
bilateral economic and military assistance, 245, 248
budget, 2001-2012, 224 (table)
Dodd-Frank Act and, 101
Economic Support Fund program, 233
Egypt, 233, 245, 252, 254
global health, 245, 248
Haiti, 233, 288
international financial institutions, 245, 248
international peacekeeping, 245
Israel, 228, 245, 293
Millennium Challenge Account program aid appropriations, 250
FY 2010, 156, 245
FY 2011, 156
Pakistan, 233, 236–238, 252, 253–254, 270, 272–273
USAID, 243, 245, 253
See also Foreign policy
Foreign Corrupt Practices Act, 660
Foreign Intelligence and Information Commission, 248
Foreign Intelligence Surveillance Act (FISA), 205, 206, 209, 551
extension, 215–217
overhaul, 251
Foreign policy, 223–259, 690, 698–701
action chronology, 2009-2010, 232–248
Afghanistan (*See* Afghanistan war)
Arab Spring, 223–224
budget actions
FY 2009 state-foreign operations funding, 232–233
FY 2009 supplemental appropriations, 233
FY 2010 state-foreign operations funding, 243–245
FY 2011 state-foreign operations funding, 248, 249–250
FY 2012 state-foreign operations funding, 252–254
FY 2013 state-foreign operations funding, 258
Iran, 224–225, 232, 238–241, 243, 255–258
Iraq, 225, 234–235 (box), 236 (box) (*See also* Iraq war)
Israel and the Palestinians, 225, 228
pivot toward Asia, 228
Syria, 223–225
See also Foreign aid
Foreign Relations Committee, Senate, 644, 846
New START treaty, 290
ranking members and chairs, 643, 662
Russian trade normalization, 201
State Department reauthorization, 241
Susan Rice and, 227 (box)
Foreign Service, 241, 242, 250
Foreign tax provisions, 480
Foreign trade and business, 192
agreements, 192
Andean Trade Preference Act, 194 (box), 197, 198
China, 191, 192, 193–194
Colombia, 193, 195, 197–198
North American Free Trade Agreement (NAFTA), 195
Panama, 193, 194 (box), 195–196, 198–199
Russia, 191, 201
South Korea, 193, 195–197
budget bills, 156
economic policy, 74, 191
Export-Import Bank
Iran sanctions, 240
reauthorization, 200
fast-track rules, 196
Generalized System of Preferences (GSP), 194 (box), 199
importation of prescription drugs, 461, 462
measures package, 2012, 200–201
sanctions, 238–241, 243, 255–258, 308, 311
Trade Adjustment Assistance Act (TAA), 74, 83, 194 (box), 196, 199–200
trade balances, 191, 192 (table)
trade policy, 192
Forests and forest products
Senate committees, 843–844
U.S. Forest Service, 129
Formaldehyde emissions, 379–380
Formaldehyde Standards for Composite Wood Products Act, 380
For-profit career colleges, 488 (box)
Fortenberry, Jeff (R-Neb.), 458 (box), 849
Fox News, 435, 651
Foxx, Virginia (R-N.C.), 850
adult literacy, 492
community service programs, 604–605
Puerto Rico political status, 619
student aid, 488
Frank, Barney (D-Mass.), 68, 77, 88, 338
2010 budget negotiations, 244
committees, 851
executive bonuses, 532
executive pay, 533
Fannie and Freddie executive pay, 510

Financial Services Committee, 646, 664
foreclosure aid, 509
Internet gambling, 566
Maxine Waters ethics probe, 675
mortgage insurance, 503
mortgage regulation, 502–503
Section 8 vouchers, 506
Franken, Al (D-Minn.), 14, 17, 642, 848
Franklin D, Roosevelt Presidential Library and Museum, 615
Franks, Trent (R-Ariz.), 852
abortion, 579
missile defense, 276, 308
F-22 Raptor Fighter, 133, 265–266, 267, 273, 275, 276–277
appropriations
FY 2010, 281–283
FY 2011, 294
procurement, 278
Fraud, voter, 680
Frazier, Lynn, 44
Freddie Mac. *See* Federal Home Loan Mortgage Corporation (Freddie Mac)
Free Application for Federal Student Aid, 478
Freedom of Information Act (FOIA), 271, 272, 602
Freeh, Louis J., 70–71
Frelinghuysen, Rodney P. (R-N.J.), 377, 849
Friends of Angelo, 652
Frooman, Michael, 195 (box)
Fudge, Ann, 143
Fudge, Marcia (D-Ohio), 482
Furman, Jason, 49
Future Combat Systems, 278, 281, 284, 294, 303, 307

Gaddafi, Muammar, 223, 224, 250, 300, 689, 701, 704
Galbraith, Gatewood, 30
Gallegly, Elton (R-Calif.), 853
Gallup Polls, 27, 702
Gambling
Internet, 566
background, 338
House action, 338
Senate action, 338–339
112th Congress work on, 357–358
Native American casinos, 618
See Internet, gambling
Game Change, 646 (box)
Gang of Eight, 246, 247
Gang of Six, 164, 429
Gang prevention, 491–492
GAO. *See* Government Accountability Office (GAO)
Garamendi, John (D-Calif.), 305
2013 defense authorization, 308
Gardner, Cory (R-Colo.), 460
Garland, Merrick B., 711, 712
Garrett, Scott (R-N.J.)
covered bonds, 507
mortgage insurance, 503
mortgage lender regulation, 503
Gas. *See* Gasoline; Natural gas; Oil
Gasoline
biofuels, 308, 311, 444
taxes, 133
Gates, Robert M. (secretary of defense), 22, 153, 173, 227 (box), 263, 264–265, 267, 270, 274 (box), 296, 297, 704
"don't ask, don't tell," 288, 289
F-35 engine, 295
nomination by Obama, 705 (box), 706
Gawker, 671 (box)
GDP. *See* Gross domestic product (GDP)
Geithner, Timothy F., 48, 66 (figure), 160, 161, 422 (box), 709
bank stress tests, 694
2009 debt ceiling increase, 134
fiscal cliff, 186, 187
LIBOR scandal and, 72
nomination by Obama, 705 (box), 706
tax problems, 706
Genachowski, Julius, 323, 333
Gender-based wage discrimination, 528–529
General government
about, 597, 604
America COMPETES Act, 607–609
American community survey, 635–636
American-made U.S. flags, 616–617
community service programs, 604–605
Constellation space program, 626–627
contractors, 630
cybersecurity research, 615
deceptive use of "census," 614
domestic partner benefits, 603–604, 623
earthquake hazard, 611
e-mail records protection, 614–615
excess public properties, 634–635
FDR memorabilia, 615–616
Federal employee intelligence leaks, 622
Federal Reserve audit, 633
Federal science programs, 609–610
Federal teleworking, 601
Federal worker pay, 600–601
Federal worker software sharing, 603
Federal workforce pensions, 621
FEMA, 611–612. 626
filing Federal regulations, 615
FTC and National Gallery, 636
GAO authority, 634
government agency efficiency, 612
government spending accountability, 633
Hatch Act, 622
Hurricane Sandy, 597, 625–626
immigration status on census, 614
improper payments, 612–613, 634
Indian casino land, 618
Indian health service, 617
Indian tribes recognition, 617–618
information overclassification, 613
Mark Twain Commemorative Coin, 629–630
merit-based pay plan, 600
NASA, 605–607
national flood insurance, 610–611, 624–625
National Women's History Museum, 616
Native Americans, 617
native Hawaiian government, 618–619
OMB performance standards, 633–634
outlays for, 598

parental leave for Federal workers, 602–603
Peace Corps volunteer protection, 624
plain writing, 613–614
political debate, 598–599
Postal Service, 601, 627–629
presidential records, 616
Puerto Rico political status, 619–620
regulatory oversight, 631–632
restrictions on regulations, 632–633
small business Federal contracting, 630–631
tax delinquents and Federal work, 624
whistleblower protection, 601–602, 623
Generalized System of Preferences (GSP), 194 (box), 199
General Motors Corp., 48, 61, 63–64, 65, 76, 703
bankruptcy, 63–64
franchise dealerships, 131
Obama and, 694
General Services Administration (GSA)
appropriations, 131
government spending accountability, 633
public park or recreation area transfers, 635
Generic drugs, 461, 462
Geneva Conventions, 279, 707
Geoghegan, Pat, 65
George, Esther, 59
Gephardt, Richard (D-Mo.), 134, 665
Gephardt rule, 134, 665
Germany
economic crisis of 2007-2008 and, 55
Holocaust survivors, 580
Gerrymandering, 4
Ghailani, Ahmed, 314
Gibbs, Bob (R-Ohio), 390, 855
Gibson, Chris (R-N.Y.), 43
Giffords, Gabrielle (D-Ariz.), 10, 27, 43, 458
committees, 854
NASA, 607
shooting, 643 (box)
solar energy technology, 380
Gillespie, Ed, 36
Gillibrand, Kirsten (D-N.Y.), 17, 26, 30, 844
committees, 843
nutrition bill, 469
Gingrey, Phil (R-Ga.), 852
Gingrich, Newt (R-Ga.), 36, 37, 661 (box), 702
Ginsburg, Ruth Bader, 10, 21, 593, 594, 666
gender-based wage discrimination, 528
liberal positions, 584, 585, 586, 590
Giovagnoli, Mary, 556
Global climate change, 607
budget bills, 245
HR 2454—H Rept 111-137, Part 1
committee action on, 369–370
floor action on, 370–371
HR 2454 stalls, 2009, 367–368
Obama address on, 892–893
Obama policy, 695–696
Global Hawk surveillance drones, 182, 310, 312
Global health, 245, 248, 253
Global impact of the economic crisis of 2007-2008, 55, 58–60
GMAC/Ally Financial, 65
Gohmert, Louie (R-Texas), 309
COPS, 562
Golden parachutes, 84, 98
Goldman Sachs, 63, 70, 77, 195
Gold Plan, Affordable Care Act, 437
Gonzalez, Alberto R., 653
Goodlatte, Robert W. (R-Va.), 647, 675, 853
impeachment of Federal judges, 558
journalism sources, 559
undocumented children, 557
Goodwin, Carte P. (D-W.Va.), 26
unemployment compensation, 524
Goolsbee, Austan, 49
GOP. *See* Republican Party
Gordon, Bart (D-Tenn.), 373, 664, 854
NASA, 608
Science and Technology Committee, 646
Gore, Al (vice president), 921 (table)
plain language in government, 613
Government. *See* Federal government (general); State and local government
Government Accountability Office (GAO), 530, 603, 627, 634
ACORN defunding, 680
appropriations
FY 2010, 128
FY 2011, 154
FY 2012, 175
border entry points, 219
defense acquisition rules, 268
Defense of Marriage Act, 669
Dodd-Frank Act and, 89, 94
F-35 engine, 299
report on electronic waste, 379
STOCK Act, 668
student punishment, 481
Government agency efficiency, 612
Government Customer Service Improvement Act of 2012, 633
Government Efficiency, Effectiveness, and Performance (GPRA) Modernization Act, 612
Government Efficiency through Small Business Contracting Act of 2012, 630
Government National Mortgage Association (Ginnie Mae), 68
Government Printing Office, 856
appropriations
FY 2010, 128
FY 2012, 175
pocket edition Constitution, 670
Stop the OverPrinting (STOP) Act, 670
Government Spending Accountability Act (2013), 633
Gowdy, Trey (R-S.C.), 853
GPRA. *See* Government Efficiency, Effectiveness, and Performance (GPRA) Modernization Act
Graham, Lindsay (R-S.C.), 122, 364, 366, 367
Abu Ghraib prison, 271
appellate judgeships, 576, 577
2013 budget negotiation, 181
Guantánamo Bay, Cuba, 315
Iran sanctions, 256
Iraq withdrawal, 699
New START treaty, 291
offshore drilling, 373

2012 state-foreign operations funding, 253
undocumented children, 557
Gramm-Leach-Bliley Act of 1999, 95
Gramm-Rudman-Hollings anti-deficit law, 685
Granger, Kay (R-Texas)
committees, 849
state department funding, FY 2010, 243
Granholm, Jennifer, 711
Grassley, Charles E. (R-Iowa), 86
Affordable Care Act, 429
appellate judgeships, 577
Children's Health Insurance Program, 446
committees, 846, 847
Dodd-Frank Act, 90
E-Verify system, 211
executive bonuses, 531
Finance Committee, 644
Holder held in contempt of Congress, 573, 574
job creation and protection, 527
Judiciary Committee, 662
justice leadership, 549
Medicare payments to physicians, 452
Pakistan aid, 237
Patent law, 570
Patriot Act, 215
STOCK Act, 666, 667
Timothy Geithner nomination, 706
TV coverage of court proceedings, 565–566
Violence Against Women Act, 572
Graves, Sam (R-Mo.), 854
ethics probe, 654
Small Business Committee, 647, 664
small business Federal contracting, 630
Graves, Tom (R-Ga.), 26
Grayson, Alan (D-Ill.), 36
Grayson, Trey, 24
Great Britain
Bank of England, 72
LIBOR scandal, 72
Great Recession. *See* Economic crisis (2007-2008)
Greece, 51, 55
Greenhouse gas emissions, 5, 151, 175, 363–364, 386–387
cap-and-trade model for reducing, 369
Clean Air Act Amendments, 372–373
Green the Capitol initiative, 670
regulation, 5, 151, 175
Green schools bill, 380–381
Green the Capitol initiative, 670
Gregg, Judd (R-N.H.), 87, 338, 662, 845
Afghanistan aid, 244
Budget Committee, 644
Cash for Clunkers, 272
debt ceiling increase, 134, 141
debt commission bill, 127
National Commission on Fiscal Responsibility and Reform, 143
nomination by Obama, 708
Postal Service retiree benefits, 601
public safety workers, 534
Griffin, Tim (R-Ark.), restrictions on regulations, 632
Griffith, Parker (R-Ala.), 18
Grijalva, Raúl M. (D-Ariz.), 853
federal lands bill, 398
hunting and fishing regulations, 400–401
Gross domestic product (GDP)
deficit as percentage of, 125
FY 2010 budget and, 126
FY 2011 budget and, 136
National Commission on Fiscal Responsibility and Reform recommendations, 143
taxes and other revenues as percentage of GDP, 1935-2013, 149 (table)
Ground-based Midcourse Defense system, 308
Ground Combat Vehicle, 294, 303, 307
GSA. *See* General Services Administration (GSA)
Guam, 298, 648
construction workers minimum wage, 530
Guang-cheng, Chen, 228
Guantánamo Bay, Cuba, 10, 211, 267, 383
appropriations
FY 2009, 122, 270
FY 2010, 129
FY 2013, 307–308
Director of National Intelligence and, 248
military commissions act, 316
military tribunals, 285
plans for closure of, 316
recidivism, 316
release of detainees from, 266, 278, 292, 299
restrictions on transferring detainees from, 129, 130, 173, 210, 243–244, 271, 292, 301, 307, 314–316
Gubernatorial elections, 18, 25, 30, 44
2009 special, 931
2010, 932–940
2012, 942–949
special, 941
Guinta, Frank (R-N.H.), 43
Gulf of Mexico oil spill, 139, 288
Guns and gun control, 10, 175, 692
about, 559–560
Amtrak, 133
concealed, 575–576
concealed handguns, 575–576
Eric Holder, 706–707
Giffords shooting, 643 (box)
national parks and wildlife refuges, 84, 85
Sonia Sotomayor, 712
Guthrie, Brett (R-Ky.), student aid, 477–478
Gutierrez, Luis V. (D-Ill.)
affordable housing, 510
Puerto Rico political status, 619, 620
Gutiérrez, Luis V. (D-Ill.), 851

Habitat for Humanity, 652
Hagan, Kay R. (D-N.C.), 844
tobacco regulation, 449
Hahn, Janice (D-Calif.), 30, 674
Haiti, 139
children, 565
foreign aid to, 233, 288

Hall, John J. (D-N.Y.), 855
Hall, Ralph M. (D-Texas), 373, 647, 854
  NASA, 608
  Science, Space, and Technology Committee, 664
Halligan, Caitlin J., 576–577
Halperin, Mark, 646 (box)
Hamdan v. Rumsfeld, 316
Hammill, Drew, 644 (box)
HAMP. *See* Home Affordable Modification Program (HAMP)
Hampton, Cynthia, 651, 672
Hampton, Douglas, 651–652, 671–672
  Tom Coburn ethics probe, 672
Hanabusa, Colleen, 26
Handguns. *See* Guns and gun control
Hanna, Richard (R-N.Y.), 458 (box)
Hardest Hit Fund, 64
Harkin, Tom (D-Iowa), 411
  budget negotiations (2011), 139
  committees, 844, 847
  education, 484
  FDA user fees, 461
  Health, Education, Labor, and Pensions Committee, 643, 662
  labor union regulations, 538
  Medicaid and education spending bill, 2010, 453
  minimum wage, 540
  No Child Left Behind, 473
  Ryan White HIV/AIDS Act reauthorization, 453
  student aid, 478
  unions, 533, 534
  war supplemental (2010), 286
Harman, Jane (D-Calif.), 30, 395, 852
  ethics probe, 653
  gun control, 643 (box)
Harper, Gregg (R-Miss.), 852, 856
  Election Assistance Commission, 682
  pocket edition Constitution, 670
Harris, Andy (R-Md.), 854
Harrison, John C., 549
Hartzler, Vicky (R-Mo.), 300
Hastert, J. Dennis (R-Ill.), 29 (box)
Hastert rule, 29 (box), 31
Hastings, Alcee L. (D-Fla.), 394, 853
  defense authorization (2010), 276
  ethics probe, 673–674
  impeachment of Federal judges, 559
  restrictions on regulations, 632
  shooting ranges on public lands, 400–401
Hastings, Richard "Doc" (R-Wash.), 392, 394, 397, 853
  Native Hawaiian government, 619
  Natural Resources Committee, 647, 664
  Puerto Rico political status, 620
Hatch, Carl (D-N.M.), 622
Hatch, Orrin G. (R-Utah), 846
  additional Utah seat, 650
  Affordable Care Act, 430, 435
  appellate judgeships, 576
  Children's Health Insurance Program, 446
  community service programs, 605
  Finance Committee, 662
  hate crimes, 554
  impeachment of Federal judges, 558
  journalism sources, 559
  New START treaty, 291
  Patent law, 561
  undocumented children, 557
  unions, 539
  welfare law, 544
Hatch Act modernization, 622
Hate crimes, 553–555
  laws, 277, 554
Hate Crimes Prevention Act (2009), 554
Hayden, Michael V., 227 (box)
Hayes, Thomas, 72
H-2B immigrants, 541
Head Start, 82
  See also Education
Health, Education, Labor, and Pensions Committee, Senate, 411, 534, 605, 644, 846–847
  Affordable Care Act, 427, 428
  physical education in schools, 490 (box)
  ranking members and chairs, 643, 662
  tobacco regulation, 449
Health and Human Services Department, U.S. (HHS), 544
  Affordable Care Act, 422 (box)
    state-run exchanges, 436
    temporary high-risk pool, 438
  antibullying website, 492
  appointments, 707–708
  appropriations
    FY 2010, 131
    FY 2011, 155
    FY 2012, 175
    FY 2013, 184
  Indian Health Service, 129, 443, 445
Health and medical care, 82, 419–470
  abortion (*See* Abortion)
  action chronology
    2009-2010, 421–454
    2011-2012, 455–464
  childhood obesity, 420
  devices tax, 424 (box), 432, 443
  drugs and pharmaceuticals (*See* Drugs and pharmaceutical industry)
  flu (*See* Flu, pandemic)
  food and nutrition (*See* Food and nutrition)
  foreign aid, 245, 248
  global health, 245, 248, 253
  HIV/AIDS, 132, 154, 155, 248, 419, 420 (figure), 452–453
  Indian Health Service, 129, 443, 445
  information technology, 83
  insurance (*See* Health insurance)
  lead pipes, 378
  National Commission on Fiscal Responsibility and Reform recommendations, 144
  outlays, 2001-2012, 422 (figure)
  pandemic flu preparation, 122, 270, 272
  reserve fund request, 2010, 125
  study, veterans', 445
  tax deduction, 444
Health Care and Education Reconciliation Act of 2010, 476
Health care overhaul, 174, 691–694
  historical efforts at, 421

Obama address to Congress on, 430 (box)
See also Affordable Care Act
Health care workers
home health aides, 540–541
National Commission on Fiscal Responsibility and Reform recommendations, 144
See also Physicians
Health insurance
Children's Health Insurance Program (*See* Children's Health Insurance Program (CHIP))
COBRA, 83
Consumer Operated and Oriented Plan (CO-OP), 437, 457 (box)
executive compensation deduction, 444
health care overhaul, 691–694
historical efforts, 421
Medicaid (*See* Medicaid)
Medicare (*See* Medicare)
military, 303, 312, 428
private, 421, 423 (box), 425, 444
reform (*See* Affordable Care Act)
state-run exchanges, 436–437
subsidies, 422, 423 (box), 425, 432
W-2 reporting, 445
See also Affordable Care Act
Heck, Joseph J. (R-Nev.), 854
Medicare payments to physicians, 464
Hedge fund registration, 98
Heilemann, John, 646 (box)
Heitkamp, Heidi (D-N.D.), 41
Heller, Dean (R-Nev.), 30, 41
HELP. *See* Health, Education, Labor, and Pensions Committee, Senate
Helping Families Save Their Homes Act of 2009, 500
Hensarling, Jeb (R-Texas), 5 (table), 78
committees, 168, 843
foreclosure aid, 509
government-sponsored enterprises, 512
national flood insurance, 611
2010 war supplemental, 286
Herger, Wally (R-Calif.), 855
contractors withholding rule, 630
Heritage Action, 200, 259
Herrera Beutler, Jaime (R-Wash.), 631
Herseth Sandlin, Stephanie (D-S.D.), 855
HHS. *See* Health and Human Services Department, U.S. (HHS)
Higgerson, David P., 206 (figure)
Higher education
American Graduation Initiative, 697
college campus fire safety, 482
college savings plans, 481, 487 (box)
Deposit Restricted Qualified Tuition Program Act of 2010, 413
Diversity Visa Program, 489
Hope scholarship credit, 83
student aid (*See* Student aid)
tuition credit, 189
Higher Education Act of 1965, 476, 478, 488
High-risk pool, Affordable Care Act, 438
High speed rail, 133, 156
Hill, Baron P. (D-Ind.), 370
illegal immigrants, 561
Hill, Rick (R-Mont.), 44
Hill, The, 674, 685
Hillary: The Movie, 677 (box)
Hinojosa, Ruben (D-Texas), 850
Hispanics
in Congress, 1947-2011, 34 (table)
presidential election of 2008, 35
presidential election of 2012, 704
racial profiling of, 556
HIV/AIDS
appropriations, 2011, 154, 155
global funding, 248
name-based reporting, 453
national testing goal, 453
needle exchange programs and, 132
Ryan White HIV/AIDS Act, 419, 420 (figure), 452–453
Hochul, Kathy (D-N.Y.), 30
Hodes, Paul W. (D-N.H.), e-mail records protection, 615
Hoekstra, Peter (R-Mich.), 647, 854
2010 intelligence authorization, 247
Holden, Tim (D-Pa.), 849
Holder, Eric J., Jr., 285, 315, 705 (box)
in contempt of Congress, 552, 573–574
Guantánamo detainees, 561
justice leadership, 549
law and law enforcement, 568
nomination by Obama, 706–707
Holds, secret, 640
Holmes Norton, Eleanor (D-D.C.), 633
Holocaust survivors, 580
Holt, Rush D. (D-N.J.), 276, 394, 395
charter schools, 491
government spending accountability, 633
Home Affordable Modification Program (HAMP), 64, 509–510
Homebuyer tax credit, 79 (box), 83, 503–505
Home health aides, 540–541
Home improvement rebates, 506
Homeland security, 205–219
action chronology, 2009-2010, 208–213
Central Intelligence Agency and, 227 (box)
chemical plant security, 207, 208, 212
Coast Guard reauthorization, 207, 214, 218–219
cybersecurity, 207, 214, 217–218, 298 (box)
Director of National Intelligence and, 227 (box)
Foreign Intelligence Surveillance Act (FISA), 205, 206, 209
extension, 215–217
Guantánamo Bay, Cuba (*See* Guantánamo Bay, Cuba)
Patriot Act, 133, 205–206, 208–209, 214–215
U.S. ambassador to United Nations and, 224, 226–227 (box)
wiretapping, 205, 208–209, 214, 215–217
See also Border security; Homeland Security Department, U.S. (DHS); Transportation Security Administration (TSA)
Homeland Security and Governmental Affairs Committee, House, 647, 851–852
D.C. representation, 648–649
ranking members and chairs, 646, 662, 664
Homeland Security and Governmental Affairs Committee, Senate, 644, 847
Presidential Appointment Efficiency and Streamlining Act, 668
ranking members and chairs, 643–644, 662

Homeland Security Department, U.S. (DHS)
appointments, 710
appropriations
FY 2010, 129, 209–212
FY 2011, 154
FY 2012, 174, 252
FY 2013, 183
Patriot Act, 133, 205–206
Home loans and mortgages
assistance programs, 79 (box)
Countrywide Financial Corp., 652–653
Dodd-Frank Act and, 100–101
Fannie and Freddie executive pay, 510
Fannie Mae and Freddie Mac, 48, 53, 67–68
foreclosures, 53–54, 64, 509–510
government-sponsored enterprises, 511–512
homebuyer tax credit, 503–505
insurance, 503
interest rates, 54
lender regulation, 502–503
predatory lending, 100–101
relief assistance, 500–502
STOCK Act, 668
subprime crisis, 53–54, 90
Troubled Asset Relief Program (TARP) and, 61, 64
Homeowners' Defense Act of 2009, 610
Home Ownership and Equity Protection Act of 1994, 100
Home Star Energy Retrofit Act of 2010, 506
Homosexuals
Defense of Marriage Act, 182, 289, 313
House Office of General Counsel, 669–670
marriage of, 44, 242, 300, 301, 305, 308
in the military, 19, 22, 264–265, 267, 288–289, 291, 299–300, 308
State Department employees, 242
Honda, Michael M. (D-Calif.), 669
Honeywell, 143
Hope for Homeowners program, 79 (box), 500, 502, 532
Hope scholarship credit, 83
Horow, Michael E., 574
Hospitals and health care facilities
acquired infections, 441, 442
additional Medicare hospital payments, 441
community health centers, 442
Medicare hospital payroll tax, 422, 424 (box), 426, 443
nonprofit, 444
physician-owned, 441
reimbursement for preventable readmission, 441
House Administration Committee, 852
Architect of the Capitol, 651
Election Assistance Commission, 682
ranking members and chairs, 646, 664
House GOP Sequester Replacement Reconciliation Act, 544
Household debt service ratio, 52
Household wealth, 51
House Interior-Environment Appropriations Subcommittee, 383
House of Representatives, U.S.
committees (*See* specific committees)
conference committees, 639
Congress (*See* Congress, U.S.)
cut-as-you-go rules, 664–665
discharge petitions since 1931, 872
elections (*See also* Congressional elections)
1928–2012, 950–955
2010, 23–24, 932–940
2012, 42–44, 942–949
by region, 43 (table)
Gephardt rule, 134, 665
Green the Capitol initiative, 670
key votes (*See* Congressional votes)
leadership, 843
111th Congress, 645–647
112th Congress, 663–665
members (*See* Congress, members of)
operating budget, 155
pay and benefits (*See* Congressional pay and benefits)
pay-as-you-go rules, 126–127, 141, 142, 451, 664–665, 697
redistricting (*See* Redistricting)
rules, 127, 647, 664–665
suspension, 640
transition teams, 661 (box)
U.S.-made goods in the Capitol, 651
voting (*See* Congressional votes)
See also Congress, U.S.
Housing
action chronology
2009-2010, 500–508
2011-2012, 509–512
affordable, 510
assistance outlays, 2001-2012, 466 (figure)
"cash for clunkers," 506
covered bonds, 507–508
drywall safety, 508, 511
funding, 498–499, 499 (box)
homebuyer tax credit, 79 (box), 83
home improvement rebates, 506
homeless children and youth, 512
leadership for, 499 (box)
loans (*See* Home loans and mortgages)
policy, 497–512
Section 8, 121, 156, 506
Section 8 vouchers, 505–506, 505 (box)
subprime mortgage crisis, 53–54, 90, 497–498
TARP programs, 64
Housing and Economic Recovery Act, 67
Housing and Urban Development Department, U.S. (HUD), 100–101
appointments, 709
appropriations
FY 2010, 131
FY 2011, 156
FY 2012, 172
FY 2013, 185
emergency mortgage relief, 509
Neighborhood Stabilization Program, 500
secretary, 499 (box)
Section 8 voucher program, 121, 156
See also Housing
Hoyer, Steny (D-Md.), 5 (table), 22, 80, 663
Affordable Care Act, 436, 460
budget negotiations (2011), 152
child nutrition bill, 467

committees, 843
D.C. representation, 650
Eric Massa ethics probe, 655
executive bonuses, 532
Export-Import Bank reauthorization, 200
Federal worker pay, 621
fiscal cliff, 186
majority leader, 645
national flood insurance, 611
PMA Group, 655
statutory pay-as-you go rules, 126
war supplemental (2010), 289
HUD. *See* Housing and Urban Development Department, U.S. (HUD)
Huelskamp, Tim (R-Kan.), 305
Huffington Post, 674
Hugler, Edward C., 711
Human embryos, 131
Human immunodeficiency virus (HIV). *See* HIV/AIDS
Human services. *See* Health and Human Services Department, U.S. (HHS)
Human spaceflight, 607
Hunger. *See* Food assistance programs; Welfare and social services
Hunter, Duncan (R-Calif.), 491, 647, 850
Affordable Care Act, 428
"don't ask, don't tell," 299–300
Hunting and fishing regulations, 400–401
Huntsman, John, Jr., 37
Hurricane Irene, 170
Hurricane Katrina, 139, 154, 205, 208, 288, 511, 598–599, 611
increased Medicaid matching funds, 439
Hurricane Rita, 139, 288
Hurricane Sandy, 10, 33, 39, 205, 207 (box), 499 (box), 597, 625–626
supplemental funds, 2013, 189–190
2012 presidential election, 702, 704
Hurst, Brooks, 654
Hurt, Robert (R-Va.)
foreclosure aid, 509
government-sponsored enterprises, 512
Hussein, Saddam, 234 (box)
Hutchison, Kay Bailey (R-Texas), 377, 845
Children's Health Insurance Program, 446
Commerce, Science, and Transportation Committee, 644, 662
gender-based wage discrimination, 529
Violence Against Women Act, 572
Hyde, Henry J. (R-Ill.), 432 (box)
Hyde amendment, 432–433 (box)
Hydropower, 397

ICE. *See* Immigration and Customs Enforcement (ICE)
Icebreaker ships, 218–219
Illegal drugs
Coast Guard and, 207, 214, 218–219
Mexico-U.S. border and, 208
needle exchange programs, 132, 175
penalties for crack cocaine, 562
Illegal immigrants, 19
Affordable Care Act, 430, 438
budget bills, 182, 208
Census Bureau counting of, 614
children, 556
Children's Health Insurance Program, 446, 447
Coast Guard and, 207, 214, 218–219
detention of, 577–578
DREAM Act and, 7
E-Verify program and, 129, 210, 211
smuggling of, 561
Illinois, 709
Rod Blagojevich, 17, 647–648, 650, 652, 675
Roland W. Burris, 17, 26, 648, 650, 652, 675
IMF. *See* International Monetary Fund (IMF)
Immigration
about, 556
highly skilled legal immigrants, 582
housing assistance, 506
status on census, 614
student visas, 489–490
visa mills, 489–490
Immigration and Customs Enforcement (ICE), 140
appropriations
FY 2010, 211, 213
FY 2011, 154
Guantánamo Bay detainees and, 316
Improper Payments Elimination and Recovery Act (2010), 612–613, 634
Improvised explosive device (IED) attacks, 279, 284, 307
Incandescent light bulbs, 395
Incest, abortion funding for, 131, 432 (box)
Income taxes. *See* Taxes
Incumbents in congressional elections, 12 (table), 24–25
Independent Payment Advisory Board (IPAB), 184, 440, 457, 460
Independent voters, 23
Indiana, 704
Indian Affairs Committee, Senate, 644, 847
ranking members and chairs, 643, 662
Indian Arts and Crafts Amendment Act (2010), 563
Indian casino land, 618
Indian Health Care Improvement Reauthorization and Extension Act of 2009, 443, 617
Indian Health Service, 129, 443, 445, 617
Indian Reorganization Act of 1934, 618
Indian tribes, recognition of, 617–618
Individual mandate, Affordable Care Act, 419, 423 (box), 426, 430 (box), 438
Individual rights, 590–591
Industrial boilers, 388
Ineligibility Clause, U.S. Constitution, 672, 684
Inflation
Consumer Price Index (CPI), 187, 188
rates, 1996–2012, 50 (table)
Information overclassification, 613
Inglis, Bob (R-S.C.), 373
Inhofe, James M. (R-Okla.), 372, 378, 846
Environment and Public Works Committee, 644, 662
FEMA, 612
Guantánamo Bay, Cuba, 315
John Bryson nomination, 709
military construction appropriations (2010), 285
State Department reauthorization, 243

Initial public offerings (IPOs), 667
Inouye, Daniel K. (D-Hawaii), 5 (table)
  Appropriations Committee, 643, 662
  budget negotiations (2012), 161
  committees, 843, 844
  death of, 662
  debt limit legislation, 137, 137 (box)
  defense appropriations (2010), 282
  defense appropriations (2012), 305
  president pro tempore, 642
  Race to the Top, 480
  war supplemental (2009), 271
  war supplemental (2010), 286
Insider trading, 667–668
Inslee, Jay (D-Wash.), 44
Inspector General Act, 602
Institute of Medicine, 422 (box)
Insurance
  disability insurance outlays, 2001-2012, 466 (figure)
  Federal Insurance Office, 98–99
  health (*See* Health insurance)
  Iran sanctions, 256–257
  mortgages, 503
  pensions, 486
  unemployment compensation (*See* Unemployment compensation)
  See also Federal Deposit Insurance Corporation (FDIC)
Intellectual property
  Colombia, 197
  cybersecurity, 217
  Internet piracy, 358
  Panama, 198–199
  satellite and cable programming, 336
  South Korea, 197
Intelligence activities and agencies
  appropriations
    FY 2010, 133, 245–248
    FY 2011 and 2012, 250–251
    FY 2013, 254–255
  Central Intelligence Agency (*See* Central Intelligence Agency (CIA))
  contractors, 247–248
  covert agents, 248
  Director of National Intelligence, 227 (box), 246–248
  Federal Bureau of Investigation (*See* Federal Bureau of Investigation (FBI))
  inspector general, 247
  interrogation of military detainees, 246, 248
  wiretaps (*See* Wiretapping)
Intelligence Committee, House, 246, 647, 854
  Cybersecurity, 217
  Foreign Intelligence Surveillance Act, 216
  ranking members and chairs, 646, 662, 664
Intelligence Committee, Senate, 246, 644, 848
  FY 2011 intelligence authorization, 251
  ranking members and chairs, 643, 662
Intelligence Reform and Terrorism Prevention Act of 2004, 602
Interest rates
  1996-2012, 50 (table)
  credit card, 84–85
  Federal Reserve actions during the financial crisis and recession, 56, 60
  home mortgage, 54
  LIBOR scandal and, 72
Interfaith Center on Corporate Responsibility, 680
Interior Department, U.S., 383
  appointments, 710
  appropriations
    FY 2010, 128, 129–130
    FY 2012, 173
    FY 2013, 183–184
  Bureau of Reclamation, 173
  leadership, 367
  outer continental shelf legislation, 392
Interior-Environment bill, 385
  House floor action, 403–404
  major provisions, 402–403
  provisions, 402–403
Internal Revenue Service (IRS)
  Affordable Care Act tax reporting requirement repeal, 456 (box)
  appropriations
    FY 2010, 131
    FY 2012, 174
    FY 2013, 183
  "economic substance," 444
  health coverage W-2 reporting, 445
  information reporting, 444
  Small Business Jobs Act of 2010 and, 102, 103
International Commission on Holocaust Era Insurance Claims, 580
International Committee of the Red Cross, 276, 279
International Crisis Group, 230
International Emergency Economic Powers Act (IEEPA), 240
International Labor Organizations (ILO), 197
International Maritime Organization, 218
International Monetary Fund (IMF), 72, 101
  appropriations
    FY 2009, 122, 270, 272
    FY 2009 supplemental, 233
    FY 2010, 131, 244, 245
    FY 2012, 176, 252
  Timothy Geithner, 706
International terrorism. *See* Terrorism and counterterrorism
International trade. *See* Foreign trade and business
International Trade Commission (ITC), 196, 197, 198
Internet
  access, disability rights and, 479 (box)
  advertising, 685
  cybersecurity, 207, 214, 217–218
  cyberstalking, 567
  gambling, 566
    background, 338
    House action, 338
    Senate action, 338–339
    112th Congress work on, 357–358
  as new media, 4, 152
  piracy, 358–359
  schemes, 563
  social media, 110, 671 (box)
  Wiki Leaks, 251
Interrogation of military detainees, 246, 248
Interstate commerce. *See* Business and industry
Interstate Recognition of Notarizations Act of 2010, 339

Iowa, 703
IPAB. *See* Independent Payment Advisory Board (IPAB)
Iqbal, Javaid, 591
Iran, 224–225, 232
  Central Bank, 241, 301
  cybersecurity, 217
  Revolutionary Guard Corps, 257
  sanctions, 238–241, 243, 255–258, 308, 311
  See also Middle East
Iran Freedom and Counter-Proliferation Act, 255
Iran Threat Reduction and Syria Human Rights Act, 255
Iraq, 225, 249
  Elaf Islamic Bank sanctions, 256
  foreign policy toward, 234–235 (box), 236 (box)
  Iraq Security Forces Fund, 153
  See also Middle East
Iraq Body Count, 235 (box)
Iraq war, 10, 225, 263–264
  Abu Ghraib prison photos and, 235 (box)
  appropriations
    FY 2009, 16, 122
    FY 2010, 133, 138–139, 279
    FY 2011, 138, 153
    FY 2013, 184
  Commander's Emergency Response Program, 153, 284, 295, 304, 307
  congressional action, 2009, 235 (box)
  costs of, 235 (box)
  Obama on, 699–700
  U.S. casualties, 236 (box)
  U.S. troop presence, 2009-2011, 234 (box)
Ireland, 51
IRS. *See* Internal Revenue Service (IRS)
"Is DoD's New Pay System Fair?", 600
Isakson, Johnny (R-Ga.), 848
  homebuyer tax credit, 504–505
  New START treaty, 290
  Peace Corps volunteer protection, 624
  Select Ethics Committee, 645, 662
  unemployment compensation, 523
Israel
  foreign aid to, 233, 245, 293
  Iron Dome antimissile defense system, 293, 312
  Palestinians and, 225, 228, 254
  See also Middle East
Israel, Steve (D-N.Y.), 663
Issa, Darrell (R-Calif.)
  ACORN defunding, 680
  Alaska bypass, 629
  committees, 853
  D.C. representation, 649
  deceptive use of "census," 614
  Federal Reserve audit, 633
  Federal teleworking, 601
  government spending accountability, 633
  on Holder held in contempt of Congress, 573
  Hurricane Sandy, 626
  Hurricane Sandy supplemental funds, 190
  Oversight and Government Reform Committee, 647, 664
  parental leave for Federal workers, 603
  Postal Service, 627
  student aid, 478
  tax delinquents and Federal work, 624
  tobacco regulation, 448
  Violence Against Women Act, 572
Italy, 51, 55

Jackson, Jesse L., Jr. (D-Ill.), 653, 675–676
Jackson, Jonathan, 653
Jackson, Lisa, 367
Jackson-Lee, Sheila (D-Texas), 852
  bullying and gang prevention, 492
  Foreign Intelligence Surveillance Act, 216
  regulatory oversight, 632
  Violence Against Women Act, 573
Jackson-Vanik amendment, 201
Jahr, Mark, 499 (box)
Japan, 51
  foreign policy toward, 228
  relations with China, 228
  trade agreements, 192
Jefferson, Thomas, president, 35, 702
Jefferson, William J. (D-La.), 660
Jeffords, James M. (D-Vt.), 18
Jim Crow laws, 567
Jindal, Bobby, 30
Job creation legislation, 521
Jobs for Main Street Act of 2009, 14, 85, 527
Johanns, Mike (R-Neb.), 384, 396, 680
Johnson, Bill (R-Ohio), 855
Johnson, Charles E., 707
Johnson, Eddie Bernice (D-Texas), 854
  Science, Space, and Technology Committee, 664
Johnson, Hank (D-Ga.)
  concealed handguns, 576
  pricing floors, 564
  restrictions on regulations, 632
Johnson, Henry C., Jr. (D-Ga.), 852
Johnson, Ron (R-Wis.), 107
  Affordable Care Act, 460
Johnson, Sam (R-Texas), 855
Johnson, Tim (D-S.D.), 844, 845
  Banking, Housing, and Urban Affairs Committee, 662
  Ethics Committee, 643
  Iran sanctions, 258
Johnson, Timothy V. (R-Ill.), 849
Joint Chiefs of Staff, 22, 275 (box), 706
  Afghanistan war insider attacks, 230
Joint Committees, 856
Jones, James L., Jr., 226 (box)
Jones, Walter B. (R-N.C.), 300
  Afghanistan war, 313
Jordan, Jim (R-Ohio), 383, 853
Journalism sources, 559
JP Morgan Chase, 54, 63
  losses by, 71–72, 105
  MF Global and, 71
Judicial Watch, 673
Judiciary Committee, House, 852
  antibullying and gang prevention, 491–492
  D.C. representation, 649–650
  Foreign Intelligence Surveillance Act, 216
  Patriot Act, 215
  ranking members and chairs, 646, 662, 664

Judiciary Committee, Senate, 847
  Arlen Spector, 644–645
  Corruption Prosecution Improvement Act, 666
  ranking members and chairs, 643, 662
Judiciary Subcommittee on Immigration Refugees, and Border Security, Senate, 556
Jumpstart Our Business Startups Act (JOBS), 110
Justice, military. *See* Military tribunals
Justice Department, U.S. (DOJ)
  Alan Mollohan ethics probe, 654
  antibullying website, 492
  appropriations
    FY 2009, 127
    FY 2010, 130–131
    FY 2011, 152–153
    FY 2012, 171–172
    FY 2013, 182
  Attorney General Eric J. Holder, Jr., 285, 315, 705 (box)
    nomination by Obama, 706–707
  border-related law enforcement, 206, 213
  disability rights, 479 (box)
  Jane Harman ethics probe, 653
  Tom DeLay ethics probe, 660
Justice leadership, 549
Juvenile Accountability Block Grant Reauthorization, 491–492

Kagan, Elena, 10, 20–21, 712
  confirmation of, 552, 553
  liberal positions, 584, 585, 586, 588, 590
Kaine, Tim, 18, 42
Kanjorski, Paul E. (D-Pa.), 851
Kanka, Megan, 567
Kaptur, Marcy (D-Ohio), 645
  ethics probe, 655–656
  U.S.-made goods in the Capitol, 651
Karzai, Hamid, 225, 229, 700
Kashkari, Neel, 77
Kaufman, Ted (D-Del.), 17
Kazran, Sam, 674
Keenan, Douglas, 72
Keep All Students Safe Act, 481
Kelly, Jess, 43
Kelly, Mark, 10
Kemp, Jack, 921 (table)
Kennedy, Anthony M., 455 (box), 584, 586, 588, 590, 591, 592, 594, 669
Kennedy, Edward M. (D-Mass.), 6, 10, 425, 433 (box), 456 (box), 605, 693
  community service programs, 604
  death of, 18, 19, 643
  education, 473
  hate crimes, 554
  tobacco regulation, 448, 449
  unions, 533, 534
  universal health care, 427, 436
Kennedy, John F., president, 18, 668
Kennedy, Patrick J. (D-R.I.), 605
Kent, Samuel B.
  impeachment of, 557–558
  resignation of, 553
Kenya, 314
Kerry, John F. (D-Mass.), 337, 364, 366, 367, 845, 846
  Congressional deficit committee, 168
  disability rights, 259
  Foreign Relations Committee, 643, 662
  greenhouse gas emisisons, 376
  Iran sanctions, 258
  Kerry-Boxer bill, 372
  mortgage relief assistance, 502
  New START treaty, 290
  Pakistan aid, 236, 237
  as Senate Foreign Relations Committee Chair, 226 (box)
  State Department reauthorization, 241
Kerry, John F. (Secretary of State), 224, 226 (box)
Kerry-Boxer bill, 372
Keystone XL pipeline, 109, 364–365, 390–392, 696
Khan, Abdul Qadeer, 237
Kildee, Dale (D-Mich.), 850
  public safety workers, 534
Killefer, Nancy, 707
Kilpatrick, Carolyn Cheeks (D-Mich.), 655, 658
Kilroy, Mary Jo (D-Ohio), 604
Kind, Ron (D-Wis.), 469
King, Angus, 35
King, Peter T. (R-N.Y.)
  committees, 647, 852
  Domestic Nuclear Detection Office, 210
  Homeland Security Committee, 664
  Hurricane Sandy supplemental funds, 190
King, Steve (R-Iowa), 313, 491
  Affordable Care Act, 459
  antibullying and gang prevention, 492
  Democracy Is Strengthened by Casting Light on Spending in Elections (DISCLOSE) Act, 679
  Republican Steering Committee, 665
  Violence Against Women Act, 573
Kingston, Jack (R-Ga.), 412, 849
  fiscal 2012 appropriations, 575
  nutrition bill, 469
  war supplemental (2010), 287
Kinzinger, Adam (R-Ill.), 661 (box)
Kircher, Kerry, 669
Kirk, Mark Steven (R-Ill.), 26
  budget negotiations (2010), 243, 244
  Central Bank of Iran, 301
  defense authorization (2011), 293
  "don't ask, don't tell," 289
  Iran sanctions, 243, 257
  Mark Twain Commemorative Coin, 629–630
  New START treaty, 291
Kirk, Paul G., Jr. (D-Mass.), 18
  Affordable Care Act, 425
Kirk, Ron, 195 (box)
Kissinger, Henry A., 290
Kline, John (R-Minn), 850
  charter schools, 491
  child nutrition bill, 467
  education, 473, 475, 484
  Education and the Workforce Committee, 647, 664

labor union regulations, 538
minimum wage, 541
unions, 539
Klobuchar, Amy (D-Minn.), 379
committees, 845, 846, 848
Koch, Charles, 36
Koch, David, 36
Koch Industries, 36
Kohl, Herb (D-Wis.), 412, 844, 847, 848
COPS, 561–562
railroad mergers, 564
Special Aging Committee, 643, 662
Krueger, Alan B., 49
Kucinich, Dennis J. (D-Ohio)
budget negotiations (2011), 139
committees, 853
Democracy Is Strengthened by Casting Light on Spending in Elections (DISCLOSE) Act, 679
restrictions on regulations, 632
use of force in Libya, 250
war supplemental (2010), 287
Kuwait, 234 (box), 264
Kyl, John (R-Ariz.), 5 (table), 22, 338
Affordable Care Act, 430
budget negotiations (2012), 161
committees, 843
Congressional deficit committee, 168
D.C. representation, 649
estate taxes, 147
executive bonuses, 532
journalism sources, 559
minority whip, 642, 662
New START treaty, 290–291
Patent law, 570
Patriot Act, 209

Labor, Department of (DOL)
appointments, 710–711
appropriations
FY 2010, 131
FY 2011, 155
FY 2012, 175
FY 2013, 184
Labor and pensions
about, 515–516, 517
COBRA, 525–527
Education Jobs Fund, 528
executive bonuses, 531–532
executive pay, 530–531
gender-based wage discrimination, 528–529
job creation and protection, 527–528
minimum wage for Guam construction workers, 530
minimum wage for U.S. Territory workers, 529–530
public safety workers, 534
shareholder oversight of executive pay, 532–533
Unemployment Compensation, 517–524
union card check, 533–534
wage parity, 529
Labor leadership, 518
Labor unions
collective bargaining, 309
election timeline, 538
Employee Free Choice Act, 711
foreign trade agreements, 193, 195, 196, 197, 198
organizing rules, 539
rail and aviation elections, 539–540
regulations for, 537–539
Russian trade normalization and, 201
union card check, 533–534
See Labor unions
Lacker, Jeffrey, 59
LaHood, Ray, 323, 324, 349, 351, 704, 705 (box), 709–710
Highway Trust Fund, 341
Lamborn, Doug (R-Colo.), 853
New START treaty, 300
Lame duck sessions of Congress, 7, 9, 22, 138, 857–859
Land and Water Conservation Fund, 183–184
Landrieu, Mary L. (D-La.), 371, 680, 844, 847, 848
drywall safety, 508
ethics probe, 652
FEMA, 597
minimum wage, 541
national flood insurance, 611
public safety workers, 534
Small Business and Entrepreneurship Committee, 643, 662
Langevin, James R. (D-R.I.), 850
Lankford, James (R-Okla.), 853
critical minerals legislation, 399
Lantos, Tom (D-Calif.), 646
Larsen, Rick (D-Wash.), 275
Larson, John B. (D-Conn.), 5 (table), 22
committees, 843
Democratic Caucus, 663
Democratic Caucus ranking members and chairs, 645
Latham, Tom (R-Iowa), 383, 849
La Tourette, Steve (R-Ohio), 320
unions, 539
Lautenberg, Frank R. (D-N.J.), 342, 399, 846
Mexico City policy, 244, 248, 258
2012 state-foreign operations funding, 253
Lavrov, Sergey, 290
Law and law enforcement
abortion, 578–579
about, 547–548, 553, 568
administrative changes to Federal courts, 566
animal crush videos, 562–563
apology for slavery and segregation, 567
appellate judgeships, 576–577
attorneys fees, 579–580
bankruptcy judgeships, 565
caller ID spoofing, 563
child pornography, 581–582
Community Oriented Policing Services (COPS) program, 153, 171, 552, 561–562, 568, 575
concealed handguns, 575–576
COPS authorization, 561–562
cyberstalking, 567
detention of illegal immigrants, 577–578
drug traffickers, 580–581
elderly and disabled refugees, 583
firearms, 559–560
Fiscal 2012 appropriations, 574–575

Guantánamo detainees, 560–561
Haitian children, 565
hate crimes, 553–555
highly skilled legal immigrants, 582
Holder in contempt of Congress, 573–574
Holocaust survivors, 580
immigration, 556
impeachment of Federal judges, 557–559
Internet gambling, 566
Internet schemes, 563
journalism sources, 559
legal settlements, 555–556
low-immigration regions, 582–583
major accomplishments, 548–551
missing persons, 564
partisan battles, 552
Patent law overhaul, 561, 568–571
penalties for crack cocaine, 562
pricing floors, 564
prison deaths, 578
property rights, 579
railroad mergers, 564
same-sex couples, 581
sex tourism, 566–567
smuggling of illegal immigrants, 561
Social Security lawsuits, 565
trade secrets, 580
treatment of suspected terrorists, 578
on tribal lands, 563–564
TV coverage of court proceedings, 565–566
undocumented children, 556–557
Violence Against Women Act, 571–573
witness protection programs, 565
Lawrence Berkeley National Laboratory, 708
Lead pipes, 378
Leahy, Patrick J. (D-Vt), 5 (table), 336
appellate judgeships, 576
committees, 843, 844, 847
defense appropriations (2010), 282
defense authorization (2012), 301
Foreign Intelligence Surveillance Act, 217
Guantánamo Bay, Cuba, 315
Guantánamo detainees, 560
hate crimes, 554–555
hate crimes laws, 277
Hurricane Sandy, 626
journalism sources, 559
Judiciary Committee, 643, 662
justice leadership, 549
Patent law, 561, 569, 570
Patriot Act, 206, 209, 215
president pro tempore, 662
STOCK Act, 666, 667
Violence Against Women Act, 572
Leaking Underground Storage Tank Trust Fund, 342, 543
Leal Garcia, Humberto, 593
Lee, Barbara (D-Calif.), 139
Afghanistan war bill, 230
defense appropriations (2013), 313
defense authorization (2013), 309
use-of-force law, 300
war supplemental (2010), 287
Lee, Christopher (R-N.Y.), 30
sexual misadventures and resignation, 671 (box)
Stop the OverPrinting (STOP) Act, 670
Lee, Mike (R-Utah)
disability rights, 259
Foreign Intelligence Surveillance Act, 217
Senate rules, 662
Legal Services Corporation, 153
Legal settlements, 555–556
Legislative branch. *See* Congress, U.S.
LeHand, Missy, 616
Lehman Brothers, 60, 63, 67, 69
Lehrner, Lawrence, 676
LeMieux, George (R-Fla.), 18, 102
Lets Move! campaign, 490 (box)
Levin, Carl (D-Mich.), 274 (box)
Air National Guard, 311
Armed Services Committee, 642, 662
committees, 844, 847
defense acquisition rules, 268
defense authorization (2011), 292
defense authorization (2012), 301
Iran sanctions, 258
unemployment compensation, 522
Levin, Sander M. (D-Mich.), 855, 856
unemployment compensation, 522, 523, 527
Ways and Means Committee, 646, 664
welfare law, 544
Lew, Jacob, 49, 157, 161
Lewis, Jerry (R-Calif.), 664
budget negotiations (2009), 121, 122
committees, 646, 849
defense appropriations (2010), 281
Guantánamo Bay, Cuba, detainees, 210, 211, 243–244
opposes Omnibus appropriations, 382–383
war supplemental (2009), 270
Lewis, John (D-Ga.), 663, 843, 855
LIBOR. *See* London Interbank Offered Rate (LIBOR)
Library of Congress, 856
appropriations
FY 2010, 128
FY 2012, 175
FY 2013, 184
Libya, 223, 226 (box), 305, 689, 692, 701, 704
Benghazi attack, 224, 249, 690
use of force in, 250
See also Middle East
Lieberman, Joseph (I-Conn.), 18, 35, 81
Abu Ghraib prison, 271
ACORN defunding, 680
Affordable Care Act, 434
climate bill, 364, 366, 367
committees, 844, 847
cybersecurity research, 615
D.C. representation, 648–649
D.C. school vouchers, 490–491
defense appropriations (2010), 282
domestic partner benefits, 604
"don't ask, don't tell," 291
Federal employee domestic partnerships, 623
FEMA, 612
F-35 fighter, 277

greenhouse gas emissions, 373, 375–376
Guantánamo Bay, Cuba, 315
Harry Reid and, 644
Homeland Security and Governmental Reform Committee, 643–644, 662
impeachment of Federal judges, 559
Postal Service, 628
presidential campaign (2000), 921 (table)
prisoner abuse photos, 122
same-sex couples, 581
STOCK Act, 666
war supplemental (2010), 288–289
Lifetime spending limits, Affordable Care Act, 424 (box), 440
Light bulbs, 395
Lilly Ledbetter Fair Pay Act (2009), 517, 528, 548, 550
Lincoln, Abraham, president, 13, 704
Lincoln, Blanche (D-Ark.), 23, 25, 369, 662
Agriculture, Nutrition, and Forestry Committee, 643
child nutrition bill, 466
committees, 843, 846
Dodd-Frank Act, 91, 92
estate taxes, 147
Line-item veto, 915–916
Lingle, Linda, 618–619
Lipinski, Daniel (D-Ill.), 854
Literacy, adult, 492
Littoral Combat Ships, 138, 278, 283, 303, 306, 312
Liu, Goodwin, 576
Loans. *See* Home loans and mortgages; Student aid
Lobbyists and lobbying, 18, 691
Democracy Is Strengthened by Casting Light on Spending in Elections (DISCLOSE) Act, 678
Doug Hampton, 652, 671–672
House ethics probe, 655
Tom Daschle, 707
See also specific organizations
LoBiondo, Frank A. (R-N.J.), 855
defense authorization (2011), 292
Locke, Gary F., 323, 704, 705 (box), 708–709
Loebsack, Dave (D-Iowa), 604
restrictions on regulations, 632
Lofgren, Zoe (D-Calif.), 852, 854
Charles Rangel ethics probe, 659
Democracy Is Strengthened by Casting Light on Spending in Elections (DISCLOSE) Act, 678
Eric Massa ethics probe, 655
home loans and mortgages, 501–502
illegal immigrants, 577
legal immigrants, 582
Maxine Waters ethics probe, 656
Patent law, 571
Standards of Official Conduct Committee, 646
student visas, 489
Violence Against Women Act, 573
London Interbank Offered Rate (LIBOR), 72
Lone wolf provision, Patriot Act, 214, 215
Long-term care, 442
"Look back trigger," 524
Loran-C program, 210, 211
Lorillard Tobacco Co., 448, 449
Lott, Trent (R-Miss.), 646 (box)
Loughner, Jared Lee, 643 (box)
Louisiana, Affordable Care Act increased matching funds for, 439
Lowenthal, Terri Ann, 614
Lowery, Nita M. (D-N.Y.)
Afghanistan aid, 248
committees, 849
family-planning funding, 243, 258
Low-immigration regions, 582–583
Low Income Home Energy Assistance Program, 138
Low-level nuclear waste., 379
LPD-17 San Antonio-class amphibious ship, 278, 283, 306–307
Lucas, Frank D. (R-Okla.), 849
Agriculture Committee, 647, 664
Luetkemeyer, Blaine (R-Mo.), Mark Twain Commemorative Coin, 630
Lugar, Richard G. (R-Ind.), 41
committees, 846
Foreign Relations Committee, 644, 662
New START treaty, 290
Pakistan aid, 236, 237
State Department reauthorization, 241
undocumented children, 557
Lungren, Daniel E. (R-Calif.), 645, 852
Administration Committee, 647, 664
Defense of Marriage Act, 669
Democracy Is Strengthened by Casting Light on Spending in Elections (DISCLOSE) Act, 678
Lynch, Stephen F. (D-Mass.), 601, 853
domestic partner benefits, 603
FDR memorabilia, 616
Postal Service, 628

M-1 Abrams tanks, 304
Mack, Connie (R-Fla.), 381, 851
Mad cow disease, 196
Madison, James, president, 35, 702
Madison Amendment, 685
Madoff, Bernard, 90
Magnitsky, Sergei, 201, 202
Making Home Affordable program, 53
Making Work Pay tax credit, 80, 81–82, 82–83, 124, 125
Malaria, 245, 248
Malloy, Dan, 25
Maloney, Bill, 30
Maloney, Carolyn B. (D-N.Y.), 78, 664, 856
deceptive use of "census," 614
National Women's History Museum, 616
Malpractice, medical, 144, 424 (box), 430 (box), 442
Management and Budget, Office of (OMB), 49, 143, 603, 612, 633–634
PAYGO rules, 142
request (2010), 125
request (2011), 157
sequestration report, 685
Manchin, Joe, III (D-W. Va.), 25, 30
budget negotiation (2013), 181
Postal Service, 628
Mandatory spending, 120
Manned Ground Vehicle program, 278
Manufacturing
American-made flags, 616–617
"black liquor," 444

BPA restrictions, 411
Export-Import Bank reauthorization, 200
foreign trade agreements
Colombia, 198
South Korea, 196
Manzullo, Donald A. (R-Ill.), 851
March of Dimes, 629–630
Marijuana
legalized, 44
scheduling of synthetic drugs, 463
Marine Corps, U.S.
Expeditionary Fighting Vehicle, 303
F-35 alternative engine, 266
V-22 tilt-rotor Osprey aircraft, 312
Market basket updates, Affordable Care Act, 441
Market Transparency and Taxpayer Protection Act of 2011, 512
Markey, Betsy (D-Colo.), 604
Markey, Edward J. (D-Mass.)
committees, 850, 853, 855
disability rights, 479 (box)
drinking-water and wastewater systems security, 212
electric grid protection, 382
HomeStar progam, 381
broadband access, 333, 335
electric grid bill, 382
mining bill, 399–400
medical device testing and safety, 462
Natural Resources Committee, 664
on nuisance dust, 397
regulating coal waste, 390
renewable energy loans, 395
restrictions on regulations, 632
Select Engery Independence and Global Warming Committee, 646
waste containment amendment, 390
Mark Twain Commemorative Coin, 629–630
Marriage
Defense of Marriage Act, 182, 289, 313
House Office of General Counsel, 669–670
of military members, 300, 301, 305, 308
same-sex, 242, 300, 301, 305, 308
Marshall, Kate, 30
Martin, Billy, 675
Martinez, Mel (R-Fla.), 18, 709
Special Aging Committee, 645
Maryland, 654
Massa, Eric (D-N.Y.), 26
ethics probe, 654–655
sexual misadventures and resignation, 671 (box)
Massachusetts v. EPA, 372
Massie, Thomas (R-Ky.), 44
Matheson, Jim (D-Utah), 43
Matsui, Doris (D-Calif.), 335
McAuliffe, Terry, 18
McBroom, Cathy, 557–558
McCain, John (R-Ariz.), 11, 11 (table), 36, 38
Armed Services Committee, 644, 662
biofuels, 311
Bipartisan Campaign Reform Act, 677 (box)
border security funding bill, 212
budget negotiations (2009), 81
climate change, 599
committees, 844
copper mining, 396
D.C. representation, 648–649
death of Muammar Gaddafi, 701
defense appropriations (2010), 282
defense authorization (2011), 292
disability rights, 259
"don't ask, don't tell," 289
election (2008), 702
importation of prescription drugs, 461
Internet services, 333
Joseph Lieberman support of, 643–644
nuclear as renewable energy, 371
Postal Service, 628
Ray LaHood nomination, 710
Stanley McChrystal, 275 (box)
Syrian rebels, 224
McCain-Feingold Act, 677 (box)
McCarran-Ferguson Act, 432
McCarthy, Carolyn (D-N.Y.), 850
community service programs, 604
concealed handguns, 576
regulatory oversight, 631
McCarthy, Kevin (R-Calif.), 5 (table), 21, 843
majority whip, 663
McCaskill, Claire (D-Mo.), 336
committees, 844, 847
debt limit legislation, 137 (box)
defense authorization (2010), 276
executive pay, 531
Federal worker software sharing, 603
GAO authority, 634
impeachment of Federal judges, 558
Postal Service, 628
McCaul, Michael T. (R-Texas)
committees, 852
Pakistan aid, 236–237
McChrystal, Stanley, 230, 274 (box), 700
McClintock, Tom (R-Calif.), 395, 853
McConnell, Michael, 588
McConnell, Mitch (R-Ky.), 9, 22, 151, 388, 690, 698
Affordable Care Act, 425, 433, 457 (box), 459, 459 (box)
appellate judgeships, 577
budget negotiations (2009), 81
budget negotiations (2011), 113, 151
budget negotiations (2012), 35
continuing resolutions (2012), 170
debt limit legislation, 137 (box)
debt limit negotiations (2011), 162–164
Democracy Is Strengthened by Casting Light on Spending in Elections (DISCLOSE) Act, 679
fiscal cliff, 186–187, 188–189
Guantánamo Bay, Cuba, 315
Guantánamo detainees, 560
Harry Reid's remarks about Obama, 646 (box)
job creation legislation, 106
Keystone Pipeline, 390
labor union regulations, 538
law and law enforcement, 548

Medicare payments to physicians, 451, 464
minority leader, 642, 662
as minority leader, 5 (table), 22, 27, 843
National Commission on Fiscal Responsibility and Reform, 143
New START treaty, 290
opposition to the Affordable Care Act, 15
Patriot Act, 215
payroll tax cut, 109
Senate rules, 662, 663
small business assistance legislation, 2010, 102
STOCK Act, 667
student aid, 486
tax increases, 113
trade authority, 192
unemployment compensation, 536
war supplemental (2009), 271
McCormack, Ellen, 616
McCotter, Thaddeus (R-Mich.), 44, 843
Republican Policy Committee, 645, 663
McCrery, Jim (R-La.), 647
McCrory, Pat, 44
McDermott, Jim (D-Wash.), 338, 855
Internet gambling, 566
McDonald, Michael, 216
McDonnell, Bob, 18, 38
McGovern, Jim (D-Mass.), 276
Afghanistan war, 300, 310
child nutrition bill, 467
PMA Group, 655
war supplemental (2010), 287
McHenry, Patrick T. (R-N.C.), 853
mortgage lender regulation, 503
McHugh, John M. (R-N.Y.), 17
Armed Services Committee, 647
defense acquisition rules, 268
McIntyre, Mike (D-N.C.), 458, 849
McKeon, Howard P. (R-Calif.), 850
Armed Services Committee, 647, 664
defense authorization (2012), 299
defense authorization (2013), 309
green schools bill, 380
missile defense, 273
McKinney, Cynthia (D-Ga.), 644 (box)
McKinney-Vento Homeless Assistance Act (1987), 635
McMahon, Linda, 36
Media. *See* Communications
Medicaid, 15
Affordable Care Act expansion, 20, 421, 423 (box), 426, 432, 435, 439
cost savings, 441–442
appropriations
FY 2010, 131, 139–140
FY 2012, 175
FY 2013, 184
budget actions
2009-2010, 83–84
2011, 28
2012, 34
Affordable Care Act, 421
eligibility, 439
federal matching funds, 439
for U.S. territories, 439
income eligibility rules, 439
increased matching funds for Louisiana, 439
Independent Payment Advisory Board, 184
National Commission on Fiscal Responsibility and Reform recommendations, 144
outlays, 2001-2012, 420 (figure)
premium assistance, 442
prescription drug rebates, 442
reimbursements for primary care, 439
spending bill, 2010, 453–454
state-run exchanges, 437
See also Children's Health Insurance Program (CHIP)
Medical care. *See* Health and medical care
Medical devices
FDA review, 461, 462
tax, 424 (box), 432, 443
user fee, 463
Medical ethics
abortion (*See* Abortion)
malpractice (*See* Medical malpractice)
Medical malpractice, 144
Affordable Care Act, 424 (box), 430 (box), 442
Medical personnel. *See* Health care workers; Physicians
Medicare, 9, 19
Advantage program, 426, 430–431, 440, 441
Affordable Care Act, 20, 422, 434, 440–441
prescription drug coverage gap, 424 (box), 426, 440–441
appropriations
FY 2010, 131
FY 2012, 175
FY 2013, 184
2011 budget negotiations and, 28
2012 budget negotiations and, 34
creation of, 421, 436
hospital payroll tax, 422, 424 (box), 426, 443
Independent Payment Advisory Board, 457, 460
Independent Payment Advisory Board (IPAB), 184, 440
National Commission on Fiscal Responsibility and Reform recommendations, 144
outlays, 2001-2012, 420 (figure)
Part B premiums, 441
Part D, 444
physician payments, 108, 109, 127, 133, 148, 284, 419–420, 463–464
Rand Paul and, 25
reimbursements, 32
trust fund, 112
Medvedev, Dmitry, 290
Meehan, Patrick (R-Pa.), 852
Meeks, Gregory W. (D-N.Y.), 851
Megan's Law, 567
Melson, Kenneth, 574
Members of Congress. *See* Congress, members of
Menendez, Robert (D-N.J.), 371
Central Bank of Iran, 301
Children's Health Insurance Program, 446
committees, 843, 845, 846
Democratic Senatorial Campaign Committee, 642, 661

immigration, 556
Iran sanctions, 257, 311
Pakistan aid, 237
Mephedrone, 463
Merit-based pay plan, 600
Merit Systems Protection Board (MSPB), 623
Merkley, Jeff (D-Ore.), 217
MetLife Bank, 54, 69
Mexico City policy, 131, 176, 185, 244, 248, 252, 258
2012 state-foreign operations funding and, 253
Mexico-U.S. border area, 271
Border Patrol hiring, 287
entry points, 219
fence, 129, 208, 211
International Boundary Water Commission, 233
National Guard troops at, 212, 292
MF Global, 70–71
Mica, John L. (R-Fla.), 341, 390, 396, 636, 647, 855
Transportation and Infrastructure Committee, 664
unions, 539
Michaud, Michael H. (D-Maine), 855
Middle Class Tax Relief and Job Creation Act (2012), 520, 621
Middle East, 60, 249
Arab Spring, 223–224, 249, 700–701
Muslim Brotherhood, 223, 252, 701
no-fly zones, 250, 701
See also specific countries
Midwestern states, floods of 2008, 139, 288
See also specific states
Miers, Harriet, 574, 647
Mikulski, Barbara (D-Md.), 844, 847
community service programs, 605
minimum wage, 541
wage parity, 529
Milestone Decision Authority, 269
Military affairs. *See* Defense policy
Military aid. *See* Foreign aid
Military aircraft. *See specific aircraft*
Military base closings. *See* Base realignment and closure (BRAC)
Military construction
FY 2009, 16, 269
FY 2010, 131, 284–285
FY 2011, 155, 294, 297–298
FY 2012, 175–176, 252, 304
FY 2013, 184, 312
Military health care and hospitals
Agent Orange, 139, 288
appropriations
FY 2009, 270
FY 2010, 284
FY 2011, 294
FY 2012, 307
FY 2013, 312
post-traumatic stress disorder, 235 (box)
Tricare program, 303, 312, 428
Military housing, appropriations, 285, 294, 298, 304
Military justice. *See* Military tribunals
Military pay and benefits
concurrent receipt, 279
increase
2009, 269
2010, 284
2011, 292, 293, 294, 297
2012, 303, 307
2013, 312
Military personnel
abortion services, 308, 310–311
appropriations, 2009, 280
authorizations for force levels
FY 2009, 16
FY 2011, 294
FY 2012, 303
health care and hospitals (*See* Military health care and hospitals)
homosexual, 19, 22, 264–265, 267, 288–289, 299–300, 308
marriage of, 300, 301, 305, 308
pay and benefits (*See* Military pay and benefits)
post-traumatic stress disorder (PTSD) in, 235 (box)
retirement, 133
Military tribunals, 285, 309
Milk and dairy products, 128
Milken Institute, 71
Millender-McDonald, Juanita (D-Calif.), 646
Millennium Challenge Corporation, 156, 245, 250
Miller, Aaron David, 701
Miller, Brad (D-N.C.), 854
Patent law, 571
Miller, Candice S. (R-Mich.)
border entry points, 219
committee, 852
Miller, Gary G. (R-Calif.), 851
Miller, George (D-Calif.), 397, 850
Affordable Care Act, 428
affordable housing, 510
charter schools, 491
child nutrition bill, 466
community service programs, 605
education, 473, 477, 483
Education and Labor Committee, 646, 664
gender-based wage discrimination, 528
green schools bill, 380
labor union regulations, 538
minimum wage, 540
restrictions on regulations, 632
student aid, 489
student punishment, 481
unions, 533
Miller, Jeff (R-Fla.), 664, 855
hunting and fishing regulations, 400–401
Miller, Joe, 24
Mineral resources and mining
coal, 399, 708, 710
conflict minerals from the Congo, 101
copper, 395–396
Ken Salazar, 710
mine safety, 101
mining on public lands bill, 399
offshore drilling, 374–376, 394
payments for resource extraction, 101

Mine Resistant Ambush Protected (MRAP) vehicles, 153, 269, 279, 282, 284, 297, 304, 307
Minimum wage
 about, 516, 540
 American Samoa workers, 541
 for Guam construction workers, 530
 H-2B immigrants, 541
 home health aides, 540–541
 for U.S. Territory workers, 529–530
Minority-serving institutions, 479
Miranda warnings, 247, 279, 593
Mirelson, Doc, 607
Missile defense, 273–274, 276, 284, 302, 306
 Alaska and California, 311
 East Coast site, 308
 ground-based Midcourse Defense system, 308
 Israel's Iron Dome, 293, 312
Missing persons, 564
Mitchell, George, 228
Mitchell, Harry E. (D-Ariz.), 855
Mohammed, Khalid Sheikh, 307, 315, 316
Mollohan, Alan B. (D-W.Va.), 849
 ethics probe, 654
Money Market Investor Funding Facility, 57
Monroe, James, president, 35, 702
Moody's Investors Service, 162
Moore, Dennis (D-Kan.), 851
Moore, Mikael, 675
Moran, Brian, 18
Moran, James P. (D-Va.), 18, 849
 ethics probe, 655–656
 Green the Capitol initiative, 670
 Iran sanctions, 243
 nutrition bill, 469
Moran, Jerry (R-Kan.), same-sex couples, 581
Moreno, Carlos, 711
Morgan Stanley, 72
"Morning after" pill, 422 (box)
Mortgage Reform and Anti-Predatory Lending Act of 2009, 502–503
Mortgages. *See* Home loans and mortgages
Mourdock, Richard E., 41
Moving Ahead for Progress in the 21st Century (MAP-21) Act of 2012, 340–341, 485, 491
Moynihan, Daniel, 585
Mozilo, Angelo, 652
Mubarak, Hosni, 223, 224, 249, 250, 700–701
Mueller, Robert S., III
 Guantánamo detainees, 561
 justice leadership, 549
 Supreme Court, 591
Mullen, Mike, 230, 288
Multiple Peril Insurance Act, 611
Mulvaney, Mick (R-S.C.)
 committees, 854
 2013 defense appropriations, 312–313
 small business Federal contracting, 630–631
Murkowski, Lisa (R-Alaska), 24, 371, 845
 appellate judgeships, 576–577
 "don't ask, don't tell," 289
 emissions prohibition modification, 384
 Energy and Natural Resources Committee, 644, 662
Murphy, Christopher S. (D-Conn.), 36
 missing persons, 564
Murphy, Patrick J. (D-Pa.)
 defense authorization (2011), 292
 Democracy Is Strengthened by Casting Light on Spending in Elections (DISCLOSE) Act, 679
 war supplemental (2010), 288–289
Murray, Patty (D-Wash.), 40, 378
 committees, 844, 847
 Congressional deficit committee, 168
 Democratic Caucus Secretary, 642, 661
 Medicaid-education supplemental, 140
 Veterans Affairs Committee, 662
Murtha, John (D-Pa.), 26
 budget negotiations (2009), 122
 defense appropriations (2010), 281–282
 ethics probe, 655–656
 F-22 fighter, 277
 2009 war supplemental, 272
Muslim Brotherhood, 223, 252, 701
Myanmar, 201, 228
Myrick, Sue Wilkins (R-N.C.)
 committees, 854
 2013 intelligence authorization, 255

Nadler, Jerrold (D-N.Y.), 852
 abortion, 579
 concealed handguns, 576
 D.C. representation, 649
 Foreign Intelligence Surveillance Act, 216
 restrictions on regulations, 632
 same-sex couples, 581
NAFTA. *See* North American Free Trade Agreement (NAFTA)
Naftiran Intertrade Company, 238
Napolitano, Grace F. (D-Calif.), 207 (box), 397, 853
Napolitano, Janet, 205, 206 (figure), 208, 705 (box)
 considered for Supreme Court appointment, 711
 immigration, 556
 nomination by Obama, 710
NARA. *See* National Archives and Records Administration (NARA)
NASA. *See* National Aeronautics and Space Administration (NASA)
National Aeronautics and Space Administration (NASA), 21, 82, 605–607
 appropriations
  FY 2010, 130
  FY 2011, 153
  FY 2012, 171
  FY 2013, 182
 collaborations with China banned, 153, 171
National Aeronautics and Space Administration Authorization Act (2010), 605
National ambient air quality standards (NAAQS), 398
National Animal Identification System, 412, 413
National Archives and Records Administration (NARA), 615
National Association of Counties, 380
National Association of Insurance Commissioners, 99

National Association of Manufacturers, 161
Democracy Is Strengthened by Casting Light on Spending in Elections (DISCLOSE) Act, 678
Export-Import Bank reauthorization, 200
National Bankers Association, 657, 675
National Broadband Plan, 323, 340
National Coalition for Syrian Revolutionary and Opposition Forces, 701
National Commission on Fiscal Responsibility and Reform, 142–144, 697
National Council on Disability, 668
National Credit Union Administration (NCUA), 69, 92
increase in deposit insurance, 500
National Earthquake Hazards Reduction Program, 611
National Economic Council (NEC), 49
National Education Association (NEA)
antibullying and gang prevention law, 492
Arne Duncan and, 477 (box)
D.C. school vouchers, 481
National Endowment for the Arts, 151
National Environmental Policy Act, 184
National Federation of Independent Business, 169
National Flood Insurance Program, 190, 610–611, 624–625
National Flood Insurance Program Reextension Act (2010), 611
National Foundation for American Policy, 582
National Governors Association, 467
National Guard, 140, 152, 279–280, 281
appropriations, 294, 307
FY 2010, 133, 273
at the U.S.-Mexico border, 212, 292
National Institute of Standards and Technology (NIST), 608, 609
cybersecurity standards, 218
National Institutes of Health (NIH), 82
National Iranian Oil Company, 256
National Iranian Tanker Company, 256
National Labor Relations Act (1935), 540
National Labor Relations Board (NLRB), 105–106, 175, 184, 537–538
National Legal and Policy Center, 654, 655
Nationally Recognized Statistical Rating Organizations, 99
National Mediation Board (NMB), 33, 539
National Mortgage Settlement, 499 (box)
National Museum and Library Services Board, 668
National Nuclear Security Administration (NNSA), 138, 152, 279, 294, 303
National parks and monuments, 84, 85
National Park Service, 383
National Public Radio (NPR), 155
ACORN defunding, 680
National Republican Congressional Committee, 645, 663, 843
National Republican Senatorial Committee, 642, 843
National Retail Federation, 193
National Rifle Association (NRA), 10, 551
Democracy Is Strengthened by Casting Light on Spending in Elections (DISCLOSE) Act, 678
Sonia Sotomayor, 712
National Right to Life Committee, 433 (box), 678
National Science Foundation (NSF), 82, 608, 609
appropriations, FY 2009, 121
cybersecurity programs, 218
e-waste grants, 379
Presidential Appointment Efficiency and Streamlining Act, 668
National Security Act of 1947, 246, 602
National Security Agency (NSA)
appropriations
FY 2010, 246
FY 2013, 254
FY 2011 and 2012, 251
wiretapping, 216
National Security Council, 227 (box)
National security letters, 209
National Security Personnel System (NSPS), 600
National Service Reserve Corps, 604
National Telecommunications and Information Administration (NTIA), 325
National Women's History Museum, 616, 636
Native Americans, 555
apology to, 617
casinos, 618
Indian Affairs Committee, Senate, 644, 847
ranking members and chairs, 643, 662
Indian Health Care Improvement Act, 443
Indian Health Service, 129, 443
law enforcement on tribal lands, 563
women married to non-native men, 572
Native Hawaiian government, 618–619
NATO. *See* North Atlantic Treaty Organization (NATO)
Natural disasters
Hurricane Katrina, 139, 154, 205, 208, 288
Hurricane Rita, 139, 288
Superstorm Sandy, 10, 33, 39, 205, 207 (box)
2012 presidential election, 702, 704
supplemental funds, 2013, 189–190
See Disaster relief
Natural gas, 708
David Vitter ethics probe, 672
George W. Bush ties, 363
Iran, 240, 241
Natural Hazards Risk Reduction Act, 611
Natural Resources Committee, House, 647, 853
ranking members and chairs, 646, 664
Natural Resources Defense Council, 709
Natural resources outlays, 364 (figure)
Navy, U.S.
appropriations
FY 2011, 138
FY 2013, 312
DDG-51 Arleigh Burke-class destroyer, 283, 303, 306, 312
F-35 alternative engine, 266
Littoral Combat Ships, 138, 278, 283, 303, 306, 312
shipbuilding authorizations, 278, 283, 303, 306, 312
submarines, 283, 303, 312
warplanes, 278
NCUA. *See* National Credit Union Administration (NCUA)
NEA. *See* National Education Association (NEA)
Neal, Richard E. (D-Mass.), 855
NEC. *See* National Economic Council (NEC)
Needle exchange programs, 132, 175
Neighborhood Stabilization Program, 101, 500, 509

Nelson, Ben (D-Neb.), 35, 41, 81, 844
  Affordable Care Act, 421, 431, 433 (box), 435
  appellate judgeships, 576
  "Cornhusker kickback," 435
  Elena Kagan nomination, 712
Nelson, Bill (D-Fla.), 371, 846
  drywall safety, 508
Netanyahu, Benjamin, 225, 228
Net neutrality, 320, 331–334
Neugebauer, Randy (R-Texas), 851
Nevada
  Shelley Berkley ethics probe, 676
  Yucca Mountain, 173, 183, 377–378, 394–395
NewMexico, 708
New START (Strategic Arms Reduction Treaty), 7, 22, 138, 152, 232, 267, 289–291, 300, 303–304, 309
New Starts and Small Starts projects, 325
New York
  Acquisition Fund, 709
  gubernatorial elections, 25
  Shaun Donovan, 709
New York Carib News Foundation, 655
New York Times
  on Alan B. Mollohan, 654
  on Charles Rangel, 658
  on Guantánamo Bay detainees, 314
  Robert B. Reich, 698
  Shelley Berkley ethics probe, 676
  on unmanned aerial vehicles, 255
Nicotine. *See* Tobacco
Nightline, 651
NIH. *See* National Institutes of Health (NIH)
NIST (National Institute of Standards and Technology), 608
Nixon, Richard, president, 216
  plain writing, 613
NLRB. *See* National Labor Relations Board (NLRB)
NMB. *See* National Mediation Board (NMB)
NNSA. *See* National Nuclear Security Administration (NNSA)
Nobel Peace Prize, 689, 690 (figure), 699, 888–892
No Child Left Behind Act of 2002, 696–697, 709
  executive action on, 485
  reauthorization of, 473, 477 (box), 483–484, 491
  waivers for, 474–475
Noem, Kristi (R-S.D.), 396
No-fly list, 211, 316
No-fly zones, 250, 701
Nominations and confirmations, 690–691, 704–712
  Agriculture, 410, 711
  attorney general, 706–707
  Bureau of Consumer Financial Protection, 69
  Commerce, 323, 708–709
  Consumer Financial Protection Bureau, 104, 105–106, 690
  Defense, 264–265, 274 (box), 706
  economic leadership, 48–49, 54
  Education, 709
  Energy, 367, 708
  Environmental Protection Agency, 367
  Federal Communications Commission, 323, 354
  Federal Reserve, 86 (box)
  Health and Human Services, 707–708
  Homeland Security, 710
  Housing and Urban Development, 709
  Interior, 367, 710
  John E. Bryson, 323
  judicial, 20–21, 691 (*See also* Supreme Court, U.S.)
    Elena Kagan, 10, 20–21
    Sotomayor, Sonia, 10, 16–17, 21, 711–712
  Julius Genachowski, 323
  Ken Salazar, 367
  Labor, 710–711
  Lisa Jackson, 367
  Presidential Appointment Efficiency and Streamlining Act, 668–669
  Ray LaHood, 323
  recess, 105–106
  Secretary of State, 226 (box), 704–705
  Tom Vilsack, 410
  Transportation, 709–710
  Treasury, 323, 338, 706
  Veterans Affairs, 710
  See also specific nominees and presidents
Nonprofits. *See* Charities and non-profit organizations
North American Free Trade Agreement (NAFTA), 195
North Atlantic Treaty Organization (NATO), 224, 229, 230, 300, 700
North Carolina, 704
Northern Mariana Islands, 648
North Korea, 699
Northwest Airlines, 207 (box), 208
Norton, Eleanor Holmes (D-D.C.), 490, 855
  D.C. representation, 649
Norton, Jane, 24
Notarization, 339, 915–916
NRA. *See* National Rifle Association (NRA)
NSF. *See* National Science Foundation (NSF)
NSPS. *See* National Security Personnel System (NSPS)
Nuclear power, 278–279
  Domestic Nuclear Detection Office, 210
  Iran and, 225, 240–241
  New Strategic Arms Reduction Treaty (START), 7, 22, 138, 152, 232, 267, 289–291, 300, 303–304
  Pakistan and, 238
Nuclear Regulatory Commission, 173
Nuclear waste, 173, 183, 377–378, 394–395
  low-level, 379
Nuclear weapons
  appropriations, 278–279, 294, 303–304, 307
  delivery vehicles, 313
Nugent, Richard B. (R-Fla.), 854
Nuisance dust, 396
Nunes, Devin (R-Calif.), 397
Nunnelee, Alan (R-Miss.), 460
Nussle, Jim (R-Iowa), 661 (box)
Nutrition. *See* Food and nutrition
Nye, Glenn C. (D-Va.), 854

Obama, Barack, president
  abortion, 579
  address at Cairo University in Egypt, 699, 883–888
  address on accepting the Nobel Peace Prize, 699, 888–892
  address on climate change, 892–893
  address to Congress on health care, 430 (box)

Afghanistan policy, 229–231, 700
agricultural legislation, 407
appellate judgeships, 576, 577
approval ratings, 692, 698
Arab Spring, 700–701
bank stress tests, 694–695
budget battles, 2011-2012, 697–698
budget requests
FY 2009, 122
FY 2010, 125–126
FY 2011, 112, 135–136, 150
FY 2012, 157–159
FY 2013, 177–180
cabinet, 705 (box)
caller ID spoofing, 563
campaign finance, 551
campaign spending, 36
climate change, 695–696
community service programs, 604
congressional election (2010) and, 6–7, 22–23
contractors withholding rule, 630
cybersecurity research, 615
debt limit negotiations (2011), 28, 160–167
decline of public financing in 2008, 36 (box)
defense policy, 263–266
doctrine, 699
domestic partner benefits, 604
domestic policy, 689–690, 692–698
economic crisis of 2007–2008 and, 60–61
economic leadership, 48–49
economic policy, 47
economic stimulus package, 47, 61, 66, 325, 691, 692–693
education, 473–474, 485
election (2008), 3, 10, 11 (table), 689, 924, 925
election (2012), 11, 11 (table), 35–40, 926
electoral votes, 927
statement on winning, 912–914
energy policies, 363, 365
excess public properties, 634
executive actions, 122
executive pay, 531
extension of Bush tax cuts, 144–146
federal employee domestic partnerships, 623
federal unemployment benefits extension, 29–30
federal worker pay, 600, 622
federal worker pension contributions, 541, 542–543
financial services regulatory reform, 20
first inaugural address, 877–879
first year agenda, 13
fiscal 2012 appropriations, 575
fiscal cliff talks with Boehner, 187–188
foreign policy, 223–231, 690, 698–701
gender-based wage discrimination, 528
governors during first term of, 956–957
Guantánamo detainees, 560
Harry Reid's remarks about, 646 (box)
health care overhaul, 419, 691–692, 693–694 (*See also* Affordable Care Act)
highspeed rail development, 340
Holder held in contempt of Congress, 574
homeland security policy, 205
Hurricane Sandy, 598, 625, 626
immigration, 556
inauguration of, 515, 689
Indian health service, 617
Iraq war policy, 699–700
job creation and protection, 527
job creation plan, 2010, 106–107
journalism sources, 559
justice leadership, 549
labor union regulations, 537
law and law enforcement, 547, 568
Lily Ledbetter Pair Pay Act, 550
minimum wage, 529
NASA, 605, 606, 608
National Commission on Fiscal Responsibility and Reform, 142–144
national infrastructure bank, 340
negotiations with Boehner, 692, 697
Nobel Peace Prize, 689, 690 (figure), 699, 888–892
nominations and appointments (*See* Nominations and confirmations)
111th Congress and, 13–26
112th Congress and, 27–44
partisanship under, 4, 552
patent law, 568, 569
personality, 692
plain writing, 613
pocket veto, 650
policy on Guantánamo Bay, 130
presidential records, 616
public housing, 505 (box)
pulls plug on Yucca Mountain program, 377
reelection of, 113, 692, 702–704
Republicans and, 689–690
resignation from Senate, 17
same-sex couples, 581
sequester and, 29
shortfalls, 689–692
signs farm bill extension, 414
signs Omnibus appropriations, 382
signs transportation measure, 2012, 387
Solyndra bankruptcy, 395
speech on climate change bill, 370
statement on death of Osama bin Laden, 905–906
State of the Union address
2009, 879–883
2010, 893–899
2011, 899–905
2012, 906–912
student aid, 486
Supreme Court, 584, 585, 586
TARP and auto company bailouts, 694
teachers, 495 (box)
trade policy, 191
Troubled Asset Relief Program (TARP) and, 694
unemployment compensation, 524, 535
unions, 533
vetoes, 339, 915–916
Wall Street reform, 695
whistleblower protection, 602

Obama, Michelle, 13, 465
 Capital Hill dress code, 644 (box)
 childhood obesity, 420
 Lets Move! campaign, 490 (box)
Obamacare. *See* Affordable Care Act
Oberstar, James L. (D-Minn.), 22, 24, 87, 324, 326, 341, 385, 664, 855
 FEMA, 611
 Transportation and Infrastructure Committee, 646
Obesity
 childhood, 420, 465–467
 restaurant menu labeling, 443
Obey, David R. (D-Wis.), 86, 383, 664
 Afghanistan war, 231
 Appropriations Committee ranking members and chairs, 645
 budget negotiations (2009), 121
 budget negotiations (2011), 137, 139
 committees, 849
 Guantánamo Bay, Cuba detainees, 210
 Medicaid and education spending bill, 2010, 454
 pocket veto, 650
 Race to the Top, 480–481
 war supplemental (2009), 270
 war supplemental (2010), 286, 287
OCC. *See* Office of the Comptroller of the Currency (OCC)
OCE. *See* Office of Congressional Ethics (OCE)
O'Connor, Sandra Day, 10
 appointment of, 585
Odierno, Ray, 275
O'Donnell, Christine, 24, 25
OECD. *See* Organisation for Economic Co-operation and Development (OECD)
Office of Congressional Ethics (OCE), 653, 656, 673, 674
 See also Congressional ethics probes
Office of Credit Ratings, 99
Office of Federal Housing Enterprise Oversight, 67
Office of Financial Research, 92, 93
Office of General Counsel, House, 669–670
Office of Government Ethics, 666
Office of Housing Counseling, 100
Office of Investor Advocate, 101
Office of National Counterintelligence Executive, 580
Office of Personnel Management (OPM)
 Affordable Care Act, 425
 Affordable Care Act state-run exchanges, 436–437
 appropriations, FY 2010, 131
Office of Science and Technology Policy, 152, 171
 See also Science and technology
Office of Surface Mining, 403
Office of Sustainable Housing and Communities, 499 (box)
Office of the Comptroller of the Currency (OCC), 69, 695
 Dodd-Frank Act and, 94
 Financial Stability Oversight Council and, 92
 JP Morgan Chase and, 71
Office of the Director of National Intelligence (DNI), 227 (box), 246–248, 251, 254
 insider threat detection program, 251
Office of Thrift Supervision (OTS), 94
Offsets, Dodd-Frank Act, 89, 99
Offshore drilling, 374–376, 394
O'Hayre, John, 613
Ohio, 703
Oil, 708
 biofuels, 308
 David Vitter ethics probe, 672
 George W. Bush ties, 363
 Gulf of Mexico oil spill, 139, 205, 288
 Iranian, 238–241, 256
 Keystone XL pipeline, 109, 364–365, 390–392, 696
 offshore drilling, 374–376, 394
Oil Spill Liability Trust Fund, 376
O'Keefe, James, 680
Oliver, John W. (D-Mass.), 849
Olson, Pete (R-Texas), 373
OMB. *See* Management and Budget, Office of (OMB)
Omnibus appropriations, 382–383, 529
O'Neill, Thomas P. (D-Mass.), 49
OneUnited Bank, 656, 675
Operation Fast and Furious, 171, 549, 552, 568, 575
"Operation Twist," 57–58
OPM. *See* Office of Personnel Management (OPM)
Orderly liquidation, 93
Oregonian, 673
Organisation for Economic Co-operation and Development (OECD), 196
Ornstein, Norman J., 27
Orszag, Peter S., 49
Ortiz, Solomon P. (D-Texas), 850
Outer Continental Shelf Lands Act, 394
Outlays for Agriculture (chart), 408
Outlays for Energy (chart), 265
Overseas Contingency Operations (OCO), 252, 284, 294–295, 304, 307, 312
Oversight and Government Reform Committee, House, 542, 544, 573, 647, 853
 cybersecurity bills, 218
 ranking members and chairs, 646, 664
 tobacco regulation, 448

PACE. *See* Property-assisted clean energy (PACE) loans
Packer, Winsome, 673–674
PACs. *See* Political action committees (PACs)
Pakistan, 122, 131, 176
 Afghanistan war and, 231
 Counterinsurgency Fund, 152, 237, 270, 304–305
 foreign aid to, 233, 236–238, 252, 253–254, 270, 272–273, 310
 Taliban in, 229
 unmanned aerial vehicles in, 255
 See also Middle East
Palazzo, Steven M. (R-Miss.), 854
 same-sex marriage, 308
Palestine Liberation Organization, 253
Palestinian Authority, 254
Palestinians, 225, 228, 249
Palin, Sarah, 6, 921 (table)
Pallone, Frank, Jr. (D-N.J.), 850
 Ryan White HIV/AIDS Act reauthorization, 453
 tobacco regulation, 448
Panama, 74
 intellectual property, 198–199
 trade agreements, 193, 194 (box), 195–196, 198–199

Panetta, Leon E., 188, 246, 249, 263
  CIA director, 227 (box), 706
  defense authorization (2013), 309
  defense secretary, 265, 274 (box), 296
  nomination by Obama, 705 (box)
Paper and Stop the OverPrinting (STOP) Act, 670
Parental leave for federal workers, 602–603
Partisanship, 7, 7 (table), 8–9, 552
  111th Congress, 13–14
  112th Congress, 27
  risk of modern, 4
Passport cards, 244
Pastor, Ed (D-Ariz.), 377
Pata, Jacqueline, 617
Patent and Trademark Office, 571
Patent and Trademark Office (PTO), 568
Patent law overhaul, 561, 568–571
Patents, biologic drug, 442
Paterson, David A., 453
"Path to Prosperity, The," 156
Patient Protection and Affordable Care Act (2010), 584, 602, 617
Patrick, Deval, 18, 25
USA Patriot Act, 133, 205–206, 208–209, 548, 550, 568
  business records provision, 214, 215
  four-year extension, 215
  lone wolf provision, 214, 215
  roving wiretaps, 214, 215
  short-term extension, 209, 215
Paul, Rand (R-Ky.), 23, 24, 25
  2011 budget negotiations, 160
  classification and regulation of food or dietary supplements as drugs, 461
  education, 484
  elderly and disabled refugees, 583
  Federal Reserve audit, 633
  Iran sanctions, 256
  Patriot Act, 215
  Postal Service, 628
  regulatory oversight, 631
  Senate rules, 662
Paul, Ron (R-Tex.), 24, 37, 851
  Dodd-Frank Act, 92
  use-of-force law, 300
Paulson, Henry M., 48, 77, 657
Pawlenty, Tim, 702
Pay-as-you-go (PAYGO) rules, 126–127, 141, 142, 451, 664–665, 697
Payment in Lieu of Taxes, 485
Payne, Donald M. (D-N.J.), 44, 658, 851
  ethics probe, 655
Payroll taxes, 8–9, 30, 32, 74, 543
  forgiveness, 87
  Medicare hospital, 422, 424 (box), 426, 443
  reductions
    2010, 79 (box)
    2011, 108–110, 146
    2012, 172
Peace Corps, 241, 242
  volunteer protection, 624
Peacekeeping activities, 245
Pease provision, 146
Pell grants, 82
  funding for, 478, 479, 486–487
  FY 2011, 135, 136, 138, 155
  FY 2012, 167, 175
  2010 war supplemental, 287
  See also Student aid
Pelosi, Nancy (D-Calif.), 4
  Affordable Care Act, 15, 422–423, 427, 431, 432 (box), 435
  budget negotiations (2009), 121
  budget negotiations (2010), 123, 126
  budget negotiations (2011), 151, 152
  Capitol Hill dress code, 644 (box)
  Charles Rangel ethics probe, 659
  child nutrition bill, 467
  committees, 843
  cybersecurity research, 615
  David Wu ethics probe, 673
  debt limit negotiations (2011), 162, 164
  Democracy Is Strengthened by Casting Light on Spending in Elections (DISCLOSE) Act, 678
  education jobs fund, 479
  energy negotiations, 370
  Eric Massa ethics probe, 654
  estate taxes, 147
  extension of Bush tax cuts, 145
  foreign trade agreements, 193, 197
  Green the Capitol initiative, 670
  health care fund, 485
  homebuyer tax credit, 505
  home loans and mortgages, 500–501
  Jane Harman ethics probe, 653
  jobs creation bill, 85
  Medicaid and education spending bill, 2010, 453
  minority leader, 663
  as minority leader, 21–22
  National Commission on Fiscal Responsibility and Reform, 143
  online disclosure of expenditures, 650–651
  pay-as-you go rules, 126, 141
  photo, 516
  Speaker of the House, 645, 661 (box)
  as Speaker of the House, 5 (table), 14, 843
  STOCK Act, 666, 667
  war supplemental (2010), 287
  waterboarding, 246
Pence, Mike (R-Ind.), 5 (table), 44
  committees, 843
  Iran sanctions, 239
  Republican Conference, 645
  State Department reauthorization, 242
Pennsylvania, 703
Pension Benefit Guaranty Corporation (PBGC), 144, 486, 543
Pensions and retirement
  federal employee (*See* Federal employees)
  income, 83
  military, 133, 279
  outlays, 2001-2012, 466 (figure)
  Social Security (*See* Social Security)
Pentagon
  Afghanistan war and, 229–230

appropriations
FY 2010, 133, 280
FY 2011, 139, 293
FY 2012, 172–173
FY 2013, 180, 307
audit, 301
costs of Iraq war to, 235 (box)
Milestone Decision Authority, 269
Pakistan counterinsurgency funds, 122
Perdue, Beverly, 44
Perkins Loan Program, 478
Perry, Rick, 37
presidential campaign, 702
Peters, Gary (D-Mich.), 381, 682
home loans and mortgages, 502
Peterson, Collin C. (D-Minn.), 370, 849
Agriculture Committee, 645, 664
Petraeus, David H., 227 (box), 274–275 (box)
Petri, Thomas E. (R-Wis.), 855
Petroleum. *See* Oil
Pharmaceutical Research and Manufacturers of America, 462
Philip Morris USA, 448
PhRMA, 431
Physicians
medical malpractice, 144, 424 (box), 430 (box), 442
Medicare payments to, 108, 109, 127, 133, 148, 284, 419–420, 450–452, 463–464
-owned hospitals, 441
Pierluisi, Pedro R., 619
Pigford v. Glickman, 413
Pilling, David, 192
Pilot training and air safety, 332
Pingree, Chellie (D-Maine), 292
community service programs, 604
Pinsonat, Bernie, 24
Pipeline and Hazardous Materials Safety Administration, 401
Piracy, Internet, 358–359
Pitts, Joseph R. (R-Pa.), 851
CLASS act repeal, 457
Plain Language in Government Communications Act, 613–614
Plain writing, 613–614
Planned Parenthood Federation of America, Inc., 8, 151, 152, 155, 184
Democracy Is Strengthened by Casting Light on Spending in Elections (DISCLOSE) Act, 678
Platinum Plan, Affordable Care Act, 437
Platts, Todd R. (R-Pa.), 602, 853
education spending, 484
whistleblower protection, 601
Pledge to America, 134
Plutonium 238, 608
PMA Group, 655–656
PNC, 54
Pocket edition Constitution, 670
Pocket veto, 650
Poe, Ted (R-Texas), 305
Afghanistan war, 313
American community survey, 636
bankruptcy judgeships, 565
COPS, 562
Violence Against Women Act, 573
Poland, 278, 293
Polar Sea (ship), 218–219
Polar Star (ship), 218–219
Polio, 245
Polis, Jared (D-Colo.), 390
Political action committees (PACs), 36
Political committees, 843
Political parties
affiliations of presidents, 1789-2015, 929–930
victorious in presidential races, 1860-2012, 922–923
See also Democratic Party; Republican Party
Political year (2009), 17–18
administration-related vacancies, 17
gubernatorial elections, 18
party switches, 18
Senate vacancies, 17–18
Political year (2010), 30
financial services regulatory reform, 20
GOP surge, 23
health care reform, 19–20
House elections, 23–24
Kagan confirmed, 20–21
lame duck surprise, 22
organization the next Congress, 21–22
preelection gridlock, 21
seat shift in Senate, 19
Senate elections, 24–25
special elections, 26
state elections, 25
Political year (2011)
cutting the budget, 28
debt limit increase, 28–29
getting to fiscal 2012, 29
governorships, 31
House special elections, 31
round one on spending, 27–28
sequester, 29
turning to jobs, 30–31
Political year (2012)
budgets and spending, 31–32
fiscal cliff, 34–35
GOP priorities frustrated, 34
gubernatorial races, 44
House elections, 42–43
laws, 32–33
presidential election, 35–40
Senate elections, 40–42
special House elections, 43–44
statehouse races, ballot initiatives, 44
unfinished legislation, 33–34
Politico, 651–652, 675
Pollock, Jef, 42
Pomeroy, Earl (D-N.D.), 855
Ponzi schemes, 90
Porteous, G. Thomas, Jr., 553
conviction of, 557
impeachment of, 558
Portman, Rob (R-Ohio), 38
Congressional deficit committee, 168
Presidential Appointment Efficiency and Streamlining Act, 668

Portugal, 51, 55
Postal Reform Act, 627
Postal Reorganization Act, 601
Postal Service
congressional members disclaimers in mailings, 685
overhaul, 627–629
retiree benefit, 601
Post Office Department, U.S. *See* Postal Service
Post-traumatic stress disorder (PTSD), 235 (box)
Potholm, Erik, 41
Poverty
Affordable Care Act
Basic Health Plan, 437
employer vouchers, 438–439
limit on out-of-pocket costs, 437–438
tax credits for lower-income households, 437
housing, 497, 505–506, 505 (box), 506
income security outlays, 2001-2012, 466 (figure)
Medicaid, 15
Affordable Care Act and, 20, 421, 439
appropriations
FY 2010, 131, 139–140
FY 2012, 175
FY 2013, 184
budget actions
2009-2010, 83–84
2011, 28
2012, 34
Affordable Care Act, 421
Independent Payment Advisory Board, 184
National Commission on Fiscal Responsibility and Reform recommendations, 144
outlays, 2001-2012, 420 (figure)
Ryan White HIV/AIDS Act, 419, 420 (figure), 452–453
social services (*See* Welfare and social services)
student aid, 487(box)
Temporary Assistance to Needy Families (TANF), 110, 181
Powell, Colin L., 290
Pratt, Erich, 560
Predatory lending, 100–101
Preexisting conditions and Affordable Care Act, 422, 424 (box), 430 (box), 439
Pregnancy
abortion (*See* Abortion)
teen, 131
WIC program (*See* Women, Infants, and Children (WIC) program)
Preschool education. *See* Head Start
Presidential Appointment Efficiency and Streamlining Act, 668–669
Presidential debt panel, 142–144
Presidential election (2008), 3, 702, 924, 925
Joseph Lieberman, 643–644
Presidential election (2012), 9–12, 35–40, 702–704, 926
electoral votes, 927
Presidential Election Campaign Fund, 154, 682
Presidential elections
Presidential Election Campaign Fund, 154, 682
1789-2012 summary, 919–921
Presidential Records Act (1978), 616
Presidents, U.S., party affiliations, 1789-2015, 929–930
Prevent Deceptive Census Look Alike Mailings Act (2010), 614
Price, David E. (D-N.C.)
border security supplemental spending, 2010, 140, 206
2013 budget negotiations, 181
committees, 849
Guantánamo Bay, Cuba detainees, 210
Presidential Election Campaign Fund, 682
Price, Tom (R-Ga.), 843
ethics probe, 672–673
home loans and mortgages, 500
New START treaty, 309
Section 8 vouchers, 506
Pricing floors, 564
Primary Dealer Credit Facility, 56
Principal Reduction Alternative, 64
Printing, Joint Committee on, 856
pocket edition Constitution, 670
Print media and publishing
on the Afghanistan war, 230–231
ethics probes and, 651, 652
on the home mortgage market, 67–68
on the LIBOR scandal, 72
on trade partnerships, 192
"Prior user" defense, 570
Prison deaths, 578
Program integrity initiatives, 123
Project labor agreements, 176
Property-assisted clean energy (PACE) loans, 501 (box)
Property rights, 579
Propriety trading, 69, 95
ProPublica, 67–68
Protecting Academic Freedom in Higher Education Act, 488
Protecting Cyberspace as a National Asset Act of 2010, 615
Pryor, Mark (D-Ark.), 412
committees, 845, 847
disability rights, 479 (box)
domestic partner benefits, 604
national flood insurance, 624
same-sex couples, 581
unions, 533
Pryzbyl, Michael, 206 (figure)
PTO (U.S. Patent and Trademark Office), 568
Public Broadcasting Service (PBS), 155
Public housing. *See* Section 8 housing
Public Housing Capital Fund, 156
Public Housing Operating Fund, 156
Public Interest Research Group, 678
Public lands, 183–184, 398–399
Public laws, 2009-2012, 961–1004
Public opinion. *See* Gallup Polls
Public option, Affordable Care Act, 425, 429, 430 (box), 434
Public-Private Investment Program, TARP, 64
Public safety workers, 534
Puerto Rico, 648
Affordable Care Act, 439
political status of, 619–620
Puerto Rico Democracy Act (2010), 619
Punishment, student, 481
Putin, Vladimir V., 201
Putnam, Adam H. (R-Fla.), 645
national flood insurance, 611
Puzey, Kate, 624

Qatar, 224
Quantitative easing (QE), 57–58
Quayle, Benjamin (R-Ariz.), 854
Quayle, Dan, 921 (table)
Quigley, Mike (D-Ill.), 573
Quorums, live, 640

Racalto, Joe, 655
Race to the Top program, 175, 287, 473–474, 480–481, 492–494, 696
Rahall, Nick J., II (D-W.Va.), 43, 387
  committees, 853, 855
  Natural Resources Committee, 646
  Transportation and Infrastructure Committee, 664
Railroads
  American Association of, 564
  Amtrak, 133, 325, 341, 710
  high speed, 133, 156
  mergers, 564
  Rail and Aviation Union Elections, 539
  retirement benefits, 83
Railway Labor Act (2010), 539
Rangel, Charles B. (D-N.Y.), 21, 646
  censured for misconduct, 22, 642
  ethics probe, 655, 657–659, 657 (box)
  foreign trade agreements, 193
  unemployment compensation, 523
Rangel, Charles B. (D-N.Y.), 324
Rapanos v. United States, 380
Rape, abortion funding for, 131, 432 (box)
Reagan, Ronald, president, 692
  Mexico City policy, 131
  nomination of Kennedy by, 584
  plain writing, 613
  presidential records, 616
RealtyTrac, 64
Reapportionment Act of 1929, 648
Rebuild America Jobs Act, 107–108
Recess appointments, 105–106
Recession. *See* Economic crisis (2007-2008)
Recidivism, Guantánamo Bay detainees, 316
Recognizing Educational Success, Professional Excellence, and Collaborative Teaching (RESPECT) Project, 495 (box)
Reconciliation, budget, 120
Recycling electronic products, 379
Recycling electronic products, 379
Redistricting, 4, 10, 36, 42, 42 (box), 43
RedState.org, 152
Red Tape Reduction and Small Business Job Creation Act (2012), 632
Reducing Over-Classification Act (2010), 613
Reed, Jack (D-R.I.)
  committees, 845
  2010 war supplemental, 286
Reed, Tom (R-N.Y.), 26
Regulation and deregulation, 74, 695
  banking, 15–16, 20, 68–70
  Basel III, 70
  derivatives, 89, 92, 97, 104–105
  end users and, 105
  environmental (*See* Environmental protection)
  financial (*See* Dodd-Frank Wall Street Reform and Consumer Protection Act)
  mortgages, 67–68
  tobacco, 15, 419, 448–450
  utilities, 401
Regulatory oversight, 631–632
Rehabilitation Act of 1973, 529
Rehberg, Denny (R-Mont.), 41, 849
  Affordable Care Act, 459
  fiscal 2012 appropriations, 575
  nutrition bill, 469
Reich, Robert B., 698
Reid, Harry (D-Nev.), 8, 9, 40, 77, 338, 366, 480
  Affordable Care Act, 15, 425, 427, 432–433 (box), 433–434, 436, 456, 459 (box)
  appellate judgeships, 576, 577
  budget negotiations (2009), 121
  budget negotiations (2011), 151
  budget negotiations (2012), 172
  budget negotiations (2013), 180
  cloture motions by, 6
  committees, 843, 844
  community service programs, 605
  compromise with Mitch McConnell, 27
  congressional pay, 683
  2012 continuing resolutions, 170
  cybersecurity, 207, 218, 298 (box)
  D.C. representation, 650
  debt ceiling increase, 141
  debt limit legislation, 137
  2011 debt limit negotiations, 160–167
  Democracy Is Strengthened by Casting Light on Spending in Elections (DISCLOSE) Act, 678, 679, 681, 682
  disability rights, 259
  Dodd-Frank Act, 90, 92
  Energy-Water bill, 378
  executive bonuses, 532
  executive branch nominations and, 105, 106
  Export-Import Bank reauthorization, 200
  financial reform and, 20
  fiscal cliff, 188
  Hastert rule and, 31
  immigration status on census, 614
  ineligibility clause, 684
  jobs creation bill, 2010, 86–87, 527
  Joseph Lieberman and, 644
  Keystone Pipeline, 390
  law and law enforcement, 548
  majority leader, 5 (table), 13, 22, 642, 661, 843
  Medicaid and education spending bill, 2010, 140, 454
  Medicare payments to physicians, 450–451, 464
  National Commission on Fiscal Responsibility and Reform, 143
  national flood insurance, 625
  New START treaty, 290
  opposition to Roland W. Burris, 18
  Patriot Act, 215
  payroll tax cut, 109
  public safety workers, 534
  reelection in 2010, 23, 24
  remarks about Obama, 646 (box)
  Rod Blagovich, 647–648

Senate rules, 662, 663
STOCK Act, 667
student aid, 485–486
tax cuts, 148
tax increases, 113
tobacco regulation, 449
unemployment compensation, 522, 523, 526, 536
unions, 540
wage parity, 529
Reid, Jack (D-R.I.), 844
REINS (Executive in Need of Scrutiny) Act (2013), 631
Reliance Industries, Ltd., 241, 243
Religion. *See* Churches and religious groups
Rell, Jodi M., 25
Renewable energy
PACE loans, 501 (box)
programs, 125, 183
Republican Conference, 642, 645, 662, 843
Republican National Committee (RNC), 614, 646 (box)
Republican National Convention, 644
Republican Party
Affordable Care Act and, 19–20
control of redistricting, 42 (box)
defeat in 2012, 40, 702–704
election of 2010, 22–23
governors, 25
Hastert rule and, 29 (box), 31
independent voters and, 23
key votes (*See* Congressional votes)
leadership (*See* Congress, U.S.)
modern partisanship and, 4
Pledge to America, 134
state elections
2010, 25
2012, 44
switches, 18
Tea Party movement and, 6–7, 21, 23, 24
Republican Policy Committee, 642, 645, 662, 663, 843
Republican Steering Committee, 665, 843
Resolution Copper, 395–396
RESPECT (Recognizing Educational Success, Professional Excellence, and Collaborative Teaching) Project, 495 (box)
Restaurant menu labeling, 443
Restore Online Shoppers' Confidence Act (2010), 563
Restore Our Future, 36
Revenue. *See* Taxes
Reyes, Silvestre (D-Texas), 664
committees, 854
drug traffickers, 581
intelligence authorization (2010), 246
Jane Harman ethics probe, 653
Select Intelligence Committee, 646
Rhee, Michelle, 477 (box)
Rice, Susan E., 224, 226–227 (box), 249
Rich, Marc, 707
Richardson, Bill, 708
Richardson, Laura (D-Calif.), 394, 852
ethics probe, 656, 674
Rigell, Scott (R-Va.), 305
Rivlin, Alice, 143
R.J. Reynolds Tobacco Co., 448, 449
RNC (Republican National Committee), 614
Roberts, John G., Jr., 689
Affordable Care Act, 419, 455 (box), 456
appointment of, 586, 587, 588, 589, 590, 591, 592
Supreme Court, 584
Roberts, Pat (R-Kan.), 844
Agriculture, Nutrition, and Forestry Committee, 662
Robert T. Stafford Disaster Relief and Emergency Assistance Act (1988), 626
Robo-signing, 54
Rockefeller, John D., IV (D-W.Va.), 845, 846
Affordable Care Act, 429
Children's Health Insurance Program, 446
Commerce, Science, and Transportation Committee, 643, 662
expansion of broadband, 335, 354, 357, 358
FAA extension legislation, 351–352
FAA reauthorization bill, 330
Guantánamo Bay, Cuba, 315
John Bryson nomination, 709
net neutrality, 333
Postal Service, 628
satellite TV rebroadcasting rules, 336
Roe, David P. (R-Tenn.), 850
Roe v. Wade, 433 (box)
Rogers, Harold (R-Ky.)
Appropriations Committee, 664
border security, 206–207, 211
budget negotiations (2009), 122
budget negotiations (2011), 151
committees, 849
Patent law, 571
war supplemental (2009), 271
Rogers, Mike (R-Mich.)
committees, 852, 854
cybersecurity, 217
Foreign Intelligence Surveillance Act, 216
Guantánamo detainees, 561
Select Intelligence Committee, 664
Rohrabacher, Dana (R-Calif.), 664, 851
Roll, John M., 643 (box)
Romer, Christina D., 49
Romney, Mitt, 9, 11, 11 (table), 33, 34, 35, 177, 691, 692, 926
auto industry bailout, 694
Benjamin Netanyahu and, 225
campaign spending, 36
on Dodd-Frank, 68
election loss, 39, 702
electoral votes, 927
fall campaign, 38–39
primary opponents, 37
slow start in the 2012 campaign, 37–38, 702
student aid, 485
Rooney, Tom (R-Fla.)
committees, 849
COPS, 562
defense appropriations (2011), 296
defense authorization (2013), 309
Roosevelt, Franklin D., president, 22, 216, 702, 915
memorabilia of, 615, 616
Roosevelt, Theodore, president, 421

Roskam, Peter (R-Ill.), 843
Ros-Lehtinen, Ileana (R-Fla.)
  committees, 647, 851
  Foreign Affairs Committee, 664
  Holocaust survivors, 580
  Iran sanctions, 256
  Pakistan aid, 237
  Peace Corps volunteer protection, 624
  State Department reauthorization, 242
Ross, Dennis A. (R-Fla.), 853
  Federal worker pension contributions, 542
  Federal workforce pensions, 621
Ross, Mike (D-Ark.), 428, 458
Roubideauz, Yvette, 617
Rove, Karl, 36
Roving wiretaps, 214, 215
Royal Bank of Scotland, 72
Royce, Edward R. (R-Calif.), 664, 851
  mortgage lender regulation, 503
RtxTec, 461
Rubin, Robert E., 600
Rubio, Marco (R-Fla.), 38
Rules and Administration Committee, Senate, 644, 848
  ranking members and chairs, 643, 662
Rules Committee, House, 647, 853–854
  ranking members and chairs, 646, 664
Rumsfeld, Donald H., 274 (box), 710
Runyan, Jon (R-N.J.), 855
Ruppersberger, C. A. Dutch (D-Md.)
  committees, 854
  cybersecurity, 217
  Foreign Intelligence Surveillance Act, 216
  intelligence authorization (2013), 254
  Select Intelligence Committee, 664
Rural schools, 491
Rural Utilities Service (RUS), 325
Rush, Bobby L. (D-Ill.), 390, 850
Russia
  cybersecurity, 217
  New Strategic Arms Reduction Treaty (START), 7, 22, 138, 152, 232, 267, 289–291, 300, 303–304, 309
  trade relations with, 191, 201
Ryan, Leo J. (D-Calif.), 643 (box)
Ryan, Paul (R-Wis.), 9, 341
  Budget Committee, 646, 664
  budget negotiations (2011), 32
  budget negotiations (2012), 156, 159, 161
  budget resolution (2013), 177
  committees, 850
  fiscal cliff, 187
  Medicare cuts, 420
  National Commission on Fiscal Responsibility and Reform, 143
  omnibus appropriations (2011), 150
  patent law, 571
  pay-as-you go rules, 127
  presidential campaign (2012), 38, 703, 921 (table)
  student aid, 486–487
Ryan White HIV/AIDS Act, 419, 420 (figure), 452–453
Saban, Haim, 653
Sabato, Larry J., 23
Safe, Accountable, Flexible, and Efficient Transportation Equity Act, 324, 326
Safer Oil and Natural Gas Drilling Technology Research and Development Program, 377
Safety
  college campus fire, 482
  food, 411–412
  mine, 101
  pipeline, 401
  public safety workers, 534
SAFRA (Student Aid and Fiscal Responsibility Act), 476, 477
Salazar, Ken (D-Colo.), 17, 24, 367, 705 (box)
  David Vitter ethics probe, 672
  ineligibility clause, 684
  Secretary of the Interior, 710
Saleh, Ali Abdullah, 223
Same-sex marriage, 44, 300, 301, 305, 308, 581
  Defense of Marriage Act, 182, 289, 313
    House Office of General Counsel, 669–670
Samuelson, Robert J., 54
Sanchez, Linda T. (D-Calif.), 851, 854
  Ethics Committee, 664, 674
  minimum wage, 541
Sanchez, Loretta (D-Calif.), 664, 850
  cyberstalking, 567
  missile defense, 308
Sanders, Bernard (I-Vt.), 18, 846
  Affordable Care Act, 434
  budget negotiations (2011), 151
  committees, 846, 847
  Dodd-Frank Act, 91
  drug marketing rights, 461
  milk subsidies, 128
San Joaquin Valley, water access in, 397
Santorum, Rick (R-Pa.), 37
  presidential campaign, 702
Santos, Juan Manuel, 195, 197
Sarbanes, John (D-Md.), 601
Satellite Home Viewer Extension and Reauthorization Act of 2004, 335
Satellite Television Extension and Localism Act (STELA), 335
  background, 335
  final action, 337
  House and senate floor action, 335–336
  House committee action, 335
Saudi Arabia, 224, 701
Sayyad, Sam, 711
SBA. *See* Small Business Administration (SBA)
Scalia, Antonin, 586, 589, 591, 592, 593
Schakowsky, Janice D. (D-Ill.), 854
  National Commission on Fiscal Responsibility and Reform, 143
Schiff, Adam B. (D-Cal.)
  COPS, 562
  impeachment of Federal judges, 558
Schlafly, Phyllis, 616
Schmidt, Jean (R-Ohio), 849
Scholarships. *See* Student aid

Scholarships for Opportunity and Results (SOAR) Act of 2011, 490
School lunch/breakfast programs, 420, 465–467
Schools
  antibulllying and gang prevention, 491–492
  charter, 477 (box), 480, 484, 490, 491, 709, 882
  for-profit career colleges, 488 (box)
  green, 380–381
  improvement strategies, 485
  physical education report, 490 (box)
  rural, 491
  State Fiscal Stabilization Fund, 82
  student punishment, 481
  Title 1 grants, 484
  Title I grants, 155, 175
  voucher program, Washington D.C., 121, 481, 490–491
  See also Education
Schrader, Kurt (D-Ore.), 854
  regulatory oversight, 631
  small business Federal contracting, 631
Schumer, Charles (D-N.Y.), 5 (table)
  Affordable Care Act, 429
  appellate judgeships, 577
  border security funding, 212
  committees, 847, 848
  Democracy Is Strengthened by Casting Light on Spending in Elections (DISCLOSE) Act, 678, 679
  Democratic Caucus Vice Chair, 642, 661
  elderly and disabled refugees, 583
  immigration, 556
  Joint Committee appointments, 856
  journalism sources, 559
  Rules and Administration Committee, 643, 662
  student visas, 489
  on tax cuts, 3 (figure)
  TV coverage of court proceedings, 566
  witness protection programs, 565
Schwartz, Allyson Y. (D-Pa.), 464
Schwarzenegger, Arnold, 25
Schweitzer, Brian, 44
Science, Technology, Engineering, and Math (STEM) Master Teacher Corps, 495 (box)
Science and technology
  budget bills, 127, 130–131, 152–153, 171–172, 182
  cybersecurity, 207, 214, 217–218
  human embryos destruction, 131
  immigrant visas, 489
  recycling electronic products, 379
  space exploration, 152
  See also Office of Science and Technology Policy
Science and Technology/Science, Space and Technology Committee, House, 606, 647, 854
  cybersecurity bill, 218
  global warming, 373
  ranking members and chairs, 646, 664
  solar energy technology, 380
Science and Technology Subcommittee on Energy and Environment, 378
Scott, David (D-Ga.), 849
Scott, Robert C. (D-Va.), 852
  child pornography, 582
  cocaine penalties, 562
  hate crimes, 554
  prison deaths, 578
Scott, Tim (R-S.C.)
  labor union regulations, 537–538
  unions, 539
Search warrants, 209
Sears, Leah Ward, 711
Sebelius, Kathleen, 705 (box), 707–708
  Affordable Care Act, 422 (box), 433, 459 (box)
  nomination by Obama, 707–708
  tax problems, 708
SEC. *See* Securities and Exchange Commission (SEC)
Secret holds, 640
Section 8 housing, 121, 156, 506
Section 529 plans, 481, 487(box)
Secure Federal File Sharing Act (2009), 603
Secure Rural Schools law, 485
Securing Annuities for Federal Employees Act of 2012, 621
Securing the Cities initiative, 210
Securities and Exchange Commission (SEC)
  appropriations
    FY 2010, 131
    FY 2011, 154
    FY 2012, 174
    FY 2013, 183
  credit rating agencies and, 99–100
  derivatives regulation, 97–98
  Dodd-Frank Act and, 68, 69, 90, 91, 104–105
  Financial Stability Oversight Council and, 92
  hedge fund registration, 98
  investor protections, 101
  MF Global and, 71
  STOCK Act, 665–668
Securities Industry and Financial Markets Association, 161
Securitization, 101
Segregation, apology for, 567
Selfridge Air National Guard Base, 311
Senate, U.S.
  committees (*See* specific committees)
  conference committees, 639
  confirmations legislation, 668–669
  elections
    2010, 24–25, 932–940
    2012, 40–42, 942–949
  filibusters (*See* Filibusters and cloture votes)
  leadership, 843
    111th Congress, 642–645
    112th Congress, 661–663
  members (*See* Congress, members of)
  online disclosure of expenditures, 650–651
  operating budget, 155
  organization, 111th Congress, 642–645
  pay and benefits (*See* Congressional pay and benefits)
  political committees, 843
  rules, 662–663
    suspension, 640
  vacancies, 2009, 17–18
  voting (*See* Congressional votes)
  See also Congress, U.S.

Sensenbrenner, F. James, Jr. (R-Wis.), 647
  committees, 853, 855
  D.C. representation, 649
  Patent law, 571
  Patriot Act, 215
  property rights, 579
September 11, 2001 terrorist attacks, 39, 65, 232
  Foreign Intelligence Surveillance Act and, 216
  Patriot Act and, 205, 208
Sequestration, 29, 113, 116–117, 120, 160, 177, 186, 189, 263
  congressional pay and, 685
  OMB report, 685
Serrano, Jose E. (D-N.Y.), 849
  Puerto Rico political status, 620
Service Employees International Union, 143
Sessions, Jeff (R-Ala.), 371
  Afghanistan war bill, 231
  appellate judgeships, 576
  Budget Committee, 662
  committees, 845, 847
  debt limit legislation, 137 (box)
  defense appropriations (2010), 282
  E-Verify system, 210
  hunting and fishing regulations, 400–401
  journalism sources, 559
  Judiciary Committee, 645
  nondefense discretionary spending, 126
  Patent law, 571
  Postal Service, 629
  undocumented children, 557
Sessions, Pete (R-Texas), 843, 854
  National Republican Congressional Committee, 645, 663
Sestak, Joe, 18
Setting New Priorities in Education Spending Act, 483–484
Sex education, 132, 175
  Affordable Care Act, 443
Sex tourism, 566–567
Sexual harassment, 673–674
Sexual orientation discrimination, 242, 264–265, 267, 288–289, 291, 299–300
Shaheen, Jean (D-N.H.), 845, 846
  abortion services for military members, 310–311
Shalala, Donna E., 600
Shareholders
  oversight of executive pay, 532–533
  Shareholder Protection Act, 679–680
Shea-Porter, Carol (D-N.H.), 600
Shelby, Richard C. (D/R-Ala.), 5
  Banking, Housing, and Urban Affairs Committee, 644, 662
  committees, 844
  credit card restrictions, 84
  Dodd-Frank Act, 90, 91
  Hurricane Sandy, 625
  Iran sanctions, 239
  minimum wage, 541
  STOCK Act, 666
Shepard, Matthew, 553
Sherman, Brad (D-Calif.), 36, 43, 851
  Iran sanctions, 238
Sherrod, Shirley, 410
Shimkus, John (R-Ill.), 395, 851
Shinseki, Eric K., 705 (box), 710
Ships and shipping
  budget bills, 278
  Coast Guard (*See* Coast Guard, U.S.)
  Iran sanctions, 256–257
  Navy (*See* Navy, U.S.)
Shuler, Heath (D-N.C.), 21, 663, 854
Shultz, George P., 290
Shuster, Bill (R-Pa.), 855
Sign-on letters, 645 (box)
Silver Plan, Affordable Care Act, 437
Simpson, Alan K. (R-Wyo.), 143, 697
Simpson, Michael K. (R-Idaho), 383, 849
60 Minutes, 665, 667
Skelton, Ike (D-Mo.), 24, 664, 850
  Armed Services Committee, 645–646
  defense acquisition rules, 268
  detainee release, 292
  missile defense, 274
Skilling, Jeffrey, 592, 666
Skilling v. United States, 666
Slaughter, Louise M. (D-N.Y.), 853, 854
  regulatory oversight, 631
  Rules Committee, 646, 664
  STOCK Act, 667
  unemployment compensation, 523
Slavery, apology for, 567
Small business
  Affordable Care Act, 422, 423 (box)
    simple cafeteria plans, 445
    tax credits, 438
  crowd-funding, 110
  federal contracting, 630–631
  regulation easing, 110
  Small Business Jobs Act of 2010, 102–103
  TARP Public-Private Investment Program, 64
  tax preferences, 485–486
  tax reporting requirement, 169
  See also Business and industry; Small Business Administration (SBA)
Small Business Administration (SBA)
  appropriations, 131
  Securities Purchase Program, 64–65
  See also Small business
Small Business and Entrepreneurship Committee, Senate, 644, 848
  ranking members and chairs, 643, 662
Small Business Committee, House, 647, 854
  ranking members and chairs, 646, 664
Small Business Job Protection Act, 487(box)
Small Business Jobs Act of 2010, 102
Small Business Lending Fund, 102
Small Business Opportunity Act of 2014, 631
Small Business Reauthorization Act of 1997, 630
Smith, Adam (D-Wash.), 850
  Armed Services Committee, 664
  detainee releases, 299
  F-35 fighters, 308
  military tribunals, 309

Smith, Christopher H. (R-N.J.)
  committees, 851
  sex tourism, 567
  State Department reauthorization, 242
Smith, Gordon H. (R-Ore.), 645
Smith, Lamar (R-Texas)
  attorneys fees, 579–580
  child pornography, 582
  cocaine penalties, 562
  committees, 647, 852
  D.C. representation, 649
  drug traffickers, 581
  Foreign Intelligence Surveillance Act, 216
  impeachment of Federal judges, 558
  journalism sources, 559
  Judiciary Committee, 664
  legal immigrants, 582
  low-immigration regions, 582
  Patent law, 569, 571
  student visas, 489
  trade secrets, 580
Smithsonian Institution, 129
Smolinski, Billy, 564
Smuggling of illegal immigrants, 561
SNAP. *See* Supplemental Nutrition Assistance Program (SNAP)
"Sneak and peek" search warrants, 209
Snowden, Edward, 194 (box)
Snowe, Olympia (R-Maine), 11, 12, 35, 41, 81
  Affordable Care Act, 429
  algal blooms, 379
  Children's Health Insurance Program, 446
  committees, 848
  Democracy Is Strengthened by Casting Light on Spending in Elections (DISCLOSE) Act, 679
  Dodd-Frank Act, 90, 91, 92
  "don't ask, don't tell," 289
  Medicaid and education spending bill, 2010, 454
  Small Business and Entrepreneurship Committee, 644
  unemployment compensation, 522, 524
Snyder, Vic (D-Ark.), 850
SOAR (Scholarships for Opportunity and Results) Act of 2011, 490
Social media, 110, 671 (box)
Social Security, 9
  cost-of-living benefit increases, 188
  cost of living changes proposed for, 542–543
  creation of, 436
  lawsuits, 565
  National Commission on Fiscal Responsibility and Reform recommendations, 144
  outlays for, 516
  retiree assistance, 2010, 83
  retirement age, 143, 157
  tax reduction, 110
  See also Payroll taxes
Solar energy technology, 380
Solar Technology Roadmap Committee, 380
Solid Waste Agency of Northern Cook County v. U.S. Army Corps of Engineers, 380
Solis, Hilda (D-Calif.), 17, 704, 705 (box), 710–711
  minimum wage, 518, 541
Solyndra, 170
Sotomayor, Sonia, 10, 16–17, 21, 711–712
  confirmation of, 552, 553
  liberal positions, 584, 585, 586, 590–591
Souder, Mark (R-Ind.), 26
  Affordable Care Act, 428
  sexual misadventures and resignation, 671 (box)
Souter, David H., 10, 16, 584, 585, 586, 711
South America. *See specific countries*
Southern Media & Opinion Research, 24
South Korea, 74
  foreign policy toward, 228
  intellectual property, 197
  trade agreements, 193, 195–197
Space, Zack (D-Ohio), 370
Space exploration, Constellation space program, 605, 606, 607, 626–627
Spain, 51, 55
Special Aging Committee, Senate, 645, 848
  ranking members and chairs, 643, 662
Special elections, 6, 30, 43–44, 931, 941
Special interest groups. *See* Lobbyists and lobbying
Special Supplemental Nutrition Program for Women, Infants, and Children. *See* Women, Infants, and Children (WIC) program
Specter, Arlen (D-Pa.), 14, 17, 81
  committees, 847
  Dodd-Frank Act, 90
  journalism sources, 559
  Judiciary Committee, 644–645
  Patent law, 561
  Patriot Act, 209
  railroad mergers, 564
  switch from Republican to Democrat, 18
  unions, 533
Spending ceiling. *See* Budget, U.S.
Sperling, Gene B., 49
Spratt, John M., Jr. (D-S.C.), 24
  Budget Committee, 646, 664
  2011 budget negotiations, 137
  committees, 850
  National Commission on Fiscal Responsibility and Reform, 143
Stabenow, Debbie (D-Mich.), 322, 843, 844, 845
  Agriculture, Nutrition, and Forestry Committee, 662
  child nutrition bill, 466
  Medicare payments to physicians, 450–451
  unemployment compensation, 523
Stafford loan program, 485–486
Standard & Poor's credit rating, 698
Standards of Official Conduct Committee, House, 22, 647, 655–656, 854
  ethics probes (*See* Congressional ethics probes)
  ranking members and chairs, 646
  See also Ethics Committee, House
Stark, Fortney Pete (D-Calif.), 855
  ethics probe, 654
START treaty. *See* New Strategic Arms Reduction Treaty (START)
State and Local Funding Flexibility Act, 483

State and local government
  Affordable Care Act state-run exchanges, 436–437
  economic policies, 55
  governors during Obama's first term, 956–957
  gubernatorial elections, 18, 25, 30, 44, 942–949
State Criminal Alien Assistance Program, 575
State Department
  appropriations
    FY 2009, 130, 232–233
    FY 2010, 127, 132, 243–245
    FY 2011, 155, 248, 249–250
    FY 2012, 176, 252–254
    FY 2013, 184–185, 258
  reauthorization bill, 2010, 241–243
State Fiscal Stabilization Fund, 82
State Innovation Pilot Act of 2011, 475
State of the Union address
  2010, 893–899
  2011, 899–905
  2012, 906–912
State-run exchanges, Affordable Care Act, 436–437
Stearns, Cliff (R-Fla.), 664, 851
  concealed handguns, 576
Steele, Michael, 646 (box)
Steinberg, James, 226 (box)
STEM Education Coordination Act, 609–610
STEM Jobs Act of 2012, 489
STEM (Science, Technology, Engineering, and Math) Master Teacher Corps, 495 (box)
Stern, Andy, 143
Stevens, Christopher J., 39, 224, 690
Stevens, John Paul, 10, 20, 584, 586, 712
Stevens, Ted (R-Alaska), 644
Stiglitz, Joseph, 65
Stimulus packages. *See* Economic stimulus packages
Stivers, Steve (R-Ohio), 512
STOCK (Stop Trading on Congressional Knowledge) Act
  background, 665–666
  final action, 667
  House action, 667
  major provisions, 667–668
  Senate action, 666–667
Stock market. *See* Stocks, bonds, and securities
Stocks, bonds, and securities
  deleveraging, 52–53
  economic crisis of 2007-2008 and recovery of, 53, 55
  Federal Reserve crisis-related programs for, 56–57
  initial public offerings (IPOs), 665–668
  insider trading, 667–668
  investor protection, 101
  securitization, 101
  STOCK Act, 665–668
  tax-exempt bonds, 83, 87
  toxic assets, 60
  Troubled Asset Relief Program (TARP) and, 6, 14, 47, 48, 60–61, 62–63
Stop the OverPrinting (STOP) Act, 670
Stop the Student Loan Interest Rate Hike Act of 2012, 485–486
Stop Trading on Congressional Knowledge Act. *See* STOCK (Stop Trading on Congressional Knowledge) Act
Strategic Arms Reduction Treaty (START), 7, 22, 138, 152, 232, 267, 289–291, 300, 303–304, 309
Stress tests, bank, 69–70, 694–695
Strickland, Ted, 25
Studds, Gerry E. (D-Mass.), 658
Student aid
  ACORN defunding, 680
  action, 2009, 61, 83
  American Recovery and Reinvestment Act of 2009 and, 61
  college savings accounts, 481, 487(box)
  Deposit Restricted Qualified Tuition Program Act of 2010, 413
  direct student loans, 476, 478, 479
  funding for, 479
  interest rates, 32–33, 485–486
  Pell grants, 82, 135, 136, 155, 167, 175
  reconciliation bills, 125, 476, 477–478
  reserve funds, 125
  rules for, 488–489, 488 (box)
  Stop the Student Loan Interest Rate Hike Act of 2012, 485–486
  tuition credit, 189
  See also Higher education
Student Aid and Fiscal Responsibility Act (SAFRA), 476, 477
StudentFirst, 477 (box)
Student Success Act, 484
Student Visa Reform Act of 2012, 489
Stupak, Bart (D-Mich.), 850
  Affordable Care Act, 431, 432 (box), 433 (box), 435
Stutzman, Marlin (R-Ind.), 26, 855
Stuxnet, 255
Styrofoam, 670
Subcontracting Transparency and Reliability Act (2012), 630
Submarines, 283, 303, 312
Subsidies
  farm, 469
  health care, 422, 423 (box), 425, 432
Sudan, 241
Suicide and bullying, 492
Summers, Lawrence, 49, 75, 709
SunTrust, 54, 69
Supplemental Appropriations Act of 2008, 519, 520
Supplemental Nutrition Assistance Program (SNAP), 33, 61, 82, 171, 407, 413, 466, 468
  child nutrition bill, 466–467
Supreme Court
  about, 584–586
  business law, 593–594
  confirmations by, 585
  criminal law and procedure, 591–593
  election law, 586–587
  environmental law, 594
  first amendment, 589–590
  health care legislation, 586–587
  individual rights, 590–591
Supreme Court, U.S.
  Affordable Care Act individual mandate, 419, 423 (box), 455 (box)
  Anthony M. Kennedy, 669
  John Roberts, 419
  Obama appointments
    Elena Kagan, 10, 16, 20–21, 712
    Sonia Sotomayor, 10, 16, 21, 711–712

retirements
David Souter, 10, 16, 711
John Paul Stevens, 10, 20, 712
Ruth Bader Ginsburg, 10, 21
Samuel A. Alito, Jr., 669
See also Supreme Court cases; *specific justices by name*
Supreme Court cases
American Insurance Association v. Garamendi (2003), 580
American Tradition Partnership v. Bullock (2012), 588
Apprendi v. New Jersey (2000), 591
Arizona Christian School Tuition Organization v. Winn (2011), 589–590
Arizona Free Enterprise Club's Freedom Club PAC v. Bennett (2012), 588
Arizona v. United States (2012), 590
Atlantic Corp. v. Twombly (2007), 591
AT&T Mobility v. Concepcion (2011), 593
Austin v. Michigan State Chamber of Commerce (1990), 588, 677 (box)
Bartlett v. Strickland (2009), 589
Bilski v. Kappos (2010), 594
Brown v. Entertainment Merchants Association (2011), 589
Carcieri v. Salazar (2009), 618
Chamber of Commerce of the United States v. NLRB (2012), 539
Chamber of Commerce v. Whiting (2011), 594
Christian Legal Society v. Martinez (2010), 590
Citizens United v. Federal Election Commission (2010), 36, 551, 586–589, 677, 678, 682
Cobell v. Salazar (2010), 555
Crawford v. Metropolitan Government of Nashville and Davidson County (2009), 594
Davis v. Federal Election Commission (2008), 587
District Attorney's Office v. Osborne (2009), 592
District of Columbia v. Heller (2008), 590, 649
Doe v. Reed (2010), 588
Electric Power Co. v. Connecticut (2011), 594
Entergy Corp v. Riverkeeper (2009), 594
Federal Aviation Administration v. Cooper (2012), 591
Federal Communications Commission v. Fox Television Stations (2012), 589
Federal Election Commission v. Wisconsin Right to Life (2003), 587
Florence v. Board of Chosen Freeholders of Burlington County (2012), 591
Graham v. Florida (2010), 591
Hamdan v. Rumsfeld (2006), 316
Harrington v. Richter (2011), 592
Herring v. United States (2009), 592
Holder v. Humanitarian Law Project (2010), 589
Hosanna-Tabor Evangelical Lutheran Church and School v. Equal Employment Opportunity Commission (2012), 590
Janus Capital Group v. First Derivative Traders (2011), 593
Kelo v. City of New London (2005), 579
Lafler v. Cooper (2012), 592
Leal Garcia v. Texas (2011), 593
Ledbetter v. Goodyear Tire and Rubber Company (2007), 528
Leegin Creative Leather Products Inc. v. PSKS Inc. (2007), 564
McConnell v. Federal Election Commission (2003), 587–588
McDonald v. City of Chicago (2010), 590
Melendez-Diaz v. Massachusetts (2009), 592
Miller v. Alabama (2012), 591
Missouri v. Frye (2012), 592
Montejo v. Louisiana (2009), 593
National Association of Manufacturers v. NLRB (2012), 539
National Federation of Independent Business v. Sebelius (2012), 586
Northwest Austin Municipal Utility District No. 1 v. Holder (2009), 586–587, 588
Perdue v. Kenny A. (2010), 591
Perry v. New Hampshire (2012), 592
Pigford v. Glickman (2010), 555
PLIVA v. Mensing (2011), 594
Premo v. Moore (2011), 592
Ricci v. DeStefano (2009), 590
Roe v. Wade (1973), 433 (box)
Sackett v. EPA (2012), 594
Safford Unified School District #1 v. Redding (2009), 591
Salazar v. Buono (2010), 589
Shelby County v. Holder (2013), 588–589
Skilling v. United States (2010), 592, 593, 666
Skinner v. Switzer (2011), 592
Snyder v. Phelps (2009), 589
Southern Union Co. v. United States (2012), 591
United States v. Alvarez (2012), 589
United States v. Jones (2012), 592
United States v. Stevens (2010), 562, 589
United States v. Windsor (2013), 669
Wal-Mart Stores v. Dukes (2011), 593
Surface Transportation Authorization, 324–327, 340–344
Highway Funding Formula, 327
Senate Committee Action, 326
Short-Term Extensions, 326–327
Surface Transportation Board, 564
Surveillance powers
Foreign Intelligence Surveillance Act (FISA), 205, 206, 209
extension, 215–217
overhaul, 251
Global Hawk surveillance drones, 182, 310, 312
USA Patriot Act, 133, 205–206, 208–209
business records provision, 214, 215
four-year extension, 215
lone wolf provision, 214, 215
roving wiretaps, 214, 215
short-term extension, 209, 215
Sutton, Rep. Betty, 321–322
Suu Kyi, Aung San, 228
Switzerland, 72
Synthetic drug scheduling, 463
Syria, 223–225, 692, 701
sanctions, 257
See also Middle East

TAA. *See* Trade Adjustment Assistance Act (TAA)
Taj, Syed, 44
Take Back Washington, 309
Taliban, 10, 225, 229, 700
Talk-radio, 4
TANF. *See* Temporary Assistance to Needy Families (TANF)
Tanner, John S. (D-Tenn.), 855
Tanning tax, 444
Tanzania, 314

Targeted Investment Program, 63
TARP. *See* Troubled Assets Relief Program (TARP)
Tarullo, Daniel K., 70
Tauscher, Ellen O., 17
Taxation, Joint Committee on (JCT), 82, 103, 147, 856
  Affordable Care Act, 426
Taxes, 120
  Affordable Care Act, 20, 424 (box), 426, 456 (box)
    additional Medicare hospital insurance, 443
    credits for small business, 438
    excise tax on high-cost health plans, 443
    individual mandate, 419, 423 (box), 426
    medical devices, 424 (box), 432, 443
    subsidies, 422, 423 (box), 425
  alternative minimum tax, 80–81, 82, 83, 124, 127, 146, 187
    exemptions, 136
  American Recovery and Reinvestment Act of 2009 and, 61
  American Taxpayer Relief Act of 2012, 67, 520, 622, 684
  business (*See* Business taxes)
  capital gains, 146, 189
  contractor tax withholding repeal, 169
  credits
    adoption, 444
    Affordable Care Act, 437, 438
    child, 80, 83, 124, 136, 146
    Earned-Income, 80, 83
    homebuyer, 79 (box), 83, 503–505
    Making Work Pay, 80, 81–82, 82–83, 124, 125
    medical expenses, 444
    therapeutic discovery projects, 445
  cuts, 7, 9, 16, 22, 66, 79 (box)
    2009-2010, 82–83
    extension of Bush, 7, 9, 66–67, 112, 124, 135–136, 144–146, 698
  delinquents, 624
  dividends and capital gains, 146
  "economic substance," 444
  estate, 146–147
  exempt bonds, 83, 87
  federal land and, 485
  fiscal cliff and, 188
  foreign tax provisions, 480
  health insurance W-2 reporting, 445
  higher education savings accounts, 481, 487(box)
  homebuyer tax credit, 503–505
  information reporting, 444
  mortgage interest deductions, 498
  motor fuel, 133
  pay-as-you-go rules, 126
  payroll, 8–9, 30, 32, 74, 79 (box), 108–110, 146, 172
    forgiveness, 87
    Medicare hospital, 422, 424 (box), 426, 443
  as percentage of GDP, 1935-2013, 149 (table)
  problems
    Charles Rangel, 657–659
    Kathleen Sebelius, 708
    Timothy Geithner, 706
    Tom Daschle, 707
  reporting requirement, 169
  small businesses, 485–486
  tanning, 444
  tobacco, 445, 447–448
Tax extenders bill, 521
Taxpayers for Common Sense, 121
Tax Relief, Unemployment Insurance Reauthorization, and Job Creation Act of 2010, 66, 520, 524
Taylor, Gene (D-Miss.), 850
  national flood insurance, 611
Teacher Incentive Fund, 495 (box)
Teachers
  American Federation of Teachers, 492
  appropriations, FY 2011, 140–141
  Encouraging Innovation and Effective Teachers Act of 2012, 484
  initiatives focused on, 484
  layoffs, 139
  Medicaid and education spending bill, 2010, 454
  performance-based pay programs, 709
  RESPECT Project, 495 (box)
  STEM Master Teacher Corps, 495 (box)
Tea Party movement, 6–7, 8, 21, 23, 24, 151, 517, 636, 697
  Affordable Care Act, 433 (box)
  debt limit negotiations (2012), 160, 163, 164
  House transition and, 661 (box)
  Senate rules, 662
  Troubled Asset Relief Program (TARP) and, 61
Teenagers. *See* Adolescents and youth
Telecommunications
  broadband access, 334–335, 334–335l, 356
  Broadband Technology Opportunities Program, 333
  caller ID spoofing, 563
  Federal Communications Commission (FCC), 144, 563
  foreign trade pacts, 197, 198
  Internet piracy, 357–359
  laws, 320
  leadership, 323
  Lifeline program, 335
  National Broadband Plan, 334–335
  net neutrality, 355–356
  net neutrality, 331–334
  Open Internet Advisory Committee, 334
  Open Internet Order, 334
  overhaul, 354–355
  satellite and cable programming, 357–358
  Spectrum Auction, 356–357
Television
  campaign ads on public, 681 (box)
  coverage of court proceedings, 565
  satellite and cable programming, 335–337
Telework Enhancement Act, 601
Temporary Assistance for Needy Families (TANF), 110, 181, 544, 556
Temporary Extension Act of 2010, 520, 522, 526
Temporary Payroll Tax Cut Continuation Act of 2011, 520, 536
Tenth Amendment Center, 309
Term Asset-Backed Securities Loan Facility (TALF), 57, 65
Term Auction Facility, 56
Term Securities Lending Facility, 56
Territories, U.S.
  Affordable Care Act, 439
  minimum wage, 529–530

Terrorism and counterterrorism, 10, 39, 65, 207 (box), 302
Benghazi attack, 224
competitive analysis council, 251
Miranda warnings and, 247
Northwest Airlines attempted bombing, 207 (box), 208
Risk Insurance, 98
Taliban, 10, 225, 229, 700
Times Square attempted bombing, 208
treatment of suspected, 578
waterboarding, 246
wiretapping and, 205–206, 208–209
Tester, Jon (D-Mont.), 41, 411
budget negotiation (2013), 181
hunting and fishing regulations, 400–401
Postal Service, 628
Textiles and apparel, 198
Brazil, 468–469
Pakistan aid and, 237
Therapeutic discovery projects, 445
Thomas, Clarence, 586, 591
Thomas, Sidney R., 712
Thomasina E. Jordan Indian Tribes of Virginia Federal Recognition Act, 617
Thompson, Bennie (D-Miss.), 658, 852
ethics probe, 655
Homeland Security Committee, 646, 664
unions, 540
Thompson, Glenn (R-Pa.), 849
Thompson, John (R-Wisc.), 25
Thompson, Mike (D-Calif.), 854
Osama bin Laden death report, 251
Thompson, Tommy G. (R-Wisc.), 41
Thornberry, Mac (R-Texas), 664, 850
Thrift Savings Plan, 448, 450
Thune, John (R-S.D.), 277, 478
child nutrition bill, 466
community service programs, 605
Republican Conference, 642, 662
Thurmond, Strom (R-S.C.), 646 (box)
Tiahrt, Todd (R-Kan.), 270, 383
ethics probe, 655–656
Tiberi, Patrick J. (R-Ohio), 855
Tierney, John F. (D-Mass.), 43, 853
charter schools, 491
TIGER. *See* Transportation Investment Generating Economic Recovery (TIGER)
Tipton, Scott (R-Colo.), 854
Titus, Dina (D-Nev.), 604
Tobacco
advisory committee, 450
flavor additives, 450
penalties, 450
product claims, 450
product information, 450
regulation, 15, 419, 448–450
taxes, 445, 447–448
user fees, 450
warning labels, 449–450
Tombin, Earl Ray, 30
Tonko, Paul (D-N.Y.), 381
critical minerals legislation, 399
Toomey, Patrick J. (R-Pa.), 18, 160
climate change, 599
Congressional deficit committee, 168
Hurricane Sandy, 625
Towns, Edolphus (D-N.Y.), 664, 853
efficiency of government agencies, 612
Federal worker software sharing, 603
Oversight and Government Reform Committee, 646
tobacco regulation, 448
Toxic assets, 60, 64, 76
Toxic Substances Control Act (PL 94-469), 399
Trade. *See* Foreign trade and business
Trade Adjustment Assistance Act (TAA), 74, 83, 194 (box), 196, 199–200
Trade Adjustment Assistance program, 478
Trade secrets, 580
Training, job, 199–200
Trains. *See* Railroads
Trans-Atlantic Trade and Investment Partnership (TIPP), 192
Transition Adjustment Assistance, 49
Trans-Pacific Partnership (TPP) agreement, 192
Transportation, 319–359, 387 (box), 486
action chronology
FY 2009-2010, 321–339
FY 2011-2012, 340–359
air (*See* Air transportation; Federal Aviation Administration (FAA))
American Recovery and Reinvestment Act of 2009 and, 61
budget outlays, 32, 82
Cash for Clunkers program, 64, 79
cost for families, 499 (box)
Surface Transportation Authorization, 324–327, 340–344
See also Commerce
Transportation, Department of (DOT)
appointments, 709–710
appropriations
FY 2010, 131
FY 2012, 172
FY 2013, 185
Federal Highway Trust Fund, 32, 87, 133, 172, 185
high-speed rail, 133, 156
Transportation and Infrastructure Committee, House, 324, 341, 539, 647, 855
National Women's History Museum, 616
ranking members and chairs, 646, 664
Transportation Infrastructure Finance and Innovation Act, 341
Transportation Investment Generating Economic Recovery (TIGER), 156, 172, 185, 340
Transportation Security Administration (TSA)
appropriations
FY 2010, 129, 210, 211
FY 2011, 154
bargaining rights of, 540
no-fly list, 210
Treasury Department, U.S.
appointments, 706

appropriations
FY 2010, 131
FY 2011, 154
bank stress tests, 69–70
Dodd-Frank Act and, 91
Fannie Mae and Freddie Mac bailout, 511 (box)
Federal Reserve large-scale asset purchases and, 57–58
Internet gambling, 338
leadership, 48
Making Home Affordable program, 53
Maxine Waters ethics probe, 675
orderly liquidation of failing institutions, 93
presidential election campaign fund, 682
sanctions by, 256
Small Business Jobs Act of 2010, 102–103
Standard and Poor's rating, 160
tobacco permits, 448
Troubled Asset Relief Program (TARP) administration of, 62–63, 695
Treaties and international agreements
Andean Trade Preference Act, 194 (box), 197, 198
disability rights, 258–259
foreign trade, 74, 195
North American Free Trade Agreement (NAFTA), 195, 229, 230, 300, 700
North Atlantic Treaty Organization (NATO), 224
Strategic Arms Reduction Treaty (START), 7, 22, 138, 152, 232, 289–291, 309
Tribal lands, law enforcement on, 563–564
Tricare program, 303, 312, 428
Troubled Assets Relief Program (TARP), 6, 14, 29–30, 47, 48, 60–61, 74, 75, 154, 321, 485, 509, 530–531, 694, 695, 751
bank bailouts, 62–63
budget appropriations (2010) and, 125
continuing efforts to curb, 78
credit market programs, 64–65
criticism of, 65
Democracy Is Strengthened by Casting Light on Spending in Elections (DISCLOSE) Act, 678
end of, 89, 99
executive compensation and, 65
funds released, 75–78
housing programs, 64
money diverted from, 85–86
OneUnited Bank, 657
public opinion of, 62
restrictions, 2009-2010, 84
Truman, Harry S., president, 693
health care overhaul, 421
Truth in Caller ID Act, 563
TSA. *See* Transportation Security Administration (TSA)
Tubbs Jones, Stephanie (D-Ohio), 646
Tuberculosis, 245, 248
Tuition credit. *See* Student aid
Tulafono, Togiola, 530
Tully, Grace, 615
Tully Archive, 615
Tunisia, 223, 249, 700
See also Middle East
Turley, Jonathan, 558
Turner, Bob (R-N.Y.), 30
Turner, Michael R. (R-Ohio), 850
missile defense, 274
New START treaty, 309
nuclear weapons, 313
Twenty-first Century Communications and Video Accessibility Act of 2010, 479 (box)
21st century Postal Service Act, 628
Twitter, 4, 6, 671 (box)

UC. *See* Unemployment Compensation (UC)
Udall, Mark (D-Colo.), 377
committees, 845, 846
Foreign Intelligence Surveillance Act, 217
Postal Service, 628
Ullyot, John, 289
Ultra-Deepwater and Unconventional Natural Gas and Other Petroleum Resources Program, 376
Underbanked consumers, 99
Undocumented children, 556–557
Unemployment
adult literacy, 492
economic crisis of 2007-2008 and, 52
2010 election and, 23
for-profit colleges and, 488 (box)
rate, 23, 47, 691
1996-2012, 50 (table)
2011, 74
2012, 179
Trade Adjustment Assistance programs, 74, 83
Unemployment compensation (UC), 22
about, 517–518, 535
background, 519
federal benefits extension, 29–30, 61, 66, 79 (box), 83, 146
lapses in, 524
outlays, 2001-2012, 466 (figure)
program, 520
Unemployment Compensation Extension Act of 2008, 520
Unemployment Compensation Extension Act of 2009, 504
Unemployment Compensation Extension Act of 2010, 520
Unemployment rate, 515
Unemployment Trust Fund (UTF), 519
Unions. *See* Labor unions
United Auto Workers, 196
United Kingdom. *See* Great Britain
United Nations
Convention on the Rights of Persons with Disabilities, 259
Human Rights Council, 252
Palestinians and, 228
panel on climate change, 252
peacekeeping activities, 245
Population Fund, 176, 185, 252
U.S. ambassador to, 224, 226–227 (box)
United States v. Windsor, 669–670
Universal health insurance. *See* Affordable Care Act
Universal Service Fund (USF), 334
University of Virginia Center for Politics, 23
Upton, Fred (R-Mich.), 851
Congressional deficit committee, 168

Energy and Commerce Committee, 664
generic drug applications, 462
Medicare payments to physicians, 464
U.S. Agency for International Development (USAID), 243, 245, 253
U.S. Bank, 54
USAID. *See* U.S. Agency for International Development (USAID)
USDA. *See* Agriculture Department, U.S. (USDA)
Use-of-force law, 300
Utah, 648–650
Utilites regulations, 401

Van Hollen, Chris (D-Md.), 602
Budget Committee, 664
budget negotiations (2012), 161
campaign finance, 551
committees, 850
Congressional deficit committee, 168
Democracy Is Strengthened by Casting Light on Spending in Elections (DISCLOSE) Act, 678
Democratic Congressional Campaign Committee, 645, 663
Pakistan aid, 237
Presidential Election Campaign Fund, 682
whistleblower protection, 601
Velázquez, Nydia M. (D-N.Y.), 854
Puerto Rico political status, 619
Small Business Committee, 646, 664
small business Federal contracting, 630
Venezuela, 239
Venture capital, 147–148
Veterans Affairs, Department of (VA), 108
appointments, 710
appropriations, 125
FY 2009, 131
FY 2010, 131, 288
FY 2011, 139, 155, 297
FY 2012, 175–176
FY 2013, 184
health study, 445
outlays for, 280 (figure)
Veterans Affairs Committee, House, 647, 848, 855
ranking members and chairs, 646, 664
Veterans Affairs Committee, Senate, 643, 644
ranking members and chairs, 662
Veterans Benefits Administration, 155, 297
Veterans Health Administration, 176, 297
Veterans health care and hospitals, 280
Veto. *See* Line-item veto; Pocket veto
VH-71 presidential helicopter, 133, 276, 278, 281–283
Vice, Daniel, 559
Vietnam War, 4, 139, 288
Vilsack, Thomas J., 410, 705 (box), 711
Violence Against Women Act, 33, 552, 568, 571–573
Virginia, 703
Virgin Islands, 648
Visclosky, Peter J. (D-Ind.), 655–656, 849
ethics probe, 655–656
Vitter, David (R-La.), 75, 77, 384
community service programs, 605
congressional pay, 683
ethics probe, 672
Hillary Clinton nomination as Secretary of State and, 226 (box), 705
Hurricane Sandy, 625
immigration status on census, 614
ineligibility clause, 684
nutrition bill, 469
Vocker, Paul A., 69
Voinovich, George V. (R-Ohio), 102
"don't ask, don't tell," 289
travel documents, 244
unemployment compensation, 522
Volcker, Paul, 49, 92, 695
Volcker rule, 69, 92
Voting
congressional votes (*See* Congressional votes)
fraud, 680
House elections (*See* Congressional elections)
Rights Act, 588
Senate elections (*See* Congressional elections)
Vouchers, Affordable Care Act employer, 438–439
Voyager Expanded Learning, 652
V-22 tilt-rotor Osprey aircraft, 312

Wages
discrimination
about, 550
gender-based, 528–529
for Federal workers, 600–601
merit-based pay plan, 600
parity in, 529
Wagoner, Rick, Jr., 694
Walberg, Tim (R-Mich.), 850
minimum wage, 541
Walden, Greg (R-Ore.), 851
Walker, Scott, 41, 44
Wall Street Journal
employee payroll tax cut, 109
fiscal cliff, 187
John Corzine, 70
LIBOR-rate scandal, 72
Wall Street Reform and Consumer Protection Act. *See* Dodd-Frank Wall Street Reform and Consumer Protection Act
Walmart Foundation, 49
Walsh, Joe (R-Ill.), 42, 854
government spending accountability, 633
Walz, Tim (D-Minn.), 682
Warner, Mark (D-Va.), 161
OMB performance standards, 633
"War on coal" (Obama), 399–400
War Powers Act, 701
War Powers Resolution, 1973, 139, 287
Warren, Elizabeth (D-Mass.), 41, 69, 105
Washington, D.C. *See* District of Columbia
Washington Institute for Near East Policy, 239
Washington Mutual Bank, 656
Washington Post
on Afghanistan war, 230–231
on congressional pay, 685
on D.C. representation, 650

on Eric Massa, 655
on Jane Harman, 653
Wasserman Schultz, Debbie (D-Fla.), 651
Wastewater treatment, 212, 381
Water
Army Corps of Engineers, 128
budget bills, 183–184
California, 397
Clean Water Act, 173, 184, 380
Clean Water and Drinking Water State Revolving Funds, 184, 381, 385
drinking, 154, 173, 212
hydropower, 397
pollution, 212, 381, 389
security regulation, 212
U.S.-Mexico International Boundary Water Commission, 233
waste, 212, 381
Waterboarding, 246
Waters, Maxine (D-Calif.), 851
ethics probe, 656–657, 674–675
Section 8 vouchers, 506
Watson, Diane E. (D-Calif.), 853
Watt, Melvin L. (D-N.C.), 665, 851
Fannie and Freddie executive pay, 510
Patent law, 571
restrictions on regulations, 632
Violence Against Women Act, 573
Waxman, Henry (D-Calif.), 333, 370, 393
emissions legislation, 370
Waxman, Henry A. (D-Calif.), 36, 370
Affordable Care Act, 428, 457 (box)
Children's Health Insurance Program, 445
committees, 850, 851
energy amendments, 382
Energy and Commerce Committee, 646, 664
on energy legislation, 387–388
home improvement rebates, 506
national ambient air quality standards (NAAQS), 398
tobacco regulation, 448, 449
Ways and Means Committee, House, 647, 855
Affordable Care Act, 427
foreign trade agreements, 193, 196, 199
Pete Stark ethics probe, 654
ranking members and chairs, 646, 664
Russian trade normalization, 201–202
tax cuts and health insurance program expansion, 80
Wealth, household, 51
Weapons
guns and gun control (*See* Guns and gun control)
improvised explosive device (IED), 279, 284, 307
nuclear (*See* Nuclear weapons)
Weapon Systems Acquisition Reform Act of 2009, 301
Weather Assistance Program, 82
Webb, Jim (D-Va.), 844, 846
executive pay, 532
Guantánamo Bay, Cuba, 315
State Department reauthorization, 243
war supplemental (2010), 288
Webster, Daniel (R-Fla.), 635
Weill, Jim, 466
Weiner, Anthony (D-N.Y), 30, 671 (box)
COPS, 562
Weinstein, Jason, 574
Welch, Peter (D-Vt.), 632
Welfare and social services
action chronology, 2009-2010
changes in law, 544
food assistance programs (*See* Food assistance programs)
Low Income Home Energy Assistance Program, 138
Section 8 housing voucher program, 121, 156
Supplemental Nutrition Assistance Program (SNAP), 33, 61, 82, 171
Temporary Assistance for Needy Families (TANF), 110, 181, 544, 556
Temporary Assistance to Needy Families (TANF), 110, 181
Wells Fargo, 54
Weprin, David I., 30
Western Hemisphere Travel Initiative, 210
Westmoreland, Lynn A. (R-Ga.), 854
Wexler, Robert (D-Fla.), 26
drywall safety, 508
Whistleblower Protection Enhancement Act (2012), 601, 623
Whistleblowers, 251, 601, 623
White, Jesse, 648
White, Ryan, 419, 453
White-Ginder, Jeanne, 420 (figure)
Whitehouse, Sheldon (D-R.I.), 846, 847, 848
Democracy Is Strengthened by Casting Light on Spending in Elections (DISCLOSE) Act, 681, 682
foreclosure aid, 510
White House Conference on Bullying Prevention, 492
Whitfield, Edward (R-Ky.), 396, 851
national ambient air quality standards (NAAQS), 398
WIC. *See* Women, Infants, and Children (WIC) program
Wicker, Roger (R-Miss.), 301
unions, 540
Wiki Leaks, 251
Wildfires, California, 139, 288
Wilkerson, Donna, 557–558
Williams, David L., 30
Williams, Sidney, 656
Wilson, Joe (R-S.C.), 4, 430 (box), 850
ethics probe, 653–654
Wind energy, 381
Windsor, Edith, 669
Winnefeld, James A., Jr., 275 (box)
Win Without War, 309
Wiretapping, 205–206, 208–209
Foreign Intelligence Surveillance Act, 215–217
roving, 214
Wisconsin, 703
Witness protection programs, 565
Wittman, Robert J. (R-Va.), 850
Base Realignment and Closure (BRAC), 308
Wolf, Frank R. (R-Va.), 849
counterterrorism competitive analysis council, 251
Guantánamo detainees, 561

Pakistan Counterinsurgency Fund, 304
2009 war supplemental, 270
Wolf, Martin, 55
Women
abortion and (*See* Abortion)
in Congress, 1947-2011, 33 (table)
equal pay, 517, 528, 548, 550
sex crimes against (*See* Rape)
Violence Against Women Act, 33
WIC program (*See* Women, Infants, and Children (WIC) program)
Women, Infants, and Children (WIC) program, 413, 468, 469, 470
appropriations
FY 2010, 128
FY 2011, 152
FY 2012, 171
child nutrition bill, 465
Wood, Diane Pamela, 711, 712
Woolsey, Lynn (D-Calif.), 377, 850
education, 484
restrictions on regulations, 632
Worker, Homeownership and Business Assistance Act (2009), 520, 521
Works Progress Administration (WPA), 622
World Bank, 131, 233, 245
World Trade Organization, 192, 193
Brazil and, 469
General Agreement on Services, 197
Russia and, 201
Russian trade normalization and, 201
WPA (Works Progress Administration), 622
Wright, Jim (D-Texas), 644 (box)
Wu, David (D-Ore.), 43, 854
ethics probe, 673
sexual misadventures and resignation, 671 (box)
Wyden, Ron (D-Ore.), 338
committees, 845, 846
Foreign Intelligence Surveillance Act, 217, 251
intelligence authorization (2013), 255
whistleblowers, 251
wiretapping, 206

Yarmuth, John (D-Ky.), 675
Yellen, Janet, 54
Yemen, 223, 249, 700
unmanned aerial vehicles in, 255
See also Middle East
Yingling, Edward L., 92
Young, C. W. Bill (R-Fla.)
committees, 849
ethics probe, 655–656
war supplemental (2009), 270–271
Young, Don (R-Alaska), 647, 853
ethics probe, 673
Young Americans for Liberty, 309
Young & Rubicam Brands, 143
Yucca Mountain, Nevada, 173, 183, 377–378, 394–395

Zients, Jeffrey, 49, 179
Zimmerman, Gabriel, 643 (box)